CASES AND MATERIALS

CORPORATE FINANCE

SIXTH EDITION

by

WILLIAM W. BRATTON
Peter P. Weidenbruch, Jr., Professor of Business Law
Georgetown University Law Center

FOUNDATION PRESS
75TH ANNIVERSARY

THOMSON

WEST

© 1972, 1979, 1987, 1993, 2003 FOUNDATION PRESS
© 2008 By FOUNDATION PRESS
　　　　395 Hudson Street
　　　　New York, NY 10014
　　　　Phone Toll Free 1–877–888–1330
　　　　Fax (212) 367–6799
　　　　foundation–press.com
Printed in the United States of America

ISBN 978–1–59941–225–2

TEXT IS PRINTED ON 10% POST
CONSUMER RECYCLED PAPER

PREFACE TO THE SIXTH EDITION

This Sixth Edition updates, expands, and reorganizes.

The updating requires no special explanation. This Edition incorporates developments in law, in practice, and in legal and economic theory.

Expansions will be most apparent in Parts I and II. In Part I the materials on derivatives and options have been taken a step farther with an exposition of put-call parity and a presentation on the empty voting phenomenon. Part II now includes a long overdue section on securitization and a not overdue but necessary section on credit derivatives.

The reorganization follows from conversations with users of the book and developments in my own pedagogy. This Edition attempts to present its concepts and materials in an order that makes it unnecessary to refer to materials coming later in the course when explaining today's topic. Although the goal is not reached, it is approached.

Here is a more particular explanation. In Victor Brudney and Marvin Chirelstein's original conception, Part I was a succinct presentation of the basic elements of valuation, introduced with *Atlas Pipeline*, but otherwise conducted with little reference to legal materials. They expanded Part I in the Third Edition, moving up front materials on the CAPM and EMH from the back of the book. I added more explanatory material when I joined with the Fourth Edition. In the Fifth Edition, I revised Part I to reflect what I had been doing all along in my teaching, moving forward *duPont v. Universal* from the section on mergers. I also added the *LeBeau* case, less for its contributions to the law of appraisal than for its nuts and bolts exposition of valuation techniques. *LeBeau* turned out to be awkward in the teaching, however. To explain what was going on, I had to tell the story of *Harris v. Rapid-American*, and that's a hard story to tell to a listener who has not read the case. I decided that the rest of the materials on appraisal valuation should follow *duPont v. Universal* into Part I.

Part I was always burdened by another problem—*Atlas Pipeline*. Some users have told me that they think it is a great introductory case. Others have asked me when I finally will be deleting it. I myself taught it some years and omitted it others. Its persistence owed more to my inability to find a table-setting case as a substitute than to anything else. When I taught *Atlas* again last year I decided it had to go. The Chandler Act, chapter X, and the mandatory SEC report lie so far in the past as to denude the case of pedagogical plausibility, not to mention the alienation and confusion that ensues when one tries to explain them, along with the basic outline of insolvency reorganization, on the first day of class. At the same time, bankruptcy reorganization has receded as a source of legal materials on valuation. It is all process now. What judicial valuation we get today comes from the Delaware courts under § 262. I concluded that Part I should use appraisal valuation and its primary conceptual sticking points as a running theme, a legal counterpoint to the exposition of valuation basics. The table-setter is now *Tri-Continental v. Battye* and its treatment of the problem of a market discount to fundamental value. Its an old chestnut, but one that has the benefit of remaining good law. The discount versus value theme is picked up and developed in the later appraisal cases and the excerpt from Reiner Kraakman's wonderful piece on premiums and discounts in mergers. To complete the reorganization, I moved efficient markets from the back of Part I to the front. This seems counterintuitive—Part I should start with the time value of money and discounting. I don't disagree. This is a second-best (maybe third-best) solution. Here is my thinking. *Battye* introduces the closed-end fund discount, which is a core topic in EMH literature. At the same time, there really never was a good place to put the EMH. Its earlier place at the end of Part I, as a coda, made analytic sense. But I kept finding myself making references forward to it when discussing fundamentals. In fact, I taught it out of order–after CAPM but before derivatives–even though that made no analytic sense. My solution is to put it first, so that the market pricing problematic gets presented and discussed before the course proceeds to value fundamentals. EMH's operative concept–that information moves prices–is quite intuitive, so the shift implicates no special pedagogical challenges. My doubts about the shift go primarily to the accuracy of the implicit representation made to the students in the course's first two or so hours. When the course starts with discounting there is no room for illusions about the level of difficulty confronting the uninitiated. Information and market prices, although by no means easy, lack the brutality of numbers.

The other organizational change concerns what used to be Part III, the Part on capital structure built around Modigliani and Miller. That Part originally followed a Part II that contained very little on debt. The debt materials grew in the Fourth Edition, after debt returned from the back room of practice to the front lines of policy debate in the 1980s. There it remains and continues to grow. As Part II got longer and longer, it began to feel odd to talk M-M and high leverage long after the contracts and the doctrine on debt had been discussed in class. So I have pulled M-M forward as a theoretical introduction to the debt materials, which has been the order of my teaching for years anyway. The debt-equity materials from old Part III are now integrated into Part II. As a consequence, preferred stock and convertibles have been raised to the dignity of a separate Part–they follow in their usual place, now as Part III. What was left of old Part III all concerns common stock, and now is conjoined with executive pay and blockholders as a separate Part IV on special problems related to equity finance.

I can assure those who find these innovations uncongenial that the old threads of points remain in place. The book can be taught in the old sequence without an encounter of significant friction. Indeed, the intent remains as before–this book presents a menu of possibilities rather than a mandated syllabus.

The revision benefits from conversations with Jose Gabilondo, Caroline Gentile, Mitu Gulati, Kim Krawiec, Don Langevoort, Joe McCahery, Fred McChesney, Troy Paredes, and Frank Partnoy. My thanks to Stephanie Lyerly, Georgetown Law 2008, for research assistance.

I have one regret. The Depression-era mentality that combined financial conservatism and a belief that responsible regulators could derive right answers in cases of financial conflict is barely evident in this Sixth Edition. *Atlas* is gone; *Consumers Power* is gone along with the Holding Company Act itself. But a casebook editor must accept his universe. I do not doubt that the cycle will turn and that the law of finance will return to these postures at some time in the future. I just hope not to be present to see the precipitating events.

W.W.B.

Washington, D.C.
July, 2007

*

ACKNOWLEDGMENTS

It is with appreciation that acknowledgment is made to the publishers and authors who gave permission for the reproduction of excerpts of the following materials:

American Bar Association. Section on Business Law

Revised Model Simplified Indenture, The Business Lawyer, vol. 55, no. 3, May 2000

Model Stock Purchase Agreement

American Economic Association. American Economic Review and Journal of Economic Perspectives

Andrade, Mitchell and Stafford, New Evidence and Perspectives on Mergers

Easterbrook, Two Agency Cost Explanations of Dividends

Jensen, Agency Costs of Free Cash Flow, Corporate Finance and Takeovers

Holmstrom and Kaplan, Corporate Governance and Merger Activity in the United States: Making Sense of the 1980s and 1990s

Lintner, Distributions of Incomes of Corporations Among Dividends, Retained Earnings and Taxes

Myers, Capital Structure

Shleifer and Summers, The Noise Trading Approach to Finance

Cardozo Law Review

Buffett, The Essays of Warren Buffett: Lessons for Corporate America

Rock, The Dark Side of Relational Investing

Columbia Law Review

Kraakman, Taking Discounts Seriously: The Implications of "Discounted" Share Prices as an Acquisition Motive. This article originally appeared at 88 Colum. L. Rev. 891 (1988). Reprinted by permission.

Duke Law Journal

Yablon, Poison Pills and Litigation Uncertainty © 1989

Financial Accounting Foundation

Summaries of FASB Statement No. 141, Business Combinations, and Statement No. 142, Goodwill and Other Intangible Assets, copy righted by the Financial Accounting Standards Board, 401 Merritt 7, P.O. Box 5116, Norwalk, Connecticut 06856, U.S.A. Portions are reprinted with permission. Complete copies of these documents are available from FASB

Financial Analysts Journal

Modigliani and Pogue, An Introduction to Risk and Return: Concepts and Evidence

Georgetown Law Journal

Bratton, The New Dividend Puzzle, vol. 93, no. 3 © 2005

Thompson, Exit, Liquidity, and Majority Rule: Appraisal's Role in Corporate Law , vol. 84, no. 1 © 1995

Harvard Law Review Association

Andrews, The Stockholder's Right to Equal Opportunity in the Sale of Shares

Brudney and Chirelstein, Fair Shares in Corporate Mergers and Takeovers

Irwin/McGraw-Hill

Brealey, Myers and Allen, Principles of Corporate Finance, 8th ed. © 2006

Ross, Westerfield and Jaffe, Corporate Finance, 5th ed. © 1999

John Wiley & Sons, Inc.

Grayson, The Use of Statistical Techniques in Capital Budgeting, in Robichek, ed., Financial Research and Management Decisions © 1967. Reprinted by permission of John Wiley & Sons, Inc.

Journal of Law and Economics and The University of Chicago

Gompers and Lerner, The Use of Covenants: An Empirical Analysis of Venture Capital Partnership Agreements. Copyright 1996 by The University of Chicago. All rights reserved

Journal of Legal Studies

Bebchuk, The Sole Owner Standard for Takeover Policy © 1988

Schwartz, The Fairness of Tender Offer Prices in Utilitarian Theory © 1988

MacMillan Publishing Company

Bierman and Smidt, The Capital Budgeting Decision (1966) © 1966

Michigan Law Review

Ayer, Rethinking Absolute Priority After Ahlers © 1989

National Bureau of Economic Research

Durand, Costs of Debt and Equity Funds for Business: Trends and Problems of Measurement © 1952

Oxford University Press, Coffee, Lowenstein, and Rose-Ackerman, eds. (1987), Knights, Raiders, and Targets: The Impact of Hostile Takeovers © 1987 by Center for law and Economics, Columbia University

Herman and Lowenstein, The Efficiency Effects of Hostile Takeovers

Pearson Education, Inc., Upper Saddle River NJ

Alexander, Sharpe and Bailey, Fundamentals of Investments, 3rd ed. © 2001

Van Horne, Financial Management and Policy, 12th ed. © 2001

Quorum Books, an imprint of Greenwood Publishing Company, Inc., Westport, CT. Marc I. Steinberg, ed., Tender Offers: Developments and Commentaries © 1985 by Marc I. Steinberg

Sargent, Do the Second-Generation Takeover Statutes Violate the Commerce Clause?

Richard D. Irwin, Inc.

Lorie, Dodd and Kimpton, The Stock Market: Theories and Evidence © 1985

San Diego Law Review

Volk, Leicher, and Koloski, Negotiating Business Combination Agreements–The "Seller's" Point of View

Southern California Law Review

Huang and Knoll, Corporate Finance, Corporate Law and Finance Theory, 45 Southern California Law Review 175–192 (2000) reprinted with the permission of the Southern California Law Review

Texas Law Review Association

Coates, Takeover Defenses in the Shadow of the Pill: A Critique of the Scientific Evidence © 2000

Lupica, Asset Securitization, The Unsecured Creditor's Perspective © 1998

University of Chicago Press

Baird and Rasmussen, Boyd's Legacy and Blackstone's Ghost

University of Pennsylvania Law Review

David A. Skeel, Creditor's Ball, The "New" Corporate Governance in Chapter 11 © 2003

Michael L. Wachter, Takeover Defense When Financial Markets are (Only) Relatively Efficient © 2003

Wadsworth Publishing Company, Inc.

Alchian and Allen, University Economics (3rd ed. 1972) © 1972

Lewellen, W.G., The Cost of Capital (1969) © 1969

Wake Forest Law Review

Thomas and Martin, The Determinants of Shareholder Voting on Stock Option Plans

Yale Journal on Regulation

Romano, A Guide to Takeovers: Theory, Evidence, and Regulation © 1992 by the YALE JOURNAL ON REGULATION, P.O. Box 208215, New Haven, CT 06520–8215. Reprinted from Vol. 9 by permission. All rights reserved

Yale Law Journal and Fred B. Rothman & Company

Easterbrook and Fischel, Corporate Control Transactions

Fischel, The Economics of Lender Liability, from The Yale Law Journal, vol. 99, pp 131-154

The Yale Law Journal Company, Inc.

   Subramanian, Fixing Freezeouts, from The Yale Law Journal, Vol. 115, 2–7

SUMMARY OF CONTENTS

Preface to the Sixth Edition --- iii
Acknowledgements --- vii
Table of Cases --- xxxi

PART I VALUING THE FIRM AND ITS SECURITIES

Introduction -- 1

Section A. Market Value and Fundamental Value ----------------- 6

1. Introduction -- 6
2. Market Efficiency -- 15
   (A) The Efficient Market Hypothesis ------------------------------------- 15
   (B) Behavioral Finance: The Noise Trading Approach and Other
       Alternatives to the Efficient Market Hypothesis ------------------- 26

Section B. Elements of Fundamental Value ------------------------ 38

1. The Time Value of Money --- 38
2. Expected Returns --- 47
   (A) The Composition of "Returns" --- 48
   (B) Future Returns and Probability Distributions --------------------- 58
3. Risk and the Capitalization Rate -- 63
   (A) Risk as Degree of Dispersion -- 64
   (B) Comparable Firms and Market Capitalization Rates: The
       Price/Earnings Ratio -- 71
   (C) Measures of Risk—The Capital Asset Pricing Model and Beta   83
4. Premiums and Discounts in Mergers and Acquisitions --------------- 120
5. Risk Reduction through Hedging --------------------------------------- 153
   (A) Risk Exposure -- 154
   (B) Hedging --- 156
   (C) Option Strategies and Put–Call Parity --------------------------- 165
   (D) Call Option Valuation -- 171
   (E) Regulation of Derivatives-- 173

PART II DEBT FINANCING

Introduction -- 205

Section A. Capital Structure and Leverage -------------------------- 214

1. Leverage and Value-- 215
   (A) The Cost of Capital and the Value of the Firm----------------- 215
   (B) The Modigliani–Miller Position and the Revised Concept of
       Optimal Capital Structure -- 221

Section B. Basic Terms and Concepts 240

1. Introduction 240
2. Corporate Trust and the Trust Indenture Act of 1939 248
3. The Bondholder and the Going Concern 253
   (A) The Promise to Pay 253
   (B) Promises That Protect the Value of the Promise to Pay 268

Section C. Security And Seniority 281

1. Mortgage Bonds 282
2. Leases 284
3. Subordination 286
4. Asset Securitization 287
   (A) Overview 288
   (B) Accounting Treatment 294
   (C) Transaction Structure 296
   (D) Bankruptcy Risks 299

Section D. High Leverage Restructuring 304

1. Leverage and Management Discipline 304
2. The Rise, Decline, and Reappearance of Leveraged Restructuring 308
3. Event Risk and Bond Contracts 320

Section E. Debtor Distress 341

1. Altering the Bond Contract–Amendment and Exchange, Coercion and Holding Out 341
2. Credit Derivatives 359
3. Creditor Protection in Law 373
   (A) Regulation of Capital Structure 374
   (B) Corporate Law Legal Capital Rules 383
   (C) Fraudulent Conveyance Law 392
   (D) Fiduciary Duty 406

Section F. Insolvency Reorganization 411

1. Introduction: The Reorganization Bargain and the Limits of the Parties' Bargaining Freedom 411
   (A) Reorganization By Judicial Proceeding 411
   (B) The Parameters of the Bankruptcy Bargain 413
2. The Rise and Decline of Absolute Priority 414
   (A) Absolute Priority Under the Bankruptcy Act of 1938 415
   (B) The Bankruptcy Act of 1978 431
3. Reorganization under the Bankruptcy Code 434
   (A) Overview 434
   (B) Absolute Priority Under Chapter 11 448
   (C) The New Value Exception 455

4. The Move to Creditor Control --- 468
5. Rethinking the System --- 477
   (A) Rethinking Creditors' Rights–The Common Pool and the
       Creditors' Bargain --- 477
   (B) Rethinking the Reorganization Process–Alternative Ap-
       proaches--- 479

PART III FINANCING WITH HYBRID SECURITIES

Introduction --- 485

Section A. Preferred Stock Financing ---------------------------------- 485

1. Rights and Preferences --- 485
   (A) Preferred Stock Defined --- 485
   (B) The Preferred Stock Contract --- 487
   (C) Issuer Motivations and Holder Expectations --------------------------- 493
2. Claims to Dividends --- 495
   (A) Preferred Stock Dividend Provisions ------------------------------------ 495
   (B) Board Discretion to Withhold Payment --------------------------------- 496
3. Claims to Principal, Including Arrearages -- 502
   (A) Alteration By Amendment --- 502
   (B) Alteration By Merger --- 521

Section B. Convertible Securities and Warrants -------------------- 546

Introduction --- 546
1. Terms and Valuation -- 547
   (A) The Value of a Call Option -- 547
   (B) Convertible Bond Features and Valuation Variables ----------------- 548
2. Conflicts of Interest -- 559
   (A) Protective Contract Provisions --- 559
   (B) Duties Implied in Law --- 579

Section C. Venture Capital Finance ----------------------------------- 596

PART IV EQUITY CAPITAL STRUCTURE—PAYOUT POLI-
CY AND OWNERSHIP STAKES

Introduction --- 619

Section A. Payout Policy—Dividends, Repurchases, and Re-
tained Earnings -- 620

Introduction --- 620
1. Cash Dividends and Dividend Policy --- 621
   (A) A Theory of Stock Valuation --- 621
   (B) The Role of Dividend Policy -- 624
2. Applicable Legal Standards --- 639
3. Stock Dividends-- 656
4. Restructuring by Dividend—Spin Offs and Tracking Stock ---------------- 664

(A) Spin Offs 665
(B) Tracking Stock 666
5. Repurchase of Outstanding Shares 668
(A) The Economics of Share Repurchases 668
(B) Repurchases—Fiduciary and Disclosure Obligations 675

Section B. Equity Ownership and the Value of the Firm 697

1. Executive Stock Options 699
Introduction 699
(A) Stock Options and Shareholder Value 699
(B) Fiduciary Duties 711
2. Blockholding 728
(A) Blockholding, Corporate Governance, and Shareholder Value .. 728
(B) Regulation of Blockholders 734

PART V MERGERS AND ACQUISITIONS

Introduction 765

Section A. The Move to Merge 767

Section B. Accounting and Taxes 778

1. Accounting for Mergers—Purchase, Pooling, and Accounting for
     Goodwill 778
(A) Purchase Versus Pooling 779
(B) Revised Purchase Treatment 780
2. Tax Treatment of Mergers 786

Section C. The Merger Agreement 791

Section D. Formal Aspects of Merger 806

1. The Mechanics of the Process 806
(A) Classical Mergers 806
(B) Sale of Assets—An Alternative to the Classical Merger 808
(C) Share Purchase and Share Exchange 809
(D) Triangular Mergers 810
(E) De Facto Mergers 812
2. Appraisal 826

Section E. Fairness and Disclosure 830

Introduction 830
1. Freeze–Outs and Buyouts: Fair Dealing, Fair Price, and the Ap-
     praisal Remedy 832
Introduction 832
(A) Freeze–Outs 832
(B) Management Buyouts 905
Introduction 905

2. The Duty of Care --- 919
3. Disclosure Duties -- 933
   (A) State Fiduciary Law --- 933
   (B) Federal Disclosure Rules: The Materiality Of Soft Information 945

Section F.   The Tender Offer ------------------------------------- 977

Introduction --- 977
1. Why Tender Offers? Economic Welfare and Regulatory Strategies -- 979
   (A) The Proponents' View -- 979
   (B) The Opponents' View --- 983
   (C) The Intermediate View --- 989
2. Bidder Tactics, Policy Alternatives, and the Williams Act ------------- 991
   (A) Bidder Incentives --- 991
   (B) The Market and Sole Owner Standards ------------------------------- 993
   (C) The Williams Act -- 998
3. Management Defenses and Fiduciary Duties ----------------------------- 1024
   (A) Defensive Tactics -- 1024
   (B) Defensive Tactics and the Duty of Loyalty ------------------------ 1036
4. State Antitakeover Legislation --------------------------------------- 1124
   (A) First Generation Statutes -- 1125
   (B) Second Generation Statutes --------------------------------------- 1126
   (C) Third Generation Statutes -- 1132

APPENDICES

App.

   A.   FINANCIAL CONTRACT FORMS -- A–1

   B.   STATE CORPORATE CODES --- B–1

   C.   THE BANKRUPTCY CODE --- C–1

   D.   PROVISIONS OF THE FEDERAL SECURITIES LAWS AND RULES PROMULGATED THEREUNDER --- D–1

   E.   THE BINOMIAL AND BLACK–SCHOLES OPTION PRICING MODELS ----------- E–1

   F.   TABLES -- F–1

INDEX -- I–1

*

TABLE OF CONTENTS

PREFACE TO THE SIXTH EDITION -- iii
ACKNOWLEDGMENTS -- vii
TABLE OF CASES -- xxxi

PART I VALUING THE FIRM AND ITS SECURITIES

Introduction -- 1

Section A. Market Value and Fundamental Value ------------------- 6

1. Introduction -- 6
   Tri-Continental Corp. v. Battye ------------------------------------- 6
   Note: Funds -- 11
   Note: Merger Appraisal Rights and the Closed–End Fund Discount 13
2. Market Efficiency --- 15
   (A) The Efficient Market Hypothesis ---------------------------- 15
       Brealey, Myers, and Allen, Principles of Corporate Finance ----- 15
       Note: Speculative Efficiency, Allocative Efficiency, and Incentive Problems -- 20
       Note: Empirical Testing of the EMH --------------------------- 22
   (B) Behavioral Finance: The Noise Trading Approach and Other Alternatives to the Efficient Market Hypothesis ---------------- 26
       Shleifer and Summers, The Noise Trader Approach to Finance 27
       Note: Behavioral Theory -------------------------------------- 32
       Note: Bubbles and Crashes ----------------------------------- 34

Section B. Elements of Fundamental Value ----------------------- 38

1. The Time Value of Money --- 38
   Alchian and Allen, University Economics ------------------------- 39
   Note: The Role of Discounting in Bond Valuation ---------------- 44
   Note: Discounting in Capital Budgeting Decisions --------------- 45
2. Expected Returns --- 47
   (A) The Composition of "Returns" ------------------------------ 48
       Warren Buffett, The Essays of Warren Buffett: Lessons for Corporate America --- 48
       Note: Accounting Earnings, "Owner Earnings," and Net Cash Flows --- 53
   (B) Future Returns and Probability Distributions --------------- 58
       Grayson, The Use of Statistical Techniques in Capital Budgeting -- 59
3. Risk and the Capitalization Rate ------------------------------------- 63
   (A) Risk as Degree of Dispersion ------------------------------- 64
       Lewellen, The Cost of Capital -------------------------------- 64
       Note: Risk and Return Characteristics of Different Securities -- 70
   (B) Comparable Firms and Market Capitalization Rates: The Price/Earnings Ratio -- 71

Francis I. duPont & Co. v. Universal City Studios, Inc. 71
Universal City Studios, Inc. v. Francis I. duPont & Co. 77
Note: Inferred Capitalization Rates and Constant Growth
  Valuation 80
Note: Price/Earnings Ratios and Investment Strategy 83
(C) Measures of Risk—The Capital Asset Pricing Model and Beta 83
  (1) Portfolio Theory 84
    (a) portfolio selection 84
      Sharpe, Portfolio Theory and Capital Markets 84
    (b) diversification as a means of reducing risk 91
    (c) choosing a "best portfolio"—the critical ratio and the
      separation theorem 94
      *Lintner, A Model of a Perfectly Functioning Securities
      Market* 94
      *Lorie, Dodd and Kimpton, The Stockmarket: Theories
      and Evidence* 96
  (2) The Capital Asset Pricing Model 98
    (a) derivation 99
      *Modigliani and Pogue, An Introduction to Risk and
      Return: Concepts and Evidence* 99
      Note: CAPM 106
    (b) using beta in valuation 107
      Cede & Co. v. Technicolor, Inc. 108
      Note: The Judicial Role in Appraisal 111
      *Brealey, Myers, and Allen, Principles of Corporate
      Finance* 112
      Note: Shareholder Value, Risk Aversion, and Risk
      Neutrality 115
    (c) empirical testing and multiple factor models 116
4. Premiums and Discounts in Mergers and Acquisitions 120
  *Kraakman, Taking Discounts Seriously: The Implications of "Dis-
  counted" Share Prices as an Acquisition Motive* 120
  Note: Downward–Sloping Demand 127
  Rapid–American Corp. v. Harris 127
  Problem 132
  Note: Premiums, Discounts, and Merger Gain 133
  Le Beau v. M.G. Bancorporation, Inc. 136
  Note: Valuation Concepts Introduced in Le Beau 146
  Note: The Implicit Minority Discount 149
  Note: The Marketability Discount 150
5. Risk Reduction through Hedging 153
  (A) Risk Exposure 154
  (B) Hedging 156
    (1) Forward Contracts 156
    (2) Futures Contracts 158
    (3) Swaps 159
    (4) Options 163
  (C) Option Strategies and Put–Call Parity 165
    (1) Using Options 165
      Note: Financial Engineering 171
  (D) Call Option Valuation 171
    (1) Determining Factors 171
    (2) The Binomial and Black–Scholes Option Pricing Models.... 173
      Alexander, Sharpe, and Bailey 173

(E) Regulation of Derivatives -- 173
   (1) Counterparty Relationships ------------------------------- 174
     Caiola v. Citibank, N.A. ------------------------------- 174
     Note: Swaps --- 182
   (2) Hedging and Corporate Law Rights and Duties ------------- 186
     Brane v. Roth --- 186
     Note: Hedging, Shareholder Value, The CAPM, and the
       Irrelevance Hypothesis ------------------------------ 189
     *Deephaven Risk Arb Trading Ltd. v. UnitedGlobalCom
       Inc.* -- 190
     Note: Empty Voting ------------------------------------- 195
   (3) Systemic Risk and Transparency -------------------------- 196
     (a) the scope of the problem ----------------------------- 196
       Chairman Alan Greenspan, Remarks at the 36th Annual Conference on Bank Structure and Competition of the Federal Reserve Bank of Chicago ----------------- 196
       Note: Unexpected Volatility --------------------------- 199
     (b) regulatory possibilities and responses --------------------- 202

PART II DEBT FINANCING

Introduction --- 205
Eliasen v. Itel Corporation --- 205
Note: Priority of Claim -- 212

Section A. Capital Structure and Leverage --------------------------- 214

1. Leverage and Value -- 215
 (A) The Cost of Capital and the Value of the Firm --------------------- 215
   Durand, Costs of Debt and Equity Funds for Business: Trends and Problems of Measurement ------------------------------------- 216
 (B) The Modigliani–Miller Position and the Revised Concept of Optimal Capital Structure --- 221
   (1) The M–M Thesis and Its Assumptions ----------------------- 221
     Van Horne, Financial Management and Policy ----------- 222
   (2) Relaxing M–M's Assumptions ----------------------------- 225
     (a) institutional constraints ------------------------------- 226
     (b) taxes --- 227
       Van Horne, Financial Management and Policy --------- 227
       Note: Taxation and the M–M Theorem ------------------ 229
     (c) bankruptcy costs ------------------------------------- 231
     (d) agency costs --- 233
       Note: Fiduciary Law and Capital Structure -------------- 235
     (e) information asymmetries ------------------------------- 235
       Myers, Capital Structure ----------------------------- 236
       Note: The Pecking Order ----------------------------- 238

Section B. Basic Terms and Concepts -------------------------------- 240

1. Introduction -- 240
2. Corporate Trust and the Trust Indenture Act of 1939 ----------------- 248
  Elliott Associates v. J. Henry Schroder Bank & Trust Co. ------------- 248
  Note: The Trust Indenture Act of 1939 ----------------------------- 251

3. The Bondholder and the Going Concern ------------------------------- 253
   (A) The Promise to Pay --- 253
        1 Dewing, The Financial Policy of Corporations ----------------- 253
        Note: Redemption Rights and Duties ------------------------------ 255
        Morgan Stanley & Co., Inc. v. Archer Daniels Midland Co. ------ 258
        Note: Refunding Cases --- 265
        Note: Bondholder Remedies Upon Default -------------------------- 267
   (B) Promises That Protect the Value of the Promise to Pay ----------- 268
        (1) Business Covenants -- 268
             (a) debt contracts and debtor misbehavior ----------------- 268
             (b) principal covenants ----------------------------------- 270
             (c) commentaries -- 274
        (2) Judicial Interpretation of Covenants ------------------------ 274
             Sharon Steel Corp. v. The Chase Manhattan Bank, N.A. ----- 274
             Note: Boilerplate Indenture Terms ------------------------- 279

Section C.   Security And Seniority ------------------------------- 281

1. Mortgage Bonds -- 282
2. Leases -- 284
3. Subordination --- 286
4. Asset Securitization -- 287
   (A) Overview --- 288
        *Lupica, Asset Securitization: The Unsecured Creditor's Per-
          spective* --- 288
        Note: Risk and Return -- 293
   (B) Accounting Treatment --- 294
   (C) Transaction Structure -- 296
   (D) Bankruptcy Risks --- 299
        In re LTV Steel Company, Inc. -------------------------------- 300
        Note: Subsequent Proceedings ----------------------------------- 303
        Note: Policy Debates --- 304

Section D.   High Leverage Restructuring -------------------------- 304

1. Leverage and Management Discipline ---------------------------------- 304
   *Jensen, Agency Costs of Free Cash Flow, Corporate Finance and
     Takeovers* --- 306
2. The Rise, Decline, and Reappearance of Leveraged Restructuring --- 308
   *Holmstrom and Kaplan, Corporate Governance and Merger Activity
     in the United States: Making Sense of the 1980s and 1990s* ------ 309
   Note: The High Leverage Restructurings of the 1980s ---------------- 315
   Note: The Private Equity Restructurings of the 2000s --------------- 317
3. Event Risk and Bond Contracts --------------------------------------- 320
   Metropolitan Life Insurance Company v. RJR Nabisco, Inc. --------- 323
   Note: The Aftermath of the RJR Nabisco Restructuring --------------- 335
   Note: Spin Offs -- 335
   Note: Fiduciary Theory, Good Faith Duties, and Other Bases for
     Judicial Protection of Bondholders ------------------------------- 336
   Note: Lender Liability Compared ------------------------------------ 339

Section E. Debtor Distress 341

1. Altering the Bond Contract–Amendment and Exchange, Coercion and Holding Out 341
   Aladdin Hotel Co. v. Bloom 342
   Note: Amendment Under the Trust Indenture Act 346
   Katz v. Oak Industries Inc. 348
   Note: Coerced Votes and Hold Outs 356
   Note: Vulture Investors 358
   Note: Prepackaged Bankruptcy 359
2. Credit Derivatives 359
   Eternity Global Master Fund Limited v. Morgan Guaranty Trust Company of New York 359
   Note: Credit Derivatives 368
3. Creditor Protection in Law 373
   (A) Regulation of Capital Structure 374
       (1) Public Utilities 374
       (2) Investment Companies 375
       (3) Margin Requirements 378
       (4) Bank Capital 380
   (B) Corporate Law Legal Capital Rules 383
       (1) The Stated Capital Requirement 383
       (2) Dividends and Distributions 385
           (a) traditional statutes 385
               Klang v. Smith's Food & Drug Centers, Inc. 387
               Note: Restrictions on Distributions 391
           (b) new model statutes 392
   (C) Fraudulent Conveyance Law 392
       Wieboldt Stores, Inc. v. Schottenstein 394
       Note: Fraudulent Conveyance Avoidance of Leveraged Buy-outs 403
   (D) Fiduciary Duty 406
       Credit Lyonnais Bank Nederland N.V. v. Pathe Communications Co. 406
       Note: Pre–Bankruptcy Fiduciary Duties to Creditors 407

Section F. Insolvency Reorganization 411

1. Introduction: The Reorganization Bargain and the Limits of the Parties' Bargaining Freedom 411
   (A) Reorganization By Judicial Proceeding 411
   (B) The Parameters of the Bankruptcy Bargain 413
2. The Rise and Decline of Absolute Priority 414
   (A) Absolute Priority Under the Bankruptcy Act of 1938 415
       Ayer, Rethinking Absolute Priority After Ahlers 415
       Note: A Contrasting Account 419
       Consolidated Rock Products Co. v. Du Bois 420
       Note: The Aftermath of the Consolidated Rock Products Company Case 427
       Note: Issues Under Absolute Priority 428

Note: The Composition Tradition and the Best Interest of Creditors Standard 430
(B) The Bankruptcy Act of 1978 431
House Report No. 95–595 432
3. Reorganization under the Bankruptcy Code 434
(A) Overview 434
In re Zenith Electronics Corporation 434
Note: Proceedings Under Chapter 11 443
(B) Absolute Priority Under Chapter 11 448
House Report No. 95–595 448
Excerpt From Debates on Bankruptcy Reform Act of 1978 450
Note: Issues Under the Code 452
Note: Empirical Results—Deviations From Absolute Priority ... 454
(C) The New Value Exception 455
Bank of America National Trust and Savings Association v. 203 North LaSalle Street Partnership 458
Note: The New Value Exception 466
4. The Move to Creditor Control 468
Skeel, Creditor's Ball: The "New" New Corporate Governance in Chapter 11 468
Note: Restrictions on Executive Pay 476
5. Rethinking the System 477
(A) Rethinking Creditors' Rights–The Common Pool and the Creditors' Bargain 477
(B) Rethinking the Reorganization Process–Alternative Approaches 479
(1) Market–Based Proposals 479
(a) cash auction 479
(b) securities market test 481
(c) options 481
(d) judicially–supervised auction 482
(2) Contractual Proposals 482
(a) automatic conversion 482
(b) contractual choice 483

PART III FINANCING WITH HYBRID SECURITIES

Introduction 485

Section A. Preferred Stock Financing 485

1. Rights and Preferences 485
(A) Preferred Stock Defined 485
(B) The Preferred Stock Contract 487
(C) Issuer Motivations and Holder Expectations 493
2. Claims to Dividends 495
(A) Preferred Stock Dividend Provisions 495
(B) Board Discretion to Withhold Payment 496
(1) Cumulative Preferred 496
(2) Noncumulative Preferred 497
(3) Issuer Tender and Exchange Offers to Holders of Preferred in Arrears 498

Eisenberg v. Chicago Milwaukee Corp. ----------------------------- 498
    Note: Denver Tramway -- 501
  (4) Board Discretion and Voting Control ----------------------- 501
3. Claims to Principal, Including Arrearages ------------------------- 502
  (A) Alteration By Amendment ----------------------------------- 502
    (1) Liquidation Provisions----------------------------------- 502
      Goldman v. Postal Telegraph------------------------------ 504
      Note: Junior Hold Ups ---------------------------------- 506
    (2) Redemption Provisions ---------------------------------- 510
      Bowman v. Armour & Co. ------------------------------ 511
      Bowman v. Armour & Co. ------------------------------ 519
      Note: Bowman --- 521
  (B) Alteration By Merger -------------------------------------- 521
    Bove v. The Community Hotel Corporation of Newport, Rhode Island --- 521
    Note: The Investment Value Doctrine ----------------------- 527
    Rothschild International Corporation v. Liggett Group Inc. ------ 529
    Note: Drafting -- 533
    Note: "De Facto" Theories --------------------------------- 535
    Note: Preferred Class Voting in Respect of Mergers----------- 536
    Note: Fairness Scrutiny Under Delaware Law --------------- 538
    Dalton v. American Investment Co.------------------------- 541
    Note: FLS Holdings --------------------------------------- 543
    Note: Judicial Review of Recapitalizations and Mergers Impairing the Rights of Preferred Stockholders ------------------- 544

Section B.   Convertible Securities and Warrants ----------------- 546

Introduction -- 546
1. Terms and Valuation-- 547
  (A) The Value of a Call Option-------------------------------- 547
  (B) Convertible Bond Features and Valuation Variables ------------- 548
    (1) Traditional Convertibles ------------------------------- 548
      (a) elements of convertible bond value --------------------- 548
      (b) the conversion premium------------------------------- 550
      (c) issuer call rights ----------------------------------- 551
        Note: The Convertible Bond Puzzle ------------------- 552
    (2) Variations on the Traditional Convertible --------------------- 555
      (a) original issue discount convertibles----------------------- 555
      (b) puttable convertibles --------------------------------- 555
      (c) equity–linked securities ------------------------------ 555
      (d) floating price ("toxic") convertibles -------------------- 556
2. Conflicts of Interest --- 559
  (A) Protective Contract Provisions ----------------------------- 559
    Note: Implied in Fact Antidilution Protection----------------- 561
    HB Korenvaes Investments, L.P. v. Marriott Corporation -------- 563
    Note: Convertible Hedges --------------------------------- 575
    Note: Interpretation Contra Proferentum ------------------- 575
    Note: Convertible Bond Contracts--------------------------- 577
  (B) Duties Implied in Law------------------------------------- 579
    Van Gemert v. Boeing Co. --------------------------------- 579
    Note: Van Gemert's Operative Theory----------------------- 583

Broad v. Rockwell International Corp. ------------------------------- 584
Note: Fair and Unfair Dividends ---------------------------------- 592
Note: Fair and Unfair Mergers ----------------------------------- 594

Section C.   Venture Capital Finance -------------------------- 596

Equity–Linked Investors, L.P. v. Adams --------------------------- 596
Note: Venture Capital Finance ----------------------------------- 609
Note: Cases for Comparison -------------------------------------- 614

PART   IV   EQUITY CAPITAL STRUCTURE—PAYOUT POLICY AND OWNERSHIP STAKES

Introduction -- 619

Section A.   Payout Policy—Dividends, Repurchases, and Retained Earnings -- 620

Introduction -- 620
1. Cash Dividends and Dividend Policy ---------------------------- 621
   (A) A Theory of Stock Valuation ----------------------------- 621
        (1) Dividend Capitalization Model --------------------- 621
        (2) The Retention Ratio ------------------------------- 623
   (B) The Role of Dividend Policy ----------------------------- 624
        (1) Traditional Dividend Practice --------------------- 625
             Lintner, Distributions of Incomes of Corporations Among Dividends, Retained Earnings and Taxes ------------ 625
             Note: Payout Practices ---------------------------- 628
        (2) Dividends as a Financing Decision—The Dividend Puzzle-- 629
             (a) dividend policy under the irrelevance hypothesis ------- 630
             (b) taxes, other imperfections, and the low payout hypothesis -------------------------------------- 632
        (3) Information Asymmetries, Signaling, and Pecking Order Theory --- 634
        (4) Management Dividend Policies and Agency Theory --------- 636
2. Applicable Legal Standards ----------------------------------- 639
   Berwald v. Mission Development Company ---------------------- 640
   Note: Dividends and "Corporate Opportunity" ----------------- 644
   Wertheim Schroder & Co. Incorporated v. Avon Products, Inc. -------- 645
   Note: Special Dividends ------------------------------------- 651
   Note: Disclosure on the Downside --------------------------- 652
   Note: Dividends and Conflicts of Interest ------------------- 653
3. Stock Dividends -- 656
   Lewellen, The Cost of Capital ----------------------------- 656
   Note: Explaining Stock Splits and Stock Dividends ----------- 658
   Note: Stock Dividends As Information and the Regulation of Disclosure --- 659
   New York Stock Exchange, Listed Company Manual ----------- 659
   Note: Reverse Splits and Fractional Shares ------------------ 661
4. Restructuring by Dividend—Spin Offs and Tracking Stock ----------- 664
   (A) Spin Offs --- 665
   (B) Tracking Stock -- 666

5. Repurchase of Outstanding Shares 668
    (A) The Economics of Share Repurchases 668
        (1) Repurchase Transactions 668
        (2) Theoretical Irrelevance Between Dividends and Repurchases 669
        (3) Agency Costs and Information Asymmetries 671
        (4) Taxation 671
            Note: Repurchases—Volume and Stated Purpose 672
    (B) Repurchases—Fiduciary and Disclosure Obligations 675
        (1) The Scope of the Problem 675
        (2) Fiduciary Duties 677
            Kahn v. United States Sugar Corporation 677
            Note: Regulation of Repurchases 683
            Note: Greenmail and Defensive Repurchases 684
        (3) Federal Securities Laws—Repurchase Tender Offers 686
            Note: Federal Regulation of Repurchase Tender Offers 687
        (4) Federal Securities Laws—Open Market Repurchases 689
            (a) manipulation—Securities Exchange Act Section 9(a)(2) 690
            (b) safe harbor for potentially manipulative repurchases .. 692
                Note: OMRs and Market Transparency 693
        (5) Dividends, Repurchases, and Corporate Governance 694
            Bratton, The New Dividend Puzzle 694

Section B.   Equity Ownership and the Value of the Firm 697

1. Executive Stock Options 699
    Introduction 699
    (A) Stock Options and Shareholder Value 699
        Thomas and Martin, The Determinants of Shareholder Voting on Stock Option Plans 701
        Note: After Exercise 705
        Note: The Executive Pay Debate 706
        Note: Regulatory Environment 710
    (B) Fiduciary Duties 711
        Lewis v. Vogelstein 711
        Note: Regulation of Stock Options 720
        Ryan v. Gifford 723
        Note: Spring–Loading 726
2. Blockholding 728
    (A) Blockholding, Corporate Governance, and Shareholder Value .. 728
        (1) Blockholders as Monitors 728
        (2) Comparative Corporate Governance: Market Versus Blockholder Systems 729
        (3) Implications 731
            Note: The New Blockholders—Activist Hedge Funds 733
    (B) Regulation of Blockholders 734
        (1) Regulation as a Barrier to Blockholding 734
        (2) Fiduciary Regulation of Blockholders 736
            (a) noncontrolling blockholders 736

Rock, Controlling the Dark Side of Relational Investing --- 736
   (b) controlling blockholders ------------------------------------- 741
       Levco Alternative Fund v. The Reader's Digest Association, Inc. --- 741
       Note: The Tele–Communications–AT&T Merger ------- 743
       Note: Regulatory Barriers: The "One Share, One Vote" Controversy ------------------------------------- 746
       Perlman v. Feldmann -------------------------------------- 747
       Note: The Proposed Rule of Equal Opportunity --------- 755
       Note: Regulation of Control Sales After Feldmann ------ 758

PART V MERGERS AND ACQUISITIONS

Introduction -- 765

Section A. The Move to Merge ------------------------------------- 767

Andrade, Mitchell, and Stafford, New Evidence and Perspectives on Mergers --- 767
Note: Mergers and Value Creation ------------------------------------- 771

Section B. Accounting and Taxes ------------------------------ 778

1. Accounting for Mergers—Purchase, Pooling, and Accounting for Goodwill --- 778
   (A) Purchase Versus Pooling ------------------------------------ 779
   (B) Revised Purchase Treatment ------------------------------- 780
       Financial Accounting Standards Board Summary of Statement No. 141, Business Combinations. --------------- 780
       Questions --- 783
       Financial Accounting Standards Board Summary of Statement No. 142, Goodwill and Other Intangible Assets. ---------- 783
       Note: Testing Goodwill for Impairment -------------------- 785
2. Tax Treatment of Mergers -- 786
   Carney, Mergers & Acquisitions: Cases and Materials (2d ed. 2007) 786

Section C. The Merger Agreement ------------------------------ 791

Volk, Leicher & Koloski, Negotiating Business Combination Agreements—The "Seller's" Point of View ----------------------------- 791
IBP, Inc. v. Tyson Foods, Inc. --- 793

Section D. Formal Aspects of Merger ----------------------------- 806

1. The Mechanics of the Process -------------------------------------- 806
   (A) Classical Mergers --- 806
       (1) Stock for Stock Merger ----------------------------------- 806
       (2) Small Scale Merger --------------------------------------- 806
       (3) Classical Merger with Cash Consideration ------------- 807
       (4) Parent Subsidiary Mergers ------------------------------ 807
   (B) Sale of Assets—An Alternative to the Classical Merger --------- 808

(C) Share Purchase and Share Exchange ---------------------------------- 809
(D) Triangular Mergers --- 810
(E) De Facto Mergers --- 812
    Farris v. Glen Alden Corp. -------------------------------------- 812
    Note: A Pennsylvania Triangular Merger --------------------------- 818
    Hariton v. Arco Electronics, Inc. ------------------------------ 818
    Note: Other Consequences of De Facto Merger --------------------- 824
    Note: Successor Liability -- 825
2. Appraisal -- 826
  Thompson, Exit, Liquidity, and Majority Rule: Appraisal's Role in
    Corporate Law -- 826
  Note: Reform -- 829

Section E.   Fairness and Disclosure -------------------------------- 830

Introduction -- 830
1. Freeze–Outs and Buyouts: Fair Dealing, Fair Price, and the Appraisal Remedy -- 832
  Introduction -- 832
  (A) Freeze–Outs -- 832
    (1) Alternative Perspectives ----------------------------------- 833
      Brudney & Chirelstein, Fair Shares in Corporate Mergers
        and Takeovers --- 833
      Easterbrook and Fischel, Corporate Control Transactions -- 837
    (2) Fiduciary Duties --- 843
      (a) business purpose -------------------------------------- 843
        Coggins v. New England Patriots Football Club, Inc. --- 844
        Note: Business Purpose and Fairness ------------------- 849
      (b) fair dealing and fair price -------------------------- 849
        Weinberger v. UOP, Inc. ----------------------------- 849
        Note: Market Price As a Measure of the Value of
          Subsidiary Stock ----------------------------------- 864
        Note: Clarifying Weinberger -------------------------- 865
        Note: Kahn v. Lynch Communication Systems ----------- 869
        In re Siliconix Incorporated Shareholders Litigation --- 873
        Glassman v. Unocal Exploration Corp. --------------- 881
        In re Pure Resources, Inc., Shareholders Litigation ----- 884
        Subramanian, Fixing Freezeouts --------------------- 892
        Note: The Siliconix Cases ---------------------------- 897
    (3) Appraisal Exclusivity -------------------------------------- 898
      Note: Interrelations Between Fairness Claims and Ap-
       praisal Actions --- 902
  (B) Management Buyouts -- 905
    Introduction --- 905
    In re Topps Co. Shareholders Litigation ---------------------- 907
    Note: Umpiring the Going Private Process ---------------------- 915
    Note: The Fairness Opinion ------------------------------------ 918
2. The Duty of Care --- 919
  Cede & Co. v. Technicolor, Inc. ----------------------------------- 920
  Note: The Remand in Cede v. Technicolor --------------------------- 929
  Note: The Duty of Care and Merger Negotiations -------------------- 931

3. Disclosure Duties 933
  (A) State Fiduciary Law 933
      Emerald Partners v. Berlin 934
      Emerald Partners v. Berlin 938
      Note: Further Proceedings 939
      Note: The Status of the Fiduciary Duty to Disclose 939
  (B) Federal Disclosure Rules: The Materiality Of Soft Information 945
      Starkman v. Marathon Oil Co. 947
      Basic Incorporated v. Levinson 957
      Note: Misrepresentations, Silence, Mergers and Other Soft
      Information 972
      Note: Materiality and Context 975
      Note: Sources of Legal Obligations to Disclose on the Part of
      Non–Transactors 976

Section F.   The Tender Offer 977

Introduction 977
1. Why Tender Offers? Economic Welfare and Regulatory Strategies .. 979
  (A) The Proponents' View 979
      Romano, A Guide to Takeovers: Theory, Evidence, and Regula-
      tion 979
      Securities and Exchange Commission Report of Recommenda-
      tions of Advisory Committee on Tender Offers Separate
      Statement of Frank H. Easterbrook and Gregg A. Jarrell 982
  (B) The Opponents' View 983
      Herman and Lowenstein, The Efficiency Effects of Hostile
      Take–Overs 983
      Note: The Board Veto 987
  (C) The Intermediate View 989
      Wachter, Takeover Defense When Financial Markets are (Only)
      Relatively Efficient 989
      Note: Adaptation 990
2. Bidder Tactics, Policy Alternatives, and the Williams Act 991
  (A) Bidder Incentives 991
  (B) The Market and Sole Owner Standards 993
  (C) The Williams Act 998
      (1) Bidder Disclosure 999
          Flynn v. Bass Bros. Enterprises, Inc. 1000
          Note: Bidder Disclosure 1004
      (2) Target Disclosure 1005
          Note: Target Disclosure 1006
      (3) Undistorted Choice for Target Shareholders 1008
          (a) withdrawal and proration 1008
          (b) equal treatment 1010
              Note: The All Holders Rule and the Sec's Rulemaking
              Authority 1010
              Gerber v. Computer Associates International, Inc. 1011
              Note: Case for Comparison 1016
              Note: Friendly Acquisitions and the Amendment of
              Rule 14d–10 1016
              Note: Rule 14e–5 1017
          (c) coverage problems 1019
              Note: Defining (and Not Defining) ''Tender Offer'' 1022

3. Management Defenses and Fiduciary Duties ----------------------------------- 1024
   (A) Defensive Tactics -- 1024
       (1) Defenses Requiring Amendment of the Corporate Charter 1024
       (2) Defenses Not Requiring Amendment of the Corporate
           Charter --- 1026
           (a) poison pills: terms and effects ----------------------------- 1027
           (b) the shadow pill and interactions between pills and
               other defensive provisions -------------------------------- 1030
               *Coates, Takeover Defenses in the Shadow of the Pill: A
               Critique of the Scientific Evidence* ----------------------- 1030
               Note: Stonewalling With a Staggered Board -------------- 1034
       (3) Empirical Studies of Defensive Tactics and Shareholder
           Value -- 1034
   (B) Defensive Tactics and the Duty of Loyalty ------------------------------ 1036
       (1) Introduction: Defensive Tactics and Business Judgment ---- 1037
       (2) The Operation of the Unocal Standard ---------------------------- 1040
           (a) poison pills --- 1040
               Moran v. Household International, Inc. ------------------- 1040
               Carmody v. Toll Brothers, Inc. ---------------------------- 1045
               Note: No Hand Pills -- 1051
               Note: The Blasius Rule ------------------------------------- 1052
               Note: Shareholder Protests --------------------------------- 1053
               Note: Corporate Law's Structural Limits on Antitake-
               over Defenses -- 1054
           (b) structural coercion --- 1054
           (c) all cash–all shares tender offers --------------------------- 1056
       (3) The Revlon Auction Duty -- 1058
           Revlon, Inc. v. MacAndrews & Forbes Holdings, Inc. -------- 1058
           Note: Mills v. Macmillan -------------------------------------- 1062
           Note: The Revlon Auction ------------------------------------- 1065
       (4) The Evolution of Unocal and Revlon ---------------------------- 1066
           Paramount Communications, Inc. v. Time Inc. --------------- 1066
           Paramount Communications Inc. v. QVC Network Inc. ------- 1079
           Note: The "Revlon" Duty After Paramount -------------------- 1096
           Unitrin, Inc. v. American General Corp. ----------------------- 1098
           Note: Preclusive Effect --------------------------------------- 1104
           Note: Chesapeake Corp. v. Shore ----------------------------- 1105
           Note: Unocal or Blasius? -------------------------------------- 1110
           Omnicare, Inc. v. NCS Healthcare, Inc. ----------------------- 1111
           Note: Lockups --- 1120
           Note: Comments on the Delaware Antitakeover Cases ------ 1123
4. State Antitakeover Legislation -- 1124
   (A) First Generation Statutes --- 1125
   (B) Second Generation Statutes --- 1126
       (1) Legislation -- 1126
       (2) Constitutionality --- 1129
   (C) Third Generation Statutes --- 1132
       (1) The Delaware Statute --- 1132
       (2) Pennsylvania --- 1132
       (3) Poison Pills and Staggered Boards ---------------------------- 1133
       (4) Constituency Statutes -- 1133

(5) Constitutionality --- 1134

Amanda Acquisition Corp. v. Universal Foods Corp. --------- 1134

Note: Antitakeover Statutes and Shareholder Value -------- 1143

APPENDICES

App.

A. FINANCIAL CONTRACT FORMS -------------------------------------- A–1

Revised Model Simplified Indenture ------------------------------- A–3
Note Purchase Agreement -- A–37
Preferred Stock Charter Provisions------------------------------- A–95
Model Stock Purchase Agreement --------------------------------- A–107
Wachtell, Lipton, Rosen & Katz preferred Shareholder Rights Plan --- A–163

B. STATE CORPORATE CODES--------------------------------------- B–1

Provisions of the Revised Model Business Corporation Act ---------------- B–5
Provisions of the Delaware and New York Statutes ------------------------ B–55

C. THE BANKRUPTCY CODE-- C–1

D. PROVISIONS OF THE FEDERAL SECURITIES LAWS AND RULES PROMULGAT-
ED THEREUNDER --- D–1

E. THE BINOMIAL AND BLACK–SCHOLES OPTION PRICING MODELS ---------- E–1

Alexander, Sharpe, and Bailey, Fundamentals of Investments ------------ E–1

F. TABLES --- F–1

INDEX --- I–1

TABLE OF CASES

Principal cases are in bold type. Non-principal cases are in roman type. References are to Pages.

Abbey v. E.W. Scripps Co., 1995 WL 478957 (Del.Ch.1995), 899

AC Acquisitions Corp. v. Anderson, Clayton & Co., 519 A.2d 103 (Del.Ch.1986), 1056

ACE Ltd. v. Capital Re Corp., 747 A.2d 95 (Del.Ch.1999), 1123

Adams v. United States Distributing Corp., 184 Va. 134, 34 S.E.2d 244 (Va.1945), 503

Agranoff v. Miller, 791 A.2d 880 (Del.Ch. 2001), 150

Alabama By–Products Corp. v. Neal, 588 A.2d 255 (Del.Supr.1991), 904

Aladdin Hotel Co. v. Bloom, 200 F.2d 627 (8th Cir.1953), **342,** 347

Alleco, Inc. v. IBJ Schroder Bank & Trust Co., 745 F.Supp. 1467 (D.Minn.1989), 281

Allied Capital Corp. v. GC–Sun Holdings, L.P., 910 A.2d 1020 (Del.Ch.2006), 281

Amalgamated Sugar Co. v. NL Industries, Inc., 644 F.Supp. 1229 (S.D.N.Y.1986), 1054

Amanda Acquisition Corp. v. Universal Foods Corp., 877 F.2d 496 (7th Cir. 1989), **1134**

American Hardware Corp. v. Savage Arms Corp., 37 Del.Ch. 59, 136 A.2d 690 (Del. Supr.1957), 1053

Andaloro v. PFPC Worldwide, Inc., 2005 WL 2045640 (Del.Ch.2005), 112

Anderson v. Cleveland–Cliffs Iron Co., 87 N.E.2d 384, 40 O.O. 130 (Ohio Com.Pl. 1948), 503

Angelo, Gordon & Co., L.P. v. Allied Riser Communications Corp., 805 A.2d 221 (Del. Ch.2002), 410

Anuhco, Inc. v. Westinghouse Credit Corp., 883 S.W.2d 910 (Mo.App. W.D.1994), 340

Aon Financial Products, Inc. v. Societe Generale, 476 F.3d 90 (2nd Cir.2007), 371

Applebaum v. Avaya, Inc., 812 A.2d 880 (Del. Supr.2002), 661

Appraisal of Ford Holdings, Inc. Preferred Stock, Matter of, 698 A.2d 973 (Del.Ch. 1997), 533

Arizona Western Ins. Co. v. L. L. Constantin & Co., 247 F.2d 388 (3rd Cir.1957), 495

Armstrong v. Marathon Oil Co., 32 Ohio St.3d 397, 513 N.E.2d 776 (Ohio 1987), 905

Arnaud v. Stockgrowers State Bank of Ashland, Kansas, 268 Kan. 163, 992 P.2d 216 (Kan.1999), 152

Arnold v. Society for Sav. Bancorp, Inc. (Arnold II), 678 A.2d 533 (Del.Supr.1996), 939, 940

Arnold v. Society for Sav. Bancorp, Inc. (Arnold I), 650 A.2d 1270 (Del.Supr.1994), 939, 940

Arnold v. Society for Sav. Bancorp, Inc., 1993 WL 526781 (Del.Ch.1993), 1096

Arnold Graphics Industries, Inc. v. Independent Agent Center, Inc., 775 F.2d 38 (2nd Cir.1985), 825

Asarco Inc. v. Court, 611 F.Supp. 468 (D.N.J. 1985), 1054

Aspen Advisors LLC v. United Artists Theatre Co., 861 A.2d 1251 (Del.Supr.2004), 595

Atlas Tool Co., Inc. v. C.I.R., 614 F.2d 860 (3rd Cir.1980), 825

Atrium High Point Ltd. Partnership, In re, 189 B.R. 599 (Bkrtcy.M.D.N.C.1995), 454

Aztec Co., In re, 107 B.R. 585 (Bkrtcy. M.D.Tenn.1989), 453

Balsamides v. Protameen Chemicals, Inc., 160 N.J. 352, 734 A.2d 721 (N.J.1999), 152

Bank of America Nat. Trust and Sav. Ass'n v. 203 North LaSalle Street Partnership, 526 U.S. 434, 119 S.Ct. 1411, 143 L.Ed.2d 607 (1999), **458,** 466, 467

Bank of New York v. BearingPoint, Inc., 824 N.Y.S.2d 752 (N.Y.Sup.2006), 273

Barkan v. Amsted Industries, Inc., 567 A.2d 1279 (Del.Supr.1989), 1065

Barney & Carey Co., In re, 170 B.R. 17 (Bkrtcy.D.Mass.1994), 453

Baron v. Allied Artists Pictures Corp., 337 A.2d 653 (Del.Ch.1975), 501

Barrett v. Denver Tramway Corporation, 53 F.Supp. 198 (D.Del.1943), 501

Basic Inc. v. Levinson, 485 U.S. 224, 108 S.Ct. 978, 99 L.Ed.2d 194 (1988), **957,** 973, 974, 975, 976, 1006

Bay Plastics, Inc., In re, 187 B.R. 315 (Bkrtcy.C.D.Cal.1995), 403

Beloff v. Consolidated Edison Co. of New York, 300 N.Y. 11, 87 N.E.2d 561 (N.Y. 1949), 491

Benchmark Capital Partners IV, L.P. v. Vague, 2002 WL 1732423 (Del.Ch.2002), 537

Bennett v. Propp, 41 Del.Ch. 14, 187 A.2d 405 (Del.Supr.1962), 685

Bergsoe Metal Corp., In re, 910 F.2d 668 (9th Cir.1990), 341

Berwald v. Mission Development Co., 40 Del.Ch. 509, 185 A.2d 480 (Del.Supr. 1962), **640**

Blackmore Partners, L.P. v. Link Energy LLC, 2005 WL 2709639 (Del.Ch.2005), 616

Blackmore Partners, L.P. v. Link Energy LLC, 864 A.2d 80 (Del.Ch.2004), 615

Blasius Industries, Inc. v. Atlas Corp., 564 A.2d 651 (Del.Ch.1988), 1052, 1053, 1110

Blitch v. Peoples Bank, 246 Ga.App. 453, 540 S.E.2d 667 (Ga.App.2000), 153

Blumenthal v. Di Giorgio Fruit Corp., 30 Cal.App.2d 11, 85 P.2d 580 (Cal.App. 1 Dist.1938), 491

BNE Massachusetts Corp. v. Sims, 32 Mass. App.Ct. 190, 588 N.E.2d 14 (Mass.App.Ct. 1992), 82

BNS Inc. v. Koppers Co., Inc., 683 F.Supp. 458 (D.Del.1988), 1134

Bomarko, Inc. v. International Telecharge, Inc., 794 A.2d 1161 (Del.Ch.1999), 150

Borruso v. Communications Telesystems Intern., 753 A.2d 451 (Del.Ch.1999), 150, 152

Bove v. Community Hotel Corp. of Newport, R. I., 105 R.I. 36, 249 A.2d 89 (R.I.1969), **521,** 527, 537

Bowman v. Armour & Co., 17 Ill.2d 43, 160 N.E.2d 753 (Ill.1959), 511, **519,** 521

Brane v. Roth, 590 N.E.2d 587 (Ind.App. 1 Dist.1992), **186,** 189

Breslav v. New York & Queens Elec. Light & Power Co., 249 A.D. 181, 291 N.Y.S. 932 (N.Y.A.D. 2 Dept.1936), 491

Broad v. Rockwell Intern. Corp., 642 F.2d 929 (5th Cir.1981), **584**

Broad v. Rockwell Intern. Corp., 614 F.2d 418 (5th Cir.1980), 592, 594, 595

Brown v. Halbert, 271 Cal.App.2d 252, 76 Cal.Rptr. 781 (Cal.App. 1 Dist.1969), 758

Bryson Properties, XVIII, In re, 961 F.2d 496 (4th Cir.1992), 466

B.S.F. Co. v. Philadelphia Nat. Bank, 42 Del. Ch. 106, 204 A.2d 746 (Del.Supr.1964), 560

BT Securities Corporation, Matter of, 1994 WL 710743 (S.E.C. Release No.1994), 182, 184

Burton v. Exxon Corp., 583 F.Supp. 405 (S.D.N.Y.1984), 509

Business Roundtable v. S.E.C., 905 F.2d 406, 284 U.S.App.D.C. 301 (D.C.Cir.1990), 746

Caiola v. Citibank, N.A., New York, 295 F.3d 312 (2nd Cir.2002), **174**

Cargo Partner AG v. Albatrans, Inc., 352 F.3d 41 (2nd Cir.2003), 826

Carmody v. Toll Bros., Inc., 723 A.2d 1180 (Del.Ch.1998), **1045,** 1051, 1052, 1054

Case v. Los Angeles Lumber Products Co., 308 U.S. 106, 60 S.Ct. 1, 84 L.Ed. 110 (1939), 456

Cavalier Oil Corp. v. Harnett, 564 A.2d 1137 (Del.Supr.1989), 130, 151, 152, 904

Cede & Co. v. JRC Acquisition Corp., 2004 WL 286963 (Del.Ch.2004), 148

Cede & Co. v. Technicolor, Inc., 684 A.2d 289 (Del.Supr.1996), 112, 116, 134

Cede & Co. v. Technicolor, Inc., 634 A.2d 345 (Del.Supr.1993), **920, 929,** 932

Cede & Co. v. Technicolor, Inc., 1990 WL 161084 (Del.Ch.1990), **108,** 147

Cede & Co. v. Technicolor, Inc., 542 A.2d 1182 (Del.Supr.1988), 902, 904

Cede & Co. v. Technicolor, Inc., 2003 WL 23700218 (Del.Ch.2003), 111

Cede & Co., Inc. v. MedPointe Healthcare, Inc., 2004 WL 2093967 (Del.Ch.2004), 118, 148

Cheff v. Mathes, 41 Del.Ch. 494, 199 A.2d 548 (Del.Supr.1964), 685, 1038, 1039

Chesapeake Corp. v. Shore, 771 A.2d 293 (Del.Ch.2000), 1105

Chevron United StatesA., Inc. v. Natural Resources Defense Council, Inc., 467 U.S. 837, 104 S.Ct. 2778, 81 L.Ed.2d 694 (1984), 1011

Chicago, Milwaukee, St. Paul and Pacific R. Co., Matter of, 784 F.2d 831 (7th Cir. 1986), 428

Cinerama, Inc. v. Technicolor, Inc., 663 A.2d 1156 (Del.Supr.1995), 134

Cinerama, Inc. v. Technicolor, Inc., 663 A.2d 1134 (Del.Ch.1994), 929

Citron v. E.I. Du Pont de Nemours & Co., 584 A.2d 490 (Del.Ch.1990), 866, 869

City Capital Associates Ltd. Partnership v. Interco Inc., 551 A.2d 787 (Del.Ch.1988), 1056

City Capital Associates Ltd. Partnership v. Interco, Inc., 696 F.Supp. 1551 (D.Del. 1988), 1134

City of (see name of city)

Class Plaintiffs v. City of Seattle, 955 F.2d 1268 (9th Cir.1992), 358

Cofman v. Acton Corp., 958 F.2d 494 (1st Cir.1992), 561, 562

Coggins v. New England Patriots Football Club, Inc., 397 Mass. 525, 492 N.E.2d 1112 (Mass.1986), 833, **844,** 849, 899

Colonial Ford, Inc., In re, 24 B.R. 1014 (Bkrtcy.D.Utah 1982), 359

Colorado Springs Spring Creek General Imp. Dist., In re City of, 177 B.R. 684 (Bkrtcy. D.Colo.1995), 359

Columbus Mills, Inc. v. Kahn, 259 Ga. 80, 377 S.E.2d 153 (Ga.1989), 899

CompuDyne Corp. v. Shane, 453 F.Supp.2d 807 (S.D.N.Y.2006), 559

Condec Corp. v. Lunkenheimer Co., 43 Del. Ch. 353, 230 A.2d 769 (Del.Ch.1967), 1053

Consolidated Rock Products Co. v. Du Bois, 312 U.S. 510, 61 S.Ct. 675, 85 L.Ed. 982 (1941), **420,** 429, 430

Continental Airlines Corp. v. American General Corp., 575 A.2d 1160 (Del.Supr.1990), 596

Cottle v. Standard Brands Paint Co., 1990 WL 34824 (Del.Ch.1990), 683, 684

Cowles Foundation v. Empire Inc., 589 F.Supp. 669 (S.D.N.Y.1984), 577, 594, 595

Coyne v. MSL Industries, Inc., 1976 WL 765 (N.D.Ill.1976), 688

Craddock–Terry Co. v. Powell, 181 Va. 417, 25 S.E.2d 363 (Va.1943), 503

Credit Lyonnais Bank Nederland, N.V. v. Pathe Communications Corp., 1991 WL 277613 (Del.Ch.1991), 338, **406,** 408

Credit Managers Ass'n of Southern California v. Federal Co., 629 F.Supp. 175 (C.D.Cal. 1985), 403

Cross v. Communication Channels, Inc., 116 Misc.2d 1019, 456 N.Y.S.2d 971 (N.Y.Sup. 1982), 849

Cruden v. Bank of New York, 957 F.2d 961 (2nd Cir.1992), 267

C–T of Virginia, Inc., In re, 958 F.2d 606 (4th Cir.1992), 391

C–T of Virginia, Inc. v. Euroshoe Associates Ltd. Partnership, 953 F.2d 637 (4th Cir. 1992), 403

CTS Corp. v. Dynamics Corp. of America, 481 U.S. 69, 107 S.Ct. 1637, 95 L.Ed.2d 67 (1987), 1129, 1132, 1134

Dalton v. American Inv. Co., 490 A.2d 574 (Del.Ch.1985), 509, 511, **541,** 543

Dart v. Kohlberg, Kravis, Roberts & Co., 1985 WL 21145 (Del.Ch.1985), 535, 538, 539, 540

Deephaven Risk Arb Trading Ltd. v. UnitedGlobalCom, Inc., 2005 WL 1713067 (Del.Ch.2005), **190**

Deutsche Bank AG v. AMBAC Credit Products, LLC, 2006 WL 1867497 (S.D.N.Y. 2006), 371

D & F Const. Inc., Matter of, 865 F.2d 673 (5th Cir.1989), 453

Dibble v. Sumter Ice and Fuel Co., 283 S.C. 278, 322 S.E.2d 674 (S.C.App.1984), 83

Digex Inc. Shareholders Litigation, In re, 789 A.2d 1176 (Del.Ch.2000), 761

Dodge v. Ford Motor Co., 204 Mich. 459, 170 N.W. 668 (Mich.1919), 640

Doft & Co. v. Travelocity.com Inc., 2004 WL 1152338 (Del.Ch.2004), 150

Dowling v. Narragansett Capital Corp., 735 F.Supp. 1105 (D.R.I.1990), 899

Drage v. Santa Fe Pacific Corp., 1995 WL 396370 (Ohio App. 8 Dist.1995), 357

Drexel Burnham Lambert Products Corp. v. MCorp, 1991 WL 165941 (Del.Super.1991), 162

Dynamics Corp. of America v. CTS Corp., 805 F.2d 705 (7th Cir.1986), 1054

Eastern Gas and Fuel Associates, Matter of, 30 S.E.C. 834 (S.E.C. Release No.1950), 528

Edgar v. MITE Corp., 457 U.S. 624, 102 S.Ct. 2629, 73 L.Ed.2d 269 (1982), 1125, 1126, 1130, 1131, 1132

Eisenberg v. Chicago Milwaukee Corp., 537 A.2d 1051 (Del.Ch.1987), **498,** 684, 876

Eliasen v. Itel Corp., 82 F.3d 731 (7th Cir.1996), **205**

Elliott Associates v. J. Henry Schroder Bank & Trust Co., 838 F.2d 66 (2nd Cir.1988), **248**

Elliott Associates, L.P. v. Avatex Corp., 715 A.2d 843 (Del.Supr.1998), 536

Emerald Partners v. Berlin, 726 A.2d 1215 (Del.Supr.1999), **934**

Emerald Partners v. Berlin, 840 A.2d 641 (Del.Supr.2003), 939

Emerald Partners v. Berlin, 787 A.2d 85 (Del.Supr.2001), **938,** 939, 944

English v. Artromick Intern., Inc., 2000 WL 1125637 (Ohio App. 10 Dist.2000), 153

Epstein v. MCA, Inc., 50 F.3d 644 (9th Cir. 1995), 1016

Equity Group Holdings v. DMG, Inc., 576 F.Supp. 1197 (S.D.Fla.1983), 818

Equity–Linked Investors, L.P. v. Adams, 705 A.2d 1040 (Del.Ch.1997), **596,** 609, 611, 613, 1097

Eternity Global Master Fund Ltd. v. Morgan Guar. Trust Co. of N.Y., 375 F.3d 168 (2nd Cir.2004), **359,** 371, 372

Fait v. Hummel, 333 F.3d 854 (7th Cir.2003), 614

Farm Credit of Cent. Florida, ACA v. Polk, 160 B.R. 870 (M.D.Fla.1993), 454

Farris v. Glen Alden Corp., 393 Pa. 427, 143 A.2d 25 (Pa.1958), **812,** 825, 830

Federal United Corp. v. Havender, 24 Del.Ch. 318, 11 A.2d 331 (Del.Supr.1940), 523

FGC Holdings Ltd. v. Teltronics, Inc., 2005 WL 2334357 (Del.Ch.2005), 490

Field v. Trump, 850 F.2d 938 (2nd Cir.1988), 1020, 1022

Financial Industrial Fund, Inc. v. McDonnell Douglas Corp., 474 F.2d 514 (10th Cir. 1973), 976

First Western Bank Wall v. Olsen, 621 N.W.2d 611 (S.D.2001), 153

Fitzgerald v. Fahnestock & Co., Inc., 286 A.D.2d 573, 730 N.Y.S.2d 70 (N.Y.A.D. 1 Dept.2001), 826

Flamm v. Eberstadt, 814 F.2d 1169 (7th Cir. 1987), 973, 976

Fleet Factors Corp., United States v., 901 F.2d 1550 (11th Cir.1990), 341

FLS Holdings, Inc. Shareholders Litigation, In re, 1993 WL 104562 (Del.Ch.1993), 543

Flynn v. Bass Bros. Enterprises, Inc., 744 F.2d 978 (3rd Cir.1984), **1000**

Ford v. Courier–Journal Job Printing Co., 639 S.W.2d 553 (Ky.App.1982), 83

Fort Howard Corp. Shareholders Litigation, In re, 1988 WL 83147 (Del.Ch.1988), 917

Francis I. duPont & Co. v. Universal City Studios, Inc., 312 A.2d 344 (Del. Ch.1973), **71**, 80, 82

Geiger v. American Seeding Mach. Co., 124 Ohio St. 222, 177 N.E. 594 (Ohio 1931), 503

Georgia–Pacific Corp. v. Great Northern Ne-koosa Corp., 731 F.Supp. 38 (D.Me.1990), 1054

Gerber v. Computer Associates Intern., Inc., 303 F.3d 126 (2nd Cir.2002), **1011**, 1016, 1017, 1019

Gerdes v. Reynolds, 28 N.Y.S.2d 622 (N.Y.Sup.1941), 755

Geren v. Quantum Chemical Corp., 832 F.Supp. 728 (S.D.N.Y.1993), 336

Geyer v. Ingersoll Publications Co., 621 A.2d 784 (Del.Ch.1992), 338, 408

Gimbel v. Signal Companies, Inc., 316 A.2d 619 (Del.Supr.1974), 809

Glassman v. Unocal Exploration Corp., 777 A.2d 242 (Del.Supr.2001), **881**, 898

Glazer v. Formica Corp., 964 F.2d 149 (2nd Cir.1992), 976

Glinert v. Wickes Companies, Inc., 1990 WL 34703 (Del.Ch.1990), 595

Goldman v. Postal Telegraph, 52 F.Supp. 763 (D.Del.1943), **504,** 506

Goldstein v. S.E.C., 451 F.3d 873, 371 U.S.App.D.C. 358 (D.C.Cir.2006), 12, 735

Gonsalves v. Straight Arrow Publishers, Inc., 1996 WL 696936 (Del.Ch.1996), 82

Grand Metropolitan Public Ltd. Co. v. Pills-bury Co., 558 A.2d 1049 (Del.Ch.1988), 1057

Green v. Hamilton Intern. Corp., 493 F.Supp. 596 (S.D.N.Y.1979), 578

Guaranty Trust Co. of New York v. Chase Nat. Bank of City of New York, 302 N.Y. 658, 98 N.E.2d 474 (N.Y.1951), 429

Guttmann v. Illinois Cent. R. Co., 189 F.2d 927 (2nd Cir.1951), 497, 498

Halsey, Stuart & Co. Inc., Matter of, 30 S.E.C. 106 (S.E.C. Release No.1949), 690, 691

Hanson Trust PLC v. SCM Corp., 774 F.2d 47 (2nd Cir.1985), 1022, 1023, 1024

Harff v. Kerkorian, 347 A.2d 133 (Del.Supr. 1975), 592, 595

Hariton v. Arco Electronics, Inc., 40 Del. Ch. 326, 182 A.2d 22 (Del.Ch.1962), **818,** 824, 825

Harris v. Carter, 582 A.2d 222 (Del.Ch.1990), 755

Harris v. Union Elec. Co., 787 F.2d 355 (8th Cir.1986), 265

Harris v. Union Elec. Co., 622 S.W.2d 239 (Mo.App. E.D.1981), 265

Harris Trust and Sav. Bank v. E–II Holdings, Inc., 722 F.Supp. 429 (N.D.Ill.1989), 281

HB Korenvaes Investments, L.P. v. Marriott Corp., 1993 WL 257422 (Del.Ch. 1993), 336, **563**, 575, 579, 592, 593

Healthco Intern., Inc., In re, 208 B.R. 288 (Bkrtcy.D.Mass.1997), 405, 407, 408

HealthExtras, Inc. v. SG Cowen Securities Corp., 2004 WL 97699 (S.D.N.Y.2004), 559

Hennepin County 1986 Recycling Bond Litigation, In re, 540 N.W.2d 494 (Minn. 1995), 266

Herald Co. v. Seawell, 472 F.2d 1081 (10th Cir.1972), 685

HMO–W Inc. v. SSM Health Care System, 234 Wis.2d 707, 611 N.W.2d 250 (Wis. 2000), 153

Honigman v. Green Giant Co., 208 F.Supp. 754 (D.Minn.1961), 755

Hyde Park Partners, L.P. v. Connolly, 839 F.2d 837 (1st Cir.1988), 1134

IBP, Inc. v. Tyson Foods, Inc., In re, 789 A.2d 14 (Del.Ch.2001), **793**

Indu Craft, Inc. v. Bank of Baroda, 47 F.3d 490 (2nd Cir.1995), 340

In re (see name of party)

Integra Realty Resources, Inc., In re, 198 B.R. 352 (Bkrtcy.D.Colo.1996), 403

International Broth. of Teamsters General Fund v. Fleming Companies, Inc., 975 P.2d 907 (Okla.1999), 1053

IRA for Benefit of Oppenheimer v. Brenner Companies, Inc., 107 N.C.App. 16, 419 S.E.2d 354 (N.C.App.1992), 899

Ivanhoe Partners v. Newmont Min. Corp., 535 A.2d 1334 (Del.Supr.1987), 1055

Ivanhoe Partners v. Newmont Min. Corp., 533 A.2d 585 (Del.Ch.1987), 879

IXC Communications, Inc., In re v. Cincinnati Bell, Inc., 1999 WL 1009174 (Del.Ch. 1999), 1122

Jade Oil & Gas Co., 44 S.E.C. 45 (1969)

Jamie Securities Co. v. The Ltd., Inc., 880 F.2d 1572 (2nd Cir.1989), 578

Jedwab v. MGM Grand Hotels, Inc., 509 A.2d 584 (Del.Ch.1986), 539

Jewel Recovery, L.P. v. Gordon, 196 B.R. 348 (N.D.Tex.1996), 405

John Hancock Mut. Life Ins. Co. v. Carolina Power & Light Co., 717 F.2d 664 (2nd Cir.1983), 265

Johnson v. Bradley Knitting Co., 228 Wis. 566, 280 N.W. 688 (Wis.1938), 491

Johnson v. Trueblood, 629 F.2d 287 (3rd Cir. 1980), 1038

Jones v. St. Louis Structural Steel Co., 267 Ill.App. 576 (Ill.App. 4 Dist.1932), 503

Kahn v. Lynch Communication Systems, Inc. (Lynch II), 669 A.2d 79 (Del.Supr.1995), 869

Kahn v. Lynch Communication Systems, Inc., 638 A.2d 1110 (Del.Supr.1994), 869

Kahn v. United States Sugar Corp., 1985 WL 4449 (Del.Ch.1985), **677,** 683, 684, 688

Kahn on Behalf of DeKalb Genetics Corp. v. Roberts, 679 A.2d 460 (Del.Supr.1996), 685

Kaiser Aluminum Corp. v. Matheson, 681 A.2d 392 (Del.Supr.1996), 575, 578

Kaiser Steel Corp., In re, 952 F.2d 1230 (10th Cir.1991), 405

Kass v. Eastern Air Lines, Inc., 1986 WL 13008 (Del.Ch.1986), 357

Katz v. Oak Industries Inc., 508 A.2d 873 (Del.Ch.1986), **348,** 356, 357

Keller v. Wilson & Co., 21 Del.Ch. 391, 190 A. 115 (Del.Supr.1936), 523

Kern v. Chicago & E. I. R. Co., 6 Ill.App.3d 247, 285 N.E.2d 501 (Ill.App. 1 Dist.1972), 495

Kessler v. General Cable Corp., 92 Cal.App.3d 531, 155 Cal.Rptr. 94 (Cal.App. 2 Dist. 1979), 595

Kirschner Brothers Oil, Inc. v. Natomas Co., 185 Cal.App.3d 784, 229 Cal.Rptr. 899 (Cal.App. 1 Dist.1986), 535

Klang v. Smith's Food & Drug Centers, Inc., 702 A.2d 150 (Del.Supr.1997), **387,** 391

K.M.C. Co., Inc. v. Irving Trust Co., 757 F.2d 752 (6th Cir.1985), 339, 340

Knapp v. North Am. Rockwell Corp., 506 F.2d 361 (3rd Cir.1974), 825

Koppel v. Middle States Petroleum Corp., 197 Misc. 479, 96 N.Y.S.2d 38 (N.Y.Sup.1950), 495

Kowal v. International Business Machines Corporate Securities Litigation, 163 F.3d 102 (2nd Cir.1998), 652

Kupetz v. Wolf, 845 F.2d 842 (9th Cir.1988), 403

Laird v. I. C. C., 691 F.2d 147 (3rd Cir.1982), 849

Langfelder v. Universal Laboratories, Inc., 163 F.2d 804 (3rd Cir.1947), 503

Lawson Mardon Wheaton, Inc. v. Smith, 160 N.J. 383, 734 A.2d 738 (N.J.1999), 150, 152

Lear Corp. Shareholder Litigation, In re, 926 A.2d 94 (Del.Ch.2007), 916

Le Beau v. M. G. Bancorporation, Inc., 1998 WL 44993 (Del.Ch.1998), **136,** 146, 147, 148, 149

Lerro v. Quaker Oats Co., 897 F.Supp. 1131 (N.D.Ill.1995), 1016

Levco Alternative Fund Ltd. v. Reader's Digest Ass'n, Inc., 803 A.2d 428 (Del. Supr.2002), **741**

Leverso v. Lieberman, 18 F.3d 1527 (11th Cir.1994), 358

Levien v. Sinclair Oil Corp., 261 A.2d 911 (Del.Ch.1969), 644

Lewis v. Vogelstein, 699 A.2d 327 (Del.Ch. 1997), **711**

Lindner Fund, Inc. v. Waldbaum, Inc., 604 N.Y.S.2d 32, 624 N.E.2d 160 (N.Y.1993), 941

Lionel Corp., In re, 722 F.2d 1063 (2nd Cir. 1983), 452

L. L. Constantin & Co. v. R. P. Holding Corp., 56 N.J.Super. 411, 153 A.2d 378 (N.J.Super.Ch.1959), 495

Lohnes v. Level 3 Communications, Inc., 272 F.3d 49 (1st Cir.2001), 561

Lorenz v. CSX Corp., 1 F.3d 1406 (3rd Cir. 1993), 594

Loudon v. Archer–Daniels–Midland Co., 700 A.2d 135 (Del.Supr.1997), 943

LTV Steel Company, Inc., In re, 2001 WL 1822360 (N.D.Ohio 2001), 304

LTV Steel Company, Inc., In re, 274 B.R. 278 (Bkrtcy.N.D.Ohio 2001), **300**

Lumber Exchange Ltd. Partnership, In re, 125 B.R. 1000 (Bkrtcy.D.Minn.1991), 466

Lynch v. Vickers Energy Corp. (Lynch I), 429 A.2d 497 (Del.Supr.1981), 873

Lynch v. Vickers Energy Corp., 383 A.2d 278 (Del.Supr.1977), 933

Lynch v. Vickers Energy Corp., 351 A.2d 570 (Del.Ch.1976), 933

Maffia v. American Woolen Co, 125 F.Supp. 465 (S.D.N.Y.1954), 503

Malone v. Brincat, 722 A.2d 5 (Del.Supr. 1998), 879, 943

Malpiede v. Townson, 780 A.2d 1075 (Del. Supr.2001), 932

Marx v. Computer Sciences Corp., 507 F.2d 485 (9th Cir.1974), 976

Matter of (see name of party)

Matthews v. Groove Networks, Inc., 2005 WL 3498423 (Del.Ch.2005), 533

McDermott Inc. v. Lewis, 531 A.2d 206 (Del. Supr.1987), 538

McMullen v. Beran, 1999 WL 1135146 (Del. Ch.1999), 1097

Meckel v. Continental Resources Co., 758 F.2d 811 (2nd Cir.1985), 578

Mellon Bank, N.A. v. Metro Communications, Inc., 945 F.2d 635 (3rd Cir.1991), 404

Mellor, In re, 734 F.2d 1396 (9th Cir.1984), 445

Mendel v. Carroll, 651 A.2d 297 (Del.Ch. 1994), 761, 763

Mentor Graphics Corp. v. Quickturn Design Systems, Inc., 728 A.2d 25 (Del.Ch.1998), 1105

Merritt–Chapman & Scott Corp. v. New York Trust Co., 184 F.2d 954 (2nd Cir.1950), 578

Metropolitan Life Ins. Co. v. RJR Nabisco, Inc., 716 F.Supp. 1504 (S.D.N.Y. 1989), **323,** 336, 340

MFS/Sun Life Trust–High Yield Series v. Van Dusen Airport Services Co., 910 F.Supp. 913 (S.D.N.Y.1995), 404, 405

Miami Center Associates, Ltd., In re, 144 B.R. 937 (Bkrtcy.S.D.Fla.1992), 453

Mills Acquisition Co. v. Macmillan, Inc., 559 A.2d 1261 (Del.Supr.1989), 1062, 1065, 1122

Minstar Acquiring Corp. v. AMF Inc., 621 F.Supp. 1252 (S.D.N.Y.1985), 1054

MM Companies, Inc. v. Liquid Audio, Inc., 813 A.2d 1118 (Del.Supr.2003), 1110

Monarch Beach Venture, Ltd., In re, 166 B.R. 428 (C.D.Cal.1993), 453

MONY Group, Inc. Shareholder Litigation, In re, 853 A.2d 661 (Del.Ch.2004), 195

Moody v. Security Pacific Business Credit, Inc., 971 F.2d 1056 (3rd Cir.1992), 405

Moran v. Household Intern., Inc., 500 A.2d 1346 (Del.Supr.1985), **1040,** 1054, 1056

Morgan Stanley & Co., Inc. v. Archer Daniels Midland Co., 570 F.Supp. 1529 (S.D.N.Y.1983), **258,** 265

Morris v. American Public Utilities Co., 14 Del.Ch. 136, 122 A. 696 (Del.Ch.1923), 491

M.P.M. Enterprises, Inc. v. Gilbert, 731 A.2d 790 (Del.Supr.1999), 136

Mueller v. Howard Aircraft Corp., 329 Ill. App. 570, 70 N.E.2d 203 (Ill.App. 1 Dist. 1946), 578

Mullen v. Academy Life Ins. Co., 705 F.2d 971 (8th Cir.1983), 899

Munford, Inc., Matter of, 98 F.3d 604 (11th Cir.1996), 405

Mutual Sav. Life Ins. Co. v. James River Corp. of Virginia, 716 So.2d 1172 (Ala. 1998), 266

Nite Lite Inns, In re, 17 B.R. 367 (Bkrtcy. S.D.Cal.1982), 429, 452

North American Catholic Educational Programming Foundation, Inc. v. Rob Gheewalla, 2006 WL 2588971 (Del.Ch.2006), 410

Northway, Inc. v. TSC Industries, Inc., 512 F.2d 324 (7th Cir.1975), 945

Norwest Bank Worthington v. Ahlers, 485 U.S. 197, 108 S.Ct. 963, 99 L.Ed.2d 169 (1988), 456, 466

Octagon Gas Systems, Inc. v. Rimmer, 995 F.2d 948 (10th Cir.1993), 300

Omnicare, Inc. v. NCS Healthcare, Inc., 818 A.2d 914 (Del.Supr.2003), **1111,** 1122

Orban v. Field, 1997 WL 153831 (Del.Ch. 1997), 506

Orban v. Field, 1993 WL 547187 (Del.Ch. 1993), 616

Outlook/Century, Ltd., In re, 127 B.R. 650 (Bkrtcy.N.D.Cal.1991), 466

Page Mill Asset Management v. Credit Suisse First Boston Corp., 2000 WL 335557 (S.D.N.Y.2000), 338

Panter v. Marshall Field & Co., 646 F.2d 271 (7th Cir.1981), 1008, 1038

Paramount Communications Inc. v. QVC Network Inc., 637 A.2d 34 (Del.Supr. 1994), **1079,** 1096, 1120, 1122

Paramount Communications, Inc. v. Time Inc., 571 A.2d 1140 (Del.Supr. 1989), **1066**

Parkinson v. West End St. Ry. Co., 173 Mass. 446, 53 N.E. 891 (Mass.1899), 560

Paskill Corp. v. Alcoma Corp., 747 A.2d 549 (Del.Supr.2000), 13, 149

Penn Central Securities Litigation, In re, 367 F.Supp. 1158 (E.D.Pa.1973), 818

Perl v. IU Intern. Corp., 61 Haw. 622, 607 P.2d 1036 (Hawai'i 1980), 899

Perlman v. Feldmann, 219 F.2d 173 (2nd Cir.1955), **747,** 755, 758

Petry v. Harwood Electric Co., 280 Pa. 142, 124 A. 302 (Pa.1924), 503

Phelps Dodge Corp. v. Cyprus Amax Minerals Co., 1999 WL 1054255 (Del.Ch.1999), 1122

Phillips v. LCI Intern., Inc., 190 F.3d 609 (4th Cir.1999), 974

Piemonte v. New Boston Garden Corp., 377 Mass. 719, 387 N.E.2d 1145 (Mass.1979), 82

Pittelman v. Pearce, 8 Cal.Rptr.2d 359 (Cal. App. 2 Dist.1992), 595

Pittsburgh Terminal Corp. v. The Baltimore & Ohio R. Co., 680 F.2d 933 (3rd Cir. 1982), 578, 593

Plaine v. McCabe, 797 F.2d 713 (9th Cir. 1986), 1004

Polaroid Corp. v. Disney, 862 F.2d 987 (3rd Cir.1988), 1010

Polk v. Good, 507 A.2d 531 (Del.Supr.1986), 685

Popp Telcom v. American Sharecom, Inc., 210 F.3d 928 (8th Cir.2000), 899

Porter v. Texas Commerce Bancshares, Inc., 1989 WL 120358 (Del.Ch.1989), 905

PPM America, Inc. v. Marriott Corp., 820 F.Supp. 970 (D.Md.1993), 336

Prescott, Ball & Turben v. LTV Corp., 531 F.Supp. 213 (S.D.N.Y.1981), 578

Pritchard v. Mead, 155 Wis.2d 431, 455 N.W.2d 263 (Wis.App.1990), 899

Procter & Gamble Co. v. Bankers Trust Co., 925 F.Supp. 1270 (S.D.Ohio 1996), 183

Production Resources Group, L.L.C. v. NCT Group, Inc., 863 A.2d 772 (Del.Ch.2004), 408

Providence & Worcester Co. v. Baker, 378 A.2d 121 (Del.Supr.1977), 1054

Pryor v. United States Steel Corp., 794 F.2d 52 (2nd Cir.1986), 1009

Public Service Co. of New Hampshire v. Consolidated Utilities and Communications, Inc., 846 F.2d 803 (1st Cir.1988), 446

Pullman Const. Industries Inc., In re, 107 B.R. 909 (Bkrtcy.N.D.Ill.1989), 466

Pure Resources, Inc., Shareholders Litigation, In re, 808 A.2d 421 (Del.Ch. 2002), **884**

PWS Holding Corp., In re, 228 F.3d 224 (3rd Cir.2000), 404, 405

Quickturn Design Systems, Inc. v. Shapiro, 721 A.2d 1281 (Del.Supr.1998), 1051, 1052, 1054

Rabinowitz v. Kaiser–Frazer Corp., 111 N.Y.S.2d 539 (N.Y.Sup.1952), 267
Rabkin v. Hunt Chemical Corp., 498 A.2d 1099 (Del.Supr.1985), 865, 866, 868, 899
Rabkin v. Olin Corp., 1990 WL 47648 (Del. Ch.1990), 869, 870
Radol v. Thomas, 772 F.2d 244 (6th Cir. 1985), 1006
Ramirez v. Amsted Industries, Inc., 86 N.J. 332, 431 A.2d 811 (N.J.1981), 826
Rapid–American Corp. v. Harris, 603 A.2d 796 (Del.Supr.1992), **127,** 133, 149
Rath v. Rath Packing Co., 257 Iowa 1277, 136 N.W.2d 410 (Iowa 1965), 824
Rauch v. RCA Corp., 861 F.2d 29 (2nd Cir. 1988), 535
Reiss v. Financial Performance Corp., 738 N.Y.S.2d 658, 764 N.E.2d 958 (N.Y.2001), 562
Reiss v. Financial Performance Corp., 279 A.D.2d 13, 715 N.Y.S.2d 29 (N.Y.A.D. 1 Dept.2000), 562
Reiss v. Pan American World Airways, Inc., 711 F.2d 11 (2nd Cir.1983), 976
Revco D.S., Inc., In re, 118 B.R. 468 (Bkrtcy. N.D.Ohio 1990), 405
Revlon, Inc. v. MacAndrews & Forbes Holdings, Inc., 506 A.2d 173 (Del.Supr. 1985), 616, 911, 916, **1058,** 1062, 1065, 1066, 1097, 1122
Revlon, Inc. v. Pantry Pride, Inc., 621 F.Supp. 804 (D.Del.1985), 1004
Revlon, In re, CCH Fed.Sec.L.Rep. para. 84,006 (1986), 1007
Rigel Corp. v. Cutchall, 245 Neb. 118, 511 N.W.2d 519 (Neb.1994), 152
Roeder v. Alpha Industries, Inc., 814 F.2d 22 (1st Cir.1987), 976
Rosenblatt v. Getty Oil Co., 493 A.2d 929 (Del.Supr.1985), 865, 866, 869, 873
Rothschild Intern. Corp. v. Liggett Group Inc., 474 A.2d 133 (Del.Supr. 1984), 503, 509, **529,** 533, 535, 613
RP Acquisition Corp. v. Staley Continental, Inc., 686 F.Supp. 476 (D.Del.1988), 1134
Ryan v. Gifford, 918 A.2d 341 (Del.Ch. 2007), **723**

Sanders v. Cuba R. Co., 21 N.J. 78, 120 A.2d 849 (N.J.1956), 498
Sanders v. Wang, 1999 WL 1044880 (Del.Ch. 1999), 722
Sarrouf v. New England Patriots Football Club, Inc., 397 Mass. 542, 492 N.E.2d 1122 (Mass.1986), 82
Schneider v. Lazard Freres & Co., 159 A.D.2d 291, 552 N.Y.S.2d 571 (N.Y.A.D. 1 Dept. 1990), 918

Schnell v. Chris–Craft Industries, Inc., 285 A.2d 437 (Del.Supr.1971), 1053
Schreiber v. Burlington Northern, Inc., 472 U.S. 1, 105 S.Ct. 2458, 86 L.Ed.2d 1 (1985), 1009, 1011
S.E.C. v. Carter Hawley Hale Stores, Inc., 760 F.2d 945 (9th Cir.1985), 1024
S.E.C. v. Zandford, 535 U.S. 813, 122 S.Ct. 1899, 153 L.Ed.2d 1 (2002), 976
Securities and Exchange Commission v. Texas Gulf Sulphur Co., 401 F.2d 833 (2nd Cir.1968), 976
Shamrock Holdings, Inc. v. Polaroid Corp., 559 A.2d 278 (Del.Ch.1989), 740
Sharon Steel Corp. v. Chase Manhattan Bank, N.A., 691 F.2d 1039 (2nd Cir. 1982), **274,** 279, 280, 281, 577
Shenandoah Life Ins. Co. v. Valero Energy Corp., 1988 WL 63491 (Del.Ch.1988), 265
Shintom Co., Ltd. v. Audiovox Corp., 888 A.2d 225 (Del.Supr.2005), 495
Shoe–Town, Inc. Stockholders Litigation, In re, 1990 WL 13475 (Del.Ch.1990), 919
Sieg Co. v. Kelly, 568 N.W.2d 794 (Iowa 1997), 136, 152
Siegman v. Palomar Medical Technologies, Inc., 1998 WL 118201 (Del.Ch.1998), 487
Siliconix Inc. Shareholders Litigation, In re, 2001 WL 716787 (Del.Ch.2001), **873,** 897, 898
Simons v. Cogan, 542 A.2d 785 (Del.Ch.1987), 594, 595
Sinclair Oil Corp. v. Levien, 280 A.2d 717 (Del.Supr.1971), 509, 644
Singer v. Magnavox Co., 380 A.2d 969 (Del. Supr.1977), 831
Smith v. Van Gorkom, 488 A.2d 858 (Del. Supr.1985), 919, 931
Snyder, Matter of, 967 F.2d 1126 (7th Cir. 1992), 466
Sound Radio, Inc., Matter of, 93 B.R. 849 (Bkrtcy.D.N.J.1988), 452
South Carolina Nat. Bank v. Stone, 749 F.Supp. 1419 (D.S.C.1990), 358
Squires v. Balbach Co., 177 Neb. 465, 129 N.W.2d 462 (Neb.1964), 496
SS & C Technologies, Inc., Shareholders Litigation, In re, 911 A.2d 816 (Del.Ch.2006), 917
Staffin v. Greenberg, 672 F.2d 1196 (3rd Cir. 1982), 976
Stahl v. Apple Bancorp, Inc., 1990 WL 114222 (Del.Ch.1990), 1053
Stahl v. Apple Bancorp, Inc., 579 A.2d 1115 (Del.Ch.1990), 1053
Stanton v. Republic Bank of South Chicago, 144 Ill.2d 472, 163 Ill.Dec. 524, 581 N.E.2d 678 (Ill.1991), 153
Starkman v. Marathon Oil Co., 772 F.2d 231 (6th Cir.1985), **947,** 974, 975, 1006
State Nat. Bank of El Paso v. Farah Mfg. Co., Inc., 678 S.W.2d 661 (Tex.App.-El Paso 1984), 340
State Teachers Retirement Bd. v. Fluor Corp., 654 F.2d 843 (2nd Cir.1981), 976

Steinberg v. Amplica, Inc., 233 Cal.Rptr. 249, 729 P.2d 683 (Cal.1986), 901

Stepak v. Schey, 51 Ohio St.3d 8, 553 N.E.2d 1072 (Ohio 1990), 899, 905

Stephenson v. Plastics Corp. of America, 276 Minn. 400, 150 N.W.2d 668 (Minn.1967), 578

St. Louis Southwestern Ry. Co. v. Loeb, 318 S.W.2d 246 (Mo.1958), 496

Stringer v. Car Data Systems, Inc., 314 Or. 576, 841 P.2d 1183 (Or.1992), 899

Stroud v. Grace, 606 A.2d 75 (Del.Supr.1992), 1050, 1053

Sturgeon Petroleums, Ltd. v. Merchants Petroleum Co., 147 Cal.App.3d 134, 195 Cal. Rptr. 29 (Cal.App. 2 Dist.1983), 901

Sturges v. Knapp, 31 Vt. 1 (Vt.1858), 250

Sullivan Money Management, Inc. v. FLS Holdings Inc., 1992 WL 345453 (Del.Ch. 1992), 536

Sunstates Corp. Shareholder Litigation, In re, 788 A.2d 530 (Del.Ch.2001), 496

Swanson v. Wabash, Inc., 577 F.Supp. 1308 (N.D.Ill.1983), 1018

Swope v. Siegel–Robert, Inc., 243 F.3d 486 (8th Cir.2001), 153

Tanzer v. International General Industries, Inc., 379 A.2d 1121 (Del.Supr.1977), 849

Taylor v. First Union Corp. of South Carolina, 857 F.2d 240 (4th Cir.1988), 976

Tele–Communications, Inc. Shareholders Litigation, In re, 2005 WL 3642727 (Del.Ch. 2005), 743

Terry v. Penn Central Corp., 668 F.2d 188 (3rd Cir.1981), 818

Thorpe by Castleman v. CERBCO, Inc., 676 A.2d 436 (Del.Supr.1996), 759, 761, 809

TLX Acquisition Corp. v. Telex Corp., 679 F.Supp. 1022 (W.D.Okla.1987), 1134

Topps Co. Shareholders Litigation, In re, 926 A.2d 58 (Del.Ch.2007), **907**, 915

Tranel, In re, 940 F.2d 1168 (8th Cir.1991), 447

Treves v. Menzies, 37 Del.Ch. 330, 142 A.2d 520 (Del.Ch.1958), 503

Tri–Continental Corp. v. Battye, 31 Del. Ch. 523, 74 A.2d 71 (Del.Supr.1950), **6,** 13, 23, 149

Trident Center v. Connecticut General Life Ins. Co., 847 F.2d 564 (9th Cir.1988), 267

Tri–Star Pictures, Inc., Litigation, In re, 634 A.2d 319 (Del.Supr.1993), 941, 943

TSC Industries, Inc. v. Northway, Inc., 426 U.S. 438, 96 S.Ct. 2126, 48 L.Ed.2d 757 (1976), 945

TS Industries, Inc., In re, 117 B.R. 682 (Bkrtcy.D.Utah 1990), 359

Turner v. Bituminous Cas. Co., 397 Mich. 406, 244 N.W.2d 873 (Mich.1976), 826

Tyson Foods, Inc., In re, 919 A.2d 563 (Del. Ch.2007), 726

Tyson Foods, Inc. v. McReynolds, 865 F.2d 99 (6th Cir.1989), 1134

Union Illinois 1995 Inv. Ltd. Partnership v. Union Financial Group, Ltd., 847 A.2d 340 (Del.Ch.2004), 118

United California Bank v. Prudential Ins. Co. of America, 140 Ariz. 238, 681 P.2d 390 (Ariz.App. Div. 1 1983), 340

United Sav. Ass'n of Texas v. Timbers of Inwood Forest Associates, Ltd., 484 U.S. 365, 108 S.Ct. 626, 98 L.Ed.2d 740 (1988), 429, 444

United States v. _____ (see opposing party)

Unitrin, Inc. v. American General Corp., 651 A.2d 1361 (Del.Supr.1995), **1098,** 1104, 1105, 1106, 1110

Universal City Studios, Inc. v. Francis I. duPont & Co., 334 A.2d 216 (Del.Supr. 1975), **77**

Unocal Corp. v. Mesa Petroleum Co., 493 A.2d 946 (Del.Supr.1985), 685, 740, 1039, 1054, 1055, 1056, 1057, 1058, 1066, 1099, 1104, 1105, 1110, 1111, 1122

Vadnais Lumber Supply, Inc., In re, 100 B.R. 127 (Bkrtcy.D.Mass.1989), 404

Valente v. PepsiCo, Inc., 454 F.Supp. 1228 (D.Del.1978), 1005

Valuation of Common Stock of Libby, McNeill & Libby, In re, 406 A.2d 54 (Me. 1979), 82

Van Gemert v. Boeing Co., 553 F.2d 812 (2nd Cir.1977), 583

Van Gemert v. Boeing Co., 520 F.2d 1373 (2nd Cir.1975), 578, **579,** 593

VantagePoint Venture Partners 1996 v. Examen, Inc., 871 A.2d 1108 (Del.Supr.2005), 538

VFB LLC v. Campbell Soup Co., 482 F.3d 624 (3rd Cir.2007), 406

Wabash Ry. Co. v. Barclay, 280 U.S. 197, 50 S.Ct. 106, 74 L.Ed. 368 (1930), 497, 498

Walker v. Action Industries, Inc., 802 F.2d 703 (4th Cir.1986), 689

Walt Disney Co. Derivative Litigation, In re, 907 A.2d 693 (Del.Ch.2005), 721

Walt Disney Co. Derivative Litigation, In re, 825 A.2d 275 (Del.Ch.2003), 721

Walter J. Schloss Associates v. Arkwin Industries, Inc., 472 N.Y.S.2d 605, 460 N.E.2d 1090 (N.Y.1984), 899

Walter J. Schloss Associates v. Chesapeake and Ohio Ry. Co., 73 Md.App. 727, 536 A.2d 147 (Md.App.1988), 899

Warner Communications Inc. v. Chris–Craft Industries, Inc., 583 A.2d 962 (Del.Ch. 1989), 536, 537

Weigel Broadcasting Company v. Lloyd C. Smith, 1996 WL 714630 (Ill.App. 1 Dist. 1996), 153

Weinberger v. UOP, Inc., 457 A.2d 701 (Del.Supr.1983), 82, 111, 118, **849,** 865, 866, 867, 899, 901, 930

Wells v. Shearson Lehman/American Exp., Inc., 127 A.D.2d 200, 514 N.Y.S.2d 1 (N.Y.A.D. 1 Dept.1987), 918

Wertheim Schroder & Co., Inc. v. Avon Products, Inc., 1993 WL 126427 (S.D.N.Y.1993), **645**

Western Foundry Co. v. Wicker, 403 Ill. 260, 85 N.E.2d 722 (Ill.1949), 491

Wieboldt Stores, Inc. v. Schottenstein, 94 B.R. 488 (N.D.Ill.1988), **394,** 403, 404, 405

Yeager v. Paul Semonin Co., 691 S.W.2d 227 (Ky.App.1985), 899

Zahn v. Transamerica Corp., 162 F.2d 36 (3rd Cir.1947), 496

Zahn v. Yucaipa Capital Fund, 218 B.R. 656 (D.R.I.1998), 403

Zenith Electronics Corp., In re, 241 B.R. 92 (Bkrtcy.D.Del.1999), **434,** 443, 446, 447, 453

Zetlin v. Hanson Holdings, Inc., 421 N.Y.S.2d 877, 397 N.E.2d 387 (N.Y.1979), 758

Zimmerman v. Home Shopping Network, Inc., 1990 WL 140890 (Del.Ch.1990), 559

Zirn v. VLI Corp. (Zirn II), 681 A.2d 1050 (Del.Supr.1996), 939, 941

Zirn v. VLI Corp. (Zirn I), 621 A.2d 773 (Del.Supr.1993), 939, 940

Zupnick v. Goizueta, 698 A.2d 384 (Del.Ch. 1997), 721

*

CORPORATE FINANCE

*

PART I

VALUING THE FIRM AND ITS SECURITIES

INTRODUCTION

Valuation—of the corporate firm and of its securities—is a theme that pervades and loosely unifies the cases and readings collected in this book, both those legal in character and those oriented to economics and business. Many of the most interesting legal issues in the field of corporate finance in some sense require an answer to the question of how much the firm and its securities are worth. That the question is partly one of definition takes nothing away from its complexity. That the question will not admit of a verifiable answer once the definitional problems are worked out detracts neither from its importance nor its frequency of occurrence.

1. *Valuation and the Objective of the Firm.*

Valuation and value maximization are of central importance to those who manage a corporation's business and finances. Ordinary equity investors expect management to enhance their economic welfare through stock ownership—for that reason the investor pays her money; for that reason the investor takes her chance; the investor admits no other assumption. Accordingly, for the equity investor the objective of the firm can be stated easily: it is to maximize the firm's value to its stockholders, subject to whatever constraints may be imposed externally. It is, of course, far from self-evident that corporate managers actually behave in accordance with this norm. Moreover, a substantial body of opinion supports a contrary assumption. Nevertheless, value maximization is a useful organizing principle. It provides a basis for further discussion of corporate goals and management behavior, and conforms reasonably closely to investors' expectations.

Even as we adopt this description of the firm's objective, we immediately have to refine it. When we speak of "maximizing the value of the corporation" or "shareholder value" what is the relevant measure of worth? Should we focus on the firm's after-tax profits? Or should we look at earnings per share, or dividends, or rate of return on equity, or growth prospects, to name a few of the better known standards?

For at least three reasons it appears that none of these measures is sufficiently comprehensive and unambiguous to serve our purpose. First, when we assert that the firm should (for example) "maximize profits," there remains the question whether we mean *current* or *future* profits. Is a modest profit this year as good as, or worse or better than, a much larger profit at a later time? To answer, we must know exactly how much larger and how much later, since "profits" comprehend both possibilities. Second, once we focus on future profits we must recognize that the future is uncertain. What should be done to reflect this factor of investment risk? Is the expectation of a small but relatively safe profit as good as, or worse or better than, the expectation of a large but relatively risky one? This question cannot be answered by reference only to a norm of profit maximization; something must also be known about investors' attitudes towards risk-taking. Taken by itself, therefore, the familiar profit-maximizing standard leaves open important questions about timing and risk. Third comes the question as to how the term "profit" is to be defined—the familiar profit-maximizing standard lacks a clearly established definition. Does it refer to the accounting definition of "income" (in all of its notorious variations with all attendant risk of audit failure), or to some other concept of annual accretion? "Earnings per share," "dividends," and other profit-related standards suffer from most or all of the same ambiguities and insufficiencies. The term "growth", in addition, lacks a clear referent. It reasonably might be taken to refer to growth in sales volume or asset size, neither of which will always benefit the company's shareholders. And if the definition is redirected to mean "growth of profits," we encounter the same problems of timing, risk, and definition.

How can these ambiguities be avoided? Let us return to our first postulate about the firm's proper objective—that the firm's goal should be to maximize its shareholders' economic welfare. What matters, on this view, is not profits, earnings, dividends, or growth *as such*, but the ability of the company's shareholders, through the ownership of its shares, to acquire goods and services in the amounts and at the times that produce the largest measure of individual satisfaction. The important question is: How can the firm most directly aid its shareholders in achieving their personal wealth objectives?

Under one view, we respond by saying that the aim of the firm should be to maximize the market price per share of its stock—that is, to achieve the highest market value for the company's common shares. If the market price of the stock is maximized, the stockholder's wealth is necessarily maximized as well—which means that the holder's opportunity (whether through spending or saving) to acquire the satisfactions that wealth provides is likewise at an optimum.

But is it clear that present share price maximization necessarily entails the maximization of the value of the firm? A manager who, left in isolation, might make a long term investment that maximizes the value of the firm also might forego that investment to boost accounting earnings in the near term, thereby supporting the stock price and maintaining good relationships with the shareholders. Alternatively, the manager might make aggressive accounting decisions that improve earnings per share and raise the stock price, only later to stumble into destabilizing compliance problems. Reference to the shareholder interest fails to provide a clear signal in either case, for here the interests of shareholders with near term time horizons stand at odds with those holding for the long term. It is noted that, once this issue is posed, most observers recommend the long term view.

Whatever the time horizon, the standard is shareholder value maximization. Accepting the standard does not, however, tell us how to go about doing the maximizing. Our attention thus returns to management. Let us assume that it knows how to produce the firm's widgets competitively. But if maximum share value is accepted as the firm's goal, then to complete its job management still will need a valuation model for the shares as well as a business plan for the factory. The factors upon which share value depends must be known, or at least assumed, if the managers are effectively to pursue the maximization objective. For example, if value is a function of asset size, then the firm's managers should do all they can to increase assets; if it is a function of the firm's capital structure, or of its dividend or earnings patterns, different decision criteria might be relevant.

2.   *Valuation and Trading Markets—The Relationship of Fundamental Value and Market Value.*

How do market prices impact the exercise of valuing the firm? Valuations occur when business actors trade producing assets as well as when they manage assets on a going concern basis. Whether the investment is an entire firm, a security, or some other asset, a valuation will occur before the closing of a purchase transaction. Where there exists an active and extensive market in which securities or assets are bought and sold, the price set in the market by its many buyers and sellers can come to signal the value for all transacting parties.

Does the same result follow for valuations in legal contexts? The same economic data that determine valuations in business transactions come to bear in legal valuation. But legal valuations, like all legal determinations, are sensitive to normative contexts. As a result, legal valuation takes on special characteristics. It usually is conceived as an exercise in assimilating detailed economic data in sizable quantities and in designing theoretical equipment with which the data can be reduced to a defensible value figure. The value figure, once derived, takes on objective significance as the fundamental or "intrinsic" value of the firm, security, or asset. What direction should the legal inquiry into "intrinsic value" take when a trading market exists in the asset or security in question? Should the market price be taken as the best measure of fundamental value? Much will depend on whether information flows between the firm and the financial community are adequate. Assuming that investors are fully and accurately informed, is it likely, or indeed, inevitable, that the values of the firm and its traded securities will be identical?

When judges undertake a separate search for "intrinsic" value even though an adequately informed "market" value can be derived, they assume that the market does not accurately measure the value to which the law attaches consequences, or measures inadequately for the purpose of vindicating the legal norm. The judge inquires into "intrinsic" value independent of market price of securities to determine the existence or non-existence of a fact—value—which triggers certain legal consequences. A significant body of commentary questions this approach. It draws on economic theory to assert that market prices of the firm's securities are the best available indicators of value. But other equally sophisticated economic theory shows that market prices and intrinsic values do not necessarily coincide. Under this approach market prices and enterprise values persistently diverge because investors in securities act on different premises than purchasers of assets. Alternatively, investors are seen as unwise, uneducated, emotional, cognitively deficient, or otherwise inclined to react to irrelevant variables. As a result, investors must bear not only business, and possibly financial risks, but also the hazards of an unstable market in which real values are often disregarded. Part I of this book describes both of these economic perspectives on market prices and intrinsic values and sets out some notable exemplars of judicial valuation.

3.   *Valuation and the Market for Corporate Control.*

The mergers and acquisitions market triggers much of the policy interest and most of the litigation respecting corporate finance. The shareholders of firms targeted for acquisition routinely receive a premium consideration amounting to 20 to 50 percent of the antecedent market value of the firm's equity capital. What elements of value support (and justify) these premium payments? They might result from "synergistic" value added due to the combination of the target and acquiring firms. If that is the case, does it follow that a target shareholder should or should not have a legal right to a proportionate share of the gain arising from the merger? On the other hand, merger premiums could reflect discounts in the market price of the target stock. In that event, the market value of a share of the firm's stock by definition is less than its pro rata share of intrinsic value. Such a discount could follow from poor management at the target or the market's failure accurately to value the firm. Alternatively, acquiring firms might pay premiums because they are purchasing control and control has a value independent of the elements of value attached to a single share. If that is the case, what are the implications for the legal rights of a shareholder in a target firm? Should the shareholder, in legal contemplation an "owner" of the firm, have a proportionate right to a share of control value? Finally, if it is management's job to maximize the value of the firm and a potential offeror is offering a premium payment, should management have a legal duty to cooperate with the sale, and, indeed, to assure that the firm is sold to the highest valuing user? These issues are taken up in Parts I and V.

4.   *Valuation and Financial Contracting.*

This book's exploration of value and the role of law in its maximization also encompasses financial contracts. It is often asserted that the appropriate solution to disputes over corporate value is not legal intervention but deregulation to get the assets in question to the highest valuing user through the mechanism of free contract. Thus, the study of valuation in matters of corporate finance requires consideration of contracts as value maximizing tools. The legal materials that follow frequently deal with conflicts among various classes of claimants within a given firm—common stockholders, preferred stockholders, bondholders, and managers—where the stakes are the firm's value. These "pie splitting" contests turn out to be difficult to resolve. Traditionally, legal decisionmakers have brought a mix of contract and fairness concepts to bear. In the materials that follow, "contract" and "fairness" sometimes vie for primacy of place in the allocation of slices of value among conflicting claimants. The trend of the law lies emphatically on contract's side, as decisionmakers retreat from direct review of business judgments, even in conflict of interest situations. Moreover, when a contract fails to resolve a conflict courts now prefer process solutions to substantive pronouncements. The meaning of "fairness" in the law of corporate finance still presents an important question, but the answer evolves dynamically over time.

5. *Valuation and the Firm's Capital Structure, Dividend, and Risk Management Policies.*

Presumably, if a firm has only common stock outstanding, the value of the firm should equal the value of its common stock on the market. But suppose the firm has securities outstanding in addition to common stock. How is the firm's value calculated now? Consider two firms which are alike except that A has only common stock outstanding while B has long-term bonds and preferred stock outstanding as well as common shares. Even though A and B possess the same economic operating characteristics, is it possible that the aggregate market value of B's shares might be higher or lower than A's shares because of the presence of senior securities having a limited but prior claim on the income stream? Put otherwise, do the senior securities imply risk-return characteristics for B's common shares different than those that relate directly to B's business activities? If so, might the value of B's shares be penalized or enhanced, relative to A's?

Similarly, if B follows a more generous dividend policy than A, paying out a larger proportion of its annual earnings to stockholders, may this factor alter investors' outlooks and induce a preference for the securities of one firm over the other? Or if B uses devices like forward contracts and commodities future contracts to hedge the risks attending the business it conducts, or if B uses devices like swap contracts with financial institutions to hedge its financial risks, will B have enhanced its value in the view of stock market investors? More generally, apart from the firm's business and investment policies, are there aspects of financial practice, whether in respect to capital structure, dividends, or risk management, which independently affect the value of the firm or its securities? These issues are considered in Parts II and IV.

6. *Value Maximization and Law.*

Finally, let us assume that we can derive a sound theory of valuation of firms and their securities. Should the law and legal regulators employ the theory to encourage or require managers to produce higher firm and security values? If the answer to this question is "yes," what is the cheapest and most effective mode of implementing such regulation and what are its allocative consequences? If the answer is "no," and such regulation turns out to be inappropriate, what factor is responsible? Is regulation inappropriate because market forces suffice to encourage higher values? Or is value maximization such a complex objective as to make effective legal regulation impracticable? Or does our basic assumption that maximization of the value of the stock is the appropriate goal for corporate managers turn out to be too simplistic in some contexts because of conflicts of interest between the various constituents of the corporation—not only the shareholders and managers but also bondholders and other creditors? Or, finally, do even the most soundly conceived theories of valuation, when applied in practical contexts, turn out to have serious shortcomings? These questions recur in the materials collected in this book.

SECTION A.   MARKET VALUE AND FUNDAMENTAL VALUE

Most people experience the valuation of firms as observers of the securities markets. Much of business law is directed to protecting those markets' integrity. The massive apparatus of the federal securities laws seeks to assure that market value reflects fundamental value by mandating disclosure of material information and restraining manipulative conduct on the part of market actors. This book in large measure leaves those matters over to the Securities Regulation course. Here a different problem looms large. Assuming that the market price follows from an adequate base of information and is otherwise untainted, how reliably does it measure the firm's fundamental value? This Section addresses that question, in effect beginning the book with a "macro" view of firm valuation. Section B will proceed to the "micro" side of the matter, unpacking elements that go into firm valuations and analytical context in which value is estimated.

1.   INTRODUCTION

Tri-Continental Corp. v. Battye

Supreme Court of Delaware, 1950.
74 A.2d 71.

General Shareholdings Corporation, a Delaware corporation (referred to hereinafter as General), was merged into its parent company, Tri–Continental Corporation, a Maryland corporation (referred to hereinafter as Tri–Continental), as of October 1, 1948. Pursuant to Section 61 of the Delaware General Corporation Law * * * certain common stockholders of General objected to the terms of the merger and complied with the statutory requirements to register their objection. Thereafter, the Vice Chancellor determined the common shareholders of General entitled to a valuation of and payment for their shares and appointed an appraiser to determine the value of the common shares of General as of October 1, 1948.

* * *

The appraiser fixed the value of General's common stock on October 1, 1948 at $4.08 per share. [The stockholders] excepted to the appraiser's report. The Vice Chancellor sustained the exceptions and fixed the value of General's common stock at $4.62 per share. From the order of the Vice Chancellor fixing the value of the common stock of General, Tri–Continental appealed.

■ WOLCOTT, JUDGE, delivering the opinion of the Court:

Section 61 of the General Corporation Law Code 1935 * * * provides that upon the merger of a corporation, stockholders who object to the merger and who fulfill the statutory requirements to register their objection shall be paid the value of their stock on the date of the merger, exclusive of any element of value arising from the expectation or accomplishment of the merger. The meaning of the word "value" under this section of the Corporation Law has never been considered by this court. * * *

The basic concept of value under the appraisal statute is that the stockholder is entitled to be paid for that which has been taken from him, viz., his proportionate interest in a going concern. By value of the stockholder's proportionate interest in the corporate enterprise is meant the true or intrinsic value of his stock which has been taken by the merger. In determining what figure represents this true or intrinsic value, the appraiser and the courts must take into consideration all factors and elements which reasonably might enter into the fixing of value. Thus, market value, asset value, dividends, earning prospects, the nature of the enterprise and any other facts which were known or which could be ascertained as of the date of merger and which throw any light on future prospects of the merged corporation are not only pertinent to an inquiry as to the value of the dissenting stockholders' interest, but must be considered by the agency fixing the value.

* * * [S]ince intrinsic or true value is to be ascertained, the problem will not be settled by the acceptance as the sole measure of only one element entering into value without considering other elements. For example, * * * market value may not be taken as the sole measure of the value of the stock. So, also, since value is to be fixed on a going-concern basis, the liquidating value of the stock may not be accepted as the sole measure.

General was a regulated closed-end investment company with leverage, and was engaged in the business of investing in the stock market generally seeking to acquire and hold a cross-section of the stock market. Investments were made by General primarily with the possibility of capital appreciation in view. General's portfolio held diversified investments, practically all of which fell within the class of marketable securities readily liquidated.

A regulated close-end investment company is of a peculiar nature. The common stockholder of a closed-end company has no right at any time to demand of the company his proportionate share of the company's assets.[1] A regulated investment company is required to distribute all of its income from dividends and interest to its stockholders but, in so doing, pays no tax on the amounts so distributed. It also has the option of distributing net long-term capital gains to its stockholders or retaining them and paying a flat 25% tax. As in the case of individuals, a regulated investment company has the right to deduct capital losses from its capital gains.

On September 30, 1948, the day preceding the merger, General had outstanding debentures and preferred stock equaling in value 60.8% of the total assets of the company, leaving 39.2% of the company's assets applicable to the common stock. This condition of General made applicable the principle of leverage. Simply stated, this meant that since the debentures and preferred stock of General were a fixed liability, the same amount of assets at all times was required to be set off against them. The result of this unalterable fact was that if the stock market declined, thus decreasing the value of the assets of General, all of the decrease fell upon the common stock. On the other hand, when the stock market rose, thus increasing the value of General's assets, all of the increase accrued to the benefit of the common stock.

39.2% common stock

* * *

The closed-end feature and leverage have a direct effect on the market value of the common stock of closed-end investment companies. When the market price of the common stock moves into a certain price range in relation to its net asset value, upward leverage disappears and the stock sells on the market at a lower price than its net asset figure. This fact, together with the inability of the common stockholder to withdraw his proportionate interest in the assets of the company, has consistently resulted in a lower market value of the common stock in comparison with its net asset value. This difference between the net asset value and the market value of the common stock of a closed-end investment company is known as discount.

The record discloses that the common stock of General, prior to the merger, was selling within the price range which brought discount into play. The appraiser found the discount rate applicable to General to be 25%. This rate of discount is accepted for the purposes of this case since the parties do not argue that this finding was error.

Discount, therefore, may be applied to net asset value to determine on any day a theoretical or constructed market value of the common stock of a closed-end investment company with leverage. On September 30, 1948, the net asset value of the common stock of General was $4.90 per share and, if the discount of 25% is applied to that figure, a market value of General's common stock on that day of $3.67 per share is constructed.

The appraiser considered various factors which all agree should be considered in valuing the common stock of General. Those factors were:

1. In contradistinction, the stockholders of the so-called open-end company have the right at the close of business on designated days to demand from the company their proportionate share of the company's assets.

The nature of the enterprise, i.e., a regulated closed-end investment company; leverage; discount; net asset value; market value; management; earnings and dividends; expenses of operation; particular stockholdings in General's portfolio; and a favorable tax situation which General had.

The appraiser found that the factors of management, earnings and dividends, expenses of operation, and the particular stockholdings of General, under the circumstances, were not entitled to be debited or credited in arriving at a value for the common stock. It is not necessary to review his reasons, for the parties are agreed that his findings in this respect were correct. Since, however, earnings and dividends of a corporation are ordinarily of prime importance in valuing common stock, we feel, in order to avoid future confusion, that we should state briefly why they are not of much importance in this case. The reason is that General was an investment company with large leverage which meant that normal income of the company necessarily went in large part to the servicing of the senior debentures and preferred stock, leaving a relatively small amount left to be paid out in dividends to the common. Actually, dividends on the common stock of General in the past were negligible, nor were the prospects for the future materially brighter.

The favorable tax situation of General was found by the appraiser to be worth 29 cents to each share of common stock. This finding is not urged as error. The favorable tax situation resulted from realized losses in 1948 and loss carryovers which would have enabled General to take profits gained before the end of 1948 * * * without paying a 25% capital gains tax or distributing the proceeds to its stockholders who would then be taxed on them.

The appraiser found that, at the time of merger and prior thereto, there was no actual market of General's common stock uninfluenced by the merger and, accordingly, excluded actual market value of the stock as a factor to enter into the final determination of value. This was not error, nor would it have been error had the appraiser constructed a hypothetical uninfluenced market value by discounting the net asset value of the common stock on the day of merger and given some effect to it in his final valuation. Had there been an actual market value uninfluenced by the merger in existence, it would have been error to disregard it, but the absence of such an element does not require the construction of a hypothetical market value to be given effect in the final determination of value.

A great deal of argument in this cause has turned around the phrase 'net asset value' which is simply a mathematical figures representing the total value of the assets of General less the prior claims. The net asset value of the common stock of General could be determined as of any date by computing the total market value of the securities in the portfolio, adding to that sum the cash in the company's possession, deducting the total of the outstanding liabilities, debentures and preferred stock, and dividing the final result by the number of common shares outstanding.

However, since the value of dissenting stock is to be fixed on a going-concern basis, the taking of the net asset value as the appraisal value of the stock obviously is precluded by the rule. This is so because, primarily, net asset value is a theoretical liquidating value to which the share would be entitled upon the company going out of business. Its very nature indicates that it is not the value of stock in a going concern.

Furthermore, since we are called upon to fix the value of common stock in a closed-end investment company with leverage, an additional reason exists for the refusal to fix the value of that stock at its net asset value. This reason is that the common stockholder of a closed-end company can never withdraw his proportionate interest from the company as long as it is a going concern. He can obtain his full proportionate share of the company's assets, or the net asset value of his stock, only upon liquidation of the company.[2] He cannot obtain the net asset value of his common stock by sale of the stock because of discount which is always applicable when the stock of the closed-end investment company is selling within the necessary price range, and which prevents the sale of the common stock except at a price less than the net asset value.

Since, therefore, net asset value is, in reality, a liquidating value, it cannot be made the sole criterion of the measure of the value of the dissenting stock. The appraiser, therefore, properly concluded that net asset value as of September 30, 1948 should not be taken as the basis for arriving at the appraisal value. He preferred, and we think correctly, to construct an asset value on the basis of month-end averages of the portfolio securities over a reasonable period of time. This method resulted in an asset figure of $5.15 per share of common stock of General. * * *

To the per share asset value of $5.15 so determined, the appraiser added 29 cents, the value of the favorable tax situation of General, to each share of its common stock. The result of $5.44 is called by the appraiser the "fair asset value" of a share of the common stock of General. The appraiser then arrived at the true or intrinsic value of a common share of General by applying the discount to the fair asset value of $5.44, and arrived at a value of $4.08 per share for the common stock of General. [The appraiser also determined that the state of the stock market was "normal," so that the fund's leverage had no impact, positive or negative, on its value.]

The Vice Chancellor adopted the findings of the appraiser in every particular, but disagreed with him as to the method of arriving at the value of the common share from those findings. He differed with the method of arriving at value used by the appraiser primarily because he was of the opinion that discount "has exclusive application to the question of but one element of value, namely, market value." With this as his premise, he reached the conclusion that the appraiser, in discounting the fair asset value of $5.44, had in fact constructed a market value of the common share, and had committed error when he gave 100% weight to that constructed market value.

2. Actually, net asset value of common stock of a closed-end company could never, as a practical matter, be obtained since liquidation would be accompanied by expense and would probably result in driving the market down through the sudden sale of large blocks of stock, thus automatically decreasing the net asset value.

The Vice Chancellor was of the opinion that net asset value unaltered by the discount factor must be considered as an independent element of value [and] that constructed market value and net asset value should be fairly weighted in order to determine the value of the shares involved. Recognizing that the weighting of different elements of value necessarily is arbitrary, he gave a weight of 40% to net asset value and a weight of 60% to constructed market value, reaching the conclusion that the value of a common share of General was $4.62.

We do not agree with the Vice Chancellor in this respect * * *. [The court took the position that the appraiser's $4.08 did not amount to a "constructed market value" because it grossed up the asset value to include the 29 cent tax benefit, a benefit that only could only be realized against future capital gain offsets. It thus amounted to a hidden, prospective element of going concern value rather than an element of net asset value. A "constructed market value," in contrast, implied a slightly different calculation—the 25 percent discount applied directly to net asset value with no gross up in respect of the tax benefit.]

The dissenting stockholder is entitled to receive the intrinsic value of his share in a going concern. This can mean only that he is entitled to receive that sum which represents the amount he would have received as a stockholder in one way or another as long as the company continued in business. Since we are dealing with a regulated closed-end investment company with leverage from which the stockholder cannot withdraw his proportionate interest, and since dividends on the stock of such companies are of small importance, it follows that the only way in which a common stockholder of a going closed-end company with leverage can obtain the value of his stock is by the sale of it on the market. Furthermore, whenever he seeks to do so, he, by force of circumstances, must sell at a discount, whenever this is an operating element.

The conclusion is, therefore, inescapable that the full value of the corporate assets to the corporation is not the same as the value of those assets to the common stockholder because of the factor of discount. * * * Discount is an element of value which must be given independent effect in the valuing of common stock of regulated closed-end investment companies with leverage, and is not confined solely to the construction of a hypothetical market value.

* * *

We believe that the appraiser was correct in his method of determining value and in the result reached by him. * * *

A mandate will be entered reversing the order of the Vice Chancellor and directing him to give effect to the valuation of the appraiser.

NOTE: FUNDS

General Shareholdings was an "investment company" within the meaning of the Investment Company Act of 1940. Under the Act's definition, 15 U.S.C. § 80a–3, an investment company is (1) a securities issuer that is engaged primarily in the business of investing, reinvesting, or trading in securities, or (2) a securities issuer engaged in the business of investing, reinvesting, owning, holding, or trading in securities and owning investment securities constituting more than 40 percent of the value of its total assets. The Investment Company Act imposes registration, disclosure, and governance requirements. Generally, investment companies are created and marketed by separate firms in the business of providing them financial advisory services pursuant to contracts. A companion statute, the Investment Advisers Act of 1940 imposes registration, disclosure and governance requirements on these firms. See 15 U.S.C. 80b–1(11). Under § 15 of the Investment Company Act, 15 U.S.C. § 80a–15, the advisory contract between the advisor and the fund can be no longer than two years in duration and must be terminable at any time by the fund.

The Investment Company Act, speaking broadly, covers funds whose shares are offered and sold to the general public. Again speaking broadly, there are two varieties of funds, closed-end and open-end. General Shareholdings was a closed-end fund. Like any business corporation, it took in capital in exchange for shares and then invested the capital for an open-ended duration. Unlike conventional "operating companies," of course, closed-end funds invest in securities rather than directly in producing assets. See 15 U.S.C. § 80a–23 for special rules governing closed-end funds. The other type of fund is a mutual fund. This also invests in marketable securities, but does so subject to a durational limitation—the shareholders may redeem their shares for net asset value. See 15 U.S.C. § 80a–22 for rules governing redemption terms. Because mutual funds must be prepared to meet redemptions, they tend to invest in liquid securities on a short-term time horizon.

Compare private equity funds and hedge funds. These also are investment companies within the Investment Company Act definition, and they are organized and promoted by advisers within the Advisers Act definition. But they enjoy exemptions from regulation, and thus lie for the most part outside the bounds of federal regulation of investment companies and their advisers. They are exempt from the Investment Company Act of 1940 because they either have 100 or fewer beneficial owners and do not offer their securities to the public, see 15 U.S.C. § 80a–3(c)(1), or because their investors are all qualifying wealthy individuals or institutions, id. § 80a–3(c)(7). For their status under the Investment Advisers Act of 1940, 15 U.S.C. § 80b–1–8b–21, see Goldstein v. SEC, 451 F.3d 873 (D.C.Cir.2006), which vacates and remands the SEC's "Hedge Fund Rule," see Registration Under the Advisers Act of Certain Hedge Fund Advisers, 69 Fed. Reg. 72,054 (Dec. 10, 2004) (codified at 17 C.F.R. §§ 275, 279). The SEC has imposed an antifraud rule on these advisers' dealings with investors or potential investors. See Rule 206(4)–8 under the Advisers Act. There is no private right of action, however.

Private equity funds and hedge funds thus occupy the same largely unregulated space. They also appeal the same class of investors—investment institutions like pension funds and university endowments and rich, sophisticated individuals. Both also lever their portfolios. Until recently, we could distinguish hedge funds from private equity funds by the characteristics of their investments. Private equity, the successor to the leveraged buyout funds of the 1980s, takes companies private, investing long-term in their equity from a control position. Hedge funds, in contrast, play securities markets worldwide. Private equity firms possess expertise in company analysis. Hedge funds, in contrast, employ "numbers guys" expert in complex market arbitrage. Different hedge funds concentrate on different market plays. Some specialize in securities of distressed firms. Others make directional bets on the movement of currency exchange or interest rates. Still others pursue convertible arbitrage, going long in a convertible bond and shorting the underlying common stock. Many follow market momentum, moving in groups in and out of asset classes world wide. Recently, some have taken up risky lending, funding leveraged buyouts and firms in bankruptcy reorganization, and trading in junk bonds and credit derivatives. The tie that binds the hedge funds (and private equity) together, despite the variety of investment styles, is their promise to deliver above-market returns, a task that becomes harder and harder as more funds pursue the same strategies.

Where closed-end funds have indefinite durations and capital in open-end funds is redeemable at any time, durations vary with private equity funds and hedge funds. Everything depends on the governing contract. Contracts governing private equity investment tend to lock up investments for five years, with some contracts going as far as ten years. These long-term arrangements facilitate large, illiquid, and long-term equity positions. Contracts governing investment in hedge funds typically lock up investor capital for six months, although some now impose terms of two years or longer. There is an emerging zone in which hedge funds with longer-term durations become indistinguishable from private equity funds.

NOTE: MERGER APPRAISAL RIGHTS AND THE CLOSED–END FUND DISCOUNT

1. Battye *Reaffirmed.*

The Delaware Supreme Court once again took up the appraisal of a closed-end investment company in **Paskill Corp. v. Alcoma Corp.**, 747 A.2d 549 (Del.2000). The parties to the proceeding agreed on a base figure derived from the company's net asset value but disputed some adjustments mooted by the defense. Specifically, the defendant (a) estimated and subtracted closing costs that would be incurred in realizing the cash value of the company's real estate holdings, and (b) estimated and deducted deferred federal, state, and other taxes that would be incurred upon the realization of capital gains on the company's securities holdings. The Court of Chancery rejected the deduction of real estate closing costs on the ground that none of the company's assets had been for sale at the time of the merger, but accepted the deduction of the estimated future tax liabilities. The Supreme Court reversed and remanded. Following *Battye*, it ruled that the company must be valued on a going concern rather than liquidation basis, and that the projected tax liabilities had been deducted improperly.

2. *Explaining the Closed–End Fund Discount.*

Kraakman, Taking Discounts Seriously: The Implications of "Discounted" Share Prices as an Acquisition Motive, 88 Colum. L.Rev. 891, 902–05 (1988), describes the closed-end fund discount, and competing explanations therefor:

"Like mutual funds (or 'open-end' companies), closed-end funds are investment companies. Like ordinary corporations, however, closed-end funds issue shares that trade publicly and are not redeemable against their issuers. Many closed-end funds hold diversified portfolios of publicly-traded stocks and issue shares that are themselves traded on major stock exchanges. The financial press regularly publishes dual market prices for both the shares of exchange-traded funds and the net asset value (per share) of their securities portfolios. The interesting feature of these dual prices is that they frequently diverge. Compared with the market value of their portfolios, funds often trade at discounts and occasionally trade at premia. While start-up funds generally begin trading at premia, their share prices subsequently drop relative to their asset values. Thereafter, discounts on seasoned funds of 20% or more, persisting for five years or longer, have been common in the recent past. * * *

"Although there have been numerous investigations of discounts on closed-end funds, none has satisfactorily accounted for their origins. Discounts are certainly not due to misinformation about the value of fund assets, nor are they attributable to management expenses or trading costs, which are generally modest. Tax liabilities may explain some discounting behavior, but even this is uncertain. Thus, the larger portion of the variance in discounts is fair game for informed conjecture. Not surprisingly, competing explanations divide along the familiar lines of the market-or-manager dichotomy. On the market side, discounts are usually attributed either to gross market inefficiencies or to our failure to understand the true structure of investor returns on closed-end funds. On the manager side, discounts are often ascribed to doubts about future performance, which are usually linked to the investment skills of fund managers but might relate to other risks of misinvestment or expropriation as well. As might be expected, moreover, each genre of discount explanation has significant drawbacks. In particular, the market-based accounts seem to challenge basic hypotheses in financial economics, while agency cost theories have difficulty explaining why the past performance of funds is only a modest predictor of discounts. If there is a significant risk of agency losses, it has not yet materialized—or at least not since the Great Depression.

"Regardless of the origins of discounts, however, the market demonstrates a rational if uneven response to the existence of large discounts. Discounts rapidly disappear when closed-end funds announce plans to liquidate or merge with mutual funds. Further, funds with larger discounts are more likely to liquidate or 'open' than those with smaller discounts, whether openings occur on management's initiative or in response to threats of proxy contests or takeovers. Thus, discounts are an important stimulus for fund reorganizations and also explain in part the overwhelming market preeminence that mutual funds enjoy over their closed-end competitors. But despite the apparent advantages of the mutual form, many large closed-end funds have weathered years of steep discounts without reorganization, presumably because the costs of proxy contests or hostile takeovers would have exceeded the gains."

Hamermesh and Wachter, The Short and Puzzling Life of the "Implicit Minority Discount" in Delaware Appraisal Law, 155 U.Pa.L.Rev. ____ (forthcoming 2007), offers a different view of the discount, opting for an agency cost explanation. They cite Jonathan Berk and Richard Stanton, Managerial Ability, Compensation, and the Closed End Fund Discount, 62 J. Fin. 529 (2007), for the proposition that closed-end fund discount stems from a trade off between management ability and management fees. In the view of the authors, it follows that the closed-end fund discount differs not at all from any other management-related factor that has the effect of depressing the value of the firm.

Does the appraisal outcome respecting the application of the closed-end fund discount depend on the explanation for the discount? What is the difference for fair value in an appraisal between saying that the discount stems from persistent market pricing irrationality and saying that the discount stems from agency costs?

3. *Trading Markets and the Availability of Appraisal.*

General Shareholdings had close to 3,000 shareholders and was traded on the New York Curb Exchange, the predecessor of today's NASDAQ market. Ironically, given that posture, its shareholders would not have appraisal rights if the case came up today. Generally, under Delaware Corporation Law § 262, target shareholders may dissent from a merger and request an appraisal only when the firm's shares are not publicly traded, or the consideration in the merger is cash or anything other than publicly traded stock. Thus, when a publicly traded firm merges and the consideration is stock, appraisal rights do not obtain. (For a more detailed description of the availability of voting and appraisal rights in mergers, see infra Part V.) In most cases, the statutory provision of appraisal rights in mergers deems the market price to be sufficiently reliable to protect the shareholders' interests. How safe is that assumption? The materials that follow take up that question.

2.   MARKET EFFICIENCY

When we turn to the particulars of value calculations in Section B, we will find that market prices and market-determined rates of return are never far away. Even in the case of a close corporation, the ascertainment of a present value will in the end require reference to market prices of comparable firms. That reliance implicates a question: Do those market prices of shares of publicly traded companies manifest accurate, or at least adequate, valuations of the companies' going concern assets?

The efficient market hypothesis (EMH) of financial economics bears on the answer to the question. The EMH has been the leading proposition of financial economics for more than four decades. In the classic statement, Fama, Efficient Capital Markets: A Review of Theory and Empirical Work, 25 J. Fin. 383 (1970), an efficient market is one in which security prices always fully reflect available information. The EMH asserts that real world securities markets are efficient within the meaning of Fama's statement. This powerful assertion is described in the excerpt that follows.

(A) THE EFFICIENT MARKET HYPOTHESIS

Brealey, Myers, and Allen, Principles of Corporate Finance

(8th ed. 2006), pp. 333–341.

13.2   WHAT IS AN EFFICIENT MARKET?

A Startling Discovery: Price Changes Are Random

As is so often the case with important ideas, the concept of efficient capital markets stemmed from a chance discovery. In 1953 Maurice Kendall, a British statistician, presented a controversial paper to the Royal Statistical Society on the behavior of stock and commodity prices.[2] Kendall had expected to find regular price cycles, but to his surprise they did not seem to exist. Each series appeared to be "a 'wandering' one, almost as if once a week the Demon of Chance drew a random number . . . and added it to the current price to determine the next week's price." In other words, prices seemed to follow a *random walk*.

---

2. See M.G. Kendall, "The Analysis of Economic Time–Series, Part I. Prices," *Journal of the Royal Statistical Society,* 96 (1953), pp. 11–25. Kendall's idea was not wholly new. It had been proposed in an almost forgotten doctoral thesis written 53 years earlier by a French doctoral student, Louis Bachelier. Bachelier's accompanying development of the mathematical theory of random processes an- ticipated by 5 years Einstein's famous work on the random Brownian motion of colliding gas molecules. See L. Bachelier, *Theorie de la Speculation*, Gauthier–Villars, Paris, 1900. Reprinted in English (A.J. Boness, trans.) in P.H. Cootner (ed.), *The Random Character of Stock Market Prices,* M.I.T. Press, Cambridge, Mass., 1964, pp. 17–78.

If you are not sure what we mean by *random walk,* you might like to think of the following example. You are given $100 to play a game. At the end of each week a coin is tossed. If it comes up heads, you win 3 percent of your investment; if it is tails, you lose 2.5 percent. Therefore your capital at the end of the first week is either $103.00 or $97.50. At the end of the second week the coin is tossed again. Now the possible outcomes are:

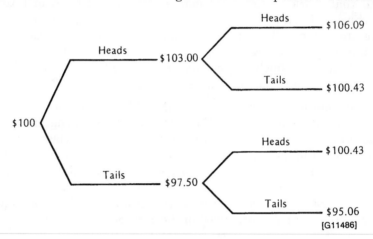

[G11486]

This process is a random walk with a positive drift of .25 percent per week.[3] It is a random walk because successive changes in value are independent. That is, the odds each week are 50 percent, regardless of the value at the start of the week or of the pattern of heads and tails in the previous weeks.

If you find it difficult to believe that there are no patterns in share price changes, look at the two charts in Figure 13.1. One of these charts shows the outcome from playing our game for 5 years; the other shows the actual performance of the Standard and Poor's Index for a 5–year period. Can you tell which one is which?[4]

---

3. The drift is equal to the expected outcome: $(\frac{1}{2})(3) + (\frac{1}{2})(-2.5) = .25\%$.

4. The bottom chart in Figure 13.1 shows the real Standard and Poor's Index for march 1997 to March 2002; the top chart is a series of cumulated random numbers. Of course, 50 percent of you will have guessed right, but we bet it was just a guess. A similar comparison between cumulated random numbers and actual price series was first suggested by H.V. Roberts, "Stock Market 'Patterns' and Financial Analysis: Methodological Suggestions," *Journal of Finance,* 14: 1–10 (March 1959).

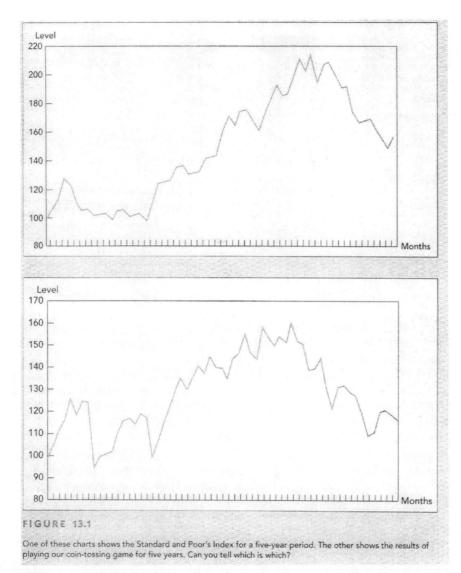

FIGURE 13.1

One of these charts shows the Standard and Poor's Index for a five-year period. The other shows the results of playing our coin-tossing game for five years. Can you tell which is which?

When Maurice Kendall suggested that stock prices follow a random walk, he was implying that the price changes are independent of one another just as the gains and losses in our coin-tossing game were independent. Figure 13.2 illustrates this. Each dot shows the change in the price of Microsoft stock on successive days. The circled dot in the southeast quadrant refers to a pair of days in which a 1 percent increase was followed by a 1 percent decrease. If there was a systematic tendency for increases to be followed by decreases, there would be many crosses in the southeast quadrant and few in the northeast quadrant. It is obvious from a glance that there is very little pattern in these price movements, but we can test this more precisely by calculating the coefficient of correlation between each day's price change and the next. If price movements persisted, the correlation would be significantly positive; if there was no relationship, it would be 0. In our example, the correlation between successive price changes in Microsoft stock was +.025; there was a negligible tendency for price rises to be followed by further rises.[5]

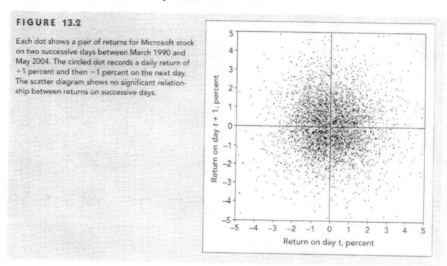

FIGURE 13.2

Each dot shows a pair of returns for Microsoft stock on two successive days between March 1990 and May 2004. The circled dot records a daily return of +1 percent and then −1 percent on the next day. The scatter diagram shows no significant relationship between returns on successive days.

Figure 13.2 suggests that Microsoft's price changes were effectively uncorrelated. Today's price change gave investors almost no clue as to the likely change tomorrow. Does that surprise you? If so, imagine that it were not the case and that changes in Microsoft's stock price were expected to persist for several months. Figure 13.3 provides an example of such a predictable cycle. You can see that an increase in Microsoft's stock price started last month, when the price was $50, and it is expected to carry the stock price to $90 next month. What will happen when investors perceive this bonanza? It will self-destruct. Since Microsoft stock is a bargain at $70, investors will rush to buy. They will stop buying only when the stock offers a normal rate of return. Therefore, as soon as a cycle becomes apparent to investors, they immediately eliminate it by their trading.

Three Forms of Market Efficiency

You should now see why prices in competitive markets must follow a random walk. If past prices could be used to predict future price changes, investors could make easy profits. But in competitive markets easy profits don't last. As investors try to take advantage of the information in past prices, prices adjust immediately until the superior profits from studying past price movements disappear. As a result, all the information in past prices will be reflected in *today's* stock price, not tomorrow's. Patterns in prices will no longer exist and price changes in one period will independent of changes in the next. In other words, the share price will follow a random walk.

---

5. The correlation coefficient between successive observations is known as the *autocorrelation coefficient*. An autocorrelation of +.025 implies that, if Microsoft stock price rose by 1 percent more than average yesterday, your best forecast of today's price change would be a rise of .025 percent more than average.

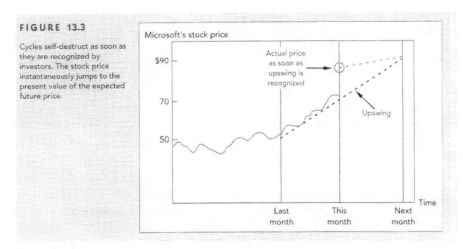

FIGURE 13.3

Cycles self-destruct as soon as they are recognized by investors. The stock price instantaneously jumps to the present value of the expected future price.

In competitive markets today's stock price must already reflect the information in past prices. But why stop there? If markets are competitive, shouldn't today's stock price reflect *all* the information that is available to investors? If so, securities will be fairly priced and security returns will be unpredictable, whatever information you consider.

Economists often define three levels of market efficiency, which are distinguished by the degree of information reflected in security prices. In the first level, prices reflect the information contained in the record of past prices. This is called the *weak* form of efficiency. If markets are efficient in the weak sense, then it is impossible to make consistently superior profits by studying past returns. Prices will follow a random walk.

The second level of efficiency requires that prices reflect not only past prices but all other published information, such as you might get from reading the financial press. This is known as the *semistrong* form of efficiency. If markets are efficient in this sense, then prices will adjust immediately to public information such as the announcement of the last quarter's earnings, a new issue of stock, a proposal to merge two companies, and so on.

Finally, we might envisage a *strong* form of efficiency, in which prices reflect all the information that can be acquired by painstaking fundamental analysis of the company and the economy. In such a market we would observe lucky and unlucky investors, but we wouldn't find any superior investment managers who can consistently beat the market.

Efficient Markets: The Evidence

In the years that followed Maurice Kendall's discovery, financial journals were packed with tests of the efficient-market hypothesis. To test the weak form of the hypothesis, researchers measured the profitability of some of the trading rules used by analysts who claim to find patterns in security prices. They also employed statistical tests such as the one we described when looking for patterns in the returns of Microsoft stock. * * * It appears that throughout the world there are few patterns in week-to-week returns.

To analyze the semistrong form of the efficient market hypothesis, researchers have measured how rapidly security prices respond to different items of news, such as an earnings or dividend announcement, news of a takeover, or macroeconomic information. * * *

* * *

A study by Patell and Wolfson shows just how fast prices move when new information becomes available.[10] They found that, when a firm publishes its latest earnings or announces a dividend change, the major part of the adjustment in price occurs within 5 to 10 minutes of the announcement.

Tests of the strong form of the hypothesis have examined the recommendations of professional security analysts and have looked for mutual funds or pension funds that could predictably outperform the market. Some researchers have found a slightly persistent outperformance, but just as many have concluded that professionally managed funds fail to recoup the costs of management. * * *

It would be surprising if some managers were not smarter than others and could earn superior returns. But it seems difficult to spot the smart ones, and the top-performing managers one year have about an average chance of falling on their face the next year. * * *

[E]vidence on strong form efficiency has proved to be sufficiently convincing that many professionally managed funds have given up the pursuit of superior performance. They simply "buy the index," which maximizes diversification and minimizes the costs of managing the portfolio. * * *

NOTE: SPECULATIVE EFFICIENCY, ALLOCATIVE EFFICIENCY, AND INCENTIVE PROBLEMS

1. *Speculative Efficiency and Allocative Efficiency.*

Different claims are made respecting the meaning of the market efficiency assertion. The more modest claim is that prices react *quickly*. This confines the hypothesis to a statement about the promptness with which information thought by investors to be relevant in pricing shares of stock (including information which does not necessarily relate to the "intrinsic value" of the firm) is reflected in prices—and the resultant inability of investors to make advantageous purchases or sales systematically by acquiring information before it is reflected in prices. This is the "speculative" or "no bargains" version of the hypothesis. It has an important, testable implication: Stale information is of no value in making money.

There is a stronger, separate claim that has a much weaker basis of empirical support. This asserts that prices react *correctly*. There is, in other words, a definite relationship between the market prices of securities and the "true" value of the firm. This is the "intrinsic value" or "allocative efficiency" version of the EMH. This version goes beyond the claim that market prices promptly reflect all available

---

10. See J.M.Patell and M.A.Wolfson, "The Intraday Speed of Adjustment of Stock Prices to Earnings and Dividend Announce- ments," *Journal of Financial Economics* 13 (June 1984), pp. 223–252.

information to assert that the price also reflects rational treatment of that information by market actors. In other words, only value-relevant information shows up in the price. Tobin points out that the validity of the intrinsic value version "is by no means implied by" the validity of the "no-bargains" version. Tobin, On the Efficiency of the Financial System, 153 Lloyd's Bank Review 1, 5 (July 1984). The allocative efficiency assertion has two further, testable implications. First, prices should neither overreact nor underreact to particular news. Second, since price equals intrinsic value, the price should not move at all in the absence of news relevant to the value of the security. Restating this point, prices should not react to changes in demand or supply respecting the security. Shleifer, Inefficient Markets: An Introduction to Behavioral Finance 5 (2000).

The two versions of the hypothesis have different ramifications in legal contexts. To the extent that speculative efficiency is found to obtain, views about the need for regulation to protect disadvantaged investors against advantaged professionals and others may change. The implications of the allocative efficiency claim reach more broadly. Some of these implications are deregulatory. If market prices in fact reflect fundamental value, then any cause of action that results in judicial revaluation of a publicly traded security appears to be substantively unsound. On the other hand, the allocative efficiency assertion arguably justifies heightened legal intervention to protect the market pricing process from misinformation, insufficient information, or manipulation.

2. *Incentive Problems and Modifications.*

There is an incentive problem bound up in the process by which relevant information becomes impounded in the "efficient" market price. If the mechanism for effecting discovery and "instantaneous" absorption of information by the market is the eager search by thousands of aggressively competing investors and analysts, the hypothesis contemplates systematic expenditure of funds by such persons to discover information with which, by the hypothesis, a profit cannot be made systematically. A problem arises. Why would anyone who believes the market is efficient incur these expenses? But, then, if no one incurs these expenses, how will the relevant information become "promptly" available so as to make the market efficient?

Of course, proponents of the hypothesis never asserted that all "available" information is in fact instantaneously and costlessly available to all investors. Two assumptions lay beneath their assertion that the price "fully reflects" all information: that the price is set at the margin, and that the market behaves "as if" the information were in fact available to all investors. Even so, the EMH had to be modified to avoid the incentive problem. Unmodified, it seemed implausible.

The result was modification of the assertion that the market price reflects the information level of the best informed trader and restatement of the market efficiency assertion as a matter of degree. The breakthrough article was Grossman and Stiglitz, On the Impossibility of Informationally Efficient Markets, 70 Am.Econ. Rev. 393 (1980). The Grossman and Stiglitz model drops the assumption of competitive equilibrium and substitutes a picture of an "equilibrium degree of disequilibrium." In this model, prices only partially reflect the information level of the most sophisticated trader. The price becomes more informative as the number of well-informed individuals trading the security increases. The price is completely accurate only if all traders have full information. Id. at 393–395. Given this model, there is nothing inconsistent about having efficient markets and security analysis at the same time. Gilson and Kraakman, The Mechanisms of Market Efficiency, 70 Va.L.Rev. 549, 622–626 (1984), expands on this approach. Their analysis focuses on the market for information and the differential costs (and prices) of different kinds of information. They suggest that the securities market has varying degrees of efficiency in reflecting information in price, depending on differences in the cost of discovery and speed of absorption of different kinds of information. They also relate those differences to the operation of different identified market mechanisms—(1) universally informed trading, most closely approximated with respect to old price information and big news stories like presidential election results, (2) professionally informed trading, (3) derivatively informed trading, which occurs when traders without information act in response to the observed behavior of those with information, and (4) uninformed trading.

NOTE: EMPIRICAL TESTING OF THE EMH

1. *The Joint Hypothesis Problem.*

A significant theoretical objection has been lodged against the claim that the EMH has been verified. Fama terms this the "joint-hypothesis problem." Fama, supra, at 1575–1576. According to Gordon and Kornhauser, Efficient Markets, Costly Information and Securities Research, 60 N.Y.U.L.Rev. 761, 771–772 (1985):

> "[U]nfortunately the efficient market hypothesis cannot be tested in a straightforward way. It is not a hypothesis subject to relatively simple observation, such as 'all the balls in the urn are white.' The basic data, prices and price changes, are interpretable only through the lens of a larger model of investor behavior and market processes. Thus we cannot test the validity of the efficient market hypothesis alone; every test of EMH also assumes some particular theory of what the 'right' price for an asset is. These asset pricing models establish the benchmark of 'normal' returns in order to determine the efficiency of the market. Consequently, every empirical test of the efficient market hypothesis is a 'joint test' of both the hypothesis and an asset pricing model. If the test yields evidence consistent with market efficiency, it also yields evidence consistent with the asset pricing model. If however, the test yields anomalous evidence, either the market is inefficient or the asset pricing model used is incorrect (or possibly both EMH and the pricing model are wrong). Understanding EMH therefore requires that we consider the asset pricing models that have been used to test it."

Note that opponents as well as proponents of the EMH run into the joint hypothesis problem. If a proponent does an empirical test which claims to show allocative efficiency while using the leading asset pricing model, the Capital Asset Pricing Model (CAPM) (see infra Part I), as a measure of value, an opponent can object on the ground that the CAPM is itself questionable. If an opponent produces a study claiming that a strategy exploiting stale information earns a positive cash flow on average over time, proponents can respond that the positive returns are merely compensation for risk bearing and can suggest a model of risk and return that will support their position. Schleifer, supra, pp. 5–7.

2. *First-Generation Results.*

In 1978, Michael Jensen famously stated that "there is no proposition in economics which has more solid empirical evidence supporting it than the Efficient Markets Hypothesis." Jensen, Some Anomalous Evidence Regarding Market Efficiency, 6 J. Fin. Econ. 95 (1978). The statement seemed accurate at the time.

The empirical tests to which Jensen referred mostly addressed the weak and semi-strong versions of the EMH. Few have attempted to validate the strong form, which heroically presupposes that information and trading costs are zero. "Since there are surely positive information and trading costs, the extreme version of the * * * hypothesis is surely false." Fama, Efficient Capital Markets: II, 46 J.Fin.1575

(1991). The strong version also is flatly contradicted by the persistence of insider trading for high profits. Empirical literature on insider trading confirms that insiders can, in fact, earn extranormal trading profits. Seyhun, Insiders' Profits, Costs of Trading, and Market Efficiency, 16 J.Fin. Econ. 189 (1986).

The weak form of the hypothesis has the strongest empirical support. The first-generation empirical studies are directed to the random walk point. They show that generally technical strategies do not yield systematic profits and that on any given day the price of stock is as likely to rise after a previous day's increase as after a previous day's decline. See, e.g., Fama, The Behavior of Stock Market Prices, 38 J. Bus. 34 (1965). First-generation tests also yield some support for the semi-strong form's prediction of speculative efficiency. The tests employ event study methodology to measure the speed with which the market price adjusts to new information (such as announcements of stock splits, dividends or earnings reports, or takeovers or mergers). They show quick adjustments and support the assertion that individuals cannot systematically acquire and use the information before the price reflects it. Other studies reveal the market's acute, if not just as speedy, perception of ambiguous or misleading information in statements permitted by generally accepted accounting principles (e.g., by reflecting the "actual" rather than the higher or lower reported earnings made possible by changed accounting methods). Still other studies show that if risk is held constant, mutual funds, presumed to be the most sophisticated and diligent investors, do not outperform each other or the market. For summaries, see Gilson and Kraakman, supra, at 555.

3. *The Empirical Case Against the Hypothesis.*

In the 1980s, Jensen's statement about the evidence favoring the EMH was contradicted by studies showing stock prices behaving in "anomalous" ways not conforming to EMH predictions. These phenomena include the following:

• **The Closed–End Fund Discount.** Whatever place *Tri-Continental v. Battye*, supra, should hold in the context of the law of mergers, it discusses a valuation problem that stands front and center in the line of empirical reproaches to the EMH. We will see that the fundamental value of most firms is difficult to measure. Closed-end funds holding portfolios of publicly traded securities present a rare case in which fundamental value can be measured easily. The fundamental value of a closed-end fund that pays dividends equal to the dividends on the stocks in its portfolio is the value of its portfolio. Yet, securities issued by these funds persistently trade at variance with their net asset values—usually at a discount but sometimes at a premium. The consensus view is that these discounts cannot be explained in terms of fundamental value factors, despite attempts to account for them in terms of the agency costs of fund management or in terms of tax liabilities. See De Long, Shleifer, Summers and Waldmann, Noise Trader Risk in Financial Markets, 98 J.Pol.Econ. 703, 728 (1990).

For a theoretical model to the contrary, see Jonathan Berk and Richard Stanton, Managerial Ability, Compensation, and the Closed End Fund Discount, 62 J. Fin. 529 (2007). The model assumes that, on average, managers can, by correctly picking stocks, generate returns in excess of their fees, but that, while managers sign long term contracts with the fund, the fund cannot prevent the managers from leaving. They argue that the resulting uncertainties about the tradeoff between management ability and fees in future fund performance provide a rational explanation for at least a part of the observed pattern of premiums and discounts

• **Small Firms.** Smaller corporations tend to have high abnormal rates of return. See Symposium, 12 J.Fin.Econ. 3 (1983). This "small firm effect" is tied to a "January effect"—a pattern of abnormally high returns in early January. See Thaler, Anomalies: Weekend, Holiday, Turn of the Month and Intraday Effects, 1

J.Econ.Perspectives 169 (1987); Thaler, Anomalies: The January Effect, 1 J.Econ.Perspectives 197 (1987).

• **Volatility.** A number of studies show that stock prices overreact to changes in fundamentals. Cutler, Poterba and Summers, What Moves Stock Prices? 15 J.Portfolio Management 4, 9 (1989), suggests the "difficulty of explaining as much as half the variance in aggregate stock prices on the basis of publicly available news bearing on fundamental values." Jacobs and Levy, On the Value of "Value," Fin. Analysts J. 47, 48 (1988), finds that value as measured by a dividend discount model is "but a small part of the security pricing story." Shiller, Do Stock Prices Move Too Much to be Justified by Subsequent Dividends? 71 Amer.Econ.Rev. 421, 432–33 (1981), suggests that "stock price volatility over the past century appears to be far too high to be attributed to new information about future real dividends if uncertainty about future dividends is measured by the sample standard deviations of real dividends around their long run exponential growth path." See also Roll, R2, 42 J.Fin. 541 (1988). French and Roll, Stock Return Variances: The Arrival of Information and the Reaction of Traders, 17 J.Fin. Econ. 17 (1986), shows that return volatility is greater when the market is open than when it is closed. This finding implies that the market makes its own news—news not keyed to fundamental value points. Finally, it seems that including a stock in the S & P 500 always causes its price to spike upward. Wurgler and Zhuravskaya, Does Arbitrage Flatten Demand Curves for Stocks? (Harvard University Working Paper 1999). Stock prices depart from fundamental value in all of these cases, resulting in a negative implication for the allocative efficiency assertion.

• **Timing.** There are a number of documented patterns in stock returns over weekends, holidays, and different calendar periods. One is the "week-end effect": a pattern of systematic negative returns on Mondays. See Keim and Stanbaugh, A Further Investigation of the Week End Effect on Stock Returns, 39 J.Fin. 819 (1984); Schatzberg and Datta, The Weekend Effect and Corporate Dividend Announcements, 15 J.Fin.Research 69 (1992). There also is a "holiday effect." Ariel, High Stock Returns before Holidays: Existence and Evidence on Possible Causes, 45 J.Fin. 1611 (1990), shows that over one third of the total return accruing to the market portfolio from 1963 to 1982 was earned on the eight yearly trading days falling before holiday closings. Even the core EMH assertion respecting fundamental analysis and the rapidity of price changes has been questioned. Stice, The Market Reaction to 10–K and 10–Q Filings and to Subsequent *The Wall Street Journal* Earnings Announcements, 66 Accounting Rev. 42 (1991), shows that in cases where earnings results are reported first in an SEC filing with the press announcement coming several days later, the market reaction comes only upon the subsequent announcement to the media.

• **Weather.** Hirschliefer and Shumway, Good Day Sunshine: Stock Returns and Weather, 58 J. Fin. 1009 (2003), finds a significant positive correlation between morning sunshine and stock returns in twenty-six countries. Rain and snow, however, are unrelated to returns.

• **Serial Correlations.** Other studies show positive and negative serial correlations of stock prices over different periods of time. Over short periods of time, from a week, a month, six months, or a year, price changes tend to persist. Jegadeesh and Titman, Returns to Buying Winners and Selling Losers: Implications for Stock Market Efficiency, 48 J. Fin. 65 (1993). Over periods of longer than a year, in contrast, stock returns display a negative serial correlation. De Bondt and Thaler, Does the Stock Market Overreact? 40 J. Fin. 793 (1985). Note that these findings contradict not only to the semi-strong version of the EMH, but also the random walk model. For critical discussions of this work, see Fama, Efficient

Capital Markets: II, 46 J.Fin. 1575, 1609 (1991); Malkiel, Is the Stock Market Efficient? 243 Science 1313, 1314 (1989).

● **Contrarian Investment Strategies**. A related body of studies shows that "value" investing strategies produce high returns over time. Fama and French, The Cross–Section of Expected Stock Returns, 47 J.Fin. 427 (1992), compares portfolios with a low ratio of stock market value of equity to book value of equity to portfolios of firms with high ratios. High market to book firms tend to be "growth" firms whose stocks are favored by the market, while low market to book firms are inexpensive "value" stocks. Fama and French show that historically, portfolios of high market to book stocks earn significantly lower returns than do value portfolios. Lakonishok, Shleifer and Vishny, Contrarian Investment, Extrapolation, and Risk, 49 J.Fin. 1541 (1994), adds that high market to book firms have a higher market risk than do low market to book firms. The implication is that stale information can be predictive of returns. The results also suggest that growth stock investors suffer from a cognitive limitation: They overreact optimistically to the recent history of good news about those stocks, paying too much on the assumption that past earnings growth can be extrapolated into the indefinite future. At the same time, they overreact in the negative to the stocks of firms that have suffered recent reverses. Lakonishok, Shleifer, and Vishny assert that institutional investors make the same mistake, confusing investment in stocks with outstanding performance records in recent periods with "prudent" investment.

● **Sentiment.** A number of investigations look to investor sentiment to explain serially correlated returns. Baker and Wurgler, Investor Sentiment and the Cross–Section of Stock Returns, 61 J. Fin.1645 (2006), lays out a history of sentimental ups and downs in different stock market sectors since 1961. They then test stock returns across high sentiment (bull) and low sentiment (bear) markets. They find that in low sentiment markets small firms, newly listed firms, highly volatile firms, and unprofitable firms earn high subsequent returns. When sentiment is high, the size effect disappears. For new, volatile, and unprofitable firms, the pattern reverses–what the authors describe as "sign-flipping predictive power."

4. *Continuing Debate.*

Fama and French, Multi–Factor Explanations of Market Pricing Anomalies, 51 J. Fin. 55 (1996), Fama and French, Size and Book-to-Market Factors in Earnings and Returns, 50 J. Fin. 131 (1995), and Fama and French, Common Risk Factors in the Returns on Stocks and Bonds, 33 J. Fin. Econ. 427 (1993), propose an alternative explanation for some of the foregoing results. Their explanation is well-aligned with the EMH even as it follows from their attack on the CAPM, infra Part I. They assert that (a) the CAPM has failed to provide an asset pricing model adequate to the task of interpreting the foregoing results in a coherent risk-return framework, and (b) market equity and book to market equity can be substituted as variables proving that growth stock and value stock risk and return are related positively. More specifically, they show that value stocks show higher returns because they are more risky. Conversely, large stocks earn lower returns because they are safer. Growth stocks earn lower average returns because they represent hedges against market to book risk. By thus showing a direct connection between risk and market returns, Fama and French purport to reconfirm the rationality of stock pricing. See also Malkiel, The Efficient Market Hypothesis and Its Critics, 17 J. Econ. Perspectives 59 (2003)(contending that markets are more efficient than the critics would have us believe and insisting that anomalies do not create portfolio trading opportunities yielding extraordinary risk adjusted returns).

Lakonishok, Shleifer, and Vishny, supra, respond to Fama and French. They question whether the book to market ratio captures a cogent measurement of risk and contend that there is no direct evidence that value stocks carry more risk. They also show affirmatively that value stocks do not underperform during times of distress. Their test leads them to conclude, unlike Fama and French, that the market picks up its pricing mistakes only very slowly over a five year period—it in effect continues to extrapolate from the past performance of both glamour and value issues, eventually correcting its irrational evaluation toward the end of the period.

(B) BEHAVIORAL FINANCE: THE NOISE TRADING APPROACH AND OTHER ALTERNATIVES TO THE EFFICIENT MARKET HYPOTHESIS

The EMH assumes (1) that to the extent that investors trade irrationally, their trades are random and cancel each other out, and (2) that to the extent irrational investors' trades correlate with one another and do not cancel out, they are met in the market by rational arbitrageurs whose trades eliminate their influence on prices. See Shleifer, supra, p. 2. Arbitrage means finding two things that are essentially the same but priced differently in the market. The arbitrageur buys the cheaper and sells the more expensive. The market is efficiently priced when all arbitrage opportunities have been exhausted.

The empirical work discussed in the preceding Note has prompted the EMH's critics to mount a direct theoretical attack on the foregoing assumptions. If the critics' attack on the validity of the assumptions is on the mark and the EMH is wrong, then a question arises: If competition among diverse investors and arbitrage does not keep stock prices close to fundamental value, conceived in terms of discounted flows of future dividends, what factors *do* determine stock prices? The critics respond with a new body of stock pricing theory. Drawing on the empirical findings, this work focuses on psychological factors, "noise" trading, and fads in investment styles.

Such speculation is not new. There were insightful conjectures about the behavior of market actors long before the current interest in the nature and import of efficient markets. The most famous of these is a metaphor set out in Keynes, General Theory of Employment, Interest and Money 156 (1936):

" * * * professional investment may be likened to those newspaper competitions in which the competitors have to pick out the six prettiest faces from a hundred photographs, the prize being awarded to the competitor whose choice most nearly corresponds to the average preferences of the competitors as a whole; so that each competitor has to pick, not those faces which he himself finds prettiest, but those which he thinks likeliest to catch the fancy of the other competitors, all of whom are looking at the problem from the same point of view. It is not a case of choosing those which, to the best of one's judgment, are really the prettiest, nor even those which average opinion genuinely thinks the prettiest. We have reached the third degree where we devote our intelligences to anticipating what average opinion expects the average opinion to be. And there are some, I believe, who practice the fourth, fifth and higher degrees."

Shleifer and Summers, The Noise Trader Approach to Finance

4 J.Econ. Perspectives 19, 19–22, 23–26 (1990).

* * * Our approach rests on two assumptions. First, some investors are not fully rational and their demand for risky assets is affected by their beliefs and sentiments that are not fully justified by fundamental news. Second, arbitrage—defined as trading by fully rational investors not subject to such sentiment—is risky and therefore limited. The two assumptions together imply that changes in investor sentiment are not fully countered by arbitrageurs and so affect security returns. We argue that this approach to financial markets is in many ways superior to the efficient markets paradigm.

* * * The efficient markets hypothesis obtains only as an extreme case of perfect riskless arbitrage that is unlikely to apply in practice. * * * [T]he investor sentiment/limited arbitrage approach yields a more accurate description of the financial markets * * *.

* * *

The Limits of Arbitrage

We think of the market as consisting of two types of investors: "arbitrageurs"—also called "smart money" and "rational speculators"—and other investors. Arbitrageurs are defined as investors who form fully rational expectations about security returns. In contrast, the opinions and trading patterns of other investors—also known as "noise traders" and "liquidity traders"—may be subject to systematic biases. In practice, the line between arbitrageurs and other investors may be blurred, but for our argument it helps to draw a sharp distinction between them, since the arbitrageurs do the work of bringing prices toward fundamentals.

Arbitrageurs play a central role in standard finance. They trade to ensure that if a security has a perfect substitute—a portfolio of other securities that yields the same returns—then the price of the security equals the price of that substitute portfolio. If the price of the security falls below that of the substitute portfolio, arbitrageurs sell the portfolio and buy the security until the prices are equalized, and vice versa if the price of a security rises above that of the substitute portfolio. When the substitute is indeed perfect, this arbitrage is riskless. As a result, arbitrageurs have perfectly elastic demand for the security at the price of its substitute portfolio. Arbitrage thus assures that relative prices of securities must be in line for there to be no riskless arbitrage opportunities. Such riskless arbitrage is very effective for derivative securities, such as futures and options, but also for individual stocks and bonds where reasonably close substitutes are usually available.

Although riskless arbitrage ensures that relative prices are in line, it does not help to pin price levels of, say, stocks or bonds as a whole. These classes of securities do not have close substitute portfolios, and therefore if for some reason they are mispriced, there is no riskless hedge for the arbitrageur. For example, an arbitrageur who thinks that stocks are underpriced cannot buy stocks and sell the substitute portfolio, since such a portfolio does not exist. The arbitrageur can instead simply buy stocks in hopes of an above-normal return, but this arbitrage is no longer riskless. If the arbitrageur is risk-averse, his demand for underpriced stocks will be limited. With a finite number of arbitrageurs, their combined demand curve is no longer perfectly elastic.

Two types of risk limit arbitrage. The first is fundamental risk. Suppose that stocks are selling above the expected value of future dividends and an arbitrageur is selling them short. The arbitrageur then bears the risk that the realization of dividends—or of the news about dividends—is better than expected, in which case he loses on his trade. Selling "over-valued" stocks is risky because there is always a chance that the market will do very well. Fear of such a loss limits the arbitrageur's original position, and keeps his short-selling from driving prices all the way down to fundamentals.

The second source of risk that limits arbitrage comes from unpredictability of the future resale price * * *. Suppose again that stocks are overpriced and an arbitrageur is selling them short. As long as the arbitrageur is thinking of liquidating his position in the future, he must bear the risk that at that time stocks will be even more overpriced than they are today. If future mispricing is more extreme than when the arbitrage trade is put on, the arbitrageur suffers a loss on his position. Again, fear of this loss limits the size of the arbitrageur's initial position, and so keeps him from driving the price all the way down to fundamentals.

Clearly, this resale price risk depends on the arbitrageur having a finite horizon. If the arbitrageur's horizon is infinite, he simply sells the stock short and pays dividends on it in all the future periods, recognizing that the present value of those is lower than his proceeds from the short sale. But there are several reasons that it makes sense to assume that arbitrageurs have short horizons. Most importantly, arbitrageurs have to borrow cash or securities to implement their trades, and as a result must pay the lenders per period fees. These fees cumulate over the period that the position remains open, and can add up to large amounts for long term arbitrage. The structure of transaction costs thus induces a strong bias toward short horizons * * *. In addition, the performance of most money managers is evaluated at least one year and usually once every few months, also limiting the horizon of arbitrage. As a result of these problems, resources dedicated to long-term arbitrage against fundamental mispricing are very scarce.

* * *

These arguments that risk makes arbitrage ineffective actually understate the limits of arbitrage. After all, they presume that the arbitrageur knows the fundamental value of the security. In fact, the arbitrageur might not exactly know what this value is, or be able to detect price changes that reflect deviations from fundamentals. In this case, arbitrage is even riskier than before.

* * *

Substantial evidence shows that, contrary to the efficient markets hypothesis, arbitrage does not completely counter responses of prices to fluctuations in uninformed demand. Of course, identifying such fluctuations in demand is tricky, since price changes may reflect new market information which changes the equilibrium price at which arbitrageurs trade. Several recent studies do, however, avoid this objection by looking at responses of prices to changes in demand that do not plausibly reflect any new fundamental information because they have institutional or tax motives.

* * *

Investor Sentiment

Some shifts in investor demand for securities are completely rational. Such changes could reflect, for example, reactions to public announcements that affect future growth rate of dividends, risk, or risk aversion. Rational demand changes can also reflect adjustment to news conveyed through the trading process itself. Finally, rational demand changes can reflect tax trading or trading done for institutional reasons of the types discussed above.

But not all demand changes appear to be so rational; some seem to be a response to changes in expectations or sentiment that are not fully justified by information. Such changes can be a response to pseudo-signals that investors believe convey information about future returns but that would not convey such information in a fully rational model * * *. An example of such pseudo-signals is advice of brokers or financial gurus. We use the term "noise traders" to describe such investors * * *. Changes in demand can also reflect investors' use of inflexible trading strategies or of "popular models" * * *. One such strategy is trend chasing. Although these changes in demand are unwarranted by fundamentals, they can be related to fundamentals, as in the case of overreaction to news.

These demand shifts will only matter if they are correlated across noise traders. If all investors trade randomly, their trades cancel out and there are no aggregate shifts in demand. Undoubtedly, some trading in the market brings together noise traders with different models who cancel each other out. However, many trading strategies based on pseudo-signals, noise, and popular models are correlated, leading to aggregate demand shifts. The reason for this is that judgment biases afflicting investors in processing information tend to be the same. Subjects in psychological experiments tend to make the same mistake; they do not make random mistakes.

Many of these persistent mistakes are relevant for financial markets. For example, experimental subjects tend to be overconfident * * * which makes them take on more risk. Experimental subjects also tend to extrapolate past time series, which can lead them to chase trends * * *. Finally, in making inferences experimental subjects put too little weight on base rates and too much weight on new information * * *, which might lead them to overreact to news.

* * *

A look at how market participants behave provides perhaps the most convincing evidence that noise rather than information drives many of their decisions. Investors follow market gurus and forecasters, such as Joe Granville and "Wall Street Week." Charging bulls, Jimmy Connors and John Houseman all affect where and how people entrust their money.

* * *

So-called "technical analysis" is another example of demand shifts without a fundamental rationalization. Technical analysis typically calls for buying more stocks when stocks have risen (broke through a barrier), and selling stocks when they fall through a floor.

* * *

There can be little doubt that these sorts of factors influence demand for securities, but can they be big enough to make a difference? The standard economist's reason for doubting the size of these effects has been to posit that investors trading on noise might lose their money to arbitrageurs, leading to a diminution of their wealth and effect on demand * * *. Noise traders might also learn the error of their ways and reform into rational arbitrageurs.

However, the argument that noise traders lose money and eventually disappear is not self-evident. First, noise traders might be on average more aggressive than the arbitrageurs—either because they are overoptimistic or because they are overconfident—and so bear more risk. If risk-taking is rewarded in the market, noise traders can earn higher expected returns even despite buying high and selling low on average. The risk rewarded by the market need not even be fundamental; it can be the resale price risk arising from the unpredictability of future noise traders' opinions. With higher expected returns, noise traders as a group do not disappear from the market rapidly, if at all.

Of course, higher expected returns because of higher risk come together with a greater variance of returns. Noise traders might end up very rich with a trivial probability, and poor almost for sure. Almost for sure, then, they fail to affect demand in the long run. But in principle, either the expected return or the variance effect can dominate.

Learning and imitation may not adversely affect noise traders either. When noise traders earn high average returns, many other investors might imitate them, ignoring the fact that they took more risk and just got lucky. Such imitation brings more money to follow noise traders strategies. Noise traders themselves might become even more cocky, attributing their investment success to skill rather than luck. As noise traders who do well become more aggressive, their effect on demand increases.

The case against the importance of noise traders also ignores the fact that new investors enter the market all the time, and old investors who have lost money come back. These investors are subject to the same judgment biases as the current survivors in the market and so add to the effect of judgment biases on demand.

These arguments suggest that the case for long run unimportance of noise traders is at best premature. In other words, shifts in the demand for stocks that do not depend on news or fundamental factors are likely to affect prices even in the long run.

Explaining the Puzzles

When arbitrage is limited, and investor demand for securities responds to noise and to predictions of popular models, security prices move in response to these changes in demand as well as to changes in fundamentals. Arbitrageurs counter the shifts in demand prompted by changes in investor sentiment, but do not eliminate the effects of such shifts on the price completely.

＊ ＊ ＊

The effects of demand shifts on prices are larger when most investors follow the finance textbooks and passively hold the market portfolio. In this case, a switch in the sentiment of some investors is not countered by a change of position of all the market participants, but only of a few arbitrageurs. The smaller the risk bearing capacity of arbitrageurs, the bigger the effect of a sentiment shift on the price. A simple example highlights this point. Suppose that all investors are sure that the market is efficient and hold the market portfolio. Now suppose that one investor decides to hold additional shares of a particular security. Its price is driven to infinity.

This approach fits very neatly with the conventional nonacademic view of financial markets. On that view, the key to investment success is not just predicting future fundamentals, but also predicting the movement of other active investors. Market professionals spend considerable resources tracking price trends, volume, short interest, odd lot volume, investor sentiment indexes and numerous other gauges of demand for equities. Tracking these possible indicators of demand makes no sense if prices responded only to fundamental news and not to investor demand. They make perfect sense, in contrast, in a world where investor sentiment moves prices and so predicting changes in this sentiment pays. The prevalence of investment strategies based on indicators of demand in financial markets suggests the recognition by arbitrageurs of the role of demand.

Not only do arbitrageurs spend time and money to predict noise trader moves, they also make active attempts to take advantage of these moves. When noise traders are optimistic about particular securities, it pays arbitrageurs to create more of them. These securities might be mutual funds, new share issues, penny oil stocks, or junk bonds: anything that is overpriced at the moment.

＊ ＊ ＊

When they bet against noise traders, arbitrageurs begin to look like noise traders themselves. They pick stocks instead of diversifying, because that is what betting against noise traders requires. They time the market to take advantage of noise trader mood swings. If these swings are temporary, arbitrageurs who cannot predict noise trader moves simply follow contrarian strategies. It becomes hard to tell the noise traders from the arbitrageurs.

NOTE: BEHAVIORAL THEORY

1. *Shorting the Stock.*

Assume that you discern that the shares of ABC Corp. are overpriced at the present price of $25 with the correct price being $18. You also believe that the market price in the long run will approximate fundamental value. You accordingly predict that ABC shares will decline. You can profit on the projection by selling 1,000 shares you do not presently own and covering the position later when the shares sell for $18. The profit on the play will be $7,000, the difference between the $25,000 proceeds of the sale and the $18,000 cost of covering the position later by buying the shares at the lower price of $18. To sell shares you do not own is to "short" the stock.

Shorting is easy to do, but the process has its complications. One opens a short position by borrowing the shares to be sold from a broker. (The broker draws on inventories of shares that it holds in street name for its customers.) At this point one pockets the proceeds of sale, owing the broker not that amount but the number of shares sold. One covers by buying the number of shares owed in the market. During the period the position is open one must pay the broker any dividends paid on the stock; the broker in turn pays that amount over to its customer. In theory one can hold the position open indefinitely so long as the broker has a customer holding ABC stock who has permitted the broker to borrow it.

Under stock exchange rules, the short customer must hold the proceeds of sale in an account with the broker. (A short customer with bargaining power might be able to negotiate for some income return on this sum during the time the position is open.) The customer also must post a "margin"—a percentage of sale proceeds (say 30 or 50 percent) in addition to the proceeds of sale. This is collateral to cover the possibility of loss in the event the stock goes up and stays up. Let us say that you post a $12.50 per share margin on the ABC short sale and that ABC stock goes up to $37.50. The increase exhausts the margin. At that point you face a margin call— you must stake additional cash or close out the position.

2. *The Limits of Arbitrage.*

A pure arbitrage play requires that the mispriced security have a close substitute security which is not also mispriced. Given an overpriced security, the arbitrageur shorts the overpriced issue and hedges by purchasing the correctly priced substitute. For some securities, such as derivatives like futures and options, close substitutes are available. But for stocks and bonds as a whole there is no substitute portfolio and therefore no riskless hedge for the arbitrageur. Individual securities, in contrast, often do have close substitutes. But arbitrage still carries a risk of unexpected good news on the short position and unexpected bad news on the long position. Shleifer, supra, pp. 13–14. In addition, under the noise trader approach, arbitrage is limited because noise traders driven by sentiment affect stock prices and sentiment is unpredictable. Note also that the trading capacity of arbitrageurs who play with borrowed capital will be constrained by a shock in noise demand that not only moves prices away from fundamental value but makes lenders nervous, causing a credit cut back. Shleifer and Vishny, The Limits of Arbitrage, 52 J. Fin. 35 (1997). These points have been applied (1) to suggest that stocks will have higher returns than their fundamentals warrant because stocks will be subject to larger fluctuations of investor sentiment than bonds and thus will command enlarged risk premiums, and (2) to explain the persistence of closed-end fund discounts. See De Long, Shleifer, Summers & Waldmann, Noise Trader Risk in Financial Markets, 98 J.Pol.Econ. 703, 724–730 (1990); Lee, Schleifer & Thaler, Investor Sentiment and the Closed–End Fund Puzzle, 46 J.Fin. 75 (1991).

3. *Psychological Bases.*

Kahneman and Riepe, Aspects of Investor Psychology, 24 J. Portfolio Mgt. 52 (1998), catalogs several ways in which investors deviate from maxims of economic rationality when they make decisions: (a) When assessing risky investments people do not take a neutral look at projected outcomes. Instead they gauge the possible gains and losses from subjective reference points that vary from situation to situation. They also display risk aversion that causes them to be reluctant to sell stocks which lose value and demand super premiums for risky investments. (b) Investors do not make Bayesian probability assessments. They tend instead to make predictions by taking a short history or small set of facts and expanding it into a broader picture. This behavior pattern, termed the "representativeness heuristic," leads people to perceive patterns in random sequences. See Kahneman and Tversky, On the Psychology of Prediction, 80 Psychological Rev. 237 (1973). Representativeness leads to the overreactions and underreactions documented in the empirical literature on growth and value stocks. (c) The manner in which an investment choice is framed can influence investor choice. Assume that stocks have long-term positive returns but that recent short term stock market results have been volatile. When the former fact is stressed, investors weight stocks more heavily in their portfolios than they do when the latter point is stressed.

4. *Theoretical Extensions and Current Debates.*

Barberis, Shleifer and Vishny, A Model of Investor Sentiment, 49 J. Fin. Econ. 307 (1998), pulls together much of the foregoing in a formal model. The model combines representativeness and a related phenomenon, conservatism, defined as slow updating of models in the face of new evidence. It depicts investors with a given information set about a stock. When they receive favorable news about the firm's earnings, they fail to give the news due weight in valuing the firm. As a result, the stock price underreacts to the news and displays a short term trend. As time passes and investors are confronted repeatedly with similar favorable news, they give up the old model and due to representativeness, adopt a new model that shows earnings in an upward trend. In making the shift they underestimate the probability that the past good news has resulted from chance rather than from the causal sequence depicted in the new model. As a result, the stock price now overreacts to the good news.

Compare Daniel, Hirshleifer, and Subramanyam, Investor Psychology and Security Market Under-and Overreactions, 53 J. Fin. 1839 (1998), which offers an alternative explanation. This model looks at the market's well-informed price setters and suggests two flaws: (a) overconfidence, which causes them to exaggerate the precision of their private signals about a stock's value, and (b) biased self-attribution, which causes them to underestimate the significance of public signals about value, especially when it contradicts their private signals. Compare also Hong and Stein, A Unified Theory of Underreaction, Momentum Trading, and Overreaction in Asset Markets, 54 J. Fin. 2143 (1999). This model depicts two types of irrational investors: (a) newswatchers, who receive private signals about value but who do not learn from market prices; and (b) momentum investors, who have no private information and trade on the basis of recent changes in price. Both types influence price, as new private information diffuses to be reinforced by momentum trading.

The number of EMH supporters in the financial economic community appears to be dwindling rapidly. Consider the positions of one of the leaders, Eugene Fama. In 1998, in Fama, Market Efficiency, Long–Term Returns, and Behavioral Finance, 49 J. Fin. Econ. 283 (1998), he was quite critical of the many studies of long-term market pricing anomalies. Some, he said, may be explained as rational market pricing. Many others can be attributed to chance and tend to disappear when measured pursuant to alternative statistical approaches. The foregoing models, meanwhile, did not in his view succeed in explaining wider terrain of empirical results showing stock price over-or underreaction. His more recent work takes a more neutral posture. See Fama and French, Disagreement, Tastes, and Asset Prices, 83 J. Fin. Econ. 667 (2007), which explores the potential for misinformed investors and investor tastes to influence stock prices.

5. *Implications for Legal Policy.*

What are the implications of the noise trading approach for legal policy making? For discussion, see Dunbar and Heller, Fraud on the Market Meets Behavioral Finance, 31 Del. J. Corp. L. 455 (2006); Fisher, Does Efficient Market Theory Help Us Do Justice in a Time of Madness? 54 Emory L. J. 843 (2005); Langevoort, Taming the Animal Spirits of the Stock Markets, A Behavioral Approach to Securities Regulation, 97 Nw. U. L. Rev. 135 (2002); Langevoort, Half–Truths: Protecting Mistaken Inferences By Investors and Others, 52 Stan. L. Rev. 1499 (1999); Stout, How Efficient Markets Undervalue Stocks: CAPM and ECMH Under Conditions of Uncertainty and Disagreement, 19 Cardozo L. Rev. 475 (1997); Hill, Why Financial Appearances Might Matter: An Explanation for "Dirty Pooling" and Some Other Types of Financial Cosmetics, 22 Del. J. Corp. L. 141 (1997); Langevoort, Selling Hope, Selling Risk: Some Lessons for Law From Behavioral Economics About Stockbrokers and Sophisticated Customers, 84 Cal. L. Rev. 627 (1996); Stout, Are Stock Markets Costly Casinos? Disagreement, Market Failure, and Securities Regulation, 81 Va. L. Rev. 611 (1995); Langevoort, Theories, Assumptions, and Securities Regulation: Market Efficiency Revisited, 140 U.Pa.L.Rev. 851 (1992).

Given noise trading and a market price that need not reflect fundamental values, how should the law characterize the duties of corporate managers to shareholders? Should they maximize the stock price, or maximize the value of the firm, taken as the discounted value of future cash flows? In the absence of a generally accepted theory of asset pricing and noise trading, maximum stock price and maximum firm value will not necessarily be identical. Ayres, Back to *Basics:* Regulating How Corporations Speak to the Market, 77 Va.L.Rev. 945, 993–994 (1991), suggests that since different shareholders may have different objectives and corporate practices respecting information disclosure can impact on their interests, firms should "announce their planned quantity and quality of corporate speech then allow shareholders to sort themselves by voting with their feet—investing in those corporations that provide their preferred package of speech and divesting their holdings in corporations that do not." For a contrasting view, see Hu, Risk, Time, and Fiduciary Principles in Corporate Investment, 38 UCLA L.Rev. 277, 290–291 (1990).

NOTE: BUBBLES AND CRASHES

1. *Equity Markets at the Millennium.*

On December 5, 1996, Federal Reserve Chairman Alan Greenspan used the term "irrational exuberance" to describe the behavior of investors in the stock market. In the eyes of many, the term still applied—only more so—four years later.

The Dow, which stood at 3,600 in early 1994, had risen to 11,700 by the opening of trading in 2000. As Robert J. Shiller noted in *Irrational Exuberance* (2000), basic economic indicators had not come close to tripling during this period. U.S. personal income and gross domestic product had risen 30 percent, with half of that increase due to inflation. Corporate profits had done better. They doubled between the recession year 1992 and 1997 and rose 60 percent between 1994 and 2000. But stock prices had far outstripped them. In January 2000, the P/E ratio for the S & P Composite Index—taken as a function of current market price over an inflation corrected 10 year average of past earnings—stood at an all time high of 44.3. The previous high was 32.6, reached in September 1929. Id. at 4–8.

Evidence on dividend yields told a similar story. From 1946 to the mid 1990s, the dividend yield on the S & P 500 tended toward 4 cents on the dollar. In the mid–1990s it dropped to 2 cents. By mid 1998 it was 1.5 cents. Cornell, The Equity Risk Premium: The Long–Run Future of the Stock Market 160 (1999). The story was told again in terms of Tobin's Q and gross domestic product. Tobin's Q is a value measure of the ratio of the market value of the firm's equity over the replacement cost of its assets. One study showed an average level of 0.72 for this ratio from 1926 to 1997, with 90 percent of the ratios for individual firms during the period falling in a range between 0.40 and 1.35. At the end of 1997, however, the average Tobin's Q across the market had gone over 1.60. Similarly, from 1926 to 1996 the average ratio of total stock market equity to gross domestic product was 0.54, exceeding 1.0 only in 1929. By April 1998, the value of stocks had run the ratio to 1.8. Id. at 164.

These statistics signaled that stock prices had ceased to reflect fundamental value. Shiller and others believed that the markets were experiencing a classic speculative bubble. Shiller identified a number of "precipitating" structural factors that contributed to its appearance. These included a wide range of things: demographics—the maturation of the baby boomers, the arrival of the Internet, changes in pension plans and pension investment and the rise of mutual funds, low inflation, the political consensus favoring low taxes and consequent expectations of capital gains cuts, reverence for business success, the spread of and social acceptability of gambling, and a decline in the quality of professional investment advice. Shiller, supra, pp. 17–43. Said Shiller, the combined effect of these factors was amplified though a feedback loop. This was a "naturally occurring Ponzi process" through which investor confidence, buoyed up by past price increases, bid stock prices farther up. The rising prices enticed more investors into the market, and they bid the prices up even more. More investors come in, and the process repeated itself—again and again. Id. at 44–68. The feedback process, said Shiller, was not merely a matter of arithmetical chart-making projecting an upward rise. The bubble reflected changes in the culture's overall thought patterns. The cultural changes contributing to the overvaluation had been shaped by the news media, with their obsession with market records of various kinds, their short-termism, their delight in bandwagons, and their appetite for stories about the "new era" economy. Id. at 69–102. Unsurprisingly, the EMH had no place in Shiller's account.

Significantly, the high market prices had their defenders. They made two arguments. We will see in Section B, infra, that on a dividend theory of valuation, Present Value (PV)= d/r-g, where d is the current period dividend, the r is the capitalization rate and g is the growth rate of the dividend stream. If PV rises markedly and in so doing reflects fundamental value, then one of two things must have happened (or perhaps both). Either projections of g in future periods have risen markedly, or the capitalization rate presently applied has dropped markedly due to a decline in the riskless rate of return, in the risk attending the stock, or in investors' level of risk aversion. The leading defenses of late 1990s markets followed this logic. It was argued (a) that we had a new economy that would produce indefinite and significant increases in productivity and earnings growth, and (b) that common stocks were less risky than formerly thought and the risk premium built into equity capitalization rates would decline significantly in future periods. Looking back on those arguments in 2007, one can only wonder what people were thinking. But the stories stand for an important point: fundamental value stories always accompany irrational run ups in market prices.

2.   *The Crash of 1987 and the Correction of 2000–2001.*

Price bubbles tend to be associated with subsequent market crashes. On this view, a crash is an abrupt correction of a speculatively and irrationally inflated price. The stock market crash of 1929 and the crash of seventeenth century Dutch tulip prices are oft-stated examples of this. But a crash can occur without an antecedent bubble. The October 1987 stock market crash is an example. In early October 1987, the Dow Jones average was at approximately 2600. Then, on October 19, the Dow Jones fell by more than 500 points on unprecedented trading volume. Before the end of the month, the Dow was trading under 1800—a drop of about one third on the month. Prices did not rebound immediately, but did return to pre-crash levels in 1988.

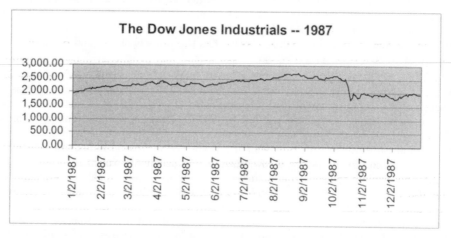

Compare the picture at the turn of the 21st century. Observers in 2000 expressed the hope that inflated equity prices would correct slowly over time rather than suddenly in a crash. Whether such expectations were fulfilled depended on the market sector. The chart that follows compares monthly closes of the S & P 500 index, the Dow Jones Technology index, and the Dow Jones Telecommunications index for the period 1995 to 2005. All three peaked in 2000 and thereafter declined until 2003. The indices otherwise had very different behavior patterns. Neither the S & P 500 nor the telecommunications index can be said to have crashed, however irrational some of the exuberance that fueled gains in the late 1990s. In contrast, the technology index starkly presents a picture of bubble followed by crash.

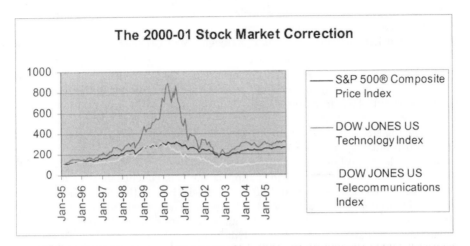

The 2000-01 Stock Market Correction

— S&P 500® Composite Price Index

— DOW JONES US Technology Index

DOW JONES US Telecommunications Index

As technology stocks hit the stratosphere beginning in 1998, very few observers were citing the EMH for the proposition that the prices reflected fundamental value. The damage already had been done in 1987. Some observers explained that crash by referring to technical factors rather than changes in economic fundamentals. Three factors dominated these discussions. See generally, Report of the Presidential Task Force on Market Mechanisms (1988) (the "Brady Report"): (a) Observers noted that an imbalance of sell orders had exhausted market liquidity. Once the exchange hit its capacity, prices fell drastically. But this does not work as a complete explanation, for prices did not rebound once liquidity was restored. See Harris, The Dangers of Regulatory Overreaction to the October 1987 Crash, 74 Cornell L.Rev. 927, 933 (1989). (b) Observers blamed arbitrage between index futures and the stock market, and the "program trading" mechanism for executing the orders of arbitrageurs. But, according to Harris, supra, this explanation also was unpersuasive: "Arbitrage only serves to link the two markets together. * * * [It] cannot explain the sell order submitted in the first place." (c) Observers blamed the use of a "price insensitive" strategy called "portfolio insurance." Portfolio insurance is a dynamic hedging strategy pursuant to which an investor tries to maintain a synthetic put option on a portfolio. A put option is an option to sell a security at a stated exercise price. If one buys a stock and a put on the stock simultaneously, down-side risk on the stock holding is reduced—if the stock drops below the exercise price on the put, one exercises the put and thus receives the difference between the exercise price and the depressed stock price less the cost of the put. Under the synthetic option strategy, one buys stock or stock index futures when the market is rising and sells stock when the market falls. Specifically, one gets down-side protection by short-selling a proportion of the shares held and placing the proceeds, plus the cost of the put in a safe security. The idea is that the portfolio's value does not fall below a fixed value called the "strike price," and that the portfolio also does not perform worse than the market as a whole. To maintain the synthetic option, the strike price must constantly change with the market. Thus the strike price goes up with the market, locking in the holders' gains. But, with a market drop, the owner of the insurance has to sell more shares short (or more index risk). These orders add to selling pressure in the market. On the day of the crash, portfolio insurance schemes caused waves of institutional selling.

Subsequent studies cast doubt the conclusion that sell orders stemming from portfolio insurance caused the crash. See Brennan and Schwartz, "Portfolio Insurance and Financial Market Equilibrium," 62 J.Bus. 455 (1989). The $6 billion of portfolio insurance outstanding amounted to less than 0.2 percent of the $3.5

trillion of equity value in existence at dawn on October 19. Sales pressure of this magnitude does not, taken alone, account for a 20 percent loss of value. See Gennotte and Leland, Market Liquidity, Hedging and Crashes, 80 Amer.Econ.Rev. 99 (1990).

Shleifer and Summers, supra, at 29, also refuse to ascribe the crash to portfolio insurance. They explain it in terms of "positive feedback trading"—the tendency to chase the trend. The dramatic rise in the 1987 market to a peak in August as investors chased the trend; then downside positive feedback trading caused the crash, once it started, to go deep. Id. at 28–30. This, in effect, returns us to the Keynesian beauty contest, but with a contemporary title. Seyhun, Overreaction or Fundamentals: Some Lessons from Insiders' Response to the Market Crash of 1987, 45 J. Finance 1363 (1990), provides support for this conclusion with a study of insider stock purchases before and after the crash. Before the crash there was no increase in insider selling activity. But after the crash insiders bought their own firms' stocks in record numbers. This implies that fundamentals were not driving the market and that "overreaction" contributed to the crash.

SECTION B.   ELEMENTS OF FUNDAMENTAL VALUE

Valuation comes down to three basic points: (1) money has a time value; (2) value is cash in your pocket, not numbers on a page; and (3) people are risk averse. This Section takes up each point in turn.

1.   THE TIME VALUE OF MONEY

To say that money has a time value is to say that a dollar paid in the future is worth less than a dollar today. To make an investment is to part with money today in exchange for a return payment (or series of payments) in the future. Valuation is the exercise of appraising the future payment or payment held out by a potential investment. The exercise thus entails the translation of the future value into present value—the future returns must be *discounted*. Discounting is fundamental to the valuation process. It is important that there be no confusion about how this process works.

One knows intuitively that a dollar to be paid in the future is worth less than a dollar payable today, but it may be worthwhile to advance two related arguments which support that intuition. First, as long as investors or consumers are willing to borrow funds at a positive rate of interest, money has a time value. The owner of $1,000 today can, if he wishes, deposit that sum in a federally insured savings account at 5.5 percent and have $1,055 at the end of a year. It follows that an individual would not be indifferent if offered a choice of receiving $1,000 today and $1,000 a year from now; he or she would always prefer $1,000 today, since that amount, deposited at interest, will grow to be a larger sum by the end of the year's waiting period. This is true, moreover, even if receipt of the future payment is a guaranteed certainty, i.e., even when risk is wholly absent.

Secondly, even if an individual desires to expend funds on consumption goods and is not interested in saving, it is reasonable to assume that a greater value is placed on present consumption than on future consumption. $1,000 worth of consumption today is better than $1,000 worth of consumption a year from now; satisfaction is pleasant, abstention less so. Hence an individual can be induced to forego current consumption only if paid for forbearance by the promise of greater satisfaction at a future date. But if nothing can be gained by waiting, one may as well indulge. Again, therefore, an individual would not be indifferent as between $1,000 today and $1,000 a year from now; the former would be preferred in almost every case. For both of these reasons, amounts to be received in the future must be discounted by some factor (rate of return or capitalization rate) if one wishes to ascertain their present worth.

Now a word about the usage of the terms "discount," "capitalization," and "multiplier" in the valuation literature. As a matter of practice, the terms "discount" or "discounting" are commonly used in reference to a finite set of future payments, e.g., the rents to be received from a 10–year lease. When the future payments are expected to continue in perpetuity— e.g., dividends on a share of stock—the terms "capitalization" or "capitalizing" are generally employed. One would say, for example, that the present value of $1,000 a year for 10 years is determined by "discounting" the stream of payments at a given interest rate, while the present value of $1,000 a year forever is determined by "capitalizing" the stream of payments at a given rate. The term "multiplier" refers to the reciprocal of the capitalization rate. Thus, if an 8 percent capitalization rate is assumed, the multiplier is 12.5 (i.e., $8/100 \times 12.5 = 1$); and the present value of $1,000 a year in perpetuity is $12.5 \times $1,000$ or $12,500.

Alchian and Allen, University Economics*

179–185 (3d ed. 1972).

The *more distant* the deferred service (or income, or goods), the *lower* its present price. At an interest rate of 6 percent, the current price of $1 deferred a year is 94 cents—the amount that will grow at 6 percent in one year to $1. This is given by the formula

$$p_1 = \frac{A}{(1 + r)} = \frac{\$1.00}{(1 + .06)} = \$.943.$$

[315a]

To get the present price for $1 deferred *two* years, simply repeat the above operation. If $1 deferred one year is now worth 94 cents, then deferring the dollar an additional year again reduces its present value by the same proportion. For two years, this is $.943 \times .943 = .890$. A dollar due in two years is worth 89 cents today.

This can be expressed by noting that at 6 percent per year 89 cents will grow in one year to 94 cents, and then in the second year the 94 cents will grow to exactly $1. This can be written in algebraic form

$$p_2 (1 + r)(1 + r) = A.$$

* From University Economics, Elements of Inquiry, Third Edition, by Armen A. Alchian and William R. Allen. © 1972 by Wadsworth Publishing Company, Inc., Belmont, California 94002. Reprinted by permission of the publisher.

where p represents the price now that will in two years grow at the 6 percent annual rate of interest to the amount A. Solving for p_2, we get

$$p_2 = \frac{A}{(1 + r)\,(1 + r)} = \frac{A}{(1 + r)^2} = \frac{\$1.00}{(1.06)^2} = \$.890.$$

[316a]

Two years' discounting is measured by the factor $1/(1 + .06)^2 = .890$; three years of discounting is obtained by multiplying the future amount due in three years by $1/(1.06)^3 = .839$. The present value of $1 deferred t years from today is obtained by use of the "present value factor" $1/(1.06)^t$. Multiplying an amount due at the end of t years by this present-value factor gives the present value (or present price, or discounted value) of the deferred amount, A, due in t years. A set of these present-value factors is given in Table 11-1 for various rates of interest and years of deferment. The present-value factor decreases as t is larger: the farther into the future an amount is deferred, the lower is its *present* value. This is in no way dependent upon an assumption of inflation of prices.

TABLE 11-1. Present Value of a Future $1: What a Dollar at End of Specified Future Year is Worth Today   PV of $1 * future pmt = PV

Year	3%	4%	5%	6%	7%	8%	10%	12%	15%	20%	Year
1	.971	.962	.952	.943	.935	.926	.909	.893	.870	.833	1
2	.943	.925	.907	.890	.873	.857	.826	.797	.756	.694	2
3	.915	.890	.864	.839	.816	.794	.751	.711	.658	.578	3
4	.889	.855	.823	.792	.763	.735	.683	.636	.572	.482	4
5	.863	.823	.784	.747	.713	.681	.620	.567	.497	.402	5
6	.838	.790	.746	.705	.666	.630	.564	.507	.432	.335	6
7	.813	.760	.711	.665	.623	.583	.513	.452	.376	.279	7
8	.789	.731	.677	.627	.582	.540	.466	.404	.326	.233	8
9	.766	.703	.645	.591	.544	.500	.424	.360	.284	.194	9
10	.744	.676	.614	.558	.508	.463	.385	.322	.247	.162	10
11	.722	.650	.585	.526	.475	.429	.350	.287	.215	.134	11
12	.701	.625	.557	.497	.444	.397	.318	.257	.187	.112	12
13	.681	.601	.530	.468	.415	.368	.289	.229	.162	.0935	13
14	.661	.577	.505	.442	.388	.340	.263	.204	.141	.0779	14
15	.642	.555	.481	.417	.362	.315	.239	.183	.122	.0649	15
16	.623	.534	.458	.393	.339	.292	.217	.163	.107	.0541	16
17	.605	.513	.436	.371	.317	.270	.197	.146	.093	.0451	17
18	.587	.494	.416	.350	.296	.250	.179	.130	.0808	.0376	18
19	.570	.475	.396	.330	.277	.232	.163	.116	.0703	.0313	19
20	.554	.456	.377	.311	.258	.215	.148	.104	.0611	.0261	20
25	.478	.375	.295	.232	.184	.146	.0923	.0588	.0304	.0105	25
30	.412	.308	.231	.174	.131	.0994	.0573	.0334	.0151	.00421	30
40	.307	.208	.142	.0972	.067	.0460	.0221	.0107	.00373	.000680	40
50	.228	.141	.087	.0543	.034	.0213	.00852	.00346	.000922	.000109	50

Each column lists how much a dollar received at the end of various years in the future is worth today. For example, at 6 percent per year a dollar to be received ten years hence is equivalent in value to $.558 now, in other words, $.558 invested now at 6 percent, with interest compounded annually, would grow to $1.00 in ten years. Note that $1.00 to be received at the end of fifty years is, at 6 percent, worth today just about a nickel. And at 10 percent it is worth only about .8 of one cent, which is to say that 8 mills (.8 of a cent) invested now would grow, at 10 percent interest compounded annually, to $1.00 in fifty years. Similarly $1,000 in fifty years is worth today $8.52, and $10,000 is worth today $85—all at 10 percent rate of interest. * * * Why not make that investment? Formula for entry in table is $1/(1 + r)^t$. (No inflation is involved in this table).

FUTURE AMOUNTS CORRESPONDING
TO GIVEN PRESENT VALUES

Instead of working from future amounts to present values, we can derive for any annual rate of interest the future amount that will be purchasable for any present value. How much will $1 paid now purchase if the future amount is due in one year, or in two years, or in three years? At 15 percent per year, $1 will be worth $1.15 in one year. And at 15 percent for the next year, that $1.15 will in turn grow to $1.32. Hence, $1 today is the present price or value of $1.32 in two years. In terms of our formula, this can be expressed

$$p_2(1 + r)(1 + r) = A.$$
$$\$1(1.15)(1.15) = \$1(1.32) = \$1.32.$$

If the future amount is deferred three years, the term (1.15) enters three times, and if deferred t years, it enters t times. For three years, the quantity (1.15) is multiplied together three times, denoted $(1.15)^3$, and equals 1.52. Therefore, in three years $1 will grow to $1.52. In general, the formula is

$$p_t(1 + r)^t = A$$

for any present payment, p_t that is paid for an amount A available t years later. The multiplicative factor $(1 + r)^t$ is called the *future-value* (or *amount*) *factor*. Values of this future-amount factor for different combinations of t and r are given in Table 11-2. For example, at 6 percent in five

TABLE 11-2. Compound Amount of $1: Amount to Which $1 Now Will Grow by End of Specified Year at Compounded Interest

Year	3%	4%	5%	6%	7%	8%	10%	12%	15%	20%	Year
1	1.03	1.04	1.05	1.06	1.07	1.08	1.10	1.12	1.15	1.20	1
2	1.06	1.08	1.10	1.12	1.14	1.17	1.21	1.25	1.32	1.44	2
3	1.09	1.12	1.16	1.19	1.23	1.26	1.33	1.40	1.52	1.73	3
4	1.13	1.17	1.22	1.26	1.31	1.36	1.46	1.57	1.74	2.07	4
5	1.16	1.22	1.28	1.34	1.40	1.47	1.61	1.76	2.01	2.49	5
6	1.19	1.27	1.34	1.41	1.50	1.59	1.77	1.97	2.31	2.99	6
7	1.23	1.32	1.41	1.50	1.61	1.71	1.94	2.21	2.66	3.58	7
8	1.27	1.37	1.48	1.59	1.72	1.85	2.14	2.48	3.05	4.30	8
9	1.30	1.42	1.55	1.68	1.84	2.00	2.35	2.77	3.52	5.16	9
10	1.34	1.48	1.63	1.79	1.97	2.16	2.59	3.11	4.05	6.19	10
11	1.38	1.54	1.71	1.89	2.10	2.33	2.85	3.48	4.66	7.43	11
12	1.43	1.60	1.80	2.01	2.25	2.52	3.13	3.90	5.30	8.92	12
13	1.47	1.67	1.89	2.13	2.41	2.72	3.45	4.36	6.10	10.7	13
14	1.51	1.73	1.98	2.26	2.58	2.94	3.79	4.89	7.00	12.8	14
15	1.56	1.80	2.08	2.39	2.76	3.17	4.17	5.47	8.13	15.4	15
16	1.60	1.87	2.18	2.54	2.95	3.43	4.59	6.13	9.40	18.5	16
17	1.65	1.95	2.29	2.69	3.16	3.70	5.05	6.87	10.6	22.2	17
18	1.70	2.03	2.41	2.85	3.38	4.00	5.55	7.70	12.5	26.6	18
19	1.75	2.11	2.53	3.02	3.62	4.32	6.11	8.61	14.0	31.9	19
20	1.81	2.19	2.65	3.20	3.87	4.66	6.72	9.65	16.1	38.3	20
25	2.09	2.67	3.39	4.29	5.43	6.85	10.8	17.0	32.9	95.4	25
30	2.43	3.24	4.32	5.74	7.61	10.0	17.4	30.0	66.2	237	30
40	3.26	4.80	7.04	10.3	15.0	21.7	45.3	93.1	267.0	1470	40
50	4.38	7.11	11.5	18.4	29.5	46.9	117	289	1080	9100	50

This table shows to what amounts $1.00 invested now will grow at the end of various years, at different rates of growth compounded annually. For example, $1.00 invested now will grow in thirty years to $5.74 at 6 percent. In other words, $5.74 due thirty years hence is worth now exactly $1.00 at a 6 percent rate of interest per year. * * * The entries in this table are the reciprocals of the entries in Table 11-1; that is, they are the entries of Table 11-1 divided into 1. * * *

years, the future-amount factor is 1.34, which means that a present payment of $1 will buy, or grow to, the future amount $1.34 at the end of five years. Notice that the entries in Table 11–2 are simply the reciprocals of the entries in Table 11–1.

PRESENT CAPITAL VALUE FOR SERIES OF FUTURE AMOUNTS

For a sequence of amounts due at future times, we can find a present value. Just as we add up the costs of individual items in a market basket of groceries, we add the present values of each of the future amounts due. That sum is the present value of the whole series of amounts due at various future dates.

This series might be compared with an oil well that each year on December 31 spurts out one gallon of oil that sells for $1. To simplify the problem, let's first suppose that the series of dollars (spurts of oil) continues for only two years. If the interest rate is 6 percent, the present value of $1 deferred one year is 94 cents (see Table 11–1, column of .06 rate of interest for one year); and the present value of $1 due in two years is 89.0 cents (see the same table, same column, but now read the entry for year 2). The sum of the present capital values of both amounts due is the sum of 94.3 cents and 89.0 cents, which is $1.83. To say that the rate of interest is 6 percent per year is equivalent to saying that you can exchange $1.83 today for the right to receive $1 in one year *and* another dollar in two years.

Suppose the sequence is to last three years, with three $1 receipts. The aggregate present value is augmented by the present value of the dollar due in the third year. At a 6 percent rate of interest, this third dollar has a present value of 83.9 cents (see Table 11–1). Therefore, the present value of the three-year series is $2.67 (given in Table 11–3).

The present value of a series of amounts due is called the *capital value* of the future receipts. Capital value is the current *price* of the rights to the stream (series) of receipts.

Some technical jargon will be convenient for subsequent analyses. The sequence of future amounts due is called an *annuity*, a word that suggests *annual* amounts. A two-year sequence is a two-year annuity. A person who has purchased the right to a stream of future annuities or amounts due—for example, his pension benefits—is sometimes called an *annuitant*.

What is the present capital value of a four-year annuity? The fourth year's $1 has a present value of 79.2 cents, which, when added to the present value of a three-year annuity of $1 a year, gives $3.46. A five-year annuity would have a present value of $4.21, because the dollar received at the end of the fifth year is now worth 74.7 cents. Proceed to the end of ten years, and you will find (in Table 11–3) that at 6 percent interest the present capital value of a ten-year annuity of $1 each year is $7.36.

TABLE 11–3. Present Value of Annuity of $1, Received at End of Each Year   PVAof $1 * future annual puts=PVA

Year	3%	4%	5%	6%	7%	8%	10%	12%	15%	20%	Year
1	0.971	0.960	0.952	0.943	0.935	0.926	0.909	0.890	0.870	0.833	1
2	1.91	1.89	1.86	1.83	1.81	1.78	1.73	1.69	1.63	1.53	2
3	2.83	2.78	2.72	2.67	2.62	2.58	2.48	2.40	2.28	2.11	3
4	3.72	3.63	3.55	3.46	3.39	3.31	3.16	3.04	2.86	2.59	4
5	4.58	4.45	4.33	4.21	4.10	3.99	3.79	3.60	3.35	2.99	5
6	5.42	5.24	5.08	4.91	4.77	4.62	4.35	4.11	3.78	3.33	6
7	6.23	6.00	5.79	5.58	5.39	5.21	4.86	4.56	4.16	3.60	7
8	7.02	6.73	6.46	6.20	5.97	5.75	5.33	4.97	4.49	3.84	8
9	7.79	7.44	7.11	6.80	6.52	6.25	5.75	5.33	4.78	4.03	9
10	8.53	8.11	7.72	7.36	7.02	6.71	6.14	5.65	5.02	4.19	10
11	9.25	8.76	8.31	7.88	7.50	7.14	6.49	5.94	5.23	4.33	11
12	9.95	9.39	8.86	8.38	7.94	7.54	6.81	6.19	5.41	4.44	12
13	10.6	9.99	9.39	8.85	8.36	7.90	7.10	6.42	5.65	4.53	13
14	11.3	10.6	9.90	9.29	8.75	8.24	7.36	6.63	5.76	4.61	14
15	11.9	11.1	10.4	9.71	9.11	8.56	7.60	6.81	5.87	4.68	15
16	12.6	11.6	10.8	10.1	9.45	8.85	7.82	6.97	5.96	4.73	16
17	13.2	12.2	11.3	10.4	9.76	9.12	8.02	7.12	6.03	4.77	17
18	13.8	12.7	11.7	10.8	10.1	9.37	8.20	7.25	6.10	4.81	18
19	14.3	13.1	12.1	11.1	10.3	9.60	8.36	7.37	6.17	4.84	19
20	14.9	13.6	12.5	11.4	10.6	9.82	8.51	7.47	6.23	4.87	20
25	17.4	15.6	14.1	12.8	11.7	10.7	9.08	7.84	6.46	4.95	25
30	19.6	17.3	15.4	13.8	12.4	11.3	9.43	8.06	6.57	4.98	30
40	23.1	19.8	17.2	15.0	13.3	11.9	9.78	8.24	6.64	5.00	40
50	25.7	21.5	18.3	15.8	13.8	12.2	9.91	8.30	6.66	5.00	50

An annuity is a sequence of annual amounts received at annual intervals. This table shows with each entry how much it takes today to buy an annuity of $1 a year at the rates of interest indicated. For example, an annuity of $1 a year for twenty years at 6 percent interest could be purchased today with $11.40. This amount would, if invested at 6 percent, be sufficient to yield some interest which, along with some depletion of the principle in each year, would enable a payout of exactly $1 a year for twenty years, at which time the fund would be completely depleted. And $1,000 a year for twenty years would, at 6 percent compounded annually, cost today $11,400, which is obviously 1,000 times as much as for an annuity of just $1. * * *

If we extended the series to twenty years (still with $1 at the end of each year) at 6 percent per year, the present capital value would increase to $11.40. Notice that the *present* value of the *last half* of that series (the ten amounts due in the eleventh through the twentieth years) is only $4.04 (= 11.40 − 7.36). At a 6 percent interest rate. $4.04 *today* will buy you $1 a year for ten years, beginning at the end of the eleventh year.

Table 11–3 gives the present value of each separate future payment in the annuity. For convenience, Table 11–3 gives the present value of annuities of various lengths, where the payment *at the end* of each year is $1. Look at the entry for two years at 6 percent. It is the sum of .943 and .890, based on the data of Table 11–1. For an annuity lasting fifty years, the entry is 15.8—which says that a fifty-year annuity of $1 per year, with the first payment coming at the end of one year, has a present capital value of only $15.80 (at 6 percent).

Even an annuity that lasted forever (called a *perpetuity*), or for as long as you and your heirs desire, would have a finite capital value—namely, $16.67 (at 6 percent interest).

A second thought will remove the mystery from the fact that an infinitely long series of $1 amounts due yearly has a finite (limited) price today. To get a perpetual series of payments of $1 every year, all one has to do is keep $16.67 on deposit in a bank, if he can get 6 percent per year. Every year the interest payment of $1 can be taken out, and this can be done forever. In effect you pay $16.67 today to purchase an infinitely long sequence. But (from Table 11–3) you can also see that the first fifty years of receipts (a fifty-year annuity) has a present value of $15.80. Hence, the remaining infinitely long series of $1 receipts, beginning fifty years from now, is worth today only about 87 cents. Distant events have small present values!

NOTE: THE ROLE OF DISCOUNTING IN BOND VALUATION

The holder of a bond receives a fixed set of cash payments—an interest payment each year until the bond matures and the face value (or *principal*) of the bond in addition to the final interest payment on the date of maturity.

Suppose that in May 2008 you invest in a 12 percent U.S. Treasury bond due in May 2013. The bond has a coupon rate of 12 percent and a face value of $1000. Assume that this means you will get an interest payment of .12 x 1000 or $120 on an annual basis until 2013. When the bond matures in May 2013 you get the last interest payment of $120, along with the principal of $1000. The bond thus throws off the following series of payments:

2009	2010	2011	2012	2013
$120.00	$120.00	$120.00	$120.00	$1,120.00

How much will you be required to pay for this series of payments in the bond market in May 2008? We can determine that by reference to the returns provided by comparable bonds in the mid–2008 bond market. Assume that in mid 2008, treasury bonds with a five-year maturity were priced to return 6 percent. Accordingly, valuation of the 12 percent bond means discounting the projected series of cash flows at 6 percent.

The formula for this exercise usually is stated as follows:

$$PV = \sum_{t=1}^{5} \frac{A_t}{(1+r)^t}$$

The key to understanding the formula is the sigma—Σ. In this context it means "the sum of." The formula directs the calculator to take the sum of a series of amounts A being paid over time, each divided by $(1+r)^t$ where the number of payments and years is 5 and the first payment is received at the end of year 1:

$$PV = \frac{120}{1+r} + \frac{120}{(1+r)^2} + \frac{120}{(1+r)^3} + \frac{120}{(1+r)^4} + \frac{1,120}{(1+r)^5}$$

$$= \frac{120}{1.06} + \frac{120}{(1.06)^2} + \frac{120}{(1.06)^3} + \frac{120}{(1.06)^4} + \frac{1,120}{(1.06)^5}$$

$$= \$1,252.74$$

Since it is customary to state bond prices as a percentage of face value, this 12 percent bond would be quoted at 125.27–125.27 percent of the face value of 1000.

We can reverse the inquiry and solve for the rate of return yielded by the 12 percent bond given a market price of $1252.74. Here we seek the value of r that solves the following:

$$\$1252.74 = \frac{120}{1+r} + \frac{120}{(1+r)^2} + \frac{120}{(1+r)^3} + \frac{120}{(1+r)^4} + \frac{1,120}{(1+r)^5}$$

The value of r is the discount rate that brings the stated series of flows to the given present value of $1252.74. We know it to be 6 percent, having worked the calculation the other way. On these numbers the 6 percent rate of r is the bond's *yield to maturity* or *internal rate of return*. In cases where the rate of r is not known in advance, the figure traditionally was determined by trial and error reference to the present value tables or by reference to a bond book showing different values of r for different coupons and maturity dates. Today these calculations can be done on a standard desktop computer with a program such as Excel.

The foregoing calculation makes a significant limiting assumption when it stipulates that interest payments are made annually. In fact, Treasury bonds make coupon payments semiannually. This means that a holder of the 12 percent bond would receive $60 every six months rather than $120 every year. The real world 12 percent Treasury that pays semiannually is worth slightly more than the hypothetical bond paying annually because $60 of each 12 percent annual coupon is received six months earlier.

The present value calculation can be adjusted to accommodate semi-annual payments. Generally, when interest is paid (or compounded) more than once a year, instead of dividing the future payment by $(1+r)^t$, present value is determined as follows:

$$PV = \sum_{t=1}^{5} \frac{A_t}{(1 + r/m)^{mt}}$$

As before, A_t is the future payment, r is the discount rate and t the future year; m is the number of times a year interest is paid or compounded. Since A_t now is $60 and the number of yearly payments is 2, it follows that the 12 percent bond paying semiannually presents a series of 10 interest payments to be discounted on a six month basis as follows:

$$PV = \frac{60}{1.03} + \frac{60}{(1.03)^2} + * * * + \frac{60}{(1.03)^9} + \frac{1,060}{(1.03)^{10}}$$

NOTE: DISCOUNTING IN CAPITAL BUDGETING DECISIONS

The discounting process plays a central part not only in valuing the firm as a whole and in valuing an individual security issued by a firm but in developing a systematic approach to a firm's internal process of investment decision making. The term "capital budgeting decision" refers to the evaluation of particular investment projects which are under consideration by the firm's managers. Such projects can range in size from the purchase of a single new machine to the acquisition of another company. In every case, large or small, the question is whether the project is worthwhile on an economic basis. What standards of evaluation should management employ in making this determination? This Note considers three alternative methods—net present value, internal rate of return, and payback.

1. *The Net Present Value Method.*

Under the net present value (NPV) approach to capital budgeting, the decision entails (a) estimating the returns that can be expected to be realized from the investment over time, and (b) discounting those projected returns to present value. The investment can be viewed as acceptable if the present value of the estimated returns equals or exceeds the cash outlay required to finance it. The investment can be compared with available alternatives on the same basis. To illustrate, assume that a firm is considering the purchase of a new machine costing $18,000. The machine's useful life will be 5 years, at the end of which time its value will be zero. The new machine is expected to add $5,600 after taxes to the firm's annual income throughout the 5–year period. Under the NPV method, we first discount the expected cash inflows of $5,600 per year at an appropriate discount rate—let us assume 10 percent—to establish the present value of those inflows. The result is compared to the required outlay of $18,000 to determine whether the investment has a positive *net* present value.

- NPV = Discounted sum of expected inflows minus cost

↑ value needs to be positive

Resorting to Table 11–3, supra, it turns out that the present value of the anticipated inflows is $21,224 (3.79 × $5,600). Since the investment has a NPV of $3,224 ($21,224 − $18,000), it is acceptable and the outlay should be made.

NPV = 21,224 − 18,000
= 3,224 → positive,
investable

Management thus easily can resolve its decision problem if it is able to estimate the future returns of an investment project, if it knows the project's out-of-pocket cost, and if it can apply an appropriate rate of discount (the word "if" being repeated for emphasis). Managers wanting to maximize the value of the enterprise should accept all investment projects having a positive NPV because the effect of such acceptance is to replace cash assets with tangible, producing assets of greater worth. Obviously, management should reject all projects having a negative NPV. Finally, if two "acceptable" projects are for some reason mutually exclusive, a choice between them can be made by comparing their present values relative to their required cash outlays.

2. *The Internal Rate of Return Method.*

There is an alternative formulation, usually referred to as the internal-rate-of-return (IRR) method of project evaluation, which also involves discounting. Using the same illustration, under the IRR method we would first establish what rate of discount serves to equate the anticipated inflows of $5,600 per year for 5 years with the required cash outlay of $18,000. The result is compared to the required rate of return—here 10 percent—to determine whether the net yield on the investment is positive.

don't use the one provided, calculate
PV of cash flow at IRR − cost

- Sum of expected flows discounted at IRR minus cost = 0

The annuity tables in Appendix F tell us that the expected yield on the investment in the new machine is roughly 17 percent (i.e., $5,600 per year for 5 years discounted at 17 percent equals $18,000). Since this exceeds the 10 percent rate which the firm is assumed to require on investments of this character, the project is plainly acceptable.

If IRR > required rate of return → acceptable

The NPV and IRR methods differ in some respects. The principal difference involves the implied rate of return on invested capital. The IRR method assumes that the project cost of $18,000 invested at 17 percent will compound in such a way as to release $5,600 at the end of each of the next five years. The NPV method implies compounding at the required rate of return, here 10 percent. That is, it assumes that the NPV at 10 percent ($3,224) plus the cost ($18,000), or $21,224, if invested at 10 percent will compound in such a way as to release $5,600 at the end of each of the next five years. The two methods will not necessarily produce the same accept-reject result. Conflicting signals can result if the choice is between two mutually exclusive projects, one of which involves a larger investment but a smaller rate of return than the other, or a project whose cash flows over time vary between positive and negative. Conservative text writers prefer the NPV method. Entrepreneurs are said to prefer the IRR method. For a fuller comparison see Van Horne, Financial Management and Policy 143–146 (11th ed. 1998); Brealey, Myers, and Allen, Principles of Corporate Finance 93–99 (8th ed. 2006).

Despite the differences, the NPV and IRR methods of project evaluation frequently produce the same "accept" or "reject" signal. Note that both methods take account of the *timing* of cash inflows and outflows over the entire life of the investment. Thus, both give the factor of delay (or anticipation) in the realization of expected inflows appropriate weight.

3. *The Payback Method.*

Another commonly used method of project evaluation—the payback method—is usually thought to be inadequate because it fails to take account of timing and ignores the need to discount all expected flows. Under the payback method, an investment is deemed acceptable if within a certain maximum period of time arbitrarily set by management the expected cash inflows produced by the investment equal the original cash outlay which the investment requires. If in the above illustration management sets the payback period at 3 years, the new machine would be rejected (3 x $5,600 < $18,000), even though the discounted cash flow methods show that the contrary decision is correct. Similarly, if the machine produced expected returns of $9,000 per year for only 2 years, automatic application of the payback method would lead to acceptance even though the net present value or the net yield of the investment is plainly negative. One would not expect the payback method to be employed so blindly, of course, but the examples do illustrate the point that a disregard of timing may result in error.

2.   EXPECTED RETURNS

The mechanics of discounting describe the formal framework of valuation theory. To fill that framework with substantive content, we need to determine (1) the quantity and duration of the stream of expected returns to be discounted and (2) the discount rate.

With respect to the determination of the amount to be discounted—variously referred to as inflows, income, profits, earnings, returns, or yield—two general questions can be raised. First, what is (or ought to be) meant by the term "returns" in the context of investment valuation? In the illustration used in the preceding Note, should the expectation of $5,600 per year be taken to refer to accounting income, or to some broader, or narrower, concept of enrichment? Second, is it appropriate to utilize a single-valued estimate of expected returns, or should the investor or appraiser somehow attempt to take account of the full range of possible outcomes, insofar as they can be foreseen? Should $5,600 per year be assumed to represent the "best estimate" of probable returns, a conservative estimate, the absolute minimum that can be expected, or something else? These questions are taken up, in order, in the materials that follow.

(A) THE COMPOSITION OF "RETURNS"

Warren Buffett, The Essays of Warren Buffett: Lessons for Corporate America

19 Cardozo L. Rev. 1, 180–87 (1997).
(Lawrence Cunningham, ed.).

[The following, entitled "Owner Earnings and the Cash Flow Fallacy," originally appeared in the 1986 Annual Report of Berkshire Hathaway, Inc.]

[Many business acquisitions require] major purchase-price accounting adjustments, as prescribed by generally accepted accounting principles (GAAP). The GAAP figures, of course, are the ones used in our consolidated financial statements. But, in our view, the GAAP figures are not necessarily the most useful ones for investors or managers. Therefore, the figures shown for specific operating units are earnings before purchase-price adjustments are taken into account. In effect, these are the earnings that would have been reported by the businesses if we had not purchased them.

* * *

First a short quiz: below are abbreviated 1986 statements of earnings for two companies. Which business is the more valuable?

	Company O	Company N
	(000s Omitted)	
Revenues	$677,240	$677,240
Cost of Goods Sold:		
Historical costs, excluding depreciation	$341,170	$341,170
Special non-cash inventory costs		4,979[1]
Depreciation of plant and equipment	8,301	13,355[2]
	349,471	359,504
Gross Profit	$327,769	$317,736
Selling & Admin. Expense	$260,286	$260,286
Amortization of Goodwill		595[3]
	260,286	260,881
Operating Profit	$67,483	$56,855
Other Income, Net	4,135	4,135
PreTax Income	$71,618	$60,990
Applicable Income Tax:		
Historical deferred and current tax	$31,387	$31,387
Non–Cash Inter-period Allocation Adjustment		998[4]

	Company O	Company N
	(000s Omitted)	
	31,387	32,385
Net Income	$40,231	$28,605

*(Numbers (1) through (4) designate items discussed later * * *.)*

As you've probably guessed, Companies O and N are the same business—Scott Fetzer. In the "O" (for "old") column we have shown what the company's 1986 GAAP earnings would have been if we had not purchased it; in the "N" (for "new") column we have shown Scott Fetzer's GAAP earnings as actually reported by Berkshire.

It should be emphasized that the two columns depict identical economics—i.e., the same sales, wages, taxes, etc. And both "companies" generate the same amount of cash for owners. Only the accounting is different.

So, fellow philosophers, which column presents truth? Upon which set of numbers should managers and investors focus?

Before we tackle those questions, let's look at what produces the disparity between O and N. * * *.

The contrast between O and N comes about because we paid an amount for Scott Fetzer that was different from its stated net worth. Under GAAP, such differences—such premiums or discounts—must be accounted for by "purchase-price adjustments." In Scott Fetzer's case, we paid $315 million for net assets that were carried on its books at $172.4 million. So we paid a premium of $142.6 million.

The first step in accounting for any premium paid is to adjust the carrying value of current assets to current values. In practice, this requirement usually does not affect receivables, which are routinely carried at current value, but often affects inventories. Because of a $22.9 million LIFO reserve and other accounting intricacies, Scott Fetzer's inventory account was carried at a $37.3 million discount from current value. So, making our first accounting move, we used $37.3 million of our $142.6 million premium to increase the carrying value of the inventory.

Assuming any premium is left after current assets are adjusted, the next step is to adjust fixed assets to current value. In our case, this adjustment also required a few accounting acrobatics relating to deferred taxes. * * * I will skip the details and give you the bottom line: $68.0 million was added to fixed assets and $13.0 million was eliminated from deferred tax liabilities. After making this $81.0 million adjustment, we were left with $24.3 million of premium to allocate.

   * * *

The final accounting adjustment we needed to make, after recording fair market values for all assets and liabilities, was the assignment of the residual premium to Goodwill (technically known as "excess of cost over the fair value of net assets acquired"). This residual amounted to $24.3 million. Thus, the balance sheet of Scott Fetzer immediately before the acquisition, which is summarized below in column O, was transformed by the purchase into the balance sheet shown in column N. In real terms, both balance sheets depict the same assets and liabilities—but, as you can see, certain figures differ significantly.

	Company O	Company N
	(000s Omitted)	
Assets		
Cash and Cash Equivalents	$3,593	$3,593
Receivables, net	90,919	90,919
Inventories	77,489	114,764
Other	5,954	5,954
Total Current Assets	177,955	215,230
Property, Plant, and Equipment, net	80,967	148,960
Investments in the Advances to Unconsolidated Subsidiaries and Joint Ventures	93,589	93,589
Other Assets, including Goodwill	9,836	34,210
	$362,347	$491,989
Liabilities		
Notes Payable and Current Portion of Long–Term Debt	$4,650	$4,650
Accounts Payable	39,003	39,003
Accrued Liabilities	84,939	84,939
Total Current Liabilities	128,592	128,592
Long-term Debt and Capitalized Leases	34,669	34,669
Deferred Income Taxes	17,052	4,075
Other Deferred Credits	9,657	9,657
Total Liabilities	189,970	176,993
Shareholder's Equity	172,377	314,996
	$362,347	$491,989

The higher balance sheet figures shown in column N produce the lower income figures shown in column N of the earnings statement presented earlier. This is the result of the asset write-ups and of the fact that some of the written-up assets must be depreciated or amortized. The higher the asset figure, the higher the annual depreciation or amortization charge to earnings must be. The charges that flowed to the earnings statement because of the balance sheet write-ups were numbered in the statement of earnings shown earlier:

1. $4,979,000 for non-cash inventory costs resulting, primarily, from reductions that Scott Fetzer made in its inventories during 1986; charges of this kind are apt to be small or non-existent in future years.

2. $5,054,000 for extra depreciation attributable to the write-up of fixed assets; a charge approximating this amount will probably be made annually for 12 more years.

3. $595,000 for amortization of Goodwill; this charge will be made annually for 39 more years in a slightly larger amount because our

purchase was made on January 6 and, therefore, the 1986 figure applies to only 98% of the year.

4. $998,000 for deferred-tax acrobatics that are beyond my ability to explain briefly (or perhaps even non-briefly); a charge approximating this amount will probably be made annually for 12 more years.

It is important to understand that none of these newly-created accounting costs, totaling $11.6 million, are deductible for income tax purposes. [The tax rule has changed. *See* I.R.C. § 197.] The "new" Scott Fetzer pays exactly the same tax as the "old" Scott Fetzer would have, even though the GAAP earnings of the two entities differ greatly. And, in respect to operating earnings, that would be true in the future also. However, in the unlikely event that Scott Fetzer sells one of its businesses, the tax consequences to the "old" and "new" company might differ widely.

By the end of 1986 the difference between the net worth of the "old" and "new" Scott Fetzer had been reduced from $142.6 million to $131.0 million by means of the extra $11.6 million that was charged to earnings of the new entity. As the years go by, similar charges to earnings will cause most of the premium to disappear, and the two balance sheets will converge. However, the higher land values and most of the higher inventory values that were established on the new balance sheet will remain unless land is disposed of or inventory levels are further reduced.

What does all this mean for owners? Did the shareholders of Berkshire buy a business that earned $40.2 million in 1986 or did they buy one earning $28.6 million? Were those $11.6 million of new charges a real economic cost to us? Should investors pay more for the stock of Company O than of Company N? And, if a business is worth some given multiple of earnings, was Scott Fetzer worth considerably more the day before we bought it than it was worth the following day?

If we think through these questions, we can gain some insights about what may be called "owner earnings." These represent (a) reported earnings plus (b) depreciation, depletion, amortization, and certain other non-cash charges such as Company N's items (1) and (4) less (c) the average annual amount of capitalized expenditures for plant and equipment, etc. that the business requires to fully maintain its long-term competitive position and its unit volume. (If the business requires additional working capital to maintain its competitive position and unit volume, the increment also should be included in (c). However, businesses following the LIFO inventory method usually do not require additional working capital if unit volume does not change.)

Our owner-earnings equation does not yield the deceptively precise figures provided by GAAP, since (c) must be a guess—and one sometimes very difficult to make. Despite this problem, we consider the owner earnings figure, not the GAAP figure, to be the relevant item for valuation purposes—both for investors in buying stocks and for managers in buying entire businesses. We agree with Keynes's observation: "I would rather be vaguely right than precisely wrong."

The approach we have outlined produces "owner earnings" for Company O and Company N that are identical, which means valuations are also identical, just as common sense would tell you should be the case. This result is reached because the sum of (a) and (b) is the same in both columns O and N, and because (c) is necessarily the same in both cases.

And what do Charlie [Munger] and I, as owners and managers, believe is the correct figure for the owner earnings of Scott Fetzer? Under current circumstances, we believe (c) is very close to the "old" company's (b) number of $8.3 million and much below the "new" company's (b) number of $19.9 million. Therefore, we believe that owner earnings are far better depicted by the reported earnings in the O column than by those in the N column. In other words, we feel owner earnings of Scott Fetzer are considerably larger than the GAAP figures that we report.

That is obviously a happy state of affairs. But calculations of this sort usually do not provide such pleasant news. Most managers probably will acknowledge that they need to spend something more than (b) on their businesses over the longer term just to hold their ground in terms of both unit volume and competitive position. When this imperative exists—that is, when (c) exceeds (b)—GAAP earnings overstate owner earnings. Frequently this overstatement is substantial. The oil industry has in recent years provided a conspicuous example of this phenomenon. Had most major oil companies spent only (b) each year, they would have guaranteed their shrinkage in real terms.

All of this points up the absurdity of the "cash flow" numbers that are often set forth in Wall Street reports. These numbers routinely include (a) plus (b)—but do not subtract (c). Most sales brochures of investment bankers also feature deceptive presentations of this kind. These imply that the business being offered is the commercial counterpart of the Pyramids—forever state-of-the-art, never needing to be replaced, improved or refurbished. Indeed, if all U.S. corporations were to be offered simultaneously for sale through our leading investment bankers—and if the sales brochures describing them were to be believed—governmental projections of national plant and equipment spending would have to be slashed by 90%.

"Cash Flow," true, may serve as a shorthand of some utility in descriptions of certain real estate businesses or other enterprises that make huge initial outlays and only tiny outlays thereafter. A company whose only holding is a bridge or an extremely long-lived gas field would be an example. But "cash flow" is meaningless in such businesses as manufacturing, retailing, extractive companies, and utilities because, for them, (c) is always significant. To be sure, businesses of this kind may in a given year be able to defer capital spending. But over a five-or ten-year period, they must make the investment—or the business decays.

Why, then, are "cash flow" numbers so popular today? In answer, we confess our cynicism: we believe these numbers are frequently used by marketers of businesses and securities in attempts to justify the unjustifiable (and thereby to sell what should be the unsalable). When (a)—that is, GAAP earnings—looks by itself inadequate to service debt of a junk bond or justify a foolish stock price, how convenient it becomes for salesmen to focus on (a) + (b). But you shouldn't add (b) without subtracting (c): though dentists correctly claim that if you ignore your teeth they'll go away, the same is not true for (c). The company or investor believing that the debt-servicing ability or the equity valuation or an enterprise can be measured by totaling (a) and (b) while ignoring (c) is headed for certain trouble.

* * *

Accounting numbers of course, are the language of business and as such are of enormous help to anyone evaluating the worth of a business and tracking its progress. Charlie and I would be lost without these numbers: they invariably are the starting point for us in evaluating our own businesses and those of others. Managers and owners need to remember, however, that accounting is but an aid to business thinking, never a substitute for it.

NOTE: ACCOUNTING EARNINGS, "OWNER EARNINGS," AND NET CASH FLOWS

[handwritten: accounting return + financial return]

1. *Depreciation.*

Let us return to the machine hypothesized in the Note on Capital Budgeting, supra. As noted, the machine costs $18,000 fully installed and has a useful life of five years after which its value is zero. We now add some additional details. Total annual additional revenues attributable to the installation of the machine are projected as $12,600. Annual direct costs of operating and maintaining the machine will be $6,000. The company uses straight-line depreciation, which comes to $3,600 per year for the machine. The company pays annual income taxes at a marginal rate of 33 1/3 percent of its net earnings for accounting purposes.

Given these additional facts what is the appropriate figure to be discounted for investment analysis under Warren Buffett's concept of "owner earnings"? The answer is still $5,600 per year.

The derivation of $5,600 follows from Buffett's formula. Two of its components come to bear here with particular importance. First, the accounting earnings in Buffett's (a) are *after* tax. For valuation purposes, taxes paid are no different from out-of-pocket operating expenses: Since they never reach the investor they are not "returns" to be discounted. Second, amounts deducted for depreciation in calculating net accounting earnings are not deducted for valuation purposes.

The derivation works as follows:

[handwritten: annual]

	$12,600	additional revenues
minus	6,000	direct costs *of operating machine annually*
	6,600	earnings before depreciation and taxes
minus	3,600	depreciation
	3,000	net earnings
minus	1,000	income tax *per yr*
	$ 2,000	net earnings after tax

[handwritten right margin: 12,600 − 6,000 − 1,000 = 5,600 not NPV (needs to be disc) annual cf; annual additional revenue − annual cost of operating − tax]

Note that if either of net earnings before tax or net earnings after tax is employed as the expected return figure in the capital budgeting exercise, then at a 10 percent discount rate the investment looks like a loser.

We adjust as follows:

	$ 2,000	net earnings after tax
plus	3,600	depreciation
	$ 5,600	net cash flow

Why is the depreciation added back? The accounting process takes account of the cost implicated in the progressive exhaustion of plant, equipment, and other long-lived assets by annually offsetting a proportion of the assets' original cost against the firm's operating revenues. The straight-line method of depreciation, which involves dividing the cost of the asset (less salvage value) by the number of years of its expected useful life, results in a level annual allowance. This is deducted as an expense regardless of the actual rate of physical exhaustion. Other methods, such as the declining-balance method, accelerate cost-recovery by requiring higher allowances in the earlier years and lower allowances in the later years of useful life. Either way, the capital investment in the asset is gradually converted into a current expense as the asset is used up in the generation of revenues during its useful life. An economic truth is bound up in this treatment: The exhaustion of asset is indeed a cost incurred in generating the revenues over time.

Valuation also deducts the cost of the asset. But it does so *as of the time capital is invested* in the asset. So, where the calculation of accounting earnings means deducting the $18,000 cost in five installments of $3,600 over five years, in the capital budgeting calculation the entire $18,000 is deducted at Day 1: NPV = Sum of discounted expected returns *minus* cost of asset. To deduct depreciation from the expected return figure in a valuation is to deduct the cost of the asset twice.

2. Scrap Value.

Let us change the facts of the problem and stipulate that the machine has an estimated scrap value of $3,000. How does this change the NPV calculation?

Cost $18,000 − Scrap $3,000 = $15,000 to be depreciated over five years or $3,000 per year. The revised expected annual net cash flow figure emerges as follows:

	$12,600	additional revenues
minus	6,000	direct costs
	6,600	earnings before depreciation and taxes
minus	3,000	depreciation
	3,600	net earnings
minus	1,200	income tax
	$ 2,400	net earnings after tax
plus	3,000	depreciation
	$ 5,400	net cash flow

(handwritten left margin) $12,600 − 6,000 − 1,200 = [400]

(handwritten left margin) have to minus D first and do all those steps to figure out the appropriate income tax

(handwritten annotation next to net earnings) 3600 * 33.3% = 1,200

(handwritten annotation) PV of 5-yr cash cash = 5,400 each @ 10%

Using Table 11–3, the present value of the flows is $5,400 × 3.79 = $20,466.

(handwritten left margin) NPV = 20,466 + 3,000 / 1.10⁵ − 18,000

This NPV calculation is not yet complete, however. At termination of use in Year 5 the machine will be worth $3,000. For valuation purposes this is the substantive equivalent of a cash inflow paid five years in the future. Using Table 11–1, we discount the flow at 10 percent: $3,000 x .620 = $1,860.

NPV = discounted sum of net cash flows $20,466 + present value of scrap $1,860 − cost $18,000 = $22,326 − $18,000 = $4,326

The result is intuitively satisfying: The machine is worth more ($4,326) with a scrap value than without ($3,224).

3. Reinvestment.

Let us revert to the no scrap value version of the problem and add a further fact. In addition to ordinary maintenance costs, already included in the $6,000 direct costs figure, the machine will need a $3,000 special maintenance overhaul at the end of Year 3. This is the sort of cost picked up in Buffett's formula under category (c)—it is a capital expenditure for plant and equipment necessary for the maintenance of competitive position and unit volume. It figures into the NPV calculation as a cash outflow in Year 3. To make the adjustment we go to Table 11–3 and find the negative present value of $3,000 in 3 years at 10 percent: $–3,000 x .751 = $–2,253. The NPV goes down as follows:

NPV = $3,224 – 2,253 *just minus the value*
    = $971

Note that here the valuation exercise adjusts for future wear and tear, even as it adds back accounting's depreciation expense. As Buffett notes, accounting depreciation *would* serve as a proxy for future replacement expenditures if an amount exactly equal to the depreciation allowance is annually reinvested to maintain the income-producing capacity of the asset or firm. But such an outcome occurs only accidentally and certainly not in most cases. When it does not, as Buffett also notes, the net earnings figure, however accurate as an accounting matter, is inadequate from the standpoint of valuation. It is too high if the sum of depreciation and other non-cash accounting deductions is less than category (c) capital expenditures; it is too low if the total non-cash earnings deductions are greater than the category (c) expenditures.

The student should not read too much into Buffett's complaints about "cash flow" valuation. The figure yielded by his (a) plus (b) minus (c) formula is ? commonly called the "net cash flow." Buffett complains not about discounted cash flow valuation in theory but in practice, where intermediaries peddling going-concern assets seem to have a habit of forgetting to make the deduction for the category (c) capital expenditures. For commentary on Buffett and accounting, see Johnson, Accounting in Favor of Investors, 19 Cardozo L.Rev. 637 (1997).

4. *Valuing a Firm.*

Now we take up the valuation of an entire firm. What computations or adjustments which have not thus far figured into the valuation of machine with a five year expected life will be required?

Suppose we set up a hypothetical firm, ABC Corporation, by extrapolating from the machine problem. We multiply the machine's expected future return figure by 10,000. This yields $56,000,000, which we stipulate as ABC Corporation's expected future annual return. But there is a *caveat*: The $56,000,000 figure represents Buffett's (a) plus (b); no deduction respecting Buffett's (c) has yet been made.

Assuming a 10 percent discount rate, can we simply take the machine's $21,224 net present value figure and multiply it by 10,000 to yield a plausible hypothetical value of $212,240,000 for ABC Corp.? $212.24 million represents a multiple of only 3.8 on the $56,000,000 projected annual cash flow. This seems like an implausibly low value for a contemporary firm. A corrective assumption needs to be made respecting the *duration* of the payment stream. The machine was stipulated to have five year useful life, so its valuation entailed discounting only five future payments plus any scrap value. Firms, in contrast, are valued as perpetuities, at least absent a stipulation of a planned future cessation of operation and liquidation.

Table 11–3 does not quite take us to perpetuity, but it does allow us to discount a 50 year payment stream. At 10 percent, $56,000,000 x 9.91 = $554,960,000. The extension of this figure from 50 years to infinity actually is quite simple. For a perpetuity,

PV = Future cash flow ÷ capitalization rate *r*

perpetuity: $PV = \dfrac{\text{annual cash flow}}{r}$

PV = $56,000,000 ÷ .10

PV = $560,000,000

This $560,000,000 figure is presumptively too high, however. Recall that we have not yet made a downward adjustment for Buffett's category (c)—projected annual capital expenditures for new or replacement plant and equipment necessary to maintain competitive position and unit volume.

To see why a downward adjustment must be made, let us go back to the $18,000 machine (assuming no scrap value and no Year 3 retooling) and value it as a perpetuity instead of as a five year wasting asset. If we are going to model this $5,600 annual positive cash flow as a flow that never stops, we are going to have to make a deduction for all future category (c) costs respecting the equipment that produces the flow. Under the problem's assumptions, the machine is going to have to be replaced by a new machine every five years. Let us assume these new machines will have a constant cost equal to today's cost of $18,000. The arithmetic still gets complicated: The discounted perpetual $5,600 has to be offset against the negative present value of a cash outflow of $18,000 at the end of each of Years 5, 10, 15, 20, and so on. (Alternatively, the $3,224 NPV of the five year wasting asset can be discounted as a sequence of payments received at five-year intervals.)

[handwritten in margin: net cash flow per yr = 56,000,000 - 10,000,000 = 46,000,000]

We are now ready to return to ABC Corp. and make a conforming adjustment in respect of Buffet's category (c). We assume that the category (c) outflows will average $10,000,000 per year. The net cash flow amount is therefore $46,000,000 and the capitalized value $460,000,000 at 10 percent.

5. Adjusting for Growth.

ABC Corp., as just hypothesized, is a firm whose assets and flows stay at a constant level, like a single machine that runs forever. A robust valuation model will have to take an additional step and allow for managers who, in addition to maintaining and replacing existing assets, *expand* the firm's operations by investing in additional plant and equipment or other firms, whether by raising new capital or retaining and reinvesting a large portion of its annual cash flows.

The expansion case can be handled by extending our previous analysis. Assume that ABC Corp. plans to purchase an additional production facility at the end of Year 1. The new facility will cost $10,000,000 and will be financed out of ABC Corp's. internally generated cash flows. ABC Corp's. managers use Buffett's categories and make the following projection respecting the cash flows to be generated by the new facility:

[handwritten in margin: owners earning per yr (cost not accounted for)]

(a) additional accounting earnings $13,000,000 plus (b) depreciation $2,000,000 minus (c) cost of maintenance and replacement $3,000,000 = $12,000,000 net cash flow.

No further expansion is in view for ABC Corp. Therefore net cash flows for ABC Corp in Year 2 and in every year thereafter are expected to be $46,000,000 + $12,000,000 = $58,000,000.

Once again, the goal of valuation requires that we define "earnings" as the anticipated *net* cash inflows of the firm. Since $10,000,000 is to be reinvested at the end of the Year 1, net flows for Year 1 must be reduced by that amount. ABC Corp's "earnings" available as investment returns in Year 1 will therefore be $46,000,000 minus the $10,000,000 reinvested or $36,000,000. We in effect have expanded the (c) deduction to encompass not only retention of cash flows for repair and replacement but also for expansion. The correct value is thus the present value of $36,000,000 at the end of the first year plus the present value of $58,000,000 starting in the second year and continuing in perpetuity. Still assuming a 10

*[handwritten in margin: Not 58,000,000 coz expense made at the end of yr 1.
Yr 1 = 46,000,000 - 10,000,000 = 36,000,000]*

percent capitalization rate, we add to the present value of the Year 1 flow the present value of the expanded firm as if it were a payment made at the end of Year 2:

$$\text{NPV} = \$36,000,000 \, (.909) + \$58,000,000 \, /(.10)(.909)$$
$$= \$32,724,000 + \$527,220,000 = 559,944,000$$

Reduction of the first year's "earnings" by $10,000,000 is the critical point to observe. If the $10,000,000 reinvested by the firm *were* included in the first year's earnings for valuation purposes, a double-counting error would result. The income to be earned *on* the $10,000,000 expansion is fully reflected in the value of the enterprise when the expected cash flows of $12,000,000 are capitalized from Year 2 to infinity. To add in the *cost* of those expected flows as well would be to count the same quantity twice, and thus to overstate the firm's value.

6. *Earnings and Dividends.*

Summing up, net present value is calculated on the basis of "net cash flow," rather than the so-called "accounting earnings" presented in a corporation's financial statements. The economic value of an investment project is measured in terms of its returns in cash or cash equivalents and not by numbers printed on a page. Securities analysts using financial statements can generally adjust accounting earnings to arrive at an annual cash flow figure by adding back to accounting earnings non-cash charges incurred but not paid during the reporting period, e.g., depreciation, depletion, and amortization. These annual cash flow figures, netted for capital and other expenditures, can then be used in projecting expected annual net cash flows to be discounted in the present value calculation.

The foregoing formulation holds true where the firm's expansion plans call for the retention and reinvestment of a fraction of its annual cash flows each year for an indefinite period. Thus, for valuation purposes the term "earnings" should refer to the difference between the cash flows realized from operations and the amount retained by the company both to replace existing assets *and* to acquire new income-producing assets. To be sure, net cash flows can be expected to increase as the result of a decision to retain and reinvest a portion of the company's income annually; hence it now becomes appropriate to capitalize a growing, rather than a constant, stream of future returns. But because the company intends (for the foreseeable future) to reinvest a portion of those future returns in additional assets, it is necessary to reflect the negative value of the intended outlays by deducting them from the larger anticipated inflows.

In all examples in this Note, the term "net cash flow" can be described as the amount of returns from operations which is *not* required by the firm for plant replacement or reinvestment. As such, "net cash flow" should be viewed as excess capital, to be returned to shareholders as periodic dividends. One may conclude that, from the shareholder's point of view, net cash flows and dividends are identical quantities, and that what the holder of publicly traded shares really capitalizes when valuing the firm is the amount annually available for distribution to shareholders. Bluntly stated, the value of the firm is equal to the present value of what the owners can expect to get out of it, neither more nor less.

7. *Economic Value Added.*

We have seen that valuing a firm means discounting future net cash flows. Now consider a further application marketed by the consultancy Stern Stewart as an evaluative tool–Economic Value Added or EVA. EVA holds out a yardstick for determining the quality of a firm's earnings in a given period, or, in the words of

Stern Stewart, "the financial performance measure that comes closer than any other to capturing the true economic profit of an enterprise."

EVA = Net Operating Profit After Taxes (NOPAT) minus Capital Charge

NOPAT = Sales minus operating expenses minus taxes. Note that this a cash flow measure. Sales less operating expenses yields a figure that does not deduct depreciation or amortization. No deduction is made for interest expense because the cost of debt is factored out in the capital charge.

Capital Charge = Total Capital x Cost of Capital. Ascertaining this figure can involve complications and judgment calls. We will keep it simple and define total capital as the sum of the firm's debt and equity capital as booked on the balance sheet and the cost of capital as the weighted average of the cost of debt and equity capital.

Now let us plug in some numbers.

Firm ABC–results for year 200X:
Sales: $100,000,000
Operating expenses: $75,000,000
Effective tax rate: 30%

NOPAT: ℃
= 100,000,000 − 75,000,000
− (100,000,000−75,000,000)*0.3

NOPAT	= (100,000,000—75,000,000)* (1–0.30)
	= $17,500,000
	Total debt: 50,000,000 at 8%
	Total equity: 50,000,000 at 12%
	Weighted Average Cost of Capital = 10%
Capital Charge	= (50,000,000 + 50,000,000) * 0.10
	= $10,000,000
EVA	= 17,500,000—10,000,000
	= $7,500,000

To value a firm using EVA, one projects amounts of EVA for future periods and discounts the sums back using the weighted average cost of capital as the value of r. The present sum of invested capital is then added to the discounted present value of projected future EVA. This approach contrasts with the dividend-based approach to valuation posed in the previous note (6) because it does not ask whether or not the value added has been distributed to the shareholders.

(B) FUTURE RETURNS AND PROBABILITY DISTRIBUTIONS

Up to this point, we have been discussing expected returns as if "returns" could be expressed as a single-valued estimate of future cash flows. Thus, in deciding whether the firm should invest $18,000 in a new machine, we simply discounted the expected flows of $5,600 per year back to the present date and then compared the result with the required outlay to determine whether the investment possessed a positive net present value. The input data consisted of only a single-figure estimate of annual future returns, the amount of the required outlay, and an appropriate rate of discount. With annuity tables, the necessary computation could be accomplished easily.

But a statement of investor expectations solely in the form of a single-figure estimate of future returns is incomplete. As the future is uncertain, investments will seldom yield an amount precisely equal to this anticipated return. Our single-figure estimate of returns should therefore not be taken to mean that no more and no less than $5,600 annually is actually expected to be realized from the investment. Yet if that is not the intention, just what do we mean by positing the $5,600 figure to the exclusion of all others?

The discussion that follows addresses the firm's individual capital budgeting decisions. However, it is just as relevant to the valuation of the firm as a whole and the valuation of the firm's various securities.

Grayson, The Use of Statistical Techniques in Capital Budgeting

Financial Research and Management Decisions, Robichek ed. 1967, pp. 98–107.

At the heart of any capital budgeting decision is a forecast of future events, regardless of whether that forecast is explicit or implicit. A typical forecast is a single figure, usually labeled "best estimate" or "most likely."

Let's take a closer look at this single figure. How confident is the forecaster of that figure? Is he very certain, very uncertain, or somewhere in between? And what does he really mean by the words, best estimate or most likely? Has he already reduced his "true" best estimate by some amount to reflect risk? Is he truly giving us the most likely figure, which is the *mode* ? Is he really thinking through some internal calculus of a weighted average figure, the *mean* ? Or, does he perhaps typically select the middle figure, the *median* ? It's hard to say. Moreover, in some situations, which measure is inferred can make quite a difference in the investment decision.

Thus, the single forecasted figure limits the decision analysis in two ways. First, we do not know the uncertainty surrounding that figure, that is, we do not know the "probability distribution"—the range of the forecast and the probability estimates associated with figures within that range. Second, we do not know for sure whether his best estimate is really the mode, median, or mean. For both reasons, we would like, therefore, to have the forecaster give us not just one estimate, but a *range* of estimates and associated *probabilities*—a probability distribution.

A probability distribution, in its simplest form, could consist of only a few estimates. One popular form consists of three figures: the "optimistic, most likely, and pessimistic," or the "high, low, and best guess" estimates.

	Annual Sales
Forecast	(Units)
Optimistic	100,000
Most likely	75,000
Pessimistic	50,000

Some improvement has been made over the single forecast figure. More information has been obtained on the range of possible outcomes, but some information that may be critical is ignored. For example, *could* the firm sell less than 50,000 units? This might well mean a substantial loss for the firm, or bankruptcy for smaller firms, and a decision maker would undoubtedly want to know how likely this occurrence is. Moreover, how likely is the "most likely" estimate in the forecaster's mind? Is the optimistic forecast very improbable, or close to the most likely forecast? Or, are all three forecasts equally likely? It would be quite helpful, therefore, if the forecaster would describe for us more accurately his *degree of confidence* in his forecasts, or describe his feelings as to the probability of these estimates occurring.

Forecast	Units	Probability
Optimistic	100,000	.30
Most likely	75,000	.60
Pessimistic	50,000	.10

Clearly, more information is available now. This information may be used to advantage (1) in subsequent profitability calculations and (2) in assessing more clearly the effects of risk on the value of the investment to the decision maker. If attaching probabilities to this simple three-figure forecast is a gain in analysis, it is an appealing step to ask our forecaster to give us his estimates of the entire range of figures that might occur—the entire probability distribution as shown in Fig. 5.1.

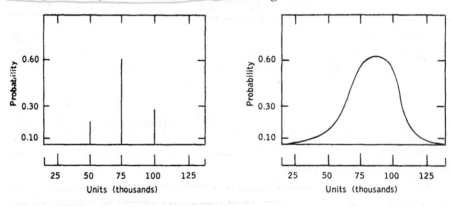

FIG. 5.1. *Left:* three-figure estimate; *right:* entire probability distribution.
[A5505]

Now, even more information is available for the decision maker. Granted that this may be valuable information, says a businessman, how can such probability distributions be obtained? This is a subject to which theorists have been devoting a great deal of attention in recent years, and with some success.

What has restrained the use of probability theory in business decision making for many years has been the classical "frequency" concept of probability. Briefly, this concept indicates that no statement *whatsoever* can be made about the probability of any single event. In fact, the classical view holds that one can only talk about probability in a very long-run sense, given that the occurrence or nonoccurrence of the event can be repeatedly observed over a *very large number of times under independent identical conditions.*

Though this concept is a useful mathematical formulation for theoretical purposes, its use in business situations is severely restricted to a few applications—large-scale production runs, insurance, gambling—where the events to be forecasted are repeated again and again over a long run with "nearly constant" underlying probabilities. I submit that most business decisions are exactly the opposite—little (or no) prior experience on which to draw, lack of ability to repeat the event, and inability to create independent, identical conditions over time. Also, businessmen are interested quite often in predicting single events. Of what use, then, is probability theory for most business decisions?

Well, not all theorists agree with the point of view expressed above. In recent years another view of probability has revived, that is, the personalistic view, which holds that it makes a great deal of sense to talk about the probability of a *single event,* without reference to the repeatability, long-run frequency concept. It is perfectly valid, therefore, to talk about the probability of rain tomorrow, the probability of sales reaching a certain level next year, or the probability that earnings per share will exceed $2.50 next year, or five years hence. Such probability assignments are called *personal or subjective probabilities.*

" * * * on a personalistic view of probability, strictly interpreted, no probability is unknown to the person concerned, or, at any rate, he can determine probability only by interrogating himself * * * "

With this view, *uncertainty estimates can be made for every business decision, in an explicit fashion.* This is a powerful concept, and has tremendous implications for improving decision making procedures.

The usual first reaction of businessmen to this idea is that this procedure seems highly subjective, and they want *objective* probabilities. Though a detailed rebuttal of this objection takes quite a while to develop, a quick reply is that in real life there are no truly objective probabilities. All probabilities are subjective.

It is perfectly true that if there is a great amount of "objective" data, say on interest rates in the past, then these data should be considered and will *strongly influence* the subjective probability assignments to future interest rates. In fact, research has shown that two decision makers with roughly the same objective data or past experience, will assign to a future event roughly the same subjective probability if they believe the future will be similar to the past. *But,* if one forecaster thinks that there may be a structural shift in the economy, or has a direct pipeline to the Federal Reserve Board's thinking, *he may alter or throw away past data in making his probability assignment, and it is perfectly valid for him to do so.*

* * * Assuming for the purposes of this article that you accept this concept for the moment, a natural question is how can these probability assignments be obtained?

As stated previously, if there are large amounts of historical data, these should be strongly considered. This is where descriptive statistics and statistical inference become important. Past data can be organized in various ways to generate frequency distributions, index numbers, time series, regression, and correlation analysis. Certain central tendencies of the data can be described, such as the mean, median, or mode. And various measures can be used to describe the variation around these central tendencies and the shape of the distribution—standard deviation, variance, skewness, and kurtosis.

Such statistical analysis of past data may be extremely useful in making predictions of the future, for, under certain conditions, we may be willing to view the past data as a *sample* from an underlying process. And statistics have a lot to say about what the next sample in the future may look like. But, keep in mind, such past and present figures are only useful insofar as they are presumed to be representative of the future.

But what if the forecaster does not wish merely to project the past into the future? Or, even more compelling, what if there are *few or no data* relevant to the future. Perhaps the event to be predicted is almost unique—a completely new product. How can his probability assignments be obtained? There are several possible ways.

The simplest is by direct assessment. Ask the forecaster to write down or draw a probability distribution that describes *his* predictions. If he is very, very certain, then his distribution may look like Fig. 5.2.

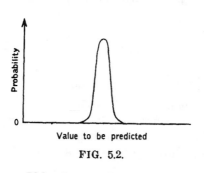
Value to be predicted
FIG. 5.2.

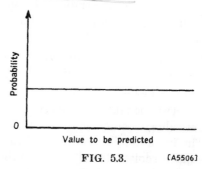
Value to be predicted
FIG. 5.3.   [A5506]

If he is completely uncertain, if he thinks that all values are equally likely, then the distribution will look like Fig. 5.3.

In a typical situation, the forecaster will be neither very certain nor very uncertain, but somewhere in between as in Fig. 5.4. * * *

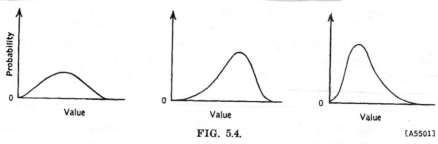
Value   Value   Value
FIG. 5.4.   [A5501]

Some persons find it difficult to assess directly an entire numerical distribution, but can express their feelings more easily by using a mixture of language and numbers. For example, a typical statement might be:

"Well, I would guess there's about a 50–50 chance that the market share will be between 25% and 35%, and it could go as high as 40%, or even as low as 20%. Who knows? But I'd say that there's only a slight chance of that—oh, only about a 1 in 20 chance. When you get right down to it, my best guess is about 28%."

From this, a probability distribution can be described, using the quantitative estimates and making inferences about the intervening points. After it is drawn, the forecaster can examine the distribution and make any alterations he wishes before adopting it.

* * *

Expected Monetary Value

Assuming that probability assignments are made to future events, what can be done with them? The next step typically is to multiply the probabilities times the monetary values of the possible events to get the "expected monetary value" of the investment.

Let us use the earlier simple illustration and assume for the moment that unit sales return a present monetary value of $1 each. In effect, we weight the value of the possible events by the probability that the events will be realized. The sum is the "weighted average" value of the investment.

Forecast	Profit	Probability	Expected Monetary Value
Optimistic	$100,000	⨯ .30	$30,000
Most likely	75,000	⨯ .60	45,000
Pessimistic	50,000	⨯ .10	5,000
			$80,000

The $80,000 expected monetary value figure becomes a figure with which we can work in our extended decision analysis. We can compare two decisions, and *generally speaking,* we would tend to prefer that decision that has the highest expected monetary value.

3. RISK AND THE CAPITALIZATION RATE

As Grayson suggests above, the factor of expected returns can be identified as the arithmetic mean of the possible outcomes of an investment, with each such outcome being weighted by the probability of its occurrence. Given a choice among a number of investment projects, an investor will always prefer the one that offers the highest expected return, *provided* that the various projects under consideration are alike in degree of risk. The proviso is critically important. If Project A offers higher expected returns than Project B, but is also in some sense riskier, the investor may find that she fears the added risk even more than she likes the greater return and decide that B is the better choice from her standpoint. While investors no doubt react intuitively to such matters in most cases, financial managers and others serving in a capacity that calls for a formal appraisal would presumably wish to quantify, or at least to isolate, the risk factor. Accordingly, how should risk be measured? If probability distributions yield a statistical measure of the expected monetary value of future returns, do they also yield a statistical measure of risk? How should the adverse effect of risk be allowed for in the valuation process?

(A) RISK AS DEGREE OF DISPERSION

Lewellen, The Cost of Capital

Ch. 2 (1969).

THE UTILITY FUNCTION

A convenient vehicle for examining the nature of [investors'] attitudes is what an economist would term a "utility function". This is simply a representation of the satisfaction which investors can be thought of as deriving from different amounts of wealth. Although it could be described in mathematical terms, the graphical representation shown in Figure 2–1 will suffice for our purposes here. The various levels of wealth, in dollars, that an individual might conceivably experience are plotted on the horizontal axis and the enjoyment—the inner glow—he would feel at each level is plotted on the vertical scale. * * *

FIGURE 2–1. *An investor's utility function.*

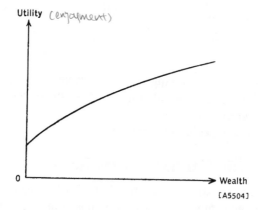

Despite its necessarily abstract nature, the utility function pictured above was not chosen at random. The fact that the curve, while steadily rising, falls away to the right at higher and higher levels of wealth conveys two important—and by now reasonably well accepted—features of the typical investor's attitudes: (1) the more money he has, the happier he is; (2) but equal successive increments to his wealth imply progressively smaller increments to his total utility.

The first of these is perhaps the easier to accept * * * Since in the business world, people attempt to make money, little more need be said to justify a rising utility function. Actually, the arguments to be made below do not require that the curve continually rise—just that it never turn downward. As long as additional wealth is no *dis*advantage to the investor, this will be a legitimate assumption.

The other point—i.e., that the curve is in fact a curve rather than a straight line—may have less logical appeal. As it turns out, this is merely an expression of the familiar economic principle of diminishing marginal returns. An individual eventually becomes somewhat satiated with his wealth. The second million he acquires, while still worth having, is not quite as valuable to him as the first million, since the latter has already provided him with most of the material satisfactions he wanted out of life. Three summer homes do not really generate half again the happiness of two.

    * * *

If such intuitive arguments are not wholly convincing, there is considerable empirical evidence to support them. Our discussion is leading up to the conclusion that a utility function of the type illustrated implies that investors dislike risk—and we have clear indications of risk aversion in the real world. We observe that people buy insurance; we see that they diversify their investment portfolios instead of putting all their funds into a single stock; we notice businessmen requiring larger prospective returns from ventures that are highly uncertain than they do from safer investments; and we see corporate bonds rated as grade "B" in terms of the ability of the issuer to meet the required payments selling at a lower price than those rated "Aaa." Thus, visible economic behavior is consistent with aversion to risk on the part of investors—and our curve, as we shall see, provides the underlying rationale for just such an attitude. In that respect, it is offered here as a rough, but valid, approximation of the wealth-utility responses of most security purchasers. * * *

RISK AND RETURN

Using this framework, then, let us examine the manner in which an individual would appraise the attractiveness of an investment opportunity whose outcome is uncertain. Since any such investment is basically a form of gambling, we may cast our analysis in a simple betting context for purposes of illustration. Consider the following circumstance: An individual whose total wealth amounts to $1,000 is offered the chance to bet $100 on the outcome of a coin toss. If the coin comes up heads, he wins $100; if it shows tails, he loses $100. The coin is "fair" so that the probabilities of winning and losing are both equal to one-half. The question therefore is: Will this be an attractive proposition?

We can answer that question by looking at his utility function in the region of $1,000 initial wealth. He perceives the possible results of the bet to be as shown in Figure 2–2. At the moment, he has a thousand dollars and enjoys the level of satisfaction denoted by $U(1,000)$. That is, the goods and services he could purchase with those funds would provide him with that much "utility." If he accepts the bet and wins, his wealth rises to $1,100 and his satisfaction to $U (1,100)$. If he loses, his wealth declines to $900 and his satisfaction to $U (900)$. Should he gamble?

FIGURE 2-2. *Utility response to changes in wealth.*

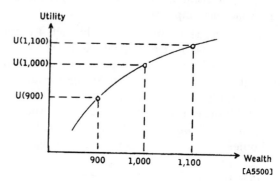

The answer clearly is no. Although the bet is fair in money terms, it is not fair with respect to what the money means to him. The additional satisfaction he would obtain by winning—the difference between $U (1,100)$ and $U (1,000)$—is less than the pain he would be subjected to in losing—the difference between $U (1,000)$ and $U (900)$. He will bet only if the amount he stands to win is sufficiently greater than his possible loss that the two increments on the *utility* scale are equal, as illustrated in Figure 2-3, where:

$$U (1,130) - U (1,000) = U (1,000) - U (930). \qquad (2\text{-}1)$$

A coin toss having the following outcomes *would* be acceptable: heads, he wins $130; tails, he loses $70. That situation could be achieved by making it a condition of the bet that the other party first pay our man $30 and then flip the coin. In this light, $30 can be interpreted as the "risk premium" necessary to induce participation. It measures the monetary equivalent of our investors "risk aversion" to the indicated set of uncertain outcomes.
* * *

FIGURE 2-3. *An acceptable bet.*

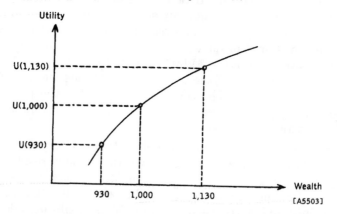

DISPERSION AND RISK PREMIUMS

If all this seems reasonable in the context of a single gamble, what can our utility function tell us about the relative attractiveness of different bets? Let us suppose our man with $1,000 is confronted with an additional opportunity. Someone else offers him a heads-or-tails bet in which the stakes now are $200 instead of only $100. We may characterize his reactions by Figure 2–4. If he accepts the first bet, the difference between the utility he stands to gain and that which he stands to lose is

$$\Delta U_1 = [U(1,100) - U(1,000)] - [U(1,000) - U(900)]. \qquad (2\text{-}2)$$

$= 100 - 100 = 0 \quad (\text{negative})$

FIGURE 2–4. *Comparison of two gambles.*

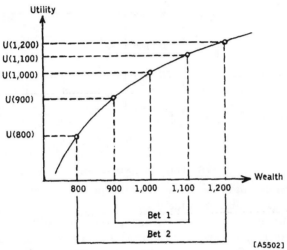

In the case of the second bet:

$$\Delta U_2 = [U(1,200) - U(1,000)] - [U(1,000) - U(800)]. \qquad (2\text{-}3)$$

Both of which, of course, are negative. By the nature of the curve, however, it will always be true that uU_2 exceeds (is more negative than) uU_1. The larger the bet—the greater the spread of its possible outcomes for a given monetary expected value—the less attractive it is.[1] An investor therefore must not only be "paid" something to take an even bet; he must be paid more the wider its range of consequences. Thus, he would be indifferent between the two bets if the terms were as in Figure 2–5, where the stipulation is that

$$U(1,130) - U(1,000) = U(1,000) - U(930) \qquad (2\text{-}4)$$
$$U(1,250) - U(1,000) = U(1,000) - U(850). \qquad (2\text{-}5)$$

$130 - 70 = 60 \quad (2\text{-}4) \quad 60/2 = 30$

$250 - 150 = 100 \quad (2\text{-}5) \quad 100/2 = 50$

His companions would have to pay him $30 to get him to take number 1,

---

1. Put differently, the greater the spread of the dollar outcomes, the more negative is the expected *utility* value of the bet.

Implicit in our discussion is the proposition that a "fair" gamble is one with an expected value of zero in utility terms.

but $50 to take number 2 with its higher stakes.* In order to analyze the relative attractiveness of different investments, then, we must recognize not only the expected value of their outcomes but also the relative *dispersion* of the probability distribution associated with each. Fortunately, there is a convenient mathematical measure of that dispersion which we can make use of in our subsequent discussions of alternative financing decisions under uncertainty.

FIGURE 2-5. *Comparison of two acceptable bets.*

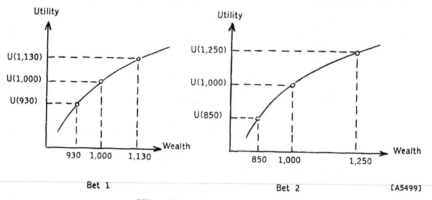

WHY GAMBLE AND INVEST?

The objection might be raised at this point that something must be wrong with the preceding arguments, since they in effect imply that no one in the community would ever either gamble or invest. How can the existence of both activities be explained if we are really to believe that utility functions of the sort described adequately depict individual attitudes?

Take gambling first—in particular, the penny-ante poker game or similar small-stakes endeavors. We can fit these into our mold with only a minor stretching of the analysis. The rationale would be that the range of possible dollar wins and losses is so small in relation to the players' total wealth that they simply are not sufficiently sensitive to the utility implications to react adversely. The difference between the gain in utility from winning, say, $5 if you have a good night with the cards and the utility loss implied by ending up $5 in the hole on a bad night is just not great enough to notice, much less worry about. If you feel you are as likely to win as to lose such an amount—i.e., you play poker as well as anyone else in the game—you will play despite the minor utility consequences. Few of us, however, will stay in the game when the pots reach $500 per hand. By that time, the happiness connected with winning and the pain produced by losing are far enough out of balance that we abstain. The same phenomenon, of course, is observed where investments in common stocks are concerned. Most people are willing to put only a portion of their total

* [Ed. Note] Logically, the risk premium associated with doubling the bet would have to be *more* than twice the risk premium for the initial bet—i.e. more than $60. Reference in the text to a $50 premium is simply an oversight.

wealth into equities, keeping some of their funds in savings accounts or similar secure investments.[2]

Another reason for gambling is that the process itself has some "utility." It's fun to get together * * * and match wits. Poker is only the excuse for doing so. If you happen to lose a few dollars every once in a while, you regard that as merely the price of an evening's entertainment. Perhaps a better reason, however, is that you may in fact believe that your chances of winning are better than your chances of losing. You have faith in your ability at cards. You perceive yourself in the situation depicted in Figure 2–3 above where the potential win is $130 while the loss is only $70, so that in utility terms the gamble *is* sensible. This may be the attitude of most so-called "professional" gamblers. They think they know something that their adversaries do not and therefore are willing to participate in the game.

The same reasoning can be extended to investing. The expectation of the investor is that, on average, there *is* an opportunity to profit. The "bet" is weighted in his favor—its expected monetary value is positive. Empirical evidence, of course, supports that attitude. People *do* make money in the market if for no other reason than the fact that most firms whose shares are traded are themselves earning a profit from operations. Stock prices seem to be generally rising over time and, while the risks we are concerned with here are clearly present, so are attractive opportunities. The question for us, then, is the manner in which these two aspects of an investment are balanced in an investor's mind.

EXPECTED VALUE AND VARIANCE

The utility function approach described above suggests that the answer lies in an examination of the two features of the probability distribution of investment outcomes which measure "return" and "risk"—the expected monetary value of the investment and its degree of dispersion. The former, as was indicated, is defined simply as the average outcome of the opportunity: the sum of each possible result weighted by its probability of occurrence. Thus, an investment whose characteristics are as shown below has an expected value equal to $1,000.

Possible Outcome, x	Probability of Occurrence, Pr(x)	x · Pr(x)
$ 900	¼	$ 225
1,000	½	500
1,100	¼	275
		$1,000

This parameter, which is commonly called the "mean" of the distribution, will hereafter be denoted * * * by a bar over the pertinent variable, e.g., x.

---

2. This continuing analogy between investing and gambling may not be entirely appreciated by the investment community. The following quotation attributed to the Dallas *Times–Herald* may be pertinent: "If you bet on a horse, that's gambling. If you bet you can make three spades, that's entertainment. If you bet AT&T will go up three points, that's business. See the difference?"

Similarly, the extent of the possible spread of a set of such outcomes is measured by a parameter termed its "variance" and defined as the [sum of the squares] of the deviations from the mean, also weighted by their respective probabilities:

Possible x	Pr(x)	x–x̄	(x–x̄)²	[Pr(x)][(x–x̄)²]
$ 900	¼	−100	10,000	2,500
1,000	½	0	0	0
1,100	¼	+100	10,000	2,500
			Variance =	5,000

The greater the potential variation in the results, the larger will be this parameter. Squaring any negative deviations ensures that relationship.

* * *

The point of calculating the variance, it should be emphasized, is that the typical investor's utility function tells us that the greater the range of the consequences of a gamble, the less attractive it becomes. The utility disadvantages of the losses become progressively more severe in relation to the benefits of the profits. For that reason, variance is a convenient proxy measure of the size of the relevant "risk premiums."

NOTE: RISK AND RETURN CHARACTERISTICS OF DIFFERENT SECURITIES

1. *Variance and Standard Deviation.*

The Lewellen discussion describes the psychological roots of risk aversion and shows why economists and financial theorists generally express the idea of investment risk in terms of the dispersion of the expected outcomes about their mean or average value. The statistical concepts commonly used to measure the *degree* of dispersion, and hence of risk, are "variance" and (perhaps more often) "standard deviation." As indicated above, variance is defined with respect to a set of outcomes as the sum of the squares of the deviations from the mean, multiplied in each instance by the probability of occurrence. Standard deviation is the square root of variance. Thus, if variance is 5,000 in Lewellen's example above, standard deviation is the square root of 5,000, or 70.71.

2. *Real World Risks and Returns.*

Empirical studies of investments in real world securities markets confirm the foregoing theoretical assertions about risk and return. Brealey, Myers & Allen, Principles of Corporate Finance 149,159–160 164–165 (8th ed. 2006), measures the historical performance of portfolios of treasury bills, long-term treasury bonds, and common stocks from 1900 to 2003. Here are the annual average rates of return:

Portfolio	Average Nominal Annual Rate of Return (percent per year)	Average Real Annual Rate of Return (percent per year)
Treasury bills	4.1	1.
Government bonds	5.2	2.3
Common stocks	11.7	8.5

The standard deviations and variances for the portfolios were as follows:

Portfolio	Standard Deviation σ	Variance σ^2
Treasury bills	2.8	7.9
Government bonds	8.2	68.0
Common stocks	20.1	402.6

(handwritten annotation: as risk ↑, σ ≠ σ² ↑)

As the level of risk increases across the portfolios, so do the returns and risks. Note that Treasury bills and Treasury bonds show variance and standard deviation despite the absence of default risk because the real value of their returns remains subject to inflation risk.

Would you expect the 20.1 standard deviation for the stock portfolio across the entire century to be higher or lower than the figure for a shorter period? Compare the results respecting stock market variability in each decade since 1931:

Decade	Market Standard Deviation σ_m
1931–1940	37.8
1941–1950	14.0
1951–1960	12.1
1961–1970	13.0
1971–1980	15.8
1981–1990	16.5
1991–2003	14.8

One point of controversy respecting these results should be noted. In the view of some, the historical rates of return on common stock are *higher* than their risk characteristics should justify.

(B) COMPARABLE FIRMS AND MARKET CAPITALIZATION RATES: THE PRICE/EARNINGS RATIO

We have seen PV = A/r and that r is risk sensitive. The greater the volatility, the higher the r, the greater the required rate of return, and the lower the present value. We have also seen that risk/return tradeoffs implicate subjective responses. How then does one produce an "objective" valuation?

Appraisers often quantify the risk that the estimated stream of earnings will not be realized by reference to the risk which the market attributes to comparable firms or to comparable securities of comparable firms. Use of comparable securities and firms as yardsticks appears to entail less "subjectivity" than the other modes of measuring risk discussed previously, because it draws on market data rather than pure abstraction. But the process by no means eliminates reliance on subjective judgments, including a judgment of what other company or companies are comparable.

Francis I. duPont & Co. v. Universal City Studios, Inc.

Court of Chancery of Delaware, 1973.
312 A.2d 344.

■ DUFFY, JUSTICE.

This is the decision upon exceptions to an Appraiser's final report determining the value of minority shares in a corporation absorbed in a short form merger.

A.

On March 25, 1966 Universal Pictures Co. (Universal) was merged into Universal City Studios, Inc. (defendant) under 8 Del.C. § 253. [The merger was] effected by MCA, Inc., the common parent. MCA owned 92% of Universal and 100% of defendant. The minority stockholders of Universal were offered $75 per share which plaintiffs rejected and then perfected their appraisal rights.

On March 29, 1973 the Appraiser filed a final report, in which he found the value of the Universal stock to be $91.47 per share. Both parties filed exceptions and this is the decision thereon after briefing and oral argument.

B.

The parties' ultimate disagreement is, of course, over the value of the stock. Plaintiffs submit that the true value is $131.89 per share, defendant says it is $52.36. The computations are as follows:

Plaintiffs

Value Factor	Value	Weight	Result
Earnings	$129.12	70%	$ 90.38
Market	144.36	20%	28.87
Assets	126.46	10%	12.64
	Value per share		$131.89

Defendant

Value Factor	Value	Weight	Result
Earnings	$ 51.93	70%	$ 36.35
Dividends	41.66	20%	8.33
Assets	76.77	10%	7.68
	Value per share		$ 52.36

Appraiser

Value Factor	Value	Weight	Result
Earnings	$ 92.89	80%	$ 74.31
Assets	85.82	20%	17.16
	Value per share		$ 91.47

* * *

C.

* * *

Defendant takes exception to the Appraiser's failure to find that in the years prior to merger the industry was declining and that Universal was ranked near its bottom. And it argues that Universal was in the business of producing and distributing feature motion pictures for theatrical exhibition. It contends that such business, generally, was in a severe decline at the time of merger and that Universal, in particular, was in a vulnerable position because it had failed to diversify, its feature films were of low commercial quality and, unlike other motion picture companies, substantially all of its film library had already been committed to distributors for television exhibition. In short, defendant pictures Universal as a weak ("wasting asset") corporation in a sick industry with poor prospects for revival.

The stockholders see a different company. They say that Universal's business was indeed the production and distribution of feature films, but not merely for theatrical exhibition. They argue that there was a dramatic increase in the television market for such feature films at the time of the merger. This new market, they contend, gave great new value to a fully amortized film library and significantly enhanced the value of Universal's current and future productions. They equate the television market to the "acquisition of a new and highly profitable business whose earnings potential was just beginning to be realized at the time of the merger." Finally, say plaintiffs, the theatrical market itself was recovering in 1966. Thus, they paint the portrait of a well situated corporation in a rejuvenated industry.

The Appraiser agreed with the stockholders that the theatrical market was recovering and that the new television market had favorable effects and would continue to provide a ready market for future films to be released by Universal. However, he declined to give the stockholders the benefit of all inferences as to specific value factors which they maintained those conclusions required.

D.

I first consider earnings. Both parties disagree, for different reasons, with the result of the Appraiser's analysis of Universal's earnings as a value factor. He concluded that Universal's earnings value should be derived by calculating the mean average of earnings per share for the years 1961 through 1965, the five years preceding the merger.[4] So doing, he arrived at average earnings of $5.77 per share. He then adopted a multiplier of 16.1, which is the average price earnings ratio of nine motion picture companies,[5] to capitalize Universal's earnings.

The stockholders accept the multiplier selected by the Appraiser but argue that he should have used the 1965 earnings of $8.02 per share rather than the mean average of the five years preceding the merger. * * *

* * *

It is established Delaware law that for appraisal purposes earnings are to be determined by averaging the corporation's earnings over a reasonable period of time. In re Olivetti Underwood Corp., Del.Ch., 246 A.2d 800 (1968); Sproborg v. City Specialty Stores, 35 Del.Ch., 560, 123 A.2d 121

---

4. Those earnings per share were:

1961	$3.32
1962	4.96
1963	6.22
1964	6.32
1965	8.02

5. Those companies were Columbia, MGM, Paramount, Republic, 20th Century Fox, United Artists, M.C.A., Walt Disney, and Warner Brothers.

(1956). The determination must be based upon historical earnings rather than on the basis of prospective earnings. Application of Delaware Racing Association, Del.Supr., 213 A.2d 203 (1965). The five-year period immediately preceding the merger is ordinarily considered to be the most representative and reasonable period of time over which to compute the average. Application of Delaware Racing Association, supra; In re Olivetti Underwood Corporation, supra.

Our cases have recognized that an appraiser, in certain circumstances, may justify adjusting average earnings by eliminating "unusual and isolated" items from reported earnings or, in a "most unusual situation" by limiting or expanding the number of years over which the average is taken. Adams v. R.C. Williams & Company, 39 Del.Ch. 61, 158 A.2d 797 (1960). But I agree with the Appraiser's finding that no such situation has been shown here.

The stockholders argue that averaging past earnings is proper only when the earnings history has been erratic. In support of that proposition, Mr. Stanley Nabi, managing partner of a NYSE brokerage house and an investment and financial analyst, testified that the accepted practice among security analysts is to capitalize present earnings, and to give the trend of earnings important consideration in the selection of the multiplier. The stockholders argue that Universal's earnings history was not erratic but, in fact, had a steady and rapid growth. They contend that the Appraiser therefore should have used the current (1965) earnings as the figure to be capitalized.

This argument is not persuasive even if Mr. Nabi's testimony as to the accepted practice among security analysts for capitalizing earnings is conceded to be correct. Whatever that practice may currently be, the policy of Delaware law is that averaging earnings over the five years immediately preceding the merger should be the rule and not the exception. In short, a choice among alternative techniques for capitalizing earnings has been made and no persuasive conceptual reason has been shown to change that choice now.

The stockholders also argue that Universal's earlier earnings, particularly those of 1961, were not representative of Universal's earning power at the time of merger because television was a relatively minor factor in such earnings. They offered a number of alternatives to the Appraiser and, on the exceptions, press their contention that he should have used 1965 earnings of $8.02 per share.

I do not agree with the shareholders that the "pre–1965 earnings had become an anachronism" at the time of merger. I view Universal's situation at that time as one of change in the nature of its market, not in the fundamental nature of its business. It was undoubtedly clear at the time of merger that the new television market had contributed substantially to Universal's earnings and would continue to do so for at least the short term. It was also evident that television presented a relatively permanent new market. But I do not think it realistic to say that that market was of such a revolutionary character as to assure for time without end either a trend of increasing earnings or a comparatively high level of earnings.

Compare Adams v. R.C. Williams & Company, supra. The fact is that, with or without the television market, Universal's earning experience over the long term remains subject to the variables in its managerial and artistic talent, the ability and ingenuity of competitors and the uncertainties of public tastes in entertainment.

Certainly the figures show, as plaintiffs argue, that the trend in earnings was on the rise from 1961 through 1965 but that is not a reason in law for abandoning the averaging approach required under *Delaware Racing* and other Supreme Court decisions, nor does it provide a basis for eliminating any one year as unusual or isolated under *Adams*. The trend has significance in the choice of the multiplier.

* * *

I conclude, therefore, that the Appraiser correctly used the mean average of earnings for the five years immediately preceding the merger.

Defendant agrees that the earnings to be capitalized is the five-year average of $5.77 per share, but says that the Appraiser erred in adopting as a multiplier the industry price earnings ratio (16:1). It argues that even if such ratio were appropriate, the correct figure is not more than 12.7 and it contends that the maximum multiplier permitted under our case law is 10, except under special circumstances not present here. Plaintiffs do not except to the Appraiser's multiplier. Specifically, defendant says a multiplier of 9 is fair both in terms of Universal's prior history and its position in that industry.

Admittedly many of the cases and treatises approve a multiplier of 10 or thereabouts. But that is based largely on the economics and pricing structure of an earlier day and, under the circumstances here present, the use of any such number would be artificial.

* * *

The earnings value (16.1 $\times$ $5.77 = $92.89) determined by the Appraiser will be approved.

E.

I turn now to asset value. Plaintiffs say that at the time of merger the net figure was $126.46, defendant says it was $76.77, the Appraiser determined it to be $85.82.

The parties have argued at some length their respective views of the adjustments which should be made to Universal's book value, but I do not propose to discuss each of these in detail. * * *

I conclude that for appraisal purposes a share of Universal stock should be assigned an asset value of $91.72.

F.

The Appraiser declined to include market value of Universal stock as a value factor because there was not a reliable market for it and none could be constructed. Defendant agrees with that conclusion. Plaintiffs urged the Appraiser to find a reconstructed value of $144 a share.

The Delaware law is that in the absence of a reliable market for stock, a reconstructed market value "must be given consideration", if one can be made. Application of Delaware Racing Association, supra.

I agree with plaintiffs that, on a comparative basis, Universal's financial performance was more impressive than that of MCA, but I am not persuaded that a reliable basis for valuation can be established by applying MCA price earnings ratio to Universal's 1965 earnings. Certainly there was a market for MCA shares and Universal's earnings and experience contributed to whatever value that buyers and sellers in that market placed upon MCA at any given time. But to reach through the MCA curtain and find Universal, is to grasp at shadows, and to attempt to divine (in this case where we deal with hard dollars) what buyers would have paid for Universal had they the chance, is to substitute fantasy for fact. This simply involves too much speculation about too many intangibles. Accordingly, market value will not be included as an appraisal index.

G.

Defendant urged the Appraiser to capitalize the historical dividends of Universal and assign to them an independent value of $41.66 for appraisal purposes. He declined to do so. Plaintiffs agree.

I agree with the Appraiser's conclusion, based upon Felder v. Anderson, Clayton & Co., supra, that dividends largely reflect the same value as earnings and so should not be separately considered. *Delaware Racing,* with its policy and history of "no dividends", was obviously a unique case entirely unlike that presented here.

H.

Finally, I consider the weighting factor, an issue as to which the parties are in least disagreement. The views of the Appraiser and the parties are as follows:

Value Factor	Plaintiffs	Defendant	Appraiser
Earnings	70%	70%	80%
Assets	10%	10%	20%
Market value	20%	—	—
Dividend Distribution	—	20%	—

As this table shows, the parties agree on the weight which should be assigned to earnings and assets, respectively. They differ on allocation of the remaining 20% which each argues should be assigned to separate factors, both of which the Appraiser and the Court have rejected. The Appraiser, in effect, divided the 20% equally between the two components he used.

In my own view, a more precise division of that 20% should be made by applying to it a factor derived from the allocations about which the parties agree. I think this is particularly desirable because both sides agree that earnings are entitled to seven times as much weight as assets. Applying such factors (7/8 for earnings, 1/8 for assets) to the remaining 20%, I conclude that the earnings percentage should be increased by 17.5%, while the asset percentage should be increased by 2.5%.

* * *

I conclude that the value of a share of Universal stock on the date of merger should be determined to be as follows:

Value Factor	Value	Weight	Result
Earnings	$92.89	87.5%	$81.28
Assets	91.72	12.5%	11.47
		Value per share	$92.75

———

Universal City Studios, Inc. v. Francis I. duPont & Co.

Supreme Court of Delaware, 1975.
334 A.2d 216.

■ McNEILLY, JUSTICE.

* * * The prospective financial condition of the subject corporation and the risk factor inherent in the corporation and the industry within which it operates are vital factors to be considered in arriving at a realistic present earnings value. These considerations are manifested in the valuation process through the choice of a capitalization factor, or multiplier. The multiplier will be low if the financial outlook for a corporation is poor, or high if prospects are encouraging. When the multiplier is computed with the past earnings record (in this case $5.77 per share), the resultant figure is deemed to best approximate the present earnings value of a share of stock. The multiplier adopted by the Appraiser and the Court below was 16.1 and that figure, as well as the means used to arrive at such number, are the primary issues upon which appellant bases its appeal.

* * *

The appellees assert that the 16.1 figure should be affirmed. The appellant contends that improper criteria were used by the Appraiser and the Court in determining the multiplier and that the figure is impermissibly high. For this latter proposition, appellants cite Professor Dewing, whose works in the past have been accorded deferential treatment in Delaware. At page 388 of his work, "The Financial Policy of Corporations," (5th Ed.1953) Professor Dewing states that a multiplier of 10 is the highest value that can be assigned to a business. We, however, do not find such a view to be persuasive, but instead concur with the findings of Swanton, supra, (where a multiplier of 14 was fixed), which recognized that Professor Dewing's capitalization chart was not the "be-all and end-all," and it did not "freeze the subject matter for all time," especially since "contemporary financial history" reveals a "need for flexibility." (at 246).

* * * We agree with the appellant insofar as the 16.1 figure is arrived at through precise mathematical calculations involving the price-earnings ratios of these nine other companies. We disagree however that this was the sole consideration * * *

[handwritten margin note: In arriving at the M. in addition to considering the PE ratio of comparable companies, some other factors should also be considered (and the lower court did so)]

* * * The Chancellor included a table in the opinion which showed that in 1961, earnings per share were $3.32, and that the earnings steadily increased until in 1965, they were at $8.02 per share. The record shows that during these years, none of the companies except Disney could show a steady growth trend. Within the industry, there was pronounced volatility of earnings, with years of deficit and decline. Universal, on the other hand, was able to show a steady growth, even during the period of 1962 and 1963, when the industry was suffering greatly. As for the "predictability" of certain of its television income, the Chancellor was taking cognizance of the Appraiser's report, which specified that Universal was to receive "substantial future income" in the sum of over $48,000,000 as a result of the leasing of major portions of its film library to television networks. Such commitments were labeled "guaranteed" by the Appraiser, and he noted that they would result in net earnings from television of at least $16.63 per share over the following four years. Further income could be expected from renewal of television contracts as well as from release of future films and subsequent leases to television. The evidence presented was sufficient to warrant a departure from Dewing's capitalization chart. The steady upward trend in Universal's earnings and the vast amount of money guaranteed to inure to Universal are persuasive factors indicating future economic success and stability. * * * It is true that a corporation in the motion picture industry, such as Universal, is subject to the whims of public taste and the artistic talents of its employees. Fluctuation in earnings is indeed a trademark of the motion picture industry and Universal was as vulnerable to non-acceptance of its theatrical productions as any other company. However, as of the date of the merger, Universal had exhibited a better earnings picture than any other motion picture company and had, through its television contracts, provided a buffer which would tend to offset for several years any theatrical losses. Therefore a relatively high multiplier was warranted.

There are other factors not alluded to in the opinion which support a high multiplier in this case. The years of 1964 and 1965 showed a marked resurgence for the motion picture industry after a long period of slumping profits due to competition from television. The stock market reflected the turnaround of the industry by rising from the stock price index of 49 in 1963 (the mean price of Columbia, MGM, 20th Century Fox, United Artists, Paramount, Warner Brothers) to a mean of about $64 per share figure in 1966. Further, on March 25, 1966, the Dow Jones and Standard and Poors Indices showed an average price to earnings ratio of approximately 17.3, 17.4. Universal's growth rate during the years 1961 through 1965 amounted to 142 per cent or a compound rate of 25 per cent a year. This record, showing no yearly volatility, was far superior to those other companies within the industry and was also superior to the rate of growth of the stocks listed in the Dow Jones and Standard and Poors Indices.

Appellant contends that the use of the average price earnings ratio of the nine other companies in the industry was improper in that those companies were not comparable and did not reflect the corporate managerial policies which were unique to Universal. Alternatively, it is contended that if companies within the industry were to be used in arriving at a multiplier, only those companies which were financially and otherwise comparable should have been used. In addition, appellant contends it was error as a matter of law for the average industry price earnings ratio to have been computed on the basis of one day's market price. We disagree.

* * *

There being no valid market price for Universal's stock, and therefore no valid price-earnings ratio, the Appraiser was without a fixed mathematical method whereby factors relating solely to Universal's own stability and growth potential could be given effect in the form of a multiplier. Therefore, the Appraiser referred to the industry price-earnings ratio on the date of the merger as a starting point in the fixing of a multiplier. The use of price-earnings ratios of comparable businesses on the date of merger as a factor in evaluating another company, and here as a vital first step in arriving at a multiplier, is reasonable and has support in Delaware case law. * * * The five-year average was adopted because the market was in a boom phase. Though the motion picture industry was in a period of rejuvenation at the time of Universal's merger, a look at the price-earnings ratios over the five-year period preceding the merger as compared with the 16.1 average on the date of merger, reveals figures not disproportionate. * * * The determination of value as of the day of merger being the Court's endeavor, it is appropriate that the price-earnings ratios of comparable companies, serving as barometers of risk within the industry, be referred to solely on the day of merger in the absence of extraordinary deviation from the past price-earnings record.

As for the appellant's contention that error was committed below by the use of certain non-comparable companies in arriving at the 16.1 figure, we are not persuaded to reverse. The "imponderables of the valuation process" and the concomitant broad discretion traditionally granted to evaluators of corporate shares of stock, compel an acceptance of the method of determining a multiplier unless there is a clear abuse of discretion amounting to an error at law, i.e., such as the use of only one value factor at the expense of other factors. *Tri Continental,* supra.

* * *

True, some of the companies were more diversified than Universal, and some produced more award winning movies than Universal. Nevertheless, all nine companies were heavily engaged in the production and distribution of motion pictures and were therefore subject to the same public moods and reactions that affected Universal. We note that, based on its past record and managerial plans for the future, Universal was in a position to suffer less than other companies from woes generally affecting the industry. We are not prepared to delineate one or more companies within the same industry as Universal, as being non-comparable, when influxes applicable to one are applicable to all, but register in varying degrees as measured by financial growth or depletion. * * *

* * * [W]e conclude that the 16.1 figure reached below is within the range of reason.

* * *

Affirmed.

NOTE: INFERRED CAPITALIZATION RATES AND CONSTANT GROWTH VALUATION

1. *Inferring Capitalization Rates from Price/Earnings Ratios of Comparable Firms.*

DuPont v. Universal illustrates a judicial attempt to set a capitalization rate by reference to price/earnings ratios of a set of "comparable" firms. The Advisory Report of the Securities and Exchange Commission in the insolvency reorganization under Chapter X of **Jade Oil & Gas Co.,** 44 S.E.C. 56 (1969), shows us a more extreme use of the same methodology.

Jade Oil arose under Chapter X of the Bankruptcy Act of 1938 (since replaced by Chapter 11 of the Bankruptcy Code of 1978). Chapter X (like present Chapter 11), involved failed business enterprises whose operating income had proved insufficient to meet the contractual claims of their creditors. Chapter X (like present Chapter 11) protected the assets of these companies by barring their creditors from immediately enforcing their claims through foreclosure proceedings or otherwise. Instead, under Chapter X the enterprise continued, at least for the time being, while an effort was made to develop a plan of financial readjustment. The plan had to satisfy two legal standards. First, it had to be "feasible"—that is, a solvent future had to be a likely possibility for the reorganized firm. Second, it had to be "fair and equitable"—that is, it had to respect absolutely priorities of the securities in the firm's capital structure. Accordingly, the court's task was to decide whether, and in what amounts, the claims of various individual and classes of creditors were valid, whether the firm was viable, and whether the value of the reorganized firm was sufficient to satisfy those claims.

Chapter X required that, prior to judicial approval and submission to security holders, the reorganization plans were to be referred to the Securities and Exchange Commission for an advisory report to be sent to affected security holders and creditors. The Commission's report was not binding on the court, and the Commission had no right to appeal the court's determination, though it might join in appeals taken by others.

In *Jade Oil* the SEC was reporting on a small bankrupt oil company—a highly risky enterprise described as a "wildcatter." Jade explored for oil in unproven, unproductive areas in which leases could be procured at low cost. One lucky strike meant riches for all. But Jade had not had any lucky strikes for a while. Revenues from existing properties were expected to decline from $1 million per year to $660,000 per year in five years. The SEC objected to a reorganization plan formulated by Jade's bankruptcy Trustee which projected a series of new oil strikes that would return a growing revenue stream—from $66,000 in Year 1 to $678,000 in Year 5. The Trustee had capitalized the growing stream of net cash flows that resulted with a multiplier of 33. Said the SEC Report:

> In arriving at a capitalization rate, the Trustee notes that in his sample of 15 comparable companies the average cash flow is on the average capitalized at 37 times. He concludes therefore that 3% is the appropriate rate at which to capitalize Jade's prospective cash flow, or 33 times the anticipated average cash flow of $577,660 for 1970–1974. We think it impossible to derive a capitalization rate valid or acceptable for Chapter X purposes from a market in capitalized hope dominated by the pursuit of long shots. * * *

Moreover, the Trustee's concept of striking and using some industry-wide "average" is extremely dubious. One of the Trustee's sample of 15 companies sells for 10 times cash flow, and, at the other extreme, another sells for 450 times cash flow. There is not even the semblance of a clue as to which rate is appropriate, and "averaging" such disparate numbers contributes nothing to a rational resolution of the issue. The Trustee himself recognizes that there is something questionable about averaging the odds. He notes that small oil and gas companies tend to sell at multiples much higher than larger ones, and therefore begins by looking for small oil and gas companies comparable to Jade. He finds 15, four of which he considers unrepresentative because the multiples at which they sell seem too high. For those very high multiples he substitutes the arbitrarily chosen multiple of 50. Of those the Trustee regards as acceptable, one sells at 10 times cash flow while another sells at 41 times. In the face of the vast range of multipliers, we consider market prices an unreliable guide to value and fairness.

Was the SEC correct to reject the valuation? If the market really did capitalize the earnings (or cash flows) of such companies at a 3 percent rate, would not Jade's senior security holders have received a windfall as a result of the SEC's "under appraisal" of the company's value? On the other hand, assuming that small wildcatters did sell in the market at 33 times their *current* cash flows, was the Trustee proceeding on a sound theoretical basis when applying that multiplier to Jade's *prospective* cash flows? Or is there a fallacy in applying current price/earnings ratios to anticipated future earnings? If Jade's net cash flows could be expected to grow at a rate of, say, 15 percent a year indefinitely (as the Trustee's projections suggested), what would be the present value of those flows if capitalized at a rate of 3 percent? Finally, and in the same vein, why should small oil and gas companies tend to sell at higher multiples than larger ones?

When reference is made to "comparable firms" in deriving capitalization rates in valuation, one has to be careful in ascertaining what projections actors in the marketplace are making respecting those comparable firms. One often hears of "glamour" stocks selling at price/earnings multiples of 50 (or higher). Does that mean that the market actually views such companies as a 2 percent risk? If not, how could the "true" rate of capitalization be inferred?

The answer is that since the market is engaged in capitalizing *future* (not past or even solely current) earnings, the capitalization rate cannot be observed directly or determined precisely. Thus the ratio of current earnings to the present price of a company's shares represents the market capitalization rate only if current earnings are expected to continue unchanged into the future. If earnings are expected to grow as time goes by, then the company's capitalization rate is necessarily greater than that implied by the current price/earnings ratio.

2. *The Perpetual Growth Model.*

A standard formula (sometimes termed the "Gordon Growth Model") was developed to reflect growth yields in capitalization rates. Under the formula, the capitalization rate applicable to the company's shares is obtained by adding the current dividend rate to the rate at which dividends are expected to grow in the indefinite future. To illustrate, assume that X Corp. has current and expected earnings of $5 a share after provision is made for the maintenance and replacement of existing assets. Assume further that X, having identified a profitable opportunity, decides to expand its capital each year for the foreseeable future by retaining and reinvesting 60 percent of its annual earnings in additional plant and equipment—as a result of which future earnings and dividends (d) are expected to grow (g) at a constant rate of 10 percent. Assume, finally, that the current market price (MP) of X shares is \$100. The capitalization rate r would be:

$$r = \frac{d}{MP} + g$$

[handwritten: → paid out from now on]

where d/MP is equal to the current dividend yield and g is the expected growth rate. In numerical terms:

$$r = \frac{\$2}{\$100} + 10\% = 12\%$$

[handwritten in left margin: $2 = current dividend = 5 60% reinvested = 5 x 0.6 = 3 5 - 3 = $2]

Stated otherwise, if current dividends of \$2 a share are expected to grow perpetually at a compound rate of 10 percent, the present value of the stream of future returns, discounted at a rate of 12 percent, is \$100. What then does it mean to say that X Corp. stock is selling at 20 times current earnings (\$100/\$5)? This convenient shorthand expression presumably implies that the market expects earnings and dividends to grow substantially in the future. But it tells us nothing *directly* about the rate of capitalization applicable to the company's shares.

We can solve for the present value of the stock given the dividend, capitalization rate, and growth rate, as follows:

$$MP = \frac{d}{r - g}$$

The apparent precision of the above calculations should not disguise the very real difficulty of ascertaining what rate of growth the market actually anticipates. Information about the market's expectations is hard to come by. There is, however, no way to avoid the task of making an estimate if market capitalization rates of comparable companies are to be used for valuation purposes.

3. Weinberger, *the Delaware Block, and the Primacy of Experts in Appraisal Proceedings.*

The court in *duPont v. Universal* rules that where Delaware precedent diverges from securities market practice respecting valuation, the Delaware precedent controls. **Weinberger v. UOP, Inc.**, 457 A.2d 701 (Del.1983), retreats from this privileging of law over economics:

> * * * [T]he standard "Delaware block" or weighted average method of valuation, formerly employed in appraisal and other stock valuation cases *shall no longer exclusively control such proceedings*. We believe that a more liberal approach must include proof of value by any techniques or methods which are generally considered acceptable in the financial community and otherwise admissible in court * * *. * * * This will obviate the very structured and mechanistic procedure that has heretofore governed such matters. * * * Fair price obviously requires consideration of all relevant factors involving the value of a company.

It should be noted that Delaware does not foreclose the possibility of the block's use. See, e.g., Gonsalves v. Straight Arrow Publishers, Inc., 1996 WL 696936 (Del.Ch.)(Allen, Ch.), in which the court adopts both a block-weighted presentation and an earnings calculation based on a five-year past average, both offered by the expert for the issuer. Other states also continue to regard block-weighting as appropriate. See Piemonte v. New Boston Garden Corp., 377 Mass. 719, 387 N.E.2d 1145 (1979); Sarrouf v. New England Patriots Football Club, Inc., 397 Mass. 542, 492 N.E.2d 1122 (1986); BNE Massachusetts Corp. v. Sims, 32 Mass.App.Ct. 190, 588 N.E.2d 14 (1992); In re Valuation of Common Stock of Libby, McNeill and

Libby, 406 A.2d 54 (Me.1979); Dibble v. Sumter Ice and Fuel Co., 283 S.C. 278, 322 S.E.2d 674 (1984); Ford v. Courier–Journal Job Printing Co., 639 S.W.2d 553 (Ky.App.1982). So too has the Comptroller of the Currency with respect to dissenters from mergers involving national banks. See Austin, Commercial Bank Dissenters' Appraisals, 101 Banking L.J. 302, 318–319 (1984). See also Schaefer, The Fallacy of Weighting Asset Value and Earnings Value in the Appraisal of Corporate Stock, 55 S.Cal.L.Rev. 1031 (1982).

NOTE: PRICE/EARNINGS RATIOS AND INVESTMENT STRATEGY

Assume that you have capital to invest and a choice between two stocks, one with a high price/earnings ratio and the other with a low price/earnings ratio. All other things are equal. Which stock do you choose?

A "value" investor will choose the low P/E stock, reasoning as follows. A high P/E does more than signal that earnings growth is expected. It concretely evidences that the market already has bid up the price in anticipation of that future growth. If the market price now fully reflects the increase projected, then there is no reason to expect the price to rise further. Moreover, to the extent the market is likely to overreact to the good news, the high P/E issue might be overpriced and due for a downward price correction. With a low P/E stock, the market by definition is not expecting significant earnings growth. If the price accurately reflects the expectation and the expectation is based on full information, rationally analyzed, then this stock is not going up either. But suppose the price reflects faulty analysis, cognitive bias, or errant sentiment? If the market is undervaluing the company for reasons unrelated to fundamental value, the low P/E stock could present an attractive investment opportunity.

When is a high P/E too high? Market analysts use the "price to earnings growth ratio" or "PEG" to identify overpriced issues. The PEG numerator is the P/E based on earnings for the most recent 12 months; the denominator is the median of the analyst's 3 to 5 year growth projections for the company's earnings. A PEG of 1 signals a price that accurately reflects projected growth; a PEG above 1 implies an overpriced stock; and a PEG below 1 implies an underpriced stock.

Here are some PEGs reported by the Wall Street Journal Data Group for DJIA stocks in April 2007:

	Recent Price	P/E	Median Projected Earnings Increase	PEG
Caterpillar	71.82	13.3	14.5	0.9 $13.3/14.5 = 0.91$
Home Depot	39.21	13.9	12	1.2
General Electric	35.13	17.2	10	1.4
Exxon Mobil	79.76	11.7	5.6	2.1
Pfizer	26.97	17.8	5	3.6

The reader can check the accuracy of the implied price predictions by referring to today's market price report.

(C) MEASURES OF RISK—THE CAPITAL ASSET PRICING MODEL AND BETA

The Capital Asset Pricing Model (CAPM, pronounced cap-m) is a powerful, if much-disputed, theoretical analysis of asset pricing in the capital markets. It was developed by finance academics decades ago to offer a measure of the "risk" of an enterprise and its securities different from a measure relying on the standard deviation or variance of the particular firm's expected earnings. The CAPM's central notion is that the self-referential quantification of a firm's (or asset's) expected returns that comes with calculating the variance or standard deviation does not provide an adequate basis for relating risks and returns; a firm's returns and their variance need to be related to the return and variance of the market as a whole.

The CAPM rests on a series of assumptions, drawn from portfolio theory, about the risk-return tradeoffs made by rational actors in the securities markets. Discussion of the model accordingly must be prefaced with a discussion of portfolio theory and investment diversification.

(1) Portfolio Theory

(a) portfolio selection

Sharpe, Portfolio Theory and Capital Markets

20–33 (1970).

* * *

Portfolio theory assumes that an investor is willing to choose among portfolios solely on the basis of these two measures [i.e., the expected value and the "spread" of the probability distribution]. Formally, it assumes that each pair summarizes a particular probability distribution. In practice such distributions need not be stated explicitly. The theory may be just as useful if predictions are provided directly and intuitively as if they are stated "scientifically."

To make clear the formal meanings, when referring to a portfolio, the two measures will be denoted:

E_p = expected (predicted) rate of return for a portfolio

σ_p = standard deviation (uncertainty) of rate of return for a portfolio.*

* * *

The desirability of a portfolio is expressed by the values of E_p and σ_p. * * * The theory assumes that any investor would consider [two portfolios with the same expected return and standard deviation] equivalent—he would just as soon have one as the other. This may not be strictly true in every instance. As always, abstraction may lead to error. But the chance of error may be small; and the error, if made, may not be serious.

---

* [Ed. Note] "The manner in which the standard deviation measures the 'spread' of a probability distribution is particularly accurate if the distribution is *normal;* i.e., follows the familiar bell-shaped curve. In such a case:

"The chances are roughly 2 out of 3 that the actual outcome will be between $(E - \sigma)$ and $(E + \sigma)$.

"The chances are roughly 95 out of 100 that the actual outcome will be between $(E - 2\sigma)$ and $(E + 2\sigma)$."

Any portfolio can be represented by a point on a graph such as that shown in Fig. 2–4. Standard deviation of rate of return is plotted on the horizontal axis, and expected rate of return is plotted on the vertical axis.[2]

FIGURE 2–4.

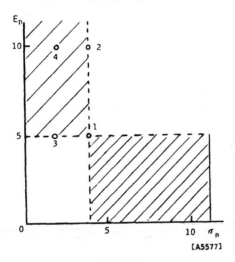

[A5577]

How does an investor choose among alternative portfolios? The following rules are assumed to apply for any investor:

1.   If two portfolios have the same standard deviation of return and different expected returns, the one with the larger expected return is preferred.

2.   If two portfolios have the same expected return and different standard deviations of return, the one with the smaller standard deviation is preferred.

3.   If one portfolio has a smaller standard deviation of return and a larger expected return than another, it is preferred.

The rules may be summarized succinctly:

4. E_p is *good*: other things equal, more is preferred to less.

5. σ_p is *bad:* other things equal, less is preferred to more.

Assumption 5 is often termed *risk aversion*. A large body of evidence indicates that almost everyone is a risk averter when making important decisions. Clear counter-examples are rarely found. A day at the horse races provides something besides risk and probable loss, and even the ardent fan seldom takes his entire earnings to the track.

Figure 2–5 shows the distributions of rate of return for four portfolios; their E_p and σ_p values are plotted in Fig. 2–4. Among other things, the assumptions about investor preferences imply that:

2.   Some reverse the arrangement, plot-   horizontal. * * *
ting σ_p on the vertical axis and E_p on the

Portfolio 2 is preferred to portfolio 1 (rules 1, 4).

Portfolio 3 is preferred to portfolio 1 (rules 2, 5).

Portfolio 4 is preferred to portfolio 1 (rules 3, 4, and 5).

Graphically, the rules assert that for any investor:

FIGURE 2-5

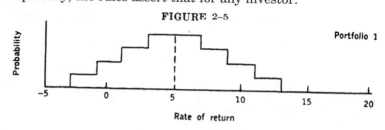

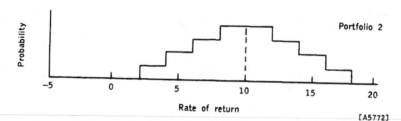

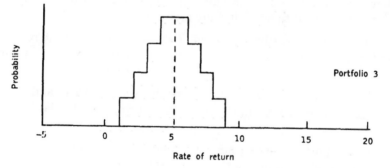

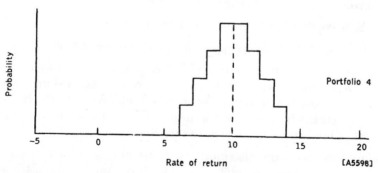

Portfolios represented by points lying to the northwest of the point representing a portfolio are better (i.e., preferred).

Portfolios represented by points lying to the southeast of the point representing a portfolio are worse (i.e., the original portfolio is preferred).

Portfolios represented by points lying in the lightly shaded area in Fig. 2–4 are preferred to portfolio 1, but portfolio 1 is preferred to all those represented by points lying in the darkly shaded area.

The major results of portfolio theory follow directly from the assumption that investors like E_p and dislike σ_p. Of course, more can be said about the preferences of any *given* investor. How strong is his dislike for σ_p vis-à-vis E_p? How much uncertainty is he willing to accept to enhance his prospects for a likely rate of return?

The feelings of a particular investor can usefully be represented by a family of *indifference curves*. Consider Fig. 2–6. The lightly shaded area [to the left of the curve] contains all the points representing portfolios that Mr. T prefers to portfolio 1. The darkly shaded area [to the right] contains all the points representing portfolios that he considers inferior to portfolio 1. The curve that divides the region contains all the points representing portfolios that he considers equivalent to portfolio 1; he has no preferences among them—he is *indifferent* about the choice.

FIGURE 2–6

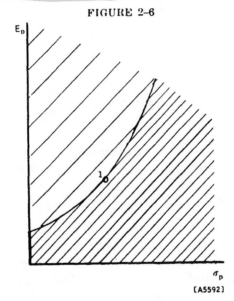

[A5592]

As long as E_p is desired and σ_p is not, every indifference curve will be upward-sloping. Generally, each curve will become steeper as E_p and σ_p increase.

The indifference curve in Fig. 2–6 captures some of Mr. T's feelings. But to represent the manner in which he would make choices in a great variety of circumstances, many more curves are required. Figure 2–7 repeats the curve of Fig. 2–6 as I_1. In addition it shows another curve derived by starting with portfolio 2. Since portfolio 2 is preferred to portfolio 1, every point on I_2 must be preferred to every point on I_1. This follows from the concept of indifference and minimal requirements for rational choice. Indifference curves may not cross.

The number of indifference curves is almost limitless. Only a selected few are shown in graphical examples. It is conventional to label those shown in order of preference. Thus points on I_2 are preferred to those on I_1; points on I_3 are preferred to those on I_2, etc.

A set of indifference curves summarizes the preferences of a given individual. Figure 2–8 shows two extreme cases. Mr. Fearless is oblivious to risk; Mr. Chicken is oblivious to everything except risk.

FIGURE 2–7

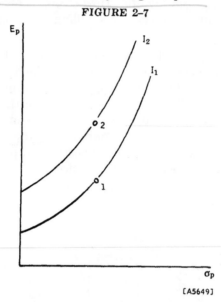

[A5649]

Figure 2–9 shows more common cases. Mr. Birch is relatively conservative, requiring substantial increases in E_p to induce him to accept greater uncertainty (σ_p). Mr. Flynn is more adventuresome. Neither likes uncertainty, but Mr. Birch dislikes it more (relative to his preference for E_p).

Consider Mr. Z. His preferences are shown by the indifference curves in Fig. 2–10. Many portfolios are available to him. Their E_p and σ_p values may be shown by a group of points in the figure. Such points will entirely fill the shaded area. Which will Mr. Z prefer? Obviously the one shown by point B.

The decision illustrated in Fig. 2–10 can be broken into three separate phases: security analysis, portfolio analysis, and portfolio selection.

Security analysis is an art. It requires predictions about the future prospects of securities * * *. These predictions must take into account both uncertainty and interrelationships. In particular, they must be suitable for use in the next phase.

FIGURE 2-8

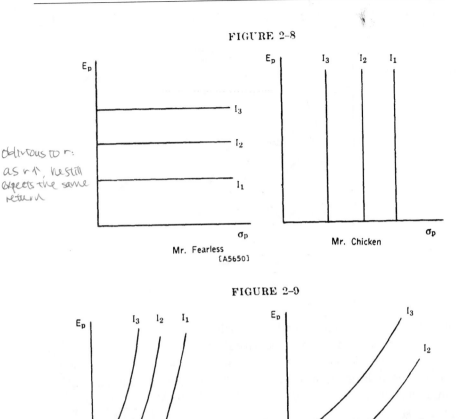

Oblivous to r: as r↑, he still expects the same return

Oblivous to everything except risk: although r stays the same, expects higher & higher return

Mr. Fearless
[A5650]

Mr. Chicken

FIGURE 2-9

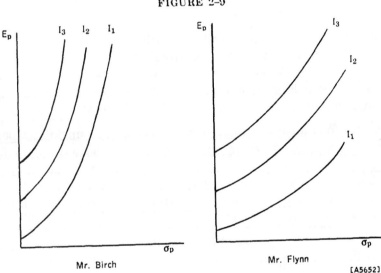

Mr. Birch

Mr. Flynn
[A5652]

Portfolio analysis produces predictions about portfolios. The predictions, in the form of E_p and σ_p estimates, are derived entirely from the predictions about securities produced in the first phase. No artistry is required, just computation.

Portfolio selection is the final phase. Given the available E_p, σ_p combinations, the investor, or someone knowing his preferences, selects the best.

The first phase requires the skills of a seer. The last requires knowledge of a specific investor's preferences. Portfolio analysis requires only technical skills. One person (e.g., the investor) can, of course, do the entire job. But comparative advantage may dictate a division of labor.

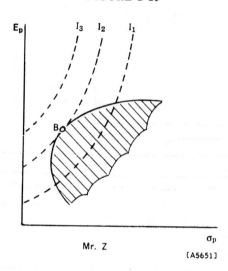

FIGURE 2-10

Mr. Z

[A5651]

Portfolio theory is concerned primarily with the task of portfolio analysis. Given predictions about securities, what E_p, σ_p combinations can be obtained by the proper choice of a portfolio? The answer to such a question will be a large number of points (e.g., several million) entirely filling an area such as the shaded region of Fig. 2–10.

The portfolio analyst cannot normally choose the single best portfolio for a given investor. But he can reject certain possibilities. In particular, he can reject any portfolio not represented by a point on the upper border of the region. This is illustrated in Fig. 2–11. Portfolio *e dominates* portfolio *I*; it has a larger E_p and the same σ_p. Portfolio *e* is said to be an *efficient portfolio;* portfolio *I* is inefficient.

FIGURE 2-11

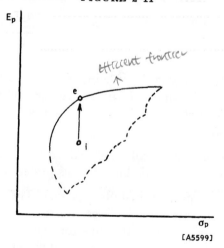

efficient frontier

[A5599]

The upper border of the region of available E_p, σ_p combinations is called the *efficient frontier*. The portfolios whose E_p, σ_p values are plotted on the frontier comprise the set of efficient portfolios.

(b) diversification as a means of reducing risk

Why is Sharpe's discussion carried on in terms of *portfolios* of securities rather than individual stocks? Indeed, why do most investors invest in combinations of securities—a little bit of this and a little bit of that—instead of putting everything they have into the single "best" security available in the market? The answer—as everyone knows intuitively—is that it is somehow dangerous to put all your eggs in one basket. As a result, equity investors usually prefer to hold securities of companies in different industries, or to accomplish the same end by owning shares of a mutual fund which affords participation in a widely varied portfolio. Can this preference be expressed in systematic terms?

The advantage of diversification (and of mutual funds) can be illustrated as follows. Suppose investors can purchase the stock of Warco, which manufactures weapons, and of Peaceco, which builds low-income housing. Both stocks sell at the same price. Performance of Warco depends on the size of the defense budget, as indicated in the following table:

Event	Probability of event	Warco Return
Large Defense Budget	⅓	12%
Medium–Size Defense Budget	⅓	8%
Small Defense Budget	⅓	4%

Performance of Peaceco depends on non-defense government expenditures, which are always inversely proportional to defense expenditures, e.g., a large defense budget means a small non-defense budget and low earnings for Peaceco. Peaceco's performance can be related directly to the size of the defense budget, as indicated in the following table:

Event	Probability of event	Peaceco Return
Large Defense Budget	⅓	4%
Medium–Size Defense Budget	⅓	8%
Small Defense Budget	⅓	12%

If an investor decides on a portfolio divided equally between Warco and Peaceco, the following results can be expected:

put your money in half & half : 8 when neutral, 8 good, 8 bad → SD is brought down to 0

Event	Prob.	Warco Return	Peaceco Return	Average Return
Large Defense Budget	⅓	12%	4%	8%
Medium–Size Defense Budget	⅓	8%	8%	8%
Small Defense Budget	⅓	4%	12%	8%

Because Warco and Peaceco *always* react in *exactly* opposite ways to the same event, the return on a portfolio composed equally of both securities does not vary *at all*. Accordingly, if we assume that the size of the defense budget is the only event of significance to either company, an equal investment in both stocks produces an absolutely certain 8 percent return. By contrast, an investment in either company by itself, while it produces the same *expected* rate of return (8 percent), also produces the risk that the actual rate may fall substantially short of the expected rate. Recall that investors are assumed to be averse to risk, i.e., the loss of utility associated with a possible decline in their fortunes is never wholly compensated by the gain in utility associated with a possible rise in their fortunes, where the possible rise and possible decline are equal in dollar amount. Under this assumption, an investor will always prefer a stock (or portfolio of stocks) which offers a certain return of 8 percent to a stock which offers a 1/3 chance of 4 percent, a 1/3 chance of 8 percent, and a 1/3 chance of 12 percent. It follows that the investor will feel better off if his or her wealth is divided equally between Warco and Peaceco than if either stock is acquired alone or both stocks are acquired in a proportion other than the prescribed 50–50.

Another way of expressing this concept is to say that the expected return of a portfolio divided equally between two securities is equal to the average of the expected return from each security. The *risk* of such portfolio, however, is not necessarily the average of the individual risks. If individual securities react differently to the same future events, the risk of the portfolio as a whole will be less than the average of the individual risks. As shown, a portfolio that combines Warco and Peaceco in equal proportion is entirely *free* of risk; at the same time, expected dollar income is *unreduced*. Of course, the opportunity to get an 8 percent return on Warco and Peaceco would not last very long. Once the market became aware of the advantage of combining them, the prices of both stocks would be bid up until their expected yields approximated the yield on riskless securities such as government bonds. But the investor who first perceived the advantage would get the benefit of the rise.

In the real world, of course, a portfolio consisting of Warco and Peaceco would continue to have substantial risk, even if one accepted the "fact" that the net incomes of the two companies are negatively correlated. The reason is that, like most common stocks, the market prices of *both* Warco and Peaceco will rise and fall with the ups and downs of the market *as a whole.* The market reacts to news having nothing directly to do with particular companies—indeed, it has been variously estimated that between one-third and one-half of the variability of most stocks listed on the New York Stock Exchange is attributable to events which occasion price changes in the entire market (i.e., political and economic developments of all sorts) or that a security's unsystematic risk ranges from 40 percent to 50 percent or more of its total risk. Some stocks are highly responsive to market ups and downs, others less so. But there is no stock whose movements are inversely correlated with the market, or which is wholly unaffected by changes in the general level of market prices.

What this means, in effect, is that the risk, or variability, in the performance of a stock or a portfolio must be divided into two components. The first, called "independent" or "unsystematic" variability, relates to events that are unique to the firm itself—management strength, labor problems, research plans, and so on. The second, called "market" or "systematic" variability, relates to price changes occasioned by movements in the market as a whole. Diversification—the act of combining Warco and Peaceco—is reduces the *independent* variability of a stock or portfolio, but it can do little to reduce the risk attributable to *market* variability.

It does not follow that diversification is unimportant. Quite the contrary: since independent variability can be reduced to (or near) zero by diversifying "efficiently," the only risk which an investor in stocks is actually obliged to take, and hence the only risk for which he can expect to be compensated by a high rate of return, is that of market variability—the one risk element that cannot be diversified away. Put another way, the existence of independent variability in a portfolio means that its owner is accepting a risk that could be avoided through better diversification, and is doing so without any compensating increase in expected income. In summary, the object of diversification is to eliminate independent variability from the portfolio. Even when this is done, however, portfolios will still differ in degree of market risk, and hence will fall at different points on the efficient frontier.

How *many* securities should an investor hold to achieve "efficient" diversification? While the average number of stocks owned by individual investors will be only three or four in many cases, institutional investors such as mutual funds often maintain hundreds or thousands of different stocks in their portfolios, as well as a variety of corporate and government bonds. Some financial writers have estimated that diversification beyond 20 or 30 securities cannot reduce risk by a meaningful amount, and that the quality of the diversification, i.e., the degree of interrelatedness among the securities selected, is significantly more important than the quantity. A little diversification, then, can go a long way. The point has practical implications since a portfolio containing 200 securities presumably costs more to manage than one containing 20 or 30. If relatively little reduction in risk is accomplished by holding the larger number, the additional management expense may not be worthwhile. On the other hand, index funds provide investment mechanisms offering investors a relatively low-cost means to participate in portfolios that replicate the widely diversified market portfolio (or some other selected portfolio configuration of risk and return).

(c) choosing a "best portfolio"—the critical ratio and the separation theorem

Looking back at Sharpe's Figure 2–11, it appears that only those portfolios which lie on the upper border of the shaded region (e.g., portfolio *e*) should be regarded by investors as acceptable. A portfolio represented by a point on what Sharpe terms the "efficient frontier" offers a greater return for a given level of risk than any portfolio not so represented and hence should be preferred by investors, just as portfolio *e* would be preferred to portfolio *I* in Figure 2–11.

Suppose, however, that we designate another point on the efficient frontier—call it portfolio *n*. By hypothesis, portfolios *e* and *n* are equally "efficient." Is there any basis for asserting that one is better than the other? Since each portfolio lies at a different point on the upper border in Figure 2–11, either *e* offers a greater return *but* is riskier than *n*, or *n* offers a greater return *but* is riskier than *e*. Neither has the advantage in both categories at once. Accordingly, it would seem that the choice between *e* and *n* is very much a matter of the individual investor's personal preference for greater return as opposed to greater risk, an idea which is portrayed in Figure 2–10.

Sharpe and others argue that the availability of riskless assets (U.S. treasury bills, insured savings accounts) makes it possible to name one of the two portfolios as "best"—that is, to regard portfolio *e* or *n* as superior to the other (and possibly to all other portfolios on the efficient frontier)— even recognizing that investors differ widely in their willingness to bear risk.

Lintner, A Model of a Perfectly Functioning Securities Market

Economic Policy and the Regulation of Corporate Securities (Manne, ed. 1969). 150–154.

Investor Response to a Given Set of Stock Prices

Consider then the individual investor facing *any* possible set of current prices for different stocks in the market which he might hold. The probability distribution of ending price-plus-dividend for each stock divided by the current price gives him an expected rate of return and risk-of-return for each stock and each percentage mix or portfolio of different stocks. Think of some one possible stock portfolio offering, say, an expected return of 8% with a risk of 12%. If the investor puts all his funds in this portfolio this would be his expected return and risk on all his assets. If the riskless rate is 5%, he *could* get 5% with no risk on all his assets. Splitting his funds equally between bonds and this portfolio would give him an overall expected return of $(8 + 5)/2 = 6 \frac{1}{2}\%$ with an overall return risk of 6%. In general, even if this investor confines his attention to combining just this one stock portfolio with bills, he can vary his return and risk on his investable assets within wide limits by shifting the relative amount he holds in cash and the amount (including borrowing if he wishes, subject to margin limits) invested in this stock mix.

Suppose there is another stock portfolio offering an expected return of 10% with a risk of 15%. Would our investor prefer it? He clearly would. The reason is that a combination of *this* portfolio and government bonds (of appropriate maturity) which had the same expected return on his total investable funds would involve less risk, than the combination of this riskless asset with the first portfolio;[1] correspondingly, a combination of this second portfolio and the riskless asset which would show the same risk on all his investable funds would show a larger expected overall return.[2]

In general, the investor will always be able to duplicate the expected return on investable funds at lower overall risk by finding another stock portfolio which has a larger *"critical ratio"* of expected excess stock portfolio return to stock portfolio risk. (Excess portfolio return is the portfolio return less the return on the riskless asset). In our examples, the (10–5)/15 = 1/3 for our second stock portfolio is preferred to the ratio (8–5)/12 = 1/4 for the first. Under the conditions we are working with, this single ratio summarizes the desirability of alternative stock portfolios to the investor. But with any given joint probability distribution over a set of stocks, the investor can form a very large number of different possible stock portfolios by varying the subset of stocks he tentatively considers including, and even with each subset, by varying the percentage mix among the stocks. In principle, in his own self-interest he will search over all these possible stock portfolios (mixes) offered in the market and find the mix with the highest critical ratio.

After he has found the best stock mix, he can then determine *how much* (in dollars or as a percentage of his investable funds) he wants to invest in *this* stock portfolio, holding the remainder in the riskless asset (or borrowing). Analytically it turns out that risk averters (in the sense we used the term above) necessarily require larger and larger increments of expected return to feel as well off as they bear more and more risk. If an investor's return requirement per unit of added risk is greater than that offered by the best stock portfolio he sees in the market, he simply buys no stock. If the requirement is initially less than that offered by this portfolio, he buys some and continues to shift funds into this portfolio until his (increasing) return requirement as he bears more and more risk no longer is less than (and hence equals) the return-risk tradeoff offered by this best portfolio in the market.

1. This investor could get an expected return of 6½% by putting 70% of his funds in bills at 5% and 30% of his funds in this stock mix—the same expected return as the 50–50 split between bills and the first stock portfolio. But with the first stock mix, his corresponding risk was .5(12%) = 6%, while now he has a risk of only .3(15%) = 4.5% on his total investable funds.

2. The investor had an overall return risk of 6% with a 50–50 investment in the first portfolio and bills; he would have the same overall risk of 6% on his entire investable funds by placing 40% of the funds in the second stock portfolio. His expected return on all his investable funds with the latter portfolio would be * * * [7%] which is greater than the 6% he had using the first portfolio.

Lorie, Dodd and Kimpton, The Stockmarket: Theories and Evidence

(2nd ed.1985).
pp. 122–126.

A natural extension of the Markowitz analysis was to consider the problem of building portfolios which included riskless assets and portfolios purchased in part with borrowed funds, as well as portfolios of risky assets paid with the investor's equity.

Recall that the efficient frontier for portfolios made up of many risky assets is typically concave from below in the plane whose axes are risk (as measured by the standard deviation) and expected return. For any given period, there are assets whose rates of return can be predicted with virtual certainty—except for times of nuclear holocausts, natural disasters, and revolution. Most investors have confidence that they can accurately predict the rate of return on federal government securities for any period which is equal to their maturity. For example, Treasury bills maturing in one year have a precisely predictable rate of return for one year.*

The introduction of riskless assets into portfolios has interesting consequences. In the following diagrams, the return on a risk-free asset is designated by R_f on the vertical axis. Sharpe and Tobin stated that if this alternative exists, it is possible to select portfolios at any given point on line R_fB defined by the return on the riskless asset and the point of tangency with the efficient frontier of portfolios with risky assets (Figure 8–11.) This follows from the discussion of asset combinations.

* * *

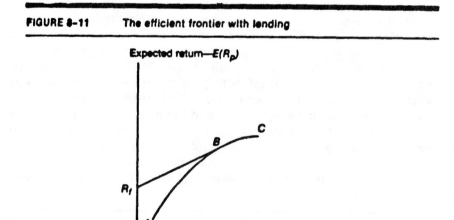

FIGURE 8-11   The efficient frontier with lending

---

* For government securities with periodic interest payments, the prediction of the rate of return to maturity is somewhat less certain, since the rates that will exist when interest payments have to be reinvested cannot be known with certainty.

Investing entirely in the risk-free asset is possible, investing entirely in the risky assets at the point of tangency is possible; and achieving portfolios at any point on a straight line between these points is also possible. Portfolios on this line are preferred to portfolios on curve AB, consisting solely of risky assets, since the former provide more return for given risk.

Sharpe further showed that one can hold efficient portfolios on line R_f B beyond the point of tangency if borrowing is allowed. If it is assumed that one can borrow to buy financial assets at a rate similar to what the investor receives on the risk-free assets, the efficient portfolios beyond the point of tangency lie on a linear extrapolation of the line to the point of tangency (Figure 8–12). Any point on line R_fBD is now attainable by combining the portfolio of risky assets at point B with the riskless asset, or by levering portfolio B by borrowing and investing the funds in B. Portfolios on R_fBD are preferred to portfolios between A and B and between B and C, since they offer greater return for a given level of risk or less risk for a given level of return. The efficient frontier is now entirely linear. R_fBD is Sharpe's capital market line. It relates the expected return on an efficient portfolio to its risk as measured by the standard deviation.

In Figure 8–12, there is only one portfolio of *risky* assets that is optimal, and it is the same for all investors. Since only one portfolio of risky assets is optimal, it must be the market portfolio. That is, it includes all assets in proportion to their market value.

* * *

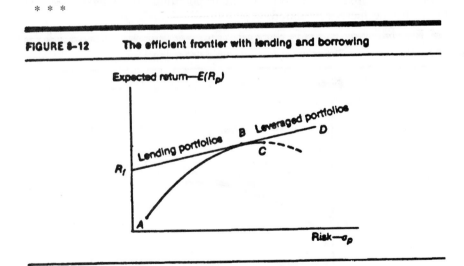

FIGURE 8-12   **The efficient frontier with lending and borrowing**

In Sharpe's model, individual preferences will determine only the amount of borrowing or lending. The fact that this choice is independent of the optimal combination of risky assets is called the "separation theorem."

Two qualifications should be noted. If only lending is allowed, the separation theorem will not hold. For example, in Figure 8–14, the efficient set of portfolios is not limited to those on line R_fM. It also includes portfolios of risky assets between *M* and *C*. A particular investor might prefer one of the latter to portfolios on R_fM. In other words, there is no single optimum combination of risky assets.

FIGURE 8-14   **The efficient frontier with no borrowing**

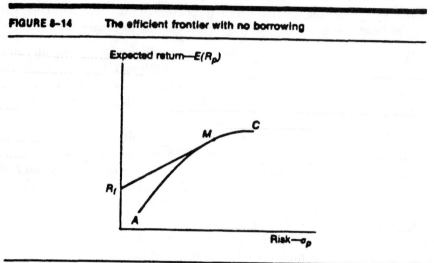

The second qualification is that the efficient frontier for portfolios of risky assets can have linear segments. If the frontier is linear at the point of tangency, once again there is more than one optimum portfolio of risky assets. This is illustrated in Figure 8–15. Portfolios *B* and *C*, and all those on the line between them, are efficient portfolios of risky assets. Their returns are perfectly correlated.

FIGURE 8-15   **The efficient frontier with a linear segment**

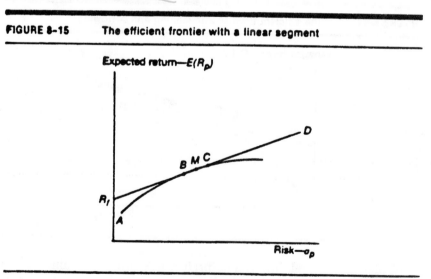

(2) The Capital Asset Pricing Model

As suggested above, financial theory makes an important distinction between the "systematic" and the "unsystematic" risk that inheres in every security. Unsystematic risk—the tendency of a stock to react to events that particularly affect the company, such as product market conditions, technological developments, management changes, strikes, or new legal regulations—can be largely "washed away" by mixing the security with other securities in a diversified portfolio. With Warco and Peaceco, supra, each depends for its profitability on the size of the defense budget, but since each reacts oppositely to the same event, the risk that the defense budget will be high (disfavoring Peaceco) or low (disfavoring Warco) can be wholly eliminated by combining both securities in a single portfolio. This can be done, moreover, without any sacrifice in expected return.

But even if a Warco–Peaceco portfolio existed in the market, the fact is that the portfolio would *still* contain risk. This would be true because of the tendency of *all* stocks to fluctuate with changes in the overall level of the stock market. The important point is that this element of systematic risk is *unaffected* by diversification. Thus, the systematic risk of a portfolio is simply the average of the systematic risks of all the securities included in that portfolio.

The distinction between systematic and unsystematic risk leads directly to the formulation of a "benchmark" against which the performance of a portfolio can be measured. This benchmark is referred to as the Capital Asset Pricing Model, a concept that is explained in the excerpt following.

(a) derivation

Modigliani and Pogue, An Introduction to Risk and Return: Concepts and Evidence

30 Fin.Anal.J. 68 (March/April, 1974).
30 Fin.Anal.J. 69 (May/June, 1974).

5. The Risk of Individual Securities

* * * In the previous section we concluded that the systematic risk of an individual security is that portion of its total risk (standard deviation of return) which cannot be eliminated by combining it with other securities in a well diversified portfolio. We now need a way of quantifying the systematic risk of a security and relating the systematic risk of a portfolio to that of its component securities. This can be accomplished by dividing security return into two parts: one dependent (i.e., perfectly correlated), and a second independent (i.e., uncorrelated) of market return. The first component of return is usually referred to as "systematic", the second as "unsystematic" return. Thus we have

Security Return =   Systematic Return
                       + Unsystematic Return.   (4)

Since the systematic return is perfectly correlated with the market return, it can be expressed as a factor, designated beta (β), times the market return, R_m. The beta factor is a market sensitivity index, indicating how sensitive the security return is to changes in the market level. The unsystematic return, which is independent of market returns, is usually represented by a factor epsilon (ε). Thus the security return, R, may be expressed

$$R = \beta R_m + \varepsilon. \tag{5}$$

For example, if a security had a β factor of 2.0 (e.g., an airline stock), then a 10 per cent market return would generate a systematic return for the stock of 20 per cent. The security return for the period would be the 20 per cent plus the unsystematic component. The unsystematic component depends on factors unique to the company, such as labor difficulties, higher than expected sales, etc.

The security returns model given by Equation (5) is usually written in a way such that the average value of the residual term, ε, is zero. This is accomplished by adding a factor, alpha ($\yen$), to the model to represent the average value of the unsystematic returns over time. That is, we set $l' = \yen + l$ so that

$$R = \alpha + \beta R_m + \varepsilon, \tag{6}$$

where the average l over time is equal to zero.

The model for security returns given by Equation (6) is usually referred to as the "market model". Graphically, the model can be depicted as a line fitted to a plot of security returns against rates of return on the market index. This is shown in Exhibit 7 for a hypothetical security.

The beta factor can be thought of as the slope of the line. It gives the expected increase in security return for a one per cent increase in market return. In Exhibit 7, the security has a beta of 1.0. Thus, a ten per cent market return will result, on the average, in a ten per cent security return. The market-weighted average beta for all stocks is 1.0 by definition.

The alpha factor is represented by the intercept of the line on the vertical security return axis. It is equal to the average value over time of the unsystematic returns (ε) on the stock. For most stocks, the alpha factor tends to be small and unstable. (We shall return to alpha later.)

Using the definition of security return given by the market model, the specification of systematic and unsystematic risk is straighforward—they are simply the standard deviations of the two return components.

The systematic risk of a security is equal to β times the standard deviation of the market return:

$$\text{Systematic Risk} = \beta \sigma_m. \tag{7}$$

The unsystematic risk equals the standard deviation of the residual return factor l:

$$\text{Unsystematic Risk} = \sigma_e. \tag{8}$$

Given measures of individual security systematic risk, we can now compute the systematic risk of portfolio. It is equal to the beta factor for the portfolio, β_p, times the risk of the market index, σ_m:

$$\text{Portfolio Systematic Risk} = \beta_p \sigma_m. \tag{9}$$

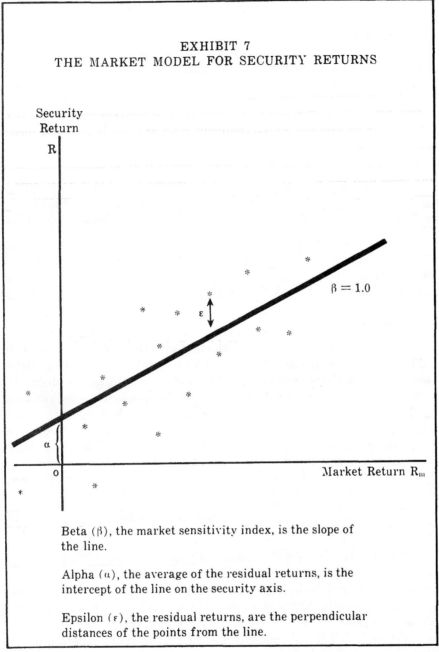

EXHIBIT 7
THE MARKET MODEL FOR SECURITY RETURNS

Beta (β), the market sensitivity index, is the slope of
the line.

Alpha (α), the average of the residual returns, is the
intercept of the line on the security axis.

Epsilon (ϵ), the residual returns, are the perpendicular
distances of the points from the line.

[B9959]

The portfolio beta factor in turn can be shown to be simply an average
of the individual security betas, weighted by the proportion of each security
in the portfolio, or

$$\beta_p = \sum_{j=1}^{N} X_j \beta_j, \tag{10}$$

where

X_j = the proportion of portfolio market value represented by security j

N = the number of securities.

Thus the systematic risk of the portfolio is simply a weighted average of the systematic risk of the individual securities. If the portfolio is composed of an equal dollar investment in each stock * * * the β_p is simply an unweighted average of the component security betas.

The unsystematic risk of the portfolio is also a function of the unsystematic security risks, but the form is more complex. The important point is that with increasing diversification this risk can be reduced toward zero.

The main results of this section can be summarized as follows: First, * * * roughly 40 to 50 per cent of total security risk can be eliminated by diversification. Second, the remaining systematic risk is equal to the security β times market risk. Third, portfolio systematic risk is a weighted average of security systematic risks.

The implications of these results are substantial. First, we would expect realized rates of return over substantial periods of time to be related to the systematic as opposed to total risk of securities. Since the unsystematic risk is relatively easily eliminated, we should not expect the market to offer a risk premium for bearing it. Second, since security systematic risk is equal to the security beta times σ_m (which is common to all securities), beta is useful as a *relative* risk measure. The β gives the systematic risk of a security (or portfolio) relative to the risk of the market index. * * *

* * *

6. The Relationship Between Expected Return and Risk: The Capital Asset Pricing Model

The first part of this article developed two measures of risk: one is a measure of total risk (standard deviation), the other a relative index of systematic or nondiversifiable risk (beta). The beta measure would appear to be the more relevant for the pricing of securities. Returns expected by investors should logically be related to systematic as opposed to total risk. Securities with higher systematic risk should have higher expected returns.

The question to be considered now is the form of the relationship between risk and return. In this section we describe a relationship called the "Capital Asset Pricing Model" (CAPM), which is based on elementary logic and simple economic principles. The basic postulate underlying finance theory is that assets with the same risk should have the same expected rate of return. That is, the prices of assets in the capital markets should adjust until equivalent risk assets have identical expected returns.

To see the implications of this postulate, let us consider an investor who holds a risky portfolio with the same risk as the market portfolio (beta equal to 1.0). What return should he expect? Logically, he should expect the same return as that of the market portfolio.

Let us consider another investor who holds a riskless portfolio (beta equal to zero). The investor in this case should expect to earn the rate of return on riskless assets such as treasury bills. By taking no risk, he earns the riskless rate of return.

Now let us consider the case of an investor who holds a mixture of these two portfolios. Assuming he invests a proportion X of his money in the risky portfolio and $(1 - X)$ in the riskless portfolio, what risk does he bear and what return should he expect? The risk of the composite portfolio is easily computed when we recall that the beta of a portfolio is simply a weighted average of the component security betas, where the weights are the portfolio proportions. Thus the portfolio beta, β_p, is a weighted average of the beta of the market portfolio and the beta of the risk-free rate. However, the market beta is 1.0, and that of the risk-free rate is zero. Therefore

$$\beta_p = (1 - X) \cdot 0 + \times \cdot 1,$$
$$= X. \tag{11}$$

Thus β_p is equal to the fraction of his money invested in the risky portfolio. If 100 per cent or less of the investor's funds is invested in the risky portfolio, his portfolio beta will be between zero and 1.0. If he borrows at the risk-free rate and invests the proceeds in the risky portfolio, his portfolio beta will be greater than 1.0.

The expected return of the composite portfolio is also a weighted average of the expected returns on the two-component portfolios; that is,

$$E(R_p) = (1 - X) \cdot R_f + \times \cdot E(R_m), \tag{12}$$

where $E(R_p)$, $E(R_m)$, and R_r are the expected returns on the portfolio, the market index, and the risk-free rate. Now, from Equation (11) we know that X is equal to β_p. Substituting into Equation (12), we have

$$E(R_p) = (1 - \beta_p) \cdot R_F + \beta_p \cdot E(R_m),$$

or

$$E(R_p) = R_F + \beta_p \cdot (E(R_m) - R_F). \tag{13}$$

Equation (13) is the Capital Asset Pricing Model (CAPM), an extremely important theoretical result. It says that the expected return on a portfolio should exceed the riskless rate of return by an amount which is proportional to the portfolio beta. That is, the relationship between return and risk should be linear.

The model is often stated in "risk-premium" form. Risk premiums are obtained by subtracting the risk-free rate from the rates of return. The expected portfolio and market risk premiums (designated $E(r_p)$ and $E(r_m)$ respectively) are given by

$$E(r_p) = E(R_P) - R_F \tag{14a}$$

$$E(r_m) = E(R_m) - R_F. \tag{14b}$$

Substituting these risk premiums into Equation (13), we obtain

$$E(r_p) = \beta_P \cdot E(r_m). \tag{15}$$

In this form, the CAPM states that the expected risk premium for the investor's portfolio is equal to its beta value times the expected market risk premium.

     We can illustrate the model by assuming that short-term (risk-free) interest rate is 6 per cent and the expected return on the market is 10 per cent. The expected risk premium for holding the market portfolio is just the difference between the 10 per cent and the short-term interest rate of 6 per cent, or 4 per cent. Investors who hold the market portfolio expect to earn 10 per cent, which is 4 per cent greater than they could earn on a short-term market instrument for certain. In order to satisfy Equation (13), the expected return on securities or portfolios with different levels of risk must be:

Expected Return for Different Levels of Portfolio Beta

the smaller the β, the less risky it is, the lower the expected return

Beta	Expected Return
0.0 → safe, earn risk-free rate	6%
0.5 → below mkt, earn less than expected return on mkt	8%
1.0	10%
1.5	12%
2.0 } above the mkt β → earn higher than expected mkt return	14%

[margin notes:]
$Rf = 6\%$ $E(Rm) = 10\%$

$E(Rp) = Rf + Bp(E(Rm) - Rf)$

$E(Rp) = 6\% + 0.5(10\% - 6\%) = 8\%$

$β < 1 = $ less risky than the mkt as a whole
$β > 1 = $ riskier than the mkt

     The predictions of the model are inherently sensible. For safe investments ($\beta = 0$), the model predicts that investors would expect to earn the risk-free rate of interest. For a risky investment ($\beta > 0$) investors would expect a rate of return proportional to the market sensitivity (β) of the investment. Thus, stocks with lower than average market sensitivities (such as most utilities) would offer expected returns less than the expected market return. Stocks with above average values of beta (such as most airline securities) would offer expected returns in excess of the market.

     * * *

     In our development of CAPM we have made a number of assumptions that are required if the model is to be established on a rigorous basis. These assumptions involve investor behavior and conditions in the capital markets. The following is a set of assumptions that will allow a simple derivation of the model.

(a) The market is composed of risk-averse investors who measure risk in terms of standard deviation of portfolio return. This assumption provides a basis for the use of beta-type risk measures.

(b) All investors have a common time horizon for investment decision making (e.g., one month, one year, etc.). This assumption allows us to measure investor expectations over some common interval, thus making comparisons meaningful.

(c) All investors are assumed to have the same expectations about future security returns and risks. Without this assumption, the analysis would become much more complicated.

(d) Capital markets are perfect in the sense that all assets are completely divisible, there are no transactions costs or differential taxes, and borrowing and lending rates are equal to each other and the same for all investors. Without these conditions, frictional barriers would exist to the equilibrium conditions on which the model is based.

While these assumptions are sufficient to derive the model, it is not clear that all are necessary in their current form. It may well be that several of the assumptions can be substantially relaxed without major change in the form of the model. A good deal of research is currently being conducted toward this end.

While the CAPM is indeed simple and elegant, these qualities do not in themselves guarantee that it will be useful in explaining observed risk-return patterns. In Section 8 we will review the empirical literature on attempts to verify the model.

* * *

8.   Tests of the Capital Asset Pricing Model

The major difficulty in testing the CAPM is that the model is stated in terms of investors' expectations and not in terms of realized returns. The fact that expectations are not always realized introduces an error term, which from a statistical point of view should be zero *on the average,* but not necessarily zero for any single stock or single period of time.

* * *

Summary of Test Results

We will briefly summarize the major results of the empirical tests.

1. The evidence shows a significant positive relationship between realized returns and systematic risk. However, the slope of the relationship (K_1) is usually less than predicted by the CAPM.

2. The relationship between risk and return appears to be linear. The studies give no evidence of significant curvature in the risk-return relationship.

3. Tests that attempt to discriminate between the effects of systematic and unsystematic risk do not yield definitive results. Both kinds of risk appear to be positively related to security returns. However, there is substantial support for the proposition that the relationship between return and unsystematic risk is at least partly spurious—that is, it partly reflects statistical problems rather than the true nature of capital markets.

Obviously, we cannot claim that the CAPM is absolutely right. On the other hand, the empirical tests do support the view that beta is a useful risk measure and that high beta stocks tend to be priced so as to yield correspondingly high rates of return.

NOTE: CAPM

1. *Arbitrage.*

Why would rates of return on stocks converge on the market line predicted by the CAPM? The answer is arbitrage in the market, with returns falling on the market line amounting to the equilibrium result. Van Horne, Financial Management and Policy 93–94 (11th ed. 1998), explains the role arbitrage plays: "[I]n competitive financial markets arbitrage will ensure that riskless assets provide the same expected return. Arbitrage simply means finding two things that are essentially the same and buying the cheaper and selling, or selling short, the more expensive. The model is based on the simple notion that security prices adjust as investors form portfolios in search of arbitrage profits. When such profit opportunities have been exhausted, security prices are said to be in equilibrium. In this context, a definition of market efficiency is the absence of arbitrage opportunities, their having been eliminated by arbitragers."

CAPM predicts that when a security is priced based on a rate of return higher than predicted, arbitrage players will see that a lower rate is appropriate and will buy the stock. Since the price in the long run will reflect the lower rate, all other things being equal, the present price is too low. Conversely, when the price follows from a rate of return lower than predicted, the price is too high and the players will sell the stock.

2. *Deriving the Beta.*

A. Kolbe, J. Read, Jr., and G. Hall, The Cost of Capital: Estimating the Rate of Return for Public Utilities 68–69(1984), tells us more about where the beta comes from:

> An asset's beta combines the volatility of the asset's returns and the correlation of those returns with other assets into a single measure. The first factor in beta is the width of the average swing in the asset's value relative to the average swing in the portfolio's value. This can be measured by the standard deviation of the asset's returns divided by the standard deviation of the portfolio's returns. The second factor in beta is the correlation between the asset's moves and the portfolio's moves. A correlation of -1 implies the asset's returns *always* move up when the portfolio's returns move up. A correlation of 1 implies the asset's returns always move *down* when the portfolio's return moves *up*. A correlation of 0 implies the asset and the portfolio move independently of each other. The product of the correlation and the ratio of the standard deviations is the asset's beta *with respect to that portfolio*.

> An important conclusion of the CAPM is that all investors hold the "market portfolio," a portfolio consisting of shares of all stocks. One way to understand this conclusion is to note that such a portfolio would provide maximum diversification. Investors would calculate each asset's beta with respect to "the market." Few investors literally hold the market. However, the returns of well-diversified portfolios are highly correlated with market movements. Thus asset betas measured relative to the market are attractive general measures of asset risk. Betas measured with respect to the market are also the sole measure of asset risk in the CAPM.

Thus an asset's beta depends on the correlation of its rate of return with the market's rate of return and on the size of its standard deviation (its variability) relative to the market's.

Ideally, the market portfolio used in calculating the beta would include all assets—stocks, bonds, and real estate. As a practical matter, stock indexes are used. Results can differ significantly with the choice of stock index. Van Horne, Financial Management and Policy 74–75 (11th ed. 1998).

For an excellent step-by-step exposition of the process of beta derivation, consult Thompson, Demystifying the Use of Beta in the Determination of the Cost of Capital and an Illustration of Its Use in Lazard's Valuation of Conrail, 25 J. Corp. L. 213 (1999).

3. *Calculating the Return on the Market Portfolio.*

The CAPM assumes that the return on the market portfolio equals the risk free rate of return plus a risk premium: $r_m = r_f$ + risk premium. In real world securities markets these numbers change all the time. How is the volatility dealt with in applications of the CAPM?

The practice is to take the current return on treasury securities as the risk free rate of return. But opinions differ as to whether reference should be made to returns on Treasury bills or long or intermediate term treasury bonds. Obviously, results can differ depending on the choice made. Van Horne, supra, pp. 72–73. Opinion also differs about the derivation of the risk premium (return on the market minus risk free rate of return). Under the most prominent line of practice under the CAPM, an historical average is used. The figure yielded varies depending on the length of history included in the calculation. Consider this example: Robert Shiller derives a 6 percent risk premium from stock price data for the period 1870–1998; the Ibbotsen yearbook derives a 9.4 percent figure for 1926–1998. See Welch, Views of Financial Economists On the Equity Premium and On Professional Controversies, 73 J. Bus. 501 (2000). Welch presents the results of a survey of the opinions of financial economists as to the appropriate long term equity risk premium. The result is a consensus forecast of 7 percent on a thirty year time horizon. Shortening the time horizon to one year causes the consensus figure to go down 0.5 percent to 6.5 percent.

If we take Welch's 30 year figure together with the 4.8 percent return on 6 month treasury bills in mid 2007, the model yields the following:

$$r_m = r_f (2007) + \text{normal risk premium (30 year horizon)}$$
$$= .048 + .07 = .118 \text{ or } 11.8\%$$

(b) *using beta in valuation*

Recall that the present value of a perpetual series of cash flows is expressed as follows:

$$PV = \sum_{t=1}^{\infty} \frac{A_t}{(1+r)^t}$$

In discussing valuation we first introduced the idea of discounting—the exercise of dividing A_t by $(1 + r)^t$. Next we discussed the problematics of estimating the future values of A_t. We then turned to the subject of risk, the factor that determines the value of r. Our concern has been the value of r ever since. We have looked at cases that dealt with r by indirection, applying multiples drawn from market data on comparable companies. The CAPM (along with betas derived from past stock price movements) here proves very useful because it permits an analyst a means to derive a value of r tailored to the firm being valued. It is widely used to fill in a value of r in real world valuations—of firms, securities, and portfolios and in capital budgeting.

Cede & Co. v. Technicolor, Inc.
Court of Chancery of Delaware, 1990.
1990 WL 161084 (Del.Ch.).

■ ALLEN, CHANCELLOR.

[This section 262 appraisal action concerned the friendly 1983 merger of Technicolor Inc. into a shell corporation controlled by Ronald Perelman for $23 per share. Technicolor pursued a number of related lines of business. Its main revenues and profits came from its Professional Services Group, which processed motion pictures. Lesser lines of business included a Videocassette Duplicating Division, a Consumer Photo Processing Division, which operated a film processing business, and the Standard Manufacturing Co., which manufactured film slicers. Technicolor also ran One Hour Photo (OHP), a chain of one-hour film development stores. OHP was a recent, capital-intensive expansion program that proved a drain on profits. Technicolor's stock had been trading at 22 when OHP was begun in 1981. By late 1982, when Perelman began bidding for the company, the stock had declined to the $8 to $10 range.]

An appraisal action is a judicial, not an inquisitorial, proceeding. The parties, not the court, establish the record and the court is limited by the record created. The statutory command to determine fair value is a command to do so in a judicial proceeding, with the powers and constraints such a proceeding entails. Accepting that the expert testimony has been so structured as to largely foreclose the court from accepting parts of one [discounted cash flow (DCF)] model and sections of the other, it follows that the court must decide which of the two principal experts has the greater claim overall to have correctly estimated the intrinsic value of [the company's] stock at the time of the merger. Having decided that question, it will be open to me to critically review the details of that expert's opinion in order to determine if the record will permit, and judicial judgment require, modification of any inputs in that model. What the record will not permit is either a completely independent judicially created * * * model or a pastiche composed of bits of one model and pieces of the other.

For good reasons aside from technical competence, one might be disinclined to do so. Simply to accept one expert's view or the other would have a significant institutional or precedential advantage. The DCF model typically can generate a wide range of estimates. In the world of real transactions (capital budgeting decisions for example) the hypothetical, future-oriented, nature of the model is not thought fatal to the DCF technique because those employing it typically have an intense personal interest in having the best estimates and assumptions used as inputs. In the litigation context use of the model does not have that built-in protection. On the contrary, particularly if the court will ultimately reject both parties DCF analysis and do its own, the incentive of the contending parties is to arrive at estimates of value that are at the outer margins of plausibility—that essentially define a bargaining range. If it is understood that the court will or is likely to accept the whole of one witness's testimony or the other, incentives will be modified. While the incentives of the real world applications of the DCF model will not be replicated, at least the parties will have incentives to make their estimate of value appear most reasonable. This would tend to narrow the range of estimates, which would unquestionably be a benefit to the process.

[Chancellor Allen discussed his decision to accept, with modifications, the capitalization rate provided by the defendants' appraiser, Professor Rappaport:]

Professor Rappaport used the Capital Asset Pricing Model (CAPM) to estimate Technicolor's costs of capital as of January 24, 1983. That model estimates the cost of company debt (on an after tax basis for a company expected to be able to utilize the tax deductibility of interest payments) by estimating the expected future cost of borrowing; it estimates the future cost of equity through a multi-factor equation and then proportionately weighs and combines the cost of equity and the cost of debt to determine a cost of capital.

The CAPM is used widely (and by all experts in this case) to estimate a firm's cost of equity capital. It does this by attempting to identify a risk-free rate for money and to identify a risk premium that would be demanded for investment in the particular enterprise in issue. In the CAPM model the riskless rate is typically derived from government treasury obligations. For a traded security the market risk premium is derived in two steps. First a market risk premium is calculated. It is the excess of the expected rate of return for a representative stock index (such as the Standard & Poor 500 or all NYSE companies) over the riskless rate. Next the individual company's 'systematic risk'—that is the nondiversified risk associated with the economy as a whole as it affects this firm—is estimated. This second element of the risk premium is, in the CAPM, represented by a coefficient (beta) that measures the relative volatility of the subject firm's stock price relative to the movement of the market generally. The higher that coefficient (i.e., the higher the beta) the more volatile or risky the stock of the subject company is said to be. Of course, the riskier the investment the higher its costs of capital will be.

The CAPM * * * cannot, of course, determine a uniquely correct cost of equity. Many judgments go into it. The beta coefficient can be measured in a variety of ways; the index rate of return can be determined pursuant to differing definitions, and adjustments can be made, such as the small capitalization premium, discussed below. But the CAPM methodology is certainly one of the principal "techniques or methods * * * generally considered acceptable [for estimating the cost of equity capital component of a discounted cash flow modeling] in the financial community * * *." Weinberger v. UOP, Inc. at 713.

In accepting Professor Rappaport's method for estimating Technicolor's costs of capital, I do so mindful of the extent to which it reflects judgments. That the results of the CAPM are in all instances contestable does not mean that as a technique for estimation it is unreliable. It simply means that it may not fairly be regarded as having claims to validity independent of the judgments made in applying it.

With respect to the cost of capital aspect of the discounted cash flow methodology (in distinction to the projection of net cash flows and, in most respects, the terminal value) the record does permit the court to evaluate some of the variables, used in that model chosen as the most reasonable of the two (i.e., Professor Rappaport's) and to adjust the cost of capital accordingly. I do so with respect to two elements of Professor Rappaport's determination of costs of equity for the various Technicolor divisions. These businesses were all (excepting One Hour Photo, Consumer Photo Processing and Standard Manufacturing) assigned a cost of equity of 22.7% and a weighted average cost of capital of 20.4%. The remaining businesses were assigned a cost of equity of 20.4% and a weighted average cost of capital of 17.3%.

In fixing the 22.7% cost of equity for film processing and other businesses Professor Rappaport employed a 1.7 beta which was an estimate published by Merrill Lynch, a reputable source for December 1982. That figure seems intuitively high for a company with relatively stable cash flows. Intuition aside, however, it plainly was affected to some extent by the striking volatility in Technicolor's stock during the period surrounding the announcement of [a] proposal to acquire Technicolor for $23 per share. Technicolor stock rapidly shot up to the $23 level from a range of $9 to $12 in which it traded for all of September and the first week of October. Technicolor stock was thus a great deal more volatile than the market during this period. Applying the same measure of risk—the Merrill Lynch published beta—for September yields a significantly different beta measurement: 1.27. Looking at other evidence with respect to Technicolor betas I conclude that 1.27 is a more reasonable estimate of Technicolor's stock beta for purposes of calculating its cost of capital on January 24, 1983, than 1.7, even though that latter figure represents a December 1982 estimation.

The second particular in which the record permits and my judgment with respect to weight of evidence requires a modification of Mr. Rappaport's cost of capital calculation relates to the so-called small capitalization effect or premium. This refers to an unexplained inability of the capital asset pricing model to replicate with complete accuracy the historic returns of stocks with the same historic betas. The empirical data show that there is a recurring premium paid by small capitalization companies. This phenomena was first noted in 1981 and has been confirmed. The greatest part of the additional return for small cap companies appears to occur in January stock prices. No theory satisfactorily explaining the phenomena has been generally accepted.

Professor Rappaport classifies Technicolor as a small capitalization company and expressed the view that its cost of equity would include a 4% premium over that generated by the CAPM.

The question whether the premium can be justified in this instance is difficult because of the inability of academic financial economists to generate an accepted theory of the phenomenon. While Technicolor may qualify as a small cap company, the particulars of its situation are different from many small cap companies. It was an old, not a new company. It existed in a relatively stable industry—motion picture film processing. That industry was an oligopoly and Technicolor was a leader. It had "brand name" identification. Do these distinctive characteristics that Technicolor had in common with many giant capitalization companies, matter at all in terms of the "small cap" anomaly? One cannot say. Yet the impact of a 4% increase in the cost of equity (yielding a 3.44% increase in the cost of capital of the Film Processing & Videocassette divisions) would be material to the value of the company and the appraisal value of a share. In these circumstances, I cannot conclude that it has been persuasively shown that the statutory fair value of Technicolor stock would more likely result from the inclusion of a small capitalization premium than from its exclusion. In this circumstance, I conclude it should not be considered.

Thus, in summary, I find Professor Rappaport's calculation of a cost of capital follows an accepted technique for evaluating the cost of capital; it employs that technique in a reasonable way and, except for the two particulars noted above, in a way that is deserving of adoption by the court. Applying these adjustments they lead to a cost capital of 15.28% for the main part of Technicolor's cash flow and 14.13% for the One Hour Photo related cash flows.

NOTE: THE JUDICIAL ROLE IN APPRAISAL

Weinberger, taken together with the legislative change that eliminated the requirement of a court-appointed appraiser in appraisal proceedings, elevates the role of expert appraisers employed by the parties. An increase in detail and complexity of appraisal cases has resulted. A question arises concerning the role to be played by the judge in sifting through the voluminous and technical expert evidence.

Chancellor Chandler describes the adjudication of fair value as follows in Cede & Co. v. Technicolor, Inc., 2003 WL 23700218 (Del.Ch.), at 2:

> [I]t is one of the conceits of our law that we purport to declare something as elusive as *the* fair value of an entity on a given date * * *. Experience in the adversarial, battle of the experts' appraisal process under Delaware law teaches one lesson very clearly: valuation decisions are impossible to make with anything approaching complete confidence. Valuing an entity is a difficult intellectual exercise, especially when business and financial experts are able to organize data in support of wildly divergent valuations for the same entity. For a judge who is not an expert in corporate finance, one can do little more than try to detect gross distortions in the experts' opinions. This effort should, therefore, not be understood, as a matter of intellectual honesty, as resulting in *the* fair value of a corporation on a given date. The value of a corporation is not a point on a line, but a range of reasonable values, and the judge's task is to assign one particular value within this range as the most reasonable value in light of all of the relevant evidence and based on considerations of fairness.

Vice–Chancellor Strine seconds the point in Andaloro v. PFPC Worldwide, Inc., 2005 WL 2045640 (Del.Ch.), at 2:

> In coming to my valuation, I have had to stagger through a sandstorm of contending arguments, on all points great and small. Many of these playground tussles involve issues that emerge in the actual application of broad corporate finance principles that are commonly taught in academic institutions. The real world nitty-gritty use of those principles brings to the fore problems of measurement and theory that academics, and frankly, even real world business people, have no rational reason to solve because they seek to use corporate finance principles to reach a reliable approximation of a range of values from which rational investment decisions can be made. The process of appraisal calling for the court to derive a single best estimate of value based on the "expert input" of finance professionals paid to achieve diametrically opposite objectives tends, regrettably, to surface minor, granular issues of this kind, which are not well addressed in the academic literature. The trial record in this case has more than its share of these minute disputes and the literature cited to me has done little to convince me that there are clear-cut answers to most of them.

Chancellor Allen, in the principal case, suggested that a process approach reminiscent of a baseball arbitration might ameliorate the burden. On appeal, in **Cede & Co. v. Technicolor, Inc.**, 684 A.2d 289, 300 (Del.1996), however, the Delaware Supreme Court suggested a more capacious approach:

> Upon remand, it is within the Court of Chancery's discretion to select one of the parties' valuation models as its general framework, or fashion its own * * *. The Court of Chancery has properly recognized that its choice of framework does not require it to adopt any one expert's model, methodology, or mathematical calculations in toto.

Brealey, Myers, and Allen, Principles of Corporate Finance

215–217 (8th ed. 2006).

The **company cost of capital** is defined as the expected return on a portfolio of all the company's existing securities. It is the opportunity cost of capital for investment in the firm's assets, and therefore the appropriate discount rate for the firm's average-risk projects.

If the firm has no significant amount of debt outstanding, then the company cost of capital is just the expected rate of return on the firm's stock. Many large, successful companies fit this special case, including Microsoft. [We estimate] that investors require a return of 12.9 percent from Microsoft common stock. If Microsoft is contemplating an expansion of the firm's existing business, it would make sense to discount the forecasted cash flows at 12.9 percent.

The company cost of capital is *not* the correct discount rate if the new projects are more or less risky than the firm's existing business. Each project should be evaluated at its *own* opportunity cost of capital. * * * For a firm composed of assets A and B, the firm value is

Firm value = PV(AB) = PV(A) + PV(B) = sum of separate asset values

Here PV(A) and PV(B) are valued just as if they were mini-firms in which stockholders could invest directly. Investors would value A by discounting its forecasted cash flows at a rate reflecting the risk of A. They would value B by discounting at a rate reflecting the risk of B. The two discount rates will, in general, be different. * * *

If the firm considers investing in a third project C, it should also value C as if C were a mini-firm. That is, the firm should discount the cash flows of C at the expected rate of return that investors would demand to make a separate investment in C. *The true cost of capital depends on the use to which the capital is put.*

This means that Microsoft should accept any project that more than compensates for the *project's beta*. In other words, Microsoft should accept any project lying above the upward-sloping line that links expected return to risk in Figure 9.1. If the project is high-risk, Microsoft needs a higher prospective return than if the project is low-risk. Now contrast this with the company cost of capital rule, which is to accept any project *regardless of its risk* as long as it offers a higher return than the *company's* cost of capital. In terms of Figure 9.1, the rule tells Microsoft to accept any project above the horizontal cost-of-capital line, i.e., any project offering a return of more than 12.9 percent.

FIGURE 9.1

A comparison between the company cost of capital rule and the required return under the capital asset pricing model. Microsoft's company cost of capital is about 12.9 percent. This is the correct discount rate only if the project beta is 1.70. In general, the correct discount rate increases as project beta increases. Microsoft should accept projects with rates of return above the security market line relating required return to beta.

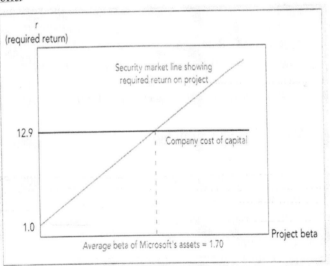

It is clearly silly to suggest that Microsoft should demand the same rate of return from a very safe project as from a very risky one. If Microsoft used the company cost of capital rule, it would reject many good low-risk projects and accept many poor high-risk projects. It is also silly to suggest that just because another company has a low company cost of capital, it is justified in accepting projects that Microsoft would reject.

The notion that each company has some individual discount rate or cost of capital is widespread, but far from universal. Many firms require different returns from different categories of investment. Discount rates might be set, e.g., as follows:

Category	Discount Rate, %
Speculative ventures	30
New products	20
Expansion of existing business	15 (company cost of capital)
Cost improvement, known technology	10

Restating the foregoing, the expected return on a given firm's stock, as measured by beta, is not necessarily the rate of return appropriate in the capital budgeting analysis for a new project. A project more risky than the firm's present set of assets calls for a higher required rate of return.

Let us say that the stock of Firm XYZ has a beta of 1.5, and that the risk free rate of return is 5 percent and the long term return on the market is 12 percent. The rate of return on XYZ stock can be calculated as follows:

$$5\% + 1.5 (12\% - 5\%) = 16.5\%$$

Now assume that XYZ plans to invest in a new line of business. The investment will cost $5,500,000 and is expected to return an infinite annual net cash flow of $1 million. The new line of business is riskier than XYZ's present line of business. Firms in the same line of business possessing capital structures similar to XYZ have betas of 2.0, which in turn imply a rate of return of 19 percent: $5\% + 2.0 (12\% - 5\%) = 19\%$.

Now compare the results of net present value analyses using the rate of return on XYZ's common stock and the rate of the return on the shares of companies with assets at a risk level comparable to that of the proposed project:

XYZ cost of equity capital:

A/r = PV

$1,000,000/0.165 = $6,060,606 minus $5,500,000 = $560,606

Comparable asset cost of equity capital:

$1,000,000/0.19 = $5,263,157.8 minus $5,500,000 = $-236,842.20

Failing to adjust the required rate of return to the risk level of the asset results in a false positive.

Ascertaining a project beta can be a complicated business. Even if there are publicly traded firms of the same asset class, their stock returns need not be directly comparable. Suppose, for example, that the firms in the asset class are heavily levered but that XYZ has no debt. The comparable firms' stock betas will reflect the added risk bound up in their capital structures, a risk factor that will not be replicated in respect of an investment in the same type of asset by XYZ. The analyst accordingly must go through the exercise of "delevering" the comparables to ascertain a beta appropriate for the capital budgeting exercise at XYZ. Delevering looks toward a beta for the asset in isolation, rather than the asset as contained in a particular corporate structure. Alternatively, the particular project could have risk properties that change over time—some projects are more risky in their early years and safer later, or vice versa. In such a case, the project beta would be adjusted over time, with different required rates of return for different periods.

Finally, in some cases, there will be no publicly traded firms to provide a ready yardstick. Here the analyst must exercise his or her own judgment. Brealey, Myers and Allen, supra, at 223–26, make three suggestions in this case. First, if the project holds out downside possibilities, it is better to work out an adjustment in the expected amount of A_t than to gross up the value of r. Second, cyclical projects call for a higher rate of return. Third, projects with high fixed costs are riskier.

NOTE: SHAREHOLDER VALUE, RISK AVERSION, AND RISK NEUTRALITY

Brealey, Myers, and Allen employ the CAPM in capital budgeting to distinguish different projects in accordance with their different risk levels. But they elsewhere have reminded us that "a good project is a good project is a good project." Does this imply that a firm's managers should invest in all "good projects" regardless of their high betas? The implication of the "capital market line" is that given the right return, the firm's stockholders will be indifferent if management takes on riskier projects so long as the expected return was appropriately high. Alternatively, should managers disregard the implications of the capital market line and distinguish among the pool of good projects, selecting those that fit into a preexisting risk profile understood by investors in the marketplace on the theory that they thereby protect the "expectations" of those investors? Are company managers in some sense "bound" by the risk-preferences of the company's stockholders, or even by those of the larger community of potential stockholders, to the extent that such composites can be ascertained? Or should managers be left free to exercise their own preferences, leaving it to investors to make suitable judgments about the policies of the companies whose shares they buy and sell? In the latter event, is it proper for management to expand, contract, or otherwise alter the company's business objectives once those goals have been established in investor's minds, or should they seek to maintain a constant level of business risk so as to relieve investors of the need to make frequent reassessments?

Financial economics takes an emphatic position respecting these questions. Managers should avoid trying to ascertain their shareholders' actual risk preferences and assume that the shareholders want all good high return projects to be selected regardless of the level of risk. Managers, in other words, should the managers assume that the shareholders are *risk neutral*.

Portfolio theory and the CAPM combine to justify this answer. Recall that portfolio theory remits the risk averse investor to diversify fully. If too much risk remains, it can be reduced by balancing the risky portfolio with risk free securities. It follows that shareholder risk aversion does not justify managers who turn down high return/high risk projects which pass inspection under the CAPM. These managers are sacrificing shareholder value. Risk aversion no doubt is the prime motivation of such managers. But, under the foregoing analysis it is not the shareholders' risk aversion that is doing the motivating. Instead, the managers take low risk/low return projects so as to reduce the personal career risk that attends business failure.

Such risk averse behavior is deemed to impose "agency costs" on the share-holders. It is perfectly rational. Managers invest human capital in their firms. Unlike capital invested in stocks, this capital cannot be diversified fully and risk-adjusted with treasury securities. Risk averse but suboptimal investment decisions can follow. The recommended correctives are stepped up monitoring by outside directors and institutional shareholders along with compensation arrangements that align the managers' interests with those of their risk neutral shareholders, in particular, generous stock option packages. For further analysis along these lines see Hu, Risk, Time, and Fiduciary Principles in Corporate Investment, 38 UCLA L.Rev. 277, 282–83 (1990).

(c) empirical testing and multiple factor models

1.   *Empirical Results.*

As Modigliani and Pogue point out, the empirical evidence never supported the view that "CAPM is absolutely right." But the early test results were broadly supportive. They showed a linear relationship between risk (measured by beta) and return even as Modigliani and Pogue acknowledged that the slope of the relationship was less than the theory predicted. The empirical capital market line was too flat—low beta stocks had higher returns than predicted and high beta stocks had lower returns. Notably, the early study showing a positive correlation of beta with average stock returns covered only the period through 1969.

Under later studies covering 1963 to 1990, the relation between beta and average market return disappeared. See Fama and French, The Cross–Section of Expected Stock Returns, 47 J. Fin. 427 (1992); Lakonishok and Shapiro, Systematic Risk, Total Risk and Size as Determinants of Stock Market Returns, 10 J. Banking & Fin. 115 (1986). The later results by no means signal rejection of the idea that risk sensitivities determine rates of return and that statistical analysis can provide important information about risk sensitivities. But they do reject the notion that price relates *solely* to the single risk sensitivity embodied in the security's market risk or beta, and thus seriously challenge any absolutist claims advanced by CAPM proponents. Fama and French back up this criticism by presenting factors other than beta that successfully explain the portion of security returns beta does not capture. They isolate two such additional risk sensitivities. The first is a *small firm effect* identified in statistical tests of the CAPM: Holding beta constant, stocks with small market capitalizations provide higher returns than large capitalization stocks. Cede & Co. v. Technicolor, supra, provides an example in which this discount shows up in an appraisal proceeding. The second risk sensitivity is based on a given stock's ratio of book value to market value: Holding beta constant, stocks with high ratios of book-to-market value have rates of return higher than could be explained by the CAPM. This phenomenon is sometimes called the "value premium," due to the association between high book-to-market and so-called value stocks. Looking at the period 1963 to 1994, Fama and French show that small firm stocks returned on average an extra 3.2 percent over large firm stocks and that high book-to-market stocks returned on average an extra 5.4 percent over low book to market stocks. See Fama and French, Size and Book to Market Factors in Earnings and Returns, 50 J. Fin. 131

(1995). (Fama and French also show a negative correlation between stock return and firm size. See Fama and French, Common Risk Factors in the Returns on Stocks and Bonds, 17 J. Fin. Econ. 3 (1993)).

The original CAPM assumed homogeneous investor expectations. Further studies relaxed that assumption but substituted another—that even if investors disagree in their prediction for returns on a given investment, the weighted average of investor expectations equals the true expected values of the next period's payoffs, so that prices are set as if there is complete agreement. Fama and French, Disagreement, Tastes, and Asset Prices, 83 J. Fin. Econ. 667 (2007), relaxes the fall back assumption and looks into the price effects of investor disagreement and asset tastes, otherwise using CAPM as the framework of inquiry. They conclude that investor differences can have potentially significant effects on prices.

2. *The Three Factor Model.*

Based on the foregoing results, Fama and French present a modified model that corrects for CAPM's failure to predict market capitalization rates for small firm stocks and stocks with a high ratio of book value to market value. The model incorporates factors measuring size sensitivity ("small minus big") and sensitivity to difference in book-to-market ("high minus low") in addition to market beta.

To see how the model works, let us first restate the CAPM to solve for a given stock's market risk premium. The CAPM solves for the stock's overall rate of return as follows:

$$r = r_f + \beta \, (r_m - r_f)$$

We can rearrange the equation to solve for the stock's expected risk premium:

$$r - r_f = \beta \, (r_m - r_f)$$

Having done that we can turn to the three factor equation, which solves for a given stock's risk premium as follows:

$$r - r_f = \beta_{market} \, (r_{market \; factor}) + \beta_{size} \, (r_{size \; factor}) + \beta_{book\text{-}to\text{-}market} \, (r_{book\text{-}to\text{-}market \; factor})$$

The $r_{market \; factor}$ is the long term market risk premium used in the standard CAPM. The $r_{size \; factor}$ is the "small minus big" factor for the market as a whole: The return on small firm stocks minus the return on large firm stocks, a 3.2 percent difference in the Fama and French calculation. The $r_{book\text{-}to\text{-}market \; factor}$ is the "high minus low" factor for the market as a whole: The return on stocks with a high ratio of book value to market value minus the return on stocks with low book to market ratios, a 5.4 percent difference in the Fama and French calculation. The β_{market} is the standard CAPM market-based risk factor; the β_{size} measures a given stock's sensitivity to the size factor; and $\beta_{book\text{-}to\text{-}market}$ measures a given stock's sensitivity to the book-to-market factor.

Fama and French, Industry Costs of Equity, 43 J. Fin. Econ. 153, 172–73 (1997), calculates factor sensitivities for baskets of stocks from different industries. The results for six of the industries are set out below. The market betas are the standard CAPM factors—a beta of less than 1 means less risky than the market as a whole, a beta of more than one means more risky than the market as a whole. The size and book-to-market betas work a little differently. Consider the book-to-market sensitivity figure for automotive industry of .60. This implies that an increase of 1 percent in the market return on this factor accompanies an increase in the return on automotive stocks of .60 percent. It works differently with computer stocks, where a 1 percent market increase implies a decrease of computer stock returns of .49 percent. For drug stocks the decrease is .63 percent.

	β_{market}	β_{size}	$\beta_{book-to-market}$	Three factor risk premium	CAPM risk premium
Automotive	1.10	.17	.60	9.39	5.13
Computers	.90	.17	-.49	2.49	5.29
Drugs	.84	-.25	-.63	.09	4.71
Energy	.96	-.35	.21	4.93	4.32
Telcoms	.79	-.23	.35	5.17	3.39
Utilities	.79	-.20	.38	5.41	3.39

To go from the sensitivity figures to the risk premium figures one has to interpolate Fama and French's figures for r—the market risk premium of 5.2 percent for the CAPM and conventional beta, the 3.2 percent difference for the size beta, and the 5.4 percent difference for the book-to-market beta. The three factor expected risk premium results when the sensitivity figure is multiplied by its respective market risk factor and the results are added up. See Brealey, Myers, and Allen, Principles of Corporate Finance 204 (8th ed. 2006).

Valuations employing the three factor model have been showing up in Delaware appraisal actions. The courts, invoking *Weinberger*, have accepted them as state-of-the-art methodology. See, e.g., Cede & Co., Inc. v. Med-Pointe Healthcare, Inc., 2004 WL 2093967, at 18; Union Illinois 1995 Inv. Ltd. P'ship v. Union Fin. Group, Ltd., 847 A.2d 340, 362 (Del.Ch.2004).

The theoretical jury is still out, however. High statistical debate continues in the finance journals. Beta's defenders suggest that Fama and French's results may be due to data-snooping biases. See, e.g., Conrad, et al, Value versus Glamour, 58 J. Fin. 1969 (2003); Kothari, et al., Another Look at the Cross–Section of Expected Stock Returns, 50 J. Fin. 185 (1995). See also Black, Estimating Expected Return, 49 Financial Analysts J. 36 (1993). Loughran, Book-to Market Across Firm Size, Exchange, and Seasonality, 32 J. Fin. & Quan. Anal. 249 (1997), launches a major challenge to the Fama and French book-to-market findings for the period 1963–1995. Fama and French, The Value Premium and the CAPM, 61 J. Fin. 2163 (2007), counterattacks. They concede the point about book-to-market for the period after 1963, but substitute the P/E ratio as a metric for distinguishing value stocks from growth stocks, and reinstate their prior statistical finding of a value premium. They also show that book-to-market retains its statistical cogency for the period 1926–1963. Ang and Chen, The CAPM Over the Long Run, working paper (2005), claims to show that the CAPM beta does capture the value premium during the period 1926 to 1963. Fama and French concede this, but show a residuum of variation in beta unrelated to size going unrewarded.

For a review of the literature on asset pricing theory, see Campbell, Asset Pricing at the Millennium, 55 J.Fin. 1515 (2000).

3. *Arbitrage Pricing Theory.*

Stephen Ross's arbitrage pricing theory (APT) strikes off in a different direction. Like the CAPM, it assumes that unsystematic risk is diversified out. Unlike the CAPM, it does not look to the securities market for a measure of systematic risk. It instead defines systematic risk in terms of macroeconomic factors external to the securities market that cannot be diversified out—commodities price risk, interest rate risk, and so forth. The risk premium on a given stock depends on the macroeconomic factors to which it is sensitive. Different stocks will be sensitive to different factors at different rates. Unfortunately, the model does not identify the macroeconomic factors.

Ross, Westerfield and Jaffe, Corporate Finance 283–285 (5th ed. 1999) compares the APT with the CAPM:

"[T]he APT * * * can handle multiple factors while the CAPM ignores them. * * * [A] multi-factor model is probably more reflective of reality. That is, one must abstract from many market-wide and industry-wide factors before the unsystematic risk of one security becomes uncorrelated with the unsystematic risks of other securities. Under this multi-factor version of the APT, the relationship between risk and return can be expressed as:

$$R = R_F + (R_1 - R_F)\beta_1 + (R_2 - R_F)\beta_2 + (R_3 - R_F)\beta_3 + \ldots + (R_K - R_F)\beta_K$$
$$(11.6)$$

In this equation, β_1 stands for the security's beta with respect to the first factor, β_2 stands for the security's beta with respect to the second factor, and so on. For example, if the first factor is GNP, β_1 is the security's GNP beta. The term R_1 is the expected return on a security (or portfolio) whose beta with respect to the first factor is 1 and whose beta with respect to all other factors is zero. Because the market compensates for risk, $(R_1 - R_F)$ will be positive in the normal case. (An analogous interpretation can be given to R_2, R_3, and so on.)

"The equation states that the security's expected return is related to the security's factor betas. The intuition in equation (11.6) is straightforward. Each factor represents risk that cannot be diversified away. The higher a security's beta with regard to a particular factor is, the higher is the risk that the security bears. In a rational world, the expected return on the security should compensate for this risk. The above equation states that the expected return is a summation of the risk-free rate plus the compensation for each type of risk that the security bears.

"As an example, consider a study where the factors were monthly growth in industrial production (IP), change in expected inflation (UEI), unanticipated inflation (UI), unanticipated change in the risk-premium between risky bonds and default-free bonds (URP), and unanticipated change in the difference between the return on long-term government bonds and the return on short-term government bonds (UBR). Using the period 1958–1984, the empirical results of the study indicated that the expected monthly return on any stock, R_S, can be described as

$$R_s = 0.0041 + 0.0136\beta_{IP} - 0.0001\beta_{EI} - 0.0006\beta_{UI} + 0.0072\beta_{URP} - 0.0052\beta_{UBR}$$

"Suppose a particular stock had the following betas: $\beta_{IP} = 1.1$, $\beta_{EI} = 2$, $J_{UI} = 3$, $\beta_{URP} = 0.1$, $\beta_{UBR} = 1.6$. The expected monthly return on that security would be

$$R_S = 0.0041 + 0.0136 \times 1.1 - 0.0001 \times 2 - 0.0006 \times 3 + 0.0072 \times 0.1 - 0.0052 \times 1.6 = 0.0095$$

Assuming that a firm is unlevered and that one of the firm's projects has risk equivalent to that of the firm, this value of 0.0095 (i.e., 95%) can be used as the monthly discount rate for the project. (Because annual data is often supplied for capital budgeting purposes, the annual rate of 0.120 ($[1.0095]^{12} - 1$) might be used instead.)

"Because many factors appear on the right hand side of [the APT] equation * * *, the APT formulation has the potential to measure expected returns more accurately than does the CAPM. However, as we mentioned earlier, one cannot easily determine which are the appropriate factors. The factors in the above study were included for reasons of both common sense and convenience. They were not derived from theory."

Brealey, Myers and Allen, supra at 200, summarize the difference between APT and CAPM as follows: "You can think of the factors in arbitrage pricing as representing special portfolios of stocks that tend to be subject to common influence. If the expected risk premium on each of these portfolios is proportional to the portfolio's market beta, then the arbitrage pricing theory and the capital asset pricing model will give the same answer. In any other case they will not." For an exercise in making the APT operational, see Elton, Gruber and Mei, "Cost of Capital Using Arbitrage Pricing Theory: A Case Study of Nine New York Utilities," 3 Fin. Markets, Institutions and Instruments 46 (1994).

4. PREMIUMS AND DISCOUNTS IN MERGERS AND ACQUISITIONS

Kraakman, Taking Discounts Seriously: The Implications of "Discounted" Share Prices as an Acquisition Motive

88 Colum.L.Rev. 891 (1988).
pp. 893–905, 907–911, 913, 925–930.

I. An Overview of Acquisition Gains

Three possibilities might occur to an observer who first learned that acquirers routinely pay large premia over share price for the assets of target firms: (1) acquirers may be discovering more valuable uses for target assets; (2) share prices may "underprice" these assets; or, finally, (3) acquirers may simply be paying too much. These same possibilities point to a useful typology of current explanations of acquisition gains. A broad class of "traditional" gains hypotheses assumes that acquirers can create or claim new value to pay for acquisition premia. These explanations accord with the assumption that informed share prices fully reflect asset values. They include all ways in which acquirers might expect to increase the net cash flows of targets, for example, by improving management or redeploying assets. A second class of "discount" hypotheses asserts that while acquirers' bid prices reflect real private gains, these gains result because share prices discount the underlying value of target assets. Finally, a third and more troubling class of "overbidding" hypotheses questions whether bid prices and takeover premia reflect real opportunities for acquisition gains at all. Under these theories, managers of acquiring firms may misperceive or misvalue targets out of "hubris," or they may pursue distinctly managerial interests such as corporate growth at great cost to shareholder interests.

The extent to which this third class of acquisition hypotheses might explain takeover premia remains a difficult issue. Nevertheless, a prosperous acquisitions market and a large empirical literature both suggest that most acquisitions do generate private gains, at least as measured by their impact on share prices. Target shareholders earn large returns in the form of premia, while shareholders of acquiring firms do not seem to suffer losses and may also register gains. Since a primary role for private gains in motivating takeovers seems likely, inquiry must turn to the traditional and discount hypotheses. The question thus becomes: What mix of opportunities can explain these gains and the size of acquisition premia?

A. *Traditional Gains Hypotheses*

Most traditional accounts of motives and gains in the acquisitions literature favor active and resourceful acquirers who seek to increase cash flows from target assets through the redeployment or better management of these assets. The reorganization of assets can lead to synergy benefits, while new management may slash operating costs and increase returns in a variety of ways. In either case, acquisitions create both private gains for the participating parties and net social gains. In addition, there are less prominent, if no less traditional, accounts of how acquisitions might create private gains by imposing costs on third parties. Acquirers might exploit monopoly power,[10] or breach "implicit contracts" between target shareholders and creditors, employees, or incumbent managers.[11]

---

10. Indirect evidence strongly suggests that market power is not an important acquisition motive. See Eckbo, Horizontal Mergers, Collusion, and Stockholder Wealth, 11 J.Fin.Econ. 241, 251–68 (1983).

11. Among the most provocative revisionist accounts of private gains in takeovers are implicit contract theories that locate private gains in the redistribution of surplus from nonshareholder factors of target firms to acquiring firms. Thus, several commentators portray takeovers as a species of shareholder opportunism vis-a-vis incumbent managers. * * * This view suggests that acquirers profit in part by breaching implicit agreements to pay incumbent managers deferred compensation or to provide other perquisites. Professors Shleifer and Summers generalize the implicit contract perspective to other major corporate factors including employees and creditors. * * *

Two further accounts of acquisition gains straddle the line between traditional and discount hypotheses. One of these is a "private information" theory, which assumes that the market may be uninformed about the real value of target assets. In this case, acquirers who privately learn key information can exploit true discrepancies between share prices and asset values. The possibility of such information is a traditional caveat to the identification of share prices and asset values. Yet its practical significance seems largely limited to friendly transactions. Short of hiring informers, hostile acquirers lack access to inside information about targets. In addition, evidence that unsuccessful bids fail to increase the share prices of target firms over the long run also suggests that hostile bids do not release key inside information.

The second of these accounts concerns the import of tax savings for acquisition premia. The tax hypothesis may be either a traditional or a discount hypothesis depending on the nature of the asserted tax gain. In most instances, it is a traditional hypothesis that turns on corporate-level tax savings. Acquirers are said to garner significant tax gains by stepping up the basis on target assets, transferring valuable operating loss carry-overs ("NOLs"), or increasing their interest deductions by borrowing against target assets. These forms of the tax hypothesis are variations on the better management theory, although here management is tax management and the potential savings at issue are purely distributional gains. Recent studies suggest that each of these corporate-level tax gains has played some role in acquisitions and, more importantly, in management buyouts. Yet, apart from leveraged buyouts, their role seems to have been modest in the recent past; tax effects seldom appear to have been primary motives for acquisitions.

* * *

B. *Discount Hypotheses*

True discount hypotheses rely on neither private information nor a traditional inquiry into how acquirers might extract larger net cash flows from target assets. The discount claim assumes that acquisition premia reflect the existing value of target assets, a value that may be much higher than the pre-bid market value of target shares. A discount hypothesis must explain why these values differ. Apart from specialized tax claims, two broad explanations of discounts are possible: the misinvestment hypothesis and the market hypothesis.

The misinvestment hypothesis comes closest to traditional accounts of takeover gains. This account locates discrepancies between share prices and asset values in a rational mistrust of managers' future investment decisions. As such, it belongs to the broader family of agency cost theories. Unlike accounts of manager-shareholder conflict over operating slack and perquisites, however, the misinvestment hypothesis follows more recent analyses of manager-shareholder conflict over the distribution of corporate returns. In this view, managers exercise discretionary control over what

Professor Jensen terms "free cash flows"—those cash flows exceeding the investment requirements of the firm's existing projects. If managers are reluctant to distribute these cash flows and are unable—or unwilling—to discover profitable new investments, shareholders must inevitably price firms at below informed appraisals of their asset values.

Although the misinvestment hypothesis is conceptually related to traditional accounts of acquisition gains arising from improvements in the operational management of target firms, there is an important difference. Ongoing mismanagement of targets' assets reduces their cash flows. Thus, low share prices may accurately mirror the value of mismanaged target assets; there may be no discounts. By contrast, under the misinvestment hypothesis, discounts can arise even though targets' assets are put to their best uses. These discounts, which acquirers can exploit, result from the ongoing or expected misinvestment of surplus cash flows that exceed targets' operating requirements. Acquiring firms can profit, then, merely by purchasing discounted shares at any price up to the full value of targets' assets.

The alternative discount hypothesis—the market hypothesis—fits less easily with standard accounts of the securities market. In this view, share prices may discount asset values for reasons endogenous to the formation of market prices. Financial economics conventionally assumes that share prices are best estimates, given available information, of the present value of expected corporate cash flows available for distribution to shareholders. Thus, share prices should fully capitalize the value of corporate assets in the hands of existing managers. In real markets, this assumption is an approximation; it is unlikely to be either precisely correct or, given the sensitivity of share prices to new information, wholly misguided. It is a very good approximation in the standard view. By contrast, the market hypothesis asserts that discounts arise because share prices are sometimes very poor estimates of the expected value of corporate assets.

Modern objections to identifying share prices with asset values typically fall into two classes. The first class includes "valuation" challenges that question whether a single valuation model can apply across the markets for shares and firms or within the share market itself. Even if traders in both the asset and share markets value corporate assets similarly, share prices might nonetheless discount asset values simply because assets and shares differ in ways that matter to traders. For example, the share prices of firms holding liquid assets might discount asset values if traders placed an intrinsic value on the right to liquidate firms in the asset market—a right that minority shareholders in these firms would necessarily lack. Alternatively, overlapping clienteles of traders within the securities market might have heterogeneous demands for timing, magnitude, or tax attributes of shareholder distributions. In this case, shares might sell at either a discount or a premium relative to asset values.

The second and more prominent class of objections to equating share prices with asset values challenges the price setting role of informed traders. Thus, there is a growing theoretical literature on "mispricing" behavior, which argues that uninformed traders may introduce persistent biases or cumulative noise into share prices or that speculative trading might lead to positive or negative price "bubbles." Large-scale noise trading—arising from misconceived strategies, erroneous valuation assumptions, fashion and fads, or simple pleasure in trading—might distort share prices and generate discounts or premia through the sheer pressure of trading. In addition, some commentators suggest that noise trading further distorts share prices by encouraging informed traders to speculate on noise and by imposing "noise trader risk" on all traders in a noisy market. Finally, noise theorists find evidence of mispricing in the long-term price behavior of both individual firms and the entire market.

* * * What remains uncertain is how effectively share prices estimate the full present value of corporate cash flows, as distinct from predicting near-term share prices, and how large residual mispricing effects are likely to be. The market hypothesis simply asserts that recurrent discrepancies between share prices and asset values can explain major portions of at least some acquisition premia.

Stepping back from the market hypothesis, then, it is apparent that neither this account nor the misinvestment theory of acquisition gains is easily evaluated. * * * Fortunately, however, one task does not require such an evaluation: namely, examining the discount claim in its own right as a motive for acquisitions. Evidence of discounts can support either hypothesis. * * *

II.   The Case for Discounts

Market discounts must satisfy three conditions to be meaningful. First, potential acquirers and market professionals must be able to form reliable asset or break up values for the firm "as is;" that is, as its component assets are already managed and deployed. Asset values in this sense are particularly credible when assets can be separated from the functions of top management. Thus, natural resources or established corporate divisions may lend themselves to reliable valuation, while start-up projects or undeveloped investment opportunities might be impossible to value with confidence. Second, share prices must fall significantly below asset values. And third, potential acquirers must accept appraisals within the consensus range as useful—perhaps as minimal—estimates of what target assets will be worth to themselves and competing bidders.

Although these conditions are difficult to test, the case for discounts is nonetheless persuasive. Certain specialized firms that hold easily priced assets provide direct evidence of discounting. In addition, pervasive discounting can explain much recent acquisition behavior, including breakup acquisitions, management buyouts, and the sheer size of takeover premia. Finally, support for discounts can be found in many forms of corporate restructuring, including the wave of share repurchases and recapitalizations that swept American corporations during the mid–1980s.

A.   Discounts on Specialized Firms

Specialized firms whose shares clearly trade below the value of their assets provide direct evidence of discounting. * * * The closed-end investment fund is the best example of such a firm, and discounts on closed-end funds have long been viewed as important anomalies by financial economists. Yet discounts appear to be common among holding companies and natural resource companies, which are also firms that possess easily accessible and seemingly reliable asset values. Thus, even though reliable appraisals are not readily available for most firms, the suggestion is clear: If discounts appear wherever we are able to detect them, we have good reason to suspect that they may occur elsewhere. * * *

* * *

B. *Acquisition Behavior*

Given a basic presumption in favor of discounts, the discount claim becomes an intuitively attractive explanation over a broad spectrum of corporate activity. In particular, it accords well with at least two aspects of acquisition behavior where traditional hypotheses falter. One is the sheer size of premia in hostile acquisitions and management buyouts. The other is the recent prominence of break up acquisitions that exploit perceived differences between the share prices and asset values of conglomerate firms.

Consider first the size of acquisition premia. In recent years, premia have averaged about 50% of share value in management buyouts and 50% or more in hostile acquisitions. Most studies suggest that acquisitions of all kinds are either zero or positive net present value transactions on average. Thus, assuming that most acquirers reasonably expect to recover their premia costs, the obvious question is: How can they be so sure? Apart from possible tax gains, which few commentators believe to dominate premia, we are left to choose among market discounts and the usual suspects including the displacement of inefficient management, synergy gains, or the exploitation of private information. * * *

An evaluation of these assumptions shows the superiority of the discount claim. Large premia are easily explained if reliable appraisals of large firms can reveal the existence of market discounts. Under these circumstances, acquirers can calculate discounts with standard appraisal techniques and thereby learn, within the limits of appraisal error, whether the bulk of their premia costs are a simple purchase of assets at their existing values. That is, acquirers learn that their premia costs largely pay for assets that are worth the price if they merely continue to perform as they have in the past. By contrast, the synergy and better management hypotheses require acquirers to value novel and still hypothetical changes in targets' operating assets, while the information hypothesis demands that acquirers routinely discover dramatic good news relative to market expectation about targets.

* * *

Many commentators implicitly recognize the difficulty of valuing hypothetical changes by surmising that the cost of searching for opportunities to extract operating gains is a principal determinant of takeover activity. But this assumption encounters institutional difficulties. Casual evidence of several kinds suggests that acquirers rely heavily upon routine appraisals of the existing value of target assets rather than farsighted assessments of their potential value. Investment bankers deploy standard valuation programs in advising their clients; second bidders enter bidding contests on short notice; and outside analysts offer roughly similar and often accurate predictions of acquisition values as soon as firms are rumored to be "in play." Moreover, the rapid convergence of offer prices in auctions suggests common criteria for estimating value that seem unlikely to result from operating gains. Of course, consensus in the acquisitions market might also follow if first bidders fully revealed common opportunities for exploiting operating gains through their offers. But precisely because operating gains are complex and potentially unique to particular firms, this prospect seems unlikely. * * *

Finally, the discount claim can help to explain breakup acquisitions. Breakup acquisitions, whether hostile or friendly, present a clear analogy to the liquidation of closed-end investment funds. Where discounted funds hold portfolios of stocks, breakup targets are typically conglomerates holding several divisions that acquirers can resell piecemeal with their managements and markets intact. Although the prima facie likelihood of immediate operating gains from conglomerate breakups is greater than the likelihood of similar gains from management buyouts or acquisitions of natural resource firms, conglomerates still would have to impose enormous costs on their operating divisions for acquirers to generate 50% premia merely by eliminating the conglomerate structure. Operating gains in breakup acquisitions more plausibly occur—as in management buyouts—at the time when corporate assets are resold. Acquirers expect profits from the breakup and resale of target divisions, and these profits, in turn, may reflect the synergy or management gains that are available to the third-party purchasers of target assets. Standing alone, however, these resale profits seem unlikely to explain large initial premia paid to target shareholders. Acquirers and their financial backers cannot predict *ex ante* the synergy and management gains of end purchasers. Once again, operating gains would have to be improbably large to support prepayments of 50% premia, particularly since these gains must be divided between acquirers and end purchasers in negotiated transactions. While breakups may ultimately generate large operating or synergy gains, then, the discount claim presents a more compelling account of initial premia.

* * *

IV. Discounts as an Acquisition Motive

A. *Joint Gains*

The most important way in which discounts can prompt takeovers is in combination with other sources of acquisition gains such as operating gains or private information. Only large discounts can trigger takeovers in isolation if, as I have argued, target shareholders ordinarily capture most of the value of discounts. Nevertheless, small gains from other sources might transform firms with modest discounts into attractive targets, provided that these ancillary gains are—unlike discounts—uniquely available to particular acquirers. This possibility assumes that acquirers are able to capture most unique gains for their own accounts. Like pre-bid purchases on the open market, such gains give first bidders a strategic edge. They are unavailable to rival bidders, and they are likely to be invisible or at least difficult to value for defending managers or the market at large.

A simple example can clarify how such appropriate gains might affect acquisition decisions on the margin. Suppose that a target trades at a 30% discount below its asset value of $500,000,000, and that an acquirer can purchase 10% of the target's stock at the discounted price. In addition, assume that a tender offer for the remaining 90% must be priced at the target's pro rata asset value in order to discourage management resistance, including the solicitation of rival bids. In this case, a potential bidder would anticipate a gross return of $15,000,000 (0.10 × 0.30 × $500,000,000) from the target's discount. Thus, if the expected costs of a successful bid—including professional fees, financing and solicitation costs, contingent liabilities, defensive tactics, and transition expenses—totaled, say, $20,000,000, no acquirer would bid on the basis of the target's discount alone. If, however, an acquirer expected even minor synergy gains (on the order of $10,000,000) in addition to discount gains, a hostile bid would become an attractive proposition.

[I]f large discounts can offset premia and subsidize first-stage transaction costs, even uncertain synergies or management gains might suffice to motivate buyout syndicates or breakup acquirers. Thus, the joint-gains hypothesis can accommodate conflicting evidence about the "real" motive behind these transactions and explain one of their most puzzling features: why buyers pay "second premia" when breakup assets are resold, buyout targets go public, or residual shares in recapitalized firms appreciate in the market. Second premia on this account are merely the rewards of forecasting previously uncertain operating gains.

NOTE: DOWNWARD–SLOPING DEMAND

Booth, Discounts and Other Mysteries of Corporate Finance, 79 Calif.L.Rev. 1055 (1991), stresses that the misinvestment and market explanations of discounts are not mutually exclusive. According to Booth, id. pp. 1058–1059, "both explanations are nothing more than alternative formulations of the same basic truth: stocks, like other commodities have downward-sloping demand curves. In other words, the price of a share for purposes of the trading market is established by the lowest-valuing current shareholder or, stated another way, the highest-valuing potential shareholder while the price of a share for the purposes of a tender offer or other acquisition is set by the highest-valuing current shareholder or highest-valuing bidder." Stout, Are Takeover Premiums Really Premiums? Market Price, Fair Value, and Corporate Law, 99 Yale L.J. 1235 (1990), also suggests that takeover premiums stem from heterogeneous investor beliefs and downward sloping demand.

Rapid–American Corp. v. Harris

Supreme Court of Delaware, 1992.
603 A.2d 796.

■ MOORE, JUSTICE.

[Rapid–American Corp. ("Rapid") was a publicly held conglomerate that received 99 percent of its revenues and most of its income from three wholly-owned subsidiaries: (1) McCrory Corp., a retailer, contributing more than half of Rapid's net sales and profits, (2) Schenley Industries, a distiller, contributing 25 percent of Rapid's net sales and profits, and (3) McGregor–Duniger, Inc., a clothing manufacturer, contributing less than 1 percent of Rapid's net sales and profits. Rapid was heavily leveraged, capitalized with close to 75 percent long and short term debt.

[In 1974, Rapid's CEO and Chairman, Meshulam Riklis, began purchasing its shares in the open market. Two corporate vehicles conducted the purchases: Kenton Corp. ("Kenton"), controlled by Riklis, and American Financial Corp. ("AFC"), controlled by Carl Lindener. Rapid also contemporaneously repurchased large blocks of its own shares, causing Riklis' control of Rapid's outstanding shares to increase. By 1980, Kenton and AFC controlled 46.5 percent of Rapid's outstanding stock. That year, Rapid agreed to merge with Kenton into a newly reformed, privately-held Rapid, owned 60 percent by Riklis and 40 percent by Lindener. Rapid's other shareholders received a package worth $28. including a $45 face amount 10 percent subordinated debenture, and $3.25 cash.

[Harris, who owned 58,400 shares, brought an appraisal proceeding and sought $73 per share. The Chancery court awarded $51 per share plus simple interest. Both sides appealed.]

I.

* * *

Rapid employed an independent Transaction Review Committee ("TRC") to evaluate the merger price. The TRC retained Bear Stearns & Co. to provide financial advice. The TRC also employed Standard Research Consultants ("SRC") to determine, among other things, the fairness of the proposed transaction to Rapid's shareholders. Arthur H. Rosenbloom, SRC's head consultant and expert witness at trial, led the investigation. The examination continued for approximately six months. SRC ultimately concluded that the $28.00 compensation package was fair to Rapid's shareholders.

SRC's valuation technique considered Rapid on a consolidated basis. It evaluated Rapid based on an analysis of earnings and dividends. *Harris,* slip op. at 7. SRC calculated price/earnings ratios for each subsidiary and adjusted its figures to include certain dividend ratios. It figured each subsidiaries' contribution to the parent's operating income for a set period of time to calculate Rapid's ultimate value. SRC then tested its figures against various established financial ratios of similarly situated corporations. Id.

Harris retained Willamette Management Associates, Inc. ("WMA") to evaluate the merger consideration. In contrast to SRC's technique, WMA separately evaluated each of Rapid's subsidiaries. WMA reasoned that its "segmented" approach to valuation was particularly appropriate because of the difficulty of finding a conglomerate comparable to Rapid.

* * *

The Court of Chancery adopted WMA's comparative analysis. Id. at 19. It examined each of Rapid's subsidiaries as a separate entity. Id. It then compared the subsidiaries to a group of comparable publicly-traded companies. Id.

WMA examined the financial statements of the subsidiaries and the comparables to develop certain pricing multiples. Id. at 20. These multiples were based on revenues, pre-interest and tax earnings, earnings "before depreciation, amortization, interest and taxes [and] tangible book value of invested capital * * *." Id. WMA specifically treated each subsidiary and comparable on a debt-free basis in an effort to factor out the vagaries of "managerial discretion" and to treat the companies on a "level playing field." Id. The analysis yielded a market value of invested capital for each segment. Id. The trial court also considered an average of the subsidiaries' financials for the five years preceding the merger, but placed special emphasis on the twelve months before the merger. Id. at 20–21. After calculating the market value of invested capital for each segment, the court subtracted out the market value of all senior debt and preferred equity to calculate the value of each segment's common equity. Id. at 13, 21. The trial court also considered "various parent-level" factors. Id.

The Vice Chancellor rejected WMA's inclusion of a "control premium" in its final evaluation of each Rapid subsidiary. Id. at 21–22. It found that the addition of a "control premium" violated Delaware law. Id. at 29, 35, 38. The court reasoned that the "control premium" contravened the proscription against weighing factors affecting valuation "at the shareholder level." Id. at 29.

II.

* * *

We now turn to the specific merits of Rapid's appeal to determine whether the trial court abused its discretion. We first consider Rapid's claim that the court's "segmented" valuation technique violated Delaware law because it supposedly assessed Rapid's value on a liquidation basis instead of considering it as a going concern. Rapid argues that the court's valuation approach was identical to the liquidation technique rejected in Bell v. Kirby Lumber Corp., Del.Ch., 395 A.2d 730 (1978), modified, Del.Supr., 413 A.2d 137 (1980).

* * *

Bell best illustrates the law. Kirby Lumber Corporation ("Kirby"), the company subject to the appraisal in *Bell,* was a manufacturing concern primarily engaged in the production of lumber and plywood. *Bell,* 395 A.2d at 732. Kirby also held a vast acreage of timberland. Id. at 733. Kirby harvested the timber on a "sustained yield" basis to maintain a steady and constant supply of natural resources for its wood production operations. Id.

The dissenting shareholders argued that the court should have evaluated Kirby on its acquisition value. Id. at 735–36. They claimed that Kirby's natural resources were much more valuable than its worth as an on-going concern. Id. The dissenters thus maintained that the court should have set Kirby's "fair value" at the price a third party would have paid for the company instead of relying on an evaluation of earnings or market price. Id.

The trial court rejected the dissenters' argument. Id. at 736. It reasoned that the liquidation value incorrectly assumed that Kirby would not have continued in its pre-merger form as an on-going concern. Id. This Court affirmed. *Bell*, 413 A.2d at 142. We agreed that the dissenters' liquidation approach violated the statute and improperly failed to consider Kirby's value apart from its acquisition value. Id.

* * *

We find nothing in the record to convincingly support the claim that the court's "segmented" valuation technique was either identical or even similar to the liquidation approach rejected in *Bell*. The modified WMA valuation explicitly considered Rapid's subsidiaries as going concerns. See *Harris*, slip op. at 34–35. It placed special emphasis on financial data cumulated from operating results and not liquidation values. Id. at 19–22.

The "segmented" technique itself also did not manifest a liquidation analysis. Instead, the "segmented" approach best mirrored economic reality. Indeed, even Riklis admitted that "Rapid's value is best found in the sum of its parts." Id. at 10.

* * *

III.

We now consider the merits of Harris' cross-appeal. The trial court determined the publicly traded equity ("PTE") value of Rapid's shares after adopting WMA's "segmented" comparative valuation technique. See *Harris*, slip op. at 22–38. The court, however, refused to add a "control premium" to the PTE for each of Rapid's operating subsidiaries. The court, citing [Cavalier Oil Corp. v. Harnett, 564 A.2d 1137 (Del.1989)], reasoned that adding a "control premium" violated 8 Del.C. § 262 because it contravened the general proscription against weighing any additional factors affecting valuation "at the shareholder level." Id. at 29, 35, 38.

* * * Harris maintains that WMA's valuation technique only compared its subsidiaries' PTE's with the individual shares of similar corporations trading in the market. He notes that the market price of these comparable corporations are discounted and do not reflect a control premium. Harris concludes that the trial court effectively treated Rapid as a minority shareholder in its wholly-owned subsidiaries. Harris contends that the trial court gave the new, privately-held Rapid, a windfall at his expense.

* * *

We disagree with the trial court's characterization of the "control premium" in this case as an impermissible shareholder level adjustment.

Its reliance on *Cavalier* and *Bell* is misplaced. The "control premium" Harris urged the trial court to adopt represented a valid adjustment to its valuation model which "applied a [bonus] at the company level against all assets * * *." *Cavalier,* 564 A.2d at 1144.

    * * *

Tri–Continental recognized that a court had the authority to discount the value of the enterprise at the corporate level. 74 A.2d at 76. The company appraised in *Tri–Continental* was a leveraged closed-end mutual fund. Id. at 73. The court understood that the shares of a leveraged closed-end mutual fund ordinarily trade at a discount of its underlying assets. Id. at 76. The court concluded:

> [T]he full value of the corporate assets to the corporation is not the same as the value of those assets to the common stockholder because of the factor of discount. To fail to recognize this conclusion * * * is to fail to face the *economic facts* and to commit error.

Id. (Emphasis added).

Cavalier also recognized the importance of assigning a realistic market value to the appraised corporation. 564 A.2d at 1144. * * * The court, however, rejected shareholder level discounting. It found that an appraisal explicitly considering the minority discount at the shareholder level both injects speculative elements into the calculation, and more importantly:

> [F]ail[s] to accord to a minority shareholder the full proportionate value of his shares [which] imposes a penalty for lack of control, and unfairly enriches the majority shareholders who may reap a windfall from the appraisal process by cashing out a dissenting shareholder, a clearly undesirable result.

Id. at 1145.

Rapid misses the fundamental point that Harris was not claiming a "control premium" at the shareholder level. Harris urged the trial court to add a premium at the parent level to compensate all of Rapid's shareholders for its 100% ownership position in the three subsidiaries. WMA's valuation technique arrived at comparable values using the market price of similar shares. These shares presumptively traded at a price that discounted the "control premium."

The trial court's decision to reject the addition of a control premium within the WMA valuation model placed too much emphasis on market value. * * * Recent price changes in the stock market dramatically illustrate the defects of an *overstated* reliance on market price to determine a corporation's intrinsic value in an appraisal proceeding. * * *

Rapid was a parent company with a 100% ownership interest in three valuable subsidiaries. The trial court's decision to exclude the control premium at the *corporate level* practically discounted Rapid's entire inherent value. The exclusion of a "control premium" artificially and unrealistically treated Rapid as a minority shareholder. Contrary to Rapid's arguments, Delaware law *compels* the inclusion of a control premium under the unique facts of this case. Rapid's 100% ownership interest in its subsidiaries was clearly a "relevant" valuation factor and the trial court's rejection of the "control premium" implicitly placed a disproportionate emphasis on pure market value. See *Weinberger,* 457 A.2d at 712–13; *Munds,* 172 A. at 456.

We also reject Rapid's implicit claim that the inclusion of a "control premium" violates our decision in *Bell.* Rapid seems to contend that a "control premium" is only payable when the corporation is liquidated. It concludes that the addition of a "control premium" incorrectly inflates Rapid's worth to an acquisition value instead of pricing its inherent value as a going concern.

We reject Rapid's arguments because *Bell* is easily distinguishable on its facts. Unlike *Bell,* the WMA valuation technique did not assume that an acquiror would liquidate Rapid. WMA's valuation technique added the "control premium" to reflect market realities. Rapid may have had a different value as a going concern if the court had considered that it enjoyed a 100% interest in its three major subsidiaries.

We recognize that the term "control premium" may be misleading here. The past decade has proven that an acquiror is often willing to pay a "control premium" in return for a majority interest in a corporation. Nonetheless, the WMA valuation technique utilized the control premium as a means of making its valuation more realistic. Under the circumstances presented here, the trial court was under a duty to assess the value of Rapid's full ownership in its subsidiaries.

* * *

Accordingly, we reverse the Court of Chancery and remand. The court must consider the "control premium," together with all other traditional valuation elements, and determine what, if any, additional value is to be ascribed to Harris' stock above the $51.00 per share initial finding.

* * *

On remand, the Chancery Court awarded the plaintiffs the "control premium" they requested—$23 per share for a total value per share of $73. Harris v. Rapid–American Corp., 1992 WL 69614 (Del.Ch.).

PROBLEM

At what point does a permissible "segmented" analysis become an impermissible liquidation approach? At what point does the valuation depart from permissible "corporate level" considerations into impermissible "shareholder level" territory? Consider the following problem.

Conglom Corp. operates three wholly owned subsidiaries, Manufacturing Corp. (M), Retail Corp. (R), and Timber Corp. (T). M and R each contribute approximately 40 percent of Conglom's sales and profits. T contributes 20 percent. Conglom has no significant parent level business. Conglom's stock trades at 30; the total market value of the stock is $100 million. Then, Nasticorp mounts a hostile tender offer for $45 cash per share, a total of $150 million. Conglom's managers encourage the shareholders not to tender because $45 is "too low." Nasticorp acquires 85 percent of Conglom's stock. In a subsequent second step merger, the consideration is set at $45. Before execution of the merger agreement, Nasticorp retains investment bankers who, after exhaustive study, determine the value of Conglom to be $150 million, after subtracting its debt at market value. They value M at $60 million, R at $60 million, and T at $30 million on a "going concern" basis. Shareholder (S) brings an appraisal proceeding under section 262.

A disgruntled former employee of Nasticorp leaks a document to S. This internal memorandum is a study of Conglom conducted prior to the takeover. This describes a "reorganization plan" pursuant to which Nasticorp will sell R and T in the corporate asset market after the acquisition. According to the memo, (1) Nasticorp expects to realize between $60 and $70 million for T and $55 to $65 million for R, and (2) Nasticorp will retain M because it is a good "fit" with its other manufacturing businesses; given the fit, M is worth $70 million to Nasticorp.

S introduces the memorandum as evidence of Conglom's value. Should the court admit the memorandum? If the memorandum is relevant evidence, what role should it play in the valuation? Is projected sale price of T of $60 to $70 million a part of the *ex ante* going concern value of T or a "liquidation" figure? Does one have to know what the potential acquirers would do with the assets? Can S assert the $70 million figure for T on a "control premium" theory?

Suppose S introduces evidence that Conglom's managers were considering an arm's length sale of T for $60 to $70 million with a subsequent dividend of the proceeds to its shareholders? Is this evidence of "going concern" value?

Suppose Nasticorp introduces evidence that Conglom's value is $150 million based on a comparison with three "comparable" conglomerates, each of which operates a retail, manufacturing and timber subsidiary. Does this submission block consideration of a higher "segmented" valuation submitted by S's expert?

What would the result be if the Delaware block approach is taken? How would the asset value of Conglom be calculated, and what weight should it take in the block?

Suppose the firm being appraised has a single operating division wholly owned by a parent doing no other business. May the court include a control premium in its appraisal?

NOTE: PREMIUMS, DISCOUNTS, AND MERGER GAIN

1. *Constituents of Premiums.*

What value factors comprise the control premiums awarded by the court *Rapid-American*? Reconsider Kraakman's discussion of the constituents of takeover premiums, supra. If the control premiums awarded in *Rapid–American* are made up of the same elements as the takeover premiums in Kraakman's discussion, are they not impermissible elements of value "arising from the accomplishment or expectation of the merger" within section 262? Does the determination of whether a premium arises from the merger depend on its particular components? If the premium stems from perceptions of management misinvestment or expectations of other synergistic gains, is it impermissible in an appraisal proceeding, while a premium due to market pricing imperfections may be awarded? In that case, given Kraakman's discussion, how workable is the distinction between value elements arising from the merger and value elements independent of the merger?

For the argument that the interpolation of premiums in appraisal cases has gone farther than market economics can sustain, see Booth, Minority Discounts and Control Premiums in Appraisal Proceedings, 57 Bus. Law. 127 (2001).

2. *Value as of the Date of the Merger.*

The Delaware Supreme Court again discussed the distinction between value elements arising from the merger and value elements independent of the merger in **Cede & Co. v. Technicolor, Inc.,** 684 A.2d 289 (Del.1996). This was the delayed appeal of Chancellor Allen's 1990 appraisal of Technicolor, see supra Section B.3. The appraisal proceeding, held in abeyance pending determination of Cinerama's personal liability action, revived upon the termination of the liability action in the defendants' favor. See Cinerama v. Technicolor, 663 A.2d 1156 (Del.Supr.1995).

The appeal addressed only one question—whether the firm to be appraised was "Kamerman's Technicolor" or "Perelman's Technicolor."

Kamerman's Technicolor was the going concern under the business plan of the incumbent CEO and board. This plan centered on Technicolor's principal business, theatrical film processing. Kamerman and his team also had entered the field of rapid consumer film processing by establishing a network of stores offering one-hour film development. The business, named One Hour Photo ("OHP"), required Technicolor to invest about $150 million. Technicolor announced this ambitious venture in May 1981, and on the date of the announcement, its stock rose to a high of $22.13. But OHP turned out to be an expensive failure. For the fiscal year ending June 1982, Technicolor reported an eighty percent decline of consolidated net income—from $17.073 million to $3.445 million. Its stock fell to a low of $8.37.

Perelman's Technicolor was Technicolor after implementing Ronald Perelman's business plan. Perelman acquired control of Technicolor through a friendly tender offer and second step merger. The Court describes these transactions and the business plan as follows, 684 A.2d at 293:

"The Court of Chancery made a factual finding that, 'upon acquiring control' of Technicolor, Perelman and his associates 'began to dismember what they saw as a badly conceived melange of businesses.' Perelman testified: 'Presumably we made the evaluation of the business of Technicolor before we made the purchase, not after.' That evaluation assumed the retention of the Professional and Government Services Groups and the disposition of OHP [and a number of smaller unsuccessful divisions].

"Consequently, immediately after becoming Technicolor's controlling share-holder, MAF 'started looking for buyers for several of the [Technicolor] divisions.' Bear Stearns & Co. was also retained by MAF in December 1982 to assist it in disposing of Technicolor assets. A target date of June 30, 1983 was set for liquidating all of Technicolor's excess assets. As of December 31, 1982, MAF was projecting that $54 million would be realized from asset sales. In December 1982, the Board of Technicolor notified its stockholders of a special shareholders meeting on January 24, 1983. At the meeting, the Technicolor shareholders voted * * * in favor of the proposed merger. MAF and Technicolor completed the merger."

The Supreme Court ruled as follows, 684 A.2d at 298–300:

"The Court of Chancery * * * excluded any value that was admittedly part of Technicolor as a going concern on the date of the merger, if that value was created by substituting new management or redeploying assets during the transient period between the first and second steps of this two-step merger, i.e., Perelman's Plan. The Court of Chancery reasoned that valuing Technicolor as a going concern, under the Perelman Plan, on the date of the merger, would be tantamount to awarding Cinerama a proportionate share of a control premium, which the Court of Chancery deemed to be both economically undesirable and contrary to this Court's holding in Bell v. Kirby Lumber Corp., Del.Supr., 413 A.2d 137, 140–42 (1980). See also Rapid–American Corp. v. Harris, Del.Supr., 603 A.2d 796, 805–07 (1992). Thus, the Court of Chancery concluded 'that value [added by a majority acquiror] is not ... a part of the "going concern" in which a dissenting shareholder has a legal (or equitable) right to participate.'

"In Kirby and its progeny, including Technicolor I, this Court has explained that the dissenter in an appraisal action is entitled to receive a proportionate share of fair value in the going concern on the date of the merger, rather than value that is determined on a liquidated basis. Bell v. Kirby Lumber Corp., 413 A.2d at 142; * * * accord Rapid–American Corp. v. Harris, 603 A.2d at 802–03. Thus, the company must first be valued as an operating entity. Cavalier Oil Corp. v. Harnett, 564 A.2d at 1144. In that regard, one of the most important factors to consider is the 'nature of the enterprise' that is the subject of the appraisal proceeding. Rapid–American Corp. v. Harris, 603 A.2d at 805 * * *.

"In a two-step merger, to the extent that value has been added following a change in majority control before cash-out, it is still value attributable to the going concern, i.e., the extant 'nature of the enterprise,' on the date of the merger. See Rapid–American Corp. v. Harris, 603 A.2d at 805. The dissenting shareholder's proportionate interest is determined only after the company has been valued as an operating entity on the date of the merger. Cavalier Oil Corp. v. Harnett, 564 A.2d at 1144 * * *. Consequently, value added to the going concern by the 'majority acquiror,' during the transient period of a two-step merger, accrues to the benefit of all shareholders and must be included in the appraisal process on the date of the merger. See Rapid–American Corp. v. Harris, 603 A.2d 796 * * *.

"In this case, the question in the appraisal action was the fair value of Technicolor stock on the date of the merger, January 24, 1983, as Technicolor was operating pursuant to the Perelman Plan. The Court of Chancery erred, as a matter of law, by determining the fair value of Technicolor on the date of the merger 'but for' the Perelman Plan; or, in other words, by valuing Technicolor as it was operating on October 29, 1982, pursuant to the Kamerman Plan. By failing to accord Cinerama the full proportionate value of its shares in the going concern on the date of the merger, the Court of Chancery imposed a penalty upon Cinerama for lack of control. Cavalier Oil Corp. v. Harnett, 564 A.2d at 1145; accord Rapid–American Corp. v. Harris, 603 A.2d at 805–07; Bell v. Kirby Lumber Corp., 413 A.2d at 140–42.

"The 'accomplishment or expectation' of the merger exception in Section 262 is very narrow, 'designed to eliminate use of pro forma data and projections of a speculative variety relating to the completion of a merger.' Weinberger v. UOP, Inc., 457 A.2d at 713. That narrow exclusion does not encompass known elements of value, including those which exist on the date of the merger because of a majority acquiror's interim action in a two-step cash-out transaction. Cf. In re Shell Oil Co., 607 A.2d at 1218–19. '[O]nly the speculative elements of value that may arise from the "accomplishment or expectation" of the merger' should have been excluded from the Court of Chancery's calculation of fair value on the date of the merger. Weinberger v. UOP, Inc., 457 A.2d at 713 * * *. The Court of Chancery's determination not to value Technicolor as a going concern on the date of the merger under the Perelman Plan, resulted in an understatement of Technicolor's fair value in the appraisal action. * * *

  * * *

"Upon remand, it is within the Court of Chancery's discretion to select one of the parties' valuation models as its general framework, or fashion its own, to determine fair value in the appraisal proceeding. See Rapid–American Corp. v. Harris, 603 A.2d at 804. * * * "

3. *Evidence of Real World Transactions.*

Return to the Problem preceding this Note and change the facts. Suppose immediately after the closing of the merger and prior to the trial of the appraisal proceeding, the surviving corporation receives an unsolicited communication from a broker representing a potential buyer of R's assets. A deal is quickly concluded and R's assets sold for $66 million—a figure 10 percent higher than the figure in the valuation. Should this 10 percent premium be relevant in the appraisal valuation? On similar facts, **Sieg Co. v. Kelly**, 568 N.W.2d 794 (Iowa Supr.1997), holds that such a premium need not be considered under the Iowa appraisal statute. The dissenting shareholders, said the court, are entitled to compensation for the loss of their "opportunity to share in the company's future prospects; they are not entitled to actually share in the realization of those future prospects." Thus the fact of sale and payment does not automatically trigger entitlement to a *pro rata* share in the context of the appraisal proceeding. The *Sieg* court acknowledged a possible basis for admitting the evidence, however: The dissenter might get evidence of the sale price admitted as probative of the value of the company's future prospects as of the time of the merger. But that was not the basis for admission asserted in the case.

M.P.M. Enterprises, Inc. v. Gilbert, 731 A.2d 790 (Del.1999), presents the converse problem. This is a rare case of an arm's-length transaction in which the appraisal plaintiff managed to establish a fair value much in excess of the merger price. The corporate defendant, MPM, appealed, contending that the Chancery Court had abused its discretion in refusing to compare the figures resulting from the DCF analysis that yielded the high figure to the lower merger price and the amounts of some prior offers. The Supreme Court found no abuse of discretion, 731 A.2d at 797:

> "* * * A merger price resulting from arms-length negotiations where there are no claims of collusion is a very strong indication of fair value. But in an appraisal action, that merger price must be accompanied by evidence tending to show that it represents the going concern value of the company rather than just the value of the company to one specific buyer. In this case, MPM failed to present this additional evidence with respect to either the merger or the prior offers. This led the Court of Chancery to decide that these values were of only marginal relevance, if any. In our view, this determination was not an abuse of discretion."

Le Beau v. M.G. Bancorporation, Inc.

Court of Chancery of Delaware, 1998.
1998 WL 44993.

■ Jacobs, Vice Chancellor.

     * * *

I.   FACTS

A.   The Parties and the Merger

The Petitioners are shareholders who owned 18,151 shares of common stock of MGB before the Merger. The Respondents are Southwest Bancorp, Inc. ("Southwest") and its subsidiary, MGB. Before the Merger, MGB was a Delaware-chartered bank holding company headquartered in Worth, Illinois. MGB had two operating Illinois-chartered bank subsidiaries, Mount Greenwood Bank ("Greenwood") and Worth Bancorp, Inc.

("WBC"). Both banks served customers in the southwestern Chicago metropolitan area. MGB owned 100% of Mount Greenwood and 75.5% of WBC.

Before the Merger, Southwestern owned 91.68% of MGB's common shares. On November 17, 1993, MGB was merged into Southwest in a "short form" merger under 8 Del. C. § 253. Because the Merger was accomplished unilaterally, neither MGB's board of directors nor its minority shareholders were legally required to, or did, vote on the transaction. MGB's minority shareholders were offered $41 in cash per share in the Merger. The Petitioners rejected that offer, electing instead to pursue their statutory appraisal rights.

To assist it in setting the Merger price, Southwest engaged Alex Sheshunoff & Co. Investment Bankers ("Sheshunoff") to determine the "fair market value" of MGB's minority shares. In a report submitted to Southwest on or about October 28, 1993, Sheshunoff determined that the fair market value of MGB's minority shares was $41 per share as of June 30, 1993. Thereafter, a stockholders breach of fiduciary duty damage action was filed attacking the Merger, and this appraisal proceeding was also commenced. On July 5, 1995, this Court issued an Opinion in the companion class action, holding that Sheshunoff had performed its appraisal in a legally improper manner. The basis for the Court's conclusion was that Sheshunoff had determined only the "fair market value" of MGB's minority shares, as opposed to valuing MGB in its entirety as a going concern and determining the fair value of the minority shares as a pro-rata percentage of that value.

B. The Petitioners' Valuation

* * * At trial the Petitioners' expert witness, David Clarke ("Clarke"), testified that as of the Merger date the fair value of MGB common stock was at least $85 per share. In arriving at that conclusion, Clarke used three distinct methodologies to value MGB's two operating bank subsidiaries: (I) the comparative publicly-traded company approach, (ii) the discounted cash flow ("DCF") method, and (iii) the comparative acquisition technique. Clarke then added a control premium to the values of the two subsidiaries to reflect the value of the holding company's (MGB's) controlling interest in those subsidiaries.[3] Lastly, Clarke then added the value of MGB's remaining assets to the sum of his valuations of the two subsidiaries, to arrive at an overall fair value of $85 per share for MGB.

What follows is a more detailed description of how Clarke performed his valuation(s) of MGB.

1. Comparative Company Approach

Clarke's comparative publicly-traded company approach involved five steps: (1) identifying an appropriate set of comparable companies, (2)

---

3. The Petitioners had instructed Clarke that Delaware law mandated such a premium at the subsidiary level, relying on Rapid-American v. Harris, 603 A.2d 796, 804–05 (1992). In Rapid–American the Supreme Court of Delaware held that the trial court had erred by failing to include a "control premium" in valuing the subsidiaries of a holding company that was the subject of an appraisal. * * *

identifying the multiples of earnings and book value at which the comparable companies traded, (3) comparing certain of MGB's financial fundamentals (e.g., return on assets and return on equity) to those of the comparable companies, (4) making certain adjustments to those financial fundamentals, and (5) adding an appropriate control premium. After completing the first four steps, Clarke arrived at a value for WBC of $33.059 million ($48.02 per share), and for Greenwood of $20.952 million ($30.44 per share). Clarke next determined that during the period January 1989 to June 1993, acquirors of controlling interests in publicly-traded companies had paid an average premium of at least 35%. On that basis, Clarke concluded that a 35% premium was appropriate, and applied that premium to the values he had determined for Greenwood and WBC, to arrive at fair values of $43.3 million ($62.90 per share) for WBC and $27.1 million ($39.37 per share) for Greenwood, respectively. Clarke then valued MGB's 75.5% controlling interest in WBC at $32.691 million ($47.49 per share), and MGB's 100% interest in Greenwood at $27.1 million ($39.37 per share), under his comparative company approach.

2. Discounted Cash Flow Approach

Clarke's DCF valuation analysis involved four steps: (1) projecting the future net cash flows available to MGB's shareholders for ten years after the Merger date, (2) discounting those future cash flows to present value as of the Merger date by using a discount rate based on the weighted average cost of capital ("WACC"), (3) adding a terminal value that represented the present value of all future cash flows generated after the ten year projection period, and (4) applying a control premium to the sum of (2) and (3).

Clarke did not create his own cash flow projections. He used the projections made by Sheshunoff at the time of the Merger, because Southwest's own management had accepted those projections when they fixed the Merger price. Clarke also accepted Sheshunoff's ten year projection period, because he independently had concluded that it would require ten years for MGB's cash flows to stabilize. Based on a 1996 Ibbotson Associates ("Ibbotson") study of the banking industry, Clarke concluded that the appropriate "small stock" premium to be used in the capital asset pricing model ("CAPM") to determine MGB's discount rate (WACC), was 1%, and that the appropriate discount rate (WACC) for MGB was 12%. Applying that 12% discount rate, Clarke calculated the present value of WBC's future cash flows to be $17.251 million, and WBC's terminal value to be $14.824 million. Applying that same 12% discount rate, Clarke arrived at a present value of $10.937 million, and a terminal value of $9.138 million, for Greenwood.

Applying the same 35% control premium to those values of the two subsidiaries, Clarke calculated MGB's 75.5% interest in WBC at $33.824 million or $49.14 per share; and MGB's 100% interest in Greenwood at $28.3 million, or $41.11 per share.

3. Comparative Acquisition Approach

Clarke's third valuation approach, the comparative acquisition method, focused upon multiples of MGB's last twelve months earnings and its tangible book value. Those multiples were determined by reference to the prices at which the stock of comparable companies had been sold in transactions involving the sale of control. Unlike the comparative company and DCF valuation approaches, this method did not require adding a control premium to the values of the subsidiaries because under that methodology, the parent holding company's controlling interest in the subsidiaries was already accounted for.

In valuing MGB under his third approach, Clarke identified three transactions involving community banks in the relevant geographic area that occurred within one year of the Merger. He also considered data published by The Chicago Corporation in its September 1993 issue of Midwest Bank & Thrift Survey. From these sources, Clarke determined that (I) control of WBC could be sold for a price between a multiple of 14 times WBC's last twelve months' earnings and 200% of WBC's tangible book value, and that (ii) control of Greenwood could be sold for a price between a multiple of 12 times Greenwood's last twelve months' earnings and 175% of its tangible book value. Giving equal weight to these two sets of values, Clarke valued MGB's 75.5% interest in WBC at $28.8 million (75.5% x $38.1 million) or $41.84 per share, and MGB's 100% interest in Greenwood, at $22.9 million, or $33.27 per share.

4.   MGB's Remaining Assets

Having valued MGB's two subsidiaries, Clarke then determined the fair value of MGB's remaining net assets, which included (I) a $6.83 million note payable by Southwest, (ii) certain intangibles that Clarke did not include in his valuation, (iii) $78,000 in cash, and (iv) other assets worth $2000. These assets totaled $6.91 million, from which Clarke subtracted liabilities of $96,000 to arrive at a net asset value of $6.814 million ($9.90 per share) for MGB's remaining assets.

5.   Fair Value Computation

Clarke then added the values he had determined under each of his valuation methodologies, for (I) MGB's 75.5% interest in WBC, (ii) MGB's 100% interest in Greenwood, and (iii) MGB's 100% interest in its remaining assets. Under his comparative publicly-traded method, Clarke concluded that MGB's value was $76.59 per share with no control premium, and $96.76 per share with a control premium. Under his DCF approach, Clarke determined that MGB's value was $74.75 per share with no control premium, and $100.15 per share with a control premium. And under his comparative acquisitions method, Clarke concluded that MGB's minimum fair value was $85 per share, which represented the median of the values described above.

C.   The Respondents' Valuation

At trial the * * * Respondents relied upon the testimony of Mr. Robert Reilly ("Reilly"),[5] who opined that as of the Merger date, the fair value of

---

5. Reilly is an expert in performing business valuations. He was formerly the Na- tional Director of Valuation Services for De- loitte and Touche and is an accredited senior

MGB common stock was $41.90 per share—only 90 cents per share more than Sheshunoff's $41 valuation. Reilly arrived at that result by performing two separate valuations: a DCF analysis and a "capital market" analysis. Reilly did not include any control premium, having determined that a control premium was inappropriate in valuing a holding company such as MGB.

1. DCF Analysis

Reilly's DCF analysis consisted of: (1) projecting MGB's future net cash flows available to shareholders for a period of five years after the Merger date, (2) determining an appropriate discount rate and discounting those future cash flows back to the Merger date, and (3) adding a terminal value that represented the present value of all future cash flows beyond the five year projection period. Reilly used a five year period, because in his opinion any longer interval would be too speculative. Relying on a 1992 Ibbotson study that was not specific to the banking industry, he also concluded that 5.2% was the appropriate small stock size premium to use in the CAPM for purposes of determining the WACC for MGB.

In determining an appropriate discount rate, Reilly concluded that MGB was subject to certain company-specific risks, namely, litigation involving its data processor (BYSIS) and MGB's dependence upon a single key supplier. Reilly quantified those risks at four percentage points, and on that basis concluded that the appropriate discount rate for MGB was 18%. Applying that 18% discount rate to MGB's future cash flows, Reilly valued MGB at $29.220 million, or $42.45 per share, on the basis of his DCF approach.

2. Capital Market Method

Reilly's second method for valuing MGB was the "capital market" method, which involved: (1) identifying a portfolio of guideline publicly-traded companies, (2) identifying appropriate pricing multiples for those companies, (3) using the multiples for the guideline companies to calculate the appropriate pricing multiples for MGB[6] and (4) applying the multiples to the corresponding financial indicators for MGB. By this method, Reilly concluded that MGB was worth $28.4 million, or $41.26 per share, at the time of the Merger.

---

appraiser and a certified public accountant. The Petitioners claim that Reilly's entire valuation should be rejected because Reilly had no significant experience in valuing banks or bank holding companies, and was therefore not competent to value bank holding companies. Although the Court ultimately rejects Reilly's valuations, it is for reasons that concern the merits of his valuation approaches, not his expertise.

6. Reilly's pricing multiples were all related to the market value of invested capital ("MVIC"). Reilly computed the ratios of MVIC to: (1) earnings before interest and taxes ("EBIT"); (2) earnings before interest, depreciation and taxes ("EBIDT"); (3) debt free net income ("DFNI"); (4) debt free cash flow ("DFCF"); (5) interest incomes; and (6) total book value of invested capital ("TBVIC").

Reilly then averaged his DCF and capital market valuations, to arrive at an ultimate fair value for MGB of $41.90 per share.[1]

* * *

III. ANALYSIS

* * *

A. MGB's Fair Value

* * * [T]his Court determined in its earlier Opinion that Sheshunoff's $41 valuation was impermissible under 8 Del. C. § 262, because it was an appraisal not of the entire corporation as a going concern but only of a minority block of its shares. Presumably that is why the Respondents chose not to rely upon the Sheshunoff valuation or to call Sheshunoff personnel as trial witnesses. Instead, Respondents elected to rely solely upon Reilly's valuation, which resulted in the same $41 per share value that Sheshunoff had arrived at by a valuation approach found to be improper.

The fact that Reilly's per share fair value determination serendipitously turned out to be only 90 cents per share more than Sheshunoff's legally flawed $41 valuation, cannot help but render Respondent's valuation position highly suspect and meriting the most careful judicial scrutiny. As a matter of plain common sense, it would appear evident that a proper fair value determination based upon a going concern valuation of the entire company, would significantly exceed a $41 per share fair market valuation of only a minority block of its shares. If Respondents choose to contend otherwise, it is their burden to persuade the Court that $41.90 per share

1. [Ed. Note] The Court included the following chart summarizing the valuation evidence:

Valuation in $'000's:	WBC	75.5% of WBC	Greenwood	Other Assets	Total	Per Share
Petitioners (Clarke)						
Comparative Publicly–Traded Method:	33,059	24,960	20,952	6,814	52,726	76.59
With Control Premium:	43,300	32,692	27,100	6,814	66,606	96.76
DCF Method:	32,075	24,217	20,079	6,814	51,110	74.25
With Control Premium:	44,800	33,824	28,300	6,814	68,938	100.15
Comparative Acquisitions Method:	38,100	28,800	22,900	6,814	58,514	85.00=-fair value
Respondents (Reilly)						
Capital Market Method:					28,400	41.26
DCF Method:					29,220	42.45
					Average:	41.90=-fair value
Sheshunoff (Updated) (Without Control Premium)						
Adjusted Book Value:						64.13
Adjusted Earnings						76.80

represents MGB's fair value. The Court concludes that the Respondents have fallen far short of carrying their burden, and independently determines that the fair value of MGB at the time of the Merger was $85 per share.

1.   The Validity of Reilly's "Capital Market" Approach

The Court first addresses whether Reilly's capital market approach is legally permissible. That valuation approach (to repeat) involved deriving various pricing multiples from selected publicly-traded companies, and then applying those multiples to MGB, resulting in a valuation of $41.26 per share.

The Petitioners argue that Reilly's capital market valuation method is impermissible because it includes a built-in minority discount. The valuation literature, including a treatise co-authored by Reilly himself, supports that position, and Respondents have introduced no evidence to the contrary. Nor did the Respondents establish that Reilly's capital market method is generally accepted by the financial community for purposes of valuing bank holding companies, as distinguished from other types of enterprises. Reilly determined the ratio of MVIC to other financial measures such as EBIT, EBIDT, DFNI, DFCF, Interest Income, and TBVIC—ratios that the record indicates are not used to value banks.

Because Reilly's capital market method results in a minority valuation, and the Respondents have failed to establish that that approach is generally accepted in the financial community to value banks or bank holding companies, the Court must conclude that in this specific case Reilly's capital market approach is improper, and must be rejected.[18]

2.   The Parties' Respective Applications of the Comparative Publicly–Traded and DCF Valuation Methodologies

The Court next considers (I) whether Clarke properly applied his comparative company analysis to MGB, and (ii) whether both sides' experts properly applied their respective DCF analyses to MGB. The validity per se of these two valuation methodologies is not in dispute.

a.   Comparative Company Approach

A primary issue dividing the parties concerns the companies chosen as "comparable" to the corporation being appraised. A determination of that kind is necessarily fact intensive.

In performing his comparative company analysis, Clarke selected as comparables, banks having financial ratios, geographic locations, and demographic factors similar to those of MGB's two bank subsidiaries. Reilly, on the other hand, included companies that operated outside MGB's geographic location, in different economic environments, and in different lines of business. Where the valuation exercise rests upon data derived from companies comparable to the company being valued, it stands to reason that the more "comparable" the company, the more reliable will be the

---

18. This conclusion should not be read as a categorical, matter-of-law determination that Reilly's capital market approach is an inappropriate method to value banks. The opposite may be true, but in this specific case the Respondents failed to discharge their burden of proof on that issue.

resulting valuation information. The Court concludes that in this case it was sounder practice to use as comparables suburban banks located in the same geographic area (as Clarke did), rather than banks located outside of WBC's and Greenwood's immediate areas (as Reilly did). Accordingly, I find Clarke's comparable companies to be superior to Reilly's.

Another key difference between the parties' comparative publicly-traded company approaches is that Clarke used the price-to-earnings and price-to-book value financial multiples, whereas Reilly used multiples based upon the market value of invested capital ("MVIC"). Relying upon various valuation authorities and publications, the Petitioners argue that where the enterprise being valued is a bank, the relevant ratios are price-to-earnings and price-to-book value. Reilly disagreed. He opined that it is more appropriate to compare the different financial measures as a fraction of MVIC, because that approach eliminates the distortions inherent in Clarke's financial ratios. Reilly did not elaborate on what those distortions were, however, nor did he point to specific cases where MVIC was considered an appropriate financial measure of a bank or bank holding company. Given this record, the Respondents have not persuaded the Court that MVIC is widely accepted in the financial community as a measure of the value of a bank or bank holding company.[21] Clarke's financial measures are generally accepted in the financial community for valuing banks, and the Court accepts them.

A third major difference between the parties' comparative company approaches is that Clarke used historical financial data going back five years before the Merger, whereas Reilly used historical financial data going back 2.75 years. In performing bank valuations, five year historical information is typically used. Reilly's position was that the banking industry had changed dramatically during the five years before the Merger, such that it was not appropriate to rely upon financial data going back that far.

At the heart of this dispute are the experts' differing assumptions about MGB's future growth prospects. The Respondents paint a bleak picture of MGB's future prospects for increasing its revenues; the Petitioners argue that MGB's future prospects were far brighter. Petitioners agree that a company's more recent historical economic averages are a good indicator of its future growth rate, but emphasize that a firm's financial trends are often more reliably evidenced by its performance over the past five years. I concur. Petitioners have demonstrated that MGB's historical performance, whether over the past five years, three years, or twelve months before the Merger, indicated significant future growth. * * *

A fourth major difference between the parties' comparative company analyses is that Reilly relied upon comparable company stock prices on the day before the Merger, whereas Clarke used price quotations six weeks before the Merger. Because the merger date (more specifically, the date before the public announcement of a merger) is normally the time that is

---

21. The use of MVIC as a tool to value other kinds of enterprises is, of course, widely accepted. See, Rapid–American Corp. v. Harris, 603 A.2d 796 (1992). Again, the Court's conclusion that MVIC has not been shown to be an appropriate measure of a bank's value is fact-specific to this case, and by virtue of the Respondent's failure of proof.

relevant, and because the Petitioners made no effort to justify Clarke's use of stock prices going back six weeks before the Merger, the Court cannot accept Clarke's comparative company valuation, despite the validity of the technique itself. Clarke's use of six week old pre-merger stock prices represents a departure from the norm without demonstrated justification.

To summarize, Reilly's capital market approach must be rejected because it was not shown to be generally accepted in the financial community for bank valuation purposes. Clarke's comparative company valuation must be rejected because it was improperly applied in this specific case. Accordingly, the only valuation methodologies remaining to be considered are (I) Reilly's and Clarke's DCF valuations and (ii) Clarke's comparative acquisition analysis.

b.   The Parties' DCF Analyses

The difference between Clarke's 12% discount rate and Reilly's 18% discount rate is attributable primarily to their different estimates of MGB's cost of equity capital, and their different assessments of the company specific risks confronting MGB at the time of the Merger. Reilly selected an equity risk premium based upon a 1992 Ibbotson study indicating that an appropriate small stock premium factor was 5.2%. Clarke relied on a 1996 Ibbotson study indicating that a premium of 1% was appropriate. The problem with the 1992 Ibbotson study was that it is not specific to the banking industry. The problem with the 1996 Ibbotson study is that although it was specific to the banking industry, the Petitioners have not shown that the data contained in that study (and relied upon by Clarke) was in existence as of the Merger date. The Court, therefore, is unable to accept the 1996 Ibbotson study, and the 12% discount rate derived therefrom.

Reilly's 18% discount rate is also flawed, however, because it rests on the unsupported assumption that at the time of the Merger, MGB was subject to certain material risks that required a steep discount of MGB's projected future cash flow. Reilly placed great emphasis upon MGB's dependence upon one key supplier and upon the pending litigation involving BYSIS, MGB's data process server as a basis to conclude that MGB involved abnormal business risk to a potential acquiror. The underlying evidence that these "risks" were material is unpersuasive. No document contemporaneous with the Merger shows that Southwest's or MGB's management or boards viewed these developments as material risks. Importantly, nowhere in its valuation report did Sheshunoff allude to those risks. That fact significantly diminishes the credibility of a Southwest employee's litigation-driven trial testimony that management viewed these risks as significant. Of considerable importance also is that Sheshunoff concluded that a 10% discount factor (2% lower than Clarke's) was appropriate, and management accepted that discount assumption. Accordingly, the Court concludes that Reilly's 18% discount rate is inappropriately high and not supported by the record.

The final major difference between the parties' DCF analyses is that Clarke projected ten years of future cash flows at a constant growth rate of

4% using many of Sheshunoff's projections; whereas Reilly projected future cash flows for only five years, at a growth rate that decreased after the fifth year, using his (Reilly's) own projections. Sheshunoff used a ten year projection period for future cash flows, and assumed a constant rate of growth. Because Sheshunoff performed its valuation at the time of the Merger, without the benefit of hindsight and when no litigation was pending, and management accepted its assumptions, the Court accepts Sheshunoff's DCF assumptions (except for its minority discount) as more appropriate than Reilly's litigation-driven (and extremely conservative) assumptions.

Because neither side has supported certain key DCF valuation assumptions by a preponderance of persuasive evidence, the Court is unable to accept either Clarke's or Reilly's discounted cash flow valuations. That leaves Clarke's comparative acquisition approach, which the Court turns to next.

2. The "Control Premium" Question and the Validity of Clarke's Comparative Acquisition Approach

Having rejected Clarke's DCF and comparative company valuations, both of which involved directly adding a control premium to the values of MGB's two subsidiaries, the Court need not decide whether the direct addition of a premium is or is not mandated by Rapid–American. Nonetheless, the Court must address the control premium issue, but in a different context. That is, the Court must decide whether Clarke's comparative acquisition valuation, in which a control premium is implicit, is proscribed by § 262. I conclude that it is not.

In Rapid-American Corp. v. Harris, [Del.Supr., 603 A.2d 796, 806–07 (1992)],the Delaware Supreme Court held that in valuing a holding company for § 262 appraisal purposes, it was appropriate to include a control premium as an element of the fair value of the majority-owned subsidiaries. * * *

The Respondents argue that Rapid–American turned on the "unique fact" that its subsidiaries were involved in three different industries. I do not read Rapid–American to hold that that "unique" fact was in any way critical to the result. The Respondents' construction of that case is too narrow. What the Supreme Court ruled is that a holding company's ownership of a controlling interest in its subsidiaries is an independent element of value that must be taken into account in determining a fair value for the parent company. Thus, the rationale of Rapid–American applies to MGB, and the Respondents have not shown otherwise.

The Respondents also challenge Clarke's comparative acquisition approach on a different basis. Pointing to the command in 8 Del. C. § 262(h) that fair value must be determined "exclusive of post-merger events or other possible business combinations," the Respondents urge that any valuation method that includes a control premium as an element of "fair value" necessarily represents post-merger synergies proscribed by § 262(h). I cannot agree. The (implicit) control premium at issue here is not the product of post-merger synergies. Rather, that control premium reflects an independent element of value existing at the time of the merger, flowing from the fact that the parent company owned a controlling interest in its subsidiaries at that point in time. Therefore, Clarke's comparative acquisition valuation cannot be invalidated on that basis either.

Because the Respondents have not challenged Clarke's comparative acquisition approach on any valid ground, and because the Court has rejected the parties' valuations based on their other methodologies, by process of elimination the only evidence of MGB's fair value is the $85 per share Clarke arrived at by the comparative acquisition method. Having no other adjudicated basis to value MGB, the Court would be justified in accepting $85 per share as the fair value of MGB, and does so—but not by default or uncritically.

The Court is mindful that $85 per share is more than double the Merger price. The Court is also aware of its role under § 262, which is to determine fair value independently. In discharging that institutional function as an independent appraiser, the Court should, where possible, test the soundness of its valuation conclusion against whatever reliable corroborative evidence the record contains. On that score the record falls far short of perfection. Limited corroborative evidence is available, however, in the form of Sheshunoff's 1993 fair market valuation, (I) adjusted by Clarke to exclude Sheshunoff's minority discount and (ii) updated by Clarke to reflect value data as of November 17, 1993, the date of the Merger. When Sheshunoff's 1993 valuation is adjusted in that manner, the resulting value of MGB is $48,504,664 or $70.46 per share with no control premium. If (for purposes of illustration) a 20% control premium were added, the resulting value would be $56,842,796.80 or $82.57 per share; and if the premium were 35%, the resulting value would be $63,096,394.40, or $91.66 per share. The $85 per share fair value based upon Clarke's comparative acquisition approach fits comfortably within that (hypothetical) range of values.

NOTE: VALUATION CONCEPTS INTRODUCED IN *LE BEAU*

1. *Adjusting for Nonconstant Growth.*

Neither expert in *Le Beau* uses a constant growth model to derive DCF. Instead, each assumes that cash flows will grow for a limited period only, with flat returns thereafter. This approach reflects the conventional wisdom that firms go through life cycles. They grow faster than the economy as a whole during the early part of their lives; later they match the economy's growth. Valuation models reflecting this scenario can be more complicated than the two phase growth/no growth models in *Le Beau*. For example, a projection could assume a period of supergrowth, followed by a period of normal growth. A third period of growth slower than that of the economy or a third period of no growth might be added. See Brigham, Gapenski & Ehrhardt, Financial Management: Theory and Practice 338–345(9th ed. 1999).

Nonconstant growth scenarios mean increased arithmetical detail. Assume a firm the dividend of which is expected to grow at a 14 percent rate for 10 years with no further growth thereafter. The present value calculation can be expressed as follows:

$$PV = \sum_{t=1}^{10} \frac{D_0\,(1.14)^t}{(1+r)^t} + \sum_{t=11}^{\infty} \frac{D_{10}\,(1.00)^{t-10}}{(1+r)^t}$$

Let us lay out the numbers, assuming a 16 percent discount rate and a dividend of $2 at t_0. The first 10 years look like this:

Year	Dividend $g=14\%$	PV of Dividend $r=16\%$
1	$ 2.28	$ 1.97
2	2.60	1.93
3	2.96	1.90
4	3.38	1.87
5	3.85	1.83
6	4.39	1.80
7	5.00	1.77
8	5.71	1.74
9	6.50	1.71
10	7.41	1.68
PV(first 10 years)=		$ 18.20

Note that since the discount rate is higher than the rate of dividend growth, the present value of each growing dividend declines steadily.

To derive a terminal value we find the PV of the dividends expected from Year 11 to infinity. This is a two step exercise. First, we find the expected value of the stock as of the end of year 10:

PV = A/r
    = $7.41/0.16
    = 46.3402

Next we find the present value of that Year 10 stock price:

PV_{10} = $\dfrac{46.3402}{(1.16)^{10}}$

PV_{10} = 10.5046

The present value of the stock is the sum of the present values of the 10 year growing payment stream ($18.20) and the no-growth perpetuity that begins to flow after Year 10:

$$PV_0 = \$18.20 + 10.504 = \$28.70.$$

2. *Terminal Value.*

The *Le Beau* valuations manifest a conservative variation on the theme just described. Both assume *no* growth after the early period (whether or five or ten years). This approach shows up in many contemporary cases. **Cede & Co. v. Technicolor,** 1990 WL 161084 (Del.Ch.) describes the underlying intuition:

"[This approach] assumes * * * that for every company its particular set of comparative advantages establish, as of any moment, a future period of some greater or lesser length during which it will be able to earn rates of return that exceed its cost of capital. Beyond that point, the company (as of the present moment of valuation) can expect to earn no returns in excess of its cost of capital and therefore, beyond that point, no additional shareholder value will be created. [This] is an application of elementary notions of neo-classical economics: profits above the cost of capital in an industry will attract competitors, who will over some time period drive returns down to the point at which returns equal the cost of capital. * * * The existence of such a point in time does not mean that there is no value attributed to the period beyond that point, but rather that there is no further value growth."

The "terminal value" approach to DCF valuation reflects the sensible notion that it is unsafe to project perpetual growth in a competitive world. But is it possible that a terminal value derived from discounting a constant payment stream may result in undervaluation at many companies? The answer appears to be "yes." To see why, compare two possible justifications for a perpetual growth projection: (1) perpetual growth in market share at the expense of competing firms, and (2) perpetual growth in lockstep with the growth of the economy as a whole. Many valuation experts calculate terminal values that include a perpetual growth factor based on economy-wide factors. Such projections have been accepted in Delaware appraisals. Consider in this regard, **Cede & Co. v. JRC Acquisition Corp.**, 2004 WL 286963 (Del.Ch.), an appraisal in the wake of a short form merger of JR Cigar. The dissenting shareholder projected a 5 percent perpetual growth, despite general decline in the cigar market, citing an array of possible developments dismissed by the court as speculative. But the court did allow a lower perpetual growth rate of 2.5 to 3.5. Interestingly, this lower perpetual growth assumption was proposed by the respondent, through its expert, the economist Greg Jarrell. Said the court, id. at 8: "The problem with ascertaining a growth rate in perpetuity is that it is an inherently speculative enterprise. Jarrell, under questioning by the Court, was refreshingly candid when he stated: 'Who knows what the growth rate in perpetuity is going to be. It's a judgment call.' The experts, and ultimately the Court, are asked to surmise what rate a company will grow at five years into the future. This is hardly an exact science. In this type of circumstance it is difficult (if not impossible) for litigants to 'prov[e] their respective valuation positions by a preponderance of the evidence.' Nevertheless, the Court must assess whether one expert's judgment is more defensible than the other. And, on this record, it appears that Jarrell's judgment that JR Cigar's growth rate in perpetuity is at or slightly above the rate of inflation is more credible. Jarrell used a range of 2.5% (roughly equal to the long-term rate of inflation in 2000) to 3.5% in his DCF analysis. In my opinion, the upper end of that range is appropriate and fair. Using a rate of 3.5% accounts for the possibility, however marginal, that JR Cigar may be able to expand in an otherwise declining domestic market for cigars and cigarettes."

See also Cede & Co., Inc. v. MedPointe Healthcare, Inc., 2004 WL 2093967 (Del.Ch.)(combining expected inflation and a modest company growth into a perpetual growth factor).

3. *Comparing the Valuation Methods in* Le Beau.

The *comparative company comparisons* described in *Le Beau* extrapolate from two sources: (1) the comparable firms' price earnings ratios, and (2) their ratios of price to book value. The *capital market comparisons* are based on the "Market Value of Invested Capital" (MVIC) of the comparable firms. Exactly how MVIC is calculated depends on whether the "invested capital" in question is the equity capital only or the equity capital plus the debt capital. If it is the equity:

MVIC = common stock market price x number of common shares outstanding

When the debt is brought into the MVIC calculation it is either measured by a trading price from the bond market or by balance sheet book value. (Is it clear which MVIC calculation has been submitted in *Le Beau*?) The MVIC provides the basis for a series of pricing multiples when set over a series of cash flow figures. MVIC also is set over the book value of invested capital. The *comparative acquisition* approach differs markedly from the capital market and company comparisons. Where the latter approaches are based on the stock prices of comparable banks, the acquisition comparison looks at sale prices of comparable banks in the market for banks as going concern assets. Each valuation technique shares a methodology. Each relies on a *multiple* derived from hard numbers generated by comparable firms. The multiple is taken back to a hard number appearing on the books of the firm being valued. By hypothesis, if the comparable firms really are comparable, the value figure yielded by the multiple is credible.

DCF valuation differs in that the values of the flows to be discounted are soft. They are projections generated by an appraiser, sometimes an outside expert and other times, as in *Le Beau*, the firm's insiders. (The capitalization rate, in contrast, is extrapolated from comparable firms.) The diminished credibility stemming from the subjective nature of the values discounted is counterbalanced by situational sensitivity. Only the DCF approach allows adjustment for the firm's particular prospects.

Given strengths and weaknesses across the board, the practice of conducting a series of calculations under different methodologies appears to make sense. For an empirical test of the accuracy of real world DCF projections made by managers of firms undergoing leveraged buyouts, see Kaplan and Ruback, The Valuation of Cash Flow Forecasts: An Empirical Analysis, 50 J.Fin. 1059 (1995). The DCF projections in the sample were within an average of 10 percent of the market values of the completed transactions.

NOTE: THE IMPLICIT MINORITY DISCOUNT

In **Paskill Corp. v. Alcoma Corp.**, 747 A.2d 549, 556–57 (Del. Supr. 2000), the Supreme Court read *Le Beau* together with *Tri-Continental v. Battye*, supra, making a conceptual association between the premium recognized in the latter and the discount imposed in the former:

"The combined argot of law and economics requires periodic explication. *Tri-Continental* has been construed by this Court as standing for the proposition that an appraisal valuation must take into consideration the unique nature of the enterprise. In *Tri-Continental*, this Court held that the Court of Chancery had the authority to discount asset values at the corporate level, in appropriate circumstances, as a means of establishing the fair value of the entire corporation as a going concern. Read in the proper context, *Tri-Continental* was an acknowledgment that the Court of Chancery was vested with the authority to make a discount of the subject corporation's fair asset value at the corporate level because it constituted a proper application of an accepted methodology for arriving at the proper valuation of the unique corporate enterprise, i.e., in *Tri-Continental*, the Delaware Block Method was applied to value a regulated closed-end investment company with leverage that was engaged in investing in a cross-section of the stock market. Similarly, [in *LeBeau*] this Court recently upheld the Court of Chancery's conclusion that a corporate level comparative acquisition approach to valuing a company, which included a control premium for a majority interest in a subsidiary, was a relevant and reliable methodology to use in an appraisal proceeding to determine the fair market value of shares in a holding company."

The Court's association of *Tri-Continental* and *Le Beau* invites a question: Does the control premium awarded in *Rapid-American* and *Le Beau* always imply a correlative discount? That is, if holding company shareholders are entitled to compensation for the control value of each subsidiary company, should not minority shareholders of a publicly traded operating company receive a similar gross up in an appraisal proceeding? In either case, the premium would be measured by the amount to be yielded in a hypothetical arms' length sale to a third party.

The Delaware courts have been awarding such a gross up in respect of this "minority discount" in appraisals of operating companies, no longer limiting the award to the holding company-subsidiary fact pattern. The rule of thumb is 30 percent. Interestingly, the award is only granted in respect of valuations based on multiples of publicly traded comparable company stocks. No upward adjustment is made in DCF valuations. See Doft & Co. v. Travelocity.com Inc., 2004 WL 1152338 (Del.Ch.), at 11. See also, Agranoff v. Miller, 791 A.2d 880, 887 (Del.Ch.2001); Borruso v. Communications Telesystems Int'l, 753 A.2d 451, 459 (Del.Ch.1999); Bomarko v. International Telecharge, Inc., 794 A.2d 1161, 1186 n. 11 (Del.Ch.1999), aff'd, 766 A.2d 437 (Del.2000). For discussion of the law relating to minority discounts, see Coates, "Fair Value" as an Avoidable rule of Corporate Law: Minority Discounts in Conflict Transactions, 147 U.Pa. L. Rev. 1251 (1999).

Hamermesh and Wachter, The Short and Puzzling Life of the "Implicit Minority Discount" in Delaware Appraisal Law, 155 U.Pa.L.Rev. ___ (forthcoming 2007), enters a vigorous dissent to the practice. The gross up amounts to a windfall, in the view of the authors, because merger premiums stem for the most part from anticipated synergistic gains. They reason that pre-merger market price does not incorporate a discount. The authors acknowledge that acquirers pay premiums to acquire control and that control blocks command premiums, but they argue that these control premiums do not in turn imply a minority discount. Control shares, they argue, sell for more because they worth more; furthermore, their added value should not be considered a part of the firm's going concern value. Here the authors cite to Pratt, et al., Valuing a Business 349 (4th ed. 2000), for an account of the elements contributing to control block premium: (1) the nature and magnitude of nonoperating assets; (2) the nature and magnitude of discretionary expenses; (3) management quality; (4) the nature and magnitude of opportunities not being exploited by the business, and (5) the potential for easy integration of the business of the company into that of an acquirer. Hamermesh and Wachter assert that four of the five factors should not occasion recovery in an appraisal proceeding. They characterize factors (1) and (2) as agency cost items, items that in their view are always are factored as negatives into the firm's going concern value. The dissenting shareholder having bought the stock at a price adjusted downward to take agency costs into account, the appraisal proceeding should not open an opportunity for their recovery. They view item (3), which looks to management improvement after the merger, as a noncompensable item of gain arising in respect of the merger. Item (5) is similarly noncompensable because it amounts to a synergy. They treat item (4) differently, however, at least to the extent an unexploited business opportunity is viewed is seen as a possible source of value within the scope of the firm's business plan prior to the merger.

NOTE: THE MARKETABILITY DISCOUNT

In the case of a close corporation, does the lack of marketability justify a deduction? Or is the dissenter entitled to an aliquot share of the value of the firm? **Lawson Mardon Wheaton, Inc. v. Smith**, 160 N.J. 383, 734 A.2d 738 (1999), an appraisal in respect of a recapitalization engineered by the insiders of a close corporation, discusses these questions as follows, 734 A.2d at 747–750:

" * * * [It] is useful to understand the distinction between a marketability discount and a minority discount. Some courts confuse those terms. A minority discount adjusts for lack of control over the business entity on the theory that non-controlling shares of stock are not worth their proportionate share of the firm's value because they lack voting power to control corporate actions. Edwin T. Hood et al., Valuation of Closely Held Business Interests, 65 UMKC L.Rev. 399, 438 (1997) * * *. A marketability discount adjusts for a lack of liquidity in one's interest in an entity, on the theory that there is a limited supply of potential buyers for stock in a closely-held corporation. * * * Even controlling interests in nonpublic companies may be eligible for marketability discounts, as the inability to convert the stock interest into cash applies regardless of control. * * *

* * *

"The appraisal remedy today serves a minority shareholder protection role, sometimes providing liquidity to shareholders, but most often operating to protect minority shareholders who are cashed out of their investment. The remedy fulfills this function ex ante, deterring insiders from engaging in wrongful transactions, and ex post, providing a remedy to minority shareholders who are subjected to such transactions. * * * Accordingly, the statute should be liberally construed in favor of the dissenting shareholders. * * *

" * * * [E]quitable considerations have led the majority of states and commentators to conclude that marketability and minority discounts should not be applied when determining the fair value of dissenting shareholders' stock in an appraisal action. Although there is no clear consensus, the use of a fair value standard, combined with the application of equitable principles, has resulted in a majority of jurisdictions holding that a dissenting shareholder is entitled to her proportional share of the fair market value of the corporation. * * *

"Courts rejecting the discount have concluded that it injects speculation into the appraisal process, fails to give the minority shareholder the full proportionate value of his shares, and encourages corporate squeeze-outs. * * * Other commentators, however, believe that marketability discounts are appropriate in appraising dissenters' shares since they compensate for the high risks inherent in small family-owned businesses or for the lack of liquidity caused by the limited pool of buyers. * * * '[A] respectable minority of states, including Ohio, Indiana, and Kansas accept the view that a minority discount is appropriate in valuing shares in a dissenters' rights proceedings.' [1 John R. MacKay II, New Jersey Business Corporations, p 9–10(c)(2) (2d ed. 1996)(citations omitted)].

"We find most persuasive those cases holding that marketability discounts should not be applied in determining the 'fair value' of a dissenting shareholder's share in an appraisal action. The appraisal remedy originally was viewed as a solution to the potential gridlock problems of corporate unanimity. * * * A rule that imposes a discount on the exiting dissenting shareholder 'fail[s] to accord to a minority shareholder the full proportionate value of his shares ... [and] enriches the majority shareholder who may reap a windfall from the appraisal process by cashing out a dissenting shareholder....' [Cavalier Oil Corp. v. Harnett, 564 A.2d 1137, 1145 (Del.1989)]. Such a rule also penalizes the minority for taking advantage of the protection afforded by the appraisal statute. * * *

" * * * Of course, there may be situations where equity compels another result. Those situations are best resolved by resort to the "extraordinary circumstances" exception in 2 ALI Principles, § 7.22(a) * * *:

   * * * Such circumstances require more than the absence of a trading market in the shares; rather, the court should apply this exception only when it finds that the dissenting shareholder has held out in order to exploit the transaction

giving rise to appraisal so as to divert value to itself that could not be made available proportionately to other shareholders. . . . * * *

"[W]e do not believe the record in this case supports a finding of 'extraordinary circumstances.' The dissenters in this case wanted liquidity for their stock and wanted to sell their stock in a corporation now controlled by new management in whom they lacked confidence. That is not an 'extraordinary circumstance.' In fact, most appraisal cases involving family-held corporations concern family feuds. To find such circumstances extraordinary would be inconsistent with the purpose of the Appraisal Statute."

Compare with *Lawson Marden* the same court's treatment of a marketability discount in **Balsamides v. Protameen Chemicals, Inc.**, 160 N.J. 352, 734 A.2d 721 (1999). There it sustained a 35 percent marketability discount in a valuation incident to a judicially mandated buyout prompted by an action for dissolution for oppression. The court distinguished valuations of stock for tax or "equitable distributions" from valuations in appraisal actions and sustained the discount on equitable grounds. The purchaser, it reasoned, was the victim of the seller's oppressive actions and would, if ever eventually a seller of the stock "suffer the full effect of any marketing difficulties."

Finally, compare, **Borruso v. Communications Telesystems International**, 753 A.2d 451 (Del.Ch.1999). *Borruso* was an appraisal proceeding concerning a cashout merger of a 95 percent owned subsidiary (WXL) into its parent (CTS). Both of the parties' experts began with WXL's earnings for the most recent 12 months and applied a multiplier derived from comparable publicly traded companies to yield a Market Value of Invested Capital (MVIC). The defendant asked for a 20 percent marketability discount. Delaware has taken the majority view on marketability discounts, rejecting them in Cavalier Oil Corp. v. Harnett, 564 A.2d 1137, 1145 (Del.1989). But *Borruso* introduces some complications into the picture, suggesting that in the proper case a marketability discount might be deducted from the control premium:

"To the extent [defendant] is arguing for the application of a 'corporate level' discount to reflect the fact that all shares of WXL shares were worth less because there was no public market in which to sell them, I read Cavalier Oil as prohibiting such a discount. This is simply a liquidity discount applied at the 'corporate level.' Even if taken 'at the corporate level' (in circumstances in which the effect on the fair value of the shares is the same as a 'shareholder level' discount) such a discount is, nevertheless, based on trading characteristics of the shares themselves, not any factor intrinsic to the corporation or its assets. It is therefore prohibited. [Defendant] argues, alternatively, that [its expert's] discount is justified on the basis of * * * testimony about the existence of studies showing that privately held corporations sell at valuation multiples substantially lower than publicly held corporations. I agree with [defendant] that, if the record supported this assertion, Cavalier Oil would not prevent taking such studies into account in determining the fair value of shares of a privately held corporation. Unquestionably, it would be appropriate to use a lower control premium than I have because the size of that premium is based substantially or entirely on data derived from sales of publicly traded companies.

"The record in this matter is not adequate, however, to support the application of such a discount."

For more caselaw, see Sieg Co. v. Kelly, 568 N.W.2d 794 (Iowa Supr. 1997)(discount for lack of marketability inappropriate); Rigel Corp. v. Cutchall, 245 Neb. 118, 511 N.W.2d 519 (1994)(neither a minority discount nor deduction for lack of marketability appropriate in appraisal of 20 percent block of shares in close corporation); Arnaud v. Stockgrowers State Bank of Ashland, Kansas, 268 Kan. 163,

992 P.2d 216 (1999)(holding in appraisal prompted by a 1 to 400 reverse stock split that neither minority nor marketability discount appropriate); Swope v. Siegel–Robert, Inc., 243 F.3d 486 (8th Cir.2001)(rejecting minority discount in appraisal context under Missouri law); First Western Bank Wall v. Olsen, 621 N.W.2d 611 (S.D.2001)(rejecting minority discount in appraisal context); HMO–W Inc. v. SSM Health Care System, 234 Wis.2d 707, 611 N.W.2d 250 (2000)(same); Blitch v. Peoples Bank, 246 Ga.App. 453, 540 S.E.2d 667 (2000)(same). But see Weigel Broadcasting Co. v. Smith, 1996 WL 714630 (Ill.App.), an appraisal proceeding prompted by a 1 to 1,750 share reverse stock split. The split had the effect of cashing out for $115 outsiders holding blocks of less than 1,750 shares. The court, following Stanton v. Republic Bank of South Chicago, 144 Ill.2d 472, 163 Ill.Dec. 524, 581 N.E.2d 678 (1991), sustained the imposition of a 50 percent discount in respect of the minority holders' illiquid status. English v. Artromick Int'l, 2000 WL 1125637 (Ohio App. 10 Dist.), also sustains application of a minority discount on the ground that the Ohio statute contemplates the deduction by requiring determination of "fair cash value," as opposed to the "fair value" required by other state codes.

5.   RISK REDUCTION THROUGH HEDGING

Risk reduction through diversification works better for investors in securities than for managers of going concerns in manufacturing or services. Diversification costs investors little and leaves their flexibility unimpaired. For corporate managers, in contrast, it implies the drastic and questionable step of organizing a conglomerate firm. Managers, accordingly, employ other techniques to reduce risk.

Imagine a company in the business of harvesting trees and manufacturing building products. Many factors beyond the control of its managers may combine to reduce its future cash flows—among them price changes in capital, product and labor markets, changes in tax rates and currency exchange rates, and changes in technology. Management can hedge some of these risks.

Consider the following downside possibilities:

• Prices of standardized products sold by the company, here lumber, may fall.

• Prices of standardized products used by the company as raw materials, here energy, may rise. Assume that this producer is located in the Pacific Northwest and uses hydroelectric power, that most competing producers use oil, and the price of oil falls while that of hydroelectric power remains unchanged. The competitors' costs now decline, causing a decline in product prices.

• Currency exchange rates may rise or fall. (1) Assume the company has entered into a contract to sell lumber to a German firm, payment to be received in Euros in 120 days. If the dollar rises and the Euro falls during the interim, the contract is less valuable. (2) Assume that the company has contracted to purchase new production equipment from a Japanese firm, payment to be made in yen in 90 days. If the yen rises and the dollar falls during the interim, the cost of the equipment will rise. (3) Assume that the company's principal competitors are Canadian firms. If the Canadian dollar falls relative to the United States dollar in a given market, the Canadian firms gain a price advantage.

• Interest rates may rise or fall. (1) Assume the company has variable rate debt outstanding. If interest rates rise, the company's cost of capital rises with them. (2) Assume that the company has fixed rate debt outstanding that is noncallable or callable at a premium. If interest rates fall, the company's cost of capital is higher than necessary, and perhaps higher than that of a competitor with a capital structure suited to take advantage of the rate decline. (3) Assume that most of the company's products are used in domestic building construction. If interest rates rise, building starts will fall, decreasing the demand for the company's product.

All of the above risk factors—commodity prices, exchange rates, and interest rates—have been subject to increased volatility during the past four decades. Retail prices rose more sharply during the post-war period than during any period for which records have been kept; foreign exchange markets became more volatile after the breakdown of the Bretton Woods system of fixed exchange rates in the early 1970s; interest rates underwent especially sharp swings from 1979 until the mid–1980s; commodities prices rose sharply after the 1970s oil shock and then declined sharply after 1979. See Rawls and Smithson, The Evolution of Risk Management Products, in Chew (ed.), The New Corporate Finance: Where Theory Meets Practice pp. 349–355 (1993). The more volatile these risks, the greater the chance of financial distress from causes independent of the production and marketing strategies to which managers devote most of their attention. Financial instruments and strategies that contain these risks and thus in theory increase the value of the firm's net cash flows have evolved accordingly. The principal hedging devices are forward contracts, futures contracts, swaps, and options.

(A) RISK EXPOSURE

Estimates of risk exposure, like all exercises in valuation, must account for time factors as well possible future changes in amounts. More particularly, a payment stream's sensitivity to changes in interest rates will vary depending on its *duration*, calculated in terms of its weighted average time to maturity.

The duration of a bond that pays interest annually, makes no prepayments, and has three years to maturity would be calculated as follows, where PV(A) is the discounted present value of each annual interest payment; PV(P) is the discounted present value of the principal payment at maturity; and V is the sum of the present values of the payments:

$$\text{Duration} = \frac{PV(A_1)}{V} \times 1 + \frac{PV(A_2)}{V} \times 2 + \frac{PV(A_3)}{V} \times 3 + \frac{PV(P_3)}{V} \times 3$$

The calculation renders each payment as a proportion of the total present value of the stream and then multiplies the proportionate payment figure by the number of years until it is received. The results are then added. The duration of a three year bond paying an 8 percent coupon, given an 8 percent rate of return, is 2.788 years, as follows (using table 11–1 supra):

$$\frac{74.08}{1000} \times 1 + \frac{68.56}{1000} \times 2 + \frac{63.52}{1000} \times 3 + \frac{794}{1000} \times 3 = 2.788$$

*[handwritten:] coupon: 1000 * 0.08 = 80*
PV(A₁) = 80/1.08 = 74.08
PV(A₂) = 80/1.08² = 68.56
PV(A₃) = 80/1.08³ = 63.52
PV(P₃) = 1000/1.08³ = 794

Compare a three year bond paying a 12 percent coupon, given the same 8 percent rate of return. Although its payments and maturity come on the same dates, its duration is slightly shorter because a larger proportion of the cash flows are received earlier:

$$\frac{111.11}{1103} \times 1 + \frac{102.84}{1103} \times 2 + \frac{95.28}{1103} \times 3 + \frac{794}{1103} \times 3 = 2.705$$

Once duration has been calculated, different payment or liability streams can be compared directly for purposes of sensitivity to changes in interest rates. The duration calculation effectively reduces the different streams to zero interest payment instruments for purposes of comparison. The percentage change in the value of a payment stream (yV/V) can be expressed in terms of a percentage change in the discount rate (y(1+r)/1+r)) and the duration of the security as follows:

$$\frac{\Delta V}{V} = \frac{\Delta(1+r)}{(1+r)} \times \text{Duration}$$

Assume that the required rate of return for the two bonds increases by 2 percentage points. The percentage changes in value are as follows:

8 percent bond: 12 percent bond:

$$\frac{.02}{1.08} \times 2.78 = .0516 \qquad \frac{.02}{1.08} \times 2.705 = .050$$ *better, less sensitive to Δs in interest rate*

As intuition would indicate, the bond with the slightly longer duration loses slightly more value, 5.1 percent as opposed to 5.0 percent.

The concept of duration facilitates measurement of the interest rate risk exposure of financial institutions, such as banks and savings and loans, that mismatch the maturities of their assets and liabilities in the ordinary course of business. As the above numbers indicate, the tendency to incur liabilities with shorter terms than the durations of investments will cause these firms to lose value as interest rates increase.

For all firms, the concept of duration facilitates the matching of liabilities incurred in respect of new investments with the investments' income streams. If the income stream projected for a new asset and the new liability have the same duration, the value of both will be equally affected by changes in interest rates.

Complex techniques that ascertain the *risk profile* of a firm measure the change in value of the firm expected to accompany a given change in a financial price (V/P). In essence these are computer simulation models that check the responsiveness of a firm's cash flows to changes in interest and exchange rates and commodities prices. The managers employing these models make base case assumptions for the above factors and then project the firm's flows on that basis. Then they consider alternative values for interest rates, exchange rates, or commodity prices, thereby obtaining new cash flow forecasts under the changed assumptions.

Outside observers will not have access to the projected flow data necessary for these appraisals. Accordingly, outsiders work with models based on historical stock price data. These employ statistical methodology similar to CAPM, but result in multiple betas—measures of the sensitivity of the firm's market rate of return to changes in interest rates, exchange rates, and commodity prices.

(B) HEDGING

Firms can hedge against significant risks with "on balance sheet" transactions. One such device is the matching of the duration of assets and liabilities suggested above. The risk of competitive disadvantage due to exchange rate fluctuations, such as the price disadvantage abroad stemming from a rise in the dollar, might be dealt with either by borrowing in a competitor's currency or moving production abroad.

"Off balance sheet" transactions—forward contracts, futures contracts, swaps, and options—provide a more flexible means to the same end.

(1) Forward Contracts

A forward contract is a contract of sale at a price set presently with delivery and payment specified to occur at a future date. If the price of the thing traded rises higher than the sale (or "exercise") price on the date of delivery, the buyer (or "owner") has made a profit; if the market price is less than the exercise price, the owner has lost. Delivery of the thing need not be required—the contract may be *derivative* and involve a money settlement calculated with reference to the market price of the thing. With a derivative forward, we have a "maturity" date instead of a delivery date; no payment is made until the maturity date. If the market price rises above the exercise price, the owner receives the difference and the other party (or "maker") makes the payment; if the market price falls below the exercise price, the owner makes the payment; if the exercise price and the market price are equal on the maturity date, neither party makes a payment.

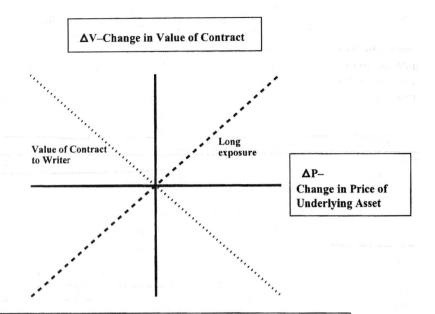

△V–Change in Value of Contract

Value of Contract to Writer

Long exposure

△P– Change in Price of Underlying Asset

A Forward Contract's Hedge of a Long Position: Changes in the value of the asset held long are plotted on the horizontal line. Changes in the value of the forward contract are plotted on the vertical line. The point of intersection represents the value of the underlying asset and of the contract on the date the contract is entered into. First follow the heavy dashed line--this represents the value of the asset to the writer--in the upper right quadrant, the value goes up as the asset price goes up; in the lower left quadrant the value goes down as the price goes down. The forward contract's value changes on a mirror image basis. The writer is out of the money on the forward in the lower right quadrant, where the writer shows a gain on the asset. The writer is in the money on the forward in the upper left quadrant, where the writer has taken a loss on the asset.

Note that a derivative forward contract entails an assumption of risk by each party—extreme price changes can lead, in theory, to massive gains or losses on the contract for either. But such a contract need not entail speculation if used as a means to hedge an underlying exposure. To see this point, return to the forest products company described above. If the price of lumber drops, the firm loses value. But the firm can limit its exposure to lumber price declines by selling forward contracts in lumber with exercise prices based on the current price. If the market price falls below the exercise price, the company will collect the difference. That sum will offset the loss on its inventories stemming from the price decline. If the market price rises above the exercise price, the company will have to make a payment to the owner of the contract (presumably a lumber purchaser), but it also will have an inventory of lumber to sell at the higher price. Note that the hedge thus limits the company's profit increase on a price rise even as it limits its exposure in the event of a price decline.

The forward contracts most widely used by nonfinancial companies are foreign exchange forwards. In the case of the forest products firm described above, such a contract could hedge against the exposure created by its Euro denominated receivable for goods sold due in 120 days and its yen denominated payable for equipment purchased due in 90 days. Forward contracts also are used to hedge against interest rate risk. For example, a firm that plans to enter into a three month loan in six months' time can lock in an interest rate by buying a forward rate agreement from a bank, keyed a benchmark rate such as to the London Interbank Offered Rate (LIBOR) at the time of the contract—if LIBOR rises above the rate set, the bank pays the difference; if LIBOR falls, the firm pays the bank (but borrows at a lower rate than anticipated).

(2) Futures Contracts

Originally, futures contracts were forward contracts made with respect to agricultural commodities. They facilitated (and still facilitate) hedging by agricultural producers and dealers. Today's agricultural futures still require delivery of the commodity if left to run until maturity. But the seller of the future (who has a "short" position and need not be a farmer) can avoid that result by buying the other side of the contract prior to the delivery date (just prior to the maturity date the price will be that of the current (or "spot") price of the commodity). The physical delivery option, although rarely exercised today, still performs the critical function of establishing the pricing relationship between the futures and the spot market. Romano, A Thumbnail Sketch of Derivative Securities and Their Regulation, 55 Md. L. Rev. 1, 8 (1996).

As with a forward contract, the seller of the future will profit if the spot price is lower than the exercise price. If the seller (who has a "short" position) is a farmer, the gain on the contract will offset the loss caused by the price decline upon sale of the crop. The buyer of the futures contract (who has a "long" position) profits if the spot price is higher than the exercise price.

Today, futures contracts trade on organized exchanges, and futures are created in respect of financial products in addition to commodities. (By now, financial futures constitute 80 percent of the total number of contracts written.) The exchanges facilitate liquidity by providing standardized assets, exercise dates, and contract sizes. To limit default risk with respect to the contracts, the exchanges have developed two devices. First, all contracts are "marked to market" at the end of each trading day—that is, profits and losses on each contract are calculated and netted out daily. If the daily closing spot price of the commodity is below the exercise price, the seller realizes a profit and the buyer realizes a loss. The next day, the exercise price of the contract will be the previous day's closing spot price. Traded futures, then, amount to seriatim forward contracts with daily settling of yesterday's contract followed by rewriting of today's contract. See Black, The Pricing of Commodity Contracts, 3 J. Fin. Econ. 167 (1976). With forward contracts, in contrast, no settlement occurs until the maturity date. Extreme volatility thereby can give rise to substantial default risk by a party whose bet has gone wrong and whose exposure has not been properly hedged.

Second, the commodities exchanges impose minimum capital requirements on their participants. Buyers and sellers of futures contracts are required to maintain margin accounts. Gains on the account holders' contracts are added to the account at the end of the day and losses are subtracted. If losses cause the account to fall below a specified minimum amount, either the account is replenished with new capital or it is closed out, eliminating default.

Financial futures contracts perform hedging functions for financial institutions in the same way that commodities futures contracts reduce the risks of firms that deal in commodities. Consider an insurance company holding a well-diversified $200 million portfolio of common stocks. The firm projects that the stock market will fall and as a result decides temporarily to shift the capital to treasury bills. It can of course sell the portfolio and reinvest. But it can replicate that result at a lower transaction cost by selling the right amount of S & P 500 index futures contracts: if the market falls, the futures contracts pay a sum that approximates the loss on the company's stock portfolio; if the market rises, the rise in the value of the portfolio offsets the loss on the futures contract. Similarly, consider a bank that maintains an inventory of government bonds for resale to its customers. This customer service function entails a risk of loss on the inventory. The bank can hedge the risk by selling treasury bond futures. Portfolio managers who frequently shift funds in search of higher yields find that stock index futures offer a faster, cheaper, and more liquid means of taking positions than does the conventional purchase of a long position in a portfolio of stocks. Volume has risen as a result.

Prices of commodities futures contracts derive from prices for present sales. They are adjusted for the time differential for three reasons: (1) the buyer earns interest on the deferred price payment during the contract period, (2) the buyer avoids the incurrence of storage costs during the contract period, (3) the seller may have a "convenience yield"—a benefit from having the commodity in inventory during the contract period. The result is that:

Futures price =

Spot price $\times (1 + r)^t$ + PV (storage costs) − PV (convenience yield)

The time value will, of course, derive from the contract's duration. Storage and convenience factors will depend on the particular commodity.

For a financial future, such as a contract to deliver the stock index at the maturity date, no adjustment need be made for storage and convenience. But an adjustment will be made for the dividends expected to be paid by the stocks in the index during the life of the contract:

Stock index futures price =

Present index price $\times (1 + r)^t$ − maturity value of dividends expected over time[t]

(3) Swaps

A swap is a financial exchange over time between two parties (the "counterparties"), either of cash flows over time or amounts calculated with reference to cash flows over time.

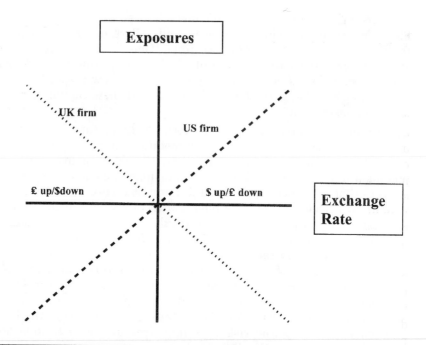

Exposures

UK firm

US firm

£ up/$down

$ up/£ down

Exchange Rate

The Economics Underlying a Currency Swap: The point of intersection is the pound/dollar exchange rate on the date the swap is entered into. The U.S. firm, which has a future obligation to pay in pounds, is benefitted as the dollar rises against the pound and injured as the pound rises against the dollar. The converse obtains for a UK firm, which has a future obligation to pay in dollars. The swap matches the exposures and the benefits so that neither party suffers either a benefit or detriment due to exchange rate fluctuations. As a practical matter, the parties contract separately with a financial institution, which performs the matching function as it constructs a portfolio of swap transactions.

The first swaps were on balance sheet transactions called *parallel loans*. For example, a British company would make a loan in pounds to an American company, which would make a loan of dollars of equal value to the British company. The two loans would have parallel payment dates. The arrangement enabled each counterparty to hedge its exposure to exchange rate fluctuation through the assumption of a debt in the other's currency. The problem was that both loans appeared on both balance sheets, and default by one counterparty did not release the other. These arrangements soon were displaced by a derivative device performing the same function called a *currency swap*. Under a fixed rate currency swap, the counterparties agree to exchange cash flows over a set period based on a fixed exchange rate between the dollar and the pound. If the dollar then declines relative to the pound on the markets, the British counterparty paying the dollars is benefitted; if the pound declines, the American party paying the pounds is benefitted. If one party defaults on a payment, the other party is released from its obligation. The parties may or may not exchange the principal amounts on the origination and maturity dates; if no principal is exchanged the principal amount is "notional." This swap in effect amounts to a series of foreign exchange forward contracts. The hedging principle is the same as with forwards—here the U.S. exporter transfers its foreign exchange risk to a foreign firm that has the opposite exposure.

Interest rate swaps generally entail an exchange of fixed for floating coupon payments. Return again to the forest products company described above and assume that it has a five year borrowing that pays semi-annually at a fixed 10 percent rate that it wishes to transform into a floating rate obligation. It would enter into a swap contract for the notional amount of its borrowing, keyed to the floating rate on the six month LIBOR. The substance of the contract is that the forest products company pays the LIBOR rate and receives the fixed rate. Assume that the LIBOR is 10 percent on the origination date. If, six months later, on the first settlement date, the LIBOR has dropped to 8½ percent, the forest products company (which still owes a payment on its 10 percent loan) will receive a "difference check" based on the 1½ percent spread from the counterparty; if instead the LIBOR rises to 11½ percent, the forest products company makes the payment. Note that here, unlike a currency swap, only the difference is exchanged; thus, if LIBOR remains at 10 percent, neither party makes a payment. The swap amounts to a series of interest rate forward contracts.

There are many variations on the theme presented by the above "plain vanilla" interest rate swap. Under an "amortizing" swap, the notional amount decreases over time in the manner of an amortized loan payment schedule; under an "accumulation" or "accreting" swap, the notional amount increases over time. Under a "basis" swap, each side of the swap is pegged to a different floating rate. Under a "callable" swap, the fixed-rate payer has an option to terminate the contract early; under a "puttable" swap, the floating rate payer has an option to terminate early. An option on a swap, or "swaption," gives a right to enter into a swap on stated terms at a later date. An interest rate swap also can be combined with an term, called a "cap" or a "floor," that fixes a maximum or minimum interest rate payment for the swap's floating side. Since the floating rate payer must pay for the benefit of the cap, it has an cost incentive to combine it with a floor—when combined, a cap and a floor become a "collar." The menu of risks with respect to which swaps have been structured also has expanded—firms have used swaps to protect themselves against real estate price fluctuations, changes in creditworthiness, and changes in tax rates. See Romano, supra, pp. 47–48; Hu, Hedging Expectations: "Derivative Reality" and the Law and Finance of the Corporate Objective, 73 Tex. L. Rev. 985, 1010 (1995).

The default risk on a swap lies between that on a forward contract and that on a futures contract. The forward entails the greatest credit risk because the performance period extends to the length of the contract. The future entails the least credit risk because the futures exchanges reduce the performance period to one day and require market participants to maintain margin accounts. Swaps require periodic performance on an intermediate timetable, usually quarterly or semiannually. Accordingly, they entail some credit risk. Historically, swap contracts have mitigated this default risk with "early termination" provisions triggered by a counterparty's bankruptcy, insolvency, or payment default. The disadvantaged party in effect cuts its losses and avoids future losses that could result from rate or price changes that increase the magnitude of future payment defaults. See Drexel Burnham Lambert Products Corp. v. MCorp., 1991 WL 165941.

Section 560 of the Bankruptcy Code, enacted in 1990, exempts these early terminations from the automatic stay provision in section 365 of the Code. The 1990 amendment to the Bankruptcy Code also assures the effectiveness of a "netting" provision commonly included in swap agreement termination clauses. Pursuant to the netting provision, the solvent counterparty can terminate and net out all outstanding swaps with the insolvent counterparty. The netting provision is designed to prevent the bankruptcy estate from selectively affirming those swaps that are in the money while disaffirming unfavorable contracts. Congress extended this treatment in the Bankruptcy Abuse Prevention and Consumer Protection Act of 2005, which added section 561 to the Bankruptcy Code. This shields contractual rights under a wide range of "master netting agreements" from the automatic stay. More specifically, the section covers rights arising: (1) from the rules of a derivatives clearing organization, multilateral clearing organization, securities clearing agency, securities exchange, securities association, contract market, derivatives transaction execution facility, or board of trade, (2) under the common law, or (3) by reason of normal business practice.

Most credit risk respecting swaps is borne by financial intermediaries. Currency and interest rate swaps differ from the early parallel loans in that the hedging counterparties do not contract with one another. Instead, an intermediary enters into a swap with one party, and then either offsets the position with a counter transaction with another party, hedges the exposure with a financial futures contract, or simply takes the risk. The results are that the intermediaries' capital bears the default risk and that more heavily capitalized commercial banks have displaced investment banks as the market's principal intermediaries. To stay competitive as derivative dealers, securities firms have organized well-capitalized, AAA rated, special purpose derivatives subsidiaries.

Legal uncertainty respecting swaps, particularly in respect of the contingency of counterparty insolvency, is mitigated through the use of a standard form contract developed by the International Swaps and Derivatives Association, a trade association of swaps dealers. Counterparties fill in key terms as to price, duration, and quantity on a deal-by-deal basis.

Unlike futures and options, swaps are not exchange-traded. Indeed, under the standard form, they are neither tradable nor assignable without each counterparty's consent. To the extent a secondary market in swaps exits, it ordinarily involves the unwinding of positions through the creation of a mirror image contract that in effect cancels the original (this avoids any taxable income that would be realized on a direct cancellation and settlement). Many counterparties to swaps also mark their positions to market for internal risk monitoring purposes.

(4) Options

An option gives its owner a right to buy or sell an asset at a future date for a price specified on the date of origination. A *call option* gives the owner the right to buy an asset in the future at a specified exercise or "strike" price; a "European" call can be exercised only on the maturity date; an "American" call can be exercised on or before the exercise date. A *put option* gives the owner the right to sell an asset in the future at the striking price, and can appear in either the European or American variant.

The seller of a call option receives money up front in exchange for assuming an obligation to sell the stock at the exercise price if the option holder decides to purchase it. The seller of a put option also receives cash up front, but in exchange for assuming an obligation to buy the stock at the exercise price if the option holder decides to sell it. The seller of a call profits if the stock price stays low; the holder of a call profits only if the stock price rises. The seller of a put profits if the stock price rises; the holder of a put profits if the stock price stays low.

Considered as devices for hedging, options differ from forwards, futures, and swaps in two related respects. Forwards, futures, and swaps have symmetric payoff distributions—changes in underlying prices lead to equal gains or losses on both sides. Options have asymmetric payoff distributions. Consider a call option on common stock. If the stock rises, the holder of the option gains; if the stock falls the holder does not gain but does not have to pay the difference between the striking price and the lower price of the stock on the maturity date to the writer of the option. The second difference follows from the difference in the payoff pattern. With forwards, futures, and swaps, money changes hands only on the maturity date. With options, the holder has to pay up front for the privilege of obtaining the benefit of an asymmetric payoff distribution. This payment is the option *premium*. Reconsider the holder of a call option on common stock. If the stock rises above the striking price, the holder's profit equals the difference between the stock price on the maturity date and the exercise price minus the premium paid. If the stock falls below the striking price, the holder has lost the premium.

The costs and payoffs of calls and puts work as follows:

STOCK PRICE HIGHER THAN EXERCISE PRICE

	CALL	PUT
	(1)	(3)
HOLDER:	CAPITAL GAIN PREMIUM OUT OF POCKET	RIGHT WORTHLESS PREMIUM OUT OF POCKET
	(2)	(4)
WRITER:	CAPITAL LOSS PREMIUM IN POCKET	OBLIGATION COSTLESS PREMIUM IN POCKET

<u>STOCK PRICE LOWER THAN EXERCISE PRICE</u>

	<u>CALL</u>	<u>PUT</u>
HOLDER:	(1) RIGHT WORTHLESS PREMIUM OUT OF POCKET	(3) CAPITAL GAIN PREMIUM OUT OF POCKET
WRITER:	(2) OBLIGATION COSTLESS PREMIUM IN POCKET	(4) CAPITAL LOSS PREMIUM IN POCKET

More particularly, as the stock (or other asset) price rises above the striking price:

(1) the holder (or buyer) of a call, who has the right to buy the stock at the lower price, gains the difference in value (minus the premium);

(2) the writer (or seller) of a call, who has the obligation to sell the stock at the lower price, loses the difference in value (but has already gained the premium);

(3) the holder (or buyer) of a put, who has the right to sell the stock at the lower striking price has a worthless right, since the holder will prefer to sell the shares at the higher market price (and will also have lost the premium paid for the right); and

(4) the writer (or seller) of a put has an obligation to buy the stock at the lower exercise price, but the obligation never comes due because the exercise of the right does not profit the holder (and the writer also will have gained the premium paid for the right).

As the stock (or other asset) price falls below the striking price:

(1) the holder (or buyer) of a call, who has the right to buy the stock at the higher striking price has a worthless right, since the holder will prefer to buy the shares at the lower market price (and will also have lost the premium paid for the right);

(2) the writer (or seller) of a call, who has the obligation to sell the stock at the higher market price, has an obligation to sell that never comes due because the exercise of the right does not profit the holder (and the writer also will have gained the premium paid for the right);

(3) the holder (or buyer) of a put, who has the right to sell the stock at the higher striking price gains the difference in value (minus the premium already paid for the right); and

(4) the writer (or seller) of a put has an obligation to buy the stock at the higher striking price loses the difference in value (but has already gained the premium).

The Options Clearing Corporation ("OCC") serves as the clearing-house for all domestically traded stock options, functioning similarly to the clearinghouses of the futures exchanges. The OCC is an intermediary in all transactions and guarantees the seller's performance. Trades are cleared

through OCC member firms, which must meet minimum capital requirements and maintain margin accounts with the OCC.

(C) OPTION STRATEGIES AND PUT–CALL PARITY

(1) Using Options

Investors can achieve a range of payoffs by combining puts and calls,
with or without also holding the underlying stock.

Here are prices for calls and puts on Microsoft stock quoted by Yahoo
finance at 11:47 am on May 3, 2007. All of the options were to expire on
January 18, 2008. Microsoft's stock was selling for $30.96.

Strike Price	Call	Put
15	16.20	0.11
20	11.45	0.10
25	6.90	0.33
27.50	4.70	0.63
30	2.91	1.28
32.50	1.53	2.39
35	0.70	4.55
40	0.12	11.20

- **Protective Put.** Consider simultaneously taking a long position in
Microsoft at $30.96 and buying a put on the stock with a strike price of
$30. If at the put's expiration in 8 ½ months the stock is selling for $25 the
investor still has something approximating her initial investment of $30.96,
yielded through the exercise of the put at $30, minus the $1.28 premium
paid on the put. The premium amounts to payment for the hedge, in effect
a form of loss insurance. If at the put's expiration the stock is selling for
$35, the investor's portfolio is of course worth $35, with the put expiring
unexercised and the $4.04 profit being reduced by the $1.28 spent on the
put.

- **Covered Call.** Now consider simultaneously taking a long position
in a share of Microsoft and selling a call on the stock. The stock is
purchased at $30.96 with the call having an exercise price of $35 and a
duration of 8 ½ months. If at the call's expiration the stock is selling for
$34, the call expires unexercised and the investor has enhanced her gain of
$3.04 by the $0.70 premium received. If at the call's expiration the stock is
selling for $40, the holder exercises the call. The investor's gain is $4.04
plus the $0.70 premium received, but the additional $5 gain on the stock
has been foregone. Why make this play? The investor has traded off upside
gain above the exercise price for enhanced returns on more modest gain
scenarios (and slightly mitigated the loss on downside scenarios). In effect,
the investor has bound herself to sell at $35.

- **Straddle.** An investor makes a straddle by simultaneously buying a
put and a call on a stock, each with the same strike price and exercise date.
Say that our investor buys six $35 calls for $0.70 each and six $35 puts for
$4.55 each a total investment of $31.50. Consider two possible outcomes—

Microsoft is selling for $45 in January; Microsoft is selling for $25 in January. The investor has $60 either way, almost a 100 percent return on her investment. Her returns go up more and more as Microsoft moves higher or lower. Now consider an alternative outcome. Microsoft moves in a band between 30 and 36 during the ensuing 8 ½ months and ends up at $35. Both options expire worthless and the investor is out of pocket the entire $31.50. Had she put $30.96 into a long holding of Microsoft stock, she would have been in the money to the extent of $4.04. A straddle amounts to a bet on volatility: the investor wins on the upside and the downside, but only if the swings are sufficiently extreme to cover the option premiums.

Now reverse the view and consider the positions of the writer of the two options. The straddle writer is betting against volatility. If the stock stays close to $35 during the option period, the writer puts the premium in her pocket, enhancing returns in a quiet market.

If the straddle player projects volatility but with a higher downside probability, she can make a "strip," combining two puts and one call. A projection of volatility with the chances weighted on the upside signals a "strap," combining two calls and one put.

- **Collar.** Now consider a risk averse investor who has just invested $30.96 in a share of Microsoft. She can limit her downside risk for the next 8 ½ months to $27.50 if she is willing to spend $0.63 on the put. She can finance this insurance at no cost if she also is willing to limit her upside for the period to $4.04 by selling a call with a $35 strike price for $0.70. Does this make sense? Perhaps. If the $35 cap is reached, she still has a 13.04 percent return on her 8 ½ month investment, with downside scenarios protected by a no cost insurance policy for outcomes under $27.50.

Now consider a different case for a collar. A large corporation is considering initiating a takeover of another firm. The first stage in the campaign entails the purchase of a block of the target's stock not to exceed 4 percent. But the firm will not be in a position to commence purchases for three months. It is in effect short in the target's stock—any price increase injures it. It can ameliorate the problem by purchasing calls and selling puts. It will be covered by the call if the stock goes up. Any loss on the put amounts to a wash—it will be buying the stock at a lower price than budgeted. The position replicates the payoff of a forward contract to purchase an asset.

At this point compare calls and puts to forwards, futures, and swaps for their relative utility as hedging devices. Forwards, futures, and swaps have low upfront transaction costs: no premium is paid, and competition keeps bid-asked spreads small. The insurance cost of forwards, futures, and swaps comes when gain is foregone on an upside scenario; with a correct hedge and well functioning markets, downside risk is limited to the counterparty's credit risk. The purchase of a put or a call, in contrast, implies a substantial upfront cost in the form of the premium. As the Microsoft figures show, premiums vary depending on whether the option is "at the money" or "in the money"—with the striking price equal to or lower than the market price at the time of purchase, or "out of the money"—with the striking price greater than the market price at the time of purchase. The premium will be lower in the latter case, but the downside protection the right offers also will be lower. A collar solves the problem by combining the sale of a call and purchase of a put, each with the same striking price. The out of pocket cost of the premium on the purchase of the put roughly matches the premium received on the sale of the call; the upfront cost thereby is eliminated.

(2) Put–Call Parity

Return to the protective put described above and assume that such a position is established in respect of a stock selling for $100, and that the put, which expires in one year, has a strike price of $100. The investment's posture is depicted below. As the stock rises over $100, the investor gains along the broken line in the northeast quadrant; as the stock goes lower than $100 the put protects the investor from the decline. In effecting the position, the investor pays the $100 stock price plus the price of the put.

(1) Protective Put / Call plus Treasury

Change in Value

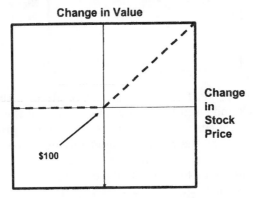

$100

Change in Stock Price

Now try something else with the same stock selling for $100. An investor can buy a call with an exercise price of $100 and a duration of one year, and a zero coupon U.S. treasury maturing in one year and paying $100 at maturity. The call puts the investor in the same position with respect to stock price increases as does the stock plus put combination—as the stock goes up the value moves up the broken line in the northeast quadrant. The risk free $100 arriving in one year has the same effect as the put—the investment's downside is limited to $100. In effecting the position, the investor pays the present value of $100 in one year discounted at the risk free rate of return + the price of the call. Note that the present value of the treasury security just happens to be the present value of the exercise price of the call option expiring in one year.

The point is that these two very different-looking investments put the investor into the same payoff position. This result has an important implication: if economic result is the same, then the two positions should have the same cost. (If a price differential were to open up between the two investments, arbitrage investors would close the gap.) Accordingly, for a given option exercise price and stock price and a given option duration:

● Stock price + value of put = PV of call exercise price + value of call (1)

This relationship is termed *put-call parity*. All factors must be precisely aligned for equality to obtain—exercise price, stock price, and option duration. In addition, the relationship obtains only for European calls—the positions must be held until the expiration.

To explore the implications of put-call parity, let us rearrange as follows:

● Stock price = Value of call — value of put + PV of call exercise price (2)

(2)

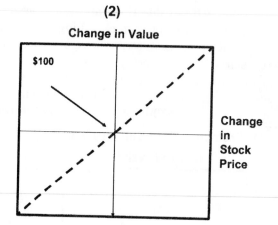

This says that one replicates an investment position in the stock by buying a call on the stock and simultaneously selling a put of the same duration (to subtract the negative cash outflow represented by the price of the put is to sell the put and pocket the premium) and buying a zero coupon bond due on the expiration date. How can this be? Consider three scenarios—at expiration, the stock sells for $200, $100, or $50.

Stock at $200: Here the holder of the position on the right side of the equation matches the left side result of a $100 gain on the stock by exercising the call; the treasury bond supplies the $100 call price; the put expires out of the money.

Stock at $100: Here the holder of the right side position matches the left side result with the mature treasury; both options expire unexercised at the money.

Stock at $50: Here the call expires out of the money and the right side investor owes $50 on the put. The mature treasury supplies that $50 and another $50 besides, netting the investor out at the same $50 as would result from a direct investment in the stock.

Note that any dividend payments on the stock disrupt the parity.

Now let us rearrange once more:

● Stock price — value of call = PV of call exercise price — value of put (3)

The left side of this version has the investor buy the stock and simultaneously sell a call option (subtracting the negative cash outflow represented by the price of the call is the equivalent of selling the call and pocketing the premium). The strategy is familiar—this is the covered call

(3)

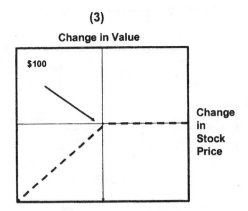

Change in Value

described above. Under put-call parity, the covered call is the equivalent of buying the zero coupon treasury and simultaneously selling a put.

Stock at $200: Here the left side investor has the covered call—$100 plus the call premium, and does not benefit from the price increase. The right side investor has the $100 treasury plus the put premium. The equation thus posits that the two premiums are equal in amount.

Stock at $100: Here both investors are in exactly the same place, the difference being that the left side investor's $100 now comes from the stock rather than the call proceeds.

Stock at $50: Here the left side investor has stock worth $50 plus the call premium. The right side investor must pay $50 on the put but can cover that with the $100 bond, leaving $50 plus the put premium.

Graph (3) depicts the position. Either way, as the stock goes down, the investor is out of pocket. Upside is limited to $100. The reward for this bet against the stock price is the option premium, from the sale of the call on the left side of the equation and the sale of put of the right side. Notice that each rearrangement implies two investment strategies holding out the same result.

Now let us rearrange to ascertain the equivalent of the purchase of a put. Recall that to buy a put is to be in the money as the stock price goes down. Here is the put-call parity equivalent:

Value of put = PV of call exercise price + value of call — stock price (4)

The right side reconstructs the "naked" put position as follows: Purchase the call, invest the present value of the call exercise price in a treasury, and short the stock. To see how this works, note that shorting the stock yields funds to finance the much of the purchase of the treasury and the purchase of the call, but, by hypothesis, does not quite cover the out of pocket cost of the right side position.

Stock at $200: Here the right side must cover the $200 open short position but can achieve that by exercising the call, with the bond supplying the call price. When the smoke clears, she has a net loss in the amount of the call premium, which equates with the position of the left side

(4)

Change in Value

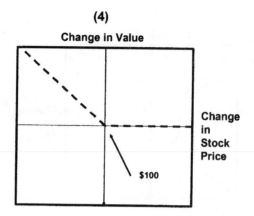

Change in Stock Price

$100

investor, whose put has expired out of the money, leaving her net out of pocket the cost of the put.

Stock at $100: Here the left side investor has a worthless put and once again is out of pocket its purchase price. The right side investor has a worthless call, a short position needing to be covered with $100 and $100 from the bond to supply the funds. Her net loss is the price of the call.

Stock at $50: Here the right side investor owes $50 on the short position, but receives $100 on the bond, leaving $50 minus the cost of the call, which expires unexercised. On the left side, the investor exercises the put and pockets $50, but must subtract the premium on the put. Both net out with $50 minus the cost of the option.

Finally, let us rearrange to put the call option on the left side:

Value of call = Value of put + Stock price — PV of call exercise price (5)

(5)

Change in Value

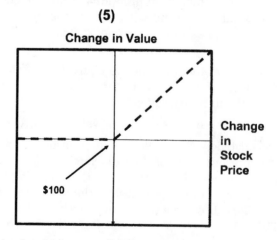

Change in Stock Price

$100

To see why this should be, recall that a call holds out an upward ride on the stock, with no downside risk other than the risk of being out of the pocket in the amount of the premium. The right side of the equation reconstructs that dynamic. The elimination of the downside risk factor means giving up the cost of the put. The present investment in the stock assures gain in the event that the stock rises. The short sale of the treasury funds most of the purchase of the stock. If the stock goes down, the put covers the loss. If the stock goes up, the investor on the right side of the equation owns the stock. But the short sale of the treasuries still needs to be covered.

Stock at $200: Here the right side investor has a worthless put and a share of stock worth $200. The investor also has an open short position on the treasury, the covering of which will cost $100. She nets out with $100 minus the cost of the put. The left side investor exercises the call, pocketing $200 minus the $100 exercise price, netting out with $100 minus the cost of the call.

Stock at $100: Here the left side investor has a worthless call and is out of pocket in the amount of premium paid. The right side investor has $100 on the stock but must cover the $100 short position on the bond. She is out of pocket the premium paid on the worthless put.

Stock at $50: Here the left side investor once again has a worthless call and is out of pocket in the amount of premium paid. The right side investor has stock worth $50 plus a put worth $50, but must cover the $100 short position on the bond. She once again nets out minus the cost of the put.

NOTE: FINANCIAL ENGINEERING

An investor who buys a call, sells a put, and buys a zero coupon bond due at the call's expiration date is said to have a "synthetic" position in the stock. Other derivative contracts can be combined to effect different synthetic replications. For instance, a series of forwards can amount to a future or a swap. Or a "synthetic" call option can be constructed by a portfolio that combines a forward contract with a position in a treasury. These two points—that two hedging devices can be combined to replicate the payoff result of a third, and that two traditional financial instruments can be combined to create the payoff effect of a hedging device—lead us to the concept of *financial engineering*. "Financial engineers" combine traditional balance sheet financial instruments and off balance sheet derivative devices to create risk and return configurations *otherwise unavailable*. The list of such devices is a list of exotic names, such as the swaptions, caps, floors, and collars mentioned above, and in addition, captions, floortions, spreadtions, and look-backs. The list is still growing. These devices tend to be embodied in customized over-the-counter contracts between end users and large financial intermediaries, either money center banks or large brokerages.

(D) CALL OPTION VALUATION

(1) Determining Factors

Put-call parity poses equivalences without actually going so far as to model the value of the option. We now lay out the factors that determine that figure.

Return to the $100 call option described above and assume that the stock is trading for $120 with six months to go before expiration. We can readily see that this in-the-money option will trade for at least $20. Will it trade for more than $20? With six months left to go and a possibility that the stock will go above $120, a price higher than $20 makes sense. How high can the option go? The upper limit is set by the stock price—who would pay more than $120 to buy an option to purchase stock selling for

$120? Let's say the option sells for $25 with the stock price at $120. Here are some terms: the $20 difference between the exercise price and the stock price is called the "intrinsic" or "theoretical" value of the option. The $5 difference between the intrinsic value and the market price is termed the "time premium." Now let's say that the price of the stock is $80. When the price of the stock is lower than the exercise price of the option, the option has a zero theoretical value. But as long as the option continues to be exercisable after the date on which it is being valued, it is possible for its market value to be greater than its theoretical value. Even though the stock price is $20 less than the exercise price, the option has value because the stock still may rise above $100 during the remaining six months of the option's life. For a given option, how much value depends on how far out of the money the option is, the amount of time remaining, and expectations respecting the stock. Note that in May 2007, with Microsoft at $30.96, an 8 ½ month option to buy at $40 costs 12 cents.

Summarizing, the value of the call will lie in a region between an upper boundary set by the stock price and a lower boundary set by intrinsic value—the price of the stock minus the exercise price of the call.

The latter combination was first envisioned in the famous Black–Scholes option pricing model. Black and Scholes solved the puzzle of valuing the option premium with the following insight: a call option is a levered investment in the underlying stock that (1) profits its holder on an in-the-money scenario with a payoff resembling that of a forward contract to buy, and (2) so limits its holder's risk on an out-of-the-money scenario as to resemble the risk-return characteristics of a riskless treasury security. (The particular combination of stock and debt that must be maintained to replicate the option must the adjusted as the price of the stock changes. The varying number of shares is called the hedge ratio or delta ratio.) For more on the Black–Scholes model, see Appendix E, infra.

Under Black–Scholes, five factors determine the value of a call option:

Stock price. The higher the stock price, the higher the value of the call.

Exercise price. The higher the exercise price, the lower the value of the call.

Duration. The longer the time to the expiration date, the higher the value of the call.

Risk free rate of return. The higher the risk free rate of return, the higher the value of the call. What accounts for this factor, given that, as we have seen with both stocks and bonds, the higher the risk free rate of return, the higher the discount rate, and the lower the value of the security? One can see this two ways. First, note that another element of value, the exercise price, entails a cash outflow in the future. A cash payout in the future has a negative present value. The higher the risk free rate of return, the higher the discount rate, the lower the negative present value of the outflow, and the higher the value of the option. Alternatively, recall that:

Value of call = Value of put + Stock price — PV of call exercise price (5)

We conceived of the "minus PV of call exercise price" factor as an open short position on a treasury security. As the risk free rate of return increases, the maturity value of the treasury security declines, with the right side investor's short obligation declining with it.

Volatility of stock. The more volatile the stock price, the higher the call value. What accounts for this factor, given that because investors are risk averse, the greater the variance in the stream of payments, the less their value? The explanation lies in the lower boundary of option value—the proposition that the market value of the option can never go below zero. Return to the call option with an exercise price of $100 on a stock with a current price of $80. Now make a limiting assumption—the stock will have one of two prices at the expiration of the call at a 50–50 probability: $75 or $125. If the stock turns out to be worth only $75 the option is worthless. But, despite that possibility, the option has a present value because the stock may be worth $125. Now let us change the limiting assumption. The stock will be worth $50 or $150. On this new fact pattern the stock is more volatile. But the option is worth more. Changing the lower of the two possible stock prices from $75 to $50 does not make the option any less valuable because the option is worth zero in either event. But the increase in the upper price from $125 to $150 makes the option worth more when it is in the money. Thus, assuming the same mean return, the wider the dispersion of possible returns on the company's assets, the greater the value of the option, because it cannot be worth less than zero but can constitute a claim on the upper end of the dispersion.

The five factors identified above were first combined into a formula for valuing options in Black and Scholes, The Pricing of Options and Corporate Liabilities, 81 J.Pol.Econ. 637 (1973). Relying on the insight that an investor can create a riskless hedge by buying shares of stock and simultaneously selling options on the stock, their formula sets the value of an option at any one time as a function of the relation among current value of the underlying security, the exercise price of the option, the short term interest rate, the time until expiration, and the variance of the expected return on the stock.

Black and Scholes contributed a powerful insight about the interrelationship of senior and junior securities along with their valuation formula. Once a corporation sells debt, they asserted, its stock represents a call on the firm's assets. The firm's equity literally has an option: It can repay the debt and buy back the firm, the exercise price of the option being the principal amount of the debt; in the alternative, it can default and leave the firm to the debt holders. This insight, taken together with the option pricing model, implies that the conflict of interest between the debt and the equity is sharper than previously assumed.

(2) The Binomial and Black–Scholes Option Pricing Models

Alexander, Sharpe, and Bailey
Fundamentals of Investments.
3d edition, 2001, pages 618–623, 625–631.

Appendix E
(E) REGULATION OF DERIVATIVES

In 1993, Professor Merton Miller commented on the growth in the creation and use of derivative instruments during the previous twenty years:

The combined set of futures and options contracts and the markets, formal and informal, in which they are transferred has * * * been likened to a gigantic insurance company—and rightly so. Efficient risk-sharing is what much of the futures and options revolution has been all about. And that is why the term "risk management" has come increasingly to be applied to the whole panoply of instruments and institutions that have followed in the wake of the introduction of foreign exchange futures in * * * 1972. Honesty requires one to acknowledge, however, that this essentially benign view of the recent great innovative wave is not universally shared by the general public or even by academic economists.

Miller, Financial Innovation: Achievements and Prospects, in Chew (ed.), The New Corporate Finance: Where Theory Meets Practice 343–444 (1993).

Miller understated the point. By the fourth quarter of 2006, according to the Bank for International Settlements, the notional amount basis of all derivative instruments turned over on derivatives exchanges internationally was $431 trillion. Risk management respecting derivatives continues to be discussed by business and regulatory actors worldwide.

The regulatory problem is multifaceted. Section (1) below takes up counterparty relationships and the problems arising within them when hedging activity proceeds outside the framework of "correct" risk reduction. Hedging devices can create unintended or unforeseen risks if conducted on the basis of faulty premises or with a counterparty headed toward financial distress. In addition, derivative instruments lend themselves to speculative use: for more active position takers and dealers, activity in derivatives entails the assumption of significant risk for the chance of extraordinary returns. Section (2) takes up the converse problem that arises respecting "plain vanilla" hedging for the purpose of reducing risk. The question concerns the impact of risk reduction activities on shareholder value and concomitant implications for the corporate law duty of care. Section (3) considers risks that derivative trading activity holds out for the financial stability of the economy as a whole.

(1) *Counterparty Relationships*

Caiola v. Citibank, N.A.

United States Court of Appeals for the Second Circuit, 2002.
295 F.3d 312.

BEFORE: Sack, B.D. Parker, Jr., and Gibson, Circuit Judges.

■ Parker, Circuit J.

Plaintiff-appellant Louis S. Caiola brought federal securities fraud and state law claims against defendant-appellee Citibank, N.A., New York arising from extensive physical and synthetic investments. The District Court (Denise L. Cote, *Judge*) granted Citibank's motion to dismiss the Complaint under Federal Rule of Civil Procedure 12(b)(6), finding that Caiola lacked standing under Rule 10b–5 to allege a violation of section

10(b) of the Securities Exchange Act of 1934 (the "1934 Act") because he was not a purchaser or seller of securities, his synthetic transactions were not "securities" as defined by the 1934 Act, and he failed to plead material misrepresentations. * * * *Caiola v. Citibank, N.A.*, 137 F.Supp.2d 362 (S.D.N.Y.2001). Caiola appealed. We find that Caiola sufficiently alleged both purchases and sales of securities and material misrepresentations for purposes of Rule 10b–5 and therefore reverse and remand.

BACKGROUND

Because the Complaint was dismissed under Rule 12(b)(6), we accept its factual allegations for purposes of this appeal. The allegations in the Complaint are as follows. Caiola, an entrepreneur and sophisticated investor, was a major client of Citibank Private Bank, a division of Citibank, from the mid–1980s to September 1999. * * *

Beginning in the mid–1980s, Caiola undertook high volume equity trading, entrusting funds to Citibank who in turn engaged various outside brokerage firms. Caiola specialized in the stock of Philip Morris Companies, Inc. ("Philip Morris") and regularly traded hundreds of thousands of shares valued at many millions of dollars. To hedge the risks associated with these trades, Caiola established option positions corresponding to his stock positions.

As Caiola's trades increased in size, he and Citibank grew increasingly concerned about the efficacy of his trading and hedging strategies. Caiola's positions required margin postings of tens of millions of dollars and were sufficiently large that the risks to him were unacceptable unless hedged. But the volume of options necessary to hedge effectively could impact prices and disclose his positions—effects known as "footprints" on the market. In early 1994, Citibank proposed synthetic trading. A synthetic transaction is typically a contractual agreement between two counterparties, usually an investor and a bank, that seeks to economically replicate the ownership and physical trading of shares and options. The counterparties establish synthetic positions in shares or options, the values of which are pegged to the market prices of the related physical shares or options. The aggregate market values of the shares or options that underlie the synthetic trades are referred to as "notional" values and are treated as interest-bearing loans to the investor. As Citibank explained to Caiola, synthetic trading offers significant advantages to investors who heavily concentrate on large positions of a single stock by reducing the risks associated with large-volume trading. Synthetic trading alleviates the necessity of posting large amounts of margin capital and ensures that positions can be established and unwound quickly. Synthetic trading also offers a solution to the "footprint" problem by permitting the purchase of large volumes of options in stocks without affecting their price.

Taking Citibank's advice, Caiola began to engage in two types of synthetic transactions focusing on Philip Morris stock and options: equity swaps and cash-settled over-the-counter options. In a typical equity swap, one party (Caiola) makes periodic interest payments on the notional value of a stock position and also payments equal to any decrease in value of the shares upon which the notional value is based. * * * The other party (Citibank) pays any increase in the value of the shares and any dividends, also based on the same notional value.

For example, if Caiola synthetically purchased 1000 shares of Philip Morris at $50 per share, the notional value of that transaction would be $50,000. Because this notional value would resemble a loan from Citibank, Caiola would pay interest at a predetermined rate on the $50,000. If Philip Morris's stock price fell $10, Caiola would pay Citibank $10,000. If the stock price rose $10, Citibank would pay Caiola $10,000. Citibank also would pay Caiola the value of any dividends that Caiola would have received had he actually owned 1000 physical shares.

Caiola also acquired synthetic options, which were cash-settled over-the-counter options. Because these options were not listed and traded on physical exchanges, their existence and size did not impact market prices. Caiola and Citibank agreed to terms regarding the various attributes of the option in a particular transaction (such as the strike price, expiration date, option type, and premium). They agreed to settle these option transactions in cash when the option was exercised or expired, based on the then-current market price of the underlying security.

Caiola and Citibank documented their equity swaps and synthetic options through an International Swap Dealers Association Master Agreement ("ISDA Agreement") dated March 25, 1994. The ISDA Agreement established specific terms for the synthetic trading. After entering into the ISDA Agreement, Caiola, on Citibank's advice, began to enter into "coupled" synthetic transactions with Citibank. Specifically, Caiola's over-the-counter option positions were established in connection with a paired equity swap, ensuring that his synthetic options would always hedge his equity swaps. This strategy limited the amount he could lose and ensured that his risks would be both controllable and quantifiable.

Citibank promised Caiola that as his counterparty it would control its own risks through a strategy known as "delta hedging." Delta hedging makes a derivative position, such as an option position, immune to small changes in the price of an underlying asset, such as a stock, over a short period of time. *See* John C. Hull, *Options Futures, and Other Derivatives* 311–12 (4th ed.2000). The "delta" measures the sensitivity of the price of the derivative to the change in the price of the underlying asset. Specifically, "delta" is the ratio of the change in the price of the derivative to that of the underlying asset. Thus, if an option has a delta of .5, a $1 change in the stock price would result in a $.50 change in the option price. Caiola's synthetic positions contained a number of components, such as a stock position plus one or more option positions. For each of these coupled or integrated transactions a "net delta" was calculated which helped Citibank determine the amount of securities necessary to establish its "delta core" position. By maintaining a "delta core" position in the physical market, Citibank could achieve "delta neutrality," a hedge position that would offset Citibank's obligations to Caiola.

Effective delta hedging is a sophisticated trading activity that involves the continuous realignment of the hedge's portfolio. Because the delta changes with movements in the price of the underlying asset, the size of the delta core position also constantly changes. Although a certain delta core position might sufficiently hedge Citibank's obligations at one point, a different delta core position may become necessary a short time later. Thus, as markets fluctuate, the net delta must be readjusted continuously to ensure an optimal exposure to risk. * * * Citibank told Caiola that as his counterparty it would continuously adjust its delta core positions to maintain delta neutrality. Also, Caiola routinely altered his transactions to account for their effect on Citibank's delta core positions. This arrangement was satisfactory so long as Citibank adhered to its delta hedging strategy, which involved comparably small purchases in the physical market. However, if Citibank fully replicated Caiola's stock and option positions in the physical market instead of delta hedging, the benefits of synthetic trading would disappear and he would be exposed to risks that this strategy was designed to avoid.

Each synthetic transaction was governed by an individualized confirmation containing a number of disclaimers. A confirmation for Caiola's purchase of 360,000 cash-settled over-the-counter options dated December 9, 1998 ("Confirmation"), for instance, provides that each party represents to the other that "it is not relying on any advice, statements or recommendations (whether written or oral) of the other party," that each is entering the transaction "as principal and not as an agent for [the] other party," and that "[Caiola] acknowledges and agrees that [Citibank] is not acting as a fiduciary or advisor to [him] in connection with this Transaction." Further, the ISDA Agreement and accompanying Schedule, which governed the overall synthetic relationship, provides:

> This Agreement constitutes the entire agreement and understanding of the parties with respect to its subject matter and supersedes all oral communication and prior writings with respect thereto.

> [Caiola] has such knowledge and experience in financial, business and tax matters that render him capable of evaluating the merits and risks of this Agreement and the Transactions contemplated hereunder; [Caiola] is able to bear the economic risks of this Agreement and the Transaction contemplated hereunder; and, after appropriate independent investigations, [Caiola] has determined that this Agreement and the Transactions contemplated hereunder are suitable for him....

In October 1998, Citicorp, Citibank's parent company, merged with Travelers Group, Inc. ("Travelers"). Caiola feared that Salomon Smith Barney ("SSB"), a Travelers affiliate, might become involved in his account. At a November 18, 1998 meeting, Citibank informed Caiola that SSB would become involved in Caiola's synthetic equities trading. At this meeting, Caiola stated that he did not wish to become a client of SSB and that, unless his relationship with Citibank were to continue as it had previously existed, he would terminate it. Citibank assured Caiola then and subsequently that their relationship would continue unchanged and, specifically, that his synthetic trading relationship with Citibank would remain unaltered by SSB's involvement.

Relying on these assurances, Caiola maintained his account at Citibank * * *. From January 1999 through March 1999, Caiola bought and sold more than twenty-two million options, established a swap position involving two million shares of Philip Morris stock with a notional value of eighty million dollars, and paid Citibank millions of dollars in commissions and interest.

However, after November 1998, and contrary to its representations and unknown to Caiola, Citibank had secretly stopped delta hedging and transformed Caiola's synthetic portfolio into a physical one by executing massive trades in the physical markets that mirrored Caiola's synthetic transactions. In other words, when Caiola sought to open an integrated synthetic position in shares of synthetic stock and synthetic options, Citibank, instead of delta hedging, simply executed physical trades on stock and options.[2] These transactions, Caiola alleges, exposed him to the risks— "footprints" and a lack of liquidity—that synthetic trading was intended to avoid.

On March 12, 1999, Citibank told Caiola that it intended to early exercise certain options in his portfolio for physical settlement, a demand inconsistent with a synthetic relationship. One week later Citibank for the first time refused to establish a synthetic option position Caiola requested. Growing concerned, on March 26, 1999, Caiola inquired and was told that SSB was unwilling to assume the risks associated with synthetic trading. During this time period, although Caiola had taken a large position in Philip Morris stock that was declining in value, he wrote options expecting to recoup his losses and to profit from an anticipated rise in the value of the shares. The strategy, Caiola claims, failed because Citibank had secretly and unilaterally terminated synthetic trading. This termination cost Caiola tens of millions of dollars because the price of Philip Morris rebounded as he had expected.

At this point, Caiola investigated and discovered that Citibank had ceased treating his investments synthetically as early as November 1998. Two Citibank officers informed Caiola that "many" of his trades had been executed on the physical market, although they had been submitted and accepted by Citibank as synthetic transactions. * * **

* * * [A]s Citibank executed certain option transactions during this unwind period, Citibank sent Caiola confirmations reflecting that the transactions were for physical, instead of cash, settlement. Caiola also was told by a Citibank official that it was holding hundreds of thousands of physical shares of Philip Morris stock in his account and that Citibank had

---

2. Caiola offers the following illustration: For example, on March 9, 1998[sic], Mr. Caiola submitted an order to establish a synthetic position consisting of (i) a long position in 2 million notional shares of Philip Morris stock; (ii) a long position in 2 million synthetic Philip Morris put options, and (iii) a short position in 2 million synthetic Philip Morris call options. Had Citibank still been delta hedging, it would only have needed to purchase approximately 100,000 shares of Philip Morris stock to adjust its delta core position as a result of this transaction. But, as publicly available trading records reveal, Citibank actually bought huge quantities of real physical options on the American Option Exchange in order to open this position.

executed certain unwind transactions by going to the physical market to sell millions of options and shares. Finally, when Citibank failed to completely unwind a certain swap position, it told Caiola that hundreds of thousands of physical shares—for which he had no hedge protection and was financially responsible—were being sold on his behalf.

In July 2000, Caiola sued Citibank alleging violations of section 10(b) and Rule 10b–5. He also asserted state law claims for fraud, breach of fiduciary duty, and breach of contract. * * *

Citibank moved to dismiss under Rule 12(b)(6) on the grounds that * * * the synthetic transactions were not "securities," and that the confirmations established that neither party was entitled to rely on the representations of the other. *See* Fed.R.Civ.P. 12(b)(6). The District Court granted Citibank's motion. *Caiola v. Citibank, N.A.*, 137 F.Supp.2d 362, 367–73 (S.D.N.Y.2001).

* * *

DISCUSSION

I. Standing Under Rule 10b–5

Caiola alleges that Citibank committed securities fraud in violation of section 10(b) and Rule 10b–5. * * * Citibank argues that the Complaint fails to allege two of these elements: a purchase or sale of securities and reliance.

A. The Purchase or Sale of Securities

* * *

2. Synthetic Transactions as Securities

The District Court * * * concluded—without distinguishing between options and swaps—that Caiola failed to allege the purchase or sale of a security because his synthetic transactions were not "securities." * * *

Caiola's synthetic transactions * * * involved two distinct instruments: cash-settled over-the-counter options and equity swaps. The two must be analyzed separately. * * *

a. Cash–Settled Over-the-Counter Options

The anti-fraud provisions of the federal securities laws cover options on securities. Section 3(a)(10) of the 1934 Act defines "security" to include "any put, call, straddle, option, or privilege on any security, certificate of deposit, or group or index of securities (including any interest therein or based on the value thereof)...." 15 U.S.C. § 78c(a)(10) (2000). * * *

* * * Options have been covered under section 10(b) since the 1934 Act was amended in 1982. Securities Exchange Act of 1934 Amendments of 1982, Pub.L. No. 97–303, 96 Stat. 1409 (1982). The parties dispute whether cash-settled over-the-counter options on the value of a security are covered by section 10(b). We hold that they are.

The Supreme Court has cautioned that "[i]n searching for the meaning and scope of the word 'security' ... the emphasis should be on economic reality." *United Hous. Found. v. Forman,* 421 U.S. 837, 848, 95 S.Ct. 2051, 44 L.Ed.2d 621 (1975) (quoting *Tcherepnin v. Knight,* 389 U.S. 332, 336, 88 S.Ct. 548, 19 L.Ed.2d 564 (1967)). The definition of security is construed in a "flexible" manner, so as to "meet the countless and variable schemes devised by those who seek the use of the money of others on the promise of profits." *SEC v. W.J. Howey Co.,* 328 U.S. 293, 299, 66 S.Ct. 1100, 90 L.Ed. 1244 (1946). * * *

Under section 3(a)(10) "security" includes (I) an option on any "security," (ii) an option on any "certificate of deposit," and (iii) an option on any "group or index of securities." Therefore, "option" under section 3(a)(10) is not limited to "conventional" exchange-traded options. It applies to both exchange-traded as well as over-the-counter options and does not distinguish between physically-settled and cash-settled options. Nor does the definition distinguish between options documented as swaps as opposed to options documented in some other fashion.

We find further support for our conclusion in section 3(a)(10)'s definition of "security" to include an option on any "group or index of securities." An option on a security can be physically settled by delivery of physical stock. An index of securities, however, is simply a benchmark against which financial performance is measured. An option on an index of securities is settled by cash since physical delivery is not possible. * * * Consequently, the right to take possession does not define an "option" under section 3(a)(10), which covers options that can be physically delivered as well as those that cannot.

Both the District Court and Citibank rely heavily on *Procter & Gamble* for their conclusion that cash-settled over-the-counter options are not securities. *Procter & Gamble,* however, held that a very different type of transaction—swaps linked to the price of Treasury notes—were not securities. The plaintiff in *Procter & Gamble* argued that even though the instrument in question was technically an interest rate swap, it had option-like features and thus could be characterized as an "option on a security" under section 3(a)(10). *Procter & Gamble,* 925 F.Supp. at 1280–81. The court, however, rejected this argument because the swap "did not give either counterparty the right to exercise an option or to take possession of any security." *Id.* at 1282. The District Court imported this language from *Procter & Gamble,* finding it dispositive. *Caiola,* 137 F.Supp.2d at 370 (quoting *Procter & Gamble,* 925 F.Supp. at 1282). Unlike the plaintiff's argument in *Procter & Gamble* that an interest rate swap with option-like features could be characterized as an option on a security, Caiola's transactions involve the much more straightforward question of whether a cash-settled over-the-counter option on Philip Morris stock—similar to options commonly traded on the market—is an option on a security. *Procter & Gamble* does not address this issue.

Further, *Procter & Gamble* concluded that a critical feature of an option was the right to exercise and to take possession of the security because the parenthetical "based on the value thereof" in section 3(a)(10) applied only to the immediately preceding phrase, "group or index of securities" and not to "any security." *Procter & Gamble,* 925 F.Supp. at 1281–82. We believe this conclusion is incorrect, and we decline to follow its lead. We hold that the parenthetical applies to "any security." The text of the statute itself includes cash-settled options by defining "option" to include an option on a "group or index of securities." This provision is sufficiently clear that a resort to legislative history is not necessary. * * * A contrary reading would mean that the statute illogically both includes and excludes cash-settled options in the same sentence. In other words, there is no basis for reading into the term "option" as used in the phrase "option . . . on any security" a limitation requiring a particular method of settlement—a limitation that clearly does not apply to "option" as used in the phrase "option . . . on any . . . index of securities." The *Procter & Gamble* court's application of the parenthetical also produced the odd consequence that Rule 10b–5 would cover options based on the value of two securities but not options based on the value of single security. We do not agree with this interpretation * * *.

b. Equity Swaps

* * * In December 2000, Congress enacted the CFMA to, among other things, clarify the status of swap agreements under the securities laws. CFMA § 2, 114 Stat. at 2763A–366. Sections 302 and 303 of the CMFA define "swap agreements" and then expressly exclude them from the definition of "securities," but amend section 10(b) to reach swap agreements. *Id.* §§ 302, 303, 114 Stat. at 2763A–452. Had Caiola entered into his synthetic stock transactions after the enactment of the CFMA, they clearly would now be covered under Rule 10b–5. To prevail on a retroactivity argument, Caiola faces a substantial burden. * * *

We find it unnecessary to resolve whether Caiola has overcome this hurdle because he failed to raise the issue properly in the District Court and we generally do not consider arguments not raised below. * * *
* * *

c. Reasonable Reliance

Relying on various provisions of the ISDA Agreement and the Confirmation, Citibank argues that a reasonable investor of Caiola's sophistication would not have relied upon Citibank's oral misrepresentations in light of the disclaimers. In particular, the Confirmation specifically provided that Caiola would not be relying on Citibank's advice or recommendations, that he would make his own investment decisions, and that Citibank would not be his fiduciary or advisor.

We are not persuaded that these disclaimers barred Caiola from relying on Citibank's oral statements. A disclaimer is generally enforceable only if it "tracks the substance of the alleged misrepresentation. . . ." *Grumman Allied Indus., Inc. v. Rohr Indus., Inc.,* 748 F.2d 729, 735 (2d Cir.1984). The disclaimer provisions contained in the Confirmation fall well short of tracking the particular misrepresentations alleged by Caiola. *See Mfrs. Hanover Trust Co. v. Yanakas,* 7 F.3d 310, 316 (2d Cir.1993) * * *. Caiola specifically alleges that Citibank offered false assurances that after the Travelers merger the parties' existing trading relationship would not change and that Citibank would continue to act as a delta hedging counterparty. The disclaimer in the Confirmation states only in general terms that neither party relies "on any advice, statements or recommendation (whether written or oral) of the other party." This disclaimer is general, not specific, and says nothing about Citibank's commitment to delta hedging.

Finally, we deem irrelevant Citibank's contention that the disclaimers meant that it owed Caiola no duty to disclose its hedging strategy. Whether Citibank had such a duty in the first instance is irrelevant because Caiola alleges that Citibank chose to disclose its hedging strategy. Caiola alleges that Citibank affirmatively spoke and, in doing so, made material misrepresentations concerning this strategy * * *.

Assuming Caiola can prove these allegations, the lack of an independent duty is not, under such circumstances, a defense to Rule 10b–5 liability because upon choosing to speak, one must speak truthfully about material issues. * * * Once Citibank chose to discuss its hedging strategy, it had a duty to be both accurate and complete.

* * *

NOTE: SWAPS

1. *Swaps Dealers.*

Exchange-traded futures and stock options have established places within the system of federal market regulation. The SEC regulates "securities," which include stocks, bonds, and options. The Commodity Futures Trading Commission regulates "futures," which include exchange traded futures on commodities, instruments, and indices. After a period of regulatory confusion, it has been settled that neither regulatory field covers swaps. The confusion is understandable. Viewed literally, swaps are contracts between private parties governed by the contract law the parties select (most likely, New York law in a domestic transaction and British law in an international transaction). Since they originate over-the-counter and are not traded in a market, they arguably implicate neither the federal securities laws nor the federal commodities trading laws. Commentators accordingly criticized the SEC's ruling that swaps are securities in its enforcement proceeding against Bankers Trust in *In the Matter of BT Securities Corporation,* Release No. 33–7124, Release No. 34–35136, CCH Fed. Secs. L. Rep. ¶ 85,477, January 4, 1995. See Hu, Illiteracy and Intervention: Wholesale Derivatives, Retail Mutual Funds, and the Matter of Asset Class, 84 Geo. L.J. 2319, 2336–2339 (1996); Romano, supra, p. 67–70. But note that under the CFMA's amendment of section 10(b) to prohibit "any manipulative or deceptive device or contrivance" in connection with "the purchase or sale of any ... security-based swap agreement" an SEC enforcement action remains an active possibility in a subclass of disputes between institutional swap dealers and their customers.

Note also that jurisdictional objections did not arise with respect to a second disciplinary proceeding instituted against Bankers Trust in respect of its swaps practices in the early 1990s, this one by the Federal Reserve Board. The proceeding resulted in a settlement under which Bankers Trust was required to adhere to stricter standards of management oversight and information provision to swap customers. More generally, banking regulators directly exercise supervisory authority over the swaps market through bank examinations, reporting requirements, and capital requirements. But this oversight obtains only where a bank serves as the institutional counterparty. Securities firms compete with the banks through special purpose swaps subsidiaries, which in turn come under indirect control of the SEC. For discussion, see Romano, supra, pp. 59–64. For further discussion of the regulation of counterparty relationships and the place of derivatives in the context of the federal securities and commodities trading regimes, see Partnoy, The Shifting Contours of Global Derivatives Regulation, 12 U.Pa.J. Int'l Econ. 421 (2001); Huang, A Normative Analysis of New Financially Engineered Derivatives, 73 S.Cal.L.Rev. 471 (2000).

2. *Proceedings Respecting Bankers Trust.*

Bankers Trust became famous for questionable treatment of its swaps clients in several cases in the early 1990s involving "leveraged swaps." The court in **Procter & Gamble Co. v. Bankers Trust Co.**, 925 F.Supp. 1270, 1276–77 (S.D.Ohio 1996), describes two of these transactions:

"In the 5s/30s swap transaction, BT agreed to pay P & G a fixed rate of interest of 5.30% for five years on a notional amount of $200 million. P & G agreed to pay BT a floating interest rate. For the first six months, that floating rate was the prevailing commercial paper ('CP') interest rate minus 75 basis points (0.75%). For the remaining four-and-a-half years, P & G was to make floating interest rate payments of CP minus 75 basis points plus a spread. The spread was to be calculated at the end of the first six months (on May 4, 1994) using the following formula:

$$\text{Spread} = (98.5 * [5 \text{ year CMT}] - 30 \text{ T Price})$$

$$\frac{5.78\%}{100}$$

In this formula, the '5 year CMT' (Constant Maturity Treasury) represents the yield on the five-year Treasury Note, and the '30 T Price' represents the price of the thirty-year Treasury Bond. The leverage factor in this formula meant that even a small movement up or down in prevailing interest rates results in an incrementally larger change in P & G's position in the swap.

"The parties amended this swap transaction in January 1994; they postponed the date the spread was to be set to May 19, 1994, and P & G was to receive CP minus 88 basis points, rather than 75 basis points, up to the spread date.

"In late January 1994, P & G and BT negotiated a second swap, known as the 'DM swap', based on the value of the German Deutschemark. The Confirmation for this swap is dated February 14, 1994. For the first year, BT was to pay P & G a floating interest rate plus 233 basis points. P & G was to pay the same floating rate plus 133 basis points; P & G thus received a 1% premium for the first year, the effective dates being January 16, 1994 through January 16, 1995. On January 16, 1995, P & G was to add a spread to its payments to BT if the four-year DM swap rate ever traded below 4.05% or above 6.01% at any time between January 16, 1994, and January 16, 1995. If the DM swap rate stayed within that band of interest rates, the spread was zero. If the DM swap rate broke that band, the spread would be set on January 16, 1995, using the following formula:

$$\text{Spread} = 10 * [4\text{–year DM swap rate} - 4.50\%]$$

The leverage factor in this swap was shown in the formula as ten.

"P & G unwound both of these swaps before their spread set dates, as interest rates in both the United States and Germany took a significant turn upward, thus putting P & G in a negative position vis-a-vis its counterparty BT. BT now claims that it is owed over $200 million on the two swaps, while P & G claims the swaps were fraudulently induced and fraudulently executed, and seeks a declaratory verdict that it owes nothing."

Proctor and Gamble's securities fraud claims were dismissed on the ground that the swaps were not "securities" within the meaning of the federal securities laws. The court also rejected the claim that a fiduciary relationship existed between the counterparties. It did not, however, dismiss Proctor & Gamble's New York law claims of common law misrepresentation and breach of the contract law good faith duty. The parties eventually settled the case. See also In the Matter of BT Securities Corporation, Release No. 33–7124, Release No. 34–35136, CCH Fed. Secs. L. Rep. ¶ 85,477, January 4, 1995 (describing questionable activities of actors at Bankers Trust in connection with leveraged swap transactions entered into with Gibson Greetings).

3. *Enron and the Equity Swaps that Weren't.*

Equity swaps like those entered into between Caiola and Citibank are quite common. They are typically are entered into for short and intermediate terms between financial institutions and executives holding underdiversified stakes in their own companies' stocks. Under the swap, the executive gets the benefit of diversification without having to sell the stock and realize a taxable gain. But the payouts of this swap work the other way from those of the Caiola–Citibank transactions. If the stock subject to the swap goes up during the period of the swap, the executive pays the bank the amount of the price increase. Since the executive's own block of stock has gone up as well, the transaction is a wash so far as the executive is concerned. If the stock goes down, the bank pays the amount of the decrease to the executive. The bank in turn hedges its downside risk on the stock by selling the stock short or purchasing a put option on the stock. Recall that, in order to borrow the shares, the short party must provide cash collateral. The party lending the shares and holding the cash collateral pays interest on the cash, at rate slightly under LIBOR. The bank pays this interest over to its swap customer, but at an even lower rate, pocketing a spread (around 30 basis points, depending on the customer). This in effect is the bank's fee. These swaps can become complex—the executive may swap for the return on some other investment, for example the return on a market portfolio such as the S & P 500 on a portfolio of bonds.

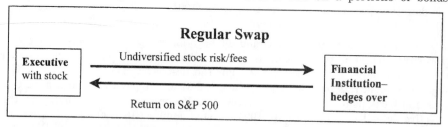

Equity swaps figured centrally in the Enron scandal of 2001–2002, but not equity swaps with the economics of those in *Caiola* or those described above. Enron had a large exposure to downside risk on large block positions of publicly traded equity it held in its "merchant" portfolio. Enron needed hedges of theses exposures to protect its income statement. (Enron accounted the holdings for as trading securities, which meant that any unrealized increases and decreases in the market values of the blocks flowed through to Enron's net earnings.)

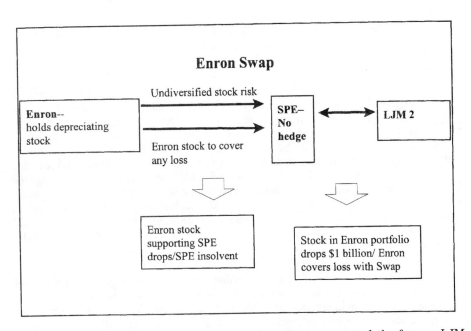

Enron and its chief financial officer, Andrew Fastow, created the famous LJM limited partnerships to find a counterparty to enter into equity swaps respecting these stock positions. LJM raised equity capital in the private placement market. It then set up a series of Special Purpose Entities (SPEs), set up so that they could act as independent entities capable of entering into swap transactions with Enron. The entities, called the "Raptors," were funded with nominal equity capital from LJM. Each entered into a paper exchange with Enron: The SPE received original issue common stock of Enron, then flying high on the stock exchange, in exchange for its own promissory notes. These paper exchanges amounted to $1.2 billion. Thus stuffed with Enron stock, the SPEs entered into swaps with Enron. The SPEs acted in the position of the financial institution. But they did not make hedging contracts to cover their exposure in the event the stock subject to the swap lost value. Such contracts would have been expensive if available at all. Instead, the Enron common stock (issued in exchange for the SPE notes) used to fund the SPEs was to cover any SPE loss on the swap.

The Enron portfolio stocks under the swap did lose value—quite a bit of value. Enron set up the swaps just as the subject stock prices hit peaks. Using numbers stated in Dean Powers' Report on Enron, the value of the portfolio under the swaps fell by $1.1 billion across five fiscal quarters, so that the SPEs owned Enron $1.1 billion under the contracts. Enron, using the new "fair value" accounting, marked the value of its rights under the swap contracts to market for income statement purposes. (Enron's reported numbers were lower than the later Powers figures: Enron's Annual Report for 2000 showed a $500 million gain on the swap contracts which exactly offset its loss on the stock portfolio). This $500 million made up about one third of Enron's earnings for 2000 (prior to restatement in 2001).

Problems arose. The Enron common used to fund the SPEs with capital to support the swaps also started falling. Where its value fell below the SPE's exposure on the swap, the SPE was technically insolvent. There resulted a series of improvised restructurings of the transactions, carried out by Enron's middle managers and concealed from its board of directors.

Worse, the whole transaction structure followed from a very faulty premise. The stock protected by the swaps—issues of speculative high tech and energy companies—was not going to go back up. The SPEs had not hedged, so under the deal, their losses on the stock would have to be covered by the stock issued by Enron.

To see why these swaps lie at the core of the scandal, collapse all the steps into one transaction. Here Enron was issuing its own common to itself (the SPE being its alter ego in economic substance) to cover its own income statement loss, thereby increasing its own net earnings by a total over the life of the swaps by a figure in excess of $500 million; $1.1 billion according to the Powers Report. This is something a firm may not do under the most basic rules of accounting. Indeed, this is something that may not be done under the most basic rules of capitalism. One issues stock to raise capital and then uses the capital to do business and generate income. One cannot skip the step, and enter the capital stock directly into income. As we have seen, the value of a firm stems from its ability to take the capital and earn money over time; its stock market capitalization reflects projections of its ability so to do. Here Enron perverted the system, using its market capitalization—the value of its common—to support the value of its common.

At CEO Ken Lay's direction, Enron folded the SPEs and the swaps in the third quarter of 2001, restating past earnings downward by almost $600 million. Enron had at least noted the arrangement in the footnotes to its 2000 Annual Report. The Report mentioned the hedges, and stated that Enron owed the SPEs "premiums" totaling $36 million. Further: "Enron recognized revenues of approximately $500 million related to the subsequent change in the market value of these derivatives, which offset market value changes in certain ... investments...." However, the Report did not go on the tell how the SPEs would be covering its $500 million loss exposure.

Nor did the Annual Report explain why "premiums" were due and owing. The Powers Report cleared that up later. Fastow had negotiated a deal for LJM that guaranteed a windfall profit out of each SPE even before a single swap was put in place. The SPE would write a put on its Enron common and sell the put to Enron. Enron would pay a premium on the put at the market rate for such a contract. The SPE transferred the premium to LJM an immediate return on capital. For example, with LJM1 and the Talon SPE, this was a $41 million payment, making for a 193 percent annualized return on the LJM investment.

For more on Enron, see Bratton, Enron and the Dark Side of Shareholder Value, 76 Tul. L. Rev. 1275 (2002).

(2) Hedging and Corporate Law Rights and Duties

Brane v. Roth

Court of Appeals of Indiana, First District, 1992.
590 N.E.2d 587.

■ Ratliff, Chief Judge.

STATEMENT OF THE CASE

Paul H. Brane, Kenneth Richison, Ralph Dawes, and John Thompson (collectively "directors") appeal the award of $424,038.89 plus interest for Porter Roth, et al. (collectively "shareholders"), in an action against them as directors of the LaFontaine Grain Co-op ("Co-op"). We affirm.

* * *

FACTS

This case involves a shareholders' action against the directors of a rural grain elevator cooperative for losses Co-op suffered in 1980 due to the directors' failure to protect its position by adequately hedging in the grain market. Paul Brane, Kenneth Richison, Ralph Dawes, and John Thompson were directors of Co-op in 1980. Eldon Richison was Co-op's manager that year who handled the buying and selling of grain. Approximately ninety percent of Co-op's business was buying and selling grain. The directors met on a monthly basis reviewing the manager's general report and financial reports prepared by Virginia Daihl, Co-op's bookkeeper. The directors also discussed maintenance and improvement matters and authorized loan transactions for Co-op. Requests for additional information on the reports were rare. The directors did not make any specific inquiry as to losses sustained in 1980.

The records show that Co-op's gross profit had fallen continually from 1977. After a substantial loss in 1979, Co-op's CPA, Michael Matchette, recommended that the directors hedge Co-op's grain position to protect itself from future losses. The directors authorized the manager to hedge for Co-op. Only a minimal amount was hedged, specifically $20,050 in hedging contracts were made, whereas Co-op had $7,300,000 in grain sales.

On February 3, 1981, Matchette presented the 1980 financial statement to the directors, indicating a net profit of only $68,684. In 1982, Matchette informed the directors of errors in his 1980 financial statement and that Co-op had actually experienced a gross loss of $227,329. * * * The directors consulted another accounting firm to review the financial condition of Co-op. CPA Rex E. Coulter found additional errors in Matchette's 1980 financial statement, which increased the gross loss to $424,038. * * * Coulter opined that the primary cause of the gross loss was the failure to hedge.

The court entered specific findings and conclusions determining that the directors breached their duties by retaining a manager inexperienced in hedging; failing to maintain reasonable supervision over him; and failing to attain knowledge of the basic fundamentals of hedging to be able to direct the hedging activities and supervise the manager properly; and that their gross inattention and failure to protect the grain profits caused the resultant loss of $424,038.89. * * *

DISCUSSION AND DECISION

* * *

[The trial court correctly applied] the standard of care set forth in IND.CODE § 23–1–2–11. In 1980, I.C. § 23–1–2–11 provided that a director shall perform his duties in good faith in the best interest of the corporation and with such care as an ordinarily prudent person in a like position would use in similar circumstances. The statute allows the director to rely upon information, reports, and opinions of the corporation's officers and employees which he reasonably believes to be reliable and competent, and public accountants on matters which he reasonably believes to be within such person's professional competence. * * *

   * * *

   Under [the "clearly erroneous"] standard of review, we find that there was probative evidence that Co-op's losses were due to a failure to hedge. Coulter testified that grain elevators should engage in hedging to protect the co-op from losses from price swings. * * * One expert in the grain elevator business and hedging testified that co-ops should not speculate and that Co-op's losses stemmed from the failure to hedge. * * *

   Further evidence in the record supports the court's findings and its conclusions that the directors breached their duty by their failure to supervise the manager and become aware of the essentials of hedging to be able to monitor the business which was a proximate cause of Co-op's losses. Although the directors argue that they relied upon their manager and should be insulated from liability, the business judgment rule protects directors from liability only if their decisions were informed ones. See Hanson Trust PLC v. ML SCM Acquisitions, Inc. (2d Cir.1986), 781 F.2d 264, 275 * * *.

   In W & W Equipment Co. v. Mink (1991), Ind.App., 568 N.E.2d 564, trans. denied, we stated that "a director cannot blindly take action and later avoid the consequences by saying he was not aware of the effect of the action he took. A director has some duty to become informed about the actions he is about to undertake." * * * Here, the evidence shows that the directors made no meaningful attempts to be informed of the hedging activities and their effects upon Co-op's financial position. Their failure to provide adequate supervision of the manager's actions was a breach of their duty of care to protect Co-op's interests in a reasonable manner. * * * The business judgment rule does not shield the directors from liability.

   * * * [In Coddington v. Canaday (1901), 157 Ind. 243, 61 N.E. 567] our supreme court held that directors are not liable for mere errors of judgment, but that they are liable for losses occurring through their gross inattention to the business or their willful violation of their duties. * * * The Coddington case points out particular duties which were breached by bank directors, such as the duties of: knowing the company's general financial condition, knowing its solvency position, checking or preventing improvident or dishonest conduct of managers, examining corporate records and knowing the manner in which business is conducted, and supervising managers. * * * [T]he court determined the bank directors were grossly inattentive to the business and willfully violated their duties. The directors argue that this language requires "gross negligence" before liability is exacted. We disagree with the directors' interpretation and also note that * * * the proper standard of care is that set forth in I.C. § 23–1–2–11, which is not a gross negligence standard. The trial court's reference to Coddington reinforces the findings of the particular breaches of duties here and does not imply that a finding of gross negligence by Co-op's directors was necessary. Furthermore, the reference to Coddington shows the trial court required more than errors in judgment before finding the directors were negligent. It was necessary that the trial court here decide

whether the directors acted as ordinarily prudent persons in like positions in similar circumstances would have acted. The trial court applied that standard correctly. * * *

   * * *

■ GARRARD, J., concurs.

■ SULLIVAN, J., concurs in result.

NOTE: HEDGING, SHAREHOLDER VALUE, THE CAPM, AND THE IRRELEVANCE HYPOTHESIS

Brane v. Roth, read broadly, implies that a well-advised board of directors should take a proactive stance toward hedging the risks of enterprise. But note that the Co-op in *Brane*, a membership corporation, was by definition closely held. Its equity participants accordingly were disabled from diversifying their investments. Even if the *Brane* ruling is appropriate for such a firm, does it follow that it would be appropriate for a publicly held corporation? Could one plausibly argue that it would not be on the ground that a thorough-going hedging strategy would not enhance value for the shareholders of a publicly held corporation?

Portfolio theory and the CAPM, when taken together with the "irrelevance hypothesis" described infra Part II, section A, provide a basis for a powerful three-pronged argument against such an "insurance" approach to risk management. See Duffie, Futures Markets 228–31 (1989). First, to the extent that the risks to be hedged are unsystematic, the shareholders themselves can and presumably will eliminate them through diversification. Second, the shareholders themselves can deal with aversion to any residual systematic risk by including the appropriate amount of "riskless" treasury securities in their portfolios. Third, to the extent that a particular source of systematic risk can be identified within the firm, shareholders not wishing to bear the risk may be able to construct their own "home-made" hedges with the result that the unhedged firm and the hedged firm have the same long run value. Note that the third prong of the argument, based on the irrelevance hypothesis, presumably applies to closely held firm like the co-operative in *Brane v. Roth* as well as to publicly held companies.

If the argument is correct, then the fully hedged firm in fact is less valuable than the unhedged firm to the extent of the transaction costs of hedging. The argument also invites us to ascribe appearances of aggressive corporate hedging to management self-interest. Under this view, managers who cannot diversify their investments of human capital hedge at the shareholders' expense toward the end of providing themselves with a stable institutional environment. Much hedging of "exchange rate risk," for example, is conducted by multinational firms not to protect against disruption of actual financial transactions but to protect the firm's annual earnings figure from downward adjustment pursuant to GAAP. See Hu, Hedging Expectations: "Derivative Reality" and the Law and Finance of the Corporate Objective, 73 Tex. L. Rev. 985 (1995).

The argument against hedging is confronted in Hu, supra, in Romano, A Thumbnail Sketch of Derivative Securities and Their Regulation, 55 Md. L. Rev. 1 (1996), and in Krawiec, Derivatives, Corporate Hedging, and Shareholder Wealth: Modigliani–Miller Forty Years Later, 1998 U.Ill.L. Rev. 1039. Professors Hu and Romano note sticking points in applying the financial economic theories on which the argument is based and point out that we do not yet have conclusive empirical evidence on the connection between hedging and firm value. Hu's view, tentatively expressed, is that there is a risk that corporate hedging does proceed contrary to the interests of shareholders. For correctives he looks to the concept of shareholder expectations and disclosure policy. Shareholder expectations are critical here because they may differ—for example, some shareholders in natural resource companies may be seeking to speculate on volatile commodity prices, while others may prefer that those risks be hedged away. Managers, say Hu, should try to align their policies with their shareholders' expectations (to the extent that such expectations can be ascertained), and, in addition, should publicly disclose the major components of their hedging strategy.

Romano, supra, seconds the disclosure point. But she also takes pains to present a number of points "suggestive," id. at 39–39, of the proposition that corporate hedging has a value. These include (1) signaling—with full hedging the shareholders are better positioned to surmount the problem of information asymmetry and ascribe business reversals to management performance rather than to uncontrollable external shocks; (2) management compensation—the fully hedged firm justifiably can pay fixed compensation at a lower rate because it offers a less volatile working environment; and (3) investment policy—given that financing through internally generated cash flows is cheaper than new debt or equity financing, shocks to the firm's internal cash flows can cause it to forego good investment opportunities.

Professor Krawiec mounts a more sustained attack on the irrelevance hypothesis. She reviews the empirical evidence and concludes that, although it leaves open many questions, it is "generally consistent" with the proposition that hedging can enhance shareholder value. 1998 U.Ill.L.Rev. at 1082. She goes on to note that conglomerate mergers and derivatives hedging present two distinguishable types of corporate risk-reducing behavior and to show that empirical evidence of the wealth reduction due to conglomerate merger has provided the primary basis for the academic attack on the value of derivative hedging. She identifies seven means by which firm-level risk reduction can enhance shareholder value, id. at 1043: (1) if firm-level hedging reduces systematic risk; (2) if there are transaction costs associated with risky firms; (3) if the firm's investment policy fluctuates with its cash flows; (4) if agency costs can be reduced through firm-level risk reduction; (5) if hedging is a cost-effective substitute for vertical integration as a strategy for assuring a reliable input or output source; (6) if there are tax savings associated with reducing firm-level risk; and (7) if the firm's shareholders are not diversified. She concludes that the value of hedging varies from firm to firm.

Empirical support for the shareholder value assertion can be found in Adam and Fernando, Hedging, Speculation, and Shareholder Value, 81 J. Fin. Econ. 283 (2006). The paper looks at derivative positions taken by the firms in the gold mining industry over a ten year period and finds that the portfolios produced substantial positive cash flows rather than netting out as hedging washes. The managers in effect incorporate their views about the direction of market prices into their hedging programs. Interestingly, there was no evidence of increased systematic risk for the firms in the sample.

Deephaven Risk Arb Trading Ltd. v. UnitedGlobalCom Inc.

Court of Chancery of Delaware, 2005.
2005 WL 1713067.

■ PARSONS, VICE CHANCELLOR.

Plaintiff, Deephaven Risk Arb Trading, Ltd. ("Deephaven"), is an investment fund and claims to have brought this action as a stockholder of UnitedGlobalCom, Inc., a Delaware corporation ("UGC"). * * *

    * * *

I. FACTS

Deephaven is an investment fund that utilizes market-neutral investment strategies designed to deliver risk-adjusted returns with low volatility.
Market-neutral strategies seek to capture mispricings or spreads between
related capital instruments without being exposed to absolute price movements. These objectives are often achieved by combining long and short
positions.

UGC is a large international broadband communications provider. On
January 12, 2004, UGC announced a $1 billion rights offering (the "Rights
Offering"). On the record date of the Rights Offering, UGC had outstanding 293,107,030 shares of Class A common stock ("Class A" or "Stock"),
8,198,016 shares of Class B common stock ("Class B") and 303,123,542
shares of Class C common stock ("Class C"). The Class A stock was
publicly traded on the NASDAQ National Market and widely held. Liberty
Media Corporation owned all of the Class B and Class C shares, giving it
approximately 55% of the outstanding common stock and 92% of the
cumulative voting power.

* * *

A. Deephaven's Dealings in UGC Stock and Rights

Following the announcement of the Rights Offering on January 12,
2004, Deephaven began actively trading UGC Stock. To do so, Deephaven
utilized at least five brokerage accounts, at Barclays, Deutsche Bank,
Goldman Sachs, Morgan Stanley and Salomon Smith Barney. It was often
Deephaven's practice to borrow UGC shares in one of its accounts with the
intention of short-selling them to itself in another Deephaven account. The
result of that type of transaction is that Deephaven's purchase and sale
prices are identical and no economic interest in UGC Stock is created—that
is, Deephaven is not exposed to fluctuations in the value of UGC shares.
Not all of Deephaven's UGC trades, however, were matched short-sales and
purchases. Beginning January 13, 2004, and in earnest on January 22,
Deephaven amassed a substantial net short position across its accounts.
For example, on February 18, 2004, just two days before the final results of
the Rights Offering were released, Deephaven was net short 4,615,071
shares of UGC.

Throughout that period, however, Deephaven's Barclays account consistently held a long position in UGC Stock. On January 13, 2004, Deephaven established a position of 2,050,000 shares in the Barclays account and
that figure swelled to a high of 9,338,592 on March 3. In fact, aside from a
three day period between March 5 and March 8, following the liquidation of
the UGC position in its Barclays account, Deephaven held UGC shares long
in the Barclays account at all times between January 13 and August 23,
2004. In addition to buying and selling UGC shares, Deephaven also

actively participated in the market for rights, purchasing millions of rights on the open market.

B.   The Rights Offering

* * *

Under the terms of the Rights Offering, each right entitled its holder to a basic subscription privilege and an oversubscription privilege. Each share of Class A stock entitled stockholders to receive .28 rights and approximately 83 million Class A rights were distributed. The basic subscription privilege of each full Class A right allowed the holder to purchase one share of Class A stock at a price of $6.00—a 40% discount to the then-current market price of approximately $10.00. The oversubscription privilege also entitled rightsholders who had exercised their basic subscription privilege in full to purchase additional shares of Stock. The number of shares available for oversubscription was to be equal to the number of shares made available by rightsholders that failed to exercise their basic subscription privileges. In other words, UGC sought to sell all of the Stock offered in the rights offering either through basic subscriptions or a combination of basic and oversubscriptions.

[The rights were distributed on January 21, 2004, and were freely tradable on the NASDAQ. The Rights Offering had its expiration date extended to February 12. To subscribe to the Rights Offering, stockholders were required to deliver a rights certificate together with payment of the full subscription price before the expiration date. Stockholders wishing to exercise their rights, but who were unable to deliver rights certificates by the expiration date were required to provide full payment and a notice of guaranteed delivery before expiration. Before the expiration date, Deephaven submitted 5,190,700 rights certificates, a request for 1 million oversubscription rights, and full payment for the requested shares.

[On February 13, 2004, UGC issued a press release announcing preliminary results—Class A rightsholders have subscribed for approximately 63.7 million shares pursuant to the basic subscription privilege and approximately 66.8 million shares pursuant to the oversubscription privilege. Based on these preliminary figures, Deephaven stood to receive the entire 1 million shares it requested from oversubscription rights. A week later, however, UGC issued a final press release stating that it had received subscriptions for approximately 82 million of the 83 million rights, leaving only about 1 million shares available for oversubscription. The February 13 press release explained the discrepancy by stating that the February 13 press release had excluded shares subscribed pursuant to the guaranteed delivery procedure. In the final allocation, Deephaven received just 34,603 oversubscription shares based on its exercised position of 5,190,700 basic rights and its request for 1,000,000 oversubscription rights.

[Deephaven's counsel thereafter wrote to UGC to express its concern over the sudden change in available rights and to request that all relevant files, documents, and other information be preserved. UGC responded with a denial of any "wrongful actions after the delivery deadline."

[Deephaven then wrote to UGC demanding inspection of certain categories of UGC's books and records pursuant to 8 Del. C. § 220 (Deephaven's "Demand Letter"). Specifically, the Demand Letter requested eleven categories of documents relating to various aspects of the Rights offering and the manner in which it was executed. UGC resisted the demand, and this action followed.]

II. ANALYSIS

* * *

1. Is ownership of individual shares of stock negated by a net short position?

  * * *

At the time of the Rights Offering, Deephaven held over 4 million UGC shares long in its Barclays account. At the same time, Deephaven's net position across all of its brokerage accounts was more than 4 million shares short. According to UGC, because Deephaven was net short, "Deephaven did not own any UGC stock; it owed over 4 million shares to others." In other words, UGC contends that if an investor simultaneously holds a long position in a security and a larger short position in the same security, the investor does not "own" the shares held long. UGC offers no authority for this proposition, however, and it is unsupported by either the statute or practical considerations.

  * * *

Section 220 is a summary proceeding. Historically, only record holders had standing to seek inspection rights. Proof that the plaintiff was a stockholder of record generally ended that portion of the analysis. For example, it has been held that "§ 220 does not require that a shareholder have a 'direct' economic interest in the stock she owns of record to be entitled to enforce the inspection right." In addition, record holders have inspection rights "even though the possibility exists that a stockholder may later be divested of this stock in some other proceeding or be declared in some future proceeding to be holding his stock contrary to law or private agreement."

The statute was amended in 2003 to, among other things, extend inspection rights to beneficial owners of stock. In describing the pertinent portion of the legislation, the bill explains: "inspection rights are extended to a person who beneficially owns stock through either a voting trustee or a nominee who holds the stock of record on behalf of such person." Importantly, neither the newly-amended statute nor the legislation itself indicates an intent to create two classes of inspection rights: one for record holders and one for beneficial holders. I interpret the 2003 amendment to afford to beneficial holders all § 220 rights previously held by record holders. Therefore, established law that record holders need not have an economic interest in stock to have inspection rights applies with equal force to beneficial holders such as Deephaven.

Practically, requiring an analysis of why and under what circumstances a § 220 plaintiff came to hold a company's shares could significantly complicate the nature of this summary and often expedited proceeding. To give effect to UGC's position potentially would force courts to undertake a complex analysis to determine the plaintiff's financial position net of stock, options and other derivatives. One can imagine cases in which financial experts might be necessary to make such a determination. Moreover, the specter of being forced to disclose sophisticated and proprietary trading techniques could have a chilling effect on the use of § 220 by a substantial segment of stockholders. Finally, unlike in other situations such as voting, the § 220 analysis includes its own safeguard against plaintiffs with economic incentives that are not aligned with other stockholders: the proper purpose analysis. For all of these reasons, I see no grounds to discount Deephaven's beneficial ownership of UGC shares held at Barclays because it also held off-setting short positions.

2. Is a purchaser of one's own short sales a beneficial owner?

UGC argues that "[a]s a short seller, Deephaven was not a beneficial owner of UGC stock" and that "Deephaven's transfer of shares and cash from one pocket to the other pocket does not alter its status as a short seller and does not establish beneficial ownership." UGC's argument has two components. First, UGC argues that because a short sale involves borrowing shares in order to sell them, the short seller never "owns" the shares and never becomes a "beneficial owner." UGC then argues that Deephaven's transfer of borrowed shares to another of its brokerage accounts did not change their status as borrowed shares.

The first component of UGC's argument raises the interesting question of whether one who merely borrows shares, and does not sell them, becomes a beneficial owner. One would think not, but for present purposes the Court need not answer that question. It is sufficient to note that under Delaware law a purchaser of shares from a short seller is a beneficial owner. This result enables short selling in modern markets without necessitating quasi-title searches in connection with each stock purchase. The remaining question is whether Deephaven's short-sales to itself constitute normal sales or, as UGC argues, some other type of transfer. UGC's position is without merit. All transfers of Stock into Deephaven's Barclays account involved an exchange of cash for Stock. More importantly, once in the Barclays account, the shares were not linked to, or otherwise encumbered by, the short positions in the other Deephaven accounts. Once Deephaven paid for the shares in its Barclays account, it had all of the rights of ownership, including the right to dispose of them and to receive the corresponding subscription rights. UGC's interpretation would differentiate between stockholders that purchased shorted shares on the open market and those that purchased such shares from themselves. I question the wisdom of treating those two situations differently in determining beneficial ownership. Therefore, I hold that regardless of the method Deephaven used to finance the shares in its Barclays account, having paid for and held them, Deephaven beneficially owned the shares and had the necessary standing to bring this action.

NOTE: EMPTY VOTING

Deephaven's undertaking of an informational probe under § 220 from a net short position held out little apparent threat to the conduct of business at UGC. But the exercise of shareholder rights, particularly voting rights, by holders thus situated can have disturbing implications.

Consider the recent case of the proposed acquisition of King Pharmaceutical by Mylan Laboratories. As often happens when a merger agreement is concluded, the shares of the target, King, rose substantially, while those of the acquirer, Mylan, fell. Perry Corp., a large hedge fund, held a large stake in King, and favored the merger. Carl Icahn, in contrast, held a large stake in Mylan, and opposed the merger. Perry acquired 9.9 percent of Mylan's shares for the purpose of voting them in favor of the merger. Perry simultaneously entered into equity swaps with Wall Street firms, thus taking a short position that fully hedged its exposure to a decline in Mylan's share price. Understandably, Icahn was much upset by the prospect that a Mylan holder thus situated might be in a position to influence the outcome of the vote.

Mylan eventually abandoned the King deal due to adverse facts uncovered during due diligence. See Kahan and Rock, Hedge Funds in Corporate Governance and Corporate Control, (University of Pennsylvania Institute for Law and Economics Research Paper No. 06–16, available at: http://ssrn.com/abstract=919881). But the issue raised by Perry's voting position persists. Perry, like Deephaven in the principal case, had no direct economic interest in Mylan even as it held 10 percent of the votes on the merger. Indeed, because its economic stake lay in a long position in the target's shares, its interest arguably was adverse to that of Mylan's other stockholders. Hu and Black, The New Vote Buying: Empty Voting and Hidden Morphable Ownership, 79 S. Cal. L. Rev. 811, 875–86 (2006), calls this situation "empty voting." Note that swaps are not the only means to the end of uncoupling the vote from the underlying equity interest—short positions in stock can be effected through the purchase of puts, the sale of a single stock futures contract, or by a simultaneous short sale of the stock itself.

Note also that an empty voter's incentives will vary depending on its investment position. For example, if Hedge Fund X had a substantial short position in King stock upon the merger's announcement, it would have had an incentive to take the same position in Mylan stock as Perry for the purpose of voting against the merger. As to those empty votes, Carl Icahn presumably would have had no objection.

Thus do votes on mergers hold out a prospect of keenly conflicting incentives on the part of hedged investors. In re MONY Group Shareholder Litigation, 853 A.2d 661 (Del.Ch.2004), describes a famous case of this. AXA, a large French insurer, entered into a merger agreement with MONY, the target. A number of hedge funds with substantial long positions in MONY objected on the ground that the price was too low. Meanwhile, AXA had issued convertible bonds to raise the cash for the merger consideration. The bond contract priced the option to convert into AXA common in the money, and the option's value quickly rose because AXA's stock went up after the announcement of the deal. But the bond contract also provided that the bonds would be redeemed at a small premium in the event the merger failed. Holders of the bonds accordingly had a high-powered incentive to support the merger, and bought MONY stock in order to vote in favor. At the same time, one of the hedge funds that was opposing the deal shorted the bonds, thereby enhancing its payoff in the event of the merger's defeat. (The merger eventually passed by a small margin.)

Martin and Partnoy, Encumbered Shares, 2005 U. Ill.L. Rev. 775, sets out a range of situations in which offsetting positions can skew voting incentives. Assume that X Fund holds a significant number of Y Corp. shares and that the outcome of an upcoming shareholder vote will materially impact the price of Y's stock. How will X Fund's incentives differ from those of a holder whose only pertinent interest is a long position in Y stock:

1. If X's long position is offset by an equal number of short sales of Y stock?

2. If X purchases at-the-money put options on an equal number of Y shares?

3. If X sells call options on an equal number of Y shares?

4. If X sells put options on an equal number of Y shares?

5. If X purchases call options on an equal number of Y shares?

6. If X has a substantial holding of bonds issued by Y Corp.?

7. If X has shorted a substantial number of bonds issued by Y Corp?

What, if anything, should be done about empty voting? Hu and Black recommend an overhaul of the federal securities laws to import transparency respecting the overall investment positions of large holders. Martin and Partnoy make a more radical recommendation, proposing a rule under which shares held by stockholders who lack "the otherwise homogenous incentives generated by 'pure' share ownership" would not be entitled to vote.

(3) Systemic Risk and Transparency

(a) the scope of the problem

Chairman Alan Greenspan, Remarks at the 36th Annual Conference on Bank Structure and Competition of the Federal Reserve Bank of Chicago

May 4, 2000.

* * *

It seems undeniable that in recent years the rate of financial innovation has quickened. Many in fact argue that the pace of innovation will increase yet further in the next few years as financial markets increasingly intertwine and facilitate the integration of the new technologies into the world economy. As we stand at the dawn of the twenty-first century, the possible configurations of products and services offered by financial institutions appear limitless. There can be little doubt that these evolving changes in the financial landscape are providing net benefits for the large majority of the American people. The rising share of financial services in the nation's national income in recent years is a measure of the contribution of the newer financial innovations to America's accelerated economic growth.

Derivatives * * * have been in the forefront of the recent financial expansion, fostering the financing of a wider range of activities more efficiently and with improved management and control of the associated risks.

Fear of Change

Nonetheless, some find these developments worrisome or even deeply troubling. The rapid growth and increasing importance of derivative instruments in the risk profile of many large banks has been a particular concern. Yet large losses on over-the-counter derivatives have been few.

Derivatives possibly intensified the losses in underlying markets in the liquidity crisis during the third quarter of 1998, but they were scarcely the major players. Credit losses on derivatives spiked but remained well below those experienced on banks' loan portfolios in that episode.

Derivatives credit exposures, as you all know, are quite small relative to credit exposures in traditional assets, such as banks' loans. In the fourth quarter of last year, for example, banks charged off $141 million of credit losses from derivatives—including options, swaps, futures, and forwards-or only 0.04 percent of their total credit exposure from derivatives. This in part reflects the fact that in some derivative contracts, most notably in interest rate swaps, there is no principal to be exchanged and thus no principal at risk. In comparison, net charge-offs relative to loans were 0.58 percent in that quarter—also small but, nonetheless, almost fifteen times as much. In the third quarter of 1998, at the height of the recent financial turmoil, the loan charge-off rate at U.S. banks was $4\frac{1}{2}$ times that of derivatives.

In a similar vein, concerns of highly leveraged positions caused by derivatives have led to fears of "excessive leverage." But leverage, at least as traditionally measured, is not a particularly useful concept for gauging risk from derivatives. A firm might acquire an interest rate cap, for example, to hedge future interest rate uncertainty and hence to reduce its risk profile. Yet if the cap is financed through debt, measured leverage increases. Thus, although one may harbor concerns about the overall capital adequacy of banks and other participants in derivatives markets and their degree of leverage, the advent of derivatives appears to make measures of leverage more difficult to interpret but not necessarily more risky. To be sure, the unfamiliar complexity of some new financial instruments and new activities, or the extent to which they facilitate other kinds of risk-taking, cannot be readily dismissed even by those of us who view the remarkable expansion of finance in recent years as a significant net benefit.

What I suspect gives particular comfort to those of us most involved with the heightened complexity of modern finance is the impressive role private market discipline plays in these markets. Importantly, derivatives dealers have found that they must maintain strong credit ratings to participate in the market. Participants are simply unwilling to accept counterparty credit exposures to those with low ratings. Besides requiring a strong capital base and high credit ratings, counterparties in recent years have increasingly insisted both on netting of exposures and on daily posting of collateral against credit exposures. U.S. dealers, in particular, have rapidly expanded their use of collateral to mitigate counterparty credit risks. In these programs, counterparties typically agree that, if exposures change over time and one party comes to represent a credit risk to the other, the party posing the credit risk will post collateral to cover some (or all) of the exposure. These programs offer market participants a powerful tool for helping control credit risk, although their use does, as we all know, pose significant legal and operational issues.

Legitimate Concerns

Despite the commendable historical loss record and effective market discipline, there are undoubtedly legitimate concerns and avenues for significant improvement of risk management practices. Moreover, during the recent phenomenal growth of the derivatives market, no significant downturn has occurred in the overall economy to test the resilience of derivatives markets and participants' tools for managing risk. The possibility that market participants are developing a degree of complacency or a feeling that technology has inoculated them against market turbulence is admittedly somewhat disquieting.

Such complacency is not justified. In estimating necessary levels of risk capital, the primary concern should be to address those disturbances that occasionally do stress institutional solvency—the negative tail of the loss distribution that is so central to modern risk management. As such, the incorporation of stress scenarios into formal risk modeling would seem to be of first-order importance. However, the incipient art of stress testing has yet to find formalization and uniformity across banks and securities dealers. At present most banks pick a small number of ad hoc scenarios as their stress tests. And although the results of the stress tests may be given to management, they are, to my knowledge, never entered into the formal risk modeling process.

Additional concern derives from the fact that some forms of risk that we understand to be important, such as liquidity and operational risk, cannot at present be precisely quantified, and some participants do not quantify them at all, effectively assuming them to be zero. Similarly, the present practice of modeling market risk separately from credit risk, a simplification made for expediency, is certainly questionable in times of extraordinary market stress. Under extreme conditions, discontinuous jumps in market valuations raise the specter of insolvency, and market risk becomes indistinct from credit risk.

Of course, at root, effective risk management lies in evaluating the risk models upon which capital allocations and economic decisions are made. Regardless of the resources and effort a bank puts into forecasting its risk profile, it ought not make crucial capital allocation decisions based on those forecasts until their accuracy has been appraised. Yet forecast evaluation, or "backtesting," procedures to date have received surprisingly little attention in both academic circles and private industry.

Quite apart from complacency over risk-modeling systems, we must be careful not to foster an expectation that policymakers will ultimately solve all serious potential problems and disruptions. Such a conviction could lull financial institutions into believing that all severe episodes will be handled by their central bank and hence that their own risk-management systems need not be relied upon. Thus, over-reliance on public policy could lead to destabilizing behavior by market participants that would not otherwise be observed—what economists call moral hazard.

There are many that hold the misperception that some American financial institutions are too big to fail. I can certainly envision that in times of crisis the financial implosion of a large intermediary could exacerbate the situation. Accordingly, the monetary and supervisory authorities would doubtless endeavor to manage an orderly liquidation of the failed entity, including the unwinding of its positions. But shareholders would not be protected, and I would anticipate appropriate discounts or "haircuts" for other than federally guaranteed liabilities.

As we consider potential shortcomings in risk management against the backdrop of an absence of significant credit losses in derivatives, one is compelled to ask: Has the financial system become more stable, or has it simply not been tested?

Probability distributions estimated largely, or exclusively, over cycles that do not include periods of financial stress will underestimate the likelihood of extreme price movements because they fail to capture a secondary peak at the extreme negative tail that reflects the probability of the occurrence of extreme losses. Further, because the experience during crises indicates heightened correlations of price movements, joint distributions estimated over periods that do not include severe turbulence would inaccurately estimate correlations between asset returns during such episodes. The benefits of diversification will accordingly be overestimated.

Another aspect of the system that may not have been appropriately tested is the set of credit risk modeling systems that have evolved alongside the growth in derivatives. Such models embody procedures for gauging potential future exposure. Prevailing prices will doubtless change in the future, so counterparties must assess whether those contracts with small or even negative current values now have the potential to result in large positive market values and, hence, a potential credit loss on default. Do such calculations adequately account for the possibility of prolonged disruptions or recessions? Are assumptions relating exposures to default probabilities sufficiently inclusive? These and other support columns underlying estimation of potential future exposure should continue to be examined under a critical light.

NOTE: UNEXPECTED VOLATILITY

There follow descriptions of two cases where bond market volatility caused sudden and destabilizing losses on derivatives. The first is the one mentioned by Alan Greenspan—the 1998 collapse and bail out of Long Term Capital Management, L.P.("LTCM"). The second, a series of cases not dissimilar in substance, occurred in the bond markets of 1994. Both cases were much cited when a negative shock disrupted the credit markets in the summer of 2007.

1. *The LTCM Collapse.*

"Hedge funds" are investment companies that privately and exclusively place their equity shares with sophisticated, wealthy individuals and financial institutions, remaining exempt from regulation under the Investment Company Act.

LTCM was a premier hedge fund. Its principals included John Meriwether, who earlier had pioneered fixed income arbitrage at Salomon Bros., David Mullins, a former Harvard economics professor and Federal Reserve vice chairman, and the Nobel prize winning economists Myron Scholes and Robert Merton. LTCM had a range of investments, but the core of its portfolio was made up of arbitrage positions based on computer models of market behavior patterns. More particularly, LTCM specialized in detecting temporary price discrepancies between different types of debt securities and predicting the direction of price movements based on models derived from past market behavior. In 1998 its models indicated a price discrepancy between U.S. treasuries—thought to be overpriced—and a range of other bonds, including junk bonds, mortgage-backed securities, and European government bonds—all thought to be underpriced. LTCM accordingly shorted U.S. treasuries and went long in the other bonds.

Unfortunately, LCTM's models did not allow for the sequence of events that played out in practice in 1998. Many stock markets worldwide were plunging. Then, in mid-August, Russia devalued the ruble and defaulted on its debt. A worldwide flight to quality resulted. Investors bought U.S. treasuries, causing their yields to fall and prices to rise, and simultaneously sold riskier debt like junk bonds and European government issues. Meanwhile, the fall in the rate on treasuries caused domestic mortgage interest rates to fall, causing some mortgage-backed securities to lose value. As a result, LTCM's bets all went in the wrong direction at once. Had the firm not been highly levered, it might have been in a position to ride out the storm and wait for the pricing pattern predicted in its models to reassert itself. But LTCM was very, very highly levered.

Part of LTCM's problem lay in the fact that it was not the only firm making arbitrage plays based on computer models. As more and more players got into that game, yields on particular bets declined. To keep up a high yield on equity invested—routinely 40 percent per year before the trouble—LTCM borrowed heavily to finance a higher volume of bets. At one point LCTM's assets exceeded its equity capital by 100 times, with borrowing providing the rest of the stakes. Its assets shrank as the bets went wrong—as of August 1998 LTCM had a balance sheet of $125 billion of assets, 54 times its equity capital base of $2.3 billion. By September, when its lenders made margin calls, LTCM's assets had shrunk to $80 billion and its capital to $600 million.

A bail out followed. Fifteen leading financial institutions drawn from among LTCM's lenders loaned an additional $3.5 billion. They took 90 percent of LTCM's equity in exchange. The bailout was brokered by Federal Reserve Chair Alan Greenspan. He later stressed that it was not undertaken to benefit LTCM's principals but to minimize a systemic threat to world financial markets that would result from a default on LTCM's mountain of debt.

Lax lending practices were implicated. LTCM's principals had potent reputations and a brilliant track record, making financial institutions eager to lend to the firm. LTCM insisted on secrecy respecting its positions, so as to avoid sharing yields with imitators. So eager were the lenders that they accepted this condition and loaned billions without requiring basic information about LTCM's assets and positions. Nor did they require LTCM to maintain a level of equity capital sufficient to support its positions.

2. *Events in 1994.*

● **Bond markets.** In early 1994 bond markets were bullish worldwide, and many actors speculated on further price increases. Many of the speculators were hedge funds. Some of the larger hedge funds had invested heavily in internationally diversified portfolios of bonds, borrowing most of the capital on a short term basis from banks. The funds, which expected bond prices to rise, were taking advantage of an interest rate spread. In addition, banks and securities firms aggressively wrote call options on bonds to the hedge funds and other bond speculators. The banks and brokerages that wrote the options carried inventories of bonds to hedge their exposure on the options in case of price increases. But these long positions in bonds did not fully cover the options written. Instead, the long positions were set pursuant to delta hedge programs derived from the Black–Scholes model. These programs signal adjustments in the long positions as prices move up and down. As prices move up, more bonds must be purchased to cover the increasingly in-the-money options (approaching full coverage as the market price approaches the striking price). As prices move down, bonds are sold because fewer are needed to cover the options as they move out-of-the-money, and the bond portfolio is losing value in any event.

In February 1994, the Federal Reserve Bank raised short term interest rates for the first time since 1989. This had the expected effect of causing bond prices to fall rapidly in the United States and the unexpected effect of causing bond prices to fall rapidly in Europe as well. The hedge funds had to start selling European bonds to cover margin calls on their loans. Meanwhile, as bond prices fell, the delta hedge programs of the firms that had written the now out-of-money calls triggered massive sales of their own bond inventories. This added to the downward price pressure. Losses were aggravated across the board because execution of the sell orders could not keep up with the changes in price. In addition, many of the speculators who had bought bond call options had paid for the premiums by simultaneously selling puts. As prices fell, the value of the puts rose rapidly, opening up a large potential loss exposure. To cover this exposure, the put writers had to sell their own bonds into the falling market, adding more selling pressure.

On another front, the largest hedge fund had placed a large bet that the dollar would rise against the yen. But a threatened trade war between the United States and Japan caused the yen to move upward sharply at the same time the bond markets fell. This resulted in additional selling pressure in the bond market because the fund had to raise cash to meet loan calls resulting from its foreign exchange loss.

• **Money funds and structured notes.** Losses stemming from the break in interest rates showed up in other quarters as 1994 continued. For example, some money funds had invested in derivatives to boost their yields during the period of low rates. One vehicle was the "structured note" issued by AAA government sponsored issuers like Fannie Mae, Freddie Mac, and the Federal Home Land Bank (which had $44.3 billion of structured notes outstanding in 1994). Unlike conventional fixed-income securities, structured notes pay returns based on changes in an underlying index or formula. For example, the interest rate on a note might rise or fall in inverse relation to the Federal Home Land Bank's cost of funds; or, with a "dual index floater" the interest rate reset provision is tied to more than one index so that a change in the relationship between the two indexes can result in the value of the instrument falling below face value. Many of these instruments offered high yields during periods of stable or falling rates, but low yields or no yield as the rates rose in 1994. The result for money funds holding significant positions was a fall in per share value below $1. Seeking to preserve the funds' reputation as safe investments, many advisors (among them Bank of America and Fleet Financial) made voluntary cash infusions into their funds so as to keep the share value at $1. Others did not. Also, Orange County, California went bankrupt as the result of losses on these securities.

3. *Systemic problems.*

The failure of LTCM and its lenders and the failure of the banks, brokerage firms, and investment advisors in the 1994 bond market follow from limitations on strategies and hedging devices they employed. See Hu, Misunderstood Derivatives: The Causes of Informational Failure and the Promise of Regulatory Incrementalism, 102 Yale L.J. 1457, 1476–80 (1993), which points out, first, that Black–Scholes models depend on projections of future volatility, and the uncertainty inherent in such projections leads to wide margins of error in pricing and hedging; second, that the adjustments required by sophisticated hedging techniques derived from option pricing models become impossible in chaotic, illiquid markets; and, third, competition leads banks to market new derivative products so quickly that they have little time to assess proper pricing and hedging strategies for their products, much less to assess the risk of their derivative positions as a whole (some of which, however, may be mitigated by portfolio effects).

Hu goes on to suggest, id. at 1481–95, factors that may contribute to systematic underinvestment in the development of risk information respecting new derivative products. First, information flow within the marketplace makes it difficult for the firms which invest in the development of derivative products to appropriate all the gains. Second, a cognitive bias against the recognition of low probability catastrophic events may impair decisionmaking respecting derivatives. Third, there are agency problems—employees engaged in derivative operations have career incentives to emphasize rewards and downplay risks, and senior managers often lack the technical wherewithal to monitor their activities (and, in the case of banks, suffer the disincentives that result from the presence of the federal safety net).

(b) *regulatory possibilities and responses*

A number of problems respecting effective risk management within financial institutions recur in the above examples—lack of transparency, excessive leverage, and insufficient internal controls. These problems are compounded when attention turns to the matter of an appropriate regulatory response. Competition among the various international financial marketplaces could make vigorous regulation by any one jurisdiction pointless. A regulatory roadblock in one jurisdiction can result in a change of the contracting venue with the result that local financial institutions lose business to foreign competitors. The subject matter, moreover, is hard to grasp, much less effectively to regulate. The value of an over-the-counter derivative at any given time must be ascertained by application of a theoretical model. But the models are in an ongoing process of change and refinement, and, as we saw with LTCM, the transacting parties have little incentive to make their techniques public.

● **Governance.** Leading governance "recommendations" are found in the Derivatives Policy Group Report: Framework for Voluntary Compliance, CCH Fed. Secs. L. Rep. ¶ 86,607 (March 9, 1995). Six large securities firms formed the Derivatives Policy Group (DPG) at the suggestion of then SEC Chairman Arthur Levitt. With Levitt and Mary Schapiro, then chairman of the CFTC, as "official sector contacts," the DPG report envisages a regulatory framework based on coordination between the firms and the SEC and CFTC. It breaks down into four "components":

(1) Management controls. These guidelines are directed to the firms' boards to assure effective risk monitoring and measurement and effective

external audit and verification processes. More specifically, the board (or equivalent authority) is to (a) set written guidelines addressing the scope of permitted OTC derivatives activity and setting acceptable levels of credit and market risk, and (b) establish an independent monitoring and verification process within the firm.

(2) *Reporting.* The firms are to submit periodically to the agencies a new series of quantitative reports covering credit risk exposure. These will identify, *inter alia*, credit concentration in the firm's portfolio through the identification of the firm's top 20 net exposures on a counterparty by counterparty basis.

(3) *Evaluation of risk in relation to capital.* These guidelines set out a framework for reporting each firm's aggregate credit exposure related to OTC derivatives activity. They address a calculative problem. Each firm's risk to capital exposure must be measured by a quantitative model that is the firm's proprietary information. The guidelines contemplate that each firm will employ its own model, but report in accordance with a defined market stress scenario. Since the market stress scenario will be based on backward-looking statistics, the guidelines contemplate additional back up estimates of possible loss that could ensue in the event of low probability events that carry a high risk of loss.

(4) *Counterparty relationships.* These guidelines contain standards of conduct for professional intermediaries who deal with nonprofessional counterparties. They assert that these relationships are arms' length and not advisory, but go on to impose risk standards built on a norm of good faith disclosure of risks, valuations, quotations.

The "stress-testing" mentioned in paragraph (3) above reemerged as a focus of concern three years later in discussions that followed the LTCM bailout. Two new groups were formed to grapple with the problem of derivative risk, also in the wake of LTCM: a President's Working Group on Financial Markets (PWG) made up of representatives from the securities, commodities, and bank regulatory agencies, and Counterparty Risk Management Policy Group made up of industry leaders.

A May 1999 PWG Report recommends, *inter alia*, (1) that financial institutions enhance their practices respecting counterparty risk management and disclose information concerning their exposure to highly leveraged institutions such as hedge funds; (2) that the development of means to assure public disclosure of information respecting hedge funds, in particular value-at-risk or stress test results; (3) that regulators of broker-dealers and futures commission merchants be given expanded authority over the firms' unregulated affiliates; and (4) that regulators take up the problem of creating incentives to encourage offshore financial centers to comply with international standards.

The PWG pronounced again in 2007 with a set of "Principles and Guidelines regarding Private Pools of Capital." These address concerns stemming from the growing prominence of hedge funds in the derivative market. Self-regulation and counterparty vigilance continue as the themes. Here the "overarching principles" articulated by the PWG:

The vitality, stability, and integrity of our capital markets are a shared responsibility between the private and public sectors. Market discipline most effectively addresses systematic risks posed by private pools of capital. Supervisors should use their existing authorities with respect to creditors, counterparties, investors, and fiduciaries to foster market discipline on private pools of capital. Investor protection concerns can be addressed most effectively through a combination of market discipline and regulatory policies that limit direct investment in such pools to more sophisticated investors.

● **Disclosure.** The income statements of securities firms separately reported the results of derivative activities for the first time only in 1993. The Financial Accounting Standards Board (FASB) now imposes derivative reporting requirements on all firms. These rules have evolved rapidly (and controversially). Under FAS No. 133, which became effective for calendar years beginning January 1, 2001, there is a shift to a mark-to-market model of derivative accounting. This entails (a) reporting of all derivatives as assets or liabilities measured at their fair value, and (b) fair-value measurement of changes in value in earnings in the period of the change, unless the instrument is designated as a hedge of an asset, liability, or firm commitment. In the case of a hedge, deferred reporting of gains and losses will be available. The criterion governing qualification for hedge treatment is whether the hedging relationship is "effective in achieving offsetting changes in fair value or cash flows." The FAS rules are highly technical, and much criticized. See, e,g., Lesak, FASB's Folly: A Look at the Misguided New Rules on Derivatives Valuation and Disclosure, 29 Loy. U. Chi. L.J. 649 (1998).

PART II

Debt Financing

INTRODUCTION

Most financing is debt financing, at least for established, stable firms. This Part presents and examines the economics of debt-equity relations and the rules, contractual and otherwise, that govern the distribution of risks and rewards between lenders and corporate borrowers. Section A takes up the economics of debt financing, posing answers to the question as to why established firms tend to raise new capital through borrowing. Section B sets out the basic terms of an unsecured debt deal. Section C looks at security and seniority, in particular mortgage bonds and asset securitization. Section D describes the phenomenon of high leverage restructuring. Section E turns to debtor distress outside of bankruptcy, discussing the legal framework surrounding contractual workouts, the positive law of creditor protection, and credit derivatives. Section F completes the story of the relationship between the distressed corporate borrower and its lenders with a look at chapter 11 reorganization.

This is the first of two Parts devoted to the relationships of senior and junior securityholders. The treatment continues in Part III, which takes up the hybrid securities—preferred stock and convertible bonds.

Eliasen v. Itel Corporation

United States Court of Appeals, Seventh Circuit, 1996.
82 F.3d 731.

Before POSNER, CHIEF JUDGE, and KANNE and EVANS, CIRCUIT JUDGES.

■ POSNER, CHIEF JUDGE.

Three years ago Itel Corporation, which owned all the common stock plus 78 percent of the Class B debentures of the Green Bay & Western Railroad Company, sold the railroad. The owners of the remaining Class B debentures, who are the plaintiffs in this class action against Itel, claim to be entitled to share in the proceeds of the sale over and above the $1,000 face value of each debenture that they received when, in accordance with the terms of their debenture certificates, the debentures were repaid out of the proceeds of the sale. They argue that in refusing to honor their claim

Itel has converted property that is rightfully theirs, in violation of both federal and state law under a variety of legal theories unnecessary to discuss. The district judge granted Itel's motion to dismiss, ruling that the debentures did not entitle the holders to more than $1,000 per debenture. * * *

A debenture, as the word is normally used in the legal and financial communities of the United States, and as it was normally used a century ago as well, when the debentures involved in this suit were first issued, is a type of bond, specifically a bond unsecured by a lien. * * * Ordinarily, when a corporation is sold, the proceeds above what is needed to pay off creditors, including bondholders—including therefore debenture holders—go to the shareholders, as the residual claimants to the corporation's assets. The plaintiffs argue that, contrary to the norm, the Class B debentures in the Green Bay & Western Railroad Company were intended to be the equivalent of shares of stock, while the shares of stock were intended to be the equivalent of debentures. They ask us to look behind the labels of these instruments to the economic reality.

Each debenture certificate is a contract between the railroad and the debenture holder, and parties to a contract can agree to use words in a nonstandard sense. But it does not help the plaintiffs' case that they are unable to direct us to any other instance in U.S. corporate history in which the word "debenture" has been used to denote an equity interest. Convertible debentures, that is, debentures convertible into stock upon the coming to pass of stated conditions, have by virtue of their conversion feature an equity hue; but the debentures issued by the Green Bay & Western Railroad are not convertible. A treatise gives an example of where the term "debenture" has been interpreted to mean preferred stock. 6 *Fletcher Cyclopedia of the Law of Private Corporations* § 2649.1, p. 27 (1989 rev. ed.). But there is much less space between a conventional debenture and preferred stock than between a conventional debenture and common stock, since preferred stock normally is "maxed out" at its stated par value, * * * just like the Class B debentures if Itel's interpretation is accepted.

To determine whether the interpretation is correct requires an examination of the history and terms of the securities. The Green Bay & Western Railroad was created, under a different name, in 1866. It went broke ten years later and again in 1888, emerging from the second bankruptcy exactly one century ago, in 1896, with a radically new capital structure. The first mortgagees, who had foreclosed on the railroad's property, received all the capital stock of the new company—25,000 shares with a par value of $100 each. The second mortgagees and old shareholders received the Class B debentures—7,000 debentures each with a face value, as we have said, of $1,000. They also received, in exchange for investing $600,000 of new money, 600 Class A debentures with a face value of $1,000 each. None of the three classes of securities specified either maturity dates or a fixed entitlement to income, and only the capital stock had voting rights.

Although the debentures do not create a fixed entitlement to interest or dividends, they do provide for the allocation of any annual dividends that the board of directors decides to declare. The dividends are to go to the holders of the Class A debentures until those investors have received 2.5 percent of the face value of the debenture, then to the shareholders until they have received 2.5 percent of the par value of their stock, and then to the holders of the Class A debentures and the shareholders, pro rata, until the two groups have received a total of 5 percent of the face value of the Class A debentures and of the par value of the stock. Any money left after these distributions is to go to the holders of the Class B debentures. In simplest terms, then, the Class B debenture holders are entitled to any dividends that exceed what is necessary to give the shareholders and the Class A debenture holders 5 percent of the face amount of their securities.

In the event of a sale or reorganization of the company, the Class B debenture certificate specifies the following distribution of the proceeds after payment of all liens and charges: the first $600,000 to the holders of the Class A debentures, the next $2.5 million to the shareholders, and either the rest—or the first $7 million of the rest—to the holders of the Class B debentures. Which is the issue in this case.

> Each Class B debenture certificate states that the Green Bay & Western Railroad Company certifies that this is one of a series of seven thousand of its Class B Debentures, in the sum of ONE THOUSAND DOLLARS each, aggregating in all the sum of Seven Million Dollars, *which sum of One Thousand Dollars will be payable to the bearer hereof* as follows: viz., only in the event of a sale or reorganization of the Railroad and property of said Company, and then only out of any net proceeds of such sale or reorganization which may remain after payment of any liens and charges upon such railroad or property, and after payment of Six Hundred Thousand Dollars to the holders of a series of Debentures known as Class A, issued or to be issued, by said Company, and the sum of Two Million Five Hundred Thousand Dollars to and among the stockholders of said Company. *Any such net proceeds remaining after such payments shall be distributed pro rata to and among the holders of this series of Class B Debentures.* [Emphasis added.]

Itel argues that the first clause that we have italicized makes clear that the only entitlement of the holders of Class B debentures is to $1,000 per debenture. The plaintiffs argue that the last sentence in the quoted passage, which we have also italicized, makes clear that any proceeds from a sale over and above all liens and charges, $600,000 to the holders of the class A debentures, and $2.5 million to the shareholders, go to the holders of the Class B debentures, making them in effect the equity owners of the railroad. On Itel's reading the shareholders have a debt-like claim to the par value of their stock (the $2.5 million) that is subordinate only to the other creditor interests, including the Class A debentures but excluding the Class B debentures, but they also have the normal equity interest, which comes into play after the Class B debenture holders are paid their $7 million.

The question of what happens after the Class B debenture holders receive the full face value of their debentures cannot arise unless at the time of sale or reorganization the net value of the company exceeds $10.1

million, the sum of the face or par values of the three classes of security. That happy eventuality must have seemed remote in 1896, for the debentures and other documents of the 1896 reorganization do not make clear provision for it. Nevertheless the presumption in 1896 as now was (is) that the residual, unprovided-for value of a corporation belongs to the shareholders rather than to the holders of debentures or other bonds. The first clause that we italicized in the Class B debenture reinforces the presumption, for it states flatly that the holder's right in the event of a sale or reorganization of the railroad is to receive the face amount of the debenture, $1,000. The sentence on which the plaintiffs rely can easily be read as merely specifying the mode of distribution among the Class B debenture holders in what must have seemed the likely event that the proceeds of the sale were insufficient to give them the full $7 million.

It is true that on Itel's interpretation the Class B debenture holders got very little in the reorganization. They got no right to any income unless the board of directors decided to declare a dividend larger than 5 percent of the combined face value of the Class A debentures and par value of the common stock, that is, more than 5 percent of $3.1 million ($155,000). And if the railroad was never sold or reorganized, the debenture holders would never get their principal back. But remember that the recipients of the Class B debentures were the junior mortgagees, and the shareholders, of a bankrupt railroad. They may have gotten little in exchange for the surrender of their interests in the railroad because those interests were worth little. *Eliasen v. Green Bay & Western R.R.*, 569 F.Supp. 84, 90 (E.D.Wis. 1982), aff'd. without opinion, 705 F.2d 461 (7th Cir.1983). The junior mortgagees had not been paid anything on their mortgages for the fourteen years preceding the reorganization. *Leuw v. Green Bay & Western R.R.*, No. 89–CV–53, slip op.at 6 (Wis.Cir.Ct. Feb. 1, 1993). To the extent that these investors did not merely exchange their old interests for new ones but also contributed new value to the railroad, as they did, they were compensated by receiving Class A debentures. Those debentures were entitled to priority both in the distribution of the railroad's income and in the eventuality of a sale or reorganization. The new shareholders, having in their previous capacity as first mortgagees already foreclosed on the railroad, received both voting control and a bond-like entitlement to $2.5 million in the event that a sale or reorganization yielded net proceeds after all liens and charges of at least $3.1 million, plus (on Itel's interpretation) what must have seemed the remote possibility of an additional return should the railroad be sold and reorganized at a time when it had attained a net worth in excess of $10.1 million.

Itel's interpretation makes better economic sense than the plaintiffs' because it is more consistent with the creation and maintenance of proper incentives for operating the railroad in such a way as to maximize its value. (This is relevant because most commercial transactions are designed to be value-maximizing.) Only the shareholders had been given voting rights. Only the shareholders, therefore, could control the management of the corporation. If they had no right to any part of the gain from increasing the value of the corporation above $3.1 million, the level that would just cover their fixed entitlement to $2.5 million, they would have had little zeal for developing the railroad to the level it reached when it was sold in 1993. We do not know the sale price, because Itel sold the Green Bay & Western Railroad together with another railroad for a combined price of $64 million. The plaintiffs claim that $43 million is the minimum amount of the sale price fairly allocable to the Green Bay, which if so would entitle the Class B debenture holders, under the plaintiffs' theory of the case, to roughly $40 million. The plaintiffs, recall, own 22 percent of those debentures.

A corporate structure in which the bondholders, for that is what the plaintiffs think the shareholders are—holders of 25,000 bonds worth $100 apiece—have all the voting rights, and the shareholders, who are what the plaintiffs consider the Class B debenture holders to be, have no voting rights, is anomalous. * * * See Frank H. Easterbrook and Daniel R. Fischel, "Voting in Corporate Law," 26 *J.Law & Econ.* 395, 403–05 (1983). And yet this inverted corporate structure would not be crazy if at the time it was created the possibility that the railroad would ever be worth at least $10.1 million was so remote that the shareholders, even if they were the residual claimants, would have no incentive to maximize the value of the railroad, beyond trying to create a cushion to protect their $2.5 million bond-like entitlement. As Easterbrook and Fischel point out, corporate indentures frequently shift voting rights to creditor groups when financial distress attenuates the shareholders' interests and makes the creditors the de facto residual claimants to the value of the corporation's assets. *Id.* at 404–05. Throughout most of the history of the railroad it has been the Class B debenture holders who have been the real equity owners, because until the railroad attained a net value of $10.1 million (which for all we know has not yet occurred) any increase in value would enure to the benefit of those investors. But this is an argument for having given the Class B debenture holders the voting rights and hence control of the corporation, which the reorganization plan and the debenture certificates did not do. The only way to give the shareholders, who do control the corporation, a robust incentive to maximize the railroad's value is to give them an equity kicker above the Class B debenture holders' entitlement, and so the debenture contract can be presumed to have done this.

Another reason to doubt that the debenture holders received an equity interest is that the shareholders, being in control of the corporation as a consequence of their voting rights, could so easily circumvent that interest. Before a sale or reorganization of the railroad the value of the debentures would be depressed because the holders would have no right to force either a sale of the railroad or a declaration of dividends in an amount that would give any part of the railroad's income to the debenture holders. The owners of the stock could therefore buy up the debentures cheap, so that, when the railroad was sold, the stockholders (now also the debenture holders) would obtain the benefits of the equity interest nominally held, under the plaintiffs' interpretation, by the debenture holders. And indeed when Itel bought the railroad's common stock it also bought 78 percent of the Class B debentures.

So uncertain was the right of the debenture holders to income from the corporation that the Tax Court ruled, in a decision upheld by this court in

Green Bay & W.R. Co. v. Commissioner, 147 F.2d 585 (7th Cir.1945), that the railroad could not deduct payments to either class of debenture holders as interest. Instead it had to treat these payments for tax purposes as dividends (the term, as it happens, used in the debentures themselves). But this is just to say that the debenture holders have no interest entitlement. It does not address the question of their entitlement in the event of a sale. This is obvious from the fact that the court treated the Class A debenture holders the same as the Class B holders, even though it is indisputable that the former are entitled only to the face value of their debentures in the event of a sale.

So the tax case cannot do much for the plaintiffs and neither can *Biltchik v.Green Bay & W.R. Co.*, 250 Wis. 177, 26 N.W.2d 633 (1947), despite its tantalizing dictum that the provision "as to distribution on liquidation puts the holders of the Class B Debentures on the footing of stockholders of an ordinary corporation. It makes them, instead of the stockholders, the owners of the equity of the corporation." *Id*. 26 N.W.2d at 635. The issue in *Biltchik* was whether the railroad's board of directors had any duty to declare a dividend large enough to give the Class B debenture holders some income. The court held that the board had no such duty as long as it used the railroad's income for proper purposes. The court pointed out that the Class B debenture holders might benefit indirectly if the railroad rather than paying generous dividends plowed back its earnings into improvements, since that would make the railroad worth more in the event it was sold. If the railroad was already worth $10.1 million, such improvements would not benefit the Class B debenture holders directly if their entitlement in the event of a sale or reorganization is capped at $7 million, although it would do so indirectly, by increasing the probability that they would be paid in full should the railroad ever be sold. But it is fairly plain that the railroad was worth much less than $10.1 million at the time of *Biltchik*. See *id*. 26 N.W.2d at 635. So the cap was not material and the court's passing remark about the status of the Class B debenture holders cannot be considered authoritative.

Even if as we believe Itel has the better of the argument when consideration is limited to the text of the Class B debenture, should consideration be so limited? Since the debenture makes no explicit provision for the allocation of the net proceeds of sale above $10.1 million, and since the last sentence that we quoted from the debenture certificate, the sentence on which the plaintiffs pitch their case, provides at least some support for it, there is enough ambiguity to permit the consideration of extrinsic evidence, that is, evidence outside the text of the Class B debenture itself. Itel implicitly acknowledges this by pointing out that these debentures were issued in exchange for interests that probably had little value.

The first item of extrinsic evidence that the plaintiffs want us to consider is the text of the Class A debenture. It is almost identical to that of the Class B debenture, except that the first sentence of the Class A debenture, of course, states the entitlement of the holders of that debenture to their $1,000 rather than the entitlement of the Class B debenture holders to their $1,000. Like the Class B debenture, the Class A debenture goes on to specify the order of distribution, including the payment to the holders of the Class B debentures of the surplus after satisfaction of the entitlements of the Class A debenture holders and the shareholders. Since the first sentence of the Class A debenture does not mention the Class B debenture holders, there is nothing to qualify the last sentence—the sentence that taken by itself appears to give the entire surplus, with no $7 million cap, to those debenture holders. That sentence is not found, however, in the description of the Class A debentures that appears in the articles of incorporation of the reorganized firm. And to the holder of a Class A debenture the only important thing is his entitlement, and not, after his entitlement has been satisfied, how any surplus above the amount necessary to satisfy it is to be divided between other classes of investor. It would be odd for the owner of a Class B debenture to look to the text of *another* debenture for the statement of his rights (though, granted, initially the holders of the two classes of debentures were the same people—the railroad's Second mortgagees and former shareholders). No one reading the Class B debenture, with its flat statement that it entitles the holder to $1,000 if the railroad is ever sold or reorganized, would suppose that it entitled the holder to more—to almost six times as much, in fact, if the plaintiffs' estimate of the sale price of the railroad is correct.

The plaintiffs point to a series of statements that the railroad made, some in the two cases that we discussed, some in other cases, others in Submissions to the SEC and the ICC, which the plaintiffs construe as admissions that the Class B debenture holders are the residual owners of the railroad. So far as appears, however, these statements (contradicted, incidentally, by others, which do refer to the $7 million cap) were made at a time when the railroad was worth less than $10.1 million, so that the question of the entitlement to any surplus value above that was academic. In the 1940s, when *Biltchik* and the tax case were decided, the market value of the Class B debentures was only $120, implying that the net worth of the railroad may have been as little as $3,940,000 ($.6 million plus $2.5 million plus 7,000 x $120). If so, the Class B debenture holders were the real equity owners, because, had the railroad been sold then at that price, they would have received the entire net proceeds minus the $3.1 million reserved for the Class A debenture holders and the shareholders.

Despite what we have just said, the value of the railroad cannot be inferred directly from the market value of the Class B debentures. That market value would have been depressed by the inability of the debenture holders to force a sale or a distribution of income to them. The court in *Biltchik* thought the railroad worth more, about $5 million—or so we infer from 26 N.W.2d at 635. This estimate may well have been more realistic. But it is still far below the point at which the Class B debenture holders would be paid in full in the event the railroad was sold.

The plaintiffs presented no evidence of the value of the railroad at any of the times when the statements on which they rely were made, although it appears that as late as 1986 the railroad was worth no more than $8.4 million. *Leuw v. Green Bay & Western R.R.*, supra, slip op. at 21, 48. Itel had acquired its interest in the railroad–100 percent of the common stock and 78 percent of the Class B debentures—in 1978 for a total of $8 million. (Because it had bought securities of the railroad rather than the railroad itself, its purchase did not trigger the entitlement of the debenture holders to be paid out.) The plaintiffs' claim that the railroad was sold for at least $43 million in 1993 appears to be grossly exaggerated. Itel had paid $61 million for the Fox River Valley Railroad, the railroad it sold together with the Green Bay & Western Railroad for $64 million in 1993.

Remarks, even considered statements, that the Class B debenture holders were the real equity owners of the Green Bay, made at the time when they *were* the real though not formal equity owners, are not highly probative of what their status would be if the residual value of the railroad rose above the face amount of those debentures. The plaintiffs want a trial but have cited no evidence that would rebut the presumption from the text and history and economic logic of the Class B debenture that it caps the holders' entitlement at $7 million. No jury would be permitted to speculate that this debenture was really a share of stock.

* * * In effect the parties have recast the issue on appeal as whether we should grant summary judgment for the defendant. We should and do. The judgment is therefore Affirmed.

NOTE: PRIORITY OF CLAIM

1. *The Meaning of Seniority.*

What makes a senior claim "senior"? The security holder's investment contract may be viewed as describing (a) a claim to share in that cash flow stream and in any liquidating distribution, and (b) a right to affect the conduct of the enterprise to protect and enhance the value of that claim. The claims of a firm's various investment securities upon its cash flows and assets are defined in their respective investment contracts. The contracts state the amount of the claims and prescribe their priority vis-a-vis other claims. Thus, typically, a senior debt claim (e.g., principal or interest on a bond) has a right to payment which must be satisfied before the next most junior claim (e.g., preferred stock dividends or liquidating distributions) may be paid. The preferred stock has a comparable prior claim to dividends and in liquidation over the common stock.

Technically the claim of the debt is an obligation, since generally it represents a promise to pay principal and interest, which on default the creditor may enforce. In contrast, the preferred stock's claim is only a priority against the claims of other stockholders. It is embodied in a negative covenant, which becomes enforceable only if the common or other juniors seek to distribute earnings or assets to themselves.

A necessary corollary to the priority of a claim is the existence of a ceiling or limit on its amount: The stated maximum amount of the claim to cash flows or assets must be satisfied before the next claim in the hierarchy is entitled to any portion of the flows or assets. No more than that amount need (or may) be diverted from the stream of cash flows or from the assets to the prior claim, no matter what the growth of the stream or assets. The limited character of the "senior" claims contrasts with the open-ended residual character of the common stock claim. The common stock is exposed to the greatest risk because it receives distributions only after all other claims are satisfied. But it also has the opportunity to reap the greatest rewards because it is entitled to all amounts available in excess of the prior limited claim of the seniors.

The contracts creating the capital structure of the Green Bay & Western, discussed in the principal case, break the standard mold just described. The Class B debentures, nominally senior to the common as "debentures," have the junior and residual right respecting the distribution of cash flows—"dividends" payable when, as, and if declared by the board with no ceiling as to amount. The last quoted sentence of the debenture appears to hold out an equivalent treatment respecting proceeds on sale of the firm—all sums remaining after payment of fixed sums to prior classes. Does the combination of uncapped rights respecting dividends and apparently uncapped rights respecting proceeds on sale dictate the conclusion that the Class B should be treated as the residual interest holder?

2. *Control Rights.*

Accompanying the common stock's greater exposure to risk and greater opportunity for benefit is its control of the enterprise. While the "control" of dispersed common stock over management is problematic, it can be significant when compared to the power of voteless senior securities. With control of the election of management comes the possibility of influencing critical decisions respecting the firm's levels of risk and the growth or contraction of its cash flows and assets. More particularly, voting control (a) offers the opportunity to influence the determination of the portions, if any, of the cash flows or assets to be distributed to the firm's different classes of security holders; (b) enables the common stock's management representatives to determine the creation of new priority claims on cash flows and assets (e.g., bonds or preferred stock); (c) carries possible influence over determination of the risk-return characteristics of the business undertaken by the firm; and (d) in a distress situation enables the common's management representatives to set the terms by which existing claims are altered pursuant to a refinancing or recapitalization. Management's power to seek such alterations, even though usually subject to the consent of the holders of outstanding senior securities, can be tantamount to the power to compel them.

The common stockholders of the Green Bay & Western held all of the aforementioned rights. Do you agree with the court's suggestion that control rights cannot coherently be coupled with a senior and capped claim to the firm's cash flows?

3. *Allocational Conflict.*

Legal issues arise when junior security holders, generally common stockholders, exercise their control powers to benefit themselves at the expense of senior claimants. Since the seniors' and juniors' legal rights are embodied in investment contracts (which, in the case of stock, include provisions from the corporate code of the chartering state), the issues in the first instance involve the interpretation of contracts and statutes. Sometimes, the junior security holders wield their power to injure the interests of senior security holders during prosperous times, as where additional senior capital is borrowed to invest in riskier projects or to fund a return of capital to the common stockholders. Here, if the senior claimants have not reserved contract rights against the injurious course of conduct, the legal question will be whether such a right should be implied in fact or in law. More often, the setting for senior-junior conflict is one of economic adversity. The company has experienced operating losses over an extended period, and default on senior obligations is imminent or may already have occurred. In this context the common stockholders, through their management representatives, may seek to rebargain the relationship with the senior security owners to preserve an economic interest in the enterprise at a minimum sacrifice. The seniors, on the other hand, will prefer a strict enforcement of their contract rights, even if that entails extinguishing the common stockholders' interest and possibly a liquidation of the corporation. A tug-of-war follows. In this conflict the common stockholders often have the advantage both of having drafted (through their representatives, and without serious or direct bargaining by the seniors) the original investment contract and, by comparison with the seniors, of controlling the enterprise thereafter. As a consequence the seniors can occupy a weaker negotiating position than the common, and sometimes even may be subject to its dictates. In either event, legal constraints on the rebargaining process matter critically for the seniors, in addition to issues of contract interpretation. On the other hand, today's bankruptcy reorganization context enhances the seniors' opportunity to take meaningful control, often forcing the common into the junior position contemplated by the contract regime.

Section A.   Capital Structure and Leverage

One of the most widely debated issues in financial theory is whether the value of the firm can be enhanced through appropriate engineering of its capital structure. Can a firm finance its investments with an appropriate amount of senior securities in addition to common shares and thereby enhance the welfare of its common shareholders?

Under the traditional view, including bonds or other senior securities in the corporation's capital structure, when kept within appropriate limits, increases the total value of the firm and advantages common stockholders. Beyond some point of maximum advantage, however, additional increments of debt or other fixed obligations have the opposite effect and reduce firm value and hence the value of common shares. Under the traditional view, then, capital structure is relevant to the value of the firm and the issue of debt and equity in roughly optimal proportions is a significant task of financial management.

The belief that there is an advantage in financing with one mix of securities rather than another was challenged by financial economists—most notably, Franco Modigliani and Merton Miller (M–M) in their Nobel Prize winning article, The Cost of Capital, Corporation Finance and the Theory of Investment, 48 Amer.Econ.Rev. 261 (1958). Briefly stated, the M–M analysis, which extended an earlier discussion by Durand, argued that the value of the firm is independent of its capital structure and is determined solely by capitalizing its expected stream of operating income at a discount rate appropriate to its asset base's business risk; the external arrangement of claims against the income stream can have no influence on the value placed on that stream by the market. Restating, capital structure is irrelevant to the value of the firm. To see this point, think of the firm as a pie. The assertion is that the size of the pie is determined by the production function itself—the firm's technology, physical facilities, management and employee expertise, and marketing strategy. The capital structure merely slices the pie, with different patterns of slices never affecting the pie's size. If this view is correct, then, unless extraneous factors intervene, management should cease searching for an optimal capital structure and concentrate on other goals.

We will see in this Section that this "irrelevance" argument, while powerful, has proved unable to support a complete theory of firm value and capital structure. The allocation of claims to slices of the pie turns out to be causally connected to the size of the pie, due to effects on the incentives of the actors who create the pie, information asymmetries, regulation, tax, and other factors. Discussions of the M–M thesis in the end produced new theories about the benefits of including debt in corporate capital structures. These revived theories of optimal capital structure entail examining particular benefits and detriments stemming from debt financing—bankruptcy costs, tax benefits, asserted corporate governance or "agency cost" factors, and informational content.

1. LEVERAGE AND VALUE

(A) THE COST OF CAPITAL AND THE VALUE OF THE FIRM

As a matter of formal definition, the cost of capital for a firm is a discount rate with the property that an investment with a rate of return above this rate will raise the value of the firm and an investment with a rate of return below the rate will lower the value of the firm. How is this critical rate of return determined in the context of new investment? Assume that Corporation A is investing $100,000,000 in Investment X, a new plant to be financed entirely by a new issue of debentures with a coupon rate of 10 percent. Is that 10 percent cost of debt the appropriate cost of capital to be employed as the discount rate in a Net Present Value calculation respecting Investment X? It would appear that so long as Investment X generates returns at a rate above that 10 percent, the firm is more valuable. Yet this approach is problematic for two reasons. First, it looks at the firm in the abstract, as a separate entity, rather than looking at the firm from the point of view of its shareholders' financial interest. Second, it compares Investment X only to the out of pocket cost of its own financing rather than to competing investments that Corporation A could have made had it not devoted $100,000,000 to Investment X. To determine whether Investment X makes the firm more valuable to its shareholders, a cost of capital must be employed that reflects this $100,000,000 opportunity cost. If Investment X's rate of return is less than the return on the alternative, the firm's value is not enhanced. This investment alternative need not be a competing project. Both conceptually and practically, a firm's own securities represent a real investment opportunity. Outstanding common can be repurchased by the firm whenever internally generated funds exceed the amounts needed for new investment projects, or, in this case, with the proceeds of a newly financed $100,000,000.

It follows that the shareholders' rate of return is the standard for the firm's cost of capital rather than the firm's overall cost of debt, senior equity, and junior equity. Thus, Investment X enhances firm value if it returns more than the rate of return on the common stock.

As we saw in Part I, the rate of return on a firm's common stock must be derived by inference, even though the stock's price is concretely set by a trading market. Present common stock rates of return (as opposed to present market prices) are subject to all the indeterminacies and intractabilities of valuation in a world with an uncertain future. No empirically verifiable figure will be available to the firm's managers at any particular time. It accordingly is unsurprising that most firms adopt a rule of thumb figure based on past performance for the cost they will attach to their use of capital, and employ it as a discount rate in present value calculations.

Having taken the analysis this far, we emerge in a position to state the issue for discussion in this Section. Return to Corporation A and Investment X. Let us assume that management has determined that Investment X has a positive net present value, having discounted its projected returns by the rate of return on Corporation A's common, which we stipulate to be 14 percent. As stated, management has access to debt capital at 10 percent. The question is whether it automatically is the case that the firm is more valuable to its shareholders if Investment X is financed with that 10 percent debt capital rather than with the $100,000,000 proceeds of a new issue of common stock, or, if available, retained earnings from operations.

The materials that follow address this question.

Durand, Costs of Debt and Equity Funds for Business: Trends and Problems of Measurement

(National Bureau of Economic Research, Inc.).
Haverford College, June 19–21, 1952.

TABLE I
Balance Sheet of the ABC Manufacturing Company

Assets		$30,000,000
Liabilities		
Total Current	$ 6,000,000	
Common stock, 1,000,000 shares at $15 per share	15,000,000	
Surplus	9,000,000	
	$24,000,000	
Total		$30,000,000

Income Statement of the ABC Manufacturing Company

Net operating income	2,500,000
Dividends paid	2,000,000
Transferred to Surplus	500,000
Earnings per share	$2.50
Dividends per share	$2.00

* * *

Could a corporation [whose balance sheet and income statement are summarized in Table I] profitably finance additional plant by issuing $10 million of 4 percent bonds, provided the expansion were expected to earn $800,000 annually, or 8 percent? The estimated income after the proposed expansion is shown below:

Net income, current operations	$2,500,000
[Net income, proposed operations ($800,000 less $400,000 interest)]	400,000

Net income	$2,900,000
Dividends (old rate)	2,000,000
	$ 900,000

But if the bond issue could be arranged, would the stockholders consider the transaction attractive? The expansion has the advantage of increasing the prospective earnings from $2.50 a share to $2.90. It also has the disadvantage of increasing the risk because the proposed bond issue is so large that dividends might be curtailed for several years—even if the expected earnings were realized; and the entire financial position of the company might be jeopardized if earnings fell off sharply.

* * *

* * * Suppose, for example, that 12½ percent, or eight times earnings, is considered a fair capitalization rate as long as the company remains debt free, and that an increase to 15 percent, or six and two-thirds times earnings, is considered an adequate adjustment to compensate for the risk of carrying $10 million in debt. These assumed rates are completely arbitrary * * * [It is sufficient for the present argument merely to assume that the stockholders consider the rates satisfactory.] The necessary stock appraisals can then be made easily, as shown below. These calculations imply that the proposed expansion is inadvisable.

Earnings per share from current operations	$ 2.50
Multiplier	8
Investment value per share	$20.00
Projected earnings after expansion	$ 2.90
Multiplier	6⅔
Investment value	$19.33

Because the stockholders suffer a decline in the investment value of their holdings, the small increase in earnings is not sufficient to compensate for the additional risk.

Required Return

The preceding example showed that the risks incurred in borrowing may discourage investment, even though the rate of return on the new investment exceeds the interest cost of borrowed money. Specifically, the possibility of earning 8 percent in this example did not justify borrowing at only half that rate. But a still higher rate of return would have justified the investment. The following calculations show how to ascertain a rate that is just high enough to offset the risk. It is assumed that the risk will be just offset if the prospective per share earnings capitalized at 15 percent maintain the value of the common stock at $20.00.

Required value of stock per share	$20.00
Capitalization rate	.15
Required earnings, per share	3.00
Required earnings, 1,000,000 shares	3,000,000
Earnings previously available	2,500,000

Additional earnings required	500,000
Interest charges	400,000
Required earnings before interest	900,000
Rate of required earnings	9%

The required rate of earnings—9 percent for this example—is in a sense the cost to this corporation of borrowing the needed money. Of course, it is not an out-of-pocket cost, but a sort of opportunity cost—the minimum rate that the new investment must earn without being actually disadvantageous to the stockholders. But perhaps this is too broad an interpretation of cost, and the reader is, therefore, free to choose for himself. * * * For the remainder of this paper, the required rate of earnings will be referred to as the *required return* and will be abbreviated, RR. * * *

Although the RR discussed above refers to bond financing, there is also a RR when a corporation sells stock, and sometimes even when it finances expansion with cash retained from operations. If the stockholders in the previous example had been deterred from authorizing the proposed expansion because the expected returns were inadequate to justify the inherent risk incurred by bond financing, they might have considered preferred stock, common stock, and perhaps a judicious combination of common stock and bonds. Would the expected return have been sufficient to justify any of these alternatives? And if not, what rate of return would have been sufficient? * * * When capital is raised by a common stock issue, the old stockholders will suffer a dilution of earning power and hence a dilution of investment value unless the new investment is capable of earning enough to maintain per-share earnings at the old level. The RR depends upon the old level of earnings and the price at which the new shares must be sold. If the stockholders of the ABC Company wanted to raise $10 million by selling 500,000 shares on the market at $20.00, the new investment would have to earn $1,250,000 or 12½ percent to avoid dilution of earnings. Hence 12½ percent is the RR.

II. The Problem of Security Appraisal

It should be clear enough that any practical application of the principles of the RR necessitates a sound, effective, and generally acceptable system of security appraisal. Yet at present, no such system exists. Naturally some differences of opinion concerning details may always be expected. But present differences run much deeper than details. On the single question of capitalizing earnings, involved in most appraisal methods, there appear to be two systems in current use that arise from fundamentally different assumptions, lead to substantially different results in calculating the RR, and have radically different implications for financial policy. An analysis of these two systems will therefore prove illuminating and will further highlight the need of providing a sound conceptual groundwork for research on investment problems and the costs of capital.

The accompanying sample balance sheet and income statement contain enough data to illustrate the fundamental difference between the two methods of capitalizing earnings. This hypothetical company is financed partly with bonds, partly with common stock; and the problem at hand is to estimate the value of the common stock on the assumption that the bonds, which are well protected, sell in the market at par. Since the purpose of the illustration is to focus attention on the problem of capitalizing earnings, questions of assets and book value will be neglected entirely, and the important matter of the corporate income tax will be deferred for later treatment.

Balance Sheet of the PDQ Manufacturing Company [Abridged]

Assets		$30,000,000
Liabilities		
Total Current	$5,000,000	
Bonded debt, 4 percent debentures	5,000,000	
Common stock, 1,500,000 shares at $10 per share	15,000,000	
Earned surplus	5,000,000	
Total		$30,000,000

Income Statement of the PDQ Manufacturing Company

Sales	$30,000,000
Cost of goods sold	28,000,000
Net operating income	2,000,000
Interest	200,000
Net income	$1,800,000

One approach, hereafter called the NOI Method, capitalizes net operating income and subtracts the debt as follows:

Net operating income	$2,000,000
Capitalization rate, 10%	× 10
Total value of company	20,000,000
Total bonded debt	5,000,000
Total value of common stock	15,000,000
Value per share, 1,500,000 shares	$10.00

The essence of this approach is that the total value of all bonds and stock must always be the same—$20 million in this example—regardless of the proportion of bonds and stock. Had there been no bonds at all, for example, the total value of the common stock would have been $20 million, and had there been $2.5 million in bonds, the value would have been $17.5 million. Hereafter, the total of all stocks and bonds will be called the "total investment value" of the company.

The alternative approach, hereafter called the NI Method, capitalizes net income instead of net operating income. The calculations are as follows:

Net operating income	$2,000,000
Interest	200,000
Net income	1,800,000
Capitalization rate, 10%	× 10
Total value of common stock	18,000,000
Value per share, 1,500,000 shares	$12.00

Under this method, the total investment value does not remain constant, but increases with the proportion of bonds in the capital structure. In the table below, three levels of bond financing are assumed: $5 million, $2.5 million, and no bonds at all. At each level, the value of the stock is

Assumed amount of bonds	None	$ 2,500,000	$ 5,000,000
Value of common stock	$20,000,000	19,000,000	18,000,000
Total investment value	$20,000,000	$21,500,000	$23,000,000

obtained, as above, by capitalizing at 10 percent the residual income after bond interest. The implied relation in this table is that an increase of $2.5 million in bonded debt (total capitalization remaining constant) produces a corresponding increase of $1.5 million in total investment value. However, such a relationship cannot continue indefinitely as the proponents of the NI Method clearly point out. As the debt burden becomes substantial, the bonds will slip below par, and the stock will cease to be worth ten times earnings.

* * *

* * * The most obvious difference between the two methods is that the NI Method results in a higher total investment value and a higher value for the common stock except for companies capitalized entirely with stock. For such companies the two methods give identical results provided the same capitalization rate is used. This difference alone marks the NI Method as more liberal than the NOI Method, but the distinction between the optimism of the NI Method and the pessimism of the NOI Method will grow sharper as the discussion progresses. The NI Method, it will appear, takes a very sanguine view of the risks incurred in business borrowing; the NOI Method takes a more sober view.

Proponents of the NOI Method argue that the totality of risk incurred by all security holders of a given company cannot be altered by merely changing the capitalization proportions. Such a change could only alter the proportion of the total risk borne by each class of security holder. Thus if the PDQ Company had been capitalized entirely with stock—say 2,000,000 shares instead of 1,500,000—the stockholders would have borne all the risk. With $5 million in bonds in lieu of the additional 500,000 shares, the bondholders would have incurred a portion of this risk. But because the bonds are so well protected, this portion would be small—say in the order of 5 or ten percent. Hence the stockholders would still be bearing most of the risk, and with 25 percent fewer shares the risk per share would be substantially greater.[8]

8. This proposition can be stated rigorously in terms of mathematical expectation. In brief, the argument runs along the following lines. The future income of a company has a definite, though perhaps unknown, mathematical expectation. If this income is to be divided up among types of security holder according to some formula, the income of each type will also have a definite mathematical expectation. Finally, the sum of the mathematical expectations for each type will necessarily equal the total for the entire income *no matter how that income is divided up.*

In spite of the logical merits of this proposition, the basic assumption may be objectionable. One of my critics opines that the

The advocates of the NI Method take a position that is somewhat less straightforward. Those who adhere strictly to this method contend: first, that *conservative* increases in bonded debt do not increase the risk borne by the common stockholders; second, that a package of securities containing a *conservative* proportion of bonds will justifiably command a higher market price than a package of common stock alone.

The first contention seems to have little merit; it runs counter to the rigorous analysis offered by the advocates of the NOI Method; and it seems to imply that the security holders of a business can raise themselves by their own bootstraps.[9] The second contention appears to be correct, however, and it certainly merits critical analysis.

(B) THE MODIGLIANI–MILLER POSITION AND THE REVISED CONCEPT OF OPTIMAL CAPITAL STRUCTURE

(1) The M–M Thesis and Its Assumptions

The net operating income approach to enterprise valuation stressed by Durand was further elaborated in Modigliani and Miller, "The Cost of Capital, Corporation Finance and the Theory of Investment," 48 Am.Econ. Rev. 261 (1958). M–M are famous for two propositions. Proposition 1 begins with Durand and asserts that the market values of the firm's debt D and equity E add up to the total value of the firm V. Myers, Capital Structure, 15 J. Econ. Perspectives 81, 84–85 (2001), describes how M–M carry that proposition out to its logical conclusion:

[handwritten: V (firm value) $= D + E$]

"Proposition 1 also says that each firm's cost of capital is a constant, regardless of the debt ratio. The cost of capital is a standard tool of practical finance, so it's worth writing out the formula. Let r_D and r_E be the cost of debt and the cost of equity—that is, the expected rates of return demanded by investors in the firm's debt and equity securities. The overall (weighted-average) cost of capital depends on these costs and the market-value ratios of debt and equity to overall firm value.

$$\text{Weighted Average Cost of Capital} =$$
$$r_A = r_D D/V + r_E E/V$$

The weighted average cost of capital r_A is the expected return on a portfolio of all the firm's outstanding securities. * * *

"The weighted average cost of capital r_A is, according to Modigliani and Miller, a constant. Also, debt has a prior claim on the firm's assets and earnings, so the cost of debt is always less than the cost of equity. Suppose we solve the equation for the cost of equity.

$$r_E = r_A + (r_A - r_D)D/E$$

---

totality of risk is increased when a business borrows and that even the NOI Method is optimistic.

9. The argument * * * implies that a business can incur any amount of debt without increasing the proprietors' risk. Recog- nizing that this is a practical absurdity, the advocates of the NI Method say merely that a business can incur a limited amount of debt without increasing the proprietors' risk. * * *

In other words, the cost of equity—the expected rate of return demanded by equity investors—increases with the market-value debt-equity ratio D/E. The rate of increase depends on the spread between the overall cost of capital r_A and the cost of debt r_D. This equation is Modigliani and Miller's Proposition 2. It shows why 'there is no magic in financial leverage.' Any attempt to substitute 'cheap' debt for 'expensive' equity fails to reduce the overall cost of capital because it makes the remaining equity still more expensive—just enough more expensive to keep the overall cost of capital constant."

Van Horne, Financial Management and Policy

256–260 (12th Ed. 2002).

TRADITIONAL APPROACH

The **traditional approach** to valuation and leverage assumes that there is an optimal capital structure and that the firm can increase the total value of the firm through the judicious use of leverage. The approach suggests that the firm initially can lower its cost of capital and raise its total value through leverage. Although investors raise the equity-capitalization rate, the increase in k_e [the cost of equity] does not offset entirely the benefit of using "cheaper" debt funds. As more leverage occurs, investors increasingly penalize the firm's equity capitalization rate until eventually this effect more than offsets the use of "cheaper" debt funds.

In one variation of the traditional approach, shown in Fig. 9–2, k_e is assumed to rise at an increasing rate with leverage, whereas k_o [the firm's overall cost of capital] is assumed to rise only after significant leverage has occurred. At first, the weighted-average cost of capital declines with leverage because the rise in k_e does not offset entirely the use of cheaper debt funds. As a result, the weighted-average cost of capital, k_o, declines with moderate use of leverage. After a point, however, the increase in k_e more than offsets the use of cheaper debt funds in the capital structure, and k_o begins to rise. The optimal capital structure is the point at which k_o bottoms out. In the figure, this optimal capital structure is point X. Thus the traditional position implies that the cost of capital is not independent of the capital structure of the firm and that there is an optimal capital structure.

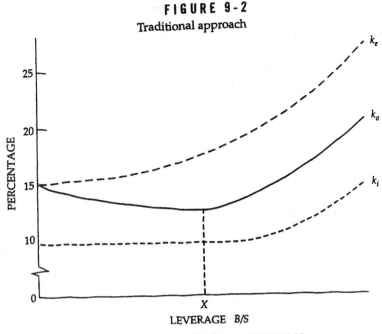

FIGURE 9-2
Traditional approach

MODIGLIANI–MILLER POSITION

Modigliani and Miller (MM) advocate that the relationship between leverage and the cost of capital is explained by the net operating income approach. They make a formidable attack on the traditional position by offering behavioral justification for having the cost of capital, k_o, remain constant throughout all degrees of leverage. As their assumptions are extremely important, it is necessary to spell them out.

1. Capital markets are perfect. Information is costless and readily available to all investors. There are no transaction costs, and all securities are infinitely divisible. Investors are assumed to be rational and to behave accordingly.

2. The average expected future operating earnings of a firm are represented by subjective random variables. It is assumed that the expected values of the probability distributions of all investors are the same. The MM illustration implies that the expected values of the probability distributions of expected operating earnings for all future periods are the same as present operating earnings.

3. Firms can be categorized into "equivalent return" classes. All firms within a class have the same degree of business risk. As we shall see later, this assumption is not essential for their proof.

4. The absence of corporate income taxes is assumed. MM remove this assumption later.

Simply put, the Modigliani–Miller position is based on the idea that no matter how you divide up the capital structure of a firm among debt, equity, and other claims, there is a conservation of investment value. That is, because the total investment value of a corporation depends upon its underlying profitability and risk, it is invariant with respect to relative changes in the firm's financial capitalization. Thus, the total pie does not change as it is divided into debt, equity, and other securities. The sum of the parts must equal the whole; so regardless of financing mix, the total value of the firm stays the same, according to MM. * * *

HOMEMADE LEVERAGE

The support for this position rests on the idea that investors are able to substitute personal for corporate leverage, thereby replicating any capital structure the firm might undertake. Because the firm is unable to do something for its stockholders (leverage) that they cannot do for themselves, capital structure changes are not a thing of value in the perfect capital market world that MM assume. Therefore, two firms alike in every respect except capital structure must have the same total value. If not, arbitrage will be possible, and its occurrence will cause the two firms to sell in the market at the same total value.

Illustration. Consider two firms identical in every respect except that Company A is not levered, while Company B has $30,000 of 12 percent bonds outstanding. According to the traditional position, Company B may have a higher total value and lower average cost of capital than Company A. The valuation of the two firms is assumed to be the following:

		Company A	Company B
O	Net operating income	$10,000	$10,000
F	Interest on debt	_____	3,600
E	Earnings available to common stockholders	$10,000	$6,400
k_e	Equity-capitalization rate	0.15	0.16
S	Market value of stock	$66,667	$40,000
B	Market value of debt	_____	30,000
V	Total value of firm	$66,667	$70,000
k_o	Implied overall capitalization rate	15%	14.3%
B/S	Debt-to-equity ratio	0	75.0%

MM maintain that this situation cannot continue, for arbitrage will drive the total values of the two firms together. Company B cannot command a higher total value simply because it has a financing mix different from Company A's. MM argue that by investing in Company A, investors in Company B are able to obtain the same dollar return with no increase in financial risk. Moreover, they are able to do so with a smaller investment outlay. Because investors would be better off with the investment requiring the lesser outlay, they would sell their shares in Company B and buy shares in Company A. These **arbitrage transactions** would continue until Company B's shares declined in price and Company A's shares increased in price enough to make the total value of the two firms identical.

Arbitrage Steps. If you are a rational investor who owns 1 percent of the stock of Company B, the levered firm, worth $400 (market value) you should

1. Sell the stock in Company B for $400.

2. Borrow $300 at 12 percent interest. This personal debt is equal to 1 percent of the debt of Company B, your previous proportional ownership of the company.

3. Buy 1 percent of the shares of Company A, the unlevered firm, for $667.67.

Prior to this series of transactions, your expected return on investment in Company B's stock was 16 percent on a $400 investment, or $64. Your expected return on investment in Company A is 15 percent on a $666.67 investment, or $100. From this return you must deduct the interest charges on your personal borrowings, so your net dollar return is

Return on investment in Company A	$100
Less interest ($300 × 0.12)	36
Net return	$ 64

Your net dollar return, $64, is the same as it was for your investment in Company B; however, your cash outlay of $366.67 ($666.67 less personal borrowings of $300) is less than the $400 investment in Company B, the levered firm. Because of the lower investment, you would prefer to invest in Company A under the conditions described. In essence, you "lever" the stock of the unlevered firm by taking on personal debt.*

The action of a number of investors undertaking similar arbitrage transactions will tend to drive up the price of Company A shares, lower its k_e, drive down the price of Company B, and increase its k_e. This arbitrage process will continue until there is no further opportunity for reducing one's investment outlay and achieving the same dollar return. At this equilibrium, the total value of the two firms must be the same. The principle involved is simply that investors are able to reconstitute their former positions by offsetting changes in corporate leverage with changes in personal leverage. Unless a company is able to do something for investors that they cannot do for themselves, value is not created.

* * *

(2) Relaxing M–M's Assumptions

Does the M–M Theorem predict the behavior of firms in the real world? If not, why is the M–M Theorem celebrated as the cornerstone of economic learning on capital structure? Consider the observations of Huang and Knoll, Corporate Finance, Corporate Law and Finance Theory, 74 So. Cal.L.Rev. 179–180 (2000):

* [Ed. Note] Suppose, however, that an investor borrows to buy stock in levered firm B, thus apparently doubling the leverage effect by adding his or her own to the corporation's borrowing. Will the investor then have succeeded in outrunning investors in A shares and hence be willing to pay a premium for that opportunity? The answer (which the reader is left to illustrate for himself or herself) is that the investor can accomplish the same results by simply borrowing more to buy an equivalent proportionate stock interest in A. Once again, therefore, the inducement to pay a premium for B is non-existent, at least theoretically.

"When it first appeared, commentators vigorously debated the Theo-rem's significance. The debate was not whether the theorem was a com-pletely accurate picture of reality (after all, even its staunchest defenders acknowledged that our economy had taxes), but whether it captured the essential features well enough so that its conclusion was roughly correct. Over time, the consensus has developed that the theorem does not accu-rately capture reality and so its conclusion is incorrect. Surprisingly, it is precisely the inaccuracy of the M & M Theorem's assumptions that makes it the foundation of modern corporate finance.

* * *

"The explanatory power of the M & M Theorem comes from turning it upside down: If capital structure can affect the value of the firm, it must work through one or more of the four M & M assumptions. That is to say, the only ways that capital structure can increase value are by lowering taxes, providing access to cheaper borrowing, releasing valuable informa-tion, or improving cash flow. We call this idea the Reverse M & M Theorem.

"The crucial insight provided by the M & M Theorem is that it tells us where to look to understand capital structure. If we want to understand how firms raise capital, we need to look at taxes, borrowing costs, informa-tion, and cash flows. Any explanation why some firms tend to use or avoid particular capital structures must, therefore, focus on exploiting the fail-ures to satisfy the M & M assumptions. In this way, the Reverse M & M Theorem is an important organizing principle for modern corporate finance because it tells us what types of arguments can explain capital structure policies. At a very general level, the most commonly invoked explanations for capital structures are as follows:

> Taxes: Relaxing the assumption of no taxes implies that capital struc-ture can create value by reducing taxes. This opens the way for explanations based on tax asymmetries.
>
> Inefficient markets: Relaxing the efficiency assumption implies that individuals can have different information and different opinions as to how much a security is worth. This has led to explanations based upon signaling and heterogeneous expectations.
>
> Imperfect markets: Relaxing the assumption of perfect capital markets means that capital structure can create value by changing investment policy. This has led to explanations based on agency costs."

(a) institutional constraints

M–M assume that corporate and homemade leverage are perfect substi-tutes, and in a world without frictions such would be the case. In the real world, the risk profiles and behavior patterns of corporate borrowers and individual borrowers will be different, even assuming that the individuals' borrowings are secured by portfolios of common stock issued by the same corporate borrowers. Individual borrowers are likely to be more risk averse than corporate borrowers, limiting the scope of the homemade leverage corrective. One reason for this is that individuals who borrow to buy stock, unlike corporate actors borrowing to buy hard assets, tend to be subject to unlimited liability. They also are subject to margin calls triggered by market price declines. The uncontrollable aspect of these mandatory pre-payments can constrain the incentive to borrow. Contrariwise, individual borrowing secured by stock may be perceived as riskier than direct borrowing by the corporate issuers of the stock. All the factors that contribute to the special volatility of stock markets, discussed in Part I, supra, bear more strongly on the individual's stock portfolio than the corporate borrower's asset base. Higher volatility means higher borrowing costs.

Of course, financial institutions may borrow to hold equities and perform the arbitrage function instead of individual investors. A financial institution will more closely resemble the behavior pattern and risk-return profile of a corporate borrower. This more secure posture will ameliorate the foregoing limitations on the availability of homemade leverage. But financial institutions do not operate free of constraints. The equity portfolios of institutions like pension funds and life insurance companies are often restricted by regulators. Such investors may be limited to a list of issuers meeting certain quality standards, such as only a "safe" amount of leverage. The limitation decreases the capacity for homemade equity. Only with unregulated institutions like the hedge funds do we finally approach the financial economic ideal of a pure arbitrageur.

(b) taxes

Van Horne, Financial Management and Policy

261–263, 264–266 (12th Ed.2002).

CORPORATE TAXES

The advantage of debt in a world of **corporate taxes** is that interest payments are deductible as an expense. They elude taxation at the corporate level, whereas dividends or retained earnings associated with stock are not deductible by the corporation for tax purposes. Consequently, the total amount of payments available for both debtholders and stockholders is greater if debt is employed.

To illustrate, suppose that the earnings before interest and taxes are $2,000 for companies X and Y, and they are alike in every respect except in leverage. Company Y has $5,000 in debt at 12 percent interest, whereas Company X has no debt. If the tax rate (federal and state) is 40 percent for each company, we have

	Company X	Company Y
Earnings before interest and taxes	$2,000	$2,000
Interest—income to debtholders	0	600
Profit before taxes	2,000	1,400
Taxes	800	560
Income available to stockholders	$1,200	$840
Income to debtholders plus income to stockholders	$1,200	$1,440

Thus, total income to both debtholders and stockholders is larger for levered Company Y than it is for unlevered Company X. The reason is that debtholders receive interest payments without the deduction of taxes at the corporate level, whereas income to stockholders is after corporate taxes have been paid. In essence, the government pays a subsidy to the levered company for the use of debt. Total income to all investors increases by the interest payment times the tax rate. In our example, this amounts to $600 × 0.40 = $240. This figure represents a tax shield that the government provides the levered company * * *.

* * * [T]he greater the amount of debt, the greater the tax shield and the greater value of the firm, all other things the same. Thus, the original MM proposition as subsequently adjusted for corporate taxes suggests that an optimal strategy is to take on a maximum amount of leverage. Clearly, this is not consistent with the behavior of corporations, and alternative explanations must be sought.

* * *

CORPORATE PLUS PERSONAL TAXES

* * * [T]he presence of taxes on personal income may reduce or possibly eliminate the corporate tax advantage associated with debt. If returns on debt and on stock are taxed at the same personal tax rate, however, the corporate tax advantage remains. This can be seen by taking our earlier example and applying a 30 percent personal tax rate to the debt and stock returns:

	Company X	Company Y
Debt income	0	$600
Less personal taxes of .30		− 180
Debt income after personal taxes	0	420
Income available to stockholders	$1200	$840
Less personal taxes of .30	− 360	− 252
Stockholders income after personal taxes	840	588
Income to debt holders and stockholders after personal taxes	$840	$1008

Although the total after-tax income to debt holders and stockholders is less than before, the tax advantage associated with debt remains.

* * *

* * * Therefore, the corporate tax advantage of debt remains exactly the same if debt income and stock income are taxed at the same personal tax rate.

Dividends versus Capital Gains. We know that stock income is comprised both of dividends and capital gains * * *. Dividend income by and large is taxed at the same personal tax rate as interest income. Capital gains are often taxed at a lower rate. Sometimes the differential is explicit in that the tax rate is less. Even when capital gains are taxed at the same rate as ordinary income, however, there is an advantage to the capital gain. For one thing, it is postponed until the security is sold. For those who give appreciated securities as gifts to charitable causes, the tax may be largely avoided, as it is if a person dies. For these reasons, the effective tax on capital gains in a present value sense is less than that on interest and dividend incomes. As a result, the corporate tax advantage associated with corporate debt is reduced. * * *

* * * If the company is concerned with only after-tax income to the investor, it would finance either with debt or with stock, depending upon the relative values of t_{pd} [personal income tax on debt income] and t_c [corporate income tax]. If the personal tax rate on debt income exceeds the corporate tax rate, the company would finance with stock, because the after-tax income to the investor would be higher. If t_{pd} is less than t_c, however, it would finance with debt, because after-tax income to the investor would be greater here. If t_{pd} equals t_c, it would be a matter of indifference whether debt or stock were employed.

NOTE: TAXATION AND THE M–M THEOREM

1. *Taxes and Homemade Leverage.*

The "tax shield" referred to by Van Horne has been shown to be worth (on average) 10 or 13 percent (depending on the measuring yardstick) of the market value of the firm's stock. The figure can rise to 20 percent after a leveraged buyout. See Graham, How Big are the Tax Benefits of Debt? 55 J. Fin. 1901 (2000).

The tax shield is a shield that homemade leverage cannot duplicate or overcome. As has been seen, a corporation with bonds outstanding can deduct all interest payments in computing its taxable income. By contrast, a corporation with an all-stock capital structure computes its taxable income without deducting dividends, and without regard to interest payments made at the shareholder level by shareholders who are borrowing. If a corporate tax rate of 50 percent is assumed, the comparative results can be illustrated as follows:

CORP. A

100,000 shares, par value $50

E/s before tax	E/s after tax	Probability of occurrence
$12	$6	$\frac{1}{3}$
$ 8	$4	$\frac{1}{3}$
$ 4	$2	$\frac{1}{3}$

CORP. B

50,000 shares, par value $50
$2.5 million bonds at 5%

E/s before tax	E/s after tax	Probability of occurrence
$21.50 ($24—$2.50)	$10.75	$\frac{1}{3}$

$13.50 ($16—$2.50)	$ 6.75	⅓
$ 5.50 ($ 8—$2.50)	$ 2.75	⅓

The expected value of *A's* after-tax earnings is thus $4 per share; that of *B*, $6.75 per share. Assume a multiplier of 12.5 for *A*, so that the market value of a share of *A* is $50. Now, however, it can no longer be asserted that a *B* share will also sell at only $50 despite higher expected earnings, since the investor cannot duplicate the *B* income stream by engaging in personal leverage and buying 2 shares of *A*. Thus, if an investor borrows $50 at 5% and purchases a second share of *A*, he achieves the following result after allowing for the $2.50 interest charges he will owe on the loan:

Earnings on 2 A shares	Probability of occurrence
$9.50 [(2 × $6)—$2.50]	⅓
$5.50 [(2 × $4)—$2.50]	⅓
$1.50 [(2 × $2)—$2.50]	⅓

While the spread of probable outcomes is the same on 2 shares of *A* as on 1 share of *B*, the expected return on *A* is $1.25 less than on *B* ($6.75—$5.50) and indeed the investor is clearly worse off by that amount at every possible outcome. It follows that investors will pay more for *B* than for *A* and hence that corporate leverage will attract a premium once taxes are taken into account.

2. *Clientele Effects.*

There is an argument, made in Miller, Debt and Taxes, 32 J. of Fin. 261 (1977), that the interplay of income tax on investors and the tax consequences of the corporate interest deduction combined with shifting investor clienteles will make capital structure irrelevant for individual firms. Myers, Capital Structure, 15 J. Econ. Perspectives 81, 87–88 (2001), explains this tax economics:

" * * * [T]he corporate-level tax advantages of debt could be partly offset by the tax advantage of equity to individual investors, namely, the ability to defer capital gains and then to pay taxes at a lower capital gains rate. The tax rate on investors' interest and dividend income is higher than the effective tax rate on equity income, which comes as a mixture of dividends and capital gains. Corporations should see this relatively low effective rate as a reduction in the cost of equity relative to the cost of debt.

"The tax advantages of equity to investors could, in some cases, offset the value of interest tax shields to the corporation. For example, suppose Firm X's shareholders are in the top individual tax bracket, paying about 40 percent on a marginal dollar of interest or dividends received. However, the firm pays no dividends, so equity income comes entirely as capital gains. Suppose the effective rate on capital gains is 8 percent. (The top-bracket capital gains rate is now 20 percent, and can be deferred until shares are sold and the gains realized.) Then the taxes paid on $100,000 of Firm X's income are: 1) $35,000 in corporate taxes, 2) about $5,000 of (deferred) capital gains taxes (about 8 percent of the corporate income of $65,000).

"Now Firm X borrows $1 million at 10 percent and repurchases and retires $1 million of equity. It pays out $100,000 per year in interest but saves $35,000 in taxes. But investors receive $100,000 *more* in interest income and $65,000 *less* in capital gains. Their taxes go up by $40,000—5,000 = $35,000. There is no net gain once both corporate and individual taxes are considered.

"If these effective tax rates applied generally to the marginal investors in debt and equity securities, we would predict the equilibrium described by Miller * * *. The equilibrium is reached in the following way. As the supply of debt from all corporations expands, investors with higher and higher tax brackets have to be enticed to hold corporate debt, and to receive more of their income in the form of interest rather than capital gains. Interest rates rise as more and more debt is issued, so corporations face rising costs of debt relative to their costs of equity. Eventually the after-tax cost of debt becomes so high that there is no gain from further borrowing. The supply of debt increases until there is no further net tax advantage. At that point, the effects of personal and corporate taxes cancel out, and Modigliani and Miller's Proposition 1 holds despite the tax-deductibility of interest.

"But actual tax rates do not appear to support this equilibrium. * * * Nevertheless, interest tax shields should still be extremely valuable."

(c) bankruptcy costs

The more highly levered the firm, the greater the risk of bankruptcy. Bankruptcy implies significant costs. These begin with the out of pocket costs of administration and legal assistance, which as a rule of thumb take between 3 and 7 percent of the value of a the bankrupt firm, depending on its size. See Weiss, Bankruptcy Resolution: Direct Costs and Violation of Priority of Claims, 27 J. Fin. Econ. 285 (1990); Ang, Chua and McConnell, The Administrative Costs of Corporate Bankruptcy, 37 J.Fin. 219 (1982); Warner, Bankruptcy Costs: Some Evidence, 32 J. Fin. 337 (1977). These "direct" costs are accompanied by "indirect" costs, which are greater in amount but harder to measure. Generally, indirect costs of bankruptcy are operating inefficiencies of reorganizing firms stemming from their financial distress. They include costs attributable to reluctance of creditors to permit sale of some assets to obtain cash with which better to exploit other assets, difficulty of raising additional capital for profitable projects, reluctance of suppliers (including skilled labor) and customers to continue dealing with the distressed firm except on more expensive terms. See Altman, A Further Empirical Investigation of the Bankruptcy Cost Question, 39 J. Fin. 1067 (1984) (finding lost profits to be 12.2 percent of the value of retailing firms and 23.7 percent of the value of manufacturing firms). Finally, bankruptcy costs encompass reductions in value stemming from liquidations of assets at distressed prices. To the extent the firm's debt claimants receive anything less than payment in full, they share in bearing these costs with the firm's equity.

As between a levered and an unlevered firm, it is the levered firm whose value suffers from the possibility of bankruptcy and these attendant costs. Its value presumably declines by the negative present value of expected bankruptcy costs. As the firm becomes more levered, the probability that the bankruptcy will occur increases. This detracts from the firm's value and offsets the value of the tax deduction attending the debt. As the expected negative impact increases, the firm's cost of capital will rise. Creditors will respond by increasing interest rates, in effect shifting bankruptcy costs back to the firm's equity holders. Because bankruptcy costs represent a dead weight loss, the firm's equity investors will be unable to diversify away these costs, a result that occurs even if we assume that the market equilibration process is efficient. Accordingly, as the bankruptcy risk caused by debt rises, the cost of equity capital rises in response.

At some point simultaneous increases in the cost of equity and the cost of debt will cause the firm's overall cost of capital to rise. As leverage increases, bankruptcy becomes more likely, causing the required rate of return on the common stock to rise at an increasing rate. Imposition of this risk penalty on the common begins to outweigh the tax benefits of the debt. Van Horne, Financial Management and Policy 269–270 (12th ed. 2002), describes the effect as follows:

" * * * Our earlier discussion of taxes and capital structure concluded that leverage is likely to result in a net tax advantage * * *. If we allow for bankruptcy costs and if the probability of bankruptcy increases at an increasing rate with leverage, extreme leverage is likely to be penalized by investors. In a world of both taxes and bankruptcy costs, it is likely that there would be an optimal capital structure. Whereas the net tax effect would have a positive influence on value, bankruptcy costs would exert a negative influence. The value of the firm would increase as leverage was first employed because of the tax advantage of debt. Gradually, however, the prospect of bankruptcy would become increasingly important. This, together with the tax shield uncertainty, would cause the value of the firm to increase at a decreasing rate. As more and more leverage was undertaken, the bankruptcy effect eventually would offset the tax effect, and the value of the firm would decline. * * *

"The joint effect of taxes and bankruptcy costs is illustrated in Fig. 10–6. * * * The optimal capital structure by definition is the point at which the value of the firm is maximized. Thus, we have a tradeoff between the positive linear tax effects associated with leverage and the nonlinear expected bankruptcy costs that come when leverage is pushed beyond a point. While taxes and bankruptcy costs are probably the most important imperfections when it comes to capital structure decisions, there are others which bear on the problem."

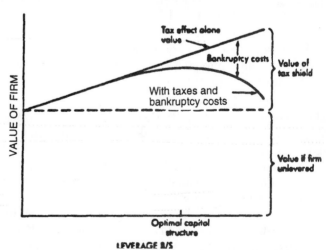

Figure 10-6
Value of firm
with taxes and
bankruptcy costs

(d) agency costs

Agency theory, first articulated by Jensen and Meckling in Theory of the Firm: Managerial Behavior, Agency Costs and Ownership Structure, 3 J. Fin. Econ. 305 (1976), broke from the irrelevance model of capital structure. It relaxed Modigliani and Miller's assumptions of perfect information and an absence of costly contracts, and thereby made possible a microeconomic account of the capital structures that we observe in practice. This account is known as "trade off theory"—the agency costs of debt rise as leverage increases and at some point outweigh the tax and other benefits of debt. One of these costs is the cost of bankruptcy identified supra. Agency theory identifies three additional costs of debt to be traded off:

• **Asset substitution**. Equity holders can increase the value of their interest in the firm at the expense of the debt if the firm disposes of the assets it holds at the time the money is borrowed and substitutes riskier assets. This opportunistic predilection follows from applying the Black–Scholes option pricing model to the firm as a whole. See Black and Scholes, The Pricing of Options and Corporate Liabilities, 81 J.Pol.Econ. 637 (1973). Under Black–Scholes, equities are viewed as combinations of options to buy and sell a firm's assets. Stockholders, in effect, hold an option to buy back the firm from the holders of the firm's debt. The stock, accordingly, is valued as an option. As we saw in Part I, supra, the value of an option increases with the volatility of the firm's stream of net cash flows. Given borrowing, therefore, stockholders will want the firm to switch to investments in high-variance projects. These could be projects less valuable to the firm, considered as a whole, than substitute projects with lower variance.

The point may be illustrated by assuming that a corporation with assets initially valued at $90 million issued $40 million face amount of 10% debt, but that the present value of its assets is only $45 million and they earn just enough to pay interest on the debt. Expected earnings (dispersion and probability) are as follows:

Earnings/ (Loss)	Probability	Expected Value
$5 million	25%	$1.25 million
$4 million	50%	$2.00 million
$3 million	25%	$ .75 million
		$4.00 million

The owners of the equity are given the opportunity to sell the assets and reinvest in much riskier assets having expected earnings of:

Earnings/ (Loss)	Probability	Expected Value
$10 million	50%	$5 million
− $2 million	50%	− $1 million
		$4 million

Although the expected return is $4 million in each case, the equity owners have little to lose and a great deal to gain in returns from switching from the old assets to the new investment. Correspondingly, the debt holders are disadvantaged. The market value of the stock will rise and of the debt will fall. (The price impact of such behavior by the common stock may be derived from the Black–Scholes formula.) Contract provisions in the firm's capital structure that prevent this asset substitution therefore cause the firm to be more valuable than it otherwise would be, given the presence of debt.

For a detailed discussion of the Black–Scholes model, see Appendix E, infra.

• **Underinvestment.** Where the firm's ability to repay its debt depends on positive returns from new investments, the firm's equity holders have an incentive to cause the firm to turn down certain kinds of profitable investment opportunities. Assume that the firm's projected cash flows from existing assets are insufficient to pay down existing debt. A new investment opportunity comes along with a positive net present value. The firm's equity holders have an incentive to cause the firm to make the investment only if its net present value exceeds the face value of the debt. Otherwise, the project will benefit only the creditors. Given limited liability, the equity holders might as well walk away. See Myers, Determinants of Corporate Borrowing, 5 J. Fin. Econ. 147 (1977). This underinvestment incentive causes the firm, taken as a whole, to forego profitable investments. Provisions to prevent underinvestment in the firm's capital structure therefore cause the firm to be more valuable than it otherwise would be.

Bankruptcy, asset substitution, and underinvestment become more problematic and generate larger and larger agency costs as the firm's leverage increases. Similarly, the risks of these costs in respect of a particular loan become greater as the loan's term becomes longer.

• **Contracting and Monitoring Costs.** The foregoing possibilities arising from the presence of debt—for transferring value from the firm's debtholders to its equityholders and for disincentives to productive use of the firm's assets and opportunities—trigger costs which the firm (and its equity) ultimately must bear, detracting from the firm's value. As we will see later, debtholders use financial contracts to protect themselves from agency costs (although not with complete success). These protections take the form of security interests in the firm's property and of business covenants. These ameliorative devices are costly to the firm and restrict its discretion to operate its business. Debt contracts imply out-of-pocket costs incurred by the firm at the time of the loan. Lenders also incur out of pocket costs when they enter into contracts. Even if the borrowing firm is not required to compensate those costs directly, the lenders presumably will look for compensation in the interest paid on the loan, shifting the cost back to the borrowing firm. In addition, even given the protection of a contract, a rational lender will monitor its borrower on an ongoing basis during the life of the loan. To be meaningful, the debt contract has to be enforced and enforcement implies monitoring. Where contract protections are absent or ineffective, monitoring becomes still more important. Even with a complete set of covenants, a lender cannot control the investment and production decisions essential to the long-term maintenance of the borrowing firm's cash flows. The lender, thus at risk, must be ready to sell at the earliest sign of trouble, and therefore must monitor. Lenders anticipate these costs in the interest rate on the loan. The higher the probable monitoring costs, the higher the interest rate, and the lower the value of the firm to its shareholders, all other things being equal.

Monitoring costs, like bankruptcy costs, imply a limit on the amount of debt that a firm optimally may issue. As the amount of debt in the capital structure increases, lender monitoring will become more intense. The cost to the firm per unit of borrowed capital accordingly increases. Monitoring costs thus join bankruptcy costs as a factor that decreases the value of firms with high leverage capital structures.

NOTE: FIDUCIARY LAW AND CAPITAL STRUCTURE

If institutional arrangements and tax considerations suggest that there can be an optimal capital structure, does a management which fails substantially—by some criteria and measure of substantiality yet to be developed—to create such capital structure violate its duty to its stockholders? If not, why not? If so, may management's obligation be policed by imposing (1) liability for failure to borrow "enough," or an order directing management to borrow more; or (2) liability for borrowing "too much," or an order directing management to reduce debt? For a case sustaining the assertion of a duty of care violation in a related situation—the decision whether to reduce risk by hedging exposure to price fluctuations, see Brane v. Roth, supra Part I.

Consider in connection with the foregoing questions an often-derived empirical result. Studies of determinants of actual debt ratios consistently find that, within a given industry, the most profitable companies tend to borrow the least. High profit, in other words, means low debt and a failure to exploit the tax shield of the interest deduction. The result obtains not only in domestic corporations but in Britain, Germany, France, Japan, and Canada. See Wald, How Firm Characteristics Affect Capital Structure: An International Comparison, 22 J. Fin. Research 161 (1999); Rajan and Zingales, What Do We Know About Capital Structure? Some Evidence from the International Data, 50 J. Fin.1421 (1995). Should we assume, based on the results, that managers of the best-performing firms are negligent, with a tendency to forego maximization of shareholder value? Or should the results lead us to question the trade off theory and look again at the benefits of conservative debt-equity ratios?

(e) information asymmetries

M–M also assume perfect information. In the real world, investors operate at a significant informational disadvantage to securities issuers. Absent verification, rational investors will discount self-serving statements managers make about the value of firms. This information asymmetry creates opportunities for issuers to use capital structure changes to convey information about the profitability and risk of the firm. As between borrowing and equity financing, borrowing signals management's confidence in the firm's soundness. Borrowing credibly can communicate management's view that conditions are better than the stock price reflects because of the penalties held out by the bankruptcy system in the event of failure to pay. The greater the asymmetry in information between managers and investors, the greater the likely stock price reaction to a particular financing announcement. Debt issues are thought to signal good news, where common stock issues signal bad news. Meanwhile, the implication is that capital structure has relevance for the value of the firm. Indeed, there emerges a "pecking order" theory of finance: retained earnings first, debt second, and new equity a distant third.

Myers, Capital Structure

15 J. Econ. Perspectives 81, 91–93 (2001).

We now look at the capital structure decision from a different point of view, the pecking order theory of Myers and Majluf[, Corporate Financing and Investment Decisions When Firms Have Information That Investors Do Not Have, 13 J.Fin.Econ. 187] (1984) and Myers[, The Capital Structure Puzzle, 39 J.Fin. 575] (1984). Myers and Majluf analyzed a firm with assets-in-place and a growth opportunity requiring additional financing. They assumed perfect financial markets, except that investors do not know the true value of either the existing assets or the new opportunity. Therefore, investors cannot precisely value the securities issued to finance the new investment.

Assume the firm announces an issue of common stock. That is good news for investors if it reveals a growth opportunity with positive net present value. It is bad news if managers believe the assets-in-place are overvalued by investors and decide to try to issue overvalued shares. (Issuing shares at too low a price transfers value from existing shareholders to new investors. If the new shares are overvalued, the transfer goes the other way.)

Myers and Majluf (1984) assumed that managers act in the interest of existing shareholders, and refuse to issue undervalued shares unless the transfer from "old" to new stockholders is more than offset by the net present value of the growth opportunity. This leads to a pooling equilibrium in which firms can issue shares, but only at a marked-down price. Share prices fall not because investors' demand for equity securities is inelastic, but because of the information investors infer from the decision to issue; it turns out that the bad news (about the value of assets in place) always outweighs the good. Some good firms whose assets-in-place are *under*valued at the new price will decide not to issue even if it means passing by an opportunity with a positive net present value.

The prediction that announcement of a stock issue will immediately drive down stock price was confirmed by several studies, including Asquith and Mullins[, Equity Issues and offering Dilution, 15 J.Fin.Econ. 61] (1986). The average fall in price is about 3 percent, that is, 3 percent of the pre-issue market capitalization of the firm. (The falls in price are much larger fractions of the amounts issued.)

This price drop should not be interpreted as a transaction cost or compared to the underwriting spreads and other expenses of stock issues. On average, the companies which issue shares do so at a fair price.

However, the companies that decide to issue are, on average, worth less than the companies that hold back. Investors downgrade the prices of issuing firms accordingly.

The price drop at announcement should be greater where the information asymmetry—in this case, the manager's information advantage over outside investors—is large. * * *

Now suppose the firm can issue either debt or equity to finance new investment. Debt has the prior claim on assets and earnings; equity is the residual claim. Investors in debt are therefore less exposed to errors in valuing the firm. The announcement of a debt issue should have a smaller downward impact on stock price than announcement of an equity issue. For investment-grade issues, where default risk is very small, the stock price impact should be negligible. [Studies] confirm this prediction.

Issuing debt minimizes the information advantage of the corporate managers. Optimistic managers, who believe the shares of their companies are undervalued, will jump at the chance to issue debt rather than equity. Only pessimistic managers will want to issue equity—but who would buy it? If debt is an open alternative, then any attempt to sell shares will reveal that the shares are not a good buy. Therefore equity issues will be spurned by investors if debt is available on fair terms, and in equilibrium only debt will be issued. Equity issues will occur only when debt is costly—for example, because the firm is already at a dangerously high debt ratio where managers and investors foresee costs of financial distress. In this case, even optimistic managers may turn to the stock market for financing.

This leads to the pecking order theory of capital structure:

1) Firms prefer internal to external finance. (Information asymmetries are assumed relevant only for external financing.)

2) Dividends are "sticky," so that dividend cuts are not used to finance capital expenditure, and so that changes in cash requirements are not soaked up in short-run dividend changes. In other words, changes in net cash show up as changes in external financing.

3) If external funds are required for capital investment, firms will issue the safest security first, that is, debt before equity. If internally generated cash flow exceeds capital investment, the surplus is used to pay down debt rather than repurchasing and retiring equity. As the requirement for external financing increases, the firm will work down the pecking order, from safe to riskier debt, perhaps to convertible securities or preferred stock, and finally to equity as a last resort.

4) Each firm's debt ratio therefore reflects its cumulative requirement for external financing.

The preference of public corporations for internal financing, and the relative infrequency of stock issues by established firms, have long been attributed to the separation of ownership and control, and the desire of managers to avoid the "discipline of capital markets." * * * Myers and Majluf (1984) suggest a different explanation: Managers who maximize market value will avoid external equity financing if they have better information than outside investors and the investors are rational. The pecking order theory explains why the bulk of external financing comes from debt. It also explains why more profitable firms borrow less: not because their target debt ratio is low—in the pecking order they don't have a target—but because profitable firms have more internal financing available. Less profitable firms require external financing, and consequently accumulate debt.

NOTE: THE PECKING ORDER

1.   *Trade Off, Pecking Order, and Real World Patterns.*

The foregoing discussions of taxes, bankruptcy costs, and agency costs suggest a "trade off" theory of capital structure. Up to some point, debt brings tax benefits and can reduce agency costs, but debt in increasing amounts implies increasing costs from potential bankruptcy and conflicts of interest. The optimal mix lies at the point where the benefit of the last dollar of debt just offsets the countervailing costs. It follows that when a firm has a suboptimally large amount of debt, it should adjust its capital structure by issuing new equity. Pecking order theory adjusts this picture by reference to information asymmetries, suggesting that new issues of equity entail heavy costs, costs with a magnitude sufficient to overwhelm the trade off calculation. Which presents the more accurate picture of real world practice?

The behavior of real world firms respecting new issues of equity raises a sticking point for both theories. Simply, firms raise capital by selling new common stock when their stock prices are high. See Baker and Wurgler, Market Timing and Capital Structure, 57 J. Fin. 1 (2002). They also tend to let their capital structures drift with their stock prices, failing to adjust in the wake of highs and lows. See Welch, Capital Structure and Stock Returns, 112 J. Pol. Econ. 106 (2004).

The trade off theory predicts the opposite. If the trade off was motivating firms, debt would be the preferred mode of finance given a high stock price, all other things being equal. As the stock price rises, the proportion of equity in the firm's capital structure rises with it. This makes the firm's existing debt less risky and hence more valuable. By hypothesis, such a firm has fallen below the optimum and needs to adjust with new borrowing. At the same time, a firm with a dropping stock price is left with too much debt and should adjust with a new equity offering.

New equity combined with a high stock price fits a little better with the pecking order. If the high price means overvalued stock, then the information asymmetry is likely to be a salient pricing factor and the time would seem ripe to take advantage. Unfortunately, this is not quite what the pecking order predicts. Under the pecking order, the high-priced potential issuer sees that the market will take the new issue as a negative signal and punish it by bidding down its stock. It accordingly resolves doubts by taking on more debt. Under the pecking order, new equity means the firm's back is against the wall—the debt markets must have shut out the firm due to poor performance before new equity financing makes sense.

Thus Baker and Wurgler, supra, suggest that equity issuers time the market, looking for the confluence of a high stock price and an irrational stock market that will ignore the negative signal. Others suggest that the information asymmetry problem is dynamic in time—at some times the firm's inside information is less at variance with the information informing the stock price than at other times. When the market is well-informed and the stock price high, the firm takes advantage and goes to the market. See, e.g., Lucas and McDonald, Equity Issues and Stock Price Dynamics, 45 J.Fin. 1019 (1990). Dittmar and Thakor, Why Do Firms Issue

Equity?, 62 J. Fin. 1 (2007), make a third suggestion. In their view, managers and stockholders want the stock price to stay up and keep going up in the long run. At the same time, their views may differ as to the quality of the project being financed with the new capital. New equity will cause the stock price to go down when there's a difference of view—"heterogeneous prior beliefs" in the authors' words. Managers thus go to the equity markets when they expect agreement with their appraisal of the project.

2. *New Issues and IPOs.*

How do the statistics that follow bear on the questions just posed?

Loughran and Ritter, The New Issues Puzzle, 50 J. Fin. 23 (1995), reports on a study of 4,753 companies which went public between 1970 and 1990 and 3,702 seasoned public companies which issued new stock between 1970 and 1990 (with utilities excluded). Both classes of issuer significantly underperformed relative to nonissuing firms for five years after the offering date. The average annual return on a buy and hold basis for IPOs was 5 percent (compared to 11.8 percent for a class of matching firms with the same market capitalization); the average annual returns for the seasoned issuers was 7 percent (compared to 15.3 percent for a class of nonissuing matching firms). In other words, 44 percent more would have to be invested in issuing firms than in nonissuing firms to produce the same return five years later.

Loughran and Ritter suggest that the results are consistent with a market where firms take advantage of brief windows of opportunity to issue equity—that is, new stock is sold during periods when the issuing firms are substantially over-valued. Why, given that the IPO overvaluation phenomenon has been known for years do investors still sign up? They seem, id. at 47, "to be systematically misestimating the probability of finding a big winner." The data on the seasoned issuers backs existing studies showing a stock price drop of around 3 percent at the time the offering is announced. Loughran and Ritter note however that their results imply that the adjustment is not nearly large enough—the price drop should not be 3 but 33 percent! See also Jain and Kini, The Post–Issue Operating Performance of IPO Firms, 49 J. Fin. 1699 (1994)(showing that firms in which the IPO entrepreneurs retain a higher ownership percentage demonstrate superior performance); Loughran and Ritter, The Operating Performance of Firms Conducting Seasoned Equity Offerings, 52 J.Fin. 1823 (1997)(showing that performance of companies making seasoned equity offerings peaks at the time of the offering and declines in the four following years).

Brav and Gompers, Myth or Reality? The Long–Run Underperformance of Initial Public Offerings: Evidence from Venture and Nonventure Capital–Backed Companies, 52 J. Fin. 1791 (1997), presents some complicating evidence on IPOs. This study divides IPO firms between those backed by venture-capital firms and a class of mostly smaller firms without venture capital backing and shows that the underperformance documented by the Loughran and Ritter study stems mostly from the latter group. Brav and Gompers also compare the performance of IPO firms to that of nonissuing firms of similar size and find that IPO firms perform no worse than do similar nonissuers. They speculate that this small firm performance effect could be due to greater vulnerability to external shocks, investor sentiment, or aggravated information asymmetries. They conclude that the inquiry should be directed to the identification of the types of factors that cause the broader class of small firms to underperform and that IPO firms should not be treated as a different group.

3. *An Empirical Challenge.*

Fama and French, Financing Decisions: Who Issues Stock?, 76 J. Fin. Econ. 549 (2005), presents an alternative picture of equity financing behavior. Pecking order advocates look for validation in the relative absence of seasoned equity offerings. Fama and French argue that equity finance needs to be understood in a broader context that includes private placements of common stock, convertible debt, warrants, direct purchase plans, rights, issues, and employee equity grants. Moreover, gross issues of equity through these avenues need to be adjusted to a figure net of share repurchases. They take a large sample of firms. For the period 1993 to 2002, they find (1) for small firms that 73.7 percent are net issuers of equity, and that the equity issues average 12.6 percent of net assets compared to 6.4 percent for new issues of debt; and (2) for large firms that 66.5 percent are net issuers of equity, and that the equity issues average 7.5 percent of net assets compared to 7.9 percent for new issues of debt. Most firms issue and repurchase every year. The upshot is that firms have many ways to increase the equity portion of their capital structures that sidestep the information asymmetry problem. Fama and French claim, id., at 551: "[t]he pecking order, as the stand-alone model of capital structure * * * is dead. * * * This does not mean that the asymmetric information problem disappears. But its implications become quite limited: firms do not follow the pecking order in financing decisions; they simply avoid issuing equity in ways that involve asymmetric information problems." See also Frank and Goyal, Testing the Pecking Order Theory of Capital Structure, 67 J. Fin.Econ. 217 (2003).

Section B.   Basic Terms and Concepts

1.   Introduction

There follows an introduction to some principal terms, forms, and practices respecting debt financing.

• **Long–Term Promissory Notes.** Bonds, debentures, and notes are long-term promissory notes. No inherent or legally recognized definition distinguishes one from the other. As a matter of historical practice, bonds and debentures are long-term obligations issued under indentures, bonds generally being secured obligations and debentures being unsecured obligations. Under the historical practice, notes may be long-term or short-term obligations, but in either case are not issued pursuant to an indenture. Recent practice has changed this. Today, "notes" often are issued pursuant to indentures as unsecured long term obligations. But they tend to be intermediate term securities, coming due in ten years or less, where "debentures" tend to mature in ten years or more.

A bond, debenture or note is simply a promise by the borrower to pay a specified amount on a specified date, together with interest at specified times, on the terms and subject to the conditions spelled out in a governing indenture or note agreement. Bonds, debentures, and notes are, then, promissory notes issued pursuant to and governed by longer contracts. Some of the governing terms and conditions will be set out on the face of the promissory note itself. Most terms, however, will be in the contract that governs the instrument and will be merely referred to on its face. The note incorporates the contract by reference.

Historically, bonds were issued in bearer form. Coupons giving the holder the right to each scheduled interest payment literally were attached to the bond to be clipped and turned into the issuer for payment. The benefit of a bearer instrument is anonymity, but it carries a concomitant risk of loss or theft. In the post-war era, the practice in this country changed, and registered bonds became the dominant form. Registered bonds, like common stock, are issued in the owner's name. The issuer, or its agent (usually the indenture trustee), keeps a registry of the owners of the issue, and remits payments of interest, prepayments of principal, and principal payments to the registered owner. Registered bonds are negotiable and transferable, with the concomitant recording of the transfer on the books of the issuer. Under the Internal Revenue Code § 163(f), issuers are denied interest deductions for bearer securities issued after 1982. As a result, new bearer bonds are not issued in this country.

Financial and legal writing use "bond" as a generic term for all long term debt securities. The practice will be followed here, although "debenture" and "note" will be used where particular contexts require.

● **Indentures.** An indenture is a contract entered into between the borrowing corporation and a trustee. The trustee administers interest and principal payments, and monitors and enforces compliance with other obligations on behalf of the bondholders. The indenture defines the assorted obligations of the borrower, the rights and remedies of the holders of the bonds, and the role of the trustee.

The borrower contracts with a trustee rather than directly with the bondholders so as to permit the bonds to be sold in small denominations to large numbers of scattered investors. Given widespread ownership in small amounts, unilateral monitoring and enforcement by each holder is not cost effective. The device of the trust solves this problem.

Trust indentures date back to financing of nineteenth century railroads, the earliest large-scale, long-term debt financings. Railroad entrepreneurs were forced to sell mortgage notes to many persons, since no one person was willing or able to furnish all of the funds to be raised. These bonds had to be made marketable and tradable while simultaneously carrying a lien against the mortgaged property. Each of the widely disbursed bondholders had to be given mortgage security on the railroad's assets without at the same time being granted an individual fractional interest in the collateral. The solution was to convey the mortgaged assets, under a trust indenture, to someone as trustee for the equal and ratable benefit of each of the holders. By the turn of the twentieth century, the device of the trust indenture was extended to cover unsecured borrowing by large industrial corporations.

The "bonds" and the "indenture" need to be conceptually distinguished. The bonds set out a promise to pay that runs to the bondholders. The indenture is a bundle of additional promises (including a backup promise to pay) that run to the trustee. The bondholders are third party beneficiaries of the promises in the indenture. Even though the promises in the bonds run directly to the holders, the bonds are subject to the indenture and therefore may be enforced directly by the holders only to the extent that the indenture allows. Indentures generally constrain the unilateral enforcement rights of small holders, channeling enforcement through the central agency of the trustee. The device of the trust indenture, then, not only facilitates enforcement by the widely scattered holders, but also restrains such enforcement. It facilitates borrowing in small amounts from large numbers of widely scattered lenders not only by constraining the issuer as against the holders, but by protecting the issuer from the holders.

Where, as in a private placement of notes to an insurance company or pension fund or a long-term loan by a bank, the loan is large enough to make direct monitoring and enforcement cost effective, the trust device is not employed. Such a note is issued pursuant to a "note agreement" or "loan agreement" entered into between the borrower and lender directly.

• **Terms of Indentures.** In many respects, trust indentures do not change much from decade to decade. The following summary of their contents from 1 A. Dewing, The Financial Policy of Corporations 173–74 (5th ed. 1953), remains accurate:

" * * * This rather elaborate document has, ordinarily, six important sets of provisions, some of which are mere recapitulations or elaborations of statements made in the primary contract, the bond, and some are provisions only indirectly referred to in the bond. There is, first, the set of provisions summarizing the amounts of money and the future date of payment, the interest rate and the time of interest payment—provisions which acknowledge that the bondholder is a creditor of the corporation entitled to the payment of his loan with interest. Furthermore, if the payment of the debt may be anticipated by the corporation, the fact will be clearly stated, together with the specific mechanism of prepayment which shall insure fairness to all the scattered bondholders. The second set of provisions describes the character and the extent of the property against which the bondholder may levy in order to satisfy his debt. If there is no such property, the agreement will categorically state that fact. Thirdly, there is a set of provisions which represents the special covenants accepted by the corporation which insure the preservation of the value of the corporate property, during the long period while the debt shall endure. The corporation will pay its taxes, make the necessary repairs, set aside adequate reserves for depreciation, replace worn-out or obsolete equipment, protect its franchises or patent rights; it will not give a prior lien to the property reserved for the bondholders. The corporation agrees not to permit the wastage or destruction of the property covered by the agreement. Fourthly, there is a set of provisions which defines with a high degree of precision the exact course the bondholders, acting individually or together, must pursue in order to levy on the corporation, as general creditors, or to levy on the specific property, if any, set aside for the security of the bonds issued under the indenture. Again, fifthly, there are provisions describing the duties and the obligations of the trustee. These clauses define with precision what he can and what he cannot do, on behalf both of the corporation and of the individual and collective bondholders. Finally—as a matter of tradition because the trustee could not legally do otherwise—there is a covenant on the part of the bondholders, acting through the trustee, that when the corporation has paid back the original loans—the face of the bonds—and has met the successive payments of interest, the lien or claims of the bondholders will cease and the corporation will no longer be bound by any of the promises of the bonds or the supplementary agreement."

Traditionally, the third item on Dewing's list—protective provisions—appears in stronger, more complex versions in indentures governing debentures than in indentures governing bonds (narrow definition). The holder of a bond relies on the security of pledged assets in addition to the earning power of the going concern. The holder of a debenture has no mortgage on particular property and relies on the going concern. Provisions of indentures, the so-called "business covenants," protect this reliance and thereby protect the debenture's value. The most important of these provisions limit the issuer's power (a) to pledge its free assets to other creditors, (b) to incur additional debt on a parity with, or superior to, the debentures, and (c) to make dividends or other payments to holders of its stock.

The terms and protective provisions in indentures accreted over a long period, reflecting the accumulated experience of generations of lawyers. Four decades ago the American Bar Foundation sponsored a Corporate Debt Financing Project to reform the complex and convoluted terms of indentures and offered a standardized form of the most conventional covenants and provisions. Its efforts have produced model incorporating forms of indentures, standard or "model" indenture provisions (sometimes with alternatives), and "negotiable" provisions for terms most likely to vary with particular borrowings. See Model Debenture Indenture (1965) and related Sample Incorporating Indenture; Model Debenture Indenture Provisions—All Registered Issues (1967) and related Sample Incorporating Indenture; Commentaries on both the 1965 and 1967 products. A more recent Model Simplified Indenture (text and accompanying notes in 38 Bus.Law. 741 (1983)), based on a form originally prepared by Morey W. McDaniel, simplifies the language of frequently used provisions. A Revised Model Simplified Indenture has appeared (text and notes in 55 Bus. Law. 1115 (2000)).

Sections of the Revised Model Simplified Indenture are set out in Appendix A.

• **Duration.** The bond's face states a due date. But ascertaining a bond's maturity often is a complicated matter that cannot be settled by a simple reference to the face of the bond. Most bond issuers must make "sinking fund" payments—prepayments of principal in advance of the due date. A bond subject to these mandatory prepayments has, in substance, serial maturities.

Complicating matters, many bonds are redeemable, in whole or in part, at the option of the borrowing corporation. The redeeming issuer is said to "call" the bond. In other words, the indenture provides for prepayments of principal at the option of the issuer in addition to the prepayments of principal that the issuer is required to make. Sinking fund payments disadvantage the borrower, while redemption payments disadvantage the lender. Sinking fund and redemption provisions are treated at greater length infra.

• **Creditworthiness and Credit Ratings.** Issuers pay two firms, Moody's and Standard & Poor's, to rate their debt for creditworthiness. The firms assess the likelihood of default. The ratings do not cover risk due to changes in interest rates. Under Moody's rating system "high grade" is Aaa and Aa; "medium grade" is A and Baa; "low grade," or "junk" is Ba and B; Caa and Ca is lower still; C is in default. A 1, 2 or 3, added to a Moody's rating functions like a plus or a minus, with a 1 being a plus. Standard & Poor's rates between AAA and D (default). Junk is below BBB.

A firm's credit rating tends to determine its mode of debt finance. Large firms with investment-grade credit ratings tend to borrow at the short and long end of the maturity spectrum. Firms with speculative rating tend to borrow for the intermediate term. Guedes and Opler, The Determinants of the Maturity of Corporate Debt Issues, 51 J.Fin. 1809 (1996); Barclay and Smith, The Maturity Structure of Corporate Debt, 50 J. Fin. 609 (1995).

Partnoy, The Siskel and Ebert of Financial Markets?: Two Thumbs Down for the Credit Rating Agencies, 77 Wash.U.L.Q. 619 (1999), argues that the informational quality of the ratings has gone down in recent years. That view is widely shared. Under the Credit Agency Reform Act of 2006, 15 U.S.C. § 78o–7, the SEC has implemented registration, record keeping, financial reporting, and oversight rules.

• **Variations.** (a) *Floating rate bonds.* A floating interest rate reduces the risk of interest rate volatility, and such issues are particularly likely to appear during inflationary periods. A floating rate is adjusted periodically to keep current with changes in the lender's short term cost of funds. Coupon payments are a function of the value of a stated interest rate index, such as the Treasury bill interest rate, the 30–year treasury bond rate, or LIBOR (the London interbank offered rate) at the time the payment is due. The floating rate can be subject to a floor or a ceiling. There are many variations on the theme. In recent years, floating rate corporate lending has concentrated in the riskier sectors—loans to private equity buyouts or distressed firms. Floating rate loans in this sector (at 1 1/4 or 1 1/2 percent above LIBOR) are termed "leveraged loans."

(b) *Zero coupon bonds.* These are bonds that pay a lump sum at maturity and no interest at all. They therefore are offered at very deep discounts. As single-payment vehicles, they are attractive to investors wishing to lock up yield over a specified period or wishing to obtain a precise duration instrument. "Original issue discount bonds," are similar. These bonds are issued at a very low interest rate and hence also sell at a deep discount at original issue.

(c) *Convertible bonds.* Convertible bonds are debentures or notes that can be changed at the holder's option into a specified number of shares of the issuer's common stock. These "hybrid" securities combine the downside protection of senior status with the upside potential of common stock. See infra Part III.B.

● **Public Offerings and Private Placements.** When bonds are offered to the public, the issuer and underwriters must comply with the registration requirements of the Securities Act of 1933. In addition, the execution of a trust indenture conforming with the requirements of the Trust Indenture Act of 1939 is mandatory for public offerings. The compliance process requires substantial lead time, although large issuers can shortcut the registration process through the shelf registration device provided for in Rule 415 under the 1933 Act. The company registers a large quantity of securities for future issue—up to two years in advance. When it wishes to offer and sell some of these preregistered securities, it files an amendment with the SEC containing details about the securities on offer. Under this system, new debt securities can be publicly marketed in a matter of days. Transaction costs are lowered and the issuer gains timing flexibility. The public debt markets hold out economies of scale respecting flotation costs for large issues of bonds only. Krishnasami, Spindt, and Subramaniam, Information Asymmetry, Monitoring, and the Placement Structure of Corporate Debt, 51 J. Fin. Econ. 407 (1999).

Issuers too small to gain access to the public debt markets and issuers too small to qualify for shelf registrations may issue long-term debt in the private placement market. Both the 1933 Act, in section 4(2) and Rule 144 thereunder, and the 1939 Act, in section 304, contain exemptions for securities that are not offered to the general public. Under these sections, registration of the issue and the qualification of a trust indenture can be avoided if the offer and sale of the bonds is limited to a small number of sophisticated institutional investors.

"Private placements," transactions taking advantage of these exemptions, constitute a substantial portion of all issues of long-term debt. Private placements involve face-to-face negotiations between the issuer and an institutional purchaser or group of purchasers. The process can be concluded quickly and relatively cheaply. The compliance and incidental expenses of public offerings are avoided. Terms can be tailored to meet the borrower's situation and needs. Funds can be disbursed at intervals to meet the borrower's specific financing needs.

Before the development of the junk bond market, described below, private placements, along with long-term loans from banks, were the only available source of long term debt financing for small and medium sized issuers whose debt was rated Ba, B, or below. These issuers remain prominent in the private placement market. As a result, the face amount of each issue of debt sold in a private placement transaction can be smaller than that sold in a public offering. Large corporate borrowers also enter the private placement market—when the available terms are as favorable as those on offer in the public market.

Private placement note agreements for small and medium sized issuers tend to contain tighter, more complex business covenants than do trust indentures governing public issue debentures and notes. From the lender's point of view, a private placement represents a long-term commitment of capital to a smaller issuer—a less secure investment than those on offer in the public trading market. Such a loan imports high risk; strict covenants lessen the risk. Tighter monitoring does so also. Thus, the private placement lender can be expected to do its own careful study of the borrower before committing to lend. The absence of public disclosure requirements creates an environment conducive to frank discussion of the borrower's prospects. The monitoring continues during the life of the loan: private placement note agreements tend to provide for more extensive periodic reports than do public indentures.

From the borrower's point of view, strict business covenants are not only inconvenient, they also create the possibility of a contractual barrier to beneficial new investment activity. Given such a barrier, and a good new investment, a waiver of the covenant solves the problem. In the case of publicly traded debentures, the costs of collecting the consents requisite for the waiver may be substantial and a consideration often is expected. In contrast, with a single or small group of institutional investors it is mechanically more feasible to obtain the lender's waiver and a consideration generally is not demanded. Indeed, periodic renegotiation of terms according with the changing circumstances of the borrower is not uncommon in private placement relationships. Private placement noteholders are likely to be responsive to changes that the borrower perceives will enhance its economic well being.

Traditionally, life insurance companies have been the largest lenders in the private placement market. Pension funds also participate heavily. The life companies are constrained by credit quality controls imposed by the National Association of Insurance Commissioners. These constitute six credit categories, numbered 1 through 6, with investment grade being 1 and 2. Lender reserve requirements increase as the borrower's credit rating goes down. As a result many life companies do not lend below grades 1 and 2, making such lenders less of a factor in the private placement market.

As between publicly issued debt, bank borrowing, and private placements, there is a rule of thumb as to which borrowers use which mode of financing. The highest quality borrowers go to the public markets; medium quality borrowers go to the banks for term loans; the lowest quality must resort to the private placement market. For empirical verification, see Denis and Mihov, The Choice Among Bank Debt, Non–Bank Private Debt, and Public Debt: Evidence from New Corporate Borrowings, 70 J. Fin. Econ. 3 (2003).

- **Rule 144A.** Rule 144A, promulgated under the 1933 Act in 1990, permits trading of private placement notes among institutional investors meeting stated qualifications. The resulting Rule 144A market imports liquidity to private placement investment, blurring the distinction between publicly-and privately offered debt. Rule 144A also provides foreign issuers an inexpensive means of access to United States debt markets.

Many new issues under Rule 144A, however, come from investment grade firms which find that the Rule 144A market facilitates the sale of debt securities at more advantageous prices, more favorable terms, and at lower transaction costs than do traditional private placements or public offerings. These issuers make what in substance amounts to public offerings underwritten by investment banks. As a result, the Rule 144A market has become a full-scale third market positioned between the public and private alternatives. As in the public markets, the rating agencies play the critical informational role. In addition, many 144A securities are converted into public securities through *ex post* registrations or exchange offers.

● **Junk Bonds.** Forty years ago the private placement market was the only alternative to bank borrowing for small and medium sized issuers looking for long-term debt capital. The public markets were foreclosed to these lower grade companies. This changed with the development of a "junk bond" market constituted of publicly traded low-grade debt.

In the bond market, "junk" means "below investment grade." All junk bonds are high yield/high risk instruments. There are two subcategories, "fallen angels" and original issue junk bonds. Fallen angels are bonds that had investment grade status at the time of original issue but that suffer later down-grading due to increased default risk respecting their issuers.

Junk bonds have been controversial. During the 1980s they were associated with Michael Milken and the Drexel Burnham Lambert firm. Together Milken and Drexel put together an extensive network of junk bond issuers and purchasers in the 1970s and 1980s. In the mid-and late-1980s these Drexel junk issues became the financing engine for the period's high leverage corporate restructurings. But the junk bond market collapsed in 1989, due to a wave of defaults, an impending recession, and new regulatory constraints on the portfolios of institutional bond purchasers. The junk bond default rate went from 4 percent of issues in 1989 to 10 percent in 1990–1991. New issues dried up. In February 1990, Drexel went down as well, under pressure from government regulators for securities law violations. Milken, pursued by Rudolph Giuliani, then a Manhattan U.S. Attorney, spent time in jail.

Unlike Drexel, the junk bond market recovered. New issues began to reappear in 1992, and the market has been growing ever since. See infra, Part II.D.

● **Short Term Borrowing.** Many firms require outside financing to handle short intervals in which cash inflows fall short of cash outflows. For example, a manufacturer may incur cash costs of production in advance of its principal selling season, causing a time lag between the time the expenses have to be paid and the time the sales revenues that cover them are realized. Short term borrowing, that is, borrowing for a term of less than one year, is the financial solution to the problem.

There are many modes of short-term borrowing. The firm can arrange for a line of credit with a bank. This may involve a formal commitment of up to one year and a commitment fee. The interest rate probably will float at a percentage over the prime rate. The borrower may have to keep a "compensating balance" at the bank. This is literally an account at the bank in which the borrower deposits cash flow. It will be a low interest or non-interest bearing account, and thus will provide the bank additional return on the loan.

The line of credit may be secured by a "floating lien" on the borrower's accounts receivables or inventories. With a receivables financing arrangement, the bank will lend up to a stated percentage of the firm's receivables. On default, the bank collects the proceeds of the receivables, but has a deficiency claim against the borrower if the proceeds of the receivables fall short of the principal amount of the loan. Under a "factoring" arrangement, the receivable is discounted and sold to the lender. The lender collects the proceeds and has no recourse against the borrower. Other techniques are employed when inventory is used as security.

Large, highly rated firms requiring short term financing can issue commercial paper. This consists of promissory notes maturing within 270 days. Some commercial paper is issued through a handful of major dealers, who purchase it and resell it in a market dominated by institutional investors. The largest issuers bypass the dealers and sell to the institutions directly. Rates are lower than those prevailing on bank lines of credit.

2. CORPORATE TRUST AND THE TRUST INDENTURE ACT OF 1939

Elliott Associates v. J. Henry Schroder Bank & Trust Co.

United States Court of Appeals, Second Circuit, 1988.
838 F.2d 66.

■ ALTIMARI, CIRCUIT JUDGE:

[The case involved an indenture which required the issuer to give 50 days notice to the Trustee of an issue of convertible debentures before redeeming the debentures, "unless a shorter notice shall be satisfactory to the [t]rustee." The provision was designed to give the Trustee enough time to handle the mechanics of sending notice of redemption to the debenture holders within the time prescribed for such notice to them. If the Trustee required less time for the mechanics, it was authorized to waive—that is, shorten—the 50 day period within which the issuer was to inform the Trustee of its proposed redemption; the notice period for the bondholders would not be affected by the waiver. In this case, if the Trustee did not shorten the 50 day period, the redemption would have occurred on a date *after* an interest payment was due on the debentures; on the other hand, if the Trustee shortened the 50 day period, the issuer could redeem *before* the interest payment date, and thus save itself one semi annual interest payment. The Trustee shortened the notice period because the mechanics of the particular redemption were simple and could easily be handled within a shorter period. The notice provision, including the waiver clause, was modeled on the American Bar Foundation Model Indenture, and it apparently was the regular practice of Trustees to shorten the notice period in circumstances in which they did not need the full period to handle the mechanics. In a debenture holder's class action against the Trustee for shortening the notice period, the Court of Appeals affirmed the holding of the District Court that "the trustee's waiver did not constitute a breach of any duty owed to the debenture holders—under the indenture or otherwise—because a trustee's pre-default duties are limited to those duties expressly provided in the indenture." The court of Appeals (Altimari, J.) went on as follows.]

Thus, it is clear from the express terms of the Act and its legislative history that no implicit duties, such as those suggested by Elliott, are imposed on the trustee to limit its pre-default conduct.

It is equally well-established under state common law that the duties of an indenture trustee are strictly defined and limited to the terms of the indenture, see, e.g., Green v. Title Guarantee & Trust Co., 223 A.D. 12, 227 N.Y.S. 252 (1st Dep't), aff'd, 248 N.Y. 627, 162 N.E. 552 (1928); Hazzard v. Chase National Bank, 159 Misc. 57, 287 N.Y.S. 541 (Sup.Ct.N.Y.County 1936), aff'd, 257 A.D. 950, 14 N.Y.S.2d 147 (1st Dep't), aff'd, 282 N.Y. 652, 26 N.E.2d 801, cert. denied, 311 U.S. 708 (1940), although the trustee must nevertheless refrain from engaging in conflicts of interest. See United States Trust Co. v. First National City Bank, 57 A.D. 285, 394 N.Y.S.2d 653 (1st Dep't 1977), aff'd, 45 N.Y.2d 869, 410 N.Y.S.2d 680 (1978).

In view of the foregoing, it is no surprise that we have consistently rejected the imposition of additional duties on the trustee in light of the special relationship that the trustee already has with both the issuer and the debenture holders under the indenture. See Meckel v. Continental Resources Co., 758 F.2d 811, 816 (2d Cir.1985); In Re W.T. Grant Co., 699 F.2d 599, 612 (2d Cir.), cert. denied, 464 U.S. 822 (1983); Browning Debenture Holders' Comm. v. DASA Corp., 560 F.2d 1078, 1083 (2d Cir.1977). As we recognized in *Meckel,*

> [a]n indenture trustee is not subject to the ordinary trustee's duty of undivided loyalty. Unlike the ordinary trustee, who has historic common-law duties imposed beyond those in the trust agreement, *an indenture trustee is more like a stakeholder whose duties and obligations are exclusively defined by the terms of the indenture agreement.*

758 F.2d at 816 (citing Hazzard v. Chase National Bank, supra) (emphasis added). We therefore conclude that, so long as the trustee fulfills its obligations under the express terms of the indenture, it owes the debenture holders no additional, implicit pre-default duties or obligations except to avoid conflicts of interest.

  * * *

  * * * It is clear that Schroder complied with the letter and spirit of the indenture when it waived compliance with the full 50–day notice. Schroder was given the discretion to waive full notice under appropriate circumstances, and we find that it reasonably exercised that discretion.

To support its argument that Schroder was obligated to consider the impact of the waiver on the interest of the debenture holders, Elliott relies on our decision in Dabney v. Chase National Bank, 196 F.2d 668 (2d Cir.1952), as suppl'd, 201 F.2d 635 (2d Cir.), cert. dismissed per stipulation, 346 U.S. 863 (1953). *Dabney* provided that

> the duty of a trustee, not to profit at the possible expense of his beneficiary, is the most fundamental of the duties which he accepts

when he becomes a trustee. It is part of his obligation to give his beneficiary his undivided loyalty, free from any conflicting personal interest; an obligation that has been nowhere more jealously and rigidly enforced than in New York where these indentures were executed. "The most fundamental duty owed by the trustee to the beneficiaries of the trust is the duty of loyalty. * * * In some relations the fiduciary element is more intense than in others; it is peculiarly intense in the case of a trust." We should be even disposed to say that without this duty there could be no trust at all.

196 F.2d at 670 (footnotes omitted) (citations omitted); see United States Trust Co. v. First National City Bank, 57 A.D.2d 285, 394 N.Y.S.2d 653, 660–61 (1st Dept.1977), aff'd 45 N.Y.2d 869, 410 N.Y.S.2d 680 (1978) (adopting *Dabney*). *Dabney* arose, however, in an entirely different factual context than the instant case.

The *Dabney* court examined the conduct of a trustee who knew or should have known that the company for whose bonds it served as trustee was insolvent. While possessing knowledge of the company's insolvency, the trustee proceeded to collect loan obligations from the company. The court held that the trustee's conduct in this regard constituted a breach of its obligation not to take an action which might disadvantage the debenture holders while providing itself with a financial advantage, i.e., the trustee engaged in a conflict of interest. See 196 F.2d at 673. Thus, while *Dabney* stands for the proposition that a trustee must refrain from engaging in conflicts of interest, it simply does not support the broader proposition that an implied fiduciary duty is imposed on a trustee to advance the financial interests of the debenture holders during the period prior to default. Because no evidence was offered in the instant case to suggest that Schroder benefitted, directly or indirectly, from its decision to waive the 50–day notice, and thus did not engage in a conflict of interest, it is clear that *Dabney* is inapposite to the instant appeal.

Revised Model Simplified Indenture, Appendix A

Article 7 (Duties of the trustee).

NOTE: CORPORATE TRUST

Notwithstanding the title "trustee," the norms determining the care and fidelity to which indenture trustees were held prior to enactment of the Trust Indenture Act of 1939 derived more from the terms of the Indenture (and its exculpatory clauses) than from any legally imposed fiduciary obligations. The dominance of the "contract" over the "trust" aspects of the indenture trustee's duties at common law, which is reflected in *Elliott Associates,* has not been uniformly accepted. Since Sturges v. Knapp, 31 Vt. 1 (1858), the leading early case, the decisions reveal wide variations in the conception of the trustee's role. Commentators have summarized the law as follows:

"Some courts have held that relationships between Trustees and investors are fiduciary. York v. Guaranty Trust Co. of New York, 143 F.2d 503 (2d Cir.1944), reversed on other grounds, 326 U.S. 99 (1945). Others have resolved controversies by drawing principles from the law of agency, regarding Trustees as agents for investors. First Trust Co. of Lincoln v. Carlsen, 129 Neb. 118, 261 N.W. 333 (1935). A third line of cases sees the indenture as essentially a contract, the terms of which exclusively define the rights and duties of Trustees. Hazzard v. Chase Nat. Bank of the City of New York, 159 Misc. 57, 287 N.Y.S. 541 (Sup.Ct.1936). The fourth approach is to regard Trustees as partaking of the characteristics of more than one relationship, such as those of both depositary and ordinary Trustees. Dunn v. Reading Trust Co., 121 F.2d 854 (3d Cir.1941).

"An examination of authorities in the corporate trust field reveals a similar divergence of opinion. Some regard Trustees solely as a fiduciary, subject to the rules of trust law in general. G.G. Bogert & G.T. Bogert, The Law of Trust and Trustee, 64–65 (2d ed. 1968); Palmer, Trusteeship under the Trust Indenture, 41 Colum.L.Rev. 193 (1941). Others see the indenture as an instrument *sui generis,* combining elements of various legal relationships, particularly contract and trust, but being identical with none. Kennedy, Corporate Trust Administration 1, note 9, at 18–25; Posner, The Trustee and the Trust Indenture: A Further Study, 46 Yale L.J. 737, 794 (1937)."

Campbell and Zack, Put a Bullet in the Poor Beast * * *. 32 Bus.Law. 1705, 1723, note 56 (1977).

For discussion of the operation of trust indentures, see Landau and Krueger, Corporate Trust Administration and Management (5th ed. 1998). For a *de novo* policy review of the entire institution of corporate trust, see Amihud, Garbade, and Kahan, A New Governance Structure for Corporate Bonds, 51 Stan. L. Rev. 447 (1999). Amihud, Garbade, and Kahan would discard the ministerial trustee of traditional corporate trust in favor of an actor with incentives actively to monitor the firm and the power not only to enforce but to renegotiate the promises in the indenture.

NOTE: THE TRUST INDENTURE ACT OF 1939

The Trust Indenture Act of 1939 (15 U.S.C. § 77aaa, et seq.) protects bondholders by requiring that publicly-issued bonds be issued pursuant to a trust indenture conforming to specific standards. In addition to regulating the terms of trust indentures, the Act sets standards for the eligibility and qualification of trustees, including conflict of interest standards.

Prior to the Act, the trustee's duties were not defined and performed so as effectively to protect the bondholders' interest. According to the Securities and Exchange Commission Report on the Study and Investigation of the Work, Activities, Personnel and Functions of Protective and Reorganization Committees, Part VI (1936) 3:

"* * * [A]n examination of the provisions of modern trust indentures and their administration by trustees will show that [the bondholders'] reliance [on the trustee to enforce their rights] is unfounded. It will show that typically the trustees do not exercise the elaborate powers which are the bondholders' only protection; that they have taken virtually all of the powers designed to protect the bondholders, but have rejected any duty to exercise them; and that they have shorn themselves of all responsibilities which normally trusteeship imports. The 'so-called trustee' which is left is merely a clerical agency and a formal instrument which can be used by the bondholders when and if enough of them combine as specified in the indenture."

The Act was extensively amended in 1990. For critical, commentary on the level of protection for bondholders afforded by the Act, see Lev, The Indenture Trustee: Does It Really Protect Bondholders? 8 U. Miami. Bus. L. Rev. 47 (1999) and Amihud, Garbade & Kahan, supra.

TRUST INDENTURE ACT, AS AMENDED **1990**, SECTION **315**, APPENDIX **D**

Senate Report No. 101–155

101st Congress, 1st Session, 1989.

Title IV—Trust Indenture Reform Act of 1939

C. *Conflicts of interest*

[The amended Act] would make significant changes to the Act's method for determining conflict of interest. In the Act's present form, the existence of any of the nine relationships described in section 310(b) at any time indenture securities are outstanding requires the trustee either to remove the conflict or to resign within 90 days. This requirement is an outgrowth of the 1936 Report and reflected Congress' concern about instances of abuses involving relationship between the obligor and the trustee. However, each of the instances of abuse cited in the 1936 Report arose in situations in which there had been a default on the bonds. In the cases described in the Report, the trustees took steps to protect their own financial interests, instead of protecting the interests of the bondholders. There is no indication in the legislation history of the TIA that Congress was concerned about abuses by trustees prior to a default. In its memorandum in support of the legislation, the Commission has stated that, in the absence of default, the indenture trustee's duties are essentially ministerial, consisting largely of maintaining security holders' lists and transmitting interest payments to holders. The Commission has said that prior to default, there is no incentive for a trustee, even one with a technical conflict of interest, to withhold these services. Furthermore, there is no historical evidence showing a trustee in dereliction of its duties in the absence of default.

At the time of default, however, the character of the trustee's duties becomes critically different. At that time, inconsistent loyalties in the trustee, whether to holders of other securities of the obligor, to the obligor or to an underwriter, are unacceptable. Insistence on independence after a default is necessary to permit the indenture trustee to take vigorous action for the enforcement of rights under the indenture.

The Act's current conflicts standard, disqualifying a trustee from service if a conflict exists without regard to default or the character of the trustee's duties, may unnecessarily restrict an institutional trustee's ability both to act as trustee and to engage in other legitimate business activities.

* * *

[The amended Act] would recognize the differences in a trustee's duties before and after default by removing these and other restrictions on trustees pre-default conduct. This would be accomplished by making the event of default the time at which conflicts defined by section 310(b) become disabling relationships. To prevent evasion, grace and notice provisions within the indenture would be disregarded for the purpose of determining when a default occurs. In view of the added significance of the existence of a default, the legislation would require the obligor to certify annually whether a default exists under the indenture.

In a significant change from the existing statutory scheme, a creditor relationship would become a prohibited conflict of interest. The omission of the creditor relationship as a disqualification to serve as an indenture trustee has been the source of the criticism under the existing statute. No conflict could be clearer than that between the interests of a trustee with significant loans to a corporate borrower, for example, and that corporation's bondholders. On default, a trustee/creditor may become a competitor for funds of the corporation and, thus, in a relation adverse to the rights of the bondholders. Because most institutional trustees are commercial banks, a creditor relationship with the obligor is an ordinary occurrence. * * *

3.   THE BONDHOLDER AND THE GOING CONCERN

(A) THE PROMISE TO PAY

1 Dewing, The Financial Policy of Corporations

(5th Ed. 1953) 172–174.

Attitude Toward Bonded Debt.—The intent of bonds is that they should be paid. The difference between bonded debt and bank loans is merely the period during which the loan shall remain outstanding. The bank expects the loan to be paid when due; the investor expects the bond to be paid when due. Yet, in view of the longer life of the bond, there has [sic] developed, through the years, two distinctly different attitudes which a corporation management may take with reference to long-term debt. In the one case the management may look upon corporate debt, and the bonds issued to represent it, as the evidence of borrowed capital; and inherent in the nature of borrowed capital is the obvious fact that the equivalent in money, once borrowed, must be returned at a later time. Debt, however distant its due date, must be paid. The other point of view ignores the strict legal implication of debt. A corporate management regards the issue of bonds as a device to give investors a favored participation in the fortunes of the enterprise in return for the willingness, on the part of investors, to accept a low fixed return. The explicit implications of the debt can be ignored; in the continuing success of the corporation, new debt can be incurred to refund the old and if the corporation is not a success, the debt holders can be paid only out of the dying body of the corporation. In the event of failure, the debt holders must take their fortunes along with the stockholders, except that they will be paid first out of the proceeds of liquidation or be given prior rights in any attempt to rehabilitate the business. The one point of view looks upon the bondholders as creditors beyond the pale of the corporation—outsiders who have lent capital which must be returned; the other point of view looks upon bondholders as joint heirs in the corporate fortunes—participants in the success or failure who have been given preferential rights in the common hazard.

Revised Model Simplified Indenture, Appendix A

Exhibit A (Debenture form).

Section 1 of the debenture form sets out the issuer's promise to repay at interest. This promise is modified in sections 5, 6, 7 and 8. Section 6 is the provision for sinking fund payments—mandatory prepayments of principal by the issuer. Sections 5 and 7 provide for redemption rights—prepayments of principal at the issuer's option.

Note Purchase Agreement, Appendix A

Exhibit 1 (Form of Senior Note).

The following materials describe the dynamics of redemption and sinking fund provisions.

Van Horne, Financial Management and Policy

(12th ed. 2002) pp. 595–597.

CALL FEATURE AND REFUNDING

* * * [T]he call feature * * * gives the issuer the option to buy back a debt instrument at a specified price before maturity. The price at which this occurs is known as the *call price*. When a bond is callable, the call price usually is above the par value of the bond and decreases over time. Frequently, the call price in the first year is established at 1 year's interest above the face value of the bond. If the coupon rate is 9 percent, the initial call price may be $109 ($1,090 per $1,000 face value).

Forms of the Provision

The call feature itself may take several forms. The security may be **immediately callable**, which simply means that the instrument may be bought back by the issuer at the call price at any time. Even here, the investor is partially protected from a call because the initial call price is above the face value of the bond. Moreover, there are a number of expenses and inconveniences associated with refunding a bond issue which must be factored in by the borrower before a decision to call a bond issue is made. However, should interest rates decline significantly, the issuer may wish to call the bond. Rather than being immediately callable, the call provision may be **deferred** for a period of time. This means that the instrument cannot be called during the deferment period; thus, the investor is protected from a call.

Though many corporate bond issues have a call feature, the relative use of the provision varies over time. When interest rates are low and investors demand what corporations regard as too high a premium in yield, noncallable bonds are issued. This was the case in the 1990s, when most bond issues were noncallable. This experience contrasts with that of the 1970s, when almost all were callable. When corporate bonds are callable, they usually provide the investor with deferred call protection. For a long-term industrial bond issue, the typical deferment period is ten years, whereas for a public utility it is five years.

The call provision gives the company flexibility. If interest rates should decline significantly, it can call the bonds and refinance the issue at a lower interest cost. Thus, the company does not have to wait until the final maturity to refinance. In addition, the provision may be advantageous to the company if it finds any of the protective covenants in the bond indenture to be unduly restrictive.

Refunding versus Redemption

The deferment period protects the investor from early call. * * * However, * * * [i]n most bond indentures, call deferment is restricted to business situations where a refunding takes place. By **refunding**, we mean refinancing the bond issue with a new bond issue at lower interest cost.

However, many bond issues can be **redeemed** provided the source of the redemption is not a refunding. It may be the issuer has excess liquidity, or it could sell assets. It might issue common stock or be acquired in a merger. As long as the funds used to redeem the bond issue do not come from a new one, the investor has no deferred call protection. * * * The line of demarcation between a call and a redemption is blurred. For example, if a company redeems a bond issue out of cash and later issues bonds to restore its liquidity, is it a redemption or a call? Sometimes legal redress is sought; but seldom does the investor win.

Value of Call Privilege

Although the call privilege is beneficial to the issuing corporation, it works to the detriment of investors. If interest rates fall and the bond issue is called, they can invest in other bonds only at a sacrifice in yield to maturity. Consequently, the call privilege usually does not come free to the borrower. Its cost, or value, is measured at the time of issuance by the difference in yield on the callable bond and the yield that would be necessary if the security were noncallable. This value is determined by supply and demand forces in the market for callable securities. When interest rates are high and expected to fall, the call feature is likely to have significant value. Investors are unwilling to invest in callable bonds unless such bonds yield more than bonds that are noncallable, all other things the same. In other words, they must be compensated for assuming the risk that the bonds might be called. On the other hand, borrowers are willing to pay a premium in yield for the call privilege in the belief that yields will fall and that it will be advantageous to refund the bonds.

When interest rates are low and expected to rise, the call privilege may have a negligible value in that the company might pay the same yield if there were no call privilege. The key factor is that the borrower has to be able to refund the issue at a profit and that cannot be done unless interest rates drop significantly, for the issuer must pay the call price—which is usually at a premium above par value—as well as the flotation costs involved in refinancing. If there is no probability that the borrower can refund the issue at a profit, the call privilege is unlikely to have a value.

NOTE: REDEMPTION RIGHTS AND DUTIES

1. *The Make-Whole Premium.*

A contract form embodying the call privilege, as described by Van Horne, can be found in section 5 of the debenture form appended to the Revised Model

Simplified Indenture, Appendix A. The drafter filling in the year and percentage figures for a 20 year, 9 percent bond would take the following steps:

(a) Divide 9.00 by 20, yielding .45.

(b) Set the premium for the first 12 month period at 9 percent.

(c) Set the premium for the second 12 month period at 9 minus 0.45 or 8.55 percent.

(d) Set the premium for the third 12 month period at 8.55 percent minus 0.45 percent or 8.1 percent, and so on through Year 19.

Note that the MSI redemption provision contains no refunding limitation.

Note also that the premium calculated in accordance with the above procedure may not fully compensate the lender in event of a drop in interest rates. If rates drop markedly, then a premium of 9 or less percent of face value may be less than the diminution in yield to the lender upon the reinvestment of the prepaid principal amount in new bonds. Private placement lenders have averted this problem by revising the form of call provision. The new provision permits call at the issuer's option without a refunding limitation, but includes a "make whole" premium that fully compensates for declines in interest rates. The Model Form Note Purchase Agreement drafted by the insurance company Private Placement Enhancement Project defines the amount of the make whole premium as follows:

> an amount equal to the excess, if any, of the Discounted Value of the Remaining Scheduled Payments with respect to the Called Principal * * * over the amount of such Called Principal, *provided* that the Make–Whole Amount may in no event be less than zero.

Under the form's definitions, the discounting of the scheduled future payments of interest and principal on the called principal amount employs a factor equal to the current reported yields on U.S. treasury securities having a maturity equal to the remaining weighted average life to maturity of the called principal. The use of the risk free rate of return in the discounting exercise assures a maximal make whole amount; it is up to the borrower to negotiate for a more favorable formula utilizing the U.S. treasury figure as a base and adding on an additional factor. The proviso against a negative make-whole amount protects the lender against the possibility that increases in the risk free rate could result in a call price lower than face value.

Klein, Anderson & McGuinness, The Call Provision of Corporate Bonds: A Standard Form in Need of Change, 18 J. Corp. L. 653 (1993), suggests a number of modifications in risk allocation bound up in the standard make-whole provision.

For full-dress prepayment language including provision for a make-whole premium, see Appendix A, Note Purchase Agreement, Section 8.

2. *Distinguishing Call Rights from Sinking Fund Duties.*

A *sinking fund* is a bond prepayment provision under which the issuer must repay the principal in installments over the course of the issue's life. Calls and sinking fund payments are both *prepayments* of principal prior to maturity. Calls are at the option of the issuer; sinking fund payments are mandated by the bond contract. Consult the debenture form appended to the Revised Model Simplified Indenture and compare section 6, which sets up the sinking fund (called a "mandatory redemption") with the call provisions in sections 5 and 7.

Sinking fund payments usually are made to the indenture trustee. Decades ago, trust indentures provided that these monies remain on deposit with the trustee until the bonds' maturity. The trustee would hold and reinvest the funds. Upon the issue's maturity the amount on deposit would be used to pay down the issue as a whole. Today's trust indentures provide that the payment flow through to the bondholders when made. Sinking fund payments tend to come due annually on the anniversary of the first issue of the bonds. Often an increasing percentage of the total amount of the issue is due each year to maturity. No premium is payable. In effect, then, bonds requiring sinking fund payments have serial maturities. Failure to make a payment is an event of default. See Revised Model Simplified Indenture, section 6.01.

Bond issuers usually get an option as to the mode of satisfying their sinking fund obligations: The issuer can either (a) pay in cash at the face amount of amount of bonds redeemed, or (b) repurchase bonds in the market and present to the trustee a face amount of repurchased bonds equal to the amount of the sinking fund payment due. The trustee may either select the bonds to be redeemed by lot or spread the payment *pro rata* across the issue as a whole. See Revised Model Simplified Indenture, sections 3.01, 3.02. The market price of the bonds will determine the issuer's choice between payment in cash and presentation of repurchased bonds. If interest rates have risen and the bonds are trading below face value, the issuer will find it advantageous to repurchase the bonds at a discount to get a sinking fund payment credit equal to the greater face value. If rates have fallen since original issue and the bonds are selling at a premium, the issuer will find it advantageous to pay in cash. In the latter case, the bondholders' payment "mandate" works against their interest, for they must reinvest the prepaid amount at the lower prevailing interest rate.

Why then do bond investors tend to insist on sinking fund provisions? Says Brigham, Gapenski and Ehrhardt, Financial Management: Theory and Practice (9th ed. 1999): "[S]ecurities that provide for a sinking fund and continuing redemption are regarded as being safer than bonds without sinking funds, so adding a sinking fund provision to a bond issue will lower the interest rate on the bond."

3.   *Redemption at the Holders' Option.*

Occasionally bonds are redeemable at par at the holder's option, or "puttable." The put protects the investor from a rise in interest rates and concomitant price decline. The duration of such a right can be expected to be limited. A narrowly tailored variation on the put right, termed a "poison put" is conditioned on the occurrence of an event, such as a tender offer or merger, that adversely affects the value of the bonds. Contrariwise, issuers sometimes reserve the right to redeem all or part of the issue without premium where the bond contract stipulates that the bondholders must approve a stipulated transaction—a merger, for example—and the bondholders withhold their approval.

4.   *Sweeps.*

Shorter term loans by banks commonly contain mandatory prepayment provisions conditioned on borrower business choices. Where the particular choice is adverse to the bank's interest such a provision, termed a sweep, performs the same function as a business covenant. A subsequent borrowing, equity offering, or asset sale triggers a duty to pay down all or part of the loan, with the sweep provision tying the magnitude of the triggering event to a percentage of the loan to be paid down—for example an asset sale exceeding a stated amount or percentage of net assets triggers a duty to pay down 50 percent of the loan. In the case of a sweep covering subsequent borrowing or equity issuance, the provision signals that both the bank and the borrower see the loan as an interim feature of the borrower's capital structure—the deal contemplates that the subsequent financing takes out the bank. In contrast, an asset sale sweep plays the more conventional agency cost control function. Note finally that a prepayment also can be achieved under a conventional negative covenant—the lender waives the covenant in exchange for a negotiated prepayment out of the proceeds of the asset sale. The difference is that under a conventional covenant, the result obtains only as the outcome of a renegotiation, where under a sweep it follows as a matter of right.

5. *Explaining the Pattern.*

It has been suggested that call and sinking fund provisions help to solve the agency costs problems of debt—information asymmetry as between issuer and bondholder, and the issuer's incentive to invest in riskier projects or not to invest at all. See Kao and Wu, Sinking Funds and the Agency Costs of Corporate Debt, 25 Financial Rev. 95 (1990); Barnea, Haugen & Senbet, A Rationale for Debt Maturing Structure and Call Provisions in the Agency Theoretic Framework, 35 J. Finance 1223 (1980). But, as the following case shows, these provisions can create agency costs of their own.

Morgan Stanley & Co., Inc. v. Archer Daniels Midland Co.

United States District Court, Southern District of New York, 1983.
570 F.Supp. 1529.

■ SAND, DISTRICT JUDGE.

This action * * * arises out of the planned redemption of $125 million in 16% Sinking Fund Debentures ("the Debentures") by the defendant ADM Midland Company ("ADM") scheduled to take place on Monday, August 1st, 1983. Morgan Stanley & Company, Inc. ("Morgan Stanley") brings this suit under § 10(b) of the Securities Exchange Act of 1934, * * * and other state and federal laws * * *. Morgan Stanley seeks a preliminary injunction enjoining ADM from consummating the redemption as planned * * *. Both parties * * * now cross-move for summary judgment.

FACTS

In May, 1981, Archer Daniels issued $125,000,000 of 16% Sinking Fund Debentures due May 15, 2011. * * * The Debentures state in relevant part:

> The Debentures are subject to redemption upon not less than 30 nor more than 60 days' notice by mail, at any time, in whole or in part, at the election of the Company, at the following optional Redemption Price (expressed in percentages of the principal amount), together with accrued interest to the Redemption Date * * *, all as provided in the Indenture: If redeemed during the twelve-month period beginning May 15 of the years indicated:

Year	Percentage	Year	Percentage
1981	115.500%	1991	107.750%
1982	114.725	1992	106.975
1983	113.950	1993	106.200
1984	113.175	1994	105.425
1985	112.400	1995	104.650
1986	111.625	1996	103.875
1987	110.850	1997	103.100
1988	110.075	1998	102.325
1989	109.300	1999	101.550
1990	108.525	2000	100.775

and thereafter at 100%; provided, however, that prior to May 15, 1991, the Company may not redeem any of the Debentures pursuant to such option from the proceeds, or in anticipation, of the issuance of any indebtedness for money borrowed by or for the account of the Company or any Subsidiary (as defined in the Indenture) or from the proceeds, or in anticipation of a sale and leaseback transaction (as defined in Section 1008 of the Indenture), if, in either case, the interest cost or interest factor applicable thereto (calculated in accordance with generally accepted financial practice) shall be less than 16.08% per annum.

The May 12, 1981 Prospectus and the Indenture pursuant to which the Debentures were issued contain substantially similar language. The Moody's Bond Survey of April 27, 1981, in reviewing its rating of the Debentures, described the redemption provision in the following manner:

"The 16% sinking fund debentures are nonrefundable with lower cost interest debt before April 15, 1991. Otherwise, they are callable in whole or in part at prices to be determined."

The proceeds of the Debenture offering were applied to the purchase of long-term government securities bearing rates of interest below 16.089%.

ADM raised money through public borrowing at interest rates less than 16.08% on at least two occasions subsequent to the issuance of the Debentures. On May 7, 1982, over a year before the announcement of the planned redemption, ADM borrowed $50,555,500 by the issuance of $400,000,000 face amount zero coupon debentures due 2002 and $100,000,000 face amount zero coupon notes due 1992 (the "Zeroes"). The Zeroes bore an effective interest rate of less than 16.08%. On March 10, 1983, ADM raised an additional $86,400,000 by the issuance of $263,232,500 face amount Secured Trust Accrual Receipts, known as "Stars," through a wholly-owned subsidiary, Midland Stars Inc. The Stars carry an effective interest rate of less than 16.08%. The Stars were in the form of notes with varying maturities secured by government securities deposited by ADM with a trustee established for that purpose. There is significant dispute between the parties as to whether the Stars transaction should be treated as an issuance of debt or as a sale of government securities. We assume, for purposes of this motion, that the transaction resulted in the incurring of debt.

In the period since the issuance of the Debentures, ADM also raised money through two common stock offerings. Six million shares of common stock were issued by prospectus dated January 28, 1983, resulting in proceeds of $131,370,000. And by a prospectus supplement dated June 1, 1983, ADM raised an additional $15,450,000 by issuing 600,000 shares of common stock.

Morgan Stanley, the plaintiff in this action, bought $15,518,000 principal amount of the Debentures at $1,252.50 per $1,000 face amount on May 5, 1983, and $500,000 principal amount at $1,200 per $1,000 face amount on May 31, 1983. The next day, June 1, ADM announced that it was calling for the redemption of the 16% Sinking Fund Debentures, effective August 1, 1983. The direct source of funds was to be the two ADM common stock offerings of January and June, 1983. The proceeds of these offerings were delivered to the Indenture Trustee, Morgan Guaranty Trust Company, and deposited in a special account to be applied to the redemption. * * *

Prior to the announcement of the call for redemption, the Debentures were trading at a price in excess of the $1,139.50 call price. * * *

* * * [P]laintiff contends that the proposed redemption is barred by the express terms of the call provisions of the Debenture and the Indenture Agreement * * *. The plaintiff's claim is founded on the language contained in the Debenture and Trust Indenture that states that the company may not redeem the Debentures "from the proceeds, or in anticipation, of the issuance of any indebtedness * * * if * * * the interest cost or interest factor * * * [is] less than 16.08% per annum." Plaintiff points to the $86,400,000 raised by the Stars transaction within 90 days of the June 1 redemption announcement, and the $50,555,500 raised by the Zeroes transaction in May, 1982—both at interest rates below 16.08%—as proof that the redemption is being funded, at least indirectly, from the proceeds of borrowing in violation of the Debentures and Indenture agreement. The fact that ADM raised sufficient funds to redeem the Debentures entirely through the issuance of common stock is, according to the plaintiffs, an irrelevant "juggling of funds" used to circumvent the protections afforded investors by the redemption provisions of the Debenture. Plaintiff would have the Court interpret the provision as barring redemption during any period when the issuer has borrowing [sic] at a rate lower than that prescribed by the Debentures, regardless of whether the direct source of the funds is the issuance of equity, the sale of assets, or merely cash on hand.

    * * *

DISCUSSION

    * * *

* * * Even if we were to assume, *arguendo,* that Morgan Stanley had made out a claim for irreparable harm, it has failed to meet the additional criteria necessary for the issuance of a preliminary injunction.

With respect to the likelihood of success on the merits, defendant's interpretation of the redemption provision seems at least as likely to be in accord with the language of the Debentures, the Indenture, and the available authorities than is the view proffered by the plaintiff. We first note that the one court to directly address this issue chose to construe the language in the manner set forth in this action by the defendant. Franklin Life Insurance Co. v. Commonwealth Edison Co., 451 F.Supp. 602 (S.D.Ill. 1978), aff'd per curiam on the opinion below, 598 F.2d 1109 (7th Cir.), rehearing and rehearing en banc denied, id., cert. denied, 444 U.S. 900 (1979). While plaintiff is correct in noting that this Circuit is not bound by this decision, and while this case can no doubt be distinguished factually on a number of grounds, none of which we deem to be of major significance, *Franklin* is nevertheless persuasive authority in support of defendant's position.

Defendant's view of the redemption language is also arguably supported by The American Bar Foundation's Commentaries on Model Debenture Indenture Provisions (1977), from which the boilerplate language in question was apparently taken verbatim. In discussing the various types of available redemption provisions, the Commentaries state:

> [I]nstead of an absolute restriction [on redemption], the parties may agree that the borrower may not redeem with funds borrowed at an interest rate lower than the interest rate in the debentures. *Such an arrangement recognizes that funds for redemption may become available from other than borrowing,* but correspondingly recognizes that the debenture holder is entitled to be protected for a while against redemption if interest rates fall and the borrower can borrow funds at a lower rate to pay off the debentures.

Id. at 477 (emphasis added). We read this comment as pointing to the *source* of funds as the dispositive factor in determining the availability of redemption to the issuer—the position advanced by defendant ADM.

Finally, we view the redemption language itself as supporting defendant's position. The redemption provision in the Indenture and the Debentures begins with the broad statement that the Debentures are "subject to redemption * * * at any time, in whole or in part, at the election of the company, at the following optional Redemption Price * * *." Following this language is a table of decreasing redemption percentages keyed to the year in which the redemption occurs. This broad language is then followed by the narrowing provision "provided, however * * * the Company may not redeem any of the Debentures pursuant to such option from the proceeds, or in anticipation, of the issuance of any indebtedness" borrowed at rates less than that paid on the Debentures.

While the "plain meaning" of this language is not entirely clear with respect to the question presented in this case, we think the restrictive phrasing of the redemption provision, together with its placement after broad language allowing redemption in all other cases at the election of the company, supports defendant's more restrictive reading.

Morgan Stanley asserts that defendant's view would afford bondholders no protection against redemption through lower-cost borrowing and would result in great uncertainty among holders of bonds containing similar provisions. In its view, the "plain meaning" of the redemption bondholders of these bonds and the investment community generally, is that the issuer may not redeem when it is contemporaneously engaging in lower-cost borrowing, regardless of the source of the funds for redemption. At the same time, however, the plaintiff does not contend that redemption through equity funding is prohibited for the life of the redemption restriction once the issuer borrows funds at a lower interest rate subsequent to the Debenture's issuance. On the contrary, plaintiff concedes that the legality of the redemption transaction would depend on a factual inquiry into the magnitude of the borrowing relative to the size of the contemplated equity-funded redemption and its proximity in time relative to the date the redemption was to take place. Thus, a $100 million redemption two years after a $1 million short-term debt issue might be allowable, while the same redemption six months after a $20 million long-term debt issue might not be allowable.

This case-by-case approach is problematic in a number of respects. First, it appears keyed to the subjective expectations of the bondholders; if it *appears* that the redemption is funded through lower-cost borrowing, based on the Company's recent or prospective borrowing history, the redemption is deemed unlawful. The approach thus reads a subjective element into what presumably should be an objective determination based on the language appearing in the bond agreement. Second, and most important, this approach would likely cause greater uncertainty among bondholders than a strict "source" rule such as that adopted in *Franklin,* supra.

Plaintiff's fear that bondholders would be left "unprotected" by adoption of the "source" rule also appears rather overstated. The rule proposed by defendant does not, as plaintiff suggests, entail a virtual emasculation of the refunding restrictions. An issuer contemplating redemption would still be required to fund such redemption from a source other than lower-cost borrowing, such as reserves, the sale of assets, or the proceeds of a common stock issue. Bondholders would thus be protected against the type of continuous short-term refunding of debt in times of plummeting interest rates that the language was apparently intended to prohibit. See *Franklin,* supra, 451 F.Supp. at 609. Moreover, this is not an instance where protections against premature redemption are wholly absent from the Debenture. On the contrary, the Debentures and the Indenture explicitly provide for early redemption expressed in declining percentages of the principal amount, depending on the year the redemption is effected.

* * *

For all of the above reasons, and on the record now before us, plaintiff's application for preliminary injunctive relief is hereby denied.

ON MOTION FOR SUMMARY JUDGMENT

■ SAND, DISTRICT JUDGE.

* * * [W]e now grant the motion of [ADM] for partial summary judgment on the contract claims * * *.

Contract Claims

The plaintiff's contract claims arise out of alleged violations of state contract law. Section 113 of the Indenture provides that the Indenture and the Debentures shall be governed by New York law. Under New York law, the terms of the Debentures constitute a contract between ADM and the holders of the Debentures, including Morgan Stanley. * * * The relevant contract terms are printed on the Debentures and, by incorporation, in the Indenture.[2]

We note as an initial matter that where, as here, the contract language in dispute is a "boilerplate" provision found in numerous debentures and indenture agreements, the desire to give such language a consistent, uniform interpretation requires that the Court construe the language as a matter of law. See Sharon Steel Corp. v. Chase Manhattan Bank, N.A., 691 F.2d 1039, 1048–49 (2d Cir.1982) (applying New York law), cert. denied, 460 U.S. 1012, 103 S.Ct. 1253, 75 L.Ed.2d 482 (1983). * * *

In Franklin Life Insurance Co. v. Commonwealth Edison Co., 451 F.Supp. 602 (S.D.Ill.1978), aff'd per curiam on the opinion below, 598 F.2d 1109 (7th Cir.), rehearing and rehearing en banc denied, id., cert. denied, 444 U.S. 900 (1979), the district court found, with respect to language nearly identical to that now before us, that an early redemption of preferred stock was lawful where funded directly from the proceeds of a common stock offering.

Morgan Stanley argues, however, that *Franklin* was incorrectly decided and should therefore be limited to its facts. We find any attempt to distinguish *Franklin* on its facts to be wholly unpersuasive. * * *

* * *

Morgan Stanley contends * * * that *Franklin* was wrongly decided, as a matter of law, and that a fresh examination of the redemption language in light of the applicable New York cases would lead us to reject the "source" rule. In this regard, Morgan Stanley suggests a number of universal axioms of contract construction intended to guide us in construing the redemption language as a matter of first impression. * * *

We find these well-accepted and universal principles of contract construction singularly unhelpful in construing the contract language before us. * * *

2. ADM argues that, because Morgan Stanley holds less than 25% of the outstanding Debentures, it has no standing under § 507(2) of the Indenture to maintain its contract claims. Section 507(2) provides that no Debenture holder shall have the right to institute suit with respect to the Indenture unless the holders of not less than 25% of the outstanding Debentures first request the Trustee to institute proceedings in its own name. Such limitations on the rights of bondholders to seek legal relief are not enforceable, however, where the face of the bond does not give adequate notice of the restriction. Friedman v. Airlift International, Inc., 44 A.D.2d 459, 355 N.Y.S.2d 613 (1st Dep't 1974). The ADM Debentures do not explicitly mention the restrictions contained in § 507. In any event, we view the intervention in this action by the Indenture Trustee, Morgan Guaranty, as a waiver of § 507 to the extent applicable.

Not only do the rules of contract construction provide little aid on the facts before us, but we find the equities in this action to be more or less in equilibrium. Morgan Stanley now argues, no doubt in good faith, that the redemption is unlawful under the Indenture. Nevertheless, as we noted in our prior opinion, Morgan Stanley employees were fully aware of the uncertain legal status of an early call at the time they purchased the ADM Debentures. To speak of upsetting Morgan's "settled expectations" would thus be rather misleading under the circumstances. By the same token, however, it is also clear that ADM had no expectations with respect to the availability of an early redemption call until the idea was first suggested by Merrill Lynch.

Because we find equitable rules of contract construction so unhelpful on the facts of this case, the decision in *Franklin* takes on added importance. * * * Moreover, we note that the decision in *Franklin* preceded the drafting of the ADM Indenture by several years. We must assume, therefore, that the decision was readily available to bond counsel for all parties. * * * While *Franklin* was decided under Illinois law and is therefore not binding on the New York courts, we cannot ignore the fact that it was the single existing authority on this issue, and was decided on the basis of universal contract principles. Under these circumstances, it was predictable that *Franklin* would affect any subsequent decision under New York law. * * *

Finally, we note that to cast aside the holding in *Franklin* would, in effect, result in the very situation the Second Circuit sought to avoid in *Sharon Steel, supra.* In that case, the Court warned that allowing juries to construe boilerplate language as they saw fit would likely result in intolerable uncertainty in the capital markets. To avoid such an outcome, the Court found that the interpretation of boilerplate should be left to the Court as a matter of law. *Sharon Steel,* supra, 691 F.2d at 1048. While the Court in *Sharon Steel* was addressing the issue of varying interpretations by juries rather than by the courts, this distinction does not diminish the uncertainty that would result were we to reject the holding in *Franklin.* Given the paramount interest in uniformly construing boilerplate provisions, and for all the other reasons stated above and in our prior Opinion, we chose to follow the holding in *Franklin.*[4]

---

4. We note in this regard that the "source" rule adopted in *Franklin* in no sense constitutes a license to violate the refunding provision. The court is still required to make a finding of the true source of the proceeds for redemption. Where the facts indicate that the proposed redemption was indirectly funded by the proceeds of anticipated debt borrowed at a prohibited interest rate, such redemption would be barred regardless of the name of the account from which the funds were withdrawn. Thus, a different case would be before us if ADM, contemporaneously with the redemption, issued new, lower-cost debt and used the proceeds of such debt to repurchase the stock issued in the first instance to finance the original redemption. On those facts, the redemption could arguably be said to have been indirectly funded through the proceeds of anticipated lower-cost debt, since ADM would be in virtually the same financial posture after the transaction as it was before the redemption—except that the new debt would be carried at a lower interest rate. Here, by contrast, there is no allegation that ADM intends to repurchase the common stock it issued to fund the redemption. The issuance of stock, with its concomitant effect on the company's debt/equity ratio, is exactly the type of substantive

NOTE: REFUNDING CASES

1. *Following Morgan Stanley v. ADM.*

Harris v. Union Electric Co., 622 S.W.2d 239 (Mo.Ct.App.1981), concerned a refunding limitation similar to that in *Morgan Stanley v. Archer Daniels Midland.* Here the refunding limitation was set out in the supplemental indenture governing an issue of bonds and contained a parenthetical excepting redemptions from a "maintenance fund." This maintenance fund was set up under earlier supplemental indentures and was intended to force a partial redemption to the extent that the issuer failed to devote 15 percent of any year's earnings to property maintenance. Unfortunately for the bondholders, the earlier supplemental indentures limited neither the source of the money that went into the maintenance fund nor the occasion for its use. The issuer sold a new issue of bonds at a lower coupon rate, put the proceeds in the maintenance fund, and redeemed the original bonds at face value out of the maintenance fund. It thereby avoided not only the refunding limitation but a redemption premium also provided for in the supplemental indenture. The court found the language in the supplemental indenture to be unambiguous on its face and ruled for the issuer. The court made this ruling despite the fact that contextual evidence, including the subjective understanding of officers of the issuer, showed that no one involved with the transactions foresaw that the maintenance fund could be used to circumvent the refunding limitation. See also John Hancock Mutual Life Insurance Co. v. Carolina Power & Light Co., 717 F.2d 664 (2d Cir.1983). But cf. Harris v. Union Electric Co., 787 F.2d 355 (8th Cir.1986), where the failure to make the fragility of call protection clear in a prospectus was held to underpin liability for a violation of Rule 10b–5. Similarly, Blanc and Gordon, Reforming the Unbargained Contract: Avoiding Bondholder Claims for Surprise Par Calls, 55 Bus. Law. 317 (1999), argues for detailed advance disclosure of all situations in which issuers may call bonds.

Shenandoah Life Insurance Co. v. Valero Energy Corp., 1988 WL 63491 (Del.Ch.), took up another variation on the theme. There the issuer did a debt financing at a lower rate simultaneously with an equity financing. The proceeds of the equity financing were segregated and applied to the redemption of an issue of 16 3/4 percent debt subject to a six year bar of refunding "by the application * * * indirectly of [borrowed] moneys." The court held that the fact that the new equity was integrated with an equally large debt financing did not cause the redemption "indirectly"

financial transaction the proceeds of which may be used for early redemption.

Moreover, we fail to see how, on the facts of this case, the redemption could be argued to be a refunding from the proceeds of lower-cost debt. The Zeroes transaction occurred over a year before the redemption and appears completely unrelated to it. The proceeds of that transaction were used to purchase government securities that remain in ADM's portfolio. The Stars transaction, while closer in time, similarly is not fairly viewed as the source of the redemption, given that the proceeds of that transaction were applied directly to reducing ADM's short-term debt. To view the redemption as having been funded *indirectly* "from the proceeds" of the Stars transaction would require us to ignore the *direct* source of the refunding, the two ADM common stock issues.

to be funded with cheaper debt. The Chancellor read the word "indirectly" narrowly: "the inclusion of that phrase is intended to reach situations in which the underlying economic reality of the completed transaction is the functional equivalent of a direct loan for the purposes of effectuating a redemption and nothing more."

Mutual Savings Life Insurance Co. v. James River Corp., 716 So.2d 1172 (Ala.1998), shows that repurchase by tender offer also provides the issuer a means to circumvent application of a clause restricting refunding "directly or indirectly" from the proceeds of cheaper borrowing. The trust indenture containing the clause governed an issue of 10.75 percent debentures due 2018. The indenture did not, however, explicitly prohibit or otherwise regulate bond repurchases, by tender offer or otherwise. Taking advantage of this omission, the issuer made a "simultaneous tender and call" (or "STAC")—that is, it made a tender offer for the bonds priced slightly above the call price and simultaneously called the bonds. The tender offer was funded by the proceeds of a new issue of 6.75 percent medium term notes. Unsurprisingly, given the simultaneous call at a slightly lower price, the tender offer was accepted by the holders of 98 percent of the outstanding bonds. The remaining 2 percent of the bonds then were redeemed pursuant to the call, the call being funded with the proceeds of the sale of a new issue of preferred stock, a source of funds not prohibited under the refunding limitation.

The bondholder plaintiff asked the court to take a substance over form approach, viewing the STAC as a single transaction and thereby establishing a basis for applying the refunding limitation. The court, however, put the burden of showing specific language in the contract on the bondholder and refused to collapse the two transactions into one. The result of finding two separate transactions was, of course, to place the tender offer funded by lower cost borrowing outside of the purview of the refunding limitation. The court also held that the combination of the call and tender offer did not amount to impermissible coercion.

2. *Ruling for the Bondholders.*

In **In re Hennepin County 1986 Recycling Bond Litigation**, 540 N.W.2d 494 (Minn.1995), the bondholders got the benefit of the doubt. The case concerned the interplay of two redemption provisions. The first was a conventional provision for issuer call at a premium. The right was to become exercisable only on the tenth anniversary of the bonds' original issue, with the bonds to be nonredeemable prior to that time. The second was tied to the bonds' security arrangements. The bonds, issued in 1986, were secured by a bank letter of credit scheduled to expire in 1992. The contract provided for mandatory redemption in the event that a new letter of credit was not provided in 1992. In 1992, the municipal issuer determined not to renew the letter of credit for the purpose of effecting redemption and refunding at a substantially lower interest rate.

The Minnesota Supreme Court held the bond contract to be ambiguous on the critical point whether a redemption triggered by the security provision could be used to circumvent the ten year redemption prohibition. The Court resolved the ambiguity in the bondholders' favor. It reasoned that the mandatory redemption tied to the letter of credit was "intended for the protection of the bondholders" in the event an unforeseen contingency put their investment at risk. Meanwhile, the other redemption provisions manifested an apparent risk allocation respecting interest rate changes. Upsetting that allocation, said the court, made no sense. See also Trident Center v. Connecticut General Life Insurance Co., 847 F.2d 564 (9th Cir.1988).

NOTE: BONDHOLDER REMEDIES UPON DEFAULT

Revised Model Simplified Indenture, Appendix A

Article 6 (Defaults and remedies)

These provisions determine the bondholders' rights in the event of the issuer's failure to perform one or more of its promises to pay.

The provisions make distinctions between payment defaults, section 6.01(1) and (2), and failure to perform other promises in the indenture, such as business covenants, section 6.01(3). First, under section 6.02, in order for acceleration of the bonds to follow as the result of the "default," the default must be an "event of default," and, under the last paragraph of section 6.01, covenant defaults are not events of default unless the issuer has failed to cure the default 60 days after receipt of notice from the trustee.

Second, payment defaults may be the subject of a direct lawsuit by an individual bondholder, pursuant to section 6.07. This section is declaratory of a bondholder right provided for in section 316(b) of the Trust Indenture Act. But this unwaivable provision for a direct bondholder action goes only to separate skipped payments of interest and principal. It does not carry into a unilateral bondholder right to accelerate in respect of a payment default so as to perfect a right to sue for the entire principal amount of the bond. See section 6.02. Direct bondholder actions in respect of defaults other than payment defaults are subject to the "no action" clause in section 6.06. This requires that, as a prerequisite to a direct action, the plaintiff bondholder (1) assemble a group of the holders of 25 percent of the outstanding bonds, (2) make a group demand on the trustee that the trustee pursue the action, and (3) that the trustee fail to comply with the bondholders' demand. Such "no action" clauses are enforceable, although they are strictly construed. See Cruden v. Bank of New York, 957 F.2d 961 (2d Cir.1992). Courts also excuse compliance with the provision in the rare case where the bondholder can make out a showing of trustee incompetence, whether by virtue of negligence or a conflict of interest. See, e.g., Rabinowitz v. Kaiser–Frazer Corp., 111 N.Y.S.2d 539 (Supr.Ct.1952) (compliance excused where trustee loans to issuer facilitated the transaction that caused the event of default). In addition, no action clauses do not block bondholder suits against the trustee itself. Cruden v. Bank of New York, supra.

For a set of default provisions drafted for a private placement, see Appendix A, Note Purchase Agreement, sections 11 and 12, Exhibit A.

(B) PROMISES THAT PROTECT THE VALUE OF THE PROMISE TO PAY

(1) Business Covenants

Note Purchase Agreement, Appendix A

Sections 9 and 10, Exhibit A

(a) debt contracts and debtor misbehavior

Once a loan closes, the borrower's expectations are substantially fulfilled. It has possession of the capital and the discretion to invest it. The lender expects repayment at interest and has a contract right to this effect. But, having parted with the capital, it ultimately must rely on the borrower's conduct of its business for the fulfillment of its expectations. Much can happen to impair the lender's position during the life of the loan. Business reverses can diminish the borrower's ability to pay. In addition, the borrower can make business decisions that have the effect of making payment of the loan less likely even as they have the effect of enhancing the positions of its stockholders and managers. Obviously, the best protection against these risks is full security. The unsecured long term lender foregoes this protection, exchanging a higher rate of return for additional risks of nonperformance. These additional risks can be made more manageable if provisions respecting the course and conduct of the borrower's business are included in the debt contract. Such promises cannot assure business success. But they can give the lender the option of calling a default in the event of business reverses or opportunistic conduct by the borrower.

The option of calling a default does not assure payment either. But, as the cases that follow in this part will show, it has a value nevertheless. The borrower in default has a choice—it can cure the default, seek the protection of a bankruptcy proceeding, or make the lender an offer of a substitute performance in exchange for a waiver. If the default occurs when the borrower is not in a situation of extreme distress, the borrower will not necessarily see a bankruptcy proceeding as in its best interests. Accordingly, in the right case, the right to call a default can be a substantial guarantee of performance. In distress situations, performance of the contract will not be a practical possibility. But, depending on the circumstances, contract rights can enhance the lender's position in the event of a recapitalization outside of bankruptcy.

Fischel, The Economics of Lender Liability, 99 Yale L.J. 131, 134–135 (1989), describes the interrelated problems of business failure and debtor misbehavior:

"The effect of exogenous events such as dramatic changes in market or industry conditions (i.e., a recession or a sharp decline in the price of oil) is clear. These events can significantly affect the probability of default and the likely recovery if a default occurs.

"The effect of debtor misbehavior is also straightforward. Debtors have an incentive to engage in several types of misbehavior once a loan has been made.

"(1) *Asset withdrawal.* Once a lender contributes capital to a firm, the borrower has an incentive to withdraw assets from the firm by, for example, declaring a dividend for the amount of the loan. This harmful incentive structure is exacerbated in situations involving extensions of credit to firms with limited liability;

"(2) *Risky investment policy.* The existence of debt creates an incentive for borrowers to invest in riskier projects. This incentive arises because the lender bears the downside risk if the project turns out poorly, but he does not share in the upside potential if the project turns out well. In other words, before the loan was made, the borrower bore the costs of risky investments that failed; now these costs are shared with the lender. Before and after the extension of credit, however, the borrower alone obtains the benefit from risky investments that succeed.

"This incentive to invest in risky projects is a direct function of the amount the borrower has at risk—the size of the equity cushion. In the extreme case in which the value of the firm equals the value of outstanding debt, the firm has nothing to lose and everything to gain by adopting a 'shoot the moon' investment strategy;

"(3) *Claim dilution.* The value of debt is a function, *inter alia,* of the amount of other debt. The greater the amount of debt of the same or higher seniority, the lower the value of debt. Thus a borrower can reduce the value of outstanding debt by issuing more debt and thereby diluting the claims of existing creditors; and

"(4) *Underinvestment.* The creation of debt imposes an additional claimant on the firm's income stream. This additional claim can result in the borrower failing to invest in a profitable investment project if too much of the benefit from the project will accrue to the lender. In this event, the value of outstanding debt will again be reduced because of the borrower's actions.

"At first blush, the two types of events that can adversely affect lenders after credit has been extended—exogenous events and debtor misbehavior—seem completely unrelated. In reality, however, there is a close relationship between the two. As exogenous events adversely affect the borrower, the probability of debtor misbehavior increases. This point can best be illustrated by a simple numerical example: Consider a hypothetical company with capital of $200, consisting of equal $100 contributions of debt and equity. Now assume that the company suffers a $100 decline in value as a result of a recession. The remaining $100 of value is just enough to pay off the lender.

"Although debtor misbehavior did not cause the $100 decline in value, this decline will have a profound effect on the borrower's incentives. For example, as discussed above, the borrower's incentive to invest in risky projects increases as the value of the debt falls, because the borrower now has less of its own funds at risk. Returning to the example, the borrower would not have been likely to have accepted a project with a negative net present value of less than $100 when the firm was worth $200 because the borrower would bear the loss. However, once the value of the firm has fallen to $100, the borrower might be willing to invest in a project with some upside potential even if its expected value is negative because the loss is borne by the lender. Furthermore, if the value of the firm falls below $100, the borrower may even reject some positive net present value projects due to the underinvestment problem. Because the benefits of the investment in this situation go to the lender, the borrower has no incentive to proceed.

"Similarly, the probability that the declaration of a dividend or an increase in the amount of outstanding debt will hurt existing creditors is a function of the value of the borrower not represented by debt. The lower the equity cushion, the greater the probability that these actions will harm existing creditors. Thus, if the equity cushion is eroded or eliminated entirely, as in the above example by adverse market or industry developments, actions such as withdrawal of assets will impose greater harm on existing creditors."

As Fischel states, the unsecured lender finds its ultimate protection in the borrower's "equity cushion." Business covenants are designed to keep the equity cushion in place and make it available to generate loan payments. In so doing, they regulate, directly and indirectly, the borrower misbehavior Fischel describes.

(b) principal covenants

There follows a description of the principal business covenants.

• **Restriction on dividends and other payments to shareholders.** This covenant is directed both to the problems of "asset withdrawal" and "underinvestment" identified by Fischel. It restricts transfers of corporate assets to shareholders, whether by way of a dividend or by redemption or repurchase of outstanding stock. The restriction typically operates by reference to the borrower's level of profits: It sets a base date and permits dividends and redemptions only to the extent of cumulative earnings after that date, and then only up to a given percentage or amount. Credit might be given for the proceeds of the sale of new equity.

• **Restriction on additional debt.** This covenant is one of the two principal means of protecting the lender against claim dilution. Lenders are best served neither by a blanket permission for new debt nor a categorical prohibition of new debt. On the one hand, to the extent that additional debt is issued, the number of claims on the equity cushion increase. The risk of insolvency likewise increases, and the lender's position in a bankruptcy proceeding is proportionately impaired. On other hand, additional debt can benefit existing lenders by providing the borrower with additional capital that permits its business to grow and thereby make existing lenders more secure. Debt covenants, therefore, tend to regulate rather than prohibit the incurrence of new debt, allowing it when justified by the economic state of the enterprise. These covenants tend to set out ratios of total debt to net assets and ratios of earnings available to pay debt to debt service costs, and permit new debt to be incurred to the extent that the tests are met.

Debt covenants also tend to restrict transactions that lenders view as the functional equivalent of borrowing, such as financial leases and the guaranties of the obligations of others. Debt covenants also can make distinctions between short-term borrowing and long-term debt and between subordinated and unsubordinated debt. For example, the borrowing window can be made larger for new debt issues subordinated to the issue covered by the covenant. The cumulation of factors and precise regulations can result in a very complicated exercise in contract drafting.

By regulating the conditions in which the borrower can incur additional debt, the lender indirectly discourages risky investment policy—risky debt and risky investments tend to be concomitants. Note also that the greater the covenant's complication and the tighter its restriction, the more likely that the borrower may request a waiver of the covenant so as to be able to pursue a legitimate investment opportunity. Accordingly, strict debt covenants tend to appear only where a later waiver is feasible, as in a private placement.

• **Restriction on mortgages and liens.** This covenant is the other principal barrier to claim dilution. Unsecured creditors look only to the borrower's unencumbered property—if the property is subject to mortgages, security interests, and other liens, it is not available to pay their claims in a liquidation. Secured creditors, moreover, are accorded priority in a bankruptcy reorganization to the extent of the value of the property covered by their liens. Contracts governing unsecured debt, accordingly, tend to restrict the creation of new liens. There are two modes of drafting such a restriction. The first is a direct and sweeping prohibition, subject to negotiated exceptions. Exceptions are most likely to be granted for purchase money security interests. This rigid drafting technique is more likely to be employed in a private placement than in a public offering. The second is the "negative pledge" covenant. This comparatively simple provision states that no lien will be created unless that lien also equally and ratably secures the debentures or notes covered by the provision. This version tends to show up in indentures covering public issues. Bjerre, Secured Transactions Inside Out: Negative Pledge Covenants, Property, and Perfection, 84 Cornell L. Rev. 305 (1999), argues that negative pledge provisions should be enforceable specifically provided that the beneficiary has made an advance notice filing in the manner of the filing made to perfect the lien of a mortgage or security interest.

Sale and leaseback transactions, which take assets presently owned by the borrower and available to pay the lender and transfer title to them to a third party, are the functional equivalents of liens from the lender's point of view. Separate sale and leaseback prohibitions are common in all debt contracts.

• **Restriction on mergers and sales of assets.** A merger with another operating company can work to the detriment of the lender, even though the surviving corporation is a larger firm. Claim dilution can follow if the merger partner is highly leveraged. If the partner has a riskier line of business, the merger accomplishes a detrimental shift to a risky investment policy. Similar problems can follow from the sale of all or substantially all of the borrower's assets. In contrast, a merger into or sale of assets to a shell acquisition subsidiary organized by a conservatively managed firm may be a matter of indifference or benefit to the lender. Covenants dealing with prospective mergers and acquisitions range from very loose to very strict. With public issues, mergers and sales of all or substantially all assets may be permitted subject to the assumption of the debt by the surviving or purchasing corporation. Private placements are likely to impose tighter constraints—a transaction will be permitted only so long as the survivor or purchaser can demonstrate compliance with every covenant and test in the debt contract. There are other available modes of regulating these transactions. For example, they may be permitted subject to a right of redemption in the bondholders.

Piecemeal sales of assets present problems of asset withdrawal and risky investment policy. Any sale of producing assets raises a question respecting the adequacy and reinvestment of the proceeds. Moreover, a firm that sells off pieces of itself over a period of time and reinvests the proceeds in a different line of business can effect a change to a riskier asset base. Covenants regulating these transactions may put a book value or fair value cap on the aggregate annual permissible amount of assets sold, along with a fair value standard to govern the terms of permitted sales.

• **Restriction on investments.** There does not appear to be such a thing as a meaningful affirmative promise to invest capital competitively at an acceptable risk level. Smith and Warner, On Financial Contracting: An Analysis of Bond Covenants, 7 J. Financial Econ. 117, 153 (1979), explains the problem: " * * * [P]roduction/investment policy is very expensive to monitor. Stockholder use (or misuse) of production/investment policy frequently involves not some explicit act, but the failure to take a certain action (e.g., failure to accept a positive net present value project). It is expensive even to ascertain when the firm's production/investment policy is not optimal, since such a determination depends on magnitudes which are difficult to observe. The high monitoring costs which would be associated with restrictive production/investment covenants, including the potential legal costs associated with bondholder control, dictate that few production/investment decisions will be contractually proscribed. For the firm's owners to go very far in directly restricting the firm's production/investment policy would be inefficient."

A lender can, however, cost-effectively impose a prohibition against some varieties of risky investment. Investment covenants prohibit liquid investments (for example, portfolios of common stocks or futures contracts) other than safe, short-term investments such as treasury securities or certificates of deposit. They thereby indirectly require the borrower to devote its capital to its going concern or to new going concerns. Note that such a covenant, taken together with a dividend covenant, also indirectly addresses the underinvestment problem. The investment covenant restricts the set of available investments for the borrower's free cash flow, while the dividend covenant blocks the payment of the free cash flow to the shareholders. Given spare cash and no attractive reinvestment opportunities in the going concern, the prepayment of the bonds is left as the best use of the free capital.

Managers are especially likely to resist restriction of their discretion to make investments. Accordingly, these covenants are likely to appear only in private placement transactions in which the lender has substantial bargaining power.

● **Maintenance of financial condition.** Some lenders impose financial maintenance tests. These tend to set a minimum level of net worth (assets minus liabilities), either as a dollar amount or a ratio. A net worth test establishes the smallest equity cushion that the lender must tolerate and functions as an early warning of distress. If the borrower fails to meet the test, it must either raise equity capital or go into default. Tests of working capital (current assets minus current liabilities) also appear, either as dollar amounts or ratios. Here failure to meet the test gives the lender an early warning of a possible liquidity crisis.

● **Maintenance of business and property.** These covenants contain affirmative promises to stay in the same line of business and keep property insured and in good repair.

● **Reporting provisions**. Recall that, but for the mandatory disclosure system of the federal securities laws, a holder of common stock seeking basic financial information respecting the issuer has the burden under state law to make an inspection demand, and then perfect in court a right to go to the firm's offices to extract information. In contrast, debt contracts customarily facilitate ongoing monitoring by the holders by requiring the borrower to provide periodic financial reports to the lender, along with certification that the borrower is complying with the contract's terms. This provision also may stipulate that the borrower follow generally accepted accounting principles, have an annual audit conducted by a national accounting firm and, in the case of a private placement, send the lender a copy of the annual auditor's letter. In a private placement, an inspection right also may be included.

These innocuous-looking, ministerial covenants have triggered numerous disputes in recent years. Record numbers of firms have been required to restate their financials as accounting compliance standards have tightened in the wake of the Enron and WorldCom scandals. Restatements of past financials often take time to work out, with the result that the subject firm becomes delinquent in filing its quarterly or annual financial statements. The reporting covenants contain filing deadlines, with failure to file ripening into a default. See Bank of New York v. BearingPoint, Inc., 13 Misc.3d 1209, 824 N.Y.S.2d 752 (N.Y. Supp. 2006). Aggressive bondholders, with the hedge funds in the lead, do not hesitate to take the procedural steps leading to the acceleration of the issue of bonds. The result is a defensive solicitation of waivers of the default by the issuer, an exercise that calls for a cash payment to the consenting bondholders. In an extreme case, bank creditors may demand even more, such as governance changes or removal of the CEO.

(c) commentaries

When and as to which firms are covenants most likely to show up in a debt contract? Billett, et al., Growth Opportunities and the Choice of Leverage, Debt, Maturity, and Covenants, 52 J. Fin. 697 (2007), studies the incidence of covenants in the debt issues of a large sample of firms across the last four decades. They find that protection is increasing in leverage and firm growth opportunities and decreasing in the proportion of short-term debt.

For model firms and commentaries thereon, see Committee on Trust Indentures and Indenture Trustees, ABA Section of Business Law, Model Negotiated Covenants and Related Definitions, 61 Bus. Law. 1439 (2006); American Bar Foundation, Commentaries on the Model Debenture Indenture Provisions (1971). For additional commentary, see Bratton, Bond Covenants and Creditor Protection: Economics and Law, Theory and Practice, Substance and Process, 7 Eur. Bus. Org. L. Rev. 39 (2006); Baird and Rasmussen, Private Debt and the Missing Lever of Corporate Governance, 154 U. Pa. L. Rev. 1209 (2006); Lloyd, Financial Covenants in Commercial Loan Documentation: Uses and Limitations, 58 Tenn.L.Rev. 335 (1991); McDaniel, Are Negative Pledge Clauses in Public Debt Issues Obsolete?, 39 Bus.Law. 867 (1983); Simpson, The Drafting of Loan Agreements: A Borrower's Viewpoint, 28 Bus.Law. 1161 (1973).

(2) Judicial Interpretation of Covenants

Sharon Steel Corp. v. The Chase Manhattan Bank, N.A.

United States Court of Appeals for the Second Circuit, 1982.
691 F.2d 1039, cert. denied, 460 U.S. 1012, 103 S.Ct. 1253, 75 L.Ed.2d 482 (1983).

■ Before FEINBERG, CHIEF JUDGE, and NEWMAN and WINTER, CIRCUIT JUDGES.

■ RALPH K. WINTER, CIRCUIT JUDGE:

[UV Industries, Inc. ("UV") had around $155 million of long term debt outstanding pursuant to five separate indentures. Each indenture provided for redemption at a premium prior to maturity, and contained a "successor obligor" provision allowing UV to assign its debt to a corporate successor which purchased "all or substantially all" of UV's assets.

[UV operated three lines of business: (1) Federal Electric, which generated 61 percent of UV's operating revenues and 81 percent of its profits, and constituted 44 percent of the book value of UV's assets; (2) oil and gas properties, which generated 2 percent of its revenues and 6 percent of its profits, and constituted 5 percent of its book value; and (3) Mueller Brass, which generated 38 percent of its revenues and 13 percent of its profits and constituted 34 percent of the book value of its assets.

[In early 1979 UV submitted to its shareholders a plan to sell Federal for $345 million cash and then, within 12 months, sell the rest of its assets and liquidate. UV's shareholders approved the plan and the sale of Federal was consummated by the end of March. UV contracted to sell the oil and gas properties for $135 million cash in July. UV made an $18 per share dividend to its shareholders in April, after agreeing with the trustees of the bonds to set aside $155 million to pay down the bonds. Then, in November, UV changed course. It entered into an asset purchase agreement with Sharon Steel Corp. pursuant to which Sharon would purchase the rest of UV's assets, which by then constituted Mueller Brass and $322 million in cash, in exchange for $107 million cash and $411 million face amount of Sharon's subordinated debentures.

[The sale to Sharon included an agreement that Sharon assume all of UV's liabilities *including* the obligations outstanding under the five indentures. Sharon and UV took the position that Sharon was purchasing "all or substantially all" of UV's assets within the meaning of the successor obligor clauses. Sharon and UV executed the supplemental indentures provided for in the successor obligor clauses and tendered them to the indenture trustees. The trustees refused to sign, and instead issued notices of default and brought actions for redemption of the debentures.]

1.   *The Successor Obligor Clauses*

Sharon Steel argues that Judge Werker erred in not submitting to the jury issues going to the meaning of the successor obligor clauses. We disagree.

Successor obligor clauses are "boilerplate" or contractual provisions which are standard in a certain genre of contracts. Successor obligor clauses are thus found in virtually all indentures. Such boilerplate must be distinguished from contractual provisions which are peculiar to a particular indenture and must be given a consistent, uniform interpretation. As the American Bar Foundation Commentaries on Indentures (1971) ("*Commentaries*") state:

> Since there is seldom any difference in the intended meaning [boilerplate] provisions are susceptible of standardized expression. The use of standardized language can result in a better and quicker understanding of those provisions and a substantial saving of time not only for the draftsman but also for the parties and all others who must comply with or refer to the indenture, including governmental bodies whose approval or authorization of the issuance of the securities is required by law.

Id.

Boilerplate provisions are thus not the consequence of the relationship of particular borrowers and lenders and do not depend upon particularized intentions of the parties to an indenture. There are no adjudicative facts relating to the parties to the litigation for a jury to find and the meaning of boilerplate provisions is, therefore, a matter of law rather than fact.

Moreover, uniformity in interpretation is important to the efficiency of capital markets. As the Fifth Circuit has stated:

> A large degree of uniformity in the language of debenture indentures is essential to the effective functioning of the financial markets: uniformity of the indentures that govern competing debenture issues is what makes it possible meaningfully to compare one debenture issue with another, focusing only on the business provisions of the issue (such as

> the interest rate, the maturity date, the redemption and sinking fund provisions in the conversion rate) and the economic conditions of the issuer, without being misled by peculiarities in the underlying instruments.

Broad v. Rockwell International Corp., 642 F.2d 929, 943 (5th Cir.), cert. denied, 454 U.S. 965 (1981). Whereas participants in the capital market can adjust their affairs according to a uniform interpretation, whether it be correct or not as an initial proposition, the creation of enduring uncertainties as to the meaning of boilerplate provisions would decrease the value of all debenture issues and greatly impair the efficient working of capital markets. Such uncertainties would vastly increase the risks and, therefore, the costs of borrowing with no offsetting benefits either in the capital market or in the administration of justice. Just such uncertainties would be created if interpretation of boilerplate provisions were submitted to juries sitting in every judicial district in the nation.

Sharon also argues that Judge Werker erred in rejecting evidence of custom and usage and practical construction as to the meaning of the successor obligor clauses. While custom or usage might in some circumstances create a fact question as to the interpretation of boilerplate provisions, the evidence actually offered by Sharon simply did not tend to prove a relevant custom or usage. * * *

We turn now to the meaning of the successor obligor clauses. Interpretation of indenture provisions is a matter of basic contract law. As the *Commentaries* at 2 state:

> The second fundamental characteristic of long term debt financing is that the rights of holders of the debt securities are largely a matter of contract. There is no governing body of statutory or common law that protects the holder of unsecured debt securities against harmful acts by the debtor except in the most extreme situations * * * [T]he debt securityholder can do nothing to protect himself against actions of the borrower which jeopardize its ability to pay the debt unless he * * * establishes his rights through contractual provisions set forth in the * * * indenture.

Contract language is thus the starting point in the search for meaning and Sharon argues strenuously that the language of the successor obligor clauses clearly permits its assumption of UV's public debt. Sharon's argument is a masterpiece of simplicity: on November 26, 1979, it bought everything UV owned; therefore, the transaction was a "sale" of "all" UV's "assets." * * *

Sharon's literalist approach simply proves too much. If proceeds from earlier piecemeal sales are "assets," then UV continued to own "all" its "assets" even after the Sharon transaction since the proceeds of that transaction, including the $107 million cash for cash "sale," went into the UV treasury. If the language is to be given the "literal" meaning attributed to it by Sharon, therefore, UV's "assets" were not "sold" on November 26 and the ensuing liquidation requires the redemption of the debentures by UV. Sharon's literal approach is thus self-defeating.

* * *

Sharon argues that the sole purpose of successor obligor clauses is to leave the borrower free to merge, liquidate or to sell its assets in order to enter a wholly new business free of public debt and that they are not intended to offer any protection to lenders. On their face, however, they seem designed to protect lenders as well by assuring a degree of continuity of assets. Thus, a borrower which sells all its assets does not have an option to continue holding the debt. It must either assign the debt or pay it off. * * * The single reported decision construing a successor obligor clause, B.S.F. Company v. Philadelphia National Bank, 42 Del.Ch. 106, 204 A.2d 746 (1964), clearly held that one purpose of the clause was to insure that the principal operating assets of a borrower are available for satisfaction of the debt.

Sharon seeks to rebut such inferences by arguing that a number of transactions which seriously dilute the assets of a company are perfectly permissible under such clauses. For example, UV might merge with, or sell its assets to, a company which has a minuscule equity base and is debt heavy. They argue from these examples that the successor obligor clause was not intended to protect borrowers from the kind of transaction in which UV and Sharon engaged.

We disagree. In fact, a substantial degree of protection against diluting transactions exists for the lender. Lenders can rely, for example, on the self-interest of equityholders for protection against mergers which result in a firm with a substantially greater danger of insolvency. So far as the sale of assets to such a firm is concerned, that can occur but substantial protection exists even there since the more debt heavy the purchaser, the less likely it is that the seller's equityholders would accept anything but cash for the assets. A sale to a truly crippled firm is thus unlikely given the self-interest of the equityholders. After a sale, moreover, the lenders would continue to have the protection of the original assets. * * *

Sharon poses hypotheticals closer to home in the hope of demonstrating that successor obligor clauses protect only borrowers: *e.g.*, a transaction involving a sale of Federal and the oil and gas properties in the regular course of UV's business followed by an $18 per share distribution to shareholders after which the assets are sold to Sharon and Sharon assumes the indenture obligations. To the extent that a decision to sell off some properties is not part of an overall scheme to liquidate and is made in the regular course of business it is considerably different from a plan of piecemeal liquidation, whether or not followed by independent and subsequent decisions to sell off the rest. A sale in the absence of a plan to liquidate is undertaken because the directors expect the sale to strengthen the corporation as a going concern. A plan of liquidation, however, may be undertaken solely because of the financial needs and opportunities or the tax status of the major shareholders. In the latter case, relatively quick sales may be at low prices or may break up profitable asset combinations, thus drastically increasing the lender's risks if the last sale assigns the public debt. In this case, for example, tax considerations compelled completion of the liquidation within 12 months. The fact that piecemeal sales in the regular course of business are permitted thus does not demonstrate that successor obligor clauses apply to piecemeal liquidations, allowing the buyer last in time to assume the entire public debt.

We hold, therefore, that protection for borrowers as well as for lenders may be fairly inferred from the nature of successor obligor clauses. The former are enabled to sell entire businesses and liquidate, to consolidate or merge with another corporation, or to liquidate their operating assets and enter a new field free of the public debt. Lenders, on the other hand, are assured a degree of continuity of assets.

Where contractual language seems designed to protect the interests of both parties and where conflicting interpretations are argued, the contract should be construed to sacrifice the principal interests of each party as little as possible. An interpretation which sacrifices a major interest of one of the parties while furthering only a marginal interest of the other should be rejected in favor of an interpretation which sacrifices marginal interests of both parties in order to protect their major concerns.

Of the contending positions, we believe that of the Indenture Trustees and Debentureholders best accommodates the principal interests of corporate borrowers and their lenders. Even if the UV/Sharon transaction is held not to be covered by the successor obligor clauses, borrowers are free to merge, consolidate or dispose of the operating assets of the business. Accepting Sharon's position, however, would severely impair the interests of lenders. Sharon's view would allow a borrowing corporation to engage in a piecemeal sale of assets, with concurrent liquidating dividends to that point at which the asset restrictions of an indenture prohibited further distribution. A sale of "all or substantially all" of the remaining assets could then be consummated, a new debtor substituted, and the liquidation of the borrower completed. * * * We hold, therefore, that boilerplate successor obligor clauses do not permit assignment of the public debt to another party in the course of a liquidation unless "all or substantially all" of the assets of the company at the time the plan of liquidation is determined upon are transferred to a single purchaser.

* * *

Since we do not regard the question in this case as even close, we need not determine how the substantiality of corporate assets is to be measured, what percentage meets the "all or substantially all" test or what role a jury might play in determining those issues. Even when the liquid assets (other than proceeds from the sale of Federal and the oil and gas properties) are aggregated with the operating properties, the transfer to Sharon accounted for only 51% of the total book value of UV's assets. In no sense, therefore, are they "all or substantially all" of those assets. The successor obligor clauses are, therefore, not applicable. UV is thus in default on the indentures and the debentures are due and payable. For that reason, we need not reach the question whether the April Document was breached by UV.

* * *

3. *The Redemption Premium*

Judge Werker held that the redemption premium under the indentures need not be paid by UV. His reasoning was essentially that UV defaulted under the indenture agreement and that the default provisions provide for acceleration rather than a redemption premium. We do not agree. The acceleration provisions of the indentures are explicitly permissive and not exclusive of other remedies. We see no bar, therefore, to the Indenture Trustees seeking specific performance of the redemption provisions where the debtor causes the debentures to become due and payable by its voluntary actions.

This is not a case in which a debtor finds itself unable to make required payments. The default here stemmed from the plan of voluntary liquidation approved on March 26, 1979, followed by the unsuccessful attempt to invoke the successor obligor clauses. The purpose of a redemption premium is to put a price upon the voluntary satisfaction of a debt before the date of maturity. While such premiums may seem largely irrelevant for commercial purposes in times of high interest rates, they nevertheless are part of the contract and would apply in a voluntary liquidation which included plans for payment and satisfaction of the public debt. We believe it undermines the plain purpose of the redemption provisions to allow a liquidating debtor to avoid their terms simply by failing to take the steps necessary to redeem the debentures, thereby creating a default. We hold, therefore, that the redemption premium must be paid. See Harnickell v. Omaha Water Co., 146 A.D. 693, 131 N.Y.S. 489 (1st Dep't 1911), aff'd, 208 N.Y. 520, 101 N.E. 1104 (1913).

* * *

CONCLUSION

We affirm Judge Werker's dismissal of Sharon's amended complaint and award of judgment to the Indenture Trustees and Debentureholders on their claim that the debentures are due and payable. We reverse his dismissal of the claim for payment of the redemption premium * * *.

NOTE: BOILERPLATE INDENTURE TERMS

1. *Economic Efficiency.*

Sharon Steel asserts a tie between contractual uniformity and economic efficiency. But is contractual uniformity always efficient? A contrasting line of thinking suggests that bond contracts may be particularly prone to suboptimal evolution over time precisely because uniformity has a value. The suggestion arises by analogy to the economics of technology. This learning identifies "network externalities." These arise where, as with telephone and drive operating systems, a technology's value increases with the number of users. Such systems can get "locked in" over time. That is, an inferior technology with a large and valuable user group persists, shutting out a superior technology because the transition costs for the user group as a whole are greater than the benefits held out by technological improvement. The QWERTY typewriter keyboard is the most famous example of this. Standardized contracts may create a species of this problem. The tried and true contract term, familiar to practitioners and users and perhaps the subject of judicial interpretation, survives where an innovative term might better serve the contracting parties. See Klausner, Corporations, Corporate Law, and Networks of Contracts, 81 Va.L.Rev. 757 (1995); Kahan and Klausner, Standardization and Innovation in Corporate Contracting (Or the "Economics of Boilerplate"), 83 Va.L. Rev. 713 (1997). For criticism of the approach, see Lambert, Path Dependent Inefficiency in the Corporate Contract: The Uncertain Case With Less Certain Implications, 23 Del. J. Corp. L. 1077 (1998).

A contrasting discussion of business covenants stresses incidental efficiency consequences. The covenant's beneficiary must monitor the borrower, which in turn ameliorates information asymmetries and benefits the creditor group as a whole. See Rajan and Winton, Covenants and Collateral as Incentives to Monitor, 50 J. Fin. 1113 (1995); Triantis and Daniels, The Role of Debt in Interactive Corporate Governance, 83 Cal. L. Rev. 1073 (1995); Berlin and Loeys, Bond Covenants and Delegated Monitoring, 43 J.Fin. 397 (1988). See also Smith and Warner, On Financial Contracting, An Analysis of Bond Covenants, 7 J. Financial Econ. 117 (1979).

The two lines of analysis should not be viewed as mutually exclusive.

2. *Contract Interpretation.*

Consider the following "rules" or "maxims" of contract interpretation. How does each come to bear in the context of the interpretation of a trust indenture? Is the interpretation of a note agreement governing a private placement between a single borrower and a single lender a substantively different exercise?

- The court should protect the expectations of the parties.
- The court should interpret contract language in accordance with its generally prevailing meaning. Restatement (Second) Contracts, § 203(3)(a).
- An interpretation giving effect to all terms of an agreement should prevail over an interpretation leaving a part with an unreasonable or ineffective meaning. Restatement (Second) Contracts, § 202(1)–(2).
- The contract should be interpreted against the drafter.
- The court should give effect to the plain meaning of the provision.
- Contract provisions should be interpreted in light of all the circumstances.
- Where the parties attach different meanings to a provision, it is interpreted in accordance with the meaning attached by one of them, if at the time the contract was entered into, that party had no reason to know of a different meaning attached by the other party, and the other had reason to know of the meaning attached by the first party. Restatement (Second) Contracts, § 201(2)(b).

For discussion of the rules as applied to debt contracts, see Riger, The Trust Indenture as Bargained Contract: The Persistence of Myth, 16 J.Corp.L. 211 (1991); Bratton, The Interpretation of Contracts Governing Corporate Debt Relationships, 5 Cardozo L.Rev. 371 (1984).

For theoretical discussion of approaches to the interpretation of contracts among sophisticated business parties, compare Schwartz and Scott, Contract Theory and the Limits of Contract Law, 113 Yale L. J. 541 (2003), with Choi and Gulati, Contract as Statute, 104 Mich. L. Rev. 1129 (2006). Schwartz and Scott argue that courts should avoid a contextual approach, like that taken in jurisprudence under article 2 of the Uniform Commercial Code, and instead stick to the text. Businesses, they say, prefer courts to adhere to the ordinary meanings of words. Courts accordingly should expand the evidentiary base only at the parties' request. Choi and Gulati, looking at boilerplate terms like the one at issue in *Sharon Steel*, argue that textualism can lead to incorrectly interpreted boilerplate clauses. They argue for historical context as a guide, by analogy to statutory interpretation. That is, the original drafter's intent should determine the matter. Interestingly, they object to the approach taken in *Sharon Steel* as an errant attempt to discern a "welfare maximizing" result.

3. *Additional Cases.*

Sharon Steel is a case in which indenture trustees used covenants in attempting to protect bondholders against rapid-fire transactions in the market for corporate assets. The courts' approaches to interpretation in these cases have varied. Compare Alleco, Inc. v. IBJ Schroder Bank & Trust Co., 745 F.Supp. 1467 (D.Minn.1989) (shell corporation organized by party controlling target (that had sold off all its operating assets and held only liquid assets) incurs debt to finance successful tender offer for stock of target and merges shell into target causing target to assume shell's debt; dividend covenant in target debt contract held to apply to subsequent repayment of shell's debt even though as a formal matter the target had not paid a dividend or redeemed any stock), with Harris Trust and Savings Bank v. E–II Holdings, Inc., 722 F.Supp. 429 (N.D.Ill.1989) (literal reading of indenture reporting provisions blocks trustee demand for additional information necessary to determine whether dividend paid to new control party to provide funds to repay acquisition indebtedness amounted to event of default). For a case that stands for the proposition that only a full set of covenants provides effective protection, see Allied Capital Corp. v. GC–Sun Holdings, L.P., 910 A.2d 1020 (Del.Ch.2006)(holding that a covenant prohibiting the incurrence of "indebtedness for borrowed money" from an affiliate did not cover a transaction that transferred the borrower's assets to the affiliate in exchange for an equity interest in the affiliate).

SECTION C.   SECURITY AND SENIORITY

Up to now, we have been assuming that debt is unsecured—that the promise to pay creates only a contract right against the borrower firm. If the borrower defaults, the lender goes to court to enforce the promise. The court renders a judgment in favor of the lender. The lender, if still unpaid at this point, then levies execution on the judgment. This creates a judgment lien. Only at this point does the contract right ripen into a direct claim on the borrower's property. The lender, still unpaid, forecloses on the lien, the property is sold, and the proceeds are applied to the satisfaction of the debt.

The lender can acquire a direct interest in the borrower's property ex ante by having the borrower pledge assets as security for the performance of the promise to pay. If the assets are goods or intangible property or rights, the pledge takes the form of a security interest under article 9 of the Uniform Commercial Code. A security interest is a conditional and intangible property interest—the borrower retains possession, but if it defaults on the promise the lender can take possession of the property, have it sold, and have the proceeds of the sale applied against the unpaid debt. If the collateral is real estate, a lien on the collateral is created under a mortgage, and the real property law of the state in which the collateral is located governs. (In states where the mortgage form does not accord the lender a power of sale over the property, the security instrument will be a deed of trust; a multi-state form will accordingly be drafted as a "mortgage and deed of trust.") Whether the security takes the form of a security interest or mortgage, a bankruptcy adjudication will stay foreclosure of the lien. But the bankruptcy regime does provide a priority for secured over unsecured claims to the extent of the value of the property securing the debt.

Security makes a loan less risky and thus is traded off for a lower rate of interest and an easier set of covenants. Questions arise as to why or in what circumstances lenders should require security rather than a higher interest rate, or alternatively, protection through business covenants. In a perfect, M–M world the lender would be indifferent. Whether we should expect such a condition to obtain in the real world is the subject of considerable debate. A variety of considerations have been explored in the literature, such as the fact that some kinds of property are more fungible (less firm-specific) and therefore less costly for debtors and creditors to secure than others; some kinds of business are more costly to monitor than others, so that security is sought in lieu of explicit monitoring obligations; or some enterprises are so risky that any rational interest demand to compensate for the risk would be too high, and therefore the lender must reduce risk by taking security. For debate over the economic rationale of secured debt, see, e.g., Carlson, Secured Lending as a Zero–Sum Game, 19 Cardozo L. Rev. 1635 (1998); Baird, The Importance of Priority, 82 Cornell L. Rev. 1420 (1998); Schwartz, Taking the Analysis of Security Seriously, 80 Va. L. Rev. 2073 (1994); LoPucki, The Unsecured Creditor's Bargain, 80 Va. L. Rev. 1887 (1994); Shupack, Solving the Puzzle of Secured Transactions, 41 Rutgers L.Rev. 1067 (1989); Buckley, The Bankruptcy Priority Puzzle, 72 Va.L.Rev. 1393 (1986); Schwartz, The Continuing Puzzle of Secured Debt, 37 Vanderbilt L.Rev. 1051 (1984); Levmore, Monitors and Freeriders in Commercial and Corporate Settings, 92 Yale L.J. 49 (1982); Schwartz, Security Interests and Bankruptcy Priorities: A Review of Current Theories, 10 J. Legal Stud. 1 (1981).

The materials that follow describe in detail four variants on the theme of security and priority in corporate finance—mortgage bonds, financial leases, subordination, and asset securitization.

1. MORTGAGE BONDS

With rare exceptions, corporate bonds and debentures constitute unconditional promises to pay principal at a fixed time and interest on fixed dates. However, not all bonds and debentures rank equally as claims upon the enterprise. One frequently encountered variation affecting the priority of the bondholders' claims is the mortgage bond. Holders of the mortgage bonds are secured as to the payment of principal and interest by a pledge or mortgage of described assets of the debtor, and thus have a prior claim to payment against other creditors with respect to the mortgaged assets or their proceeds.

The mortgage bond is an obligation secured by specified property which either is made subject to the obligee's lien by the mortgage (although technically the obligor continues to hold title) or, in some states, is technically transferred to the obligee to be held solely as security for the repayment of the debt. In theory, the mortgagee of a corporate mortgage, like the mortgagee of a simple home mortgage, applies the security in payment of the defaulted debt by foreclosure on the mortgaged property in a proceeding which results in a sale. The mortgagee may purchase the property at the sale, which ideally is an auction at which competitive bidding is designed, at least formally, to assure a fair price. Whether the property is sold to the obligee or otherwise, its proceeds are applied in payment of the obligation.

To the extent that the property subject to a corporate mortgage is an integral part of a going concern, it generally has a higher monetary value if it continues to be a part of the going concern than if it is sold for cash, piecemeal or *in toto*. Hence, even when mortgage foreclosure is technically an available remedy of the bondholders, it as a practical matter functions to enable them to acquire new participations in the continuing enterprise in a bankruptcy reorganization rather than to force the sale of the liened property to third persons for cash.

A corporation's mortgage bonds may be issued in different classes having different liens and terms, such as maturity dates, interest rates, call premiums; each class may be secured by specific property dedicated exclusively to it, or by a lesser—i.e., junior—lien on the same property that secures other bonds, or, as often happened with railroads, by a combination of the two security arrangements. In the case of different liens on the same property, the rank of its lien in the hierarchy determines the order of the bond's priority in payment from the proceeds of the mortgaged property.

Mortgages may be closed-end, in which case no bonds in addition to those initially issued against the mortgaged property may be created with that property as the subject of a first mortgage. Any subsequent mortgage on that property must be only a secondary lien on it, subject to the primary claim of the closed mortgage. If the borrowing corporation wishes to borrow additional funds on the first mortgage, it must pledge other property. A closed-end mortgage thus assures the lender that no other lender can acquire a primary lien on the pledged property, but by the same token it deprives the borrower of the opportunity to borrow additional amounts on that property at the relatively low interest rates available for a first mortgage. That deprivation is not trivial if improvements or additions have been made during the period of the mortgage or the property can support a larger first mortgage than it carries. The open-end mortgage is a device to permit additional bonds to be issued as a first lien on property already subject to a first lien securing outstanding bonds. The additional bonds may be issued from time to time, in different series, and at different interest rates. Since an open-end mortgage permits creation of larger debt on property which is already mortgaged, an existing lender may subsequently find its security diluted. To avoid undue dilution of the security, protective limits are set on the quantity of new first mortgage bonds that may be issued against the security of already mortgaged property. Generally, the limits are defined in terms of the proportions which property and earnings shall bear respectively to total amount of bonds and interest.

Thus, the open-end mortgage may provide that additional bonds may only be issued up to 60 percent of the cost of unencumbered property additions, or with interest charges which, when taken together with all other mortgage bond interest charges, are covered at least two times by the borrower's operating earnings.

When lenders require not only the security of presently pledged property but also of after-acquired property, provision must be made to subject newly acquired property to the lien of the mortgage. When such a clause is contained in a mortgage, the debtor may be hard-pressed to obtain additional credit, notwithstanding its acquisition of additional property. To avoid the restrictive effect of an after-acquired property clause, the issuer may resort to a variety of devices, the cleanest, if most expensive, of which is to redeem the outstanding bond issue. It may also be possible for the issuer to induce an exchange of outstanding bonds for new bonds or to persuade the bondholders to modify the restrictions. More elaborate avoidance devices (which more sophisticated creditors proscribe), entail the acquisition of additional property through subsidiaries, or the leasing, rather than the purchase, of additional property or the use of a purchase money mortgage. Occasionally merger or consolidation with another corporation may permit avoidance of after-acquired property clauses.

The mortgage may be secured not only by a pledge of the property but also by a pledge of the income from the property. Since, however, the debtor imperatively requires the use of that income, the pledge is subject to a retraction or defeasance clause which authorizes application of the income for the operation of the property. Since the income is generated after the date of the mortgage, it constitutes a form of after-acquired property, and is theoretically subject to application for the benefit of the mortgagee in the event of default. The conceptual and practical difficulties attending efforts to resolve the conflicting claims to ownership of the income (as it actually comes into the debtor's possession) by the debtor and its general creditors, on the one hand, and on the other hand by the mortgagee who has not yet foreclosed, are legion.

In addition to the security aspects of a mortgage bond, there usually are covenants designed to protect the property and to insure its appropriate maintenance or replacement in order to preserve its value as security.

When the property securing a mortgage bond is itself an investment security such as bonds or stocks the instrument is called a collateral trust bond. Generally the pledge takes the form of a transfer of title to a trustee but the obligor corporation retains substantial control over the pledged property and enjoys the income from it so long as there is no default on the bonds themselves. Another form of security—for either debt or equity—issued to public investors in increasing amounts by operating companies and financial institutions is a participation in a specific pool of the firm's assets. This arrangement is discussed in Section 4 infra.

2.   LEASES

Entering into a "financial lease" has many of the elements of secured borrowing. The lessee takes the position of the borrower. The lessor, which may be a financial institution, takes the place of the lender. Large items of equipment, such as railroad rolling stock, airplanes, and machines used in mining are financed through financial leases.

The lessee, which gets the use of the leased asset, promises to make rental payments under the lease. The lease extends over most of the economic life of the asset and will either be noncancellable or cancellable only upon reimbursement of any losses incurred by the lessor. It also probably will be a "net" lease—the lessee promises to maintain and insure the property and pay the property taxes. The lease payments are tax deductible as business expenses. But the lessee does not get the tax benefits of the depreciation on the property—these go to the lessor. The lessor not only takes the tax benefits of depreciation, but has the security that having title to the property brings. From the lessor's point of view, the lease is profitable if the stream of rental payments, discounted on an after tax basis, are greater than the present cost of the leased property.

There are many variations on the theme of financial leasing. Under a "leveraged lease," the lessor borrows part of the purchase price of the leased property, using the leased property and the stream of payments under the lease as security for the loan. To achieve a nonrecourse basis for the loan, the financial institution in the position of lessor will have an "owner trust" established to take title to the property and serve as the nominal lessor. The financial institution is the beneficiary of the trust.

Another form of leasing entails the use of equipment trust certificates. This form is used primarily by railroads and airlines to finance their acquisition of rolling stock and airplanes. Typically the equipment is bought by the trustee, a financial institution, from the manufacturer who builds it in accordance with the specifications of the using railroad or airline. The trustee pays for the equipment with funds it receives in small part from the user, but in large part from the proceeds of its issuance of equipment trust certificates to outside investors. The trustee leases the equipment to the railroad or airline at a rental calculated to pay the investors an annual return plus annual repayment of a portion of the principal. The equipment secures the obligation to repay the certificate holders. When the last principal payment is made, which is to occur with the last rental payment, the certificates are retired and the equipment belongs to the railroad or airline. The duration of these leases varies according to the equipment involved. Since the equipment is essential and is for the operations of all enterprises in the industry, it has a ready market value, and therefore can be financed at relatively favorable terms to the user.

"Sale and leaseback" transactions occur when a business wishes to realize cash on a piece of real estate but continues to operate the facility located thereon. The property is sold to a financial purchaser simultaneously with the execution of a long-term lease from the purchaser to the seller.

Finally, "operating leases" should be distinguished from financial leases. Operating leases are short term, cancellable leases where the lessor services the equipment. Vehicles and office equipment often are obtained on this basis.

3.   Subordination

Revised Model Simplified Indenture, Appendix A

Article 11

These materials often distinguish "seniors" from "juniors." The terms are relative and context sensitive. Sometimes the seniors include all claimants with a priority—all debt along with preferred stock, with the common stock being the junior interest. Sometimes the seniors are debt and the juniors are the equity, including preferred stock. Sometimes the seniors are the secured creditors and the juniors the unsecured (or "general") creditors. Finally, sometimes the seniors are unsecured creditors whose claims have not been voluntarily subordinated by contract to other debt claims, and the juniors are unsecured creditors whose claims have been subordinated. When a note delivered by the borrower in a private placement or bank term loan is denominated a "Senior Note," it denotes seniority in this last sense—a "senior" note is not a secured note; "senior" means "not subordinated." A subordinated obligation, whether a note or debenture, will so state in its title. The subordination provisions will be set out in the governing indenture or note purchase agreement, and referenced on the debenture or note form.

Borrowers issue subordinated debt to access or conserve borrowing room in their capital structures. Sometimes a firm needing additional long-term funds may find that its capital structure will not support further senior (that is, unsubordinated) borrowing. Such a firm could of course raise additional equity capital, but, as we have seen, such a financing may be viewed as a last resort. An intermediate type of instrument known as a subordinated debenture (or note) may solve the problem. Subordinated obligations are unconditional promises to pay principal and interest at specified dates, and in that sense, do not differ from conventional, unsecured debt securities. However, by the subordination agreement, either (a) payment of principal and interest is deferred until senior debt has been paid (called complete subordination), or (b) payment of principal and interest is deferred only in the event of default on senior debt, liquidation, dissolution, bankruptcy, or reorganization (sometimes called inchoate or insolvency subordination). Complete subordination is found more often in private subordination agreements than in publicly issued subordinated debt, which is more likely to be of the insolvency or inchoate variety.

In bankruptcy proceedings both subordinated debt and senior debt enter their claims as general creditors of the firm. But, to the extent that the assets distributed in the proceeding fail to satisfy the senior claims, the subordination agreement entitles the senior creditors to receive the assets of the debtor which otherwise would be distributable to the subordinated creditors. This is called the "double dividend." The subordination agreement assigns the subordinated lender's bankruptcy claim to the senior creditors. The seniors are entitled to take all of the distributions otherwise payable to the subordinated claimants until such point a they are "paid in full." At such point as the seniors are paid in full, the subordinated claimant becomes subrogated to the seniors' remaining claims (if any), collecting on both the seniors' claims and its own claim. Subordination, then, may be viewed as a set of contingent assignments of bankruptcy claims. Critically, the subordinated lender will be subordinated only to such classes of senior claims as are specifically identified in the subordination agreement. The custom is to make only financial creditors beneficiaries of the subordination agreement, leaving out the trade creditors.

Typically, the debentures will be made subordinate to existing or future borrowed funds. Even so, if the subordination is inchoate, the subordinated obligation is an otherwise unconditional promise to pay at a fixed time. So long as there occur none of the conditions that trigger payment deferral, the inchoate subordinated debenture may be due (or prepaid) at a point of time prior to the maturity date of senior debt, which may later find itself not fully paid off.

Notwithstanding the possibility of such temporally prior payment, the subordinated debenture is effectively junior to the designated senior borrowings and therefore commands a higher interest rate. On the other hand, it is debt and therefore ranks ahead of preferred stock and carries a lower interest rate than the dividend rate required for a preferred stock. Moreover, since the interest is deductible for federal income tax purposes, it holds out a substantial economic advantage to the borrower over preferred stock as a means of obtaining long-term capital.

For discussion of subordinated debt, see Carlson, A Theory of Contractual Debt Subordination and Lien Priority, 38 Vand.L.Rev. 975 (1985); Calligar, Subordination Agreements, 70 Yale L.J. 376 (1961); Everett, Subordinated Debt—Nature, Objectives and Enforcement, 44 B.U.L.Rev. 487 (1964); Johnson, Subordinated Debentures: Debt That Serves As Equity, 10 J.Fin. 1 (1955).

4. ASSET SECURITIZATION

Hypothesize a firm that has short term and long term intangible assets, such as accounts receivable or installment loans (with the firm as the lender). Carrying these assets on its balance sheet involves a funding cost to the firm because it must maintain capital—liability, equity, or some combination of the two—at a cost, a cost that increases with the term of the asset. The firm can reduce the carrying costs of these assets by using them as security for a line of credit, in that way converting their collateral value into immediate liquidity. (This is what drives much government securities repurchase activity.) This allows the firm to enjoy the current economic use of the assets (albeit at the interest cost of the loan for which they serve as security) without having to wait for the receivables and the installments to mature into cash.

Traditionally, the firm had two alternative means of doing this in credit markets. It could grant a lender a UCC article 9 floating lien on the receivables, booking the loan from the lender as a liability on the right side of its balance sheet and initially booking the loan proceeds as "cash" on the left side of its balance sheet. Alternatively, the firm could sell the receivables for a lump-sum to a finance company, called a "factor." This way the firm received ready cash for use in its business in exchange for its contract rights (discounted by the factor to reflect both any credit risk of the receivables and any time delay in their cash flows); the balance sheet effect of factoring would be to change only asset entries (substituting cash for the sold assets on the balance sheet) without adding leverage by forcing the firm to book a new liability. Much like factoring, asset securitization tries to capture the collateral value of asset receivables without increasing the firm's balance-sheet liabilities, in so doing reducing the duration of the firm's assets. Like factoring, securitization involves the sale of accounts receivable or another asset generating a predictable revenue stream. Smooth streams are better than lumpy ones, but both types can be securitized. The trick with securitization is that the firm also taps the public credit markets even as it borrows on an off-balance sheet basis.

Unlike factoring (or collateralized borrowing using the asset receivables as security), the borrowing can occur in public credit markets made up of anonymous investors, thereby widening a firm's supply of credit providers. The vehicle used to reach this segment of the credit market is a shell entity, called a "special purpose entity" (SPE), "special purpose vehicle" (SPV), or "special purpose corporation" (SPC). Although organized by the firm seeking financing (termed the "originator" because it sources the receivables, loans, or other assets), the SPE is a separate legal entity whose sole function is to intermediate cash flow (both from the receivables and the resulting financing) and the holding preferences of investors and other counterparties. The originator sells its receivables or other illiquid assets to the SPE, producing the same effect on the firm's balance sheet as in the factoring example above. The SPE pays for this exchange by issuing its own securities in public credit markets. These are termed "asset-backed securities" (ABS) because they are backed by cash flows from the originator's former receivables (or other assets). Importantly, though, the ABS may have cash flow and risk characteristics quite different from those of the underlying receivables, an effect made possible through the use of internal and external credit enhancements that affect the investment quality of the ABS. The SPE may also sell residual interests (in the nature of equity) in the receivables pool or a blend of debt and residual participations. Because of its advantages in liquefying a firm's balance sheet, securitization has become a multi-trillion dollar business.

(A) OVERVIEW

Lupica, Asset Securitization: The Unsecured Creditor's Perspective

76 Tex. L. Rev. 595, 599–616 (1998).

II.   Structured Finance Defined

Securitization has been defined as a "structured process whereby loans and other receivables are packaged, underwritten, and sold in the form of securities." The firm originally owning and selling the receivables is a financing-seeking firm, commonly referred to as the "originator,"and the purchasing and securities issuing entity is generally an affiliated special purpose corporation (SPC). SPCs are generally organized in one of two forms: either as a "pay-through" entity or as a "pass-through" entity. A pay-through entity is the transferee of receivables and the issuer of fixed-income securities. The return on these securities is based upon the transferred receivables' anticipated cash flow. A pass-through entity is typically a type of trust that serves as a conduit for the sale of the receivables to investors, with the receivables' payments merely passing through the trust.

The sale of the receivables by an originator to an SPC returns a lump sum cash payment to the originator. Once sold, the receivables' debtors pay on their accounts, either directly to the SPC as servicer, or through a servicing agent who in turn transfers the payment to the SPC. The SPC issues securities backed by the receivables' cash flow (known as asset-backed securities or ABS) to investors in the capital markets.

Asset-backed securities can be roughly characterized as either real-estate related or non-real-estate related. Real-estate related asset-backed securities, known as mortgage-backed securities, or MBS, are securities backed by the payments on loans secured by residential or commercial real estate. Non-real-estate ABS are backed by the cash flow on any non-real-estate related receivables.

The market for non-real-estate-related asset-backed securities is relatively new compared to the MBS market. The early on-real-estate-related, quasi-securitizations involved the issuance of standard accounts-receivable-backed commercial paper fully supported by letters of credit. Following these early transactions, firms became increasingly more creative and began securitizing automobile loans, leases, and credit card receivables. As the market for ABS has expanded in recent years, issuers have become even more imaginative with respect to the type of receivables securitized. Examples of recently issued ABS include bond issuances backed by unpaid real estate taxes, securities backed by hotel and hospitality receivables, taxi cab medallion-backed securities, securities backed by the excess spread from previously issued credit card securitizations, securities backed by health-care receivables, and securities backed by government-contract receivables.

In addition, new types of entities have been originating securitization transactions in recent years. Many banks, thrifts, and finance companies, at the urging of investment bankers, have transitioned from being "portfolio lenders" to being substantial issuers of asset-backed securities. Similarly, business entities with poor credit ratings and those entities who, because of high interest rates, are reluctant to borrow money conventionally from banks are increasingly turning to securitization as a way to secure capital at lower cost.

* * *

[In the] prototype of securitization * * * the originator is a corporation and the assets securitized are accounts receivable. Such a structure also assumes that the SPC is a corporate subsidiary of the originator formed for the exclusive purpose of purchasing the originator's pool of assets and then issuing securities backed by these assets in either the public or private markets.

III.   Why Firms Securitize Assets

Firms securitize their assets for the same reason firms borrow money: to raise money for either special projects or working capital. Rational firms choosing to securitize their assets rather than use them as collateral for a secured loan conclude, on balance, that securitization's net benefits exceed the benefits of the possible financing alternatives. These benefits include improving liquidity, increasing diversification of funding sources, lowering the effective interest rate, improving risk management, and achieving accounting-related advantages. Further, firms may securitize their assets because of the persuasive influence of professional advisors who stand to benefit financially from an increasing number of securitization transactions.

* * *

B.   Improvement of Liquidity

All originators who securitize their assets enjoy an improvement in asset liquidity management. By definition, the process of securitization transforms future payments into instant cash, and this transformation allows entities to recognize immediately the value of these assets for a variety of uses, including current business needs. The sale of assets, even at a discount, results in a lump sum cash payment to the originator.

There are many positive consequences of a firm's increased liquidity. In the case of originators with trade creditors, enhanced liquidity may permit a more fluid cycling of inventory, thus increasing the chance that a firm may become able to pay its suppliers' invoices as they become due. Because in many cases suppliers of inventory are unsecured trade creditors, this cash infusion may improve their chance of repayment.

The transformation of a future payment stream into immediate cash may further enable an originator to pursue a potentially profitable project or merely meet its regular obligations. Cash represents generalized purchasing power and is needed by businesses to invest in research and development, to pay dividends to shareholders, and to engage in other long-term investments, a need not always satisfied by a firm's erratic payment stream of receivables. These investments, in turn, may enable a firm to grow in profitability and, therefore, be in a better position to pay its creditors—including its unsecured creditors—when the firm's debts become due. Cash flow concerns are often paramount in management's mind, and the ability to readily transform assets into cash may provide a firm with a competitive advantage, both for long-term development planning and for short-term credit problem resolution.

C.   Diversification of Funding Sources

Even firms ordinarily able to get financing may be able to tap a new market of investors through securitization; individuals and institutional investors who would not ordinarily invest in an originator directly may be willing to invest in that originator's asset-backed securities. This potential market expansion is important for rapidly growing firms that have exhausted their typical funding sources or whose typical funding sources are offering financing at prohibitively high rates.

Moreover, a firm may find that due to the presence of restrictive covenants in the documentation of existing financing arrangements, securitization is the only possible way for it to raise funds; a bad credit history or a lack of a financial track record has a limiting effect on alternative financing methods that rely on the firm's credit rating.

Diversification of funding sources may also improve the originator's overall credit rating; a firm with a diversity of funding options generally has somewhat higher credit quality than a firm that solely utilizes commercial lending financing sources. Credit ratings reflect the likelihood that investors will be repaid their investment, plus interest, on time and on the terms described in the transaction's offering documents, and provide investors with a means to compare a variety of investment products. The lower a security is rated, the higher risk it is deemed to be and thus the higher return paid. As such, lower rated securities result in more expensive funding for their issuers. In some cases, a firm may find it financially prudent to engage in a securitization in order to improve its credit rating and then to return to the traditional commercial finance market as a better credit risk.

D.   Improved Risk Management

Risk management is often a fundamental objective of securitizing firms. Unlike traditional lending arrangements, a successful securitization is dependent upon investors' satisfaction with the quality of the assets backing the ABS, not the credit quality of the originator.

In a traditional lending arrangement, the same institution originates the loan, structures the terms, bears the credit risk, provides the funds, and services the collection of principal and interest. As such, whatever risks the borrower offers are fully absorbed by the lender. These risks include the possibility that the value of the collateral will decline, the potential for nonpayment or late payment of the underlying collateral, the prospect of the borrower becoming subject to unexpected (or expected) liability, the uncertainty of interest rate fluctuation, any fallibility associated with the borrower's previous borrowing record, the uncertainty associated with a limited borrowing history, and the potential of borrower's bankruptcy. These risks are commonly referred to as "event risks." Secured lenders address the issue of risk by reviewing the debtor's likelihood of default and evaluating the borrower's character, repayment capacity, and economic and financial projections for the entire term of the loan. This may involve the ongoing monitoring of the debtor's business behavior and practices.

The ABS investors, in contrast to secured lenders, do not bear all of the risks associated with the originator and its business and instead rely upon risk-containing measures that are made a part of the transaction. For example, credit enhancement allows the party providing the letter of credit or guaranty to bear a portion of the risk of nonpayment or late payment, in exchange for a fee. In addition, when an originator securitizes its highest quality assets it minimizes the ABS investors' risk. Conversely, the risk exposure of the firm's other creditors is heightened by this asset division. Furthermore, because there are no unknown or uncertain events in the future that could alter the quality of the ABS investors' investment, the investors are not subject to the vagaries of the originator's business behavior, and their risk exposure is limited to the obvious risks associated with the assets in the pool.

* * *

E.   Funding at More Favorable Rates

Because securitizing originators can better manage event risks, securitization enables most firms to fund their operations at a lower effective interest rate than through a secured borrowing arrangement. [Right hand side (RHS)] funding can be very costly if a firm has a large quantity of debt on its books, little or no financing track record or financial history, or lacks exposure to a broad base of investors.

An originator can obtain this lower effective rate because the capital markets do not consider its creditworthiness in pricing the rate of return for the securitization of a firm's receivables. Rather, the quality of the underlying assets determines the rate. In cases where the originator's credit rating is deficient, the capital markets (meaning the rating agencies) may give a higher credit rating to the asset-backed securities issued by the SPC than to the securities issued by the originator directly. This translates into a lower effective interest rate. Because the quality of the asset-backed security issued depends upon the quality of the payment stream of the underlying assets, it is the character and quality of the assets that are under the rating agencies' intense scrutiny.

The diminished possibility that ABS investors will be affected by the originator's potential for bankruptcy also improves the chance that the markets will view an originator's ABS more favorably than its direct debt issuances. Ideally, securitization transactions are structured so that the securitized assets are "bankruptcy remote." In such a case, if the integrity of the transaction's structure is not compromised, the assets transferred by the originator to the SPC and used to back the asset-backed securities will be deemed not to be part of the originator's bankruptcy estate should the originator fold. Thus, because of the severance of the credit risk to the originator from the credit of the ABS and because of the bankruptcy-remote nature of the transaction's structure, smaller, less established, or more financially debilitated firms may be able to fund themselves through a securitization on net terms similar to those offered to larger, more established and financially sound firms. This in turn may enable certain firms to expand at a more rapid pace by utilizing a less expensive source of funds for operations and long-term development.

F.   Accounting–Related Advantages

Securitization further allows a firm to isolate a pool of financial assets and match them with liabilities with similar maturities, tenor, and price. If a firm decides to take advantage of this financing option as part of its overall financing strategy, it reduces the necessity to hedge its funding obligations to eliminate a mismatch in asset and liability term and interest rate. This arrangement may prove to be advantageous to customers and other creditors because the credit risk of the securitized asset pool is segregated from the rest of the firm's assets, thus decreasing the risk of interest rate fluctuation and a resulting disruption in the firm's cash flow.

A related advantage to securitization is its treatment under the accounting rules as compared with other forms of financing. Generally Accepted Accounting Principles (GAAP), established by the Financial Accounting Standards Board (FASB), are the body of rules applicable to many securitizing firms. [A] transfer of assets in connection with a structured finance transaction [can] be treated as a sale for accounting purposes * * * . This type of transfer is known as an off-balance sheet sale and offers a firm enormous flexibility in raising capital, without risking a violation of covenants and restrictions potentially found in its other financing documents.

NOTE: RISK AND RETURN

Two points are in order about the risk and return characteristics of the asset-backed securities issued by the SPE to fund the purchase of the originator's receivables. First, these receivables form the primary basis for the financial returns expected by the holders of the SPE's asset-backed securities. It follows that these receivables must yield a predictable revenue stream to qualify for securitization. The quality of the asset's revenue stream depends on the attending risks of payment delay and payment default, which in turn depend on the creditworthiness of the obligors on the receivables. A cognizable risk of default in the receivables pool does not by itself prevent securitization; indeed, commercial lenders like banks build in the foreseeability of such credit losses, for example through a loan-loss reserve. So long as a payment/nonpayment ratio of the receivables can be quantified, this default risk can be priced by prospective investors, as reflected in the asset-backed security's coupon rate. At some point, though, an asset's risk-level is so high as to make it unsuited to securitization. More particularly, if the risk level of the asset-backed securities would be higher than that of the originator firm taken as a whole, the total cost of securitized debt financing will be greater than that of direct borrowing by the originator. Thus, asset securitization will not be efficient. Finally, scale matters here too because the complex transaction structure implicates significant fixed legal, accounting, and compliance costs. For this reason, the value of the assets being securitized tends to exceed $100,000,000. Securitizations of small amounts tend to be structured not by the originator but by "conduit" issuers maintained by banks and investment bankers. The conduit issuers draw assets from multiple originators to create scale economies from large receivables pools.

Second, although the receivables provide the primary source of cash flow for repayment of the asset-backed securities, the risk and return structure of the SPE's issuances is independent from that of the underlying receivables. This is so because the SPE repackages the cash flow and supports it with credit enhancements. A typical SPE issuance includes at least one senior class of debt (usually investment-grade) supported by one or more junior classes of debt and other securities. The ability of these junior securities to bear unforeseen losses on the receivables' cash flow works as an internal credit enhancement for the investment-grade tranche. In addition, as Professor Lupica notes, originators also use external credit enhancements to ameliorate the risk that the SPE's assets prove insufficient to cover its obligations. These devices include letters of credit issued by banks and surety bonds issued by insurance companies. The originator can also boost the investment quality of asset-backed securities by making an additional capital contribution to the issuing SPE, purchasing a minority stake in the SPE's equity, or making a subordinated loan. Guarantees by the originator are rare in the private sector. In contrast, government sponsored originators like the Federal Home Loan Mortgage Corp. (Freddie Mac) and the Federal National Mortgage Association (Fannie Mae), guarantee principal and interest payments for all of their collateralized mortgage obligations.

Caveat. This all sounds nice and neat, but actors in markets for asset-backed securities have been known to make mistakes. Consider the Bear Stearns firm in mid–2007 as it announced that two large hedge funds it advised had lost all of their equity value, even as the hedge funds had specialized in investing in AA and AAA debt securities. How could that happen? The debt securities in question were asset-backed issues, the backing assets being subprime mortgages—loans to the riskiest homeowners, loans made in a consumer market that had not even existed five years earlier, loans made to purchase homes at the peak of a bubble real estate market. The AA and AAA ratings were granted on the assumption that default rates would remain low. The primary lenders had sorted out the riskiest of their loans in advance and kept them out the securitizations, and the rating agencies assumed that even given defaults the prices of the homes under the mortgages in the securitizations would keep rising so as fully to cover the risk. See Norris, Market Shock: AAA Rating May Be Junk, N.Y. Times, July 20, 2007, at C1. They assumed incorrectly. Note also that even as the textbooks tell us that securitization presupposes a reliable payment stream, with reliability amounting to an extrapolation from past performance, here the securitization industry facilitated a new lending market that had no track record. It in effect promised high returns for low risk. Bear Stearns and its hedge fund clients learned the hard way that there is no such thing. Others also are learning this lesson—shares of firms in the business of providing credit enhancement to securitizations (e.g.,, MBIA, Ambac) fell sharply in mid–2007.

(B) ACCOUNTING TREATMENT

Recall that asset securitization may be superior to borrowing on the balance sheet not only because the cost of credit may be lower, but also because securitization increases the firm's liquidity without increasing its balance sheet leverage. If the transaction is structured properly, the SPE's debt obligation will be treated under Generally Accepted Accounting Principles (GAAP) on an off-balance sheet basis and the originator will not have to book the liability. Instead, the transfer of the assets to (and return of proceeds from) the SPE is booked as a sale of assets. Generally speaking, three conditions must be fulfilled if the securitization is to yield this accounting benefit to the originator.

First, the transfer of the SPE assets must be effected as a "true sale." Indeed a successfully structured securitization must achieve true sale under multiple legal regimes—the common law of contract, UCC article 9, and bankruptcy law, as well as under GAAP. Generally, a transfer of assets to a SPE looks more like a sale and less like a cover for secured borrowing to the extent that the transfer vests the economic benefits and detriments of ownership in the SPE. This is accomplished to the extent that (a) the SPE has no recourse against the originator in the event an asset fails to yield its expected return, (b) the originator has no right to participate in any surplus value yielded by the assets after the discharge of the SPE's obligations, and (c) the entire purchase price for the assets is paid up front without being subject to adjustments for subsequent financing costs to the SPE. SFAS No. 140, the GAAP provision governing the treatment of securitization, has a true sale rule that looks to "surrender of control" over the assets, surrender of control meaning that the transferee has the right to pledge or exchange the assets. But, since SFAS No. 140 also requires the SPE to be a passive liquidating vehicle without discretion to sell or dispose of the assets, the pledge or exchange test is directed to the holders of beneficial (equity) interests in the SPE rather than to the SPE itself.

A transaction looks less like a sale if the originator continues to bear responsibility for collecting the receivables. Unfortunately, this may be the allocation of duties that makes the most cost sense. In fact, originators customarily continue to service the securitized assets. SFAS No. 140, resolves the accounting ambiguity with an explicit sanction of originator servicing along with a set of rules governing the accounting treatment of the servicing contract. The custom in transaction documentation is to allocate the servicing cost to the SPE, vest decisionmaking power over the assets in the SPE, and provide that the servicing arrangement is terminable by the SPE. See Schwarcz, Structured Finance: The New Way to Securitize Assets, 11 Cardozo L. Rev. 607, 621–26 (1990).

Second, the SPE must be set up as a "bankruptcy remote" entity. In the words of SFAS No. 140, paragraph 9, the transferred assets must have been "isolated from the transferor—put presumptively beyond the reach of the transferor and its creditors, even in bankruptcy or other receivership." Note that here the accounting rule tracks the basic assumptions of the SPE lenders, who are banking on exclusive recourse to the SPE's assets. Asset securitization holds out a lower cost of capital than direct borrowing by the originator firm only to the extent that the asset pool in the SPE is effectively separated from that of the originator. Only separation at law and in economic substance between the originator and the SPE will immunize the holders of the SPE's asset-backed securities from any credit risks of the originator. Bankruptcy remoteness means that in the event that the originator becomes bankrupt, the SPE and its assets are kept separate from the bankruptcy proceeding.

Legal risk enters into the credit picture at this point. A bankruptcy court conceivably could use its equitable powers to consolidate the SPE into the originator's proceeding. This result would be a disaster from the point of view of the SPE's debt holders, who might have to share their security with the originator's larger creditor population. Asset securitizations accordingly are set up so as to minimize the chance that a bankruptcy court might characterize the sale of assets to the SPE as either a disguised form of secured financing by the originator or a fraudulent conveyance. In addition, SPEs tend to carry special corporate governance provisions that constrain their ability to resort to bankruptcy.

GAAP seems to contemplate the residuum of legal uncertainty. The SPE assets need only be "presumptively" beyond the reach of the originator's creditors. SFAS No. 140, paragraph 27, elaborates further, showing that a standard rather than a rule governs on this matter:

> The nature and extent of supporting evidence required for an assertion in financial statements that transferred financial assets have been isolated * * * depend on the facts and circumstances. All available evidence that either supports or questions an assertion shall be considered. That consideration includes making judgments about whether the contract or circumstances permit the transferor to revoke the transfer. It may also involve making judgments about the kind of bankruptcy or other receivership into which a transferor or SPE might be placed, whether the transfer of financial assets would be likely to be deemed a true sale at law, whether the transferor is affiliated with the transferee, and any other factors appropriate under applicable law.

Third, the structure of the SPE must "qualify" under SFAS No. 140. No particular form of legal entity is contemplated—it may be a "trust or other legal vehicle." But its governing documents must limit its ability to do business and hold property to a list of tasks appropriate only to the narrow purpose of a passive conduit entity. In addition, under SFAS No. 140, paragraphs 35–36, the SPE must be "demonstrably distinct" from the originator:

> A qualifying SPE is demonstrably distinct from the transferor only if it cannot be unilaterally dissolved by any transferor, its affiliates, or its agents and * * * at least 10 percent of the fair value of its beneficial interests is held by parties other than any transferor, its affiliates, or its agents.

The 10 percent test means that 10 percent of the equity interest in the SPE must be held by parties other than the originator.

(C) TRANSACTION STRUCTURE

With the accounting rules in mind, let us take a look at a hypothetical asset securitization. In the following example, General Manufacturing Inc. (General) is an originator which securitizes a pool of receivables using two separate SPEs, one on-balance sheet and one off-balance sheet: General

Manufacturing Receivables (Receivables) and General Manufacturing Owner Trust (Owner Trust), respectively. Because Receivables is a wholly owned subsidiary of General, it is consolidated onto General's balance sheet. Receivables acts as a conduit for the transfer of the receivables between General and Owner Trust. Owner Trust is the qualifying SPE which issues the asset-backed securities. (Owner trusts tend to be used for securitizations of auto, student, home equity, and equipment loans.)

An industrial concern, General sells large machines to customers who pay over time at interest without posting collateral for these credit obligations. General has decided to securitize $1 billion face amount of these accounts receivable. The transfer of the contracts comes in two steps. First, General transfers the contracts to Receivables, in exchange for cash consideration. (For simplicity, let's assume that Receivables funds its acquisitions of the receivables from pre-existing cash reserves.) Next, Receivables transfers the same $1 billion of contracts over to Owner Trust, which in turn transfers the same cash consideration. The Owner Trust is created pursuant to an Owner Trust Agreement entered into between Receivables and a bank or trust company. The Owner Trust is a conduit that exists to take title to the receivables and borrow the money to pay for them on an off-balance sheet basis so far as concerns General and Receivables. It sells secured notes, entering into a trust indenture for the benefit of the noteholders with a second bank or trust company. The receivables and cash flows generated by the contract rights—the Owner Trust Estate—secure the notes.

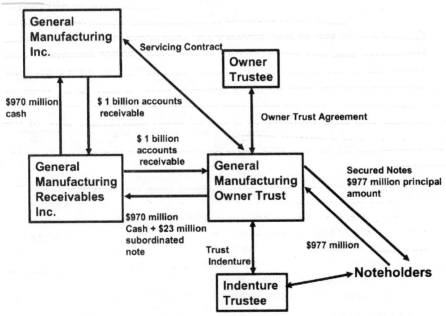

Let's look more closely at each leg of the transfer. General transfers $1 billion face amount and gets back $970 million from receivables. The $30 million shortfall follows from a projection that the default rate on General's receivables is just less than 3 percent. (If the track record were close to a default rate of 5 percent, the proceeds to General would drop to $950 million.) Note also the slight discrepancy between the $970 million proceeds to the originator and the $977 million raised in the debt financing. The additional $7 million raised by the Owner Trust stays with it as additional security. Finally, the Owner Trust issues a $23 million note to Receivables that is subordinated to the secured notes sold to the public. This sops up any residual upside return on the receivables after the investors in the asset-backed securities have been paid off in full. In other words, if the receivables outperform the estimated 3 percent default rate, e.g. the entire face amount of $1 billion is paid off, excess financial return will build up in the Owner Trust to the extent that cash flow ex post exceeds what was projected. The subordinated note directs that excess return to Receivables, not to any of the holders of the Owner Trust's securities. This is a case for complete subordination, which assures both an absence of cash flows back to Receivables while the secured notes are outstanding and, in the event the Owner Trust becomes insolvent, that Receivables' debt claim will be junior to that of the secured noteholders. Finally, under the servicing contract between the Owner Trust and General, General collects the payments on the receivables and remits them to the Owner Trust, which passes them on to the indenture trustee. From the point of view of the customers who owe General for goods purchased, it is as if the securitization had never occurred.

Under the Owner Trust, a depositor (Receivables) transfers assets to the Trust in exchange for a consideration. This occurs when the Trust is first established, before the debt securities are issued. Receivables transfers a nominal amount to the Owner Trust in exchange for Trust Certificates created and issued pursuant to the Owner Trust Agreement. The exchange establishes Receivables as the beneficiary of the Trust. The Owner Trust Agreement will provide that Receivables pay all expenses incurred by the Trustee in the course of administering the trust. Note that as a result of this arrangement, should the $7 million cash cushion placed in the Trust remain at termination, Receivables picks up this value along with any proceeds under the subordinated notes. In theory, equity capital also can be raised for the Owner Trust through the sale of additional Trust Certificates to Receivables, or through their sale to third parties. Finally, under SFAS No. 140, at least 10 percent of the Trust Certificates must be held by third parties in order for the Trust to be a qualified SPE.

The Owner Trust form imports certainty respecting administration. There also are out of pocket cost advantages—in New York the legal entity of the Owner Trust is complete upon execution and delivery of the Owner Trust Agreement and deposit of a nominal amount in the Trust; neither state filing nor annual franchise payments will be necessary. Delaware, in contrast, has instituted a filing regime incorporating nominal fees. See Del. Statutory Trust Act, 12 Del. Code § 3801 et seq. Delaware also has created a state taxation regime that is favorable to asset securitization. Accordingly, many qualifying SPEs are sited in Delaware. This is often done on a nominal basis—the owner trust will be sited in New York or another state, with a second, shadow owner trust sited in Delaware though the agency of the trustee bank's separately incorporated Delaware subsidiary.

Depending on its structure, the Owner Trust may be taxed as a separate taxpayer or qualify for pass-through status under federal income tax law, such that only the investors—and not the entity—pay tax. Generally, a business entity may elect its tax status—as a separate taxpayer or a pass-through—under the check-the-box regime instituted in 1997 in the Internal Revenue Code. Pass-through status lets the interest and other tax deductions of an SPE flow through to the tax returns of an SPE's owners or the holders of its beneficial interests. For example, the Owner Trust would avoid an entity-level tax if it qualifies as a tax-recognized "grantor trust." Often used for the securitizations of non-revolving receivables (like auto loans), a grantor trust passes through the cash flows from its receivables pool to the trust's certificate holders. A grantor trust also passes through related tax attributes—deductions and liability for income tax—to these holders. However, certain restrictions apply to a business entity's election to be taxed as a pass-through. The Owner Trust employed in the hypothetical provides flexibility by issuing different classes of securities with varying maturities. Only certain kinds of pass-through entities, however, may issue securities of different classes with different maturities. For example, pass-through treatment for the Owner Trust may be available if it is restructured as a partnership, so long as it is not a publicly-traded one, which, like a corporation, is taxed as a separate person. Unless the Owner Trust meets one of these safe-harbors for pass-through treatment, then the Owner Trust would be liable for income tax at the entity-level, although it could deduct its interest and other business expenses. There also are special federal tax provisions allowing specially-designed SPEs—real estate mortgage investment conduits (REMICs) and financial asset securitization investment trusts (FASITs)–to issue multiple debt securities and retain pass through status. See Feaslee & Nirenberg, Federal Income Taxation of Securitization Transactions (2001); Davidson, et al., Securitization: Structuring and Investment Analysis 20–21 (2003).

(D) BANKRUPTCY RISKS

As noted earlier, careful structuring of the asset transfer arrangement to resemble an arm's-length sale does not by itself eliminate bankruptcy risk. Assume that the originator does not seek off-balance sheet treatment of the securitized debt and, accordingly, conducts its asset securitizations through a wholly owned subsidiary—an entity like Receivables in the hypothetical transaction above. If the originator were to go into bankruptcy reorganization while controlling the board of this wholly owned subsidiary, it could have a powerful incentive as Debtor in Possession to cause the SPE board of directors to make a parallel chapter 11 filing so as to return the SPE assets to the originator's bankruptcy estate. SPE charters attempt to constrain the ability of the SPE to make a voluntary bankruptcy petition. They do this by requiring (a) that the SPE actually be insolvent before filing a bankruptcy petition and (b) that a bankruptcy petition be approved by independent directors who are stipulated to owe fiduciary duties to the SPE's creditors rather than its stockholders. Schwarcz, supra, at 615; Ellis, Securitization Vehicles, Fiduciary Duties, and Bondholders Rights, 24 J.Corp. L. 295, 309 (1999).

Substantive consolidation with an originator bankruptcy proceeding remains possible, even assuming the foregoing provisions work as intended. The SPE could be forced into bankruptcy involuntarily by a creditor of its own. That risk can be reduced only by constraining the SPE's ability to assume indebtedness in addition to the debt incident to the asset securitization. In the alternative, the court in an originator bankruptcy could conceivably order consolidation of a solvent SPE. The factors coming to bear on that decision include (a) the severability and identification of the assets in question, (b) the presence or absence of balance sheet consolidation, (c) a pattern of commingling of assets, (d) compliance with formalities by the SPE, and (e) separation of location and management. Schwarcz, supra at 615–17.

A dictum in Octagon Gas Systems v. Rimmer, 995 F.2d 948 (10th Cir.1993), destabilized the securitization industry by questioning the efficacy of bankruptcy remoteness. The same question has been asked repeatedly in the commentary, see Lupica, supra; Carlson, The Rotten Foundations of Securitization, 39 Wm. & Mary L. R. 1055 (1998); Frost, Asset Securitization and Corporate Risk Allocation, 72 Tul. L. Rev. 101 (1997); Hill, Securitization: A Low–Cost Sweetner for Lemons, 74 Wash.U.L.Q. 1061 (1996). Does the case that follows further destabilize the legal background?

In re LTV Steel Company, Inc.

United States Bankruptcy Court, N.D. Ohio, 2001.
37 Bankr.Ct.Dec. 137.

■ William T. Bodoh, Bankruptcy Judge.

[Debtor, a large steel company, filed for Chapter 11 reorganization for a second time in 2000. Debtor created a wholly owned subsidiary known as LTV Sales Finance Co. ("Sales Finance") for the purpose of conducting asset-backed securitizations or structured financings ("ABS").]

Abbey National is a large financial institution located in the United Kingdom. Debtor and Abbey National entered into an ABS transaction in October 1994. To effectuate this agreement, Debtor then entered into an agreement with Sales Finance which purports to sell all of Debtor's right and interest in its accounts receivables ("receivables") to Sales Finance on a continuing basis. Abbey National then agreed to loan $270,000,000 to Sales Finance in exchange for Sales Finance granting Abbey National a security interest in the receivables. On the date Debtor's petition was filed, Chase Manhattan Bank ("Chase Manhattan") was Abbey National's agent for this credit facility.

[Another wholly-owned subsidiary, LTV Steel Products, LLC ("Steel Products"), entered into a $30,000,000 securitization of LTV's inventories with a group of banks led by Chase Manhattan.]

Neither Sales Finance nor Steel Products is a debtor in this proceeding. Nevertheless, Debtor filed a motion with the Court on December 29, 2000 seeking an interim order permitting it to use cash collateral. This cash collateral consisted of the receivables and inventory that are ostensibly owned by Sales Finance and Steel Products. Debtors [sic] stated to the Court that it would be forced to shut it doors and cease operations if it did not receive authorization to use this cash collateral. A hearing was held on Debtor's cash collateral motion on December 29, 2000 as part of the first day hearings.

Abbey National was not present at the cash collateral hearing. However, the Court notes that Abbey National had actual notice of the hearing * * * .

On December 29, 2000, Debtor and Chase Manhattan reached an agreement regarding an interim order permitting Debtor to use the cash collateral. Chase Manhattan did not formally consent to the entry of this order, as it could not secure Abbey National's consent to the form of the order, but Chase Manhattan did negotiate some of the terms of the order and did not raise an objection to its entry by the Court. The Court determined that entry of the interim order was necessary to permit Debtor to continue business operations, that the interests of Abbey National and all other creditors who had an interest in the cash collateral were adequately protected by the order, and that entry of the order was in the best interests of the estate and creditors of the estate. Accordingly, the Court entered the order tendered by Debtor, the relevant provisions of which are summarized below:

1. Recognition that there is a dispute between Debtor and the secured lenders of Sales Finance and Steel Products as to whether the transactions between Debtor and those entities were true sales or disguised financing vehicles;

2. An order requiring the secured lenders to turn over to Debtor the cash proceeds of the inventory and receivables which are to be used to provide working capital for Debtor;

3. Recognition that in the event the Court determines these transactions to be true sales, the secured lenders whose cash collateral was used will be entitled to administrative expense claims against the estate;

4. Adequate protection was provided to the secured lenders in the form of senior liens on the inventory and receivables and weekly interest payments to the lenders at pre-petition non-default rates.

* * * Abbey National asks the Court to modify the interim cash collateral order nunc pro tunc * * * . [Abbey argues (1) there is no basis for the Court to determine that the receivables which are Abbey National's collateral are property of Debtor's estate and (2) that even if the receivables are property of Debtor's estate, that its interests are not adequately protected because the pre-petition receivables are diminishing at a rapid rate and will soon be depleted.]

Abbey [argues] that the receivables which constitute its collateral are not property of Debtor's estate, and thus this Court lacked jurisdiction to enter the interim order. * * *

Section 541(a) of the Bankruptcy Code provides that upon the filing of a bankruptcy petition an estate is created consisting of "all legal or equitable interests of the debtor in property as of the commencement of the case." 11 U.S.C. § 541(a)(1). The estate created by the filing of a Chapter 11 petition is very broad, and property may be included in Debtor's estate even if Debtor does not have a possessory interest in that property. * * *

Abbey National contends that the interim order is flawed because, on its face, the transaction between Debtor and Sales Finance is characterized as a true sale. Therefore, Abbey National argues, since Debtor sold its interests in the receivables to Sales Finance, Debtor no longer has an interest in the receivables and they are not property of the estate. However, Abbey National has admitted to the Court * * * that the ultimate issue of whether Debtor actually sold the receivables to Sales Finance is a fact-intensive issue that cannot be resolved without extensive discovery and an evidentiary hearing.

We find Abbey National's argument for "emergency" relief to be not well taken for several reasons. First, Abbey National's position in this regard is circular: we cannot permit Debtor to use cash collateral because it is not property of the estate, but we cannot determine if it is property of the estate until we hold an evidentiary hearing. * * * Because the determination of this issue must await further discovery, we decline to grant Abbey National relief from the interim order.

Furthermore, there seems to be an element of sophistry to suggest that Debtor does not retain at least an equitable interest in the property that is subject to the interim order. Debtor's business requires it to purchase, melt, mold and cast various metal products. To suggest that Debtor lacks some ownership interest in products that it creates with its own labor, as well as the proceeds to be derived from that labor, is difficult to accept. Accordingly, the Court concludes that Debtor has at least some equitable interest in the inventory and receivables, and that this interest is property of the Debtor's estate. This equitable interest is sufficient to support the entry of the interim cash collateral order.

Finally, it is readily apparent that granting Abbey National relief from the interim cash collateral order would be highly inequitable. The Court is satisfied that the entry of the interim order was necessary to enable Debtor to keep its doors open and continue to meet its obligations to its employees, retirees, customers and creditors. Allowing Abbey National to modify the order would allow Abbey National to enforce its state law rights as a secured lender to look to the collateral in satisfaction of this debt. This circumstance would put an immediate end to Debtor's business, would put thousands of people out of work, would deprive 100,000 retirees of needed medical benefits, and would have more far reaching economic effects on the geographic areas where Debtor does business. However, maintaining the current status quo permits Debtor to remain in business while it searches for substitute financing, and adequately protects and preserves Abbey National's rights. The equities of this situation highly favor Debtor. As a result, the Court declines to exercise its discretion to modify the interim order * * * .

* * *

The final argument Abbey National has raised in support of its motion is that its interests in the collateral are not adequately protected. Specifically, Abbey National contends that the pre-petition receivables in which Abbey National has an interest are being depleted at a rate of $10,000,000 per day, and that the receivables will be entirely consumed in short order. Additionally, Abbey National asserts that the interim order diminished the value of Abbey National's liens. * * *

Abbey National's contentions that its interest is not adequately protected can be boiled down to a simple issue. Prior to the filing of Debtor's petition, the outstanding balance on Abbey National's loan to Sales Finance was approximately $224,800,000. This loan to Sales Finance was secured by the receivables transferred to Sales Finance, and this financing arrangement was rated AAA by Standard & Poors. However, the terms of the interim order have altered the nature of Abbey National's liens. Under the terms of the interim order, Abbey National and the other secured lenders have been granted liens on Debtor's post-petition inventory and receivables. Abbey National's loan is thus now secured by inventory and assets which do not have a AAA rating, and Abbey National must now share its liens with Debtor's other secured lenders.

We find Abbey National's arguments to be not well taken. First, we find Abbey National's contention that its collateral is being consumed at a rate of $10,000,000 per day to be disingenuous. It is true that the pre-petition receivables are being used by Debtor to purchase and manufacture more steel. However, Debtor's use of the pre-petition receivables will inevitably lead to an increase in the value of post-petition receivables and inventory, in which Abbey National has a security interest.

This conclusion is amply supported by the affidavit of John T. Delmore, Debtor's Assistant Controller. Mr. Delmore's affidavit indicates that as of January 15, 2001, there was a sufficient equity cushion in both post-petition inventory and receivables to provide adequate protection to all of Debtor's secured lenders. The amount of the respective equity cushions equaled 39% for the receivables lenders and 179% for the inventory lenders. Furthermore, it appears that Debtor's business will continue to generate additional post-petition receivables and inventory sufficient to protect Abbey National's interest in the near future. Because we find that Abbey National's interest in cash collateral is adequately protected by an equity cushion and by the other terms of the interim order, the Court declines to exercise its discretion to modify the interim order * * *.

NOTE: SUBSEQUENT PROCEEDINGS

Abbey National soon settled with LTV. Under the settlement, the loans to Abbey National and Chase were paid down, releasing the collateral for the benefit of LTV as Debtor in Possession. Simultaneously, however, Abbey National and Chase funded the takeout loan. The takeout loan was accorded a bankruptcy super priority. See In re LTV Steel Co., 2001 WL 1822360 (N.D.Ohio).

NOTE: POLICY DEBATES

Let us take another look at the hypothetical securitization described above and conduct a substance over form review. General, in order to take advantage of a lower cost of borrowing, transfers assets to a bankruptcy remote borrowing entity. The structure makes sense to General's shareholders because the interest cost advantage positive exceeds the negatives of the discount on the sale price of the receivables and the transaction costs. General's shareholders also get another significant benefit: General achieves off-balance sheet status for the borrowing even as it in the end holds onto the lion's share of the debt's tax advantage. Has value been created? How would Durand and Modigliani and Miller answer this question? If the value to those holding claims in General's capital structure must in the end come from General's producing assets, and if pieces of paper cannot by themselves create value, then must not the value added for the benefit of General's shareholders come at the expense of some other claimant group in its capital structure?

Critics of securitization argue that other claimants suffer as a result of securitizations. See Lupica, supra; LoPucki, The Death of Liability, 106 Yale L. J. 1 (1996). More particularly, in the event of insolvency, general creditors of the originator come away with less than otherwise would have been the case. Of course, some general creditors, in particular unsecured financial creditors, have an opportunity to price the risk of asset depletion through securitization ex ante in the interest rate and to negotiate for covenants that constrain asset depletion. The commentators accordingly focus on "nonadjusting" creditors—tort claimants and trade creditors who do not get a chance to bargain for a rate and for whom covenant negotiation is either not cost effective or impossible. Finally, as the debtor claimed in LTV, it is possible that a bankrupt originator needs to reclaim the securitized assets in order to continue as a viable going concern. If the bankruptcy court cannot recapture the assets, chapter 11's purpose of preserving value for the benefit of the creditor group as a whole is frustrated.

Securitization's defenders make a two part response. First, nothing nefarious is going on, at least in mainstream transactions. The originator gets back fair value for the assets transferred to the SPE, and nothing about the transaction structure creates a special risk of after the fact asset dissipation by the originator. See Schwarcz, The Alchemy of Asset Securitization, 1 Stan.J.L. Bus. & Fin. 133 (1994). Second, value really is created by unbundling whole assets into separate risk and cash flow streams such that market intermediaries with different comparative advantages can make the most of the assets as repackaged into asset-backed securities. The separation of the collateral pool into a different entity lowers the lenders' monitoring costs. Id.; Hill, supra. Where the originator is in a regulated industry, as is the case with banks, regulatory costs are reduced. Id. For an intermediate position that in the main sustains securitization but allows a narrow exception for consolidation of abusive transactions, see Lubben, Beyond True Sales: Securitization and Chapter 11, 1 NYU J.L. & Bus. 89 (2004).

SECTION D.   HIGH LEVERAGE RESTRUCTURING

1.   LEVERAGE AND MANAGEMENT DISCIPLINE

Return to Section A, supra, and the "trade off" account of capital structure optimality articulated in the shadow of M–M's irrelevance hypothesis and its balancing of benefits (tax and signaling) against detriments (bankruptcy and agency costs). We turn now to a more controversial factor that falls on the benefit side. This governance benefit of debt accrues in the context of the agency relationship between shareholders and managers rather than in the context of the conflicting interests of debt and equity.

Managers in pursuit of institutional stability have an incentive to borrow too little. A low leverage capital structure leaves management with considerable discretion respecting the investment of excess earnings generated by operations. To the extent that management pursues enterprise security and ease of life in exercising that discretion, the result can be reinvestment of capital in suboptimal projects. At the same time, a bias toward a low leverage capital structure can mean that management turns down profitable new projects. High leverage, in contrast, reduces management's zone of discretion. In order to keep up payments on the debt and avoid bankruptcy the managers must run a lean and efficient operation. High leverage accordingly becomes associated with good governance.

This argument for high leverage as a device for improved corporate governance was articulated two decades ago with reference to the financial practices then prevailing in large firms. The strategy was financial self sufficiency, which entailed a bias in favor of retained earnings financing. Donaldson, Managing Corporate Wealth 57–58 (1984), reported as follows on managers and their attitudes toward debt:

"Corporate managers considered a variety of factors as they set these debt limits. Among them were: the needs of the business; the need for a substantial reserve for both offensive and defensive use; the use of debt by close competitors in the funding of competitive strategy; the opinions of the capital-market power centers—bankers, analysts, and credit rating agencies; and the managers' own subjective sense of the riskiness of any given amount of debt. The ultimate risk with which the managers were concerned was the loss of independence and control consequent upon falling into the hands of 'those damn banks.' As the executive who described the banks in these terms went on to say:

They will cut you off and they will be cold-blooded as hell. I don't want to be in the position where our money market center can control me.

"Listening to these comments, it is hard to remember that the speaker is a top executive in a large, mature, and profitable corporation—not a sidewalk entrepreneur. Yet many of his peers in other companies expressed the same concerns although they phrased them more elegantly.

　　　* * *

"Short of the extreme event of losing control, the value of a conservative debt limit was seen to lie in its ability to guarantee continued funding flexibility (through debt and equity) in the face of competitive uncertainty. Access to the capital markets *regardless of conditions* was the key consideration. Of course, the level of debt deemed conservative was to some degree a function of need and experience. New levels of debt brought on by urgent competitive spending priorities could and did become the new conservatism, if found to be tolerable over an extended period of time. However, beneath these judgments was management's abiding concern for organizational survival. As one executive remarked:

> The debt policy [of our company] reflects a primary emphasis on freedom—that if we maintain the debt limits we have set, we will be free from bank restrictions and the banks will not inhibit our activities. This, along with our earnings goals are *parts of the whole concept of a desirable quality of life* for management. (Emphasis added.)"

The conservative attitude toward debt described by Donaldson came to be seen as a symptom of management in derogation of shareholder value. The association of the two began when M–M articulated the tax-adjusted version of their position. Miller, The Modigliani–Miller Propositions After Thirty Years, 2 J. Econ. Perspectives 99, 112 (1988), recalls the appearance of the management critique:

> "In many ways this tax-adjusted MM proposition provoked even more controversy than the original invariance one, which could be, and often was, shrugged off as merely another inconsequential paradox from some economists' frictionless dreamworld. But this one carried direct and not very flattering implications for the top managements of companies with low levels of debt. It suggested that the high bond ratings of such companies, in which the management took so much pride, may actually have been a sign of their incompetence; that the managers were leaving too much of their stockholders' money on the table in the form of unnecessary corporate income tax payments, payments which in the aggregate over the sector of large, publicly held corporations clearly came to many billions of dollars."

Stating Miller's point more broadly, management's desire to be self sufficient and secure comes at the cost of maximum return on capital invested. If outside debt financing gives rise to management insecurity, then stepped-up debt financing should cause management to perform more productively. From an agency cost point of view, then, debt does more than perform a financial signaling function. See Grossman and Hart, Corporate Financial Structure and Managerial Incentives, in McCall (Ed.), The Economics of Information and Uncertainty, at pp. 108–110, (1982). The leading articulation of this perspective came from Professor Michael Jensen, in what he termed "the control hypothesis:"

Jensen, Agency Costs of Free Cash Flow, Corporate Finance and Takeovers

76 Amer. Econ. Rev. (Papers and Proceedings) 323–325 (1986).

Managers have incentives to cause their firms to grow beyond the optimal size. Growth increases managers' power by increasing the resources under their control. It is also associated with increases in managers' compensation, because changes in compensation are positively related to the growth in sales. * * * The tendency of firms to reward middle managers through promotion rather than year-to-year bonuses also creates a strong organizational bias toward growth to supply the new positions that such promotion-based reward systems require.

* * *

Free cash flow is cash flow in excess of that required to fund all projects that have positive net present values when discounted at the relevant cost of capital. Conflicts of interest between shareholders and managers over payout policies are especially severe when the organization generates substantial free cash flow. The problem is how to motivate managers to disgorge the cash rather than investing it at below the cost of capital or wasting it on organization inefficiencies.

The agency costs of debt have been widely discussed, but the benefits of debt in motivating managers and their organizations to be efficient have been ignored. I call these effects the "control hypothesis" for debt creation.

* * *

Debt creation, without retention of the proceeds of the issue, enables managers to effectively bond their promise to pay out future cash flows. Thus, debt can be an effective substitute for dividends, something not generally recognized in the corporate finance literature. By issuing debt in exchange for stock, managers are bonding their promise to pay out future cash flows in a way that cannot be accomplished by simple dividend increases. In doing so, they give shareholder recipients of the debt the right to take the firm into bankruptcy court if they do not maintain their promise to make the interest and principal payments. Thus debt reduces the agency costs of free cash flow by reducing the cash flow available for spending at the discretion of managers. These control effects of debt are a potential determinant of capital structure.

Issuing large amounts of debt to buy back stock also sets up the required organizational incentives to motivate managers and to help them overcome normal organizational resistance to retrenchment which the payout of free cash flow often requires. The threat caused by failure to make debt service payments serves as an effective motivating force to make such organizations more efficient. Stock repurchase for debt or cash also has tax advantages. * * *

Increased leverage also has costs. As leverage increases, the usual agency costs of debt rise, including bankruptcy costs. The optimal debt-equity ratio is the point at which firm value is maximized, the point where the marginal costs of debt just offset the marginal benefits.

The control hypothesis does not imply that debt issues will always have positive control effects. For example, these effects will not be as important for rapidly growing organizations with large and highly profitable investment projects but no free cash flow.

* * *

The control function of debt is more important in organizations that generate large cash flows but have low growth prospects, and even more important in organizations that must shrink. In these organizations the pressures to waste cash flows by investing them in uneconomic projects is most serious.

2. THE RISE, DECLINE, AND REAPPEARANCE OF LEVERAGED RESTRUCTURING

A distinction needs to made between the agency costs of leverage described in Section A, supra, and the agency benefits described immediately above. The agency costs are inevitable concomitants of high leverage. The agency benefits just described may not be similarly intrinsic to high leverage capital structures. They instead may be limited to a time and place—the restructuring of American firms during the 1980s by means of leveraged hostile takeovers and leveraged buyouts.

A **leveraged buyout** (LBO) is an acquisition of a company (the "target") financed by borrowed funds. The target's assets are used to secure the loans. The party or parties "bought out" are the target's common stockholders. The target can be a wholly owned subsidiary of a larger firm, a close corporation, or a publicly held corporation. In the latter case, the LBO is sometimes called a "going private" transaction. The purchaser is usually a partnership led by a professional management buyout firm and funded by a group of institutional investors. Often, the target's managers have substantial participations in the acquiring partnership and stay on as managers after the closing. These transactions are referred to as **management buyouts** (MBOs) and make up a large subset of LBOs.

Prior to 1984, most LBO targets were small and medium sized companies, often unwanted divisions and subsidiaries of conglomerate firms. The idea was that the managers of these divisions would do a better job post buyout, finding ways to cut costs and compete more effectively. They would be freed of the conglomerate's hierarchical governance constraints, driven by the need to generate the cash necessary to service the buyout debt, and encouraged by the upside incentive of substantial stock ownership. Under the usual LBO timetable, cash flows from operations were expected to repay a large piece of the LBO debt in about 5 years. After retiring the debt, a company could be taken public again in a transaction called a **reverse LBO**. The resultant influx of cash from the sale of stock to the public would afford the principals a spectacular profit, and, indeed, many of these early LBOs were highly successful.

In the mid–1980s LBO activity expanded, encompassing buyouts of large, diversified firms, including many publicly held corporations. Where banks were the principal providers of funds in the smaller, first-generation LBOS, in the larger deals of the late 1980s they were replaced by investment bankers who financed with large junk bond offerings (and also took equity positions themselves). The massive debt loads that resulted could not be serviced solely from the cash flow of continuing operations. So, in addition to staff reductions and other cost cutting, going-concern assets were sold to pay down the debt. The distinction between LBO and hostile takeover activity also became blurred. Hostile takeovers were financed by the same investment bankers and junk bonds as LBOs and resulted in the same post-closing economies and divestitures. At the same time, a number of LBOs proceeded without the participation of incumbent management, taking on a hostile aspect. Contrariwise, many LBOs were initiated as defensive moves by managers seeking bullet-proof protection from the threat of a hostile takeover. The term **leveraged restructuring** applied across-the-board.

The aggregate of all obligations, public and private (other than those of financial intermediaries) can be expressed as a percentage of gross national product to yield an aggregate national debt equity ratio. This figure stayed around 140 percent from 1945 to 1983, a ratio that had been stable as far back into the nineteenth century as data are available except during the Depression era. The figure began increasing in 1983, rising to 190 in 1989 before falling back during the retrenchment of the early 1990s. The increase occurred because businesses increased their leverage in relation to net worth, breaking longstanding financing patterns in so doing. Much of the increase stemmed from the joint appearance of the leveraged restructuring and the junk bond.

We now consider the policy implications of the leveraged restructurings of the 1980s. Specifically, were the restructurings beneficial or detrimental to the wider economy? If they were detrimental, was there any effective way to regulate them, or would the costs of any such regulation outweigh the benefits? The prevailing opinion today is that the benefits outweighed the detriments. That view is well-summarized in the discussion that follows.

Holmstrom and Kaplan, Corporate Governance and Merger Activity in the United States: Making Sense of the 1980s and 1990s

15 J. Econ. Perspectives 121, 127–132, 136–137 (2001).

Do LBOs and Leveraged Takeovers Provide Productivity Gains?

When large-scale hostile takeovers appeared in the 1980s, many voiced the opinion that they were driven by investor greed; the robber barons of Wall Street had returned to raid innocent corporations. Today, it is widely accepted that the takeovers of the 1980s had a beneficial effect on the corporate sector and that efficiency gains, rather than redistributions from stakeholders to shareholders, explain why they appeared.

The overall effect of takeovers on the economy is hard to pin down, because so many factors are involved. For example, the mild resurgence in productivity levels in the 1980s and greater boost in the second half of the 1990s is consistent with corporate governance boosting productivity—but it is consistent with other explanations as well.

One can try to assess whether the combination of takeovers, debt, and hostility is likely to have improved efficiency by looking at the evidence on leveraged buyouts. With the use of high leverage and strong incentive mechanisms (described below), LBOs can be viewed as an extreme manifestation of the changes reshaping the corporate sector in the 1980s. If LBOs increased value, it seems likely that the shift in corporate governance increased value in other areas of the economy, too.

Leveraged buyouts were associated with three large changes in corporate governance. First, LBOs changed the incentives of managers by providing them with substantial equity stakes in the buyout company. Because of high leverage, it was cheaper to give managers a high ownership stake. The purpose was to give managers the incentive to undertake the buyout, to work hard to pay off the debt, and to increase shareholder value. If successful, buyout company managers could make a great deal of money. Kaplan * * * reports that the chief executive officers of the leveraged buyouts increased their ownership stake by more than a factor of four, from 1.4 percent before the leveraged buyout to 6.4 percent after. Management teams, overall, experienced a similar increase. In the early 1980s, this approach to management compensation was fundamentally different from the prevailing practice.

Second, the high amount of debt incurred in the leveraged buyout transaction imposed strong financial discipline on company management. It was no longer possible for managers to treat capital as costless. On the contrary, failure to generate a sufficient return on capital meant default on the borrowed funds. This situation contrasts sharply with the perceived cost of capital in firms with a low degree of leverage. Because dividends are discretionary, and often determined by management, the price of equity is much less tangible than the price of debt.

Third, leveraged buyout sponsors or investors closely monitored and governed the companies they purchased. The boards of the LBO companies were small and dominated by investors with substantial equity stakes.

The empirical evidence supports the view that leveraged buyouts improved efficiency. In the first half of the 1980s, buyout companies experienced improved operating profits (both absolutely and relative to their industry) and few defaults * * *. However, the leveraged buyout experience was different in the latter half of the 1980s. Roughly one-third of the leveraged buyouts completed after 1985 subsequently defaulted on their debt, some spectacularly * * *. These defaults led many to question the existence of efficiency gains.

But even for the late 1980s, the evidence is supportive of the efficiency story. The reason for the defaults was not that profits didn't improve, but that they didn't improve by enough to pay off the enormous quantities of debt that had been taken on. For example, Kaplan and Stein[, The Evolution of Buyout Pricing and Financial Structure in the 1980s, 108 Q.J.Econ. 313] (1993) find that, overall, the larger leveraged buyouts of the later 1980s also generated improvements in operating profits despite the relatively large number of defaults. Even for deals that defaulted, Andrade and Kaplan[, How Costly Is Financial (Not Economic) Distress? Evidence From Highly Leveraged Transactions That Became Distressed, 53 J.Fin. 1443](1998) find that the leveraged buyout companies retained the same value they had attained before the leveraged buyout. In other words, the net effect of the leveraged buyout and default on capital value was slightly positive.

The case of Federated Department Stores illustrates this effect. The leveraged buyout firm Campeau acquired Federated in 1988, in is sometimes considered in the popular press to be the nadir of leveraged in the 1980s * * *. On January 1, 1988, Federated's debt and equity traded at $4.25 billion. From that point until it emerged from bankruptcy in February 1992, Federated returned roughly $5.85 billion in value, adjusted for changes in the Standard and Poor's 500. In other words, Federated was worth $1.6 billion more after being purchased by Campeau than it would have been if it had matched the S & P 500. But unfortunately for Campeau, it paid $7.67 billion for Federated, and so went bust.

If leveraged buyouts increased value, why did so many companies default? The likely answer is that the success of the LBOs of the early 1980s attracted entrants and capital. Those entrants understood the basic LBO insights. The entrants bid up the prices of the leveraged buyouts. As a result, much of the benefit of the improved discipline, incentives, and governance accrued to the selling shareholders rather than to the post-buyout LBO investors. The combined gains remained positive, but the distribution changed.

Why Did Financial Markets Become More Active in the 1980s?

The evidence in the previous section points to efficiency gains as the driving force behind the 1980s merger and takeover wave. What was the underlying source of these efficiencies and why did corporate governance capitalize on them in the 1980s and not earlier? Jensen * * * takes the view that the 1980s takeovers were ultimately caused by a failure in the internal governance mechanisms of U.S. corporations. The problems were a long time in coming. Ever since the 1930s, management incentives had become weaker as corporations had become larger, management ownership had shrunk and shareholders had become more widely dispersed. No one watched management the way J.P. Morgan and other large investors did in the early part of the twentieth century. Boards, which were supposed to be the guardians of shareholder rights, mostly sided with management and were ineffective in carrying out their duties. One of the big drawbacks of the corporation, according to Jensen, was that it could and did subsidize poorly performing divisions using the cash generated from successful ones, instead of returning the "free cash flow" to the investors.

According to Jensen[, The Modern Industrial Revolution, 48 J. Fin. 831] (1993), corporate mismanagement in the 1970s finally caused capital markets to react. The large windfall gains from the oil crisis that were spent on excessive oil exploration and diversification were a concrete trigger. But changes in technology and regulation more broadly had led to a large amount of excess capacity in many U.S. industries. Managers were unwilling to pare down their operations or simply to exit as long as they had the financial resources to continue. In the early and mid–1980s, the capital markets finally found the instruments to reduce excess capacity. Leveraged acquisitions, leveraged buyouts, hostile takeovers, and stock buybacks were successful in eliminating free cash flow, because the debt service requirements that usually accompanied them prodded managers to find ways to generate cash to make interest payments.

Impressed by the performance of the LBOs in the early 1980s, Jensen[, The Eclipse of the Public Corporation, Harv. Bus. Rev., no. 5, p. 61] (1989) went so far as to forecast that in most cases these new organizational forms would soon eclipse the corporation. Among the main benefits of leverage buyout associations run by firms like Kravis, Kohlberg and Roberts was that they didn't permit cross-subsidization.

There is little doubt that the elimination of excess capacity played an important role in the takeovers of the 1980s, particularly in industries like oil. It is less clear, however, that excess capacity was the primary driver of the takeover wave in the way Jensen suggests. The excess capacity explanation makes some strong predictions about investment. Specifically, if firms involved in takeovers and buyouts were spending too much money on capital expenditures, then after the corporate control transaction, these companies should spend less. The evidence for this is mixed. Kaplan[, The Effects of Management Buyouts on Operations and Value, 24 J.Fin.Econ. 217](1989) and Kaplan and Stein[, The Evolution of Buyout Pricing and Financial Structure in the 1980s, 108 Q.J.Econ. 313] (1993) find that management buyout firms do make large cuts in capital expenditures. However, Servaes[, Do Takeover Targets Overinvest? 7 Rev. Fin. Stud. 253] (1994) finds no evidence that targets of all takeovers, of hostile takeovers, and of going-private transactions were overinvesting in capital expenditures before the takeover. Furthermore, there do not appear to be significant changes in the ratio of capital expenditures to sales for firms that went through takeovers in the 1980s * * *.

Also, it is not obvious that self-interest alone was the reason why managers didn't exit industries with excess capacity or didn't return free cash flow. Free cash flow is not an accounting number and how much cash should be returned to investors depends on the estimated returns from internal investments. It is plausible that some management and board decisions stemmed from uncertainty about returns and competitive position in a changed market environment. Moreover, returning cash to investors was not part of the prevailing management culture at the beginning of the 1980s. Managers were supposed to have a surplus of investment ideas, not a shortage. (Witness the difficulties that today's fund managers have with this same issue.)

A second explanation of why takeovers appeared in the 1980s, offered by Shleifer and Vishny[, The Takeover Wave of the 1980s, Science, Aug 17, 1990, p. 745], is that "the takeover wave of the 1980s was to a large extent a response to the disappointment with conglomerates" that had been assembled in the previous merger and acquisition wave in the 1960s. In their view, corporate America in the 1980s "returned to specialization." Companies sold unrelated businesses and expanded into related businesses. "To a significant extent the 1980s reflect the deconglomeration of American business. Hostile takeovers and leveraged buyouts ... facilitated this process." In other words, the 1960s conglomeration wave was a mistake, at least in hindsight, a fact that managers were slow or unwilling to recognize until capital markets began to exert pressure on them.

Again, this argument has strong implications. If mergers were about deconglomeration, then it should be true that corporate diversification decreased values and deconglomeration increased values in the 1980s, and that U.S. business became substantially less diversified in the 1980s after the wave of deconglomeration. The evidence on these implications is mixed.

In influential pieces, Lang and Stulz[, Tobin's Q, Corporate Diversification, and Firm Performance, 102 J. Pol. Econ. 1248] (1994) and Berger and Ofek[, Diversification's Effect on Firm Value, 37 J.Fin.Econ. 39] (1995) find that diversified firms in the United States traded at a discount to single-segment firms in the 1908s and early 1990s. These articles suggest that diversification destroys value. * * *

More recent evidence, however, suggests that at least half of the diversification discount (and potentially a good deal more of it) can be attributed to the fact that diversifying firms are different. Many of the targets were discounted before they were acquired and became part of the diversified firm (Graham, Lemmon and Wolf, [Does Corporate Diversification Destroy Value?, working paper] 2000). Similarly, acquirers apparently trade at a discount before making diversifying acquisitions (Campa and Kedia, [Explaining the Diversification Discount, working paper] 1999). But the most difficult finding to explain is that the combined gain to bidder and target shareholders at an acquisition announcement is always positive on average in every study we have seen, even in diversifying acquisitions.

While U.S. businesses did become less diversified during the 1980s, the extent of the decrease remains unclear. * * * Mitchell and Mulherin[, The Impact of Industry Shocks on Takeover and Restructuring Activity, 41 J.Fin. Econ. 193] (1996) find that takeover activity in the 1980s clustered in particular industries at particular points in time. In contrast, takeover activity in the 1960s and 1970s exhibited no such clustering. To them, the 1980s seem less about breaking up conglomerates than about restructuring certain industries.

Stein[, forthcoming in Handbook of the Economics of Finance] (2001) summarizes the large and conflicting body of evidence on diversification and its value implications. One of the main observations is that it was primarily the poorly performing conglomerates that were taken over and restructured (Berger and Ofek, [supra]). In that respect, conglomerates may not be any different from other firms that perform poorly * * *. Overall, these empirical results suggest that deconglomeration played a role in the 1980s takeovers, but was probably not the primary driver.

Donaldson[,Corporate Restructuring](1994) provides yet another perspective on the 1980s wave of takeovers and mergers. He argues that in the 1980s the balance of power shifted from corporate stakeholders to shareholders, because of a rise in the number of institutional shareholders. From 1980 to 1996, large institutional investors nearly doubled their share of ownership of U.S. corporations from under 30 percent to over 50 percent * * *. Meanwhile, individual ownership declined from 70 percent in 1970, to 60 percent in 1980, to 48 percent in 1994 * * *. The shift towards institutional ownership and the resulting shift in power are keys for understanding why the takeovers appeared in 1980s. Donaldson calls the 1980s the "decade of confrontation."

One of the important effects of greater institutional ownership was on takeovers. Fund managers were more interested in squeezing out higher returns and less loyal to incumbent management than individual investors. Institutional investors were often the key sellers of larger blocks of shares in takeovers. This made takeovers easier. Institutional investors also supported takeovers by being large investors in the buyout funds and in the market for high-yield bonds.

We believe the 1980s takeover wave was caused by a combination of the factors mentioned above. Without a large increase in pension assets, which concentrated financial power, it is less likely that there would have been a willingness and ability to support multi-billion dollar takeovers. The scale and scope of the 1980s takeover wave was a product of the increased size of the financial markets. On the other hand, there must also have been significant inefficiencies in the way corporations were run. Without inefficiencies, the purpose of takeovers would have been missing.

The source of the inefficiencies remains open to debate. Jensen * * * thought that the problem was a poorly designed governance system, but despite his strong endorsement, the leveraged buyout form has not continued to spread. In the 1990s, the largest public corporations have become even larger and many of them have been exceptionally successful. The privatization movement has stopped * * *.

Why Did Corporate Governance and Mergers in the 1990s Look So Different?

At the end of the 1980s, the takeover and merger wave ended. Takeover volume, going private volume, and the use of leverage declined substantially in 1990. At the time, anti-takeover legislation and jurisprudence, overt political pressure against leverage, the collapse of the high yield bond market, and a credit crunch were among the explanations proffered for the decline * * *. Since then, both the political pressure against leverage and the credit crunch have abated and the noninvestment-grade bond market has recovered. Yet, neither the use of extreme leverage nor hostility have come close to their 1980s levels, suggesting that anti-takeover legislation has had an effect.

* * *

Taken as a whole, the evidence strongly suggests that U.S. corporations have voluntarily pursued shareholder-friendly policies in the 1990s. This provides the most plausible explanation of why hostile takeovers and leveraged buyouts largely disappeared in the 1990s—they were no longer needed. A telling piece of anecdotal evidence on the change in the corporate mind-set comes from a statement on corporate governance by the Business Roundtable (1997). Up until 1995, the Business Roundtable consistently opposed hostile takeovers and raiders as well as substantial changes in corporate governance practices. In 1997, the Business Roundtable changed its position to read "the paramount duty of management and the board is to the shareholder and not to ... other stakeholders." * * *

We believe management's acceptance of the shareholders' perspective was greatly aided by lucrative stock option plans, which allowed executives to reap big financial benefits from increased share prices. As a result, the restructuring of corporate America continued in the 1990s on much more amicable terms than in the 1980s.

Another reason why the 1990s merger wave differed from the 1980s wave likely has to do with different stages of the restructuring process. In the 1980s, restructuring was just beginning. The focus was on forcing corporate assets out of the hands of managers who could not or did not want to use them efficiently. The results included takeovers and restructurings of companies with excess capacity as well as bust-up takeovers of inefficient conglomerates. Hostility and leverage were important accompaniments. The 1990s appear to have been more of a build-up wave with assets reconfigured to take advantage of growth opportunities in new technologies and markets. This logic also fits with the evidence of increased use of equity in place of debt to do deals in the 1990s.

The move towards shareholder and market preeminence is also apparent in the way corporations have reorganized themselves. There has been a broad trend towards decentralization. Large companies are trying hard to become more nimble and to find ways to offer employees higher-powered incentives. At the same time, external capital markets have taken on a larger share of the reallocation of capital. The large volume of mergers is evidence in point. * * *

NOTE: THE HIGH LEVERAGE RESTRUCTURINGS OF THE 1980S

1. *Questions.*

Do Holmstrom and Kaplan, in course of putting forward the cost-benefit case in favor of the leveraged restructurings of the 1980s, assert that leveraged restructuring continues to be the best available governance device for the reform of a suboptimally managed firm? If high leverage is not useful as a governance tool today, why not? Because the necessary incentive alignment for success can be achieved by other means, such as a combination of stock options and institutional stock ownership? Would not high leverage import and even stronger incentive for success? Or do the agency and bankruptcy costs of high leverage outweigh its positive incentive effects? If the costs of leverage are prohibitively high in the first decade of the 21st century, why were they not prohibitively high in the 1980s? Consider again Holmstrom and Kaplan's case for efficiency gains respecting the large number of restructured companies that defaulted in the late 1980s and early 1990s. They deem these restructurings efficient because the firms' assets increased in value even though the assets net of the increase remained substantially less than the buyout debt. What is the operative concept of efficiency?

In line with the foregoing questions, note also that the high leverage capital structure of the classic LBO is not intended to be permanent. An LBO's final phase comes when the restructured firm's owners cash in on their work by selling their equity stake to the public. According to Kaplan, The Staying Power of Leveraged

Buyouts, 29 J.Fin. Econ. 287 (1991), the median time an LBO remains private is 6.82 years.

2. *Regulatory Responses.*

The 1980s restructuring movement prompted a number of significant changes to corporate law, state antitakeover and constituency statutes most prominent among them. The topic of high leverage, narrowly defined, was repeatedly investigated and discussed by lawmakers. But, in the end, very little lawmaking occurred. The principal legislative responses were as follows:

(a) *Legal Investment Laws and Other Regulation of Lending Institutions.* Portfolios of junk bonds held by federally insured savings and loan institutions played a role in the savings and loan crisis of the late 1980s and early 1990s. Congress responded with Section 222 of the Financial Institutions Reform, Recovery and Enforcement Act of 1989, 103 Stat. 183. This added section 28(d) to the Federal Deposit Insurance Act, 12 U.S.C. § 1831e(d), providing that thrift institutions may not "acquire or retain any corporate debt security not of investment grade," and providing further that the FDIC shall require divestment of such securities as were held at the time of the statute's enactment "as quickly as may prudently be done, and in any event not later than July 1, 1994."

Mandated divestment of thrift portfolios was accompanied by stricter scrutiny of bank portfolios. In 1989, the federal banking agencies—the Office of the Comptroller of the Currency, the Treasury, the FDIC and the Board of Governors of the Federal Reserve System—coordinated their definition of "highly leveraged transactions" in order to facilitate the work of bank examiners and comparative analysis of bank performance. The definition went through different versions until 1992, when the agencies discontinued its use, while continuing to monitor the banks' risk exposure.

The states also tightened credit standards. Connecticut, for example, revised its legal investment laws for insurance companies, defining "high yield obligations" as below investment grade and restricting such obligations as are registered under the 1933 Act to 10 percent of an insurance company's assets and limiting investment in the high yield obligations of a particular issuer to 1 percent of assets. Conn.Public Act No. 91–262 §§ 3(c), 4(c) (1991).

These constraints on institutional purchasers of junk bonds became effective in the immediate aftermath of the junk bond market crash of 1989–1990. Observers at the time attributed to them an important role in the cessation of leveraged restructuring. See, e.g., Miller, Leverage, 46 J. Finance 479, 487–488 (1991).

(b) *Tax Laws.* Federal income tax law responsive to merger and acquisition activity dates back to the conglomerate merger movement of the 1960s.

Congress in 1969 added section 279 to the Internal Revenue Code, which limits the deductibility of interest on "corporate acquisition indebtedness" where such interest exceeds $5 million a year. "Corporate acquisition indebtedness" includes obligations used to provide consideration for the acquisition of the stock or operating assets of another corporation if (1) the indebtedness is subordinated to the claims of general creditors or of other unsecured creditors, (2) the indebtedness is convertible into stock of the issuing corporation, and (3) the debt-equity ratio of the issuing corporation is in excess of 2:1, or interest on total indebtedness is not covered at least three times by projected earnings. In the view taken by Congress, for tax purposes at least, the standards last named drew the line between true debt and disguised equity. That line did not prevent significant increases in the issuance of acquisition-related junk bonds.

In 1987, Congress, concerned about the restructuring movement, considered but did not enact bills that would have added more bite to section 279. Finally, in 1989, Congress enacted legislation designed to deal with some perceived but narrowly defined tax abuses in leveraged transactions. The Revenue Reconciliation Act of 1989, among other things, limited the current deductibility of high yield original issue discount debt interest, I.R.C. §§ 163(e)(5) and 163(I), and limited the deductibility of interest paid to certain tax exempt payees, I.R.C. § 163(j).

National tax policy is often designed to induce alterations in business practices. The willingness of Congress in 1969 and again in 1989 to limit the deductibility of debt interest in certain restricted circumstances suggests that the corporate interest deduction may not be wholly invulnerable to legislative modification or even to outright repeal. Would repeal make sense as a matter either of economic or of tax policy? Since interest and dividends both represent divisions of the net earnings on invested capital, it can be argued with some force that no distinction should be made between them, and that interest charges should be included as part of the company's taxable net income. The effect would, of course, be to increase the cost of capital for many corporate enterprises, and presumably to reduce private investment, but the tax system would at least then be neutral as between debt and equity financing.

What about a legislative move in the opposite direction, i.e., by allowing a deduction for all forms of distribution to security owners? It has been urged that the corporate tax itself—rather than the distinction between interest and dividends—is the true source of "unneutrality." See Lent, Bond Interest Deduction And The Federal Corporation Income Tax, 2 Nat'l Tax.J. 131, 141 (1949).

NOTE: THE PRIVATE EQUITY RESTRUCTURINGS OF THE 2000S

Leveraged restructurings almost disappeared between 1990 and 1994. Tight credit and recession were the primary causes. Regulatory constraints on institutional bond portfolios also played a role. Between 1995 and 2000, leveraged restructuring reappeared as a minor segment of the wider merger market. Then, beginning at the turn of the century, leveraged restructuring made a notable reappearance, this time under the rubric of "private equity."

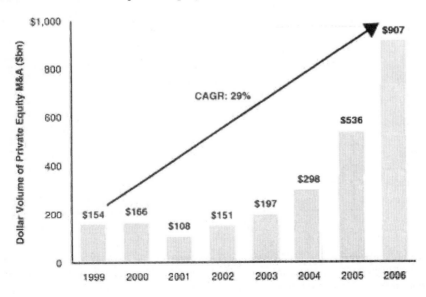

The three Figures in this Note come from the SEC Form S–1 filed by the Blackstone Group in connection with its 2007 initial public offering of equity securities. Blackstone shows in the first figure that the dollar amount of private equity acquisitions rose from $154 billion in 1999 to $907 billion in 2006, showing a 29 percent cumulative annual growth rate. In the second figure, Blackstone shows that the percentage of M & A activity emanating from the private equity sector increased in tandem. Private equity deals went from 4.9 percent of the overall merger market in 1999 to 25.5 percent in 2006, showing a 27 percent cumulative annual growth rate. Moreover, between 2005 and 2007 the average buyout tripled in size to weigh in at $1.3 billion. One obvious reason for the increase in the size and number of deals is that institutional investors found that the sector offered attractive returns and were anxious to invest more and more capital in private equity funds. As more and more capital has flowed into the sector, funds have gotten bigger and do more and bigger deals. Another facilitating factor has been the emergence of so-called "club deals." Prior to 2005, a private equity deal meant that a single fund provided the equity capital for the restructured firm. Even the biggest funds in the sector were limited to smaller targets as result. Now leading private equity firms join together in consortiums, taking larger firms private. (Critics allege that these buyout clubs make it much less likely that a competing bidder will appear.) As of mid 2007, record-breaking deals are still frequent events.

Thus has equity capital been readily available for private equity buyouts. But the debt side of the equation remains the sector's *sine qua non.* Readily available credit at low interest rates has filled this bill, and indeed, may be deemed the fuel propelling the private equity engine. In mid–2007 risk premium of junk bonds over U.S. Treasuries reached an historic low of 2.63 percent, compared to a 20–year average of 5.42 percent. At the same time, merger premiums generally have been lower than in the 1980s. Where the earlier rule of thumb was 30 to 50 percent premium, in recent years 20 percent deals have been common.

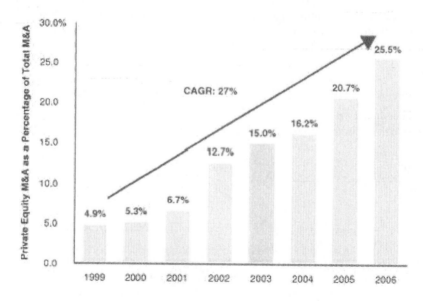

Importantly, levels of debt at buyout targets remain a notch lower than in the 1980s. Blackstone reports that, assuming a target with an enterprise value of $1 billion, a typical transaction would entail an equity investment of $300 million and

$700 million of debt. This 30–70 target compares with a 1980s rule of thumb of 20–80 or 10–90. On the other hand, there is evidence that the capital structures of restructured companies have gotten riskier. The average ratio of cash flow to interest cost was 3.4 in deals closing in 2004, 2.4 in 2006 deals, and 1.7 in 2007 deals. At the same time, lenders have eased the terms of the debt, with some deals having terms resembling the terms of late 1980s deals. As an example, consider "pay in kind toggle" bonds that give the borrower an option to defer paying interest until maturity, with the deferred sums paying a higher rate. Pay in kind, or "PIK," terms were emblematic of late 1980s leveraged capital structures that got into trouble after the economy turned in 1989. In addition, in the mid 2000s, more and more private equity loans are "covenant lite," omitting debt covenants and ratio tests. In the first quarter of 2007, global covenant-lite loan volume reached $48 billion, compared with $24 billion recorded for the whole of 2006. Such contracts are particularly likely to be seen respecting firms with cyclical businesses. Even some private placements now are covenant lite—16 percent in 2006, up from 4 percent a year earlier. The lenders are trading off protection for higher rates, rates that the borrowers still find attractive in the low rate environment.

The basic outlines of recent private equity buyouts otherwise track those of 1980s deals. The debt is raised through senior loans from commercial banks, public offerings of junk bonds, and private placements. The buyout groups look to improve operating performance over a five year period, pay down some of the debt, and then offer the equity to the public.

Here are Blackstone's upside projections for its hypothetical $1 billion buyout. If the company is sold in five years in a $1.3 billion public offering, the annual growth of the value of the firm is 6 percent over the initial $1 billion. But the value of the equity investment will have doubled, showing a 15 percent annual rate of return. If the company manages to use some of its operating cash flow to pay down $300 million of borrowing, the equity investment triples and the annual internal rate of return is 25 percent. Here is the downside: if the company gets into difficulty and has an enterprise value of $850 million at the end of the five year period and has not paid down any debt, that 15 percent decline implies a 50 percent loss on the private equity investment. See Blackstone Group L.P., Form S–1, SEC File 333–141504, filed March 22, 2007, at 115. Such are the properties of leverage.

The model has worked well for Blackstone. The third Figure shows Blackstone's calculation of the annual return, net of fees, for its private equity funds. The first set of bars tracks the funds from inception in 1987 until December 30, 2006 and shows a 22.8 percent return as compared with 11 percent for the S & P 500. The second set of bars makes the same comparison for 2002–2006. Here Blackstone returns 26.2 percent compared to the index's 6.1 percent. Id. at 123.

Does all of this imply a bright future for Blackstone and other firms in the industry? What kind of a signal does its IPO send? If the IPO is a negative signal, then perhaps we should read the history of leveraged restructuring to describe a cyclical sector that experiences periods of boom followed by sharp troughs. At the end of the 1980s the consensus view was that there had been too much leveraged buyout capital chasing a decreasing stock of good deals. While returns on transactions from early in the decade came in quite positive, the record for deals closed late in the decade was mixed. Early in the summer of 2007, many expressed the view that even as new deals broke records, the party would be over soon enough,

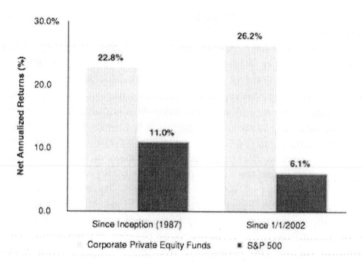

whether the terminating event was an economic downturn, a credit crunch, the collapse of a high-profile private equity deal, or some combination of the foregoing. By the end of the summer of 2007, all three events had occurred.

3.   EVENT RISK AND BOND CONTRACTS

The target of an LBO emerges in all cases with a markedly higher debt-equity ratio. That higher leverage increases the default risk respecting indebtedness incurred *prior* to the LBO. The LBO thus is precisely the sort of transaction against which traditional business covenants are directed. Indeed, where the LBO target has preexisting debt protected by covenants, the LBO group is forced to redeem the protected bonds to prevent the transaction from triggering an event of default. Where, however, the LBO target's existing long-term debt contracts do not contain effective covenants, the LBO group has no incentive to redeem the bonds. Left to ride, the bonds undergo a substantial diminution in value as a result of increased default risk. That lost value in effect is transferred to the stockholders whose interests are repurchased at a premium in the LBO.

Such wealth transfers were common events in the 1980s. Downgradings because of the risk of leveraged restructuring—called "event risk" by the bond-rating agencies—were everyday events. By mid–1987, the median grade for an industrial bond was a speculative BB; in 1982 the median grade had been A. Institutional bondholders complained loudly, but the financial community as whole took the disruption in stride. The numbers explained why. Bondholder losses in the individual case were spectacular— one-day drops of 20 percent were not uncommon. But stockholder gains in LBO and takeover premiums were more spectacular still—Unocal's bondholders lost $170 million while its stockholders received $2.8 billion. On average, bondholder losses were far outstripped by stockholder gains. While the wealth transfer effect was a real benefit to equityholders in restructurings, it was not enough of a boon to have driven the restructuring movement as a whole.

Bratton, Corporate Debt Relationships: Legal Theory in a Time of Restructuring, 1989 Duke L.J. 139–42, explains why the bonds were unprotected:

Bondholders would not have suffered wealth transfers if the contracts governing their bonds had contained restrictions against additional debt. With covenants prohibiting the transactions, those in control would have had to "take out" the bondholders by prepaying the old debt in order to take on new debt. Unfortunately for bondholders, by 1985 trust indentures governing the long-term unsecured debt of large corporations usually did not contain these restrictions.

This practice reflected a change from earlier contracting patterns, a change unnoticed in legal and economic commentary on debt contracts until the wealth transfers highlighted it. For most of this century, contracts governing long-term debt restricted subsequent substantial indebtedness, along with subsequent dividends and liens. Until recently, investors considered these provisions central to the bargain. They served as a substitute for security, protecting debtholders' interest in issuer earning streams from issuer misbehavior. In financial economic terms, the provisions insulated holders from agency costs. The degree of constraint depended on each issuer's credit standing. Better credits with access to public bond markets faced fewer restraints than smaller issuers making private placements. The best credits issued debt with no restraints other than a debt covenant.

This pattern continued until the mid–1970s. Since then, new public, unsecured debt of large industrials has tended to contain only a "negative pledge" against additional secured debt and a covenant prohibiting the sale and leaseback of issuer assets. Debt and dividend covenants have disappeared, surviving to restrain only smaller issuers.

When large restructurings commenced, the affected bondholders lacked defenses, but did not seem to know their exposure. Apparently everyone, except for the handful of lawyers and underwriters directly involved and perhaps a few traders and portfolio managers, thought that debt contracts still took the traditional form, or at least supplied some minimal protection.

The covenants had disappeared because they seemed unnecessary. Before 1985, economic prosperity combined with management's dominant governance position to make large corporations look reliable as unsecured borrowers. Whatever the turns of the business cycle, management seemed unlikely to seek to benefit stockholders by abusing bondholders. Management wanted growth and security—goals best realized with conservative leverage and retained-earnings financing. Moreover, managers had passed up opportunities to injure bondholders even when debt contracts posed no obstacle. According to the conventional wisdom, such opportunistic conduct would lead creditors in future financings to impose unfavorable terms, the costs of which would outweigh the benefits of present wealth transfers.

The assumption that management held an unassailable position ultimately led to questions about the need for covenants. Covenants became a subject of bargaining. Management characterized covenants as an unnecessary and costly backstop for the bondholders' position. Since the costs were real and the bondholders confident, management won the point.

The restructuring movement has shattered the managerialist assumptions behind the covenantless debt contract. The financial markets have proved that the manager-emperors had no clothes. Power over investment and financing has shifted to the capital markets. Corporate reputation—the unprotected bondholders' backstop—has proved ineffective. Managers' and stockholders' incentives to maintain good reputations in the capital markets do not have the staying power of contract promises; they shift along with power and money. Exiting stockholders and managers care nothing about a corporate entity's future financing costs. Managers battling to stay on might indeed care, but have more immediate problems. As Jensen and Meckling noted in 1976, and bondholders discovered in 1985, sainthood does not have infinite benefits, and agency costs do not reduce to zero.

Succeeding instances of restructuring injury in the late 1980s caused institutional bondholders to insist on contractual protections against event risk. Termed "super poison puts" or "event risk provisions,"these appeared in 40 percent of new investment-grade bonds issued in 1990. Crabbe, Event Risk: An Analysis of Losses to Bondholders and "Super Poison Put" Bond Covenants, 46 J. Finance 689 (1991). The protection came from a right to put the bonds back to the issuer at par, or in a few instances from an upward interest rate adjustment tied to a change in credit rating. The right, whether a put or a rate adjustment, was "triggered" by defined events, generally mergers and acquisitions (including LBOs), significant changes in the composition of the board of directors, and downward rate adjustments to below investment grade. A "dual trigger" provision appeared most frequently. Under this, the bondholder protective provision was triggered by the combination of a defined takeover related event and a fall in the bonds' rating. Kahan and Klausner, Anti–Takeover Provisions in Bonds: Bondholder Protection or Management Retrenchment? 40 UCLA L.Rev. 931 (1993).

As we have seen, the restructuring wave subsided abruptly at the end of 1989, due to a combination of default, recession, tight credit, and a smaller pool of appropriate targets. Bond contract protection against event risk subsided as well. Kahan and Klausner reported in 1993 that dual trigger antitakeover provisions (along with other forms of antitakeover covenant protection) appeared with substantially diminished frequency beginning in 1991. Bond buyers made a clear cut risk return decision when choosing between issues with and without protection. Around early 1990, inclusion lowered the average bond yield by 24 basis points. The price effect grew in magnitude as the bond rating declined—for a Baa bond the spread was 65.7 basis points. But, because high leverage restructuring almost disappeared in the early 1990s, those who bought the higher yielding, riskier bonds appeared to have made a good deal. Conditions changed later in the decade, however.

Chava, et al., Agency Costs and the Pricing of Bond Covenants (working paper 2004), available at http://ssrn.com/abstract=611801, looks at a database of bond contracts to report the following respecting the incidence of poison puts:

Period	Percentage of Contracts with Poison Puts
1980–89	19.7
1990–94	26.1
1995–99	46.4
2000–03	96.2

The increase in usage just happens to track the rise in prominence of private equity restructuring. Even as today's private equity financing implicates lower leverage than did deals in the 1980s, it still entails rating downgrades for unprotected debt, and downgrades still trigger bond sell-offs. Indeed, increased bond market participation by foreign institutions subject to portfolio constraints has aggravated the magnitude of such shocks. See Bratton, Bond Covenants and Creditor Protection: Economics and Law, Theory and Practice, Substance and Process, 7 Eur. Bus. Org. L. Rev. 29 (2006).

Note that the above figures imply the existence of large numbers of unprotected bonds, albeit in diminishing numbers. In addition, too much should not be made of the raw numbers. It has been reported in a number of cases that narrow drafting has rendered the puts useless. For instance, a put covering a sale to a "person" or "firm" has been deemed not to cover a sale to a private equity club, which is a collection of "persons" or "firms." (One awaits a litigation on the resulting issue of bond contract interpretation.) Note also that in the "covenant lite" deals, reported supra, the debt investors in private equity restructurings are making the same trade off of protection for yield that caused poison puts to disappear in the early 1990s.

Metropolitan Life Insurance Company v. RJR Nabisco, Inc.

United States District Court, Southern District of New York, 1989.
716 F.Supp. 1504.

■ WALKER, DISTRICT JUDGE:

I. INTRODUCTION

The corporate parties to this action are among the country's most sophisticated financial institutions, as familiar with the Wall Street investment community and the securities market as American consumers are with the Oreo cookies and Winston cigarettes made by defendant RJR Nabisco, Inc. (sometimes "the company" or "RJR Nabisco"). The present action traces its origins to October 20, 1988, when F. Ross Johnson, then the Chief Executive Officer of RJR Nabisco, proposed a $17 billion leveraged buy-out ("LBO") of the company's shareholders, at $75 per share. Within a few days, a bidding war developed among the investment group led by Johnson and the investment firm of Kohlberg Kravis Roberts & Co. ("KKR"), and others. On December 1, 1988, a special committee of RJR Nabisco directors, established by the company specifically to consider the competing proposals, recommended that the company accept the KKR proposal, a $24 billion LBO that called for the purchase of the company's outstanding stock at roughly $109 per share.[1]

* * * The Court agreed to hear the present action—filed even before the company accepted the KKR proposal—on an expedited basis, with an eye toward March 1, 1989, when RJR Nabisco was expected to merge with the KKR holding entities created to facilitate the LBO. On that date, RJR Nabisco was also scheduled to assume roughly $19 billion of new debt. After a delay unrelated to the present action, the merger was ultimately completed during the week of April 24, 1989.

Plaintiffs now allege, in short, that RJR Nabisco's actions have drastically impaired the value of bonds previously issued to plaintiffs by, in effect, misappropriating the value of those bonds to help finance the LBO and to distribute an enormous windfall to the company's shareholders. As a result, plaintiffs argue, they have unfairly suffered a multimillion dollar loss in the value of their bonds.[4]

* * *

For the reasons set forth below, this Court agrees with defendants. There being no express covenant between the parties that would restrict the incurrence of new debt, and no perceived direction to that end from covenants that are express, this Court will not imply a covenant to prevent the recent LBO and thereby create an indenture term that, while bargained for in other contexts, was not bargained for here and was not even within the mutual contemplation of the parties.

II. BACKGROUND

* * *

A. *The Parties:*

Metropolitan Life Insurance Co. ("MetLife"), incorporated in New York, is a life insurance company that provides pension benefits for 42 million individuals. According to its most recent annual report, MetLife's assets exceed $88 billion and its debt securities holdings exceed $49 billion. * * * MetLife is a mutual company and therefore has no stockholders and is instead operated for the benefit of its policyholders. * * * MetLife alleges that it owns $340,542,000 in principal amount of six separate RJR Nabisco debt issues, bonds allegedly purchased between July 1975 and July 1988. Some bonds become due as early as this year, others will not become due until 2017. The bonds bear interest rates of anywhere from 8 to 10.25

1. [Ed. Note. The Court's footnote 8:] On February 9, 1989, KKR completed its tender offer for roughly 74 percent of RJR Nabisco's common stock (of which approximately 97% of the outstanding shares were tendered) and all of its Series B Cumulative Preferred Stock (of which approximately 95% of the outstanding shares were tendered). Approximately $18 billion in cash was paid out to those stockholders. KKR acquired the remaining stock in the late April merger through the issuance of roughly $4.1 billion of pay-in-kind exchangeable preferred stock and roughly $1.8 billion in face amount of convertible debentures. See Bradley Reply Aff. ¶ 2.

4. * * * No one disputes that, subsequent to the announcement of the LBO, the RJR Nabisco bonds lost their "A" ratings.

percent. MetLife also owned 186,000 shares of RJR Nabisco common stock at the time this suit was filed. * * *

Jefferson–Pilot Life Insurance Co. ("Jefferson–Pilot") is a North Carolina company that has more than $3 billion in total assets, $1.5 billion of which are invested in debt securities. * * * Jefferson–Pilot alleges that it owns $9.34 million in principal amount of three separate RJR Nabisco debt issues, allegedly purchased between June 1978 and June 1988. Those bonds, bearing interest rates of anywhere from 8.45 to 10.75 percent, become due in 1993 and 1998. * * *

RJR Nabisco, a Delaware corporation, is a consumer products holding company that owns some of the country's best known product lines, including LifeSavers candy, Oreo cookies, and Winston cigarettes. The company was formed in 1985, when R.J. Reynolds Industries, Inc. ("R.J. Reynolds") merged with Nabisco Brands, Inc. ("Nabisco Brands"). In 1979, and thus before the R.J. Reynolds–Nabisco Brands merger, R.J. Reynolds acquired the Del Monte Corporation ("Del Monte"), which distributes canned fruits and vegetables. From January 1987 until February 1989, co-defendant Johnson served as the company's CEO. KKR, a private investment firm, organizes funds through which investors provide pools of equity to finance LBOs. * * *

B. The Indentures:

The bonds implicated by this suit are governed by long, detailed indentures, which in turn are governed by New York contract law.[10] * * * [U]nderwriters ordinarily negotiate the terms of the indentures with the issuers. Since the underwriters must then sell or place the bonds, they necessarily negotiate in part with the interests of the buyers in mind. Moreover, these indentures were not secret agreements foisted upon unwitting participants in the bond market. No successive holder is required to accept or to continue to hold the bonds, * * * indeed, plaintiffs readily admit that they could have sold their bonds right up until the announcement of the LBO. * * * Instead, sophisticated investors like plaintiffs are well aware of the indenture terms and, presumably, review them carefully before lending hundreds of millions of dollars to any company.

Indeed, the prospectuses for the indentures contain a statement relevant to this action:

> The Indenture contains no restrictions on the creation of unsecured short-term debt by [RJR Nabisco] or its subsidiaries, no restriction on the creation of unsecured Funded Debt by [RJR Nabisco] or its subsidiaries which are not Restricted Subsidiaries, and no restriction on the payment of dividends by [RJR Nabisco].

* * * Further, as plaintiffs themselves note, the contracts at issue "[do] not impose debt limits, since debt is assumed to be used for productive purposes." * * *

---

10. Both sides agree that New York law controls this Court's interpretation of the indentures, which contain explicit designations to that effect. * * *

[The court noted that two of the issues of RJR Nabisco debt held by MetLife had originally been governed by debt covenants that would have been violated by the debt to be issued in connection with the LBO, but that MetLife had agreed to amend the contracts to remove the covenants. One issue was a private placement entered into between Del Monte and MetLife in 1975, the other was a private placement entered into between Reynolds and MetLife in 1976. The Del Monte notes had been assumed by Reynolds in 1979. In 1983, MetLife agreed to amend the note agreement to delete its business covenants in exchange for a guaranty of the debt by the parent corporation. MetLife gave up the protection of the business covenants in the 1976 Reynolds notes at Reynolds' request in 1985. Reynolds needed to incur additional debt in connection with the consummation of its merger with Nabisco, and offered to exchange debentures issued under a public indenture for the private placement notes. MetLife agreed to the exchange despite the fact that the new notes had the same interest rate but no business covenant protection because (1) it was participating in a new financing in connection with the merger, and (2) the "debenturized" notes offered in exchange could be sold to the public.

[The court also noted that the problem of the LBOs' effects on bond value had been discussed in internal MetLife memoranda circulated in 1982 and 1985. The 1982 memorandum discussed an LBO in which MetLife had participated and also had held existing bonds which had been downgraded. Said the memorandum:

> "Questions have * * * been raised about our ability to force payouts in similar future situations, particularly when we would not be participating in the buyout financing. * * * A method of closing this apparent 'loophole' * * * would be through a covenant dealing with a change in ownership. Such a covenant is standard in financings with privately-held companies. * * * It provides the lender with * * * some type of special redemption."

The 1985 memorandum discussed the general absence of business covenants in public indentures, noted that the lack of covenants had caused MetLife holdings to lose value in 10 or 15 takeover or LBO situations, predicted that the problem would continue, and suggested that "appropriate language" be included in new indentures.

[The court stressed that the documents "highlight the risks" inherent in the market and that sophisticated investors such as MetLife (and Jefferson–Pilot) "would be hard-pressed to plead ignorance of these market risks."]

These documents must be read in conjunction with plaintiffs' Amended Complaint. That document asserts that the LBO "undermines the foundation of the investment grade debt market * * *," that, although "the indentures do not purport to limit dividends or debt * * * [s]uch covenants were believed unnecessary with blue chip companies * * *", * * * that "the transaction contradicts the premise of the investment grade market * * *", * * * and, finally, that "[t]his buy-out was not contemplated at the time the debt was issued, contradicts the premise of the investment grade ratings that RJR Nabisco actively solicited and received, and is inconsistent with the understandings of the market * * * which [p]laintiffs relied upon." * * *

Solely for the purposes of these motions, the Court accepts various factual assertions advanced by plaintiffs: first, that RJR Nabisco actively solicited "investment grade" ratings for its debt; second, that it relied on descriptions of its strong capital structure and earnings record which included prominent display of its ability to pay the interest obligations on its long-term debt several times over, * * * and third, that the company made express or implied representations not contained in the relevant indentures concerning its future creditworthiness. * * * In support of those allegations, plaintiffs have marshaled a number of speeches made by co-defendant Johnson and other executives of RJR Nabisco.[18] In addition, plaintiffs rely on an affidavit sworn to by John Dowdle, the former Treasurer and then Senior Vice President of RJR Nabisco from 1970 until 1987. In his opinion, the LBO "clearly undermines the fundamental premise of the [c]ompany's bargain with the bondholders, and the commitment that I believe the [c]ompany made to the bondholders * * * I firmly believe that the company made commitments * * * that require it to redeem [these bonds and notes] before paying out the value to the shareholders." * * *

III.   DISCUSSION

At the outset, the Court notes that nothing in its evaluation is substantively altered by the speeches given or remarks made by RJR Nabisco executives, or the opinions of various individuals—what, for instance, former RJR Nabisco Treasurer Dowdle personally did or did not "firmly believe" the indentures meant. * * * The parol evidence rule bars plaintiffs from arguing that the speeches made by company executives prove defendants agreed or acquiesced to a term that does not appear in the indentures. See West, Weir & Bartel, Inc. v. Mary Carter Paint Co., 25 N.Y.2d 535, 540, 307 N.Y.S.2d 449, 452, 255 N.E.2d 709, 712 (1969) * * *.

The indentures at issue clearly address the eventuality of a merger. They impose certain related restrictions not at issue in this suit, but no restriction that would prevent the recent RJR Nabisco merger transaction. * * * The indentures also explicitly set forth provisions for the adoption of new covenants, if such a course is deemed appropriate. * * * While it may be true that no explicit provision either permits or prohibits an LBO, such contractual silence itself cannot create ambiguity to avoid the dictates of the parol evidence rule, particularly where the indentures impose no debt limitations.

_ **18.** See, e.g., Address by F. Ross Johnson, November 12, 1987, * * * ("Our strong balance sheet is a cornerstone of our strategies. It gives us the resources to modernize facilities, develop new technologies, bring on new products, and support our leading brands around the world."); Remarks of Edward J. Robinson, Executive Vice President and Chief Financial Officer, February 15, 1988, * * * at 1 ("RJR Nabisco's financial strategy is * * * to enhance the strength of the balance sheet by reducing the level of debt as well as lowering the cost of existing debt."); Remarks by Dr. Robert J. Carbonell, Vice Chairman of RJR Nabisco, June 3, 1987, * * * ("We will not sacrifice our longer-term health for the sake of short term heroics.").

Under certain circumstances, however, courts will, as plaintiffs note, consider extrinsic evidence to evaluate the scope of an implied covenant of good faith. * * * However, [in *Sharon Steel*] the Second Circuit has established a different rule for customary, or boilerplate, provisions of detailed indentures used and relied upon throughout the securities market, such as those at issue.[20] * * *

A.   *Plaintiffs' Case Against the RJR Nabisco LBO:*

   1.   Count One: The implied covenant:

      * * *

A plaintiff always can allege a violation of an express covenant. If there has been such a violation, of course, the court need not reach the question of whether or not an *implied* covenant has been violated. That inquiry surfaces where, while the express terms may not have been technically breached, one party has nonetheless effectively deprived the other of those express, explicitly bargained-for benefits. In such a case, a court will read an implied covenant of good faith and fair dealing into a contract to ensure that neither party deprives the other of "the fruits of the agreement." See, e.g., Greenwich Village Assoc. v. Salle, 110 A.D.2d 111, 115, 493 N.Y.S.2d 461, 464 (1st Dep't 1985). See also Van Gemert v. Boeing Co., 553 F.2d 812, 815 ("*Van Gemert II*") (2d.Cir.1977). Such a covenant is implied only where the implied term "is consistent with other mutually agreed upon terms in the contract." Sabetay v. Sterling Drug, Inc., 69 N.Y.2d 329, 335, 514 N.Y.S.2d 209, 212, 506 N.E.2d 919, 922 (1987). * * * Viewed another way, the implied covenant of good faith is breached only when one party seeks to prevent the contract's performance or to withhold its benefits. See Collard v. Incorporated Village of Flower Hill, 75 A.D.2d 631, 632, 427 N.Y.S.2d 301, 302 (2d Dep't 1980). As a result, it thus ensures that parties to a contract perform the substantive, bargained-for terms of their agreement. See, e.g., Wakefield v. Northern Telecom, Inc., 769 F.2d 109, 112 (2d Cir.1985) (Winter, J.)

In contracts like bond indentures, "an implied covenant * * * derives its substance directly from the language of the Indenture, and 'cannot give the holders of Debentures any rights inconsistent with those set out in the Indenture.' *[Where] plaintiffs' contractual rights [have not been] violated, there can have been no breach of an implied covenant.*" Gardner & Florence Call Cowles Foundation v. Empire Inc., 589 F.Supp. 669, 673 (S.D.N.Y. 1984), vacated on procedural grounds, 754 F.2d 478 (2d Cir.1985) (quoting Broad v. Rockwell, 642 F.2d 929, 957 (5th Cir.) (en banc), cert. denied, 454 U.S. 965, 102 S.Ct. 506, 70 L.Ed.2d 380 (1981)) (emphasis added).

---

20.   To a certain extent, this discussion is academic. Even if the Court did consider the extrinsic evidence offered by plaintiffs, its ultimate decision would be no different. * * * More important, those representations are improperly raised under the rubric of an implied covenant of good faith when they cannot properly or reasonably be construed as evidencing a binding agreement or acquiescence by defendants to substantive restrictive covenants. * * *

The parole evidence rule of course does not bar descriptions of either the background of this suit or market realities consistent with the contracts at issue.

Thus, in cases like Van Gemert v. Boeing Co., 520 F.2d 1373 (2d Cir.), cert. denied, 423 U.S. 947 (1975) (*"Van Gemert I"*), and Pittsburgh Terminal Corp. v. Baltimore & Ohio Ry. Co., 680 F.2d 933 (3d Cir.), cert. denied, 459 U.S. 1056 (1982)—both relied upon by plaintiffs—the courts used the implied covenant of good faith and fair dealing to ensure that the bondholders received the benefit of their bargain as determined from the face of the contracts at issue. In *Van Gemert I*, the plaintiff bondholders alleged inadequate notice to them of defendant's intention to redeem the debentures in question and hence an inability to exercise their conversion rights before the applicable deadline. The contract itself provided that notice would be given in the first place. * * * Faced with those provisions, defendants in that case unsurprisingly admitted that the indentures specifically required the company to provide the bondholders with notice. See id. at 1379. While defendant there issued a press release that mentioned the possible redemption of outstanding convertible debentures, that limited release did not "mention even the tentative dates for redemption and expiration of the conversion rights of debenture holders." Id. at 1375. Moreover, defendant did not issue any general publicity or news release. Through an implied covenant, then, the court fleshed out the full extent of the more skeletal right that appeared in the contract itself, and thus protected plaintiff's bargained-for right of conversion.[21]

I also note, in passing, that *Van Gemert I* presented the Second Circuit with "less sophisticated investors." Id. at 1383. Similarly, the court in *Pittsburgh Terminal* applied an implied covenant to the indentures at issue because defendants there "took steps to prevent the Bondholders from receiving information which they needed *in order to receive the fruits of their conversion option should they choose to exercise it.*" *Pittsburgh Terminal,* 680 F.2d at 941 (emphasis added).

The appropriate analysis, then, is first to examine the indentures to determine "the fruits of the agreement" between the parties, and then to decide whether those "fruits" have been spoiled—which is to say, whether plaintiffs' contractual rights have been violated by defendants.

The American Bar Foundation's *Commentaries on Indentures* ("the *Commentaries*"), relied upon and respected by both plaintiffs and defendants, describes the rights and risks generally found in bond indentures like those at issue:

> The most obvious and important characteristic of long-term debt financing is that the holder ordinarily has not bargained for and does not expect any substantial gain in the value of the security to compensate for the risk of loss * * * [T]he significant fact, *which accounts in part for the detailed protective provisions of the typical long-term debt financing instrument,* is that *the lender (the purchaser of the debt security) can expect only interest at the prescribed rate plus the eventual return of the principal.* * * * Short of bankruptcy, *the debt security*

---

21. Since newspaper notice, for instance, was promised in the indenture, the court used an implied covenant to ensure that meaningful, reasonable newspaper notice was provided. See id. at 1383.

> *holder can do nothing to protect himself against actions of the borrower which jeopardize its ability to pay the debt unless he * * * establishes his rights through contractual provisions set forth in the debt agreement or indenture.*

Id. at 1–2 (1971) (emphasis added).

A review of the parties' submissions and the indentures themselves satisfies the Court that the substantive "fruits" guaranteed by those contracts and relevant to the present motions include the periodic and regular payment of interest and the eventual repayment of principal. * * * According to a typical indenture, a default shall occur if the company either (1) fails to pay principal when due; (2) fails to make a timely sinking fund payment; (3) fails to pay within 30 days of the due date thereof any interest on the date; or (4) fails duly to observe or perform any of the express covenants or agreements set forth in the agreement. * * *[23] Plaintiffs' Amended Complaint nowhere alleges that RJR Nabisco has breached these contractual obligations; interest payments continue and there is no reason to believe that the principal will not be paid when due.

[T]his Court holds that the "fruits" of these indentures do not include an implied restrictive covenant that would prevent the incurrence of new debt to facilitate the recent LBO. To hold otherwise would permit these plaintiffs to straightjacket the company in order to guarantee their investment. These plaintiffs do not invoke an implied covenant of good faith to protect a legitimate, mutually contemplated benefit of the indentures; rather, they seek to have this Court create an additional benefit for which they did not bargain.

Although the indentures generally permit mergers and the incurrence of new debt, there admittedly is not an explicit indenture provision to the contrary of what plaintiffs now claim the implied covenant requires. That absence, however, does *not* mean that the Court should imply into those very same indentures a covenant of good faith so broad that it imposes a new, substantive term of enormous scope. This is so particularly where, as here, that very term—a limitation on the incurrence of additional debt— has in other past contexts been expressly bargained for; particularly where the indentures grant the company broad discretion in the management of its affairs, as plaintiffs admit, * * * particularly where the indentures explicitly set forth specific provisions for the adoption of new covenants and restrictions, * * * and *especially* where there has been no breach of the

---

23. Plaintiffs originally indicated that, depending on the Court's disposition of the instant motions, they might seek to amend their complaint to allege that "they are not equally and ratably secured under the [express terms of the] 'negative pledge' clause of the indentures." * * * On May 26, 1989, shortly before this Opinion was filed, the Court granted defendants' request to assert a counterclaim for a declaratory judgment that those "negative pledge" covenants have not been violated by the post-LBO financial structure of RJR Nabisco. This counterclaim was advanced in response to notices of default by plaintiffs based on matters not raised in the Amended Complaint.

The Court of course will not now determine whether an alleged implied covenant flowing from a "negative pledge" provision has been breached. That inquiry necessarily must follow the Court's determination of whether or not the "negative pledge" provision has been expressly breached.

parties' bargained-for contractual rights on which the implied covenant necessarily is based. While the Court stands ready to employ an implied covenant of good faith to ensure that such bargained-for rights are performed and upheld, it will not, however, permit an implied covenant to shoehorn into an indenture additional terms plaintiffs now wish had been included. See also Broad v. Rockwell International Corp., 642 F.2d 929 (5th Cir.) (en banc) (applying New York law), cert. denied, 454 U.S. 965 (1981) (finding no liability pursuant to an implied covenant where the terms of the indenture, as bargained for, were enforced).[25]

Plaintiffs argue in the most general terms that the fundamental basis of all these indentures was that an LBO along the lines of the recent RJR Nabisco transaction would never be undertaken, that indeed *no* action would be taken, intentionally or not, that would significantly deplete the company's assets. Accepting plaintiffs' theory, their fundamental bargain with defendants dictated that nothing would be done to jeopardize the extremely high probability that the company would remain able to make interest payments and repay principal over the 20 to 30 year indenture term—and perhaps by logical extension even included the right to ask a court "to make sure that plaintiffs had made a good investment." *Gardner,* 589 F.Supp. at 674. But as Judge Knapp aptly concluded in *Gardner,* "Defendants * * * were under a duty to carry out the terms of the contract, but not to make sure that plaintiffs had made a good investment. The former they have done; the latter we have no jurisdiction over." Id. Plaintiffs' submissions and MetLife's previous undisputed internal memoranda remind the Court that a "fundamental basis" or a "fruit of an agreement" is often in the eye of the beholder, whose vision may well change along with the market, and who may, with hindsight, imagine a different bargain than the one he actually and initially accepted with open eyes.

The sort of unbounded and one-sided elasticity urged by plaintiffs would interfere with and destabilize the market. And this Court, like the parties to these contracts, cannot ignore or disavow the marketplace in which the contract is performed. Nor can it ignore the expectations of that market—expectations, for instance, that the terms of an indenture will be

---

25. The cases relied on by plaintiffs are not to the contrary. They invoke an implied covenant where it proves necessary to fulfill the explicit terms of an agreement, or to give meaning to ambiguous terms. See, e.g., Grad v. Roberts, 14 N.Y.2d 70, 248 N.Y.S.2d 633, 636, 198 N.E.2d 26, 28 (1964) (court relied on implied covenant to effect "performance of [an] option agreement according to its terms"); Zilg v. Prentice–Hall, Inc., 717 F.2d 671 (2d Cir.1983), cert. denied, 466 U.S. 938, 104 S.Ct. 1911, 80 L.Ed.2d 460 (1984). In *Zilg,* the Second Circuit first described a contract which, on its face, established the publisher's obligation to publish, advertise and publicize the book at issue. The court then determined that "the contract in question establishes a relationship between the publisher and author which implies an obligation upon the former to make certain [good faith] efforts in publishing a book it has accepted notwithstanding the clause which leaves the number of volumes to be printed and the advertising budget to the publisher's discretion." 717 F.2d at 679. In other words, the court there sought to ensure a meaningful fulfillment of the contract's express terms. See also *Van Gemert I,* supra; *Pittsburgh Terminal,* supra. In the latter two cases, the courts sought to protect the bondholders' express, bargained-for rights.

upheld, and that a court will not, *sua sponte,* add new substantive terms to that indenture as it sees fit. The Court has no reason to believe that the market, in evaluating bonds such as those at issue here, did not discount for the possibility that any company, even one the size of RJR Nabisco, might engage in an LBO heavily financed by debt. That the bonds did not lose any of their value until the October 20, 1988 announcement of a possible RJR Nabisco LBO only suggests that the market had theretofore evaluated the risks of such a transaction as slight.

* * * To support their argument that defendants have violated an implied covenant, plaintiffs contend that, since the October 20, 1988 announcement, the bond market has "stopped functioning." * * * They argue that if they had "sold and abandoned the market [before October 20, 1988], the market, if everyone had the same attitude, would have disappeared." * * * What plaintiffs term "stopped functioning" or "disappeared," however, are properly seen as natural responses and adjustments to market realities. Plaintiffs of course do not contend that no new issues are being sold, or that existing issues are no longer being traded or have become worthless.

To respond to changed market forces, new indenture provisions can be negotiated, such as provisions that were in fact once included in the 8.9 percent and 10.25 percent debentures implicated by this action. New provisions could include special debt restrictions or change-of-control covenants. There is no guarantee, of course, that companies like RJR Nabisco would accept such new covenants; parties retain the freedom to enter into contracts as they choose. But presumably, multi-billion dollar investors like plaintiffs have some say in the terms of the investments they make and continue to hold. And, presumably, companies like RJR Nabisco need the infusions of capital such investors are capable of providing.

Whatever else may be true about this case, it certainly does not present an example of the classic sort of form contract or contract of adhesion often frowned upon by courts. In those cases, what motivates a court is the strikingly inequitable nature of the parties' respective bargaining positions. See generally, Rakoff, Contracts of Adhesion: An Essay in Reconstruction, 96 Harv.L.Rev. 1173 (1982). Plaintiffs here entered this "liquid trading market," * * * with their eyes open and were free to leave at any time. Instead they remained there notwithstanding its well understood risks.

Ultimately, plaintiffs cannot escape the inherent illogic of their argument. On the one hand, it is undisputed that investors like plaintiffs recognized that companies like RJR Nabisco strenuously opposed additional restrictive covenants that might limit the incurrence of new debt or the company's ability to engage in a merger. Furthermore, plaintiffs argue that they had no choice other than to accept the indentures as written, without additional restrictive covenants, or to "abandon" the market. * * *

Yet on the other hand, plaintiffs ask this Court to imply a covenant that would have just that restrictive effect because, they contend, it reflects precisely the fundamental assumption of the market and the fundamental basis of their bargain with defendants. If that truly were the case here, it is difficult to imagine why an insistence on that term would have forced the plaintiffs to abandon the market. The Second Circuit has offered a better explanation: "[a] promise by the defendant should be implied only if the court may rightfully assume that the parties would have included it in their written agreement had their attention been called to it * * * *Any such assumption in this case would be completely unwarranted.*" Neuman v. Pike, 591 F.2d 191, 195 (2d Cir.1979) (emphasis added, citations omitted).

In the final analysis, plaintiffs offer no objective or reasonable standard for a court to use in its effort to define the sort of actions their "implied covenant" would permit a corporation to take, and those it would not.[28] Plaintiffs say only that investors like themselves rely upon the "skill" and "good faith" of a company's board and management, * * * and that their covenant would prevent the company from "destroy[ing] * * * the legitimate expectations of its long-term bondholders." * * * As is clear from the preceding discussion, however, plaintiffs have failed to convince the Court that by upholding the explicit, bargained-for terms of the indenture, RJR Nabisco has either exhibited bad faith or destroyed plaintiffs' *legitimate,* protected expectations.

* * * [This court] concludes that courts are properly reluctant to imply into an integrated agreement terms that have been and remain subject to specific, explicit provisions, where the parties are sophisticated investors, well versed in the market's assumptions, and do not stand in a fiduciary relationship with one another.

2. Count Five: In Equity:

Count Five substantially restates and realleges the contract claims advanced in Count I. * * * [These] equity claims cannot survive defendants' motion for summary judgment.

In their papers, plaintiffs variously attempt to justify Count V as being based on unjust enrichment, frustration of purpose [or] an alleged breach of something approaching a fiduciary duty * * *. Each claim fails. * * *

* * * [P]laintiffs advance a claim that remains based, their assertions to the contrary notwithstanding, on an alleged breach of a fiduciary duty.[33]

28. Under plaintiffs' theory, bondholders might ask a court to prohibit a company like RJR Nabisco not only from engaging in an LBO, but also from entering a new line of business—with the attendant costs of building new physical plants and hiring new workers—or from acquiring new businesses such as RJR Nabisco did when it acquired Del Monte.

33. * * * [C]ases relied upon by plaintiffs to support their "In Equity" Count focus on fraudulent schemes or conveyances. See, e.g., United States v. Tabor Court Realty Corp., 803 F.2d 1288, 1295 (3d Cir.1986) (explaining lower court's findings in United States v. Gleneagles Investment Co., 565 F.Supp. 556 (M.D.Pa.1983)); Pepper v. Litton, 308 U.S. 295, 296, 60 S.Ct. 238, 84 L.Ed.

281 (1939) ("The findings by the District Court, amply supported by the evidence, reveal a scheme to defraud creditors * * * "); Harff v. Kerkorian, 347 A.2d 133, 134 (Del. 1975) (bondholders limited to contract claims in absence of " 'fraud, insolvency, or a violation of a statute.' ") (citation omitted). Moreover, if the Court here were confronted with an insolvent corporation, which is not the case, the company's officers and directors might become trustees of its assets for the protection of its creditors, among others. See, e.g., New York Credit Men's Adjustment Bureau v. Weiss, 278 A.D. 501, 503, 105 N.Y.S.2d 604, 606 (1st Dep't 1951), aff'd, 305 N.Y. 1, 110 N.E.2d 397 (1953).

If not based on a fiduciary duty and the other equitable principles addressed by the

Defendants go to great lengths to prove that the law of Delaware, and not New York, governs this question. Defendants' attempt to rely on Delaware law is readily explained by even a cursory reading of Simons v. Cogan, 549 A.2d 300, 303 (Del.1988), the recent Delaware Supreme Court ruling which held, *inter alia,* that a corporate bond "represents a contractual entitlement to the repayment of a debt and does not represent an equitable interest in the issuing corporation necessary for the imposition of a trust relationship with concomitant fiduciary duties." Before such a fiduciary duty arises, "an existing property right or equitable interest supporting such a duty must exist." Id. at 304. A bondholder, that court concluded, "acquires no equitable interest, and remains a creditor of the corporation whose interests are protected by the contractual terms of the indenture." Id. Defendants argue that New York law is not to the contrary, but the single Supreme Court case they cite—a case decided over fifty years ago that was not squarely presented with the issue addressed by the *Simons* court—provides something less than dispositive support. See Marx v. Merchants' National Properties, Inc., 148 Misc. 6, 7, 265 N.Y.S. 163, 165 (1933). For their part, plaintiffs more convincingly demonstrate that New York law applies than that New York law recognizes their claim.[34]

Regardless, this Court finds *Simons* persuasive, and believes that a New York court would agree with that conclusion. In the venerable case of Meinhard v. Salmon, 249 N.Y. 458, 164 N.E. 545 (1928), then Chief Judge Cardozo explained the obligations imposed on a fiduciary, and why those obligations are so special and rare:

> Many forms of conduct permissible in a workaday world for those acting at arm's length, are forbidden to those bound by fiduciary ties. A trustee is held to something stricter than the morals of the market place. Not honesty alone, but the punctilio of an honor the most sensitive, is then the standard of behavior.

Id. at 464 (citation omitted). Before a court recognizes the duty of a "punctilio of an honor the most sensitive," it must be certain that the complainant is entitled to more than the "morals of the market place," and the protections offered by actions based on fraud, state statutes or the panoply of available federal securities laws. This Court has concluded that

Court, plaintiffs' claim, in effect, asks this Court to use its broad equitable powers to fashion a new cause of action that would adopt precisely the same arguments the Court rejected in Count I.

34. The indenture provision designating New York law as controlling,* * * would, one might assume, resolve at least the issue of the applicable law. In quoting the relevant indenture provision, however, plaintiffs omit the proviso "except as may otherwise be required by mandatory provisions of law." P.Mem. at 52, n. 46. Defendants, however, fail to argue that the internal affairs doctrine, which they assert dictates that Dela-

ware law controls this question, is such a "mandatory provision of law." Nor do defendants respond to plaintiffs' reliance on First National City Bank v. Banco Para El Comercio, 462 U.S. 611, 621, 103 S.Ct. 2591, 2597, 77 L.Ed.2d 46 (1983) ("Different conflicts principles apply, however, where the rights of third parties *external* to the corporation are at issue.") (emphasis in original, citation omitted). Ultimately, the point is academic; as explained below, the Court would grant defendants summary judgment on this Count under either New York or Delaware law.

the plaintiffs presently before it—sophisticated investors who are unsecured creditors—are not entitled to such additional protections.

Equally important, plaintiffs' position on this issue * * * provides no reasonable or workable limits, and is thus reminiscent of their implied covenant of good faith. Indeed, many indisputably legitimate corporate transactions would not survive plaintiffs' theory. With no workable limits, plaintiffs' envisioned duty would extend equally to trade creditors, employees, and every other person to whom the defendants are liable in any way. Of all such parties, these informed plaintiffs least require a Court's equitable protection; not only are they willing participants in a largely impersonal market, but they also possess the financial sophistication and size to secure their own protection.

* * *

NOTE: THE AFTERMATH OF THE RJR NABISCO RESTRUCTURING

When the LBO closed in March 1990, RJR Nabisco had $29 billion of debt and a debt-equity ratio of 23:1. Within two months, KKR realized that RJR Nabisco would default on its debt absent a recapitalization. A multi-phase deleveraging of the firm, including open-market repurchases and exchange offers, began in July 1990. The cash for this debt reduction was provided by the $5.7 billion proceeds of the sale of Del Monte and several European subsidiaries. RJR also redeemed an issue of increasing rate notes held by institutions with the proceeds of a new loan. In addition, KKR invested $1.5 billion in new common stock. By the end of 1990, RJR Nabisco had $18.7 billion of debt outstanding.

In 1991 KKR commenced a new junk bond retirement program. The cash came from a public common stock offering and new debt financing. There followed an exchange offer of common stock for outstanding convertible preferred and preferred issued in the earlier debt retirement program. By the end of 1991, debt was below $15 billion and RJR lost its junk bond rating. The reduction in interest costs resulted in positive accounting earnings for the year. Anders, Merchants of Debt: KKR and the Mortgaging of American Business 263–271 (1992).

KKR sold its remaining RJR shares in 1995, showing a profit of only $60 million on a $3.1 billion investment. The brunt of the opportunity cost was borne by KKR's equity partners rather than by KKR itself. KKR had put up only $126 million of the $3.1 billion, and had earned more than $500 million in transactions, advisor, management, and investors fees. Brigham, Gapenski, and Ehrhardt, Financial Management: Theory and Practice 1012–1013 (9th ed. 1999).

NOTE: SPIN OFFS

High leverage restructurings are not the only form of event risk. Consider a plan effected by the Marriott Corp. in 1992–1993. Marriott, which both owned hotels and managed hotels owned by others, split the two lines of business into two separately owned corporations. It shifted its management business to a new entity called Marriott International ("International") and declared a one-to-one dividend of the International shares (a "spin off"). Its real estate and almost all of its debt remained behind, and that corporation was renamed Host Marriott ("Host"). Under the separation, pro forma based on 1992 figures for the company as a whole, International had annual sales of $7.4 billion and operating cash flow of $500 million; Host had annual sales of $1.7 billion and operating cash flow of $350 million, much of which would have to be devoted to annual interest payments of $225 million per year. See HB Korenvaes Investments, L.P. v. Marriott Corp., infra Part III.B; PPM America, Inc. v. Marriott Corp., 820 F.Supp. 970 (D.Md.1993).

The announcement of the spin off caused Marriott's stock price to rise from 17 1/8 to 21 7/8. But the bond market got nervous. Marriott's bonds immediately lost $360 million in market value; its twenty year bond lost 30 percent of its value. One investment banking house estimated market-wide losses in the wake of the Marriott announcement at $11 billion. Subsequent changes in terms of the deal, made in response to lawsuits and pressure from institutional investors, reduced the bond-holder loss. But Marriott's debt securities remained $194.6 million below their pre-announcement value.

According to Parrino, Spinoffs and Wealth Transfers: The Marriott Case, 43 J. Fin. Econ. 241 (1997), the bondholder losses incident to the Marriott spin off were not exceeded (or even equaled) by stockholder gains. Parrino adjusts the stock price increase at the time of the spin off for shareholder gains experienced in the industry as a whole. The adjusted gains are only $80.6 million, less than the bondholder losses of $194.6 million. Perrino attributes the decline in the total value of the firm to transaction costs and inefficiencies related to the spin off.

How might one draft a covenant to protect a debt issue from this species of event risk? See Stark, Rahl and Seegers, "Marriott Risk": A New Model Covenant to Restrict Transfers of Wealth from Bondholders to Stockholders, 1994 Colum. Bus. L. Rev. 503. Assuming the Marriott bondholders did not have the benefit of such a covenant, can this spin off be distinguished from RJR Nabisco's leveraged restructuring for purposes of a claim of breach of a good faith duty? **Geren v. Quantum Chemical Corp.**, 832 F.Supp. 728 (S.D.N.Y.1993), suggests a negative response. The issuer in *Geren* declared a special cash dividend of $50 per share, causing its shareholders' equity to decrease from $748 million to negative $406 million and the market value of its existing bonds to decrease by 50 percent. The issuer funded the dividend by issuing $1.221 billion of new debt. The court refused to interpolate a good faith duty, rejecting the bondholders' attempt to distinguish the RJR Nabisco buyout as a "more justifiable transaction."

NOTE: FIDUCIARY THEORY, GOOD FAITH DUTIES, AND OTHER BASES FOR JUDICIAL PROTECTION OF BONDHOLDERS

1. *Fiduciary Versus Good Faith Duty.*

It is impossible to draft express protection against the open horizon of risky contingencies that are necessarily entailed in long-term relational contracts, and, at the same time, to leave management free to get on with the job of maximizing value. The possibilities of opportunistic behavior by management to the advantage of the equity and the disadvantage of the debt inevitably remain substantial. Those possibilities could be narrowed by judicially imputed covenants of good faith to govern the parties in their ongoing contractual relationship, or by judicially imposed fiduciary restrictions on the behavior of management and the equity holders vis-a-vis the debt holders.

As *Met Life v. RJR Nabisco* indicates, even if adumbrations from received contract doctrine are the source of such judicial power, difficult problems remain in determining the substance of good faith obligations. What, for example, are the limits of opportunistic behavior by the management and the equity that good faith permits? Where should the judge look to find those limits, apart from the language of the contract, which is the beginning of the inquiry? In the institutional circumstances of the bargain? In the particular circumstances of the parties' particular agreement? In economic theory? In psychology? In moral reasoning? In all of the above?

Similar problems arise if the fiduciary notion is invoked to protect the bond-holders. If the "fiduciary" is identified as the equity holders as a group, then one group of dispersed investors is being asked to serve as a fiduciary for another group with respect to their conflicting claims under relational contracts which do not specify all the circumstances in which conflict may arise. If management is identified as the "fiduciary," an agent selected by one group to work for it is being asked to resolve conflicting claims of that group against another group which had no role in the agent's selection. Is fiduciary theory responsive to these conflicts? What should the resolving courts use as the measure of the extent to which the designated fiduciary may adversely affect the beneficiary if the fiduciary represents each of the two conflicting claimants? Do managers engaged in self dealing or other self-aggrandizing conduct owe a duty to bondholders with respect to such behavior?

There is also the question of how the "fiduciary" obligation differs from the "good faith" obligation. At the poles, the differences seem clear enough. The fiduciary obligation, in its purest version, not only prohibits the fiduciary from dealing with the beneficiary's property so as to effect benefits for itself at the expense of the beneficiary (whether by way of causing loss or denying gain to the beneficiary), but also forbids the fiduciary from thus benefitting itself even if the beneficiary is not injured thereby. The "good faith" restrictions on behavior of parties to a contract start from the conception that each party is expected to derive some gains and some sacrifices in the course of their contractual relationship. As the fiduciary obligation is diluted to permit the fiduciary not only to derive some gains from use of the beneficiary's property, but thereby to deprive the beneficiary of the full gain from the transaction, the court is obliged to define the limits on the gain-sharing. And as the duty of good faith is detached from a rigid connection to an express provision of the contract, the court becomes obliged to set limits on the extent to which bondholders may be injured consistently with "good faith." In many cases, the two criteria will produce the same result.

But, despite this area of overlap, fiduciary restrictions plainly demand more restraint from the fiduciary than do good faith obligations from a contracting party. Fiduciary theory contemplates a dependent relationship in which the fiduciary serves only the interest of the beneficiary, as opposed to its own interests, when dealing with the beneficiary's assets. In contrast, the relationship of common stockholders to bondholders, although consensual, is adversarial in origin and operation. It lacks the essential import of a fiduciary or agency relationship: one party acting primarily, if not solely for the other under the other's nominal direction or control. It contemplates open-ended discretion and self-dealing with the common assets by the common stockholder without any need for bondholder consent. Nor is the bondholder entitled to share in control or gains other than those provided by the terms of the contract. The common stockholder is given the discretion to (and is expected to) take the risks involved in seeking to maximize the value of the common assets for its own benefit, subject only to the restrictions of the contract (and of "law").

Arguably, the obligation to return a fixed amount at a fixed date (along with interest in the interim) itself limits the stockholder's use of the bondholder's investment. Hence, for the bargain between them to be productive during the period of the loan, the stockholders must be free, at least in their regular operations, from the indeterminate restrictions that are implicit in a fiduciary relationship. That interest must be paid and the loan must be renewed or repaid may act as sufficient constraints on stockholder strategic behavior to reduce the need for fiduciary—albeit not contractual—restraints during the loan's term. About the only obligation that separates a fiduciary from an arms-length contracting party that generally may be imposed on the common stock vis-a-vis the bondholders (or preferred stockholders) is the obligation to disclose when seeking a change in the contract. And it is not clear how or why that obligation differs from the "good faith" obligation of contracting parties to each other.

Finally, in both law and economics, the nature of the bondholder's relationship to the borrower, its common stockholders, and its managers undergoes a change when the borrower becomes insolvent, or insolvency becomes immediately foreseeable. At this point, business judgments that maximize value from the common stockholder's point of view may not maximize value if viewed in the abstract. In theory, the corporate law system of stockholder-directed fiduciary duties collapses at this point, and the directors make decisions that maximize the value of the corporate entity, and thus benefit the bondholders. See Credit Lyonnais Bank Nederland, N.V. v. Pathe Communications Corp., 1991 WL 277613 at 42 & n. 55 (Del.Ch.1991); Geyer v. Ingersoll Publications Co., 621 A.2d 784 (Del.Ch.1992).

2. *The Nature of the Good Faith Duty.*

According to the *Metlife v. RJR Nabisco* opinion, with a bond contract, "an implied covenant * * * derives its substance directly from the language of the Indenture, and 'cannot give the holders of Debentures any rights inconsistent with those set out in the Indenture.' [Where] plaintiffs' contractual rights [have not been] violated, there can have been no breach of an implied covenant."

Under this characterization what does contractual good faith duty add, if anything, to enforcement of the contract in accord with its literal terms? **Page Mill Asset Management v. Credit Suisse First Boston Corp.**, 2000 WL 335557 (S.D.N.Y.), addresses this question as follows: "[T]he implied covenant is not distinct from the underlying contract, see Geler v. National Westminster Bank USA, 770 F.Supp. 210, 215 (S.D.N.Y.1991), and therefore '[a]s a general rule, [t]he cause of action alleging breach of [the implied covenant] is duplicative of a cause of action alleging breach of contract.' OHM Remediation Servs. Corp. v. Hughes Env'l Sys., Inc., 952 F.Supp. 120, 124 (S.D.N.Y.1997) * * *. Therefore, breach of contract claims and breach of the implied covenant claims may be maintained simultaneously only if the damages sought by the plaintiff for breach of the implied covenant are not 'intrinsically tied to the damages allegedly resulting from breach of contract.' Canstar v. J.A. Jones Constr. Co., 212 A.D.2d 452, 453, 622 N.Y.S.2d 730, 731 (1st Dep't 1995)."

3. *A "Supertrustee."*

Amihud, Garbade & Kahan, A New Governance Structure for Corporate Bonds, 51 Stan. L. Rev. 447 (1999), suggests that process problems, in particular the difficulty of amending a public bond contract, figure significantly in the marketplace persistence of bonds lacking effective contractual protection. The article suggests that protected bonds might reappear in the marketplace if the process problems were solved. Toward this end, it proposes a "supertrustee." This figure would occupy the position of an indenture trustee but carry expanded powers. The expanded powers would mimic those of a lead lender in a private placement. The supertrustee would have the duty and power to monitor, renegotiate, and enforce bond covenants, including access to confidential company information. In a distress situation, the supertrustee would renegotiate the covenants unilaterally. The bondholders, correspondingly, would lose the right to direct or replace the supertrustee. The supertrustee would be subject to liability for failure to monitor, but would receive business judgment protection for its renegotiation and enforcement decisions. Complex incentive compensation devices are suggested.

Supertrustee bonds, like bonds with poison put options, would yield less than comparable bonds. Which would institutional fund managers be likely to choose? Note also that prior to the mid–1970s, publicly traded bonds were subject to extensive business covenants. Why was this not prevented by process problems?

4. *Commentary.*

Commentary on bondholder protection takes a range of positions on the questions set out above. Fiduciary duties to bondholders are advocated in McDaniel, Bondholders and Stockholders, 1988 J.Corp.Law 205, McDaniel, Bondholders and Corporate Governance, 41 Bus.Law. 413 (1986), Mitchell, The Fairness Rights of Corporate Bondholders, 65 N.Y.U.L.Rev. 1165 (1990), and Barkey, The Financial Articulation of a Fiduciary Duty to Bondholders with Fiduciary Duties to the Stockholders of the Corporation, 20 Creighton L.Rev. 47 (1986). A contractual good faith duty with power to substitute for covenants and constrain opportunism in respect of bonds issued prior to the appearance of new event risks is advocated in Brudney, Corporate Bondholders and Debtor Opportunism: In Bad Times and Good, 105 Harv.L.Rev. 1821 (1992), Bratton, Corporate Debt Relationships: Legal Theory in a Time of Restructuring, 1989 Duke L.J. 92, and Bratton, The Economics and Jurisprudence of Convertible Bonds, 1984 Wis.L.Rev. 667. A contractual good faith duty without the power to substitute for covenants is recognized in Schwarcz, Rethinking a Corporation's Obligations to Creditors, 17 Cardozo L. Rev. 607 (1996); Coffee, Unstable Coalitions: Corporate Governance As a Multi–Player Game, 78 Geo.L.J. 1495 (1990), and Tauke, Should Bonds Have More Fun? A Reexamination of the Debate Over Corporate Bondholder Rights, 1989 Colum.Bus.Rev. 1. Hurst and McGuinness, The Corporation, the Bondholder and Fiduciary Duties, 10 J.L. & Commerce 187 (1991), also argues against judicial intervention, recommending that bondholders get stricter covenants, keep themselves informed and, in extreme cases, invoke the fraudulent conveyance laws. Economic analysts have tended to argue against judicial intervention. See Kahan, The Qualified Case Against Mandatory Terms in Bonds, 89 Nw.U.L.Rev. 565 (1995); Kanda, Debtholders and Equityholders, 21 J. Legal Stud. 431 (1992); Lehn and Poulsen, The Economics of Event Risk: The Case of Bondholders in Leveraged Buyouts, 15 J.Corp.L. 197 (1990); Lehn and Poulsen, Contractual Resolution of Bondholder–Stockholder Conflicts in Leveraged Buyouts, 34 J.L. & Econ. 645 (1991). Finally, Smith, The Efficient Norm for Corporate Law: A Neotraditional Interpretation of Fiduciary Duty, 98 Mich. L. Rev. 214 (1999), takes a contingent position, arguing that in most cases judicial intervention will not be efficient, but that intervention would be justified where the bondholders could show that management's action made the firm worse off.

NOTE: LENDER LIABILITY COMPARED

1. *The Good Faith Duty.*

K.M.C. Co. v. Irving Trust Co., 757 F.2d 752 (6th Cir.1985), is a leading case holding a lender to have violated the good faith duty in the course of performing its debt contract. The bank lender in the case refused, without any notice, to advance the last $800,000 on a line of credit of $3.5 million to a debtor in shaky condition. Whether the debtor was so shaky as to be at the point of collapse was a disputed point. The bank had discretion to refuse the advance, but the loan agreement was silent on whether, and how much advance notice was required before it exercised such discretion. A jury decided that the failure to give notice (and thus give the debtor an opportunity to obtain other financing) by a lender which was fully secured, violated the lender's obligation of good faith, and rendered the lender liable for the debtor's subsequent collapse. The Court of Appeals upheld the jury verdict, reasoning that (1) the implied notice requirement was necessary to give the borrower time to obtain alternate financing, for without it the borrower's continued existence would be entirely at the whim or mercy of the lender, (2) the lender needed a valid business reason to avoid the notice requirement, (3) the good faith constraint also covered the loan's demand provision, and (4) the fact that the lender was fully secured weighed heavily in the good faith determination.

Another leading lender liability case is **State National Bank of El Paso v. Farah Manufacturing Co.,** 678 S.W.2d 661 (Tex.App.1984), in which a group of banks invoked a contract provision to block the return of an ousted chief executive officer. One year later the officer returned and restored the borrower to a prosperity that contrasted with its losses under the management of the bank approved CEO. The borrower recovered $19 million from the banks on the claim, *inter alia,* that they fraudulently imposed the provision, having never intended to call a default in the first place. See also United California Bank v. Prudential Insurance Co., 140 Ariz. 238, 681 P.2d 390 (App.1983) (liability for failure to close real estate takeout financing). See also Indu Craft, Inc. v. Bank of Baroda, 47 F.3d 490 (2d Cir.1995); Anuhco, Inc. v. Westinghouse Credit Corp., 883 S.W.2d 910 (Mo.Ct.App.1994).

K.M.C., Farah, and similar cases, make for an interesting contrast with *RJR Nabisco.* In *Nabisco,* the borrower takes an action that reduces the value of the lenders' claims, but the good faith duty does not come to bear to protect the lenders. Lender defense against such conduct turns out to be a matter for the drafter of the bond contract. In the lender liability cases, the lenders have protected themselves with contract rights but the borrowers successfully invoke the good faith duty to claim that the exercise of the rights results in inappropriate injury.

The comparison gives rise to some questions. Should the law deal with cases of borrower injury by following the pattern of cases of borrower opportunism and putting the burden of self protection on the victim? If the borrower is to be protected by a good faith constraint on the lender but the lender is not to be likewise protected, does a consistency problem arise? If so, does the legitimate imposition of lender liability imply bondholder protection in cases of borrower opportunism? Or, can some material distinction be articulated between the unprotected borrower and the unprotected bondholder or other lender, so as to justify differential treatment? Or should the inconsistency be taken as a signal that lender liability should be rolled back forthwith?

2. *Legislative Responses to Lender Liability.*

The legislatures of a number of states have rolled back lender liability with new statutes of frauds. In lender liability cases, borrowers frequently allege that a lender has breached an oral agreement to lend, refinance an existing loan or refrain from pursuing a contractual remedy. Under the new statutes, actionable "credit agreements" must be in writing and signed by both parties; the term "credit agreement" is defined broadly to include agreements to lend, or otherwise extend credit, to forbear repayment or exercise of remedies, to enter into a new agreement, or make any other financial accommodation. The Florida statute, Fla. Stat. § 687.0304 (2007), further provides that a "credit agreement may not be implied from the relationship, fiduciary or otherwise, of the creditor and the debtor."

3. *Liability as a Controlling Party.*

Lenders can be held for losses sustained or liabilities incurred by borrowers if the lender is deemed to be in "control" of the borrower. Unlike stockholders in control, lenders in control do not have limited liability. See Douglas–Hamilton,

Creditor Liabilities Resulting from Improper Interference with the Management of a Financially Troubled Debtor, 31 Bus.Law. 343 (1975). Conventional business covenants and other negative regulations of borrower conduct are not deemed to be "control" for this purpose. See Lloyd, Financial Covenants in Commercial Loan Documentation: Uses and Limitations, 58 Tenn.L.Rev. 335, 352–353 (1991).

The control concept also shapes lender liability for toxic waste cleanup expenses under the Comprehensive Environmental Response Compensation and Liability Act ("CERCLA"), 41 U.S.C. §§ 9601–9657. CERCLA imposes liability on "any person who at the time of disposal of any hazardous substance owned or operated any * * * facility at which such hazardous substances were disposed of," 42 U.S.C. § 9607(a)(2), but excludes from the definition of "owner or operator" any "person, who, without participating in the management of a * * * facility, holds indicia of ownership primarily to protect his security interest in the * * * facility." United States v. Fleet Factors Corp., 901 F.2d 1550 (11th Cir.1990), imposed liability on a secured lender that took an active role in business decisions respecting a facility during the course of the liquidation of the defaulting borrower's business. Subsequent cases took a more cautious approach. See, e.g., In re Bergsoe Metal Corp., 910 F.2d 668, 672–673 (9th Cir.1990). Further relief from liability came with the Asset Conservation, Lender Liability and Deposit Insurance Protection Act of 1996, 42 U.S.C. § 9601(20)(E), which protects lenders taking possession after foreclosure provided they sell, release or divest at the earliest practicable time.

SECTION E. DEBTOR DISTRESS

1. ALTERING THE BOND CONTRACT–AMENDMENT AND EXCHANGE, COERCION AND HOLDING OUT

Promises in bond contracts, like promises in all contracts, can be amended or their performance can be waived. Sometimes debt issuers request amendments or waivers during good times. For instance, an issuer subject to a tight set of business covenants might need a waiver to do a financing or make an investment outside of the framework permitted by the debt contract. As noted above, the process of collecting bondholder consents to such waivers is much less onerous with private placements than with public issues.

Amendments and waivers are particularly likely to be requested by issuers in financial difficulty. When a bond issuer encounters serious distress, lessening its debt obligations is the most obvious means of alleviating the problem. If the bondholders can be induced to lower the interest rate, forgive a payment default, waive a prepayment or prepayments, waive or amend one or more business covenants, consent to some combination of the foregoing, or exchange their bonds for some less onerous package of securities, the "distress" is diminished or even eliminated without the expense and uncertainty of a bankruptcy proceeding.

Various terms describe the process of revising debt obligations to avoid distress—"workout," "composition," "restructuring," "recapitalization." Whatever the term, the distressed issuer takes advantage of the fact that its debt obligations sell at a deep discount from face value. There are a number of standard techniques. If the debt is publicly traded and the issuer has some free cash flow, it can take the simple step of repurchasing the bonds on the market at the discounted price, thereby reducing its debt carrying cost. Such a cash repurchase also might be done by means of a public tender offer, or in the case of privately held debt, by face to face negotiation. More often, the issuer does not have the spare cash to repurchase the debt, and must deal with publicly traded debt by means of an "exchange offer." This is a public offer to the holders of the debt, the consideration for which is new debt securities with scaled down rights, equity securities, cash, or a mix of the three. With privately held debt, an equivalent offer would be the subject of a face to face negotiation. Either way, the issuer must offer the bondholders a package with a value higher than the current trading value of the bonds. In exchange for the increase in present value, the bondholders give up their contract right to full payment, and possibly other contract rights. The process may or may not involve a direct amendment of outstanding debt contracts.

Two problems recur in workout situations. First, particularly in the case of exchange offers, questions arise as to whether the context allows the bondholders to make an effective choice. As the materials that follow show, issuers can work elements of coercion into exchange offers and bond amendment processes, whether or not they control a voting majority of the bonds. And, in any event, the issuer's power to determine the timing of the restructuring or amendment and to overstate the gloomy consequences of a failure to acquiesce in it offers dispersed bondholders a distorted choice and puts them at a substantial bargaining disadvantage.

Second, if a bargaining arrangement that entails aggregative action (e.g., an exchange or repurchase offer) or collective action (e.g., a majority vote that binds a minority) by bondholders to approve a proposed readjustment is vulnerable to debtor opportunism, a bargaining arrangement that permits holdouts creates an added possibility of failure of the readjustment. If the necessary majority exchanges its bonds or consents to the amendment a benefit may flow to the non-consenting minority. By refusing to consent, these holders will be left holding bonds carrying rights to full principal and coupon—although they incur the risk that they will not be paid until later and may be paid less than the amount offered in the proposed readjustment. They therefore have an incentive to hold out, but at a risk. If too many hold out, a bargaining impasse results, and the recapitalization fails to garner sufficient consents. The issuer proceeds to a more costly bankruptcy, having lost the chance to substitute an advantageous revised capital structure. This is not necessarily good news for the bondholders. Franks and Torous, A Comparison of Financial Recontracting in Distressed Exchanges and Chapter 11 Reorganizations, 33 J. Fin. Econ. 349 (1994), surveys a sample of distressed firms to find a creditors' recovery rate of 80 cents on the dollar in out of court restructurings compared to a rate of 51 cents on the dollar in chapter 11.

Aladdin Hotel Co. v. Bloom

United States Court of Appeals, Eighth Circuit, 1953.
200 F.2d 627.

■ GARDNER, CHIEF JUDGE. As originally brought this was in form a class action in which Josephine Loeb Bloom as plaintiff sought for herself and

other minority bondholders of the Aladdin Hotel Company similarly situated equitable relief. She named as defendants Aladdin Hotel Company, a
corporation, Charles O. Jones, Inez M. Jones, Charles R. Jones, Kathryn
Dorothea Jones, Barbara Ann Jones and Mississippi Valley Trust Company,
a corporation. She alleged that the class whom she purported to represent
consisted of approximately 130 members who were the owners of a minority in value of certain bonds issued by the Aladdin Hotel Company, and that
the object of the action was to obtain an adjudication of claims which
affected specific property involved in the action and that common questions
of law and fact affecting the rights of the parties constituting the class were
involved; that on September 1, 1938, the Aladdin Hotel Company executed
and delivered a series of 647 bonds aggregating in principal amount the
sum of $250,000.00. The bonds on their face were made payable September
1, 1948, with interest to that date at 5 per cent per annum payable only out
of net earnings and with interest at the rate of 8 per cent per annum from
maturity until paid; that the Hotel Company to secure payment of said
bond issue executed its deed of trust by which it mortgaged certain real
estate owned by it in Kansas City, Missouri; that the mortgage also covered
furnishings and fixtures in the hotel property owned by the Aladdin Hotel
Company; that the Mississippi Valley Trust Company was named as trustee
in said deed of trust; that the bonds and deed of trust contained provision
empowering the bondholders of not less than two-thirds principal amount
of the bonds, by agreement with the Hotel Company to modify and extend
the date of payment of said bonds provided such extension affected all
bonds alike. She then alleged that she was the owner of some of said bonds
of the total principal amount of $3500; that the defendants, other than the
Hotel Company and the Mississippi Valley Trust Company, were all members of the so-called Jones family and during the period from May 1, 1948
to the time of the commencement of this action they were the owners of a
majority of the stock of the Hotel Company and controlling members of its
Board of Directors and dominated and controlled all acts and policies of the
Hotel Company; that they were also the owners and holders of more than
two-thirds of the principal amount of said bonds, being the owners of more
than 72 per cent thereof; that they entered into an agreement with the
Hotel Company June 1, 1948 to extend the maturity date of said bonds
from September 1, 1948 to September 1, 1958. It was also alleged that
other changes were similarly made, on various dates, in the provisions of
the trust deed but as the trial court deemed them immaterial we pretermit
reciting them here in detail. It was alleged that the defendant Mississippi
Valley Trust Company certified the modifications as provided in the trust
deed; that the purported changes were made on application of the Hotel
Company and with the consent of the holders of two-thirds in principal
value of the outstanding bonds; that no notice of said application for
change in the due date of the bonds was given to the mortgage bondholders
and that plaintiff did not consent nor agree to the modification. She then
alleged that the modifications were invalid because not made in good faith
and were not for the equal benefit of all bondholders but were made
corruptly for the benefit of the defendants and such modification deprived
plaintiff and the other mortgage bondholders of their rights and property;

that said modification extended for ten additional years the powers and compensation of the Mississippi Valley Trust Company as trustee; that the Mississippi Valley Trust Company is made defendant because it is a party to the aforesaid modifications and waivers and participated in effecting them and because it benefitted by aforesaid modifications, waivers and certifications. * * * Plaintiff prayed for a declaratory judgment declaring and holding that the purported modifications, waivers and certifications are illegal, inequitable and void; that she and all other bondholders of the defendant Aladdin Hotel Company have judgment against defendant Aladdin Hotel Company for the principal amount of the bonds held by each of them with interest thereon at 8 per cent per annum (allowing said defendant credit thereon, however, for the 5 per cent per annum interest paid thereon) from September 1, 1948 until the payment of such principal and interest.

On trial the court dismissed as to all individual defendants, including the Mississippi Valley Trust Company, and made findings that the amendments benefitted the Hotel Company and the Joneses but did not benefit the bondholders; that all bondholders were entitled to notice of any proposed amendments; that the Joneses acting as the Hotel Company's officers and as majority bondholders, had a legal duty to exercise an honest discretion in extending the bonds; that the power to postpone the maturity date of the bonds could not be legally recognized in the majority bondholders under the facts of this case; that the decree, however, should be limited to a money judgment because that would grant plaintiff full relief. * * *

In seeking reversal the Hotel Company in substance contends * * * that the modification of the provisions of the trust deed extending the time of maturity of the bonds was effected in strict compliance with the provisions of the contract of the parties and hence was binding on all the bondholders * * *.

The trust deed contained provision that,

"In the event the Company shall propose any change, modification, alteration or extension of the bonds issued hereunder or of this Indenture, such change, if approved by the holders of not less than two-thirds in face amount of the bonds at the time outstanding, shall be binding and effective upon all of the holders of the then outstanding bonds, provided, however, that such modification, change, alteration or extension shall affect all of the outstanding bonds similarly."

The bonds, including those held by plaintiff, contained the following:

"The terms of this bond or of the Indenture securing the same may be modified, extended, changed or altered by agreement between the Company and the holders of two-thirds or more in face amount of bonds of this issue at the time outstanding. Any default under the Indenture may be waived by the holders of two-thirds or more in face amount of the bonds at the time outstanding."

The bonds also contained the following provision:

"For a more particular description of the covenants of the Company as well as a description of the mortgaged property, of the nature and extent of the security, of the rights of the holders of the bonds and of the terms and conditions upon which the bonds are issued and secured, reference is made to said General Mortgage Deed of Trust."

It appears without dispute that the modification here under consideration was made in strict compliance with the provisions contained in the trust deed and by reference embodied in the bonds. The Hotel Company made the application to the trustee and it was approved by the holders of more than two-thirds in face amount of the bonds at the time outstanding. When this application for modification was made to the trustee he was guided in his action by the terms of the contract between the parties. That contract made no provision for notice. It required that such application have the approval of those holding two-thirds or more in face value of the bonds. The only other limitation contained in the contract with reference to the power to modify its terms was to the effect that "such modification, change, alteration or extension shall affect all of the outstanding bonds similarly." The modification did affect all outstanding *bonds* similarly and it is important, we think, to observe that the contract does not require that such modification affect all *bondholders* similarly. What effect this change might have on various bondholders might depend upon various circumstances and conditions with which the trustee was not required to concern itself. The so-called Joneses were the controlling stockholders of the Hotel Company and were its officers and the court found that the alteration was advantageous to the Hotel Company. It was doubtless effected primarily to benefit the financial standing and operating efficiency of the hotel. It does not follow, however, that such modification was prejudicial to the bondholders. Their security was greatly improved in value by the management and it is inconceivable that the Joneses should deliberately act to the prejudice or detriment of the bondholders when they held and owned some 72 per cent of the entire outstanding bond issue. It is urged that because the Joneses were acting in a dual capacity they became trustees for the other bondholders and that as such it was incumbent upon them to do no act detrimental to the rights of the bondholders. The rights of the bondholders, however, are to be determined by their contract and courts will not make or remake a contract merely because one of the parties thereto may become dissatisfied with its provisions, but if legal will interpret and enforce it. Monticello Bldg. Corp. v. Monticello Inv. Co., 330 Mo. 1128, 52 S.W.2d 545; Minneapolis–Moline Co. v. Chicago M. St. P. & P.R. Co., 8 Cir., 199 F.2d 725. There is no question that the provision in the trust deed and bonds was a legal provision which violated no principle of public policy nor private right. The sole ground for holding the modification extending the time for payment void is that no notice was given the minority bondholders. If the Joneses had not been acting in a dual capacity, then, we assume, the modification, effected as it was with the approval of the holders of two-thirds of the face value of the outstanding bonds, would have been held good. It is conceded that under such circumstances no notice would have been necessary. We think the situation must be viewed realistically. No notice was required so far as the parties to the contract were concerned. Their rights must be determined by their contract and not by any equitable doctrine, and notice to the other bondholders could have served no possible purpose. Litigants have no standing in a court of equity where a remedy at law is available. The holders of more than two-thirds of the face value of the bonds could not have been prevented from approving the proposed change even had notice been given and the acts of the parties must be determined in relation to the terms of their contract. It follows that no prejudice could have been suffered by plaintiff or her grantors by the fact that notice of the proposed change or modification was not given them.

We have searched the record with great care and find no substantial evidence warranting a finding of bad faith, fraud, corruption or conspiracy of the Joneses. When Charles O. Jones became manager of the hotel properties in 1944 no interest had been paid on the bonds prior to that date. The Hotel Company paid the interest to all bondholders in 1944 and the interest has been paid each year since. Numerous improvements were made in the hotel property at an expense of over $300,000. At the time the Joneses took over the management in 1944 the Company had a deficit of $70,000 and a balance due of $24,000 on the first mortgage of $50,000, all of which has been paid off, and the gross income of the hotel has increased from $219,000 in 1944 to $600,000 in 1951, and the book value of the stock has increased from $384,000 in 1944 to $916,000 in 1951. The properties covered by the trust deed were at the time of the trial of the proximate value of $1,000,000.

* * *

The judgment appealed from is * * * reversed and the cause is remanded to the trial court with directions to dismiss plaintiff's complaint.

NOTE: AMENDMENT UNDER THE TRUST INDENTURE ACT
Revised Model Simplified Indenture, Appendix A
Article 9 (Amendments)

———

Trust Indenture Act of 1939, as amended 1990   NPA 817
Section 316   RMSI 89

(a) The indenture to be qualified

(1) shall automatically be deemed (unless it is expressly provided therein that any such provision is excluded) to contain provisions authorizing the holders of not less than a majority in principal amount of the indenture securities or if expressly specified in such indenture, of any series of securities at the time outstanding (A) to direct the time, method, and place of conducting any proceeding for any remedy available to such trustee, or exercising any trust or power conferred upon such trustee, under such indenture, or (B) on behalf of the holders of all such indenture securities, to consent to the waiver of any past default and its consequences; or

(2) may contain provisions authorizing the holders of not less than 75 per centum in principal amount of the indenture securities or if

expressly specified in such indenture, of any series of securities at the time outstanding to consent on behalf of the holders of all such indenture securities to the postponement of any interest payment for a period not exceeding three years from its due date.

For the purposes of this subsection and paragraph (3) of subsection (d) of section 315, in determining whether the holders of the required principal amount of indenture securities have concurred in any such direction or consent, indenture securities owned by any obligor upon the indenture securities, or by any person directly or indirectly controlling or controlled by or under direct or indirect common control with any such obligor, shall be disregarded, except that for the purposes of determining whether the indenture trustee shall be protected in relying on any such direction or consent, only indenture securities which such trustee knows are so owned shall be so disregarded.

(b) Notwithstanding any other provision of the indenture to be qualified, the right of any holder of any indenture security to receive payment of the principal of and interest on such indenture security, on or after the respective due dates expressed in such indenture security, or to institute suit for the enforcement of any such payment on or after such respective dates, shall not be impaired or affected without the consent of such holder, except as to a postponement of an interest payment consented to as provided in paragraph (2) of subsection (a), and except that such indenture may contain provisions limiting or denying the right of any such holder to institute any such suit, if and to the extent that the institution or prosecution thereof or the entry of judgment therein would, under applicable law, result in the surrender, impairment, waiver, or loss of the lien of such indenture upon any property subject to such lien.

Section 316 of the Trust Indenture Act restricts the power of majorities of bondholders to defer or forgive principal and interest payments. It was enacted as a response to process abuses that occurred in Depression-era recapitalizations. A subset of the trust indentures of the era did not limit majoritarian amendment power. Under those clauses, majorities often were induced to make modifications which were seriously detrimental to all the bondholders, without a comparable sacrifice being made by the debtor's stockholders, and sometimes without there even being any necessity for the particular concession extracted. In some cases the vote of the bondholders for the modification was obtained by misinformation or inadequate information from biased sources. In other cases, as in *Aladdin Hotel v. Bloom,* votes were cast by bondholders with interests adverse to others of their class.

How does section 316(a) of the Act affect the structure of the workout in *Oak Industries,* which follows? Does section 316 assure bondholders an opportunity to maximize the value of their bonds in distress situations? If not, what problem do the bondholders face, and how should the problem be solved?

Finally, compare Note Purchase Agreement, section 17, Appendix A. Does the private placement treatment of differ materially from that of the Trust Indenture Act?

Katz v. Oak Industries Inc.

Court of Chancery of Delaware, 1986.
508 A.2d 873.

■ ALLEN, CHANCELLOR.

* * *

Plaintiff is the owner of long-term debt securities issued by Oak Industries, Inc. ("Oak"), a Delaware corporation; in this class action he seeks to enjoin the consummation of an exchange offer and consent solicitation made by Oak to holders of various classes of its long-term debt. As detailed below that offer is an integral part of a series of transactions that together would effect a major reorganization and recapitalization of Oak. The claim asserted is in essence, that the exchange offer is a coercive device and, in the circumstances, constitutes a breach of contract. This is the Court's opinion on plaintiff's pending application for a preliminary injunction.

I.

The background facts are involved even when set forth in the abbreviated form the decision within the time period currently available requires.

Through its domestic and foreign subsidiaries and affiliated entities, Oak manufactures and markets component equipments used in consumer, industrial and military products (the "Components Segment"); produces communications equipment for use in cable television systems and satellite television systems (the "Communications Segment") and manufactures and markets laminates and other materials used in printed circuit board applications (the "Materials Segment"). During 1985, the Company has terminated certain other unrelated businesses. As detailed below, it has now entered into an agreement with Allied–Signal, Inc. for the sale of the Materials Segment of its business and is currently seeking a buyer for its Communications Segment.

Even a casual review of Oak's financial results over the last several years shows it unmistakably to be a company in deep trouble. During the period from January 1, 1982 through September 30, 1985, the Company has experienced unremitting losses from operations; on net sales of approximately $1.26 billion during that period * * * it has lost over $335 million * * *. As a result its total stockholders' equity has first shriveled (from $260 million on 12/31/81 to $85 million on 12/31/83) and then disappeared completely (as of 9/30/85 there was a $62 million deficit in its stockholders' equity accounts) * * *. Financial markets, of course, reflected this gloomy history.[2]

2. The price of the company's common stock has fallen from over $30 per share on December 31, 1981 to approximately $2 per share recently. * * * The debt securities that

Unless Oak can be made profitable within some reasonably short time it will not continue as an operating company. Oak's board of directors, comprised almost entirely of outside directors, has authorized steps to buy the company time. In February, 1985, in order to reduce a burdensome annual cash interest obligation on its $230 million of then outstanding debentures, the Company offered to exchange such debentures for a combination of notes, common stock and warrants. As a result, approximately $180 million principal amount of the then outstanding debentures were exchanged. Since interest on certain of the notes issued in that exchange offer is payable in common stock, the effect of the 1985 exchange offer was to reduce to some extent the cash drain on the Company caused by its significant debt.

About the same time that the 1985 exchange offer was made, the Company announced its intention to discontinue certain of its operations and sell certain of its properties. Taking these steps, while effective to stave off a default and to reduce to some extent the immediate cash drain, did not address Oak's longer-range problems. Therefore, also during 1985 representatives of the Company held informal discussions with several interested parties exploring the possibility of an investment from, combination with or acquisition by another company. As a result of these discussions, the Company and Allied–Signal, Inc. entered into two agreements. The first, the Acquisition Agreement, contemplates the sale to Allied–Signal of the Materials Segment for $160 million in cash. The second agreement, the Stock Purchase Agreement, provides for the purchase by Allied–Signal for $15 million cash of 10 million shares of the Company's common stock together with warrants to purchase additional common stock.

The Stock Purchase Agreement provides as a condition to Allied–Signal's obligation that at least 85% of the aggregate principal amount of all of the Company's debt securities shall have tendered and accepted the exchange offers that are the subject of this lawsuit. Oak has six classes of such long term debt.[3] If less than 85% of the aggregate principal amount of such debt accepts the offer, Allied–Signal has an option, but no obligation, to purchase the common stock and warrants contemplated by the Stock Purchase Agreement. An additional condition for the closing of the Stock Purchase Agreement is that the sale of the Company's Materials Segment contemplated by the Acquisition Agreement shall have been concluded.

Thus, as part of the restructuring and recapitalization contemplated by the Acquisition Agreement and the Stock Purchase Agreement, the Company has extended an exchange offer to each of the holders of the six classes

are the subject of the exchange offer here involved (see note 3 for identification) have traded at substantial discounts.

3. The three classes of debentures are: 13.65% debentures due April 1, 2001, 10½% convertible subordinated debentures due February 1, 2002, and 11⅞% subordinated debentures due May 15, 1998. In addition, as a result of the 1985 exchange offer the company has three classes of notes which were issued in exchange for debentures that were tendered in that offer. Those are: 13.5% senior notes due May 15, 1990, 9⅝% convertible notes due September 15, 1991 and 11⅜% notes due September 15, 1990.

of its long-term debt securities. These pending exchange offers include a Common Stock Exchange Offer (available only to holders of the 9 5/8% convertible notes) and the Payment Certificate Exchange Offers (available to holders of all six classes of Oak's long-term debt securities). The Common Stock Exchange Offer currently provides for the payment to each tendering noteholder of 407 shares of the Company's common stock in exchange for each $1,000 9 5/8% note accepted. The offer is limited to $38.6 million principal amount of notes (out of approximately $83.9 million outstanding).

The Payment Certificate Exchange Offer is an any and all offer. Under its terms, a payment certificate, payable in cash five days after the closing of the sale of the Materials Segment to Allied–Signal, is offered in exchange for debt securities. The cash value of the Payment Certificate will vary depending upon the particular security tendered. In each instance, however, that payment will be less than the face amount of the obligation. The cash payments range in amount, per $1,000 of principal, from $918 to $655. These cash values however appear to represent a premium over the market prices for the Company's debentures as of the time the terms of the transaction were set.

The Payment Certificate Exchange Offer is subject to certain important conditions before Oak has an obligation to accept tenders under it. First, it is necessary that a minimum amount ($38.6 million principal amount out of $83.9 total outstanding principal amount) of the 9 5/8% notes be tendered pursuant to the Common Stock Exchange Offer. Secondly, it is necessary that certain minimum amounts of each class of debt securities be tendered, together with consents to amendments to the underlying indentures.[4] Indeed, under the offer one may not tender securities unless at the same time one consents to the proposed amendments to the relevant indentures.

The condition of the offer that tendering security holders must consent to amendments in the indentures governing the securities gives rise to plaintiff's claim of breach of contract in this case. Those amendments would, if implemented, have the effect of removing significant negotiated protections to holders of the Company's long-term debt including the deletion of all financial covenants. Such modification may have adverse consequences to debt holders who elect not to tender pursuant to either exchange offer.

Allied–Signal apparently was unwilling to commit to the $15 million cash infusion contemplated by the Stock Purchase Agreement, unless Oak's long-term debt is reduced by 85% (at least that is a condition of their obligation to close on that contract). Mathematically, such a reduction may not occur without the Company reducing the principal amount of outstanding debentures (that is the three classes outstanding notes constitute less

---

4. The holders of more than 50% of the principal amount of each of the 13.5% notes, the 9⅝% notes and the 11⅝% notes and at least 66⅔% of the principal amount of the 13.65% debentures, 10½% debentures, and 11⅞% debentures, must validly tender such securities and consent to certain proposed amendments to the indentures governing those securities.

than 85% of all long-term debt). But existing indenture covenants * * * prohibit the Company, so long as any of its long-term notes are outstanding, from issuing any obligation (including the Payment Certificates) in exchange for any of the debentures. Thus, in this respect, amendment to the indentures is required in order to close the Stock Purchase Agreement as presently structured.

Restrictive covenants in the indentures would appear to interfere with effectuation of the recapitalization in another way. Section 4.07 of the 13.50% Indenture provides that the Company may not "acquire" for value any of the 9 5/8% Notes or 11 5/8% Notes unless it concurrently "redeems" a proportionate amount of the 13.50% Notes. This covenant, if unamended, would prohibit the disproportionate acquisition of the 9 5/8% Notes that may well occur as a result of the Exchange Offers; in addition, it would appear to require the payment of the "redemption" price for the 13.50% Notes rather than the lower, market price offered in the exchange offer.

In sum, the failure to obtain the requisite consents to the proposed amendments would permit Allied–Signal to decline to consummate both the Acquisition Agreement and the Stock Purchase Agreement.

* * *

II.

* * *

As amplified in briefing on the pending motion, plaintiff's claim is that no free choice is provided to bondholders by the exchange offer and consent solicitation. Under its terms, a rational bondholder is "forced" to tender and consent. Failure to do so would face a bondholder with the risk of owning a security stripped of all financial covenant protections and for which it is likely that there would be no ready market. A reasonable bondholder, it is suggested, cannot possibly accept those risks and thus such a bondholder is coerced to tender and thus to consent to the proposed indenture amendments.

It is urged this linking of the offer and the consent solicitation constitutes a breach of a contractual obligation that Oak owes to its bondholders to act in good faith. Specifically, plaintiff points to three contractual provisions from which it can be seen that the structuring of the current offer constitutes a breach of good faith. Those provisions (1) establish a requirement that no modification in the term of the various indentures may be effectuated without the consent of a stated percentage of bondholders; (2) restrict Oak from exercising the power to grant such consent with respect to any securities it may hold in its treasury; and (3) establish the price at which and manner in which Oak may force bondholders to submit their securities for redemption. * * *[6]

6. It is worthy of note that a very high percentage of the principal value of Oak's debt securities are owned in substantial amounts by a handful of large financial institutions. Almost 85% of the value of the 13.50% Notes is owned by four such institutions (one investment banker owns 55% of that issue); 69.1% of the 9⅝% Notes are owned by four financial institutions (the same investment banker owning 25% of that

III.

* * *

I turn first to an evaluation of the probability of plaintiff's ultimate success on the merits of his claim. I begin that analysis with two preliminary points. The first concerns what is not involved in this case. To focus briefly on this clears away much of the corporation law case law of this jurisdiction upon which plaintiff in part relies. This case does not involve the measurement of corporate or directorial conduct against that high standard of fidelity required of fiduciaries when they act with respect to the interests of the beneficiaries of their trust. Under our law—and the law generally—the relationship between a corporation and the holders of its debt securities, even convertible debt securities, is contractual in nature.

* * *

Arrangements among a corporation, the underwriters of its debt, trustees under its indentures and sometimes ultimate investors are typically thoroughly negotiated and massively documented. The rights and obligations of the various parties are or should be spelled out in that documentation. The terms of the contractual relationship agreed to and not broad concepts such as fairness define the corporation's obligation to its bondholders.[7]

Thus, the first aspect of the pending Exchange Offers about which plaintiff complains—that "the purpose and effect of the Exchange Offers is to benefit Oak's common stockholders at the expense of the Holders of its debt"—does not itself appear to allege a cognizable legal wrong. It is the obligation of directors to attempt, within the law, to maximize the long-run interests of the corporation's stockholders; that they may sometimes do so "at the expense" of others (even assuming that a transaction which one may refuse to enter into can meaningfully be said to be at his expense does not for that reason constitute a breach of duty). It seems likely that corporate restructurings designed to maximize shareholder values may in some instances have the effect of requiring bondholders to bear greater risk of loss and thus in effect transfer economic value from bondholders to stockholders. See generally, Prokesch, Merger Wave: How Stocks and Bonds Fare, N.Y. Times, Jan. 7, 1986, at A1, col. 1; McDaniel, Bondholders and Corporate Governance, 41 Bus.Law. 413, 418–423 (1986). But if courts are to provide protection against such enhanced risk, they will require either legislative direction to do so or the negotiation of indenture provisions designed to afford such protection.

issue) and 85% of the 11⅜% Notes are owned by five such institutions. Of the debentures, 89% of the 13.65% debentures are owned by four large banks; and approximately 45% of the two remaining issues is owned by two banks.

7. To say that the broad duty of loyalty that a director owes to his corporation and ultimately its shareholders is not implicated in this case is not to say, as the discussion below reflects, that as a matter of contract law a corporation owes no duty to bondholders of good faith and fair dealing. See, Restatement of Law, Contracts 2d, § 205 (1979). Such a duty, however, is quite different from the congeries of duties that are assumed by a fiduciary. See generally, Bratton, The Economics and Jurisprudence of Convertible Bonds, 1984 Wis.L.Rev. 667.

The second preliminary point concerns the limited analytical utility, at least in this context, of the word "coercive" which is central to plaintiff's own articulation of his theory of recovery. If, *pro arguendo,* we are to extend the meaning of the word coercion beyond its core meaning—dealing with the utilization of physical force to overcome the will of another—to reach instances in which the claimed coercion arises from an act designed to affect the will of another party by offering inducements to the act sought to be encouraged or by arranging unpleasant consequences for an alternative sought to be discouraged, then—in order to make the term legally meaningful at all—we must acknowledge that some further refinement is essential. Clearly some "coercion" of this kind is legally unproblematic. Parents may "coerce" a child to study with the threat of withholding an allowance; employers may "coerce" regular attendance at work by either docking wages for time absent or by rewarding with a bonus such regular attendance. Other "coercion" so defined clearly would be legally relevant (to encourage regular attendance by corporal punishment, for example). Thus, for purposes of legal analysis, the term "coercion" itself—covering a multitude of situations—is not very meaningful. For the word to have much meaning for purposes of legal analysis, it is necessary in each case that a normative judgment be attached to the concept ("inappropriately coercive" or "wrongfully coercive", etc.). But, it is then readily seen that what is legally relevant is not the conclusory term "coercion" itself but rather the norm that leads to the adverb modifying it.

In this instance, assuming that the Exchange Offers and Consent Solicitation can meaningfully be regarded as "coercive" (in the sense that Oak has structured it in a way designed—and I assume effectively so—to "force" rational bondholders to tender), the relevant legal norm that will support the judgment whether such "coercion" is wrongful or not will, for the reasons mentioned above, be derived from the law of contracts. I turn then to that subject to determine the appropriate legal test or rule.

Modern contract law has generally recognized an implied covenant to the effect that each party to a contract will act with good faith towards the other with respect to the subject matter of the contract. See, Restatement of Law, Contracts 2d, § 205 (1981); Rowe v. Great Atlantic and Pacific Tea Company, N.Y.Ct.Apps., 46 N.Y.2d 62, 412 N.Y.S.2d 827, 830, 385 N.E.2d 566, 569 (1978). The contractual theory for this implied obligation is well stated in a leading treatise:

> If the purpose of contract law is to enforce the reasonable expectations of parties induced by promises, then at some point it becomes necessary for courts to look to the substance rather than to the form of the agreement, and to hold that substance controls over form. What courts are doing here, whether calling the process "implication" of promises, or interpreting the requirements of "good faith", as the current fashion may be, is but a recognition that the parties occasionally have understandings or expectations that were so fundamental that they did not need to negotiate about those expectations. When the court "implies a promise" or holds that "good faith" requires a party not to violate those expectations, it is recognizing that sometimes silence says

more than words, and it is understanding its duty to the spirit of the bargain is higher than its duty to the technicalities of the language. Corbin on Contracts (Kaufman Supp.1984), § 570.

It is this obligation to act in good faith and to deal fairly that plaintiff claims is breached by the structure of Oak's coercive exchange offer. Because it is an implied *contractual* obligation that is asserted as the basis for the relief sought, the appropriate legal test is not difficult to deduce. It is this: is it clear from what was expressly agreed upon that the parties who negotiated the express terms of the contract would have agreed to proscribe the act later complained of as a breach of the implied covenant of good faith—had they thought to negotiate with respect to that matter. If the answer to this question is yes, then, in my opinion, a court is justified in concluding that such act constitutes a breach of the implied covenant of good faith.

* * *

With this test in mind, I turn now to a review of the specific provisions of the various indentures from which one may be best able to infer whether it is apparent that the contracting parties—had they negotiated with the exchange offer and consent solicitation in mind—would have expressly agreed to prohibit contractually the linking of the giving of consent with the purchase and sale of the security.

IV.

Applying the foregoing standard to the exchange offer and consent solicitation, I find first that there is nothing in the indenture provisions granting bondholders power to veto proposed modifications in the relevant indenture that implies that Oak may not offer an inducement to bondholders to consent to such amendments. Such an implication, at least where, as here, the inducement is offered on the same terms to each holder of an affected security, would be wholly inconsistent with the strictly commercial nature of the relationship.

Nor does the second pertinent contractual provision supply a ground to conclude that defendant's conduct violates the reasonable expectations of those who negotiated the indentures on behalf of the bondholders. Under that provision Oak may not vote debt securities held in its treasury. Plaintiff urges that Oak's conditioning of its offer to purchase debt on the giving of consents has the effect of subverting the purpose of that provision; it permits Oak to "dictate" the vote on securities which it could not itself vote.

The evident purpose of the restriction on the voting of treasury securities is to afford protection against the issuer voting as a bondholder in favor of modifications that would benefit it as issuer, even though such changes would be detrimental to bondholders. But the linking of the exchange offer and the consent solicitation does not involve the risk that bondholder interests will be affected by a vote involving anyone with a financial interest in the subject of the vote other than a bondholder's interest. That the consent is to be given concurrently with the transfer of the bond to the issuer does not in any sense create the kind of conflict of interest that the indenture's prohibition on voting treasury securities contemplates. Not only will the proposed consents be granted or withheld only by those with a financial interest to maximize the return on their investment in Oak's bonds, but the incentive to consent is equally available to all members of each class of bondholders. Thus the "vote" implied by the consent solicitation is not affected in any sense by those with a financial conflict of interest.

In these circumstances, while it is clear that Oak has fashioned the exchange offer and consent solicitation in a way designed to encourage consents, I cannot conclude that the offer violates the intendment of any of the express contractual provisions considered or, applying the test set out above, that its structure and timing breaches an implied obligation of good faith and fair dealing.

One further set of contractual provisions should be touched upon: Those granting to Oak a power to redeem the securities here treated at a price set by the relevant indentures. Plaintiff asserts that the attempt to force all bondholders to tender their securities at less than the redemption price constitutes, if not a breach of the redemption provision itself, at least a breach of an implied covenant of good faith and fair dealing associated with it. The flaw, or at least one fatal flaw, in this argument is that the present offer is not the functional equivalent of a redemption which is, of course, an act that the issuer may take unilaterally. In this instance it may happen that Oak will get tenders of a large percentage of its outstanding long-term debt securities. If it does, that fact will, in my judgment, be in major part a function of the merits of the offer (i.e., the price offered in light of the Company's financial position and the market value of its debt). To answer plaintiff's contention that the structure of the offer "forces" debt holders to tender, one only has to imagine what response this offer would receive if the price offered did not reflect a premium over market but rather was, for example, ten percent of market value. The exchange offer's success ultimately depends upon the ability and willingness of the issuer to extend an offer that will be a financially attractive alternative to holders. This process is hardly the functional equivalent of the unilateral election of redemption and thus cannot be said in any sense to constitute a subversion by Oak of the negotiated provisions dealing with redemption of its debt.

Accordingly, I conclude that plaintiff has failed to demonstrate a probability of ultimate success on the theory of liability asserted.

V.

An independent ground for the decision to deny the pending motion is supplied by the requirement that a court of equity will not issue the extraordinary remedy of preliminary injunction where to do so threatens the party sought to be enjoined with irreparable injury that, in the circumstances, seems greater than the injury that plaintiff seeks to avoid. Eastern Shore Natural Gas Co. v. Stauffer Chemical Co., Del.Supr., 298 A.2d 322 (1972). That principal has application here.

Oak is in a weak state financially. Its board, comprised of persons of experience and, in some instances, distinction, have approved the complex and interrelated transactions outlined above. It is not unreasonable to accord weight to the claims of Oak that the reorganization and recapitalization of which the exchange offer is a part may present the last good chance to regain vitality for this enterprise. I have not discussed plaintiff's claim of irreparable injury, although I have considered it. I am satisfied simply to note my conclusion that it is far outweighed by the harm that an improvidently granted injunction would threaten to Oak.

For the foregoing reasons plaintiff's application for a preliminary injunction shall be denied.

It is so ordered.

NOTE: COERCED VOTES AND HOLD OUTS

1. *Identifying the Bondholders' Problem.*

Roe, The Voting Prohibition in Bond Workouts, 97 Yale L.J. 232 (1987), asks (1) whether section 316(b) of the Trust Indenture Act should be repealed because denial of the sufficiency of majority action to alter core terms of indenture provisions is unnecessarily costly in contemporary markets dominated by institutional intermediaries, and (2) whether the evils at which the unanimity requirement is addressed—inadequate information, insider control of the bond issue, and largely unsophisticated individuals as investors in bonds—any longer exist in sufficient force to be worth the cost of precluding inexpensive pre-bankruptcy workouts by majority action without judicial supervision.

Roe suggests that section 316 exacerbates the bondholder's problem by creating holdout potential.

But the bondholder's problem can occur even where, as in *Katz v. Oak Industries,* the issuer side-steps section 316 by structuring the payment terms of the offer as an exchange and limiting amendment of the indenture to promises other than payment terms. Assume a distressed issuer and an issue of bonds trading for $500. The issuer offers these holders a package worth $550, and, as in *Oak Industries,* attaches an exit consent. The bondholders believe the intrinsic value of the bonds to be $600, and could obtain that figure in a workout given a small number of holders and a face to face negotiation. If a given bondholder does not exchange, but the requisite majority does exchange, the stripped bond will be worth $450. Here, Coffee and Klein, Bondholder Coercion: The Problem of Constrained Choice in Debt Tender Offers and Recapitalizations, 58 U.Chi.L.Rev. 1207 (1991), notes that the rational bondholder, unable to negotiate for more than $550, will tender for less than it believes the bonds to be worth. On these facts, the coercing party is not the holdout, but the issuer.

On the other hand, the potential holdout does create a problem for bondholders if the debtor's condition is so precarious that failure of the proposed workout will result in insolvency reorganization. To a greater or lesser extent, insolvency reorganization adds costs to the enterprise and therefore diminishes the amounts distributable to pre-bankruptcy claimants. If the power to hold out (that is, to decline to accept the proposed readjustment) is exercised by holders of a large portion of the debt so as to preclude the readjustment and the debtor is forced into bankruptcy reorganization, presumably all bondholders are worse off than if the proposed readjustment had been accepted.

Under what circumstances are potential holdouts likely to become actual holdouts, so as to endanger, or indeed preclude, the readjustment? Consider three scenarios. Under the first, a few bondholders believe that the readjustment price is too low, and seek to raise it for all bondholders by declining the tendered price. A second scenario involves a holdout who owns enough bonds to seek a voice in, or control of, the reorganized enterprise. Depending on the form of this governance intervention, this holder may achieve a greater return than the other bondholders receive. A third scenario also involves a holdout seeking a greater return than the other bondholders receive. This actor is a "bondmailer" who expects the vast bulk of the bondholders to accept the readjustment while it gets bought off by the issuer. Alternatively this actor might simply wait to take a larger claim (e.g., for $1,000) than those who accepted the $550 claim in any ensuing bankruptcy. In the first scenario, assuming a small number of holdouts, disruption occurs only with the assistance of section 316(b) of the Trust Indenture Act. The second scenario does not implicate section 316(b); it is the inevitable concomitant of a trading market in bonds. Holdout activity under the third scenario is indeed aided by section 316(b), and creates a larger possibility of failure of the workout because of the holdout's willingness to gamble with his, and the others,' money. The question is whether the cost of allowing such holdouts is greater than the benefits section 316(b) offers to those dispersed investors who are otherwise obliged to act collectively, and therefore are likely to be offered lower payouts in the proposed readjustment than if the section were repealed.

2. *Cash Payments.*

If instead of a tender offer at a premium to induce the bondholders to consent to elimination of protective covenants, the issuer offers simple cash payments (and retention of their bonds) to all who consent to such amendments and a bondholder challenges the offer, how will *Katz v. Oak Industries* apply? Does the cash offer make this case distinguishable, by analogy to the prohibition against the purchase and sale of the votes of stockholders? Kass v. Eastern Air Lines, Inc., 1986 WL 13008, 12 Del.J.Corp.L. 1074 (Del.Ch.1986), aff'd, 518 A.2d 983 (Del.1986), sanctions vote buying in the context of an offer made publicly to all bondholders on the same terms, but suggests that a paid solicitation to a limited number of bondholders might violate a good faith duty. Accord: Drage v. Santa Fe Pacific Corp., 1995 WL 396370 (Ohio Ct. App.).

Kahan and Tuckman, Do Bondholders Lose from Junk Bond Covenant Changes?, 66 J. Bus. 499 (1993), studies 58 consent solicitations in which an issuer of widely held debt requested the modification of existing covenants. The average payment offered in those solicitations exchanging the consent for cash was $20.51 per $1,000 face value. Evidence of the result of the solicitation was found for 52 of the cases, and in 83 percent of these the solicitation succeeded. A statistical survey of the prices of the issues showed that 29 of 42 issues, or 69 percent had positive abnormal returns around the time of the announcement of the transaction: The average abnormal bond return was 2.34 percent, while the average abnormal return for the stock of the issuer was 9.5 percent. Thus, the study showed that the solicitations increased the value of both the debt and the stock.

3. *Commentary.*

For differing analyses of, and proposed solutions for, the bondholders' problem, see Roe, supra, Coffee and Klein, supra, Kahan, The Qualified Case Against Mandatory Terms in Bonds, 89 Nw.U.L.Rev. 565 (1995); Brudney, Corporate Bondholders and Debtor Opportunism: In Bad Times and Good, 105 Harv.L.Rev. 1821 (1992), and Gertner and Scharfstein, A Theory of Workouts and the Effects of Reorganization Law, 46 J.Fin. 1189 (1991).

There is also an empirical literature. Some of the studies look at bank creditors. They show that so long as banks are fully secured they are unlikely to make concessions respecting payment but will relax covenants. Where distress is severe, the banks do make significant concessions and bank concessions make a successful public debt restructuring more likely. James, Bank Debt Restructurings and the Composition of Exchange Offers in Financial Distress, 51 J. Fin. 711 (1996); Asquith, Gertner, and Scharfstein, Anatomy of Financial Distress: An Examination of Junk Bond Issuers, 109 Q.J.Econ. 625 (1994). The latter paper also shows that firms making significant asset sales tend to avoid Chapter 11. Gilson, Transactions Costs and Capital Structure Choice: Evidence from Financially Distressed Firms, 52 J. Fin. 161 (1997), shows that out-of-court restructurings do not in general result in significant reductions in the proportion of debt in the capital structure. Finally, the holdout problem does not seem to be so severe as to prevent the accomplishment of restructurings respecting public debt, particularly given use of coercive devices like exit consents. Id.; Helwege, How Long Do Junk Bonds Spend in Default? 54 J. Fin. 341 (1999).

NOTE: VULTURE INVESTORS

There is an active market for trading claims of distressed companies. Major actors in this market are termed "vulture investors." These are wealthy individuals and hedge funds that speculate in the securities of distressed firms. Some vultures are passive investors who seek to profit by identifying undervalued claims. Others are "bondmailers" who buy blocks of claims and then hold out for premium distributions in reorganizations. Still others seek to profit by intervening in the management of the distressed firm. The question arises whether the benefits of governance improvements initiated by the third group outweigh the costs of disruption initiated by the second group.

Hotchkiss and Mooradian, Vulture Investors and the Market for Control of Distressed Firms, 43 J. Fin. Econ. 401 (1997), shows that the benefits can be substantial, without denying that bondmail can cause problems. The authors study 288 firms in distress between 1980 and 1993. They find vulture activity in 60 percent of the cases, with given vultures often accumulating more than one-third of the outstanding claims. These blockholding vultures can take seats on the board (28 percent of the cases) or become CEO or a majority stockholder (16.3 percent). In cases of active involvement the study shows evidence of better results. In other cases, the signal can be more ambiguous.

Do vulture investors who buy deeply-discounted bonds after default lack equity in legal contemplation as compared to investors who bought earlier at face value? **Leverso v. SouthTrust Bank of AL., N.A.**, 18 F.3d 1527 (11th Cir.1994), considers this question in the context of review of a post-default settlement agreement among a class of bondholders and an indenture trustee. The agreement included a distribution plan allocating the net settlement funds among the bondholders according to a pro rata share of the bondholders' cost basis, or the amount each bondholder paid for the bonds. Under this plan, bondholders who paid a higher amount for their bonds during the initial offering would receive a larger settlement than bondholders who paid a lesser amount in the secondary market after the initial offering and after the default. The district court approved the settlement, following Class Plaintiffs v. City of Seattle, 955 F.2d 1268 (9th Cir.), cert. denied, 506 U.S. 953 (1992), and South Carolina National Bank v. Stone, 749 F.Supp. 1419 (D.S.C.1990). The court of appeals reversed on the authority of the language of the trust indenture, 18 F.3d at 1534: "The plain language of several sections of the trust indenture, including the default section, unambiguously provides for each bond to be treated as every other bond. Nowhere in the trust indenture are distinctions made according to when the bond was purchased, the amount that was paid, or the circumstances under which it was purchased. Indeed, the terms of the trust indenture repeatedly state that no priority or distinction is to be made among the bonds.''

NOTE: PREPACKAGED BANKRUPTCY

The Bankruptcy Code contemplates the "prepackaged bankruptcy," a hybrid procedure that begins as a workout and ends as a chapter 11 reorganization. Section 1126(b) of the Bankruptcy Code, 11 U.S.C. § 1126(b), permits an issuer to conduct a binding vote on a plan of reorganization prior to filing for bankruptcy. In addition, section 1102(b)(1) allows a prepetition creditors committee to act as the committee in bankruptcy if it is representative of the claims and interests in the case, and section 1121(a) allows the debtor to file a plan with its chapter 11 petition. See Trost, Business Reorganization Under Chapter 11 of the New Bankruptcy Code, 34 Bus.Law. 1309, 1325 (1979). The statutory "prepackaged" bankruptcy, duly recognized by the courts, see In re TS Industries, Inc., 117 B.R. 682 (Bankr.D.Utah 1990); In re Colonial Ford, Inc., 24 B.R. 1014 (Bankr.D.Utah 1982), has influenced recapitalization practice. It allows a corporation in distress to take advantage of the chapter 11 creditor consent standard of two thirds in amount and one half in number. The debtor collects the consents to the plan before it files under chapter 11. When it files, it presents the preapproved reorganization plan for quick confirmation. With luck, the process is completed in a few months, or even more quickly.

This technique has the advantage of circumventing the holdout problem. The bankruptcy framework not only reduces the number of necessary consents, it provides that plans meeting its legal standards can be "crammed down" on nonconsenting creditors and classes of creditors. There also is a tax advantage. An exchange of old debt for new debt outside of bankruptcy by a solvent but distressed debtor results in its realization of cancellation of indebtedness income. In contrast, under Internal Revenue Code § 108(a), an economically equivalent recapitalization conducted in the bankruptcy context does not realize this income.

Prepackaged bankruptcies are very common. Between 1991 and 1997, they constituted 11.3 percent of the total bankruptcy filings made by publicly-traded companies. Eisenberg & LoPucki, Shopping for Judges: An Empirical Analysis of Venue Choice in the Bankruptcy Reorganization of Large Chapter 11 Reorganizations, 84 Cornell L.Rev. 967 (1999). See also LoPucki, Courting Failure: How Competition for Big Cases Is Corrupting the Bankruptcy Courts (2005). But as those figures imply, the practice is by no means universal. Some debtors still attempt to recapitalize privately, deterred by litigation uncertainties and possibilities of business impairment which remain intrinsic to the chapter 11 process. For example, a disclosure statement circulated in a prepackaged consent solicitation is subject to subsequent judicial review and rejection. A rejection leaves the debtor inside the chapter without a confirmed plan. See In re Colorado Springs Spring Creek Gen. Imp. Dist., 177 B.R. 684, 691 (Bankr.D.Colo.1995).

2. CREDIT DERIVATIVES

Eternity Global Master Fund Limited v. Morgan Guaranty Trust Company of New York

United States Court of Appeals, Second Circuit, 2004.
375 F.3d 168.

■ JACOBS, CIRCUIT JUDGE.

Plaintiff–Appellant Eternity Global Master Fund Limited ("Eternity" or "the Fund") purchased credit default swaps ("CDSs" or "the CDS contracts") from Defendants–Appellees Morgan Guaranty Trust Company of New York and JPMorgan Chase Bank (collectively, "Morgan") in October 2001. Eternity appeals from a final judgment entered in the United States District Court for the Southern District of New York (McKenna, J.), dismissing with prejudice its complaint alleging breach of contract * * *.

* * * For the reasons set forth below, we * * * reverse the dismissal of the contract claim and remand for further proceedings.

BACKGROUND

On behalf of its investors, Eternity trades in global bonds, equities and currencies, including emerging-market debt. During the relevant period, Eternity's investment portfolio included short-term Argentine sovereign and corporate bonds. In emerging markets such as Argentina, a significant credit risk is "country risk," i.e., "the risk that economic, social, and political conditions and events in a foreign country will adversely affect an institution's financial interests," including "the possibility of nationalization or expropriation of assets, government repudiation of external indebtedness, ... and currency depreciation or devaluation." Credit risk can be managed, however. Banks, investment funds and other institutions increasingly use financial contracts known as "credit derivatives" to mitigate credit risk. * * *

I

By way of introduction, we briefly review the terminology, documentation, and structure of Eternity's credit default swaps.

A.   Terminology

A credit default swap is the most common form of credit derivative, i.e., "[a] contract which transfers credit risk from a protection buyer to a credit protection seller." Protection buyers (here, Eternity) can use credit derivatives to manage particular market exposures and return-on-investment; and protection sellers (here, Morgan) generally use credit derivatives to earn income and diversify their own investment portfolios. Simply put, a credit default swap is a bilateral financial contract in which "[a] protection buyer makes periodic payments to ... the protection seller, in return for a contingent payment if a predefined credit event occurs in the reference credit," i.e., the obligation on which the contract is written.

Often, the reference asset that the protection buyer delivers to the protection seller following a credit event is the instrument that is being hedged. But in emerging markets, an investor may calculate that a particular credit risk "is reasonably correlated with the performance of [the sovereign] itself," so that (as here) the investor may seek to isolate and hedge country risk with credit default swaps written on some portion of the sovereign's outstanding debt.

In many contexts a "default" is a simple failure to pay; in a credit default swap, it references a stipulated bundle of "credit events" (such as bankruptcy, debt moratoria, and debt restructurings) that will trigger the protection seller's obligation to "settle" the contract via the swap mechanism agreed to between the parties. The entire bundle is typically made subject to a materiality threshold. The occurrence of a credit event triggers the "swap," i.e., the protection seller's obligation to pay on the contract according to the settlement mechanism. "The contingent payment can be based on cash settlement . . . or physical delivery of the reference asset, in exchange for a cash payment equal to the initial notional [i.e., face] amount [of the CDS contract]." A CDS buyer holding a sufficient amount of the reference credit can simply tender it to the CDS seller for payment; but ownership of the reference credit prior to default is unnecessary. If a credit event occurs with respect to the obligation(s) named in a CDS, and notice thereof has been given (and the CDS buyer has otherwise performed), the CDS seller must settle. Liquidity in a secondary market increases the usefulness of a CDS as a hedging tool, though the limited depth of that market "can make it difficult to offset . . . positions prior to contract maturity."

B. Documentation

The principal issue dividing the parties is whether the CDS contracts at issue are ambiguous in any material respect. * * *

In this case, we assess ambiguity in the disputed CDS contracts by looking to (i) the terms of the three credit default swaps; (ii) the terms of the International Swaps and Derivatives Association's ("ISDA" or "the Association") "Master Swap Agreement," on which those swaps are predicated, (iii) ISDA's 1999 Credit Derivatives Definitions—which are incorporated into the disputed contracts; and (iv) the background "customs, practices, [and] usages" of the credit derivatives trade. Because customs and usages matter, and because documentation promulgated by the ISDA was used by the parties to this dispute, we briefly review some relevant background.

The term "derivatives" references "a vast array of privately negotiated over-the counter . . . and exchange traded transactions," including interest-rate swaps, currency swaps, commodity price swaps and credit derivatives—which include credit default swaps. A derivative is a bilateral contract that is typically negotiated by phone and followed by an exchange of confirmatory faxes that constitute the contract but do not specify such terms as events of default, representations and warranties, covenants, liquidated damages, and choice of law. These (and other) terms are typically found in a "Master Swap Agreement," which, prior to standardization efforts that began in the mid–1980s, "took the form of separate 15–to 25–page agreements for each transaction."

Documentation of derivatives transactions has become streamlined, chiefly through industry adherence to "Master Agreements" promulgated by the ISDA. In 1999, Eternity and Morgan entered the ISDA Multicurrency–Cross Border Master Agreement, which governs, inter alia, the CDS transactions disputed on appeal. Each disputed CDS also incorporates the 1999 ISDA Credit Derivatives Definitions, the Association's first attempt at a comprehensive lexicon governing credit derivatives transactions. Last year, due to the rapid evolution of "ISDA documentation for credit default swaps," the Association began market implementation of the 2003 Credit Derivatives Definitions, which evidently constitutes a work in progress.

C.   Eternity's Credit Default Swaps

Eternity's Global Master Fund is managed by HFW Capital, L.P., including its Chief Investment Officer, Alberto Franco. In 2001, Franco engaged Morgan to facilitate Eternity's participation in the Argentine corporate debt market. Fearing that a government debt crisis would impair the value of Eternity's Argentine investments, Franco sought to hedge using credit default swaps written on Argentine sovereign bonds. In October 2001, the Fund entered into three such contracts. Each CDS incorporated (i) the ISDA Master Swap Agreement, and (ii) the 1999 ISDA Definitions. The total value of the contracts was $14 million * * *.

Except as to value and duration, the terms were virtually identical, as follows:

(i) Eternity would pay Morgan a fixed periodic fee tied to the notional value of each respective credit default swap.

(ii) The swaps would be triggered upon occurrence of any one of four credit events—as defined by the 1999 ISDA Credit Derivative Definitions—with respect to the Argentine sovereign bonds: Failure to pay, Obligation Acceleration, Repudiation/Moratorium, and Restructuring.

(iii) Each CDS called for physical settlement following a credit event, specifically: (a) Upon notification (by either party to the other) of a credit event, and confirmation via two publicly available sources of information (e.g., the Wall Street Journal), and (b) delivery to Morgan of the requisite amount of Argentine sovereign bonds, (c) Morgan would pay Eternity par value for the obligations tendered. * * *

The parties dispute whether any of certain actions taken by Argentina with respect to its debt obligations in November and December 2001 constituted a credit event. The district court thought not, and dismissed Eternity's contract claim at the pleading stage. * * *

II

* * *

The contracts at issue were signed in October 2001. By then, international financial markets had been speculating for months that Argentina might default on its $132 billion in government and other public debt. At an August 2001 meeting of bondholders in New York, Morgan acknowledged the possibility of a sovereign-debt default and advised that it was working with the Argentine government on restructuring scenarios. On October 31, 2001—after the effective date of the swap contracts at issue on this appeal—Morgan sent Eternity a research report noting that there was a "high implied probability of [a] restructuring" in which bondholders would likely receive replacement securities with a less-favorable rate of return. One day later, Argentine President Fernando de la Rua asked sovereign-bond holders to accept lower interest rates and longer maturities on approximately $95 billion of government debt.

On November 19, 2001, the Argentine government announced that a "voluntary debt exchange" would be offered to sovereign-bond holders. According to various public decrees, willing bondholders could exchange their obligations for secured loans that would pay a lower rate of return over a longer term, but that would be secured by certain federal tax revenues. So long as the government made timely payments on the loans, the original obligations would be held in trust for the benefit of Argentina; if the government defaulted, however, bondholders would have recourse to the original obligations, which were to "remain effective" for the duration of their life-in-trust. From late November through early December 2001, billions of dollars in sovereign bonds were exchanged for the lower-interest loans.

The complaint alleges that the debt exchange amounted to a default because local creditors had no choice but to participate, and that the financial press adopted that characterization. On November 8, 2001 Eternity served the first of three notices on Morgan asserting that the planned debt exchange was a restructuring credit event as to all three CDS contracts; but Morgan demurred.

On December 24, newly-installed interim President Adolfo Rodriguez Saa—appointed by the Argentine Congress on December 23 to replace President de la Rua—announced a public-debt moratorium. On December 27, Morgan notified Eternity that the moratorium constituted a credit event and subsequently settled the outstanding $2 million and $9 million credit default swaps (otherwise set to terminate on October 22, 2006 and March 31, 2002, respectively). According to Morgan, the third swap (valued at $3 million) had expired without being triggered, on December 17, 2001.

It is undisputed that the December 24 public-debt moratorium was a trigger of Eternity's outstanding swaps; in Eternity's view, however, the voluntary debt exchange had triggered Morgan's settlement obligations as early as November 8, 2001, as the Fund had been insisting throughout November and December of that year. In that same period, Eternity asked Morgan to liquidate the swaps on a secondary market. Notwithstanding Morgan's representations in February 2001 regarding the existence of a secondary market for the CDSs, it refused to quote Eternity any secondary-market pricing, though it did offer to "unwind" the contracts by returning the premiums Eternity had paid from October through November 2001.

DISCUSSION

* * *

I

* * * The district court concluded that * * * the plain meaning of the CDS contracts conveyed the parties' unambiguous intention to exclude the voluntary debt exchange from the bundle of government actions that could qualify as a restructuring credit event. We disagree.

The question is whether at this stage it can be decided as a matter of law that the voluntary debt exchange was not a "restructuring credit event" covered by the Fund's CDS contracts with Morgan. Resolution of that issue turns on what the CDS contracts say. * * * But resolution of the dispositive question—whether the parties intended that an event such as the voluntary debt exchange would qualify as a restructuring credit event—is not possible at this early stage of the litigation.

A.   The 1999 ISDA Definition of "Restructuring" and the Terms of Argentina's Voluntary Debt Exchange

* * * By their terms, Eternity's credit default swaps could be triggered by any of four credit events: Failure to Pay, Obligation Acceleration, Repudiation/Moratorium, and Restructuring. To flesh out these terms, Eternity and Morgan incorporated by reference the 1999 ISDA Credit Derivatives Definitions. Eternity concedes that Argentina's voluntary debt exchange is a credit event only if it qualifies as a restructuring under § 4.7 of the 1999 Definitions:

> "Restructuring" means that, with respect to one or more Obligations, including as a result of an Obligation Exchange, ... any one or more of the following events occurs * * *: (i) a reduction in the rate or amount of interest payable or the amount of scheduled interest accruals; (ii) a reduction in the amount of principal or premium payable at maturity or at scheduled redemption dates; (iii) a postponement or other deferral of a date or dates for either (A) the payment or accrual of interest or (B) the payment of principal or premium; (iv) a change in the ranking in priority of payment of any Obligation, causing the subordination of such Obligation; or (v) any change in the currency or composition of any payment of interest or principal.

The "obligations" relevant to Eternity's credit default swaps are Argentine sovereign bonds.

* * *

B.   The Voluntary Debt Exchange as a Restructuring Credit Event

Eternity contends that Argentina's voluntary debt exchange qualifies as a restructuring credit event in four ways: (i) as an obligation exchange under § 4.9 of the 1999 Definitions that constituted a "restructuring" under § 4.7; and even if not an obligation exchange, as an (ii) extension, and/or (iii) deferral, and/or (iv) subordination of the original obligations such that those obligations were restructured within the meaning of § 4.7. Morgan counters, and the district court agreed, that the voluntary debt exchange was not a restructuring within the meaning of the CDS contracts because it was not an obligation exchange, nor did it affect the payment, value, or priority of the original obligations.

(i) The voluntary debt exchange as an "Obligation Exchange"

Under the 1999 Definitions, an "Obligation Exchange" is "the mandatory transfer ... of any securities, obligations or assets to holders of Obligations in exchange for such Obligations. When so transferred, such securities, obligations or assets will be deemed to be Obligations." 1999

Definitions, § 4.9. Section 4.7 states that an "Obligation Exchange" can qualify as a restructuring, and further provides:

> If an Obligation Exchange has occurred, the determination as to whether one of the events described under Section 4.7(a)(I) to (v) has occurred will be based on a comparison of the terms of the Obligation immediately before such Obligation Exchange and the terms of the resulting Obligation immediately following such Obligation Exchange.

Thus if the voluntary debt exchange is an "Obligation Exchange," then it is a restructuring if the terms of the Secured Loans—as compared with the terms of the exchanged sovereign bonds—indicate that "one of the events [that constitutes a restructuring under § 4.7] has occurred." Morgan concedes that such a comparison would show that the voluntary debt exchange was a restructuring credit event: The secured loans undeniably provide a lower return over a longer maturity than the original bonds, two features that qualify as restructuring occurrences under § 4.7.

Morgan argues, however, that because § 4.9 of the 1999 Definitions states that an "Obligation Exchange" is a "mandatory transfer" of one set of obligations for another, and because participation in the government's debt exchange program was "voluntary," a comparison of the two instruments is irrelevant.

The term "mandatory transfer" as it appears in § 4.9 of the ISDA definitions is not self-reading, and is therefore ambiguous if it could suggest more than one meaning when viewed objectively, in the context of each CDS agreement and the "customs, practices, [and] usages ... as generally understood" in the credit derivatives trade. Morgan makes the intuitively appealing argument that a "mandatory transfer" cannot be an exchange offered on "voluntary terms." The district court was persuaded by this argument, citing Black's Law Dictionary * * *.

Eternity makes the less obvious but plausible argument that to credit-risk protection buyers such as itself, a "mandatory transfer" includes any obligation exchange achieved by "economic coercion," regardless of its classification as "voluntary" or "mandatory" by the initiating party. According to Black's, "economic coercion" is "[c]onduct that constitutes improper use of economic power to compel another to submit to the wishes of one who wields it." Black's Law Dictionary 252 (7th ed.1999). Assuming that the government's debt exchange was economically coercive, "voluntary" participation by the "coerced" bondholders appears to resemble "mandatory" action. At the same time, from Argentina's perspective, the exchange may have been voluntary in fact, i.e., the government may have had the intention to honor its debt obligations to nonparticipants without delay or reduction. But Argentina's characterization—which is self-serving—does not control, particularly when one considers Eternity's allegation that Morgan was an architect of the debt exchange. A proper interpretation of the CDS contracts must be drawn from the contract language and, where necessary, from other indicia of the parties' intent. Section 4.9 is silent as to whose perspective dictates whether an obligation exchange has occurred (e.g., the issuer or the holder, or the investment press or community), and the parties' competing interpretations are plausible. We cannot resolve that ambiguity at this stage, as the district court took no submissions on the customs and usages of the credit derivatives industry, and the parties point us to no definitive source that resolves the difficulty.

Although the CDS contracts are silent on the precise meaning of "mandatory transfer," the ISDA has not ignored the issue. In its complaint, Eternity refers to a draft "User's Guide" to the 1999 Definitions, publication of which appears to have been tabled indefinitely. The draft guide explained that the "reference to 'mandatory transfer' in [the] definition of ['Obligation Exchange'] . . . should be read as clarifying rather than restricting the Restructuring definition and should not be read to mean that the optional exchange of Obligations for other assets cannot constitute a Restructuring." The User's Guide to the 1999 Definitions was never formally promulgated, but it does indicate that, (at least) as of the time Eternity purchased the credit default swaps, the meaning of "mandatory transfer" was perhaps more open-ended than Morgan contends.

Finally, in drawing its conclusion that the voluntary debt exchange was not an obligation exchange, the district court appears to have relied on its observation that Eternity "made a choice "to participate in the voluntary debt exchange. Any such reliance was misplaced. Whether Eternity actually owned Argentina's sovereign bonds (and whether it chose to participate in the government's debt swap if it did) is irrelevant to whether the exchange was a restructuring credit event under the disputed CDS contracts. The swaps were triggered if the government defaulted on its own debt obligations, i.e., upon the occurrence of a "credit event" with respect to those obligations as a class. The CDS contracts did not require or contemplate that the credit protection buyer (here, Eternity) would hold the reference bonds except as may become necessary to exercise the put. Thus, if the Argentine government's voluntary debt exchange was a restructuring within the meaning of the 1999 Definitions, the CDS contracts were triggered; any election Eternity might have made with respect to its own bond holdings does not matter.

We go on to consider Eternity's arguments that the government's debt exchange was a restructuring even if it was not an obligation exchange.

(ii) The effect of the voluntary debt exchange on Argentina's original debt obligations

Under the 1999 Definitions, a restructuring credit event occurs when any one of five enumerated events "occurs, is agreed [to] . . . or is announced" with respect to an "obligation" upon which a credit default swap is written. 1999 Definitions, supra, § 4.7(a). These include: (i) a reduction in the rate of payable interest or principal on the obligation; (ii) a postponement of payment on interest or principal; and (iii) a subordination of the obligation that did not exist prior to the occurrence of the restructuring credit event. Eternity contends that each of these three events "occurred" with respect to certain classes of Argentine sovereign bonds as a consequence of the government's voluntary debt exchange.

The district court held that "under the terms of the 'voluntary debt exchange,' the obligations submitted into the Trust . . . themselves remained unchanged." That observation may be sound as far as it goes. But § 4.7 provides that a restructuring results if any event defined in the section "occurs" with respect to "one or more obligations." Thus, the proper inquiry is whether the debt exchange caused a restructuring to occur with respect to any of the Argentine sovereign bonds. For the purpose of this analysis, it is useful to consider separately the impact of the debt exchange on obligations that were exchanged pursuant to the government's "voluntary" offer (participating obligations), and on those retained by sovereign-bond holders who elected to forgo the government's program (nonparticipating obligations). To negative the possibility that there was a restructuring credit event, it must be clear that none of the "events" described in § 4.7 occurred with respect either to the participating obligations or to the nonparticipating obligations.

(a) Participating Obligations

Participating obligations were ultimately deposited with the Central Bank of the Republic of Argentina * * *. [The loans that replaced the bonds tendered in the exchange were governed by a Secured Loan Agreement; a Trust Agreement governed the status of the obligations tendered.] Eternity contends that a restructuring credit event occurred with respect to tendered obligations because their terms were extended and/or payment was suspended for the duration of their life-in-trust.

* * * [Eternity further contends that the terms governing the exchange effectively suspended Argentina's liability on the bonds held in trust] because (i) former bondholders could not enforce the original instruments while they were held in trust; and (ii) Argentina's role as both beneficiary and obligor on the trust assets suspended, at least temporarily, any enforceable legal obligation created by those debt instruments. We think that there is a question, at least on the present record, as to whether this trust mechanism constituted "postponement or other deferral of a date or dates for payment of those obligations," within the meaning of § 4.7(a)(iii).

* * *

(b) Nonparticipating obligations

Eternity alleges that at some point during the voluntary debt exchange process, Argentina's Economy Minister announced that the "restructured loans held domestically will have the highest priority for payment." According to Eternity, this announcement "effectively" subordinated the original obligations to the secured loans, and was thus a credit event under § 4.7, which includes "a change in the ranking in priority of payment of any Obligation, causing the subordination of such Obligation." 1999 Definitions § 4.7(a)(iv). Morgan disagrees, primarily on the ground that there is no language in the "Domestic Exchange that changes the rank in priority of payment on the existing Obligations."

* * * Section 4.7(a)(iv) of the 1999 Definitions, which says that "subordination" is a reduction "in the ranking in priority of payment of any Obligation," does not in terms exclude policy declarations such as the one allegedly announced by Argentina's Economy Minister. True, "subordina-

tion" may denote more limited circumstances, such as a formal, contractual subordination of a particular debt. But that reading is not compelled by the wording of § 4.7(a)(iv).

The ISDA promulgated a "Restructuring Supplement" to the 1999 Definitions in April 2001 which included * * * a provision that speaks directly to the definition of "subordination" under § 4.7(a)(iv):

> For purposes of Sections [sic] 4.7(a)(iv), "a change in the ranking in priority of payment of any Obligation, causing the subordination of such Obligation," means only the following: an amendment to the terms of such Obligation or other contractual arrangement pursuant to which the requisite percentage of holders of such Obligations ("Subordinated Holders") agree that, upon the liquidation, dissolution, reorganization or winding up of the Reference Entity, claims of holders of any other Obligations will be satisfied prior to the claims of Subordinated Holders. For the avoidance of doubt, the provision of collateral, credit support or credit enhancement with respect to any obligation will not, of itself, constitute a change in the ranking in priority of payment of any Obligation causing the subordination of such Obligation.

The Eternity/Morgan CDS contracts incorporate the 1999 Definitions, but do not appear to incorporate the Restructuring Supplement, which must be invoked specifically. If the Supplement had been included, the subordination issue would likely be settled (in Morgan's favor); but the version of § 4.7(a)(iv) in use here is insufficiently clear as to whether subordination can be effected by policy statements such as the one cited by Eternity. Eternity and Morgan will have to resolve the issue in discovery or, if necessary, before a trier of fact.

NOTE: CREDIT DERIVATIVES

1. *The Contracts and the Counterparties.*

Credit derivatives, developed in the 1990s, are contracts that condition one party's obligation to pay on the occurrence of a "credit event" (such as a default or a credit rating downgrade) on a debt contract. In this Note the counterparties will be categorized as the "risk seller" and the "risk buyer." (A number of alternative terms show up in practice—the risk seller is also the "protection buyer" and the risk buyer is the "protection seller.") Each contract involves a third party whose non-performance causes a credit event to occur; this party is the "reference entity" and the specific obligation upon which its performance is relevant is the "reference obligation" or "reference asset." In effect, one counterparty sells insurance to the other counterparty against the default of a third party. Historically, such contracts have been termed financial guarantees.

Broadly speaking, the risk sellers in credit derivative contracts are banks and bond investors—entities in need of protection from credit risk. If a borrower (reference entity) defaults, these entities suffer the loss of the borrower's promised payments; if, short of default, a borrower's creditworthiness deteriorates, the loans and bonds in their portfolios decline in value. Historically, banks and bond investors holding large amounts of illiquid debt instruments have used other means to manage credit risk, like loan underwriting standards, diversification, securitization, and loan sales. Credit derivatives compensate for perceived shortcomings in these mechanisms. A bank that diversifies its risk by selling a loan may destabilize its relationship with the borrower. It is difficult, for example, to sell a loan and simultaneously maintain confidentiality respecting a client's financial records. A credit derivative lets the bank reduce its exposure while maintaining the relationship. Selling a bond or note also can trigger adverse tax or accounting results; derivatives avoid these tax and accounting realizations. Administrative costs also are lower. Finally, credit derivatives assist banks in meeting capital adequacy requirements.

Commercial banks and insurance companies also figure prominently among the risk buyers. Credit derivatives allow them to diversify their credit exposures. For example, Bank A specializes in lending to cyclical Industry X, and possesses valuable expertise respecting Industry X; Bank B specializes in lending to counter-cyclical Industry Y and possesses valuable expertise respecting Industry Y. The loan portfolios of both banks are underdiversified. A beneficial portfolio effect would follow if Bank A owned Industry Y loans and Bank B owned Industry X loans. But diversification through direct lending requires a substantial investment by Bank A in information respecting Industry Y and by Bank B respecting Industry X. Credit derivatives offer an attractive alternative. Bank B buys a part of the risks of the portfolio held by Bank A, and vice versa, each paying a fee to the other and each avoiding the costs of restructuring their own portfolios. Both banks have diversified their risks. Both also have diversified their returns—for Bank A, the fees generated as risk buyer respecting Bank B's portfolio is a return from Bank B's portfolio.

Corporations, money managers, mutual funds, and pension funds also are credit derivative risk buyers, joined by the hedge funds as the largest buy-side sector. For some of these entities, credit derivatives allow access to credit markets otherwise off-limits by regulation. In addition, some risk buyers use credit derivatives when executing arbitrage strategies–they might, for example, be exploiting pricing discrepancies between bank loans and subordinated debt of the same issuer.

There are four major types of credit derivatives: credit default swaps, total return swaps, credit spread options, and credit-linked debt. Each of these contracts allow one party to transfer to another party a credit risk associated with a debt obligation.

Credit default swaps, which make up 95 percent of the market, amount to contingent put options. Here is a simple example. Assume that the reference obligation is a bond trading at face value and maturing in two years. The risk seller holds the bond. It agrees to make quarterly payments to the risk buyer for two years, calculated as a stated number of basis points on the face value of the reference obligation. The risk seller is the owner of the swap and, in exchange for its quarterly payments, it gets the right, in the event of a payment default on the bond, to put the bond to the risk buyer in exchange for the bond's par value and the interest payments. If the bond never defaults, the risk seller's yield is the payment stream on the bond minus the fixed payments on the swap. If the bond does default, the risk seller is in exactly the same position it would have been in had the bond never defaulted—the promised payments on the bond minus the fixed payments on the swap.

This hypothetical swap fully hedges the bondholder-risk seller—its long position in the bond now is matched by a short position through the swap. The swap puts the risk buyer into a long position on the bond. (To hedge, the risk buyer needs to short the bond. To effect that hedge, it borrows the bond in the repo markets. This carries the duty to pay the interest on the bond but also entails lending the face value of the bond. The difference between the outflow of the payment stream on the bond and the (lower) interest received on the loan is the cost of the hedge.)

In practice, the risk seller usually is not fully hedged and the risk buyer does not take on the full market risk of the reference obligation. The reason is that the derivative contract's term usually is shorter than that of the reference obligation. Contracts also can be much more complicated than the one just hypothesized. An entire portfolio of bonds or loans may be covered, with the risk seller receiving a payoff if more than a pre-specified number of bonds defaults.

Total return swaps are contracts in which the risk seller sends the payment stream on a reference asset, through an intermediary, to the risk buyer. Both counterparties are likely to be banks. The risk buying bank, in return for payment stream on the reference asset, gives the risk selling bank a guaranteed loan paying a specified fixed or floating cash flow that is not related to the creditworthiness of the reference asset. The risk seller transfers to the risk buyer the "total return" on the reference asset, including not only the payments actually received but in addition any appreciation in the reference asset's market value. The risk buyer takes the risk of a decline in the principal value of the reference asset in addition to that attached to the stated periodic payments: It agrees to pay the risk seller the difference between the face value of the contract and the dealer price of the reference asset, which of course moves downward in the event of negative changes in the credit profile of the reference entity. Note that the dealer price of the reference asset also declines if market sentiment causes credit spreads to widen. Herein lies the basic difference between a total return swap and a credit default swap—the credit default swap protects against loss in value due to specified credit events where the total return swap protects against loss in value irrespective of cause. Total return swaps thus replicate the results of loan sales.

Credit spread options require the risk buyer to make a payment to the risk seller in the event a "credit spread" widens enough to reach a "trigger point." A credit spread might be the difference between the risk-free interest rate and the interest rate paid by the reference entity (or reference obligation). Alternatively, the credit spread can be the difference between the yields of debt securities of two different issuers or two obligations of the same issuer bearing different maturities. Whatever the two securities defining the credit spread, the trigger point will tend to be reached in the event of a downgrade in the reference entity's credit rating. This device being an option rather than a swap, the risk seller pays a premium to the risk buyer and obtains a right to sell the reference asset to the risk buyer if the spread reaches the trigger point.

Credit-linked notes incorporate the risk insurance features of credit derivatives directly into debt securities. Here the risk seller is the note issuer (borrower) and the risk buyer is the note purchaser (lender). As with conventional debt securities, the issuer promises to pay periodic interest and to repay principal at maturity. But the principal also becomes due if a credit event, such as a deterioration of a specified financial variable, occurs prior to maturity. In the latter event, a reduced principal amount becomes due. In effect, then, the credit linked note's issuer (borrower) purchases credit insurance from the note holder (lender); in return, the holder earns a higher yield than would be available on a plain vanilla debt security of the same issuer. *Credit-linked deposits* are similar. Here the risk seller is a bank and the risk buyer is a bank depositor. The risk buyer deposits a principal amount into an account with the risk seller, agreeing to forfeit some or all of the account balance should there occur a specified credit event at a reference entity. The forfeitable deposit insures the risk seller; the risk buyer gets a premium yield on the deposit.

Synthetic Collateralized Debt Obligations. Recall that the securitization process can entail the collection of existing debt obligations of various issuers into an SPE that in turn issues its own debt securities. Such an arrangement can be replicated synthetically with credit default swaps. Here the SPE enters into credit default swaps as the risk buyer with counterparties wishing to sell the risk of given corporate debt issues. The SPE then issues its own debt securities, which are backed by the payment stream on the swaps.

2.   Eternity Global *and the ISDA Agreement.*

Argentina had a good reason to make its "self serving" description of the exchange offer as voluntary—a mandatory exchange would have amounted to an event of default under the contracts in question. It took the position that the security of the dedicated tax revenues made the substitute obligations the economic equivalents of the original bonds despite the reduction in interest rate. The rating agencies and a number of analysts disagreed on the ground that Argentina's tax revenues were declining rapidly. The analysts also rejected the "voluntary" characterization on the ground that a nontendering bondholder would be subject to greater risk than a tendering bondholder. See Faiola, Argentine Debt Downgraded, Wash. Post, Nov. 7, 2001 at E1. The exchange was in fact mandatory for some holders, in particular Argentina's domestic banks, which were ordered to participate. In addition, Argentina did state its intent to treat untendered bonds on a subordinated basis. See Salmon, Sovereign Markets Await Court Verdicts, Euromoney, May 2002 at 34.

The ISDA sided with the Morgan on the question raised in the case and eliminated the term "Obligation Exchange" from the 2003 revision of the definition of "Restructuring." For further discussion of the case, see Choi & Gulati, Contract as Statute, 104 Mich. L. Rev. 1129, 1142–1144 (2006).

A 2003 Fitch Report on synthetic collateralized debt obligations identified 112 credit events between 2000 and January 1, 2003. Of these, 94.5 percent resulted either from the "Bankruptcy" or "Failure to pay" triggers, while only 3.3 percent fell under "Restructuring." Note that the derivatives in question in *Eternity Global* did not contain the "Bankruptcy" credit event—sovereign borrowers, unlike corporate borrowers, have no bankruptcy option.

For other litigation respecting an ISDA credit swap contract respecting a sovereign obligation, see Aon Financial Products, Inc. v. Societe Generale, 476 F.3d 90 (2d Cir.2007).

Finally, note a point made in the *Eternity Global* opinion—the risk sellers do not necessarily own the bonds covered by the swap. This can lead to problems when, in the wake of a credit event, they have to procure the bonds to put them to the risk buyer. Strange things can happen in the bond market at that point. Risk sellers needing the bonds go in to the market on buy side, driving up the price of a newly defaulted bond. **Deutsche Bank v. AMBAC Credit Products, LLC**, 2006 WL 1867497 (S.D.N.Y.), bears on this phenomenon. There Deutsche Bank was both a risk seller and a risk buyer respecting bonds of a newly bankrupt company. On its risk buy side, it was awaiting bonds put by its risk sellers. On its risk sell side it needed the bonds to put them over its risk buyer. The put bonds came in slowly from Deutsche Bank's risk sellers, causing it to miss a contractual due date for putting its bonds to its own risk buyer. The buyer took the position that the failure to meet the due date was a failure of condition that discharged its obligation on the swap. The court agreed, rejecting Deutsche Bank's reference to an industry practice of late delivery and claimed violation of a good faith duty.

The ISDA announced a new cash settlement protocol in 2006. Assuming it is effective, the *AMBAC Credit* problem should not recur.

3.   *Risks and Policy Questions.*

Credit derivatives hold out a number of significant risks.

First come the inherent risks—credit and counterparty risk. Credit risk—the risk of default (or other triggering event) respecting the reference asset—is assumed by the risk buyer. It must be dealt with the old fashioned way—through diligence:

The risk buyer should carefully evaluate and monitor the reference asset. Counter-party risk—the risk that the risk buyer will default on the derivative contract–is assumed by the risk seller. For the risk seller this implies review and monitoring of the risk buyer's financial condition.

Next come two avoidable risks, termed "strategic" and "operational." Strategic risk is the risk of speculative use by imprudent, aggressive traders—hedge funds, primarily—looking for high short-term returns. Derivative speculation also implies liquidity risk. Credit derivatives are over-the-counter (OTC) instruments—as opposed to exchange-traded instruments. If a bet goes wrong, there will not necessarily be recourse to fast exit in a trading market. (This is not a problem when the derivative is used for hedging purposes.) Operational risk is the risk of improper implementation. Credit derivative contracts are complex and have evolved very rapidly. It follows that agents of risk buyers may commit without fully understanding the contract's features and the degree of risk assumed. Either way, diligence once again is the palliative. Risk buying calls for considered decisionmaking by senior managers and boards of directors and strict internal controls.

The credit derivatives market has in fact experienced growing pains. *Eternity Global Master Fund v. Morgan Guaranty Trust* shows that standard documentation is not yet free of ambiguity on critical terms. The International Swaps and Derivatives Association responded to the case by modifying the forms. It also is developing a uniform procedure for settlement in the wake of a credit event. Meanwhile, the dealer firm infrastructures have not kept up with market volume, resulting in widespread confirmation delays. The Federal Reserve intervened in 2005, and the traders now report substantial progress toward the creation of an automated market for less complicated transactions.

Credit derivatives also hold out legal risks. Due to their relative novelty, the underlying concepts and basic terms of OTC derivative contracts have not been tested in the courts. Risk sellers accordingly need to be aware that a counterparty facing large losses may resort to legal defenses to avoid paying on the contract. See Norman Menachem Feder, Deconstructing Over-the-Counter Derivatives, 2002 Colum. Bus. L. Rev. 677, 717 (2002); Robert S. Neal, Credit Derivatives: New Financial Instruments for Controlling Credit Risk, Economic Review of the Federal Reserve Bank of Kansas City; Second Quarter 1996, 15, 25.

Despite the risks, credit derivative usage has increased substantially. The credit derivatives market, nonexistent in 1993, had a $20 billion notional amount by 1995. Id. at 15. The 1997–1998 Asian credit crisis enhanced the instruments' reputation—they were held to have "performed more efficiently * * * than the underlying bond market." André Scheerer, Credit Derivatives: An Overview of Regulatory Initiatives in the U.S. and Europe, 5 Fordham J. Corp. & Fin. L. 149, 152 (2000). By 2000, the credit derivatives market was estimated to have reached a notional $1.5 trillion. Ian Bell & Petrina Dawson, Synthetic Securitization: Use of Derivative Technology for Credit Transfer, 12 Duke J. Comp. & Int'l L. 541, 551 (2002). Things really took off thereafter. The International Swaps and Derivatives Association reported a 44 percent increase on notional amounts in the first half of 2004, compared with a 33 percent growth reported during the second half of 2003. In 2004, the British Bankers Association predicted the global market to rise to $8.2 trillion notional amount by the end of 2006. It underestimated. The notional amount outstanding in 2006 was $17.1 trillion. As of June 30, 2007, the figure was $26 trillion.

Do credit derivatives create systemic problems? Arguments go back and forth. Partnoy and Skeel, The Promise and Perils of Credit Derivatives, 76 U. Cinn. L. Rev. 1019 (2007), catalogs the benefits and detriments as follows. On the benefit side, (1) credit derivatives assist banks in diversifying risks and serve as shock absorbers during credit crises; (2) credit derivatives import more liquidity into the banking system by facilitating lending at lower risk; (3) credit derivatives are entered into under an efficient standardized form that is monitored and improved by a vigilant trade group; and (4) credit derivatives provide an additional informational window into the creditworthiness of a given borrower. On the detriment side, (1) credit derivatives reduce the incentives of banks to monitor their borrowers (the case of Enron is cited); (2) credit derivatives create opportunities for strategic play respecting distressed companies; (3) the credit derivative market is opaque; and (4) credit derivatives add to systemic risk, primarily due to positions taken by hedge funds in search of short-term profits.

As to detriment point (2), the authors mention the Towers Automotive bankruptcy of 2004. Towers, in distress, needed concessions from its bank lenders respecting the property securing the loan. The banks were willing to accommodate it. But a hedge fund in the lending group refused to go along and bankruptcy followed. It was claimed that the hedge fund refused because bankruptcy enhanced the value of its short position in the company's stock. The hedge fund denied the allegation. See Sender, Hedge Funds Shake Up Lending Arena, Wall. St. J., July 18, 2005. Note that credit derivatives played no role in this interesting story.

Here are some questions asked by Treasury Assistant Secretary for Financial Institutions Emil Henry at the Federal Reserve Bank of Atlanta on April 18, 2006, available at http://www.treas.gov/press/releases/js4187.htm:

"Regarding systemic risks, I am on record suggesting that Treasury should stay abreast of systemic concerns. I believe our time is best spent addressing the nexus of hedge funds and the OTC derivatives markets, especially credit derivatives. There has been much superb effort by policy makers outside the Treasury and private groups to address this market segment. Many of these efforts are focused on market infrastructure and operational risk. And there has been significant progress.

"But there is [sic] broader financial stability issues associated with credit derivatives, particularly as it regards hedge funds. Many questions need to be explored:

- Where are financial institutions in danger of getting their risk management rubric wrong? Namely, are some credit derivative transactions becoming so complex that internal risk models * * * are unreliable when it comes to certain trades? * * *
- What are the unintended consequences of hedge fund growth on competition for lending and the provision of private equity?
- Do our largest financial institutions properly value and disclose their derivative exposure?
- Do large counterparties take false comfort in their individual exposure to and collateral with an individual hedge fund when there is little transparency on the broader financial community's aggregate exposure to that very same fund?
- Is the settlement infrastructure—even with recent attention and modification—able to handle the current volume of activity?
- Can the regulatory regime keep pace with the quickly evolving marketplace?
- Will our oversight system devolve into tacit acceptance of the risk metrics they are provided by large counterparties for the most complex transactions?
- As prime brokerage grows to meet the needs of the hedge fund community, will such providers increase leverage and relax collateral requirements as these are their principal means of competition?"

3. CREDITOR PROTECTION IN LAW

Our legal system for the most part leaves the problem of risky capital structure for solution in the marketplace. We leave it to managers to decide what level of debt is best for their stockholders and to creditors to decide whether to lend, and, if so, on what terms. We then provide an elaborate bankruptcy regime to pick up the pieces ex post in cases where these accumulated business judgments go wrong. But there also are select zones in which positive law intervenes to control business judgments relating to capital structure, whether by limiting amounts of debt, mandating a minimum equity floor, or constraining the opportunistic behavior of highly levered borrowers.

(A) REGULATION OF CAPITAL STRUCTURE

We have seen that derivatives create new possibilities for excessive risk taking with potential adverse consequences for investors and the stability of the economy as a whole. We also have seen that regulatory responses center on disclosure mandates and self regulation pursuant to broad governance standards articulated by government agencies or industry groups.

Regulators in the past employed stricter means in confronting situations where risky capital structure was thought to implicate the public interest.

(1) Public Utilities

One method was direct ex ante control by an administrative agency operating under a broad legislative standard. This was the approach taken with public utilities holding service monopolies. Monopoly provision implied a public need for price regulation. Price regulation in turn meant regulatory review of the utility's cost basis, and the costs in question included the utility's cost of capital. The utility went a state public commission to request a given rate, requesting a financial return on its service that covered its costs, including the cost of borrowing, and also provided a reasonable return for its equity investors. It followed that the regulator, as it sought to protect the public from excessive rates, needed to control the utility's capital structure decisions. Movement toward competitive service provision and accompanying deregulation over the last 30 years makes such regulation less salient. The thing to note is that these regimes exist less to control corporate financial risk *per se*, than as an incident of price regulation.

Compare the Public Utility Holding Company Act of 1935 (PUHCA), 15 U.S.C. § 79 et seq., repealed by § 1263 of the Energy Policy Act of 2005, Pub. L. 109–58, 119 Stat. 594, a federal statute that covered electric utilities operating across state lines. The PUCHA was enacted during the Depression, when many of the complicated and highly levered public utility holding company capital structures created during the 1920s proved dysfunctional. Under the PUCHA, the SEC dismantled and reorganized the pyramid structures and regulated the revised capital structures on an ongoing basis. The PUCHA, then, was expressly directed to risk control. Section 6 provided that utilities could issue securities only with the permission of the SEC. Section 7(d) provided that a request to issue securities would be denied, *inter alia*, if the SEC found that "(1) the security is not reasonably adapted to the security structure of the declarant and other companies in the same holding-company system; (2) the security is not reasonably adapted to the earning power of the declarant; or (3) financing by the issue and sale of the particular security is not necessary or appropriate to the economical and efficient operation of a business in which the applicant lawfully is engaged or has an interest." What exactly constituted "reasonable adaptation" or a "necessary or appropriate" financing was left to the risk preferences of the SEC.

(2) Investment Companies

Another Depression-era statute, the Investment Company Act of 1940, follows a different strategy, imposing a hard ratio test in the manner of a debt covenant. In § 18 (a), 15 U.S.C. § 80a–18(a), it provides for closed-end investment companies as follows:

> Sec. 18. (a) It shall be unlawful for any registered closed-end company to issue any class of senior security, or to sell any such security of which it is the issuer, unless—
>
> (1) if such class of senior security represents an indebtedness—
>
> (A) immediately after such issuance or sale, it will have an asset coverage of at least 300 per centum; and
>
> (B) provision is made to prohibit the declaration of any dividend (except a dividend payable in stock of the issuer), or the declaration of any other distribution, upon any class of the capital stock of such investment company, or the purchase of any such capital stock, unless, in every such case, such class of senior securities has at the time of the declaration of any such dividend or distribution or at the time of any such purchase an asset coverage of at least 300 per centum after deducting the amount of such dividend, distribution, or purchase price, as the case may be, except that dividends may be declared upon any preferred stock if such senior security representing indebtedness has an asset coverage of at least 200 per centum at the time of declaration thereof after deducting the amount of such dividend * * *.
>
> * * *
>
> (2) if such class of senior security is a stock—
>
> (A) immediately after such issuance or sale it will have an asset coverage of at least 200 per centum;
>
> (B) provision is made to prohibit the declaration of any dividend (except a dividend payable in common stock of the issuer), or the declaration of any other distribution, upon the common stock of such investment company, or the purchase of any such common stock, unless in every such case such class of senior security has at the time of the declaration of any such dividend or distribution or at the time of any such purchase an asset coverage of at least 200 per centum after deducting the amount of such dividend, distribution or purchase price, as the case may be * * *.

Section 18(a)'s provision for open-end companies is stricter, blocking senior securities entirely but allowing bank borrowing subject to the 300 percent test:

> (f)(1) It shall be unlawful for any registered open-end company to issue any class of senior security or to sell any senior security of which it is the issuer, except that any such registered company shall be permitted to borrow from any bank: *Provided*, That immediately after any such borrowing there is an asset coverage of at least 300 per centum for all borrowings of such registered company: *And provided further*, That in the event that such asset coverage shall at any time fall below 300 per centum such registered company shall, within three days thereafter (not including Sundays and holidays) or such longer period as the Commission may prescribe by rules and regulations, reduce the amount of its borrowings to an extent that the asset coverage of such borrowings shall be at least 300 per centum.

To what extent, if at all, do these categorical limitations on leverage for investment companies mitigate or avert the risks of leverage? In considering this question, note that § 12 of the Investment Company Act, 15 U.S.C. § 80a–12, substantially restrains registered investment companies from (1) purchasing securities on margin, (2) effecting short sales, and (3) acquiring more than limited percentages of the securities of other investment companies.

Why does the Congress constrain leverage in investment company capital structures but not the capital structures of industrial companies? Are there institutional factors affecting management of investment companies which cause unrestrained leverage to create risks for the company's senior security holders and public stockholders that are not encountered by investors in industrial enterprises? Consider the following excerpts from Part Three of the SEC Report on Investment Trusts and Investment Companies 1593–1595, 1668(1939), a Report upon which many of the provisions of the Investment Company Act of 1940 are based:

"* * * A person purchasing senior securities in an investment company is in effect lending money to the investment company for the use of the common stockholders to invest or to speculate in securities, similar in many ways to a broker's loan to a customer for use in a margin account.

"Yet the customary protection in this situation demanded by a broker is in strong contrast to the protection usually afforded senior security holders by investment companies, even by those investment companies sponsored by brokers. The broker ordinarily keeps daily supervision over the status of a customer's margin account and can long before the account reaches the point of being 'under water' compel the customer to supply additional collateral. If additional collateral is not supplied, the broker can sell out the customer's securities in a few hours and fully protect his loan. When the asset value of the investment company has dropped to a dangerously low point, e.g., the preferred stock may actually be 'under water', the senior security holder, particularly the preferred stockholder, ordinarily cannot demand more collateral or that the underlying securities be sold and his claim paid off. If he holds a bond he is almost entirely helpless until its due date, while if he holds a preferred stock, he must await the dissolution of the company, which dissolution is largely determined by the holders of the common stock. Regardless of the extent to which the senior securities are 'under water,' the common stockholder usually continues to manage the funds on which the senior securities have a prior claim. In such a situation the multiple security structure tends to encourage a speculative policy on the part of the common stock management, since speculative transactions at such a point may, with the aid of leverage, reestablish positive values for the common stock and cannot do any substantial damage to the already existing negative values.

* * *

"* * * [I]n the financing of investment companies, senior securities apparently have been used for the purpose of obtaining from the public the major part of the capital contribution, while the control of the enterprise has been retained by the sponsors with small proportionate investments through ownership of common stock. Thus, the complex capital structure usually gives rise to another crucial element of conflict within the investment company field; the general public holding the major part of the senior securities has the greatest stake in the enterprise, while the sponsors or insiders, having a much smaller stake, control the enterprise.

* * *

"The difference in rights and claims awarded the senior and equity securities, respectively, in the multiple-security company subjects the company to pressure in favor of a speculative investment policy. The impetus toward abnormal capital accretion arises from two attributes of the senior-equity structure: (a) The need of such investment companies to maintain a level of earnings and profit greater than the average yield on a diversified list of high-grade investments in order to meet the fixed interest and dividend requirements of the senior securities; and (b) The fact that the bulk of the large profits possibly accruing from a policy of speculation with the total funds of the company will inure to the sponsors while the possibility of loss to the sponsor is limited to its comparatively small investment in the company."

The phenomenon adverted to in the SEC Report on Investment Companies is generalized in agency theory as the "asset substitution" problem.

Why should an investment company that invests in low risk securities be subject to the same leverage test as a company with a risky portfolio? Does the restriction of leverage impose a cost upon investors in investment company stocks—loss of the opportunity to adjust to a desired risk-return relationship by investing in a "conservative" portfolio with a high return while levering the portfolio—with no offsetting benefit? These questions suggest a way to end-run the rule—just borrow up to the limit and invest in a risky portfolio. Alternatively, can the managers of investment companies replicate the risk-return characteristics of a levered capital structure by entering into derivative contracts, such as swap agreements? Consider in this regard the "synthetic" levered position in Philip Morris stock maintained by the plaintiff in *Caiola v. Citibank*, supra, Part I. Finally, how can the Investment Company Act limit the risks to which managers may subject investors without regulating portfolio decisions as well as financing decisions?

Note that hedge funds and private equity funds, which are open only to sophisticated investors meeting a statutory standard, now comprise an important segment of financial intermediaries. Leverage is one this sector's primary attractions. Note also that investors not meeting the statutory standard can enter this market indirectly by purchasing "funds of funds" that register under the Investment Company Act and invest in diversified portfolios of hedge funds. What signal results for federal regulatory policy? Repeal of §§ 18(a) and 12, or further extension of capital structure controls for the protection of small investors?

(3) Margin Requirements

Section 7 of the Securities Exchange Act (15 U.S.C. § 78g) empowers the Federal Reserve Board (FRB) to regulate the supply of credit available for buying securities (or selling them short) by limiting the loan value of securities. To implement § 7, the FRB has promulgated regulations prescribing permissible margin on loans or extensions of credit by brokers and dealers (Regulation T, 12 C.F.R. part 220), banks and others (Regulation U, 12 C.F.R. part 221). The regulations cover transactions in exchange listed and NASDAQ equities, debt securities, and convertible securities. To implement the Foreign Bank Secrecy Act (which amended § 7), the FRB also promulgated Regulation X (12 C.F.R. part 224) making it unlawful for any U.S. citizen to borrow from any lender anywhere if the borrowing would have violated margin requirements had it been made in the United States.

The difference between the loan value specified by the FRB and the market price of the securities represents the margin which the investor must furnish out of his own resources when he invests. Thus, if the margin requirement were 70 percent (the maximum loan value being 30 percent), an individual who purchased 100 shares of a stock selling at $50 a share, "on margin," would be permitted to borrow no more than $1,500 from his or her broker.

The FRB does not require that the margin level be maintained at the level it specifies—currently 50 percent—once the initial purchase has been made, but the rules of the stock exchanges do prescribe margin maintenance levels for customers' accounts. The New York Stock Exchange and the NASD require that margin never fall below 25 percent—i.e., that a customer's indebtedness to this broker never exceed 75 percent of the value of the cash and securities held in his or her account. If stock values decline below the permitted minimum, the customer will receive a margin call from his broker and be asked to post additional collateral. Many brokerages impose higher maintenance levels–30 percent, 40 percent, or higher depending on the security in question.

This is also Depression-era regulation. The impetus for margin requirements came from the stock market crash of 1929 and the feeling that excessive use of security credit had in some part been responsible for pushing stock prices to unrealistically high levels. As stock prices began to slide, lenders who had made security loans on as little as 10 percent margin grew apprehensive and issued calls for more collateral, which their customers were frequently unable to provide. This led to the quick liquidation of customers' portfolios as lenders attempted to retrieve some portion of their loans, and thereby induced a swifter and more severe decline in prices than might otherwise have occurred. The evidence is mixed (see Moore, Stock Market Margin Requirements, 74 J.Pub.Econ. 158 (1966)) on whether margin requirements do contribute to a healthier securities market by suppressing speculative zeal during boom periods and avoiding forced sales in periods of contraction.

A secondary purpose of the margin rules was to protect individual investors against themselves. (HR Rep. No. 1383, 73rd Cong. 2d Sess. (1934) p. 8). It has also been suggested that the margin requirements protect broker solvency by setting limits on the extent to which competition may drive brokers to make unsafe loans. With respect to each of these objectives, the FRB at one point recommended to Congress that there no longer remains sufficient justification for maintaining securities margins at levels substantially higher than needed to protect brokers and lenders against loss from customer default. The FRB recommended that the task of setting margin requirements to protect brokers and lenders be delegated to the various stock exchanges and over-the-counter regulatory bodies with coordination responsibilities vested with the SEC and CFTC. See Federal Reserve Board, A Review and Evaluation of Federal Margin Regulations, CCH Fed.Sec.L.Rep., ¶ 83,728.

Should the Congress have acted on the FRB's recommendation? Do the margin regulations, which do *not* impose restrictions on borrowing in order to purchase straight (i.e., nonconvertible) debt securities, distort the supply schedules of loan and equity funds in the market, and tend to channel more investments into senior securities than would otherwise be made? If so, do the margin regulations thereby interfere with efficient allocation of capital, albeit in the interest of a kind of distributive equity?

Why are there no governmentally imposed margin requirements on other kinds of investment, e.g., real estate? What attitude on the part of investors in highly leveraged assets do the margin requirements appear to assume?

Is the unrestrained authority to issue warrants incompatible with restrictions on the purchase of securities on margin? Does the answer turn on whether the margin restrictions are designed more to preserve the stability of stock market prices against speculative "excesses" than to preserve or protect the security holder from bankruptcy?

Is it possible for an investor to be exposed to more risk with a portfolio financed without borrowing than with a portfolio financed by borrowing 80 percent of the amount needed to purchase the securities, say, by taking positions in derivatives? If so, are the margin regulations justifiable on risk minimization grounds?

(4) Bank Capital

The Investment Company Act's leverage limits amount to a one-time only/one-size-fits-all regulatory intervention of questionable effectiveness. Today, this looks more and more like an historical holdover. Bank capital regulation, in contrast, remains a constant focus of attention and a dynamic area of regulation.

Banks present special problems. They are highly levered by nature–their depositors are, after all, creditors. They invest in loans, which are risky. But the depositors have little incentive to monitor the level of risk the banks undertake because their deposits are insured by the federal government. A risk of opportunism follows–a bank may be tempted to engage in high risk/high return investments and externalize the risk of failure on the government. The government emerges with a keen interest in the soundness of the banks. This interest arises in part from its concern for economic stability and in part from a direct financial stake. When a large bank gets into distress, the federal government sometimes enters the picture as the lender of last resort, engineering a "bail out." In the event of total failure, it emerges as the largest creditor.

The Congress has delegated rule-making responsibility for bank capital adequacy to the Board of Governors of the Federal Reserve (bank holding companies) and the Office of the Comptroller of the Currency (national banks). The Federal Reserve and OCC in turn take the view that bank capital adequacy must be dealt with on a global basis through the Basel Committee on Banking Supervision, composed of central bankers and other bank regulators from thirteen countries. The Basel Committee, established in 1974, promulgated its first set of rules ("Basel I") in 1988, followed by a revised set of rules in 2005 ("Basel II").

Tarullo, International Harmonization of Banking Regulation and Agency Accountability 8–10 (working paper, March 2007), describes the analytical framework within which a regulator sets a minimum capital requirement and the approaches taken by the federal regulators and Basel I:

" * * * Setting the requirements involves two distinct, though related, steps. The first is to determine the appropriate metric with which to calculate the requirements for each bank. This metric is generally a ratio of capital to assets. The second step is to set a minimum value for that ratio.

"The first step entails deciding both what qualifies as 'capital' and how 'assets' should be measured. The former decision implicates the regulatory purpose of assuring an appropriate buffer against loss. So, for example, the question arises as to whether certain long-term subordinated debt should qualify as 'capital.' The latter decision implicates the regulatory concern with the potential for bank losses to develop, since most bank insolvencies are associated with deterioration in the quality of the loans and other extensions of credit made by the bank. Thus the question arises whether off-balance-sheet items such as contingent letters of credit should be considered 'assets' for regulatory purposes. Another key issue is whether and how, in determining a capital ratio, the bank's assets should be 'risk-weighted' to take account of the fact that different assets pose very different risks of loss.

"The second step in establishing capital requirements–setting the minimum value of the ratio of 'capital' to 'assets'–necessitates identifying the optimal amount of bank stability (i.e., reduction in the likelihood of failure) to be achieved through regulation. Imposition of very high capital requirements could reduce the risk of failure to very small levels by drastically limiting the amount banks can lend or requiring extremely high levels of creditworthiness among borrowers. But this would largely eliminate the socially useful role of banks in intermediating between savers and users of capital. Banks dislike any requirement that they hold more capital than they maintain for business purposes, because the resulting constraints on lending deny them profit opportunities.

"At a conceptual level the optimal trade-off is fairly easy to state: Capital requirements should be established at a level that equalizes the marginal returns (e.g., the social benefits of reduced costs of costly bank failures) and the marginal costs (e.g., the social costs of reduced lending) of the regulation. In practical terms, measuring the marginal costs and benefits of an adjustment in minimum capital regulation falls somewhere between a highly imprecise, and an infeasible, undertaking. Accordingly, the capital levels actually required by bank regulators are generally regarded as–depending on one's perspective–arbitrary or a matter for the experienced 'feel' of supervisory agencies.

"In part because of the uncertainties associated with the entire enterprise and in part because of political compromises, there are currently three different forms of minimum required capital ratios in the United States. One is a 'leverage limit'–a simple ratio of 'tangible equity' to total assets. The other two requirements derive from the first Basel capital accord. Both use as the denominator in the ratio an asset figure that is adjusted for the risk associated with each asset. All assets are grouped into four categories of riskiness based solely on the nature of the debtor (bank, corporation, sovereign, etc.). The numerators in the two ratios (and thus the minimum required ratios themselves) differ. One is calculated solely by reference to the bank's core capital; the other allows a broader range of items on the bank's balance sheet to qualify as 'capital.' ''

Tarullo, id. at 17–18, further describes the risk related approach to capital requirements under Basel I:

" * * * Banks had to meet two minimum ratios, one based on its 'Tier 1,' or core, capital and the other based on its 'Tier 2,' capital, which was defined more broadly. These ratios, 4% and 8% respectively, were both based on a risk-weighting of the bank's assets. All its assets were assigned to one of four risk categories–0%, 20%, 50%, and 100%. Assets considered essentially risk-free, such as U.S. Government securities, were weighted at 0% and thus added nothing to a bank's total of risk-weighted assets. Assets weighted at 100%, which included most of the bank's non-mortgage loans to corporations and individuals, were added to the denominator of the ratios in their full book value. Off-balance-sheet items such as lines of credit and performance bonds, although not 'assets' in an accounting sense, were converted to 'asset equivalents' and added to the denominator because they also posed a risk of loss to the bank.

"Each Basel Committee country and, eventually, nearly one hundred others implemented the thirty pages of rules in the Basel I agreement into domestic banking regulations. This landmark in international regulatory convergence prompted change in the supervisory practice of even the most sophisticated bank regulators. However, even at its inception, it was apparent that Basel I was a rather crude mechanism for regulating capital levels. The use of just four categories of risk created substantial imprecision in risk assessment. The allocation of assets based solely on the character of the borrower (e.g., corporation, commercial bank, sovereign) was at odds with the actual credit risk posed by individual borrowers. There was no mechanism for adjusting the risk weight of a loan whose repayment became more uncertain because of the deteriorating financial condition of the borrower."

Tarullo describes the Basel II framework as follows, id. at 20–21:

"The final 'Revised Framework' establishes two different methods for calculating minimum capital requirements. The 'standardized' approach, intended to apply to small and medium-sized banks, retains the structure of Basel I but makes a number of changes to address its specific problems. The 'internal-ratings-based' approach (IRB), intended to apply to larger banks, has by far the more important implications for banking regulation and international cooperation. The Basel Committee has explained that it adopted the IRB approach in order to relate capital regulation requirements more directly to the actual risks posed by the bank's assets–that is, to overcome a fundamental objection to Basel I. Its essence is that banks can use their own internal models to calculate the risk associated with a particular asset, based on data specific to particular borrowers (and, as appropriate, different forms of borrowing by the same entity). These ratings are recalibrated regularly. The values generated by the internal model are then to be converted into risk weights through complicated formulas devised by the Committee; there are separate formulas for different kinds of exposures (corporate, sovereign, bank, retail). There is a parallel set of rules for securitization exposures.

"Thus the IRB approach is a kind of hybrid. It relies on a bank's own assessment of the riskiness of its credit exposures, and so attempts to enlist the expertise and information of the banks themselves in setting capital requirements. However, it places extensive requirements on the structure and operation of the bank's model. Moreover, it reserves to regulators, rather than to the banks' credit risk models, the designation of the formula for calculating the capital set-aside required by the risk rating for an asset."

The evolution from Basel I to Basel II demonstrates the difficulty of imposing minimum capital standards across an entire industry. Basel I improves on one-size-fits-all rules keyed to the right side of the balance sheet by calibrating the capital structure test to the riskiness of the assets on the left side. But, because even that approach proved too crude in a world where banks invest in complex financial products, Basel II leaves the job of measuring the riskiness of the assets over to the regulated entities themselves. Basel II thus delivers bank capital regulation to the self-regulatory end point already chosen for derivatives. Is this trade off between regulatory sensitivity and enforceability plausible? Where will a bank's reporting incentives lie in a recessionary economy?

(B) CORPORATE LAW LEGAL CAPITAL RULES

State corporation statutes contain provisions that regulate capital structure for the benefit of creditors and senior security holders. These "legal capital" rules seek to protect the seniors' equity cushion by restricting the corporation's discretion to make distributions to equityholders. The rules have been on the books for a more than a century, and have the appearance of a substantial body of corporate law. But they are generally understood to be ineffective as a shield to protect creditors from debtor opportunism. In form, the legal capital rules operate notwithstanding the solvency of the enterprise, and thereby in theory serve the function of a dividend covenant in an indenture, note agreement, or preferred stock contract. But, in fact, the rules do little more than block distributions to the shareholders of insolvent corporations. They thus in effect anticipate the constraint of fraudulent conveyance law.

Today the prevailing view is that creditors' and preferred stockholders' interests are better left to regulation through negotiated contracts than to regulation by positive law. This section's introduction to the legal capital rules is included to show why this view prevails. For further reading, see Herwitz and Barrett, Accounting for Lawyers (4th ed. 2006); Manning and Hanks, A Concise Textbook on Legal Capital (3d ed. 1990); Kummert, State Statutory Restrictions on Financial Distributions by Corporations to Shareholders, 59 Wash.L.Rev. 187 (1984); Hackney, The Financial Provisions of the Model Business Corporation Act, 70 Harv.L.Rev. (1957).

(1) *The Stated Capital Requirement*

The corporation statutes of all states contemplate (1) that *some* consideration will be paid by stockholders for the stock issued to them, (2) that the consideration will be of a *quality* which is acceptable under statutory specifications, and (3) that the *amount* of consideration will be "sufficient" or "adequate" as tested by some standard. One standard of adequacy, of course, could be the board of directors' good faith willingness to accept as adequate what the subscriber offers in exchange for its shares. The historical statutory standard instead has required the amount paid for the stock to equal the "par value" thereof as set in the firm's charter, or, alternatively, the "stated value" thereof, as set by a resolution of the board of directors in a case where the firm's charter does not set a par value. In either case, issued stock will show up on the firm's balance sheet at the par or stated value.

Problems arise under these statutes if the corporation agrees to accept less in actual value for its stock than the amount stated on its books. The agreed consideration paid by the stockholder may be given an inflated value by the corporation and be accepted in exchange for stock of par value equal to the inflated value ("watered" stock), either because the interests of the promoters are so served, or because the stockholder and the corporation are otherwise not dealing at arm's length. Or, the stock may be issued for no measurable consideration (i.e., as a bonus); or it may be issued for cash which is less than its par value (i.e., at a discount). In any of those circumstances, there may have been complete disclosure, or in any event nothing misleading, as between the stockholder paying the consideration and the promoters and executives of the corporation duly authorized to issue the stock. Hence, as a matter of tort or contract law, there is no basis for any action by the corporation against the stockholder.

The corporate books will record the consideration at a specified amount on the asset side of the balance sheet, and will reflect on the liability side of the balance sheet an amount of capital with respect to the stock issued therefor. Under the traditional statutory scheme, the amount of capital is viewed either as a representation to those extending credit or as legally imposed assurance to third parties—creditors and stockholders alike—of the receipt of something of value equal to that amount, and of the dedication of that economic value to the enterprise's long range effort to earn profits and pay its debts.

Hence, notwithstanding the fact that as between the purchasing stock-holder and the issuing corporation no one may be misled, the "adequacy" of the consideration paid by a stockholder for the stock is measured by the par value or the amount of capital "stated" to be represented by the issued shares. If the amount of the consideration (in money or in tangible or intangible property valued by the board of directors) is equal to par or the capital stated, the stockholder has fulfilled not merely the contract, but such obligations as external regulation imposes. If, however, the amount of the consideration is less than par or the stated capital, then, notwithstand-ing the fact that the stockholder may have complied with its contract with the corporation, the stockholder has failed to meet legal obligations to relying creditors or, possibly, to third party claimants generally.

The consequences attending a failure to meet the pay-in requirement were never satisfactorily worked out in the caselaw. Solution of this problem required the following:

(1) Identification of the nature of the misrepresentation or misleading appearance created by the inaccurate statement of the transaction on the corporate books. Is it with respect to the value entered as an asset, or to the statement of the amount of capital, or both?

(2) Determination of who should be liable and in what amount. Should liability be imposed upon the directors or upon the recipients of watered stock or both, and if upon either or both, should liability turn on whether they know or have reason to know of the water?

(3) Determination of the party to whom liability should run and in what amount. Should liability run only to creditors, on the theory that capital is in some way a symbol of a fund held in trust for them; or on a theory of fraud, should liability run only to those creditors who rely on the misrepresentation; or should it also run to fellow stockholders on the

theory of a statutory obligation to all persons interested in the enterprise; or should liability be to the corporation at large, notwithstanding its willingness to accept less consideration than it appears to have agreed upon? Should stockholders be liable only to make good the water or for all the corporate indebtedness? And in any event, should the remedy against them permit cancellation of their stock?

In recent years watered stock problems have rarely produced litigation, because of the ease with which they may be avoided in planning. The expedient is simple. The par or stated value required by the firm's fundamental documents does not have to equal the stock's original issue price or intrinsic value. The amount is left to the drafter's discretion. It can range from 1 cent or a fraction of 1 cent upward. Accordingly, nothing in the legal capital rules stops a firm whose stock has a par value of $1 but a market price of $100 from selling an additional share for $10.

Legislative efforts to eliminate the concepts of stated capital and par value, such as those embodied in the latest version of the Model Business Corporation Act, have not yet taken root in a number of states, including Delaware. In those jurisdictions "watered stock" problems may still call for special planning when stock is issued for property or services—as in corporate acquisitions of, or mergers with, going concerns, or in the incorporation of going concerns formerly conducted as sole proprietorships or partnerships.

(2) Dividends and Distributions

(a) traditional statutes

Historically, legal capital schemes have employed three methods of defining the funds available for dividends: (1) a balance sheet test that prohibits distributions except from surplus, (2) an income statement test that prohibits payments except from current or past net profits, and (3) an insolvency test.

● **Balance Sheet Test.** Traditional legal capital schemes employ the balance sheet as the basis for regulating distributions of corporate assets to shareholders. The distributions covered by the statutes include dividends, stock repurchases, and any other transactions entailing a net outflow of assets to shareholders.

In general, under the "balance sheet" test, distributions are prohibited if, after giving effect to the transaction, the firm's total assets would be less than the sum of its liabilities (including preferred stock liquidation price) and its "stated capital" account. "Stated capital" is a dollar figure representing the number of outstanding shares multiplied by their "par value." Par value is set in the certificate of incorporation. As noted above, the amount is left to the drafter's discretion (ranging upward from a fraction of 1 cent) and may be less than the original issue price of the stock. In the alternative, a firm's charter can specify that its stock will not have a par value. Where the firm issues no par stock, stated capital is determined by multiplying the stock's "stated value"—a dollar figure designated by the board at the time of the stock's issue—by the number of outstanding shares. The particular stated value figure, like the par value figure, is within the firm's discretion. Where shares are issued for a consideration greater than their par or stated value, the difference between the par or stated value and the consideration received is entered into a separate surplus account. Traditionally, this is termed the "capital surplus" account. On a contemporary balance sheet, this account may be termed "additional paid in capital" or "capital in excess of par."

Restating the basic legal capital test, distributions are permitted out of "surplus" accounts—whether additional paid in capital or retained earnings—but may not be made out of stated capital. The surplus accounts thus equal total assets minus the sum of liabilities and stated capital. This is the simplest of the stated capital tests in the statutes. Del.Corp.L. § 170; N.Y.Bus.Corp.L. § 510.

The following balance sheet serves to illustrate the test:

ABC Corp.

Total assets	$10,000,000

Liabilities

Accounts payable	$ 2,000,000
Funded debt	2,000,000

Shareholders' Equity

Common stock, 1,000,000 shares outstanding, par value $1 per share	$ 1,000,000	*Stated Capital*
Additional paid in capital	4,000,000	*Paid in Capital*
Retained earnings	1,000,000	
Total liabilities and equity	$10,000,000	

Based on this balance sheet, the common stock appears to have been issued originally for $5 per share. Stated capital here is the $1,000,000 "common stock" entry. The $4,000,000 additional paid in capital represents the difference between the stock's $1 par value and the $5 received for each share on original issue. Now we apply the basic test. The maximum dividend a firm may make is the amount by which total assets are greater than liabilities plus stated capital. Total assets = $4,000,000 liabilities + $1,000,000 stated capital + allowable dividend. ABC may make a maximum dividend of $5,000,000.

Restating the test, dividends may only be made out of surplus accounts: $4,000,000 additional paid in capital + $1,000,000 retained earnings = $5,000,000 total surplus accounts. ABC may make a maximum dividend of $5,000,000.

● **Net Profits Test.** Under the "net profits" or "earned surplus" standard, dividends and distributions are limited to amounts carried in the enterprise's balance sheet as "earned surplus" or "retained earnings." MBCA § 45(a). In theory, this standard relieves the firm of the necessity to compute or recompute "capital," and limits its dividends or distributions to some form of profits, current or accumulated. In practice, under both generally accepted accounting principles and the statutes, it is possible to alter the earned surplus account by drawing on capital surplus or including (or excluding) some capital transactions.

Some states employing a balance sheet test, Delaware included, provide a significant exception to the rule against distributions where stated capital is impaired. This allows dividends to the extent of the firm's earned profits during the dividend year or the previous year, regardless of the absence of a surplus. Del.Corp.L. § 170(a). Such distributions are called "nimble dividends."

● **Insolvency.** Finally, most corporation laws include an equity insolvency restriction against dividends and other distributions to shareholders. Equity insolvency occurs when a debtor cannot meet its obligations as they become due. The statutes provide, first, that a firm already insolvent in the equity sense may make no distributions to shareholders, and second, that a solvent firm may not make a distribution if, as a result, the firm would be left insolvent in an equity sense.

Klang v. Smith's Food & Drug Centers, Inc.

Supreme Court of Delaware, 1997.
702 A.2d 150.

■ VEASEY, CHIEF JUSTICE:

* * *

Smith's Food & Drug Centers, Inc. ("SFD") is a Delaware corporation that owns and operates a chain of supermarkets in the Southwestern United States. Slightly more than three years ago, Jeffrey P. Smith, SFD's Chief Executive Officer, began to entertain suitors with an interest in acquiring SFD. At the time, and until the transactions at issue, Mr. Smith and his family held common and preferred stock constituting 62.1% voting control of SFD. Plaintiff and the class he purports to represent are holders of common stock in SFD.

On January 29, 1996, SFD entered into an agreement with The Yucaipa Companies ("Yucaipa"), a California partnership also active in the supermarket industry. Under the agreement, the following would take place:

> (1) Smitty's Supermarkets, Inc. ("Smitty's"), a wholly-owned subsidiary of Yucaipa that operated a supermarket chain in Arizona, was to merge into Cactus Acquisition, Inc. ("Cactus"), a subsidiary of SFD, in exchange for which SFD would deliver to Yucaipa slightly over 3 million newly-issued shares of SFD common stock;

> (2) SFD was to undertake a recapitalization, in the course of which SFD would assume a sizable amount of new debt, retire old debt, and offer to repurchase up to fifty percent of its outstanding shares (other than those issued to Yucaipa) for $36 per share; and

> (3) SFD was to repurchase 3 million shares of preferred stock from Jeffrey Smith and his family.

SFD hired the investment firm of Houlihan Lokey Howard & Zukin ("Houlihan") to examine the transactions and render a solvency opinion. Houlihan eventually issued a report to the SFD Board replete with assurances that the transactions would not endanger SFD's solvency, and would not impair SFD's capital in violation of 8 Del.C. § 160. On May 17, 1996, in reliance on the Houlihan opinion, SFD's Board determined that there existed sufficient surplus to consummate the transactions, and enacted a resolution proclaiming as much. On May 23, 1996, SFD's stockholders voted to approve the transactions, which closed on that day. The self-tender offer was over-subscribed, so SFD repurchased fully fifty percent of its shares at the offering price of $36 per share.

* * *

A corporation may not repurchase its shares if, in so doing, it would cause an impairment of capital, unless expressly authorized by Section 160.[4] A repurchase impairs capital if the funds used in the repurchase exceed the amount of the corporation's "surplus," defined by 8 Del.C. § 154 to mean the excess of net assets over the par value of the corporation's issued stock.[5]

Plaintiff asked the Court of Chancery to rescind the transactions in question as violative of Section 160. * * *

In an April 25, 1996 proxy statement, the SFD Board released a pro forma balance sheet showing that the merger and self-tender offer would result in a deficit to surplus on SFD's books of more than $100 million. A balance sheet the SFD Board issued shortly after the transactions confirmed this result. Plaintiff asks us to adopt an interpretation of 8 Del.C. § 160 whereby balance-sheet net worth is controlling for purposes of determining compliance with the statute. Defendants do not dispute that SFD's books showed a negative net worth in the wake of its transactions with Yucaipa, but argue that corporations should have the presumptive right to revalue assets and liabilities to comply with Section 160.

---

4. Section 160(a) provides:

(a) Every corporation may purchase, redeem, receive, take or otherwise acquire, own and hold, sell, lend exchange, transfer or otherwise dispose of, pledge, use and otherwise deal in and with its own shares; provided, however, that no corporation shall:

(1) Purchase or redeem its own shares of capital stock for cash or other property when the capital of the corporation is impaired or when such purchase or redemption would cause any impairment of the capital of the corporation, except that a corporation may purchase or redeem out of capital any of its own shares which are entitled upon any distribution of its assets, whether by dividend or in liquidation, to a preference over another class or series of its stock, or, if no shares entitled to such a preference are outstanding, any of its own shares, if such shares will be retired upon their acquisition and the capital of the corporation reduced in accordance with §§ 243 and 244 of this title.

5. Section 154 provides, "Any corporation may, by resolution of its board of directors, determine that only a part of the consideration ... received by the corporation for ... its capital stock ... shall be capital.... The excess ... of the net assets of the corporation over the amount so determined to be capital shall be surplus. Net assets means the amount by which total assets exceed total liabilities. Capital and surplus are not liabilities for this purpose."

Plaintiff advances an erroneous interpretation of Section 160. We understand that the books of a corporation do not necessarily reflect the current values of its assets and liabilities. Among other factors, unrealized appreciation or depreciation can render book numbers inaccurate. It is unrealistic to hold that a corporation is bound by its balance sheets for purposes of determining compliance with Section 160. Accordingly, we adhere to the principles of Morris v. Standard Gas & Electric Co. [63 A.2d 577 (1949)] allowing corporations to revalue properly its assets and liabilities to show a surplus and thus conform to the statute.

It is helpful to recall the purpose behind Section 160. The General Assembly enacted the statute to prevent boards from draining corporations of assets to the detriment of creditors and the long-term health of the corporation. That a corporation has not yet realized or reflected on its balance sheet the appreciation of assets is irrelevant to this concern. Regardless of what a balance sheet that has not been updated may show, an actual, though unrealized, appreciation reflects real economic value that the corporation may borrow against or that creditors may claim or levy upon. Allowing corporations to revalue assets and liabilities to reflect current realities complies with the statute and serves well the policies behind this statute. * * *

Plaintiff contends that SFD's repurchase of shares violated Section 160 even without regard to the corporation's balance sheets. Plaintiff claims that the SFD Board was not entitled to rely on the solvency opinion of Houlihan, which showed that the transactions would not impair SFD's capital given a revaluation of corporate assets. The argument is that the methods that underlay the solvency opinion were inappropriate as a matter of law because they failed to take into account all of SFD's assets and liabilities. In addition, plaintiff suggests that the SFD Board's resolution of May 17, 1996 itself shows that the transactions impaired SFD's capital, and that therefore we must find a violation of 8 Del.C. § 160. We disagree, and hold that the SFD Board revalued the corporate assets under appropriate methods. * * *

* * * Houlihan reached [its conclusion that the merger and self-tender offer would not impair SFD's capital] by comparing SFD's "Total Invested Capital" of $1.8 billion—a figure Houlihan arrived at by valuing SFD's assets under the "market multiple" approach—with SFD's long-term debt of $1.46 billion. This comparison yielded an approximation of SFD's "concluded equity value" equal to $346 million, a figure clearly in excess of the outstanding par value of SFD's stock. * * *

Plaintiff contends that Houlihan's analysis relied on inappropriate methods to mask a violation of Section 160. Noting that 8 Del.C. § 154 defines "net assets" as "the amount by which total assets exceeds total liabilities," plaintiff argues that Houlihan's analysis is erroneous as a matter of law because of its failure to calculate "total assets" and "total liabilities" as separate variables. In a related argument, plaintiff claims that the analysis failed to take into account all of SFD's liabilities, i.e., that Houlihan neglected to consider current liabilities in its comparison of SFD's "Total Invested Capital" and long-term debt. Plaintiff contends that the SFD Board's resolution proves that adding current liabilities into the mix shows a violation of Section 160. The resolution declared the value of SFD's assets to be $1.8 billion, and stated that its "total liabilities" would not exceed $1.46 billion after the transactions with Yucaipa. As noted, the $1.46 billion figure described only the value of SFD's long-term debt. Adding in SFD's $372 million in current liabilities, plaintiff argues, shows that the transactions impaired SFD's capital.

We believe that plaintiff reads too much into Section 154. The statute simply defines "net assets" in the course of defining "surplus." It does not mandate a "facts and figures balancing of assets and liabilities" to determine by what amount, if any, total assets exceeds total liabilities. The statute is merely definitional. It does not require any particular method of calculating surplus, but simply prescribes factors that any such calculation must include. Although courts may not determine compliance with Section 160 except by methods that fully take into account the assets and liabilities of the corporation, Houlihan's methods were not erroneous as a matter of law simply because they used Total Invested Capital and long-term debt as analytical categories rather than "total assets" and "total liabilities."

We are satisfied that the Houlihan opinion adequately took into account all of SFD's assets and liabilities. Plaintiff points out that the $1.46 billion figure that approximated SFD's long-term debt failed to include $372 million in current liabilities, and argues that including the latter in the calculations dissipates the surplus. In fact, plaintiff has misunderstood Houlihan's methods. The record shows that Houlihan's calculation of SFD's Total Invested Capital is already net of current liabilities. Thus, subtracting long-term debt from Total Invested Capital does, in fact, yield an accurate measure of a corporation's net assets.

* * * In cases alleging impairment of capital under Section 160, the trial court may defer to the board's measurement of surplus unless a plaintiff can show that the directors "failed to fulfill their duty to evaluate the assets on the basis of acceptable data and by standards which they are entitled to believe reasonably reflect present values." In the absence of bad faith or fraud on the part of the board, courts will not "substitute [our] concepts of wisdom for that of the directors." Here, plaintiff does not argue that the SFD Board acted in bad faith. Nor has he met his burden of showing that the methods and data that underlay the board's analysis are unreliable or that its determination of surplus is so far off the mark as to constitute actual or constructive fraud. Therefore, we defer to the board's determination of surplus, and hold that SFD's self-tender offer did not violate 8 Del.C. § 160.

On a final note, we hold that the SFD Board's resolution of May 17, 1996 has no bearing on whether the transactions conformed to Section 160. The record shows that the SFD Board committed a serious error in drafting the resolution: the resolution states that, following the transactions, SFD's "total liabilities" would be no more than $1.46 billion. In fact, that figure reflects only the value of SFD's long-term debt. Although the SFD Board was guilty of sloppy work, and did not follow good corporate practices, it does not follow that Section 160 was violated. The statute requires only that there exist a surplus after a repurchase, not that the board memorialize the surplus in a resolution. The statute carves out a class of transactions that directors have no authority to execute, but does not, in fact, require any affirmative act on the part of the board. The SFD repurchase would be valid in the absence of any board resolution. A mistake in documenting the surplus will not negate the substance of the action, which complies with the statutory scheme.

NOTE: RESTRICTIONS ON DISTRIBUTIONS

1. *Defining "Distribution."*

Only "distributions" come within the purview of the legal capital rules. Whether or not a transaction constitutes a "distribution" within the meaning of the statute can be a subject of dispute, as in **C–T of Virginia, Inc. v. Barrett**, 958 F.2d 606 (4th Cir.1992). The question there was whether the payments to tendering stockholders in an LBO constituted a "distribution" within the meaning of the Virginia statute. The statute defined distribution as a "direct or indirect transfer of money * * * or incurrence of indebtedness by a corporation to or for the benefit of its shareholders in respect of any of its shares." The court, commenting that "[a] corporate acquisition, structured as a merger, is simply a different animal from a distribution," held that the payment was not a distribution. The encumbering of the corporation's assets was not an "incurrence of indebtedness" within the meaning of the statute, even though the closing of the loan transaction occurred simultaneously with the closing of the merger, because the management of the firm promoting the LBO was identical with that of the pre-merger LBO target. Furthermore, said the court, the fact that all phases of the transaction closed simultaneously meant that the debt was not incurred "for the benefit of the shareholders" within the meaning of the statute.

2. *Statutory Interpretation.*

Statutory restrictions on dividends and distributions are infected by the intrinsic ambiguity of the terms they use. To the extent that the legal meanings of terms like "assets," "liabilities," "capital," "surplus," "earned surplus," "retained earnings," and "net profits" are not determined by reference to generally accepted accounting principles, management (and common stock) can legitimately manufacture sources for, and make payments of, dividends or distributions that result in little protection for seniors. Thus, without the consent, or possibly even the knowledge, of the seniors, it is possible for management (sometimes common stockholder consent is required) simply to write up the value of assets on the books so as to create a form of distributable surplus. *Klang* shows even where the issuer is constrained to follow GAAP, a court disinclined to find a statutory violation may allow an asset write up by implication.

Other balance sheet adjustments that increase stated capital occur within the purview of GAAP. For example, the equity capital statement on a corporation's balance sheet may be manipulated to make available sources for distributing dividends that are rooted in contributed capital and do not reflect current or historical accumulation of profits. The net result is that the traditional statutes create a flimsy shield for seniors against the distribution of assets to juniors notwithstanding behavior by management that is consistent with the statutes.

(b) new model statutes

Wide recognition of the shortcomings of the legal capital rules has prompted a law reform movement. The Revised Model Business Corporation Act (RMBCA) includes a streamlined set of legal capital rules that abandon most of the traditional concepts.

The RMBCA extensively revises the rules on shareholder distributions. The Act retains an equity insolvency test. RMBCA § 6.40(c)(1). Concurrent with it, the Act employs a net worth test. RMBCA § 6.40(c)(2). This is, at bottom, a balance sheet insolvency test, providing that a corporation may not make a distribution to shareholders if its total assets do not exceed its total liabilities, plus total liquidation preferences. With the addition of liquidation preferences, the Act adjusts its net worth concept to deviate from balance sheet solvency under generally accepted accounting principles. It specifies that the dollar amounts of the sum of all the outstanding preferred stock's liquidation preferences shall be considered a liability in the net worth calculation.

The RMBCA does not incorporate the concepts of par and stated capital and does not differentiate among surpluses. A corporation may still affix a par value to shares or create legal capital, but for the purpose of regulating distributions, such actions are meaningless. See RMBCA § 2.02(b)(2)(iv). The concept of watered stock disappears along with par, and stock purchasers are simply obligated to pay the contractually ordered price for their shares. Directors have a responsibility under the RMBCA and fiduciary law to ensure that the price they demand is fair relative to other shareholders.

Sensing difficulties with an entanglement of accounting concepts within the statute, the drafters of the RMBCA require only that the accounting system used be reasonable. The Act appears to favor a system that imbues a reviewing court with discretion instead of a system that purports to mandate certain accounting principles as law.

(C) FRAUDULENT CONVEYANCE LAW

Uniform Fraudulent Transfer Act

§ 4.   Transfers Fraudulent as to Present and Future Creditors

(a) A transfer made or obligation incurred by a debtor is fraudulent as to a creditor, whether the creditor's claim arose before or after the transfer was made or the obligation was incurred, if the debtor made the transfer or incurred the obligation:

[handwritten: actual fraud] (1) with actual intent to hinder, delay, or defraud any creditor of the debtor; or

[handwritten: Constructive fraud] (2) without receiving a reasonably equivalent value in exchange for the transfer or obligation, and the debtor:

   (i) was engaged or was about to engage in a business or a transaction for which the remaining assets of the debtor were unreasonably small in relation to the business or transaction; or

(ii) intended to incur, or believed or reasonably should have believed that he would incur, debts beyond his ability to pay as they became due.

Bankruptcy Code, 11 U.S.C. § 548. Fraudulent transfers and obligations

(a)(1) The trustee may avoid any transfer (including any transfer to or for the benefit of an insider under an employment contract) of an interest of the debtor in property, or any obligation (including any obligation to or for the benefit of an insider under an employment contract) incurred by the debtor, that was made or incurred on or within 2 years before the date of the filing of the petition, if the debtor voluntarily or involuntarily—

(A) made such transfer or incurred such obligation with actual intent to hinder, delay, or defraud any entity to which the debtor was or became, on or after the date that such transfer was made or such obligation was incurred, indebted; or

(B)(i) received less than a reasonably equivalent value in exchange for such transfer or obligation; and (ii)(I) was insolvent on the date that such transfer was made or such obligation was incurred, or became insolvent as a result of such transfer or obligation; (II) was engaged in business or a transaction, or was about to engage in business or a transaction, for which any property remaining with the debtor was an unreasonably small capital; (III) intended to incur, or believed that the debtor would incur, debts that would be beyond the debtor's ability to pay as such debts matured; or (IV) made such transfer to or for the benefit of an insider, or incurred such obligation to or for the benefit of an insider, under an employment contract and not in the ordinary course of business.

* * *

(d)(2) In this section—

(A) "value" means property, or satisfaction or securing of a present or antecedent debt of the debtor, but does not include an unperformed promise to furnish support to the debtor or to a relative of the debtor;

(B) a commodity broker, forward contract merchant, stockbroker, financial institution, financial participant, or securities clearing agency that receives a margin payment * * * takes for value to the extent of such payment;

(C) a repo participant or financial participant that receives a margin payment * * * or settlement payment * * * in connection with a repurchase agreement, takes for value to the extent of such payment;

(D) a swap participant or financial participant that receives a transfer in connection with a swap agreement takes for value to the extent of such transfer; and

(E) a master netting agreement participant that receives a transfer in connection with a master netting agreement or any individual contract covered thereby takes for value to the extent of such transfer, except that, with respect to a transfer under any individual contract covered thereby, to the extent that such master netting agreement participant otherwise did not take (or is otherwise not deemed to have taken) such transfer for value.

Wieboldt Stores, Inc. v. Schottenstein

United States District Court, Northern District of Illinois, 1988.
94 B.R. 488.

■ HOLDERMAN, DISTRICT JUDGE:

Wieboldt Stores, Inc. ("Wieboldt") filed this action on September 18, 1987 under the federal bankruptcy laws, 11 U.S.C. §§ 101 et seq., the state fraudulent conveyance laws, Ill.Rev.Stat. ch. 59, ¶ 4, and the Illinois Business Corporation Act, Ill.Rev.Stat. ch. 32, ¶ 1.01 et seq. Pending before the court are numerous motions to dismiss this action under Rules 9(b), 12(b)(2), 12(b)(6) and 19 of the Federal Rules of Civil Procedure.

* * *

Wieboldt's complaint against the defendants concerns the events and transactions surrounding a leveraged buyout ("LBO") of Wieboldt by WSI Acquisition Corporation ("WSI"). WSI, a corporation formed solely for the purpose of acquiring Wieboldt, borrowed funds from third-party lenders and delivered the proceeds to the shareholders in return for their shares. Wieboldt thereafter pledged certain of its assets to the LBO lenders to secure repayment of the loan.

* * *

[Wieboldt operated a chain of twelve department stores in the Chicago area. In 1982 it had 4,000 employees and annual sales of $190,000,000. Its stock was listed on the New York Stock Exchange. But, after 1979, Wieboldt showed no profit and continued operations only by periodically selling assets to generate working capital.

[After 1982, Wieboldt was controlled by Julius and Edmond Trump, holding through a vehicle called MBT Corporation (collectively, the "Trump interests"), and Jerome Schottenstein and affiliates (collectively, the "Schottenstein interests"). The Trump and Schottenstein interests (collectively, the "controlling shareholders") each held approximately 15% of Wieboldt's outstanding shares.

[In January 1985, WSI proposed a tender offer for all outstanding Wieboldt shares for $13.50 per share. Wieboldt's Board of Directors agreed to cooperate. WSI then spent most of 1985 arranging debt financing for the transaction.

[By October 1985 WSI had funding commitments from three lenders: Household Commercial Financial Services ("HCFS"), BA Mortgage and International Realty Corporation ("BAMIRCO"), and General Electric Credit Corporation ("GECC"). The lenders knew that WSI intended to use the proceeds of the financing to (1) purchase tendered shares of Wieboldt stock; (2) pay surrender prices for Wieboldt stock options; and (3) eliminate preexisting debt of Wieboldt owed to Continental Illinois National Bank ("CINB") and secured by Wieboldt real estate.

[WSI needed approximately $38,000,000 to purchase the Wieboldt stock in the tender offer. The HCFS loan to WSI was to provide these funds. This loan was to be secured by all of Wieboldt's real estate other than its main store property at One North State Street, Chicago.

[WSI needed an additional sum in excess of $30,000,000 to pay off CINB and lift the mortgage on the One North State Street property. The BAMIRCO loan was to provide most of this. This loan was to be secured by a first mortgage on One North State Street. WSI structured this transaction through an intermediary limited partnership ("ONSSLP") set up between WSI and a real estate broker. Specifically, One North State Street was to be conveyed to ONSSLP by Wieboldt for $30,000,000, the purchase money to be loaned by BAMIRCO and a mortgage given back. The $30,000,000 would then be applied to pay down Wieboldt's obligations to CINB.

[Unfortunately, the $30,000,000 sale of One North State Street did not generate sufficient funds to pay off all the CINB obligations. The GECC commitment of a line of credit not to exceed $35,000,000 provided these additional funds. This transaction was structured as a sale of Wieboldt's customer charge card accounts. In addition to the sale of the charge card accounts, this "accounts purchase agreement" required Wieboldt to pledge all of its accounts receivable as additional security.]

The Board of Directors was fully aware of the progress of WSI's negotiations. The Board understood that WSI intended to finance the tender offer by pledging a substantial portion of Wieboldt's assets to its lenders, and that WSI did not intend to use any of its own funds or the funds of its shareholders to finance the acquisition. Moreover, although the Board initially believed that the tender offer would produce $10 million in working capital for the company, the members knew that the proceeds from the LBO lenders would not result in this additional working capital.

Nevertheless, in October, 1985 the Board directed Mr. Darrow* and Wieboldt's lawyers to work with WSI to effect the acquisition. During these negotiations, the Board learned that HCFS would provide financing for the tender offer only if Wieboldt would provide a statement from a nationally recognized accounting firm stating that Wieboldt was solvent and a going concern prior to the planned acquisition and would be solvent and a going concern after the acquisition. Mr. Darrow informed WSI that Wieboldt would only continue cooperating in the LBO if HCFS agreed not to require this solvency certificate. HCFS acceded to Wieboldt's demand and no solvency certificate was ever provided to HCFS on Wieboldt's behalf.

On November 18, 1985 Wieboldt's Board of Directors voted to approve WSI's tender offer, and on November 20, 1985 WSI announced its offer to purchase Wieboldt stock for $13.50 per share. By December 20, 1985 the tender offer was complete and WSI had acquired ownership of Wieboldt

---

* [Ed. Note] A Wieboldt director.

through its purchase of 99% of Wieboldt's stock at a total price of $38,462,164.00. All of the funds WSI used to purchase the tendered shares were provided by HCFS and were secured by the assets which BAMIRCO and GECC loan proceeds had freed from CINB obligations.

[Certain of Wieboldt's creditors commenced an involuntary liquidation proceeding against Wieboldt under chapter 7 of the Bankruptcy Code (the "Code") in September 1986. On the same day, Wieboldt filed a voluntary reorganization proceeding pursuant to chapter 11.

[Thereafter Wieboldt brought this action against (1) the controlling shareholders and Wieboldt's officers and directors, (2) other Wieboldt shareholders who owned and tendered more than 1,000 shares in response to the tender offer (the "Schedule A shareholders"), and (3) the lenders who funded the tender offer and associated purchase of One North State Street. In its complaint, Wieboldt alleged that WSI's tender offer and the resulting LBO was a fraudulent conveyance under the federal bankruptcy statute and the Illinois fraudulent conveyance laws. The various defendants move to dismiss the complaint under Rule 12(b)(6) on the grounds that Wieboldt has failed to state a claim.]

1.   *Applicability of Fraudulent Conveyance Law.*

Both the federal Bankruptcy Code and Illinois law protect creditors from transfers of property that are intended to impair a creditor's ability to enforce its rights to payment or that deplete a debtor's assets at a time when its financial condition is precarious. Modern fraudulent conveyance law derives from the English Statute of Elizabeth enacted in 1570, the substance of which has been either enacted in American statutes prohibiting such transactions or has been incorporated into American law as a part of the English common law heritage. See Sherwin, "Creditors' Rights Against Participants in a Leveraged Buy-out," 72 Minn.L.Rev. 449, 465–66 (1988).

The controlling shareholders, insider shareholders, and some of the Schedule A shareholders argue that fraudulent conveyance laws do not apply to leveraged buy-outs. These defendants argue (1) that applying fraudulent conveyance laws to public tender offers effectively allows creditors to insure themselves against subsequent mismanagement of the company; (2) that applying fraudulent conveyance laws to LBO transactions and thereby rendering them void severely restricts the usefulness of LBOs and results in great unfairness; and (3) that fraudulent conveyance laws were never intended to be used to prohibit or restrict public tender offers.

Although some support exists for defendants' arguments,[13] this court cannot hold at this stage in this litigation that the LBO in question here is entirely exempt from fraudulent conveyance laws. Neither Section 548 of the Code nor the Illinois statute exempt such transactions from their statutory coverage. Section 548 invalidates fraudulent "transfers" of a debtor's property. Section 101(50) defines such a transfer very broadly to

---

13.   See, e.g., Baird & Jackson, "Fraudulent Conveyance Law and Its Proper Domain," 38 Vand.L.Rev. 829 (1985).

include "every mode, direct or indirect, absolute or conditional, voluntary or involuntary, of disposing of or parting with property or with an interest in property, including retention of title as a security interest." 11 U.S.C. § 101(50). Likewise, the Illinois statute applies to gifts, grants, conveyances, assignments and transfers. Ill.Rev.Stat. ch. 59, ¶ 4. The language of these statutes in no way limits their application so as to exclude LBOs.

In addition, those courts which have addressed this issue have concluded that LBOs in some circumstances may constitute a fraudulent conveyance. * * * Defendants have presented no case law which holds to the contrary.[14]

The court is aware that permitting debtors to avoid all LBO transfers through the fraudulent conveyance laws could have the effect of insuring against a corporation's subsequent insolvency and failure. *Anderson Industries, Inc.* 55 B.R. at 926; see also Baird & Jackson, supra, n. 11 at 839. * * *

2. *The Structure of the Transaction.*

Although the court finds that the fraudulent conveyance laws generally are applicable to LBO transactions, a debtor cannot use these laws to avoid any and all LBO transfers. In this case, certain defendants argue that they are entitled to dismissal because the LBO transfers at issue do not fall within the parameters of the laws. These defendants argue that they are protected by the literal language of Section 548 of the Code and the "good faith transferee for value" rule in Section 550.[15] They contend, initially, that they did not receive Wieboldt property during the tender offer and, secondarily, that, even if they received Wieboldt property, they tendered their shares in good faith, for value, and without the requisite knowledge and therefore cannot be held liable under Section 550.

The merit of this assertion turns on the court's interpretation of the tender offer and LBO transactions. Defendants contend that the tender offer and LBO were composed of a series of interrelated but independent transactions. They assert, for example, that the transfer of property from HCFS to WSI and ultimately to the shareholders constituted one series of several transactions while the pledge of Wieboldt assets to HCFS to secure

14. Cf. Credit Managers Ass'n of Southern California v. Federal Company, 629 F.Supp. 175, 179 (C.D.Cal.1985), in which a California court expressed reservations about extending fraudulent conveyance law to leveraged buyouts but specifically reserved the issue in its decision.

15. While Section 548 defines the nature of the transactions that are avoidable by the debtor, Section 550 places limits on Section 548 by defining the kind of transferee from whom a debtor may recover transferred property. Section 550(a) permits a trustee to recover fraudulently transferred property from

1. the initial transferee;

2. the entity for whose benefit such transfer was made; or

3. an immediate or mediate transferee of such initial transferee (a "subsequent transferee").

11 U.S.C. § 550(a). Section 550(b) states that a trustee may *not* recover from

1. a subsequent transferee who takes the property for value, in good faith, and without knowledge of the voidability of the transfer; or

2. an immediate or mediate good faith transferee of such a transferee.

11 U.S.C. § 550(b).

the financing constituted a second series of transactions. Under this view, defendants did not receive the *debtor*'s property during the tender offer but rather received *WSI*'s property in exchange for their shares.

Wieboldt, on the other hand, urges the court to "collapse" the interrelated transactions into one aggregate transaction which had the overall effect of conveying Wieboldt property to the tendering shareholders and LBO lenders. This approach requires the court to find that the persons and entities receiving the conveyance were direct transferees who received "an interest of the debtor in property" during the tender offer/buyout, and that WSI and any other parties to the transactions were "mere conduits" of Wieboldt's property. If the court finds that all the transfers constituted one transaction, then defendants received property from Wieboldt and Wieboldt has stated a claim against them.

Few courts have considered whether complicated LBO transfers should be evaluated separately or collapsed into one integrated transaction. However, two United States Courts of Appeals opinions provide some illumination on this issue. See Capes v. Wolf, 845 F.2d 842 (9th Cir.1988); United States v. Tabor Court Realty, 803 F.2d 1288 (3d Cir.1986), cert. denied McClellan Realty Co. v. United States, ___ U.S. ___ (1987).

* * *

Neither of these two cases involved transactions which were identical to the WSI–Wieboldt buyout. However, the *Capes* and *Tabor Court* opinions are nonetheless significant because the courts in both cases expressed the view that an LBO transfer—in whatever form—was a fraudulent conveyance if the circumstances of the transaction were not "above board." *Capes,* 845 F.2d at 847. Thus, even though the court in *Capes* declined to hold the selling shareholders liable, there was no showing in *Capes* that the shareholders intended to defraud [the debtor company's] creditors nor even that the purchaser intended to finance the takeover by leveraging the company's assets. On the other hand, the court in *Tabor Court* found the LBO lender liable because it participated in the negotiations surrounding the LBO transactions and knew that the proceeds of its loan to [the corporation effecting the LBO] would deplete the debtor's assets to the point at which it was functionally insolvent under the fraudulent conveyance and bankruptcy laws. These cases indicate that a court should focus not on the formal structure of the transaction but rather on the knowledge and intent of the parties involved in the transaction.

Applying this principle to defendants' assertions, it is clear that, at least as regards the liability of the controlling shareholders, the LBO lenders, and the insider shareholders, the LBO transfers must be collapsed into one transaction. The complaint alleges clearly that these participants in the LBO negotiations attempted to structure the LBO with the requisite knowledge and contemplation that the full transaction, tender offer and LBO, be completed.[20] The Board and the insider shareholders knew that

---

20. Although many of the allegations in the complaint refer to the state of mind and activities of the Board of Directors, these allegations may fairly be imputed to the controlling shareholders. The controlling shareholders nominated a majority of the directors

WSI intended to finance its acquisition of Wieboldt through an LBO * * * and not with any of its own funds * * *. They knew that Wieboldt was insolvent before the LBO and that the LBO would result in further encumbrance of Wieboldt's already encumbered assets. * * * Attorneys for Schottenstein Stores apprised the Board of the fraudulent conveyance laws and suggested that they structure the LBO so as to avoid liability. * * * Nonetheless, these shareholders recommended that Wieboldt accept the tender offer and themselves tendered their shares to WSI. * * *

Wieboldt's complaint also alleges sufficient facts to implicate the LBO lenders in the scheme. HCFS, BAMIRCO and GECC were well aware of each other's loan or credit commitments to WSI and knew that WSI intended to use the proceeds of their financing commitments to purchase Wieboldt shares or options and to release certain Wieboldt assets from prior encumbrances. * * * Representatives of the lenders received the same information concerning the fraudulent conveyance laws as did the Board of Directors. * * *

The court, however, is not willing to "collapse" the transaction in order to find that the Schedule A shareholders also received the debtor's property in the transfer. While Wieboldt directs specific allegations of fraud against the controlling and insider shareholders and LBO lenders, Wieboldt does not allege that the Schedule A shareholders were aware that WSI's acquisition encumbered virtually all of Wieboldt's assets. Nor is there an allegation that these shareholders were aware that the consideration they received for their tendered shares was Wieboldt property. In fact, the complaint does not suggest that the Schedule A shareholders had any part in the LBO except as innocent pawns in the scheme. They were aware only that WSI made a public tender offer for shares of Wieboldt stock. * * * Viewing the transactions from the perspective of the Schedule A shareholders and considering their knowledge and intent, therefore, the asset transfers to the LBO lenders were indeed independent of the tender offer to the Schedule A shareholders.

This conclusion is in accord with the purpose of the fraudulent conveyance laws. The drafters of the Code, while attempting to protect parties harmed by fraudulent conveyances, also intended to shield innocent recipients of fraudulently conveyed property from liability. Thus, although Subsection (a) of Section 550 permits a trustee to avoid a transfer to an initial transferee or its subsequent transferee, Subsection (b) of that Section limits recovery from a subsequent transferee by providing that a trustee may not recover fraudulently conveyed property from a subsequent transferee who takes the property in good faith, for value, and without knowledge that the original transfer was voidable. Subsection (b) applies, however, only to subsequent transferees.

Similarly, the LBO lenders and the controlling and insider shareholders of Wieboldt are direct transferees of Wieboldt property. Although WSI participated in effecting the transactions, Wieboldt's complaint alleges that

to their positions on the Board. In addition, many of the individuals who served on the Board were "insiders" to Schottenstein Stores, Inc. or MBT Corporation.

WSI was a corporation formed solely for the purpose of acquiring Wieboldt stock. The court can reasonably infer from the complaint, therefore, that WSI served mainly as a conduit for the exchange of assets and loan proceeds between LBO lenders and Wieboldt and for the exchange of loan proceeds and shares of stock between the LBO lenders and the insider and controlling shareholders. On the other hand, the Schedule A shareholders are not direct transferees of Wieboldt property. From their perspective, WSI was the direct transferee of Wieboldt property and the shareholders were merely indirect transferees because WSI was an independent entity in the transaction.

* * *

3. *The Elements of a Fraudulent Conveyance.*

As discussed above, the transfers to and between the debtor and the LBO lenders, controlling shareholders, and insider shareholders are subject to the provisions in Section 548(a) of the Code and Section 4 of the Illinois statute. The court now must determine whether Wieboldt's complaint states sufficient facts to allege the elements of these causes of action.

a.   Section 548(a)(1)

In order to state a claim for relief under Section 548(a)(1) of the Code, a debtor or trustee must allege (1) that the transfer was made within one year before the debtor filed a petition in bankruptcy, and (2) that the transfer was made with the actual intent to hinder, delay or defraud the debtor's creditors. 11 U.S.C. § 548(a)(1). * * * Although defendants do not dispute that the LBO transfers occurred within a year of the date on which Wieboldt filed for bankruptcy, they vigorously assert that Wieboldt has failed to properly allege "intent to defraud" as required by Section 548(a)(1).

"Actual intent" in the context of fraudulent transfers of property is rarely susceptible to proof and "must be gleaned from inferences drawn from a course of conduct." In re Vecchione, 407 F.Supp. 609, 615 (E.D.N.Y. 1976). A general scheme or plan to strip the debtor of its assets without regard to the needs of its creditors can support a finding of actual intent. * * * In addition, certain "badges of fraud" can form the basis for a finding of actual intent to hinder, delay or defraud. 4 Collier on Bankruptcy ¶ 548.02[5] (15th ed. 1987).[24]

Counts I and III of Wieboldt's complaint state a claim under Section 548(a)(1). Count I, which Wieboldt brings against the controlling and insider shareholders, states that these defendants exchanged their shares with the actual intent to hinder, delay or defraud Wieboldt's unsecured creditors. * * * Count III states that the State Street defendants received Wieboldt's interest in One North State Street property with the actual

---

24. For example, when a debtor conceals a fact or makes false pretenses, reserves rights in the property which is transferred, or creates a closely held corporation to receive the transfer, or when the value of the transfer is unconscionably greater than the consideration received for it, the transaction is said to bear the "badge of fraud." 4 Collier on Bankruptcy ¶ 548.02[4] (15th ed. 1987).

intent to defraud Wieboldt's unsecured creditors. * * * The complaint also states generally that the LBO Lenders and the controlling and insider shareholders structured the LBO transfers in such a way as to attempt to evade fraudulent conveyance liability. * * *

b. Section 548(a)(2)

Unlike Section 548(a)(1), which requires a plaintiff to allege "actual fraud," Section 548(a)(2) requires a plaintiff to allege only constructive fraud. A plaintiff states a claim under Section 548(a)(2) by alleging that the debtor (1) transferred property within a year of filing a petition in bankruptcy; (2) received less than the reasonably equivalent value for the property transferred; and (3) either (a) was insolvent or became insolvent as a result of the transfer, (b) retained unreasonably small capital after the transfer, or (c) made the transfer with the intent to incur debts beyond its ability to pay. 11 U.S.C. § 548(a)(2).

Defendants argue that Wieboldt's allegation of insolvency is insufficient as a matter of law to satisfy the insolvency requirement in Section 548(a)(2)(B)(I). Section 101(31)(A) of the Code defines "insolvency" as a condition which occurs when the sum of an entity's debts exceeds the sum of its property "at a fair valuation." 11 U.S.C. § 101(31)(A). Wieboldt's complaint alleges that the corporation was insolvent in November, 1985 "in that the fair saleable value of its assets was exceeded by its liabilities when the illiquidity of those assets is taken into account." * * *

Wieboldt's allegations satisfy the "insolvency" requirement of Section 548(a)(2)(B)(I). Defendants' attempt to distinguish Wieboldt's phrase "fair saleable value" from Section 101(31)(A)'s "fair valuation" is, as Wieboldt suggests, "hyper-technical." * * *. "Fair valuation" is near enough in meaning to "fair value of saleable assets" to defeat defendants' motion to dismiss. * * * In addition, Wieboldt did not destroy its claim of insolvency by characterizing its assets as "illiquid" at the time of the transfer. In determining "fair valuation," a court must consider the property's intrinsic value, selling value, and the earning power of the property. * * *. Assets may be reduced by the value of the assets that cannot be readily liquidated. * * * The complaint meets the financial condition test of Section 548(a)(2)(B)(I).

Finally, defendants claim that Wieboldt cannot state a claim under Section 548(a)(2) because it received "reasonably equivalent value" in the transfer to the shareholders and the conveyance of the One North State Street property. Wieboldt granted a security interest in substantially all of its real estate assets to HCFS and received from the shareholders in return 99% of its outstanding shares of stock.[25] * * * This stock was virtually

---

25. Defendants argue that WSI (and not Wieboldt) received the outstanding shares of Wieboldt stock. However, a court analyzing an allegedly fraudulent transfer must direct its attention to "what the Debtor surrendered and what the Debtor received, irrespective of what any third party may have gained or lost." In re Ohio Corrugating Co., 70 B.R. 920, 927 (Bkrtcy.N.D.Ohio 1987). As discussed in Section C.2. of this opinion, the court considers the tender offer and buyout transfers as one transaction for the purposes of this motion.

worthless to Wieboldt. * * * Wieboldt received less than a reasonably equivalent value in exchange for an encumbrance on virtually all of its non-inventory assets, and therefore has stated a claim against the controlling and insider shareholders.

Likewise, the court need not dismiss Wieboldt's Section 548(a)(2) claim against the State Street defendants on the grounds that Wieboldt received reasonably equivalent value in exchange for its One North State Street property. The effect and intention of the parties to the One North State Street conveyance was to generate funds to purchase outstanding shares of Wieboldt stock. Although Wieboldt sold the property to ONSSLP for $30 million,[26] and used the proceeds to pay off part of the $35 million it owed CINB, Wieboldt did not receive a benefit from this transfer. * * * Defendants knew that the conveyance would neither increase Wieboldt's assets nor result in a net reduction of its liabilities. In fact, all parties to the conveyance were aware that the newly unencumbered assets would be immediately remortgaged to HCFS to finance the acquisition. * * * According to the complaint, therefore, Wieboldt received less than reasonably equivalent value for the conveyance of the One North State Street property and has stated a claim against the State Street defendants under Section 548(a)(2).

In sum, Counts II and IV of Wieboldt's complaint state a claim under Section 548(a)(2). Defendants' motions to dismiss these counts are denied.

c.   Illinois Fraudulent Conveyance Law

Under Section 544(b) of the Code, a trustee may avoid transfers that are avoidable under state law if there is at least one creditor at the time who has standing under state law to challenge the transfer. 11 U.S.C. § 544(b). Wieboldt utilizes this section to pursue a claim under the Illinois fraudulent conveyance statute, Ill.Rev.Stat. ch. 59, § 4.

The Illinois fraudulent conveyance statute is similar to Section 548 of the Code. The statute provides that:

> Every gift, grant, conveyance, assignment or transfer of, or charge upon any estate, real or personal, * * * made with the intent to disturb, delay, hinder or defraud creditors or other persons, * * * shall be void as against the creditors, purchasers and other persons.

Ill.Rev.Stat. ch. 59, § 4 (1976). Illinois courts divide fraudulent conveyances into two categories: fraud in law and fraud in fact. Tcherepnin v. Franz, 475 F.Supp. 92, 96 (N.D.Ill.1979). In fraud in fact cases, a court must find a specific intent to defraud creditors; in fraud in law cases, fraud is presumed from the circumstances. Id.

[The court ruled that Count VIII of Wieboldt's complaint stated a claim for fraud in law and denied defendants' motion to dismiss.]

---

26. In reality, Wieboldt conveyed the property to ONSSLP as beneficiary of a land trust with Boulevard Bank as trustee.

NOTE: FRAUDULENT CONVEYANCE AVOIDANCE OF LEVERAGED BUYOUTS

1. *Constructive Fraud and Form versus Substance.*

LBOs and other high leverage restructurings proceed against a cognizable legal risk of subsequent fraudulent conveyance attack. No controversy surrounds the proposition that avoidance should follow upon a finding of actual intent to defraud—the first ground pursued in *Wieboldt Stores.* Controversy does surround the second ground pursued in the case—constructive fraud on the theory that payments to the equity holders taken out are transfers for inadequate consideration leaving the corporation either insolvent or with unreasonably small capital.

Courts have differed on the constructive fraud proposition. The essential "transfer for inadequate consideration" emerges only if, as in *Wieboldt Stores,* the court applies a "substance over form" analysis. The constituent transactions are collapsed into a whole. The shell corporation that purchases the stock is disregarded so that the LBO debt is viewed as incurred by the target for the purpose of repurchasing its own stock. A second analytical step then must be taken: the payment to the target stockholders must be deemed to have no value to the target and its creditors. In effect, the payment is characterized as a dividend rather than as a purchase of stock for value. (Spins offs also have been characterized as constructive fraud in the event of the parent corporation's later bankruptcy. See, e.g., In re Integra Realty Resources, Inc., 198 B.R. 352 (Bankr.D.Colo.1996). Since these transactions are dividends in form, they require no "substance over form" analysis.)

Wieboldt Stores embodies the majority view. **Kupetz v. Wolf**, 845 F.2d 842 (9th Cir.1988), is the leading case among the minority which resist treatment of LBOs as constructive fraud. The court there in effect required a showing of intent to defraud: The LBO had been "above board" and the selling shareholders had no awareness of the insiders' financing arrangements. See also Credit Managers Association of Southern California v. Federal Co., 629 F.Supp. 175 (C.D.Cal.1985). Compare In re Bay Plastics, Inc., 187 B.R. 315 (Bankr.C.D.Cal.1995), which proceeds to constructive fraud scrutiny, collapsing the constituent corporations and distinguishing *Kupetz* on the ground that here the selling shareholders knew of the LBO arrangements. See also Zahn v. Yucaipa Capital Fund, 218 B.R. 656 (D.R.I. 1998). **C–T of Virginia, Inc. v. Euroshoe Associates Ltd. Partnership,** 953 F.2d 637 (4th Cir.1992), also takes a view favorable to LBOs. The court construed the Virginia fraudulent conveyance statute (which requires receipt by the debtor of "consideration deemed valuable" in order to justify a conveyance of assets) to be satisfied if "anything of value" is received. The acquiring company invested $4 million and borrowed approximately $26 million (which was assumed by the target) to pay off the target's stockholders a total of approximately $30 million. The court concluded that the $4 million of new investment met the test of "anything of value."

2. *Constructive Fraud and Public Policy.*

What policy gloss should be applied to high leverage restructurings for purposes of determining the application of fraudulent conveyance law?

Under an optimistic description articulated in the 1980s, leveraged restructurings are efficiency-driven transactions that provide corporate governance benefits. The payment to the equity holders amounts to a remedy for past suboptimal reinvestment of earnings by entrenched managers. The fixed coupon on the debt prevents future suboptimal capital investment. Meanwhile, tax benefits accrue to the restructured corporation. High leverage presents no problem because the capital markets will make sure that only corporations well suited to high leverage are selected: mature, noncyclical industries are best. Although some bankruptcies inevitably will occur, they will not be as costly as some fear: the interested actors will work out low cost contract solutions to the problem of defaulted loans. The preexisting creditors do sustain a short-run injury, but in the long run they benefit from improved management. They can in any event protect themselves by adjusting the terms of their contracts. See, e.g., Baird and Jackson, Fraudulent Conveyance Law and its Proper Domain, 38 Vand.L.Rev. 829 (1985). Compare Baird, Fraudulent Conveyances, Agency Costs, and Leveraged Buyouts, 20 J. Legal Studies 1 (1991), which takes a more equivocal position, leaving open the ultimate policy question respecting the costs and benefits of a creditor protective legal rule.

Under a more pessimistic description of LBOs, we cannot assume the existence of across-the-board governance benefits. Many LBOs have amounted to classic market speculations. The market is that for corporate assets, bought and sold on a going concern basis. The story is that speculators in the late 1980s took advantage of loose lending practices to bid up the prices of corporate assets and turn quick profits. No particular governance benefits accrued: it does not take a business genius to shut down a factory and lay off employees. Nor did actors in the financial markets act with acuity: many LBOs occurred in weak, cyclical segments where default was inevitable, as *Wieboldt Stores* demonstrates. For a discussion endorsing constructive fraud treatment, see Zaretsky, Fraudulent Transfer Law as the Arbiter of Unreasonable Risk, 46 S.C.L.Rev. 1165 (1995).

It should be noted that constructive fraud analysis does not preclude a showing of countervailing benefits to the debtor firm stemming from the LBO. In connection with the question whether the debtor firm received "fair consideration" in the LBO, courts have considered evidence of "indirect" benefits such as better management, synergistic effects of new corporate relationships, and tax benefits. New lines of credit also have been considered, at least where directly connected to new business opportunities. The party seeking to validate the transaction has the burden to show just how much these benefits were worth, however. See Mellon Bank, N.A. v. Metro Communications, Inc., 945 F.2d 635 (3d Cir.1991); MFS/Sun Life Trust v. Van Dusen Airport Services Co., 910 F.Supp. 913 (S.D.N.Y.1995).

3. *The Scope of Constructive Fraud Avoidance.*

Does the theory of constructive fraud articulated in *Wieboldt Stores* presumptively apply to every highly leveraged restructuring that at some point is followed by a bankruptcy reorganization? Or is avoidance risk limited to a highly-risky class of marginal transactions?

(a) *Valuation.* Determining whether a transaction leaves a debtor insolvent or with unreasonably small capital means valuing the debtor firm. The cases look at the debtor as a going concern at the time of the transaction and take a flexible approach. Balance sheet tests are avoided; cash flow projections are employed. See, e.g., In re PWS Holding Corp., 228 F.3d 224 (3d Cir.2000).

(b) *The meaning of "unreasonably small capital."* There is no fixed test, but it is clear that a point prior to insolvency is contemplated. The cases treat inadequate capitalization as a fact question for determination in the particular context. According to the court in In re Vadnais Lumber Supply, Inc., 100 B.R. 127, 137 (Bankr.D.Mass.1989), the court looks "to the ability of the debtor to generate enough cash from operations or asset sales to pay its debts and sustain itself." The standard "encompasses difficulties which are short of insolvency in any sense but are likely to lead to insolvency at some time in the future." Close scrutiny of the parties' pre-closing cash flow projections tends to be crucial. The courts review them for "reasonableness," looking to see if they allowed some margin for error. In re Healthco Int'l, Inc., 208 B.R. 288, 302 (Bankr.D.Mass.1997); MFS/Sun Life Trust v. Van Dusen Airport Services Co., supra, at 943; Moody v. Security Pac. Bus. Credit, Inc., 971 F.2d 1056, 1064 (3d Cir.1992).

(c) *Causation.* Implicitly, the transfer, and the denuded capitalization that results from it, must lead to default, and default must be a reasonably foreseeable result of the transfer. Supervening business reverses can break the nexus to the business circumstances at the time of the transfer under scrutiny. See, e.g., In re PWS Holding Corp., supra; Moody v. Security Pacific Business Credit, Inc., 971 F.2d 1056 (3d Cir.1992).

(d) *Remedies.* Fraudulent conveyance law calls for the "avoidance of the transfer." It is not always clear what sort of a decree this should lead to in the context of an LBO bankruptcy. Difficult questions come up respecting recoupment of payments made to holders of publicly-traded shares and cancellation of the LBO debt. The Examiner's Report in **In re Revco D.S.,** 118 B.R. 468 (Bankr.N.D.Ohio 1990) recommended that, as in *Wieboldt Stores,* the selling shareholders of the target not be pursued. The report suggested that the interests of the LBO participants be dealt with through the analytical device of a constructive unwind of the merger of the target and the LBO promoters' shell corporation. Under this approach, the LBO lenders' claims in bankruptcy are reconstructed as claims of creditors to the LBO shell corporation; the bankruptcy claims of the LBO promoters are treated as claims of the stockholders of the shell; and the reconstructed shell is treated as the owner of all the stock of the bankrupt corporation. This treatment detaches the LBO debt from the bankrupt corporation. The analysis in effect returns the bankrupt corporation to solvency and permits its preexisting creditors to be paid in full. Any value left over goes to interest holders in the constructive shell, first to the lenders, and then to the equity participants. In substance this amounts to equitable subordination of the LBO participants' claims.

In re Kaiser Steel Corp., 952 F.2d 1230 (10th Cir.1991), imposes a statutory barrier to recovery of amounts paid to the selling shareholders. Kaiser Steel Resources, Inc., formerly known as Kaiser Steel Corp., sought to retrieve amounts paid out to former Kaiser Steel shareholders in connection with a leveraged buyout. Kaiser claimed that these payments constituted a fraudulent conveyance. The defense was that a Bankruptcy Code exemption, section 546(e), precluded the trustee from avoiding "settlement payments" made by or to stockbrokers, financial institutions, and clearing agencies. The court held that the section 546(e) exemption encompassed amounts paid to the shareholders in the LBO, and accordingly prevented Kaiser from unwinding the transaction. The holding is controversial and has been read narrowly. Courts want to see a clear connection to the clearance and settlement system. See, e.g., Jewel Recovery, L.P. v. Gordon, 196 B.R. 348 (N.D.Tex. 1996), declining to apply the exemption to a closely-held firm. Other courts are overtly hostile. For example, In re Munford, Inc., 98 F.3d 604 (11th Cir.1996), declines to apply the exception to payments made to public stockholders by a bank.

4. *A Leveraged Spin Off.*

In 1996 Campbell Soup wanted to unload two underperforming divisions, Vlasic pickles and Swanson frozen dinners. It did so by combining a spin off with a cash for assets sale. It formed a shell subsidiary and caused the subsidiary to borrow $500 million from banks. The subsidiary then purchased Vlasic and Swanson from Campbell for $500 million cash. After the purchase closed, Campbell spun off the subsidiary, emerging with the cash and without Vlasic and Swanson. The spun off company, however, fell into distress and ended up in chapter 11 within three years. There its assets were sold off for less than the original $500 million ($504 million realized from 1999 to 2001 discounted back to $385 million in 1996 dollars). A successor representing the interests of the spun off firm's creditors sued Campbell, claiming that the original sale of the divisions for $500 million had been a fraudulent conveyance. In **VFB LLC v. Campbell Soup Co.**, 482 F.2d 624 (3d Cir.2007), the court held that the plaintiff had failed to meet the burden of proving that the deal had not been for "reasonably equivalent value." The Court did note that Campbell had driven a very hard bargain in what amounted to a self-dealing transaction with the pre-spin off subsidiary. It also noted that Campbell had been massaging the books of Vlasic and Swanson for years in violation of GAAP as it groomed them for borrowing and independent status. Even so, the conditions that led to insolvency had arisen after the spin off.

(D) FIDUCIARY DUTY

It is clear that managers of a healthy firm owe fiduciary duties to their shareholders. It is clear that the trustee of a firm in bankruptcy owes a fiduciary duty to the creditors. It also is clear that at some point between these two extremes the identity of the beneficiary of the duty shifts from equity to debt. What is not clear is where this tipping point is reached as the firm goes from financial distress to insolvency and on to reorganization. Some recent bankruptcy caselaw suggests that the tipping point may be reached when the board of directors approves an ill-advised LBO or spin off.

Credit Lyonnais Bank Nederland N.V. v. Pathe Communications Co.

Delaware Court of Chancery, 1991.
1991 WL 277613 at 42 & n. 55.

■ ALLEN, CHANCELLOR.

[W]here a corporation is operating in the vicinity of insolvency, a board of directors is not merely the agent of the residue risk bearers, but owes its duty to the corporate enterprise.

The possibility of insolvency can do curious things to incentives, exposing creditors to risks of opportunistic behavior and creating complexities for directors. Consider, for example, a solvent corporation having a single asset, a judgment for $51 million against a solvent debtor. The judgment is on appeal and thus subject to modification or reversal. Assume that the only liabilities of the company are to bondholders in the amount of $12 million. Assume that the array of probable outcomes of the appeal is as follows:

	Expected Value
25% chance of affirmance ($51mm)	$ 12.75
70% chance of modification ($4mm)	2.8
5% chance of reversal ($0)	0
Expected Value of Judgment on Appeal	$ 15.55

Thus, the best evaluation is that the current value of the equity is $3.55 million. ($15.55 million expected value of judgment on appeal $12 million liability to bondholders). Now assume an offer to settle at $12.5 million (also consider one at $17.5 million). By what standard do the directors of the company evaluate the fairness of these offers? The creditors of this solvent company would be in favor of accepting either a $12.5 million offer or a $17.5 million offer. In either event they will avoid the 75% risk of insolvency and default. The stockholders, however, will plainly be opposed to acceptance of a $12.5 million settlement (under which they get practically nothing). More importantly, they very well may be opposed to acceptance of the $17.5 million offer under which the residual value of the corporation would increase from $3.5 to $5.5 million. This is so because the litigation alternative, with its 25% probability of a $39 million outcome to them ($51 million—$12 million $39 million) has an expected value to the residual risk bearer of $9.75 million ($39 million x 25% chance of affirmance), substantially greater than the $5.5 million available to them in the settlement while in fact the stockholders' preference would reflect their appetite for risk, it is possible (and with diversified shareholders likely) that shareholders would prefer rejection of both settlement offers.

But if we consider the community of interests that the corporation represents it seems apparent that one should in this hypothetical accept the best settlement offer available providing it is greater than $15.55 million, and one below that amount should be rejected. But that result will not be reached by a director who thinks he owes duties directly to shareholders only. It will be reached by directors who are capable of conceiving of the corporation as a legal and economic entity. Such directors will recognize that in managing the business affairs of a solvent corporation in the vicinity of insolvency, circumstances may arise when the right (both the efficient and the fair) course to follow for the corporation may diverge from the choice that the stockholders (or the creditors, or the employees, or any single group interested in the corporation) would make if given the opportunity to act.

NOTE: PRE–BANKRUPTCY FIDUCIARY DUTIES TO CREDITORS

The proposition that fiduciary duties extend to creditors in a zone of distress prior to a formal bankruptcy filing has generated much controversy in recent years. The revival of high leveraged restructuring fuels the debate.

In re Healthco Int'l, 208 B.R. 288 (Bankr.D.Mass.1997), demonstrates the duty's expansive possibilities. This was a chapter 7 proceeding stemming from an unsuccessful LBO. Here the bankruptcy trustee asserted a state law breach of fiduciary duty claim against the members of the board of directors who had approved the transaction. The Court reasoned as follows, 208 B.R. at 300–02:

"The Trustee asserts a claim which belonged to Healthco, not its creditors. The Trustee contends the defendants breached their fiduciary duties owed to Healthco. Any Healthco claim is an interest in property which passed to the bankruptcy estate. [11 U.S.C. § 541(a)(1) (1994).] The Trustee can bring any suit Healthco could have brought, including suits against directors and controlling shareholders for breach of fiduciary duty. In complaining that directors authorized a transaction which unduly weakened Healthco, the Trustee is not asserting the claim of creditors. He alleges Healthco was the victim of poor management causing damage to the corporation which necessarily resulted in damage to its creditors by diminishing the value of its assets and increasing its liabilities.

"Nor are the defendants correct in stating their obligations were limited to looking out for the interests of stockholders. Normally, what is good for a corporation's stockholders is good for the corporation. But that was hardly true here if the Trustee establishes the LBO left Healthco insolvent or with unreasonably small capital. When a transaction renders a corporation insolvent, or brings it to the brink of insolvency, the rights of creditors become paramount. In those circumstances, notwithstanding shareholder consent, a representative of the corporation may recover damage from the defaulting directors.

"The courts of Delaware, the state of Healthco's incorporation, agree with these principles. * * * [I]t has been ruled the directors of an insolvent Delaware corporation breach their fiduciary duties to creditors, even in the absence of formal insolvency proceedings, when they authorize fraudulent conveyances which cause the corporation to be insolvent in fact. [See Geyer v. Ingersoll Publications Co., 621 A.2d 784 (Del.Ch.1992).]

* * *

"Requiring directors to look out for the interests of creditors as well as stockholders involves no irreconcilable conflict, as contended by defendants. It is merely an incident of the fiduciary obligations owed by directors to their corporation. A distribution to stockholders which renders the corporation insolvent, or leaves it with unreasonably small capital, threatens the very existence of the corporation. This is prejudicial to all its constituencies, including creditors, employees, and stockholders retaining an ownership interest. Surely it is not asking too much of directors that they honor their obligations of loyalty and care to avoid the corporation's destruction."

Cases like *Healthco Int'l* have resulted in pressure on Delaware to get the genie back into the bottle. Vice–Chancellor Strine takes up this task in in **Production Resources Group, LLC v. NCT Group, Inc.**, 863 A.2d 772, 787–93 (2004), putting the following gloss on *Credit Lyonnaise*:

" * * * [D]irectors–as fiduciaries in equity–are primarily focused on generating economic returns that will exceed what is required to pay bills in order to deliver a return to the company's stockholders who provided equity capital and agreed to bear the residual risk associated with the firm's operations. Somewhat oddly, a decision of this court that attempted to emphasize that directors have discretion to temper the risk that they take on behalf of the equity holders when the firm is in the 'zone of insolvency' has been read by some as creating a new body of creditor's rights law. The *Credit Lyonnais* decision's holding and spirit clearly emphasized that directors would be protected by the business judgment rule if they, in good faith, pursued a less risky business strategy precisely because they feared that a more risky strategy might render the firm unable to meet its legal obligations to creditors and other constituencies.

"The obligation of directors in that context of high risk and uncertainty, said Chancellor Allen, was not 'merely [to be] the agent of the residue risk bearers' but rather to remember their fiduciary duties to 'the corporate enterprise' itself, in the sense that the directors have an obligation 'to the community of interest that sustained the corporation.... ' and to preserve and, if prudently possible, to maximize the corporation's value to best satisfy the legitimate claims of all its constituents, and not simply to pursue the course of action that stockholders might favor as best for them. In other words, *Credit Lyonnais* provided a shield to directors from stockholders who claimed that the directors had a duty to undertake extreme risk so long as the company would not technically breach any legal obligations. By providing directors with this shield, creditors would derive a clear benefit because directors, it can be presumed, generally take seriously the company's duty to pay its bills as a first priority.

"Creative language in a famous footnote in *Credit Lyonnais* was read more expansively by some, not to create a shield for directors from stockholder claims, but to expose directors to a new set of fiduciary duty claims, this time by creditors. To the extent that a firm is in the zone of insolvency, some read *Credit Lyonnais* as authorizing creditors to challenge directors' business judgments as breaches of a fiduciary duty owed to them. Some cases in the courts of other jurisdictions have embraced this reading.

"This view of the common law of corporations is not unproblematic. Arguably, it involves using the law of fiduciary duty to fill gaps that do not exist. Creditors are often protected by strong covenants, liens on assets, and other negotiated contractual protections. The implied covenant of good faith and fair dealing also protects creditors. So does the law of fraudulent conveyance. With these protections, when creditors are unable to prove that a corporation or its directors breached any of the specific legal duties owed to them, one would think that the conceptual room for concluding that the creditors were somehow, nevertheless, injured by inequitable conduct would be extremely small, if extant. Having complied with all legal obligations owed to the firm's creditors, the board would, in that scenario, ordinarily be free to take economic risk for the benefit of the firm's equity owners, so long as the directors comply with their fiduciary duties to the firm by selecting and pursuing with fidelity and prudence a plausible strategy to maximize the firm's value.

"Fortunately, this case does not require me to explore the metaphysical boundaries of the zone of insolvency. Instead, it requires me to apply a more well-settled line of authority, albeit a line of authority that is perhaps less well understood.

"When a firm has reached the point of insolvency, it is settled that under Delaware law, the firm's directors are said to owe fiduciary duties to the company's creditors. This is an uncontroversial proposition and does not completely turn on its head the equitable obligations of the directors to the firm itself. The directors continue to have the task of attempting to maximize the economic value of the firm. That much of their job does not change. But the fact of insolvency does necessarily affect the constituency on whose behalf the directors are pursuing that end. By definition, the fact of insolvency places the creditors in the shoes normally occupied by the shareholders-that of residual risk-bearers. Where the assets of the company are insufficient to pay its debts, and the remaining equity is underwater, whatever remains of the company's assets will be used to pay creditors, usually either by seniority of debt or on a pro rata basis among debtors of equal priority.

"In insolvency, creditors, as residual claimants to a definitionally-inadequate pool of assets, become exposed to substantial risk as the entity goes forward; poor decisions by management may erode the value of the remaining assets, leaving the corporation with even less capital to satisfy its debts in an ultimate dissolution. The elimination of the stockholders' interest in the firm and the increased risk to creditors is said to justify imposing fiduciary obligations towards the company's creditors on the directors. A strand of authority (by no means universally praised) therefore describes an insolvent corporation as becoming akin to a trust for the benefit of the creditors. This line of thinking has been termed the 'trust fund doctrine.' Under a trust fund approach, the directors become trustees tasked with preserving capital for the benefit of creditors who are deemed to have an equity-like interest in the firm's assets.

" * * * [T]he transformation of a creditor into a residual owner does not change the nature of the harm in a typical claim for breach of fiduciary duty by corporate directors. Two examples will illustrate this. Assume that a corporation, say an airline, is already insolvent but that it has ongoing operations. A well-pled claim is made by one of the company's many creditors that the directors have engaged in self-dealing. Is this claim a direct claim belonging to the corporation's creditors as a class, or the specific complaining creditor, such that any monetary recovery would go directly to them, or it? I would think that it is not. Instead, because of the firm's insolvency, creditors would have standing to assert that the self-dealing directors had breached their fiduciary duties by improperly harming the economic value of the firm, to the detriment of the creditors who had legitimate claims on its assets. No particular creditor would have the right to the recovery; rather, all creditors would benefit when the firm was made whole and the firm's value was increased, enabling it to satisfy more creditor claims in order of their legal claim on the firm's assets. In other words, even in the case of an insolvent firm, poor decisions by directors that lead to a loss of corporate assets and are alleged to be a breaches of equitable fiduciary duties remain harms to the corporate entity itself. Thus, regardless of whether they are brought by creditors when a company is insolvent, these claims remain derivative, with either shareholders or creditors suing to recover for a harm done to the corporation as an economic entity and any recovery logically flows to the corporation and benefits the derivative plaintiffs indirectly to the extent of their claim on the firm's assets. The reason for this bears repeating-the fact of insolvency does not change the primary object of the director's duties, which is the firm itself. The firm's insolvency simply makes the creditors the principal constituency injured by any fiduciary breaches that diminish the firm's value and logically gives them standing to pursue these claims to rectify that injury. Put simply, when a director of an insolvent corporation, through a breach of fiduciary duty, injures the firm itself, the claim against the director is still one belonging to the corporation.

"Likewise, the fact that a firm has become insolvent after the acts that are alleged to have been fiduciarily improper does not convert a claim belonging to the corporation into one belonging to creditors, allowing them to proceed directly against the directors. Assume as a second example that a creditor alleges that the firm has become insolvent because of directorial mismanagement. The creditor's claim clearly alleges that because of director misconduct the firm itself has become less valuable. The later fact of insolvency does not transform the nature of the claim; it simply changes the class of those eligible to press the claim derivatively, by expanding it to include creditors."

See also Angelo, Gordon & Co., L.P. v. Allied Riser Communications Corp., 805 A.2d 221 (Del.Ch.2002) (employing the business judgment rule in evaluating conduct of board of distressed issuer subject to the duty); North American Catholic Educational Programming Foundation, Inc. v. Rob Gheewalla, 2006 WL 2588971 (Del.Ch.) (rejecting a direct action for breach of fiduciary duty respecting self dealing transactions where the corporation was in the zone of insolvency, but holding open the possibility that a "trust fund theory" might support a direct claim in the case of an insolvent firm).

Much commentary criticizes the zone of insolvency duty. See, e.g., Lipson, Directors' Duties to Creditors: Power Imbalance and the Financially Distressed Corporation, 50 UCLA L. Rev. 1189 (2003). Campbell and Frost, Managers' Fiduciary Duties in Financially Distressed Corporations: Chaos in Delaware (and Elsewhere), 32 J. Corp. L. 491 (2007), makes the blunt corrective suggestion that bankruptcy filing serve as the bright line, with uniform fiduciary duties across the pre-bankruptcy period.

SECTION F.   INSOLVENCY REORGANIZATION

1.   INTRODUCTION: THE REORGANIZATION BARGAIN AND THE LIMITS OF THE PARTIES' BARGAINING FREEDOM

(A) REORGANIZATION BY JUDICIAL PROCEEDING

We have seen that private, out-of-court reorganizations are thought to maximize the returns of holders of the distressed firm's equity. But we also have seen that private compositions proposed by distressed firms do not always command the assent of a sufficient number of creditors. In the latter event, a bankruptcy proceeding becomes the maximizing choice for the firm's equity holders and managers.

A bankruptcy filing brings immediate benefits to the debtor. Bankruptcy carries an automatic stay of creditor enforcement proceedings. The stay halts a "race to the courthouse" by individual creditors pursuing contractual remedies for default. Left unstayed, the race results in foreclosures in the case of secured debt, and money judgments followed by levy of execution in the case of unsecured debt. Liquidation of the debtor follows as a practical matter. Such a disorganized, piecemeal liquidation is likely to result in a loss of value to the group of creditors as a whole.

In theory, then, a bankruptcy proceeding benefits the firm's creditors because it preserves the firm's value. It follows that the proceeding should be structured so as to maximize the total value available for distribution among the creditors.

At this point difficult choices come up for the parties involved.

● **Continuation or liquidation.** The first choice concerns the disposition of the firm's assets. Depending on the facts of the case, value might be maximized by reorganizing the firm as a going concern and replacing its *ex ante*, debt-heavy, capital structure with a more feasible set of claims. Alternatively, the firm might be sold for cash as a going concern, or even closed down and liquidated piece by piece.

This choice would not have to be made if markets for the assets of distressed firms were perfect. Given perfect markets, the debtors' assets costlessly and instantly could be transferred to the highest valuing user or users in exchange for cash and corporate reorganization as we know it would not have to exist. All claimants could be paid off in cash in order of priority and there would be no need to argue over the value of the assets or the capital structure of the reorganized enterprise. But, since transfers in markets for the assets of distressed firms have not, historically, been considered a reliable means of value maximization, the reorganization process has evolved so as to leave the assets in the hands of the present claimants and avoid their sale for cash to third parties. This requires that the creditor's claims be satisfied in a form other than cash, specifically, in new participations in the going concern. The claimants receive varied forms of securities in the reorganized enterprise—mortgage debt, unsecured debt, subordinated debt, convertible debt or preferred stock, common stock and warrants. The allocation of these new participations in accordance with old priorities depends on the going concern value of the enterprise. The reorganization system, both under pre–1978 bankruptcy law and under chapter 11 of the Bankruptcy Reform Act of 1978 (the "Bankruptcy Code"), provides for the determination of this value without reference to market measures of the value of the firm or its separate assets. In addition, the system contemplates that the claimants will bargain over these matters—both the value of the enterprise and its assets and the value and composition of the packages of new securities offered in satisfaction of the old claims.

A prominent line of commentary questions this approach. We will see that it suggests that the system would provide a better means to the end of realizing maximum value if it were revised to rely on market sales of the firm's assets or, in the alternative, to rely on means of setting value based on the behavior of transacting parties rather than on judicial determinations or structured negotiations.

• **Priorities.** Once a choice as to the disposition of the firm's assets has been made, the value thus maximized (and calculated) must be distributed among the firm's interest holders. Now choices must be made respecting the status of the firm's competing claimants. The bankruptcy reorganization process contemplates that the claimants bargain over the scope, validity and priority of their claims. The resulting negotiations, as we saw in the case of out-of-court recapitalizations, can produce strategic behavior, often at the expense of public investors. But strategic behavior is treated differently in the bankruptcy context, for here the negotiation leads to and culminates in a legal proceeding. The court approves, or requires modification of, the proposed bargain, and orders its implementation.

This system of court supervised recapitalization entails two types of rules: (a) Rules which prescribe and set limits on the bargaining processes in which the dispersed claimants are permitted to engage [e.g. who may speak, and how to determine who may speak, for which groups of claimants? How are the bargains reached by representatives to be communicated and approved by the members of each group?]; and, (b) Rules which set limits on the substantive bargains the parties may reach [e.g. how much participation may a senior class be permitted to yield (for *all* the seniors) over the protest of some of its members to an opportunistically behaving junior class?]

At this point, a powerful incentive-based argument can be made for a substantive rule that wipes out the insolvent firm's equity interest. If the debtor's commitment to performance of its promise to pay is to have any force, some punishment must follow upon default on the promise. A distributional rule of absolute priority of claim is suggested. But a strict absolute priority rule can have perverse effects on the *ex ante* behavior of the distressed firm's managers and equity holders, encouraging risky investment projects and undue delay of bankruptcy filings. Hart, Different Approaches to Bankruptcy, NBER Working Paper 7921 (Sept. 2000). We will see that the bankruptcy system takes an equivocal position on this choice.

(B) THE PARAMETERS OF THE BANKRUPTCY BARGAIN

The creditors' bond contracts generally provide that when the debtor defaults in the payment of interest or principal, the bondholder has a right to demand and receive principal and accrued interest in cash. It follows that in bankruptcy the quantitative measure of a claim's priority in the distribution of the available assets is its principal and accrued interest, as if matured.

The process of satisfying the claim, thus defined, is complicated by the system's allowance of payment in units other than cash. Issues of equivalence arise: whether the security, or package of securities, being accepted in satisfaction of the claim is equivalent to the cash award called for by the matured claim. The claimants may disagree as to whether the proposed new participations in fact meet their claims. Such allocative disputes also can extend to the value of the enterprise. The more value that appears, the more room opens for participation by junior claimants.

Disputes over matters of value in bankruptcy tend to be made as moves in larger allocative contests in which junior claimants seek recoveries at the expense of seniors. Consider a firm at the edge of insolvency, with debts roughly equaling liquidation value. The firm's creditors will advocate immediate liquidation, since liquidation will satisfy their claims even as it leaves nothing for the firm's equity holders. The shareholders, in contrast, may want a long proceeding: unless a need for speed follows from the nature of the bankrupt business, the shareholders have the upside potential during the period of pendency while the creditors have the downside risk. Generally, delay favors juniors, particularly shareholders and their management representatives. By delaying, they continue the enterprise with the creditors' capital, subjecting unsecured creditors to the risks of the enterprise (which during reorganization are, in effect, equity or junior debt risks).

Delay at the instance of the juniors substantially impairs the seniors' expectations. The seniors presumably invested for a cash return, accepting a limited return in exchange for priorities to income and principal. Prompt completion of the readjustment and resumption of cash flow best fulfills their expectations. In contrast, time often costs the juniors nothing—they face partial or total elimination if the seniors' claims are honored at face amounts. Hence the juniors may delay both the initiation and completion of reorganization both as a bargaining lever and in hope that the firm's values will increase with time and the turn of the business cycle.

The senior's awkward bargaining position can give rise to a disagreement among members of a senior class as to whether, notwithstanding their entitlement to full payment, they should waive that claim and accept less. Many members of a senior class may be willing to settle for less than is their legal right in order to settle quickly. There is no doubt that 100 percent of a class of creditors can make such a settlement, even though the concession is prompted by the juniors' nuisance power. But, as we have seen, public bond contracts are regulated by section 316(b) of the Trust Indenture Act, and will not permit a majority of the bondholders to approve an amendment that reduces the principal amount payable, or alters more than trivially the payment of interest. Privately issued notes tend to opt for the same rule by contract.

Should bankruptcy law give a majority of a senior class the power to bind a minority to accept less than payment in full? Until 1978, when chapter X of the Bankruptcy Act of 1938 was repealed, both courts and Congress nominally declined to allow such majoritarian settlements. The reasons for thus imposing a rule of "absolute priority" in lieu of requiring unanimous acceptance of the bargain (and thus nominally refusing to allow a majority to bind a minority to accept less in "value" than the amount of its claim) were to be found in the conditions under which bargaining between classes of security holders had proceeded in reorganizations prior to 1938. The earlier "equity receivership" procedure had been corrupted by conflicts of interest among representatives of the bargaining groups, as well as by arrangements between senior creditors and stockholders which circumvented the legal rights and economic expectations of intermediate claimants. No less important, the strategic position of juniors in the bargaining had given them such substantial negotiating advantages over seniors that, as a class, the latter were generally induced to enter into reorganization bargains which were more forced upon them than "free", in the classic market sense of a bargain between willing and able buyers and sellers.

Absolute priority survives under the present Bankruptcy Code, but not as an absolute proposition. The Code, as amended in 1978, provides room for majorities of senior classes to make concessions to juniors, subject to modest disclosure rules. In so doing it assumes that the process rules governing bankruptcy proceedings succeed in opening a space for uncoerced contracting. Absolute priority remains in background as a prominent point on the negotiating landscape: It persists as the legal standard governing the confirmation of reorganization plans that fail to garner the requisite consents and are judicially ordered to be crammed down on nonconsenting classes.

The materials that follow take up the reorganization bargain in three modules. The first looks at history, tracing the development of the absolute priority concept in bankruptcy law. The second concentrates on doctrine, showing the influence of absolute priority policy in the decision of selected valuation questions under the present Bankruptcy Code. The third concentrates on policy, describing proposals for reform of the system.

2. THE RISE AND DECLINE OF ABSOLUTE PRIORITY

The law of corporate reorganization has been described in terms of a tension between the need to respect the pre-bankruptcy bargain, and the harshness of the bargain's after the fact vindication. Baird and Jackson,

Bargaining After the Fall and the Contours of the Absolute Priority Rule, 55 U.Chi.L.Rev. 738, 738 (1988), citing Blum, The Law and Language of Corporate Reorganizations, 17 U.Chi.L.Rev. 565 (1950). Different resolutions of this tension have been set during the history of bankruptcy law. The materials that follow draw on this historical evolution in presenting the absolute priority concept.

(A) ABSOLUTE PRIORITY UNDER THE BANKRUPTCY ACT OF 1938

Ayer, Rethinking Absolute Priority After *Ahlers*

87 Mich.L.Rev. 963, 969–977 (1989).

* * * The [absolute priority] rule arose in the context of the equity receivership. The equity receivership, in turn, is bound up with the building of the railroads. From the Civil War until World War II, investors repeatedly built railroads that could not generate operating revenues sufficient to service their debt. Picture a railroad that borrows $100 to lay down rail lines and build stations, selling $100 worth of bonds and giving the creditor-bondholder a senior mortgage on all the plant and equipment. Suppose the interest rate is 5%: Thus, the road needs $5 of revenue per year just for debt service. Suppose the railroad also owes an additional $20 to junior, unsecured trade creditors. Suppose the railroad generates only $4 a year of income above operating costs. One way of interpreting these numbers is to say that the plant and equipment are "worth" no more than $80—$4 per year capitalized at 5%. One solution to the problem would be simply to "give" the railroad to the bondholders. They lose $20 on their $100 investment, but they capture the whole value of the enterprise, and junior interests, including trade creditors and stockholders, are extinguished.

But the equity receivership didn't work that way. Instead, a "creditor," often in collusion with management, would file a proceeding in federal court, alleging that the debtor was unable to pay its debts as they matured. He would ask the court to use its equity power to administer the property for the satisfaction of claims, and to appoint a receiver to keep the business going in the meantime: hence, "equity receivership." The debtor would consent. Eventually, the receiver would "sell" the assets to a "new" entity—typically a reshuffling of the old investors. The price would be lower than the amount of the senior debt—in the current example, the buyers might agree to pay $30 for a railroad "worth" $80. The money would go to senior bondholders, but they would receive less than the total of their claim ($100) and less even than the nominal worth of the road ($80). Unsecured creditors would be eliminated, but the "new" entity, controlled by stockholders of the "old," would emerge with a company worth $80, for which they had paid only $30.

One may well ask why creditors would ever assent to such a deal, let alone collude in it. There are two reasons. One is the price of justice: old shareholders found out that they could always raise objections which, however invalid, might cost time and money to litigate. So seniors often found it cheaper to buy them off than to insist on their rights. A far more important reason is that the typical reorganization was controlled by "managers"—insiders who had an interest both in bonds and in stock. For the insider-managers, it didn't matter if they lost on bonds if they gained on stock. This approach is innocent enough for those who hold both bonds and stock, but it is devastating to those who do not. In particular, this approach damages two groups. One is the unsecured trade creditors. The other group is the noninsider bondholders, not part of the management ring, who don't hold stock and who don't have the inducement of the managers to trade away their bond interest.[31]

This *modus vivendi* collapsed during the Great Depression under the weight of the investor protective legislation implemented by the New Deal. Those regulatory changes have become so pervasive that they are almost part of the air we breathe. To understand the absolute priority rule, it is necessary to recognize that it emerged first as a primitive pre-statutory effort to regulate receiverships in the judicial process.

In the chronicle of case law, the critical juncture is *Northern Pacific Railway Co. v. Boyd,* decided 5–4 by the Supreme Court in 1913.[33] Boyd was a general creditor of the Northern Pacific Rail*road*. The "Road" asserted that it was not liable, in that all of its property had been transferred (via receivership) to the Northern Pacific Rail*way*.[34] Boyd then sued the Railway, which, of course, claimed that it was insulated in that it had purchased the assets via a bona fide receivership. But by the Court's account, the receivership sale was in fact a transfer engineered by the old bondholders and stockholders from themselves and to themselves, "squeezing out" the intermediate unsecured debt. The Court held that such a sale cannot defeat the claim of a nonassenting creditor. As against him the sale is void in equity, regardless of the motive with which it is made. As the Court put it: "[I]f purposely or unintentionally a single creditor was not paid, or provided for in the reorganization, he could assert his superior rights against the subordinate interests of the old stockholders in the property transferred to the new company."[36]

                     * * *

The decision sent chills of terror down the spines of the corporate reorganization bar.[37] * * *

---

31. For a dramatic instance of court-sanctioned minority victimization, see Aladdin Hotel Co. v. Bloom, 200 F.2d 627 (8th Cir.1953).

33. 228 U.S. 482 (1913). * * *

34. The flummery over name changes in equity receiverships may account for one of the more cherished arcana in the Bluebook—the distinction between the abbreviation used in citing the name of a Railroad (R.R.) and that used in citing the name of a

Railway (Ry.). A Uniform System of Citation R. 10.2.2(a) (14th ed. 1986).

36. 228 U.S. at 504.

37. "The *Boyd* case was received by the reorganization bar and bankers with something akin to horror. It has been a nightmare to the lawyer who presents a decree for the sale of property to a reorganization committee." Rosenberg, Reorganization—The Next Step, 22 Colum.L.Rev. 14 (1922). See generally Cravath, The Reorganization of Corporations; Bondholders' and

In any event, absolute priority thereafter passed into the language and lore of the corporate lawyer. But ingrained practice seems to have proved stronger than writ, as reorganization lawyers developed elaborate schemes to circumvent or emasculate the rule. Thus, counsel developed the practice of getting the reorganization court to bless the deal, with the intent of barring later objections. Some courts seem to have assumed (in the teeth of *Boyd*) that acceptance by a substantial majority of senior creditors gave evidence of the fairness of the plan.[44] And reorganization managers learned how to engineer the process so as to discourage dissent. Fifteen years after *Boyd,* two scholars were able to argue that corporate practice recognized two priority rules—a rule of absolute priority, à la *Boyd,* and a rule of "relative" priority, functioning in practice much like the informal "share" scheme that obtained before *Boyd.*[46] * * * Moreover, Congress complicated matters during the Great Depression by adopting legislation to supplant the equity receivership * * *[47]

That was the situation as it stood when the Supreme Court decided *Case v. Los Angeles Lumber Products Co.* in 1939.[48] The facts of *Case* are simple: the debtor holding company had liabilities of $3.8 million and held a subsidiary that owned the Los Angeles Shipyard and Drydock—an asset valued at $830,000. The plan was to cancel old securities and issue new ones in their place. Some twenty-three percent of the new securities would go to the former stockholders. Both lower courts confirmed the plan, but a unanimous Supreme Court reversed.

The case is both historically and doctrinally important. In terms of political history, the case marks a milestone in the career of Justice William O. Douglas, who wrote the opinion for the unanimous Court. Douglas had served on the Court less than a year at the time of the decision, having come from the chairmanship of the Securities and Exchange Commission. At the SEC, he was one of the principal architects of the New Deal corporate law reforms, and one of the authors of Chapter X of the Bankruptcy Act. His opinion adopts much of the substance of an *amicus* brief filed by the SEC.

As an instance of decisionmaking strategy, the case is noteworthy because it is the first major absolute priority case in which the Court interprets a statute. And indeed, Justice Douglas' interpretation has become so rooted in the culture of the law that it is a surprise to note just

Stockholders' Protective Committees; Reorganization Committees, and the Voluntary Recapitalization of Corporations, in Some Legal Phases of Corporate Financing, Reorganization and Regulation 191–98 (The Association of the Bar of the City of New York ed. 1917).

44. Jameson v. Guaranty Trust Co., 20 F.2d 808, 815 (7th Cir.1927); Samuels v. Northeastern Pub. Serv. Co., 20 Del.Ch. 204, 211, 174 A. 127, 130 (Del.Ch.1934).

46. Bonbright & Bergerman, supra, note 42. Bonbright, who first embraced the relative-priority alternative, later repented and called for "the strictest feasible enforcement of the absolute-priority idea." 2 J. Bonbright, The Valuation of Property 868 n. 64 (1937).

47. Particularly, Act of March 3, 1933, ch. 204 § 77, 47 Stat. 1467, 1474 (repealed 1978); Act of June 7, 1934, ch. 424, § 77B, 48 Stat. 911 (repealed 1938) (corporate reorganizations). * * *

48. 308 U.S. 106, rehg. denied, 308 U.S. 637 (1939).

how attenuated it is. For the statute—Bankruptcy Act, section 77B, the precursor of Chapter X—nowhere states that claims must be paid by a principle of absolute priority. Instead, Justice Douglas deploys a provision in subsection (f), which provides that a plan must be "fair and equitable." These words, Justice Douglas writes, "are words of art which prior to the advent of Section 77B had acquired a fixed meaning through judicial interpretations in the field of equity receivership reorganizations."[55] Strictly speaking, this is poppycock, and Justice Douglas knew it. None of the Supreme Court's absolute priority cases used that particular phrase in that particular way. Indeed, Justice Douglas himself cites only one prior use of the term in case law, and that is in an appellate opinion which the Supreme Court later overturned.[56] On the other hand, the question was at least open, and it was reasonable to infer that the drafters intended to import at least some kind of absolute priority rule into Section 77B.

But what kind of rule? Substantively, the remarkable fact about *Case* is that over ninety percent of all bondholders had accepted the plan. Justice Douglas held that this fact was "immaterial on the basic issue of its fairness."[59] The only possible inference was that this time, the Supreme Court meant business.

Case interpreted old Section 77B, already superseded before the Supreme Court issued its opinion.[60] But the Court soon made clear that the "fair and equitable" language also applied under the superseding Chapter X.[61] * * *

The Court [in *Case* and *Consolidated Rock Products Co.*, which follows] thus established absolute priority as the ruling principle in Chapter X. That would have finished the story (until the coming of the Bankruptcy Act of 1978) except that Chapter X was not the only pre–1978 source of reorganization law. Rather, there were—indeed there long had been—two separate strains of reorganization law, existing side-by-side in uneasy harness. One evolved from the law of equity receivership and crystallized in Chapter X, as just described. The other grew out of the common law remedy of composition, whereby creditors and debtor together agree to "compose"— or scale down—the debtor's debts. A common law composition might be binding on all creditors who agreed to it, but it was not binding on dissenters. As early as 1874, American bankruptcy law provided a scheme whereby a compromise accepted by a majority of creditors might be binding on all, including dissenters. In 1938, Congress acknowledged this tradition by embodying it in Chapter XI of the Chandler Act.

---

55.   308 U.S. at 115.

56.   Flershem v. National Radiator Corp., 64 F.2d 847, 852 (3d Cir.1933), modified sub nom. First Natl. Bank of Cincinnati v. Flershem, 290 U.S. 504 (1934) (cited in 308 U.S. at 118 n. 9). Justice Douglas also cited a number of variants of the phrase. See 308 U.S. at 118.

59.   308 U.S. at 115.

60.   *Case* was argued October 18, 1939, and decided on November 6, 1939. The Chandler Act, repealing § 77B and replacing it with Chapter X, was adopted June 22, 1938. See Chandler Act, ch. 575, 52 Stat. 883 (1938).

61.   See Marine Harbor Properties, Inc. v. Manufacturers Trust Co., 317 U.S. 78, 85 (1942).

The line between "compositions" and equity receiverships had never been clear, but a vulgar oversimplification, adequate for present purposes, is that the composition cases involved small businesses and face-to-face dealings between owner-managers, on the one hand, and vendor-creditors, on the other. The receivership cases, by contrast, involved publicly-traded, mortgage-backed debt and limited-liability corporations. Perhaps more important, the cases emerged from different cultures, each habituated to its own way of going about its task. No one can be certain of the influence that the competing principles of equity receivership and common law composition had upon the development of absolute priority doctrine. It is safe to conclude, however, that each laid an independent foundation for the ultimate bankruptcy structure.

Under the Bankruptcy Act, the Court encountered recurrent difficulties over the years in determining just which chapter was appropriate for any particular case.[70] For our purposes, the important point is this: The absolute priority rule had never been a principle of composition law. Quite the contrary, the point was that a creditor might be bound to anything he agreed to in a composition.

This was part and parcel of the theory of composition: if you had to pay the full going concern value of the enterprise to your creditors, even though they might agree to accept less, composition was never possible. This might have been acceptable public policy to an enterprise like a publicly-held corporation, where the equity ownership might come and go. It was less palatable in the case of the typical Chapter 11 debtor—a sole proprietorship or a closely-held "family" corporation.

NOTE: A CONTRASTING ACCOUNT

Baird and Rasmussen, Boyd's Legacy and Blackstone's Ghost, 1999 Sup. Ct. Rev. 393, 404–405, puts a different gloss on the history of the equity receivership and the railroad reorganizations of the late nineteenth century:

"The reorganization committee would decide how much each claimant should receive in the reorganized railroad. After negotiating this plan of reorganization, the reorganization committee would attend the sale of the railroad. The market was sufficiently illiquid that the winning bidder would inevitably be the reorganization committee, and the amount bid would typically be only a fraction of the value of the railroad, measured on a going-concern basis. Those who participated in the reorganization would receive what the plan awarded them; those who did not would only get their share of what the assets fetched at the court sale. As a result, anyone who did not participate in the process would receive nothing or only a fraction of the amount of his claim.

"The equity receivership depended upon the active cooperation of the old shareholders because they were the ones who actively managed the railroad and kept its books. They would have no incentive to orchestrate the reorganization if its effect would be to wipe out their interests completely. The reorganization, at the very least, could not leave them worse off than if they did nothing other than pray

---

70. See SEC v. United States Realty & Improvement Co., 310 U.S. 434 (1940); General Stores Corp. v. Shlensky, 350 U.S. 462

(1956); SEC v. American Trailer Rentals, 379 U.S. 594 (1965).

that things would get better. Moreover, the old shareholders were one of the few sources of new capital. As a result, equity receiverships usually produced a plan of reorganization that allowed the shareholders to retain an equity interest in the railroad, an opportunity often conditioned on their willingness to contribute new funds to the cash-strapped enterprise.

"The equity receivership provided a way in which investors could organize themselves and overcome the collective action problem from holdouts. Crucial was the ability to conduct a sale in which the reorganization committee could make a winning bid for less than the going-concern value of the assets. It often had the effect of leaving shareholders in place, even though intervening creditors were not being paid in full. This vehicle worked because the judicial sale created a new owner who took the assets free of all preexisting claims. The bargaining among the committees allowed people to sort out priorities that might not have been clear.

"The investors, as a group, were sophisticated parties and repeat players who believed that the system worked to their benefit. A creditor with a nonrecourse junior lien on a spur line could not complain about the rights of the shareholders in the reorganized entity and indeed would not want to, given that its only chance of being paid anything was if it actively participated on a reorganization committee. Most of the general creditors were suppliers with ongoing relationships with the railroad. Several rules (such as the six-month rule and the doctrine of necessity) had the effect of paying such general creditors in full, even though the railroads were typically worth far less than what the secured creditors were owed. Those who objected tended to be people like Boyd who possessed an off-beat claim."

For criticism of Baird and Rasmussen's revision, see Lubben, Railroad Receiverships and Modern Bankruptcy Theory, 89 Cornell L. Rev. 1420 (2004). Lubben collects data on early 20th century railroad equity receiverships to see how effective the process proved in alleviating distress. He finds the process ineffective—the railroads came out of reorganization with "typical capital structures such as those that might be found in a non-bankrupt railroad." For criticism in turn of Lubben's evaluative standard, see Rasmussen, Empirically Bankrupt, 2007 Colum. Bus. L. Rev. 179.

Consolidated Rock Products Co. v. Du Bois

Supreme Court of the United States, 1941.
312 U.S. 510, 61 S.Ct. 675, 85 L.Ed. 982.

■ Mr. Justice Douglas delivered the opinion of the Court.

This case involves questions as to the fairness under § 77B of the Bankruptcy Act * * * of a plan of reorganization for a parent corporation (Consolidated Rock Products Co.) and its two wholly owned subsidiaries— Union Rock Co. and Consumers Rock and Gravel Co., Inc. The District Court confirmed the plan; the Circuit Court of Appeals reversed. 114 F.2d 102. We granted the petitions for certiorari because of the importance in the administration of the reorganization provisions of the Act of certain principles enunciated by the Circuit Court of Appeals.

The stock of Union and Consumers is held by Consolidated. Union has outstanding in the hands of the public $1,877,000 of 6% bonds secured by an indenture on its property, with accrued and unpaid interest thereon of $403,555—a total mortgage indebtedness of $2,280,555. Consumers has outstanding in the hands of the public $1,137,000 of 6% bonds secured by an indenture on its property, with accrued and unpaid interest thereon of $221,715—a total mortgage indebtedness of $1,358,715. Consolidated has outstanding 285,947 shares of no par value preferred stock and 397,455 shares of no par common stock.

The plan of reorganization calls for the formation of a new corporation to which will be transferred all of the assets of Consolidated, Union, and Consumers free of all claims. The securities of the new corporation are to be distributed as follows:

Union and Consumers bonds held by the public will be exchanged for income bonds and preferred stock of the new company. For 50 per cent of the principal amounts of their claims, those bondholders will receive income bonds secured by a mortgage on all of the property of the new company; for the balance they will receive an equal amount of par value preferred stock. Their claims to accrued interest are to be extinguished, no new securities being issued therefor. Thus Union bondholders for their claims of $2,280,555 will receive income bonds and preferred stock in the face amount of $1,877,000; Consumers bondholders for their claims of $1,358,715 will receive income bonds and preferred stock in the face amount of $1,137,000. Each share of new preferred stock will have a warrant for the purchase of two shares of new $2 par value common stock at prices ranging from $2 per share within six months of issuance, to $6 per share during the fifth year after issuance.

Preferred stockholders of Consolidated will receive one share of new common stock ($2 par value) for each share of old preferred or an aggregate of 285,947 shares of new common.

A warrant to purchase one share of new common for $1 within three months of issuance will be given to the common stockholders of Consolidated for each five shares of old common. * * *

* * *

The bonds of Union and Consumers held by Consolidated, the stock of those companies held by Consolidated, and the intercompany claims (discussed hereafter) will be cancelled. * * *

* * * The District Court did not find specific values for the separate properties of Consolidated, Union, or Consumers, or for the properties of the enterprise as a unit. The average of the valuations (apparently based on physical factors) given by three witnesses at the hearing before the master were $2,202,733 for Union as against a mortgage indebtedness of $2,280,555; $1,151,033 for Consumers as against a mortgage indebtedness of $1,358,715. Relying on similar testimony, Consolidated argues that the value of its property, to be contributed to the new company, is over $1,359,000, or exclusive of an alleged good will of $500,000, $859,784. These estimated values somewhat conflict with the consolidated balance sheet (as at June 30, 1938) which shows assets of $3,723,738.15 and liabilities (exclusive of capital and surplus) of $4,253,224.41. More important, the earnings record of the enterprise casts grave doubts on the soundness of the estimated values. No dividends were ever paid on Consolidated's common stock; and except for five quarterly dividends in 1929 and

1931, none on its preferred stock. For the eight and a half years from April 1, 1929, to September 30, 1937, Consolidated had a loss of about $1,200,000 before bond interest but after depreciation and depletion. And except for the year 1929, Consolidated had no net operating profit, after bond interest and amortization, depreciation and depletion, in any year down to September 30, 1937. Yet on this record the District Court found that the present fair value of all the assets of the several companies, exclusive of good will and going concern value, was in excess of the total bonded indebtedness, plus accrued and unpaid interest. And it also found that such value, including good will and going concern value, was insufficient to pay the bonded indebtedness plus accrued and unpaid interest and the liquidation preferences and accrued dividends on Consolidated preferred stock. It further found that the present fair value of the assets admittedly subject to the trust indentures of Union and Consumers was insufficient to pay the face amount, plus accrued and unpaid interest of the respective bond issues. In spite of that finding, the District Court also found that "it would be physically impossible to determine and segregate with any degree of accuracy or fairness properties which originally belong to the companies separately"; that as a result of unified operation properties of every character "have been commingled and are now in the main held by Consolidated without any way of ascertaining what part, if any thereof, belongs to each or any of the companies separately"; and that, as a consequence, an appraisal "would be of such an indefinite and unsatisfactory nature as to produce further confusion."

The unified operation which resulted in that commingling of assets was pursuant to an operating agreement which Consolidated caused its wholly owned subsidiaries to execute in 1929. Under that agreement the subsidiaries ceased all operating functions and the entire management, operation and financing of the business and properties of the subsidiaries were undertaken by Consolidated. The corporate existence of the subsidiaries, however, was maintained and certain separate accounts were kept. Under this agreement Consolidated undertook, *inter alia*, to pay the subsidiaries the amounts necessary for the interest and sinking fund provisions of the indentures and to credit their current accounts with items of depreciation, depletion, amortization and obsolescence. Upon termination of the agreement the properties were to be returned and a final settlement of accounts made, Consolidated meanwhile to retain all net revenues after its obligations thereunder to the subsidiaries had been met. It was specifically provided that the agreement was made for the benefit of the parties, not "for the benefit of any third person." Consolidated's books as at June 30, 1938, showed a net indebtedness under that agreement to Union and Consumers of somewhat over $5,000,000. That claim was cancelled by the plan of reorganization, no securities being issued to the creditors of the subsidiaries therefor. The District Court made no findings as respects the amount or validity of that intercompany claim; it summarily disposed of it by concluding that any liability under the operating agreement was "not made for the benefit of any third parties and the bondholders are included in that category."

We agree with the Circuit Court of Appeals that it was error to confirm this plan of reorganization.

I. On this record no determination of the fairness of any plan of reorganization could be made. Absent the requisite valuation data, the court was in no position to exercise the "informed, independent judgment" (National Surety Co. v. Coriell, 289 U.S. 426, 436) which appraisal of the fairness of a plan of reorganization entails. Case v. Los Angeles Lumber Products Co., 308 U.S. 106. * * * There are two aspects of that valuation problem.

In the first place, there must be a determination of what assets are subject to the payment of the respective claims. This obvious requirement was not met. The status of the Union and Consumers bondholders emphasizes its necessity and importance. According to the District Court the mortgaged assets are insufficient to pay the mortgage debt. There is no finding, however, as to the extent of the deficiency or the amount of unmortgaged assets and their value. It is plain that the bondholders would have, as against Consolidated and its stockholders, prior recourse against any unmortgaged assets of Union and Consumers. The full and absolute priority rule of Northern Pacific Ry. Co. v. Boyd, 228 U.S. 482, and Case v. Los Angeles Lumber Products Co., supra, would preclude participation by the equity interests in any of those assets until the bondholders had been made whole. Here there are some unmortgaged assets, for there is a claim of Union and Consumers against Consolidated—a claim which according to the books of Consolidated is over $5,000,000 in amount. If that claim is valid, or even if it were allowed only to the extent of 25% of its face amount, then the entire assets of Consolidated would be drawn down into the estates of the subsidiaries. In that event Union and Consumers might or might not be solvent in the bankruptcy sense. But certainly it would render untenable the present contention of Consolidated and the preferred stockholders that they are contributing all of the assets of Consolidated to the new company in exchange for which they are entitled to new securities. On that theory of the case they would be making a contribution of only such assets of Consolidated, if any, as remained after any deficiency of the bondholders had been wholly satisfied.

* * * Consolidated makes some point of the difficulty and expense of determining the extent of its liability under the operating agreement and of the necessity to abide by the technical terms of that agreement in ascertaining that liability. But equity will not permit a holding company, which has dominated and controlled its subsidiaries, to escape or reduce its liability to those subsidiaries by reliance upon self-serving contracts which it has imposed on them. A holding company, as well as others in dominating or controlling positions (Pepper v. Litton, 308 U.S. 295), has fiduciary duties to security holders of its system which will be strictly enforced. See Taylor v. Standard Gas & Electric Co., 306 U.S. 307. * * *

So far as the ability of the bondholders of Union and Consumers to reach the assets of Consolidated on claims of the kind covered by the operation agreement is concerned, there is another and more direct route which reaches the same end. There has been a unified operation of those several properties by Consolidated pursuant to the operating agreement. That operation not only resulted in extensive commingling of assets. All management functions of the several companies were assumed by Consolidated. The subsidiaries abdicated. Consolidated operated them as mere departments of its own business. Not even the formalities of separate corporate organizations were observed, except in minor particulars such as the maintenance of certain separate accounts. In view of these facts, Consolidated is in no position to claim that its assets are insulated from such claims of creditors of the subsidiaries. To the contrary, it is well settled that where a holding company directly intervenes in the management of its subsidiaries so as to treat them as mere departments of its own enterprise, it is responsible for the obligations of those subsidiaries incurred or arising during its management. * * * We are not dealing here with a situation where other creditors of a parent company are competing with creditors of its subsidiaries. If meticulous regard to corporate forms, which Consolidated has long ignored, is now observed, the stockholders of Consolidated may be the direct beneficiaries. Equity will not countenance such a result. A holding company which assumes to treat the properties of its subsidiaries as its own cannot take the benefits of direct management without the burdens.

We have already noted that no adequate finding was made as to the value of the assets of Consolidated. In view of what we have said, it is apparent that a determination of that value must be made so that criteria will be available to determine an appropriate allocation of new securities between bondholders and stockholders in case there is an equity remaining after the bondholders have been made whole.

There is another reason why the failure to ascertain what assets are subject to the payment of the Union and Consumers bonds is fatal. There is a question raised as to the fairness of the plan as respects the bondholders *inter sese*. While the total mortgage debt of Consumers is less than that of Union, the net income of the new company, as we have seen, is to be divided into two equal parts, one to service the new securities issued to Consumers bondholders, the other to service those issued to Union bondholders. That allocation is attacked here by respondent as discriminatory against Union, on the ground that the assets of Union are much greater in volume and in value than those of Consumers. It does not appear from this record that Union and Consumers have individual earnings records. If they do not, some appropriate formula for at least an approximate ascertainment of their respective assets must be designed in spite of the difficulties occasioned by the commingling. Otherwise the issue of fairness of any plan of reorganization as between Union and Consumers bondholders cannot be intelligently resolved.

In the second place, there is the question of the method of valuation. From this record it is apparent that little, if any, effort was made to value the whole enterprise by a capitalization of prospective earnings. The necessity for such an inquiry is emphasized by the poor earnings record of this enterprise in the past. Findings as to the earning capacity of an enterprise are essential to a determination of the feasibility as well as the fairness of a plan of reorganization. Whether or not the earnings may reasonably be expected to meet the interest and dividend requirements of the new securities is a *sine qua non* to a determination of the integrity and practicability of the new capital structure. It is also essential for satisfaction of the absolute priority rule of Case v. Los Angeles Lumber Products Co., supra. Unless meticulous regard for earning capacity be had, indefensible participation of junior securities in plans of reorganization may result. * * *

* * * It is plain that valuations for other purposes are not relevant to or helpful in a determination of that issue, except as they may indirectly bear on earning capacity. * * * The criterion of earning capacity is the essential one if the enterprise is to be freed from the heavy hand of past errors, miscalculations or disaster, and if the allocation of securities among the various claimants is to be fair and equitable. * * * Since its application requires a prediction as to what will occur in the future, an estimate, as distinguished from mathematical certitude, is all that can be made. But that estimate must be based on an informed judgment which embraces all facts relevant to future earning capacity and hence to present worth, including, of course, the nature and condition of the properties, the past earnings record, and all circumstances which indicate whether or not that record is a reliable criterion of future performance. A sum of values based on physical factors and assigned to separate units of the property without regard to the earning capacity of the whole enterprise is plainly inadequate. * * * But hardly more than that was done here. The Circuit Court of Appeals correctly left the matter of a formal appraisal to the discretion of the District Court. The extent and method of inquiry necessary for a valuation based on earning capacity are necessarily dependent on the facts of each case.

II.   The Circuit Court of Appeals held that the absolute priority rule of Northern Pacific Ry. Co. v. Boyd, supra, and Case v. Los Angeles Lumber Products Co., supra, applied to reorganizations of solvent as well as insolvent companies. That is true. Whether a company is solvent or insolvent in either the equity or the bankruptcy sense, "any arrangement of the parties by which the subordinate rights and interests of the stockholders are attempted to be secured at the expense of the prior rights" of creditors "comes within judicial denunciation." Louisville Trust Co. v. Louisville, N.A. & C. Ry. Co., 174 U.S. 674, 684. And we indicated in Case v. Los Angeles Lumber Products Co., supra, that that rule was not satisfied even though the "relative priorities" of creditors and stockholders were maintained (pp. 119–120).

The instant plan runs afoul of that principle. In the first place, no provision is made for the accrued interest on the bonds. This interest is entitled to the same priority as the principal. * * * In the second place, and apart from the cancellation of interest, the plan does not satisfy the fixed principle of the *Boyd* case even on the assumption that the enterprise as a whole is solvent in the bankruptcy sense. The bondholders for the principal amount of their 6% bonds receive an equal face amount of new 5% income bonds and preferred stock, while the preferred stockholders receive new common stock. True, the relative priorities are maintained. But the bond-holders have not been made whole. They have received an inferior grade of securities, inferior in the sense that the interest rate has been reduced, a contingent return has been substituted for a fixed one, the maturities have been in part extended and in part eliminated by the substitution of preferred stock, and their former strategic position has been weakened. Those lost rights are of value. Full compensatory provision must be made for the entire bundle of rights which the creditors surrender.

The absolute priority rule does not mean that bondholders cannot be given inferior grades of securities, or even securities of the same grade as are received by junior interests. Requirements of feasibility of reorganiza-tion plans frequently necessitate it in the interests of simpler and more conservative capital structures. And standards of fairness permit it. * * * Thus it is plain that while creditors may be given inferior grades of securities, their "superior rights" must be recognized. Clearly, those prior rights are not recognized, in cases where stockholders are participating in the plan, if creditors are given only a face amount of inferior securities equal to the face amount of their claims. They must receive, in addition, compensation for the senior rights which they are to surrender. If they receive less than that full compensatory treatment, some of their property rights will be appropriated for the benefit of stockholders without compen-sation. That is not permissible. The plan then comes within judicial denunciation because it does not recognize the creditors' "equitable right to be preferred to stockholders against the full value of all property belonging to the debtor corporation." * * *

Practical adjustments, rather than a rigid formula, are necessary. The method of effecting full compensation for senior claimants will vary from case to case. As indicated in the *Boyd* case (228 U.S. at p. 508) the creditors are entitled to have the full value of the property, whether "present or prospective, for dividends or only for purposes of control," first appropriat-ed to payment of their claims. But whether in case of a solvent company the creditors should be made whole for the change in or loss of their seniority by an increased participation in assets, in earnings or in control, or in any combination thereof, will be dependent on the facts and require-ments of each case.[1] So long as the new securities offered are of a value

1. In view of the condition of the record relative to the value of the properties and the fact that the accrued interest is cancelled by the plan, it is not profitable to attempt a detailed discussion of the deficiencies in the alleged compensatory treatment of the bond-holders. It should, however, be noted as re-spects the warrants issued to the old common stockholders that they admittedly have no equity in the enterprise. Accordingly, it should have been shown that there was a necessity of seeking new money from them and that the participation accorded them was not more than reasonably equivalent to their contribution. Kansas City Terminal Ry. Co. v. Central Union Trust Co., supra; Case v. Los Angeles Lumber Products Co., * * * In the latter case we warned against the dilution of creditors' rights by inadequate contributions by stockholders. Here that dilution takes a rather obvious form in view of the lower price at which the stockholders may exercise the warrants. Warrants exercised by them would dilute the value of common stock purchased by bondholders during the same period. Fur-thermore, on Consolidated's estimate of the equity in the enterprise, the values of the new common would have to increase many fold to reach a value which exceeds the war-rant price by the amount of the accrued interest.

equal to the creditors' claims, the appropriateness of the formula employed rests in the informed discretion of the court.

The Circuit Court of Appeals, however, made certain statements which if taken literally do not comport with the requirements of the absolute priority rule. It apparently ruled that a class of claimants with a lien on specific properties must receive full compensation out of those properties, and that a plan of reorganization is *per se* unfair and inequitable if it substitutes for several old bond issues, separately secured, new securities constituting an interest in all of the properties. That does not follow from Case v. Los Angeles Lumber Products Co., supra. If the creditors are adequately compensated for the loss of their prior claims, it is not material out of what assets they are paid. So long as they receive full compensatory treatment and so long as each group shares in the securities of the whole enterprise on an equitable basis, the requirements of "fair and equitable" are satisfied.

Any other standard might well place insuperable obstacles in the way of feasible plans of reorganization. Certainly where unified operations of separate properties are deemed advisable and essential, as they were in this case, the elimination of divisional mortgages may be necessary as well as wise. Moreover, the substitution of a simple, conservative capital structure for a highly complicated one may be a primary requirement of any reorganization plan. There is no necessity to construct the new capital structure on the framework of the old.

Affirmed.

NOTE: THE AFTERMATH OF THE CONSOLIDATED ROCK PRODUCTS COMPANY CASE

Under the amended plan of reorganization which became effective February 23, 1945, each Union Rock bondholder received $1,000 principal amount in new bonds and 892 shares of new common stock for each $1,000 principal amount of Union Rock bonds and all accumulated interest; Consumers Rock bondholders received $1,000 principal amount in new bonds and 832 shares of new common stock for each $1,000 principal amount of Consumers Rock bonds and all accumulated interest. Consolidated Rock's preferred stockholders received 2.236 shares of new common for each share of old preferred, and its common stockholders were wiped out. A total of $2,944,000 principal amount of new bonds and 3,196,091 shares of common stock (par value $1 per share) were issued in the reorganization. How does the value reflected by the principal amount of bonds and par value of stock thus issued compare with the value of the enterprise discussed in the Court's opinion?

The new common stock was denied the right to receive dividends until after the principal amount of new bonds outstanding was reduced to $1,250,000.

The $2,944,000 principal amount of new bonds bearing annual interest at 3%, plus 2% if earned, were retired through sinking fund operations over the period between 1945 and 1951.

The prices of the bonds and of the stock of the reorganized company from the time the latter was first quoted, and the earnings per share applicable to the common stock, were as follows:

	BONDS High	BONDS Low	COMMON STOCK High	COMMON STOCK Low	EARNINGS PER SHARE
1944					.05
1945	89½	81			.02
1946	90	74			.12
1947	83	75			.21
1948	88	78			.24
1949	91	86	1	⅝	.08
1950			1⅛	¾	.20
1951			1⅝	1⅛	.18
1952			1.73	1.20	.13
1953			1.92	1.21	.26

NOTE: ISSUES UNDER ABSOLUTE PRIORITY

1. *The Definition of the Claim.*

Assuming the priority status of a claim has been duly recognized, how is the precise amount of the claim calculated? Under both the Bankruptcy Act of 1938 and the present Bankruptcy Code, the quantitative measure of a claim's priority is its principal and accrued interest as if matured. The maturing of the claim results either from the express terms of the investment contract, which typically accelerate maturity on default (see e.g., In The Matter of Chicago, Milwaukee, St. Paul and Pacific Railroad Company, 784 F.2d 831 (7th Cir.1986)), or from the formal "sale" of the debtor's property and liquidation of the debtor, on which the older form of equity receivership proceedings was predicated.

There have, however, been many suggestions for measuring claims of senior securities and the limits of permissible settlements of those claims, by criteria other than principal plus accrued interest. On one theory, the claims of investors in a particular class of securities might be measured by reference to the market values of the outstanding securities of the class prior to approval of the petition for reorganization. It is also possible to affect the measure of the claim of a bond by reference to its due date or to "pure" interest rates at the time of reorganization. For example, a $1000 bond due in 2033 might have a lesser claim in an insolvency reorganization in 2008 than an equivalent $1000 bond (with the same interest rate and security) due in 2009. Or a 6 percent debenture might have a larger claim than a 4 percent debenture, or the claim of each debenture might be less when the prime rate is 10 percent than when it is 5 percent, without regard to the financial condition of the particular debtor and the degree of risk of the particular debenture. The theory, with regard to interest rates, would be that insolvency and the reorganization process should not improve the position of the 4 percent debenture holder vis-a-vis the 6 percent debenture holder, or, if money rates have risen, of both of them vis-a-vis the stockholders, over what those positions would have been had the firm prospered and the debt remained outstanding. The 4 percent and 6 percent debenture holders should not be entitled to the principal amounts of their debentures, with which they can buy 8 percent bonds at current money rates. By the same token, if money rates have fallen (e.g., to 3 percent), insolvency should not injure the debenture holder by reducing his 6 percent claim to its principal amount, which can purchase only a 3 percent debenture. In short, those changes in the value of the outstanding debentures attributable solely to factors external to the risks of the particular enterprise (e.g., changes in money rates) should not be altered or offset in a reorganization process which is occurring by reason of the materialization of the risks of the enterprise.

2. *Postpetition Interest.*

Under the current Bankruptcy Code, which continues the earlier treatment, the general rule is that accrual of interest on debt securities and dividends on preferred stock stops upon filing of the petition. But, as between some classes of security holders accrual appears to be required. More particularly, as between secured and unsecured claimants, accrual is required on the secured claim but only to the extent that the value of the security exceeds the value of the claim secured. See 11 U.S.C. § 506(b); United Savings Ass'n v. Timbers of Inwood Forest, 484 U.S. 365 (1988). In addition, in straight bankruptcy liquidations, accrual is required for the benefit of unsecured creditors where the debtor is solvent. 11 U.S.C. § 726(a)(5). Is there any valid rationale for making distinctions in the accrual of postpetition interest, (a) depending upon whether the context is a straight bankruptcy liquidation or a reorganization, (b) between intra-class and inter-class claims, or (c) between various kinds of inter-class claims (e.g., tax claims)?

3. *Full Satisfaction—Cash Equivalent or Reasonable Prospect.*

As may be inferred from the *Consolidated Rock Products Co.* case, even if the claim of the senior security holders could not be reduced under the rule of absolute priority without the unanimous consent of the class, questions arose as to whether, in order for the bargain to meet the standard, a payoff in securities of the reorganized enterprise was required to consist of immediate cash equivalents in the amount of the claim. Occasional commentators and even less occasional decisions suggested that full satisfaction under the absolute priority rule should require payment in immediate cash equivalents, not merely in securities having a face amount which equals the cash claim. See Friendly, Some Comments on the Corporate Reorganizations Act, 48 Harv.L.Rev. 39, 77–78 (1934); Guaranty Trust Co. v. Chase Nat. Bank, 302 N.Y. 658, 98 N.E.2d 474 (1951).

But the prevailing view has been that "full satisfaction" was given if the surrendering senior security holders "receive, for their total claim, a par amount of the claims for which they were exchanged" even though not immediately equal to that amount in cash. See, e.g., Missouri Pacific R.R. Reorganization, 290 I.C.C. 477, 555 (1954), plan approved 129 F.Supp. 392 (E.D.Mo.1955), aff'd 225 F.2d 761 (8th Cir.1955), cert. denied 350 U.S. 959 (1956); In re Nite Lite Inns, 17 B.R. 367 (Bankr.S.D.Cal.1982)(rejecting argument that securities issued under plan could not be sold for an amount equal to the judicial valuation). Or in words of Frank, Epithetical Jurisprudence and the Work of the Securities and Exchange Commission in the Administration of Chapter X of the Bankruptcy Act, 18 N.Y.U.L.Q.Rev. 317, 340 (1941), "the new securities should be intrinsically sound, so that there is a reasonable prospect that they will have values equal to their face amounts, or in the case of stocks, equal to the values put upon them for reorganization purposes. If the securities seem not likely to meet this test, in our opinion, a greater amount must be issued to the senior security holders * * *."

Estimates of expected value are matters about which reasonable people may disagree. However, reorganization plans approved by administrative agencies and courts during the history of Chapter X almost consistently overestimated the expected value of the payout, and therefore almost consistently underpaid the claim. The implication was that, in reality, Chapter X payouts reflected disagreement with the rule that seniors be paid in full.

4. *Loss of Senior Status.*

In the Consolidated Rock Products case, Justice Douglas indicated that senior creditors were permitted to receive securities of the same quality as those awarded to junior creditors in satisfaction of their claims, but in that event, seniors were to be "adequately compensated for the loss of their prior claims." The present Bankruptcy Code, § 1129(b), seems to perpetuate the same mandate for unsecured creditors (while requiring secured creditors to receive debt securities to the extent of their secured claims, at least when the secured class dissents from the plan). How is such adequate compensation to be effected?

Note that if the payoff of claims were required to be made in immediate cash equivalents, there arguably would be no need for (or right to) such compensation. If, for example, the holder of a defaulted 8 percent secured bond in the amount of $1000 receives in full satisfaction of his claim a new 6 percent unsecured $1000 debenture at a time when the prime money rate is at the 5 percent level, and the new bond sells for $1000 or more, there is no need to "compensate" for the loss of secured position and the diminution of the coupon rate, since the bondholder could sell his new debenture at once for at least $1000.

On the other hand, if the payoff is to be made in securities which are not the immediate cash equivalent of the claim, the question arises as to how, in the forced sharing of the risks of the continuing enterprise, the seniors should be compensated for loss of a preferred position. An effort can be made to quantify the value of the seniors' loss, whether of a secured position or a sinking fund or a fixed interest obligation, and to compensate them by a corresponding increase in the value of new participations. Presumably, compensation for assuming a relatively riskier position vis-a-vis the participating juniors implies a higher return, either in the form of a higher coupon or dividend rate or in the form of a larger share of the new securities being awarded.

Thus, assume that an enterprise with outstanding debt of $1 million in 5 percent secured bonds and $1 million in 4 percent unsecured debentures is to be reorganized, and that it is valued in going concern terms at $1,500,000. If only common stock were to be issued in the reorganization, compensatory treatment would require the bondholders to receive proportionately more than the debenture holders, owing to the loss of their pledged security and higher interest claim. The problem is how to quantify the value of the loss and the value of the appropriate compensation therefor.

Consider the following allocation. If the pledged security were found to have a "value" of $800,000, the seniors would be entitled to 8/15 of the common stock plus some added portion of the common stock for the loss of their secured position. In any event, even if 8/15 of the common stock had an immediate cash value of $800,000 and were allocated to the 5 percent bonds, the bondholders would have an unsatisfied claim of $200,000 and the unsecured 4 percent debentures would have a claim of $1,000,000. Would the remaining 7/15 of the common stock be divided in the ratio of 2 to 10, or (by reason of the seniors' lost interest superiority) 1 to 4? Would the latter be compensatory for the loss of a higher interest rate? Or would the seniors be entitled to still more compensation because they are being exposed to the same risk and return as the juniors?

NOTE: THE COMPOSITION TRADITION AND THE BEST INTEREST OF CREDITORS STANDARD

There is a tradition of composition in bankruptcy proceedings which began under section 12 of the Bankruptcy Act (52 Stat. 840, repealed in 1938) and was continued in chapter XI of the Bankruptcy Act until its repeal by the 1978 Act. Under section 12, a majority in number and interest of the creditors of an enterprise were authorized to force a minority to accept a composition proposed by the debtor which resulted in the creditors receiving less than full payment, even though the debtor retained otherwise distributable assets. The limits on the power of the majority thus to force a minority to accept less than its full claim were contained in section 12(d) which provided that a composition should only be confirmed by the Court if, among other things, "it is for the best interests of the creditor." That standard was carried forward into section 366 of chapter XI (11 U.S.C. § 766). The "best interests" standard was retained on the assumptions that chapter XI would be the reorganization vehicle for small business bankruptcies in which bank and trade creditors would tend to have adequate information about the debtor's business and its owner's character and potential and could cooperate when making concessions. Chapter X and the absolute priority rule, in contrast, were intended for proceedings respecting larger firms with dispersed classes of security holders and attendant collective action problems.

Under the "best interests" standard, one—if not indeed the principal—limitation on the majority's power to make concessions for the claims of all unsecured creditors was that the composition offer the creditors a distribution of not less than they would realize in a straight bankruptcy liquidation. That was the limit to which the bankrupt's capacity (a) to collude with some creditors at the expense of others, or (b) to force the acquiescence of all the creditors in a detrimental composition by delaying and frustrating the collection and distribution of assets by concealment and diversion.

The "best interest" standard survived the repeal of chapter XI and reappeared in the Bankruptcy Act of 1978, 11 U.S.C. § 1129(a)(7), as the liquidation standard limiting the majority's power to make concessions in all reorganization proceedings.

(B) THE BANKRUPTCY ACT OF 1978

In 1978, Congress repealed chapter X and enacted the present Bankruptcy Code. The Code abandons the absolute priority rule for all reorganization bargains accepted by at least two-thirds in amount and more than one-half in number of the allowed claims of each creditor class, and two-thirds in amount of any class of equity participants. The Code contemplates (§ 1125) that full disclosure (in documents judicially determined to be adequate for the purpose) will be made to the affected voters of each class in soliciting their approval for a plan, and that such disclosure will be sufficient to legitimate the results of the bargaining—i.e., acceptance of a plan by the requisite majorities in numbers and amounts—which will thereupon become enforceable against all members of the class.

The Code, although contemplating bargaining over a plan by representatives of claimants and the debtor, limits the bargaining process in significant ways. First, the Code sets limits on how much can be conceded by the majority. Liquidation value is the floor set on the permissible concessions (§ 1129(a)(7)). Moreover, when the plan is not accepted by the requisite numbers and amounts of each class, the absolute priority rule still applies to measure the limits of a permissible reorganization plan with respect to the non-acquiescing class (§ 1129(b)). The Code's drafters, however, expected that most plans would be "accepted" by the requisite numbers and amounts of each class.

The Code also contains restrictions designed to favor submission of only the debtor's (§ 1121) plan for acceptance. In addition, committees of classes of claimants can consist only of persons appointed by the court and are intended to be the persons with the largest claims in the class. Finally, the Code curtails the role of both the SEC, eliminating its advisory reports to security holders, and the trustee. A trustee (or examiner to investigate the debtor's affairs and possible prior mismanagement or malefaction) may, but is not required to, be appointed.

The 1978 Act resulted from and responded to decades of criticism of the 1938 Act and, in particular, the absolute priority rule. Compare Posner, The Political Economy of the Bankruptcy Reform Act of 1978, 96 Mich. L. Rev. 47 (1997), with the story told in the following legislative history. Posner argues that the 1978 Bankruptcy Code reflects the interests of three groups—corporate managers (who disliked being replaced by a trustee), large corporate lenders, and the bankruptcy bar.

House Report No. 95–595

95 Cong., 1st Sess., 1977, pp. 221–224.

Chapter X requires application of the absolute priority rule as a standard for confirmation of a plan. Under that rule, senior creditors must be paid in full under the plan before junior creditors or stockholders may receive anything. In 1938, when public securities were usually senior bonds and corporations were more often privately held, the absolute priority rule prevented abuses of the public's rights by insiders of a corporation in reorganization. Today, public classes are more likely to be subordinated debenture holders and stockholders, and the protection of senior classes inures to the benefit of private creditors, often financing consortiums, that have nearly as much influence over the operation of a business as the inside shareholders did in an earlier day. Application of the absolute priority rule under chapter X has more recently led to the exclusion rather than the protection of the public.

Further, the application of that rule requires a full going concern valuation of the business. Though valuation is theoretically a precise method of determining the creditors' and stockholders' rights in a business, more often the uncertainty of predicting the future, required in any valuation, is a method of fudging a result that will support the plan that has been proposed. As Peter Coogan has aptly noted, such a valuation is usually "a guess compounded by an estimate". In a reorganization where time is of the essence, the length and uncertainty of the valuation process is no longer justified in every case.

* * *

* * * Under chapter X, the financial standard for confirmation is the absolute priority rule. Under that rule, creditors are entitled to be paid according to the going-concern value of the business, which is usually higher than the liquidation value of the business, because assets in operation can usually earn more than assets sold for scrap. Under chapter XI,

however, creditors are entitled only to the liquidation value of the business. The plan may be confirmed if creditors receive at least what they would receive under a liquidation of the business. The debtor, that is, stockholders, are able to retain for themselves the difference between liquidation value and going-concern value.

The establishment of the two chapters in 1938 was most likely due not only to the desire to differentiate both procedures and standards for small private companies versus large public ones, but also to the inability of Congress or the bankruptcy community, both the bar and academia, to decide what it was that creditors were ultimately entitled to receive: liquidation or going-concern value. They finessed the issue by the adoption of two chapters.

* * *

The consolidated chapter is chapter 11 of proposed title 11. It adopts much of the flexibility of chapter XI of current law, and incorporates the essence of the public protection features of current chapter X. The areas of greatest importance are the financial standard for confirmation; the court hearing on the plan and the report on the plan to creditors and stockholders; the right to propose a plan; and the appointment of a trustee.

II. The Financial Standard

The premise of the bill's financial standard for confirmation is the same as the premise of the securities law: parties should be given adequate disclosure or relevant information, and they should make their own decision on the acceptability of the proposed plan * * * [of] reorganization. The bill does not impose a rigid financial rule for the plan. The parties are left to their own to negotiate a fair settlement. The question of whether creditors are entitled to the going-concern or liquidation value of the business is impossible to answer. It is unrealistic to assume that the bill could or even should attempt to answer that question. Instead, negotiation among the parties after full disclosure will govern how the value of the reorganizing company will be distributed among creditors and stockholders. The bill only sets the outer limits on the outcome: it must be somewhere between the going-concern value and the liquidation value.

Only when the parties are unable to agree on a proper distribution of the value of the company does the bill establish a financial standard. If the debtor is unable to obtain the consents of all classes of creditors and stockholders, then the court may confirm the plan anyway on request of the plan's proponent, if the plan treats the nonconsenting classes fairly. The bill defines "fairly" in terms of the relative rights among the classes. Simply put, the bill requires that the plan pay any dissenting class in full before any class junior to the dissenter may be paid at all. The rule is a partial application of the absolute priority rule now applied under chapter X and requires a full valuation of the debtor as the absolute priority rule does under current law. The important difference is that the bill permits senior classes to take less than full payment, in order to expedite or insure the success of the reorganization.

3.   Reorganization under the Bankruptcy Code

(A) OVERVIEW

In re Zenith Electronics Corporation

United States Bankruptcy Court, D. Delaware, 1999.
241 B.R. 92.

■ Mary F. Walrath, Bankruptcy Judge.

This case is before the Court on the request of Zenith Electronics Corporation ("Zenith") for approval of its Disclosure Statement and confirmation of its Pre–Packaged Plan of Reorganization filed August 24, 1999 ("the Plan"). The Plan is supported by Zenith's largest shareholder and creditor, LG Electronics, Inc. ("LGE"), and the holders of a majority of the debentures issued by Zenith pre-petition ("the Bondholders"). The Plan is opposed by the Official Committee of Equity Security Holders ("the Equity Committee") and numerous shareholders, including Nordhoff Investments, Inc. ("Nordhoff")(collectively, "the Objectors"). For the reasons set forth below, we overrule the objections, approve the Disclosure Statement and will confirm the Plan, if modified in accordance with this Opinion.

I.   *FACTUAL BACKGROUND*

Zenith has been in business for over 80 years. It was a leader in the design, manufacturing, and marketing of consumer electronics for many years. In recent years it has experienced substantial financial difficulties. It incurred losses in 12 of the last 13 years.

In 1995 Zenith persuaded one of its shareholders, LGE which held approximately 5% of its stock, to invest over $366 million in acquiring a total 57.7% stake in the company. Notwithstanding that investment, and loans and credit support in excess of $340 million provided subsequently by LGE, Zenith's financial condition continued to deteriorate. Zenith suffered net losses in 1996 of $178 million, in 1997 of $299 million and in 1998 of $275 million.

In late 1997, the Asian financial crisis and the continuing losses at Zenith, caused LGE (and Zenith) to question LGE's ability to continue to support Zenith and Zenith's need to reorganize. LGE retained McKinsey & Co. ("McKinsey") to evaluate its investment in Zenith and to suggest improvements Zenith could make in its operations and focus. Zenith hired an investment banking firm, Peter J. Solomon Company ("PJSC") in December, 1997, and a new CEO, Jeff Gannon, in January 1998. Under Mr. Gannon, Zenith made substantial operational changes, including a conversion from manufacturer to a marketing and distribution company which outsourced all manufacturing. Zenith's manufacturing facilities were sold or closed in 1998 and 1999. While those operational changes did have some effect on stemming the losses, they were insufficient to eliminate them. Contemporaneously, PJSC evaluated Zenith's assets on a liquidation and going concern basis.

In early 1998, Zenith also attempted to attract a strategic investor or purchaser of part or all of its business or assets. Because of its financial condition, Zenith was advised that it could not raise money through the issuance of more stock or debt instruments. Zenith's strategy was to identify companies which might have an interest and then to have Zenith's CEO approach the target's CEO to discuss the possibilities. Several meetings were conducted with such entities.[4] No offers were received for a sale of substantial assets or business divisions; nor were any offers of equity investments received.

In April 1998, LGE proposed a possible restructuring of its debt and equity in Zenith, contingent on substantial reduction of the bond debt and elimination of the shareholder interests. Zenith appointed a Special Committee of its Board of Directors to evaluate the restructuring proposal and to conduct negotiations on behalf of Zenith. After agreement was reached with the Special Committee, negotiations proceeded with the Bondholders' Committee. Ultimately the restructuring proposal was reduced to a pre-packaged plan of reorganization.

A Disclosure Statement and Proxy Statement–Prospectus for the solicitation of votes on the Plan was prepared and reviewed by the SEC. Discussions with the SEC over the requirements of the Disclosure Statement started in August 1998. On July 15, 1999, after numerous revisions, the SEC declared the Disclosure Statement effective. On July 20, 1999, Zenith mailed the Plan and Disclosure Statement to the Bondholders and others entitled to vote on the Plan. After voting was completed on August 20, 1999, the Bondholders had voted in favor of the Plan by 98.6% in amount and 97.01% in number of those voting. LGE and Citibank, a secured creditor, had also voted to accept the Plan. Zenith immediately filed its chapter 11 petition on August 24, 1999. At the same time, Zenith filed its Plan and Disclosure Statement and sought prompt approval of both. A combined Disclosure Statement and confirmation hearing was scheduled for September 27 and 28, 1999.

An ad hoc committee of minority shareholders sought a postponement of the confirmation hearing, which was denied. We did, however, grant its motion for appointment of an official committee of equity holders, over the objection of Zenith, LGE and the Bondholders' Committee. We did so to give the equity holders an opportunity to conduct discovery and present their arguments against confirmation of the Plan.

II. *DISCUSSION*

As an initial matter, the Equity Committee objects to the adequacy of the Disclosure Statement * * *. * * *

A. *Approval of the Disclosure Statement*

4. For example, Mr. Gannon met with representatives of Microsoft, Intel, General Instrument, Hitachi, Philips, RCA/Thompson, Sony, Sun Microsystems and Texas Instruments. Several other companies were contacted, but none expressed sufficient interest to warrant a meeting.

Typically, under chapter 11 of the Bankruptcy Code, the court approves the debtor's disclosure statement before it, and the plan of reorganization, are sent to creditors and others entitled to vote on the plan. Section 1125(b) provides:

> (b) An acceptance or rejection of a plan may not be solicited after the commencement of the case under this title from a holder of a claim or interest with respect to such claim or interest, unless, at the time of or before such solicitation, there is transmitted to such holder the plan or a summary of the plan, and a written disclosure statement approved, after notice and a hearing, by the court as containing adequate information.

11 U.S.C. § 1125(b). *See also*, Fed. R. Bankr.P. 3017 & 3018.

However, Congress recognized the validity of votes solicited pre-bankruptcy (a practice which had developed under Chapter X of the Bankruptcy Act). Section 1126(b) provides:

> (b) For the purposes of subsections (c) and (d) of this section, a holder of a claim or interest that has accepted or rejected the plan before the commencement of the case under this title is deemed to have accepted or rejected such plan, as the case may be, if—

> (1) the solicitation of such acceptance or rejection was in compliance with any applicable nonbankruptcy law, rule, or regulation governing the adequacy of disclosure in connection with such solicitation; or

> (2) if there is not any such law, rule, or regulation, such acceptance or rejection was solicited after disclosure to such holder of adequate information, as defined in section 1125(a) of this title.

11 U.S.C. § 1126(b).

Zenith asserts that the Disclosure Statement meets both criteria. We agree.

* * *

In this case, the SEC was required to approve the Disclosure Statement because the Plan provides for the issuance of new securities to the Bondholders. The SEC did approve the Disclosure Statement on July 15, 1999, as containing adequate information (after 11 months of discussions and numerous amendments).

We conclude that the Disclosure Statement, having been approved by the SEC as containing adequate information, complies with the provisions of section 1126(b)(1).

* * *

Even if it did not fit the provisions of section 1126(b)(1), the Disclosure Statement does contain sufficient information to comply with section 1126(b)(2) and 1125(a). The Disclosure Statement is almost 400 pages. It contains numerous financial statements and historical information about Zenith. It has lengthy descriptions of Zenith's efforts to restructure its operations and finances and alternatives to the proposed Plan. It describes

LGE's relationship to Zenith. It provides valuation information and a liquidation analysis.

Further, Zenith is a public company. Consequently, substantial information about its finances and operations is publicly available. It files periodic statements with the SEC, and media attention to its plight has been intense.

In considering the adequacy of a disclosure statement, it is important to keep in mind the audience. Here, those entitled to vote on the Plan are sophisticated, institutional investors. They have competent professionals assisting them in analyzing and testing the information provided by Zenith. They have also been involved in negotiations with Zenith and LGE for over a year before voting on the Plan. Significant documents and information (in addition to the Disclosure Statement) were made available to the Bondholders' Committee and its professionals during that time.

Finally, there is no suggestion that the Disclosure Statement contains false information—only that certain additional information was not included. What the Equity Committee asserts is missing, however, is not uncontested, concrete facts, but rather the Equity Committee's interpretation of those facts or duplicative information.[8] We do not believe that such "information" must be included in the Disclosure Statement.

* * *

B. *Confirmation of the Plan*

* * *

2. *The value of Zenith.*

The valuation issue in this case is somewhat unique. It is not presented in connection with determining whether the Plan complies with section 1129(a)(7): the Equity Committee concedes that on a liquidation under chapter 7 the shareholders will receive nothing. PJSC estimates the liquidation value of Zenith at $170 million; creditors' claims exceed $545 million.

The value of Zenith as a going concern is, however, disputed and is relevant to the issues of whether the Plan is fair and equitable and proposed in good faith. * * *

PJSC values Zenith as a going concern at $310 million, while the Equity Committee's experts value it at $1.05 billion. The significant difference in the experts' conclusions is the value attributed to the VSB technology developed by Zenith ($155 million according to PJSC, $833 million according to E & Y).[16]

---

8. For example, neither LGE nor the Bondholders' Committee were required to include its analysis of the value of Zenith's assets in Zenith's Disclosure Statement. Zenith included its own, performed by PJSC, and that was sufficient.

16. The experts used essentially the same methodology to calculate the value of Zenith's consumer electronics business and tuner technology. Their values are not significantly different: PJSC values the consumer electronics business at $95 million; E & Y values it at $150 million. PJSC values the tuner technology at $60 million; E & Y values it at $62.6 million.

The VSB technology is (or will be) used for the transmission of digital television signals via airwaves ("terrestrial broadcast") as opposed to cable or satellite transmission. The FCC has determined that the VSB technology (which is patented by Zenith) will be the standard for terrestrial broadcast. However, terrestrial broadcast only accounted for approximately 25.7% of the television market in the United States in 1997 and its market share is projected to fall to 14% by 2007. (Cable represented 66.7% of the market in 1997 and satellite represented 7.5%). * * * No standard has been set in most of the rest of the world and VSB is competing with other technology, most notably COFDM.

Digital televisions are being manufactured but, because digital transmission is not currently available, the market is still new. The cost of the products is high and the demand is low. However, because the FCC has picked VSB as the standard and digital transmission will be required in the future, the value of Zenith's VSB technology is significantly more than current sales. It is because of this that both experts' valuations are, of necessity, speculative.

Both parties' experts used the discounted cash flow method to value the VSB technology. They relied on the same industry experts' reports on the acceptance rates of the technology and the size of the domestic and foreign markets to calculate expected future sales.

PJSC's valuation uses a discount rate for the domestic market of 25%, which was selected from the middle of the range of rates for venture funds and hedge funds. Further, PJSC compared risk inherent in the VSB technology to start-up biotech firms, which have a new product near regulatory approval but without any established sales. For the foreign markets, PJSC used discount rates of 40% and 55%, to reflect the additional risks inherent in whether the country had adopted, or was likely to adopt, the VSB standard.

In contrast, the Equity Committee's valuation expert from E & Y used a discount rate of 17% for the domestic market (with adjustments similar to PJSC's for the foreign market). E & Y also used the capital asset pricing model to determine that discount rate, but selected different companies for comparison. The Plan proponents believe the E & Y discount rate is grossly understated, noting that its discount rate is the same as Microsoft's.

We agree with the conclusion of PJSC that the discount rate for Zenith is more appropriately 25% than 17%. Zenith, although an established company in the consumer electronics industry, has clearly not been a leader in recent years. It is no Microsoft and no source of capital would view it as such. In fact, its inability to raise capital, at any rate, is one of the reasons it is in chapter 11 today. Further, the technology being assessed is new and untried in the market. There are significant risks inherent in its future: the risk that the FCC may change its decision on the standard for terrestrial broadcast, the risk that consumers may not embrace the new technology, the certainty that revenues will not be significant until digital is being broadcast and the products incorporating that technology are readily available and cheaper. We conclude that PJSC properly assessed the risk inherent in this technology by comparing it to hedge funds and biotech companies.

The other significant difference in the valuations of the two experts is the royalty rate which Zenith will be able to charge for use of the technology. PJSC (and Zenith itself) assert that Zenith can charge only $5 per unit while E & Y asserts that it can charge a percentage of each unit's sale price (4.5%). We agree with Zenith that the percentage royalty rate is faulty.

Zenith has consistently projected royalty rates of $3 to $7 per unit. When Zenith retained Price Warehouse (in 1997, before the restructuring began) to evaluate the VSB business, Price Waterhouse concluded that $5 per unit was reasonable. Zenith's conclusion that a flat fee is appropriate is also supported by the market. In this industry, royalty rates are typically flat rates, not percentage rates. The direct competitor for VSB technology in the European market (COFDM) is also priced as a flat fee ($3.50 per unit). In contrast, E & Y relied on comparables that are not even in this industry. Therefore, we agree with Zenith's (and PJSC's) conclusion that a flat fee royalty of $5 per unit is appropriate rather than a percentage rate.

We conclude that the total value of the VSB technology, as determined by PJSC, is reliable. We, therefore, accept its conclusion that the value of Zenith as a going concern is $310 million. Consequently, we conclude that there is no equity in the company, even on a going concern basis.

3. *Fair and Equitable*

Where a class of creditors or shareholders has not accepted a plan of reorganization, the court shall nonetheless confirm the plan if it "does not discriminate unfairly and is fair and equitable." 11 U.S.C. § 1129(b)(1). Fair and equitable treatment with respect to a class of equity interests— the sole non-accepting class in this case—means either the class receives or retains property equal to the value of its interest or no junior interest receives or retains anything under the plan. *Id.* at § 1129(b)(2)(C).

In the instant case we find that both alternatives are satisfied. No class junior to the common shareholders is receiving or retaining anything under the Plan. Further, based on our conclusion of the value of Zenith as a going concern, the shareholders are receiving the value of their interests under the Plan—nothing.

a. *Treatment of Bondholders*

The Equity Committee asserts, however, that the Plan's treatment of the Bondholders violates the fair and equitable requirements of the Code. Specifically, the Plan provides that if Bondholders do not accept it, they will receive nothing under the Plan and the Plan proponents will seek cramdown pursuant to section 1129(b) as to them. In contrast, if the Bondholders accept the Plan, they will be entitled to a pro rata distribution of $50 million of the new 8.19% Senior Debentures. The Equity Committee asserts that this treatment is unfair because (1) if the Plan proponents are correct in their valuation of Zenith, Bondholders are not entitled to any distribution and offering them something for their vote in favor of the Plan is not appropriate, and (2) the shareholders were not offered a similar deal.

There is no prohibition in the Code against a Plan proponent offering different treatment to a class depending on whether it votes to accept or reject the Plan. *See, e.g., In re Drexel Burnham Lambert Group, Inc.,* 140 B.R. 347, 350 (S.D.N.Y.1992) (plan which provided warrants to accepting classes but not to rejecting class was not unfairly discriminatory and could be confirmed).[21] One justification for such disparate treatment is that, if the class accepts, the Plan proponent is saved the expense and uncertainty of a cramdown fight. This is in keeping with the Bankruptcy Code's overall policy of fostering consensual plans of reorganization and does not violate the fair and equitable requirement of section 1129(b).

Nor were the votes of the Bondholders solicited in bad faith (and subject to disqualification) as a result of the above provision. *See* 11 U.S.C. § 1126(e). The case cited by the Equity Committee to support its position is easily distinguishable. *See In re Featherworks Corp.,* 25 B.R. 634, 641 (Bankr.E.D.N.Y.1982), *aff'd,* 36 B.R. 460 (E.D.N.Y.1984). In the *Featherworks* case, the Court disallowed the change of vote by one unsecured creditor after it had received a payment outside the Plan, from an insider of the Debtor, which resulted in it receiving a greater recovery on its claim than any other unsecured creditor. 25 B.R. at 641. In this case, the distribution in question is going to all creditors in the same class, is being made pursuant to the Plan, and is fully disclosed to all interested parties. Disqualification of the vote of that entire class is not mandated.

There is similarly no prohibition against the Bondholders receiving different (and better) treatment than the shareholders receive under the Plan. In fact, the cramdown provisions of the Code mandate that the Bondholders be treated better than the shareholders. In the absence of the Bondholders receiving payment in full or consenting, the shareholders may not receive anything under the Plan. 11 U.S.C. § 1129(b)(2)(B). Thus, it is not fundamentally unfair for the Bondholders to have been offered a distribution under the Plan in exchange for their assent to the Plan, while the shareholders were not.

b.   *Retention of stock by LGE*

The Equity Committee also asserts that the Plan violates the absolute priority rule, as recently articulated by the United States Supreme Court, by allowing LGE to obtain the stock of Zenith without subjecting it to sale on the open market. *See Bank of America v. 203 North LaSalle Street Partnership,* 526 U.S. 434, 119 S.Ct. 1411, 143 L.Ed.2d 607 (1999). The *203 North LaSalle* case, however, is distinguishable from the instant case. In that case, the plan gave the shareholders the exclusive right to "buy" the

---

21. *Cf. In re AOV Industries, Inc.,* 792 F.2d 1140 (D.C.Cir.1986) (court denied confirmation of plan which required creditors to release claims against plan funder in order to receive distribution). The Court in *AOV* denied confirmation because the plan provided unequal treatment to creditors *within* the same class where only one creditor in that class had a direct claim against the plan funder. Here all creditors within the Bondholder class are being treated the same.

equity, without giving creditors a similar right or allowing the market to test the price. 119 S.Ct. at 1422. The Supreme Court held that because shareholders were receiving the exclusive right to bid for the equity, and creditors were not being paid in full, this violated section 1129(b)(2)(B). *Id.* at 1424.

In this case, all creditor classes have accepted the Plan and there is no objection to confirmation by any creditor. Thus, the absolute priority rule embodied in section 1129(b)(2)(B) is not even applicable. Rather, section 1129(b)(2)(C) is the applicable section in this case.

Further, in this case, it is not a shareholder who is being given the right to buy equity, it is LGE in its capacity as a substantial secured and unsecured creditor who is being given that right. In fact, if the Plan were to allow the minority shareholders the right to bid on the equity, as they urge, it would present the same problem as the *203 North LaSalle* plan did. The Supreme Court in *203 North LaSalle* did not say that a plan which allowed a senior secured creditor to buy the equity violated the Code; in fact, it suggested that the plan in that case violated the absolute priority rule because it did *not* let the creditor bid on the equity.

It is not appropriate to extend the ruling of the *203 North LaSalle* case beyond the facts of that case. To do so would require in all cases that a debtor be placed "on the market" for sale to the highest bidder. Such a requirement would eliminate the concept of exclusivity contained in section 1121(b) and the broad powers of the debtor to propose a plan in whatever format it desires. For example, section 1123(a)(5) specifically allows a debtor to propose a plan which allows the debtor to retain all or part of its property, to transfer all or part of its property, to merge or consolidate its business with others, to sell all or part of its property (subject to or free of liens), to satisfy or modify liens, and to cancel, modify or issue securities. The restriction on the debtor's right to propose a plan contained in the *203 North LaSalle* case should be limited to the facts of that case—where the absolute priority rule encompassed in section 1129(b)(2)(B) is violated.

The instant Plan does not violate the absolute priority rule articulated in section 1129(b)(2)(B) or (C) because all creditor classes have accepted the Plan and LGE is not retaining any interest because of its shareholder status. LGE is obtaining the equity in Zenith because of its status as a creditor, senior in right to the minority shareholders.

* * *

4. *Good Faith*

The Objectors also assert that the Plan cannot be confirmed because it violates the requirement of the Bankruptcy Code that the Plan be "proposed in good faith and not by any means forbidden by law." 11 U.S.C. § 1129(a)(3).

The good faith standard requires that the plan be "proposed with honesty, good intentions and a basis for expecting that a reorganization can be effected with results consistent with the objectives and purposes of the Bankruptcy Code." *In re Sound Radio, Inc.,* 93 B.R. 849, 853 (Bankr.D.N.J. 1988). * * *

We easily conclude that Zenith's Plan is proposed in good faith under the general requirements of the Bankruptcy Code. It is proposed with the legitimate purpose of restructuring its finances to permit it to reorganize successfully. The fact that Zenith is a financially troubled company cannot be disputed; its substantial losses in the last decade attest to that. Even with its operational restructuring (which significantly reduced the losses), Zenith needs more. Readjustment of its debt structure and forgiveness of a substantial amount of its debt is necessary for it to operate profitably and to position itself in the market to take advantage of the technology it owns. This reorganization is exactly what chapter 11 of the Bankruptcy Code was designed to accomplish.

a. *Compliance with Delaware Corporate Law*

Both the Equity Committee and Nordhoff argue, however, that the Plan must not only comply with the provisions of the Code, but must meet the standards for approval of such a transaction under Delaware corporate law. We agree that section 1129(a)(3) does incorporate Delaware law (as well as any other applicable nonbankruptcy law).

In evaluating a transaction between a controlling shareholder and its corporation, the Delaware courts require a showing that the transaction is entirely fair. *See, e.g., Kahn v. Tremont Corp.,* 694 A.2d 422 (Del.1997); *Weinberger v. UOP, Inc.,* 457 A.2d 701 (Del.1983) * * *.

i. *Fair process*

The initial argument of the Objectors, and notably Nordhoff, that LGE has not met the Delaware standard appears to be premised on the assertion that LGE required that Zenith file bankruptcy in order to take advantage of the Code's cramdown (and other) provisions. However, as Judge Walsh stated in *In re PPI Enterprises (U.S.), Inc.:* "As other courts have noted, it is not 'bad faith' for debtors to file for bankruptcy in order to take advantage of a particular provision of the Code." 228 B.R. 339, 345 (Bankr.D.Del.1998) (citations omitted). * * *

* * *

* * * [W]e do not find that LGE's position as a significant creditor and shareholder unduly influenced the process. Throughout the negotiation of the restructuring, Zenith and LGE had separate counsel and other professionals. Zenith properly appointed a Special Committee of its Board of Directors (which did not include any LGE appointees) to negotiate with LGE. Further, LGE did not object or impede Zenith's efforts to find a different strategic investor or purchaser and, in fact, introduced Zenith to some targets. Finally, any undue influence which LGE might have had over Zenith was countered by the Bondholders participation (through separate professionals) in negotiating the Plan.

Further, we disagree with the Equity Committee's assertion that there was no effort to consider other alternatives. Mr. Gannon testified to his substantial efforts to obtain another investor or buyer. No alternative was forthcoming after eighteen months. Further, none of the Equity Committee's witnesses could identify any concrete offer or alternative to the LGE proposal that would afford creditors or shareholders a better return. The only alternative posited by them was to deny confirmation of the Plan and try to market the company while it is in bankruptcy. * * *

The Equity Committee asserts that it is significant that the Special Committee did not obtain an opinion attesting to the fairness of the process. We do not find this to be fatal. The Court is the ultimate arbiter of the fairness of the transaction. * * *

We have already concluded that the disclosure requirements of the Code have been met by the Disclosure Statement issued by Zenith. * * *

Finally, the Equity Committee argues that the failure of Zenith or LGE to have any meaningful negotiations with the minority shareholders renders the process unfair. We disagree. Since PJSC determined that there was no equity in the company, asking the minority shareholders for input into the financial restructuring of the company would have been futile. * * *

ii. *Fair price*

With respect to the issue of fair price, we start with the value of Zenith which we found above, $310 million. * * * [W]e conclude that the PJSC valuation included all aspects necessary to determine the value of Zenith and, therefore, the fairness of the price paid by LGE for it. * * *

Under the restructuring proposal, LGE is acquiring 100% of the equity of Zenith, which will still owe $67 million to Citibank and $50 million to the Bondholders. The net equity of the company is therefore $193 million ($310 million less the assumed debt of $117 million). In exchange, LGE is relinquishing $200 million of debt, investing up to an additional $60 million in capital funds, and exchanging $175 million in claims for the Mexican plant (valued at $40 million) plus a note for $135 million paid over time. We conclude that LGE is paying a fair price for the equity in the new Zenith.

* * *

III. *CONCLUSION*

For all the foregoing reasons, we conclude that the objections of the Equity Committee and Nordhoff to approval of the Disclosure Statement should be overruled. We further conclude that the Plan satisfies the requirements of sections 1123 and 1129 of the Bankruptcy Code and may be confirmed * * *.

NOTE: PROCEEDINGS UNDER CHAPTER 11

1. *Choice of Forum.*

It is not without significance that *Zenith* is a decision of the Bankruptcy Court of the District of Delaware in respect of a prepackaged proceeding. During the 1990s this court became a favorite choice of public corporations filing under chapter 11. In 1999 for example, 41 percent of public corporation filings were in Delaware, made by firms holding 69 percent of the total assets of publicly held firms making filings in the year. Rasmussen and Thomas, Timing Matters: Promoting Forum Shopping by Insolvent Corporations, 94 Nw. U. L. Rev. 1357 (2000). The firms seek a debtor-friendly environment; their lawyers seek a court inclined toward liberality respecting fees. Delaware is thought to serve both functions. Rasmussen and Thomas approve of such forum shopping on the ground that judicial responsiveness enhances value. They would, however, change the system to allow firms to commit in advance in their charters to file for bankruptcy only in designated venues, the idea being that advance specification would build in responsiveness to creditor interests as well. For a more equivocal view of the phenomenon, see Eisenberg and LoPucki, Shopping for Judges: An Empirical Analysis of Venue Choice in the Bankruptcy Reorganizations of Large, Publicly Held Companies, 84 Cornell L.Rev. 967 (1999).

2. *The Debtor in Possession.*

Under chapter 11, the firm becomes a "debtor in possession." 11 U.S.C. § 1101(1). No trustee is appointed, and the pre-bankruptcy managers remain in place. The automatic stay provided for in section 362 of the Code keeps the creditors in check. The restructuring of the business is facilitated by the power to continue to perform favorable executory contracts and repudiate contracts deemed unfavorable. 11 U.S.C. § 365. Contracts are approved or repudiated subject to judicial scrutiny on a business judgment basis. When a contract is repudiated, the non-breaching party can file a claim for damages in the proceeding. An automatic administrative priority for the claims of lenders providing new financing is facilitated through section 364's provision for ordinary course financing for the debtor in possession. A lender thus situated shares pro rata with other claimants holding administrative priorities. 11 U.S.C. § 507(a)(1). If additional incentives are needed to secure credit, the bankruptcy court may authorize a super priority. 11 U.S.C. § 364(c).

Thus protected and financed, management continues to operate the business. In theory, its possession of office can be terminated and a trustee appointed by the bankruptcy court upon motion by a party in interest and a finding of fraud or gross mismanagement, or a finding that the appointment otherwise is in the best interests of creditors and the estate. See 11 U.S.C. § 1104. But the presumption lies with management and a trustee is unlikely to be appointed as a practical matter.

Management's control of the bankruptcy proceeding also derives from its power to draft and propose a plan of reorganization. Under section 1121(c) of the Code, the debtor has the exclusive right to propose a plan during the first 120 days of the proceeding and any extensions the court permits, subject to an outer limit of 18 months. See 11 U.S.C. § 1123(d)(2)(A). Debtors who have run out of time, whether due to nonreceipt of an extension after 120 days or to the expiration of 18 months, may still file a plan, but no longer have the exclusive right to do so. Any party in interest, which includes the trustee, a creditor's committee, an equity security holders' committee, a creditor, an equity security holder, or any indenture trustee, may also file a plan.

3. *Secured Claims and Adequate Protection.*

The Bankruptcy Code strikes a complicated balance between the secured party's right to repossess on default and the estate's need to use the collateral in connection with the reorganization. The automatic stay extends to collateral given by the debtor. 11 U.S.C. § 362(a). The stay may not be lifted if the debtor has an equity in the collateral or the collateral is necessary for an effective reorganization. 11 U.S.C. § 362(d)(2). In other words, the stay can be lifted only if the creditor's claim is greater than the value of the property and there is no prospect of an effective reorganization. United Savings Ass'n v. Timbers of Inwood Forest Ass'n, 484 U.S. 365 (1988). But the stay is subject to a qualification. The estate is privileged to keep the collateral only if it provides "adequate protection" for the collateral itself or its value. If the secured party can show a lack of "adequate protection" of its "interest in [the] property," the court must lift the stay. 11 U.S.C. § 362(d)(1). This "adequate protection" must extend to the value of the collateral. If, for example, the value of the collateral is depreciating during the term of the stay, the secured party is entitled to compensation. This can come in the form of additional security or cash payments. 11 U.S.C. § 362(1), (2). Where the debtor has a substantial equity cushion, however, that equity is deemed adequate to protect the secured party. In re Mellor, 734 F.2d 1396, 1400 (9th Cir.1984). The automatic stay will be lifted only if the creditor can show that its claim is greater than the value of the property and that provision of substitute security or other relief will be inadequate. See 11 U.S.C. § 361.

Does the "adequate protection" requirement imply an award of post-petition interest to the secured party to compensate for lost use of the property during the term of the stay? A unanimous Supreme Court held that it does not in United Savings Ass'n v. Timbers of Inwood Forest Associates, supra. There, an underse-cured claimant argued that the phrase "interest in property" in section 362 includes the secured party's right to take immediate repossession of the defaulted security and apply it to repayment of the debt. Adequate protection of that right is reimbursement for the use of the foregone proceeds—in effect, interest. The Court rebutted the argument by reference to section 506(b) of the Code, which provides explicitly for post-petition interest, but only for *over* secured creditors "to the extent that an allowed secured claim is secured by property the value of which * * * is greater than the amount of such claim."

Note that application of section 362 entails the valuation of the collateral. As of what time should the value be calculated? Courts have employed each of (1) the date of the bankruptcy petition, (2) a later date fixed as the time at which the secured creditor would have realized value in the foreclosure that would have proceeded absent bankruptcy, and (3) the time of the determination.

4.   *Committees and Classes.*

The Code compensates for its diminution of judicial and administrative over-sight by enhancing the governance role of creditors' committees. The Code charges the members of such committees with the protection of the interests they represent, specifying that the committee consult with the debtor's managers, investigate its finances and prospects, and participate in the formulation of the plan. 11 U.S.C. § 1103(c). The Code requires the appointment of a committee of unsecured credi-tors by the United States Trustee promptly upon adjudication. Active monitors are sought: the Code articulates a preference for larger claimants with representative claims. 11 U.S.C. § 1102(b)(1). Historically, this resulted in committees dominated by bank creditors. LoPucki and Whitford, Bargaining Over Equity's Share in the Bankruptcy Reorganization of Large Publicly Held Companies, 139 U.Pa.L.Rev. 125, 155 (1990). More recently, hedge funds have been taking a prominent role in bankruptcy governance. In any event, insiders are precluded from membership. Bankruptcy Rule 1007(d). Equity committees are optional. According to LoPucki and Whitford, id. at 159–160, equityholders of insolvent debtors greatly enhance their chance of recovering an award by electing a committee to represent them in the bargaining.

Under chapter 11, creditors have "claims" and equityholders have "interests." The Code contemplates that claims and interests be separated into "classes" for purposes of confirmation, and that each member of a "class" be treated in the same way by the plan. 11 U.S.C. § 1123(a)(4). The Code does not, however, require that all similar claims or interests be placed in the same class. Instead, it sets out a negatively phrased rule: a claim or interest may be placed in a particular class "only if such claim or interest is substantially similar to the other claims or interests of such class." 11 U.S.C. § 1122(a). Thus, holders of debentures and trade creditors can be placed in different classes even though both are general creditors. It follows that a plan treating substantially similar claims in a different manner presupposes the placement of the claimants in a different class. Class formation by the intermediaries who conduct the proceeding thus becomes a stage of a wider allocational politics.

5. *Disclosure.*

The plan's proponent must provide those voting with "adequate information" by means of a disclosure statement before soliciting consents. This regime of mandatory disclosure contrasts sharply with that administered by the SEC under the federal securities laws. In bankruptcy, "adequate information" is a relative proposition. It is defined as "information of a kind, and in sufficient detail, as far as is reasonably practicable in light of the nature and history of the debtor and the condition of the debtor's books and records, that would enable a hypothetical reasonable investor typical of holders of claims or interests of the relevant class to make an informed judgment about the plan." 11 U.S.C. § 1125(a)(1). The "typical" investor is defined in section 1125(a)(2) in terms of a "relationship with the debtor" and an "ability to obtain information" similar to that of other members of the class.

Compliance with the standard is a matter of bankruptcy court discretion. The system provides this flexibility with a view to the different characteristics of different proceedings—some debtors are larger and more complicated than others, some creditor groups are better informed than others, speed matters more in some proceedings, and costs vary. 7 Collier on Bankruptcy ¶ 1125[02](15th ed. 2005).

In *Zenith*, the prepackaged bankruptcy framework triggers a requirement of SEC approval. Under § 1126(b), consents solicited outside of the § 1125 disclosure regime must conform with applicable nonbankruptcy law, which on the facts of the case meant the federal securities laws. If the proceeding is not prepackaged, the disclosure statement is exempted from registration requirements under the federal and state securities laws. Section 1125(e) adds a safe harbor from the antifraud provisions of the securities laws, conditioned on a solicitation "in good faith and in compliance with the applicable provisions of this title." See Public Service Co. v. Consolidated Utilities and Communications, 846 F.2d 803 (1st Cir.1988). The SEC still has a privilege to be heard on the issue of whether a disclosure statement contains adequate information. 11 U.S.C. § 1125(d). But the SEC does not undertake an active role in chapter 11 cases on it own motion. It has indicated a willingness to respond to "specific requests made by the bankruptcy judge and the U.S. trustee for advice with respect to matters within its area of special expertise, such as, for example, the adequacy of information contained in a disclosure statement." Commissioner Beavis Longstreth, The Securities and Exchange Commission's Role in Bankruptcy Reorganization Proceedings, November 21, 1983, CCH Fed.Sec.L.Rep. ¶ 83,463.

6. *Approval.*

Once the court approves the disclosure statement, the statement and proposed plan are disseminated to each class for a vote. Acceptance or rejection of a plan is assessed as to each class. For creditor acceptance, two thirds of amount and more than one half in number is required. 11 U.S.C. § 1126(c). The requirement for equity holders is two thirds in amount. 11 U.S.C. § 1126(d). The percentage requirements are calculated only as among those who actually voted.

If a plan proposes that a certain class is not entitled to any payment or compensation, the class is automatically deemed to have not accepted the plan. 11

U.S.C. § 1126(g). Contrariwise, classes "unimpaired" within the meaning of section 1124 of the Code are automatically deemed to have accepted the plan. Solicitation of their votes is not required for approval. 11 U.S.C. § 1126(f). "Unimpaired" claims or interests meet one of three definitions set out in section 1124. Either, (1) the plan "leaves unaltered the legal, equitable and contractual rights to which such claim or interest entitles the holder of such claim or interest;" (2) the plan reinstates the claim or interest by curing any default (other than a default under an ipso facto or bankruptcy clause), reinstating its maturity, and otherwise leaving unaltered the holder's rights under the claim; or (3) the plan pays cash in the allowed amount of a claim or liquidation preference of an interest.

7. *Confirmation Requirements.*

The following are the principal requirements that must be met for a plan to be confirmed:

(a) *Good Faith*. The plan must have been proposed in good faith and not in violation of any law. 11 U.S.C. § 1129(a)(3). We see in *Zenith* that this includes Delaware fiduciary law. Do the Delaware standards applied in the case add anything to the fairness standards implied by § 1129? Are the Delaware standards, which were designed for the benefit of minority shareholders, consistent in purpose and effect with absolute priority?

(b) *Feasibility*. The court must conclude that confirmation is not likely to be followed by liquidation or further financial reorganization, "unless such liquidation or reorganization is proposed in the plan." 11 U.S.C. § 1129(a)(11).

(c) *Best Interest of Creditors*. Each holder of a claim or interest of each impaired class must have either accepted the plan, or, in the alternative, be provided with the liquidation value of his claim. 11 U.S.C. § 1129(a)(7)(A). In other words, if the plan does not provide for each member of a class to receive at least what would have been obtained had the debtor been liquidated under chapter 7, a single negative vote defeats the plan. Application of this "best interest" test entails two valuations. First, the court must determine how much the dissenter is receiving under the plan, discounting to present value as necessary. Then the court must construct a hypothetical liquidation of the debtor, as of the effective date of the plan. The plan's proponent generates these calculations in the first instance; it must provide the creditors a liquidation analysis in an understandable form as part of the solicitation process. In re Tranel, 940 F.2d 1168, 1172 (8th Cir.1991).

Should the proponent's liquidation analysis be contested, room opens to argue over whether liquidation value means the value (1) produced by sale of the entire enterprise as scrap (i.e., piece by piece), (2) produced by sale of the entire enterprise as a going concern, or (3) produced by a combination of sale of some divisions as going concerns and others as scrap, or by some intermediate process. Even if scrap value is the goal, the search could be for the higher of the present value of the proceeds of (1) an orderly liquidation over a number of years, or (2) an instantaneous distress sale. Thus the ascertainment of "liquidation" value can implicate uncertainties as to the period over which sales of properties can be effected, the prices and terms of those sales, the credit-worthiness of the buyers, the cost of maintaining some piece of the debtor's organization over the period necessary to effect the sales, and the discount rates to be applied to both estimated receipts and estimated expenses in order to produce a "present value." It follows that a process seeking the liquidation value of a corporation with public investors could entail estimates of a range of expectations not likely to be much narrower than that involved in determining going concern values.

(d) *Class Vote*. Each class must have accepted the plan or be unimpaired by the plan. 11 U.S.C. § 1129(a)(8). This requirement can be avoided, and the plan "crammed down" on a dissenting class, if the plan satisfies the absolute priority rule, as laid down in section 1129(b). But even if the plan satisfies the "cram down" test in section 1129(b), at least one class must have accepted the plan, not including acceptance by any insider group. 11 U.S.C. § 1129(a)(10).

(B) ABSOLUTE PRIORITY UNDER CHAPTER 11

House Report No. 95–595
95th Cong., 1st Sess, 1977, pp. 408–418.

§ 1129.   Confirmation of Plan

Specifically, the court may confirm a plan over the objection of a class of secured claims if the members of that class are unimpaired or if they are to receive under the plan property of a value equal to the allowed amount of their secured claims, as determined under proposed 11 U.S.C. 506(a). The property is to be valued as of the effective date of the plan, thus recognizing the time-value of money. As used throughout this subsection, "property" includes both tangible and intangible property, such as a security of the debtor or a successor to the debtor under a reorganization plan.

The court may confirm over the dissent of a class of unsecured claims, including priority claims, only if the members of the class are unimpaired, if they will receive under the plan property of a value equal to the allowed amount of their unsecured claims, or if no class junior will share under the plan. That is, if the class is impaired, then they must be paid in full or, if paid less than in full, then no class junior may receive anything under the plan. This codifies the absolute priority rule from the dissenting class on down.

With respect to classes of equity, the court may confirm over a dissent if the members of the class are unimpaired, if they receive their liquidation preference or redemption rights, if any, or if no class junior shares under the plan. This, too, is a codification of the absolute priority rule with respect to equity. * * *

One requirement applies generally to all classes before the court may confirm under this subsection. No class may be paid more than in full.

The partial codification of the absolute priority rule here is not intended to deprive senior creditor[s] of compensation for being required to take securities in the reorganized debtor that are of an equal priority with the securities offered to a junior class. Under current law, seniors are entitled to compensation for their loss of priority, and the increased risk put upon them by being required to give up their priority will be reflected in a lower value of the securities given to them than the value of comparable securities given to juniors that have not lost a priority position.

Finally, the proponent must request use of this subsection. The court may not confirm notwithstanding nonacceptance unless the proponent requests and the court may then confirm only if subsection (b) is complied with. The court may not rewrite the plan.

A more detailed explanation follows:

* * *

The procedure followed is simple. The court examines each class of claims or interests designated under section 1123(a)(1) to see if the requirements of section 1129(b) are met. If the class is a class of secured claims, then [* * * certain] tests * * * must be complied with in order for confirmation to occur. * * * While section 1129(a) does not contemplate a valuation of the debtor's business, such a valuation will almost always be required under section 1129(b) in order to determine the value of the consideration to be distributed under the plan. Once the valuation is performed, it becomes a simple matter to impose the criterion that no claim will be paid more than in full.

* * *

* * * [W]hen an impaired class [of unsecured claims] that has not accepted the plan is to receive less than full value under the plan * * *, the plan may be confirmed * * * if the class is not unfairly discriminated against with respect to equal classes and if junior classes will receive nothing under the plan. The second criterion is the easier to understand. It is designed to prevent a senior class from giving up consideration to a junior class unless every intermediate class consents, is paid in full, or is unimpaired. This gives intermediate creditors a great deal of leverage in negotiating with senior or secured creditors who wish to have a plan that gives value to equity. One aspect of this test that is not obvious is that whether one class is senior, equal, or junior to another class is relative and not absolute. Thus from the perspective of trade creditors holding unsecured claims, claims of senior and subordinated debentures may be entitled to share on an equal basis with the trade claims. However, from the perspective of the senior unsecured debt, the subordinated debentures are junior.

This point illustrates the lack of precision in the first criterion which demands that a class not be unfairly discriminated against with respect to equal classes. From the perspective of unsecured trade claims, there is no unfair discrimination as long as the total consideration given all other classes of equal rank does not exceed the amount that would result from an exact aliquot distribution. Thus if trade creditors, senior debt, and subordinate debt are each owed $100 and the plan proposes to pay the trade debt $15, the senior debt $30, and the junior debt $0, the plan would not unfairly discriminate against the trade debt nor would any other allocation of consideration under the plan between the senior and junior debt be unfair as to the trade debt as long as the aggregate consideration is less than $30. The senior debt could take $25 and give up $5 to the junior debt and the trade debt would have no cause to complain because as far as it is concerned the junior debt is an equal class.

However, in this latter case the senior debt would have been unfairly discriminated against because the trade debt was being unfairly overcompensated; of course the plan would also fail unless the senior debt was unimpaired, received full value, or accepted the plan, because from its perspective a junior class received property under the plan. Application of the test from the perspective of senior debt is best illustrated by the plan that proposes to pay trade debt $15, senior debt $25, and junior debt $0. Here the senior debt is being unfairly discriminated against with respect to the equal trade debt even though the trade debt receives less than the senior debt. The discrimination arises from the fact that the senior debt is entitled to the rights of the junior debt which in this example entitle the senior debt to share on a 2:1 basis with the trade debt.

Finally, it is necessary to interpret the first criterion from the perspective of subordinated debt. The junior debt is subrogated to the rights of senior debt once the senior debt is paid in full. Thus, while the plan that pays trade debt $15, senior debt $25, and junior debt $0 is not unfairly discriminatory against the junior debt, a plan that proposes to pay trade debt $55, senior debt $100, and junior debt $1 would be unfairly discriminatory. In order to avoid discriminatory treatment against the junior debt, at least $10 would have to be received by such debt under those facts.

The criterion of unfair discrimination is not derived from the fair and equitable rule or from the best interests of creditors test. Rather it preserves just treatment of a dissenting class from the class's own perspective.

* * *

Excerpt From Debates on Bankruptcy Reform Act of 1978

Cong.Rec. pp. H. 11,104–11,105 (Sept. 28, 1978).

Although many of the factors interpreting "fair and equitable" are specified in paragraph (2), others, which were explicated in the description of section 1129(b) in the House report, were omitted from the House amendment to avoid statutory complexity and because they would undoubtedly be found by a court to be fundamental to "fair and equitable" treatment of a dissenting class. For example, a dissenting class should be assured that no senior class receives more than 100 percent of the amount of its claims. While that requirement was explicitly included in the House bill, the deletion is intended to be one of style and not one of substance.

Paragraph (2) provides guidelines for a court to determine whether a plan is fair and equitable with respect to a dissenting class. It must be emphasized that the fair and equitable requirement applies only with respect to dissenting classes. Therefore, unlike the fair and equitable rule contained in Chapter X and section 77 of the Bankruptcy Act under section 1129(b)(2), senior accepting classes are permitted to give up value to junior classes as long as no dissenting intervening class receives less than the amount of its claims in full. If there is no dissenting intervening class and the only dissent is from a class junior to the class to which value * * * [has] been given up, then the plan may still be fair and equitable with respect to the dissenting class, as long as no class senior to the dissenting class has received more than 100 percent of the amount of its claims.

Paragraph (2) contains three subparagraphs, each of which applies to a particular kind of class of claims or interests that is impaired and has not accepted the plan. Subparagraph (A) applies when a class of secured claims is impaired and has not accepted the plan. The provision applies whether or not section 1111(b) applies. The plan may be crammed down notwithstanding the dissent of a secured class only if the plan complies with clause (i), (ii), or (iii).

Clause (i) permits cram down if the dissenting class of secured claims will retain its lien on the property whether the property is retained by the debtor or transferred. It should be noted that the lien secures the allowed secured claim held by such holder. The meaning of "allowed secured claim" will vary depending on whether section 1111(b)(2) applies to such class.

If section 1111(b)(2) applies then the "electing" class is entitled to have the entire allowed amount of the debt related to such property secured by a lien even if the value of the collateral is less than the amount of the debt. In addition, the plan must provide for the holder to receive, on account of the allowed secured claims, payments, either present or deferred, of a principal face amount equal to the amount of the debt and of a present value equal to the value of the collateral.

For example, if a creditor loaned $15,000,000 to a debtor secured by real property worth $18,000,000 and the value of the real property had dropped to $12,000,000 by the date when the debtor commenced a proceeding under chapter 11, the plan could be confirmed notwithstanding the dissent of the creditor as long as the lien remains on the collateral to secure a $15,000,000 debt, the face amount of present or extended payments to be made to the creditor under the plan is at least $15,000,000, and the present value of the present or deferred payments is not less than $12,000,000. The House report accompanying the House bill described what is meant by "present value".

Clause (ii) is self explanatory. Clause (iii) requires the court to confirm the plan notwithstanding the dissent of the electing secured class if the plan provides for the realization by the secured class of the indubitable equivalence of the secured claims. The standard of "indubitable equivalence" is taken from In re Murel Holding Corp., 75 F.2d 941 (2d Cir.1935) (Learned Hand, Jr.).

Abandonment of the collateral to the creditor would clearly satisfy indubitable equivalence, as would a lien on similar collateral. However, present cash payments less than the secured claim would not satisfy the standard because the creditor is deprived of an opportunity to gain from a future increase in value of the collateral. Unsecured notes as to the secured claim or equity securities of the debtor would not be the indubitable equivalent. With respect to an oversecured creditor, the secured claim will never exceed the allowed claim.

* * *

Subparagraph (B) applies to a dissenting class of unsecured claims. The court must confirm the plan notwithstanding the dissent of a class of impaired unsecured claims if the plan provides for such claims to receive property with a present value equal to the allowed amount of the claims. Unsecured claims may receive any kind of "property," which is used in its broadest sense, as long as the present value of the property given to the holders of unsecured claims is equal to the allowed amount of the claims. Some kinds of property, such as securities, may require difficult valuations by the court; in such circumstances the court need only determine that there is a reasonable likelihood that the property given the dissenting class of impaired unsecured claims equals the present value of such allowed claims.

Alternatively, under clause (ii), the court must confirm the plan if the plan provides that holders of any claims or interests junior to the interests of the dissenting class of impaired unsecured claims will not receive any property under the plan on account of such junior claims or interests. As long as senior creditors have not been paid more than in full, and classes of equal claims are being treated so that the dissenting class of impaired unsecured claims is not being discriminated against unfairly, the plan may be confirmed if the impaired class of unsecured claims receives less than 100 cents on the dollar (or nothing at all) as long as no class junior to the dissenting class receives anything at all. Such an impaired dissenting class may not prevent confirmation of a plan by objection merely because a senior class has elected to give up value to a junior class that is higher in priority than the impaired dissenting class of unsecured claims as long as the above safeguards are met.

NOTE: ISSUES UNDER THE CODE

1. *Cash Value and Liquidation.*

Does the 1978 Bankruptcy Act require the pay-out to claimants in a reorganization to be close to, if not actually in, immediate cash value? The words of sections 1124, 1129(a), and 1129(b) suggest this. But the courts have not taken up the suggestion. In re Nite Lite Inns, 17 B.R. 367 (Bankr.S.D.Cal.1982), rejects a creditor's objection that the securities issued under the plan could not be sold for the amount of value assigned by the court. See also In re Sound Radio, Inc., 93 B.R. 849, 855 (Bankr.D.N.J.1988).

The same mode of thinking leads courts to favor reorganization over cash sale. See In re The Lionel Corp., 722 F.2d 1063 (2d Cir.1983), where the court, applying section 363(b) of the Code, ruled that a cash sale of assets out of the ordinary course of business had to be supported by a business justification other than the interests of the creditors. In an extreme case, a protracted reorganization proceeding ultimately fails, and the debtor goes into liquidation with the value of the creditors' claims severely compromised. For a case study, see Weiss and Wruck, Information Problems, Conflicts of Interest, and Asset Stripping: Chapter 11's Failure in the Case of Eastern Airlines, 48 J. Fin. 55 (1998).

2. *Unfair Discrimination.*

The House Report's discussion of section 1129(b)'s concept of "unfair discrimination" draws on the concept of "exact aliquot distribution." It thereby implies a rule of *pro rata* treatment across creditors of equivalent seniority. Under such a rule, a plan would be discriminatory if, for example, it provided that members of a class of trade creditors more per dollar of claim than members of separately organized class of unsecured bondholders.

But like *Zenith*, supra, the cases under the Code do not read the concept of unfair discrimination to be so strict. Literally the Code prohibits only "unfair" discrimination. By implication it thereby allows for discriminatory departures from *pro rata* treatment so long as they are not "unfair." The justification is that the plan allocates a "surplus" over liquidation value to which all creditors have not made a proportionate contribution. 7 Collier on Bankruptcy ¶ 1129.04[3][b] (15th ed. 2004). Some discrepancies in treatment have violated the rule, but they have been extreme. See In re Barney & Carey Co., 170 B.R. 17 (Bankr.D.Mass. 1994)(disallowing a plan granting 100 percent over 10 years to an unsecured class guaranteed by insiders and 15 percent in 90 days to the trade creditors).

A leading case, In re Aztec Co., 107 B.R. 585 (Bankr.M.D.Tenn.1989), offers a four part test. Unfair discrimination depends on (1) whether the discrimination has a reasonable basis, (2) whether the debtor can confirm a plan that does not discriminate, (3) whether the discrimination is in good faith; and (4) how the plan treats the classes discriminated against. For a critical discussion, see Markell, A New Perspective on Unfair Discrimination in Chapter 11, 72 Am. Bankr. L.J. 227 (1998).

3. *Risk Shifting.*

Senior creditors successfully have raised a claim of "unreasonable risk shifting" under the Code. These cases have involved single-asset firms. More particularly, real estate developers hold the equity in the single-purpose corporate owner of an office building. The building has a secured creditor with a claim exceeding the value of the building; general creditor claims are small in amount. The equity interest proposes a plan that (1) pays off the general creditor class with near-term cash payments constituting a substantial percentage of its claims, and (2) holds the secured creditor to a secured debt interest with a term materially longer than that of the original loan. The general creditor class approves the plan, while the secured creditor dissents. The secured creditor has successfully asserted in a number of these cases that the plan violates absolute priority by according the juniors relatively certain value in the near future while shifting to the seniors the distant future risks respecting the debtor's operations and financial performance. In re D & F Construction Inc., 865 F.2d 673 (5th Cir.1989); In re Monarch Beach Venture, Ltd., 166 B.R. 428 (C.D.Cal.1993); In re Miami Center Assocs., Ltd., 144 B.R. 937 (Bankr.S.D.Fla.1992). Note that, by definition, the senior makes this argument after the court already has found that the plan to be feasible and that the secured debt interest allocated to the senior amounts to "payment in full." The finding of "unreasonable risk shifting" trumps those findings, implying either that a higher discount rate should have been applied to the senior's participation or that the plan in fact is not feasible.

4. *Contracting Out.*

Lenders with bargaining power sometimes get borrowers to agree to waive rights under bankruptcy law, most prominently the protection of the automatic stay. We have seen that a conceptually-related contracting out of the bankruptcy regime occurs in asset securitization transactions. There the parties seek to make the SPV "bankruptcy remote," through contract: The SPV's charter requires (a) that the SPV actually be insolvent before filing a bankruptcy petition, and (b) that a bankruptcy petition be approved by independent directors who are stipulated to owe fiduciary duties to the SPV's creditors rather than its stockholders.

The foregoing arrangements give rise to the question whether some or all of the Code's provisions are mandatory. The caselaw on waivers of the automatic stay is split. Compare In re Atrium High Point Ltd. Partnership, 189 B.R. 599 (Bankr. M.D.N.C.1995)(sustaining a waiver), with Farm Credit, ACA v. Polk, 160 B.R. 870 (M.D.Fla.1993)(refusing to enforce). Academic commentary tends to approve contractual modifications. See, e.g., Tracht, Contractual Bankruptcy Waivers: Reconciling Theory, Practice, and Law, 82 Cornell L. Rev. 301 (1997)(arguing for presumptive validity). Schwarcz, Rethinking Freedom of Contract: A Bankruptcy Paradigm, 77 Tex. L. Rev. 515 (1999), sounds a note of caution, suggesting that in a subclass of cases, waivers likely to harm nonconsenting creditors should be unenforceable.

5.   *Feasibility and Post–Proceeding Performance.*

High leverage tends to be rule for post-bankruptcy capital structures. One study finds the median ratio of long term debt to long term debt and equity of emerging firms to be 0.47. Gilson, Transactions Costs and Capital Structure Choice: Evidence from Financially Distressed Firms, 52 J.Fin. 161 (1997). Hotchkiss, Postbankruptcy Performance and Management Turnover, 50 J.Fin. 3 (1995), studies a sample of firms filing between 1979 to 1988 to show that 40 percent experience operating losses in the first three years following bankruptcy and 32 percent eventually return to bankruptcy or conduct an out of court reorganization. Retention of pre-bankruptcy management substantially increases the chance that this will happen. On the other hand, 70 percent of the firms replace their CEO prior to emergence from the chapter.

NOTE: EMPIRICAL RESULTS—DEVIATIONS FROM ABSOLUTE PRIORITY

How is the 1978 Act working? Empirical studies of bankruptcy proceedings confirm that it operates substantially as planned. Priority is respected, even though absolute priority does not determine the results of bankruptcy distributions.

Altman and Eberhart, Do Seniority Provisions Protect Bondholders' Investments?, J. Portfolio Mgt., Summer 1994, p. 67, surveys 91 bankruptcies between 1980 and 1992 to show the following average trading prices for securities issued at emergence from chapter 11: (a) In respect of secured claims, $102.24, (b) in respect of senior unsecured claims, $77.78, (c) in respect of senior subordinated claims, $21.32, (d) in respect of subordinated claims, $30.71.

To what extent does the payout pattern implicate deviations from absolute priority benefitting the equity? LoPucki and Whitford, Bargaining Over Equity's Share in the Bankruptcy Reorganization of Large, Publicly Held Companies, 139 U. Pa. L. Rev. 125, 194–196 (1993), reports the results of a study of the forty-three largest publicly held corporations reorganized between 1979 and 1988. It finds (a) that negotiation determines the results of most proceedings, and that cram downs and judicial adjudication of absolute priority are rare; and (b) that shareholders of insolvent corporations regularly get a share of the distribution, although the share "almost invariably" is a small one when measured as a percentage of the total distribution, rarely exceeding 10 percent. With one exception among the insolvent companies covered in the study, equity participated in the distribution only so long as the general creditors received at least 14 percent on their claims. Id. at 143.

Eberhart, Moore & Roenfeldt, Security Pricing and Deviations from the Absolute Priority Rule in Bankruptcy Proceedings, 45 J. Finance 1457 (1990), report on a similar study of 30 large bankruptcy proceedings commenced between 1979 and 1986. The study finds that the deviations from absolute priority (the amount paid to common divided by total distribution) range from zero to 35 percent, with an average of 7.57 percent. The creditors were paid less than they were owed in 24 of the 30 cases; in these "creditor deficit" distributions, the deviation from absolute priority averaged 9.87 percent. Weiss, Bankruptcy Resolution: Direct Costs and Violation of Priority of Claims, supra, reports the results of a study of 37 bankruptcy proceedings, finding that absolute priority is violated in 29 (or 78 percent) of the cases. In 3 of these cases the equity received a minimal cash settlement; in 15 the equity received 25 percent or less of the equity of the reorganized company; in 12 the equity received more than 25 percent of the new equity. Introducing a geographic distinction, Weiss finds that equity holders are treated better in the New York bankruptcy courts. See also Weiss, Bankruptcy in Corporate America: Direct Costs and Enforcement of Claims, J.Leg.Econ, July 1992, p. 79.

What normative implications arise from these findings? Does a 7 or 10 percent deviation from absolute priority amount to a problem? If so why? Because the cost of debt capital goes up to the extent that the system builds in deviations from absolute priority? Because the deviations violate the expectations of investors in debt securities? Because the returns do not justify the costs of the cumbersome system of collective bargaining? White, Measuring Deviations from Absolute Priority in Chapter 11 Bankruptcy, J.Leg.Econ., July 1992, p. 71, considers whether the data described above imply that the equity receives a comparatively small slice of the pie ("crumbs off the table") or a slice large enough to cause creditors to be less willing to lend. She concludes, id. p. 76, that the equity receive a small share of the payout even when the creditors receive little or nothing "and then receive a sharply increasing share as creditors' payoff rate rises." In cases where the creditors receive less than 90 percent of their claims, the payoff to the equity averages 10 percent of the creditors' claims, while the creditors receive an average of 42 percent of their claims. The creditors, it follows, would have averaged 24 percent more had strict priority been followed, suggesting a "substantial" deviation.

Contrast with these findings an observation made by LoPucki and Whitford. They find that the bargaining dynamic between seniors and juniors in chapter 11 does not turn on projected difficulties with valuation: "In nearly every case, the negotiators knew the company was insolvent and that equity would be entitled to nothing in an adjudication." LoPucki and Whitford, supra, 139 U.Pa.L.Rev. at 195. The key factors behind the practice of awards for equity are aggressive, effective representation for the equity, on the one hand, and the "desire to have a consensual plan," id., on the other. This is partly economic—a trade off in recognition of the juniors' ability to make trouble—and partly cultural—a product of relationships in the bankruptcy community combined with a sharing norm. Finally, compare the results of Betker, Management's Incentives, Equity's Bargaining Power, and Deviations from Absolute priority in Chapter 11 Bankruptcies, 68 J. Bus. 161 (1995). Betker shows that deviations from absolute priority increase as the firm is closer to solvency, and tend to be larger where the CEO has substantial shareholdings. Deviations tend to be smaller as the proportion of bank and secured claims increases, and when the debtor in possession loses the exclusive right to present the plan.

(C) THE NEW VALUE EXCEPTION

Under both the 1938 Act and the 1978 Act, the old equity often has insisted that it is entitled to participate if it contributes "new value" in exchange for common stock of the new enterprise. The 1938 Act's absolute priority regime permitted such contributions, at least in theory. But the learning thereunder was hostile to new value contributions that consisted of intangibles (such as experience with the enterprise, financial standing in the community and continuity of management), presumably because such contributions were too ephemeral and too easily overvalued to permit them to underpin the participations proposed. Cf. Case v. Los Angeles Lumber Products Co., 308 U.S. 106 (1939). The notion was expressed, however, that new participations could be offered to the old equity if the enterprise required capital and the contributors offered cash or cash equivalents.

The Supreme Court first took up the status of new value contributions under the 1978 Act in **Norwest Bank Worthington v. Ahlers,** 485 U.S. 197 (1988), which concerned the reorganization of a family farm. The farmer owed more than $1 million to a bank, secured by the farmland, equipment, crops, livestock and proceeds. The farmer's reorganization plan provided that the farmer retain the equity in the farm in exchange for a promise to contribute labor, experience, and expertise. A unanimous Supreme Court found that the farmer's undertaking did not meet the requisites of the 1938 Act's *Los Angeles Lumber* exception, 485 U.S. at 204–205:

> "Viewed from the time of approval of the plan, respondents' promise of future services is intangible, inalienable, and, in all likelihood, unenforceable. * * * Unlike 'money or money's worth,' a promise of future services cannot be exchanged in any market for something of value to the creditors *today.* In fact, no decision of this Court or any Court of Appeals, other than the decision below, has ever found a promise to contribute future labor, management, or expertise sufficient to qualify for the *Los Angeles Lumber* exception to the absolute priority rule. In short, there is no way to distinguish between the promise respondents proffer here and those of the shareholders in *Los Angeles Lumber;* neither is an adequate consideration to escape the absolute priority rule."

Ahlers, however, did not answer the central question respecting new value contributions under the 1978 Act: Whether they are permissible at all over the objection of a dissenting class of creditors in a cramdown under section 1129(b).

Assuming a substantial cash contribution, why would 1129(b) entail a bar, whether on a *per se* or conditional basis, to a new value proposal?

Consider the following hypothetical bankruptcy proceeding. The creditors' claims total $110. The debtor advances a plan under which the business is valued on a going concern basis at $100 and pursuant to which the holders of the firm's equity propose to contribute $20 in cash for all of the reorganized firm's common stock. Let us assume (in accord with the majority view on the point) that the $20 cash contribution must be directed to the immediate benefit of the bankruptcy estate and the old creditors rather than put into escrow for the eventual benefit of the reorganized going concern. Given an absolute priority regime requiring payment in full to the old creditors, they receive $10 of the $20 contribution. A question regarding incentives arises: Why would the old equity make a cash contribution only to see all or part of it flow right the pockets of its old creditors?

Four possible explanations suggest themselves.

First, the old equity could be making its contribution in order to secure private benefits only it can access. As we will see, in the litigated cases the old equity often desires to maintain continuity of ownership in the reorganizing firm so as to hold on to tax benefits.

Second, the old equity could be making its contribution on the assumption that the $100 valuation is too low, and the reorganized firm will be worth at least $120 net of payment of an additional $10 cash to the creditors.

Third, a cash contribution for the benefit of the old creditors could be rational for the equity even if the firm is worth only $100 viewed in the abstract, because the equity views the firm's value from the point of view of a holder of an option to repurchase the firm from the debt. This scenario presupposes that the firm's possible future performances include low probability but high upside results.

Fourth, a $20 offer could be rational because, in the language of the cases, "control" has a value that does not necessarily show up in a going concern valuation of the firm viewed in the abstract. Such a control premium presupposes private benefits available to any party acquiring or maintaining control.

Finally, any or all of these incentives could combine so as to motivate a particular new value bid.

Whatever the motivation, it is hard to see why the hypothesized transaction should be objectionable, since it facilitates payment in full to the creditors. But plausible objections can be raised in an absolute priority context. To see why, let us change the facts so as to increase the amount of creditor claims to $150, and provide that the entire $20 contribution flow through to the old creditors. Although in this scenario the new value proposal still provides value to the creditors, here they are not paid in full under the plan. At the same time, the old equity appears to be seeking something of value from the bankrupt firm when it buys the new equity— something that can variously be described as private benefits, option value, or control value. A substantive objection arises at this point: To the extent the old equity has paid less than 100% of this "value," it has received value from the firm even though creditors have not been paid in full. Prima facie, this violates absolute priority.

Process objections also can arise to the extent that the new value transaction has been made on a one-sided basis. Given large numbers of creditors with small stakes, the quality of the bargaining process will depend on the effectiveness of the class representatives. Given a single bank creditor, the plan formation process is more likely to have resembled an arm's length negotiation. In either event, the Code skews the process context to bestow bargaining power on the equity by giving the debtor an exclusive right to present a plan. As process infirmities accumulate, the new value plan can be questioned on the ground that it yields less value for the creditors' benefit than a would have been yielded by an arm's length sale of the new equity a sole owner.

These objections came before the Supreme Court in the case that follows.

Bank of America National Trust and Savings Association v. 203 North LaSalle Street Partnership

Supreme Court of the United States, 1999.
526 U.S. 434, 119 S.Ct. 1411, 143 L.Ed.2d 607.

■ JUSTICE SOUTER delivered the opinion of the Court.

The issue in this Chapter 11 reorganization case is whether a debtor's prebankruptcy equity holders may, over the objection of a senior class of impaired creditors, contribute new capital and receive ownership interests in the reorganized entity, when that opportunity is given exclusively to the old equity holders under a plan adopted without consideration of alternatives. We hold that old equity holders are disqualified from participating in such a "new value" transaction by the terms of 11 U.S.C. § 1129(b)(2)(B)(ii), which in such circumstances bars a junior interest holder's receipt of any property on account of his prior interest.

I

Petitioner, Bank of America National Trust and Savings Association (Bank), is the major creditor of respondent, 203 North LaSalle Street Partnership (Debtor or Partnership), an Illinois real estate limited partnership. The Bank lent the Debtor some $93 million, secured by a nonrecourse first mortgage on the Debtor's principal asset, 15 floors of an office building in downtown Chicago. In January 1995, the Debtor defaulted, and the Bank began foreclosure in a state court.

In March, the Debtor responded with a voluntary petition for relief under Chapter 11 of the Bankruptcy Code * * *. The Debtor's principal objective was to ensure that its partners retained title to the property so as to avoid roughly $20 million in personal tax liabilities, which would fall due if the Bank foreclosed. * * * The Debtor proceeded to propose a reorganization plan during the 120–day period when it alone had the right to do so * * *. The Bankruptcy Court rejected the Bank's motion to terminate the period of exclusivity to make way for a plan of its own to liquidate the property, and instead extended the exclusivity period for cause shown, under § 1121(d).

The value of the mortgaged property was less than the balance due the Bank, which elected to divide its undersecured claim into secured and unsecured deficiency claims under § 506(a) and § 1111(b). * * * Under the plan, the Debtor separately classified the Bank's secured claim, its unsecured deficiency claim, and unsecured trade debt owed to other creditors. See § 1122(a).[7] The Bankruptcy Court found that the Debtor's available

---

7. Indeed, the Seventh Circuit apparently requires separate classification of the deficiency claim of an undersecured creditor from other general unsecured claims. See In

assets were prepetition rents in a cash account of $3.1 million and the 15 floors of rental property worth $54.5 million. The secured claim was valued at the latter figure, leaving the Bank with an unsecured deficiency of $38.5 million.

So far as we need be concerned here, the Debtor's plan had these further features:

(1) The Bank's $54.5 million secured claim would be paid in full between 7 and 10 years after the original 1995 repayment date.[8]

(2) The Bank's $38.5 million unsecured deficiency claim would be discharged for an estimated 16% of its present value.[9]

(3) The remaining unsecured claims of $90,000, held by the outside trade creditors, would be paid in full, without interest, on the effective date of the plan.[10]

(4) Certain former partners of the Debtor would contribute $6.125 million in new capital over the course of five years (the contribution being worth some $4.1 million in present value), in exchange for the Partnership's entire ownership of the reorganized debtor.

The last condition was an exclusive eligibility provision: the old equity holders were the only ones who could contribute new capital.

The Bank objected and, being the sole member of an impaired class of creditors, thereby blocked confirmation of the plan on a consensual basis. See § 1129(a)(8). The Debtor, however, took the alternate route to confirmation of a reorganization plan, forthrightly known as the judicial "cramdown" process for imposing a plan on a dissenting class. § 1129(b). * * *

There are two conditions for a cramdown. First, all requirements of § 1129(a) must be met (save for the plan's acceptance by each impaired class of claims or interests, see § 1129(a)(8)). * * * Critical among them are the conditions that the plan be accepted by at least one class of impaired creditors, see § 1129(a)(10), and satisfy the "best-interest-of-creditors" test, see § 1129(a)(7). Here, the class of trade creditors with impaired unsecured claims voted for the plan, * * * and there was no issue of best interest. Second, the objection of an impaired creditor class may be

---

re Woodbrook Associates, 19 F.3d 312, 319 (1994). Nonetheless, the Bank argued that if its deficiency claim had been included in the class of general unsecured creditors, its vote against confirmation would have resulted in the plan's rejection by that class. The Bankruptcy Court and the District Court rejected the contention that the classifications were gerrymandered to obtain requisite approval by a single class, * * * and the Court of Appeals agreed * * *. The Bank sought no review of that issue, which is thus not before us.

8. Payment consisted of a prompt cash payment of $1,149,500 and a secured, 7-year note, extendable at the Debtor's option. * * *

9. This expected yield was based upon the Bankruptcy Court's projection that a sale or refinancing of the property on the 10th anniversary of the plan confirmation would produce a $19-million distribution to the Bank.

10. The Debtor originally owed $160,000 in unsecured trade debt. After filing for bankruptcy, the general partners purchased some of the trade claims. Upon confirmation, the insiders would waive all general unsecured claims they held. * * *

overridden only if "the plan does not discriminate unfairly, and is fair and equitable, with respect to each class of claims or interests that is impaired under, and has not accepted, the plan." § 1129(b)(1). As to a dissenting class of impaired unsecured creditors, such a plan may be found to be "fair and equitable" only if the allowed value of the claim is to be paid in full, § 1129(b)(2)(B)(i), or, in the alternative, if "the holder of any claim or interest that is junior to the claims of such [impaired unsecured] class will not receive or retain under the plan on account of such junior claim or interest any property," § 1129(b)(2)(B)(ii). That latter condition is the core of what is known as the "absolute priority rule."

The absolute priority rule was the basis for the Bank's position that the plan could not be confirmed as a cramdown. * * * The Bankruptcy Court approved the plan nonetheless * * *. The District Court affirmed, * * * as did the Court of Appeals.

The majority of the Seventh Circuit's divided panel found ambiguity in the language of the statutory absolute priority rule, and looked beyond the text to interpret the phrase "on account of" as permitting recognition of a "new value corollary" to the rule. * * * According to the panel, the corollary, as stated by this Court in Case v. Los Angeles Lumber Products Co., 308 U.S. 106, 118, 60 S.Ct. 1, 84 L.Ed. 110 (1939), provides that the objection of an impaired senior class does not bar junior claim holders from receiving or retaining property interests in the debtor after reorganization, if they contribute new capital in money or money's worth, reasonably equivalent to the property's value, and necessary for successful reorganization of the restructured enterprise. * * *

We granted certiorari * * * to resolve a Circuit split on the issue. * * * We do not decide whether the statute includes a new value corollary or exception, but hold that on any reading respondent's proposed plan fails to satisfy the statute, and accordingly reverse.

II

* * * [The] classic formulation [of the "new value corollary"] occurred in Case v. Los Angeles Lumber Products Co., in which the Court spoke through Justice Douglas in this dictum:

> "It is, of course, clear that there are circumstances under which stockholders may participate in a plan of reorganization of an insolvent debtor.... Where th[e] necessity [for new capital] exists and the old stockholders make a fresh contribution and receive in return a participation reasonably equivalent to their contribution, no objection can be made....

> "[W]e believe that to accord 'the creditor his full right of priority against the corporate assets' where the debtor is insolvent, the stockholder's participation must be based on a contribution in money or in money's worth, reasonably equivalent in view of all the circumstances to the participation of the stockholder." 308 U.S., at 121–122, 60 S.Ct. 1.

Although counsel for one of the parties here has described the Case observation as " 'black-letter' principle," it never rose above the technical level of dictum in any opinion of this Court * * *. * * * Hence the controversy over how weighty the Case dictum had become, as reflected in the alternative labels for the new value notion: some writers and courts * * * have spoken of it as an exception to the absolute priority rule, * * * while others have characterized it as a simple corollary to the rule * * *.

Enactment of the Bankruptcy Code in place of the prior Act might have resolved the status of new value by a provision bearing its name or at least unmistakably couched in its terms, but the Congress chose not to avail itself of that opportunity. * * *

[The legislative history] does nothing to disparage the possibility apparent in the statutory text, that the absolute priority rule now on the books as subsection (b)(2)(B)(ii) may carry a new value corollary. Although there is no literal reference to "new value" in the phrase "on account of such junior claim," the phrase could arguably carry such an implication in modifying the prohibition against receipt by junior claimants of any interest under a plan while a senior class of unconsenting creditors goes less than fully paid.

III

Three basic interpretations have been suggested for the "on account of" modifier. The first reading is proposed by the Partnership, that "on account of" harks back to accounting practice and means something like "in exchange for," or "in satisfaction of". On this view, a plan would not violate the absolute priority rule unless the old equity holders received or retained property in exchange for the prior interest, without any significant new contribution; if substantial money passed from them as part of the deal, the prohibition of subsection (b)(2)(B)(ii) would not stand in the way, and whatever issues of fairness and equity there might otherwise be would not implicate the "on account of" modifier.

This position is beset with troubles, the first one being textual. Subsection (b)(2)(B)(ii) forbids not only receipt of property on account of the prior interest but its retention as well. See also §§ 1129(a)(7)(A)(ii), (a)(7)(B), (b)(2)(B)(i), (b)(2)(C)(i), (b)(2)(C)(ii). A common instance of the latter would be a debtor's retention of an interest in the insolvent business reorganized under the plan. Yet it would be exceedingly odd to speak of "retain[ing]" property in exchange for the same property interest, and the eccentricity of such a reading is underscored by the fact that elsewhere in the Code the drafters chose to use the very phrase "in exchange for," § 1123(a)(5)(J) (a plan shall provide adequate means for implementation, including "issuance of securities of the debtor ... for cash, for property, for existing securities, or in exchange for claims or interests"). It is unlikely that the drafters of legislation so long and minutely contemplated as the 1978 Bankruptcy Code would have used two distinctly different forms of words for the same purpose. * * *

The second difficulty is practical: the unlikelihood that Congress meant to impose a condition as manipulable as subsection (b)(2)(B)(ii) would be if "on account of" meant to prohibit merely an exchange unaccompanied by a substantial infusion of new funds but permit one whenever substantial funds changed hands. "Substantial" or "significant" or "considerable" or like characterizations of a monetary contribution would measure it by the Lord Chancellor's foot, and an absolute priority rule so variable would not be much of an absolute. Of course it is true (as already noted) that, even if old equity holders could displace the rule by adding some significant amount of cash to the deal, it would not follow that their plan would be entitled to adoption; a contested plan would still need to satisfy the overriding condition of fairness and equity. But that general fairness and equity criterion would apply in any event, and one comes back to the question why Congress would have bothered to add a separate priority rule without a sharper edge.

Since the "in exchange for" reading merits rejection, the way is open to recognize the more common understanding of "on account of" to mean "because of." This is certainly the usage meant for the phrase at other places in the statute, see § 1111(b)(1)(A) (treating certain claims as if the holder of the claim "had recourse against the debtor on account of such claim"); § 522(d)(10)(E) (permitting debtors to exempt payments under certain benefit plans and contracts "on account of illness, disability, death, age, or length of service"); § 547(b)(2) (authorizing trustee to avoid a transfer of an interest of the debtor in property "for or on account of an antecedent debt owed by the debtor"); § 547(c)(4)(B) (barring trustee from avoiding a transfer when a creditor gives new value to the debtor "on account of which new value the debtor did not make an otherwise unavoidable transfer to . . . such creditor"). So, under the commonsense rule that a given phrase is meant to carry a given concept in a single statute, see Cohen v. De La Cruz, 523 U.S. 213, 219–220, 118 S.Ct. 1212, 140 L.Ed.2d 341 (1998), the better reading of subsection (b)(2)(B)(ii) recognizes that a causal relationship between holding the prior claim or interest and receiving or retaining property is what activates the absolute priority rule.

The degree of causation is the final bone of contention. We understand the Government, as amicus curiae, to take the starchy position not only that any degree of causation between earlier interests and retained property will activate the bar to a plan providing for later property, but also that whenever the holders of equity in the Debtor end up with some property there will be some causation; when old equity, and not someone on the street, gets property the reason is res ipsa loquitur. An old equity holder simply cannot take property under a plan if creditors are not paid in full.

There are, however, reasons counting against such a reading. If, as is likely, the drafters were treating junior claimants or interest holders as a class at this point, * * * then the simple way to have prohibited the old interest holders from receiving anything over objection would have been to omit the "on account of" phrase entirely from subsection (b)(2)(B)(ii). On this assumption, reading the provision as a blanket prohibition would leave "on account of" as a redundancy, contrary to the interpretive obligation to try to give meaning to all the statutory language. * * * One would also have to ask why Congress would have desired to exclude prior equity categorically from the class of potential owners following a cramdown. Although we have some doubt about the Court of Appeals's assumption * * * that prior equity is often the only source of significant capital for reorganizations, see, e.g., Blum & Kaplan, The Absolute Priority Doctrine in Corporate Reorganizations, 41 U. Chi. L.Rev. 651, 672 (1974); Mann, Strategy and Force in the Liquidation of Secured Debt, 96 Mich. L.Rev. 159, 182–183, 192–194, 208–209 (1997), old equity may well be in the best position to make a go of the reorganized enterprise and so may be the party most likely to work out an equity-for-value reorganization.

A less absolute statutory prohibition would follow from reading the "on account of" language as intended to reconcile the two recognized policies underlying Chapter 11, of preserving going concerns and maximizing property available to satisfy creditors, see Toibb v. Radloff, 501 U.S. 157, 163, 111 S.Ct. 2197, 115 L.Ed.2d 145 (1991). Causation between the old equity's holdings and subsequent property substantial enough to disqualify a plan would presumably occur on this view of things whenever old equity's later property would come at a price that failed to provide the greatest possible addition to the bankruptcy estate, and it would always come at a price too low when the equity holders obtained or preserved an ownership interest for less than someone else would have paid.[26] A truly full value transaction, on the other hand, would pose no threat to the bankruptcy estate not posed by any reorganization, provided of course that the contribution be in cash or be realizable money's worth, just as Ahlers required for application of Case's new value rule. Cf. Ahlers, supra, at 203–205, 108 S.Ct. 963; Case, 308 U.S., at 121, 60 S.Ct. 1.

IV

Which of these positions is ultimately entitled to prevail is not to be decided here, however, for even on the latter view the Bank's objection would require rejection of the plan at issue in this case. It is doomed, we can say without necessarily exhausting its flaws, by its provision for vesting equity in the reorganized business in the Debtor's partners without extending an opportunity to anyone else either to compete for that equity or to propose a competing reorganization plan. Although the Debtor's exclusive opportunity to propose a plan under § 1121(b) is not itself "property" within the meaning of subsection (b)(2)(B)(ii), the respondent partnership in this case has taken advantage of this opportunity by proposing a plan under which the benefit of equity ownership may be obtained by no one but old equity partners. Upon the court's approval of that plan, the partners were in the same position that they would have enjoyed had they exercised an exclusive option under the plan to buy the equity in the reorganized

26. Even when old equity would pay its top dollar and that figure was as high as anyone else would pay, the price might still be too low unless the old equity holders paid more than anyone else would pay, on the theory that the "necessity" required to justify old equity's participation in a new value plan is a necessity for the participation of old equity as such. On this interpretation, disproof of a bargain would not satisfy old equity's burden; it would need to show that no one else would pay as much. * * * No such issue is before us, and we emphasize that our holding here does not suggest an exhaustive list of the requirements of a proposed new value plan.

entity, or contracted to purchase it from a seller who had first agreed to deal with no one else. It is quite true that the escrow of the partners' proposed investment eliminated any formal need to set out an express option or exclusive dealing provision in the plan itself, since the court's approval that created the opportunity and the partners' action to obtain its advantage were simultaneous. But before the Debtor's plan was accepted no one else could propose an alternative one, and after its acceptance no one else could obtain equity in the reorganized entity. At the moment of the plan's approval the Debtor's partners necessarily enjoyed an exclusive opportunity that was in no economic sense distinguishable from the advantage of the exclusively entitled offeror or option holder. This opportunity should, first of all, be treated as an item of property in its own right. Cf. In re Coltex Loop Central Three Partners, L. P., 138 F.3d, at 43 (exclusive right to purchase post-petition equity is itself property); In re Bryson Properties, XVII, 961 F.2d, at 504; Kham & Nate's Shoes No. 2, Inc. v. First Bank, 908 F.2d 1351, 1360 (C.A.7 1990); D. Baird, The Elements of Bankruptcy 261 (rev. ed. 1993) ("The right to get an equity interest for its fair market value is 'property' as the word is ordinarily used. Options to acquire an interest in a firm, even at its market value, trade for a positive price"). While it may be argued that the opportunity has no market value, being significant only to old equity holders owing to their potential tax liability, such an argument avails the Debtor nothing, for several reasons. It is to avoid just such arguments that the law is settled that any otherwise cognizable property interest must be treated as sufficiently valuable to be recognized under the Bankruptcy Code. See Ahlers, 485 U.S., at 207–208, 108 S.Ct. 963. Even aside from that rule, the assumption that no one but the Debtor's partners might pay for such an opportunity would obviously support no inference that it is valueless, let alone that it should not be treated as property. And, finally, the source in the tax law of the opportunity's value to the partners implies in no way that it lacks value to others. It might, indeed, be valuable to another precisely as a way to keep the Debtor from implementing a plan that would avoid a Chapter 7 liquidation.

Given that the opportunity is property of some value, the question arises why old equity alone should obtain it, not to mention at no cost whatever. The closest thing to an answer favorable to the Debtor is that the old equity partners would be given the opportunity in the expectation that in taking advantage of it they would add the stated purchase price to the estate. But this just begs the question why the opportunity should be exclusive to the old equity holders. If the price to be paid for the equity interest is the best obtainable, old equity does not need the protection of exclusiveness (unless to trump an equal offer from someone else); if it is not the best, there is no apparent reason for giving old equity a bargain. There is no reason, that is, unless the very purpose of the whole transaction is, at least in part, to do old equity a favor. And that, of course, is to say that old equity would obtain its opportunity, and the resulting benefit, because of old equity's prior interest within the meaning of subsection (b)(2)(B)(ii). Hence it is that the exclusiveness of the opportunity, with its protection against the market's scrutiny of the purchase price by means of competing bids or even competing plan proposals, renders the partners' right a property interest extended "on account of" the old equity position and therefore subject to an unpaid senior creditor class's objection.

It is no answer to this to say that the exclusive opportunity should be treated merely as a detail of the broader transaction that would follow its exercise, and that in this wider perspective no favoritism may be inferred, since the old equity partners would pay something, whereas no one else would pay anything. If this argument were to carry the day, of course, old equity could obtain a new property interest for a dime without being seen to receive anything on account of its old position. But even if we assume that old equity's plan would not be confirmed without satisfying the judge that the purchase price was top dollar, there is a further reason here not to treat property consisting of an exclusive opportunity as subsumed within the total transaction proposed. On the interpretation assumed here, it would, of course, be a fatal flaw if old equity acquired or retained the property interest without paying full value. It would thus be necessary for old equity to demonstrate its payment of top dollar, but this it could not satisfactorily do when it would receive or retain its property under a plan giving it exclusive rights and in the absence of a competing plan of any sort. Under a plan granting an exclusive right, making no provision for competing bids or competing plans, any determination that the price was top dollar would necessarily be made by a judge in bankruptcy court, whereas the best way to determine value is exposure to a market. * * * This is a point of some significance, since it was, after all, one of the Code's innovations to narrow the occasions for courts to make valuation judgments, as shown by its preference for the supramajoritarian class creditor voting scheme in § 1126(c) * * *. In the interest of statutory coherence, a like disfavor for decisions untested by competitive choice ought to extend to valuations in administering subsection (b)(2)(B)(ii) when some form of market valuation may be available to test the adequacy of an old equity holder's proposed contribution.

Whether a market test would require an opportunity to offer competing plans or would be satisfied by a right to bid for the same interest sought by old equity, is a question we do not decide here. It is enough to say, assuming a new value corollary, that plans providing junior interest holders with exclusive opportunities free from competition and without benefit of market valuation fall within the prohibition of § 1129(b)(2)(B)(ii).

The judgment of the Court of Appeals is accordingly reversed * * *.

■ JUSTICE THOMAS, with whom JUSTICE SCALIA joins, concurring in the judgment.

I agree with the majority's conclusion that the reorganization plan in this case could not be confirmed. However, I do not see the need for its unnecessary speculations on certain issues and do not share its approach to interpretation of the Bankruptcy Code. I therefore concur only in the judgment.

* * *

The meaning of the phrase "on account of" is the central interpretive question presented by this case. This phrase obviously denotes some type of causal relationship between the junior interest and the property received or retained—such an interpretation comports with common understandings of the phrase. See, e.g., The Random House Dictionary of the English Language 13 (2d ed.1987) ("by reason of," "because of"); Webster's Third New International Dictionary 13 (1976) ("for the sake of," "by reason of," "because of"). It also tracks the use of the phrase elsewhere in the Code. * * * Regardless how direct the causal nexus must be, the prepetition equity holders here undoubtedly received at least one form of property—the exclusive opportunity—"on account of" their prepetition equity interest. Since § 1129(b)(2)(B)(ii) prohibits the prepetition equity holders from receiving "any" property under the plan on account of their junior interest, this plan was not "fair and equitable" and could not be confirmed. That conclusion, as the majority recognizes is sufficient to resolve this case. Thus, its comments on the Government's position taken in another case and its speculations about the desirability of a "market test" are dicta binding neither this Court nor the lower federal courts.

* * *

■ JUSTICE STEVENS, dissenting.

Prior to the enactment of the Bankruptcy Reform Act of 1978, this Court unequivocally stated that there are circumstances under which stockholders may participate in a plan of reorganization of an insolvent debtor if their participation is based on a contribution in money, or in money's worth, reasonably equivalent in view of all the circumstances to their participation. * * * I believe the Court should now definitively resolve the question and state that a holder of a junior claim or interest does not receive property "on account of" such a claim when its participation in the plan is based on adequate new value.

* * *

NOTE: THE NEW VALUE EXCEPTION

1. *The New Value Exception.*

203 North LaSalle leaves open the question whether the new value exception survives the enactment of the 1978 Bankruptcy Act. A number of lower courts held that the Bankruptcy Act of 1978 effected elimination of the exception. See In re Bryson Properties, XVIII, 961 F.2d 496, 503–505 (4th Cir.1992); In re Outlook/Century, Ltd., 127 B.R. 650 (Bankr.N.D.Cal.1991); In re Lumber Exchange Ltd. Partnership, 125 B.R. 1000 (Bankr.D.Minn.1991). Other courts have been more receptive to new value contributions, applying a two part test. The new capital must (1) represent a substantial contribution, and (2) equal or exceed the value of the new interest in the corporation. The first leg of the test, "substantiality," involves the comparison of the contribution with the amount of pre-petition claims and the amount of debt discharged under the plan. See Matter of Snyder, 967 F.2d 1126 (7th Cir.1992); In re Pullman Construction Industries, 107 B.R. 909, 936–937, 948–950 (Bankr.N.D.Ill.1989). The courts have applied the test strictly. A sample of 202 chapter 11 proceedings filed after *Ahlers* found that new value plans were confirmed in only five. Carlson and Williams, The Truth About the New Value Exception to Bankruptcy's Absolute Priority Rule, 21 Cardozo L. Rev. 1303 (2000).

2. *The Market Test.*

Note that although *203 North LaSalle* requires a market test, it leaves open its precise form. It presumably could either entail a public auction of the new equity or a lapse of the debtor's exclusive right to present a plan. Whichever mode is employed, to what extent is the market test likely to solve the new value problem?

The test's impact should vary with the circumstances.

Consider a single asset case as in *203 North LaSalle*. Assume the office building is worth $100, the bank creditor is owed $150, and tax benefits held out by continued ownership are worth $20 to the equityholders but of no value to anyone else. Here, at first glance, the market test seems pointless since the tax benefit is nontransferable. But the test will still have an allocative effect if the bank may credit-bid for the new equity using its general creditor's claim of $50. (For the argument in favor of such a bank bid, see Markell, LaSalle and the Little Guy, 16 Bankr. Dev. J. 345, 357–58 (2000).) If the bank can bid, the effect of the market test is to shift bargaining power from the debtor to the bank and thereby allocate a substantial part of the $20 tax benefit to the bank. This result replicates the result that would obtain in a world without bankruptcy protection. There the secured lender's foreclosure power imports a power to deprive the borrower of its tax benefits, and would result in a negotiation between lender and borrower to slice the $20 pie. See Adler, The Emergence of Markets in Chapter 11: A Small Step on North LaSalle Street, 8 Sup. Ct. Econ. Rev. 1 (2000).

Now compare the case of a classic close corporation operated as a going concern by a sole owner. Assume that the firm's hard assets are worth $100 and have been mortgaged to a bank owed $150. There is an additional $20 of going concern value bound up in the firm specific expertise of the owner and the good will arising therefrom. Assume that the owner makes a new value offer of $5 for the reorganized firm's equity. The results of a market test will vary with the nature of the synergy between the owner and the asset. If the synergy easily could be replicated by a third party, a competing bidder might appear. Even if the synergy cannot be replicated, a creditor or a third party still could interpose a bid in an attempt to force the owner to part with a larger portion of the going concern value with the bidder. Adler, supra, at 12–14.

In both of the foregoing cases, assuming the bank can credit bid, the primary effect of the market test is to transfer bargaining power from the debtor to the bank. Such an effect reverses the assumption that informed the division between chapters X and XI under the 1938 Act. There it was thought that a single, secured bank creditor of a small business could protect itself in the reorganization bargaining context and did not need absolute priority protection. Furthermore, since the good will of the business inhered in the person of the debtor, the bank would not in any event be able to bargain its way to a share of it. Is it safe to assume that the 1978 Act's drafters intended a significant shift in the posture of the close corporation and the bank creditor when they combined the two chapters?

Finally, compare a hypothetical bankruptcy of a publicly-traded corporation, possessed of assets of a type traded in the market for going concerns. Let us assume that the plan asserts a going concern value of $100, that the creditors' claims total $150 and that a management group owns 50 percent of the common stock with the rest of the stock is publicly traded. The managers offer $20 for the stock of the reorganized firm. The court, following *203 North LaSalle*, orders an auction, pursuant to which any and all comers get chance to look over the company.

If no bid higher than $20 appears, there arises a strong circumstantial case in the plan's favor. If the plan were substantially undervaluing the firm or $20 were cognizably less than the value of the new equity for some other reason, a competing bid should have shown up. At the same time, an open bidding process conducted for the purpose of raising money for the benefit of the creditors ameliorates their bargaining disadvantage.

Now suppose that higher bids do appear and a third party takes the new equity for $30. The foregoing benefits still obtain. But we should not assume that perfection has been achieved. If, for example, the firm as whole could be sold at or near $130 cash, a single creditor with bargaining power would doubtless prefer a liquidating sale to a continued participation. Contrariwise, if asset values in the firm's industry are severely but temporarily depressed at the time of the sale, the long-term effect still could be to finesse the creditors out of $20 on their $150 claim.

4.   THE MOVE TO CREDITOR CONTROL

Skeel, Creditor's Ball: The "New" New Corporate Governance in Chapter 11

152 U. Pa. L. Rev. 917, 920–23, 925–27, 928, 930–32, 934–39, 945–47 (2003).

I.   Ch–Ch–Changes

The late 1980s and early 1990s were both the best and the worst of times for large-scale corporate reorganization in America. The enactment of the 1978 Bankruptcy Code had taken off the fetters that stymied corporate bankruptcy for forty years. Chapter X of the Chandler Act—the chapter designed for large corporations under the old Bankruptcy Act—replaced the managers of a debtor that filed for bankruptcy with a court-appointed trustee. Chapter 11 of the new 1978 Code, by contrast, authorized the managers to continue operating the business and gave them the exclusive right to propose a reorganization plan. The number of large Chapter 11 cases soared, but there were also a growing number of complaints about the very provisions that had restored bankruptcy's luster. Chapter 11 seemed to give too much control to the debtor's managers, enabling them to stiff-arm creditors and drag out the bankruptcy cases for inordinate periods of time. Managers were playing with creditors' money, and large cases often lasted several years or more.

The worst offender was Eastern Airlines (Eastern). Although it was clear to just about everyone that Eastern should be sold, Eastern's CEO Frank Lorenzo postponed the inevitable for several years as Eastern's value deteriorated. In the end, Eastern's assets were liquidated at a fraction of what they had been worth at the outset of the bankruptcy case.

With Eastern as their poster child, critics began to call for major changes to Chapter 11. In the bankruptcy literature, a vibrant debate developed as to whether Chapter 11 should be replaced by a faster, more market-oriented alternative.

And then a funny thing happened. The most obvious problems with Chapter 11—the endless cases and absence of market discipline—started to disappear. Within a few years, there were more auctions in bankruptcy, and claims trading sometimes simulated a market for corporate control. In the past several years, the changes have been even more dramatic. In most large cases, the same creditors who seemed so helpless only a few years ago are now calling most of the shots. Chapter 11 is still remarkably debtor friendly by international standards, but creditors now exert much more influence over a case than at any time in recent history. The result is faster cases that rely more on asset sales and the market for corporate control than on negotiations to move the restructuring process along.

How did everything change so fast? In part, the transformation reflects a change in the profile of American business. Unlike the businesses that traditionally landed in bankruptcy—railroads, in the nineteenth century, or industrial firms thereafter—many contemporary businesses depend on knowledge and ideas rather than on hard assets. Because these companies' most important assets can walk out the door at any moment, they cannot afford to negotiate for months or years toward an eventual restructuring. They must resolve their difficulties immediately; often, the only way to do this is to sell key assets at or shortly after the time of bankruptcy. In addition, markets for assets, and even for entire companies, are much more liquid than ever before.

More importantly, several remarkable contractual developments have been intertwined with this shift in the nature of American business. First, lenders increasingly have used their post-petition financing agreements to shape the governance of the Chapter 11 case. The second contractual strategy takes a direct appeal to managers' wallets. By crafting "pay to stay" agreements that depend heavily on bonuses based on the speed of the reorganization or the price obtained in asset sales, creditors have given managers dramatically different incentives than they had in the 1980s.

These contractual changes have shifted the ethos of bankruptcy in ways that go beyond the contracts themselves. Although bankruptcy law does not formally authorize creditors to displace the company's directors, creditors have increasingly exercised de facto control. Directors are now more likely to respond, for instance, to creditors' not-so-subtle threat that " 'sooner or later we'll own the company and we're not going to re-elect you so you should get out now.' "

* * *

A.   Debtor in Possession Financing: Creditors' New Power Tool

When commentators distinguish Chapter 11 from other countries' corporate reorganization laws, they increasingly point to DIP financing as a crucial benefit of Chapter 11. The magical provision is Section 364, which authorizes the bankruptcy court to roll out the red carpet for a lender that is willing to make a new loan to the debtor. First, the court can treat the DIP loan as an administrative expense, which puts it behind only existing, secured lenders in the priority hierarchy. Second, if the debtor has unencumbered assets, the court can give the DIP lender a security interest in those assets, thus putting the DIP lender on the same footing as the company's secured creditors. Finally, if most or all of the debtors' assets are already spoken for, Section 364 provides its most dramatic option of all: the court can give the DIP lender a so-called "priming lien"—that is, a security interest that takes priority even over existing security interests in the same collateral.

* * *

The large firms that filed for bankruptcy in the 1980s often had a large amount of unsecured debt and comparatively little secured debt. As a result, when they filed for bankruptcy, the cash generated by the business was not all spoken for, and the debtor could use this cash to finance the reorganization effort. The large companies that have filed for bankruptcy more recently have often relied more heavily on secured debt prior to bankruptcy, and thus have less cash with which to work. Lenders have responded to the greater importance of post-petition financing and to creditors' concerns about the Chapter 11 process by using the terms of DIP loans to shape the Chapter 11 case.

The financing of the US Airways bankruptcy is a particularly striking illustration of the recent trend. At the outset of its reorganization, US Airways entered into an agreement to borrow up to $740 million from the Retirement Systems of Alabama—$240 million up front, $300 million during the case, and $200 million after US Airways was to emerge from Chapter 11. The lender assured its influence over the airline's governance and paved the way to take over after bankruptcy, by bargaining for five seats on the twelve-member board of directors and a promise of 37.5% of the stock of the newly reorganized company. The US Airways financing thus was structured as a partial takeover. In many cases, the lender is not planning to take over the company. But even in these cases, the lenders frequently use their DIP financing agreement to constrain the debtor's managers' wiggle room. It is not an overstatement to say that the terms of the debtors' post-petition financing regularly set the course, and even the outcome, of the Chapter 11 cases.

B.   Keeping the Managers' Nose to the Grindstone: Executive Compensation in Chapter 11

Creditors' other new governance lever has been executive compensation. As with DIP financing agreements, creditors have relied on clear, simple targets to prevent managers from frittering away a company's value during a bankruptcy. Before the managers of a debtor can be encouraged to preserve rather than squander firm value, however, they often must be persuaded to stay.

Managerial compensation arrangements are designed to address each of these issues. Start with managers' willingness to stay with the sinking ship. The payments used to entice managers to stick around during a bankruptcy are usually referred to as "retention bonuses" or "pay to stay." It is not hard to appreciate why a debtor's managers might welcome the "pay to stay" strategy; indeed, the debtor's managers are ordinarily the ones who put forward the proposal. From the creditors' perspective, on the other hand, the decision to approve these bonuses is more complicated. After all, there is something a bit odd about begging the same managers who navigated the firm into bankruptcy to keep up the good work. Despite their reservations, however, creditors increasingly have concluded that they are better off paying to keep the debtor's existing managers in place. * * *

* * *

Now, simply paying managers to stay does not necessarily ensure they will reorganize the company efficiently. This is where pay-for-performance, the second new innovation in bankruptcy compensation, comes into play. Rather than paying managers a straight cash salary in Chapter 11, creditors have insisted in recent cases that the managers' compensation be tied to the company's progress under Chapter 11. The most straightforward strategy for rewarding managers who handle the case expeditiously is to base their compensation, at least in part, on the speed of the reorganization.

Another pay-for-performance strategy comes into play if the debtor is expected to sell some or all of its assets in connection with the Chapter 11 case. Creditors can maximize the managers' incentive to obtain the highest price possible by giving them a piece of the action, and this is exactly what they have done in a number of recent cases. In the Enron bankruptcy, for instance, the compensation scheme is designed to give the managers bonuses for quickly selling the debtor's assets. In other cases, managers' bonuses have been based not on the speed, but on the price they obtained in the asset sale.

* * *

C. Who's on First? Controlling the Board of Directors in Chapter 11

* * *

Not so long ago, most observers assumed that a company's directors were, or at least should be, beholden to the company's shareholders in Chapter 11, just as they are outside of bankruptcy. Based on this reasoning, shareholders sometimes asked for the right to hold a shareholders' meeting in order to elect a new set of directors during the Chapter 11 case. Courts were generally sympathetic to these requests, except in cases where the shareholders seemed intent on derailing the reorganization process. The related issue of whether existing directors continue to listen to shareholders, or turn their ears to creditors, after the company files for bankruptcy is more subtle; it is not always easy to determine a director's loyalties, and the empirical data are mixed. While directors sometimes seem to take their cues from shareholders, this was not always the case.

In the early years of the new millennium, many observers have forgotten all about the old assumption that shareholders call the directorial tune in Chapter 11. Observers sometimes assume, for instance, that a new manager cannot be brought on without the creditors' "approval." Strictly speaking, this is not true. Creditors' powers are much less direct. To appreciate the precise nature of creditors' influence, as well as its limits, we should briefly consider the leverage creditors have at their disposal.

* * *

Creditors have two principal ways to influence the board once the debtor files for bankruptcy. First, creditors can threaten to ask the court to appoint a trustee unless the CEO or one or more board members is replaced by a manager—often a corporate restructuring officer—who is more acceptable to the creditors. This is a powerful threat, but it is also both blunt and indirect. Replacing the debtor's managers with a trustee is a draconian step—a step that courts are quite reluctant to take in the absence of fraud or other extraordinary circumstances. Nor, in most cases, do creditors really want a trustee, since the case would slow to a crawl while the trustee educated herself about the debtor's business. The credibility of the creditors' threat (as in all games of "chicken") therefore depends on their confidence that the debtor's directors are more worried about the appointment of a trustee than are the creditors.

The creditors' second strategy is * * * to make clear to the directors that the creditors are the ones who will be holding the company's stock after the reorganization, and that they intend to dump any recalcitrant directors once they take over. This threat is more direct, but it is also rather distant if the reorganization process is going to be lengthy.

In the absence of a direct way for creditors to take control of the board, directorial norms play a crucial role in Chapter 11 governance. To the extent creditors now have implicit veto power over directorial changes, this influence suggests that directorial norms have shifted as creditors have made increasing use of DIP financing agreements and tailored compensation arrangements.

    * * *

II.   The Virtues of the "New" New Bankruptcy Governance
    * * *

We need only recall the concerns of the 1980s and early 1990s to appreciate the systemwide benefits of creditors' increased influence over bankruptcy governance. No longer do we hear complaints about endless extensions of the debtor's exclusivity period and cases that go on forever. Nor do debtors' managers cling to highly unrealistic hopes of reorganizing the firm in essentially its existing form: the terms of the debtor's post-petition financing force it to sell assets that are worth more in a buyer's hands, and performance-based executive compensation arrangements encourage managers to move more briskly through the Chapter 11 process. Now, it is in the managers'—not just creditors'—interests to reorganize as promptly as possible.

To this point, I have focused almost entirely on the ex post effects of the creditors' new governance levers, their effect once the company has encountered financial distress. But these levers have attractive ex ante effects as well. An important benefit of the deviations from absolute priority made possible by Chapter 11 is that they encourage managers of a troubled firm to file for bankruptcy, rather than delaying as long as possible and destroying value as they fend off the inevitable. But the prospect that shareholders will receive something, even if the firm fails, gives managers and shareholders an incentive to take excessive risks while the company is healthy.

If used effectively, the creditors' new governance levers can preserve the ex ante benefit of deviations from absolute priority while reducing their downside. Overall, they diminish the likelihood of deviations from absolute priority by reining in the debtor's managers. At the same time, managers know they will be paid well in Chapter 11 if creditors view them as part of the solution to the company's woes, rather than as emblematic of its problems. The knowledge that they will be reassessed at the outset of the bankruptcy case may make managers less anxious to take value-destroying risks while the company is still solvent. To be sure, there is a risk that managers will respond by pursuing projects for which they are indispensable. But the existing evidence suggests that there may be limits to managers' abilities (and perhaps even their inclination) to entrench themselves in this fashion.

At its best, then, the "new" new bankruptcy governance offers a simple and dramatically effective market-based response to the problems that plagued large-scale corporate reorganization a decade ago.

III.   Top Heavy: The Downsides of the DIP Financing Lever

Chapter 11's generous treatment of DIP financing raises closely related concerns, which stem from the priority status of this interim financing. The first and most obvious concern—the one prior commentators have tended to emphasize—is the possibility that DIP financing will promote overinvestment. The risk of overinvestment is the dark side of DIP financing's principal benefit that super-priority can counteract creditors' unwillingness to fund even desirable projects if the borrower is insolvent. Although DIP financing makes it possible to fund positive present value projects, thus solving a debtor's underinvestment problems, it can also be used to fund negative present value projects, since the lender is protected by its priority status in both contexts.

The question raised by the overinvestment concern is whether courts or other decision makers can distinguish between good DIP financing arrangements (the underinvestment context) and bad ones (the overinvestment context), and thus maximize the benefits of DIP financing and control its costs. The principal focus here is on screening—the initial decision whether, and on what terms, to authorize the DIP financing. But the growing use of DIP financing as a governance lever has underscored the fact that the DIP lender is not simply a passive supplier of capital. Its heightened prominence in major cases raises a second issue: to the extent they are calling the shots, or helping to call the shots, do DIP financiers have appropriate decision making incentives during the Chapter 11 case? I will start with this question and then return to consider some of the problematic terms that are currently being included in DIP financing agreements.

* * *

* * * Because [DIP financiers] face a downside risk if the debtor's fortunes are volatile, but their upside potential is fixed, DIP financiers have an incentive to minimize volatility and to compress the debtor's risk profile. In Chapter 11, the simplest way to do this is to convert most or all of the debtor's assets to cash through sales. It is important not to overstate the point. If the debtor's business is truly viable, and the lender hopes to continue its lending relationship with the firm, the desire for future business will counteract the impulse toward liquidation. If the debtor is not viable, on the other hand, liquidation may be just what the doctor ordered. On the margin, however, there is a risk that DIP lenders will put pressure on the debtor to liquidate too many assets prematurely if they are calling the shots.

    * * *

To the extent DIP lenders become too quick to liquidate, this impulse could not only lead to inefficient liquidation; it could undermine a salutary effect of large scale Chapter 11 cases that I will refer to as the "antitrust benefit." What I mean by "antitrust benefit" is simply that the failure of a prominent company can roil the competitive structure of an industry. If the industry is already relatively concentrated, the disappearance of a major company might leave a small number of companies that have significant market share. In the airline industry, for instance, if United, US Airways, and perhaps one or two of the other troubled airlines were liquidated or absorbed into their healthier peers, the industry could become increasingly monopolistic. By providing a way for existing companies to reorganize in stand-alone form, Chapter 11 supplies a benefit that has received surprisingly little attention from bankruptcy commentators. Further, once we focus on the antitrust benefit of Chapter 11, it immediately becomes apparent that recent complaints that WorldCom and other firms have gotten an unfair competitive benefit from bankruptcy are misguided.

If Chapter 11 was replaced with, say, mandatory auctions, the antitrust benefit could disappear. In an auction, the most likely bidders are other companies in the same industry. This is not always the case, of course, but in an auction regime, regulators would more frequently be faced with the decision whether to exclude industry bidders (and perhaps set the stage for piecemeal liquidation as a result) or to permit an industry bid that could ratchet up industry concentration.

To this point, I have lingered over the troublesome incentives of a DIP lender who faces at least some downside risk. However, if the lender is fully protected, there is a different concern: although a fully protected lender is less likely to have a bias toward liquidation, it may, in a sense, be indifferent to the fate of the firm. After all, the lender's collateral assures that it will get paid even if Chapter 11 fails to produce a sensible allocation of the debtor's assets. Once again, I do not want to overstate my point. In an increasingly competitive DIP financing market, lenders would not want to earn a reputation for regularly presiding over needlessly sinking ships. And a lender that wishes to continue lending to the debtor after bankruptcy, as a significant number of DIP lenders do, will have at least some concern for maximizing the value of the debtor's assets. * * *

A final issue is the use of DIP financing agreements to bring about a takeover of a Chapter 11 firm. While these transactions are grounds more for applause than for concern, there is a risk that a takeover bidder that enters the picture as a source of DIP financing will use the DIP financing agreement to effectively preclude other bidders. In these cases, the DIP financing agreement may serve not just to cause a change in control, but also to dictate its terms.

So, just how serious are these concerns? Overall, the emergence of DIP financing agreements as a central text of Chapter 11 is a welcome advance, for all of the reasons I briefly described in the last part. But, in at least some cases, the fetters are too tight; the restrictions enshrined in the DIP financing agreement will have perverse effects as the case progresses.

* * *

In short, courts should be especially wary when the debtor obtains DIP financing from an existing lender and should invalidate provisions that enhance the status of a prepetition loan. Provisions that lock in a change of control and stiff arm alternative bidders are also suspect. In each case, judicial discretion is likely to be the simplest and most realistic device for responding to the concerns posed by existing DIP financing agreements.

IV. Fine–Tuning the Second Governance Lever: Executive Pay

* * *

* * * Pre-bankruptcy retention bonuses raise both efficiency and fairness concerns. Whether one emphasizes efficiency or fairness, the chief concern is the agency cost of managers focusing on their own interests rather than what is best for the company. The company's directors are in effect paying their own kind when they pay retention bonuses to top managers, and one can't help suspecting that some will use retention bonuses as one last opportunity to ensure themselves a big payday.

As it turns out, existing law already provides a mechanism for challenging pre-bankruptcy pay packages that look more like handouts than efforts to retain key executives. Fraudulent conveyance law authorizes the bankruptcy court to reverse a transfer made by an insolvent debtor if the debtor did not receive "reasonably equivalent" value in exchange. If I sell my house to my sister for $1 before filing for bankruptcy, the transaction will be voided as a fraudulent conveyance. Although the facts are more subtle, one can make the same kind of argument about excessively generous pre-bankruptcy retention bonuses. * * *

Turn now to retention bonuses that are put in place after the company files for bankruptcy. Post-petition pay packages raise the same kinds of concerns as pre-bankruptcy bonuses, but with some very important differences. The key distinction is that the directors cannot unilaterally implement a bonus program once the company has filed for bankruptcy; the program must be presented to the bankruptcy court for approval. This means that creditors have the right to file formal objections; and, in practice, creditors weigh in long before the formal hearing. As a result, with post-petition pay packages, there is much less reason to worry that managers are helping themselves at the expense of the business than there is with pre-bankruptcy compensation plans.

The one concern that does loom large in the bankruptcy context is the perception of fairness. Particularly troubling to many is the possibility that managers could make even more money in bankruptcy than they did while the company was healthy. One prominent bankruptcy lawyer put it this way: " 'In an enterprise [PSINet, a networking company] where catastrophic amounts of money were lost, the notion that people should have to be compensated over and above what they were already getting is offensive.' "

What does this mean for judicial oversight of bankruptcy bonus plans? The short answer is that courts should not simply rubber stamp any proposed plan, but should exercise a stronger presumption of approval than they do with pre-bankruptcy bonus packages. The presumption should be especially strong if most or all of the company's creditors support the plan. Of course this does not mean that the current post-petition pay arrangements are optimal; rather, they are likely to be superior to straight cash compensation.

NOTE: RESTRICTIONS ON EXECUTIVE PAY

The Bankruptcy Abuse Prevention and Consumer Protection Act of 2005 adds § 503(c) to the Bankruptcy Code to exclude certain payments to executives from the category of allowed administrative expenses. Section 503(c) excludes the following:

(1) a transfer made to, or an obligation incurred for the benefit of, an insider of the debtor for the purpose of inducing such person to remain with the debtor's business, absent a finding by the court based on evidence in the record that–

(A) the transfer or obligation is essential to retention of the person because the individual has a bona fide job offer from another business at the same or greater rate of compensation;

(B) the services provided by the person are essential to the survival of the business; and

(C) either–

(i) the amount of the transfer made to, or obligation incurred for the benefit of, the person is not greater than an amount equal to 10 times the amount of the mean transfer or obligation of a similar kind given to nonmanagement employees for any purpose during the calendar year in which the transfer is made or the obligation is incurred; or

(ii) if no such similar transfers were made to, or obligations were incurred for the benefit of, such nonmanagement employees during such calendar year, the amount of the transfer or obligation is not greater than an amount equal to 25 percent of the amount of any similar transfer or obligation made to or incurred for the benefit of such insider for any purpose during the calendar year before the year in which such transfer is made or obligation is incurred;

(2) a severance payment to an insider of the debtor, unless—

(A) the payment is part of a program that is generally applicable to all full-time employees; and

(B) the amount of the payment is not greater than 10 times the amount of the mean severance pay given to nonmanagement employees during the calendar year in which the payment is made; or

(3) other transfers or obligations that are outside the ordinary course of business and not justified by the facts and circumstances of the case, including transfers made to, or obligations incurred for the benefit of, officers, managers, or consultants hired after the date of the filing of the petition.

5. RETHINKING THE SYSTEM

As we have seen, the law of corporate reorganization rests on a judgment that claimants against a distressed firm can realize greater value through a recapitalization than through a liquidation or a sale of the going concern to a third party or parties. That judgment having been made, the law then defines the amount and priority of each claim, and provides rules to guide the allocation of participations in the reorganized firm among the claimants. A particular case within this system turns on a determination of the value of the firm. First, going concern value must be greater than liquidation value for reorganization to be an appropriate alternative. Second, particular allocations of interests in the reorganized firm depend on a prior determination of the total value being allocated.

We also have seen that the Bankruptcy Code seeks to leave the final determination of value to negotiation and majoritarian vote instead of to judicial decree and full payment, and in so doing, retreats one step from absolute priority. Commentaries since its enactment question both continuing adherence to the idea that recapitalization preserves value that liquidation destroys, and its mode of solving the problem of valuation and allocation. Ironically, much of this work pursues the program of enhancing the status of absolute priority as the bankruptcy system's governing norm. Some commentaries also assert that the system's structured bargaining process unduly subordinates what ought to be the system's primary goal— the provision of an optimal capital structure for the reorganized firm.

(A) RETHINKING CREDITORS' RIGHTS–THE COMMON POOL AND THE CREDITORS' BARGAIN

The new defense of absolute priority has its roots in an economic model of bankruptcy advanced by Professor Thomas Jackson. In this account, bankruptcy is a legal response to the economic problems of debt collection. The creditors are viewed as economic actors with rights in a common pool of assets. Given debtor distress, individual creditor action to pursue rights in the pool under nonbankruptcy law undercuts the broader goal to preserve and maximize the aggregate value of the pool. See Jackson, The Logic and the Limits of Bankruptcy 10–32 (1986).

The assertion that the exclusive focus of the bankruptcy system should be optimal asset deployment leads to the assertion that the system should not focus on, or perhaps even address distributional questions. Instead, the system should defer to substantive nonbankruptcy law and leave in place the prebankruptcy rights established in the common pool. Jackson, supra, at 21–27. Since the prebankruptcy rights are primarily matters of contract, the bankruptcy system's distributional norm should be contractually deter-mined. The law should be shaped by reference to the "creditors' bargain"—the result that the creditors contracted for and, therefore had reason to expect, at the time they extended credit. These "prebankruptcy entitle-ments" include contracted for priorities. Impairment of these entitlements in bankruptcy should occur only to the extent necessary to maximize net asset distribution to the creditors as a group. See Jackson, supra, ch. 9; Jackson and Scott, On the Nature of Bankruptcy: An Essay of Bankruptcy Sharing and the Creditors' Bargain, 75 Va.L.Rev. 155 (1989). Thus does the economic model of bankruptcy return us to the distributional principle that dominated before the enactment of the present Bankruptcy Code—absolute priority.

Economists reiterate this view. In the economic picture of debt and equity, productivity advantages flow from the uncompromising imposition of downside risk on the equity. Firms prosper in part because the equity, as holder of the residual upside claim, presses the managers to produce efficiently. On the downside, the equity still presses for efficient production because, as the holder of the residual risk of loss, it will be wiped out in the event of failure. At the same time, to borrow money is to commit to pay future cash flow to the debt. If that commitment is to have force, there must be punishment in the event of default. In addition, by increasing the return to creditors in distress situations, absolute priority encourages them to lend. Any relaxation of absolute priority disrupts this system of produc-tion incentives. See Hart, Different Approaches to Bankruptcy, NBER Working Paper 7921 (2000); Weiss, Bankruptcy Resolution: Direct Costs and Violation of Priority of Claims, 27 J. Financial Econs. 285, 286 (1990).

A number of responses have been made in defense of the Bankruptcy Code's more relaxed approach. One comes from economists who point out that a hard rule wiping out the equity can lead to unproductive strategic behavior on management's part prior to bankruptcy. When the sharehold-ers have nothing to lose, it becomes rational for their management agents to invest in a highly risky project in hope of a big return that restores value to the equity. Alternatively, management will have an incentive to delay the bankruptcy filing at the creditors' expense.

Legal commentators defending the *status quo* argue that since all valuation—market, judicial, or other—is approximate, fairness consider-ations do not compel strict compliance with absolute priority, particularly in light of the fact that deviations from absolute priority in large firm bankruptcies have been modest. LoPucki and Whitford, Bargaining Over Equity's Share in the Bankruptcy Reorganization of Large Publicly Held Companies, 139 U.Pa.L.Rev. 125 (1990). Alternatively, it has been argued that "bankruptcy law is a response to the many aspects of financial distress—moral, political, personal, social and economic—and, in particular, to the grievances of those who are affected by financial distress." Korobkin, Rehabilitating Values: A Jurisprudence of Bankruptcy, 91 Colum.L.Rev. 717, 721 (1991). Under this view, the bankruptcy system provides a process for the ongoing treatment of fundamentally incommensurate values. The bankrupt firm is not merely a pool of assets to be maximized for the creditors' account, but an "evolving and dynamic enterprise" with diverse aims. Id. at 722.

But LoPucki and Whitford, supra, also recognize that the system permits juniors to delay proceedings to capture nuisance value from make-weight legal positions and that reorganization plans tend siphon value to juniors with this power in mind. They make a reform suggestion for dealing with the hold up problem—a "preemptive cram down." This relies on the Code's provision in § 105(a) for court power to "issue any order * * * that is necessary or appropriate to carry out the provisions in this title." The bankruptcy judge would make a finding early in the proceeding that the equity interests would not be entitled to any property in a cram down. This frees the collective bargaining process from the threat of an equity hold up.

(B) RETHINKING THE REORGANIZATION PROCESS– ALTERNATIVE APPROACHES

Critics of the bankruptcy system also have proposed a number of alternative modes of reorganization. Some of these question the conventional wisdom that the market is likely systematically to undervalue the reorganized enterprise and the new securities issued upon the effectiveness of the plan. See Blum, The Law and the Language of Corporate Reorganization, 17 U.Chi.L.Rev. 565, 567–568 (1950). Other critics question the conventional wisdom that preservation of the value of the firm in the face of the creditors' collective action problem necessitates resort to a collective process.

(1) *Market–Based Proposals*

(a) *cash auction*

Some question the assumption that sales of the assets of distressed firms tend to sacrifice value and suggest that we abandon the recapitalization solution and instead rely on the market for corporate assets, sold on a going concern basis. The distressed enterprise would be valued in this market, and sold for cash. The cash would be distributed to the claimants in the order of their priority. Such a system would avoid both judicial valuation and the need for dispersed creditor and junior security holders to bargain collectively over value or a revised capital structure. The only significant disputes remaining for resolution within the bankruptcy system would concern the validity, scope, and priority of claims. See Jackson, supra, ch. 9 (1986) and Baird, The Uneasy Case for Corporate Reorganization, 15 J. Legal Studies 127 (1986).

Baird and Rasmussen, The End of Bankruptcy, 55 Stan. L. Rev. 751 (2002), argues that developments in bankruptcy practice (see Skeel, supra) amount to real world movement in this direction. "Corporate reorganizations," they claim, "have all but disappeared." Chapter 11 today, they argue, serves less as a forum for negotiation over the distressed firm's future among stakeholders than a convenient venue for selling assets and dividing up the proceeds. Even where the proceeding entails more than an asset sale, the lenders tend to be in control when the filing is made and the proceeding merely implements the deal already set. Even if this were not true, they contend, chapter 11 matters less than it used to because distressed firms carry less going concern surplus than once was the case. This follows from the shift to a service based economy—the business methods of a failed services firm imply little value added.

Note that a cash auction system would cure the traditional bias against liquidation and in favor of continuation (to the extent that developments in practice have not cured the problem already). Adler, A Theory of Corporate Insolvency, 72 N.Y.U.L.Rev. 343 (1997), discusses alternative means of correcting the bias, for example, a requirement of a supermajority creditor vote in favor of continuation. Hansen and Thomas, Auctions in Bankruptcy: Theoretical Analysis and Practical Guidance, 18 Int'l Rev. L. & Econ. 159 (1998), make a contrasting process suggestion. They would give the debtor in possession 120 days to propose a plan without any possibility of an extension, and another 60 days to obtain the requisite confirmations. In the event of failure to meet the deadline, an auction would proceed.

The cash auction proposal is highly controversial. LoPucki and Whitford, Corporate Governance in the Bankruptcy of Large Publicly Held Companies, 141 U.Pa.L.Rev. 669, 753–767 (1993), reconfirms the conventional wisdom that operation under judicial protection better preserves value than does a sale of assets. LoPucki and Whitford point out that preparations for an effective quick sale of a large corporation would take around a year, that substantial fees would be incurred, and that the market for assets still may be too undeveloped to produce bids that approximate the firm's going concern value. Shleifer and Vishny, Liquidation Values and Debt Capacity: A Market Equilibrium Approach, 47 J. Finance 1343 (1992), confirms this view. They suggest that most firm assets are specialized and not redeployable. The assets are illiquid in the sense that they have no reasonable use other than "the one they are destined for." The highest valuing users therefore are as likely to be in the same industry. If distress at the bankrupt firm is industry wide, there may be constraints on the purchasing capacity of other firms in the industry. Thus the sale price may not be close to the value in best use, and operation under bankruptcy protection may be the least costly strategy. Pulvino, Do Asset Fire Sales Exist? An Empirical Investigation of Commercial Aircraft Transactions, 53 J.Fin. 939 (1998), provides strong empirical backing for these assertions with a study of transfer prices for used narrow-body aircraft. The study shows that seller airlines with limited borrowing capacity sell planes at a 14 percent discount to average market price and that purchasers benefit from a 30 percent discount during market recessions. See also Lang and Stulz, Contagion and Competitive Intra–Industry Effects of Bankruptcy Announcements, 32 J.Fin.Econ. 45 (1992). Finally, LoPucki and Doherty, Bankruptcy Fire Sales (working paper 2007), compares the prices for which 30 large public companies were sold under Bankruptcy Code § 364 between 2000 and 2004 with the values of 30 similar companies whose chapter 11 reorganization plans were confirmed during the same period. They find that the firms in the sale sample sold for an average of 35 percent of book value, while the firms in the reorganization sample emerged from the chapter retaining 80 percent of their book value and then, in post-reorganization stock trading, showed an average market capitalization value of 91 percent of book value. They conclude that sale yielded only about half of reorganization value.

(b) securities market test

The reform proposition set out in Roe, Bankruptcy and Debt: A New Model for Corporate Reorganization, 83 Colum.L.Rev. 527 (1983), also sets value by means of a market transaction. But this proposal would avoid a cash-for-assets sale and retain recapitalization as a central aspect of bankruptcy reorganization. Roe would simplify the process substantially by (1) requiring a capital structure consisting only of common stock, and (2) offering a segment of the new common stock for sale to, and trading by, the public. The price established in the public sale provides the basis for the valuation of the enterprise as a whole. The value being thus set, the remaining common stock is distributed to the claimants in order of priority. Once again, judicial valuation and collective bargaining over value are avoided.

(c) options

The foregoing proposals would improve on the present system only to the extent that the auction or market transactions on which they rely provide a more accurate means of valuation. Were the market open to substantial imperfections—such as price volatility based on supply and demand swings not related to fundamental value, or informational problems or manipulation—then the proposal's viability would be open to substantial question. Professor Lucian Bebchuk offers another alternative. This also is designed to avoid valuation by decree or by collective bargaining. But, unlike the previous alternatives, it does not rely on market transactions. Bebchuk's reorganization plan hands the firm and the claimants options instead of unconditioned ownership interests. The parties are then given time to ascertain the value of the options. The firm, in effect, becomes an investment opportunity for the claimants. The burden to establish a value flows to the claimants themselves.

More specifically, Bebchuk would place the securities of the reorganized firm in the hands of the seniors, subject to a call at the firm's option. The call price would be the amount of the seniors' claim. The junior creditors would receive an option to purchase the firm's securities, the option price being set at the amount of the seniors' claims. Thus, if the juniors determined the value of the firm to be greater than the seniors' claims, they would exercise their option. The proceeds of the exercise would be used by the firm to redeem the firm's securities from the seniors. The juniors would profit to the extent of the difference between the value of the firm and the value of the seniors' claim. Similarly, the equity would have an option to purchase the firm's securities for a price equal to the senior and junior creditors' claims. The model allows for complicating factors such as more than three levels of claim and option exercise by less than all the claimants at a given level. Bebchuk, A New Approach to Corporate Reorganizations, 101 Harv. L. Rev. 775 (1988).

(d) judicially–supervised auction

Bebchuk's options proposal would confront a problem in operation: Suppose the creditors do not have the cash to exercise the options? Aghion, Hart, and Moore, The Economics of Bankruptcy Reform, 8 J.L. Econ. & Org. 523 (1992), and Aghion, Hart and Moore, Improving Bankruptcy Procedure, 72 Wash. U. L. Q. 849 (1994), open up the model to confront the problem. These models return the judge to a central role, arguing that its authority can be used in the proper case to remove the management team or effect a combination with another firm. In this model, the bankruptcy judge solicits bids for the firm, which can come in any form—cash, or securities of a recapitalized entity (the form of bid likely to be submitted by the incumbent managers). The bidding is open for three months. The creditors, who have the entire interest in the case of an insolvent firm, then take a vote and decide which bid they wish to accept. If the bids show that the company is solvent, then the equity holders receive Bebchuk-type options; options also come into the model where multiple classes of creditors are present. If a cash bid comes in, the judge uses it to establish a minimum value for the firm. If that bid is greater than the amount owed to the seniors, then the juniors participate in the distribution. But if the juniors like a noncash bid better, they will have to find the cash to exercise their options. That problem also will come up when there is no cash bid. But, so long as the option is divisible among the holders, those who have cash sources can exercise; and, in larger bankruptcies, a market in the options can develop, permitting those lacking cash to sell into the market to realize on their value of the option.

(2) Contractual Proposals

The foregoing proposals all share the present bankruptcy system's assumption that collective action problems among the group of creditors necessitate resort to a mandatory collective legal proceeding as a value preserving aid to reorganization. Some commentators reject this assumption and argue for private ordering solutions to the problem of debtor distress.

(a) automatic conversion

Adler, Financial and Political Theories of American Corporate Bankruptcy, 45 Stan. L.Rev. 311 (1993), sets out an elaborate model for a self-adjusting capital structure that would avoid the necessity and considerable costs of reorganization. Adler's solution is to replace-conventional debt with a different form of senior participation, termed "chameleon equity." Pursuant to this, the holder receives a creditor's right to a fixed payment stream but possesses no right to accelerate or collect individually on default. But default does result in the automatic cancellation of the firm's equity, with the residual equity interest passing to the lowest tier of fixed claims on default, while the firm remains subject to higher priority fixed claims. Note that this "chameleon equity" is not debt at all, but a variant of preferred stock.

Adler notes that the existing legal system creates significant disincentives and barriers to employment of chameleon equity by a firm. Id. at 333–341. Prime among them is the Internal Revenue Code's provision for the deduction of interest but not dividends. In addition, the priority position of a senior chameleon equity claimant could be safe only with a prohibition of subsequent incurrence of debt by the issuer and resort to bankruptcy on default; corporate law does not facilitate the necessary absolute guarantee. Involuntary creditors present a further problem. For further development of the approach, see Adler, Finance's Theoretical Divide and the Proper Role of Insolvency Rules, 67 So. Cal. L. Rev. 1107 (1994). See also Bradley and Rosenzweig, The Untenable Case for Chapter 11, 101 Yale L.J. 1043 (1992).

(b) contractual choice

Other contractual proposals begin with the familiar assertion that contracting parties will do a better job of reaching efficient outcomes than will a mandatory distributional system. For a moderate proposal in this vein, consider Rasmussen, Debtor's Choice: A Menu Approach to Corporate Bankruptcy, 71 Texas L.Rev. 51 (1992). Rasmussen would provide that corporations select in their charters from among a "menu" of different modes of bankruptcy. The menu would include, *inter alia,* chapter 11, chapter 7 liquidation, no bankruptcy (with the possibility of a contingent equity capital structure), and any bankruptcy regime designed by the firm itself. Schwartz, A Contract Theory Approach to Business Bankruptcy, 107 Yale L.J. 1807 (1998), offers a more thorough-going contract-based conception. Schwartz draws on technical models from financial economics to assert that creditors can contract *ex ante* (1) to determine whether the postinsolvency firm should be liquidated or put through reorganization, and (2) to determine a postinsolvency scheme of distribution (including the postinsolvency capital structure). Such a postinsolvency distribution would be designed so as to align properly the preinsolvecy investment incentives of the equity and would not necessarily eliminate the equity interest.

Warren and Westbrook, Contracting Out of Bankruptcy: An Empirical Intervention, 118 Harv. L. Rev. 1197 (2005), enters an empirical objection to this line of analysis. They find that around one-quarter of creditors did not adjust the interest rates of their claims on a creditor-by-creditor basis, and that an additional 6 percent of debt was held in very small amounts. It follows, say the authors, that contractarian bankruptcy fails a basic feasibility test—too many creditors do not negotiate contracts in the first place. For a riposte, see Rasmussen, Empirically Bankrupt, 2007 Colum. Bus. L. Rev. 179.

PART III

Financing With Hybrid Securities

INTRODUCTION

Hybrid securities combine attributes of debt and equity. Preferred stock does this by starting with an equity interest and building on financial rights and preferences. Convertible bonds do this by starting with a debt contract and incorporating a privilege to reconstitute the contract rights as an equity interest. Both types give rise to conflicts of interest with the common stockholders and present special problems for the drafter. Section A presents preferred stock and the corporate law that governs preferred stockholders' rights. Section B takes up convertibles. Section C turns to venture capital finance, a form of relational equity investment that utilizes convertible preferred stock as its vehicle of choice.

Section A. Preferred Stock Financing

1. Rights and Preferences

(A) PREFERRED STOCK DEFINED

Preferred stock is described as a senior security offering the holder a constant payment stream resembling a bond's while simultaneously holding out to the issuer the flexibility respecting periodic payments characteristic of common stock. This description prompts a question: How can an investment simultaneously perform as a fixed income security and, short of insolvency, leave management with the discretion to withhold payments? The answer is that an investment cannot do both at once, at least in an absolute sense. Where a debt security is absolute respecting its promised payment stream (outside of severe financial distress), preferred stock is contingent and not necessarily a "fixed income" security at all. To understand preferred stock's risk and return characteristics is to grasp the difference between a contract right that is fully enforceable (outside of bankruptcy) and a contract preference that yields different monetary results across the range of different business contingencies (outside of bankruptcy).

Let us begin a more particular description of preferred stock with the authorizing language of the Delaware Corporation Law (DCL), in section 151(a):

> Every corporation may issue one or more classes of stock * * * any or all of which classes * * * may have such voting powers, full or limited, or no voting powers, and such designations, preferences and relative, participating, optional or other special rights, and qualifications, limitations or restrictions thereof, as shall be stated and expressed in the certificate of incorporation or of any amendment thereto, or in the resolution or resolutions providing for the issue of such stock adopted by the board of directors pursuant to authority expressly vested in it by provisions of its certificate of incorporation. * * *

See also Revised Model Business Corporation Act (RMBCA) § 6.01; New York Business Corporation Law (NYBCL) § 501.

Delaware § 151(a) hands the drafter of the corporate charter a blank slate on which to fill in the rights of different classes of equity participants—rights which by definition concern periodic returns, capital payouts on (or prior to) liquidation, and voting. On the blank slate the drafter may parse those rights among multiple classes of stock as he or she sees fit. To be "preferred" stock is to be a class of stock with a "preference" or "special right" as against another class of stock, with the preference or right going to periodic returns, capital payouts, or both.

The statute offers no further instructions as to the nature or form of preferred stock's rights. It instead remits us to the particular terms of a given firm's charter, an amendment thereto, or a board resolution pursuant to an authorization in the charter or an amendment, there to ascertain the particular package of rights attending a given class of stock. Section 151(a) does not even require such a class to be designated as "preferred." It could be, and often is, called Common A or Common B, as the drafter chooses.

Preferred stock, however vaguely defined in the foregoing, can be clearly distinguished from a junior debt security like a subordinated debenture. Whatever economic similarities the two may have, the preferred is *stock*. It therefore is booked with the common on the balance sheet in the shareholders' equity section, while the debenture shows up as a liability. Dividends on preferred are treated for tax purposes as a distribution of net profits to shareholders rather than as a deductible cost of doing business, as occurs with interest payments on the debentures. Furthermore, because the preferred is stock, payment of a dividend or redemption could run afoul of legal capital rules. In many states dividends may not be paid unless the enterprise has some form of surplus or earnings available therefor. And no return of capital may be made on dissolution unless assets are available after all debts have been satisfied. In addition, even though no law *per se* prohibits a payment of interest or repayment of principal on a debenture in a distress situation, fraudulent conveyance law may prevent the same payment being made respecting preferred. Finally, under 1129(b) of the

Bankruptcy Code a class of subordinated debentures can claim absolute priority over a class of preferred.

(B) THE PREFERRED STOCK CONTRACT

Any meaningful and more detailed profile of rights attending classes of preferred stock, in particular rights held relative to other classes of stock, follows not from corporate law but from corporate finance practice. As with debt securities, with preferred stock the contract defines rights in the first instance. Note that DCL § 151(a) also permits a corporate charter to authorize new classes of preferred, and hence new preferred stock contracts, on an open-ended basis. Under such a "blank check," the terms of a given issue are fixed by subsequent resolution of the board of directors without requiring a shareholder vote. See Siegman v. Palomar Medical Technologies, 1998 WL 118201 (Del.Ch.) (interpreting a blank stock charter provision providing for the issuance of preferred stock in "classes" not to authorize several "series" of preferred thereafter issued by the board). A preferred stock financing thereby can go forward as expeditiously as a debt financing. (The blank check authorization figures critically in the creation of "poison pills," where the Board unilaterally creates preferred stock and issues rights to purchase it on terms contrived to impede or effectively preclude a takeover.)

Certificate of Incorporation of General Technology, Inc.

Board Resolution providing for Series A Preferred

Appendix A → Back

(1) Financial Terms

For purposes of exposition, consider the package of rights and privileges characteristic of the preferred issued in public trading markets by large firms a half century ago (and prominently featured in caselaw through the 1980s). These issues tended to be nonparticipating (or "straight") cumulative preferred stock, redeemable only at the issuer's option. More particularly, given this package of rights and preferences:

- Upon liquidation, after payment in full to all creditors, the preferred has a priority payout over the common capped at the amount paid in per share at original issue.

- From period to period, the preferred has a priority over the common with respect to the payment of dividends, the priority being stated either as a fixed percentage of the amount originally paid in or as a fixed number of dollars per share per period. This priority embodies only a contingent and negative right—so long as the full preferred dividend is not paid, the issuer may not pay a dividend on the common; so long as the common receives no dividend, no contractual default occurs respecting the preferred.

- The "cumulative" feature of the dividend imports additional (but still negative) teeth to the priority—no common dividends may be paid until all preferred dividends skipped in past periods have been paid.

- The limitation of redemption rights to the issuer means that the holders' original capital investment, like that of the common stockholders, could stay with the firm indefinitely to be returned as a practical matter only on liquidation.

The package of rights thus described is representative only. Nothing in corporate law requires that an issue of preferred be nonparticipating, cumulative, and redeemable only by the issuer.

Preferred stock contracts vary in the force of their compulsion to make dividend payments. At one extreme, they can provide for a mandatory and fully cumulative dividend. In such a case, the issuer makes a promise to pay in addition to a priority, intensifying the preferred's resemblance to debt. At the other extreme lies preferred with a discretionary and wholly noncumulative dividend. Here the preferred's payment stream takes on a contingent, speculative quality.

There is less variance in practice respecting liquidation rights. Preferred stock contracts generally provide, in the event of dissolution of the enterprise, for the payment to the preferred prior to any distribution to the common stockholders of a specified sum plus an amount equal to all dividends in arrears, and if dissolution is voluntary, often a premium. As to redemption, preferred contracts usually provide for redemption at the issuer's option at a specific price plus an amount equal to all dividends in arrears and a premium. Mandatory sinking fund payments which retire the issue on a set schedule became common in the wake of the high inflation of the late 1970s and early 1980s. Such a redemption schedule makes a class of preferred more closely resemble debt. Preferred stock contracts may contain additional protective provisions designed to minimize risk of nonpayment, such as business covenants and the protective voting provisions described below.

Preferred stock rights and preferences thus described serve the purpose of protecting the preferred holders' prior claims to dividends and principal should the enterprise shrink. But the preferred stock contract also may embody an opportunity to share in the growth of the enterprise. Indeed, in an expanding economy, preferred stock lacking such a feature is not likely to offer a particularly attractive investment. The usual device for offering such an opportunity, while preserving priority in the event of contraction, is the conversion privilege—the right of the stockholder to convert the preferred stock into common stock by exchanging a share of preferred for a specified number of shares of common, or at a designated value for as many shares of common as may be purchased at specified prices. See Part III, Section B, infra. Alternatively, the charter can provide that the preferred "participate," that is, that it share (perhaps on a pro rata basis) in any dividends paid to the common after payment of the preferred's fixed priority. The charter also could provide for participation with the common in liquidation after repayment of the preferred's fixed liquidation preference. Such additional rights make the preferred more closely resemble equity. On the terms of preferred stock generally, see Buxbaum, Preferred Stock—Law and Draftsmanship, 42 Calif.L.Rev. 243 (1954).

(2) *Voting Rights*

Formally the preferred stockholder is an "owner" with an "equity" interest, like a common stockholder. In some states, if the charter says nothing respecting voting rights the preferred may be entitled to vote like a holder of common stock. Return to DCL section 151(a), quoted above, and note that it accords the drafter of the charter complete discretion respecting the assignment of voting rights among classes of stock, so long of course, as the drafter in the end vests complete voting rights in one class or across the classes. "Preferred" stock, then, may or may not be voting stock as the charter provides. See also RMBCA § 6.01(c); NYBCL §§ 501, 613.

Where preferred serves as a means of external finance for a seasoned company, it generally is not given significant voting power. Thus the issue of publicly traded, nonparticipating cumulative preferred hypothesized above plausibly could be nonvoting. Since the stock is issued and held as a fixed income security, a given holder's interest in directing the affairs of the enterprise is not significantly different from that of a bondholder. This preferred stockholder, like a bondholder, has a prior and limited claim on earnings of the going concern and on assets in liquidation. Like a bondholder, its participation generally may be terminated by redemption at the option of the common. Like a bondholder, its interest in the enterprise differs materially from that of the common stock, which is the residual claimant of the benefits of operations and the first to sustain the burdens of loss.

(a) *voting and contingent voting preferred*

Many corporate charters provide the preferred full voting rights on a share by share basis. But significant voting power does not necessarily follow from the grant. If, for example, there are 1,000,000 common shares outstanding and 100,000 shares in the preferred class, control effectively lies with the common interest. Although sharing full voting rights, the preferred would not necessarily even have a representative on the board of directors. (A different alignment of interests obtains when preferred is issued in close corporation capital structures and in venture capital financing. In these situations, preferred classes often hold voting control.)

Many corporate charters ameliorate the problem of preferred board representation by providing the preferred with a class vote for the election of a specified number of directors (and possibly on other matters) upon the occurrence of failure to pay a specified number of preferred dividends. The operative notion is that interruption of the payment stream substantially increases the interest of the preferred respecting governance of the firm. Voting power is bestowed upon the preferred by class, rather than by share, in recognition of the likelihood that the number of common shares exceeds the number of preferred. The magnitude of the voting power thus contingently accorded also depends on the number of board seats. A majority of board seats shifts control to the preferred. In the alternative, and more commonly, the charter provides voice in the boardroom short of control by according a class vote for one or two seats on the board.

Corporate codes do not require these contingent voting rights. But mandates can be found in stock exchange rules. For example, the New York Stock Exchange requires corporations whose preferred stock is listed on the Exchange to accord preferred classes the power to elect "at least two directors upon default of the equivalent of six quarterly dividends"—NYSE Listed Company Manual, § 313.00. Default is defined as the failure to pay an aggregate (rather than a consecutive) number of quarterly dividends. The American Stock Exchange makes a similar requirement "no later than two years after an incurred default in the payment of fixed dividends." AMEX Listing Standards, Policies and Requirements, § 124.

Default in the payment of dividends is not the only contingency upon which voting rights might be predicated. Violation of other protective provisions in the preferred stock contract, such as minimum sinking fund requirements, limitations on dividends payable to junior securities, prohibitions against creating senior securities, or business covenants may provide the occasion for class voting rights in the preferred. (In theory, bondholders also could be accorded such rights in the charter. See DCL § 221; NYBCL § 518(c).)

Charter provisions extending particularized voting rights to preferred holders give rise to questions of interpretation. As an example, consider **FGC Holdings Ltd. v. Teltronics, Inc.**, 2005 WL 2334357 (Del.Ch.), which concerned Series B preferred stock of Teltronics issued pursuant to a Certificate of Designation (CD) that provided the holders the right to elect one member of a five-seat board as follows:

> 4(b) The holders of the Series B Preferred Stock, voting separately as one class, shall have the exclusive and special right at all times to elect one (1) director ("[the Series B director]") to the Board of Directors of the Corporation provided, however, that so long as any shares of Series B Preferred Stock are outstanding, the Board of Directors shall not consist of more than five (5) members. * * * Upon the written request of the holders of record of at least a majority of the Series B Preferred Stock then outstanding, the Secretary of the Corporation shall call a special meeting of the holders of Series B Preferred Stock for the purpose of (i) removing any [Series B director] elected pursuant to this Section 4(b) and/or (ii) electing a director to fill a vacancy of the directorship authorized to be filled by the holders of Series B Preferred Stock pursuant to this Section 4(b). Such meeting shall be held at the earliest practicable date. A vacancy in the directorship to be elected by the holders of Series B Preferred Stock pursuant to this Section 4(b) may be filled only by vote or written consent in lieu of a meeting of the holders of a majority of the shares of Series B Preferred Stock then outstanding and may not be filled by the remaining directors.

The Series B originally had been issued to an institutional investor that made use of the right to vote a representative onto the fifth board seat. It later transferred the Series B to a second investor that chose not to take the board seat owing to a conflict of interest arising from a simultaneous interest in Teltronics debt securities. The second investor then transferred the Series B to the plaintiff venture capitalist, who claimed an immediate right to take a board seat, taking the position that CD § 4(b) accorded a right to elect the fifth director at any time. Teltronics resisted, contending the board was full after a recent annual meeting at which the common had filled all five board seats. The Series B holder responded that the CD implicitly limited the common to a maximum of four seats and that the fifth seat never should have been filled, The Chancery Court split the difference, holding the CD to "(i) limit the total size of the board to five directors; (ii) create one Series B directorship along with four common directorships; and (iii) allow the common stockholders to elect a provisional fifth common director in the event the Series B stockholders choose not to elect a Series B director, subject to the Series B stockholders' right to elect a Series B director at any time." It followed that one of the five directors would have to go. The identification of that director was up to the issuer, which should have noted the limiting contingency respecting the tenure of one member of its slate before the fact. In addition, the Series B was found not to have knowingly or intentionally waived its right to elect the fifth director.

(b) Voting on Amendments

The preferred stock contract is located in the corporate charter. Statutory provisions governing corporate charters accordingly are incorporated in the preferred stock contract. The results are a little surprising. If, as usually is the case, the common stockholders have most of the votes, the statute gives them (and their management representatives) the power to amend the charter to restructure the preferred stock contract's allocation of risks and returns to the disadvantage of the preferred. The asset priority embodied in the liquidation preference of preferred stock accordingly is subject to amendment (RMBCA §§ 10.03, 10.04; DCL § 242; NYBCL §§ 801–804). Similarly amendable is the income priority embodied in the preferential claim to dividends (see e.g., Johnson v. Bradley Knitting Co., 228 Wis. 566, 280 N.W. 688 (1938); Blumenthal v. Di Giorgio Fruit Corp., 30 Cal.App.2d 11, 85 P.2d 580 (1938); Western Foundry Co. v. Wicker, 403 Ill. 260, 85 N.E.2d 722 (1949)). So too is the amendment process available to modify protective features of the preferred stock contract which are designed to increase the likelihood of the payment of dividends and of the liquidation or redemption priority (such as a sinking fund provision or a special provision restricting the payment of dividends to common stock), and other features which affect its investment value, such as a noncallable feature, the redemption price, or the conversion rights or voting rights. See e.g. Morris v. American Pub. Util. Co., 14 Del.Ch. 136, 122 A. 696 (1923); compare Breslav v. New York & Queens Elec. Light & P. Co., 249 App.Div. 181, 291 N.Y.S. 932 (2d Dept.1936), aff'd without opinion, 273 N.Y. 593, 7 N.E.2d 708 (1937) with Beloff v. Consolidated Ed. Co., 300 N.Y. 11, 87 N.E.2d 561 (1949) and N.Y. § 801(b)(12).

A considerable body of case law addresses efforts to amend or alter preferred stock contracts. Typically, in these cases, the downside risks against which the preferred purchased its priorities and protections will have materialized, to the disadvantage of the common. For example, inadequate earnings over many years will have caused successive preferred dividends to have been skipped. With no curative business upturn in sight, the cumulated dividends in arrears depress the value of the common. The common then seeks to amend the charter (1) to acquire a larger share of future returns by eliminating the preferreds' right to arrears and reducing their promised or expected future returns, and (2) to increase the preferreds' risks for the future by modifying or eliminating the protective features of the investment contract. Alternatively, an opportunity may have arisen to merge or sell all the firm's assets at a price or on terms relatively favorable to the common, with the rights of the preferred respecting dividends or redemption interfering with the transaction's consummation. Here again elimination of preferred rights benefits the common, whether in connection with the distribution of the assets of the enterprise on liquidation following an asset sale, or with the distribution of new participations in a substantially changed enterprise following a merger. In all of these cases management will contend (perhaps accurately) that the proposed transaction is necessary or appropriate for the enhancement of the firm's value. The question then arises whether concomitant alteration of the preferred stock contract is equally necessary and appropriate. Most of the cases in this Section pose this question in one form or another. Results vary.

Meanwhile, it follows that a class of preferred with no voting rights whatsoever is the rough equivalent of an issue of bonds under a contract providing for amendment at the issuer's option without the bondholder consent. Indeed, an issue of preferred with full voting rights is not much better off so long as the preferred can cast only a minority of the votes and charter amendments are approved by the stockholder group as whole.

Corporate codes address this problem by granting preferred stockholders the right to vote as a class on charter amendments which adversely affect their interests. This statutory class voting right in effect grants the preferred a veto and appears to be mandatory. Occasions for it are specified in some detail in RMBCA § 10.04, and include increase in the par value or number of outstanding shares or the issue of prior preferred stock. The matters for a class vote appear in a more generalized statement in DCL § 242(b)(2), which prescribes class voting on those charter amendments which would increase or decrease the par value or aggregate number of authorized shares, or "alter or change the powers, preferences or special rights of the shares of such class so as to affect them adversely." See also NYBCL § 804.

Some statutes add an express provision for a class vote where stockholder approval is sought for a merger or consolidation which adversely affects the rights of the preferred. See RMBCA § 11.04(f); NYBCL § 903(a)(2). We will see in this part that where the statute does not make such provision, as in the case of Delaware's merger statute, the question arises whether a class vote can be implied from the right to vote as a class on charter amendments.

Finally, note that under DCL § 151(a), read together with §§ 242 and 251, preferred holders need not rely on the state statute to provide for protective class vote respecting a charter amendment or merger. Preferred class votes protecting the rights created in the charter can be vested in the charter itself.

(C) ISSUER MOTIVATIONS AND HOLDER EXPECTATIONS

Return to the nonparticipating cumulative preferred stock hypothesized above. Why would a fixed income investor purchase such a security in a world offering a menu of bonds and debentures? And why would an issuer finance with straight preferred instead of an issue of subordinated debentures? Hunt, Williams and Donaldson, Basic Business Finance 360–361 (5th ed. 1974), offers the classic advice:

"The impression created is that of a limited commitment on dividends coupled with considerable freedom in the timing of such payments. In reality, experience with preferred stocks indicates that the flexibility in dividend payments is more apparent than real. The management of a business which is experiencing normal profitability and growth desires to pay a regular dividend on both common and preferred stock because of a sense of responsibility to the corporate owners and/or because of the necessity of having to solicit further equity capital in the future. The pressure for a regular common dividend in many cases assures the holder of a preferred stock that his regular dividend will not be interrupted, even in years when profits are insufficient to give common shareholders a comparable return, for it is very damaging to the reputation of a common stock (and therefore its price) if preferred dividend arrearages stand before it. The fact that most preferred issues are substantially smaller in total amount than the related common issue means that the cash drain of a preferred dividend is often less significant than the preservation of the status of the common stock.

"The result is that management comes to view the preferred issue much as it would a bond, establishing the policy that the full preferred dividend must be paid as a matter of course. The option of passing the dividend still exists, but it is seen as a step to be taken only in case of unusual financial difficulty. * * * The primary advantage of the preferred stock becomes identical with that of a bond, namely, the opportunity to raise funds at a fixed return which is less than that realized when the funds are invested. On the other hand, the dividend rate on preferred stock is typically above the interest rate on a comparable bond and may have the additional disadvantage of not developing a tax shield. Of course, the bond [has] a sinking fund [where the preferred redeemable only at the issuer's option does not], so that the *burden* of bond and preferred stock may not be greatly different.

"The differential in cost between a preferred stock and an alternative debt issue may be considered a premium paid for the option of postponing the fixed payments. If management is reluctant to exercise this option, it is likely that the premium will be considered excessive. However, the closer a company gets to its recognized debt limits, the more management is likely to appreciate the option to defer the dividend on a preferred stock issue and be willing to pay a premium for this potential defense against a tight cash position."

Would you recommend a nonparticipating preferred to a senior member of your own family with fixed income investment objectives? Cottle, Murray and Block, Graham and Dodd's Security Analysis 470–474 (5th ed. 1988), repeats the cautionary advice of the classic Graham and Dodd text. For Graham and Dodd, the preferred stock contract is "fundamentally unsatisfactory" for the fixed income investor. Accordingly, preferred makes an appropriate fixed income investment only if contractual weakness is offset by strength in the issuing company. They recommend that a preferred issuer have all the properties of an issuer of an investment grade bond, "with an added margin of safety to offset the discretionary feature in the payment of dividends * * * so large that the directors will be expected to declare the dividend as a matter of course." Preferred of less than investment grade quality should be accompanied by some form of participation in periodic return in addition to the conventional fixed dividend preference.

Shifting back to the point of view of the security's issuer, the deductibility of interest payments gives debt a relative cost advantage over preferred. The tax differential has contributed to a relative decline in the use of preferred as a financing vehicle. Its issuance by large and mid-sized firms accordingly tends to be related to constrained debt capacity—by adding preferred to their balance sheets highly levered issuers increase the size of the equity cushion. This can improve the issuer's base for future debt financing, satisfy a regulator, or do both. More particularly, preferred stock financing tends to be employed by firms, such as public utilities and banks, the capital structures of which are subject to government regulation. They issue preferred to satisfy legally mandated debt equity ratios. For example, banks and bank holding companies, pressed by regulatory agencies to expand equity their capital base, issue large quantities of preferred, both short-and long-term. Preferred also tends to be issued to bolster the equity capital of firms near distress. It was, for example, widely employed in the recapitalization programs of firms having difficulty meeting the obligations assumed in high leverage restructurings undertaken during the 1980s. As with the banks, the objective is to increase the firm's equity cushion with the minimum possible dilution of the upside potential of the common stock.

Heinkel and Zechner, The Role of Debt and Preferred Stock as a Solution to Adverse Investment Incentives, 25 J. Fin. & Quant. Anal. 1 (1990), offer theoretical confirmation of these observations with an agency model. This shows that preferred creates incentives for the firm's common holders to invest, and thus ameliorates the underinvestment problem that follows from the issuance of debt. A new issue of preferred counters the agency costs of debt, and thereby not only enhances the firm's debt capacity but increases the overall value of the firm.

In some cases a tax advantage figures into preferred stock financing. This can offset the advantages of the lack an issuer deduction for dividend payments. Under the intercorporate dividend exclusion, I.R.C. §§ 243, 244, corporate taxpayers pay tax on only 30 percent of dividends received, meaning an effective marginal rate of .3 x .35 or 10.5 percent. Preferred stock accordingly can offer a more attractive investment opportunity than unsecured bonds to insurance companies and other institutional investors that are subject to federal corporate income tax. Such a corporate preferred issue could sell at a lower yield than the same company's bonds. Short-term floating rate preferred with dividend rates tied to short-term interest rates also make use of the intercorporate dividend exclusion. This paper is often issued by banks and sold to corporations with excess cash available for short term investment, for which it makes an attractive alternative to short term debt instruments.

Finally, in the mid 1990s investment bankers put the corporate trust device to use in inventing tax deductible preferred. Here the corporation raising the capital issues bonds to a special purpose trust. The trust in turn raises the capital to pay for the bonds by issuing preferred stock to corporate taxpayers. The ultimate credit on the deal takes an interest deduction while the ultimate sources of capital get the intercorporate dividend exclusion. By the end of 1997 more than 285 of these issues were outstanding; they had raised $27 billion. Khanna and McConnell, MIPS, QUIPS AND TOPrS: Old Wine in New Bottles, 11 J. Applied Corp. Fin. 39 (1998).

2.   CLAIMS TO DIVIDENDS

(A) PREFERRED STOCK DIVIDEND PROVISIONS

A great variety of delineations of dividend priority occurs in preferred stock contracts. At one extreme, the contract can make a promise to pay, providing that dividends shall be paid if appropriate surplus exists (Arizona Western Ins. Co. v. L.L. Constantin & Co., 247 F.2d 388 (3d Cir.1957); cf. L.L. Constantin & Co. v. R.P. Holding Corp., 56 N.J.Super. 411, 153 A.2d 378 (Ch.Div.1959) (interpreting the same charter language to be insufficiently explicit to overcome the directorial discretion that the statute authorizes)). At the opposite extreme lies preferred with a noncumulative priority (i.e., a priority that only blocks dividends to common during the current payment period and does not call for cumulation of past skipped dividends even if the enterprise was profitable). Intermediate forms most frequently encountered are fully cumulative preferred (i.e., the failure to pay dividends in any period, whether or not the enterprise had earnings during that period, does not relieve the enterprise of the obligation to pay those unpaid dividends before common dividends can be paid) and the preferred which is cumulative only if earned (i.e., unpaid dividends only cumulate or accrue if they have not been paid for periods for which there were earnings), a contingency which leaves wide room for dispute. See e.g., Kern v. Chicago & Eastern Ill. R.R. Co., 6 Ill.App.3d 247, 285 N.E.2d 501 (1972); Koppel v. Middle States Petroleum Corp., 197 Misc. 479, 96 N.Y.S.2d 38 (Sup.Ct.N.Y.County 1950). Finally, nothing prevents a firm from issuing "no dividend" preferred with a preference respecting liquidation only. See Shintom Co., Ltd. v. Audiovox Corporation, 888 A.2d 225 (Del.Supr.2005).

In addition to its limited preference—both to dividends and to assets—preferred stock may participate along with common stock in residual earnings and assets. The extent of such participation is a matter of contract and will vary with the needs of the corporation for capital and the marketability of its stock at the time when capital is needed. See e.g., Zahn v. Transamerica Corp., 162 F.2d 36 (3d Cir.1947). In the absence of contractual provision for participation, however, the majority view is that a preferred stock is limited by the amount of its priority as to dividends, and as to assets in liquidation, and is not entitled to share in residual earnings or assets. See St. Louis Southwestern Ry. Co. v. Loeb, 318 S.W.2d 246 (Mo.1958); Squires v. Balbach Co., 177 Neb. 465, 129 N.W.2d 462 (1964).

(B) BOARD DISCRETION TO WITHHOLD PAYMENT

In all cases other than that of mandatory dividend preferred, directors have discretion to withhold payment of dividends. Should courts or legislatures fashion standards limiting the exercise of that discretion, or are market incentives sufficient to channel such discretion in productive directions? Should the same standards confine directors' discretion to withhold dividends on non-cumulative preferred as on fully cumulative preferred?

(1) Cumulative Preferred

The priority attached to an issue of fully cumulative preferred has to be drafted with utmost care if management discretion respecting payment of the dividend is actually to be constrained. For a case in which the drafter's efforts fall short of the mark, see **In re Sunstates Corp. Shareholder Litigation**, 788 A.2d 530 (Del.Ch.2001). This concerned an issue of cumulative preferred issued under a charter providing that in the event of arrears "the Corporation shall not * * * make any purchase of stock ranking as to dividends junior or pari passu" to the preferred. The issuer stopped dividends on the preferred and thereafter caused a wholly owned insurance subsidiary to repurchase 70 percent of the issuer's own common stock and 30 percent of the issue of preferred.

The Delaware Chancery Court made short shrift of the preferreds' substance-over-form argument, 788 A.2d at 531–32 & n.2:

"The clause at issue clearly and unambiguously applies the special limitation against share repurchases only to [the issuer parent] and not to its subsidiary entities. Construing that clause strictly, as I must, and recognizing that 'nothing should be presumed in [its] favor,' it would be impermissible for me to find that the limitation also governs actions by [the issuer's] subsidiaries. The result may be, as plaintiffs argue, that [the issuer] was able to avoid the restriction by the simple means of channeling the repurchases through its subsidiaries. Nevertheless, no one who studied the certificate of incorporation should ever have had any other expectation. If the special limitation had been meant to apply to the actions of [the issuer's] subsidiaries, the certificate of incorporation could easily have said so.

"Fifty years ago, the fallacy of plaintiffs' argument was recognized in the seminal law review article by Richard M. Buxbaum, Preferred Stock—Law and Draftsmanship, 42 Cal. L.Rev. 243, 257 (1954). In discussing problems in drafting financial restriction clauses in preferred stock contract, Professor Buxbaum stated as follows: 'As to all these clauses, *it is vital that all payments, distributions, acquisitions, etc. include those of the subsidiaries; otherwise the provisions can be totally avoided*' (emphasis added)."

(2) Noncumulative Preferred

The discretion question has been litigated extensively in respect of noncumulative preferred. The facts giving rise to these disputes work along the following lines. No dividends are paid on either the noncumulative preferred or the underlying common for many years. During this period the corporation may be profitable—but because the business is capital intensive, management retains all earnings available for dividends. Then, when conditions improve, management starts the dividend flow again. The noncumulative preferred is paid its limited annual dividend, and the common, whose the dividend is not subject to a limitation once the preferred is paid, is paid a much larger dividend. The preferred argues that, on these facts, "noncumulative" does not have its literal meaning.

The leading cases, Wabash Railway Co. v. Barclay, 280 U.S. 197 (1930) (Holmes, J.) and **Guttmann v. Illinois Central R. Co.**, 189 F.2d 927 (2d Cir.1951) (Frank, J.), cert. denied, 342 U.S. 867 (1951), rule against the preferred. Judge Frank, in *Guttmann*, opted for literalism even while recognizing that the noncumulative arrangement opens possibilities for opportunistic manipulation for the benefit of the common:

"Here we are interpreting a contract into which uncoerced men entered. Nothing in the wording of that contract would suggest to an ordinary wayfaring person the existence of a contingent or inchoate right to arrears of dividends. The notion that such a right was promised is, rather, the invention of lawyers or other experts, a notion stemming from considerations of fairness, from a policy of protecting investors in those securities. But the preferred stockholders are not—like sailors or idiots or infants—wards of the judiciary. As courts on occasions have quoted or paraphrased ancient poets, it may not be inappropriate to paraphrase a modern poet, and to say that 'a contract is a contract is a contract.' To be sure, it is an overstatement that the courts never do more than carry out the intentions of the parties: In the interest of fairness and justice, many a judge-made legal rule does impose, on one of the parties to a contract, obligations which neither party actually contemplated and as to which the language of the contract is silent. But there are limits to the extent to which a court may go in so interpolating rights and obligations which were never in the parties' contemplation. In this case we consider those limits clear.

"In sum, we hold that, since the directors did not 'abuse' their discretion in withholding dividends on the non-cumulative preferred for any past years, (a) no right survived to have those dividends declared, and (b) the directors had no discretion whatever to declare those dividends subsequently.

"From the point of view of the preferred stockholders, the bargain they made may well be of a most undesirable kind. Perhaps the making of such bargains should be prevented. But, if so, the way to prevent them is by legislation, or by prophylactic administrative action authorized by legislation, as in the case of the S.E.C. in respect of securities, including preferred stocks, whether cumulative or noncumulative, issued by public utility holding companies or their subsidiaries. The courts are not empowered to practice such preventive legal medicine, and must not try to revise, extensively, contracts already outstanding and freely made by adults who are not incompetents."

Judge Frank also indicated that some commentators had interpreted the noncumulative feature to bar accruals only for years in which the corporation has no earnings. The New Jersey courts were prominent advocates of this interpretation. Under this approach, retained earnings serve to create a dividend credit for preferred stockholders which must be satisfied before dividends can be paid on the common. In **Sanders v. Cuba Railroad Co.**, 21 N.J. 78, 120 A.2d 849 (1956), the Supreme Court of New Jersey (Jacobs, J.) rejected an opportunity to realign itself with the *Wabash Railway* and *Guttmann* decisions:

"This much is quite apparent—if the common stockholders, who generally control the corporation and will benefit most by the passing of the dividends on the preferred stock, may freely achieve that result without any dividend credit consequences, then the preferred stockholders will be substantially at the mercy of others who will be under temptation to act in their own self-interest. See Note, Dividend Rights of Non–Cumulative Preferred Stock, 61 Yale L.J. 245, 251 (1952); Note, Right of Non–Cumulative Preferred Stockholders to Back Dividends Earned But Unpaid, 74 U.Pa.L.Rev. 605, 608 (1926). While such conclusion may sometimes be compelled by the clear contractual arrangements between the parties there is no just reason why our courts should not avoid it whenever the contract is silent or is so general as to leave adequate room for its construction. In any event, New Jersey's doctrine has received wide approval in legal writings and there does not seem to be any present disposition in this court to reject it or limit its sweep in favor of the Supreme Court's approach in the Wabash Railway case."

The case appears to remain good law in New Jersey.

Why would anyone buy non-cumulative preferred stock? The form does survive, but in venture capital finance, discussed infra, Section C, where the preferred stockholder either takes or shares control with the firm's insiders.

(3) Issuer Tender and Exchange Offers to Holders of Preferred in Arrears

Eisenberg v. Chicago Milwaukee Corp.

Delaware Court of Chancery, 1987.
537 A.2d 1051.

■ JACOBS, VICE-CHANCELLOR

[The Chicago Milwaukee (CMC) had effectively sold off most of its business in 1985 and thereafter held approximately $300 million in cash and real estate appraised at $90 million while it sought a new business or businesses. It had outstanding approximately 2.5 million shares of common stock and 464,000 shares of noncumulative preferred stock with an annual dividend preference of $5 per share (approximately $2.34 million annually) and an aggregate liquidation preference of approximately $46,400,000. The company declined to pay dividends on the preferred during the years in which it sought a new line of business. By reason of the cessation of preferred dividends, the preferred stockholders elected two of the company's ten directors. The eight common stock directors and their affiliates owned no appreciable amount of the preferred, but did own approximately 41 percent of the common stock.

[The preferred stock traded during the period from 1985 to October 16, 1987 at prices ranging between $52.50 and $80.25, gradually declined in price during 1987 and reached its low of $52.50 on October 16. On Black Monday, October 19, 1987, the stock dropped to $42.50. By October 27 the price had declined to $41.50. The directors, deciding to take advantage of the sharp price decline, caused the company to make a tender offer for its preferred stock at $55 per share and announced that the company would move to delist the stock. Holders of the preferred sought to enjoin the tender offer on the grounds that (1) the tender solicitation materials were misleading in failing, among other things, to disclose the conflict of interest of the common stock directors and their purpose to take advantage of the price drop resulting after Black Monday, and (2) the tender offer was improperly coercive.

[On the claim that the materials were misleading, the court started with the premise that the corporation and its directors owed the preferred the "exacting duty of disclosure imposed upon corporate fiduciaries" and found, as claimed by the plaintiffs, that duty not to have been met. On the coercion claim, the court also rested on fiduciary theory and reasoned as follows.]

The plaintiff argues that the Offer is inequitably coercive, because: (i) it was purposefully timed to coincide with the lowest market price for the Preferred since 1983, (ii) the offer occurs against the background of an announced Board policy of not paying dividends, despite CMC's present ability to do so, and (iii) CMC has announced that it intends to seek the delisting of the Preferred shares.

The defendants respond that the Offer, while perhaps "coercive" in the sense that its economic merits may make it more attractive to tender than not to tender, is not "actionably" coercive, because the defendants have committed no wrongful or inequitable coercive act.

In these circumstances the coercion issue is not easy to decide. To be sure, the directors have timed the Offer to coincide with the lowest Preferred stock price levels since 1983. They have also made a business judgment (one that at this stage must be presumed valid) not to pay dividends on, or to redeem, the Preferred. Given those circumstances, Preferred stockholders may perceive, not unreasonably, that unless they tender, they may not realize any return on or value for their investment in the foreseeable future. In that sense the offer does have coercive aspects. And the coercion may be attributed, at least to some extent, to acts of the directors (namely, their timing of the Offer and their no-dividend policy) rather than to market forces alone.

If these were the only relevant circumstances (and if proper disclosure was made of all material facts), the Court would have difficulty concluding, at least on this preliminary record, that the Offer is inequitably coercive. In what sense do corporate directors behave inequitably if they cause the corporation to offer to purchase its own publicly-held shares at a premium above market, even if the market price is at an historic low? So long as all material facts are candidly disclosed, the transaction would appear to be voluntary. The only arguable inequity is that if the offer is successful, it may result in a decrease in the number and market value of the outstanding shares and in the number of shareholders. That state of affairs, in turn, would create the possibility that shares not tendered will be delisted and/or deregistered. However, that possibility and its disclosure in the offering materials, without more, has been held to be not wrongfully coercive. See Klein v. Soundesign Corp., supra, at 8; Fisher v. Plessey Co., 559 F.Supp. 442, 451 (S.D.N.Y.1983).

In this case, however, the defendants have done more than simply acknowledge the possibility of delisting and deregistration; they have told the Preferred stockholders that CMC "*intends to request* delisting of the Shares from the NYSE." (Emphasis added.) It is that disclosure which tips the balance and impels the Court to find that the Offer, even if benignly motivated, operates in an inequitably coercive manner.

CMC's directors are fiduciaries for the Preferred stockholders, whose interests they have a duty to safeguard, consistent with the fiduciary duties owed by those directors to CMC's other shareholders and to CMC itself. Those directors have disclosed that they intend to seek to eliminate a valuable attribute of the Preferred stock, namely, its NYSE listing. That listing is the source of that security's market value, and its elimination will adversely affect the interests of nontendering Preferred shareholders. On what basis are the defendants, as fiduciaries, entitled to do that? Defendants do not claim that they are obliged to seek delisting in order to protect a paramount interest of the corporation or an overriding interest of the common stockholders. What they seem to argue is that the criticized disclosure is not coercive because it is not material, because if the criteria for listing are no longer met, the stock will be delisted automatically, irrespective of and without regard to any action of the directors.

That argument has two infirmities. First, it is inconsistent with the Offer to Purchase, which discloses that if the listing criteria are no longer met, the NYSE "would consider" delisting the shares. That disclosure does not say that delisting will be automatic. Second, if the defendants are correct in their argument that delisting will occur automatically as a matter of law, then they need not disclose that CMC "intends to request delisting." Such a disclosure is unnecessary and, therefore, misleading. The only apparent purpose of such a disclosure would be to induce shareholders to tender by converting a possibility of delisting into a likelihood or certainty. On that basis it must be concluded that the Offer is inequitably coercive.

NOTE: *DENVER TRAMWAY*

In **Barrett v. Denver Tramway Corporation**, 53 F.Supp. 198 (D.Del.1943), affirmed, 146 F.2d 701 (3d Cir.1944), abnormal wartime earnings created a potential source of large dividends for the common stock of Denver Tramway Corporation, dividends that could be distributed only if the arrearages on the preferred could be eliminated. The corporation effectively cancelled the preferred's arrearages by authorizing a new prior preferred stock and offering to exchange two shares of the new stock for each share of the old preferred. The new preferred carried no dividend arrearages. Each prior preferred share carried a liquidation price equal to about one half the sum of the liquidation price plus the arrearage on each old share. Dividends on the new stock were comparably scaled to produce approximately the same dividends on two shares of new preferred as were provided on one share of old. Those holders of old preferred who accepted the offer could expect dividends from the bulging earnings. Those who did not accept the offer remained with their old preferred, whose claims were subordinate to those of the new preferred, and were therefore unable to receive dividends if these new preferred were not fully paid. The common stock gambled on the whip-saw effect to induce the exchange and thus eliminate the arrearage obstacle to the flow of dividends to it—and it won. When dissident holders of old preferred challenged the scheme as unfair (even if technically conforming to the Delaware statute), the court (Leahy, J.) reluctantly held the scheme not to be unfair under Delaware caselaw.

(4) *Board Discretion and Voting Control*

Suppose the holders of a class of cumulative preferred stock gain the right under the charter to elect a majority of the board of directors if the issuer defaults in the payment of six quarterly dividends. The defaults occur and the preferred holders elect themselves to the board. The new board returns the corporation to profitability. But the preferreds' board members never declare the payment of the preferred dividends in arrears. So doing would cause the vote to revert to the common stock and possibly cost them their control. Would the common stockholders at some point have a right to have these board elections declared invalid?

This was the question in **Baron v. Allied Artists Pictures Corp.**, 337 A.2d 653 (Del.Ch.1975). Holders of preferred stock of Allied Artists Pictures had been electing the board for ten years when a class of common holders sought to avoid the election. As of that 1974 election, preferred arrearages exceeded $280,000. A corporation called Kalvex held 52 percent of the preferred and thereby controlled the corporation even though the holding amounted only to 7.5 percent of the total equity. Kalvex nominated the board and top officers of Allied; these nominees drew annual salaries from Allied totalling $402,088, including $100,000 for the president. But Allied also had returned to profitability under Kalvex control, recently having produced hits like *Cabaret* and *Papillon*.

The board had been disabled from paying dividends for a number of years under the terms of a tax deficiency settlement with the IRS. One final payment was pending under this at the time of the 1974 board election. As of the fiscal year ended June 30, 1973, Allied's capital surplus available for dividend payments amounted to only $118,000.

The court sustained the 1974 election, subject to an ultimate limit on the preferred stockholders' hegemony:

"Plaintiff stresses that he is not asking the Court to compel the payment of the dividend arrearages, but only that a new election be held because of the preferred board's allegedly wrongful refusal to do so. * * *

"Plaintiff * * * asks for a ruling that a board of directors elected by preferred shareholders whose dividends are in arrears has an absolute duty to pay off all preferred dividends due and to return control to the common shareholders as soon as funds become legally available for that purpose, regardless of anything else. * * *

"When the yearly hit-and-miss financial history of Allied from 1964 through 1974 is considered along with the Internal Revenue obligation during the same time span, I cannot conclude, as a matter of law, that Allied's board has been guilty of perpetuating itself in office by wrongfully refusing to apply corporate funds to the liquidation of the preferred dividend arrearages and the accelerated payment of the Internal Revenue debt. Thus I find no basis on the record before me to set aside the 1974 annual election and to order a new one through a master appointed by the court.

* * *

"It is clear, however, that Allied's present board does have a fiduciary duty to see that the preferred dividends are brought up to date as soon as possible in keeping with prudent business management.

* * *

"This is particularly true now that the Internal Revenue debt has been satisfied in full and business is prospering. It cannot be permitted indefinitely to plough back all profits in future commitments so as to avoid full satisfaction of the rights of the preferred to their dividends and the otherwise normal right of the common stockholders to elect corporate management. While previous limitations on net income and capital surplus may offer a justification for the past, continued limitations in a time of greatly increased cash flow could well create new issues in the area of business discretion for the future."

3.   CLAIMS TO PRINCIPAL, INCLUDING ARREARAGES

(A) ALTERATION BY AMENDMENT

(1) Liquidation Provisions

The preferred stock contract typically provides that on the "liquidation, dissolution or winding up" of the corporation, the preferred stockholder is entitled to payment of a specified amount before any assets are distributable to common stockholders or to holders of any other junior security. The "principal" amount thus distributable is generally equal to the par value or the amount paid on the original issuance of the preferred stock, but it need not be equal to either. In addition to the "principal" amount of the claim, the preferred stock contract usually entitles the holder to priority of payment of all dividend arrearages on dissolution, and to a premium if the dissolution is voluntary. Payment is usually required to be made in cash.

The protective significance of the liquidation preference is diminished by the fact that as a practical matter the protection offered most likely is sought when it least likely is available—when the enterprise is insolvent. The liquidation preference's protective capacity also is diminished by the narrow scope courts attribute to the typical language in which it is embodied. Thus questions have been raised as to what conduct or acts invoke the liquidation preference, and whether in the given case the liquidation preference triggered is voluntary (with premium) or involuntary. Does the customary language prescribing a preference in the event of any "liquidation, dissolution or winding up," cover the sale of substantially all the assets, so that on such a sale, the preferred class can assert a right to receive distribution of the proceeds, as against the "corporation's" claim to retain the proceeds and engage in new business activities? See Treves v. Menzies, 37 Del.Ch. 330, 142 A.2d 520 (1958); Maffia v. American Woolen Co., 125 F.Supp. 465 (S.D.N.Y.1954); Rothschild International Corporation v. Liggett Group Inc., infra. Or is still other action—e.g., dissolution or distribution of assets—required before the clause is triggered? See Craddock–Terry Co. v. Powell, 181 Va. 417, 25 S.E.2d 363 (1943); Geiger v. American Seeding Machine Co., 124 Ohio St. 222, 177 N.E. 594 (1931).

Similar problems of interpretation arise with respect to whether the conventional language of the liquidation preference clause covers a merger of the preferred stockholder's corporation into another corporation, in which the preferred stockholder and common stockholder of the old corporation each received common stock of the surviving corporation. Compare Petry v. Harwood Electric Co., 280 Pa. 142, 124 A. 302 (1924) with Rothschild Int'l Corp. v. Liggett Group, Inc., infra, Anderson v. Cleveland–Cliffs Iron Co., 87 N.E.2d 384, 394–396 (Ohio C.P.1948) and Adams v. United States Distributing Corp., 184 Va. 134, 149–151, 34 S.E.2d 244, 251–252 (1945). Can the charter lawfully provide that, notwithstanding express statutory provisions authorizing and prescribing the consequences of mergers and sales of assets, such transactions trigger the preferred stock liquidation preference? Compare Jones v. St. Louis Structural Steel Co., 267 Ill.App. 576 (1932); Langfelder v. Universal Laboratories, Inc., 163 F.2d 804 (3d Cir.1947). The answer in Delaware is yes. See the cases in the Note on drafting after Rothschild Int'l Corp. v. Liggett Group, Inc., infra.

Compare the constituencies authorized to vote on a merger (RMBCA § 11.04; DCL § 251; NYBCL § 903); sale of assets (RMBCA § 12.02; DCL § 271; NYBCL § 909); dissolution (RMBCA § 14.02(e); DCL § 275; NYBCL §§ 1001–1002), and amendment (RMBCA §§ 10.03(e), 10.04; NYBCL §§ 803, 804; DCL § 242(b)(2)).

Goldman v. Postal Telegraph

United States District Court, District of Delaware, 1943.
52 F.Supp. 763.

■ Leahy, District Judge. Diversity and the requisite amount establish jurisdiction.

* * *

Postal Telegraph, Inc., incorporated under the laws of Delaware in 1939 (herein called "Postal"), agreed to transfer to Western Union Telegraph Company (herein called "Western Union"), another Delaware corporation, all its assets. At the time of the agreement plaintiff owned 500 shares of non-cumulative preferred stock of Postal which, by the terms of Postal's certificate of incorporation, entitled all preferred stockholders to a payment of $60 a share on liquidation before any distribution could be made to its common stockholders. On July 5, 1943, defendant Postal proposed to its stockholders three resolutions authorizing (1) the sale of all its assets to Western Union, conditioned upon the approval by Postal's stockholders of an amendment to its certificate of incorporation referred to in (2); (2) the amendment of Postal's certificate of incorporation so as to provide that the holders of defendant's non-cumulative preferred stock would receive in lieu of $60 per share on liquidation one share of Western Union B stock;* and (3) formal dissolution of Postal. At the stockholders' meeting held on August 10, 1943, these resolutions were passed by a requisite vote over plaintiff's express objection. This suit followed.

The Postal–Western Union agreement provides that for the transfer of all the assets of Postal to Western Union, Postal will receive as part consideration 308,124 shares of Class B stock of Western Union. The entire amount of Class B stock to be received from Western Union will have a value substantially less than the aggregate liquidation preference of the preferred stock of Postal. Consequently, under its certificate of incorporation Postal's common stockholders—whose equity is deeply under water—would be entitled to receive nothing if ordinary liquidation occurred. Subject to various adjustments which do not have my immediate attention, Western Union will assume approximately $10,800,000 of Postal's liabilities. Postal's economic position is shown by its steady losses, aggregating over $13,500,000 from February 1, 1940, to May 31, 1943. These losses have been financed, in part, by advances from the Reconstruction Finance

---

* [Ed. Note] The amendment added the following to the provisions of the certificate of incorporation dealing with the rights of preferred stockholders:

"Provided, however, that notwithstanding the provisions of the next preceding paragraph in this subdivision (e) contained, if substantially all of the assets of the Corporation or of its operating subsidiaries are sold to the Western Union Telegraph Company then upon any liquidation, dissolution or winding up of the affairs of the Corporation the holders of

shares of the Non–Cumulative Preferred Stock shall be entitled to receive for each share out of the assets of the Corporation (in lieu of the cash payments in said next preceding paragraph specified) one share of the Class B Stock of the Western Union Telegraph Company before any distribution or payment shall be made to the holders of shares of Common Stock; but they shall be entitled to no further or other participation in any distribution or payment."

Corporation. In facing further corporate existence, two courses were open to Postal: (a) To submit to government ownership or (b) to seek some type of merger with or absorption by Western Union.

In order to complete the proposed transfer of assets to Western Union, the vote of a majority of the outstanding stock of Postal was required under the Delaware law, sec. 65. See Rev.Code of Delaware of 1935, c. 65, Sec. 2097. Postal's outstanding preferred was 256,769.9 and the number of shares of common was 1,027,076.6. Hence, if all the preferred voted in favor of the plan, it would still be necessary to obtain the affirmative vote of approximately 400,000 shares of common. In order to obtain such vote, Postal's directors determined it advisable that the preferred's rights on liquidation be modified, so as to provide that out of the 308,124 shares of Class B stock of Western Union to be received by Postal, 256,770 shares would be distributed share for share for each of Postal's preferred and the balance of the Class B—51,354 shares—would be distributed to Postal's common stockholders, which was to be in the ratio of 1/20 of a share of Class B Western Union stock for each share of common stock of Postal.

As part of the plan, Western Union would also change its present 1,045,592 shares of capital stock into an equal number of shares of Class A stock without par value, which stock would be entitled to a non-cumulative dividend of $2 per share in each year before any dividends could be paid upon the Class B stock. After such dividend payment, the Class A and Class B stock are to participate on an equal basis in any dividends.

* * * Plaintiff here seeks, on behalf of himself and all other non-assenting shareholders, to enforce the liquidating rights which he contends are secured to him by the certificate of incorporation of Postal prior to the adoption of the resolution to amend it under Sec. 26. Defendant moved to dismiss on the ground that the complaint failed to state a cause of action.

* * *

[Plaintiff contends] that defendant could not agree to sell its assets conditioned upon the power of the corporation to amend its certificate of incorporation as a part of the transaction. There is no merit to this view. When the statute provides the amendment may be made from time to time, when and as desired, it means the amendment may be effectuated at any time; and there is no limitation with respect to the circumstances or the exigencies of the situation upon the exercise of the power. See Havender v. Federal United Corp., 23 Del.Ch. 104, 2 A.2d 143; 11 A.2d 331; Hartford Accident, etc., Co. v. Dickey Clay Co., Del.Ch., 24 A.2d 315.

Craddock–Terry Co. v. Powell, 181 Va. 417, 25 S.E.2d 363, relied on by plaintiff, is distinguishable. In the Craddock & Co. case the corporation sought, in connection with the contract for the sale of its assets, to force the minority to take shares in the buyer corporation which were of a lesser value than the seller corporation's stockholders were entitled to receive under the liquidation provisions of the latter's certificate of incorporation. In that case, no attempt was made to pursue the statutory provisions for amendment; an attempt was made to accomplish by the contract of sale itself the alteration of the seller corporation's stockholders' preference rights. It is one thing to alter a preference pursuant to valid statutory authority; it is another to ignore a grant of power and attempt to accomplish the same result without the benefit of statutory reclassification.

In the case at bar, I see no reason why a Delaware corporation cannot agree to sell its assets conditioned upon the seller corporation amending its certificate of incorporation as a part of the transaction. In fact, such a condition may well become a part of the urgent necessities of a particular transaction. Here, for example, 256,770 shares of preferred, if entitled to $60 a share on dissolution, would be entitled to receive approximately $15,000,000 on liquidation. The present value of the Class B stock of Western Union to be received by Postal in exchange for its assets, at about $19 a share, admittedly amounts to only $4,888,000. If the preferential right of $60 a share remains unaltered, it would be impossible in this case to obtain the vote of the common stockholders in favor of the sale and dissolution, because there could not possibly be any rational basis, under the circumstances, for the common stock voting in approval. One thing is certain. Nothing can be accomplished, either in law or in life, by calling the recalcitrants names. The reality of the situation confronting Postal's management called for some inducement to be offered the common stockholders to secure their favorable vote for the plan. It seems to me of little moment whether that approval was voiced at one or two meetings. The fact is something had to induce the common stockholders to come along. This court and the Delaware courts have recognized the strategic position of common stock to hamper the desires of the real owners of the equity of a corporation, and the tribute which common stock exacts for its vote under reclassification and reorganization. Cf. MacCrone v. American Capital Corp., D.C.Del., 51 F.Supp. 462, at page 469; and MacFarlane v. North American Cement Corporation, 16 Del.Ch. 172, 180, 157 A. 396. And, as stated, separate meetings of Postal's stockholders could have been called to (a) amend under Sec. 26 and (b) approve a sale of assets under Sec. 65; for purposes of convenience and the saving of expense, both steps were taken at one meeting. Nothing in the Delaware law forbids such a procedure. Secs. 26 and 65 contain no limitations on the time or the necessary circumstances which must exist for the exercise of the grant of majority power given under the statutes, except the procedural ritual contained in those statutes.

Accordingly, I conclude for the reasons hereinabove mentioned that defendant's motion to dismiss has merit. A form of decree for my consideration may be submitted upon notice.

NOTE: JUNIOR HOLD UPS

1. *Orban v. Field.*

Like *Goldman*, **Orban v. Field**, 1997 WL 153831 (Del.Ch.), involves a contest between the preferred and the common respecting the division of the proceeds of sale of a distressed preferred stock issuer. But in *Orban* the balance of voting power between preferred and common is reversed. Significantly, the result in the case also changes.

Before the events in question in the case, the issuer, Office Mart, had three series of stock outstanding. The series and voting rights (each share carried one vote) were distributed as follows: Series A convertible preferred (23 percent), Series B convertible preferred (63 percent), and common (14 percent). The preferred was held by a small number of institutional investors. The overwhelming majority of the common was held by the plaintiff, Orban. Orban had served as the company's promoter at its start up in 1987 and purchased his stock at that time for $15,000. The Series A preferred was initially issued at start up for $2.95 million. The Series B was initially issued in 1988 for $17.08 million.

Office Mart proved to be chronically short of capital. In 1990, the company met this need by offering to its shareholders on a pro rata basis a package of three year secured notes and common stock purchase warrants carrying a right to acquire 40 percent of its fully diluted equity. A group of Series B holders accepted this offer and became creditors of the company. But their notes quickly fell into arrears and in 1991 more warrants were issued to the noteholders in exchange for a deferral of interest payments.

A more elaborate recapitalization followed later in 1991. Pursuant to this, the notes were canceled and replaced by a combination of new Series C nonconvertible preferred and common stock (2.1 million shares constituting more than 50 percent of the outstanding common stock), along with a reduction of the exercise price of the existing common stock purchase warrants. As a result of this, the pre-recapitalization common had its percentage ownership reduced from 14 percent to 3 percent (leaving Orban with 2.54 percent of the votes), and the Series A and Series B preferred had their percentages reduced to 10.5 percent and 36.9 percent.

The 1991 recapitalization ran into a technical snag. Office Mart did not have a large enough number of authorized shares in its charter to support the issue of the new shares and to provide a reserve of shares for the ownership rights created by the new convertible preferred and warrants. The board decided to forego the expense of a charter amendment and instead to do a proportionate reduction in the number of shares outstanding. Orban subsequently was asked to surrender certificates for 874,708 shares. Orban failed to return these certificates, however.

Office Mart's ongoing search for capital next led to acquisition negotiations. A stock-for-stock merger into Staples, Inc. structured as a tax free pooling of interests was announced early in 1992. The merger consideration was 1.093 million shares of Staples common worth around $35 million. The Staples common was to be distributed to the Series A, B, and C preferred in accordance with their preferences. Since the preferences exhausted the consideration, the common would receive nothing. For tax purposes, the merger agreement required the approval of 90 percent of each class of stock. Orban's unreturned certificates created a problem at this point. He had no incentive to vote in favor of the merger but literally could be deemed to hold more than 10 percent of the outstanding common. Orban seized the moment and demanded $4 million in exchange for the certificates. The board refused, and instead engineered the exercise of a sufficient number of existing warrants to dilute Orban's holding to under 10 percent. This was achieved by means of (a) a charter amendment increasing the authorized shares, (b) exercise price reductions respecting the warrants, and (c) a non pro rata redemption of Series C preferred. The Series C redemption siphoned $3 million to the warrant holders to provide them with the cash exercise price. The cash thus came right back to the company when the warrants were exercised.

The result, when the shooting stopped, was that the entire merger consideration went to those who, prior to the recapitalization, had held Series A and B preferred and notes and the simultaneous approval of the merger by 90 percent of the common stock. Significantly, however, the recapitalization had no effect on the distribution of the merger proceeds—assuming respect for preferences, the common would have had no merger proceeds had the recapitalization never occurred.

The theory of Orban's subsequent lawsuit was that, even though the common stock was under water, Orban's stock had a value because of the requirement of a 90 percent vote, and that the destruction of that value by the board's dilutive maneuvering amounted to a breach of fiduciary duty to the common. On motion for summary judgment, Chancellor Allen ruled for the defendants, reasoning as follows:

"For purposes of this motion for summary judgment, I will assume that the business judgment rule is not applicable to the actions challenged by Mr. Orban's breach of fiduciary duty claim. Unquestionably in this instance the board of directors exercised corporate power—most pointedly in authorizing a non-pro-rata redemption of preferred shares for the purpose of funding the exercise by holders of preferred stock of warrants to buy common stock. That act was directed against the common stock who found themselves with a certain leverage because of the requirements for pooling treatment. A board may certainly deploy corporate power against its own shareholders in some circumstances—the greater good justifying the action—but when it does, it should be required to demonstrate that it acted both in good faith and reasonably. * * *

" * * * [I]t is important to note that there is no evidence, or even remaining allegation, that the November recapitalization was part of a scheme to deprive the common stockholders of consideration in the subsequent merger. The recapitalization was legally effectuated by the Board, validly altering the existing ownership structure of the company.[25] Certainly, when viewed as an isolated event, the recapitalization [was] authorized appropriately, and if it were to be tested under a fairness test, it would satisfy that standard. * * *

"Once Orban attempted to use a potential power to deprive the transaction of pooling treatment, the Board was inevitably forced to decide whether it would support the common stock's (Mr. Orban's) effort to extract value from the preferred position or whether it would seek to accomplish the negotiated transaction, which it believed to be the transaction at the highest available price.

"Certainly in some circumstances a board may elect (subject to the corporation's answering in contract damages) to repudiate a contractual obligation where to do so provides a net benefit to the corporation. * * * But it would be bizarre to take this fact of legal life so far as to assert, as Mr. Orban must, that the Board had a duty to common stock to refrain from recognizing the corporation's legal obligations to its other classes of voting securities.

"To resolve this situation, the Board decided not to negotiate with Mr. Orban, but rather to effectuate the transaction as intended, respecting the preferential rights of the preferred stockholders. In my opinion, it cannot be said that the Board breached a duty of loyalty in making this decision. Whereas the preferred stockholders had existing legal preferences, the common stockholders had no legal right to a portion of the merger consideration under Delaware law or the corporate charter. The Staples' transaction appeared reasonably to be the best available transaction. Mr. Orban's threat to impede the realization of that transaction by the corporation

---

25. The recapitalization was approved by Mr. Orban as a director and ratified by a majority of Office Mart's shareholders. As was discussed above, this Court has already determined that Mr. Orban had no legal right to a class vote on the recapitalization. Ordinarily, the approval of disinterested directors and shareholder ratification would provide the recapitalization with the protection of the business judgment rule.

was thwarted by legally permissible action that was measured and appropriate in the circumstances. * * * "

Questions: Were there any contract rights to the preferred that would have been breached by an allocation to the common? Does the court assert that the preferred had a *right* to have its liquidation preference satisfied first out of the proceeds of the merger? If the charter did not provide explicitly that a merger should be treated as a liquidating event, would not the board have had the option of allocating some of the merger consideration to the common? Consider *Rothschild v. Liggett Group*, infra, and *Dalton v. American Investment Co.*, infra.

2. *Burton v. Exxon.*

Compare **Burton v. Exxon Corp.**, 583 F.Supp. 405 (S.D.N.Y.1984). Here a controlling stockholder, holding all the common and an entire issue of first preferred, sought to dissolve the corporation, and a shareholder holding second preferred sought to enjoin the dissolution on the ground that continuance of the corporation eventually would result in dividend payments on the second preferred. Exxon held all of the first preferred stock and 90 percent of the common stock of Eurgasco, a corporation formed during the 1930s to explore for oil and gas in Eastern Europe. Eurgasco had never paid any dividends on any of its stock. By 1977, dividend arrearages on the first preferred amounted to $6.5 million. Plaintiff owned shares of an issue of second preferred stock on which arrearages totaled $2.3 million in 1977.

Eurgasco's only reason for continued existence was the prosecution of claims for compensation of assets nationalized by the Hungarian government after World War II. Between 1977 and 1980, Eurgasco received $9 million in total payment of these claims and earned $823,000 of interest income on these funds. Between 1977 and 1980, Eurgasco declared a series of large dividends, all of which were paid in compliance with its charter to Exxon as the holder of the first preferred. By the time the stream of claims payments stopped in 1980, Eurgasco had $2.8 million left. Its board, comprised of Exxon nominees, determined to dissolve it. This would result in the entire $2.8 million being paid to Exxon as first preferred holder, since the stock still had $2.8 million of dividend arrearages plus a liquidation preference of $2.3 million. But the votes of two-thirds of the holders of the second preferred were required to approve the dissolution, and most of these holders either voted no or failed to return proxies. As a result, Exxon filed a petition for judicial dissolution in the Delaware courts. Plaintiff brought a federal action to enjoin the dissolution proceeding, claiming breaches of fiduciary duty.

The court, applying *Sinclair v. Levien*, infra, Part IV. A, held that the dividend payments constituted self dealing on the part of Exxon. The test, it said, "is not whether the minority stockholders were entitled to the item transferred but whether the minority stockholders were excluded from, or damaged by, the transfer * * * to the * * * majority stockholder." The fact that the charter did not entitle plaintiffs to dividend payments did not block the self dealing finding, but was "important only in so far as deciding whether the dividend decision was intrinsically fair."

The plaintiff claimed that the dividends were unfair on the theory that, given prevailing interest rates in the late 1970s, the rate of return on reinvested funds exceeded the rate of arrearage accruals, permitting Eurgasco to reinvest the funds so as to cause the eventual payment of arrearages on both issues of preferred. The court rejected the claim and ruled that the dividends were intrinsically fair, and that the plaintiff's case against the dissolution proceeding accordingly was moot. The court gave two reasons. First, high returns on reinvested funds were not certain at the time the decision to make the dividends was made in 1977. At the rate levels prevailing in 1977, it would have taken until 2024 to pay down all the arrearages. That the higher rates prevailing in 1978–1983 would have brought forward the payoff date to 1991 did not change matters. Second, the board owed fiduciary duties to the first preferred as well as the second preferred. Had the board decided to retain the funds, the first preferred might have successfully claimed a breach of fiduciary duty. Citing *Baron v. Allied Artists,* the court stated that "[i]n keeping with prudent business management, the board of directors does have a fiduciary duty to see that preferred dividend arrearages are brought up to date as soon as possible."

Suppose you were the judge presiding over Exxon's Delaware proceeding to dissolve Eurgasco. How would you rule?

(2) *Redemption Provisions*

Corporation statutes authorize the inclusion in the charter of power to redeem classes of stock. See RMBCA § 6.01, NYBCL § 512, DCL § 151(b). The power to redeem or "call" the stock is the power to compel the stock's return in exchange for cash or property. It is no more an inevitable incident of an issue of preferred than it is of an issue of common, and must be provided for expressly in the charter. The power to redeem should not be confused with a stockholder "put"—a unilateral option in the stockholder to compel repurchase either as a direct obligation or as an upstream conversion. Whether the right is in the issuer or the holder, its exercise will be subject to the statutory constraints on corporate distributions which might impair capital or be made from sources other than an appropriate surplus. See, e.g., Model Business Corporation Act (MBCA) §§ 66, 67, NYBCL § 513, DCL § 160, 243. A redemption or put exercise also can be constrained by contractual restrictions on distributions.

When is an issuer likely to exercise a right to redeem a preferred issue? The answer to this question tracks the answer to the same question respecting the right to redeem debt. From the issuer's point of view (and, therefore, that of the common stock) the fixed claim on earnings represented by preferred stock becomes onerous when interest rates fall below the rates implied in the preferred's dividend preference. At that point, it may be in the corporation's interest to replace the outstanding preferred stock with a senior security carrying the lower, current rate of interest or dividends. In the alternative, the redemption power may be invoked to benefit the common stock by relieving the corporation of other obligations to the preferred, such as business covenants in the preferred stock contract. Or, tax considerations may lead the issuer to refund an issue of preferred with an issue of debt. Finally, the redemption power enables the corporation to compel, or to frustrate, the exercise of a conversion privilege.

There is no legal requirement for the redemption price to be any minimum amount, but as a practical matter it is not likely to be less than the issue price of the stock. Indeed, to the extent that the stock represents a desirable investment when issued, and will only be redeemed when it represents an even more desirable investment, the holder regards the corporation's unilateral power to redeem with disfavor. Accordingly, the redemption price generally includes a premium above the issue price to compensate the investor for the loss of a desirable investment.

Finally, it should be noted that, paralleling the structure of debt contracts, preferred stock contracts often contain sinking fund provisions—scheduled mandatory redemptions of stated numbers of shares. These provisions, like redemption provisions, are subject to legal constraints on corporate distributions. Sinking fund preferred has been much more common (along with floating rate preferred) since the late 1970s, when rising and volatile interest rates caused perpetual preferred issues to have a poor market reception. See Gombola and Ogden, Effects of a Sinking Fund on Preferred Stock Marketability: A Probit Analysis, 27 Q.J.Bus.Econ. 41 (1988) (reporting that sinking fund provisions enhance the marketability of preferred). For a look at the predicament of a holder of perpetual preferred issued in the early 1960s—a period of low interest rates—in the late 1970s and early 1980s—a period of high rates, see Dalton v. American Investment Co., infra.

Bowman v. Armour & Co.   *(reversed)*

Superior Court, Cook County, 1959.

■ Opinion of SBARBARO, J.

On January 11, 1955, plaintiff, Johnston A. Bowman, brought this action against the defendants for a declaratory judgment that an amendment to Armour's articles of incorporation and action taken pursuant thereto was illegal, unfair and unconstitutional. * * * The amendment in question, which was duly presented to Armour's stockholders on December 7, 1954, changed the redemption provisions of Armour's $6 Cumulative Convertible Prior Preferred Stock (herein called "Prior Stock") from $115 per share plus accumulated dividends to the date of redemption to a price of $120 per share payable in 5% debentures of a like principal amount maturing on November 1, 1984, and one warrant for the purchase of one share of common stock of the Company. This amendment also waived the preemptive rights of the common stock as to the shares to be issued upon the exercise of these warrants. The stockholders adopted this amendment by the affirmative vote of the holders of 352,922 shares of Prior Stock, or 70.6% of the 500,000 shares of Prior Stock authorized and outstanding on that date, and 81.7% of the shares of common stock outstanding on that date.

The evidence showed that the amendment was adopted as part of a plan for the retirement of the Prior Stock, and the proxy material furnished to the stockholders stated that if the amendment were adopted, the Company would promptly issue its notice of redemption in order to effectuate the plan. Thus, in accordance with the articles of incorporation as amended by the stockholders, the Board of Directors of the Company, at a meeting held on December 7, 1954, after the stockholders' meeting, authorized the issuance of the debentures and warrants, called the Prior Stock for redemption on December 21, 1954, and authorized the issuance of a notice of such redemption to each Prior Stockholder. * * *

The rights of the Prior Stockholders were determined by a contract, the terms of which are found in the articles of incorporation of the

Company and in the provisions of the Illinois Business Corporation Act which was in force at the time when the Prior Stock was issued. Tennant versus Epstein, 356 Ill. 26, 189 N.E. 864 (1934). Thus the issue is drawn: Did the Act authorize the amendment in question? For the same contract creating a right may, by other terms and conditions, make the right defeasible by appropriate action of the stockholders. Plaintiffs are bound by their contract and cannot be heard to question action taken in accordance therewith, whether such action be taken by the stockholders or by the Company. Western Foundry Co. versus Wicker, 403 Ill. 260, 85 N.E.2d 722, 8 A.L.R.2d 878 (1949).

"The rights of the holders of the preferred stock—their so-called preemptive rights, their rights to retain their shares as against a call thereof, and their rights as to dividends—are all purely contractual. If no term of the contract authorizes a change in such rights as originally stated, then they cannot be changed. Statutes in existence when the stock is issued (and perhaps also those in existence when stock is acquired by individual shareholders) are, however, a part of the contract, and if such statutes authorize a change, then any seemingly absolute statement of such rights in other parts of the contract necessarily is to be read as subject to the changes so authorized, and such rights cannot properly be described as 'vested' in any sense which implies that they are not subject to such changes. That principle is plain and elementary." Zobel versus American Locomotive Co., 44 N.Y.S.2d 33, 35–36 (S.Ct.N.Y.1943).

Section 52 of the Business Corporation Act provides, in part:

"Right to Amend Articles of Incorporation: A corporation may amend its articles of incorporation, from time to time, in any and as many respects as may be desired, provided that its articles of incorporation as amended contain only such provisions as might be lawfully contained in original articles of incorporation if made at the time of making such amendment, and, if a change in shares or an exchange or reclassification of shares is to be made, such provisions as may be necessary to effect such change, exchange or reclassification as may be desired and is permitted by this Act.

"In particular, and without limitation upon such general power of amendment, a corporation may amend its articles of incorporation, from time to time, so as: * * * (g) To change the designation of all or any part of its shares, whether issued or unissued, and to change the preferences, qualifications, limitations, restrictions, and the special or relative rights in respect of all or any part of its shares, whether issued or unissued."

Section 14 of the Act provides, in part:

"Authorized Shares. Each corporation shall have power to create and issue the number of shares stated in its articles of incorporation. Such shares may be divided into one or more classes, any or all of which classes may consist of shares with par value or shares without par value, with such designations, preferences, qualifications, limitations, restrictions and such special or relative rights as shall be stated in the articles of incorporation." (This section goes on to set forth, "without limiting the authority herein contained," certain classes of stock which a corporation may issue.)

It is my opinion that Section 52(g), especially when read together with the introductory paragraphs of Sections 14 and 52 quoted above, clearly authorize the adoption of the amendment by Armour's stockholders. In adopting Section 52, the General Assembly used the broadest language at its disposal to allow amendments to the articles of incorporation of Illinois companies. I do not see how I can carve out from this broad grant of authority the action taken by Armour and its stockholders in 1954. A plain mandate from the Legislature may not be treated so lightly by the judiciary. * * *

The rule that a person buying into a corporation does so with the assumed knowledge that his contract may be changed by appropriate action of the stockholders is not a harsh rule. It is one of the fundamental concepts of Illinois corporate law that protection against arbitrary action is found in the requirement that a two-thirds majority of those affected by the amendment must vote in favor of it in order to have it adopted. This may result in a form of paternalism as charged by plaintiffs, but to hold otherwise would be to ask the judiciary to indulge in a judicial paternalism that would be limitless.

* * *

Next presented is plaintiff's contention that even if the plan may be said to have been authorized by the literal expressions of the Business Corporation Act, I should declare it ineffective as to them because it is unfair and contrary to equity and good conscience. They cite the well-known rule of law that the exercise of a statutory grant of power is always subject to the historical process of an equity court to judge whether there has been an oppressive exercise of the power granted. About this rule there can be no question, if it is properly understood and applied. The rule in Illinois, as in most other states, is that a recapitalization effected in accordance with power conferred by a corporation act may not be interfered with unless actual or constructive fraud is proved. Western Foundry Co. versus Wicker, supra; Kreicker versus Naylor Pipe Company, 374 Ill. 364, 29 N.E.2d 502 (1940); see Hofeller versus General Candy Corporation, 275 Ill.App. 89 (1934). And when fraud such as this is urged as a basis for upsetting a recapitalization, it must be of such a nature as to impel the conclusion that it emanated from acts of bad faith or reckless indifference to the rights of others interested, rather than from an honest error of judgment. Barrett versus Denver Tramway Corporation, 146 F.2d 701, 706–707 (3d Cir.1944), and cases therein cited. This again may be traced to a common sense and democratic concept that barring unusual circumstances not here present, stockholders of a corporation know what is in their best interest. However, since the fairness of this action by the Company has been so strongly assailed and so vigorously defended, I feel I should discuss the evidence on this subject.

From the elaborate testimony and stipulations introduced by the parties, the following facts appear:

(1) Armour has had for many years and undoubtedly will have for many years in the future a heavy long-term debt which requires substantial annual interest and sinking fund payments.*

* [Ed. Note] According to the Illinois Supreme Court opinion, infra, in 1954, prior to the proposed plan of recapitalization, Armour's capital structure (in thousands of dollars) contained:

Long Term Debt	$124,699
Prior Stock	50,000
Common Stock	20,329
Capital and Paid in Surplus	33,619
Earned Surplus	134,079
	$362,726

(2) Armour has had for many years and undoubtedly will have for many years in the future a need to spend substantial amounts of money each year for modernization and maintenance of its plants as well as for desirable diversification.

(3) Inflation required Armour to invest more and more funds into its working capital. This condition has existed for many years and will undoubtedly continue in the future.

(4) The earnings of Armour have been sporadic.**

(5) As a result of these factors, there was a shortage of funds with which to conduct the company's business. This fact is further testified to by the extensive current bank loans which the Company has had outstanding ever since 1946.

(6) Because of this shortage of funds, the dividend payments on the Prior Stock were often omitted, and there were dividends in arrears for seventeen of the twenty years during which the Prior Stock was outstanding. As of November 1, 1954, there were arrearages on the Prior Stock of $18.50 per share.*** Courts are not unaware of the problems posed by

** [Ed. Note] Armour's net income, as disclosed in appellee's brief in the Illinois Supreme Court and Moody's Manual of Industrials was as follows (in thousands of dollars):

Year	Total	Per Share of Common	Year	Total	Per Share of Common
1945	$ 9,172	$1.41	1953	10,339	1.81
1946	30,291	4.27	1954	1,557	.35
1947	30,950	4.91	1955	10,108	2.49
1948	(1,966)	(1.22)	1956	13,867	3.60
1949	588	(.60)	1957	3,370	.56
1950	19,039	3.94	1958	5,560	1.19
1951	16,029	3.20	1959	14,067	2.73
1952	7,140	1.02	1960	16,221	3.10

*** [Ed. Note] The history of Armour's dividend payments is as follows (from appellee's brief and Moody's Manual of Industrials):

	Preferred		Common
	Dividends Paid	Arrearages	Cash Div. Paid
1945	$ 6.00	$28.50	—
1946	9.50	25.00	—
1947	31.00	—	—
1948	6.00	—	$.90
1949	3.00	3.00	—
1950	—	9.00	—
1951	6.00	9.00	—
1952	3.00	12.00	—
1953	6.00	12.00	—
1954	—	18.00	—
1955 to 1959			None

continuing arrearages in preferred stock dividends. For example, in Zogel versus American Locomotive Co. supra, the court said, at page 35:

"The existence of a large amount of unpaid cumulative dividends may well be and in many cases is detrimental to the interests of a company, and no showing is here made which enables the court to say that that is not true in this case."

Again, in Hottenstein v. York Ice Machinery Corporation, 136 F.2d 944, 952–953 (3d Cir.1943), the court said: "As a practical matter we know that it is difficult to refinance corporate indebtedness when there are heavy arrearages of accumulated dividends outstanding. A corporation so situated reasonably may expect litigation and its concomitant miseries."

(7) During the twenty years when the Prior Stock was outstanding, the common stock received a total of $1.60 per share in dividends. The Company was faced with two unhappy groups of stockholders.

These problems had been under consideration by the officers and directors of the Company for at least several years prior to 1954. In early 1954, Wertheim & Co., through Milton Steinbach, was commissioned by the President of the Company to analyze the plans which had been submitted by stockholders and to devise a plan of recapitalization which would alleviate the Company's financial difficulties. They arrived at this plan which was presented to the Board of Directors (in substantially the same form as ultimately adopted) in September of 1954. The Board acted upon it with the results herein set forth.

It appears that the plan of recapitalization had the following effects on the Company:

(1) The plan will result in more funds becoming available to the Company because of a tax saving of up to $1,560,000 annually. This tax saving occurs because of the different tax treatment given to interest on debentures as compared with dividends on preferred stock.

(2) The plan will result in additional equity capital being invested in the Company upon the exercise of the warrants. Testimony showed that $2,250,000 or more has already been received by the Company from this source and that up to $8,000,000 total may be similarly received.

(3) The elimination of the accrued dividends and conversion possibility (about which more will be said later) benefitted the company and placed the common stock in a better position to enable it to reflect in market value the earnings of the company. This will help the common to become a fit vehicle for equity financing and acquisitions in the future.*

It is my opinion, therefore, that the plan of recapitalization adopted by Armour resulted in an improvement both in the capital structure of the

---

* [Ed. Note] Appellee's brief in the Illinois Supreme Court urged the fairness of the recapitalization in large part as a predicate to raising equity capital in the future. The brief said:

"Armour could not have raised additional capital through new long-term debt because the restrictive provisions of the existing debt would prevent * * * Armour from incurring any additional

Company and in the operating end of the Company. This was the main reason for its adoption. I turn now to analyze the changes wrought by the plan on the former Prior Stockholder, comparing the one share of Prior Stock he held before the adoption of the plan with the $120 of debentures and one warrant he held after.

(1) His annual return from his investment is unchanged, but there is a much greater assurance of payment now because interest must be paid on the debentures if earned, but payment of dividends was a discretionary act on the part of the Board of Directors. Also, the coverage is greater on the debentures: Armour had to earn $6,250,000 before taxes to pay dividends on the Par Stock in full, but it has to earn only $3,000,000 before taxes to pay interest on the debentures in full.

(2) The holders of the Prior Stock had no right to return of capital except at Armour's option. On the other hand, the debentures will mature on November 1, 1984, and there are elaborate sinking fund provisions to protect this maturity.

(3) One share of Prior Stock could be converted into six shares of common stock at the option of the holder. This right of conversion was terminated on December 21, 1954, and the debentures are not convertible.

debt with a maturity of more than one year, except subordinated debt, and except certain deferred payment obligations for the purchase price of property.

"Prior to the plan of recapitalization, Armour could not have raised additional capital by common stock financing without engaging in an unorthodox financing of the most flagrant nature due to the low price at which the common stock would have had to be sold. Armour's shareholders would not have permitted Armour to try to raise additional capital by this means.

" * * *

"A major purpose of the plan was to increase the value of the common stock by improvement of Armour's capital structure so that ultimately it could be used as a means of equity financing. Armour believed this objective could be accomplished by the combined elimination of the conversion privilege and existing preferred dividend arrearages, and by the benefit obtained from tax saving.

* * * [T]he conversion privilege of six for one threatened a radical dilution of the common stock from approximately four million to seven million shares and that this possibility operated as depressant on the value of the common stock.

* * *

"In addition to this possible use of the common stock for equity financing in the future, the warrants issued in redemption of the Prior Stock resulted in Armour raising additional equity capital. Each warrant gave the holder thereof an option to purchase one share of common stock at the following prices: $12.50 per share during the years 1954–1956, $15 per share during the years 1957–1959, $17.50 per share during the years 1960–1961, and $20.00 per share during the years 1962–1964. Between the date of issuance of these warrants and the trial below, $2,250,000 in additional equity capital had been raised by the exercise of these warrants and there existed the possibility that a total of $6,000,000 would be raised by this means."

According to Moody's Manual of Industrials, Armour's assets (per books) decreased from some $470,000,000 at the end of 1954 to some $398,000,000 at the end of 1960. During that period, no new long term debt was incurred and no new equity capital was sought, or (except by reason of exercise of employee stock options and the warrants issued in the recapitalization) obtained.

The evidence showed that no share of Prior Stock had ever been converted into common; that at no time could such conversion have ever taken place without loss to the holder in terms of market value; and that at all times since the adoption of the plan, the new package received for one share of Prior Stock could have been sold and more than six shares of common bought with the proceeds on the open market.* I am convinced that the conversion privilege was never realistic or attractive.** The directors knew this and the stockholders apparently did also. The directors were also of the opinion that the conversion privilege operated to depress the value of the common stock and to prevent its use as a vehicle for acquisition and equity financing. I cannot find that the removal of the conversion right was in any respects unfair.

* [Ed. Note] The market prices of Armour's common and preferred stocks and 5% debentures and warrants were as follows (according to Moody's Manual for Industrials):

	H L 1960	H L 1959	H L 1958	H L 1957
Debentures	90–81⅜	86½–79	80–69½	78½–62½
Common	42⅜–29	37⅜–23	24⅝–12⅛	16⅝–10⅜
Warrants	29½–15¼	22⅜–11⅜	12⅞–4⅝	6½–3½

	H L 1956	H L 1955	H L 1954
Debentures	87½–70¼	85–78¼	80½–77½
Common	24–15¾	18–13½	14⅞–8⅝
Warrants	11⅞–4¼	8¼–5½	8–4⅝
Preferred	–	–	106¾–85¾

During 1951–1953 the preferred stock ranged in price (annually) between approximately 77 and 95 and the common stock between approximately 8½ and 12½.

** [Ed. Note] To test the correctness of this conclusion, consider the following possible dispersion of earnings per share (e/sh) and probabilities (Pr.) for Armour's common and preferred on three contingencies—events A, B and C:

	COMMON			PREFERRED		
	I 1 share	II 6 shares		III 1 sh. w/o conversion right	IV 1 share converted	V best choice
	e/sh Pr.	e/sh Pr.		e/sh Pr.	e/sh	e/sh Pr.
Event A	$4 × .2= .8	$24 × .2= 4.8		$6 × .2= 1.2	$24	$24 × .2= 4.8
Event B	$2 × .3= .6	$12 × .3= 3.6		$6 × .3= 1.8	$12	$12 × .3= 3.6
Event C	0 × .5= 0	0 × .5= 0		$4 × .5= 2.0	0	$ 4 × .5= 2.0
Mean	$1.4	$8.4		$5	$ 8.4	$10.4

The "best choice" for the holder of the convertible preferred who looks to the future (Col. V) offers protection on the down side (by refraining from converting) combined with gain on the upside (by converting whenever in the future the contingencies look most favorable). At any given time, the convertible preferred should sell at a price higher than six shares of common. The reason for this is that at any given time, the conversion privilege has value (compare Col. IV with Col. III); and, assuming a known dividend policy, the value of the preferred exceeds the value of six common because its claim on the expected earnings will not go below $4, (to that extent making its owner better off than the owner of six shares of common stock) and its opportunity to share in all earnings above $6 leaves its owner no worse off than the owner of six shares of common stock. The entitlement of the holder to protection against exposure to the worst part of the dispersion and to share in the best part is a value that is not eliminated by comparing the constantly higher price of the preferred with the price of six shares of common.

(4) After the plan, the Prior Stockholder had no right to the $18.50 dividends which had accrued on his share of Prior Stock of $100 stated value, but he did have $120 of debentures and the warrant. There was nothing unfair about this change. Armour's earned surplus was not supported by cash or liquid securities which would have been available for the payment of these accrued dividends. The Company's need for cash and its continuing heavy bank loans outstanding have been referred to above. The dividends on the Prior Stock could not be paid out of bricks and mortar, and the cash needs of the Company were such that it was within the discretion of the Board of Directors to withhold the payment of further cash dividends. The retention of this cash for operations, to meet the payments required on the long-term debt and to furnish needed funds for other corporate purposes outlined above is something that is committed to the directors' discretion.

The many other points raised by the plaintiffs concerning the fairness of the plan have been considered, but I do not believe that any extension of these remarks is necessary. Suffice it to say that the burden is on the plaintiffs to show that unfairness which would require me to hold the plan invalid. Dratz versus Occidental Hotel Co., supra. This burden has not been sustained. "True, plaintiffs say that the plan is so unfair to the preferred stockholders in favor of the common stockholders that it amounts to fraud, but as has been indicated above, that is here nothing more than an emphatic way of saying that as a matter of business judgment plaintiffs would rather keep what they now have. No actual bad faith is shown, and neither is there such unfairness, if any, as would justify an inference of fraud." Zobel versus American Locomotive Co. supra, * * *.

The former Prior Stockholders received in exchange for their stock marketable securities of the Company with a much greater assurance of annual return and a somewhat higher market value. The plan as noted above, redounded to the benefit of the Company. I think it was fair to all concerned. 98 ½% of the Prior Stock has been exchanged in accordance with this plan. The holders of these shares apparently agree with me.

From what has been said, it is also clear that plaintiffs have not been deprived of rights without the due process of law within the purview of the fourteenth amendment to the Federal Constitution or the similar provisions of the state constitution. Dratz versus Occidental Hotel Co., supra; Goldman versus Postal Telegraph Inc., supra.

Further, the Western Foundry Co. case, supra, laid to rest any doubt that defeasible rights of preferred stockholders are not "vested." They may constitutionally be altered by appropriate corporate and stockholder action. The reason for this is that it is not unconstitutional to alter a right which the stockholder consented in advance to have alterable. So long as the rights of the stockholder lie within the confining box of stock ownership, he cannot complain of action taken in accordance with statutory power. Only by giving the plaintiffs a status as creditors—which was done in this case— can they escape from these limitations of the stockholder-corporation relationship. See Langfelder versus Universal Laboratories, 163 F.2d 804, 807 (3d Cir.1947); Mayfield versus Alton Ry. Gas & Electric Co., 198 Ill. 528, 65 N.E. 100 (1902). * * *

Bowman v. Armour & Co.

Supreme Court of Illinois, 1959.
17 Ill.2d 43, 160 N.E.2d 753.

■ HERSHEY, J.

The language of subparagraph (g) of section 52, authorizing amendment of articles of incorporation makes rights and privileges of preferred stock defeasible to the extent that amendments are authorized. The question here is not one of the existence of the power to amend nor is the question here one of the authority to divest certain rights and privileges. Rather, the question is whether this quoted language gives to Armour the right to amend to the extent that holders of the prior shares are required to surrender their ownership in said stock and accept in lieu thereof the earnings bonds as specified.

The amendment, whether it is viewed as effecting a purchase of the prior stock with bonds or as a compulsory redemption thereof, obviously contemplates that the fundamental relationship of stockholder as between the holders of the prior stock and Armour will be changed and the prior stockholders will become mere creditors of the company.

A share of stock in a corporation is a unit of interest in the corporation and it entitles the shareholder to an aliquot part of the property or its proceeds to the extent indicated. The interest of a shareholder entitles him to participate in the net profits in proportion to the number of his shares, to have a voice in the selection of the corporate officers and, upon dissolution or liquidation, to receive his portion of the property of the corporation that may remain after payment of its debts. A change in preferences, qualifications or relative rights may increase or decrease the right to participate in profits, the right to participate in distribution of the assets of the corporation on dissolution or liquidation, or other indicia of ownership manifest by the ownership of corporate stock. But the change here contemplated is more than that; it is a compulsory redemption or a purchase of the stock rather than a divestiture of certain rights and privileges.

The plan of recapitalization here is not a divestiture of rights or privileges or an increase or decrease in relative rights of shares but it is, as we have said, a compulsory redemption or purchase that results in a change of the status of the shareholder from that of a shareholder to that of a creditor. The ownership of some equity in the corporation is not modified or changed leaving some resulting ownership, but it is liquidated and a corporate owner prior to the amendment finds that subsequent to the amendment he is a creditor.

A corporation has no inherent right to redeem its preferred stock and can do so only if authorized by law. Fletcher Cyclopedia, Corporations, vol.

11, Permanent Ed., sec. 5309. Section 14 of our Business Corporation Act provides for the issuance of preferred shares and further provides that the same may be redeemed "at not exceeding the price fixed by the articles of incorporation. * * * " The articles of Armour expressly provided that the prior stock could be redeemed at a price of $115 per share plus accrued dividends.

* * *

It is the position of the plaintiffs that the only way the stock can be redeemed is by compliance with the provisions of the article and the payment in dollars of the sum therein provided. The plaintiffs assert that the word "price," as used in the statute, is definable only to mean money and not bonds or other evidences of debt.

* * *

The word "price" is used in the redemption language of section 14 and is also found in section 15 of the Business Corporation Act with reference to the issuance of preferred or special shares in a series. It is there provided that there may be variations between series of stock as to price. Further, in section 18 of the Business Corporation Act, the word "price" is not found, and in that section it is obvious that when the legislature wished to broaden the meaning of the term it did not use the word "price" but used the word "consideration" and defined it to include many things—money, property, labor or services actually performed.

A consideration of these sections can lead us only to the conclusion that when the legislature makes reference to the payment of money it uses the word "price." When it is concerned with a broader definition it found adequate words to express its intention.

* * *

It seems to us to be evident that the effect of the amendment here sought to be sustained was, in fact, a purchase with bonds by the Armour Company of its own outstanding preferred stock without the consent of the owners of said stock. While the Business Corporation Act does, under certain circumstances, permit a corporation to purchase its own stock, it can do so only when the shareholder is willing to sell, and no amendment passed with the approval of a two-thirds vote of the shareholders can force him to sell.

Further, that section 52(g) should be construed as we have indicated is made more clear by referring to the express safeguards found in the Business Corporation Act applicable to merger. Section 61 expressly provides that on merger the shares of each merging corporation may be converted into shares or other securities or obligations of the corporation. Section 70 provides safeguards for shareholders who may dissent from the merger by permitting them to obtain the fair market value of their shares. To construe section 52 as to authorize the recapitalization plan here under consideration would mean that a minority shareholder would not have the protection on recapitalization that the legislature has provided on merger, even though the recapitalization plan could more drastically affect his interest than would a merger. It is obvious to us that the legislature did not intend to authorize a recapitalization program by amendment of the nature and to the extent of the one here involved but, rather, by the language of section 52(g) contemplated only changes in relative rights, privileges, restrictions or limitations.

* * *

For the reasons stated, the decree of the superior Court of Cook County is reversed and the cause is remanded to that court for the entry of a decree in accordance with the views here expressed. * * *

NOTE: *BOWMAN*

In the final disposition of the case in December 1959, the plaintiff and those stockholders participating in the suit received 7.26 shares of common stock for each surrendered share of preferred. The number of common shares was computed by adding to the 6 shares attributable to the conversion right 1.26 shares reflecting stock dividends between 1954 and 1959.

Note that the Illinois statute accorded the preferred a class vote on the amendment and 70.6% of the 500,000 shares voted in favor. Why did the preferred assent to an amendment that transferred value to the common? By hypothesis, the holders must not have understood the amendment's financial implications. One wonders whether Armour's management submitted them proxy statement designed to exacerbate or to diminish their confusion. Would it have made a difference if most of the preferred had been held by sophisticated investment institutions? Such might be the case today.

Note that *Bowman* also antedates the judicial implication of a private right of action under Rule 14a–9 in respect of misleading proxy statements. Perhaps the threat of such an action would have prompted a differently drafted proxy statement in this case—one pointing out the detrimental aspects of the amendment. More generally, do the disclosure requirements in the proxy rules promulgated by the Securities and Exchange Commission under Section 14 of the Securities Exchange Act provide the preferred stockholder with information sufficient to induce a critical assessment of the terms of a recapitalization plan? Does the answer turn on the rigor with which the rules require disclosure of future oriented information such as the magnitude or duration of improvements in earnings anticipated by management or of the magnitude of benefits expected to flow to the common stockholders or management from the recapitalization proposal, or the reasons for the proposed alterations?

(B) ALTERATION BY MERGER

Bove v. The Community Hotel Corporation of Newport, Rhode Island

Supreme Court of Rhode Island, 1969.
105 R.I. 36, 249 A.2d 89.

■ JOSLIN, J.

[The plaintiffs held shares of $100 par value, 6 percent cumulative preferred stock of The Community Hotel Corporation of Newport, Rhode Island. Dividends on the 4,335 outstanding shares of the stock had not been declared for 24 years; dividend arrearages totaled $645,000, or $148.75 per share.

[The board of Community Hotel organized a shell corporation called Newport Hotel Corp. and caused Community Hotel to agree to merge into it. Under the merger, each of Community Hotel's outstanding 6 percent preferred shares, together with all accrued dividends, would be converted into 5 shares of Newport common; each share of Community Hotel's outstanding 2,106 shares of common stock would be converted into one share of Newport common. Under section 7–5–3 of the Rhode Island statute, the merger required the approval of the holders of two thirds of each class of stock.

[The court affirmed a judgment denying the issuance of an injunction against the accomplishment of the merger.]

It is true, of course, that to accomplish the proposed recapitalization by amending Community Hotel's articles of association under relevant provisions of the general corporation law would require the unanimous vote of the preferred shareholders, whereas under the merger statute, only a two-third vote of those stockholders will be needed. Concededly, unanimity of the preferred stockholders is unobtainable in this case, and plaintiffs argue, therefore, that to permit the less restrictive provisions of the merger statute to be used to accomplish indirectly what otherwise would be incapable of being accomplished directly by the more stringent amendment procedures of the general corporation law is tantamount to sanctioning a circumvention or perversion of that law.

The question, however, is not whether recapitalization by the merger route is a subterfuge, but whether a merger which is designed for the sole purpose of cancelling the rights of preferred stockholders with the consent of less than all has been authorized by the legislature. The controlling statute is § 7–5–2. Its language is clear, all-embracing and unqualified. It authorizes any two or more business corporations *which were or might have been organized* under the general corporation law to merge into a single corporation; and it provides that the merger agreement shall prescribe " * * * the terms and conditions of consolidation or merger, the mode of carrying the same into effect * * * *as well as the manner of converting the shares of each of the constituent corporations into shares or other securities of the corporation resulting from or surviving such consolidation or merger,* with such other details and provisions as are deemed necessary."[3] (italics ours) Nothing in that language even suggests that the legislature intended to make *underlying purpose* a standard for determining permissibility. Indeed, the contrary is apparent since the very breadth of the language selected presupposes a complete lack of concern with whether the merger is designed to further the mutual interests of two existing and nonaffiliated corporations or whether alternatively it is pur-

---

3. The quoted provision is substantially identical to the Delaware merger statute (Del.Rev.Code (1935) C. 65, § 2091) con-strued in Federal United Corp. v. Havender, 24 Del.Ch. 318, 11 A.2d 331.

posed solely upon effecting a substantial change in an existing corporation's capital structure.

Moreover, that a possible effect of corporate action under the merger statute is not possible, or is even forbidden, under another section of the general corporation law is of no import, it being settled that the several sections of that law may have independent legal significance, and that the validity of corporate action taken pursuant to one section is not necessarily dependent upon its being valid under another. * * *

We hold, therefore, that nothing within the purview of our statute forbids a merger between a parent and a subsidiary corporation even under circumstances where the merger device has been resorted to solely for the purpose of obviating the necessity for the unanimous vote which would otherwise be required in order to cancel the priorities of preferred shareholders. * * *

A more basic problem, narrowed so as to bring it within the factual context of this case, is whether the right of a holder of cumulative preferred stock to dividend arrearages and other preferences may be cancelled by a statutory merger. That precise problem has not heretofore been before this court, but elsewhere there is a considerable body of law on the subject. There is no need to discuss all of the authorities. For illustrative purposes it is sufficient that we refer principally to cases involving Delaware corporations. * * *

* * * [The Court contrasted the Delaware Supreme Court's decision in Keller v. Wilson & Co., 21 Del.Ch. 391, 190 A. 115 (1936), which ruled that the statutory power authorizing stockholders to amend charters did not permit an amendment cancelling accrued dividends on preferred stock, with its 1940 decision in Federal United Corp. v. Havender, 24 Del.Ch. 318, 11 A.2d 331 (1940), which ruled that the Delaware merger statute did authorize cancellation of such accruals by merger with a wholly-owned subsidiary, even though the effect of the merger was identical to that of a prohibited charter amendment. The Court then continued:]

The *Havender* approach is the one to which we subscribe as being the sounder, and it has support in the authorities. * * *

The plaintiffs do not suggest, other than as they may have argued that this particular merger is a subterfuge, that our merger statute will not permit in any circumstances a merger for the sole reason that it affects accrued, but undeclared, preferred stock dividends. Rather do they argue that what should control is the date of the enactment of the enabling legislation, and they point out that in *Havender,* Federal United Corp. was organized and its stock was issued subsequent to the adoption of the statute authorizing mergers, whereas in this case the corporate creation and the stock issue preceded adoption of such a statute. That distinguishing feature brings into question what limitations, if any, exist to a state's authority under the reserved power to permit by subsequent legislation corporate acts which affect the preferential rights of a stockholder. More specifically, it raises the problem of whether subsequent legislation is repugnant to the federal and state constitutional prohibitions against the passage of laws impairing the obligations of contracts, because it permits elimination of accumulated preferred dividends by a lesser vote than was required under the law in existence at the time of the incorporation and when the stock was issued.

The mere mention of the constitutional prohibitions against such laws calls to mind Trustees of Dartmouth College v. Woodward, 17 U.S. 518, 4 Wheaton 518, 4 L.Ed. 629, where the decision was that a private corporation charter granted by the state is a contract protected under the constitution against repeal, amendment or alteration by subsequent legislation. Of equal significance in the field of corporation law is Mr. Justice Story's concurring opinion wherein he suggested that application of the impairment clause upon acts of incorporation might be avoided if a state legislature, coincident with granting a corporate charter, reserved as a part of that contract the right of amendment or repeal. With such a reservation, he said, any subsequent amendment or repeal would be pursuant, rather than repugnant, to the terms of the contract and would not therefore impair its obligation.

Our own legislature was quick to heed Story's advice, * * * and since at least as far back as 1844 the corporation law has read in substance as it does today viz., " * * * The charter or articles of association of every corporation hereafter created may be amended or repealed at the will of the general assembly." Section 7–1–13.

       * * *

The plaintiffs * * * insist that any legislation, if enacted subsequent to the creation of a corporation and the issuance of its preferred stock, may not be a source of authority for corporate action which deprives a holder of his stock or of its preferential rights or of the dividends accrued thereon. An attempt to do so, they say, constitutes an unconstitutional exercise of the reserved power. On this issue, as on most others in this case, the authorities are not in accord.

On the one side, there is a body of law which speaks of the threefold nature of the stockholder's contract and, while agreeable to an exercise of the reserved power affecting only the contractual relationship between the state and the corporation, rejects as unconstitutional any exercise which affects the relationship between the stockholder and the corporation or between the stockholders inter sese. Wheatley v. A.I. Root Co., 147 Ohio St. 127, 69 N.E.2d 187; Schaad v. Hotel Easton Co., 369 Pa. 486, 87 A.2d 227. Under this view, subsequent legislation purporting to permit a corporate act to cancel accrued preferred dividends would obviously be an improper exercise of the power inasmuch as the essence of a preferred stockholder's contract is its definition of his relationship with the corporation and with the other stockholders vis-à-vis such matters as the distribution of the profits of the enterprise or the division of its capital and surplus account in the event of liquidation.

The other side of the argument considers that the question is primarily one of statutory construction and that so long as the statute authorizes the corporate action, it should make no difference whether its enactment preceded or postdated the birth of the corporation or the issuance of its stock. The basis for this viewpoint is that the terms of the preferred stockholder's contractual relationship are not restricted to the specifics inscribed on the stock certificate, but include also the stipulations contained in the charter or articles of association as well as the pertinent provisions of the general corporation law. One of those provisions is, of course, the reserved power; and so long as it is a part of the preferred shareholder's contract, any subsequent legislation enacted pursuant to it, even though it may amend the contract's original terms, will not impair its obligation in the constitutional sense. It is as if the stock certificate were inscribed with the legend "All of the terms and conditions hereof may be changed by the legislature acting pursuant to the power it has reserved in G.L.1956, § 7–1–13."

    * * *

On the basis of our own precedents we conclude that the merger legislation, notwithstanding its effect on the rights of its stockholders, did not necessarily constitute an improper exercise of the right of amendment reserved merely because it was subsequent.

    * * * [P]laintiffs also contend that [the merger] is unfair and inequitable to them, and that its consummation should, therefore, be enjoined. By that assertion they raise the problem of whether equity should heed the request of a dissenting stockholder and intervene to prevent a merger notwithstanding that it has received the vote of the designated proportions of the various classes of stock of the constituent corporations.

    * * *

This case involves a merger, not a recapitalization by charter amendment, and in this state the legislature, looking to the possibility that there might be those who would not be agreeable to the proposed merger, provided a means whereby a dissatisfied stockholder might demand and the corporation be compelled to pay the fair value of his securities. G.L.1956, §§ 7–5–8 through 7–5–16 inclusive. Our inquiry then is to the effect of that remedy upon plaintiff's right to challenge the proposed merger on the ground that it is unfair and inequitable because it dictates what shall be their proportionate interests in the corporate assets. Once again there is no agreement among the authorities. Vorenberg, "Exclusiveness of the Dissenting Stockholder's Appraisal Right," 77 Harv.L.Rev. 1189. See also Annot. 162 A.L.R. 1237, 1250. Some authorities appear to say that the statutory remedy of appraisal is exclusive. Beloff v. Consolidated Edison Co., 300 N.Y. 11, 87 N.E.2d 561; Hubbard v. Jones & Laughlin Steel Corp., D.C., 42 F.Supp. 432. Others say that it may be disregarded and that equity may intervene if the minority is treated oppressively or unfairly, Barnett v. Philadelphia Market Co., 218 Pa. 649, 67 A. 912; May v. Midwest Refining Co., 1 Cir., 121 F.2d 431, cert. denied 314 U.S. 668, 62 Sup.Ct. 129, 86 L.Ed. 534, or if the merger is tainted with fraud or illegality, Adams v. United States Distributing Corp., 184 Va. 134, 147, 34 S.E.2d 244, 250, 162 A.L.R. 1227; Porges v. Vadsco Sales Corp., 27 Del.Ch. 127, 32 A.2d 148. To these differing views must also be added the divergence of opinion on whether those in control or those dissenting must bear the burden of establishing that the plan meets whatever the required standard may be. Vorenberg, supra; 77 Harv.L.Rev. 1189, 1210–1215.

In this case we do not choose as between the varying views, nor is there any need for us to do so. Even were we to accept that view which is most favorable to plaintiffs we still would not be able to find that they have been either unfairly or inequitably treated. The record insofar as it relates to the unfairness issue is at best sparse. In substance it consists of the corporation's balance sheet as of September 1967, together with supporting schedules. That statement uses book, rather than the appraised, values, and neither it nor any other evidentiary matter in any way indicates, except as the same may be reflected in the surplus account, the corporation's earning history or its prospects for profitable operations in the future.

Going to the figures we find a capital and surplus account of $669,948 of which $453,000 is allocable to the 4,530 issued and outstanding shares of $100 par value preferred stock and the balance of $216,948 to surplus. Obviously, a realization of the book value of the assets in the event of liquidation, forced or otherwise, would not only leave nothing for the common stockholders, but would not even suffice to pay the preferred shareholders the par value of their stock plus the accrued dividends of $645,000.

If we were to follow a rule of absolute priority, any proposal which would give anything to common stockholders without first providing for full payment of stated value plus dividend accruals would be unfair to the preferred shareholders. It could be argued that the proposal in this case violates that rule because an exchange of one share of Community Hotel's preferred stock for five shares of Newport's common stock would give the preferred shareholders securities worth less than the amount of their liquidation preference rights while at the same time the one to one exchange ratio on the common would enrich Community Hotel's common stockholders by allowing them to participate in its surplus.

An inherent fallacy in applying the rule of absolute priority to the circumstances of this case, however, is its assumption that assets would be liquidated and that nothing more than their book value will be realized. But Community Hotel is not in liquidation. Instead it is a going concern which, because of its present capitalization, cannot obtain the modern debt-financing needed to meet threatened competition. Moreover, management, in the call of the meeting at which it was intended to consider and vote on the plan, said that the proposed recapitalization plan was conceived only " * * * after careful consideration by your Board of Directors and a review of the relative values of the preferred and common stocks by the independent public accountants of the Corporation. The exchange ratio of five new common shares for each share of the existing preferred stock was determined on the basis of the book and market values of the preferred and the inherent value of the unpaid preferred dividends." Those assertions are contained in a document admitted as an exhibit and they have testimonial value.

When the varying considerations—both balance sheet figures and management's assertions—are taken into account, we are unable to conclude, at least at this stage of the proceedings, that the proposed plan is unfair and inequitable, particularly because plaintiffs as dissidents may avail themselves of the opportunity to receive the fair market value of their securities under the appraisal methods prescribed in § 7–5–8 through § 7–5–16 inclusive.

The plaintiffs argue that due consideration will not be given to their dividend accruals under the appraisal. We do not agree. Jeffrey v. American Screw Co., 98 R.I. 286, 201 A.2d 146, requires that the securities of a dissident invoking the statute must be appraised by a person "versed in the intricacies of corporate finance." Such a person will find when he looks to *Jeffrey* for guidance that the evaluation process requires him to consider " * * * all relevant value factors including market value, book value, asset value, and other intrinsic factors probative of value." Certainly, unpaid dividend arrearages fall within that directive and are a relevant factor to be considered in arriving at the full and fair cash value of the plaintiffs' preferred stock. While we make no decision one way or the other on the exclusiveness of appraisal as a remedy for a dissident, we do decide that its availability is an element or a circumstance which equity should weigh before intervening. When that is done in this case, we find no ground for intervention.

For the reasons stated, the judgment appealed from is affirmed.

NOTE: THE INVESTMENT VALUE DOCTRINE

The *Bove* court rejects the proposition that liquidation value should be taken as a measure of the value of the rights of the preferred. This gives rise to a problem, whether in the context of an appraisal proceeding or a determination whether good faith or fiduciary duties owed to the preferred have been violated. How, from a valuation perspective, is a court to determine whether a reallocation of rights (and hence of value) is or is not fair? It is often asserted that the allocative problems attending equity recapitalization are intractable when reviewed for fairness *ex post*. Historical precedent arguably falsifies that claim.

The Public Utility Holding Company Act of 1935 called for a breakup of the huge public utility holding companies which had been assembled during the previous two decades. Generally speaking, it sought to restrict their operations to one or more systems whose operations were integrated and confined to a single State and States contiguous thereto. It also had as one of its major objectives the simplification of the corporate and capital structures of holding company systems and the redistribution of voting power among security holders on a fair and equitable basis.

The volume and complexity of the corporate and capital structures which were required to be simplified and the nature and scope of the geographical dispersion of the properties required to be integrated presented difficult and novel problems. The SEC had the task of resolving these problems. Opponents of the legislation had asserted that the law would cause dumping and forced liquidation of securities, demoralizing the trading markets. They characterized the integration and simplification requirements as a "death sentence." The Congress, on the other hand, contemplated that this program should not and need not destroy any legitimate investment values. It gave the SEC a mandate to bring about the required integration and simplification in keeping with that objective.

Compliance with the integration and simplification requirements took various forms. They included liquidations, mergers and consolidations, separation of large systems into smaller, integrated systems, divestment of nonutility properties unrelated to the utility business, sale of nonretainable utility properties to other systems with whose properties they could be integrated, sale of the securities of nonretainable subsidiaries to the public at competitive bidding or pursuant to a rights offering to stockholders of the parent company and distribution of securities pro rata among stockholders.

The Commission was authorized to approve a simplification plan under Section 11(e) of the Act only if, *inter alia,* it found the plan to be "fair and equitable" (15 U.S.C. § 79k), the same formula which Congress had formerly embedded in Section 77 (11 U.S.C. § 205) and Section 77B (48 Stat. 912) of the Bankruptcy Act, and later inserted in Chapter X of the Bankruptcy Act. In ruling upon simplification plans, the Commission developed a so called "investment value" doctrine to implement the "fair and equitable" standard contained in Section 11. That doctrine was designed to meet the problem created by the disparity—often substantial— between the "value" of a security when assessed as a continuing claim on a going concern and the value of the corporate assets to which the same security would, by its terms, be entitled to receive in a liquidation, recapitalization, merger, or other form of corporate readjustment compelled by Section 11. To honor the contractual provision might be to entitle the security holder in a given case to more (or less) than the going-concern value of the security she is being forced to surrender. But except for the compulsion of Section 11, senior-security holders might not have the right to force, and junior-security holders might not have the desire to make, the proposed readjustment. And the regulatory compulsion of Section 11, unlike the compulsion of bankruptcy, was not a contingency contemplated in allocating risk and return in the senior security contract.

The investment-value doctrine rested on the assumption that Congress did not intend enforcement of the overriding public policy of holding-company simplification to have its effect visited on one class with a corresponding windfall to another class of security holders, or to result in shifting investment values from one class of security holders to another. On that premise, both the SEC and the Supreme Court concluded that the Act (1) in effect, overrode the security contract—i.e., precluded a mandated corporate readjustment from being a "maturing" event under the security contract, even though the particular form of readjustment occurring was a contingency apparently explicitly provided for in the contract, and (2) required surrendering security holders to receive the long-term going-concern values which their securities had when the act compelled their surrender—i.e., their claims were to be measured by their going-concern values rather than by the formal requirements of their contracts or by some other norm.

The "investment value" standard (as invoked in In the Matter of Eastern Gas and Fuel Associates, 30 S.E.C. 834 (1950), approved and enforced 90 F.Supp. 955 (D.Mass.)) is illustrated, and advocated, in Note, A Standard of Fairness for Compensating Preferred Shareholders in Corporate Recapitalizations, 33 U.Chi. L.Rev. 97 (1965), as follows:

"Consider, for example, a strong corporation which expects to have $100,000 in earnings available annually for its shareholders and which has 10,000 shares of common and 10,000 shares of 5%, $100–par preferred each with $20 of arrears. The investment value of the preferred shares would be the sum of the value of the contract without arrears and the value of the arrears, determined as follows:

(1) The value of the contract without arrears is derived from the preferred dividend requirement of $50,000 per year. The value of this right is the present value of $50,000 per year in perpetuity, capitalized at a rate which properly reflects the risk of not earning the dividend. Because the corporation is strong and the risk is small, a proper capitalization rate might be 7%. The value of the contractual right to dividends is thus $714,073.

(2) The second component of the preferred shares' investment value is the value of the arrears. If the company earns $100,000 annually and pays $50,000 in preferred dividends, $50,000 will be available for payments on the arrears. Assuming depreciation charges sufficient to maintain the plant at a level necessary to earn $100,000 and assuming a willing board of directors, if the entire sum is devoted to that purpose the arrears will be paid off in four years ($20 on each of 10,000 shares; $200,000 total arrearage accruals). The present value of $50,000 per year for four years must be determined. Since the risk of not earning this sum is greater than the risk of not earning the first $50,000 of the corporation's expected annual income, it should be capitalized at, perhaps, 10%. Thus, the present value of the arrears is $158,493, and the total value of the preferred rights is $872,566.

The preferred should be given either cash or securities of this value. If the new capital structure is to consist of one class of securities such as common stock, the preferred should be given a percentage of that stock equal to the ratio of the preferred's investment value to the value of the entire equity. The value of the entire equity is determined by capitalizing the expected annual earnings available for the equity interest, $100,000, in perpetuity at the appropriate rate considering the risk of not achieving those earnings (e.g., 8 ½%). On this basis, the total equity is worth $1,176,405 and the preferred would be entitled to 74% of the new single class of stock to be issued. If more than one class of securities is to be issued, the preferred should be given the most senior package of shares which will, if present expert expectations are realized, have a market value equal to the preferred's present investment value. The expected market value of the new shares is estimated in the same manner in which the investment value of the old shares was determined. The earnings attributable to the new shares are capitalized at a rate which the market would probably require of a security of similar quality in a similarly-situated company."

Rothschild International Corporation v. Liggett Group Inc.

Supreme Court of Delaware, 1984.
474 A.2d 133.

■ HORSEY, JUSTICE.

This appeal is from a summary judgment Order of the Court of Chancery dismissing a purported class action filed by the owners of 7% cumulative preferred stock in Liggett Group, Inc. ("Liggett"), a Delaware corporation. The suit arises out of a combined tender offer and reverse cash-out merger whereby the interests of the 7% preferred shareholders were eliminated for a price of $70 per share, an amount $30 below the liquidation preference stated in Liggett's certificate of incorporation. Plaintiff-appellant asserts claims for breach of contract and breach of fiduciary duty based on the non-payment of the $30 premium.

I

Plaintiff, Rothschild International Corp., filed a class action in the Court of Chancery on behalf of 7% cumulative preferred stockholders of Liggett against defendants Liggett, Grand Metropolitan Limited ("GM"), a corporation of England, GM Sub Corporation ("GM Sub"), a Delaware corporation formed for the purpose of acquiring Liggett, and GM Sub II, a wholly-owned Delaware subsidiary of GM. The class was to consist of those 7% shareholders who tendered their preferred stock for $70 per share in response to GM's tender offer and those who did not so tender and were cashed out for the same per share price in the subsequent merger of GM Sub II into Liggett.*

On motion by defendants, GM was dismissed as a party to the action for lack of personal jurisdiction; similarly, the case against GM Sub II was dismissed as GM Sub II had ceased to exist by virtue of its merger into Liggett in August, 1980. After such dismissal, but during the pendency of plaintiff's motion for class certification, both sides moved for summary judgment on the merits of plaintiff's claims. Upon consolidation of the motions and presentation of oral argument, the Court granted defendants' motion for summary judgment.

On appeal, plaintiff contends that the takeover of Liggett via the combined tender offer and merger in essence effected a liquidation of the company thus warranting payment to the holders of the 7% preferred stock of the $100 liquidation value set forth in Liggett's charter. Plaintiff's breach of contract and breach of fiduciary duty claims are premised on a single assertion—that GM's plan of acquisition was equivalent to a liquidation. However, as we view the record, the transaction did not involve a liquidation of Liggett's business. Hence, we must affirm.

II

A.

There is no dispute of facts. Liggett's certificate of incorporation provided that "[i]n the event of any liquidation of the assets of the Corporation (whether voluntary or involuntary) the holders of the 7% Preferred Stock shall be entitled to be paid the par amount of their 7% Preferred shares and the amount of any dividends accumulated and unpaid thereon. * * * "[1] Under the terms of Liggett's charter, each share of the 7% security carried a $100 par value. Plaintiff makes two interrelated

---

* [Ed. Note] According to the trial court (Rothschild International Corporation v. Liggett Group, Inc., 463 A.2d 642, at 644), "Under the terms of Liggett's charter, the 7% Preferred had no right to vote as a class on a merger proposal. As a consequence, even though less than 40% of the 7% Preferred tendered their shares in response to the offer, GM Sub's combined acquisition of an overwhelming majority of both Liggett's common stock and the $5.25 Convertible Preferred gave it sufficient voting power to approve a follow up merger proposal whereby all remaining shareholders of Liggett other than GM Sub were eliminated in return for the payment of cash for their shares."

1. The certificate also provided that its 7% Cumulative Preferred stock could not be redeemed, called or converted into any other security. The stock also guaranteed a fixed 7% return per annum.

arguments: (1) that the economic effect of the merger was a liquidation of Liggett's assets "just as if [Liggett] were sold piece meal to Grand Met"; and (2) that any corporate reorganization that forcibly liquidates a shareholder's *interests* is tantamount to a liquidation of the *corporation* itself. From this, plaintiff argues that it necessarily follows that defendants' failure to pay the preferred shareholders the full liquidation price constituted a breach of Liggett's charter. We cannot agree with either argument.

Preferential rights are contractual in nature and therefore are governed by the express provisions of a company's certificate of incorporation. Stock preferences must also be clearly expressed and will not be presumed. See Wood v. Coastal States Gas Corp., Del.Supr., 401 A.2d 932 (1979); Ellingwood v. Wolf's Head Oil Refining Co., Del.Supr., 88 A.2d 743 (1944). See also Hibbert v. Hollywood Park, Inc., Del.Supr., 457 A.2d 339 (1983); Shanghai Power Co. v. Delaware Trust Co., Del.Ch., 316 A.2d 589, 594 (1974).

Liggett's charter stated that the $100 liquidation preference would be paid only in the event of "any liquidation of the assets of the Corporation." The term "liquidation", as applied to a corporation, means the "winding up of the affairs of the corporation by getting in its assets, settling with creditors and debtors and apportioning the amount of profit and loss." W. Fletcher, Corporations § 7968 (1979). See Sterling v. Mayflower Hotel Corp., Del.Supr., 93 A.2d 107, 112 (1952).

Our view of the record confirms the correctness of the Chancellor's finding that there was no "liquidation" of Liggett within the well-defined meaning of that term. Clearly the directors and shareholders of Liggett determined that the company should be integrated with GM, not that the corporate assets be liquidated on a "piece meal" basis. The fact is that Liggett has retained its corporate identity. Having elected this plan of reorganization, the parties had the right to avail themselves of the most effective means for achieving that result, subject only to their duty to deal fairly with the minority interests.

Thus, we must construe Liggett's liquidation provision as written and conclude that the reverse cash-out merger of Liggett did not accomplish a "liquidation" of Liggett's assets. Only upon a liquidation of its assets would Liggett's preferred shareholders' charter rights to payment of par value "spring into being." Rothschild International Corp. v. Liggett Group, Del.Ch., 463 A.2d 642, 647 (1983).

Sterling v. Mayflower Hotel Corp., supra, is in point on this issue. There, this Court held that a merger is not equivalent to a sale of assets. In so holding, the Court followed the well-settled principle of Delaware Corporation Law that "action taken under one section of that law is legally independent, and its validity is not dependent upon, nor to be tested by the requirements of other unrelated sections under which the same final result might be attained by different means." Orzeck v. Englehart, Del.Supr., 195 A.2d 375, 378 (1963).

It is equally settled under Delaware law that minority stock interests may be eliminated by merger. And, where a merger of corporations is permitted by law, a shareholder's preferential rights are subject to defeasance. Stockholders are charged with knowledge of this possibility at the time they acquire their shares. *Federal United Corp. v. Havender,* Del. Supr., 11 A.2d 331, 338 (1940). Accord, *Langfelder v. Universal Laboratories, Inc.,* D.Del., 68 F.Supp. 209 (1946), aff'd 3rd Cir., 163 F.2d 804, 806–807 (1947); *Hottenstein v. York Ice Machinery Corp.,* 3rd Cir., 136 F.2d 944, 950 (1943).

Plaintiff claims that reliance on *Sterling* and *Havender* for a finding that Liggett was not liquidated is misplaced. To support this claim, plaintiff variously argues: (1) that as *Sterling* and *Havender* predated cash mergers, they are not dispositive as to whether a Liggett-like takeover could constitute a liquidation; (2) that the relied-on authorities viewed a merger as contemplating the continuance of a stockholder's investment in the corporate enterprise; and (3) that because of the *Sterling/Havender* view of a merger and the unique features of the 7% preferred stock, the 7% shareholders could reasonably expect to be paid the $100 liquidation preference in any circumstance effecting a total elimination of their investment in Liggett.

The short answer to plaintiff's arguments is that, as a matter of law, stock issued or purchased prior to the Legislature's authorization of cash mergers does not entitle the stockholder to any vested right of immunity from the operation of the cash merger provision. *Coyne v. Park & Tilford Distillers Corp.,* Del.Supr., 154 A.2d 893 (1959). Further, it is settled that the State has the reserved power to enact laws having the effect of amending certificates of incorporation and any rights arising thereunder. *Id.* at 897. As plaintiff is charged with knowledge of the possible defeasance of its stock interests upon a merger, *Singer v. Magnavox Co.,* Del.Supr., 380 A.2d 969, 978 (1977), plaintiff cannot successfully argue for relief on the basis of the uniqueness of the 7% stock and the stockholders' "reasonable expectations" theory.

B.

Plaintiff also claims that Liggett and GM, acting through its subsidiary GM Sub, breached their fiduciary duties to accord to the 7% shareholders fair and equitable terms of conversion. Simply stated, plaintiff argues that, irrespective of whether a de facto liquidation occurred, "[a]ny payment less than the full liquidation price was not 'entirely fair' to the 7% Preferred stockholders."

We agree with the Chancellor that plaintiff's "fairness" argument presumes a *right* of the 7% shareholders to receive full liquidation value and does not *per se* raise the issue of the intrinsic fairness of the $70 price offered at the time of the tender offer and merger. However, even assuming *arguendo* that plaintiff did present a fairness issue, it is well settled that "the stockholder is entitled to be paid for that which has been taken from him, *viz.,* his proportionate interest in a going concern." *Tri–Continental Corp. v. Battye,* Del.Supr., 74 A.2d 71, 72 (1950). Moreover, the measure of "fair value" is not "liquidation value." Rather, the 7% shareholders were entitled only to an amount equal to their proportionate interests in Liggett as determined by "all relevant factors." 8 Del.C. § 262; Weinberger v. UOP, Inc., Del.Supr., 457 A.2d 701 (1983); Tri–Continental Corp. v. Battye, supra.

Thus, having reviewed the transaction, we find that the Chancellor did not err as a matter of law in granting defendants' motion for summary judgment.

* * *

Affirmed.

NOTE: DRAFTING

1. Drafting into Liquidation Value: *Groove Networks*.

The drafter can avoid the problem encountered by the preferred stockholders in *Liggett* and secure recovery of liquidation value in the event of a merger. The charter simply needs to provide that a merger or sale of all or substantially all the assets triggers the liquidation preference. **Matthews v. Groove Networks**, 2005 WL 3498423 (Del.Ch.), concerned preferred issued under a charter that got the holders to that result subject to a slight glitch. The liquidation preference applied to a "Liquidation Event," and "Liquidation Event" included "any reorganization, merger or consolidation" in addition to "any liquidation, dissolution, or winding up." The liquidation preference went on to state that, in the event of a merger, the preferred stockholders were to be paid from "Distributable Assets." Distributable Assets were then defined as the company's assets, "whether from capital, surplus or earnings." Finally, the charter clarified the definition of Distributable Assets, stating: "In the event of a sale of a Majority of the Assets, the Distributable Assets shall be the net proceeds of such sale." But there was no corollary statement clarifying what constituted Distributable Assets in the event of a merger.

The issuer was sold in a cash out merger and applied the liquidation preference with the result that all of the merger proceeds went to the preferred. A common stockholder challenged the distribution, contending that merger consideration was not intended to be part of the assets of the corporation within the meaning of the Distributable Assets definition, noting that in a cash out merger the proceeds come from the acquiring corporation and strictly speaking are not assets of the corporation; as a result, the liquidation preference did not govern the distribution of merger consideration. Chancellor Chandler ruled in the issuer's favor, holding that the liquidation preference covered the merger.

2. Capping the Payout at Liquidation Value: *Ford Holdings*.

Now take up the converse question. Can a preferred stockholder's right to a statutory appraisal in the event of a merger be cut off by a charter provision that caps the amount payable in a merger at liquidation value plus accrued dividends? **In re Appraisal of Ford Holdings, Inc. Preferred Stock**, 698 A.2d 973 (Del.Ch. 1997), sustains the cap.

The preferred stock issuer was Ford Motor's subsidiary, Ford Holdings, Inc. ("Holdings"). Two series of preferred were in question: (1) Cumulative Preferred, and (2) Flexible Rate Auction Preferred ("Auction Preferred"). Both classes were nonconvertible and nonredeemable, had cumulative dividends, and had liquidation preferences equal to par plus any accumulated and unpaid dividends. The Cumulative Preferred stock bore a stated dividend, payable quarterly. The Auction Preferred employed a financing technique designed to afford Holdings the benefit of equity capital bearing a short-term floating rate.

Ford, wishing to cash out various classes of Holdings preferred, caused Holdings to be merged into a wholly owned subsidiary, Ford Holdings Capital Corporation. Several preferred holders dissented and sought appraisal under DCL § 262. Holdings argued that under the language of the Certificate of Designations ("Designations"), the preferred holders were entitled only to the consideration therein provided. The holders argued that appraisal rights are mandatory.

The Court ruled as follows, 698 A.2d at 977–79:

"One question to be resolved * * * is whether purchasers of preferred stock can, in effect, contract away their rights to seek judicial determination of the fair value of their stock, by accepting a security that explicitly provides either a stated amount or a formula by which an amount to be received in the event of a merger is set forth. * * *

" * * * [T]his case deals only with the appraisal remedy for preferred stock and preferred stock is a very special case. As is well understood, preferred stock can have characteristics of both debt and equity. To the extent it possesses any special rights or powers and to the extent it is restricted or limited in any way, the relation between the holder of the preferred and the corporation is contractual. * * * While, as part of that contract, an issuer will owe the limited duty of good faith that one contractual party always owes to the other, with respect to those special preferences, etc., the issuer owes no duty of loyalty to the holders of the preferred. * * *

"The general rule applies as with all contracting parties: that which is a valid contract will be enforced either specifically or through a damages action, unless the contract violates positive law or its non-performance is excused. I cannot conclude that a provision that establishes the cash value of a preferred stock in the event of a cash-out merger would violate the public policy reflected in Section 262, given the essentially contractual nature of preferred stock. Thus, the relevant question in this case is whether the instruments establishing the rights and preferences of these various series of preferred stocks do contractually limit the right of a holder to seek judicial appraisal in the event of a cash-out merger.

"I start with a preliminary generality. Since Section 262 represents a statutorily conferred right, it may be effectively waived in the documents creating the security only when that result is quite clearly set forth when interpreting the relevant document under generally applicable principles of construction. * * * Secondly, I note that ambiguity in these matters ought to be construed against the issuer who, as the analysis below certainly indicates, had it within its power clearly to establish the result for which it here contends. Kaiser Alum. Corp. v. Matheson, Del.Supr., 681 A.2d 392 (1996).

"The rights of stockholders of the Cumulative Preferred in the event of a merger are clearly stated in [a] provision [that] specifically identifies the consideration that preferred shareholders will receive upon a cash-out merger of the type which occurred * * *. It states explicitly that shareholders will be paid the liquidation preference—a specific, pre-determined dollar amount—and accrued and unpaid dividends—also a specifically determinable amount. The last phrase of the provision, stating that the holder is entitled to the consideration specified 'and no more', reinforces the conclusion that the shareholders are not entitled to anything additional.

"It is my judgment, then, that the terms of the Designations of the Cumulative Preferred clearly describe an agreement between the shareholders and the company regarding the consideration to be received by the shareholders in the event of a cash-out merger. * * * The shareholders can not now come to this court seeking additional consideration in the merger through the appraisal process. * * *

"The rights of the Auction Preferred * * * shareholders in the event of a cash-out merger are not as clearly expressed as those of the Cumulative Preferred shares. Most notably, there is no provision specifically governing (and limiting) 'Rights on ... Cash-out Merger.' There are two interrelated provisions in the Designations which the corporation claims bear upon the rights of the shareholders to receive money in a cash-out merger. * * *

"Paragraph 5(d)(iii) assures that the preferred shareholders will be able to vote as a class to prevent the corporation from engaging in a merger that a majority of holders find disadvantageous, but that the class loses that power if the preferred receive specified consideration—the liquidation preference ($100,000), a merger premium, if any is authorized, and accumulated and unpaid dividends. Thus, the provision implies that the class has no need for class vote protection—no risk of exploitation—if the preferred receives in the merger consideration equal to the liquidation value, etc. Such an implication would of course be consistent with an understanding that that consideration was all that the preferred was entitled to receive. While this implication is possible, it is not clear or compelled. The voting provisions are, in the end, voting provisions. The stipulated absence of a class vote is too frail a base upon which to rest the claim that there has been a contractual relinquishment of rights under Section 262 or, to state it differently, that the consideration that acts to remove the rights to a class vote also is conclusively established to be the 'fair value.'

"Clear and direct drafting, of the type found in Section 4 of the Designation of the Cumulative Preferred, can implement a term conclusively fixing merger consideration of preferred. But the court may not cut stockholders off from a statutory right by the level of indirection that the company's argument requires.

"Two principles mentioned above support the determination that the 'fair value' of Series D Preferred is not contractually limited by the terms of the Designation. The first is the principle that statutory rights should ordinarily be waived only by clear affirmative words or actions. * * * The second is the principle that holds that ambiguity in a contractual document should be construed against the party that had the power to avoid the ambiguity. See Kaiser Alum. Corp. v. Matheson, Del.Supr., 681 A.2d 392 (1996)."

NOTE: "DE FACTO" THEORIES

1. The reasoning of *Rothschild v. Liggett* is extended to defeat the proposition that a merger constitutes a redemption of preferred stock in Rauch v. RCA Corp., 861 F.2d 29 (2d Cir.1988), and Dart v. Kohlberg, Kravis, Roberts & Co., 1985 WL 21145 (1985).

2. In **Kirschner Bros. Oil, Inc. v. Natomas Co.,** 185 Cal.App.3d 784, 229 Cal.Rptr. 899 (1986), preferred holders in pursuit of a class veto of a transaction unsuccessfully advanced a "de facto" argument. The merger agreement in question provided for the acquisition of the issuer by reverse triangular merger of an acquisition subsidiary of the acquirer into the issuer. The merger agreement provided that the preferred receive preferred stock of a new holding company formed in connection with the transaction. Class votes by both the preferred and common of the issuer were provided for. But the merger agreement also provided that in the event the preferred did not approve the transaction by class vote, the transaction would go forward anyway; the preferred would be left outstanding, holding stock of an issuer the common stock of which was held by the acquirer.

Here the control parties took advantage of a provision of the California statute excusing the requirement of a class vote by preferred shares of surviving corporations the rights and preferences of which were left unchanged by the merger. The preferred argued that in the context of a reverse triangular merger they should not be deemed shareholders of the "surviving corporation," but de facto, holders of shares of the transferor. The court held against them, and also held that the transaction structure did not constitute a breach of fiduciary duty.

NOTE: PREFERRED CLASS VOTING IN RESPECT OF MERGERS

1. *Class Voting Provisions and Their Limitations.*

As we have seen, state business corporation laws now ordinarily require class voting as a condition to certificate amendments that alter preferred stockholders' rights and preferences. See DCL § 242(b)(2); RMBCA § 10.04. These provisions somewhat ameliorate fairness problems respecting adjustment of preferred stockholders' rights. State corporation statutes are less thoroughgoing in their provision for preferred class votes in respect of mergers and acquisitions, however. Recall that the issuer in *Bove*, supra, evaded a statute requiring a unanimous preferred class vote for a direct certificate amendment by engineering a merger pursuant to which a two-thirds class vote sufficed.

2. *Warner v. Chris–Craft*

Delaware has permitted a more extreme version of this move. **Warner Communications Inc. v. Chris–Craft Industries, Inc.**, 583 A.2d 962 (Del.Ch.1989), concerned a merger consummated without class voting that adversely affected the rights of a class of preferred. The holder of the preferred claimed a right to a class vote under two charter provisions. The first provided that a two-thirds vote of the particular class of preferred was necessary for the issuer to "amend, alter or repeal any of the provisions of the Certificate of Incorporation or By–Laws * * * so as to affect adversely any of the preferences, rights, powers or privileges" of the class of preferred. The second provided that a two thirds class vote of all outstanding shares of preferred "shall be necessary to alter or change any rights, preferences or limitations of the Preferred stock so as to affect the holders of all such shares adversely * * *." Chancellor Allen held that neither provision applied to merger votes. As to the first provision, the impairment of rights stemmed from the conversion of the stock pursuant to a merger under § 251 of the Delaware statute rather than from an "amendment" or "repeal" under § 242. The second provision was not so narrowly phrased. But, because it tracked language in § 242 (read by the court to apply only to direct amendments and not to provide for class voting rights in mergers), it was held inapplicable. The court ascribed to the drafter the "general understanding" that Delaware's merger and certificate amendment provisions operate separately under the "bedrock doctrine of independent legal significance." Given this, said the court, it is "extraordinarily unlikely" that the provision could have been intended to apply to mergers. See also Sullivan Money Management, Inc. v. FLS Holdings Inc., CCH Fed.Sec.L.Rep. ¶ 97,292, 1992 WL 345453 (Del.Ch.1992).

If the second provision was not intended to apply to mergers, then why did the drafter put it in the charter? Do clients pay drafters to replicate the results of the naked application of the DCL interpreted under the doctrine of independent legal significance or do they pay to have those results reversed with investor-protective results?

3. *Elliott Associates v. Avatex*

The Delaware Supreme Court distinguished *Warner v. Chris–Craft* in a later "case of first impression," **Elliott Associates, L.P. v. Avatex Corp.**, 715 A.2d 843

(Del.Supr.1998). The preferred stock issuer there, Avatex, was not performing well. Like the issuer in *Bove v. Community Hotel*, supra, it effected a recapitalization by creating a wholly owned shell subsidiary (called "Xetava") and engineering a merger with the subsidiary as surviving corporation. Pursuant to the merger, Avatex's charter was eliminated and its First Series Preferred stockholders received 73 percent of the common stock of the survivor. Under the Avatex charter, the preferred had no right to vote, except on any "amendment, alteration or repeal" of the charter "whether by merger, consolidation or otherwise," that "materially and adversely" affected the rights of the preferred. The preferred claimed a right to a two-thirds class vote. Avatex resisted, claiming that as in *Warner v. Chris–Craft*, it was only the conversion of the stock as a result of the merger, and not the amendment, alteration or repeal of the certificate, that would adversely affect the preferred stockholders. The Chancery Court agreed, 583 A.2d 962, and denied the class vote. The Supreme Court reversed, 715 A.2d at 847–51:

"It is important to keep in mind, however, that the terms of the preferred stock in Warner were significantly different from those present here, because in Warner the phrase 'whether by merger, consolidation or otherwise' was not included. The issue here, therefore, is whether the presence of this additional phrase in the Avatex certificate is an outcome-determinative distinction from Warner.

" * * * Nevertheless, the heart of the Warner rationale, which we must address here, is that it was not the amendment, alteration or repeal of the Warner certificate that adversely affected the Warner * * * stock. The Chancellor held that it was only the conversion of the Warner [preferred] to Time [preferred] that caused the adverse effect, and, moreover, that the conversion was permissible under 8 Del. C. § 251, which (unlike 8 Del. C. § 242) does not require a class vote on a merger. Further, the Chancellor held that no contractual protection of the Warner [preferred] provided for a class vote on a merger. * * *

" * * * Here the First Series Preferred stock of Avatex is converted to common stock of the surviving corporation, Xetava, a newly formed corporation admittedly a wholly owned subsidiary of Avatex created for the sole purpose of effecting this merger and eliminating the rights of the Avatex First Series Preferred. In Warner, the Warner [preferred] also received a new security—Time [preferred]—a senior security issued by the surviving corporation, Time (renamed Time Warner). This was accomplished by using TW Sub, Time's wholly-owned subsidiary, as the merger partner of Warner. Since we do not reach the question of the economic quality of the transaction, it makes no difference for purposes of this analysis (as plaintiffs argue) that in Warner there were two distinct acts that operated independently— that the substitution of charters was between Warner and TW Sub and the exchange of shares was between Warner and Time. The operative events here are that the proposed downstream merger of Avatex into Xetava results in the conversion of Avatex stock to Xetava stock and the elimination 'by merger' of the certificate protections granted to the Avatex First Series Preferred. Thus, it is both the stock conversion and the repeal of the Avatex certificate that causes the adverse effect to the First Series Preferred. In Warner, it was only the stock conversion that caused the adverse effect because the phrase, 'whether by merger, consolidation or otherwise' was not present."

A more recent case, Benchmark Capital Partners IV, L.P. v. Vague, 2002 WL 1732423 (Del.Ch.), followed *Warner v. Cris–Craft* where the charter provided for a class vote respecting corporate actions that "materially adversely change the rights, preferences and privileges" of the preferred. For commentary, see Smith, Independent Legal Significance, Good Faith, and the Interpretation of Venture Capital

Contracts, 40 Willamette L. Rev. 825 (2004); Bratton, Gaming Delaware, 40 Willamette L. Rev. 853 (2004).

4. *What Law Applies?*

VantagePoint Venture Partners 1996, LP v. Examen, Inc., 871 A.2d 1108 (Del.Supr.2005), involved the merger of a Delaware corporation whose business was situated in California. A class of preferred possessed 20 percent of the votes at the meeting on the merger, without class voting. The charter did not provide for a class vote. Had it done so, the plaintiff, the holder of 85 percent of the preferred, would have been in a position to block the deal. So the plaintiff filed an action in the California Superior Court seeking a declaration that the issuer was a quasi-California corporation pursuant to California Corporations Code § 2115, which defines foreign corporations for which the California statute has an outreach effect as those foreign corporations, half of whose voting securities are held of record by persons with California addresses, that also conduct half of their business in California as measured by a formula weighing assets, sales, and payroll factors. If the issuer was a quasi-California corporation, it would be subject to California Corporations Code § 1201(a), which held out a class vote to the preferred. The Delaware Supreme Court held that, under the internal affairs doctrine, Delaware law applied, and did so as a constitutional proposition:

> The internal affairs doctrine is not, however, only a conflicts of law principle. Pursuant to the Fourteenth Amendment Due Process Clause, directors and officers of corporations "have a significant right . . . to know what law will be applied to their actions" and "[s]tockholders . . . have a right to know by what standards of accountability they may hold those managing the corporation's business and affairs." [McDermott Inc. v. Lewis, 531 A.2d 206, 216, 217 (Del.Supr.1987).] Under the Commerce Clause, a state "has no interest in regulating the internal affairs of foreign corporations." [Id. at 217.] Therefore, this Court has held that an "application of the internal affairs doctrine is mandated by constitutional principles, except in the 'rarest situations,' "e.g., when "the law of the state of incorporation is inconsistent with a national policy on foreign or interstate commerce."

5. *Drafting Practice.*

Note, Arrearage Elimination and the Preferred Stock Contract: A Survey and a Proposal for Reform, 9 Cardozo L.Rev. 1335, 1345–53, 1361–70 (1988), presents the results of a survey of the contracts governing 97 preferred stock issues of 52 industrial corporations chartered in Delaware. Only 14 percent of the issues had provisions for a class vote in respect of a merger.

Fifty-two percent of the issues surveyed were listed on the New York Stock Exchange and thus subject to the Exchange's listing requirement of a two-thirds supermajority class vote for adverse certificate amendments. NYSE Company Manual, A–281 (1984). But only about one half of these listed stocks actually included the supermajority provision, presumably because of a liberal policy of granting exceptions on the part of the Exchange. Of the listed stocks, 22 percent provided for merger class votes.

NOTE: FAIRNESS SCRUTINY UNDER DELAWARE LAW

1. *Dart v. KKR.*

The Delaware Chancery Court was asked to apply fairness scrutiny, the treatment accorded to a class of preferred in connection with a management buyout in **Dart v. Kohlberg, Kravis, Roberts & Co.**, 1985 WL 21145 (Del.Ch.1985). The claim survived a motion to dismiss.

The preferred stock in question was first issued by Amstar Corp. in 1967. It initially sold for $12.50 per share, and was entitled to a $0.68 per share annual dividend. The Certificate provided for redemption at the issuer's option for $13.125 per share, and entitled the holders to $12.50 upon liquidation. The Certificate also provided that no change could be made of any of the express terms of the preferred stock which would adversely affect the holder of the stock without an affirmative vote of two-thirds of the holders of the stock.

In 1982 and 1983 two other corporations began accumulating significant positions in Amstar common. As a result, Amstar's managers began looking for a friendly acquisition partner. They entered into discussion with KKR Associates. In October 1983 Amstar and KKR Associates entered into an agreement pursuant to which KKR would form an acquisition subsidiary which would merge into Amstar. The common stockholders of Amstar would receive $47 cash for their shares; KKR Associates would be left with the common stock of Amstar; management would receive stock options designed to leave it holding 8 percent of the stock of Amstar post-merger.

Initially, the merger agreement made no provision for the preferred. It later was amended to provide for a cash out of the preferred at $8 per share (a premium over the then market price), subject to an affirmative vote by two-thirds of the holders of the preferred. But only 60 percent of the preferred cast affirmative votes. As a result, the preferred was not cashed out and remained outstanding as a security of a privately held and heavily indebted Amstar.

The court discussed the plaintiff's claim as follows:

"Although the plaintiff has not shown any legal basis for his claim that the preferred stockholders should have been permitted to vote as a separate class on the entire merger, inequitable action does not become permissible simply because it is legally possible. Schnell v. Chris–Craft Industries, Inc., Del.Supr., 285 A.2d 437 (1971). Although everything done by defendants may have been in strict compliance with the letter of Delaware law, it is possible that the totality of actions resulted in an impermissible inequity to the holders of the preferred stock. The difficulty with the challenged transaction is that it was highly leveraged and a majority of the preferred stockholders ended up still owning their shares although they preferred to be bought out. The assets of the corporation were used as sole security for the loans obtained for the purpose of buying out the common stock and the public preferred stockholders were left holding their shares in a corporation which, as a result of the transaction, has a much greater debt and therefore perhaps a lessened ability to pay preferred dividends. Such a leveraged buy-out calls for judicial scrutiny to prevent possible abuse. On the present record, therefore, which does not contain the fruits of full discovery, it can be at least reasonably inferred that plaintiff has a cause of action, however imperfectly stated and however speculative, as to the allegations which attack the leveraged buy-out and its effect on the preferred stockholders."

2. *The Jedwab Standard.*

If the fairness question in *Dart* came up for adjudication how would the court determine the fairness (or unfairness) of the leveraged buyout respecting the preferred? Consider application of the standard of scrutiny in respect of fiduciary duty to preferred stockholders articulated by Chancellor Allen, in **Jedwab v. MGM Grand Hotels, Inc.**, 509 A.2d 584, 594–595 (Del.Ch.1986):

"[W]ith respect to matters relating to preferences or limitations that distinguish preferred stock from common, the duty of the corporation and its directors is essentially contractual and the scope of the duty is appropriately defined by reference to the specific words evidencing that contract; where however the right asserted is not to a preference as against the common stock but rather a right shared equally with the common, the existence of such right and the scope of the correlative duty may be measured by equitable as well as legal standards.

"With this distinction in mind the Delaware cases which frequently analyze rights of and duties towards preferred stock in legal (i.e., contractual) terminology (e.g., Wood v. Coastal States Gas Corp., supra; Judah v. Delaware Trust Company, Del.Supr., 378 A.2d 624 (1977); Rothschild International Corp. v. Liggett Group, Inc., supra) may be made consistent with those cases that apply fiduciary standards to claims of preferred shareholders (e.g., David J. Greene & Co. v. Schenley Industries, Inc., Del.Ch., 281 A.2d 30 (1971); Lewis v. Great Western United Corporation, Del.Ch., C.A. No. 5397, Brown, V.C. (September 15, 1977)).

* * *

"Assuming that plaintiff and the other preferred shareholders have a 'right' recognized in equity to a fair apportionment of the merger consideration (and such a right to require directors to exercise appropriate care) it becomes material to know what legal standard is to be used to assess the probability that a violation of that right will ultimately be proven. Plaintiff asserts that the appropriate test is one of entire or intrinsic fairness. That test is the familiar one employed when fiduciaries elect to utilize their power over the corporation to effectuate a transaction in which they have an interest that diverges from that of the corporation or the minority shareholders. See, Weinberger v. UOP, Inc., supra; Gottlieb v. Heyden Chemical Corp., Del.Supr., 91 A.2d 57 (1952).

"Our Supreme Court has made it quite clear that the heightened judicial scrutiny called for by the test of intrinsic or entire fairness is not called forth simply by a demonstration that a controlling shareholder fixes the terms of a transaction and, by exercise of voting power or by domination of the board, compels its effectuation. (The apparent situation presented in this action.) It is in each instance essential to show as well that the fiduciary has an interest with respect to the transaction that conflicts with the interests of minority shareholders. Aronson v. Lewis, Del.Supr., 473 A.2d 805, 812 (1984). Speaking in the context of a parent dealing with a controlled but not wholly-owned subsidiary our Supreme Court has said:

> The basic situation for the application of the rule [requiring a fiduciary to assume the burden to show intrinsic fairness] is the one in which the parent has received a benefit to the exclusion and at the expense of the subsidiary.

> * * *

"A parent does indeed owe a fiduciary duty to its subsidiary when there are parent-subsidiary dealings. However, this alone will not evoke the intrinsic fairness standard. This standard will be applied only when the fiduciary duty is accompanied by self-dealing—the situation when a parent is on both sides of a transaction with its subsidiary. Self-dealing occurs when the parent, by virtue of its domination of the subsidiary, causes the subsidiary to act in such a way that the parent receives something from the subsidiary to the exclusion of, and detriment to, the minority stockholders of the subsidiary. Sinclair Oil Corporation v. Levien, Del.Supr., 280 A.2d 717, 720 (1971)."

What benefit did the majority in *Dart* receive "to the exclusion and at the expense" of the preferred?

Dalton v. American Investment Co.

Delaware Court of Chancery, 1985.
490 A.2d 574.

[This case concerned the 1980 acquisition of American Investment Company ("AIC") by a wholly owned subsidiary of Leucadia, Inc. AIC had 5.5 million common shares outstanding and two issues of preferred. The plaintiffs held noncallable 5½ percent Series B having a stated redemption and liquidation value of $25. Because of increases in interest rates after the issue of the Series B in 1961, the stock, which had no trading market, had a market value of less than $9 during the events in question.

[AIC had been on the market for an acquirer before Leucadia came along. Two years earlier, Household Finance Corporation ("HFC") offered to acquire AIC for a total consideration of $75 million, distributed $12 per share to the common and $25 per share to the preferred. The deal aborted when the Justice Department objected on antitrust grounds. Thereafter, the President of AIC, Brockmann, continued to market the company, alluding to the book value of the common stock, about $13.50, as the basis on which a successful offer should be made.

[Leucadia's initial offer was $13 for the common and nothing for the preferred. Brockmann then suggested that "something should be done" for the preferred, and Leucadia added an offer to increase the dividend rate on the preferred from 5½ percent to 7 percent and set up a sinking fund to retire the stock over 20 years.

[The merger negotiations also involved a third party interested in purchasing some of AIC's receivables. The deal included a sale of $130 million of these receivables to the third party for $120 million cash. As a result, AIC came to Leucadia with a pot of cash containing much more than the $72.2 million purchase price. All of the directors of AIC owned common; their holdings collectively amounted to 12 percent of the outstanding common. One director held preferred. No preferred class vote was held. In the pooled vote for the merger, the Series B holders voted 170,000 of the 280,000 shares outstanding against the merger.]

Plaintiffs suggest that what Brockmann and the other directors did was note that HFC had offered to pay a total of $75.7 million to acquire AIC, broken down into components of $66.5 million for the common ($12 per share × roughly 5.5 million shares) and $9.2 million for the total of the two series of preferred ($25 per share × some 361,000 shares). They say that simple arithmetic shows that AIC's 1980 book value of $13.50 for the common shares multiplied by the 5.5 million common shares outstanding worked out to approximately $75 million. Since it was not necessary for a potential acquirer to cash out the preferred shareholders in order to gain control of the company, and since the AIC board viewed the offer of HFC to purchase the preferred shares at their redemption value of $25 per share as having been a potential "Christmas present" to the preferred shareholders anyway, plaintiffs charge that what Brockmann did, with the board's ultimate approval, was to suggest the book value of the common stock as the starting point for any merger offer so as to assure that the whole of any new offer would go totally to the owners of the common shares.

* * *

In sum, plaintiffs contend that the failure of the defendant directors to treat their interests evenhandedly with those of the common shareholders has damaged them financially by leaving them as minority shareholders in a de-listed company and as the owners of an unmarketable preferred stock paying only a meager return when measured by present-day standards. They charge that the defendant directors knowingly took the action which has served to lock them in as preferred shareholders of AIC when, had they properly exercised the fiduciary duty of fair dealing owed to all shareholders, they could have extricated the plaintiffs at a fair price as well. For this alleged wrong, plaintiffs demand monetary damages.

* * *

[D]efendants point out that Leucadia's view of the preferred shares as "cheap debt", and the fact that Leucadia was well aware that it could accomplish its goal of acquiring AIC without the need to purchase the preferred shares, left Brockmann and the other members of AIC's board with absolutely no leverage with which to negotiate a pay-out for the preferred. Moreover, had they attempted to do so once Leucadia made its offer, two consequences were possible—both being fraught with danger insofar as AIC's board was concerned.

First, if AIC's board had attempted to persuade Leucadia to reduce its $13 per share for the common by some portion in order that the difference might be used to cash out the preferred shareholders, such conduct could have been viewed as a breach of the fiduciary duty of fair dealing owed to the common shareholders and subjected the board members to suit for this reason. Alternatively, such an effort by the AIC board might have caused Leucadia to believe that it could acquire the common shares for less than $13 per share, in which event Leucadia might have reduced its offer for the common and still offered nothing for the preferred—again subjecting the board to potential suit by the common shareholders. And, of course, there was always the possibility that if AIC's board rejected the proposal for its failure to include a price for the preferred shares, Leucadia could have backed off and gone the tender offer route for the common shares so as to acquire control in that manner and bring about a merger under its own terms at some later date.

[The court reasoned that the "Hobson's choice defense raised by the defendant directors * * * misses the point" and that case turned on "the factual determination of whether or not Leucadia's offer was made in response to a solicitation by Brockmann and the other director defendants."]

When the trimmings of precedent and fiduciary duty are brushed aside, plaintiffs' argument, reduced to its simplest terms, is (1) that between the HFC proposal in 1978 and the Leucadia merger in 1980 the price per share for the common stock was increased from $12 to $13 per share while the preferred shareholders went from $25 per share to no cash consideration whatever, and (2) that during the interval between the two events Brockmann and the AIC board were soliciting offers at book value, or $13.50, for the common shares while seeking nothing for the preferred. From these two premises plaintiffs proceed to the conclusion that the difference between the HFC and Leucadia proposals was necessarily a direct result of the efforts by the AIC board to increase the cash consideration from the common stock with knowledge that such an increase would be at the expense of the preferred shares. Having thus bridged the gap to arrive at this factual conclusion, plaintiffs then plug it into the legal principle which holds that it is improper for those in a fiduciary position to utilize the merger process solely to promote the interests of one class of shareholders to the detriment, and at the expense, of the members of a minority class of shareholders. Thus plaintiffs reach their final position that they have been injured monetarily by the failure of the defendant directors to adhere to their fiduciary duty to deal fairly with all shareholders in a merger context.

[The court ruled against the plaintiffs on a finding of causation. Reviewing the evidence on the formulation of the Leucadia offer, it found that the offer had been determined by the offeror's business interests and had not been "made in direct response to a veiled solicitation by Brockmann."]

NOTE: *FLS HOLDINGS*

Can the problem posed by the treatment of preferred stockholders in the position of those in *Dalton* be solved through the appointment of a special negotiator who represents their interests? From what source would the negotiator derive bargaining power?

Consider comments made by Chancellor Allen in his review of a settlement in **In re FLS Holdings, Inc. Shareholders Litigation**, 1993 WL 104562 (Del.Ch.). FLS Holdings, a steel manufacturer, underwent a leveraged buyout in 1988 and performed badly thereafter. By 1991 it was unable to make periodic payments on its debt. Its two classes of common stock were closely held by its managers, some of its employees, and the LBO promoters, Goldman Sachs and Citibank. A new class of preferred stock had been issued to former common stockholders of the company in the back end of the LBO merger. This stock had a liquidation preference of $53.33, and a 17.5 percent dividend preference, payable in kind (that is, in additional newly issued preferred stock) until 1994. As a result of in kind dividend payments, 1.6 million preferred shares were outstanding by 1993, representing an investment of $80 million at original issue prices and carrying a liquidation preference of $94.7 million.

Bankruptcy loomed in 1992, and Goldman Sachs went looking for a potential buyer for FLS. Kyoei Steel, Ltd. approached Goldman and offered to pay $43.2 million for the firm's equity—$10 per share or $5 million for the common, and $27 per share or $38.2 million for the preferred—and to pay 100 cents on the dollar to the holders of its debt. A back and forth between Kyoei and its representative and the FLS board and Goldman as its representative followed. Goldman and the board negotiated for a larger overall consideration and a more "fair" allocation between the common and the preferred. At each stage of the negotiations the amount payable to the common increased, while the amount payable to the preferred stayed about the same. Eventually, a merger agreement was signed providing $15 million for the common and $38.4 million for the preferred. The preferred had no class vote in the projected merger.

Then, at the due diligence stage, Kyoei discovered $24 million of hidden environmental, pension and other liabilities. More negotiations followed. The parties agreed to a $15 million price reduction—$5.6 million from the common and $9.4 million from the preferred. The final price for the common was $17.90 per share (a total of $9 million) and for the preferred was $18.124 per share (a total of $29.01 million). These sums amounted to a return of 54 percent of the common's original investment and 62 percent of the value of the stock surrendered by the preferred in the back end of the LBO merger.

The board paid Salomon Brothers $400,000 for a fairness opinion respecting the payment to the preferred. Salomon examined other restructurings of distressed firms that entailed allocations between the preferred and the common. Said Solomon, the 75.5 percent of the total consideration paid to the preferred here compared favorably with the median payout of 68.7 percent in the other restructurings.

Chancellor Allen declined to approve a litigation settlement under which the attorneys representing the class of preferred received $200,000 and the preferred received no additional money consideration. The asserted nonpecuniary benefits to the preferred obtained by the attorneys amounted to enhanced disclosure of the terms of the merger and a notice describing their option of a section 262 appraisal.

The Chancellor discounted the value of the Salomon opinion because it failed to indicate the relative size of the investments of the preferred and common in the restructuring transactions used as a basis for comparison. He appraised the merits of the plaintiffs' claim as follows:

"In allocating the consideration of this merger, the directors, although they were elected by the common stock, owed fiduciary duties to both the preferred and common stockholders, and were obligated to treat the preferred fairly. See Eisenberg v. Chicago Milwaukee Corp., Del.Ch., 537 A.2d 1051, 1062 (1987); Jedwab v. MGM Grand Hotels, Del.Ch., 509 A.2d 584, 593–94 (1986). That standard is, of course, a somewhat opaque one that, unless procedures are employed that are sufficient in themselves to give reasonable assurance of fairness, may require a reviewing agency to make a highly specific inquiry of the company and the transaction.

"In preliminarily assessing plaintiffs' claim, I note first that here no mechanism employing a truly independent agency on the behalf of the preferred was employed before the transaction was formulated. Only the relatively weak procedural protection of an investment banker's *ex post* opinion, was available to support the position that the final allocation was fair. * * *

* * *

"If this case proceeds to an adjudication of the merits of plaintiffs' claims, defendants will bear the burden of proving that the allocation was fair to the preferred. * * * "

NOTE: JUDICIAL REVIEW OF RECAPITALIZATIONS AND MERGERS IMPAIRING THE RIGHTS OF PREFERRED STOCKHOLDERS

Consider a case where an issue of preferred stock is held by a sole owner—whether an industrial firm, an investment institution, or a sophisticated individual investor. So long as that sole owner has a class vote by statute or charter provision, no fairness issue is likely to arise when the issuer proposes an alteration of the preferred's rights and preferences. The holder can use its veto to bring the issuer to the bargaining table and the institution of free contract provides adequate protection. Presumably, the situation is substantially similar if the preferred is held by a small number of sophisticated investors protected by a class vote.

But the situations in the cases in this chapter have been very different. In many cases, particularly with respect to mergers, the preferred class has not even had the benefit of a class vote, so that even sole owners or small groups of institutional investors have been left with no contract protection. In most of the cases the preferred has been held by a dispersed group, so that even where a class vote has been available, its efficacy has not always been manifest.

With widely held preferred, even where the investment contract expressly provides for the possibility of alteration by a class vote, one doubts that the alteration feature of the contract was pressed on the investors' attention when the stock was sold. Nor is there any reason to believe that investors' attention often is called to the possibility of effecting alterations by contrived merger. Hence, for courts to find buried in the contracts drafted by the commons' representatives the preferreds' *consent*, even to the power of a majority of the class, to amend or merge or "voluntarily" exchange arrears out of existence or otherwise alter particular preferences or protection, cannot be to suggest that the preferred holders actually bargained for those terms and expected to experience an impairment of their contract rights. Nor can it imply a finding that the terms were communicated to, or understood by, those buying the stock—except possibly by the osmotic process that makes the market an efficient discounter not only of economic information and contingencies, but of legal changes and potential for maneuver.

Despite the apparent cognitive failure, one still reasonably could counsel judicial restraint. Under this approach, the preferred holders' problem is best left to market solution over time. By hypothesis, across generations of preferred stock contracts, the weak points and anomalies are identified. To the extent the realization of investor community expectations depends on a change in drafting practice, the change is incorporated as the contract forms evolve. But a question arises, based on the cases in this chapter: How well does this evolutionary process appear to have worked? The preferred holders' problem has been a corporate law constant for a century, with no across-the-board drafting solution yet in sight.

In the alternative, the courts could confront the politics of the readjustment process and consider imposing limits on "rebargaining." The preferred comes to the process at a disadvantage of economic position as against the common. This stems from the negative impact of delay in payment on the preferred holders, with their fixed income expectations. Dispersed preferred holders are also at a disadvantage in the *process* of bargaining in a recapitalization. Indeed, the preferred stock recapitalizations seen in most of the cases in this chapter may be described as bargains only by a loose euphemism. Not much real bargaining seems to take place. Inevitably the plan originates with management. Even where the preferred has a class vote, the proxy apparatus is in control of management, which thus has the advantage of primary access to the finances and facilities to solicit consents and the ability to control the information disclosed to those solicited, as well as ability to time the plan on short notice.

It may be an overstatement to suggest that common stockholders can impose their will unilaterally on preferred holders when they propose a recapitalization, particularly given the rise of the institutional investor and the use of preferred in venture capital investment. But it cannot be denied that there is considerably greater freedom of action for the common stockholders and substantially less protection for the preferred holders than is present for seniors in insolvency reorganization. As an observer of the process has remarked, "through the bargaining leverage of common stockholdings" preferred holders have regularly "been euchred, cajoled, coerced, elbowed and traded out of their legal rights." Accordingly, there is much to be said for judicial intervention in, if not actual supervision of the process.

Courts have recognized that these process problems import a justification for setting limits on the recapitalization bargain. Yet the cases in this chapter fall short of providing a reliable protective rule or standard. The chief difficulty appears to have been the courts' inability to formulate criteria for determining the appropriate limits of the bargain. See Brudney, Standards of Fairness and the Limits of Preferred Stock Modifications, 26 Rutgers L.Rev. 445 (1973). This inevitably implicates the question of substantive fairness of the transaction.

The Delaware courts remit all complaints respecting alteration of preferred rights and preferences to the law of contract. We have seen that the reference to contract often (but not always) leads to a result favoring the issuer. But is it clear in these cases as a matter of contract interpretation that the parties "intended" or "expected" tribute to the paid by the preferred? Alternatively, contract law imports a duty of good faith which constrains an extreme deprivation of the expectations of one party where the action in question is not essential to the accomplishment of the counterparty's expectations. Might not the good faith rubric, originally articulated for "relational" contracting situations, appropriately constrain issuer extractions from preferred in recapitalizations and mergers?

In alternative, courts could bring to bear the fiduciary framework of majority-to-minority fiduciary duty, which imposes a burden of proof on the majority in the wake of a showing of majority self dealing. The majority-minority framework of review goes on to open the door for the majority to justify its actions by showing a valid business purpose—that is, that the action enhances the value of the firm as a whole, with no alternative course of action less oppressive to the minority interest being available. Would this sequence of inquiry provide a workable basis for determining the fairness of a recapitalization or merger? See Mitchell, The Puzzling Problem of Preferred Stock (And Why We Should Care About It), 51 Bus. Law. 443 (1996); Note, Protection For Shareholder Interests in Recapitalizations of Publicly Held Corporations, 58 Col.L.Rev. 1030, 1066–7 (1958).

Carrying the analogy to majority-to-minority fiduciary duty out one additional step, courts also could apply process scrutiny along the lines developed in cash-out merger cases, see infra, Part V. This approach, in fact, is suggested in the *FLH* opinion, supra. Under this, the recapitalization would be vulnerable to fairness review unless the preferred got a place at the negotiating table, represented by its own counsel and economic advisor. Note, however, that a significant limit on protective power of this device is suggested in *FLH*. In Delaware, such a constructed negotiation would extend to the "equity" value of the preferred only; rights and preferences, being outside of the Delaware fiduciary regime, presumably would not be on the table as mandatory subjects of bargaining.

SECTION B.   CONVERTIBLE SECURITIES AND WARRANTS

INTRODUCTION

Convertibility is a contractual privilege that allows one class of securities to be exchanged for another. How it is used more particularly is up to the drafter. A "convertible bond" is a bond that incorporates the privilege of conversion into the issuer's common stock. An issue of preferred stock may similarly be made convertible into issuer common. But common stock is not the only available underlying security. Bonds can be made convertible into preferred stock of the issuer or common stock of a subsidiary or sister corporation. (Technically, debt that is convertible into stock of an issuer other than the debtor is called "exchangeable" debt.) Nor need the conversion option lie only with the holder; bonds convertible at the option of the issuer also appear. Finally, there have been security contracts that contemplate conversion of a junior security into a senior security. These are known as "upstream" convertibles. Many state codes expressly permit them. See, e.g., NYBCL § 519; N.J.Statutes § 14A:7–9(1); DCL § 151(e).

A "warrant" is a long-term option on the common stock of a corporation granted for consideration by the corporation itself. A conversion privilege added to a bond or a share of preferred includes the economic substance of a warrant, for it similarly grants the holder a long-term option on the issuer's common stock. Alternatively, an issuer can take a straight bond, attach a warrant, and sell the two as a package called a "bond-warrant unit" at a cost of capital comparable to that of a convertible debt issue. The warrant portions of the unit may or may not be detachable, i.e., the debt and warrant portions may or may not separate into two distinct securities.

Like preferred stock, convertibles and bonds with attached warrants are "hybrids"—they combine features of debt and equity in a single security. The option that effects the combination gives rise to distinct problems of valuation. Its attachment and sale also gives the issuer distinct opportunities to hinder and frustrate the holders' expectations. Convertibles and warrants accordingly present special problems of contract drafting, and give rise to a constant flow of litigation in which holders ask judges to intervene to protect them from issuer opportunism.

1. TERMS AND VALUATION

Convertibles combine a debt (or preferred stock) interest with an equity option. Many different combinations of debt and equity interests with varying contractual terms fit within the definition. In all cases the combination makes for a complex exercise in valuation.

(A) THE VALUE OF A CALL OPTION

Options come in a number of sizes and shapes. Convertibles and warrants, which embody a call on *the issuer* to sell stock to the holder, should be distinguished from the option which is a "call" on a *third party* to sell (or a "put" to a third party to buy) stock of a named issuer to (or from) the option holder. The latter options, which tend to have short durations, do not represent an overhang on the common stock of an issuer since they do not require issuance of any more stock. They nevertheless provide a useful beginning point for a presentation of convertible bond valuation. Consult the presentation supra, Part I.

(B) CONVERTIBLE BOND FEATURES AND VALUATION VARIABLES

The presentation that follows comes in two parts. The first part describes a traditional convertible bond–a fixed interest debt security with the attributes of a traditional bond that may be converted into common stock at the option of the holder. The second part describes a number of contemporary variations on the traditional theme.

(1) *Traditional Convertibles*

The issuer incorporating a conversion privilege into its bonds grants a future claim on its equity. For investors, the future claim gives convertible bonds the advantage of combining desirable features of straight bonds, such as fixed income payments and principal repayment, with the upside potential of common stock. In exchange for the future equity claim, bondholders customarily accept subordinated status and a coupon rate lower than that of an equivalent straight bond—100 basis points or more depending on interest rate levels. To issuers, these concessions give convertibles advantages over straight debt, such as cost savings, increased future capacity to incur senior debt, and greater flexibility to advance the interests of the common stockholders. The value of the conversion privilege has been said to stem from these mutual perceptions of advantage.

Figure: The Traditional Convertible Bond

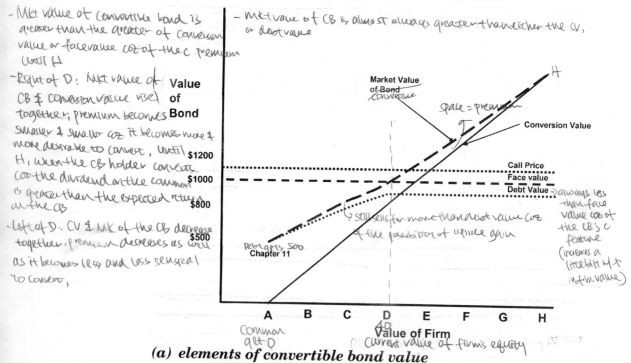

(a) *elements of convertible bond value*

The Figure illustrates the upside and downside interrelations of the three constituent elements of value—debt value, conversion value, and conversion premium—for a typical convertible bond at various possible values of the issuing corporation. The hypothetical bond has a 20 year term. Conversion is optional with the holder at any time over the entire term of the bond. The issuer may redeem the bond for its face value plus a small premium at any time during the term. The coupon rate is 200 basis points below the rate available on a comparable nonconvertible bond.

Debt value is the value of an equivalent straight bond with the same coupon rate. It is sensitive to the variables dominant in straight bond valuation, such as interest rate levels and the issuer's equity cushion. **Conversion value** is the value of the amount of common stock into which the bond can be converted. It depends on the market value of the underlying common stock and the price, the **conversion price**, at which the bonds, taken at their face value, are convertible. The conversion price is commonly set 10 to 20 percent above the market price of the underlying common stock at the time of original issue. The conversion price may remain constant for the life of the conversion privilege, or could be stepped up (or down) at stated intervals. The **conversion ratio** expresses the number of shares of common stock the bondholder receives upon conversion. For example, a bond with a face value of $1000 and a conversion price of $50 has a conversion ratio of 20. More generally,

$$\text{Conversion Ratio} = \frac{\text{Face Value}}{\text{Conversion Price}}$$

Conversion value = CR * Price trading currently.

If the conversion price is a constant, conversion value is subject to the same determinants as the stock price, and goes up and down in lockstep with it. Although arbitrage possibilities prevent the bond from selling below the higher of debt or conversion value, nothing prevents it from selling above the higher of these two values. **Conversion premium** is the amount by which market value exceeds debt or conversion value. If we characterize the conversion privilege as a long-term option on the underlying common, the premium represents the option's value.

Assume that the bond illustrated in the Figure is priced, issued, and sold for its $1000 face value with a conversion price of $50. Assume further that at the time of the bond's issue the issuer's stock is trading at $40 and the issuer's value is at D. Debt value at issue is $900, reflecting the convertible's lower coupon rate. Conversion value is $800, reflecting that the $50 conversion price exceeds the $40 market price of the underlying common. The premium at issue is $100, the difference between the higher of debt or conversion value and the initial $1000 market price. Valuation at issue reflects the expectation that the issuer's value will increase substantially during the early years of the bond's term.

Looking to the right of D in the Figure, we see the bond's conversion value and market value rising in tandem with higher issuer values, illustrating the convertible bond's upside potential. Debt value, in contrast, is limited by a fixed coupon rate and does not rise significantly. (If the Figure were to show the convertible's value as a function of different levels of prevailing interest rates, rather than of different firm values, then movement to the right on the horizontal axis would cause the debt value line to drop.) As issuer values increase, the market behavior of the convertible increasingly mirrors the market behavior of the underlying common stock and the premium accordingly becomes progressively smaller. Eventually, at H, the issuer's value and the dividend payout on the underlying common have increased so much that the expected return on the underlying common exceeds the expected return on the bonds. As a result, the premium disappears and the holders convert.

We see the bond's downside market behavior by looking to the left of D. Conversion value declines in tandem with the issuer's value and the premium disappears as the decline in value becomes extreme. Debt value, protected by the bond contract, shows more stability and resilience. At B, the bond's market value has fallen so far as to have become nearly contiguous with debt value; this is the "bond floor." As the issuer's value goes into extreme decline to the left of B, even the bond floor begins seriously to give way. With the issuer's value at A, we reach the end of the line—a hypothetical bankruptcy liquidation pursuant to which the holders of the convertible issue receive $500 per bond and the stockholders receive nothing.

(b) the conversion premium

We have seen that calculating the conversion value, given a constant conversion price, is a matter of valuing the underlying common, and that calculating the debt value is a matter of straight bond valuation. Valuing the conversion premium, in contrast, is a matter of valuing the conversion privilege. Sorting out the interrelated variables which constitute and affect the premium is the central problem of convertible bond valuation.

The premium has been said to arise from investors' perception that advantages lie in having two imperfectly correlated elements of value—debt value and conversion value—combined in the same security. One advantage of the combination comes from the bond's limited downside risk. The downside risk of holding the bond is less than that of holding the amount of common into which it is convertible because debt value provides a floor should issuer values decline. This floor also gives the convertible greater price stability than the underlying common possesses. (One therefore can expect a positive correlation between the size of the premium and the size of the variance in the price movements of the underlying stock.)

The limited downside risk causes the bond to sell for more than its conversion value even when we are to the right of D in the Figure, where higher issuer values cause conversion value to surpass debt value. But since the relative importance of bond floor protection decreases as issuer values increase, the premium also decreases as issuer values increase.

Another advantage comes from the bondholder's potential upside participation. The bond in the Figure still sells at a premium to the left of D, even though debt value exceeds conversion value at these lower issuer values. This premium results not from bond floor downside protection but from the market's hopes that conversion value has upside potential. Since this upside potential's relative importance decreases as issuer values decrease, the premium diminishes so as to disappear entirely when bankruptcy liquidation is reached at A.

The premium also results from the convertible's income stream. So long as the convertible's coupon rate exceeds the underlying common's dividend payout rate, it is a more advantageous holding than the common. Indeed, so long as the coupon rate exceeds the dividend rate, arbitrage possibilities will prevent the bond from selling as low as conversion value, except immediately prior to declaration of a dividend or an adverse change in conversion terms. Given the stated condition, the bond always sells above its conversion value and the investor will not find it optimal to convert at any time prior to maturity, since conversion would result in the premium's destruction. Conversely, as is the case in the Figure, if the dividend payout rate eventually exceeds the coupon rate at higher issuer values, the premium will be entirely eliminated. At that point, voluntary conversion should occur, preventing the occurrence of a negative premium.

The premium is also sensitive to the conversion privilege's durability— the longer its life, the greater its value. Conversely, the premium is reduced if the issuer retains the power to shorten the duration of the conversion privilege. Issuers customarily retain this power in the form of a call (or redemption) right—the right to pay off the bond prior to maturity at the call price, usually fixed at par plus a small premium.

(c) issuer call rights

Call rights will reduce the size of the conversion premium in varying degrees depending upon the likelihood that the issuer actually will exercise them. Issuer call policies in turn depend on a number of factors, including bond contract provisions, market restraints on management actions, and, at bottom, management awareness.

Some issuers reserve the right to call issues of convertible bonds at any time. Other convertible issues are made noncallable for a stated number of years from the date of original issue. In either case, the issuer eventually can exercise its call right to force conversion at such time as issuer growth causes conversion value to exceed the call price. Since conversion value is the higher figure, the bondholder converts before the redemption date. On the redemption date both bond and conversion privileges disappear and are replaced with the right to claim the call price. Needless to say, the conversion premium disappears also.

Forced conversion through call advances stockholder interests: if the total value of the issuer is the sum of the value of the debt and equity claims upon it, then permitting convertibles further to appreciate in value as the issuer grows permits the bondholders' claim on the issuer's equity to increase at the stockholders' expense.

In theory, then, a stockholder optimal call policy dictates call as soon as the bond's conversion value exceeds its call price. In the real world, however, such a call policy would have to permit conversion value to rise somewhat higher to assure that a drop in the market price of the stock during the period between the call and the redemption date (usually between 30 and 60 days) does not discourage voluntary conversion and force the issuer to cash out bondholders on the redemption date. It is thought that a stock price 20 percent in excess of the call price ought to provide a sufficient cushion. But actual issuer call practices entail more significant delays—the median issuer delays call until conversion value exceeds call price by over 40 percent. Ingersoll, An Examination of Corporate Call Policy on Convertible Securities, 32 J.Fin. 463 (1977). The question arises whether the issuers are waiting too long. This would seem surprising in view of issuers' assiduous reservation of the contractual right to pursue a stockholder optimal policy. Asquith and Mullins, Convertible Debt: Corporate Call Policy and Voluntary Conversion, 46 J. Finance 1273 (1991), offers an explanation for the delay of issuer calls. The tax deductibility of the interest on the uncalled bond builds a cash flow bias in favor of delayed call until the dividend payments on the stock are higher than the after tax cost of the debt. Asquith, Convertible Bonds Are Not Called Late, 50 J.Fin. 1275 (1995), follows up with a duration study and finds that the median delay period is only four months.

The call problem illustrates the riskiness of investment in the conversion premium. According to one analyst, it is an average of six times more risky than investment in the underlying common. The same analyst tells us that the investors exact a high rate of return for bearing this risk. These market statistics indicate that the bargain embodied in convertible securities, although peculiar in some particulars, at bottom is sound because an efficient market correctly perceives the risk and requires a commensurately big return.

Premium protected convertibles have appeared, but not in large numbers. Protection comes in the form of a promise by the issuer to pay one-half of the bond's remaining coupon payments in the event the bond is converted after a set date. This makes early call unlikely, but implies a considerable sacrifice of issuer flexibility. See Calamos, Convertible Securities 42–43 (1998).

Based on the foregoing, would you expect convertible bond prices to be more or less volatile than prices of straight bonds? Prices of common stocks? Beatty, Lee and Chen, On the Nonstationarity of Convertible Bond Betas: Theory and Evidence, 28 Q.Rev.Econs. & Bus. 15 (1988) reports on an empirical study of the price behavior of a sample of 97 convertible bonds traded between 1976 and 1979. The convertible prices and returns were compared to those of the bond and stock markets. Twenty of the 97 issues exhibited the characteristics of equities; 77 of the 97 issues exhibited the characteristics of debt securities.

NOTE: THE CONVERTIBLE BOND PUZZLE

1. *Traditional Explanations.*

Why do issuers finance with convertible bonds when they could sequence debt and equity finance in other, possibly cheaper ways?

One old fashioned line of explanation emphasizes the debt portion of the convertible. Under this, the convertible is a mode of "cheap debt" financing utilized by an issuer seeking to take advantage of the rate differential from a straight bond. The "equity kicker" was added so that the issuer can save on out-of-pocket costs during an investment-intensive time. Under an alternative, equally old-fashioned explanation, convertibles are a mode of delayed equity finance. Under this, the issuer ultimately wants to finance with common stock but dislikes the condition of the equity market at the time it needs the capital. A convertible bond makes particularly good sense to this issuer during the early period when it is investing the capital raised. During this period the project will not yet be throwing off cash flows and contributing to higher earnings per share. Thus, even if equity market conditions were favorable, common stock financing could cause earnings per share to decline during the early period by increasing the number of shares of stock in circulation before the new cash flows from the project come on line to increase earnings per share. The issuer happily charges the cost of the convertible debt from its earnings and pockets the income tax deduction, knowing that it can force conversion later on when it is less harmful to its EPS.

One problem with the latter explanation is that the issuer, instead of issuing a convertible, could sell straight debt and later refinance the debt by selling common stock. This two step approach mimics the convertible's debt-to-equity feature while holding out an advantage. With two steps, the common stock refunding occurs at the same time the convertible issuer would use call to force conversion. The common stock sale goes forward at the later market price, where the forced conversion is at the conversion price, which is by definition at a significant discount from the common stock's later market price. The two step approach accordingly is materially less dilutive of the value of the equity. See Klein, The Convertible Bond: A Peculiar Package, 123 U.Pa.L.Rev. 547 553–560 (1975). If the additional transaction costs bound up in doing the financing in two steps rather than one (see Mayers, Why Firms Issue Convertible Bonds: The Matching of Financial and Real Investment Options, 47 J.Fin.Econ. 83 (1998)), and are less than the cost of the additional dilution tied to the convertible, then the two step approach leaves the common stockholders better off than does convertible bond financing. The fact the convertible means additional dilution also raises doubts about the first, "cheap debt" explanation. The issue cheaper debt is not to get a free lunch—the common stockholders pick up the tab in the form of dilution.

The inadequacy of the traditional explanations gives rise to a "convertible bond puzzle." Successive generations of financial economists have addressed its solution.

2. *Information-Based Explanations.*

One line of financial economics accounts for the issuance of convertible debt on a signaling theory. This approach leads to a conclusion in line with the traditional "deferred equity financing" explanation. See Triantis and Triantis, Conversion Rights and the Design of Financial Contracts, 72 Wash. U. L. Q. 1231, 1239 (1994). The base point lies in the comparison between the convertible debt offering and an immediate offering of common stock. The problem with the common stock offering is that it sends a negative signal respecting the issuer's prospects to the financial markets. See Part II, Section A, supra. Issuing short-term debt, in contrast, signals that insiders view the firm's prospects optimistically. See Diamond, Debt Maturity Structure and Liquidity Risk, 106 Q. J. Econ. 709 (1991); Flannery, Asymmetric Information and Risky Debt Maturity Choice, 41 J. Fin. 19 (1986). The issuer of short-term debt refinances it with cheaper long term debt or equity later on, when the inside information has been revealed to the market. Convertible debt performs the same function, but removes uncertainty about the appropriate time for equity refinancing—short-term debt comes due at a date certain; convertible call is at the issuer's option. See Triantis and Triantis, supra, at 1236–37. Stein, Convertible

Bonds as Backdoor Equity Financing, 32 J. Fin. Econ. 3 (1992), suggests that firms' selection among straight debt, convertible debt, and new common facilitates a separating equilibrium in the securities markets: High quality firms issue straight debt and capture the gains of the private information; low quality firms issue equity; medium quality firms are concerned about financial distress but send a positive signal with a convertible issue.

Mayers, supra, extends this information asymmetry analysis in a somewhat counter-intuitive direction. Mayers suggests that convertible bond financing might make sense given the prospect of *future* investment by management in a project the quality of which is presently unknown. The convertible proves useful in respect of two problems posed by that future investment opportunity. On the one hand, management might devote internal cash flows to the project even though it turned out to be of poor quality. As compared to present common stock financing, present convertible bond financing makes this less likely by diverting internal cash flows to outside bondholders on downside scenarios. On the other hand, if the investment turned out to be a good one management might have difficulty obtaining low cost equity financing. Call of the convertibles facilitates this on a flexible timetable.

3. *Agency-Based Explanations.*

Agency cost explanations look at convertibles as debt financing with an equity option. See Triantis and Triantis, supra, at 1239. The idea is that the option feature dampens the incentives of the firm's managers to make investment and financing decisions that transfer wealth from debt to equity. Spatt & Sterbenz, Incentive Conflicts, Bundling Claims, and the Interaction among Financial Claimants, 48 J. Fin. 513 (1993), takes this approach in proposing a solution to the question as to why investors tend to prefer convertibles to detachable bond-warrant units. Spatt and Sterbenz work from a precedent model set out in Green, Investment Incentives, Debt, and Warrants, 13 J. Fin. Econ. 115 (1984). Green addressed the investment incentive problem that arises from the combination of debt and equity in a capital structure—the priority position and fixed claim of the debt creates an incentive for the equity to invest in riskier projects that are suboptimal from the point of view of the firm as a whole. Green showed that financing with a correct balance of warrants and bonds reorients the incentive picture so the equity has an incentive to invest to maximize the value of the firm. The warrants benefit from increased risk; the debt benefits from decreased risk; the equity's interests lie in the middle. With the right balance, the equity makes optimal investments.

Spatt and Sterbenz relax Green's assumptions and introduce an open time horizon and public trading of the firm's securities. If the equity buys warrants, the resulting project selection is riskier and the debt loses value; if the equity buys debt, the project selection is less risky and the warrants lose value. A double squeeze results as the prices of both the debt and the warrants are discounted to reflect the downside possibility. Convertibles solve the problem because they bundle the warrant together with the debt—the equity cannot purchase one claim without purchasing the other.

4. *Other Explanations.*

For an institutional approach that contrasts with both the agency and the information asymmetry theories, see Dent, The Role of Convertible Securities in Corporate Finance, 21 J.Corp.L. 241 (1996). Dent stresses the role of management preferences in shaping the terms of convertible transactions and also notes significant differences between private placements and public offerings.

A "clientele effect" on the demand side also may operate in convertible debt markets. Convertibles may attract at least two distinct groups of investors who might not otherwise be brought into the corporate fold: (1) those who because of legal restrictions must contemplate a debt instrument or a preferred stock, but who are willing to assume a subordinate position in a highly leveraged capital structure because of the possibility of gain through the accompanying conversion, warrant, or option; and (2) those sophisticated investors in common stock whose primary interest is the option, which is made more attractive because it is attached to a debt investment with more permissive margin requirements and a steadier cash flow than are available for common stock, and a lower commission rate on the purchase.

(2) Variations on the Traditional Convertible

(a) original issue discount convertibles

An original issue discount (OID) bond is sold at a discount to its face value at original issue because its coupon payments are set at a rate lower than the market rate of return. An extreme case is a zero coupon bond that pays no interest prior to maturity and sells at a very deep discount–say $500 for a bond with a maturity value of $1000. Assuming no change in the issuer's risk profile and no change in prevailing interest rates, the market value of the bond will gradually increase over its lifetime, approaching $1000 at maturity. During this period the issuer will deduct an imputed interest charge (the discount amortized over the life of the bond) on its corporate tax return–a happy posture in view of the fact that there is no cash outflow to the bondholders prior to maturity. The holders are less favored—they pay an imputed annual interest charge on their tax returns even though the investment yields no cash flow prior to maturity. (The issuer can ameliorate the holder's resulting liquidity problem by paying a nominal coupon during the bond's life, issuing the bond at a slightly less deep discount.) Convertible OID bonds are particularly attractive to issuers: If the stock goes up as anticipated, the obligation to make up the discount in cash never comes due.

(b) puttable convertibles

In the mid–1980s the Merrill Lynch firm invented Liquid Option Yield Notes or "LYONs." LYONs are long-term OID bonds giving the holder an option to put the bond back to the issuer at the end of five years. (Alternatively, the put can be incorporated at regular intervals during the life of the bond.) The put price is set at original issue based on a five year yield to maturity projection. Here is an example. In 1993, Motorola issued LYONs due in 2013 for $639. The bonds were puttable in five years at $715. The $715 put price implied a yield to maturity of 2 1/4 percent, figure that followed from prevailing rates on five year borrowings of comparable credits. See Calamos, Convertible Securities 38 (1998). The put potentially shortens the issue's maturity and as a result cushions the market price of the bond from decreases in interest rates and decreases in the price of the underlying stock. At the same time, the holder retains the full benefit of the equity upside.

(c) equity–linked securities

These are variations on the theme of convertible preferred stock. They depart from the traditional pattern with a mandatory conversion feature—

automatic conversion to common stock at a set future date, payable either in cash or common stock at the issuer's option. Automatic conversion cuts off bond floor protection and thus implies higher risk. These securities also tend to impose caps on the equity upside—they participate in stock price increases only up to the cap. The give-back for these concessions is a higher yield of periodic payments. The issuer may reserve call rights, pegged at the cap price plus a premium. Downside protection depends on the terms of the issue. Some provide full principal protection, others partial protection, others one-to-one downside participation with the common. Durations tend to be intermediate—say, three or four years. Equity linked securities have names that differ depending on the sponsoring investment bank and the bundle of rights. Donaldson Lufkin Jenrette markets PACERS—preferred adjusted to equity redeemable stock; Morgan Stanley markets PERCS—preferred equity redemption cumulative stock; Merrill Lynch markets PRIDES—preferred redemption increased dividend equity securities; and so on.

Here is an example. X Corp. in 2007 issues PERCs due in 2010. X's stock, which pays no dividend, is selling for $25. The PERCs are sold for $25 each, and pay an annual mandatory dividend of $0.625 (2½ percent). The cap is set at $40. There is no principal protection. At the end of 3 years, assume the stock is selling for $20, $40, or $55. On both the $20 and $40 scenarios, the PERC holder has done well as compared to a holder of the common. They hold securities with identical market prices, but where the common made no periodic payments, the PERC holder had a 2½ percent yield. On the $55 scenario the $40 cap bites the PERC holder, who traded off $15 in capital appreciation for $0.625 in annual dividends. Note a similarity to the covered call play described in Part I, supra. In effect, the PERC holder has bought the stock and simultaneously sold an out-of-the money call with a $40 exercise price; the yield on the PERC is the functional equivalent of the pocketing of the premium on the call.

(d) floating price ("toxic") convertibles

As we have seen, a traditional convertible bond has a single, unchanging conversion price, set at a premium to the stock price at original issue. The typical issuer of a traditional convertible is a firm with good prospects that has a new project about which the insiders are confident. The insiders, however, have a problem in credibly communicating their confidence in the firm's prospects to the securities markets. They would prefer to fund the new project with equity, but fear that the markets will take the financing as a signal of an insider view that the stock is overvalued and respond by bidding down the stock price. A traditional convertible bond issue solves the problem. Because the issue entails an irrevocable commitment to pay on the borrowing in the event the stock never rises high enough to put the conversion privilege in the money, it credibly signals confidence in the firm's financial soundness. At the same time, the combination of the issue's fixed conversion price and the issuer's call rights limits the negative dilution impact on the existing stockholders. Once conversion value rises above the call price by a comfortable margin, the issuer calls the bonds, transforming the capital into equity without the negative cash flow consequences or refunding costs of a cash redemption.

Now let us put ourselves in the position of skeptical potential investor and ask some questions. Suppose the issuer has high hopes for the new project but at the same time sees a cognizable chance of failure. It does not see financial distress as a likely result, but does see a distinct possibility of a languishing stock price in the event the project fails to come in a winner. Under the pecking order theory of finance, see Part II, Section A, supra, the issuer will resort to new equity financing only as a last resort when distress actually is upon it. Given that, the potential purchaser has reason to wonder whether the convertible presents a good deal. If the stock price languishes, the conversion privilege never will be in the money. Meanwhile, the purchaser has bought a debt security with a coupon yield a notch lower than that payable on a straight bond issued by a comparable credit.

How can the issuer persuade the skeptic? A floating conversion price appears useful: Under this arrangement, a stock price decline triggers a reduction in the conversion price (and an increase in the conversion ratio), calculated to preserve the market value of the convertible holder's equity interest. Assume, as an example, that a $1000 convertible is originally issued with a conversion price of $10 with the stock trading at $10. Conversion value is $1000. Assume the stock drops to $5. Given a fixed price, a decline in the stock price puts the conversion privilege deeply out of the money. But if the conversion price is adjusted downward to $5, the conversion privilege retains its value of $1000. The value retention comes at the expense of the firm's stockholders, of course. Where at $10 the $1000 convertible bought 100 shares; now it buys 200 shares, diluting their interest.

Why would a holder bother to convert on downside scenarios if conversion value remains fixed at $1000? Better to collect the interest on the debt and bide one's time. To address this problem, let us modify the contract to provide for a discounted conversion price–say 20 percent below the stock price—and put a time limit on the discount's availability. With this arrangement, conversion can be expected during the period in which the discount is available. To the extent the discounted conversion window is opened early in the life of the security, the convertible security's economics are radically transformed. Now the convertible is a conduit to an early conversion to common stock. The duration of the debt portion can be expected to be short because the holders will convert to grab the discount. This holds out a benefit to the issuer on downside scenarios where a traditional convertible means being stuck paying the debt. With the discounted floating conversion price, the debt disappears even if the stock price declines. Where the traditional convertible signals confidence in financial strength, this arrangement signals financial weakness. It amounts to a discounted equity offering.

Large quantities of floating price convertibles were issued beginning in the mid–1990s along the lines just described. The contract sets the discounted conversion price by reference to the range of the issuer's stock price during a defined "look back period," at either the average price or the lowest price. If the look back period price falls below the original price, the conversion price is reduced accordingly. But no upward adjustment is made if the stock price rises above its level on the original issue date. Conversion is not permitted at the time of original issue. Instead the contract specifies a lock-up period during which conversion is prohibited. Upon the expiration of the lock-up period, the number of converted shares that can be resold into the public trading market in any given period (probably defined as monthly) is capped by reference to the trading volume of the stock. As a result, conversion takes place gradually. But the overall timetable can be expected to be rapid. Indeed, some contracts provide for acceleration of the timetable in the event the stock price declines below a set floor. Finally, the debt portion of many of these instruments does not hold out interest in cash. The bonds instead are pay-in-kind, with periodic return coming in the form of more floating price convertibles. Finally, the contract provides that all unconverted bonds must be converted at maturity.

Add all of this up and this convertible is an equity issue at a price to be determined in the future. Even though there is promise to pay, no cash payment ever is made and none of the agency problems of debt—asset substitution, underinvestment, and bankruptcy costs—are implicated. (Packaging as debt still matters because debt status carries a bankruptcy priority.) The convertible holder still bears a risk at an extreme downside. The conversion price adjustment avails it nothing if the stock price falls to $0. As a practical matter, a stock price drop to $1 signals the investment's failure because at $1 delisting can be expected to follow.

What type of company would find this package to present an attractive mode of financing? Given the built in dilution of the interest of the existing stockholders, it must be a firm in need of capital but with no available financing alternatives. Such a firm by definition is facing distress—exactly the firm fingered as an equity issuer by the pecking order theory. So long as the capital is absolutely necessary and there really is no alternative, the existing stockholders presumably should view the deal favorably. Hillion and Vermaelen, Death Spiral Convertibles, 71 J. Fin. Econ. 381 (2004), test this proposition, surveying 467 issues of floating price convertibles issued from 1994 to 1998. They report that the issuers are small, young, and risky. So risky that the stock of 85 percent of the issuers lost value in the year following the convertible financing, with the average across the sample amounting to a 34 percent decline (in the midst of a stock market that otherwise was overheated on the upside). In addition, the convertible issuers when compared to comparable firms show significant declines in return on assets and operating cash flow over assets. A question arises as to whether the price declines stem from poor prospects, the dilution factor imported by the convertible, or both. Hillion and Vermaelen, controlling for accounting based measures of performance, attribute much of the decline in the issuer's stock prices to the price discount feature. They conclude that floating price convertibles are indeed a "last resort" mode of finance— equity with sweeteners for managers facing financial distress and having no alternative.

The question is whether these strapped issuers get a reasonable deal. Floating price convertibles tend to issued as PIPEs–"private interests in public equity." This is a private equity submarket in which a fund with a short term investment horizon purchases a minority equity stake in a publicly traded company. (Mainstream private equity deals, in contrast, involve majority stakes on an intermediate or long term in firms taken private.) In this submarket, the hedge funds join the private equity firms as investors. A problem arises. If the market in the issuer's stock is thick enough to allow the convertible holders to short the stock prior to conversion, the holders have every incentive so to do, if only for the purpose of hedging their long equity position. Indeed, the contract may permit this explicitly. The question is whether the holders' shorting activity triggers downward movement in the issuer stock that causes the stock to trade below its intrinsic value. Unfortunately, this result benefits the convertible holders because the conversion price adjustment holds them harmless. They end up with a larger proportion of the equity of the firm than they would have held given an accurate stock price. The risk of holder opportunism is correspondingly high.

In a number of well-publicized cases, hedge fund short selling is alleged to have caused the stock price to decline below intrinsic value. Floating rate convertibles as a result bear appellations like "toxic convertibles," "death spiral convertibles," and "junk equity." There also have been both SEC enforcement actions and private litigations respecting undisclosed short-selling connected with PIPE issues. The short-selling in question was carried out by PIPE investors *prior* to the public announcement of the PIPE transaction. The SEC takes the position that news of the transaction is material nonpublic information. See GAO Report, 05–244, available at: http://www.gao.gov/new.items/d05244. See also CompuDyne v. Shane, 453 F.Supp.2d 807 (S.D.N.Y.2006); HealthExtras v. SG Cowen Securities Corp., 2004 WL 97699 (S.D.N.Y.)

It should be noted that there is a less toxic variant on the floating price theme—the convertible reset. Here the conversion price also is set at a discount from the stock price, but the conversion price does not float. Instead it is reset a limited number of times during the live of the bond. Typically, there is only one reset that occurs 30 to 60 days after original issue. For a dispute respecting a reset provision, see Zimmerman v. Home Shopping Network, Inc., 1990 WL 140890 (Del.Ch.1990).

2.   CONFLICTS OF INTEREST

(A) PROTECTIVE CONTRACT PROVISIONS

Revised Model Simplified Indenture, Article 10

Appendix A

Imagine a convertible bond (or warrant) issued without any contract provision for the adjustment of the terms of the option in the event of changes in the issuer's capital structure. The bond has a conversion price of $20. The stock price rises to $20 from $15 at the time of original issue. Now the issuer splits its common stock two-for-one. The price of a share of stock drops to $10, destroying much of the value of the conversion privilege. The issuer could achieve the same result through four consecutive quarterly 25 percent stock dividends (assuming the stock's value stays constant during the period). If the issuer were to mount a successful rights offering to its existing common stockholders, it could cause the common stock price to fall to $10, provided that it priced the shares offered below $10 and sold a sufficient number. In sum, conversion value is destroyed when the issuer increases the number of common shares outstanding without proportionately increasing their value.

Conversion value also is destroyed whenever, as with a dividend, the issuer disgorges assets for less than equivalent consideration. Total destruction of conversion value occurs when the issuer, the underlying common, or both cease to exist altogether. Any number of voluntary issuer actions can accomplish this—a recapitalization, merger, or liquidation and dissolution. The traditional view is that as a matter of law, the conversion privilege is diminished or lost in all of these cases if the contract does not provide for its survival. Compare B.S.F. Co. v. Philadelphia Nat'l Bank, 204 A.2d 746 (Del.1964); Parkinson v. West End. St. Ry., 173 Mass. 446, 53 N.E. 891 (1899) (Holmes, J.).

These dilutive or destructive actions are so easy to effect and impair the bond's conversion value so substantially (in the case of a warrant, they can destroy the security's value completely), that provisions protecting against them are found in most convertible bond and warrant contracts. These "anti-dilution" provisions protect against dilutive and partially destructive actions by triggering proportionate reductions in the conversion price. Conversion value remains unaffected by the action as a result. They protect against destructive events such as mergers, recapitalizations, and liquidations by creating a right to convert into the securities or other consideration being distributed to the common stockholders in connection with the particular transaction. They also often provide for advance notice of dilutive and destructive actions. This is a lesser order of protection: like notice in advance of a call, it permits the holder to realize on the bond's conversion value prior to the consummation of the issuer action. It provides only cold comfort where, as in cases that follow, the conversion price exceeds the conversion value.

Note that antidilution protection covers only conversion value. Most antidilution provisions address decreases in the value of the securities to be received upon conversion by preserving the value that would have been obtained had the bond been converted immediately prior to the event in question. They do not protect the full economic value of the bond— conversion value plus conversion premium. For an argument that the prevailing approach fails to protect the full value of the option and that contract forms should make reference to the Black–Scholes option pricing model, see Glover, Solving Dilution Problems, 51 Bus. Law. 1241, 1251–55 (1996). For a rebuttal, see Woronoff and Rosen, Understanding Anti-Dilution Provisions in Convertible Securities, 74 Ford. L. Rev. 129 138–39 (2005).

It is safe to assume that the governing contract in every one of the cases that follows in this section contained "standard" antidilution language. How effective were these provisions in preserving the value of the option for which the holders bargained?

NOTE: IMPLIED IN FACT ANTIDILUTION PROTECTION

Holders of convertible bonds and warrants lacking antidilution protection or containing incomplete, nonstandard provisions have not fared well in the courts.

Lohnes v. Level 3 Communications, Inc., 272 F.3d 49 (1st Cir.2001), exemplifies such a case. It concerns a warrantholder seeking a downward adjustment of the exercise price in the wake of a 2 for 1 stock split conducted as a 100 percent stock dividend. The warrant had antidilution provisions, but none of these were addressed directly to stock splits or stock dividends. The warrant did have the following provision:

> *Reorganizations and Reclassifications.* If there shall occur any capital reorganization or reclassification of the Common Stock, then, as part of any such reorganization or reclassification, lawful provision shall be made so that the Holder shall have the right thereafter to receive upon the exercise hereof the kind and amount of shares of stock or other securities or property which such Holder would have been entitled to receive if, immediately prior to any such reorganization or reclassification, such Holder had held the number of shares of Common Stock which were then purchasable upon the exercise of this Warrant.

The holder argued that the 2 for 1 stock split was a "reorganization or reclassification" within the meaning. The First Circuit rejected the argument.

The same court was more forgiving in **Cofman v. Acton Corp.**, 958 F.2d 494 (1st Cir.1992), where it relaxed a century-old caselaw prohibition against antidilution protection by implication. The case concerned a settlement agreement pursuant to which the payees (the "Partnership") received a right to a future payment from Acton Corp. The contract read as follows:

> [T]he Partnership shall be entitled to receive, upon written demand made within the three years following the execution of the Settlement Agreement (the "Exercise Date"), the following one time payment: the sum of "X" times a multiple of 7,500 where "X" equals the "price" of one share of Acton Corporation's common stock on the Exercise Date less $7.00. The "price" on the Exercise Date shall be equal to the average closing price of one share of the common stock of Acton Corporation on the American Stock Exchange for any period, selected by the Partnership, consisting of thirty (30) consecutive trading days prior to the Exercise Date.

Within the three year period, Acton conducted a one-for-five reverse stock split and the Partnership claimed a right to a payment based on the stock price after the split, an amount five times higher than would have been payable absent the reverse split.

The court affirmed a ruling in favor of Acton, 958 F.2d at 497:

> "No doubt recognizing this symbiosis, when the district court inquired, as later did we, whether Acton could have avoided all liability under the agreement simply by increasing the number of shares, counsel answered affirmatively. The court characterized his proffered concession as 'gallant.' We can only say that if this particular counsel would have been too gallant to make a claim, surely someone less chivalrous could have been found. How could so meaningless an undertaking have

been considered a sweetener? It is a fundamental principle that a contract is to be construed as meaningful and not illusory. As the court said in *Clark,* 270 Mass. at 153, 169 N.E. 897,

> The construction of a written instrument to be adopted is the one which appears to be in accord with justice and common sense and the probable intention of the parties. It is to be interpreted as a business transaction entered into by practical men to accomplish an honest and straightforward end."

But the court also distinguished convertible debentures, id. at 958, n. 5:

"We do not pause over Partnership's sought analogy to convertible debentures, where the rule is that anti-dilution must be expressly stated. *Broad v. Rockwell International Corp.,* 642 F.2d 929, 940–45 (5th Cir.) (en banc), *cert. denied,* 454 U.S. 965, 102 S.Ct. 506, 70 L.Ed.2d 380 (1981); *Parkinson v. West End Street Ry.,* 173 Mass. 446, 53 N.E. 891 (1899). These are formal, and complicated commercial structures, prepared with care for the general public. Purchasers have the bonds in any event. Here we have a simple agreement between individuals, not even assignable."

Cofman v. Acton was followed over a vigorous dissent in **Reiss v. Financial Performance Corp.,** 279 A.D.2d 13, 715 N.Y.S.2d 29 (2000), a case involving a privately negotiated stock purchase warrant lacking an antidilution clause and a reverse stock split. The issuer, which had voluntarily initiated the split, asked for an implied in law upward adjustment of the exercise price. The Appellate Division majority agreed, 715 N.Y.S.2d at 34,

"[T]o the extent that the warrants may be viewed as not containing an implicit requirement for the proportional adjustment of Financial's stock upon a split or reverse-split, it means that the parties omitted what is undeniably an essential term of the agreement. Contrary to the dissent's contention, a provision dealing with this eventuality is essential since it fundamentally affects both the number of shares that may be purchased and the price to be paid. In a circumstance where an essential term is omitted, section 204 of the Restatement of the Law (Second) of Contracts is instructive. That section provides:

> When the parties to a bargain sufficiently defined to be a contract have not agreed with respect to a term which is essential to a determination of their rights and duties, a term which is reasonable in the circumstances is supplied by the court.

Here, following the Restatement approach, the only reasonable term would be the one consistent with the self-evident expectations of the parties when the warrants were executed, namely, a term requiring a proportional adjustment of both the number of shares that may be purchased and their price."

The New York Court of Appeals reversed, however. Reiss v. Financial Performance Corp., 97 N.Y.2d 195, 764 N.E.2d 958, 738 N.Y.S.2d 658 (2001). The court noted that it might be different if a holder asked for protection:

"It may be that Reiss would be entitled to a remedy if Financial performed a forward stock split, on the theory that he 'did not intend to acquire nothing' (Cofman, 958 F.2d, at 497). We should not assume that one party intended to be placed at the mercy of the other (*Wood v. Duff–Gordon,* 222 N.Y. 88, 91, 118 N.E. 214 [1917]). It does not follow, however, that Financial should be given a comparable remedy to save it from the consequences of its own agreements and its own decision to perform a reverse stock split."

HB Korenvaes Investments, L.P. v. Marriott Corporation

Del.Ch., 1993.
CCH Fed. Sec. L. Rep. ¶ 97,773, 1993 WL 257422.

■ ALLEN, CHANCELLOR

In this action holders of Series A Cumulative Convertible Preferred Stock of Marriott Corporation seek to enjoin a planned reorganization of the businesses owned by that corporation. The reorganization involves the creation of a new corporate subsidiary, Marriott International, Inc. ("International"), the transfer to International of the greatest part of Marriott's cash-generating businesses, followed by the distribution of the stock of International to all of the holders of Marriott common stock, as a special dividend.

* * *

For the reasons that follow, I conclude that plaintiffs have not shown a reasonable likelihood of success with respect to those aspects of their claims that appear to state a claim upon which relief might be granted. * * *

I.

* * *

(a) *The Company*

Marriott Corporation, as presently constituted, is in the business (1) of owning and operating hotels, resorts, and retirement homes, (2) of providing institutional food service and facilities management, and (3) of operating restaurants and food, beverage and merchandise concessions at airports, tollway plazas and other facilities. Its common stock has a present market value of approximately $2.6 billion. In December 1991 Marriott issued $200,000,000 face amount of convertible preferred stock bearing an 8 1/4% cumulative dividend, the stock owned by plaintiffs. Marriott has substantial debt, including Liquid Yield Option Notes ("LYONS") with an accreted value of $228 million; and long-term debt of $2.732 billion. According to its proxy statement, the book value of Marriott's assets is $6.560 billion.

In the fiscal year ending January 1, 1993 Marriott's sales were $8.722 billion; earnings before interest, taxes, depreciation and amortization (EBITDA) was $777 million; earnings before interest and corporate expenses was $496 million; and net income was $85 million. * * * Each common share has received an annual cash dividend of $0.28 per share and the preferred stock dividends have been paid over its short life.

(b) *The terms of the preferred stock in brief*

The preferred stock is entitled to an 8 1/4% cumulative dividend and no more. It ranks prior to the common stock with respect to dividends and distribution of assets. It has in total, a face amount of $200,000,000 and that, plus the amount of any unpaid cumulated dividends, "and no more" is the amount of its liquidation preference. The corporation may, at its option, redeem any or all of the preferred stock after January 15, 1996, at prices set forth in the certificate.

The preferred stock is convertible at the option of the holder into common stock at a conversion price set forth in the certificate. Generally that means that every $50.00 face amount share of preferred stock may be converted into 2.87 shares of common stock. The certificate provides a mechanism to adjust the conversion price "in case the Corporation shall, by dividend ... distribute to all holders of Common Stock ... assets (including securities).... "

The value of the right to convert is protected by a notice provision.
* * *

There are no express restrictions on the payment of dividends other than the requirement that the quarterly dividend on the preferred must be paid prior to the distribution of dividend payments to common stock.

(c) *Announcement of the proposed transaction*

On October 5, 1993, Marriott announced a radical rearrangement of the legal structure of the Company's businesses. The restructuring was said to be designed to separate Marriott's "ownership of real estate ... and other capital intensive businesses from its management and services businesses." * * * The latter constitute Marriott's most profitable and fastest growing business segments. As indicated above, following this transfer Marriott intends to "spin-off" this new subsidiary by distributing all its stock as a dividend to Marriott's common stockholders.

(d) *Marriott International*

International is anticipated to be highly profitable from its inception and to be well positioned for future growth. It is expected to pay to its common stockholders the same dividend that has been paid to Marriott's common stock. [International will operate or franchise—under long-term contracts—hotels, motels and other properties owned by Host Marriott and others.]

According to its pro forma balance sheet for the quarter ending March 26, 1993, after the distribution (and assuming the Exchange Offer described below * * * is effectuated) International will have assets of $3.048 billion, long-term debt of $902 million, and shareholders equity of $375 million. * * *

Had International, with all the assets it will hold, been operated as a separate company in 1992, it would have had sales of $7.787 billion, earnings before interest and corporate expenses of $331 million and net income of $136 million. * * * Marriott's adviser, S.G. Warburg & Company, has estimated that in 1993 International will have sales of $8.210 billion, and EBIT of $368 million.

(e) *Host Marriott*

Marriott's remaining assets will consist of large real estate holdings and Marriott's airport and tollway concession business. Marriott will be renamed Host Marriott ("Host"). The assets retained by Host have a value of several billion dollars but will be burdened with great debt and produce little cash-flow after debt service. * * *

Assuming the Exchange Offer * * * is effectuated, after the special dividend Host will have, according to its pro forma balance sheet as of March 26, 1993, assets of $3.796 billion, long-term debt of $2.130 billion and shareholders' equity of $516 million. * * * Host's pro forma income statement for the fiscal year ending January 1, 1993, would reflect sales of $1.209 billion, earnings before corporate expenses and interest of $152 million, interest expense of $196 million, corporate expenses of $46 million, and a net loss of $44 million. * * *

* * *

(f) *Future operation of Host and International*

If the special dividend is distributed, International and Host will formally constitute two separate corporate entities. They will, however, share a large number of relationships. * * * International will have long-term agreements to manage many of Host's hotel properties and other real estate assets. International will have a right to share in the proceeds of some of Host's asset sales in lieu of receiving base management fees, as well as a right of first refusal in any sale of Host's airport and toll-road concessions. * * *

As discussed below International will extend a $630 million line of credit to Host's subsidiary Host Marriott Hospitality, Inc. ("HMH"). * * * For ten years after the special dividend, International will have the right to purchase 20% of Host's common stock if any person acquires more than 20% or announces a tender offer for 30% or more of Host's common stock. The two companies will have common management * * *. There will be a non-competition agreement between the two companies.

(g) *Bondholders' suits lead to modified transaction*

* * * Marriott's bondholders reacted strongly against the proposed special dividend. The transaction will of course remove very substantial assets and even more cash flow from their debtor and will, in the circumstances, substantially increase the risk associated with the bondholders' investment, or so it was thought.

* * *

On March 11, 1993, Marriott reached a settlement with the bondholder class action plaintiffs. The settlement, if effectuated, would require Marriott to cause the Host subsidiary HMH to offer to exchange for existing bonds new bonds (Exchange Bonds) with a longer average maturity and bearing an interest rate 100 basis points higher than the existing bonds. The Exchange Bonds will include restrictive covenants that greatly limit opportunities for HMH to transfer cash to Host. Host's airport and toll road concession businesses, representing the preponderant part of its operating assets, and 40% of its cash-flow, will be transferred to a subsidiary of HMH. A $630 million credit line will be provided by International to HMH, but it cannot be drawn on to pay preferred dividends. One effect of the Exchange Offer, and the transfers it contemplates, is to restrict further Host's ability, as a practical matter, to pay dividends to the preferred stock.

Shortly after the Exchange Offer settlement Marriott announced for the first time that it was intended that, following the special dividend, Host would not pay dividends on its preferred stock. On March 15, 1993, Host announced in an S.E.C. filing that:

It is the Company's present intention following the Distribution to declare dividends on its preferred stock only to the extent earnings equal or exceed the amount of such dividends. Since Host Marriott is expected to report book losses following the Distribution, this policy would lead to an indefinite suspension of dividends on the Company's preferred stock. * * *

(h) *Plaintiffs' acquisition of preferred stock and short sales of common*

Plaintiffs began for the first time to purchase substantial amounts of Marriott's preferred stock following the announcement of the special dividend.

Since the preferred stock is convertible at the option of the holder into 2.87 shares of Marriott common stock and bears a dividend of 8 1/4% on its stated (liquidation) value of $50 per share, the market value of a share of preferred stock includes two possible components of value: the value of the conversion right and the value of the preferences. The presence of a presently exercisable conversion right will assure that the market value of the preferred will not fall below the market value of the security or property into which the preferred might convert, in this case 2.87 shares of common stock (less transaction costs of the conversion). The stated dividend, the dividend preference and the liquidation preference and other features of the preferred will ordinarily assure that the preferred trades at some premium to the value of the conversion right.

In this instance plaintiffs have acquired a majority of the shares of the preferred stock. Plaintiffs, however, did not simply acquire preferred stock. The record shows that each of the plaintiffs, except one, have hedged their risk by entering short sales contracts with respect to Marriott common stock. In this way plaintiffs have isolated their risk to that part of the preferred stock trading value represented by that stock's preference rights. Any change in the market price of the preferred stock caused by movement in the value of the underlying common stock will in their case be offset by change in the extent of their obligations under the short sales contracts.

(i) *Marriott common and preferred stock price changes*

The prices of both Marriott common stock and Marriott preferred stock have increased substantially since the announcement of the special dividend. On the last trading day before the announcement of the transaction Marriott's common stock closed at $17.125 per share. The day of the announcement the price increased to $19.25 and by June 4, 1993 it had reached $25.75, for a total increase of approximately 50.3%. * * *

The price of Marriott preferred stock closed on the last trading day before the announcement at $62.75, which represented a premium of

$13.54 over the value of the 2.8736 common shares into which each preferred share could convert. The day of the announcement the preferred stock increased to $68.875. On June 4, 1993 the price of the preferred stock closed at $77.00 per share, an increase of 22.8% over the pre-announcement market price. The premium that the preferred stock commanded over the common into which it could convert (i.e., the market value of the preferences) however, had by June 4th, shrunk, to $3.00.

Thus while both common stock and preferred stock have experienced substantial increases in the market value of their securities, because of the impact of their hedging strategy, plaintiffs are in a different position than are non-hedged holders of preferred stock. The reduction of the premium at which the preferred stock trades has resulted in losses on their short sales, leading some plaintiffs, as of June 4, 1993, to net unrealized losses on their investments.

For example, plaintiff, The President and Fellows of Harvard College, ("Harvard") as of June 4, 1993 owned 480,300 shares of preferred stock, which were purchased for $33,580,108 and which had a market value on that day of $37,724,801. Thus, this plaintiff has an unrealized profit of $4,144,693 on its investment in the preferred stock. Harvard also entered into short sales of 1,338,300 shares of Marriott common stock, approximately 2.8 times the number of preferred shares it purchased. It received $30,949,383 on these short sales. The cost to cover these short sales, however, has increased to $34,609,056, or $3,659,673 more than was received on the sales, representing an unrealized loss in that amount. Thus, as of June 4, 1993, although the value of the preferred stock owned by this plaintiff has increased in value by over $4 million, the total value of its investment position has increased by only $485,020.[9]

II.

Plaintiffs' Account

[The plaintiffs argued that (1) absent conversion into Marriott common prior to the consummation of the spin-off, the preferred would end up with a right to convert into more than 50 percent of the Host common, (2) that the conversion privilege therefore threatened the Marriott family's control over Host, and (3) that Marriott's March 15, 1993 announcement of its intention to suspend dividends on the preferred after the spin-off was intended to solve this problem by forcing conversions.]

V.

The Section 5(e)(iv) Claim

I turn now to analysis of that which I regard as the centrally important certificate provision, Section 5(e)(iv). That section affords protection

---

9. At least two other plaintiffs have entered into similar transactions. AKT Associates L.P., had as of June 4, 1993, an unrealized profit on its preferred stock of $2,033,495 and increased cost to cover short sales of $2,036,777 for an unrealized loss of $3,282. * * * HB Korenvaes Investments, L.P. had an unrealized gain of $3,555,648 on its preferred and a loss of $3,793,089 on its short position for an unrealized loss of $237,441. * * *

against dilution of the conversion component of the market value of the preferred stock by providing an adjustment to the conversion price when the corporation declares a dividend of assets, including securities. The principle * * * is that when the assets of the firm are depleted through a special distribution to shareholders, the preferred will be protected by the triggering of a conversion price adjustment formula. Under Section 5(e)(iv) the number of shares into which the preferred can convert will be proportionately increased in order to maintain the value of the preferred's conversion feature. The principle seems clear enough; the realization of it will inevitably involve problems.

(a) Section 5(e)(iv) of the certificate of designation requires Marriott, when effectuating a special dividend, to leave sufficient net assets in the corporation to permit that Section to function as intended to protect the pre-disposition value of the preferred stock.

The language of the certificate of designation is as follows:

5. *Conversion Rights.* * * * (a) Shares of Convertible Preferred Stock shall be convertible at any time into fully paid and nonassessable shares of Common Stock at a conversion price of $17.40 per share of Common Stock (the "Conversion Price").

* * *

(e) The conversion Price shall be adjusted from time to time as follows: (iv) *In case the Corporation shall, by dividend or otherwise, distribute to all holders of its Common Stock ... assets* (including securities ...), *the Conversion Price shall be adjusted* so that the same shall equal the price determined by multiplying the Conversion Price in effect immediately prior to the close of business on the date fixed for the determination of stockholders entitled to receive such distribution by a fraction of which the numerator shall be the current market price per share (determined as provided in subsection (vi) below) of the Common Stock on the date fixed for such determination less the then fair market value (as determined by the Board of Directors, whose determination shall be conclusive and shall be described in a statement filed with the transfer agent for the Convertible Preferred Stock) of the portion of the evidences of indebtedness or assets so distributed applicable to one share of Common Stock and the denominator shall be such current market price per share of the Common Stock, such adjustment to become effective immediately prior to the opening of business on the day following the date fixed for the determination of stockholders entitled to receive such distribution. (*emphasis added*)

Thus, stated simply, whenever Marriott distributes assets to its common stockholders this provision protects the value of the preferred conversion right by reducing the conversion price. * * * What is intuitively apparent is that in a narrow range of extreme cases, a dividend of property may be so large relative to the corporation's net worth, that following the distribution, the firm, while still solvent, will not represent sufficient value to preserve the pre-dividend value of the preferred's conversion right.

Appended to this opinion are three hypothetical cases in which the Section 5(e)(iv) formula is employed. Case 1 involves a dividend of 40% of the issuing corporation's net asset value. Case 2 is a dividend of 90% of net asset value. Case 3 displays the consequences of a dividend of 95% of asset value. Given the assumptions of the examples (i.e. preferred conversion rights equal 9.1% of total pre-distribution value), only in the last case does the Section 5(e)(iv) formula fail to function.*

* [Ed. Note] The Appendix is as follows:

APPENDIX
CASE I

* * *

Assume a company, Corporation Y, with $1 billion in assets and no debts. It has 10 million shares of common stock and 1 million shares of cumulative convertible preferred stock having a face amount and liquidation preference of $100 million. The preferred is convertible into common stock at a price of $100 face amount per common share or into 1 million common shares, in total. The certificate of designation contains a provision identical to Section 5(e)(iv).

Assume further that the capital markets operate efficiently and the common stock trades at price reflecting Corporation Y's asset values on a fully diluted basis.

Under these assumptions at time [T1], Current Market Price ("CMP") is determined as follows:

$$CMP = \frac{\$1 \text{ billion}}{11 \text{ million shares}} = \$90.9091 \text{ per share}$$

Preferred Conversion Value = 1 million shares x $90.9091 = $90,909,100

* * *

At time [T2] Corporation Y declares a dividend of assets with a fair market value of $400 million or $40 per outstanding common share, leaving the company with $600 million in assets.

The conversion price would be adjusted by the same formula as applies in Section 5(e)(iv):

$$ACP = \frac{CP \text{ x } (CMP - FMV)}{CMP}$$

Where: ACP=Adjusted Conversion Price; CP=Conversion Price; FMV=Fair Market Value; CMP=Current Market Price common stock

$$ACP = \frac{100 \text{ x } (\$90.9091 - \$40)}{\$90.9091} = \$56.0000$$

The preferred would become convertible into 1,785,710 common shares,

$$\frac{\$100,000,000 \text{ x } 1 \text{ common share}}{\$56.0000} = 1,785,710 \text{ common shares}$$

with an aggregate value of $90,908,900,

$$\frac{\$600,000,000 \text{ x } 1,785,710 \text{ converted shares}}{11,785,710 \text{ common shares}} = \$90,908,900$$

Thus in this case the anti-dilution provision of the certificate would serve to preserve the economic value of the preferred stock despite the diversion of 40% of Corporation Y's net worth out of the company.

In light of the mathematical effect demonstrated in the appended examples, a court that must construe Section 5(e)(iv) is required to conclude, in my opinion, that Marriott has voluntarily and effectively bound itself not to declare and distribute special dividends of a proportion that would deprive the preferred stockholders of the protection that provision was intended to afford. In providing a mechanism to maintain pre-distribution value (putting to one side for the moment, how pre-distribution value is determined) the issuer impliedly but unmistakably and necessarily

CASE II

Now assume alternatively that Corporation Y declares a special dividend to its common stockholders of $900 million of its assets or $90 per outstanding share.

The conversion price adjustment formula would work to adjust the conversion price from $100 to 1.00 per share:

$$ACP = \frac{\$100 \times \$90.0991 - \$90}{\$90.9091} = \$1.0000$$

The preferred would become convertible into 100,000,000 shares, (91% of all common stock) at [T2].

$$\frac{\$100,000,000 \times 1 \text{ common share}}{\$1.0000} = 100,000,000 \text{ shares}$$

But the aggregate value of the preferred portion would remain unchanged at $90,909,091:

$$\frac{100,000,000 \text{ converted shares}}{110,000,000 \text{ common shares}} \times \$100,000,000 = \$90,909,091$$

Thus, on these assumptions, even if 90% of Corporation Y's assets are distributed to the common stockholders, the conversion value of the preferred is maintained at its pre-distribution level by the Section 5(e)(iv) gross-up provision.

CASE III

When the special dividend is so large that insufficient equity remains in Corporation Y to maintain the value of the preferred upon conversion the gross up provisions will fail to work. In such a situation the gross-up equation provides for a negative adjusted conversion price and is therefore meaningless.

For example: If Corporation Y declared a dividend of $950 million of its assets, the gross-up equation would give the following result:

$$ACP = \frac{CP \times (CMP - FMV)}{CMP}$$

$$ACP = \frac{\$100 \times (\$90.9091 - \$95.00)}{\$90.9091} = -(\$4.999)$$

Thus, a distribution of $950 million leaves only $50 million in assets in the corporation, making it impossible for the preferred to maintain its pre-distribution conversion value of $90.909 million. For that reason it also causes Section 5(e)(iv) to fail to work meaningfully.

undertook to refrain from declaring a dividend so large that what is left in the corporation is itself worth less than the pre-distribution value of the preferred stock. No other interpretation of the certificate of designation gives the language of Section 5(e)(iv) its intended effect in all circumstances. Thus, were the facts of Case 3 the facts of this case, I would be required to find that the special dividend violated the rights of the preferred stockholders created by the certificate of designation.

Such a holding would not be inconsistent with those cases that hold that rights of preference are to be strictly construed * * *. This strict construction perspective on the interpretation of certificates of designation has long been the law of this jurisdiction and others. While that principle does define the court's approach to construction and interpretation of the documents that create preferred stock, that principle does not excuse a court from the duty to interpret the legal meaning of the certificate of designation. * * * Thus where the *necessary implication* of the language used is the existence of a right or a duty, a court construing that language is duty bound to recognize the existence of that right or that duty. See Sullivan Money Management, Inc. v. FLS Holdings, Inc., Del.Ch., C.A. 12731, Jacobs, V.C. (Nov. 20, 1992), aff'd 628 A.2d 84 (June 18, 1993).

(b) Plaintiffs have failed to introduce evidence from which it could be concluded at this time that it is reasonably probable that they will prevail on a claim that the special dividend violates Section 5(e)(iv).

(i) *The value that Section 5(e)(iv) intends to protect is the market value of the conversion feature at the time the board authorizes a special dividend transaction.*

The determination that Section 5 of the certificate creates by necessary implication an obligation on the part of the corporation to leave sufficient value in the corporation following a special dividend to permit the protections it creates to function with the intended effect, raises the further question, what value does Section 5 intend to protect. Plainly it is the value of the conversion feature, that is what all of Section 5 is about, but measured at what point in time?

On the last day of trading before the announcement of the special dividend, Marriott's common stock closed at $17.125. The preferred's *conversion feature*, (its right to convert into 11,494,400 common shares) had a value at that time of $196,842,000. Beginning the first trading day after the announcement of the special dividend, Marriott common stock rose greatly in price. By May 21, 1993, it had increased to approximately $26.00 per share and the value of the preferred's conversion right had increased to $298.5 million. * * *

Plaintiffs' position is that this value, as effected by the prospect of the dividend attacked, is the value that must be left in the corporation.

I cannot accept this interpretation of what good faith adherence to the provisions of the certificate requires of Marriott. Section 5(e)(iv) operates to prevent the confiscation of the value of the preferred conversion right through a special dividend. By necessary implication it limits the board's discretion with respect to the size of special dividends. But that limitation is one that has its effect when it is respected by the board of directors at the time it takes corporate action to declare the dividend.[17] If, when declared, the dividend will leave the corporation with sufficient assets to preserve the conversion value that the preferred possesses at that time, it satisfies the limitation that such a protective provision necessarily implies. That is, Section 5(e)(iv) does not, in my opinion, explicitly or by necessary implication grant the preferred a right to assurance that any increase in the value of their conversion rights following the authorization of a special dividend be maintained.

(ii) *Plaintiffs have failed to introduce evidence that establishes a reasonable probability of their proving that the net value remaining in Host after distribution of the special dividend is or is reasonably likely to be insufficient to maintain the pre-distribution value of the preferred's conversion right.*

[The plaintiffs' expert valued Host's equity at less than $200 million, but did so on the basis of Hosts' financial structure as contemplated in October 1992, prior to the settlement of the bondholder litigation.]

A discounted cash flow valuation of Host produced by [Wolfensohn, Inc., an expert retained by Marriott] on April 20, 1993 and based on the assumption that the Exchange Offer will be effectuated, produced a range of values from $270 million (assuming a 14% discount rate; and a multiple of 7 times EBITDA) to $884 million (assuming a 12% discount rate and a multiple of 9 times EBITDA) with a middle case of $567 million (assuming a 13% discount rate and a multiple of 8 times EBITDA.) * * *

S.G. Warburg's valuation of Host, dated May 6, 1993, estimated the trading value of Host, assuming the Exchange Offer closes, at $1.38 to $2.84 per share or an aggregate of $179 million to $368 million. Warburg also estimated that the summary business value of Host would be in the range of $551 to $830 million or $4.25 to $6.40 per share.

The lower end of S.G. Warburg's estimate of the likely range of trading values for Host stock falls below the $196.8 million that represents the value of plaintiffs' conversion rights prior to the announcement of the distribution. Unspecified assertions by plaintiffs' expert that "major assumptions used in the discounted cash flow analysis are inappropriate" and that companies used for comparison are not comparable to Host, do not, however, provide a basis upon which to conclude that it is more likely that Host's common stock will have a value in the lower end of this range of values rather than in the higher part. The mere possibility that this will be the case is not enough to support the grant of a preliminary injunction. I assume the shape of a graph of the probabilities of any of these values in the range being "correct" would form a bell shaped curve. That is to say it is more likely that, upon more exhaustive analysis or with a more definitive

---

17. I put aside, as not involved here, any attempt to affect market prices before taking such actions.

valuation technique, the intrinsic value of Host would be the mean number of these ranges rather than either expressed limit of them. These higher probability mean estimates are all in excess of $196 million.

Thus, I am unable to conclude that plaintiffs have shown a sufficient probability of demonstrating that the protective functions of Section 5(e)(iv) will be frustrated by the size of the special dividend to justify the issuance of an injunction preventing the effectuation of the planned reorganization of Marriott.

(c) Plaintiffs have not shown that defendants have breached (or are about to breach) the agreed upon formula for implementing Section 5(e)(iv).

* * *

* * * Marriott intends to first determine "with reference to all relevant factors" the "intrinsic values" of International and Host. Then the fraction of the value of a Marriott share represented by International would be determined by dividing International's "intrinsic value" by the sum of the intrinsic values of International and Host. This fraction would then be multiplied by the current trading value of Marriott to determine the fair market value (per share) of International and thus of the distribution. Therefore, the fair market value of the distribution (i.e., International) is treated by the board's proposed valuation method *as fraction of the market value of Marriott prior to the distribution* of the dividend. The premise of this methodology is the assertion that as long as Host common stock trades at some positive value, the fair market value of International for purposes of applying Section 5(e)(iv) must be less than the current market value of Marriott; the whole (Marriott) cannot be less than the sum of its parts (International plus Host).

Defendants claim that this method of determining fair market value is consistent with the certificate and that it reaches a determination of the fair market value of the distribution that can meaningfully be compared to the current market value of Marriott. Indeed, they assert that any alternative technique which yields a value for International that is higher than the market value of Marriott must (as long as Host trades at a positive value) be faulty.

Plaintiffs contend that defendants' approach is inconsistent with the contract language. They say that it is designed to hide the fact that the special dividend is so large that the conversion price adjustment formula cannot work properly with respect to it.

Plaintiffs point out that the conversion price adjustment formula requires as a numerator the current per share market price of Marriott (determined over a 30 day period) less the *"then fair market value"* (expressed as a per share figure) of the assets distributed.[19] This number

---

19. I need not express a view as to whether the "then" is best read as (I) the time of the distribution (record date) or (ii) the time period during which the market value of Marriott stock is determined under the formula. In all events the "then fair market" is to be decided "by the Board of Directors, whose determination shall be concan be well estimated, it is claimed, by reference to the "when-issued" market which will, for a week or so before the distribution, establish a good proxy for the market value of the assets distributed.[20]

Plaintiffs claim that the method of determining the fair market value of International which defendants propose to employ is an attempt to manipulate Section 5(e)(iv), by artificially limiting the "fair market value" of the assets to be distributed (International's common stock) to a fraction of Marriott's total value despite the fact that Section 5(e)(iv) makes no mention of such a limitation. Plaintiffs rely on the language of the certificate which states explicitly that the board must determine the fair market value of the assets to be distributed, to support their argument that the board is required to determine this value without placing a ceiling on it of the value of Marriott.

In my opinion, Marriott's proposed technique for determining the values to employ in the contractual formula is one valid way to do what the company is contractually bound to do. It follows that this claim presents no grounds to justify the issuance of a preliminary injunction.

It is, of course, the case that plaintiffs' alternative technique might seem superior to some, in that it looks to a direct market measure of the value of the distribution. While that has appeal, it is also true that the different measuring times that this technique implies (see supra. n. 20) itself makes it possible that it would cause the adjustment formula to produce a negative number. Given the multiple factors that affect public securities markets, this could be true, even if far more equity were left in Host than the value of the preferred. Thus, there is good reason to reject plaintiffs' proposal even though it has appealing aspects.

Defendants' intended technique for estimating the "fair market value applicable to one share" would appear to serve the purpose of the section. As explained above, the equation is intended to operate to reduce the conversion price by the same percentage that the total assets of the company are being reduced. Assuming again that Host will have some positive net worth, it is clear that less than 100% of the assets of Marriott are being distributed. Therefore, in such a case the conversion price should be reduced by less than 100%. The method adopted by the company for determining applicable fair market value would, if fairly and competently applied, provide for the adjustment of the conversion price in a manner that effectuates the purposes of the clause. The certificate of course confers

clusive," so long as made in good faith I would add.

20. Plaintiffs express the view that it is quite possible that the when issued price for International will be in excess of the market price of Marriott, but if one is assuming contemporaneous measurement and one assumes Host will be solvent (which appears to be the case) it is difficult to see why that would be the case. Marriott common stock captures the full value of International before the distribution plus some additional value of

a solvent Host. Thus if Host is solvent it does seem illogical for a market to assign a higher value to International then to Marriott. The possibility of different measuring periods (the certificate language contemplates that the current market value of Marriott be measured over a thirty day period commencing forty five days before the distribution) would introduce a possibility for the when issued market for International to be higher on any particular day than the value of Marriott common stock over the measuring period.

broad discretion on Marriott in implementing the formula of Section 5(e)(iv) and makes its choices "conclusive." While that grant may too imply a duty of commercial good faith, the facts adduced do not suggest that the employment of the formula by defendants has been other than in good faith.

NOTE: CONVERTIBLE HEDGES

The plaintiffs in *Korenvaes* implemented convertible hedge strategies. This is a common practice—there are hedge funds that specialize in it. Note that the plaintiffs shorted an amount of Marriott stock roughly equal to the amount underlying the Marriott convertible preferred. The full hedge signals a bearish strategy on Marriott common—the plaintiffs sought to profit on the short sales with the long position in the convertible hedging the short position in the event of a dramatic increase in Marriott's stock price. The investment results in the case show that the hedge worked more or less as planned.

The trick to the hedge lies in the fact that the priority position and yield on the convertible causes it to hold value relative to the common in the event of a stock price decline; contrariwise, the preferred reacts positively to an increase in the stock price but often does not increase in value at a rate equaling that of the stock. It follows that the convertible makes a suitable hedge for a short on the stock. (Hedges built on short positions at less than one-to-one coverage of the stock underlying the convertible serve to protect the investment in the convertible from volatility in the underlying stock.)

Assume an issuer with a stock price at $50 and an 8 percent convertible bond priced at $100 convertible into two shares. The stock pays an annual dividend of $1. Let us short two shares and leave the position open for one year. The short sale yields $100, which we roll over into the purchase of 1 bond.

If the stock price falls to $25, we are in the money $50 on the short position. The convertible will fall as well, but less precipitously, say, to $82. We net out $32 ahead. Note that the 8 percent yield on the convertible is greater than the 2 percent dividend stream on the stock. Interest payments on the convertible will have more than covered dividends owed on the stock during the period the short position is open–$8 minus $2 = $6. Total gain then is $38, which is pretty nifty in view of the fact that the capital invested is limited to that otherwise in our margin account. Now consider a stock price increase to $75. We are out of pocket $50 on the short position. But the convertible will have risen with the stock, say, to $134. The $34 gain on the convertible plus the $6 net on interest cushions the $50 loss on the stock. We net $10 out of pocket.

Players in this game employ convertible valuation models that permit precise advance estimation of the relative interplay of market prices. The large number of players imports liquidity to convertible issues that otherwise would suffer from thin markets. But not all convertibles are created equal so far concerns suitability for hedging. Here are two rules of thumb: (1) the closer the convertible's market price to debt value the better, for then the convertible falls much less steeply than does the stock; and (2) the lower the conversion premium relative to the bond price the better. The latter rule follows from the premium's fragility relative to external events like takeovers. See Calamos, supra, at 296–97, 305.

NOTE: INTERPRETATION *CONTRA PROFERENTUM*

Kaiser Aluminum Corp. v. Matheson, 681 A.2d 392 (Del.Supr.1996), applies the old maxim of interpretation against the drafter to a set of preferred stock antidilution provisions. The result is a ruling against the issuer.

The issue in question was Kaiser Aluminum's Preferred Redeemable Increased Dividend Equity Securities ("PRIDES"), issued in 1994. The PRIDES were convertible into .8333 shares of common stock at the option of the holder prior to December 31, 1997; from December 31, 1997, each share of PRIDES converted automatically into one share of common. The PRIDES had 4/5 vote per share and voted with the common, and were redeemable prior to December 31, 1997 at a ratio based on the market price of the common subject to a minimum redemption value of .8333 shares of common for each share of PRIDES.

Kaiser, two-thirds owned by Maxxam, launched a dual class common recapitalization prior to December 31, 1997. Under the recapitalization, its existing single class of common was to be turned into two classes of common with disparate voting rights. The charter was to be amended to create one class of Class A Common shares ("New Class A") with full voting rights and to authorize the issuance of an additional 250 million shares of new, low-voting common stock ("New Common") possessing voting rights of 1/10 vote per share. Current holders of existing common would receive .33 shares of New Class A and .67 shares of New Common for each share of existing common. Kaiser also proposed "carry over" treatment for the PRIDES—each share of PRIDES would convert after December 31, 1997 into .33 shares of New Class A and .67 of New Common. But a class of PRIDES-holding plaintiffs intervened, requesting and receiving an injunction against the recapitalization on the ground that they could not under the charter be forced to take the New Class A and the New Common.

Section 3(d)(i) of the charter read as follows:

(i) If the Corporation shall either:

(1) pay a dividend or make a distribution with respect to Common Stock [defined in the charter as "fully paid and non-assessable shares of common stock of the Corporation"] in shares of Common Stock,

(2) subdivide or split its outstanding shares of Common Stock into a greater number of shares,

(3) combine its outstanding shares of Common Stock into a smaller number of shares, or

(4) issue by reclassification of its shares of Common Stock any shares of common stock of the Corporation then, in any such event, [the conversion rates] in effect immediately prior thereto shall each be adjusted so that the holder of a share of PRIDES shall be entitled to receive, on the conversion of such share of PRIDES, the number of shares of Common Stock of the Corporation which such holder would have owned or been entitled to receive after the happening of any of the events described above had such share of PRIDES been converted ... immediately prior to the happening of such event....

The plaintiffs' theory was that the use of the capitalized term "Common Stock" in the "then in any such event" clause of § 3(d)(i) meant that they had to be provided with Kaiser common stock as existing prior to any recapitalization. Kaiser contended that the provision should be read so that the PRIDES holders received *pro rata* whatever the holders of the underlying security received in the recapitalization.

The problem with Kaiser's reading, said the Delaware Supreme Court, was that it presupposed use of lower case "common stock" in the "then in any such event" clause. It compared the parallel language in § 10.06 of the Model Simplified Indenture, noting that the MSI language sufficed to achieve the result sought by

Kaiser. In contrast to the Kaiser charter, the MSI shifts to the undefined term "capital stock" in the "then" cause:

If the Company:

* * *

(5) issues by reclassification of its Common Stock [defined as "Common Stock of the Company as it exists on the date of this Indenture as originally signed"] any shares of its capital stock, then the conversion privilege and the conversion price in effect immediately prior to such action shall be adjusted so that the Holder of a Security thereafter converted may receive the number of shares of capital stock of the Company which he would have owned immediately following such action if he had converted the Security immediately prior to such action.

But if § 3(d)(i) of the Kaiser charter did not suffice to carry the conversion privilege over so that the holders received *pro rata* what the common received under the recapitalization, for what then did it provide? It was, said the court "hopelessly unclear" and not easily explicable. Resort to extrinsic evidence of intent to clarify the ambiguity was disfavored for the reasons stated in *Sharon Steel*, Part II, Section B, supra. As a "last resort" the court invoked the principle of interpretation against the drafter:

We agree that "[w]hile debtor corporations are not the actual drafters of bond contracts, they are in a much better position to clarify the meaning of ... contract terms in advance of disputes than are investors generally." Tauke [Should Bonds Have More Fun? A Reexamination of the Debate Over Corporate Bondholder Rights, 1989 Colum. Bus. Rev. 1, 87 (1989)]. The issuer is "better able to clarify unclear bond contract terms in advance so as to avoid future disputes and therefore should bear the drafting burden that the contra proferentum principle would impose upon it." Id. at 89 * * *. Moreover, when faced with an ambiguous provision in a document such as the Certificate, the Court must construe the document to adhere to the reasonable expectations of the investors who purchased the security and thereby subjected themselves to the terms of the contract. Rhone–Poulenc, 616 A.2d at 1196.

We caution against this principle becoming "a short-cut for avoiding the sometimes difficult tasks of determining expectations.... " Tauke, 1989 Colum. Bus. Rev. at 88. Certificates of Designation and indentures are necessarily complex documents prepared by sophisticated drafters. They require some effort and careful thought to understand. In the normal course of events, the four corners of the document will yield a result which is consistent with reasonable expectations. See William W. Bratton, Jr., The Interpretation of Contracts Concerning Corporate Debt Relationships, 5 Cardozo L.Rev. 371, 379 (1984). We apply the contra proferentum principle here only as a last resort because the language of the Certificate presents a hopeless ambiguity, particularly when alternative formulations indicate that these provisions could easily have been made clear.

NOTE: CONVERTIBLE BOND CONTRACTS

1. *Additional Issues of Interpretation.*

Anti-dilution provisions give rise to endless interpretive problems. Many cases concern whether a particular issuer action is within a particular contingency provided for in the contract, and thus protected or unprotected. See, e.g., Gardner and Florence Call Cowles Foundation v. Empire Inc., 589 F.Supp. 669 (S.D.N.Y. 1984)(whether reverse triangular cashout merger falls within antidilution provision directed to distribution of securities or indebtedness); Prescott, Ball & Turben v. LTV Corp., 531 F.Supp. 213 (S.D.N.Y.1981) and Stephenson v. Plastics Corp. of America, 276 Minn. 400, 150 N.W.2d 668 (1967) (whether a spin off of a subsidiary is a "dividend" or "capital reorganization"). Other cases raise the question whether the agreement is to be read to preserve the option holder's proportionate interest in the enterprise by altering the price or rate at which his security is convertible to stock to reflect proposed alterations in the structure of the enterprise (e.g., stock splits, capital distributions, etc.), or should be read to force the holder to elect either to exercise the option or to suffer the dilution when an alteration in capital structure is proposed. See e.g., Pittsburgh Terminal Corporation v. The Baltimore and Ohio Railroad Company, 680 F.2d 933 (3d Cir.1982); Meckel v. Continental Resources Co., 758 F.2d 811 (2d Cir.1985); Merritt–Chapman & Scott Corp. v. New York Trust Co., 184 F.2d 954 (2d Cir.1950). As already noted, the latter alternative is effected by providing, instead of an adjustment of the conversion price or rate, that the bondholder shall receive notice of the proposed alteration and be required to exercise his conversion option or forego the proposed distribution within the noticed period. Problems created by the interplay between the call provisions and the conversion privilege also are illustrated in Jamie Securities Co. v. The Limited, Inc., 880 F.2d 1572 (2d Cir.1989); Mueller v. Howard Aircraft Corp., 329 Ill.App. 570, 70 N.E.2d 203 (1946); Green v. Hamilton Int'l Corp., 493 F.Supp. 596 (S.D.N.Y.1979) (invoking Rule 10b–5); and Van Gemert v. The Boeing Co., infra. Generally, the burden to draft against specific contingencies is imposed by courts on the bondholder. Should the burden of specificity instead lie with the issuer, as held in *Matheson*, supra?

2. *Good Faith Provisions.*

The limitations on the effectiveness of standard form antidilution clauses have not escaped the notice of the corporate bar. Many private placement debt contracts contain a so-called "good faith" anti-dilution provision. This catches all actions not otherwise covered which "materially and adversely affect the conversion rights of the holders." See Kaplan, Piercing the Corporate Boilerplate: Anti–Dilution Clauses in Convertible Securities, 33 U.Chi.L.Rev. 1, 18 n. 27 (1965). In theory this shifts the risk of dilution and destruction back to the issuer.

3. *Issue of Additional Common Stock.*

How should the convertible bond contract deal with a subsequent issue in an arms length transaction of common stock for a price lower than the conversion price? Fifty years ago standard antidilution provisions in bonds issued by mature publicly traded companies employed a "conversion price" formula. Under this, the conversion price was adjusted downward whenever stock was sold below the conversion price pursuant to a weighted-average formula. The idea was that the conversion privilege was an option on a specified portion of the issuer's earnings. The operative theory of injurious dilution later changed. The contracts then provided for downward adjustment of the conversion price only in response to below market offerings of new stock and rights to existing common stockholders. The new theory was that the contract should (a) protect not a percentage claim on earnings but the current market level of conversion value and conversion premium, and (b) operate only when stockholders receive a benefit at the bondholders expense (which presumably is impossible if the offering is made at the market price) and that otherwise there should be parity of treatment. See Kaplan, supra, at 18; Bratton, The Economics and Jurisprudence of Convertible Bonds, 1984 Wis. L.Rev. 667, 687.

Compare the drafting practice in venture capital deals. There a subsequent issue of stock below the conversion price can trigger a "full ratchet" that lowers the conversion price to the price yielded in the subsequent stock issue, with potentially drastic effects on relative equity interests. Woronoff and Rosen, supra, at 146–47, defend this approach on the ground that start up investments hold out significant information asymmetries as between inside entrepreneurs and outside capitalists. The ratchet, they point out, comes into play when the firm was overvalued at the time the convertible was issued and has the beneficial effect of evening the informational playing field ex post.

4. *Drafting Practice.*

Kahan, Anti–Dilution Provisions in Convertible Securities, 2 Stan. J.L. Bus. & Fin. 147 (1995), reports on a survey of indenture provisions governing 49 convertible bonds issued in 1993. The results show a trend toward more effective, if not perfect coverage, of dilution risks attending dividends and mergers.

Significantly, most issues now provide anti-dilution protection for noncash dividends, using the same adjustment formula discussed in the *Marriott* case, supra. About half of the indentures also apply the formula to large cash dividends on the condition that the aggregate amount of annual dividends exceed a stated percentage of the market value of the outstanding common stock. The threshold percentages in the indentures range from 4 to 25 percent with a 14 percent average. Market price common stock repurchases, in contrast, do not trigger adjustments—no doubt because the reduction in the number of common shares outstanding attending such repurchases assures that they are not dilutive. About half of the indentures, however, do provide for adjustments in the case of common stock repurchases by means of a self tender offer at a premium. Like the cash dividend adjustment provisions, these tend to be triggered when aggregate self-tender payments exceed a stated percentage of the market value of the outstanding common stock.

(B) DUTIES IMPLIED IN LAW

Does the inclusion of a conversion privilege in a bond import a status change, so that the convertible bondholder benefits from an issuer fiduciary duty where the holder of a straight bond does not? If so, does the duty extend only to actions impairing the value of the conversion privilege and not to actions impairing the bond's debt value? If no fiduciary duty obtains, does the conversion privilege's susceptibility to easy impairment give rise to a contractual good faith duty that supports judicial intervention to restrain issuer action materially diluting or otherwise impairing the value of the conversion privilege? Finally, does the interest in the corporation's equity carried by the conversion privilege import bondholder standing to enforce management duties to the corporation by means of a derivative action?

The cases that follow deal with these questions.

Van Gemert v. Boeing Co.

United States Court of Appeals, Second Circuit, 1975.
520 F.2d 1373, cert. denied, 423 U.S. 947 (1975).

■ OAKES, CIRCUIT JUDGE:

This appeal is from a judgment dismissing the amended complaint in a consolidation class action brought by nonconverting holders of The Boeing Company's "4 1/2% Convertible Subordinated Debentures, due July 1, 1980." The complaint was jurisdictionally based on the Securities Exchange Act of 1934 as amended * * * and the principles of pendent jurisdiction.

The gist of the complaint was that the appellants and their class had inadequate and unreasonable notice of Boeing's intention to redeem or "call" the convertible debentures in question and were hence unable to exercise their conversion rights before the deadline in the call of midnight, March 29, 1966. Their damage lay in the fact that the redemption price for each $100 of principal amount of debentures was only $103.25, while under the conversion rate of, at a minimum, two shares of common stock for each $100 of principal amount of debentures, the stock was worth $316.25 on March 29, 1966, the cut-off date for the exercise of conversion privileges, or within 30 days thereafter, $364.00. The named appellants number 56, and the total loss alleged is over $2 million.

[The debentures had been issued pursuant to a rights offering made by Boeing to holders of its common stock to purchase $100 of debentures for each 23 shares held. The Chase Manhattan Bank ("Chase") was indenture trustee and the debentures were listed on the New York Stock Exchange ("NYSE").]

The Indenture itself, a 113–page printed booklet, provides in Art. V, § 5.02, as follows:

> In case the Company shall desire to exercise the right to redeem all or any part of the debentures, as the case may be, pursuant to Section 5.01, it shall publish prior to the date fixed for redemption a notice of such redemption at least twice in an Authorized Newspaper, the first such publication to be not less than 30 days and not more than 90 days before the date fixed for redemption. Such publication shall be in successive weeks but on any day of the week....[6]

The Indenture also provided that debenture-holders who registered their bonds would receive notice by mail of any redemption call by the Boeing directors.

While the prospectus for the debenture issue did not refer to any registration rights, it did state that redemption could occur "on not less than 30 days' and not more than 90 days' published notice."

[Under the listing agreement entered into between Boeing and NYSE, Boeing had a duty to publicize any action taken pertaining to the rights of the debenture holders. The necessary publicity was more particularly defined in the NYSE Company Manual as a general news release containing in the case of redemption, information as to the rate of conversion and date and time of expiration of the conversion privilege. The Manual also required of notice of a call to the NYSE itself.

[At the time Boeing called the bonds, it complied with Indenture's requirement of published notice and also mentioned the call in a general new release. The news release did not, however, provide information as to the conversion rate or expiration time, as required by the NYSE rules.]

There was, in short, no general news release as called for by the Listing Agreement as amplified in the Company Manual until on the eve of

---

6. An "Authorized Newspaper" is defined as one published at least five days a week and of general circulation in the borough of Manhattan, N.Y. * * *

expiration of the conversion rights, March 25, 1966, it appeared that $10,849,300 face amount of debentures over one-half of those outstanding at that time remained unconverted. At that point Boeing issued a press release and then * * * the Company republished its earlier advertisement * * * and additional advertisements were placed. This later action had what the court below termed a "dramatic and widespread rippling effect." Some $9,305,000 of debentures were converted on March 28 and 29. The ripples, however, had not spread to the appellants' class by the midnight deadline on the 29th; they literally went to sleep with $1.5 million of debentures that were worth $4 million if only converted.

* * * [A]lmost all of [the] notices or items were in fine print, buried in the multitude of information and data published about the financial markets and scarcely of a kind to attract the eye of the average lay investor or debenture holder. On March 9, 1966, the listing in the New York Times for the convertible debentures read, for example: "Boeing cv 41/2 s 80." The change on March 10 was to "Boeing 41/2 s 80 cld," giving the investor in Dubuque or Little Rock or Lampasas only 19 days to pick up this change and figure that "cld" meant "called." Proof of the inadequacy of these notices lies in the fact that, despite the dramatic disparity between the value of the debentures unconverted and the conversion stock, over one-half of the debentures outstanding on the date of the first notice remained unconverted until the general publicity release on the eve of expiration of the conversion privilege.

Because the appellants place some emphasis on the fact, although we do not reach their contention of unreasonable notice based on it, we should mention that Boeing made no attempt to mail notice to the original subscribers (which could have been done at concededly nominal expense), and neither Boeing nor Chase inquired of or gave notice to collecting banks which had tendered for collection coupons bearing the payment dates of July 15, 1965, or January 15, 1966, the last two coupons before the redemption, either of which might have had some beneficial effect.

* * *

The claim that Boeing is civilly liable under federal law for violation of the NYSE Listing Agreement and Section A10 of the Company Manual is a colorable one. * * *

* * *

Nevertheless, we do not now take the position that appellees advance and the court below apparently accepted, that violation of an exchange rule cannot under any circumstances give rise to civil liability under the federal acts. Such a position would be in conflict with our own most recent statements on this subject as well as some of the developing case law. * * *

* * *

The notice Boeing gave, we hold, had two deficiencies. First, Boeing did not adequately apprise the debenture holders what notice would be given of a redemption call. Investors were not informed by the prospectus or by the debentures that they could receive mail notice by registering their debentures, and that otherwise they would have to rely primarily on finding one of the scheduled advertisements in the newspaper or on keeping a constant eye on the bond tables. Second, the newspaper notice given by Boeing was itself inadequate.

The first factor we think highly significant. Many of the debenture holders might well have decided to register their bonds, had the significance of registration, or of the failure to register, been brought home in the materials generally available to the purchasers of the debentures. No detailed information as to notice was given on the face of the debentures, even in the fine print. The debentures stated simply:

> The debentures are subject to redemption, as a whole or in part, at any time or times, at the option of the Company, in not less than 30 nor more than 90 days' prior notice, as provided in the Indenture ...

There was no indication that registration would mean that a debenture holder would receive mail notice. Nor was there any indication of the extent of newspaper notice to be provided either as to the papers that would be used or how often the notice would be published. Debenture holders were simply referred by the debenture, as well as by the prospectus, to the 113–page Indenture Agreement, which, to be sure, was available to debenture holders or prospective purchasers upon request, but which was not circulated generally with the warrants or debentures.

[While] the newspaper notice actually given * * * may have conformed to the requirements of the Indenture it was simply insufficient to give fair and reasonable notice to the debenture holders.

The duty of reasonable notice arises out of the contract between Boeing and the debenture holders, pursuant to which Boeing was exercising its right to redeem the debentures. An issuer of debentures has a duty to give adequate notice either on the face of the debentures * * * or in some other way, of the notice to be provided in the event the company decides to redeem the debentures. Absent such advice as to the specific notice agreed upon by the issuer and the trustee for the debenture holders, the debenture holders' reasonable expectations as to notice should be protected.

For less sophisticated investors (it will be recalled that warrants for the purchase of debentures were issued to all Boeing shareholders), putting the notice provisions only in the 113–page Indenture Agreement was effectively no notice at all. It was not reasonable for Boeing to expect these investors to send off for, and then to read understandingly, the 113–page Indenture Agreement referred to in both the prospectus and the debentures themselves in order to find out what notice would be provided in the event of redemption.

Boeing could very easily have run more than two advertisements in a single paper prior to the eleventh hour (March 28), at which time it issued its belated news release and advertised for the third time in the Wall Street Journal and for the first time in the New York Times. Moreover, in the same period that the debentures were in the process of being redeemed, Boeing was preparing for its annual meeting (to be held April 24). Proxy materials were being prepared throughout March and were finally mailed sometime between March 24 and March 30. Management could readily have arranged the redemption dates and the proxy mailing so that notice of the redemption dates could have been included in the envelope with the proxy materials. Thus at no extra cost except that of printing brief notices, at least all Boeing shareholders would have received mail notice, and presumably a significant number of the plaintiff class owned Boeing common stock, as well as debentures, in 1966. Had Boeing attempted such mail notice, or mail notice to original subscribers, and also given further newspaper publicity either by appropriate news releases or advertising earlier in the redemption period, we would have a different case and reasonable and sufficient notice might well be found.

* * *

What one buys when purchasing a convertible debenture in addition to the debt obligation of the company incurred thereby is principally the expectation that the stock will increase sufficiently in value that the conversion right will make the debenture worth more than the debt. The debenture holder relies on the opportunity to make a proper conversion on due notice. Any loss occurring to him from failure to convert, as here, is not from a risk inherent in his investment but rather from unsatisfactory notification procedures. * * * The debenture holder's expectancy is that he will receive reasonable notice and it is his reliance on this expectancy that the courts will protect. See generally Fuller & Perdue, The Reliance Interest in Contract Damages, 46 Yale L.J. 52, 373 (1936–37). * * * Had there been proper publication, a reasonable investor undoubtedly would have taken action to prevent the loss occurring to him.

Of course, it may be suggested that the appellee corporation itself was not the beneficiary of the appellants' loss; rather, the corporate stockholders benefited by not having their stock watered down by the number of shares necessary to convert appellants' debentures. But an award against Boeing will in effect tend to reduce pro tanto the equity of shareholders in the corporation and thus to a large extent those who were benefited, one might almost say unjustly enriched, will be the ones who pay appellants' loss.

NOTE: *VAN GEMERT'S* OPERATIVE THEORY

Van Gemert remanded the case to the District Court for a determination of damages. In an appeal of that determination, **Van Gemert v. The Boeing Co.,** 553 F.2d 812 (2d Cir.1977), another panel of the same court offered further advice on the rationale of the case:

" * * * In our prior decision, we did not rely on a mutual mistake between the parties in expressing the terms of their agreement. Neither did we find unilateral mistake on the part of the debenture holders occasioned by Boeing's fraud. We did find significant, however, the fact that the debentures did not explicitly set forth the type of notice which appellants could expect if Boeing decided to call the bonds. Without such a declaration, we held as a matter of law that appellants were entitled to expect that Boeing would employ a method of notification reasonably calculated to inform the debenture holders of the call. In doing so, we merely applied the settled principle, 'that in every contract there is an implied covenant that neither party shall do anything which will have the effect of destroying or injuring the right of the other party to receive the fruits of the contract. . . . ' Kirke La Shelle Co. v. Paul Armstrong Co., 263 N.Y. 79, 87, 188 N.E. 163, 167 (1933). Simply stated, every contract contains the implied requirement of good faith and fair dealing. Boeing was found liable therefore because it breached its contract with appellants, and damages were awarded. * * * ''

Broad v. Rockwell International Corp.

United States Court of Appeals, Fifth Circuit (en banc), 1981.
642 F.2d 929, cert. denied, 454 U.S. 965 (1981).

■ Randall, Circuit Judge:

This case, which is before us for rehearing en banc, turns on the construction of an indenture dated as of January 1, 1967 (the "Indenture"). The original parties to the Indenture were Collins Radio Company, an Iowa corporation ("Collins"), and The Chase Manhattan Bank (National Association), a national banking association ("Chase"). The Indenture governed the terms of $40,000,000 principal amount of 4 7/8 Convertible Subordinated Debentures due January 1, 1987 (the "Debentures"), which were issued by Collins in January 1967. By means of a supplemental indenture executed in May 1970, United States Trust Company of New York, a New York corporation (the "Trust Company"), succeeded Chase as Trustee under the Indenture.

The events that triggered this lawsuit occurred in the fall of 1973, when Rockwell International Corporation, a Delaware corporation ("Rockwell"), acquired Collins in a cash merger. The central question in the case is this: In what form did the conversion rights of the holders of the Debentures survive the merger under the terms of the Indenture?

David Broad brought this class action on behalf of himself and all others who at the time of the merger were holders of the Debentures. He sued Rockwell, Collins, the controlling persons of both, and the Trust Company, alleging that the defendants breached the terms of the Indenture, breached their respective fiduciary duties, and violated various provisions of the federal securities laws. The district court granted a directed verdict in favor of the defendants at the close of Broad's case-in-chief, holding that (1) the defendants' interpretation of the Indenture and their actions in accord with that interpretation were correct and nonactionable as a matter of state law, and (2) for a number of reasons, no reasonable jury could have found violations of the federal securities laws based on the evidence Broad had adduced at trial. A panel of this court affirmed as to the directed verdict on the federal securities counts, but reversed and remanded on the pendent state-law claims; a majority of the full court, however, vacated the panel's decision * * * and ordered that the appeal be reheard en banc. Broad v. Rockwell International Corp., 614 F.2d 418, vacated and rehearing en banc granted, 618 F.2d 396 (5th Cir.1980).

On rehearing en banc, we agree with the panel that the district court acted properly in directing a verdict on the federal securities claims * * *. We disagree, however, with the panel's construction of the Indenture, and hold instead that the district court properly construed that document's provisions. Accordingly, for the reasons set out herein, we affirm the judgment of the district court.

[Collins manufactured radio communications and aircraft navigation equipment. When the Debentures were first issued in 1967, its common stock was trading for $60. The conversion price, meanwhile, was $72.50. Beginning in 1969, however, Collins business declined rapidly. During 1971 its stock never traded above $21 and sold for as little as $9 3/4. The Debentures reached a low of around $600. In August 1971, with Collins on the verge of bankruptcy, Rockwell made a $35 million equity investment in Collins and guaranteed an additional $20 million of indebtedness, simultaneously taking control of Collins' board of directors. In 1973, Rockwell commenced a friendly tender offer for Collins' common stock for $25 per share and purchased 75 percent of the outstanding shares. It thereafter merged Collins into itself. Under the Merger Plan, each share of common received $25 per share. The merger was approved by a two-thirds shareholder vote, as required by the law of Iowa, Collins' state of incorporation.

[The Debentures proved to be a sticking point. The Trust Company consulted outside counsel respecting the rights of the debentureholders. Counsel opined that their rights were not free from doubt, and that a court conceivably could hold that under the Indenture they were entitled to a right to convert into shares of common of the survivor of the merger, Rockwell. Meanwhile, Rockwell proposed a supplemental indenture providing that the holders have the right to convert only into the amount of cash that would have been payable under the Merger Plan—an unfavorable trade of the $72.50 conversion price for $25 cash.

[The Trust Company resisted executing Rockwell's supplemental indenture because of the legal uncertainty. But, under considerable pressure from Rockwell and a promise of indemnity in respect of any resulting liability judgment, the Trust Company eventually assented.]

* * * [O]n November 14, 1973, the merger was effected, and a supplemental indenture between Rockwell and the Trust Company was executed, effective as of November 1, 1973. The supplemental indenture provided that Rockwell would assume Collins' obligations on the Debentures. Specifically, it provided that after the merger, the holders of the Debentures had the right to convert the debentures into that which they would have received in the Merger Plan had they converted immediately before the merger's effective date. * * * Rockwell has consistently interpreted this to mean that the Debentures could be converted into cash, but not into the common stock of either Rockwell or Collins; the conversion rate was $344.75 in cash for each $1000 in principal amount of Debentures surrendered.

* * *

As a matter of law, be it the law of New York [the Indenture contained a choice of law clause designating New York law] or any other jurisdiction with which we are acquainted, the Indenture either is or is not ambiguous. It either does or does not adequately demonstrate the intent of the parties from its own four corners. We cannot emphasize too strongly that the resolution of this issue is for the district court in the first instance, rather than for a jury; and because it is a question of law, we review the district court's decision with the full freedom to substitute our own judgment for that of the court below. The opinions of the many lawyers who have reviewed the Indenture before this litigation reached this court may be quite relevant for some other purposes e. g., for determining the defendants' good faith or the lack thereof. We may, but certainly need not, find the force of their legal reasoning compelling, and adopt it as our own. But on the initial and often determinative question of whether the contract sufficiently demonstrates the intent of the parties so as to be enforceable only by reference to the four corners of the document, it does not matter at all how many lawyers have in the past pronounced this contract to be ambiguous or unambiguous. Neither does it matter in whose behalf, or with what motives, or when, they made such arguments. We note that virtually every case involving the interpretation of a contract comes to us with two sets of lawyers and two sets of clients with sharply differing views of the meaning of the contract. But interpreting contracts is ultimately the business of the courts.

* * *

The structure of the Indenture is fairly typical of convertible debenture indentures generally. See American Bar Foundation, Model Debenture Indenture Provisions All Registered Issues 1967, reprinted in Commentaries at 19 & passim (1971). As might be expected, there is an article of the Indenture devoted wholly to the conversion rights of the holders of the Debentures, and a section within that article which addresses the possibility of a merger of Collins with another company: Article Four of the Indenture is entitled "Conversion of Debentures," and the next-to-last section of that Article, Section 4.11, is described in the Indenture's table of contents as governing the "(c)ontinuation of the conversion privilege in case of a consolidation, merger or sale of assets." We note that there is no provision in the Indenture which explicitly mandates that the holders of the Debentures should have a continuing right to convert into common stock after a merger. Aside from his few arguments based on the language of Section 4.11, Broad basically argues his case by implication from more general language that is not specifically addressed to the merger context. But because Section 4.11 is more specifically addressed to the merger context than any other provision of the Indenture, we begin our discussion with that particular provision, to see if the language thereof clearly and unambiguously conveys the intent of the parties.

Section 4.11 provides, in pertinent part, as follows:

In case of any consolidation of (Collins) with, or merger of (Collins) into, any other corporation ... , the corporation formed by such consolidation or the corporation into which (Collins) shall have been merged ... shall execute and deliver to the (Trust Company) a supplemental indenture ... providing that the holder of each Debenture then outstanding shall have the right (until the expiration of the conversion right of such Debenture) to convert such Debenture into the kind and amount of shares of stock and other securities and property receivable upon such consolidation (or) merger ... by a holder of the number of shares of Common Stock of (Collins) into which such Debenture might have been converted immediately prior to such consolidation (or) merger....

Parsing this section into logical units, we note that it serves two purposes. First, it specifies what the Trust Company and Collins' successor must do in the event of a merger in which Collins is not the surviving company: they must execute a supplemental indenture that will formally provide for the conversion rights of the holders of Debentures after the merger. There is no question in this case but that Rockwell and the Trust Company complied with this directive, for they did execute a supplemental indenture detailing the post-merger conversion rights of the holders of Debentures. Rather, the question is whether the interpretation they have placed on the language of the Indenture and the supplemental indenture that after the merger, the holder of a Debenture would have the right to convert a Debenture in the principal amount of $1000 only into $344.75 in cash fairly and adequately accords to the holders of Debentures their valid rights under the Indenture.

The second part of Section 4.11 provides by its terms that after the merger, the holder of each Debenture shall have the right to convert that Debenture into something but what? It cannot be Collins Common Stock, for there will be no more of that after the merger. It therefore must be something else other than Collins Common Stock. The nature of the "something else" into which the holder of a Debenture can convert his Debenture is specified by reference to what the holders of the Collins Common Stock received in the merger: he can convert into the kind of "shares of stock and other securities and property" that the holders of Collins Common Stock received as part of the Merger Plan. * * *

　　　　　　* * *

* * * Section 4.11 gives us a formula for computing the quantity of the "something else." There are two variables in the formula: the conversion price of the Debentures immediately prior to the merger, and the quantity of the "something" received by the holders of Collins Common Stock in exchange for each share they surrendered as part of the Merger Plan. Section 4.11 directs that we first determine the number of shares of Collins Common Stock that a holder of Debentures would have been entitled to receive had he converted his Debentures immediately prior to the merger. As of the date of the merger, nothing had happened to trigger any of the conversion price adjustment provisions set out elsewhere in Article Four of the Indenture. Therefore, the conversion price originally specified when the Debentures were issued $72.50 was still in effect at the time of the merger. At this conversion price, the Debentures were convertible immediately prior to the merger at the rate of 13.79 shares of Collins Common Stock per $1000 in principal amount of the Debentures surrendered.

The formula next provides that we take the quantity of the "something" that was received by the holders of Collins Common Stock in the merger in exchange for each share of Common Stock they surrendered ($25 cash), and multiply that "something" by the number of shares of Collins

Common Stock into which the Debentures would have been convertible (13.79 shares per $1000 Debenture). The result is that each $1000 principal amount of Debenture is convertible into $344.75 cash (13.79 × $25).

Under the plain language of Section 4.11, then, we are compelled to the conclusion that Rockwell and the Trust Company correctly fulfilled their duties to execute a supplemental indenture providing for the post-merger conversion rights of the holders of Debentures; further, they correctly calculated those rights as specified by the terms of Section 4.11. Unless there is some compelling reason that we should not give the language of this Section its plain meaning, Broad's breach of contract claim must fail.

* * *

Broad's first argument against giving the language of Section 4.11 its plain meaning is based indirectly on the "and other securities and property" clause. Broad concedes that under New York law, the term "property" includes cash within its scope. But, he argues, the parties could not have intended at the time of the Indenture's execution that the right to convert into cash could be substituted for the right to convert into Collins Common Stock. As support for this argument, he notes that Collins was incorporated under the laws of Iowa, and that as of 1967, when the Indenture was executed, Iowa law did not permit a merger in which the shareholders of the merged company received only cash in exchange for their shares. Rockwell and the Trust Company concede that such a merger was not possible under Iowa law until 1970.

The actual language of Section 4.11, however, is entirely inconsistent with Broad's argument. If the intent of the parties was that the right to convert into Collins Common Stock would be replaced in the event of a merger with a right to convert into only common stock of another company, then the phrase "and other securities and property" would be meaningless surplusage with no effect. Under the New York rules of contract construction discussed above, contracts should be construed so as to give meaning to all provisions. The phrase "and other securities and property" can only have meaning if the contract is interpreted to mean that the parties intended that the holders of Debentures should be entitled to convert into whatever types of compensation the holders of Collins Common Stock could receive under the state law governing mergers at any given point in time.

We note as well that it would be entirely inconsistent with the tone and purpose of the remainder of the Indenture which was drafted to provide, insofar as humanly possible, for every imaginable contingency to impute to the parties an intent to freeze as of the year 1967 the nature of the property into which the Debentures were convertible. If that were in fact their intent, it would have ill served the holders of the Debentures.

* * *

* * *

Broad next argues that the Indenture elsewhere provides an absolute, unabridgeable right to convert into Collins Common Stock at any time while the Debentures are outstanding. He first points to Section 4.01, which provides in pertinent part as follows:

Subject to and upon compliance with the provisions of this Article Four, at the option of the holder thereof, any Debenture … may, at any time (while the Debentures are outstanding) be converted … into fully paid and non-assessable shares … of Common Stock of (Collins)….

Broad would have us read the "at any time" language as precluding the effect we would otherwise give to the language of Section 4.11.

In the first place, if there were any conflict between the above-quoted language of Section 4.01 and Section 4.11, the latter would control under principles of New York contract law, since of the two sections, Section 4.11 is more specifically addressed to the merger context. But in fact there is no conflict. Broad's suggested construction would make sense only if we were to ignore the introductory phrase of Section 4.01 "(s)ubject to and upon compliance with the provisions of this Article Four." Section 4.11 is part of Article Four, and Section 4.01, by its very terms, is explicitly made subject to that article. Thus, the "at any time" language of Section 4.01 is implicitly qualified by reference to Section 4.11 to mean "at any time except in the merger context, at which point Section 4.11 becomes applicable."

* * *

We conclude, after examining the entire Indenture in addition to those portions discussed specifically above, that the district court was correct in its conclusion that the Indenture is unambiguous. * * *

* * *

Broad's persistent complaint has been that the Debentures' conversion feature was suddenly and arbitrarily liquidated, without permission or compensation. While the conversion feature has not technically been eliminated, since the holders of the Debentures retain the right to convert into $344.75 in cash for each $1000 principal amount of Debentures, it is true that the merger did eliminate the possibility that the holders of the Debentures would benefit as a result of the future profitability of the Collins business, just as the merger eliminated that possibility for the holders of Collins Common Stock. A purchaser of Debentures, however, takes the risks inherent in the equity feature of the security, risks that are shared with the holders of Collins Common Stock. One of those risks is that Collins might merge with another company which is effectively the risk that any individual investor's assessment of the value of Collins Common Stock, based on Collins' prospects for the future, will be replaced by the collective judgment of the marketplace and the other investors in Collins who might vote in favor of the merger. This like the risk that Collins' future operations might be lackluster, with the result that conversion might never be economically attractive is simply a risk inherent in this type of investment.

* * *

As we understand New York law, every contract governed by the laws of that State necessarily contains an implied-by-law covenant to act fairly and in good faith in the course of performing the contract. E. g., Rowe v.

Great Atlantic & Pacific Tea Co., 46 N.Y.2d 62, 68, 385 N.E.2d 566, 569, 412 N.Y.S.2d 827, 830 (1978); Van Gemert v. Boeing Co., 520 F.2d 1373, 1383–85 (2d Cir.), cert. denied, 423 U.S. 947, 96 S.Ct. 364, 46 L.Ed.2d 282 (1975), appeal after remand, 553 F.2d 812, 815 (2d Cir.1977) (applying New York law). The panel that first heard this case thought the Indenture to be ambiguous on the question of the conversion rights remaining with the holders of Debentures after a merger, and held that the evidence produced by Broad prior to the directed verdict raised a jury question as to whether Broad and the Trust Company had dealt fairly and in good faith with the holders of Debentures in the light of that ambiguity. 614 F.2d at 429–30. Having reached a different conclusion than the panel did on the ambiguity issue, we are compelled to a different result on the good faith and fair dealing issue as well.

We note first that this implied covenant of good faith and fair dealing cannot give the holders of Debentures any rights inconsistent with those explicitly set out in the Indenture. "(W)here the instrument contains an express covenant in regard to any subject, no covenants are to be implied with respect to the same subject...." Burr v. Stenton, 43 N.Y. 462, 464 (1871). "It is ... well established in New York that, where the expressed intention of contracting parties is clear, a contrary intent will not be created by implication." Neuman v. Pike, 591 F.2d 191, 194 (2d Cir.1979) (citing and applying New York law). The covenant is breached only when one party to a contract seeks to prevent its performance by, or to withhold its benefits from, the other. Collard v. Incorporated Village of Flower Hill, 75 A.D.2d 631, 632, 427 N.Y.S.2d 301, 302 (2d Dep't 1980). The mere exercise of one's contractual rights, without more, cannot constitute such a breach. See Mutual Life Insurance Co. v. Tailored Woman, Inc., 309 N.Y. 248, 254, 128 N.E.2d 401, 403 (1955).

Broad relies here, as he did in the district court and before the panel, on the Van Gemert case cited above. * * *

We do not find the Van Gemert opinions of particular relevance to the case at bar. The "loss," if any, suffered by the holders of Debentures was certainly not the result of unsatisfactory administrative procedures in the Indenture; rather, this case turns on the question of substantive rights that are basic to the nature of the contract. The risk of merger was inherent in the investment made by the holders of Debentures. Rockwell and the Trust Company did nothing that could be described as "destroying or injuring the right of the other party to receive the fruits of the contract," because under our holding in * * * this opinion, the benefits that the holders of Debentures received were all the rights to which they were contractually entitled. Indeed, had Rockwell conferred on the holders of Debentures rights significantly greater than those set out in the Indenture, it might have faced claims by its own shareholders for waste and corporate mismanagement. * * *

* * * [The panel also] held that Rockwell owed the holders of Debentures a fiduciary duty of good faith and fair dealing because it controlled both parties to the 1973 merger. But the panel also held that if, on remand, the jury were to find that Rockwell had fully complied with its obligations

under the Indenture, its fiduciary obligations also would have been discharged as a matter of law. * * *

* * *

[T]he judgment of the district court is AFFIRMED.

■ HENDERSON, CIRCUIT JUDGE, concurring in part and dissenting in part:

Despite the majority's thorough and exhaustive review of the law of contracts, I adhere to the conclusion reached by the panel the indenture is ambiguous.[1] It does not clearly contemplate the plaintiffs' conversion rights in the event of a cash-out merger. I would therefore remand the case for a trial to determine the intent of the parties. * * *

The plaintiffs maintain that upon merger Rockwell was required by § 14.01 of the indenture to "expressly assume" all of Collins' obligations, including the § 4.01 duty to exchange the debentures for stock. The majority finds this construction precluded by § 4.11. I see no necessary conflict between § 4.11 and § 4.01. A jury could read the indenture to provide that after a merger a debentureholder had conversion rights under at least two sections: a § 4.11 right to convert into what the Collins shareholders received, and a § 4.01 right to convert into the "Common Stock of the Company," "the Company" being Rockwell, § 14.02. In stock-for-stock mergers these options would be similar, if not the same. Here however they are distinct. The plaintiffs simply insist that the § 4.11 right is not exclusive. This is a fair interpretation of the contract, and the jury might adopt it.

---

1. My conclusion is based on what I perceive to be "holes" in the contract not my "instinct for the disposition of equity," ante at 947. Nonetheless, I cannot agree with the majority's assessment of the fairness of the outcome of this case * * *. Convertible debentures are a wholly different investment vehicle from common stocks, and are, contrary to the assertion of the majority, presumably purchased by persons with different views of the future. The current price of any security reflects the market's collective judgment of its prospects, with all possibilities discounted for their probability. Conversion rights will be exercised only if profitable, so the probability that the underlying stock will exceed the conversion price is a determinant of the value of a convertible security. But if the stock price stays down, the debentureholder's primary concern will be his interest income. The owners of stock, on the other hand, carry the entire burden of any decline in the value of their shares. All equityholders hope for a bright tomorrow, but the convertible debentureholder, who is also a corporate creditor, pays for protection against a gloomy future. Debentureholders accept low interest precisely because they want upside partic-ipation without downside risk. The effect of the court's decision is to retain the low interest rate payable to the plaintiffs while denying them a right to participate in increases in the value of Collins' business. And the value of the conversion right has not only been frozen, it has been rendered practically worthless.

The purchase and sale of a convertible debenture, like that of any other security, is at heart an allocation of risks. Presumably the parties to the indenture considered the likelihood that the market interest rate and the market price of Collins shares would fluctuate during the life of the debentures. They supposedly had different expectations. But this case would not be here if all that was involved was the effect of the market. The question we face is whether the contract ordained that the right to convert into equity could be eliminated. Perhaps the parties did consider the possibility and factored that into the price of the debentures. If they did, so be it. I, like the court, do not suggest that we alter anyone's contract. Were it relevant, however, I would dispute the majority's statement that this merger treated shareholders and debentureholders identically.

A brief comment on "the 'Iowa law' argument" * * *. Iowa did not permit cash-out mergers when the debentures were issued, and the plaintiffs suggest that the buyers could have safely assumed that after any merger they would still be entitled to convert into an equity interest in some going business. * * * To be sure, specific provisions of the indenture enabled Collins to force the debentureholders to accept cash at any time, but only through liquidation, in which event the debtholders would have been entitled to receive full compensation prior to any distribution to equityholders, or through redemption, for about three times what the court now holds the debentureholders are due.

The majority notes that in reading the indenture, "Due consideration must be given to the purpose of the parties in making the contract, and fair and reasonable interpretation consistent with that purpose must guide the courts in enforcing the agreement." * * * The equity kicker, the whole point of a convertible security, was arguably the price insisted upon by buyers willing to accept a substantially reduced rate of interest. * * * It seems unlikely that the debenture buyers, or for that matter the seller, thought this participation would be as short-lived as it turns out to have been. In any case I am not convinced by the court's treatment of the matter. * * * In fact, to quote the majority opinion, "Had the parties to the contract wished to fashion such a bizarre provision, they certainly would have done so in a more explicit fashion." * * *

NOTE: FAIR AND UNFAIR DIVIDENDS

Return to the spin off described in the *Marriott* case, supra. Suppose Marriott had an issue of convertible bonds outstanding the antidilution provisions of which made no provision or adjustment in respect of spin offs or cash dividends, so long as the action resulted in no impairment of the issuer's stated capital. (Such ill-drafted provisions were common prior to the 1980s.) Suppose further that, in fact, no impairment of Marriott's stated capital resulted from the spin off. Does such a spin off present a case for implied-in-law intervention on a good faith theory where the merger in *Broad* does not? Is there any difference between cases involving mergers and cases involving large dividends, so far as concerns the expectations of the parties? Consider the authority afforded by the following two cases.

Harff v. Kerkorian, 347 A.2d 133 (Del.Supr.1975), reversing 324 A.2d 215 (Del.Ch.1974), concerned $1.75 cash dividend paid by MGM, its first dividend in four years. A holder of 5 percent convertible subordinated debentures of MGM, which lacked antidilution protection respecting the dividend, brought (1) a derivative action alleging that the dividend damaged MGM by depleting its capital, and (2) a class action alleging that the dividend impaired the debentures' conversion value and had caused their market price to decline. The Delaware Supreme Court sustained the Chancery's dismissal of the derivative action on the ground that as holders of options to buy stock, convertible bondholders lack standing to bring derivative actions. But the Supreme Court reversed the Chancery's dismissal of the class action, on the ground that the complaint had alleged fraud:

"* * * [P]aragraph 22 alleged:

'22. The $10,500,000 dividend was conceived and effectuated by the individual defendants fraudulently and in breach of their fiduciary duties for the personal benefit of Kerkorian.'

"The claim of fraud is thus clearly sounded in the complaint; and it permeates the plaintiffs' position *vis a vis* the Indenture limitations: the plaintiffs argue that the 'dividend was wrongfully declared'; that this 'tort claim is wholly unrelated to and unaffected by any contract rights that the plaintiffs may have under the Indenture Agreement'; that the directors 'were not merely negligent but were guilty of wrongful acts'; that 'here, tortious acts have been committed'; that the 'alleged wrongful declaration of a dividend is a tort'; that if 'special circumstances are necessary [to enable debenture holders to assert a right not included in the Indenture], * * * the intentional looting of a corporation clearly qualifies as such.'

"While the plaintiffs' demonstrated reluctance to use the word 'fraud' is remarkable, there can be no doubt that the issue of fraud is sufficiently asserted to require trial of that issue."

Pittsburgh Terminal Corp. v. The Baltimore and Ohio R. Co., 680 F.2d 933 (3d Cir.), cert.denied, 459 U.S. 1056 (1982), combined the fact pattern of *Marriott* with that of *Van Gemert*. The B & O railroad, 99 percent owned by the Chesapeake & Ohio railroad, wanted to separate its non-railroad related assets to develop them free of interference from the Interstate Commerce Commission. B & O transferred the assets to a wholly owned subsidiary and then made a dividend of the subsidiary shares. It did not give notice of the dividend to holders of its outstanding 4.5 percent convertible debentures due 2010. This was a conscious decision—B & O did not want the debentureholders to convert and pick up a share of the spun off shares, ostensibly to avoid registration expenses respecting the spun off stock. The indenture did not contain a notice requirement.

In a plurality opinion, Judge Gibbons ruled that B & O had both a fiduciary and a good faith duty to speak, either of which supported a 10b–5 action:

" * * * [W]e are here dealing with securities having an equity option feature. Maryland follows the settled rule that a control stockholder owes a fiduciary obligation not to exercise that control to the disadvantage of minority equity participants. * * *. Similarly, Maryland directors must act as fiduciaries to all equity participants. * * * Although no Maryland case has been called to our attention presenting the precise issue of fiduciary obligations to holders of securities containing stock options, we would be very much surprised if Maryland or any other state would today hold that no such obligations were owed by an issuer of such securities and its directors. Moreover the scope of the obligation of the fiduciary depends upon the nature of the interest of the beneficiary. If the beneficiary of a fiduciary duty needs information in order intelligently to protect that interest, the withholding of it, especially when withholding it confers advantage upon others (in this case C & O * * *), is an obvious breach of duty.

"The 1956 Indenture under which B & O borrowed the sums evidenced by the convertible debentures was made in New York and the loan transaction completed there. B & O's obligation, therefore, is a New York contract. The law of that state is 'that in every contract there is an implied covenant that neither party shall do anything which will have the effect of destroying or injuring the right of the other party to receive the fruits of the contract * * *.' Kirke La Shelle Co. v. Paul Armstrong Co., 263 N.Y. 79, 87, 188 N.E. 163, 167 (1933). See Van Gemert v. Boeing Co., 553 F.2d 812, 815 (2d Cir.1977); Restatement (Second) of Contracts § 205 (1981). Defendants in this case took steps to prevent the Bondholders from receiving information which they needed in order to receive the fruits of their conversion option should they choose to exercise it. As a matter of New York contract law, B & O had a duty to speak."

Judge Adams dissented, repeating the good faith rationale of *Broad v. Rockwell Int'l*, supra. A subsequent panel of the same court signaled agreement with the dissent. Lorenz v. CSX Corp., 1 F.3d 1406 (3d Cir.1993).

NOTE: FAIR AND UNFAIR MERGERS

1.   *Variations on the Theme of Cashout Merger.*

Return to the Figure depicting convertible bond values, supra. In *Broad*, the value of Collins at the time of the merger was, roughly speaking, at point B. Suppose a cash out merger occurs at point D or point E. Does the fact that the lost premium now is substantial make the case distinguishable?

Compare **Cowles Foundation v. Empire Inc.**, 589 F.Supp. 669, vacated on other grounds, 754 F.2d 478 (2d Cir.1985), another cash out merger case. There the conversion price was $48.75 and the consideration in the merger was $27 in cash and debentures. But, unlike in *Broad*, the takeover of the issuer of the convertibles proceeded by means of a reverse triangular merger. Thus the issuer survived the merger as a wholly owned subsidiary of the acquirer. The parties allowed the bondholders to retain the right to convert into its common stock. Although that stock was no longer publicly traded, there remained a possibility for participation in its appreciation—a possibility foreclosed in *Broad* by the direct merger of Collins into Rockwell. Was the *Cowles* merger fair where the *Broad* merger was not?

The facts **Simons v. Cogan**, 542 A.2d 785, 790–791 (Del.Ch.1987), affirmed, 549 A.2d 300 (Del.1988), are similar to those of *Cowles*, but bear comparison. *Simons* concerned 8½ percent subordinated debentures of Knoll International ("Knoll"), convertible into its Class A common stock at a $19.20 conversion price. More than 90 percent of the issuer's voting stock was held by a parent corporation, Knoll Holding. In 1986–1987, the parent mounted a tender offer and second step merger to cash out the minority shareholders of Knoll. The tender offer and merger price was $12 per share. Knoll survived the merger, but as a wholly owned subsidiary. In connection with the merger, Knoll issued a supplemental indenture providing that upon conversion of the debentures, the holders would receive $12 cash instead of Knoll common stock.

On the day before the announcement of the cash-out transaction, Knoll's class A common traded for 9 1/4 and the debentures traded at 86. The plaintiffs alleged that the debentures declined in value upon the announcement of the supplemental indenture, trading at 73 1/4 immediately thereafter. The Supreme Court opinion reports, 549 A.2d at 301, that an "additional" supplemental indenture was executed that increased the interest rate on the debentures from 8½ percent to 9⅞ percent. The opinion does not specify the time at which this "additional" accommodation of the bondholders was announced. Thus its relationship with the asserted drop in the market price of the debentures is unclear.

Assume that no additional supplemental indenture had been issued and the merger caused the bonds to drop to 73 1/4. Why did the bonds' price drop—due to loss of debt value, conversion value, or premium? Was the lost value captured by the stockholders or parent corporation? Was the transaction unfair?

Why would the issuer provide the "additional" supplemental indenture? Would an interest rate increase make the bondholders whole for their loss in respect of the merger? Would the approach taken by the court in *Broad* make it more or less likely that future issuers will offer stepped up interest rates to convertible bondholders who lose value due to mergers?

Glinert v. Wickes Companies, Inc., 1990 WL 34703 (Del.Ch.) takes a similar approach to the claims of a class of warrantholders. The holders advanced fiduciary and good faith claims against a reclassification precedent to a merger that limited the upside potential of equity not held by insiders, thus wiping out the value of their options.

2. *The Prevailing View.*

Cowles, like *Broad,* declined to intervene against the merger on either a fiduciary or good faith theory. See also Pittelman v. Pearce, 6 Cal.App.4th 1436, 8 Cal.Rptr.2d 359 (1992) (leveraged buyout); Kessler v. General Cable Corp., 92 Cal.App.3d 531, 155 Cal.Rptr. 94 (2d Dist.1979)(no cause of action for loss of the value of their conversion rights where acquiring company has acquired 95 percent of outstanding stock so as to cause cessation of public market for the stock). *Simons* brought Delaware into line with the overall approach, dispelling any doubts about the meaning of the *Harff v. Kerkorian* reversal. Said the Chancery opinion:

" * * * [T]here exists a body of judicial opinion willing to extend the protection offered by the fiduciary concept to the relationship between an issuer and the holders of its convertible debt securities. These seeds, however, have fallen upon stones. None of the appellate opinions actually represent a holding so extending that concept and, indeed, each of those cases evidence the fact that prevailing judicial opinion remains to the contrary.

* * *

"The tide has no doubt long run away from a world of hard and fast rules with predictable outcomes and towards a world in which it is common for courts to evaluate specific behavior in the light cast by broadly worded principles. Working amid such flows, however, courts must be wary of the danger to useful structures that they entail. To introduce the powerful abstraction of 'fiduciary duty' into the highly negotiated and exhaustively documented commercial relationship between an issuer of convertible securities and the holders of such securities would, or so it now appears to me, risk greater insecurity and uncertainty than could be justified by the occasional increment in fairness that might be hoped for."

Should a court which finds all contracts to have been complied with by the merger nevertheless impose an overriding restriction of fairness? Should the concept of fairness be the same in arms-length mergers as in parent-subsidiary mergers? How should the bondholders be compensated for unfair treatment? By valuing the lost possibility of gain under the conventional option pricing formula? Consider also the extension of the conversion privilege to the stock of the acquirer, diluted to reflect the ratio of cash received in the merger to the market price of the acquirer's stock.

3. *Appraisal Rights.*

May a class of warrantholders that is dissatisfied with the proceeds of a merger proceed to a statutory appraisal under DCL § 262? **Aspen Advisors LLC v. United Artists Theatre Company**, 861 A.2d 1251 (Del.Supr.2004), holds no. The warrants' exercise price was $10 and the cashout merger consideration was $14. The warrant contract provided that in the wake of the merger each warrant would be exercisable into the difference between the merger consideration and the exercise price—$4. No appraisal rights were provided for. The court commented as follows:

A warrantholder is only entitled to the rights of a shareholder—including statutory appraisal rights—after they make an investment in the corporation in accordance with the terms of the warrant and thereby expose themselves to the risks that are incident to stock ownership. * * * These Warrantholders did not take that economic risk. Therefore, the Court of Chancery properly determined that the Warrantholders "relegated themselves to the protections afforded them by the Warrants," which "do not include a silent, interstitial right to a remedy akin to statutory appraisal, but lacking the key trade-off inherent in that legislative remedy, the required eschewal of the merger consideration."

The court distinguished *Continental Airlines Corp. v. American General Corp.*, 575 A.2d 1160 (Del.1990), which held that a warrantholder had a contractual right to receive the "same fair price established in post-merger proceedings" for its warrants that the stockholders had actually received as merger consideration. Such a right followed from the fact that a class of stockholders had successfully pursued a post-merger class action proceeding that increased the amount of merger consideration. It did not import stockholder standing to the warrantholders.

SECTION C.   VENTURE CAPITAL FINANCE

Equity–Linked Investors, L.P. v. Adams

Court of Chancery of Delaware, 1997.
705 A.2d 1040.

■ ALLEN, CHANCELLOR.

The case now under consideration involves a conflict between the financial interests of the holders of a convertible preferred stock with a liquidation preference, and the interests of the common stock. The conflict arises because the company, Genta Incorporated, is on the lip of insolvency and in liquidation it would probably be worth substantially less than the $30 million liquidation preference of the preferred stock. Thus, if the liquidation preference of the preferred were treated as a liability of Genta, the firm would certainly be insolvent now. Yet Genta, a bio-pharmaceutical company that has never made a profit, does have several promising technologies in research and there is some ground to think that the value of products that might be developed from those technologies could be very great. Were that to occur, naturally, a large part of the "upside" gain would accrue to the benefit of the common stock, in equity the residual owners of the firm's net cash flows. (Of course, whatever the source of funds that would enable a nearly insolvent company to achieve that result would also negotiate for a share of those future gains—which is what this case is about). * * *

* * *

* * * Plaintiff is Equity–Linked Investors, L.P. (together with its affiliate herein referred to as Equity–Linked), one of the institutional investors that holds Genta's Series A preferred stock. Equity–Linked also holds a relatively small amount of Genta's common stock, which it received as a dividend on its preferred. The suit challenges the transaction in which Genta borrowed on a secured basis some $3,000,000 and received other significant consideration from Paramount Capital Asset Management, Inc., a manager of the Aries Fund (together referred to as "Aries") in exchange for a note, warrants exercisable into half of Genta's outstanding stock, and

other consideration. The suit seeks an injunction or other equitable relief against this transaction.

* * * [F]rom a realistic or finance perspective, the heart of the matter is the conflict between the interests of the institutional investors that own the preferred stock and the economic interests of the common stock * * *. * * * [T]he facts out of which this dispute arises indisputably entail the imposition by the board of (or continuation of) economic risks upon the preferred stock which the holders of the preferred did not want, and * * * those facts do not constitute a breach of duty. While the board in these circumstances could have made a different business judgment,[2] in my opinion, it violated no duty owed to the preferred in not doing so. The special protections offered to the preferred are contractual in nature. See Ellingwood v. Wolf's Head Oil Refining Co., Del.Supr., 38 A.2d 743, 747 (1944). The corporation is, of course, required to respect those legal rights. But, aside from the insolvency point just alluded to, generally it will be the duty of the board, where discretionary judgment is to be exercised, to prefer the interests of common stock—as the good faith judgment of the board sees them to be—to the interests created by the special rights, preferences, etc., of preferred stock, where there is a conflict. See Katz v. Oak Industries, Inc., Del. Ch., 508 A.2d 873, 879 (1986). The facts of this case, as they are explained below, do not involve any violation by the board of any special right or privilege of the Series A preferred stock, nor of any residual right of the preferred as owners of equity.

* * * [T]hat is, I think, the heart of this matter. But the case has been presented, not as a preferred stock case, but as a "Revlon" case. * * * Relying upon the teachings of Paramount Communications v. QVC Network, Del.Supr., 637 A.2d 34 (1993), plaintiff argues that the board did not satisfy the relevant legal test because, it says, defendants did not search for the best deal. Specifically, the board did not ask the holders of the preferred stock what they would have paid for the consideration given by Genta to Aries. The preferred, plaintiff says, would have "paid more" and that would have benefitted the common or all equity. For the reasons set forth below * * * I conclude that the directors * * * breached no duty owed to the corporation or any of the holders of its equity securities.

I.

A. The Company: Genta was started in 1988 by Dr. Thomas Adams who has served since as its CEO and Chairman. It is in the bio-pharmaceutical business with its principle facility in San Diego. It has three components. First, it owns various intellectual property rights with respect to a genetic research area known as "antisense". Its antisense activities involve research, development, and testing directed towards developing a treatment

---

2. See Credit Lyonnais Bank Nederland, N.V. v. Pathe Communications Corp., Del. Ch., C.A. No. 12150, Allen, C. (Dec. 30, 1991) Mem. Op. at n. 55 (where foreseeable financial effects of a board decision may importantly fall upon creditors as well as holders of common stock, as where corporation is in the vicinity of insolvency, an independent board may consider impacts upon all corporate constituencies in exercising its good faith business judgment for benefit of the "corporation").

for certain cancers. It has developed no commercial products from its intellectual properties. Second, through a wholly owned subsidiary, JBL Scientific Inc., Genta manufactures generic chemicals, pharmaceuticals, and intermediate products used by bio-pharmaceutical companies, including its own antisense business. It has a positive cash flow. Thirdly, Genta owns a 50% interest in a joint venture with SkyePharma PLC, which is involved in the development of a new oral drug delivery technology. It has not yet produced a positive cash flow. Indeed, both the antisense and drug delivery products are still entirely at the development stage. The company has never made a profit and has expended almost $100 million on research, development, and overhead since its founding. While this sounds bleak, nevertheless, it is the case that some of its technologies, if they could be developed into marketable products, would be exceptionally useful and valuable.

* * *

B.   Capital Structure: As of January 28, 1997, the capital structure of Genta comprised 39,991,626 shares of common stock; 528,100 shares of Series A preferred stock; and 1,424 shares of Series C preferred stock outstanding. The original investment by the common stock had been about $58 million. The Series A preferred had originally invested $30 million. Something less than $10 million had been raised from later classes of preferred, much of which had subsequently been converted to common stock. The Series A preferred stock was issued in 1993 at $50 per share. It carries a $50 per share liquidation premium ($30 million in total). It had a dividend paid in common stock for the first two years and earns a $5 per share cumulative dividend, payable if, as, and when declared for subsequent years. In the event of a "fundamental change," holders of Series A preferred stock would have an option to have their shares redeemed by the company at $50 per share, plus accrued dividends. Among events that would constitute a "fundamental change" would be a delisting of Genta stock on the Nasdaq.[6] More important for this case, Genta was contractually obligated to redeem the Series A shares on September 23, 1996 with cash or common stock and, if common stock, to use its best efforts to arrange a public underwriting of the common stock. This obligation, and the factors which prevented the redemption from occurring, occasioned the long negotiation with the holders of the preferred stock discussed below.

In addition to the foregoing, the preferred had certain governance rights. For example, the holders were entitled to notice of board meetings and were to be given rights to inspect corporate books and visit and observe board meetings.

6. A fundamental change would occur if there were a change in voting power of the company greater than 60%, a merger or transfer of the joint venture, or a substantial reduction of the public market for Genta common stock, as would occur in the event of a delisting from Nasdaq. An occurrence of a fundamental change due to a delisting from Nasdaq became a realistic threat as of December 1996. In the event of a fundamental change, the Series A shareholders would become creditors of the company and could potentially require the company to enter into bankruptcy proceedings.

C.   Chronic Financial Problems: The lack of a product that generates substantial positive cash flows, coupled with an active research and development agenda, has lead to a notable (later, a somewhat desperate) search for sources of new investment capital. Genta engaged in a series of small equity placements in 1995 and 1996. * * * By the spring of 1996, it became quite apparent that as of September the company would have insufficient cash to redeem the preferred with cash and, that while common stock would be available, the company's good faith efforts to arrange a firm commitment underwriting of that stock would in all likelihood have no reasonable prospect of success. Genta's board retained Alex. Brown & Sons Incorporated ("Alex. Brown") to advise and assist the company in dealing with its inability to provide either cash or an assured underwriting of its common stock. In addition, the company asked Alex. Brown to attempt to locate potential sources of equity financing * * *.

D.   Series A Committee Organized: In July 1996, plaintiff and five other investors holding Series A stock created the Series A Preferred Ad Hoc Committee to act as a bargaining agent with the company. [Meetings among the Committee, company officers, and Alex. Brown followed. Alex. Brown proposed a combination of (1) a cash sale of the antisense business and JBL, (2) a purchase by Genta of SkyePharma's interest in the joint venture in exchange for a placement in SkyePharma of a majority holding of Genta common, (3) an exchange of a minority holding of Genta common for all of the preferred. The Series A committee rejected this, along with other proposals that contemplated a disposition of assets without also providing for an immediate cash distribution. The Committee took the position if a suitable transaction were not proposed, the preferred would just as soon] "wait and see if [Genta would] run out of money and then get [delisted]. . . . " A delisting would give the preferred stock the legal right to the liquidation preference, allowing them to place the company into bankruptcy. [The company, meanwhile, had made its distressed circumstances known to the public in a series of press releases.]

* * *

E.   Genta's Inability to Redeem or Convert Preferred: In September, Genta gave the Series A holders an option to convert their shares into common stock, but could provide no underwriting in any event. Genta offered to effectuate the conversion or to permit the preferred stock simply to remain outstanding for the time. Due to the low market price of Genta's common stock, (less than $1 per share) an immediate conversion into common stock was not an economically attractive option. Only 10% of the Series A stockholders elected to convert into common stock without an underwriting. The remaining Series A shareholders continued to negotiate with Genta concerning its restructuring proposal.

F.   Multiple Track Investigations: [During October and November, Genta engaged LBC Capital Resources, Inc. ("LBC") to find a new source of equity capital. Alex. Brown, which remained involved, made a second recapitalization proposal to the Committee. This proposal, like its predecessor, failed to provide for outright sales of Genta's assets followed by a distribution of proceeds. Accordingly, the Series A committee rejected it as well. The Genta board, meanwhile, opposed a proposed sale of the antisense assets being advocated by the Committee. Such a sale, said the board, would result in the breach of a contract with a third party, Gen–Probe. In addition, the proposed purchaser, Isis, had refused to assume any of Genta's liabilities.]

* * * On November 14, 1996, Genta issued a Form 10–Q stating that:

The Company will run out of its existing cash resources in December of 1996. Substantial additional sources of financing will be required in order for the Company to continue its planned operations thereafter.... If such funding is unavailable, the Company will be required to consider [various alternatives] ... including, discontinuing its operations, liquidation or seeking protection under the federal bankruptcy laws.

On November 18, Genta's common stock price closed at $.31 per share. As a result, on November 19, Nasdaq announced that Genta's common stock would be delisted unless by December 3 it submitted a plan with respect to how it would comply with Nasdaq's listing requirements concerning net worth. * * *

[Meanwhile, LBC's search had yielded a potential equity investor, Aries. LBC proceeded to discuss a deal with Aries on the working assumption that Genta could issue up to 60 million additional shares of common stock without triggering the "fundamental change" provision of the preferred stock designations and obligating Genta to repurchase the preferred.]

G. **Aries Proposal**: Dr. Rosenwald [the CEO of Aries] presented the following financing proposal to Genta at the November 26 meeting. Aries would lend Genta between $5–6 million in exchange for a secured note plus securities consisting of a new class of preferred stock (special preferred stock with embedded alternative rights convertible into common stock at $.10 per share) and warrants to buy common stock at an exercise price of $.10 per share. The letter setting forth this proposal stipulated that Aries's immediate control of the Genta board was a non-negotiable term of the proposed transaction.[21]

Adams responded that Genta sought (1) a two tiered financing (i.e., some immediate cash infusion), (2) a higher exercise price on any warrants ($.25 per share) granted in consideration of the second tier financing, and (3) a more limited board presence, permitting Aries to designate only one director and two observers. Two days later, Aries agreed to the two tiered financing structure and a $.20 second tranche exercise price for the warrants. It continued to insist upon a contract right to designate a majority of the board.[22]

---

21. Aries, which typically makes non-passive investments, has a history of assisting in successful turn arounds of financially troubled bio-pharmaceutical companies.

22. After further negotiations, discussed below, Aries agreed to a forfeiture of board control in the event that additional second tier financing was not arranged by Aries for Genta. In addition, Aries agreed to an increase in the exercise prices for the first and second tranches to $.15 and $.30 per share respectively.

H.   December Negotiations: [Aries and Genta continued to negotiate during December, with Rosenwald making a formal presentation to the Genta board on December 30. A confidentiality rule prevailed—neither Alex. Brown nor the Series A committee had knowledge of Aries' interest in Genta, the proposed transaction, the ongoing negotiations, or the board presentation. The first disclosure occurred after the board's January 28 meeting.

[The Series A committee, meanwhile, made a formal restructuring proposal to Genta. This entailed (1) the sale of JBL for cash with proceeds escrowed for the preferred, (2) the sale of the antisense assets with most proceeds being held for the preferred and the remainder made available to the common provided certain performance conditions were met, and (3) the sale of the rest of Genta to SkyePharma for (a) $3 million in SkyePharma stock to be distributed to the preferred, and (b) a 29 percent interest in the joint venture of which 20 percent was to go to the Genta common. The Committee proposal offered no solution to the problem of the Gen–Probe contract.]

As of December 20, it had become apparent that Genta might be forced into bankruptcy if it did not fairly promptly effectuate one of the transactions on the table. Genta's bankruptcy counsel attended its December 20 board meeting at which the status of Genta's negotiations and the ongoing Nasdaq delisting proceedings were discussed. As expected, on December 21, Nasdaq denied Genta's request for continued listing, but the actual delisting was temporarily suspended until after a formal hearing could be held on January 23.

* * *

I.   January 1997: [The board considered all options at its January 13 meeting, including a possible chapter 11 filing and a revised proposal that the Series A committee had put on the table. The revised proposal provided less for the common than had its predecessor, reflecting unfavorable revisions in the terms of some of the proposed asset sale transactions. After the meeting, the Alex. Brown representative noted that the proposal's "punitive" treatment of the common made it unlikely that it ever could garner the vote of the common required by section 271. Thereafter, in advance of a meeting on January 26, the board members received LBC's informal written evaluation of the Committee proposal and the Aries transaction, which concluded that Aries was the "fairer" choice. Adams also submitted an analysis according to which Genta possessed a $59 million going concern value.]

On January 23, Genta and an Aries representative participated in the anticipated Nasdaq delisting hearing. As a result of the hearing, Nasdaq decided again to postpone the threatened delisting of Genta's stock. Genta was, however, informed that it would be delisted in the future unless it increased its net tangible assets and met other requirements.[34]

---

34. On February 4, 1997, after the challenged Aries transaction had already been entered into and announced, Genta was removed from the Nasdaq National Market and was instead listed on the Nasdaq Small-Cap Market. At that time, Genta was in-

As of the January 26 meeting, it had become clear that Genta had to complete a financing transaction rapidly, or else face bankruptcy. Recognizing that Genta would not have sufficient cash for its payroll due on February 1, Genta's bankruptcy lawyers had begun preparing the necessary papers to file for bankruptcy on January 29. At this juncture, faced with an imminent decision, Dr. Adams informed the board that he opposed the [Series A] restructuring proposal in its present form.[35] [Meanwhile, the Aries offer was set to expire as of January 28.]

J.   Aries Transaction: On January 28, 1997, the Genta board unanimously approved the Aries transaction. [The letter of intent that the board approved at the meeting called for a two-step financing.] The first step, which by the time of trial of this case had already occurred, involved Aries loaning Genta $3 million in cash. In exchange, Aries received convertible secured bridge notes with a $3 million face value, 7.8 million Class A warrants with a $.001 per share exercise price, and 12.2 million Class B warrants with a per share exercise price of $.55.[40] The bridge notes are immediately convertible into 600,000 shares of Series D convertible preferred stock with a $10 stated value per share.[41] In the event that Aries converts this preferred stock, Aries would receive 20 million shares of Genta common stock. Together the transaction offers Aries the right to acquire 40 million shares of Genta common stock—a controlling interest in the company.

In addition to this consideration in the form of debt and equity, Aries received an immediate contractual right to require the Genta board to cause a sufficient number of its designees to be added to the board so as to constitute a majority of the board.[43] In the event that Aries does not satisfy its future obligations to raise additional capital (the second tier financing),

---

formed that it would be removed from the SmallCap listing as well unless it increased its net tangible assets by April 7, 1997.

35.   Director Klem [the other inside director] had concluded as well that the final Series A proposal was unacceptable, identifying five key problems: the impact on the common stockholders, the plan to escrow the JBL proceeds in a manner which could enable the Series A holders to force Genta into bankruptcy, the remaining Gen–Probe issue, the fact that it would be unfair to give an estimated $85 million in value (on his assumption about values based on the data supplied by LBC) to the Series A holders while the common received zero value, and the failure to resolve the threat of a future Nasdaq delisting. In his opinion, the Aries proposal would give the common stockholders between $1 to $2 in value per share.

40.   Both the A and B warrants are immediately exercisable and have a term of five years. The effective average price of these warrants is actually $.15 per share of

common stock, not $.25. I conclude this because, pursuant to the financing agreement, the failure of Genta's stockholders to approve the transaction would constitute an event of default, entitling Aries to convert up to $300,000 of its secured debt into three hundred million shares of Genta common stock (or in that event 90% of the common). In effect, this coercive default provision guarantees stockholder approval, which may be required under Nasdaq listing standards. Once the Aries deal has received stockholder approval, or there has been a decision that such approval is not required, all of the warrants can be exchanged for new warrants with the same terms, but convertible at $.15 per share.

41.   The initial conversion price for such notes is $5 per share. The Series D preferred stock is then convertible into common stock at $.15 per share.

43.   Aries has not exercised this right yet, and has indicated that it does not intend to do so while this litigation is pending.

however, this right will terminate. That is, pursuant to the terms of the second tranche of this financing, Aries has agreed to use its "best efforts" to arrange between $2.5 to $12 million in additional financing for Genta.[44] If, within six months following the effective date of the agreement, Aries has not located at least $3.5 million of additional financing for the company, it will lose its right to designate a majority of the board. The agreement does not state the minimum terms upon which an acceptable financing can be made in order to satisfy Aries's obligation, but requires board approval and permits Genta to opt for alternative financing if it is available on preferable terms.

In addition to the financial terms of the deal, Aries represented to Genta that it did not intend to liquidate the company and would use its best efforts to continue Genta's antisense business. Aries did not make any representations or side agreements concerning the continued employment of Dr. Adams or other Genta board members. To the contrary, the testimony is that Dr. Adams told Aries that it should consider hiring a new CEO.

K. Equity–Linked's March 3 Proposal: Immediately prior to the hearing in this action, Equity Linked delivered a proposal to Genta that offered to extend a $3.6 million loan to Genta on the same terms as those reflected in the Aries transaction. This offer appears to have been an attempt by plaintiff to demonstrate that it would have been willing to do the same deal on terms at least as favorable as those offered by Aries.

II.

The broad question is whether the foregoing facts constitute a breach of duty by the directors of Genta. The theory of the original complaint was that the Aries transaction represented a bad faith exercise of corporate power; that the purpose of the transaction was simply to protect the employment of the incumbent officers * * *.

The claim now is that the board "transferred control" of the company and that in such a transaction it is necessary that the board act reasonably to get the highest price, which this board did not do. Plaintiff urges that the special duty recognized in Revlon, Inc. v. MacAndrews & Forbes Holding, Inc., Del.Supr., 506 A.2d 173 (1986), arose here because (1) Aries has a contract right to designate a majority of the Genta board and (2) Aries acquired warrants that if exercised would give it the power to control any election of the Genta board. Thus, this transaction is seen as similar to the noted case of Paramount Communications Inc. v. QVC Network Inc., Del.Supr., 637 A.2d 34 (1993). Plaintiff claims that the board hid the fact that control might be for sale, instead of announcing it and creating price competition respecting it. In support of the assertion that the board could have done better for common stockholders, like themselves, plaintiff points to the litigation produced alternative proposal of the Series A preferred

44. Specifically, Aries agreed to use its "best efforts" to effect the purchase of a minimum of 25 up to a maximum of 75 "units," which will be sold at $100,000 per unit. Such units will have three components, including $70,000 of senior secured convertible notes, 3,000 shares of preferred stock, and 333,334 warrants. The notes and warrants will both have an exercise price of at least $.30 per share of common stock.

stock. The idea is that this alternative is financially a little better and that if the directors would have met their "Revlon duty" then, this or another better alternative would have come to light. In this way, plaintiff claims the interests of all holders of equity securities would have been better off because Genta would have gotten greater value.

* * * [I]t is my opinion * * * that the Genta board fully satisfied its obligations of good faith and attention with respect to the Aries transaction. * * *

A.

"Revlon Duties" and a Change in Corporate Control: In Paramount Communications, Inc. v. QVC Network Inc., the Delaware Supreme Court considered a series of cases dealing with the fiduciary duties of corporate directors when directors authorize a transaction that has the effect of changing corporate control. The most prominent of these was the 1986 opinion in Revlon, Inc. v. MacAndrews & Forbes Holding, Inc. That case had been widely thought to announce special directorial duties in the event of a "sale" of the corporation. The specific character of that rule however was not entirely clear, but it was generally taken to be that in certain circumstances (loosely a "sale" of the company) directors must maximize the current value of the corporation's stock; they may not exercise a judgment to choose less when more is offered. But this broad generalization masks more questions than it answers. In fact the meaning of Revlon—specifically, when its special duties were triggered, and what those duties specifically required—were questions that repeatedly troubled the bench and the bar in the turbulent wake of the Revlon decision. * * *

* * *

This existing uncertainty respecting the meaning of "Revlon duties" was substantially dissipated by the Delaware Supreme Court's opinion in Paramount. The case teaches a great deal, but it may be said to support these generalizations at least: (1) where a transaction constituted a "change in corporate control", such that the shareholders would thereafter lose a further opportunity to participate in a change of control premium, (2) the board's duty of loyalty requires it to try in good faith to get the best price reasonably available (which specifically means that the board must at least discuss an interest expressed by any financially capable buyer), and (3) in such context courts will employ an (objective) "reasonableness" standard of review (both to the process and the result!) to evaluate whether the directors have complied with their fundamental duties of care and good faith (loyalty).

* * *

B.

Application of Paramount to the Aries Transaction: The questions that Paramount frames for this case are essentially two. First, is the Aries transaction a "change in corporate control" that triggers special directorial duties and that requires enhanced judicial review, under a reasonableness standard. Second, if it is, do the facts found, set forth above, constitute either (1) bad faith or insufficiently informed action or (2) unreasonable action given the type of transaction that was under consideration.

1. Does the Aries transaction trigger special board duties? I assume for purposes of deciding this case, without deciding, that the granting of immediately exercisable warrants, which, if exercised, would give the holder voting control of the corporation, is a transaction of the type that warrants the imposition of the special duties and special review standard of Paramount.

2. What are the special duties that are triggered? The duties that devolve upon the board when it approves a transaction having a change in corporate control effect (and here I mean specifically, as in Paramount, where corporate action plays a necessary part in the formation of a control block where one did not previously exist), is to take special efforts to be well informed of alternatives, and to approve only a transaction that seeks reasonably to maximize the current value of the corporation's equity. That is the gist of the Revlon state: to act reasonably to maximize current, not some future, value. * * * The enhanced information obligation, occasioned by the gravity of the triggering transaction, may be satisfied through an auction, through a "market check," or perhaps in other ways, but it is fundamental that the board's effort to be informed must be active and reasonable.

3. Have the director-defendants failed to reasonably attempt to advance the current interests (or value) of the holders of the corporation's equity securities? The board did not negotiate with the preferred stock with respect to a transaction of the kind it was attempting to find elsewhere. Thus the question: Did this violate the board's duty to be especially active and reasonable in searching for relevant information? Secondly, assuming, without deciding, that the March 3 proposal by the preferred stock was on better terms than the Rosenwald/Aries deal—in that it offered a somewhat greater first tranche credit—has the board failed reasonably to maximize the current value of the firm's equity?

In my opinion, the answer to both of these questions is no.

With respect to the first question, even though no offer was made to the preferred to permit them to acquire control, I cannot conclude that the board was not fully informed of the company's relevant alternatives (i.e., relevant to the board's good faith business plan) by the time it authorized the Aries transaction. The ultimate choice for the board was correctly understood. It was not between the Aries transaction and an alternative similar transaction at a "higher price" or on better terms, of which the board did not know because of its inattention (or otherwise). The real choice was between (1) a transaction that attempted to finance a future for the company in which products might be developed and brought to market, and (2) a transaction that treated the enterprise (perhaps correctly) as a failed effort and would therefore involve the sale of its assets and a distribution of the proceeds, largely if not entirely, to the preferred stock.[49]

---

49. It is not part of the court's responsibility to evaluate which course of action was wiser from the point of view of the convertible preferred or the common. I would have

After a lot of effort the board saw this choice as the choice between accepting the Aries transaction, on one hand, which offered some prospect of further credit being raised, some bio-tech expertise being brought to bear by the investor, and some meaningful enhancement of the prospects of the company for survival, product development, and ultimate financial success, and, on the other hand, accepting the final, take it or leave it proposal of the Series A preferred stock, which meant that the common would get essentially nothing and the corporation would never see the future benefit of the exploitation of its intellectual property.

The charge of failure to search appropriately for alternatives that would have been more beneficial to the owners of the company's equity securities is deeply unconvincing on the evidence. The evidence is completely inconsistent with the notion that some other (third) party, who was unknown, would have offered a better deal to Genta. The board, with the advice and assistance of professional advisors, had thoroughly explored that possibility. The more plausible supposition is that if the board had gone back to the Series A preferred stock once its deal with Aries was substantially negotiated, the preferred would likely have authorized a proposal like the one that the holders ultimately put forth in the litigation, which I will assume is in certain respects superior. Nevertheless, I conclude that the board's failure to afford the preferred stock an opportunity to meet or exceed the Aries proposal was quite reasonable in the circumstances (some reasonable minds may have thought it likely to be futile and wasteful).

The Genta board had been dealing with the preferred stock for some time in a rather intense way. The board knew, or had good reason to believe it knew, what were the business goals of the preferred with respect to its investment in Genta. The preferred quite certainly were interested in taking as much money out of Genta as possible, as soon as possible.

* * *

Moreover, the Series A knew that management was looking for financing. There were press releases to that effect. Yet they were unwilling to put in more money. The preferred is of course not to be criticized for that. They have every right to send no good dollars after bad ones. Indeed, they had the right to withhold necessary consents to salvage plans unless their demands were satisfied. But when plaintiff now contends that the Genta board was required by fiduciary duty to the company's common stockholders to go back to the Series A preferred after finding an investor willing to do what the Series A sought to prevent, I cannot agree. * * *

It was quite reasonable for the Genta board to conclude that, if the policy of the board was to try to find a way to finance further research and development in order to attempt to benefit the residual owners of the firm,

to accept the notion that the holders of the preferred stock are in the only position to say with authority what is in their best interest. Equally clearly, the common had an adverse interest to the preferred if the preferred didn't want (as they apparently did not want) to role the dice on the future.

that any proposal that transferred corporate control or potential control to the preferred stock was a highly dubious way to achieve that goal.

Why a Revlon auction or other bidding with the preferred anticipating would not maximize value of the common stock in the situation faced by Genta's board: A bidding contest between the Series A and a new investor interested in developing Genta's intellectual property would be a poor way to attempt to maximize either the present value or some future value of the common stock in these particular circumstances, I assume, as the facts allow, that the Series A liquidation premium is greater than the liquidation value of the firm—but that the preferred stock has no legal right to force a liquidation. In that event, the preferred would have a bidding advantage and would use it to deprive the common of their power to exploit the preferred that the common currently possesses. Assume, for example, that the present value of the firm's prospects as a going concern would be only $9 million (net), which is also its liquidation value. Assume that in an open bidding contest, a well informed bidder will offer the company something less than 3 million for a 51% interest (i.e., $9mm + $3mm = $12mm divided by 2 = $6mm; but since in liquidation the common stock would be worthless, the bidder would be unlikely to bid the maximum $6mm value on these assumptions). Assume such a $3mm bid would permit the common stock some further opportunity to see a payoff in the company labs and in the marketplace. Now assume that a bidding contest occurs in which the preferred takes part. What will probably happen? The preferred's aim might be simply to liquidate the company and take all of the net proceeds and apply it to its preference. This will prevent its exploitation by the common and cut its losses. To accomplish that goal, the preferred could easily pay in an auction up to $21 million ($30 million liquidation preference minus present net liquidation value) because that amount would go into the company's treasury but could be immediately restored to the preferred when it exercised its voting power to cause the liquidation of the firm.

To generalize, the existence of a "below water" liquidation preference would allow the preferred to out bid an arm's length bidder for Genta's assets and defeat an attempt to exploit the company's properties (and not incidentally, an attempt to exploit the preferred in its current situation) for the benefit of the common stock. What the board did, in effect, was to try on behalf of the common to exploit the preferred—by imposing risks on them without proportionate opportunity for rewards. That the preferred is open to this risk legally, is a function of the terms of its security. I think it is perfectly permissible for the board to choose this course in these circumstances. To engage in a Revlon auction or otherwise allow the preferred to out bid a third party, would be to defeat this legitimate strategy.

* * *

With respect to the second question, if we assume that Genta's board was operating under the unusual gravitational pulls of planet Revlon, we must acknowledge that the board is supposed in such "sale of control" circumstances, to have the single aim of maximizing the present value of the firm's equity. That requirement is very clear when, for example, one bidder, offers an all cash deal and another offers all cash as well, but less money. It is tolerably clear when one bidder offers cash and another offers cash and widely traded securities, the package being worth less when measured by dependable markets. But what that requirement means in this setting, where (1) the transaction is not a merger or tender offer with a "price" per share at all, and (2) the transaction (or alternatives now advanced) are not otherwise easily reduced to a present value calculation, is not obvious. What is clear is that the Genta board was striving to maximize the possibility of the common stock participating in some "upside" benefit from the commercial development of the company's intellectual properties. It is clear too that the course it took to do that arguably was superior to an alternative in which the preferred acquired control, because the preferred had a financial incentive to liquidate the firm immediately, thus depriving the common of any current value. Thus, unlike two competing cash transactions or transaction in which widely traded securities are offered, the alternatives that plaintiff poses are rich with legitimate, indeed unavoidable, occasions for the exercise of good faith business judgment. Where judgment is inescapably required, all that the law may sensibly ask of corporate directors is that they exercise independent, good faith and attentive judgment, both with respect to the quantum of information necessary or appropriate in the circumstances and with respect to the substantive decision to be made.

This principle has application here. The Genta board had a business goal of trying to maintain an equity participation for the common stock in its promising intellectual properties. It mattered to this strategy who was the controlling shareholder. While the Genta board hardly could (or at all events did not) negotiate binding provisions assuring that its goal would be obtained, it could and did exercise an informed good faith judgment concerning it. It took steps demonstrating its good faith efforts. First, it negotiated with Dr. Rosenwald for the second tranche of financing. Second, it received an undertaking from Dr. Rosenwald that he did not intend to liquidate the company and would try to develop the antisense business. Third, the economic incentives of Aries were inherently different than those of the Series A preferred stock and the board could recognize and depend to some extent on those differences. That is, the Series A inherently have some interest in protecting their liquidation preference. Aries, like other owners of only common, has an incentive to employ the remaining capital and that which can be raised, to commercially exploit Genta's properties.

* * *

In short, the facts of this case clearly do not look like a situation in which, from the common stock's perspective, "there is no tomorrow," and the board ought not be recognized as having discretion to prefer what it sees as a "longer term value" over a higher present value. The court would have no basis to conclude that the immediate value of the common would in fact be greater had an alternative of the kind presented by the preferred somehow been put in place in January.

Thus, I conclude in the circumstances disclosed by the balance of the credible evidence, that the Genta board concluded in good faith that the corporation's interests were best served by a transaction that it thought would maximize potential long-run wealth creation and that in the circumstances, including the potential insolvency of the company and the presence of a $30 million liquidation preference, the board acted reasonably in pursuit of the highest achievable present value of the Genta common stock, by proceeding as it did.

NOTE: VENTURE CAPITAL FINANCE

1. *Venture Capital Investment.*

Equity–Linked Investors v. Adams is a case about a venture capital deal gone sour. Such situations are not unusual. One-third of venture capital issuers end up insolvent. Another third limp along, generating enough cash to pay expenses, especially the insiders' salaries, but never generating enough profit to support a public offering of common stock. Another third succeeds, reaching the initial public offering stage and generating substantial returns for venture capital investors— enough to compensate them for the high risk and illiquidity of their overall venture capital portfolios. Dent, Venture Capital and the Future of Corporate Finance, 70 Wash. U.L.Q. 1029, 1034 (1992). The issuer in *Adams* partakes of the traits of all three groups. It had gone public and conducted a second round of venture capital finance only then to go into a stall.

Venture capital commitments rose substantially in the 1990s with the amount of committed capital increasing twentyfold during the course of the decade. By 2000, the peak year, there were 228 venture capital funds with a total committed capital of $67.7 billion. The tech boom thereupon collapsed and the sector thereafter underwent severe contraction.

Gompers and Lerner, The Use of Covenants: An Empirical Analysis of Venture Capital Partnership Agreements, 39 J.L. & Econ. 463, 465–69 (1996), describes the venture capital industry:

"Entrepreneurs often develop ideas that require substantial capital to implement. Most entrepreneurs do not have sufficient funds to finance these projects themselves and must seek outside financing. Start-up companies that lack substantial tangible assets, expect several years of negative earnings, and have uncertain prospects are unlikely to receive bank loans or other debt financing. Venture capitalists finance these high-risk, potentially high-reward projects, purchasing equity stakes while the firms are still privately held. Venture capitalists have backed many high-technology companies, including Microsoft, Intel, Lotus, Apple Computer, and Genentech, as well as a substantial number of service firms.

"Whether the firm is in a high-or low-technology industry, venture capitalists are active investors. They monitor the progress of firms, sit on boards of directors, and mete out financing based on the attainment of milestones. Venture capitalists retain the right to appoint key managers and remove members of the entrepreneurial team. In addition, venture capitalists provide entrepreneurs with access to consultants, investment bankers, and lawyers.

"The first modern venture capital firm, American Research and Development (ARD), was formed in 1946. A handful of other venture funds were established in the decade after ARD's formation. Most, like ARD, were structured as publicly traded closed-end funds. The first venture capital limited partnership, Draper,

Gaither, and Anderson, was formed in 1958. Imitators soon followed, but limited partnerships accounted for a minority of the venture pool during the 1960s and 1970s. The remainder of venture capital organizations were either closed-end funds or small business investment companies (SBICs), federally guaranteed risk-capital pools that proliferated during the 1960s. The annual flow of money into new venture funds during these years never exceeded a few hundred million dollars and usually was much less.

"Funds * * * flowing into the venture capital industry and the number of active venture organizations increased dramatically during the late 1970s and early 1980s.* * *

"The single most important factor accounting for the increase in money flowing into the venture capital sector was the 1979 amendment to the 'prudent man' rule governing pension fund investments. Prior to that date, the Employee Retirement Income Security Act of 1974 prohibited pension funds from investing substantial amounts of money in venture capital or other high-risk asset classes. The Department of Labor's clarification of the rule explicitly allowed pension managers to invest in high-risk assets, including venture capital. The rule change opened the door to pensions' tremendous capital resources. * * * [I]n 1978, when $424 million was invested in new venture capital funds, individuals accounted for the largest share (32 percent). Pension funds supplied just 15 percent. Eight years later, when more than $4 billion was invested, pension funds accounted for more than half of all contributions.

"An associated change during the 1980s was the increasing role of investment advisers. During the late 1970s and early 1980s, almost all pension funds invested directly in venture funds. Because venture capital was a small portion of their portfolios, few resources were devoted to monitoring and evaluating these investments. During the mid–1980s, investment advisers (often referred to as 'gatekeepers') entered the market to advise institutional investors about venture investments. The gatekeepers pooled resources from their clients, monitored the progress of existing investments, and evaluated potential new venture funds. By 1991, one-third of all pension fund commitments were made through an investment adviser. One-fifth of all money raised by new funds came through an investment adviser.

"A final change in the venture capital industry during this period was the rise of the limited partnership as the dominant organizational form. In a venture capital limited partnership, the venture capitalists are general partners and control the fund's activities. The investors serve as limited partners. Investors monitor the fund's progress, attend annual meetings, but cannot become involved in the fund's day-to-day management if they are to retain limited liability. Venture partnerships have predetermined, finite lifetimes (usually 10 years, though extensions are often allowed). Most venture organizations raise funds every 2–5 years. * * * [P]artnerships have grown from 40 percent of the venture pool in 1980 to 81 percent in 1992."

2. *Securities and Documentation.*

Although there is no one-size-fits-all term sheet for venture capital transactions, one can expect them to involve the private placement of equity securities (or debt securities convertible into equity securities). Convertible preferred stock usually is the security issued. In some deals, this states a fixed dividend preference, often noncumulative; other deals employ participating preferred incorporating a fixed dividend preference and pro rata participation with the common above the preference amount.

An issue of venture capital convertible preferred is likely to be sold pursuant to a Stock Purchase Agreement and an Investors' Rights Agreement entered into between the company, usually referred to as the "entrepreneur" in this context, and the venture capital investors. The Stock Purchase Agreement sets the terms and conditions of the private placement. The Investors' Rights Agreement sets out registration rights respecting the purchased securities and rights of first refusal respecting subsequent issues of securities. This Agreement also sets out governance rights for the venture capitalist, including rights to information and the right to inspect the issuer's premises, and also may include strict business covenants. The dividend, liquidation, redemption, and voting rights of the preferred stock will, of course, be placed in the issuer's charter.

These contracts' primary job is to align the incentives of both the entrepreneur and the venture capitalist toward success and, in the event of success, to provide for gain sharing and access to liquidity for the venture capitalist. The operative expectation is that if the project is successful, the venture capitalist realizes its investment yield by cashing out by participating in an initial public offering. Thereafter the entrepreneur is left in control of the firm. The contract protects the venture capitalist's upside interest in the terms of the conversion privilege attached to the preferred and the provision of registration rights facilitating later exit via the public trading markets. The contract also likely will provide for mandatory conversion of venture capital preferred in the event of a qualifying IPO. "Qualification" means that the IPO passes quality tests keyed to the stock price, the amount of proceeds, or the resulting market capitalization. This assures that the venture capitalist does indeed exit and leave the entrepreneur in unchallenged control.

An IPO is not the only available means of upside exit for the venture capitalist. Sale of the going concern to a third-party firm also is an option. In this case the venture capital preferred remains unconverted and the board of the start up negotiates with the board over the purchaser over the terms of a merger. The National Venture Capital Association reports that from 1996 to 2004 there were more exits by sale than by IPO in 7 of 9 years. See Hellman, IPOs, Acquisitions, and the Use of Convertible Securities in Venture Capital, 81 J. Fin. Econ. 649 (2006).

Concerns about the entrepreneur's incentives also loom large on the upside. These are addressed by allocating the entrepreneur's equity interest in the firm's growth in the form of options to take common stock that vest over time. Sequential option vesting diminishes any temptation to abandon the project prior to the IPO phase. In those cases where the entrepreneur does not have boardroom control, the contingent payoff arrangement also imports a high-powered incentive to remain in the good graces of the venture capitalist and any outside directors.

Venture capital contracts treat downside scenarios by shaping priorities. A start up firm creating no value and running out of capital goes into bankruptcy, probably to be liquidated once there. Alternatively, if the start up has no significant debt, a liquidation is conducted privately. Either way, the risk of complete failure is intrinsic to venture capital investment. Venture capital firms moderate it by staging the entrepreneur's draw downs of capital, by diversifying their portfolios of investments in startup firms, by syndicating investments in particular firms, and by closely monitoring their positions. When a particular investment does turn out to be a complete failure, the contract structures priorities to allocate any crumbs left on the table to the venture capitalist. But these will not amount to much.

As *Equity-Linked Investors v. Adams* shows, poor or mediocre performance short of complete failure presents a less tractable problem, one resembling that of preferred stock issued by underperforming mature issuers. Poor results can mean that venture capital is cut off, given staged investment. Venture capital preferred tends to take an intermediate term, with a duration of four to six years. When the time is up, redemption rights become exercisable. The mediocre performer still limping along either finds replacement capital, is sold to a third party, or is liquidated. In any case, the interests of the entrepreneur and the venture capitalist can come into sharp conflict, with the former desiring continuation and a chance for an upside recovery and the latter desiring termination and the present realization of any value on the table.

3. *Control Arrangements.*

Sometimes the entrepreneur so needs venture capital that it cedes both a majority of stock and control of the boardroom to the venture capitalist. If the portfolio company succeeds, control returns to the entrepreneur when the venture capitalist sells its stock in an initial public offering (IPO). Black and Gilson, Venture Capital and the Structure of Capital Markets: Banks Versus Stock Markets, 47 J. Fin.Econ. 243, 253, 255–56, 260–61 (1998), discusses the resulting contracting problems. The primary problem for solution is the entrepreneur's lack of assurance against opportunistic retention of control by venture capitalist through undue delay of the IPO. They suggest that an "implicit contract" backed by reputational constraints and financial incentives assures the entrepreneur that the venture capitalist will voluntarily surrender the reins. See also Hellman, The Allocation of Control Rights in Venture Capital Contracts, 29 Rand J. Econ. 57 (1998).

How often does the venture capitalist get complete control? Kaplan and Stromberg, Financial Contracting Theory Meets the Real World: An Empirical Study of Venture Capital Contracts, 70 Rev. Econ. Stud. 281 (2003), gathers contracting data from venture capital investments in 118 start ups made by 14 venture capital firms. Kaplan and Stromberg find that one party, venture capitalist or entrepreneur, controls the board in only 38 percent of their cases. In this subset, the venture capitalist takes control in two thirds of the cases and the entrepreneur takes control in one third of the cases. In the remaining 62 percent of the cases, they report that neither side takes control. Instead, each party designates a director for a seat or seats. They then are to agree on a candidate to fill the remaining seat or seats. The third party director takes the arbitrator's role in the event of disputes. Boardroom control accordingly is shared.

Kaplan and Stromberg also have data on voting control. Venture capital transactions tend to provide separate voting schemes for board election and for other matters on which shareholders vote, with the latter proceeding on a one vote per share basis. Voting control over matters like charter amendments and mergers thus goes to the actor, entrepreneur or venture capitalist, holding the largest number of shares. Here are Kaplan and Stromberg's figures respecting the allocation of these votes for all rounds of financing: In 70.8 percent of the cases, the venture capitalist controls a majority of the votes, assuming no performance-based stock allocations to the entrepreneur ever come to vest. Given full vesting, the number of cases in which venture capitalist controls a majority decreases to 55.8 percent. Entrepreneur controls in 11.6 percent of the cases, rising to 23.1 percent given full vesting. Neither party controls in 17.6 percent, rising to 21.1 given full vesting.

Smith, The Exit Structure of Venture Capital, 53 UCLA L. Rev. 315 (2005), reviews the documents governing 367 startups that made SEC filings in connection with IPOs. He finds that the charter vests sole control in one party in 38 percent of the cases, with the venture capitalist receiving control in 77 percent of the sole control subset. These results more or less track those of Kaplan and Stromberg. But, as to the other cases, Smith produces a contrasting picture of the practice. According to Smith, entrepreneurs tend to start out in control of the board of directors, with venture capitalists taking voting control as they contribute more and more capital through staged draw downs during the start up process. He also finds no evidence of shared control arrangements, even though the documents do tend to expressly allocate one set of board seats to the venture capitalist, a second set of board seats to the entrepreneur, and leave open the allocation of a third seat or set of seats occupying a tie breaking position. According to Smith, the documents provide for voting by all shareholders voting as a single class on the open seat or seats. Given a conflict, it follows that control in the end goes to party possessing the voting majority.

4. *Venture Capital Exposure to Entrepreneur Opportunism.*

Adams, in which the entrepreneur has clear control of both the boardroom and the votes, presents an unusual case. In the more usual case of a split board with a tie-breaking director, opportunistic stripping of preferred rights and preferences to benefit the entrepreneur seems unlikely. Given an extended dispute, the venture capitalist will be safe as long as it has voting control at shareholders' meetings, and in most cases it will have the votes.

But there remain, as in *Adams*, a significant number of minority-vote venture capitalists. To what extent are they threatened by opportunism from majority vote entrepreneurs due to their status as preferred holders? The primary limitations on exposure are built into the transactions' overall economic structure. These deals have an intermediate duration, with the entrepreneur being required to raise cash to redeem the preferred in the event of an unfavorable outcome. So the window for opportunism opens in only a minority of cases and stays open for only a short period. Of course, *Adams* shows how a majority-vote entrepreneur can strip value even during this short period.

The degree to which value and rights can be stripped in this minority of cases depends on fine points of contracting practice. In a first round financing, covenants in the investor rights agreement should provide adequate protection for the venture capitalist. In a second round financing without an investor rights agreement, as in *Adams*, the venture capitalist must rely on the charter. The standard venture capital preferred contract forms provide for class votes in respect of adverse charter amendments, increases in the number of authorized shares, and the authorization of preferred classes of higher priority. Mergers are treated separately under a one-size-fits-all term. A merger is treated as a liquidation, triggering a right to redeem the preferred if the "stockholders of the Company immediately prior to [closing of the transaction] own less than 50% of the Company's voting power" thereafter. If the merger is treated as a liquidation, a class vote also is provided for. If the merger is not treated as a liquidation, no class vote is provided for.

This one-size-fits-all term is fairly effective, even as it falls a step short of perfection. The term manifestly is designed to overrule *Rothschild v. Liggett*, supra, the Delaware ruling that a cash out merger is not a liquidation. Where all of the shares of transferor firm in the merger are cashed out, the term manifestly achieves its intended purpose. The preferred liquidation rights become immediately exercisable and the preferred gets a class vote that allows it to veto the merger. But the preferred with a minority of the overall shares will not be protected under this provision in all cases.

5. *Entrepreneur Exposure to Venture Capital Opportunism.*

Opportunism is a problem whenever there is a majority stockholder. Since the venture capitalist has a voting majority most of the time, the entrepreneur is a potential victim. Indeed, by the numbers, he or she is the most likely victim. Here is the scenario of woe. The start up has created value, but not enough to support exit through an IPO or a lucrative third party sale. The venture capitalist has liquidity needs and loses patience, using its control power to force a third party sale yielding a modest sum. The sale is structured as a merger and the charter treats mergers as liquidations. All of the proceeds accordingly go to the venture capitalist because the liquidation value of the preferred exceeds the merger consideration. The purchaser has no use for the entrepreneur, and terminates his or her employment. The entrepreneur emerges with at best crumbs off the table, looking for work. The venture capitalist walks away with the value, value created by the entrepreneur.

The venture capitalist of course takes the position that a deal is deal. Fried and Ganor, Agency Costs of Venture Capital Control in Startups, 81 N.Y.U.L.Rev. 967 (2006), respond that venture capitalist eagerness to sell can implicate welfare losses. In their picture, the venture capitalist may have an incentive to favor a low-risk, low value exit over a high-risk, high value strategy that would maximize value for the shareholders as a group. They contend that the standard remedies against value-destroying exercises of control power—fiduciary duties, shareholder voting, appraisal rights, and reputational concerns–will avail the entrepreneur little.

How likely is that a venture capitalist will force a sale to a buyer that will so misuse the start up assets so as to sacrifice welfare in the long run? How likely is it that the entrepreneur behind a start up that fails to make the LBO stage and is worth less the redemption value of the venture capital preferred will argue in good faith that his or her continued control maximizes economic welfare?

NOTE: CASES FOR COMPARISON

1. *Fait v. Hummel.*

Fait v. Hummel, 333 F.3d 854 (7th Cir.2003), shows that appropriately drafted contracts can facilitate the transfer of control from the entrepreneur to venture capital investors in the event of substandard performance.

The case concerned Pentech, a pharmaceutical company in the business of developing drugs. Pentech issued Series A preferred shares to a number of investors, pursuant to an investor rights agreement that gave them the right of first refusal on any newly issued stock. The agreement also gave the Series A the right to elect two of Pentech's five board members and the power to elect four out of five for a period of 2 years if Pentech violated certain covenants in the agreement. Pentech went on to violate the covenants and the Series A holders exercised their rights to elect four of the five directors. As a result, Fait, Pentech's founder, lost his seat on the board. The preferred also removed Pentech's CEO, El–Rashidy. El–Rashidy thereupon resigned from the board. (Fait and El–Rashidy together owned two-thirds of Pentech's common stock.) This left a board of four, all nominated by the Series A. Three of the four directors held no Series A and thus were "independent" of the Series A.

Pentech was close to insolvency and needed new equity capital. The "independent" and thus "disinterested" majority of the board approved an offer of 4,220,921 new shares of common stock for $1/share. The Series A holders exercised their right of first refusal under the investor rights agreement and bought all of the shares. Fait attacked the stock offering as an invalid self-dealing transaction. Fait claimed that the deal unfairly diluted the interest of the common shareholders and that the $1/share price was inadequate. Fait also claimed that Pentech would have been better off selling junior preferred stock to a new investor, Julphar Pharmaceuticals. Julphar had been discussing the possibility of buying up to $20 million worth of junior preferred stock from Pentech, but the talks had broken down. Fait claimed that the board gave up on the deal prematurely, preferring a stock offering that gave the Series A permanent control.

The Seventh Circuit, applying Illinois law, concluded that Fait had not met the burden of proving that the offering was not fair. Fait's theory was that the stock offering failed as a self-dealing transaction because the disinterested directors who approved it lacked knowledge of all material facts. More particularly, Fait argued that the disinterested directors, whose expertise lay in pharmaceuticals, lacked the requisite business knowledge and should have hired outside experts. The court, noting that the directors knew quite a bit about the company and its financial situation, ruled that Fait had not met his burden of proof.

2. *Blackmore Partners v. Link Energy.*

Blackmore Partners, L.P. v. Link Energy LLC, 864 A.2d 80 (Del.Ch.2004), makes an interesting comparison with the principal case.

Link Energy LLC emerged from the Chapter 11 restructuring of EOTT Energy Partners LP. In the reorganization, a class of unsecured 11 percent noteholders with a $235 million claim received a new issue of 9 percent notes with a face value of $104 million and a pro rata share of Link Energy equity units; EOTT common received 3 percent of Link Energy's equity units; and the rest of the Link Energy Equity units were distributed to its other unsecured creditors.

Link's performance upon emergence from the Chapter disappointed its managers. They announced that they were considering alternatives to continuing operation and engaged Lehman Brothers Inc. as an advisor. Link soon thereafter agreed to sell its assets and business to Plains All American Pipeline, L.P. for $290 million. Under the terms of the Link LLC operating agreement the board of directors had the power to effectuate that transaction without a vote of unit holders. Link thereafter duly sold substantially all of its assets, ceased all of its principal business, and proceeded to wind up.

Prior to the asset sale, Link issued a press release disclosing the negotiations and stating that any proceeds of sale would be used to pay its creditors. As to the equity units, the release stated: "Based on current projections, the company's management believes that its unit holders would receive a minimal amount, if any, after payment of, or otherwise making provision for, all of its liabilities, obligations and contingencies, which are substantial. There can be no assurance, however, that there will be any funds to distribute to unit holders." The press release also stated that "[t]his sale is in Link Energy's long-term best interest in order to protect the value of the assets, the needs of our customers, and the jobs of our employees."

The market responded quickly: the next day price of the equity units dropped from $5 to $1. They went on down to $0.20 before trading was halted. Unit holders, including the plaintiff, promptly contacted management about the possibility of "alternate transactions." But management closed on the asset sale within a few weeks. Of the $290 million proceeds, $265 million was used repay debt, including the 9 percent notes. In addition to the value of the principal and the accrued interest, the 9 percent note holders also received their pro rata share of the $25 million remaining from the sale of Link's assets. This $25 million kicker was described as consideration for the note holders waiving covenants in the notes that required any purchaser of Link's assets to assume the notes.

The complaint alleged that the Link board members violated fiduciary duties owed to the equity holders by approving the sale of substantially all of Link's assets to Plains. Two distinct, but related, claims were raised. First, the complaint alleged that the board favored the 9 percent note holders, to whom it did not owe a fiduciary duty, at the expense of the unit holders, by approving the distribution them of the $25 million excess consideration. Second, the complaint alleged that the board failed to maximize unit holder value in a sale of control transaction and, therefore, violated its duty of loyalty under *Revlon*.

Affirming the Chancery Court's denial of the defendants' motion to dismiss, the Delaware Supreme Court reasoned as follows, 864 A.2d at 85–86:

"Once a board of directors determines to sell the corporation in a change of control transaction, its responsibility is to endeavor to secure the highest value reasonably attainable for the stockholders. * * * [T]he board's actions must be evaluated in light of the relevant circumstances to determine whether they were undertaken with due diligence and in good faith. If no breach of duty is found, the board's actions are entitled to the protections of the business judgment rule. * * *

"The complaint alleges, and for purposes of this motion the court assumes as true, that the Director Defendants approved a transaction that disadvantaged the holders of Link's equity units. Until the announcement of the transaction, the units had significant, if not substantial, trading value. Indeed, there is a basis in the complaint to infer that the value of Link's assets exceeded its liabilities by least $25 million. Moreover, the facts alleged support an inference that Link was neither insolvent nor on the verge of re-entering bankruptcy. Yet, as a result of the transaction at issue, those units were rendered valueless.

"In the circumstances, the allegation that the Defendant Directors approved a sale of substantially all of Link's assets and a resultant distribution of proceeds that went exclusively to the company's creditors raises a reasonable inference of disloyalty or intentional misconduct. * * * [B]ased only the facts alleged and the reasonable inferences that the court must draw from them, it would appear that no transaction could have been worse for the unit holders and reasonable to infer, as the plaintiff argues, that a properly motivated board of directors would not have agreed to a proposal that wiped out the value of the common equity and surrendered all of that value to the company's creditors.

"In an analogous case, Chancellor Allen recognized '[t]he broad principle that if directors take action directed against a class of securities they should be required to justify' their action. [Orban v. Field, 1993 WL 547187, at *9 (Del.Ch. Dec. 30, 1993).] Thus, while on a more complete record, it may appear that the Director Defendants took no such action or were justified in acting as they did, this court cannot now conclude that the complaint does not state a claim for breach of the duty of loyalty * * *."

In **Blackmore Partners, L.P. v. Link Energy LLC**, 2005 WL 2709639 (Del.Ch.), the Chancery Court later granted the defendants' motion for summary judgment, having found as a fact that Link was insolvent during the events in question. The plaintiff's theory was treated as follows:

"The plaintiff claims that Chancellor Allen's decision in Orban v. Field requires 'that when a board approves a transaction that favors one corporate constituency over another, they lose, at least as an initial matter, the cloak of business judgment protection.' But the plaintiff's reliance on Orban for the proposition that the company owed the Unit holders a higher duty of care in this case is misplaced.

"It is doubtless true, as Chancellor Allen noted in Orban, that a board deploying corporate power against a class of shareholders must specially demonstrate that it acted reasonably and in good faith. But that duty, though important, is limited to circumstances where the board uses the very levers of corporate power against its own shareholders in order to achieve some purportedly higher end. In Orban itself, for example, the board did not simply make a business decision that hurt shareholders while repaying creditors, but engaged in an elaborate maneuver in which the defendant company intentionally diluted a major shareholder to a position where he was powerless to stop a merger favored by the directors. In the face of such overwhelming force, it was clearly appropriate for the court to require the board to demonstrate the reasonableness and good faith of its action on a full evidentiary record. And even in that case, the court eventually upheld the board's action as necessary in otherwise pressing circumstances.

"This case stands in sharp contrast to Orban. The corporate action complained of here, though it did result in Unit holders being left with no residual value, did not involve the use of corporate power against a shareholder class in the sense of Orban. The defendants did not act 'solely or primarily for the express purpose of depriving a shareholder of effective enjoyment of a right conferred by law.' Crucially, the Unit holders, by charter, did not even retain the right to vote on the sale of substantially all of Link's assets. Thus, no extraordinary efforts were needed to secure approval, or to stop a vote, for no such approval or vote was necessary. In such a case, it seems plain that Orban's enhanced scrutiny does not apply. It is a test designed for different circumstances, ones raising the omnipresent specter of management entrenchment.

"Even if one were to apply Orban to this case, however, the defendants meet the enhanced standard required by that case. Link was insolvent, teetering on the brink of bankruptcy. At any moment, the provider of its chief credit facility could have forced it into default. Business prospects were declining, reducing daily the amount of consideration the company could hope for in any non-bankruptcy alternative. Finally, no better transaction was available. These corporate interests are every bit as compelling as those that were served in Orban."

PART IV

EQUITY CAPITAL STRUCTURE—PAYOUT POLICY AND OWNERSHIP STAKES

INTRODUCTION

This Part returns to the question whether the value of the firm can be enhanced through appropriate engineering of its capital structure, a question already taken up in Part II's discussion of debt policy. Now the focus turns to the common stock and two topics that bear importantly on the value of the firm. This first topic, considered in Section A, is *payout policy*, where the question is whether one or another payout pattern figures into an optimal corporate financial policy. Does the common's market price respond favorably to relatively high dividend payment rates and a record of dividend stability, or are low dividends and a higher rate of reinvestment preferred by investors? Alternatively, will investors reward the stock of a firm that avoids distributing excess cash flow in the form of dividends and instead devotes the cash to open market repurchases of common stock? Addressing these questions requires a return to the irrelevance hypothesis of Modigliani and Miller. The second topic, considered in Section B, is *equity ownership*, where the question is whether widely dispersed common stock ownership depresses firm value. Is the equity ownership pattern embodied in the so-called "Berle and Means" corporation, with its separation of ownership and control, suboptimal because it both discourages monitoring of management and lowers management's performance incentives? Or, in the alternative, is widely dispersed equity ownership the best available ownership structure because it supports and accompanies deep trading markets which in turn import liquidity? Many today take the position that complete separation of ownership and control does indeed lead to suboptimal management. Two palliatives are advocated. The first, taken

619

up in Section B.1 is management equity compensation. The second, taken up in Section B.2 is blockholding.

SECTION A.   PAYOUT POLICY—DIVIDENDS, REPURCHASES, AND RETAINED EARNINGS

INTRODUCTION

How much should a corporation pay out to its shareholders in annual cash dividends, and how much should it retain for reinvestment? Are there "maximizing rules" that ought to be observed by company management in setting the corporation's dividend rate? Does the market respond favorably to, and will it pay a premium for, relatively high dividend payment rates and a record of dividend stability, or are low dividends and a higher rate of reinvestment preferred by investors? In addition, what form should corporate distributions take? Many corporations return more capital to their shareholders through stock repurchases than through regular or special cash dividends. What are the relative merits of these distribution procedures, and which, if any, is to be preferred?

Like the capital structure question, the relationship of payout policy to firm value has been debated by financial theorists. It remains a "puzzle" to some extent. See Black, The Dividend Puzzle, 2 J. Portfolio Mgt. 5 (1976); Feldstein and Green, Why Do Companies Pay Dividends?, 73 Amer. Econ. Rev. 17 (1983). The issue is whether payout policy is an active variable which affirmatively affects share prices, or simply a means of distributing funds for which management can find no competitive employment. If the former, identification of an optimal payout rate should be a matter of urgent concern to financial managers. If the latter, dividends and repurchases may be treated as a "mere detail" to be determined by the availability of competitive investment projects which otherwise preempt the use of corporate funds.

As with discussions of capital structure, discussions of payout policy implicate problems of corporate governance. There is an agency cost problem bound up in the payout decision. Managers seeking comfort and security have an incentive to reinvest corporate cash flows suboptimally, thereby setting payouts too low from the shareholders' point of view. Payout policy can make this agency problem harder to solve to the extent that optimal dividends and repurchases require more or less cash than the firm requires to make only competitive investments. Finally, as with discussions of capital structure, information asymmetries between insiders and outsiders bear on discussions of payout policy. Like changes capital structure, dividends and repurchases "signal" management expectations about future performance.

The first section below discusses the economics of the dividend, to be followed by a section on the dividend's legal treatment. Thereafter, the materials turn to two variations on the standard cash dividend–stock dividends and spin offs. The final section takes up the economics and law of stock repurchases. But some background points need to be established first. Specifically, we return to the role of dividends in stock valuation.

1. CASH DIVIDENDS AND DIVIDEND POLICY

(A) A THEORY OF STOCK VALUATION

(1) Dividend Capitalization Model

What do investors "really" capitalize when they buy shares—dividends or earnings? The emphatic answer of classical financial economics is dividends. These are the only tangible returns produced by a share of common stock. Earnings are mere numbers on a page. The stock market puts on a positive value on a stock only to the extent cash is expected in the future. A stock that never will pay out any cash is only a piece of paper and has no value. Earnings retention positively impacts value only to the extent the project in which the retained capital is invested is expected to contribute to those increased future cash payouts.

There is a standard objection to this line of thinking: What about capital appreciation? So long as the stock price goes up, investors care nothing of dividends. Accordingly, earnings matter. The firm reinvests the earnings, and the reinvested capital causes the stock to keep going up. Investors rely not on dividend payouts but a liquid market that permits them to cash out at will.

Classic financial economics has an answer to these objections. Why would a rational investor part with money in the expectation that the stock will go up? The rational investor sees that future cash payments are the only source of value. If the firm's dividends are expected to stay at their present level indefinitely, then the rational investor will value the stock as a bond without a maturity date–a perpetual annuity. Accordingly, the investor expects capital appreciation only on a projection of an increasing dividend stream.

But suppose this rational investor only expects to hold the stock for one year. Why would dividends matter given this short holding period? The answer is that a one year investor looking for a capital gain must be assuming the existence of a future investor who will be willing to pay the appreciated sum. A rational future buyer will part with that appreciated price only if he or she projects a future stream of cash payments of a magnitude sufficient to support the higher price. If this future buyer in turn expects to hold for one year, he or she also must be assuming the existence of a future investor projecting a future stream of payments of a magnitude sufficient to support the higher price.

Lewellen, Cost of Capital (1969) 92–93, completes the story:

> It should not be necessary to carry the game further to make the intended point. If we keep repeating this process—which in principle we should do in order to predict the successive [price increases]—we eventually reach a situation in which the formula for *PV* is an infinite stream of (presumably growing) discounted dividend payments and the

last relevant resale price is indefinitely far in the future. Indeed, once we get past 25 or 30 years of inflows in such an analysis, the subsequent dividends as well as that ultimate price can be ignored because, for any meaningful discount rate K, they add virtually nothing to our estimate of PV. As a result, we end up with an expression for the worth of a share of stock in a world where investors actively seek capital gains, which is paradoxically nothing more than the present value of the firm's per-share dividend payments during the foreseeable future. It is incontrovertible that the only thing investors receive in return for purchasing securities is a series of dividend payments plus a terminal capital gain. All we need accept is this almost tautological view of the securities market and the conclusion above follows automatically. Investors in fact "buy" dividends. Their capital gains are merely the product of anticipated higher future dividends.

Thus does classical finance theory employ a *dividend capitalization model* of share valuation. The model assumes that the present value of a share of stock is equal to the value of all future dividend payments, capitalized at a rate reflecting the market's view of the risks associated with the firm's expected income stream. If we take a highly simplified situation in which the firm's earnings remain constant over time and are fully distributed each year as dividends (i.e., there is no reinvestment), the market value of the shares can be determined by the usual formula for perpetual annuities:

$$PV = \frac{d}{1 + k} + \frac{d}{(1 + k)^2} + \frac{d}{(1 + k)^3} + \ldots = \frac{d}{k}$$

where PV is the market value of a share, d is the expected constant dividend, and k is the market capitalization rate. If the expected dividend is $2 a year in perpetuity and the market capitalization rate is 8 percent, the value of each share is $25 ($2 ÷ .08).

Suppose, however, that the firm decides to retain a portion of its earnings each year. As the amounts retained are invested in additional income-producing assets, stockholders can expect a growing, rather than a constant, stream of future dividends. While the dividend capitalization formula remains applicable in concept, the annual growth factor must also be taken into account. If we represent the ratio of retained earnings to total earnings by the symbol b and the rate of return on such reinvested earnings by the symbol r, the firm's dividends (as well as its earnings and retentions) will grow continuously at a rate of $g = br$. Under these circumstances the annuity formula must be altered to reflect the fact that the stream of dividend payments is expanding at the annual rate of g:

$$pv = \frac{d}{1 + k} + \frac{d(1 + g)}{(1 + k)^2} + \frac{d(1 + g)^2}{(1 + k)^3} + \ldots$$

As the dividend payments are not constant, the above formula must take each dividend into account separately, and the resulting statement is long and awkward. In consequence, financial writers customarily use the following substitute formula, which is equivalent in mathematical terms but considerably more manageable:

$$PV = \frac{d}{k-g} = \frac{d}{k-br}$$

This formula, termed the "Gordon Growth Model," simply says that market value is equal to the firm's current dividend capitalized at a rate $k-g$. To illustrate, assume the firm's current earnings are $5 per share; that it plans to retain 60 percent of its earnings this year and every year; that the expected return on its investments is 16.67 percent; and that the market capitalization rate is 12 percent. The current dividend is thus $2 (i.e., .40 × $5), and the expected growth rate is 10 percent (i.e., .60 × .1667). The value of the firm's shares is:

$$\frac{\$2}{.12 - .10} = \frac{\$2}{.02} = \$100$$

(2) *The Retention Ratio*

A more substantial question can now be considered. How much of its annual earnings *should* the firm retain for reinvestment? Most firms do retain and reinvest some portion of their annual earnings, in many instances the greater portion. The result, as stated, is that dividends can be expected to grow instead of staying constant. While this sounds all to the good, it must be remembered that when funds are retained for reinvestment the *current* dividend is necessarily reduced by the amount held back. Stockholders must give up some dividend income today for the sake of larger dividends in the future; they cannot have it both ways. The question is how to determine the *retention rate* that maximizes shareholder wealth. Which of all the possible dividend streams that might be generated— smaller today but larger later, *much* smaller today but *much* larger later, etc.—has the greatest present value to the company's shareholders? For the moment we will defer discussion of the possibility of raising money by issuing new securities and assume that retained earnings represent the company's only source of additional funds.

A solution to the retention rate problem can be found in the relationship between the internal rate of return obtainable from the firm's investment projects and the rate at which the firm's dividends are capitalized by investors in the market. Briefly stated, retention of earnings is justified if the proposed investment offers a yield in excess of the dividend capitalization rate—if, in the customary notation, r (internal rate of return) exceeds k (dividend capitalization rate). Under these circumstances, the value of the company's shares is maximized by retaining 100 percent of earnings and reducing the current dividend to zero since all funds retained can be reinvested at better than the market rate of return. This relationship between r and k ($r > k$) presumably prevails in the case of "true" growth companies—IBM in the 1960s, Google today. As a result, shares of such companies often sell at very high multiples of current earnings, reflecting the expectation of super-normal profits.

In contrast, if $r < k$, share price is maximized when the retention rate is zero and earnings are distributed as dividends. A positive rate of retention under these conditions would reduce the value of the company's stock; if the company cannot invest funds at a rate of k or better, it should not be investing internally.

The same logic governs the answer to the retention question if $r = k$. If the firm's investment opportunities promise a rate of return exactly equal to the market capitalization rate, market price per share should be insensitive to the retention ratio. The argument is that funds distributed as dividends can be invested by the stockholders at a rate (k) equal to the firm's internal rate of return, either by purchasing additional shares of the firm itself or by acquiring shares of comparable firms. In this third situation, reinvestment brings about an expansion in assets, earnings, and dividends, but the firm has no investment opportunities which promise yields above the normal rate of return. Accordingly, the stockholders gain (or lose) nothing through changes in the firm's retention policy; the market price of their stock remains the same at any retention rate, at least in theory.

All of this merely restates the general rule that ought to govern management's capital budgeting decisions. The standard prescription is that all investment opportunities should be accepted which have a positive net present value, i.e., which promise a rate of return in excess of the company's cost of capital. Thus, the basic comparison is again between r and k.

With these principles in mind, we turn to the debate over dividend policy. We drop the assumption that the company is restricted to retained earnings as a source of funds and assume that it can finance investment projects from external as well as internal sources. Which course is best from the standpoint of shareholder value enhancement? Should the company maintain its current dividend rate and finance its investments by issuing new securities? Or, when a good investment comes along should it cut back on current dividends and finance the investment out of retained earnings? In terms of the formulas above, which approach minimizes k?

(B) THE ROLE OF DIVIDEND POLICY

Economists have been debating dividend policy for decades. Under the traditional view, investors prefer a stable pattern of dividends, and dividend increases in some circumstances can cause firm value to increase. The Modigliani–Miller irrelevance proposition challenged this traditional view of dividend policy, just as it challenged the traditional view on capital structure. Under the irrelevance proposition, dividend policy makes no difference to firm value. But the irrelevance proposition itself came to be questioned in the process of being applied in a real world with taxes and market imperfections, continuing the parallel to the capital structure debate. The process of questioning gave rise to a third point of view. Under this view, low dividends maximize firm value.

(1) Traditional Dividend Practice

Lintner, Distributions of Incomes of Corporations Among Dividends, Retained Earnings and Taxes

46 American Economic Review, 97, 99–106 (1956).

What then can be said in any general way regarding the dividend policies of this diverse group of 28 companies? Several features of central importance stand out clearly. With the possible exception of 2 companies which sought a relatively fixed percentage pay-out, consideration of what dividends should be paid at any given time turned, first and foremost in every case, on the question whether the existing rate of payment should be changed. In studying 196 company-years of dividend action (28 companies, seven years, 1947–1953), we found no instance in which the question of how much should be paid in a given quarter or year was considered without regard to the existing rate as an optimum problem in terms of the interests of the company and/or its stockholders at the given time, after the manner suggested by the usual theoretical formulations of such problems in static terms, even when expectations are considered. Rather, there would be serious consideration of the second question of just how large the change in dividend payments should be only after management had satisfied itself that a change in the existing rate would be positively desirable. Even then, the companies' existing dividend rate continued to be a central bench mark for the problem in managements' eyes. On the basis of our field observations, the dependent variable in the decision-making process is the change in the existing rate, not the amount of the newly established rate as such.

It was equally clear that these elements of inertia and conservatism—and the belief on the part of many managements that most stockholders prefer a reasonably stable rate and that the market puts a premium on stability or gradual growth in rate—were strong enough that most managements sought to avoid making changes in their dividend rates that might have to be reversed within a year or so. This conservatism and effort to avoid erratic changes in rates very generally resulted in the development of reasonably consistent patterns of behavior in dividend decisions. The principal device used to achieve this consistent pattern was a practice or policy of changing dividends in any given year by only part of the amounts which were indicated by changes in current financial figures. Further partial adjustments in dividend rates were then made in subsequent years if still warranted. This policy of progressive, continuing "partial adaptation" tends to stabilize dividend distributions and provides a consistency in the pattern of dividend action which helps to minimize adverse stockholder reactions. At the same time it enables management to live more comfortably with its unavoidable uncertainties regarding future developments—and this is generally true even during at least a considerable part of most cyclical declines, since the failure of dividends to reflect increasing earnings fully and promptly during the preceding upswing leaves more cushion in the cash flow position as earnings start to decline.

Within this context of the decision-making process, it became clear that any reason which would lead management to decide to change an existing rate—and any reason which would be an important consideration in determining the amount of the change—had to seem prudent and convincing to officers and directors themselves and had to be of a character which provided strong motivations to management. Consequently, such reasons had to involve considerations that stockholders and the financial community generally would know about and which management would expect these outside groups to understand and find reasonably persuasive, if not compelling. Current net earnings meet these conditions better than any other factor. Earnings are reported frequently and receive wide publicity in the financial press. Most officers and directors regarded their stockholders as having a proprietary interest in earnings, and many urged the stockholders' special interest in getting earnings in dividends, subject to their interest in regularity of payment. The managements we interviewed very generally believed that, unless there were other compelling reasons to the contrary, their fiduciary responsibilities and standards of fairness required them to distribute part of any substantial increase in earnings to the stockholders in dividends. Even the executives in the minority who were most inclined to view the interests of the company as distinct from those of the stockholders, and who seemed least concerned with their responsibility to frame dividend policy in the best interests of the stockholders as such, were generally concerned with the decline in favorable proxies and in the weakening of their personal positions which they believed would follow any failure to reflect a "fair share" of such added earnings in dividends. Similarly, managements felt that it was both fair and prudent for dividends to the shareholders to reflect some part of any substantial or continued decline in earnings, and that under these circumstances stockholders would understand and accept the cut.

In contrast with earnings, other considerations and aspects of the companies' positions were thought to be less generally known, less widely understood, and less generally and sympathetically recognized by stockholders as factors which should have an important bearing upon dividend distributions. Moreover, no other consideration was nearly as consistently important year by year and company by company. Such things, for instance, as indenture provisions restricting dividends, debts to be discharged at specific dates, or tight liquidity positions were important in particular instances, but dividend decisions were dominated by such considerations rather than by earnings in line with an established policy in less than five percent of the company-years studied, and these exceptions were not clustered in any particular years. In part this finding reflects the general prosperity of the postwar period, but a large part of the explanation almost certainly lies deeper. A prudent foresighted management will always do its best to plan ahead in all aspects of financial policy to avoid getting into such uncomfortable situations where dividends *have* to be cut substantially below those which the company's previous practice would lead stockholders to expect on the basis of current earnings. Stockholder reactions in such situations have been sufficiently vigorous and effective in enough companies that the fear of such a reaction is an effective "burr under the saddle" to all managements, including those which have never been in such difficulty themselves. We might add that a policy geared to considerations other than earnings would have to be explained and justified first on one thing and then on another. Even if there were a perfectly consistent underlying rationale to such a policy, it would be difficult to explain in simple, understandable and persuasive terms, and would probably seem erratic, *ad hoc* or "academic." Moreover, as shown below, companies have generally framed policies (or systematic patterns of behavior) geared to earnings which do quite generally take care of these other considerations in what they regard as a reasonably satisfactory manner.

* * *

Special comment is required, however, regarding the bearing of the magnitude and profitability of current investment opportunities and the ease or stringency of current liquidity positions on each year's dividend decisions within the framework of these two standards. As already indicated, each company's target pay-out ratio and speed-of-adjustment factor reflected the cyclical movements of investment opportunities, working capital requirements, and fund flows in its previous experience along with the other considerations mentioned. Moreover, the standards ran in terms of net earnings as reported to stockholders and many used LIFO accounting for much of their inventories. Generally speaking, after these standards had been established or embodied in informal understandings, the company lived with them and undertook all of its financial planning and capital budgeting in the light of these standards of dividend behavior. Managements deliberately planned ahead so that carrying through their established dividend policy would not involve them in unduly short liquidity positions. Management was generally in a position and was willing to draw down on working capital to help meet such requirements. In general, management's standards with respect to its current liquidity position appeared to be very much more flexible than its standards with respect to dividend policy, and this flexibility frequently provided the buffer between reasonably definite dividend requirements in line with established policy and especially rich current investment opportunities. If investment opportunities were particularly abundant and could not be financed with the funds currently available after dividends had been increased in line with established policies, the remaining investment projects which could be undertaken only through outside financing were re-examined to make sure that they were sufficiently desirable as to justify the company in having recourse to outside capital. If so, the necessary capital was raised and the projects were undertaken; if not, the projects were abandoned. In the companies which as a matter of policy would not go to the outside market except in most extreme circumstances, the capital budget year by year was simply cut to fit the available funds.

In this connection it must be recognized that net earnings generally increase much more than in proportion to increased volume (and similarly on declines). Even though dividend rates are increased somewhat in line with policy described, the current pay-out ratio will decline with increased profits and under this pattern of behavior retained earnings fluctuate still more than in proportion. Marked fluctuations in working capital require-ments and investment outlays are consequently "automatically" provided for under this form of conservative dividend behavior to a very considerable extent at least. This fact, together with the marked dependence of capital budgets upon the availability of internal funds (even when outside funds are used) shown in all the studies of this subject, go far to explain the finding that investment requirements as such very generally had relatively little direct effect in modifying the pattern of dividend behavior, except in a limited number of special situations well scattered over the years studied.

NOTE: PAYOUT PRACTICES

1. *Lintner's Results.*

The practices described in Lintner's study have persisted, according to later research. See Fama and Babiak, Dividend Policies: An Empirical Analysis, 63 J. Amer. Statistical A'ssn. 1132 (1968); DeAngelo, DeAngelo, and Skinner, Dividends and Losses, 47 J. Fin. 1837 (1992); Sung and Urrutia, Long–Term and Short–Term Causal Relations Between Dividends and Stock Prices: A Test of Lintner's Dividend Model and the Present Value Model of Stock Prices, 18 J. Fin. Res. 171 (1995); Jagannathan, Stephens, and Weisbach, Financial Flexibility and the Choice Be-tween Dividends and Stock Repurchases, 57 J. Fin. Econ. 355 (2000). The practice is endorsed by no less an authority than Warren Buffett:

> Shareholders of public corporations understandably prefer that dividends be consistent and predictable. Payments, therefore, should reflect long-term expec-tations for both earnings and returns on incremental capital. Since the long-term corporate outlook changes only infrequently, dividend patterns should change no more often.

Buffett, The Essays of Warren Buffett, 19 Cardozo L. Rev. 5, 127 (1997).

2. *No Payout Firms.*

Fama and French, Disappearing Dividends: Changing Firm Characteristics or Lower Propensity to Pay?, 60 J. Fin. Econ. 3 (2001), presents the results of a survey of dividend payouts by publicly traded companies from 1973 to 1999. The study shows that firms have become much less likely to pay dividends. In 1973, 52.8 percent of publicly traded companies paid dividends; in 1978 the figure was 66.5 percent; in 1998 only 20.8 percent paid dividends. Fama and French show that this change is less the result of cessation of payments by dividend-paying firms than the result of the fact that companies which have gone public in recent years are unlikely ever to start paying dividends. More particularly, dividend payers on average are 10 times larger than nonpayers and tend to be more profitable. Dividend payers tend to invest annually an amount equal to their pre-interest earnings, where nonpayers invest more than their earnings, do more R and D, and have a higher ratio of market value of assets to book value. Across the period of the study, an increasing percentage of publicly traded companies displays the characteristics of nonpaying firms—low earnings, strong investments, and small size. (Indeed, Fama and French show that the profitability of newly-listed firms as compared to all listed firms has fallen drastically during the period under study.) At the same time, the characteris-tics of dividend paying firms remain stable after 1978, while firms with lower profitability and abundant growth opportunities tend to start paying dividends at a much lower rate than formerly. More generally, firms that have never paid dividends are much less likely to start paying than they were before 1978. Fama and French conclude that the lower propensity to pay is "general."

Interestingly, the lower propensity to pay dividends is unrelated to the much-discussed increase in open market repurchases of shares, see infra, this Section A. Fama and French show that the set of repurchasing firms for the most part overlaps with the set of dividend paying firms. Increased repurchases thus have had the effect of increasing the total payout of the paying firms.

DeAngelo, DeAngelo and Skinner, Are Dividends Disappearing? Dividend Concentration and the Consolidation of Earnings, 72 J. Fin. Econ. 425 (2004), replicates the Fama and French results—100 percent of firms with at least $1 billion in real earnings paid dividends in 1978, whereas 85.7 percent paid dividends in 2000. But the authors also enter a *caveat*. Dividends paid by industrial firms increased over 1978–2000, both in nominal and in real terms (by 224.6 percent and 22.7 percent respectively). The decline in the number of payers occurred mostly among small firms, and so had a minor impact on aggregate numbers. At the same time, the 25 largest payers increased their dividends substantially. This group, made up of established firms, supplied 54.9 percent of aggregate industrial dividends in 2000. The dividends these firms paid in 2000 exceeded their 1978 level by $9.2 billion in real terms.

(2) Dividends as a Financing Decision—The Dividend Puzzle

Under the traditional dividend practice just described, the firm sets its dividend payout level as a fixed amount rather than as a fixed percentage of earnings yielding a fluctuating amount. The operative notion is that shareholders react favorably to a stable dividend policy and unfavorably to volatility, and that a departure from the preferred pattern will result in a suboptimal market price for the company's shares. Significantly, under this approach, the firm increases its dividend only once it is clear that the new, higher payout level can be sustained against negative shocks to cash flow. In the event of such a shock, the firm should (if possible) borrow to maintain the dividend until relief comes in the form of a cyclical recovery. As earnings grow, therefore, the shareholder payout does not rise pro rata with the earnings. Contrariwise, in periods of earnings decline, the payout could be higher than the earnings.

The traditional dividend practice does not synchronize well with the wisdom about reinvestment policy described above. Under the textbook advice, corporate cash flows should be reinvested only if management has a project that promises a rate of return r greater than the cost of its equity capital k. Absent such a project, management should pay out earnings as dividends, or, in the alternative, devote earnings to repurchases of the corporation's shares. In contrast, under traditional dividend practice, cases can arise where internally generated cash flows are not to be distributed as dividends, even though $k>r$ for all available new investments. The traditional practice makes an apparent invitation to reinvest earnings in suboptimal projects (putting to one side for the moment the possibility of using the free cash flow to repurchase shares on the open market). A different problem arises when a firm has a large set of available investments as to which $r>k$. Where management exhausts or chooses not to pursue outside sources of finance, the necessary cash for investment becomes available only if the dividend is cut. Under traditional payout practice, the firm either finds outside financing or foregoes the investment rather than cut its dividend. This is the "dividend puzzle." Financial economics suggests a number of alternative solutions.

(a) dividend policy under the irrelevance hypothesis

Modigliani and Miller (M–M) assert in Dividend Policy, Growth and the Valuation of Shares, 34 J. Bus. 411 (1961), that, *once the investment decision of the firm is made known to investors,* the dividend-payout ratio is irrelevant in the valuation process. The value of the firm, they argue, depends solely upon the earning power of its assets. This value is unaffected by how the firm finances its activities, whether by retaining earnings (i.e., withholding dividends) or by selling new securities (i.e., paying dividends, but issuing stock or bonds to obtain funds needed for investment). The net wealth of the company's shareholders, who are (or ought to be) indifferent between a dollar of dividend income and a dollar of capital gain, is said to be the same under either financing procedure. Far from being the subject of an independent policy decision, therefore, dividends (in this view) should simply be a means of disposing of the firm's "residual" cash assets—funds left over after all of the firm's financing needs have been met.

To illustrate the "irrelevance-of-dividends" thesis, assume that X Corporation has outstanding 100,000 shares of common stock and no long-term debt; that it earns $1,000,000 annually, or $10 per share, all of which it normally pays out in dividends; and that its stock normally sells at $100, reflecting a 10 percent capitalization rate. Assume further that management identifies a new investment opportunity (involving the same degree of risk as present operations) which will require an immediate outlay of $1,000,000 and is expected to generate earnings of $200,000 annually in perpetuity. If the investment is made, X's earnings are expected to increase to $1,200,000. As the company has no further investment plans, all earnings from the expanded operation will be distributed as dividends. What financing procedure should X adopt consistent with the goal of maximizing shareholder wealth? Three possibilities exist:

• **Retained earnings.** X could distribute no dividends to its shareholders this year and use its current earnings of $1,000,000 to finance the new investment. In that event, the expected dividends for all future years will be $1,200,000 or $12 per share. Capitalizing these future dividends at a 10 percent rate, the present value of a share of X will be $120.

• **New stock issue.** X could pay a dividend of $1,000,000 to its shareholders and finance the new investment by selling $1,000,000 of additional common stock. Present shareholders of X would receive a current cash dividend of $10 per share. Their wealth would consist of the $10 dividend plus the value of the X stock *after* the proposed stock issue and the new investment. The value of X stock, in turn, will depend on the number of additional shares that must be sold to raise $1,000,000. If n = the number of shares to be sold and P = the price per share, then

$$n \times P = \$1,000,000.$$

We know that the issue price of the new X shares will be 10 times the expected dividend per share (given a capitalization rate of 10 percent). Hence:

$$P = 10 \times \$1,200,000/100,000 + n.$$

The expected dividends still rise to $1,200,000 to reflect the new investment, but the number of shares outstanding is increased by n to reflect the new stock issue.

When these equations are solved for n and for P (by substituting the right-hand side of the second equation into the first), it turns out that n = 9090.9 and P = $110. Thus, X can finance the new investment by selling 9090.9 shares for $110 per share. Future dividends will be $1,200,000/109,-090.9, or $11 per share. At the 10 percent capitalization rate, the value of X stock will be $110 per share. Accordingly, for each X share that they now own, present shareholders will have a $10 cash dividend plus $110 in share value, or total wealth of $120 per share, just as above.

● **Bond issue.** X could pay a dividend of $1,000,000 to its shareholders and finance the new investment by issuing $1,000,000 of bonds. At 5 percent interest, after the interest charge of $50,000 X's earnings (and dividends) would be $1,150,000, or $11.50 per share. If the market continues to capitalize X's dividends at a rate of 10 percent, then the wealth of present shareholders would include the $10 current dividend and X stock with a value of $115 per share, for a total of $125, making this financing procedure better than either of the others. On the other hand, M–M argue that the dividend capitalization rate must rise (owing to the greater risk resulting from the issuance of bonds) to offset exactly the increase in expected dividends, so that share value would be the same as with an all-equity capital structure, i.e., $110 per share. In the latter event, the present shareholders of X would have total wealth per share of $120, just as in the first two alternatives.

If the total wealth figure is the same with all three financing procedures, shareholders will be indifferent to the company's dividend policy and will be just as happy whether the company finances the new investment out of retained earnings or by issuing new securities. Thus, suppose X decides to obtain the needed funds by withholding current dividends. A shareholder who wants cash income to meet consumption needs can either sell some stock or borrow from his or her broker using securities as collateral. Shareholders who prefer to reinvest their dividends will have had that done for them by the corporation. On the other hand, suppose X elects to pay the current dividend, and then recoups those funds by issuing new securities. Again, a shareholder who prefers consumption will have received a cash payment and can use it for that purpose, while shareholders who prefer to save can reinvest their dividends by buying more X securities or securities of a comparable company. Ignoring brokerage costs, and assuming (in accordance with M–M's earlier argument) that corporate leverage has no advantage, it appears that the manner in which X's earnings stream is split between dividends and retention does not affect the value of the firm even when investor preferences for saving or consumption are taken into account.

(b) taxes, other imperfections, and the low payout hypothesis

Like M–M's hypothesis of the irrelevance of capital structure, M–M's hypothesis of the irrelevance of dividends rests on strong assumptions. As the assumptions are relaxed, dividend and earnings retention policy becomes relevant to shareholder value. As before, the M–M model assumes perfect markets with no transaction costs. Once that assumption is relaxed, external finance, whether through debt or equity, carries higher transaction costs per unit of capital raised than does earnings retention. External financing is not perfectly divisible, as M–M assume—small deals simply are not cost effective. Nor can "homemade dividends" be effected without frictions. To sell stock to satisfy a preference for present consumption means incurring a brokerage fee. Once again, perfect divisibility does not obtain—the minimum sale is one share and round lot sales are cheaper per share.

The M–M model also assumes that investors have perfect information and act rationally. Given those assumptions, and assuming earnings retention only so long as $r>k$, an investor will prefer earnings retention to a dividend and will be indifferent between earnings retention if $r = k$ respecting reinvested capital. A real world investor might opt for the "bird in the hand" preferring \$1 to be paid out rather than retained where $r = k$. The economists call this the "bird in the hand fallacy" but given real world imperfections, including the propensity of insiders to self deal, a strong argument can be made for its rationality. Indeed, a real world investor acting under uncertainty might prefer \$1 to be paid out even given a plausible claim that $r>k$ for reinvested funds.

The taxless world is the strongest assumption behind the dividend irrelevance hypothesis. What happens to the analysis when federal income taxes are introduced? As we have seen, the tax code differentiates between interest payments and dividends. Interest is deductible, dividends are not. This means that a corporation that finances its investments by issuing bonds will have less tax to pay and will have a larger after-tax income than a corporation that raises capital by issuing stock. Since its after-tax income will be larger, a levered (interest-paying) corporation is certain to be worth more than an unlevered (dividend-paying) corporation, everything else being equal, even if one accepts in full the M–M position that leverage of itself makes no difference to the value of the firm.

But this does not quite end the tax story. If debt is better than stock because of the interest deduction, why don't all firms maintain as high a debt/equity ratio as possible? Why don't they all add debt to their capital structure up to the point where there is a cognizable probability of bankruptcy? The fact, of course, is that they do not. Indeed, it is a common observation that most firms prefer to draw on *retained earnings* to finance the replacement or expansion of their assets and that the issuance of long-term debt is only the second choice. Thus, external financing, even through debt, is usually resorted to only when internally generated cash-flows are insufficient to cover investment requirements. Why should this be so?

Once again, the tax system provides a clue. As the reader knows, the Internal Revenue Code imposes a shareholder-level tax on corporate dividends at the regular progressive personal rates. Accordingly, if the firm's individual stockholders paid tax on dividends at a higher rate than the corporate rate, then the saving resulting from the corporate interest deduction would be outweighed by the dividend tax. In that event, as the following illustration shows, retained earnings rather than debt would represent the preferred source of financing.

Assume a firm earned $15 a share this year and now wants to invest in a new project that will cost precisely $15. To finance the project entirely through debt the firm would first distribute the $15 of earnings as a dividend and then "recapture" the amount distributed by issuing a $15 bond. While interest on the bond will be deductible, the saving in corporate tax—which will accrue annually and (we may assume) in perpetuity—has to be compared with the tax payable by the shareholders on the current dividend. Suppose the dividend tax would be at a 60 percent rate, or $9. If the bond coupon is 8 percent, or $1.20, the corporate tax (assume it is 50 percent) saving is 60 cents a year in perpetuity. When this saving is capitalized at the same 8 percent rate at which the bond interest is capitalized, its present value is $7.50 ($0.60 × 12.5), which is $1.50 less than the tax paid on the dividend. It follows that where the shareholders of a corporation are taxable at a higher rate than the corporation itself, they are likely to be better off if the corporation holds back dividends and finances out of retained earnings than if it distributes the dividend and finances by issuing debt. While the retained earnings will ultimately be taxed when the shares are sold (at the lower capital gains rate), this factor in many cases will not be great enough to outweigh the immediate tax cost of the dividend even when the corporate interest deduction is taken into account.

Suppose, however, that the new project which the above firm has in view will require an investment that *exceeds* the year's earnings—let's say the required investment is $25 a share rather than $15. In respect of the additional $10, the tax law plainly offers an inducement to finance by issuing debt. Here the firm takes the corporate-level interest deduction without any offsetting cost in the form of a current dividend. Since *future* interest payments on the "new" capital are deductible, while future dividends on such new capital are not, the firm will normally prefer to issue a $10 bond rather than an additional $10 of new common stock and will presumably do so if the new debt does not create a serious risk of bankruptcy.

As suggested, the observable financing pattern followed by most corporations—resorting first to retained earnings, second to external debt, and last to new equity—has largely conformed to the pattern of incentives and penalties contained in the tax law.

The low payout theorists took this pattern as the basis for a generalization. If dividends are taxed more heavily than capital gains, then the firm should pay the lowest possible cash dividend. The firm thereby transforms the dividends into capital gains taxed at a lower rate. Given two equivalent firms, one of which offers returns in the form of capital gains with the other paying cash dividends, the dividend-paying firm would have the higher cost of equity capital. Moreover, suboptimal reinvestment of cash flows is not necessarily implied by a low payout policy. To the extent that the firm does not have a competitive investment available, it should still avoid paying a dividend and instead repurchase outstanding shares.

The foregoing account presupposes a top individual tax rate higher than the top corporate tax rate and a significant rate shift in respect of individuals' capital gains. The Internal Revenue Code's base rates fit this description, with a top individual rate of 38.6 percent and a top corporate rate of 34 percent, with the individual top rate temporarily dropping to 35 percent under the tax reduction legislation of 2001. The Jobs and Growth Tax Relief Reconciliation Act of 2003 temporarily aligns tax rates on shareholder capital gains and dividend income at a maximum 15 percent, departing from the classical rate preference for capital gains. This makes dividends more attractive, but does not completely eliminate the tax bias favoring capital gains: If the firm retains earnings and does not pay a dividend, the shareholders benefit from a deferral of the 15 percent tax. (In the late 1980s a different rate structure prevailed under the Tax Reform Act of 1986. Individual tax rates then were significantly *lower* than the maximum corporate rate of 34 percent. Under that tax picture, it was in many cases beneficial for the corporation to distribute its earnings as dividends and then recapture the amounts distributed by issuing interest-bearing debt, thus in effect substituting the lower individual for the higher corporate marginal tax rate.)

A number of factors further complicate the tax picture. Significant segments of the shareholding community have tax reasons to prefer dividends. Some shareholders, such as pension funds and not-for-profit institutions, are tax exempt. In addition, corporations that hold shares can take advantage of the inter-corporate dividend exclusion and pay corporate income tax on only 30 percent of any dividends received.

Generally, however, tax paying shareholders with long-term investment perspectives can be expected to favor earnings retention. Management, which has institutional reasons to want to retain earnings, can be expected to continue to cater to this segment of the shareholding population. Graham and Kumar, Do Dividend Clienteles Exist? Evidence on Dividend Preferences of Retail Investors 61 J. Fin. 1305 (2006), confirms that retail investors as a group prefer nondividend paying stocks to dividend paying stocks. But even here there are exceptions–within the retail investor group, older and low-income investors prefer dividend paying stocks; looking only at dividend paying stocks, retail investors as a group prefer high dividend yield stocks over low dividend yield stocks.

(3) Information Asymmetries, Signaling, and Pecking Order Theory

Consider that, despite the apparent tax advantage of financing out of retained earnings, the market in practice has historically reacted unfavorably when corporations *reduced* their dividend payments to acquire new assets. Does this mean that the tax advantages of corporate leverage outweigh those associated with retained earnings, or possibly, that the latter are in reality less significant than the above illustration implies? Or does the market, because it dislikes uncertainty, pay a premium for dividends and dividend stability? Or do dividends have an informational component to which investors react, perhaps irrationally? How do dividend policy and earnings retention policy interact with the firm's objectives and constraints respecting external finance? Do factors in addition to taxation explain the preference for earnings retention over external finance and for new debt finance over new equity finance? These and related issues are examined in the materials that follow.

Recall the pecking order theory of Myers and Majluf, Corporate Financing and Investment Decisions When Firms Have Information that Investors Do Not Have, 13 J.Fin.Econ. 187 (1984), and Myers, The Capital Structure Puzzle, 39 J.Fin. 575 (1984), discussed in Part II.A, supra. Under the pecking order, information asymmetries cause firms to avoid financing with new common stock: outsiders in the market will assume that new equity financing means that the insiders doing the financing believe the stock to be overvalued. In addition, earnings retention is the favored mode of finance—because it is internal, information asymmetries do not impair it. The result tracks the tax pecking order just discussed—retention first, borrowing next, equity last.

The information-based pecking order has limitations. For example, management is not always free to retain earnings and cut the dividend because information asymmetries constrain dividend policy. Dividends, like the different modes of external finance, have a signaling effect. An increase in dividends is said to signal management's favorable expectations about the future profitability of the firm; a decrease signals unfavorable expectations. It follows that dividends are "sticky," so that dividend cuts are not used to finance capital expenditure and changes in cash requirements are not soaked up in short-run dividend changes.

Asquith and Mullins, Signaling with Dividends, Repurchases and Equity Issues, pp. 15–16 (1984) (Research Paper 75th Anniversary Colloquium Series Harvard Business School), describes the informational content of dividend changes:

> There are reasons for the efficacy of dividends as signals. Dividend announcements are backed by hard, cold cash. The firm must generate this cash internally or convince the capital markets to supply it. Alternative communications may lack the credibility that comes from saying it with cash. Investors may suspect that statements from management are backed by the ghostwriting of well paid public relations specialists. They may feel that financial statements have been skillfully massaged by the financial staff. In addition, dividend decisions tend to be future oriented as opposed to accounting statements which document past performance.

> Besides credibility, dividends also have the advantage of simplicity and visibility. Many other announcements are, at the same time, complex and detailed in focus. They require time and expertise to

decipher. In contrast, few investors fail to notice and understand a check in the mail. An empty mailbox is also easily interpreted. As simple numerical signals, dividends facilitate comparative analysis unlike statements by management which may be difficult to calibrate. Simplicity is especially advantageous for investors holding many firms' shares to achieve the benefits of diversification. Further, dividend signals convey information without releasing sensitive details which may be useful to competitors.

Hard cash in the mail, then, is good sign. Good enough that dividend increases on average trigger a 1 percent stock price uptick. See Asquith and Mullins, supra; Aharony and Swary, Quarterly Dividend and Earnings Announcements and Stockholder Returns: An Empirical Analysis 35 J. Fin. 1 (1980).

There is a puzzling aspect to the signaling effect attributed to changes in dividends. If management increases dividends, it either foregoes a better use for the funds or distributes the funds because it has no better use for them. The dividend recipient cannot tell from the mere act of paying dividends which circumstances underpin the distribution—whether management sees the future optimistically or has no better use for the funds. If management has no better use for the funds, the dividend signals the opposite information from that which is thought by the "signaling" theorists and the market to be conveyed. And if the dividend is paid notwithstanding management's foregoing a profitable opportunity to do so, the signal is no more accurate. DeAngelo, DeAngelo and Skinner, Reversal of Fortune: Dividend Signaling and the Disappearance of Sustained Earnings Growth, 40 J.Fin.Econ. 341 (1996), offers an interesting insight about the meaning to be drawn from a dividend increase. It may be good news but it is not a signal of increased earnings in the future. It instead should be read together with the traditional payout pattern to signal something less— management's confidence that the payout level thus reached can be sustained.

Similar obscurities, if not inaccuracies, attend the decision to reduce or withhold dividends—a decision which except for unusual growth situations is read by the market unfavorably rather than to reflect management's expectation for favorable new investment. Denis and Sarin, The Information Content of Dividend Changes, 29 J.Fin. & Quant. Anal. 567 (1994), confirm this, reporting an average 6 percent stock price decline in the three days surrounding an announcement of a cut.

If, as appears to be the case, there is little doubt that the market reads increases favorably and cuts unfavorably, can management be said to be culpably misleading if it foresees the opposite, or at any rate a different, consequence from that perceived by the market, but does not so state?

(4) Management Dividend Policies and Agency Theory

The pecking order theory, while cogent, rests on the heroic assumption that managers design capital structures to maximize value for the firm's existing shareholders. Agency theory, in contrast, looks at managers as maximizers of their own welfare and looks to corporate governance and financing practice to ameliorate the resulting costs.

The traditional payout policy implies an agency cost. The goal of a "stable" payout means that dividend increases lag behind increases in earnings. A "stable" payout policy accordingly could invite reinvestment in projects where $r<k$—projects that detract from the value of the firm even as they satisfy management's desire to build an empire. Consider the report of Donaldson, Managing Corporate Wealth (1984), pp. 51–54, on the attitudes of managers prior to the leveraged restructurings of the 1980s:

" * * * Top management teams recognized the importance of dividends as a signal of financial well-being and as a measure of cash-flow volatility. They knew that unexpected discontinuities conveyed a disconcerting prospect of a management surprised by events and not in full control. Consequently they stressed the importance of dividend continuity and emphasized strongly the need for growth to keep pace with earnings and general inflation. However, as these managers thought about dividend policy they were concerned less directly with their shareholders than with the flow of funds within the firm. Thus they concentrated on dividend payout targets instead of dividends per share.

" * * * The implications of this orientation are apparent in the financial planning documents of a company whose profit margins were below the *Fortune* 500 average. From the shareholders' perspective, it would be reasonable to assume that the company's payout would be inversely proportional to its profitability, on the theory that the better the earnings performance, the more justification and opportunity for reinvestment. In reality, the president argued just the reverse in a document circulated to his four top executives:

> * * * [Our performance is below average; it must and can be improved; we are confident of our ability to accomplish our goals; therefore, we are justified in asking our shareholders to make an above-average reinvestment of earnings to fund it.

Such self-confident managers assume that the shareholders will agree with their optimistic views and, in time of need, they lean toward the highest acceptable target earnings-retention ratio consistent with the continuity of dividends per share. Indeed, these top managers generally preferred to keep their payouts as low as possible in the belief that 'we can make better use of the money than our shareholders can,' given reinvestment opportunities and the personal tax advantages of undistributed earnings. None sought to increase payouts as a deliberate policy. All spoke often about the need for a reasonable or fair dividend policy—thereby suggesting that in the absence of such concerns, internal pressures would result in lower payouts."

Is a dividend policy shaped by the considerations described by Donaldson likely to be optimal from the point of view of a shareholder? Recall that the leveraged restructurings of the 1980s were justified as drastic remedies to the problem of self-serving financing and investment decisions made by managers. Management's preference for a low but safe level of debt was but one practice held out to be in need of correction. Its tendency to pay a low dividend and retain an excessive amount of earnings was another. Professor Michael Jensen made the leading theoretical statement of this point. Jensen, Agency Costs of Free Cash Flow, Corporate Finance and Takeover, 76 Amer. Econ. Rev. 323 (1986), asserts that a firm with substantial available internally generated funds, or free cash flows, will tend to overinvest them, accepting marginal investment projects. That is, management tends to reinvest earnings in investments where $r<k$. Jensen connects this point to the dividend policy debate. All other things being equal, an increase in the dividend will reduce the extent of suboptimal investment and increase the value of the firm. According to Jensen, then, dividends matter, and high dividends may be preferable to low dividends depending on the set of investments available to the firm. See also Lang and Litzenberger, Dividend Announcements: Cash Flow Signaling vs. Free Cash Flow Hypothesis? 24 J. Fin. Econ. 181 (1989) (empirical study supporting both free cash flow and signaling explanations).

It should be noted that the recognition of the presence of agency costs does not, taken alone, require the conclusion that the traditional dividend payout pattern is suboptimal. Easterbrook, Two Agency–Cost Explanations of Dividends, 74 Amer. Econ. Rev. 650 (1984), offers a contrasting agency cost explanation of the pattern described by Lintner. Easterbrook starts with the point that managers' risk aversion causes them to prefer levels of debt which are suboptimal from a shareholder point of view. If managers were forced to go to the capital markets to borrow, effective monitoring would occur and the level of debt would rise. Easterbrook posits that dividends play a role in causing this to occur, id. at 655, 657:

"The role of dividends in starting up the monitoring provided by the capital market is easy to see. An example of the role of dividends in making risk adjustments may help. Suppose a firm has an initial capitalization of 100, of which 50 is debt and 50 equity. It invests the 100 in a project. The firm prospers, and earnings raise its holdings to 200. The creditors now have substantially more security than they started with, and correspondingly the residual claimants are paying the creditors a rate of interest unwarranted by current circumstances. They can correct this situation by paying a dividend of 50 while issuing new debt worth 50. The firm's capital continues to be 200, but the debt-equity ratio has been restored, and the interest rate on the original debt is again appropriate to the creditors' risk.

"Expected, continuing dividends compel firms to raise new money in order to carry out their activities. They therefore precipitate the monitoring and debt-equity adjustments that benefit stockholders. Moreover, even when dividends are not accompanied by the raising of new capital, they at least increase the debt-equity ratio so that shareholders are not giving (as much) wealth away to bondholders. In other words, dividends set in motion mechanisms that reduce the agency costs of management and that prevent one group of investors from gaining, relative to another, by changes in the firm's fortunes after financial instruments have been issued. The future is always anticipated imperfectly in these contracts, so there will always be some need for *ex post* adjustments and supervision, and dividends play a role in these adjustments."

Easterbrook's sanguine view of traditional dividend policy is seconded from a different agency cost perspective in La Porta, et al., Agency Problems and Dividend Policies around the World, 55 J.Fin. 1 (2000). This study compares dividend payout rates of firms in the United States, Britain, the Continent of Europe, and East Asia, and finds significantly higher payouts in Britain and the United States. The explanation is that high agency costs stemming from ineffective governance do indeed mean a lower dividend payout rate. The authors suggest that the higher payouts in this country and Britain stem from governance systems that do a better job of protecting the shareholder interest. This does not imply a claim that domestic shareholders can direct dividend payments. The claim instead is that the combination of our proxy and board election system, our disclosure requirements, our institutional investor monitoring, our allowance of take-overs, and our regime of fiduciary law together compel managers to share a larger portion of corporate returns than do the less strict governance systems in most other industrial countries. See also Pinkowitz, Stulz, and Williamson, Does the Contribution of Corporate Cash Holdings and Dividends to Firm Value Depend on Governance? A Cross-country Analysis. 61 J. Fin. 2725 (2006).

DeAngelo and DeAngelo, The Irrelevance of the MM Dividend Irrelevance Theorem,79 J. Fin. Econ. 293 (2006), takes the point that animates the agency discussion–that the payout-retention decision has critical shareholder value implications—back to the theoretical square one of the M–M irrelevance hypothesis. They note that M–M's irrelevance conclusion follows from an assumption that 100 percent of free cash flow is paid out in every period, an assumption that elides the payout/retention decision. Once the payout/retention decision is brought to the center of the theory, payout policy matters in the same sense that investment policy does. Furthermore, only when payout policy is optimized will the dividend model of firm valuation work and the present value of distributions equal the present value of project cash flows.

2. APPLICABLE LEGAL STANDARDS

Both the Modigliani–Miller hypothesis on the irrelevance of dividends as against retention and the pecking order theory assume a firm in which the interests of the stockholders are perfectly aligned with those of the managers making the dividend decision. If, as agency theory asserts, management's interests diverge from those of the stockholders, then a basic assumption of both of these theories is negated. The different assumptions implicate different legal norms. If the interests are mutual, then a dispute over investment or dividend policy presumably reflects differences only of business judgment, and management should enjoy the wide discretion allowed under the business judgment rule. If the interests diverge, then the breadth of managerial discretion allowed by the business judgment rule suggests that the choice of an optimal dividend policy should be restrained, or stimulated. Such a restraint or stimulus could arise either in the form of irate shareholders exercising their voting rights, or of "penalties" for inefficiency imposed by the capital markets, presumably through lower prices for the company's shares and takeovers. But if these governance correctives are unlikely to be fully effective, then, despite relative superiority of our system of correctives to alternatives in Europe and Asia, it appears American managers have some degree of discretion to define their own goals and to behave accordingly. See Berle and Means, The Modern Corporation and Private Property (1932); Roe, Strong Managers, Weak Owners: The Political Roots of American Corporate Finance (1994). In view of this uncertainty, Jensen's critique remains relevant. Is it safe to assume that management's investment decisions are guided by "scientific" capital budgeting principles (or their practical equivalent) and that new investment projects are accepted or rejected only in response to considerations most likely to enhance the value of the company's outstanding shares?

From a legal standpoint, selection of a dividend policy is almost entirely within the business judgment zone of management discretion, subject to the caveat that management must make reference to the health of the business and avoid reference to constituency interests in justifying decisions to retain. See Dodge v. Ford Motor Co., 204 Mich. 459, 170 N.W. 668 (1919). Statutory surplus requirements (supra, Part II) must be met when dividends are paid, but this is rarely a problem for large, publicly held corporations whose balance sheets almost always contain sizable quantities of retained earnings. Nevertheless, as the cases that follow suggest, the law is not without some further impact on corporate distribution policy, especially when that policy is suspected of having manipulative or other illicit goals in view.

Berwald v. Mission Development Company

Supreme Court of Delaware, 1962.
40 Del.Ch. 509, 185 A.2d 480.

■ SOUTHERLAND, CHIEF JUSTICE.

Plaintiffs, owners of 248 shares of the stock of Mission Development Corporation, brought suit to compel the liquidation of Mission and the distribution of its assets to its stockholders. Mission answered and filed a motion for summary judgment, based on affidavits and depositions. Plaintiffs tendered no contradictory proof. The Vice Chancellor granted the motion and the plaintiffs appeal.

The facts are as follows:

Defendant, Mission Development, is a holding company. Its sole significant asset is a block of nearly seven million shares of Tidewater Oil Company. Tidewater is a large integrated oil company, qualified to do business in all the States of the Union. It is controlled, through Mission Development and Getty Oil Company, by J. Paul Getty.

Mission Development was formed in 1948 for the purpose of acquiring a block of 1,416,693 shares of Tidewater common stock then owned by Mission Corporation, a Nevada corporation. Its avowed purpose was to invest only in Tidewater stock, and in furtherance of this purpose to acquire additional stock to fortify its position in Tidewater. Accordingly, Mission of Delaware issued to Mission of Nevada 2,833,386 shares of its common stock and received the block of Tidewater stock held by Mission. Appropriate orders under the Investment Company Act were obtained from the Securities and Exchange Commission. The shares of both Mission Development and Tidewater are listed on the New York Stock Exchange.

Mission of Delaware will be hereinafter referred to as "Mission".

From 1948 to 1951 Mission acquired an additional 1,050,420 shares of Tidewater. Thereafter, and by 1960, Mission's holdings of Tidewater, through a 100% stock dividend and annual stock dividends of five per cent, increased to 6,943,957 shares.

In 1954 Tidewater discontinued the payment of cash dividends, thus effecting a discontinuance of Mission's income. Mission, as above noted, received thereafter until 1960 an annual 5% stock dividend, but Mission's proportionate ownership of Tidewater was not thereby increased, and its management accordingly deemed it unwise to distribute the shares as a dividend, since to do so would have decreased its proportionate ownership of Tidewater.

As hereafter shown, Tidewater's discontinuance of cash dividends was prompted by the adoption in 1954 of a policy of corporate expansion and modernization. The use of its available cash for this purpose left it without funds for dividends.

Later in the same year, Tidewater proposed to its stockholders to exchange shares of its cumulative $1.20 preferred stock for shares of its common stock held by the stockholders. Getty Oil Company and Mission were excluded from this offer.

All of the foregoing facts were reported to Mission stockholders by letter of J. Paul Getty, President of the corporation, dated April 11, 1955.

We pause to note that some of the plaintiff's stock in Mission Development was bought in 1956 and 1959.

In 1960 Tidewater discontinued the practice of distributing stock dividends. In the same year it submitted to its stockholders an exchange offer similar to the one made in 1955, again excluding Getty Oil and Mission.

From September 1960 to and including August 1961 Getty Oil Company acquired 510,200 shares of Mission. Some of these were purchased off the market.

In November 1960 this suit was filed.

As above indicated, plaintiffs seek to compel a complete or partial liquidation of the defendant and the distribution of its assets, either through the medium of a winding-up receivership, or by means of a court order compelling the management to distribute, or to offer to distribute, at least part of the Tidewater shares in exchange for Mission shares.

The extreme relief of receivership to wind up a solvent going business is rarely granted. To obtain it there must be a showing of imminent danger of great loss resulting from fraud or mismanagement. Hall v. John S. Isaacs, etc., Inc., Del.Ch., 163 A.2d 288, 293. Like caution is dictated in considering an application to compel a corporation to make a partial distribution.

Since no showing is made of fraud or mismanagement inflicting injury upon the corporation, what is the basis of plaintiff's case?

Plaintiff's argument proceeds as follows:

There is an inherent conflict of interest between the controlling stockholder of Mission, Mr. J. Paul Getty, and the minority stockholders. This arises out of the dividend policy of Tidewater. Because of high income taxes, Mr. Getty, it is said, is not interested in receiving dividends; he is interested in acquiring more shares of Tidewater. To achieve this end, it is charged, he has caused Tidewater to discontinue all dividends and to announce, in 1960, that no dividends could be expected for five years. The necessary effect of this policy, plaintiffs say, was to depress the market value of Mission shares, and enable Mr. Getty to buy more Mission shares at an artificially low price, at the expense of Mission's minority stockholders. This, plaintiffs charge, is just what he has done, as is proved by Getty Oil's purchases of stock in 1960 and 1961. Thus he and Mission have inflicted a serious wrong upon the minority stockholders.

It is quite true that in some cases the interests of a controlling stockholder and of the minority stockholders in respect of the receipt of dividends may conflict, because of the existence of very high income taxes. See Cases and Materials, Baker and Cary, p. 1375. And in some cases this may work hardship on the minority. But we find no such situation here.

It is plain that the whole argument based on a charge of conflict of interest rests upon the claim that Tidewater's dividend policy, and its public announcement of it, were designed to serve the selfish interest of Mr. Getty and not to further its own corporate interests. If the opposite is true—if Tidewater's policy was adopted in furtherance of its own corporate interest—then Mission's stockholders have not been subjected to an actionable wrong and have no complaint. The fact of Mr. Getty's purchase of Mission Development stock then becomes irrelevant.

What does the record show with respect to Tidewater's dividend policy?

In the ten years prior to 1953 Tidewater's expenditure for capital improvements did not exceed $41,100,000 in any one year. Shortly prior to 1954 Tidewater began to expand and modernize its facilities. In February 1955 it closed and subsequently sold its obsolete refinery at Bayonne, New Jersey, and built a new and modern refinery in New Castle County, Delaware at a cost in excess of $200,000,000. Also, it commenced and still continues the expansion and modernization of its refinery facilities at Avon, California, and the increase of its crude oil and natural gas resources. As of November 3, 1960, the budget for new capital projects to be begun in 1961 was $111,000,000.

It is unnecessary to elaborate the point. It is entirely clear from the facts set forth in the affidavits that Tidewater's cash has since 1960 been largely devoted to capital improvements and that, in the opinion of management, funds were not available for dividends. These facts are uncontradicted, and they constitute a refutation of the basic argument of plaintiffs that dividends were discontinued to enable J. Paul Getty to buy Mission stock at a depressed price.

Some point is sought to be made of the unusual action of the Tidewater management in announcing that dividends could not be expected for five years. As defendant's counsel says, this was done out of common fairness to its stockholders and to prospective purchasers of its stock.

It is earnestly argued that plaintiffs should be allowed to go to trial and adduce testimony on the issue of the selfish motives of the controlling stockholder. Plaintiffs say that they could show by expert testimony that the market price of Mission common was artificially depressed.

It is first to be noted that the record of market prices put in by the plaintiffs themselves fails to show any drop in prices coincident with or closely following the announcement of the cessation of dividends. Plaintiffs reply that this fact is meaningless because at that time the market was steadily going up, and say that expert testimony will establish this. The answer to this argument is that if plaintiffs had such proof, they should have come forward with it. "In such a situation, a duty is cast upon the plaintiff to disclose evidence which will demonstrate the existence of a genuine issue of fact * * * if summary judgment * * * is to be denied." Frank C. Sparks Co. v. Huber Baking Co., 9 Terry 9, 48 Del. 9, 96 A.2d 456, 459.

There are other facts in this case that support the conclusion above indicated. The sole corporate purpose of Mission is and has been to hold Tidewater stock. Any investor in its shares could readily ascertain this fact. Because of this he knows, or should know, that he is buying for growth and not for income.

Some point is made of the exclusion of Mission from the exchange offers made by Tidewater to its stockholders in 1954 and 1960. Obviously, for Mission Development to have been included in the exchange would have defeated the very purpose of its corporate existence.

However the various arguments are put they come to this: Plaintiffs are in effect seeking to wind up the corporation, either wholly or partially, because it is doing exactly what it was lawfully organized to do.

We think the plaintiffs have failed to make a case.

The judgment below is affirmed.

* * *

Why would anyone buy shares of Mission Development Co. in the first place? If you fancy Tidewater Oil, why not own its shares and receive its dividends directly? Broad hint: Under I.R.C. § 243 a corporation (Mission) which receives a dividend from another corporation (Tidewater) was at that time allowed to deduct 85 percent of such dividend from its gross income (today the deduction is 70 percent). Since the corporate tax was then 52 percent, intercorporate dividends were taxed at the effective rate of only 7.8 percent, i.e., 52 percent of 15 percent. Individuals owning stock in the recipient corporation were taxed at capital gain rates when they sold those shares. The capital gain tax was half the tax on ordinary dividend income, however, and prior to 1969 it could not exceed 25 percent.

NOTE: DIVIDENDS AND "CORPORATE OPPORTUNITY"

In **Sinclair Oil Corp. v. Levien,** a minority stockholder of Sinclair's 97%–owned Venezuelan subsidiary (Sinven) brought an action for damages and an accounting on the ground that Sinclair had injured Sinven by causing it to distribute "excessive" dividends for the purpose of financing Sinclair's worldwide exploration activities. The plaintiff stressed that between 1960 and 1966 Sinven had paid out $108 million in dividends, which was $38 million more than its earnings during that period. While the plaintiff and other public stockholders received their proportionate share of such dividends, the plaintiff argued that Sinven was thereby effectively disabled from undertaking new investments of its own, and was, in effect, thrown into partial liquidation to serve its parent's need for cash.

The plaintiff was successful in obtaining an accounting order in the Court of Chancery, 261 A.2d 911 (Del.Ch.1969). On appeal, the Supreme Court of Delaware reversed (280 A.2d 717 (1971)), stating (at 719–722):

"The Chancellor held that because of Sinclair's fiduciary duty and its control over Sinven, its relationship with Sinven must meet the test of intrinsic fairness. The standard of intrinsic fairness involves both a high degree of fairness and a shift in the burden of proof. Under this standard the burden is on Sinclair to prove, subject to careful judicial scrutiny, that its transactions with Sinven were objectively fair. Guth v. Loft, Inc., 23 Del.Ch. 255, 5 A.2d 503 (Del.Sup.1939); Getty Oil Co. v. Skelly Oil Co., supra.

"Sinclair argues that the transactions between it and Sinven should be tested, not by the test of intrinsic fairness with the accompanying shift of the burden of proof, but by the business judgment rule under which a court will not interfere with the judgment of a board of directors unless there is a showing of gross and palpable overreaching. * * *

"A parent does indeed owe a fiduciary duty to its subsidiary when there are parent-subsidiary dealings. However, this alone will not evoke the intrinsic fairness standard. This standard will be applied only when the fiduciary duty is accompanied by self-dealing—the situation when a parent is on both sides of a transaction with its subsidiary. Self-dealing occurs when the parent, by virtue of its domination of the subsidiary, causes the subsidiary to act in such a way that the parent receives something from the subsidiary to the exclusion of, and detriment to, the minority stockholders of the subsidiary. * * *

"Consequently, it must be determined whether the dividend payments by Sinven were, in essence, a self-dealing by Sinclair. The dividends resulted in great sums of money being transferred from Sinven to Sinclair. However, a proportionate share of this money was received by the minority shareholders of Sinven. Sinclair received nothing from Sinven to the exclusion of its minority stockholders. As such, these dividends were not self-dealing. We hold therefore that the Chancellor erred in applying the intrinsic fairness test as to these dividend payments. The business judgment standard should have been applied.

"We conclude that the facts demonstrate that the dividend payments complied with the business judgment standard. * * * The motives for causing the declaration of dividends are immaterial unless the plaintiff can show that the dividend payments resulted from improper motives and amounted to waste. The plaintiff contends only that the dividend payments drained Sinven of cash to such an extent that it was prevented from expanding.

"The plaintiff proved no business opportunities which came to Sinven independently and which Sinclair either took to itself or denied to Sinven. As a matter of fact, with two minor exceptions which resulted in losses, all of Sinven's operations have been conducted in Venezuela, and Sinclair had a policy of exploiting its oil properties located in different countries by subsidiaries located in the particular countries.

"From 1960 to 1966 Sinclair purchased or developed oil fields in Alaska, Canada, Paraguay, and other places around the world. The plaintiff contends that these were all opportunities which could have been taken by Sinven. The Chancellor concluded that Sinclair had not proved that its denial of expansion opportunities to Sinven was intrinsically fair. He based this conclusion on the following findings of fact. Sinclair made no real effort to expand Sinven. The excessive dividends paid by Sinven resulted in so great a cash drain as to effectively deny to Sinven any ability to expand. During this same period Sinclair actively pursued a company-wide policy of developing through its subsidiaries new sources of revenue, but Sinven was not permitted to participate and was confined in its activities to Venezuela.

"However, the plaintiff could point to no opportunities which came to Sinven. Therefore, Sinclair usurped no business opportunity belonging to Sinven. Since Sinclair received nothing from Sinven to the exclusion of and detriment to Sinven's minority stockholders, there was no self-dealing. Therefore, business judgment is the proper standard by which to evaluate Sinclair's expansion policies.

" * * * Accordingly, Sinclair's decision, absent fraud or gross overreaching, * * * must be upheld."

On the remand, Sinclair was found liable to Sinven on another count for breach of a contract involving inter-company transactions, in the amount of approximately $5,250,000. 314 A.2d 216 (Del.Ch.1973).

Wertheim Schroder & Co. Incorporated v. Avon Products, Inc.

United States District Court, Southern District of New York, 1993.
1993 WL 126427 (S.D.N.Y.).

■ LEISURE, DISTRICT JUDGE.

[Avon is one of the world's leading manufacturers and marketers of beauty products. After a period of expansion, it determined to retreat and developed a restructuring program. As a part of this, the Avon board decided that, in an effort to conserve cash needed to retire debt, Avon's annual cash dividend on its common stock would be reduced from $2 to $1 per share. However, Avon's financial adviser, Morgan Stanley & Co. ("Morgan Stanley"), advised that a significant decrease in Avon's stock price would follow. Morgan Stanley recommended that, at the time Avon announced the dividend reduction, Avon should also announce the issuance of a new class of stock, PERCS, which would provide shareholders with the option of continuing to receive the $2 per share dividend in exchange for a limitation on capital appreciation.

[In June 1988, Avon simultaneously announced a dividend cut from $2 to $1 and a one-to-one exchange offer of up to 18 million shares (25 percent of the total) of the common stock for PERCS. The key component of the PERCS was the continuation of the prior annual dividend of $2 per year in exchange for a limitation on capital appreciation. Avon effectuated the limitation on capital appreciation by incorporating an Optional Redemption into the terms of the PERCS. The Optional Redemption allowed Avon to redeem the PERCS at any time during their term in accordance with a fixed schedule of prices, known as the "Call Price." The Call Price would be set at levels significantly above the market price of the Avon common stock at the time the PERCS were issued and could be paid in either cash or Avon common stock. Thus, if the market price of the Avon common stock rose above the Call Price, Avon would be able to effect an Optional Redemption of the PERCS prior to the end of their term at a value below the then-current market price of Avon common stock.]

The rationale behind the issuance of PERCS was that yield-oriented investors, instead of selling their common stock, would be willing to exchange their shares for PERCS, thereby maintaining the $2 annual dividend in exchange for a limitation on capital appreciation. However, there was a concern that the PERCS would not appeal to investors if there was the potential that they would be excluded from any large dividend payout made on the common stock while the PERCS were outstanding, or would be excluded from the consideration received by common stockholders in a merger involving Avon. In order to alleviate the concern that common stockholders might receive some benefit that the PERCS holders would have received if they had retained their common shares, Avon incorporated an Accelerated Redemption provision into the terms of the PERCS. Under this provision, it was agreed that (1) in the event Avon "shall pay" a common stock dividend at a "cumulative rate per annum equal to or greater than $1.50 per share"; or (2) in the event Avon was involved in a merger, consolidation, or similar extraordinary transaction during this period, the Accelerated Redemption provision would be triggered and PERCS holders would be entitled to a one-for-one exchange for common stock (or cash equivalent), plus the payment of a specified premium and accrued and unpaid dividends.

[Assuming that neither an Optional nor an Accelerated Redemption occurred, a Final Redemption would occur on September 1, 1991, with each PERCS being exchanged for one common share. The terms upon which the PERCS were issued were set forth in an Amendment to Article IIIB of Avon's Certificate of Incorporation ("Article IIIB"). The exchange offer of common shares for PERCS was fully subscribed. Thereafter, plaintiff Wertheim Schroder, an investment banking firm, became a substantial investor in PERCS.

[On February 7, 1991, Avon declared a first quarter common stock dividend of $0.35 per share payable on March 1. At the same time, Avon declared a special dividend of $3.00 per share to be paid on September 16, 1991 to common shareholders of record on September 4, 1991. In addition, Avon indicated that in the future it would continue to declare and pay regular quarterly common stock dividends at the rate of $0.35. On March 1 Avon paid the quarterly dividend of $0.35 announced on February 7. The quarterly dividend of $0.35 was paid again on June 1, 1991. On June 3, 1991, Avon exercised the Optional Redemption of all PERCS.

[Wertheim Schroder claims that the declaration of the dividend increase on February 7, 1991 and/or the payment of the March 1, 1991 dividend triggered the Accelerated Redemption provision, and that Avon has failed to honor the terms of that provision. In the alternative, Wertheim Schroder states a claim of violation of the duty of good faith. Defendant Avon moves for summary judgment.]

* * *

The language of Article IIIB at issue in this summary judgment motion is contained in the Accelerated Redemption provision of the PERCS which states in relevant part:

> In the event ... the Corporation shall pay any regular quarterly cash dividend or any other cash dividend with respect to the shares of its Common Stock at a cumulative rate per annum equal to or greater than $1.50 per share, then the Corporation shall redeem all outstanding shares of [the PERCS] ... on the business day next preceding the date fixed as the record date for the determination of holders of shares of Common Stock entitled to receive such cash dividend.

* * * [T]he Court finds that there are ambiguities contained in the Accelerated Redemption provision which preclude summary judgment on the issue of whether the declaration of February 7, 1991 and/or the subsequent dividend payment on March 1, 1991 triggered the Accelerated Redemption provision.

A.   THE DIVIDEND PAYMENT OF MARCH 1, 1991 AS THE TRIGGERING EVENT

* * *

The * * * phrase "cumulative rate per annum" * * * is ambiguous as to whether the declaration of a $3.00 special dividend in February 1991, during the term of the PERCS, allows such dividend to immediately become part of the "cumulative rate per annum" of that particular year even though the payment of the dividend would not take place until September 1991, after the term of the PERCS had expired.

* * * Avon argues that * * * it is abundantly clear from the language of the provision itself that it is only the payment of a dividend, not the declaration of such dividend, which is relevant for purposes of determining whether the Acceleration Provision has been triggered. However, the Court finds that, according to the language of the provision, it is not simply the payment of the dividend of $1.50 or more that triggers the provision, but rather the provision also includes the payment of a smaller dividend at an annual rate of $1.50 or more. Thus, once a payment has been made, it is the method of calculating the rate per annum which becomes the pivotal focus of the inquiry.

While Avon argues that until a dividend is paid it cannot be part of the "cumulative rate per annum," the Court finds that the terms of the

Accelerated Provision do not unambiguously support this position. By defendant's own interpretation of the contractual language, the calculation of the "cumulative rate per annum" would include future undeclared quarterly dividends. For example, if the first quarter dividend for 1991 was $0.35 and there was no declaration of the special dividend or declaration of other future quarterly dividends, then clearly the "cumulative rate per annum" would be $1.40, even though the rate would be based upon three future quarterly dividends of $0.35 for that year which were undeclared at that point in time.

Similarly, the Court also rejects Avon's contention that the language unambiguously indicates that prospective payments of dividends in 1991 which will occur after Final Redemption are automatically excluded from the cumulative rate. Using the same example as above, the fact that the fourth quarter payment of $0.35 would take place after the date for Final Redemption of the PERCS in 1991 would not mean that such payment is not included in the "cumulative rate per annum" for that year. Therefore, in calculating the dividend rate of March 1, 1991 as $1.40, one would include the quarterly dividend payment of $0.35 projected for December 1991, even though such payment would be after the Final Redemption date. * * *

Avon's real contention is that the payment of the quarterly dividend on February 7, 1991 must be treated separately from the declared, but unpaid, $3.00 special dividend for purposes of calculating the "cumulative rate per annum." In other words, Avon argues that the mere declaration of a separate special dividend to be paid at a later date cannot be treated as part of the payment of the regular quarterly dividend for purposes of calculating the rate per annum. The reasoning behind this distinction is that the language of the provision states that Accelerated Redemption is triggered when "the Corporation shall pay any regular quarterly cash dividend or any other cash dividend ... at a cumulative rate per annum equal to or greater than $1.50 per share." Thus, the contention is that the payment of a regular quarterly dividend allows for the inclusion of such a dividend in the calculation of the "rate per annum" (by multiplying that dividend by four), but a declared special dividend is a separate consideration that does not become part of the cumulative calculation until it is paid.

While defendant Avon has asserted a reasonable interpretation of the contractual language, the Court finds that it is not the only reasonable interpretation of the language of the provision. A reasonable factfinder could conclude, as Wertheim Schroder contends, that there is no basis for allowing projected but undeclared and unpaid quarterly dividends to be included in the "cumulative rate per annum," while a simultaneous declared but unpaid special dividend is not included. The plain meaning of the terms of the provision does not preclude finding that when a corporation pays a quarterly dividend and also has declared that a special dividend will be paid at a later date during that same year, both dividends immediately become part of the cumulative dividend rate for that year despite the fact that the special dividend has not yet been paid. In other words, a reasonable person could conclude that "cumulative rate per annum" is determined by multiplying the last quarterly dividend by four and adding to that any declared special dividends that would be paid prospectively in the twelve-month period. * * *

The ability for such an interpretation to survive a summary judgment motion is strengthened by the fact that after the February 7 declaration of the special dividend on the common stock, Avon had a legally binding obligation to pay the special dividend. * * * [See] Staats v. Biograph Co., 236 F. 454, 458 (2d Cir.1916) (when Board of Directors declares a dividend and makes a public announcement of that fact, it cannot thereafter rescind the dividend); Jaques v. White Knob Copper & Dev. Co., 260 A.D. 640, 641, 23 N.Y.S.2d 326, 328 (1st Dep't 1940) ("The relationship between a corporation and a stockholder with respect to the latter's share of a dividend declared by the corporation is that of debtor and creditor. At any time after the date fixed for payment of each dividend, a holder of stock may maintain an action at law to recover the sum due."); * * *. Given that once Avon declared the special dividend on February 7 it had a legal obligation to pay that dividend on the announced future date, an investor could reasonably conclude that, at the time Avon made its first quarterly dividend payment on March 1, 1991, that the payment was being made at a "cumulative rate" for 1991 which now included not only future quarterly dividends for 1991, but also the mandatory special dividend to paid out on September 16, 1991. Thus, one could reasonably interpret the annual dividend rate, as of March 1, 1991, to be $4.40 per share.

B. THE FEBRUARY 7, 1991 DECLARATION AS THE TRIGGERING EVENT

In addition to alleging that the March 1 payment was the triggering event, plaintiff Wertheim Schroder also argues that, given the ambiguity in the terms of the Accelerated Redemption provision, one could interpret the provision as stating that Accelerated Redemption was triggered by the declaration of the special dividend on February 7. The basis for plaintiff's alternative interpretation is the ambiguity in the term "shall pay." Plaintiff contends that the use of the term "shall pay"—as opposed to language such as "pays" or "has paid"—indicates that the provision is triggered by a future intention or obligation to pay. Thus, plaintiff claims that, since the declaration of a dividend constitutes a future intention or obligation to pay, a reasonable interpretation of the Accelerated Provision is that a dividend becomes part of the "cumulative rate per annum" at the time Avon declares that it "shall pay" such a dividend, rather than at the time the actual payment is made.

The Court finds that this alternative argument can be viewed as a reasonable interpretation of the contractual provision. The word "shall", in its normal usage, is used inter alia "to express what is inevitable or what seems to be fated or decreed or likely to happen in the future." Webster's Third New International Dictionary 2085 (1981). * * *

If Avon wished to make clear that the Accelerated Redemption was only triggered upon actual payment of an offending dividend, rather than the mere declaration of such a dividend, it could have used language such as "in the event the Corporation pays" or "in the event the Corporation has paid." * * * [T]he Court finds that the ambiguity creates a reasonable basis for a difference of opinion as to whether the February 7 declaration triggered Accelerated Redemption.

Avon argues, inter alia, that interpreting the provision in such a way that Accelerated Redemption is triggered is untenable because "the effect of adopting Wertheim's interpretation of the Accelerated Redemption provision is to require Avon to redeem the PERCS at a price substantially above the price at which the securities were callable, thus providing a windfall for PERCS holders and fundamentally undermining the economic arrangement underlying the PERCS, which provided for enhanced dividends to PERCS holders in exchange for a limitation on the potential appreciation of their securities." * * *

The Court emphasizes that on a motion for summary judgment "the judge's function is not himself to weigh the evidence and determine the truth of the matter but to determine whether there is a genuine issue for trial." Anderson v. Liberty Lobby, Inc., 477 U.S. 242, 249 (1986). Thus, the Court is not assessing the relative strength of either party's interpretation of the PERCS agreement. * * *

C. GOOD FAITH AND FAIR DEALING

Assuming arguendo that Avon did not violate the express terms of the PERCS provisions, Wertheim Schroder contends that Avon's "purposeful manipulation of its dividend to circumvent Accelerated Redemption" was a breach of the covenant of good faith and fair dealing. The covenant of good faith and fair dealing is implied in all contracts governed by New York law [and] "is violated when a party to a contract acts in a manner that, although not expressly forbidden by any contractual provision, would deprive the other of the right to receive the benefits under their agreement." Don King Productions, Inc. v. Douglas, 742 F.Supp. 741, 767 (S.D.N.Y.1990).

In support of its contention that Avon purposefully manipulated the dividend process to the disadvantage of PERCS investors, plaintiff Wertheim Schroder notes that Avon had never before deferred a dividend payment for such an extended period of time. Plaintiff's expert states that there is no apparent precedent in the industry for such a dividend deferral. Thus, plaintiff argues that Avon's invariable practice of declaring and paying dividends in the normal course was an underlying assumption of the investment agreement and that Avon altered this procedure solely for the purpose of depriving plaintiff of benefits that it reasonably expected to receive under the investment agreement. See Report of Avon's Special Committee, at 6 ("In order to avoid paying this premium and to preserve Avon's optional redemption rights, the Special Committee recommends that the special dividend be declared as soon as possible, but made payable to holders of record as of September 4, 1991 (immediately after the final redemption of the PERCS).") According to plaintiff, this declaration of the extraordinary dividend, inter alia, allowed Avon to boost the common stock price and then choose to pay for the Optional Redemption of the PERCS with common stock whose value was inflated by the declaration of a special dividend which had not yet been paid. The alleged result of this procedure was that PERCS holders received fewer common shares on Optional Redemption than they would have received under an Optional Redemption without the impact of the declaration of the special dividend. * * *

Drawing all inferences in plaintiff's favor, the Court finds that plaintiff has raised genuine issues of material fact as to whether Avon's conduct, with respect to the timing of the declaration of the special dividend and payment of that dividend, improperly deprived plaintiff of benefits which were reasonably expected under the terms of the PERCS and, as a result, constituted a breach of the covenant of good faith and fair dealing.

NOTE: SPECIAL DIVIDENDS

The special dividend, employed by Avon in the principal case, holds out a potential solution to the problem of the sticky dividend. Putting the impact on the PERCS to one side, Avon made its $3.00 declaration as a "special" because it did not want the market to read it as a commitment to a higher "regular" dividend. Thus do many firms separate their declarations, distinguishing regular from special dividends, disgorging temporary cash flows by dividend without committing to a permanent increase. The "special" designation tells the shareholders that repetition should not be expected. See Brickley, Shareholder Wealth, Information Signaling and the Specially Designated Dividend: An Empirical Study, 12 J. Fin. Econ. 187 (1983). Since the designation is defensive, there is no reason to expect the market to disbelieve or misunderstand it. Nor is this suggestion merely hypothetical. DeAngelo, DeAngelo, and Skinner, Special Dividends and the Evolution of Dividend Signaling, 57 J. Fin. Econ. 309 (2000), shows that prior to the 1970s, firms routinely used special dividends to disgorge temporary cash flows. From 1927 to 1949, special dividends averaged 9.8 percent of the total dividend payout, and from 1927 to the 1950s, 26.2 percent of dividend paying firms paid specials. Specials were used flexibly. They came and went without stickiness, and cuts of specials triggered no negative market response, at least where the special was an isolated event.

But specials did die out. Where in the 1940s, 61.7 percent of NYSE companies paid at least one special, in the early 1990s only 4.9 percent paid one. Id. at 315. Specials, as vehicles for paying occasional cash, more or less disappeared by the 1970s. DeAngelo, DeAngelo, and Skinner, conclude that specials died out because they over time failed to serve the occasional cash payment function. Firms that paid specials did so with regularity–27.9 percent of firms paying specials did so 90 percent of the time; 56.8 percent of firms paying specials did so more frequently than every other year. Id. at 311, 322. Reductions in specials tended to be accompanied by increases in the regular dividend, so that the firms' overall payouts remained unaffected. Dividend practice, then, evolved toward homogeneity by the 1970s. The authors conclude that the decline of specials should be correlated with the rise of institutional stockholding: In the 1960s and 1970s, these new, sophisticated shareholders saw that specials merely substituted for regulars and held out no benefits. Id. at 337–38.

Does any of the foregoing imply that a firm with extra cash for which it has no productive use could not use the device of a special dividend? Increased use of specials after 2000 signals that the device remains useful.

NOTE: DISCLOSURE ON THE DOWNSIDE

Kowal v. International Business Machines Corp., 163 F.3d 102 (2d Cir.1998), concerned IBM's disclosure practices in advance of a substantial dividend cut. During 1991 and 1992, IBM's revenues were declining drastically and a restructuring was commenced. Through the third quarter of 1992, IBM maintained a quarterly dividend of $1.21 per share. In the face of continued questions and speculation about a dividend cut, IBM spokespersons expressed confidence in the firm's ability to maintain the dividend. The spokespersons made statements such as the following:

(a) IBM's chief financial officer on September 30:

So I will say again what I've said before. I have no plan, no desire, and I see no need to cut the dividend. If you want to say to me—well, what if you run ten years without covering the dividend, will you have a problem? I expect I will … I mean, unless they change the accounting rules a lot. So we have to get back to an earnings level that does cover our dividend. But I see no short term problems at all.

(b) The same officer on October 15:

We have no plans nor need to do anything about the dividend. Our results in the third quarter although below our expectations in terms of cash flow are not a major hit to us. And we fully expect our cash flow … to be much higher than they were last year. And sufficient to cover the dividend in 1992.

(c) The PR director on October 15, took the following question:

[S]ince as you point out you can't forecast sales and you can't forecast economic environment but you still believe that even if you don't have any major changes, the economy—you'll be able to cover the dividend next year?

His answer was: "I think from your planning point of view the answer to that is yes."

Finally, on December 15, 1992, IBM announced that it was "unsure of its ability to maintain the dividend at current levels." In response to this announcement, the price of IBM's stock decreased 6 3/4 points, from 62 7/8 to 56 1/8. On January 26, 1993, IBM's board of directors voted to cut the dividend from $1.21 per share to $.54 per share. In July, 1993, IBM cut its dividend again, to $.25 per share.

The plaintiffs' class action complaint under Rule 10b–5 alleged that from September 30, 1992 to December 14, 1992, IBM disseminated false and misleading information to investors. The Second Circuit, per Judge Walker, affirmed a dismissal of the complaint. Said the Second Circuit,

"The decisive issue in this case is the [requirement that plaintiffs] prove that IBM made a false statement or omission of material fact. A statement is material only if there is a 'substantial likelihood that the disclosure of the omitted fact would have been viewed by the reasonable investor as having significantly altered the "total mix" of information made available.' Basic v. Levinson, 485 U.S. 224, 231–32, 108 S.Ct. 978, 99 L.Ed.2d 194 (1988) (quoting TSC Indus., Inc. v. Northway, Inc., 426 U.S. 438, 449, 96 S.Ct. 2126, 48 L.Ed.2d 757 (1976)).

"The statements challenged by plaintiffs are expressions of optimism or projections about the future. Each statement plaintiffs challenge in this action concerns an uncertain future event—the payment of dividends. Statements that are opinions or predictions are not per se inactionable under the securities laws. * * * Statements regarding projections of future performance may be actionable under Section 10(b) or Rule 10b–5 if they are worded as guarantees or are supported by specific statements of fact, * * * or if the speaker does not genuinely or reasonably believe them, see Time Warner, 9 F.3d at 266; In re Donald Trump Casino Secs. Litig., 7 F.3d 357, 368 (3d Cir.1993). None of these conditions applies in this case.

"First, the challenged statements regarding the future payment of dividends were predictions or opinions, and not guarantees. This conclusion is compelled by both the facts and the law. Under New York law, corporations cannot guarantee the payment of dividends because the directors of a corporation owe a duty to shareholders to declare dividends only when it is in the best interests of the corporation to do so. * * * Moreover, the power to declare dividends is traditionally vested in a corporation's board of directors. * * * Indeed, in the case of IBM, the corporation's publicly-filed Certificate of Incorporation confers the power to declare dividends exclusively on IBM's board. Thus * * * IBM's management lacked the actual or apparent authority to guarantee the dividend, and it would be unreasonable for the market to have interpreted the statements at issue as anything other than an individual's prediction about the future. Accordingly, we conclude that the challenged statements are, as a matter of law, opinions and not guarantees.

"Plaintiffs' claim also fails because plaintiffs can point to no material misrepresentations in any of the statements at issue. The challenged statements were neither false nor misleading. After each of the challenged statements were made, IBM maintained its dividend at its prior level. * * *

* * *

"Plaintiffs argue that even if IBM's statements were true when made, the company had a duty to [update] the dividend statements at issue because its position on the dividend materially changed on November 25, 1992, when [the Chief Financial Officer] revealed to representatives of the Michigan Pension Fund that IBM's dividend was, as appellants put it, 'vulnerable and likely to be cut.' * * *

* * *

"A duty to update may exist when a statement, reasonable at the time it is made, becomes misleading because of a subsequent event. See Time Warner, 9 F.3d at 267; In re Burlington Coat Factory Secs. Litig., 114 F.3d 1410, 1431 (3d Cir.1997). However, there is no duty to update vague statements of optimism or expressions of opinion. See San Leandro, 75 F.3d at 811. * * *

"The statements at issue here were not material and 'lack the sort of definite positive projections that might require later correction.' Time Warner, 9 F.3d at 267; see also San Leandro, 75 F.3d at 811 (finding no duty to update 'subdued general comments' of optimism). The challenged statements are vague expressions of opinion which are not sufficiently concrete, specific or material to impose a duty to update."

NOTE: DIVIDENDS AND CONFLICTS OF INTEREST

1. *The Scope of the Problem.*

If some managers exercise a systematic preference for retaining earnings over payment of dividends, a dispute over investment policy or dividend policy may reflect conflicts of interest, as well as differing business judgments. In that event, the legal norm for assessing the propriety of a particular investment/dividend policy may involve conventional fiduciary considerations as well as business judgment. These questions are presented in their most acute form when dividend policy is determined by controlling stockholders, who are likely to be less concerned than "outside" stockholders with the impact of dividend policy on near-term share prices, and less dependent upon cash dividends from the enterprise. As suggested in the *Mission Development* case, controlling shareholders, having power to modify dividend policy as they choose, may actually prefer a dividend policy which reduces, or does not increase, near-term share prices, but saves them from a tax at ordinary income rates or enables them to purchase minority-held shares more cheaply. La Porta et al., supra, confirm this point from a comparative perspective when they report lower dividend payout rates in European and Asian countries where block-holding patterns of share ownership prevail.

Different questions come up respecting firms where ownership and control are separated. As agency theory suggests, management's preference for the quiet life and lower levels of risk (and return) in conducting the firm's business may lead to dividend and reinvestment decisions that are suboptimal from a shareholder point of view. Do Jensen's concerns about suboptimal reinvestment of free cash flow survive in the wake of the restructuring movement of the 1980s? As with capital structure more generally, should we view the era of restructuring as a successful shock therapy respecting suboptimal reinvestment policy? Where thirty years ago managers' reputations depended on company growth, evaluations today are keyed to shareholder value. Reputational incentives now tend to encourage more care in the choice of new investment opportunities and in the framing of payout policy.

We can see that the experience of the 1980s ameliorated the problem of suboptimal reinvestment. But has the problem of suboptimal payout policy completely gone away? Why, for example, have we seen no sign of change in traditional dividend payout pattern? And why has the percentage of publicly held firms paying dividends fallen drastically in recent years? The materials on stock repurchases, infra, will provide only partial assurance of improvements in management practice. Wall Street, in fact, has complained loudly about low dividend levels in recent years, as cash flows increased with economic expansion after 2004 but neither payout levels nor reinvestment activity kept pace. Interestingly, the recent management behavior pattern does not prompt claims of suboptimal reinvestment. These days, the firms hold the extra capital in cash and cash equivalents even as they lag in stepping up payouts.

Does the pattern of conflicting interests give force to Easterbrook's suggestion, supra, that stockholder preference for dividends reflects the notion that such a policy reduces agency costs? Certainly, to the extent that payment of dividends requires management to look to the market for capital, it substitutes capital market actors for dispersed stockholders as monitors of management's behavior. But Easterbrook's analysis leaves open the question whether the level of payments emerging is suboptimally low. If it is, questions arise about the effectiveness of law's grant of substantial discretion to management and the backstop system of governance constraints. For the view that market controls are adequate to deal with management's dividend discretion, see Fischel, The Law and Economics of Dividend Policy, 67 Va.L.Rev. 699 (1981).

2. *Mandatory Payouts.*

Consider the draconian suggestion that management should be forced to pay out all or some substantial and designated portion of earnings as dividends. A. Rubner, The Ensnared Shareholder 133–36 (1965); Brewster, The Corporation and Economic Federalism, in The Corporation in Modern Society 72, 81 (E. Mason, ed. 1960). This is a simple suggestion, but it leads quickly to the complicated problem of developing the legal and economic standards by which to determine and measure the mandated payout. If the payout of all earnings were required, management would have to go to the capital market for all the cash needed to expand or meet competition—with explanations that are costly in either case. If payout of only some portion of earnings were required, there would remain the problem of defining appropriate and enforceable criteria for selecting the proper amount. As we saw above, economic theory does not offer a determinate answer to the question of the proper amount. An arbitrarily selected percentage could be decreed as a fall back, but would present problems of its own.

3. *Shareholder Dividend Options.*

Compare a less draconian suggestion made in Goshen, Shareholder Dividend Options, 104 Yale L. J. 881 (1995), expanding on an earlier suggestion made in Fox, Finance and Industrial Performance in a Dynamic Economy 383–400 (1987). Under this, public corporation shareholders are accorded a right to receive a *pro rata* share of each year's earnings in cash, or, in the alternative, to receive a *pro rata* stock dividend that in effect reinvests a *pro rata* share of earnings.

Goshen offers a multistep argument in support of this mandatory dividend option. Shareholders, he says, are unlikely to make suboptimal dividend and reinvestment decisions; therefore, a dividend option will cause capital to move in the direction of its best use. The option would not cause material disruption to existing corporate financing practices, provided of course that management has been doing a good job of reinvesting earnings. Says Goshen, the expected return on such a company's stock is already impounded in the stock price, and so, presumably, each investor in its shareholder group is satisfied with the rate of return; holders dissatisfied with the return already will have sold. So where legitimate growth prospects are on offer (or where no growth is on offer but a level of internally generated working capital is necessary to maintain cash flows), the shareholders can be expected to grasp the maximizing course and permit earnings retention. Of course, some firms reinvest suboptimally, and as to these some step up in the amount of firm borrowing can be expected. The danger of high leverage is minimal since the payout mandate bound up in the dividend option is contingent on the existence of earnings. Goshen acknowledges that coordination problems could cause shareholders to force a payout above the minimal reinvestment amount necessary to preserve the business. He makes a technical adjustment to solve the problem: Each shareholder who opts for retention does so conditioned on the a minimum percentage of other shareholders deciding to do the same thing; failure to meet the shareholder's stated threshold cancels the retention decision. Each shareholder thus will "reveal her true retention preference and avoid reinvesting in a firm with insufficient working capital." Id. at 924–25.

The dividend option assumes that shareholders will make a better payout decision because their attention is focused by their staked capital and the possibility of gain and loss, while managers' decisions are clouded by conflicting interests. Do the contrasting incentives in fact imply that shareholders are the better decision-makers? Or would shareholders exercising their dividend options merely bring to bear all the factors pointed to in the literature of stock market pricing imperfections? Is it safe to predict that a shareholder who is by definition under-informed, but who is possessed of a pure financial incentive, will make reinvestment decisions superior to those of a better-informed manager with a complex of motives? One suspects that results would vary from company to company—some deadwood management teams would get a dose of needed discipline, other conscientious and talented teams would be forced to borrow more than an optimal amount or simply to pass on good opportunities the value of which proved difficult to communicate credibly. See Bratton, Dividends, Noncontractibility, and Corporate Law, 19 Cardozo L. Rev. 409 (1997).

4. *Enhanced Disclosure Requirements.*

Must we conclude that, although traditional corporate law fails to put adequate restraints on management's powers respecting dividend policy, there is good reason to conclude that the law cannot be reformed so as to impose any effective additional restrictions? Brudney, Dividends, Discretion, and Disclosure, 66 Va.L.Rev. 85, 85–86 (1980), suggests that the situation calls for stepped up disclosure rules: "The inability to impose feasible limits on management's discretion in making the dividend decision underscores the significance of defining the extent of management's obligation to convey the information content of the dividend decision. Questions about the adequacy of management's disclosure arise from the essential ambiguity of signals given by the mere act of declaring or altering a dividend and from the potential, if not intrinsic, conflicts of interest between management and stockholders over dividend policy. That combination of intrinsic ambiguity and divergence of interest invites the examination of compelling management to communicate more clearly the meaning of its dividend action."

3. Stock Dividends

Lewellen, The Cost of Capital
Chapter 8 (1969).

Stock Dividends and Splits

Is it possible for a firm to increase its total market value simply by changing the number of shares it has outstanding? Logic—and the weight of current scholarly opinion—would suggest a negative reply. Given the firm's investments, the level of its borrowing, and therefore its aggregate after-interest-and-tax profit prospects, it should make no difference how many pieces of paper it happens to hand out to its owners. The product

$$V_s = \text{(price per share)} \times \text{(number of shares)}$$

should be a constant. Two shares of stock promising $5 a year should not sell for more in total than one share promising $10. The same argument— in reverse—is the basis for the stock repurchase discussion * * * [below]. If a corporation uses its redundant cash to remove some of its shares from the market and retire them, the price of those remaining should rise correspondingly to reflect higher per-share future income prospects.

Why, then, do firms occasionally split their stock and pay stock dividends—and why does it often seem that the share prices involved do not fall quite in proportion? Thus, it is not unusual to see a $60 stock which is split two-for-one end up selling for more than $30 afterward. One answer commonly given is that, by lowering the shares' price range, the market for them is broadened to include more small investors. People who will not consider a $60 stock because it is "high-priced" will buy it if it trades near $30 instead. They will be attracted to the opportunity to buy what in market terminology is called a "round lot"—100 shares—for $3,000, whereas they would not think of buying 50 shares at $60. If this sounds a little bizarre, there does seem to be some truth in it. A possible reason is that the brokerage commissions on a round lot are smaller per share so that there *is* a slight saving on such purchases as compared with "odd lots" of less than 100 shares. Since this saving is fairly small, however, the main factor seems to be purely psychological. Enough people appear to like lower-priced shares that the firm does get some benefit out of keeping the trading range of its stock at an appropriate level through periodic splits.

A more rational sort of explanation for the same phenomenon involves the effect of stock splits on investors' expectations. The market may interpret the act of splitting in itself as an indication that the firm's subsequent earnings and dividends are likely to be higher than were previously anticipated. The firm in a sense is telling the world that the time has come to bring its share price down to a more manageable level because it looks as though even further increases will soon be forthcoming. This alerts investors to the company's bright future and—if the brightness is in fact there and has just not been fully appreciated before—a price increase is a logical result. In that respect, a stock split may be said to contain implicitly some useful information about management's confidence in the firm's prospects.

An even more concrete way of expressing that confidence, of course, is to raise the company's cash dividend simultaneously. This seems the most likely justification for any hopes that a corporation's total market value will increase, particularly in the case of a stock dividend. If a firm "pays" a 5 percent stock dividend—giving its shareholders one additional piece of paper for every 20 they now own—but does not adjust its per-share cash dividend payment downward by the same fraction, the effect is to augment its owners' aggregate annual cash income by 5 percent. It would therefore come as no surprise if it turned out that the per-share price of the company's stock held steady. The basis for such a result, however, is the behavior of the relevant cash payments rather than the presence of extra stock certificates. The firm could achieve the same objective by skipping the latter entirely and simply raising its per-share cash payout.

As an illustration, consider the situation of a company which has been paying $5 per share cash dividend every year for many years. Its earnings have fluctuated, but have exhibited no tendency to grow over time and there is no expectation of higher dividends to come. Its current stock price is $50. Suddenly, one of its products catches on with consumers and it becomes clear that earnings will jump to a new level that will permit dividends to be raised to—and maintained at—$5.25 a share. If the firm increases its payout in that manner, a new stock price of $52.50 can be anticipated. If instead it issues a 5 percent stock dividend and keeps the cash payment at $5.00, the price should continue to be $50. Either way, every original shareholder will own stock worth a total of $52.50, will be receiving $5.25 annually in cash dividends, and will eventually have to pay tax on a $2.50 capital gain. But the cause of these happy circumstances is the improvement in the firm's profit position and thereby in its ability to generate income for its owners—not an increase in the number of pieces of paper those individuals have in their safety deposit boxes.

By way of comic relief, the following news item from the December 20, 1965, *Wall Street Journal* suggests the confusion which often attends discussions of the efficacy of stock dividends. As a charitable gesture, the company and the executive involved will be allowed to remain anonymous:

The XXX Corporation today declared a 2.5 percent stock dividend payable February 1 to stock of record January 3. It is the first dividend declared by the company since it was formed in 1945. John Doe, Senior Vice–President for Finance, said: "This has been a very good financial year and we felt we should recognize this by a stock dividend to our shareholders. Because of our equipment program, we felt we shouldn't pay it in cash."

Wouldn't a 5 percent dividend have been twice as good?

NOTE: EXPLAINING STOCK SPLITS AND STOCK DIVIDENDS

1. *Stock Splits.*

The two standard explanations of stock splits—management signaling and the return of the stock price to a "normal" trading range—have been the subject of debate.

There is empirical support for the downward price adjustment explanation. Lamoureux and Poon, The Market Reaction to Stock Splits, 42 J. Fin. 1347 (1987), finds that the number of shareholders tends to increase after a split. Lakonishok and Lev, Stock Splits and Stock Dividends: Why, Who and When, 42 J. Fin. 913 (1987), confirms the price adjustment explanation with a study of stock split and stock dividend activity during the period 1963 to 1982. The study shows that during the five years preceding the split, a 70 percent gap tends to open up between the stock prices of splitting firms and control firms. After the split, the price gap narrows and then vanishes. Mason and Shelor, Stock Splits: An Institutional Investor Preference, 33 Fin. Rev. 33 (1998), finds that institutional investors are attracted to firms about to split their stock.

The signaling explanation is the subject of an analytical objection. If the split is a signal that the company is undervalued, then the market must extract some cost in the case of a false signal. Otherwise it would be impossible to distinguish an undervalued splitting stock from an overvalued splitting stock. But no such cost appears, and the signal could be a negative one in any event—the split could reflect management's judgment that the price has peaked. See Lamoureux and Poon, supra, at 1348. The Lakonishok and Lev study, supra, at 922, provides a partial rebuttal to this objection. Splitting firms have higher dividend growth than non-splitting firms during both the pre-and post-split periods. In the post-split period, the most dramatic increase in dividends occurs during the first quarter after the split. This leads to the conclusion that a split signals "mildly good news"—the firm's presplit earnings will stabilize at the newly reached plateau. See also Pilotte and Manuel, The Market's Response to Recurring Events: The Case of Stock Splits, 41 J. Fin. Econ. 111 (1996); Mason and Shelor, Stock Splits: An Institutional Investor Preference, 33 Fin. Rev. 33 (1998)(showing a tendency for institutions to favor stocks with pre-split characteristics).

Byun and Rozeff, Long-run Performance after Stock Splits,1927 to 1996, 58 J. Fin. 1063 (2003), provides mixed evidence on firms that split their stock, using a large database. They find that the shares of firms conducting 2 to 1 split do in fact display positive abnormal returns in succeeding years. A larger sample of firms conducting 25 percent or larger splits, however, shows no significant over-performance.

2. *Stock Dividends.*

Lakonishok and Lev, supra, report that the number of firms issuing stock dividends declined steadily, from 13.45 percent in 1968 to 4.48 percent in 1982. They also find that firms issuing stock dividends enjoy only slightly higher preannouncement earnings growth than do control firms. Stock price appreciation tends to occur around the announcement date. Lakonishok and Lev explain this by referring to an additional empirical finding: the stock dividend announcement tends to be followed by a relatively large cash dividend increase. Id. at 923–25. They conclude that stock dividends are not just small stock splits. The traditional explanation that managers consider them to be a temporary substitute for cash dividends, although unpersuasive as an economic justification for stock dividends, may be accurate. Notwithstanding this point, managers apparently believe that the market does not reduce stock prices even if cash dividends are not effectively increased upon distribution of a stock dividend. See Eiseman and Moses, Stock Dividends: Management's View, 34 Fin.Anal.J. 77 (July–August 1978); Woolridge, Ex Date Stock Price Adjustment to Stock Dividends: A Note, 38 J. Finance 247 (1983).

NOTE: STOCK DIVIDENDS AS INFORMATION AND THE REGULATION OF DISCLOSURE

The preceding discussion suggests that stock dividends are often intended to express the distributing corporation's optimistic outlook: "business is good and getting better, but we want to retain our cash assets to use for expansion." Additional shares give a kind of recognition to the fact that the company is profitable and has attractive investment opportunities on hand.

Suppose that just the opposite is true for DotBomb, Inc. Dotbomb has yet to generate a positive operating cash flow. It continues as a going concern by drawing on the proceeds of an initial public offering conducted last year. Dotbomb's business plan is not succeeding and it may not be viable once that cash runs out. Its stock price has fallen from 25 to 5. Suppose Dotbomb's board, which at least officially remains optimistic, decides to communicate its optimism and generate investor interest by declaring a series of 5 percent quarterly stock dividends. Could Dotbomb's managers thereby obscure the real state of affairs? How well, and how directly, do the regulations of the NYSE, below, deal with the assumed vice?

New York Stock Exchange, Listed Company Manual

Section 703.02 (last modified, July 1, 1998).

Stock Dividends—Many listed companies find it preferable at times to pay dividends in stock rather than cash, particularly in those cases in which a substantial part of earnings is retained by the company for use in its business. In order to guard against possible misconception by the shareowners of the effect of stock dividends on their equity in the company, and of their relation to current earnings, the Exchange has adopted certain standards of disclosure and accounting treatment.

Distinction between a Stock Dividend, a Partial Stock Split, and a Stock Split in Exchange Policy:

Stock Dividend—A distribution of less than 25% of the outstanding shares (as calculated prior to the distribution).

Partial Stock Split—A distribution of 25% or more but less than 100% of the outstanding shares (as calculated prior to the distribution).

Stock Split—A distribution of 100% or more of the outstanding shares (as calculated prior to the distribution).

Accounting Treatment—In accordance with generally accepted accounting principles, the following accounting treatment is required for the various distributions:

Stock Dividend—Capitalize retained earnings for the fair market value of the additional shares to be issued. Fair market value should closely approximate the current share market price adjusted to give effect to the distribution.

Partial Stock Split—Requires capitalization of paid-in capital (surplus) for the par or stated value of the shares issued only where there is to be no change in the par or stated value. In those circumstances where the distributions of small stock splits assume the character of stock dividends through repetition of issuance under circumstances not consistent with the intent and purpose of stock splits, the Exchange may require that such distributions be accounted for as stock dividends, i.e., capitalization of retained earnings.

Stock Split—Requires transfer from paid-in capital (surplus) for the par or stated value of the shares issued unless there is to be a change in the par or stated value.

Avoidance of the Word "Dividend"—A stock split is frequently effected by means of a distribution to shareholders upon the same authority, and in the same manner as a stock dividend. However, in order to preserve the distinction between a stock split and a stock dividend, the use of the word "dividend" should be avoided in any reference to a stock split when such a distribution does not result in the capitalization of retained earnings of the fair market value of the shares distributed. Such usage may otherwise tend to obscure the real nature of the distribution. Where legal considerations require the use of the word "dividend", the distribution should be described, for example, as a "stock split effected in the form of a stock dividend."

Notice to Shareholders with Stock Dividend Distribution—A notice should be sent to shareholders with the distribution advising them of the amount capitalized in the aggregate and per share, the relation of such aggregate amount to current earnings and retained earnings, the account or accounts to which such aggregate has been charged and credited, the reason for issuance of the stock dividend, and that sale of the dividend shares would reduce their proportionate equity in the company.

———

The SEC, in Securities Exchange Act Release No. 8268 (March 7, 1968), proposed a new rule 10b–12, which would have made a failure to follow the substance of the NYSE rule a "manipulative or deceptive device or contrivance in connection with the purchase or sale of a security within the meaning of Section 10(b)." Does the fact that the proposed Rule 10b–12 was never adopted, mean that a sequence of stock dividends not in conformity with the NYSE Rule 703.02 could not violate the securities acts' antifraud rules? Suppose a corporation's financial statements accounted for a series of four stock distributions (two of 10% and two of 25%, characterized as "stock split * * * dividends") over a period of years by transfers to capital from capital surplus, in the absence of earned surplus. Would this treatment be misleading (in violation of either Sections 11, 12 or 17 of the Securities Act of 1933 or Rule 10b–5) if it purported to follow generally accepted accounting principles? Compare Matter of Monmouth Capital Corporation, 44 S.E.C. 626 (July 14, 1971) and S.A.Rel. No. 5255 (June 1, 1972), CCH Fed.Sec.L.Rep. ¶ 72,146, suggesting that where companies do not have retained or current earnings "declaration of a dividend not warranted by the business condition of a company is characteristic of a manipulative scheme."

With the above requirements contrast the statutory provisions authorizing stock dividends to be underpinned by a transfer to capital from surplus (MBCA §§ 18, 45(d); NYBCL § 511). Do these statutes permit a transfer from capital surplus even if the corporation has earned surplus? Do these statutes prescribe the amount of the charge to either type of surplus? If a corporation has sufficient authorized, but unissued, shares, a stock dividend may in most states be declared simply by action of the board of directors, without need for a stockholders' vote (RMBCA § 6.23; NYBCL § 511; DCL §§ 170, 173).

On the other hand, a stock split may require stockholders' action as well as board action. This is because in the case of par value shares amendment of the charter will normally be required. In the case of no-par shares, a stock split may be effected by charter amendment (RMBCA §§ 10.03, 10.04; NYBCL § 801). But the same result may often be achieved by action of the board alone. Even with par value shares, so long as the charter has sufficient additional authorized shares, the board may effect what the NYSE calls a "stock split effected by a stock dividend."

NOTE: REVERSE SPLITS AND FRACTIONAL SHARES

Applebaum v. Avaya, Inc., 812 A.2d 880 (Del.Supr.2002), involved the interpretation of DCL § 155 in connection with a reverse stock split of Avaya, Inc. Avaya descended from AT & T by means of two spin offs—first the spin off of Lucent from AT & T, and second the spin off of Avaya from Lucent. One result of this was a large number of holders of less than 100 shares. Over 3.3 million common stockholders owned fewer than 90 shares of Avaya. The company accordingly incurred disproportionately large costs of maintaining shareholder accounts and printing and mailing annual disclosure and proxy documents.

The Avaya board determined to reduce the number of holders through a reverse stock split. It presented, and the stockholders approved, a proposal authorizing the board to engage in one of three alternative transactions: (1) a reverse 1–for–30 stock split followed immediately by a forward 30–for–1 stock split; (2) a reverse 1–for–40 stock split followed immediately by a forward 40–for–1 stock split; or (3) a reverse 1–for–50 stock split followed immediately by a forward 50–for–1 stock split (the "Transaction," "Proposed Transaction,"or the "Reverse/Forward Split"). The choice among the three would depend on market conditions. Whichever transaction was chosen, the Reverse Split will occur at 6:00 p.m., followed by a Forward Split one minute later.

Stockholders who did not hold the minimum number of shares necessary to survive the initial Reverse Split would be cashed out and receive payment for their resulting fractional interests. Avaya would compensate them by either combining the fractional interests and selling them as whole shares on the open market or by paying them the value of their fractional interests based on the trading price of the stock averaged over a ten-day period preceding the Reverse Split. Stockholders owning a sufficient amount of stock to survive the Reverse Split would not have their fractional interests cashed out. Once the Forward Split occurred, their fractional holdings would be converted back into whole shares of stock. Thus, assuming that Stockholder A owned 15 shares, Stockholder B owned 45 shares, and Avaya initiated a Reverse 1–for–30 Stock Split, the following would result. A would possess a fractional interest equivalent to ½ a share which would be cashed out. B would hold 1 whole share and a fractional interest equivalent to ½ a share. B would remain a stockholder—when Avaya executed the accompanying Forward 30–for–1 Stock Split, B's interest in 1½ shares would be converted into 45 shares of stock, the same amount that held prior to the Transaction.

The plaintiff, Applebaum, a holder of 27 shares, challenged the Transaction as a violation of DCL § 155, which provided as follows:

Fractions of shares. A corporation may, but shall not be required to, issue fractions of a share. If it does not issue fractions of a share, it shall (1) arrange for the disposition of fractional interests by those entitled thereto, (2) pay in cash the fair value of fractions of a share as of the time when those entitled to receive such fractions are determined or (3) issue scrip or warrants in registered form (either represented by a certificate or uncertificated) or in bearer form (represented by a certificate) which shall entitle the holder to receive a full share upon the surrender of such scrip or warrants aggregating a full share. A certificate for a fractional share or an uncertificated fractional share shall, but scrip or warrants shall not unless otherwise provided therein, entitle the holder to exercise voting rights, to receive dividends thereon and to participate in any of the assets of the corporation in the event of liquidation. The board of directors may cause scrip or warrants to be issued subject to the conditions that they shall become void if not exchanged for certificates representing the full shares or uncertificated full shares before a specified date, or subject to the conditions that the shares for which scrip or warrants are exchangeable may be sold by the corporation and the proceeds thereof distributed to the holders of scrip or warrants, or subject to any other conditions which the board of directors may impose.

The Delaware Supreme Court rejected the challenge. As to a claim based on differential treatment between those in the positions of Stockholders A and B:

"Applebaum correctly notes that Avaya stockholders are not treated equally in the Proposed Transaction. The disparate treatment, however, does not arise by issuing fractional shares selectively. It occurs through the selective disposition of some fractional interests but not others. The provisions of Section 155 do not forbid this disparate treatment. While principles of equity permit this Court to intervene when technical compliance with a statute produces an unfair result, equity and equality are not synonymous concepts in the Delaware General Corporation Law. Moreover, this Court should not create a safeguard against stockholder inequality that does not appear in the statute. Here there is no showing that Applebaum was treated inequitably."

The Transaction's provision for ex post disposition of the fractional shares on the market also passed muster:

"[The corporation has a] responsibility under Section 155(1) to 'arrange' for the disposition of fractional interests. Since fractional shares cannot be listed on the major stock exchanges, the corporation must arrange for their aggregation in order to sell them. Aggregation is normally performed by affording to the stockholder an election to sell the fractional share or to purchase an additional fraction sufficient to make up a whole share. The elections are forwarded to a trust company or other agent of the corporation who matches up the purchases and sales and issues certificates for the whole shares or checks for payment of the fractional shares.

"The general practice requires the corporation to act as an intermediary to package the fractional interests into marketable shares. If the corporation were not permitted to do so, the fractional interests of the cashed-out stockholders would be dissipated through the transaction costs of finding other fractional holders with whom to combine and sell fractional interests in the market."

Nor was the Transaction's alternative allowance of a price based on an ex ante 10–day market range objectionable:

"The corporation owes its cashed-out stockholders payment representing the 'fair value' of their fractional interests. The cashed-out stockholders will receive fair value if Avaya compensates them with payment based on the price of Avaya stock averaged over a ten-day period preceding the Proposed Transaction. While market price is not employed in all valuation contexts, our jurisprudence recognizes that in many circumstances a property interest is best valued by the amount a buyer will pay for it. The Vice Chancellor correctly concluded that a well-informed, liquid trading market will provide a measure of fair value superior to any estimate the court could impose."

Finally, section 155's requirement of a "fair price" did not implicate appraisal rights for Applebaum. The court distinguished section 155 precedents that resulted in value inquiries in reverse stock split cases involving close corporations:

"Although the Reverse/Forward Split will cash out smaller stockholders, the transaction will not allow the corporation to realize a gain at their expense. Unlike the more typical 'freeze-out' context, the cashed-out Avaya stockholders may continue to share in the value of the enterprise. Avaya stockholders can avoid the effects of the proposed transaction either by purchasing a sufficient amount of stock to survive the initial Reverse Split or by simply using the payment provided under Section 155(2) to repurchase the same amount of Avaya stock that they held before the transaction.

"The Reverse/Forward Split merely forces the stockholders to choose affirmatively to remain in the corporation. Avaya will succeed in saving administrative costs only if the board has assumed correctly that the stockholders who received a small interest in the corporation through the Lucent spin off would prefer to receive payment, free of transaction costs, rather than continue with the corporation. The Transaction is not structured to prevent the cashed-out stockholders from maintaining their stakes in the company. A payment based on market price is appropriate because it will permit the stockholders to reinvest in Avaya, should they wish to do so.

    * * *

"The valuation of a stockholder's interest as a 'going concern' is necessary only when the board's proposal will alter the nature of the corporation through a merger. * * * When a minority stockholder is confronted with a freeze-out merger, the Section 262 appraisal process will prevent the proponents of the merger from 'reaping a windfall' by placing the full value of the company as a going concern into the merged entity while compensating the dissenting stockholder with discounted consideration.

"Avaya will not capture its full going-concern value in the Reverse/Forward Split. As the Vice Chancellor noted, if the cashed-out stockholders were awarded the value of the company as a going concern, they, rather than the corporation, would receive a windfall. The cashed-out stockholders could capture the full proportionate value of the fractional interest, return to the market and buy the reissued stock at the market price, and realize the going concern value a second time should Avaya ever merge or otherwise become subject to a change of control transaction."

4. RESTRUCTURING BY DIVIDEND—SPIN OFFS AND TRACKING STOCK

American firms have a history of combination followed by unbundling. The combinations were the conglomerate mergers of the 1960s and 1970s. The unbundling began in the wake of 1980s takeovers. The story accompanying the unbundling was that conglomerate mergers had sacrificed value and that subsequent takeovers unlocked that value.

Much evidence confirms the story. Study after study shows that diversification destroys value. Berger and Ofek, Diversification's Effect on Firm Value, 37 J. Fin. Econ. 89 (1995), puts this "diversification discount" at 15 percent in a study of firms in the period 1986–1991. Confirming this finding, the market rewards firms that divest unrelated subsidiaries. See, e.g., Desai and Jain, Firm Performance and Focus: Long–Run Stock Market Performance Following Spin Offs, 54 J. Fin. Econ. 75 (1999). Subsequent performance improvements register at the divesting company. In addition, asset sales that improve the focus of the selling firm have been shown to be factor in improved operating performance over subsequent years. See John and Ofek, Asset Sales and Increase in Focus, 37 J. Fin. Econ. 105 (1995).

Why does conglomeration destroy value? According to the prevailing explanation, the value loss stems from the conglomerate firm's overinvestment in its unrelated subsidiaries—the unrelated subsidiaries underperform and must be subsidized by better performing divisions. See Berger and Ofek, Bustup Takeovers of Value–Destroying Diversified Firms, 51 J. Fin. 1175 (1996). Unbundling stops the flow of cash to poor performers. It also allows for better incentivized managers and imports transparency, facilitating monitoring by the board. The top-team's management skills also may be better suited to the firm's core assets than to the unrelated divisions.

A contrasting account looks to market pricing and finds that expected future returns of diversified firms are different from those of single purpose firms. The diversified firms' different expected returns dictate a higher discount rate. The "diversification discount" follows from the use of a higher discount rate. This accounts for the discount without reference to agency costs and governance shortcomings. See Lamont and Polk, The Diversification Discount: Cash Flows Versus Returns, 56 J. Fin. 1693 (2001). Here the problem lies in otherwise explaining the application of a higher discount rate. A showing of increased risk would suffice, but conglomerates presumably reduce risk by collecting uncorrelated cash flows. Market mispricing has been suggested accordingly. The mispricing could follow from informational shortcomings–conglomerate complexity makes the value hard to see. It also could be due to behavioral shortcomings–market price setters have an irrational aversion to complex entities. This explanation still holds out the possibility that bust up mergers or voluntary spin offs can enhance value. The difference is that the motivation is market-based rather than governance-based.

Whichever explanation one prefers, we have witnessed an era of corporate downsizing. In the 1980s, downsizing tended to occur as a consequence of highly leveraged buyouts of firms' publicly held equity interests. Downsizing continued through the 1990s, even though highly leveraged cash buyouts of equity were relatively rare during the decade beginning in 1989.

The downsizing trend's persistence after the (temporary) disappearance of leveraged restructuring followed partly from a change in the conventional wisdom respecting good business practice. Given a mature firm, a reduction in size rather than an increase in size came to signal the presence of effective managers. Reputational incentives changed accordingly. Far from having to be forced by outside pressure to make divestitures and personnel cuts, managers at many firms carried them out as a part of the business plan. In the prevailing wisdom, good managers should concentrate their energies on core businesses they know well and dispose of peripheral lines of business.

(A) SPIN OFFS

The spin off has emerged as a means commonly employed to effect conglomerate unbundling. A spin off entails a parent corporation's divestiture of a subsidiary through the declaration of a dividend of the subsidiary's common stock to its shareholders. If the parent's stock is publicly held, the spin off results in two publicly held firms, the ownership groups of which begin in identity but differentiate themselves over time as ownership turns over through stock trading. The volume of spin off activity increased in the 1990s. Famous firms such as AT & T, ITT, General Motors, Pepsico, Sears Roebuck, Viacom, and Westinghouse made use of the device. According to a 1995 J.P. Morgan study, spin offs resulted in the appearance of 112 new concerns appeared between 1992 and 1995. Furthermore, says the study (looking at 77 spin offs conducted between 1985 and 1995), the spun off companies outperformed the market by an average of 20 percent during their first 18 months. In addition, the parent companies outperformed the market by 5 to 6 percent during the period between the announcement and the spin off.

Explanations of the spin off phenomenon focus on two points. The first is the changing management incentive picture. In the present environment, it is a rise in the stock price rather than an increase in the size of the firm that enhances the reputation of the CEO. More tangibly, many corporate incentive compensation schemes have been revised to depend more closely on stock price performance. See infra, Section B. Furthermore, in the standard fact pattern, the spun off company is a laggard performer and its divestiture tends to follow or accompany a program of management retrenchment and job reduction. Either way, the responsible CEO is rid of a problem. The second explanation concerns tax effects. Spin offs hold out a tax advantage over other forms of divestiture. With the repeal of the General Utilities Doctrine, the spin off has emerged as the only way that a corporation can divest assets and avoid incurring capital gains tax. Under § 355 of the Internal Revenue Code, a spin off will be tax free to both the corporation and its shareholders if, among other things, it is for a valid business purpose and includes 80 percent of the common stock of a subsidiary owned for at least five years. Firms contemplating spin offs customarily condition consummation on the procurance of a ruling from the Internal Revenue Service as to the transaction's tax-free status.

A *caveat* also must be entered. The announcement and consummation of a spin off can trigger new problems. Unsurprisingly, if a spun off company is deemed to be weak, then its stock can be expected to decline. Indeed, the withdrawal of the support of free cash flow from other companies within a conglomerate may give rise to unforeseen problems for newly independent components, as occurred with pieces of ATT and ITT after unbundling.

(B) TRACKING STOCK

Some firms claim to have unlocked some (if not all) of the shareholder value accessible through a spin off through the creation of "tracking stock" (also called "letter" or "target" stock). Tracking stock is a class of common stock that is linked in the charter to the earnings and cash flows of a particular division or subsidiary of the issuer. Tracking stock schemes include the production of new financial reports keyed the performances of the divisions tracked, facilitating separate analysis of each. The idea follows from the line of economics that looks to market mispricing to explain the conglomerate discount. It is thought that linking different classes of the issuer's stock to the performance of its different subdivisions makes the issuer's operations more transparent to the outside investor, unlocking equity value that formerly was invisible.

Unlike a spin off, a tracking stock scheme does not entail the declaration of a dividend of the shares of an existing subsidiary. Instead, the issuer carves out a new class of its own common by means of a charter amendment; a stock dividend of the new class follows the adoption of the amendment.

Tracking stock charter provisions tend to be minimal in their definition of tracking stockholder rights. As to dividends, they describe only an upper limit—a maximum "available dividend amount" defined by reference to what the state legal capital rules would allow to be distributed if the tracking stock were issued by a stand-alone firm. The practical result appears to be that the issuer's board retains discretion over both the tracking stock dividend stream and the division of dividend flows between the tracking stock and the issuer's other class (or classes) of common. Tracking stock liquidation rights tend to be defined in terms of the relative market capitalizations of the different classes of the firm's stock at the time of the liquidation. Unequal voting rights also are common—one class receives a fixed number of votes per share, while the voting rights of the other class or classes fluctuate depending on the relative market capitalizations of the classes. Might the market values of the different classes be open to manipulation under such a scheme? See Hass, Directorial Fiduciary Duties in a Tracking Stock Equity Structure: The Need for a Duty of Fairness, 94 Mich. L. Rev. 2089 (1996).

Hass, supra, at 2105–07, offers the following summary of the investment banking community's description of the advantages of tracking stock schemes:

"Use of tracking stocks in an attempt to unlock stockholder value is thought to be particularly expedient with respect to a diversified parent corporation that is operating one or more growth businesses, on the one hand, and one or more declining, out-of-favor or even stable (yet financially uninspiring) businesses, on the other hand. The belief of such a corporation—often sparked, fueled and fanned by its investment bankers—is that the marketplace is simply failing to understand and fully appreciate (and thus value) all the businesses operated by that diversified corporation. Accordingly, in determining the trading value of that corporation's conventional common stock, the financial community is placing too much weight on declining businesses operated by the corporation and not enough on the growth businesses. The net effect of the financial community's naivete is its undervaluation of the corporation as a while.

" * * * The belief (and hope) of a corporation implementing a tracking stock equity structure is that the financial marketplace will value shares of each class of tracking stock as if they were shares of a stand alone corporation primarily engaging in the business of the particular business group to which such class is linked. Once these stocks begin trading like stocks of separate, stand-alone corporations, it is anticipated that the combined trading value of the two tracking stocks will be greater than that of the former conventional common stock. Or so the theory goes."

Would you expect market practice to bear out the theory's prediction? If the parts are worth more than the whole, where does that increased value come from? Could an equivalent increase be effected without a tracking stock scheme simply through the adoption of a more transparent scheme of financial reporting?

There was a short-lived craze in 1999–2000 in which "old economy" companies which had developed a "dot com" or other high technology division floated a tracking stock for the division so as to get the benefit in the run up of stock prices for "new economy" companies. Even so, some institutional shareholders were unenthusiastic about tracking stock recapitalizations. Because management retained legal control over the whole (and, presumably, the bondholders retained their claim on the whole), tracking stock traded at a discount from the value that could be realized through a full-scale spin off. A study released in 1999 confirmed the negative view. The study looked at all tracking stocks for a three-year period ending in 1998 and found negative excess returns. The study showed no boost for the parent company stocks either. Nor, finally, did the purported heightened transparency result in more accurate predictions by analysts of tracking stock companies. McGough, Tracking Stocks Fail to Justify Their Buzz, Wall St. J., April 25, 2000, p. C1. There are conflicting studies, however.

In any event, the tracking stock craze ended after 2000. Since then, many tracking stock issuers have reverted to conventional capital structures.

5. Repurchase of Outstanding Shares

(A) THE ECONOMICS OF SHARE REPURCHASES

(1) Repurchase Transactions

Dividends are not the only way to distribute excess cash to shareholders. A corporation can, in the alternative, repurchase its own shares. Once repurchased, shares may be placed in the corporation's "treasury," an accounting zone where they are authorized and issued but no longer outstanding. Treasury shares may be reissued. Alternatively, reacquired shares may be retired, at which point they remain authorized by the charter but are neither issued nor outstanding. Some minor differences in accounting treatment attend the choice between treasury status and retirement.

There are three types of transactions pursuant to which shares may be repurchased:

• **Open market repurchase (OMR).** The corporation announces an intention to repurchase its shares in the open market, usually (1) stating a time period in over which it intends to act as a buyer, (2) stating a ballpark number of shares that it expects to repurchase, and (3) qualifying the foregoing statements by stating that the number of shares actually repurchased will depend on market conditions. Time periods for open market repurchase programs tend to be long, ranging from several months to several years. The average percentage of shares targeted is 6.6 percent. Ikenberry, Lakonishok and Vermaelen, Market Underreaction to Open Market Share Repurchases, 39 J. Fin. Econ. 181, 185 (1995).

• **Repurchase tender offer (RTO).** The corporation makes a public offer to its shareholders to repurchase a set number of shares at a premium over the market price, usually 15 to 20 percent. The shareholders decide whether or not to tender into the offer. The time period is short—under the rules under 1934 Act § 13(e), the offer must be held open for at least 20 business days. The amount of shares repurchased averages at around 15 percent of the number outstanding. Vafeas, Determinants of the Choice between Alternative Share Repurchase Methods, 12 J. Acct. Auditing & Fin. 101 (1997).

Today, most RTOs are structured as "Dutch auctions." Under this procedure, the corporation, instead of announcing one price, announces a series of prices at which it is willing to repurchase shares. Shareholders interested in selling then submit offers stating the number of shares they desire to sell at each of the stated prices. The corporation, having collected the offers, calculates the lowest single price that yields the number of shares it desires to repurchase, and accepts at that price the offers made at that price and all lower prices.

The Dutch auction mode has emerged as the dominant RTO practice because it tends to yield a lower overall purchase price. Fried, Insider Signaling and Insider Trading with Repurchase Tender Offers, 67 U. Chi. L. Rev. 421, 431–32 (2000), illustrates why: "ABC Corp. offers to repurchase 100 of its 200 shares for any price between $9 and $10. Fifty shares are tendered at $9, 50 shares are tendered at $9.50, and 50 shares are tendered at $10. ABC purchases 100 shares for $9.50. In a fixed price RTO at $10, ABC would attract 150 shares, and repurchase 100 for $10 each. Thus ABC Corp. would spend $50 (100x$.50) more repurchasing the shares through the fixed price RTO."

• **Directly negotiated repurchase.** The corporation negotiates in private to repurchase all or part of the shares held by one more shareholders. As a practical matter, the selling shareholder will hold a large block of stock, and the negotiated price will be at a premium over the market price. One subset of this type of repurchase is "greenmail," where the seller accumulates the block in the open market and threatens a takeover; the issuer then repurchases the block at a premium to defuse the takeover threat.

(2) *Theoretical Irrelevance Between Dividends and Repurchases*

In theory, assuming perfect markets and no taxation, it makes no difference to the value of the firm to its shareholders whether the firm chooses to distribute a stated amount of funds as a dividend or distribute the funds by means of a share repurchase. Of course, with a repurchase a distinction does open up within the firm's group of shareholders. With a dividend, each is treated *pro rata*. With a share repurchase, the shareholders emerge in two groups—those who have chosen to sell and take the cash and those who have chosen to hold and receive no cash. But, in theory (and given the above assumptions), no economic discrimination obtains as between the two groups.

To see this, consider two hypothetical firms, Corporation D and Corporation R. At t=0 Corporation D and Corporation R are identical in all respects. They operate the same business in adjoining identical markets and do not compete with one another. Each has 1,000,000 common shares outstanding and no debt. All shareholders of both firms have identical preferences and are fully informed.

Each firm will produce $10,000,000 of net cash flows per year indefinitely. Neither firm will ever grow. The $10,000,000 cash flow is net of all amounts necessary to keep the corporation's production function fully operational and competitive. The market requires a 10 percent rate of return for the common stock of both corporations.

Corporation D will pay out all of its net cash flows as dividends at the end of each year. Given the above assumptions, the value of a share of Corporation D common at t=0, the beginning of Year 1, is easily calculated as follows:

$10,000,000 ÷ 1,000,000 shares = $10 annual dividend per share

$$PV_{D\ share} = \frac{d}{k-g} = \frac{\$10}{.10-0} = \$100$$

The total market value of Corporation D's equity is $100 x 1,000,000 shares = $100,000,000.

At t=0 Corporation R breaks ranks with Corporation D and announces that in Year 1 it will pay no dividend. Instead, at the end of Year 1 it will take its annual net cash flow of $10,000,000 and devote it to an OMR of its shares. In all years thereafter, Corporation R will pay out its net cash flow in the form of a dividend.

What is the value of a share of Corporation R common at t=0? Looking forward, the total present equity value of Corporation R is the sum of the present value of the two pies into which Corporation R will be splitting its equity at the end of Year 1:

Repurchase Pie: $10,000,000 in one year at 10 percent

PV_{RP} = $10,000,000 ÷ 1.1 [Future Value factor for 1 year at 10 percent from Table 11–2, supra]

PV_{RP} = $9,090,909

Holder Pie: $10,000,000 perpetuity beginning at end Year 2 at 10 percent

PV_{HP} = $10,000,000 ÷ .10 ÷ 1.1

PV_{HP} = ($10,000,000 ÷ .10 = $100,000,000) ÷ 1.1 = $90,909,091

The whole is equal to the sum of the parts:

PV_R = $9,090,909 + $90,909,091 = $100,000,000

Since the PV of Corporation R's equity is $100,000,000, given 1,000,000 shares outstanding,

$$PV_{R\ share} = \$100 = PV_{D\ share}$$

At t=0, then, the repurchase announcement creates no divergence in the value of the two firms.

But exactly what is going to happen to the value of a Corporation R share when the $10,000,000 is used to repurchase shares at the end of Year 1 and how is equality then maintained between (a) the value of the equity of Corporations D and R, and (b) the selling and holding shareholders of R?

The answer to these questions depends on the number of shares Corporation R will be able to repurchase with its pot of $10,000,000 at the end of Year 1. Since we are assuming that all of Corporation R's shareholders have identical preferences and expectations, including a 10 percent required annual return on their investment, the number is ascertainable. Selling R shareholders will require a 10 percent return for Year 1, assuming a $100 investment at t=0. Accordingly, Corporation R shareholders will sell for $110 per share.

Corporation R repurchases as follows:

$10,000,000 ÷ $110 = 90,910 shares (rounding up one fractional share)

What is the per share value of the 909,090 shares remaining outstanding?

Since there will be fewer shares splitting the same $10,000,000 pie, the value of a holding share will rise—but only once the repurchase is concluded at the end of Year 1:

$10,000,000 ÷ 909,090 = $11 annual dividend per share

$$V_{\text{H share end Year 1}} = \$11 \div .10 = \$110$$

The value of a holding share of Corporation R at t=0 is of course lower. Given a 10 percent rate of return:

$$PV_{\text{H share}} = \$110 \div 1.1 = \$100$$

To sum up, given the assumptions, all shareholders of Corporation D and Corporation R are in exactly the same present value situation whether or not their firm is making a dividend or a repurchase and whether or not the shareholder is selling or holding. The foregoing presentation adapts numbers set out in Brealey and Myers, Principles of Corporate Finance 449–452 (6th ed. 2000).

(3) Agency Costs and Information Asymmetries

As with our foregoing encounters with irrelevance hypotheses, we must caution that the irrelevance result follows from heroic assumptions. As we relax the assumptions, possibilities arise for value differentials and for unequal results. For example, if Corporation R does a privately negotiated repurchase at a premium from an insider shareholder, we have a wealth transfer from the nonselling shareholders to the seller. The opposite result obtains if Corporation R's management has inside information of an upside result and repurchases before the information is known to the public. Note also that, given the signaling effect of dividend policy, Corporation R might have some trouble at the time of its repurchase announcement at t=0, since the repurchase means cutting the dividend. If the market reacts to the information by increasing the required return on R's stock, then Corporation D's equity emerges (at least temporarily) with a higher value than that of Corporation R.

(4) Taxation

Tax differentials also loom large as we relax assumptions. Traditionally, dividends are taxed as ordinary income, while repurchases trigger a capital gains tax on the selling shareholders at a lower rate. Corporation D's Year 1 dividend payout of $10,000,000 is taxed to the shareholder group as a whole at ordinary income rates, with the top rate currently varying between 38.6 percent and 35 percent. Corporation R's Year 1 repurchase triggers capital gains tax to the selling shareholders at the difference between their tax bases and yield on sale. To the extent the selling shareholders have held for a long term, they pay this tax at the capital gains rate, which currently tops out at 20 percent. Looking at aggregate tax payments and assuming no tax free shareholders, all payments at the top rate, and all long term holds, the dividend triggers a transfer of $3,960,000 to the IRS where the repurchase triggers a transfer of $2,000,000. An open market repurchase program accordingly holds out a tax benefit when compared to a regular dividend. Persistent shareholder demand for a steady dividend stream in the teeth of this rate differential is a principal component of the dividend "puzzle."

The Jobs and Growth Tax Relief Reconciliation Act of 2003 (the "JGTRRA") temporarily aligns tax rates on shareholder capital gains and dividend income at a maximum 15 percent, departing from the classical rate preference for capital gains and ameliorating the tax system's long-standing bias against dividends. The JGTRRA changes the tax ramifications of a firm's choice between dividends and repurchases without completely denuding repurchases of their tax benefit. On the face of it, D's year 1 dividend triggers a shareholder tax of $1,500,000 and R's repurchase triggers a capital gains transfer of $1,500,000. This rate parity does not imply equal tax payments for all, however. To the extent the shareholders selling into the repurchase have bases higher than zero, they pay less than 15 percent in capital gains tax with respect to the proceeds of their sales. In addition, the nonselling shareholders at R benefit from a tax deferral on the $10–per-share rise in the value of the stock. The value of the deferral declines with the tax rate, but remains cognizable regardless.

NOTE: REPURCHASES—VOLUME AND STATED PURPOSE

1. *Rising Volume.*

Increasing employment of open market stock repurchase programs has been one the most significant trends in corporate finance during the past two decades. Jagannathan, Stephens and Weisbach, Financial Flexibility and the Choice between Dividends and Stock Repurchases, 57 J. Fin. Econ. 355, 356–57 (2000), reports that between 1985 and 1996 "the number of open market repurchase program announcements by U.S. industrial firms has increased 750% from $15.4 billion to $113 billion. Correspondingly, dividends have only risen by a factor of just over two during the same period; aggregate dividends for all industrial firms listed on Compustat have risen from $67.6 billion to $141.7 billion. Repurchases are clearly an increasingly important method of paying out cash to shareholders." In addition, over the period 1985 to 1996, "aggregate actual share repurchases by industrial firms total between $249 billion and $339 billion. This corresponds to 53 to 72% of announced repurchase levels and 20 to 27% of aggregate dividends. * * * Overall, repurchases have not replaced dividends as the primary payout vehicle. Even in 1996, which was the largest year for repurchases in this sample, dividends amounted to more than double the total actual share repurchases and 126% of the total announced share repurchases. Firms are still generally increasing dividends every year; the fact that they are doing so and not increasing repurchases even faster suggests that there is still a dividend puzzle."

The repurchase tide continues to rise. In the first quarter of 2007, firms in the S & P 500 bought back shares worth a record $117.1 billion, an increase of 17.5 percent over the previous year.

2. *Flexibility—Repurchases Versus Dividends.*

How can we explain the changing payout pattern? Recall Fama and French's finding, supra, that dividend payers and repurchasers are for the most part the same set of firms. The more particular question, then, concerns an increasing tendency to supplement dividend payouts with repurchases. Jagannathan, Stephens, and Weisbach, supra, conclude that the emerging payout pattern follows from the traditional wisdom about dividends described by Lintner, supra. That is, managers avoid cutting dividends; therefore, they increase dividends only when they perceive the increase to be backed by a stable cash flow. Since dividends represent a permanent commitment, they are made from what management views as permanent, reliable cash flows. Repurchase is the mode favored for cash flows management views as temporary. Repurchases imply no future commitment and thus preserve financial flexibility. Where a given firm's dividend payout pattern is smooth, aggregate repurchases tend to be volatile. They are sensitive to the business cycle, rising disproportionately during booms and declining drastically during recessions. Guay and Harford, The Cash–Flow Permanence and Information Content of Dividend Increases Versus Repurchases, 57 J. Fin. Econ. 385 (2000), confirms this picture, and adds a point about signaling effects—investors will note whether the cash is paid out by dividend or repurchase and accordingly adjust their estimate of the permanence of the firm's cash flows.

3. *Management Motivations.*

Given the above, why did repurchase activity increase so markedly in the late 1980s and 1990s? Presumably, earlier managers also had to grapple with permanent and temporary cash flows. The key to an answer probably lies in the fact that the recent increase in OMRs is incremental—in addition to dividends. Before the mid 1980s, firms were less likely to distribute this additional, temporary cash and instead reinvested it. We thus can ascribe a causative role to the 1980s restructuring movement and emergent managerial notions of shareholder value enhancement. The pattern of stepped up payouts also suggests a concomitant decrease in $r<k$ investment (at least among firms making payouts).

The foregoing answer is not fully satisfactory, however. "Shareholder value enhancement" surely is a key management concern today. But it does not taken alone provide a basis for a credible account of a financial development as significant as this one. One suspects there may be something more in this for management than the satisfaction of transferring wealth to its investors in a mode holding out tax advantages. More fully to explain the increasing prominence of repurchases in more recent years, especially OMRs, we must make reference to three additional aspects of repurchases.

● **Stock price undervaluation.** The conventional wisdom holds that repurchase announcements credibly signal management's view that its stock is undervalued. A simple press release stating that management believes its stock to be undervalued is of course not credible. To repurchase the stock, in contrast, is to incur the cost of investing in the stock. It should follow that shares of firms with OMR programs outperform the market. This story is a bit counterintuitive, since repurchasing firms tend to be the established, large capital firms whose shares are the least likely to be mispriced in the market. Vermaelen, Common Stock Repurchases and Market Signaling: An Empirical Study, 9 J. Fin. Econ. 139 (1981). But there is empirical support for the story in the finding that repurchases are negatively correlated with antecedent stock returns. Stephens and Weisbach, Actual

Share Reacquisitions in Open–Market Purchase Programs, 53 J. Fin. 313 (1998). There also is a well-documented tendency for the stock price to rise around 3 to 3.5 percent in response to the announcement. Ikenberry, Lakonishok and Vermaelen, Market Underreaction to Open Market Share Repurchases, 39 J. Fin. Econ. 181 (1995), shows positive abnormal returns for the four years *after* the repurchase program announcement, especially for firms with a low ratio of market-to-book value.

Note, however, that the announcement of an OMR program does not commit management to purchase any shares. A corporate repurchase "announcement" does not necessarily embody an accurate near-term projection of management conduct respecting inflows and outflows of stock from the corporate treasury. There can be a considerable time lag between the announcement of an intention to repurchase and the actual completion of the program. For example, the programs of $176 billion "announced" in 1996 compared with a 1996 total of "completed" programs $30.8 billion. Indeed, Stephens and Weisbach, supra, at 314, report that a substantial number of firms making such announcements in fact do not repurchase a single share. On the other hand, the volume of repurchases announced and the volume of repurchases consummated tend to get closer over time. Over the eight years from 1989 to 1996, 85 percent of announced repurchases were completed.

The discrepancy between announced volume and consummated repurchases detracts from the credibility of the signal. Compare a repurchase tender offer (RTO), which has a short timetable and, under section 13 of the 1934 Act, entails a commitment to purchase. It accordingly sends a stronger signal, particularly when the firm's insiders commit not to tender into the offer. The studies show an 8 percent stock rise connected to RTOs, compared to 3.5 percent with open market repurchases. Fried, supra, at 444. D'Mello and Shroff, Equity Undervaluation and Decisions Related to Repurchase Tender Offers: An Empirical Investigation, 50 J. Fin. 2399 (2000), takes a retrospective look at a group of firms that conducted RTOs and finds that the stock of 74 percent in fact was underpriced on the market.

● **Leverage Ratio Adjustment.** Distribution of funds by repurchase, like a distribution of funds by dividend, will effect the firm's capital structure, all other things being equal. More particularly, a repurchase reduces the firm's equity capitalization and increases its debt-to-equity ratio. Firms whose debt-to-equity ratios are below their target levels accordingly are more likely to repurchase stock. See Dittmar, Why Do Firms Repurchase Stock? 73 J. Bus. 331 335 (2000). The larger the proportion of stock repurchased, the more the repurchase program resembles a high leverage restructuring. With high leverage, the effect is to transfer wealth from existing creditors to the firm's equityholders.

● **Stock Price Dilution and Management Stock Options.** The recent rise in repurchase activity has occurred in tandem with an increase in the use of the stock option as a form of management compensation. The correlation admits of a positive interpretation. Stock compensation is supposed to align management incentives with those of the shareholders, and, as noted above, an increase in repurchases implies a decrease in reinvestment of earnings in $r<k$ projects. By implication, the new distribution pattern follows from the realigned incentives.

But there is an alternative, darker interpretation. The value of an option is negatively related to the level of future dividend payments: Recall from the chapter on convertible securities that as between retention (even where $r<k$) and payment as a dividend the dividend payment detracts from the value of an option because the optionholder does not share in the dividend. Repurchases, in contrast, provide a way for a firm to distribute cash without diluting the per share value of its stock and thereby injuring its optionholders relative to its shareholders. The stock price

preservation effect (indeed, the above-mentioned stock price enhancement effect) thus makes the choice of a repurchase over a dividend particularly attractive to a manager holding a significant amount of stock options. At the same the time, the return of repurchased stock to the treasury provides an inventory for issue upon exercise of the stock options. To the extent a repurchase program brings in a number of shares equal to the number under option, EPS remains the same net of the option exercises and the options cause no overall dilution in the value of the stock.

Note an additional negative implication: to the extent managers exercising stock options hew to a firm target respecting reduction in the number of shares outstanding, they would proceed with repurchases despite a conviction that the market overvalues the stock being repurchased. Such repurchases benefit the exiting shareholders at the expense of the shareholders remaining.

For empirical studies showing that the probability of stock repurchase is positively correlated with stock options and the probability of a dividend strongly negatively correlated, see Jolls, The Role of Compensation in Explaining the Stock–Repurchase Puzzle (Harvard Law School Working Paper 1998); Fenn and Liang, Corporate Payout Policy and Managerial Stock Incentives, 60 J. Fin. Econ. 45 (2001). Aggregate numbers respecting shares issued also support this assertion. The firms making up the Standard & Poor's 500 were net issuers of shares in nine of the ten years 1987 through 1996. Although in 1996 these firms bought back 1 billion shares, they more than made up by issuing 2.9 billion shares (exclusive of shares issued in acquisitions).

(B) REPURCHASES—FIDUCIARY AND DISCLOSURE OBLIGATIONS

(1) *The Scope of the Problem*

Although at one time there was a question whether the corporation had power (in the sense of intra vires) to repurchase its stock, corporate codes in the United States fairly uniformly vest such power in the corporation. (Corporations still lack the power in some other countries. The trend abroad, as seen in countries like Britain and Japan, is to amend the corporations statute to permit repurchases.) However, because a repurchase is economically a distribution of assets to stockholders, restrictions comparable to those that apply to payment of dividends apply to repurchase—both contractual (in the corporate charter or debt instruments) and statutory. See NYBCL §§ 513–516, 719; Del.Corp.Law §§ 160, 172, 174, 243. The questions raised by those restrictions are of some significance for close corporations, but do not often arise in the case of large publicly held enterprises.

Legal questions respecting the repurchases by large firms stem from the fact that, unlike dividends, they do not put income *pro rata* into the hands of stockholders. This creates a potential for both unequal treatment of stockholders and concealment of information. Repurchases accordingly give rise to a variety of interrelated problems of substantive fairness, process, and disclosure. The severity of the problem varies with the process context—privately negotiated repurchase, RTO, or OMR.

Privately negotiated repurchases carry a particularly high risk of abuse by virtue of overpayment for the stock repurchased. These transactions are by definition "side deals" effected between managers and favored shareholders. The selling shareholders may be "bailing out." Alternatively, management may be purchasing at a premium above market solely to preserve its control and access to perquisites.

Repurchase tender offers carry a diminished risk of abuse because they are more transparent and open to the shareholder group as a whole. Moreover, 80 percent of RTOs do not involve defense against a pending or threatened hostile tender offer. Yet there is still cause for concern. Professor Jesse Fried sees reason for suspicion in the comparison between RTOs and OMRs. Repurchasing firms have a choice between the two. An OMR holds out greater flexibility, lower transaction costs, and diminished regulatory risk. Why then would a firm mount an RTO? Fried argues that the signaling explanation for RTOs, described above, cannot be taken as complete. If the firm's stock really were worth more than the offer price, no one would tender into RTOs and the stock price response to the announcement of an RTO would be higher than the 8 percent average reported. The key to explaining why firms choose RTOs, he asserts, lies in the fact the managers own shares for their own accounts: "[B]y conducting an RTO with a repurchase price below the stock's actual value, and not tendering, insiders can indirectly buy the public's shares at a low price. And by conducting an RTO with a repurchase price above the actual value, and tendering, insiders can indirectly sell their stock to the nontendering public at a high price. * * * [I]nsiders can achieve substantially the same result as tendering by selling their stock in the market after the RTO is announced." See Fried, Insider Trading With Repurchase Tender Offers, 67 U. Chi. L. Rev. 421, 453 (2000).

OMRs arguably present a lower risk of abuse. The risk of over- or underpayment remains, but the problem is ameliorated by use of the trading market to set the price. The selling shareholder still could have cause to complain of a low price—transparency is far from complete and the repurchasing firm has a clear information advantage. But the practice of making an antecedent public announcement of the OMR program at least puts the seller on notice of the repurchasing firm's presence in the market. The firm's view that the stock is underpriced is implicit in the notice. The seller, moreover, is uncoerced. The remaining, nonselling shareholders also could have cause to complain, in cases where the repurchases turn out to be high priced. A management overly zealous to repurchase could choose an inopportune time, or divert capital away from $r>k$ investments. As noted above, the excess of zeal might stem from a perceived need to husband shares for issue in connection with its own overly-generous stock option plan. But, at least arguably, the place for diagnosis and cure may be the stock option plan rather than the OMR program. At least management is holding equity in the firm in some form, and any dissatisfied shareholders are free to sell into a market buoyed by the repurchases. It also has been argued that management's informational advantage imports an economic justification for OMRs. The corporation's bargain purchase drives the market price in the correct direction. See Stewart, Should a Corporation Repurchase Its Own Stock? 31 J.Fin. 911 (1976).

Despite the foregoing, OMRs prompt serious substantive questions. Would management's incentives be better aligned if it distributed all excess cash by dividend? Do considerations of fairness bear in favor of the *pro rata* mode of distribution? If the market undervalues the stock, and even given the fullest permissible disclosure the market still evaluates the stock at less than management does, is it proper for management (even assuming no interest in private benefits) to use corporate assets to favor one set of stockholders (the non-sellers) over another (the sellers) by causing the corporation to make a "bargain" purchase on the market? If market efficiency is enhanced thereby, does that result come at the cost of behavior that is not consonant with fairness norms? If repurchase thus results in favoring one group of stockholders over another, does the fact that management often purchases corporate stock for itself at bargain prices prior to announcing an OMR further complicate the problem? See Lee, Mikkelson and Partch, Managers' Trading Around Stock Repurchases, 47 J. Fin. 1947 (1992).

(2) *Fiduciary Duties*

Kahn v. United States Sugar Corporation

Delaware Court of Chancery, 1985.
1985 WL 4449.

■ HARTNETT, VICE CHANCELLOR.

This suit was brought as a class action challenging a leveraged cash tender offer made by United States Sugar Corporation ("U.S. Sugar") and a trust existing under its Employee Stock Ownership Plan (the "ESOP") to the corporation's stockholders. It was commenced in September of 1983 and on October 18, 1983, an application for a preliminary injunction enjoining the consummation of the offer was denied. * * *

I find from all the properly admissible evidence that there was a breach of fiduciary duty by the defendants because the disclosures made in the tender offer solicitation materials did not disclose with complete candor all the material facts a stockholder needed to make a fully informed decision as to whether to accept the tender offer. I also conclude that the tender offer was coercive. I further find that it would be impossible to rescind the transaction and that, therefore, an award of damages is the only possible remedy. I find that the amount of damages is $4 per share.

I

* * * The named plaintiffs represent the class of minority, public shareholders of U.S. Sugar who tendered their shares in response to the tender offer by U.S. Sugar and the ESOP. Defendants are U.S. Sugar, the ESOP, and the members of the Board of Directors of U.S. Sugar.

At the time of the tender offer U.S. Sugar was a public company with almost 5 million shares outstanding and its shares were held of record by more than 2,000 shareholders. The shares traded on the over-the-counter market, but only 28% of the outstanding shares were held by the public.

The other 72% were owned either by charitable organizations established by Charles Stewart Mott, the founder of U.S. Sugar, or by members of the Mott family (collectively, the "Mott Interests"). The Board of Directors consisted of 14 persons of whom eight were either members of the Mott family or trustees of Mott charities or family trusts. Three were part of management.

* * *

The tender offer came about because the Mott Interests wished to reduce their holdings in U.S. Sugar but did not wish to relinquish their aggregated ability to exercise majority control over the company. The market price for U.S. Sugar stock was already considered to be depressed due to the world sugar glut and the sale of a substantial block of stock would have likely depressed it still further: It was therefore decided that a leveraged tender offer for 75% of the outstanding shares (over 3.5 million shares) was the best means of facilitating the wishes of the Mott Interests, while not depressing the market. Additionally, this tender offer would allow public shareholders to share in the tender offer and thus take advantage of a premium above market price.

Because the Mott Interests planned to tender a substantial number of shares while still retaining majority control, they had competing desires to both receive the highest possible tender offer price and still leave U.S. Sugar as a viable company not unduly burdened with debt. It is asserted by the defendants that these competing interests would tend to assure that those public shareholders who tendered their shares in response to the tender offer would receive as high a price as feasible for their shares, while also assuring that shareholders who did not choose to tender would not be locked into an overburdened corporation. Be that as it may, although more than 93% of the publicly held shares were tendered, more than 42% of the 2,000 shareholders chose not to be completely cashed out but elected to retain some portion of their holdings.

The ESOP was formed as a part of the tender offer plan. It purchased over one million shares at $68 per share with funds borrowed from U.S. Sugar. It was planned that the ESOP would repay U.S. Sugar from the annual tax deductible contributions made to the ESOP by the company.

There being no independent directors on U.S. Sugar's Board, no independent committee of directors could be appointed to review the tender offer and to negotiate on behalf of the public shareholders. However, the existence of the conflicts of interest was disclosed in the tender offer statement.

The tender offer was not intended to be merely the first step of a two-step elimination of public shareholders because those shareholders who did not tender their shares were not to be cashed out in a merger following the tender offer. A substantial number of shares are presently outstanding and held by public shareholders, and there continues to be a market for the trading of U.S. Sugar shares, although it has been trading at a lesser price than it did before the tender offer.

Prior to the challenged transaction, U.S. Sugar was virtually debt free. Chemical Bank, the corporation's traditional bank, was approached and was requested to advance $300 million, $250 million of which was to be used to finance the tender offer while the remaining $50 million would be used for working capital. Chemical Bank determined that U.S. Sugar would generate sufficient cash flow to service such a loan and that its assets would be sufficient to repay the loan in the event a foreclosure became necessary. Using conservative projections as to sugar yields, number of acres planted, etc., it also decided that sufficient cash would be generated to service the debt. The bank further determined that on a "worse case" basis, assuming a foreclosure sale, the assets would be worth at least $369 million (approximately $75 per share.) Chemical Bank, for its loan purposes, concluded that the current market value of U.S. Sugar's assets indicated a real net worth of more than $400 million (more than $80 per share). The replacement cost of U.S. Sugar's assets was estimated by the corporation in 1983 to be over $631 million ($130 per share).

Plaintiffs assert that U.S. Sugar's management disregarded information it had as to the value of its assets and instead arrived at the proposed tender offer price by considering only the price range which could be paid off by a projected cash flow over ten years. This range was $60 to $70 per share.

While consideration of the tender offer price range was still taking place, U.S. Sugar retained First Boston Corporation ("First Boston") to render a fairness opinion on the offering price. It was paid $650,000 for its three weeks of work. Initially First Boston was only informed of the range being considered for the tender offer by the corporation and was not informed of the actual tender offer price of $68 until the Friday before it delivered its opinion on Tuesday, September 13, 1983. In the fairness opinion issued by First Boston it opined that the $68 per share was fair to the public shareholders from a financial point of view.

First Boston was originally engaged to represent the public shareholders, as well as to give an opinion as to fairness. Its representative role was never carried out; it was not asked to recommend an independently arrived at fair price; it did not engage in any negotiations over the offering price with U.S. Sugar; it did not consult with any representatives of the minority shareholders; nor did it solicit outside offers to purchase.

Bear, Stearns & Co. ("Bear, Stearns") was retained to represent the ESOP and U.S. Sugar. It was asked to opine that the price to be offered in the tender offer was reasonable to the ESOP. It was also asked to determine whether after the proposed transaction the fair market value of U.S. Sugar's assets would exceed its liabilities by at least $50 million.

The determination that the corporation's assets had a fair market value which would exceed liabilities by at least $50 million after the tender offer was completed was necessary to allow the Board to make a finding that U.S. Sugar's capital would not be impaired, a finding required by Delaware law. This determination was called for because the distribution to be made under the tender offer would be greater than the net book value of the corporation's assets.

Bear, Stearns did negotiate on behalf of the ESOP. It was responsible for the setting of the offering price at $68 rather than $70 which the officers of U.S. Sugar had originally determined should be the offering price. The $68 price followed Bear, Stearns' decision that the fair price range was between $62 and $68 per share and that any higher price would be unfair to the ESOP.

The Offer to Purchase ("Tender Offering Statement") was sent to the stockholders by U.S. Sugar and the ESOP about September 20, 1983. In response, 1,288,210 shares were tendered by public stockholders. Of the then outstanding publicly held shares only 89,108 were not tendered.

While a different plan might have achieved the objectives of the Mott Interests without involving the public stockholders, I find that the tender offer, as made, required substantial acceptance by the public stockholders if the objectives of the majority stockholders were to be achieved.

II

Plaintiffs contend that the Tender Offering Statement was misleading or coercive and concealed or buried facts [including internal studies of the company's asset value and valuations by First Boston and Bear, Stearns] which, if disclosed, might have led stockholders to conclude that the $68 price was inadequate * * *.

Plaintiffs also assert that the Tender Offering Statement contained disclosures which created the impression that U.S. Sugar's management had arrived at the $68 price based mainly upon the independent valuation opinion of First Boston, that First Boston had been allowed to do a thorough valuation study with no restraints placed upon it, and that the interests of the public shareholders had been adequately represented by First Boston in the process of determining the terms of the offer. These disclosures are claimed to be false and misleading because certain alleged facts were omitted: (1) that U.S. Sugar's management, and not First Boston's, had arrived at the $68 price and that First Boston had never suggested a price which it felt was fair but merely opined as to the fairness of the price suggested by management; (2) that the $68 price was derived from a consideration of the amount which could comfortably be borrowed and repaid rather than from any evaluation of U.S. Sugar's true worth; (3) that management would have paid up to $70 per share if Bear, Stearns had not represented that no price above $68 would be reasonable for the ESOP to pay; (4) that First Boston had accepted a representation that the sale of U.S. Sugar to a third party would not be considered and therefore had made no attempt to solicit outside offers; and (5) that after the meeting of the Board of Directors at which it was unanimously determined that $68 per share was a fair price, Stewart Mott, a director and son of the founder of U.S. Sugar, decided not to tender any of the shares registered in his name.

The tender offer and the disclosures in the Tender Offering Statement are further asserted by the plaintiffs to have been coercive because the shareholders were told that they had a choice between tendering at $68 per share or retaining their stock, which after the transaction would no longer be listed on any exchange, would yield no dividends for a minimum of three years, and would represent ownership in a company burdened by substantial debt.

Plaintiffs claim that the fair value of U.S. Sugar at the time of the tender offer was $122 per share which they claim was the liquidation value of the assets. They request that the Court find that the defendants breached their fiduciary duties by not disclosing all germane facts with complete candor and by structuring a coercive tender offer. They claim that the appropriate remedy is an award of money damages measured by the difference between the $68 tender offering price and $122 which they claim was the true value of the shares at the time of the tender offer, plus prejudgment interest.

On the other hand, defendants contend that the tender offer was not coercive, that all germane facts were fully disclosed and that, in light of this, U.S. Sugar was under no duty to offer any particular price since the shareholders had all the information necessary to make an informed decision whether to accept or to reject the offer. The defendants further assert that the $68 price was fair to the public shareholders and that it was properly arrived at by the financial consultants retained by U.S. Sugar.

III

I find, from the facts adduced at trial, that the disclosures in the Tender Offer Statement did not fully comply with the requirements for disclosure with complete candor which are mandated by Delaware law. Singer v. Magnavox Co., 380 A.2d 969 (Del.Supr.1977); Smith v. Van Gorkom, 488 A.2d 858 (Del.Supr.1985); and Rosenblatt v. Getty Oil Company, 493 A.2d 929 (Del.Supr.1985).

There was a failure to clearly indicate in the proxy materials that the book value of the land, which was the principal asset of U.S. Sugar, was based primarily on the 1931 acquisition costs of the land and that in 1982 the internal real estate department of the corporation had rendered an informal opinion to management that the fee simple holdings of land was in excess of $408 million ($83 per share). The tender offer proxy materials also failed to adequately disclose that a Cash Flow Terminal Value Study prepared by First Boston had shown estimated values as high as $100.50 per share; that Bear, Stearns had made some estimates of value of up to $78 per share; and that First Boston did not actually prepare a thorough valuation study without restraints.

I also find that there was a failure to adequately disclose the methods used to arrive at the $68 tender offer price, especially because it was, for all practical purposes, chosen because that is what the ESOP and the corporation could afford to pay to service the loan obtained to finance the tender offer.

I also find that the method used to select the tender offer price was not likely to assure that the public minority stockholders would receive the true value of their shares and, as will be seen, they did not. The tender offer price, unfortunately, was, in essence, arrived at by determining how much debt the corporation could safely and prudently assume. The public stockholders had to either accept this price and tender their shares or to hold on to their shares only to find, because of the large loan which was to be used to pay for the shares tendered, that their shares would dramatically decline in value with no prospects for any dividends for at least three years.

In some circumstances a corporation is under no obligation to offer a particular tender offer price. Joseph v. Shell Oil Co., 482 A.2d 335 (Del.Ch. 1984). Here, however, because of the highly leveraged nature of the transaction it was coercive and therefore defendants had an obligation to offer a fair price.

I acknowledge that the directors of U.S. Sugar were faced with a most difficult scenario because the majority shareholders desired to sell a substantial portion of their shares and yet insisted on retaining control of the corporation. The only feasible way to accomplish this was for the corporation to buy its own shares by the means of a leveraged tender offer. If the price offered had been fair there would not be any problem. The price offered, however, was not fair and it should have been selected with a greater emphasis on the true value of the corporation.

I do not, however, find the statements in the proxy statement setting forth the results which would likely occur if a stockholder did not tender to have been inadequate, improper or coercive. The proxy materials merely set forth that which was obvious: the minority stockholders who did not tender their shares would end up owning shares with a greatly diminished value because of the large debt being created to finance the tender offer.

* * *

Having found that there was a breach of fiduciary duty, I must now find a remedy.

IV

Plaintiffs seek, as damages, the difference between the fair value of the shares and the $68 offering price, plus pre-judgment interest. They correctly point out that it would be impossible now to rescind the transaction.

Most of the testimony adduced at trial relating to value was produced by experts retained by the litigants who expressed their opinion of the fair and intrinsic value of U.S. Sugar's stock at the time of the tender offer. Analyses of U.S. Sugar were performed on behalf of the plaintiffs by Professor James E. Walter and on behalf of the defendants by Mr. Francis C. Schaffer, Mr. W. Stanley Hanson, Jr., First Boston and Bear, Stearns.

A review of this testimony clearly shows the reason that testimony as to value by experts is of such limited use to a trier of fact.

* * *

VIII

The * * * testimony of the expert witnesses * * * is in hopeless disagreement. Each expert presented impressive credentials. Each expressed an opinion as to value based on dozens of value judgment assumptions. While each assumption was based on some data, almost all of the assumptions were fairly debatable and reasonable men using the same data could conclude that a different percentage multiple, or per acreage figure, etc., should be used.

Quite frankly, there is no rational way that I as the trier of fact could conclude that one expression of value was best. All had flaws, all were based on personal assumptions and opinions and all were expressed by obviously knowledgeable and experienced experts who were retained by one side or the other.

* * *

After considering and weighing all the conflicting testimony, the many value judgments and assumptions (some of which were invalid), and the credentials and demeanor of the witnesses, I conclude that the fair value of the assets of U.S. Sugar at the time of the tender offer was $72 per share. The damages, therefore, are equal to $4 per share ($72 less the $68 tender offer price).*

NOTE: REGULATION OF REPURCHASES

1. *Coercion.*

Any tender offer at a premium over market price entails an application of pressure on the offerees. Given that fact, what differentiates a "coercive" RTO, such as that in *Kahn,* from a permissibly "uncoercive" RTO?

Cottle v. Standard Brands Paint Co., CCH Fed.Sec.L.Rep. ¶ 95,306 (Del.Ch. 1990), expands on the concept of impermissible coercion:

"A claim for coercion must state that the plaintiffs, the tendering stockholders, 'were wrongfully induced by some act of the defendants to sell their shares for reasons unrelated to the economic merits of the sale.' Ivanhoe Partners v. Newmont Mining Corp., Del.Ch., 533 A.2d 585, 605, aff'd Del.Supr., 535 A.2d 946, 1334 (1987). Thus, a two-tier tender offer in which the buyer plans to freeze out non-tendering stockholders, giving them subordinated securities in the back end, is coercive. Unocal Corp. v. Mesa Petroleum Co., Del.Supr., 493 A.2d 946, 956 (1985). Similarly, a 'tender offered structured and timed so as to effectively deprive stockholders of the ability to choose a competing offer—also at a fair price—that the shareholders might have found preferable' is coercive. Ivanhoe, 533 A.2d at 605 * * *.

"Actionable coercion does not exist, however, simply because a tender offer price is too good to pass up. Id. Further, a self-tender at a premium above the shares' market price does not appear to be actionably coercive, even if paying that premium may adversely affect the market value of the remaining outstanding shares, provided that the offering materials make full disclosure of such an adverse effect. Eisenberg v. Chicago Milwaukee Corp., Del.Ch., 537 A.2d 1051, 1061–62 (1987)."

* [Ed. Note] The litigation was later settled. $4,719,708 (calculated as $3.50 per share to holders of 1,348,488 shares) plus interest from February 11, 1986 was to be paid; and from that sum, lawyers' fees and expenses were to be paid in the amount of $1,179,927.

Is the courts last statement, based on a reading of *Eisenberg v. Chicago Milwaukee,* supra, Part III, consistent with the coercion finding in *Kahn?*

The *Cottle* case concerned an RTO conducted in the immediate aftermath of the 1987 crash. Early in 1987, the issuer had rejected an outside $28 per share offer for the stock. After the crash, the stock traded for around $16. The offer was structured as a Dutch auction at a price of $25 to $28 per share. The offering materials stated that (1) the shares' post offering price was expected to be less than the tender offer price, and (2) the only way the holders could be assured of maximizing the value of their holdings was by tendering all shares at the minimum $25 price.

The court found no infirmities in the Dutch auction structure. It did not, said the court, "function much differently from an ordinary tender offer at $25.00." The timing of the offer did not provide a basis for a coercion case either, because plaintiff, unlike the plaintiff in *Kahn,* failed to make an adequate allegation that the offering price was unfair.

2. *Investment Companies.*

Repurchase of stock by closed-end investment companies (which tend to trade at a discount to the sum of the market value of the securities in their portfolios) presents a sufficiently acute opportunity for abuse to cause Congress in § 23(c) of the Investment Company Act of 1940 to prohibit such repurchases except by public tender solicitations or on the exchanges or similarly "open" markets (with an uncertain, but advance, disclosure requirement) or under other circumstances permitted by the Commission. A fair catalogue of the repurchase practices apparently found to exist and considered improper by the Commission may be inferred from its Regulation § 270.23c–1, and from its admonition in Inv.Co.Act.Rel. No. 3548 (Oct. 3, 1962) against repurchase, notwithstanding full disclosure, "if the issuer has failed to declare dividends on its stock even though substantial earnings are available for this purpose."

NOTE: GREENMAIL AND DEFENSIVE REPURCHASES

1. *Defining the Problem.*

In contrast to the foregoing cases, which concern low-price repurchases for the benefit of insiders, a fiduciary problem respecting a high-price repurchase for the benefit of insiders arises when management spends corporate funds to purchase corporate stock to preserve its control by buying off a "raider" or "greenmailer." The resulting conflict of interest problem goes beyond that bound up in the question as to over-or underpayment. If corporate funds are spent to fend off the "raider" or "greenmailer"—whether by OMRs, an RTO, or negotiated repurchase from the "raider"—the stockholders are denied the benefit of at least one potential tender offer or new controller, and possibly others. If the repurchase price equals or exceeds the market price, the question arises whether the loss to non-selling stockholders is worth the gain to them of the prevention of the "raider's" success (assuming the existence of the gain). The harm thought to attend the "raider's" success is either (a) the possibility of too low a future bid price by the "raider" for the remainder of the company's stock, or (b) the disadvantages (by overreaching or incompetence) to be imposed on the company by the "raider's" expected conduct, as compared to that expected of incumbent management. The "loss" derives not merely from the expenditure of corporate cash for a premium, but from the impact of elimination of the threat of the "raider" on the price of the stock. See e.g., Dann and DeAngelo, Standstill Agreements, Privately Negotiated Stock Repurchases and the Market for Corporate Control, 11 J.Fin.Econ. 275 (1983); Bradley and Wakeman, The Wealth Effects of Targeted Share Repurchases, 11 J.Fin.Econ. 301 (1983).

If the "raider" contemplated purchase of 100 percent of the stock in a tender offer, the questions arise not only (1) whether the repurchase price per share for less than 100 percent of the stock is higher than the tender offer would have been, but (2) whether the surviving stockholders are, as a result of the repurchase, worse off than they would have been if they could have sold to the bidder.

Some economic studies defend greenmail on the statistical ground the investment made by a potential hostile offeror leads to positive returns for the target shareholders, and that these positive returns exceed the negative returns that result from the announcement of a greenmail repurchase. See generally, Macey and McChesney, A Theoretical Analysis of Corporate Greenmail, 95 Yale L.J. 13 (1985); McChesney, Transaction Costs and Corporate Greenmail: Theory, Empirics, and a Mickey Mouse Case Study, 14 Managerial & Decision Econ. 131 (1993). Since the possibility of greenmail encourages the hostile offeror's initial investment, it was argued that greenmail should not be prohibited. Other studies support a different conclusion. If, after the greenmail transaction, no subsequent offeror shows up, the target shareholders' initial gains are lost. See Ang and Tucker, The Shareholder Wealth Effects of Corporate Greenmail, 11 J. Fin. Res. 265 (1988).

Based on the foregoing statement of the problem, the issue in a greenmail case could be phrased in cost-benefit terms, so that the propriety of the repurchase at a premium turns on whether it was made at an economically "fair" price (i.e., in some sense, was "worth" it). In contrast, courts in the leading cases have permitted the answer to turn on whether management could reasonably have believed that the "raider" would have caused more damage to the corporation than the cost of the repurchase. See e.g., Herald Co. v. Seawell, 472 F.2d 1081 (10th Cir.1972); Bennett v. Propp, 41 Del.Ch. 14, 187 A.2d 405 (Sup.Ct.1962); Cheff v. Mathes, 41 Del.Ch. 494, 199 A.2d 548 (Sup.Ct.1964). The inquiry in the cases is heavily tilted in management's favor by the trial procedure—i.e., the bought-out "raider" is either not available to testify (about allegedly pernicious purposes) (cf. Cheff v. Mathes, supra) or may act to support the integrity of the buy-out, or modify the arrangements to dilute its impropriety (cf. Polk v. Good, 507 A.2d 531 (Del.1986)). Even if the so-called burden of proof is said to be on the directors to "justify" the purchase, it is easily carried so long as the courts defer to the directors' business judgment. When a majority of the board consists of outsiders (i.e., persons not visibly affiliated in interest with management), the assumption is that they are sufficiently disinterested to justify judicial review of their behavior under, in the earlier cases, a very permissive version of the business judgment rule (Cheff v. Mathes, supra; Bennett v. Propp, supra), or in later cases a somewhat tighter version (cf. Unocal Corp. v. Mesa Petroleum Co., supra, 493 A.2d at 955; Polk v. Good, 507 A.2d 531 (Del. 1986)).

2.   *Unocal Review versus Business Judgment Scrutiny.*

Kahn v. Roberts, 679 A.2d 460 (Del.1996), concerned the privately negotiated repurchase of one third of the Class A voting stock of DeKalb Genetics Corp. The selling shareholders were a branch of the controlling Roberts family, the members of which branch had been shut out of top executive positions in the firm. The sellers had professed dissatisfaction with the firm's management and had suggested that the firm be sold. Instead, the Board formed a special committee of independent directors to negotiate the repurchase of their stock. The committee, acting on the advice of an independent investment banker, effected the repurchase for $40 per share. The plaintiff claimed that the repurchase was a defensive one and therefore a breach of fiduciary duty. The Delaware Supreme Court rejected the claim:

"The threshold question is determining the standard of judicial review of the directors' decision to repurchase one-third of DeKalb's outstanding shares. The

Unocal standard applies if the directors initiated the repurchase in response to a threat to corporate policy related to a potential change in control of the corporation. In re Santa Fe Pacific Corp. Shareholder Litig., Del.Supr., 669 A.2d 59, 71 (1995); Stroud v. Grace, Del.Supr., 606 A.2d 75, 82 (1992).

* * *

" * * * [T]he factual circumstances do not warrant the application of Unocal * * *. This is not the case where one-third of the outstanding shares are being sought by a third party, or a self-tender for those shares was made in the face of a third party bid for control. Such situations might bring about a change in control and be closer to the Unocal paradigm. Cf. Santa Fe, 669 A.2d at 65, 71–72 (Unocal applicable in hostile tender offer situation). Here the corporation sought to repurchase its own shares in a situation where there was no hostile bidder. Nothing in the record indicates that there was a real probability of any hostile acquiror emerging or that the corporation was 'in play.' * * *

"Absent an actual threat to corporate control or action substantially taken for the purpose of entrenchment, the actions of the board are judged under the business judgment rule. * * * The repurchase was approved after the board established an independent committee, consulted with legal and financial advisors and considered its options over the course of several meetings. Cf. Smith v. Van Gorkom, Del.Supr., 488 A.2d 858, 874 (1985). Further analysis of the repurchase is unnecessary to sustain the board's decision as a sound exercise of business judgment."

3. *Tax Legislation.*

Greenmail became a political issue during the white-hot phase of the 1980s' corporate control market. Direct prohibitions were introduced in Congress, but not enacted. See H.R. 2172, 100th Cong., 1st Sess.; S. 1324, 100th Cong., 1st Sess. But a tax disincentive was enacted in 1987 as § 5881 of the Internal Revenue Code. This imposes a 50 percent excise tax on profit realized in a greenmail transaction. The tax is imposed in addition to corporate or personal income tax, resulting in an effective rate of 84 percent or more. Greenmail is defined as consideration transferred by a corporation to repurchase its stock from a shareholder for less than two years who made or threatened a tender offer, unless the acquisition is pursuant to an offer made on the same terms to all shareholders. For criticism, see Gilson, Drafting an Effective Greenmail Prohibition, 88 Colum. L. Rev. 329 (1988); Zelinsky, Greenmail, Golden Parachutes and the Internal Revenue Code: A Tax Policy Critique of Sections 280G, 4999 and 5881, 35 Vill. L. Rev. 131 (1990).

(3) *Federal Securities Laws—Repurchase Tender Offers*

RTOS, whether made defensively against third party tender offers or otherwise, generate for the issuer's security holders needs for disclosure (particularly as to the issuer's purposes, plans, and proposals), and relief from sales pressure comparable to (although far from identical with) those generated by third party tender offers. To meet those needs, the Securities Exchange Commission promulgated Rule 13e–4 which, it will be noted, contains both disclosure requirements and substantive restrictions on the manner of making the tender offer. The Commission's authority under either Section 13 or Section 14 to impose such substantive requirements has been the subject of debate.

Securities Exchange Act. Section 13(e) and Rule 13e–4, Appendix D

Paragraphs (c), (d), (e) and (f) of Rule 13e–4 prescribe requirements for filing, disclosing, and disseminating information, and restricting the manner of making the tender offer. In general, the regulations track those applying to third party tender offers: (1) the offer must be held open for at least 20 business days; (2) the offerees have withdrawal rights the period of the offer; (3) the required pro rata purchase must be made soon after the period of the offer; and (4) under a "best price" rule, where the issuer increases the consideration offered after the tender offer is commenced, the issuer is required to pay the increased consideration to all security holders. See Rule 13e–4(f).

Rule 13e–4 also prohibits, for the ten business days after termination of the offer, any purchases by the issuer, or by persons in a control relationship with the issuer, of the securities which are the subject of the tender offer. Similarly, in the context of exchange offers, the Rule prohibits purchases by the issuer of any security being offered pursuant to the exchange offer, or any security of the same class and series as, or any right to purchase, any such security. Market activity in these securities may affect the market price for the security which is the subject of the tender offer, or the security offered pursuant to an exchange offer. See Securities Exchange Act Rel. No. 16,112 (August 16, 1979).

The information required to be disclosed under Rule 13e–4 and Schedule TO, 17 C.F.R. 240.1d–100, consists, among other things, of the usual financial statements, including income statements, balance sheets, and ratios of earnings to fixed charges for the two most recent fiscal years and the latest interim period and for the corresponding interim period for the prior year; earnings and book value per share; and a pro forma presentation disclosing the effect of the tender offer on the figures for the most recent fiscal year and for the latest year-to-date interim period, where material. In addition, information is required about the source of funds for the repurchase, the purposes of the tender offer, and any plans or proposals which relate to or would result in an extraordinary corporate transaction such as a merger, a sale or transfer of a material amount of assets, a material change in dividend rates or policies or indebtedness or capitalization, any change in the board, or any acquisition or disposition by the issuer of additional securities of the issuer, any other material change in the issuer's corporate structure of business, and any defensive changes in the issuer's charter or securities structure making it less vulnerable to take-over. Rule 13e–4(e)(3) requires disclosure of material changes in already disclosed information.

NOTE: FEDERAL REGULATION OF REPURCHASE TENDER OFFERS

1. *Repurchases During Third Party Tender Offers.*

Rule 13e–1 applies to issuers whose shares currently are subject to a third party tender offer. It prohibits market repurchases by such an issuer unless the issuer files with the SEC an information statement describing, *inter alia*, the venue and terms of the transactions, the purpose of the transactions, and the source of funds.

Does this disclosure rule adequately address the problems arising when the issuer repurchases stock during the period of a third party tender offer? Whether, during that period, the issuer should be denied the freedom of making OMRs and be confined to the restrictions entailed in making a competing RTO (in effect restricting its management to more equal competitive terms with the third party bidder) is the subject of discussion in Bradley and Rosenzweig, Defensive Stock Repurchases, 99 Harv. L. Rev. 1377 (1986); Note, 38 Stan. L. Rev. 701 (1986); see also Gordon and Kornhauser, Takeover Defense Tactics: A Comment on Two Models 96 Yale L. J. 295 (1986); Bradley and Rosenzweig, Defensive Stock Repurchases and The Appraisal Remedy 96 Yale L. J. 322 (1986).

2. *Purchases and Sales by Managers of Repurchasing Firms.*

Does Rule 13e–4 regulate purchases and sales by managers of firms making RTOs for their own accounts? Should it? Fried, supra, proposes a "disclose/delay" rule to reduce insiders' ability to use RTOs for private gain. The rule would require insiders to disclose whether and to what extent they are participating in the RTO, and, in the case of Dutch auction RTOs, the prices at which they are tendering their shares. In addition, insiders would be prohibited from selling stock outside the RTO for six months beginning with the announcement of the RTO.

Would Fried's rule have constrained the insiders in *Kahn v. U.S. Sugar* supra?

3. *Disclosure of Projections and Soft Information.*

Suppose ABC Corp. makes an RTO for 15 percent of its shares for $25 with the market price at $21. ABC's Schedule TO contains financials showing substantial increases in sales and earnings of around 15 percent per year for recent years and periods and estimating similar increased earnings for the current fiscal year. The Schedule also states that ABC believes repurchase at $25 to be in its best interest; that the repurchased shares will be held in treasury for future acquisitions; and that no director of officer of the firm would be tendering into the offer or selling shares in the market during the period of the offer. Finally, ABC makes the following statement:

> Neither the Company nor the Board of Directors makes any recommendation that stockholders tender or refrain from tendering any or all of their shares. Each stockholder must make his own decision whether to tender or to remain a holder of Common Stock.

The offer closes, fully subscribed. In the first fiscal year after the closing of the offer, ABC's earnings rise 30 percent. Nine months after the closing of the offer, XYZ Corp. announces a friendly tender offer for ABC for $50 per share.

Plaintiff, who sold into the offer, sues under Rule 13e–4, claiming that ABC failed to disclose its internal projections respecting its increased earnings in the year after the offer.

Does Rule 13e–4 require such disclosure? Should it?

On substantially similar facts, in a case arising under Rule 10b–5, **Coyne v. MSL Industries**, CCH Fed.Sec.L.Rep. ¶ 95,451 (N.D.Ill.1976), ruled that "known facts and plans" had to be disclosed but not predictions: "a present plan of future corporate activity may be a material existing fact, but mere speculation is not. Corporate insiders need not give investors the benefit of expert financial analysis or educated guesses and predictions. Insiders need not volunteer economic forecasts."

Walker v. Action Industries, Inc., 802 F.2d 703 (4th Cir.1986), cert. denied 479 U.S. 1065 (1987), similarly declines to require disclosure of an RTO issuer's internal sales and earnings projections which, if "hard," would plainly have been material. The decision relies heavily on the fact that neither Rule 13e–4, nor the regulations authorizing projections in registration statements and proxy materials require disclosure of projections—notwithstanding that the plaintiff's claim appears to have been based on Rule 10b–5.

Even if management is not required to disclose internal projections in the ordinary course of business, does commencement of an RTO amount to an extraordinary event justifying special rules? What problems would arise if "soft" internal projections be were classified as "material" in connection with RTOs? Would disclosure tend to discourage tenders? Or would shareholders discount disclosures as signals without credibility? Or, on a signaling theory, do shareholders rationally assume that management conducting an RTO expects materially improved results? Does it depend on whether or not insiders are tendering into the offer?

(4) Federal Securities Laws—Open Market Repurchases

Suppose the management of X Corp. wishes to embark on an merger and acquisition program, using X Corp. common as currency. It reasonably considers that the company's stock is undervalued on the market, where it is priced at 32. It believes that once the market focuses on the stock, the stock's price will rise to 60.

Some questions:

(a) Is it in the interest of the company's shareholders for the company to initiate an OMR program and bid the price up to its true value? If so, should the company disclose its intention to do so, or as with the discovery of any undervalued situation, would not the company defeat its purpose if it made a prior announcement of its intentions? If management honestly believes that the market undervalues X Corp. stock and that acquisitions can be carried out more easily, or more cheaply, if a better "price-structure" is established, presumably on a permanent basis (and there is no showing of an intention to create a mere temporary run up) should the law leave OMRs unregulated? Or should the law make it impossible for a company to undertake OMRs without prior notice?

(b) If the true value of X Corp. is only 32, how can the company hope to benefit by overpaying for the shares? Unless it plans to issue false statements about its prospects and accomplishments, will not the market price fairly quickly settle back to the earlier level? If so, and management's OMR causes a temporary run up in the price, has the price been "manipulated" during the that period? If so, should the law prohibit the OMR program?

(c) Even if the stock price does not settle back down to its earlier level in the wake of management's OMRs, do such purchases, even if disclosed in advance to the public, inject into the market an artificiality which detracts from the role of the market as the register of equilibrium between a willing seller and a willing buyer? Is management's judgment—whether as a faithful fiduciary or as an errant fiduciary—a "legitimate" pricing factor comparable to the judgments of buyers and sellers seeking to advance their economic interests as investors? Is management's self-interest apt to inject a bias in the OMR program which should be irrelevant to the market's pricing mechanism—e.g., to keep the price higher than the stock's value justifies in order to win the approval of stockholders? If any of the foregoing questions elicits a "yes" answer, should the law completely prohibit OMRs?

(d) If the disparity between management's judgment as to the stock's value and the market's evaluation of the stock is to be reduced, is it more appropriate to use corporate cash to affect the price than to disclose information which will bring the price into line? Are there limits to the disclosure which is permissible when made to bring the price of the stock up to management's judgment of an appropriate price? Or, even if full disclosure could be made, would the market valuation ever reflect it fully? Signaling theory tells us that mere disclosure is not credible unless backed with a cost. Liability respecting a good faith but unrealized projection would impose just such a cost, but perhaps not a cost managers and their shareholder insurers rationally would be willing to bear. Instead the OMR itself imports the measure of credibility, because if management turns out to be wrong about the stock's value it will have bought the stock at a premium. But how accurate is the signal?

These questions make it clear that even if we remain unconcerned with the substantive inequality incident to OMRs' division of the shareholder group into underinformed sellers and nonsellers, we still need to ask question about OMRs' effect on the trading market: Should the law deem market buying activity by an issuer to "correct" its stock price to be a form of market manipulation?

(a) manipulation—Securities Exchange Act Section 9(a)(2)

Management repurchases resemble certain classic forms of stock price manipulation. In both cases, after all, purchases are being made to increase the stock price. The resemblance has given rise to questions respecting the applicability of the sections of the 1934 Act that prohibit stock price manipulation. Consider section 9(a)(2), which provides:

> "It shall be unlawful for any person, directly or indirectly, by the use of the mails or any means or instrumentality of interstate commerce, or of any facility of any national securities exchange, or for any member of any national securities exchange—* * * to effect, alone or with one or more other persons, a series of transactions in any security registered on a national securities exchange * * * creating actual or apparent active trading in such security, or raising or depressing the price of such security, for the purpose of inducing the purchase or sale of such security by others."

In **Halsey, Stuart & Co., Inc.**, 30 S.E.C. 106, 110–112 (1949), the Securities and Exchange Commission said the following in the course of applying section 9(a)(2):

> "A manipulation may be accomplished without wash sales, matched orders, or other fictitious devices. Actual buying with the design to create activity, prevent price falls, or raise prices for the purpose of inducing

others to buy is to distort the character of the market as a reflection of the combined judgments of buyers and sellers, and to make of it a stage-managed performance. Whether or not his belief is, in good faith, that the free market has undervalued the securities, the manipulator's design in raising prices is to create the appearance that a free market is supplying demand whereas the demand in fact comes from his planned purpose to stimulate buyers' interest. It is of utmost materiality to a buyer under such circumstances to know that he may not assume that the prices he pays were reached in a free market; and the manipulator cannot make sales not accompanied by disclosure of his activities without committing fraud."

Section 9(a)(2), thus interpreted, arguably would apply to a conventional OMR program which was not disclosed to the public. The 1934 Act's antifraud provisions also arguably would apply to such a program. *Halsey, Stuart*, supra, also asserted the SEC's view that such overlapping applications can obtain.

Does antecedent disclosure of an OMR program by itself deflect section 9(a)(2) and the antifraud rules? Can there be manipulative behavior which, although disclosed, artificially affects market prices? The SEC has asserted both that such behavior exists and that it is empowered to prohibit the behavior. In Rel. No. 34–17222 (Oct. 10, 1980)(discussing a proposed but unadopted version of Rule 13e–2) the SEC stated:

" * * * Disclosure is unlikely to prevent manipulative conduct from having improper effects on the market since market manipulation is not solely a matter of deception and cannot be cured solely by preventing deception. For example, an issuer that every day participated in the opening and closing transactions in its securities could significantly and improperly affect the price of those securities despite the fact that its conduct was fully disclosed. Similarly, disclosure of an issuer repurchase program that involved purchases that dominated the market would not eliminate the effects of that domination. Disclosure of an issuer's efforts to drive the price of its securities up or to maintain it at artificial levels, by engaging several brokers to bid against one another or through other measures, would not cure the ill effects of such a manipulation. Moreover, given the often considerable fluctuations in market conditions and the rapid pace at which market transactions occur, it is questionable whether full and timely disclosure of certain practices could ever be made in a fashion that would protect the markets and investors as fully or efficiently as can more direct prohibitions on manipulative practices. * * * "

Thus holding § 9(a)(2) to apply on this basis as a substantive provision is to invite controversy. In the view of many, Congress in enacting such anti-manipulative provisions did not empower the Commission to promulgate substantive rules which restrict behavior or forbid transactions; instead it empowered only rules which define and enforce disclosure requirements. Alternatively, even if Congress empowered substantive rulemaking, the scope of the permissible substantive rules should be limited to proscribing behavior which causes injury to investors only by reason of its misleading or deceptive import.

(b) safe harbor for potentially manipulative repurchases
Securities Exchange Act. Rule 10b–18, Appendix D

In 1968, Congress added § 13(e) to the 1934 Act to give the SEC authority to make comprehensive rules with respect to share repurchases. The Commission did not succeed in promulgating antimanipulative rules thereunder for OMRs until the adoption in 1984 of Rule 10b–18.

To take advantage of the safe harbor provided by Rule 10b–18, an issuer or affiliated purchaser has to comply with all stated conditions. The conditions are designed to prevent the issuer from dominating the trading market in its shares, constraining repurchase executions on a day-to-day basis: Only one broker may be used per day; the issuer may not make the opening transaction, and purchases must cease ten to thirty minutes before the close, depending on the depth of the market in the stock; no purchase price may exceed the greater of the highest independent published bid and the last independent sale price; and purchases may not exceed 25 percent of daily trading volume.

In Securities Exchange Act Release No. 19244 (November 17, 1982), promulgating Rule 10b–18, the Commission stated as follows:

"The Commission has recognized that issuer repurchase programs are seldom undertaken with improper intent, may frequently be of substantial economic benefit to investors, and, that, in any event, undue restriction of these programs is not in the interest of investors, issuers, or the market-place. Issuers generally engage in repurchase programs for legitimate business reasons and any rule in this area must not be overly intrusive. Accordingly, the Commission has endeavored to * * * avoid complex and costly restrictions that impinge on the operation of issuer repurchase programs.

" * * * Accordingly, the Commission * * * has determined that a safe harbor is the appropriate regulatory approach * * *.

"The Commission wishes to stress, however, that the safe harbor is not mandatory nor the exclusive means of effecting issuer purchases without manipulating the market. As a safe harbor, new Rule 10b–18 will provide clarity and certainty for issuers and broker-dealers who assist issuers in their repurchase programs. If an issuer effects its repurchases in compliance with the conditions of the rule, it will avoid what might otherwise be substantial and unpredictable risks of liability under the general anti-manipulative provisions of the federal securities laws. * * *

" * * * In order to make it clear that Rule 10b–18 is not the exclusive means to effect issuer repurchases, paragraph (c) of the rule provides that no presumption shall arise that an issuer or affiliated purchaser has violated Section 9(a)(2) or Rule 10b–5 if the purchases do not meet the conditions of paragraph (b).

* * *

"The Commission has reconsidered the question of whether a general antifraud provision is necessary in this context and has concluded that it is not. The sole purpose of the rule as adopted is to provide a safe harbor from liability under the anti-manipulative provisions of the Act. For that reason, the Commission has determined not to include a general antifraud provision in Rule 10b–18.

"Proposed Rule 13e–2 would have required issuers and affiliated purchasers that sought to repurchase more than two percent of the issuer's stock during any twelve-month period publicly to disclose certain specified information prior to effecting any purchases of the issuer's stock. In addition, those persons would have been required to disclose the specified information to any exchange on which the stock was listed for trading or to the NASD if the stock was authorized for quotation in NASDAQ.

* * *

"The proposed disclosure requirements were not intended to be coextensive with other disclosure obligations. Nevertheless, the Commission is persuaded that the obligation to disclose information concerning repurchases of an issuer's stock should depend on whether the information is material under the circumstances, regardless of whether such purchases are made as part of a program authorized by a company's board of directors or otherwise. The Commission has therefore determined not to adopt the specific disclosure requirements contained in paragraph (d) of proposed Rule 13e–2, even as a safe harbor. Other relevant provisions of the federal securities laws and existing policies and procedures of the various self-regulatory organizations impose disclosure responsibilities that appear to be sufficient to ensure that investors and the marketplace in general receive adequate information concerning issuer repurchases. * * * "

NOTE: OMRS AND MARKET TRANSPARENCY

Managers believe they can time their OMR purchases to beat the market. OMR firms report that they keep track of their traders' success or failure in so doing, rewarding those who succeed as they execute their program repurchases. The literature of external confirmation is thin, however. Data are lacking due to the federal securities laws' failure to require OMR firms to break out the results of their trades in a separate disclosure. OMR proponents point to two indirect confirmations: (1) OMR programs tend to be announced after periods of relatively poor stock performance, (2) they tend to be executed when the stock trades at the low end of its long-term price range, and (3) the average 3 to 3.5 percent uptick in the stock price triggered by the OMR program announcement. The one direct study tests data provided voluntarily by 68 firms (out of 478 firms solicited). See Cook et al., On the Timing and Execution of Open Market Repurchases (Nov. 2000) (unpublished working paper), at http:// ssrn.com/abstract=251854. The study tests the firms' repurchases against a benchmark of highs and lows of their stock prices. Results are mixed. Some firms, particularly NYSE firms, show timing skill, outperforming their benchmarks; other firms, particularly NASDAQ firms, underperform. Another result in the study should be noted. The 10b–18 safe harbor is widely but not slavishly utilized. Forty-one percent of the firms surveyed exceeded the volume limits on at least one occasion. The trades in the sample exceeded the pricing and timing limits around 25 percent of the time. Issuers apparently do this in pursuit of bargains.

If the Rule 10b–18 trading restrictions so constrain the OMR firm's trading activities as to counteract the usual market response to informed trading, then might they not also prevent the firm from beating the market systematically? The consistent price uptick of 3 to 3.5 percent during an OMR announcement period suggests otherwise. But a second question arises immediately: Might we see different announcement period results under a stricter regulatory regime? Prior to 2004, neither the federal securities laws nor the stock exchange rules required ongoing ex post disclosure of purchases under OMR programs. OMR firms took advantage of this blackout and moved by stealth. In a sample of 54 firms, these firms waited an average of 17 days after an OMR announcement before buying any stock, minimizing the cost of the post-announcement uptick and they only executed trades on about one-third of the available trading days during the life of the program. See Cook, et al., An Analysis of SEC Guidelines for Executing Open Market Repurchases, 76 J. Bus. 289, 295 (2003). Beginning in 2004, the SEC required firms to report their repurchases on a quarterly basis. The periodic and ex-post character of this disclosure requirement leaves open considerable room for stealth.

Compare additional restrictions imposed by the London Stock Exchange's listing rules. These broaden the time reference of the trading constraint, blocking repurchases at a price greater than 5 percent above the average market value of the stock during the antecedent 10 business days. They also impose long blackout periods: two months before annual earnings reports and one month before quarterly reports. Finally, trading results have to be disclosed almost immediately. This makes it difficult to take advantage of an undervalued stock price. Post-announcement excess returns for firms conducting OMRs on the London Stock Exchange are only 1.14 percent—one-third of the U.S. amount.

From all of this it follows that some of the advantage of OMRs over dividends derives from the fact that OMR executions proceed by stealth. It follows that some of the advantage would disappear if market regulations brought transparency to issuer trades. Fried, Informed Trading and False Signaling with Open Market Repurchases, 93 Cal. L. Rev.1323 (2005), makes a case for just such a reform, suggesting that firms be required to disclose their purchase orders *before* execution by their brokers.

Finally, remember that even as OMR proponents cite bargain repurchases and show some evidence, nothing guarantees that OMR firms always make bargain repurchases. Adverse selection is a constant possibility in a skewed stock market.

(5) *Dividends, Repurchases, and Corporate Governance*

Bratton, The New Dividend Puzzle
93 Geo. L. J. 845, 890–94 (2005).

Economic theory posits irrelevance for payout decisions. In an ideal world in which managers never self-serve and all shareholders are fully informed, the choice between dividends and repurchases implicates neither gain nor loss. But, in the second-best world we inhabit, the decision as to the mode of payout implies cost-benefit tradeoffs.

A number of these cost-benefit factors figured into the historical shift from dividends to repurchases. Tax certainly must be mentioned, but not because managers altruistically shape payout policy to minimize shareholder tax liabilities. Rather, the tax bias favoring repurchases caused actors in the investment community to favor the change, effectively expanding the zone of management discretion. The normative drift to shareholder-value maximization had a similar effect. The shareholder-oriented mindset of the 1990s was shaped during the investor revolt of the 1980s against suboptimal reinvestment of marginal dollars by managers. The restructuring battles of the 1980s succeeded in disrupting management's habit of reflexive investment in poor projects. But shareholders, still wary of a management bias toward reinvestment, welcomed any transfer of cash out of the firm. With payout assured and suboptimal investment avoided, shareholders asked no further questions about the mode of payout chosen. The door was open for managers to shift a portion of the total payout to repurchases in lockstep with their desire to obscure the costs of their stock option exercises. Regulatory developments also figured into the change. The SEC opened its door to repurchases in 1984 by promulgating the Rule 10b–18 safe harbor for OMRs. Like shareholders, it then stopped asking questions.

How do the costs and benefits of different payout methods compare today? If we put taxation to one side for the moment, the case in favor of repurchases rests on two points. First, the flexibility of OMR programs facilitates the disgorgement of free cash flows that otherwise might be retained suboptimally. Second, firms can beat the market in their own shares and purchase undervalued stock. But the stock option overlay triggers questions about both claimed advantages. Although OMRs are flexible, it must be questioned whether, absent side benefits to management, their availability alone assures payout of free cash flows. If we answer the question in the negative, we get the counterfactual suggestion that the overall payout rate in recent years would have been lower absent stock options.

Similar questions arise for the bargain repurchase assertion. Managers holding stock options have every reason to execute repurchases at advantageous prices. But to the extent that earnings management determines the amount of cash devoted to repurchases from quarter to quarter, there is less reason to assume purchase price acuity. If the quarterly earnings per share calculation signals for repurchases, the OMR program presumably proceeds even in a market that is at a cyclical high point. Stock option economics compound the problem: The dilutive effect of an exercise of stock options increases with the market price. Increased dilution signals more repurchases to protect earnings per share, whether or not the market is overpriced. To be sure, officers executing an OMR program in such a market will still endeavor to trade at times when the price falls to the low end of the current range. But on average, repurchases under such conditions will not both provide an advantage to long-term shareholders and improve the earnings per share.

One point emerges, regardless of how payout policy might have developed in the 1990s absent the stock option bonanza: The shift to repurchases should not be read as a governance success story. Because repurchases held out tax benefits to most shareholders, there was no reason for outside monitors to ask hard questions about flexibility and adverse selection nor to inquire about the motivational effects of stock option valuation on earnings management. With tax-rate parity, the governance system needs to start the questioning process.

Once shareholders and outside commentators have asked these questions, the special dividend emerges as a viable answer. The shareholders of a firm that diverts its surplus profits into special dividends instead of repurchases get three benefits. First, the shareholders no longer bear an adverse-selection risk with respect to the prices paid for repurchased shares. Second, they get the benefit of transparency with respect to the dilution cost of managers' stock options. And third, they receive more meaningful reports of earnings per share. But they also incur two costs. First, they lose the benefit of management's short-term market trading advantage. Second, the tax system returns to the picture, and taxpaying shareholders lose the ability to defer taxes on sums paid out. If the adverse-selection and trading-advantage possibilities cancel each other out, then the matter comes down to a trade-off between transparency and tax deferral. The outcome of this trade-off is unclear, but the point to note is that transparency has a value. Wider appreciation of the costs of equity compensation schemes could beneficially affect boardroom judgments respecting compensation, holding out the possible dollars-and-cents benefit of a decrease in management compensation.

Thus, we return to the corporate governance system with a cost-benefit question on the table. The trade-offs have to be considered case by case. A series of qualitative assessments comes to bear on each firm's managers, investment opportunities, incentive pay structure, and stock price. Is the governance system constituted so that the issue will be joined?

At present, the answer is probably no: the system will likely let the matter pass. The payout decision lies in the ultimate redoubt of management discretion, at least as a question of corporate law. * * * [C]orporations tend in practice to back into their dividend and repurchase decisions. Spare cash for distribution comes to the table by a process of deduction. The business plan, new investments, and liquidity take first priority. The dividend payout comes next, with aversion to present or future dividend cuts constraining the zone of discretion. Cash for OMRs is released at the final step. The deductive sequence leaves the board of directors in the traditional rubber-stamp position. Management has no incentive to institute a review of the basic assumptions, especially because of the convenient linkage between OMRs and stock option value. Nor should we look to outside directors to make disruptive suggestions. Despite the linkage to stock options, not one decision in the sequence falls into the emerging category of subjects reserved for separate examination by independent directors: auditor approval, board nominations, and executive compensation. As to the last, shareholder approval is emerging as the norm for all equity compensation schemes. Yet the SEC has traditionally blocked shareholder input on dividend and repurchase decisions.

The federal securities laws aid and abet the system by enveloping payout policy in black boxes. OMR program execution implicates ongoing reporting only on an ex-post, quarterly basis. Indeed, prior to 2004, firms were not even required to break out totals, even on an annual basis. Dividends declared and paid have always been public information, of course. But nondisclosure otherwise still tends to be the rule for decisions respecting payout and reinvestment. Warren Buffett comments as follows on management communications respecting dividend and reinvestment decisions:

> Dividend policy is often reported to shareholders, but seldom explained. A company will say something like, "Our goal is to pay out 40% to 50% of earnings and to increase dividends at a rate at least equal to the rise in the CPI." And that's it—no analysis will be supplied as to why that particular policy is best for the owners of the business. Yet allocation of capital is crucial to business and investment management.

Buffett's comment is descriptive of practice under the mandatory disclosure system, which has never mandated meaningful disclosure of dividend and reinvestment decisions. A disclosure regime more skeptical of the incentives driving payout and reinvestment decisions would require firms to identify the different investment projects adopted and funded in a given period and state the amount invested. Unfortunately, such a rule would entail a systemic overhaul.

A lesser level of transparency keyed to the mode of payout could be achieved without root-and-branch reform. Here we put investment policy to one side and concentrate on enhanced transparency and responsiveness respecting choice between OMRs and dividends. OMRs, like stock options, can be reviewed by independent directors and sent to the shareholders for annual ratification. The accompanying proxy statements can set out the record of past repurchases and their correlation with stock option exercises. These added disclosures could move payout policy to a higher place on the board's agenda, triggering confrontation with attendant cost-benefit questions.

At a minimum, boards should look carefully at the market before their firms buy back stock and should monitor the market while programs are being executed. They also should pay attention to the trading behavior of the officers they monitor. If the officers are selling the firm's stock, then the firm should not be buying it. And if some officer sales should be put down to benign purposes—for example, sales for the purpose of diversifying an officer's personal portfolio—then the benign number of sales per period can and should be stated in advance.

SECTION B.   EQUITY OWNERSHIP AND THE VALUE OF THE FIRM

The discussion in Part II connected capital structure and corporate governance, suggesting that some capital structures do a better job than others in reducing agency costs. The more particular suggestion was that high leverage imports discipline in management, thereby enhancing firm value. But that suggestion became subject to significant qualifications. Although today debt financing signals strength and management confidence, actors no longer look to high leverage as the best available means to align incentives within the firm. Leveraged restructuring now is seen as a shock therapy that effected the transition from the managerialism of the post war period, which became moribund in the 1970s, to today's regime of shareholder value enhancement. In the eyes of many, today's managers have substituted shareholder value maximization for corporate growth as the yardstick by which they measure their own success. There accordingly is less need than formerly to incentivize them by wielding the sticks of hostile takeovers and high leverage. Now we hold out a carrot in the form of stock options.

This does not go to say that the takeover has no place in the overall incentive structure, see Part V, Section F, infra. But, today, when something needs to be done about incompetence, sloth, or private benefit-seeking in the management suite, we hear the shareholder voice expressed in the matter. Sometimes this occurs in the form of actual dialogue with management. On other occasions shareholders voice their views in connection with votes respecting board seats, shareholder proposals, or charter and by law amendments. Formerly such exercises were thought to be futile. Now the shareholder voice can be influential. Its effective, if not directive, expression is facilitated by the concentration of shares in institutional hands. This has ameliorated, if not solved, the collective action problem which historically constrained shareholder intervention in corporate governance under separated ownership and control.

Equity ownership figures into this new account of governance, management incentives, and value enhancement at two critical junctures. First, the account holds out the carrot in the form of equity compensation. Second, the account looks to concentrated shareholding to hold out the stick, reducing agency costs by making enhanced shareholder monitoring cost beneficial.

In this section we take up these connections between equity ownership and effective management. Both connections implicate questions and problems. With management stock options, the questions go to matters of structure and degree. How many shares must be vested in management to get the desired incentive effect and how should options on those shares be structured and priced? With concentrated shareholding the question concerns the incentives of holders of large blocks of stock. These actors perform a monitoring function only so long as they do not take management positions (along with accompanying compensation and perquisites). But why should a blockholder bother to monitor for the benefit of the shareholder group as a whole if the only returns for its efforts are shared *pro rata*? So doing arguably is irrational, implying that blockholder monitors take their returns in the form of what economists call "private benefits," known to lawyers as self dealing transactions.

Legal questions in these contexts arise in traditional fiduciary territory. Executive stock options implicate the duty of care and the "waste" standard applied to executive compensation under the duty of loyalty. Blockholders are subject the general strictures on self-dealing transactions. In addition, when the blockholder has control power, it becomes subject to the special scrutiny of majority-minority fiduciary duties.

1. EXECUTIVE STOCK OPTIONS

INTRODUCTION

Consider a simple model of optimal capital structure articulated by the economist Oliver Hart. Hart takes up the problem of management incentives, shifting the focus away from high leverage and toward the dividend stream. He makes two assumptions—no taxes and managers who derive no private benefits from control of assets. Hart asserts that optimal management performance easily can be achieved with an all equity capital structure and a simple incentive compensation system. The managers' compensation depends entirely on the dividend: Incentive compensation I should = $\pi(d)$, where π is a small positive number and d is the dividend. If the payment also includes a portion of the proceeds L of liquidation or sale (or other transfer) of the going concern to a third party—$I = \pi[d,L]$—the manager can be expected at any time and on any performance state to make an optimal decision respecting the firm's continuance as a going concern. No debt is needed in order to align management incentives with the interests of the firm's equity. See Hart, Firms, Contracts, and Financial Structures 101–06 (1995).

Given Hart's assumptions, his theory manifestly is correct. It overcomes the agency problems stemming from the separation of ownership and control by giving management a financial interest identical to that of the shareholders. Problems come up, as usual, when the assumptions are relaxed. Managers do derive private benefits from asset management—they have subjective reasons for holding on to their jobs in addition to their financial interests. They therefore may be disinclined to let go of control positions despite the payment of $\pi[L]$ on sale or liquidation. But the biggest problem, as Hart points out, concerns the magnitude of the bribe π required align management incentives with those of the outside equity holders. The necessary π is unfeasibly large.

To restate Hart's point, to solve the incentive problems of separated ownership and control by vesting an equity interest in management, you have to pay the managers more than they are worth. If we grant the equity interest in the form of stock options do we open a route to incentive compatibility without having to pay too much? Or does the problem of excessive pay persist? Indeed, do stock option plans today pay too much without even solving the incentive problem?

(A) STOCK OPTIONS AND SHAREHOLDER VALUE

During the 1990s, stock options rose to coequal status with salary in executive compensation. Average total remuneration for CEOs in S & P 500 firms (adjusted for inflation using 2002 dollars) increased from about $850,000 in 1970 to over $14 million in 2000, falling to $9.4 million in 2002. The Black–Scholes value of options on the grant date rose from close to 0 in 1970 to over $7.0 million in 2000, falling to $4.4 million in 2002. In 2000, then, stock options made up one-half of the average CEO pay package. The rest was comprised of cash compensation, restricted stock, retirement benefits, and payouts long-term cash bonus plans.

In their broad outlines executive stock options are not materially different from the publicly traded options described in Part I supra. The three most important terms governing any stock option grant are the number of shares covered, the strike (or exercise) price, and the duration. As a matter of corporate practice, the strike price tends to be the "at the money"—that is, the stock price at the time of the option's issue. According to Murphy, Executive Compensation, in Handbook of Labor Economics 2485 (1999), 95 percent of all options granted today are priced this way. The duration tends to be ten years.

To see the incentive effect, compare a manager on straight salary with a manager receiving the same total compensation, but evenly divided between a salary and a stock option plan. A straight salary is not incentive compatible because it is paid irrespective of the firm's results, good or bad, for a given period. Furthermore, the all-salary executive will have a subjective risk return response respecting new corporate investment that differs from that of most of the firm's shareholders. The executive has an undiversified human capital investment in the firm and therefore will be risk averse; risky investments may destabilize the institution and jeopardize his or her job security. To the extent that the shareholders are fully diversified they will be much less risk averse, favoring a competitive high risk/high return investment lying outside of the executive's more parochial risk preferences. (Note that to the extent that the risks attending a given investment cause the firm's beta to rise, diversified shareholders still may display risk aversion and will not perfectly embody the "risk neutral" investor often assumed in financial economics. The theoretical response is the separation theorem, described supra, Part I. This advises the fully diversified, risk averse investor to hold a portfolio divided between equities and riskless treasuries. When the firm makes the risky investment and raises its beta, the risk averse investor adjusts by increasing the proportion of treasuries.)

There are three reasons why the manager receiving salary and stock options will be more attuned to the shareholders' interest than the manager on salary only. First, options tie the level of pay to corporate performance. Although the present value of the option plus salary equals the amount paid to the all-salary executive, future realization of the option's value depends on the extent to which the stock price rises above the strike price. The more shareholder value the executive creates the higher that future payoff. Such a "pay for performance" scheme could be structured as a cash bonus keyed to profits, of course. This brings us to the second incentive-aligning effect of a stock option. By awarding stock, as opposed to cash, the option plan expands the commonality of interest between the manager and the shareholders. Of course, the manager is still underdiversified—even with the stock options, a disproportionately large portion of the manager's wealth is staked in the firm, inducing risk aversion respecting firm investments. This brings us to the third incentive-aligning effect of the option. Because the equity participation comes under option, rather than

simply as a direct grant of new shares, volatility enhances the participation's value where volatility detracts from the value of a share held
outright in an underdiversified portfolio. Taken alone, the option would
make a manager risk-prone. But taken as a part of larger package including
firm specific investment of human capital, it in theory has the less drastic
effect of shifting the manager's subjective risk return responses in the
direction of the ideal of risk neutrality.

As we saw with the option embedded in a convertible bond, however,
there is no such thing as a free lunch. Shareholders pay for executive stock
options when their stock is diluted on the options' exercise. The firm with
executives holding options differs from the firm with salaried executives
because its shareholders must share the increase in the value of the stock
with the option holders. Sharing with the executives decreases the proportion of the larger pie allocable to the shareholders. Thus, the stock option
plan enhances the value of the outside shareholders' shares only to the
extent that the value of the incremental management effort induced by the
option plan exceeds the cost of the dilution. Thomas and Martin, infra, at
36, point out another cost. As the shares under option are exercised,
management can come to have significant voting power. In 1998, for
example, stock under active options constituted 13.2 percent of total
publicly traded equity. If, in a given firm, the managers exercise and hold
and end up with 13.2 percent of the votes, they can vote as a block and
influence the outcomes of close votes. Given a 90 percent supermajority
provision, for example, they have a veto.

Thomas and Martin, The Determinants of Shareholder Voting on Stock Option Plans
35 Wake Forest L. Rev. 31, 40–46 (2000).

[T]he critics of pay for performance have become more numerous in
the past few years. Accepting the idea that giving executives stock interests
in the company will incentivize them to work harder to improve the
company does not end the debate over the appropriate level of their
compensation. Even if managers' pay should be tied to increases in stock
prices during the relevant time period, and these increases can be attributed to the efforts of the managers, "the question is still open as to what
portion of that additional wealth should be paid to the CEO." Thus, even if
the theory of pay for performance is accepted, this only marks the beginning of the inquiry.

Several crucial questions about incentive pay remain unanswered. For
example, if an executive is highly motivated by $1 million in stock options,
then will she be more motivated and work harder if the board awards her
$2 million in stock options? If so, will the improvement in performance be
worth the additional cost? Do executives (or boards) even understand the
incentives provided by stock options? In order to understand the incentives
generated by stock options, executives must understand how different
actions and events affect the value of their options. Valuing a stock option
requires using the Black–Scholes formula and is not an intuitive process.

How do the executive's incentives change over time? Will the board of directors need to give her higher levels of stock options next year in order to maintain her incentives at that time? Or do executives develop the habit of working hard to grow the company, so that they will keep working hard no matter what the pay? Do social comparisons matter, so that if executives at one company get pay increases, while those at a second company do not, the latter's efforts decrease? If so, this suggests that the absolute level of pay may be less important than relative pay levels.

On a more practical level, a lack of correlation frequently exists between pay and performance. For example, CEO pay increased an average of 9.4% in 1991, while their companies' corporate profits declined 7% and median stock prices fell 7.7%. In a similar vein, CEO compensation in the 1980s increased 212%, while earnings per share rose only 78%. These statistics illustrate how the rhetoric of pay for performance may not correspond to reality.

There are also many design problems in pay for performance contracts. Many so-called performance-based compensation packages do not base remuneration on the actual performance of the executive or the corporation. Instead, pay is based on economic indicators, which may not accurately reflect how an executive is performing. For example, stock price increases may be caused by market fluctuations and not by the efforts of a company's management.

Existing types of pay for performance compensation packages may not appropriately align an executive's pay with her company's performance from the shareholders' perspective. To understand this point, it is first necessary to explain a bit about the valuation of stock options. Under current practices, CEOs are typically awarded stock options with a ten year duration and an exercise price equal to the current stock price for the company's common stock ("at the money" options). The value of these options is sensitive to the price of the company's stock, but the value of one option is less than the value of one share of the company's stock.[45] Thus, for the same ex ante value transfer, the board of directors can award an executive a larger number of stock options than stock shares.[46] Awarding stock options rather than stock will greatly increase the pay to performance sensitivity of the executive's pay because of the leverage effect of stock options.[47]

45. If the value of the common stock changes, then the value of the stock option changes, too. The amount of the change that occurs is the option's delta. An option's delta, that is the change in the value of the option for a derivative change in the stock's price, is less than one.

46. See [Brian J. Hall, A Better Way to Pay CEOs?, in Executive Compensation and Shareholder Value: Theory and Evidence 35, 40 (Jennifer N. Carpenter & David L. Yermack eds., 1999)]. In the example that Hall used, the board could award three times as many stock options as shares of stock for the same ex ante value transfer. Id.

47. Perhaps the best way to illustrate the additional leverage created by stock options is with an example. Hall compared the value of a one million share transfer where the stock was trading at $1.00 per share with the value of an equivalent value (ex ante) transfer of three times as many stock options. Id. If the company's stock price rose from $1.00 per share to $1.25 per share, he calculated that the value of the stock would rise by $0.25 million, whereas the value of

However, the sensitivity of pay to performance could be further increased by awarding "out of the money" options or indexed options. Out of the money options are even more sensitive to changes in the company's stock price than at the money options. This means that a board can award even more out of the money options than it can at the money options to achieve the same ex ante value. The leverage effect of out of the money options will be greater than that of at the money options.[50] Similar logic applies to the use of indexed options rather than at the money options.[51]

Shareholders would much prefer that boards award CEOs out of the money or indexed options than at the money options, because they "raise the hurdle" for CEOs. The out of the money option forces the CEO to raise the stock price by substantially more than its current level in order for the option to have value when it is exercised. The indexed option requires the company to beat the stock market before there is any payoff to the CEO. In fact, these types of options are rarely used today.

Stock option repricing is another point of shareholder concern.[55] Companies claim that stock options lose their incentive value if the stock price falls far enough below the exercise price that there is little chance the executive will exercise the option. Thus, they claim that the incentive effects of this form of compensation no longer exist. To restore these incentives, companies drop the exercise price of these existing options to the current level of their stock price, thereby "repricing" them.

Shareholder critics claim that option repricing is an egregious abuse of their rights.[56] These investors argue that the alignment of shareholder and

the options would increase by $0.43 million. See id.

50. The intuition is that the board can award more of the lower valued, out of the money stock options than at the money options for the same ex ante value. If the company's stock price increases, the value of the out of the money options increases more than the value of the at the money options. See Hall, supra, note [46], at 42.

51. Indexed options have exercise prices that rise with a market index change. See id. at 43. Executives only make money on indexed options if the company's stock price rises by more than the market index. See id. Each option is therefore worth substantially less than at the money options, and, as a result, the board can award more of them for the same ex ante value. The net effect is to increase the sensitivity of executive pay to company performance. See id.

55. * * *

Ruxton found that, out of the 1189 firms in the S & P Super 1500 covered in her study, only 36 firms, or 3%, repriced stock options in 1998. [Kathy B. Ruxton, Investor Responsibility Research Ctr., Executive Pay 1998 13, 18 (1999).] Most of these firms were in the Technology Sector, with 20 of the 36 firms being from that industry group. See id. Most technology firms are in the S & P 600 SmallCap index. While these numbers are fairly low, Ruxton pointed out that the practice could become much more widespread if there were a sustained decline in the stock markets. Id. at 19.

56. See Graef S. Crystal, In Search of Excess 176 (1991); Charles M. Yablon, Overcompensating: The Corporate Lawyer and Executive Pay, 92 Colum. L. Rev. 1867, 1880 (1992). With repricing, no downside risk exists for an executive whose salary purportedly depends on his company's performance. * * * However, under Treasury Department regulations, stock options that have been revalued will not be classified as performance-based compensation for purposes of the deductibility limit:

[I]f the amount of compensation the employee will receive under the grant or award is not based solely on an increase in the value of the stock after the date of grant or award (e.g., in the case of re-management incentives only exists if executives are unrewarded when stock prices fail to rise or fall. Shareholders further complain that they do not enjoy similar treatment for their stock when the price of the company's shares falls.[58]

Stock option compensation may lead managers to manipulate earnings or other accounting figures so as to insure that the company meets or exceeds analysts' expectations and that the company's stock price rises. Executives holding options also have a tendency to avoid dividends and engage in share repurchases. This raises important questions about whether managers are running the company to increase the value of their stock options or to raise the value of the common stock held by the shareholders. This issue may be critical at certain times in the corporation's life cycle, such as when deciding to take the company public. Managers may bring the company to market too quickly in order to realize immediate value for their stock options.

Numerous other criticisms have been levied against pay for performance. These complaints include: many performance-based compensation packages use inadequate accounting indicators to measure the company's performance,[62] pay for performance packages based on attaining economic performance measures may lead managers to engage in unethical behavior to insure that the company meets performance goals, and the derivatives market can be used by executives to trade stock options for fixed payment streams based on factors other than the company's performance.

Many companies argue that the alleged "abuses" are necessary parts of incentive pay. Option repricing, for example, is claimed to be needed to insure that managers continue to have incentives to perform even if their company's stock price drops after the grant of their original options. This is particularly important, companies say, where the decline in stock prices is caused by economic factors beyond executives' control.

Other criticisms can be addressed through an appropriately designed pay for performance package. For instance, the criticism that stock options may reward executives even though the rise in the stock's price was due to

stricted stock, or an option that is granted with an exercise price that is less than the fair market value of the stock as of the date of the grant), none of the compensation attributable to the grant or award is qualified performance-based compensation. . . .

Treas. Reg. § 162.27(e)(2)(vi)(A) (as amended in 1995)* * *.

58. A related practice is called the reload option. "Reload provisions issue new options to replace shares sold to pay the exercise price of exercised options. The new options are granted at fair market value with a term equal to the remaining term on the option exercised." [Kevin J. Murphy, Executive Compensation, in Handbook of Labor Economics 2485, 2508 n. 27 (Orley Ashenfelter & David Card eds., 1999).] This gives executives a "heads I win, tails we start over" deal. * * *

62. * * * For example, using return on equity as an indicator can lead to management "subtly manipulating" various discretionary responsibilities to award themselves higher compensation without providing any long-term benefit to the company. [Joshua A. Kreinberg, Note, Reaching Beyond Performance Compensation in Attempts to Own the Corporate Executive, 45 Duke L.J. 138, 152 (1995).] Thus, shareholders may be lulled into a false sense of security by compensation classified as performance-based and will be less likely to investigate pay practices.

market factors can be taken care of by using an indexed option.[67] Critics' concerns that management will manipulate the short-term price of the company's stock can be overcome by requiring executives to hold their stock for longer periods of time. Stock options can be made to have a downside risk for executives by using a "purchased stock option."[69] Finally, the government could prohibit executives from using derivative instruments as a way of realizing immediate value on their stock options.

NOTE: AFTER EXERCISE

1. *Sell or Hold?*

Upon exercise of a stock option, which would be better from the point of view of incentive alignment—sale of the stock or long-term holding of the stock? Which is better from the point of view of the manager thus compensated? As rational economic actors, managers can be expected to have a tendency to sell so as to diversify their portfolios. Ofek and Yermack, Taking Stock: Equity–Based Compensation and the Evolution of Managerial Ownership, 55 J. Fin. 1367 (2000), show that many executives do exactly that. They show that managers break into two groups, those with high ownership stakes (in terms of the number of shares held) and those with low stakes. Those already owning significant stakes sell their existing shares as new options are granted and move deeper into the money. The offset sales neutralize the incentive impact of the new options. Executives with low ownership positions are more likely to hold after exercise, so that the option plan does result in their taking a long equity position in the firm.

Downside executive sales of stock purchased through option plans figured prominently in the scandals of 2001–2002. Enron presented the most famous case. There executives sold as the company failed, even as the company's ESOP was locked down ostensibly on administrative grounds. Note that in accord with the above discussion, ongoing executive stock sales can be expected whether the news is good or bad.

Does immediate disclosure of the fact of the sale (without exceptions or loopholes) solve any problem? Should executives be required to hold onto all or a fixed percentage of the stock they purchase? Should employee ESOPs pursue a full diversification policy, or do the same incentive concerns that inform discussion of executive compensation also apply to employees?

2. *Risk Reduction with Derivatives.*

There are two types of derivative transactions widely utilized by executives to reduce the risk attached to their long positions in their company's stock. One is the equity swap. This is a swap contract entered into with a financial institution under which the executive pays the stock's dividends to the counterparty for the contract term and the gain in the stock's value at the end of the term. In exchange, the

---

67. See [Steven A. Bank, Devaluing Reform: The Derivatives Market and Executive Compensation, 7 DePaul Bus. L.J. 301, 312 (1995).] An indexed option is one where "the exercise price of the option is adjusted to the price movements of a designated index such as the Standard & Poor's 500 or to an index more narrowly tailored to the company's industry group." Id. * * *

69. Id. A purchased stock option is simply an option that requires the executive to pay a significant amount of money before it is granted, thus resulting in a real loss if the price of the stock falls below the exercise price. See id.

counterparty pays the executive the income from either a portfolio constituted of treasuries or a diversified portfolio of stocks and also pays any gain in portfolio value over the period. The executive compensates for any loss in value in the diversified portfolio and the counterparty compensates for any loss in value to the stock. The economic effect is that for the period of the swap contract the executive holds the diversified portfolio. In the alternative, the executive could enter into a "zero-cost collar." This is a straddle—the executive buys a put on his or her company stock; the put is financed by a simultaneous sale of a call option on the stock. For the period of the straddle, the risk of a capital loss is avoided (as is the incentive of a gain in the stock price).

Even as executives enter into these derivative contracts, the salary that they collect qualifies as performance-based for purposes of corporate tax deduction. Note also that even as the executives transfer the risk of holding their firms' stock, they avoid having to pay a capital gains tax because they still own the stock. Even better, they retain their voting power in the company. Bank, Devaluing Reform: The Derivatives Market and Executive Compensation, 7 DePaul Bus. L.J. 301, 314, 318–320 (1995).

Bettis, Bizjak and Lemmon, Insider Trading in Derivative Securities: An Empirical Examination of the Use of Zero–Cost Collars and Equity Swaps by Corporate Insiders, SSRN File No. 99060527.pdf (1999), studied 89 such swaps and collars entered into by stockholding executives and concluded (a) that the transactions cover an average of one-third of the stock held by the executives, (b) that these transactions provide a relatively cheap way of undoing the incentive effect of the stock option plan, and (c) these transactions tend to be employed after significant run ups in the company stock price.

NOTE: THE EXECUTIVE PAY DEBATE

1. *Pay without Performance.*

Bebchuk and Fried, Pay without Performance: The Unfulfilled Promise of Executive Compensation (2004), repeats many points made by Thomas and Martin, but in a much more critical mode. Bebchuk and Fried's normative base point is a model of the arm's length bargain. They make a crucial assumption—that an arm's length deal would tightly tie pay to performance: executive pay packages should reward an executive a sum in excess of his or her reservation price, should contain terms that encourage the executive to increase the value of the firm, and should avoid terms that reduce the value of the firm. Compensation packages, they assert, do not conform to the model because top managers possess influence over independent directors. Restating the point, top managers use power to extract rents, defined as benefits better than those available under an arm's length bargain.

Bebchuk and Fried point out that governance institutions are ill-suited to foster arm's bargaining between top managers and their corporate employers. Four factors, all well-known to students of corporate governance, contribute to this debility. First, the board itself is weak because outside directors tend to be loyal to or dominated by the CEO due to process infirmities like large numbers and CEO chairmanship, interlocks, and financial dependence. Second, most firms lack a substantial large outside shareholder, the financial interest of whom would influence bargaining over pay. Third, oversight by large institutional shareholders tends to lead to more sensitive pay arrangements and some firms have fewer large institutional shareholders than do others. Fourth, antitakeover arrangements insulate most managers from the discipline otherwise imposed by the market for corporate control. In Bebchuk and Fried's view, the checks built into the system do not suffice to correct this imbalance and assure that the shareholder interest dominates.

On stock options, Bebchuk and Fried question exercise prices, numbers granted, and vesting rules. Their main complaint goes to price. Only 5 percent of companies price options out of the money, that is, below the market price of the stock at grant, despite the give up in the incentive effect. The practice of leaving the price fixed for the life of the option also diminishes the incentive effect. A fixed price rewards the executive for market wide and sector wide upward price movement in addition to upward movement due to the company's own performance (said to account for only 30 percent of stock growth on average). Because the market tends to rise over time, a pay off is virtually guaranteed. Indexing would solve the problem. The exercise price would be reset upward and downward over time to filter out changes attributable to the market or sector. Alternatively, vesting could be conditioned on meeting a fixed performance target. Neither palliative is seen in practice, despite the obvious opportunity cost in terms of incentive effect.

As to the numbers granted, Bebchuk and Fried think that fewer would be better. According to empirical evidence they cite, the positive incentive effect declines as the number granted increases, so that the benefits of the last option granted may be less than the cost. They also criticize the practice of reloading. Under this, a new option automatically is granted every time an option is exercised. This lets the executive lock in protection against a subsequent decline in the stock price, perversely turning stock price volatility into a source of personal profit.

Under the prevailing practice, once the option vests, the exercising executive is free to sell the underlying stock. According to Bebchuk and Fried, executives do sell 90 percent of the stock purchased upon exercise. No nefarious intentions need be read in. We have seen that they sell to diversify their portfolios, acting no differently from other rational investors. But Bebchuk and Fried object to the concession of free transfer, arguing that restraints on alienation and on hedging would tie the executive's interest more closely to long term value creation within the firm. And, although bad motives need not be read in, nefarious deeds do occur. Executives use inside information to time their sales. Here too correction would be easy–executives should be forced to disclose their sales in advance.

Bebchuk and Fried object even more strongly to restricted stock grants. Pay consultants and commentators have been recommending this as a healthy alternative to options. Because options gain in value as the firm's stock becomes more volatile, they perversely tie executive wealth to stock volatility. Awarding the stock outright avoids that problem. Bebchuk and Fried accept this reasoning, subject to the caveat that the executive be prohibited from selling the stock. But they also note that alienation can be restrained with options just as easily. And they enter a loud objection: Restricted stock is an option with an exercise price of zero and there is no reason to believe zero is an optimal exercise price. To see their point, compare the award of an option to buy 100 shares at $100 and an outright grant of 100 shares, both awarded with the stock trading for $100. Assume that the stock price declines to $80 on the day after the grant and stays at $80 forever because the firm is badly managed. The holder of the option is wiped out; the holder of the stock emerges with 80 cents on the dollar despite poor performance. (It can be noted that many firms did move to restricted stock after the stock market fell in 2000.)

Bebchuk and Fried also criticize add ons like retirement pensions, deferred compensation, post retirement perquisites, and consulting fees. All of these are performance insensitive and, prior to an SEC rules amendment in 2006, were buried in disclosures of supplemental retirement plans rather than placed up front in the compensation table included in the annual proxy statement.

Finally, executives also draw down much of their pay under cash bonus plans. These could be structured to condition rewards on the stock price, but tend not to be. Bonus rewards frequently depend on meeting targets within the payees' control that have no necessary connection with performance improvement at the bottom line—targets such as spending all the funds in an annual budget, or, worse, closing an acquisition. When performance targets are not met, they often are lowered ex post. There also are bonuses on entry and exit. Bonuses for signing are unsurprising, assuming a competitive market for the best managers. Bonuses for leaving, whether by firing, retirement, or acquisition, are a little more disturbing, competitive market or not. The average severance package equals three or more years of compensation, with only two percent of firms reducing it in the event the CEO finds new work. Firing, argue Bebchuk and Fried, should not be a cash bonanza.

2.   The Defense.

Defenders of the practice respond to the critics at three levels. The first level presents a full dress defense of prevailing practice. The second level steps back to admit process infirmities, but to reject the unequal bargaining power description. The third level steps farther back still to admit management empowerment but to argue that the system is robust nonetheless.

The full dress defense, put forward by Professor Kevin Murphy and others, draws on the economic relationship between risk and return to describe prevailing compensation practice as a fair trade. See Hall and Murphy, Stock Options for Undiversified Executives (working paper, Nov. 2002), available at: http://ssrn.com/abstract=252805. This analysis turns on comparison of outside and insider option valuation. From the firm's point of view, the cost of an executive stock option is the cash consideration the firm would receive from a third party investor for the same contingent interest in the stock. But third party investors and firm employees differ in a critical respect as option buyers. Third party investors are fully diversified and positioned to hedge the risk attending the option position. See Murphy, Explaining Executive Compensation: Managerial Power Versus the Perceived Cost of Stock Options, 69 U.Chi.L. Rev. 847, 859–60 (2002). They accordingly are risk neutral, where employees are underdiversified and risk adverse. It follows that the option's value to the employee is less than its value to the third party. It further follows that an option makes no sense when considered as pure compensation in comparison to cash: In order to constitute $1 of pay in the eyes of the employee, option compensation must be increased to make up for the employee's valuation discount. The option thereby costs the firm more than the $1 in value the employee receives. An option nevertheless might make sense as incentive compensation. But the overall terms of an arm's length option package should be expected to reflect the employee's risk aversion. This explains terms that otherwise could be seen as giveaways, such as exercise prices set at the money rather than at a discount, the failure to index the exercise price, and the allowance of both early exercise and stock sales after exercise.

This fair deal emerges only on a critical assumption—that the employee's compensation objective and the firm's incentive objective may be traded off without any further scrutiny of the resulting contract's incentive properties. This contrasts sharply with Bebchuk and Fried's assumption that an arm's length deal tightly ties pay to performance and avoids harm to the firm.

Next comes a process defense mooted to counter the charge of executive empowerment. This begins with the same assertion as the fair deal defense—stock options, viewed as compensation, fail to pass the cost benefit test. The follow up assertion is that board members fail to appreciate the costs. They incorrectly believe stock options to be a bargain mode of compensation, overvaluing options in comparison to cash payments by underestimating the options' economic cost to the shareholders whose stakes they dilute. See Jensen and Murphy, Remuneration: Where We've Been, How We Got to Here, What are the Problems, and How to Fix Them 24–25 (Harv. NOM Working Paper No. 04–28, 2004), *available at* http://ssrn.com/abstract=561305.

Jensen and Murphy use this point to account for a number of practices. For example, during the 1990s, firms continued to grant the same number of stock options year after year even as their stock prices doubled, causing the value of incentive grants to balloon. Had pay plans been laser focused on performance sensitivity, numbers of options would have been cut back as the market rose. Contrariwise, when the market fell after 2000, option value went down in lockstep with it. Had the value of the grants been the center of attention rather than absolute numbers of shares granted, further adjustments would have been required. (Indeed, if management were all powerful, the market decline by itself should have caused a gross up in the numbers.) For Jensen and Murphy, this "free lunch" fallacy does a better job of accounting for prevailing practices than executive empowerment. They also look to lack of sophistication to explain the absence of indexing: Prior to 2005, firms were required under GAAP to expense the value of indexed options from their earnings, while no deduction was required for fixed price, unindexed options. It follows that boards gave up performance sensitivity not because they were dominated but because they were naively fixated on earnings per share and the applicable GAAP was badly articulated.

The third defense makes still more concessions. Management power is hard to deny. Many defenders, including Jensen and Murphy, accordingly concede it a place in the institutional description. Some even concede that some managers take excessive rewards, that equity compensation is more liquid than shareholders would want, and that perverse incentives have cropped up in the form of accounting manipulation. The dispute goes to the normative implications of the diagnosis of systemic imperfection. Here is the question: To what extent does the system succeed or fail in cost effectively channeling the energy of empowered managers to productive ends that serve the shareholder interest? To answer the question is to make a judgment call. Defenders of the practice make a three-part case for relative success.

The first part of the defensive case takes a broad view and looks at the bright side. Shareholders, it is said, should be pleased with the way things have gone since 1990. Returns, measured net of the cost of executive compensation, have been generally higher since the switch to option-based compensation. And the shift did succeed in aligning management interests with those of the shareholders to a greater extent than in the past.

Defenders also point to governance improvements initiated in the 1990s—boards became smaller and more independent, shareholders became more vigilant, compensation committees became the norm, and federal disclosure regulations required greater transparency than ever before. Shareholders apparently welcomed the shift to option compensation as they enjoyed the bull market of the 1990s. In contrast, a much smaller net pay increase to management during the 1980s triggered a populist backlash, due to the association of high salaries with layoffs, plant closings, and downsizing.

Finally, the defenders argue that problems with executive compensation after 2000 mainly concerned a few cases of abuse, and that any breakdowns due to the strain of the 1990s boom market have been addressed quickly. Cases where high pay and poor performance coincide can be identified statistically and dealt with accordingly. The existence of bad apples does not compel the conclusion that the whole economy suffers from governance problems.

NOTE: REGULATORY ENVIRONMENT

1. *Taxation.*

The move to pay for performance stems partly from changes in the regulatory environment, changes which in turn responded to public dissatisfaction with sharp increases in executive pay during the 1980s. Internal Revenue Code § 162(m), enacted in 1993, disallows deductions for nonperformance related compensation of over $1 million for the CEO and four other highest paid executives.

The overwhelming majority of stock options are "nonqualified" for federal tax purposes. That is, the executive realizes ordinary income at the time of exercise at the difference between the stock price at that time and the exercise price. The corporation, meanwhile, deducts an equal amount as a business expense. No income is realized by the executive at the time of granting or vesting. "Incentive stock options" are a separate tax category, laden with qualifications. If the plan qualifies, the executive realizes no income upon exercise of the option; if the executive holds an additional year after exercise, capital gains tax is paid at the time of the sale of the stock. Unfortunately for managers, incentive stock option treatment is subject to a cap of $100,000 per employee measured in terms of the fair market value of stock purchased upon exercise. To qualify, the plan also must have been submitted for shareholder ratification.

2. *Accounting.*

Prior to the reporting year beginning in 2007, GAAP permitted conventional stock options to be granted without the corporation recording an expense on its income statement, as long as the option price at grant was not below the stock price and even as the cost was deducted for tax purposes. In 1993, the FASB proposed rules which would have required the value of stock options to be treated as compensation expense on the income statement. But the FASB withdrew the proposal after blocking legislation was introduced in the House and Senate. It instead issued SFAS No. 123, Accounting for Stock–Based Compensation, which encouraged expensing the value of options but permitted corporations to continue the practice of footnote disclosure. The footnote described the impact the options would have had on net income and earnings per share had the rules required expensing of the options at fair value. This accounting treatment had the inadvertent effect of discouraging indexed options. Since indexed options do not have a fixed exercise price they fell outside of FAS No. 123's safe harbor. In any event, by 2004 more than 750 reporting companies had taken up FASB's invitation to expense voluntarily the fair value of their option grants. The number of volunteers increased substantially in the wake of reporting Enron, Worldcom, Tyco, and other large firms.

The scandals altered the political environment, clearing the way for mandatory expensing under SFAS No. 123, Accounting for Stock–Based Compensation (revised 2004). Revised SFAS No. 123 requires reporting companies to "measure the cost of employee services received in exchange for an award of equity instruments based on the grant-date fair value of the award." For stock options, the cost will be recognized over the vesting period. A stock option's grant-date fair value is estimated using option-pricing models "adjusted for the unique characteristics of those instruments (unless observable market prices for the same or similar instruments are available)." If an option is modified after the grant date, incremental compensation cost will be recognized in an amount equal to the excess of the fair value of the modified award over the fair value of the original award immediately before the modification.

3. *SEC Reports and Corporate Governance.*

Rules on executive compensation disclosure, adopted by the SEC in 1992 require, inter alia, that the reporting company compare its financial performance to an industry benchmark and produce a report by the compensation committee explicitly identifying qualitative and quantitative performance measures used in evaluating managers. See Executive Compensation Disclosure, Exchange Act Release No. 33–6962, 34–31327, IC–19032 (Oct. 21, 1992). The SEC, reacting to post-Enron debates over executive pay, revisited these rules in 2006. See Executive Compensation and Related Person Disclosure, Rel. Nos. 33–8732A; 34–54302A, IC–27444A (Aug. 29, 2006). The revision calls for an introductory discussion and analysis of the firm's compensation policies and a more extensive report on total pay packages, current and deferred.

Bebchuk and Fried offer an additional, longer menu of governance improvements. Some of these would tweak the present system so as to make it more likely that the shareholder voice registers inside boardrooms. For example, they contend that the shareholder vote could be made more meaningful, with separate votes on different segments of compensation plans giving shareholders the opportunity to pinpoint objectionable provisions. Bebchuk and Fried, supra, at 197. Other proposals on their menu are more radical and would empower the shareholders, fundamentally changing the system. For example, binding shareholder initiatives on compensation could be permitted. Id. at 198. More than that, the board could lose its legally vested agenda control over important corporate legislation so that shareholders could remove entrenching provisions. Id. at 211–12. Finally, shareholders could have access to the ballot. Id. at 210. See also Bebchuk, The Case for Increasing Shareholder Power,118 Harv. L. Rev. 833 (2005).

(B) FIDUCIARY DUTIES

Lewis v. Vogelstein

Court of Chancery of Delaware, 1997.
699 A.2d 327.

■ ALLEN, CHANCELLOR.

This shareholders' suit challenges a stock option compensation plan for the directors of Mattel, Inc., which was approved or ratified by the shareholders of the company at its 1996 Annual Meeting of Shareholders. Two claims are asserted.

First, and most interestingly, plaintiff asserts that the proxy statement that solicited shareholder proxies to vote in favor of the adoption of the 1996 Mattel Stock Option Plan ("1996 Plan" or "Plan") was materially incomplete and misleading, because it did not include an estimated present value of the stock option grants to which directors might become entitled under the Plan. Thus, the first claim asserts that the corporate directors had, in the circumstances presented, a duty to disclose the present value of future options as estimated by some option-pricing formula, such as the Black–Scholes option-pricing model.

Second, it is asserted that the grants of options actually made under the 1996 Plan did not offer reasonable assurance to the corporation that it would receive adequate value in exchange for such grants, and that such grants represent excessively large compensation for the directors in relation to the value of their service to Mattel. For these reasons, the granting of the option is said to constitute a breach of fiduciary duty.

* * *

Pending is defendants' motion to dismiss the complaint for failure to state a claim upon which relief may be granted. * * *

For the reasons set forth below I conclude that there is no legal obligation for corporate directors who seek shareholder ratification of a plan of officer or director option grants, to make and disclose an estimate of present value of future options under a plan of the type described in the complaint. There is, therefore, no basis to conclude that failure to set forth such estimate constitutes a violation of any board obligation to set forth all material facts in connection with a ratification vote. Second, I conclude that the allegations of the complaint are not necessarily inconsistent with a conclusion that the 1996 Plan constitutes a waste of corporate assets. Thus, the complaint may not be dismissed as failing to state a claim.

I.

The facts as they appear in the pleading are as follows. The Plan was adopted in 1996 and ratified by the company's shareholders at the 1996 annual meeting. It contemplates two forms of stock option grants to the company's directors: a one-time grant of options on a block of stock and subsequent, smaller annual grants of further options.

With respect to the one-time grant, the Plan provides that each outside director will qualify for a grant of options on 15,000 shares of Mattel common stock at the market price on the day such options are granted (the "one-time options"). The one-time options are alleged to be exercisable immediately upon being granted although they will achieve economic value, if ever, only with the passage of time. It is alleged that if not exercised, they remain valid for ten years.[2]

With respect to the second type of option grant, the Plan qualifies each director for a grant of options upon his or her re-election to the board each year (the "Annual Options"). The maximum number of options grantable to a director pursuant to the annual options provision depends on the number of years the director has served on the Mattel board. Those outside directors with five or fewer years of service will qualify to receive options

---

2. As to the term of the one-time options there exists a material dispute of relevant fact. The complaint alleges those options are valid for ten years. Defendants assert however that a reading of the Plan itself certainly establishes that in fact the options expire *sixty days after an outside director ceases to be a member of Mattel's board or in ten years whichever occurs first.* Thus, according to defendants, the value of the options only continues while the grantee is serving on the board and is, presumably, affected by their motivational effect. This fact if true would render these options very difficult to value under option pricing theory. The procedural setting of the motion requires me to assume that plaintiff's allegation is correct.

on no more than 5,000 shares, while those with more than five years service will qualify for options to purchase up to 10,000 shares. Once granted, these options vest over a four year period, at a rate of 25% per year. When exercisable, they entitle the holder to buy stock at the market price on the day of the grant. According to the complaint, options granted pursuant to the annual options provision also expire ten years from their grant date, whether or not the holder has remained on the board.

When the shareholders were asked to ratify the adoption of the Plan, as is typically true, no estimated present value of options that were authorized to be granted under the Plan was stated in the proxy solicitation materials.

II.

As the presence of valid shareholder ratification of executive or director compensation plans importantly affects the form of judicial review of such grants, it is logical to begin an analysis of the legal sufficiency of the complaint by analyzing the sufficiency of the attack on the disclosures made in connection with the ratification vote.

A. Disclosure Obligation:

I first note a preliminary point: The complaint's assertion is not simply that the ratification of the 1996 Plan by the Mattel shareholders was ineffective because it was defective. If that were the whole of plaintiff's theory, the effect of any defect in disclosure under it would be only to deny to the board the benefits that ratification bestows in such a case. *See In re Wheelabrator Tech., Inc. Shareholders Litig.*, Del.Ch., 663 A.2d 1194 (1995). The thrust of the allegation, however, is that in seeking ratification and in, allegedly, failing fully to disclose material facts, the board has committed an independent wrong. Despite the fact that shareholder approval was not required for the authorization of this transaction and was sought only for its effect on the standard of judicial review, there is language in Delaware cases dealing with "fair process", suggesting that a misdisclosure may make available a remedy, even if the shareholder vote was not required to authorize the transaction and the transaction can substantively satisfy a fairness test. *Cf. In re Tri–Star Pictures, Inc., Litig.*, 634 A.2d 319, 333 (1993) (nominal damages available for misdisclosure in all events.)

In all events, in this instance, the theory advanced is that the alleged non-disclosure itself breaches a duty of candor and gives rise to a remedy. The defect alleged is that *the shareholders were not told the present value of the compensation to the outside directors that the Plan contemplated i.e.,* the present value of the options that were authorized. It is alleged that the present value of the one-time options was as much as $180,000 per director and that that "fact" would be material to a Mattel shareholder in voting whether or not to ratify the board's action in adopting the 1996 Plan. According to plaintiff, the shareholders needed to have a specific dollar valuation of the options in order to decide whether to ratify the 1996 Plan. Such a valuation could, plaintiff suggests, be determined by application of formulas such as the widely-used option-pricing model first devised by

Professors Fischer Black and Myron Scholes.[6] Plaintiff urges that this court should hold that because no such valuation was provided to the shareholders, the proxy statement failed to disclose material matter and was, therefore, defective.

B. Disclosure of Estimated Present Value of Options to be Granted:

Estimates of option values are a species of "soft information" that would be derived from sources such as the specific terms of a plan (including when and for how long options are exercisable), historical information concerning the volatility of the securities that will be authorized to be optioned, and debatable assumptions about the future. Permissible and mandated disclosure of "soft information"—valuation opinions and projections most commonly—are problematic for federal and state disclosure law. Such estimates are inherently more easily subject to intentional manipulation or innocent error than data concerning historical facts. Such estimates raise threats to the quality and effectiveness of disclosure not raised by disclosure of historical data.

As the terms of the options granted under the 1996 Plan demonstrate, option-pricing models, when applied to executive or director stock options, are subject to special problems. Significant doubt exists whether the Black–Scholes option-pricing formula, or other, similar option-pricing models, provide a sufficiently reliable estimate of the value of options with terms such as those granted to the outside directors of Mattel.[8]

First, the Black–Scholes formula assumes that the options being valued are issued and publicly traded. Publicly-traded options have certain common characteristics that are important in assessing their value. Steven Huddart & Mark Lang, *Employee Stock Exercises: An Empirical Analysis*, 21 J.ACCT. & ECON. 1, 9 (1996). The options granted to the Mattel directors under the Plan include restrictive terms that are different from those of typical, publicly-traded options and which may effect their value. Importantly, for instance, the directors' options are not assignable.

Second, the Black–Scholes model overstates the value of options that can be exercised at any time during their term because it does not take into account the cost-reducing effect of early exercise. Huddart & Lang at 18. The Mattel directors' one-time options are not options that are exercisable on a set date. They can be exercised at any time after the grant for a period, according to plaintiff, of up to ten years.

---

6. Fischer Black & Myron Scholes, *The Pricing of Options and Corporate Liabilities,* 81 J.POL.ECON. 637 (1973).

8. For example, the term of such an option—a critical variable in estimating present value—is uncertain because it *expires when exercised, at any time during its life,* rather than at a fixed period at its maturity. *See also* footnote 2, regarding the dispute in this case concerning whether options terminate sixty days after any director to be em-

ployed by Mattel. Such a provision would also make calculation of a present value of the option grant difficult since the probability of a directors' termination at any (or every) point during the ten year term is impossible to know and very hard to responsibly estimate. Thus, one of the vital components of an option-pricing formula, the life of the option, appears quite problematic in instances of this sort.

Third, the value of publicly-traded options and restricted options responds very differently to increased volatility of the price of the underlying stock. The volatility of the stock price is one of the important variables in the Black–Scholes formula. ROSS, ET AL., CORPORATE FINANCE 629–31 (3d ed. 1993). Publicly-traded options increase in value as the price volatility of the underlying stock increases. The value of options of the type granted to the Mattel directors, on the other hand, arguably decreases with increased volatility, because the holders are more likely to exercise the options early since they cannot be traded. Nalin Kulatilaka & Alan J. Marcus, *Valuing Employee Stock Options,* FIN.ANALYSTS J. Nov.-Dec. 1994, at 46, 51.[9]

Plaintiff argues that option pricing techniques are sufficiently developed so that the Financial Accounting Standards Board ("FASB") requires that financial statements state a value of options granted to directors according to a stock-option pricing model. Thus, they assert, the same information should be given to shareholders by directors seeking ratification. There are salient differences, however, between financial statement disclosure of an estimated value of stock options under a plan and disclosure for the purpose of shareholder ratification of adoption of the plan. For instance, financial statements are compiled at the end of the fiscal year, *when the value of the options granted can be assessed with greater certainty,* than is possible at the time the option plan is authorized or ratified since the market price at time of issue is known at that later point.

More broadly, it may be the case that good public policy recommends the disclosure to shareholders of estimates of present value (determined by one technique or another) of options that may be granted as compensation to senior officers and directors, when feasible techniques produce reliable estimates. But while it is unquestionably the case that corporation law plays an important part in the development of public policy in the area of directors' legal relations to corporations and shareholders, including disclosure law, it does not follow that the fiduciary duty of corporate directors is the appropriate instrument to determine and implement sound public policy with respect to this technical issue.

What makes good sense—good policy—in terms of *mandated corporate disclosure* concerning prospective option grants involves not simply the moral intuition that directors should be candid with shareholders with respect to relevant facts, but inescapably involves technical judgments concerning what is feasible and helpful in varying circumstances. Judgments concerning what disclosure, if any, of estimated present values of options should be mandated are best made at this stage of the science, not

---

9. *Cf.* Regulation S–K, Item 402(b) (mandating that companies report the value of compensation paid to executives in stock options, but not requiring that the value be arrived at by using an option-pricing formula). It should be noted that in this instance the utility of the Black–Scholes or a similar option-pricing formula would also be reduced if the outside directors' options do, in fact, expire sixty days after the directors terminate their employment with Mattel. Because the Plan has not been submitted to the court in a manner that permits its specific provisions to be interpreted, it is not possible at this point to conclude whether this would be another shortcoming of this method of pricing the options.

by a court under a very general materiality standard, but by an agency with finance expertise. An administrative agency—the Securities and Exchange Commission—has a technical staff, is able to hold public hearings, and can, thus, receive wide and expert input, and can specify forms of disclosure, if appropriate. It can propose rules for comment and can easily amend rules that do not work well in practice. As just one example, any option-pricing formula premised on the assumptions that underlie Professors Black and Scholes's model would be concerned with the expected volatility of the stock over the term of option. How that volatility is itself estimated would be a significant factor in any standardized disclosure regime. But this certainly is not the type of inquiry that the judicial process is designed optimally to address. Clearly, determining whether disclosure of estimates of the present value of options ought to be mandated, and how those values ought to be calculated, is not a subject that lends itself to the blunt instrument of duty of loyalty analysis.

In all events, for these reasons, I conclude that, given the tools currently used in financial analysis, a careful board or compensation committee may customarily be expected to consider whether expert estimates of the present value of option grants will be informative and reliable to itself or to shareholders. And if such estimates are deemed by the board, acting in good faith, to be reliable and helpful, the board may elect to disclose them to the shareholders, if it seeks ratification of its actions. But, such "soft information" estimates may be highly problematic and not helpful at all, as for example would likely be the case here, if the options terminate two months after the holder leaves Mattel's board, instead of continuing for ten years, as defendants assert. *See supra* note 2.

* * * I conclude that the allegations of failure to disclose estimated present value calculations fails to state a claim upon which relief may be granted. Where shareholder ratification of a plan of option compensation is involved, the duty of disclosure is satisfied by the disclosure or fair summary of all of the relevant terms and conditions of the proposed plan of compensation, together with any material extrinsic fact within the board's knowledge bearing on the issue. The directors' fiduciary duty of disclosure does not mandate that the board disclose one or more estimates of present value of options that may be granted under the plan. Such estimates may be an appropriate subject of disclosure where they are generated competently, and disclosed in a good faith effort to inform shareholder action, but no case is cited in which disclosure of such estimates has been mandated in order to satisfy the directors' fiduciary duty and I lack sufficient confidence to break that fresh ground. *Absent allegations of intentional manipulation,* where shareholder ratification of a plan of stock option compensation is sought, what may constitute appropriate disclosure respecting estimated present (or other) values of such options grantable under the plan is a subject better left to the judgment of the Securities and Exchange Commission and, subject to that regulatory regime, the judgment of the board seeking such approval.

III.

* * * I turn to the motion to dismiss the complaint's allegation to the effect that the Plan, or grants under it, constitute a breach of the directors' fiduciary duty of loyalty. * * * [T]he Plan * * * constitutes self-dealing that would ordinarily require that the directors prove that the grants involved were, in the circumstances, entirely fair to the corporation. *Weinberger v. U.O.P., Inc.,* Del.Supr., 457 A.2d 701 (1983). However, it is the case that the shareholders have ratified the directors' action. That ratification is attacked only on the ground just treated. Thus, for these purposes I assume that the ratification was effective. The question then becomes what is the effect of informed shareholder ratification on a transaction of this type (*i.e.,* officer or director pay).

A.   Shareholder Ratification Under Delaware Law:

* * *

* * * [I]nformed, uncoerced, disinterested shareholder ratification of a transaction in which corporate directors have a material conflict of interest has the effect of protecting the transaction from judicial review except on the basis of waste. *Keenan v. Eshleman,* Del.Supr., 2 A.2d 904 (1938); *Gottlieb v. Heyden Chem. Corp.,* Del.Supr., 91 A.2d 57, 58 (1952); *Steiner v. Meyerson,* Del.Ch., C.A. No. 13139, 1995 WL 441999, Allen, C. (July 18, 1995).

B.   The Waste Standard:

* * * Roughly, a waste entails an exchange of corporate assets for consideration so disproportionately small as to lie beyond the range at which any reasonable person might be willing to trade. * * * Most often the claim is associated with a transfer of corporate assets that serves no corporate purpose; or for which no consideration at all is received. Such a transfer is in effect a gift. If, however, there is *any substantial* consideration received by the corporation, and if there is a *good faith judgment* that in the circumstances the transaction is worthwhile, there should be no finding of waste, even if the fact finder would conclude *ex post* that the transaction was unreasonably risky. Any other rule would deter corporate boards from the optimal rational acceptance of risk, for reasons explained elsewhere. * * * Courts are ill-fitted to attempt to weigh the "adequacy" of consideration under the waste standard or, *ex post*, to judge appropriate degrees of business risk.

C.   Ratification of Officer or Director Option Grants:

Let me turn now to the history of the Delaware law treating shareholder ratification of corporate plans that authorize the granting of stock options to corporate officers and directors. What is interesting about this law is that while it is consistent with the foregoing general treatment of shareholder ratification—*i.e.,* it appears to hold that informed, non-coerced ratification validates any such plan or grant, unless the plan is wasteful—in its earlier expressions, the waste standard used by the courts in fact was not a waste standard at all, but was a form of "reasonableness" or proportionality review.

1. *Development of Delaware law of option compensation:* It is fair to say I think that Delaware law took a skeptical or suspicious stance towards the innovation of stock option compensation as it developed in a major way following World War II. *See, e.g., Kerbs, et al. v. California Eastern*

Airways, Inc., Del.Supr., 90 A.2d 652 (1952); *Gottlieb v. Heyden Chem. Corp.,* Del.Supr., 91 A.2d 57 (1952); *Id.,* 90 A.2d 660 (1952); *Id.,* Del.Ch., 99 A.2d 507 (1953). Such skepticism is a fairly natural consequence of the common law of director compensation and of the experience that corporate law judges had over the decades with schemes to water stock or to divert investors funds into the hands of promoters or management.

The early Delaware cases on option compensation established that, even in the presence of informed ratification, in order for stock option grants to be valid a two part test had to be satisfied. First it was seen as necessary that the court conclude that the grant contemplates that the corporation will receive "sufficient consideration." *E.g., Kerbs,* at 90 A.2d 652, 656 (1952). "Sufficient consideration" as employed in the early cases does not seem like a waste standard: "Sufficient consideration to the corporation may be, *inter alia,* the retention of the services of an employee, or the gaining of the services of a new employee, *provided there is a reasonable relationship between the value of the services . . . and the value of the options . . .* " *Kerbs* at 656 (emphasis added).

Secondly it was held early on that, in addition, the plan or the circumstances of the grant must include "conditions or the existence of circumstances *which may be expected to insure* that the contemplated consideration will in fact pass to the corporation." *Kerbs* at 656 (emphasis added). Elsewhere the Supreme Court spoke of "circumstances which may reasonably be regarded as *sufficient to insure* that the corporation will receive that which it desires . . .". *Id.* at 657 (emphasis added).

This (1) weighing of the reasonableness of the relationship between the value of the consideration flowing both ways and (2) evaluating the sufficiency of the circumstances to insure receipt of the benefit sought, seem rather distant from the substance of a waste standard of judicial review. Indeed these tests seem to be a form of heightened scrutiny that is now sometimes referred to as an intermediate or proportionality review. *Cf. Unocal Corp. v. Mesa Petroleum, Co.,* Del.Supr., 493 A.2d 946 (1985); *Paramount Communications v. QVC Network,* Del.Supr., 637 A.2d 34 (1993).

In all events, these tests were in fact operationally very problematic. Valuing an option grant (as part of a reasonable relationship test) is quite difficult, even under today's more highly developed techniques of financial analysis. This would be especially true where, as this case exemplifies, the options are tied to and conditioned upon a continued status as an officer or director. Even more problematic is valuing—or judicially reviewing a judgment of equivalency of value of—the future benefits that the corporation hopes to obtain from the option grant. There is no objective metric to gauge *ex ante* incentive effects of owning options by officers or directors. Beyond this operational problem, the approach of these early option cases may be thought to raise the question, why was it necessary for the court reviewing a stock option grant to conclude that the circumstances "insure" that the corporation will receive the benefits it seeks to achieve. In other contexts, even where interested transactions are involved, a fair (*i.e.,* valid and enforceable) contract might contemplate payment in exchange for a probability of corporation benefit. A corporation, for example, certainly could acquire from an officer or director at a fair price a property interest that had only prospective commercial value.

In *Beard v. Elster*, Del.Supr., 160 A.2d 731 (1960), the Delaware Supreme Court relaxed slightly the general formulation of *Kerbs, et al.,* and rejected the reading of *Kerbs* to the effect that the corporation had to have (or insure receipt of) *legally cognizable* consideration in order to make an option grant valid. The court also emphasized the effect that approval by an independent board or committee might have. It held that what was necessary to validate an officer or director stock option grant was a finding that a reasonable board could conclude from the circumstances that the corporation may reasonably expect to receive a proportionate benefit. A good faith determination by a disinterested board or committee to that effect, at least when ratified by a disinterested shareholder vote, entitled such a grant to business judgment protection (*i.e.,* classic waste standard). * * * After *Beard,* judicial review of officer and director option grants sensibly focused in practice less on attempting independently to assess whether the corporation in fact would receive proportionate value, and more on the procedures used to authorize and ratify such grants. But *Beard* addressed only a situation in which an independent committee of the board functioned on the question.

2. *Current law on ratification effect on option grants:* A substantive question that remains however is whether in practice the waste standard that is utilized where informed shareholders ratify a grant of options adopted and recommended by a self-interested board *is* the classical waste test (*i.e.,* no consideration; gift; no person of ordinary prudence could possibly agree, etc.) or whether, in fact, it *is a species of intermediate review* in which the court assesses reasonableness in relationship to perceived benefits.

The Supreme Court has not expressly deviated from the "proportionality" approach to waste of its earlier decision, although in recent decades it has had few occasions to address the subject. In *Michelson v. Duncan,* Del.Supr., 407 A.2d 211 (1979), a stock option case in which ratification had occurred, however, the court repeatedly referred to the relevant test where ratification had occurred as that of "gift or waste" and plainly meant by waste, the absence of *any consideration* (" ... when there are issues of fact as to the *existence of consideration,* a full hearing is required regardless of shareholder ratification." 407 A.2d at 223). Issues of "sufficiency" of consideration or adequacy of assurance that a benefit or proportionate benefit would be achieved were not referenced.

The Court of Chancery has interpreted the waste standard in the ratified option context as invoking not a proportionality or reasonableness test a la *Kerbs* but the traditional waste standard referred to in *Michelson.* * * *

In according substantial effect to shareholder ratification these more recent cases are not unmindful of the collective action problem faced by shareholders in public corporations. These problems do render the assent that ratification can afford very different in character from the assent that a single individual may give. In this age in which institutional shareholders have grown strong and can more easily communicate, however, that assent, is, I think, a more rational means to monitor compensation than judicial determinations of the "fairness," or sufficiency of consideration, which seems a useful technique principally, I suppose, to those unfamiliar with the limitations of courts and their litigation processes. In all events, the classic waste standard does afford some protection against egregious cases or "constructive fraud."

* * *

* * * Where under any state of facts consistent with the factual allegations of the complaint the plaintiff would be entitled to a judgment, the complaint may not be dismissed as legally defective. * * * Yet it cannot be the case that allegations of the facts of any (or every) transaction coupled with a statement that the transaction constitutes a waste of assets, necessarily states a claim upon which discovery may be had; such a rule would, in this area, constitute an undue encouragement to strike suits. Certainly some set of facts, if true, may be said as a matter of law not to constitute waste. For example, a claim that the grant of options on stock with a market price of say $5,000 to a corporate director, exercisable at a future time, if the optionee is still an officer or director of the issuer, constitutes a corporate waste, would in my opinion be subject to dismissal on motion, despite the contextual nature of judgments concerning waste. *See Steiner v. Meyerson,* Del.Ch., C.A. No. 13139, 1995 WL 441999, Allen, C. (July 18, 1995); *Zupnick v. Goizueta,* Del.Ch., 698 A.2d 384, Jacobs, V.C. (1997). In some instances the facts alleged, if true, will be so far from satisfying the waste standard that dismissal is appropriate.

This is not such a case in my opinion. Giving the pleader the presumptions to which he is entitled on this motion, I cannot conclude that no set of facts could be shown that would permit the court to conclude that the grant of these options, particularly focusing upon the one-time options, constituted an exchange to which no reasonable person not acting under compulsion and in good faith could agree. In so concluding, I do not mean to suggest a view that these grants are suspect, only that one time option grants to directors of this size seem at this point sufficiently unusual to require the court to refer to evidence before making an adjudication of their validity and consistency with fiduciary duty. Thus, for that reason the motion to dismiss will be denied. It is so Ordered.

NOTE: REGULATION OF STOCK OPTIONS

1. *Questions.*

Would it be violation of the duty of care for a board of directors to approve a sale of the company without reviewing a full-dress valuation of the company by an outside expert? Would it be violation of the duty of care for a board of directors to approve the purchase of another company at a premium without review of a valuation of the target? Would it be violation of the duty of care for a board of directors to approve a stock option plan creating options on a number of shares of stock equal to 5 percent of the company's outstanding shares without review of a valuation of the stock options? Why or why not are stock options are different from mergers so far as concerns the necessity of valuation information in the boardroom?

The foregoing questions are more likely to prompt affirmative answers in the wake of **In re The Walt Disney Company Derivative Litigation**, 825 A.2d 275 (Del.Ch.2003). There Chancellor Chandler famously denied a motion to dismiss a "good faith" based claim arising from the actions of Michael Eisner and the Disney board in connection with the hiring and termination of Michael Ovitz. The thrust of the complaint was that the Disney board played no role when Eisner agreed to a no fault termination of Ovitz at a cost to the company of $140 million. The Disney charter had the duty of care exculpatory clause permitted by DCL 102(b)(7). The section's exculpation does not extend acts in bad faith, opening the door to a quasi-care challenge. Eisner and the Disney board succeeded in deflecting the claim after an extensive trial. See In re The Walt Disney Company Derivative Litigation, 907 A.2d 693 (Del.Ch.2005), aff'd, 906 A.2d 27 (Del.Supr.2006). Chancellor Chandler's opinion implies a warning to future boards respecting procedures followed when approving executive compensation packages, 907 A.2d at 697:

> As I will explain in painful detail hereafter, there are many aspects of defendants' conduct that fell significantly short of the best practices of ideal corporate governance. Recognizing the protean nature of ideal corporate governance practices, particularly over an era that has included the Enron and WorldCom debacles, and the resulting legislative focus on corporate governance, it is perhaps worth pointing out that the actions (and the failures to act) of the Disney board that gave rise to this lawsuit took place ten years ago, and that applying 21st century notions of best practices in analyzing whether those decisions were actionable would be misplaced.

> Unlike ideals of corporate governance, a fiduciary's duties do not change over time. How we understand those duties may evolve and become refined, but the duties themselves have not changed, except to the extent that fulfilling a fiduciary duty requires obedience to other positive law. This Court strongly encourages directors and officers to employ best practices, as those practices are understood at the time a corporate decision is taken. But Delaware law does not-indeed, the common law cannot-hold fiduciaries liable for a failure to comply with the aspirational ideal of best practices, any more than a common-law court deciding a medical malpractice dispute can impose a standard of liability based on ideal-rather than competent or standard-medical treatment practices, lest the average medical practitioner be found inevitably derelict.

2. *Waste.*

In **Zupnick v. Goizueta**, 698 A.2d 384 (Del.Ch.1997), Coca Cola's board granted Goizueta, its retiring CEO, options to purchase 1 million shares. The governing document stated that the grant was in respect of past services; there was no promise of continued availability to consult by Goizueta. The options, moreover, were immediately exercisable. The plaintiff's derivative action claimed the grant to be waste, there being no consideration for it as a contract law proposition. The Chancery Court dismissed the complaint, reasoning as follows, 698 A.2d at 387–389:

> "Any analysis of the waste claim must begin with 8 *Del. C.* § 157. That statute authorizes a Delaware corporation to create and issue * * * options to purchase its shares. It also provides that in the absence of actual fraud, 'the judgment of the directors as to the consideration for the issuance of such ... options and the sufficiency thereof shall be conclusive.' 8 *Del. C.* § 157. That is, so long as there is any consideration for the issuance of shares or options, the sufficiency of the consideration fixed by the directors cannot be challenged in the absence of actual fraud. Only where it is claimed that the issuance of shares or options was entirely

without consideration will § 157 not operate as 'a legal barrier to any claim for relief as to an illegal gift or waste of corporate assets in the issuance of stock options.' *Michelson v. Duncan*, 407 A.2d at 224.

* * *

"Normally, stock options issued to employees are made exercisable at some future date after their issuance, in order to motivate the recipient to continue to perform valuable service for the corporation. * * * That is, the consideration for stock options is often the reasonable prospect of obtaining the employee's valued future services. But that is not the only permissible form of consideration for a grant of stock options. Under certain limited circumstances, stock options may also be issued as a form of compensation for an employee's past services. * * * Nor is there any proscription against using options as a form of executive compensation. If a board may properly award a bonus in the form of cash, then *a fortiori* it may award an immediately exercisable option that is the equivalent of cash. * * *

"In this case, the pleaded facts establish (for present purposes) that reasonable, disinterested directors could have concluded—and in this instance did conclude—that Goizueta's past services were of that character and that the resulting benefit to the corporation was of that magnitude. * * * This case, therefore, falls within a recognized exception to the common law rule that otherwise generally prohibits retroactive executive compensation. As thus viewed, the fact that the options might have become exercisable immediately had Goizueta chosen to retire is, from a legal standpoint, of no consequence."

When, in light of this ruling could a stock option grant ever constitute waste?

3. *The Importance of Careful Drafting.*

Sanders v. Wang, 1999 WL 1044880 (Del.Ch.), concerned a Key Employee Stock Ownership Plan (KESOP) of Computer Associates (CA). The KEPSOP in its § 3.1 authorized a Compensation Committee "to grant up to 6,000,000 shares of Common Stock to the Participants." The grant was conditioned on CA meeting performance targets keyed to the stock price. The Committee issued 20.25 million shares, justifying its action on the ground that CA had split its stock 3 times since the KESOP had set the 6 million figure. Plaintiffs sued to have the grants beyond 6 million set aside and the Delaware Chancery court denied the defendants' motion to dismiss:

"In analyzing the terms of the Plan, I find they are not susceptible to varying interpretations under any reasonable analysis that could lead to the conclusion that the board had the authority to award excess shares over the limitation found in § 3.1. When the language is 'clear and unequivocal, a party will be bound by its clear meaning.' Section 3.1 could not be more clear in limiting the total share grant under the Plan. While § 6.2 gives the board authority to interpret and administer the Plan, I can not find that the board could reasonably ignore a clear six million share limit in order to authorize an award of 20.25 million shares.

"Further, while § 3.3 explicitly permits any stock splits to be reflected when calculating performance targets, *no other provisions or language* explicitly support the proposition that the § 3.1 limit may be contravened or unilaterally adjusted for these same stock splits. The presence of this § 3.3 authorization and the corresponding and conspicuous absence of a provision authorizing alteration of § 3.1 reinforces my conclusion that the Plan's clear language provided *no power* to alter the limitations in § 3.1 based on any stock split criteria.

"Finally, § 1.1 does not state objectives that, read along with the board's § 6.2 discretion, justify ignoring the § 3.1 share ceiling in order to achieve these objectives. * * * I must conclude that § 3.1 and its plain meaning is, in fact, integral to understanding the Plan's intent. It is as much a part of understanding how the drafters and the approving shareholders intended the Plan to operate and the purpose of this Plan as any other particular provision.

"As a practical matter, my rough calculations indicate that even under the strictest reading of the Plan, the three Participants will together still receive nearly $320 million. $320 million is no mere bagatelle. I find it remarkable that defendants would have me believe that CA's shareholders would consider that $320 million for three individuals failed to 'encourage, recognize, and reward sustained outstanding individual performance by certain key employees.' "

Ryan v. Gifford

Delaware Court of Chancery, 2007.
918 A.2d 341.

■ CHANDLER, CHANCELLOR.

On March 18, 2006, *The Wall Street Journal* sparked controversy throughout the investment community by publishing a one-page article, based on an academic's statistical analysis of option grants, which revealed an arguably questionable compensation practice. Commonly known as backdating, this practice involves a company issuing stock options to an executive on one date while providing fraudulent documentation asserting that the options were actually issued earlier. These options may provide a windfall for executives because the falsely dated stock option grants often coincide with market lows. Such timing reduces the strike prices and inflates the value of stock options, thereby increasing management compensation. This practice allegedly violates any stock option plan that requires strike prices to be no less than the fair market value on the date on which the option is granted by the board. Further, this practice runs afoul of many state and federal common and statutory laws that prohibit dissemination of false and misleading information.

* * *

Maxim Integrated Products, Inc. is a technology leader in design, development, and manufacture of linear and mixed-signal integrated circuits used in microprocessor-based electronic equipment. From 1998 to mid–2002 Maxim's board of directors and compensation committee granted stock options for the purchase of millions of shares of Maxim's common stock to John F. Gifford, founder, chairman of the board, and chief executive officer, pursuant to shareholder-approved stock option plans filed with the Securities and Exchange Commission. Under the terms of these plans, Maxim contracted and represented that the exercise price of all stock options granted would be no less than the fair market value of the company's common stock, measured by the publicly traded closing price for Maxim stock on the date of the grant. Additionally, the plan identified the board or a committee designated by the board as administrators of its terms.

[Plaintiff Ryan, a Maxim shareholder, filed a derivative action against Gifford and the members of the compensation committee, alleging that nine specific grants were backdated between 1998 and 2002, on the ground that they were too fortuitously timed to be explained as simple coincidence.]

* * *

As practices surrounding the timing of options grants for public companies began facing increased scrutiny in early 2006, Merrill Lynch conducted an analysis of the timing of stock option grants from 1997 to 2002 for the semiconductor and semiconductor equipment companies that comprise the Philadelphia Semiconductor Index. Merrill Lynch measured the aggressiveness of timing of option grants by examining the extent to which stock price performance subsequent to options pricing events diverges from stock price performance over a longer period of time. "Specifically, it looked at annualized stock price returns for the twenty day period subsequent to options pricing in comparison to stock price returns for the calendar year in which the options were granted." In theory, companies should not generate systematic excess return in comparison to other investors as a result of the timing of options pricing events. "[I]f the timing of options grants is an arm's length process, and companies have [not] systematically taken advantage of their ability to backdate options within the [twenty] day windows that the law provided prior to the implementation of Sarbanes Oxley in 2002, there shouldn't be any difference between the two measures." Merrill Lynch failed to take a position on whether Maxim actually backdated; however, it noted that if backdating did not occur, management of Maxim was remarkably effective at timing options pricing events.

With regard to Maxim, Merrill Lynch found that the twenty-day return on option grants to management averaged 14% over the five-year period, an annualized return of 243%, or almost ten times higher than the 29% annualized market returns in the same period.

* * *

Plaintiff contends that all defendants breached their fiduciary duties to Maxim and its shareholders. [The shareholder-approved plans bound the board to set the exercise price according to the terms of the plans. The plan allowed the board to designate a committee to approve the plans, and the committee approved option grants.] Plaintiff alleges that from 1998 to 2002, the board actively allowed Maxim to backdate at least nine option grants issued to Gifford, in violation of shareholder-approved plans, and to purposefully mislead shareholders regarding its actions. As a result of the active violations of the plan and the active deceit, plaintiff contends that Maxim received lower payments upon exercise of the options than would have been received had they not been backdated. Further, Maxim suffers adverse effects from tax and accounting rules. The options priced below the stock's fair market value on the date of the grant allegedly bring the recipient an instant paper gain. At the time, such compensation had to be treated as a cost to the company, thereby reducing reported earnings and resulting in overstated profits. This likely necessitates revision of the company's financial statements and tax reporting. Moreover, Gifford, the recipient of the backdated options, is allegedly unjustly enriched due to receipt of compensation in clear violation of the shareholder-approved plans.

* * *

* * * [T]he complaint here alleges bad faith and, therefore, a breach of the duty of loyalty sufficient to rebut the business judgment rule and survive a motion to dismiss. * * *

In *Stone v. Ritter,* [911 A.2d 362, 370 (Del.2006),] the Supreme Court of Delaware held that acts taken in bad faith breach the duty of loyalty. Bad faith, the Court stated, may be shown where "the fiduciary intentionally acts with a purpose other than that of advancing the best interests of the corporation, where the fiduciary acts with the intent to violate applicable positive law, or where the fiduciary intentionally fails to act in the face of known duty to act, demonstrating a conscious disregard for his duties." Additionally, other examples of bad faith might exist. These examples include any action that demonstrates a faithlessness or lack of true devotion to the interests of the corporation and its shareholders.

Based on the allegations of the complaint, and all reasonable inferences drawn therefrom, I am convinced that the intentional violation of a shareholder approved stock option plan, coupled with fraudulent disclosures regarding the directors' purported compliance with that plan, constitute conduct that is disloyal to the corporation and is therefore an act in bad faith. Plaintiffs allege the following conduct: Maxim's directors affirmatively represented to Maxim's shareholders that the exercise price of any option grant would be no less than 100% of the fair value of the shares, measured by the market price of the shares on the date the option is granted. Maxim shareholders, possessing an absolute right to rely on those assurances when determining whether to approve the plans, in fact relied upon those representations and approved the plans. Thereafter, Maxim's directors are alleged to have deliberately attempted to circumvent their duty to price the shares at no less than market value on the option grant dates by surreptitiously changing the dates on which the options were granted. To make matters worse, the directors allegedly failed to disclose this conduct to their shareholders, instead making false representations regarding the option dates in many of their public disclosures.

I am unable to fathom a situation where the deliberate violation of a shareholder approved stock option plan and false disclosures, obviously intended to mislead shareholders into thinking that the directors complied honestly with the shareholder-approved option plan, is anything but an act of bad faith. It certainly cannot be said to amount to faithful and devoted conduct of a loyal fiduciary. Well-pleaded allegations of such conduct are sufficient, in my opinion, to rebut the business judgment rule and to survive a motion to dismiss.

* * *

[Defendants contend that the statute of limitations bars plaintiff's claims because none of the challenged transactions occurred within the past three years. Plaintiff responds that the doctrine of fraudulent concealment tolls the statute of limitations in this case.]

Defendants argue that there is no fraudulent concealment since Merrill Lynch based its report on public disclosures and plaintiff bases his complaint on the Merrill Lynch report. That is, defendants insist that Ryan, through investigation, could have discovered the same information that Merrill Lynch discovered. This defense is unconvincing. Shareholders may be expected to exercise reasonable diligence with respect to their shares, but this diligence does not require a shareholder to conduct complicated statistical analysis in order to uncover alleged malfeasance. The above-mentioned facts, in conjunction with an alleged affirmative cover up, convince me that the actions were fraudulently concealed and, thus, defendants may not rely on the statute of limitations as a defense. Inaccurate public representations as to whether directors are in compliance with shareholder-approved stock option plans constitute fraudulent concealment of wrongdoing sufficient to toll the statute of limitations.[60]

* * *

Finally, defendants contend that plaintiff's claim for unjust enrichment fails because there is no allegation that Gifford exercised any of the alleged backdated options and, therefore, Gifford did not obtain any benefit to which he was not entitled to the detriment of another. This defense is contrary both to the normal concept of remuneration and to common sense.

NOTE: SPRING–LOADING

In **In re Tyson Foods, Inc. Consolidated Shareholder Litigation**, 919 A.2d 563 (Del.Ch.2007), the plaintiffs alleged that the Compensation Committee of Tyson Foods, at the behest of several board members, "spring-loaded" options granted under Tyson's Stock Incentive Plan. The Committee had complete discretion as to when and to whom they would distribute option awards, subject to an instruction to consult with and receive recommendations from the CEO. The plaintiffs alleged that, at all relevant times, the Plan required that the price of the

---

60. Further, the existence of fraudulent concealment is supported by the fact that no one noticed these patterns for at least six years. Though most alleged backdating occurred more than four years ago, before the birth of Sarbanes–Oxley, challenges to this compensation method are a recent phenomena, and most of the current litigation is born from the Merrill Lynch report and other articles like it, the earliest of which seem to have been published in 2005. The literature on the opportunistic timing of option grants-and the more recent literature on backdating-have focused on post-and pre-grant stock returns as their tool for detecting and investigating abnormal patterns in option grants. In particular, to detect patterns that could be the result of backdating, this research examined whether post-grant returns tended to be positive, whether pre-grant returns tended to be negative, and whether post-grant returns tended to exceed pre-grant returns. Post-and pre-grant returns have then been the tool used by this research to investigate the variables correlated with grant manipulation as well as to estimate the incidence of such manipulation. See, e.g., Lucian Bebchuk, Yaniv Grinstein & Urs Peyer, *Lucky CEOs* (Harvard Law and Economics, Working Paper Series No. 566, 2006), *available at* http:// papers . ssrn. com/ sol 3 / papers. cfm? abstract_ id= 945392 (citing David Yermack, *Good Timing: CEO Stock Option Awards and Company News Announcements,* 52 J. of Fin. 449 (1997)); Erik Lie, *On the Timing of CEO Stock Option Awards,* 51 Mgmt. Sci. 802 (2005); M.P. Narayanan and Hasan Nejat Seyhun, *The Dating Game: Do Managers Designate Option Grant Dates to Increase Their Compensation? Review of Financial Studies* (U. Mich. Working Paper Series, 2006), *available at* http:// ssrn. com/ abstract = 896164).

option be no lower than the fair market value of the company's stock on the day of the grant.

The Committee awarded options on 2.8 million shares just before Tyson issued press releases likely to drive stock prices higher. Four instances of allegedly well-timed option grants were identified: (1) the day after a grant at $15 Tyson disclosed an agreement to sell a division, causing the stock price to rise to $16.53 in less than six days; (2) the day after a grant at $11.50 Tyson publicly cancelled a $3.2 billion deal to acquire IBP, Inc., causing the stock to rise to $13.47; (3) two weeks after a grant Tyson announced quarterly earnings more than double those expected by analysts, causing the stock price to rise to $11.90; and (4) one week after a grant at $13.33 a Tyson earnings announcement caused the stock price to rise to $14.25.

Defendants' motion to dismiss was denied as follows, 919 A.2d 591–93:

"As plaintiffs' allegations against these directors are insufficient to suggest a lack of independence, plaintiffs must demonstrate that the grant of the 2003 options could not be within the bounds of the Compensation Committee's business judgment. A severe test faces those seeking to overcome this presumption: '[W]here a director is independent and disinterested, there can be no liability for corporate loss, unless the facts are such that no person could possibly authorize such a transaction if he or she were attempting in *good faith* to meet their duty.'

"Whether a board of directors may in good faith grant spring-loaded options is a somewhat more difficult question than that posed by options backdating, a practice that has attracted much journalistic, prosecutorial, and judicial thinking of late. At their heart, all backdated options involve a fundamental, incontrovertible lie: directors who approve an option dissemble as to the date on which the grant was actually made. Allegations of springloading implicate a much more subtle deception.

"Granting spring-loaded options, without explicit authorization from shareholders, clearly involves an indirect deception. A director's duty of loyalty includes the duty to deal fairly and honestly with the shareholders for whom he is a fiduciary. It is inconsistent with such a duty for a board of directors to ask for shareholder approval of an incentive stock option plan and then later to distribute shares to managers in such a way as to undermine the very objectives approved by shareholders. This remains true even if the board complies with the strict letter of a shareholder-approved plan as it relates to strike prices or issue dates.

"The question before the Court is not, as plaintiffs suggest, whether spring-loading constitutes a form of insider trading as it would be understood under federal securities law.[77] The relevant issue is whether a director acts in bad faith by authorizing options with a market-value strike price, as he is required to do by a shareholder-approved incentive option plan, at a time when he *knows* those shares are actually worth more than the exercise price. A director who intentionally uses inside knowledge not available to shareholders in order to enrich employees while

77. * * * Academic commentary on the relationship between spring-loading and insider trading is decidedly mixed. *See, e.g.,* Victor Fleischer, *Options Backdating, Tax Shelters, and Corporate Culture* 9 n. 27 (Univ. of Colo. Legal Studies Working Paper Series, Working Paper No. 06–38, 2006), *available at* http:// ssrn. com/ abstract = 939914; Stephen Bainbridge, Spring-loaded Options and Insider Trading, on ProfessorBa-inbridge.com, http:// www. professor bainbridge. com / 2006/ 07/ spring loaded_ op_ 1. html (July 10, 2006) (presenting argument of Iman Anabtawi that spring-loaded options constitute a form of insider trading or breach of fiduciary duty); Larry E. Ribstein, Options and Insider Trading, on Ideoblog, http:// bus movie. typepad . com/ ideoblog / 2006/ 07/ options_ and_ ins. html (July 11, 2006) (refuting Anabtawi's insider trading argument).

avoiding shareholder-imposed requirements cannot, in my opinion, be said to be acting loyally and in good faith as a fiduciary.

"This conclusion, however, rests upon at least two premises, each of which should be (and, in this case, has been) alleged by a plaintiff in order to show that a spring-loaded option issued by a disinterested and independent board is nevertheless beyond the bounds of business judgment. First, a plaintiff must allege that options were issued according to a shareholder-approved employee compensation plan. Second, a plaintiff must allege that the directors that approved spring-loaded (or bullet-dodging) options (a) possessed material non-public information soon to be released that would impact the company's share price, and (b) issued those options with the intent to circumvent otherwise valid shareholder-approved restrictions upon the exercise price of the options. Such allegations would satisfy a plaintiff's requirement to show adequately at the pleading stage that a director acted disloyally and in bad faith and is therefore unable to claim the protection of the business judgment rule. Of course, it is conceivable that a director might show that shareholders have expressly empowered the board of directors (or relevant committee) to use backdating, spring-loading, or bullet-dodging as part of employee compensation, and that such actions would not otherwise violate applicable law. But defendants make no such assertion here.

"Plaintiffs have alleged adequately that the Compensation Committee violated a fiduciary duty by acting disloyally and in bad faith with regard to the grant of options. * * * "

2. Blockholding

(A) BLOCKHOLDING, CORPORATE GOVERNANCE, AND SHAREHOLDER VALUE

(1) Blockholders as Monitors

Even as institutional shareholders take a leading role in monitoring management conduct and enforcing governance norms, significant frictions continue to impede their performance as monitors and enforcers. The institutions became more active as they came to hold larger proportionate stakes of publicly-traded shares. In theory, larger stakes per institution mean higher expected returns from costs incurred to monitor individual firms in a given institution's portfolio. See Bernard S. Black, Shareholder Passivity Reexamined, 89 Mich. L. Rev. 520, 524–25, 585–89 (1990). But levels of ownership concentration have risen to a point sufficient only to prompt sporadic activity. Institutions tend to intervene in the affairs of firms with well-publicized problems. They are less likely to engage in constant monitoring designed to prevent problems from arising in the first place. Nor, when institutions do intervene, do they do so in direct but costly modes like proxy contests. Instead the institutions put the pressure on through informal communication, which costs relatively little. Finally, if we put to one side the new activist hedge funds, discussed below, the most aggressive institutions are public and labor pension funds, the managers of which have complex political agendas rather than pure financial incentives.

Constraints on institutional activity stem from the same shareholder collective action problem that caused ownership and control to separate in the first place. More particularly, a free rider problem makes costly activism irrational for investment institutions in the "for profit" sector. An institutional shareholder which does not invest in intervention gets the same increased returns as an institution which does invest—the stock price goes up for everybody. Unfortunately, the passive institution shows a better bottom line result because it saves the cost of intervening. Given this problem, a diversified financial institution will be unlikely to have a financial incentive to take the lead in investing aggressively in governance intervention. The best explanation for such institutional activism as we do see in practice lies in selective incentives such as reputation. See Edward B. Rock, The Logic and (Uncertain) Significance of Institutional Shareholder Activism, 79 Geo. L.J. 445, 473–74 (1991). At the same time, while it is clear that stepped up monitoring holds out long run financial benefits for investors as a whole, it is not at all clear that cost-intensive intervention holds out short and intermediate term returns sufficient to induce investment by a profit-seeking institution. Underperforming companies tend to be publicly identified in the ordinary course, and in such cases institutions already will be informally (and cheaply) communicating their criticisms to their managers.

Recognition of these difficulties has led proponents of intensified shareholder participation to advocate the desirability of a large blockholding as a mode of relational investing. The model blockholder is the legendary Warren Buffett, a fundamental value investor who takes large, underdiversified, long-term positions, monitors carefully, does not attempt to interfere with the formulation or implementation of the business plan, but does intervene in a crisis. Thus modeled, the blockholding investor has an adequate incentive for active monitoring. It is less clear, however, whether there are any incentives that might induce conventional investment institutions to make large block investments. Relational investors of the type hypothesized have appeared only rarely in the history of American capitalism. Blockholding implicates two important sacrifices. First, a blockholder institution is underdiversified, making its investments riskier than those of its competitors. Second, large blocks are less liquid than small stakes, and illiquidity also imports higher risk. To compensate for this risk, a blockholder needs a source of reliable returns, returns exceeding those produced by the diversified portfolios of competing investment institutions. Some unconventional investment institutions, the activist hedge funds, discussed below, appear to be breaking the pattern of passivity.

(2) Comparative Corporate Governance: Market Versus Blockholder Systems

Proponents of intensified institutional monitoring have looked abroad for real world models that reinforce their recommendation. It was hoped in particular that practices in Germany and Japan would show that aggressive monitoring by investment institutions holding large equity stakes can generate sufficient financial rewards and need not be deterred by free riding. Mark Roe's leading study looks at the investment and monitoring practices of large banks in Germany and Japan and finds significant bank shareholdings and governance input. Roe, Strong Managers, Weak Owners: The Political Roots of American Corporate Finance (1994).

Extensive discussions of comparative corporate governance have followed Roe's lead. From these there emerges a widely accepted picture which divides the countries of the industrial world into two types. One type, of which the United States and Britain are the leading exemplars, is the market corporate governance system. The other type, of which countries in Continental Europe and Japan are the leading exemplars, is the blockholder system.

The features of market corporate governance systems are familiar to readers of this book. Market systems are characterized by dispersed equity holding, a portfolio orientation among equity holders, and a broad delegation to management of discretion to operate the business. Two productivity disadvantages result from this structure. The first disadvantage is the shareholder-management agency problem. Collective action problems prevent close monitoring of management performance by widely dispersed shareholder owners holding small stakes. Imperfect performance incentives result for managers, who may rationally sacrifice shareholder value to pursue their own agendas. Market systems address this management incentive problem with four corrective mechanisms: incentive pay, the hostile takeover, shareholder legal rights against management self-dealing, and the inclusion of outside monitors on boards of directors voted on by the shareholders. Institutional activism in turn ameliorates shortcomings in the operation of the correctives. The second productive disadvantage of the market system is a time-horizon cost that stems from the shareholders' tendency to rely on short-term performance numbers, and, indeed, to invest with short-term time horizons. This problem has been attributed to information asymmetries. Management has superior information respecting investment policy and the firm's prospects, but this information tends to be either soft or proprietary and therefore cannot credibly be communicated to actors in trading markets. At the same time, market systems fail to provide clear-cut protections to managers who make firm-specific investments of human capital, a failure due in part to these systems' reliance on takeovers, proxy fights, and boardroom coups to control agency costs.

Market systems have countervailing advantages. Their shareholders can cheaply reduce their risk through diversification. Relative to public shareholders in blockholder systems, they receive high rates of return. Market systems' deep trading markets facilitate greater shareholder liquidity. These capital markets also facilitate corporate finance, providing management with greater flexibility as to the type and sources of new capital than do the markets in blockholder systems. More generally, they provide an environment relatively more conducive to management entrepreneurship, as reflected in increased investment in new technologies.

Blockholder systems are characterized by majority or near-majority holdings of stock held in the hands of one, two, or a small group of large investors. Blockholder systems, like market systems, leave management in charge of the business plan and operations. But large-block investments imply a closer level of shareholder monitoring. In addition, the coalescence of voting power in a small number of hands means earlier, cheaper intervention in the case of management failure. The other primary benefit of blockholder systems stems from the blockholders' ability to access information about operations. This decreased information asymmetry permits blockholders to invest more patiently. The longer shareholder time-horizon in turn frees management to invest for a long term and creates a more secure environment for firm-specific investments of human capital by the firm's managers.

There are corresponding costs and limitations. Where the blockholder is a firm, internal agency costs can constrain its effectiveness as monitor. Indeed, whatever the identity of the blockholder, its heightened oversight incentive does not appear in practice to result in sharp oversight of management investment policy. Freedom to make long-term investments thus often means pursuit of growth in market share at the cost of a sub-optimal rate of return on equity investment. Trading markets in blockholder countries tend to be thinner and less transparent than in market system countries, and firms in search of financing encounter a more restricted range of alternatives. Meanwhile, the blockholders themselves forego the benefits of diversification and, given thin trading markets, liquidity and the possibility of easy exit through sale. Finally, there is a shortage of loyalty. Blockholders, having sacrificed diversification and liquidity, extract a return in the form of private benefits yielded through self-dealing or insider trading. Legal regimes in blockholder states facilitate this *quid pro quo* with lax protection of minority shareholder rights and lax securities market regulation. This in turn chills the development of robust trading markets.

(3) Implications

The comparison of market and blockholder systems holds out positive and negative implications for the proposition that blockholding should be encouraged in domestic firms. On the positive side, blockholding does hold out gains through more intensive monitoring. On the negative side lies a cognizable risk of perverse effects. Recall that proponents look to block-holders as tougher institutional monitors who avoid the governance weak-ness of conventional institutional shareholders, with their free rider prob-lems. A problem arises once an institution or other investor has put cash on the table to form a block. It will immediately be looking for tangible returns. At this point, the speculative and long-term nature of the gains on offer from governance participation holds out little satisfaction. To get near term returns, the blockholder, rather than engaging in patient public-regarding monitoring and problem solving, rationally will look for compen-sation for its investment and the cost of monitoring in the form of side payments from management. Since these by definition would not be shared with competing institutions in the shareholder group, they would solve the free rider problem as well as the returns specification problem.

Comparative governance studies have not uncovered any easy solutions to this private benefits problem. Roe's leading study of Germany looks at the investment and monitoring practices of Germany's large banks but not at the practices of other German blockholders, such as the rich families who control many German firms. The study finds significant bank share-holdings and governance input, but not the sort of institutional monitoring being envisioned for institutions in the United States. German bank monitors have not taken an activist role in effecting investment and divestment policies keyed to shareholder value. When they do monitor they tend to take a lender's point of view, intervening on the financial downside.

Nor has the comparison with Japan produce a direct solution to domestic governance problems. Like the German universal bank, the Japanese main bank engages in crisis monitoring from the lender's perspective. For enhanced returns on their equity holdings, Japanese banks historically have looked to captive lender-borrower relationships and insider trading, rather than to public-regarding monitoring. J. Mark Ramseyer, Columbian Cartel Launches Bid for Japanese Firms, 102 Yale L.J. 1927, 2013–14 (1993). A different Japanese phenomenon—cross shareholding (and resulting monitoring) among nonfinancial firms in *keiretsu* organizations—also has been studied. But this has not filled the bill either. These relationships came to be described as a means to the end of stabilizing long-term relational contracts among members of vertical production combines. Gilson and Roe, Understanding the Japanese Keiretsu: Overlaps Between Corporate Governance and Industrial Organization, 102 Yale L.J. 871, 874–875 (1993). As such they offered no immediate precedent for financial institutions in the United States.

Summing up, the question for the United States is whether blockholding importing significant domestic governance improvements is compatible with the fundamental precepts of the system of corporate law and securities regulation that support the market system, specifically, the duty of loyalty and the prohibition of insider trading.

Policy discussions prompted by the comparison of the two systems proceed abroad as well. Observers in Europe's blockholder countries now debate the question as to the desirability of creating a shareholder-protective legal regime resembling that of the United States. The proponents of reform look primarily to securities law as the means to the end of deeper equity trading markets, proposing (and enacting) regulations that would enhance transparency respecting both issuers and the markets on which their shares are traded. One question is whether such disclosure and insider trading rules would suffice by themselves to foster an environment conducive to dispersed shareholding. Self-dealing transactions between blockholders and firms that do not involve purchases and sales of shares on securities exchanges may independently discourage dispersed shareholding. Accordingly, discussants in countries like Germany, France, and the Netherlands have gone much farther and suggested corporate law reforms. This agenda features direct controls on blockholders, such as the one share, one vote rule, self-dealing constraints to protect outside shareholders, and voting caps and limits on the proportion of capital held by designated investors. The residual question for Europe is whether meaningful reform along these lines could destabilize the incentives that sustain Europe's blockholder monitoring regime, inadvertently causing the blocks to dissipate by cutting off the holders' sources of return.

NOTE: THE NEW BLOCKHOLDERS—ACTIVIST HEDGE FUNDS

In recent years, hedge funds have emerged as aggressive blockholders at many firms. See Kahan and Rock, Hedge Funds in Corporate Governance and Corporate Control, 155 U. Pa. L. Rev. 1021 (2007). The funds target companies and take large positions in their stock (typically between 5 and 10 percent of the shares outstanding). These firms, like Warren Buffett's Berkshire, are underdiversified. Like Berkshire, they profess to be "value" investors. Their relational approach, however, is quite different. They publicly criticize their investee's business plans and governance practices and confront their managers, demanding action enhancing shareholder value. When one hedge fund announces a 5 or 10 percent position in company, others follow, forming a "wolf pack" that sometimes has the voting power to force management to address its demands. The demands, in turn, likely include one or more actions assuring a quick return on investment–sale of the company at a premium, unbundling of the company through the sale or spin off of a large division, or a large cash payment to the shareholders in the form of a special dividend or share repurchase. The activists pack their biggest punch at small companies at which their investments translate into large voting blocks. But they also have confronted giants like General Motors, McDonald's, and Time Warner.

Not everyone approves. The critics ask why, as between a team of managers who have been running a firm for years and an outside activist looking for above-market returns in the current period, the activist's judgment about the best way to run the business should command respect. Hedge fund pressure on present and potential targets is thought negatively to constrain investment policy, skewing managers away from promising but difficult to value projects toward less promising but more easily valued projects. Where an activist extracts a payout financed by debt, the ongoing cash drain could leave the target vulnerable to distress in the economy's next downturn.

The shareholder value norm is cited in defense. Cash payouts, say the activists, should be applauded: Managers should pay out capital for which the company has no good use, turning the job of reinvestment over to capital markets better suited to the task. Meanwhile, the activist funds operate subject to constraints. Wolf pack voting does not necessarily predetermine a hostile engagement's outcome. An alternative business plan must persuade the wider community of institutional investors and informational intermediaries, which can be counted on to reject unsound, short-term interventions.

Bratton, Hedge Funds and Governance Targets, 95 Geo.L.J. 1375 (2007), collects information on 130 domestic firms identified in the business press from 2002 to 2006 as investment targets of "activist" hedge funds, surveying the funds' demands, their tactics, and the results of their interventions for the targets' governance and finance. The results rebut two allegations made by the hedge funds' critics. The interventions neither amount to near-term hold ups nor revive the 1980s leveraged restructuring. The activists' time horizon is not short-term—they typically invest for an intermediate term of two years or longer. During that time, they employ the proxy system with remarkable, perhaps unprecedented, success. Here is the typical scenario. The activist hedge fund quietly buys a 5 percent stake in the target's stock, and then reveals itself in 1934 Act filings, presenting the target's managers with demands for redirection of the firm's business plan and governance improvements. A proxy contest for a board seat or seats also is threatened. In most cases the proxy contest never actually occurs because target management backs down in the face of the threat and makes a significant concession to the activist's demands. This can be a large cash payout to the shareholders, sale of a division or other property, or sale of the whole firm. In cases where a full solicitation occurs, the activists tend to win, having gained the support of the mainstream institutions. One way or the other, the activist ended up on the board of directors in 40 percent of the sample.

Although the pattern of engagement includes large cash payouts, this is not a return to the high leverage, bust up takeovers of the 1980s. Large payouts were made by only a minority of the firms surveyed, with borrowing as the mode of finance in only minority of the payout cases. Today's pattern is more moderate than that that characterized the hostile tender offers of 20 years ago. Engagements in the 1980s tended to have all or nothing outcomes–either the raider took over the firm, the firm went private or otherwise paid off its shareholders with the proceeds of a leveraged restructuring, or the firm stayed independent, perhaps after making a greenmail payment. Today's activism triggers changes in control only in a minority of cases; when control does change it tends to mean a sale to a third party rather than to the activist. Today's cash payouts, while substantial, do not imply radical transformation of the targets' capital structures.

The cases that conclude with the activist on the board amount to an experiment in blockholding–a new variation on the blockholder theme. The activist fund enters the boardroom both as a substantial shareholder and as a past adversary. The question is whether the adversity gives way to constructive engagement. With boardroom entry come fiduciary duties to the entity as a whole and an implicit commitment to pursue the value agenda in a cooperative framework, much as Warren Buffet always has done. At the same time, the activists' independence and financial stakes imply a more critical stance toward management initiatives than heretofore forthcoming from independent outside directors. This new blockholder is more distanced from management and arguably better positioned to approach corporate governance's theoretical ideal of a vigorous outside monitor. Whether the activists succeed in thus mediating between their agendas as fund managers and as boardroom fiduciaries remains to be seen. As yet, at any rate, there are no signs of self-dealing abuses. For a case where board membership means only that the fight continues inside the firm, see In re Topps. Co. Shareholders Litigation, infra Part V.E.

It also remains to be seen whether the new activists will alter permanently the balance of power between managers and shareholders. The separation of ownership and control will yield only to the extent that clear cut financial incentives encourage shareholder intervention. The study's review of financial results at the target firms in the sample does not confirm the presence of such incentives. A comparison of the results on the investments in the sample and results of the market as a whole do not show the activists, as portfolio managers, to have been beating the market.

(B) REGULATION OF BLOCKHOLDERS

(1) Regulation as a Barrier to Blockholding

Proponents of blockholding in domestic corporations have to explain why, relative to Europe and East Asia, it has not been the dominant mode of domestic shareholding in the past. The leading explanation is that domestic regulation discourages blockholding. The following regulations have been singled out. It is argued that they unnecessarily discourage the formation of large blocks, and in particular make it costly for investment institutions to take large block positions. See, e.g., Roe, A Political Theory of American Corporate Finance, 91 Colum. L. Rev.10, 26–27 (1991).

● Section 13(d) of the Williams Act, 15 U.S.C. § 78m(d). This section imposes disclosure requirements imposed on holders of more than 5 percent of a class of securities.

● Section 15 of the 1933 Act, 15 U.S.C. § 77o, and § 20(a) of the Exchange Act, 15 U.S.C. § 78(a). These sections impose liability on controlling persons for securities law violations of controlled persons.

● Section 16(b) of the 1934 Act, 15 U.S.C. § 78p. This section imposes liability for profits received on shares held less than 6 months by holders of 10 percent of any class of equity security.

● Sections 18(d) and 23 of the Investment Company Act, *see* 15 U.S.C. §§ 80a–18(d), 23(a), 23(b). These sections impose restrictions on capital structures and incentive compensation for advisors of investment companies.

● Portfolio diversification requirements under ERISA.

Regulation FD, promulgated in 2000 should be added to the list. Regulation FD prohibits selective disclosure by issuers of material nonpublic information to, inter alia, investment advisers as defined in § 202(a)(11) of the Investment Advisers Act of 1940 and institutional investment managers as defined in § 13(f)(5) of the Exchange Act.

What offsetting benefits flow from these regulations? How does one trade off these benefits against the cost of discouraging blockholding?

It can be noted that these regulations have not constrained the hedge fund activists. They use § 13(d) to their advantage, making it a conduit for public attacks on target managers. They hold for longer than 6 months. Their funds are open to sophisticated investors and hence not subject to the Investment Company Act. See 15 U.S.C. § 80a–3(c)(1),(7). And they need not register under the Investment Advisors Act. See 15 U.S.C. § 80b–1–8b–21; Goldstein v. SEC, 451 F.3d 873 (D.C. Cir. 2006).

An opponent of stepped up blockholding (and the hedge fund activists) might comment that a cost benefit discussion of the regulations singled out above would be too narrowly confined. The real regulatory question respecting the encouragement or discouragement of blockholding concerns two additional bodies of regulation—the ban of insider trading under 1934 Act section 10(b) and rule 10b–5 and restrictions on self dealing transactions under the state law duty of loyalty. Under this line of reasoning, absent substantial curtailment of these regulations, no material expansion of blockholding can be expected. As to such a more fundamental deregulatory initiative, the further argument is that the market system's benefits—thick trading markets and liquidity—depend on these regulations. Accordingly, their costs are vastly outweighed by their benefits. Some assert these points to be the main regulatory implication of the comparative corporate governance inquiry. This is known as the "law matters" thesis. See Bratton and McCahery, Comparative Corporate Governance and the Theory of the Firm: The Case Against Global Cross Reference, 38 Colum. J. Transnat'l L. 213 (1999); Coffee, The Future as History: The Prospects for Global Convergence in Corporate Governance and Its Implications, 93 Nw. U. L. Rev. 641 (1999). Proponents of this view cite a body of recent comparative empirical studies which suggest that the degree of protection a country's legal system provides for outside investors has an important effect on its corporate governance system. Strong protection of minority interests and insider trading restrictions are associated with deeper, more efficient securities markets, greater liquidity, and a lower cost of capital. For a summary of these results, see La Porta et al., Investor Protection and Corporate Governance, 58 J. Fin. Econ. 3 (2000). For an attack on the "law matters" view, based on British law, see Cheffins, Does Law Matter? The Separation of Ownership and Control in the United Kingdom, 30 J. Leg. Stud. 459 (2001).

(2) Fiduciary Regulation of Blockholders

(a) noncontrolling blockholders

The ideal blockholder of corporate governance theory takes a substantial but noncontrolling stake in the firm's equity, say 10 percent of the common stock. The blockholder then proceeds in the manner of Warren Buffett, taking a seat (or two) on the board, making constructive suggestions and monitoring but intervening only in a crisis. The blockholder takes its returns in the form of an increase in the stock price. But, in the real world, blockholders, even 10 percent blockholders, may not be so patient. Like the hedge funds, they may look to quick fixes like asset sales and large cash payouts. Alternatively, they may look for profits from insider trading and self dealing transactions.

Relationships within Japanese *keiretsu* are the preeminent case of returns through self dealing. Within *keiretsu*, member firms make small block investments in one another, say 2 to 10 percent of one anothers' common stock, with ten or twenty firms being associated in the informal organization. There emerge patterns of cross holdings among most of Japan's large firms. These become quite complex as suppliers, customers, and financial firms take mutual stakes in one another, many belonging to more than one *keiretsu*. Buyer-seller and financial relationships follow the stock ownership pattern.

Such buyer-seller relationships are not exclusive to Japan, as the following excerpt shows. The excerpt also focuses on a feature that characterized some domestic blockholder relationships in the past: Issuing firms seek to induce blockholder investments when they are threatened with a hostile takeover. This point goes for Japan also—*keiretsu* cross holdings amounting to 40 percent or more of an issuer's outstanding stock taken together with mutual loyalty within the organization, effectively blocks hostile takeover activity.

Rock, Controlling the Dark Side of Relational Investing
15 Cardozo L. Rev. 987, 991–999 (1994).

Consider this problematic scenario: In exchange for buying a large block of specially tailored preferred stock at a low price (what I will refer to as "sweetheart preferred"), a relational investor agrees to protect incumbent management from a hostile takeover or other outside interference with business as usual. In this regard, consider the following examples.

1. Corporate Partners and Polaroid

In the spring of 1988, at a time when Polaroid stock was trading for between $30 and $35 per share, Shamrock Holdings, Inc. ("Shamrock") accumulated slightly less than 5% of Polaroid's stock. In June, Shamrock contacted Polaroid in an effort to arrange a meeting to "establish the ground work for a good relationship with the company."

To "protect" Polaroid's shareholders from an anticipated tender offer from Shamrock, the Board of Directors erected a number of defenses [including an employee stock ownership plan and an OMR program.]

In September 1988, Shamrock commenced a tender offer, offering $42 per share in cash for all outstanding shares of Polaroid's common stock, conditioned upon the tendering of 90% of the shares and judicial invalidation of the ESOP. * * *

After Polaroid established its ESOP and while it was planning its share repurchase, Corporate Partners, an investment fund managed by Lazard Freres & Co., entered the picture. According to its promotional literature, Corporate Partners was in the business of protecting management from hostile tender offers * * *.

* * * On January 30, 1989, Polaroid sold $300 million of special preferred stock to Corporate Partners and its investment partners.

Polaroid issued two special series of preferred stock to Corporate Partners: $100 million of Series B Cumulative Convertible Preferred Stock with annual cumulative cash dividends of 11%; and $200 million of Series C Cumulative Convertible Preferred Stock with annual cumulative payment-in-kind dividends of 11.5%. In addition, Polaroid issued seven-year warrants for 635,000 shares of common stock, exercisable at $50 per share (Polaroid's self-tender price).

Both series of preferred stock had the right to vote with the common stock and, in aggregate, represented just under 10% of the votes. As part of the purchase, Corporate Partners agreed to a number of restrictions. Specifically, Corporate Partners agreed not to

> (I) deposit any voting securities in a voting trust, (ii) solicit proxies or become a participant in a proxy solicitation, (iii) form a group for the purpose of acquiring, holding, voting or disposing of voting securities or (iv) otherwise act, alone or in concert with others, to seek to affect or influence control of the Company.

Moreover, Corporate Partners agreed not to sell its shares to a third party (though it apparently retained the right to tender into a Shamrock offer).

The preferred stock contained both put and call provisions. Polaroid had the option of calling both classes in seven years in cash at par. Polaroid could call the preferred early in the event of a final judicial determination or settlement of the Kodak litigation. In the event that someone other than Shamrock acquired control of Polaroid, Corporate Partners had an option to sell the shares back to Polaroid at a price reflecting an annual rate of return of 28–30%. Finally, Corporate Partners had the right to name two directors.

In March 1989, after Polaroid had placed 14% of its shares in an ESOP, 10% of its shares with Corporate Partners, and had launched an $800 million self-tender (16 million shares at $50 per share), Shamrock abandoned its takeover bid and negotiated a peace treaty. Shamrock and Polaroid agreed that Shamrock would withdraw its tender offer and proposed proxy contest, agree to a ten-year standstill, and withdraw all pending litigation, in return for Polaroid's promise to distribute to shareholders a portion of its proceeds from the Kodak litigation and a payment of $25 million ($20 million as reimbursement of expenses and $5 million as a nonrefundable advance payment for radio and television advertising time on Shamrock's affiliated radio and/or television stations). After the agreement was announced, Polaroid stock dropped $4.50, to $36 per share.

On October 7, 1991, just over two and one-half years after Corporate Partners purchased preferred stock for $300 million, Polaroid bought it all back for $420 million ($280 million in cash and $140 million in convertible subordinated debentures). Adding to this the nearly $30 million in dividends that were due quarterly in cash on the Series B preferred stock, Corporate Partners' profit on its $300 million investment approached $150 million, an annual return of nearly 20%. * * *

2. Some Other Examples?

Corporate Partners' investment in Polaroid is not an isolated example of sweetheart preferred. In the 1980s, Warren Buffett was Corporate Partners' chief competitor as management's savior. In 1987, Salomon faced a bid for control from Ronald Perelman. Salomon was vulnerable because its stock had dropped and, more troubling, Minorco had publicly disclosed that it wanted to sell its 14% block of common stock. To "protect" itself, Salomon bought back the Minorco block at a premium above market value, and then turned around and sold Buffett a new issue of special preferred stock carrying 12% of the votes for $700 million. A rather skeptical commentator estimated that on the open market, the preferred, which receives a dividend of 9% per year plus the same opportunity for gains as the common shareholders, would have sold for between $850 million and $1.2 billion.

* * *

B. Keeping the Relations Happy

Another problematic scenario: The relational investor acquires a large block of stock in the firm, perhaps on the open market, and designates a number of directors. Everyone now understands that the relational investor has the power to replace incumbent managers if it becomes unhappy with their performance. Shortly thereafter, the relational investor becomes one of the firm's largest suppliers, outpacing all competitors in securing the firm's business.

1. Du Pont and General Motors

The Du Pont Company's investment in General Motors ("GM") provides, for some, an attractive model for corporate governance—a potential alternative to the Berle & Means corporation. The story is well known, but worth summarizing. In 1917, Du Pont acquired about 23% of GM stock at a time when GM was a distant second in the automobile industry. At the same time, Pierre du Pont, then Chairman of the Board of Du Pont, also became Chairman of the Board of GM. By the end of 1920, after a badly managed postwar expansion and a significant recession, GM was on the brink of bankruptcy. At that time, Pierre du Pont, who had withdrawn from active management of Du Pont in 1919, became President of GM. During the next two and one-half years, he devoted himself full-time to reorganizing and restructuring GM, turning over the presidency to Alfred P. Sloan, Jr., in May 1923. By 1928, GM had replaced Ford as the leading American automobile company.

From one perspective, this seems to be the paradigm of good relational investing. A large shareholder, by virtue of its holdings in the firm, actively monitors managers and, when necessary, steps in to replace bad managers and to reorganize the firm. Pierre du Pont's scrutiny of GM was an example of "continuous and textured monitoring."

But even in this paradigm case, there is more to the story. Du Pont's holdings of GM gave rise to a major antitrust case, leading to forced divestiture. The courts' opinions describe a different, and potentially more troubling, aspect of the relationship.

Pierre du Pont and his long time business associate and the treasurer of Du Pont, John Raskob, first invested in GM in 1914, becoming directors in 1915. In 1917, when Raskob recommended that Du Pont acquire a significant interest in GM, his memo identified two principal reasons. Not only would the investment be profitable, but also "our interest in the General Motors Company will undoubtedly secure for us the entire Fabrikoid [an artificial leather], Pyralin, paint and varnish business of those companies, which is a substantial factor."

* * *

2. A More Recent Example?

In early 1989, Transco Energy Company, an oil and gas concern, sold Corporate Partners $125 million of a special issue of 9.25% convertible preferred stock entitled to vote with common stock, representing 9% of the votes, in connection with Transco's acquisition of Texas Gas Transmission Corp. (a natural gas pipeline system being auctioned by CSX Corp.).

Over the subsequent months, Transco and related entities paid Lazard Freres the following fees: in May 1989, $937,500 plus expenses for financial advisory services in connection with the private placement of the 9.25% preferred as well as $3,500,000 for investment banking services in connection with the acquisition of Texas Gas; in August 1989, $707,441 plus expenses for financial services in connection with the sale of certain onshore oil and gas properties; and in September 1989, $8,048,455 plus expenses in connection with the sale of certain other assets, and another $500,000 in connection with other asset sales.

Subsequently, in 1990, Transco engaged Lazard as its agent in the sale of a natural gas field in Louisiana for a fee of .66% of the ultimate sales price. In June 1992, that property was sold for $82 million, resulting in an additional fee of $541,200 for Lazard. Thus, from 1989 through 1992, Lazard received $14,234,596 in investment banking fees (plus expenses) from its involvement with Transco.

One does not know whether Corporate Partners' investment in Transco led to the Lazard assignment, whether Lazard's long-time representation of Transco led to the Corporate Partners investment, or whether the events were entirely unrelated. Corporate Partners maintains that they were unrelated. But the Transco/Lazard/Corporate Partners relationship effectively illustrates the potential for using investment banking fees to keep a relational investor happy. Perhaps it is a recognition of this difficulty that has led Ali Wambold (co-Managing Director of Corporate Partners and a partner in Lazard) to maintain that "the Corporate Partners fund is completely separate from Lazard's investment banking business . . . to prevent potential conflicts of interest."

———

Were any fiduciary duties violated in the foregoing examples? In Shamrock Holdings, Inc. v. Polaroid Corp., 559 A.2d 278 (Del.Ch.1989), the Delaware Chancery, applying *Unocal* proportionality scrutiny, declined to enjoin the sale of the preferred to Corporate Partners. Rock, supra, at 1011–1012, reports finding one case where the Chancery Court did enjoin a preferred stock sale:

"Packer v. Yampol, [1986 WL 4748 (Del.Ch.)], shows just how much a plaintiff must prove. Vice Chancellor Jacobs enjoined the issuance of supervoting preferred to one Yampol, the Chairman, CEO, and 17% shareholder of Graphic Scanning Corp. ('Graphic'), and to a third party recruited by Yampol. Plaintiffs argued that the preferred stock was issued to entrench Yampol in response to rumors of a hostile tender offer. Yampol countered that the stock was issued to raise necessary capital.

"Consider the evidence the court recounts. First, Yampol had a long history of sleazy self-dealing transactions with Graphic. Second, the court did not consider any of the directors of Graphic to be independent of Yampol. Third, plaintiffs somehow came up with a memo to Yampol from his lawyers at Paul Weiss Rifkind Warton & Garrison which recommended the issuance of the preferred stock because 'the issuance of the Series A and Series B stock gives Mr. Yampol effective veto power over any proposed plan of merger which is presented for shareholder vote.' Fourth, not only had Graphic never used supervoting preferred stock to raise capital, although it had used just about every other means, but Graphic had not even hired an investment banker to seek alternative sources of capital. Based on this very strong evidence of self-dealing, the absence of independent directors, and an utterly implausible alternative explanation, the court enjoined the issuance of the supervoting preferred.

"The Delaware courts' approach to the issuance of sweetheart preferred thus follows familiar patterns. If the process appears to be arm's length, and there is evidence of hard bargaining, the court will not second-guess the judgment of directors. The court is most likely to intervene when there is substantial evidence of self-dealing. While this approach may be reasonably effective at preventing egregious self-dealing of the sort present in Packer v. Yampol, it is peculiarly useless in preventing the sort of bad relational investing previously described.

"When a bad relational investor implicitly or explicitly offers to protect bad management from interference or displacement in return for sweetheart preferred, hard arm's length bargaining over the magnitude and terms of the protection is to be expected, and, therefore, will be no evidence whatsoever that the stock was issued for valid corporate purposes. * * *"

(b) controlling blockholders

One teaching of the comparative governance literature is that in countries where blockholding predominates in equity capital structures, the blockholders tend to control the board of the directors of their firms. Such controlling blockholders are quite familiar in domestic capital structures. The paradigm case arising when a founder or group of founders takes the firm public, retaining substantial stock holdings. At present Bill Gates is the best known blockholder of this type.

The materials that follow take up two problematic situations which recur in connection with controlling blockholders. Both situations concern a subset of controlling blockholders—those who control the membership of the board of directors but hold less than an absolute voting majority of the stock. The first situation carries on the takeover defense theme developed in the preceding materials: The blockholder whose control is threatened engineers a recapitalization that vests it with voting control. The second situation arises when a controlling blockholder sells the block at a premium, simultaneously transferring control of the board.

1. *Majority–Minority Fiduciary Duty*

Levco Alternative Fund v. The Reader's Digest Association, Inc.

Supreme Court of Delaware, 2002.
803 A.2d 428.

■ Before WALSH, BERGER, and STEELE, JUSTICES.

(1) This is an expedited appeal from the Court of Chancery following denial of an application for a preliminary injunction. The appellants-plaintiffs below are Class A non-voting shareholders of Reader's Digest Association, Inc.("RDA"), a Delaware corporation, who seek to prevent the

implementation of a recapitalization of RDA scheduled for shareholder vote on August 14, 2002. * * *

(2) The recapitalization plan at issue calls for RDA to: (I) purchase all the shares of its Class B voting stock at a premium ratio of 1.24 to 1 with the newly issued common stock at one vote per share; (ii) recapitalize each share of the Class A non-voting stock into one share of the new voting common stock; (iii) create a staggered Board of Directors; and (iv) eliminate the ability of shareholders to act by written consent.

(3) The key to the recapitalization proposal is the agreement by RDA to purchase 3,636,363 shares of Class B Voting Stock owned by the DeWitt Wallace–Reader's Digest Fund and the Lila Wallace Reader's Digest Fund (the "Funds") at $27.50 per share for an aggregate purchase price of approximately $100 million. The Funds currently control 50 percent of the Class B voting stock. Following the recapitalization, the funds will hold 14 percent of the new voting stock.

* * *

(7) Appellants * * * assert that the directors, including the Special Committee, were subject to the control of the Funds and were thus required to demonstrate the entire fairness of the transaction. Appellants further contend that the directors breached their duty of care. Rejecting the entire fairness claim, the Court of Chancery ruled that regardless of where the burden of proof reposed, the evidence does not support the view that plaintiffs would ultimately succeed in demonstrating that the activities of the Special Committee did not result in a "fair and genuinely negotiated price." In our view the record does not support that conclusion.

(8) * * * [W]e think it significant here that the initial burden of establishing entire fairness rests upon the party who stands on both sides of the transaction. Kahn v. Lynch Comm. Sys., Inc., 638 A.2d 1110, 1117 (Del.1994). That burden may shift, of course, if an independent committee of directors has approved the transaction. Emerald Partners v. Berlin, 726 A.2d 1215, 1221 (Del.1999). While we agree with the Court of Chancery that the independent committee who negotiated the recapitalization believed it was operating in the interests of the corporation as an entity, we conclude that the committee's functioning, to the extent it was required to balance the conflicting interests of two classes of shareholders, was flawed both from the standpoint of process and price.

(9) With respect to the unfair dealing claim, the Special Committee never sought, nor did its financial advisor, Goldman Sachs, ever tender, an opinion as to whether the transaction was fair to the Class A shareholders. Goldman Sachs directed its fairness opinion to the interests of RDA as a corporate entity. Given the obvious conflicting interests of the shareholder classes, the conceded absence of an evaluation of the fairness of the recapitalization on the Class A shareholders is significant. While the Class A shareholders received voting rights, their equity interests decreased by at least $100 million without either their consent or an objective evaluation of the exchange. In short, while the Special Committee believed, perhaps in good faith, that the transaction was in the best interests of the corporation,

arguably, it never focused on the specific impact upon the Class A shareholders of RDA's payment of $100 million to the Class B shareholders.

(10) With respect to the premium paid to the Class B shareholders, given RDA's tenuous financial condition, having recently committed to a large acquisition, incurring additional debt in order to pay $100 million to the Class B shareholders is a matter of concern. The net result of the transaction was to significantly reduce the post-capitalization equity of the corporation. To the extent that the directors did not secure sufficient information concerning the effect of the recapitalization premium on the Class A holders, a serious question is raised concerning the discharge of their duty of care. Kahn v. Tremont Corp., 694 A.2d 422, 430 (Del.1997).

(11) When seeking a preliminary injunction, a plaintiff must demonstrate a reasonable probability of success on the merits and that some irreparable harm will occur in the absence of the injunction. * * *

(12) We are not required, nor was the Court of Chancery, to determine the final merits of appellants' claims but, in our view, they stand a reasonable probability of success. It is unquestioned that the appellants will be irreparably harmed. While future monetary relief may be available, the issuance of the shares contemplated by the recapitalization may place a practical remedy beyond judicial reach.

NOTE: THE TELE–COMMUNICATIONS–AT&T MERGER

In re Tele–Communications Shareholders Litigation, 2005 WL 3642727 (Del.Ch.), concerned the stock-for-stock merger of Tele–Communications, Inc. (TCI) into AT&T. TCI had a dual class common capital structure, with common A being held publicly and thinly traded, and supervoting common B being held by insiders. Under the merger, each A share was exchanged for .7757 of a share of AT&T common, and each B share was exchanged for .8533 of a share of AT&T common. The Chancery Court described the conflict of interest and the standard of review as follows: "As in both *FLS* and *Levco*, the interests of two distinct classes significantly diverged in this transaction, by over $350 million at closing. As in *FLS*, no single shareholder possessed more than 50% of the vote, but the financial interests of a number of directors holding large amounts of [common B] shares significantly diverged from the interests of their constituent shareholders. Because a clear and significant benefit of nearly $300 million accrued primarily (over 84% of the total [common B] premium proceeds) to such directors controlling such a large vote of the corporation, at the expense of another class of shareholders to whom was owed a fiduciary duty, then a standard of entire fairness applies."

The plaintiffs' action for breach of fiduciary duty survived the defendants' motion to dismiss despite an overwhelming ratification of the merger by the TCI common A. The Court found infirmities in the process conducted by the special committee that approved the deal. The Court strictly reviewed the committee's justification for the premium paid to the common B:

"Plaintiffs * * * have presented data showing the trading prices and volumes of [the A and the B] from January 1997 to the announcement of the transaction. According to such data, during those approximately eighteen months the historical [B] premium was 10% or greater only during a single five-trading day interval.

" * * * The DLJ [the investment banker advising the Board] board book presented four precedents of premiums paid for high-vote stock, one of which was the Bell Atlantic/TCI failed merger. Without examining in detail the symmetry of each precedent with the AT & T transaction, I note that a salient factor was quickly glossed over. During the presentation of these four precedents, DLJ expressly confirmed that a premium for high-vote stock was not the norm * * *.

"The lingering question that the Special Committee failed to ask was how less common are such high vote premiums than equal treatment? The four precedents arguably supporting a high-vote premium could be in a universe of ten sales or one hundred sales. In fact, plaintiffs have presented approximately twenty transactions taking place from 1990 to 1998 in which publicly traded high-vote and low-vote stock were treated equally (in one additional transaction, the low-vote stock received a premium). These transactions create a large universe in which not even one high-vote stock received a premium. Reasonably construing the record in the light most favorable to the plaintiffs, the Special Committee was simply inadequately informed in respect to such high-vote precedents."

2. *Dual Class Common Recapitalizations*

Dual class common recapitalizations were common in the 1980s. Stock exchange rules bar them today. They retain interest as an example of blockholder manipulation of capital structure.

Dual class common recapitalizations usually involved the creation of a new class of supervoting common stock and the alignment of the supervoting stock with insiders and the regular voting stock with the public shareholders. In the alternative, they involved the creation of a new class of limited voting common stock and its alignment with the public holders. The result was a new capital structure, with the public class holding a diminished control interest and in many cases an enhanced financial interest, and the inside class holding primary voting rights and in many cases a diminished financial interest.

Supervoting rights can be attached by adding more votes per share to the supervoting class or by attaching a majority of the seats on the board to the supervoting class. Once such stock has been distributed to the blockholder or inside group, the publicly held class becomes a limited voting class automatically. Other means to the same end can be employed. For instance, a scheme can place a class of full voting stock carrying no financial rights with the insiders while transforming the existing stock into nonvoting stock. The insiders retain a financial interest to the extent of their prior holdings of the public class. The bottom line is the same. The insiders get unassailable power to elect a majority of the board. In many cases, the public shareholders get a step up in the dividend payout on the limited voting common in exchange.

The transformation from a single class, publicly held capital structure to a dual class division of voting and economic rights can be accomplished in a number of ways. In an exchange offer recapitalization, the shareholders approve a charter amendment providing for a class of common carrying, for example, 10 votes per share but receiving a 10 percent lower dividend. The supervoting common carries severe restrictions on transfer, violation of which causes the stock to be transformed into common of the low voting class. Then a one-time one-to-one exchange offer is made to the entire body of shareholders. The public shareholders have no reason to exchange, due to the payment stream incentive attached to the old common and the transfer disincentive attached to the new. Gordon, Ties That Bond: Dual Class Common Stock and the Problem of Shareholder Choice, 76 Cal.L.Rev. 3, 40–41 (1988), sets out this scenario and shows that given a 10 vote per share supervoting class, a blockholder or insider group holding 9.091 percent of the common can gain majority voting power, provided that it exchanges all its shares and none of the public holders exchange theirs. In the alternative, the recapitalization can be effected by means of a dividend. Here again the charter is amended to authorize a new supervoting class of common again carrying strict restrictions providing for automatic conversion to low voting common in the event of a transfer. It may or may not carry a diminished dividend. The stock is distributed upon a one-to-one dividend declaration. No automatic change in voting power results since each public holder holds a share of supervoting stock. Control shifts as the public shareholders at the time of the dividend gradually trade their stock. Each trade causes conversion into lowvoting stock, causing the proportion of lowvoting stock held publicly to rise over time. In addition, the transfer restriction on the supervoting stock makes its acquisition by a hostile offeror impossible. Gordon, supra, at pp. 41–42. See also Jarrell and Poulsen, Dual–Class Recapitalizations as Antitakeover Mechanisms: The Recent Evidence, 20 J. Financial Econs. 129, 135–136 (1988). Note that under either approach, this mode of defense presupposes a blockholder or an inside group holding a substantial, but less than majority block of common. Management groups controlling well under 10 percent blocks but desiring absolute security from attack tend to sponsor MBOs.

Dual class recapitalizations had their supporters. They pointed out that shareholder consent is required to effect the necessary charter amendment and that the exchange offer mode gives the shareholders a second opportunity to exercise choice. At another level, the dual class recapitalizations were compared to management buyouts, see Gilson, Evaluating Dual Class Common Stock: The Relevance of Substitutes, 73 Va.L.Rev. 807, 811–823 (1987), and a productivity defense articulated. The subject firms tended to be high growth enterprises dependent on the energies and skills of the blockholder or inside group, in contrast to the mature, low growth subjects of MBOs. Absent the reorganization, the insiders would be less willing to accept the best investment opportunities. The announcement of the recapitalization was thus a positive signal. Since the public shareholders retained a substantial financial interest, they gained. See Partch, The Creation of a Class of Limited Voting Common Stock and Shareholders' Wealth, 18 J. Financial Econs. 313 (1987). See also Fischel, Organized Exchanges and the Regulation of Dual Class Common Stock, 54 U.Chi.L.Rev. 119 (1987).

The many detractors of dual class recapitalizations focused on the fact that the result was classic management entrenchment with all attendant agency costs. They also alleged a wealth transfer. Voting control has a well-documented value, see Lease, McConnell and Mikkelson, The Market Value of Control in Publicly Traded Corporations, 11 J. Financial Econs. 439 (1983), and here the insiders acquired it for a suspect consideration. The shareholders' consent to the transfer was not effectively given. The first step charter amendment suffered the infirmities of a corporate governance provision procured through proxy solicitation—the managers had agenda control, and no individual shareholder had an economic incentive to mount a counter attack. See Gordon, supra, pp. 42–47. Furthermore, subsequent exchange offers were coercive. The dividend advantage attached to the low voting stock put the public holders in an awkward position. If a given public holder accepted the offer and took the high voting stock but the other public holders refused the offer, the accepting holder in effect granted a dividend subsidy to the others. Ruback, Coercive Dual–Class Exchange Offers, 20 J. Financial Econs. 153 (1988). Lured by the carrot and hit with the stick, the rational holder declined the offer, even though exchange by all the holders would eliminate the dividend subsidy and at least delay any control transfer. See also Seligman, Equal Protection in Shareholder Voting Rights: The One Common Share, One Vote Controversy, 54 Geo. Wash.L.Rev. 687 (1987).

Did dual class recapitalizations transfer value from public shareholders to insiders? As with other takeover defense maneuvers, a collection of empirical studies offer conflicting results. Some studies found small stock price gains, others found no wealth effect, others documented negative returns. Gordon, supra, at 39, surveyed the conflicting evidence and concluded that the transactions on balance had negative wealth effects. He explained the wealth neutral statistical results in terms of a trade off: the recapitalization signals positive investment opportunities, but detracts from the value of the public stock. The shareholders thus were deprived of an upside opportunity.

NOTE: REGULATORY BARRIERS: THE "ONE SHARE, ONE VOTE" CONTROVERSY

For many years, the New York Stock Exchange maintained and enforced a "one share, one vote" rule. Thus a dual class recapitalization came at the cost of delisting from the NYSE. Neither the American Stock Exchange nor the National Association of Securities Dealers imposed a similarly strict requirement. In 1984, the NYSE declared a moratorium on enforcement of its rule in the wake of a dispute with General Motors, one of its larger issuers. GM desired to issue a class of stock with lower voting rights in connection with the acquisition of a data services firm controlled by Ross Perot. The NYSE, in turn, desired to hold onto its base of issuers, for whom AMEX or OTC trading had become a viable alternative. The NYSE proposed a dilution of its rule. But this needed SEC approval. The SEC attempted to mediate a uniform one share, one vote rule among the NYSE, AMEX and NASD. When the negotiations failed, the SEC commenced a rule-making proceeding of its own. The result was Exchange Act Rule 19c–4, which barred all national securities exchanges and the NASDAQ from listing stock of a firm that takes action that nullifies, restricts, or disparately reduces the voting rights of existing shareholders. See Exchange Act Rel. Nos. 25,891, 25,891A, CCH Fed.Sec. L.Rep. ¶ 84,247 (1988). Each of the NYSE, AMEX and NASD was compelled to adopt the rule.

The SEC's rulemaking authority respecting 19c–4 was challenged successfully in Business Roundtable v. SEC, 905 F.2d 406 (D.C.Cir.1990). The court took the position that § 19(c) of the 1934 Act, on which the SEC relied for rulemaking authority, does not provide a sufficiently broad delegation of corporate governance rulemaking power. The SEC rule thus lost its mandatory force. The AMEX and NASD thereafter withdrew the SEC rule from their books, although not required to do so.

In 1994, the NYSE finally abandoned adherence to Rule 19c–4, adopting a more "flexible" policy. Nonvoting stock is not prohibited. But recapitalizations that move single class voting structures to insider dual class structures are barred: "Voting rights of existing shareholders of publicly traded common stock * * * cannot be disparately reduced or restricted through any corporate action or issuance. Examples of such corporate action or issuance include, but are not limited to, the adoption of time phased voting plans, the adoption of capped voting rights plans, the issuance of super voting stock, or the issuance of stock with voting rights less than the per share voting rights of the existing common stock through an exchange offer." NYSE Company Manual 313.00 (last modified Aug. 21, 2006). Existing dual class structures are grandfathered. The NASDAQ now has a similar rule. See NASD Rule 4351 (2006).

Note that the NYSE rule inhibits restructurings that take existing firms from full voting to dual class without prohibiting IPO firms from having dual class capital structures. In fact, new dual class firms do appear, with the supervoting class held by the insiders not being publicly traded.

Gompers, Ishii, and Metrick, Extreme Governance: An Analysis of Dual–Class Firms in the United States, working paper May 2007, available at http://ssrn.com/abstract=562511, reports that today about 6 percent of U.S. publicly traded companies have more than one class of common stock. These firms constitute about 8 percent of the market capitalization of all firms. For about 85 percent of dual-class firms, there is at least one untraded class of common stock, and the untraded class almost always has superior voting rights to the traded class. Thus, almost all of the firms are virtually immune to a hostile takeover. On average, the insiders have 60 percent of the voting rights and 40 percent of the cash-flow rights, and for almost 40 percent of the firms, insiders have more than half of the voting rights (thus providing effective control) but less than half of the cash-flow rights. The authors' statistical analysis shows strong evidence that firm value is positively associated with insiders' cash-flow rights, and a significant negative relation between insider voting rights and firm value.

3.   *Sale of Control*

Perlman v. Feldmann

United States Court of Appeals, Second Circuit, 1955.
219 F.2d 173, cert. denied, 349 U.S. 952, 75 S.Ct. 880, 99 L.Ed. 1277 (1955).

■ CLARK, CHIEF JUDGE. This is a derivative action brought by minority stockholders of Newport Steel Corporation to compel accounting for, and restitution of, allegedly illegal gains which accrued to defendants as a result of the sale in August, 1950, of their controlling interest in the corporation. The principal defendant, C. Russell Feldmann, who represented and acted for the others, members of his family,[10] was at that time not only the

---

10.   The stock was not held personally by Feldmann in his own name, but was held by the members of his family and by personal corporations. The aggregate of stock thus had

dominant stockholder, but also the chairman of the board of directors and the president of the corporation. Newport, an Indiana corporation, operated mills for the production of steel sheets for sale to manufacturers of steel products, first at Newport, Kentucky, and later also at other places in Kentucky and Ohio. The buyers, a syndicate organized as Wilport Company, a Delaware corporation, consisted of end-users of steel who were interested in securing a source of supply in a market becoming ever tighter in the Korean War. Plaintiffs contend that the consideration paid for the stock included compensation for the sale of a corporate asset, a power held in trust for the corporation by Feldmann as its fiduciary. This power was the ability to control the allocation of the corporate product in a time of short supply, through control of the board of directors; and it was effectively transferred in this sale by having Feldmann procure the resignation of his own board and the election of Wilport's nominees immediately upon consummation of the sale.

The present action represents the consolidation of three pending stockholders' actions in which yet another stockholder has been permitted to intervene. Jurisdiction below was based upon the diverse citizenship of the parties. Plaintiffs argue here, as they did in the court below, that in the situation here disclosed the vendors must account to the nonparticipating minority stockholders for that share of their profit which is attributable to the sale of the corporate power. Judge Hincks denied the validity of the premise, holding that the rights involved in the sale were only those normally incident to the possession of a controlling block of shares, with which a dominant stockholder, in the absence of fraud or foreseeable looting, was entitled to deal according to his own best interests. Furthermore, he held that plaintiffs had failed to satisfy their burden of proving that the sales price was not a fair price for the stock per se. Plaintiffs appeal from these rulings of law which resulted in the dismissal of their complaint.

The essential facts found by the trial judge are not in dispute. Newport was a relative newcomer in the steel industry with predominantly old installations which were in the process of being supplemented by more modern facilities. Except in times of extreme shortage Newport was not in a position to compete profitably with other steel mills for customers not in its immediate geographical area. Wilport, the purchasing syndicate, consisted of geographically remote end-users of steel who were interested in buying more steel from Newport than they had been able to obtain during recent periods of tight supply. The price of $20 per share was found by Judge Hincks to be a fair one for a control block of stock, although the over-the-counter market price had not exceeded $12 and the book value per share was $17.03. But this finding was limited by Judge Hincks' statement that "[w]hat value the block would have had if shorn of its appurtenant power to control distribution of the corporate product, the evidence does

amounted to 33% of the outstanding Newport stock and gave working control to the holder. The actual sale included 55,552 additional shares held by friends and associates of Feldmann, so that a total of 37% of the Newport stock was transferred.

not show." It was also conditioned by his earlier ruling that the burden was on plaintiffs to prove a lesser value for the stock.

Both as director and as dominant stockholder, Feldmann stood in a fiduciary relationship to the corporation and to the minority stockholders as beneficiaries thereof. Pepper v. Litton, 308 U.S. 295, 60 S.Ct. 238, 84 L.Ed. 281; Southern Pac. Co. v. Bogert, 250 U.S. 483, 39 S.Ct. 533, 63 L.Ed. 1099. His fiduciary obligation must in the first instance be measured by the law of Indiana, the state of incorporation of Newport. Rogers v. Guaranty Trust Co. of New York, 288 U.S. 123, 136, 53 S.Ct. 295, 77 L.Ed. 652; Mayflower Hotel Stockholders Protective Committee v. Mayflower Hotel Corp., 89 U.S.App.D.C. 171, 193 F.2d 666, 668. Although there is no Indiana case directly in point, the most closely analogous one emphasizes the close scrutiny to which Indiana subjects the conduct of fiduciaries when personal benefit may stand in the way of fulfillment of trust obligations. In Schemmel v. Hill, 91 Ind.App. 373, 169 N.E. 678, 682, 683, McMahan, J., said: "Directors of a business corporation act in a strictly fiduciary capacity. Their office is a trust. Stratis v. Andreson, 1926, 254 Mass. 536, 150 N.E. 832, 44 A.L.R. 567; Hill v. Nisbet, 1885, 100 Ind. 341, 353. When a director deals with his corporation, his acts will be closely scrutinized. Bossert v. Geis, 1914, 57 Ind.App. 384, 107 N.E. 95. Directors of a corporation are its agents, and they are governed by the rules of law applicable to other agents, and, as between themselves and their principal, the rules relating to honesty and fair dealing in the management of the affairs of their principal are applicable. They must not, in any degree, allow their official conduct to be swayed by their private interest, which must yield to official duty. Leader Publishing Co. v. Grant Trust Co., 1915, 182 Ind. 651, 108 N.E. 121. In a transaction between a director and his corporation, where he acts for himself and his principal at the same time in a matter connected with the relation between them, it is presumed, where he is thus potential on both sides of the contract, that self-interest will overcome his fidelity to his principal, to his own benefit and to his principal's hurt." And the judge added: "Absolute and most scrupulous good faith is the very essence of a director's obligation to his corporation. The first principal duty arising from his official relation is to act in all things of trust wholly for the benefit of his corporation."

In Indiana, then, as elsewhere, the responsibility of the fiduciary is not limited to a proper regard for the tangible balance sheet assets of the corporation, but includes the dedication of his uncorrupted business judgment for the sole benefit of the corporation, in any dealings which may adversely affect it. Young v. Higbee Co., 324 U.S. 204, 65 S.Ct. 594, 89 L.Ed. 890; Irving Trust Co. v. Deutsch, 2 Cir., 73 F.2d 121, certiorari denied 294 U.S. 708, 55 S.Ct. 405, 79 L.Ed. 1243; Seagrave Corp. v. Mount, 6 Cir., 212 F.2d 389; Meinhard v. Salmon, 249 N.Y. 458, 164 N.E. 545, 62 A.L.R. 1; Commonwealth Title Ins. & Trust Co. v. Seltzer, 227 Pa. 410, 76 A. 77. Although the Indiana case is particularly relevant to Feldmann as a director, the same rule should apply to his fiduciary duties as majority stockholder, for in that capacity he chooses and controls the directors, and thus is held to have assumed their liability. Pepper v. Litton, supra, 308

U.S. 295, 60 S.Ct. 238. This, therefore, is the standard to which Feldmann was by law required to conform in his activities here under scrutiny.

It is true, as defendants have been at pains to point out, that this is not the ordinary case of breach of fiduciary duty. We have here no fraud, no misuse of confidential information, no outright looting of a helpless corporation. But on the other hand, we do not find compliance with that high standard which we have just stated and which we and other courts have come to expect and demand of corporate fiduciaries. In the often-quoted words of Judge Cardozo: "Many forms of conduct permissible in a workaday world for those acting at arm's length, are forbidden to those bound by fiduciary ties. A trustee is held to something stricter than the morals of the market place. Not honesty alone, but the punctilio of an honor the most sensitive, is then the standard of behavior. As to this there has developed a tradition that is unbending and inveterate. Uncompromising rigidity has been the attitude of courts of equity when petitioned to undermine the rule of undivided loyalty by the 'disintegrating erosion' of particular exceptions." Meinhard v. Salmon, supra, 249 N.Y. 458, 464, 164 N.E. 545, 546, 62 A.L.R. 1. The actions of defendants in siphoning off for personal gain corporate advantages to be derived from a favorable market situation do not betoken the necessary undivided loyalty owed by the fiduciary to his principal.

The corporate opportunities of whose misappropriation the minority stockholders complain need not have been an absolute certainty in order to support this action against Feldmann. If there was possibility of corporate gain, they are entitled to recover. In Young v. Higbee Co., supra, 324 U.S. 204, 65 S.Ct. 594, two stockholders appealing the confirmation of a plan of bankruptcy reorganization were held liable for profits received for the sale of their stock pending determination of the validity of the appeal. They were held accountable for the excess of the price of their stock over its normal price, even though there was no indication that the appeal could have succeeded on substantive grounds. And in Irving Trust Co. v. Deutsch, supra, 2 Cir., 73 F.2d 121, 124, an accounting was required of corporate directors who bought stock for themselves for corporate use, even though there was an affirmative showing that the corporation did not have the finances itself to acquire the stock. Judge Swan speaking for the court pointed out that "The defendants' argument, contrary to Wing v. Dillingham [5 Cir., 239 F. 54], that the equitable rule that fiduciaries should not be permitted to assume a position in which their individual interests might be in conflict with those of the corporation can have no application where the corporation is unable to undertake the venture, is not convincing. If directors are permitted to justify their conduct on such a theory, there will be a temptation to refrain from exerting their strongest efforts on behalf of the corporation since, if it does not meet the obligations, an opportunity of profit will be open to them personally."

This rationale is equally appropriate to a consideration of the benefits which Newport might have derived from the steel shortage. In the past Newport had used and profited by its market leverage by operation of what the industry had come to call the "Feldmann Plan." This consisted of securing interest-free advances from prospective purchasers of steel in return for firm commitments to them from future production. The funds thus acquired were used to finance improvements in existing plants and to acquire new installations. In the summer of 1950 Newport had been negotiating for cold-rolling facilities which it needed for a more fully integrated operation and a more marketable product, and Feldmann plan funds might well have been used toward this end.

Further, as plaintiffs alternatively suggest, Newport might have used the period of short supply to build up patronage in the geographical area in which it could compete profitably even when steel was more abundant. Either of these opportunities was Newport's, to be used to its advantage only. Only if defendants had been able to negate completely any possibility of gain by Newport could they have prevailed. It is true that a trial court finding states: "Whether or not, in August, 1950, Newport's position was such that it could have entered into 'Feldmann Plan' type transactions to procure funds and financing for the further expansion and integration of its steel facilities and whether such expansion would have been desirable for Newport, the evidence does not show." This, however, cannot avail the defendants, who—contrary to the ruling below—had the burden of proof on this issue, since fiduciaries always have the burden of proof in establishing the fairness of their dealings with trust property. Pepper v. Litton, supra, 308 U.S. 295, 60 S.Ct. 238; Geddes v. Anaconda Copper Mining Co., 254 U.S. 590, 41 S.Ct. 209, 65 L.Ed. 425; Mayflower Hotel Stockholders Protective Committee v. Mayflower Hotel Corp., 84 U.S.App.D.C. 275, 173 F.2d 416.

Defendants seek to categorize the corporate opportunities which might have accrued to Newport as too unethical to warrant further consideration. It is true that reputable steel producers were not participating in the gray market brought about by the Korean War and were refraining from advancing their prices, although to do so would not have been illegal. But Feldmann plan transactions were not considered within this self-imposed interdiction; the trial court found that around the time of the Feldmann sale Jones & Laughlin Steel Corporation, Republic Steel Company, and Pittsburgh Steel Corporation were all participating in such arrangements. In any event, it ill becomes the defendants to disparage as unethical the market advantages from which they themselves reaped rich benefits.

We do not mean to suggest that a majority stockholder cannot dispose of his controlling block of stock to outsiders without having to account to his corporation for profits or even never do this with impunity when the buyer is an interested customer, actual or potential, for the corporation's product. But when the sale necessarily results in a sacrifice of this element of corporate good will and consequent unusual profit to the fiduciary who has caused the sacrifice, he should account for his gains. So in a time of market shortage, where a call on a corporation's product commands an unusually large premium, in one form or another, we think it sound law that a fiduciary may not appropriate to himself the value of this premium. Such personal gain at the expense of his coventurers seems particularly reprehensible when made by the trusted president and director of his company. In this case the violation of duty seems to be all the clearer because of this triple role in which Feldmann appears, though we are unwilling to say, and are not to be understood as saying, that we should accept a lesser obligation for any one of his roles alone.

Hence to the extent that the price received by Feldmann and his codefendants included such a bonus, he is accountable to the minority stockholders who sue here. Restatement, Restitution §§ 190, 197 (1937); Seagrave Corp. v. Mount, supra, 6 Cir., 212 F.2d 389. And plaintiffs, as they contend, are entitled to a recovery in their own right, instead of in right of the corporation (as in the usual derivative actions), since neither Wilport nor their successors in interest should share in any judgment which may be rendered. See Southern Pacific Co. v. Bogert, 250 U.S. 483, 39 S.Ct. 533, 63 L.Ed. 1099. Defendants cannot well object to this form of recovery, since the only alternative, recovery for the corporation as a whole, would subject them to a greater total liability.

The case will therefore be remanded to the district court for a determination of the question expressly left open below, namely, the value of defendants' stock without the appurtenant control over the corporation's output of steel. We reiterate that on this issue, as on all others relating to a breach of fiduciary duty, the burden of proof must rest on the defendants. Bigelow v. RKO Radio Pictures, 327 U.S. 251, 265–266, 66 S.Ct. 574, 90 L.Ed. 652; Package Closure Corp. v. Sealright Co., 2 Cir., 141 F.2d 972, 979. Judgment should go to these plaintiffs and those whom they represent for any premium value so shown to the extent of their respective stock interests.

The judgment is therefore reversed and the action remanded for further proceedings pursuant to this opinion.

■ Swan, Circuit Judge. With the general principles enunciated in the majority opinion as to the duties of fiduciaries I am, of course, in thorough accord. But, as Mr. Justice Frankfurter stated in Securities and Exchange Comm. v. Chenery Corp., 318 U.S. 80, 85, 63 S.Ct. 454, 458, 87 L.Ed. 626, "to say that a man is a fiduciary only begins analysis; it gives direction to further inquiry. To whom is he a fiduciary? What obligations does he owe as a fiduciary? In what respect has he failed to discharge these obligations?" My brothers' opinion does not specify precisely what fiduciary duty Feldmann is held to have violated or whether it was a duty imposed upon him as the dominant stockholder or as a director of Newport. Without such specification I think that both the legal profession and the business world will find the decision confusing and will be unable to foretell the extent of its impact upon customary practices in the sale of stock.

The power to control the management of a corporation, that is, to elect directors to manage its affairs, is an inseparable incident to the ownership of a majority of its stock, or sometimes, as in the present instance, to the ownership of enough shares, less than a majority, to control an election. Concededly a majority or dominant shareholder is ordinarily privileged to sell his stock at the best price obtainable from the purchaser. In so doing he acts on his own behalf, not as an agent of the corporation. If he knows or has reason to believe that the purchaser intends to exercise to the detriment of the corporation the power of management acquired by the purchase, such knowledge or reasonable suspicion will terminate the dominant shareholder's privilege to sell and will create a duty not to transfer the power of management to such purchaser. The duty seems to me to resemble the obligation which everyone is under not to assist another to commit a tort rather than the obligation of a fiduciary. But whatever the nature of the duty, a violation of it will subject the violator to liability for damages sustained by the corporation. Judge Hincks found that Feldmann had no reason to think that Wilport would use the power of management it would acquire by the purchase to injure Newport, and that there was no proof that it ever was so used. Feldmann did know, it is true, that the reason Wilport wanted the stock was to put in a board of directors who would be likely to permit Wilport's members to purchase more of Newport's steel than they might otherwise be able to get. But there is nothing illegal in a dominant shareholder purchasing from his own corporation at the same prices it offers to other customers. That is what the members of Wilport did, and there is no proof that Newport suffered any detriment therefrom.

My brothers say that "the consideration paid for the stock included compensation for the sale of a corporate asset", which they describe as "the ability to control the allocation of the corporate product in a time of short supply, through control of the board of directors; and it was effectively transferred in this sale by having Feldmann procure the resignation of his own board and the election of Wilport's nominees immediately upon consummation of the sale." The implications of this are not clear to me. If it means that when market conditions are such as to induce users of a corporation's product to wish to buy a controlling block of stock in order to be able to purchase part of the corporation's output at the same mill list prices as are offered to other customers, the dominant stockholder is under a fiduciary duty not to sell his stock, I cannot agree. For reasons already stated, in my opinion Feldmann was not proved to be under any fiduciary duty as a stockholder not to sell the stock he controlled.

Feldmann was also a director of Newport. Perhaps the quoted statement means that as a director he violated his fiduciary duty in voting to elect Wilport's nominees to fill the vacancies created by the resignations of the former directors of Newport. As a director Feldmann was under a fiduciary duty to use an honest judgment in acting on the corporation's behalf. A director is privileged to resign, but so long as he remains a director he must be faithful to his fiduciary duties and must not make a personal gain from performing them. Consequently, if the price paid for Feldmann's stock included a payment for voting to elect the new directors, he must account to the corporation for such payment, even though he honestly believed that the men he voted to elect were well qualified to serve as directors. He can not take pay for performing his fiduciary duty. There is no suggestion that he did so, unless the price paid for his stock was more than its value. So it seems to me that decision must turn on whether finding 120 and conclusion 5 of the district judge are supportable on the evidence. They are set out in the margin.[1]

Judge Hincks went into the matter of valuation of the stock with his customary care and thoroughness. He made no error of law in applying the principles relating to valuation of stock. Concededly a controlling block of stock has greater sale value than a small lot. While the spread between $10 per share for small lots and $20 per share for the controlling block seems rather extraordinarily wide, the $20 valuation was supported by the expert testimony of Dr. Badger, whom the district judge said he could not find to be wrong. I see no justification for upsetting the valuation as clearly erroneous. Nor can I agree with my brothers that the $20 valuation "was limited" by the last sentence in finding 120. The controlling block could not by any possibility be shorn of its appurtenant power to elect directors and through them to control distribution of the corporate product. It is this "appurtenant power" which gives a controlling block its value as such block. What evidence could be adduced to show the value of the block "if shorn" of such appurtenant power, I cannot conceive, for it cannot be shorn of it.

The opinion also asserts that the burden of proving a lesser value than $20 per share was not upon the plaintiffs but the burden was upon the defendants to prove that the stock was worth that value. Assuming that this might be true as to the defendants who were directors of Newport, they did show it, unless finding 120 be set aside. Furthermore, not all the defendants were directors; upon what theory the plaintiffs should be relieved from the burden of proof as to defendants who were not directors, the opinion does not explain.

The final conclusion of my brothers is that the plaintiffs are entitled to recover in their own right instead of in the right of the corporation. This appears to be completely inconsistent with the theory advanced at the outset of the opinion, namely, that the price of the stock "included compensation for the sale of a corporate asset." If a corporate asset was sold, surely the corporation should recover the compensation received for it by the defendants. Moreover, if the plaintiffs were suing in their own right, Newport was not a proper party. The case of Southern Pacific Co. v. Bogert, 250 U.S. 483, 39 S.Ct. 533, 63 L.Ed. 1099, relied upon as authority for the conclusion that the plaintiffs are entitled to recover in their own right, relates to a situation so different that the decision appears to me to be inapposite.

I would affirm the judgment on appeal.

---

1. "120. The 398,927 shares of Newport stock sold to Wilport as of August 31, 1950, had a fair value as a control block of $20 per share. What value the block would have had if shorn of its appurtenant power to control distribution of the corporate product, the evidence does not show."

"5. Even if Feldmann's conduct in cooperating to accomplish a transfer of control to Wilport immediately upon the sale constituted a breach of a fiduciary duty to Newport, no part of the moneys received by the defendants in connection with the sale constituted profits for which they were accountable to Newport."

NOTE: THE PROPOSED RULE OF EQUAL OPPORTUNITY

1. *Readings of the Case.*

Perlman v. Feldmann has been interpreted narrowly by some commentators, broadly by others. Often the decision is explained by grouping it with "looting" cases such as Gerdes v. Reynolds, 28 N.Y.S.2d 622 (Sup.Ct.1941), in which the control shares of an investment company were sold at a premium to purchasers who used their position of dominance to loot the corporation, selling portfolio securities and appropriating the proceeds. Finding that the seller knew or should have known of the danger of looting, which did in fact occur, the court held the seller liable for the premium received on the sale of the control shares and for the amount of the corporation's losses. See also Harris v. Carter, 582 A.2d 222 (Del.Ch.1990) (imposing a duty of care on the selling stockholder as a matter of Delaware law). *Feldmann* is said to be based on similar considerations, with the harm to the corporation being loss of opportunities for Feldmann-plan financing and other benefits. See Hill, The Sale of Controlling Shares, 70 Harv.L.Rev. 986, 989 (1957). A different, though related, explanation for the outcome in *Feldmann* stems from the fact that the premium paid for Feldmann's stock was in reality payment of a premium price for Newport's steel output. It is said the decision can best be understood as holding that stockholders must be allowed to share equally in profits resulting from strong market demand whether such profits are realized through sale of the product or sale of stock. See Manning, The Shareholder's Appraisal Remedy, 72 Yale L.J. 223, 225 (1962).

Under a more expansive view of the case, the court's opinion reflects a belief that control is a corporate asset, or is held in trust for the corporation, and cannot be sold for private gain. As a result, the decision should be read as requiring the controller-fiduciary to disgorge the amount received in excess of the investment value of his shares shorn of control. Berle, "Control" in Corporate Law, 58 Col.L.Rev. 1212 (1958); Jennings, Trading in Corporate Control, 44 Calif.L.Rev. 1 (1956). But see, Honigman v. Green Giant Co., 208 F.Supp. 754 (D.Minn.1961), aff'd, 309 F.2d 667 (8th Cir.1962), cert. denied 372 U.S. 941 (1963).

2. *Andrews' Rule of Equal Opportunity.*

The interpretation of the *Feldmann* decision that became the focal point for discussion of the fiduciary duties of control blockholders appeared in Andrews, The Stockholder's Right to Equal Opportunity in the Sale of Shares, 78 Harv.L.Rev. 505, 515–18 (1965):

"The rule to be considered can be stated thus: whenever a controlling stockholder sells his shares, every other holder of shares (of the same class) is entitled to have an equal opportunity to sell his shares, or a pro rata part of them, on substantially the same terms. Or in terms of the correlative duty: before a controlling stockholder may sell his shares to an outsider he must assure his fellow stockholders an equal opportunity to sell their shares, or as high a proportion of theirs as he ultimately sells of his own * * *.

"Now let us look briefly at what the rule means. First, it neither compels nor prohibits a sale of stock at any particular price; it leaves a controlling stockholder wholly free to decide for himself the price above which he will sell and below which he will hold his shares. The rule only says that in executing his decision to sell, a controlling stockholder cannot sell pursuant to a purchase offer more favorable than any available to other stockholders. Second, the rule does not compel a prospective purchaser to make an open offer for all shares on the same terms. He can offer to purchase shares on the condition that he gets a certain proportion of the total. Or he can even make an offer to purchase 51 per cent of the shares, no more and no less. The only requirement is that his offer, whatever it may be, be made equally or proportionately available to all stockholders.

"Obviously if a purchaser offers to buy only 51 per cent of the shares, and the offer must be made equally available to all stockholders, no stockholder accepting the offer can count on selling all his shares. There are established mechanics for dealing with this situation. The purchaser makes a so-called tender offer, indicating the price at which he wants to buy and how many shares, and inviting all stockholders to tender their stock if they wish to sell at that price. If more shares are tendered than the purchaser is willing to take, then he purchases pro rata from each tendering stockholder. * * *

"The asserted right would prevent just what happened in Feldmann: a private sale by a controlling stockholder at a price not available to other stockholders. But there are two modes of compliance with the rule: either the purchaser can extend his offer to all stockholders, or the seller can offer participation in the sale to his fellow stockholders. A sale is prevented from taking place only when the purchaser is unwilling to buy more than a specified percentage of the shares, and the seller will sell only if he can sell out completely. Indeed, even under these circumstances it is an overstatement to say the rule would prevent a sale taking place, since the minority stockholders may consent to the sale. They may even sell to the purchaser at a lower price than what he pays the controlling stockholder, provided they are adequately informed of what is going on. Thus the rule only operates to prevent a sale when (1) the purchaser is unwilling to purchase more shares, (2) the seller insists on disposing of all his shares, and (3) the minority stockholders are unwilling to stay in the enterprise under the purchaser's control.

        * * *

" * * * There is a substantial danger that following a transfer of controlling shares corporate affairs may be conducted in a manner detrimental of the interests of the stockholders who have not had an opportunity to sell their shares. The corporation may be looted; it may just be badly run. Or the sale of controlling shares may operate to destroy a favorable opportunity for corporate action. Recent events confirm that gross mismanagement may follow a sale of controlling shares.

"The equal opportunity rule does not deal directly with the problem of mismanagement, which may occur even after a transfer of control complying with the rule; but enforcement of the rule will remove much of the incentive a purchaser can offer a controlling stockholder to sell on profitable terms. Indeed, in the case of a purchasing looter there is nothing in it for the purchaser unless he can buy less than all the shares; there is no profit in stealing from a solvent corporation if the thief owns all the stock. But the controlling stockholder will be loath to sell only part of his shares (except at a price that compensates him for all of his shares) if he expects the purchaser to destroy the value of what he keeps. The rule forces the controlling stockholder to share equally with his fellow stockholders both the benefits of the price he receives for the shares he sells and the business risks incident to the shares he retains. This will tend strongly to discourage a sale of controlling shares when the risk of looting, or other harm to the corporation, is apparent; and it will provide the seller with a direct incentive to investigate and evaluate with care when the risks are not apparent, since his own financial interest continues to be at stake."

3. *Ongoing Debates.*

Easterbrook and Fischel, Corporate Control Transactions, 93 Yale L.J. 698, 703–15 (1982), makes a famous critique of Andrews' equal opportunity proposal. They argue that, assuming full diversification, equityholders will not view having to forego gain in respect of a particular blockholder control sale as a cognizable injury to their expectations. In the long run, a diversified shareholder ends up on the winning side as well as the losing side in respect of these deals, and therefore prefers the legal rule promoting the largest aggregate amount of investment gain, so long as each transaction leaves each investors' *ex ante* holding value unimpaired. Sharing rules discourage transactions which create gain and therefore should be discouraged. Moreover, when courts intervene they do so *ex post*; they are not in a position to recreate the risk-discounted projections that determine the behavior of the parties to the block sale transaction. They have no basis with which to allocate gains between risk bearing and risk sharing parties. See also Javaras, Equal Opportunity in the Sale of Controlling Shares: A Reply to Professor Andrews, 32 U.Chi.L.Rev. 420 (1965); Manne, Mergers and the Market for Corporate Control, 73 J. Pub. Econ. 110 (1965).

Andrews anticipated some of these arguments, affirming that a sale of control shares may have advantageous effects to the corporation and its shareholders—as when inefficient managers are replaced by a purchaser who can, or believes he can, do better. Andrews concedes that the prevention of sales in such circumstances "would be a high price to pay for the prevention of harm in other cases," but denies that the rule would have that effect.

Which is the better view? Would an equal opportunity rule chill the movement of going concern assets to higher valuing users? If so, are the resulting costs outweighed by the benefits of deterring transactions driven by access to private benefits?

The incentive to pay a premium derives from either (or both) the expectation of diverting assets to the new controlling blockholder or the expectation of exercising control so as to enhance the value of all shareholders' (including the new blockholder's) pro-rata interest in the enterprise. To the extent that diversion of assets is the principal incentive (see Meeker and Joy, Price Premiums for Controlling Shares of Closely Held Bank Stock, 53 J. Bus. 297 (1980)), the premium represents the capitalized value of the power of blockholders thus to appropriate corporate property for themselves, by reason presumably of the porous restraints otherwise imposed upon them by law. See Brudney, Equal Treatment of Shareholders in Corporate Distributions and Reorganizations, 71 Calif.L.Rev. 1072, 1122–1126 (1983). Cf. Barclay and Holderness, Private Benefits from Control of Public Corporations, 25 J.Fin.Econ. 371 (1989) (empirical study of 63 block trades between 1978 and 1982 involving at least 5 percent of the common stock of NYSE or Amex firms, concluding that the premium represents the value of corporate benefits accruing to the blockholder alone). To the extent that the principal incentive is pro-rata gain, as Andrews has pointed out, the buyer of the control block should not be willing to pay more per share for the minimum number of shares needed for control than for the balance of the shares.

Assuming both incentives, the propriety of allowing the payment of a premium to a selling blockholder implicates a determination whether the amount by which the purchasing blockholder is likely to augment the value of the firm (by innovation and reduction of agency costs) exceeds the amount of firm value the purchaser diverts to itself. See Hamilton, Private Sale of Control Transactions: Where We Stand Today, 36 Case Western Reserve L.Rev. 248 (1985). See also Levmore, A Primer on the Sale of Corporate Control, 65 Tex.L.Rev. 1061 (1987). Is it also relevant to consider the possibility, if not the probability, that the new blockholder will divert more than did the predecessor? In any event is the blockholder entitled to more than "fair" compensation for services in reducing agency costs? While the amount of that compensation is hard to determine, the question is whether in theory the blockholder is entitled to any more (i.e., requires any more as an incentive), and whether in practice is likely to take any more.

The ultimate question is whether the net benefits of a sharing rule (that overdeters some beneficial transactions) are equal to, greater, or less than the net benefits of a free sale rule (that underdeters harmful transactions). Bebchuk, Efficient and Inefficient Sales of Corporate Control, 109 Q.J.Econ. 957 (1994) works through the problem. In Bebchuk's analysis, a free transfer rule allows some inefficient transfers to take place because the higher value placed on the stock by the purchaser may stem from a greater ability to extract private rents; contrariwise, an efficient transfer may not take place in a free transfer regime if the private control benefits projected by a potential purchaser are significantly smaller than those accruing to the selling holder. An equal opportunity rule, in contrast, prevents all inefficient transfers. But it at the same time prevents a wider range of efficient transfers than does a free transfer rule because, given the sharing requirement, the control seller sometimes will be better off not selling despite the fact that the firm as a whole will be more valuable in the hands of the potential purchaser. The severity of the efficiency problem under a free transfer rule thus depends on the magnitude of the difference of the private control benefits available to sellers and buyers; under the equal opportunity rule the severity of the efficiency problem depends on the absolute level of private control benefits enjoyed by potential sellers. Thus, in theory, if potential sellers and buyers of control do not greatly differ so far as concerns the realization of private control benefits, a free transfer regime will be more efficient. But the ultimate determination depends on empirical evidence. Compare Kahan, Sales of Corporate Control, 9 J. L. Econ. & Org. 368 (1993); Elhauge, The Triggering Function of Sale of Control Doctrine, 59 U.Chi.L.Rev. 1465 (1992).

In the absence of empirical proof, should the answer to the cost benefit question turn on the assumptions one makes about acquisitive behavior when corporate control changes hands? Or is a middle ground possible? Does the following set of empirical results provide a basis for answers to foregoing questions? Holderness & Sheehan, The Role of Majority Shareholders in Publicly Held Corporations: An Exploratory Analysis, 20 J.Fin.Econ. 317 (1988), measures the returns to minority shares of 21 listed companies that announced sales of majority blocks from 1978 to 1982. Such stock had statistically significant abnormal returns of 9.4 percent during the 30 days surrounding the announcement and 5.5 percent for the two days surrounding the announcement. Exactly what does the fact that the market expects increased returns tell us about the benefits and costs of the sale of control? An increase in the stock price indicates the market's assessment of a probable increase in the payment stream, but not the mode of increase in the payment stream—whether increased dividend payout, future tender offer for the minority shares, or cash out merger at a premium over the market price.

NOTE: REGULATION OF CONTROL SALES AFTER *FELDMANN*

1. *The Majority View.*

With the exception of Brown v. Halbert, 271 Cal.App.2d 252, 76 Cal.Rptr. 781 (1969), most cases since *Perlman v. Feldmann* have rejected a requirement that the seller of a control block account to other stockholders for the premium received, at least in the absence of good reason to believe, or to investigate whether, the buyer is a looter or the buyer has a structural conflict of interest with the seller's business. The leading case is **Zetlin v. Hanson Holdings, Inc.**, 48 N.Y.2d 684, 421 N.Y.S.2d 877, 397 N.E.2d 387 (1979), in which the plaintiff challenged the sale of a 44.4 percent control block at a 100 percent premium over market. The New York Court of Appeals rejected the plaintiff's suggestion of an equal opportunity rule with the following comment: "This rule would profoundly affect the manner in which controlling stock interests are now transferred. It would require, essentially, that a controlling interest be transferred only by means of an offer to all stockholders, i.e., a tender offer. This would be contrary to existing law and if so radical a change is to be effected it would best be done by the Legislature."

2.   *Block Sale as Corporate Opportunity.*

In **Thorpe v. CERBCO, Inc.**, 676 A.2d 436 (Del.Supr.1996), a proposed block sale was held to violate the corporate opportunity doctrine. Even so, the Delaware Supreme Court concluded that no damages were owing.

CERBCO was a holding company with one profitable subsidiary, Insituform East, Inc. ("East"). The continued profitability of East was in doubt, however, because its regional license to conduct its primary business was about to expire. This license to exploit a process used in the in-place repair of pipes was obtained from Insituform of North America, Inc. ("INA").

CERBCO had two classes of stock. Class A was entitled to one vote per share, and Class B was entitled to 10 votes per share. In addition, the B shares were empowered to elect 75 percent of the board of directors. The Erikson brothers constituted CERBCO's controlling group of shareholders, owning 247,564 or 78 percent of the outstanding B, and 111,000 or 7.6 percent of the outstanding A, which meant they owned 24.6 percent of the total equity while exercising voting control with 56 percent of the total votes. The Eriksons also constituted two of the four members of CERBCO's board. East's capital structure was similar, with 318,000 Class B shares having ten votes and electing 75 percent of the board and 4.3 million Class A shares having one vote each. CERBCO owned 1.1 million shares of the A (26 percent of the outstanding A shares) and 93 percent of the B.

INA explored the possibility of purchasing the assets of East. Krugman, INA's Chairman, retained Drexel, Burnham, Lambert & Company ("Drexel") to advise him. Krugman met with the Eriksons to discuss the matter in their representative capacities as officers and directors, unaware of CERBCO's capital structure and the Eriksons' control. The Eriksons made a counterproposal that involved the Eriksons' selling their controlling interest in CERBCO to INA. Krugman was led to believe that the Eriksons would permit only the transaction involving their sale of CERB-CO stock to INA. Thereafter, INA had Drexel perform comparative financial projections of various transactions by which it might gain control of East. Drexel's work up suggested that, while a direct purchase of CERBCO's East stock had a higher initial cost than a purchase of the Eriksons' holdings, in certain respects it would be preferable since the indebtedness of Capital Copy, one of CERBCO's subsidiaries, would not be assumed in the latter transaction.

The Ericksons did not inform CERBCO's outside directors that INA had originally approached them with the intention of buying East from CERBCO. But the Ericksons did sign a letter of intent with INA to sell their controlling interest in CERBCO for $6 million. That transaction never closed, however. Negotiations broke down over issues of indemnification and litigation expenses.

The plaintiffs' derivative action claimed that the Eriksons had diverted from CERBCO the opportunity to sell East to INA. The Supreme Court applied the corporate opportunity doctrine as follows:

" * * * When CERBCO's president, Krugman, approached the Eriksons, he did so to inquire about INA's purchase of CERBCO's shares in East, not the purchase of the Eriksons' shares in CERBCO. Since the Eriksons were approached in their capacities as directors, their loyalty should have been to the corporation. The

Chancellor correctly found that the Eriksons had breached that duty of loyalty through self-interest in subsequent actions. The Eriksons should have informed the CERBCO board of INA's interest in gaining control of East since INA originally wanted to deal with CERBCO. * * *

"Once INA had expressed an interest in acquiring East, CERBCO should have been able to negotiate with INA unhindered by the dominating hand of the Eriksons. * * * The Eriksons were entitled to profit from their control premium and to that end compete with CERBCO but only after informing CERBCO of the opportunity. Thereafter, they should have removed themselves from the negotiations and allowed the disinterested directors to act on behalf of CERBCO.

"After finding a breach of the duty of loyalty, the Chancellor tested the defendants' actions for entire fairness, but this test is an unwieldy instrument to use in circumstances such as the breach of duty that occurred here. * * * We find the corporate opportunity doctrine to be a better framework than entire fairness analysis for addressing the Eriksons' duties as directors. * * *

    * * *

"Generally, the corporate opportunity doctrine is applied in circumstances where the director and the corporation compete against each other to buy something, whether it be a patent, license, or an entire business. This case differs in that both the Eriksons and CERBCO wanted to sell stock, and the objects of the dispute, their respective blocks of stock to be sold, were not perfectly fungible. In order for the Eriksons and CERBCO to compete against one another, their stock must have been rough substitutes in the eyes of INA. * * *

"The Chancellor thoroughly examined the evidence presented by the parties to determine that only one transaction presented a serious alternative to an Erikson–INA deal. This one viable alternative involved the sale of all of CERBCO's East stock for a price of $12.8 million. * * *

"Because the alternative transaction would have been covered by § 271, the Eriksons had the statutory right as shareholders to veto this transaction. Given their power, the Eriksons would obviously never allow CERBCO to enter a transaction against their economic interests. Damages cannot be awarded on the basis of a transaction that has a zero probability of occurring due to the lawful exercise of statutory rights.

"It is true that the Eriksons breached their fiduciary duties and that damages flowing from that breach are to liberally calculated. * * * Section 271 must, however, be given independent legal significance apart from the duty of loyalty. Cf. Orzeck v. Englehart, Del.Supr., 195 A.2d 375, 377 (1963)(compliance with one provision of the General Corporation Law protects actions from invalidation). While the failure of CERBCO to sell East to INA is certainly related to the Eriksons' faithlessness, that failure did not proximately result from the breach. Instead the Eriksons' § 271 rights are ultimately responsible for the nonconsummation of the transaction. Even if the Eriksons had behaved faithfully to their duties to CERBCO, they still could have rightfully vetoed a sale of substantially all of CERBCO's assets under § 271. Thus, the § 271 rights, not the breach, were the proximate cause of the nonconsummation of the transaction. Accordingly, transactional damages are inappropriate.

"While this denial of transactional damages may seem incompatible with our decision to award damages for the breach of fiduciary duty, the two holdings are reconcilable. * * * While the Eriksons did have a duty to present [the] opportunity to CERBCO, they had no responsibility to ensure that a transaction was consummated. Any INA–CERBCO transaction would have required a shareholder vote and the Eriksons were entitled to pursue their own interests in voting their shares. The failure of INA and CERBCO to reach an agreement was proximately caused by the Eriksons' ability to block the transaction, not by the Eriksons' breach of the duty of loyalty. Consequently, no liability arises from the breach for the inability of CERBCO to take advantage of the opportunity to sell its control of East to INA."

The court, having thus denied "transactional damages," nevertheless awarded "incidental damages" against the Eriksons. These included disgorgement of a $75,000 fee received by the Eriksons from INA pursuant to a letter of intent and reimbursement of costs incurred by CERBCO in connection with the performance of the letter of intent.

In **In re Digex Inc. Shareholders Litigation**, 789 A.2d 1176 (Del. Ch. 2000), the minority shareholders of a valuable subsidiary pressed a corporate opportunity claim against a troubled parent corporation. A suitor interested in the subsidiary instead purchased the parent, depriving the minority shareholders of the subsidiary of a potential opportunity to be cashed out. Citing *Thorpe v. CERBCO* the court ruled that the opportunity taken belonged to the shareholders and not to the subsidiary as a corporation and rejected the claim.

3. *Blockholders and Third Party Offerors.*

Does a control blockholder have a duty to sell into a third party offer benefitting the other shareholders? **Mendel v. Carroll**, 651 A.2d 297 (Del.Ch. 1994), holds that it does not, on the facts of the case. A small group of members of the Carroll Family members controlled between 48 percent and 52 percent of the stock of Katy Industries, Inc. ("Katy"). The Carrolls made an offer to buy out the minority shares for $25.75, which offer was approved by Katy's investment bankers, Goldman Sachs, and a special committee of the board of directors. A merger agreement was negotiated and a proxy statement was mailed. Then Pensler proposed to the board a friendly offer to purchase all shares of Katy for $29, subject to a number of conditions. This resulted in the temporary withdrawal of the Goldman Sachs opinion on, and the special committee endorsement of, the Carroll offer. Thereafter, Pensler made a new offer at $27.80. The Pensler offer was conditioned on the execution of a Stock Option Agreement providing for the purchase by Pensler of 1.8 million authorized but unissued shares at the merger consideration. Exercise of the option would have reduced the voting power of the Carrolls from the current level of 50.6 percent to approximately 40 percent and thus would make feasible stockholder approval of the Pensler transaction. The plaintiffs sought an order directing the board to grant to Pensler an option to purchase up to 20 percent of Katy's outstanding common stock at $27.80 per share. The plaintiffs' theory was that when the Katy board had accepted the terms of a $25.75 cash out merger proposed by the Carrolls, the company was put up "for sale," putting the board under a duty to make a good faith effort to get the best available value for the stockholders.

Unfortunately for the plaintiffs, the court determined that the Pensler offer was not the best available value:

" * * * The gist of plaintiffs' complaint is that the minority shareholders could get more cash for their stock in a Pensler cash deal than they would have gotten in the proposed $25.75 Carroll Group deal. Thus, plaintiffs would contend that * * * the board is * * * under a current obligation to take the radical step of intentionally diluting the control of the controlling block of stock.

"In my opinion, this view is mistaken. I apprehend in the facts recited above no threat of exploitation or even unfairness towards a vulnerable minority that might arguably justify discrimination against a controlling block of stock. Plaintiffs see in the Carroll Group's unwillingness to sell at $27.80 or to buy at that price, a denial of plaintiffs' ability to realize such a price, and see this as exploitation or breach of duty. This view implicitly regards the $27.80 per share price and the Carroll Family Merger price of $25.75 as comparable sorts of things. But they are legally and financially quite different. *It is, for example, quite possible that the Carroll $25.75 price may have been fair, even generous, while the $27.80 Pensler price may be inadequate.* If one understands why this is so, one will understand one reason why the injunction now sought cannot be granted.

"The fundamental difference between these two possible transactions arises from the fact that the Carroll Family already in fact had a committed block of controlling stock. Financial markets in widely traded corporate stock accord a premium to a block of stock that can assure corporate control. Analysts differ as to the source of any such premium but not on its existence. Optimists see the control premium as a reflection of the efficiency enhancing changes that the buyer of control is planning on making to the organization. Others tend to see it, at least sometimes, as the price that a prospective wrongdoer is willing to pay in order to put himself in the position to exploit vulnerable others, or simply as a function of a downward sloping demand curve demonstrating investors' heterogeneous beliefs about the subject stock's value. In all events, it is widely understood that buyers of corporate control will be required to pay a premium above the market price for the company's traded securities.

"The law has acknowledged, albeit in a guarded and complex way, the legitimacy of the acceptance by controlling shareholders of a control premium. * * *

"The significant fact is that in the Carroll Family Merger, the buyers were not buying corporate control. With either 48% or 52% of the outstanding stock they already had it. Therefore, in evaluating the fairness of the Carroll proposal, the Special Committee and its financial advisors were in a distinctly different position than would be a seller in a transaction in which corporate control was to pass.

"The Pensler offer, of course, was fundamentally different. It was an offer, in effect, to the controlling shareholder to purchase corporate control, and to all public shareholders, to purchase the remaining part of the company's shares, all at a single price. It distributed the control premium evenly over all shares. Because the Pensler proposed $27.80 price was a price that contemplated not simply the purchase of non-controlling stock, as did the Carroll Family Merger, but complete control over the corporation, it was not fairly comparable to the per-share price proposed by the Carroll Group.

" * * * When the Katy board or its Special Committee evaluated the Carroll Family Merger, it was obligated to take note of the circumstance that the proposal was being advanced by a group of shareholders that constituted approximately 50% of all share ownership, and who arguably had the power to elect the board. In this circumstance, in my opinion, the board's duty was to respect the rights of the Carroll Family, while assuring that if any transaction of the type proposed was to be accomplished, it would be accomplished only on terms that were fair to the public shareholders and represented the best available terms from their point of view. * * *

" * * *[If] the board were to approve a proposed cash-out merger, it would have to bear in mind that the transaction is a final-stage transaction for the public shareholders. Thus, the time frame for analysis, insofar as those shareholders are concerned, is immediate value maximization. The directors are obliged in such a situation to try, within their fiduciary obligation, to maximize the current value of the minority shares. In this respect the obligation is analogous to the board's duty when it is engaged in a process of 'selling' the corporation, as for example in the recent Paramount Communications Inc. v. QVC Network Inc., Del.Supr., 637 A.2d 34 (1994). But the duty is somewhat different because of the existence of the controlling Carroll Family block.

"The Carroll Family made it clear throughout these events that, for the most part, its members were completely uninterested in being sellers in any transaction. No part of their fiduciary duty as controlling shareholders requires them to sell their interest. See Bershad v. Curtiss–Wright Corp., Del.Supr., 535 A.2d 840 (1987); Jedwab v. MGM Grand Hotels, Inc., Del.Ch., 509 A.2d 584 (1986) (self sacrifice not required). The board's fiduciary obligation to the corporation and its shareholders, in this setting, requires it to be a protective guardian of the rightful interest of the public shareholders. But while that obligation may authorize the board to take extraordinary steps to protect the minority from plain overreaching, it does not authorize the board to deploy corporate power *against* the majority stockholders, in the absence of a threatened serious breach of fiduciary duty by the controlling stock.

"To acknowledge that the Carroll Family has no obligation to support a transaction in which they would in effect sell their stock is not, of course, to suggest that they can use their control over the corporation to effectuate a self-interested merger at an unfair price. See Weinberger v. U.O.P., Inc., Del.Supr., 457 A.2d 701 (1983). There is nothing in the present record, however, that suggests to me that the $25.75 price the Carroll Group proposed to pay for the public shares was an inadequate or unfair price for the non-controlling stock. For the reasons stated above, the fact that Pensler was willing to pay more for all of the shares does not, logically, support an inference that the Carroll proposal for the non-controlling public shares was not fair.

"Thus, while I continue to hold open the possibility that a situation might arise in which a board could, consistently with its fiduciary duties, issue a dilutive option in order to protect the corporation or its minority shareholders from exploitation by a controlling shareholder who was in the process or threatening to violate his fiduciary duties to the corporation, such a situation does not at all appear to have been faced by the Katy board of directors."

Questions. Suppose the board had gone forward to grant the stock option to Pensler. Does the reasoning in *Mendel* dictate a finding of a breach of fiduciary duty? Could the board employ the proposed rule of equal opportunity to sustain its business judgment?

Consider the following hypothetical. ABC Corporation is controlled by X, who owns 52 percent of the stock. The market value of 100 percent of ABC's stock is $100 million; in addition, the ABC stock has been definitively valued for appraisal purposes as having a total value of $100 million. Y Corporation, seeking a synergistic gain, makes a public offer for 100 percent of the shares for $150 million. X refuses to sell, and as a result Y withdraws the offer. Do the minority shareholders of ABC have a cause of action against X in respect of the refusal to sell? If not, should they?

4. *State Corporate Codes.*

Successful hostile takeovers entail the creation of control blocks. Legislatures in some states, seeking to constrain takeover activity, have effected changes in regulation of the conduct of purchasers of control blocks. Under the "control share" antitakeover statutes enacted in a number of jurisdictions during the 1980s, a majority of the disinterested shareholders must, in some cases, approve the purchase of a control block prior to consummation of a subsequent merger giving the purchaser 100 per cent of the target's stock. In other states they must approve the attachment of voting rights to the stock after the purchase. One state, Pennsylvania, has added a "profit disgorgement" provision under which a party that acquires 20 percent of a firm's stock and disposes of the stock within 18 months must turn any profit realized on the disposition to the firm.

PART V

MERGERS AND ACQUISITIONS

INTRODUCTION

Ideally, a firm that acquires another firm does so for exactly the same reason that a firm purchases a new piece of machinery (even though the factors entering into the decision to purchase an entire firm may be more numerous and complex). The decision to invest rests upon the expectation that the future returns to existing shareholders, discounted to present value at a rate which reflects the risks, will exceed the amount presently invested. If this expectation is communicated to and believed by a sufficient number of investors, the shares of the acquiring company will rise to reflect the anticipation of greater returns. The projection of expected returns and the calculation of an appropriate discount rate each has its difficulties. But the elements of the calculations are presumably unaffected by the size of the investment project being considered.

The decision to acquire another firm also entails financial, tax, and legal factors that rarely come to bear on a small scale capital budgeting decision. The cost of capital problems bound up in financing a major acquisition are of greater complexity than those involved in financing normal asset acquisitions. Accounting procedures for acquisitions or mergers also are complex, expanding the range of variables affecting future reports of earnings. And, the income tax laws affect the decision to merge in a manner not encountered in simpler settings. Finally, as a legal matter, the economic importance of a merger decision raises urgent questions respecting management's skill, judgment, and loyalty to shareholder interests.

From the point of view of the acquiring corporation, the initial inquiry concerns the diligence applied in determining the transaction's basic terms—whether "too much" is being paid. More particularly, the question is whether the consideration flowing from the acquiring firm is greater than the sum of (1) the acquired corporation's value apart from the merger and (2) any value added to the resulting corporation by the combination. In ascertaining the latter value, the questions arise whether there are any effective bases for quantifying "synergistic" or other gains expected to arise from the merger and whether there are rational norms available to guide the division of the gain between the parties. Suppose that A and B are merging, with A contributing risky earnings of 3 and B contributing equally risky earnings of 1. The managers of A and B assert that the combined enterprise is expected to earn 6 due (for example) to the elimination of duplicated expenses. From the point of view of A's shareholders, two questions arise. First, how has the asserted additional value of 2 been apportioned between the shareholders of A and B? A's management needs to have fulfilled its duty of care in respect of the division of gain in the merger bargain. Second, there arises a question as to the credibility of value projection and the very existence of the gains held out for the acquiring corporation's shareholders. Managers motivated by self interest or fear might be paying for increased size (and the resultant presumed perquisites to management) and increased assurance of continuity of tenure rather than for shareholder value. Alternatively, acquiring firm managers might be irrationally chasing trends, encouraged by investment bankers seeking fees.

From the point of view of the acquired corporation, the initial inquiry also concerns care—whether enough is being received for the value given up, apart from any increased efficiency or profitability flowing from the merger, and whether synergistic or other gains are being appropriately divided. There is also a question of loyalty—whether management (or those in control) received a side payment or other premium for consenting to the acquisition. If circumstances or legal rules place power over the merger decision in a given individual or group, one realistically can expect that its exercise will not always go uncompensated. Thus the sales price sometimes will be less than it would otherwise be, by an amount which exceeds the side payment to management or other controlling persons.

Volumes of studies address these questions—whether stockholders of acquired companies are under paid, fully paid, or over paid, whether stockholders of acquiring companies gain or lose notwithstanding payment of premiums to selling shareholders, and whether acquiring companies have proved more efficient or more profitable than non-acquiring companies of comparable size and risk. The studies try to affirm or deny the existence of systematic management biases. But, although the literature is voluminous, and the debate tendentious, the findings (except for consistent gains to stockholders of acquired companies) are inconclusive.

The corporate law of mergers and acquisitions is concerned primarily with prescribing the procedures for effecting these transactions. The law designates the organs of the corporation which must consider and approve them. In so doing it recognizes frictions and imperfections in the linkage between management and stockholders in the decision making process. It accordingly imposes occasional constraints on the freedom of management in making merger bargains, including obligations to disclose essential information to security holders. Legal standards measuring the propriety of merger bargains and forcing disclosure largely tend to protect or benefit stockholders on the sellers' side of the transaction, presumably because problems of fair division more often arise when business ownership is terminated for cash or securities than when it is extended to embrace additional operating assets.

SECTION A. THE MOVE TO MERGE

Andrade, Mitchell, and Stafford, New Evidence and Perspectives on Mergers

15 J. Econ. Perspectives 103, 104–109 (2001).

A recent strand of the literature * * * has tried to address the issue of why mergers occur by building up from the two most consistent empirical features of merger activity over the last century: 1) mergers occur in waves; and 2) within a wave, mergers strongly cluster by industry. These features suggest that mergers might occur as a reaction to unexpected shocks to industry structure. We believe this arena is a potentially fruitful one to explore from both a theoretical and empirical point of view. It also seems to correspond to the intuition of practitioners and analysts that industries tend to restructure and consolidate in concentrated periods of time, that these changes occur suddenly, and that they are hard to predict. However, identifying industry shocks and documenting their effect is challenging.

In this paper, we provide evidence that merger activity in the 1990s, as in previous decades, strongly clusters by industry. Furthermore, we show that one particular kind of industry shock, deregulation, while important in previous periods, becomes a dominant factor in merger and acquisition activity after the late 1980s and accounts for nearly half of the merger activity since then. In fact, we can say without exaggeration or hyperbole that in explaining the causes of mergers and acquisitions, the 1990s were the "decade of deregulation."

* * *

Mergers in the 1990s: What's New?

* * * [W]e document merger activity using the stock database from the Center for Research in Security Prices (CRSP) at the University of Chicago. * * *

Figure 1
Aggregate Merger Activity

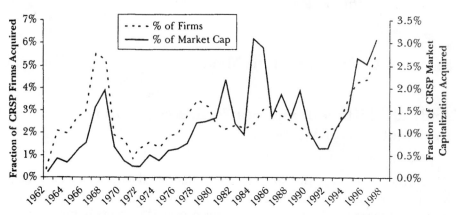

Figure 1 displays two different measures of annual merger activity. The dotted line represents the number of firms acquired during the year expressed as a fraction of the beginning-of-year number of firms in CRSP. The solid line gives a sense for the values involved, obtained by dividing the aggregate dollar value of mergers over the year by the total beginning-of-year market capitalization of the firms listed on CRSP. The evidence is entirely consistent with the well-known view that there have been three major waves of takeover activity since the early 1960s. Interestingly, the 1960s wave contained many more deals, relative to the number of publicly available targets, than the 1980s. However in dollar terms, the 1980s were far more important, as large multi-billion dollar deals became common. On a value-weighted basis, the 1980s were truly a period of massive asset reallocation via merger, and as reported by Mitchell and Mulherin[, The Impact of Industry Shocks on Takeover and Restructuring Activity, 41 J. Fin.Econ. 193] (1996), nearly half of all major U.S. corporations received a takeover offer. It is astounding that the merger and acquisition activity in the 1990s seems to be even more dramatic and widespread, with number of deals comparable to the 1960s, and values similar to the 1980s.

For the remainder of the paper, we will focus on the 26 years beginning in 1973 * * *. This results in about 4,300 completed deals. Table I reports key descriptive statistics and characteristics for our merger sample, broken down by decade.

The evidence in Table I suggests that mergers in the 1980s and 1990s are different in many ways. The first key distinction is the overwhelming use of stock as a method of payment during the latter decade. About 70 percent of all deals in the 1990s involved stock compensation, with 58 percent entirely stock financed. These numbers are approximately 50 percent more than in the 1980s.

Table I
Characteristics and Descriptive Statistics by Decade, 1973–1998

	1973–1979	*1980–1989*	*1990–1998*	*1973–1998*
N	789	1,427	2,040	4,256
All Cash	38.3%	45.3%	27.4%	35.4%
All Stock	37.0%	32.9%	57.8%	45.6%
Any Stock	45.1%	45.6%	70.9%	57.6%
Hostile Bid at Any Point	8.4%	14.3%	4.0%	8.3%
Hostile Bid Successful	4.1%	7.1%	2.6%	4.4%
Bidders/Deal	1.1	1.2	1.0	1.1
Bids/Deal	1.6	1.6	1.2	1.4
Own Industry	29.9%	40.1%	47.8%	42.1%
Premium (Median)	47.2%	37.7%	34.5%	37.9%
Acquirer Leverage > Target Leverage	68.3%	61.6%	61.8%	62.9%
Acquirer Q > Target Q	68.4%	61.3%	68.3%	66.0%
Relative Size (Median)	10.0%	13.3%	11.2%	11.7%
Fraction of Acquirer Announcement Returns <—5%	14.9%	17.0%	19.4%	17.5%
Fraction of Acquirer Announcement Returns > 5%	9.6%	11.3%	10.7%	11.1%

Perhaps related to the predominance of stock financing, note the virtual disappearance of hostility in the takeover market. We define a bid as hostile if the target company publicly rejects it, or if the acquirer describes it as unsolicited and unfriendly. Only 4 percent of transactions in the 1990s involved a hostile bid at any point, compared to 14 percent in the 1980s, and a hostile bidder acquired less than 3 percent of targets. Consistent with this more "friendly" atmosphere, the average transaction in the 1990s involved only one bidder, and 1.2 rounds of bidding, far less than during the 1980s.

The evidence for the 1980s by itself is interesting, because it suggests that the hostility of takeover activity during that time was less severe than generally believed. Mitchell and Mulherin (1996) report that 23 percent of the firms in their sample receive a hostile bid at some point during the 1980s; however, their sample only includes firms listed in the Value Line Investment Survey, which are generally larger, better-known companies. During the same period, only 14 percent of the firms in our sample receive a hostile offer. Since we include all publicly traded firms, the contrast in these two results suggests that hostile activity was practically nonexistent among the smaller, lesser-known companies.

Table 2
Top Five Industries Based on Average Annual Merger Activity

1970s	*1980s*	*1990s*
Metal Mining	Oil & Gas	Metal Mining
Real Estate	Textile	Media & Telecom.
Oil & Gas	Misc. Manufacturing	Banking
Apparel	Non–Depository Credit	Real Estate
Machinery	Food	Hotels

Finally, the 1990s continue a trend, begun in the 1970s, of an ever-increasing percentage of mergers where both parties are in the same industry (defined at the 2—digit SIC code level), now nearly half. The picture of mergers in the 1990s that emerges is one where merging parties, often in closely related industries, negotiate a friendly stock swap.

Of the recent empirical findings highlighted in the literature, one of the most interesting is the presence of industry clustering in merger activity. * * * Although merger and acquisition activity, as discussed above, occurs in readily identifiable waves over time, these waves are not alike, in fact, the identity of the industries that make up each merger boom varies tremendously. A simple way to see that is to compare the level of merger activity in each industry over time. If we rank industries in each decade by the market values of all acquired firms, and then correlate these rankings across decades, we find that the correlations are negligible—that is, industries that exhibit high levels of merger activity in one decade, are no more likely to do so in other decades. As Table 2 illustrates, there is no overlap between the top five industries, ranked by merger values, of the 1980s and 1990s.

If mergers come in waves, but each wave is different in terms of industry composition, then a significant portion of merger activity might be due to industry-level shocks. Industries react to these shocks by restructuring, often via merger. These shocks are unexpected, which explains why industry-level takeover activity is concentrated in time, and is different over time, which accounts for the variation in industry composition for each wave. Examples of shocks include: technological innovations, which can create excess capacity and the need for industry consolidation; supply shocks, such as oil prices; and deregulation.

The view that merger activity is the result of industry-level shocks is not new. * * * However, recently there has been evidence successfully tying mergers to specific shocks. Mitchell and Mulherin (1996) show that deregulation, oil price shocks, foreign competition, and financial innovations can explain a significant portion of takeover activity in the 1980s. * * *

Of the shocks listed above, deregulation is an ideal candidate for analysis. First, it creates new investment opportunities for the industry. Second, it potentially removes long-standing barriers to merging and consolidating, which might have kept the industry artificially dispersed. Finally, it is fairly well-defined in time and in terms of parties affected, so empirically we know where and when to look.

We classify the following industries as having undergone substantial deregulation since 1973: airlines (1978), broadcasting (1984 and 1996), entertainment (1984), natural gas (1978), trucking (1980), banks and thrifts (1994), utilities (1992) and telecommunications (1996). We define a ten-year period around each of these events (three years before to six years after) as a ''deregulation window.'' Figure 2 displays, for each year, the percentage of total merger activity represented by mergers in industries in the deregulation window. During most of the 1980s, this percentage hovers around 10–15 percent. After 1988, however, deregulated industries account for nearly half of all annual deal volume, on average. This is consistent with the evidence in Table 2 that banking and media/telecommunications are two of the most active industries in the 1990s.

It is clear that deregulation was a key driver of merger activity over the last ten years. Whether rightly or wrongly—and the jury is still out on the efficiency benefits and value enhancements brought about in these industries—the fact is that deregulation precipitated widespread consolidation and restructuring of a few industries in the 1990s, frequently accomplished through merger.

In our view, the industry shock explanation for mergers has added substantially to our understanding of mergers, not so much how mergers create value, but rather why and when they occur. * * *

NOTE: MERGERS AND VALUE CREATION

1. *Merger Waves: 1980s, 1990s, 2000s.*

The merger wave of the 1980s peaked with the RJR Nabisco buyout of 1988— then the biggest deal ever—and then subsided during the 1989–1992 recession. Merger and acquisition activity bottomed out in 1992. The 1990s merger wave followed. Activity rose continuously through 2000 along with an expanding economy. The volume of transactions matched levels seen in the 1980s in 1994, and new volume records were set in each succeeding year through 2000. Volume fell off when recession struck in 2001. By mid 2002, the market had came to a virtual halt. The trough persisted until mid–2003, when a new wave began.

The 1980s merger wave was characterized by bust-up transactions. The targets often were conglomerate firms. The acquirers often were hostile offerors. The consideration paid tended to be cash, a substantial portion of which was borrowed. After the closing of the transaction, pieces of the conglomerate were sold for cash in the market for going concern assets, the proceeds being used to pay down portions of the acquisition debt.

Transaction patterns in the 1990s merger market differed substantially from those prevailing in the 1980s. Where "restructuring" described deals in the 1980s, in the 1990s "growth" returned as an explanation—but growth (and competitive position) within a given line of business or closely related line of business. Mergers in the technology, media, and telecommunications sectors, which constituted 50 percent of the volume in the latter part of the decade, fit this description in particular. Other transactions followed more from a search for cost savings—in a time of low inflation and intense price competition managers seeking earnings growth had nowhere else to look. By combining companies in the same line of business, managers sought to use newly found market power to buy raw materials more cheaply; they sought to achieve cost savings by combining distribution pipelines; or they simply eliminated duplicative operations. Thus did health care companies under increasing cost-pressure combine in pursuit of economies of scale. Banks and financial services companies also combined in pursuit of economies of scale and enhanced competitive position.

Buzzwords like "market power" and "globalization" summed up the conventional wisdom in the 1990s acquisition market. Size counted. Indeed, the very volume of merger activity generated more activity all by itself. In many industries, one had to acquire, cut a friendly deal to be acquired, or be left out in the cold worrying about being acquired. The same forces that drove domestic transactions also prompted a wave of cross-border combinations. In industries like automotive, communications, drugs, finance, engineering, oil, and tires, transnational companies formed through merger became commonplace.

Patterns of financing and pricing also changed in the 1990s. With stock prices relatively high, common stock reemerged as the most prominent form of consideration—deals with all stock consideration were not uncommon. But debt still played a role in many transactions. Indeed, lending banks steadily expanded the profile of an acceptable deal as the 1990s progressed and low interest rates kept down the cost of the debt. At the same time, a significant portion of the cash consideration in many deals came from the participants' own cash reserves. Finally, while substantial premiums approaching 50 percent still were paid in some deals, the high premium no longer served as a strong pricing norm. In 1996 the average acquisition premium was only 28 percent. Indeed, a number of larger combinations, particularly in the financial and communications sectors, were termed "mergers of equals"— that is, they proceeded without any significant premium being paid to the transferor shareholders.

Most 1990s transactions were friendly, with hostile transactions occurring in diminished numbers. The pattern also differed from that of the 1980s. In the 1990s, hostile bidders tended to be larger firms than the targets, and included blue chip companies like H.F. Ahmanson, General Electric, Hilton, IBM, Johnson & Johnson, and Wells Fargo. These giants looked for strategic mergers, started with fat knock out bids, and then proceeded with patience. Unsolicited bidders won about one half of the time, up from a 35 percent rate of victory in 1988. Hostile activity was most pronounced in sectors where acquisitions came to be deemed necessary for corporate survival: Companies "jumped" other companies' pending deals, making an unsolicited bid where competitors had announced combinations. Finally, an uptick in hostile activity in 1999–2000 should be noted. It was fueled by price declines for many "old economy" firms disfavored by market actors then besotted with technology stocks.

Heavily leveraged acquisitions fueled by the prospect of short-term returns in the market for corporate assets still occurred in the 1990s, but at a much reduced level. Where one-third of the deals in the 1980s market fit this description, such deals generated only four to five percent of merger volume for most of the 1990s. High stock prices, bank limits on lending to highly leveraged deals, and the proliferation of strategic mergers among cash rich companies inhibited LBO activity. The junk bond market proved much tighter than in the 1980s, forcing participants to contribute much more equity than formerly. Furthermore, "corporate restructuring" by means of workforce downsizing and divestiture of unrelated lines of business came to occur as an integral (and voluntary) part of business plans. It nevertheless remained closely connected to merger activity. As mentioned above, same-industry combinations meant reductions in personnel performing duplicative functions.

The 1990s merger wave crested in 2000, when volume peaked at $3.48 trillion world-wide and $1.83 trillion in the United States. But volume began to fall in that year's fourth quarter. There followed a trough that extended until the second half of 2003, a period of economic recession and market uncertainty. In 2001, global merger and acquisition activity dropped 50 percent to $1.7 trillion, with the U.S. market falling 57 percent to $795.5 billion. The market bottomed out in 2002, depressed by weak stock markets, weak economies, and accounting scandals. Global volume fell an additional 28 percent that year. Domestic activity fell another 41 percent to $447.8 billion, the lowest level since 1994 and a 74 percent fall from the

2000 peak. The weak stock market inhibited buyers from using stock as currency while sellers resisted deals at low prices.

During the downturn, the energy and financial services sectors remained the most active, with oil and natural gas capturing the leading market share in domestic deals. Consumer products firms also continued to make acquisitions. Companies also continued to divest noncore businesses as large asset sales continued across the board. The market also focused on distressed firms—internet destinations accounted for 34 percent of acquisitions spending in 2001. Finally, leveraged buyout firms, now termed "private equity," reappeared as prominent buy-side players. Unlike ordinary firms producing goods and services, these financial houses were stuffed with cash and thus positioned to buy. Low interest rates also contributed, allowing the private equity firms to court larger targets. Lower premiums also figured into the private equity revival—20 percent has been a common premium in recent years.

The market revived in the second half of 2003 along with national economies and stock markets. Mega deals reappeared in 2004, as global volume rose 41 percent to $1.95 trillion, and domestic volume went up more than 50 percent to $875 billion. The industries pushing the biggest deals were health care, software, utilities and telecommunications. Even so, CEOs and investors remained wary recreating the bad deals of the 1990s. This led to long deal processes, extensive due diligence, and many failed deals. Private equity firms retained their front and center place in the market, with their $300 billion of deals making up 15 percent of overall volume, as compared to 4 percent in 2000. Private equity volume increased more than 60 percent between 2003 and 2004.

The new wave rose higher in 2005 and 2006. The 2006 global total was a record $3.79 trillion, of which the U.S. share was $1.7 trillion. As in the 1990s, most mergers were horizontal, combining two similar firms in the pursuit of cost cutting rather than combining different companies with the goal of diversification. Big combinations once thought not to be feasible emerged, spurred by the combination of the lowest takeover premiums in 20 years and slack in antitrust regulation. Soaring commodity prices also contributed. Active sectors included the oil and gas industry, health care, high technology, and real estate. But dealmakers stressed the market's breadth—all sectors were affected. Low world-wide interest rates continued to encourage deal-making. Excess corporate cash also became an important facilitator. As economies rebounded, cash came to represent approximately 10 percent of corporate assets. Companies used cash for about 58 percent of what they were buying, with stock representing the remainder. Private-equity deal volume also continued to rise notably, making up 27 percent of the U.S. market in 2006. However, concerns arose over the large amounts of debt being placed on some companies in private-equity deals, signaling potential problems for this segment in the future.

2. Do Mergers Create, Destroy, or Merely Transfer Value? Empirical Results.

An acquiring corporation is an investor of capital who conducts a valuation of a potential investment. Valuation, as we know, is a tricky business. Some assume that acquiring managers make cognizably accurate appraisals most of the time—that value in fact is present to support the premium, despite inevitable uncertainty. There also is a view to the contrary. Under this, the acquiring firms have a tendency to overvalue target firms—value in fact may not be present much of the time.

Which of the two views finds support in empirical studies of the financial effects of acquisition transactions?

Andrade, Mitchell and Stafford, supra, at 109, describe the results of studies that inquire into the question whether acquisition transactions create value for the shareholders of the constituent companies. The leading studies in this vast literature employ the technique of statistical analysis of the firms' stock prices in the days surrounding the merger announcement. These "event windows" are either three days or twenty days. The box below summarizes results reported by Andrade, Mitchell and Stafford, id. at 110:

	1980-89	1990-98	1973-98
Target			
3 day window	16%	15.9%	16%
20 day window	23.9%	23.3%	23.8%
Acquirer			
3 day window	-0.4%	-1.0%	-0.7%
20 day window	-3.1%	-3.1%	-3.8%
Combined			
3 day window	2.6%	1.4%	1.8%

What inferences should be drawn from this picture of "average abnormal returns" over the event windows? First, the averages for the 1980s and 1990s merger waves are remarkably similar, despite the two decades' different transactional patterns. Second, target firm shareholders are consistent winners. Third, acquiring firm shareholders appear to be modest losers. Fourth, overall gains are similarly modest. Other event studies have reached very similar results. See Jarrell, Brickley and Netter, The Market for Corporate Control: The Empirical Evidence Since 1980, 2 J.Econ. Perspectives 49 (1988).

Acquiring firm losses can be made less disturbing with a reference to portfolio theory. Most bidder shareholders own their shares in diversified portfolios. They thus stand on both sides of the deal and so are indifferent to the division of gain as between bidder and target. So long as the combined result for the bidder and the target nets out positive, everything is fine. And such was the case until the late 1990s: from 1973 to 1998, the combined 3 day window result averaged a positive 1.8 percent; from 1980 to 1989, the average was 2.6 percent; and from 1990 to 1998 the figure was 1.4 percent. Andrade, Mitchell & Stafford, supra at 109.

Unfortunately, a cluster of mergers in the late 1990s reversed the 1.8 percent long term positive. Moeller, Schlingemann, and Stulz, Wealth Destruction on A Massive Scale? A Study of Acquiring Firm Returns in the Recent Merger Wave, 60 J. Fin. 757 (2005), marshals some shocking three-day announcement returns. They show that from 1980 to 1990, bidder firms' shares lost an aggregate $4 billion, and from 1990 to 1997 they gained $24 billion. From 1998 to 2001, however, they lost $240 billion, bringing down the 1990 to 2001 result to a $216 billion bidder loss. The 1998 to 2001 numbers are so bad that they make for a negative combined result of $134 billion for bidders and targets in the period. The negative dominoes fall from there. Where in the 1980s combined returns were a positive $12 billion, from 1991 to 2001 the combined loss was $90 billion. That nets out to a $78 billion loss for 1980 to 2001.

The disastrous results stem from 87 deals out of a total of 4,136 in the authors' sample. The large loss deals were more likely to be hostile tender offers and more likely to be in the same industry, but neither result is statistically significant. The most prominent common feature among the bidding firms is prior acquisition behavior. They are serial acquirers with high market valuations that had made value enhancing acquisitions. Moeller, Schingemann, and Stulz suggest that the pattern of success caused an increase in the managers' zone of discretion. The managers then push the acquisition pattern too far and the market withdraws its support.

Does the form of consideration paid to the target firm shareholders make a difference? Here distinguish an all cash acquisition from an acquisition in which the consideration is common stock of the acquiring firm. Recall that when a mature firm issues new common stock, the market reads the financing as a signal that the issuer's managers believe its stock price to have reached a peak. Consider some additional numbers from Andrade, Mitchell and Stafford, supra, at 112, which distinguish mergers from 1973 to 1998 in which some acquirer common stock is issued as consideration from mergers in which no stock is issued. Given a twenty day window, in stock mergers the acquiring firm's stock has a negative 6.3 percent abnormal return, the target a 20.8 percent positive return, with the combined firms negative 0.6 percent; in no stock deals the targets are positive 27.8 percent, the acquirer negative 0.2 percent and the combined companies positive 5.3 percent. It thus appears that target shareholders do better when they receive no acquirer common, that acquirer shareholders do much worse when common is issued, and that common stock consideration can wipe out any gain for the combined firms.

Studies limited to three and twenty day windows around the announcement date have obvious limitations as measures of merger value creation. They proxy the reactions and expectations of investors on the scene for economic events which must unfold over time. Presumably, measures of the subsequent performance of the emerging firm can tell us more about a merger's success or failure. Loughran and Vijh, Do Long–Term Shareholders Benefit from Corporate Acquisitions? 52 J. Fin. 1765 (1997), calculates long-term abnormal returns for acquiring firms, based on the five year period after closing for mergers from 1970 to 1989. For stock deals they show a negative abnormal return of 24.2 percent; for cash mergers they show a positive abnormal return of 18.5 percent. See also Rau and Vermaelen, Glamour, Value and the Post–Acquisition Performance of Acquiring Firms, 49 J. Fin. Econ. 223 (1998)(using a three year window to show that friendly acquisitions underperform relative to hostile acquisitions). For a contrasting set of results based on a three year window and a different methodology, see Mitchell and Stafford, Managerial Decisions and Long Term Stock Performance, 73 J. Bus. 287 (2000). Here acquiring firms issuing stock suffer a negative 9 percent abnormal return and acquiring firms not issuing stock suffer a negative 1.4 percent return. Caveat: These long-term studies employ a range of statistical techniques and are methodologically controversial. Since we have no generally accepted model of "expected returns" for given firms across three or five year periods, estimates of long term "abnormal" returns suffer from considerable imprecision.

3. *Management Motivations.*

If merger and acquisition activity often destroys or transfers value, how do we explain it?

● **Hubris.** Roll, Empirical Evidence on Takeover Activity and Shareholder Wealth, in Coffee, Lowenstein and Rose–Ackerman, eds., Knights, Raiders, and Targets: The Impact of the Hostile Takeover, 241, 249–250 (1988), ascribes the phenomenon of overpayment in mergers to the hubris of the acquiring firms' managers:

"A recent paper of mine [Roll, The Hubris Hypothesis of Corporate Takeovers, 59 J.Bus. 197 (1986)] advances a behavioral explanation for the takeover phenomenon. My argument is that bidding firm managers intend to profit by taking over other firms, possibly because they *believe* that synergy is present, that the target has inefficient management, etc. Their intentions are not fulfilled, however, because the market price already reflects the full value of the firm, (i.e., there is actually no synergy nor inefficient management involved). Why, then, do bidding firms persist in their pursuit of the target? Because the *individual* decision makers in the bidding firm are infected by overweaning pride and arrogance (hubris) and thus persist in a belief that their own valuation of the target is correct, despite objective information that the target's true economic value is lower.

"The hubris explanation is heavily dependent on improper recognition of the 'winner's curse,' a concept familiar to scholars of bidding theory. The idea of the winner's curse is simple: Whoever makes the winning bid for a valuable object is likely to be a bidder with a positive valuation error. In auctions with only a few bidders, the winner is likely to have made the biggest (positive) error. Optimal-bidding theory recognizes this problem and prescribes a lower bid than the valuation in general. The extent of downward bias in the bid depends on the variability in the bidder's distribution of values, perhaps subjectively determined, and the number of competitors.

* * *

"Hubris cannot be the sole explanation of the takeover phenomenon because it implies that every bid announcement should elicit a price decline in the bidding firm's shares. Some papers have even found an average increase. Furthermore, if all bids were inspired by hubris, stockholders could easily stop them by the simple expedient of a prohibition in the corporate charter. On the other hand, a strict prohibition would be irrelevant to a fully diversified shareholder since a hubris-driven takeover is a wealth transfer, from one of his or her issues to another (ignoring the deadweight takeover costs). We do not observe such stringent antibid charter provisions, which must imply that stockholders at least believe that an occasional bid by a firm might have positive individual and aggregate benefits."

● **Bounded Rationality.** Fanto, Braking the Merger Momentum: Reforming Corporate Law Governing Mega–Mergers, 49 Buff. L. Rev. 249 (2001), describes the managers of acquirers as "quasi-rational." In this picture, the mega mergers of the 1990s stemmed less from dispassionate financial analysis than from psychological momentum. The CEOs felt pressure to imitate competitors already doing large transactions. Boards of directors in turn felt compelled to go along with the CEO, particularly a CEO with a good track record for effecting mergers. The business press fed the momentum by describing each new transaction in hyperbolic terms. The momentum then carried along financial professionals and investors. Fanto, Quasi–Rationality in Action: A Study of Psychological Factors in Merger Decision–Making, 62 Ohio St. L.J. 1333 (2001), turns to behavioral psychology for a particular explanation, showing evidence of, inter alia, myopia, status quo bias, and over optimism, in the documentation surrounding the late–1990s mega mergers.

● **Self Interest.** Others suggest that management self interest plays a causative role. Morck, Shleifer and Vishny, supra, combine management self-interest and management concern for the market value of the firm. In their view, the particular mix of motivations varies with the transactional circumstances. Managers, they say, are more likely to overbid where they detect personal benefits. This is a situation where the acquisition contributes to long term firm growth, enhances job security, or enables the manager to diversify the risk on human capital. Id. at 31–32. Morck, Shleifer and Vishny accompany their description with an empirical study of 326 acquisitions consummated between 1975 and 1987, and report on several situations where acquiring firms systematically overpay. Specifically, returns to the shareholders of bidding firms are lower where managers pursue unrelated diversification and buy growth. For a complementary hypothesis—that managers have special incentives to stay on the bidding side of the mergers and acquisitions market—see Agrawal and Walking, Executive Careers and Compensation Surrounding Takeover Bids, 49 J. Finance 985 (1994). This study finds (1) that takeovers occur more frequently in industries in which CEOs have significant positive abnormal compensation; (2) that target CEOs are more likely to be replaced when a bid succeeds than when it fails, and that those who lose their jobs tend to fail to find an equivalent position during the three years following the bid; and (3) that CEOs who are retained after a bid experience salary gains no better than others in their industry, and that post-bid changes in their salaries tend to be negatively related to the amount of their pre-bid excess compensation.

Morck, Shleifer and Vishny, supra, at 33–34, 45–47, also find that firms with bad managers do much worse with their acquisitions than do firms with good managers. See also Lang, Stulz, and Walkling, Managerial Performance, Tobin's Q and the Gains from Successful Takeovers, 24 J. Financial Econ. 137 (1989) (using the ratio of firm market value to replacement cost of assets as a measure of management quality, and shows that well managed companies earn significant positive returns when they acquire poorly managed companies and that poorly managed companies earn significant negative returns when they acquire well managed companies).

• **Overvalued Stock.** Recall that cash deals consistently yield better performance statistics than to stock deals. The economists Shleifer and Vishny take this point as the basis for a general theory of mergers. Shleifer and Vishny, Stock Market Driven Acquisitions, 70 J. Fin. Econ.295 (2003). The theory emerges from a model that assumes that mergers create no value and substitutes a motivational account grounded entirely in market mispricing. Mergers leading to abnormal negative bidder returns emerge as rational for both parties.

The model yields a taxonomy of merger motivations. Under the model, stock acquisitions occur when there are large numbers of overvalued firms available to be bidders and also numbers of less overvalued potential targets. Since the potential bidder's stock is overvalued, its long-term returns are going to be negative at all events. Such a bidder can acquire a target at a premium and benefit its own shareholders as well as the target shareholders, so long as the long-term returns on its stock in the wake of the merger are not as low as they would have been had the merger not been made. Although the target shareholders get the short-term gain, the bidder shareholders benefit long term by having their capital claim enhanced. Restating the model's point, it makes sense to use overvalued stock as a currency to buy assets more attractively priced than one's own. So doing cushions the inevitable collapse of the overvalued firm's stock. Of course, the overvalued firm cannot sell the merger to the marketplace in these terms. Accordingly, the market must perceive a synergy, making the merger look attractive in the short-term. Under the conditions described, even conglomerate mergers can make sense.

Within the model, a cash acquisition presupposes an undervalued target. This follows from the assumption that no value follows from the merger itself. Given the assumption, there is no reason to spend good money on a target absent undervaluation. The necessary conditions invite target resistance: Since the target shares are by definition undervalued, the return on holding them is higher than the return on the cash consideration. It follows that potential bidders often must resort to hostile tactics and that target resistance can benefit target shareholders.

Shleifer and Vishny take their typology into history. The 1960s and 1970s come forth as a period of bidder overvaluation with the theory of the conglomerate merger operating to supply the short-term synergy. In the 1980s target market values were low, cash deals became salient, and Jensen's free cash flow story supplied the short term synergy. Rising stock prices rather than regulation choked off the cash pattern in the 1990s, bringing back stock mergers initiated by overvalued bidders.

4. *Regulatory Implications.*

Does the phenomenon of the bad merger have implications for the law regulating mergers and acquisitions? If merger transactions should be regulated, who should do the regulating—courts or shareholders? Dent, Unprofitable Mergers: Toward a Market–Based Legal Response, 80 Nw.U.L.Rev. 777 (1986), proposes that courts enjoin bids causing significant declines in bidder stock prices. Coffee, Regulating the Market for Corporate Control: A Critical Assessment of the Tender Offer's Role in Corporate Governance, 84 Colum.L.Rev. 1145, 1269–72 (1984), suggests approval by acquiring firm shareholders in all cases. Finally, Fanto, supra, at 1389–1401, suggests that the mandatory disclosure system needs to be adjusted to address the cognitive limitations of corporate decisionmakers. Companies would be required to enumerate reasons for and against the transaction in considerable detail; investment bankers giving opinion would be required to take into account negative consequences and costs.

SECTION B.   ACCOUNTING AND TAXES

1. ACCOUNTING FOR MERGERS—PURCHASE, POOLING, AND ACCOUNTING FOR GOODWILL

Under the "purchase" method of accounting for business combinations, the assets and liabilities of the acquired company are recorded on the books of the acquiring company at their fair values as of the date of the combination. Any difference between the total value of the consideration paid by the acquiring company and the fair value of the tangible and identifiable intangible assets of the acquired firm is recorded as goodwill. Prior to 2001, under the American Institute of Certified Public Accountants (AICPA) APB Opinion No. 17 (1970), goodwill was deemed to have a limited useful life. Accordingly, like any other asset whose value disappears over time, its cost was amortized year-by-year against the income of the combined enterprise.

Between 1970 and 2001, the AICPA's APB Opinion No. 16 (1970) made available an alternative method of accounting for business combinations, but only where the combination was effected by an exchange of voting stock. Under this "pooling" method, the combination was treated not as a purchase but as a joining or "marriage" of two previously separated entities. The amounts at which assets and liabilities were recorded on the books of the acquired company (for the most part at historical cost under GAAP) were carried forward without change in the accounts of the acquiring company. Neither the fair value of the acquired company's assets nor any premium above that figure paid in the transaction was recognized on the emerging firm's balance sheet. As a consequence, the income of the combined firm was reduced neither by an increased depreciation allowance resulting from the upward revaluation of tangible assets nor by amortization of an amount attributable to the acquired company's goodwill.

Under the Financial Accounting Standards Board's (FASB) Statement No. 141 (2001), the purchase method must be employed for all business combinations initiated after June 30, 2001. The books of firms resulting from pooling combinations initiated before that date will not be required to be restated, however. At the same time, under FAS No. 142 (2001), goodwill no longer is required to be amortized after January 1, 2002. Instead it is to be reviewed for impairment periodically, and written off as a loss at such time as it is deemed to be impaired.

(A) PURCHASE VERSUS POOLING

Under purchase accounting, the acquired firm's tangible assets, identifiable intangible assets, and liabilities are recorded on the acquiring firm's books at fair value as at date of the combination. As a result, in the years after the transaction the reported income of the acquirer is decreased by depreciation charges taken in respect of the "stepped-up" value of the acquired firm's tangible assets. In addition, purchase treatment requires that the excess of the consideration paid by the acquiring firm above the net amount of the fair value of the acquired firm's assets—in effect the merger premium—be booked on the asset side of acquiring firm's balance sheet as goodwill. Under APB Opinion No. 17, this intangible asset had to be amortized against net earnings over a period not to exceed forty years. The earnings statement of the acquiring firm includes the earnings of the acquired firm only from the effective date of the acquisition. Prior to 2001, purchase accounting was unpopular with the managers of acquiring firms due to the general requirement for amortization of all intangibles. To the extent purchase treatment meant booking goodwill on the acquirer's balance sheet, future reported earnings were reduced.

Under pooling treatment, the owners of two going concerns were viewed as having combined their firms by combining their stock interests. In effect, they each swapped their stock in the constituent firm for stock issued by the surviving, combined entity. The balance sheets of the constituent firms were combined without adjustments of prior book values of assets. There occurred no write up to fair value of the assets of the acquired firm and no recording of a goodwill amount in respect of acquisition premium. The acquiring firm's future reported income accordingly was not reduced by the amount of amortized goodwill. Indeed, under pooling, the merger often resulted in a step up in reported earnings. The constituent firms' income statements were combined from the beginning of the year in which the transaction took place. As a result, the acquiring firm's earnings sometimes included the income of the target for a pre-acquisition period.

Pooling, which as a practical matter was available only for stock-for-stock transactions, was employed extensively in the "mergers of equals" of the 1990s. Under APB Opinion No. 16 firms seeking pooling treatment needed to satisfy a set of twelve qualifications. These included the following:

• The combination had to be effected by the issue of voting common stock in exchange for at least 90 percent of the voting common stock of acquired company or for all of its net assets. No pro rata distribution of cash or other consideration to the holders of the 90 percent could be made. But, where less than 100 percent and more than 90 percent of the stock was acquired the remaining shares could be left outstanding as a minority interest or be acquired for cash or other consideration.

• Each of the combining companies had to be autonomous, and could not have been a subsidiary or division of any other corporation within two years before initiation of the combination.

• The combination had to be effected in a single transaction or be completed under a specific plan within one year, unless delayed by governmental intervention or litigation. Taken together with the requirement that the combining firms be independent of each other, this condition made it difficult to get pooling treatment for mergers following hostile takeovers. Independence meant that a combining firm could not hold more than 10 percent of the voting common of another combining firm. This made it difficult to engineer a pooling if a hostile offer or preparatory series of open market purchases resulted in a block of more than 10 percent. Once a holder of a greater than 10 percent block, the acquirer had to go forward and purchase the requisite 90 percent as a part of the same plan within one year.

• The merger plan could not provide for any contingent future additional consideration.

• The acquiring firm could have no plan to dispose of a significant part of the combined assets within two years, except to sell duplicate facilities, excess capacity, and assets that would have been sold in the ordinary course of business by a constituent firm. Here the idea was to discourage post merger asset sales at amounts in excess of book value executed for the purpose of pumping up reported earnings.

• Specific rules sought to assure that no ancillary program of recapitalization or stock repurchase disturbed the transaction's status as a genuine "pooling" of the constituent firms' voting stock. These restricted, *inter alia* (a) stock repurchases for the purpose of warehousing treasury stock for use as consideration in combinations, (b) stock repurchases or other retirements of stock after consummation of the combination, and (c) changes in the voting rights or other rights of the constituent firms common stockholders by antecedent recapitalization or by terms incident to the combination.

(B) REVISED PURCHASE TREATMENT

Financial Accounting Standards Board
Summary of Statement No. 141, Business Combinations.
pp. 5–8, June 2001.

Reasons for Issuing This Statement

Under Opinion 16, business combinations were accounted for using one of two methods, the pooling-of-interests method (pooling method) or the purchase method. Use of the pooling method was required whenever 12 criteria were met; otherwise, the purchase method was to be used. Because those 12 criteria did not distinguish economically dissimilar transactions, similar business combinations were accounted for using different methods that produced dramatically different financial statement results. Consequently:

Analysts and other users of financial statements indicated that it was difficult to compare the financial results of entities because different methods of accounting for business combinations were used.

Users of financial statements also indicated a need for better information about intangible assets because those assets are an increasingly important economic resource for many entities and are an increasing proportion of the assets acquired in many business combinations. While the purchase method recognizes all intangible assets acquired in a business combination (either separately or as goodwill), only those intangible assets previously recorded by the acquired entity are recognized when the pooling method is used.

Company managements indicated that the differences between the pooling and purchase methods of accounting for business combinations affected competition in markets for mergers and acquisitions.

Differences Between This Statement and Opinion 16

The provisions of this Statement reflect a fundamentally different approach to accounting for business combinations than was taken in Opinion 16. The single-method approach used in this Statement reflects the conclusion that virtually all business combinations are acquisitions and, thus, all business combinations should be accounted for in the same way that other asset acquisitions are accounted for-based on the values exchanged.

This Statement changes the accounting for business combinations in Opinion 16 in the following significant respects:

This Statement requires that all business combinations be accounted for by a single method—the purchase method.

* * *

* * * [T]his Statement requires disclosure of the primary reasons for a business combination and the allocation of the purchase price paid to the assets acquired and liabilities assumed by major balance sheet caption. When the amounts of goodwill and intangible assets acquired are significant in relation to the purchase price paid, disclosure of other information about those assets is required, such as the amount of goodwill by reportable segment and the amount of the purchase price assigned to each major intangible asset class.

This Statement does not * * * fundamentally change the guidance for determining the cost of an acquired entity and allocating that cost to the assets acquired and liabilities assumed * * *. * * *

How the Changes in This Statement Improve Financial Reporting

The changes to accounting for business combinations required by this Statement improve financial reporting because the financial statements of entities that engage in business combinations will better reflect the underlying economics of those transactions. In particular, application of this Statement will result in financial statements that:

Better reflect the investment made in an acquired entity—the purchase method records a business combination based on the values exchanged, thus users are provided information about the total purchase price paid to acquire another entity, which allows for more meaningful evaluation of the subsequent performance of that investment. Similar information is not provided when the pooling method is used.

Improve the comparability of reported financial information—all business combinations are counted for using a single method, thus, users are able to compare the financial results of entities that engage in business combinations on an apples-to-apples basis. That is because the assets acquired and liabilities assumed in all business combinations are recognized and measured in the same way regardless of the nature of the consideration exchanged for them.

Provide more complete financial information—the explicit criteria for recognition of intangible assets apart from goodwill and the expanded disclosure requirements of this Statement provide more information about the assets acquired and liabilities assumed in business combinations. That additional information should, among other things, provide users with a better understanding of the resources acquired and improve their ability to assess future profitability and cash flows.

* * *

How the Conclusions in This Statement Relate to the Conceptual Framework

* * *

The Board * * * noted that FASB Concepts Statement No. 1, Objectives of Financial Reporting by Business Enterprises, states that financial reporting should provide information that helps in assessing the amounts, timing, and uncertainty of prospective net cash inflows to an entity. The Board noted that because the purchase method records the net assets acquired in a business combination at their fair values, the information provided by that method is more useful in assessing the cash-generating abilities of the net assets acquired than the information provided by the pooling method.

Some of the Board's constituents indicated that the pooling method should be retained for public policy reasons. For example, some argued that eliminating the pooling method would impede consolidation of certain industries, reduce the amount of capital flowing into certain industries, and slow the development of new technology. Concepts Statement 2 states that a necessary and important characteristic of accounting information is neutrality. In the context of business combinations, neutrality means that the accounting standards should neither encourage nor discourage business combinations but rather, provide information about those combinations that is fair and evenhanded. The Board concluded that its public policy goal is to issue accounting standards that result in neutral and representationally faithful financial information and that eliminating the pooling method is consistent with that goal.

QUESTIONS

1. How does the exercise of writing up the assets to fair value and booking the premium make the acquiring firm's balance sheet "more useful in assessing the cash-generating abilities of the net assets acquired"? Would an appraiser make reference to the balance sheet at all? If it makes sense to write up the acquired firm's assets to fair value because an acquisition has occurred, does it make sense to leave the acquiring firm's assets on the balance sheet at historical cost?

2. Did the defenders of pooling make a plausible argument when they asserted that the pooling method encouraged consolidation in some industries, increased the flow of capital into those industries, and encouraged the development of new technology? If stocks are priced efficiently on the market is anyone fooled by the earnings and asset differentials between combined firms displayed under purchase treatment and combined firms displayed under pooling treatment? Studies of stock market reactions reach conflicting results. For a discussion see Hill, Why Financial Appearance Might Matter: An Explanation for "Dirty Pooling" and Some Other Types of Financial Cosmetics, 22 Del. J. Corp. L. 141 (1997).

Financial Accounting Standards Board
Summary of Statement No. 142, Goodwill and Other Intangible Assets.

pp. 5–7, June 2001.

    * * *

Differences Between This Statement and Opinion 17

This Statement changes the unit of account for goodwill and takes a very different approach to how goodwill and other intangible assets are accounted for subsequent to their initial recognition. Because goodwill and some intangible assets will no longer be amortized, the reported amounts of goodwill and intangible assets (as well as total assets) will not decrease at the same time and in the same manner as under previous standards. There may be more volatility in reported income than under previous standards because impairment losses are likely to occur irregularly and in varying amounts.

This Statement changes the subsequent accounting for goodwill and other intangible assets in the following significant respects:

Acquiring entities usually integrate acquired entities into their operations, and thus the acquirers' expectations of benefits from the resulting synergies usually are reflected in the premium that they pay to acquire those entities. However, the transaction-based approach to accounting for goodwill under Opinion 17 treated the acquired entity as if it remained a stand-alone entity rather than being integrated with the acquiring entity; as a result, the portion of the premium related to expected synergies (goodwill) was not accounted for appropriately. This Statement adopts a more aggregate view of goodwill and bases the accounting for goodwill on the units of the combined entity into which an acquired entity is integrated (those units are referred to as reporting units). Opinion 17 presumed that goodwill and all other intangible assets were wasting assets (that is, finite lived), and thus the amounts assigned to them should be amortized in determining net income; Opinion 17 also mandated an arbitrary ceiling of 40 years for that amortization. This Statement does not presume that those assets are wasting assets. Instead, goodwill and intangible assets that have indefinite useful lives will not be amortized but rather will be tested at least annually for impairment. Intangible assets that have finite useful lives will continue to be amortized over their useful lives, but without the constraint of an arbitrary ceiling.

Previous standards provided little guidance about how to determine and measure goodwill impairment; as a result, the accounting for goodwill impairments was not consistent and not comparable and yielded information of questionable usefulness. This Statement provides specific guidance for testing goodwill for impairment. Goodwill will be tested for impairment at least annually using a two-step process that begins with an estimation of the fair value of a reporting unit. The first step is a screen for potential impairment, and the second step measures the amount of impairment, if any. However, if certain criteria are met, the requirement to test goodwill for impairment annually can be satisfied without a remeasurement of the fair value of a reporting unit.

In addition, this Statement provides specific guidance on testing intangible assets that will not be amortized for impairment and thus removes those intangible assets from the scope of other impairment guidance. Intangible assets that are not amortized will be tested for impairment at least annually by comparing the fair values of those assets with their recorded amounts.

* * *

How the Changes in This Statement Improve Financial Reporting

The changes included in this Statement will improve financial reporting because the financial statements of entities that acquire goodwill and other intangible assets will better reflect the underlying economics of those assets. As a result, financial statement users will be better able to understand the investments made in those assets and the subsequent performance of those investments. The enhanced disclosures about goodwill and intangible assets subsequent to their acquisition also will provide users with a better understanding of the expectations about and changes in those assets over time, thereby improving their ability to assess future profitability and cash flows.

How the Conclusions in This Statement Relate to the Conceptual Framework

The Board concluded that amortization of goodwill was not consistent with the concept of representational faithfulness * * *. The Board concluded that nonamortization of goodwill coupled with impairment testing is consistent with that concept. The appropriate balance of both relevance and reliability and costs and benefits also was central to the Board's conclusion that this Statement will improve financial reporting.

　　* * *

NOTE: TESTING GOODWILL FOR IMPAIRMENT

The test for goodwill impairment under FAS No. 142 operates in two steps.

Step One: The fair value of the reporting unit is ascertained and compared to the amount carried on the balance sheet in respect of the unit. If the unit's fair value is greater than the carrying amount, the review process ceases. If the unit's fair value is less than the balance sheet amount, the process proceeds to Step 2.

Step Two: The "implied" fair value of the good will of the reporting unit is ascertained and compared to the balance sheet amount of good will. The fair value of the unit is allocated to the unit's assets and liabilities as if the unit was being purchased for the first time. The excess of total fair value over the sum of the fair value applied to the assets is the "implied" fair value of the good will. If that amount is less than the balance sheet amount of good will, the difference constitutes an impairment loss. This loss is charged to operations.

Valuation Techniques: SFAS No. 157, Fair Value Measurements ii–iii (Sept. 2006), provides guidance on fair value calculations for accounting purposes. The FASB describes the overall approach as follows:

The definition of fair value retains the exchange price notion in earlier definitions of fair value. This Statement clarifies that the exchange price is the price in an orderly transaction between market participants to sell the asset or transfer the liability in the market in which the reporting entity would transact for the asset or liability, that is, the principal or most advantageous market for the asset or liability. The transaction to sell the asset or transfer the liability is a hypothetical transaction at the measurement date, considered from the perspective of a market participant that holds the asset or owes the liability. Therefore, the definition focuses on the price that would be received to sell the asset or paid to transfer the liability (an exit price), not the price that would be paid to acquire the asset or received to assume the liability (an entry price).

This Statement emphasizes that fair value is a market-based measurement, not an entity-specific measurement. Therefore, a fair value measurement should be determined based on the assumptions that market participants would use in pricing the asset or liability. As a basis for considering market participant assumptions in fair value measurements, this Statement establishes a fair value hierarchy that distinguishes between (1) market participant assumptions developed based on market data obtained from sources independent of the reporting entity (observable inputs) and (2) the reporting entity's own assumptions about market participant assumptions developed based on the best information available in the circumstances (unobservable inputs). The notion of unobservable inputs is intended to allow for situations in which there is little, if any, market activity for the asset or liability at the measurement date. In those situations, the reporting entity need not undertake all possible efforts to obtain information about market participant assumptions. However, the reporting entity must not ignore information about market participant assumptions that is reasonably available without undue cost and effort.

2. TAX TREATMENT OF MERGERS

Carney, Mergers & Acquisitions: Cases and Materials (2d ed. 2007)

pp. 56–61.

While taxation of corporate acquisitions is often the subject of a separate law school course, it is important for those who do not take that course to have at least a basic understanding of the issues involved.[1] This section must begin with a distinction between acquisitions—a generic term—and reorganizations—which generally covers only those transactions where no taxable event is recognized.[2] It must also note the distinction between acquisitive "reorganizations," the subject of this book, and bankruptcy "reorganizations."

Shareholders of a target company would, in many cases, prefer a taxfree reorganization, because this allows them to defer recognition of taxable gain until they dispose of the consideration (normally equity securities of the buyer) received in the reorganization. There may be cases where this is not a major consideration, and cash, which is fully taxable, would be more appealing. This may occur when the target corporation's shares have not appreciated significantly over a long period of time, so many shareholders will not recognize significant gains if they sell in a taxable transaction. It may also occur when the cash price is high enough to compensate most shareholders for the taxes they will incur.

Under modern accounting for acquisitions, buyers will have to record assets acquired either through a merger or asset purchase on their books at fair market value. In many cases this value may be well above the book value at which the assets were carried on the seller's books. Writing up assets to their fair market value increases the buyer's depreciation expense and lowers reported earnings. To the extent the buyer can keep the asset valuation lower, it can record the balance of the purchase price as good will, which is not subject to depreciation or amortization. Sellers also prefer not to have much of the purchase price allocated to depreciable assets, because they may suffer depreciation recapture, which leads to payment of taxes on these gains at ordinary income rates. Sellers would prefer allocation to non-depreciable assets, such as land or goodwill, which permits capital gain

---

1. Good brief reviews of this topic can be found in Howard E. Abrams and Richard L. Doernberg, Federal Corporate Taxation (2002), Chaps. 9–10 and in Barnet Phillips IV and Robert P. Rothman, Structuring Corpo-rate Acquisitions—Tax Aspects, Tax Management Portfolio No. 770.

2. Tax-free reorganizations are covered in Internal Revenue Code of 1986, 26 U.S.C. § 368 (hereinafter I "Code").

treatment, taxable at a lower rate.[3] Because of the two levels of taxation that a seller will face in a taxable asset sale, at both the corporate level and then at the shareholder level if the selling firm is liquidated and the sale proceeds distributed to the shareholders, this method is rarely employed.

The buyer's consideration of the preferable form of acquisition may be altered by the presence of tax loss carryovers in the selling corporation. A corporation that has suffered a series of tax losses may carry those losses forward as a deduction against future taxable income. If the buying corporation acquires the shares of the target and keeps it as a separate entity, these tax loss carryovers will remain available to offset future income of the acquired corporation, and of its parent if tax returns are filed on a consolidated basis.[4] A purchase of all the assets of the target in a taxable transaction does not transfer the tax loss carryovers, while a purchase of assets in a tax-free reorganization does transfer them, as does any form of tax-free reorganization that meets certain requirements.[5]

The result of these incentives is that choice of form can have a significant influence on the ultimate price of the transaction. Selling shareholders will demand a higher price in a taxable transaction, and a buyer seeking tax benefits from increased depreciation deductions may be willing to pay more in cash.[6]

i. TAXABLE TRANSACTIONS

Asset purchases in a taxable transaction involve a bidder purchasing the assets of a target for cash and the subsequent liquidation of the target, which distributes the cash to its shareholders. In this case the transaction would be subject to taxation at two levels. If the sale price of the assets exceeds their basis, the selling corporation has recognized taxable income to this extent, taxable at its current rate. When the selling corporation liquidates, the shareholders are again taxed on this distribution, to the extent it exceeds their basis in their shares.[7] This result can't be avoided by first liquidating through an in-kind distribution to shareholders, who then sell the assets to the purchasing corporation.[8]

---

3. This subject is governed by Code § 1060 in the event the agreement does not allocate the purchase price.

4. 26 C.F.R. 1.1502–11 (hereinafter "Regs."). The availability of a share exchange under § 11.03 of the Model Business Corporation Act facilitates such transactions.

5. Code § 381(a)(2). There are, however, limitations on the use of net operating loss carryforwards by the acquiring or surviving corporation. Among other things, there must be satisfaction of continuity of business requirements. (Code § 382(c)) For other limitations, see Code § 383.

6. This is borne out by some empirical studies, which show weighted average abnormal returns to target shareholders of 7.7% in mergers, while similar returns for sharehold-

ers in tender offers (which are always for cash), averaged 29.1%. The early evidence is summarized in Michael C. Jensen & Richard S. Ruback, The Market for Corporate Control: The Scientific Evidence, 11 J. Fin. Econ. 5, 10–14 (1983).

7. Code §§ 331 and 1001.

8. On liquidation, the corporation would recognize a gain under Code § 336, and the shareholders would be taxed on the difference between the fair market value of the assets and their basis in their stock under Code § 334(a). For an example, see Abrams & Doernberg, supra, note 1 at § 9.01.

Share purchases for cash involve only one level of taxation for the target corporation and its shareholders—the gain received by shareholders, measured by the excess of the purchase price over their individual basis in shares.[9] Similarly, a merger in which target shareholders received cash or debt is a taxable transaction, triggering capital gains treatment for target shareholders. At present there is a maximum tax of 15% on long-term capital gains,[10] but there is no assurance this rate will remain in effect indefinitely.

Acquiring corporations in taxable acquisitions recognize no taxable income in an acquisition of either assets or stock. They have a basis in either the assets or stock equal to the price paid.[11] However, if stock is purchased, the value of the assets is not stepped up to the amount of the purchase price, because the assets remain in the same corporation.

ii.   TAX–FREE REORGANIZATIONS

General. Shareholders who dispose of shares in a tax-free reorganization do not recognize gain or loss to the extent they receive "qualifying consideration."[12] Similarly, the target corporation in a tax-free reorganization recognizes no gain or loss.[13] The buying corporation acquires shares in a tax-free reorganization at the same basis as the selling shareholders.[14] It acquires assets from the target in a tax-free reorganization at the same basis as the selling corporation's basis.[15] There are three important types of tax-free reorganizations, discussed below.

"A" Reorganizations. The statutory merger or consolidation—the "A" reorganization—is the most flexible form of reorganization. Any form of consideration may be used—provided the continuity of interest doctrine—discussed below—is satisfied. The only disadvantage of this form is that the merger must be between the acquiring and acquired corporations.[16] This creates difficulties for many acquiring firms, because the triangular merger—between a subsidiary of the acquiring firm and the target—is often preferred * * *. In a triangular merger (the "(a)(2)(D) transaction"), the consideration paid is often shares of the parent corporation, but this triggers special rules not applicable when the merger is directly between the bidder and the target. In triangular mergers of this type, only stock of the parent, and not of the acquisition subsidiary, may be used to satisfy the continuity of interest requirement discussed below. Different rules apply to "reverse triangular" mergers, which are not discussed here. An "A" reorganization need not involve solely stock of the acquiring corporation as the consideration, although a significant amount—discussed below under the continuity of interest concept—must be stock. The balance is "boot." Shareholders in the selling corporation are subject

---

9.   Code § 1001.

10.   Code § 1(h).

11.   Code § 1012.

12.   Code § 354.

13.   Code § 361 (a) & (b).

14.   Code § 362(b).

15.   Id.

16.   Code § 368(a)(1)(A).

to taxation on boot received, but only to the extent of their gains on the entire transaction.[17]

"B" Reorganizations. The exchange of voting stock of the target constituting control of 80% of the outstanding voting stock plus 80% of all nonvoting classes of stock solely for voting stock of the acquiring corporation or its parent is perhaps the least flexible form of reorganization.[18] Whether the acquisition is "solely" for voting stock of the buyer may turn on whether the buyer has previously purchased any of the target's shares for cash, and whether these purchases should be integrated with the exchange.[19] Receipt of any non-qualifying consideration ("boot") destroys the tax-free status of the reorganization.[20] Thus, the bidder's assumption of a target corporation liability guaranteed by a shareholder constitutes boot that violates the "solely" requirement.[21] Because so many transactions involving publicly traded companies involve the bidder's prior acquisition of some target stock for cash, the use of "B" reorganizations seems to be largely confined to the acquisition of closely held corporations. Until the 1980s, share exchanges were purely voluntary transactions, but the 1984 revision of the Model Business Corporation Act provides for share exchanges by corporate action.[22] Thus, if the required vote is obtained from the shareholders as a class, the exchange will be effected for all shares in the class. But this does not make it easier to use a share exchange for public corporations, because each shareholder has the right to dissent from the share exchange and be paid the fair value of his or her shares, thus destroying the "B" reorganization.[23]

"C" Reorganizations. The last major form of reorganization is the exchange of substantially all of a corporation's assets solely for voting stock of the acquiror.[24] But the interpretation of "solely for voting stock" of the buyer is much more flexible than in "B" reorganizations. Virtually all active businesses have some debt obligations; the inability of a buyer to assume these obligations in the course of a reorganization would render this form virtually useless. Accordingly, assumption of seller corporation debt is disregarded in a "C" reorganization. Further, up to 20% of the total consideration paid in a "C" reorganization may be in a form other than common stock of the buyer ("boot"). As previously discussed under "A" reorganizations, receipt of "boot" will be taxable to the shareholder. However, for purposes of determining how much "boot" has been paid, the value of seller corporation indebtedness assumed must be included in the

17. Code § 356(a). While the general rule is that any gain recognized is taxable as capital gain, boot will be taxed as a dividend at ordinary income rates to the extent of retained earnings in the target corporation, if the exchange "has the effect of the distribution of a dividend."

18. Code § 368(a)(1)(B).

19. Most cases have held that earlier cash purchases absolutely violate the "solely for" requirement. See, e.g., Howard v. Commissioner, 238 F.2d 943 (7th Cir.1956); Chapman v. Commissioner, 618 F.2d 856 (1st Cir.

1980), cert. dismissed 451 U.S. 1012 (1981), and Heverly v. Commissioner, 621 F.2d 1227 (3d Cir.1980).

20. Turnbow v. Commissioner, 368 U.S. 337 (1961).

21. Rev. Rul. 79–4, 1979–1 C.B. 483.

22. Model Bus. Corp. Act ("MBCA") § 11.02.

23. MBCA § 13.02.

24. Code § 368(a)(1)(C).

calculation of "boot." Because there will be many cases where the debt assumed exceeds 20% of the total purchase price, the use of boot may be effectively precluded. The final requirement for a "C" reorganization is that the plan of reorganization must require the selling corporation to liquidate and distribute the stock and other consideration received, plus any remaining assets, to its shareholders.[25]

Continuity of Interest. In order for a transaction to qualify as a "reorganization," a substantial portion of the consideration paid must be in the form of stock of the acquiring corporation or its parent, with the rules spelled out with more specificity with respect to "B" and "C" reorganizations, as discussed above.[26] The stock may be either preferred or common, voting or non-voting, or participating or non-participating preferred.[27] In "A" reorganizations, there is no specific statutory requirement, and one case held that if 38% of the consideration were stock, that satisfied the continuity of interest requirement.[28] In both "B" and "C" reorganizations, the Code provides that 100% of the consideration must be voting stock of the issuer, subject to the "boot" allowed in a "C" reorganization.[29] These rules represent a codification of previous judge-made rulings that for all acquisitive reorganizations, the shareholders of the target corporation retain a significant equity interest in the corporation following the transaction. The focus is on the stock received as a proportion of total consideration received—not on the proportion of the bidder's stock held by target shareholders.[30] If the target shareholders intend to sell the bidder's stock in the market immediately after closing, the continuity of interest requirement will not be met, because of the "step transaction" doctrine that folds together all planned steps into a single transaction.

Business Purpose. Regulations requiring the existence of a business purpose (other than tax avoidance) for the acquisition codify earlier judicial decisions in this area.[31] This requirement is normally not difficult to satisfy where the acquisition is on an arms' length basis, and is most frequently problematic where the corporations are under common ownership or control.

Continuity of Business Enterprise. The regulations require that the acquiring corporation must either continue a line of the target's historic business or use a significant part of the target's assets in any business.[32] This is one way in which the Code prevents the acquisition of a corporation simply to take advantage of its net operating loss carryforwards, and "trafficking in net operating losses."

---

25. Code § 268(a)(2)(G).

26. Regs. § 1.368–2(a).

27. See John A. Nelson Co. v. Helvering, 296 U.S. 374 (1935). "Participating" preferred stock is preferred which, after payment of its fixed dividend, shares in additional dividends on some basis with the common stock.

28. Nelson v. Helvering, supra.

29. Code §§ 368(a)(1)(B) and 368(a)(1)(C).

30. See, e.g., Helvering v. Minnesota Tea Co., 296 U.S. 378 (1935).

31. Regs. H 1.368–1(b), 1.368–1(c) and 1.368–2(g).

32. Regs. § 1.368–1(d).

SECTION C. THE MERGER AGREEMENT
American Bar Association, Model Stock
Purchase Agreement (1995)
Appendix A

The ABA's Model Stock Purchase Agreement represent's a buyer's first draft in a heavily-negotiated acquisition of a closely held corporation. Such transactions are customarily concluded as stock purchases rather than as mergers. The stock purchase mode reduces transaction costs and results in the target firm's emergence in the desirable position of wholly-owned subsidiary of the acquiror. Most of the items on the menu of representations and warranties and closing conditions contained in the Model Agreement will be replicated in any set of acquisition documents, whether the mode is merger, asset sale, or stock sale.

Volk, Leicher & Koloski, Negotiating Business Combination Agreements—The "Seller's" Point of View

33 San Diego L. Rev. 1077, 1123–1126 (1996).

The seller will be most concerned about provisions of the merger agreement that could allow the purchaser not to close the transaction based on events or circumstances that are not within the seller's control. The purchaser, on the other hand, will want to make sure that the business it acquires is the one it expected. The provisions discussed below are among the most heavily negotiated in any merger agreement.

A. Material Adverse Change Clauses and Related Matters

Given the fact that parties to a business combination transaction sign a merger agreement several months (or longer) prior to the closing of the transaction, there is a risk that during such period the seller will lose some of its value. A purchaser will seek to condition its obligation to consummate the transaction on the absence of a material adverse change (MAC) in the seller. MAC clauses are often the subject of intense negotiation between the seller and the purchaser. Ideally, the seller would like to force the purchaser to accept all risk of such a change. Certain merger agreements between parties in the same industry, where the purchaser already faces the same business risks as the seller, contain no MAC condition or a very limited MAC condition. More typically, the parties negotiate a MAC clause that leaves some of the risk with the seller. The purchaser would, ideally, prefer to be able to avoid closing if, between the signing and the closing of the merger agreement, there is:

any circumstance, change in, or effect on, the Seller or any subsidiary of the Seller that, individually or in the aggregate with all other circumstances, changes in, or effects on, the Seller or its subsidiaries: (a) is, or could be, materially adverse to the business, operations, assets or liabilities, results of operations or the condition (financial or otherwise) of the Seller and its subsidiaries taken as a whole or (b) could materially adversely affect the ability of the Purchaser to operate or conduct the business of the Seller in the manner in which it is currently operated or conducted by the Seller.

The seller, on the other hand, will seek to limit the MAC clause in several ways. First, the seller will want to remove the word "could" in clause (b) and any reference to prospects, in order to avoid any possibility that the purchaser can get out of the agreement based on its subjective view of future events. In addition, the seller may wish to remove clause (b) entirely because without the "could" it is merely a restatement of what is covered in clause (a). In addition, the type of effects covered by clause (b) could include events or circumstances relating solely to the purchaser, which should be explicitly excluded. Other possible exclusions to ask for are: (1) an exclusion for changes that affect the seller's industry as a whole (especially if the purchaser is in the same industry), or the economy as a whole; and (2) an exclusion for changes resulting from the announcement or consummation of the transaction. The latter can be especially important in vertical mergers because the customers of the acquired company may be competitors of the acquiror.

A "back-door" MAC condition may be accomplished through the use of a "bring-down" condition (that the representations are true as if made on the closing date). In the case of an agreement with broad representations, this would have an effect similar to that of including a MAC condition.

B. Due Diligence Issues

The seller (especially if it is a public company) should resist provisions that permit the acquiror to forgo closing based on the results of any due diligence or similar investigation after the signing of the acquisition agreement. In general, the effect of such a provision (unless the threshold of problems that would allow the buyer not to close is very high) would be to grant the buyer an option to purchase the company. The failure of the transaction to close after a definitive agreement has been entered into may brand the company as "damaged goods," which, at the least, would give significant leverage to the acquiror in any pre-closing negotiations.

The seller should also resist any attempt by the acquiror to include a so-called "10b–5 representation" in the acquisition agreement. The name "10b–5 representation" comes from Rule 10b–5 promulgated under the Securities Exchange Act of 1934. The representation, following the general anti-fraud language of Rule 10b–5, provides that the acquisition agreement "does not contain any untrue statement of a material fact or omit to state any material fact necessary to make the statement contained herein not misleading." Such a representation broadens the applicability of the other representations and does not merely duplicate the rules provided by the securities laws with respect to the transfer of corporate stock. Mere duplication does not occur because of the prima facie case required, and the defenses (including those provided by the applicable statutes of limitations) available with respect to the statutory rules differ from those applicable by contract. In fact, the seller will usually wish to demand language indicating that the buyer has had the opportunity to perform due diligence, is satisfied with the results, and, most importantly, can refuse to close based only on the untruth of the representations and warranties made in the agreement (at signing and, to the extent provided in the bring-down condition, again at closing). In addition, the seller should seek to include language by which the acquiror explicitly acknowledges that it understands that it is not to rely on anything not contained within the agreement and related disclosure schedule, even if provided to the acquiror during the due diligence investigation. However, it is generally appropriate for a seller that is a public company to make a representation that its filings with the Securities and Exchange Commission "did not, at the time they were filed, contain any untrue statement of a material fact or omit to state a material fact required to be stated therein or necessary in order to make the statements therein, in light of the circumstances under which they were made, not misleading." In effect, the seller is representing that it has complied with duties imposed on it by the securities laws as a result of its status as a public company. This representation will usually be accompanied by a representation that such filings were in proper form and otherwise prepared and filed in accordance with the securities laws.

C.   Antitrust Issues

The Hart–Scott–Rodino Antitrust Improvements Act requires parties involved in certain types of business combination transactions to supply specific information to the Antitrust Division of the Department of Justice and the Federal Trade Commission prior to the consummation of a merger. Such information will be used in determining whether the proposed transaction will have any anti-competitive effects that would require the transaction to be terminated or restructured.

Depending on the level of risk that the combined company may be required to divest certain assets, the seller may wish to include language in the acquisition agreement that binds the purchaser to go through with the transaction notwithstanding such requirements (a "hell or high water" provision) or that otherwise sets, in advance, a threshold of what the purchaser is willing to do. The purchaser may be unwilling to agree to a "hell or high water" requirement for fear that, once the regulatory authorities know that it has agreed to do anything it takes to complete the transaction, the purchaser will lose all of its bargaining power with respect to the regulators.

IBP, Inc. v. Tyson Foods, Inc.

Court of Chancery of Delaware, 2001.
789 A.2d 14.

■ STRINE, VICE CHANCELLOR.

This post-trial opinion addresses a demand for specific performance of a "Merger Agreement" by IBP, Inc., the nation's number one beef and number two pork distributor. By this action, IBP seeks to compel the "Merger" between itself and Tyson Foods, Inc., the nation's leading chicken distributor, in a transaction in which IBP stockholders will receive their choice of $30 a share in cash or Tyson stock, or a combination of the two.

The IBP–Tyson Merger Agreement resulted from a vigorous auction process that pitted Tyson against the nation's number one pork producer, Smithfield Foods. To say that Tyson was eager to win the auction is to slight its ardent desire to possess IBP. During the bidding process, Tyson was anxious to ensure that it would acquire IBP, and to make sure Smithfield did not. By succeeding, Tyson hoped to create the world's preeminent meat products company—a company that would dominate the meat cases of supermarkets in the United States and eventually throughout the globe.

During the auction process, Tyson was given a great deal of information that suggested that IBP was heading into a trough in the beef business. Even more, Tyson was alerted to serious problems at an IBP subsidiary, DFG, which had been victimized by accounting fraud to the tune of over $30 million in charges to earnings and which was the active subject of an asset impairment study. Not only that, Tyson knew that IBP was projected to fall seriously short of the fiscal year 2000 earnings predicted in projections prepared by IBP's Chief Financial Officer in August, 2000.

By the end of the auction process, Tyson had come to have great doubts about IBP's ability to project its future earnings, the credibility of IBP's management, and thought that the important business unit in which DFG was located—Foodbrands—was broken.

Yet, Tyson's ardor for IBP was such that Tyson raised its bid by a total of $4.00 a share after learning of these problems. Tyson also signed the Merger Agreement, which permitted IBP to recognize unlimited additional liabilities on account of the accounting improprieties at DFG. It did so without demanding any representation that IBP meet its projections for future earnings, or any escrow tied to those projections.

After the Merger Agreement was signed on January 1, 2001, Tyson trumpeted the value of the merger to its stockholders and the financial community, and indicated that it was fully aware of the risks that attended the cyclical nature of IBP's business. In early January, Tyson's stockholders ratified the merger agreement and authorized its management to take whatever action was needed to effectuate it.

During the winter and spring of 2001, Tyson's own business performance was dismal. Meanwhile, IBP was struggling through a poor first quarter. Both companies' problems were due in large measure to a severe winter, which adversely affected livestock supplies and vitality. As these struggles deepened, Tyson's desire to buy IBP weakened.

This cooling of affections first resulted in a slow-down by Tyson in the process of consummating a transaction, a slow-down that was attributed to IBP's on-going efforts to resolve issues that had been raised about its financial statements by the Securities and Exchange Commission ("SEC"). The most important of these issues was how to report the problems at DFG, which Tyson had been aware of at the time it signed the Merger

Agreement. Indeed, all the key issues that the SEC raised with IBP were known by Tyson at the time it signed the Merger Agreement. The SEC first raised these issues in a faxed letter on December 29, 2000 to IBP's outside counsel. Neither IBP management nor Tyson learned of the letter until the second week of January, 2001. After learning of the letter, Tyson management put the Merger Agreement to a successful board and stockholder vote.

But the most important reason that Tyson slowed down the Merger process was different: it was having buyer's regret. Tyson wished it had paid less especially in view of its own compromised 2001 performance and IBP's slow 2001 results.

By March, Tyson's founder and controlling stockholder, Don Tyson, no longer wanted to go through with the Merger Agreement. He made the decision to abandon the Merger. His son, John Tyson, Tyson's Chief Executive Officer, and the other Tyson managers followed his instructions. Don Tyson abandoned the Merger because of IBP's and Tyson's poor results in 2001, and not because of DFG or the SEC issues IBP was dealing with. Indeed, Don Tyson told IBP management that he would blow DFG up if he were them.

After the business decision was made to terminate, Tyson's legal team swung into action. They fired off a letter terminating the Agreement at the same time as they filed suit accusing IBP of fraudulently inducing the Merger that Tyson had once so desperately desired.

* * *

In this opinion, I address IBP's claim that Tyson had no legal basis to avoid its obligation to consummate the Merger Agreement, as well as Tyson's contrary arguments. * * *

I. *Factual Background*

* * *

The Merger Agreement Negotiations

* * *

Late on December 30, IBP sent Tyson's negotiators the disclosure schedules to the Merger Agreement, which had been drafted by IBP's General Counsel Hagen. These schedules included a Schedule 5.11 that expressly qualified Section 5.11 of the Merger Agreement, which reads as follows:

> Section 5.11. *No Undisclosed Material Liabilities.* Except as set forth in *Schedule 5.11* the Company 10–K or the Company 10–Qs, there are no liabilities of the Company of any Subsidiary of any kind whatsoever, whether accrued, contingent, absolute, determined, determinable or otherwise, and there is no existing condition, situation or set of circumstances which could reasonably be expected to result in such a liability, other than:
>
> (a) liabilities disclosed or provided for in the Balance Sheet;

(b) liabilities incurred in the ordinary course of business consistent with past practice since the Balance Sheet Date or as otherwise specifically contemplated by this Agreement;

(c) liabilities under this agreement;

(d) other liabilities which individually or in the aggregate do not and could not reasonably be expected to have a Material Adverse Effect.

Schedule 5.11 itself states:

No Undisclosed Material Liabilities

Except as to those potential liabilities disclosed in Schedule 5.12, 5.13, 5.16 and 5.19, the Injunction against IBP in the Department of Labor Wage and Hour litigation (requiring compliance with the Wage and Hour laws), and *any further liabilities (in addition to IBP's restatement of earnings in its 3rd Quarter 2000) associated with certain improper accounting practices at DFG Foods, a subsidiary of IBP, there are none.*

On a later conference call between Tyson and IBP negotiators, Hagen told the Tyson participants that Schedule 5.11 was intended to cover the DFG issues discussed by Shipley in the December 29 conference call. The Tyson negotiators accepted the Schedule, based on prior discussions between Tyson in-house counsel Hudson and Tyson Finance Vice President Leatherby.

* * *

The Merger Agreement's Basic Terms and Structure

[The Merger Agreement contemplated a friendly tender offer by Tyson for $30 that would give IBP shareholders the choice of taking cash or an exchange of $30 worth of Tyson stock (subject to a collar). The Cash Offer would close by February 28, 2001 unless closing conditions set forth in an Annex to the Merger Agreement were not satisfied. If the conditions to the Cash Offer were not met, Tyson would proceed with a "Cash Election Merger" to close on or before May 15, 2001 unless the closing conditions set forth in Annex III of the Merger Agreement were not satisfied. Under this, IBP stockholders would receive $30 in cash, $30 in Tyson stock (subject to a collar), or a combination.]

The Annexes to the Agreement contain certain language that is substantively identical regarding Tyson's duty to close the transactions. That language provides:

[E]xcept as affected by actions specifically permitted by this Agreement, the representations and warranties of the Company contained in this Agreement (x) that are qualified by materiality or Material Adverse Effect shall not be true at and as of the scheduled expiration of the Offer as if made at and as of such time (except in respect of representations and warranties made as of a specified date which shall not be true as of such specified date), and (y) that are not qualified by materiality or Material Adverse Effect shall not be true in all material respects at and as of the scheduled expiration date of the Offer as if made at and as of such time (except in respect of representations and

warranties made as of a specific date which shall not be true in all material respects as of such specified date).

The previously described Section 5.11 is one of the representations and warranties referenced above. Primarily implicated in this case are the following representations and warranties:

Section 5.07. *SEC Filings.* (a) The Company has delivered or made available to Parent (i) the Company's annual report on Form 10–K for the year ended December 25, 1999 (the *"Company 10–K"*), (ii) its quarterly report on Form 10–Q for its fiscal quarter ended September 23, 2000, its quarterly report on Form 10–Q for its fiscal quarter ended June 24, 2000 (as amended) and its quarterly report on Form 10–Q for its fiscal quarter ended March 25, 2000 (together, the *"Company 10–Qs"*), (iii) its proxy or information statements relating to meetings of, or actions taken without a meeting by, the stockholders of the Company held since January 1, 1998, and (iv) all of its other reports, statements, schedules and registration statements filed with the SEC since January 1, 1998.

(b) As of its filing date, each such report or statement filed pursuant to the Exchange Act did not contain any untrue statement of a material fact or omit to state any material fact necessary in order to make the statements made therein, in the light of the circumstances under which they were made, not misleading.

(c) Each such registration statement, as amended or supplemented, if applicable, filed pursuant to the Securities Act of 1933, as amended (the *"Securities Act"*), as of the date such statement or amendment became effective did not contain any untrue statement of a material fact or omit to state any material fact required to be stated therein or necessary to make the statements therein not misleading.

Section 5.08. *Financial Statements.* The audited consolidated financial statements of the Company included in the Company 10–K and unaudited consolidated financial statements of the Company included in the Company 10–Qs each fairly present, in all material respects, in conformity with generally accepted accounting principles applied on a consistent basis (except as may be indicated in the notes thereto), the consolidated financial position of the Company and its consolidated subsidiaries as of the dates thereof and their consolidated results of operations and changes in financial position for the periods then ended (subject to normal year-end adjustments in the case of any unaudited interim financial statements). For purposes of this Agreement, *"Balance Sheet"* means the consolidated balance sheet of the Company as of December 25, 1999 set forth in the Company 10–K and *"Balance Sheet Date"* means December 25, 1999.

Section 5.09. *Disclosure Documents.* (a) Each document required to be filed by the Company with the SEC in connection with the transactions contemplated by this Agreement (the *"Company Disclosure Documents"*), including, without limitation, (I) the Exchange Schedule 14D–9 (including information required by Rule 14f–1 under the Exchange

Act), the Schedule 14D–9/A (including information required by Rule 14f–1 under the Exchange Act) and (iii) the proxy or information statement of the Company containing information required by Regulation 14A under the Exchange Act (the *"Company Proxy Statement"*), if any, to be filed with the SEC in connection with the Offer or the Merger and any amendments or supplements thereto will, when filed, comply as to form in all material respects with the applicable requirements of the Exchange Act except that no representation or warranty is made hereby with respect to any information furnished to the Company by Parent in writing specifically for inclusion in the Company Disclosure Documents.

(b) At the time the Schedule 14D–9/A, the Exchange Schedule 14D–9 and the Company Proxy Statement or any amendment or supplement thereto is first mailed to stockholders of the Company, and, with respect to the Company Proxy Statement only, at the time such stockholders vote on adoption of this Agreement and at the Effective Time, the Schedule 14D–9/A, the Exchange Schedule 14D–9 and the Company Proxy Statement, as supplemented or amended, if applicable, will not contain any untrue statement of a material fact or omit to state any material fact necessary in order to make the statements made therein, in the light of the circumstances under which they were made, not misleading. At the time of the filing of any Company Disclosure Document other than the Company Proxy Statement and at the time of any distribution thereof, such Company Disclosure Document will not contain any untrue statement of a material fact or omit to state a material fact necessary in order to make the statements made therein, in the light of the circumstances under which they were made, not misleading. The representations and warranties contained in this *Section 5.09(b)* will not apply to statements or omissions included in the Company Disclosure Documents based upon information furnished to the Company in writing by Parent specifically for use therein.

(c) Neither the information with respect to the Company or any Subsidiary that the Company furnishes in writing to Parent specifically for use in the Parent Disclosure Documents (as defined in *Section 6.09(a)*) nor the information incrporated (sic) by reference from documents filed by the Company with the SEC will, at the time of the provision thereof to Parent or at the time of the filing thereof by the Company with the SEC, as the case may be, at the time of the meeting of the Company's stockholders, if any, contain any untrue statement of a material fact or omit to state any material fact required to be stated therein or necessary in order to make the statements made therein, in the light of the circumstances under which they were made, not misleading.

Section 5.10. *Absence of Certain Changes.* Except as set forth in *Schedule 5.10* hereto, the Company 10–K or the Company 10–Qs, since the Balance Sheet Date, the Company and the Subsidiaries have conducted their business in the ordinary course consistent with past practice and there has not been:

(a) any event, occurrence or development of a state of circumstances or facts which has had or reasonably could be expected to have a Material Adverse Effect. . . .

Sections 5.07–5.09 therefore warrant the material accuracy of IBP's 1999 10–K and its 10–Qs for the first three quarters of 2000 (the "Warranted Financials"). Viewed literally and in isolation, these representations can be read as providing Tyson with a right not to close if IBP had to restate the Warranted Financials on account of the earnings charges at DFG that clearly related to past conduct that occurred during the periods covered by the Warranted Financials. Meanwhile, § 5.10 protected Tyson in the event IBP suffered a Material Adverse Effect, as defined in the Agreement.

III.   *Resolution of the Parties' Merits Arguments*

* * *

The Merger Agreement's terms are to be interpreted under New York law. * * *

* * *

B.   *Do the DFG Charges to Earnings Evidence a Breach of Warranty?*

1.   *The Merger Agreement Does Not Unambiguously Assign the DFG–Related Risks*

The first question I address is whether the DFG-related problems of IBP were a risk that was contractually accepted by Tyson, through the inclusion of Schedule 5.11. The parties have starkly different views of whether the reference to DFG in Schedule 5.11 operates to qualify all of the representations and warranties in the Agreement. Tyson contends that Schedule 5.11 has no effect on any representation and warranty other than that contained in § 5.11 of the Agreement. There are no Schedules 5.07–5.09 attached to the Agreement that operate to qualify §§ 5.07–5.09 explicitly. And §§ 5.07, 5.08, and 5.09 are, by their own terms, unqualified by reference to Schedule 5.11, and generally stand for the proposition that IBP warranted that the Warranted Financial Statements were accurate in all material respects and comported with GAAP. Tyson thus claims that these "flat" representations were plainly breached when IBP restated the Warranted Financial Statements to record the additional losses at DFG.

In support of this argument, Tyson points out that the parties knew how to qualify representations and warranties when they wished to do so. For example, § 5.16 in the Agreement is a representation regarding IBP's compliance with its legal obligations. The Agreement contains no Schedule 5.16, but § 5.16 expressly references Schedules 5.11, 5.12, and 5.19. Likewise, the Agreement's disclosure schedule states that "[i]tems disclosed for any one section of this Disclosure Schedule are deemed to be disclosed for all other sections of this Disclosure Schedule to the extent that it is reasonably apparent that such disclosure is applicable to other such section(s)." Had the drafters wished to provide that each Schedule would qualify each representation and warranty, this language could have been easily altered to accomplish that purpose plainly. * * *

* * * As a general matter, the strength of Tyson's interpretation—its simplicity and laser beam focus on the language of §§ 5.07–5.09—is also its weakness. When these sections are considered in light of the overall Agreement and the undisputed factual context in which the parties were contracting, the Tyson reading becomes far less than compulsory.

I begin at § 5.11 itself. That section says that "[e]xcept as set forth in Schedule 5.11 [or the Warranted Financials], there are no liabilities of the Company or any Subsidiary of any kind whether accrued, contingent, absolute, determinable or otherwise. . . . " Schedule 5.11 itself states that in addition to what was disclosed in the Warranted Financials, there may be "*further liabilities* (in addition to IBP's *restatement of earnings* in its 3rd Quarter 2000) associated with certain *improper accounting practices* at DFG Foods." Taken together, § 5.11 and Schedule 5.11 use the term "liabilities" in a broad and imprecise manner that would not be used by an accountant. Certainly, Schedule 5.11 can reasonably be read to include additional charges to earnings associated with improper accounting practices at DFG within the term, along with any other liabilities—such as litigation risks—associated with those practices.

Section 5.11 expressly contemplates that scheduled liabilities of this nature are not reflected in the Warranted Financials, but will be in addition to those contained in the Warranted Financials, *regardless of when the events giving rise to the liabilities arose.* Tyson largely acknowledges that this is the most reasonable reading of § 5.11 and Schedule 5.11.

But it argues that the fact that IBP could recognize potentially unlimited liabilities because of *past* accounting improprieties at DFG does not mean that DFG was free to restate the Warranted Financials without breaching the Agreement. That is, what was contractually important to the parties was the particular document in which such liabilities were publicly disclosed, rather than the magnitude of such liabilities. To be specific, under Tyson's reading, IBP was free to take a charge to earnings of $45 million in its fourth quarter 2000 10–Q, even if that charge related to accounting improprieties that had taken place in prior periods. What IBP was not permitted to do was to disclose an identical charge as a restatement to the Warranted Financials because that would violate the "flat" warranties in §§ 5.07–5.09.

The record reveals that this sort of hair-splitting has no rational commercial purpose. * * *

Tyson's interpretation is one that would be "unreal to men of business and practical affairs." New York law disfavors a reading of a contract that produces capricious and absurd results, in favor of a reading that is reasonable in the commercial context in which the parties were contracting.

To rebut this conclusion, Tyson has argued that §§ 5.07–5.09 "look to the past" and "do not identify future risks." Meanwhile, Schedule 5.11 is supposedly forward-looking and only "warrants that there are no contingencies that may result in IBP obligations in the future to a third party (such as litigation against the company) other than those disclosed in the [Warranted Financials] and Schedule 5.11."

There are several reasons why this construction is not mandated. First, as noted, the term "liabilities" in Schedule 5.11 seems to clearly encompass charges to earnings of the kind taken in the third quarter 2000 10–Q so long as those charges resulted from the same kind of *past* accounting irregularities that produced the initial charges. Second is Tyson's past and future reading of the Agreement. Tyson contends that its past/future construction makes sense because a restatement of past financial statements adversely affects market perception and subjects the company to fraud suits by investors, as it did here. Supposedly, Tyson did not want to accept this sort of risk. Yet, by its own argument, Tyson admits that Schedule 5.11 allocates to Tyson the risk of any liability that arose from "improper accounting practices" at DFG, including liability from lawsuits based on the practices. Tyson's logic is simply sliced too thin to sustain a finding that its construction is the only reasonable one.

Perhaps most importantly, Tyson's argument fails to address Schedule 5.11's reference to Schedule 5.13. Schedule 5.13 discloses that IBP is engaged in an "inventory accounting method dispute" with the Internal Revenue Service, and that the "issue of past years has yet to be formally resolved" and "[t]ax years 1992 to date are still open." Sections 5.07–5.09 do not cross-reference Schedule 5.13. Under Tyson's argument, it could walk away from the contract if the IRS determines that IBP's inventory accounting methods used in the Warranted Financials was improper and that a restatement of them is required. That reading of the Agreement therefore produces a silly result, which supports IBP's contention that §§ 5.07–5.09 cannot be read woodenly in isolation from the other provisions of the Agreement.

* * * [T]he Annexes to the Agreement * * * are of great significance because they govern the circumstances under which Tyson was free to abandon its Cash and Exchange Offers, as well as the Merger. Each of the applicable Annexes provides that Tyson may refuse to close if the representations and warranties in the Agreement are not true "except as affected by actions specifically permitted by" the Merger Agreement. IBP argues that this proviso is essentially a contract-specific articulation of the New York law principle that more specific sections of a contract govern over more general ones, when there is an inconsistency between the two.

According to IBP, Schedule 5.11 specifically permits IBP to recognize further liabilities on account of the accounting improprieties at DFG. Thus, according to IBP, the Annexes protect IBP by ensuring that its specific contractual right to do so does not result in a technical breach of a more general representation and warranty that permits Tyson to walk. IBP supports this contention by pointing to the Model Stock Purchase Agreement produced by the American Bar Association's Committee on Negotiated Acquisitions. The Committee Commentary states:

> The Sellers may also request that the 'bring down' clause [*i.e.*, the Annexes] be modified to clarify that the Buyer will not have a 'walk right' if any of the Sellers' representations is rendered inaccurate as a

result of an occurrence specifically contemplated by the acquisition agreement. The requested modification entails inserting the words 'except as contemplated or permitted by this Agreement' (or some similar qualification). [*Model Stock Purchase Agreement*, 1995 A.B.A. Sec. Bus. L. § 7, at 163.]

* * * [I]t seems more commercially reasonable to read the proviso in the Annexes, as IBP does, as a safe-guard that ensures that more specific aspects of the representations and warranties in the Agreement will govern over the more general, when giving literal effect to both the general and specific provisions produces an unreasonable result.

* * * [I]f forced to choose, I would find that IBP's reading of the Agreement is the one that is most reasonable in view of the overall language and structure of the Agreement, and commercial setting within which the parties were operating. * * * Tyson argues that it came out of a hotly contested auction with an option, rather than an obligation, to purchase IBP, having silently pocketed an almost sure walk-away right. By contrast, the IBP reading continues to give wide scope to §§ 5.07–5.09, but merely qualifies their application when necessary to give effect to a more specific provision of the contract.

* * *

D.   *Was Tyson's Termination Justified Because IBP Has Suffered a Material Adverse Effect?*

Tyson argues that it was also permitted to terminate because IBP had breached § 5.10 of the Agreement, which is a representation and warranty that IBP had not suffered a material adverse effect since the "Balance Sheet Date" of December 25, 1999, except as set forth in the Warranted Financials or Schedule 5.10 of the Agreement. Under the contract, a material adverse effect (or "MAE") is defined as "any event, occurrence or development of a state of circumstances or facts which has had or reasonably could be expected to have a Material Adverse Effect" ... "on the condition (financial or otherwise), business, assets, liabilities or results of operations of [IBP] and [its] Subsidiaries taken as whole.... "

Tyson asserts that the decline in IBP's performance in the last quarter of 2000 and the first quarter of 2001 evidences the existence of a Material Adverse Effect. It also contends that the DFG Impairment Charge constitutes a Material Adverse Effect. And taken together, Tyson claims that it is virtually indisputable that the combination of these factors amounts to a Material Adverse Effect.

* * *

The resolution of Tyson's Material Adverse Effect argument requires the court to engage in an exercise that is quite imprecise. The simplicity of § 5.10's words is deceptive, because the application of those words is dauntingly complex. On its face, § 5.10 is a capacious clause that puts IBP at risk for a variety of uncontrollable factors that might materially affect its overall business or results of operation as a whole. Although many merger contracts contain specific exclusions from MAE clauses that cover declines in the overall economy or the relevant industry sector, or adverse weather or market conditions, § 5.10 is unqualified by such express exclusions.

IBP argues, however, that statements in the Warranted Financials that emphasize the risks IBP faces from swings in livestock supply act as an implicit carve-out, because a Material Adverse Effect under that section cannot include an Effect that is set forth in the Warranted Financials. I agree with Tyson, however, that these disclaimers were far too general to preclude industry-wide or general factors from constituting a Material Adverse Effect. Had IBP wished such an exclusion from the broad language of § 5.10, IBP should have bargained for it. At the same time, the notion that § 5.10 gave Tyson a right to walk away simply because of a downturn in cattle supply is equally untenable. Instead, Tyson would have to show that the event had the required materiality of effect.

The difficulty of addressing that question is considerable, however, because § 5.10 is fraught with temporal ambiguity. By its own terms, it refers to any Material Adverse Effect that has occurred to IBP since December 25, 1999 unless that Effect is covered by the Warranted Financials or Schedule 5.10. Moreover, Tyson's right to refuse to close because a Material Adverse Effect has occurred is also qualified by the other express disclosures in the Schedules. * * * Taken together, these provisions can be read to require the court to examine whether a MAE has occurred against the December 25, 1999 condition of IBP as adjusted by the specific disclosures of the Warranted Financials and the Agreement itself. This approach makes commercial sense because it establishes a baseline that roughly reflects the status of IBP as Tyson indisputably knew it at the time of signing the Merger Agreement.

But describing this basic contractual approach is somewhat easier than applying it. For example, the original IBP 10–K for FY 1999 revealed the following five-year earnings from operations and earnings per share before extraordinary items:

	1999	1998	1997	1996	1995
Earnings from Operations (in thousands)					
$	528,473	373,735	226,716	322,908	480,096
Net Earnings Per Share					
$	3.39	2.21	1.26	2.10	2.96

The picture that is revealed from this data is of a company that is consistently profitable, but subject to strong swings in annual EBIT and net earnings. * * *

The original Warranted Financials in FY 2000 also emphasize that swings in IBP's performance were a part of its business reality. For example, the trailing last twelve month's earnings from operations as of the end of third quarter of FY 2000 were $462 million, as compared to $528 million for full year 1999, as originally reported. In addition, the third quarter 10–Q showed that IBP's earnings from operations for the first 39 weeks of 2000 were lagging earnings from operations for the comparable period in 1999 by $40 million, after adjusting for the CFBA Charges.

* * *

* * * [T]he contractual language must be read in the larger context in which the parties were transacting. To a short-term speculator, the failure of a company to meet analysts' projected earnings for a quarter could be highly material. Such a failure is less important to an acquiror who seeks to purchase the company as part of a long-term strategy. To such an acquiror, the important thing is whether the company has suffered a Material Adverse Effect in its business or results of operations that is consequential to the company's earnings power over a commercially reasonable period, which one would think would be measured in years rather than months. It is odd to think that a strategic buyer would view a short-term blip in earnings as material, so long as the target's earnings-generating potential is not materially affected by that blip or the blip's cause.

* * *

Practical reasons lead me to conclude that a New York court would incline toward the view that a buyer ought to have to make a strong showing to invoke a Material Adverse Effect exception to its obligation to close. Merger contracts are heavily negotiated and cover a large number of specific risks explicitly. As a result, even where a Material Adverse Effect condition is as broadly written as the one in the Merger Agreement, that provision is best read as a backstop protecting the acquiror from the occurrence of unknown events that substantially threaten the overall earnings potential of the target in a durationally-significant manner. A short-term hiccup in earnings should not suffice; rather the Material Adverse Effect should be material when viewed from the longer-term perspective of a reasonable acquiror. In this regard, it is worth noting that IBP never provided Tyson with *quarterly* projections.

When examined from this seller-friendly perspective, the question of whether IBP has suffered a Material Adverse Effect remains a close one. IBP had a very sub-par first quarter. The earnings per share of $.19 it reported exaggerate IBP's success, because part of those earnings were generated from a windfall generated by accounting for its stock option plan, a type of gain that is not likely to recur. On a normalized basis, IBP's first quarter of 2001 earnings from operations ran 64% behind the comparable period in 2000. If IBP had continued to perform on a straight-line basis using its first quarter 2001 performance, it would generate earnings from operations of around $200 million. This sort of annual performance would be consequential to a reasonable acquiror and would deviate materially from the range in which IBP had performed during the recent past.

Tyson says that this impact must also be coupled with the DFG Impairment Charge of $60.4 million. That Charge represents an indication that DFG is likely to generate far less cash flow than IBP had previously anticipated. At the very least, the Charge is worth between $.50 and $.60 cents per IBP share, which is not trivial. It is worth even more, says Tyson, if one realizes that the Rawhide Projections* portrayed Foodbrands as the

---

* [Ed. Note] The Rawhide Projections were a set of near and intermediate term projections for IBP generated internally by members of an MBO-group at an early stage of the IBP sale process.

driver of increased profitability in an era of flat fresh meats profits. This deficiency must be considered in view of the overall poor performance of Foodbrands so far in FY 2001. The Rawhide Projections had targeted Foodbrands to earn $137 million in 2001. * * * As of the end of the first quarter, Foodbrands had earned only $2 million, and thus needed another $135 million in the succeeding three quarters to reach its Rawhide Projection. * * *

As a result of these problems, analysts following IBP issued sharply reduced earnings estimates for FY 2001. Originally, analysts were predicting that IBP would exceed the Rawhide Projections in 2001 by a wide margin. After IBP's poor first quarter, some analysts had reduced their estimate from $2.38 per share to $1.44 a share. * * * [T]his was a sharp drop.

Tyson contends that the logical inference to be drawn from the record evidence that is available is that IBP will likely have its worst year since 1997, a year which will be well below the company's average performance for all relevant periods. * * *

     * * *

I am confessedly torn about the correct outcome. * * *

In the end, however, Tyson has not persuaded me that IBP has suffered a Material Adverse Effect. By its own arguments, Tyson has evinced more confidence in stock market analysts than I personally harbor. But its embrace of the analysts is illustrative of why I conclude that Tyson has not met its burden.

As of May 2001, analysts were predicting that IBP would earn between $1.50 to around $1.74 per share in 2001. The analysts were also predicting that IBP would earn between $2.33 and $2.42 per share in 2002. These members are based on reported "mean" or "consensus" analyst numbers. Even at the low end of this *consensus* range, IBP's earnings for the next two years would not be out of line with its historical performance during troughs in the beef cycle. As recently as years 1996–1998, IBP went through a period with a three year average earnings of $1.85 per share. At the high end of the analysts' consensus range, IBP's results would exceed this figure by $.21 per year.

This predicted range of performance from the source that Tyson vouches for suggests that no Material Adverse Effect has occurred. Rather, the analyst views support the conclusion that IBP remains what the baseline evidence suggests it was—a consistently but erratically profitable company struggling to implement a strategy that will reduce the cyclicality of its earnings. Although IBP may not be performing as well as it and Tyson had hoped, IBP's business appears to be in sound enough shape to deliver results of operations in line with the company's recent historical performance. Tyson's own investment banker still believes IBP is fairly priced at $30 per share. The fact that Foodbrands is not yet delivering on the promise of even better performance for IBP during beef troughs is unavailing to Tyson, since § 5.10 focuses on IBP as a whole and IBP's performance as an entire company is in keeping with its baseline condition.

Section D. Formal Aspects of Merger

1. The Mechanics of the Process

We turn now to the mechanical processes for completing mergers and acquisitions under state corporate codes, in particular the Delaware Corporation Law (DCL) and the Revised Model Business Corporation Act (RMBCA). These statutes make it possible to combine corporations utilizing any of three techniques—merger, purchase of assets, and purchase of shares. The statutes also allow for different types of consideration to be paid to the shareholders of the transferor firm. They may receive stock or other securities of the acquiring firm, stock or other securities of a firm other than the acquiring firm, cash, or a mix of any of the foregoing. Attendant rights and duties can differ substantially depending on the mode of combination employed and type of consideration paid.

(A) CLASSICAL MERGERS

(1) Stock for Stock Merger

We begin with the classical merger. Assume Acquirer (A) combines with Target (T), by a direct merger of T into A, pursuant to which T disappears and all of its assets and liabilities pass by operation of law to A. A has 1,000,000 common shares outstanding and T has 400,000 common shares outstanding. The shares of each of A and T are listed on a national securities exchange. The consideration received by the T shareholders is A common stock, to be distributed on a one-to-one basis. The A common distributed to the T shareholders has full voting rights.

Under DCL § 251(c), the board of directors of each of A and T must submit the merger for shareholder approval. The same dual shareholder votes are required under RMBCA §§ 11.04(b),(g), and 6.21(f). Delaware, however, does not hold out appraisal rights for either A shareholders or T shareholders who dissent from this merger. Under the "market out" provision of DCL § 262, holders of shares listed on a national securities exchange or the NASDAQ receive no appraisal rights. RMBCA § 13.02(b)(1)(I) contains a similar limitation, but goes on to list a series of special cases in which appraisal rights become available to T holders even though T is publicly traded. More particularly, under RMBCA § 13.02(b)(4), T holders receive appraisal rights if T's shares or assets are (1) being acquired by a firm or affiliate of a person or firm possessing 20 percent of the voting power of T during the preceding year or the right to elect a quarter of the T board during the preceding year, and (2) being acquired by a person or affiliate of a person who was during the prior year a T senior officer or T director and who receives in the merger "a financial benefit not generally available to other shareholders as such."

(2) Small Scale Merger

Contrast a different classical merger. Here A acquires a close corporation (CC). CC has 150,000 common shares issued and outstanding. These shares are held among seven individuals and are not publicly traded. The consideration in the merger is A common stock, distributed on a one-to-one basis. Under the DCL, the shareholders of A have no vote in this transaction. Under DCL § 251(f), where the effect of the merger is that the number of common shares of A issued and outstanding increases by 20 percent or less, no vote of A shareholders is required. Under DCL § 262(b)(1), shareholders thus situated receive no appraisal rights. The treatment of T differs. T shareholders still must approve the merger under DCL § 251(c). In addition they receive appraisal rights under § 262(a), for nothing in § 262(b) takes away the appraisal rights of shareholders of closely held transferor corporations. Voting at T works the same way under RMBCA § 11.04, and also works the same way under at A under RMBCA §§ 11.04(g) and 6.21(f), pursuant to which no shareholder vote is required for share issuances of 20 percent or less of A stock. Under RMBCA § 13.02(a),(b) appraisal rights are available to the T shareholders by virtue of the fact that their vote is required and their T stock is not publicly traded; under the same criteria, A shareholders have no appraisal rights.

(3) Classical Merger with Cash Consideration

Return now to the original stock-for-stock merger between A and T, both with publicly traded stock, but change the facts so that T shareholders receive cash for their shares at a 30 percent premium over the market price. Here again A shareholders lose their vote under DCL § 251(f) and with it their appraisal rights. Under § 251(f) the acquiring firm's shareholders get a vote only when the merger neither (1) increases the common stock by more than 20 percent, (2) effects a charter amendment, nor (3) otherwise affects the status or rights of acquirer shares outstanding immediately prior to the merger. The T shareholders continue to have a vote. Indeed, in Delaware, the transferor firm's shareholders always have a vote on mergers consummated under § 251. In this transaction they also have appraisal rights because the consideration is cash. Under DCL § 262(b)(2), the appraisal rights taken away under the public trading exception come back if the consideration in the merger is anything other than shares of the survivor or of another publicly traded company. RMBCA § 11.04(g) works like DCL § 251(f) to obviate a vote at A; not having a vote, the A shareholders have no appraisal rights under § 13.01(a). RMBCA § 11.04(b) tracks Delaware's treatment of the T shareholders respecting the vote. Appraisal rights work differently, however. The RMBCA's "market out" provision applies in a cash deal; appraisal rights come back only if the consideration is debt securities or stock in an entity that is not publicly traded. The T shareholders accordingly do not have appraisal rights here. RMBCA § 13.02(b)(2), (b)(3).

(4) Parent Subsidiary Mergers

Under DCL § 253, where the acquiring corporation owns at least 90 percent of the outstanding shares of each class of the transferor's outstanding shares, it may effectuate a merger of the subsidiary into itself by means of a resolution of its board of directors. No vote of the transferor's shareholders is necessary. At the same time, § 253(d) and § 262(b)(3) provide that appraisal rights always obtain for any minority shareholders of the transferor in respect of such a merger. RMBCA § 11.05 similarly provides for a merger of a 90 percent-owned subsidiary by virtue of action taken in the parent's boardroom. RMBCA § 13.02 provides for appraisal rights for any minority shareholders of the transferor subsidiary, but does so pursuant to a different drafting scheme. Under § 13.02, the minority shareholders of the subsidiary have appraisal rights by virtue of the fact that the parent held more than 20 percent of the voting power of the subsidiary. It follows that in any parent-subsidiary merger, the minority shareholders of the subsidiary have appraisal rights despite a public trading market in the subsidiary shares and without regard the consideration paid in the merger. Note that the effect of this provision is to strengthen the hand of shareholders left in the back end of a two step, front end loaded hostile tender offer (or shareholders holding out in the case of a single step all shares tender offer). Delaware is not so liberal—where less than 90 percent of the shares are owned by the parent and the minority shares continue to have a public market, minority shareholders receiving publicly traded stock can lose their appraisal rights under the public trading exception.

(B) SALE OF ASSETS—AN ALTERNATIVE TO THE CLASSICAL MERGER

We will now reconstitute the classical stock-for-stock combination of A and T as a sale of assets and assumption of liabilities. To achieve this, A and T enter into an Asset Purchase Agreement pursuant to which T agrees to sell all of its assets to A in exchange for 400,000 A shares. Without more, upon consummation of such a the sale, T would emerge as a closed-end investment company holding 400,000 A shares. To avoid the emergence of T as a blockholder, A will require T to dissolve and distribute the 400,000 A shares to its shareholders. A also will assume T's liabilities pursuant to a collateral "assumption agreement." Once all of this has taken place, A emerges exactly as it emerged pursuant to the classical stock for stock merger, as the successor to T's going concern with 400,000 of its shares held by T's former shareholders. But under the DCL the A shareholders have no vote on the transaction even though their approval would be required had the merger mode been employed. (It is noted that if A's charter did not authorize the 400,000 additional shares issued in the merger, an A shareholder vote would be required to amend the charter to increase the number of authorized shares.) In the contemplation of the statute, in this transaction A invests in the assets purchased; investment decisions are allocated to the board of directors under DCL § 141(a). Under DCL § 271(a), however, the T shareholders' vote is required because "all or substantially all" of the corporation's assets are being sold or exchanged. On the other hand, no appraisal rights obtain in respect of asset sales under DCL § 262—the appraisal statute covers "mergers" only. Of course, in this case it makes no difference, for T's shareholders would have no appraisal rights in a merger under Delaware's public trading exception. A difference would show up if we rewrote the deal to substitute cash for stock consideration. In a cash merger, the T shareholders always have appraisal rights. In a cash for assets sale of the going concern no appraisal rights obtain, although the T shareholders' vote is required.

Model Act treatment differs. The RMBCA brings the foregoing stock-for-assets combination of A and T into precise alignment with its treatment of the classical stock-for-stock merger. Under RMBCA § 6.21(f) a vote of A shareholders is required. This section of the RMBCA tracks the rules of the securities exchanges—NYSE Rule 312.03, AMEX Rule 712(b), and NAS-DAQ Rule 4310(c)(25)(H)(i)—in requiring a shareholder vote whenever in a single transaction or series of transactions and for a consideration other than cash, an issuer issues shares comprising more than 20 percent of the voting power outstanding immediately prior to the issuance. These provisions resemble DCL § 251(f), but have the effect of expanding the class of acquisitions requiring approval of the acquirers' shareholders. No appraisal rights would be available for either T or A shareholders under the RMBCA's public trading exception. But, where the public trading exception does not apply, the RMBCA holds out appraisal rights for the transferor shareholders in an asset sale. See RMBCA § 13.02(a)(3).

As under Delaware law, the T shareholders must approve the transaction under RMBCA 12.02(a). But § 12.02(a) departs from the Delaware pattern by decreasing the class of asset sales in which a transferor vote is required. Section 12.02(a) sets out a new articulation of what constitutes a sale of "all or substantially" all of a firm's assets. Under this a disposition requires a vote only if it "would leave the corporation without a significant continuing business activity." A brightline test is attached:

> If a corporation retains a business activity that represented at least 25 percent of total assets at the end of the most recently completed fiscal year, and 25 percent of either income from continuing operations before taxes or revenues from continuing operations for that fiscal year, * * * the corporation will conclusively be deemed to have retained a significant continuing business activity.

In the Official Comment to this section, its drafter asserts that the section sets out a standard "comparable" to that articulated in Delaware cases like Gimbel v. Signal Cos., 316 A.2d 619 (Del.1974), and Thorpe v. CERBO, Inc., 676 A.2d 436 (Del.1996). Both of these cases, as the drafter notes, stress that the line between a small-scale asset sale not requiring a vote and a sale of "all or substantially all" assets is not determinable by a strict mathematical standard but instead depends on the sale's qualitative effect of the corporation's business. The drafter does not note, however, that in eschewing a mathematical test, the Delaware courts chart a course in a markedly different direction from that followed by § 12.02 and its 25 percent test. *Thorpe v. CERBCO*, for example, holds a sale of an asset constituting 68 percent of the firm's business to amount to "substantially all" so as to require a vote. Under § 12.02, the opposite result would obtain.

(C) SHARE PURCHASE AND SHARE EXCHANGE

An acquiring firm could approach a stock-for-stock acquisition of a transferor from a different direction by appealing to T's shareholders directly. If such a "voluntary share exchange" were to occur between A and T's shareholders, A would offer to swap a share of its stock in exchange for each share of T's stock held by T's shareholders. If all T shareholders agreed to make the exchange, A would emerge holding 100 percent of T's stock with T's shareholders holding 400,000 A shares. This result differs significantly from that of the above-described classical merger. Here T survives as A's wholly-owned subsidiary where in a classical merger T disappears as its business is subsumed into A. The wholly-owned subsidiary result usually is thought to be superior since it minimizes detail work respecting successorship to T's contracts and brings A the benefits of limited liability so far as concerns any hidden or contingent future liabilities of T. But this advantageous result is not easily obtained by means of a voluntary exchange. A cooperative exchange process tends as a practical matter to presuppose the support of T's board of directors. Absent such support, a voluntary share exchange goes forward only as a hostile tender offer. Whether the offer is friendly or hostile, its voluntary terms invite holding out by the less cooperatively inclined actors amongst the T shareholders.

In Delaware, a voluntary stock-for-stock share exchange requires no formal shareholder approval on either side, so long as A has enough authorized shares. The target corporation, after all, is not itself a party to the transaction. The acquirer offers to purchase the target's shares from its shareholders, each of whom decides whether he or she wishes to sell. There are no voting or appraisal rights since no corporate action by the target corporation occurs and its shareholders are not compelled to exchange their shares. Shareholder protection rests on the individual right to sell or retain shares. Under RMBCA § 6.21(f) a different result obtains respecting a vote of A's shareholders. Since A is issuing stock carrying greater than 20 percent voting rights, the A shareholders' approval is required. A avoids that result by changing the consideration on offer to cash or perhaps a class of nonvoting common (provided it is authorized in its charter).

With the "compulsory share exchange" the RMBCA provides A with a more direct route to an acquisition of T as a wholly-owned subsidiary. Under this form of acquisition, all shareholders (or shareholders of a particular class of shares) of T must transfer their shares to A for the consideration set forth in a "plan of share exchange." So long as the exchange involves all classes of T shares, T emerges as A's wholly-owned subsidiary. Under RMBCA § 11.03, the consideration need not be A common; cash or other securities also can be exchanged. Under RMBCA § 11.04, the approval process is the same as that for a merger. Thus, the T shareholders get a vote, while an A shareholder vote depends on the consideration and ancillary contractual arrangements. Under RMBCA § 13.02 appraisal rights also work in tandem for mergers and share exchanges, so that the public trading exception precludes them for an A–T stock-for-stock share exchange, including an exchange for cash consideration.

(D) TRIANGULAR MERGERS

The DCL makes no provision for compulsory share exchanges. The reason is that practitioners easily can effectuate the same result—an acquisition in which the target emerges as a wholly-owned subsidiary—by setting up a "triangular merger."

Traditional corporate codes restricted the consideration payable in mergers to shares, securities, or obligations of the surviving corporation. As a result, mergers could have only two parties. In the 1960s and 1970s, merger consideration provisions were amended not only to authorize the use of cash or other property as merger consideration, but also explicitly to sanction the use of shares or securities of any corporation. There resulted three-party mergers in which the acquiring corporation creates a shell subsidiary and places its own shares (or other consideration to be used in the merger) in the subsidiary in exchange for the issue of 100 percent of the subsidiary's common stock. The target then merges with the shell subsidiary rather than directly with the acquirer parent, with the parent shares (or other assets) placed in the subsidiary serving as merger consideration for the target shareholders. The target emerges as the acquirer's wholly-owned subsidiary, as in a compulsory share exchange.

Triangular mergers are done in two ways, forward and reverse. In a forward triangle the target merges into the acquisition subsidiary and the target shareholders receive the parent shares (or other consideration) held by the subsidiary. In addition, the acquisition subsidiary changes its corporate name to the name of the target upon consummation. Thus does the subsidiary remain wholly-owned by the acquiring parent, emerging in possession of the assets and subject to the liabilities of the target. A reverse triangle is used when, as almost invariably is the case, business or tax considerations demand that the target remain in continuous existence. Here the acquisition subsidiary merges into the target. The plan of merger provides that the target's shares are "converted" into the parent shares (or other consideration) held by the acquisition subsidiary. The shares of the acquisition subsidiary held by the parent are similarly "converted" into 100 percent of the outstanding shares of the target. Upon consummation, the target is the nominal survivor to the merger with its assets and liabilities intact. In substance, of course, the target has been acquired by the parent, which emerges holding all of the target's outstanding shares.

Let us return to A and T and their stock for stock combination, structuring the deal as a reverse triangle between A Sub and T and assuming that A has sufficient shares authorized in its charter. Under DCL § 251, the transferor party to the merger is A Sub and T is the survivor; A itself is not a party to the merger. As a result the A shareholders have neither voting nor appraisal rights on any state of facts. The T shareholders have a vote even though they technically are holders of the survivor's shares. A close reading of DCL § 251(f) shows that the section is carefully drafted to avoid causing removal of voting rights of target shareholders in reverse triangles. Since the T is publicly traded, its shareholders have no appraisal rights under § 262. As before, if we change the merger consideration to cash, the T shareholders regain appraisal rights. Shifting over the RMBCA, we once again encounter some points of difference. First, under § 6.21(g), the issuance of the 400,000 shares to A Sub with a view to use in a merger is an action requiring A shareholder approval. Second, T shareholders will be subject to the "market out" provision in a cash deal and get no appraisal rights. Third, under § 13.02(4), a blockholding or control relationship between A and T could prevent the application of the "market out" and trigger appraisal rights in the T shareholders.

(E) DE FACTO MERGERS

Farris v. Glen Alden Corp.

Supreme Court of Pennsylvania, 1958.
393 Pa. 427, 143 A.2d 25.

■ COHEN, JUSTICE. We are required to determine on this appeal whether, as a result of a "Reorganization Agreement" executed by the officers of Glen Alden Corporation and List Industries Corporation, and approved by the shareholders of the former company, the rights and remedies of a dissenting shareholder accrue to the plaintiff.

Glen Alden is a Pennsylvania corporation engaged principally in the mining of anthracite coal and lately in the manufacture of air conditioning units and fire-fighting equipment. In recent years the company's operating revenue has declined substantially, and in fact, its coal operations have resulted in tax loss carryovers of approximately $14,000,000. In October 1957, List, a Delaware holding company owning interests in motion picture theaters, textile companies and real estate, and to a lesser extent, in oil and gas operations, warehouses and aluminum piston manufacturing, purchased through a wholly owned subsidiary 38.5% of Glen Alden's outstanding stock.[1] This acquisition enabled List to place three of its directors on the Glen Alden board.

On March 20, 1958, the two corporations entered into a "reorganization agreement," subject to stockholder approval, which contemplated the following actions:

1. Glen Alden is to acquire all of the assets of List, excepting a small amount of cash reserved for the payment of List's expenses in connection with the transaction. These assets include over $8,000,000 in cash held chiefly in the treasuries of List's wholly owned subsidiaries.

2. In consideration of the transfer, Glen Alden is to issue 3,621,703 shares of stock to List. List in turn is to distribute the stock to its shareholders at a ratio of five shares of Glen Alden stock for each six shares of List stock. In order to accomplish the necessary distribution, Glen Alden is to increase the authorized number of its shares of capital stock from 2,500,000 shares to 7,500,000 shares without according preemptive rights to the present shareholders upon the issuance of any such shares.

3. Further, Glen Alden is to assume all of List's liabilities including a $5,000,000 note incurred by List in order to purchase Glen Alden stock in 1957, outstanding stock options, incentive stock options plans, and pension obligations.

---

1. Of the purchase price of $8,719,109, $5,000,000 was borrowed.

4. Glen Alden is to change its corporate name from Glen Alden Corporation to List Alden Corporation.

5. The present directors of both corporations are to become directors of List Alden.

6. List is to be dissolved and List Alden is to then carry on the operations of both former corporations.

Two days after the agreement was executed notice of the annual meeting of Glen Alden to be held on April 11, 1958, was mailed to the shareholders together with a proxy statement analyzing the reorganization agreement and recommending its approval as well as approval of certain amendments to Glen Alden's articles of incorporation and bylaws necessary to implement the agreement. At this meeting the holders of a majority of the outstanding shares, (not including those owned by List), voted in favor of a resolution approving the reorganization agreement.

On the day of the shareholders' meeting, plaintiff, a shareholder of Glen Alden, filed a complaint in equity against the corporation and its officers seeking to enjoin them temporarily until final hearing, and perpetually thereafter, from executing and carrying out the agreement.[2]

The gravamen of the complaint was that the notice of the annual shareholders' meeting did not conform to the requirements of the Business Corporation Law, 15 P.S. § 2852–1 et seq., in three respects: (1) It did not give notice to the shareholders that the true intent and purpose of the meeting was to effect a merger or consolidation of Glen Alden and List; (2) It failed to give notice to the shareholders of their right to dissent to the plan of merger or consolidation and claim fair value for their shares, and (3) It did not contain copies of the text of certain sections of the Business Corporation Law as required.[3]

By reason of these omissions, plaintiff contended that the approval of the reorganization agreement by the shareholders at the annual meeting was invalid and unless the carrying out of the plan were enjoined, he would suffer irreparable loss by being deprived of substantial property rights.[4]

The defendants answered admitting the material allegations of fact in the complaint but denying that they gave rise to a cause of action because the transaction complained of was a purchase of corporate assets as to

---

2. The plaintiff also sought to enjoin the shareholders of Glen Alden from approving the reorganization agreement and from adopting amendments to Glen Alden's articles of incorporation, certificate of incorporation and bylaws in implementation of the agreement. However, apparently because of the shortness of time, this prayer was refused by the court.

3. The proxy statement included the following declaration: "Appraisal Rights."

"In the opinion of counsel, the shareholders of neither Glen Alden nor List Industries will have any rights of appraisal or similar rights of dissenters with respect to any matter to be acted upon at their respective meetings."

4. The complaint also set forth that the exchange of shares of Glen Alden's stock for those of List would constitute a violation of the pre-emptive rights of Glen Alden shareholders as established by the law of Pennsylvania at the time of Glen Alden's incorporation in 1917. The defendants answered that under both statute and prior common law no pre-emptive rights existed with respect to stock issued in exchange for property.

which shareholders had no rights of dissent or appraisal. For these reasons the defendants then moved for judgment on the pleadings.[5]

The court below concluded that the reorganization agreement entered into between the two corporations was a plan for a *de facto* merger, and that therefore the failure of the notice of the annual meeting to conform to the pertinent requirements of the merger provisions of the Business Corporation Law rendered the notice defective and all proceedings in furtherance of the agreement void. Wherefore, the court entered a final decree denying defendants' motion for judgment on the pleadings, entering judgment upon plaintiff's complaint and granting the injunctive relief therein sought. This appeal followed.

When use of the corporate form of business organization first became widespread, it was relatively easy for courts to define a "merger" or a "sale of assets" and to label a particular transaction as one or the other. See, e.g., 15 Fletcher, Corporations §§ 7040–7045 (rev. vol. 1938); In re Buist's Estate, 1929, 297 Pa. 537, 541, 147 A. 606; Koehler v. St. Mary's Brewing Co., 1910, 228 Pa. 648, 653–654, 77 A. 1016. But prompted by the desire to avoid the impact of adverse, and to obtain the benefits of favorable, government regulations, particularly federal tax laws, new accounting and legal techniques were developed by lawyers and accountants which interwove the elements characteristic of each, thereby creating hybrid forms of corporate amalgamation. Thus, it is no longer helpful to consider an individual transaction in the abstract and solely by reference to the various elements therein determine whether it is a "merger" or a "sale". Instead, to determine properly the nature of a corporate transaction, we must refer not only to all the provisions of the agreement, but also to the consequences of the transaction and to the purposes of the provisions of the corporation law said to be applicable. We shall apply this principle to the instant case.

Section 908, subd. A of the Pennsylvania Business Corporation Law provides: "If any shareholder of a domestic corporation which becomes a party to a plan of merger or consolidation shall object to such plan of merger or consolidation * * * such shareholder shall be entitled to * * *, [the fair value of his shares upon surrender of the share certificate or certificates representing his shares]." Act of May 5, 1933, P.L. 364, as amended, 15 P.S. § 2852–908, subd. A.[6]

5. Counsel for the defendants concedes that if the corporation is required to pay the dissenting shareholders the appraised fair value of their shares, the resultant drain of cash would prevent Glen Alden from carrying out the agreement. On the other hand, plaintiff contends that if the shareholders had been told of their rights as dissenters, rather than specifically advised that they had no such rights, the resolution approving the reorganization agreement would have been defeated.

6. Furthermore, section 902, subd. B provides that notice of the proposed merger and of the right to dissent thereto must be given the shareholders. "There shall be included in, or enclosed with * * * notice [of meeting of shareholders to vote on plan of merger] a copy or a summary of the plan of merger or plan of consolidation, as the case may be, and * * * a copy of subsection A of section 908 and of subsections B, C and D of section 515 of this act." Act of May 5, 1933, P.L. 364, § 902, subd. B, as amended, 15 P.S. § 2852–902, subd. B.

This provision had its origin in the early decision of this Court in Lauman v. Lebanon Valley R.R. Co., 1858, 30 Pa. 42. There a shareholder who objected to the consolidation of his company with another was held to have a right in the absence of statute to treat the consolidation as a dissolution of his company and to receive the value of his shares upon their surrender.

The rationale of the Lauman case, and of the present section of the Business Corporation Law based thereon, is that when a corporation combines with another so as to lose its essential nature and alter the original fundamental relationships of the shareholders among themselves and to the corporation, a shareholder who does not wish to continue his membership therein may treat his membership in the original corporation as terminated and have the value of his shares paid to him. See Lauman v. Lebanon Valley R.R. Co., supra, 30 Pa. at pages 46–47. See also Bloch v. Baldwin Locomotive Works, C.P.Del.1950, 75 Pa.Dist. & Co.R. 24, 36–38.

Does the combination outlined in the present "reorganization" agreement so fundamentally change the corporate character of Glen Alden and the interest of the plaintiff as a shareholder therein, that to refuse him the rights and remedies of a dissenting shareholder would in reality force him to give up his stock in one corporation and against his will accept shares in another? If so, the combination is a merger within the meaning of section 908, subd. A of the corporation law. See Bloch v. Baldwin Locomotive Works, supra. Cf. Marks v. Autocar Co., D.C.E.D.Pa.1954, 153 F.Supp. 768. See also Troupiansky v. Henry Disston & Sons, D.C.E.D.Pa.1957, 151 F.Supp. 609.

If the reorganization agreement were consummated plaintiff would find that the "List Alden" resulting from the amalgamation would be quite a different corporation than the "Glen Alden" in which he is now a shareholder. Instead of continuing primarily as a coal mining company, Glen Alden would be transformed, after amendment of its articles of incorporation, into a diversified holding company whose interests would range from motion picture theaters to textile companies, Plaintiff would find himself a member of a company with assets of $169,000,000 and a long-term debt of $38,000,000 in lieu of a company one-half that size and with but one-seventh the long-term debt.

While the administration of the operations and properties of Glen Alden as well as List would be in the hands of management common to both companies, since all executives of List would be retained in List Alden, the control of Glen Alden would pass to the directors of List; for List would hold eleven of the seventeen directorships on the new board of directors.

As an aftermath of the transaction plaintiff's proportionate interest in Glen Alden would have been reduced to only two-fifths of what it presently is because of the issuance of an additional 3,621,703 shares to List which would not be subject to pre-emptive rights. In fact, ownership of Glen Alden would pass to the stockholders of List who would hold 76.5% of the outstanding shares as compared with but 23.5% retained by the present Glen Alden shareholders.

Perhaps the most important consequence to the plaintiff, if he were denied the right to have his shares redeemed at their fair value, would be the serious financial loss suffered upon consummation of the agreement. While the present book value of his stock is $38 a share, after combination it would be worth only $21 a share. In contrast, the shareholders of List who presently hold stock with a total book value of $33,000,000 or $7.50 a share, would receive stock with a book value of $76,000,000 or $21 a share.

Under these circumstances it may well be said that if the proposed combination is allowed to take place without right of dissent, plaintiff would have his stock in Glen Alden taken away from him and the stock of a new company thrust upon him in its place. He would be projected against his will into a new enterprise under terms not of his own choosing. It was to protect dissident shareholders against just such a result that this Court one hundred years ago in the Lauman case, and the legislature thereafter in section 908, subd. A, granted the right of dissent. And it is to accord that protection to the plaintiff that we conclude that the combination proposed in the case at hand is a merger within the intendment of section 908, subd. A.

Nevertheless, defendants contend that the 1957 amendments to sections 311 and 908 of the corporation law preclude us from reaching this result and require the entry of judgment in their favor. Subsection F of section 311 dealing with the voluntary transfer of corporate assets provides: "The shareholders of a business corporation which acquires by sale, lease or exchange all or substantially all of the property of another corporation by the issuance of stock, securities or otherwise shall not be entitled to the rights and remedies of dissenting shareholders * * *." Act of July 11, 1957, P.L. 711, § 1, 15 P.S. § 2852–311, subd. F.

And the amendment to section 908 reads as follows: "The right of dissenting shareholders * * * shall not apply to the purchase by a corporation of assets whether or not the consideration therefor be money or property, real or personal, including shares or bonds or other evidences of indebtedness of such corporation. The shareholders of such corporation shall have no right to dissent from any such purchase." Act of July 11, 1957, P.L. 711, § 1, 15 P.S. § 2852–908, subd. C.

Defendants view these amendments as abridging the right of shareholders to dissent to a transaction between two corporations which involves a transfer of assets for a consideration even though the transfer has all the legal incidents of a merger. They claim that only if the merger is accomplished in accordance with the prescribed statutory procedure does the right of dissent accrue. In support of this position they cite to us the comment on the amendments by the Committee on Corporation Law of the Pennsylvania Bar Association, the committee which originally drafted these provisions. The comment states that the provisions were intended to overrule cases which granted shareholders the right to dissent to a sale of assets when accompanied by the legal incidents of a merger. See 61 Ann.Rep.Pa.Bar Ass'n 277, 284 (1957).[7] Whatever may have been the

---

7. "The amendment to Section 311 expressly provides that a sale, lease or exchange   of substantially all corporate assets in connection with its liquidation or dissolution is

intent of the *committee,* there is no evidence to indicate that the *legislature* intended the 1957 amendments to have the effect contended for. But furthermore, the language of these two provisions does not support the opinion of the committee and is inapt to achieve any such purpose. The amendments of 1957 do not provide that a transaction between two corporations which has the effect of a merger but which includes a transfer of assets for consideration is to be exempt from the protective provisions of sections 908, subd. A and 515. They provide only that the shareholders of a corporation which acquires the property or purchases the assets of another corporation, *without more,* are not entitled to the right to dissent from the transaction. So, as in the present case, when as part of a transaction between two corporations, one corporation dissolves, its liabilities are assumed by the survivor, its executives and directors take over the management and control of the survivor, and, as consideration for the transfer, its stockholders acquire a majority of the shares of stock of the survivor, then the transaction is no longer simply a purchase of assets or acquisition of property to which sections 311, subd. F and 908, subd. C apply, but a merger governed by section 908, subd. A of the corporation law. To divest shareholders of their right of dissent under such circumstances would require express language which is absent from the 1957 amendments.

Even were we to assume that the combination provided for in the reorganization agreement is a "sale of assets" to which section 908, subd. A does not apply, it would avail the defendants nothing; we will not blind our eyes to the realities of the transaction. Despite the designation of the parties and the form employed, Glen Alden does not in fact acquire List, rather, List acquires Glen Alden, cf. Metropolitan Edison Co. v. Commissioner, 3 Cir., 1938, 98 F.2d 807, affirmed sub nom., Helvering v. Metropolitan Edison Co., 1939, 306 U.S. 522, 59 S.Ct. 634, 83 L.Ed. 957, and under section 311, subd. D[8] the right of dissent would remain with the shareholders of Glen Alden.

subject to the provisions of Article XI of the Act, and that no consent or authorization of shareholders other than what is required by Article XI is necessary. The recent decision in Marks v. Autocar Co., D.C.E.D.Pa., Civil Action No. 16075 [153 F.Supp. 768] is to the contrary. This amendment, together with the proposed amendment to Section 1104 expressly permitting the directors in liquidating the corporation to sell only such assets as may be required to pay its debts and distribute any assets remaining among shareholders (Section 1108, [subd.] B now so provides in the case of receivers) have the effect of overruling Marks v. Autocar Co., * * * which permits a shareholder dissenting from such a sale to obtain the fair value of his shares. The Marks case relies substantially on Bloch v. Baldwin Locomotive Works, 75 [Pa.] Dist. & Co.R. 24, also believed to be an undesirable

decision. That case permitted a holder of stock in a corporation which *purchased* for stock all the assets of another corporation to obtain the fair value of his shares. That case is also in effect overruled by the new Sections 311 [subd.] F and 908 [subd.] C." 61 Ann. Rep.Pa.Bar Ass'n, 277, 284 (1957).

8. "If any shareholder of a business corporation which sells, leases or exchanges all or substantially all of its property and assets otherwise than (1) in the usual and regular course of its business, (2) for the purpose of relocating its business, or (3) in connection with its dissolution and liquidation, shall object to such sale, lease or exchange and comply with the provisions of section 515 of this act, such shareholder shall be entitled to the rights and remedies of dissenting shareholders as therein provided."

We hold that the combination contemplated by the reorganization agreement, although consummated by contract rather than in accordance with the statutory procedure, is a merger within the protective purview of sections 908, subd. A and 515 of the corporation law. The shareholders of Glen Alden should have been notified accordingly and advised of their statutory rights of dissent and appraisal. The failure of the corporate officers to take these steps renders the stockholder approval of the agreement at the 1958 shareholders' meeting invalid. The lower court did not err in enjoining the officers and directors of Glen Alden from carrying out this agreement.*

Decree affirmed at appellants' cost.

NOTE: A PENNSYLVANIA TRIANGULAR MERGER

In **Terry v. Penn Central Corporation,** 668 F.2d 188, 192–194 (3d Cir. 1981), the court was concerned with whether a triangular merger involving PCC Holdings, Inc., a wholly owned subsidiary of Penn Central Corporation, and Colt Industries, Inc., in which Colt was to be merged into PCC in exchange for Penn Central stock, constituted a "merger" to which Penn Central was a party so as to trigger the voting and dissenters' appraisal rights of Penn Central stockholders. The court concluded that Penn Central was not a party to the merger between its subsidiary and Colt, and it rejected the de facto merger doctrine as a mechanism for construing the transaction and the statute so as to make Penn Central a party to the merger. The court relied upon the emphatic action of the Pennsylvania legislature immediately after the Glen Alden case in explicitly repealing the de facto merger doctrine in Pennsylvania. But its opinion alluded to circumstances in which that doctrine (which had been held applicable to a triangular merger in Penn Central Securities Litigation, 367 F.Supp. 1158 (E.D.Pa.1973)) might not be ignored by a court. For similar rejection of the de facto merger doctrine with respect to voting power of the parent's stockholders in triangular mergers, see Equity Group Holdings v. DMG, Inc., 576 F.Supp. 1197 (S.D.Fla.1983).

Hariton v. Arco Electronics, Inc.

Court of Chancery of Delaware, 1962.
40 Del.Ch. 326, 182 A.2d 22, aff'd, 41 Del.Ch. 74, 188 A.2d 123 (1963).

■ SHORT, VICE CHANCELLOR.

Plaintiff is a stockholder of defendant Arco Electronics, Inc., a Delaware corporation. The complaint challenges the validity of the purchase by Loral Electronics Corporation, a New York corporation, of all the assets of Arco. Two causes of action are asserted, namely (1) that the transaction is unfair to Arco stockholders, and (2) that the transaction constituted a de

Act of July 11, 1975, P.L. 711, 15 P.S. § 2852–311, subd. D.

   * [Ed. Note] According to Moody's Industrial Manual (1960), on April 21, 1959 Glen Alden merged List by exchange of one Glen Alden share for one List share and by issu- ance of an additional Glen Alden share to holders of each 4 Glen Alden shares; at the end of 1958, Glen Alden had outstanding approximately 1,750,000 shares and List approximately 4,210,000 shares.

facto merger and is unlawful since the merger provisions of the Delaware law were not complied with.

Defendant has moved to dismiss the complaint and for summary judgment on the ground that the transaction was fair to Arco stockholders and was, in fact, one of purchase and sale and not a merger.

Plaintiff now concedes that he is unable to sustain the charge of unfairness. The only issue before the court, therefore, is whether the transaction was by its nature a de facto merger with a consequent right of appraisal in plaintiff.

Prior to the transaction of which plaintiff complains Arco was principally engaged in the business of the wholesale distribution of components or parts for electronics and electrical equipment. It had outstanding 486,-500 shares of Class A common stock and 362,500 shares of Class B common stock. The rights of the holders of the Class A and Class B common stock differed only as to preferences in dividends. Arco's balance sheet as of September 30, 1961 shows total assets of $3,013,642. Its net income for the preceding year was $273,466.

Loral was engaged, primarily, in the research, development and production of electronic equipment. Its balance sheet shows total assets of $16,453,479. Its net income for the year ending March 31, 1961 was $1,301,618.

In the summer of 1961 Arco commenced negotiations with Loral with a view to the purchase by Loral of all of the assets of Arco in exchange for shares of Loral common stock. I think it fair to say that the record establishes that the negotiations which ultimately led to the transaction involved were conducted by the representatives of the two corporations at arms length. There is no suggestion that any representative of Arco had any interest whatever in Loral, or vice versa. In any event, Arco rejected two offers made by Loral of a purchase price based upon certain ratios of Loral shares for Arco shares. Finally, on October 11, 1961, Loral offered a purchase price based on the ratio of one share of Loral common stock for three shares of Arco common stock. This offer was accepted by the representatives of Arco on October 24, 1961 and an agreement for the purchase was entered into between Loral and Arco on October 27, 1961. This agreement provides, among other things, as follows:

1. Arco will convey and transfer to Loral all of its assets and property of every kind, tangible and intangible; and will grant to Loral the use of its name and slogans.

2. Loral will assume and pay all of Arco's debts and liabilities.

3. Loral will issue to Arco 283,000 shares of its common stock.

4. Upon the closing of the transaction Arco will dissolve and distribute to its shareholders, pro rata, the shares of the common stock of Loral.

5. Arco will call a meeting of its stockholders to be held December 21, 1961 to authorize and approve the conveyance and delivery of all the assets of Arco to Loral.

6. After the closing date Arco will not engage in any business or activity except as may be required to complete the liquidation and dissolution of Arco.

Pursuant to its undertaking in the agreement for purchase and sale Arco caused a special meeting of its stockholders to be called for December 27, 1961. The notice of such meeting set forth three specific purposes therefor: (1) to vote upon a proposal to ratify the agreement of purchase and sale, a copy of which was attached to the notice; (2) to vote upon a proposal to change the name of the corporation; and (3) if Proposals (1) and (2) should be adopted, to vote upon a proposal to liquidate and dissolve the corporation and to distribute the Loral shares to Arco shareholders. Proxies for this special meeting were not solicited. At the meeting 652,050 shares were voted in favor of the sale and none against. The proposals to change the name of the corporation and to dissolve it and distribute the Loral stock were also approved. The transaction was thereafter consummated.

Plaintiff contends that the transaction, though in form a sale of assets of Arco, is in substance and effect a merger, and that it is unlawful because the merger statute has not been complied with, thereby depriving plaintiff of his right of appraisal.

Defendant contends that since all the formalities of a sale of assets pursuant to 8 Del.C. § 271 have been complied with the transaction is in fact a sale of assets and not a merger. In this connection it is to be noted that plaintiffs nowhere allege or claim that defendant has not complied to the letter with the provisions of said section.

The question here presented is one which has not been heretofore passed upon by any court in this state. In Heilbrunn v. Sun Chemical Corporation, Del., 150 A.2d 755, the Supreme Court was called upon to determine whether or not a stockholder of the *purchasing* corporation could, in circumstances like those here presented, obtain relief on the theory of a de facto merger. The court held that relief was not available to such a stockholder. It expressly observed that the question here presented was not before the court for determination. It pointed out also that while Delaware does not grant appraisal rights to a stockholder dissenting from a sale, citing Argenbright v. Phoenix Finance Co., 21 Del.Ch. 288, 187 A. 124, and Finch v. Warrior Cement Corp., 16 Del.Ch. 44, 141 A. 54, those cases are distinguishable from the facts here presented, "because dissolution of the seller and distribution of the stock of the purchaser were not required as a part of the sale in either case." In speaking of the form of the transaction the Supreme Court observes:

"The argument that the result of this transaction is substantially the same as the result that would have followed a merger may be readily accepted. As plaintiffs correctly say, the Ansbacher enterprise [seller] is continued in altered form as a part of Sun [purchaser]. This is ordinarily a typical characteristic of a merger. Sterling v. Mayflower Hotel Corp., 33 Del. 293, 303, 93 A.2d 107, 38 A.L.R.2d 425. Moreover the plan of reorganization *requires* the dissolution of Ansbacher and the distribution to its stockholders of the Sun stock received by it for the assets. As a part of the plan, the Ansbacher stockholders are compelled to receive Sun stock.

From the viewpoint of Ansbacher, the result is the same as if Ansbacher had formally merged into Sun.

"This result is made possible, of course, by the overlapping scope of the merger statute and the statute authorizing the sale of all the corporate assets. This possibility of overlapping was noticed in our opinion in the Mayflower case.

"There is nothing new about such a result. For many years drafters of plans of corporate reorganization have increasingly resorted to the use of the sale-of-assets method in preference to the method by merger. Historically at least, there were reasons for this quite apart from the avoidance of the appraisal right given to stockholders dissenting from a merger."

Though it is said in the Heilbrunn case that the doctrine of de facto merger has been recognized in Delaware, it is to be noted that in each of the cases cited as recognizing the doctrine, namely, Drug, Inc. v. Hunt, 35 Del. 339, 168 A. 87 and Finch v. Warrior Cement Corp., supra, there was a failure to comply with the statute governing sale of assets. In both cases the sales agreement required delivery of the shares of the purchasing corporation to be made directly to the shareholders of the selling corporation. It was, of course, held in each case that no consideration passed to the selling corporation and that therefore the transaction did not constitute a sale of the assets of the selling corporation to the purchasing corporation. No such failure to comply with the provisions of the sale of assets statute is present in this case. On the contrary, as heretofore observed there was a literal compliance with the terms of the statute by this defendant.

The doctrine of de facto merger in comparable circumstances has been recognized and applied by the Pennsylvania courts, both state and federal. Lauman v. Lebanon Valley Railroad Co., 30 Pa. 42; Marks v. Autocar Co., D.C., 153 F.Supp. 768; Farris v. Glen Alden Corporation, 393 Pa. 427, 143 A.2d 25. The two cases last cited are founded upon the holding in the case first cited which was decided on common law principles. The basis for the holding in the Lauman case is not at all clear. The transaction involved was a merger of two railroads and the special Pennsylvania statute authorizing the merger made no provision for a dissenting shareholder to be allowed the fair value of his shares. The theory of the court's holding was to the effect that a shareholder could not be compelled to exchange his shares for stock in a new corporation since to do so would be to deprive him of his property without due process of law. The later Pennsylvania cases adopt the de facto merger approach and stress the requirement of dissolution and distribution of the purchaser's stock among the seller's shareholders. The Farris case demonstrates the length to which the Pennsylvania courts have gone in applying this principle. It was there applied in favor of a stockholder of the purchasing corporation, an application which our Supreme Court expressly rejected in Heilbrunn.

The right of appraisal accorded to a dissenting stockholder by the merger statutes is in compensation for the right which he had at common law to prevent a merger. Chicago Corporation v. Munds, 20 Del.Ch. 142, 172 A. 452. At common law a single dissenting stockholder could also prevent a sale of all of the assets of a corporation. 18 C.J.S. Corporations

§ 515, p. 1194. The Legislatures of many states have seen fit to grant the appraisal right to a dissenting stockholder not only under the merger statutes but as well under the sale of assets statutes. Our Legislature has seen fit to expressly grant the appraisal right only under the merger statutes. This difference in treatment of the rights of dissenting stockholders may well have been deliberate, in order "to allow even greater freedom of action to corporate majorities in arranging combinations than is possible under the merger statutes." 72 Harv.L.Rev. 1132, "The Right of Shareholders Dissenting From Corporate Combinations To Demand Cash Payment For Their Shares."

While plaintiff's contention that the doctrine of de facto merger should be applied in the present circumstances is not without appeal, the subject is one which, in my opinion, is within the legislative domain. Moreover it is difficult to differentiate between a case such as the present and one where the reorganization plan contemplates the ultimate dissolution of the selling corporation but does not formally require such procedure in express terms. The Supreme Court of Iowa in Graeser v. Phoenix Finance Co., 218 Iowa 1112, 254 N.W. 859, wherein the court considered the identical state of facts which were presented to this court in Argenbright v. Phoenix Finance Co., supra, had this to say: "We think the evidence fairly shows that, while the plan pursued contemplated the ultimate dissolution of the old Phoenix Corporations, this was not inconsistent with the sale of their corporate assets to the Phoenix Finance Corporation, in accordance with the provisions of the Delaware statute. * * * Under the agreements thus made, the cash, stock, and securities of Phoenix Finance Corporation, which were given in exchange for the assets of the St. Louis and Des Moines companies, became the property of these respective companies, and these corporations did not cease to exist, as would be the necessary result of a consolidation, but still continued in existence as corporate entities." By the same token, Arco continued in existence as a corporate entity following the exchange of securities for its assets. The fact that it continued corporate existence only for the purpose of winding up its affairs by the distribution of Loral stock is, in my mind, of little consequence. The argument underlying the applicability of the doctrine of de facto merger, namely, that the stockholder is forced against his will to accept a new investment in an enterprise foreign to that of which he was a part has little pertinency. The right of the corporation to sell all of its assets for stock in another corporation was expressly accorded to Arco by § 271 of Title 8, Del.C. The stockholder was, in contemplation of law, aware of this right when he acquired his stock. He was also aware of the fact that the situation might develop whereby he would be ultimately forced to accept a new investment, as would have been the case here had the resolution authorizing dissolution followed consummation of the sale. Argenbright v. Phoenix Finance Co., supra; Finch v. Warrior Cement Corp., supra. Inclusion of the condition in the sale agreement does not in any way add to his position to complain.

There is authority in decisions of courts of this state for the proposition that the various sections of the Delaware Corporation Law conferring authority for corporate action are independent of each other and that a given result may be accomplished by proceeding under one section which is not possible, or is even forbidden under another. For example, dividends which have accrued to preferred stockholders may not be eliminated by an amendment to the corporate charter under § 242, Title 8. Keller v. Wilson & Co., 21 Del.Ch. 391, 190 A. 115. On the other hand, such accrued dividends may be eliminated by a merger between the corporation and a wholly owned subsidiary. Federal United Corporation v. Havender, 24 Del.Ch. 318, 11 A.2d 331; Hottenstein v. York Ice Machinery Corp., D.C.Del., 45 F.Supp. 436, Id., 3 Cir., 136 F.2d 944. In Langfelder v. Universal Laboratories, D.C., 68 F.Supp. 209, Judge Leahy commented upon these holdings as follows:

" * * * Havender v. Federal United Corporation, Del.Sup., 11 A.2d 331 and Hottenstein v. York Ice Machinery Corp., D.C.Del., 45 F.Supp. 436; Id., 3 Cir., 136 F.2d 944 hold that in Delaware a parent may merge with a wholly owned subsidiary and thereby cancel old preferred stock and the rights of the holders thereof to the unpaid, accumulated dividends, by substituting in lieu thereof stocks of the surviving corporation. Under Delaware law, accrued dividends after the passage of time mature into a debt and can not be eliminated by an amendment to the corporate charter under Sec. 26 of the Delaware Corporation Law, Rev.Code 1935, § 2058. But the right to be paid in full for such dividends, notwithstanding provisions in the charter contract, may be eliminated by means of a merger which meets the standard of fairness. The rationale is that a merger is an act of independent legal significance, and when it meets the requirements of fairness and all other statutory requirements, the merger is valid and not subordinate or dependent upon any other section of the Delaware Corporation Law."

In a footnote to Judge Leahy's opinion the following comment appears:

"The text is but a particularization of the general theory of the Delaware Corporation Law that action taken pursuant to the authority of the various sections of that law constitute acts of independent legal significance and their validity is not dependent on other sections of the Act. Havender v. Federal United Corporation proves the correctness of this interpretation. Under Keller v. Wilson & Co. accrued dividends are regarded as matured rights and must be paid. But, this does not prevent a merger, good under the provisions of Sec. 59, from having the incidental effect of wiping out such dividend rights, i.e., Sec. 59 is complete in itself and is not dependent upon any other section, absent fraud. The same thing is true with most other sections of the Corporation Law."

The situation posed by the present case is even stronger than that presented in the Havender and York Ice cases. In those cases the court permitted the circumvention of matured rights by proceeding under the merger statute. Here, the stockholder has no rights unless another and independent statute is invoked to create a right. A holding in the stockholder's favor would be directly contrary to the theory of the cited cases.

I conclude that the transaction complained of was not a de facto merger, either in the sense that there was a failure to comply with one or more of the requirements of § 271 of the Delaware Corporation Law, or that the result accomplished was in effect a merger entitling plaintiff to a right of appraisal.

Defendant's motion for summary judgment is granted. Order on notice.

NOTE: OTHER CONSEQUENCES OF DE FACTO MERGER

In **Rath v. Rath Packing Co.,** 257 Iowa 1277, 136 N.W.2d 410 (1965), a challenge was made to a "Plan and Agreement of Reorganization" entered into between Rath Packing Co. (an Iowa corporation) and Needham Packing Co. (a Delaware corporation) under which Rath was to issue newly created common and preferred stock to Needham, assume all of Needham's debts and liabilities, elect two Needham officers to its Board, and change its name to Rath–Needham Corporation. Needham was to transfer all of its assets to Rath, distribute the new Rath–Needham shares to its stockholders in liquidation and then dissolve. Notwithstanding the fact that Rath was a much larger corporation than Needham, the plan contemplated that Rath would issue 5.5 shares of its common and two shares of its convertible preferred in exchange for each 5 shares of Needham common. If the new preferred were converted, the old Needham stockholders would own a majority of the outstanding shares of Rath–Needham.

On a book basis the value of Rath common as of January 2, 1965 was reduced by the amalgamation from $27.99 to $15.93 per share. Each share of Needham's common was increased in book value from $6.61 to $23.90 (if all the preferred were converted). If the preferred were not converted, Needham shareholders would enjoy a priority in liquidation slightly in excess of the book value of all Needham shares and a prior claim of approximately 80 cents a share on dividends over Rath stockholders. Shortly prior to the time the terms of the Plan were made public, Rath and Needham shares sold on the American Stock Exchange for about the same price, but almost immediately thereafter the price of Needham shares increased and Rath's decreased, so that the former sold for 50% more than the latter. Needham's and Rath's earnings per share records compared as follows:

	Rath	Needham
1961	(1.91)	.18
1962	(.83)	.80
1963	.81	.39
1964	.41	.61
1965	(3.12)	2.15

A vote of Rath stockholders was necessary in order to increase the number of authorized shares, to change the corporation's name and to elect the Needham directors. Approximately 60% of the outstanding Rath shares voted in favor of the transaction. Minority shareholders of Rath sought to enjoin the transaction on the ground that it constituted a merger, and that it had not been approved by the holders of two-thirds of the outstanding shares of Rath, as required by the Iowa Code. The Code authorized amendments of the charter, such as were called for by the Plan, by a majority vote.

The trial court accepted the *Hariton* approach, and interpreted the Iowa Code to give corporate management the option to choose between the consequences of amalgamating the two firms by the process taken and amalgamating them by a formal statutory merger. Hence it dismissed the complaint. The Iowa Supreme Court reversed and directed the issuance of an injunction against effectuation of the Plan, on the ground that the effect of the Plan was identical with that of a merger, and that the statutory voting requirements for merger had not been met. The Court rejected the *Hariton* approach, denied that the Code gave management a choice of methods in effecting a combination which produces the same continuing single enterprise as would a merger, and ruled that the merger provisions of the Code imposed constraints on the amendment provisions. The Court said (136 N.W.2d at 416–417):

"It is apparent that if the sections pertaining to amending articles and issuing stock are construed to authorize a merger by a majority vote of shareholders they conflict with the sections specifically dealing with the one matter of mergers which require a two-thirds vote of shareholders. The two sets of sections may be harmonized by holding, as we do, that the merger sections govern the matter of merger and must be regarded as an exception to the sections dealing with amending articles and issuing stock, which may or may not be involved in a merger.

"The construction we give these sections is in accord with the cardinal rule that, if reasonably possible, effect will be given to every part of a statute. * * *

"The merger sections make it clear the legislature intended to require a two-thirds vote of shareholders and accord so-called appraisal rights to dissenters in case of a merger. It is unreasonable to ascribe to the same legislature an intent to provide in the same act a method of evading the required two-thirds vote and the grant of such appraisal rights. The practical effect of the decision appealed from is to render the requirements of a two-thirds vote and appraisal rights meaningless in virtually all mergers. It is scarcely an exaggeration to say the decision amounts to judicial repeal of the merger sections in most instances of merger.

"It is obvious, as defendants' counsel frankly stated in oral argument, that corporate management would naturally choose a method which requires only majority approval of shareholders and does not grant dissenters the right to be paid the fair value of their stock. The legislature could hardly have intended to vest in corporate management the option to comply with the requirements just referred to or to proceed without such compliance, a choice that would invariably be exercised in favor of the easier method."

NOTE: SUCCESSOR LIABILITY

The question whether a nonmerger transaction constitutes a *de facto* merger to be treated as if it were a merger *de jure* may arise in contexts other than voting or appraisal claims of minority or dissenting stockholders. For example, an arrangement like that in *Hariton* may be asserted to be a *de facto* merger by creditors of the acquired corporation where less than all of the obligations of the selling corporation are assumed by the acquiring corporation and the stock of the acquiring corporation is distributed to the stockholders of the acquired corporation together with its few remaining assets. See, e.g., Arnold Graphics Indus. v. Independent Agent Center, Inc., 775 F.2d 38 (2d Cir.1985) (judgment creditor can sue successor); Knapp v. North American Rockwell Corp., 506 F.2d 361 (3d Cir.1974) (applying *Farris* in respect of product liability claim arising from machine sold by liquidated predecessor); Atlas Tool Co. v. Commissioner of Internal Revenue, 614 F.2d 860 (3d Cir.1980) (successor liable for tax obligations of liquidated firm).

Successor liability for asset purchasers obtains in different degrees in different jurisdictions. Under the traditional, most restrictive view, liability attaches where the purchaser amounts to a "continuation of the enterprise"—that is, where the successor has a commonality of management and ownership with the predecessor. On this theory, a stock for assets deal implies successor liability where a cash for assets deal does not. Under a more expansive formulation, successor liability can obtain where the successor has paid cash or for some other reason there is no continuity of ownership. See, e.g., Fitzgerald v. Fahnestock & Co., Inc., 286 A.D.2d 573, 730 N.Y.S.2d 70 (2001)(doctrine applies where successor takes the benefits of the going concern and therefore "should" assume the liabilities); Turner v. Bituminous Cas. Co., 397 Mich. 406, 244 N.W.2d 873 (1976). But cf. Cargo Partner AG v. Albatrans, Inc. 352 F.3d 41 (2d Cir. 2003)(reading the Fahnestock opinion narrowly and ruling that continuity of ownership is essential to make out a case for successor liability under New York law). California, New Jersey, Pennsylvania and Washington accept a still more expansive variant of the doctrine in products liability contexts. Under this "product line" exception, products liability can extend to the purchaser of a production facility. See, e.g., Ramirez v. Amsted Industries, Inc., 86 N.J. 332, 431 A.2d 811 (1981). For discussion, see Blumberg, The Continuity of the Enterprise Doctrine: Corporate Successorship, 10 Fla. J. Int'l L. 365 (1996); Symposium, 67 Wash.U.L.Q. 325 (1989); Schecter, Acquiring Corporate Assets Without Successor Liability: Is It a Myth? 1986 Colum.Bus.L.Rev. 137; Roe, Mergers, Acquisitions and Tort: A Comment on the Problem of Successor Corporation Liability, 70 Va.L.Rev. 1559 (1984). Finally, note that federal environmental law drastically expands the zone of successor liability.

2. APPRAISAL

See Appendix B for the statutory provisions for appraisal in Delaware and New York and under the RMBCA. Delaware General Corporation Law, § 262; New York Business Corporation Law, §§ 623 and 910; Revised Model Business Corporation Act, chapter 13.

Thompson, Exit, Liquidity, and Majority Rule: Appraisal's Role in Corporate Law

84 Geo. L.J. 1, 11–13, 18–24, 25 (1995).

Statutory appraisal provisions arose at the end of the last century as part of an effort to facilitate the business combinations of railroads and other businesses that could benefit from large pools of capital. Majority shareholders received broader authority to make decisions allowing for growth; minority investors who did not want to go along with these changes could get out and receive the fair value of their shares. While the appraisal remedy could protect against misuse of majority power to structure self-dealing or other conflict transactions, its dominant use was to provide shareholders with liquidity, a way out of a transaction that the majority had implemented. Only in appraisal's reincarnation in recent years did the focus of the remedy shift to policing majority opportunism in conflict transactions.

In the business and legal setting at the time of the first enactment of appraisal statutes, corporate enterprises had much less freedom than they do today. The general incorporation statutes that had become widespread by the 1880s usually contained substantial limits on the corporation's duration, its purposes, and its capital, reflecting societal distrust of corporations. Decision-making within even the earliest corporation permitted those in control to bind the minority, thus providing the incorporated business a more centralized decision-making apparatus than the consensus model of the typical partnership. This flexibility, however, did not extend to mergers and consolidations, which required shareholder unanimity. Such a transformation of the shares was perceived as a taking of a shareholder's property, which required each owner's consent.

* * *

The balance struck with the introduction of appraisal provided something for three groups: majority shareholders, minority shareholders, and the public. Courts commonly described the purpose of appraisal statutes as protecting minority shareholders and concluded that the statutes should be liberally construed for that purpose. In the face of such a purpose, some saw majority shareholders as having hijacked the remedy, in a process that Bayless Manning described as "perspicacious legislative agents of management" playing for the "rebound in history." If the chronological focus is only on appraisal after the merger has been implemented, the purpose, no doubt, is to protect minority shareholders. Appraisal coupled with authorization of mergers by less than a unanimous vote, however, was clearly a "lubricant to speed the spread of majoritarianism" so as to arm the majority "for vigorous maneuver" to make advantageous trades free of hold-ups by the minority. The public thus benefitted from a healthy business condition as firms could more easily adapt to new circumstances.

* * *

Through this first period the purpose of appraisal was as summarized by the comment to the Uniform Business Incorporation Act: "The majority ought to be able to carry out the policies which seem to them best, but the minority ought not to have to bear the consequences of the majority's adoption of those rather extraordinary and unexpected measures." The focus was on the minority's choice to refuse to go along, disassociate, exercise the right to retire, jump ship, or, in the words of one court, simply to say "I want out." The statute was designed to provide liquidity and thus protect the minority shareholders from a negative act: they could not be forced into a new corporation against their will. It was an instrument that permitted minority shareholders either to exercise their right to appraisal or to continue in the changed enterprise.

In this period there was less need to police majority misuse of mergers and similar transactions. * * * [L]imits on corporate authority and the judicial use of fiduciary duty to check self-dealing restricted the majority's ability to implement [a freezeout] transaction. * * * Appraisal was "not primarily a control, but an escape."

* * *

The procedures attendant to the appraisal process and the valuation standard reflected this more limited reach of majority power and of the appraisal remedy. The amount to which a minority investor was entitled was the value of the shares on the day before the transaction exclusive of any appreciation or depreciation from the triggering transaction. This phrasing is consistent with the initial view of appraisal as triggered by a transaction in which a minority shareholder was choosing to leave or to retire, having disagreed with the majority's choice to change the venture.

In that setting, the complaining minority should get the value of the shares before the transaction was proposed, which was the value of what had been taken from the shareholder. There would be no need to look at what came after the transaction because the minority would have made a choice to go in a different direction.

Similarly, the procedures that developed to perfect an appraisal right reflected this transactional setting. The exercise of appraisal could drain the corporation of cash. To prevent injustice to the entire group, management needed to know how many shareholders were going to elect this right. State legislatures' decisions to place the procedural burden on the minority seemed appropriate when the minority had the right to continue in the changed enterprise, but instead chose to retire.

Finally, appraisal was seldom seen as exclusive in this period. Some worried that it could not serve its intended purpose for the majority if it were not exclusive, and some states wrote exclusivity into their statutes, but the more common view was to focus on the cumulative nature of this remedy. It provided shareholders a choice to exit without infringing on shareholders' existing rights to block self-dealing transactions.

* * *

The appraisal remedy was retrieved from the mothballs when courts and legislatures expanded the scope of majority power to authorize actions not previously thought possible. Most important was a change permitting those in control of a corporation to implement a merger that forced minority shareholders out of the corporation in exchange for cash. A majority shareholder today can form a shell corporation with no shareholder other than itself and no assets other than the cash to be paid to squeeze out minority shareholders. The boards of directors of the shell corporation and the original corporation (who may be the very same individuals) then approve the merger of the shell corporation into the original on terms specifying that the majority shareholder will retain its stock in the original corporation and that the minority shareholders will receive cash in exchange for their shares. This disparate treatment of shareholders would have seemed impossible in earlier times because cash was not widely authorized as a permissible consideration in ordinary mergers until the 1960s. Courts interpreted the new cash merger statutes to permit disparate treatment that forced out minority shareholders. Because shareholders were being ousted anyway, appraisal served no liquidity function. Rather, this change shifted the primary use of the remedy to constrain majority overreaching.

During this same period, the liquidity purpose for appraisal in other transactions was disappearing because of statutory changes. About half of the states enacted market exceptions that withdrew appraisal rights for shares traded on a national securities exchange or when the corporation had more than 2000 shareholders. As Folk described the change: "In short, the theory [behind the stock market exception] is that, if the appraisal remedy provides a judicially created market for dissenting shareholders, such a device is unnecessary where there is already a substantial trading market." In addition, states moved to withdraw appraisal rights from shareholders of the surviving corporation if the merger did not result in any change in the surviving shareholders' shares and did not result in an increase of shares beyond twenty percent or some other threshold. Professor Folk described this change as a "major innovation" in corporate law, and indeed, it marked the effective end of the liquidity function for appraisal.

Thus, the stage was set for the use of appraisal as a remedy against opportunistic behavior by majority shareholders in mergers, but it was another fifteen years or so before appraisal was widely used in that role and even today it has not reached full maturity as a complete remedy for overreaching by the majority. * * * The Delaware Supreme Court's 1983 opinion in Weinberger v. UOP, Inc. marked the enthronement of a revitalized appraisal remedy for use as a check on majority power in cash-out settings. * * *

Any effort to apply appraisal, by a legislature or court, should begin with a recognition of when appraisal is used and how that use differs from earlier times. Modern appraisal cases typically arise from a transaction in which a majority shareholder has structured a merger or other transaction to kick the minority out of the enterprise. There are very few cases today like early merger cases in which the majority planned an expansion or other fundamental change in the enterprise and offered the minority the chance to come along, but the minority elected appraisal as a way out of the new venture.

NOTE: REFORM

1. *Substantive Modifications.*

● Should appraisal statutes be drafted to address all cases where majority shareholders seek to expel minority shareholders in exchange for cash, without "market out" exceptions? See Thompson, supra, at 54; Wertheimer, The Shareholders' Appraisal Remedy and How Courts Determine Fair Value, 47 Duke L.J. 615 (1998).

● Should the appraisal remedy cover virtually all extraordinary transactions, such as asset sales and charter amendments? Should nonvoting shareholders also have appraisal rights? See Siegel, Back to the Future: Appraisal Rights in the Twenty–First Century, 32 Harv. J. Legis. 79, 113, 133 (1995).

● Should the appraisal remedy be deemed exclusive, or should a dissenting minority shareholder have access to remedies for breach of fiduciary duty? See Thompson, supra, at 54.

● Should the concept of "fair value" be expanded to encompass gains accruing to the majority as a result of the accomplishment of the transaction?

● What forms of overreaching should a well-drafted appraisal statute address? In addition to restricting overreaching by majority shareholders, should the appraisal remedy also serve to deter slack or acceptance of side payments by managers negotiating mergers? How effective is the existing mechanism in performing this function? What is the likely impact on managerial efforts (in negotiating a merger) to maximize stockholder returns or to refrain from taking side payments of (a) the fact that the corporation (as opposed to its managers or its merger partner) is the only source of payment of fair value in an appraisal proceeding, (b) the substantive provisions of most appraisal statutes that exclude from the "fair value" to which the dissenter is entitled any of the gains from the merger?

2.   *Process Modifications.*

Thomas, Revising the Delaware Appraisal Statute, 3 Del. L.Rev. 1 (2000), makes a number of suggestions toward the end of making Delaware appraisal a more user-friendly remedy. More particularly: (a) A summary mode of proceeding should be adopted. Thomas suggests as a model the proceeding held out to shareholders seeking to inspect books and records, although he notes that discovery requests would have to be admitted in the appraisal context. He also suggests that the parties be given an option of having the valuation concluded through an arbitration proceeding. Each party would appoint one expert appraiser, with the two appraisers appointing a third expert. (b) Costs to the shareholder should be reduced through a provision for contingent shifting of the fees of lawyers and experts to the defendant. For example, the defending corporation would make an initial settlement offer. If the shareholder rejected it and proved a higher value, the defendant would be liable for the costs. Cf. NYBCL § 623(h)(7), which provides for costs where the fair value as determined "materially exceeds" the corporation's offer, and also provides for awards of costs to the corporation on a finding of a bad faith refusal to accept the corporation's fair value offer. (c) The statute should address the problem of illiquidity on the dissenting shareholders' part during the pendency of the proceeding. As under RMBCA § 13.24 and NYBCL § 623(g), the corporation should not only present an estimated fair share value, it should also pay over that value to the dissenter.

SECTION E.   FAIRNESS AND DISCLOSURE

INTRODUCTION

Ideally, the managers of each party to a merger bargain for maximum enhancement of share value. Unfortunately, transactions in the real world often fall short of the ideal. There may be a lack of identity of interest between the managers doing the "bargaining" and the public stockholders. This can be seen most easily in a case like Farris v. Glen Alden, supra. There, List, the "acquiring company," was in control of Glen Alden at the time the merger between the two took place; the List directors effectively sat on both sides of the bargaining table. The exchange rate for the publicly owned shares of Glen Alden was unilaterally determined by List's management rather than through arm's length negotiation. To be sure, unilateral decision was inevitable once List had obtained control and could not of itself constitute a violation of fiduciary duty. But given the evident, and indeed quite natural, tendency of the List directors to view their obligation to List and its stockholders as primary, and to regard Glen Alden's public stockholders as "outsiders," the value placed on the latter's interest might be expected to be as low as reasonable pessimism would allow.

It should not be surprising to find that a merger between an acquirer and a controlled target is very often challenged by the target's public stockholders. Here courts confront the question as to what constitutes "fair treatment" of the target's public or outside investors. This issue continues to be important because of the persistence of partial takeovers (through cash tender offer or other means) of public companies. Typically, the takeover process begins with a corporation's acquiring a controlling, but not a 100 percent interest, in the target. In some instances partial ownership is merely a transitory step towards full ownership and is followed fairly promptly by merger of the target, now a subsidiary, into the acquirer. In others the status of parent and subsidiary is preserved for an extended period: the parent operates the subsidiary as such through a board of directors composed of its own nominees, but then ultimately elects to merge the subsidiary into itself, thereby obtaining direct ownership of all the subsidiary's assets. Under either circumstance, the public stockholders of the merging subsidiary receive stock or other securities of the parent, or cash, for their minority shares.

The resulting fairness question is almost exclusively a feature of mergers between controlling and controlled corporations, and the cases that follow are almost all of that sort. By contrast, where merger takes place between companies that are unrelated—neither having representation on the board of the other (Hariton v. Arco Electronics, supra, is an example)—the expectation is that each side will bargain exclusively in its own interest, that the outcome will truly be an arm's length deal, and that fiduciary problems of the kind that afflict related-party dealings will not arise. Even here, however, the facts may well be otherwise. The target company's managers possess economic "power," since they alone have access to the proxy machinery and their approval is required before the acquirer's merger proposal can be placed before the target's stockholders. Some managers will insist upon personal consideration—long-term employment contracts, stock options, or the like—before consenting to approve the merger, in which event the purchase price that is finally communicated to the stockholders may well be less than all they are entitled to. More than a hint of this appears in the court's opinion in Singer v. Magnavox, 380 A.2d 969 (Del.1977), in which a target's management that was "shocked at the inadequacy of" an $8 per share bid was able soon thereafter to agree upon a $9 per share price and employment contracts.

Even if disparate formal treatment of insiders and outsiders is to be tolerated, should restraints of "fairness" with respect to the substance of the exchange be imposed? And if a test of "fairness" is the appropriate restriction to impose upon mergers, either because of a systematic divergence of interest between management and stockholders with respect to the merger decision or because of self-dealing where one of the parties to the merger controls the other, what criteria should determine fairness, and what ought to be the procedural requirements for testing compliance with those criteria?

Finally, some acquisition transactions are suboptimal from the point of view of the participating shareholders even though no conflict of interest compromises management's actions. Incompetence, miscalculation, or bargaining disadvantage can result in a flawed transaction. Yet the statutorily specified majority of the shareholders easily can be brought together to approve such a bad deal. Corporate fiduciary law has responded to this adverse selection problem in recent years. It has, first, developed a branch of the duty of care specific to the context of merger negotiations. Second, it addresses the integrity of the shareholder approval process with a full disclosure requirement. The leading cases appear in Sections 2 and 3, infra. To what extent does the resulting legal regime assure that shareholders receive top dollar when the firm is sold?

1.   Freeze-Outs and Buyouts: Fair Dealing, Fair Price, and the Appraisal Remedy

INTRODUCTION

Managers and controlling stockholders may on occasion repurchase stock in order to "take the corporation private," or freeze-out the public stockholders. Two distinguishable transaction forms have emerged: (1) Freeze-outs in which a party in control ex ante, whether a parent company or a group of stockholders, uses the transaction to transform the stakes of a group of minority equityholders into cash or fixed return securities. In this case, traditional fiduciary constraints import horizontal equity—i.e., equality of treatment for all members of the class of stockholders—more than restrictions on an agent dealing with his principal's property. Freeze-out activity has increased in recent years, due in part to the stock market decline of 2000 and the additional costs imposed on public companies under the Sarbanes–Oxley Act. (2) The management buyout, in which a group of managers who own little stock use the transaction to take control. This case implicates traditional fiduciary-agency notions—collective assets are being diverted by agents to themselves, effectively unilaterally, with no offsetting benefit to stockholders other than a "fair" price—i.e., a price that presumably gives stockholders the fairly derived present value of their stock, and produces no present gain for the management-agent, or possibly a "fair" sharing of any gain. As we saw in Part II, supra, management buyout activity also has increased in recent years.

Social welfare concerns suggest a different transactional justification in one case than in the other. The case of a freeze-out, at least where the controller is a parent corporation, is likely to involve termination of a structure which tempts the parent to overreach its subsidiary in intercompany transactions. In that circumstance the freeze-out is said to be justified by both efficiency reasons (for the parent to avoid the cost of the protective veneer to prevent successful challenges to intercompany transactions) and equitable considerations (to avoid the danger to minority stockholders of continuous over-reaching in such transactions). In the case of the management buyout, the social gain is said to result from the added incentive to management by reason of its acquisition of substantial ownership interest and the more effective monitoring of management by a small number of sophisticated equity investors.

(A) FREEZE-OUTS

Although freeze-outs often occur in close corporations, they more often occur after a corporation has acquired a controlling interest in a publicly-held corporation either by market purchases or by purchases from controlling stockholders. When the acquirer owns a large enough proportion of the subsidiary's stock to make it feasible to do so, it absorbs the subsidiary—either by merger or by liquidation—in a transaction which results in the parent acquiring all the productive assets of the subsidiary and the minority public stockholders receiving cash.

On the basic question whether the public stockholder can be *required* to accept cash or non-participating senior securities rather than a continuing participation in the merged enterprise, the cases have answered in the affirmative. Freeze-out transactions nonetheless are subjected to fiduciary scrutiny under the rubric of "entire fairness." The questions will be (a) whether in the particular case the amount of cash or securities involved can be challenged as inadequate in an action for damages or by an effort to enjoin the transaction as unfair, (b) whether, in the alternative, the transaction can be challenged for procedural unfairness in an action for damages or an injunctive proceeding, (c) whether, in the alternative, the appraisal remedy is the dissenting shareholder's sole alternative. The further question goes to division of freeze-out transactions between (a) and (b), on the one hand, and (c), on the other: Can or should any particular class of freeze-out transaction be exempted from fiduciary scrutiny and if so on what coherent principle or principles?

In addressing those questions consider whether there are valid bases for distinguishing among (a) mergers that are purely internal rearrangements which effect no change in the enterprise other than elimination of "outside" stockholders, such as the "going private" transactions illustrated by the *Coggins* case, infra, (b) mergers that are purely internal rearrangements which effect no change in the enterprise other than elimination of "outside" stockholders of a majority-owned subsidiary, but which compensate the outside stockholders with common stock of the parent company instead of cash; (c) mergers in which third parties are taking over and something new is added, such as a transfer of all the assets to a stranger in a transaction in which the controlling insiders are given stock or other participations in the combined enterprise and the outsiders are given only cash or senior securities, (d) absorption by the successful take-over bidder of previously untendered stock within a short period after the successful take-over, (e) absorption by a parent of a subsidiary which it has controlled for many years, and (f) internal rearrangements which effect no change in the enterprise other than elimination of "outside" stockholders of a majority-owned subsidiary by means of a tender offer by the parent for the bulk of the minority block of stock, with a short form merger following the tender offer's consummation.

(1) Alternative Perspectives

Brudney & Chirelstein, Fair Shares in Corporate Mergers and Takeovers

88 Harv. L. Rev. 297, 313–14, 317, 318–325 (1974).

* * * [T]he situation to be considered is one in which [Parent company] P acquires a controlling stock interest in [Subsidiary] S (by whatever

means) and then proceeds to operate S as a subsidiary. Ultimately, after a more or less extended period of affiliation, P elects to merge S into itself, paying off S's public stockholders in stock, debt or cash or some combination of the three. In these circumstances, what constitutes fair treatment of the public stockholders?

To focus our inquiry, let us assume that the stock of P (which owns 50.01 percent of S) sells at 10 times current earnings of $12 a share, or $120, just prior to the announcement of the merger, and S stock sells at 10 times current earnings of 50 cents a share, or $5. P has 1 million shares outstanding; S has 2 million-plus shares outstanding, of which the public owns 1 million and P owns the balance. P's total income and stock value are thus $12 million and $120 million. S's public shares earn $500,000 and are worth $5 million; and the sum of the separate values of the publicly owned shares of P and S is $125 million. Let us further assume that a merger between P and S will produce an enterprise worth $135 million; for whatever reason—cost economies, tax savings, or other benefits which are realized solely by virtue of the merger—P's decision to merge with S has produced an increment of $10 million in the expected combined value of the two corporations. The obvious issue of fairness is how this increment should be divided between P and the public stockholders of S.

The solution to this sharing problem depends entirely on what the concept of fiduciary obligation—which P is uniformly said to owe S—should be understood to mean in this context. In making a bargain between parent and subsidiary, is management free to consider that its primary duty is to one entity—presumably the parent—and that its duty to the other is of a secondary order? Or does fiduciary obligation imply an equal standard of responsibility, with neither entity having a superior claim to management's best efforts?

* * *

* * * [T]he plain fact is that P and S are not at arm's length and it seems incongruous to treat them as if they were. * * *

* * *

The shortcomings of the arm's-length bargain analogy suggest that it may be more appropriate to emphasize the joint character of management's responsibility to the stockholders of the two entities than to postulate a fictional bargain at arm's length. What ought to be stressed, we think, is not the idea of a make-believe bargain between strangers, but the fact that a single management team is in charge of both enterprises, and that its ultimate responsibility is to the individual investors who own those companies' shares. Taking that view, a more fitting analogy is to the legal responsibility of a trustee who undertakes to manage two (or more) trust accounts on behalf of separate beneficiaries having similar financial objectives. Where a profitable opportunity has been discovered—here the merger—the question that arises would not be one of improper self-dealing on the part of the fiduciary, for which an arm's-length standard might indeed be appropriate. Rather, the issue to be resolved would be how, or whether, a single fiduciary acting on behalf of multiple beneficiaries should be required to apportion among them the tangible benefits which his management skills produce. Suppose—to use a somewhat fanciful illustration— that a trustee has discretionary authority to manage two accounts: the first, belonging to beneficiary A, has assets of $100; the second, belonging to beneficiary B, has assets of $50. The trustee determines that a cost-saving of $10 can be realized if both accounts are joined in a single administrative unit. The question is how that saving should be apportioned by the trustee so as to comply with his fiduciary obligations to A and B.

It is too plain for argument that the $10 saving must be shared on some basis between A and B, and cannot be allocated solely to either—at least in the absence of agreement or demonstrable expectations to the contrary. Each beneficiary has a claim on the trustee's management skill, a claim which is entitled to recognition in some amount; neither can be wholly excluded from participation in the gain from the combination. On the other hand, a 50–50 apportionment of the expected gain is unwarranted because such a division would produce for B twice the percentage return on his investment account that A would get on his. Thus, if each account were credited with $5, B would earn a 10 percent return while A would earn only 5 percent. To be sure, the dollar return to both would be the same, but such an outcome seems to be unreasonable when A has twice as many dollars under management as B. The only sensible view of the trustee's obligation, we think, is one which promises each beneficiary the same return per dollar of resources managed, and this in turn requires that the administrative saving be allocated on the basis of relative account size. Thus A should receive $6.67, and B, $3.33, of the anticipated $10 gain, each thereby obtaining a 6 percent return on his investment. That indeed is the principle which determines the allocation of investment opportunities in the administration of common trust funds.

If the same considerations which govern (or ought to govern) the duty of the trustee in the illustration above are allowed to control in our parent-subsidiary merger example, the effect will be to divide the merger gain equally—not on a dollar basis, as already noted, but as a percentage of premerger values. With S shares worth $5 prior to merger and P shares worth $120, the rule of "proportionate sharing" that we have just described would entitle the S stockholders to receive the premerger value of their S shares ($5 million) plus 5/125ths of the $10 million of appreciation expected to result from the merger itself, or $400,000. The S stockholders would thus receive $5.4 million in value if paid in bonds or cash. If paid in common stock, they would receive roughly 41,667 shares of P on the exchange. With 1,041,667 shares of P outstanding after the merger, each P share would be worth $129.60, and the S stockholders would then hold P shares with a total value of $5.4 million.

On this approach, $9.6 million of the $10 million merger increment is allocated to the P stockholders and $.4 million to the S minority. The result is that both sets of stockholders earn an 8 percent return on their investment as a result of the merger—$9.60/$120 for P's owners, and $0.40/$5 for the public stockholders of S—so that an equal dollar investment in either stock will generate the same return. The outcome is thus a fair one in the respect that all investors to whom management has an obligation of trust are treated alike.

In summary, the fiduciary obligation may be envisioned in the present setting in three possible forms. The first—which reflects the prevailing body of law—apparently assumes direct arm's-length dealings between P (the entity) and the individual minority stockholders of S. Such dealings are considered fair if the price paid for the minority shares is equal to their premerger value—$5 per share in our illustration—even though a gain results from the merger itself which is retained in full by P. The second alternative assumes that the dealings are between P and an uncontrolled S, with each entity being represented by an independent bargaining agent. On that assumption a wide range of outcomes is possible, and no single outcome seems to be dictated. If a fair bargain would entail an equal dollar division of the merger gain, the S stockholders would receive $7.50 per share, which represents the premerger value of their stock in S plus their share of the half of the merger increment allocated to S. Finally, the third version of fiduciary duty (and the one here urged) entirely discards the idea of dealings between P and S or its stockholders. What is emphasized instead is the duty of management to treat all stockholders alike by giving each an equal return on his investment, whether that investment is in the shares of P or the shares of S. Under this formulation the allocation of values is fair if the S stockholders receive the premerger value of their shares ($5) plus 5/125ths of the gain attributable to the merger ($0.40), or $5.40 per share. This method provides a determinate or unique solution to the sharing problem and avoids the difficulties inherent in the artificial assumption that dealing between P and S takes place at arm's length.

Apart from whether particular circumstances may justify or require departure from the formula, the problems of practical implementation that can be foreseen seem not much greater than under present law. Where the stockholders of S receive stock of P in the merger, the proposed formula is satisfied by an exchange of shares based on the premerger value of each entity. A payout in the form of debt or cash, however, would make it necessary to place a value not merely on the shares of each entity before the merger, but on the combined entity after the merger in order to ascertain whether the S minority is adequately compensated. Since the premise of common control precludes concealment of information by either party, earnings expectations or hidden resources of the subsidiary may not be as easily obscured as on the assumption of an arm's-length bargain. To the extent that fuller disclosure may be required, some of the problems of valuation heretofore encountered by courts in testing the fairness of mergers may actually be reduced in scope. In any event, expectations of the gains from the merger are appropriate subjects for disclosure. No doubt there will always remain a substantial area for dispute about estimates of the future or about appropriate capitalization rates, and the parent's experts will always have insiders' advantages over dissident stockholders' experts in proffering such evidence. But the expanding obligation to disclose will curtail those advantages by increasing the risk to the parent if it predicates the merger terms on assumptions about the future which rest upon past or present conditions that were not adequately set forth.

Easterbrook and Fischel, Corporate Control Transactions

93 Yale L.J. 698, 703–715 (1982).

* * *

II.   Equal Treatment, Fiduciary Duty, and Shareholders' Welfare

Many scholars, and a few courts, conclude that one aspect of fiduciary duty is the equal treatment of investors. Their argument takes the following form: fiduciary principles require fair conduct; equal treatment is fair conduct; hence, fiduciary principles require equal treatment. The conclusion does not follow. The argument depends upon an equivalence between equality and fair treatment, which we have questioned elsewhere. To say that fiduciary principles require equal (or even fair) treatment is to beg the central question—whether investors would contract for equal or even roughly equal treatment.[17]

Our analysis of this question requires that a distinction be drawn between rules that maximize value *ex ante* and actions that maximize the returns of certain investors *ex post*. A simple example illustrates the point. A corporation may choose to invest its capital in one of two ventures. Venture 1 will pay $100, and the returns can be divided equally among the firm's investors. Thus, if there are 10 investors in the firm, the expected value to each investor is $10. Venture 2 will pay $150, in contrast, but only if the extra returns are given wholly to five of the ten investors. Thus, five "lucky" investors will receive $20 apiece, and the unlucky ones $10. Because each investor has a 50 percent chance of being lucky, each would think Venture 2 to be worth $15. The directors of the firm should choose Venture 2 over Venture 1 because it has the higher value and because none of the investors is worse off under Venture 2.

Now consider Venture 3, in which $200 in gains are to be divided among only five of the ten investors with nothing for the rest. If investors are risk neutral, fiduciaries should choose Venture 3 over Venture 2 (despite the fact that some investors end up worse off under Venture 3), because the expected value to each investor is $20 under Venture 3 and only $15 under Venture 2.

In sum, if the terms under which the directors obtain control of the firm call for them to maximize the wealth of the investors, their duty is to select the highest-paying venture and, following that, to abide by the rules of distribution. If unequal distribution is necessary to make the stakes higher, then duty requires inequality. The *ex post* inequality under Ven-

---

17. Lawyers beg this question with regrettable frequency. As George Stigler observed: "Since the fairness of an arrangement is a large factor in the public's attitude toward it, the lawyers as representatives of the public seek to give their schemes the sheen of justice. They employ to this end two approaches. One is to invoke any widely-held belief—on the tacit but convincing ground that any position is invulnerable against non-existent attack." Fairness is an invulnerable position; who is for unfairness? But for lawyers fairness is "a suitcase full of bottled ethics from which one freely chooses to blend his own type of justice." Stigler, The Law and Economics of Public Policy: A Plea to the Scholars, 1 J.Legal Stud. 1, 2, 4 (1972).

tures 2 and 3 is no more "unfair" than the *ex post* inequality of a lottery, in which all players invest a certain amount but only a few collect. The equal treatment of the investors going into Ventures 2 and 3, and the gains they receive from taking chances, make the *ex post* inequality both fair and desirable.[19]

We hope that our analysis of Ventures 2 and 3 above are uncontroversial. If corporate control transactions sufficiently resemble Ventures 2 and 3, this analysis supplies a guide for analyzing the fiduciary duties of corporate managers. A class of control transactions resembles Ventures 2 and 3 if: (1) control changes and financial restructurings produce gains for investors to enjoy; (2) the existence or amount of the gain depends upon unequal distribution; and (3) shareholders would prefer the unequal distribution to a more equal distribution of smaller gains from an alternative transaction (or no transaction). We address these issues in the remainder of Part II and conclude by advancing a fiduciary principle under which managers always are free to engage in transactions resembling Venture 2. For practical reasons, however, our principle prohibits transactions resembling Venture 3.

A.   *The Potential Gains From Control Transactions*

* * *

* * * The freezeout of minority shareholders may create gains when it facilitates a takeover. Transfers of control are expensive, and apart from the obvious cost of the premium over the market price necessary to induce the sale of control, the purchaser must invest considerable sums in research to determine which firms can be operated profitably after a shift in control. Transfers of control will occur only if the purchaser believes it can recoup these costs. Recoupment is difficult. Although the purchaser benefits if the share prices of the target firm appreciate after the transfer in control, this gain accrues equally to shareholders who did not sell to the purchaser. By eliminating free-riding shareholders in a freezeout, the purchaser may recoup the costs of the acquisition by appropriating the gains from the transfer of control. Such a freezeout clearly increases expected aggregate shareholders' wealth if it increases the likelihood of a profitable transfer of control.

In addition, a freezeout of minority shareholders in a longstanding subsidiary will produce gains if the value of the combined entity is greater than the sum of the separate values of the parent and the subsidiary. Such an increase in value may be attributable to economies of scale, centralized

---

19. The firm's managers could not easily justify a choice of Venture 2 or 3, followed by a "surprise" equal distribution of the proceeds among the 10 investors. In the example we posed, the firm obtained the higher returns only by agreeing to unequal distribution. It might get away with a breach of these conditions once, but Ventures 2 and 3 or their equivalent soon would become unavailable. Besides, if the firm promises to pay some investors unequally when it undertakes the venture, the managers could not be "fair" to the unlucky investors without being unfair to the lucky ones. *See* Broad v. Rockwell Int'l Corp., 642 F.2d 929, 955–60 (5th Cir.1981) (en banc) (fiduciary duties require managers to abide by bargains and disregard considerations of fairness), cert. denied, 102 S.Ct. 506 (1981).

management and corporate planning, or economies of information. Moreover, a freezeout of the minority shareholders of a subsidiary is beneficial if it reduces the cost of policing conflicts of interest and enables the firm to make additional cost-justified investments. A parent may not send new projects to a subsidiary, for example, if the parent's investors must guarantee loans to finance the projects. Under these circumstances, the parent's investors bear a proportionally greater risk of loss than the minority shareholders in the subsidiary, but they do not receive a proportionally greater share of any gains. Thus, the elimination [of] the minority shareholders can increase the likelihood that profitable new ventures will be undertaken.

Other control transactions attack agency costs directly. Although public ownership of a firm may be value-maximizing at one time, changes in the firm's line of business or financial structure may make it worthwhile for the firm to "go private" later. When firms go private they eliminate—or substantially reduce—the separation of ownership and control that creates the clash of interest between principal and agent. Other things being equal, the lower agency costs mean higher returns to investors. In addition, going-private transactions may eliminate costs attributable to public ownership, which include substantial (and increasing) expenditures for legal and auditing fees, stockholder relations and compliance with myriad disclosure obligations mandated by the SEC and organized stock exchanges. By going private, the firm can avoid these costs of compliance and reduce the risk of liability resulting from failure to comply with uncertain disclosure obligations. Moreover, the avoidance of disclosure obligations can benefit the firm if it might have to sacrifice prospective business opportunities if disclosure were required.

* * *

Some corporate control transactions that do not produce gains, however, are not always self-deterring. Looting may explain certain transfers of control. Some going-private transactions may be motivated by a desire to exploit inside information rather than to reduce agency costs. And sometimes a manager may appropriate control of a corporate opportunity even though the firm would have been able to exploit the opportunity more profitably.

At least for publicly-traded firms, the market offers information that distinguishes value-increasing control transactions from others in which looting or mismanagement may be in store. The information is contained in the price of a firm's shares. If the control change is associated with an increase in price, the investors apparently do not fear looting or other harm to the firm. If a syndicate acquires a control bloc of shares, and the price of the remaining shares *rises,* relative to the market as a whole, then the shareholders are betting on the basis of available information that the new controller will be better for their interests than the old. * * *

Fewer price signals are available in going-private transactions, because such a transaction frequently eliminates public trading of the firm's shares. Even these transactions, however, leave some traces. If the price paid to frozen-out shareholders is higher than the price that the shares commanded before the transaction, the buyer anticipates that the transaction will produce gains. There is little percentage in paying $15 for shares selling at $10. If the only purpose of the transaction is to eliminate minority shareholders, it is irrational for the controlling shareholder to pay a premium over the market price. By using corporate assets to pay minority shareholders more than their shares are worth, the controlling shareholder will have decreased the value of his own holdings and therefore be worse off as a result.

* * *

B.   *The Gains May Depend on Unequal Division*

In many cases the apportionment of the gain makes little difference to the success of the transaction. If the gain from taking over a corporation exceeds the cost incurred by the acquiror, he would be indifferent to who receives the premium that is necessary to obtain control. But the fact that apportionment is irrelevant to the acquiror in many cases does not mean that apportionment of gains is always immaterial—in some marginal cases apportionment is the decisive factor. Suppose that a prospective acquiror of control concludes that, by expending $10, he can create a 50 per cent chance of producing $30 in gains. If the prospective acquiror is risk-neutral, the transaction will go forward because the expected gains of $15 exceed the $10 cost of the transaction. If the fiduciary principle is interpreted to require the prospective acquiror to share the $20 gain in the event it is realized, however, and absorb the entire loss if the gain is not realized, the deal may become unprofitable because the costs exceed the expected gains.

In theory, the law could require sharing of the $5 expected gain, but courts could not calculate this amount because they could not observe the *ex ante* risk of failure. Moreover, a large part of the cost to the acquiror is an opportunity cost—the money the acquiror could have made by devoting his talents to other projects. Another cost is the premium required to compensate risk-averse acquirors for risk-bearing. Because it would be difficult or impossible to compute opportunity costs and risk premia in the context of litigation, it would be difficult or impossible to implement a sensible sharing rule. Even if opportunity costs could be approximated, judicial errors would arise, and beneficial control changes would be stifled.

A sharing requirement also may make an otherwise profitable transaction unattractive to the prospective seller of control. To illustrate, suppose that the owner of a control bloc of shares finds that his perquisites or the other amenities of his position are worth $10. A prospective acquiror of control concludes that, by eliminating these perquisites and other amenities, he could produce a gain of $15. The shareholders in the company benefit if the acquiror pays a premium of $11 to the owner of the controlling bloc, ousts the current managers, and makes the contemplated improvements. The net gains of $4 inure to each investor according to his holdings, and although the acquiror obtains the largest portion because he holds the largest bloc, no one is left out. If the owner of the control bloc must share the $11 premium with all of the existing shareholders, however, the deal collapses. The owner will not part with his bloc for less than a $10 premium. A sharing requirement would make the deal unprofitable to him, and the other investors would lose the prospective gain from the installation of better managers.

Other value-increasing transactions would also be deterred by a sharing requirement. First, as we have noted above, sometimes a purchase of control is profitable to the purchaser only if he can prevent minority shareholders from sharing in the gains. Freezeouts of minority shareholders after a transfer of control perform precisely this function. Second, if the controlling shareholder in a going-private transaction or merger of a subsidiary into a parent corporation must underwrite the costs of future value-increasing transactions and thereby incur a proportionally greater risk of loss than the minority shareholders in the event expectations are not realized, the deal may become unprofitable to the controlling shareholder if he must share the gains with minority shareholders if all goes well. Thus, a sharing principle in these transactions leads to a reduction in total wealth as people desist from entering into otherwise profitable transactions.

There are other ways in which the gains from corporate control transactions may depend on unequal distribution. Because investors in the firm must cooperate to transfer control, sharing creates incentives to "free ride." In a tender offer, for example, shareholders must tender rather than hold their shares if the bid is to succeed; in a merger (other than a short-form merger), they must vote favorably rather than abstain. If gains must be shared equally, however, each shareholder may find it worthwhile not to cooperate in the transaction. To illustrate, suppose that all of the gains from a tender offer must be shared equally among the investors in the target corporation and that, if there is a follow-up merger, non-tendering shareholders cannot be eliminated for less than the tender offer price. When a prospective acquiror makes a bid, the investors recognize that the acquiror can profit only to the extent it causes the value of shares to rise. If the bidder is offering $50 per share, the reasoning runs, it cannot profit unless value eventually rises above $50. Under the legal rules assumed above, it may be rational for every shareholder to spurn the $50 offer and hope that enough other shareholders tender to make the offer succeed: If there is a follow-up merger, the "fair" price cannot be less than $50 for the untendered shares. If there is no follow-up merger, the shareholder expects the price to exceed $50. Each shareholder, in other words, may attempt to take a free ride on the efforts of the bidder and other shareholders. To the extent free riding prevails, it reduces the chance that the beneficial transaction will go forward.

A final reason why the gains from beneficial transactions may depend on unequal division is that sharing rules may lead to costly attempts to appropriate greater parts of the gains. The appropriation problem arises because most gain-sharing rules do not produce completely predictable results—it is difficult to determine the "fair" price. If all investors are entitled to a "fair" share of the bounty, each will find it advantageous to claim as much as possible and fight for his claim. He would spend as much as a dollar, on the margin, to claim another dollar of the benefits. It is possible for a substantial part of the gain to be frittered away, therefore, as claimants attempt to make the argument that they are entitled to more. Fear for this eventuality may cause otherwise beneficial control transactions to fall through; in any event resources will be wasted in litigation or other skirmishings.

C. *Investors Prefer the Fiduciary Principle That Maximizes Aggregate Gains*

Do investors prefer a larger pie even if not everyone may have a larger slice in every case? We argue here that they do, for two reasons. First, their expected wealth is greatest under this interpretation of the fiduciary principle, and second, they may deal with any risk by holding diversified portfolios of investments.

Clearly, if control transactions produce gains, and if the gains depend on unequal allocation, then the expected wealth of the shareholders in the aggregate is maximized by a rule allowing unequal allocation. *All* share prices *ex ante* will be highest when the probability of a value-increasing transaction in the future is the greatest. Shareholders can realize this value at any time by selling their shares, or they can hold the shares and take the chance of gaining still more as a result of the unequal allocation of gains *ex post*.

This argument may seem to disregard the fact that many investors are risk averse—they prefer a sure $10, say, to a one in ten chance of receiving $100. On the surface, therefore, it seems that investors might benefit from equal or fair division of gains notwithstanding the loss of some gains as a result. This argument, however, ignores the lessons of modern portfolio theory. By investing in many firms simultaneously, risk averse investors can reduce the risk of losses without extinguishing profitable-but-risky transactions.

* * *

We have shown that the *ex post* inequality under Ventures 2 and 3, like the *ex post* inequality in a lottery, is not "unfair" if, *ex ante,* all investors have an equal chance to win and can eliminate risk through diversification. We now consider a potential objection to this reasoning. One might argue that this *ex ante* equality is absent in corporate control transactions because insiders systematically benefit at the expense of outsiders. Small shareholders, the argument runs, consistently will be frozen out, deprived of control premiums, and otherwise disadvantaged by insiders.

The argument loses its plausibility on close examination. One need not be wealthy to be on the "winning side" of a control transaction, and neither wealth nor status as an insider ensures being a winner. If corporation A purchases from corporation B a control block of shares in corporation C, a small (or outside) shareholder might participate in the gains by holding shares in any of the three firms. Similarly, if corporation D merges with corporation E (its long-held subsidiary) and freezes out the minority shareholders of corporation E, these shareholders may participate in the gains by holding shares of corporation D. Small shareholders also may participate in the gains resulting from tender offers, going private transactions, allocation of a corporate opportunity to a parent rather than a subsidiary, and other types of corporate control transactions, simply by holding shares in the firm that produces the gains. There is no need for the small shareholder to identify these situations in advance. By holding a diversified portfolio containing the securities of many firms, the small shareholder can ensure that he will participate in the gains produced. All shareholders therefore have a chance of receiving the gains produced by corporate control transactions—if not an equal chance, at least enough of a chance to allow diversification of the risk. There remain cases in which it is impossible for an investor to share in gains or diversify away the risk by holding stock in both firms. This would be true, for example, where one of the firms is privately held. The shareholder can minimize this non-diversifiable risk, however, by not investing in firms that are controlled by an individual or a privately-held firm.

D. *Market Value as a Benchmark Under the Fiduciary Principle*

In the circumstances we have discussed, shareholders unanimously prefer legal rules under which the amount of gains is maximized, regardless of how the gains are distributed. The ideal transaction is one like Venture 2 above, in which the gains are unequally distributed but all shareholders are at least as well off as they were before the transaction. Shareholders may also benefit from transactions in which the distribution of gains leaves some shareholders worse off than before the transaction—as in Venture 3—but there are probably few such transactions. We cannot imagine why gains would depend on making some investors worse off, and we have not encountered any example of such a transaction. In a world of costly information, investors will view Venture 2 transactions very differently from Venture 3 transactions, which would raise all-but-insuperable difficulties in determining whether the transaction produced gain. One can imagine instances, of which looting is a good example, in which the person acquiring control pays a premium to some investor(s) in order to obtain control and obliterate the remaining claims, recouping the premium without putting resources to a more productive use. A requirement that all investors receive at least the market value of their positions prior to the transactions would be a useful rule-of-thumb for separating beneficial deals from potentially harmful ones. If every investor receives at least what he had before, and some receive a premium, the transaction *must* produce gains.

(2) *Fiduciary Duties*

(a) *business purpose*

One form of legal restraint which might be imposed to prevent mergers from causing unequal treatment between outside and inside or controlling stockholders would be to require equal treatment in *form*. All stockholders in the absorbed firm would be entitled to receive the same form of participation in the continuing enterprise; none would be required to accept a different form of pay-out (e.g., cash or non-participating senior securities) than the others. The state legislatures, however, deliberately rejected such a constraint in short form merger legislation and apparently no less explicitly in long form merger statutes. This, in turn, has posed for the courts the question how to resolve any incompatibility between what some would see as the stockholders' right to remain stockholders and the statutes, which apparently permit insiders to *force* the outsiders out of the firm by giving them a cash or other non-participating pay-out. Can—or should—such legislation be interpreted narrowly to permit freeze-outs only when some economically tolerable function is served by the transaction, or is the legislation a carte blanche? If the former, how should courts define an economically tolerable function and determine whether the merger serves that function? On whom should the burden of proof be placed to demonstrate that such a function exists and could not be as well performed by procedures which do not freeze out the outside stockholders?

Coggins v. New England Patriots Football Club, Inc.

Massachusetts Supreme Judicial Court, 1986.
397 Mass. 525, 492 N.E.2d 1112.

■ LIACOS, J.

On November 18, 1959, William H. Sullivan, Jr. (Sullivan), purchased an American Football League (AFL) franchise for a professional football team. The team was to be the last of the eight original teams set up to form the AFL (now the American Football Conference of the National Football League). For the franchise, Sullivan paid $25,000. Four months later, Sullivan organized a corporation, the American League Professional Football Team of Boston, Inc. Sullivan contributed his AFL franchise; nine other persons each contributed $25,000. In return, each of the ten investors received 10,000 shares of voting common stock in the corporation. Another four months later, in July, 1960, the corporation sold 120,000 shares of nonvoting common stock to the public at $5 a share.

Sullivan had effective control of the corporation from its inception until 1974. By April, 1974, Sullivan had increased his ownership of shares from 10,000 shares of voting stock to 23,718 shares, and also had acquired 5,499 shares of nonvoting stock. Nevertheless, in 1974 the other voting stockholders ousted him from the presidency and from operating control of the corporation. He then began the effort to regain control of the corporation—an effort which culminated in this and other law suits.

In November, 1975, Sullivan succeeded in obtaining ownership or control of all 100,000 of the voting shares, at a price of approximately $102 a share (adjusted cash value), of the corporation, by that time renamed the New England Patriots Football Club, Inc. (Old Patriots). "Upon completion of the purchase, he immediately used his 100% control to vote out the hostile directors, elect a friendly board and arrange his resumption of the presidency and the complete control of the Patriots. In order to finance this coup, Sullivan borrowed approximately $5,348,000 from the Rhode Island Hospital National Bank and the Lasalle National Bank of Chicago. As a condition of these loans, Sullivan was to use his best efforts to reorganize the Patriots so that the income of the corporation could be devoted to the payment of these personal loans and the assets of the corporation pledged to secure them. At this point they were secured by all of the voting shares held by Sullivan. In order to accomplish in effect the assumption by the corporation of Sullivan's personal obligations, it was necessary, as a matter of corporate law, to eliminate the interest of the nonvoting shares."[3]

On October 20, 1976, Sullivan organized a new corporation called the New Patriots Football Club, Inc. (New Patriots). The board of directors of the Old Patriots and the board of directors of the New Patriots executed an agreement of merger of the two corporations providing that, after the merger, the voting stock of the Old Patriots would be extinguished, the nonvoting stock would be exchanged for cash at the rate of $15 a share, and the name of the New Patriots would be changed to the name formerly used by the Old Patriots. As part of this plan, Sullivan gave the New Patriots his 100,000 voting shares of the Old Patriots in return for 100% of the New Patriots stock.

General Laws c. 156B, § 78(c)(1)(iii), as amended through St.1976, c. 327, required approval of the merger agreement by a majority vote of each class of affected stock. Approval by the voting class, entirely controlled by Sullivan, was assured. The merger was approved by the class of nonvoting stockholders at a special meeting on December 8, 1976. On January 31, 1977, the merger of the New Patriots and the Old Patriots was consummated.

David A. Coggins (Coggins) was the owner of ten shares of nonvoting stock in the Old Patriots. Coggins, a fan of the Patriots from the time of their formation, was serving in Vietnam in 1967 when he purchased the shares through his brother. Over the years, he followed the fortunes of the team, taking special pride in his status as an owner. When he heard of the proposed merger, Coggins was upset that he could be forced to sell. Coggins voted against the merger and commenced this suit on behalf of those stockholders, who, like himself, believed the transaction to be unfair and illegal. A judge of the Superior Court certified the class as "stockholders of New England Patriots Football Club, Inc. who have voted against the merger * * * but who have neither turned in their shares nor perfected their appraisal rights * * * [and who] desire only to void the merger."

The trial judge found in favor of the Coggins class but determined that the merger should not be undone. Instead, he ruled that the plaintiffs are entitled to rescissory damages, and he ordered that further hearings be held to determine the amount of damages. * * *

   * * *

We conclude that the trial judge was correct in ruling that the merger was illegal and that the plaintiffs have been wronged. Ordinarily, rescission of the merger would be the appropriate remedy. This merger, however, is

---

3. These findings of fact were made by a Federal District Court judge in the unreported decision of *Pavlidis v. New England Patriots Football Club, Inc.*, No. 76–4240–S (D.Mass. July 22, 1983), aff'd in part and rev'd in part, 737 F.2d 1227 (1st Cir.1984). The trial judge in the case at bar adopted these findings as his own.

now nearly ten years old, and, because an effective and orderly rescission of the merger now is not feasible, we remand the case for proceedings to determine the appropriate monetary damages to compensate the plaintiffs. * * *

Scope of judicial review. In deciding this case, we address an important corporate law question: What approach will a Massachusetts court reviewing a cash freeze-out merger employ? This question has been considered by courts in a number of other States. * * *

The parties have urged us to consider the views of a court with great experience in such matters, the Supreme Court of Delaware. We note that the Delaware court announced one test in 1977, but recently has changed to another. In Singer v. Magnavox Co., 380 A.2d 969, 980 (Del.1977), the Delaware court established the so-called "business-purpose" test, holding that controlling stockholders violate their fiduciary duties when they "cause a merger to be made for the sole purpose of eliminating a minority on a cash-out basis." Id. at 978. In 1983, Delaware jettisoned the business-purpose test, satisfied that the "fairness" test "long * * * applicable to parent-subsidiary mergers, Sterling v. Mayflower Hotel Corp., Del.Supr., 93 A.2d 107, 109–110 (1952), the expanded appraisal remedy now available to stockholders, and the broad discretion of the Chancellor to fashion such relief as the facts of a given case may dictate" provided sufficient protection to the frozen-out minority. Weinberger v. UOP, Inc., 457 A.2d 701, 715 (Del.1983).

* * * We note that the "fairness" test to which the Delaware court now has adhered is, as we later show, closely related to the views expressed in our decisions. Unlike the Delaware court, however, we believe that the "business-purpose" test is an additional useful means under our statutes and case law for examining a transaction in which a controlling stockholder eliminates the minority interest in a corporation. * * * This concept of fair dealing is not limited to close corporations but applies to judicial review of cash freeze-out mergers. * * *

The defendants argue that judicial review of a merger cannot be invoked by disgruntled stockholders, absent illegal or fraudulent conduct. They rely on G.L. c. 156B, § 98 (1984 ed.).[12] In the defendants' view, "the Superior Court's finding of liability was premised solely on the claimed inadequacy of the offering price." Any dispute over offering price, they urge, must be resolved solely through the statutory remedy of appraisal.

We have held in regard to so called "close corporations" that the statute does not divest the courts of their equitable jurisdiction to assure that the conduct of controlling stockholders does not violate the fiduciary principles governing the relationship between majority and minority stockholders. * * *

---

12. "The enforcement by a stockholder of his right to receive payment for his shares in the manner provided in this chapter shall be an exclusive remedy except that this chapter shall not exclude the right of such stockholder to bring or maintain an appropriate proceeding to obtain relief on the ground that such corporate action will be or is illegal or fraudulent as to him." G.L. c. 156B, § 98.

The dangers of self-dealing and abuse of fiduciary duty are greatest in freeze-out situations like the Patriots merger, where a controlling stockholder and corporate director chooses to eliminate public ownership.[14] It is in these cases that a judge should examine with closest scrutiny the motives and the behavior of the controlling stockholder. A showing of compliance with statutory procedures is an insufficient substitute for the inquiry of the courts when a minority stockholder claims that the corporate action "will be or is illegal or fraudulent as to him." G.L. c. 156B, § 98. Leader v. Hycor, Inc., 395 Mass. 215, 221 (1985) (judicial review may be had of claims of breach of fiduciary duty and unfairness).

A controlling stockholder who is also a director standing on both sides of the transaction bears the burden of showing that the transaction does not violate fiduciary obligations.

* * *

Factors in judicial review. * * *

Judicial scrutiny should begin with recognition of the basic principle that the duty of a corporate director must be to further the legitimate goals of the corporation. The result of a freeze-out merger is the elimination of public ownership in the corporation. The controlling faction increases its equity from a majority to 100%, using corporate processes and corporate assets. The corporate directors who benefit from this transfer of ownership must demonstrate how the legitimate goals of the corporation are furthered. * * * Because the danger of abuse of fiduciary duty is especially great in a freeze-out merger, the court must be satisfied that the freeze-out was for the advancement of a legitimate corporate purpose. If satisfied that elimination of public ownership is in furtherance of a business purpose, the court should then proceed to determine if the transaction was fair by examining the totality of the circumstances.

The plaintiffs here adequately alleged that the merger of the Old Patriots and New Patriots was a freeze-out merger undertaken for no legitimate business purpose, but merely for the personal benefit of Sullivan. * * * Consequently, the defendants bear the burden of proving, first, that the merger was for a legitimate business purpose, and, second, that, considering totality of circumstances, it was fair to the minority.

The decision of the Superior Court judge includes a finding that "the defendants have failed to demonstrate that the merger served any valid corporate objective unrelated to the personal interests of the majority shareholders. It thus appears that the sole reason for the merger was to effectuate a restructuring of the Patriots that would enable the repayment of the [personal] indebtedness incurred by Sullivan * * *." The trial judge considered the defendants' claims that the policy of the National Football League (NFL) requiring majority ownership by a single individual or family made it necessary to eliminate public ownership. He found that "the stock ownership of the Patriots as it existed just prior to the merger fully satisfied the rationale underlying the policy as expressed by NFL Commis-

---

14. All freeze-out mergers are not alike. See Brudney and Chirelstein, A Restatement of Corporate Freezeouts, 87 Yale L.J. 1354, 1356, and sources cited (1978).

sioner Pete Rozelle. Having acquired 100% control of the voting common stock of the Patriots, Sullivan possessed unquestionable authority to act on behalf of the franchise at League meetings and effectively foreclosed the possible recurrence of the internal management disputes that had existed in 1974. Moreover, as the proxy statement itself notes, the Old Patriots were under no legal compulsion to eliminate public ownership." Likewise, the defendants did not succeed in showing a conflict between the interests of the league owners and the Old Patriots' stockholders. We perceive no error in these findings. They are fully supported by the evidence. Under the approach we set forth above, there is no need to consider further the elements of fairness of a transaction that is not related to a valid corporate purpose.

Remedy. The plaintiffs are entitled to relief. They argue that the appropriate relief is rescission of the merger and restoration of the parties to their positions of 1976. We agree that the normally appropriate remedy for an impermissible freeze-out merger is rescission. Because Massachusetts statutes do not bar a cash freeze-out, however, numerous third parties relied in good faith on the outcome of the merger. The trial judge concluded that the expectations of those parties should not be upset, and so chose to award damages rather than rescission.

* * * Ordinarily, we would remand with instructions for the trial judge to determine whether rescission would be in the corporation's best interests, but such a remedy does not appear to be equitable at this time. This litigation has gone on for many years. There is yet at least another related case pending (in the Federal District Court). Furthermore, other factors weigh against rescission. The passage of time has made the 1976 position of the parties difficult, if not impossible, to restore. A substantial number of former stockholders have chosen other courses and should not be forced back into the Patriots corporation. In these circumstances the interests of the corporation and of the plaintiffs will be furthered best by limiting the plaintiffs' remedy to an assessment of damages.

We do not think it appropriate, however, to award damages based on a 1976 appraisal value. To do so would make this suit a nullity, leaving the plaintiffs with no effective remedy except appraisal, a position we have already rejected. Rescissory damages must be determined based on the present value of the Patriots, that is, what the stockholders would have if the merger were rescinded. Determination of the value of a unique property like the Patriots requires specialized expertise, cf. Correia v. New Bedford Redevelopment Auth., 375 Mass. 360, 367 (1978) (valuation of unusual property may require unusual approach), and, while the trial judge is entitled to reach his own conclusion as to value, Piemonte v. New Boston Garden Corp., 377 Mass. 719, 731 (1979), the credibility of testimony on value will depend in part on the familiarity of the witness with property of this kind. On remand, the judge is to take further evidence on the present value of the Old Patriots on the theory that the merger had not taken place.

Each share of the Coggins class is to receive, as rescissory damages, its aliquot share of the present assets.

The trial judge dismissed the plaintiffs' claims against the individual defendants based on waste of corporate assets. The remedy we order is intended to give the plaintiffs what they would have if the merger were undone and the corporation were put back together again. The trial judge's finding that the sole purpose of the merger was the personal financial benefit of William H. Sullivan, Jr., and the use of corporate assets to accomplish this impermissible purpose, lead inescapably to the conclusion that part of what the plaintiffs otherwise would have benefitted by, was removed from the corporation by the individual defendants. We reverse the dismissal of the claim for waste of corporate assets and remand this question to the trial court. The present value of the Patriots, as determined on remand, should include the amount wrongfully removed or diverted from the corporate coffers by the individual defendants.

NOTE: BUSINESS PURPOSE AND FAIRNESS

In Tanzer v. International General Industries, Inc., 379 A.2d 1121 (Del.1977), the Delaware Supreme Court concluded that the parent's or controlling stockholders' business needs could constitute a sufficient business purpose to permit a cash-out merger. Other jurisdictions have been even more flexible in finding valid business purposes, including elimination of the household costs of servicing public stockholders and complying with federal regulations. See e.g., Cross v. Communication Channels, Inc., 456 N.Y.S.2d 971 (Sup.Ct.1982); Laird v. I.C.C., 691 F.2d 147 (3d Cir.1982)(elimination of household costs of communicating with and otherwise servicing public stockholders can constitute valid business purpose).

In view of the possibilities for discord and for agreement among the stockholders of close corporations, should the concepts, "business purpose" and "fairness" serve the same function and have the same meaning in assessing the propriety of freeze-outs (1) by controllers of close corporations, (2) by parent corporations, as in the *Weinberger* case, infra, and (3) by individual controllers of publicly held corporations, as in the *Coggins* case?

(b) fair dealing and fair price

Weinberger v. UOP, Inc.

Supreme Court of Delaware, 1983.
457 A.2d 701.

■ MOORE, JUSTICE:

This post-trial appeal was reheard en banc from a decision of the Court of Chancery. It was brought by the class action plaintiff below, a former shareholder of UOP, Inc., who challenged the elimination of UOP's minority shareholders by a cash-out merger between UOP and its majority owner, The Signal Companies, Inc. Originally, the defendants in this action were Signal, UOP, certain officers and directors of those companies, and UOP's investment banker, Lehman Brothers Kuhn Loeb, Inc. The present Chancellor held that the terms of the merger were fair to the plaintiff and the other minority shareholders of UOP. Accordingly, he entered judgment in favor of the defendants.

Numerous points were raised by the parties, but we address only the following questions presented by the trial court's opinion:

1) The plaintiff's duty to plead sufficient facts demonstrating the unfairness of the challenged merger;

2) The burden of proof upon the parties where the merger has been approved by the purportedly informed vote of a majority of the minority shareholders;

3) The fairness of the merger in terms of adequacy of the defendants' disclosures to the minority shareholders;

4) The fairness of the merger in terms of adequacy of the price paid for the minority shares and the remedy appropriate to that issue; and

5) The continued force and effect of Singer v. Magnavox Co., Del.Supr., 380 A.2d 969, 980 (1977), and its progeny.

In ruling for the defendants, the Chancellor re-stated his earlier conclusion that the plaintiff in a suit challenging a cash-out merger must allege specific acts of fraud, misrepresentation, or other items of misconduct to demonstrate the unfairness of the merger terms to the minority. We approve this rule and affirm it.

The Chancellor also held that even though the ultimate burden of proof is on the majority shareholder to show by a preponderance of the evidence that the transaction is fair, it is first the burden of the plaintiff attacking the merger to demonstrate some basis for invoking the fairness obligation. We agree with that principle. However, where corporate action has been approved by an informed vote of a majority of the minority shareholders, we conclude that the burden entirely shifts to the plaintiff to show that the transaction was unfair to the minority. See, e.g., Michelson v. Duncan, Del.Supr., 407 A.2d 211, 224 (1979). But in all this, the burden clearly remains on those relying on the vote to show that they completely disclosed all material facts relevant to the transaction.

Here, the record does not support a conclusion that the minority stockholder vote was an informed one. Material information, necessary to acquaint those shareholders with the bargaining positions of Signal and UOP, was withheld under circumstances amounting to a breach of fiduciary duty. We therefore conclude that this merger does not meet the test of fairness, at least as we address that concept, and no burden thus shifted to the plaintiff by reason of the minority shareholder vote. Accordingly, we reverse and remand for further proceedings consistent herewith.

In considering the nature of the remedy available under our law to minority shareholders in a cash-out merger, we believe that it is, and hereafter should be, an appraisal under 8 Del.C. § 262 as hereinafter construed. We therefore overrule Lynch v. Vickers Energy Corp., Del.Supr., 429 A.2d 497 (1981) (Lynch II) to the extent that it purports to limit a stockholder's monetary relief to a specific damage formula. See Lynch II, 429 A.2d at 507–08 (McNeilly & Quillen, JJ., dissenting). But to give full effect to section 262 within the framework of the General Corporation Law we adopt a more liberal, less rigid and stylized, approach to the valuation process than has heretofore been permitted by our courts. While the present state of these proceedings does not admit the plaintiff to the appraisal remedy per se, the practical effect of the remedy we do grant him will be co-extensive with the liberalized valuation and appraisal methods we herein approve for cases coming after this decision.

Our treatment of these matters has necessarily led us to a reconsideration of the business purpose rule announced in the trilogy of Singer v. Magnavox Co., supra; Tanzer v. International General Industries, Inc., Del.Supr., 879 A.2d 1121 (1977); and Roland International Corp. v. Najjar, Del.Supr., 407 A.2d 1032 (1979). For the reasons hereafter set forth we consider that the business purpose requirement of these cases is no longer the law of Delaware.

I.

The facts found by the trial court, pertinent to the issues before us, are supported by the record, and we draw from them as set out in the Chancellor's opinion.

Signal is a diversified, technically based company operating through various subsidiaries. Its stock is publicly traded on the New York, Philadelphia and Pacific Stock Exchanges. UOP, formerly known as Universal Oil Products Company, was a diversified industrial company engaged in various lines of business, including petroleum and petro-chemical services and related products, construction, fabricated metal products, transportation equipment products, chemicals and plastics, and other products and services including land development, lumber products and waste disposal. Its stock was publicly held and listed on the New York Stock Exchange.

In 1974 Signal sold one of its wholly-owned subsidiaries for $420,000,000 in cash. See Gimbel v. Signal Companies, Inc., Del.Ch., 816 A.2d 599, aff'd, Del.Supr., 816 A.2d 619 (1974). While looking to invest this cash surplus, Signal became interested in UOP as a possible acquisition. Friendly negotiations ensued, and Signal proposed to acquire a controlling interest in UOP at a price of $19 per share. UOP's representatives sought $25 per share. In the arm's length bargaining that followed, an understanding was reached whereby Signal agreed to purchase from UOP 1,500,000 shares of UOP's authorized but unissued stock at $21 per share.

This purchase was contingent upon Signal making a successful cash tender offer for 4,300,000 publicly held shares of UOP, also at a price of $21 per share. This combined method of acquisition permitted Signal to acquire 5,800,000 shares of stock, representing 50.5% of UOP's outstanding shares. The UOP board of directors advised the company's shareholders that it had no objection to Signal's tender offer at that price. Immediately before the announcement of the tender offer, UOP's common stock had been trading on the New York Stock Exchange at a fraction under $14 per share.

The negotiations between Signal and UOP occurred during April 1975, and the resulting tender offer was greatly oversubscribed. However, Signal limited its total purchase of the tendered shares so that, when coupled with the stock brought from UOP, it had achieved its goal of becoming a 50.5% shareholder of UOP.

Although UOP's board consisted of thirteen directors, Signal nominated and elected only six. Of these, five were either directors or employees of Signal. The sixth, a partner in the banking firm of Lazard Freres & Co., had been one of Signal's representatives in the negotiations and bargaining with UOP concerning the tender offer and purchase price of the UOP shares.

However, the president and chief executive officer of UOP retired during 1975, and Signal caused him to be replaced by James V. Crawford, a long-time employee and senior executive vice president of one of Signal's wholly-owned subsidiaries. Crawford succeeded his predecessor on UOP's board of directors and also was made a director of Signal.

By the end of 1977 Signal basically was unsuccessful in finding other suitable investment candidates for its excess cash, and by February 1978 considered that it had no other realistic acquisitions available to it on a friendly basis. Once again its attention turned to UOP.

The trial court found that at the investigation of certain Signal management personnel, including William W. Walkup, its board chairman, and Forrest N. Shumway, its president, a feasibility study was made concerning the possible acquisition of the balance of UOP's outstanding shares. This study was performed by two Signal officers, Charles S. Arledge, vice president (director of planning) and Andrew J. Chitiea, senior vice president (chief financial officer). Messrs. Walkup, Shumway, Arledge and Chitiea were all directors of UOP in addition to their membership on the Signal board.

Arledge and Chitiea concluded that it would be a good investment for Signal to acquire the remaining 49.5% of UOP shares at any price up to $24 each. Their report was discussed between Walkup and Shumway who, along with Arledge, Chitiea and Brewster L. Arms, internal counsel for Signal, constituted Signal's senior management. In particular, they talked about the proper price to be paid if the acquisition was pursued, purportedly keeping in mind that as UOP's majority shareholder, Signal owed a fiduciary responsibility to both its own stockholders as well as to UOP's minority. It was ultimately agreed that a meeting of Signal's Executive Committee would be called to propose that Signal acquire the remaining outstanding stock of UOP through a cash-out merger in the range of $20 to $21 per share.

The Executive Committee meeting was set for February 28, 1978. As a courtesy, UOP's president, Crawford, was invited to attend, although he was not a member of Signal's executive committee. On his arrival, and prior to the meeting, Crawford was asked to meet privately with Walkup and Shumway. He was then told of Signal's plan to acquire full ownership of UOP and was asked for his reaction to the proposed price range of $20 to $21 per share. Crawford said he thought such a price would be "generous", and that it was certainly one which should be submitted to UOP's minority shareholders for their ultimate consideration. He stated, however, that

Signal's 100% ownership could cause internal problems at UOP. He believed that employees would have to be given some assurance of their future place in a fully-owned Signal subsidiary. Otherwise, he feared the departure of essential personnel. Also, many of UOP's key employees had stock option incentive programs which would be wiped out by a merger. Crawford therefore urged that some adjustment would have to be made, such as providing a comparable incentive in Signal's shares, if after the merger he was to maintain his quality of personnel and efficiency at UOP.

Thus, Crawford voiced no objection to the $20 to $21 price range, nor did he suggest that Signal should consider paying more than $21 per share for the minority interests. Later, at the Executive Committee meeting the same factors were discussed, with Crawford repeating the position he earlier took with Walkup and Shumway. Also considered was the 1975 tender offer and the fact that it had been greatly oversubscribed at $21 per share. For many reasons, Signal's management concluded that the acquisition of UOP's minority shares provided the solution to a number of its business problems.

Thus, it was the consensus that a price of $20 to $21 per share would be fair to both Signal and the minority shareholders of UOP. Signal's executive committee authorized its management "to negotiate" with UOP "for a cash acquisition of the minority ownership in UOP, Inc., with the intention of presenting a proposal to [Signal's] board of directors * * * on March 6, 1978". Immediately after this February 28, 1978 meeting, Signal issued a press release stating:

> The Signal Companies, Inc. and UOP, Inc. are conducting negotiations for the acquisition for cash by Signal of the 49.5 per cent of UOP which it does not presently own, announced Forrest N. Shumway, president and chief executive officer of Signal, and James V. Crawford, UOP president.

> Price and other terms of the proposed transaction have not yet been finalized and would be subject to approval of the boards of directors of Signal and UOP, scheduled to meet early next week, the stockholders of UOP and certain federal agencies.

The announcement also referred to the fact that the closing price of UOP's common stock on that day was $14.50 per share.

Two days later, on March 2, 1978, Signal issued a second press release stating that its management would recommend a price in the range of $20 to $21 per share for UOP's 49.5% minority interest. This announcement referred to Signal's earlier statement that "negotiations" were being conducted for the acquisition of the minority shares.

Between Tuesday, February 28, 1978 and Monday, March 6, 1978, a total of four business days, Crawford spoke by telephone with all of UOP's non-Signal, i.e., outside, directors. Also during that period, Crawford retained Lehman Brothers to render a fairness opinion as to the price offered the minority for its stock. He gave two reasons for this choice. First, the time schedule between the announcement and the board meetings was short (by then only three business days) and since Lehman Brothers had been acting as UOP's investment banker for many years, Crawford felt that it would be in the best position to respond on such brief notice. Second, James W. Glanville, a long-time director of UOP and a partner in Lehman Brothers, had acted as a financial advisor to UOP for many years. Crawford believed that Glanville's familiarity with UOP, as a member of its board, would also be of assistance in enabling Lehman Brothers to render a fairness opinion within the existing time constraints.

Crawford telephoned Glanville, who gave his assurance that Lehman Brothers had no conflicts that would prevent it from accepting the task. Glanville's immediate personal reaction was that a price of $20 to $21 would certainly be fair, since it represented almost a 50% premium over UOP's market price. Glanville sought a $250,000 fee for Lehman Brothers' services, but Crawford thought this too much. After further discussions Glanville finally agreed that Lehman Brothers would render its fairness opinion for $150,000.

* * *

* * * [T]he Lehman Brothers team concluded that "the price of either $20 or $21 would be a fair price for the remaining shares of UOP". They telephoned this impression to Glanville, who was spending the weekend in Vermont.

On Monday morning, March 6, 1978, Glanville and the senior member of the Lehman Brothers team flew to Des Plaines to attend the scheduled UOP directors meeting. Glanville looked over the assembled information during the flight. The two had with them the draft of a "fairness opinion letter" in which the price had been left blank. Either during or immediately prior to the directors' meeting, the two-page "fairness opinion letter" was typed in final form and the price of $21 per share was inserted.

On March 6, 1978, both the Signal and UOP boards were convened to consider the proposed merger. Telephone communications were maintained between the two meetings. Walkup, Signal's board chairman, and also a UOP director, attended UOP's meeting with Crawford in order to present Signal's position and answer any questions that UOP's non-Signal directors might have. Arledge and Chitiea, along with Signal's other designees on UOP's board participated by conference telephone. All of UOP's outside directors attended the meeting either in person or by conference telephone.

First, Signal's board unanimously adopted a resolution authorizing Signal to propose to UOP a cash merger of $21 per share as outlined in a certain merger agreement and other supporting documents. This proposal required that the merger be approved by a majority of UOP's outstanding minority shares voting at the stockholders meeting at which the merger would be considered, and that the minority shares voting in favor of the merger, when coupled with Signal's 50.5% interest would have to comprise at least two-thirds of all UOP shares. Otherwise the proposed merger would be deemed disapproved.

UOP's board then considered the proposal. Copies of the agreement were delivered to the directors in attendance, and other copies had been forwarded earlier to the directors participating by telephone. They also had before them UOP financial data for 1974–1977, UOP's most recent financial statements, market price information, and budget projections for 1978. In addition they had Lehman Brothers' hurriedly prepared fairness opinion letter finding the price of $21 to be fair. Glanville, the Lehman Brothers partner, and UOP director, commented on the information that had gone into preparation of the letter.

Signal also suggests that the Arledge–Chitiea feasibility study, indicating that a price of up to $24 per share would be a "good investment" for Signal, was discussed at the UOP directors' meeting. The Chancellor made no such finding, and our independent review of the record, detailed infra, satisfies us by a preponderance of the evidence that there was no discussion of this document at UOP's board meeting. Furthermore, it is clear beyond peradventure that nothing in that report was ever disclosed to UOP's minority shareholders prior to their approval of the merger.

After consideration of Signal's proposal, Walkup and Crawford left the meeting to permit a free and uninhibited exchange between UOP's non-Signal directors. Upon their return a resolution to accept Signal's offer was then proposed and adopted. While Signal's men on UOP's board participated in various aspects of the meeting, they abstained from voting. However, the minutes show that each of them "if voting would have voted yes".

On March 7, 1978, UOP sent a letter to its shareholders advising them of the action taken by UOP's board with respect to Signal's offer. This document pointed out, among other things, that on February 28, 1978 "both companies had announced negotiations were being conducted".

Despite the swift board action of the two companies, the merger was not submitted to UOP's shareholders until their annual meeting on May 26, 1978. In the notice of that meeting and proxy statement sent to shareholders in May, UOP's management and board urged that the merger be approved. The proxy statement also advised:

> The price was determined after *discussions* between James V. Crawford, a director of Signal and Chief Executive Officer of UOP, and officers of Signal which took place during meetings on February 28, 1978, and in the course of several subsequent telephone conversations. (Emphasis added.)

In the original draft of the proxy statement the word "negotiations" had been used rather than "discussions". However, when the Securities and Exchange Commission sought details of the "negotiations" as part of its review of these materials, the term was deleted and the word "discussions" was substituted. The proxy statement indicated that the vote of UOP's board in approving the merger had been unanimous. It also advised the shareholders that Lehman Brothers had given its opinion that the merger price of $21 per share was fair to UOP's minority. However, it did not disclose the hurried method by which this conclusion was reached.

As of the record date of UOP's annual meeting, there were 11,488,302 shares of UOP common stock outstanding, 5,688,302 of which were owned by the minority. At the meeting only 56%, or 3,208,652, of the minority shares were voted. Of these, 2,953,812, or 51.9% of the total minority, voted for the merger, and 254,840 voted against it. When Signal's stock was added to the minority shares voting in favor, a total of 76.2% of UOP's outstanding shares approved the merger while only 2.2% opposed it.

By its terms the merger became effective on May 26, 1978, and each share of UOP's stock held by the minority was automatically converted into a right to receive $21 cash.

II.

A.

A primary issue mandating reversal is the preparation by two UOP directors, Arledge and Chitiea, of their feasibility study for the exclusive use and benefit of Signal. This document was of obvious significance to both Signal and UOP. Using UOP data, it described the advantages to Signal of ousting the minority at a price range of $21–$24 per share.

* * *

The Arledge–Chitiea report speaks for itself in supporting the Chancellor's finding that a price of up to $24 was a "good investment" for Signal. It shows that a return on the investment at $21 would be 15.7% versus 15.5% at $24 per share. This was a difference of only two-tenths of one percent, while it meant over $17,000,000 to the minority. Under such circumstances, paying UOP's minority shareholders $24 would have had relatively little long-term effect on Signal, and the Chancellor's findings concerning the benefit to Signal, even at a price of $24, were obviously correct. Levitt v. Bouvier, Del.Supr., 287 A.2d 671, 673 (1972).

Certainly, this was a matter of material significance to UOP and its shareholders. Since the study was prepared by two UOP directors, using UOP information for the exclusive benefit of Signal, and nothing whatever was done to disclose it to the outside UOP directors or the minority shareholders, a question of breach of fiduciary duty arises. This problem occurs because there were common Signal–UOP directors participating, at least to some extent, in the UOP board's decision-making processes without full disclosure of the conflicts they faced.[7]

---

7. Although perfection is not possible, or expected, the result here could have been entirely different if UOP had appointed an independent negotiating committee of its outside directors to deal with Signal at arm's length. See, e.g., Harriman v. E.I. duPont de Nemours & Co., 411 F.Supp. 133 (D.Del. 1975). Since fairness in this context can be equated to conduct by a theoretical, wholly independent, board of directors acting upon the matter before them, it is unfortunate that this course apparently was neither considered nor pursued. Johnston v. Greene, Del.Supr., 121 A.2d 919, 925 (1956). Particularly in a parent-subsidiary context, a showing that the action taken was as though each of the contending parties had in fact exerted its bargaining power against the other at arm's length is strong evidence that the transaction meets the test of fairness. Getty Oil Co. v. Skelly Oil Co., Del.Supr., 267 A.2d 883, 886 (1970); Puma v. Marriott, Del.Ch., 283 A.2d 693, 696 (1971).

B.

In assessing this situation, the Court of Chancery was required to:

examine what information defendants had and to measure it against what they gave to the minority stockholders, in a context in which "complete candor" is required. In other words, the limited function of the Court was to determine whether defendants had disclosed all information in their possession germane to the transaction in issue. And by "germane" we mean, for present purposes, information such as a reasonable shareholder would consider important in deciding whether to sell or retain stock.

* * *

* * * Completeness, not adequacy, is both the norm and the mandate under present circumstances.

Lynch v. Vickers Energy Corp., Del.Supr., 383 A.2d 278, 281 (1977) (Lynch I). This is merely stating in another way the long-existing principle of Delaware law that these Signal designated directors on UOP's board still owed UOP and its shareholders an uncompromising duty of loyalty.

* * *

Given the absence of any attempt to structure this transaction on an arm's length basis, Signal cannot escape the effects of the conflicts it faced, particularly when its designees on UOP's board did not totally abstain from participation in the matter. There is no "safe harbor" for such divided loyalties in Delaware. When directors of a Delaware corporation are on both sides of a transaction, they are required to demonstrate their utmost good faith and the most scrupulous inherent fairness of the bargain. Gottlieb v. Heyden Chemical Corp., Del.Supr., 91 A.2d 57, 57–58 (1952). The requirement of fairness is unflinching in its demand that where one stands on both sides of a transaction, he has the burden of establishing its entire fairness, sufficient to pass the test of careful scrutiny by the courts. Sterling v. Mayflower Hotel Corp., Del.Supr., 93 A.2d 107, 110 (1952); Bastian v. Bourns, Inc., Del.Ch., 256 A.2d 680, 681 (1969), aff'd, Del.Supr., 278 A.2d 467 (1970); David J. Greene & Co. v. Dunhill International Inc., Del.Ch., 249 A.2d 427, 431 (1968).

There is no dilution of this obligation where one holds dual or multiple directorships, as in a parent-subsidiary context. Levien v. Sinclair Oil Corp., Del.Ch., 261 A.2d 911, 915 (1969). Thus, individuals who act in a dual capacity as directors of two corporations, one of whom is parent and the other subsidiary, owe the same duty of good management to both corporations, and in the absence of an independent negotiating structure (see note 7, supra), or the directors' total abstention from any participation in the matter, this duty is to be exercised in light of what is best for both companies. Warshaw v. Calhoun, Del.Supr., 221 A.2d 487, 492 (1966). The record demonstrates that Signal has not met this obligation.

C.

The concept of fairness has two basic aspects: fair dealing and fair price. The former embraces questions of when the transaction was timed, how it was initiated, structured, negotiated, disclosed to the directors, and how the approvals of the directors and the stockholders were obtained. The latter aspect of fairness relates to the economic and financial considerations of the proposed merger, including all relevant factors: assets, market value, earnings, future prospects, and any other elements that affect the intrinsic or inherent value of a company's stock. Moore, The "Interested" Director or Officer Transaction, 4 Del.J.Corp.L. 674, 676 (1979); Nathan & Shapiro, Legal Standard of Fairness of Merger Terms Under Delaware Law, 2 Del.J.Corp.L. 44, 46–47 (1977). See Tri–Continental Corp. v. Battye, Del. Supr., 74 A.2d 71, 72 (1950); 8 Del.C. § 262(h). However, the test for fairness is not a bifurcated one as between fair dealing and price. All aspects of the issue must be examined as a whole since the question is one of entire fairness. However, in a non-fraudulent transaction we recognize that price may be the preponderant consideration outweighing other features of the merger. Here, we address the two basic aspects of fairness separately because we find reversible error as to both.

D.

Part of fair dealing is the obvious duty of candor required by Lynch I, supra. Moreover, one possessing superior knowledge may not mislead any stockholder by use of corporate information to which the latter is not privy. Lank v. Steiner, Del.Supr., 224 A.2d 242, 244 (1966). Delaware has long imposed this duty even upon persons who are not corporate officers or directors, but who nonetheless are privy to matters of interest or significance to their company. Brophy v. Cities Service Co., Del.Ch., 70 A.2d 5, 7 (1949). With the well-established Delaware law on the subject, and the Court of Chancery's findings of fact here, it is inevitable that the obvious conflicts posed by Arledge and Chitiea's preparation of their "feasibility study", derived from UOP information, for the sole use and benefit of Signal, cannot pass muster.

The Arledge–Chitiea report is but one aspect of the element of fair dealing. How did this merger evolve? It is clear that it was entirely initiated by Signal. The serious time constraints under which the principals acted were all set by Signal. It had not found a suitable outlet for its excess cash and considered UOP a desirable investment, particularly since it was now in a position to acquire the whole company for itself. For whatever reasons, and they were only Signal's, the entire transaction was presented to and approved by UOP's board within four business days. Standing alone, this is not necessarily indicative of any lack of fairness by a majority shareholder. It was what occurred, or more properly, what did not occur, during this brief period that makes the time constraints imposed by Signal relevant to the issue of fairness.

The structure of the transaction, again, was Signal's doing. So far as negotiations were concerned, it is clear that they were modest at best. Crawford, Signal's man at UOP, never really talked price with Signal, except to accede to its management's statements on the subject, and to convey to Signal the UOP outside directors' view that as between the $20–$21 range under consideration, it would have to be $21. The latter is not a surprising outcome, but hardly arm's length negotiations. Only the protection of benefits for UOP's key employees and the issue of Lehman Brothers' fee approached any concept of bargaining.

As we have noted, the matter of disclosure to the UOP directors was wholly flawed by the conflicts of interest raised by the Arledge–Chitiea report. All of those conflicts were resolved by Signal in its own favor without divulging any aspect of them to UOP.

This cannot but undermine a conclusion that this merger meets any reasonable test of fairness. The outside UOP directors lacked one material piece of information generated by two of their colleagues, but shared only with Signal. True, the UOP board had the Lehman Brothers' fairness opinion, but that firm has been blamed by the plaintiff for the hurried task it performed, when more properly the responsibility for this lies with Signal. There was no disclosure of the circumstances surrounding the rather cursory preparation of the Lehman Brothers' fairness opinion. Instead, the impression was given UOP's minority that a careful study had been made, when in fact speed was the hallmark, and Mr. Glanville, Lehman's partner in charge of the matter, and also a UOP director, having spent the weekend in Vermont, brought a draft of the "fairness opinion letter" to the UOP directors' meeting on March 6, 1978 with the price left blank. We can only conclude from the record that the rush imposed on Lehman Brothers by Signal's timetable contributed to the difficulties under which this investment banking firm attempted to perform its responsibilities. Yet, none of this was disclosed to UOP's minority.

Finally, the minority stockholders were denied the critical information that Signal considered a price of $24 to be a good investment. Since this would have meant over $17,000,000 more to the minority, we cannot conclude that the shareholder vote was an informed one. Under the circumstances, an approval by a majority of the minority was meaningless. Lynch I, 383 A.2d at 279, 281; Cahall v. Lofland, Del.Ch., 114 A. 224 (1921).

Given these particulars and the Delaware law on the subject, the record does not establish that this transaction satisfies any reasonable concept of fair dealing, and the Chancellor's findings in that regard must be reversed.

E.

Turning to the matter of price, plaintiff also challenges its fairness. His evidence was that on the date the merger was approved the stock was worth at least $26 per share. In support, he offered the testimony of a chartered investment analyst who used two basic approaches to valuation: a comparative analysis of the premium paid over market in ten other tender offer-merger combinations, and a discounted cash flow analysis.

In this breach of fiduciary duty case, the Chancellor perceived that the approach to valuation was the same as that in an appraisal proceeding. Consistent with precedent, he rejected plaintiff's method of proof and accepted defendants' evidence of value as being in accord with practice under prior case law. This means that the so-called "Delaware block" or weighted average method was employed wherein the elements of value, i.e., assets, market price, earnings, etc., were assigned a particular weight and the resulting amounts added to determine the value per share. This procedure has been in use for decades. See In re General Realty & Utilities Corp., Del.Ch., 52 A.2d 6, 14–15 (1947). However, to the extent it excludes other generally accepted techniques used in the financial community and the courts, it is now clearly outmoded. It is time we recognize this in appraisal and other stock valuation proceedings and bring our law current on the subject.

While the Chancellor rejected plaintiff's discounted cash flow method of valuing UOP's stock, as not corresponding with "either logic or the existing law" (426 A.2d at 1360), it is significant that this was essentially the focus, i.e., earnings potential of UOP, of Messrs. Arledge and Chitiea in their evaluation of the merger. Accordingly, the standard "Delaware block" or weighted average method of valuation, formerly employed in appraisal and other stock *valuation cases shall no longer exclusively control such proceedings*. We believe that a more liberal approach must include proof of value by any techniques or methods which are generally considered acceptable in the financial community and otherwise admissible in court, subject only to our interpretation of 8 Del.C. § 262(b), infra. See also D.R.E. 702– 05. This will obviate the very structured and mechanistic procedure that has heretofore governed such matters. See Jacques Coe & Co. v. Minneapolis–Moline Co., Del.Ch., 75 A.2d 244, 247 (1950); Tri–Continental Corp. v. Battye, Del.Ch., 86 A.2d 910, 917–18 (1949); In re General Realty and Utilities Corp., supra.

Fair price obviously requires consideration of all relevant factors involving the value of a company. This has long been the law of Delaware as stated in Tri–Continental Corp., 74 A.2d at 72:

> The basic concept of value under the appraisal statute is that the stockholder is entitled to be paid for that which has been taken from him, viz., his proportionate interest in a going concern. By value of the stockholder's proportionate interest in the corporate enterprise is meant the true or intrinsic value of his stock which has been taken by the merger. In determining what figure represents this true or intrinsic value, the appraiser and the courts must take into consideration all factors and elements which reasonably might enter into the fixing of value. Thus, market value, asset value, dividends, earning prospects, the nature of the enterprise and any other facts which were known or which could be ascertained as of the date of merger and which throw any light on *future prospects* of the merged corporation are not only pertinent to an inquiry as to the value of the dissenting stockholders' interest, but *must be considered* by the agency fixing the value. (Emphasis added.)

This is not only in accord with the realities of present day affairs, but it is thoroughly consonant with the purpose and intent of our statutory law. Under 8 Del.C. § 262(h), the Court of Chancery:

> shall appraise the shares, determining their *fair* value exclusive of any element of value arising from the accomplishment or expectation of the

merger, together with a fair rate of interest, if any, to be paid upon the amount determined to be the *fair* value. In determining such *fair* value, the Court shall take into account *all relevant factors* * * * (Emphasis added)

See also Bell v. Kirby Lumber Corp., Del.Supr., 413 A.2d 137, 150–51 (1980) (Quillen, J., concurring).

It is significant that section 262 now mandates the determination of "fair" value based upon "all relevant factors". Only the speculative elements of value that may arise from the "accomplishment or expectation" of the merger are excluded. We take this to be a very narrow exception to the appraisal process, designed to eliminate use of *pro forma* data and projections of a speculative variety relating to the completion of a merger. But elements of future value, including the nature of the enterprise, which are known or susceptible of proof as of the date of the merger and not the product of speculation, may be considered. When the trial court deems it appropriate, fair value also includes any damages, resulting from the taking, which the stockholders sustain as a class. If that was not the case, then the obligation to consider "all relevant factors" in the valuation process would be eroded. We are supported in this view not only by *Tri–Continental Corp.*, 74 A.2d at 72, but also by the evolutionary amendments to section 262.

Prior to an amendment in 1976, the earlier relevant provision of section 262 stated:

(f) The appraiser shall determine the value of the stock of the stockholders * * * The Court shall by its decree determine the value of the stock of the stockholders entitled to payment therefor

* * *

The first references to "fair" value occurred in a 1976 amendment to section 262(f), which provided:

(f) * * * the Court shall appraise the shares, determining their fair value exclusively of any element of value arising from the accomplishment or expectation of the merger * * *.

It was not until the 1981 amendment to section 262 that the reference to "fair value" was repeatedly emphasized and the statutory mandate that the Court "take into account all relevant factors" appeared [section 262(h)]. Clearly, there is a legislative intent to fully compensate shareholders for whatever their loss may be, subject only to the narrow limitation that one can not take speculative effects of the merger into account.

Although the Chancellor received the plaintiff's evidence, his opinion indicates that the use of it was precluded because of past Delaware practice. While we do not suggest a monetary result one way or the other, we do think the plaintiff's evidence should be part of the factual mix and weighed as such. Until the $21 price is measured on remand by the valuation standards mandated by Delaware law, there can be no finding at the present stage of these proceedings that the price is fair. Given the lack of any candid disclosure of the material facts surrounding establishment of the $21 price, the majority of the minority vote, approving the merger, is meaningless.

The plaintiff has not sought an appraisal, but rescissory damages of the type contemplated by Lynch v. Vickers Energy Corp., Del.Supr., 429 A.2d 497, 505–06 (1981) (Lynch II). In view of the approach to valuation that we announce today, we see no basis in our law for *Lynch II's* exclusive monetary formula for relief.* On remand the plaintiff will be permitted to test the fairness of the $21 price by the standards we herein establish, in conformity with the principle applicable to an appraisal—that fair value be determined by taking "into account all relevant factors" [see 8 Del.C. § 262(h), supra]. In our view this includes the elements of rescissory damages if the Chancellor considers them susceptible of proof and a remedy appropriate to all the issues of fairness before him. To the extent that *Lynch II,* 429 A.2d at 505–06, purports to limit the Chancellor's discretion to a single remedial formula for monetary damages in a cash-out merger, it is overruled.

While a plaintiff's monetary remedy ordinarily should be confined to the more liberalized appraisal proceeding herein established, we do not intend any limitation on the historic powers of the Chancellor to grant such other relief as the facts of a particular case may dictate. The appraisal remedy we approve may not be adequate in certain cases, particularly where fraud, misrepresentation, self-dealing, deliberate waste of corporate assets, or gross and palpable overreaching are involved. Cole v. National Cash Credit Association, Del.Ch., 156 A. 183, 187 (1931). Under such circumstances, the Chancellor's powers are complete to fashion any form of equitable and monetary relief as may be appropriate, including rescissory damages. Since it is apparent that this long completed transaction is too involved to undo, and in view of the Chancellor's discretion, the award, if any, should be in the form of monetary damages based upon entire fairness standards, i.e., fair dealing and fair price.

Obviously, there are other litigants, like the plaintiff, who abjured an appraisal and whose rights to challenge the element of fair value must be preserved. Accordingly, the quasi-appraisal remedy we grant the plaintiff here will apply only to: (1) this case; (2) any case now pending on appeal to this Court; (3) any case now pending in the Court of Chancery which has not yet been appealed but which may be eligible for direct appeal to this

---

* [Ed. Note] On the first remand, in Lynch v. Vickers Energy Corp. (Lynch I), the trial court valued the Vickers stock as though in an appraisal proceeding, and concluded that plaintiffs had not been damaged because they had received more than fair value for their shares. (402 A.2d 5 (Del.Ch.1980)). On appeal, the Delaware Supreme Court affirmed in part, reversed in part, and remanded (429 A.2d 497 (1981)). (Lynch II) It ruled that in a cause of action for damages for having been induced fraudulently to sell stock, the actual value of the stock is relevant in determining whether plaintiff may recover the damages he seeks. But where the claim is for a failure to make adequate disclosure in breach of fiduciary duty, plaintiff is entitled to an accounting or rescission. This can be accomplished without interfering with the completed transaction, "by ordering damages which are the monetary equivalent of rescission and which will, in effect, equal the increment in value that Vickers [the bidder] enjoyed as a result of acquiring and holding the TransOcean [the target] stock in issue" (429 A.2d at 501).

Court; (4) any case challenging a cash-out merger, the effective date of which is on or before February 1, 1983; and (5) any proposed merger to be presented at a shareholders' meeting, the notification of which is mailed to the stockholders on or before February 23, 1983. Thereafter, the provisions of 8 Del.C. § 262, as herein construed, respecting the scope of an appraisal and the means for perfecting the same, shall govern the financial remedy available to minority shareholders in a cash-out merger. Thus, we return to the well established principles of Stauffer v. Standard Brands, Inc., Del. Supr., 187 A.2d 78 (1962) and David J. Greene & Co. v. Schenley Industries, Inc., Del.Ch., 281 A.2d 30 (1971), mandating a stockholder's recourse to the basic remedy of an appraisal.

III.

Finally, we address the matter of business purpose. The defendants contend that the purpose of this merger was not a proper subject of inquiry by the trial court. The plaintiff says that no valid purpose existed—the entire transaction was a mere subterfuge designed to eliminate the minority. The Chancellor ruled otherwise, but in so doing he clearly circumscribed the thrust and effect of *Singer*. Weinberger v. UOP, 426 A.2d at 1342–43, 1348–50. This has led to the thoroughly sound observation that the business purpose test "may be * * * virtually interpreted out of existence, as it was in *Weinberger*".[9]

The requirement of a business purpose is new to our law of mergers and was a departure from prior case law. See Stauffer v. Standard Brands, Inc., supra; David J. Greene & Co. v. Schenley Industries, Inc., supra.

In view of the fairness test which has long been applicable to parent-subsidiary mergers, Sterling v. Mayflower Hotel Corp., Del.Supr., 93 A.2d 107, 109–10 (1952), the expanded appraisal remedy now available to shareholders, and the broad discretion of the Chancellor to fashion such relief as the facts of a given case may dictate, we do not believe that any additional meaningful protection is afforded minority shareholders by the business purpose requirement of the trilogy of *Singer, Tanzer, Najjar,* and their progeny. Accordingly, such requirement shall no longer be of any force or effect.

The judgment of the Court of Chancery, finding both the circumstances of the merger and the price paid the minority shareholders to be fair, is reversed. The matter is remanded for further proceedings consistent herewith. Upon remand the plaintiff's post-trial motion to enlarge the class should be granted.

* * *

Reversed and Remanded.

---

9. Weiss, The Law of Take Out Mergers: A Historical Perspective, 56 N.Y.U. L.Rev. 624, 671, n. 300 (1981).

On the remand, the Court of Chancery awarded members of the plaintiffs' class damages of $1 per share and interest from February 1, 1983, the date of the Delaware Supreme Court's en banc decision to remand. The Supreme Court upheld that award and in its order said:

"Plaintiffs contend, inter alia, that the Court of Chancery erred (a) in placing the burden of proof on them, (b) in deciding not to award rescissory damages, (c) in awarding an inadequate amount of damages, and (d) in not awarding interest on the damages from the date of the wrong. We conclude that these contentions are without merit."

The decision not to award rescissory damages was based on the Chancellor's proclaimed inability "to formulate a post merger value for a share of UOP stock [frozen out in "a long completed merger"] with a sufficient degree of certainty to put the theory to work." That inability was a function of the length of time between the merger and the decision on remand, and the resulting incalculability of the relevant variables which are essential to be taken into account in "constructing" rescissory damages for a freeze-out merger. How likely is it that rescissory damages will be calculable "with a sufficient degree of certainty to put the theory to work" in any freeze-out merger involving a parent and subsidiary each of which has substantial operating assets?

NOTE: MARKET PRICE AS A MEASURE OF THE VALUE OF SUBSIDIARY STOCK

Why not let the pre-merger value of UOP's stock serve as a fairness yardstick? Given the substantial premium over that value, should UOP stockholders be heard to complain, whether in an appraisal or fairness proceeding?

It has been suggested that there are different, if not separate, markets for the entire firm or for a control block of its stock and for small units of its stock. Whether or not those markets function separately or are so related that the efficiency of the latter market extends to the former, there is good reason to believe that the latter market is likely to be systematically distorted, and therefore an inappropriate measure of the values of parent and subsidiary at the time of their merger.

Securities analysts recognize that, particularly as the parent owns increasingly larger proportions of the total stock, the publicly traded stock of the subsidiary often sells at a discount from the price at which the same stock would have sold if there were no parent, or at less than its pro-rata share of the going concern value of the enterprise. A variety of reasons is offered for the distortion—such as the thinness of the market and the uncertainty among investors generated by the fear that in the continuing relations between the two enterprises the parent will inevitably exercise discretion (lawfully as well as unlawfully, but substantially undetectably) to divert assets to itself instead of sharing them with the subsidiary and its public stockholders. In addition to the fear of such exploitation on a continuing basis, there is the no less plausible fear that the parent will force a merger of the two companies on terms disadvantageous to the subsidiary—but which it will be difficult to challenge effectively or at tolerable cost because their propriety turns on information (e.g., predictions about the future) of a kind that has not been made public and that cannot be extracted from the parent.

There is also reason to believe that the market price of the stocks of both parent and subsidiary will be inaccurate at the time of a merger because of systematic impediments to the flow of information. The parent can, and if it contemplates absorbing the subsidiary by merger it is likely to, control both the use of accounting conventions and the release of operating or financial information so as to cause the market price of the subsidiary's stock to drop below its "intrinsic value," and the market price of its own stock to rise above its "intrinsic value," in anticipation of the merger which if assessed by the comparative stock prices will thus inaccurately measure the comparative contributions to the merger.

Finally, it may be noted that if the "give-up" by the subsidiary stockholders is to be measured by a standard of fairness which entitles them to some compensation for their contribution to the gains produced by the merger, the market will be unable adequately to measure that contribution because the relevant information is, by definition, solely within the parent's possession and therefore not reflected in the price of the subsidiary's stock. Nor can the market register, as of the time of the merger, the value of the combined enterprise, if that value depends upon (a) information not reflected in the price of the subsidiary's stock and (b) gains to be produced by aspects of the combination's operation then known only to the parent. Moreover, the market for the combined enterprise's securities may be affected by variables irrelevant to the merger—e.g., a depression in the market generally at the time of the merger.

Not only may reported earnings be understated for the subsidiary and over-stated for the parent by "legitimate" application of a variety of accounting conventions, but dividend policies and substantive decisions (maintenance) may be taken with a view to advantaging the parent in the rate of exchange in the ultimate merger. Apart from thus misstating the past, the parent may fail to state what it, but not the public, knows about the future—and time the merger when a new development in the subsidiary is about to reach fruition. The shorter the period between the decision to absorb and the initiation of the merger transaction, the easier it is to prevent discovery of the distortions in the information flow and therefore of the improper price-value relationship. It is also possible in any relatively short period for the parent to manipulate the prices of the stocks—both the subsidiary's and its own—so as to support the distortion caused by corruption of the information flow.

NOTE: CLARIFYING *WEINBERGER*

The Delaware Supreme Court clarified the meaning of *Weinberger* in two cases decided in 1985, *Rosenblatt v. Getty* and *Rabkin v. Hunt Chemical*.

1. *The Standard of Review and Disclosure Duties.*

Rosenblatt v. Getty Oil Co., 493 A.2d 929 (Del. Supr. 1985), concerned the merger of Skelly Oil Co. into Getty Oil Co., which controlled 72.6 percent of Skelly's stock. The court placed the burden of proving the fairness of the merger on Getty:

> Getty, as majority shareholder of Skelly, stood on both sides of this transaction and bore the initial burden of establishing its entire fairness. However, approval of a merger, as here, by an informed vote of a majority of the minority shareholders, while not a legal prerequisite, shifts the burden of proving the unfairness of the merger entirely to the plaintiffs. Getty, nonetheless, retained the burden of showing complete disclosure of all material facts relevant to that vote.

The plaintiffs claimed that Getty had breached its duty to the Skelly minority shareholders by failing to disclose an internal memorandum that predicted a $52 million drop in Getty's earnings. Here the Court drew a distinction from *Weinberger*:

"* * * [P]laintiffs liken this document, projecting a $52,165,000 after-tax decrease in Getty's 1976 earnings, in comparison to its 1975 earnings, to the Arledge and Chitiea report in *Weinberger,* which indicated that the majority shareholder, Signal, still considered the elimination of the minority an 'outstanding investment opportunity' even at a price higher than that actually being offered. See *Weinberger,* 457 A.2d at 705, 708, 712. However, the two reports are factually and legally different. First, it is not clear that Skelly and its negotiators were unaware of Getty's projected earnings decrease.

"Second, the Arledge–Chitiea report, used secretly by and exclusively for Signal, was prepared by two Signal directors, who were also UOP directors, using UOP information obtained solely in their capacities as UOP directors. *Weinberger,* 457 A.2d at 705. Here, the decreased earnings projection was prepared by a member of Getty's management for Getty's use as part of its annual reporting function. Moreover, there is not the slightest indication that its disclosure could have materially affected the exchange ratio negotiations. See id. at 709, 712. Third, the merger in *Weinberger* was expressly conditioned on approval of a majority of UOP's minority shareholders; here, there was no such condition. See id. at 707.

"While it has been suggested that *Weinberger* stands for the proposition that a majority shareholder must under all circumstances disclose its top bid to the minority, that clearly is a misconception of what we said there. The sole basis for our conclusions in *Weinberger* regarding the non-disclosure of the Arledge–Chitiea report was because Signal appointed directors on UOP's board, who thus stood on both sides of the transaction, violated their undiminished duty of loyalty to UOP. It had nothing to do with Signal's duty, as the majority stockholder, to the other shareholders of UOP."

The Delaware Court of Chancery had occasion to apply the standard of review articulated in *Rosenblatt* in **Citron v. E.I. Du Pont de Nemours & Co.,** 584 A.2d 490 (Del.Ch.1990). According to Vice Chancellor Jacobs, *Sinclair Oil Corp. v. Levien,* supra, Part IV, holds that the entire fairness standard is triggered when the plaintiff demonstrates "that the parent corporation stood on both sides of the transaction *and* * * * dictated its terms" (emphasis in original), while *Rosenblatt* requires only a showing that the parent corporation stood on both sides of the transaction. Thus, in a case where the merger is negotiated and approved by disinterested directors and ratified by a fully informed majority of the minority stockholders, business judgment scrutiny does not apply because the parent stands on both sides. Under *Rosenblatt,* minority stockholder ratification after disinterested director intervention operates to shift the burden of persuasion on the issue of entire fairness to the plaintiff.

2. *Appraisal Exclusivity and Procedural Fairness.*

Rabkin v. Philip A. Hunt Chemical Corp., 498 A.2d 1099 (Del.Supr.1985), elaborated on *Weinberger's* teaching respecting the exclusivity of the appraisal remedy and the significance of procedural fairness. The case involved a challenge to the merger of Hunt Corp. into Olin Corp. in July 1984. On March 1, 1983 Olin Corp. had bought 63.4 percent of the Hunt common stock for $25 per share from a holding company. At the latter's insistence, Olin undertook, at the time of its purchase on March 1, 1983, to pay at least the equivalent of $25 per share to the holders of the remaining Hunt stock if within one year thereafter it absorbed Hunt by merger, consolidation, tender offer, or the like. Although, according to the evidence obtained in discovery in the case, Olin quite plainly always had contemplated acquiring 100 percent of Hunt, it waited until after the year had run, then obtained a banker's opinion that $20 per share was fair for Hunt stock, and merged out the remaining Hunt common stock at $20 on July 5, 1984.

The merger procedure entailed a statement by Olin's CEO to Hunt's President of the terms of the merger on the evening of March 27, 1984, and the issuance on March 28 of a joint press release announcing the merger on those terms. According to the Supreme Court, Moore, J. (498 A.2d at 1103–1108):

"Later that day the Hunt Board appointed a Special Committee, consisting of the four Hunt outside directors, to review and determine the fairness of Olin's merger proposal. These directors met on April 4, 1984, and retained Merrill Lynch as their financial advisor and the law firm of Shea and Gould as legal counsel. This committee met again on three other occasions. At the May 10, 1984 meeting the Special Committee heard a presentation by the lawyers for several plaintiffs who had filed class actions on behalf of the minority shareholders to enjoin the proposed merger. A representative of Merrill Lynch advised the meeting that $20 per share was fair to the minority from a financial standpoint, but that the range of values for the common stock was probably $19 to $25 per share.

"The outside directors subsequently notified the Hunt board that they had unanimously found $20 per share to be fair but not generous. They therefore recommended that Olin consider increasing the price above $20. The next day, May 11, 1984, Olin informed the Hunt Special Committee that it had considered its recommendation but declined to raise the price. The Hunt outside directors then met again on May 14, 1984, by teleconference call, and at a meeting of the Hunt board on May 15, also held by teleconference, the Special Committee announced that it had unanimously found the $20 per share price fair and recommended approval of the merger.

"On June 7, 1984, Hunt issued its proxy statement favoring the merger. That document also made clear Olin's intention to vote its 64% of the Hunt shares in favor of the proposal, thereby guaranteeing its passage. There was no requirement of approval by a majority of the minority stockholders.

* * *

"In ordering the complaints dismissed the Vice Chancellor reasoned that:

Where, * * * there are no allegations of non-disclosures or misrepresentations, *Weinberger* mandates that plaintiffs' entire fairness claims be determined in an appraisal proceeding.

We consider that an erroneous interpretation of *Weinberger*, because it fails to take account of the entire context of the holding.

* * *

"Thus, the trial court's narrow interpretation of *Weinberger* would render meaningless our extensive discussion of fair dealing found in that opinion. In *Weinberger* we defined fair dealing as embracing 'questions of when the transaction was timed, how it was initiated, structured, negotiated, disclosed to the directors, and how the approvals of the directors and the stockholders were obtained.' 457 A.2d at 711. While this duty of fairness certainly incorporates the principle that a cash-out merger must be free of fraud or misrepresentation, *Weinberger's* mandate of fair dealing does not turn solely on issues of deception. We particularly noted broader concerns respecting the matter of procedural fairness.

* * *

" * * * Here, plaintiffs are not arguing questions of valuation which are the traditional subjects of an appraisal. Rather, they seek to enforce a contractual right to receive $25 per share, which they claim was unfairly destroyed by Olin's manipulative conduct.

* * *

"The Court of Chancery stated that '[t]he gravamen of all the complaints appears to be that the cash-out price is unfair.' However, this conclusion, which seems to be more directed to issues of valuation, is neither supported by the pleadings themselves nor the extensive discussion of unfair dealing found in the trial court's opinion. There is no challenge to any method of valuation or to the components of value upon which Olin's $20 price was based. The plaintiffs want the $25 per share guaranteed by the one year commitment, which they claim was unfairly denied them by Olin's manipulations.

* * *

"In *Weinberger* we observed that the timing, structure, negotiation and disclosure of a cash-out merger all had a bearing on the issue of procedural fairness. The plaintiffs contend *inter alia* that Olin breached its fiduciary duty of fair dealing by purposely timing the merger, and thereby unfairly manipulating it, to avoid the one year commitment * * *

" * * * Olin's alleged attitude toward the minority, at least as it appears on the face of the complaints and their proposed amendments, coupled with the apparent absence of any meaningful negotiations as to price, all have an air reminiscent of the dealings between Signal and UOP in *Weinberger*. * * *

" * * * As we read the complaints and the proposed amendments, they assert a conscious intent by Olin, as the majority shareholder of Hunt, to deprive the Hunt minority of the same bargain that Olin made with Hunt's former majority shareholder, Turner and Newall. But for Olin's allegedly unfair manipulation, the plaintiffs contend, this bargain also was due them. In short, the defendants are charged with bad faith which goes beyond issues of "mere inadequacy of price." Cole v. National Cash Credit Association, Del.Ch., 156 A. 183, 187–88 (1931). In *Weinberger* we specifically relied upon this aspect of *Cole* in acknowledging the imperfections of an appraisal where circumstances of this sort are present.

"Necessarily, this will require the Court of Chancery to closely focus upon *Weinberger's* mandate of entire fairness based on a careful analysis of both the fair price and fair dealing aspects of a transaction. We recognize that this can present certain practical problems, since stockholders may invariably claim that the price being offered is the result of unfair dealings. However, we think that plaintiffs will be tempered in this approach by the prospect that an ultimate judgment in defendants' favor may have cost plaintiffs their unperfected appraisal rights. Moreover, our courts are not without a degree of sophistication in such matters. A balance must be struck between sustaining complaints averring faithless acts, which taken as true would constitute breaches of fiduciary duties that are reasonably related to and have a substantial impact upon the price offered, and properly dismissing those allegations questioning judgmental factors of valuation. Cole v. National Cash Credit Association, 156 A. at 187–88. Otherwise, we face the anomalous result that stockholders who are eliminated without appraisal rights can bring class actions, while in other cases a squeezed-out minority is limited to an appraisal, provided there was no deception, regardless of the degree of procedural unfairness employed to take their shares. Without that balance, *Weinberger's* concern for entire fairness loses all force."

On the remand of the *Rabkin* case, Chandler, V.C., demonstrated the "degree of sophistication in such matters" that the Delaware courts are not without. He ruled that the plaintiffs failed to prove that Olin Corp. deliberately timed the cash-out merger so as to violate "its duty of fair dealing in connection with the one year price commitment." Nor had Olin otherwise violated the terms of its section 13D promise to pay a fair price to the minority if it cashed them out after a year. **Rabkin v. Olin Corp.,** CCH Fed.Sec.L.Rep. ¶ 95,255 (Del.Ch.1990).

Do the opinions of the Delaware courts in parent-subsidiary mergers suggest that procedural fairness, effected by adherence to forms that imitate arm's-length bargaining, is the crucial test of fairness in such mergers? Whatever may be the substantive standard of fairness that can be deciphered from the opinions, does its application implicate such unconstrained judicial discretion that the court's ultimate decision is the result of its perception of procedural fairness? In any event, what is the teaching of these cases for corporate counsel in staging the merger?

NOTE: *KAHN v. LYNCH COMMUNICATION SYSTEMS*

How does the standard of review articulated in *Rosenblatt v. Getty* and *Citron v. Du Pont* apply in a case where the special committee, after a period of resistance, finally accedes to the price offered by the controlling shareholder? The Delaware Supreme Court took up this problem in succeeding opinions in **Kahn v. Lynch Communication Systems, Inc.**, 638 A.2d 1110 (Del.Supr.1994)("Lynch I"), and 669 A.2d 79 (Del.Supr.1995)("Lynch II").

1. *Lynch I.*

Alcatel (S.A.), a French telecommunications and electronics firm, owned 43.3 percent of the stock of Lynch, a domestic manufacturer of telecommunications equipment. Pursuant to a stock purchase agreement, Alcatel had right to proportional representation on the Lynch board and had secured an amendment of Lynch's charter requiring an 80 percent shareholder vote to approve any business combination.

In 1986, Lynch's management determined that it required fiber optics technology to remain competitive in its field. It explored the possible acquisition of Telco Systems, which possessed the desired technology. But Alcatel, which possessed a veto under the charter, opposed the acquisition and proposed instead a combination with Celwave Systems, an indirect subsidiary of Alcatel's parent, in the business of manufacturing wire and cable.

The combination with Celwave was presented to the Lynch board at a meeting held on August 1, 1986. The Lynch CEO expressed the view that but for the Alcatel's ownership of Celwave, the company would not be of interest to Lynch. Alcatel's representatives made it clear that they desired the board to consider a Celwave combination before it considered a combination with Telco. The board unanimously agreed to appoint an Independent Committee to explore a transaction with Celwave.

Renewal of the employment contracts of Lynch's managers also came up at the meeting. The independent directors were disposed to renew the contracts, but Alcatel was opposed. One Alcatel nominee was reported to have expressed its position as follows: "[Y]ou must listen to us. We are 43 percent owner. You have to do what we tell you.... [Y]ou are pushing us very much to take control of the company. Our opinion is not taken into consideration." The independent directors responded by pointing out to the incumbent manager-directors that renewal of their contracts in the face of Alcatel's opposition would put the company in an awkward situation. The management directors thereupon left the room, and the remaining board members then voted not to renew the contracts.

Thereafter, the Independent Committee, acting on the advice of its investment banker, failed to agree with Alcatel on the exchange ratio proposed for the Celwave combination. Alcatel responded by withdrawing the proposal, simultaneously offering to acquire the remaining 57 percent of Lynch's stock for $14 per share. The Independent Committee made a counter offer of $17. Alcatel responded with $15, then $15.25, and finally $15.50. With the $15.50 offer came notice that Alcatel was ready to proceed with an unfriendly tender offer at a lower price. The Committee reviewed the alternatives earlier suggested by its counsel—a white knight deal with a third party, a share repurchase, and a shareholder rights plan. The Committee determined that the charter's supermajority requirement blocked the first alternative, and that the second and third were not feasible from a financial point of view. The Committee then recommended the $15.50 offer to the board, which unanimously approved it, the Alcatel nominees abstaining.

In the plaintiff's action for damages, the Chancery Court ruled that Alcatel was a controlling shareholder owing fiduciary duties to Lynch, but that Alcatel had not breached those duties. The Supreme Court affirmed the former ruling but reversed the latter, reasoning as follows:

"The same policy rationale which requires judicial review of interested cash-out mergers exclusively for entire fairness also mandates careful judicial scrutiny of a special committee's real bargaining power before shifting the burden of proof on the issue of entire fairness. A recent decision from the Court of Chancery articulated a two-part test for determining whether burden shifting is appropriate in an interested merger transaction. *Rabkin v. Olin Corp.*, Del.Ch., C.A. No. 7547 (Consolidated), Chandler, V.C., 1990 WL 47648, slip op. at 14–15 (Apr. 17, 1990), *reprinted in* 16 Del.J.Corp.L. 851, 861–62 (1991), aff'd, Del.Supr., 586 A.2d 1202 (1990). In *Olin*, the Court of Chancery stated:

> The mere existence of an independent special committee ... does not itself shift the burden. At least two factors are required. First, the majority shareholder must not dictate the terms of the merger. *Rosenblatt v. Getty Oil Co.*, Del.Ch., 493 A.2d 929, 937 (1985). Second, the special committee must have real bargaining power that it can exercise with the majority shareholder on an arms length basis.

Id., slip op. at 14–15, 16 Del.J.Corp.L. at 861–62.[6] This Court expressed its agreement with that statement by affirming the Court of Chancery decision in *Olin* on appeal.

"* * * [T]he performance of the Independent Committee merits careful judicial scrutiny to determine whether Alcatel's demonstrated pattern of domination was effectively neutralized so that 'each of the contending parties had in fact exerted its bargaining power against the other at arm's length.' *Id.* * * *

* * *

"The Court of Chancery properly noted that limitations on the alternatives to Alcatel's offer did not mean that the Independent Committee should have agreed to a price that was unfair: The power to say no is a significant power. It is the duty of

---

6. In *Olin*, the Court of Chancery concluded that because the special committee had been given "the narrow mandate of determining the monetary fairness of a non-negotiable offer," and because the majority shareholder "dictated the terms" and "there were no arm's-length negotiations," the burden of proof on the issue of entire fairness remained with the defendants. *Id.*, slip op. at 15, 16 Del.J.Corp.L. at 862. In making that determination, the Court of Chancery pointed out that the majority shareholder 'could obviously have used its majority stake to effectuate the merger' regardless of the committee's or the board's disapproval, and that the record demonstrated that the directors of both corporations were "acutely aware of this fact." *Id.*, slip op. at 13, 16 Del.J.Corp.L. at 861.

directors serving on [an independent] committee to approve only a transaction that is in the best interests of the public shareholders, to say no to any transaction that is not fair to those shareholders and is not the best transaction available. It is not sufficient for such directors to achieve the best price that a fiduciary will pay if that price is not a fair price. (Quoting *In re First Boston, Inc. Shareholders Litig.*, Del.Ch., C.A. 10338 (Consolidated), Allen, C., 1990 WL 78836, slip op. at 15–16 (June 7, 1990)).

* * *

"A condition precedent to finding that the burden of proving entire fairness has shifted in an interested merger transaction is a careful judicial analysis of the factual circumstances of each case. Particular consideration must be given to evidence of whether the special committee was truly independent, fully informed, and had the freedom to negotiate at arm's length. * * * 'Although perfection is not possible,' unless the controlling or dominating shareholder can demonstrate that it has not only formed an independent committee but also replicated a process 'as though each of the contending parties had in fact exerted its bargaining power at arm's length,' the burden of proving entire fairness will not shift. *Weinberger v. UOP, Inc.*, 457 A.2d at 709–10 n. 7. *See also Rosenblatt v. Getty Oil Co.*, Del.Supr., 493 A.2d 929, 937–38 (1985).

"Subsequent to *Rosenblatt*, this Court pointed out that 'the use of an independent negotiating committee of outside directors may have significant advantages to the majority stockholder in defending suits of this type,' but it does not *ipso facto* establish the procedural fairness of an interested merger transaction. *Rabkin v. Philip A. Hunt Chem. Corp.*, Del.Supr., 498 A.2d 1099, 1106 & n. 7 (1985). In reversing the granting of the defendants' motion to dismiss in *Rabkin*, this Court implied that the burden on entire fairness would not be shifted by the use of an independent committee which concluded its processes with 'what could be considered a quick surrender' to the dictated terms of the controlling shareholder. *Id.* at 1106. This Court concluded in Rabkin that the majority stockholder's 'attitude toward the minority,' coupled with the 'apparent absence of any meaningful negotiations as to price,' did not manifest the exercise of arm's length bargaining by the independent committee. *Id.*

"The Court of Chancery's determination that the Independent Committee 'appropriately simulated a third-party transaction, where negotiations are conducted at arm's-length and there is no compulsion to reach an agreement,' is not supported by the record. Under the circumstances present in the case *sub judice*, the Court of Chancery erred in shifting the burden of proof with regard to entire fairness to the contesting Lynch shareholder-plaintiff, Kahn. The record reflects that the ability of the Committee effectively to negotiate at arm's length was compromised by Alcatel's threats to proceed with a hostile tender offer if the $15.50 price was not approved by the Committee and the Lynch board. The fact that the Independent Committee rejected three initial offers, which were well below the Independent Committee's estimated valuation for Lynch and were not combined with an explicit threat that Alcatel was 'ready to proceed' with a hostile bid, cannot alter the conclusion that any semblance of arm's length bargaining ended when the Independent Committee surrendered to the ultimatum that accompanied Alcatel's final offer. * * * "

The Court remanded the case for redetermination of the entire fairness of the cash-out merger to the minority shareholders of Lynch, with the burden of proof to be on Alcatel.

2.   *Lynch II.*

On remand, the Chancellor ruled that Alcatel had sustained the burden of proving that the merger was entirely fair. The plaintiff appealed, claiming (1) that the coercion of the Independent Committee constituted a *per se* breach of fiduciary duty, compelling a finding that the transaction was not entirely fair, and (2) that the initiation, timing and negotiation of the merger were unfair, requiring a finding of unfair dealing.

The Supreme Court affirmed the Chancellor, reasoning as follows, 669 A.2d at 84–86:

"In addressing the fair dealing component of the transaction, the Court of Chancery determined that the initiation and timing of the transactions were responsive to Lynch's needs. This conclusion was based on the fact that Lynch's marketing strategy was handicapped by the lack of a fiber optic technology. Alcatel proposed the merger with Celwave to remedy this competitive weakness but Lynch management and the non-Alcatel directors did not believe this combination would be beneficial to Lynch. Dertinger, Lynch's CEO, suggested to Alcatel that, under the circumstances, a cash merger with Alcatel will be preferable to a Celwave merger. Thus, the Alcatel offer to acquire the minority interests in Lynch was viewed as an alternative to the disfavored Celwave transaction.

"Kahn argues that the Telco acquisition, which Lynch management strongly supported, was vetoed by Alcatel to force Lynch to accept Celwave as a merger partner or agree to a cash out merger with Alcatel. The benefits of the Telco transaction, however, are clearly debatable. Telco was not profitable and had a limited fiber optic capability. There is no assurance that Lynch's shareholders would have benefitted from the acquisition. More to the point, the timing of a merger transaction cannot be viewed solely from the perspective of the acquired entity. A majority shareholder is naturally motivated by economic self-interest in initiating a transaction. Otherwise, there is no reason to do it. Thus, mere initiation by the acquirer is not reprehensible so long as the controlling shareholder does not gain a financial advantage at the expense of the minority. *Cinerama, Inc. v. Technicolor, Inc.*, Del.Supr., 663 A.2d 1156, 1172 (1995); *Jedwab v. MGM Grand Hotels, Inc.*, Del.Ch., 509 A.2d 584, 599 (1986).

"In support of its claim of coercion, Kahn contends that Alcatel timed its merger offer, with a thinly-veiled threat of using its controlling position to force the result, to take advantage of the opportunity to buy Lynch on the cheap. [But] Lynch was experiencing a difficult and rapidly changing competitive situation. Its current financial results reflected that fact. Although its stock was trading at low levels, this may simply have been a reflection of its competitive problems. Alcatel is not to be faulted for taking advantage of the objective reality of Lynch's financial situation. Thus the mere fact that the transaction was initiated at Alcatel's discretion, does not dictate a finding of unfairness in the absence of a determination that the minority shareholders of Lynch were harmed by the timing. The Court of Chancery rejected such a claim and we agree.

"With respect to the negotiations and structure of the transaction, the Court of Chancery, while acknowledging that the Court in *Lynch I* found the negotiations coercive, commented that the negotiations 'certainly were no less fair than if there had been no negotiations at all' 1995 decision at 4. The court noted that a committee of non-Alcatel directors negotiated an increase in price from $14 per share to $15.50. The committee also retained two investment banking firms who were well acquainted with Lynch's prospects based on their work on the Celwave proposal. Moreover, the committee had the benefit of outside legal counsel.

"It is true that the committee and the Board agreed to a price which at least one member of the committee later opined was not a fair price. *Lynch I*, 638 A.2d at 1118. But there is no requirement of unanimity in such matters either at the Independent Committee level or by the Board. A finding of unfair dealing based on lack of unanimity could discourage the use of special committees in majority dominated cash-out mergers. * * *

" * * *[T]o be actionable, the coercive conduct directed at selling shareholders must be a 'material' influence on the decision to sell. *Id.*; *see also Eisenberg v. Chicago Milwaukee Corp.*, Del.Ch., 537 A.2d 1051, 1061–62 (1987).

"Where other economic forces are at work and more likely produced the decision to sell, as the Court of Chancery determined here, the specter of coercion may not be deemed material with respect to the transaction as a whole, and will not prevent a finding of entire fairness. In this case, no shareholder was treated differently in the transaction from any other shareholder nor subjected to a two-tiered or squeeze-out treatment. *See, e.g., Unocal Corp. v. Mesa Petroleum Co.*, Del.Supr., 493 A.2d 946, 956 (1985). Alcatel offered cash for all the minority shares and paid cash for all shares tendered. Clearly there was no coercion exerted which was material to this aspect of the transaction, and thus no finding of *per se* liability is required."

3. *The Burden of Proof.*

Note that *Lynch I* reaffirms the standard of review set out in *Rosenblatt*: Neither independent special committee review nor majority of the minority shareholder approval triggers business judgment protection for the merger; they instead shift the burden of proof to show the merger to be unfair to the plaintiff. For the view that business judgment scrutiny should be accorded in either case, see Allen, Jacobs & Strine, Function Over Form: A Reassessment of Standards of Review in Delaware Corporation Law, 56 Bus. Law. 1287, 1306–09 (2001). In the view of the authors, two of whom presently serve on the Delaware courts and one of whom formerly served, institutional investor participation, stepped up information flow due to technological advancement, and SEC oversight suffice to protect the minority shareholders.

In re Siliconix Incorporated Shareholders Litigation

Court of Chancery of Delaware, 2001.
2001 WL 716787 (Del.Ch.).

■ NOBLE, VICE CHANCELLOR.

[Plaintiff Raymond L. Fitzgerald ("Fitzgerald"), a shareholder in defendant Siliconix Incorporated ("Siliconix") challenged a stock-for-stock tender offer made by a wholly-owned subsidiary of defendant Vishay Intertechnology, Inc. ("Vishay") for the 19.6% equity interest in Siliconix that Vishay does not already own. Fitzgerald moved to enjoin preliminarily the tender.]

II.   FACTUAL HISTORY

A.   *The Parties.*

Fitzgerald has owned Siliconix stock since February 1991. His holdings have a market value in excess of $4 million.

Vishay, which is listed on the New York Stock Exchange, is a manufacturer of passive electronic components and semiconductor components. It owns 80.4% of the equity in Siliconix.

Siliconix is listed on the NASDAQ. It designs, markets, and manufactures power and analog semiconductor products. It is the leading manufacturer of power MOSFETS ("metal oxide semiconductor field effect transistors"), power integrated circuits, and analog signaling devices for computers, cell phones, fixed communications networks, automobiles, and other electrical systems. In March 1998, Daimler–Benz sold its TEMIC semiconductor division, which included an 80.4% equity interest in Siliconix, to Vishay.

Defendant Felix Zandman ("Zandman") is the chairman, chief executive officer, and controlling stockholder of Vishay.

* * *

Defendants Mark Segall ("Segall") and Timothy Talbert ("Talbert") are directors of Siliconix and served on the Special Committee formed to evaluate a Vishay proposal to acquire the minority interests in Siliconix.

B. *Background to the Tenders.*

[Siliconix suffered reverses in 2000–2001, along with the rest of the telecommunications industry. Its earnings for the first quarter of 2001 decreased by 65 percent from the those of the first quarter of 2001. In March 2000 its stock sold for $165. By December 2000 it traded for $17.]

C. *The Cash Tender Offer.*

On February 22, 2001, Vishay publicly announced a proposed, all-cash tender offer for the publicly-held Siliconix common stock at a price of $28.82 per share. It also announced that if it obtained over 90% of the Siliconix stock, it would consider a short-form merger of Siliconix into a Vishay subsidiary for the same price. Vishay determined the price by applying a 10% premium to the then market price of Siliconix stock. Vishay made no effort to value Siliconix. Fitzgerald maintains that the tender offer price of $28.82 per share was grossly inadequate and asserts that the public announcement was an effort to keep the price artificially depressed. Among other factors, he points out that the price represented a 20.1% discount from Siliconix' average closing price for the six-month period prior to the announcement of the cash tender offer.

D. *Appointment of the Special Committee.*

[The Siliconix board appointed Segall and Talbert to a Special Committee to negotiate the terms of the tender offer with Vishay. Each of the two had past business ties with Vishay and personal friendships with top Vishay executives. Talbert, in fact, was appointed to the Silconix board immediately before the tender offer announcement with a view to special committee service. The Committee engaged Lehman Brothers as financial advisor and the Heller, Ehrman law firm as counsel, neither of which had ties to Vishay. The Committee and its advisors met with Vishay in April and expressed the view that $28.82 was not a fair price.]

E.   *The Stock-for-Stock Exchange.*

In the meantime, Siliconix' stock had risen above the $28.82 per share cash offer price. Vishay management was unwilling to increase the cash offer and therefore started to consider a stock-for-stock transaction. On May 2, 2001, the Special Committee again met with Vishay. Vishay was again told that the Special Committee did not consider $28.82 per share adequate, and Vishay floated the possibility of a stock-for-stock deal. * * * Vishay drafted a merger agreement for consideration by the Special Committee, and the parties conducted on-going negotiations for several weeks about a potential merger.

On May 9, 2001, Zandman made a presentation at an analysts' conference during which he discussed not only Vishay's business but also the business of Siliconix. He spoke of Siliconix' "very good market position" and its status as "number one" in its industry. He indicated that the economic cycle was hitting the bottom, in his opinion, and reflected that Siliconix historically has emerged from downturns ahead of Vishay. He expressed his view that Siliconix was experiencing a "bottoming up," but he went on to caution that the outlook for Siliconix was unsettled.

On May 23, 2001, Vishay informed the Special Committee that it was considering proceeding with a stock-for-stock exchange offer without first obtaining the Special Committee's approval. Two days later, Vishay announced the exchange offer under which it would exchange 1.5 shares of Vishay common stock for every share of Siliconix common stock. The exchange ratio was simply the ratio of the Siliconix and Vishay stock prices as of the February 22 proposal. Unlike the February 22 cash tender announcement, the share exchange carried no market premium for the Siliconix shareholders.

* * * According to Fitzgerald, Vishay had to move quickly to take advantage of the temporary market pressure on Siliconix stock because it perceived that Siliconix' stock price and operating performance were likely to rebound with improvements in the national and global economies and that Siliconix moves in periods of recovery ahead of Vishay. Also, Vishay, according to Fitzgerald, sought to take advantage of the continuing adverse impact of the February 22 announcement on Siliconix' stock price.

Vishay disputes Fitzgerald's explanation. Vishay explains that it announced the stock-for-stock offer because of its perception of a continuing deterioration in the electronic components market generally and Siliconix' market niche in particular. The record suggests that Siliconix' sales were continuing to fall. * * *

        * * *

Vishay's offer contained a non-waivable "majority of the minority" provision providing that Vishay would not proceed with its tender offer unless a majority of those shareholders not affiliated with Vishay tendered their shares. Vishay also stated that it intended to effect a short-form merger following a successful tender offer, but it noted that it is not required to do so and that there might be circumstances under which it would not do so. Its [S–4] Registration Statement also advised the minority shareholders that if Vishay pursued the short-form merger, it would be at the same per share consideration as the exchange offer and that objecting shareholders could invoke their appraisal rights under Delaware law.

When the exchange offer was announced, Vishay was trading for $25.81, an equivalent of $38.71 per share of Siliconix. Since then, the price of Vishay has dropped to roughly $20, thereby producing an imputed value of roughly $30 for each Siliconix share. One of the reasons for the decline may have been the announcement on May 30, 2001, by Vishay of a major debt offering.

The Special Committee advised Vishay that is was unlikely to approve the 1.5 exchange ratio as fair, but the record is unclear what steps were taken to seek enhancement of the terms of the tender offer. * * *

On June 8, 2001, Siliconix filed with the Securities and Exchange Commission its Schedule 14D–9 setting forth its disclosures concerning Vishay's offer. It reported that the Special Committee has determined to remain neutral and make no recommendation with respect to the tender offer. The Special Committee never requested Lehman to prepare a fairness opinion as to the exchange offer.

* * *

III. ANALYSIS

* * *

1. *Fair Price Issues.*

In responding to a voluntary tender offer, shareholders of Delaware corporations are free to accept or reject the tender based on their own evaluation of their best interests. "That choice will normally depend upon each stockholder's individual investment objectives and his evaluation of the merits of the offer." [*Eisenberg v. Chicago Milwaukee Corp.*, Del. Ch., 537 A.2d 1051, 1056 (1987).] However, this Court will intervene to protect the rights of the shareholders to make a voluntary choice. The issue of voluntariness of the tender depends on the absence of improper coercion and the absence of disclosure violations. Thus, "as a general principle, our law holds that a controlling shareholder extending an offer for minority-held shares in the controlled corporation is under no obligation, absent evidence that material information about the offer has been withheld or misrepresented or that the offer is coercive in some significant way, to offer any particular price for the minority-held stock." [In re Ocean Drilling & Exploration Co. Shareholders Litig. ("*Ocean Drilling*"), Del. Ch., Consol. C.A. No. 11898, Chandler, V.C., mem. op. at 6–7 (Apr. 30, 1991)].

Accordingly, Vishay was under no duty to offer any particular price, or a "fair" price, to the minority shareholders of Siliconix unless actual coercion or disclosure violations are shown by Fitzgerald. In short, as long as the tender offer is pursued properly, the free choice of the minority shareholders to reject the tender offer provides sufficient protection. Because I conclude that there were no disclosure violations and the tender is not coercive, Vishay was not obligated to offer a fair price in its tender.

2. *Entire Fairness Standard.*

Fitzgerald argues that a preliminary injunction should issue because the Defendants cannot demonstrate that the transaction is entirely fair. He contends that both the fair dealing and the fair price prongs of the entire fairness standard are implicated because the Siliconix directors (including the Special Committee members) breached their duty of care and their duty of loyalty to the Siliconix shareholders. Briefly, the Siliconix board is alleged to have breached its duty of care by not carefully evaluating the proposed transaction and then developing with appropriate assistance from investment banking professionals and sharing with the stockholders a recommendation as to the response to the tender offer that would be in the shareholders' best interest. The alleged breach of the duty of loyalty flows directly from the concededly conflicted status of at least a substantial majority of the board, which certainly is not uncommon in instances where the controlling stockholder seeks to acquire the balance of the shares in the subsidiary. However, unless coercion or disclosure violations can be shown, no defendant has the duty to demonstrate the entire fairness of this proposed tender transaction.

It may seem strange that the scrutiny given to tender offer transactions is less than the scrutiny that may be given to, for example, a merger transaction which is accompanied by more general breaches of fiduciary duty by the directors of the acquired corporation. From the standpoint of a Siliconix shareholder, there may be little substantive difference if the tender is successful and Vishay proceeds, as it has indicated that it most likely will, with the short-form merger. The Siliconix shareholders may reject the tender, but, if the tender is successful and the short-form merger accomplished, the shareholder, except for the passage of time, will end up in the same position as if he or she had tendered or if the transaction had been structured as a merger, *i.e.,* as the holder of 1.5 Vishay shares for every Siliconix share held before the process began (or as someone pursuing appraisal rights) and with no continuing direct economic interest in the Siliconix business enterprise.

The difference in judicial approach can be traced to two simple concepts. The first is that accepting or rejecting a tender is a decision to be made by the individual shareholder, and at least as to the tender itself, he will, if he rejects the tender, still own the stock of the target company following the tender. The second concept is that the acquired company in the merger context enters into a merger agreement, but the target company in the tender context does not confront a comparable corporate decision because the actual target of a tender is not the corporation (or its directors), but, instead, is its shareholders. Indeed, the board of the tender target is not asking its shareholders to approve any corporate action by the tender target. That, however, does not mean that the board of the company to be acquired in a tender has no duties to shareholders.

But addressing that question in the circumstances of this case involves one in considering an anomaly. Public tender offers are, or rather can be, change in control transactions that are functionally similar to merger transactions with respect to the critical question of control over the corporate enterprise. Yet, under the corporation law, a board of directors which is given the critical role of initiating and recommending a merger to the shareholders (*see* 8 *Del. C.* § 251) traditionally has been accorded no statutory role whatsoever with respect to a public tender offer for even a controlling number of shares. * * * [T]ender offers essentially represent the sale of shareholders' separate property and such sales—even when aggregated into a single change in control transaction—require no "corporate" action and do not involve distinctively "corporate" interests.

As noted, the General Assembly has imposed specific duties on the directors of corporations entering into merger agreements, 8 *Del. C.* § 251, but it has not chosen to impose comparable statutory duties on directors of companies that are targets of tender offers.[26]

In a similar vein, Fitzgerald maintains that the Siliconix board (or perhaps its Special Committee) was required by *McMullin v. Beran,* [Del. Supr., 765 A.2d 910 (2000).] to take a position on whether the Siliconix shareholders should accept the tender and inform them of that decision and the reasons for it. * * *

McMullin teaches, *inter alia,* that in the context of a merger of a subsidiary with a third party (thereby effecting a complete sale of the subsidiary) where the controlling shareholder wants the merger to occur and the minority shareholders are powerless to prevent it: (i) the directors of the subsidiary have "an affirmative duty to protect those minority shareholders' interests"; (ii) the board cannot "abdicate [its] duty by leaving it to the shareholders alone" to determine how to respond; and (iii) the board has a duty to assist the minority shareholders by ascertaining the subsidiary's value as a going concern so that the shareholders may be better able to assess the acquiring party's offer and, thus, to assist in determining whether to pursue appraisal rights.

Many of the pertinent factors in *McMullin* are similar to the Siliconix circumstances. [But] there is one large difference: *McMullin* involved a merger of the subsidiary into a third-party, a transaction for which the subsidiary board sought the approval of the minority shareholders.

* * *

When one looks at both the *McMullin* and Siliconix transactions from the perspective of the minority shareholders, their need for (and their ability to benefit from) the guidance and information to be provided by their boards in accordance with the principles of *McMullin* is virtually indistinguishable. The most likely ultimate puzzle for the minority shareholder, as noted above, is (a) take the consideration offered or (b) seek appraisal. However, this analysis must focus on the source of the duties motivating the result in *McMullin*. The Supreme Court was careful to note

26. Fitzgerald cites *Kahn v. Lynch Communication Systems, Inc.,* Del.Supr., 638 A.2d 1110 (1994) and *Kahn v. Tremont Corp.,* Del.Supr., 694 A.2d 422 (1997), in support of his contention that the structure of the transaction requires the entire fairness analysis. Both of these cases, however, involve "self-dealing" where the controlling shareholder stood on both sides of the transactions. Here, of course, Vishay stands on only one side of the tender.

throughout its opinion that the duties involved were statutory duties imposed by 8 *Del. C.* § 251 (relating to mergers) and the "attendant" fiduciary duties. * * * I conclude that *McMullin* cannot be read to require application of the entire fairness test to evaluate the proposed transaction.

To the extent that *McMullin* may be read to require the subsidiary board to guide the minority shareholders in their decision to accept or reject a tender, I note that there may exist circumstances where there is no answer to the question of whether to accept or reject. Sometimes the facts in favor of and against acceptance of the tender will balance out. On this preliminary record, I am not persuaded that the Special Committee's decision not to take a position was not reasonably supported by the information available to it. There are a number of competing factors. For example, the tender consideration, whether in reference to the frequently mentioned $34 per share or the Lehman analysis reciting a wide range of potential values, is at the low end. On the other hand, factors such as liquidity and the possibility that the Siliconix price might decline if the Vishay offer is withdrawn may be interpreted as supporting a tender. * * *

3. *Disclosure.*

A majority stockholder, in this instance, Vishay, who makes a tender to acquire the stock of the minority shareholders owes the minority shareholders a fiduciary duty to disclose accurately all material facts surrounding the tender [*Malone v. Brincat,* Del.Supr., 722 A.2d 5, 11 (1998)]. * * *

* * *

* * * I have not found that, on this preliminary record, Fitzgerald had made the necessary showing to establish any disclosure violation. * * *

4. *Coercion.*

A tender offer is coercive if the tendering shareholders are "wrongfully induced by some act of the defendant to sell their shares for reasons unrelated to the economic merits of the sale." The wrongful acts must "[influence] in some material way" the shareholder's decision to tender. [*Ivanhoe Partners v. Newmont Mining Corp.,* Del. Ch., 533 A.2d 585, 605, aff'd., Del.Supr., 535 A.2d 1334 (1987)] I now turn to the instances alleged by Fitzgerald to constitute actionable coercion.

(a) Fitzgerald contends that the timing of Vishay's actions created coercive pricing conditions in [two] ways.

First, he alleges that the transaction was timed to take advantage of Siliconix' temporarily low price. Vishay, however, did not propose the transaction at an historic low. Indeed, the price of Siliconix, as of the time of the exchange offer, had risen significantly from its then recent low in December 2000. (The stock had been as high as $144.50 in March 2000.) Given the volatility of the Siliconix stock, like many stocks in the technology sector, it is difficult to give either credit or blame to Vishay based on any timing decision. Moreover, Vishay has provided a credible explanation that it chose to pursue the balance of the minority shares because of industry conditions and its needs to achieve the benefits of consolidation with Siliconix. * * *

Although there may be circumstances where the timing of a tender could be deemed coercive because of market conditions, they are not present here.

Second, the original tender offer of February 2000, according to Fitzgerald, was intended by Vishay to keep the Siliconix price depressed. That tender offer set forth a price per share of $28.82. If it was intended as a "cap," it was unsuccessful because Siliconix traded as high as $32.67 per share on May 23, 2001. All two-step merger transactions may be said to have some effect at "capping" the price, but an announcement, such as the one Vishay made in February (and one which Vishay apparently was lawfully entitled to make), cannot be said to have a coercive effect three months later, at least without more proof than is available at this stage of the proceedings.

* * *

(b) Vishay's failure to commit absolutely to pursue the short-form merger, following a successful tender, on the same terms as the tender, Fitzgerald argues, constitutes actionable coercion. The implicit threat is said to be that the short-form merger might be consummated on less favorable terms, and, notwithstanding the protection afforded by their appraisal rights, Siliconix shareholders will be wrongfully induced to respond favorably to the tender out of fear that they might be faced with reduced consideration in the context of the short-form merger or, perhaps worse, as Vishay has disclosed as a possibility, they may find themselves for an extended period of time or even permanently as members of an even smaller minority. The question is whether Vishay's position, and its disclosure to the Siliconix shareholders, constitutes actionable coercion. This Court has considered whether the refusal to commit to a second step merger following a tender is coercive and has concluded that it is not. I see nothing in the facts of this case to persuade to deviate from this line of authority.

(c) Fitzgerald has also observed that Vishay's Registration Statement reflects Vishay's intent to delist Siliconix shares from the NASDAQ. The threat of delisting, with its potentially significant adverse impact on liquidity, was viewed by the Court in *Eisenberg v. Chicago Milwaukee Corp.* as the final factor that led to the conclusion that the tender there was coercive.

* * *

The Registration Statement * * * provides that the Siliconix "could be" de-listed if the tender is completed but the short-form merger is not carried out. The Registration Statement refers readers to another section to explain both the reasons for, and the consequences of, a potential delisting. Unlike *Eisenberg,* where the acquirer vowed to initiate the delisting, here any delisting would depend upon the success of the Vishay tender. Thus, this is not threatening or coercive but, instead, is the disclosure of a potential (and undeniably adverse) consequence to those shareholders who do not tender, if the tender is successful. By itself, or in conjunction with, the other allegedly coercive circumstances, Fitzgerald has not demonstrated that the delisting statement constitutes coercion, at least at this preliminary stage.

* * *

IV. CONCLUSION

For the foregoing reasons, an Order denying Fitzgerald's Motion for a Preliminary Injunction will be entered.

Glassman v. Unocal Exploration Corp.

Supreme Court of Delaware (en banc), 2001.
777 A.2d 242.

■ BERGER, JUSTICE.

* * *

I. Factual and Procedural Background

Unocal Corporation is an earth resources company primarily engaged in the exploration for and production of crude oil and natural gas. At the time of the merger at issue, Unocal owned approximately 96% of the stock of Unocal Exploration Corporation ("UXC"), an oil and gas company operating in and around the Gulf of Mexico. In 1991, low natural gas prices caused a drop in both companies' revenues and earnings. Unocal investigated areas of possible cost savings and decided that, by eliminating the UXC minority, it would reduce taxes and overhead expenses.

In December 1991 the boards of Unocal and UXC appointed special committees to consider a possible merger. The UXC committee consisted of three directors who, although also directors of Unocal, were not officers or employees of the parent company. The UXC committee retained financial and legal advisors and met four times before agreeing to a merger exchange ratio of .54 shares of Unocal stock for each share of UXC. Unocal and UXC announced the merger on February 24, 1992, and it was effected, pursuant to 8 *Del. C.* § 253, on May 2, 1992. The Notice of Merger and Prospectus stated the terms of the merger and advised the former UXC stockholders of their appraisal rights.

Plaintiffs filed this class action, on behalf of UXC's minority stockholders, on the day the merger was announced. They asserted, among other claims, that Unocal and its directors breached their fiduciary duties of entire fairness and full disclosure. The Court of Chancery conducted a two day trial and held that: (I) the Prospectus did not contain any material misstatements or omissions; (ii) the entire fairness standard does not control in a short-form merger; and (iii) plaintiffs' exclusive remedy in this case was appraisal. The decision of the Court of Chancery is affirmed.

II. Discussion

The short-form merger statute, as enacted in 1937, authorized a parent corporation to merge with its wholly-owned subsidiary by filing and recording a certificate evidencing the parent's ownership and its merger resolution. In 1957, the statute was expanded to include parent/subsidiary mergers where the parent company owns at least 90% of the stock of the subsidiary. The 1957 amendment also made it possible, for the first time and only in a short-form merger, to pay the minority cash for their shares, thereby eliminating their ownership interest in the company. * * *

This Court first reviewed § 253 in *Coyne v. Park & Tilford Distillers Corporation.* [Del.Supr., 154 A.2d 893 (1959)]. There, minority stockholders of the merged-out subsidiary argued that the statute could not mean what it says because Delaware law "never has permitted, and does not now permit, the payment of cash for whole shares surrendered in a merger and the consequent expulsion of a stockholder from the enterprise in which he has invested." The *Coyne* court held that § 253 plainly does permit such a result and that the statute is constitutional.

The next question presented to this Court was whether any equitable relief is available to minority stockholders who object to a short-form merger. In *Stauffer v. Standard Brands Incorporated* [Del.Supr., 187 A.2d 78 (1962)], minority stockholders sued to set aside the contested merger or, in the alternative, for damages. They alleged that the merger consideration was so grossly inadequate as to constitute constructive fraud and that Standard Brands breached its fiduciary duty to the minority by failing to set a fair price for their stock. The Court of Chancery held that appraisal was the stockholders' exclusive remedy, and dismissed the complaint. This Court affirmed, but explained that appraisal would not be the exclusive remedy in a short-form merger tainted by fraud or illegality:

> * * * No illegality or overreaching is shown. The dispute reduces to nothing but a difference of opinion as to value. Indeed it is difficult to imagine a case under the short merger statute in which there could be such actual fraud as would entitle a minority to set aside the merger. This is so because the very purpose of the statute is to provide the parent corporation with a means of eliminating the minority shareholder's interest in the enterprise. Thereafter the former stockholder has only a monetary claim. [187 A.2d at 80.]

The *Stauffer* doctrine's viability rose and fell over the next four decades. Its holding on the exclusivity of appraisal took on added significance in 1967, when the long-form merger statute—§ 251—was amended to allow cash-out mergers. In *David J. Greene & Co. v. Schenley Industries, Inc.* [Del.Ch., 281 A.2d 30 (1971)], the Court of Chancery applied *Stauffer* to a long-form cash-out merger. *Schenley* recognized that the corporate fiduciaries had to establish entire fairness, but concluded that fair value was the plaintiff's only real concern and that appraisal was an adequate remedy. * * *

In 1977, this Court started retreating from *Stauffer* (and *Schenley*). *Singer v. Magnavox Co.* [Del.Supr., 380 A.2d 969 (1977)], held that a controlling stockholder breaches its fiduciary duty if it effects a cash-out merger under § 251 for the sole purpose of eliminating the minority stockholders. The *Singer* court distinguished *Stauffer* as being a case where the only complaint was about the value of the converted shares. * * *

Singer's business purpose test was extended to short-form mergers two years later in *Roland International Corporation v. Najjar.* [Del.Supr., 407 A.2d 1032 (1979)]. * * *

After *Roland,* there was not much of *Stauffer* that safely could be considered good law. But that changed in 1983, in *Weinberger v. UOP, Inc.* [Del.Supr., 457 A.2d 701 (1983)], when the Court dropped the business purpose test, made appraisal a more adequate remedy, and said that it was "return[ing] to the well established principles of *Stauffer* . . . and *Schenley* . . . mandating a stockholder's recourse to the basic remedy of an appraisal." * * *

By referencing both *Stauffer* and *Schenley,* one might have thought that the *Weinberger* court intended appraisal to be the exclusive remedy "ordinarily" in non-fraudulent mergers where "price . . . [is] the preponderant consideration outweighing other features of the merger." In *Rabkin v. Philip A. Hunt Chemical Corp.* [Del.Supr., 498 A.2d 1099 (1985)], however, the Court dispelled that view * * * holding that * * * appraisal is the exclusive remedy only if stockholders' complaints are limited to "judgmental factors of valuation."

Rabkin, through its interpretation of *Weinberger,* effectively eliminated appraisal as the exclusive remedy for any claim alleging breach of the duty of entire fairness. But *Rabkin* involved a long-form merger, and the Court did not discuss, in that case or any others, how its refinement of *Weinberger* impacted short-form mergers. * * *

Mindful of this history, we must decide whether a minority stockholder may challenge a short-form merger by seeking equitable relief through an entire fairness claim. Under settled principles, a parent corporation and its directors undertaking a short-form merger are self-dealing fiduciaries who should be required to establish entire fairness, including fair dealing and fair price. The problem is that § 253 authorizes a summary procedure that is inconsistent with any reasonable notion of fair dealing. In a short-form merger, there is no agreement of merger negotiated by two companies; there is only a unilateral act—a decision by the parent company that its 90% owned subsidiary shall no longer exist as a separate entity. The minority stockholders receive no advance notice of the merger; their directors do not consider or approve it; and there is no vote. Those who object are given the right to obtain fair value for their shares through appraisal.

The equitable claim plainly conflicts with the statute. If a corporate fiduciary follows the truncated process authorized by § 253, it will not be able to establish the fair dealing prong of entire fairness. If, instead, the corporate fiduciary sets up negotiating committees, hires independent financial and legal experts, etc., then it will have lost the very benefit provided by the statute—a simple, fast and inexpensive process for accomplishing a merger. We resolve this conflict by giving effect the intent of the General Assembly. In order to serve its purpose, § 253 must be construed to obviate the requirement to establish entire fairness.

Thus, we again return to *Stauffer,* and hold that, absent fraud or illegality, appraisal is the exclusive remedy available to a minority stockholder who objects to a short-form merger. In doing so, we also reaffirm *Weinberger's* statements about the scope of appraisal. The determination of fair value must be based on *all* relevant factors, including damages and elements of future value, where appropriate. So, for example, if the merger was timed to take advantage of a depressed market, or a low point in the company's cyclical earnings, or to precede an anticipated positive development, the appraised value may be adjusted to account for those factors. We recognize that these are the types of issues frequently raised in entire fairness claims, and we have held that claims for unfair dealing cannot be litigated in an appraisal. But our prior holdings simply explained that equitable claims may not be engrafted onto a statutory appraisal proceeding; stockholders may not receive rescissionary relief in an appraisal. Those decisions should not be read to restrict the elements of value that properly may be considered in an appraisal.

Although fiduciaries are not required to establish entire fairness in a short-form merger, the duty of full disclosure remains, in the context of this request for stockholder action. Where the only choice for the minority stockholders is whether to accept the merger consideration or seek appraisal, they must be given all the factual information that is material to that decision. The Court of Chancery carefully considered plaintiffs' disclosure claims and applied settled law in rejecting them. We affirm this aspect of the appeal on the basis of the trial court's decision.

In re Pure Resources, Inc., Shareholders Litigation

Court of Chancery of Delaware, 2002.
808 A.2d 421.

■ STRINE, VICE CHANCELLOR.

This is the court's decision on a motion for preliminary injunction. The lead plaintiff in the case holds a large block of stock in Pure Resources, Inc., 65% of the shares of which are owned by Unocal Corporation. The lead plaintiff and its fellow plaintiffs seek to enjoin a now-pending exchange offer (the "Offer") by which Unocal hopes to acquire the rest of the shares of Pure in exchange for shares of its own stock.

The plaintiffs believe that the Offer is inadequate and is subject to entire fairness review, consistent with the rationale of Kahn v. Lynch Communication Systems, Inc. [638 A.2d 1110 (Del.1994)] and its progeny. * * *

By contrast, the defendants argue that the Offer is a non-coercive one * * *. As such, they argue that the Offer is not subject to the entire fairness standard, but to the standards set forth in cases like Solomon v. Pathe Communications Corp. [672 A.2d 35 (Del.1996)], standards which they argue have been fully met.

* * *

I

[In 2000 Unocal spun off a unit in West Texas and combined it with Titan Exploration, Inc., an oil and gas company operating in the same region. Pure Resources, Inc. resulted, with Unocal owning 65.4% of the stock. The remaining 34.6% was held by Titan's former stockholders, including its managers, who stayed on to run Pure. Jack D. Hightower, Pure's CEO, emerged holding 6.1% of Pure's stock. Pure's managers controlled between a quarter and a third of the Pure stock not owned by Unocal, giving effect to stock purchase options.

[Under a voting agreement, Unocal was to designate five members of the Pure board, Hightower was to designate two members, with the eighth member being jointly designated. At the pertinent times, Unocal's designees were (1) Chessum, Unocal's treasurer, (2) Ling, Unocal's president and chief operating officer, (3) Laughbaum, a retired Unocal executive, (4) Maxwell, a retired Unocal executive, and (5) Williamson, an outsider. Hightower's designees were himself and Staley, Pure's chief operating officer and also a large stockholder. The joint designee was Covington, a Unocal outsider who was a personal friend of Ling.

[Under a "Business Opportunities Agreement" (BOA), Pure was limited to the oil and gas exploration and production business in certain designated areas. Unocal, however, was expressly permitted to compete with Pure in its areas of operation. In addition, the Pure managers entered into "Put Agreements" with Unocal. These gave the managers—including Hightower and Staley—the right to put their Pure stock to Unocal upon the occurrence of certain triggering events—among which would be consummation of Unocal's Offer. Upon exercise, Unocal was required to pay the managers the "per share net asset value" or "NAV" of Pure, determined under a complex formula. Pure's NAV for purposes of the Put Agreement could fall below or exceed the price of a triggering transaction, but in the latter event the triggering transaction would provide the Put holders with the right to receive the higher NAV. Finally, Pure's senior managers had severance agreements that could be triggered to provide substantial payments in the event the Offer succeeded.]

II.

[Tensions and conflicts disrupted the relationship among Pure's managers and Unocal. The Pure managers wanted aggressively to expand its operations, and received successive waivers of the BOA from Unocal to permit expansion. But the tensions did not dissipate. So Hightower suggested that Unocal should either let Pure expand as much it could profitably do or buy the rest of Pure. Unocal began looking into the feasibility of acquiring Pure in the summer of 2001. Hightower complicated this inquiry by mooting an asset securitization scheme for Pure. This "Royalty Trust" would monetize the value of certain mineral rights owned by Pure by selling portions of those interests to third parties. This would generate a cash infusion that would reduce Pure's debt and potentially give it capital to expand. Discussion of the Royalty Trust put pressure on Unocal to decide whether to proceed with an acquisition offer. Hightower, simultaneous with pushing the Royalty Trust, encouraged Unocal to make an offer for the rest of Pure. Hightower suggested that Unocal proceed by way of a tender offer, because he believed that his Put rights complicated the Pure board's ability to act on a merger proposal.

[Unocal informed the Pure board of its intention to make an Exchange Offer for the remaining Pure shares on August 20, 2002. The Pure board met the next day, with Ling and Chessum recusing themselves. The Pure board voted to establish a Special Committee, comprised of Williamson and Covington (the only two outsiders), to respond. Maxwell and Laughbaum, although not on the Committee, did not recuse themselves generally from the Pure board's process of reacting to the Offer. Hightower and Staley were excluded from the Committee because the Offer would trigger their right to receive a higher price under the NAV formula in the Put Agreements.]

The precise authority of the Special Committee to act on behalf of Pure was left hazy at first, but seemed to consist solely of the power to retain independent advisors, to take a position on the offer's advisability on behalf of Pure, and to negotiate with Unocal to see if it would increase its bid. [The Committee soon retained two financial advisors (Credit Suisse First Boston, the investment bank assisting Pure with its consideration of the Royalty Trust, and Petrie Parkman & Co., Inc., a smaller firm very experienced in the energy field) and legal advisors (Baker Botts and Potter Anderson & Corroon).]

After the formation of the Special Committee, Unocal formally commenced its Offer, which had these key features:

• An exchange ratio of 0.6527 of a Unocal share for each Pure share.

• A non-waivable majority of the minority tender provision, which required a majority of shares not owned by Unocal to tender. Management of Pure, including Hightower and Staley, are considered part of the minority for purposes of this condition, not to mention Maxwell, Laughbaum, Chessum, and Ling.

• A waivable condition that a sufficient number of tenders be received to enable Unocal to own 90% of Pure and to effect a short-form merger under 8 Del.C. § 253.

• A statement by Unocal that it intends, if it obtains 90%, to consummate a short-form merger as soon as practicable at the same exchange ratio.

As of this time, this litigation had been filed and a preliminary injunction hearing was soon scheduled. Among the issues raised was the adequacy of the Special Committee's scope of authority.

Thereafter, the Special Committee sought to, in its words, "clarify" its authority. The clarity it sought was clear: the Special Committee wanted to be delegated the full authority of the board under Delaware law to respond to the Offer. * * *

What exactly happened at this point is shrouded by invocations of privilege. But this much is clear. [Chessum and Ling intervened, bringing in Unocal's in-house counsel. The Committee's proposed resolution was redrafted] to take out any ability * * * to do anything other than study the Offer, negotiate it, and make a recommendation on behalf of Pure in the required 14D–9.

The record does not illuminate exactly why the Special Committee did not make this their Alamo. * * *

At best, the record supports the inference that the Special Committee believed some of the broader options technically open to them under their preferred resolution (e.g., finding another buyer) were not practicable. As to their failure to insist on the power to deploy a poison pill—the by-now de rigeur tool of a board responding to a third-party tender offer—the record is obscure. The Special Committee's brief suggests that the Committee believed that the pill could not be deployed consistently with the Non–Dilution Agreement protecting Unocal, but nowhere indicates how Unocal's contractual right to preserve its 65% position precluded a rights plan designed solely to keep it at that level. The Special Committee also argues that the pill was unnecessary because the Committee's ability to make a negative recommendation—coupled with Hightower's and Staley's by-then apparent opposition to the Offer—were leverage and protection enough.

[The Special Committee met on a continuous basis and asked Unocal to increase the exchange ratio from 0.6527 to 0.787. Unocal refused. So the Special Committee voted not to recommend the Offer, based on its analysis and the advice of its financial advisors. It prepared a 14D–9 containing the board's recommendation not to tender into the Offer. Hightower and Staley announced their personal present intentions not to tender, intentions that if adhered to would make it nearly impossible for Unocal to obtain 90% of Pure's shares in the Offer.]

During the discovery process, a representative of the lead plaintiff, which is an investment fund, testified that he did not feel coerced by the Offer. The discovery record also reveals that a great deal of the Pure stock held by the public is in the hands of institutional investors.

III. The Plaintiffs' Demand For A Preliminary Injunction

* * * When a transaction to buy out the minority is proposed, is it more important to the development of strong capital markets to hold controlling stockholders and target boards to very strict (and litigation-intensive) standards of fiduciary conduct? Or is more stockholder wealth generated if less rigorous protections are adopted, which permit acquisitions to proceed so long as the majority has not misled or strong-armed the minority? Is such flexibility in fact beneficial to minority stockholders because it encourages liquidity-generating tender offers to them and provides incentives for acquirers to pay hefty premiums to buy control, knowing that control will be accompanied by legal rules that permit a later "going private" transaction to occur in a relatively non-litigious manner?

At present, the Delaware case law has two strands of authority that answer these questions differently. In one strand, which deals with situations in which controlling stockholders negotiate a merger agreement with the target board to buy out the minority, our decisional law emphasizes the protection of minority stockholders against unfairness. In the other strand, which deals with situations when a controlling stockholder seeks to acquire the rest of the company's shares through a tender offer followed by a short-form merger under 8 Del.C. § 253, Delaware case precedent facilitates the free flow of capital between willing buyers and willing sellers of shares, so long as the consent of the sellers is not procured by inadequate or misleading information or by wrongful compulsion.

These strands appear to treat economically similar transactions as categorically different simply because the method by which the controlling stockholder proceeds varies. This disparity in treatment persists even though the two basic methods (negotiated merger versus tender offer/short-form merger) pose similar threats to minority stockholders. Indeed, it can be argued that the distinction in approach subjects the transaction that is more protective of minority stockholders when implemented with appropriate protective devices—a merger negotiated by an independent committee with the power to say no and conditioned on a majority of the minority vote—to more stringent review than the more dangerous form of a going private deal—an unnegotiated tender offer made by a majority stockholder. The latter transaction is arguably less protective than a merger of the kind described, because the majority stockholder-offeror has access to inside information, and the offer requires disaggregated stockholders to decide whether to tender quickly, pressured by the risk of being squeezed out in a short-form merger at a different price later or being left as part of a much smaller public minority. This disparity creates a possible incoherence in our law.

 * * *

 * * * I remain less than satisfied that there is a justifiable basis for the distinction between the Lynch and Solomon lines of cases. Instead, their disparate teachings reflect a difference in policy emphasis that is far greater than can be explained by the technical differences between tender offers and negotiated mergers, especially given Delaware's director-centered approach to tender offers made by third-parties, which emphasizes the vulnerability of disaggregated stockholders absent important help and protection from their directors.

 * * *

The absence of convincing reasons for this disparity in treatment inspires the plaintiffs to urge me to apply the entire fairness standard of review to Unocal's offer. Otherwise, they say, the important protections set forth in the Lynch line of cases will be rendered useless, as all controlling stockholders will simply choose to proceed to make subsidiary acquisitions by way of a tender offer and later short-form merger.

I admit being troubled by the imbalance in Delaware law exposed by the Solomon/Lynch lines of cases. Under Solomon, the policy emphasis is on the right of willing buyers and sellers of stock to deal with each other freely, with only such judicial intervention as is necessary to ensure fair disclosure and to prevent structural coercion. The advantage of this emphasis is that it provides a relatively non-litigious way to effect going private transactions and relies upon minority stockholders to protect themselves. The cost of this approach is that it arguably exposes minority stockholders to the more subtle form of coercion that Lynch addresses and leaves them without adequate redress for unfairly timed and priced offers. The approach also minimizes the potential for the minority to get the best price, by arguably giving them only enough protection to keep them from being structurally coerced into accepting grossly insufficient bids but not necessarily merely inadequate ones.

Admittedly, the Solomon policy choice would be less disquieting if Delaware also took the same approach to third-party offers and thereby allowed diversified investors the same degree of unrestrained access to premium bids by third-parties. In its brief, Unocal makes a brave effort to explain why it is understandable that Delaware law emphasizes the rights of minority stockholders to freely receive structurally, non-coercive tender offers from controlling stockholders but not their right to accept identically structured offers from third parties. Although there may be subtle ways to explain this variance, a forest-eye summary by a stockholder advocate might run as follows: As a general matter, Delaware law permits directors substantial leeway to block the access of stockholders to receive substantial premium tender offers made by third-parties by use of the poison pill but provides relatively free access to minority stockholders to accept buy-out offers from controlling stockholders.

In the case of third-party offers, these advocates would note, there is arguably less need to protect stockholders indefinitely from structurally non-coercive bids because alternative buyers can emerge and because the target board can use the poison pill to buy time and to tell its story. By contrast, when a controlling stockholder makes a tender offer, the subsidiary board is unlikely—as this case demonstrates—to be permitted by the controlling stockholder to employ a poison pill to fend off the bid and exert pressure for a price increase and usually lacks any real clout to develop an alternative transaction. In the end, however, I do not believe that these discrepancies should lead to an expansion of the Lynch standard to controlling stockholder tender offers.

Instead, the preferable policy choice is to continue to adhere to the more flexible and less constraining Solomon approach, while giving some greater recognition to the inherent coercion and structural bias concerns that motivate the Lynch line of cases. Adherence to the Solomon rubric as a general matter, moreover, is advisable in view of the increased activism of institutional investors and the greater information flows available to them. Investors have demonstrated themselves capable of resisting tender offers made by controlling stockholders on occasion, and even the lead plaintiff here expresses no fear of retribution. This does not mean that controlling stockholder tender offers do not pose risks to minority stockholders; it is only to acknowledge that the corporate law should not be designed on the assumption that diversified investors are infirm but instead should give great deference to transactions approved by them voluntarily and knowledgeably.

To the extent that my decision to adhere to Solomon causes some discordance between the treatment of similar transactions to persist, that lack of harmony is better addressed in the Lynch line, by affording greater liability-immunizing effect to protective devices such as majority of minority approval conditions and special committee negotiation and approval.

* * *

To be more specific about the application of Solomon in these circumstances, it is important to note that the Solomon line of cases does not eliminate the fiduciary duties of controlling stockholders or target boards in connection with tender offers made by controlling stockholders. Rather, the question is the contextual extent and nature of those duties, a question I will now tentatively, and incompletely, answer.

The potential for coercion and unfairness posed by controlling stockholders who seek to acquire the balance of the company's shares by acquisition requires some equitable reinforcement, in order to give proper effect to the concerns undergirding Lynch. In order to address the prisoner's dilemma problem, our law should consider an acquisition tender offer by a controlling stockholder non-coercive only when: 1) it is subject to a non-waivable majority of the minority tender condition; 2) the controlling stockholder promises to consummate a prompt § 253 merger at the same price if it obtains more than 90% of the shares; and 3) the controlling stockholder has made no retributive threats. Those protections—also stressed in this court's recent Aquila decision—minimize the distorting influence of the tendering process on voluntary choice. They also recognize the adverse conditions that confront stockholders who find themselves owning what have become very thinly traded shares. These conditions also provide a partial cure to the disaggregation problem, by providing a realistic non-tendering goal the minority can achieve to prevent the offer from proceeding altogether.

When a tender offer is non-coercive in the sense I have identified and the independent directors of the target are permitted to make an informed recommendation and provide fair disclosure, the law should be chary about superimposing the full fiduciary requirement of entire fairness upon the statutory tender offer process. Here, the plaintiffs argue that the Pure board breached its fiduciary duties by not giving the Special Committee the power to block the Offer by, among other means, deploying a poison pill. Indeed, the plaintiffs argue that the full board's decision not to grant that authority is subject to the entire fairness standard of review because a majority of the full board was not independent of Unocal.

That argument has some analytical and normative appeal, embodying as it does the rough fairness of the goose and gander rule. I am reluctant, however, to burden the common law of corporations with a new rule that would tend to compel the use of a device that our statutory law only obliquely sanctions and that in other contexts is subject to misuse, especially when used to block a high value bid that is not structurally coercive. When a controlling stockholder makes a tender offer that is not coercive in the sense I have articulated, therefore, the better rule is that there is no duty on its part to permit the target board to block the bid through use of the pill. Nor is there any duty on the part of the independent directors to seek blocking power. But it is important to be mindful of one of the reasons that make a contrary rule problematic—the awkwardness of a legal rule requiring a board to take aggressive action against a structurally non-coercive offer by the controlling stockholder that elects it. This recognition of the sociology of controlled subsidiaries puts a point on the increased vulnerability that stockholders face from controlling stockholder tenders, because the minority stockholders are denied the full range of protection offered by boards in response to third party offers. This factor illustrates the utility of the protective conditions that I have identified as necessary to prevent abuse of the minority.

* * *

Turning specifically to Unocal's Offer, I conclude that the application of these principles yields the following result. The Offer, in its present form, is coercive because it includes within the definition of the "minority" those stockholders who are affiliated with Unocal as directors and officers. It also includes the management of Pure, whose incentives are skewed by their employment, their severance agreements, and their Put Agreements. This is, of course, a problem that can be cured if Unocal amends the Offer to condition it on approval of a majority of Pure's unaffiliated stockholders. Requiring the minority to be defined exclusive of stockholders whose independence from the controlling stockholder is compromised is the better legal rule (and result). Too often, it will be the case that officers and directors of controlled subsidiaries have voting incentives that are not perfectly aligned with their economic interest in their stock and who are more than acceptably susceptible to influence from controlling stockholders. Aside, however, from this glitch in the majority of the minority condition, I conclude that Unocal's Offer satisfies the other requirements of "non-coerciveness." Its promise to consummate a prompt § 253 merger is sufficiently specific, and Unocal has made no retributive threats.

Although Unocal's Offer does not altogether comport with the above-described definition of non-coercive, it does not follow that I believe that the plaintiffs have established a probability of success on the merits as to their claim that the Pure board should have blocked that Offer with a pill or other measures. Putting aside the shroud of silence that cloaked the board's (mostly, it seems, behind the scenes) deliberations, there appears to have been at least a rational basis to believe that a pill was not necessary to protect the Pure minority against coercion, largely, because Pure's management had expressed adamant opposition to the Offer. Moreover, the board allowed the Special Committee a free hand: to recommend against the Offer—as it did; to negotiate for a higher price—as it attempted to do; and to prepare the company's 14D–9—as it did.

For all these reasons, therefore, I find that the plaintiffs do not have a probability of success on the merits of their attack on the Offer, with the exception that the majority of the minority condition is flawed.

[The Court went on to rule that the Offer must be preliminarily enjoined because material information relevant to the Pure stockholders' decision-making process had not been fairly disclosed.]

Subramanian, Fixing Freezeouts

115 Yale L.J., 31–45 (2005).

II. THE PROBLEM WITH EXISTING DOCTRINE

A. Opportunistic Behavior in Tender Offer Freezeouts

2. Categories of Opportunistic Behavior

The ability to freeze out the minority at some increment over the market price in a tender offer freezeout, as opposed to "fair value" in a merger freezeout, introduces the possibility of opportunistic behavior by the controller. I now describe the two basic ways in which opportunistic behavior can manifest itself.

a. Freezeout Timing

First, the controller determines the timing of a freezeout. This means that a controller can freeze out the minority when it perceives that the market price of the target stock is lower than its intrinsic value. Although insider trading restrictions prevent the most egregious forms of this kind of opportunism, the controller may be able to take advantage of smaller pieces of nonpublic information, which individually do not meet the test for materiality, but collectively give the controller greater insight than the public minority shareholders about the intrinsic value of the company.

This kind of opportunism is not possible in a merger freezeout because the court will engage in, and the [Special Committee (SC)] will bargain in the shadow of, a de novo examination of fair value. This background legal entitlement works to detach the offer price from the market price, because in entire fairness proceedings courts give little evidentiary weight to prevailing market prices. Because the controller will have little or no informational advantage over the SC, it is unable to exploit differences between market price and intrinsic value in merger-freezeout negotiations.

b. Influencing the Target's Value

A second way in which a controller might engage in an opportunistic tender offer freezeout is by influencing the value of the target, thereby altering the target's market price and, in turn, the baseline for the tender-offer-freezeout price. John Coates summarizes the three categories of this kind of behavior: underinvestment in positive net present value (NPV) projects; investment in negative NPV projects; and shirking managerial responsibilities. [John C. Coates IV, "Fair Value" as an Avoidable Rule of Corporate Law: Minority Discounts in Conflict Transactions, 147 U. Pa. L. Rev. 1251, 1316 (1999).] Each of these three categories can be further divided into reversible value reductions and nonreversible value reductions.

Value reductions that are fully reversible are difficult to come by in the real world, but are theoretically possible. Consider the case of a one-time positive NPV project, for which the only question is whether to implement the project before or after the freezeout. If the project is not completely transparent to the marketplace, a controller might rationally delay this investment until after the freezeout, in order to reap the full benefit rather than sharing the benefit with the minority. This value diversion would be difficult to detect, and, even if detected, would likely be protected by the business judgment rule, particularly if there were some plausible basis for the delay (e.g., reduced risk due to the delay).

As demonstrated by the example in the previous Subsection, this opportunistic behavior would not be possible in a merger freezeout because the opportunity presented by the positive NPV project would likely be known to the SC and to the court. It is the information asymmetry between the controller and the minority shareholders, as compared to the relative symmetry between the controller and the SC, that facilitates the controller's opportunistic behavior in a tender offer freezeout.

In contrast to the one-time positive NPV project, most value reductions are at least partially nonreversible. Take the example of managerial shirking, which reduces firm value in ways that cannot be fully recovered after the freezeout if certain corporate opportunities are time-limited. When the value reduction cannot be reversed fully, the controller's incentives are less clear, because the reduction will hurt the controller in proportion to its pre-deal stake in the target. But even with respect to these types of value reductions, it is easy to identify situations in which it is still in the controller's interest to deliberately reduce firm value pre-freezeout, provided the value reduction is at least partially reversible after the freezeout. In any particular case the controller would compare its share of the nonreversible value reduction (which is proportional to the controller's pre-freezeout stake) against the benefit that arises from a lower tender offer price.

   3.   Efficiency Implications

   * * * [One] could argue that the controller's opportunistic behavior will also be priced in the minority's initial stake. That is, minority investors will understand not only the lower price that they will receive in a freezeout under the tender offer mechanism, but also the controller's enhanced ability to exploit asymmetric information to its benefit. Over time, both of these effects will be fully priced ex ante, eliminating any unfairness to the minority and maintaining allocational efficiency.

Despite the superficial appeal of this argument, the possibility for opportunistic behavior does, in fact, yield three types of efficiency losses: through nonreversible value reductions, the facilitation of some value-reducing freezeouts, and reduced access to minority capital. I now discuss each of these effects in turn.

   a.   Nonreversible Value Reductions

   The first, most obvious, social welfare loss arises from nonreversible value reductions. * * *

   b.   Facilitating Some Inefficient Freezeouts

   A second social welfare loss arises from the possibility of buying the minority shares at less than their intrinsic value. In many cases, the gap between intrinsic value and market value might be bridged by the premium over market that the controller must pay in order to succeed in a tender offer freezeout. The empirical evidence in my companion paper indicates that, on average, premiums in post-Siliconix tender offer freezeouts are approximately 25% higher than the preannouncement market price of the target stock. While this kind of gap between intrinsic value and market value would be rare (though not implausible) in well-functioning capital markets, the controller's ability to influence the market price makes a gap of this magnitude more likely in the controlled company context.

To the extent the controller is able to buy the minority shares for less than their intrinsic value, the controller would be able to make a profit on a value-destroying (negative synergy) freezeout. To see this point, consider a company that has a higher intrinsic value as a public company than as a private company—for example, from the ability to attract managers with publicly traded stock options, the benefit of having an acquisition currency, or the advantage of analyst coverage. The controller might nevertheless decide to take the company private through a tender offer freezeout if it has the opportunity to buy the minority shares for less than their intrinsic value. The gains from the tender offer would subsidize the negative consequences of going private, even though overall social welfare is higher if the company remains publicly traded. In these cases the tender-offer-freezeout mechanism might facilitate some value-destroying (inefficient) transactions.

c.   Reduced Access to Minority Capital

The third, more subtle, social welfare loss that arises from tender offer freezeouts arises from the "lemons effect" in corporate freezeouts, first identified and described in detail by Lucian Bebchuk and Marcel Kahan. [See Lucian Arye Bebchuk & Marcel Kahan, Adverse Selection and Gains to Controllers in Corporate Freezeouts, in Concentrated Corporate Owner-ship 247 (Randall K. Morck ed., 2000).] If, as described above, the controller will freeze out the minority when the market price is lower than the intrinsic value, then minority shareholders should (rationally) receive an important signal when the controller does not freeze them out—namely, that the market price fully values or perhaps overvalues the company. Through backward induction, the minority shareholders should rationally bid down the value of the stock. In the extreme form of the Bebchuk and Kahan model, the market price of the minority shares is bid down to zero because of the negative signal that the lack of a freezeout conveys.

* * *

Of course, several real-world factors might limit the manifestation of the lemons problem. For example, while the theoretical models assume that the controlling shareholder can unilaterally freeze out the minority, in the real world minority shareholders may say no through their tender decision. If a sufficient percentage of minority shareholders refuse to tender, the controller will be unable to get to the 90% threshold that allows a short-form merger. Minority shareholders might refuse to tender even if the offer is at a substantial premium if they infer good news from the controller's tender offer itself. Similarly, if the controller only makes a tender offer when the inherent value of the firm is higher than the market value, then minority shareholders, knowing this fact ex ante, should refuse to tender in order to share in the upside that the controller signals by making a tender offer.

Other constraints are also possible. A controlling shareholder might not freeze out the minority even if the inherent value is greater than the market value if the controller has capital constraints. (Indeed, capital constraints may have caused the controller to issue the minority stake in the first place.) The absence of a freezeout by a capital-constrained controller should convey no signal to the minority, thereby preventing the adverse inference which would trigger the lemons effect. * * *

These checks are likely to prevent the extreme manifestation of the lemons effect, in which minority shares are worthless. But to the extent that the lemons effect depresses the price of minority shares, pre-IPO owners would have to sell a greater fraction of the company in order to raise the same dollar value of public capital. The increase in dilution may deter some entrepreneurs from selling a public stake, even when it would be socially desirable for the entrepreneur to do so. * * *

    * * *

B. Deterring Efficient Freezeouts Through the Merger Mechanism

In the previous Section, I demonstrated how existing doctrine encourages some inefficient tender offer freezeouts. I now discuss ways in which existing doctrine also discourages some efficient merger freezeouts. * * *

1. The Problem of Special Committee Resistance

a. With Special Committee Veto Power

* * * [T]he post-Lynch world of freezeout merger negotiations seems to require SC veto power over the transaction. To the extent that there is ambiguity about this point (discussed in the next Subsection), many controllers explicitly bestow veto power on the SC in a merger freezeout. My empirical evidence indicates that SCs have made frequent use of this veto power. In my database of all post-Siliconix freezeouts, I find that the controller withdrew in eighteen out of the eighty freezeout merger negotiations with an SC that were announced between June 2001 and April 2005, a 23% failure rate, even though the controller's first offer invariably represented a premium over the prevailing market price.

    * * *

As practitioners become more comfortable with the tender-offer-freezeout mechanism, merger freezeouts may increasingly be negotiated in the shadow of a tender-offer-freezeout threat. In a curious twist of Delaware corporate law, the controller would be subject to entire fairness review, with no burden shift, if the controller threatens a tender offer, and the SC agrees to a merger deal on the basis of the threat. But if the controller simply breaks off negotiations, a subsequent (even immediate) tender offer to the minority would seem to avoid entire fairness review. In view of these twists, a well-advised controller will engage in a kabuki dance of making a final offer, and perhaps hinting at its walk-away alternative, but not threatening the SC in a manner that would eliminate the SC's ability to say no under Lynch.

    * * *

In a regime in which the tender offer option is well understood, therefore, prices in merger freezeouts will be driven down to the predicted prices in tender offer freezeouts. * * *

2. The Problem of Deterred Deals

While the problem of blocked deals involves efficient freezeouts that are initiated by the controller but are not consummated, the problem of deterred deals involves efficient freezeouts that are never initiated. I discuss two deterrent effects: the fact that SCs in the current regime are likely to extract some part of the synergies in freezeout mergers that occur; and the possibility that entire fairness litigation acts as a "tax" on the controller's freezeout decision.

a. Through Allocation of Deal Synergies

I begin with the assumption that the likelihood that a controller will initiate a freezeout increases monotonically with the controller's expected profits from the deal. It follows that the controller should receive the full value of the synergies from the deal, in order to maximize the likelihood that controllers will initiate value-creating freezeouts. The question then becomes whether and to what extent the merger-freezeout process provides the controller with the full value of the synergies from the deal.

The overall picture on this question is that courts have been notoriously unpredictable in their approach to synergy value in entire fairness proceedings. As a starting point, courts in entire fairness proceedings generally look to the appraisal remedy, and here section 262(h) of the Delaware corporate code mandates that "fair value" in appraisal shall be determined "exclusive of any element of value arising from the accomplishment . . . of the merger." Although this language on its face would seem to exclude synergy value, Delaware courts have muddied the water considerably. Weinberger began the confusion with its holding that section 262(h) only excludes "speculative elements of value that may arise from the 'accomplishment or expectation' of the merger." While subsequent chancery court opinions have read Weinberger narrowly in order to exclude synergy value from the minority's entitlement, on the one occasion that the Delaware Supreme Court revisited Weinberger's reading of section 262(h) it confirmed its earlier holding.

In addition, there is a more subtle way in which courts might arrive at a share of the synergies. In contrast to valuation in an appraisal proceeding, courts are not bound by the statutory language of section 262(h) in an entire fairness proceeding. In particular, a court may determine that fairness requires rescissory damages, defined as what minority shareholders would receive if the freezeout transaction were rescinded. If the synergies from the deal do not depend on taking the company from public to private status, then a rescissory damages approach would provide minority shareholders with a share of the synergies from the deal.

Using either Weinberger's interpretation of section 262(h) or the flexibility inherent in an equitable remedy, then, courts have the authority to award a share of the synergies in an entire fairness proceeding. As a result, SCs bargaining in the shadow of entire fairness will be able to extract a share of the synergies as well. Reducing the controller's expected profits from the freezeout in this way deters some value-increasing freeze-outs, under the assumption that the likelihood of freezeout increases monotonically with the controller's profits from the deal.

b. Through Litigation Costs

A second factor that might deter some deals is the high likelihood of litigation costs that arises from merger-freezeout doctrine. The availability of a class action claim for entire fairness, combined with a presumption that the first to file should be named lead or co-lead counsel, creates a "race to the courthouse" in which plaintiffs' counsel will typically file multiple lawsuits in the few days (and even hours) after the freezeout merger is announced. This litigation activity imposes costs on the controlling shareholder because the controller will typically agree, in effect, to pay plaintiffs' legal fees as part of its settlement. These litigation costs do not create an ex post social welfare loss, because they merely represent a wealth transfer from the controller to plaintiffs' counsel. Rather, a social welfare loss might arise because a controller may be deterred ex ante from initiating an efficient transaction by the expected "tax" imposed by plaintiffs' counsel.

The empirical evidence indicates that this tax represents a trivial fraction of the overall value of transactions: One study of shareholder class actions in Delaware finds a fee range of 0.005% to 1.36% of the deal value, with an average fee of 0.19%. By way of comparison, the tax imposed by investment bankers, lawyers, and accountants in arms-length acquisitions is typically in the range of 1.0% to 2.0% of deal value. Therefore, while expected litigation costs might deter merger freezeouts in theory, the magnitude of the litigation costs as a percentage of deal value suggests that such deterrence, if any, should be small in practice.

NOTE: THE *SILICONIX* CASES

Many predicted that *Siliconix* would trigger an across-the-board shift in the mode of conducting freezeouts from the § 251 merger to tender offers followed by § 253 mergers. Subramanian, Post–Siliconix Freeze–Outs: Theory and Evidence, 36 J. Legal Stud. 1 (2007), shows that, while there has been a shift, it has not been as marked as predicted. Subramanian collects data from all Delaware freeze-outs executed in the 4 years after *Siliconix* was decided, a total of 76 cases. He shows that the shift in the law has had an impact but that mergers still dominate: the split between mergers and tender offers is 67 percent to 33 percent. This compares to the an 87 percent 13 percent split in the pre-*Siliconix* period, 1996 to 2001.

Special Committees were established in 49 out of the 51 merger cases and in 23 out of the 25 tender offer cases. In the merger cases, the bargaining between the committee and the controlling stockholder reached impasse in 27 percent of the cases. Tender offers proved more likely to reach consummation than did mergers–84 percent of the tender offers were completed while 75 percent of the mergers closed–but the difference was not statistically significant.

All of the tender offerors held out the same consideration in the projected follow up merger under § 253. The average rate of tender among the minority shareholders was 71 percent, but the range of results was wide–from 30 percent at the low end to 93 percent at the high end.

Subramanian's statistical analysis shows that the minority stockholders receive lower cumulative returns in tender offer cases than in merger cases: "This difference is statistically and economically meaningful and is consistent with New York City practitioner views that controlling shareholders have more bargaining power against SCs in tender-offer freeze-outs than in merger freeze-outs." Id. at 24.

Subramanian, Fixing Freeze–Outs, supra, also discusses doctrinal implications of these results. He concludes that the law would be more effective in filtering good deals from bad deals if the procedural bar was raised–"meaningful" special committee approval and approval of a majority of minority shareholders should be required, as opposed to the either/or regime under current Delaware law. But, where the process requirements are satisfied, review should proceed under the business judgment rule.

Gilson and Gordon, Controlling Controlling Shareholders, 152 U. Pa. L. Rev. 785 (2003), which would put the emphasis on a special committee endowed with veto power and overrule *Kahn v. Lynch I*, id. at 838–39:

" * * * We find the choice between a reconsideration of *Kahn I* and a reconsideration of the extension of *Solomon* to freeze-outs a close question. In the end, the weight of the considerations on both sides leads us to prefer a hybrid approach that involves reconsideration of both *Kahn I* and *Solomon*. We share the *Pure* court's conclusion that a fully empowered special committee, including the Pure anticoercion litany and the right to say 'no,' affords sufficient process so that entire fairness review in a freeze-out merger can be eliminated. Where independent directors have the power to block a freeze-out merger, but do not, it is fair to assume that the process sufficiently tracks an arm's-length negotiation which fairly relegates shareholders to their appraisal remedy. To this extent, we favor revisiting *Kahn I*.

"But what if the special committee rejects the proposed freeze-out merger and the controlling shareholder goes over the committee's head as in *Siliconix*? Here, the chancery court's extension of *Solomon* to freeze-out tender offers also should be reconsidered. If the controlling shareholder seeks to override the special committee's veto, the process no longer matches an arm's-length transaction—the minority shareholders lose the protection of their bargaining agent, and unlike in a hostile tender offer, the protection of the market for corporate control is not available. Under these circumstances, the transaction remains a *Sinclair*-like interested transaction, and entire fairness protection (here meaning 'fair price') is appropriate—an outcome consistent with the symmetric controls governing the extraction of private benefits by controlling shareholders. One particular advantage of this hybrid approach is that it strengthens the bargaining position of the special committee by giving its 'say "no"' power more bite. As the special committee's 'threat point' shifts from statutory appraisal to class-based appraisal, the conditions of arm's-length bargaining are more nearly replicated. This outcome should appeal to the concerns that animate both the *Kahn I* and *Pure* courts."

For a more favorable view of the *Siliconix* cases, see Pritchard, Tender Offers by Controlling Shareholders: The Specter of Coercion and Fair Price, Berkeley Bus. L. J. 83 (2004)(arguing that market pricing will remove any inequity after a one-time wealth transfer from minority to majority shareholders).

(3) Appraisal Exclusivity

Glassman appears once and for all to settle in Delaware the question whether appraisal should be the exclusive remedy for a minority shareholder objecting to a *short form* merger. Does it follow that the mere existence of the appraisal remedy precludes a challenge to enjoin consummation of a *long form* merger between parent and subsidiary (as well as between strangers) on grounds of illegality, unlawfulness, overreaching or fraud (i.e., deception or failure to make adequate disclosure) or otherwise? *Weinberger* and *Rabkin* show Delaware's ambiguous response to this question.

In many other states the judicial allusion to the exclusivity of the appraisal remedy as the mechanism for vindicating a dissenter's rights in a merger often suggests an exception for cases of outright fraud or deception, as well as for cases of "unlawfulness" or "illegality." See e.g., Coggins v. New England Patriots Football Club, Inc., supra. See also Popp Telcom v. American Sharecom, Inc., 210 F.3d 928 (8th Cir.2000)(permitting a fraud action to proceed subsequent to an appraisal); Abbey v. E.W. Scripps Co., 1995 WL 478957 (Del.Ch.)(Allen, Ch.)(applying Ohio law and confirming fraud exception but suggesting that exception covers only a case in which the value of the stock does not fully compensate for the loss caused by the fraud); Stepak v. Schey, 51 Ohio St.3d 8, 553 N.E.2d 1072 (1990) (fraud exception confirmed, but allegation that lock-up action prevented auction "is essentially a complaint regarding the price" making appraisal exclusive remedy); Stringer v. Car Data Systems, Inc., 314 Or. 576, 841 P.2d 1183 (1992); Walter J. Schloss Associates v. Chesapeake & Ohio Ry., 73 Md.App. 727, 536 A.2d 147 (1988); Pritchard v. Mead, 155 Wis.2d 431, 455 N.W.2d 263 (App.1990); Dowling v. Narragansett Capital Corp., 735 F.Supp. 1105 (D.R.I.1990); Columbus Mills, Inc. v. Kahn, 259 Ga. 80, 377 S.E.2d 153 (1989); IRA for Benefit of Oppenheimer v. Brenner Companies Inc., 107 N.C.App. 16, 419 S.E.2d 354 (1992); Yeager v. Paul Semonin Co., 691 S.W.2d 227 (Ky.App.1985); Mullen v. Academy Life Insurance Co., 705 F.2d 971 (8th Cir.1983) (dealing with New Jersey law); Perl v. IU International Corp., 61 Haw. 622, 607 P.2d 1036 (1980).

In New York, the uncertainty is reflected in the Legislative Finding for 1982 Amendment of section 623 of the merger law:

"The principle that the right of appraisal, if duly consummated in accordance with the statutes, is the exclusive right of the shareholder * * * has been codified, subject to the well recognized exception that this principle does not apply where the statutory procedures for appraisal are disregarded (Matter of Drosnes, 187 App.Div. 425, 175 N.Y.S. 628 (1st Dep't. 1919)), or where the transaction involved fraud or overreaching (see, Eisenberg v. Central Zone Property Corp., 306 N.Y. 58, 115 N.E.2d 652 (1953))." In 1984 the New York Court of Appeals (Walter J. Schlors Associates v. Arkwin Industries, 61 N.Y.2d 700, 460 N.E.2d 1090 (1984)) implied that although § 623(K) is effective to preclude an action for damages by a complaining shareholder, it does not preclude a shareholder who alleges grounds for which a court of equity would recognize a cause of action (e.g. fraud or breach of fiduciary duty) and makes a "primary request for equitable relief."

Similar ambiguity shows up in the statements of the drafters of the Model Act, in the explanation of the Committee on Corporate Laws of the

ABA Section on Corporation Banking and Business Law for making the remedy exclusive in § 80(d) which is embodied in § 13.02 of RMBCA as modified in the following Comment to § 13.02(b):

"* * * Section 13.02(b) basically adopts the New York formula as to exclusivity of the dissenters' remedy of this chapter. The remedy is the exclusive remedy unless the transaction is 'unlawful' or 'fraudulent.' The theory underlying this section is as follows: when a majority of shareholders has approved a corporate change, the corporation should be permitted to proceed even if a minority considers the change unwise or disadvantageous, and persuades a court that this is correct. Since dissenting shareholders can obtain the fair value of their shares, they are protected from pecuniary loss. Thus in general terms an exclusivity principle is justified. But the prospect that shareholders may be 'paid off' does not justify the corporation in proceeding unlawfully or fraudulently. If the corporation attempts an action in violation of the corporation law on voting, in violation of clauses in articles of incorporation prohibiting it, by deception of shareholders, or in violation of a fiduciary duty—to take some common examples—the court's freedom to intervene should be unaffected by the presence or absence of dissenters' rights under this chapter. Because of the variety of situations in which unlawfulness and fraud may appear, this section makes no attempt to specify particular illustrations. Rather, it is designed to recognize and preserve the principles that have developed in the case law of Delaware, New York and other states with regard to the effect of dissenters' rights on other remedies of dissident shareholders. See Weinberger v. UOP, Inc. * * *. See also Vorenberg, 'Exclusiveness of the Dissenting Stockholders' Appraisal Right,' 77 Harv.L.Rev. 1189 (1964)."

California takes a somewhat different approach. Section 1312 of the California General Corporation Law provides:

"(a) No shareholder of a corporation who has a right under this chapter to demand payment of cash for the shares held by the shareholder shall have any right at law or in equity to attack the validity of the reorganization or short-form merger, or to have the reorganization or short-form merger set aside or rescinded, except in an action to test whether the number of shares required to authorize or approve the reorganization have been legally voted in favor thereof; but any holder of shares of a class whose terms and provisions specifically set forth the amount to be paid in respect to them in the event of a reorganization or short-form merger is entitled to payment in accordance with those terms and provisions * * *.

"(b) If one of the parties to a reorganization or short-form merger is directly or indirectly controlled by, or under common control with, another party to the reorganization or short-form merger, subdivision (a) shall not apply to any shareholder of such party who has not demanded payment of cash for such shareholder's shares pursuant to this chapter; but if the shareholder institutes any action to attack the validity of the reorganization or short-form merger or to have the reorganization or short-form merger set aside or rescinded, the shareholder shall not thereafter have any right to demand payment of cash for the shareholder's shares pursuant to this chapter. The court in any action attacking the validity of the reorganization or short-form merger or to have the reorganization or short-form merger set aside or rescinded shall not restrain or enjoin the consummation of the transaction except upon 10–days prior notice to the corporation and upon a determination by the court that clearly no other remedy will adequately protect the complaining shareholder or the class of shareholders of which such shareholder is a member.

"(c) If one of the parties to a reorganization or short-form merger is directly or indirectly controlled by, or under common control with, another party to the reorganization or short-form merger, in any action to attack the validity of the reorganization or short-form merger or to have the reorganization or short-form merger set aside or rescinded, (1) a party to a reorganization or short-form merger which controls another party to the reorganization or short-form merger shall have the burden of proving that the transaction is just and reasonable as to the shareholders of the controlled party, and (2) a person who controls two or more parties to a reorganization shall have the burden of proving that the transaction is just and reasonable as to the shareholders of any party so controlled."

See Small, Corporate Combinations Under the New California General Corporation Law, 23 U.C.L.A.L.Rev. 1190, 1217 et seq. (1976); Buxbaum, The Dissenters' Appraisal Remedy, 23 U.C.L.A.L.Rev. 1229, 1244–1247 (1976).

The California Supreme Court reads the exclusivity provision broadly to preclude collateral challenges to the validity of arm's-length mergers, including post-merger suits seeking only damages because those controlling the absorbed company violated fiduciary duties (e.g. by accepting side payments) and because of fraud in the merger. The court suggests that the damages claim and the controllers' misconduct may (must?) be considered in the appraisal proceeding in determining the fair value to which the claimant is entitled. Steinberg v. Amplica, Inc., 42 Cal.3d 1198, 233 Cal.Rptr. 249, 729 P.2d 683 (1986). See also Sturgeon Petroleums, Ltd. v. Merchants Petroleum Co., 147 Cal.App.3d 134, 195 Cal.Rptr. 29 (1983).

Even where appraisal is said not to be the exclusive remedy, there remains the question whether its availability does, or should, affect the nature of the judicial assessment of the fairness of the merger. See also Bove v. Community Hotel Corp., supra Part III.A. Does the change in the concept of, and in the modes of determining, fair value in appraisal proceedings expressed in the *Weinberger* case, in the RMBCA and in the New York Business Corporation Law suggest that appraisal is an adequate substitute for other remedies and should remain exclusive? Or are there, and should there be, restrictions by way of "fairness" requirements on the terms which insiders can impose on the outside or public stockholders in a merger and remedies, *in addition to appraisal,* available to public stockholders to enforce those restrictions? Brudney and Chirelstein, Fair Shares in Mergers and Take–Overs, 88 Harv.L.Rev. 297, 304–307 (1974), respond as follows:

"In answering * * * [those questions], it is important to remember that the object of appraisal is to give dissident stockholders an opportunity to avoid the consequences of merger, not to undo the merger or to press directly for better terms. Appraisal statutes generally make explicit that the claim for which the dissenter is to be compensated in cash is the value of his shares 'exclusive of any element of value arising from the expectation or accomplishment of the merger or consolidation' * * *. [T]he appraisal process is thus designed to generate a claim on behalf of dissenting stockholders equal to the value of their shares in the old firm, just as if it had continued on its customary course without the intervention of a merger bid. Hence, where the merger is perceived as producing gains for the combined enterprise, the appraisal price by itself is inadequate to permit the subsidiary's stockholders to receive any part of those gains. By the same token, it is not the object of the appraisal proceeding to require an overreaching parent to redistribute any portion of the merger gains among the subsidiary's public stockholders. [Nor can the cashed-out objecting shareholder fairly be said to choose appraisal and its risks rather than continue with the enterprise, and therefore properly to be exposed to the limitations of the appraisal remedy.]

     * * *

     " * * * [T]he individual right of appraisal is not directly responsive to the problem of fiduciary abuse in mergers between parents and subsidiaries. Appraisal is predicated more on the conception of managerial incompetence in valuing the old enterprise and negotiating a price for it than on the notion of a conflict of interest which results in a diversion of a portion of the merger proceeds to a controlling parent. Moreover, it neither imposes its cost solely on the stockholders of the acquiring company nor seeks to reimburse all the victims of the inadequate merger price, that is, *all* the public stockholders of the acquired company. Finally, appraisal is merely an option-out alternative, and as such it focuses on the premerger value of the acquired company's shares. In short, it neither serves nor is designed to serve as a remedy for the fiduciary misbehavior at which the fairness challenge is directed."

NOTE: INTERRELATIONS BETWEEN FAIRNESS CLAIMS AND APPRAISAL ACTIONS

    1. *Appraisal and Fiduciary Actions in* Technicolor.

    In **Cede & Co. v. Technicolor, Inc.,** 542 A.2d 1182 (Del.1988), the Delaware Supreme Court addressed the following question: Whether a minority shareholder who has dissented from a cash-out merger and commenced an appraisal proceeding under DCL § 262 may pursue a later-discovered individual claim of fraud in the merger through an action for rescissory damages against the participants for breach of fiduciary duty.

    Under a special provision of the merger target's charter, a 95 percent supermajority shareholder vote was required to approve a merger unless a unanimous board of directors voted to waive the requirement and submitted the waiver for shareholder ratification. The merger had closed on the assumption that the unanimous board vote had been obtained, with 82 percent of the shares subsequently voting in favor. The plaintiff, Cinerama, in the course of discovery in respect of its appraisal action, took the deposition of a former director who claimed that he had dissented in the waiver vote and had voted against the merger. The plaintiff responded with a fraud action, claiming that the 82 percent shareholder vote was legally insufficient for approval of the merger. The plaintiff also charged multiple acts of wrongdoing and breaches of fiduciary duty in the merger, including waste, self-dealing, intentional and negligent misrepresentation, unfair dealing, and accepting a grossly unfair price for Technicolor stock.

The Supreme Court affirmed the Chancery's refusal to dismiss the action:

" * * * Given the distinctive nature of the remedies available to a cashed-out shareholder, the Chancellor properly declined to find Cinerama to lack standing to pursue its fraud claim. To rule that Cinerama, having elected to pursue an appraisal remedy under section 262, without apparent knowledge of a claim of fraud in the merger, was foreclosed from asserting a later-discovered claim of fraud in the merger, would have been clearly contrary to the teachings of *Weinberger* and *Rabkin*.

* * *

"The Chancellor correctly equated the right of a shareholder who loses share membership through misrepresentation, conspiracy, fraud, or breach of fiduciary duty to seek redress with the right of a shareholder who dissents from a merger and seeks appraisal of his shares to seek redress after discovery of allegedly wrongful conduct. Fairness and consistency require equal recourse for a former shareholder who accepts a cash-out offer in ignorance of a later-discovered claim against management for breach of fiduciary duty and a shareholder who discovers such a claim after electing appraisal rights.

"Moreover, policy considerations militate against foreclosing a shareholder electing appraisal rights from later bringing a fraud action based on after-discovered wrongdoing in the merger. Experience has shown that the great majority of minority shareholders in a freeze-out merger accept the cash-out consideration, notwithstanding the possible existence of a claim of unfair dealing, due to the risks of litigation. See Joseph v. Shell Oil Co., Del.Ch., 498 A.2d 1117, 1122 (1985). With the majority of the minority shareholders tendering their shares, only shareholders pursuing discovery during an appraisal proceeding are likely to acquire the relevant information needed to pursue a fraud action if such information exists. Such shareholders, however, would not have any financial incentive to communicate their discovered claim of wrongdoing in the merger to the shareholders who tendered their shares for the consideration offered by the majority and, by tendering, have standing to file suit. Thus, to bar those seeking appraisal from asserting a later-discovered fraud claim may effectively immunize a controlling shareholder from answering to a fraud claim."

The Court at the same time affirmed the Chancery's denial of the plaintiff's motion to amend its appraisal action to include the fraud and fiduciary claims:

" * * * [T]he necessary party defendants in a 'fraud in the merger' action are the alleged wrongdoers because it is they who arguably caused the injury and should pay any damage award. To permit Cinerama to amend its statutory appraisal action to include its fraud claims would impermissibly broaden the legislative remedy. It would also fail to bring before the Court the necessary parties for the fashioning of any appropriate relief for a fraud."

Finally, the Court ruled that it was error to require the plaintiff elect between appraisal and fiduciary remedies prior to trial:

"Cinerama should not have been barred from proceeding to trial on its alternate claims for relief. During the consolidated proceeding, if it is determined that the merger should not have occurred due to fraud, breach of fiduciary duty, or other wrongdoing on the part of the defendants, then Cinerama's appraisal action will be rendered moot and Cinerama will be entitled to receive rescissory damages. If such wrongdoing on the part of the defendants is not found, and the merger was properly authorized, then Cinerama will be entitled to collect the fair value of its Technicolor shares pursuant to statutory appraisal and its fraud action will be dismissed. Under either scenario, Cinerama will be limited to a single recovery judgment.

"Cinerama, therefore, is entitled to proceed simultaneously with its statutory and equitable claims for relief. What Cinerama may not do, however, is recover duplicative judgments or obtain double recovery."

2. *Wrongdoing and Appraisal Valuation.*

The admonition in the *Technicolor* case that a party may not assert in an appraisal proceeding "claims of wrongdoing in the merger" should not be taken as an absolute. In footnote 9 of the same opinion the court suggested that at some level, a merger price below intrinsic value signals nondisclosure on the insiders' part:

"Information and insight not communicated to the market may not be reflected in stock prices; thus, minority shareholders being cashed out may be deprived of part of the true investment value of their shares. See generally R. Clark, Corporate Law 507 (1986); Fama, Efficient Capital Markets: A Review of Theory and Empirical Work, 25 J.Fin. 383 (1970). The issue we are addressing is not the manipulation of the transaction, see *Rabkin*, 498 A.2d at 1104–05, nor the suppression or misstatement of material information by insiders defrauding the market, see Basic Inc. v. Levinson, 485 U.S. 224, 108 S.Ct. 978, 99 L.Ed.2d 194 (1988). Instead, we recognize that the majority may have insight into their company's future based primarily on bits and pieces of *nonmaterial* information that have value as a totality. See Clark, supra, at 508. It is this information that, if available in a statutory appraisal proceeding, the Court of Chancery must evaluate to determine if future earnings will affect the fair value of shares on the day of the merger. See 8 Del.C. § 262(h). To obtain this information the appraisal petitioner must be permitted to conduct a 'detailed investigation into the facts that is warranted by the acute conflict of interest and the potential for investor harm that is inherent in freeze-out transactions.' Clark, supra, at 508."

Two later cases take a further step and suggest that prior breaches of fiduciary duty have relevance to the ascertainment of intrinsic value in an appraisal. In **Cavalier Oil Corp. v. Harnett,** 564 A.2d 1137 (Del.1989) (involving a group of closed corporations), a claim for an earlier misappropriation by the parent group of a corporate opportunity that should have been shared with the subsidiary was held triable in the appraisal proceeding. The court suggested a distinction between asserting in an appraisal proceeding misbehavior by an absorbing parent corporation in the course of its prior dealings with the subsidiary (thus affecting the fair value of the latter by reason of its potential recovery from the former for such misbehavior) and claiming wrongdoing in the merger "itself," which *Technicolor* appears to forbid. In **Alabama By–Products Corp. v. Neal,** 588 A.2d 255 (Del.1991), the Delaware Supreme Court affirmed a ruling that raised the price to which the dissenting stockholders of the subsidiary were entitled from the $75.60 per share offered by the parent to $180.67 per share. The Chancellor had refused to entertain a claim for unfair dealings in the merger itself, but had admitted evidence offered in support of that claim as relevant and proper in assessing the correctness of the valuation. In the course of its opinion, the court said:

" * * * The petitioners argue that after their unfair dealing claim was properly dismissed from the appraisal proceeding, the Court of Chancery was nevertheless entitled to consider the evidence of unfair dealing for the alternative purpose for which it was introduced, i.e., to impeach the respondents' credibility. We agree.

"The respondents' argument fails to recognize the distinction between the propriety of considering an act of unfair dealing, which may relate to a party's credibility, and the impropriety of considering an action for unfair dealing in an appraisal proceeding. Although the justiciable issue in an appraisal action is a limited one, the statute specifically provides that 'all relevant factors' are to be considered by the Court of Chancery in 'determining the fair value' of shares which are subject to appraisal (* * * Cavalier Oil Corp. v. Hartnett, 564 A.2d at 1142–43; Weinberger v. UOP, Inc., 457 A.2d at 713.) There is nothing in the appraisal statute or this Court's prior holdings, including Cede, which suggests that the Court of Chancery may not consider the respondents' conduct at the time of the merger in assessing the credibility of the respondents' testimony in support of their valuation contentions in an appraisal proceeding."

3. *Question.*

In any particular state, the appraisal proceeding may be determined to be rigorously limited to a valuation process without inquiry into other "wrongs" entailed in the merger, and that process itself may be narrowly confined to ascertaining only the market price of the dissenter's stock. See Armstrong v. Marathon Oil Co., 32 Ohio St.3d 397, 513 N.E.2d 776 (1987). As the appraisal proceeding thus confines inquiry more and more narrowly, does (or should) appraisal become less the exclusive remedy for a shareholder who objects to the terms of the merger, particularly in a parent-subsidiary merger or freeze-out? Cf. Stepak v. Schey, 51 Ohio St.3d 8, 553 N.E.2d 1072 (1990). Can (or must) the value of outstanding claims for breach of fiduciary duty held at the time of the merger by the acquired corporation against its officers and directors be taken into account in the appraisal price? See Porter v. Texas Commerce Bancshares, 1989 WL 120358 (Del.Ch.).

(B) MANAGEMENT BUYOUTS

INTRODUCTION

The management buyout usually involves (a) the purchase by a newly formed company of all of a company's stock or assets for cash, (b) financing largely from institutional lenders or banks and intermediate or junior lenders, and (c) the receipt by old management and their outside equity partners of the bulk of the equity in the new company. The essence of the technique is the combination of high leverage and outside private equity together with the management team's commitment to remain with the company after the buyout in exchange for a substantial equity participation. Management acquires a potentially substantial but risky equity in a "new" firm on the expectation that earnings will be sufficient to pay off the buyout debt in the intermediate term.

The buyout is typically powered by a combination of tax incentives and the belief that the company, often a mature enterprise with substantial future earning power, is undervalued by the market. The buyout takes a public company private. (In some cases, the buyout's attractiveness is enhanced for management by its utility as a defense mechanism to a threatened takeover.) The subject "mature" companies also are said to be the prime generators of "excess" cash flows and correspondingly "wasteful" management. Significant efficiency gains are said to result from management buyouts by reason of the combined effect of (a) reduction in management discretion to waste mature companies' excess cash flow because of the need to pay interest on the debt, (b) the parallel ownership of debt and equity on monitoring costs, and (c) the added incentive to management from increased equity ownership.

The central legal issues are embedded in the question whether the public investors (of the bought-out company or of the parent) are being treated fairly. The management buyout presents the conflict of interest bound up in the taking of a "corporate opportunity:" Does management fulfill its duty to public investors if it takes for itself any or all the upside opportunities facilitated by a loan on the sole security of the firm's assets, a loan obtained in order to buy out the public for management's personal benefit? This corporate opportunity problem arises in large part because management has a significant information advantage over public investors about the value of the assets and earning prospects of the enterprise. Management can overreach the public investors on price in what can easily amount to a unilateral transaction.

The principal restraint on the temptation to overreach is the possibility of a bid from a third party. Such a bid, or the threat of such a bid, can substantially increase the premium paid to the public stockholders. Since the company's own assets underpin the buyout's financing, once the company is priced by management any other company can compete with a higher bid if it is interested in purchasing the assets. The management buyout is thus, in form at least, considerably less coercive of the public stockholders than is a going private transaction conducted by stockholders already possessed of a control block. Not that management comes to the transaction without a head start. Inside information facilitates higher leverage, and a bidding advantage. Notwithstanding the information disadvantages affecting outside bidders, if management and its associates bid more than the third party the transaction seems to be less plainly a case of taking advantage in a self-dealing transaction than if there is no other bidder at all—unless management places significant blocks in the path of third parties. Process questions accordingly arise respecting the evenness of the field opened to competitors as well as the adversity of the negotiation between the managers and the selling firm.

The courts apply fiduciary standards for management responses to hostile tender offers and management conduct of bidding competitions. Fairness to the selling public shareholders in management buyout transactions is thought to be assured by two process requirements. First, a window of time must be opened for competing bids. Second, the corporation must be represented in negotiations by a committee of independent directors that, in turn, retains its own investment bankers and counsel. Does the practice of delegating decisionmaking authority to a committee of outside directors provide an adequate guarantee against overreaching by management due to its structural and informational advantages? Does the prevention of overreaching require, as a practical matter, a *per se* rule that the outside committee sell control of the corporation to the highest bidder? If so, what procedures assure that the highest possible price is obtained for the shareholders?

In re Topps Co. Shareholders Litigation

Delaware Court of Chancery, 2007.
926 A.2d 58.

■ STRINE, VICE CHANCELLOR.*

The Topps Company, Inc. is familiar to all sports-loving Americans. Topps makes baseball and other cards (think Pokemon), this is Topps's so-called "Entertainment Business." It also distributes Bazooka bubble gum and other old-style confections, this is Topps's "Confectionary Business." Arthur Shorin, the son of Joseph Shorin, one of the founders of Topps and the inspiration for "Bazooka Joe," is Topps's current Chairman and Chief Executive Officer. Shorin has served in those positions since 1980 and has worked for Topps for more than half a century, though he owns only about 7% of Topps's equity. Shorin's son-in-law, Scott Silverstein, is his second-in-command, serving as Topps's President and Chief Operating Officer.

Despite its household name, Topps is not a large public company. Its market capitalization is less than a half billion dollars and its financial performance has, as a general matter, flagged over the past five years.

In 2005, Topps was threatened with a proxy contest. It settled that dispute by a promise to explore strategic options, including a sale of its Confectionary Business. Topps tried to auction off its Confectionary Business, but a serious buyer never came forward. Insurgents reemerged the next year, in a year when Shorin was among the three directors up for re-election to Topps's classified board. With the ballots about to be counted, and defeat a near certainty for the management nominees, Shorin cut a face-saving deal, which expanded the board to ten and involved his re-election along with the election of all of the insurgent nominees.

Before that happened, former Disney CEO and current private equity investor Michael Eisner had called Shorin and offered to be "helpful." Shorin understood Eisner to be proposing a going private transaction.

Once the insurgents were seated, an "Ad Hoc Committee" was formed of two insurgent directors and two "Incumbent Directors" to evaluate Topps's strategic direction. Almost immediately, the insurgent directors and the incumbent directors began to split on substantive and, it is fair to say, stylistic grounds. The insurgents then became "Dissident Directors."

In particular, the Ad Hoc Committee divided on the issue of whether and how Topps should be sold. The Dissident Directors waxed and waned on the advisability of a sale, but insisted that if a sale was to occur, it should involve a public auction process. The Incumbent Directors were also

---

* [Ed. Note] The bracketed sections of the report of the case are sections taken from later parts of the opinion and reinserted in forward locations.

ambivalent about a sale, but were resistant to the idea that Topps should again begin an auction process, having already failed once in trying to auction its Confectionary Business.

From the time the insurgents were seated, Eisner was on the scene, expressing an interest in making a bid [through a private equity firm he controls, The Tornante Company, LLC, in an alliance with another private equity group, Madison Dearborn Capital Partners, LLC.]. Two other financial buyers also made a pass. But Topps's public message was that it was not for sale.

Eventually, the other bidders dropped out after making disappointingly low value expressions of interest. Eisner was told by a key Incumbent Director that the Incumbent Directors might embrace a bid of $10 per share. Eisner later bid $9.24 in a proposal that envisioned his retention of existing management, including Shorin's son-in-law. Eisner was willing to tolerate a post-signing Go Shop process, but not a pre-signing auction.

The Ad Hoc Committee split 2–2 over whether to negotiate with Eisner. Although offered the opportunity to participate in the negotiation process, the apparent leader of the Dissidents refused, favoring a public auction. One of the Incumbent Directors who was an independent director took up the negotiating oar, and reached agreement with Eisner on a merger at $9.75 per share. [The Merger Agreement is not conditioned on Eisner's ability to finance the transaction, and contains a representation that Eisner has the ability to obtain such financing. But the only remedy against Eisner if he breaches his duties and fails to consummate the Merger is his responsibility to pay a $12 million reverse break-up fee.

[The "Go Shop" provision in the Merger Agreement works like this. For a period of forty days after the execution of the Merger Agreement, Topps was authorized to solicit alternative bids and to freely discuss a potential transaction with any buyer that might come along. Upon the expiration of the "Go Shop Period," Topps was required to cease all talks with any potential bidders unless the bidder had already submitted a "Superior Proposal," or the Topps board determined that the bidder was an "Excluded Party," which was defined as a potential bidder that the board considered reasonably likely to make a Superior Proposal. If the bidder had submitted a Superior Proposal or was an Excluded Party, Topps was permitted to continue talks with them after the expiration of the Go Shop Period.

[The Merger Agreement defined a Superior Proposal as a proposal to acquire at least 60% of Topps that would provide more value to Topps stockholders than the Eisner Merger. The method in which the 60% measure was to be calculated, however, is not precisely defined in the Merger Agreement, but was sought by Eisner in order to require any topping bidder to make an offer for all of Topps, not just one of its Businesses.

[Topps was also permitted to consider unsolicited bids after the expiration of the 40–day Go Shop period if the unsolicited bid constituted a Superior Proposal or was reasonably likely to lead to one. Topps could terminate the Merger Agreement in order to accept a Superior Proposal, subject only to Eisner's right to match any other offer to acquire Topps.

[The Eisner Merger Agreement contains a two-tier termination fee provision. If Topps terminated the Eisner Merger Agreement in order to accept a Superior Proposal during the Go Shop Period, Eisner was entitled to an $8 million termination fee (plus a $3.5 million expense reimbursement), in total, or approximately 3.0% of the transaction value. If Topps terminates the Merger Agreement after the expiration of the Go Shop Period, Eisner is entitled to a $12 million termination fee (plus a $4.5 million expense reimbursement), or approximately 4.6% of the total deal value.

[The Eisner Merger Agreement is subject to a number of closing conditions, such as consent to the transaction by regulatory authorities and the parties to certain of Topps's material contracts, such as its licenses with Major League Baseball and other sports leagues.

[In connection with the Eisner Merger Agreement, Shorin and Eisner entered into a letter agreement pursuant to which Shorin agreed to retire within sixty days after the consummation of the Merger and to surrender $2.8 million to which he would otherwise be entitled under his existing employment agreement in the event of a change of control of Topps. Shorin would remain a consultant to Topps for several years with sizable benefits, consistent with his existing employment agreement.]

The Topps board approved the Merger Agreement in a divided vote, with the Incumbent Directors all favoring the Merger, and the Dissidents all dissenting. Because of the dysfunctional relations on the Ad Hoc Committee, that Committee was displaced from dealing with the Go Shop process by an Executive Committee comprised entirely of Incumbent Directors.

Shortly before the Merger Agreement was approved, Topps's chief competitor in the sports cards business, plaintiff The Upper Deck Company, expressed a willingness to make a bid. That likely came as no surprise to Topps since Upper Deck had indicated its interest in Topps nearly a year and half earlier. In fact, Upper Deck had expressed an unrequited ardor for a friendly deal with Topps since 1999, and Shorin knew that. But Topps signed the Merger Agreement with Eisner without responding to Upper Deck's overture. Shortly after the Merger was approved, Topps's investment banker began the Go Shop process, contacting more than 100 potential strategic and financial bidders, including Upper Deck, who was the only serious bidder to emerge.

Suffice it to say that Upper Deck did not move with the clarity and assiduousness one would ideally expect from a competitive rival seeking to make a topping bid. Suffice it also to say that Topps's own reaction to Upper Deck's interest was less than welcoming. Instead of an aggressive bidder and a hungry seller tangling in a diligent, expedited way over key due diligence and deal term issues, the story that emerges from the record is of a slow-moving bidder unwilling to acknowledge Topps's legitimate proprietary concerns about turning over sensitive information to its main competitor and a seller happy to have a bid from an industry rival go away, even if that bid promised the Topps's stockholders better value.

By the end of the Go Shop period, Upper Deck had expressed a willingness to pay $10.75 per share in a friendly merger, subject to its receipt of additional due diligence and other conditions. Although having the option freely to continue negotiations to induce an even more favorable topping bid by finding that Upper Deck's interest was likely to result in a Superior Proposal, the Topps board, with one Dissident Director dissenting, one abstaining, and one absent, voted not to make such a finding.

After the end of the Go Shop period, Upper Deck made another unsolicited overture, expressing a willingness to buy Topps for $10.75 without a financing contingency and with a strong come hell or high water promise to deal with manageable (indeed, mostly cosmetic) antitrust issues. The bid, however, limited Topps to a remedy for failing to close limited to a reverse break-up fee in the same amount ($12 million) Eisner secured as the only recourse against him. Without ever seriously articulating why Upper Deck's proposal for addressing the antitrust issue was inadequate and without proposing a specific higher reverse break-up fee, the Topps Incumbent Directors have thus far refused to treat Upper Deck as having presented a Superior Proposal, a prerequisite to putting the onus on Eisner to match that price or step aside.

In fact, Topps went public with a disclosure about Upper Deck's bid, but in a form that did not accurately represent that expression of interest and disparaged Upper Deck's seriousness. Topps did that knowing that it had required Upper Deck to agree to a contractual standstill (the "Standstill Agreement") prohibiting Upper Deck from making public any information about its discussions with Topps or proceeding with a tender offer for Topps shares without permission from the Topps board.

[The * * * Standstill Agreement that contained the following material terms: (1) Topps would make available to Upper Deck certain information concerning the business, financial condition, operations, prospects, assets, and liabilities of Topps solely for the purpose of allowing Upper Deck to evaluate a possible transaction between Topps and itself; (2) Upper Deck agreed not to disclose the fact that such information was being provided to it or that it had entered into the Standstill Agreement, or make any public disclosure with respect to any proposed transaction between Upper Deck and Topps; and (3) Upper Deck agreed for a period of two years not to acquire or offer to acquire any of Topps's common stock by way of purchase in the open market, tender offer, or otherwise without Topps's consent, or to solicit proxies or seek to control Topps in any manner.]

The Topps board has refused Upper Deck's request for relief from the Standstill Agreement in order to allow Upper Deck to make a tender offer and to tell its side of events. A vote on the Eisner Merger is scheduled to occur within a couple of weeks.

A group of "Stockholder Plaintiffs" and Upper Deck (collectively, the "moving parties") have moved for a preliminary injunction. They contend that the upcoming Merger vote will be tainted by Topps's failure to disclose material facts about the process that led to the Merger Agreement and about Topps's subsequent dealings with Upper Deck. Even more, they argue that Topps is denying its stockholders the chance to decide for themselves whether to forsake the lower-priced Eisner Merger in favor of the chance to accept a tender offer from Upper Deck at a higher price. Regardless of whether the Topps board prefers the Eisner Merger as lower risk, the moving parties contend that the principles animating *Revlon, Inc. v. MacAndrews & Forbes Holdings, Inc.* [506 A.2d 173 (Del.1986)] prevent the board from denying the stockholders the chance to make a mature, uncoerced decision for themselves.

[When directors of a Delaware corporation seek approval for a merger, they have a duty to provide the stockholders with the material facts relevant to making an informed decision. In that connection, the directors must also avoid making materially misleading disclosures, which tell a distorted rendition of events or obscure material facts. In determining whether the directors have complied with their disclosure obligations, the court applies well-settled standards of materiality, familiar to practitioners of our law and federal securities law.

[The so-called *Revlon* standard is equally familiar. When directors propose to sell a company for cash or engage in a change of control transaction, they must take reasonable measures to ensure that the stock-holders receive the highest value reasonably attainable. Of particular pertinence to this case, when directors have made the decision to sell the company, any favoritism they display toward particular bidders must be justified solely by reference to the objective of maximizing the price the stockholders receive for their shares. When directors bias the process against one bidder and toward another not in a reasoned effort to maximize advantage for the stockholders, but to tilt the process toward the bidder more likely to continue current management, they commit a breach of fiduciary duty.]

In this decision, I conclude that a preliminary injunction against the procession of the Eisner Merger vote should issue until such time as: (1) the Topps board discloses several material facts not contained in the corporation's "Proxy Statement," including facts regarding Eisner's assurances that he would retain existing management after the Merger; and (2) Upper Deck is released from the standstill for purposes of: (a) publicly commenting on its negotiations with Topps; and (b) making a non-coercive tender offer on conditions as favorable or more favorable than those it has offered to the Topps board.

The moving parties have established a reasonable probability of success that the Topps board is breaching its fiduciary duties by misusing the Standstill in order to prevent Upper Deck from communicating with the Topps stockholders and presenting a bid that the Topps stockholders could find materially more favorable than the Eisner Merger. Likewise, the moving parties have shown a likelihood of success on their claim that the Proxy Statement is materially misleading in its current form.

    * * *

In the end, I perceive no unreasonable flaw in the approach that the Topps board took to negotiating the Merger Agreement with Eisner. I see no evidence that another bidder who expressed a serious interest to get in the game during 2006 was fended off. There is no suggestion by even the Stockholder Plaintiffs that the two other private equity firms who discussed making a bid with Topps were inappropriately treated.

Most important, I do not believe that the substantive terms of the Merger Agreement suggest an unreasonable approach to value maximization. The Topps board did not accept Eisner's $9.24 bid. They got him up to $9.75 per share-not their desired goal but a respectable price, especially given Topps's actual earnings history and the precarious nature of its business.

Critical, of course, to my determination is that the Topps board recognized that they had not done a pre-signing market check. Therefore, they secured a 40–day Go Shop Period and the right to continue discussions with any bidder arising during that time who was deemed by the board likely to make a Superior Proposal. Furthermore, the advantage given to Eisner over later arriving bidders is difficult to see as unreasonable. He was given a match right, a useful deal protection for him, but one that has frequently been overcome in other real-world situations. Likewise, the termination fee and expense reimbursement he was to receive if Topps terminated and accepted another deal-an eventuality more likely to occur after the Go Shop Period expired than during it-was around 4.3% of the total deal value. Although this is a bit high in percentage terms, it includes Eisner's expenses, and therefore can be explained by the relatively small size of the deal. At 42 cents a share, the termination fee (including expenses) is not of the magnitude that I believe was likely to have deterred a bidder with an interest in materially outbidding Eisner. In fact, Upper Deck's expression of interest seems to prove that point-the termination fee is not even one of the factors it stresses.

Although a target might desire a longer Go Shop Period or a lower break fee, the deal protections the Topps board agreed to in the Merger Agreement seem to have left reasonable room for an effective post-signing market check. For 40 days, the Topps board could shop like Paris Hilton. Even after the Go Shop Period expired, the Topps board could entertain an unsolicited bid, and, subject to Eisner's match right, accept a Superior Proposal. The 40–day Go Shop Period and this later right work together, as they allowed interested bidders to talk to Topps and obtain information during the Go Shop Period with the knowledge that if they needed more time to decide whether to make a bid, they could lob in an unsolicited Superior Proposal after the Period expired and resume the process.

In finding that this approach to value maximization was likely a reasonable one, I also take into account the potential utility of having the proverbial bird in hand. Although it is true that having signed up with Eisner at $9.75 likely prevented Topps from securing another deal at $10, the $9.75 bird in hand might be thought useful in creating circumstances where other bidders would feel more comfortable paying something like Upper Deck now says it is willing to bid. * * *

In this regard, Topps's decision to enter into the Merger Agreement with Eisner despite its having received an unsolicited indication of interest from Upper Deck a few days before the signing was also likely not an unreasonable one. This is perhaps a closer call, but the suggestion of Dissident Director Brog to respond to Upper Deck only after inking the Eisner deal bolsters this conclusion. Although the facts on this point are less than clear, as discussed, Topps appears to have had rational reason to be suspicious of Upper Deck's sincerity. Upper Deck had made proposals before, but had often appeared flaky. Moreover, Upper Deck was only expressing an interest in the Entertainment Business, not the whole company at that point. A sale of the Entertainment Business would have left Topps with a floundering Confectionary Business that it had already tried to sell once, without success. Signing up a sure thing with Eisner forced Upper Deck to get serious about the whole company, and set a price floor that Upper Deck knew it had to beat by a material amount.

* * *

The parties have presented competing versions of the events surrounding Topps's discussions with Upper Deck during the Go Shop Period, beginning with a fight over who was the first to contact the other and when the parties began discussing the Standstill Agreement, which was not executed until the start of the third week of the Go Shop Period. Neither party emerges from these arguments in an entirely positive light. * * *

In any event, I need not obsess over the behavior of the parties during the Go Shop Period. Upper Deck did finally make a formal bid for Topps at $10.75 per share two days before the close of the Go Shop. The Topps board had a fiduciary obligation to consider that bid in good faith and to determine whether it was a Superior Proposal or reasonably likely to lead to one. That is especially the case because the Topps board was duty bound to pursue the highest price reasonably attainable, given that they were recommending that the stockholders sell their shares to Eisner for cash.

* * *

* * * Upper Deck was offering a substantially higher price, and rather than responding to Upper Deck's proposal by raising these legitimate concerns, the Topps board chose to tie its hands by failing to declare Upper Deck an Excluded Party in a situation where it would have cost Topps nothing to do so. Eisner would have had no contractual basis to complain about a Topps board decision to treat Upper Deck as an Excluded Party in light of Upper Deck's 10% higher bid price.

* * *

Upper Deck came back a month later with an improved unsolicited bid. That bid again offered a price materially higher than Eisner's: $10.75 per share. That bid also was, again, not any more financially contingent than Eisner's bid; there was no financial contingency, but Topps's remedy was limited to a $12 million reverse break-up fee. This time, to address Topps's antitrust concerns, Upper Deck offered a strong "come hell or high water" provision offering to divest key licenses if required by antitrust regulators, as well as an opinion by a respected antitrust expert addressing Topps's still unspecified antitrust concerns.

* * *

The record before me clearly evidences Shorin's diffidence toward Upper Deck and his comparatively much greater enthusiasm for doing a deal with Eisner. Eisner's deal is premised on continuity of management and involvement of the Shorin family in the firm's business going forward. Upper Deck is in the same business line and does not need Shorin or his top managers.

Although Shorin and the other defendants claim that they truly desire to get the highest value and want nothing more than to get a topping bid from Upper Deck that they can accept, their behavior belies those protestations. In reaching that conclusion, I rely not only on the defendants' apparent failure to undertake diligent good faith efforts at bargaining with Upper Deck, I also rely on the misrepresentations of fact about Upper Deck's offer that are contained in Topps's public statements.

This raises the related issue of how the defendants have used the Standstill. Standstills serve legitimate purposes. When a corporation is running a sale process, it is responsible, if not mandated, for the board to ensure that confidential information is not misused by bidders and advisors whose interests are not aligned with the corporation, to establish rules of the game that promote an orderly auction, and to give the corporation leverage to extract concessions from the parties who seek to make a bid.

But standstills are also subject to abuse. Parties like Eisner often, as was done here, insist on a standstill as a deal protection. Furthermore, a standstill can be used by a target improperly to favor one bidder over another, not for reasons consistent with stockholder interest, but because managers prefer one bidder for their own motives.

In this case, the Topps board reserved the right to waive the Standstill if its fiduciary duties required. That was an important thing to do, given that there was no shopping process before signing with Eisner.

The fiduciary out here also highlights a reality. Although the Standstill is a contract, the Topps board is bound to use its contractual power under that contract only for proper purposes. On this record, I am convinced that Upper Deck has shown a reasonable probability of success on its claim that the Topps board is misusing the Standstill. As I have indicated, I cannot read the record as indicating that the Topps board is using the Standstill to extract reasonable concessions from Upper Deck in order to unlock higher value. The Topps board's negotiating posture and factual misrepresentations are more redolent of pretext, than of a sincere desire to comply with their Revlon duties.

Frustrated with its attempt to negotiate with Topps, Upper Deck asked for a release from the Standstill to make a tender offer on the terms it offered to Topps and to communicate with Topps's stockholders. The Topps board refused. That refusal not only keeps the stockholders from having the chance to accept a potentially more attractive higher priced deal, it keeps them in the dark about Upper Deck's version of important events, and it keeps Upper Deck from obtaining antitrust clearance, because it cannot begin the process without either a signed merger agreement or a formal tender offer.

Because the Topps board is recommending that the stockholders cash out, its decision to foreclose its stockholders from receiving an offer from Upper Deck seems likely, after trial, to be found a breach of fiduciary duty. If Upper Deck makes a tender at $10.75 per share on the conditions it has outlined, the Topps stockholders will still be free to reject that offer if the Topps board convinces them it is too conditional. Indeed, Upper Deck is not even asking for some sort of prior restraint preventing the Topps board from implementing a rights plan in the event of a tender offer (although Upper Deck has indicated that will begin round two of this litigation if Topps does). What Upper Deck is asking for is release from the prior restraint on it, a prior restraint that prevents Topps's stockholders from choosing another higher-priced deal. Given that the Topps board has decided to sell the company, and is not using the Standstill Agreement for any apparent legitimate purpose, its refusal to release Upper Deck justifies an injunction. Otherwise, the Topps stockholders may be foreclosed from ever considering Upper Deck's offer, a result that, under our precedent, threatens irreparable injury.

Similarly, Topps went public with statements disparaging Upper Deck's bid and its seriousness but continues to use the Standstill to prevent Upper Deck from telling its own side of the story. The Topps board seeks to have the Topps stockholders accept Eisner's bid without hearing the full story. That is not a proper use of a standstill by a fiduciary given the circumstances presented here. Rather, it threatens the Topps stockholders with making an important decision on an uninformed basis, a threat that justifies injunctive relief.

As this reasoning recognizes, one danger of an injunction based on the Topps board's refusal to waive the Standstill is that it will reduce the board's leverage to bargain with Upper Deck. Because this record suggests no genuine desire by the board to use the Standstill for that purpose, that danger is minimal. To address it, however, the injunction I will issue will not allow Upper Deck to go backwards as it were. The Merger vote will be enjoined until after Topps has granted Upper Deck a waiver of the Standstill to: (1) make an all shares, non-coercive tender offer of $10.75 cash or more per share, on conditions as to financing and antitrust no less favorable to Topps than contained in Upper Deck's most recent offer; and (2) communicate with Topps stockholders about its version of relevant events. The parties shall settle the order in good faith so as to avoid any timing inequities to either Eisner or Upper Deck, and therefore to the Topps stockholders. The injunction will not permit Upper Deck any relief from its obligations not to misuse Topps's confidential information.

NOTE: UMPIRING THE GOING PRIVATE PROCESS

Topps is one of a number of recent cases in which the Delaware Court of Chancery has been interposed in a private equity process.

Compare **In re Lear Corp. Shareholder Litigation**, 926 A.2d 94 (Del.Ch. 2007), which concerns a private equity buyout process at Lear Corp., a large, but troubled supplier of automotive interior systems. Carl Icahn, who recently had acquired 24 percent of the firm's stock, proposed the buyout to the CEO. Icahn and the CEO discussed the matter for a week. Only then did the CEO tell the rest of the board. The board then formed a Special Committee, which authorized the CEO to negotiate merger terms with Icahn. During the negotiations, Icahn only moved modestly from his initial offering price of $35, going to $36. He indicated that he would pull his offer if the board desired to conduct a pre-signing auction. But Icahn made it clear that he would allow the company to freely shop his bid after signing, during a go-shop period, but in exchange for a 3 percent termination fee. The board accepted the terms. After signing, the board's financial advisors aggressively shopped Lear to both financial and strategic buyers. None came forward with a topping bid during the go shop period. Lear thereafter was free to entertain an unsolicited superior bid. None was made.

Stockholder plaintiffs moved to enjoin the upcoming merger vote, arguing that the Lear board breached its *Revlon* duties and has failed to disclose material facts necessary for the stockholders to cast an informed vote.

Vice–Chancellor Strine rejected the *Revlon* claim but found fault with the proxy disclosure as follows:

"I largely reject the plaintiffs' claims. Although the Lear Special Committee made an infelicitous decision to permit the CEO to negotiate the merger terms outside the presence of Special Committee supervision, there is no evidence that that decision adversely affected the overall reasonableness of the board's efforts to secure the highest possible value. The board retained for itself broad leeway to shop the company after signing, and negotiated deal protection measures that did not present an unreasonable barrier to any second-arriving bidder. Moreover, the board obtained Icahn's agreement to vote his equity position for any bid superior to his own that was embraced by the board, thus signaling Icahn's own willingness to be a seller at the right price. Given the circumstances faced by Lear, the decision of the board to lock in the potential for its stockholders to receive $36 per share with the right for the board to hunt for more emerges as reasonable. The board's post-signing market check was a reasonable one that provided adequate assurance that no bidder willing to materially top Icahn existed. Thus, I conclude that it is unlikely that the plaintiffs would, after trial, succeed on their claims relating to the sale process.

"That said, I do find that a very limited injunction is in order. As noted, the Special Committee employed the CEO to negotiate deal terms with Icahn. But the proxy statement does not disclose that shortly before Icahn expressed an interest in making a going private offer, the CEO had asked the Lear board to change his employment arrangements to allow him to cash in his retirement benefits while continuing to run the company. The board was willing to do that, and even engaged a compensation consultant to generate potential options, but the consultant advised that accommodations of the type the CEO desired might draw fire from institutional investors, a factor that deterred the CEO from immediately accepting any renegotiation of his retirement benefits.

"Because the CEO might rationally have expected a going private transaction to provide him with a unique means to achieve his personal objectives, and because the merger with Icahn in fact secured for the CEO the joint benefits of immediate liquidity and continued employment that he sought just before negotiating that merger, the Lear stockholders are entitled to know that the CEO harbored material economic motivations that differed from their own that could have influenced his negotiating posture with Icahn. Given that the Special Committee delegated to the CEO the sole authority to conduct the merger negotiations, this concern is magnified. As such, an injunction will issue preventing the vote on the merger vote until such time as the Lear shareholders are apprised of the CEO's overtures to the board concerning his retirement benefits.''

A revised proxy statement later went out and the shareholders voted against the Icahn deal.

In **In re SS & C Technologies, Inc., Shareholders Litigation**, 911 A.2d 816 (Del.Ch. 2006), Vice Chancellor Lamb rejected a settlement agreement concerning the completed buyout of SS & C Technologies in a deal sponsored by Carlyle Investment Management L.L.C. Stone, SS & C's CEO, had been a key party. Stone had converted 3.92 million shares of his SS & C common stock and all of his SS & C stock options into a 31 percent equity position in the surviving entity. He also was to receive $37.25 per share for his remaining 1.95 million SS & C common shares (the same price received by the other stockholders), for total cash proceeds of approximately $72.6 million. Stone also entered into a new employment agreement, with an initial three-year term. Stone had initiated the discussions with Carlyle, and negotiated with it. Only once Stone had terms to his taste did Carlyle put a formal $37 offer on the table. And only then was the SS & C board informed. A special committee was then appointed, and, with counsel and investment banker, it negotiated with Carlyle and opened the window for other offers. None were forthcoming. The committee came back with $0.25 extra.

Said Vice–Chancellor Lamb, 911 A.2d at 820:

"These facts, on their face, raise a series of questions about both Stone's conduct and that of the board of directors. For instance, did Stone misuse the information and resources of the corporation when, acting in his official capacity but without board authorization, he hired an investment banker to help him identify a private equity partner to suit his needs? Another question is whether, given Stone's precommitment to a deal with Carlyle, the board of directors was ever in a position to objectively consider whether or not a sale of the enterprise should take place. Similarly, did Stone's general agreement to do a deal with Carlyle make it more difficult for the special committee to attract competing bids, especially from buyers not interested in having Stone own a significant equity interest in the surviving enterprise? And, did Stone's negotiation of a price range with Carlyle unfairly impede the special committee in securing the best terms reasonably available? These are only some of the important legal issues that result from the way Stone and the board of directors formulated the private equity buy-out of SS & C Technologies.

"None of these issues is adequately addressed by the plaintiffs' counsel in connection with the proposed settlement. Indeed, the plaintiffs' submissions, both written and oral, fail to come to grips with the fact that Stone had an array of conflicting interests that made him an unreliable negotiator or that the special committee was placed in a difficult position by Stone's preemptive activities. Most surprisingly, at the hearing, the plaintiffs' counsel told the court that Stone took no cash out of the deal and instead rolled all of his stock and options into equity in the new deal. Suffice it to say that a manager who has the opportunity to both take $72.6 million in cash from the transaction and roll a portion of his equity into a large equity position in the surviving entity has a different set of motivations than one who does not."

Finally, compare a famous case from the 1980s, **In re Fort Howard Corp. Shareholders Litigation**, 1988 WL 83147 (Del.Ch.1988). In *Fort Howard*, a special committee accepted the proposal of a management buyout group after opening a thirty day window in which the management offer was public information and the committee was willing to share proprietary information with interested outside bidders. No bids were solicited, however. The Delaware court raised an eyebrow at the facts that the corporation's CEO, a member of the buyout group, selected both the chair and outside counsel of the special committee, that the CEO discussed the proposal with the committee chair, and that he joined the chair in selecting the other two members of the committee. But the court sustained the procedure nevertheless. Would this sequence pass inspection today?

NOTE: THE FAIRNESS OPINION

Where no outside bids are solicited, is it sufficient that the committee's outside investment bankers opine that the consideration is "fair"? Outside fairness opinions are a necessary component of merger and acquisition transactions. Liability considerations, particularly in respect of the duty of care, have made it almost inconceivable that a board of directors would approve a sale of the firm without an outside opinion on the fairness of the price. A practical necessity such as this does not necessarily guaranty substantive adequacy, however. For criticism of practice respecting the preparation of these opinions, see Bebchuk and Kahan, Fairness Opinions: How Fair are They and What Can be Done About It? 1989 Duke L.J. 27, 53. Bebchuk and Kahan make several recommendations: (a) the courts should develop a definition of fair price and investment banks should disclose their own definitions of fair price in their opinions; (b) the weight attached to a fairness opinion should depend on whether the opinion contains information about the range of fair prices and on the sensitivity of the price estimate; and (c) courts should be sensitive to conflicts of interest on the part of the investment bankers. If the banker is paid by a contingent fee, is involved in other aspects of the transaction, or has prior dealings with the corporation, the court should discount the opinion.

Should the courts go a step farther and hold investment bankers liable for negligently prepared opinions by analogy to cases respecting accountants or attorneys? Do outside investment bankers owe a fiduciary duty of care and loyalty as agents in connection with the transaction? If so, to whom? To the special committee? The target board? The target? The shareholders of the target? A pair of New York cases suggest that a duty to the shareholders obtains. **Wells v. Shearson Lehman/American Express, Inc.,** 127 A.D.2d 200, 514 N.Y.S.2d 1 (1987), rev'd on other grounds, 72 N.Y.2d 11, 530 N.Y.S.2d 517, 526 N.E.2d 8 (1988), concerned an opinion rendered in connection with a $1.1 billion management buyout of Metromedia in 1984. Metromedia paid Shearson $750,000 for the opinion, $685,000 in brokers fees, and promised an additional $3.2 million if the merger went through. The opinion was included in proxy material sent to the shareholders. Within a year of the buyout, Metromedia sold its television assets for $2 billion. Thereafter, it sold most of its remaining assets for $2.5 billion—a total of $4.5 billion. The court denied Shearson's motion to dismiss the plaintiff's negligence complaint on an agency theory. Liability, said the court, did not depend on privity of contract between the bankers and the shareholders. This approach is reasserted in **Schneider v. Lazard Freres & Co.,** 159 A.D.2d 291, 552 N.Y.S.2d 571 (1990), an action against the firms that advised the RJR Nabisco board. The firms, which had addressed their opinions to the committee only, argued against liability as subagents of the board by making reference to the traditional idea that the board represents not the shareholders but the corporate entity. The court, rejecting the argument, said that "the sale of control of a corporation is not corporate business of the type governed by traditional principles of corporate governance * * *." Fiflis, Responsibility of Investment Bankers to Shareholders, 70 Wash.U.L.Q. 497 (1992), approves of liability to shareholders. Oesterle, Fairness Opinions as Magic Pieces of Paper, 70 Wash.U.L.Q. 541 (1992), takes the position that the firm, not the shareholder, is the client and any shareholder action for breach of the relationship should be a derivative action. Carney, Fairness Opinions: How Fair Are They and Why We Should Do Nothing About It, 70 Wash.U.L.Q. 523 (1992), argues that courts are ill suited to articulate the necessary standards of care, and that as a result, the costs of investment banker liability would outweigh the benefits. At least one Delaware court has taken the position that the special committee's investment banker is not an agent of the shareholders. In re Shoe–Town, Inc. Stockholders Litigation, 1990 WL 13475 (Del.Ch.1990).

2. THE DUTY OF CARE

The cash-out merger cases' emphasis on the board's compliance with appropriate procedures in considering the terms of the merger and in informing stockholders is replicated in shareholder challenges to arm's length mergers. The focus on the duty of care in this area begins with **Smith v. Van Gorkom,** 488 A.2d 858 (Del.1985). That case was an action by dissident stockholders of Trans Union Corporation (Trans Union) for rescission and damages on account of the merger of Trans Union with a wholly owned subsidiary of the Marmon Group Inc. (Marmon), resulting in the cash-out of Trans Union stockholders at $55 per share of stock that had never traded at more than 39 ½. The case turned on (1) whether the Trans Union board, in the exercise of its duty of care in approving the merger, had sufficiently informed itself of the "intrinsic value" of the company and of the terms and conditions of the merger to pass the test of exercise of informed business judgment in approving the merger, and (2) whether the board had complied with its fiduciary obligations under Delaware law to disclose in the proxy material which it circulated soliciting stockholder approval of the merger, "all facts germane to the transaction at issue in an atmosphere of complete candor."

The Delaware Supreme Court, reversing the Chancellor, ruled (1) that "gross negligence" is the test of propriety of Board action, (2) that the Board, which did not include an investment banker or a financial analyst, acting at a hastily called meeting which lasted only about two hours, had not sufficiently informed itself of the intrinsic value of the company or the "fairness" of the merger price (e.g., it had not obtained an outside banker's opinion or examined documentation on value) or the terms of the merger agreement; nor did it, by the time of its later meeting on January 26 formally approving the merger, cure those deficiencies; and (3) that the resulting avoidability of the merger was not cured by stockholder ratification because the proxy material soliciting stockholder approval was defective, in that among other things (a) it failed to disclose to the stockholders the board's ignorance of the intrinsic value of the company, (b) in characterizing $55 as a "substantial" premium it failed to disclose the Board's failure to assess the premium in terms of other relevant valuation techniques, and (c) in supplying material additional information in support of the merger in a supplementary Proxy Statement dated January 27, it failed to disclose that the Board had learned of that additional information only on January 26 when it formally approved the merger.

The decision focused primarily on the propriety of the Board's procedure in approving the merger. What considerations support (or oppose) a judicial preference for instructing outside directors on how to proceed in form, rather than testing their actions by substantive standards that implicate their integrity, and may entail measurements of "fairness" or the reasonableness of the business judgment as to the need for, and propriety of, the defensive maneuver?

Cede & Co. v. Technicolor, Inc.

Supreme Court of Delaware, 1993.
634 A.2d 345.

■ Before HORSEY, MOORE and HOLLAND, JJ.

■ HORSEY, JUSTICE:

I.

Prior Proceedings

This appeal from final judgment of the Court of Chancery encompasses consolidated suits: a first-filed Delaware statutory appraisal proceeding (the "appraisal action"), and a later-filed shareholders' individual suit for rescissory damages for "fraud" and unfair dealing (the "personal liability action") brought by plaintiffs, Cinerama, Inc. ("Cinerama"), a New York corporation, and Cede & Co. ("Cede"), the owner of record. The actions stem from a 1982–83 cash-out merger in which Technicolor, Incorporated ("Technicolor"), a Delaware corporation, was acquired by MacAndrews & Forbes Group, Incorporated ("MAF"), a Delaware corporation, through a merger with Macanfor Corporation ("Macanfor"), a wholly-owned subsidiary of MAF. Under the terms of the tender offer and later cash-out merger, each shareholder of Technicolor (excluding MAF and its subsidiaries) was offered $23 cash per share.

Plaintiff Cinerama was at all times the owner of 201,200 shares of the common stock of Technicolor, representing 4.405 percent of the total shares outstanding. Cinerama did not tender its stock in the first leg of the MAF acquisition commencing November 4, 1982; and Cinerama dissented from the second stage merger, which was completed on January 24, 1983. After dissenting, Cinerama, in March 1983, petitioned the Court of Chancery for appraisal of its shares pursuant to 8 *Del.C.* § 262. In pretrial discovery during the appraisal proceedings, Cinerama obtained testimony leading it to believe that director misconduct had occurred in the sale of the company. In January 1986, Cinerama filed a second suit in the Court of Chancery against Technicolor, seven of the nine members of the Technicolor board at the time of the merger, MAF, Macanfor and Ronald O. Perelman ("Perelman"), MAF's Chairman and controlling shareholder. Cinerama's personal liability action encompassed claims for fraud, breach of fiduciary duty and unfair dealing, and included a claim for rescissory damages, among other relief. Cinerama also claimed that the merger was void *ab initio* for lack of unanimous director approval of repeal of a supermajority provision of Technicolor's charter.

The defendants in the personal liability action moved to dismiss the action, arguing that Cinerama had no standing to pursue such a claim after petitioning for appraisal of its shares. The Chancellor denied the motion but ruled that after discovery was completed, Cinerama would have to elect which cause of action it wished to pursue. Cinerama filed an interlocutory appeal to this Court and we reversed. *Cede & Co. v. Technicolor, Inc.*, Del.Supr., 542 A.2d 1182 (1988) (*"Cede I"*). In Cede I this Court found the Chancellor to have committed legal error in requiring plaintiff to make an election of remedies before trial. We held that the plaintiff shareholder was entitled to pursue concurrently, through trial, its appraisal action and its personal liability action. We then remanded the case for trial of the consolidated appraisal and personal liability actions.

Following an extended trial and after further discovery, the Chancellor elected to decide first the appraisal suit. The court did so notwithstanding this Court's implicit instruction in *Cede I*. 542 A.2d at 1189, 1191.[2] By unreported decision (the "Appraisal Opinion") dated October 19, 1990, the Chancellor found the fair value of the dissenting shareholders' Technicolor stock to be $21.60 per share, as of January 24, 1983, the date of the merger. In June 1991, the court, in a second unreported decision (the "Personal Liability Opinion"), 1991 WL 111134, found pervasive and persuasive evidence of the defendant directors' breach of their fiduciary duties, but concluded that Cinerama had not met its burden of proof. On that ground, the Chancellor entered judgment for the defendants. * * *

* * * [W]e reverse and remand the personal liability action with instructions to the trial court to apply the entire fairness standard of review to the merger.

Our determination of the personal liability action renders moot Cinerama's appeal of the Appraisal Opinion and the issues raised therein. *See Cede I.*

II. FACTS

A. Background

In 1970 Technicolor was a corporation with a long and prominent history in the film/audio-visual industries. Technicolor's core business for over thirty years had been the processing of film for Hollywood movies through facilities in the United States, England and Italy. [But Technicolor's competitiveness decreased in the late 1970s and management problems cropped up.] Its major film processing laboratory was, in the words of Morton Kamerman ("Kamerman"), its Chief Executive Officer and Board Chairman,[4] "totally out of control" and it was taking losses that were "unacceptable."

---

2. Therein we stated twice that if, in the consolidated proceedings, the court should determine that the merger "should not have occurred due to fraud, breach of fiduciary duty, or other wrongdoing on the part of the defendants, then Cinerama's appraisal action will be rendered moot and Cinerama will be entitled to receive rescissory damages." Cede I, 542 A.2d at 1191. * * *

4. * * * In 1982 Kamerman was also the second largest shareholder of Technicolor stock. The Court of Chancery characterized Kamerman as a "strong-willed" chairman.

[Kamerman successfully reduced costs, and earnings increased. But then they again leveled off. Kamerman, looking to expand, proposed that Technicolor enter the field of rapid processing of consumer film by establishing a network of stores across the country offering one-hour development of film, with quality service at competitive prices. The business, named "One Hour Photo" ("OHP"), would require Technicolor to open approximately one thousand stores over the next five years and to invest about $150 million. The OHP project began in 1981, at a time when Technicolor's stock traded at around $22. The market reacted negatively to OHP, which in any evert fell behind schedule. Net income for 1982 declined 80 percent. Only 21 of 50 planned stores opened by September 1982, when the stock was trading at around $8.50.]

B. Prelude to Negotiations

In the late summer of 1982, Perelman of MAF concluded that Technicolor would be an attractive candidate for takeover by MAF. [MAF began purchasing Technicolor stock in the market and by October had acquired about 4.8 percent of the shares outstanding. Perelman, acting through an intermediary, contacted Fred Sullivan ("Sullivan"), a Technicolor director, and expressed an interest in acquiring 100 percent of Technicolor's stock for $15 per share. Sullivan set up a meeting between Perelman and Kamerman. Perelman and Kamerman met repeatedly in October, actively negotiating a deal. Perelman offered $20, while Kamerman held out for $25.] Other subjects discussed * * * included: the effect an MAF acquisition of Technicolor would have on Kamerman's employment contract with Technicolor; whether Kamerman and Sullivan would continue as directors of Technicolor; the importance to Perelman of obtaining from Kamerman and Guy M. Bjorkman ("Bjorkman"), Technicolor's two largest stockholders, binding options to purchase their and their spouses' stock holdings and their exercise of stock options; the income tax consequences of Kamerman's exercise of his options; and whether Sullivan would receive a finder's fee. [Eventually, a finder's fee of $150,000 for Sullivan was agreed upon, along with a post-merger employment contract for Kamerman. Furthermore, through] individual stock purchase agreements with Kamerman and Bjorkman and their spouses, MAF would acquire eleven percent of Technicolor's outstanding stock. MAF, through an option from Technicolor, would have the right to purchase another eighteen percent of Technicolor's authorized but unissued stock, exercisable by MAF if another bidder emerged and topped MAF's price. With such agreements in place and MAF's 4.8 percent present holdings of Technicolor, MAF would control about thirty-four percent of Technicolor's outstanding stock. Taking this evidence into account, along with Technicolor's supermajority charter provision requiring a shareholder vote of ninety-five percent of the outstanding shares for approval of a merger, the Chancellor found a probable "lock-up" by MAF of Technicolor.

[Neither Kamerman nor Sullivan disclosed the meetings nor the fact of Perelman's interest in Technicolor to any Technicolor officers and directors other than Bjorkman, whose stock Perelman wished to option, George Lewis ("Lewis"), a Technicolor director sought out by Kamerman for tax advice, John Oliphant, ("Oliphant"), the general counsel, and Wayne Powitzky ("Powitzky"), the treasurer. Indeed, Kamerman retained Goldman Sachs ("Goldman") as investment banker and Meredith Brown ("Brown") of Debevoise & Plimpton as outside legal counsel without disclosing the negotiations to any additional officers and directors. Brown and a Goldman project team flew to Los Angeles for meetings, but were permitted to consult only with the foregoing people. Only Jonathan Isham ("Isham"), a retired director who required considerable advance notice of board meetings was informed. Arthur Ryan ("Ryan"), Technicolor's President and Chief Operating Officer, although kept out of the loop by Kamerman, was tipped off by Martin Davis of Gulf & Western, who also was a friend of Perelman.]

* * * [O]n October 21, Goldman told Kamerman by telephone that a price of $20–$22 was worth pursuing. However, Goldman also suggested that Kamerman consider other possible purchasers for Technicolor. Goldman prepared an LBO model which included both an analysis of Technicolor's value and MAF's financial condition.[16]

Goldman performed no other financial study concerning Technicolor's sale to MAF, except a fairness opinion for presentation at Technicolor's board meeting of October 29. Goldman Sachs also revised its October 21 LBO analysis for presentation to the board on October 29.

On October 27, six days after Kamerman's receipt of Goldman Sachs' fairness opinion, he and Perelman reached an agreement on price by telephone. Perelman initially offered $22.50 per share for Technicolor's stock. Kamerman, responding that he could not take that bid to the board, countered with a figure of $23 per share and stated that he would recommend its acceptance to the board. Perelman agreed to $23.

That evening Kamerman instructed Technicolor's general counsel, Oliphant, to prepare a notice for the calling of a special meeting of the Board of Directors of Technicolor for New York City at 10:00 a.m., two days later, Friday, October 29. Technicolor requested the New York Stock Exchange to halt trading in its stock. The notice of special meeting did not disclose the meeting's purpose and only a few of the directors received notice of the meeting before Thursday, the 28th.

All nine directors of Technicolor attended the meeting. Three of the directors—Lewis, Isham and Bjorkman—* * * had only limited knowledge of the proposed sale of the company. Bjorkman's and Lewis' knowledge of the terms of the transaction was limited to what Kamerman had told them individually in advance of the meeting. Three other directors of Technicolor, Charles S. Simone ("Simone"), William R. Frye ("Frye") (who had formerly headed Technicolor's Consumer Processing Division), and Richard M. Blanco ("Blanco") (who was also Chief Executive Officer of Technicol-

---

16. The LBO model showed that "a $23 LBO" was feasible, taking into consideration both Technicolor's value and MAF's level of borrowing, and that $25 might be feasible. Goldman found that any price significantly higher would become "problematic" because of MAF's debt; and concluded that a price of $27 made an LBO "almost impossible."

or's Government Services Division), were told nothing of Technicolor's sale prior to the meeting.

Ryan, though also President and Chief Operating Officer, knew little except what he had learned indirectly from Davis of Gulf & Western.[18]

* * *

The Technicolor board convened on October 29 to consider MAF's proposal. Kamerman told the board of Bear Stearns' contact on behalf of MAF and then outlined the history of his negotiations with Perelman. Kamerman stated that he had received an offer from Perelman of $20 a share, that he had countered with $25 and that he, on October 27, had agreed to a sale price of $23 per share. Kamerman counseled the board that $23 was "good" because it was ten times "core" earnings of between $2.30 and $2.50 a share. Kamerman recommended that MAF's $23 per share offer be accepted in view of the present market value of Technicolor's shares. He stated that they should assume a loss of $1 per share on the One Hour Photo business. He believed that Technicolor's depressed share price rendered the company vulnerable for a takeover. Kamerman stated that accepting $23 a share was "advisable rather than shooting dice" on the prospects of Technicolor's One Hour Photo venture.

Kamerman then explained the basic structure of the transaction: a tender offer by MAF at $23 per share for all the outstanding shares of common stock of Technicolor and a second-step merger with the remaining outstanding shares converted into $23 per share, with Technicolor becoming a wholly owned subsidiary of MAF. Kamerman described MAF's proposed option to purchase up to 844,000 unissued shares of the company's common stock and MAF's proposed stock purchase agreement with Kamerman and Bjorkman and their wives.

Kamerman also outlined the terms of his proposed employment contract with MAF and stated that Technicolor would pay Sullivan a finder's fee of $150,000. He explained that he and Sullivan therefore had a financial interest in the proposed transaction.

Kamerman then turned the meeting over to Technicolor's outside counsel, Brown. Brown did not know that Sullivan, Bjorkman, Lewis and Isham had limited knowledge of the proposed sale and that Blanco, Simone and Frye had no substantial prior knowledge of the sale. Brown explained the structure of the proposed transaction, summarized the terms of the proposed merger, and reviewed the key documents involved. Brown advised the board that it was not obligated to accept Perelman's offer, or any offer for that matter, or obligated to "shop" the company.

Goldman then made an oral presentation, based on a 78–page "board book,"[20] and explained Technicolor's financial projections, stock price and

---

18. The Court of Chancery found that Ryan believed Perelman would deal with him fairly and maybe even place him in Kamerman's position. In fact, the court found that shortly after the merger in February 1983, Ryan was "promoted" after Kamerman's employment was terminated.

20. This book included median and mean values for other similar companies, a comparison of acquisitions in the motion picture business, a common stock comparison ownership data. It presented its LBO analysis and concluded with an oral opinion that a price of $23 was fair, subject to further due diligence.

After these briefings several directors suggested pushing Perelman for more money but were advised that Perelman would go no higher. One director, Simone, suggested that Kamerman solicit other offers. Board consensus appeared to be that "a bird in the hand was better than a bigger one in the bush," and it ultimately rejected Simone's suggestion.

According to the minutes of the meeting, and the trial court so found, the board unanimously approved the Agreement and Plan of Merger with MAF and recommended to the stockholders of Technicolor the acceptance of the offer of $23 per share. The board also unanimously recommended repeal of the supermajority provision of the Certificate of Incorporation. The board approved the Stock Option Agreement, Sullivan's finder's fee and Kamerman's new employment contract.

* * *

In December 1982, the board of Technicolor notified its stockholders of a special shareholders meeting on January 24, 1983, and distributed proxy statements. Attached to the proxy statement was Goldman's written fairness opinion dated November 19, 1982. At the January 24, 1983 shareholder meeting, 89 percent of the shareholders voted to repeal the supermajority amendment and in favor of the proposed merger. MAF and Technicolor completed the merger and the Technicolor directors resigned from office.

III. APPLICATION OF THE BUSINESS JUDGMENT RULE

The pivotal question in this case is whether the Technicolor board's decision of October 29 to approve the plan of merger with MAF was protected by the business judgment rule or should be subject to judicial review for its entire fairness.

* * * [The Chancellor] ruled that it was not sufficient for Cinerama to prove that the defendant directors had collectively, as a board, breached their duty of care. Cinerama was required to prove that it had suffered a monetary loss from such breach and to quantify that loss. The court expressed "grave doubts" that the Technicolor board "as a whole" had met that duty in approving the terms of the merger/sale of the company. The court, in effect, read into the business judgment presumption of due care the legal maxim that proof of negligence without proof of injury is not actionable. The court also reasoned that a judicial finding of director good faith and loyalty in a third-party, arms-length transaction should minimize the consequences of a board's *found* failure to exercise due care in a sale of a company. The Chancellor's rationale for subordinating the due care element of the business judgment rule, as applied to an arms-length, third-party transaction, was a belief that the rule, unless modified, would lead to

---

for other retailing companies, the financial performance of Technicolor and its constituent businesses, a profit and loss statement for each of Technicolor's major divisions, pro- jections for Technicolor through 1989, projections on MAF's ability to consummate the transaction, and a Standard and Poor's tear sheet on MAF.

draconian results. The Chancellor left no doubt that he was referring to this Court's decision in *Smith v. Van Gorkom*, Del.Supr., 488 A.2d 858 (1985). He stated, "In all, plaintiff contends that this case presents a compelling case for another administration of the discipline applied by the Delaware Supreme Court in *Smith v. Van Gorkom*, Del.Supr., 488 A.2d 858 (1985)."

* * *

* * * [A] shareholder plaintiff challenging a board decision has the burden at the outset to rebut the [business judgment] rule's presumption. * * * To rebut the rule, a shareholder plaintiff assumes the burden of providing evidence that directors, in reaching their challenged decision, breached any one of the *triads* of their fiduciary duty—good faith, loyalty or due care. * * * If a shareholder plaintiff fails to meet this evidentiary burden, the business judgment rule attaches to protect corporate officers and directors and the decisions they make, and our courts will not second-guess these business judgments. * * * If the rule is rebutted, the burden shifts to the defendant directors, the proponents of the challenged transaction, to prove to the trier of fact the "entire fairness" of the transaction to the shareholder plaintiff. *Nixon v. Blackwell*, Del.Supr., 626 A.2d 1366, 1376 (1993); *Mills*, 559 A.2d at 1279; *Weinberger v. UOP, Inc.*, Del.Supr., 457 A.2d 701, 710 (1983).

Under the entire fairness standard of judicial review, the defendant directors must establish to the *court's* satisfaction that the transaction was the product of both fair dealing *and* fair price. *Nixon*, 626 A.2d at 1376; *Mills*, 559 A.2d at 1279; *Weinberger*, 457 A.2d at 710. Further, in the review of a transaction involving a sale of a company, the directors have the burden of establishing that the price offered was the highest value reasonably available under the circumstances. *Mills*, 559 A.2d at 1288 * * *.

V. DIRECTOR AND BOARD DUTY OF CARE

* * *

Director Duty of Care and Board Presumption of Care

* * *

Applying the [business judgment] rule, a trial court will not find a board to have breached its duty of care unless the directors individually and the board collectively have failed to inform themselves fully and in a deliberate manner before voting as a board upon a transaction as significant as a proposed merger or sale of the company. *See Van Gorkom*, 488 A.2d at 873; *Aronson*, 473 A.2d at 812. Only on such a judicial finding will a board lose the protection of the business judgment rule under the duty of care element and will a trial court be required to scrutinize the challenged transaction under an entire fairness standard of review. *See, e.g., Van Gorkom*, 488 A.2d at 893; *Shamrock Holdings, Inc. v. Polaroid Corp.*, Del.Ch., 559 A.2d 257, 271 (1989).

The Chancellor[, h]aving assumed that the Technicolor board was grossly negligent in failing to exercise due care, * * * avoided the business judgment rule's rebuttal by adding to the rule a requirement of proof of injury. The court then found that requirement not met and, indeed, injury not provable due to its earlier finding of fair value for statutory appraisal purposes. In this manner, the court avoided having to determine whether the board had failed to "satisfy its obligation to take reasonable steps in the sale of the enterprise to be adequately informed before it authorized the execution of the merger agreement." * * *

The court found authority for its requirement of proof of injury in a seventy-year-old decision that none of the parties had relied on or felt pertinent. The trial court ruled: because the board as a deliberative body was disinterested in the transaction and operating in good faith, plaintiff bears the burden to show that any such innocent, though regrettable, lapse was likely to have injured it. *See, e.g., Barnes v. Andrews*, 298 F. 614 (S.D.N.Y.1924). * * * The court put it this way: * * * [A]s in any case in which the gist of the claim is negligence, plaintiff bears the burden to establish that the negligence shown was the proximate cause of some injury to it and what that injury was. *See Barnes v. Andrews*, 298 F. 614, 616–18 (S.D.N.Y.1924) * * *.

* * * [T]his Court has never interposed, for purposes of the rule's rebuttal, a requirement that a shareholder asserting a claim of director breach of duty of care (*or* duty of loyalty) must prove not only a breach of such duty, but that an injury has resulted from the breach *and* quantify that injury at that juncture of the case. No Delaware court has, until this case, imposed such a condition upon a shareholder plaintiff. That should not be surprising. The purpose of a trial court's application of an entire fairness standard of review to a challenged business transaction is simply to shift to the defendant directors the burden of demonstrating to the court the entire fairness of the transaction to the shareholder plaintiff, applying *Weinberger* and its progeny: *Rosenblatt*, 493 A.2d 929; *Bershad v. Curtiss-Wright Corp.*, Del.Supr., 535 A.2d 840 (1987); and *Mills*, 559 A.2d 1261. Requiring a plaintiff to show injury through unfair price would effectively relieve director defendants found to have breached their duty of care of establishing the entire fairness of a challenged transaction.

The Chancellor so ruled, notwithstanding finding from the record following trial that whether the Technicolor board exercised due care in approving the merger agreement was not simply a "close question" but one as to which he had "grave doubts." *Personal Liability Opinion* at 5–6. The trial court's doubts were based on at least five explicit predicate findings on the issue of due care: (1) that the agreement was not preceded by a "prudent search for alternatives," *id.* at 6; (2) that, given the terms of the merger and the circumstances, the directors had no reasonable basis to assume that a better offer from a third party could be expected to be made following the agreement's signing, *id.*; (3) that, although Kamerman had discussed Perelman's "approach" with several of the directors before the meeting, most of the directors had little or no knowledge of an impending sale of the company until they arrived at the meeting and only a few of them had any knowledge of the terms of the sale and of the required side agreements, *id.* at 12–13; (4) that Perelman "did, probably, effectively lock-up the transaction on October 29 when he acquired rights to buy the Kamerman and Bjorkman shares (about eleven percent together) and acquired rights under the stock option agreement to purchase stock that would equal 18 percent of the company's outstanding stock after exercise" given Technicolor's charter provision and Perelman's prior stock ownership of about five percent, *id.* at 49; and (5) that the board did not "satisfy its obligation [under *Revlon*] to take reasonable steps in the sale of the enterprise to be adequately informed before it authorized the execution of the merger agreement." *Id.* at 40. In addition, the Chancellor noted the relevance of *Revlon* in "illuminat[ing] the scope of [the] board's due care obligations ..." and implied that the Technicolor board's failure to auction the company evidenced a breach of their duty of care.[37] Id.

We adopt, as clearly supported by the record, the Chancellor's presumed findings of the directors' failure to reach an informed decision in approving the sale of the company. We disagree with the Chancellor's imposition on Cinerama of an additional burden, for overcoming the rule, of proving that the board's gross negligence caused any monetary loss to Cinerama. We turn to the court's reformulation of the rule's requirements for imposition of an entire fairness standard of review of the challenged transaction.

* * *

The Chancellor's Enlargement of the Rule to Require Cinerama to Prove Resultant Injury from the Board's Presumed Failure to Exercise Due Care

The trial court's presumed findings of fact of board breach of duty of care clearly brought the case under the controlling principles of *Van Gorkom* and its holding that the defendant board's breach of its duty of care required the transaction to be reviewed for its entire fairness. * * *

The Chancellor's reliance on *Barnes* is misguided.[39] While *Barnes* may still be "good law," *Barnes*, a tort action, does not control a claim for

---

37. The Chancellor wrote: ... the due care theory and the Revlon theory do not present two separate legal theories justifying shareholder recovery.... [B]oth theories reduce to a claim that directors were inadequately informed (of alternatives, or of the consequences of executing a merger and related agreements). An auction is a way to get information. A pre-or post-agreement market-check mechanism is another, less effective but perhaps less risky, way to get information. A "lock-up" is suspect because it impedes the emergence of information in that an alternative buyer that would pay (or would have paid) more is less likely to emerge once such an impediment is in place. * * *

39. In *Barnes*, the receiver of a failed corporation brought suit against Andrews, who was one of the corporation's former directors, for negligence in the performance of his duties. Andrews was charged with taking little, if any, active role as a director because he attended only part of one of two important board meetings. The court found Andrews to have been negligent in his inattention to his directorial duties but not liable for damages since plaintiff failed to prove that the company's insolvency actually resulted from Andrews' negligence rather than the negligence of his fellow directors. Then District Judge Learned Hand ruled:

Therefore I cannot acquit Andrews of misprision in his office, though his integrity

breach of fiduciary duty. In *Barnes*, the court found no actionable negligence or proof of loss—and granted defendant's motion for a nonsuit or grant of judgment for defendant on the merits. Here, the court was determining the appropriate standard of review of a business decision and whether it was protected by the judicial presumption accorded board action. The tort principles of *Barnes* have no place in a business judgment rule standard of review analysis.

To inject a requirement of proof of injury into the rule's formulation for burden shifting purposes is to lose sight of the underlying purpose of the rule. Burden shifting does not create *per se* liability on the part of the directors; rather, it is a procedure by which Delaware courts of equity determine under what standard of review director liability is to be judged. To require proof of injury as a component of the proof necessary to rebut the business judgment presumption would be to convert the burden shifting process from a threshold determination of the appropriate standard of review to a dispositive adjudication on the merits.

This Court has consistently held that the breach of the duty of care, without any requirement of proof of injury, is sufficient to rebut the business judgment rule. *See Mills*, 559 A.2d at 1280–81; *Van Gorkom*, 488 A.2d at 893. * * * Cinerama clearly met its burden of proof for the purpose of rebutting the rule's presumption by showing that the defendant directors of Technicolor failed to inform themselves fully concerning all material information reasonably available prior to approving the merger agreement. Our basis for this conclusion is the Chancellor's own findings, enumerated above.

* * * [W]e emphasize that the measure of any recoverable loss by Cinerama under an entire fairness standard of review is not necessarily limited to the difference between the price offered and the "true" value as determined under appraisal proceedings. Under *Weinberger*, the Chancellor may "fashion any form of equitable and monetary relief as may be appropriate, including rescissory damages." 457 A.2d at 714. The Chancellor may incorporate elements of rescissory damages into his determination of fair price, if he considers such elements: (1) susceptible to proof; and (2) appropriate under the circumstances. Id. Thus, we must reverse and remand the case to the trial court with directions to apply the entire fairness standard of review to the challenged transaction. * * *

NOTE: THE REMAND IN *CEDE* v. *TECHNICOLOR*

On the remand of *Cede & Co. v. Technicolor*, Chancellor Allen found the merger to have been entirely fair. **Cinerama, Inc. v. Technicolor, Inc.**, 663 A.2d 1134 (Del.Ch.1994). The Delaware Supreme Court subsequently affirmed his ruling. 663 A.2d 1156 (Del.Supr.1995).

is unquestioned. The plaintiff must, however, go further than to show that he should have been more active in his duties. *This cause of action rests upon a tort*, as much though it be a tort of omission as though it had rested upon a positive act. The plaintiff must accept the burden of showing that the performance of the defendant's duties would have avoided the loss, and what loss it would have avoided. Barnes, 298 F. at 616. (emphasis added)

Pursuant to the *Weinberger* formulation, Chancellor Allen took up process and price. As to process, he commented as follows:

" * * * [C]andor requires me to state that quite basically I cannot conclude that the transaction attacked was unfair to Cinerama, or other Technicolor shareholders, at all.

" * * * In large measure this judgment reflects my conclusion that (1) CEO Kamerman consistently sought the highest price that Perelman would pay; (2) Kamerman was better informed about the strengths and weaknesses of Technicolor as a business than anyone else; he was an active and experienced CEO who had designed and implemented a cost reduction program that was very beneficial and knew the businesses in which Technicolor operated; (3) Kamerman and later the board were advised by firms who were among the best in the country; (4) the negotiations lead to a price that was very high when compared to the prior market price of the stock (about a 100% premium over unaffected market price) or when compared to premiums paid in more or less comparable transactions during the period; (5) while the company was not shopped there is no indication in the record that more money was possible from Mr. Perelman or likely from anyone else; management declined to do an MBO transaction at a higher price and while I did conclude that the deal was 'probably locked up', if the value of the company at that time was or appeared to be remotely close to the value Cinerama claimed at trial, any 'lock-up' arrangement present would not have created an insuperable financial or legal obstacle to an alternative buyer. Indeed the conclusion that the transaction was probably locked up was logically and actually premised upon the belief that the $23 price was high."

Furthermore, said the Chancellor, the good faith of the directors also came to bear on the process fairness judgment:

"Nor can I, in making an overall judgment of fairness to shareholders, put out of my mind the firm conclusion that I have reached that a large majority of the board of directors had no material interest in this transaction that conflicted with the shareholders interest. Mr. Sullivan the only director with a found, material conflict fully disclosed that interest to the disinterested members of the board and the contract was thereafter approved by them."

On price, the Chancellor reasoned as follows:

" * * * Numerous reliable sources indicate that the $23 per share received constituted the highest value reasonably available to the Technicolor shareholders.

"At trial the court was presented with the results of two studies comparing the premium received in this sale with premiums received in comparable deals during the relevant period. The results provide significant evidence that the Technicolor shareholders were fully compensated for their relinquishment of control. * * *

"Additional facts strongly suggest that the $23 per share received would not have been exceeded had the Technicolor directors properly fulfilled their duties. For example, after considering engaging in an LBO, Technicolor's senior management declined to pursue the LBO and instead they sold their Technicolor shares to MAF. This fact that major shareholders, including Kamerman and Bjorkman who had the greatest insight into the value of the company, sold their stock to MAF at the same price paid to the remaining shareholders also powerfully implies that the price received was fair. * * *

" * * * The components of value in an acquisition might be considered to be two: the going concern value of the firm as currently organized and managed and the 'synergistic value' to be created by the changes that the bidder contemplates (e.g., new management, cost efficiencies, etc.). This second component will vary to some extent among bidders. It is the expectation of such synergies that allows a rational bidder to pay a premium when he negotiates an acquisition. Of course, no bidder will rationally pay more than a 100% of the expected synergy value to a seller, but in a competitive market of many buyers he may be driven to pay a substantial part of the expected synergy value in order to get the deal.

"Here even if a few dollars more might have been financially rational to a buyer, the $23 price achieved reflected a more than 'fair' allocation of synergy value to the sellers. * * * A fair price does not mean the highest price financable or the highest price that fiduciary could afford to pay. At least in the non-self-dealing context, it means a price that is one that a reasonable seller, under all of the circumstances, would regard as within a range of fair value; one that such a seller could reasonably accept."

Finally, the Chancellor made some observations about the availability of rescissory damages:

" * * * [R]escissory damages should never be awarded against a corporate director as a remedy for breach of his duty of care alone; that remedy may be appropriate where a breach of the directors duty of loyalty has been found, see Weinberger, 457 A.2d at 714 (holding that rescissory damages may be awarded if the lower court on remand finds them 'susceptible of proof and a remedy appropriate to all the issues of fairness where the directors were on both sides of the transaction and did not deal fairly with the minority shareholders'); Lynch v. Vickers Energy Corp., Del.Supr., 429 A.2d 497 (1981) (holding that rescissory damages should be awarded where a majority shareholder did not disclose material facts surrounding its tender offer), but neither principle nor authority supports the awarding of rescission or a substitute for it against one who neither participates in the deal as a principal nor, is a co-conspirator of a principal or has a material conflict of interest of another sort. * * *

"In a mechanical way, rescissory damages function to put a party in the same financial position it would have occupied prior to the initiation of a transaction which is found to be invalid or voidable. This remedy is applied when equitable rescission of a transaction would be appropriate, but is not feasible. At the most general level, this remedy is premised upon the idea that (1) the transaction whereby the party gave up an asset was wrongful in some way and (2) the nature of the wrong perpetrated is such that plaintiff is entitled to more than his 'out-of-pocket' harm, as measured by the market value of the asset at or around the time of the wrong. A review of the case law shows two prevailing 'strains' of the remedy of rescissory damages. The first grows out of, and is closely connected to, restitutionary relief. The second theory (and the more prominent one) employs a liberal application of the compensatory theory of damages against trustees who commit egregious breaches of the express terms of a trust or who self-deal.

* * *

"[T]here is no cogent evidence that the Technicolor Board, in any material respect, put their interests ahead of the shareholders negotiating the sale of the company. * * * "

NOTE: THE DUTY OF CARE AND MERGER NEGOTIATIONS

1. The 102(b)(7) Defense.

Van Gorkom, famously, precipitated a liability insurance crisis. The Delaware legislature responded by making it possible, in DCL § 102(b)(7) for corporations to amend their charters to opt out of liability for damages for violations of the duty of care. For a leading case sustaining a 102(b)(7) defense in the face of a complaint alleging a duty of care violation in respect of a merger, see **Malpiede v. Townson**, 780 A.2d 1075 (Del.2001). The care claim was rooted in the assertion that the board of directors might have used a poison pill aggressively to level the playing field between inside and outside bidders, resulting in a higher price. It was alleged in tandem with duty of loyalty claims and claimed violations of the duty to disclose. The latter claims all were dismissed on 12(b)(6) motions, leaving the care claim. The defendant having raised the 102(b)(7)defense, the Supreme Court held that there was nothing else for the Chancery to do but dismiss the complaint as a matter of law.

2.   *The Duty of Care and Entire Fairness Review.*

Cede has been criticized in many quarters, few more distinguished than Allen, Jacobs & Strine, Function Over Form: A Reassessment of Standards of Review in Delaware Corporation Law, 56 Bus. Law. 1287, 1303–04 (2001):

"The *Cede II* court cited no precedent, nor offered any explanation, for why on policy grounds duty of care claims should receive the same searching substantive review that traditionally is reserved for duty of loyalty claims. We submit that no reason in law or policy justifies that linkage.

"First, the basic rationale for entire fairness review—the difficulty of ascertaining, in non-arms-length transactions, the price at which the deal would have been effected in the market—does not apply in due care cases. 'Care cases, unlike loyalty cases, do not deprive corporations of 'neutral decision-makers.'[61] In the due care context, the plaintiff should be able to identify whatever harm flowed from the neutral decision-makers' alleged breach of care, and thereby obviate any need for judicial assessment of the substantive fairness of the board's business decision.

"Second, in care cases not involving a specific transaction, the entire fairness analysis is of little or no utility. The reason is that in non-transactional settings (e.g., uninformed or otherwise careless decisions on corporate distributions, or decisions to expand or shrink a business other than through a purchase or divestiture of an entire corporation), due care cases do not involve discrete market-based events that lend themselves to a fairness analysis. The same is true of non-transactional director conduct such as an alleged failure to monitor. Thus, the *Cede II* analytical framework is not a uniform review standard that can be applied in all breach of due care cases, which raises fundamental questions of how to locate the outer limits and contours of the *Cede II* doctrine.

"Third, the *Cede II* standard-changing and burden-shifting treatment of the duty of care is procedurally unfair to directors accused of breaching that duty, and may diminish the incentive for directors to engage in risk-taking transactions that could serve the best interests of stockholders. Under traditional (*pre-Cede II*) duty of care analysis, the plaintiff had the burden of proving that the director(s) breached the duty and that the breach proximately caused harm to the corporation and/or the shareholders. Any claim that the duty was breached would be reviewed under the gross negligence standard, and if a breach of duty and resulting harm were found, then liability would follow.

"Under *Cede II*, all the plaintiff need show now is a breach of the duty, irrespective of whether any harm resulted, to trigger a far more liability-threaten-

---

61. Lyman Johnson, *Rethinking Judicial Review of Director Care*, 24 Del. J. Corp. L. 787, 822–23 (1999) * * *.

ing procedural consequence—a change of the review standard to the more exacting entire fairness scrutiny, with the directors having the burden to negate the presumption of unfairness. Nothing in *Cede II* explains why directors accused of due care violations should be subjected to that far greater liability risk. The likely effect will be to make directors more risk averse, because they will have an incentive to refrain from risky wealth-creating transactions that as a policy matter corporate boards should be encouraged to undertake. Such risk aversion would run counter to the policy that gross negligence standard of review in due care cases is intended to promote."

For further commentary, see Symposium, *Van Gorkum* and the Corporate Board: Problem, Solution, Or Placebo, 96 Nw. U. L. Rev. 447 (2002); Johnson, Rethinking Judicial Review of Director Care, 24 Del. J. Corp. L. 787 (1999); Cunningham and Yablon, Delaware Fiduciary Duty Law After *QVC* and *Technicolor*: A Unified Standard (and the End of *Revlon* Duties?), 49 Bus. Law. 1593 (1994).

3. DISCLOSURE DUTIES

(A) STATE FIDUCIARY LAW

Lynch v. Vickers Energy Corp., 383 A.2d 278 (Del.1977), was an action for damages by a tendering stockholder against Esmark, Inc. (Esmark), its wholly owned subsidiary, Vickers Energy Corporation (Vickers), and the directors of TransOcean Oil, Inc. (TransOcean) 53.5 percent of whose common stock was owned by Vickers. The complaint charged that in a tender offer which Vickers made for the balance of TransOcean's common stock, defendants (1) made less than a full and frank disclosure in the tender offer of the value of TransOcean's net assets; and (2) coerced the minority shareholders, through use of their superior bargaining position and control over the corporate assets and processes, to sell their respective shares for a grossly inadequate price.

After trial on the merits, the Chancery Court entered judgment for defendants, ruling that plaintiff had failed to prove either actionable coercion or fraudulent misrepresentation 351 A.2d 570 (1976).

The Delaware Supreme Court, in reversing that judgment stated (383 A.2d 278 at 281):

The Court's duty was to examine what information defendants had and to measure it against what they gave to the minority stockholders, in a context in which "complete candor" is required. In other words, the limited function of the Court was to determine whether defendants had disclosed all information in their possession germane to the transaction in issue. And by "germane" we mean, for present purposes, such as a reasonable shareholder would consider important in deciding whether to sell or retain stock. Compare TSC Industries, Inc. v. Northway, Inc., 426 U.S. 438 (1976). The objective, of course, is to prevent insiders from using special knowledge which they may have to their own advantage and to the detriment of the stockholders. Compare Speed v. Transamerica Corp., D.Del., 99 F.Supp. 808, 829 (1951); Talbot v. James, 259 S.C. 73, 190 S.E.2d 759, 764 (1972); 3 Loss Securities Regulation 1433–1434.

Tested by that standard, the Supreme Court concluded, as a matter of law, that Vickers' tender offer circular was defective in that:

(i) in announcing that the value of TransOcean's net assets was "not less than $200,000,000 (approximately $15.00 per share) and could be substantially greater," it failed to disclose that defendants were in possession of estimates by the Vice President of TransOcean, a petroleum engineer, that the net asset value was between $250.8 million (approximately $20 per share) and $300 million, and

(ii) in soliciting tenders at $12 per share, the tender offer circular stated that Vickers had, pursuant to a program of open market purchases, acquired 265,000 shares of TransOcean at an average price of $11.49 per share, but failed to disclose that in connection with that purchase program Vickers had authorized open market purchases of TransOcean's shares at a price of $15 per share. The trial court had concluded that the $15 authorization price "was nothing more than a procedural convenience and not an accurate reflection of Vickers' opinion as to the true value of TransOcean's shares." Accordingly, it ruled that nondisclosure thereof was not fatal. In reversing, the Supreme Court said:

> But, again, the Court incorrectly weighed the quality of the information before it ruled on the claim of nondisclosure. Whether the authorization price accurately stated Vickers' opinion as to true value of TransOcean's shares, or whether it was a tool of convenience established to facilitate the acquisition of TransOcean's shares in a fluctuating market, is not relevant in a context involving the fiduciary obligation of full disclosure. What is important is the fact that the authorization price was germane to the terms of the tender offer, and as such it should have been disclosed to the minority shareholders.

Emerald Partners v. Berlin

Supreme Court of Delaware, 1999.
726 A.2d 1215.

■ Before WALSH, HOLLAND and BERGER, JUSTICES.

■ WALSH, JUSTICE:

In this appeal from the Court of Chancery, we review the grant of summary judgment in favor of the defendant corporation and its directors, on the ground that the plaintiffs, in their attack on a merger, had not sufficiently pled claims of entire fairness and best price. We conclude that the entire fairness claim was fairly pleaded and is intertwined with disclosure violation claims. Accordingly, we reverse as to the director defendants.

I

* * *

In October, 1987, [Craig Hall ("Hall")], at that time a holder of 52.4% of [the common stock of May Petroleum, Inc. ("May")], proposed a merger of May and thirteen sub-chapter S corporations owned by Hall that were primarily engaged in the real estate service business. The board of directors of May consisted of Hall and Berlin, the inside directors, and Florence, Sebastian and Strauss, the outside directors.

The outside directors authorized the engagement of Bear Stearns & Company ("Bear Stearns") to act as investment advisor and render a fairness opinion to the board and the May stockholders. On the basis of company valuations and the Bear Stearns fairness letter, the transaction, as eventually crafted, contemplated that Hall would receive twenty-seven million May common shares in exchange for the merger of the Hall corporations with May, increasing Hall's shareholding to 73.5% of May's outstanding common stock as reflected in the post-merger entity.

May and the Hall corporations entered into a proposed merger agreement on November 30, 1987. * * * On February 16, 1988, May issued a proxy statement to shareholders that described May, the Hall corporations and the proposed merger terms. The May shareholders approved the merger on March 11, 1988 * * *.

  * * *

Thereafter, the merger was completed on August 15, 1988. Despite the consummation of the merger, Emerald Partners continued its class and derivative claims * * *.

  * * *

II

A

Emerald Partners claims that the Court of Chancery erred in refusing to consider its entire fairness and best price claims directed against the merger and then granting summary judgment based on May's certificate of incorporation provision which tracks the language of 8 Del. C. § 102(b)(7)—Delaware's director exculpation statute. * * *

  * * *

As a matter of substantive law, the circumstances attendant upon the events leading to the negotiation of the merger would appear to implicate the entire fairness standard. Hall, as Chairman and Chief Executive Officer of both May and the Hall corporations and sole owner of the Hall corporations, clearly stood on both sides of the transaction. Additionally, at the time the parties entered the proposed merger agreement in November of 1987, Hall owned 52.4% of May common stock. Also, a breach of any one of the board of directors' triad of fiduciary duties, loyalty, good faith or due care, sufficiently rebuts the business judgment presumption and permits a challenge to the board's action under the entire fairness standard. Cinerama, Inc. v. Technicolor, Inc., Del.Supr., 663 A.2d 1156, 1162–64 (1995); In re Tri–Star Pictures, Inc., Litig., Del.Supr., 634 A.2d 319, 333 (1993).

The Court of Chancery acknowledged that Emerald Partners' complaint and briefs cited facts that "might raise a question as to the judgment and care of the defendant directors" regarding their proxy statement disclosure decisions connected with the merger. While this statement by the court was not a finding that the director defendants had breached their duty of care, Emerald Partners has made a sufficient showing through factual allegations that entire fairness should be the standard by which the directors' actions are reviewed. Such a showing shifts to the director defendants the burden to establish that the challenged transaction was entirely fair.

B

The Court of Chancery refused to consider Emerald Partners' entire fairness claim as ill-pleaded and examined the disclosure claims, standing alone. We conclude that the entire fairness and disclosure claims under these circumstances were intertwined and should not have been separately considered.

Emerald Partners contends that the February 16, 1988 proxy statement distributed in connection with, and seeking shareholder approval of, the proposed merger, contained misstatements about the merger negotiation process and misstatements or omissions regarding an investment. Specifically Emerald Partners challenges the following individual recitals in the proxy statement:

i) "[i]n connection with the Merger, the Non–Affiliated Directors have frequently held separate deliberations and have relied extensively on the advice of its independent legal counsel;"

ii) "[t]he terms of the Merger, including the exchange ratio of May Common Stock for shares of the Hall Corporations, were the result of arm's-length negotiations between representatives of the Hall Corporations and the Non–Affiliated Directors;" and

iii) the lack of disclosure regarding May's participation in the acquisition of The Singer Company and the amount of May's investment in HSSM#7 Limited Partnership reflected in the proxy statement. [HSSM#7 Limited Partnership was an entity that invested in Bilzerian Partners Limited Partnership I, a blind pool controlled by Paul Bilzerian. Bilzerian Partners successfully completed a leveraged hostile takeover of The Singer Company.]

The Court of Chancery held that the director defendants could not be found liable as a matter of law regardless of the materiality of these alleged omissions or misstatements. The court found that, throughout the relevant time period, a provision in May's certificate of incorporation protected the directors from liability for money damages for the proxy statement claims when "acting in honest pursuit of the best interests of the corporation." The court agreed with the defendants that Emerald Partners "failed to allege or reveal facts to support a conclusion that the directors acted in a manner which excepted them from the protections" of the charter provision "in deciding upon the appropriate extent of disclosure to be made in the proxy statement."

As previously noted, the Court of Chancery performed a separate analysis of both the entire fairness standard and the disclosure claim. Once the entire fairness standard has been implicated, as here, the defendants, at least initially, bear the burden of demonstrating the two basic aspects of fair dealing and fair price. Kahn v. Lynch Communication Systems, Inc., Del.Supr., 638 A.2d 1110, 1115, 1117 (1994). The burden of proof on the issue of fairness may shift. This Court has identified two scenarios that can provide the basis for shifting the burden to the plaintiff to demonstrate that the transaction complained of was not entirely fair. First, an approval of the transaction by an independent committee of directors who have real bargaining power that can be exerted in dealings with a majority shareholder who does not dictate the terms of the merger may supply the necessary basis for shifting the burden. Kahn v. Tremont Corp., Del.Supr., 694 A.2d 422, 428 (1997)* * *. Second, the approval of the transaction by a fully informed vote of a majority of the minority shareholders will shift the burden. Rosenblatt v. Getty Oil Co., Del.Supr., 493 A.2d 929, 937 (1985); see also 8 Del. C. § 144(a)(2). In all events, "[a] condition precedent to finding that the burden of proving entire fairness has shifted in an interested merger transaction is a careful judicial analysis of the factual circumstances of each case." Kahn v. Lynch, 638 A.2d at 1120.

The director defendants in this case may be able to secure the burden shifting benefit by demonstrating either sufficient independent director approval or fully informed shareholder approval. But that inquiry has been foreclosed by the Court of Chancery's grant of summary judgment and the present record does not permit this Court to resolve that issue.

The issue of the existence of a fully informed shareholder vote enforces the conclusion that dismissal of Emerald Partners' disclosure claims is inappropriate at this stage of the proceedings. Directors of Delaware corporations have a fiduciary duty to shareholders to exercise due care, good faith and loyalty whenever they communicate publicly or directly with shareholders about the corporation's affairs. Malone v. Brincat, Del.Supr., 722 A.2d 5, 10 (1998). When stockholder action is requested, directors are required to provide shareholders with all information that is material to the action being requested and "to provide a balanced, truthful account of all matters disclosed in the communications with shareholders." Id. at 12.

The Court of Chancery did not decide the issue of materiality of the alleged proxy statement misstatements or omissions but focused, instead, on the statutory protection available to the directors in the context of due care claims. Since we conclude that the disclosure claims here alleged are not so categorized, the analysis falls short. Accordingly, we reverse the grant of summary judgment on the disclosure claims.

Although we reverse the Court of Chancery's grant of summary judgment as essentially premature on the present record, we note, for the guidance of the Court of Chancery and the parties, that the shield from liability provided by a certificate of incorporation provision adopted pursuant to 8 Del. C. § 102(b)(7) is in the nature of an affirmative defense. * * * Defendants seeking exculpation under such a provision will normally bear the burden of establishing each of its elements. Here, the Court of Chancery incorrectly ruled that Emerald Partners was required to establish at trial that the individual defendants acted in bad faith or in breach of their duty of loyalty. To the contrary, the burden of demonstrating good faith, however slight it might be in given circumstances, is upon the party seeking the protection of the statute. Nonetheless, where the factual basis for a claim solely implicates a violation of the duty of care, this Court has indicated that the protections of such a charter provision may properly be invoked and applied. Arnold v. Society for Savings Bancorp. Del.Supr., 650 A.2d 1270, 1288 (1994); Zirn v. VLI Corp., Del.Supr., 681 A.2d 1050, 1061 (1996).

* * *

In sum, the grant of summary judgment in favor of the director defendants is reversed and remanded for proceedings consistent with this opinion. * * *

Emerald Partners v. Berlin

Supreme Court of Delaware, 2001.
787 A.2d 85.

■ HOLLAND, JUSTICE.

In this appeal, the appellants contend that the Court of Chancery failed to follow the mandate of this Court upon remand and erred, as a matter of law, by not conducting an entire fairness analysis in its posttrial opinion. The director defendants contend that the Court of Chancery properly declined to address any issue in its posttrial decision except for the exculpatory provision in the corporate charter that was enacted pursuant to 8 *Del. C.* § 102(b)(7). * * *

* * *

We have determined that this matter must be remanded for a second time because, once again, the Court of Chancery's consideration of the Section 102(b)(7) charter provision was premature. The same policy rationale that subjects a transaction to judicial review for entire fairness, even if the burden of persuasion shifts, requires a finding of unfairness and the basis of liability for monetary damages, before the exculpatory nature of a Section 102(b)(7) provision is examined. When the case was remanded after the last appeal to this Court, the initial focus of the Court of Chancery's posttrial opinion should have been an entire fairness analysis. The Court of Chancery erred, as a matter of law, when it failed to engage in an entire fairness analysis and, instead, simply examined the plaintiffs' claims in the context of the Section 102(b)(7) charter provision.

Upon remand, the Court of Chancery must analyze the factual circumstances, apply a disciplined balancing test to its findings on the issue of fair dealing and fair price, and articulate the basis upon which it decides the ultimate question of entire fairness. If the Court of Chancery determines that the transaction was entirely fair, the director defendants have no liability for monetary damages. The Court of Chancery should address the Section 102(b)(7) charter provision only if it makes a determination that the challenged transaction was not entirely fair. The director defendants' Section 102(b)(7) request for exculpation must then be examined in the context of the completed judicial analysis that resulted in a finding of unfairness. The director defendants can avoid personal liability for paying monetary damages only if they have established that their failure to withstand an entire fairness analysis is exclusively attributable to a violation of the duty of care.

NOTE: FURTHER PROCEEDINGS

On remand, the Court of Chancery held that the 1988 merger between May and Hall was entirely fair. The Delaware Supreme Court affirmed, **Emerald Partners v. Berlin**, 840 A.2d 641, 2003 WL 23019210 (Del.Supr.), noting as follows:

" * * * [W]e find that the many process flaws in this case raise serious questions as to the independent directors' good faith, e.g., the independent directors evidenced a 'we don't care about the risks' attitude by repeatedly failing to exclude Hall from their deliberative process and by giving Hall continuous direct and prior access to the valuation expert hired to advise the independent directors. But, the Court of Chancery found that the price was fair and this Court accords a 'high level of deference' to Court of Chancery findings based upon the evaluation of expert financial testimony. In this case, we agree with its analysis on the issue of price.

"Thus, we need not address the good faith claim because, even if the May directors would not be protected by the exculpation provision in their company's certificate of incorporation, they are not liable for any monetary damages. * * * "

NOTE: THE STATUS OF THE FIDUCIARY DUTY TO DISCLOSE

1. *Disclosure as Loyalty, Disclosure as Care, and Section 102(b)(7).*

Prior to *Emerald Partners v. Berlin*, the Delaware Supreme Court issued a series of opinions that discussed the application of § 102(b)(7)'s limitation of liability respecting violations of the duty of care to claims of breach of a fiduciary duty to disclose material facts in respect of acquisition transactions: **Zirn v. VLI Corporation**, 621 A.2d 773 (Del.1993)("*Zirn I*"), **Zirn v. VLI Corporation**, 681 A.2d 1050 (Del.1996)("*Zirn II*"), **Arnold v. Society for Savings Bancorp, Inc.**, 650 A.2d 1270 (Del.1994)("*Arnold I*"), and **Arnold v. Society for Savings Bancorp, Inc.**, 678 A.2d 533 (Del.1996)("*Arnold II*").

Zirn I concerned a shareholder's claim of "equitable fraud" respecting disclosures made in connection with a friendly tender offer followed by a cash out merger. The offer had closed after 94 percent of the shares had been tendered. The second-step merger then closed, prior to the filing of the lawsuit. The offer price had been lowered from $7 to $6.25 during the course of negotiations due to problems with a patent and a contemporaneous stock market crash. The plaintiff claimed that the materials failed accurately to state the crash's role in the price adjustment. The Chancery put the burden of proof on the plaintiff to prove that the market crash had been a primary factor. The Supreme Court disagreed:

"The requirement that a director disclose to shareholders all material facts bearing upon a merger vote arises under the duties of care and loyalty. Weinberger v. UOP, Inc., Del.Supr., 457 A.2d 701 (1983). In Rosenblatt v. Getty Oil Co., Del.Supr., 493 A.2d 929, 944 (1985), this Court adopted the materiality standard set forth by the United States Supreme Court in TSC Industries v. Northway, 426 U.S. 438, 449 (1976). * * *

"The TSC materiality standard is an objective one, measured from the point of view of the *reasonable investor*. It does not contemplate the subjective views of the directors, nor does it require that the information be of such import that its revelation would cause an investor to change his vote. * * * In determining what information is to be provided to the shareholders, a director should not be controlled by his or her own subjective views to the exclusion of an objective analysis of what the investor might consider relevant.

"In our view the Vice Chancellor departed from the TSC/Rosenblatt standard in two important respects: (1) consideration of the VLI director's subjective views and motivations, without addressing what a reasonable stockholder would consider; and (2) ruling that only a directors' primary reason for approving a merger is relevant to the stockholders.

* * *

"We conclude that the Vice Chancellor's application of the materiality test incorrectly placed upon Zirn the burden of proving that the market decline was the primary factor in rescission of the merger agreement. Upon remand, the court should apply an objective standard calculated to determine what information a reasonable VLI shareholder should possess in order to gauge the motivation for the price reduction. The consideration given by the VLI directors to a variety of factors, including the market crash, may be relevant to this inquiry but does not control it."

A § 102(b)(7) provision in the target firm's charter would not block the lawsuit:

"This provision, which purports to protect directors from monetary liability for breaches of fiduciary duty, does not shield directors from liability for equitable fraud. Moreover, the legislative history of the statute authorizing this provision, 8 Del.C. § 102(b)(7), indicates that corporations are empowered to shield directors from breaches of the duty of care, not the duty of loyalty, which also embraces the duty of disclosure that is at issue here. 1 R. Balotti & J.F. Finkelstein, The Delaware Law of Corporations and Business Organizations, § 4.19 at 4–330 (1991). Even defendants' own proxy materials note that the provision's applicability is limited to the duty of care."

Zirn I thus implied that § 102(b)(7) did not impede fiduciary claims respecting inaccurate disclosures in connection with tender offers and mergers. *Arnold I* rebutted the implication. There, despite finding a material omission in a proxy solicitation, the court went on to determine the matter based on the defendant directors' culpability. Since the omission had been in "good faith," and the record showed no "intentional violation," the § 102(b)(7) shield was effective. *Zirn*, said the court, had been different—there an "equitable fraud" claim had been argued.

The *Arnold I* court cautioned that the 102(b)(7) shield applied only to personal liability and provided no exemption from "equitable relief." It also remanded on the question whether a remedy existed against the transferor firm itself. In *Arnold II* it returned to these matters. The material omission, it said, did not render the merger void *ab initio*–that would take a violation of § 251 or § 252 rather than a breach of fiduciary duty. Nor did an action lie against the corporation–the fiduciary duty was owed by officers and directors to the corporation and its shareholders. Finally, the 102(b)(7) barrier did not imply a complete absence of judicial power to supervise disclosures respecting mergers and acquisitions–injunctive relief was always available in action prior to the transaction's consummation: "If we were to create by decisional law a form of corporate liability for damages, we would be replacing in a different form, ex post, a remedy which the General Assembly permitted the stockholders to waive, ex ante, by democratic process."

The *Zirn* plaintiff, after discovery, refocused the action on a misstatement concerning the acquired firm's problems with its patent. In *Zirn II* the court ruled that the misstatement was material, but found no prima facie case of equitable fraud. The plaintiff had neither tendered nor participated in the merger; hence the reliance element was lacking. The § 102(b)(7) clause in the charter defeated the claim at all events. While equitable fraud did not require a knowing or intentional misstatement or omission, § 102(b)(7) required bad faith: "The VLI directors lacked any pecuniary motive to mislead the VLI stockholders intentionally and no other plausible motive for deceiving the stockholders has been advanced. A good faith erroneous judgment as to the proper scope or content of required disclosure implicates the duty of care rather than the duty of loyalty."

2. *Disclosure of Merger Negotiations.*

Does a state law fiduciary duty to disclose arise on the part of a constituent corporation for the benefit of its shareholders prior to the execution and delivery of a definitive merger agreement? **Lindner Fund, Inc. v. Waldbaum, Inc.**, 82 N.Y.2d 219, 624 N.E.2d 160, 604 N.Y.S.2d 32 (1993), answers in the negative. The defendant issuer, Waldbaum, announced a definitive agreement to merge at a 100 percent premium over its market price after the markets closed on November 26, 1986. The plaintiff, which had sold a substantial block of Waldbaum stock during the previous ten days, complained that Waldbaum should have disclosed the deal at the time it reached an "agreement in principle" some days earlier. Looking to federal securities fraud cases on the materiality of merger negotiations, the court rejected the suggestion that a duty to disclose obtained as a matter of fiduciary law. The duty suggested, said the court, "is not prudent and is likely to lead to uncertainty and inappropriate market risks and losses." Furthermore, the business judgment rule protects "a corporation's officers and directors when they act in the overall best interests of all the shareholders and maintain the confidentiality of merger negotiations to avoid speculative or premature market fluctuations."

3. *Causation and Damages in Disclosure Cases.*

In re Tri–Star Pictures, Inc. Litigation, 634 A.2d 319 (Del.Supr.1993), concerned the sale of entertainment assets of Coca–Cola to Tri–Star in exchange for Tri–Star common stock. Prior to the transaction, Coca–Cola owned 36.8 percent of the common stock of Tri–Star, but controlled 56.6 percent of the stock through shareholders' agreements with a number of other large holders. The stock-for-assets transaction was priced on a book value basis. Since the unappraised Coca–Cola assets transferred had a book value of $745 million, while Tri–Star had a book value of $265 million, Coca–Cola ended up with 80 percent of the Tri–Star common. The stock Coca–Cola received had a market value of $12–13 per share, for a total of $900 to $977 million. The transaction was approved by the board and the stockholders of Tri–Star, with Coca–Cola undertaking not to vote its shares in favor unless of a majority of the other shareholders did so first. Given the control arrangements, this in effect meant that 24.4 percent of the shares not in the control group had to vote in favor.

Two months after the transaction closed, the Tri–Star board wrote down the assets purchased by $200 million. One and one half years later, Coca–Cola and Sony agreed on the sale of Tri–Star to Sony for $27 per share.

The Chancery court dismissed the plaintiffs' class action based on nondisclosures in the proxy statement respecting the stock-for-assets transaction on the ground that sufficient individual injury had not been shown. Reversing, the Supreme Court expanded as follows on the matter of loss causation in nondisclosure cases, 634 A.2d at 333–334:

"The trial court held that proof of special damages was required in a suit seeking compensatory damages for a breach of the fiduciary duty of disclosure. * * * As Cede observes, however, that is not the law in the context of a fairness case. Cede, 634 A.2d at 370–371.

" * * * In Delaware existing law and policy have evolved into a virtual *per se* rule of damages for breach of the fiduciary duty of disclosure. In Weinberger v. UOP, Inc., Del.Ch., C.A. No. 5642, Brown, C., slip op., 1985 WL 11546 (Jan. 30, 1985), aff'd, Del.Supr., 497 A.2d 792 (1985), the court awarded damages of $1.00 per share because of evidence that, if the stockholders had voted down the proposed cash-out merger on complete disclosure, the majority stockholder would have acquired plaintiffs' shares at $22 instead of $21 per share. Id., slip op. at 23–35. In reaching this decision, the former Chancellor held that because equity will not suffer a wrong without a remedy, the minority should be compensated for the wrong done to them even though a damage figure cannot be ascertained from a comparison of selected stock values with any degree of precision. Id., slip op. at 20–21.

"In Smith v. Shell Petroleum, Inc., Del.Ch., C.A. No. 8395, Hartnett, V.C., slip op., 1990 WL 186446 (Nov. 26, 1990), aff'd, Del.Supr., 606 A.2d 112 (1992), Vice Chancellor Hartnett held that an award of monetary damages was justified to remedy an injury arising from the failure to disclose oil and gas reserves that induced stockholders to accept an inadequate price in a cash out merger, because the deprivation of the stockholders' right to make an informed decision provided ample proof of the certainty of their claim. Id., slip op. at 11. And in Gaffin v. Teledyne, Inc., Del.Ch., C.A. No. 5786, Hartnett, V.C., slip op., 1990 WL 195914 (Dec. 4, 1990), the court awarded damages of $1.00 per share only after first holding that plaintiffs had shown an injury from the omission even though they were unable to demonstrate the amount of damages with certainty. Id., slip op. at 47.

"In all of these cases, the courts recognized some value associated with a stockholder's right to make an informed decision on corporate affairs. That issue is squarely raised here. But for the nondisclosure of Coca–Cola's alleged scheme to divest itself of the overvalued and ailing Entertainment Sector on Tri–Star, to improve Coca–Cola's own corporate balance sheet, the plaintiff class may very well have voted against the Transfer Agreement, effectively killing the agreement. Thus, the alleged loss suffered by the plaintiffs here is no different than that suffered by the plaintiffs in Weinberger, Gaffin or Smith—in all three cases the nondisclosure purportedly led to a diminution in the value of the plaintiffs' shares. Yet, none of those cases required the plaintiffs to prove damages at the pleading stage as an element of the *prima facie* case for breach of the fiduciary duty of disclosure.

"Although it is clear that claims for common law fraud, misrepresentation, or equitable fraud do require plaintiffs to show quantifiable damage, * * * the issues before us relate to breach of fiduciary duty, not fraud. Recently we held that damages need not always be proven in that context: [T]he absence of specific damage to a beneficiary is not the sole test for determining disloyalty by one occupying a fiduciary position. It is an act of disloyalty for a fiduciary to profit personally from the use of information secured in a confidential relationship, even if such profit or advantage is not gained at the expense of the fiduciary. The result is nonetheless one of unjust enrichment which will not be countenanced by a Court of Equity. Oberly v. Kirby, Del.Supr., 592 A.2d 445, 463 (1991). The distinction we noted in Oberly explains why no Delaware court has extended the damage rule to actions for breach of the duty of loyalty, which may embrace disclosure violations of the type alleged here.[18]"

---

18. This does not suggest, however, that the Court approves the means by which plaintiffs have sought to establish the measure of their damages. If plaintiffs seek more than nominal damages arising out of their claim for breach of the fiduciary duty of disclosure, the Court would expect that plaintiffs' present hypothetical estimates will give

The Delaware Supreme Court returned to the question of loss causation in **Loudon v. Archer–Daniels–Midland**, 700 A.2d 135, 142–43 (Del.1997). It there read *Tri-Star* narrowly, explaining its "per se" damages dictum as follows, 700 A.2d at 142–43:

" * * * Citing cases involving breaches of disclosure duties where stockholders had approved economically injurious transactions, the Court recognized a discrete set of conditions in which a damage remedy for non-disclosure would be appropriate. The particular facts of Tri–Star placed the case squarely within that context. Therefore, Tri–Star stands only for the narrow proposition that, where directors have breached their disclosure duties in a corporate transaction that has in turn caused impairment to the economic or voting rights of stockholders, there must at least be an award of nominal damages. Tri–Star should not be read to stand for any broader proposition.

"The plaintiff asserts here that the Proxy Statement issued by ADM in connection with the company's 1995 Annual Stockholder Meeting failed to disclose material facts. Plaintiff's damages claim therefore rests solely on the issue of election of directors. The circumstances recognized in Tri–Star—disclosure violations and deprivation of stockholders' economic or voting rights—that would give rise to a damages remedy are absent here. In claiming damages for directors' breach of the duty of disclosure in this instance, plaintiff takes out of context and would stretch too far the Tri–Star Court's dictum referred to above."

4. *The Reach of the State Law Fiduciary Duty to Disclose.*

In **Malone v. Brincat**, 722 A.2d 5 (Del.Supr.1998), the plaintiffs asserted a state law claim in respect of alleged material misstatements of an issuer's financial condition made in SEC filings. The Chancery Court dismissed the complaint on the ground that Delaware should not usurp or duplicate federal regulation where the disclosure issue lacks a connection to a request for shareholder action under Delaware law. The Delaware Supreme Court reversed. Said the Court, 722 A.2d at 10–11:

"The shareholder constituents of a Delaware corporation are entitled to rely upon their elected directors to discharge their fiduciary duties at all times. Whenever directors communicate publicly or directly with shareholders about the corporation's affairs, with or without a request for shareholder action, directors have a fiduciary duty to shareholders to exercise due care, good faith and loyalty. It follows a fortiori that when directors communicate publicly or directly with shareholders about corporate matters the sine qua non of directors' fiduciary duty to shareholders is honesty. * * *

"The issue in this case is not whether [the] directors breached their duty of disclosure. It is whether they breached their more general fiduciary duty of loyalty and good faith by knowingly disseminating to the stockholders false information about the financial condition of the company. The directors' fiduciary duties include the duty to deal with their stockholders honestly.

"Shareholders are entitled to rely upon the truthfulness of all information disseminated to them by the directors they elect to manage the corporate enterprise. Delaware directors disseminate information in at least three contexts: public statements made to the market, including shareholders; statements informing shareholders about the affairs of the corporation without a request for shareholder

way to the more generally accepted practice of offering expert testimony on the amount of damages actually suffered by the class.

action; and, statements to shareholders in conjunction with a request for shareholder action. Inaccurate information in these contexts may be the result of violation of the fiduciary duties of care, loyalty or good faith."

But the court cautioned that the state law duty, thus expansively defined, does not give rise to a cause of action tracking that under section 10(b) of the 1934 Act, 722 A.2d at 13–14:

" * * * In deference to the panoply of federal protections that are available to investors in connection with the purchase or sale of securities of Delaware corporations, this Court has decided not to recognize a state common law cause of action against the directors of Delaware corporations for 'fraud on the market.' Here, it is to be noted, the claim appears to be made by those who did not sell and, therefore, would not implicate federal securities laws which relate to the purchase or sale of securities.

"The historic roles played by state and federal law in regulating corporate disclosures have been not only compatible but complementary. That symbiotic relationship has been perpetuated by the recently enacted federal Securities Litigation Uniform Standards Act of 1998 [Pub.L. No. 105–353, 112 Stat. 3227]. Although that statute by its terms does not apply to this case, the new statute will require securities class actions involving the purchase or sale of nationally traded securities, based upon false or misleading statements, to be brought exclusively in federal court under federal law. The 1998 Act, however, contains two important exceptions: the first provides that an 'exclusively derivative action brought by one or more shareholders on behalf of a corporation' is not preempted; the second preserves the availability of state court class actions, where state law already provides that corporate directors have fiduciary disclosure obligations to shareholders. These exceptions have become known as the 'Delaware carve-outs.' "

The court went on to note as follows, 722 A.2d, at 13 n. 42:

"The Senate Committee Report on the Act is instructive. It states, in part:

The Committee is keenly aware of the importance of state corporate law, specifically those states that have laws that establish a fiduciary duty of disclosure. It is not the intent of the Committee in adopting this legislation to interfere with state law regarding the duties and performance of an issuer's directors or officers in connection with a purchase or sale of securities by the issuer or an affiliate from current shareholders or communicating with existing shareholders with respect to voting their shares, acting in response to a tender or exchange offer, or exercising dissenters' or appraisal rights.

S. Rep. No. 105–182, at 11–12 (May 4, 1998).

We need not decide at this time, however, whether this new Act will have any effect on this litigation if plaintiffs elect to replead. See Section (c) of the Act:

(c) Applicability.—The amendments made by this section shall not affect or apply to any action commenced before and pending on the date of enactment of this Act."

5. *Commentary.*

Allen, Jacobs & Strine, supra, at 1304–05, offer a reading of DCL § 102(b)(7) contrasting with that of *Emerald Partners v. Berlin*, supra:

"We suggest that a section 102(b)(7) defense is more properly treated as a statutory immunity than as an affirmative defense. But however the defense is treated, in our opinion it is unsound policy to impose the burden of establishing the defense on the directors. That approach undercuts the purpose of section 102(b)(7), which is to exculpate directors for duty of care claims for money damages. Imposing the burden to establish the exculpation defense upon the directors perversely requires them to disprove all of the duty of loyalty-related 'exceptions' to the defense, to be relieved of liability for due care claims. That is not how the exculpation defense should work. Rather, to the extent a complaint seeks damages against directors for claimed duty of care violations, those claims should be deemed exculpated. All other claims will by definition be duty of loyalty claims that the plaintiff traditionally has the burden to establish. The unintended result of the Emerald Partners doctrine is to make those directors who interpose the exculpation defense worse off procedurally than those who do not. That creates disincentives to raising that statutory defense, as well as the potential for meritless cases to survive motions to dismiss, thereby perpetuating costly litigation having little or no countervailing social utility.

"As an analytical matter, to establish the section 102(b)(7) defense, all that the defendant directors should be required to do is demonstrate the existence of the exculpatory charter provision. By doing that, the directors establish that they cannot be held liable for damages on account of any breaches of the duty of care. The logical procedural consequence would be that the plaintiff who seeks a monetary recovery against the directors will have the burden to plead facts that support the inference (and the eventual burden to prove at trial) that the directors engaged in non-exculpated conduct that resulted in damage."

For further commentary on the Delaware fiduciary duty to disclose, see Klock, Lighthouse or Hidden Reef? Navigating the Fiduciary Duty of Delaware Corporations' Directors in the Wake of *Malone*, 6 Stan. J. L. Bus. & Fin. 1 (2000); Hamermesh, Calling Off the *Lynch* Mob: The Corporate Director's Fiduciary Disclosure Duty, 49 Vand. L. Rev. 1087 (1996).

(B) FEDERAL DISCLOSURE RULES: THE MATERIALITY OF SOFT INFORMATION

What information must be disclosed to shareholders pursuant to the federal securities laws respecting merger and acquisition transactions and when must it be disclosed?

The particular items of information that must be disclosed in the schedules under the registration requirements of the 1933 Act or under Sections 12, 13 and 14 of the 1934 Act are presumably automatically deemed to be "material." In addition, the statutes implicitly, and regulations explicitly, request disclosure in filed statements of any other material information or additional information that is necessary to make the filed information not misleading. The disclosure requirements derived from the general antifraud provisions of the 1934 Act also either expressly or implicitly require disclosure of "material" information.

The prevailing definition of materiality comes from **TSC Industries, Inc. v. Northway, Inc.**, 426 U.S. 438 (1976), which involved a suit in respect of injuries caused by alleged falsehoods and omissions of material facts in a proxy statement issued in connection with a parent-subsidiary merger, in violation of Rule 14a–9. The District Court denied plaintiff's motion for summary judgment, but the Court of Appeals (512 F.2d 324 (7th Cir.1975)) reversed and held that the proxy material was defective as a matter of law. In reversing the Court of Appeals, the Supreme Court defined the standard of materiality for proxy statements under § 14 and Rule 14a–9 as follows (426 U.S. at 449):

> "The general standard of materiality that we think best comports with the policies of Rule 14a–9 is as follows: an omitted fact is material if there is a substantial likelihood that a reasonable shareholder would consider it important in deciding how to vote. This standard is fully consistent with *Mills* general description of materiality as a requirement that 'the defect have a significant *propensity* to affect the voting process.' It does not require proof of a substantial likelihood that disclosure of the omitted fact would have caused the reasonable investor to change his vote. What the standard does contemplate is a showing of a substantial likelihood that, under all the circumstances, the omitted fact would have assumed actual significance in the deliberations of the reasonable shareholder. Put another way, there must be a substantial likelihood that the disclosure of the omitted fact would have been viewed by the reasonable investor as having significantly altered the 'total mix' of information made available."

To what extent does the mandate to disclose "material" information, thus defined, extend to the disclosure of soft or future-oriented information, such as projections of future cash flows, or pending transactions in the market for going concerns? Nothing on the face of the statutes expressly requires or forbids disclosure of soft or future-oriented information. During the period of SEC hostility toward disclosure of such information, which ended in 1979, disclosure of such items as "other material information" was not an option. Once the SEC withdrew the disclosure bar, the mandatory disclosure question has come up repeatedly.

In cases where a reporting firm determines to make a disclosure of soft information, a statutory safe harbor provides protection from private civil actions (but not SEC enforcement actions). The safe harbor, contained in the Private Securities Litigation Reform Act of 1995, 109 Stat. 737 (codified at scattered sections of 15 U.S.C.), protects issuers, persons acting on behalf of issuers and "outside reviewers" who make "forward-looking statements," including, *inter alia*, (1) statements projecting earnings or other financial information, (2) statements of management's plans and objectives for future operations, (3) statements concerning future economic performance (including those in M D & A or results of operations), and (4) statements of the assumptions underlying or relating to any of the foregoing statements. 15 U.S.C. § 77z–2(a),(b), § 78u–5(a),(b). A forward-looking statement is protected when it is identified as such and "accompanied by meaningful cautionary statements" which identify factors which could make actual results differ materially from those projected (the "bespeaks caution" doctrine). Alternatively, protection extends to forward-looking statements that are immaterial. Finally, the plaintiff who surmounts the forgoing barriers still must prove that the statement was made with actual knowledge that the statement was false and misleading. 15 U.S.C. § 78u–5(c)(1), § 77z–2(c)(1).

The cases that follow concern a different problem—the case where a forward-looking statement of considerable interest to investors might be made but the firm's managers choose not to do so. When in so doing do they violate the federal antifraud mandates? Future oriented information entails not only traditional soft information, such as projections and appraisals, but also information about contemplated transactions that are contingent, and have varying degrees of imminence.

Analytically, there is little reason to deny that the subject soft information sometimes is material. At the same time, there is little reason to assert that it always is material. The question is how *relevant* and how *reliable* the information must be so as to justify its use by a reasonable investor in estimating the future price of the corporation's securities. At some level, any information, soft or hard, is of such little relevance, or so unreliable, or both, that an investor would not use it. At all points above that level, the rational investor finds the information useful. But the fact that a particular piece of information is in some way useful does not necessarily mean that it should or must be disclosed. Particularly where soft information is involved, there is a large range of uncertainty about the analytic inferences that may properly be made from the underlying information to the estimate of future prices and the intensity with which those estimates are held by their makers. Thus "materiality" depends not merely on the location of some minimum level of analytic utility. The question is where, beyond that point, relevance and reliability combine to require disclosure.

Starkman v. Marathon Oil Co.

United States Court of Appeals, Sixth Circuit, 1985.
772 F.2d 231.

■ MERRITT, CIRCUIT JUDGE.

Like Radol v. Thomas, 772 F.2d 244 (6th Cir.1985), this action arises out of U.S. Steel's November, 1981 acquisition and eventual merger with Marathon Oil Company. The plaintiff here, Irving Starkman, was a Marathon shareholder until selling his shares on the open market for $78 per share on November 18, 1981, the day before U.S. Steel's tender offer for 51% of Marathon's outstanding shares at $125 per share was announced. On October 31, 1981, Mobil Oil had initiated its takeover bid for Marathon, a bid which Marathon actively resisted by urging its rejection by Marathon shareholders and by seeking and eventually finding a "white knight" or alternative, friendly merger partner-tender offeror, U.S. Steel. Starkman claims that Marathon's board violated Rule 10b–5 and its fiduciary duty to him as a Marathon shareholder by failing to disclose various items of "soft" information—information of less certainty than hard facts—in its public statements to shareholders during the period after Mobil's hostile tender offer and prior to Steel's friendly tender offer. In particular, he says that Marathon should have told shareholders that negotiations were underway with U.S. Steel prior to the consummation of those negotiations in an agreement, and that internal and externally-prepared asset appraisals and five-year earnings and cash flow projections should have been disclosed to shareholders so that they could make a fully informed choice whether to sell their shares or gamble on receiving a higher price in a possible Steel–Marathon merger.

The District Court granted summary judgment for Marathon, finding that these items of soft information had either been sufficiently disclosed or were not required to be disclosed because their nondisclosure did not render materially misleading Marathon's other affirmative public statements. For the reasons stated below, we affirm the judgment of the district Court.

I. BACKGROUND

* * *

In the summer of 1981, Marathon was among a number of oil companies considered to be prime takeover targets. In this atmosphere, Marathon's top level management began preparations against a hostile takeover bid. Harold Hoopman, Marathon's president and chief executive officer, instructed the company's vice presidents to compile a catalog of assets. This document, referred to as the "Strong Report" or "internal asset evaluation," estimated the value of Marathon's transportation, refining and marketing assets, its other equipment and structures, and the value of proven, probable, and potential oil reserves as well as exploratory acreage. Hoopman and John Strong, who was responsible for combining materials received from various divisions into the final report, both testified that the Strong report was viewed as a "selling document" which placed optimistic values on Marathon's oil and gas reserves so as to attract the interest of prospective buyers and ensure that Marathon could either ward off an attempt to capture Marathon at a bargain price or obtain the best offer available.

In estimating proven, probable, and potential reserves and exploratory acreage, the Strong Report was based on information that was not available to the general public, for example in annual reports, because only the value of proven reserves was normally included in such public documents. The Strong Report defined proven reserves as those actually producing, probable reserves as reserves for properties where some production had been established and additional production was likely, and potential reserves as reserves for properties where production had not yet been established but where geologic evidence supported wildcat drilling. These reserves were valued using a discounted cash flow methodology, under which the present value of oil reserves is calculated by summing risk discounted expected net revenues from the particular field over the life of the field, and then discounted into present value by dividing by an estimated interest rate. This valuation method, a standard procedure for determining the cash value of oil and gas properties, required projections of price and cost conditions prevailing as far as 20 years into the future. For example, the Strong Report assumed that the rate of increase in oil prices would average over 9% per year from 1980–1990.

Using this methodology, the Strong Report valued Marathon's net assets at between $19 billion and $16 billion (depending on which set of interest rates was used to discount back to present value), a per share value of between $323 and $276. The value of oil and gas reserves made up $14 billion of the $19 billion estimate and $11.5 billion of the $16 billion estimate. A similar report using identical methodology was prepared in mid-July 1981 by the investment banking firm of First Boston, which had been hired by Marathon to assist in preparing for potential takeover bids. The First Boston Report was based only upon proven and probable oil reserves and was also intended to be used as a "presentation piece" to avoid a takeover or maximize the price obtained in a takeover. It placed Marathon's value at between $188 and $225 per share.

Some perspective on the values arrived at in the Strong and First Boston reports can be gained from other, publicly available appraisals of Marathon's assets prepared during 1981. The Herold Oil Industry Comparative Appraisal placed Marathon's appraised value at $199 per share, and two other reports by securities analysts said Marathon had an appraised value of between $200 and $210 per share.

Marathon's market value, however, was well below these appraised values. On October 29, 1981, Marathon closed at $63.75 per share. The next day, Mobil Oil announced its tender offer to purchase up to approximately 68% of outstanding Marathon common stock for $85 per share in cash. Mobile proposed to follow the tender offer with a going private or freezeout merger in which the remaining shareholders of Marathon would receive sinking fund debentures worth approximately $85 per share.

On October 31, 1981, Marathon's board of directors met in emergency session and unanimously decided that the Mobil offer was "grossly inadequate" and approved a vigorous campaign to persuade Marathon shareholders not to tender to Mobil, and to simultaneously seek a "white knight." On November 11 and 12, Marathon's Board made public statements to the shareholders recommending rejection of Mobil's bid as "grossly inadequate" and against the best interests of the company. We explore these statements in more detail below, as they are a primary focus of Starkman's claims of inadequate disclosure. However, at the time these statements to shareholders were made, Marathon representatives had already contacted all of the 30 to 35 companies who could possibly undertake an acquisition topping Mobil's bid, and, in particular, had begun negotiations with U.S. Steel on November 10. The Strong and First Boston reports were given to Steel on that same day, on the condition that they be kept confidential, and on November 12, Marathon's vice president for finance delivered five-year earnings forecasts and cash flow projections to Steel in Pittsburgh.

On November 17, Hoopman and David Roderick, Steel's president, reached agreement on the terms of Steel's purchase of Marathon, and, after Board approval, an agreement was signed on November 18, 1981. Under the terms of the agreement, Steel would make a tender offer for up to 31 million shares (about 51%) of Marathon stock for $125 per share in cash, to be followed by a merger proposal in which each remaining Marathon shareholder would receive one $100 face value, 12 year, 12 ½ per cent guaranteed note per share of common stock. On November 19, Steel mailed its tender offer to Marathon shareholders, and Hoopman sent a letter to

Marathon shareholders describing the two-stage deal and stating the opinion of Marathon's Board that the agreement was fair to Marathon shareholders. Steel's offer was successful, with over 91% of the outstanding shares tendered, and the second stage freezeout merger was approved by a two-thirds majority of the remaining shareholders in February, 1982.

II.   MARATHON'S PUBLIC STATEMENTS AND DISPOSITION BELOW

There are three public statements by Marathon management at issue here. First, Marathon's November 11, 1981, press release, which states, in pertinent part, that:

> Our Board of Directors has determined that Mobil Corporation's unsolicited tender offer is grossly inadequate. The offer is not in the best interests of Marathon Oil or its shareholders. It doesn't reflect current asset values and it doesn't permit the long-term investor the opportunity to participate in the potential values that have been developed.
> * * *
> We plan to do everything we possibly can to defeat this offer. We are determined to stay independent.

The next day, as required by Rule 14e–2, Marathon mailed a letter to its shareholders stating its position regarding Mobil's tender offer. The letter urged rejection of the offer, stating that Marathon's Board was "convinced that the Mobil offer is grossly inadequate and does not represent the real values of the assets underlying your investment in Marathon." The letter described a number of alternative courses of action that were being considered by the Board, including "repurchase of Marathon shares, acquisition of all or part of another company, a business combination with another company, (and) the declaration of an extra ordinary dividend and a complete or partial liquidation of the Company," and concluded by again urging rejection of Mobil's attempt to "seize control of Marathon's assets at a fraction of their value," and stating that "[w]e are convinced that you and our other shareholders would be well served if Marathon remains independent."

Attached to this letter was a copy of Marathon's Schedule 14D–9, filed pursuant to Rule 14d–9, 17 C.F.R. § 240.14d–9, in which the board informed the SEC that it had recommended rejection of the Mobil offer as "grossly inadequate." Item 4(b)(iv) of Marathon's Schedule 14D–9 listed as a factor supporting this recommendation the board's belief that based on current economic and market factors, "this is an extremely inopportune time to sell the Company and, in any event, that its shareholders would be better served if the Company were to remain independent."

Item 7 of this same schedule described "Certain Negotiations and Transactions" by Marathon:

> At a meeting of the Board of Directors held on October 31, 1981, the Board considered and reviewed the feasibility and desirability of exploring and investigating certain types of possible transactions, including, without limitation, repurchases of Company Common Shares, the

public or private sale of equity or other securities of the Company, a business combination between the Company and another company, the acquisition of a significant interest in or the entire Company or of one or more of its significant business segments by another company, a joint venture between the Company and one or more other companies, the acquisition by the Company of all or part of the business of another Company, a complete or partial liquidation of the Company or the declaration of an extraordinary dividend. After considerable discussion, the Board resolved that it was desirable and in the best interest of the Company and its shareholders to explore and investigate, with the assistance and advice of First Boston, such transactions, although the Board noted that the initiation or continuation of such activities may be dependent upon Mobil's future actions with respect to the Mobil Offer. There can be no assurance that these activities will result in any transaction being recommended to the Board of Directors or that any transaction which is recommended will be authorized or consummated.

Starkman argues that the failure of any of these communications to disclose the Strong and First Boston reports and the five-year earnings and cash flow projections constituted an omission of material facts which rendered these communications materially misleading, and that Marathon not only failed to adequately disclose its search for a white knight and its negotiations with Steel but actually gave the false impression that the Board was endeavoring to preserve Marathon as an independent entity. He argues that the Strong and First Boston reports, the five-year cash and earnings projections, and the fact of ongoing negotiations with U.S. Steel were all material facts because knowledge of them would have affected a reasonable shareholder's evaluation of the likelihood that Marathon would succeed in negotiating a higher price takeover, and thereby affect such a shareholder's decision to sell his shares. He contends that shareholders were not adequately informed of Marathon management's search for a "white knight" and of the negotiations with Steel, and that failure to disclose more information regarding these negotiations rendered statements suggesting that Marathon might remain independent materially misleading. Similarly, Starkman contends that if he had been told of the Strong and First Boston reports and the five-year earnings and cash flow projections, and also that Marathon management was using these figures in seeking an alternative bidder, then he would have anticipated a much higher bid than he did, and that failure to release this information rendered materially misleading the affirmative statements Marathon did make.

* * *

III. DISCUSSION

A. Introduction

* * *

Despite occasional suggestions by commentators, see, e.g., Bauman, Rule 10b–5 and the Corporation's Affirmative Duty to Disclose, 67 Geo.L.J. 935 (1979), and the courts, Zweig v. Hearst Corp., 594 F.2d 1261, 1266 (9th

Cir.1979), that Rule 10b–5 imposes an affirmative obligation on the corporation to disclose all material information regardless of whether the corporation has made any other statements, the established view is that a "duty to speak" must exist before the disclosure of material facts is required under Rule 10b–5. See Flynn v. Bass Brothers Enterprises, Inc., 744 F.2d 978, 984 (3d Cir.1984) (citing Chiarella v. United States, 445 U.S. 222, 235, 100 S.Ct. 1108, 1118, 63 L.Ed.2d 348 (1980); Staffin v. Greenberg, 672 F.2d 1196, 1202 (3d Cir.1982)). Provided that such a duty to speak exists, a further limitation on the duty to disclose is imposed by the requirement that only misstatements of material facts and omissions of material facts necessary to make other required statements not misleading are prohibited by Rule 10b–5. The Supreme Court's definition of "material" in the context of an alleged violation of Rule 14a–9, governing disclosure requirements in proxy statements, has been adopted for cases involving Rule 10b–5 in the tender offer context.

* * *

In structuring the disclosure duties of a tender offer target, we begin therefore with the basic proposition that only material facts—those substantially likely to affect the deliberations of the reasonable shareholder—must be disclosed, and then *only* if the nondisclosure of the particular material facts would make misleading the affirmative statements otherwise required by the federal securities laws and SEC regulations.

Our adherence to this basic proposition ensures that target management's disclosure obligations will strike the correct balance between the competing costs and benefits of disclosure. The benefits of disclosure in ensuring that shareholders who are suddenly faced with a tender offer will not be forced to respond without adequate information are clearly recognized in Section 14(e) of the Williams Act, 15 U.S.C. § 78n(e), which somewhat broadens the reach of Rule 10b–5 to statements made "in connection with any tender offer" and which provides the statutory authority for SEC rules imposing affirmative disclosure obligations on tender offer targets. On the other hand, tender offers remain essentially contests in which participants on both sides act under the "stresses of the marketplace," and "[p]robably there will no more be a perfect tender offer than a perfect trial." Electronic Specialty Co. v. International Controls Corp., 409 F.2d 937, 948 (2d Cir.1969) (Friendly, J.). Under these conditions, imposing an "unrealistic requirement of laboratory conditions," id., would place target management under the highly unpredictable threat of huge liability for the failure to disclose, perhaps inducing the disclosure of mountains of documents and hourly reports on negotiations with potential tender offerors, a deluge of information which would be more likely to confuse than guide the reasonable lay shareholder and which could interfere with the negotiation of a higher tender offer and actually reduce the likelihood that a shareholder will benefit from a successful tender offer at a premium over the market. It is with these competing considerations in mind that we turn to the particular disclosure claims made here.

B.   Assets Appraisals and Earnings Projections

We first address Starkman's contention that Marathon should have disclosed the Strong and First Boston reports and the five-year earnings projections and forecasts given to Steel. Under the authority of Section 14(e) of the Williams Act, the SEC requires a tender offer target to make two affirmative statements regarding an offer. First, Rule 14e–2 requires that the target company mail or publish a statement to its shareholders within 10 days of the tender offer stating its position (or stating it cannot take a position) and giving reasons for the position. Under Rule 14d–9, a Schedule 14D–9 must be filed with the SEC "as soon as practicable" after the recommendation letter is sent to shareholders. The information to be included in the Schedule 14D–9 is described in 17 C.F.R. § 14d–101. Significantly, although Item 4 of the Schedule 14D–9 is to contain a statement of the reasons for the target's position with respect to the offer, and Item 8 requires disclosure of any additional information as "may be necessary to make the required statements, in light of the circumstances under which they are made, not misleading" neither the shareholder recommendation letter nor the Schedule 14D–9 must contain internal asset appraisals, appraisals done by outside consultants such as First Boston, or earnings and cash flow projections.

Since there is no SEC rule specifically requiring the disclosure of this information, we must determine whether Rule 10b–5 requires its disclosure as material information, the nondisclosure of which would render misleading other statements made by Marathon. The starting point in this analysis is the underlying regulatory policy toward disclosure of such information, since regulatory rules reflect careful study of general conditions prevailing in the securities marketplace and provide guidelines upon which corporate officers and directors are entitled to rely.

The SEC's policy toward the inclusion of appraised asset valuations, projections and other "soft" information in proxy materials, tender offers and other disclosure documents has undergone a gradual evolution toward *allowing* the inclusion of such information in some special contexts, provided that the assumptions and hypotheses underlying predicted values are also disclosed.

In 1976, future earnings projections were deleted from a list of examples of potentially misleading disclosures in proxy statements in the note which followed Rule 14a–9. See Securities Act Release No. 5699, reprinted in [1975–76 Transfer Binder] Fed.Sec.L.Rep. (CCH) ¶ 80, 461 (1976). And, effective July 30, 1979, the SEC adopted a "safe harbor" rule for projections, under which a statement containing a projection of revenues and earnings would not be considered to be a materially misleading misstatement or omission for purposes of liability under the federal securities laws provided the statement was prepared with a reasonable basis and was disclosed in good faith. See Securities Act Release No. 6084 reprinted in [1979 Transfer Binder] Fed.Sec.L.Rep. (CCH) ¶ 82,117, at 81,939 (June 25, 1979).

With respect to asset appraisals, Rule 13e–3, 17 C.F.R. § 240.13e–3, requires disclosure of the information called for by Items 7, 8, and 9 of

Schedule 13E–3, 17 C.F.R. § 240.13e–100, in the context of freezeout mergers. Item 8 of Schedule 13E–3 requires disclosure of factors important in determining the fairness of such a transaction to unaffiliated shareholders, and these factors include liquidation value; Item 9 of that same schedule says that a summary of any outside appraisal must be furnished, with the summary including a discussion of the procedures and methods of arriving at the findings and recommendations of the appraisal. However, a 1979 SEC-proposed amendment under which an issuer would have to disclose any projection given to an appraisal furnisher was never adopted, see 2 Fed.Sec.L.Rep. (CCH) ¶ 23–706, at 17,245–21 through 21A, and, even more importantly, in Radol v. Thomas, 772 F.2d 244 No. 83–3598, (6th Cir.1985), we have rejected the position that SEC rules regarding freezeout mergers and proxies should determine the disclosure obligations of target management in the first stage of a two-tier tender offer.[6]

Finally, we note that until March, 1982, Regulation S–K, the source for disclosure obligations in annual reports, registration documents and other documents that must be filed with the SEC, provided in Instruction 2 to Item 2(b) that estimates of probable or possible oil and gas reserves should not be disclosed in any document publicly filed with the SEC. See Securities Act Release No. 6008, reprinted in [1978 Transfer Binder] Fed.Sec.L.Rep. (CCH) para. 81,768, at 81,104 (Dec. 19, 1978). The underlying reason was that "estimates of probable or possible reserves and any value thereof are not sufficiently reliable to be included * * * and may be misleading to investors." Id. In March, 1982, well after Steel's tender offer, Item 102 of Regulation S–K was amended to *allow* disclosure of "estimated" as well as proved reserves where such estimates have previously been provided to a person who is offering to acquire or merge with the subject company, see Securities Act Release No. 6383, reprinted in [1937–1982 Accounting Series Release Transfer Binder] Fed.Sec.L.Rep. (CCH) ¶ 72,328, at 63,003 (March 3, 1982). The Strong and First Boston reports contain estimates of probable and possible reserves, and the disclosure of this information was actually prohibited at the time of Steel's tender offer, and only *permitted* since that time.

Thus, at the time of Steel's tender offer, the SEC did not require disclosure of earnings projections in any context, and required disclosure of asset appraisals, in summary form, only in the special context of freezeout mergers, which differs markedly from the setting of a first-stage tender offer. Although the SEC allowed disclosure of projections, provided they were prepared on a "reasonable basis" and in "good faith," and also

---

6. In addition, while the note to Rule 14a–9 lists "predictions as to specific future market values" as a potentially misleading proxy statement disclosure, the SEC in 1980 authorized disclosure of good faith appraisals made on a reasonable basis in proxy contests in which a principal issue is the disposition of the issuer's assets, provided that the valuations are accompanied by "disclosure which facilitates shareholders' understanding of the basis for and limitations on the projected realizable values." Exchange Act Release No. 34–16833, reprinted in 3 Fed.Sec.L.Rep. (CCH) ¶ 24,117 (May 23, 1980). This same release cautioned, however, that where "valuations are so qualified and subject to material limitations and contingencies, inclusion in proxy soliciting material of specific realizable values may be unreasonable." 3 Fed.Sec. L.Rep. (CCH) at 17, 621–13.

allowed disclosure of similarly supported asset appraisals in some proxy contests, it forbade the disclosure of estimates of probable and potential oil and gas reserves, a major component of the Strong and First Boston appraisals. Absent compelling authority to the contrary, we are reluctant to impose liability on Marathon for failing to disclose asset appraisals based on hypothetical valuations which the SEC did not then permit to be disclosed in most contexts, particularly since Section 23(a) of the Securities and Exchange Act, 15 U.S.C. § 78w(a)(1) provides that no liability under the federal securities laws shall be imposed for "any act done or omitted in good faith, conformity with a rule, regulation, or order of the Commission."

* * *

Rather than suggesting a duty to disclose the Strong and First Boston reports, however, our cases firmly establish the rule that soft information such as asset appraisals and projections must be disclosed only if the reported values are virtually as certain as hard facts.

This Court has recently held that a target's failure to disclose an appraisal based on five-year cash flow and earnings projections and intended to be used as a selling document in ongoing merger discussions did not violate Rule 10b–5. Biechele v. Cedar Point, Inc., 747 F.2d 209 (6th Cir.1984). Chief Judge Lively's opinion for the court reasoned that the report was a "selling document" which "contained projections and speculative assumptions which were little more than predictions of future business success," and valuations based on the replacement cost of assets which could be misleading to shareholders, since they varied from balance sheet information prepared according to accepted accounting principles. Id. at 216. * * *

Our cases fully support a rule under which a tender offer target must disclose projections and asset appraisals based upon predictions regarding future economic and corporate events only if the predictions underlying the appraisal or projection are substantially certain to hold. An example is when the predictions in fact state a fixed plan of corporate activity. If a target chooses to disclose projections and appraisals which do not rise to this level of certainty, then it must also inform the shareholders as to the basis for and limitations on the projected realizable values.

The Third Circuit has enunciated a different test, under which "courts should ascertain the duty to disclose asset valuations and other soft information on a case by case basis, by weighing the potential aid such information will give the shareholder against the potential harm, such as undue reliance, if the information is released with a proper cautionary note." Flynn v. Bass Brothers Enterprises, 744 F.2d at 988. The court listed several factors the courts have considered in determining the reliability of soft information, including the qualifications of those who prepared the appraisal, the degree of certainty of the data on which it was based, and the purpose for which it was prepared. 744 F.2d at 986, 988 (compiling cases); see also Panter v. Marshall Field, 646 F.2d at 292–93.

By its very nature, however, this sort of judicial cost-benefit analysis is uncertain and unpredictable, and it moreover neglects the role of the market in providing shareholders with information regarding the target's value through competing tender offers. Our approach, which focuses on the certainty of the data underlying the appraisal or projection, ensures that the target company's shareholders will receive all essentially factual information, while preserving the target's discretion to disclose more uncertain information without the threat of liability, provided appropriate qualifications and explanations are made.

Under this standard, Marathon plainly had no duty to disclose the Strong and First Boston reports, because these reports contained estimates of the value of probable, potential and unexplored oil and gas reserves which were based on highly speculative assumptions regarding the path of oil and gas prices, recovery rates and the like over a period of thirty to fifty years. Disclosure of such estimated values could well have been misleading without an accompanying mountain of data and explanations. There is no reported case actually holding that disclosure of appraised values of oil and gas reserves is required, and several which agree with our decision that such disclosure is not required.

Similarly, Marathon had no duty to disclose the five-year earnings and cash flow projections given to Steel and First Boston. This information does not rise to the level of substantial certainty triggering a duty to disclose. *Biechele v. Cedar Point; James v. Gerber Products Corp.*, both supra.

Further, disclosure of the asset appraisals and earnings and cash flow projections was not required in order to ensure that other statements in Marathon's 14D–9 and in its letter recommending rejection of Mobil's bid were not misleading. Marathon stated that Mobil's $85 offer was "grossly inadequate" and disclosure of highly uncertain information indicating that Marathon had a net asset value of over $200 per share would only have supported this statement, and could have actually misled shareholders into thinking that the market would actually support a price of $200 per share.

C.

Starkman's contention that Marathon should have disclosed more information regarding its search for a white knight and its negotiations with Steel are equally without merit. The SEC and the courts have enunciated a firm rule regarding a tender offer target's duty to disclose ongoing negotiations: so long as merger or acquisition discussions are preliminary, general disclosure of the fact that such alternatives are being considered will suffice to adequately inform shareholders; a duty to disclose the possible terms of any transaction and the parties thereto arises only after an agreement in principle, regarding such fundamental terms as price and structure, has been reached. See Item 7 of Schedule 14D–9, 17 C.F.R. § 240.14d–101 (1984); *Greenfield v. Heublein, Inc.*, 742 F.2d 751, 756–57 (3d Cir.1984), cert. denied, 469 U.S. 1215, 105 S.Ct. 1189, 84 L.Ed.2d 336 (1985) (rejecting an "intent to merge" trigger standard); *Staffin v. Greenberg*, 672 F.2d 1196, 1207 (3d Cir.1982); *Reiss v. Pan American World Airways, Inc.*, 711 F.2d 11, 14 (2d Cir.1983).

The rationale emerging from these cases is that when dealing with complex bargaining which may fail as well as succeed and which may succeed on terms which vary greatly from those originally anticipated, the disclosure of preliminary discussions could very easily mislead shareholders as to the prospects of success, and by making public an impending offer, push the price of the target's stock toward the expected tender price, thereby depriving shareholders of the primary inducement to tender—a premium above market price—and forcing the offeror to abandon its plans or greatly increasing the cost of the offer. See Staffin v. Greenberg, 672 F.2d at 1207.

In the instant case, Marathon's shareholder recommendation letter and its Schedule 14D–9 stated that the company was considering a number of alternatives, including a merger with another firm. These statements adequately informed the shareholders of Marathon's plans. * * *

* * *

Accordingly, the judgment of the District Court is affirmed.

Basic Incorporated v. Levinson

Supreme Court of the United States, 1988.
485 U.S. 224, 108 S.Ct. 978, 99 L.Ed.2d 194.

BLACKMUN, J., delivered the opinion of the Court, in which BRENNAN, MARSHALL, and STEVENS, JJ., joined, and in Parts I, II, and III of which WHITE and O'CONNOR, JJ., joined. WHITE, J., filed an opinion concurring in part and dissenting in part, in which O'CONNOR, J., joined. REHNQUIST, C.J., and SCALIA and KENNEDY, JJ., took no part in the consideration or decision of the case.

■ JUSTICE BLACKMUN delivered the opinion of the Court.

This case requires us to apply the materiality requirement of § 10(b) of the Securities Exchange Act of 1934, 48 Stat. 881, as amended, 15 U.S.C. § 78a et seq. (1934 Act), and the Securities and Exchange Commission's Rule 10b–5, promulgated thereunder, see 17 CFR § 240.10b–5 (1987), in the context of preliminary corporate merger discussions. We must also determine whether a person who traded a corporation's shares on a securities exchange after the issuance of a materially misleading statement by the corporation may invoke a rebuttable presumption that, in trading, he relied on the integrity of the price set by the market.

I

Prior to December 20, 1978, Basic Incorporated was a publicly traded company primarily engaged in the business of manufacturing chemical refractories for the steel industry. As early as 1965 or 1966, Combustion Engineering, Inc., a company producing mostly alumina-based refractories, expressed some interest in acquiring Basic, but was deterred from pursuing this inclination seriously because of antitrust concerns it then entertained. * * * In 1976, however, regulatory action opened the way to a renewal of Combustion's interest. The "Strategic Plan," dated October 25, 1976, for Combustion's Industrial Products Group included the objective: "Acquire Basic Inc. $30 million." * * *

Beginning in September 1976, Combustion representatives had meetings and telephone conversations with Basic officers and directors, including petitioners here, concerning the possibility of a merger. During 1977 and 1978, Basic made three public statements denying that it was engaged in merger negotiations.[4] On December 18, 1978, Basic asked the New York Stock Exchange to suspend trading in its shares and issued a release stating that it had been "approached" by another company concerning a merger. * * * On December 19, Basic's board endorsed Combustion's offer of $46 per share for its common stock, * * * and on the following day publicly announced its approval of Combustion's tender offer for all outstanding shares.

Respondents are former Basic shareholders who sold their stock after Basic's first public statement of October 21, 1977, and before the suspension of trading in December 1978. Respondents brought a class action against Basic and its directors, asserting that the defendants issued three false or misleading public statements and thereby were in violation of § 10(b) of the 1934 Act and of Rule 10b–5. Respondents alleged that they were injured by selling Basic shares at artificially depressed prices in a market affected by petitioners' misleading statements and in reliance thereon. The District Court adopted a presumption of reliance by members of the plaintiff class upon petitioners' public statements that enabled the court to conclude that common questions of fact or law predominated over particular questions pertaining to individual plaintiffs. See Fed.Rule Civ. Proc. 23(b)(3). The District Court therefore certified respondents' class. On the merits, however, the District Court granted summary judgment for the defendants. It held that, as a matter of law, any misstatements were immaterial: there were no negotiations ongoing at the time of the first statement, and although negotiations were taking place when the second and third statements were issued, those negotiations were not "destined, with reasonable certainty, to become a merger agreement in principle." * * *

The United States Court of Appeals for the Sixth Circuit affirmed the class certification, but reversed the District Court's summary judgment,

---

4. On October 21, 1977, after heavy trading and a new high in Basic stock, the following news item appeared in the Cleveland Plain Dealer:

"[Basic] President Max Muller said the company knew no reason for the stock's activity and that no negotiations were under way with any company for a merger. He said Flintkote recently denied Wall Street rumors that it would make a tender offer of $25 a share for control of the Cleveland-based maker of refractories for the steel industry." * * *

On September 25, 1978, in reply to an inquiry from the New York Stock Exchange, Basic issued a release concerning increased activity in its stock and stated that

"management is unaware of any present or pending company development that would result in the abnormally heavy trading activity and price fluctuation in company shares that have been experienced in the past few days." * * *

On November 6, 1978, Basic issued to its shareholders a "Nine Months Report 1978." This Report stated:

"With regard to the stock market activity in the Company's shares we remain unaware of any present or pending developments which would account for the high volume of trading and price fluctuations in recent months." * * *

and remanded the case. 786 F.2d 741 (1986). The court reasoned that while petitioners were under no general duty to disclose their discussions with Combustion, any statement the company voluntarily released could not be " 'so incomplete as to mislead.' "Id., at 746, quoting SEC v. Texas Gulf Sulphur Co., 401 F.2d 833, 862 (C.A.2 1968) (en banc), cert. denied, sub nom. Coates v. SEC, 394 U.S. 976 (1969). In the Court of Appeals' view, Basic's statements that no negotiations were taking place, and that it knew of no corporate developments to account for the heavy trading activity, were misleading. With respect to materiality, the court rejected the argument that preliminary merger discussions are immaterial as a matter of law, and held that "once a statement is made denying the existence of any discussions, even discussions that might not have been material in absence of the denial are material because they make the statement made untrue." 786 F.2d, at 749.

The Court of Appeals joined a number of other circuits in accepting the "fraud-on-the-market theory" to create a rebuttable presumption that respondents relied on petitioners' material misrepresentations, noting that without the presumption it would be impractical to certify a class under Fed.Rule Civ.Proc. 23(b)(3). See 786 F.2d, at 750–751.

We granted certiorari, 484 U.S. ___ (1987), to resolve the split * * * among the Courts of Appeals as to the standard of materiality applicable to preliminary merger discussions, and to determine whether the courts below properly applied a presumption of reliance in certifying the class, rather than requiring each class member to show direct reliance on Basic's statements.

II

* * *

Pursuant to its authority under § 10(b) of the 1934 Act, 15 U.S.C. § 78j, the Securities and Exchange Commission promulgated Rule 10b–5.[6]

* * *

The Court previously has addressed various positive and common-law requirements for a violation of § 10(b) or of Rule 10b–5. * * * The Court also explicitly has defined a standard of materiality under the securities laws, see TSC Industries, Inc. v. Northway, Inc., 426 U.S. 438 (1976), concluding in the proxy-solicitation context that "[a]n omitted fact is material if there is a substantial likelihood that a reasonable shareholder would consider it important in deciding how to vote." Id., at 449. Acknowledging that certain information concerning corporate developments could

---

6. In relevant part, Rule 10b–5 provides:

"It shall be unlawful for any person, directly or indirectly, by the use of any means or instrumentality of interstate commerce, or of the mails or of any facility of any national securities exchange,

* * *

"(b) To make any untrue statement of a material fact or to omit to state a material fact necessary in order to make the statements made, in the light of the circumstances under which they were made, not misleading * * * in connection with the purchase or sale of any security."

well be of "dubious significance," id., at 448, the Court was careful not to set too low a standard of materiality; it was concerned that a minimal standard might bring an overabundance of information within its reach, and lead management "simply to bury the shareholders in an avalanche of trivial information—a result that is hardly conducive to informed decision-making." Id., at 448–449. It further explained that to fulfill the materiality requirement "there must be a substantial likelihood that the disclosure of the omitted fact would have been viewed by the reasonable investor as having significantly altered the 'total mix' of information made available." Id., at 449. We now expressly adopt the TSC Industries standard of materiality for the § 10(b) and Rule 10b–5 context.

III

The application of this materiality standard to preliminary merger discussions is not self-evident. Where the impact of the corporate development on the target's fortune is certain and clear, the TSC Industries materiality definition admits straightforward application. Where, on the other hand, the event is contingent or speculative in nature, it is difficult to ascertain whether the "reasonable investor" would have considered the omitted information significant at the time. Merger negotiations, because of the ever-present possibility that the contemplated transaction will not be effectuated, fall into the latter category.[9]

A

Petitioners urge upon us a Third Circuit test for resolving this difficulty.[10] * * * Under this approach, preliminary merger discussions do not become material until "agreement-in-principle" as to the price and structure of the transaction has been reached between the would-be merger partners. See Greenfield v. Heublein, Inc., 742 F.2d 751, 757 (C.A.3 1984), cert. denied, 469 U.S. 1215 (1985). By definition, then, information concerning any negotiations not yet at the agreement-in-principle stage could be withheld or even misrepresented without a violation of Rule 10b–5.

9. We do not address here any other kinds of contingent or speculative information, such as earnings forecasts or projections. See generally Hiler, The SEC and the Courts' Approach to Disclosure of Earnings Projections, Asset Appraisals, and Other Soft Information: Old Problems, Changing Views, 46 Md.L.Rev. 1114 (1987).

10. See Staffin v. Greenberg, 672 F.2d 1196, 1207 (C.A.3 1982) (defining duty to disclose existence of ongoing merger negotiations as triggered when agreement-in-principle is reached); Greenfield v. Heublein, Inc., 742 F.2d 751 (C.A.3 1984) (applying agreement-in-principle test to materiality inquiry), cert. denied, 469 U.S. 1215 (1985). Citing Staffin, the United States Court of Appeals for the Second Circuit has rejected a claim that defendant was under an obligation to disclose various events related to merger negotiations. Reiss v. Pan American World Airways, Inc., 711 F.2d 11, 13–14 (C.A.2 1983). The Seventh Circuit recently endorsed the agreement-in-principle test of materiality. See Flamm v. Eberstadt, 814 F.2d 1169, 1174–1179 (CA7) (describing agreement-in-principle as an agreement on price and structure), cert. denied, ___ U.S. ___ (1987). In some of these cases it is unclear whether the court based its decision on a finding that no duty arose to reveal the existence of negotiations, or whether it concluded that the negotiations were immaterial under an interpretation of the opinion in TSC Industries, Inc. v. Northway, Inc., supra.

Three rationales have been offered in support of the "agreement-in-principle" test. The first derives from the concern expressed in TSC Industries that an investor not be overwhelmed by excessively detailed and trivial information, and focuses on the substantial risk that preliminary merger discussions may collapse: because such discussions are inherently tentative, disclosure of their existence itself could mislead investors and foster false optimism. See Greenfield v. Heublein, Inc., 742 F.2d, at 756; Reiss v. Pan American World Airways, Inc., 711 F.2d 11, 14 (C.A.2 1983). The other two justifications for the agreement-in-principle standard are based on management concerns: because the requirement of "agreement-in-principle" limits the scope of disclosure obligations, it helps preserve the confidentiality of merger discussions where earlier disclosure might prejudice the negotiations; and the test also provides a usable, bright-line rule for determining when disclosure must be made. See Greenfield v. Heublein, Inc., 742 F.2d, at 757; Flamm v. Eberstadt, 814 F.2d 1169, 1176–1178 (CA7), cert. denied, ___ U.S. ___ (1987).

None of these policy-based rationales, however, purports to explain why drawing the line at agreement-in-principle reflects the significance of the information upon the investor's decision. The first rationale, and the only one connected to the concerns expressed in TSC Industries, stands soundly rejected, even by a Court of Appeals that otherwise has accepted the wisdom of the agreement-in-principle test. "It assumes that investors are nitwits, unable to appreciate—even when told—that mergers are risky propositions up until the closing." Flamm v. Eberstadt, 814 F.2d, at 1175. Disclosure, and not paternalistic withholding of accurate information, is the policy chosen and expressed by Congress. We have recognized time and again, a "fundamental purpose" of the various securities acts, "was to substitute a philosophy of full disclosure for the philosophy of *caveat emptor* and thus to achieve a high standard of business ethics in the securities industry." SEC v. Capital Gains Research Bureau, Inc., 375 U.S. 180, 186 (1963). * * * The role of the materiality requirement is not to "attribute to investors a child-like simplicity, an inability to grasp the probabilistic significance of negotiations," Flamm v. Eberstadt, 814 F.2d, at 1175, but to filter out essentially useless information that a reasonable investor would not consider significant, even as part of a larger "mix" of factors to consider in making his investment decision. TSC Industries, Inc. v. Northway, Inc., 426 U.S., at 448–449.

The second rationale, the importance of secrecy during the early stages of merger discussions, also seems irrelevant to an assessment whether their existence is significant to the trading decision of a reasonable investor. To avoid a "bidding war" over its target, an acquiring firm often will insist that negotiations remain confidential, see, e.g., In re Carnation Co., Exchange Act Release No. 22214, 33 SEC Docket 1025 (1985), and at least one Court of Appeals has stated that "silence pending settlement of the price and structure of a deal is beneficial to most investors, most of the time." Flamm v. Eberstadt, 814 F.2d, at 1177.

We need not ascertain, however, whether secrecy necessarily maximizes shareholder wealth—although we note that the proposition is at least disputed as a matter of theory and empirical research[12]—for this case does not concern the timing of a disclosure; it concerns only its accuracy and completeness. We face here the narrow question whether information concerning the existence and status of preliminary merger discussions is significant to the reasonable investor's trading decision. Arguments based on the premise that some disclosure would be "premature" in a sense are more properly considered under the rubric of an issuer's duty to disclose. The "secrecy" rationale is simply inapposite to the definition of materiality.

The final justification offered in support of the agreement-in-principle test seems to be directed solely at the comfort of corporate managers. A bright-line rule indeed is easier to follow than a standard that requires the exercise of judgment in the light of all the circumstances. But ease of application alone is not an excuse for ignoring the purposes of the securities acts and Congress' policy decisions. Any approach that designates a single fact or occurrence as always determinative of an inherently fact-specific finding such as materiality, must necessarily be over- or underinclusive. In *TSC Industries* this Court explained: "The determination [of materiality] requires delicate assessments of the inferences a 'reasonable shareholder' would draw from a given set of facts and the significance of those inferences to him. * * *" 426 U.S., at 450. After much study, the Advisory Committee on Corporate Disclosure cautioned the SEC against administratively confining materiality to a rigid formula.[14] Courts also would do well to heed this advice.

We therefore find no valid justification for artificially excluding from the definition of materiality information concerning merger discussions, which would otherwise be considered significant to the trading decision of a reasonable investor, merely because agreement-in-principle as to price and structure has not yet been reached by the parties or their representatives.

The Sixth Circuit explicitly rejected the agreement-in-principle test, as we do today, but in its place adopted a rule that, if taken literally, would be equally insensitive, in our view, to the distinction between materiality and the other elements of an action under Rule 10b–5:

12. See, e.g., Brown, Corporate Secrecy, the Federal Securities Laws, and the Disclosure of Ongoing Negotiations, 36 Cath. U.L.Rev. 93, 145–155 (1986); Bebchuk, The Case for Facilitating Competing Tender Offers, 95 Harv.L.Rev. 1028 (1982); Flamm v. Eberstadt, 814 F.2d, at 1177, n. 2 (citing scholarly debate). See also In re Carnation Co., Exchange Act Release No. 22214, 33 SEC Docket 1025, 1030 (1985) ("The importance of accurate and complete issuer disclosure to the integrity of the securities markets cannot be overemphasized. To the extent that investors cannot rely upon the accuracy and completeness of issuer statements, they will be less likely to invest, thereby reducing the liquidity of the securities markets to the detriment of investors and issuers alike").

14. "Although the Committee believes that ideally it would be desirable to have absolute certainty in the application of the materiality concept, it is its view that such a goal is illusory and unrealistic. The materiality concept is judgmental in nature and it is not possible to translate this into a numerical formula. The Committee's advice to the [SEC] is to avoid this quest for certainty and to continue consideration of materiality on a case-by-case basis as problems are identified."

Report of the Advisory Committee on Corporate Disclosure to the Securities and Exchange Commission 327 (House Committee on Interstate and Foreign Commerce, 95th Cong., 1st Sess.) (Comm.Print) (1977).

"When a company whose stock is publicly traded makes a statement, as Basic did, that 'no negotiations' are underway, and that the corporation knows of 'no reason for the stock's activity,' and that 'management is unaware of any present or pending corporate development that would result in the abnormally heavy trading activity,' information concerning ongoing acquisition discussions becomes material *by virtue of the statement denying their existence.*

* * *

In analyzing whether information regarding merger discussions is material such that it must be affirmatively disclosed to avoid a violation of Rule 10b–5, the discussions and their progress are the primary considerations. However, once a statement is made denying the existence of any discussions, even discussions that might not have been material in absence of the denial are material because they make the statement made untrue." 786 F.2d, at 748–749 (emphasis in original).

This approach, however, fails to recognize that, in order to prevail on a Rule 10b–5 claim, a plaintiff must show that the statements were *misleading* as to a *material* fact. It is not enough that a statement is false or incomplete, if the misrepresented fact is otherwise insignificant.

C

Even before this Court's decision in TSC Industries, the Second Circuit had explained the role of the materiality requirement of Rule 10b–5, with respect to contingent or speculative information or events, in a manner that gave that term meaning that is independent of the other provisions of the Rule. Under such circumstances, materiality "will depend at any given time upon a balancing of both the indicated probability that the event will occur and the anticipated magnitude of the event in light of the totality of the company activity." SEC v. Texas Gulf Sulphur Co., 401 F.2d, at 849. Interestingly, neither the Third Circuit decision adopting the agreement-in-principle test nor petitioners here take issue with this general standard. Rather, they suggest that with respect to preliminary merger discussions, there are good reasons to draw a line at agreement on price and structure. In a subsequent decision, the late Judge Friendly, writing for a Second Circuit panel, applied the Texas Gulf Sulphur probability/magnitude approach in the specific context of preliminary merger negotiations. After acknowledging that materiality is something to be determined on the basis of the particular facts of each case, he stated:

"Since a merger in which it is bought out is the most important event that can occur in a small corporation's life, to wit, its death, we think that inside information, as regards a merger of this sort, can become material at an earlier stage than would be the case as regards lesser transactions—and this even though the mortality rate of mergers in such formative stages is doubtless high."

SEC v. Geon Industries, Inc., 531 F.2d 39, 47–48 (C.A.2 1976). We agree with that analysis.

Whether merger discussions in any particular case are material therefore depends on the facts. Generally, in order to assess the probability that the event will occur, a factfinder will need to look to indicia of interest in the transaction at the highest corporate levels. Without attempting to catalog all such possible factors, we note by way of example that board resolutions, instructions to investment bankers, and actual negotiations between principals or their intermediaries may serve as indicia of interest. To assess the magnitude of the transaction to the issuer of the securities allegedly manipulated, a factfinder will need to consider such facts as the size of the two corporate entities and of the potential premiums over market value. No particular event or factor short of closing the transaction need be either necessary or sufficient by itself to render merger discussions material.[17]

As we clarify today, materiality depends on the significance the reasonable investor would place on the withheld or misrepresented information.[18]

---

17. To be actionable, of course, a statement must also be misleading. Silence, absent a duty to disclose, is not misleading under Rule 10b–5. "No comment" statements are generally the functional equivalent of silence. See In re Carnation Co., supra. See also New York Stock Exchange Listed Company Manual § 202.01, reprinted in 3 CCH Fed.Sec.L.Rep. ¶ 23,515 (premature public announcement may properly be delayed for valid business purpose and where adequate security can be maintained); American Stock Exchange Company Guide §§ 401–405, reprinted in 3 CCH Fed.Sec.L.Rep. ¶¶ 23, 124A–23, 124E (similar provisions).

It has been suggested that given current market practices, a "no comment" statement is tantamount to an admission that merger discussions are underway. See Flamm v. Eberstadt, 814 F.2d, at 1178. That may well hold true to the extent that issuers adopt a policy of truthfully denying merger rumors when no discussions are underway, and of issuing "no comment" statements when they are in the midst of negotiations. There are, of course, other statement policies firms could adopt; we need not now advise issuers as to what kind of practice to follow, within the range permitted by law. Perhaps more importantly, we think that creating an exception to a regulatory scheme founded on a prodisclosure legislative philosophy, because complying with the regulation might be "bad for business," is a role for Congress, not this Court. See also id., at 1182 (opinion concurring in the judgment and concurring in part).

18. We find no authority in the statute, the legislative history, or our previous decisions, for varying the standard of materiality depending on who brings the action or whether insiders are alleged to have profited. See, e.g., Pavlidis v. New England Patriots Football Club, Inc., 737 F.2d 1227, 1231 (C.A.1 1984) ("A fact does not become more material to the shareholder's decision because it is withheld by an insider, or because the insider might profit by withholding it"); cf. Aaron v. SEC, 446 U.S. 680, 691 (1980) ("scienter is an element of a violation of § 10(b) and Rule 10b–5, regardless of the identity of the plaintiff or the nature of the relief sought").

We recognize that trading (and profit making) by insiders can serve as an indication of materiality, see SEC v. Texas Gulf Sulphur Co., 401 F.2d, at 851; General Portland, Inc. v. LaFarge Coppee S.A., CCH Fed. Sec.L.Rep. (1982–1983 Transfer Binder) ¶ 99,148, p. 95,544 (ND Tex.1981). We are not prepared to agree, however, that "[i]n cases of the disclosure of inside information to a favored few, determination of materiality has a different aspect than when the issue is, for example, an inaccuracy in a publicly disseminated press release." SEC v. Geon Industries, Inc., 531 F.2d 39, 48 (C.A.2 1976). Devising two different standards of materiality, one for situations where insiders have traded in abrogation of their duty to disclose or abstain (or for that matter when any disclosure duty has been breached), and another covering affirmative misrepresentations by those under no duty to disclose (but under the ever-present duty not to mislead), would effectively collapse the materiality requirement into the analysis of defendant's disclosure duties.

The fact-specific inquiry we endorse here is consistent with the approach a number of courts have taken in assessing the materiality of merger negotiations. Because the standard of materiality we have adopted differs from that used by both courts below, we remand the case for reconsideration of the question whether a grant of summary judgment is appropriate on this record.

IV

A

We turn to the question of reliance and the fraud-on-the-market theory. Succinctly put:

> "The fraud on the market theory is based on the hypothesis that, in an open and developed securities market, the price of a company's stock is determined by the available material information regarding the company and its business. * * * Misleading statements will therefore defraud purchasers of stock even if the purchasers do not directly rely on the misstatements. * * * The causal connection between the defendants' fraud and the plaintiffs' purchase of stock in such a case is no less significant than in a case of direct reliance on misrepresentations." Peil v. Speiser, 806 F.2d 1154, 1160–1161 (C.A.3 1986).

Our task, of course, is not to assess the general validity of the theory, but to consider whether it was proper for the courts below to apply a rebuttable presumption of reliance, supported in part by the fraud-on-the-market theory. * * *

This case required resolution of several common questions of law and fact concerning the falsity or misleading nature of the three public statements made by Basic, the presence or absence of scienter, and the materiality of the misrepresentations, if any. In their amended complaint, the named plaintiffs alleged that in reliance on Basic's statements they sold their shares of Basic stock in the depressed market created by petitioners. * * * Requiring proof of individualized reliance from each member of the proposed plaintiff class effectively would have prevented respondents from proceeding with a class action, since individual issues then would have overwhelmed the common ones. The District Court found that the presumption of reliance created by the fraud-on-the-market theory provided "a practical resolution to the problem of balancing the substantive requirement of proof of reliance in securities cases against the procedural requisites of [Fed.Rule Civ.Proc.] 23." The District Court thus concluded that with reference to each public statement and its impact upon the open market for Basic shares, common questions predominated over individual questions, as required by Fed.Rule Civ.Proc. 23(a)(2) and (b)(3).

* * *

* * * [R]eliance is an element of a Rule 10b–5 cause of action. See Ernst & Ernst v. Hochfelder, 425 U.S., at 206 (quoting Senate Report). Reliance provides the requisite causal connection between a defendant's misrepresentation and a plaintiff's injury. * * * There is, however, more than one way to demonstrate the causal connection. Indeed, we previously

have dispensed with a requirement of positive proof of reliance, where a duty to disclose material information had been breached, concluding that the necessary nexus between the plaintiffs' injury and the defendant's wrongful conduct had been established. See Affiliated Ute Citizens v. United States, 406 U.S., at 153–154. Similarly, we did not require proof that material omissions or misstatements in a proxy statement decisively affected voting, because the proxy solicitation itself, rather than the defect in the solicitation materials, served as an essential link in the transaction. See Mills v. Electric Auto–Lite Co., 396 U.S. 375, 384–385 (1970).

The modern securities markets, literally involving millions of shares changing hands daily, differ from the face-to-face transactions contemplated by early fraud cases, and our understanding of Rule 10b–5's reliance requirement must encompass these differences.

> "In face-to-face transactions, the inquiry into an investor's reliance upon information is into the subjective pricing of that information by that investor. With the presence of a market, the market is interposed between seller and buyer and, ideally, transmits information to the investor in the processed form of a market price. Thus the market is performing a substantial part of the valuation process performed by the investor in a face-to-face transaction. The market is acting as the unpaid agent of the investor, informing him that given all the information available to it, the value of the stock is worth the market price." In re LTV Securities Litigation, 88 F.R.D. 134, 143 (N.D.Tex.1980).

* * *

B

Presumptions typically serve to assist courts in managing circumstances in which direct proof, for one reason or another, is rendered difficult. See, e.g., D. Louisell & C. Mueller, Federal Evidence 541–542 (1977). The courts below accepted a presumption, created by the fraud-on-the-market theory and subject to rebuttal by petitioners, that persons who had traded Basic shares had done so in reliance on the integrity of the price set by the market, but because of petitioners' material misrepresentations that price had been fraudulently depressed. Requiring a plaintiff to show a speculative state of facts, i.e., how he would have acted if omitted material information had been disclosed, see Affiliated Ute Citizens v. United States, 406 U.S., at 153–154, or if the misrepresentation had not been made, see Sharp v. Coopers & Lybrand, 649 F.2d 175, 188 (C.A.3 1981), cert. denied, 455 U.S. 938 (1982), would place an unnecessarily unrealistic evidentiary burden on the Rule 10b–5 plaintiff who has traded on an impersonal market. Cf. Mills v. Electric Auto–Lite Co., 396 U.S., at 385.

Arising out of considerations of fairness, public policy, and probability, as well as judicial economy, presumptions are also useful devices for allocating the burdens of proof between parties. See E. Cleary, McCormick on Evidence 968–969 (3rd ed. 1984); see also Fed.Rule Evid. 301 and notes. The presumption of reliance employed in this case is consistent with, and, by facilitating Rule 10b–5 litigation, supports, the congressional policy embodied in the 1934 Act. * * *

The presumption is also supported by common sense and probability. Recent empirical studies have tended to confirm Congress' premise that the market price of shares traded on well-developed markets reflects all publicly available information, and, hence, any material misrepresentations.[24] It has been noted that "it is hard to imagine that there ever is a buyer or seller who does not rely on market integrity. Who would knowingly roll the dice in a crooked crap game?" Schlanger v. Four–Phase Systems Inc., 555 F.Supp. 535, 538 (S.D.N.Y.1982). Indeed, nearly every court that has considered the proposition has concluded that where materially misleading statements have been disseminated into an impersonal, well-developed market for securities, the reliance of individual plaintiffs on the integrity of the market price may be presumed. Commentators generally have applauded the adoption of one variation or another of the fraud-on-the-market theory. An investor who buys or sells stock at the price set by the market does so in reliance on the integrity of that price. Because most publicly available information is reflected in market price, an investor's reliance on any public material misrepresentations, therefore, may be presumed for purposes of a Rule 10b–5 action.

C

* * *

Any showing that severs the link between the alleged misrepresentation and either the price received (or paid) by the plaintiff, or his decision to trade at a fair market price, will be sufficient to rebut the presumption of reliance. For example, if petitioners could show that the "market makers" were privy to the truth about the merger discussions here with Combustion, and thus that the market price would not have been affected by their misrepresentations, the causal connection could be broken: the basis for finding that the fraud had been transmitted through market price would be gone. Similarly, if, despite petitioners' allegedly fraudulent attempt to manipulate market price, news of the merger discussions credibly entered the market and dissipated the effects of the misstatements, those who traded Basic shares after the corrective statements would have no direct or indirect connection with the fraud.[29] Petitioners also could rebut

---

24. See In re LTV Securities Litigation, 88 F.R.D. 134, 144 (N.D.Tex.1980) (citing studies); Fischel, Use of Modern Finance Theory in Securities Fraud Cases Involving Actively Traded Securities, 38 Bus.Law. 1, 4, n. 9 (1982) (citing literature on efficient-capital-market theory); Dennis, Materiality and the Efficient Capital Market Model: A Recipe for the Total Mix, 25 Wm. & Mary L.Rev. 373, 374–381, and n. 1 (1984). We need not determine by adjudication what economists and social scientists have debated through the use of sophisticated statistical analysis and the application of economic theory. For purposes of accepting the presumption of reliance in this case, we need only believe that market professionals generally consider most publicly announced material statements about companies, thereby affecting stock market prices.

29. We note there may be a certain incongruity between the assumption that Basic shares are traded on a well-developed, efficient, and information-hungry market, and the allegation that such a market could remain misinformed, and its valuation of Basic shares depressed, for 14 months, on the basis of the three public statements. Proof of that sort is a matter for trial, throughout which the District Court retains the authority to amend the certification order as may be appropriate. See Fed.Rule Civ.Proc. 23(c)(1)

the presumption of reliance as to plaintiffs who would have divested themselves of their Basic shares without relying on the integrity of the market. For example, a plaintiff who believed that Basic's statements were false and that Basic was indeed engaged in merger discussions, and who consequently believed that Basic stock was artificially underpriced, but sold his shares nevertheless because of other unrelated concerns, e.g., potential antitrust problems, or political pressures to divest from shares of certain businesses, could not be said to have relied on the integrity of a price he knew had been manipulated.

V

* * *

The judgment of the Court of Appeals is vacated and the case is remanded to that court for further proceedings consistent with this opinion. It is so ordered.

■ JUSTICE WHITE, with whom JUSTICE O'CONNOR joins, concurring in part and dissenting in part.

I join Parts I–III of the Court's opinion, as I agree that the standard of materiality we set forth in TSC Industries, Inc. v. Northway, Inc., 426 U.S. 438, 449 (1976), should be applied to actions under § 10(b) and Rule 10b–5. But I dissent from the remainder of the Court's holding because I do not agree that the "fraud-on-the-market" theory should be applied in this case.

I

Even when compared to the relatively youthful private cause-of-action under § 10(b), see Kardon v. National Gypsum Co., 69 F.Supp. 512 (E.D.Pa.1946), the fraud-on-the-market theory is a mere babe. Yet today, the Court embraces this theory with the sweeping confidence usually reserved for more mature legal doctrines. In so doing, I fear that the Court's decision may have many adverse, unintended effects as it is applied and interpreted in the years to come.

A

At the outset, I note that there are portions of the Court's fraud-on-the-market holding with which I am in agreement. Most importantly, the Court rejects the version of that theory, heretofore adopted by some courts, which equates "causation" with "reliance," and permits recovery by a plaintiff who claims merely to have been harmed by a material misrepresentation which altered a market price, notwithstanding proof that the plaintiff did not in any way rely on that price. * * * I agree with the Court that if Rule 10b–5's reliance requirement is to be left with any content at all, the fraud-on-the-market presumption must be capable of being rebutted by a showing that a plaintiff did not "rely" on the market price. For

and (c)(4). See 7B C. Wright, A. Miller & M. Kane, Federal Practice and Procedure 128–132 (1986). Thus, we see no need to engage in the kind of factual analysis the dissent suggests that manifests the "oddities" of applying a rebuttable presumption of reliance in this case. * * *

example, a plaintiff who decides, months in advance of an alleged misrepresentation, to purchase a stock; one who buys or sells a stock for reasons unrelated to its price; one who actually sells a stock "short" days before the misrepresentation is made—surely none of these people can state a valid claim under Rule 10b–5. Yet, some federal courts have allowed such claims to stand under one variety or another of the fraud-on-the-market theory.

Happily, the majority puts to rest the prospect of recovery under such circumstances. A nonrebuttable presumption of reliance—or even worse, allowing recovery in the face of "affirmative evidence of nonreliance," Zweig v. Hearst Corp., 594 F.2d 1261, 1272 (C.A.9 1979) (Ely, J., dissenting)—would effectively convert Rule 10b–5 into "a scheme of investor's insurance." Shores v. Sklar, 647 F.2d 462, 469, n. 5 (C.A.5 1981) (en banc), cert. denied, 459 U.S. 1102 (1983). There is no support in the Securities Act, the Rule, or our cases for such a result.

B

But even as the Court attempts to limit the fraud-on-the-market theory it endorses today, the pitfalls in its approach are revealed by previous uses by the lower courts of the broader versions of the theory. Confusion and contradiction in court rulings are inevitable when traditional legal analysis is replaced with economic theorization by the federal courts.

In general, the case law developed in this Court with respect to § 10(b) and Rule 10b–5 has been based on doctrines with which we, as judges, are familiar: common-law doctrines of fraud and deceit. See, e.g., Santa Fe Industries, Inc. v. Green, 430 U.S. 462, 471–477 (1977). Even when we have extended civil liability under Rule 10b–5 to a broader reach than the common law had previously permitted, * * * we have retained familiar legal principles as or guideposts. See, e.g., Herman & MacLean v. Huddleston, 459 U.S. 375, 389–390 (1983). The federal courts have proved adept at developing an evolving jurisprudence of Rule 10b–5 in such a manner. But with no staff economists, no experts schooled in the "efficient-capital-market hypothesis," no ability to test the validity of empirical market studies, we are not well equipped to embrace novel constructions of a statute based on contemporary microeconomic theory.[4]

The "wrong turns" in those Court of Appeals and district court fraud-on-the-market decisions which the Court implicitly rejects as going too far should be ample illustration of the dangers when economic theories replace legal rules as the basis for recovery. Yet the Court today ventures into this

---

4. This view was put well by two commentators who wrote a few years ago:

"Of all recent developments in financial economics, the efficient capital market hypothesis ("ECMH") has achieved the widest acceptance by the legal culture. * * *

"Yet the legal culture's remarkably rapid and broad acceptance of an economic concept that did not exist twenty years ago is not matched by an equivalent degree of *understanding*." Gilson & Kraakman, The Mechanisms of Market Efficiency, 70 Va.L.Rev. 549, 549–550 (1984) (footnotes omitted; emphasis added).

While the fraud-on-the-market theory has gained even broader acceptance since 1984, I doubt that it has achieved any greater understanding.

area beyond its expertise, beyond—by its own admission—the confines of our previous fraud cases. * * * Even if I agreed with the Court that "modern securities markets * * * involving millions of shares changing hands daily" require that the "understanding of Rule 10b–5's reliance requirement" be changed, * * * I prefer that such changes come from Congress in amending § 10(b). The Congress, with its superior resources and expertise, is far better equipped than the federal courts for the task of determining how modern economic theory and global financial markets require that established legal notions of fraud be modified. In choosing to make these decisions itself, the Court, I fear, embarks on a course that it does not genuinely understand, giving rise to consequences it cannot foresee.

For while the economists' theories which underpin the fraud-on-the-market presumption may have the appeal of mathematical exactitude and scientific certainty, they are—in the end—nothing more than theories which may or may not prove accurate upon further consideration. Even the most earnest advocates of economic analysis of the law recognize this. See, e.g., Easterbrook, Afterword: Knowledge and Answers, 85 Colum.L.Rev. 1117, 1118 (1985). Thus, while the majority states that, for purposes of reaching its result it need only make modest assumptions about the way in which "market professionals generally" do their jobs, and how the conduct of market professionals affects stock prices, * * * I doubt that we are in much of a position to assess which theories aptly describe the functioning of the securities industry.

Consequently, I cannot join the Court in its effort to reconfigure the securities laws, based on recent economic theories, to better fit what it perceives to be the new realities of financial markets. I would leave this task to others more equipped for the job than we.

C

At the bottom of the Court's conclusion that the fraud-on-the-market theory sustains a presumption of reliance is the assumption that individuals rely "on the integrity of the market price" when buying or selling stock in "impersonal, well-developed market[s] for securities." * * * Even if I was prepared to accept (as a matter of common sense or general understanding) the assumption that most persons buying or selling stock do so in response to the market price, the fraud-on-the-market theory goes further. For in adopting a "presumption of reliance," the Court also assumes that buyers and sellers rely—not just on the market price—but on the "integrity" of that price. It is this aspect of the fraud-on-the-market hypothesis which most mystifies me.

To define the term "integrity of the market price," the majority quotes approvingly from cases which suggest that investors are entitled to " 'rely on the price of a stock as a reflection of its value.' " * * * But the meaning of this phrase eludes me, for it implicitly suggests that stocks have some "true value" that is measurable by a standard other than their market price. While the Scholastics of Medieval times professed a means to make such a valuation of a commodity's "worth," I doubt that the federal courts of our day are similarly equipped.

Even if securities had some "value"—knowable and distinct from the market price of a stock—investors do not always share the Court's presumption that a stock's price is a "reflection of [this] value." Indeed, "many investors purchase or sell stock because they believe the price inaccurately reflects the corporation's worth." See Black, Fraud on the Market: A Criticism of Dispensing with Reliance Requirements in Certain Open Market Transactions, 62 N.C.L.Rev. 435, 455 (1984) (emphasis added). If investors really believed that stock prices reflected a stock's "value," many sellers would never sell, and many buyers never buy (given the time and cost associated with executing a stock transaction). As we recognized just a few years ago: "[I]nvestors act on inevitably incomplete or inaccurate information, [consequently] there are always winners and losers; but those who have 'lost' have not necessarily been defrauded." Dirks v. SEC, 463 U.S. 646, 667, n. 27 (1983). Yet today, the Court allows investors to recover who can show little more than that they sold stock at a lower price than what might have been.[7]

I do not propose that the law retreat from the many protections that § 10(b) and Rule 10b–5, as interpreted in our prior cases, provide to investors. But any extension of these laws, to approach something closer to an investor insurance scheme, should come from Congress, and not from the courts.

II

Congress has not passed on the fraud-on-the-market theory the Court embraces today. That is reason enough for us to abstain from doing so. But it is even more troubling that, to the extent that any view of Congress on this question can be inferred indirectly, it is contrary to the result the majority reaches.

* * *

III

Finally, the particular facts of this case make it an exceedingly poor candidate for the Court's fraud-on-the-market theory, and illustrate the illogic achieved by that theory's application in many cases. Respondents here are a class of sellers who sold Basic stock between October, 1977 and December 1978, a fourteen-month period. At the time the class period began, Basic's stock was trading at $20 a share (at the time, an all-time high); the last members of the class to sell their Basic stock got a price of

---

7. This is what the Court's rule boils down to in practical terms. For while, in theory, the Court allows for rebuttal of its "presumption of reliance"—a proviso with which I agree, * * * in practice the Court must realize, as other courts applying the fraud-on-the-market theory have, that such rebuttal is virtually impossible in all but the most extraordinary case. * * *

Consequently, while the Court considers it significant that the fraud-on-the-market presumption it endorses is a rebuttable one, * * * the majority's implicit rejection of the "pure causation" fraud-on-the-market theory rings hollow. In most cases, the Court's theory will operate just as the causation theory would, creating a non-rebuttable presumption of "reliance" in future 10b–5 actions.

just over $30 a share. * * * It is indisputable that virtually every member of the class made money from his or her sale of Basic stock. The oddities of applying the fraud-on-the-market theory in this case are manifest. First, there are the facts that the plaintiffs are sellers and the class period is so lengthy—both are virtually without precedent in prior fraud-on-the-market cases.

Second, there is the fact that in this case, there is no evidence that petitioner's officials made the troublesome misstatements for the purpose of manipulating stock prices, or with any intent to engage in underhanded trading of Basic stock. Indeed, during the class period, petitioners do not appear to have purchased or sold any Basic stock whatsoever. * * * I agree with amicus who argues that "[i]mposition of damages liability under Rule 10b–5 makes little sense * * * where a defendant is neither a purchaser nor a seller of securities." See Brief for American Corporate Counsel Association as Amicus Curiae 13.

    * * *

Third, there are the peculiarities of what kinds of investors will be able to recover in this case. As I read the District Court's class certification order, * * * there are potentially many persons who did not purchase Basic stock until after the first false statement (October 1977), but who nonetheless will be able to recover under the Court's fraud-on-the-market theory. Thus, it is possible that a person who heard the first corporate misstatement and disbelieved it—i.e., someone who purchased Basic stock thinking that petitioners' statement was false—may still be included in the plaintiff-class on remand. How a person who undertook such a speculative stock-investing strategy—and made $10 a share doing so (if he bought on October 22, 1977, and sold on December 15, 1978)—can say that he was "defrauded" by virtue of his reliance on the "integrity" of the market price is beyond me. And such speculators may not be uncommon, at least in this case. * * *

Indeed, the facts of this case lead a casual observer to the almost inescapable conclusion that many of those who bought or sold Basic stock during the period in question flatly disbelieved the statements which are alleged to have been "materially misleading." Despite three statements denying that merger negotiations were underway, Basic stock hit record-high after record-high during the 14–month class period. * * *

And who will pay the judgments won in such actions? I suspect that all too often the majority's rule will "lead to large judgments, payable in the last analysis by innocent investors, for the benefit of speculators and their lawyers." Cf. SEC v. Texas Gulf Sulphur Co., 401 F.2d 833, 867 (C.A.2 1968) (en banc) (Friendly, J., concurring), cert. denied, 394 U.S. 976 (1969). * * *

NOTE: MISREPRESENTATIONS, SILENCE, MERGERS AND OTHER SOFT INFORMATION

1. *Misrepresentations and the Market.*

Macey and Miller, Good Finance, Bad Economics: An Analysis of the Fraud-on-the-Market Theory, 42 Stan.L.Rev. 1059, 1072, 1075–76 (1990), takes issue with the result in the case. Putting the matter into a hypothetical contract framework, Macey and Miller argue that most investors would agree in advance to permit management fraud in some cases, so long as management's actions cause the stock value to be maximized in the long run. They assert that legal intervention against management fraud is necessary only where as a result of the fraud the stock price goes up, thus externalizing the social cost of the lie. Where, as in *Basic,* the misrepresentation causes the stock price to go down, the firm's cost of capital goes up, and the cost is internalized, there should be no liability. For a response to this, see Ayres, Back to *Basics:* Regulating How Corporations Speak to the Market, 77 Va.L.Rev. 945 (1991). See also Spindler, Why Shareholders Want their CEOs to Lie More After Dura Pharmaceuticals, 95 Geo. L.J. 653 (2007); Kahan, Games, Lies, and Securities Fraud, 67 N.Y.U.L.Rev. 750 (1992). For other criticisms of fraud on the market doctrine, see Mahoney, Precaution Costs and the Law of Fraud on Impersonal Markets, 78 Va. L. Rev. 623 (1992); Carney, Limits of the Fraud on the Market Doctrine, 44 Bus. Law. 1259 (1989).

2. *Merger Negotiations and Financial Economics.*

Justice Blackmun refers to financial economics to support the "fraud on the market" theory of reliance. But what approach is counseled by the precepts of financial economics on the matter of disclosure of merger negotiations?

Consider, in connection with these questions, the opinion of Judge Easterbrook in **Flamm v. Eberstadt,** 814 F.2d 1169 (7th Cir.1987), cert. denied, 484 U.S. 853 (1987). The 10b–5 plaintiff there sold stock of a tender offer target after the tender offer but before the announcement of a competing friendly tender offer at a higher price. Plaintiff contended that the target's search for a White Knight should have been disclosed. Unlike the corporation in *Basic,* no false denials had been issued.

Judge Easterbrook, approved the price-and-structure rule as follows, pp. 1176–1177:

"[Plaintiff contends] that silence is not beneficial to all investors, that there is a conflict of interest between investors who sell before the disclosure and investors who hold, thereby receiving the benefits later on. See Ronald J. Gilson, The Law and Finance of Corporate Acquisitions 977 (1986). Perhaps so, although the corporation is not required by the securities law to favor hair-trigger sellers over other investors. From a longer perspective, however, even this conflict disappears. Investors who wanted to prescribe their managers' behavior during merger discussions would favor a rule of silence until the discussions had reached agreement on price and structure. Such discussions may occur anytime during the life of the firm. Ex ante, each investor's chance of selling during that window is small. The chance of selling for 'too little' is offset by an identical chance of buying at a bargain; every sale has a buyer and a seller. Over the long run, then, the prospect of selling for too little and buying a bargain are a wash, leaving only the prospect of receiving (or scaring away) beneficial opportunities to merge. All investors would prefer whichever approach maximized their anticipated wealth. The legal rule governing disclosure is like this hypothetical bargain among investors. It applies to all firms, to all investors be they buyers or sellers, at all times. In selecting a legal rule, a court must consider the effects on all investors in all firms, not just the effects on the plaintiff.

"Even the unlucky investors, such as Flamm, who sell their stock in a particular firm too soon can take comfort in knowing that they do not lose the whole gain. To the extent the appearance of White Knights is predictable, the probability of a White Knight appearing in this contest will be reflected in the price of the stock. Most buyers during tender offer contests are arbitrageurs, professional investors who are exceptionally knowledgeable. These professionals make money by taking risk—they take the risk that all bids will vanish (and the price fall here to $11.75) in exchange for the prospect of gain from the offer (here at $17) and the chance of a higher bid. When Flamm sold his stock, he passed to the arbitrageurs the risk that the price would fall to $11.75, or even to $17 (he received $17 3/8); the arbitrageurs did not take the risk off Flamm's shoulders for free but were compensated by the possibility (remote as of December 29!) of a higher price. Undoubtedly many arbitrageurs had learned that Goldman, Sachs was shopping for a deal. Their bids reflected the value of a potential deal, and Flamm received this value without knowing about the prospects himself. It is not right to reply that the arbitrageurs— 'speculators', transient investors—are swiping gains that 'belong' to the longer-term investors such as Flamm. Arbitrageurs must compete among themselves to buy stock. The more likely the gain from a later White Knight bid, the more any given arbitrageur is willing to pay for stock. To make a profit the arbitrageur must put his hands on the stock; to acquire the stock he must outbid other arbitrageurs, who have the same end in view; the competition ultimately passes back to Flamm and the other original investors the gains from the probability of a White Knight bid, as of December 29 (or any other date), less the premium for taking risk off Flamm's hands. Premature disclosure could have reduced the chances of an acquisition by a White Knight, and therefore reduced the bids made in the market for Flamm's stock.

"So silence pending settlement of the price and structure of a deal is beneficial to most investors, most of the time. We do not think that the securities laws war against the best interests of investors. Rule 10b–5 is about *fraud* after all, and it is not fraudulent to conduct business in a way that makes investors better off—that all investors prefer ex ante and that most prefer ex post. Cf. Dirks v. SEC, 463 U.S. 646, 653–59 (1983) (liability depends on a 'duty' to disclose, duty defined in part to ensure the welfare of investors as a group).

"We agree, too, with the conclusion of the other circuits that the benefits of certainty supply additional support for the price-and-structure rule. If disclosure must occur at an earlier date, how much earlier? That would be a fertile ground for disputation. No matter how soon the firm announced the negotiations, investors could say that it should have done so a little sooner. * * * "

Consider also the solution proposed by Professor Ayres. He places the question in a hypothetical contract model and reasons that a default rule in which corporations warrant the honesty of their statements would best suit market actors. He suggests that corporations contract out of the default rule in their certificates of incorporation by committing in advance to silence in merger negotiation situations. See Ayres, supra, at 954–956.

3.   Basic *Impact.*

Reconsider *Starkman v. Marathon* in light of *Basic.* Does the bright line exclusion for preliminary negotiations applied in *Starkman* survive *Basic* ? Would *Basic* require a different result in *Starkman* on the issue respecting the disclosure of internal appraisal reports? Should the *Starkman* court have required disclosure of the negotiations with U.S. Steel? If the case came up today, would *Basic* require disclosure of those negotiations?

Consider in this regard the court's statement in **Phillips v. LCI Intern., Inc.,** 190 F.3d 609 614 (4th Cir. 1999). There preliminary negotiations between two merger partners broke down, only to restart and proceed to fruition several months later. During the hiatus, the target's CEO stated publicly that the company "is not for sale." The district court found the statement immaterial on the ground that "[e]very investor knows or should know that at the right price, and under certain circumstances, any publicly-held company can be for 'sale.' " The circuit court disagreed, id. at 614: "This conclusion seems to us to be a variation on the infamous statement in *Flamm v. Eberstadt,* 814 F.2d 1169 (7th Cir.1987). There the court held that misstatements about merger negotiations were immaterial as a matter of law because '[a]t the right price, any corporation is for sale.' *Id.* at 1179. *Basic* substantially undercuts the force of such aphorisms. Although in *Basic* the Supreme Court did not expressly disapprove of such rationales, it did clearly state that the materiality of statements involving merger negotiations required a 'fact-specific' inquiry that 'depends on the significance the reasonable investor would place on the ... misrepresented information,' and explicitly rejected the view adopted by the *Flamm* court that merger discussions do not become material until the merger partners have agreed in principle as to price and structure."

NOTE: MATERIALITY AND CONTEXT

Is the materiality determination respecting a given transaction the same no matter what the disclosure context? Footnote 18 of Justice Blackmun's opinion indicates this—otherwise, it says, the materiality and duty to disclose inquiries begin to collapse into one another. At the same time, the opinion suggests that materiality is a factual determination focusing on probability and magnitude. The question, in effect, is whether an abstract reasonable investor would want the information without regard to context.

Can this neat analytical separation be maintained in practice? Or, given the indeterminacy of the materiality inquiry, will normative considerations going beyond the welfare of a hypothesized rational investor inevitably come into the determination? Consider the following problems:

a.   Take internal asset appraisals or earnings projections such as those at issue in the *Starkman* case. Assume that management would be comfortable in releasing this information to analysts or including the information in a selling document put together by an investment banker. But management has grounds to question the ultimate reliability of the projection. Should the projection be considered material and its disclosure be mandatory in any of the following transactions:

1.   a registration statement covering a public issue of additional shares of stock?

2.   proxy materials issued in connection with a friendly merger?

3.   proxy materials issued in connection with the merger of a 51% owned subsidiary with a parent corporation?

4.   a cash tender offer by the corporation to repurchase 15% of its outstanding shares?

5.   market purchases of stock by the corporation's top managers?

6.   filings by the corporation with the SEC under section 13(a) of the 1934 Act (e.g., on form 10K or 10Q)?

b.   Would your analysis differ if the same projection was an external analysis employed by a hostile offeror as the basis for a hostile tender offer?

c.   Now take merger negotiations comparable to those in *Basic,* and assume that the issuer has made no statement about them. Try questions 1, 3, 4, 5 and 6.

d.   Assume that a particular set of merger negotiations about which the corporation has made no disclosures has been found to be immaterial for purposes of a periodic filing under the 1934 Act because the transaction was very uncertain of accomplishment and disclosure could have caused the transaction to abort. Does it follow that insider should be allowed to trade without disclosing the negotiations because they are not material?

NOTE: SOURCES OF LEGAL OBLIGATIONS TO DISCLOSE ON THE PART OF NON–TRANSACTORS

Basic v. Levinson makes it clear that although Rule 10b–5 is aimed primarily at transactional advantages by persons who are buying or selling, it is violated when a corporation makes false statements about material facts concerning its affairs, even though the corporation is not, and does not contemplate, buying and selling or otherwise dealing in its own securities. But suppose the corporation in *Basic* had made no affirmative misstatements and instead had kept silent about the merger? Does Rule 10b–5 impose an affirmative duty to disclose material information, even though the corporation is not in the market, and therefore does not have the option of refraining from dealing in lieu of disclosure? Courts have said that it does, but have not been clear as to which language of Rule 10b–5 imposes this obligation. See Financial Industrial Fund, Inc. v. McDonnell Douglas Corp., 474 F.2d 514 (10th Cir.1973), cert. denied, 414 U.S. 874 (1973); SEC v. Texas Gulf Sulphur Co., Inc., 401 F.2d 833, 850 n. 12 (2d Cir.1968), cert. denied, 394 U.S. 976 (1969); Marx v. Computer Sciences Corp., 507 F.2d 485 (9th Cir.1974). Some courts have imposed a duty to disclose on the premise that materiality alone is enough, at least in the circumstances of merger negotiations. See, e.g., Flamm v. Eberstadt, supra; Staffin v. Greenberg, 672 F.2d 1196 (3d Cir.1982); Reiss v. Pan American World Airways, Inc., 711 F.2d 11 (2d Cir.1983). But Supreme Court caselaw undercuts this approach. In its most recent pronouncement on the ambit of section 10(b), the Court suggests that the section covers a "fraudulent scheme in which * * * securities transactions and breaches of fiduciary duty coincide." SEC v. Zandford, 535 U.S. 813 (2002). See also footnote 17 in Basic v. Levinson, supra. Similarly, earlier lower court opinions indicate that the materiality of information possessed by non-transactors does not alone implicate any duty to disclose it; some externally imposed duty to disclose must be found before materiality vel non is relevant. See Glazer v. Formica Corp., 964 F.2d 149 (2d Cir.1992) (merger); Taylor v. First Union Corp., 857 F.2d 240 (4th Cir.1988), cert. den., 489 U.S. 1080 (1989); Roeder v. Alpha Industries, Inc., 814 F.2d 22 (1st Cir.1987); State Teachers Retirement Board v. Fluor Corp., 654 F.2d 843 (2d Cir.1981).

From what source might such an external fiduciary duty arise?

SEC Regulation FD, 17 C.F.R. § 243.100, requires a reporting company to make a public disclosure upon disclosing material nonpublic information to a broker or dealer, an investment adviser, an investment company, or a company stockholder who is a reasonably foreseeable purchaser or seller. Failure so to do, however, does not per se violate Rule 10b–5. 17 C.F.R. § 243.102.

Section 409 of the Sarbanes–Oxley Act of 2002 requires issuers reporting under Section 13(a) or 15(d) of the Exchange Act to disclose to the public, on a rapid and current basis and in plain English, any additional information concerning material changes in financial condition or operations as the SEC determines, by rule, is necessary or useful for the protection of investors and in the public interest.

The New York Stock Exchange Listed Company Manual, Rule 202.05 (Aug. 21, 2006) admonishes that a "listed company is expected to release quickly to the public any news or information which might reasonably be expected to materially affect the market for its securities * * *. A listed company should also act promptly to dispel unfounded rumors which result in unusual market activity or price variations." In addition, Rule 202.01 (July 1, 1991) describes in some detail the procedures and practices with respect to timely disclosure by which listed companies are expected to be guided. Not only are companies urged to confine the dissemination of material developments to a limited group within the company, but when the developments implicate so many people, particularly outsiders, that "maintaining security * * * is virtually impossible," an immediate announcement should be made. Elaborate instruction is also provided for (a) dissemination of information to securities analysts and institutional managers particularly by keeping an "open door" policy (Rule 202.02 (July 1, 1992)), (b) dealing with rumors of unusual market activity (Rule 202.03 (July 1, 1992)), and (c) procedures for public release of information (Rule 202.06 (June 13, 1991)).

Comparable disclosure policies are contained in the American Stock Exchange Listing Standards, Policies, and Requirements, §§ 401–404, and in considerably less detail in the N.A.S.D. Manual, Rules 4310(c)(15),(16).

SECTION F.   THE TENDER OFFER

INTRODUCTION

A tender offer is an invitation addressed to all shareholders of a target corporation to tender their shares for sale at a specified price, either in cash or in securities of the tender offeror (also called the "bidder"). The offer is sometimes for 100 percent of the target company's shares and sometimes merely for a controlling block, with almost all tender offers seeking at least control of the target company.

Why did the tender offer develop in addition to the conventional form of merger as a means of transferring control? At first glance the proliferation of tender offers presents a puzzle. Tax and accounting considerations (pooling and tax free exchanges) have historically argued in favor of merger, at least over a cash purchase. In addition, to make a tender offer is to forego the opportunity to make a detailed investigation of the target. Nor can a hostile offeror procure the protective warranties and covenants which the acquirer conventionally obtains in a negotiated merger. The question posed is easily answered, however. Tender offers tend to be used when management of the target company opposes the combination or, where it does not to resist, when it is unwilling actively to sponsor the combination. The target's management may oppose the offer because it thinks the price inadequate or thinks the offeror's plans detrimental to non-tendering stockholders. Alternatively, the target management may be reluctant to lose its perquisites. The prevalence, as well as the significance, of the latter motive is suggested by the fact that larger premiums are paid in hostile takeovers than in negotiated mergers. A fair part of the difference can presumably be saved for the bidder by making appropriate overtures to the target's management in a friendly transactional context. See Hartzell, Ofek and Yermack, What's in It for Me?: Personal Benefits Obtained by CEOs Whose Firms Are Acquired, working paper (2001)(showing that CEOs accept a lower premium where transaction terms include special treatment of CEO).

The acquiring firm proceeds with a takeover for the same reason or range of reasons that motivate mergers. Thus it may envision gains from economies of scale or other synergies, or, possibly, product market dominance. Or it may see a bargain purchase because it believes there are realizable values in the target's assets or divisions which are not reflected in its market price. Whatever may be the acquirer's more particular reasons, it acts only when it views the target's stock to be undervalued in the market or it expects to use control to enhance the target's going concern value—as is evident from the necessity to pay a substantial premium above market price.

Whether hostile takeovers offer economic benefits to society remains a much debated subject. Traditional commentators view takeover bidders as financial manipulators who bootstrap acquisitions, or looters and raiders who intend to pay too little for 100 percent control and, if they get less than 100 percent, to milk the acquired company. Managerialists denounce takeovers for wasting capital and management energy better spent on internal improvements. The takeover threat, they argue, chills long-term investment and exacerbates the shareholding community's tendency to seek value maximization in the short run. Proponents of hostile takeovers see them as the best method available to displace an inefficient management. The very threat of a takeover, they argue, goads management into better performance. Takeovers benefit the shareholders of the target company because the acquirer pays them more than the market price. The acquirer also makes the firm more prosperous and valuable, benefitting society at large in addition to the shareholders.

It is generally agreed that shareholders of target companies gain significantly from successful tender offers, measured by the premiums they receive or increased stock prices. But there is dispute over whether the shareholders of acquiring companies gain much, if anything, whether measured by stock market prices or otherwise, and some doubt whether gains accrue in aggregate and on average to all stockholders. There is also dispute over whether the process results in social gain, even apart from the deadweight transaction costs of the process itself. Opponents suggest that the social cost of hostile takeovers—through displacement of employees, managers, supply arrangements, and the like—can in theory and does sometimes in practice exceed the private gains to target shareholders. They also argue that waste occurs when defending managers' spend on defensive maneuvers and divert their energies from seeking enhanced productivity for the firm. Proponents respond that target companies tend to be relatively less prosperous than others in their field. They are characterized by inadequate management, large cash flows, low dividends, and low debt; the takeover brings a stronger incentive structure and more efficient management.

Where does this back and forth leave us? Enough has been shown to confirm that hostile takeovers can serve a useful purpose in displacing (and possibly in threatening to displace) inefficient or corrupt managers, benefitting shareholders in general. But while the takeover process has been beneficial in some cases, it has been unduly costly in others, whether due to overbidding, disruption of business plans, or transaction costs. In the absence of a principled basis for differentiating the beneficial and the costly ex ante, the articulation of general rules for *all* takeovers presents a problem. The uncertainty weighs prominently in any calculus of appropriate regulation, which must inevitably balance the cost of protecting public investors (and possibly other firm participants or constituents) against the benefits accruing from such protection, if such protection increases the cost of (or otherwise impedes) the takeover process.

1.   WHY TENDER OFFERS? ECONOMIC WELFARE AND REGULATORY STRATEGIES

(A) THE PROPONENTS' VIEW

Romano, A Guide to Takeovers: Theory, Evidence, and Regulation

9 Yale J. Reg. 119, 120–24, 125–26, 129, 131–32, 143–45 (1992).

The empirical evidence is most consistent with value-maximizing, efficiency-based explanations of takeovers. Yet the thrust of regulation is to thwart and burden takeovers, as if they were non-value-maximizing wealth transfers. The sharp discrepancy between the economic understanding of takeovers and the output of the political process in this area is a function of two factors. First, the public is largely uninformed about and uninterested in takeovers. Takeover regulation is therefore low salience legislation for most voters, and interest groups are consequently able to exercise significant influence on legislators in this area. Second, there are asymmetric organizational advantages across the interest groups most affected by takeovers that favor those whom takeovers potentially harm, managers, over those whom takeovers benefit, shareholders. Managers are easier to coordinate across firms than shareholders, and they have more to lose. The organizational advantage is important because lobbyists play a significant role in educating legislators, and intuition is often at odds with the economic learning. Under such circumstances, legislators are likely to be woefully misinformed concerning the probable effects of takeovers—their education is incomplete and distorted—and predisposed to regulate.

　　* * *

I.   Theories of Takeovers and Related Transactions

One important, and undisputed, datum about acquisitive transactions should be noted from the outset: acquisitions generate substantial gains to target company shareholders. All studies find that target firms experience statistically significant positive stock price responses to the announcement of takeover attempts or merger agreements. On average, there is a 20% increase over the pre-announcement market price for mergers and a 30% increase for tender offers in the period around the takeover announcement. Abnormal returns in going-private transactions (leveraged buyouts) are of similar magnitude, ranging across studies between 20% and 37%. Without question, the announcement of a bid is good news for target shareholders. The different explanations of acquisitions that will be examined are efforts at explaining the source of these gains.

The data are more ambiguous, however, concerning acquiring firms' returns. Depending on the sample and time period, acquirers experience positive, negative, or zero abnormal returns on a bid's announcement and completion. From the acquirer's perspective, there are two classes of explanations or motivations for a takeover: value-maximizing and non-value-maximizing ones. Value-maximizing explanations view takeovers as undertaken in order to increase the equity share price of the acquiring firm. Non-value-maximizing explanations consider takeovers in diametrically opposite terms, as transactions that maximize managers' utility rather than shareholder wealth. These two explanations therefore predict a different stock price reaction, positive and negative, respectively.

* * *

There are, however, theoretically plausible reasons for not finding positive abnormal returns to bidders even when acquisitions are value-maximizing transactions. First, acquiring firms are typically much larger than target firms, making it more difficult to measure abnormal returns. Second, a bid may reveal information about the bidding firm unrelated to the particular acquisition, confounding the stock price effect. Third, if the takeover market is competitive, then bidders will earn only normal returns, as abnormal profits are competed away. Finally, for acquiring firms that have an active mergers and acquisitions program, the gain from a specific acquisition may have been anticipated in the bidder's stock price at the time the mergers and acquisitions program was announced.

* * *

A.   Value–Maximizing Efficiency Explanations

There are two efficiency explanations of takeovers: to realize synergy gains and to reduce agency costs.

1.   Synergy Gains

One value-maximizing efficiency explanation of takeovers is to achieve synergy gains: the value of the combined firm is greater than the value of the two firms (target and acquirer) separately. The increased value may be generated by real operating efficiencies, or it may be due to financial synergies.

* * *

2.   Reducing Agency Costs

A reduction in agency costs is the other efficiency explanation for takeovers. Corporate law is concerned with principal-agent problems, the alignment of managers' incentives with shareholders' interests. A takeover is, in this framework, a backstop remedy when other corporate governance devices that monitor performance, such as the board of directors, fail at effective incentive-alignment.

a.   Replacement of Inefficient Management

The most important agency cost explanation of takeovers is that they reduce managerial slack by replacing inefficient management. Manne [, Mergers and the Market for Corporate Control, 73 J. Pol. Econ. 110 (1965)] put forth this view in a classic article over 20 years ago, and it is one of the central insights in corporate law scholarship. Manne maintained that takeovers are the market for corporate control's key mechanism for disciplining managers because, unlike mergers, which require the approval of the target firm's board, the takeover bypasses target management and goes directly to the target shareholders for approval. Takeovers accordingly keep the capital market competitive, and constrain managers to work in the shareholders' interest.

* * *

b.   Free Cash Flow

An alternative explanation that views takeovers as a mechanism for reducing agency costs but does not predict management's replacement is Jensen's "free cash flow" theory. Jensen contends that a cause of takeover activity, especially in the petroleum industry, is the agency cost associated with the conflict between managers and shareholders over the payout of free cash flow. Free cash flow is cash flow in excess of the amount required to fund all of the firm's projects that have a positive net present value. If these funds are paid out to shareholders, managers will have fewer resources under their control, and will thus be unable to waste cash by investing in projects with negative net present values. In addition, eliminating free cash flow subjects managers to capital market monitoring when they need to finance new projects, further constraining their ability to undertake negative net present value transactions.

This explanation stands the financial synergy (reduction of the cost of capital) explanation on its head, both because it is the target and not the acquiring firm with excess cash, and because external financing is deemed preferable to internal financing, due to incentive problems. But in contrast to the other efficiency explanations, an acquiring firm is not needed to realize this operating improvement. Incumbent managers can eliminate free cash flow on their own through a financial restructuring, which increases the firm's leverage and pays the borrowed cash out to the shareholders. Synergy gains, by definition, require two firms, and replacing inefficient management requires a change in the management team. Hence, of the explanations analyzed thus far, only free cash flow explains an increase in value from a defensive restructuring, as well as from a takeover.

* * *

C.   Value–Maximizing Market Inefficiency Explanations

The final value-maximizing (that is, beneficial to acquirers' shareholders) explanation of takeover gains is premised on market inefficiency, the view that stock prices do not reflect firms' "fundamental value." According to this explanation, which is probably as widely-circulated in the popular press as the labor expropriation explanation, acquirers exploit market inefficiency by identifying undervalued firms, and presumably capture a large share of the gains by paying premiums below the correct valuation. There are two distinct market inefficiency explanations: general underpricing of stocks and myopia (overvaluation of current profits and excessive discounting of future profits).

1.   Underpricing

The most general version of the market inefficiency explanation of takeovers is that the capital market simply misprices securities. Acquiring firms identify undervalued securities and profit from the difference between the price they pay and the firm's true value. Given the size of the premiums received in takeovers, this explanation cannot be characterized as an expropriation explanation from current investors in targets to bidders. Because the target shareholders' gain is not a "real" gain, in that it does not depend on any operating improvements or other changes to be undertaken by the bidder in the future, this explanation is also classified separately from the efficiency-enhancing explanations of takeovers.

There is no evidence supporting the underpricing explanation of takeover gains. In particular, if this explanation was correct, then once a bidder identified a target, its price would rise and remain at the higher true value, regardless of whether the acquisition occurred. Several studies find, however, that the stock price of takeover targets that are not acquired returns to its lower pre-bid price. Takeovers therefore do not merely provide an inefficient market with the information necessary for revaluing stock prices. More generally, the large body of event studies examining numerous events in corporate finance besides acquisitions casts doubt on this explanation, as the studies are supportive of market efficiency.

2. Market Myopia

The market myopia inefficiency explanation is more sophisticated than the underpricing hypothesis. In this explanation, investors are short-sighted and behave myopically to sacrifice long-term benefits for immediate profits. As a consequence, firms that engage in long-term planning and make substantial investments in research and development (R & D) are supposedly undervalued by the market and become takeover targets. To avoid undervalued stock, managers thus also behave myopically and shift from profitable long-term investments to more easily valued short-term projects. This explanation of takeovers could be characterized as efficiency-enhancing, because the acquirer presumably gains by taking the firm private and undertaking the neglected long-term investments. As Netter suggests, it can also be given an expropriation gloss, as a "redistribution from the future" to the present. In this alternative view, the acquirers are myopic and slash R & D budgets to raise stock value.

Securities and Exchange Commission Report of Recommendations of Advisory Committee on Tender Offers Separate Statement of Frank H. Easterbrook and Gregg A. Jarrell

July 8, 1983.
(pp. 71–73).

We start from the position * * * that tender offers benefit shareholders of both bidders and targets. The premiums paid to targets do not just come out of the hide of bidders' stockholders; there is a gain when the bidders and targets are evaluated as a unit. Moreover, the evidence also shows that both the regulation of bids and the targets' defensive tactics make initial tender offers more costly to mount, and thus there will be fewer of them. As the price of anything goes up, the number purchased decreases. Regulation increases the cost (including the cost of uncertainty and risk) in making offers. Fewer offers mean fewer occasions when shareholders collect premiums, which also means that all corporations trade for less in the market because their value as future acquisitions is less.

The premiums reflect real gains to society as well as to investors. Stock prices reflect the anticipated future dividends of the stock (including profits distributed in any "final" dividend, such as the payment accompanying a merger). Profits and dividends, in turn, increase when a firm becomes more efficient or better at producing what consumers want to buy. Higher stock prices thus are based on social as well as private gains. Perhaps the gains observed in tender offers come from the fact that bidders' managers make more efficient use of the targets' resources than the targets' managers do. Resurrecting a declining business is no less productive than building a new one. The threat of tender offers also induces managers to take more care in their work, so that there are fewer declining businesses to resurrect. Perhaps the gains come from the combination of the bidders' and targets' assets, including their production, sales, and distribution networks, into more efficient units. The exact source of the gain does not matter much, so long as it is real. The market evidence tells us it is real and large. Unless the market systematically (not just occasionally) is irrational, this evidence is compelling. Thus when tender offers are not made because of regulation or defense, real value is lost.

The gains from tender offers are important for new businesses as well as existing ones. The prospective investors in a new firm want some assurance that people will be looking over the managers' shoulders, ready to step in if the managers falter badly or if there is a better use for the firm's assets. When shareholdings are diversified, it is important to find ways, such as the employment market, the tender offer, and the proxy contest, to control the agency costs of management, which scattered shareholders cannot do for themselves. (Agency costs are the full costs, in both monitoring and lost profits, that investors incur in inducing managers to act completely in the investors' interests rather than the managers' own. Agency costs are apt to rise as managers' stake in the firms' profits falls, for the smaller the managers' stake, the less they will sacrifice at the margin to obtain gains that accrue to other people.) Investors pay more for new stock with better safeguards against agency costs built in. Another way to put this is that new investments are more attractive (and hence society will invest more, increasing productivity) when tender offers are available.

(B) THE OPPONENTS' VIEW

Herman and Lowenstein, The Efficiency Effects of Hostile Take–Overs

In Coffee, Lowenstein and Rose–Ackerman (eds.) Knights, Raiders and Targets: The Impact of the Hostile Takeover 211 (1988); pp. 213 to 216.

SOME FUNDAMENTAL POSTULATES OF EFFICIENCY-ENHANCEMENT MODELS

Analyses that feature takeovers as efficiency-enhancing start with the premise that the acquiring firms' managements are striving to maximize shareholder wealth. In their search for ways of improving shareholder wealth, these managements observe that other firms are badly run or fail to put their resources to best use. These managers are thereby induced to acquire such badly managed firms* * *. They frequently and regrettably encounter target managements who go to great pains to prevent takeovers that would provide large stockholder windfalls. It would appear, then, that the *defending* managements are not striving to maximize shareholder benefits. This dichotomous treatment of the motivation of the managers of bidding and acquired firms is partially bridged by the concession that there exists one dimension—the evaluation and hiring of management services—in which managerial and stockholder interests may deviate seriously. There may be "agency costs" as the agents fail to police themselves adequately; hence the service of takeovers in keeping such agency costs under control.

The flaw in this argument is that it opens a Pandora's box and gives no reason for closing it with only "defenses against takeovers" and "agency costs" removed. If managements can so egregiously waste opportunities where stockholder wealth could be quickly and obviously increased by more than 50 percent, it will not suffice to make this an exception to management loyalty by mere assertion or reference to stock option plans.[17] If managers can openly ignore stockholder interests in the one case—an obvious and public one—the reasonable presumption to be rebutted is that they may pursue non-stockholder interests in other cases, most relevantly here, in *acquiring* other companies. Efficiency enhancement may be only a partial and special case explanation of takeovers.

If managements defending against takeovers can pursue their private ends in serious violation of shareholder interests, this also raises questions about the meaning of the "agency" relationship and the parallel asymmetry of *its* applications. If the "agent" (management) is not subject to the control of his principals in the one case, why should we assume control in other cases? If the agent himself controls or substantially influences the board of directors, the control that the board then imposes on his activities may be largely nominal. The gearing of managerial and shareholder interests via executive compensation arrangements, for example, may be illusory if the fixing of the salaries and bonuses is under the control of the agent (who may adjust them ex post facto to accomplish his goals).[19] The

17. An important alternative strand of "reductionist" analysis stresses an active managerial labor market and a labor market for directors to discipline managers. Fama, for example, elevates managerial-directorial labor markets to primacy, leaving the market for corporate control as a "last resort"; Agency Problems and the Theory of the Firm, 88 J.Pol.Econ. 288, 295 [1980]. Among its other weaknesses, the institutional premises of this alternative line of analysis seem to us far-fetched. * * *

19. W. Lewellen, Recent Evidence on Senior Executive Pay, Nat.Tax J. 161–64 [1975]; Herman, Corporate Control, Corporate Power 95–96. In a 1982 study of 140 large corporations, Carol Loomis found "some examples of consistency in which pay and performance match. But there were

agreement of the board to a new acquisition program may be as compelling an illustration of the control by the agent as board approval of management's compensation arrangements.

The recent literature in defense of takeovers treats too lightly the role of the board and the dynamics of power within the corporation. Sometimes, on occasions when the virtues of the market for corporate control are being extolled, the thoroughgoing domination of the organization by the management is stressed. At other times, when it is desired to show that the managerial interest may still be kept in line with that of the shareholders by devices such as stock option plans, reference is made to the independent directors who, according to Fama, act "as professional referees [and have the] task * * * to stimulate and oversee the competition among the firm's top managers * * *. [The] outside directors are in their turn disciplined by the market for their services which *prices* them according to their performance as referees."[21] If the board is dominated by the management and the management dominates the proxy machinery, however, the "price" will be a function of service to the controlling management. And there would seem to be no independent source of power to contract that would effectively limit the actions of the "agent." The ability of the agent to resist value enhancing takeover bids points up the fact that the agency contract is an elusive construct, which permits an evasion of the realities of corporate control and power.

The new defenses of takeovers as efficiency-enhancing also rest their case heavily on stock prices as providing reliable measures of asset and managerial worth. Efficient markets digest all available information and yield prices that show the only true valuation of the assets of each company and their potential in the hands of existing managements. Takeover bid prices thus reflect the anticipated enhancement of values based on the perceived superiority of the new management and its plans for redeployment, etc. The efficient markets hypothesis denies that the stock market could undervalue corporate assets in any meaningful way. There is, it is true, substantial evidence of information-arbitrage market efficiency, meaning that prices respond quickly to new information and "their correlations with past histories are too weak to be exploited profitably."[23] But this technical efficiency is very different from the claimed ability of the market to value stocks in accordance with the expected stream of future earnings or dividends. On the contrary, there is substantial evidence that fundamental value equilibria are special cases. Traders and institutional investors, having extremely short time horizons, are influenced by their perceptions of what other market traders and the public will be thinking of stock prospects. This is not irrational. The stock market is almost entirely a

---

many more examples of irrationality and contradiction." Peter Grace, of W.R. Grace, received, for example, a bonus of $1 million in 1981 in "recognition of his accomplishments during his 36–year tenure," a period in which the shareholders earned an annual return of 7.4 percent. Loomis, The Madness of Executive Compensation, Fortune, July 12, 1982.

21. Fama, Agency Problems and the Theory of the Firm, supra, note [17], at 293–94. Emphasis added.

23. Tobin, On the Efficiency of the Financial System, Hirsch Memorial Lecture, May 15, 1984, at 6.

secondary market, and the pricing of shares depends on extremely difficult projections of earnings and dividends on the one hand and an essentially subjective valuation process—fixing the price-earnings ratios—on the other. In the face of such uncertainty, it is not surprising that investors react by looking as much or more to each other—playing the "performance" game as it is currently called—than to the underlying fundamentals. What financial economists frequently characterize as quantifiable risks are in reality uncertainties of such large and incalculable proportions as to intimidate investors and send them scurrying to the seemingly safer ground of follow-the-leader. Such markets can be influenced by fads. The result is that stock prices do not move in any systematic relationship to changes in expected returns.[25]

There is good evidence, also, that investors who look at the value of corporate assets as a whole and as a producing entity value them different-ly than traders and passive investors.[26] No coherent explanation consistent with the efficient markets hypothesis has ever been given as to why acquiring firms will regularly pay large premia for companies whose managements they intend to retain and whose assets they have no plans to redeploy or recombine.

It may be argued, of course, that the acquisition which reduces undervaluation in trading markets is performing a valuable function, pushing market values closer to whole company values, and at the same time paying shareholders of the target firms sums reflecting those more valid market values. This may be true, but there are numerous costs involved in this rectification of prices, including both the transaction costs and, more importantly, a huge diversion of managerial effort into devising ways to reduce a vulnerability that did not grow out of managerial inefficiency. Some of the policies that may be employed to counter this threat, such as loading up on debt and "defensive acquisitions,"[28] may be seriously detrimental to the long-term interests of the shareholders. In short, it requires a giant leap to conclude that in order to correct market disequilibria we should encourage an active, day-to-day trading not merely of *shares* of firms but of the firms themselves. The main point, however, is that takeovers rooted in a market undervaluation of corporate assets are not designed to prune dead managerial wood or improve asset utilization—on the contrary, they reflect a flaw in the market machinery and valuation process. Furthermore, an acquisitions route based on undervaluation can be pursued by bad as well as good managers. In fact, it may be the preferred path for those managers who can not perform well in their own productive domains.

25. See, e.g., Goodman and Peavy, In-dustry Relative Price–Earnings Ratios as In-dicators of Investment Returns, Fin.Analysts J., July–Aug. 1983; R. Shiller, Do Stock Prices Move Too Much to be Justified by Subsequent Changes in Dividends?, 71 Am. Econ.Rev. 421 (1981); R. Shiller, Stock Prices and Social Dynamics, Cowles Found. Disc. Paper No. 719R [Oct.1984]; Wang, Some Ar-guments That the Stock Market Is Not Effi-cient, 19 U.C.Davis L.Rev. 341 (1986).

26. See M. Whitman & M. Shubik, The Aggressive Conservative Investor 51 [1979]; * * *.

28. See, e.g., Panter v. Marshall Field & Co., 646 F.2d 271 [7th Cir.1981], cert. denied, 454 U.S. 1092 (1981).

The efficiency-enhancement perspective also rests on a vision of a market for corporate control that gives only a very partial version of reality. * * * It is certainly important that by means of takeover bids outsiders can bypass managements and appeal directly to stockholders, a process that has made it possible to displace managements by operations and strategies in the financial markets. The former stability of corporate control and irrelevance of shareholder ownership and voting rights to corporate power has been badly shaken and weakened. Furthermore, the "market" has become quantitatively significant.

But several caveats are in order. The number of buyers who bid in particular takeover transactions is not large and does not meet a competitive standard. The assumption that these buyers are well informed is also implausible as a general rule, given the frequent lack of familiarity of the acquirer with the target's business, the lack of access to sometimes crucial inside knowledge, the great speed with which major decisions are frequently made, and the considerable evidence of unpleasant ex post surprises. We have also argued above that the * * * vision of the players in the market as competing managers seeking to control resources in order to manage them more efficiently is at best unproven. A substantial number of acquisitions are explained by the bidders themselves in terms of plans to enter fields with greater growth prospects, or to round out a product line, or to achieve some kind of advantage through vertical integration. Acquisitions made in connection with these strategic plans and efforts appear to be based only marginally on efficiency considerations.

The expansion of the takeover market has also brought with it numerous players who do not fit well the behavioral requirements of the efficiency-enhancement vision. There are now a substantial number of professional sharks in the business of putting companies "into play," not to acquire and manage these companies themselves, but to force bids and counterbids by unknown third parties. There are also "wolfpacks" of substantial investors now prepared to fund takeovers by plausible bidders on high yield terms. The ability to mobilize in advance vast sums for bidding in takeover contests is a significant development. It has increased the size of potential targets and reduced the size and financial requirements of potential bidders. * * *

The new institutional arrangements that are now in place are being steadily enlarged by the force of competitive pressure and short-run profitability calculations of investment bankers and investors * * *. These developments have already pushed us into a promotional environment in which the largest companies are now potentially "in play" and within the grasp of promotional interests.

NOTE: THE BOARD VETO

Those who worry that unconstrained takeovers result in net social costs suggest legal constraints. Lowenstein, for example, would deter takeovers with a 100 percent tax on all gains from the sale of stock or derivative securities held for less than one year. L. Lowenstein, What's Wrong With Wall Street: Short Term Gain and the Absentee Shareholder 202–204 (1988). Lowenstein's suggestion would cause the time perspectives of investors to veer toward the long term and would occasion greater investor participation in governance. Lipton and Rosenblum, A New System of Corporate Governance: The Quinquennial Election of Directors, 58 U.Chi.L.Rev. 187 (1991), makes a more blunt (and arguably, more pro-management) proposal. They suggest that annual director elections be replaced with quinquennial elections and that nonconsensual changes of control between elections be barred, but that major stockholders have direct access to the proxy machinery at the time of the 5 year election.

Both of the foregoing suggestions require significant law reform. But many tender offer opponents (unlike tender offer proponents) profess substantial satisfaction with the prevailing legal regime. Management defensive devices sanctioned by state codes and courts, in particular the poison pill and the staggered board, accord the target's managers a de facto veto over hostile offers. See subsection (2), which follows. Opponents of a free market in corporate control offer a spirited defense of the board veto. See Stout, The Shareholder as Ulysses: Some Empirical Evidence on Why Investors in Public Corporations Tolerate Board Governance, 152 U. Pa. L. Rev. 667 (2003); Allen, Jacobs, and Strine, The Great Takeover Debate: A Mediation on Bridging the Conceptual Divide, 69 U. Chi. L. Rev. 1067 (2002); Lipton and Rowe, Pills, Polls, and Professors: A Reply to Professor Gilson, New York University Working Paper CLB–01–006 (2001); Lipton, Pills, Polls, and Professors Redux, 69 U. Chi. L. Rev. 1037 (2002).

Supporters of the board veto advance four justifications.

• First, the board veto is the term that the target firm's shareholders would place in the charter ex ante if left to their own devices. This is because it gives the board a zone of discretion in which to act to advance their interests, whether by forestalling a change of control in a case where incumbent management remains the best team for maximizing the value of the assets or by forcing the offeror to increase its bid. In either case, the target's managers are in the best position of all interested parties to ascertain the firm's value and therefore to evaluate the adequacy of a bid.

• Second, interests of target shareholders with a short term time horizon and those with a long term time horizon often diverge in respect of a hostile offer. As between the two groups, the long term holders are more deserving of governance solicitude. The board veto permits the long term constituency's view to be given greater weight in the determination of the outcome.

• Third, in many cases a hostile tender bidder pays too much, just in many cases the acquirer in a friendly merger pays too much. Here the loss to the acquirer's shareholders may exceed the gain to the target's holders. A board veto accordingly can enhance the welfare of shareholders as a whole. Ex ante, no particular shareholder knows whether he or she will end up on the bidder or target side. Accordingly, all shareholders have an interest in a governance mechanism that introduces order and deliberation to the tender offer process so that value maximizing transactions can be sorted out from bad deals.

• Fourth, the shareholders are not the only constituents with interests at stake in hostile tender offers. Other constituents like employees and suppliers have a legitimate case for representation and the board veto opens that opportunity.

How persuasive are these justifications? For criticism, see Bebchuk, The Case Against Board Veto in Takeovers, 69 U. Chi. L. Rev. 973 (2002).

(C) THE INTERMEDIATE VIEW

Wachter, Takeover Defense When Financial Markets are (Only) Relatively Efficient

151 U. Pa. L. Rev. 787, 792–94 (2003).

If financial markets are entirely efficient—the prevailing assumption in the shareholder-choice literature—then the shareholder-choice theory of takeover jurisprudence is clearly the winning argument. If financial markets are efficient, then any hostile bid above market value moves assets to more valued uses, enriches shareholders, and, perhaps most important, disciplines managers to manage the corporation on behalf of shareholders.

The same is not true if financial markets are only relatively efficient. I use the term relatively efficient to signify the prevailing view in the financial market literature that market efficiency, like perfect competition, is an ideal that is unattainable as long as there are market frictions. Specifically, when financial markets are relatively efficient, while investors cannot expect to outperform the market on an ongoing basis, individual stock prices can still be incorrect at any point in time—either under-or overestimating the value of the corporation.

The failure of financial markets to correctly price the pro rata value of the corporation is shown primarily by the inability of existing models to generate a reliable estimate of the appropriate discount rate or market capitalization rate for equity capital on a continuing basis. This rate is a critical building block in determining the company's cost of capital, which in turn drives the firm's capital expenditure investment decisions. It is also the rate investors use to discount the future dividends that the corporation is likely to pay, hence determining the stock market valuation of the company's shares. If the market generates an incorrect or imprecise market capitalization rate, the market's valuation of the company's common stock is likewise incorrect or imprecise.

I next explore the requisite features of financial markets that can lead to the conclusion that shareholders might be better served by a legal regime of management discretion in determining the outcome of hostile tender offers. First, any underpricing of a company's share price by the financial market is temporary so that the stock price ultimately returns to the correct level. Second, due to the presence of asymmetric information, management may be better informed than the market as to the correct market capitalization rate. Third, management's superior information may be difficult to communicate to financial markets in a manner that is verifiable by the market so as to be incorporated into stock prices.

When financial markets are only relatively efficient, hostile tender offers that are above market prices but below fundamental value can succeed. Although the market for corporate control in the form of competitive bidding for target firms may mitigate this underpricing, it is unlikely to entirely eliminate it. Given these results, the signal conveyed by the market for corporate control is, at best, highly noisy and unreliable and, at worst, can distort the decisions made by managers prior to the emergence of a hostile bid.

The final critical step is to recognize that the failure to resolve agency cost difficulties is not solely a weakness of the management-discretion model. Instead, each legal regime creates its own agency problems. A shareholder-choice standard can lead managers to respond to a threat of takeovers, not by managing better, but by "managing to the anomaly." That is, the managers adopt strategies that make it less likely that the firm's stock will become underpriced, thereby making the firm less attractive to a hostile bidder, even though the effect is to reduce the ultimate value of the corporation. There are a variety of ways in which this phenomenon might be manifested.

The most straightforward example would be a company that decided to sell a particular asset that it believed was the source of the underpricing and where the sale price was below management's estimate of the true value of the asset. Another example is where managers avoid investments in firm-specific, long-lived assets for which the discount rate is dependent on firm product market data that is not verifiable by financial markets. Although the investment would increase the value of the corporation, it would make the firm more vulnerable to market mispricing and hostile tender offers. Finally, managers might invest in assets that play to market fads, in the hope that their stock would become overpriced. Adopting strategies that lead the company stock to be overvalued is the ultimate takeover defense. As an extra benefit, the inflated currency can turn the potential target into a bidder.

Should companies take such actions? What does the faithful fiduciary do? For those who believe that financial markets are always efficient, management should manage to the stock market signals. Since there are no anomalies, all signals are accurate. But if markets are only relatively efficient and managers believe, based on their own information, that certain actions reduce the ultimate value of the corporation, then the manager, as faithful fiduciary, would not make those investment decisions.

When financial markets are only relatively efficient, legal decision makers face a tradeoff. Standards promoting shareholder choice solve the agency costs of managers who might attempt to entrench themselves once a hostile bid has been made. However, those standards create incentives for managers to adopt strategies that make hostile bids less likely to occur, even if those strategies reduce the ultimate value of the corporation to the shareholders. Standards promoting management discretion have the reverse set of incentives. The current Delaware Supreme Court standard that allows for management discretion resolves the tradeoff by encouraging faithful managers to maximize the value of the corporation, but at the cost of allowing the faithless managers to entrench themselves by rejecting hostile tender offers that are truly above the firm's fundamental value.

NOTE: ADAPTATION

Compare the approach of Kahan and Rock, How I Stopped Worrying and Love the Pill: Adaptive Responses to Takeover Law, 69 U. Chi. L. Rev. 871, 899 (2002):

"What is most striking about the recent history of takeovers is that * * * the use of adaptive devices seems to work reasonably well for the participants. The level of M & A activity, the percentage of friendly versus hostile deals, the decline in efforts to adopt 'show stopping' charter amendments such as dual-class recapitalizations, and the failure of states offering extreme antitakeover measures such as dead-hand pills to attract incorporations all suggest that the intensity of managerial insecurity has been tempered, and with it managers' opposition to selling the company. For buyers, the current state seems satisfactory: Payments owed managers under incentive compensation contracts can be budgeted into the price; the amounts, while large for CEOs, are of the same order of magnitude as investment banking fees and amount to a relatively small percentage of the deal price; and market participants generally assert that deals that make economic sense get done.

"For target shareholders, the current state likewise seems satisfactory: Managers have largely adopted 'shareholder value maximization' as their mantra; target shareholders earn significant premia in friendly deals; and the market through the 1990s soared. Finally, the current state suits most potential target managers: They stand to get rich on their options and their 'golden parachute' packages should they be made redundant by an acquisition.

"Overall, political controversy over takeovers has died down and the more hyperbolic claims by the partisans—that permitting a board to block a bid amounts to 'corporate treason' or that preventing the board from blocking a bid constitutes 'a dagger aimed at the hearts' of corporations—have vanished from the public debate. In other words, the system as a whole is in an equilibrium with no substantial pressure for radical change. The only people who think that there remains a systematic problem to be solved are commentators who view the threat of managers being penalized by a hostile tender offer as an essential tool for disciplining management or who resent the high levels of compensation engendered by stock options."

2.   BIDDER TACTICS, POLICY ALTERNATIVES, AND THE WILLIAMS ACT

(A) BIDDER INCENTIVES

The economics of a tender offer encourage the tender offeror to initiate the transaction with as little notice as possible and to consummate it as quickly as possible. The bidder wishes to preclude incumbent management from preparing resistance. The incentive for prompt completion derives in part from market uncertainties and in part from business necessities. Time affords the opportunity for the market price of the target shares to move above the offering price, so as to negate the premium offered, either because of market conditions generally or because a competing tender offer, stimulated by the target's management or otherwise, might be made at a higher price. Similarly, fluctuation in interest rates for offerors which must borrow to obtain the purchase price poses a difficulty which increases with the length of the offering period. And delay increases acquisition expenses for the services of the dealer-manager, the depositary bank and others. Finally, any tie-up of the offeror's capital argues for a brief offering period. In short, enforced delay in consummating the offer can, and has been effective to, cause the offeror to terminate the offer.

A short timetable also can have a coercive effect on target shareholders, particularly when combined with an offer for less than all the target stock outstanding. Bebchuk, The Sole Owner Standard for Takeover Policy, 17 J.Legal Studies 197, 217–218 (1988) describes this situation:

" * * * Facing no restrictions, bidders would generally make offers of the Saturday Night Special type: partial offers that are open for a very brief period on a first-come, first-served basis.[36] In the face of such an offer, shareholders' situation would be pretty weak relative to that of a sole owner engaged in bargaining with the bidder.

"To start with, the brevity of the offer's period would practically rule out the possibility that a rival offer would be made before shareholders must make their tender decisions with respect to the present offer. Thus, when shareholders make their decisions, only one offer would be on the table.

"The brevity of the time a given offer is open, and the resulting absence of rival offers, would not have a devastating effect on a sole owner's position because the owner would be able to exercise an undistorted choice, and would thus accept the offer only if he concludes that acceptance is indeed his value-maximizing course of action. In reaching his decision, he would take into account the expected value of other offers that might be made later were he to reject the present offer.

"In contrast, in the face of a Saturday Night Special offer, the absence of the threat of rival offers would hurt the target's shareholders greatly. For the dispersed shareholders might be unable to reject the offer even if rejection would constitute their value-maximizing course of action—even if, for instance, they expect that rejection would lead to receiving much higher offers later on. As long as the expected post-takeover value of minority shares is lower than the bid price (which, under existing law, might well be the case even if the bid's premium is quite modest), the shareholders' decisions would be distorted in favor of tendering.

"The gap between the bid price and the expected value of minority shares would present shareholders with a 'carrot' and a 'stick,' both pushing the shareholders toward tendering. The carrot is the prospect that, since the offer is partial and on a first-come, first-served basis, tendering early would enable a shareholder to have all of his shares acquired for the bid price and thus to end up with more than his pro rata fraction of the acquisition price. The stick is the prospect that, if the shareholder does not tender or does not tender early enough, he might end up with all of his shares becoming minority shares and thus with less than his pro rata fraction of the acquisition price."

The "two-step front-end loaded" tender offer leads to similar pressures to tender. Suppose a bidder wants to acquire a target for $52 per share.

---

36. Bidders are at present prohibited from making offers that are open for a brief period or that are on a first-come, first-served basis. While bidders are free to use partial offers, they do not use them all that often * * *. This is because partial offers become more coercive than offers for all shares only when combined with a first-come, first-served structure.

The stock is trading for \$42, but the target's shareholders value the target at \$60 per share. The bidder structures the tender offer as follows: \$60 cash for 60 percent of the shares, and an announced intention to follow the tender offer with a second step merger in which the remaining 40 percent of the target's shares are exchanged for debt securities worth \$40. The weighted average value of the offer is \$52 per share. The shareholders are likely to find it rational to tender. The calculation is as follows: tendering results in the realization of at least \$52; failing to tender holds open the possibility of realizing \$60 only if this offer does not succeed and a higher offer materializes; failing to tender results in the realization of \$40 in the second step merger if the offer succeeds. Absent an ability to coordinate with the other shareholders, the rational shareholder will tender.

The target shareholder, confronted with an offer, faces a complex decision—whether to tender, not tender, or sell the shares on the open market for a lesser premium. The decision entails a comparison of the offer price (P), a projected value of the target in the event that the offer fails (T), and a projected value of the untendered shares if the offer succeeds (S).

The projection of T is a daunting task. It includes everything that goes into an *ex ante* fundamental valuation of the target and goes on to add variables. For example, once a bid is made and the firm is in play, the bidder's private valuation of the target becomes a critical piece of information. If that valuation is high, compared to P, a higher bid can be expected in the event of target shareholder resistance. A decision not to tender is indicated. If that valuation is close to P, no more can be expected from this bidder. But it does not follow that the shareholder will decide that this offer should succeed. The shareholder's willingness to accept the offer also will depend on an estimate of, first, the likelihood of the appearance of a competing bid, and, second, an estimate of the value of the company in the event that the incumbent managers stay in control. In addition, to make an estimate of S, the shareholder needs to know what the bidder plans to with the target and the remaining shares in the event of success.

A target shareholder with an informed basis for making these projections plus complete information on the terms and conditions of the offer still faces a significant information problem. It may have no way of knowing what action the other shareholders plan to take. If S is less than P, and P is less than T, then the shareholder should hold out—but only if all the other shareholders hold out. Since S is the low figure, if all the other shareholders tender the shareholder should do likewise. See Schwartz, The Fairness of Tender Offer Prices in Utilitarian Theory, 17 J. Legal Studies 165, 174–75 (1988).

Thus the bidder's interest in prompt consummation is coupled with an interest in minimum disclosure. The less the target shareholders and potential competing bidders know about the bidder, its valuation of the target, and its post-offer plans for the target, the greater the likelihood that the bidder can win control of the target for a low price.

(B) THE MARKET AND SOLE OWNER STANDARDS

Takeover proponents are not of one mind so far as concerns the implications of information asymmetries and institutional skews and consequent inequities in the allocation of takeover gain to stockholders. One school of thought advocates a "market standard." Under this, shareholders and society together maximize in the long run if the market dominates the tender offer process and the law assists the market with a rule of management passivity. The competing school of thought advocates a "sole owner" (or "single owner") standard. Under this, the appropriate price in a tender offer is measured by reference to the price that would be realized by a single owner of the assets in an arms' length negotiation. Two standards have contrasting implications respecting procedural regulation of tender offers.

Schwartz, The Fairness of Tender Offer Prices in Utilitarian Theory, 17 J. Legal Studies 165, 165–167 (1988), offers a more complete description of the two positions:

"The current debate among legal commentators about tender offers has proved difficult and inconclusive. These troubles derive in part from disagreement over the appropriate standard by which to measure the fairness of particular offers. The commentators rely, often implicitly, on two distinct standards of fairness: the 'market standard' and the 'single-owner standard.' * * *

"The market standard holds that any offer above the target's prebid market price should succeed. According to the efficient-market hypothesis the prebid market price is the present discounted value of the target's future earnings under current management. A bid above the market price implies that the bidder can increase these earnings, if bidders are informed, rational, and maximize profits. An increase in earnings from the same assets is an increase in welfare. Hence, any bid price that induces tender is fair, if economic efficiency is the standard by which the fairness of a transaction is measured.

"The single-owner standard holds that an efficient sale is one that a willing buyer and seller would make were both parties free from coercion. To understand the application of this standard here, suppose the state were to appoint 'selling agents' just to represent target shareholders in connection with takeovers. Each agent would be charged with obtaining for its set of shareholders the highest price that the traffic will bear. This charge would reflect shareholder preferences because each shareholder too would bargain for the highest price were he the sole owner of the target's business. Consequently, the measure of an efficient—that is, fair—takeover price is its resemblance to the price that would emerge from a hypothetical bargain between a potential acquirer and such a selling agent. This ideal price is referred to as the 'single-owner price.'

"The concrete implications of a choice between these standards are best introduced by an example. Let Company T have fifty shares outstanding that sell for $2 each. A bidder B believes that it can generate sufficient earnings from T's assets to give them a present value of $200; B thereupon bids $2.35 a share—$117.50 in total—for all T's shares. Let the direct costs to T's shareholders of tendering (mailing shares, rebalancing portfolios) be $.05 per share. The market standard holds that the bid should succeed because the acquisition is probably value increasing, and T's shareholders have been more than compensated for their 'losses,' which are only $2.05 per share. The single-owner standard, on the other hand, is not necessarily satisfied on these facts. According to it, T's actual or 'true' value is the reservation price of a single owner of T's assets. If this true value exceeds $117.50, as it well might, a transfer at $117.50 would be inefficient. Therefore, some single-owner adherents claim, the state should require a target's board to obtain the highest possible price. Other adherents, believing that boards have a conflict of interest (they could want to block acquisitions to retain their positions), urge the state to create institutions that would effectively bar transfers below single-owner prices.''

The two competing approaches lead to markedly different prescriptions for regulatory policy. The market standard carries a norm of management passivity in response to a hostile bid along with a recommendation for the repeal of all state antitakeover legislation and the Williams Act. The sole owner standard implies approval of the Williams Act but not of state antitakeover legislation. It also prescribes strict scrutiny of management conduct of tender offer response but not a passivity rule. Actions that defeat takeovers in order to entrench managers should not be taken, but managers should take defensive steps that maximize shareholder return.

Professor Schwartz goes on to advocate the market standard. He concludes that auctions by targets are inefficient. Since auctions increase sale prices, they decrease the incentive of potential bidders to search for mismanaged firms. And as less search occurs the takeover sanction becomes a less effective disciplinary force. Schwartz, Search Theory and the Tender Offer Auction, 2 J.L.Econ. & Org. 229 (1986). Although Schwartz recognizes that dispersed target shareholders in an unregulated environment face a hostile bid in a disadvantaged contracting position, he argues that they are not so disadvantaged as is commonly supposed. Schwartz, supra, 17 J.Legal Studies at 170–183. He contends, *inter alia,* that the possible appearance of competing bidders will encourage offerors to make high preemptive opening bids that benefit the shareholders, and that higher valuing bidders are more likely to make short-term take-it-or-leave-it offers than are lower valuing bidders. In any event, says Schwartz, id. pp. 184–185:

"The disadvantage that shareholders seemingly suffer stems from their relative inability to dissipate the bargaining power that the ability to make take it or leave it offers confers on bidders. This suggests that adherents to the single-owner standard should support reforms that are consistent with the management-passivity thesis that Easterbrook and Fischel derived from the market standard. The suggestion may seem surprising because the obvious way to make takeover prices more like single-owner prices is to empower target managers to bargain on their shareholders' behalf, but this reform has the equally obvious disadvantage that the managers may frustrate transfers that benefit shareholders in order to preserve their own positions. When managers do bargain for shareholders, they are effective largely insofar as they reduce entry costs for later bidders. These costs can be reduced by lengthening minimum-offer periods and increasing the disclosure obligations of initial offerors, reforms that do not require the participation of target managers. Because involving target management creates the risk of blocking efficient transfers, the single-owner standard is best implemented by reforms that promise to raise takeover prices without involving target managers in the takeover process. * * * "

Professor Lucian Bebchuk, responding to Schwartz, in Bebchuk, The Sole Owner Standard for Takeover Policy, 17 J.Leg. Stud. 197 (1988), makes the following challenge to the basic assumptions of the market standard, id. pp. 203–204, 206–207:

"In advocating the market standard, Schwartz's analysis concentrates on the effect that takeover policy has on the outcome of bids and thus on the allocation of target assets. From the perspective of efficiency, it is desirable that a bid succeed if and only if the acquisition would put the target's assets to a more efficient, valuable use. Let us denote by W the value of the target's assets in the bidder's hands, and by V the value of the target's assets under independent existence. From the perspective of efficiency, the acquisition is desirable if and only if $V < W$.

"Thus, it follows that to ensure efficient outcome of bids, a takeover policy should accomplish two things. First, the policy should prevent any inefficient acquisition—that is, any acquisition where $V > W$. Second, the policy should facilitate any efficient acquisition—that is, any acquisition where $V < W$.

"The problem with the sole owner standard, and the reason why Schwartz objects to it, is that it might sometimes prevent an efficient acquisition. Consider a situation in which $V < W$ and in which an acquisition would thus be efficient. The buyer offers some acquisition price P, where presumably $P < W$. Even though the acquisition would be efficient, the owner(s) might reject the price P, insist on receiving a larger fraction of the acquisition gains, and hope that the buyer will raise its offer. While the buyer might indeed raise its offer, it might also walk away because of strategic or transaction cost considerations. Thus, the potential acquisition gains of $(W–V)$ might be lost because of such 'bargaining failure.' Such a possibility exists whenever owners have the power to reject offers—whether in the corporate context or in the sole owner context.

* * *

"The point Schwartz misses is that the market standard is significantly inferior to the sole owner standard in preventing inefficient acquisitions—that is, acquisitions where $V > W$. Schwartz incorrectly believes that the market standard would prevent all such inefficient acquisitions. This belief is based on Schwartz's claim that V is best represented by the prebid market price of the target's shares. Given this proposition, whenever the offered acquisition price exceeds the prebid market price, the acquisition price—and hence also W, as the bidder will presumably offer to pay less than W—will exceed V, and the acquisition would be efficient.

"Schwartz justifies his critical proposition—that, for the purpose of identifying the efficient outcome of a bid, V is best represented by the prebid market price of the target's shares—by asserting that it follows from the semistrong version of the efficient market hypothesis. As explained below, however, this justification is inadequate because (I) Schwartz's proposition does not follow from semistrong efficiency of the capital markets, and (ii) in any event, relying on the hypothesis of semistrong efficiency in designing takeover policy is risky.

* * *

" * * * [I]t is perfectly consistent with semistrong market efficiency that, between the last prebid trading time and the time of shareholders' tender decisions, the target's shareholders would receive a substantial amount of novel information about V, the target's independent value. Because most of this novel information is likely to be in the nature of 'good news,' the estimate of V that shareholders have at the time of their tender decisions is likely to be higher than the prebid market price. Therefore, the fact that the offered acquisition price exceeds the prebid price in no way implies that the offered price also exceeds the best estimate of V available when the outcome of the bid is determined. It follows that the market standard would enable some inefficient acquisitions that the sole owner standard would prevent."

Bebchuk adds, id. p. 209:

"[T]he existing evidence does not establish, certainly not with a significant degree of confidence, the proposition that the prebid price of all takeover targets fully reflects all information publicly available at the time, hard and soft. The evidence does not rule out this proposition, and some observers might even view the evidence as supportive. But the evidence does leave us with the nontrivial chance that the proposition does not hold or holds only with important exceptions and qualifications. This possibility should not be ignored in designing takeover policy."

Bebchuk goes on to insert a competing policy concern and to question the market side's emphasis on encouraging investment in the search for targets, id. pp. 210, 212–213:

"The sole owner standard would perform better than the market standard not only in attaining efficient outcome of bids, but also in providing incentives to investment decisions. This superior effect on investment decisions is due to the fact that the sole owner standard, by providing target shareholders with a substantial fraction of the produced acquisition gains, enables investors to capture social gains that result from their investment. * * *

" * * * The gains that result from an acquisition are attributable not only to the bidder's actions; they are also attributable to individuals' prior decisions to establish, and invest in, the target. Thus, for such decisions to be socially optimal, the target's shareholders must capture the social benefits produced by their investment. Unlike the market standard, the sole owner standard would provide shareholders with a substantial fraction of the acquisition gains that are attributable to the target's existence. Thus, the sole owner standard would move us closer to attaining optimal levels of investment in given companies."

Finally Bebchuk asserts that by focusing on shareholder choice as a primary objective, the problem of managerial misconduct can be solved without leaving the shareholders defenseless. He suggests a reform that removes management from the center of the process and assists the realization of maximum tender offer prices. Tender offers would be presented to the shareholders as yes/no ballots. Shareholders would mark either their approval or disapproval of the offer depending on their satisfaction with its terms, and only offers meeting a stated approval threshold would succeed. In the alternative, the tender offer would proceed only approval by a separate vote of the target shareholders. Id. pp. 222–223. See also Bebchuk, The Case Against Board Veto in Takeovers, 69 U. Chi. L. Rev. 973 (2002).

Advocates of the sole owner standard also attack the search costs point from another angle. They point out that a first bidder that does not win the contest can recoup its search costs by tendering the block of shares it accumulates before making the bid, or by selling those shares on the market in the midst of the contest. Since search costs are not excessive in the first instance, auctions do not significantly reduce takeover activity. Furthermore, assets should go to the highest valuing user, here the bidder with the largest potential synergistic gain. Auctions facilitate that process. See Romano, supra, at 157–158. Professor Schwartz, in turn, rebuts this line of argument by reference to the economic theory of auctions in Cramton and Schwartz, Using Auction Theory to Inform Takeover Regulation, 7 J.L.Econ. & Org. 27, 27–30, 45–46 (1991).

On two points all would agree. First, governing federal and state law sometimes follows the sole owner standard but in many cases follows neither standard and favors management. Second, this debate has been exhaustively recorded in the journals. In addition to the articles mentioned above, a limited list includes, on the market standard side, F. Easterbrook and D. Fischel, The Economic Structure of Corporate Law 162–211 (1991); Schwartz, Defensive Tactics and Optimal Search, 5 J.L.Econ. & Org. 413 (1989); Easterbrook & Fischel, The Proper Role of the Target's Management in Responding to a Tender Offer, 94 Harv.L.Rev. 1161 (1981). On the sole owner side, a limited list includes Bebchuk, The Case Against Board Veto in Takeovers, Harvard Center for Law, Economics, and Business Discussion Paper No. 361 (2002); Black and Kraakman, Delaware's Takeover Law: The Uncertain Search for Hidden Value, 96 Nw.U.L.Rev. 521 (2002); Bebchuk, Toward Undistorted Choice and Equal Treatment in Corporate Takeovers, 98 Harv.L.Rev. 69 (1985); Coffee, Regulating the Market for Corporate Control: A Critical Assessment of the Tender Offer's Role in Corporate Governance, 84 Colum.L.Rev. 1145 (1984); Lowenstein, Pruning Deadwood in Hostile Takeovers: A Proposal for Legislation, 83 Colum.L.Rev. 249 (1983); Gilson, The Case Against Shark Repellant Amendments: Structural Limitations on the Enabling Concept, 34 Stan. L.Rev. 775 (1982); Gilson, A Structural Approach to Corporations: The Case Against Defensive Tactics in Tender Offers, 33 Stan.L.Rev. 819 (1981).

(C) THE WILLIAMS ACT

Special obligations are imposed upon bidders, competing bidders, and target companies by the portions of §§ 13 and 14 of the Securities Exchange Act, known as the Williams Act. These sections, first adopted in 1968, were stated to be designed to protect investors, and *not* to regulate takeovers as an economic phenomenon or to favor either incumbent management or takeover bidders. They impose two kinds of requirements—regulatory restrictions and disclosure obligations. The former, together with implementing regulations, are designed to prohibit (a) time pressure or whipsaw constraints on investors to tender (by requiring a tolerable period for the offer and prescribing minimum withdrawal rights), (b) discrimination among tendering investors, and (c) maneuvers for favorable purchase prices before or after the tender offer or short tendering. The disclosure rules are designed to enable the public investors to make intelligent investment (or disinvestment) decisions.

Securities Exchange Act §§ 13(d), 13(e), 14(d), 14(e), and 14(f), Appendix D

Section 14(d) covers tender offers whose consummation make the bidder the owner of 5 percent of the class of securities in question, and provides that no offer can be made until the bidder has filed a disclosure statement with the SEC that contains the information specified in § 13(d). Under Rule 14e–2, the target's board of directors must state its position respecting the offer within 10 business days. Section 14(e) states the standard federal antifraud rule.

Additional substantive provisions are set forth in Rules 14e–1, 14d–7, and 14d–8. Rule 14e–1 regulates the minimum length of a tender offer. Any tender offer (other than certain issuer tender offers) is required to remain open for a minimum of twenty business days from the date of commencement and for ten business days from the date of any increase or decrease in the percentage of the class being sought or any notice of increase in the offered consideration or the dealer's soliciting fee. These time periods are designed to operate concurrently. Thus, if a tender offer commences on business day 1 and the bidder increases the consideration on business day 8, the ten business day period expires during the minimum twenty business day period.

Rules 14d–7 and 14d–8 also relate to the terms under which the tender offer may be conducted. Under Rule 14d–7 a shareholder has the right to withdraw any securities tendered for the entire period the offer remains open. Rule 14d–8 enables a bidder for less than all securities of a class to vary the pro rata acceptance provisions of § 14(d)(6) and take and pay for pro rata portions of all securities deposited during the period of the offer according to the number of securities deposited by each depositor.

(1) Bidder Disclosure

The disclosure required of a third party buyer or bidder under § 13(d) and accompanying Schedule 13D and § 14(d) and accompanying Schedule TO is addressed in part to the identity and funding of the bidder and its relationship to the target and to the target's affiliates or associates. The more significant substantive requirements are addressed to the bidder's "purpose or purposes" in making the acquisition of securities and to "any plan or proposal" the bidder may have which relates to acquiring or disposing of additional securities (in the case of disclosure under § 13(d)) and to causing any extraordinary transactions such as sale of the target's assets or merger or liquidation of the target, or change in its Board or capital structure or dividend policy.* In addition, Schedule TO requires the bidder to furnish financial statements if "the bidder is other than a natural person and the bidder's financial condition is material" to the offeree's decision.

Flynn v. Bass Bros. Enterprises, Inc.

United States Court of Appeals, Third Circuit, 1984.
744 F.2d 978.

■ ADAMS, CIRCUIT JUDGE.

This appeal concerns the adequacy under federal securities law of disclosure in a tender offer by defendant Bass Brothers Enterprises, Inc. (Bass Brothers) for the outstanding shares of defendant National Alfalfa Dehydrating and Milling Company (National Alfalfa) * * *.

[At the time of the tender offer in March 1976, Bass Brothers held 61.2 percent of National Alfalfa's outstanding shares. It had acquired the stock in a series of private transactions, including a purchase of a 52 percent control block from the CEO, Charles Peterson. The tender offer, priced at $6.45 per share, was for any and all of the remaining outstanding shares.

---

* Item 4 of Schedule 13D requires:

Item 4. Purpose of Transaction

State the purpose or purposes of the acquisition of securities of the issuer. Describe any plans or proposals which the reporting persons may have which relate to or would result in:

(a) The acquisition by any person of additional securities of the issuer, or the disposition of securities of the issuer;

(b) An extraordinary corporate transaction, such as a merger, reorganization or liquidation, involving the issuer or any of its subsidiaries;

(c) A sale or transfer of a material amount of assets of the issuer or of any of its subsidiaries;

(d) Any change in the present board of directors or management of the issuer, including any plans or proposals to change the number or term of directors or to fill any existing vacancies on the board;

(e) Any material change in the present capitalization or dividend policy of the issuer;

(f) Any other material change in the issuer's business or corporate structure, including but not limited to, if the issuer is a registered closed-end investment company, any plans or proposals to make any changes in its investment policy for which a vote is required by section 13 of the Investment Company Act of 1940;

(g) Changes in the issuer's charter, by-laws or instruments corresponding thereto or other actions which may impede the acquisition of control of the issuer by any person;

(h) Causing a class of securities of the issuer to be delisted from a national securities exchange or to cease to be authorized to be quoted in an inter-dealer quotation system of a registered national securities association;

(i) A class of equity securities of the issuer becoming eligible for termination of registration pursuant to Section 12(g)(4) of the Act; or

(j) Any action similar to any of those enumerated above.

[Before proceeding with the tender offer, Bass Brothers had acquired from Prochemco, Inc, in exchange for a finders fee, two reports on National Alfalfa's history and operations, including an appraisal of its assets based on alternative hypothetical valuations. Prochemco's appraisal, which was not disclosed in Bass Brothers tender offer filing, stated that:

$6.40 could be realized through "liquidation [of National Alfalfa] under stress conditions";

$12.40 could be realized through "liquidation in an orderly fashion over a reasonable period of time";

$16.40 represented National Alfalfa's value "as [an] ongoing venture."

The tender offer also omitted reference to a second report prepared by Prochemco which gave two additional valuations: $17.28 representing the "Value per Peterson"; $7.60 representing the "Value per Prochemco."

[The tender offer stated: "Offeror did not receive any material non-public information from [National Alfalfa] with respect to its prior acquisitions of shares nor * * * does it believe it presently possesses any such information. Offeror has not been able to verify independently the accuracy or completeness of the information contained in Appendices A through E [furnished by National Alfalfa] and assumes no responsibility therefor."

[A supplement to the tender offer stated:

While the Offeror has made no independent appraisal of the value of the Company's land and makes no representation with respect thereto, in view of the foregoing factors the aggregate current fair market value of the Company's agricultural land may be substantially higher than its original cost as reflected on the books of the Company. Depending upon the respective market values for such land, stockholders could receive, upon liquidation of the Company, an amount per share significantly higher than the current book value and possibly higher than the price of $6.45 per Share offered by Offeror in the Offer. The amount received by stockholders upon liquidation of the Company would also be dependent upon, among other things, the market value of the Company's other assets and the length of time allowed for such liquidation. The Offeror has no reason to believe that the Company's management has any present intention of liquidating the Company. As noted on page 8 of the Offer to Purchase under "Purpose of This Offer: Present Relationship of Company and Offeror", Offeror does not currently intend to liquidate the Company.

[At the tender offer's close, Bass Brothers held 92 percent of the stock. A DCL § 253 merger followed. The plaintiffs, former National Alfalfa shareholders, later sued on the ground that the failure to disclose the appraisal values violated §§ 10(b) and 14(e).]

At the time Bass Brothers was making its tender offer, although courts did not generally require the disclosure of asset valuations, such disclosure was not prohibited. [The court noted that in 1976 the SEC had deleted future earnings from its list of potentially misleading disclosures and in

1978 the SEC had promulgated a safe-harbor rule for forward looking statements.]

In order to give full effect to the evolution in the law of disclosure, and to avoid in the future, at least in the Third Circuit, the problem caused by the time lag between challenged acts and judicial resolution, today we set forth the law for disclosure of soft information as it is to be applied from this date on. Henceforth, the law is not that asset appraisals are, as a matter of law, immaterial. Rather, in appropriate cases, such information must be disclosed. Courts should ascertain the duty to disclose asset valuations and other soft information on a case by case basis, by weighing the potential aid such information will give a shareholder against the potential harm, such as undue reliance, if the information is released with a proper cautionary note.

The factors a court must consider in making such a determination are: the facts upon which the information is based; the qualifications of those who prepared or compiled it; the purpose for which the information was originally intended; its relevance to the stockholders' impending decision; the degree of subjectivity or bias reflected in its preparation; the degree to which the information is unique; and the availability to the investor of other more reliable sources of information. * * *

* * *

* * * [W]e must determine whether the trial judge erred in ruling that Bass Brothers and the management of National Alfalfa had no duty to disclose the asset valuations at issue in this case. We note that despite our formulation of the current law applicable to corporate disclosure, we are constrained by the significant development in disclosure law since 1976 not to apply the announced standard retroactively,[19] but to evaluate defendants' conduct by the standards which prevailed in 1976.

* * *

A.

The shareholders contend that the Prochemco reports were material and should have been disclosed. However, employing the approach commonly followed by courts when Bass Brothers made its tender offer in early 1976, we do not find the Prochemco reports had sufficient indicia of reliability to require disclosure. Plaintiffs did not adequately establish that the reports were prepared by experts. * * * Moreover, plaintiffs did not establish that the reports had sufficient basis in fact to be reliable. * * *

The purpose for which the Prochemco reports were prepared—to attract financing for its proposed purchase of Peterson's controlling block of National Alfalfa shares—also diminishes the reliability of the reports. Further, at the time of the tender offer the valuations in the Prochemco reports were outdated.

---

19. Our reluctance to apply the new standard for disclosure retroactively is confined to the facts of this case. We do not intend to imply that in other cases based on actions occurring before the date of this opinion, the new standard necessarily is inapplicable.

Plaintiffs assert that the reliability of the reports was amply demonstrated by Bass Brothers' reliance on them and by the payment of $130,000 to Prochemco for them. The shareholders reason that "if the Prochemco reports were reliable and accurate enough for Bass Brothers to use * * * in deciding to [purchase Peterson's stock] then the existence of and valuations in the Prochemco reports were material and should have been shared with National Alfalfa's shareholders" through the tender offer. To bolster their argument, the shareholders note that after buying Peterson's stock, Bass Brothers chose not to examine any of National Alfalfa's internal asset valuations before making the tender offer.

Although it is not inconceivable that Bass Brothers may have relied on the Prochemco valuations, plaintiffs did not advance sufficient evidence to establish the point. Moreover, even if there had been some reliance on the reports, that alone would be insufficient to mandate disclosure in this case. The reports were not prepared by experts, had no adequately demonstrated basis in fact and were prepared to encourage financing to purchase Peterson's share. In light of the record before us, we cannot say that the district court erred in concluding that at the time of the tender offer Bass Brothers had no duty to disclose the Prochemco reports.

B.

Plaintiffs assert that Bass Brothers also should have disclosed its own internal valuations. To substantiate their belief that Bass Brothers commissioned a report to corroborate the information in the Prochemco report, the shareholders point to an informal typewritten list of "Items for Investigation" drawn up by Rusty Rose, a Bass Brothers consultant. The list sets forth a number of assignments to be performed by Rose. Item 2(a) states: "Have expert appraise farm land and equipment." A handwritten notation after this item states "Done—values confirmed." * * * The shareholders contend that this cryptic notation, without more, "confirms that Bass Brothers had obtained an 'expert' appraisal." Plaintiffs had ample opportunity during discovery to pursue this lead yet failed to turn up any additional evidence of a corroborating study. Presentation of this handwritten notation, alone, to the jury simply could not support a finding of fraudulent and material nondisclosure of information.

C.

The third piece of information that the shareholders claim should have been disclosed was a study prepared by Carl Schweitzer, a vice president of National Alfalfa, using various assumptions, such as the projected appreciation of National Alfalfa's land holdings, to arrive at a value per share of $12.95. At trial, Schweitzer's unrefuted testimony indicated that such a figure was, in fact, hypothetical because of the nature of the assumptions used in the calculation. Schweitzer stated that he used land values supplied by Peterson and some "unnamed people within or without of the company." Thus, plaintiffs have not established a sufficient factual basis for the valuations. Moreover, the purpose of some of these calculations was to help Peterson find a buyer for his stock. Schweitzer testified that the land values were inflated, or optimistic, so as to present the company in the best possible light to future investors. Moreover, Schweitzer admitted that neither he nor members of National Alfalfa's accounting staff had expertise with regard to land appraisal. Thus, plaintiffs were unable to produce evidence that the Schweitzer reports were sufficiently reliable to be material for shareholders confronted with the tender offer.

NOTE: BIDDER DISCLOSURE

1. *The Statement of Purpose.*

There is a body of litigation in connection with the efforts of bidders filing Schedules 13D and TO to set forth as many possible alternatives for future relationships or dealings with the target as can be envisioned, so that the bidders retain options to deal with the target as they choose and remain unconfined to particular alternatives. Another tactic to achieve similar freedom of action is to make bland statements of possibilities allegedly because the bidder is unable to be more definite (see e.g., Revlon, Inc. v. Pantry Pride, 621 F.Supp. 804 (D.Del.1985)). Comparable ambiguity attends discussion on disclosure of merger negotiations. Such statements invite a finding of inaccuracy only if the bidder takes particular action with respect to the target (e.g., merger) very shortly after the statement is made. The cases suggest that the courts have a large tolerance for bland or ambiguous statements of purpose, at least under Schedule TO.

2. *Questions.*

What information should a recipient of a tender offer seek in order to be able intelligently to make the decision whether to tender or not? If the information required by the statute with respect to the bidder's background or associates or sources of financing or future plans for the target company appeal to the offeree, should she tender any or all of his shares, or hold on to them? Should the answer be the same if the bidder is seeking only control of the target as if the bidder is seeking 100% of the target's stock and announces an intention (if it should acquire 51% or more) to cash out those who decline to tender?

Do the SEC filing requirements under §§ 13(d) and 14(d) prescribe too costly a disclosure program for the benefits provided? For example, in the case of a bidder seeking 100% control for cash, is any disclosure necessary or appropriate about the bidder, its finances or its plans (other than its ability to finance the tender offer)?

If the bid is made without prior negotiations, must the bidder disclose theretofore undisclosed values of the target which its diligence has produced? If the bid is made with the cooperation of the target's management, is the disclosure obligation more demanding? See e.g. Plaine v. McCabe, 797 F.2d 713 (9th Cir.1986). In any event, must the bidder reveal the gains which it expects to follow from its combination with the target? Is the analogy to information required in a proxy or registration statement apposite?

What is the likely impact on potential take-over attempts of the requirement that the bidder disclose future merger or liquidation plans or other major changes (or discovery values) with respect to the target company (§ 13(d)(1)(C)), which the latter's management may thereupon be free to appropriate? Is it appropriate for the bidder to formulate its future plans for merger so ambiguously that offerees will not know whether, if they decline to tender at the bid price, they will later be under pressure to accept securities of lesser value in a merger forced by the successful bidder?

Courts, in enforcing those provisions, are under conflicting pressures to cause bidders to furnish information about their plans, particularly if they seek less than all the target's stock. If all offered stock will not, or cannot, be taken by the bidder, the investor is interested in learning as much, and as explicitly, as possible about those plans. But the bidder is fearful of too much specificity, both because it may not have enough knowledge about the target to make firm commitments or precise statements which increase the risk of its liability, and because it is not anxious to educate the target's management or potential competing bidders about unexploited opportunities.

The context of a contest imposes other pressures on courts in enforcing the disclosure requirements of the Williams Act. The fact that offers must be responded to within a limited period may induce a court which is solicitous that offerees have adequate information to require more disclosure (for example, of alternatives, see e.g., Valente v. PepsiCo, Inc., 454 F.Supp. 1228 (D.Del.1978) (appraisal rights)) and clearer exposition than it would require in a less demanding situation. On the other hand, the fact of a contest puts time pressure on the parties (reducing their ability to formulate communications) and offers rebuttal opportunities which may mitigate the strictness of a requirement of "full" disclosure which would be applicable if only one party's communications were available to investors.

The continuing debate between advocates of the market and sole owner standards, provides bases for arguing both sides of many of the foregoing questions. On the market side, see, e.g., Macey and Netter, Regulation 13D and the Regulatory Process, 65 Wash. U.L.Q. 131 (1987).

Assume, for the moment, a decision to adhere to the sole owner standard. Does the Williams Act, as drafted, provide the best possible framework for realizing shareholder value? Booth, The Problem With Federal Tender Offer Law, 77 Cal. L.Rev. 707, 713–715, 738–743 (1989), suggests that the Act, by offering the target shareholders too much in the way of procedural protection, inadvertently diminishes their returns. According to Booth, the Act's assurances of withdrawal rights, proration, and receipt of the highest price offered by a given bidder lull the shareholders into tendering. Pressure to hold out and force a higher price is dissipated. Given stair-step offers (forbidden by the Act) and absent withdrawal rights (provided by the Act), the shareholders would be forced to act defensively. Assured adequate information and time to think by the Act, the shareholders should be able to defend themselves. To guard against the possibility that such a regime would overly increase the pressure to tender, Professor Booth would require the bidder to pay the highest price to all shareholders after the point at which control is obtained. Would the target shareholders do better if the decision respecting the transfer of control were removed from the market context entirely?

(2) Target Disclosure

Rule 14e–2, Appendix D

Rule 14e–2 requires the subject company to publish or send or give to security holders a statement disclosing its position with respect to the tender offer within 10 business days of the offer's commencement. The statement of position can take one of three forms: (1) a recommendation of acceptance or rejection; (2) an expression of no opinion and a neutral posture; or (3) an inability to take a position. The target also is required to state the reasons for its position and promptly notify the stockholders of any change of position. A 14e–2 statement of position is subject to § 14(d)(1) and is deemed by Rule 14d–9(f) to constitute a solicitation or recommendation within the meaning of Rule 14d–9 and § 14(d)(4). The target accordingly must file a Schedule 14D–9 with the Commission and include the information required by certain items thereof in the information disseminated to security holders. Item 4 of the Schedule (Item 1012 of Regulation M–A) serves as the vehicle by which the target satisfies its disclosure obligation under Rule 14e–2.

NOTE: TARGET DISCLOSURE

1. *Appraisals.*

Radol v. Thomas, 772 F.2d 244 (6th Cir.), cert. denied 477 U.S. 903 (1986), treats for targets the issue that Flynn v. Bass Brothers treated for bidders. The case concerned the successful two-step acquisition of Marathon by U.S. Steel, and the Strong and First Boston appraisals of the value of Marathon's assets. For the factual background, see Starkman v. Marathon, supra, Part V.E.3(B). The appraisals were included in the Schedule 13E–3 filed by Marathon in connection with the second-step merger with Steel, pursuant to Item 9 of Schedule 13E–3 (requiring that a summary of any asset appraisal prepared in connection with such a merger must be furnished). The plaintiffs, shareholders of Marathon, contended that asset appraisals also should have been disclosed in the tender offer materials earlier distributed to shareholders by Marathon and Steel, and that the failure to disclose violated Rule 10b–5, and § 14(e), constituting an omission of material facts necessary to make not misleading other affirmative statements.

The Court rejected the claim:

"In Starkman v. Marathon Oil Co., 772 F.2d 231 (6th Cir.1985), we have reaffirmed our adherence to the basic rule established by our prior decisions that tender offer materials must disclose soft information, such as these asset appraisals based upon predictions regarding future economic and corporate events, only if the predictions underlying the appraisal are substantially certain to hold. The Supreme Court's test for materiality as set forth in TSC Industries, Inc. v. Northway, Inc., 426 U.S. 438, 450, 96 S.Ct. 2126, 2132, 48 L.Ed.2d 757 (1976), is whether there is a 'substantial likelihood that, under all the circumstances, the omitted fact would have assumed actual significance in the deliberations of the reasonable shareholder.' The District Court's instructions to the jury accurately stated this general test for materiality and the specific rule in this circuit governing the duty to disclose asset appraisals, and we have, in any event, held in *Starkman* that there was no duty to disclose the asset appraisals at issue here.

"Indeed, if there was an error below on this issue, it was in allowing it to reach the jury. * * * "

The *Radol* court's treatment of Marathon's asset appraisals presumably should be reconsidered in light of Basic v. Levinson, supra, Part V.E.3(B). What should result from such a reconsideration? Does the context of a tender offer make a significant difference in the materiality determination in respect of asset appraisals?

2. *Disclosure of Defensive Negotiations.*

The SEC's posture respecting disclosure of negotiations looking toward target asset sales or defensive mergers provides a striking comparison with *Radol*. The Commission long has insisted that the existence of such negotiations be disclosed promptly. The Commission set out its position in Exchange Act Rel. No. 16,384 (Nov. 29, 1979):

"Item 7 of Schedule 14D–9 [now located as Item 1006(a) of Regulation M–A] requires disclosure with respect to certain negotiations and transactions by the subject company. As proposed for comment, Item 7 would have required disclosure of any negotiation or transaction being undertaken in response to the tender offer by the subject company which related to or would have resulted in any of the following: (1) an extraordinary transaction, such as a merger or reorganization, involving the subject company or any subsidiary of the subject company; (2) a sale or transfer of a material amount of assets of the subject company or any of its subsidiaries; (3) a tender offer for or other acquisition of subject company securities; or (4) any material change in the subject company's present capitalization or dividend policy. The proposal was criticized by commentators who were concerned that it would elicit premature disclosure of negotiations with competing bidders which could dissuade them from making an offer. It was noted that this would be harmful to security holders since they would be prevented from obtaining the highest price for their securities. In addition, concern was expressed that such disclosure may, either innocently or fraudulently, induce security holders to reject a tender offer on the basis of an unjustified inference that a competing bid is imminent.

"The Commission recognizes that premature disclosure of the matters contemplated by the proposal may be detrimental to the interests of security holders. The effective representation of the interests of security holders may at times require management to maintain confidentiality during the formative stages of negotiations. On the other hand, the major developments referred to in Item 7 can be one of the most material items of information received by security holders.

"The Commission has addressed these competing concerns by approaching disclosure of these matters at two levels. While the proposal would have required the subject company to describe negotiations in response to a tender offer which related to or would result in the specified events, new Item 7(a) [now located at Item 1006(d) of Regulation M–A] requires a statement as to whether negotiations are being undertaken or are underway with respect to such events without requiring detailed disclosure. An instruction has also been added to Item 7(a) which clarifies the extent of the disclosure required with respect to negotiations. The instruction provides that, if an agreement in principle has not been reached, the possible terms of any transaction or the parties thereto need not be disclosed if in the opinion of the Board of Directors of the subject company such disclosure would jeopardize continuation of such negotiations. In such event, disclosure that negotiations are being undertaken or are underway and are in the preliminary stages will be sufficient. Thus, security holders will be apprised that such negotiations are being held without the subject company's having to furnish disclosure which would discourage further negotiations."

The SEC has been notably aggressive in its enforcement of the requirement that targets keep Item 7 current. In In re Revlon, CCH Fed.Sec.L.Rep. ¶ 84,006 (1986), the Commission ruled that Revlon violated the Act in failing to amend its Schedule 14D–9 to note the existence of negotiations with a group interested in purchasing its cosmetic producing assets, even though terms on price and structure were far from concluded. The fact that discussions on price and structure were under way and an initial offer on the table were enough. In re Kern, CCH Fed.Sec.L.Rep. ¶ 84,342 (1988), a similar enforcement proceeding, extends the duty to outside counsel for the target where the lawyer, here the head of the mergers and acquisitions group at Sullivan & Cromwell, held all responsibility for compliance decisions.

3. *Defenses That Pretermit Actions for Inadequate Disclosure.*

In **Panter v. Marshall Field & Co.,** 646 F.2d 271 (7th Cir.1981), cert. denied, 454 U.S. 1092 (1981), target shareholders unsuccessfully brought an action under § 14(e) in respect of management defensive actions that caused a prospective hostile bid to fail to materialize. The management of Marshall Field brought an antitrust action against a merger proposed by the hostile suitor, Carter Hawley Hale (CHH). It simultaneously proceeded to expand Field's business into new geographic markets in which CHH had a significant presence. The court disposed of the 14(e) claim as follows, 646 F.2d at 283–284, 285–286:

"By denying the plaintiffs the opportunity to tender their shares to CHH, the plaintiffs claim the defendants deprived them of the difference between $42.00, the amount of the CHH offer, and $19.76, the amount at which Field's shares traded in the market after withdrawal of the CHH proposal. Total damages under this theory would exceed $200,000,000.00.

"Because § 14(e) is intended to protect shareholders from making a tender offer decision on inaccurate or inadequate information, among the elements of § 14(e) plaintiff must establish is 'that there was a misrepresentation upon which the target corporation shareholders relied * * *.' Chris–Craft Industries, Inc. v. Piper Aircraft Corp., 480 F.2d 341, 373 (2d Cir.), cert. denied, 414 U.S. 910, 94 S.Ct. 231, 38 L.Ed.2d 148 (1973). Because the CHH tender offer was withdrawn before the plaintiffs had the opportunity to decide whether or not to tender their shares, it was impossible for the plaintiffs to rely on any alleged deception in making the decision to tender or not. Because the plaintiffs were never presented with that critical decision and therefore never relied on the defendants' alleged misrepresentations, they fail to establish a vital element of a § 14(e) claim as regards the CHH $42.00 offer.

* * *

"Courts seeking to construe the provisions of the Williams Act have also noted that its protections are required by the peculiar nature of a tender offer, which forces a shareholder to decide whether to dispose of his shares at some premium over the market, or retain them with knowledge that the offeror may alter the management of the target company to its detriment. See Piper v. Chris–Craft Industries, Inc., 430 U.S. at 35, 97 S.Ct. at 946; Bucher v. Shumway, 452 F.Supp. 1288, 1294 (S.D.N.Y.1978). * * * Here there was no deadline by which shareholders were forced to tender, and by hypothesis when we are discussing market transactions, no premium over the market. Therefore Field's shareholders were simply not subjected to the proscribed pressures the Williams Act was designed to alleviate. * * * *"

(3) *Undistorted Choice for Target Shareholders*

(a) *withdrawal and proration*

Rules 14d–7 and 14d–8, Appendix D

Rule 14d–7 extends a right to withdraw tendered stock at any time during the duration of the offer. Rule 14d–8 applies to tenders for less than all of a class of shares and provides that for proration ("as nearly as may be pro rata") in a case where the number of shares tendered exceeds the number requested in the offer. A 10 day proration period is contemplated.

Suppose a bidder voluntarily extends the proration period, permitting additional tenders to an oversubscribed offer and diluting the yield to those who tendered within the original period? **Pryor v. United States Steel Corp.**, 794 F.2d 52 (2d Cir.), cert. denied 479 U.S. 954 (1986), implied a private right of action under § 14(d)(6) and sanctioned an action for damages by holders who tendered during the original period:

" * * * Prior to Section 14(d)(6), first-come, first-serve offers were often employed in two-step takeovers. Offerors placed a premium on shares amounting to a control bloc, and tender offers for less than 100% of a company's common stock were believed by Congress to confront shareholders with a difficult and time-pressured decision. Congress reasoned that shareholders might be tempted to tender without carefully weighing the offer so as to avoid missing out on a piece of the control premium. * * * Section 14(d)(6)'s mandatory minimum proration period thus affords shareholders a period of time in which to consider the offer and also to share in the control premium if a decision to tender is made. It is clear therefore that the ten-day period is a mandatory minimum.

"In addition, Section 14(d)(6) requires equal treatment of holders who tender within the proration period and thus has a non-discrimination component. Had U.S. Steel purchased a greater than pro rata share of timely-tendered shares from a particular shareholder, it would have violated Section 14(d)(6). This is evident not only in the very use of the term pro rata, but also in Section 14(d)(6)'s requirement that 'an increase in the consideration offered to security holders' automatically extends the proration period for an additional ten days. For better or for worse, Congress desired to spread any premium for control among all shareholders tendering within the proration period. This purpose cannot be achieved unless offerors are forbidden to purchase a greater than pro rata share from particular holders.

"It also follows that offerors are not free to extend the proration deadline after it has expired where the effect is to diminish the numbers of shares purchased from those who tendered before the deadline. It cannot be determined whether U.S. Steel extended the proration period for the purpose of benefitting particular shareholders. However, the result of its increasing the size of the pool after expiration of the offer is the same as if it had. The discretionary power to extend selectively the proration date after the offer has been oversubscribed entails the power to alter the size and make-up of the proration pool, which in turn enables the offeror to favor certain holders to the detriment of others. * * * "

Compare **Schreiber v. Burlington Northern, Inc.**, 472 U.S. 1 (1985), which concerned a claimed violation of § 14(e), the Williams Act's antifraud provision, in connection with a proration. In this case, the bidder made two successive offers, the first hostile and the second (made after the bidder cut a deal with the target managers) friendly. The first offer, which was rescinded, had been for 25.1 million shares at $24. The follow up offer was for only 21 million shares at $24, the bidder having agreed to purchase 4.1 million shares directly from the target on an original issue basis. As the second offer was greatly oversubscribed, shareholders who had tendered into the first offer accordingly received a diminished payment. The plaintiff claimed that the withdrawal and substitution was a "manipulation" within the meaning of § 14(e). A unanimous Supreme Court rejected the claim, holding that "manipulative" acts under § 14(e) require misrepresentation or nondisclosure.

In 1999 the SEC adopted Rule 14d–11 and amended Rule 14d–7 to allow third party bidders to elect to provide for a subsequent offering period of between 3 and 20 business days in which securities may be tendered without withdrawal rights on the part of the holders. This provision hinges on a long list of conditions and restrictions:

(1) the subsequent offer must be for all outstanding securities of the class and the same consideration must be paid in both the initial and subsequent offering periods;

(2) the initial offering period, which must have carried withdrawal rights, must have remained open for at least 20 business days;

(3) the bidder is deemed to have waived all conditions on the initial offer before the close of the initial offering period;

(4) the bidder must have both accepted and paid for all securities tendered during the initial offering period upon the period's closing and must immediately accept and pay for all securities tendered in the subsequent offering period; and

(5) the bidder must have announced the number and percentage of securities tendered into the initial offering no later than 9 a.m. on the first business day following the initial offering period's scheduled expiration.

(b) equal treatment

Rule 14d–10, Appendix D

Rule 14d–10 provides that tender offers must be open to all holders of the subject class of securities (the "all holders rule") and that the consideration paid to any one holder "during" the tender offer must equal the highest consideration paid to any other holder (the "best price" rule). Provisions similar to those in Rule 14d–10 are contained in Rule 13e–4(f)(8)–(11) governing issuer tender offers.

NOTE: THE ALL HOLDERS RULE AND THE SEC'S RULEMAKING AUTHORITY

Securities Act Rel. No. 6653 (July 11, 1986), published as Part II, No. 1186, CCH Fed.Sec.L.Rep. (July 16, 1986), discusses the bases on which the Commission relied in promulgating Rule 14d–10 and related provisions. The Release intimates that the principles underlying the Williams Act contemplate equal treatment of stockholders. If equality of treatment of stockholders is contemplated by the Williams Act, is it only as an instrument for facilitating a purpose of undistorted choice by the target stockholders? At what point does undistorted choice dictate equal treatment?

The validity of the All Holders Rule was confirmed in **Polaroid Corp. v. Disney,** 862 F.2d 987 (3d Cir.1988):

"Section 14(e) of the Williams Act proscribes 'fraudulent, deceptive, or manipulative acts * * * in connection with any tender offer.' 15 U.S.C. § 78n(e). A unanimous Court in Schreiber v. Burlington Northern, Inc., 472 U.S. 1 (1985), held that section 14(e) does not prohibit manipulative conduct unless there has been some element of deception through a material misrepresentation or omission. The Court held that '[i]t is clear that Congress relied primarily on disclosure to implement the purpose of the Williams Act' and characterized all of the Williams Act provisions as disclosure provisions. *Id.* at 8–9. *Schreiber* characterizes even section 14(d)(6), which mandates the proration of share purchases when the number of shares tendered exceeds the number of shares sought, and section 14(d)(7), which mandates the payment of the same price to all those whose shares are purchased, as 'requir[ing] or prohibit[ing] certain acts so that investors will possess additional time within which to take advantage of the disclosed information.' *Id.* at 9. It is thus possible to read *Schreiber* to imply that the All Holders Rule is beyond the SEC's authority under the Williams Act, for the Rule's purpose seems to be neither to ensure full disclosure nor to provide for an adequate time period for investors to comprehend disclosed information.

"Although *Schreiber* categorizes the proration and best price provisions of the Williams Act as relating to disclosure, these provisions are only tangentially related to ensuring that investors make fully informed decisions. While the All Holders Rule thus has little to do with ensuring complete disclosure, it is no less related to disclosure than are the proration and best price provisions. Moreover, the SEC has articulated a disclosure justification for the Rule:

> [t]he all-holders requirement would realize the disclosure purposes of the Williams Act by ensuring that all members of the class subject to the tender offer receive information necessary to make an informed decision regarding the merits of the tender offer. If tender offer disclosure is given to all holders, but some are barred from participating in the offer, the Williams Act disclosure objectives would be ineffective.

51 Fed.Reg. at 25,875 (footnote omitted). In light of the loose definition that *Schreiber* itself ascribes to the meaning of a 'disclosure' provision, the emphasis in *Schreiber* on characterizing the Williams Act as a disclosure statute *simpliciter* is of small force in an effort to invalidate the All Holders Rule. For the foregoing reasons, we are satisfied that the SEC was acting within its authority in promulgating the All Holders Rule. This conclusion is buttressed by the deference due the agency's interpretation of its enabling statute, the statute being ambiguous on the issue and the agency's interpretation being a permissible one. Chevron, U.S.A., Inc. v. Natural Resources Defense Council, Inc., 467 U.S. 837, 843 (1984).

"The holding of *Schreiber*—that misrepresentation or nondisclosure is a necessary element of a violation of section 14(e)—is not compromised by a determination that the All Holders Rule is a valid exercise of SEC rulemaking authority. The All Holders Rule is not an attempt to proscribe manipulative practices so much as an attempt to ensure that all holders of a class of securities subject to a tender offer receive fair and equal treatment. And, as explained in the SEC's release, this attempt to ensure fair and equal treatment is the purpose behind both the proration and best price provisions. 51 Fed.Reg. at 25,876."

Gerber v. Computer Associates International, Inc.

United States Court of Appeals, Second Circuit, 2002.
303 F.3d 126.

■ Before FEINBERG, KEARSE, and B.D. PARKER, CIRCUIT JUDGES.

■ B.D. PARKER, JR., CIRCUIT JUDGE.

　　* * *

BACKGROUND

[Computer Associates International, Inc. ("CA")] is in the business of designing and marketing computer software products. In July 1991, CA's chairman, Charles Wang, approached the chairman and chief executive officer of [On–Line Software International, Inc. ("On–Line")], Jack Berdy, to discuss the possibility of CA's acquiring On Line. On–Line, which Berdy founded in 1969, was also in the software business. Berdy owned 1.5 million shares of On–Line stock, representing approximately 25% of the company's outstanding shares. Berdy and Wang, as well as Sanjay Kumar, the chief operating officer of CA, negotiated extensively over the price that CA would pay for On–Line's stock.

Negotiations over the terms of a non-compete agreement proceeded concurrently with negotiations over the purchase price. CA insisted that Berdy and other On–Line executives, who would be leaving the company following the acquisition, agree not to compete with CA for a specified period of time, but Berdy initially resisted entering into a non-compete agreement. [CA offered to pay $14 per share for On–Line's stock (then trading at $10 on the NYSE) and to pay Berdy $9 million for a seven-year non-compete agreement. On–Line's board responded that the offer for the shares was too low and the $9 million too high, suggesting $16 for the shares. CA came back with $15.50 per share. In the end the parties agreed in principle on a price of $15.75, along with a $5 million, 5 year non-compete for Berdy.]

On August 15 and 16, 1991, there was an unusually large amount of trading in On–Line stock. On August 15, the stock price rose $1, and the NYSE asked On–Line about the unusual trading activity. On the morning of August 16, when the stock price rose another dollar, On–Line told the NYSE that it was in discussions with CA and that a press release might be issued shortly. Berdy told CA that On–Line was under pressure from the NYSE to issue a press release. Around noon on August 16, On Line and CA reached their agreement at $15.75 per share, On–Line told the NYSE that it would issue press release, and trading in On–Line stock was halted. Later that day, each company issued a press release announcing that it had reached an agreement with the other. CA's press release stated in relevant part that CA has reached an agreement in principle with the management of [On–Line] whereby CA will acquire all of the outstanding common stock of On–Line for $15-3/4 per share in cash. The transaction is subject to the approval of the Boards of Directors of On–Line and CA, the execution of definitive agreements and regulatory approval. On–Line's press release was very similar to CA's, except it also noted that "no assurance can be given that a transaction between On–Line and Computer Associates of any sort will occur."

[After issuing their August 16 press releases, CA and On–Line continued to negotiate the terms and conditions of their tender offer and follow-up merger. The CA board approved a Merger Agreement, a Stock Purchase and Non Competition Agreement (the "Berdy Agreement") on August 20. The On–Line board approved the Merger Agreement and recommended the transaction to its shareholders on August 21. Under the Berdy Agreement, CA paid Berdy the same $15.75 for his stock offered to the other On–Line shareholders. The Berdy Agreement also provided that Berdy could not tender his shares in the tender offer, and that, if another bidder made a better offer, CA retained an option to purchase Berdy's shares for $15.75 per share. The Berdy Agreement contained a provision prohibiting him from "engag[ing] in any business activities which are competitive with the computer software business activities of CA" for a period of five years, in consideration for which CA agreed to pay Berdy $5 million. The various agreements were executed on August 21. On August 22, CA and On–Line (1) issued a joint press release announcing that the two companies had entered into an agreement and that CA "will make a tender offer today" and conduct a follow-up merger, (2) filed with the SEC, and (3) disseminated an Offer to Purchase remaining open until September 20. A majority of the On–Line shareholders tendered and the acquisition and follow up merger were completed.

[Gerber, a tendering On–Line shareholder, brought this action individually and on behalf of a class of tendering On–Line shareholders, alleging that CA, Wang, Kumar, and Berdy had violated Section 14(d)(7) of the Securities Exchange Act of 1934, and SEC Rule 14d–10 (collectively, the "Williams Act claims"), by offering and paying $5 million more consideration to Berdy for his On–Line shares than it offered or paid to other On–Line shareholders.

[On defendants' motion for summary judgment, the District Court concluded as a matter of law that the tender offer commenced on August 16, 1991, when CA issued its first press release. The case went to trial. At the close of trial, the District Court instructed the jury, without objection, to "consider whether the payment of 5 million dollars under the so-called Berdy agreement was paid to Dr. Berdy for his On–Line shares, or his agreement not to compete, or partly for the shares and partly for the agreement not to compete." The jury returned a special verdict in favor of the plaintiff class, finding that $2.34 million of the $5 million that CA had paid to Berdy was compensation for Berdy's On–Line shares, while the remainder was legitimate consideration for the non-compete agreement.]

DISCUSSION

* * *

A. Whether the Berdy Agreement Was Executed During the Tender Offer

Defendants' arguments regarding the legal sufficiency of the Williams Act claims focus primarily on timing. * * * If defendants are correct, and the tender offer did not commence until August 22, then the Berdy Agreement preceded the tender offer and is not subject to the Best Price Rule. If Gerber is correct, and the tender offer commenced on August 16, then the Berdy Agreement was executed during the tender offer and must satisfy the Best Price Rule.

In order to determine when the tender offer commenced, we turn to SEC Rule 14d–2. In 1991, Rule 14d–2(b) provided:

> A public announcement by a bidder through a press release, newspaper advertisement or public statement which includes the information in paragraph (c) of this section with respect to a tender offer in which the consideration consists solely of cash and/or securities exempt from registration under section 3 of the Securities Act of 1933 shall be deemed to constitute the commencement of a tender offer....

Rule 14d–2(c) provided:

> The information referred to in paragraph (b) of this section is as follows: (1) The identity of the bidder; (2) The identity of the subject company; and (3) The amount and class of securities being sought and the price or range of prices being offered therefor.

Under Rule 14d–2(b), if CA's August 16 press release "include[d] the information in [Rule 14d–2(c)]," then the August 16 press release "shall be deemed to constitute the commencement of [the] tender offer." * * *

[The CA] press release includes all the information listed in Rule 14d–2(c): (1) it identifies CA as the bidder; (2) it identifies On–Line as the subject company; and (3) it identifies "all ... outstanding common stock" as the amount and class of securities being sought, and "$15–3/4 per share in cash" as the offer price. * * *

In arguing that its August 16 press release was not made "with respect to a tender offer," CA confuses the test for whether a tender offer has occurred with the test for when a tender offer commences. CA argues that, under the "totality of the circumstances" test of Hanson Trust PLC v. SCM Corp., 774 F.2d 47 (2d Cir.1985), and the eight-factor test of Wellman v. Dickinson, 475 F.Supp. 783 (S.D.N.Y.1979), the tender offer began on August 22, not August 16, because those tests were not satisfied until August 22. As the District Court correctly found, however, Hanson and Wellman both involve the issue of whether a tender offer has occurred, not when a tender offer starts, and the parties here do not dispute that a tender offer occurred. Gerber, 812 F.Supp. at 366. Rather, the only question is when the tender offer commenced, a question which is answered by Rule 14d–2(c), not by Hanson or Wellman. See Lerro v. Quaker Oats Co., 84 F.3d 239, 246 (7th Cir.1996) (noting that "our case is about 'when' rather than 'what'"). * * * [W]e have no trouble concluding that CA's August 16, 1991 press release was made "with respect to a tender offer."

CA also argues that its August 16 press release was not made "with respect to a tender offer" because the press release does not contain the words "tender offer." While the August 16 press release does not contain the words "tender offer," Rule 14d–2(c) imposes no such requirement. Because the entire purpose of that rule is to prescribe the information that a public announcement must contain in order to commence a tender offer, we deem it dispositive that the words "tender offer" are not among the Rule's prescriptions. To the extent CA asks us to graft an additional requirement onto Rule 14d–2(c), we decline to do so. "Were the label used by the acquiror determinative, virtually all of the provisions of the Williams

Act, including the filing and disclosure requirements[,] could be evaded simply by an offeror's announcement that offers to purchase [ ] stock were private purchases." Field, 850 F.2d at 944 (citation omitted).

We also reject CA's argument that the press release did not commence a tender offer because it stated that the transaction was subject to future conditions * * *. Nothing in Rule 14d–2 or Rule 14d–10 renders them inapplicable to tender offers that are subject to conditions. Indeed, CA's ultimate Offer to Purchase, which CA contends commenced the tender offer, also states that the transaction is subject to certain conditions. Our conclusion * * * is consistent with the Seventh Circuit's decision in Lerro* * *. The plaintiffs in Lerro contended that a tender offer begins "as soon as a potential bidder opens negotiation with a potential target's management," even if no public announcement has been made. Lerro, 84 F.3d at 245. The court rejected this contention, holding that, under Rule 14d–2, " 'the tender offer' means the definitive announcement, not negotiations looking toward an offer." Id. Unlike the situation in Lerro, CA's August 16 press release did not announce mere "negotiations looking toward an offer"; rather, the release stated that CA and On Line had "reached an agreement in principle." * * *

CA also contends that its August 16 press release did not commence the tender offer because CA issued that release in response to NYSE inquiries and in order to fulfill disclosure obligations. CA argues that it cannot be penalized under one provision of the Exchange Act as a result of its compliance with a disclosure obligation under another provision. We need not reach the merits of this argument for the simple reasons that the NYSE did not make any inquiries of CA on August 16 * * *. As CA acknowledges, the NYSE made inquiries of On–Line, not of CA, and did so after "unusual market activity in On–Line stock." On–Line responded to these inquiries by issuing its own press release on August 16, stating that the management of CA and On–Line had "reached agreement at $15.75 per share." Thus, CA's independent press release was not necessary to respond to the NYSE's inquiries. * * *

B. Whether Berdy Was Paid During the Tender Offer

Next, CA argues that, regardless of when the tender offer commenced, the $5 million payment to Berdy cannot violate the Best Price Rule because Berdy was paid after, and not during, the tender offer. CA relies on Rule 14d–10(a)(2), which requires a bidder to pay to any security holder pursuant to a tender offer "the highest consideration paid to any other security holder during such tender offer." While Rule 14d–2 governs the determination of when a tender offer commences, no pertinent rule or statute addresses when a tender offer concludes. CA would have us create a rigid rule equating the duration of a tender offer, for purposes of Rule 14d–10(a)(2), with the offer's self-prescribed expiration date. Such a rule would benefit CA, as its tender offer "closed" on September 20, 1991, and Berdy was not paid until September 25, 1991. We believe that the phrase "during the tender offer," however, is flexible enough to include CA's payment to Berdy, which occurred after the shares had been tendered but before any other On–Line shareholder was paid. See Epstein v. MCA, Inc., 50 F.3d

644, 654 (9th Cir.1995) ("[T]he term 'tender offer,' as used in the federal securities laws, has never been interpreted to denote a rigid period of time."), rev'd on other grounds sub nom. Matsushita Elec. Indus. Co. v. Epstein, 516 U.S. 367, 116 S.Ct. 873, 134 L.Ed.2d 6 (1996). We deem it significant that Berdy was paid before all other On–Line shareholders, so that, if Berdy was not paid "during the tender offer," then neither was any other On–Line shareholder.

More fundamentally, equating the termination of a tender offer with the offer's self-imposed expiration date, as CA would have us do, would make it all too easy to contract around the Best Price Rule. * * *

In concluding that Berdy was paid during the tender offer, we draw upon our decision in Field, 850 F.2d 938, where we looked past the labels that the parties had attached to their transactions. * * *

Like the defendants in Field, CA continuously pursued the goal of its tender offer, the acquisition of On–Line. We have already determined that the Berdy Agreement was executed during the tender offer, and a properly instructed jury determined that CA paid part of the $5 million to Berdy as compensation for his On–Line shares. Far from having abandoned its intent to acquire On–Line, CA paid Berdy in support of its tender offer. In assessing CA's intent, it is significant that Berdy was paid before all other On–Line shareholders. In purchasing a majority of the outstanding common stock of On Line, and in paying the On–Line shareholders for that stock, CA clearly intended to acquire On–Line. Thus, when CA paid Berdy in support of its continuous goal of acquiring On–Line, it did so during the tender offer. * * *

NOTE: CASE FOR COMPARISON

In **Lerro v. Quaker Oats Co.**, 897 F.Supp. 1131 (N.D.Ill.1995), a party controlling 70 percent of the stock of the target of a friendly tender offer received a perpetual and exclusive right to distribute products of the target and the offeror in designated areas. The distributorship agreement was concluded on the same day as a merger agreement between the offeror and the target, November 1. Public announcement of the deal followed the next day, November 2. Pursuant to the merger agreement, the tender offer commenced four days later, on November 4. The distributorship agreement was conditioned on the tender offer's success. The court nonetheless held it to be collateral to the tender offer—the offeror, said the court, could not be expected unconditionally to grant rights respecting products of a company it did not yet control. The court, utilizing rule 14d–2 "as the guideline for establishing the start date," 897 F.Supp. at 1135, also held that the tender offer had not yet commenced as of November 1. See also Epstein v. MCA, Inc., 50 F.3d 644 (9th Cir. 1995), rev'd on other grounds, 516 U.S. 367 (1996).

NOTE: FRIENDLY ACQUISITIONS AND THE AMENDMENT OF RULE 14D–10

Cases like *Gerber* are extremely unpopular with dealmakers. To the extent the best price rule covers side deals like that in the case, the tender offer may be blocked as means to the end of a friendly acquisition. Putting the best price rule to one side, many practitioners prefer a friendly two-step tender offer to a one-step merger. The reason is speed. In a one-step merger, SEC review of the proxy statement takes 30 to 60 days. Only once the review has been completed does the proxy statement go out to the shareholders, with the solicitation taking another month or so. In contrast, the tender offer portion of a two-step deal can be completed in as few as 20 business days. Moreover, if 90 percent or more of the shares are tendered, the bidder can go immediately to a § 253 second step merger, avoiding the necessity of conducting a proxy solicitation. Even if 90 percent of the shares are not tendered and a proxy solicitation is required, the closing of the tender offer imports transactional certainty. Assuming a good deal, it also gets most of the consideration to the target shareholders more quickly.

In 2006, the SEC amended Rule 14d–10, revising the language of the best price rule so that the best price applies only to "securities tendered in the tender offer." The new phrase is intended validate the position taken by the defendant in *Gerber*, and limit the rule to consideration for securities tendered and exclude other consideration paid in side deals even though "integral" with the tender offer. In addition, new Rule 14d–10(d)(1) provides that the rule does "not prohibit" employment benefit arrangements with target securityholders provided that the payment is in respect of past or future services or noncompetition and in an amount not based on the number of shares held by the beneficiary. Finally, there is a "non-exclusive safe harbor." Under this, the (d)(1) exemption is satisfied if an compensation committee made up of independent directors approves it.

The revised rule does not solve all regulatory problems attending a friendly tender offer, however. Problems arise for levered deals under the margin rules in Regulations U and X, which limit the amount of credit that may be extended that is secured "directly or indirectly" to purchase "margin stock." In a levered one-step merger the margin rules present no problem because the loan closes simultaneously with the merger, so that the assets of the target, rather than the target's stock, provide the security. The same would be the case in a two-step tender offer that closed simultaneously with the effectuation of a § 253 merger. The problem arises in a two-step transaction where the tender offer yields less than 90 percent of the stock, necessitating a § 251 merger and accompanying proxy solicitation in the second step. If the money paid in the tender offer is borrowed, the margin rules will apply from the closing of the tender offer until the closing of the merger. Secured borrowing accordingly will be limited to 50 percent of the value of the stock. In a private equity deal, the sponsor may make the difference with a temporary equity contribution. The equity bridge gets paid down when the second-step merger closes. There also are other, more complicated solutions to the problem.

NOTE: RULE 14E–5

Rule 14e–5 Prohibiting purchases outside of a tender offer.

(a) Unlawful activity. As a means reasonably designed to prevent fraudulent, deceptive or manipulative acts or practices in connection with a tender offer for equity securities, no covered person may directly or indirectly purchase or arrange to purchase any subject securities or any related securities except as part of the tender offer. This prohibition applies from the time of public announcement of the tender offer until the tender offer expires. This prohibition does not apply to any purchases or arrangements to purchase made during the time of any subsequent offering period as provided for in [Rule 14d–11] if the consideration paid or to be paid for the purchases or arrangements to purchase is the same in form and amount as the consideration offered in the tender offer.

* * *

(c) Definitions. For purposes of this section, the term:

* * *

(3) Covered person means:

(i) The offeror and its affiliates;

(ii) The offeror's dealer-manager and its affiliates;

(iii) Any advisor to any of the persons specified in paragraph (c)(3)(i) and (ii) of this section, whose compensation is dependent on the completion of the offer; and

(iv) Any person acting, directly or indirectly, in concert with any of the persons specified in this paragraph (c)(3) in connection with any purchase or arrangement to purchase any subject securities or any related securities * * *.

* * *

Rule 14e–5 amends and restates Rule 10b–13, originally promulgated in 1969. Securities Exchange Act Release No. 8712 (Oct. 8, 1969), offers the following justification for the original Rule:

"Where securities are purchased for a consideration greater than that of the tender offer price, this operates to the disadvantage of the security holders who have already deposited their securities and who are unable to withdraw them in order to obtain the advantage of possible resulting higher market prices. Additionally, irrespective of the price at which such purchases are made, they are often fraudulent or manipulative in nature and they can deceive the investing public as to the true state of affairs. Their consequences can be various, depending upon conditions in the market and the nature of the purchases. They could defeat the tender offer, either by driving the market price above the offer price or by otherwise reducing the number of shares tendered below the stated minimum. Alternatively, they could further the tender offer by raising the market price to the point where ordinary investors sell in the market to arbitrageurs, who in turn tender. Accordingly, by prohibiting a person who makes a cash tender offer or exchange offer from purchasing equity securities of the same class during the tender offer period otherwise than pursuant to the offer itself, the rule accomplishes the objective of safeguarding the interests of the persons who have tendered their securities in response to a cash tender offer or exchange offer; moreover once the offer has been made, the rule removes any incentive on the part of holders of substantial blocks of securities to demand from the person making a tender offer or exchange offer a consideration greater than or different from that currently offered to public investors."

The variety of practices at which Rule 14e–5 is aimed, and the reach of the rule, are suggested by the circumstances involved in **Swanson v. Wabash, Inc.,** 577 F.Supp. 1308 (N.D.Ill.1983), decided under the predecessor Rule 10b–13. In that case a target's stockholders charged that the acquiring company purchased stock options from the target's executives and stock from selected stockholders on terms that differed from the tender offer terms. The difference in terms resulted from (1) the payment by the acquiring company of 50 percent tax bonuses to the executives in order to compensate them for the tax consequences sustained on the sale of their options, and (2) arrangements between the acquirer and special stockholders to postpone the acceptance of their stock beyond expiration of the term of the tender offer until six months had elapsed from the time they had purchased it, so that they would receive long term capital gains, a postponement which was not available for the bulk of the tendering stockholders. The Court held that both the alleged transactions violated section 10b–13, which prohibited both direct and indirect purchases of securities outside the tender offer terms, and declined to dismiss the complaint.

(c) coverage problems

Rule 14d–2, Appendix D

The Securities Exchange Commission has declined to define the term "tender offer" by rule, taking the position that a bright-line definition would invite evasion by resourceful bidders. Recall from *Gerber*, supra, and its reference to Rule 14d–2, that the Commission has addressed the problem of defining when a tender offer commences. Recall also that the "public announcement" rule applied in *Gerber* referenced Rule 14d–2 as in effect in 1991, when the On–Line–CA transaction occurred. As then in effect, Rule 14d–2 also had a provision for early termination. Under this, "if within five business days of such public announcement, the bidder * * * [m]akes a subsequent public announcement stating that the bidder has determined not to continue with such tender offer" then the tender offer shall be deemed not to have commenced.

Rule 14d–2 was subsequently revised to shift the start time from press release to publication and eliminate the 5 business day early exit provision. In SEA Rel. 42055, the Commission discussed the changes in the Rule as follows:

"Currently, the tender offer rules restrict a third-party bidder's communications regarding a proposed tender offer. The restrictions on communications stem from the concept of 'commencement,' the five business day rule for cash tender offers, and the requirement that a registration statement be filed promptly for registered exchange offers. A target's communications regarding a tender offer are similarly restricted. To harmonize the treatment of communications regarding business combination transactions under the three regulatory schemes; and to promote the dissemination of information to all security holders on a more timely basis, we are modifying the definition of 'commencement' and eliminating the five business day rule and the requirement to promptly file a registration statement after announcing a registered exchange offer.

"In place of these rules, we are adopting a filing requirement for all written communications that relate to a tender offer beginning with and including the first public announcement of the transaction. As with communications subject to the Securities Act and the proxy rules, written communications must be filed on the date that the communication is made. In addition, written communications must contain a legend advising security holders to read the full tender offer or recommendation statement when it becomes available.

"Under the revised rules, 'commencement' is when the bidder first publishes, sends or gives security holders the means to tender securities in the offer. We believe that security holders need the information required by the tender offer rules when they are either asked or able to tender their securities in an offer.

"To minimize the potential for dissemination of false offers into the marketplace in the absence of the five business day rule, we are adopting new Rule 14e–8. As proposed, this rule prohibits bidders from announcing an offer: without an intent to commence the offer within a reasonable time and complete the offer; with the intent to manipulate the price of the bidder or the target's securities; or without a reasonable belief that the person will have the means to purchase the securities sought. We believe that a specific rule prohibiting such conduct is appropriate. This antifraud rule is intended as a means to prevent fraudulent and misleading communications regarding proposed offers under the new communications scheme, in addition to the existing antifraud provisions.

* * *

"The new definition continues to * * * [establish] a uniform time at which a tender offer is deemed to commence, it continues to balance the rights and obligations of bidders and targets, and it facilitates the free flow of information from both bidders and targets before that date (subject to the antifraud provisions), based on our judgment that this flow of information is in the best interests of the holders of securities. The elimination of the five business day rule and the other changes in the rule are intended to provide security holders with the broadest possible disclosure of information at the earliest date possible.

"We believe that courts would hold that any state law that conflicted with the new rule by attempting to establish a different commencement date or otherwise frustrating operation of the rule would be preempted. For instance, we believe that any state provision that made it impossible to comply with both state and federal requirements or that created obstacles to the accomplishment and execution of the full purposes and objectives of the new rule would continue to be preempted."

The revised rule leaves open a problem respecting the time of termination, a problem that becomes acute in a case like *Schreiber,* supra, where, after the commencement of a first offer, the bidder cuts a deal with insiders at the target that leads to the first offer's withdrawal and the commencement of a new friendly offer on revised terms.

The two-offer fact pattern gave rise to a problems under the earlier version of Rule 14d–2 and the best price rule in **Field v. Trump**, 850 F.2d 938 (2d Cir.1988). The target in the case (Pay'n Save) had a blockholder group (the "Strouns") that was dissatisfied with the first offer price. After commencing the offer at $22.50, the bidder (the "Trumps") commenced face-to-face negotiations with the blockholders. This led it to invoke the 14d–2 five business day rule and publicly withdraw the offer, the lapsed time amounting to 4 business days. A deal was cut, with the Strouns granting the bidder an option to purchase their stock for $23.50 plus an additional $900,000 for "expenses." The bidder then commenced a new offer for $23.50. The plaintiffs sued under § 14(d)(7), claiming that the $900,000 side deal amounted to the payment of an extra $1.50 per share in violation of the best price rule. The claim depended on an assertion that the first tender offer had not in fact been effectively terminated.

The District Court agreed with the bidder that the first offer had been cut off under Rule 14d–2. The Second Circuit disagreed:

" * * * [G]iving effect to every purported withdrawal that allows a discriminatory premium to be paid to large shareholders would completely undermine the 'best-price rule.' For example, plaintiff has alleged that the purported withdrawal of the original tender offer was intended solely to allow the Trumps to pay a premium of $1.50 per share to the Stroums that was not offered to shareholders who tendered pursuant to the 'new' tender offer announced immediately thereafter.[20] The 'best-price rule' of Section 14(d)(7) and Rule 14d–10 is completely unenforceable if offerors may announce periodic 'withdrawals' during which purchases at a premium are made and thereafter followed by 'new' tender offers. Unless successive tender offers interrupted by withdrawals can in appropriate circumstances be viewed as a single tender offer for purposes of the Williams Act, the 'best-price rule' is meaningless.

"Whether the purchase of the Stroum shares was a private purchase or part of a continuing tender offer is not determined simply by the Trumps' use of the labels 'withdrawal' and 'new' offer. * * * Indeed, we have explicitly recognized that purchases after a purported withdrawal of a tender offer may constitute a continuation of the offer in light of the surrounding circumstances. *Hanson Trust,* 774 F.2d at 58–59. Finally, Section 14(d)(7) itself explicitly treats a material change in the terms of a tender offer in the form of an increased price as a continuation of the original offer rather than as a new tender offer. Clearly, therefore, purchases of shares by an offeror after a purported withdrawal of a tender offer may constitute a continuation of the original tender offer.

"Rule 14d–2(b) is not to the contrary. That Rule merely creates a window of time during which a genuine withdrawal leaves matters for all legal purposes as though a tender offer had never been commenced. The Rule does nothing to alter the principle that the mere announcement of a withdrawal may not be effective if followed by purchases of shares and other conduct inconsistent with a genuine intent to withdraw. The Rule is also irrelevant because a bidder is always free to withdraw a tender offer. The argument advanced by defendants, if correct, would thus apply even in cases in which the provisions of Rule 14d–2(b) governing withdrawal announcements did not.

"For purposes of the 'best-price rule,' therefore, an announcement of a withdrawal is effective when the offeror genuinely intends to abandon the goal of the original offer. * * * The complaint here alleges that the Trumps' Offer to Purchase explicitly stated that the purported withdrawal

---

20. Whether the "fees and expenses" for which the Trumps paid $900,000 to the Stroums were actually incurred is irrelevant under the "best-price rule." Some or all of those sums were expended in order to obtain a premium for the Stroums, and it would thwart the purposes of Section 14(d)(7) to allow reimbursement. Moreover, we believe the "best-price rule" would be unworkable if offerors were permitted to discriminate among shareholders according to expenses that were not uniformly incurred, such as broker's or attorney's fees.

was intended to allow negotiations with the Strouns. Such negotiations indicate a continuing intent to obtain control of Pay'n Save.

"Moreover, the complaint alleges conduct from which inferences might be drawn that the Trumps had not abandoned the goal of the original offer. In determining the most appropriate analysis for evaluating the conduct of an offeror surrounding a purported withdrawal, we draw upon a suggestion of Professor Loss. He has noted that the determination of whether formally separate offerings of securities should be "integrated," and thus considered a single offering, for the purposes of the various registration exemptions, is closely analogous to the question of whether single or multiple tender offers have been made. L. Loss, Fundamentals of Securities Regulation 577 n. 33 (1983) (suggesting comparison of 'integration' problem with respect to certain exemptions under the 1933 Act with Section 202(166)(B) of the ALI's proposed Federal Securities Code, which 'treats [tender] offers as separate if they are for different classes of securities or are "substantially distinct on the basis of such factors as manner, time, purpose, price and kind of consideration" ').

"In establishing criteria to govern the integration of formally separate offerings, the SEC has identified the following factors, *inter alia,* as relevant: '(1) are the offerings part of a single of financing; (2) do the offerings involve issuance of the same class of security; (3) are the offerings made at or about the same time * * *?' Section 3(a)(11) Exemption for Local Offerings, Securities Act Release No. 4434 (Dec. 6, 1961). Analogous factors may thus point to 'integration' in the context of formally separate tender offers: (1) are the offers part of a single plan of acquisition; (2) do the offers involve the purchase of the same class of security; and (3) are the offers made at or about the same time? These factors are useful in determining the ultimate fact of whether an offeror has abandoned the goal of an initial tender offer in announcing a withdrawal of that offer. * * *

"Accepting as true the facts alleged in plaintiff's complaint, all of the listed factors weigh in favor of treating the Trumps' acquisition of Pay'n Save shares as a single tender offer. If the allegations are proven, the alleged $1.50 premium to the Strouns would violate Section 14(d)(7).

"The parties and the district court have correctly assumed that Section 14(d)(7) impliedly affords a private right of action to shareholders. In Pryor v. United States Steel Corp., 794 F.2d 52, 57–58 (2d Cir.), cert. denied, ___ U.S. ___, 107 S.Ct. 445 (1986), we held that the best-price provision's statutory neighbor, Section 14(d)(6) of the '34 Act, 15 U.S.C. § 78n(d)(6) (1982), which requires pro rata acceptance of tendered shares in oversubscribed offers, could be privately enforced. Section 14(d)(7) certainly provides at least as strong a basis for the implication of a private remedy as does Section 14(d)(6). * * * "

NOTE: DEFINING (AND NOT DEFINING) "TENDER OFFER"

1. *Street Sweeps.*

Compare the facts of *Field v. Trump* with those of **Hanson Trust PLC v. SCM Corp.,** 774 F.2d 47 (2d Cir.1985). Hanson Trust had made a $72 per share cash tender offer for shares of SCM. SCM responded by announcing a $74 per share two-step acquisition with Merrill Lynch, a white knight. This defensive proposal depended on the acquisition of two thirds of SCM's stock by Merrill. It included a lock up option under which Merrill had the right to purchase SCM's two most profitable divisions. Hanson Trust withdrew its offer in response to the lock up. The withdrawal was announced on the Dow Jones tape at 12:38 P.M. on September 11. Either immediately before or immediately after the announcement, Hanson Trust decided to make open market purchases of SCM stock with the objective of acquiring enough shares to block the defensive merger. Within two hours, on the same afternoon, Hanson Trust concluded five separately negotiated cash purchases of SCM and one open market purchase, purchasing a total of 3.1 million shares or 25 percent. All five negotiated purchases were concluded at $73.50 per share; the market price ranged between $72.50 and $73.50 during the afternoon. The sellers were arbitrageurs, who had accumulated large positions. One of the five negotiated purchases was solicited by Hanson, the others were not.

Such a program of quick and substantial post-withdrawal negotiated purchases is termed a "street sweep." Street sweeps occurred frequently during the mid 1980s.

Should street sweeps be deemed to constitute tender offers? In *Hanson Trust*, the Second Circuit ruled that the street sweep was not a tender offer. In so doing it declined to bring to bear an eight part test that had been approved by the SEC and employed by other courts, 774 F.2d at 56–57:

" * * * The borderline between public solicitations and privately negotiated stock purchases is not bright and it is frequently difficult to determine whether transactions falling close to the line or in a type of 'no man's land' are 'tender offers' or private deals. This has led some to advocate a broader interpretation of the term 'tender offer' than that followed by us in Kennecott Copper Corp. v. Curtiss–Wright Corp., supra, 584 F.2d at 1207, and to adopt the eight-factor 'test' of what is a tender offer, which was recommended by the SEC and applied by the district court in Wellman v. Dickinson, 475 F.Supp. 783, 823–24 (S.D.N.Y.1979), aff'd on other grounds, 682 F.2d 355 (2d Cir.1982), cert. denied, 460 U.S. 1069, 103 S.Ct. 1522, 75 L.Ed.2d 946 (1983), and by the Ninth Circuit in SEC v. Carter Hawley Hale Stores, Inc., supra. The eight factors are:

'(1) active and widespread solicitation of public shareholders for the shares of an issuer;

(2) solicitation made for a substantial percentage of the issuer's stock;

(3) offer to purchase made at a premium over the prevailing market price;

(4) terms of the offer are firm rather than negotiable;

(5) offer contingent on the tender of a fixed number of shares, often subject to a fixed maximum number to be purchased;

(6) offer open only for a limited period of time;

(7) offeree subjected to pressure to sell his stock; * * *

[(8)] public announcements of a purchasing program concerning the target company precede or accompany rapid accumulation of large amounts of the target company's securities.' (475 F.Supp. at 823–24).

Although many of the above-listed factors are relevant for purposes of determining whether a given solicitation amounts to a tender offer, the elevation of such a list to a mandatory 'litmus test' appears to be both unwise and unnecessary. * * *

"We prefer to be guided by the principle followed by the Supreme Court in deciding what transactions fall within the private offering exemption provided by § 4(1) of the Securities Act of 1933, and by ourselves in *Kennecott Copper* in determining whether the Williams Act applies to private transactions. That principle is simply to look to the statutory purpose. * * * [T]he question of whether a solicitation constitutes a 'tender offer' within the meaning of § 14(d) turns on whether, viewing the transaction in the light of the totality of circumstances, there appears to be a likelihood that unless the pre-acquisition filing strictures of that statute are followed there will be a substantial risk that solicitees will lack information needed to make a carefully considered appraisal of the proposal put before them."

SEC v. Carter Hawley Hale Stores, Inc., 760 F.2d 945 (9th Cir.1985), cited by the *Hanson Trust* court, applied the eight part test to reach the same result with respect to a target's repurchase of over 50 percent of its own shares on the open market.

What result does the "sole owner" standard for forming tender offer rules counsel in these situations? Should the SEC have defined "tender offer" so as to pick up these transactions and thereby extend the protection of section 14(d) to unsophisticated investors? For criticism of the SEC's approach, see Oesterle, The Rise and Fall of Street Sweep Takeovers, 1989 Duke L.J. 202.

The SEC proposed but never promulgated a rule that would have prohibited street sweeps. Even so, street sweeps did cease during the last years of the 1980s. The proliferation of poison pills and state antitakeover statutes had made piecemeal acquisitions of large blocks of target stock disadvantageous to bidders. See Oesterle, *supra* at 239–241.

2. *Reform Proposal.*

In an effort to deal with the problems generated by *Hanson* and *Carter Hawley Hale*, the Commission proposed (but did not promulgate) a new Rule 14d–11 requiring that upon commencement of a tender offer by any person (and until the expiration of 30 days after the termination of that offer in the case of bidders and 10 days after termination in the case of other persons) all persons seeking to acquire a substantial amount of the target company securities (10 percent) effect that acquisition only through a conventional tender offer. (SEA Rel. No. 24,976 (Oct. 1, 1987)). The establishment of a "cooling off" period after termination of the tender offer (compare Rule 13e–4(f)(6) providing a ten business day period for issuer tender offers) "would ensure that neither the initial bidder nor any other person could take advantage of the market activity generated by an offer to effect a rapid acquisition of securities."

3.   MANAGEMENT DEFENSES AND FIDUCIARY DUTIES

(A) DEFENSIVE TACTICS

The efforts of managers to thwart hostile takeover attempts, either in advance or in response to a bid, are limited only by the ingenuity of counsel.

(1) Defenses Requiring Amendment of the Corporate Charter

A variety of "shark repellent" charter amendments are designed to delay or complicate a successful bidder's accession to operating control. These include provisions (1) staggering the election of directors, (2) requiring "cause" for removal of directors, (3) requiring special qualifications for election to the board of directors (residence, occupation, etc.), (4) curtailing the availability of written consent action by stockholders (e.g., DCL § 228), (5) limiting the voting power per share of holders of blocks of stock of specified size, and (6) requiring super-majority (and disinterested majority) votes for removal of directors or sale of assets or merger, or for second tier mergers at prices lower than the first tier bid. The last named "fair price" provisions also are embodied in many state antitakeover statutes. They effectively preclude two-tier tender offers and raise the price for 100 percent offers. Other amendments contemplate the creation of a class of voting stock with greater voting power per share or special veto power on mergers. Occasionally, too, a charter will impose on the owner or acquirer of a specified percentage of stock, such as 20 percent, a requirement of offering to buy all the issuer's outstanding stock.

Prior to the mid–1980s, shareholders routinely voted in favor of charter amendments containing antitakeover provisions. By 1986, over 40 percent of the Fortune 500 and over 700 NYSE companies had some form of shark repellent charter amendment. See Pound, The Effects of Antitakeover Amendments on Takeover Activity: Some Direct Evidence, 30 J.L. & Econ. 353 (1987). In the latter part of the 1980s, however, shareholder preferences markedly shifted. Institutional investors came to see their interests as aligned with a vigorous takeover market. They accordingly started to vote against shark repellant charter amendments. Their opposition continues. As a result, management groups have for the most part stopped proposing such amendments. The annual number of such proposals dropped by 90 percent between 1986 and 2000. See Klausner, Institutional Shareholders' Split Personality on Corporate Governance: Active in Proxies, Passive in IPOs, 152 U. Pa. L. Rev. 755 (2003).

This creates a world in which some firms have charters laden with defensive provisions, while the charters of others lack such provisions without a practical possibility of amendment. The protected class includes the firms which put through their amendments prior to the shift in shareholder preferences in the 1980s. This class also includes firms which went public after that time but did so with fully-equipped defensive charters at the time of their IPOs. According to one study, two-thirds of IPO charters contain antitakeover provisions which could pose a significant impediment to a hostile acquisition. Daines and Klausner, Do IPO Charters Maximize firm Value? Antitakeover Protection in IPOs, 17 J. L. Econ. & Org. 83 (2001). Commentators view the latter class of firms as presenting a puzzle for economic theory. Under the famous Jensen and Meckling model of the firm, a set of shark repellents in the charter of a firm conducting an initial public offering holds out an agency cost to the purchasing shareholders. The model predicts that the IPO offering price will be bid down as a result. This in effect would allocate the cost of the shark repellent provisions to the IPO firm and its selling shareholders. The cost allocation in turn would create a disincentive toward the inclusion of such provisions in the first place. And yet most IPO charters include the full menu of terms and no significant cost effects have been detected. Conflicting inferences arise. One possibility is that the benefits of protection to the managers (and controlling shareholders) of the IPO outweigh the financial cost incurred when the IPO shares are priced. The implication of this possibility is that the IPO firm has an inefficient charter. Another possibility is that, as argued by proponents of the management veto, shark repellent provisions are efficient because they give management a stronger bargaining hand in the wake of the hostile offer. The study of Daines and Klausner, supra, supports the former hypothesis.

Note also Coates, Explaining the Variation in Takeover Defenses, 89 Cal. L. Rev. 1301 (2001), which shows that the choice of a law firm can be outcome determinative in respect of the terms in an IPO firm's charter. The number and strength of takeover defenses adopted by an IPO firm can directly depend on the takeover experience, size, and location of its law firm. More particularly, in a sample of 1991–92 IPOs, firms advised by lawyers located in Silicon Valley adopted fewer defenses; companies represented by law firms from other financial centers, firms with venture capital backing, and firms represented by high-quality underwriters adopted more defenses. By 1998, however, the Silicon Valley law firms had ridden up the antitakeover learning curve and were as likely to recommend antitakeover provisions as law firms elsewhere.

(2) Defenses Not Requiring Amendment of the Corporate Charter

There are many other devices in management's arsenal. Management can issue stock (with or without special voting power) into friendly hands, sometimes those of the trustees of an Employee Stock Ownership Plan organized for the occasion. Management also sometimes repurchases the corporation's shares to reduce both corporate cash and the number of shares outstanding, and in the case of greenmail payments, to assure the disappearance of a particular hostile bidder. Settlements reached with particular bidders or potential bidders in these and other cases entail the execution of standstill agreements that freeze the stockholding status of the bidder at or about the number of shares held at the date of the contract. "Golden parachutes" and "tin parachutes"—contracts for generous payments to management and employees, respectively, upon a change of control of the corporation—do not block takeovers. But they do make them more expensive.

Managers in the midst of takeover battles can make moves directed at particular bidders (1) by granting options to purchase valuable target property ("lock ups;" see infra this section) or target stock to preferred bidders or partners ("white knights" or "white squires"), (2) by entering into "scorched earth" sales of attractive properties, (3) by making a "pac man" counter tender offer against the bidder, or (4) by creating incompatibility between the target and the bidder by acquiring assets that would entail regulatory approval or antitrust clearance for the bidder.

Finally, it should be noted that some of the shark repellent charter provisions described above may be instituted by means of a by law amendment.

WACHTELL, LIPTON, ROSEN & KATZ PREFERRED SHAREHOLDER RIGHTS PLAN

Appendix A

The most effective and widespread advance defense that management can employ without resort to the charter amendment process is the "poison pill." This denomination covers an array of mechanisms. Some poison pill plans are issued as dividends on common stock in the form of preferred stock. Other plans are issued as rights to acquire preferred stock or rights to acquire notes. Either way, management derives the power to issue a poison pill from a "blank stock" allocation in the firm's charter. Poison pill plans also customarily provide for redemption of the poisonous rights granted for a trivial price at the instance of the target board. Once a plan is in place, its effect is to vest final decisionmaking authority in a takeover contest in the target's boardroom rather than in the marketplace because no combination goes forward unless the target board decides to redeem the pill. Decisions not to redeem result in judicial review of the decision under applicable fiduciary law.

(a) poison pills: terms and effects

Yablon, Poison Pills and Litigation Uncertainty, 1989 Duke L.J. 54, 58–62, offers a more particular description:

"The term 'poison pill' has no precise definition. It generically denotes a range of defensive techniques, usually adopted by boards of directors as amendments to company bylaws. Such amendments generally authorize creation of a new class of securities, and 'Rights' to purchase those securities. The board then makes these Rights available to stockholders by declaring a dividend of one Right per outstanding common share. At the time when the board declares the 'dividend,' the Rights have neither economic significance nor, for that matter, any physical existence.

"These Rights do, however, contain provisions that become important in the event of a hostile takeover attempt. Most common are 'flip-over' provisions, which provide that when a raider successfully obtains more than a specified percentage of a target's shares, all Right holders will, if a subsequent merger or other combination or transaction between target and raider takes place, have the right to purchase a specified amount of the raider's stock for half its market value. Also common are 'flip-in' provisions, which operate like flip-overs except that they give each Rights holder the right to purchase for the purchase price of the Right, an amount of the target company's own common stock worth twice the purchase price of the Right. For example, a flip-in, once triggered, might give each Right holder the right to buy $500 worth of target shares for $250.

"The real reason why Rights exist is to prevent the occurrence of a 'triggering event,' an event that activates flip-over or flip-in provisions. Flip-over provisions are generally triggered by events that diminish or destroy the economic value of a target's common stock (such as an acquirer's proposal of a merger in which the target stock will be canceled). In such circumstances, the Right 'flips over' and becomes a right to purchase the acquirer's common stock at a bargain price. The flip-over thus poses a powerful deterrent to any raider who seeks to acquire majority control through a tender offer and then to remove minority shareholders through a back-end merger. It does nothing, however, to deter a raider who is content to acquire control of a company without effecting a back-end merger. For that reason, many recent pills contain flip-in as well as flip-over provisions. A host of events, including, in many cases, the mere acquisition of more than fifty percent of a target's stock, can trigger a flip-in.

"Flip-ins generally provide that once a raider (or a raider's affiliate) acquires any Right, that Right becomes void and may not be exercised. Thus, a flip-in, when triggered, gives every Right holder except the raider a virtually irresistible bargain (the right to buy target stock at half the market price.) Once exercised, these rights put substantially more stock in the Right holders' hands, diluting the raider's holdings.

"The current generation of pills gives incumbent management substantial power and discretion to delay or eliminate a poison pill's deleterious effects on offerors. Many pills authorize incumbent directors to suspend the exercise of Rights for a substantial period of time following a triggering event, and almost every pill now provides that a majority of incumbent directors can cause the target corporation to redeem the Rights for a nominal price, thereby removing their deterrent effect on offerors.

"In sum, poison pills serve two fundamental objectives: (1) they provide maximum deterrence to hostile offers by severely limiting the actions that raiders can take without triggering a pill's flip-in or flip-over provisions, and (2) they give incumbent board members maximum flexibility to remove a pill's deterrent effects, if and when they decide to do so."

The bottom line result is a contingent management veto. A hostile bidder is very unlikely to close a tender offer if the target's poison pill is unredeemed, unless the bidder holds 100 percent of the target stock (and thus the entire set of poisonous options) or an amount very close to 100 percent. The veto also accords management an opportunity to negotiate on behalf of the shareholders, thereby resolving a problem of distorted choice triggered by the pill and the hostile offer.

To see the latter point, imagine that Coercive Co. is looking over two potential targets, Sitting Duck Co., and Porcupine Co. Both Sitting Duck and Porcupine have 10,000 widely dispersed shares outstanding and all the shareholders of both value their shares at $100. The shares are trading for a considerably lower price, however.

Sitting Duck has no takeover defenses in place. Coercive would like to acquire it for $94. To do so, it would structure a two-tier, front-end loaded offer as follows: $100 per share cash for 60 percent of the stock in a tender offer; $85 per share in senior securities in a second-step merger.

Porcupine, in contrast, has a poison pill that contains flip-over and flip-in provisions with a $250 exercise price. Yablon, supra, at 64, explains that the poison pill creates a new problem of distorted choice:

"Clearly, Coercive's bidding strategy for Sitting Duck would not work in a bid for Porcupine. In the first place, the strategy would involve considerably more expense when applied to Porcupine. In addition to offering $100 per share for the 60% taken in the first step and $85 per share for the remaining 40%, Coercive would trigger the flip-over rights of the 40% minority, which would require payment of $1,000,000 (4000 × $250) over and above the $940,000 that Coercive expects to pay for Porcupine's common stock. Coercive attempts to solve this problem by abandoning its two-step strategy, tendering for *all* of Porcupine's shares, and requiring, as a condition of its offer, that at least 90% of the outstanding shares (along with their accompanying Rights) be tendered. In doing so, Coercive is offering a deal with an aggregate value of $1,235,000 ((9000 × $100) + (1000 × $85) + (1000 × $250)), considerably more than the amount at which Porcupine shareholders value their stock. If the shareholders could coordinate their responses, their most rational strategy would be to tender the 90% on a pro rata basis, thus giving each share a blended value of $123.50.

"Without such coordination, however, shareholders' individual decisions result in a distorted choice that is the mirror image of the non-poison-pill scenario. In this case, if you tender and the offer succeeds, you receive $100 per share. But if you do not tender and the offer succeeds, you receive $355 per share ($85 for the share and $250 from the flip-over Right). If the offer does not succeed, it makes no difference whether you tendered or not. Accordingly, in this scenario, you reluctantly refrain from tendering, and the offer fails, even though it exceeds your and the other shareholders' valuation of Porcupine's shares.

"One important factor, however, distinguishes the two scenarios. In the poison pill scenario, Porcupine's board has the power to solve the shareholder-coordination problem by offering to redeem the pill in a negotiated transaction in which Coercive pays $123.50 for each share. Presumably, Coercive would have no objection to such a deal, since it has already offered to pay the same aggregate value for the Porcupine shares. The question, of course, is whether Porcupine's directors would have any incentive to make such a deal."

But how poisonous are most of the pills approved in corporate boardrooms? Carney and Silverstein, The Illusory Protections of the Poison Pill, 79 Notre Dame L. Rev. 179 (2003), upsets a generation of assumptions about the quantum of venom. A pill, say the authors "is only as good as the dilution of a bidder that it provides, and * * * many pills provide surprisingly little." A typical pill may add only 6 to 12 percent to the cost of an acquisition, id. at 181:

> * * * [T]ypical rights plans are less effective than conventional wisdom suggests at deterring hostile bidders, because the dilution that the bidder suffers has been examined in a static model that ends with the dilution of the bidder's initial investment. A dynamic model, in which the bidder completes the acquisition of the target after suffering dilution, produces quite a different impression. First, the ability of a rights plan to add to a bidder's costs, and thus to the amounts received

by target shareholders, is limited to the amount spent by the bidder in reaching the triggering ownership level—typically 15% of the target's stock. The obvious intuition is that even total dilution of a bidder holding 15% cannot add more than 15% to the cost of a takeover—which means that a conventional rights plan cannot raise the cost of an undervalued target to an acceptably fair price in many cases. Second, the mechanics of the typical rights plan mean that the bidder will lose only a fraction, rather than all, of that initial investment.

Subramanian, Bargaining in the Shadow of PeopleSoft's (Defective) Poison Pill, 12 Harv. Negot. L. Rev. 41 (2007), puts Carney and Silverstein's insight to use, speculating whether Oracle, in its 2004 hostile campaign against PeopleSoft, might have strengthened its hand by deliberately triggering the PeopleSoft pill.

(b) the shadow pill and interactions between pills and other defensive provisions

A poison pill, once facilitated by an appropriate stock authorization in a firm's charter, is so easily adopted by a threatened board of directors that the target firm benefits from the pill's defensive effect without even having to take the formal step of adoption. At the same time, whether adopted or potential, the pill's effectiveness as an antitakeover device can render other shark repellents irrelevant. As the following excerpt shows, however, in many circumstances a poison pill and a staggered board together make for an optimal defensive combination.

Coates, Takeover Defenses in the Shadow of the Pill: A Critique of the Scientific Evidence

79 Tex. L. Rev. 271, 288–292, 320–323, 325–327 (2000).

II.   Pill Adoptions in the Shadow of the Pill

* * *

* * * [P]ill adoption rarely has any real effect on the legal takeover vulnerability of the firm adopting a pill.

To see why, imagine you are a bidder, considering a high premium bid for a target. Imagine the target lacks a pill. Do you conclude that the target is easy to acquire, as a matter of law? Clearly not. Unless there is something unusual about the target, the target will have the ability to—and almost certainly will—adopt a pill as soon as you start your bid. For large, sophisticated targets, pill adoption can occur in a single business day: the only legal action necessary is a board meeting and approval, lawyers can keep necessary documents at the ready, and directors can meet by conference call on a few hours notice. Even for less sophisticated firms, takeover bids are subject to sufficient delay under the Williams Act and the Hart–Scott–Rodino Antitrust Improvements Act of 1976 ("HSR Act") that a target will rarely if ever be prejudiced by failing to adopt a pill in advance. Numerous targets have in fact adopted pills in response to bids, and evidence shows that targets do not allow themselves to be taken over solely because they had not adopted pre-bid pills.

* * * To be clear, the point is not that pills have no effects on bids. Rather, it is that pill adoption by particular firms prior to a bid rarely has an effect on bids because of the possibility of later adoption. It is the potential for pill adoption that achieves any deterrent effect the pill may have. Another way of putting the point is that once the Delaware Supreme Court made it clear in *Moran v. Household International* that pills were legitimate, all Delaware firms (except those few with other governance terms that would impede pill adoption) have had a shadow pill in place, witting or not. Takeovers of such firms have been restrained by a set of "shadow restrictions"—the expectation of a pill's adoption and subsequent effects—on transfer of control to a hostile bidder. The adoption of an actual pill by any given firm only brings this shadow pill into the light, but does nothing to change the odds that the target will be acquired or not. Whether the shadow pill has had an impact on bids is unknown, precisely because its existence has not been taken into account by studies of defenses.

The only limits to the ability of companies to defer pill adoption (i.e., to adopt a pill post-bid) are (a) a charter or other legal provision that bars pill adoption, (b) the risk (to managers) that an independent board might be unwilling to adopt a pill after a bid, or (c) the impending closing of a bid. However, antipill provisions are almost never found, and an independent board is more likely to be willing to adopt a pill after a bid emerges: any harm that pills do is due to entrenchment, and an independent board is able to both adopt a pill and use it to bargain for shareholders or seek better alternatives, rather than blocking the bid altogether. * * *

Among firms that have not adopted pills, some have no reason to do so, even though they legally could. As a percentage of all public firms, bids are rare, and some firms are invulnerable to hostile bids because they have controlling shareholders. Some bids consist solely of "bear hug" letters and do not include a tender offer, so a pill is unnecessary for the target to "just say no." Other bids are "bust-up" bids, launched only after the target has committed to a sale process. In such cases, if the bust-up bid is at a higher price, it will be difficult for the target to close its initial lower-priced deal, or to drop that deal and "just say no" to the bust-up bid. After some bids, targets do not bother adopting pills because doing so would be futile. The targets' other defenses leave them vulnerable to quick proxy fights, in which bidders could replace target boards, and so remove a pill. And, finally, other targets have no need to adopt pills even after bids are made because they are protected by lengthy pre-closing regulatory procedures. Bank and utility laws, for example, impose substantial delay on acquisitions; until that period begins to run out, bidders cannot close bids and targets need not worry about adopting a pill to block bids.

* * * The subset of firms for which pill adoption would have a real impact on bid outcome—firms that wait until it is almost too late—is likely to be quite small, perhaps too small for meaningful empirical analysis.

In sum, a firm that has adopted a pill is in nearly the same takeover posture as a firm that has not yet adopted a pill. Pill adoption cannot be expected to generate any significant price reactions related to the presence of a pill itself. Any price reaction to pill adoptions, then, reflects one thing, and one thing only: inferences about private information in the hands of managers of adopting companies.

* * *

III.   Shark Repellents in the Shadow of the Pill

* * *

* * * [S]upermajority requirements and fair price provisions * * * are no longer important in actual takeover fights, if they ever were. At most, such defenses impair (without eliminating) the ability of bidders to use a two-tier takeover tactic to create a prisoner's dilemma and pressure target shareholders to tender. Yet the shadow pill completely dominates these shark repellents in preventing two-tier bids. * * *

To see why the shadow pill completely dominates fair price and supermajority provisions in effect, imagine again you are a bidder, and you are unwilling or unable to win a proxy fight for the target. In that case, a pre-or post-bid pill will completely block you from acquiring more than a small toehold, regardless of whether you are willing to pay a premium price to all shareholders (in which case the fair price provision would have little or no effect), and regardless of the fact that a supermajority of shareholders would like to accept your offer. Absent a proxy fight, the shadow pill will deter any bid a supermajority or fair price provision would deter, so that regardless of whether the target has already adopted a pill, the shadow pill will deter you from bidding.

Now imagine, as a bidder, you are willing and able to win a proxy fight for the target. The necessity for the proxy fight to eliminate the pill defeats any pressure-to-tender a two-tier bid might create, accomplishing the main deterrent effect of both fair price and supermajority provisions. Put otherwise, a bidder willing and able to win a proxy fight must be uninterested in the coercive aspects of two-tier bids. Thus, the shadow pill on its own will deter any bid that fair price or super-majority provisions would deter.

Finally, imagine you have won the proxy fight. Fair price provisions almost never apply to one-step mergers between the target and a person not in control of more than the specified threshold of stock ownership, or even to two-step transactions, if the first step is approved by the target board. A bidder that has won a proxy fight may avoid a fair price provision by having the newly elected target board approve its proposed merger. Supermajority provisions usually have "board outs," and can be avoided by a victorious bidder because, once in control of the target's board, the bidder may simply remove the pill and offer all share-holders a single premium price, which will normally attract a supermajority of tenders or votes.

In sum, supermajority and fair price provisions were rendered vestigial by judicial approval and widespread adoption of the pill in the middle and late 1980s. This conclusion is supported by two pieces of empirical evidence. First, hostile two-tier bids have disappeared in the 1990s: of 4,698 deals in the SDC database in the period 1988–1999, only 52 (1.1%) were two-tier front-end loaded bids, and only 19 (0.4%) were hostile two-tier bids, with most occurring in the late 1980s, and none in the late 1990s. The decline of hostile two-tier bids has been general, despite the fact that fewer than half of large public firms have fair price or supermajority provisions. Thus, it was the shadow pill, and not shark repellents, that was the primary cause of this decline. Second, data from IRRC on the number of firms adopting fair price and supermajority provisions in the post-pill era * * * demonstrates that firms have largely ceased to adopt such defenses in the 1990s; classified boards, by comparison, have continued to grow at large firms (although most new classified boards are adopted prior to IPOs, rather than midstream).

* * *

* * * [D]efenses interact, and did so in the pre-pill era. One term can dramatically impact the effect of another term, a possibility that studies of defenses have generally failed to take seriously. The ways defenses interact is a large topic in its own right, but a few examples, focusing on what are probably the two most important structural defenses (pills and classified boards) should illustrate the point.

Suppose firm A has adopted a pill, and firm B has not. Further, suppose firm A has a classified board, and firm B does not. Initially, note the way in which the pill and the classified board interact. Without the pill, the presence or absence of a classified board is largely irrelevant, because a tender offer or open-market accumulations of stock will allow a bidder to acquire control of the target in approximately one month, the minimum time necessary to clear antitrust review and, for tender offers, to comply with the Williams Act. Even if the target board could, in theory, refuse to resign after the control acquisition has occurred, they will almost never do so * * *. Indeed, it was largely for this reason that the pill was invented.

With a classified board—if it cannot be evaded (about which more in a moment)—the pill becomes a far more effective defense than the pill alone. That is because a pill can always be removed by the target board; a bidder always has the option of removing the target board in a proxy fight. If a target's directors are all up for election each year, the pill can be removed in no more, and often much less, than a year from the bid's initiation. If the target has a classified board, by contrast, the pill is protected from such circumvention for at least, and often much more than, one year. For firms with pills, in other words, effective classified boards change a maximum time required to take over the target to the minimum time required.

All this is old hat to lawyers, and even financial economists in studying poison pills and shark repellents have assumed that firm A, with its pill and its staggered board, is less vulnerable to takeover than firm B. Interactions, however, are potentially much more complex. Suppose that firm A permits shareholders to remove directors without cause, and firm B does not, and that neither firm has a provision that prohibits the adoption of pills or a provision that would allow shareholders to act by written consent or call a special meeting. Now the legal takeover vulnerability of both firms is identical.

To see why, recall that (absent a prohibition on pills) firm B can adopt a pill at any time. Thus, the presence of a pill at firm A, and the absence of a pill at firm B, are irrelevant to its legal takeover vulnerability. Likewise, given the ability of shareholders to remove directors without cause at firm A, its staggered board is ineffective. Shareholders at both firms are in a position to mobilize (or be mobilized by a bidder) and replace the entire board at the next annual meeting. At firm B, directors are normally up for election at the next annual meeting; at firm A, shareholders (or a bidder) can remove all directors, and fill the resulting vacancies. On both counts, studies have misgauged the relative takeover vulnerability of firms A and B: traditional studies have assumed that pills and staggered boards affect takeover vulnerability, when for particular firms they often do not.

NOTE: STONEWALLING WITH A STAGGERED BOARD

As we have seen, an effectively-drafted poison pill gives the defending board a de facto veto of the tender offer. The bidder responds by mounting a proxy contest, the purpose of which is to replace the incumbents with a board that supports the tender offer and redeems the pill. The staggered board comes into the defensive strategy at this point to play its time-honored function of effecting a delay in the shift of control in the boardroom. Given a classification scheme, the successful proxy contestant does not get control of the board by electing all of the directors up for election. A board majority only can come with the second (or in some cases third) successive election.

What happens when the incumbents lose the proxy fight and the hostile bidder enters the boardroom with less than a majority of the directors? The conventional wisdom has been that the incumbents at this point throw in the towel and cut a deal with the hostile bidder. Since the shareholders support the bid, there is little to be gained by further holding out. Just such a response was forthcoming the famous AT&T–NCR proxy contest of 1991. Compare Weyerhauser's tender offer-proxy contest for control of Willamette in 2001. Weyerhauser, with a $50 offer (up from an original $48) on the table, won the proxy contest and took a third of the board seats in mid 2001, but the incumbents stayed on. Six months later, Weyerhauser raised its bid to $55, even as the incumbents tried to interest the Willamette shareholders with an alternative deal with Georgia Pacific. Finally, the shareholders showing no enthusiasm for Georgia Pacific, the incumbents reached agreement with Weyerhauser at $55.50, fourteen months after the Weyerhauser's initial offer to the Willamette board. Lipton, Pills, Polls, and Professors Redux, 69 U.Chi.L.Rev. 1037 (2002), argues that this sequence of events demonstrates the value of the board veto on the ground that the shareholders ended up with $55.50 rather than $48, a 16 percent increase. Do you agree? Should the increase to the Willamette shareholders due to the staggered board be seen as 50 cents rather than as $7.50? Could the Willamette board successfully have negotiated for a 16 percent increase on day one?

(3) Empirical Studies of Defensive Tactics and Shareholder Value

Does management deploy its arsenal of defensive weaponry so effectively that it has a "show-stopping" effect—decreasing the number of takeovers and reducing overall premiums realized by shareholders in the long run? Or do defensive tactics more delay than deter hostile bidders, so as to assist the shareholders in surmounting their collective action problem, cause bids to go up, and increase the overall amount of premiums realized? An impressive body of empirical studies addresses these questions, but reaches inconclusive results. Qualified yes answers to *both* of the questions find support. It seems that some defensive devices adopted by some firms have a positive or neutral stock price effect, while other devices adopted by other firms have negative price effects. For surveys of the literature see Coates, Takeover Defenses in the Shadow of the Pill: A Critique of the Scientific Evidence, 79 Tex. L. Rev. 271 (2000); Romano, A Guide to Takeovers: Theory, Evidence, and Regulation, 9 Yale J. Reg. 119 (1992); and Jarrell, Brickley and Netter, The Market for Corporate Control: The Empirical Evidence Since 1980, 2 J.Econ.Persp. 49 (1988).

Unsurprisingly, studies of cases where offers are defeated present the strongest value evidence against defensive tactics. Bebchuk, Coates, and Subramanian, The Anti–Takeover Power of Classified Boards: Theory, Evidence and Policy, 54 Stan. L. Rev. 887 (2002), studies hostile offers in the years 1996–2000 where the target remained independent. The study finds that during a period of 30 months following a bid, the target shareholders were on average substantially worse off in comparison with where they would have been had the board accepted the bid. Where the target is acquired, returns to its shareholders are 54 percent higher. Cotter and Zenner, How Managerial Wealth Affects the Tender Offer Process, 35 J. Fin. Econ. 63 (1994), offers a complementary finding: When an offer is defeated, the target shareholders suffer an average 21 percent stock price decline.

It is harder to show an unambiguous ex ante negative price effect respecting a given defensive device. Viewed ex ante, after all, the device also can be used to extract a higher premium. Even so, early event studies of poison pills tended to be condemnatory, but even there a contra signal showed up. Jarrell and Ryngaert, The Effect of Poison Pills on the Wealth of Target Shareholders (SEC Office of Chief Economist, Oct. 23, 1986), reported that pill adoption meant a loss 2.21 percent of the value of the firm's stock two days following adoption. Ryngaert, Effects of Poison Pills on Shareholder Wealth, 20 J.Fin. Econ. 377 (1988), reported that where the adopting firm was not the subject of takeover speculation a statistically significant negative stock price effect of .34 percent results from the adoption of a pill. With takeover speculation the negative effect was a larger 1.51 percent. On the other hand, Ryngaert reported that the least potent pills caused stock price increases. In addition, pill-adopting firms had a low average managerial ownership of 3 percent, and in the event of litigation over the pill, a pro-target decision was likely to have a negative price effect (15 of 18 cases) and a pro-bidder decision a positive effect (6 of 11). Choi, Kamma and Weintrop, The Delaware Courts, Poison Pills, and Shareholder Wealth, 5 J.L.Econ. & Org. 375 (1989), and Malatesta and Walkling, Poison Pill Securities: Stockholder Wealth, Profitability and ownership Structure, 20 J.Fin. Econ. 347 (1988), also reported significant negative price effects. But Coates, supra, mounts a powerful attack against the event study methodology deployed in this context. What matters for the stock price, he argues, is the shadow pill. Accordingly, actual pill adoption is not necessarily an event worth studying so far as the stock price is concerned. Reviewing the study results over all, Coates concludes that no case has been made out either way concerning pill adoption and shareholder value.

Studies of shark repellent charter amendments are similarly inconclusive. To take one example, Pound, The Effects of Antitakeover Amendments on Takeover Activity: Some Direct Evidence, 30 J.L. & Econ. 353 (1987), tests the effect of blanket supermajority provisions and classified board provisions, both thought to have negative wealth effects, and confirms that they dampen the frequency of subsequent takeovers. More significantly, the study shows (1) that once a takeover does occur, shareholders "protected" by shark repellents are not rewarded with higher premiums, and (2) that shark repellents do not seem to deter the incidence of front end loaded/two-step offers—the proportion of "any and all shares" offers is lower for targets with shark repellents. Pound concludes that any increase in management bargaining power does not result in shareholder wealth increases in practice. McWilliams, Managerial Share Ownership and the Stock Price Effects of Antitakeover Amendment Proposals, 45 J.Fin. 1627 (1990), makes for an interesting comparison. This is a stock price study. McWilliams' sample covers NYSE firms adopting the range of shark repellent amendments during the period 1980–1984. She finds that where the firm has a low level of managerial share ownership (10 percent or less), the shark repellent has significant positive price effect. The inference is that the dispersed shareholders of these firms rely on their managers to extract higher bids. She also finds that with higher levels of managerial share ownership, amendments have negative price effects, but that the positive effect with low ownership firms is larger than the negative effect with higher ownership firms. She concludes that on average shark repellents do not harm shareholders.

How impressed should we be with a study finding a 1 or 2 percent stock price decline in the wake of a pill or a shark repellant? The economists Comment and Schwert conclude that such showings are unimpressive: "[I]f the probability of a takeover decreases by 10% with the adoption of an antitakeover measure, and if a 50% gain is lost, then the wealth decline on adoption should be about 5%. The empirical estimates of wealth loss generally do not approach this level. Thus, the size of the average wealth decline on the adoption of an antitakeover measure is consistent with only a modest change in takeover probability." Comment and Schwert, Poison or Placebo? Evidence on the Deterrence and Wealth Effects of Modern Antitakeover Measures, 39 J. Fin. Econ. 3, 8 (1995).

(B) DEFENSIVE TACTICS AND THE DUTY OF LOYALTY

As we have seen, a tender offer, if friendly, but particularly if hostile, differs from a negotiated transaction in significant part because the seller of control is not a single knowledgeable person who can bargain about the transaction; instead of a seller we have sellers—dispersed offerees who cannot function coherently either to inquire about the facts and discover the relevant information or to negotiate the terms. If dispersed offerees should, in the interests of efficiency and equity, have an undistorted choice

comparable to (albeit not identical with) that of a sole seller about responding to the tender offer, certain bargaining disadvantages—both of information and of power—should be mitigated or eliminated. By that test, offerees
need protection against (a) the bidder, whether respecting undue pressure
or lack of information, (b) management, whether respecting failure timely
to proffer relevant information, improper rejection of the take-over bid, or
other efforts to thwart a take-over attempt, and (c) market professionals
who may manipulate the tender offer process.

The primary state-level legal rules which govern the game involved in
the takeover contest are common law teachings on the fiduciary duties of
the management of the target company to its stockholders and of the
management of the bidder company to its stockholders.

Few of the standard defensive tactics have amounted to *per se* violations of state law fiduciary duties. But many items on the menu can
generate plausible allegations of breach of fiduciary duty. Takeover litigation raises questions as to which, if any, of management's defensive tactics
is consistent with management's duties (and rights). On what grounds can
management legitimately use corporate assets to oppose a bidder (a) if the
bid is for less than all the target's stock? (b) if the bid is a cash offer for all
the target's stock by a bidder proposing a cash-out merger if it obtains a
majority of the stock? In the latter case, should management be forbidden
from taking any "defensive" steps other than disclosing its position and the
reasons therefor? Or does management have a duty to oppose two-step
takeovers which contemplate, or create a likelihood of, a cash-out after a
successful acquisition of control? In any event, does (should) management
have a duty to consider, or to seek out, "better" bids or overtures, and
therefore, at least when doing so, a right to oppose a tender offer? The
cases and materials below illustrate underlying patterns and responses
under state fiduciary law.

(1) Introduction: Defensive Tactics and Business Judgment

Two opposing possibilities present themselves when managers defend
themselves and their firms from takeovers. At one pole, these actions could
promote management's interest in entrenching itself. At the other pole,
these actions could facilitate higher values for the benefit of the shareholders. If, at the one pole, management can be found to seek *only* to
perpetuate its own hold on office or to bargain for side payments or
advantageous purchases for itself, the defensive action and any related use
of corporate assets violates elementary notions of fiduciary obligation. If, at
the other pole, management can be found to seek *only* to protect or
enhance stockholder wealth, the action and any related use of corporate
assets should be regulated only by the business judgment rule. Since both
possibilities usually are present, both intrinsic fairness scrutiny and the
business judgment rule come to bear as the duty of loyalty is articulated in
the context of takeover defense.

The triggers that govern the business judgment rule's application in
this context have been set and reset as the Delaware courts have negotiated
a route between the two poles. The first version of their test was formulat-

ed in **Cheff v. Mathes,** 41 Del.Ch. 494, 199 A.2d 548 (1964), an early greenmail case. The *Cheff* rule made a variation of the business judgment shield available to defending managers. The plaintiff had an initial burden to show that management had a personal interest in the defense of the corporation. This was not a difficult showing for a plaintiff to make, since managers defend their own corporate positions by virtue of defending the firm. Once the plaintiff made a showing of self interest, the burden shifted to the managers to show a "reasonable ground to believe a danger to corporate policy and effectiveness existed" by the presence of the proposed threat. That burden could be met "by showing good faith and reasonable investigation; the directors will not be penalized for an honest mistake of judgment, if the judgment appeared reasonable at the time the decision was made."

On the facts of *Cheff,* a board (only a minority of which had an express financial interest in entrenchment) that used corporate funds to repurchase a substantial block of stock held by a potential bidder, was held to have made an adequate showing. The board established that the potential bidder had a reputation for liquidating companies and thus constituted "a reasonable threat to the continued existence" of the corporation in its present form. This "danger" went to the integrity of the business plan and employee welfare—*corporate* as opposed to *shareholder* concerns. Any shareholder value concerns at the other pole went unmentioned.

Business judgment treatment under *Cheff* did not quite guarantee judicial sanction of any and all defensive tactics. In theory, once management made its showing of a threat and a "good faith, reasonable investigation," the burden shifted back to the plaintiff to show an improper purpose to stay in control as management's sole or predominant motive. But, the cases that followed *Cheff* showed this burden to be extremely difficult to surmount. See, e.g., Panter v. Marshall Field & Co., 646 F.2d 271 (7th Cir.1981), cert. denied, 454 U.S. 1092 (1981); Johnson v. Trueblood, 629 F.2d 287 (3d Cir.1980). The plaintiff had to make out a picture of management self-aggrandizing behavior from which it was virtually impossible for the court to avert its gaze. In *Panter,* for example, defending management successfully used a combination of antitrust litigation and selective expansion into markets occupied by the potential bidder. The case stood for the proposition that, as applied, *Cheff* permitted the "business plan," and as a result management self-interest (not to mention federal antitrust policy), to take precedence over shareholder value.

Under *Cheff,* a modicum of boardroom diligence usually was sufficient to secure the protection of the business judgment shield. Outside counsel were adept at engineering the final shift in the burden to the plaintiff by documenting a "reasonable investigation" keyed to a corporate policy and bolstering the case for "good faith" through the use of independent directors.

The resulting deference to boardroom processes was puzzling in view of the structural significance and self-dealing import of anti-takeover defenses. The rule permitted decisionmaking power in respect of the disposition of shares to be shifted from stockholders and markets to the management-controlled venue of the boardroom. Courts under *Cheff* paid small attention to (1) the difference between the justification for the business judgment rule in validating exercises of managerial decisionmaking power over normal corporate operations and its limited relevance to the interests of stockholders in the disposition of their stock in takeover bids, and (2) the incongruity of relying upon business judgment as the predicate for managerial behavior which frustrates the function of takeovers in policing management's normal exercise of business judgment.

The Delaware Supreme Court added a new element to the *Cheff* rule in **Unocal Corp. v. Mesa Petroleum Co., 493 A.2d 946 (Del.1985):**

> If a defensive measure is to come within the ambit of the business judgment rule, it must be reasonable in relation to the threat posed. This entails an analysis by the directors of the nature of the takeover bid and its effect on the corporate enterprise. Examples of such concerns may include: inadequacy of the price offered, nature and timing of the offer, questions of illegality, the impact on 'constituencies' other than shareholders (i.e., creditors, customers, employees, and perhaps even the community generally), the risk of nonconsummation, and the quality of securities being offered in exchange.

The restated test reflected dissatisfaction with *Cheff's* close to absolute business judgment shield and held out the possibility of more searching judicial scrutiny of defensive tactics.

The application of the new rule on the facts of *Unocal* itself did little to signal a shift to more searching scrutiny. Unocal's management had devised a very effective response to a $54 two-tier, front-end loaded tender offer. The offeror, Boone Pickens' Mesa Petroleum, already owned 13 percent of Unocal's stock, and tendered for an additional 37 percent. Unocal made a cash exchange offer for 49 percent of its stock outstanding conditioned on the acquisition by Mesa of the 37 percent for which it had tendered. Borrowing was to provide the source of funds for the cash consideration. The upshot would be that Mesa, upon succeeding with its tender offer, would be deprived of the borrowing base it needed for financing. Moreover, the Unocal exchange offer excluded Mesa from participation. Applying its new test, the court validated the tactic. The threat posed was a "grossly inadequate two-tier coercive tender offer coupled with the threat of greenmail." The selective exchange offer reasonably responded to the threat because it was keyed to shares left in the back-end of Mesa's proposed transaction; the exclusion of Mesa prevented Pickens from drawing down any of the funds thus designated for those shares.

The cases that follow pose the question as to the degree to which the possibility of searching scrutiny of defensive tactics under the *Unocal* rule has been realized. First, what is a cognizable "threat" within the rule? Will proposed disruption to an established business plan suffice? Or must the threat be directed to the shareholders' interest, as in the case of a coercive two-tier front-end loaded offer? If "corporate" and "constituency" interests as well as shareholder interests can be taken into account in defining the threat, how is the balance between them to be set? Second, how is a "reasonable" response defined? Is a judicially controlled rule of proportionality contemplated? Or will the establishment of a "threat" simply bring in the business judgment shield provided management employs the right procedures? Finally, to what extent does deference to management's business judgment affect the identification of a "threat" and the determination of the reasonable response?

(2) *The Operation of the Unocal Standard*

(a) *poison pills*

Moran v. Household International, Inc.

Supreme Court of Delaware, 1985.
500 A.2d 1346.

■ McNEILLY, JUSTICE:

[This case involved the legality of the adoption by Household International, Inc. (Household) of a Rights Plan "as a preventative mechanism to ward off future" raiders.]

* * *

The intricacies of the Rights Plan are contained in a 48–page document entitled "Rights Agreement". Basically, the Plan provides that Household common stockholders are entitled to the issuance of one Right per common share under certain triggering conditions. There are two triggering events that can activate the Rights. The first is the announcement of a tender offer for 30 percent of Household's shares ("30% trigger") and the second is the acquisition of 20 percent of Household's shares by any single entity or group ("20% trigger").

If an announcement of a tender offer for 30 percent of Household's shares is made, the Rights are issued and are immediately exercisable to purchase 1/100 share of new preferred stock for $100 and are redeemable by the Board for $.50 per Right. If 20 percent of Household's shares are acquired by anyone, the Rights are issued and become nonredeemable and are exercisable to purchase 1/100 of a share of preferred. If a Right is not exercised for preferred, and thereafter, a merger or consolidation occurs, the Rights holder can exercise each Right to purchase $200 of the common stock of the tender offeror for $100. This "flip-over" provision of the Rights Plan is at the heart of this controversy.

* * *

The primary issue here is the applicability of the business judgment rule as the standard by which the adoption of the Rights Plan should be reviewed. Much of this issue has been decided by our recent decision in Unocal Corp. v. Mesa Petroleum Co., Del.Supr., 493 A.2d 946 (1985). In *Unocal,* we applied the business judgment rule to analyze Unocal's discriminatory self-tender. We explained:

> When a board addresses a pending takeover bid it has an obligation to determine whether the offer is in the best interests of the corporation and its shareholders. In that respect a board's duty is no

different from any other responsibility it shoulders, and its decisions should be no less entitled to the respect they otherwise would be accorded in the realm of business judgment.

Id. at 954 (citation and footnote omitted).

[Before testing management's behavior by the business judgment rule, however, the Court examined whether there existed sufficient authority to permit management to adopt the Rights Plan. If the Board lacked that authority, no issue of business judgment remained in the case.]

Appellants vehemently contend that the Board of Directors was unauthorized to adopt the Rights Plan. First, appellants contend that no provision of the Delaware General Corporation Law authorizes the issuance of such Rights. Secondly, appellants, along with the SEC, contend that the Board is unauthorized to usurp stockholders' rights to receive hostile tender offers. Third, appellants and the SEC also contend that the Board is unauthorized to fundamentally restrict stockholders' rights to conduct a proxy contest. We address each of these contentions in turn.

[With respect to the first contention, the Court replied that the language of §§ 151(g) and 157 of the General Corporation Law of Delaware contained sufficient authority. Section 157 authorized the issuance of rights generally, and did not forbid the issuance of rights of the kind here at issue. Presumably similar logic dictated the implicit conclusion of the Court that § 151(g) authorized the issuance of blank check preferred stock generally and did not forbid the variety of blank check preferred stock here involved. And § 141(a), conferring power on the Board to manage "the business and affairs" of the corporation, adds to the authority to issue the poison pill. The flavor of the Court's logic is revealed in its observation, quoting from its Unocal opinion: "[O]ur corporate law is not static. It must grow and develop in response to, indeed in anticipating of, evolving concepts and needs. Merely because the General Corporation Law is silent as to a specific matter does not mean that it is prohibited."

[With respect to appellants' contention that "the Board is unauthorized to usurp stockholders' rights to receive tender offers by changing Household's fundamental structure," the Court concluded "that the Rights Plan does not prevent stockholders from receiving tender offers, and that the change of Household's structure was less than that which results from the implementation of other defensive mechanisms upheld by various courts."]

The fallacy of that contention is apparent when we look at the recent takeover of Crown Zellerbach, which has a similar Rights Plan, by Sir James Goldsmith. Wall Street Journal, July 26, 1985, at 3, 12. The evidence at trial also evidenced many methods around the Plan ranging from tendering with a condition that the Board redeem the Rights, tendering with a high minimum condition of shares and Rights, tendering and soliciting consents to remove the Board and redeem the Rights, to acquiring 50% of the shares and causing Household to self-tender for the Rights. One could also form a group of up to 19.9% and solicit proxies for consents to remove the Board and redeem the Rights. These are but a few of the methods by which Household can still be acquired by a hostile tender offer.[1]

In addition, the Rights Plan is not absolute. When the Household Board of Directors is faced with a tender offer and a request to redeem the Rights, they will not be able to arbitrarily reject the offer. They will be held to the same fiduciary standards any other board of directors would be held to in deciding to adopt a defensive mechanism, the same standard as they were held to in originally approving the Rights Plan. See *Unocal,* 493 A.2d at 954–55, 958.

In addition, appellants contend that the deterrence of tender offers will be accomplished by what they label "a fundamental transfer of power from the stockholders to the directors." They contend that this transfer of power, in itself, is unauthorized.

The Rights Plan will result in no more of a structural change than any other defensive mechanism adopted by a board of directors. The Rights Plan does not destroy the assets of the corporation. The implementation of the Plan neither results in any outflow of money from the corporation nor impairs its financial flexibility. It does not dilute earnings per share and does not have any adverse tax consequences for the corporation or its stockholders. The Plan has not adversely affected the market price of Household's stock.

Comparing the Rights Plan with other defensive mechanisms, it does less harm to the value structure of the corporation than do the other mechanisms. Other mechanisms result in increased debt of the corporation. See *Whittaker Corp. v. Edgar, supra,* (sale of "prize asset"), *Cheff v. Mathes, supra,* (paying greenmail to eliminate a threat), *Unocal Corp. v. Mesa Petroleum Co., supra,* (discriminatory self-tender).

There is little change in the governance structure as a result of the adoption of the Rights Plan. The Board does not now have unfettered discretion in refusing to redeem the Rights. The Board has no more discretion in refusing to redeem the Rights than it does in enacting any defensive mechanism.

The contention that the Rights Plan alters the structure more than do other defensive mechanisms because it is so effective as to make the

---

1. [Ed. Note] In contrast to the view of the Delaware Supreme Court the trial court observed, 490 A.2d at 1077–1078:

Household * * * does concede, and the evidence so indicates, that the Plan will virtually eliminate hostile two-tiered offers for Household. Unsolicited or non-management-endorsed tender offers which are not front-end loaded or conditioned by high minimum acquisition or the surrender of rights to avoid the dilution effect of the flip-over provision have little hope of succeeding. The market professionals on both sides agree that a high minimum offer for a company of Household's size has never been attempted and it is questionable that such would succeed * * * It clearly would not attract the interest of arbitrageurs or large institutional investors without whose support a hostile tender offer cannot succeed. Even a high minimum-partial offer which leaves a 5% unacquired residual may be deterred. There is apparent agreement that the primary goal of a potential acquiror is to achieve 100% ownership both for tax purposes and in order to operate the company without concern for the interests of minority shareholders.

corporation completely safe from hostile tender offers is likewise without merit. As explained above, there are numerous methods to successfully launch a hostile tender offer.

[With respect to the third contention, that the Board was "unauthorized to fundamentally restrict stockholders' rights to conduct a proxy contest," the Court said:]

The issue, then, is whether the restriction upon individuals or groups from first acquiring 20% of shares before waging a proxy contest fundamentally restricts stockholders' right to conduct a proxy contest. Regarding this issue the Court of Chancery found:

> Thus, while the Rights Plan does deter the formation of proxy efforts of a certain magnitude, it does not limit the voting power of individual shares. On the evidence presented it is highly conjectural to assume that a particular effort to assert shareholder views in the election of directors or revisions of corporate policy will be frustrated by the proxy feature of the Plan. Household's witnesses, Troubh and Higgins described recent corporate takeover battles in which insurgents holding less than 10% stock ownership were able to secure corporate control through a proxy contest or the threat of one.

Moran, 490 A.2d at 1080.

We conclude that there was sufficient evidence at trial to support the Vice–Chancellor's finding that the effect upon proxy contests will be minimal. Evidence at trial established that many proxy contests are won with an insurgent ownership of less than 20%, and that very large holdings are no guarantee of success. There was also testimony that the key variable in proxy contest success is the merit of an insurgent's issues, not the size of his holdings.

* * *

Having concluded that the adoption of the Rights Plan was within the authority of the Directors, we now look to whether the Directors have met their burden under the business judgment rule.

The business judgment rule is a "presumption that in making a business decision the directors of a corporation acted on an informed basis, in good faith and in the honest belief that the action taken was in the best interests of the company." Aronson v. Lewis, Del.Supr., 473 A.2d 805, 812 (1984) (citations omitted). Notwithstanding, in *Unocal* we held that when the business judgment rule applies to adoption of a defensive mechanism, the initial burden will lie with the directors. The "directors must show that they had reasonable grounds for believing that a danger to corporate policy and effectiveness existed. * * * [T]hey satisfy that burden 'by showing good faith and reasonable investigation. * * *'" *Unocal,* 493 A.2d at 955 (citing Cheff v. Mathes, 199 A.2d at 554–55). In addition, the directors must show that the defensive mechanism was "reasonable in relation to the threat posed." *Unocal,* 493 A.2d at 955. Moreover, that proof is materially enhanced, as we noted in *Unocal,* where, as here, a majority of the board favoring the proposal consisted of outside independent directors who have acted in accordance with the foregoing standards. *Unocal,* 493 A.2d at 955;

Aronson, 473 A.2d at 815. Then, the burden shifts back to the plaintiffs who have the ultimate burden of persuasion to show a breach of the directors' fiduciary duties. *Unocal,* 493 A.2d at 958.

There are no allegations here of any bad faith on the part of the Directors' action in the adoption of the Rights Plan. There is no allegation that the Directors' action was taken for entrenchment purposes. Household has adequately demonstrated, as explained above, that the adoption of the Rights Plan was in reaction to what it perceived to be the threat in the market place of coercive two-tier tender offers. Appellants do contend, however, that the Board did not exercise informed business judgment in its adoption of the Plan.

* * *

To determine whether a business judgment reached by a board of directors was an informed one, we determine whether the directors were grossly negligent. Smith v. Van Gorkom, Del.Supr., 488 A.2d 858, 873 (1985). Upon a review of this record, we conclude the Directors were not grossly negligent. The information supplied to the Board on August 14 provided the essentials of the Plan. The Directors were given beforehand a notebook which included a three-page summary of the Plan along with articles on the current takeover environment. The extended discussion between the Board and representatives of Wachtell, Lipton and Goldman, Sachs before approval of the Plan reflected a full and candid evaluation of the Plan. Moran's expression of his views at the meeting served to place before the Board a knowledgeable critique of the Plan. The factual happenings here are clearly distinguishable from the actions of the directors of Trans Union Corporation who displayed gross negligence in approving a cash-out merger. Id.

In addition, to meet their burden, the Directors must show that the defensive mechanism was "reasonable in relation to the threat posed". The record reflects a concern on the part of the Directors over the increasing frequency in the financial services industry of "boot-strap" and "bust-up" takeovers. The Directors were also concerned that such takeovers may take the form of two-tier offers.[14] In addition, on August 14, the Household Board was aware of Moran's overture on behalf of D–K–M. In sum, the Directors reasonably believed Household was vulnerable to coercive acquisition techniques and adopted a reasonable defensive mechanism to protect itself.

* * *

While we conclude for present purposes that the Household Directors are protected by the business judgment rule, that does not end the matter. The ultimate response to an actual takeover bid must be judged by the Directors' actions at that time, and nothing we say here relieves them of their basic fundamental duties to the corporation and its stockholders. *Unocal,* 493 A.2d at 954–55, 958; Smith v. Van Gorkom, 488 A.2d at 872–

---

14. We have discussed the coercive nature of two-tier tender offers in *Unocal,* 493 A.2d at 956, n. 12. We explained in *Unocal* that a discriminatory self-tender was reasonably related to the threat of two-tier tender offers and possible greenmail.

73; *Aronson,* 473 A.2d at 812–13; Pogostin v. Rice, Del.Supr., 480 A.2d 619, 627 (1984). Their use of the Plan will be evaluated when and if the issue arises.

* * *

Affirmed.

Carmody v. Toll Brothers, Inc.

Court of Chancery of Delaware, 1998.
723 A.2d 1180.

■ JACOBS, VICE CHANCELLOR.

At issue on this Rule 12(b)(6) motion to dismiss is whether a most recent innovation in corporate antitakeover measures—the so-called "dead hand" poison pill rights plan—is subject to legal challenge on the basis that it violates the Delaware General Corporation Law and/or the fiduciary duties of the board of directors who adopted the plan. * * *

I.   FACTS

A.   Background Leading to Adoption of the Plan

[Toll Brothers (the "company") designs, builds and markets single family luxury homes in thirteen states. It was founded in 1967, went public in 1986, and continues to enjoy increasing revenues. Its founders, Bruce and Robert Toll, still own 37.5 percent of the stock and also hold seats on the nine member board. The home building industry is highly competitive and has entered a period of consolidation through acquisition. The board, perceiving the company to be a potential acquisition target, adopted a rights plan (the "Rights Plan") in 1997 at a time when the company's stock was trading at the low end of its range of 16 to 25.]

B.   The Rights Plan

* * *

1.   The Rights Plan's "Flip In" and "Flip Over" Features

The Rights Plan would operate as follows: there would be a dividend distribution of one preferred stock purchase right (a "Right") for each outstanding share of common stock as of July 11, 1997. Initially the Rights would attach to the company's outstanding common shares, and each Right would initially entitle the holder to purchase one thousandth of a share of a newly registered series Junior A Preferred Stock for $100. The Rights would become exercisable, and would trade separately from the common shares, after the "Distribution Date," which is defined as the earlier of (a) ten business days following a public announcement that an acquiror has acquired, or obtained the right to acquire, beneficial ownership of 15% or more of the company's outstanding common shares (the "Stock Acquisition Date"), or (b) ten business days after the commencement of a tender offer or exchange offer that would result in a person or group beneficially owning 15% or more of the company's outstanding common shares. Once exercisable, the Rights remain exercisable until their Final Expiration Date (June 12, 2007, ten years after the adoption of the Plan), unless the Rights are earlier redeemed by the company.

The dilutive mechanism of the Rights is "triggered" by certain defined events. One such event is the acquisition of 15% or more of Toll Brothers' stock by any person or group of affiliated or associated persons. Should that occur, each Rights holder (except the acquiror and its affiliates and associates) becomes entitled to buy two shares of Toll Brothers common stock or other securities at half price. That is, the value of the stock received when the Right is exercised is equal to two times the exercise price of the Right. In that manner, this so-called "flip in" feature of the Rights Plan would massively dilute the value of the holdings of the unwanted acquiror.

The Rights also have a standard "flip over" feature, which is triggered if after the Stock Acquisition Date, the company is made a party to a merger in which Toll Brothers is not the surviving corporation, or in which it is the surviving corporation and its common stock is changed or exchanged. In either event, each Rights holder becomes entitled to purchase common stock of the acquiring company, again at half-price, thereby impairing the acquiror's capital structure and drastically diluting the interest of the acquiror's other stockholders.

* * * What is distinctive about the Rights Plan is that it authorizes only a specific, defined category of directors—the "Continuing Directors"— to redeem the Rights. The dispute over the legality of this "Continuing Director" or "dead hand" feature of the Rights Plan is what drives this lawsuit.

2. The "Dead Hand" Feature of the Rights Plan

In substance, the "dead hand" provision operates to prevent any directors of Toll Brothers, except those who were in office as of the date of the Rights Plan's adoption (June 12, 1997) or their designated successors, from redeeming the Rights until they expire on June 12, 2007.

According to the complaint, this "dead hand" provision has a twofold practical effect. First, it makes an unsolicited offer for the company more unlikely by eliminating a proxy contest as a useful way for a hostile acquiror to gain control, because even if the acquiror wins the contest, its newly-elected director representatives could not redeem the Rights. Second, the "dead hand" provision disenfranchises, in a proxy contest, all shareholders that wish the company to be managed by a board empowered to redeem the Rights, by depriving those shareholders of any practical choice except to vote for the incumbent directors. Given these effects, the plaintiff claims that the only purpose that the "dead hand" provision could serve is to discourage future acquisition activity by making any proxy contest to replace incumbent board members an exercise in futility.

II. OVERVIEW OF THE PROBLEM AND THE PARTIES' CONTENTIONS

* * * [O]n this motion [to dismiss] the focus of the inquiry is not whether the Rights Plan is invalid, but rather, is only whether the complaint states one or more cognizable claims of legal invalidity.

A. Overview

The critical issue on this motion is whether a "dead hand" provision in a "poison pill" rights plan is subject to legal challenge on the basis that it is invalid as ultra vires, or as a breach of fiduciary duty, or both. * * *

[The court recounted the history of *Moran* and subsequent cases. The] lesson taught by that experience was that courts were extremely reluctant to order the redemption of poison pills on fiduciary grounds. The reason was the prudent deployment of the pill proved to be largely beneficial to shareholder interests: it often resulted in a bidding contest that culminated in an acquisition on terms superior to the initial hostile offer.

Once it became clear that the prospects were unlikely for obtaining judicial relief mandating a redemption of the poison pill, a different response to the pill was needed. That response, which echoed the Supreme Court's suggestion in Moran, was the foreseeable next step in the evolution of takeover strategy: a tender offer coupled with a solicitation for shareholder proxies to remove and replace the incumbent board with the acquiror's nominees who, upon assuming office, would redeem the pill. Because that strategy, if unopposed, would enable hostile offerors to effect an "end run" around the poison pill, it again was predictable and only a matter of time that target company boards would develop counter-strategies. With one exception—the "dead hand" pill—these counterstrategies proved "successful" only in cases where the purpose was to delay the process to enable the board to develop alternatives to the hostile offer. The counterstrategies were largely unsuccessful, however, where the goal was to stop the proxy contest (and as a consequence, the hostile offer) altogether.

For example, in cases where the target board's response was either to (I) amend the by-laws to delay a shareholders meeting to elect directors, or (ii) delay an annual meeting to a later date permitted under the bylaws, so that the board and management would be able to explore alternatives to the hostile offer (but not entrench themselves), those responses were upheld.[16] On the other hand, where the target board's response to a proxy contest (coupled with a hostile offer) was (i) to move the shareholders meeting to a later date to enable the incumbent board to solicit revocations of proxies to defeat the apparently victorious dissident group, or (ii) to expand the size of the board, and then fill the newly created positions so the incumbents would retain control of the board irrespective of the outcome of the proxy contest, those responses were declared invalid.[17]

This litigation experience taught that a target board, facing a proxy contest joined with a hostile tender offer, could, in good faith, employ non-

16. See, e.g., Stahl v. Apple Bancorp, Inc., Del. Ch., 579 A.2d 1115 (1990) (upholding postponement of annual meeting to a later date permitted by bylaws to enable target board to explore alternatives to hostile offer) * * *.

17. See, Aprahamian v. HBO & Co., Del Ch., 531 A.2d 1204 (1987) (shareholders' meeting moved to later date for the purpose of defeating the apparent victors in proxy contest. Held: invalid); Blasius Indus. v. Atlas Corp., Del. Ch., 564 A.2d 651(1988) (in response to an announced proxy contest, target board amended bylaws to create two new board positions, then filled those positions to retain board control, irrespective of outcome of proxy contest. Held: invalid).

preclusive defensive measures to give the board time to explore transactional alternatives. The target board could not, however, erect defenses that would either preclude a proxy contest altogether or improperly bend the rules to favor the board's continued incumbency.

In this environment, the only defensive measure that promised to be a "show stopper" (i.e., had the potential to deter a proxy contest altogether) was a poison pill with a "dead hand" feature. The reason is that if only the incumbent directors or their designated successors could redeem the pill, it would make little sense for shareholders or the hostile bidder to wage a proxy contest to replace the incumbent board. Doing that would eliminate from the scene the only group of persons having the power to give the hostile bidder and target company shareholders what they desired: control of the target company (in the case of the hostile bidder) and the opportunity to obtain an attractive price for their shares (in the case of the target company stockholders). It is against that backdrop that the legal issues presented here, which concern the validity of the "dead hand" feature, attain significance.

     * * *

III.   ANALYSIS

     * * *

B.   The Validity of the "Dead Hand" Provision

1.   The Invalidity Contentions

The plaintiff's complaint attacks the "dead hand" feature of the Toll Brothers poison pill on both statutory and fiduciary duty grounds. The statutory claim is that the "dead hand" provision unlawfully restricts the powers of future boards by creating different classes of directors—those who have the power to redeem the poison pill, and those who do not. Under 8 Del. C. §§ 141(a) and (d), any such restrictions and director classifications must be stated in the certificate of incorporation. The complaint alleges that because those restrictions are not stated in the Toll Brothers charter, the "dead hand" provision of the Rights Plan is ultra vires and, consequently, invalid on its face.

The complaint also alleges that even if the Rights Plan is not ultra vires, its approval constituted a breach of the Toll Brothers board's fiduciary duty of loyalty in several respects. It is alleged that the board violated its duty of loyalty because (a) the "dead hand" provision was enacted solely or primarily for entrenchment purposes; (b) it was also a disproportionate defensive measure, since it precludes the shareholders from receiving tender offers and engaging in a proxy contest, in contravention of the principles of Unocal Corp. v. Mesa Petroleum Co. ("Unocal"), as elucidated in Unitrin, Inc. v. American General Corp. ("Unitrin") and (c) the "dead hand" provision purposefully interferes with the shareholder voting franchise without any compelling justification, in derogation of the principles articulated in Blasius Indus. v. Atlas Corp. ("Blasius").

     * * *

2. The Statutory Invalidity Claims

* * * [T]he complaint states legally sufficient claims that the "dead hand" provision of the Toll Brothers Rights Plan violates 8 Del. C. §§ 141(a) and (d). There are three reasons.

First, it cannot be disputed that the Rights Plan confers the power to redeem the pill only upon some, but not all, of the directors. But under § 141(d), the power to create voting power distinctions among directors exists only where there is a classified board, and where those voting power distinctions are expressed in the certificate of incorporation. Section 141(d) pertinently provides:

> ... The certificate of incorporation may confer upon holders of any class or series of stock the right to elect 1 or more directors who shall serve for such term, and have such voting powers as shall be stated in the certificate of incorporation. The terms of office and voting powers of the directors elected in the manner so provided in the certificate of incorporation may be greater than or less than those of any other director or class of directors....

The plain, unambiguous meaning of the quoted language is that if one category or group of directors is given distinctive voting rights not shared by the other directors, those distinctive voting rights must be set forth in the certificate of incorporation. In the case of Toll Brothers (the complaint alleges), they are not.

Second, § 141(d) mandates that the "right to elect 1 or more directors who shall ... have such [greater] voting powers" is reserved to the stockholders, not to the directors or a subset thereof. Absent express language in the charter, nothing in Delaware law suggests that some directors of a public corporation may be created less equal than other directors, and certainly not by unilateral board action. Vesting the pill redemption power exclusively in the Continuing Directors transgresses the statutorily protected shareholder right to elect the directors who would be so empowered. For that reason, and because it is claimed that the Rights Plan's allocation of voting power to redeem the Rights is nowhere found in the Toll Brothers certificate of incorporation, the complaint states a claim that the "dead hand" feature of the Rights Plan is ultra vires, and hence, statutorily invalid under Delaware law.

Third, the complaint states a claim that the "dead hand" provision would impermissibly interfere with the directors' statutory power to manage the business and affairs of the corporation. That power is conferred by 8 Del. C. § 141(a), which mandates:

> The business and affairs of every corporation organized under this chapter shall be managed by or under the direction of a board of directors, except as may be otherwise provided in this chapter or in its certificate of incorporation....

The "dead hand" poison pill is intended to thwart hostile bids by vesting shareholders with preclusive rights that cannot be redeemed except by the Continuing Directors. Thus, the one action that could make it practically possible to redeem the pill—replacing the entire board—could make that pill redemption legally impossible to achieve. The "dead hand" provision would jeopardize a newly-elected future board's ability to achieve a business combination by depriving that board of the power to redeem the pill without obtaining the consent of the "Continuing Directors," who (it may be assumed) would constitute a minority of the board. In this manner, it is claimed, the "dead hand" provision would interfere with the board's power to protect fully the corporation's (and its shareholders') interests in a transaction that is one of the most fundamental and important in the life of a business enterprise.

* * * The defendants [argue] that the "dead hand" provision is tantamount to a delegation to a special committee, consisting of the Continuing Directors, of the power to redeem the pill.

* * * The analogy * * * ignores fundamental structural differences between the creation of a special board committee and the operation of the "dead hand" provision of the Rights Plan. The creation of a special committee would not impose long term structural power-related distinctions between different groups of directors of the same board. The board that creates a special committee may abolish it at any time, as could any successor board.

For these reasons, the statutory invalidity claims survive the motion to dismiss.

3.   The Fiduciary Duty Invalidity Claims

Because the plaintiffs statutory invalidity claims have been found legally cognizable, the analysis arguably could end at this point. But the plaintiff also alleges that the board's adoption of the "dead hand" feature violated its fiduciary duty of loyalty. For the sake of completeness, that claim is addressed as well.

a) The Blasius Fiduciary Duty Claim

The validity of antitakeover measures is normally evaluated under the Unocal/Unitrin standard. But where the defensive measures purposefully disenfranchise shareholders, the board will be required to satisfy the more exacting Blasius standard, which our Supreme Court has articulated as follows:

> A board's unilateral decision to adopt a defensive measure touching "upon issues of control" that purposefully disenfranchises its share-holders is strongly suspect under Unocal, and cannot be sustained without a "compelling justification." [Stroud v. Grace, Del.Supr., 606 A.2d 75, 92 n. 3 (1992)].

The complaint alleges that the "dead hand" provision purposefully disenfranchises the company's shareholders without any compelling justification. The disenfranchisement would occur because even in an election contest fought over the issue of the hostile bid, the shareholders will be powerless to elect a board that is both willing and able to accept the bid, and they "may be forced to vote for [incumbent] directors whose policies they reject because only those directors have the power to change them." [Jeffrey N. Gordon, "Just Say Never" Poison Pills, Deadhand Pills and

Shareholder Adopted By–Laws: An Essay for Warren Buffett, 19 Cardozo L.Rev. 515,540 (1997)].

A claim that the directors have unilaterally "create[d] a structure in which shareholder voting is either impotent or self defeating" [Id.] is necessarily a claim of purposeful disenfranchisement. Given the Supreme Court's rationale for upholding the validity of the poison pill in Moran, and the primacy of the shareholder vote in our scheme of corporate jurisprudence, any contrary view is difficult to justify. * * * As former Chancellor Allen stated in Sutton Holding Corp. v. DeSoto, Inc. [1991 WL 80223]:

> Provisions in corporate instruments that are intended principally to restrain or coerce the free exercise of the stockholder franchise are deeply suspect. The shareholder vote is the basis upon which an individual serving as a corporate director must rest his or her claim to legitimacy. Absent quite extraordinary circumstances, in my opinion, it constitutes a fundamental offense to the dignity of this corporate office for a director to use corporate power to seek to coerce shareholders in the exercise of the vote.
>
> * * *

For these reasons, the plaintiffs Blasius-based breach of fiduciary duty claim is cognizable under Delaware law.

b) The Unocal/Unitrin Fiduciary Duty Claim

The final issue is whether the complaint states a legally cognizable claim that the inclusion of the "dead hand" provision in the Rights Plan was an unreasonable defensive measure within the meaning of Unocal. I conclude that it does.

* * * Under Unitrin, a defensive measure is disproportionate (i.e., unreasonable) if it is either coercive or preclusive. The complaint alleges that the "dead hand" provision "disenfranchises shareholders by forcing them to vote for incumbent directors or their designees if shareholders want to be represented by a board entitled to exercise its full statutory prerogatives." That is sufficient to claim that the "dead hand" provision is coercive. The complaint also alleges that that provision "makes an offer for the Company much more unlikely since it eliminates use of a proxy contest as a possible means to gain control ... [because] ... any directors elected in such a contest would still be unable to vote to redeem the pill;" and "renders future contests for corporate control of Toll Brothers prohibitively expensive and effectively impossible." A defensive measure is preclusive if it makes a bidder's ability to wage a successful proxy contest and gain control either "mathematically impossible" or "realistically unattainable." These allegations are sufficient to state a claim that the "dead hand" provision makes a proxy contest "realistically unattainable," and therefore, is disproportionate and unreasonable under Unocal.

NOTE: NO HAND PILLS

The Delaware Supreme Court endorsed the analysis of *Carmody v. Toll Brothers* in **Quickturn Design Systems, Inc. v. Shapiro**, 721 A.2d 1281 (Del.Supr.1998).

Quickturn involved "no hand" pill—a less poisonous variation on the deadhand pill theme. The pill in question had a "Deferred Redemption Provision," under which no newly elected board could redeem the pill for six months after taking office if the purpose or effect of the redemption would be to facilitate a transaction with an "Interested Person," defined as one who proposed, nominated or financially supported the election of the new directors to the board. The Supreme Court invalidated the provision, reasoning as follows, 721 A.2d at 1291–93:

"One of the most basic tenets of Delaware corporate law is that the board of directors has the ultimate responsibility for managing the business and affairs of a corporation. Section 141(a) requires that any limitation on the board's authority be set out in the certificate of incorporation. The Quickturn certificate of incorporation contains no provision purporting to limit the authority of the board in any way. The Delayed Redemption Provision, however, would prevent a newly elected board of directors from completely discharging its fundamental management duties to the corporation and its stockholders for six months. While the Delayed Redemption Provision limits the board of directors' authority in only one respect, the suspension of the Rights Plan, it nonetheless restricts the board's power in an area of fundamental importance to the shareholders—negotiating a possible sale of the corporation. Therefore, we hold that the Delayed Redemption Provision is invalid under Section 141(a), which confers upon any newly elected board of directors full power to manage and direct the business and affairs of a Delaware corporation.

* * *

"The Delayed Redemption Provision would prevent a new Quickturn board of directors from managing the corporation by redeeming the Rights Plan to facilitate a transaction that would serve the stockholders' best interests, even under circumstances where the board would be required to do so because of its fiduciary duty to the Quickturn stockholders. Because the Delayed Redemption Provision impermissibly circumscribes the board's statutory power under Section 141(a) and the directors' ability to fulfill their concomitant fiduciary duties, we hold that the Delayed Redemption Provision is invalid."

NOTE: THE *BLASIUS* RULE

Provided that neither a no hand nor dead hand pill stands in the way, the mechanism of the shareholder vote gives the patient bidder and the shareholders themselves a means to circumvent incumbent management opposition. Exchange Act § 14(a) assures the integrity of such a proxy contest, once initiated. Contrast a case where a procedural maneuver by the defending managers has the effect of *forestalling* such an exercise of the shareholder franchise. Such cases occasionally have been subjected to special judicial scrutiny. Over all, however, courts have done little to restrain directors' actions to manipulate the terms of shareholder access to (or use of) the voting process in order to thwart or impede stockholder choice.

Toll Brothers represents a case of judicial intervention to protect shareholder access to the vote. In so doing, the court acts under the rubric of **Blasius Industries, Inc. v. Atlas Corp.**, 564 A.2d 651 (Del.Ch.1988). There the Chancery Court required "compelling justification" for such Board action instead of testing it under the permissive business judgment standard. Blasius, a holder of 9.1 percent of Atlas stock, delivered to the Board a form of stockholder consent to increase the size of the board from 7 to 15 (its maximum permissible size under the Atlas charter) and elect 8 new members. The board thwarted Blasius by amending the bylaws to increase the size of the board by 2 and electing 2 new directors before the stockholder consent could be acted upon. Chancellor Allen was unable to find "compelling justification" for the board action, notwithstanding his conclusion that the board acted with appropriate care and in good faith. Concluding that the primary purpose of the board action was to prevent or impede the desires of an unaffiliated majority of the stock, he set aside the board action.

Soon after *Blasius,* the Chancellor receded from this stated concern for the protection of stockholder suffrage and reverted to a more characteristic concern for board power to protect stockholders from their own imprudent choices. In **Stahl v. Apple Bancorp, Inc.,** 579 A.2d 1115 (Del.Ch.1990), he declined to cancel a board's defensive postponement of an annual meeting where a 30 percent stockholder had mounted a proxy fight and tender offer. The board asserted that postponement would give the stockholders time to consider alternatives to the proposals—alternatives for which the board was searching at the time. The Chancellor retreated from his previously announced requirement of the need for a "compelling justification" of the board's obstruction of stockholder suffrage to a much less demanding standard. He also was unable to find that the board had acted "for the primary purpose of impairing or impeding the effective exercise of the corporate franchise." See also Stahl v. Apple Bancorp, Inc., CCH Fed.Sec.L.Rep. ¶ 95,412 (Del.Ch.1990); Stroud v. Grace, 606 A.2d 75 (Del.1992). Compare American Hardware Corp. v. Savage Arms Corp., 37 Del.Ch. 59, 136 A.2d 690 (1957) (upholding management maneuver denying stockholder choice), with Condec v. Lunkenheimer Co., 43 Del.Ch. 353, 230 A.2d 769 (1967) (preventing management from thwarting majority). But cf. Schnell v. Chris–Craft Industries, 285 A.2d 437 (Del.Sup.1971) (enjoining management from thwarting stockholder vote in circumstances comparable to *Stahl*).

NOTE: SHAREHOLDER PROTESTS

Institutional investor activists oppose poison pills, and have had success as proponents of nonbinding, precatory shareholder proposals under Rule 14a–8 that request the board to consider pill redemption. The frequency of these attacks has increased in recent years. In addition, the activist hedge funds put the pill on their governance reform agendas. Managers have retreated. The number of publicly traded companies with pill in place is said to have declined to one-third in 2007.

Some activists recently have experimented with a more aggressive mode of attack. The proponent solicits proxies to approve an amendment of the issuer's by laws under which the board must submit a poison pill plan for shareholder approval. The by law amendment also provides against unilateral subsequent amendment by means of a vote of the board. Such a by law was sustained under Oklahoma law in **International Brotherhood of Teamsters v. Fleming Cos., Inc.,** 975 P.2d 907 (Okla.1999). The same result should follow in states with corporate codes that contains a provision like that of RMBCA § 10.20(a)(2), which provides explicitly for the primacy of shareholder by laws over director amendment. The Delaware code does not contain such a provision. Instead, DCL § 109 vests by law amendment power in the shareholders and allows for director by law amendment only if there is an enabling provision in the charter. Most publicly-traded Delaware corporations have such a charter provision. The Delaware law issue that results for shareholder by laws respecting pills is whether the charter provision that enables the board to adopt and amend by laws trumps the shareholder by law's provision against unilateral amendment by the board. Opinions differ, pending a ruling by the Delaware courts. Compare Hamermesh, Corporate Democracy and Stockholder–Adopted By–Laws: Taking Back the Street?, 73 Tul. L. Rev. 409 (1998), with John C. Coffee, Jr., The Bylaw Battlefield: Can Institutions Change the Outcome of Corporate Control Contests?, 51 U. Miami L. Rev. 605 (1997).

NOTE: CORPORATE LAW'S STRUCTURAL LIMITS ON ANTITAKEOVER DEFENSES

The legality of antitakeover defenses depends in the first instance on enabling statutory provisions. Prior to *Toll Brothers* and *Quickturn*, the courts, informed by Delaware's tradition of "independent" reading of the separate provisions of state corporation law, had tended to read these liberally. The validation of poison pill plans in Moran v. Household International, Inc., supra, presents an example of this. The *Moran* court could, consistently with the language and origins of blank check preferred stock, have interpreted the provision in question to preclude its being fashioned into a poison pill. But the tradition of reading corporate statutes as broadly enabling has led even those courts that have invalidated poison pills to confirm the sufficiency of the blank check. See Asarco v. MRH Holmes A Court, 611 F.Supp. 468 (D.N.J.1985).

Outside of Delaware, statutory technicalities have been successfully invoked to invalidate defensive provisions on a few rare occasions. **Georgia–Pacific Corp. v. Great Northern Nekoosa Corp.,** 731 F.Supp. 38 (D.Me.1990), presents one of these instances in which a court reaches out for a narrow reading of a corporation statute's enabling scope. The court there invalidated a shareholder-approved charter provision requiring a 75 percent shareholder vote for the removal of a director. It made reference to the Maine statute's specific provision for removal by a two-thirds shareholder vote. In the court's view, the "specific" provision for two thirds removal took interpretive precedence over the statute's "general" allowance of supermajority voting provisions by charter or by law amendment.

Other cases invalidate defensive provisions for noncompliance with other over-arching norms deemed part of the substance of state corporation laws. A few successful attacks have been based on the ground that rights plans discriminate among holders of the same class of stock. Here a leading case is **Asarco, Inc. v. MRH Holmes A Court,** 611 F.Supp. 468 (D.N.J.1985), applying New Jersey law. The rights plan in question provided for a new series of preferred stock carrying no voting rights unless acquired by a holder of 20 percent of either the issuer's common stock or the preferred issue itself. In that event, each holder of the preferred other than the 20 percent holder received five votes on all matters. The plan was invalidated on the ground that the state statute permitted voting differentials only as among classes or series of stock. See also Minstar Acquiring Corp. v. AMF Inc., 621 F.Supp. 1252 (S.D.N.Y.1985) (nontransferable rights issue improperly discriminates against shareholders purchasing stock after record date); Amalgamated Sugar Co. v. NL Industries, Inc., 644 F.Supp. 1229 (S.D.N.Y.1986). The Delaware courts, in contrast, accept the proposition that the vote per share attached to homogenized shares of a single class may be reduced as the number of shares of a particular owner increases. See Providence & Worcester Co. v. Baker, 378 A.2d 121 (Del.1977). See also Dynamics Corp. of America v. CTS Corp., 805 F.2d 705, 717–718 (7th Cir.1986) affirmed, 481 U.S. 69 (1987).

(b) structural coercion

Observers looked to decisions applying the *Unocal* rule to teach us how to measure the dimensions or import of both the requisite threat and the appropriate response so as to be able to tell whether the latter is reasonable in relation to, or proportionate to, the former. It appeared that the *Unocal* proportionality test would derive content by an emphasis on the distinction between harm that results from bids that are structurally coercive on shareholders (e.g., two-tier front-end loaded bids) and the harm embodied in bids that are not coercive but otherwise objectionable (e.g., an all shares bid at an inadequate cash price or a price paid in currency of dubious value). That difference was said to justify different measures of proportionality in evaluating management responses. Gilson and Kraakman, Delaware's Intermediate Standard for Defensive Tactics: Is There Substance to Proportionality Review? 44 Bus.Law. 247 (1989).

This framework gave rise to difficult questions: Was the "harm" from the fact that the bid was "structurally" coercive sufficient to justify a structurally coercive or preclusive response that effectively denied the target shareholders any opportunity to accept the bid? *Unocal* intimated this result. Confirmation came with **Ivanhoe Partners v. Newmont Mining Corp.,** 535 A.2d 1334 (Del.1987). Newmont had already disposed of a first takeover attempt when Ivanhoe Partners, controlled by Boone Pickens, came along. The first potential bidder, Consolidated Gold Fields, had acquired 26 percent of Newmont's stock. It held this subject to a standstill agreement that provided, among other things, a right of first refusal to Newmont if Gold Fields should sell its stake. But it also provided for termination of the standstill at Gold Fields' option if any other party acquired 9.9 percent or more of Newmont's stock. Ivanhoe acquired 9.95 percent of Newmont's stock, giving Gold Fields the option of going forward with a takeover of Newmont. Ivanhoe made overtures to Gold Fields. Ivanhoe also made a $95 offer for 42 percent of Newmont's stock, stating an intention to pay $95 cash in a second step merger, but not specifying a committed source of financing.

Gold Fields opted to continue to cooperate with Newmont's managers. The Newmont board declared the Ivanhoe offer to be inadequate. It also approved a restructuring under which some assets were to be sold and the proceeds devoted to a dividend of $33 per share. At the same time, Newmont and Gold Fields revised their agreement to allow Gold Fields to purchase up to 49.9 percent of Newmont's stock, but to be limited to 40 percent of the seats on the board. Gold Fields, upon receiving the $33 dividend on its block of Newmont shares, took the proceeds and, in a street sweep, purchased 15.8 million Newmont shares at an average of $98 per share and increased its holdings to 49.7 percent.

The Delaware Supreme Court validated Newmont's defensive program under *Unocal*. It identified two *Unocal* threats. First, Ivanhoe's offer was coercive because it had two tiers. Second, since Ivanhoe's stock acquisition released Gold Fields from the first standstill agreement, the possibility existed that Gold Fields would attempt a two-tier acquisition, whether or not in concert with Ivanhoe, leaving a substantial number of shareholders in the back end. The defensive measures were reasonable in relation to the threat. The $33 dividend gave all the shareholders a means of participating in the value of the assets sold at an adequate price and facilitated the Gold Fields street sweep. The street sweep itself was reasonable and noncoercive. And the new standstill agreement protected Newmont's public shareholders from being squeezed out by a majority shareholder.

(c) all cash–all shares tender offers

Unocal's modification of the business judgment approach to takeover defenses also held out a possibility of strict scrutiny of defenses toward the end of maximization of shareholder value. Application of the two-step test on the facts of *Moran* and *Unocal* itself heralded no steps toward the realization of this potential. But a few such steps were taken in a subsequent series of Delaware Chancery decisions respecting all cash, all shares offers.

In **AC Acquisitions Corp. v. Anderson, Clayton & Co.,** 519 A.2d 103 (Del.Ch.1986), the bidder made an any and all shares offer of $56 and announced its intention to conduct a second-step merger at the same $56 consideration upon acquiring a majority of the target stock. The target responded by (a) commencing a self tender for 65 percent of its outstanding shares at $60, and (b) announcing an intention to sell an amount of its stock equal to 25 percent of all stock outstanding to a newly formed ESOP. Chancellor Allen ruled that this defense did not pass the *Unocal* test. The bidder had made a noncoercive offer at a fair price. Given this, the first leg of the test allowed the Board the leeway to respond to the offer by proposing an alternative restructuring plan. But the response here was not reasonable in relation to the "threat" posed. The only threat presented by this offer lay in the possibility that a majority of the shareholders might prefer an alternative to the $56 any and all offer. The response went beyond the provision of a choice, and, due to its timing, had the effect of coercively precluding the shareholders from accepting the bidder's offer. Because the $56 offer was subject to conditions, no shareholder tendering into it had an assurance of an eventual acceptance. By tendering, the shareholder precluded itself from participating in the "fat" end of the target's $60 offer. Further, a shareholder not tendering into the target's offer would run a substantial risk of having the value of its stock decline sharply, down to a $22–$31 range, if the restructuring succeeded. Given the downside, a rational shareholder would tender into the target's offer even if it thought the bidder's $56 offer to be preferable. All management had to do in order to eliminate the coercive element of its offer, said the court, was change the timing. It might, for example, have put its proposal on the table for inspection, and then waited to see whether or not 51 percent of the shareholders tendered into the hostile $56 offer.

In **City Capital Associates v. Interco Inc.,** 551 A.2d 787 (Del.Ch. 1988), Chancellor Allen brought the shareholder choice theme of *Anderson, Clayton* to a poison pill defense. The bidder made a $70 any and all shares cash offer, later raised to $74. The offer was conditioned on receipt of 75 percent of the shares and the board's redemption of a poison pill plan. The plan contained a "flip in" right to purchase target stock on a 2 for 1 basis triggered by a stockholder reaching a 30 percent ownership threshold, and a "flip over" right to purchase stock of the acquirer on a 2 for 1 basis on a subsequent merger. The target's management responded by (a) proposing a complex restructuring plan valued by its investment banker at $76 (but discounted to a figure well below $74 by the bidder's investment banker), and (b) refusing to redeem the poison pill.

Chancellor Allen took the occasion to explicate the first leg of the *Unocal* test:

" * * * [I]n the special case of a tender offer for all shares, the threat posed, if any, is not importantly to corporate policies * * * but rather the threat, if any, is most directly to shareholder interests. Broadly speaking, threats to shareholders in that context may be of two types: threats to the voluntariness of the choice offered by the offer, and threats to the substantive economic interest represented by stockholding.

" * * * It is now universally acknowledged that the structure of an offer can render mandatory in substance that which is voluntary in form. The so-called 'front-end' loaded partial offer—already a largely vanished breed—is the most extreme example of this phenomenon. * * *

" * * * Even where an offer is noncoercive, it may represent a 'threat' to shareholder interests in the special sense that an active negotiator with power, in effect, to refuse the proposal may be able to arrange an alternative transaction or a modified business plan that will present a more valuable option to shareholders. * * * Our cases, however, also indicate that in the setting of a noncoercive offer, absent unusual facts, there may come a time when a board's fiduciary duty will require it to redeem the rights and to permit shareholders to choose. * * * "

Thus, concluded Chancellor Allen, given a noncoercive offer, a target board could use a poison pill to create a window of time in which to arrange an alternative value maximizing transaction. At some point, however, the time would run out. Then the pill's only function was to prevent the shareholders from making an open choice between the two alternatives. The Chancellor ruled that the time had expired in this target's case, and its board's decision not to redeem the pill did not satisfy the *Unocal* test. In so doing, the Chancellor refused the target board's invitation to rule that its action was reasonable because its restructuring proposal was worth $2 more than the hostile bid. The values were debatable, he said, and the choice should be the shareholders'.

Finally, in **Grand Metropolitan PLC v. Pillsbury Co.,** 558 A.2d 1049 (Del.Ch.1988), the Chancery Court also decreed the redemption of poison pill rights. Here the bidder made a $63 any and all cash offer for Pillsbury, representing a 60 percent premium over market value. Management, refusing to redeem the pill, announced a restructuring centered on a spin off of the company's Burger King subsidiary. This, said management would result in value of $68 per share, after four or five years. The court ordered the pill's redemption, noting that no threat was posed to the shareholders or any other corporate constituency, 87 percent of the shares had been tendered, a reasonable shareholder very well might take $63 in 1988 instead of waiting for $68 in 1992, and, finally, two months had elapsed and no competing offers had emerged.

These opinions implied a "shareholder choice" norm under *Unocal*, at least in the case of all cash offers for all shares. Management would have no privilege to use a poison pill or other device to "just say no"—that is, to force the bidder to withdraw without offering to or procuring for the shareholders a cash alternative at a premium over market price. The Delaware Supreme Court would reject this reading of *Unocal* in *Time Warner* infra, further expanding management's room for maneuver in the face of an all cash-all shares offer (and narrowing the *Unocal* standard) in *Unitrin*, infra.

(3) The Revlon Auction Duty

Revlon, Inc. v. MacAndrews & Forbes Holdings, Inc.

Supreme Court of Delaware, 1985.
506 A.2d 173.

■ MOORE, JUSTICE:

[The opinion in this case addressed three defenses by the management of Revlon, Inc. (Revlon) against an ultimately successful takeover attempt by Pantry Pride, Inc. (Pantry Pride). The first two defenses entailed (a) the issuance by Revlon as a dividend to its stockholders of redeemable poison pill Rights (to acquire upon tender of a share of common stock a one year Note for $65 bearing interest at 12 percent) exercisable when anyone acquired 20% or more of Revlon stock (other than an acquisition of all Revlon stock for cash at not less than $65 per share) by all stockholders other than the acquiror, and (b) acquisition by Revlon of ten million shares of its common stock in exchange for its subordinated Notes and preferred stock. The last defense was a lock-up and "no-shop" agreement (including an escrowed $25 million cancellation fee) which the management of Revlon made with its white knight, Forstmann, Little, & Co. (Forstmann), in order to fend off Pantry Pride's increased bids for control.

[The Delaware Supreme Court, affirming the issuance by the trial court of a preliminary injunction against the Forstmann, Little transaction, rejected the attacks on the poison pill defense and on the repurchase of stock for Notes. Its decision rested on the ground that neither the discriminatory rights offering nor the repurchase was objectionable *per se* as a tactic, and that in the circumstances of the case each constituted a reasonable exercise of directorial business judgment in response to Pantry Pride's initial bid for control, which the Board on advice of its bankers thought (apparently correctly) to be inadequate. With respect to the third defense, it reached a different conclusion.

[The Notes issued on the repurchase of the Revlon common stock "contained covenants which limited Revlon's ability to incur additional debt, sell assets, or pay dividends unless otherwise approved by the 'independent' (non-management) members of the board." In connection with its efforts to induce Forstmann to become the white knight, Revlon indicated that its outside directors would waive those covenants and would redeem the poison pill Rights. As a result of the suggestion of waiver of the covenants, the price of those Notes began to fall in the market, and there were threats of litigation by Noteholders and of director personal liability which the directors appear to have taken seriously. In the course of the ensuing bidding war between Pantry Pride and Forstmann, in which

Pantry Pride raised its price substantially, Forstmann offered to outbid slightly Pantry Pride's then highest bid, and undertook to support the par value of the falling Notes—but only on the condition that it be given a lock-up on the assets of two of Revlon's divisions at a substantial discount from their value, and that Revlon enter into a no-shop agreement.

[The Delaware Supreme Court, after noting that the directors of Revlon had acted appropriately and within the limits of business judgment with respect to the first two defenses, observed that circumstances were altered by the time of the Forstmann lock-up and no-shop agreement, and went on to say (Moore, J.):]

However, when Pantry Pride increased its offer to $50 per share, and then to $53, it became apparent to all that the break-up of the company was inevitable. The Revlon board's authorization permitting management to negotiate a merger or buyout with a third party was a recognition that the company was for sale. The duty of the board had thus changed from the preservation of Revlon as a corporate entity to the maximization of the company's value at a sale for the stockholders' benefit. This significantly altered the board's responsibilities under the *Unocal* standards. It no longer faced threats to corporate policy and effectiveness, or to the stockholders' interests, from a grossly inadequate bid. The whole question of defensive measures became moot. The directors' role changed from defenders of the corporate bastion to auctioneers charged with getting the best price for the stockholders at a sale of the company.

This brings us to the lock-up with Forstmann and its emphasis on shoring up the sagging market value of the Notes in the face of threatened litigation by their holders. Such a focus was inconsistent with the changed concept of the directors' responsibilities at this stage of the developments. The impending waiver of the Notes covenants had caused the value of the Notes to fall, and the board was aware of the noteholders' ire as well as their subsequent threats of suit. The directors thus made support of the Notes an integral part of the company's dealings with Forstmann, even though their primary responsibility at this stage was to the equity owners.

The original threat posed by Pantry Pride—the break-up of the company—had become a reality which even the directors embraced. Selective dealing to fend off a hostile but determined bidder was no longer a proper objective. Instead, obtaining the highest price for the benefit of the stockholders should have been the central theme guiding director action. Thus, the Revlon board could not make the requisite showing of good faith by preferring the noteholders and ignoring its duty of loyalty to the shareholders. The rights of the former already were fixed by contract. Wolfensohn v. Madison Fund, Inc., Del.Supr., 253 A.2d 72, 75 (1969); Harff v. Kerkorian, Del.Ch., 324 A.2d 215 (1974). The noteholders required no further protection, and when the Revlon board entered into an auction-ending lock-up agreement with Forstmann on the basis of impermissible considerations at the expense of the shareholders, the directors breached their primary duty of loyalty.

The Revlon board argued that it acted in good faith in protecting the noteholders because *Unocal* permits consideration of other corporate constituencies. Although such considerations may be permissible, there are fundamental limitations upon that prerogative. A board may have regard for various constituencies in discharging its responsibilities, provided there are rationally related benefits accruing to the stockholders. *Unocal*, 493 A.2d at 955. However, such concern for non-stockholder interests is inappropriate when an auction among active bidders is in progress, and the object no longer is to protect or maintain the corporate enterprise but to sell it to the highest bidder.

Revlon also contended that by Gilbert v. El Paso Co., Del.Ch., 490 A.2d 1050, 1054–55 (1984), it had contractual and good faith obligations to consider the noteholders. However, any such duties are limited to the principle that one may not interfere with contractual relationships by improper actions. Here, the rights of the noteholders were fixed by agreement, and there is nothing of substance to suggest that any of those terms were violated. The Notes covenants specifically contemplated a waiver to permit sale of the company at a fair price. The Notes were accepted by the holders on that basis, including the risk of an adverse market effect stemming from a waiver. Thus, nothing remained for Revlon to legitimately protect, and no rationally related benefit thereby accrued to the stockholders. Under such circumstances we must conclude that the merger agreement with Forstmann was unreasonable in relation to the threat posed.

A lock-up is not *per se* illegal under Delaware law. Its use has been approved in an earlier case. Thompson v. Enstar Corp., Del.Ch. (1984). Such options can entice other bidders to enter a contest for control of the corporation, creating an auction for the company and maximizing shareholder profit. Current economic conditions in the takeover market are such that a "white knight" like Forstmann might only enter the bidding for the target company if it receives some form of compensation to cover the risks and costs involved. Note, Corporations–Mergers–"Lock-up" Enjoined Under Section 14(e) of Securities Exchange Act–Mobil Corp. v. Marathon Oil Co., 669 F.2d 366 (6th Cir.1981), 12 Seton Hall L.Rev. 881, 892 (1982). However, while those lock-ups which draw bidders into the battle benefit shareholders, similar measures which end an active auction and foreclose further bidding operate to the shareholders' detriment. Note, Lock-up Options: Toward a State Law Standard, 96 Harv.L.Rev. 1068, 1081 (1983).

Recently, the United States Court of Appeals for the Second Circuit invalidated a lock-up on fiduciary duty grounds similar to those here. Hanson Trust PLC, et al. v. ML SCM Acquisition Inc., et al., 781 F.2d 264 (2d Cir.1986). Citing Thompson v. Enstar Corp., supra, with approval, the court stated:

> In this regard, we are especially mindful that some lock-up options may be beneficial to the shareholders, such as those that induce a bidder to compete for control of a corporation, while others may be harmful, such as those that effectively preclude bidders from competing with the optionee bidder. 781 F.2d at 274.

In *Hanson Trust,* the bidder, Hanson, sought control of SCM by a hostile cash tender offer. SCM management joined with Merrill Lynch to propose a leveraged buy-out of the company at a higher price, and Hanson in turn increased its offer. Then, despite very little improvement in its subsequent bid, the management group sought a lock-up option to purchase SCM's two main assets at a substantial discount. The SCM directors granted the lock-up without adequate information as to the size of the discount or the effect the transaction would have on the company. Their action effectively ended a competitive bidding situation. The Hanson Court invalidated the lock-up because the directors failed to fully inform themselves about the value of a transaction in which management had a strong self-interest. "In short, the Board appears to have failed to ensure that negotiations for alternative bids were conducted by those whose only loyalty was to the shareholders." Id. at 277.

The Forstmann option had a similar destructive effect on the auction process. Forstmann had already been drawn into the contest on a preferred basis, so the result of the lock-up was not to foster bidding, but to destroy it. The board's stated reasons for approving the transactions were: (1) better financing, (2) noteholder protection, and (3) higher price. As the Court of Chancery found, and we agree, any distinctions between the rival bidders' methods of financing the proposal were nominal at best, and such a consideration has little or no significance in a cash offer for any and all shares. The principal object, contrary to the board's duty of care, appears to have been protection of the noteholders over the shareholders' interests.

While Forstmann's $57.25 offer was objectively higher than Pantry Pride's $56.25 bid, the margin of superiority is less when the Forstmann price is adjusted for the time value of money. In reality, the Revlon board ended the auction in return for very little actual improvement in the final bid. The principal benefit went to the directors, who avoided personal liability to a class of creditors to whom the board owed no further duty under the circumstances. Thus, when a board ends an intense bidding contest on an insubstantial basis, and where a significant by-product of that action is to protect the directors against a perceived threat of personal liability for consequences stemming from the adoption of previous defensive measures, the action cannot withstand the enhanced scrutiny which *Unocal* requires of director conduct. See *Unocal*, 493 A.2d at 954–55.

In addition to the lock-up option, the Court of Chancery enjoined the no-shop provision as part of the attempt to foreclose further bidding by Pantry Pride. MacAndrews & Forbes Holdings, Inc. v. Revlon, Inc., 501 A.2d at 1251. The no-shop provision, like the lock-up option, while not *per se* illegal, is impermissible under the *Unocal* standards when a board's primary duty becomes that of an auctioneer responsible for selling the company to the highest bidder. The agreement to negotiate only with Forstmann ended rather than intensified the board's involvement in the bidding contest.

It is ironic that the parties even considered a no-shop agreement when Revlon had dealt preferentially, and almost exclusively, with Forstmann throughout the contest. After the directors authorized management to negotiate with other parties, Forstmann was given every negotiating advantage that Pantry Pride had been denied: cooperation from management, access to financial data, and the exclusive opportunity to present merger proposals directly to the board of directors. Favoritism for a white knight to the total exclusion of a hostile bidder might be justifiable when the latter's offer adversely affects shareholder interests, but when bidders make relatively similar offers, or dissolution of the company becomes inevitable, the directors cannot fulfill their enhanced *Unocal* duties by playing favorites with the contending factions. Market forces must be allowed to operate freely to bring the target's shareholders the best price available for their equity. Thus, as the trial court ruled, the shareholders' interests necessitated that the board remain free to negotiate in the fulfillment of that duty.

* * *

In conclusion, the Revlon board was confronted with a situation not uncommon in the current wave of corporate takeovers. A hostile and determined bidder sought the company at a price the board was convinced was inadequate. The initial defensive tactics worked to the benefit of the shareholders, and thus the board was able to sustain its *Unocal* burdens in justifying those measures. However, in granting an asset option lock-up to Forstmann, we must conclude that under all the circumstances the directors allowed considerations other than the maximization of shareholder profit to affect their judgment, and followed a course that ended the auction for Revlon, absent court intervention, to the ultimate detriment of its shareholders. No such defensive measure can be sustained when it represents a breach of the directors' fundamental duty of care. See Smith v. Van Gorkom, Del.Supr., 488 A.2d 858, 874 (1985). In that context the board's action is not entitled to the deference accorded it by the business judgment rule. The measures were properly enjoined. The decision of the Court of Chancery, therefore, is affirmed.

NOTE: MILLS v. MACMILLAN

Mills Acquisition Co. v. Macmillan, Inc., 559 A.2d 1261 (Del.1989), describes the duties of managers in the conduct of a *Revlon* auction.

Macmillan was the target of a takeover effort by the Robert M. Bass Group. The Bass overtures were resisted by Macmillan's management (led by Evans, the CEO, and Reilly, the chief operating officer) which proposed a restructuring of the enterprise under which management, particularly Evans and Reilly, would have an immensely larger equity than they had at the outset, would acquire it "on extremely favorable terms" at the expense of the public stockholders, and would end up in control of the enterprise. The board of Macmillan and a Special Committee of the board (composed of nominal outsiders who were "hand picked" by management) relied largely on management to select and deal with the Committee's legal (Wachtell, Lipton, Rosen & Katz) and financial advisors (Lazard Freres & Co.) and to constitute the board's principal source of information of the virtues and vices of the Bass Group and their proposal. Macmillan's financial advisors valued the proposed restructuring of the enterprise as producing the equivalent of $64.15 per share for Macmillan's public common stockholders; the Special Committee's financial advisors valued the enterprise at $72.57 per share on a pre-tax basis, possibly as high as $80.00 per share, but found the restructuring at $64.15 per share to be "fair". Wasserstein, Perella and Co. Inc., the special advisors to Macmillan's management, valued the enterprise at between $63.00 and $68.00 per share but possibly as high as $80.00 per share. All concurred in recommending to the board that the Bass offers (of $64.00 per shares at first and $73.00 per share later) were inadequate, and that the restructuring was preferable to either of the Bass offers. All of this came to naught, however, when the Delaware courts enjoined the Macmillan restructuring on the ground that the Bass offers were "clearly superior."

Evans and Reilly had two responses. First, they initiated discussions with Kohlberg, Kravis, Roberts & Co. (KKR) respecting a management-sponsored buyout of the company by KKR. Second, they authorized Macmillan's investment advisors to explore a possible sale of the entire company. This procedure eventually identified six potential bidders. But the search process was motivated by the objective of repelling third party suitors unacceptable to Evans and Reilly and transferring an enhanced equity position in a restructured Macmillan to Evans and his management group.

Then Robert Maxwell and firms he controlled intervened by proposing to Evans a consensual merger between Macmillan and Maxwell at an all-cash price of $80 per share. This was $5.00 higher than any other outstanding offer. Macmillan's managers delayed responding and intensified their discussions with KKR. Maxwell eventually made an $80 per share, all-cash tender offer for Macmillan, conditioned solely upon receiving the same nonpublic information which Macmillan already had given to KKR.

Macmillan's management, acting without any significant board supervision, conducted an "auction" between Maxwell and KKR in a manner that the court found significantly favored the latter and disfavored the former. Among the "tilts" which management was found to have injected into the auction process were a tipping of KKR about the content of Maxwell's bid so that KKR could offer a better bid, and later misleading Maxwell into believing that there was no need for him to respond to the opportunity held out to him to increase his bid because his bid was then the higher of the two pending bids. Management kept the Macmillan board in ignorance of events and relevant information, occasionally actually deceiving the board. In addition, the Delaware Supreme Court found the board itself was culpably negligent in its participation in the "auction" process, at least to the extent of making voidable the transaction with KKR which it approved. The board accepted the offer of KKR (consisting of cash and securities which had a "face value" of $90.05 per share) in preference to a Maxwell offer of $90.25 per share all cash, but conditioned on invalidation of lock up and no shop agreements that Macmillan had made with KKR in connection with KKR's submission.

The Delaware Supreme Court opined as follows:

"It is clear that on * * * the day that the Court of Chancery enjoined the management-induced reorganization, and with Bass' $73 offer outstanding, Macmillan's management met with KKR to discuss a management sponsored buyout. This was done without prior board approval. By early September, Macmillan's financial and legal advisors, originally chosen by Evans, independently constructed and managed the process by which bids for the company were solicited. Although the Macmillan board was fully aware of its ultimate responsibility for ensuring the integrity of the auction, the directors wholly delegated the creation and administration of the auction to an array of Evans' hand-picked investment advisors. It is undisputed that Wasserstein, who was originally retained as an investment advisor to Macmillan's senior management, was a principal, if not the primary, 'auctioneer' of the company. While it is unnecessary to hold that Wasserstein lacked independence, or was necessarily 'beholden' to management, it appears that Lazard Freres, allegedly the investment advisor to the independent directors, was a far more appropriate candidate to conduct this process on behalf of the board. Yet, both the board and Lazard acceded to Wasserstein's, and through him Evans', primacy.

"While a board of directors may rely in good faith upon 'information, opinions, reports or statements presented' by corporate officers, employees and experts 'selected with reasonable care,' 8 *Del.C.* § 141(e), it may not avoid its active and direct duty of oversight in a matter as significant as the sale of corporate control. That would seem particularly obvious where insiders are among the bidders. This failure of the Macmillan board significantly contributed to the resulting mismanagement of the bidding process. When presumably well-intentioned outside directors remove themselves from the design and execution of an auction, then what occurred here, given the human temptations left unchecked, was virtually inevitable.

"Clearly, this auction was clandestinely and impermissibly skewed in favor of KKR. * * *

* * *

" * * * [C]ontinuing hostility toward Maxwell cannot be justified after the Macmillan board actually decided * * * to abandon any further restructuring attempts, and to sell the entire company. Although Evans [earlier] had begun negotiations with KKR * * *, the board's action in September formally initiated the auction process. Further discriminatory treatment of a bidder, without any rational benefit to the shareholders, was unwarranted. The proper objective of Macmillan's fiduciaries was to obtain the highest price reasonably available for the company, provided it was offered by a reputable and responsible bidder. At this point, there was no justification for denying Maxwell the same courtesies and access to information as had been extended to KKR. Without board planning and oversight to insulate the self-interested management from improper access to the bidding process, and to ensure the proper conduct of the auction by truly independent advisors selected by, and answerable only to, the independent directors, the legal complications which a challenged transaction faces under *Revlon* are unnecessarily intensified. * * *

"In examining the actual conduct of this auction, there can be no justification for the telephonic 'tip' to KKR of Maxwell's $89 all-cash offer following the first round of bidding held on September 26th. * * *

* * *

"Similarly, the defendants argue that the subsequent Wasserstein 'long script'—in reality another form of tip—was an immaterial and 'appropriate response' to questions by KKR, providing no tactical information useful to KKR. As to this claim, the eventual auction results demonstrate that Wasserstein's tip relayed crucial information to KKR: the methods by which KKR should tailor its bid in order to satisfy Macmillan's financial advisors. * * *

"Given the materiality of these tips, and the silence of Evans, Reilly and Wasserstein in the face of their rigorous affirmative duty of disclosure at the September 27 board meeting, there can be no dispute but that such silence was misleading and deceptive. In short, it was a fraud upon the board. * * *

* * *

"In this case, a lockup agreement was not necessary to draw any of the bidders into the contest. Macmillan cannot seriously contend that they received a final bid from KKR that materially enhanced general stockholder interests. By all rational indications it was intended to have a directly opposite effect. As the record clearly shows, on numerous occasions Maxwell requested opportunities to further negotiate the price and structure of his proposal. When he learned of KKR's higher offer, he increased his bid to $90.25 per share. * * * Further, KKR's 'enhanced' bid, being nominal at best, was a *de minimis* justification for the lockup. When one compares what KKR received for the lockup, in contrast to its inconsiderable offer, the invalidity of the agreement becomes patent. * * *

"Here, the assets covered by the lockup agreement were some of Macmillan's most valued properties, its 'crown jewels.' Even if the lockup is permissible, when it involves 'crown jewel' assets careful board scrutiny attends the decision. When the intended effect is to end an active auction, at the very least the independent members of the board must attempt to negotiate alternative bids before granting such a significant concession. * * * Maxwell invited negotiations for a purchase of the same four divisions, which KKR originally sought to buy for $775 million. Maxwell was prepared to pay $900 million. Instead of serious negotiations with Maxwell, there were only concessions to KKR by giving it a lockup of seven divisions for $865 million.

"Thus, when directors in a *Revlon* bidding contest grant a crown jewel lockup, serious questions are raised, particularly where, as here, there is little or no improvement in the final bid. * * * "

NOTE: THE *REVLON* AUCTION

1. *The Trigger.*

When is the corporation deemed to be "for sale" so as to change the directors' role from that of defender of the corporate bastion to that of an auctioneer charged with getting the best price for the stockholders? The *Revlon* formula, as modified in *Macmillan,* contains significant ambiguous components.

Is the company "for sale," so that management must conduct an auction:

a.   If, and only if, management contemplates a bust-up and sale of all or most of its assets? See *Time,* infra.

b.   If, and only if, management has proposed a transaction that results in a new management or new controlling stockholder group?

c.   If management has begun negotiations for a friendly merger but no un-friendly bid has been made? If an unfriendly, competing bid is made thereafter? As management opens and conducts negotiations, does it make a difference that the consideration in the merger is common stock of the acquiring firm rather than cash?

d.   If a third party is sought for a friendly merger after an unsolicited bid has been made?

e.   If management proposes to effect a restructuring after a hostile bid has been made?

f.   If management seeks to effect a restructuring and then an unsolicited bid is made? Barkan v. Amsted Indus., Inc., 567 A.2d 1279 (Del.1989).

Should any proposed change of control result in the company being "for sale"? If so, is the relevant change of control a change of managerial control or a change of controlling stock ownership or both? Should it be the acquisition of an actual majority of the shares or only of enough shares to give effective control? *Time,* infra, suggests that a merging enterprise is not for sale even though the old managers remain effectively entrenched in operating control, because the resulting company's widely dispersed public stockholdings keep open the technical possibility of a takeover. Is this a persuasive suggestion?

2. *The Duty.*

If the corporation is found to be for sale, will management's behavior be constrained and assessed more rigorously than under *Unocal* proportionality? The answer to this question depends in part on the determination of the permissible objective of the auction process. Should the object be the highest immediate price for stockholders? Or should some other concept of value "enhancement" be admitted, such as long term imputed value? Must the objective be stockholder gain, or can some conception of maximum return for all stakeholders be admitted?

Whatever the objective of the auction, *Revlon* requires that management conduct it "fairly." But, of course, the operational meaning of fairness will vary in accord with the choice of objective. Possibly, uncertainty as to the object of the auction explains why the Delaware courts sometimes find the process to be "fair" only if the board does not procedurally favor any bidder, and at other times find "fairness" to be satisfied notwithstanding that the board thus favors the successful bidder (by way of lock-ups, no shops, special fees, or confidential information), who is often a management affiliate or sponsor.

(4) The Evolution of Unocal and Revlon

Paramount Communications, Inc. v. Time Inc.

Supreme Court of Delaware, 1989.
571 A.2d 1140.

■ Horsey, Justice:

Paramount Communications, Inc. ("Paramount") and two other groups of plaintiffs ("Shareholder Plaintiffs"), shareholders of Time Incorporated ("Time"), a Delaware corporation, separately filed suits in the Delaware Court of Chancery seeking a preliminary injunction to halt Time's tender offer for 51% of Warner Communication, Inc.'s ("Warner") outstanding shares at $70 cash per share. The court below consolidated the cases and, following the development of an extensive record, after discovery and an evidentiary hearing, denied plaintiffs' motion. In a 50–page unreported opinion and order entered July 14, 1989, the Chancellor refused to enjoin Time's consummation of its tender offer, concluding that the plaintiffs were unlikely to prevail on the merits. In re Time Incorporated Shareholder Litigation, Del.Ch., C.A. No. 10670, Allen, C., 1989 WL 79880 (July 14, 1989).

* * *

Applying our standard of review, we affirm the Chancellor's ultimate finding and conclusion under *Unocal*. We find that Paramount's tender offer was reasonably perceived by Time's board to pose a threat to Time and that the Time board's "response" to that threat was, under the circumstances, reasonable and proportionate. Applying *Unocal*, we reject the argument that the only corporate threat posed by an all-shares, all-cash tender offer is the possibility of inadequate value.

We also find that Time's board did not by entering into its initial merger agreement with Warner come under a *Revlon* duty either to auction the company or to maximize short-term shareholder value, notwithstanding the unequal share exchange. Therefore, the Time board's original plan of merger with Warner was subject only to a business judgment rule analysis. See Smith v. Van Gorkom, Del.Supr., 488 A.2d 858, 873–74 (1985).

I

Time is a Delaware corporation with its principal offices in New York City. Time's traditional business is publication of magazines and books; however, Time also provides pay television programming through its Home Box Office, Inc. and Cinemax subsidiaries. In addition, Time owns and operates cable television franchises through its subsidiary, American Television and Communication Corporation. During the relevant time period, Time's board consisted of sixteen directors. Twelve of the directors were "outside," nonemployee directors. Four of the directors were also officers of the company. * * *

As early as 1983 and 1984, Time's executive board began considering expanding Time's operations into the entertainment industry. In 1987, Time established a special committee of executives to consider and propose corporate strategies for the 1990s. The consensus of the committee was that Time should move ahead in the area of ownership and creation of video programming. This expansion, as the Chancellor noted, was predicated upon two considerations: first, Time's desire to have greater control, in terms of quality and price, over the film products delivered by way of its cable network and franchises; and second, Time's concern over the increasing globalization of the world economy. Some of Time's outside directors, especially Luce and Temple, had opposed this move as a threat to the editorial integrity and journalistic focus of Time.[3] Despite this concern, the board recognized that a vertically integrated video enterprise to complement Time's existing HBO and cable networks would better enable it to compete on a global basis.

[In 1987, presumably stimulated by the above considerations, representatives of Time entered into negotiations with representatives of Warner Brothers for a consolidation of the two enterprises. The negotiations were complicated and protracted.]

From the outset, Time's board favored an all-cash or cash and securities acquisition of Warner as the basis for consolidation. Bruce Wasserstein, Time's financial advisor, also favored an outright purchase of Warner. However, Steve Ross, Warner's CEO, was adamant that a business combination was only practicable on a stock-for-stock basis. Warner insisted on a stock swap in order to preserve its shareholders' equity in the resulting corporation. Time's officers, on the other hand, made it abundantly clear that Time would be the acquiring corporation and that Time would control

---

3. The primary concern of Time's outside directors was the preservation of the "Time Culture." They believed that Time had become recognized in this country as an institution built upon a foundation of journalistic integrity. Time's management made a studious effort to refrain from involvement in Time's editorial policy. Several of Time's outside directors feared that a merger with an entertainment company would divert Time's focus from news journalism and threaten the Time Culture.

the resulting board. Time refused to permit itself to be cast as the "acquired" company.

Eventually Time acquiesced in Warner's insistence on a stock-for-stock deal, but talks broke down over corporate governance issues. Time wanted Ross' position as a co-CEO to be temporary and wanted Ross to retire in five years. Ross, however, refused to set a time for his retirement and viewed Time's proposal as indicating a lack of confidence in his leadership. Warner considered it vital that their executives and creative staff not perceive Warner as selling out to Time. Time's request of a guarantee that Time would dominate the CEO succession was objected to as inconsistent with the concept of a Time–Warner merger "of equals." Negotiations ended when the parties reached an impasse. Time's board refused to compromise on its position on corporate governance. Time, and particularly its outside directors, viewed the corporate governance provisions as critical for preserving the "Time Culture" through a pro-Time management at the top. See supra note 4.

Throughout the fall of 1988 Time pursued its plan of expansion into the entertainment field; Time held informal discussions with several companies, including Paramount. Capital Cities/ABC approached Time to propose a merger. Talks terminated, however, when Capital Cities/ABC suggested that it was interested in purchasing Time or in controlling the resulting board. Time steadfastly maintained it was not placing itself up for sale.

Warner and Time resumed negotiations in January 1989. The catalyst for the resumption of talks was a private dinner between Steve Ross and Time outside director, Michael Dingman. Dingman was able to convince Ross that the transitional nature of the proposed co-CEO arrangement did not reflect a lack of confidence in Ross. Ross agreed that this course was best for the company and a meeting between Ross and Munro resulted. Ross agreed to retire in five years and let Nicholas succeed him. Negotiations resumed and many of the details of the original stock-for-stock exchange agreement remained intact. In addition, Time's senior management agreed to long-term contracts.

Time insider directors Levin and Nicholas met with Warner's financial advisors to decide upon a stock exchange ratio. Time's board had recognized the potential need to pay a premium in the stock ratio in exchange for dictating the governing arrangement of the new Time–Warner. Levin and outside director Finkelstein were the primary proponents of paying a premium to protect the "Time Culture." The board discussed premium rates of 10%, 15% and 20%. Wasserstein also suggested paying a premium for Warner due to Warner's rapid growth rate. The market exchange ratio of Time stock for Warner stock was .38 in favor of Warner. Warner's financial advisors informed its board that any exchange rate over .400 was a fair deal and any exchange rate over .450 was "one hell of a deal." The parties ultimately agreed upon an exchange rate favoring Warner of .465. On that basis, Warner stockholders would have owned approximately 62%[7] of the common stock of Time–Warner.

---

7. As was noted in the briefs and at oral argument, this figure is somewhat misleading because it does not take into consideration the number of individuals who owned stock in both companies.

On March 3, 1989, Time's board, with all but one director in attendance, met and unanimously approved the stock-for-stock merger with Warner. Warner's board likewise approved the merger. The agreement called for Warner to be merged into a wholly-owned Time subsidiary with Warner becoming the surviving corporation. The common stock of Warner would then be converted into common stock of Time at the agreed upon ratio. Thereafter, the name of Time would be changed to Time–Warner, Inc.

The rules of the New York Stock Exchange required that Time's issuance of shares to effectuate the merger be approved by a vote of Time's stockholders. The Delaware General Corporation Law required approval of the merger by a majority of the Warner stockholders. Delaware law did not require any vote by Time stockholders. The Chancellor concluded that the agreement was the product of "an arms-length negotiation between two parties seeking individual advantage through mutual action."

The resulting company would have a 24–member board, with 12 members representing each corporation. The company would have co-CEO's, at first Ross and Munro, then Ross and Nicholas, and finally, after Ross' retirement, by Nicholas alone. The board would create an editorial committee with a majority of members representing Time. A similar entertainment committee would be controlled by Warner board members. A two-thirds supermajority vote was required to alter CEO successions but an earlier proposal to have supermajority protection for the editorial committee was abandoned. Warner's board suggested raising the compensation levels for Time's senior management under the new corporation. Warner's management, as with most entertainment executives, received higher salaries than comparable executives in news journalism. Time's board, however, rejected Warner's proposal to equalize the salaries of the two management teams.

At its March 3, 1989 meeting, Time's board adopted several defensive tactics.* Time entered an automatic share exchange agreement with Warner. Time would receive 17,292,747 shares of Warner's outstanding common stock (9.4%) and Warner would receive 7,080,016 shares of Time's outstanding common stock (11.1%). Either party could trigger the exchange. Time sought out and paid for "confidence" letters from various banks with which it did business. In these letters, the banks promised not to finance any third-party attempt to acquire Time. Time argues these agreements served only to preserve the confidential relationship between itself and the banks. The Chancellor found these agreements to be inconsequential and futile attempts to "dry up" money for a hostile takeover. Time also agreed to a "no-shop" clause, preventing Time from considering any other consolidation proposal, thus relinquishing its power to consider other proposals, regardless of their merits. Time did so at Warner's

---

* [Court's footnote 5.] Time had in place a panoply of defensive devices, including a staggered board, a "poison pill" * * * triggered by an acquisition of 15% of the company, a fifty-day notice period for shareholder motions, and restrictions on shareholders' ability to call a meeting or act by consent.

insistence. Warner did not want to be left "on the auction block" for an unfriendly suitor, if Time were to withdraw from the deal.

Time's board simultaneously established a special committee of outside directors, Finkelstein, Kearns, and Opel, to oversee the merger. The committee's assignment was to resolve any impediments that might arise in the course of working out the details of the merger and its consummation.

Time representatives lauded the lack of debt to the United States Senate and to the President of the United States. Public reaction to the announcement of the merger was positive. Time–Warner would be a media colossus with international scope. The board scheduled the stockholder vote for June 23; and a May 1 record date was set. On May 24, 1989, Time sent out extensive proxy statements to the stockholders regarding the approval vote on the merger. In the meantime, with the merger proceeding without impediment, the special committee had concluded, shortly after its creation, that it was not necessary either to retain independent consultants, legal or financial, or even to meet. Time's board was unanimously in favor of the proposed merger with Warner; and, by the end of May, the Time–Warner merger appeared to be an accomplished fact.

On June 7, 1989, these wishful assumptions were shattered by Paramount's surprising announcement of its all-cash offer to purchase all outstanding shares of Time for $175 per share. The following day, June 8, the trading price of Time's stock rose from $126 to $170 per share. Paramount's offer was said to be "fully negotiable."[8]

Time found Paramount's "fully negotiable" offer to be in fact subject to at least three conditions. First, Time had to terminate its merger agreement and stock exchange agreement with Warner, and remove certain other of its defensive devices, including the redemption of Time's shareholder rights. Second, Paramount had to obtain the required cable franchise transfers from Time in a fashion acceptable to Paramount in its sole discretion. Finally, the offer depended upon a judicial determination that section 203 of the General Corporate Law of Delaware (The Delaware Anti–Takeover Statute) was inapplicable to any Time–Paramount merger. While Paramount's board had been privately advised that it could take months, perhaps over a year, to forge and consummate the deal, Paramount's board publicly proclaimed its ability to close the offer by July 5, 1989. Paramount executives later conceded that none of its directors believed that July 5th was a realistic date to close the transaction.

Over the following eight days, Time's board met three times to discuss Paramount's $175 offer. The board viewed Paramount's offer as inadequate and concluded that its proposed merger with Warner was the better course of action. Therefore, the board declined to open any negotiations with Paramount and held steady its course toward a merger with Warner.

---

8. Subsequently, it was established that Paramount's board had decided as early as March 1989 to move to acquire Time. However, Paramount management intentionally delayed publicizing its proposal until Time had mailed to its stockholders its Time–Warner merger proposal along with the required proxy statements.

[C]ertain Time directors expressed their concern that Time stockholders would not comprehend the long-term benefits of the Warner merger. Large quantities of Time shares were held by institutional investors. The board feared that even though there appeared to be wide support for the Warner transaction, Paramount's cash premium would be a tempting prospect to these investors. In mid-June, Time sought permission from the New York Stock Exchange to alter its rules and allow the Time–Warner merger to proceed without stockholder approval. Time did so at Warner's insistence. The New York Stock Exchange rejected Time's request on June 15; and on that day, the value of Time stock reached $182 per share.

The following day, June 16, Time's board met to take up Paramount's offer. The board's prevailing belief was that Paramount's bid posed a threat to Time's control of its own destiny and retention of the "Time Culture." The board determined to retain its same advisors even in light of the changed circumstances. The board rescinded its agreement to pay its advisors a bonus based on the consummation of the Time–Warner merger and agreed to pay a flat fee for any advice rendered. Finally, Time's board formally rejected Paramount's offer.[11]

At the same meeting, Time's board decided to recast its consolidation with Warner into an outright cash and securities acquisition of Warner by Time; and Time so informed Warner. Time accordingly restructured its proposal to acquire Warner as follows: Time would make an immediate all-cash offer for 51% of Warner's outstanding stock at $70 per share. The remaining 49% would be purchased at some later date for a mixture of cash and securities worth $70 per share. To provide the funds required for its outright acquisition of Warner, Time would assume 7–10 billion dollars worth of debt, thus eliminating one of the principal transaction-related benefits of the original merger agreement. Nine billion dollars of the total purchase price would be allocated to the purchase of Warner's goodwill.

Warner agreed but insisted on certain terms. Warner sought a control premium and guarantees that the governance provisions found in the original merger agreement would remain intact. Warner further sought agreements that Time would not employ its poison pill against Warner and that, unless enjoined, Time would be legally bound to complete the transaction. Time's board agreed to these last measures only at the insistence of Warner. For its part, Time was assured of its ability to extend its efforts into production areas and international markets, all the while maintaining the Time identity and culture. The Chancellor found the initial Time–Warner transaction to have been negotiated at arms length and the restructured Time–Warner transaction to have resulted from Paramount's offer and its expected effect on a Time shareholder vote.

On June 23, 1989, Paramount raised its all-cash offer to buy Time's outstanding stock to $200 per share. Paramount still professed that all aspects of the offer were negotiable. Time's board met on June 26, 1989

---

11. Meanwhile, Time had already begun erecting impediments to Paramount's offer. Time encouraged local cable franchises to sue Paramount to prevent it from easily obtaining the franchises.

and formally rejected Paramount's $200 per share second offer. The board reiterated its belief that, despite the $25 increase, the offer was still inadequate. The Time board maintained that the Warner transaction offered a greater long-term value for the stockholders and, unlike Paramount's offer, did not pose a threat to Time's survival and its "culture." Paramount then filed this action in the Court of Chancery.

II

The Shareholder Plaintiffs first assert a *Revlon* claim. They contend that the March 4 Time–Warner agreement effectively put Time up for sale, triggering *Revlon* duties, requiring Time's board to enhance short-term shareholder value and to treat all other interested acquirors on an equal basis. The Shareholder Plaintiffs base this argument on two facts: (I) the ultimate Time–Warner exchange ratio of .465 favoring Warner, resulting in Warner shareholders' receipt of 62% of the combined company; and (ii) the subjective intent of Time's directors as evidenced in their statements that the market might perceive the Time–Warner merger as putting Time up "for sale" and their adoption of various defensive measures.

The Shareholder Plaintiffs further contend that Time's directors, in structuring the original merger transaction to be "take-over-proof," triggered *Revlon* duties by foreclosing their shareholders from any prospect of obtaining a control premium. In short, plaintiffs argue that Time's board's decision to merge with Warner imposed a fiduciary duty to maximize immediate share value and not erect unreasonable barriers to further bids. Therefore, they argue, the Chancellor erred in finding: that Paramount's bid for Time did not place Time "for sale"; that Time's transaction with Warner did not result in any transfer of control; and that the combined Time–Warner was not so large as to preclude the possibility of the stockholders of Time–Warner receiving a future control premium.

Paramount asserts only a *Unocal* claim in which the shareholder plaintiffs join. Paramount contends that the Chancellor, in applying the first part of the *Unocal* test, erred in finding that Time's board had reasonable grounds to believe that Paramount posed both a legally cognizable threat to Time shareholders and a danger to Time's corporate policy and effectiveness. Paramount also contests the court's finding that Time's board made a reasonable and objective investigation of Paramount's offer so as to be informed before rejecting it. Paramount further claims that the court erred in applying *Unocal*'s second part in finding Time's response to be "reasonable." Paramount points primarily to the preclusive effect of the revised agreement which denied Time shareholders the opportunity both to vote on the agreement and to respond to Paramount's tender offer. Paramount argues that the underlying motivation of Time's board in adopting these defensive measures was management's desire to perpetuate itself in office.

The Court of Chancery posed the pivotal question presented by this case to be: Under what circumstances must a board of directors abandon an in-place plan of corporate development in order to provide its shareholders with the option to elect and realize an immediate control premium? As applied to this case, the question becomes: Did Time's board, having developed a strategic plan of global expansion to be launched through a business combination with Warner, come under a fiduciary duty to jettison its plan and put the corporation's future in the hands of its shareholders?

While we affirm the result reached by the Chancellor, we think it unwise to place undue emphasis upon long-term versus short-term corporate strategy. Two key predicates underpin our analysis. First, Delaware law imposes on a board of directors the duty to manage the business and affairs of the corporation. 8 Del.C. § 141(a). This broad mandate includes a conferred authority to set a corporate course of action, including time frame, designed to enhance corporate profitability. Thus, the question of "long-term" versus "short-term" values is largely irrelevant because directors, generally, are obliged to chart a course for a corporation which is in its best interests without regard to a fixed investment horizon. Second, absent a limited set of circumstances as defined under *Revlon*, a board of directors, while always required to act in an informed manner, is not under any *per se* duty to maximize shareholder value in the short term, even in the context of a takeover.[12] In our view, the pivotal question presented by this case is: "Did Time, by entering into the proposed merger with Warner, put itself up for sale?" A resolution of that issue through application of *Revlon* has a significant bearing upon the resolution of the derivative *Unocal* issue.

A.

We first take up plaintiffs' principal *Revlon* argument, summarized above. In rejecting this argument, the Chancellor found the original Time–Warner merger agreement not to constitute a "change of control" and concluded that the transaction did not trigger *Revlon* duties. The Chancellor's conclusion is premised on a finding that "[b]efore the merger agreement was signed, control of the corporation existed in a fluid aggregation of unaffiliated shareholders representing a voting majority—in other words, in the market." The Chancellor's findings of fact are supported by the record and his conclusion is correct as a matter of law. However, we premise our rejection of plaintiffs' *Revlon* claim on different grounds, namely, the absence of any substantial evidence to conclude that Time's board, in negotiating with Warner, made the dissolution or break-up of the corporate entity inevitable, as was the case in *Revlon*.

Under Delaware law there are, generally speaking and without excluding other possibilities, two circumstances which may implicate *Revlon* duties. The first, and clearer one, is when a corporation initiates an active bidding process seeking to sell itself or to effect a business reorganization involving a clear break-up of the company. See, e.g., Mills Acquisition Co. v. Macmillan, Inc., Del.Supr., 559 A.2d 1261 (1988). However, *Revlon* duties may also be triggered where, in response to a bidder's offer, a target

---

12. Thus, we endorse the Chancellor's conclusion that it is not a breach of faith for directors to determine that the present stock market price of shares is not representative of true value or that there may indeed be several market values for any corporation's stock. We have so held in another context. See *Van Gorkom*, 488 A.2d at 876.

abandons its long-term strategy and seeks an alternative transaction involving the breakup of the company. Thus, in *Revlon,* when the board responded to Pantry Pride's offer by contemplating a "bust-up" sale of assets in a leveraged acquisition, we imposed upon the board a duty to maximize immediate shareholder value and an obligation to auction the company fairly. If, however, the board's reaction to a hostile tender offer is found to constitute only a defensive response and not an abandonment of the corporation's continued existence, *Revlon* duties are not triggered, though *Unocal* duties attach.[14] See, e.g., Ivanhoe Partners v. Newmont Mining Corp., Del.Supr., 535 A.2d 1334, 1345 (1987).

The plaintiffs insist that even though the original Time–Warner agreement may not have worked "an objective change of control," the transaction made a "sale" of Time inevitable. Plaintiffs rely on the subjective intent of Time's board of directors and principally upon certain board members' expressions of concern that the Warner transaction *might* be viewed as effectively putting Time up for sale. Plaintiffs argue that the use of a lock-up agreement, a no-shop clause, and so-called "dry-up" agreements prevented shareholders from obtaining a control premium in the immediate future and thus violated *Revlon.*

We agree with the Chancellor that such evidence is entirely insufficient to invoke *Revlon* duties; and we decline to extend *Revlon*'s application to corporate transactions simply because they might be construed as putting a corporation either "in play" or "up for sale." See Citron v. Fairchild Camera, Del.Supr., 569 A.2d 53, (1989); *Macmillan,* 559 A.2d at 1285 n. 35. The adoption of structural safety devices alone does not trigger *Revlon.*[15] Rather, as the Chancellor stated, such devices are properly subject to a *Unocal* analysis.

Finally, we do not find in Time's recasting of its merger agreement with Warner from a share exchange to a share purchase a basis to conclude that Time had either abandoned its strategic plan or made a sale of Time inevitable. The Chancellor found that although the merged Time–Warner company would be large (with a value approaching approximately $30

---

14. Within the auction process, any action taken by the board must be reasonably related to the threat posed or reasonable in relation to the advantage sought, see Mills Acquisition Co. v. Macmillan, Inc., Del.Supr., 559 A.2d 1261, 1288 (1988). Thus, a *Unocal* analysis may be appropriate when a corporation is in a *Revlon* situation and *Revlon* duties may be triggered by a defensive action taken in response to a hostile offer. Since *Revlon,* we have stated that differing treatment of various bidders is not actionable when such action reasonably relates to achieving the best price available for the stockholders. *Macmillan,* 559 A.2d at 1286–87.

15. Although the legality of the various safety devices adopted to protect the original

agreement is not a central issue, there is substantial evidence to support each of the trial court's related conclusions. Thus, the court found that the concept of the Share Exchange Agreement predated any takeover threat by Paramount and had been adopted for a rational business purpose: to deter Time and Warner from being "put in play" by their March 4 Agreement. The court further found that Time had adopted the "no-shop" clause at Warner's insistence and for Warner's protection. Finally, although certain aspects of the "dry-up" agreements were suspect on their face, we concur in the Chancellor's view that in this case they were inconsequential.

billion), recent takeover cases have proven that acquisition of the combined company might nonetheless be possible. In re Time Incorporated Shareholder Litigation, Del.Ch., C.A. No. 10670, Allen, C. (July 14, 1989), slip op. at 56. The legal consequence is that *Unocal* alone applies to determine whether the business judgment rule attaches to the revised agreement. Plaintiffs' analogy to *Macmillan* thus collapses and plaintiffs' reliance on *Macmillan* is misplaced.

B.

We turn now to plaintiffs' *Unocal* claim. We begin by noting, as did the Chancellor, that our decision does not require us to pass on the wisdom of the board's decision to enter into the original Time–Warner agreement. That is not a court's task. Our task is simply to review the record to determine whether there is sufficient evidence to support the Chancellor's conclusion that the initial Time–Warner agreement was the product of a proper exercise of business judgment. *Macmillan,* 559 A.2d at 1288.

* * * Time's decision in 1988 to combine with Warner was made only after what could be fairly characterized as an exhaustive appraisal of Time's future as a corporation. After concluding in 1983–84 that the corporation must expand to survive, and beyond journalism into entertainment, the board combed the field of available entertainment companies. By 1987 Time had focused upon Warner; by late July 1988 Time's board was convinced that Warner would provide the best "fit" for Time to achieve its strategic objectives. The record attests to the zealousness of Time's executives, fully supported by their directors, in seeing to the preservation of Time's "culture," i.e., its perceived editorial integrity in journalism. We find ample evidence in the record to support the Chancellor's conclusion that the Time board's decision to expand the business of the company through its March 3 merger with Warner was entitled to the protection of the business judgment rule. See Aronson v. Lewis, Del.Supr., 473 A.2d 805, 812 (1984).

The Chancellor reached a different conclusion in addressing the Time–Warner transaction as revised three months later. He found that the revised agreement was defense-motivated and designed to avoid the potentially disruptive effect that Paramount's offer would have had on consummation of the proposed merger were it put to a shareholder vote. Thus, the court declined to apply the traditional business judgment rule to the revised transaction and instead analyzed the Time board's June 16 decision under *Unocal*. The court ruled that *Unocal* applied to all director actions taken, following receipt of Paramount's hostile tender offer, that were reasonably determined to be defensive. Clearly that was a correct ruling and no party disputes that ruling.

In *Unocal*, we held that before the business judgment rule is applied to a board's adoption of a defensive measure, the burden will lie with the board to prove (a) reasonable grounds for believing that a danger to corporate policy and effectiveness existed; and (b) that the defensive measure adopted was reasonable in relation to the threat posed. *Unocal,* 493 A.2d 946. Directors satisfy the first part of the *Unocal* test by demonstrating good faith and reasonable investigation. We have repeatedly stated that the refusal to entertain an offer may comport with a valid exercise of a board's business judgment. See, e.g., *Macmillan,* 559 A.2d at 1285 n. 35; *Van Gorkom,* 488 A.2d at 881; Pogostin v. Rice, Del.Supr., 480 A.2d 619, 627 (1984).

Unocal involved a two-tier, highly coercive tender offer. In such a case, the threat is obvious: shareholders may be compelled to tender to avoid being treated adversely in the second stage of the transaction. Accord *Ivanhoe,* 535 at 1344. In subsequent cases, the Court of Chancery has suggested that an all-cash, all-shares offer, falling within a range of values that a shareholder might reasonably prefer, cannot constitute a legally recognized "threat" to shareholder interests sufficient to withstand a *Unocal* analysis. AC Acquisitions Corp. v. Anderson, Clayton & Co., Del. Ch., 519 A.2d 103 (1986); see Grand Metropolitan, PLC v. Pillsbury Co., Del.Ch., 558 A.2d 1049 (1988); City Capital Associates v. Interco, Inc., Del.Ch., 551 A.2d 787 (1988). In those cases, the Court of Chancery determined that whatever threat existed related only to the shareholders and only to price and not to the corporation.

From those decisions by our Court of Chancery, Paramount and the individual plaintiffs extrapolate a rule of law that an all-cash, all-shares offer with values reasonably in the range of acceptable price cannot pose any objective threat to a corporation or its shareholders. Thus, Paramount would have us hold that only if the value of Paramount's offer were determined to be clearly inferior to the value created by management's plan to merge with Warner could the offer be viewed—objectively—as a threat.

Implicit in the plaintiffs' argument is the view that a hostile tender offer can pose only two types of threats: the threat of coercion that results from a two-tier offer promising unequal treatment for nontendering shareholders; and the threat of inadequate value from an all-shares, all-cash offer at a price below what a target board in good faith deems to be the present value of its shares. See, e.g., *Interco,* 551 A.2d at 797; see also BNS, Inc. v. Koppers, D.Del., 683 F.Supp. 458 (1988). Since Paramount's offer was all-cash, the only conceivable "threat," plaintiffs argue, was inadequate value.[17] We disapprove of such a narrow and rigid construction of *Unocal,* for the reasons which follow.

---

17. Some commentators have suggested that the threats posed by hostile offers be categorized into not two but three types: "(i) *opportunity loss* * * * [where] a hostile offer might deprive target shareholders of the opportunity to select a superior alternative offered by target management [or, we would add, offered by another bidder]; (ii) *structural coercion,* * * * the risk that disparate treatment of non-tendering shareholders might distort shareholders' tender decisions; and * * * (iii) *substantive coercion,* * * * the risk that shareholders will mistakenly accept an underpriced offer because they disbelieve management's representations of intrinsic value." The recognition of substantive coercion, the authors suggest, would help guarantee that the *Unocal* standard becomes an effective intermediate standard of review. Gilson & Kraakman, Delaware's Intermediate Standard for Defensive Tactics: Is There Substance to Proportionality Review?, 44 The Business Lawyer, 247, 267 (1989).

Plaintiffs' position represents a fundamental misconception of our standard of review under *Unocal* principally because it would involve the court in substituting its judgment as to what is a "better" deal for that of a corporation's board of directors. To the extent that the Court of Chancery has recently done so in certain of its opinions, we hereby reject such approach as not in keeping with a proper *Unocal* analysis. See, e.g., *Interco,* 551 A.2d 787, and its progeny; but see TW Services, Inc. v. SWT Acquisition Corp., Del.Ch., C.A. No. 1047, Allen, C., 1989 WL 20290 (March 2, 1989).

The usefulness of *Unocal* as an analytical tool is precisely its flexibility in the face of a variety of fact scenarios. *Unocal* is not intended as an abstract standard; neither is it a structured and mechanistic procedure of appraisal. Thus, we have said that directors may consider, when evaluating the threat posed by a takeover bid, the "inadequacy of the price offered, nature and timing of the offer, questions of illegality, the impact on 'constituencies' other than shareholders * * * the risk of nonconsummation, and the quality of securities being offered in the exchange." 493 A.2d at 955. The open-ended analysis mandated by *Unocal* is not intended to lead to a simple mathematical exercise: that is, of comparing the discounted value of Time–Warner's expected trading price at some future date with Paramount's offer and determining which is the higher. Indeed, in our view, precepts underlying the business judgment rule militate against a court's engaging in the process of attempting to appraise and evaluate the relative merits of a long-term versus a short-term investment goal for shareholders. To engage in such an exercise is a distortion of the *Unocal* process and, in particular, the application of the second part of *Unocal's* test, discussed below.

In this case, the Time board reasonably determined that inadequate value was not the only legally cognizable threat that Paramount's all-cash, all-shares offer could present. Time's board concluded that Paramount's eleventh hour offer posed other threats. One concern was that Time shareholders might elect to tender into Paramount's cash offer in ignorance or a mistaken belief of the strategic benefit which a business combination with Warner might produce. Moreover, Time viewed the conditions attached to Paramount's offer as introducing a degree of uncertainty that skewed a comparative analysis. Further, the timing of Paramount's offer to follow issuance of Time's proxy notice was viewed as arguably designed to upset, if not confuse, the Time stockholders' vote. Given this record evidence, we cannot conclude that the Time board's decision of June 6 that Paramount's offer posed a threat to corporate policy and effectiveness was lacking in good faith or dominated by motives of either entrenchment or self-interest.

Paramount also contends that the Time board had not duly investigated Paramount's offer. Therefore, Paramount argues, Time was unable to make an informed decision that the offer posed a threat to Time's corporate policy. Although the Chancellor did not address this issue directly, his findings of fact do detail Time's exploration of the available entertainment companies, including Paramount, before determining that Warner provided the best strategic "fit." In addition, the court found that Time's board rejected Paramount's offer because Paramount did not serve Time's objectives or meet Time's needs. Thus, the record does, in our judgment, demonstrate that Time's board was adequately informed of the potential benefits of a transaction with Paramount. We agree with the Chancellor that the Time board's lengthy pre-June investigation of potential merger candidates, including Paramount, mooted any obligation on Time's part to halt its merger process with Warner to reconsider Paramount. Time's board was under no obligation to negotiate with Paramount. *Unocal,* 493 A.2d at 954–55; see also *Macmillan,* 559 A.2d at 1285 n. 35. Time's failure to negotiate cannot be fairly found to have been uninformed. The evidence supporting this finding is materially enhanced by the fact that twelve of Time's sixteen board members were outside independent directors. *Unocal,* 493 A.2d at 955; Moran v. Household Intern., Inc., Del.Supr., 500 A.2d 1346, 1356 (1985).

We turn to the second part of the *Unocal* analysis. The obvious requisite to determining the reasonableness of a defensive action is a clear identification of the nature of the threat. As the Chancellor correctly noted, this "requires an evaluation of the importance of the corporate objective threatened; alternative methods of protecting that objective; impacts of the 'defensive' action, and other relevant factors." In Re: Time Incorporated Shareholder Litigation, Del.Ch., 1989 WL 79880 (July 14, 1989). It is not until both parts of the *Unocal* inquiry have been satisfied that the business judgment rule attaches to defensive actions of a board of directors. *Unocal,* 493 A.2d at 954.[18] As applied to the facts of this case, the question is whether the record evidence supports the Court of Chancery's conclusion that the restructuring of the Time–Warner transaction, including the adoption of several preclusive defensive measures, was a *reasonable response* in relation to a perceived threat.

Paramount argues that, assuming its tender offer posed a threat, Time's response was unreasonable in precluding Time's shareholders from accepting the tender offer or receiving a control premium in the immediately foreseeable future. Once again, the contention stems, we believe, from a fundamental misunderstanding of where the power of corporate governance lies. Delaware law confers the management of the corporate enterprise to the stockholders' duly elected board representatives. 8 Del.C. § 141(a). The fiduciary duty to manage a corporate enterprise includes the selection of a time frame for achievement of corporate goals. That duty may not be delegated to the stockholders. *Van Gorkom,* 488 A.2d at 873. Directors are not obliged to abandon a deliberately conceived corporate plan for a short-term shareholder profit unless there is clearly no basis to sustain the corporate strategy. See, e.g., *Revlon,* 506 A.2d 173.

---

18. Some commentators have criticized *Unocal* by arguing that once the board's deliberative process has been analyzed and found not to be wanting in objectivity, good faith or deliberateness, the so-called "enhanced" business judgment rule has been satisfied and no further inquiry is undertaken. See generally Johnson & Siegel, Corporate Mergers: Redefining the Role of Target Directors, 136 U.Pa.L.Rev. 315 (1987). We reject such views.

Although the Chancellor blurred somewhat the discrete analyses required under *Unocal*, he did conclude that Time's board reasonably perceived Paramount's offer to be a significant threat to the planned Time–Warner merger and that Time's response was not "overly broad." We have found that even in light of a valid threat, management actions that are coercive in nature or force upon shareholders a management-sponsored alternative to a hostile offer may be struck down as unreasonable and non-proportionate responses. *Macmillan*, 559 A.2d 1261; *AC Acquisitions Corp.*, 519 A.2d 103.

Here, on the record facts, the Chancellor found that Time's responsive action to Paramount's tender offer was not aimed at "cramming down" on its shareholders a management-sponsored alternative, but rather had as its goal the carrying forward of a pre-existing transaction in an altered form.[19] Thus, the response was reasonably related to the threat. The Chancellor noted that the revised agreement and its accompanying safety devices did not preclude Paramount from making an offer for the combined Time–Warner company or from changing the conditions of its offer so as not to make the offer dependent upon the nullification of the Time–Warner agreement. Thus, the response was proportionate. We affirm the Chancellor's rulings as clearly supported by the record. Finally, we note that although Time was required, as a result of Paramount's hostile offer, to incur a heavy debt to finance its acquisition of Warner, that fact alone does not render the board's decision unreasonable so long as the directors could reasonably perceive the debt load not to be so injurious to the corporation as to jeopardize its well being.

C.

Conclusion

Applying the test for grant or denial of preliminary injunctive relief, we find plaintiffs failed to establish a reasonable likelihood of ultimate success on the merits. Therefore, we affirm.

Paramount Communications Inc. v. QVC Network Inc.

Supreme Court of Delaware, 1994.
637 A.2d 34.

■ Before VEASEY, C.J., and MOORE and HOLLAND, JJ.

■ VEASEY, C.J.:

In this appeal we review an order of the Court of Chancery dated November 24, 1993 (the "November 24 Order"), preliminarily enjoining

---

19. The Chancellor cited Shamrock Holdings, Inc. v. Polaroid Corp., Del.Ch., 559 A.2d 257 (1989), as a closely analogous case. In that case, the Court of Chancery upheld, in the face of a takeover bid, the establishment of an employee stock ownership plan that had a significant anti-takeover effect.

The Court of Chancery upheld the board's action largely because the ESOP had been adopted *prior* to any contest for control and was reasonably determined to increase productivity and enhance profits. The ESOP did not appear to be primarily a device to affect or secure corporate control.

certain defensive measures designed to facilitate a so-called strategic alliance between Viacom Inc. ("Viacom") and Paramount Communications Inc. ("Paramount") approved by the board of directors of Paramount (the "Paramount Board" or the "Paramount directors") and to thwart an unsolicited, more valuable, tender offer by QVC Network Inc. ("QVC"). * * *

* * * This action arises out of a proposed acquisition of Paramount by Viacom through a tender offer followed by a second-step merger (the "Paramount–Viacom transaction"), and a competing unsolicited tender offer by QVC. The Court of Chancery granted a preliminary injunction. * * *

The Court of Chancery found that the Paramount directors violated their fiduciary duties by favoring the Paramount–Viacom transaction over the more valuable unsolicited offer of QVC. The Court of Chancery preliminarily enjoined Paramount and the individual defendants (the "Paramount defendants") from amending or modifying Paramount's stockholder rights agreement (the "Rights Agreement"), including the redemption of the Rights, or taking other action to facilitate the consummation of the pending tender offer by Viacom or any proposed second-step merger, including the Merger Agreement between Paramount and Viacom dated September 12, 1993 (the "Original Merger Agreement"), as amended on October 24, 1993 (the "Amended Merger Agreement"). Viacom and the Paramount defendants were enjoined from taking any action to exercise any provision of the Stock Option Agreement between Paramount and Viacom dated September 12, 1993 (the "Stock Option Agreement"), as amended on October 24, 1993. The Court of Chancery did not grant preliminary injunctive relief as to the termination fee provided for the benefit of Viacom in Section 8.05 of the Original Merger Agreement and the Amended Merger Agreement (the "Termination Fee").

Under the circumstances of this case, the pending sale of control implicated in the Paramount–Viacom transaction required the Paramount Board to act on an informed basis to secure the best value reasonably available to the stockholders. Since we agree with the Court of Chancery that the Paramount directors violated their fiduciary duties, we have AFFIRMED the entry of the order of the Vice Chancellor granting the preliminary injunction and have REMANDED these proceedings to the Court of Chancery for proceedings consistent herewith.

* * *

I. FACTS

* * * Paramount is a Delaware corporation with its principal offices in New York City. Approximately 118 million shares of Paramount's common stock are outstanding and traded on the New York Stock Exchange. The majority of Paramount's stock is publicly held by numerous unaffiliated investors. Paramount owns and operates a diverse group of entertainment businesses, including motion picture and television studios, book publishers, professional sports teams, and amusement parks.

There are 15 persons serving on the Paramount Board. Four directors are officer-employees of Paramount: Martin S. Davis ("Davis"), Paramount's Chairman and Chief Executive Officer since 1983; Donald Oresman ("Oresman"), Executive Vice–President, Chief Administrative Officer, and General Counsel; Stanley R. Jaffe, President and Chief Operating Officer; and Ronald L. Nelson, Executive Vice President and Chief Financial Officer. Paramount's 11 outside directors are distinguished and experienced business persons who are present or former senior executives of public corporations or financial institutions.

Viacom is a Delaware corporation with its headquarters in Massachusetts. Viacom is controlled by Sumner M. Redstone ("Redstone"), its Chairman and Chief Executive Officer, who owns indirectly approximately 85.2 percent of Viacom's voting Class A stock and approximately 69.2 percent of Viacom's nonvoting Class B stock through National Amusements, Inc. ("NAI"), an entity 91.7 percent owned by Redstone. Viacom has a wide range of entertainment operations, including a number of well-known cable television channels such as MTV, Nickelodeon, Showtime, and The Movie Channel. Viacom's equity co-investors in the Paramount–Viacom transaction include NYNEX Corporation and Blockbuster Entertainment Corporation.

QVC is a Delaware corporation with its headquarters in West Chester, Pennsylvania. QVC has several large stockholders, including Liberty Media Corporation, Comcast Corporation, Advance Publications, Inc., and Cox Enterprises Inc. Barry Diller ("Diller"), the Chairman and Chief Executive Officer of QVC, is also a substantial stockholder. QVC sells a variety of merchandise through a televised shopping channel. QVC has several equity co-investors in its proposed combination with Paramount including Bell-South Corporation and Comcast Corporation.

Beginning in the late 1980s, Paramount investigated the possibility of acquiring or merging with other companies in the entertainment, media, or communications industry. Paramount considered such transactions to be desirable, and perhaps necessary, in order to keep pace with competitors in the rapidly evolving field of entertainment and communications. Consistent with its goal of strategic expansion, Paramount made a tender offer for Time Inc. in 1989, but was ultimately unsuccessful. See Paramount Communications, Inc. v. Time Inc., Del.Supr., 571 A.2d 1140 (1990) ("Time–Warner ").

Although Paramount had considered a possible combination of Paramount and Viacom as early as 1990, recent efforts to explore such a transaction began at a dinner meeting between Redstone and Davis on April 20, 1993. Robert Greenhill ("Greenhill"), Chairman of Smith Barney Shearson Inc. ("Smith Barney"), attended and helped facilitate this meeting. After several more meetings between Redstone and Davis, serious negotiations began taking place in early July.

It was tentatively agreed that Davis would be the chief executive officer and Redstone would be the controlling stockholder of the combined company, but the parties could not reach agreement on the merger price and the terms of a stock option to be granted to Viacom. With respect to price,

Viacom offered a package of cash and stock (primarily Viacom Class B nonvoting stock) with a market value of approximately $61 per share, but Paramount wanted at least $70 per share.

Shortly after negotiations broke down in July 1993, two notable events occurred. First, Davis apparently learned of QVC's potential interest in Paramount, and told Diller over lunch on July 21, 1993, that Paramount was not for sale. Second, the market value of Viacom's Class B nonvoting stock increased from $46.875 on July 6 to $57.25 on August 20. QVC claims (and Viacom disputes) that this price increase was caused by open market purchases of such stock by Redstone or entities controlled by him.

On August 20, 1993, discussions between Paramount and Viacom resumed when Greenhill arranged another meeting between Davis and Redstone. After a short hiatus, the parties negotiated in earnest in early September, and performed due diligence with the assistance of their financial advisors, Lazard Freres & Co. ("Lazard") for Paramount and Smith Barney for Viacom. On September 9, 1993, the Paramount Board was informed about the status of the negotiations and was provided information by Lazard, including an analysis of the proposed transaction.

On September 12, 1993, the Paramount Board met again and unanimously approved the Original Merger Agreement whereby Paramount would merge with and into Viacom. The terms of the merger provided that each share of Paramount common stock would be converted into 0.10 shares of Viacom Class A voting stock, 0.90 shares of Viacom Class–B nonvoting stock, and $9.10 in cash. In addition, the Paramount Board agreed to amend its "poison pill" Rights Agreement to exempt the proposed merger with Viacom. The Original Merger Agreement also contained several provisions designed to make it more difficult for a potential competing bid to succeed. We focus, as did the Court of Chancery, on three of these defensive provisions: a "no-shop" provision (the "No–Shop Provision"), the Termination Fee, and the Stock Option Agreement.

First, under the No–Shop Provision, the Paramount Board agreed that Paramount would not solicit, encourage, discuss, negotiate, or endorse any competing transaction unless: (a) a third party "makes an unsolicited written, bona fide proposal, which is not subject to any material contingencies relating to financing"; and (b) the Paramount Board determines that discussions or negotiations with the third party are necessary for the Paramount Board to comply with its fiduciary duties.

Second, under the Termination Fee provision, Viacom would receive a $100 million termination fee if: (a) Paramount terminated the Original Merger Agreement because of a competing transaction; (b) Paramount's stockholders did not approve the merger; or (c) the Paramount Board recommended a competing transaction.

The third and most significant deterrent device was the Stock Option Agreement, which granted to Viacom an option to purchase approximately 19.9 percent (23,699.000 shares) of Paramount's outstanding common stock at $69.14 per share if any of the triggering events for the Termination Fee occurred. In addition to the customary terms that are normally associated with a stock option, the Stock Option Agreement contained two provisions that were both unusual and highly beneficial to Viacom: (a) Viacom was permitted to pay for the shares with a senior subordinated note of questionable marketability instead of cash, thereby avoiding the need to raise the $1.6 billion purchase price (the "Note Feature"); and (b) Viacom could elect to require Paramount to pay Viacom in cash a sum equal to the difference between the purchase price and the market price of Paramount's stock (the "Put Feature"). Because the Stock Option Agreement was not "capped" to limit its maximum dollar value, it had the potential to reach (and in this case did reach) unreasonable levels.

After the execution of the Original Merger Agreement and the Stock Option Agreement on September 12, 1993, Paramount and Viacom announced their proposed merger. In a number of public statements, the parties indicated that the pending transaction was a virtual certainty. Redstone described it as a "marriage" that would "never be torn asunder" and stated that only a "nuclear attack" could break the deal. Redstone also called Diller and John Malone of Tele–Communications Inc., a major stockholder of QVC, to dissuade them from making a competing bid.

Despite these attempts to discourage a competing bid, Diller sent a letter to Davis on September 20, 1993, proposing a merger in which QVC would acquire Paramount for approximately $80 per share, consisting of 0.893 shares of QVC common stock and $30 in cash. QVC also expressed its eagerness to meet with Paramount to negotiate the details of a transaction. When the Paramount Board met on September 27, it was advised by Davis that the Original Merger Agreement prohibited Paramount from having discussions with QVC (or anyone else) unless certain conditions were satisfied. In particular, QVC had to supply evidence that its proposal was not subject to financing contingencies. The Paramount Board was also provided information from Lazard describing QVC and its proposal.

On October 5, 1993, QVC provided Paramount with evidence of QVC's financing. The Paramount Board then held another meeting on October 11, and decided to authorize management to meet-with QVC. Davis also informed the Paramount Board that Booz–Allen & Hamilton ("Booz–Allen"), a management consulting firm, had been retained to assess, *inter alia*, the incremental earnings potential from a Paramount–Viacom merger and a Paramount–QVC merger. Discussions proceeded slowly, however, due to a delay in Paramount signing a confidentiality agreement. In response to Paramount's request for information, QVC provided two binders of documents to Paramount on October 20.

On October 21, 1993, QVC filed this action and publicly announced an $80 cash tender offer for 51 percent of Paramount's outstanding shares (the "QVC tender offer"). Each remaining share of Paramount common stock would be converted into 1.42857 shares of QVC common stock in a second-step merger. The tender offer was conditioned on, among other things, the invalidation of the Stock Option Agreement, which was worth over $200 million by that point.[5] QVC contends that it had to commence a

---

5. By November 15, 1993, the value of the Stock Option Agreement had increased to nearly $500 million based on the $90 QVC bid. * * *

tender offer because of the slow pace of the merger discussions and the need to begin seeking clearance under federal antitrust laws.

Confronted by QVC's hostile bid, which on its face offered over $10 per share more than the consideration provided by the Original Merger Agreement, Viacom realized that it would need to raise its bid in order to remain competitive. Within hours after QVC's tender offer was announced, Viacom entered into discussions with Paramount concerning a revised transaction. These discussions led to serious negotiations concerning a comprehensive amendment to the original Paramount–Viacom transaction. In effect, the opportunity for a "new deal" with Viacom was at hand for the Paramount Board. With the QVC hostile bid offering greater value to the Paramount stockholders, the Paramount Board had considerable leverage with Viacom.

At a special meeting on October 24, 1993, the Paramount Board approved the Amended Merger Agreement and an amendment to the Stock Option Agreement. The Amended Merger Agreement was, however, essentially the same as the Original Merger Agreement, except that it included a few new provisions. One provision related to an $80 per share cash tender offer by Viacom for 51 percent of Paramount's stock, and another changed the merger consideration so that each share of Paramount would be converted into 0.20408 shares of Viacom Class A voting stock, 1.08317 shares of Viacom Class B nonvoting stock, and 0.20408 shares of a new series of Viacom convertible preferred stock. The Amended Merger Agreement also added a provision giving Paramount the right not to amend its Rights Agreement to exempt Viacom if the Paramount Board determined that such an amendment would be inconsistent with its fiduciary duties because another offer constituted a "better alternative." Finally, the Paramount Board was given the power to terminate the Amended Merger Agreement if it withdrew its recommendation of the Viacom transaction or recommended a competing transaction.

Although the Amended Merger Agreement offered more consideration to the Paramount stockholders and somewhat more flexibility to the Paramount Board than did the Original Merger Agreement, the defensive measures designed to make a competing bid more difficult were not removed or modified. In particular, there is no evidence in the record that Paramount sought to use its newly-acquired leverage to eliminate or modify the No–Shop Provision, the Termination Fee, or the Stock Option Agreement when the subject of amending the Original Merger Agreement was on the table.

Viacom's tender offer commenced on October 25, 1993, and QVC's tender offer was formally launched on October 27, 1993. Diller sent a letter to the Paramount Board on October 28 requesting an opportunity to negotiate with Paramount, and Oresman responded the following day by agreeing to meet. The meeting, held on November 1, was not very fruitful, however, after QVC's proposed guidelines for a "fair bidding process" were rejected by Paramount on the ground that "auction procedures" were inappropriate and contrary to Paramount's contractual obligations to Viacom.

On November 6, 1993, Viacom unilaterally raised its tender offer price to $85 per share in cash and offered a comparable increase in the value of the securities being proposed in the second-step merger. At a telephonic meeting held later that day, the Paramount Board agreed to recommend Viacom's higher bid to Paramount's stockholders.

QVC responded to Viacom's higher bid on November 12 by increasing its tender offer to $90 per share and by increasing the securities for its second-step merger by a similar amount. In response to QVC's latest offer, the Paramount Board scheduled a meeting for November 15, 1993. Prior to the meeting, Oresman sent the members of the Paramount Board a document summarizing the "conditions and uncertainties" of QVC's offer. One director testified that this document gave him a very negative impression of the QVC bid.

At its meeting on November 15, 1993, the Paramount Board determined that the new QVC offer was not in the best interests of the stockholders. The purported basis for this conclusion was that QVC's bid was excessively conditional. The Paramount Board did not communicate with QVC regarding the status of the conditions because it believed that the No–Shop Provision prevented such communication in the absence of firm financing. Several Paramount directors also testified that they believed the Viacom transaction would be more advantageous to Paramount's future business prospects than a QVC transaction.[7] Although a number of materials were distributed to the Paramount Board describing the Viacom and QVC transactions, the only quantitative analysis of the consideration to be received by the stockholders under each proposal was based on then-current market prices of the securities involved, not on the anticipated value of such securities at the time when the stockholders would receive them.[8]

* * * On November 19, Diller wrote to the Paramount Board to inform it that QVC had obtained financing commitments for its tender offer and that there was no antitrust obstacle to the offer. On November 24, 1993, the Court of Chancery issued its decision granting a preliminary injunction in favor of QVC and the plaintiff stockholders. This appeal followed.

II. APPLICABLE PRINCIPLES OF ESTABLISHED DELAWARE LAW

The General Corporation Law of the State of Delaware (the "General Corporation Law") and the decisions of this Court have repeatedly recog-

---

7. This belief may have been based on a report prepared by Booz–Allen and distributed to the Paramount Board at its October 24 meeting. The report, which relied on public information regarding QVC, concluded that the synergies of a Paramount–Viacom merger were significantly superior to those of a Paramount–QVC merger. QVC has labelled the Booz–Allen report as a "joke."

8. The market prices of Viacom's and QVC's stock were poor measures of their actual values because such prices constantly fluctuated depending upon which company was perceived to be the more likely to acquire Paramount.

nized the fundamental principle that the management of the business and affairs of a Delaware corporation is entrusted to its directors, who are the duly elected and authorized representatives of the stockholders. * * * Under normal circumstances, neither the courts nor the stockholders should interfere with the managerial decisions of the directors. * * *

Nevertheless, there are rare situations which mandate that a court take a more direct and active role in overseeing the decisions made and actions taken by directors. In these situations, a court subjects the directors' conduct to enhanced scrutiny to ensure that it is reasonable. The decisions of this Court have clearly established the circumstances where such enhanced scrutiny will be applied. E.g., Unocal, 493 A.2d 946; Moran v. Household Int'l, Inc., Del.Supr., 500 A.2d 1346 (1985); Revlon, 506 A.2d 173; Mills Acquisition Co. v. Macmillan, Inc., Del.Supr., 559 A.2d 1261 (1989); Gilbert v. El Paso Co., Del.Supr., 575 A.2d 1131 (1990). The case at bar implicates two such circumstances: (1) the approval of a transaction resulting in a sale of control, and (2) the adoption of defensive measures in response to a threat to corporate control.

A. The Significance of a Sale or Change of Control

When a majority of a corporation's voting shares are acquired by a single person or entity, or by a cohesive group acting together, there is a significant diminution in the voting power of those who thereby become minority stockholders. Under the statutory framework of the General Corporation Law, many of the most fundamental corporate changes can be implemented only if they are approved by a majority vote of the stockholders. Such actions include elections of directors, amendments to the certificate of incorporation, mergers, consolidations, sales of all or substantially all of the assets of the corporation, and dissolution. 8 Del. C. §§ 211, 242. 251–258, 263, 271, 275. Because of the overriding importance of voting rights, this Court and the Court of Chancery have consistently acted to protect stockholders from unwarranted interference with such rights.[11]

In the absence of devices protecting the minority stockholders,[12] stockholder votes are likely to become mere formalities where there is a majority

---

11. See Schnell v. Chris–Craft Indus., Inc., Del.Supr., 285 A.2d 437, 439 (1971) (holding that actions taken by management to manipulate corporate machinery "for the purpose of obstructing the legitimate efforts of dissident stockholders in the exercise of their rights to undertake a proxy contest against management" were "contrary to established principles of corporate democracy" and therefore invalid); Giuricich v. Emtrol Corp., Del.Supr., 449 A.2d 232, 239 (1982) (holding that "careful judicial scrutiny will be given a situation in which the right to vote for the election of successor directors has been effectively frustrated"); Centaur Partners, IV v. Nat'l Intergroup, Del.Supr., 582 A.2d 923 (1990) (holding that supermajority

voting provisions must be clear and unambiguous because they have the effect of disenfranchising the majority); Stroud v. Grace, Del.Supr., 604 A.2d 75, 84 (1992) (directors' duty of disclosure is premised on the importance of stockholders being fully informed when voting on a specific matter); Blasius Indus., Inc. v. Atlas Corp., Del. Ch., 564 A.2d 651, 659 n. 2 (1988) ("Delaware courts have long exercised a most sensitive and protective regard for the free and effective exercise of voting rights.").

12. Examples of such protective provisions are supermajority voting provisions, majority of the minority requirements, etc. Although we express no opinion on what effect the inclusion of any such stockholder

stockholder. For example, minority stockholders can be deprived of a continuing equity interest in their corporation by means of a cash-out merger. Weinberger, 457 A.2d at 703. Absent effective protective provisions, minority stockholders must rely for protection solely on the fiduciary duties owed to them by the directors and the majority stockholder, since the minority stockholders have lost the power to influence corporate direction through the ballot. The acquisition of majority status and the consequent privilege of exerting the powers of majority ownership come at a price. That price is usually a control premium which recognizes not only the value of a control block of shares, but also compensates the minority stockholders for their resulting loss of voting power.

In the case before us, the public stockholders (in the aggregate) currently own a majority of Paramount's voting stock. Control of the corporation is not vested in a single person, entity, or group, but vested in the fluid aggregation of unaffiliated stockholders. In the event the Paramount–Viacom transaction is consummated, the public stockholders will receive cash and a minority equity voting position in the surviving corporation. Following such consummation, there will be a controlling stockholder who will have the voting power to: (a) elect directors; (b) cause a break-up of the corporation; (c) merge it with another company; (d) cash-out the public stockholders; (e) amend the certificate of incorporation; (f) sell all or substantially all of the corporate assets; or (g) otherwise alter materially the nature of the corporation and the public stockholders' interests. Irrespective of the present Paramount Board's vision of a long-term strategic alliance with Viacom, the proposed sale of control would provide the new controlling stockholder with the power to alter that vision.

Because of the intended sale of control, the Paramount–Viacom transaction has economic consequences of considerable significance to the Paramount stockholders. Once control has shifted, the current Paramount stockholders will have no leverage in the future to demand another control premium. As a result, the Paramount stockholders are entitled to receive, and should receive, a control premium and/or protective devices of significant value. There being no such protective provisions in the Viacom–Paramount transaction, the Paramount directors had an obligation to take the maximum advantage of the current opportunity to realize for the stockholders the best value reasonably available.

B. The Obligations of Directors in a Sale or Change of Control Transaction

The consequences of a sale of control impose special obligations on the directors of a corporation.[13] in particular, they have the obligation of acting

protective devices would have had in this case, we note that this Court has upheld, under different circumstances, the reasonableness of a standstill agreement which limited a 49.9 percent stockholder to 40 percent board representation. Ivanhoe, 535 A.2d at 1343.

13. We express no opinion on any scenario except the actual facts before the Court, and our precise holding herein. Unsolicited tender offers in other contexts may be governed by different precedent. For example, where a potential sale of control by a corporation is not the consequence of a

reasonably to seek the transaction offering the best value reasonably available to the stockholders. The courts will apply enhanced scrutiny to ensure that the directors have acted reasonably. The obligations of the directors and the enhanced scrutiny of the courts are well-established by the decisions of this Court. * * *

In the sale of control context, the directors must focus on one primary objective—to secure the transaction offering the best value reasonably available for the stockholders—and they must exercise their fiduciary duties to further that end. The decisions of this Court have consistently emphasized this goal. Revlon, 506 A.2d at 182 ("The duty of the board . . . [is] the maximization of the company's value at a sale for the stockholders' benefit."); Macmillan, 559 A.2d at 1288 ("[I]n a sale of corporate control the responsibility of the directors is to get the highest value reasonably attainable for the shareholders."); Barkan, 567 A.2d at 1286 ("[T]he board must act in a neutral manner to encourage the highest possible price for shareholders."). * * *

In pursuing this objective, the directors must be especially diligent. * * * In particular, this Court has stressed the importance of the board being adequately informed in negotiating a sale of control: "The need for adequate information is central to the enlightened evaluation of a transaction that a board must make." Barkan, 567 A.2d at 1287. This requirement is consistent with the general principle that "directors have a duty to inform themselves, prior to making a business decision, of all material information reasonably available to them." Aronson, 473 A.2d at 812. See also Cede & Co. v. Technicolor, Inc., Del.Supr., 634 A.2d 345, 367 (1993); Smith v. Van Gorkom, Del.Supr., 488 A.2d 858, 872 (1985). Moreover, the role of outside, independent directors becomes particularly important because of the magnitude of a sale of control transaction and the possibility, in certain cases, that management may not necessarily be impartial. See Macmillan, 559 A.2d at 1285 (requiring "the intense scrutiny and participation of the independent directors").

Barkan teaches some of the methods by which a board can fulfill its obligation to seek the best value reasonably available to the stockholders. 567 A.2d at 1286–87. These methods are designed to determine the existence and viability of possible alternatives. They include conducting an auction, canvassing the market, etc. Delaware law recognizes that there is "no single blueprint" that directors must follow. Id. at 1286–87; Citron 569 A.2d at 68; Macmillan, 559 A.2d at 1287.

In determining which alternative provides the best value for the stockholders, a board of directors is not limited to considering only the

board's action, this Court has recognized the prerogative of a board of directors to resist a third party's unsolicited acquisition proposal or offer. See Pogostin, 480 A.2d at 627; Time–Warner, 571 A.2d at 1152; Bershad v. Curtiss-Wright Corp., Del.Supr., 535 A.2d 840, 845 (1987); Macmillan, 559 A.2d at 1285 n. 35. The decision of a board to resist such an acquisition, like all decisions of a properly-functioning board, must be informed, Unocal, 493 A.2d at 954–55, and the circumstances of each particular case will determine the steps that a board must take to inform itself, and what other action, if any, is required as a matter of fiduciary duty.

amount of cash involved, and is not required to ignore totally its view of the future value of a strategic alliance. See Macmillan, 559 A.2d at 1282 n. 29. Instead, the directors should analyze the entire situation and evaluate in a disciplined manner the consideration being offered. Where stock or other non-cash consideration is involved, the board should try to quantify its value, if feasible, to achieve an objective comparison of the alternatives.[14] In addition, the board may assess a variety of practical considerations relating to each alternative, including: "[an offer's] fairness and feasibility; the proposed or actual financing for the offer, and the consequences of that financing; questions of illegality; ... the risk of non-consum[m]ation; ... the bidder's identity, prior background and other business venture experiences; and the bidder's business plans for the corporation and their effects on stockholder interests." Macmillan, 559 A.2d at 1282 n. 29. These considerations are important because the selection of one alternative may permanently foreclose other opportunities. While the assessment of these factors may be complex, the board's goal is straightforward: Having informed themselves of all material information reasonably available, the directors must decide which alternative is most likely to offer the best value reasonably available to the stockholders.

C. Enhanced Judicial Scrutiny of a Sale or Change of Control Transaction

Board action in the circumstances presented here is subject to enhanced scrutiny. Such scrutiny is mandated by: (a) the threatened diminution of the current stockholders' voting power; (b) the fact that an asset belonging to public stockholders (a control premium) is being sold and may never be available again; and (c) the traditional concern of Delaware courts for actions which impair or impede stockholder voting rights (see supra note 11). In Macmillan, this Court held: When Revlon duties devolve upon directors, this Court will continue to exact an enhanced judicial scrutiny at the threshold, as in Unocal, before the normal presumptions of the business judgment rule will apply.[15] 559 A.2d at 1288. The Macmillan decision articulates a specific two-part test for analyzing board action where competing bidders are not treated equally:[16] In the face of disparate treatment, the trial court must first examine whether the directors properly perceived that shareholder interests were enhanced. In any event the board's action must be reasonable in relation to the advantage sought to be achieved, or conversely, to the threat which a particular bid allegedly poses to stockholder interests. Id. * * *

---

14. When assessing the value of non-cash consideration, a board should focus on its value as of the date it will be received by the stockholders. Normally, such value will be determined with the assistance of experts using generally accepted methods of valuation. See In re RJR Nabisco, Inc. Shareholders Litig., Del. Ch., C.A. No. 10389, Allen, C. (Jan. 31, 1989), reprinted at 14 Del. J. Corp. L. 1132, 1161.

15. Because the Paramount Board acted unreasonably as to process and result in this sale of control situation, the business judgment rule did not become operative.

16. Before this test is invoked, "the plaintiff must show, and the trial court must find, that the directors of the target company treated one or more of the respective bidders on unequal terms." Macmillan, 559 A.2d at 1288.

The key features of an enhanced scrutiny test are: (a) a judicial determination regarding the adequacy of the decisionmaking process employed by the directors, including the information on which the directors based their decision; and (b) a judicial examination of the reasonableness of the directors' action in light of the circumstances then existing. The directors have the burden of proving that they were adequately informed and acted reasonably.

Although an enhanced scrutiny test involves a review of the reasonableness of the substantive merits of a board's actions, a court should not ignore the complexity of the directors' task in a sale of control. There are many business and financial considerations implicated in investigating and selecting the best value reasonably available. The board of directors is the corporate decisionmaking body best equipped to make these judgments. Accordingly, a court applying enhanced judicial scrutiny should be deciding whether the directors made **a reasonable** decision, not **a perfect** decision. If a board selected one of several reasonable alternatives, a court should not second-guess that choice even though it might have decided otherwise or subsequent events may have cast doubt on the board's determination. Thus, courts will not substitute their business judgment for that of the directors, but will determine if the directors' decision was, on balance, within a range of reasonableness. * * *

D.   Revlon and Time–Warner Distinguished

The Paramount defendants and Viacom assert that the fiduciary obligations and the enhanced judicial scrutiny discussed above are not implicated in this case in the absence of a "break-up" of the corporation, and that the order granting the preliminary injunction should be reversed. This argument is based on their erroneous interpretation of our decisions in Revlon and Time–Warner. * * *

Based on the facts and circumstances present in Revlon, we held that "[t]he directors' role changed from defenders of the corporate bastion to auctioneers charged with getting the best price for the stockholders at a sale of the company." 506 A.2d at 182. We further held that "when a board ends an intense bidding contest on an insubstantial basis, ... [that] action cannot withstand the enhanced scrutiny which Unocal requires of director conduct." Id. at 184.

It is true that one of the circumstances bearing on these holdings was the fact that "the break-up of the company ... had become a reality which even the directors embraced." Id at 182. It does not follow, however, that a "break-up" must be present and "inevitable" before directors are subject to enhanced judicial scrutiny and are required to pursue a transaction that is calculated to produce the best value reasonably available to the stockholders. In fact, we stated in Revlon that "when bidders make relatively similar offers, or dissolution of the company becomes inevitable, the directors cannot fulfill their enhanced Unocal duties by playing favorites with the contending factions. "Id. at 184 (emphasis added). Revlon thus does not hold that an inevitable dissolution or "break-up" is necessary.

The decisions of this Court following Revlon reinforced the applicability of enhanced scrutiny and the directors' obligation to seek the best value reasonably available for the stockholders where there, is a pending sale of control, regardless of whether or not there is to be a break-up of the corporation. * * *

Although Macmillan and Barkan are clear in holding that a change of control imposes on directors the obligation to obtain the best value reasonably available to the stockholders, the Paramount defendants have interpreted our decision in Time–Warner as requiring a corporate break-up in order for that obligation to apply. The facts in Time–Warner, however, were quite different from the facts of this case, and refute Paramount's position here. In Time–Warner, the Chancellor held that there was no change of control in the original stock-for-stock merger between Time and Warner because Time would be owned by a fluid aggregation of unaffiliated stockholders both before and after the merger:

> If the appropriate inquiry is whether a change in control is contemplated, the answer must be sought in the specific circumstances surrounding the transaction. Surely under some circumstances a stock for stock merger could reflect a transfer of corporate control. That would, for example, plainly be the case here if Warner were a private company. But where, as here, the shares of both constituent corporations are widely held, corporate control can be expected to remain unaffected by a stock for stock merger. This in my judgment was the situation with respect to the original merger agreement. When the specifics of that situation are reviewed, it is seen that, aside from legal technicalities and aside from arrangements thought to enhance the prospect for the ultimate succession of [Nicholas J. Nicholas, Jr., president of Time], neither corporation could be said to be acquiring the other. **Control of both remained in a large, fluid, changeable and changing market.**

> The existence of a control block of stock in the hands of a single shareholder or a group with loyalty to each other does have real consequences to the financial value of "minority" stock. The law offers some protection to such shares through the imposition of a fiduciary duty upon controlling shareholders. **But here, effectuation of the merger would not have subjected Time shareholders to the risks and consequences of holders of minority shares. This is a reflection of the fact that no control passed to anyone in the transaction contemplated.** The shareholders of Time would have "suffered" dilution, of course, but they would suffer the same type of dilution upon the public distribution of new stock.

Paramount Communications Inc. v. Time Inc., Del. Ch., No. 10866, Allen, C. (July 17, 1989) 739 * * * (emphasis added). Moreover, the transaction actually consummated in Time–Warner was not a merger, as originally planned, but a sale of Warner's stock to Time.

In our affirmance of the Court of Chancery's well-reasoned decision, this Court held that "The Chancellor's findings of fact are supported by the record and **his conclusion is correct as a matter of law.**" 571 A.2d at

1150 (emphasis added). Nevertheless, the Paramount defendants here have argued that a break-up is a requirement and have focused on the following language in our Time–Warner decision:

> However, we premise our rejection of plaintiffs' Revlon claim on different grounds, namely, the absence of any substantial evidence to conclude that Time's board, in negotiating with Warner, made the dissolution or break-up of the corporate entity inevitable, as was the case in Revlon. Under Delaware law there are, generally speaking and **without excluding other possibilities**, two circumstances which may implicate Revlon duties. The first, and clearer one, is when a corporation **initiates an active bidding process seeking to sell itself** or to effect a business reorganization involving a clear break-up of the company. However, Revlon duties may also be triggered where, in response to a bidder's offer, a target abandons its long-term strategy and seeks an alternative transaction involving the breakup of the company.

Id. at 1150 (emphasis added).

The Paramount defendants have misread the holding of Time–Warner. Contrary to their argument, our decision in Time–Warner expressly states that the two general scenarios discussed in the above-quoted paragraph are not the only instances where "Revlon duties" may be implicated. The Paramount defendants' argument totally ignores the phrase "without excluding other possibilities." Moreover, the instant case is clearly within the first general scenario set forth in Time–Warner. The Paramount Board, albeit unintentionally, had "initiate[d] an active bidding process seeking to sell itself" by agreeing to sell control of the corporation to Viacom in circumstances where another potential acquiror (QVC) was equally interested in being a bidder.

The Paramount defendants' position that **both** a change of control **and** a break-up are **required** must be rejected. Such a holding would unduly restrict the application of Revlon, is inconsistent with this Court's decisions in Barkan and Macmillan, and has no basis in policy. There are few events that have a more significant impact on the stockholders than a sale of control or a corporate break-up. Each event represents a fundamental (and perhaps irrevocable) change in the nature of the corporate enterprise from a practical standpoint. It is the significance of **each** of these events that justifies: (a) focusing on the directors' obligation to seek the best value reasonably available to the stockholders; and (b) requiring a close scrutiny of board action which could be contrary to the stockholders' interests.

Accordingly, when a corporation undertakes a transaction which will cause: (a) a change in corporate control; **or** (b) a break-up of the corporate entity, the directors' obligation is to seek the best value reasonably available to the stockholders. This obligation arises because the effect of the Viacom–Paramount transaction, if consummated, is to shift control of Paramount from the public stockholders to a controlling stockholder, Viacom. Neither Time–Warner nor any other decision of this Court holds that a "break-up" of the company is essential to give rise to this obligation where there is a sale of control.

III.   BREACH OF FIDUCIARY DUTIES BY PARAMOUNT BOARD

We now turn to duties of the Paramount Board under the facts of this case and our conclusions as to the breaches of those duties which warrant injunctive relief.

A.   The Specific Obligations of the Paramount Board

Under the facts of this case, the Paramount directors had the obligation: (a) to be diligent and vigilant in examining critically the Paramount–Viacom transaction and the QVC tender offers; (b) to act in good faith; (c) to obtain, and act with due care on, all material information reasonably available, including information necessary to compare the two offers to determine which of these transactions, or an alternative course of action, would provide the best value reasonably available to the stockholders; and (d) to negotiate actively and in good faith with both Viacom and QVC to that end.

Having decided to sell control of the corporation, the Paramount directors were required to evaluate critically whether or not all material aspects of the Paramount–Viacom transaction (separately and in the aggregate) were reasonable and in the best interests of the Paramount stockholders in light of current circumstances, including: the change of control premium, the Stock Option Agreement, the Termination Fee, the coercive nature of both the Viacom and QVC tender offers,[18] the No–Shop Provision, and the proposed disparate use of the Rights Agreement as to the Viacom and QVC tender offers, respectively.

These obligations necessarily implicated various issues, including the questions of whether or not those provisions and other aspects of the Paramount–Viacom transaction (separately and in the aggregate): (a) adversely affected the value provided to the Paramount stockholders; (b) inhibited or encouraged alternative bids; (c) were enforceable contractual obligations in light of the directors' fiduciary duties; and (d) in the end would advance or retard the Paramount directors' obligation to secure for the Paramount stockholders the best value reasonably available under the circumstances.

The Paramount defendants contend that they were precluded by certain contractual provisions, including the No–Shop Provision, from negotiating with QVC or seeking alternatives. Such provisions, whether or not they are presumptively valid in the abstract, may not validly define or limit the directors' fiduciary duties under Delaware law or prevent the Paramount directors from carrying out their fiduciary duties under Dela-

---

18. Both the Viacom and the QVC tender offers were for 51 percent cash and a "back-end" of various securities, the value of each of which depended on the fluctuating value of Viacom and QVC stock at any given time. Thus, both tender offers were two-ti-ered, front-end loaded, and coercive. Such coercive offers are inherently problematic and should be expected to receive particularly careful analysis by a target board. See Unocal, 493 A.2d at 956.

ware law. To the extent such provisions are inconsistent with those duties, they are invalid and unenforceable. See Revlon, 506 A.2d at 184–85.

Since the Paramount directors had already decided to sell control, they had an obligation to continue their search for the best value reasonably available to the stockholders. This continuing obligation included the responsibility, at the October 24 board meeting and thereafter, to evaluate critically both the QVC tender offers and the Paramount–Viacom transaction to determine if: (a) the QVC tender offer was, or would continue to be, conditional; (b) the QVC tender offer could be improved; (c) the Viacom tender offer or other aspects of the Paramount–Viacom transaction could be improved; (d) each of the respective offers would be reasonably likely to come to closure, and under what circumstances; (e) other material information was reasonably available for consideration by the Paramount directors; (f) there were viable and realistic alternative courses of action; and (g) the timing constraints could be managed so the directors could consider these matters carefully and deliberately.

B.   The Breaches of Fiduciary Duty by the Paramount Board

The Paramount directors made the decision on September 12, 1993, that, in their judgment, a strategic merger with Viacom on the economic terms of the Original Merger Agreement was in the best interests of Paramount and its stockholders. Those terms provided a modest change of control premium to the stockholders. The directors also decided at that time that it was appropriate to agree to certain defensive measures (the Stock Option Agreement, the Termination Fee, and the No–Shop Provision) insisted upon by Viacom as part of that economic transaction. Those defensive measures, coupled with the sale of control and subsequent disparate treatment of competing bidders, implicated the judicial scrutiny of Unocal, Revlon, Macmillan, and their progeny. We conclude that the Paramount directors' process was not reasonable, and the result achieved for the stockholders was not reasonable under the circumstances.

When entering into the Original Merger Agreement, and thereafter, the Paramount Board clearly gave insufficient attention to the potential consequences of the defensive measures demanded by Viacom. The Stock Option Agreement had a number of unusual and potentially "draconian"[19] provisions, including the Note Feature and the Put Feature. Furthermore, the Termination Fee, whether or not unreasonable by itself, clearly made Paramount less attractive to other bidders, when coupled with the Stock Option Agreement. Finally, the No–Shop Provision inhibited the Paramount Board's ability to negotiate with other potential bidders, particularly QVC which had already expressed an interest in Paramount.[20]

---

19. The Vice Chancellor so characterized the Stock Option Agreement. Court of Chancery Opinion, ___ A.2d ___, slip op. at 60. We express no opinion whether a stock option agreement of essentially this magnitude, but with a reasonable "cap" and without the Note and Put Features, would be valid or invalid under other circumstances.

See Hecco Ventures v. Sea–Land Corp., Del. Ch., C.A. No. 8486, Jacobs, V.C. (May 19, 1986) (21.7 percent stock option); In re Vitalink Communications Corp. Shareholders Litig., Del. Ch., C.A. No. 12085, Chandler, V.C. (May 16, 1990) (19.9 percent stock option).

20. We express no opinion whether certain aspects of the No–Shop Provision here

Throughout the applicable time period, and especially from the first QVC merger proposal on September 20 through the Paramount Board meeting on November 15, QVC's interest in Paramount provided the **opportunity** for the Paramount Board to seek significantly higher value for the Paramount stockholders than that being offered by Viacom. QVC persistently demonstrated its intention to meet and exceed the Viacom offers, and frequently expressed its willingness to negotiate possible further increases.

The Paramount directors had the opportunity in the October 23–24 time frame, when the Original Merger Agreement was renegotiated, to take appropriate action to modify the improper defensive measures as well as to improve the economic terms of the Paramount–Viacom transaction. Under the circumstances existing at that time, it should have been clear to the Paramount Board that the Stock Option Agreement, coupled with the Termination Fee and the No–Shop Clause, were impeding the realization of the best value reasonably available to the Paramount stockholders. Nevertheless, the Paramount Board made no effort to eliminate or modify these counterproductive devices. and instead continued to cling to its vision of a strategic alliance with Viacom. Moreover, based on advice from the Paramount management, the Paramount directors considered the QVC offer to be "conditional" and asserted that they were precluded by the No-Shop Provision from seeking more information from, or negotiating with, QVC.

By November 12, 1993, the value of the revised QVC offer on its face exceeded that of the Viacom offer by over $1 billion at then current values. This significant disparity of value cannot be justified on the basis of the directors' vision of future strategy, primarily because the change of control would supplant the authority of the current Paramount Board to continue to hold and implement their strategic vision in any meaningful way. Moreover, their uninformed process had deprived their strategic vision of much of its credibility. See Van Gorkom, 488 A.2d at 872; Cede v. Technicolor, 634 A.2d at 367; Hanson Trust PLC v. ML SCM Acquisition Inc., 2d Cir., 781 F.2d 264, 274 (1986).

When the Paramount directors met on November 15 to consider QVC's increased tender offer, they remained prisoners of their own misconceptions and missed opportunities to eliminate the restrictions they had imposed on themselves. Yet, it was not "too late" to reconsider negotiating with QVC. The circumstances existing on November 15 made it clear that the defensive measures, taken as a whole, were problematic: (a) the No–

could be valid in another context. Whether or not it could validly have operated here at an early stage solely to prevent Paramount from actively "shopping" the company, it could not prevent the Paramount directors from carrying out their fiduciary duties in considering unsolicited bids or in negotiating for the best value reasonably available to the stockholders. Macmillan, 559 A.2d at 1287. As we said in Barkan: "Where a board has no reasonable basis upon which to judge the adequacy of a contemplated transaction, a no-shop restriction gives rise to the inference that the board seeks to forestall competing bids." 567 A.2d at 1288. See also Revlon, 506 A.2d at 184 (holding that "[t]he no-shop provision, like the lock-up option, while not per se illegal, is impermissible under the Unocal standards when a board's primary duty becomes that of an auctioneer responsible for selling the company to the highest bidder").

Shop Provision could not define or limit their fiduciary duties; (b) the Stock Option Agreement had become "draconian"; and (c) the Termination Fee, in context with all the circumstances, was similarly deterring the realization of possibly higher bids. Nevertheless, the Paramount directors remained paralyzed by their uninformed belief that the QVC offer was "illusory." This final opportunity to negotiate on the stockholders' behalf and to fulfill their obligation to seek the best value reasonably available was thereby squandered.

IV.   VIACOM'S CLAIM OF VESTED CONTRACT RIGHTS

Viacom argues that it had certain "vested" contract rights with respect to the No–Shop Provision and the Stock Option Agreement. In effect, Viacom's argument is that the Paramount directors could enter into an agreement in violation of their fiduciary duties and then render Paramount, and ultimately its stockholders, liable for failing to carry out an agreement in violation of those duties. Viacom's protestations about vested rights are without merit. This Court has found that those defensive measures were improperly designed to deter potential bidders, and that such measures do not meet the reasonableness test to which they must be subjected. They are consequently invalid and unenforceable under the facts of this case.

* * *

V.   CONCLUSION

The realization of the best value reasonably available to the stockholders became the Paramount directors' primary obligation under these facts in light of the change of control. * * *

It is the nature of the judicial process that we decide only the case before us—a case which, on its facts, is clearly controlled by established Delaware law. Here, the proposed change of control and the implications thereof were crystal clear. In other cases they may be less clear. The holding of this case on its facts, coupled with the holdings of the principal cases discussed herein where the issue of sale of control is implicated, should provide a workable precedent against which to measure future cases.

NOTE: THE *"REVLON"* DUTY AFTER *PARAMOUNT*

1.   *The Meaning of "Sale of Control."*

Arnold v. Society for Savings Bancorp, 1993 WL 526781, CCH Fed. Sec. L.Rep. ¶ 98,006 (Del.Ch.), rev'd on other grounds, 650 A.2d 1270 (Del.Supr.1994), suggests that we can expect little expansion of the "sale of control" trigger in the wake of *QVC*. *Arnold* concerned an arms length stock-for-stock merger of Society for Savings Bancorp into the Bank of Boston. Bancorp had put itself up for sale a year earlier, but refused all offers and stayed independent. But it also then commenced negotiations with Bank of Boston, eventually agreeing to a transaction at a price allegedly lower than a price offered in the earlier round of bidding. A plaintiff shareholder contended that an auction duty obtained respecting the Bank of Boston transaction. But the Chancellor ruled that Bancorp had effectively removed itself from the auction block and did not implicate itself under *Revlon* in pursuing a merger with Bank of Boston. No "active bidding process" was entailed. Nor did the change of control bound up in the stock-for-stock transaction suffice since the resulting group of Bank of Boston shareholders was "fluid" and "changing," no individual or entity held a control block of either participant, and nothing in the merger suggested a threat to the continuity of Bancorp's shareholders in the merged entity.

Contrariwise, no "sale of control" occurs where, through a friendly tender offer and second-step merger, an outside firm acquires 100 percent of an 87 percent-owned subsidiary firm. Here the minority shareholders lose no opportunity to participate in a change of control premium because control already is vested in the parent company. See McMullen v. Beran, 1999 WL 1135146 (Del.Ch.).

2. *A Judicial Commentary.*

In **Equity-Linked Investors, L.P. v. Adams**, 705 A.2d 1040 (Del.Ch.1997), Chancellor Allen offers the following reflections on the evolution of the *Revlon* duty:

" * * * In fact the meaning of Revlon—specifically, when its special duties were triggered, and what those duties specifically required—were questions that repeatedly troubled the bench and the bar in the turbulent wake of the Revlon decision. Reasonable minds differed. One view of the holding in Revlon was that it was premised on a duty (the duty to auction the company when it was for sale, or, less woodenly, the duty to get the best price, or the duty not to discriminate between bidders) that was different in some way from the ordinary director duties: to act in good faith pursuit of corporate welfare and to be informed and attentive. On this view, once a 'sale' of the corporation was in contemplation, 'Revlon duties' would be thought to limit the range of good faith business judgment that the board might make (e.g., board must conduct an auction; or no 'lock-up' agreements allowed; or no 'favoritism' among bidders; etc.), and afforded a reviewing court additional (fairness) grounds in any judicial review of director action. This interpretation of 'Revlon duties' was early on taken up by academic commentators and plaintiffs' attorneys and continued to resonate in some of the opinions throughout the period. See, e.g., Mills Acquisition Co. v. Macmillan, Inc., Del.Supr., 559 A.2d 1261 (1989).

"Other cases tended to 'normalize' directors' duties in these important transactions; they reflect greater deference to an independent board even in a 'sale' context, and acknowledged the necessity of an independent board to make business judgments even in that setting. Thus, these cases tended to evaluate board conduct, even in that context, in terms of the board's steps to be informed and its good faith. See, e.g., In re RJR Nabisco, Inc. Shareholders Litig., Del. Ch., C.A. No. 10389, Allen, C. (Jan. 31, 1989), Slip Op., 1989 Del.Ch. LEXIS 73 (1989). Under this more business-judgment like view, the board continued to possess substantial discretion with respect to conducting a sale. So long as it satisfied a burden to show compliance with its basic duties—independence, good faith and due attentiveness— the board's judgments would be respected. See, e.g., In re J.P. Stevens & Co., Shareholders Litig., Del. Ch., 542 A.2d 770 (1988)(upholding the grant of inducements to one bidder during an active auction); Barkan v. Amsted Indus., Inc., Del.Supr., 567 A.2d 1279 (1989)(no single template for 'selling a company'). In this view 'Revlon duties' changed things only by shifting burden of proof and persuasion and by focusing attention on present shareholder value, but it did not fundamentally interfere with the freedom of directors to make good faith business judgment.

"This existing uncertainty respecting the meaning of 'Revlon duties' was substantially dissipated by the Delaware Supreme Court's opinion in Paramount.

The case teaches a great deal, but it may be said to support these generalizations at least: (1) where a transaction constituted a 'change in corporate control', such that the shareholders would thereafter lose a further opportunity to participate in a change of control premium, (2) the board's duty of loyalty requires it to try in good faith to get the best price reasonably available (which specifically means that the board must at least discuss an interest expressed by any financially capable buyer), and (3) in such context courts will employ an (objective) 'reasonableness' standard of review (both to the process and the result!) to evaluate whether the directors have complied with their fundamental duties of care and good faith (loyalty). Thus, Paramount in effect mediates between the 'normalizing' tendency of some prior cases and the more highly regulatory approach of others. It adopts an intermediate level of judicial review which recognizes the broad power of the board to make decisions in the process of negotiating and recommending a 'sale of control' transaction, so long as the board is informed, motivated by good faith desire to achieve the best available transaction, and proceeds 'reasonably.'

"With respect to the important question of when these duties are enhanced—specifically, the duty to try in good faith to maximize current share value and the duty to reasonably explore all options (i.e., to talk with all financially responsible parties)—the court's teaching ironically narrowed the range of Revlon duties, but did not make its application necessarily clearer.[48] It narrowed the range of corporate transactions to which the principle of Revlon applies. That is, it explicitly recognized that where a stock for stock merger is involved, the business judgment of the board, concerning the quality and prospects of the stock the shareholders would receive in the merger, would be reviewed deferentially, as in other settings. See In re Santa Fe Pacific Corp. Shareholders Litig., Del.Supr., 669 A.2d 59 (1995). The holding of Paramount, however, was that where the stock to be received in the merger was the stock of a corporation under the control of a single individual or a control group, then the transaction should be treated for 'Revlon duty' purposes as a cash merger would be treated: there is no tomorrow for the shareholders (no assured long-term), the board's obligation is to make a good faith, informed judgment to maximize current share value, and the court reviews such determinations on a 'reasonableness' basis, which otherwise they would not do. How this 'change in control' trigger works in instances of mixed cash and stock or other paper awaits future cases."

Unitrin, Inc. v. American General Corp.

Supreme Court of Delaware, 1995.
651 A.2d 1361.

■ HOLLAND, JUSTICE

[American General made a public proposal for an all cash all shares purchase of Unitrin's outstanding shares for $50 3/8. The price represented a 30 percent premium over market. Unitrin's board resisted, promulgating a poison pill and authorizing a stock repurchase program that would extend to up to 10 million of the outstanding shares. Two of the outside directors owned or controlled substantial blocks of Unitrin stock; as a result, the board's combined holdings amounted to 23 percent of the shares outstanding before any repurchases.

48. This unclarity, one should be quick to note is to a large extent inherent in ex post fiduciary review and there is good reason to suppose it can be efficient.

[The board announced that its members would not participate in the repurchase program. The repurchases would, accordingly, increase their percentage ownership so as to give them a veto under a shark repellant provision in Unitrin's charter. Under the provision, business combinations with shareholders owning 15 percent or more of Unitrin's stock required a 75 percent vote.

[Five million shares were repurchased at an average slightly above the offer price before the Chancery Court, invoking *Unocal*, enjoined the repurchases at the behest of American General and a class of Unitrin shareholders. The Supreme Court reversed.]

The Court of Chancery framed the ultimate question before it as follows: "This case comes down to one final question: Is placing the decision to sell the company in the hands of stockholders who are also directors a disproportionate response to a low price offer to buy all the shares of the company for cash?" The Court of Chancery then answered that question:

> I conclude that because the only threat to the corporation is the inadequacy of an opening bid made directly to the board, and the board has already taken actions that will protect the stockholders from mistakenly falling for a low ball negotiating strategy, a repurchase program that intentionally provides members of the board with a veto of any merger proposal is not reasonably related to the threat posed by American General's negotiable all shares, all cash offer.

* * *

The Court of Chancery concluded that, although the Unitrin Board had properly perceived American General's inadequate Offer as a threat and had properly responded to that threat by adopting a "poison pill," the additional defensive response of adopting the Repurchase Program was unnecessary and disproportionate to the threat the Offer posed. * * *

* * *

The Court of Chancery found that by not participating in the Repurchase Program, the Board "expected to create a 28% voting block to support the Board's decision to reject [a future] offer by American General." From this underlying factual finding, the Court of Chancery concluded that American General might be "chilled" in its pursuit of Unitrin * * *.

* * *

* * * [R]ecently, this Court stated: "we accept the basic legal tenets," set forth in Blasius Indus., Inc. v. Atlas Corp., Del.Ch., 564 A.2d 651 (1988), that "[w]here boards of directors deliberately employ [ ] ... legal strategies either to frustrate or completely disenfranchise a shareholder vote, ... [t]here can be no dispute that such conduct violates Delaware law." Stroud v. Grace, 606 A.2d at 91. In Stroud, we concluded, however, that a Blasius analysis was inappropriate. We reached that conclusion because it could not be said that the "primary purpose" of the board's action was to interfere with or impede exercise of the shareholder franchise, and because the shareholders had a "full and fair opportunity to vote." Stroud v. Grace, 606 A.2d at 92.

This Court also specifically noted that boards of directors often interfere with the exercise of shareholder voting when an acquiror *launches both a proxy fight and a tender offer.* Id. at 92 n. 3. We then stated that such action "necessarily invoked both Unocal and Blasius" because "both [tests] recognize the inherent conflicts of interest that arise when shareholders are not permitted free exercise of their franchise." * * *

* * *

* * * The Court of Chancery concluded that Unitrin's adoption of a poison pill was a proportionate response to the threat its Board reasonably perceived from American General's Offer. Nonetheless, the Court of Chancery enjoined the additional defense of the Repurchase Program as disproportionate and "unnecessary."

The record reflects that the Court of Chancery's decision to enjoin the Repurchase Program is attributable to a continuing misunderstanding, i.e., that in conjunction with the longstanding Supermajority Vote provision in the Unitrin charter, the Repurchase Program would operate to provide the director shareholders with a "veto" to preclude a successful proxy contest by American General. The origins of that misunderstanding are three premises that are each without record support. Two of those premises are objective misconceptions and the other is subjective.

* * *

The subjective premise was the Court of Chancery's *sua sponte* determination that Unitrin's outside directors, who are also substantial stockholders, would not vote like other stockholders in a proxy contest, *i.e.,* in their own best economic interests. At American General's Offer price, the outside directors held Unitrin shares worth more than $450 million. Consequently, Unitrin argues the stockholder directors had the same interest as other Unitrin stockholders generally, when voting in a proxy contest, to wit: the maximization of the value of their investments.

In rejecting Unitrin's argument, the Court of Chancery stated that the stockholder directors would be "subconsciously" motivated in a proxy contest to vote against otherwise excellent offers which did not include a "price parameter" to compensate them for the loss of the "prestige and perquisites" of membership on Unitrin's Board. The Court of Chancery's subjective determination that the *stockholder directors* of Unitrin would reject an "excellent offer," unless it compensated them for giving up the "prestige and perquisites" of directorship, appears to be subjective and without record support. It cannot be presumed * * * that the prestige and perquisites of holding a director's office or a motive to strengthen collective power prevails over a stockholder-director's economic interest. Even the shareholder-plaintiffs in this case agree with the legal proposition Unitrin advocates on appeal: stockholders are presumed to act in their own best economic interests when they vote in a proxy contest.

* * *

The first objective premise relied upon by the Court of Chancery, unsupported by the record, is that the shareholder directors needed to implement the Repurchase Program to attain voting power in a proxy contest equal to 25%. The Court of Chancery properly calculated that if the Repurchase Program was completed, Unitrin's shareholder directors would increase their absolute voting power to 25%. It then calculated the odds of American General marshalling enough votes to defeat the Board and its supporters.

The Court of Chancery and all parties agree that proxy contests do not generate 100% shareholder participation. The shareholder plaintiffs argue that 80–85% may be a usual turnout. Therefore, *without* the Repurchase Program, the director shareholders' absolute voting power of 23% would already constitute *actual voting power greater than* 25% in a proxy contest with normal shareholder participation below 100%. * * *

The second objective premise relied upon by the Court of Chancery, unsupported by the record, is that American General's ability to succeed in a proxy contest depended on the Repurchase Program being enjoined because of the Supermajority Vote provision in Unitrin's charter. Without the approval of a target's board, the danger of activating a poison pill renders it irrational for bidders to pursue stock acquisitions above the triggering level. * * *

As American General acknowledges, a less than 15% stockholder bidder need not proceed with acquiring shares to the extent that it would ever implicate the Supermajority Vote provision. In fact, it would be illogical for American General or any other bidder to acquire more than 15% of Unitrin's stock because that would not only trigger the poison pill, but also the constraints of 8 Del.C. § 203. If American General were to initiate a proxy contest *before* acquiring 15% of Unitrin's stock, it would need to amass only 45.1% of the votes assuming a 90% voter turnout. If it commenced a tender offer at an attractive price contemporaneously with its proxy contest, it could seek to acquire 50.1% of the outstanding voting stock.

The record reflects that institutional investors own 42% of Unitrin's shares. Twenty institutions own 33% of Unitrin's shares. It is generally accepted that proxy contests have re-emerged with renewed significance as a method of acquiring corporate control because "the growth in institutional investment has reduced the dispersion of share ownership." Lucian A. Bebchuk & Marcel Kahan, A Framework for Analyzing Legal Policy Towards Proxy Contests, 78 Cal.L.Rev. 1071, 1134 (1990). * * *

* * *

The assumptions and conclusions American General sets forth in this appeal for a different purpose are particularly probative with regard to the effect of the institutional holdings in Unitrin's stock. American General's two predicate assumptions are a 90% stockholder turnout in a proxy contest and a bidder with 14.9% holdings, i.e., the maximum the bidder could own to avoid triggering the poison pill and the Supermajority Vote provision. American General also calculated the votes available to the

Board or the bidder with and without the Repurchase Program: Assuming no Repurchase [Program], the [shareholder directors] would hold 23%, the percentage collectively held by the [directors] and the bidder would be 37.9%, and the percentage of additional votes available to either side would be 52.1%. Assuming the Repurchase [Program] is fully consummated, the [shareholder directors] would hold 28%, the percentage collectively held by the bidder and the [directors] would be 42.9%, and the percentage of additional votes available to either side would be 47.1%.

American General then applied these assumptions to reach conclusions regarding the votes needed for the 14.9% stockholder bidder to prevail: first, in an election of directors; and second, in the subsequent vote on a merger. With regard to the election of directors, American General made the following calculations: Assume 90% stockholder turnout. To elect directors, a plurality must be obtained; assuming no abstentions and only two competing slates, one must obtain the votes of 45.1% of the shares. The percentage of additional votes the bidder needs to win is: 45.1% - 14.9% (maximum the bidder could own and avoid the poison pill, § 203 and supermajority) = 30.2%. A merger requires approval of a majority of outstanding shares, 8 Del.C. § 251, not just a plurality. In that regard, American General made the following calculations: Assume 90% stockholder turnout. To approve a merger, one must obtain the favorable vote of 50.1% of the shares. The percentage of additional votes the bidder needs to win is 50.1% - 14.9% = 35.2%.

Consequently, to prevail in a proxy contest with a 90% turnout, the percentage of additional shareholder votes a 14.9% shareholder bidder needs to prevail is 30.2% for directors and 35.2% in a subsequent merger. The record reflects that institutional investors held 42% of Unitrin's stock and 20 institutions held 33% of the stock. Thus, American General's own assumptions and calculations in the record support the Unitrin Board's argument that "it is hard to imagine a company more readily susceptible to a proxy contest concerning a pure issue of dollars."

The key variable in a proxy contest would be the merit of American General's issues, not the size of its stockholdings. Moran v. Household Int'l, Inc., Del.Supr., 500 A.2d 1346, 1355 (1985). If American General presented an attractive price as the cornerstone of a proxy contest, it could prevail, irrespective of whether the shareholder directors' absolute voting power was 23% or 28%. * * *

      * * *

The record appears to support Unitrin's argument that the Board's justification for adopting the Repurchase Program was its reasonably perceived risk of substantive coercion, *i.e.*, that Unitrin's shareholders might accept American General's inadequate Offer because of "ignorance or mistaken belief" regarding the Board's assessment of the long-term value of Unitrin's stock. * * *

      * * *

The Court of Chancery applied an incorrect legal standard when it ruled that the Unitrin decision to authorize the Repurchase Program was disproportionate because it was "unnecessary." The Court of Chancery stated: Given that the Board had already implemented the poison pill and the advance notice provision, the repurchase program was unnecessary to protect Unitrin from an inadequate bid.

In QVC, this Court recently elaborated upon the judicial function in applying enhanced scrutiny, citing Unocal as authority, albeit in the context of a sale of control and the target board's consideration of one of several reasonable alternatives. That teaching is nevertheless applicable here: a court applying enhanced judicial scrutiny should be deciding whether the directors made *a reasonable* decision, not *a perfect* decision. If a board selected one of several reasonable alternatives, a court should not second guess that choice even though it might have decided otherwise or subsequent events may have cast doubt on the board's determination. Thus, courts will not substitute their business judgment for that of the directors, but will determine if the directors' decision was, on balance, within a range of reasonableness. See Unocal, 493 A.2d at 955–56; Macmillan, 559 A.2d at 1288; Nixon, 626 A.2d at 1378. Paramount Communications, Inc. v. QVC Network, Inc., Del.Supr., 637 A.2d 34, 45–46 (1994). The Court of Chancery did not determine whether the Unitrin Board's decision to implement the Repurchase Program fell within a "range of reasonableness."

The record reflects that the Unitrin Board's adoption of the Repurchase Program was an apparent recognition on its part that all shareholders are not alike. This Court has stated that distinctions among types of shareholders are neither inappropriate nor irrelevant for a board of directors to make, *e.g.*, distinctions between long-term shareholders and short-term profit-takers, such as arbitrageurs, and their stockholding objectives. Id. * * *

* * *

* * * As common law applications of Unocal's proportionality standard have evolved, at least two characteristics of draconian defensive measures taken by a board of directors in responding to a threat have been brought into focus through enhanced judicial scrutiny. In the modern takeover lexicon, it is now clear that since Unocal, this Court has consistently recognized that defensive measures which are either preclusive or coercive are included within the common law definition of draconian.

If a defensive measure is not draconian, however, because it is not either coercive or preclusive, the Unocal proportionality test requires the focus of enhanced judicial scrutiny to shift to "the range of reasonableness." Paramount Communications, Inc. v. QVC Network, Inc., Del.Supr., 637 A.2d 34, 45–46 (1994). Proper and proportionate defensive responses are intended and permitted to thwart perceived threats. When a corporation is not for sale, the board of directors is the defender of the metaphorical medieval corporate bastion and the protector of the corporation's shareholders. The fact that a defensive action must not be coercive or preclusive does not prevent a board from responding defensively before a bidder is at the corporate bastion's gate.

The *ratio decidendi* for the "range of reasonableness" standard is a need of the board of directors for latitude in discharging its fiduciary duties to the corporation and its shareholders when defending against perceived threats. The concomitant requirement is for judicial restraint. * * *

* * *

A limited nondiscriminatory self-tender, like some other defensive measures, may thwart a current hostile bid, but is not inherently coercive. Moreover, it does not necessarily preclude future bids or proxy contests by stockholders who decline to participate in the repurchase. Cf. AC Acquisitions Corp. v. Anderson, Clayton & Co., Del.Ch., 519 A.2d 103 (1986) (enjoining a coercive self-tender and restructuring plan). A selective repurchase of shares in a public corporation on the market, such as Unitrin's Repurchase Program, generally does not discriminate because all shareholders can voluntarily realize the same benefit by selling. * * *

We have already determined that the record in this case appears to reflect that a proxy contest remained a viable (if more problematic) alternative for American General even if the Repurchase Program were to be completed in its entirety. Nevertheless, the Court of Chancery must determine whether Unitrin's Repurchase Program would only inhibit American General's ability to wage a proxy fight and institute a merger or whether it was, in fact, preclusive because American General's success would either be mathematically impossible or realistically unattainable. If the Court of Chancery concludes that the Unitrin Repurchase Program was not draconian because it was not preclusive, one question will remain to be answered in its proportionality review: whether the Repurchase Program was within a range of reasonableness?

The Court of Chancery found that the Unitrin Board reasonably believed that American General's Offer was inadequate and that the adoption of a poison pill was a proportionate defensive response. Upon remand, in applying the correct legal standard to the factual circumstances of this case, the Court of Chancery may conclude that the implementation of the limited Repurchase Program was also within a range of reasonable additional defensive responses available to the Unitrin Board. In considering whether the Repurchase Program was within a range of reasonableness the Court of Chancery should take into consideration whether: (1) it is a statutorily authorized form of business decision which a board of directors may routinely make in a non-takeover context; (2) as a defensive response to American General's Offer it was limited and corresponded in degree or magnitude to the degree or magnitude of the threat, (*i.e.*, assuming the threat was relatively "mild," was the response relatively "mild?"); (3) with the Repurchase Program, the Unitrin Board properly recognized that all shareholders are not alike, and provided immediate liquidity to those shareholders who wanted it.

NOTE: PRECLUSIVE EFFECT

Many now refer to the *Unocal-Unitrin* standard of review. Under this, defensive tactics withstand intermediate scrutiny if they are neither "coercive nor preclusive" and "fall within a range of reasonableness."

When is a defensive tactic "preclusive" within *Unitrin*? When it makes a hostile transfer of control impossible? If that is the case, why is a poison pill not preclusive per se? Presumably, the poison pill is not preclusive so long as the bidder and target shareholders retain the alternatives of proxy voting and pill redemption. When, then, is the transfer of control via a proxy fight precluded? Presumably, a one or two year delay caused by a staggered board does not amount to preclusion. Given any possibility of control transfer to the bidder after a proxy contest, is there any possibility that a board's refusal to redeem a poison pill could constitute a breach of fiduciary duty?

Gilson, Unocal Fifteen Years Later (And What We Can Do About It), 26 Del. J. Corp. L. 491, 501 (2001), describes *Unitrin* as the result of the Delaware Supreme Court's conclusion that proxy contests are preferable to tender offers as a means of resolving a control contest. Gilson argues that while in theory elections and tenders offers could be functional equivalents, in practice target firm manipulation, whether through timing delays, staggered boards, member qualification requirements, make elections a costly second best vehicle for control transfer. Id. at 503–504. For a case sustaining a proxy fight delaying tactic under *Unitrin*, see Mentor Graphics v. Quickturn Design Systems, 728 A.2d 25 (Del.Ch.1998). There a board faced with a proxy contest by a hostile bidder authorized a delay of a shareholders meeting called by a shareholder for 90 to 100 days after the determination of the validity of the request for a meeting. The Chancellor determined that the by law struck a "proper balance" on the facts of the case, although it arguably approached the "outer limit of reasonableness." The Chancellor also warned lawyers to refrain from continually pushing "the time-delay envelope." Comments Gilson, supra at 506: "[W]hile the impulse to lecture counsel on their duties is both laudable and continues the chancery court's useful technique of instructing counsel through dicta, the simple fact is that the Delaware courts' approach in this area operates to encourage attorneys to push the envelope precisely because there is no principle guiding the outcome."

NOTE: *CHESAPEAKE CORP. v. SHORE*

In **Chesapeake Corp. v. Shore**, 771 A.2d 293 (Del.Ch.2000), Chancellor Leo Strine confronted *Unitrin's* reading of *Unocal*.

The plaintiff, Chesapeake, had made a $16.50 all cash-all shares offer at a 40 percent premium for Shorewood Packaging (later raised to $17.25). The offer was a "Pacman" response to an earlier all cash-all shares offer by Shorewood for Chesapeake at a 41 percent premium. Unfortunately for Shorewood, Chesapeake had sounder defensive provisions. Chesapeake initiated a consent solicitation looking to the removal of a staggered board provision in Shorewood's bylaws. Anticipating this, Shorewood's board amended its bylaws to require a 66 2/3 supermajority of shareholders to amend the by laws. This was later reduced to 60 percent. Either way, with management controlling 24 percent of the stock, the supermajority provision made it mathematically impossible for a challenge to succeed assuming a 90 percent voter turnout. Assuming a 95 percent voter turnout, a challenger could in theory amend the bylaws. The question was whether *Unocal/Unitrin* permitted this variation on the "Just Say No" defense. Chancellor Strine held that it did not. He described the applicable law as follows, id. at 324–329:

"In some respects, this case unavoidably brings to the fore certain tensions in our corporation law. For example, several cases have stated that a corporate board may consider a fully-financed all-cash, all-shares, premium to market tender offer a threat to stockholders on the following premise: the board believes that the company's present strategic plan will deliver more value than the premium offer, the stock market has not yet bought that rationale, the board may be correct, and therefore there is a risk that 'stockholders might tender . . . in ignorance or based upon a mistaken belief. . . .' [*Unitrin*, 651 A.2d at 1384.] A rather interesting term has emerged to describe this threat: 'substantive coercion.' [Ronald J. Gilson & Reinier Kraakman, *Delaware's Intermediate Standard For Defensive Tactics: Is There Substance To Proportionality Review?*, 44 BUS. LAW. 247, 267 (1989).]

"One might imagine that the response to this particular type of threat might be time-limited and confined to what is necessary to ensure that the board can tell its side of the story effectively. That is, because the threat is defined as one involving the possibility that stockholders might make an erroneous investment or voting decision, the appropriate response would seem to be one that would remedy that problem by providing the stockholders with adequate information. The corporate board has, of course, many tools to accomplish that, but may legitimately need more time to ensure that it can get its message out to the marketplace.

"In addition, it may be that the corporate board acknowledges that an immediate value-maximizing transaction would be advisable but thinks that a better alternative than the tender offer might be achievable. A time period that permits the board to negotiate for a better offer or explore alternatives would also be logically proportionate to the threat of substantive coercion.

"But our law has, at times, authorized defensive responses that arguably go far beyond these categories. Paradoxically, some of these defensive responses have caused our law to adopt a view of stockholder voting capabilities that is a bit hard to reconcile. In *Unitrin,* for example, the Supreme Court held that the target Unitrin board could protect its stockholder base from an all-cash, all-shares premium tender offer from American General on the grounds that the Unitrin stockholders were susceptible to accepting an inadequate price ignorantly or mistakenly. At the same time, the Supreme Court held that it was not necessarily a disproportionate response to the American General offer for the Unitrin board to buy its stock in a selective repurchase program at a price comparable to the tender offer price (thus arguably 'substantively coercing' participants itself) even though the selective repurchase program thereby increased the percentage of the company's stock in directors' hands to as much as 28%.

"The Court held that the selective repurchase program was not *necessarily* preclusive of a successful proxy fight by the tender offeror on grounds that appear to be in tension with the Unitrin board's fear of substantive coercion. For purposes of analyzing whether American General could obtain the necessary votes to remove the Unitrin board (a majority of the quorum) or conclude a merger (a majority of the outstanding shares), the Court made certain assumptions:

- the turnout would be 90%;
- the Unitrin directors held 28% of Unitrin's stock;
- American General held 14.9% of Unitrin's stock;
- institutional investors held 42% of Unitrin's stock; and
- twenty institutions held 33% of Unitrin's stock.

"Under these assumptions, American General had to win the following majorities of the unaligned votes to prevail:

- vote on election of directors: 64.12%
- vote on a merger: 74.73%

"On their face, the required majorities, which exceed any margin ever achieved by President Franklin Roosevelt, seem to present a rather formidable and, one might daresay, preclusive barrier to the insurgent. But the Supreme Court concluded that on this evidence, the Chancery Court's determination that a successful proxy contest was not a realistic possibility could not be sustained and remanded the matter for further findings.

"In order of importance, three reasons seemed to underlie the Supreme Court's conclusion that the repurchase program might not be preclusive. First, Unitrin's stockholder base was heavily concentrated within a small number of institutional investors. This concentration 'facilitat[ed the] bidder's ability to communicate the merits of its position.' Second, the fact that the insurgent would have to receive majorities from the disinterested voters uncommon in hotly contested elections in republican democracies was of '*de minimis*' importance 'because 42% of Unitrin's stock was owned by institutional investors.' As such, the Supreme Court found that 'it is hard to imagine a company more readily susceptible [than Unitrin] to a proxy contest concerning a pure issue of dollars.' Finally, the Supreme Court was unwilling to presume that the directors' block—which was controlled almost entirely by non-management directors—would not sell for the right price or vote themselves out of office to facilitate such a sale.

"The first two premises of the Court's rejection of the Chancery Court's finding of preclusion seem somewhat contradictory to its acceptance of substantive coercion as a rationale for sweeping defensive measures against the American General bid. On the one hand, a corporate electorate highly dominated by institutional investors has the motivation and wherewithal to understand and act upon a proxy solicitation from an insurgent, such that the necessity for the insurgent to convince over 64% of the non-aligned votes to support its position in order to prevail is not necessarily preclusive. On the other, the same electorate must be protected from substantive coercion because it (the target board thinks) is unable to digest management's position on the long-term value of the company, compare that position to the view advocated by the tender offeror, and make an intelligent (if not risk-free) judgment about whether to support the election of a board that will permit them to sell their shares of stock.

"If the consistency in this approach is not in the view that stockholders will always respond in a lemming-like fashion whenever a premium offer is on the table, then a possible reading of *Unitrin* is that corporate boards are allowed to have it both ways in situations where important stockholder ownership and voting rights are at stake. In approaching the case at hand, I apply a different reading of *Unitrin*, however.

"Without denying the analytical tension within that opinion, one must also remember that the opinion did not ultimately validate the Unitrin defensive repurchase program. Rather, the Supreme Court remanded the case to the Chancery Court to conduct a further examination of the repurchase program, using the refined *Unocal* analysis the Court set forth. That analysis emphasized the need for trial courts to defer to well-informed corporate boards that identify legitimate threats and implement proportionate defensive measures addressing those threats. It was open for the court on remand to conclude, after considering the relevant factors articulated by the Supreme Court, that the repurchase program was invalid.

"I therefore believe it is open to and required of me to examine both the legitimacy of the Shorewood board's identification of 'substantive coercion' or 'stockholder confusion' as a threat and to determine whether the Supermajority Bylaw is a non-preclusive and proportionate response to that threat. Indeed, the importance to stockholders of a proper *Unocal* analysis can hardly be overstated in a case where a corporate board relies upon a threat of substantive coercion as its primary justification for defensive measures. Several reasons support this assertion.

"As a starting point, it is important to recognize that substantive coercion can be invoked by a corporate board in almost every situation. There is virtually no CEO in America who does not believe that the market is not valuing her company properly. Moreover, one hopes that directors and officers can always say that they know more about the company than the company's stockholders—after all, they are paid to know more. Thus, the threat that stockholders will be confused or wrongly eschew management's advice is omnipresent.

"Therefore, the use of this threat as a justification for aggressive defensive measures could easily be subject to abuse. The only way to protect stockholders is for courts to ensure that the threat is real and that the board asserting the threat is not imagining or exaggerating it. * * * This informational responsibility would include, one would think, the duty to communicate the company's strategic plans and prospects to stockholders as clearly and understandably as possible. If management claims that its communication efforts have been unsuccessful, shouldn't it have to show that its efforts were adequate before using the risk of confusion as a reason to deny its stockholders access to a bid offering a substantial premium to the company's market price? * * *

"This confusion rationale should also be tested against the information currently available to investors. The proliferation of computer technology and changes in the broadcast media industry have given investors access to abundant information about the companies in which they invest. The capability of corporations to communicate with their stockholders has never been greater. And the future promises even easier and more substantial information flows.

"Our law should also hesitate to ascribe rube-like qualities to stockholders. *If stockholders are presumed competent to buy stock in the first place, why are they not presumed competent to decide when to sell in a tender offer after an adequate time for deliberation has been afforded them?*

"Another related concern is the fact that corporate boards that rely upon substantive coercion as a defense are unwilling to bear the risk of their own errors. Corporate America would rightfully find it shocking if directors were found liable because they erroneously blocked a premium tender offer, the company's shares went into the tank for two years thereafter, and a court held the directors liable for the investment losses suffered by stockholders the directors barred from selling. But, because directors are not anxious to bear *any* of the investment risk in these situations, courts should hesitate before enabling them to make such fundamental investment decisions for the company's owners. It is quite different for a corporate board to determine that the owners of the company should be barred from selling their shares than to determine what products the company should manufacture. Even less legitimate is a corporate board's decision to protect stockholders from erroneously turning the board out of office.

"It is also interesting that the threat of substantive coercion seems to cause a ruckus in boardrooms most often in the context of tender offers at prices constituting substantial premiums to prior trading levels. In the case of Shorewood, for example, shareholders had been selling in the market at the pre-Chesapeake Tender Offer price, which was much lower. Did Shorewood management make any special efforts to encourage these shareholders to hold? While I recognize that the sale of an entire company is different from day-to-day sales of small blocks, one must remember that the substantive coercion rationale is not one advanced on behalf of employees or communities that might be adversely affected by a change of control. Rather, substantive coercion is a threat to stockholders who might sell at a depressed price. The stockholder who sells in a depressed market for the company's stock without a premium is obviously worse off than one who sells at premium to that depressed price in a tender offer. But it is only in the latter situation that corporate boards commonly swing into action with extraordinary measures. The fact that the premium situation usually involves a possible change in management may play more than a modest role in that difference.

"This leads to a final point. As *Unocal* recognized, the possibility that management might be displaced if a premium-producing tender offer is successful creates an inherent conflict between the interests of stockholders and management. There is always the possibility that subjectively well-intentioned, but nevertheless interested directors, will subconsciously be motivated by the profoundly negative effect a takeover could have on their personal bottom lines and careers.

"Allowing such directors to use a broad substantive coercion defense without a serious examination of the legitimacy of that defense would undercut the purpose the *Unocal* standard of review was established to serve. For many of these reasons, Professors Gilson and Kraakman–from whom our courts adopted the term substantive coercion—emphasized the need for close judicial scrutiny of defensive measures supposedly adopted to address that threat * * *

"Nothing in *Unitrin* is intrinsically inconsistent with the approach articulated by Professors Gilson and Kraakman; however, one must acknowledge that *Unitrin* mandates that the court afford a reasonable degree of deference to a properly functioning board that identifies a threat and adopts proportionate defenses after a careful and good faith inquiry. With those preliminary thoughts in mind, I turn to an examination of the Supermajority Bylaw."

The Chancellor reviewed the testimony of the parties' expert witnesses and drew the inference that "victory is not reasonably attainable for Chesapeake in the face of the Supermajority Bylaw. Finally, id. at 344, he confronted *Unitrin* on the facts:

"While I cannot deny that there is some tension between some of my analysis and the reasoning of *Unitrin*, my ultimate conclusion can be reconciled with that decision for several reasons.

"First, the Supermajority Bylaw sets a much higher barrier than the repurchase program at issue in *Unitrin*. Assuming a 90% turnout, the percentage of disinterested votes that Chesapeake must receive to amend the bylaws is far higher than had to be obtained by American General to change the board in *Unitrin*:

Unitrin	Shorewood
64.12%	88.05%

"The defendants have presented no reliable evidence to suggest that the required percentage is 'realistically' attainable. Under *Unitrin*, therefore, the Supermajority Bylaw must be considered preclusive.

"Next, the substantive coercion rationale cannot be wielded as imprecisely by the Shorewood board as was done by the defendants in *Unitrin* because the facts do not bear that rationale out in this case. Here, the early returns in the field suggest very little risk of voter confusion. Moreover, the defendants' own testimony about the company's sophisticated stockholder and analyst base and about Shorewood management's credibility with that base, as well as the defendants' arguments about their stockholders' likely voting behavior, undercut the need for any defense so extreme as the Supermajority Bylaw.

"Another critical distinction is the difference between the self-interest of the management holders in *Unitrin* and those in this case. In *Unitrin*, the directors had no material financial interests in the company other than as stockholders. Thus the Unitrin directors had no financial incentive to vote their shares simply to remain as directors. The opposite is true here, as six of the nine Shorewood directors have substantial monetary reasons to vote to keep themselves in control. Indeed, they have already announced their intention to oppose Chesapeake.

"Finally, the level of attention the Shorewood board paid to the relevant issues was grossly insufficient. *Unitrin* emphasized the need for deference to boards that make reasoned judgments about defensive measures. It in no way suggests that the court ought to sanction a board's adoption of very aggressive defensive measures when that board has given little or no consideration to relevant factors and less preclusive alternatives."

NOTE: *UNOCAL* OR *BLASIUS*?

MM Companies, Inc. v. Liquid Audio, Inc., 813 A.2d 1118 (Del.Supr.2003), offers a unitary restatement of the *Unocal/Unitrin* and *Blasius* rules. The case arose out of MM's year-long attempt to acquire Liquid Audio. MM put an offer on the table, which Liquid Audio's five-seat staggered board rejected. MM resorted to the standard tack of running an opposing slate of directors for the two seats up for election at Liquid Audio's annual meeting. Liquid Audio fought back with a variety of delays and diversions, including repeated postponement of the meeting and approval of a white knight merger. With the meeting finally scheduled and the election of the MM nominees imminent, Liquid Audio's board expanded its own size by two seats and appointed friendly nominees to both of them, classified so as not to be coming up for election. Liquid Audio's managers were concerned that one or two of the incumbent directors might resign in the wake of the election of MM's nominees, a scenario holding out a shift of control to MM given a five-seat board.

At the meeting, the Liquid Audio shareholders elected the MM nominees but rejected an MM proposal that would have added four more seats to the board and placed MM nominees thereon, shifting control to MM. MM brought an action requesting invalidation of Liquid Audio's expansion of its board, claiming violations of both *Unocal/Unitrin* and *Blasius*. The question went to which standard of review was appropriate, *Unocal/Unitrin*, *Blasius*, or both? Both, said the Delaware Supreme Court, 813 A.2d at 1131–32:

"In this case * * * the Court of Chancery was presented with the ultimate defensive measure touching upon an issue of control. It was a defensive action taken by an incumbent board of directors for the primary purpose of interfering with and impeding the effectiveness of the shareholder franchise in electing successor directors. Accordingly, the incumbent board of directors had the burden of demonstrating a compelling justification for that action to withstand enhanced judicial scrutiny *within* the *Unocal* standard of reasonableness and proportionality.

* * *

"This case presents a paragon of when the compelling justification standard of *Blasius* must be applied within *Unocal's* requirement that any defensive measure be proportionate and reasonable in relation to the threat posed. The *Unocal* standard of review applies because the Liquid Audio board's action was a 'defensive measure taken in response to some threat to corporate policy and effectiveness which touches upon issues of control.' The compelling justification standard of *Blasius* also had to be applied *within* an application of the *Unocal* standard to that specific defensive measure because the primary purpose of the Board's action was to interfere with or impede the effective exercise of the shareholder franchise in a contested election for directors.

"The Court of Chancery properly decided to examine the Board's defensive action to expand from five to seven members and to appoint two new members in acordance with the *Unocal* standard of enhanced judicial review. Initially, the Court of Chancery concluded that defensive action was not preclusive or coercive. If a defensive measure is not draconian, because it is neither coercive nor preclusive, proportionality review under *Unocal* requires the focus of enhanced judicial scrutiny to shift to the range of reasonableness.

"After the Court of Chancery determined that the Board's action was not preclusive or coercive, it properly proceeded to determine whether the Board's action was reasonable and proportionate in relation to the threat posed. Under the circumstances presented in this case, however, the Court of Chancery did not 'recognize the special [importance] of protecting the shareholder's franchise within *Unocal's* requirement that any defensive measure be proportionate and reasonable in relation to the threat posed.' Since the Court of Chancery had already concluded that the *primary* purpose of the Liquid Audio board's defensive measure was to interfere with or impede an effective exercise of the shareholder's franchise in a contested election of directors, the Board had the burden of demonstrating a compelling justification for that action.

"When the *primary purpose* of a board of directors' defensive measure is to interfere with or impede the effective exercise of the shareholder franchise in a contested election for directors, the board must first demonstrate a compelling justification for such action as a condition precedent to any judicial consideration of reasonableness and proportionately. As this case illustrates, such defensive actions by a board need not actually prevent the shareholders from attaining any success in seating one or more nominees in a contested election for directors and the election contest need not involve a challenge for outright control of the board of directors. To invoke the *Blasius* compelling justification standard of review *within* an application of the *Unocal* standard of review, the defensive actions of the board only need to be taken for the primary purpose of interfering with or impeding the effectiveness of the stockholder vote in a contested election for directors.

"The record reflects that the primary purpose of the Director Defendants' action was to interfere with and impede the effective exercise of the stockholder franchise in a contested election for directors. The Court of Chancery concluded that the Director Defendants amended the bylaws to provide for a board of seven and appointed two additional members of the Board for the primary purpose of diminishing the influence of MM's two nominees on a five-member Board by eliminating either the possibility of a deadlock on the board or of MM controlling the Board, if one or two Director Defendants resigned from the Board. That defensive action by the Director Defendants compromised the essential role of corporate democracy in maintaining the proper allocation of power between the shareholders and the Board, because that action was taken in the context of a contested election for successor directors. Since the Director Defendants did not demonstrate a compelling justification for that defensive action, the bylaw amendment that expanded the size of the Liquid Audio board, and permitted the appointment of two new members on the eve of a contested election, should have been invalidated by the Court of Chancery."

Omnicare, Inc. v. NCS Healthcare, Inc.

Supreme Court of Delaware, 2003.
818 A.2d 914.

■ Before VEASEY, CHIEF JUSTICE, WALSH, HOLLAND, BERGER and STEELE, JUSTICES, constituting the Court en Banc.

■ HOLLAND, JUSTICE, for the majority:

NCS Healthcare, Inc. ("NCS"), a Delaware corporation, was the object of competing acquisition bids, one by Genesis Health Ventures, Inc. ("Genesis''), a Pennsylvania corporation, and the other by Omnicare, Inc. (''Omnicare''), a Delaware corporation. * * *

[NCS, a provider of pharmacy services to long-term care institutions, has a dual class common capital structure, the Class A shares being entitled to 10 votes per share, the Class B shares being entitled to 1 vote per share, with the shares otherwise identical. Outcalt, the Chairman owns 202,063 shares of Class A and 3,476,086 shares of Class B. Shaw, the CEO, owns 28,905 shares of Class A and 1,141,134 shares of Class B. Outcalt and Shaw together own 65% of the voting power of NCS stock. The NCS board has two other members, Sells, a former CEO, and Osborne, a business school professor. Genesis is a healthcare provider. Omnicare is in the institutional pharmacy business. Omnicare purchased 1000 shares of NCS Class A common stock on July 30, 2002.

[There are two proceedings. One is a class action brought by NCS stockholders seeking to invalidate the merger between NCS and Genesis. Omnicare also brings a proceeding seeking to invalidate the merger agreement between NCS and Genesis on fiduciary grounds. Omnicare also challenges Voting Agreements between Genesis and Outcalt and Shaw, which irrevocably commit them to vote for the merger.]

FACTUAL BACKGROUND

[NCS entered a period of severe financial distress in 1999. Its stock dropped from $20 in early 1999 to a range of $0.09 to $0.50 in early 2001. It also defaulted on $350 million of long term debt, which was accelerated in April 2001. NCS simultaneously discussed a prepackaged bankruptcy with its creditors and searched for a third party acquirer.

[Acquisition discussions began with Omnicare. Omnicare made a bid less than the face amount of the debt and conditioned on a bankruptcy proceeding. NCS did not accept, and turned to Genesis in early 2002. Operations were improving, so the NCS directors began to look toward a transaction that would provide some recovery for NCS stockholders' equity. An independent committee was formed, comprised of the two board members, Sells and Osborne, who were neither NCS employees nor major NCS stockholders (the ''Independent Committee'').

[The terms offered by Genesis steadily improved, providing some value for the NCS shareholders as well as full payment of the senior debt. But, before negotiating a merger agreement, Genesis demanded an Exclusivity Agreement as a first step towards a completely locked up transaction. It had previously had lost a bidding war to Omnicare in another deal and harbored bitter feelings. The NCS board assented, on the recommendation of the Independent Committee, and an Exclusivity Agreement was executed and delivered, covering the period to July 31, 2002. That accomplished, Genesis put draft agreements on the table for negotiation.

[Omnicare, worried about the competitive implications of the combination of NCS and Genesis, reemerged in July. It contacted NCS to suggest a transaction in which Omnicare would retire NCS's debt at par plus accrued interest and pay the NCS stockholders $3 cash. But the Exclusivity Agreement prohibited prevented NCS from talking to Omnicare. The Independent Committee concluded that discussions with Omnicare presented an unacceptable risk that Genesis would abandon merger discussions, but instructed that Omnicare's letter be used to extract improved terms with Genesis.

[Genesis responded with substantially improved terms the next day, but also insisted that the transaction had to be approved by midnight the following day, July 28, or else Genesis would terminate and withdraw its offer. On July 28, the Independent Committee (fully informed of all material facts) voted to recommend the transaction to the full board, which convened immediately. The Board, after receiving reports and advice from its legal and financial advisors, concluded that "balancing the potential loss of the Genesis deal against the uncertainty of Omnicare's letter, results in the conclusion that the only reasonable alternative for the Board of Directors is to approve the Genesis transaction."

[The NCS/Genesis merger agreement, executed later that day, provided that: (1) the NCS stockholders would receive 1 share of Genesis common stock in exchange for every 10 shares of NCS common stock; (2) NCS would redeem its defaulted debt in accordance with its terms; (3) the merger agreement would be submitted to the stockholders regardless of whether the board continued to recommend the merger; and (4) termination under stated circumstances required NCS to pay Genesis a $6 million fee and/or Genesis's documented expenses, up to $5 million. The agreement prohibited acquisition discussions with third parties, unless (1) the third party provided an unsolicited, *bona fide* written proposal; (2) the NCS board believed in good faith that the proposal was or was likely to result in an acquisition on superior terms; and (3) the third party executed a confidentiality agreement at least as restrictive that entered into by Genesis before receiving any non-public information.

[Outcalt and Shaw, with the express approval of the board, entered into voting agreements with Genesis. These provided: (1) that Outcalt and Shaw were acting in their capacity as NCS stockholders not in their capacity as NCS directors or officers; (2) that Outcalt and Shaw would vote all of their shares in favor of the merger agreement; (3) for specific performance and an irrevocable proxy from Outcalt and Shaw to Genesis to vote their shares in favor of the merger.

[Omnicare promptly renewed its proposal, offering to buy NCS for $3.50 per share subject to a satisfactory due diligence review. Two months later it followed up with an irrevocable commitment to acquire NCS for $3.50 per share in cash. In response, the NCS board withdrew its recommendation that the stockholders vote in favor of the NCS/Genesis merger agreement. The withdrawal could not alter the result because (1) the Genesis merger agreement still had to be submitted to a stockholder vote; (2) existing contractual obligations to Genesis prevented NCS from accepting Omnicare's irrevocable merger proposal; and (3) the Outcalt and Shaw voting agreements ensured NCS stockholder approval of the Genesis merger.]

LEGAL ANALYSIS

[The Court of Chancery sustained the Genesis merger under the business judgment rule, having determined that, as a stock-for-stock transaction, it did not result in a change of control triggering *Revlon* duties. It also ruled that the NCS board had not breached its duty of care.]

The Court of Chancery's decision to review the NCS board's decision to merge with Genesis under the business judgment rule rather than the enhanced scrutiny standard of *Revlon* is not outcome determinative for the purposes of deciding this appeal. We have assumed arguendo that the business judgment rule applied to the decision by the NCS board to merge with Genesis. We have also assumed arguendo that the NCS board exercised due care * * *.

* * *

These Deal Protection Devices Unenforceable

In this case, the Court of Chancery correctly held that the NCS directors' decision to adopt defensive devices to *completely* "lock up" the Genesis merger mandated "special scrutiny" under the two-part test set forth in *Unocal*. That conclusion is consistent with our holding in *Paramount v. Time* that "safety devices" adopted to protect a transaction that did not result in a change of control are subject to enhanced judicial scrutiny under a *Unocal* analysis. The record does not, however, support the Court of Chancery's conclusion that the defensive devices adopted by the NCS board to protect the Genesis merger were reasonable and proportionate to the threat that NCS perceived from the potential loss of the Genesis transaction.

Pursuant to the judicial scrutiny required under *Unocal's* two-stage analysis, the NCS directors must first demonstrate "that they had reasonable grounds for believing that a danger to corporate policy and effectiveness existed. . . . " To satisfy that burden, the NCS directors are required to show they acted in good faith after conducting a reasonable investigation. The threat identified by the NCS board was the possibility of losing the Genesis offer and being left with no comparable alternative transaction.

The second stage of the *Unocal* test requires the NCS directors to demonstrate that their defensive response was "reasonable in relation to the threat posed." This inquiry involves a two-step analysis. The NCS directors must first establish that the merger deal protection devices adopted in response to the threat were not "coercive" or "preclusive," and then demonstrate that their response was within a "range of reasonable responses" to the threat perceived. In *Unitrin*, we stated:

● A response is "coercive" if it is aimed at forcing upon stockholders a management-sponsored alternative to a hostile offer.

● A response is "preclusive" if it deprives stockholders of the right to receive all tender offers or precludes a bidder from seeking control by fundamentally restricting proxy contests or otherwise.

This aspect of the *Unocal* standard provides for a disjunctive analysis. If defensive measures are either preclusive or coercive they are draconian and impermissible. In this case, the deal protection devices of the NCS board were *both* preclusive and coercive.

This Court enunciated the standard for determining stockholder coercion in the case of *Williams v. Geier*. A stockholder vote may be nullified by wrongful coercion "where the board or some other party takes actions which have the effect of causing the stockholders to vote in favor of the proposed transaction for some reason other than the merits of that transaction." * * *

　　* * *

Although the minority stockholders were not forced to vote for the Genesis merger, they were required to accept it because it was *a fait accompli*. The record reflects that the defensive devices employed by the NCS board are preclusive and coercive in the sense that they accomplished *a fait accompli*. In this case, despite the fact that the NCS board has withdrawn its recommendation for the Genesis transaction and recommended its rejection by the stockholders, the deal protection devices approved by the NCS board operated in concert to have a preclusive and coercive effect. Those tripartite defensive measures—the Section 251(c) provision, the voting agreements, and the absence of an effective fiduciary out clause—made it "mathematically impossible" and "realistically unattainable" for the Omnicare transaction or any other proposal to succeed, no matter how superior the proposal.

The deal protection devices adopted by the NCS board were designed to coerce the consummation of the Genesis merger and preclude the consideration of any superior transaction. The NCS directors' defensive devices are not within a reasonable range of responses to the perceived threat of losing the Genesis offer because they are preclusive and coercive. Accordingly, we hold that those deal protection devices are unenforceable.

Effective Fiduciary Out Required

[Alternatively, t]he defensive measures that protected the merger transaction are unenforceable * * * because they are invalid as they operate in this case. Given the specifically enforceable irrevocable voting agreements, the provision in the merger agreement requiring the board to submit the transaction for a stockholder vote and the omission of a fiduciary out clause in the merger agreement completely prevented the board from discharging its fiduciary responsibilities to the minority stockholders when Omnicare presented its superior transaction. * * *

Under the circumstances presented in this case, where a cohesive group of stockholders with majority voting power was irrevocably committed to the merger transaction, "[e]ffective representation of the financial interests of the minority shareholders imposed upon the [NCS board] an affirmative responsibility to protect those minority shareholders' interests." The NCS board could not abdicate its fiduciary duties to the minority by leaving it to the stockholders alone to approve or disapprove the merger agreement because two stockholders had already combined to establish a majority of the voting power that made the outcome of the stockholder vote a foregone conclusion.

The Court of Chancery noted that Section 251(c) of the Delaware General Corporation Law now permits boards to agree to submit a merger agreement for a stockholder vote, even if the Board later withdraws its support for that agreement and recommends that the stockholders reject it. The Court of Chancery also noted that stockholder voting agreements are permitted by Delaware law. * * *

Taking action that is otherwise legally possible, however, does not *ipso facto* comport with the fiduciary responsibilities of directors in all circumstances. The synopsis to the amendments that resulted in the enactment of Section 251(c) in the Delaware corporation law statute specifically provides: "the amendments are not intended to address the question of whether such a submission requirement is appropriate in any particular set of factual circumstances." Section 251 provisions, like the no-shop provision examined in QVC, are "presumptively valid in the abstract." Such provisions in a merger agreement may not, however, "validly define or limit the directors' fiduciary duties under Delaware law or prevent the [NCS] directors from carrying out their fiduciary duties under Delaware law."

* * *

* * * Instead of agreeing to the absolute defense of the Genesis merger from a superior offer, however, the NCS board was required to negotiate a fiduciary out clause to protect the NCS stockholders if the Genesis transaction became an inferior offer. By acceding to Genesis' ultimatum for complete protection *in futuro,* the NCS board disabled itself from exercising its own fiduciary obligations at a time when the board's own judgment is most important, i.e. receipt of a subsequent superior offer.

Any board has authority to give the proponent of a recommended merger agreement reasonable structural and economic defenses, incentives, and fair compensation if the transaction is not completed. To the extent that defensive measures are economic and reasonable, they may become an increased cost to the proponent of any subsequent transaction. Just as defensive measures cannot be draconian, however, they cannot limit or circumscribe the directors' fiduciary duties. Notwithstanding the corporation's insolvent condition, the NCS board had no authority to execute a merger agreement that subsequently prevented it from effectively discharging its ongoing fiduciary responsibilities.

* * *

The NCS board was required to contract for an effective fiduciary out clause to exercise its continuing fiduciary responsibilities to the minority stockholders. The issues in this appeal do not involve the general validity of either stockholder voting agreements or the authority of directors to insert a Section 251(c) provision in a merger agreement. In this case, the NCS board combined those two otherwise valid actions and caused them to operate in concert as an absolute lock up, in the absence of an effective fiduciary out clause in the Genesis merger agreement.

In the context of this preclusive and coercive lock up case, the protection of Genesis' contractual expectations must yield to the supervening responsibility of the directors to discharge their fiduciary duties on a continuing basis. The merger agreement and voting agreements, as they were combined to operate in concert in this case, are inconsistent with the NCS directors' fiduciary duties. To that extent, we hold that they are invalid and unenforceable.

■ VEASEY, CHIEF JUSTICE, with whom STEELE, JUSTICE, joins dissenting.

    * * *

Because we believe this Court must respect the reasoned judgment of the board of directors and give effect to the wishes of the controlling stockholders, we respectfully disagree with the Majority's reasoning that results in a holding that the confluence of board and stockholder action constitutes a breach of fiduciary duty. The essential fact that must always be remembered is that this agreement and the voting commitments of Outcalt and Shaw concluded a lengthy search and intense negotiation process in the context of insolvency and creditor pressure where no other viable bid had emerged. Accordingly, we endorse the Vice Chancellor's well-reasoned analysis that the NCS board's action before the hostile bid emerged was within the bounds of its fiduciary duties under these facts.

    * * *

Going into negotiations with Genesis, the NCS directors knew that, up until that time, NCS had found only one potential bidder, Omnicare. Omnicare had refused to buy NCS except at a fire sale price through an asset sale in bankruptcy. Omnicare's best proposal at that stage would not have paid off all creditors and would have provided nothing for stockholders. The Noteholders, represented by the Ad Hoc Committee, were willing to oblige Omnicare and force NCS into bankruptcy if Omnicare would pay in full the NCS debt. Through the NCS board's efforts, Genesis expressed interest that became increasingly attractive. Negotiations with Genesis led to an offer paying creditors off and conferring on NCS stockholders $24 million—an amount infinitely superior to the prior Omnicare proposals.

But there was, understandably, a sine qua non. In exchange for offering the NCS stockholders a return on their equity and creditor payment, Genesis demanded certainty that the merger would close. If the NCS board would not have acceded to the Section 251(c) provision, if Outcalt and Shaw had not agreed to the voting agreements and if NCS had insisted on a fiduciary out, there would have been no Genesis deal! Thus, the only value-enhancing transaction available would have disappeared. NCS knew that Omnicare had spoiled a Genesis acquisition in the past, and it is not disputed by the Majority that the NCS directors made a reasoned decision to accept as real the Genesis threat to walk away.

When Omnicare submitted its conditional eleventh-hour bid, the NCS board had to weigh the economic terms of the proposal against the uncertainty of completing a deal with Omnicare. Importantly, because

Omnicare's bid was conditioned on its satisfactorily completing its due diligence review of NCS, the NCS board saw this as a crippling condition * * *. As a matter of business judgment, the risk of negotiating with Omnicare and losing Genesis at that point outweighed the possible benefits. The lock-up was indisputably a sine qua non to any deal with Genesis.

A lock-up permits a target board and a bidder to "exchange certainties." Certainty itself has value. The acquirer may pay a higher price for the target if the acquirer is assured consummation of the transaction. The target company also benefits from the certainty of completing a transaction with a bidder because losing an acquirer creates the perception that a target is damaged goods, thus reducing its value.

> * * *

While the present case does not involve an attempt to hold on to only one interested bidder, the NCS board was equally concerned about "exchanging certainties" with Genesis. If the creditors decided to force NCS into bankruptcy, which could have happened at any time as NCS was unable to service its obligations, the stockholders would have received nothing. The NCS board also did not know if the NCS business prospects would have declined again, leaving NCS less attractive to other bidders, including Omnicare, which could have changed its mind and again insisted on an asset sale in bankruptcy.

> * * *

The Majority invalidates the NCS board's action by announcing a new rule that represents an extension of our jurisprudence. That new rule can be narrowly stated as follows: A merger agreement entered into after a market search, before any prospect of a topping bid has emerged, which locks up stockholder approval and does not contain a "fiduciary out" provision, is per se invalid when a later significant topping bid emerges. As we have noted, this bright-line, per se rule would apply regardless of (1) the circumstances leading up to the agreement and (2) the fact that stockholders who control voting power had irrevocably committed themselves, *as stockholders,* to vote for the merger. Narrowly stated, this new rule is a judicially-created "third rail" that now becomes one of the given "rules of the game," to be taken into account by the negotiators and drafters of merger agreements. In our view, this new rule is an unwise extension of existing precedent.

> * * *

In our view, the Majority misapplies the *Unitrin* concept of "coercive and preclusive" measures to preempt a proper proportionality balancing. Thus, the Majority asserts that "in applying *enhanced judicial scrutiny* to *defensive devices* designed to protect a merger agreement, ... a court must ... determine that those measures are not preclusive or coercive...." Here, the deal protection measures were not adopted unilaterally by the board to fend off an existing hostile offer that threatened the corporate policy and effectiveness of NCS. They were adopted because Genesis—the "only game in town"—would not save NCS, its creditors and its stockholders without these provisions.

The Majority—incorrectly, in our view—relies on *Unitrin* to advance its analysis. The discussion of "draconian" measures in *Unitrin* dealt with unilateral board action, a repurchase program, designed to fend off an existing hostile offer by American General. In *Unitrin* we recognized the need to police preclusive and coercive actions initiated *by the board* to delay or retard an existing hostile bid so as to ensure that the stockholders can benefit from the board's negotiations with the bidder or others and to exercise effectively the franchise as the ultimate check on board action. *Unitrin* polices the effect of board action on existing tender offers and proxy contests to ensure that the board cannot permanently impose its will on the stockholders, leaving the stockholders no recourse to their voting rights.

* * *

Outcalt and Shaw were fully informed stockholders. As the NCS controlling stockholders, they made an informed choice to commit their voting power to the merger. The minority stockholders were deemed to know that when controlling stockholders have 65% of the vote they can approve a merger without the need for the minority votes. Moreover, to the extent a minority stockholder may have felt "coerced" to vote for the merger, which was already a *fait accompli,* it was a meaningless coercion— or no coercion at all—because the controlling votes, those of Outcalt and Shaw, were already "cast." Although the fact that the controlling votes were committed to the merger "precluded" an overriding vote against the merger by the Class A stockholders, the pejorative "preclusive" label applicable in a *Unitrin* fact situation has no application here. Therefore, there was no meaningful minority stockholder voting decision to coerce.

In applying *Unocal* scrutiny, we believe the Majority incorrectly preempted the proportionality inquiry. In our view, the proportionality inquiry must account for the reality that the contractual measures protecting this merger agreement were necessary to obtain the Genesis deal. The Majority has not demonstrated that the director action was a disproportionate response to the threat posed. Indeed, it is clear to us that the board action to negotiate the best deal reasonably available with the only viable merger partner (Genesis) who could satisfy the creditors and benefit the stockholders, was reasonable in relation to the threat, by any practical yardstick.

An Absolute Lock-up is Not a Per Se Violation of Fiduciary Duty

We respectfully disagree with the Majority's conclusion that the NCS board breached its fiduciary duties to the Class A stockholders by failing to negotiate a "fiduciary out" in the Genesis merger agreement. What is the practical import of a "fiduciary out?" It is a contractual provision, articulated in a manner to be negotiated, that would permit the board of the corporation being acquired to exit without breaching the merger agreement in the event of a superior offer.

* * *

The Majority relies on our decision in *QVC* to assert that the board's fiduciary duties prevent the directors from negotiating a merger agreement without providing an escape provision. Reliance on *QVC* for this proposition, however, confuses our statement of a board's responsibilities when the directors confront a superior transaction and turn away from it to lock up a less valuable deal with the very different situation here, where the board committed itself to the *only* value-enhancing transaction available. * * *

The Majority also mistakenly relies on our decision in *QVC* to support the notion that the NCS board should have retained a fiduciary out to save the minority stockholder from Shaw's and Outcalt's voting agreements. Our reasoning in *QVC*, which recognizes that minority stockholders must rely for protection on the fiduciary duties owed to them by directors, does not create a *special* duty to protect the minority stockholders from the consequences of a controlling stockholder's ultimate decision unless the controlling stockholder stands on both sides of the transaction, which is certainly not the case here. * * *

NOTE: LOCKUPS

1. *Theoretical Disputes.*

A lockup is a benefit—such as a termination fee or an attractively priced option to purchase stock or going concern assets—that a target firm confers on a potential acquiring firm on the condition that the latter's proposed acquisition fails to be completed. Lockups tend to be included in friendly merger agreements. They there are said to serve the dual purposes of assuring that the potential acquiring firm is compensated for its investment in the proposed transaction and of making the target less attractive to potential rival suitors. Lockups also can show up in hostile takeovers where the target defends by inducing a friendly "white knight" firm to interpose a competing bid.

As *Paramount v. QVC* demonstrates, the courts have viewed lockups as beneficial when used in moderation but detrimental when used to excess. When, for example, a target concedes a compensatory termination fee in order to induce an acquiring firm's agreement to a merger that enhances shareholder value, the lockup is deemed benign and no breach of duty occurs. But compare a case where the target concedes a below-market option to purchase a number of newly-issued shares equaling one-third of the total of its shares outstanding. This benefit is likely to be held a breach of fiduciary duty on the ground that it forecloses the possibility of an alternate transaction paying more to the target shareholders. The unsolved problem, according to many observers, is the articulation of a clear cut test that distinguishes benign from foreclosing lockups.

The commentary also focuses on another, more fundamental problem. It has been suggested that lockups do not injure target shareholder interests to the extent that the courts have supposed. This line of analysis begins with Ayres, Analyzing Stock Lock–Ups: Do Target Treasury Sales Foreclose or Facilitate Takeover Auctions?, 90 Colum. L. Rev. 682 (1990). Ayres shows that the grant of an option of a large number of newly-issued shares to a favored bidder, taken alone, will neither preclude a rival bid nor prevent a rival bidder from outbidding the lockup beneficiary. Ayres focuses first on the position of the lockup beneficiary. It profits on its stock option only if it loses an auction for the target. That potential profit in turn affects the top price it is willing to pay in an auction for the target—the price is lower given the lockup than would have been the case be without the lockup. The beneficiary firm's reservation price declines because on some scenarios it makes more money on the lockup than it makes by winning the target. By definition, it does better with the lockup proceeds at all prices between its original reservation price and its lower, adjusted price and it does better winning the target at the adjusted reservation price and below. (Significantly, open market purchases of target stock made by a bidder prior to the bid have a different effect. Like a lockup stock option, they guarantee a profit. But, since the bidder makes the profit on these shares whether it wins or loses the auction, they do not cause a change in its reservation price.) Ayres goes on to consider the effect of the lockup on the behavior of competing third party bidders, and shows that they can adjust for the lockup's dilutive effect by lowering their own reservation prices. In the end, then, the stock option lockup neither precludes the competing bids nor changes the identity of the winner of the auction. Rather, the lockup causes only a downward adjustment in the amount of the winning bid. Id. at 695. This "auction insurance," says Ayres, also has the counter-intuitive effect of aligning the lockup beneficiary's interest with those of the target shareholders. Since they both profit from a bid at a higher reservation price, they both favor an auction. Id. at 696–97. A breach of fiduciary duty is likely only in the extreme case where the lockup insures more than 100 percent of the initial bidder's takeover risk. Such a case involves the option of a number of shares so large at a price so low as to cause the adjusted reservation prices of the each of the beneficiary and the third party bidders to fall below the level of the initial bid, leaving the target shareholders worse off. Ayres concludes that a court should evaluate each lockup in order to assure that its auction insurance cost is proportional to its benefits of auction creation. Id. at 699–706.

Ayres' analysis is extended some distance in Fraidin and Hanson, Toward Unlocking Lockups, 103 Yale L. J. 1739 (1994). Fraidin and Hanson make the controversial assertion that all lockups should be enforced subject only to business judgment scrutiny. They start with Ayres' analysis but argue that it fails to provide courts with a workable test for distinguishing benign from preclusive lockups. They go on to invoke the Coase theorem: Corporate assets will find their way to their highest valuing users if we allow corporate actors to contract free of regulatory or judicial interference. Transaction costs, of course, can prevent the realization of superior Coasean outcomes, but they present no barrier here because the incidental costs of mergers are relatively trivial compared to purchase prices. Nor do target board motivations present a problem: According to Fraidin and Hanson, a target board will be neither able nor willing to prevent the highest bidder from winning the company.

How plausible are Fraidin and Hanson's assertions? For a point by point refutation, see Skeel, A Reliance Damages Approach to Corporate Lockups, 90 Nw. U. L. Rev. 564 (1996). Compare also the analysis of Kahan and Klausner, Lockups and the Market for Corporate Control, 48 Stan. L. Rev. 1539 (1996). Kahan and Klausner seek to counter the implications of the Ayres analysis by casting new light on lockups' potential negative effects. They argue that the Ayres result—that the lockup affects the price but not the result of the auction—obtains only on the assumption that all potential bidders already have entered the bidding at the time the lockup is granted. Where potential bidders are still on the sidelines at the time of the lockup, the auction result can be altered because the lockup has an impact on the potential bidders' decisions as to whether to participate. More particularly, "first-bidder" lockups, which induce an initial bid, should be distinguished from "second-bidder" lockups, which are employed by managers dissatisfied with the identity of the first-bid firm to induce a higher valuing, "white knight" bidder to participate. Kahan and Klausner argue that second-bidder lockups should never be permitted, even though they have an auction-inducing aspect and appear to enhance shareholder value. They counter, (1) that the inducement may not be necessary, given a first bid and a higher valuing competitor, (2) that the possibility of a second-bid sweetener thus held out reduces the investment incentives of the class of potential first bidders, and (3) that the lockup's facilitation of "white knight" alternatives reduces the takeover device's ability to exact penalties on bad managers. Second-bid lockups also signal the possibility of a corrupt side-deal between the target firm's incumbent managers and the second bidder firm. Such side-deals also can occur in first-bidder situations where the lockup anticipates an unwelcome competing bid. Kahan and Klausner thus conclude that the only case that should be accorded business judgment scrutiny is a first-bidder lockup granted without anticipation of an unwelcome competing bid.

Finally, Coates and Subramanian, A Buy–Side Model of M & A Lockups: Theory and Evidence, 53 Stan. L. Rev. 307 (2000), weighs in with a set of empirical results showing that lockups matter: First, deals with lockups are more likely to proceed to closing than deals without lockups, and, second, among deals with lockups, deals with breakup fees are more likely to proceed to closing than are deals with stock option lockups. Coates and Subramanian explain these results by identifying points of distortion in the behavior of bidders, such as agency costs (bidders do not always maximize their own firms' values), endowment effects (bidders do not want to give up their deals), information asymmetries (subsequent bidders have the benefit of the first bidder's valuation), and reputation costs (bidders like look tough). The result is that the first and subsequent bidders are not interchangeable. Lockups will exacerbate this buy side stickiness, preventing higher valuing subsequent bidders from winning the target. But the message for judicial review is complex nevertheless. Coates and Subramanian accept (and expand) the standard list of lockup benefits (defraying bidder expenses and encouraging search, allocating risk, and helping solve valuation disputes). Lockups should get a "hard look", especially when they exceed 3 percent of deal value. Nor should a lockup of under 2 percent automatically be deemed benign.

Coates and Subramanian also show that Delaware decisions have directly affected contracting practice. Lockups are more common in stock-for-stock deals governed by *Unocal* than cash transactions governed by *Revlon*. Meanwhile, lockup incidence has increased–from 40 percent of deals in 1988 to 80 percent by 1998. Asset lockups, always a small minority, disappeared by the mid 1990s, reflecting the impact of *Macmillan*. Stock lockups went from a high of 40 percent of deals in 1991 to a low of 10 percent after 1996, reflecting *QVC*. Breakup fees, always the most common device, showed up in 70 percent of deals by 1998.

2. "No Talk" Clauses.

Merger agreements, like that in *Omnicare*, often contain "no talk" provisions in addition to "no shop" provisions. A no talk clause bars the managers of the transferor firm from talking to potential third-party offerors who have made or might make a higher bid. As with lock up provisions in general, no talk clauses tend to be modified by "fiduciary out" clauses providing that the board may consider superior offers when required to do so by fiduciary duty. The interrelations of no talk and fiduciary out clauses have been discussed in several recent cases.

In **Phelps Dodge Corp. v. Cyprus Amax Minerals Co.**, 1999 WL 1054255 (Del.Ch.), the Chancellor expressed doubts about a no talk clause and made a warning: A transferor board deciding not to negotiate with a third party offeror would have to meet its *QVC* duty to make an informed decision respecting the third party offer regardless of a no talk clause and whether or not a fiduciary out had been reserved. **In re IXC Communications Shareholders Litigation**, 1999 WL 1009174 (Del.Ch.), in contrast, sustained a no talk clause. But the facts of the case bore heavily on the result. First, the merger agreement containing the clause was concluded only after the transferor board conducted an active six-month market test for the best offer. clause only took effect , but with two significant qualifying conditions. Second, the no talk clause was accompanied by a fiduciary out clause allowing the board to entertain new offers. The third case is **ACE Ltd. v. Capital Re Corp.**, 747 A.2d 95 (Del.Ch.1999). Here the transferor board had not conducted a market test before entering into a merger agreement. An unsolicited higher offer came along even as a merger was about to be submitted to the shareholders for what amounted to certain approval. Once again, a no talk clause was pronounced unenforceable if unaccompanied by a fiduciary out. The clause in question was particularly restrictive, barring not only conversations with a third party offeror but any consideration of a third party offer in the target's boardroom. The merger agreement's fiduciary out also was notably restrictive. Under it, there was no fiduciary out until outside counsel opined in writing that the board had a duty to consider the third-party offer. Thus restricted, the fiduciary out did not import enforceability to the no talk clause.

NOTE: COMMENTS ON THE DELAWARE ANTITAKEOVER CASES

Black and Kraakman, Delaware's Takeover Law: The Uncertain Search for Hidden Value, 96 Nw.U.L.Rev. 521, 522–23, 526–27 (2002), reviews the cases:

" * * * *Van Gorkom* should be seen not as a business judgment rule case but as a takeover case that was the harbinger of the then newly emerging Delaware jurisprudence on friendly and hostile takeovers, which included the almost contemporaneous *Unocal* and *Revlon* decisions. *Van Gorkom's* unforgiving scrutiny of the Trans Union board's casual sale of their company anticipates Revlon's holding that a target company's board must maximize shareholder value once it decides to sell the company. Less obvious is that *Van Gorkom* also introduced the core justification for board discretion that was developed in the takeover defense cases, beginning with *Unocal* and continuing through *Moran v. Household International, Inc., Paramount Communications v. Time, Paramount Communications v. QVC Network,* and *Unitrin v. American General.* These cases all rely on *Van Gorkom's* concept of intrinsic or 'hidden' value that a hard-working board can assess, but that remains invisible to shareholders and potential acquirers.

"Crucially, this hidden value must be not only unknown to shareholders and acquirers, but unknowable—it cannot credibly be disclosed by the board. For, if hidden value were disclosable to shareholders, a simpler approach to takeover regulation would be to give the board a reasonable period of time to disclose what it knows and then let the shareholders decide whether the company should be sold. Even if hidden value is not always disclosable to shareholders, if acquirers can both see and capture this value, the target board, in most cases, would not need the power to reject all bids over shareholder objection, but only sufficient time to obtain a full price for the company in the takeover market.

* * *

"*Van Gorkom's* surface message—that a board planning to sell its company must diligently seek the best price for shareholders—is the same message that *Revlon* reiterates and refines. The subtext of *Van Gorkom,* however, is that the board of directors, and no one else, must determine the company's intrinsic value. The board cannot rely on shareholder approval to discharge its duty, nor may it rely principally on prices set by the stock market or the takeover market. Because others may miss the company's hidden value, the board must value the firm itself, preferably with an investment banker's assistance. The importance that *Van Gorkom* places on the board's efforts to value the firm sets the stage for the hidden value model and the three principal pillars of Delaware's current law of corporate takeovers: deferential to a board's decision not to sell the company and install takeover defenses, yet willing to closely examine the board's decision to sell the company for cash, yet again deferential (by pretending that the company is not being sold) if the board sells the company for stock instead of cash.

"The logic behind this two-track structure is straightforward. On the one hand, only the board can discern the company's hidden value. For this reason, a board that fails to take its role seriously—that relies on values set by the market or its shareholders instead of determining value itself—abdicates its statutory responsibility in a way that easily shades into gross negligence. On the other hand, the courts will not allow anyone, especially not shareholders, to second-guess a board that hires expert professionals and acts diligently to value the company. Thus, if such a board concludes that a hostile bid is too low, its judgment trumps shareholder preferences even if the hostile bidder offers a large cash premium over the target's market price.

"Similarly, if a diligent board deems a stock-for-stock offer more valuable than a cash offer, its opinion controls even if the acquirer offers shares with a market price far below the cash offer. The reason is again the potential for hidden value. The board knows best how to discern hidden value both in the target's stand-alone value and in its synergies with the acquirer. The board may even know best how to value the acquirer's stock. This hidden value will emerge eventually and benefit long-term shareholders who continue to hold the acquirer's shares. The board's insight into hidden value justifies its discretion to accept or reject deals.

* * *

"While the hidden value model embraces the primacy of shareholder interests and judicial deference to boards' business decisions, it takes a less conventional approach to capital market efficiency and corporate agency problems. Here, the hidden value model contrasts with an alternate model, more standard among legal and finance scholars who study takeovers, which we will call the "visible value" model. In particular, the hidden value model makes nine core assumptions that most financial economists and corporate law scholars (ourselves included) would contest. * * * "

The nine core assumptions are follows, id. at 528–533: (1) the board has good quality private information about the firm's value; (2) the board has a poor ability to communicate its value information to the shareholders; (3) the firm's hidden value significantly diverges from its market price; (4) the hidden value will remain hidden for a long time; (5) the target board's valuation can be trusted; (6) an outside investment banker credibly can verify the board's valuation claim; (7) the hidden value cannot be captured in the takeover market; (8) long term and short term shareholders' interests diverge and long term interests should control short term interests; and (9) the interests of undiversified shareholders count for more than the interests of diversified shareholders.

4.   STATE ANTITAKEOVER LEGISLATION

During the past thirty years shark repellent provisions have found their way into the business corporation laws of more than 35 states. By now these statutes have undergone three, and by some counts, four stages of evolution. They come in a variety of shapes and sizes, and lack the uniform aspect of other state corporation and Blue Sky law provisions. Management lobbying provides the motive force for this law reform movement. See, e.g., Romano, The Political Economy of Takeover Statutes, 73 Va.L.Rev. 111 (1987).

(A) FIRST GENERATION STATUTES

The first generation of antitakeover statutes followed the regulatory pattern of some Blue Sky laws and accorded a state securities administrator the power to review the adequacy of tender offer disclosure and, in some cases, the merits of the bid. The schemes thus involved a time-consuming administrative hearing process. Some of the statutes also inserted waiting periods between the time of the filing of the offer and its effectiveness—an administrative control the Williams Act avoids. The Supreme Court struck down these statutes in **Edgar v. MITE,** 457 U.S. 624 (1982). Goelzer and Cohen, The Empire Strikes Back—Post MITE Developments in State–Anti–Takeover Legislation, in Steinberg (ed.), Tender Offers: Developments and Commentaries 51–53 (1984), discuss the case:

"The Illinois Business Takeover Act, the statute at issue in *MITE,* required a tender offeror to notify the secretary of the state of Illinois twenty business days before commencement of a tender offer. The secretary of state was empowered to convene a hearing, and the tender offer could not proceed until that hearing was completed. One function of the hearing was to permit the secretary of state to review the substantive fairness of the tender offer; were an offer found 'unfair,' it could be permanently blocked.

"MITE Corp. initiated a tender offer for Chicago Rivet & Machine Co., by filing a Schedule 14D with the Securities and Exchange Commission pursuant to the Williams Act. MITE Corp. made no effort to comply with the Illinois Business Takeover Act; rather, it commenced an action in federal court challenging the constitutionality of the statute and obtained a permanent injunction against its enforcement. The Court of Appeals for the Seventh Circuit affirmed, and the Supreme Court accepted, the case for review.

"Justice White's opinion, in which only the chief justice joined entirely, held (1) that the Illinois statute unduly favored incumbent management and thus contravened the Supremacy Clause of the U.S. Constitution, because it upset the neutrality policy which is the object of federal tender offer regulation, as embodied in the Williams Act, and (2) that the statute directly restrained interstate commerce in violation of the Commerce Clause. Five justices joined in part, but not all, of the Commerce Clause holding; thus, a majority of the Court held that the Illinois statute was void, because it imposed burdens on interstate commerce that were excessive in light of Illinois' interests.

"Justice White's Commerce Clause opinion had two branches. In the first (in which only three other justices joined), he noted that the statute regulated interstate transactions taking place wholly outside of Illinois (in this case purchases by a Delaware corporation of shares owned by non-Illinois residents). Thus, the statute constituted a 'direct' restraint on interstate commerce and was, therefore, void, even without an inquiry into the state interests involved. The second branch of Justice White's Commerce Clause opinion, in which five justices concurred and which stands as the opinion of the Court, was based on Pike v. Bruce Church, Inc. In that

1970 case, the Court held that a statute which has only an incidental effect on interstate commerce is valid 'unless the burden imposed on such commerce is clearly excessive in relation to the putative local benefits.' As the Court stated in *MITE:*

> While protecting local investors is plainly a legitimate state objective, the state has no legitimate interest in protecting non-resident shareholders. Insofar as the Illinois law burdens out-of-state transactions, there is nothing to be weighed in the balance to sustain the law.

"Five of the six justices reaching the merits in *MITE* expressly held that the Act was invalid on Commerce Clause grounds, because it placed a substantial burden on interstate commerce which outweighed any local benefits.

> * * *

"Several courts, both state and federal, have applied the Supreme Court's Commerce Clause holding in *MITE* to particular state takeover statutes. These decisions, dealing with both tender offers and open market purchase programs, have been uniformly adverse to state regulation. As *MITE* has been applied to various state antitakeover statutes, it has become increasingly clear that minor variations on the Illinois theme* do not change the ultimate result."

(B) SECOND GENERATION STATUTES

(1) *Legislation*

The states responded to *MITE* with a new set of antitakeover statutes designed to circumvent the factors the case identified as objectionable. Sargent, Do the Second Generation State Takeover Statutes Violate the Commerce Clause? A Preliminary Inquiry, in Steinberg (ed.), Tender Offers: Development and Commentaries 76–83 (1984), describes the new legislation:

> * * * [I]t is almost certain that the state attempts to regulate the takeover process through Williams Act-type regulation of tender offers are unconstitutional. In other words, the first-generation state takeover statutes are probably dead.

> Some of the state legislatures, however, have not allowed the demise of these statutes to divert them from their goal of somehow regulating corporate takeovers. In fact, the repudiation of the first-generation statutes has led to the adoption of some very different forms of takeover regulation. The difference between these second-generation takeover statutes and the unconstitutional first-generation statutes reflects the distinction between state tender offer regulation and traditional state corporation law. That is, the second-generation statutes do not directly condition or restrain the tender offer or the consequent tender of shares; instead, they readjust the

---

* [Ed. Note] E.g., elimination of requirement of a preliminary filing before commencement of an offer.

target's internal ordering mechanism in a way that will have a substantial impact on what can happen after the tender offer is completed. In essence, the new direction shifts the focus from *securities regulation to corporate law;* the new statutes attempt to regulate the takeover process through regulation of the internal affairs of corporations organized under the laws of the state.

* * *

A. Ohio

In November 1982, the Ohio legislature enacted a bill requiring all acquisitions of controlling stock interests to be approved by the shareholders. This requirement applies to all control acquisitions, whether accomplished by tender offer or not, and it applies to all Ohio corporations, unless a corporation's charter excludes the corporation from the coverage of the statute.

Under this statute, the directors of the subject corporation must call a special shareholders' meeting within ten days of receipt of an acquirer's statement of intention to acquire shares sufficient to move the acquirer into a control position or from one level of control to another. At this meeting, which must be held within fifty days of receipt of the acquirer's statement of intention, the shareholders are to vote on the proposed acquisition. In order for the acquisition to proceed, it must be approved by both a majority of the voting power present at the meeting and a majority of the voting power excluding "interested shares" (primarily those owned by the acquirer and its affiliates).

The new Ohio statute thus differs from the first-generation statutes insofar as it does not regulate or otherwise condition either the tender offer itself or the tendering of shares. It shifts the focus of regulation from those phases of the takeover process to the point immediately precedent to any second-step transaction—the actual purchase of the control bloc of shares. The technique of regulation applied at this point is also quite different from those applied under the first-generation statutes to the tender offer; there are no administrative hearings, no proration or withdrawal provisions, no review of the fairness of the offering, indeed no role whatsoever for the state securities administrator. Instead, the Ohio statute draws upon the principle of shareholder approval of organic transactions to regulate this form of control transaction.

The Ohio statute does not represent, however, a complete departure from the first-generation statutes. The new approach is a form of internal affairs regulation, but by imposing conditions upon the offeror's purchase of the tendered shares, the statute will still directly affect transactions between the shareholders and the offeror. The new Maryland statute, in contrast, confines itself to the second-step transaction and has no direct effect on the tender offer. * * *

B. Maryland

The Maryland legislature enacted, in June 1983, a quite different form of takeover statute. This legislation shifted the regulatory focus entirely to the second-step transaction. It requires the successful tender offeror intending a post-tender offer "business combination" to either obtain supermajority approval from all the shareholders and from the disinterested shareholders or pay a "fair price" to all those nontendering shareholders who are forced to sell in the course of the business combination. In essence, the statute is designed to inhibit front-end—loaded, two-step takeovers, on the ground that such takeover bids are inherently coercive and unfair to nontendering shareholders.

The act is drafted very tightly to cover almost every conceivable form of business combination and to ensure that a truly "fair" price is paid to shareholders bought out in the second-step transaction. The result of this approach is the potential applicability of the fair-price/supermajority provisions to negotiated business combinations and other transactions that have nothing to do with hostile takeovers. The Maryland Act attempts to avoid this problem by granting the board of directors substantial control over when and to whom these provisions will apply. The Act thus operates something like a shark repellant, which the board, rather than the shareholders, has the authority to implement or abandon.

While the Maryland Act represents an abandonment of any attempt to regulate tender offers, it may prevent at least some partial tender offers from being made and may even reduce the aggregate number of takeover bids for Maryland corporations. This raises novel Commerce Clause questions, because these results would be achieved not through a form of securities regulation restraining the tender offeror's acquisition of shares but through corporate internal affairs regulation restricting what can be done with the shares once they have been acquired.

C. Pennsylvania

A Pennsylvania statute enacted in December 1983 represents an even more thorough exploitation of the internal affairs provisions of the general corporation law. * * *

* * * [T]he Act contains provisions similar to the fair-price/supermajority provisions of the Maryland Act and is designed to have similar effects on front-end—loaded, two-step takeovers. The Act also grants the target board substantial leverage over these provisions; second-step transactions are exempted if a majority of the board approves the transactions. Accordingly, these provisions will end up being applied only to hostile takeovers.

* * * [T]he Act requires "controlling shareholders" (persons or groups owning thirty percent of a class of voting stock) to provide notice to the other shareholders that they may obtain an appraisal—"fair" value for their shares—from the controlling shareholder. This provision should seriously inhibit partial bids for the shares of corporations subject to the Act, since it will come into play even if the bidder does not plan a second-step transaction. The board of directors also has substantial leverage over this provision, since timely adoption of an amendment to the bylaws can exempt a particular bidder from its coverage.

[D. New York (Business Corporation Law, section 912, Appendix B)

The New York statute takes a slightly different tack than the other second generation state laws. In principal part, it addresses the internal affairs of resident New York corporations (i.e., a corporation with its principal executive office and significant business operations in New York and with 10% of its voting stock owned by New Yorkers) by allocating more power to the board of directors than do conventional corporation laws. It effects that result by requiring bidders who seek to acquire ownership of 20% or more of the outstanding voting shares of a target to receive the prior approval of the target's board of directors for their purchase (or for the merger they contemplate), and failing such approval to be precluded from combining the target with the bidder's enterprise(s) for 5 years; moreover, the ultimate combination must either be approved by disinterested target stockholders or the bidder must pay a "fair" price, generally the highest price it has previously paid for such shares. The 5 year restriction may be waived by vote of disinterested shareholders to amend the target's by-laws to opt out of the statutory restriction; but even then, 18 months after its adoption must elapse before the amendment is effective. The statute also seeks to limit greenmail payments by requiring stockholder approval of them. And finally it requires more extensive disclosure (than previously required by state law) by a person who seeks to acquire more than 5% of any class of stock to be made to offerees, the target and the Attorney General at the time of, or before, the bid. The new disclosure provisions are said to produce conformity with "recent federal court decisions."]

* * *

Five states adopted statutes along the lines of the Ohio "control share" model. Only two states adopted a "redemption rights" statute like Pennsylvania's. Maryland's "fair price" provisions proved the most popular, finding their way into the statutes of thirteen other states within a few years. See Romano, supra at 117–118. The New York statute, with its "business combination" prohibition, became a model for other jurisdictions later on, in the "third generation."

(2) Constitutionality

The second round in the adjudication of the statutes' constitutionality centered on a "control share" provision adopted in Indiana. The Supreme Court sustained the statute into **CTS Corp. v. Dynamics Corp. of America,** 481 U.S. 69 (1987). The Indiana statute, like the Ohio statute, applied only to corporations incorporated in the state, and contained a provision for opting out by certificate or by law amendment or board resolution. Under the statute, an entity acquiring more than 20 percent of a corporation's stock acquired the right to vote the stock only upon the resolution of a majority of the disinterested shareholders. The necessary meeting was to be held within fifty days of the acquirer's filing of a statement with the corporation. In the event the shareholders decided against the restoration of the vote to the shares of the "control" holder, the corporation had a right to redeem the shares at fair value.

The Seventh Circuit, following *MITE,* found the statute to be unconstitutional on Commerce Clause grounds due its potential to hinder tender offers. It also, with reservations, applied the preemption rationale set out in Justice White's plurality opinion. The Supreme Court, in an opinion by Justice Powell, reversed on both grounds.

As to preemption, the Supreme Court adopted *MITE's* "broad interpretation" of the field occupied by the Williams Act only for the sake of argument. It found the Indiana statute to be consistent with the Williams Act, thus described. Unlike the Illinois statute, which favored management at the expense of bidders and therefore shareholders, the Indiana statute protected the shareholder against both parties, and thus furthered the Williams Act purpose of placing investors on an equal footing with the bidder. Said the court, 481 U.S. at 82–83:

"The Indiana Act operates on the assumption, implicit in the Williams Act, that independent shareholders faced with tender offers often are at a disadvantage. By allowing such shareholders to vote as a group, the Act protects them from the coercive aspects of some tender offers. If, for example, shareholders believe that a successful tender offer will be followed by a purchase of nontendering shares at a depressed price, individual shareholders may tender their shares—even if they doubt the tender offer is in the corporation's best interest—to protect themselves from being forced to sell their shares at a depressed price. * * * In such a situation under the Indiana Act, the shareholders as a group, acting in the corporation's best interest, could reject the offer, although individual shareholders might be inclined to accept it. The desire of the Indiana Legislature to protect shareholders of Indiana corporations from this type of coercive offer does not conflict with the Williams Act. Rather, it furthers the federal policy of investor protection."

The court dealt with the contention that the Indiana statute conflicted with the Williams Act as follows, 481 U.S. at 84–85:

"The Act does not impose an absolute 50–day delay on tender offers, nor does it preclude an offeror from purchasing shares as soon as federal law permits. If the offeror fears an adverse shareholder vote under the Act, it can make a conditional tender offer, offering to accept shares on the condition that the shares receive voting rights within a certain period of time. The Williams Act permits tender offers to be conditioned on the offeror's subsequently obtaining regulatory approval. * * *

"Even assuming that the Indiana Act imposes some additional delay, nothing in *MITE* suggested that *any* delay imposed by state regulation, however short, would create a conflict with the Williams Act. The plurality argued only that the offeror should 'be free to go forward without *unreasonable* delay.' 457 U.S., at 639 (emphasis added). In that case, the Court was confronted with the potential for indefinite delay and presented with no persuasive reason why some deadline could not be established. By contrast, the Indiana Act provides that full voting rights will be vested—if this eventually is to occur—within 50 days after commencement of the offer. This period is within the 60–day period Congress established for reinstitution of withdrawal rights in 15 U.S.C. § 78n(d)(5). We cannot say that a delay within that congressionally determined period is unreasonable."

Finally, the court asserted that if this state voting statute were preempted, then any state statutory provision that limited the free exercise power of a successful bidder, such as provisions enabling staggered boards and cumulative voting, also would be preempted.

As to the Commerce Clause, the court noted that no problem of inconsistent regulation was presented because the statute applied only to Indiana corporations. The court, going on to review the balance of benefits and burdens, emphasized that the role of the states in creating corporations, prescribing their powers, and defining the rights attached to shares, was a long-accepted part of the business landscape. "A State," said the court, 481 U.S. at 91, "has an interest in promoting stable relationships among parties involved in the corporations it charters, as well as in ensuring that investors in such corporations have an effective voice in corporate affairs." The Indiana statute, with its purpose to protect shareholders from coercive offers by enhancing their autonomy, fell into this historical zone of state interest and activity. The court then addressed the economic argument that the concern with shareholder coercion was "illusory," and that tender offers should be favored because they move assets into the most productive hands. The court responded by noting that both scholars and the SEC had recognized the coercion problem, and added, 481 U.S. at 92: "The Constitution does not require the States to subscribe to any particular economic theory." The state's interest might become attenuated if, like the statute in *MITE,* the statute applied to nonresident shareholders of nonresident corporations. But such was not the case. The court concluded by addressing the bidder's bottom line claim, 481 U.S. at 93–94:

"Dynamics' argument that the Act is unconstitutional ultimately rests on its contention that the Act will limit the number of successful tender offers. There is little evidence that this will occur. But even if true, this result would not substantially affect our Commerce Clause analysis. We reiterate that this Act does not prohibit any entity—resident or nonresident—from offering to purchase, or from purchasing, shares in Indiana corporations, or from attempting thereby to gain control. It only provides regulatory procedures designed for the better protection of the corporations' shareholders. We have rejected the 'notion that the Commerce Clause protects the particular structure or methods of operation in a * * * market.' Exxon Corp. v. Governor of Maryland, 437 U.S., at 127. The very commodity that is traded in the securities market is one whose characteristics are defined by state law. Similarly, the very commodity that is traded in the 'market for corporate control'—the corporation—is one that owes its existence and attributes to state law. Indiana need not define these commodities as other States do; it need only provide that residents and nonresidents have equal access to them. This Indiana has done. Accordingly, even if the Act should decrease the number of successful tender offers for Indiana corporations, this would not offend the Commerce Clause."

Justice White, joined by Justices Blackmun and Stevens, dissented on the Commerce Clause ground. Only Justice White took the position that the Williams Act preempted the Indiana statute.

If the issue is ever joined, will the "broad interpretation" of the Williams Act set out in *MITE* but employed in *CTS* only for the sake of argument be adopted? How would a narrower interpretation of the Williams Act affect the preemption analysis? See Amanda Acquisition v. Universal Foods, infra. How much room does *CTS* leave open for the argument that an antitakeover statute unconstitutionally burdens interstate commerce? Would a state corporate law provision requiring a 100 percent vote in a second step merger amount to such a burden? Would a provision forbidding second step mergers entirely? Would a corporate law provision forbidding public tenders for shares?

(C) THIRD GENERATION STATUTES

(1) *The Delaware Statute*

After the *CTS* decision, Delaware lawmakers went to work on the formulation of an antitakeover statute. They found a model in the "business combination" model devised in New York during the second generation. NYBCL § 912. Under this version, the rights attached to the tendered stock are not impaired, but substantial barriers are placed in the way of the consummation of the back end transaction that concludes a two-step acquisition. By now at least 27 states have adopted business combination statutes.

DCL § 203, Appendix B

PROBLEM

If section 203 had been on the books, how would the contest in each of the following cases have been affected?

1. Hanson Trust PLC v. SCM Corp.
2. Unocal v. Mesa Petroleum
3. Revlon v. MacAndrews & Forbes Holdings
4. AC Acquisitions v. Anderson Clayton
5. City Capital v. Interco

(2) *Pennsylvania*

Pennsylvania, which already had control share and redemption provisions in effect, created a stir in 1990 when it added a new "profit disgorgement" provision to its statute. Under this, unsuccessful suitors are locked into the ownership of any stock they acquire. More particularly, those holding 20 percent of the stock who dispose of the stock within 18 months of becoming 20 percent holders must disgorge to the corporation any profit realized upon the disposition. 15 Pa.Cons.Stat.Ann. § 2575. Corporations subject to the provision were given a limited time to opt out by means of a by-law amendment approved by the board. 15 Pa.Cons.Stat. Ann. § 2571(b). In 1990 Pennsylvania also added a business combination provision carrying a five year merger prohibition. This cumulation of provisions makes those Pennsylvania corporations not choosing to opt out as close to invulnerable to hostile attack as American corporations can be.

(3) Poison Pills and Staggered Boards

At least 24 states have adopted "shareholder rights plan endorsement statutes." These make explicit the board's authority to promulgate a poison pill, subject to a contrary provision in the firms charter. See, e.g., Id. Stat. § 30–1706(1). Here Maryland has pushed out the envelope, enacting a statute which authorizes "dead hand" poison pill provisions limited to 180 days. The Maryland statute also facilitates the creation of a staggered board. Where the corporation has at least three outside directors, a staggered board can be put in place by a board vote. See Md. Code Ann., Corps. & Ass'ns, §§ 2–201(c), 3–801 et seq. Massachusetts amended its statute in 1990 to mandate classified boards and staggered shareholder voting for board seats, subject to opting out by board resolution or a two thirds shareholder vote. Mass.Gen.Laws Ann., ch. 156D § 8.06.

(4) Constituency Statutes

Another variety of antitakeover statute, adopted in at least 28 states, modifies the statutory statement of the duty of loyalty by authorizing, or in at least one instance requiring, management in a control transfer situation to consider the interests of constituencies other than shareholders. According to their critics, these statutes provide management with much more additional power than is needed or appropriate to meet takeover threats. See, e.g., New York Bus.Corp.L. § 717(b); Indiana Code, § 23–1–35–1(d). For an overview of the issues, see Symposium, Corporate Malaise—Stakeholder Statutes: Cause or Cure?, 21 Stetson L.Rev. 1 (1991).

Constituency statutes accord management authority to depart from the norm of shareholder value maximization and recognize the interests of other parties, such as bondholders and employees. In so doing, they implicate a debate over corporate objectives that has been conducted many times in the past. See Dodd, For Whom Are Corporate Managers Trustees?, 45 Harv.L.Rev. 1145 (1932), and Berle, For Whom Corporate Managers Are Trustees: A Note, 45 Harv.L.Rev. 1365 (1932). Other protagonists later continued the debate in E. Mason (ed.), The Corporation in Modern Society (1959). For a discussion of the contemporary significance of the Berle/Dodd debate, see Millon, Theories of the Corporation, 1990 Duke L.J. 201.

The import of the statutes for the takeover movement lies in the virtually untrammeled discretion they vest in management, as pointed out in Hanks, Non–Stockholder Constituency Statutes, 3 Insights 20 (December 1989):

> Even if it were possible to identify the nature and extent of non-stockholders constituencies' interests, none of the statutes offers any guidance as to how much weight should be given to the interests of one constituency versus another or the weight to be given to one claim of a constituency versus other possible claims of the same constituency. Proponents of these statutes have not articulated any standard for determining "how much" of the stockholders' wealth the directors should be permitted to allocate to other groups. Do they think, for example, that under a non-stockholder constituency statute a board could cause all of the stockholders' equity (or all of the premium in a

takeover) to be paid out to the employees as a special bonus? It is evident that these statutes, especially those with open-ended language such as "any other factors the director considers pertinent," result in virtually standardless discretion. This absence of standards is likely to lead not only to greater uncertainty and unpredictability in the board-room but also to difficulty in judicial review.

But see Ryan, Calculating the "Stakes" for Corporate Stakeholders as Part of Business Decision–Making, 44 Rutgers L.Rev. 555 (1992) which proposes an analytical framework for balancing constituency conflicts. See also Millon, Redefining Corporate Law, 24 Ind.L.Rev. 223 (1991), which argues in favor of a constituent right (and right of action) at least to have its interests considered by management.

(5) Constitutionality

CTS did not offer clear guidance for testing the constitutionality of "business combination" statutes such as Delaware's, or for that matter, all features of other second generation statutes. For discussion of the open-ended aspects of the court's analysis, see, e.g., Weiss, What Lawyers Do When the Emperor Has No Clothes: Evaluating *CTS Corp. v. Dynamics Corp. of America* and Its Progeny—Part I, 78 Geo.L.J. 1655 (1990); Pinto, The Constitution and the Market for Corporate Control: State Antitakeover Statutes After *CTS Corp.*, 29 Wm. & Mary L.Rev. 699 (1988). The question is whether *CTS* stands for the proposition that the Commerce Clause and the Williams Act allow only narrowly drafted statutes keyed to protection of carefully articulated shareholder interests, or whether they allow virtual-ly any takeover block so long as it applies only to domestic corporations and does not interfere directly with the operation of the Williams Act.

The constitutionality of Delaware § 203 has been confirmed on several occasions by courts reading *CTS* to contemplate scrutiny for consonance with the Williams Act's shareholder protective purpose and going through the motions of Commerce Clause balancing. See BNS Inc. v. Koppers Co., Inc., 683 F.Supp. 458 (D.Del.1988); RP Acquisitions Corp. v. Staley Continental, Inc., 686 F.Supp. 476 (D.Del.1988); City Capital Associates v. Interco, Inc., 696 F.Supp. 1551 (D.Del.1988). But cf. Hyde Park Partners, L.P. v. Connolly, 839 F.2d 837 (1st Cir.1988) (Massachusetts statute creating one year moratorium on takeover attempts as sanction for disclo-sure violations preempted). Provisions applying to nonresident corporations have fared less well. See Tyson Foods, Inc. v. McReynolds, 865 F.2d 99 (6th Cir.1989); TLX Acquisition Corp. v. Telex Corp., 679 F.Supp. 1022 (W.D.Okl.1987).

Amanda Acquisition Corp. v. Universal Foods Corp.

United States Court of Appeals, Seventh Circuit, 1989.
877 F.2d 496, cert. denied, 493 U.S. 955, 110 S.Ct. 367, 107 L.Ed.2d 353 (1989).

■ EASTERBROOK, CIRCUIT JUDGE.

* * *

I

Amanda Acquisition Corporation is a shell with a single purpose: to acquire Universal Foods Corporation, a diversified firm incorporated in

Wisconsin and traded on the New York Stock Exchange. Universal is covered by Wisconsin's anti-takeover law. * * *

In mid-November 1988 Universal's stock was trading for about $25 per share. On December 1 Amanda commenced a tender offer at $30.50, to be effective if at least 75% of the stock should be tendered. This all-cash, all-shares offer has been increased by stages to $38.00. Amanda's financing is contingent on a prompt merger with Universal if the offer succeeds, so the offer is conditional on a judicial declaration that the law is invalid.

No firm incorporated in Wisconsin and having its headquarters, substantial operations, or 10% of its shares or shareholders there may "engage in a business combination with an interested stockholder * * * for 3 years after the interested stockholder's stock acquisition date unless the board of directors of the [Wisconsin] corporation has approved, before the interested stockholder's stock acquisition date, that business combination or the purchase of stock", Wis.Stat. § 180.726(2). An "interested stockholder" is one owning 10% of the voting stock, directly or through associates (anyone acting in concert with it), § 180.726(1)(j). A "business combination" is a merger with the bidder or any of its affiliates, sale of more than 5% of the assets to bidder or affiliate, liquidation of the target, or a transaction by which the target guarantees the bidder's or affiliates debts or passes tax benefits to the bidder or affiliate, § 180.726(1)(e). The law, in other words, provides for almost hermetic separation of bidder and target for three years after the bidder obtains 10% of the stock—unless the target's board consented before then. No matter how popular the offer, the ban applies: obtaining 85% (even 100%) of the stock held by non-management shareholders won't allow the bidder to engage in a business combination, as it would under Delaware law. * * * Wisconsin firms cannot opt out of the law, as may corporations subject to almost all other state takeover statutes. In Wisconsin it is management's approval in advance, or wait three years. Even when the time is up, the bidder needs the approval of a majority of the remaining investors, without any provision disqualifying shares still held by the managers who resisted the transaction, § 180.726(3)(b). * * * As a practical matter, Wisconsin prohibits any offer contingent on a merger between bidder and target, a condition attached to about 90% of contemporary tender offers.

Amanda filed this suit seeking a declaration that this law is preempted by the Williams Act and inconsistent with the Commerce Clause. * * *

II

* * *

A

If our views of the wisdom of state law mattered, Wisconsin's takeover statute would not survive. Like our colleagues who decided *MITE* and *CTS*, we believe that antitakeover legislation injures shareholders.[5]

---

5. Because both the district court and the parties—like the Williams Act—examine tender offers from the perspective of equity investors, we employ the same approach.

[The court then describes the benefits to shareholders of takeover premiums and the governance benefits of takeovers. It refutes management claims that successful takeover defense promotes long term investment gain by reference to stock price studies proving gain.]

Although a takeover-*proof* firm leaves investors at the mercy of incumbent managers (who may be mistaken about the wisdom of their business plan even when they act in the best of faith), a takeover-*resistant* firm may be able to assist its investors. An auction may run up the price, and delay may be essential to an auction. * * * Devices giving managers some ability to orchestrate investors' responses, in order to avoid panic tenders in response to front-end-loaded offers, also could be beneficial, as the Supreme Court emphasized in *CTS*, 481 U.S. at 92–93, 107 S.Ct. at 1651–52. ("Could be" is an important qualifier; even from a perspective limited to targets' shareholders given a bid on the table, it is important to know whether managers use this power to augment bids or to stifle them, and whether courts can tell the two apart.)

State anti-takeover laws do not serve these ends well, however. Investors who prefer to give managers the discretion to orchestrate responses to bids may do so through "fair-price" clauses in the articles of incorporation and other consensual devices. Other firms may choose different strategies. A law such as Wisconsin's does not add options to firms that would like to give more discretion to their managers; instead it destroys the possibility of divergent choices. Wisconsin's law applies even when the investors prefer to leave their managers under the gun, to allow the market full sway. Karpoff and Malatesta found that state anti-takeover laws have little or no effect on the price of shares if the firm already has poison pills (or related devices) in place, but strongly negative effects on price when firms have no such contractual devices. To put this differently, state laws have bite only when investors, given the choice, would deny managers the power to interfere with tender offers (maybe already *have* denied managers that power). See also Roberta Romano, The Political Economy of Takeover Statutes, 73 Va.L.Rev. 111, 128–31 (1987).

States could choose to protect "constituencies" other than stockholders. Creditors, managers, and workers invest human rather than financial capital. But the limitation of our inquiry to equity investors does not affect the analysis, because no evidence of which we are aware suggests that bidders confiscate workers' and other participants' investments to any greater degree than do incumbents— who may (and frequently do) close or move plants to follow the prospect of profit. Joseph A. Grundfest, a Commissioner of the SEC, showed in Job Loss and Takeovers, address to University of Toledo College of Law, Mar. 11, 1988, that acquisitions have no logical (or demonstrable) effect on employment. See also Brown & Medoff, The Impact of Firm Acquisitions on Labor, in Corporate Takeovers: Causes and Consequences 9 (A. Auerbach ed. 1988); Roberta Romano, The Future of Hostile Takeovers: Legislation and Public Opinion, 57 U.Cin.L.Rev. 457 (1988); C. Steven Bradford, Protecting Shareholders from Themselves? A Policy and Constitutional Review of a State Takeover Statute, 67 Neb. L.Rev. 459, 529–34 (1988).

B

Skepticism about the wisdom of a state's law does not lead to the conclusion that the law is beyond the state's power, however. * * * Unless a federal statute or the Constitution bars the way, Wisconsin's choice must be respected.

Preemption has not won easy acceptance among the Justices for several reasons. First there is § 28(a) of the '34 Act, 15 U.S.C. § 78bb(a), which provides that "[n]othing in this chapter shall affect the jurisdiction of the securities commission * * * of any State over any security or any person insofar as it does not conflict with the provisions of this chapter or the rules and regulations thereunder." Although some of the SEC's regulations (particularly the one defining the commencement of an offer) conflict with some state takeover laws, the SEC has not drafted regulations concerning mergers with controlling shareholders, and the Act itself does not address the subject. States have used the leeway afforded by § 28(a) to carry out "merit regulation" of securities—"blue sky" laws that allow securities commissioners to forbid sales altogether, in contrast with the federal regimen emphasizing disclosure. So § 28(a) allows states to stop some transactions federal law would permit, in pursuit of an approach at odds with a system emphasizing disclosure and investors' choice. Then there is the traditional reluctance of federal courts to infer preemption of "state law in areas traditionally regulated by the States" * * *. States have regulated corporate affairs, including mergers and sales of assets, since before the beginning of the nation.

Because Justice White's views of the Williams Act did not garner the support of a majority of the Court in *MITE*, we reexamined that subject in *CTS* and observed that the best argument for preemption is the Williams Act's "neutrality" between bidder and management, a balance designed to leave investors free to choose. This is not a confident jumping-off point, though: "Of course it is a big leap from saying that the Williams Act does not itself exhibit much hostility to tender offers to saying that it implicitly forbids states to adopt more hostile regulations, but this leap was taken by the Supreme Court plurality and us in *MITE* and by every court to consider the question since * * *. [W]hatever doubts of the Williams' Act preemptive intent we might entertain as an original matter are stifled by the weight of precedent." 794 F.2d at 262. The rough treatment our views received from the Court—only Justice White supported the holding on preemption—lifts the "weight of precedent".

There is a big difference between what Congress *enacts* and what it *supposes* will ensue. Expectations about the consequences of a law are not themselves law. To say that Congress wanted to be neutral between bidder and target—a conclusion reached in many of the Court's opinions, e.g., Piper v. Chris–Craft Industries, Inc., 430 U.S. 1, 97 S.Ct. 926, 51 L.Ed.2d 124 (1977)—is not to say that it also forbade the states to favor one of these sides. Every law has a stopping point, likely one selected because of a belief that it would be unwise (for now, maybe forever) to do more. * * * Nothing in the Williams Act says that the federal compromise among bidders, targets' managers, and investors is the only permissible one. * * *

The Williams Act regulates the *process* of tender offers: timing, disclosure, proration if tenders exceed what the bidder is willing to buy, best-price rules. It slows things down, allowing investors to evaluate the offer and management's response. Best-price, proration, and short-tender rules ensure that investors who decide at the end of the offer get the same treatment as those who decide immediately, reducing pressure to leap before looking. After complying with the disclosure and delay requirements, the bidder is free to take the shares. *MITE* held invalid a state law that increased the delay and, by authorizing a regulator to nix the offer, created a distinct possibility that the bidder would be unable to buy the stock (and the holders to sell it) despite compliance with federal law. Illinois tried to regulate the process of tender offers, contradicting in some respects the federal rules. Indiana, by contrast, allowed the tender offer to take its course as the Williams Act specified but "sterilized" the acquired shares until the remaining investors restored their voting rights. Congress said nothing about the voting power of shares acquired in tender offers. Indiana's law reduced the benefits the bidder anticipated from the acquisition but left the process alone. So the Court, although accepting Justice White's views for the purpose of argument, held that Indiana's rules do not conflict with the federal norms.

CTS observed that laws affecting the voting power of acquired shares do not differ in principle from many other rules governing the internal affairs of corporations. Laws requiring staggered or classified boards of directors delay the transfer of control to the bidder; laws requiring super-majority vote for a merger may make a transaction less attractive or impossible. 481 U.S. at 85–86, 107 S.Ct. at 1647–48. Yet these are not preempted by the Williams Act, any more than state laws concerning the *effect* of investors' votes are preempted by the portions of the Exchange Act, 15 U.S.C. § 78n(a)–(c), regulating the process of soliciting proxies. Federal securities laws frequently regulate process while state corporate law regulates substance. Federal proxy rules demand that firms disclose many things, in order to promote informed voting. Yet states may permit or compel a supermajority rule (even a unanimity rule) rendering it all but impossible for a particular side to prevail in the voting. See Robert Charles Clark, *Corporate Law* § 9.1.3 (1986). Are the state laws therefore preempted? How about state laws that allow many firms to organize without traded shares? Universities, hospitals, and other charities have self-perpetuating boards and cannot be acquired by tender offer. Insurance companies may be organized as mutuals, without traded shares; retailers often organize as co-operatives, without traded stock; some decently large companies (large enough to be "reporting companies" under the '34 Act) issue stock subject to buy-sell agreements under which the investors cannot sell to strangers without offering stock to the firm at a formula price; Ford Motor Co. issued non-voting stock to outside investors while reserving voting stock for the family, thus preventing outsiders from gaining control (dual-class stock is becoming more common); firms issue and state law enforces poison pills. All of these devices make tender offers unattractive (even impossible) and greatly diminish the power of proxy fights, success in which often depends on buying votes by acquiring the equity to which the vote is attached. See

Douglas H. Blair, Devra L. Golbe & James M. Gerard, *Unbundling the Voting Rights and Profit Claims of Common Shares,* 97 J.Pol.Econ. 420 (1989). None of these devices could be thought preempted by the Williams Act or the proxy rules. If they are not preempted, neither is Wis.Stat. § 180.726.

Any bidder complying with federal law is free to acquire shares of Wisconsin firms on schedule. Delay in completing a second-stage merger may make the target less attractive, and thus depress the price offered or even lead to an absence of bids; it does not, however, alter any of the procedures governed by federal regulation. Indeed Wisconsin's law does not depend in any way on how the acquiring firm came by its stock: open-market purchases, private acquisitions of blocs, and acquisitions via tender offers are treated identically. Wisconsin's law is no different in effect from one saying that for the three years after a person acquires 10% of a firm's stock, a unanimous vote is required to merge. Corporate law once had a generally-applicable unanimity rule in major transactions, a rule discarded because giving every investor the power to block every reorganization stopped many desirable changes. (Many investors could use their "hold-up" power to try to engross a larger portion of the gains, creating a complex bargaining problem that often could not be solved.) Wisconsin's more restrained version of unanimity also may block beneficial transactions, but not by tinkering with any of the procedures established in federal law.

Only if the Williams Act gives investors a right to be the beneficiary of offers could Wisconsin's law run afoul of the federal rule. No such entitlement can be mined out of the Williams Act, however. *Schreiber v. Burlington Northern, Inc.,* 472 U.S. 1, 105 S.Ct. 2458, 86 L.Ed.2d 1 (1985), holds that the cancellation of a pending offer because of machinations between bidder and target does not deprive investors of their due under the Williams Act. The Court treated § 14(e) as a disclosure law, so that investors could make informed decisions; it follows that events leading bidders to cease their quest do not conflict with the Williams Act any more than a state law leading a firm not to issue new securities could conflict with the Securities Act of 1933. * * * Investors have no right to receive tender offers. More to the point—since Amanda sues as bidder rather than as investor seeking to sell—the Williams Act does not create a right to profit from the business of making tender offers. It is not attractive to put bids on the table for Wisconsin corporations, but because Wisconsin leaves the process alone once a bidder appears, its law may co-exist with the Williams Act.

C

The Commerce Clause, Art. I, § 8 cl. 3 of the Constitution, grants Congress the power "[t]o regulate Commerce * * * among the several States". * * *

When state law discriminates against interstate commerce expressly— for example, when Wisconsin closes its border to butter from Minnesota— the negative Commerce Clause steps in. The law before us is not of this type: it is neutral between inter-state and intra-state commerce. Amanda therefore presses on us the broader, all-weather, be-reasonable vision of the Constitution. Wisconsin has passed a law that unreasonably injures investors, most of whom live outside of Wisconsin, and therefore it *has* to be unconstitutional, as Amanda sees things. Although Pike v. Bruce Church, Inc., 397 U.S. 137, 90 S.Ct. 844, 25 L.Ed.2d 174 (1970), sometimes is understood to authorize such general-purpose balancing, a closer examination of the cases may support the conclusion that the Court has looked for discrimination rather than for baleful effects. * * * At all events, although *MITE* employed the balancing process described in *Pike* to deal with a statute that regulated all firms having "contacts" with the state, *CTS* did not even cite that case when dealing with a statute regulating only the affairs of a firm incorporated in the state, and Justice Scalia's concurring opinion questioned its application. 481 U.S. at 95–96, 107 S.Ct. at 1652–53. The Court took a decidedly confined view of the judicial role: "We are not inclined 'to second-guess the empirical judgments of lawmakers concerning the utility of legislation,' Kassel v. Consolidated Freightways Corp., 450 U.S. [662] at 679 [101 S.Ct. 1309, 1320, 67 L.Ed.2d 580 (1981)] (BRENNAN, J., concurring in judgment)." 481 U.S. at 92, 107 S.Ct. at 1651. Although * * * scholars * * * conclude that laws such as Wisconsin's injure investors, Wisconsin is entitled to give a different answer to this empirical question—or to decide that investors' interests should be sacrificed to protect managers' interests or promote the stability of corporate arrangements.

Illinois's law, held invalid in *MITE,* regulated sales of stock elsewhere. Illinois tried to tell a Texas owner of stock in a Delaware corporation that he could not sell to a buyer in California. By contrast, Wisconsin's law, like the Indiana statute sustained by *CTS,* regulates the internal affairs of firms incorporated there. Investors may buy or sell stock as they please. Wisconsin's law differs in this respect not only from that of Illinois but also from that of Massachusetts, which forbade any transfer of shares for one year after the failure to disclose any material fact, a flaw that led the First Circuit to condemn it. Hyde Park Partners, L.P. v. Connolly, 839 F.2d 837, 847–48 (1st Cir.1988).

Buyers of stock in Wisconsin firms may exercise full rights as investors, taking immediate control. No interstate transaction is regulated or forbidden. True, Wisconsin's law makes a potential buyer less willing to buy (or depresses the bid), but this is equally true of Indiana's rule. Many other rules of corporate law—supermajority voting requirements, staggered and classified boards, and so on—have similar or greater effects on some persons' willingness to purchase stock. *CTS,* 481 U.S. at 89–90, 107 S.Ct. at 1649–50. States could ban mergers outright, with even more powerful consequences. * * * Wisconsin did not allow mergers among firms chartered there until 1947. We doubt that it was violating the Commerce Clause all those years. * * * Every rule of corporate law affects investors who live outside the state of incorporation, yet this has never been thought sufficient to authorize a form of cost-benefit inquiry through the medium of the Commerce Clause.

Wisconsin, like Indiana, is indifferent to the domicile of the bidder. A putative bidder located in Wisconsin enjoys no privilege over a firm located in New York. So too with investors: all are treated identically, regardless of residence. Doubtless most bidders (and investors) are located outside Wisconsin, but unless the law discriminates according to residence this alone does not matter. *CTS,* 481 U.S. at 87–88, 107 S.Ct. at 1648–49; Lewis v. BT Investment Managers, Inc., 447 U.S. 27, 36–37, 100 S.Ct. 2009, 2015–16, 64 L.Ed.2d 702 (1980); Exxon Corp. v. Governor of Maryland, 437 U.S. 117, 98 S.Ct. 2207, 57 L.Ed.2d 91 (1978). Every state's regulation of domestic trade (potentially) affects those who live elsewhere but wish to sell their wares within the state. A law making suppliers of drugs absolutely liable for defects will affect the conduct (and wealth) of Eli Lilly & Co., an Indiana firm, and the many other pharmaceutical houses, all located in other states, yet Wisconsin has no less power to set and change tort law than do states with domestic drug manufacturers. "Because nothing in the [Wisconsin] Act imposes a greater burden on out-of-state offerors than it does on similarly situated [Wisconsin] offerors, we reject the contention that the Act discriminates against interstate commerce." *CTS,* 481 U.S. at 88, 107 S.Ct. at 1649. For the same reason, the Court long ago held that state blue sky laws comport with the Commerce Clause. Hall v. Geiger–Jones Co., 242 U.S. 539, 37 S.Ct. 217, 61 L.Ed. 480 (1917); Caldwell v. Sioux Falls Stock Yards Co., 242 U.S. 559, 37 S.Ct. 224, 61 L.Ed. 493 (1917); Merrick v. N.W. Halsey & Co., 242 U.S. 568, 37 S.Ct. 227, 61 L.Ed. 498 (1917). Blue sky laws may bar Texans from selling stock in Wisconsin, but they apply equally to local residents' attempts to sell. That their application blocks a form of commerce altogether does not strip the states of power.

* * * This leaves only the argument that Wisconsin's law hinders the flow of interstate trade "too much". *CTS* dispatched this concern by declaring it inapplicable to laws that apply only to the internal affairs of firms incorporated in the regulating state. 481 U.S. at 89–94, 107 S.Ct. at 1649–52. States may regulate corporate transactions as they choose without having to demonstrate under an unfocused balancing test that the benefits are "enough" to justify the consequences.

To say that states have the power to enact laws whose costs exceed their benefits is not to say that investors should kiss their wallets goodbye. States compete to offer corporate codes attractive to firms. Managers who want to raise money incorporate their firms in the states that offer the combination of rules investors prefer. Ralph K. Winter, Jr., State Law, Shareholder Protection, and the Theory of the Corporation, 6 J. Legal Studies 251 (1977) * * *. Laws that in the short run injure investors and protect managers will in the longer run make the state less attractive to firms that need to raise new capital. If the law is "protectionist", the protected class is the existing body of managers (and other workers), suppliers, and so on, which bears no necessary relation to state boundaries. States regulating the affairs of domestic corporations cannot in the long run injure anyone but themselves. * * *

The long run takes time to arrive, and it is tempting to suppose that courts could contribute to investors' welfare by eliminating laws that impose costs in the short run. * * * The price of such warfare, however, is a reduction in the power of competition among states. Courts seeking to impose "good" rules on the states diminish the differences among corporate codes and dampen competitive forces. Too, courts may fail in their quest. How do judges know which rules are best? Often only the slow forces of competition reveal that information. Early economic studies may mislead, or judges (not trained as social scientists) may misinterpret the available data or act precipitously. Our Constitution allows the states to act as laboratories; slow migration (or national law on the authority of the Commerce Clause) grinds the failures under. No such process weeds out judicial errors, or decisions that, although astute when rendered, have become anachronistic in light of changes in the economy. Judges must hesitate for these practical reasons—and not only because of limits on their constitutional competence—before trying to "perfect" corporate codes.

The three district judges who have considered and sustained Delaware's law delaying mergers did so in large measure because they believed that the law left hostile offers "a meaningful opportunity for success". BNS, Inc. v. Koppers Co., 683 F.Supp. at 469. See also RP Acquisition Corp., 686 F.Supp. at 482–84, 488; *City Capital Associates,* 696 F.Supp. at 1555. Delaware allows a merger to occur forthwith if the bidder obtains 85% of the shares other than those held by management and employee stock plans. If the bid is attractive to the bulk of the unaffiliated investors, it succeeds. Wisconsin offers no such opportunity, which Amanda believes is fatal.

Even in Wisconsin, though, options remain. Defenses impenetrable to the naked eye may have cracks. Poison pills are less fatal in practice than in name (some have been swallowed willingly), and corporate law contains self-defense mechanisms. Investors concerned about stock-watering often arranged for firms to issue pre-emptive rights, entitlements for existing investors to buy stock at the same price offered to newcomers (often before the newcomers had a chance to buy in). Poison pills are dilution devices, and so pre-emptive rights ought to be handy countermeasures. So too there are countermeasures to statutes deferring mergers. The cheapest is to lower the bid to reflect the costs of delay. Because every potential bidder labors under the same drawback, the firm placing the highest value on the target still should win. Or a bidder might take down the stock and pledge it (or its dividends) as security for any loans. That is, the bidder could operate the target as a subsidiary for three years. The corporate world is full of partially owned subsidiaries. If there is gain to be had from changing the debt-equity ratio of the target, that can be done consistent with Wisconsin law. The prospect of being locked into place as holders of illiquid minority positions would cause many persons to sell out, and the threat of being locked in would cause many managers to give assent in advance, as Wisconsin allows. (Or bidders might demand that directors waive the protections of state law, just as Amanda believes that the directors' fiduciary duties compel them to redeem the poison pill rights.) Many bidders would find lock-in unattractive because of the potential for litigation by minority investors, and the need to operate the firm as a subsidiary might foreclose savings or synergies from merger. So none of these options is a perfect substitute for immediate merger, but each is a crack in the defensive wall allowing some value-increasing bids to proceed.

At the end of the day, however, it does not matter whether these countermeasures are "enough". The Commerce Clause does not demand that states leave bidders a "meaningful opportunity for success". Maryland enacted a law that absolutely banned vertical integration in the oil business. No opportunities, "meaningful" or otherwise, remained to firms wanting to own retail outlets. Exxon Corp. v. Governor of Maryland held that the law is consistent with the Commerce Clause, even on the assumption that it injures consumers and investors alike. A state with the power to forbid mergers has the power to defer them for three years. Investors can turn to firms incorporated in states committed to the dominance of market forces, or they can turn on legislators who enact unwise laws. The Constitution has room for many economic policies. "[A] law can be both economic folly and constitutional." CTS, 481 U.S. at 96–97, 107 S.Ct. at 1653–54 (Scalia, J., concurring). Wisconsin's law may well be folly; we are confident that it is constitutional.

Affirmed.

NOTE: ANTITAKEOVER STATUTES AND SHAREHOLDER VALUE

1. *Empirical Studies.*

Economists have produced a series of studies of the stock price effects of the announcement and enactment of antitakeover statutes. The results follow the ambiguous pattern of the results of similar studies of shark repellent charter provisions and dual class recapitalizations. That is, some studies support the hypothesis that defensive provisions entrench managers and increase the cost of takeovers and thus reduce the wealth of shareholders. See Ryngaert and Netter, Shareholder Wealth Effects of the Ohio Antitakeover Law, 4 J.L. Econ. & Org. 373 (1988) (passage of Ohio second generation statute causes 3.24 percent stock price decrease for firms with less than 30 percent inside ownership); Schumann, State Regulation of Takeovers and Shareholder Wealth: The Case of New York's 1985 Takeover Statute, 19 Rand J. Econ. 557 (1989) (1 percent price decrease on announcement and passage); Sidak and Woodward, Corporate Takeovers, The Commerce Clause, and the Efficient Anonymity of Shareholders, 84 Nw.U.L.Rev. 1092 (1990) (New York and Indiana; significant negative effect). Other studies support the hypothesis that defenses increase premiums, even while deterring some bids, and thereby enhance shareholder wealth. See Romano, The Political Economy of Takeover Statutes, 73 Va.L.Rev. 111 (1987) (Connecticut, Missouri, Pennsylvania; no significant effect on prices); Margotta, McWilliams & McWilliams, An Analysis of the Stock Price Effect of the 1986 Ohio Takeover Legislation, 6 J.L.Econ. & Org. 235 (1990) (no significant effect). See also Jarrell and Bradley, The Economic Effects of Federal and State Regulation of Cash Tender Offers, 23 J.L. & Econ. 371 (1980) (first generation statutes increase premiums).

Surveying some of this material, Karpoff and Malatesta, The Wealth Effects of Second–Generation State Takeover Legislation, 25 J.Fin.Econ. 291, 293 (1989), conclude that the discrepancies can be accounted for in major part by reference to the fact that "estimates of any single law's effect are heavily influenced by idiosyncratic characteristics of the researcher's event window and sample affected firms." Karpoff and Malatesta's study purports to circumvent these problems by studying the stock price effect of all new second generation statutes covered in the press through 1987, and controlling for antecedent poison pills and shark repellent charter provisions in the corporations studied. The study finds a small but statistically significant stock price decline for affected firms without antecedent pills or defensive charter provisions. Stock prices of firms with preexisting defenses experienced no significant affects.

2. *Legal Commentaries.*

How should the history of state antitakeover legislation be rated as an exercise in the evolution of economic regulation in the federal system? Some commentators take the position that the system is not working well here because this is interest group legislation enacted in disregard of the broader public interest. See, e.g., Macey, State and Federal Regulation of Corporate Takeovers: A View From the Demand Side, 69 Wash.U.L.Q. 383 (1991); Romano, The Future of Hostile Takeovers: Public Opinion and Prospects for Legislation, 57 U.Cinn.L.Rev. 457 (1988); Romano, The Political Economy of Takeover Statutes, supra. Other commentators find aspects to approve in this federal-state back and forth. See Booth, Federalism and the Market for Corporate Control, 69 Wash.U.L.Q. 411 (1991); Shipman, The Case for A Reasonable State Regulation of Corporate Takeovers: Some Observations Concerning the Ohio Experience, 57 U.Cinn.L.Rev. 507 (1988). On the preemption question, see Johnson and Millon, Misreading the Williams Act, 87 Mich.L.Rev. 1862 (1989). For the view that the statutes should be struck down under the Contract Clause, see Butler and Ribstein, State Anti–Takeover Statutes and the Contract Clause, 57 U.Cinn.L.Rev. 612 (1988).

FINANCIAL CONTRACT FORMS

Contents

FORM 1—Revised Model Simplified Indenture

Article 1 Definitions and Rules of Construction; Applicability of Trust Indenture Act

Article 2 The Securities

Article 3 Redemption

Article 4 Covenants

Article 5 Successors

Article 6 Defaults and Remedies

Article 7 Trustee

Article 9 Amendments

Article 10 Conversion

Article 11 Subordination

Article 12 Miscellaneous

Exhibit A Face of Security

FORM 2—Note Purchase Agreement

1. Authorization of Notes

2. Sale and Purchase of Notes

3. Closing

4. Conditions to Closing

5. Representations and Warranties of the Company

6. Representations of the Purchaser

7. Information as to the Company

8. Prepayment of the Notes

9. Affirmative Covenants

10. Negative Covenants

11. Events of Default

12. Remedies on Default, etc.

13. Registration, Exchange, Substitution of Notes

14. Payments on Notes

15. Expenses, etc.

16. Survival of Representations and Warranties; Entire Agreement

17. Amendment and Waiver

18. Notices

19. Reproduction of Documents

20. Confidential Information

21. Substitution of Purchaser

22. Miscellaneous

Schedule A Information Relating to Purchasers

Schedule B Defined Terms

Exhibit 1 Form of Note

Exhibit 4.4(a) Form of Opinion of Special Counsel to the Company

Exhibit 4.4(b) Form of Opinion of Special Counsel to the Purchasers

FORM 3—Preferred Stock Charter Provisions

Certificate of Incorporation of General Technology Inc.

Resolution of Board of Directors providing for the Issue of Series A Preferred Stock

FORM 4—Model Stock Purchase Agreement

Recitals

1. Definitions

2. Sale and Transfer of Shares; Closing

3. Representations and Warranties of Sellers

4. Representations and Warranties of Buyer

5. Covenants of Sellers Prior to Closing Date

6. Covenants of Buyer Prior to Closing Date

7. Conditions Precedent to Buyer's Obligation to Close

8. Conditions Precedent to Seller's Obligation to Close

9. Termination

10. Indemnification; Remedies

11. General Provisions

Ancillary Documents

FORM 5–Wachtell, Lipton, Rosen & Katz Preferred Shareholder Rights Plan

Terms of Recommended Rights Plan

Form of Plan

Exhibit A Form of Certificate of Designations of Series A

Junior Participating Preferred Stock

Exhibit B Form of Right Certificate

Exhibit C Summary of Rights to Purchase Preferred Shares

FORM 1

REVISED MODEL SIMPLIFIED INDENTURE

55 Bus. Law. 1115 (2000).

Ad Hoc Committee for Revision of the 1983 Model Simplified Indenture

INDENTURE dated as of _____, between UNIVERSAL BUSINESS CORPORATION, a [Delaware] corporation ("Company"), and GREATER BANK AND TRUST COMPANY, a [New York] [banking/trust] corporation ("Trustee").

Each party agrees as follows for the benefit of the other party and for the equal and ratable benefit of the Holders of the Company's ___% Convertible Subordinated Debentures Due _____ ("Securities"):

ARTICLE 1 *DEFINITIONS AND RULES OF CONSTRUCTION; APPLICABILITY OF THE TRUST INDENTURE ACT*

Section 1.01. Definitions. "Affiliate." Any Person controlling or controlled by or under common control with the referenced Person. "Control" for this definition means the power to direct the management and policies of a Person, directly or indirectly, whether through the ownership of voting securities, by contract, or otherwise. The terms "controlling" and "controlled" have meanings correlative to the foregoing.

"Agent." Any Registrar, Paying Agent or Conversion Agent.

"Board." The Board of Directors of the Person or any officer or committee thereof authorized to act for such Board.

"Business Day." A day that is not a Legal Holiday.

"Company." The party named as such above until a successor which duly assumes the obligations upon the Securities and under the Indenture replaces it and thereafter means the successor.

"Debt" means, with respect to any Person, (i) any obligation of such Person to pay the principal of, premium of, if any, interest on (including interest accruing on or after the filing of any petition in bankruptcy or for reorganization relating to the Company, whether or not a claim for such post-petition interest is allowed in such proceeding), penalties, reimbursement or indemnification amounts, fees, expenses or other amounts relating to any indebtedness, and any other liability, contingent or otherwise, of such Person (A) for borrowed money (including instances where the recourse of the lender is to the whole of the assets of such Person or to a portion thereof), (B) evidenced by a note, debenture or similar instrument (including a purchase money obligation) including securities, (C) for any letter of credit or performance bond in favor of such Person, or (D) for the payment of money relating to a capitalized lease obligation; (ii) any liability of others of the kind described in the preceding clause (i), which the Person has guaranteed or which is otherwise its legal liability; (iii) any obligation of the type described in clauses (i) and (ii) secured by a lien to which the property or assets of such Person are subject, whether or not the obligations secured thereby shall have been assumed by or shall otherwise be such Person's legal liability; and (iv) any and all deferrals, renewals, extensions and refunding of, or amendments, modifications or supplements to, any liability of the kind described in any of the preceding clauses (i), (ii) or (iii).

"Default." Any event which is, or after notice or passage of time would be, an Event of Default.

"Exchange Act." The Securities Exchange Act of 1934, as amended.

"Holder" or "Securityholder." A Person in whose name a Security is registered.

"Indenture." This Indenture as amended from time to time, including the terms of the Securities and any amendments.

"Officers' Certificate." A certificate signed by two Officers, one of whom must be the President, the Treasure or a Vice–President of the Company. See Sections 12.03 and 12.04.

"Opinion of Counsel." Written opinion from legal counsel who is acceptable to the Trustee. See Sections 12.03 and 12.04.

"Person." Any individual, corporation, partnership, joint venture, association, limited liability company, joint stock company, trust, unincorporated organization or government or other agency or political subdivision thereof.

"Principal" of a Security means the principal of the Security plus the premium, if any, on the Security which is due or overdue or is to become due at the relevant time.

"Proceeding." A liquidation, dissolution, bankruptcy, insolvency, reorganization, receivership or similar proceeding under Bankruptcy Law, an assignment for the benefit of creditors, any marshalling of assets or liabilities, or winding up or dissolution, but shall not include any transaction permitted by and made in compliance with Article 5.

"Representative." The indenture trustee or other trustee, agent or representative for an issue of Senior Debt.

"SEC." The U.S. Securities and Exchange Commission.

"Securities." The Securities described above issued under this Indenture.

"Senior Debt." Debt of the Company whenever incurred, outstanding at any time except (i) Debt that by its terms is not senior in right of payment to the Securities, (ii) Debt held by the Company or any Affiliate of the Company, and (iii) Debt excluded by Section 12.09.

"TIA." The Trust Indenture Act of 1939 (15 U.S.C. §§ 77aaa–77bbbb), as amended, as in effect on the date of this Indenture, except as provided in Sections 1.04 and 9.03.

"Trust Officer." Any officer or assistant officer of the Trustee assigned by the Trustee to administer its corporate trust matters or to whom a matter concerning the Indenture may be referred.

"Trustee." The party named as such above until a successor replaces it and thereafter means the successor. See also Section 11.14.

"U.S. Government Obligations." Securities that are direct, noncallable, nonredeemable obligations of, or noncallable, nonredeemable obligations guaranteed by, the United States for the timely payment of which obligation or guarantee the full faith and credit of the United States is pledged, or funds consisting solely of such securities, including funds managed by the Trustee or one of its Affiliates (including such funds for which it or its Affiliates receives fees in connection with such management).

* * *

Section 1.03. Rules of Construction. Unless the context otherwise requires:

(1) a term defined in Section 1.01 or 1.02 has the meaning assigned to it therein, and terms defined in the TIA have the meanings assigned to them in the TIA;

(2) an accounting term not otherwise defined has the meaning assigned to it in accordance with generally accepted accounting principles in the United States;

(3) "or" is not exclusive;

(4) words in the singular include the plural, and words in the plural include the singular;

(5) provisions apply to successive events and transactions;

(6) "herein," "hereof" and other words of similar import refer to this Indenture as a whole and not to any particular Article, Section or other subdivision; and

(7) "including" means including without limitation.

Section 1.04. Trust Indenture Act. The provisions of TIA Sections 310 through 317 that impose duties on any Person (including the provisions automatically deemed included herein unless expressly excluded by this Indenture) are a part of and govern this Indenture upon and so long as the Indenture and Securities are subject to the TIA. If any provision of this Indenture limits, qualifies or conflicts with such duties, the imposed duties shall control. If a provision of the TIA requires or permits a provision of this Indenture and the TIA provision is amended, then the Indenture provision shall be automatically amended to like effect.

[Any reference to a requirement under the TIA shall only apply upon and so long as the Indenture is qualified under and subject to the TIA.]

ARTICLE 2 *THE SECURITIES*

Section 2.01. Form and Dating. The Securities and the certificate of authentication shall be substantially in the form of Exhibit A, which is hereby incorporated in and expressly made a part of this Indenture. The Securities may have notations, legends or endorsements required by Section 2.11, law, stock exchange rule, automated quotation system, agreements to which the Company is subject, or usage. Each Security shall be dated the date of its authentication.

* * *

ARTICLE 3 *REDEMPTION*

Section 3.01. Notice to Trustee. If Securities are to be redeemed, the Company shall notify the Trustee of the redemption date, the Principal amount of Securities to be redeemed and the provision of the Securities permitting or requiring the redemption.

The Company may reduce the Principal amount of Securities required to be redeemed pursuant to Paragraph Six of the Securities if it notifies the Trustee of the amount of the credit and the basis for it by delivery of an Officers' Certificate. If the reduction is based on a credit for redeemed, converted or canceled Securities that the Company has not previously delivered to the Trustee for cancellation, the Company shall deliver such Securities to the Registrar before the selection of securities to be redeemed.

The Company shall give each notice provided for in this Section at least 50 days before the redemption date unless a shorter period is satisfactory to the Trustee. If fewer than all the Securities are to be redeemed, the record date relating to such redemption shall be selected by the Company and given to the Trustee, which record date shall be not less than 15 days prior to the redemption date.

Section 3.02. Selection of Securities to be Redeemed. If less than all the Securities are to be redeemed, the Trustee shall select the Securities to be redeemed by a method that complies with the requirements, if any, of any stock exchange on which the Securities are listed and that the Trustee considers fair and appropriate, which may include selection pro rata or by lot. The Trustee shall make the selection from Securities outstanding not previously called for redemption. The Trustee may select for redemption portions of the Principal of Securities that have denominations larger than $1000. Securities and portions thereof selected by the Trustee shall be in amounts of $1000 or whole multiples of $1000. Provisions of this Indenture that apply to Securities called for redemption also apply to portions of Securities called for redemption.

Section 3.03. Notice of Redemption. At least 30 days but not more than 60 days before a redemption date, the Company shall mail a notice of redemption to each Holder whose Securities are to be redeemed.

The notice shall state that it is a notice of redemption, identify the Securities to be redeemed and shall state:

(1) the redemption date;

(2) the redemption price;

(3) the conversion price;

(4) the name and address of the Paying Agent and Conversion Agent;

(5) that convertible Securities called for redemption may be converted at any time before the close of business on the Business Day immediately

preceding the redemption date (unless the redemption date is also a record date for an interest payment, in which event they may be converted at any time through the redemption date);

(6) that Holders who want to convert Securities must satisfy the requirements for conversion set forth in the Securities;

(7) that Securities called for redemption must be surrendered to the Paying Agent to collect the redemption price;

(8) that, unless the Company defaults in making such redemption payment or the Paying Agent is prohibited from making such payment pursuant to the terms of this Indenture, interest on Securities (or portion thereof) called for redemption ceases to accrue on and after the redemption date; and

(9) list the CUSIP number of the Securities and state that no representation is made as to the correctness or accuracy of the CUSIP number, if any, listed in such notice or printed on the Securities.

At the Company's request, the Trustee shall give the notice of redemption in the Company's name and at its expense.

Section 3.04. Effect of Notice of Redemption. Once notice of redemption is mailed, Securities called for redemption become due and payable on the redemption date at the redemption price. Upon surrender to the Paying Agent, such Securities shall be paid at the redemption price stated in the notice, plus accrued interest to the redemption price stated in the notice, plus accrued interest to the redemption date. Failure to give notice or any defect in the notice to any Holder shall not affect the validity of the notice to any other Holder.

Section 3.05. Deposit of Redemption Price. On or before the redemption date, the Company shall deposit with the Paying Agent (or, if the Company or any Affiliate is the Paying Agent, shall segregate and hold in trust) money sufficient to pay the redemption price of, and accrued interest on, all Securities to be redeemed on that date other than Securities or portions of Securities called for redemption which have been delivered by the Company to the Registrar for cancellation. The Paying Agent shall return to the Company any money not required for that purpose because of conversion of Securities.

Unless the Company shall default in the payment of Securities (and accrued interest) called for redemption, interest on such Securities shall cease to accrue after the redemption date. Securities called for redemption shall cease to be convertible after the close of business on the Business Day immediately preceding the redemption date (unless the redemption date is also a record date for an interest payment, in which event they may be converted through the redemption date), unless the Company shall default in the payment of such Securities on the redemption date, in which event the Securities shall remain convertible until paid (together with accrued interest).

Section 3.06. Securities Redeemed in Part. Upon surrender of a Security that is redeemed in part, the Company shall deliver to the Holder (at the Company's expense) a new Security equal in Principal amount to the unredeemed portion of the Security surrendered.

ARTICLE 4 *COVENANTS*

Section 4.01. Payment of Securities. The Company shall pay the Principal of and interest on the Securities on the dates and in the manner provided in the Securities and this Indenture. Principal and interest shall be considered paid on the date due if the Paying Agent holds in accordance with this Indenture on that date money sufficient to pay all Principal and interest then due and the Paying Agent is not prohibited from paying such money to the Holders on such date pursuant to the terms of this Indenture.

The Company shall pay interest on overdue Principal at the rate borne by the Securities; it shall pay interest on overdue Defaulted Interest at the same rate to the extent lawful.

Section 4.02. SEC Reports. The Company shall file with the Trustee within 15 days after it files them with the SEC copies of the annual reports and of the information, documents and other reports which the Company is required to file with the SEC pursuant to Section 13 or 15(d) of the Exchange Act. The Company will cause any quarterly and annual reports which it makes available to its stockholders to be mailed to the Holders. The Company will also comply with the other provisions of TIA Section 314(a). Delivery of such reports, information and documents to the Trustee is for informational purposes only and the Trustee's receipt of such shall not constitute notice or constructive notice of any information contained therein or determinable from information contained therein, including the Company's compliance with any of its covenants hereunder (as to which the Trustee is entitled to rely exclusively on Officers' Certificates).

Section 4.03. Compliance Certificate. The Company shall deliver to the Trustee, within [105] days after the end of each fiscal year of the Company, a brief certificate signed by the principal executive officer, principal financial officer or principal accounting officer of the Company, as to the signer's knowledge of the Company's compliance with all conditions and covenants contained in this Indenture (determined without regard to any period of grace or requirement of notice provided herein).

Section 4.04. Notice of Certain Events. The Company shall give prompt written notice to the Trustee and any Paying Agent of (i) any Proceeding, (ii) any Default or Event of Default, (iii) any cure or waiver of any Default or Event of Default, (iv) any Senior Debt Payment Default or Senior Debt Default Notice, and (v) if and when the Securities are listed on any stock exchange.

ARTICLE 5 *SUCCESSORS*

Section 5.01. When Company May Merge, etc. The Company shall not consolidate or merge with or into, or transfer all or substantially all of its assets to, any Person unless:

(1) either the Company shall be the resulting or surviving entity or such Person is a corporation organized and existing under the laws of the United States, a State thereof or the District of Columbia;

(2) if the Company is not the resulting or surviving entity, such Person assumes by supplemental indenture all the obligations of the Company under the Securities and this Indenture, except that it need not assume the obligations of the Company as to conversion of Securities if pursuant to Section 10.17 the Company or another Person enters into a supplemental indenture obligating it to deliver securities, cash or other assets upon conversion of Securities; and

(3) immediately before and immediately after the transaction no Default exists.

The Company shall deliver to the Trustee prior to the proposed transaction an Officers' Certificate and an Opinion of Counsel, each of which shall state that such consolidation, merger or transfer and such supplemental indenture comply with this Article 5 and that all conditions precedent herein provided for relating to such transaction have been complied with.

Section 5.02. Successor Corporation Substituted. Upon any consolidation or merger, or any transfer of all or substantially all of the assets of the Company in accordance with Section 5.01, the successor corporation formed by such consolidation or into which the Company is merged or to which such transfer is made shall succeed to, and be substituted for, and may exercise every right and power of, the Company under this Indenture and the Securities with the same effect as if such successor corporation had been named as the Company herein and in the Securities. Thereafter the obligations of the Company under the Securities and Indenture shall terminate except for (i) obligations the Company may have under a supplemental indenture pursuant to Section 10.17 and (ii) in the case of a transfer, the obligation to pay the Principal of and interest on the Securities.

ARTICLE 6 *DEFAULTS AND REMEDIES*

Section 6.01. Events of Default. An "Event of Default" occurs if:

(1) the Company fails to pay interest on any Security when the same becomes due and payable and such failure continues for a period of [30] days;

(2) the Company fails to pay the Principal of any Security when the same becomes due and payable at maturity, upon redemption or otherwise;

(3) the Company fails to comply with any of its other agreements in the Securities or this Indenture and such failure continues for the period and after the notice specified below;

(4) the Company pursuant to or within the meaning of any Bankruptcy Law:

(A) commences a voluntary case,

    (B) consents to the entry of an order for relief against it in an involuntary case,

    (C) consents to the appointment of a Custodian of it or for all or substantially all of its property, or

    (D) makes a general assignment for the benefit of its creditors; or

    (5) a court of competent jurisdiction enters an order or decree under any Bankruptcy Law that:

    (A) is for relief against the Company in an involuntary case,

    (B) appoints a Custodian of the Company or for all or substantially all of its property, or

    (C) orders the liquidation of the Company, and the order or decree remains unstayed and in effect for 60 days.

The foregoing will constitute Events of Default whatever the reason for any such Event of Default, whether it is voluntary or involuntary, a consequence of the application of Article 11, or is effected by operation of law or pursuant to any judgment, decree or order of any court or any order, rule or regulation of any administrative or governmental body.

The term "Bankruptcy Law" means title 11 of the U.S. Code or any similar Federal or state law for the relief of debtors. The term "Custodian" means any receiver, trustee, assignee, liquidator or similar official under any Bankruptcy Law.

A Default under clause (3) is not an Event of Default until the Trustee or the Holders of at least [25]% in Principal amount of the Securities notify the Company and the Trustee of the Default and the Company does not cure the Default, or it is not waived, within [60] days after receipt of the notice. The notice must specify the Default, demand that it be remedied to the extent consistent with law, and state that the notice is a "Notice of Default."

Section 6.02. Acceleration. If an Event of Default occurs and is continuing, the Trustee by notice to the Company, or the Holders of at least 25% in Principal amount of the Securities by notice to the Company and the Trustee, may declare the Principal of and accrued and unpaid interest on all the Securities to be due and payable. Upon such declaration the Principal and interest shall be due and payable immediately.

The Holders of a majority in Principal amount of the Securities by notice to the Company and the Trustee may rescind an acceleration and its consequences if the rescission would not conflict with any judgment or decree and if all existing Events of Default have been cured or waived except nonpayment of Principal or interest that has become due solely because of the acceleration.

Section 6.03. Other Remedies. If an Event of Default occurs and is continuing, the Trustee may pursue any available remedy to collect the payment of Principal or interest on the Securities or to enforce the performance of any provision of the Securities or this Indenture.

The Trustee may maintain a proceeding even if it does not possess any of the Securities or does not produce any of them in the proceeding. A delay or omission by the Trustee or any Securityholder in exercising any right or remedy accruing upon an Event of Default shall not impair the right or remedy or constitute a waiver of or acquiescence in the Event of Default. All remedies are cumulative to the extent permitted by law.

Section 6.04. Waiver of Past Defaults. The Holders of a majority in Principal amount of the Securities by notice to the Trustee may waive an existing Default and its consequences except:

(1) a Default in the payment of the Principal of or interest on any Security;

(2) a Default with respect to a provision that under Section 9.02 cannot be amended without the consent of each Securityholder affected; or

(3) a Default under Article 10.

Section 6.05. Control by Majority. The Holders of a majority in Principal amount of the Securities may direct the time, method and place of conducting any proceeding for any remedy available to the Trustee or exercising any trust or power conferred on the Trustee. However, the Trustee may refuse to follow any direction that conflicts with law or this Indenture, is unduly prejudicial to the rights of other Securityholders, or would involve the Trustee in personal liability or expense for which the Trustee has not received a satisfactory indemnity.

Section 6.06. Limitation on Suits. A Securityholder may pursue a remedy with respect to this Indenture or the Securities only if:

(1) the Holder gives to the Trustee notice of a continuing Event of Default;

(2) the Holders of at least 25% in Principal amount of the Securities make a request to the Trustee to pursue the remedy;

(3) the Trustee either (i) gives to such Holders notice it will not comply with the request, or (ii) does not comply with the request within [15 or 30] days after receipt of the request; and

(4) the Holders of a majority in Principal amount of the Securities do not give the Trustee a direction inconsistent with the request prior to the earlier of the date, if ever, on which the Trustee delivers a notice under Section 6.06(3)(i) or the expiration of the period described in Section 6.06(3)(ii).

A Securityholder may not use this Indenture to prejudice the rights of another Securityholder or to obtain a preference or priority over another Securityholder.

Section 6.07. Rights of Holders To Receive Payment. Notwithstanding any other provision of this Indenture, the right of any Holder of a Security to receive payment of Principal and interest on the Security, on or after the respective due dates expressed in the Security, or to bring suit for the enforcement of any such payment on or after such respective dates, shall not be impaired or affected without the consent of the Holder.

Notwithstanding any other provision of this Indenture, the right of any Holder of a Security to bring suit for the enforcement of the right to convert the Security shall not be impaired or affected without the consent of the Holder.

Nothing in this Indenture limits or defers the right or ability of Holders to petition for commencement of a case under applicable Bankruptcy Law to the extent consistent with such Bankruptcy Law.

Section 6.08. Priorities. After an Event of Default any money or other property distributable in respect of the Company's obligations under this Indenture shall be paid in the following order:

First: to the Trustee (including any predecessor Trustee) for amounts due under Section 7.07;

Second: to holders of Senior Debt to the extent required by Article 11;

Third: to Securityholders for amounts due and unpaid on the Securities for Principal and interest, ratably, without preference or priority of any kind, according to the amounts due and payable on the Securities for Principal and interest, respectively; and

Fourth: to the Company.

The Trustee may fix a record date and payment date for any payment to Securityholders.

Section 6.09. Undertaking for Costs. In any suit for the enforcement of any right or remedy under this Indenture or in any suit against the Trustee for any action taken or omitted by it as Trustee, a court in its discretion may require the filing by any party litigant in the suit of an undertaking to pay the costs of the suit, and the court in its discretion may assess reasonable costs, including reasonable attorneys' fees, against any party litigant in the suit, having due regard to the merits and good faith of the claims or defenses made by the party litigant. This Section does not apply to a suit by the Trustee, a suit by a Holder pursuant to Section 6.07 or a suit by Holders of more than 10% in Principal amount of the Securities.

Section 6.10. Proof of Claim. In the event of any Proceeding, the Trustee may (and, if applicable, the trustee for or holders of Senior Debt may) file a claim for the unpaid balance of the Securities in the form required in the Proceeding and cause the claim to be approved or allowed. Nothing herein contained shall be deemed to authorize the Trustee or the holders of Senior Debt to authorize or consent to or accept or adopt on behalf of any Securityholder any plan of reorganization, arrangement, adjustment, or composition affecting the Securities or the rights of any Holder thereof, or to authorize the Trustee or the holders of Senior Debt to vote in respect of the claim of any Securityholder in any Proceeding.

Section 6.11. Actions of a Holder. For the purpose of providing any consent, waiver or instruction to the Company or the Trustee, a "Holder" or "Securityholder" shall include a Person who provides to the Company or the Trustee, as the case may be, an affidavit of beneficial ownership of a Security together with a satisfactory indemnity against any loss, liability or expense to such party to the extent that it acts upon such affidavit of beneficial ownership (including any consent, waiver or instructions given by a Person providing such affidavit and indemnity).

ARTICLE 7 *TRUSTEE*

Section 7.01. Duties of Trustee.

(a) If an Event of Default has occurred and is continuing, the Trustee shall exercise such of the rights and powers vested in it by this Indenture, and use the same degree of care and skill in their exercise, as a prudent person would exercise or use under the circumstances in the conduct of its own affairs.

(b) Except during the continuance of an Event of Default:

(1) The Trustee need perform only those duties that are specifically set forth in this Indenture and no others.

(2) In the absence of bad faith on its part, the Trustee may conclusively rely, as to the truth of the statements and the correctness of the opinions expressed therein, upon certificates or opinions furnished to the Trustee and conforming to the requirements of this Indenture. However, the Trustee shall examine the certificates and opinions to determine whether or not they conform to the requirements of this Indenture.

(c) The Trustee may not be relieved from liability for its own negligent action, its own negligent failure to act or its own willful misconduct, except that:

(1) This paragraph does not limit the effect of paragraph (b) of this Section.

(2) The Trustee shall not be liable for any error of judgment made in good faith by a Trust Officer, unless it is proved that the Trustee was negligent in ascertaining the pertinent facts.

(3) The Trustee shall not be liable with respect to any action it takes or omits to take in good faith in accordance with a direction received by it pursuant to Section 6.05.

(4) The Trustee may refuse to perform any duty or exercise any right or power which would require it to expend its own funds or risk any liability if it shall reasonably believe that repayment of such funds or adequate indemnity against such risk is not reasonably assured to it.

(d) Every provision of this Indenture that in any way relates to the Trustee is subject to paragraphs (a), (b) and (c) of this Section.

(e) The Trustee shall not be liable for interest on any money received by it except as the Trustee may agree with the Company. Money held in trust by the Trustee need not be segregated from other funds except to the extent required by law.

Section 7.02. Rights of Trustee.

(a) The Trustee may rely on any document believed by it to be genuine and to have been signed or presented by the proper Person. The Trustee need not investigate any fact or matter stated in the document.

(b) Before the Trustee acts or refrains from acting, it may require an Officers' Certificate or an Opinion of Counsel. The Trustee shall not be liable for any action it takes or omits to take in good faith in reliance on the Officers' Certificate or an Opinion of Counsel. The Trustee may also consult with counsel on any matter relating to the Indenture or the Securities and the Trustee shall not be liable for any action it takes or omits to take in good faith in reliance on the advice of counsel.

(c) The Trustee may act through agents and shall not be responsible for the misconduct or negligence of any agent appointed with due care.

(d) The Trustee shall not be liable for any action it takes or omits to take in good faith which it believes to be authorized or within its rights or powers.

(e) Except in connection with compliance with TIA Section 310 or 311, the Trustee shall only be charged with knowledge of Trust Officers.

Section 7.03. Individual Rights of Trustee; Disqualification.

The Trustee in its individual or any other capacity may become the owner or pledgee of Securities and may otherwise deal with the Company or an Affiliate with the same rights it would have if it were not Trustee. Any Agent may do the same with like rights. However, the Trustee is subject to TIA Sections 310(b) and 311.

Section 7.04. Trustee's Disclaimer.

The Trustee shall have no responsibility for the validity or adequacy of this Indenture or the Securities, it shall not be accountable for the Company's use of the proceeds from the Securities and it shall not be responsible for any statement in the Securities other than its authentication.

Section 7.05. Notice of Defaults.

If a continuing Default is known to the Trustee, the Trustee shall mail to Securityholders a notice of the Default within 90 days after it occurs. Except in the case of a Default in payment on any Security, the Trustee may withhold the notice if and so long as a committee of its Trust Officers in good faith determines that withholding the notice is in the interests of Securityholders. [The Trustee shall mail to Securityholders any notice it receives from Securityholder(s) under Section 6.06, and of any notice the Trustee provides pursuant to Section 6.06(3)(i).]

Section 7.06. Reports by Trustee to Holders.

If required pursuant to TIA Section 313(a), within 60 days after the reporting date stated in Section 12.09, the Trustee shall mail to Securityholders a brief report dated as of such reporting date that complies with TIA Section 313(a). The Trustee also shall comply with TIA Section 313(b)(2).

A copy of each report at the time of its mailing to Securityholders shall be filed with the SEC and each stock exchange on which the Securities are listed.

Section 7.07. Compensation and Indemnity. The Company shall pay to the Trustee from time to time reasonable compensation for its services, including for any Agent capacity in which it acts. The Trustee's compensation shall not be limited by any law on compensation of a trustee of an express trust. The Company shall reimburse the Trustee upon request for all reasonable out-of-pocket expenses incurred by it. Such expenses shall include the reasonable compensation and out-of-pocket expenses of the Trustee's agents and counsel.

The Company shall indemnify the Trustee against any loss, liability or expense incurred by it including in any Agent capacity in which it acts. The Trustee shall notify the Company promptly of any claim for which it may seek indemnity. The Company shall defend the claim and the Trustee shall cooperate in the defense. The Trustee may have separate counsel and the Company shall pay the reasonable fees and expenses of such counsel. The Company need not pay for any settlement made without its consent, which consent shall not unreasonably be withheld.

The Company need not reimburse any expense or indemnify against any loss or liability incurred by the Trustee through gross negligence, willful misconduct or bad faith.

To secure the Company's payment obligations in this Section, the Trustee shall have a lien prior to the Securities on all money or property held or collected by the Trustee, except that held in trust to pay Principal and interest on particular Securities.

Without prejudice to its rights hereunder, when the Trustee incurs expenses or renders services after an Event of Default specified in Section 6.01(4) or (5) occurs, the expenses and the compensation for the services are intended to constitute expenses of administration under any Bankruptcy Law.

Section 7.08. Replacement of Trustee. A resignation or removal of the Trustee and appointment of a successor Trustee shall become effective only upon the successor Trustee's acceptance of appointment as provided in this Section.

The Trustee may resign by so notifying the Company. The Holders of a majority in Principal amount of the Securities may remove the Trustee by so notifying the Trustee and the Company. The Company may remove the Trustee if:

    (1) the Trustee fails to comply with Section 7.10;

    (2) the Trustee is adjudged a bankrupt or an insolvent;

    (3) a receiver or public officer takes charge of the Trustee or its property; or

    (4) the Trustee becomes incapable of acting.

If the Trustee resigns or is removed or if a vacancy exists in the office of Trustee for any reason, the Company shall promptly appoint a successor Trustee.

If a successor Trustee is not appointed and does not take office within 30 days after the retiring Trustee resigns, the retiring Trustee may appoint a successor Trustee at any time prior to the date on which a successor Trustee takes office. If a successor Trustee does not take office within [45] days after the retiring Trustee resigns or is removed, the retiring Trustee, the Company or, subject to Section 6.09, any Securityholder may petition any court of competent jurisdiction for the appointment of a successor Trustee.

If the Trustee fails to comply with Section 7.10, any Securityholder may petition any court of competent jurisdiction for the removal of the Trustee and the appointment of a successor Trustee. Within one year after a successor Trustee appointed by the Company or a court pursuant to this Section 7.08 takes office, the Holders of a majority in Principal amount of the Securities may appoint a successor Trustee to replace such successor Trustee.

A successor Trustee shall deliver a written acceptance of its appointment to the retiring Trustee and to the Company. Thereupon the resignation or removal of the retiring Trustee shall become effective, and the successor Trustee shall have all the rights, powers and duties of the Trustee under this Indenture. The successor Trustee shall mail a notice of its succession to Securityholders. The retiring Trustee shall promptly transfer all property held by it as Trustee to the successor Trustee, subject to the lien provided for in Section 7.07.

Section 7.09. Successor Trustee by Merger, etc. If the Trustee consolidates, merges or converts into, or transfers all or substantially all of its corporate trust business to, another corporation, the successor corporation without any further act shall be the successor Trustee, if such successor corporation is eligible and qualified under Section 7.10.

Section 7.10. Eligibility. This Indenture shall always have a Trustee who satisfies the requirements of TIA Sections 310(a)(1) and 310(a)(2). The Trustee shall always have a combined capital and surplus as stated in Section 12.09.

Section 7.11. Preferential Collection of Claims Against Company. Upon and so long as the Indenture is qualified under the TIA, the Trustee is subject to TIA Section 311(a), excluding any creditor relationship listed in TIA Section 311(b). A Trustee who has resigned or been removed is subject to TIA Section 311(a) to the extent indicated.

* * *

ARTICLE 9 *AMENDMENTS*

Section 9.01. Without Consent of Holders. The Company and the Trustee may amend this Indenture or the Securities without the consent of any Securityholder:

(1) to cure any ambiguity, defect or inconsistency;

(2) to comply with Section 5.01, 10.06 or 10.17; or

(3) to make any change that does not adversely affect the rights of any Securityholder.

Section 9.02. With Consent of Holders. The Company and the Trustee may amend this Indenture or the Securities with the written consent of the Holders of at least a majority in Principal amount of the Securities. However, without the consent of each Securityholder affected, an amendment under this Section may not:

[handwritten margin note: Simple majority >50% for any change except ¶2]
[handwritten margin note: (1): unanimous consent]

(1) reduce the amount of Securities whose Holders must consent to an amendment;

(2) reduce the interest on or change the time for payment of interest on any Security;

(3) reduce the Principal of or change the fixed maturity of any Security;

(4) reduce the premium payable upon the redemption of any Security [or change the time at which any Security may or shall be redeemed];

(5) make any Security payable in money other than that stated in the Security;

(6) make any change in Section 6.04, 6.07 or 9.02 (second sentence);

(7) make any change that adversely affects the right to convert any Security; or

(8) make any change in Article 11 that adversely affects the rights of any Securityholder.

It shall not be necessary for the consent of the Holders under this Section to approve the particular form of any proposed amendment, but it shall be sufficient if such consent approves the substance thereof.

An amendment under this Section may not make any change that adversely affects the rights under Article 11 of any Senior Debt unless it consents to the change.

Section 9.03. Compliance with Trust Indenture Act and Section 12.03. Every amendment to this Indenture or the Securities shall comply with the TIA as then in effect, so long as the Indenture and Securities are subject to the TIA. The Trustee is entitled to, and the Company shall provide an Opinion of Counsel and Officers' Certificate that the Trustee's execution of any amendment or supplemental indenture is permitted under this Article 9.

Section 9.04. Revocation and Effect of Consents and Waivers. A consent to an amendment or a waiver by a Holder of a Security shall bind the Holder and every subsequent Holder of that Security or portion of the Security that evidences the same debt as the consenting Holder's Security, even if notation of the consent or waiver is not made on the Security. However, any such Holder or subsequent Holder may revoke the consent or waiver as to such Holder's Security or portion of the Security if the Trustee receives the notice of revocation before the date the amendment or waiver becomes effective. After an amendment or waiver becomes effective, it shall bind every Securityholder.

The Company may, but shall not be obligated to, fix a record date for the purpose of determining the Securityholders entitled to give their consent or take any other action described above or required or permitted to be taken pursuant to this Indenture. If a record date is fixed, then notwithstanding the immediately preceding paragraph, those Persons who were Securityholders at such record date (or their duly designated proxies), and only those Persons, shall be entitled to give such consent or to revoke any consent previously given or take any such action, whether or not such Persons continue to be Holders after such record date. No such consent shall be valid or effective for more than 120 days after such record date.

Section 9.05. Notice of Amendment; Notation on or Exchange of Securities. After any amendment under this Article becomes effective, the Company shall mail to Securityholders a notice briefly describing such amendment. The failure to give such notice to all Securityholders, or any defect therein, shall not impair or affect the validity of an amendment under this Article.

The Company or the Trustee may place an appropriate notation about an amendment or waiver on any Security thereafter authenticated. The Company may issue in exchange for affected Securities new Securities that reflect the amendment or waiver.

Section 9.06. Trustee Protected. The Trustee need not sign any supplemental indenture that adversely affects its rights.

ARTICLE 10 *CONVERSION*

Section 10.01. Conversion Right and Conversion Price. A Holder of a Security may convert it into Common Stock at any time during the period stated in paragraph 9 of the Securities. The number of shares issuable upon conversion of a Security is determined as follows: Divide the Principal amount to be converted by the conversion price in effect on the conversion date. Round the result to the nearest 1/100th of a share.

The initial conversion price is stated in paragraph 9 of the Securities. The conversion price is subject to adjustment in accordance with this Article.

A Holder may convert a portion of a Security if the portion is $1000 or a whole multiple of $1000. Provisions of this Indenture that apply to conversion of all of a Security also apply to conversion of a portion of it.

"Common Stock" means the Common Stock of the Company as such Common Stock exists on the date of this Indenture.

Section 10.02. Conversion Procedure. To convert a Security, a Holder must (1) complete and sign the conversion notice on the back of the Security, (2) surrender the Security to a Conversion Agent, (3) furnish appropriate endorsements and transfer documents if required by the Trustee or Conversion Agent, (4) pay any transfer or similar tax if required, and (5) provide funds, if applicable, required pursuant to the next paragraph.

The date on which the Holder satisfies all such requirements is the conversion date. As soon as practicable, the Company shall deliver, or shall cause the Conversion Agent to deliver, upon the order of the Holder, a certificate for the number of full shares of Common Stock issuable upon the conversion and a check for any fractional share. The Person in whose name the certificate is registered shall be treated as a stockholder of record on and after the conversion date.

Any Security surrendered for conversion during the period from the close of business on the record date for any interest payment date to the close of business on the Business Day next preceding the following interest payment date shall be accompanied by payment, in New York Clearing House funds or other funds acceptable to the Company, of an amount equal to the interest otherwise payable on such interest payment date on the Principal amount being converted [; provided, however, that no such payment need be made if there shall exist at the conversion date a Default in the payment of interest on the Securities]. Notwithstanding Section 2.13, if a Holder has paid an amount equal to the interest otherwise payable in accordance with the preceding sentence and the Company thereafter defaults in the payment of interest on such interest payment date, such Defaulted Interest, together with interest thereon shall be paid to the Person who made such required payment no later than the payment date set in accordance with Section 2.13. Except as provided above in this Section 10.02, no payment or other adjustment shall be made for interest accrued on any Security converted or for dividends on any securities issued on conversion of the Security.

[Except as provided in the immediately preceding paragraph, the Company's delivery of the fixed number of shares of Common Stock into which a Security is convertible will be deemed to satisfy the Company's obligation to pay the Principal amount of the Security and all accrued interest (and original issue discount) that has not previously been (or is not simultaneously being) paid. The Common Stock is treated as issued first in payment of accrued interest (and original issue discount) and then in payment of Principal. Thus, accrued interest (and original issue discount) are treated as paid rather than cancelled.]

If a Holder converts more than one Security at the same time, the number of full shares issuable and payment pursuant to Section 10.03 upon the conversion shall be based on the total Principal amount of the Securities converted.

Upon surrender of a Security that is converted in part, the Trustee shall authenticate for the Holder a new Security equal in Principal amount to the unconverted Principal amount of the Security surrendered.

If the last day on which a Security may be converted is a Legal Holiday in a place where the Conversion Agent is located, the Security may be surrendered to the Company or the Conversion Agent on the next succeeding Business Day.

Section 10.03. Fractional Shares. The Company shall not issue a fractional share of Common Stock upon conversion of a Security. Instead, the Company shall deliver a check for an amount equal to the current market value of the fractional share. The current market value of a fraction of a share shall be determined as follows: Multiply the current market price of a full share by the fraction. Round the result to the nearest cent.

The current market price of a share of Common Stock for purposes of this Section 10.03 shall be the Quoted Price of the Common Stock on the last trading day prior to the conversion date. In the absence of such a quotation, the Board shall determine the current market price in good faith on the basis of such information as it considers reasonably appropriate.

Section 10.04. Taxes on Conversion. If a Holder of a Security converts it, the Company shall pay any documentary, stamp or similar issue or transfer tax due on the issue of shares of Common Stock upon the conversion. However, the Holder shall pay any withholding tax or any such tax that is due because the shares are issued in a name other than the Holder's name.

Section 10.05. Company to Reserve Common Stock. The Company shall at all times reserve out of its authorized but unissued Common Stock or its Common Stock held in treasury enough shares of Common Stock to permit the conversion of the Securities.

All shares of Common Stock issued upon conversion of the Securities shall be fully paid and non-assessable and free of any preemptive or other similar rights.

The Company shall endeavor to comply with all securities laws regulating the offer and delivery of shares of Common Stock upon conversion of Securities and shall endeavor to list such shares on each national securities exchange on which the Common Stock is listed.

Section 10.06. Adjustment for Change in Capital Stock. If the Company:

(1) pays a dividend or makes a distribution on its Common Stock in shares of its Common Stock;

(2) subdivides its outstanding shares of Common Stock into a greater number of shares;

(3) combines its outstanding shares of Common Stock into a smaller number of shares;

(4) makes a distribution on its Common Stock in shares of its capital stock other than Common Stock; or

(5) issues by reclassification of its Common Stock any shares of its capital stock, then the conversion privilege and the conversion price in effect immediately prior to such action shall be proportionately adjusted so that the Holder of a Security thereafter converted may receive the aggregate number and kind of shares of capital stock of the Company that the Holder would have owned immediately following such action if the Security had converted immediately prior to such action.

Each adjustment contemplated by this Section 10.06 shall become effective immediately after the record date in the case of a dividend or distribution and immediately after the effective date in the case of a subdivision, combination or reclassification.

If after an adjustment a Holder of a Security upon conversion of it may receive shares of two or more classes of capital stock of the Company, the Board, acting in good faith, shall determine the allocation of the adjusted conversion price among the classes of capital stock. After such allocation, the conversion privilege and the conversion price of each class of capital stock shall thereafter be subject to adjustment on terms comparable to those applicable to Common Stock in this Article. The term "Common Stock" shall thereafter apply to each class of capital stock and the Company shall enter into such supplemental Indenture, if any, as may be necessary to reflect such conversion privilege and conversion price.

The adjustment contemplated by this Section 10.06 shall be made successively whenever any of the events listed above shall occur.

Section 10.07. Adjustment for Rights Issue. If the Company distributes any rights, options or warrants to all holders of its Common Stock entitling them for a period expiring within 60 days after the record date mentioned below to subscribe for or purchase shares of Common Stock at a price per share less than the current market price per share on that record date, the conversion price shall be adjusted in accordance with the following formula:

$$C' = C \times \frac{O + \dfrac{N \times P}{M}}{O + N}$$

where:

C′ =   the adjusted conversion price.

C =   the current conversion price.

O =   the number of shares of Common Stock outstanding on the record date.

N =   the number of additional shares of Common Stock subject to such rights, options or warrants.

P =   the offering price per share of the additional shares.

M =   the current market price per share of Common Stock on the record date.

The adjustment contemplated by this Section 10.07 shall be made successively whenever any such rights, options or warrants are issued and shall become effective immediately after the record date for the determination of stockholders entitled to receive the rights, options or warrants. If at the end of the period during which such rights, options or warrants are exercisable, not all rights, options or warrants shall have been exercised, the conversion price shall immediately be readjusted to what it would have been if "N" in the above formula had been the number of shares actually issued.

[handwritten margin notes: "spin-off", "Partial liq.", ""Marriot""]

Section 10.08. Adjustment for Other Distributions. If the Company distributes to all holders of its Common Stock any of its assets (including, but not limited to, cash), debt securities or other securities or any rights, options or warrants to purchase assets, debt securities or other securities of the Company, the conversion price shall be adjusted in accordance with the following formula:

$$C' = C \times \frac{M - F}{M}$$

where:

> $C' =$ the adjusted conversion price.
>
> $C =$ the current conversion price.
>
> $M =$ the current market price per share of Common Stock on the record date mentioned below. *[handwritten: pre-spinoff]*
>
> $F =$ the fair market value on the record date of the assets, *[handwritten: post SO]* securities, rights, options or warrants applicable to one share of Common Stock. Fair market value shall be determined in good faith by the Board of Directors; *provided* that the Company shall obtain an appraisal or other valuation opinion in support of the Board's determination from an investment bank or accounting firm of recognized national standing if the aggregate fair market value exceeds $___ million.

The adjustment contemplated by this Section 10.08 shall be made successively whenever any such distribution is made and shall become effective immediately after the record date for the determination of stockholders entitled to receive the distribution.

This Section 10.08 does not apply to cash dividends or cash distributions paid in any fiscal year out of consolidated net income of the Company for the current fiscal year or the prior fiscal year, as shown on the books of the Company prepared in accordance with generally accepted accounting principles. Also, this Section does not apply to rights, options or warrants referred to in Section 10.07.

Section 10.09. Adjustment for Common Stock Issue. If the Company issues shares of Common Stock for a consideration per share less than the current market price per share on the date the Company fixes the offering price of such additional shares, the conversion price shall be adjusted in accordance with the following formula:

[handwritten margin note: "If the share of new issue of common is < current common share price"]

$$C' = C \times \frac{O + \dfrac{P}{M}}{A}$$

where:

> $C' =$ the adjusted conversion price.
>
> $C =$ the current conversion price.
>
> $O =$ the number of shares of Common Stock outstanding on the record date.

P = the aggregate consideration received for the issuance of such additional shares.

M = the current market price per share of Common v stock on the record date.

A = the number of shares of Common Stock outstanding immediately after the issuance of such additional shares.

O = the number of shares of Common Stock outstanding on the record date.

P = the aggregate consideration received for the issuance of such additional shares.

M = the current market price per share of Common v stock on the record date.

A = the number of shares of Common Stock outstanding immediately after the issuance of such additional shares.

The adjustment contemplated by this Section 10.09 shall be made successively whenever any such issuance is made and shall become effective immediately after the record date for the determination of stockholders entitled to receive such additional shares of Common Stock.

This Section 10.09 shall not apply to:

(1) any of the transactions described in Sections 10.07 and 10.08;

(2) the conversion of the Securities or the conversion or exchange of other securities convertible into or exchangeable for Common Stock;

(3) the issuance of Common Stock upon the exercise of rights, options or warrants issued to the holders of Common Stock;

(4) the issuance of Common Stock to the Company's employees under bona fide employee benefit plans adopted by the Board, and approved by the holders of Common Stock when required by law, but only to the extent that the aggregate number of shares excluded by this clause (4) and issued after the date of this Indenture shall not exceed 5% of the Common Stock outstanding as of the date of this Indenture;

(5) the issuance of Common Stock to stockholders of any Person that merges into the Company in proportion to their stock holdings of such Person immediately prior to such merger, upon such merger;

(6) the issuance of Common Stock in a bona fide public offering pursuant to a firm commitment underwriting; or

(7) the issuance of Common Stock in a bona fide private placement through a placement agent that is a member firm of the National Association of Securities Dealers, Inc. (except to the extent that any discount from the current market price shall exceed 20% of the then current market price).

Section 10.10. Adjustment for Convertible Securities Issue. If the Company issues any securities, rights, options or warrants convertible into or exchangeable for Common Stock (other than the Securities or securities issued in transactions described in Sections 10.07, 10.08 and 10.09) for a consideration per share of Common Stock initially deliverable upon conversion or exchange of such securities less than the current market price per share on the date of issuance of such securities, the conversion price shall be adjusted in accordance with the following formula:

$$C' = C \times \frac{O + \frac{P}{M}}{O + D}$$

where:

C' =   the adjusted conversion price.

C =   the current conversion price.

O =   the number of shares of Common Stock outstanding on the record date.

P =   the aggregate consideration received for the issuance of such securities.

M =   the current market price per share of Common Stock on the record date.

D =   the maximum number of shares of Common Stock deliverable upon conversion or exchange of such securities at the initial conversion or exchange rate.

The adjustment contemplated by this Section 10.10 shall be made successively whenever any such issuance is made and shall become effective immediately after the record date for the determination of stockholders entitled to receive such securities, rights, options or warrants. If at the end of the period during which such securities, rights, options or warrants are convertible into or exchangeable for Common Stock, not all such securities, rights, options or warrants shall have been so converted or exchanged, the conversion price shall immediately be readjusted to what it would have been if "D" in the above formula had been the number of shares actually issued upon conversion or exchange.

This Section 10.10 shall not apply to:

(1) the issuance of convertible securities to stockholders of any Person that merges into the Company, or with a subsidiary of the Company, in proportion to their stock holdings of such Person immediately prior to such merger, upon such merger;

(2) the issuance of convertible securities in a bona fide public offering pursuant to a firm commitment underwriting; or

(3) the issuance of convertible securities in a bona fide private placement through a placement agent that is a member firm of the National Association of Securities Dealers, Inc. (except to the extent that any discount from the current market price shall exceed 20% of the then current market price).

Section 10.11. Current Market Price. In Sections 10.07, 10.08, 10.09 and 10.10, the current market price per share of Common Stock on any date shall be the average of the Quoted Prices of the Common Stock for the five consecutive trading days selected by the Company commencing not more than 20 trading days before, and ending not later than, the earlier of (i) the date of such determination and (ii) the day before the "ex" date with respect to the issuance or distribution requiring such computation. The "Quoted Price" of a security shall be the last reported sales price of such security as reported by the New York Stock Exchange or, if the security is listed on another securities exchange, the last reported sales price of such security on such exchange which shall be for consolidated trading if applicable to such exchange, or as reported by the Nasdaq National Market System, or, if the security is neither so reported nor listed, the last reported bid price of the security. In the absence of one or more such quotations, the current market price shall be determined in good faith by the Board on the basis of such quotations as it considers reasonably appropriate. For the purposes of this Section 10.11, the term "ex" date, when used with respect to any issuance or distribution, shall mean the first date on which the security trades on such exchange or in such market without the right to receive such issuance or distribution.

Section 10.12. When De Minimis Adjustment May Be Deferred. No adjustment in the conversion price need be made unless the adjustment would require an increase or decrease of at least 1% in the conversion price. All calculations under this Article shall be made to the nearest cent or to the nearest 1/100th of a share, as the case may be. Any adjustments that are not made shall be carried forward and taken into account in any subsequent adjustment.

Section 10.13. When No Adjustment Required. No adjustment need be made for a transaction referred to in Sections 10.06, 10.07, 10.08, 10.09 or 10.10 if Securityholders are permitted to participate in the transaction on a basis and with notice that the Board determines to be fair and appropriate in light of the basis and notice on which holders of Common Stock are permitted to participate in the transaction.

No adjustments need be made for rights to purchase Common Stock pursuant to a Company plan for reinvestment of dividends or interest.

No adjustment need be made for a change in the par value or no par value of the Common Stock.

To the extent the Securities become convertible into cash, no adjustment need be made thereafter as to the cash. Interest will not accrue on the cash.

Section 10.14. Notice of Adjustment. Whenever the conversion price is adjusted, the Company shall promptly mail to Securityholders a notice of the adjustment. The Company shall file with the Trustee a certificate from the Company's independent public accountants briefly stating the facts requiring the adjustment and the manner of computing it. The certificate shall be conclusive evidence that the adjustment is correct, absent mathematical error.

Section 10.15. Voluntary Reduction. The Company may from time to time reduce the conversion price by any amount for any period of time if the period is at least 20 days and if the reduction is irrevocable during the period; provided, however, that in no event may the conversion price be less than the par value of a share of Common Stock.

Whenever the conversion price is reduced, the Company shall mail to Securityholders a notice of the reduction. The Company shall mail the notice at least 15 days before the date the reduced conversion price takes effect. The notice shall state the reduced conversion price and the period it will be in effect.

A reduction of the conversion price does not change or adjust the conversion price otherwise in effect for purposes of Sections 10.06 through 10.10.

Section 10.16. Notice of Certain Transactions. If:

(1) the Company takes any action that would require an adjustment in the conversion price pursuant to Section 10.06, 10.07, 10.08, 10.09 or 10.10 and if the Company does not permit Securityholders to participate pursuant to Section 10.13;

(2) the Company takes any action that would require a supplemental indenture pursuant to Section 10.17; or

(3) there is a liquidation or dissolution of the Company, the Company shall mail to Securityholders a notice stating the proposed record date for a dividend or distribution or the proposed effective date of a subdivision, combination, reclassification, consolidation, merger, transfer, lease, liquidation or dissolution. The Company shall mail the notice at least 20 days before such date. Failure to mail the notice or any defect in it shall not affect the validity of the transaction.

Section 10.17. Reorganization of the Company. If the Company is a party to a transaction subject to Section 5.01 or a merger that reclassifies or changes its outstanding Common Stock, the Person obligated to deliver securities, cash or other assets upon conversion of Securities shall enter into a supplemental indenture. If the issuer of securities deliverable upon conversion of Securities is an Affiliate of the surviving or transferee corporation, such issuer shall join in the supplemental indenture.

The supplemental indenture shall provide that the Holder of a Security may convert it into the kind and amount of securities, cash or other assets that such holder would have owned immediately after the consolidation, merger or transfer if the Security had been converted immediately before the effective date of the transaction. The supplemental indenture shall provide for adjustments that are as nearly equivalent as practicable to the adjustments provided for in this Article. The successor Company shall mail to Securityholders a notice briefly describing the supplemental indenture.

[If this Section 10.17 applies, Section 10.06 does not apply.]

Section 10.18. Company Determination Final. Any determination that the Company or the Board must make pursuant to Section 10.03, 10.06, 10.07, 10.08, 10.09, 10.10, 10.11 or 10.13 is conclusive, absent mathematical error. Not later than the date of making any such determination pursuant to Section 10.06, 10.07, 10.08, 10.09, 10.10, 10.11 or 10.13, the Company shall deliver to the Trustee an Officers' Certificate stating the basis upon which such determination was made and, if pursuant to Section 10.06, 10.07, 10.08, 10.09 or 10.10, the calculations by which adjustments under such Sections were made.

Section 10.19. Trustee's Disclaimer. The Trustee has no duty to determine when an adjustment under this Article should be made, how it should be made or what it should be. The Trustee has no duty to determine whether any provisions of a supplemental indenture under Section 10.06 or 10.17 are correct. The Trustee makes no representation as to the validity or value of any securities or assets issued upon conversion of Securities. The Trustee shall not be responsible for the Company's failure to comply with this Article. Each Conversion Agent other than the Company shall have the same protection under this Section as the Trustee.

ARTICLE 11 *SUBORDINATION*

Section 11.01. Securities Subordinated to Senior Debt. The rights of Holders to payment of the Principal of and interest on the Securities is subordinated to the rights of holders of Senior Debt, to the extent and in the manner provided in this Article 11.

Section 11.02. Securities Subordinated in Any Proceeding. Upon any Distribution in any Proceeding,

(1) any Distribution to which the Holders are entitled shall be paid directly to the holders of Senior Debt to the extent necessary to make payment in full of all Senior Debt remaining unpaid after giving effect to all other Distributions to or for the benefit of the holders of Senior Debt; and

(2) in the event that any Distribution is received by the Trustee before all Senior Debt is paid in full, such Distribution shall be applied by the Trustee in accordance with this Article 11.

Section 11.03. No Payment on Securities in Certain Circumstances. The Company shall not, directly or indirectly (other than in capital stock of the Company) pay any Principal of or interest on, redeem, defease or repurchase any of the Securities (i) after any Senior Debt becomes due and payable, unless and until all such Senior Debt shall first be paid in full or (ii) after a Senior Debt Payment Default, unless and until such Senior Debt Payment Default has been cured, waived, or otherwise has ceased to exist.

During a Payment Blockage Period, no payment of any Principal of or interest on the Securities may be made, directly or indirectly, by the Company. Unless the Senior Debt in respect of which the Senior Debt Default Notice has been given has been declared due and payable in its entirety within the Payment Blockage Period, at the end of the Payment Blockage Period, the Company shall pay all sums not paid to the Holders during the Payment Blockage Period and resume all other payments on the Securities as and when due. Defaulted Interest shall be paid in accordance with Section 2.13. Any number of Senior Debt Default Notices may be given; provided, however, that as to any issue of Senior Debt (i) not more than one Senior Debt Default Notice shall be given within a period of any [366] consecutive days, and (ii) no specific act, omission or condition that gave rise to a default that existed upon the date of such Senior Debt Default Notice (whether or not such default applies to the same issue of Senior Debt) shall be made the basis for the commencement of any other Payment Blockage Period.

If any Distribution, payment or deposit to redeem, defease or acquire any of the Securities shall have been received by the Trustee at a time when such Distribution was prohibited by the provisions of this Section 11.03, then, unless such Distribution is no longer prohibited by this Section 11.03, such Distribution shall be received and applied by the Trustee for the benefit of the holders of Senior Debt, and shall be paid or delivered by the Trustee to the holders of Senior Debt for application to the payment of all Senior Debt.

Section 11.04. Subrogation. The Holders shall not have any subrogation or other rights of recourse to any security in respect of any Senior Debt until such time as all Senior Debt shall have been paid in full. Upon the payment in full of all Senior Debt, the Holders shall be subrogated to the rights of the holders of Senior Debt to receive Distributions applicable to Senior Debt until all amounts owing in respect of the Securities shall be so paid. No Distributions to the holders of Senior Debt which otherwise would have been made to the Holders shall, as between the Company and the Holders, be deemed to be payment by the Company to or on account of Senior Debt.

If any Distribution to which the Holders would otherwise have been entitled shall have been applied pursuant to the provisions of this Article to the payment of Senior Debt, then the Holders shall be entitled to receive from the holders of such Senior Debt any Distributions received by such holders of Senior Debt in excess of the amount sufficient to pay all amounts payable on such Senior Debt to the extent provided herein.

Section 11.05. Obligations of the Company Unconditional. This Article defines the relative rights of the Holders and holders of Senior Debt. Nothing in this Indenture is intended to or shall impair, as between the Company and the Holders, the obligation of the Company, which is absolute and unconditional, to pay to the Holders the Principal of and interest on the Securities as and when the same shall become due and payable in accordance with their terms, or is intended to or shall affect the relative rights of the Holders and creditors of the Company, other than the holders of Senior Debt, nor shall anything herein or in the Securities prevent the Trustee or any Holder from exercising all remedies otherwise permitted by applicable law upon default under this Indenture, subject to the rights, if any, under this Article 11, of the holders of Senior Debt in respect of any Distribution received upon the exercise of any such remedy. If the Company fails because of this Article to pay principal of or interest on a Security on the due date, the failure is still a Default. Upon any Distribution, the Trustee and the Holders shall be entitled to rely upon any order or decree made by any court of competent jurisdiction in which the Proceeding is pending, or a certificate of the liquidating trustee or agent or other Person making any Distribution for the purpose of ascertaining the Persons entitled to participate in such Distribution, the holders of Senior Debt and other Debt of the Company, the amount thereof or payable thereon, the amount or amounts paid or distributed thereon and all other facts pertinent thereto or to this Article 11.

Section 11.06. Trustee and Paying Agents Entitled to Assume Payments Not Prohibited in Absence of Notice. The Trustee shall not at any time be charged with knowledge of the existence of any facts which would prohibit the making of any payment to or by the Trustee, unless and until a Trust Officer shall have received, no later than [] Business Day[s] prior to such payment, written notice thereof from the Company or from one or more holders of Senior Debt and, prior to the receipt of any such written notice, the Trustee, shall be entitled in all respects conclusively to presume that no such fact exists. Unless the Trustee shall have received the notice provided for in the preceding sentence, the Trustee shall have full power and authority to receive such payment and to apply the same to the purpose for which it was received, and shall not be affected by any notice to the contrary which may be received by it on or after such date. The foregoing shall not apply to any Affiliate of the Company acting as Paying Agent.

Section 11.07. Satisfaction and Discharge. Amounts deposited in trust with the Trustee pursuant to and in accordance with Article 8 and not prohibited to be deposited under Section 11.03 when deposited shall not be subject to this Article 11.

Section 11.08. Subordination Rights Not Impaired by Acts or Omissions of the Company or Holders of Senior Debt. No right of any holder of any Senior Debt established in this Article 11 shall at any time or in any way be prejudiced or impaired by any act or failure to act on the part of the Company or by any act or failure to act, in good faith, by any such holder, or by any failure by the Company to comply with the terms of this Indenture.

Section 11.09. Right to Hold Senior Debt. The Trustee is entitled to all of the rights set forth in this Article 11 in respect of any Senior Debt at any time held by it to the same extent as any other holder of Senior Debt.

Section 11.10. No Fiduciary Duty of Trustee or Securityholders to Holders of Senior Debt. Neither the Trustee nor the Holders owes any fiduciary duty to the holders of Senior Debt. Neither the Trustee nor the Holders shall be liable to any holder of Senior Debt in the event that the Trustee, acting in good faith, shall pay over or distribute to the Holders, the Company, or any other Person, any property to which any holders of Senior Debt are entitled by virtue of this Article or otherwise. Nothing contained in this Section 11.10 shall affect the obligation of any other such Person to hold such payment for the benefit of, and to pay such payment over to, the holders of Senior Debt.

Section 11.11. Distribution to Holders of Senior Debt. Any Distribution otherwise payable to the holders of the Securities made to holders of Senior Debt pursuant to this Article shall be made to such holders of Senior Debt ratably according to the respective amount of Senior Debt held by each.

Section 11.12. Trustee's Rights to Compensation, Reimbursement of Expenses and Indemnification. The Trustee's rights to compensation, reimbursement of expenses and indemnification under Sections 6.08 and 7.07 are not subordinated.

Section 11.13. Exception for Certain Distributions. The rights of holders of Senior Debt under this Article do not extend (a) to any Distribution to the extent applied to the Trustee's rights to compensation, reimbursement of expenses or indemnification or (b) to (i) securities which are subordinated to the securities distributed to the holders of Senior Debt on terms no less favorable to the holders of Senior Debt than the provisions of this Article, or (ii) Distributions under any plan approved by the court in any Proceeding.

Section 11.14. Certain Definitions. As used in this Article 11,

"Distribution" in any Proceeding means any payment or distribution of assets or securities of the Company of any kind or character from any source, whether in cash, securities or other property made by the Company, custodian, liquidating trustee or agent or any other person whether pursuant to a plan or otherwise.

"Payment Blockage Period" means the period beginning when a Senior Debt Default Notice is given to the Company and the Trustee and ending (a) when the default identified in the Senior Debt Default Notice is cured, waived or otherwise ceases to exist or (b) after [179 or fewer] days, whichever occurs first.

"Senior Debt Default Notice" means any notice of a default (other than a Senior Debt Payment Default) that permits the holders of any Senior Debt to declare such Senior Debt due and payable.

"Senior Debt Payment Default" means a default in the payment of any principal of or interest on any Senior Debt.

"Trustee" for purposes of this Article 11 includes any Paying Agent.

ARTICLE 12 *MISCELLANEOUS*

Section 12.01. Notices. Any notice by one party to the other shall be in writing and sent to the other's address stated in Section 12.09. The notice is duly given if it is delivered in Person or sent by a national courier service which provides next Business Day delivery or by first-class mail.

A party by notice to the other party may designate additional or different addresses for subsequent notices.

Any notice sent to a Securityholder shall be mailed by first-class letter mailed to its address shown on the register kept by the Registrar. Failure to mail a notice to a Securityholder or any defect in a notice mailed to a Securityholder shall not affect the sufficiency of the notice mailed to other Securityholders.

If a notice is delivered or mailed in the manner provided above within the time prescribed, it is duly given, whether or not the addressee receives it.

If the Company mails a notice to Securityholders, it shall deliver or mail a copy to the Trustee and each Agent at the same time.

A "notice" includes any communication required by this Indenture.

* * *

Section 12.09. Variable Provisions. "Officer" means the President, any Vice–President, the Treasurer, the Secretary, any Assistant Treasurer or any Assistant Secretary of the Company.

The Company initially appoints the Trustee as Registrar, Paying Agent and Conversion Agent.

The first certificate pursuant to Section 4.03 shall be for the fiscal year ending on ———, 20——.

The reporting date for Section 7.06 is ——— of each year. The first reporting date is ———.

The Trustee shall always have a combined capital and surplus of at least $——— as set forth in its most recent published annual report of condition. The Trustee will be deemed to be in compliance with the capital and surplus requirement set forth in the preceding sentence if its obligations are guaranteed by a Person which could otherwise act as Trustee hereunder and which meets such capital and surplus requirement and the Trustee has at least the minimum capital and surplus required by TIA Section 310(a)(2).

In determining whether the Trustee has a conflicting interest as defined in TIA Section 310(b)(1), the following is excluded: Indenture dated as of January 1, 20——; between the Company and Greater Bank and Trust Company, Trustee for the ——% Subordinated Debentures Due.

Senior Debt does not include:

(1) the debentures described in the preceding paragraph;

(2) the Company's ———% Convertible Subordinated Notes due ———, 20——; and

(3) the Company's subordinated guarantee of the ——% Convertible Subordinated Debentures Due ——— of [Universal Overseas Finance Corporation].

The Securities are not senior in right of payment to the foregoing debt securities of the Company.

The Company's address is:

Universal Business Corporation

1 Commerce Plaza
New York, NY 10099
Facsimile No.:
[Attention: _____]

The Trustee's address is:

Greater Bank and Trust Company
Corporate Trust Department
500 Wall Street
New York, NY 10015
Facsimile No.:
[Attention: _____]

Section 12.10. Governing Law. The laws of the State of _____ shall govern this Indenture and the Securities.

Dated: _____   UNIVERSAL BUSINESS
                                        CORPORATION
                                        By: _____
                                             Vice President

Attest:

_____
Assistant Secretary

Dated _____   GREATER BANK AND TRUST
                                        COMPANY
                                        By: _____
                                             Trust Officer

Attest:

_____
Assistant Secretary

EXHIBIT A

(Face of Security)

No. $

UNIVERSAL BUSINESS CORPORATION

promises to pay to,
or registered assigns, the principal sum of   Dollars on

% Convertible Subordinated Debenture Due
Interest Payment Dates:
Record Dates:

Dated:

Authenticated:
GREATER BANK AND TRUST
   COMPANY as Trustee

UNIVERSAL BUSINESS
   CORPORATION

By

By

     Authorized Officer

OR

By

NATIONAL BANK AND TRUST
   COMPANY, as Authenticating
   Agent

By

     Authorized Officer   (SEAL)

(Back of Security)

UNIVERSAL BUSINESS CORPORATION

   ___% Convertible Subordinated Debenture Due _____

1.   Interest. Universal Business Corporation ("Company"), a Delaware corporation, promises to pay interest on the principal amount of this Security at the rate per annum shown above. The Company will pay interest semiannually on _____ and _____ of each year. Interest on the Securities will accrue from the most recent date to which interest has been paid or, if no interest has been paid, from _____. Interest will be computed on the basis of a 360–day year of twelve 30–day months.

2.   Method of Payment. The Company will pay interest on the Securities to the Persons who are registered holders of Securities at the close of business on the record date for the next interest payment date, except as otherwise provided herein or in the Indenture even though Securities are cancelled after the record date and on or before the interest payment date. Holders must surrender Securities to a Paying Agent to collect principal payments. The Company will pay Principal and interest in money of the United States that at the time of payment is legal tender for payment of public and private debts. However, the Company may pay Principal and interest by wire transfer or check payable in such money. It may mail an interest check to a record date holder's registered address.

3.   Agents. Initially, Greater Bank and Trust Company ("Trustee"), 500 Wall Street, New York, NY 10015, will act as Registrar, Paying Agent and Conversion Agent. The Company may change any such Agent without notice. The Company or an Affiliate may act in any such capacity. Subject to certain conditions, the Company may change the Trustee.

4.   Indenture. The Company issued the Securities under an Indenture dated as of _____ ("Indenture") between the Company and the Trustee. The terms of the Securities include those stated in the Indenture and those made part of the Indenture by the Trust Indenture Act of 1939 (15 U.S.C. §§ 77aaa–77bbbb) (the "Act"). The Securities are subject to all such terms, and Securityholders are referred to the Indenture and the Act for a

statement of such terms. The Securities are unsecured subordinated general obligations of the Company limited to $_____ in aggregate principal amount.

5.   Redemption. [The Securities may not be redeemed at the option of the Company prior to (date).] The Company may redeem all the Securities at any time or some of them from time to time after [(date)] [note this date should be at least two Business Days after the last interest payment date in the period described in the preceding sentence] at the following redemption prices (expressed in percentages of principal amount), plus accrued interest to the redemption date:

If redeemed during the 12–month period beginning _____,

Year	Percentage	Year	Percentage

The Company's right to redeem securities under this Section 5 may not be exercised if and for so long as the Company has failed to pay interest on any Security when the same becomes due and payable.

6.   Mandatory Redemption. The Company will redeem $_____ principal amount of the Securities on _____ and on each _____ thereafter through _____ at a redemption price of 100% of principal amount, plus accrued interest to the redemption date.

The Company may reduce the principal amount of Securities to be redeemed pursuant to this paragraph by subtracting 100% of the principal amount (excluding premium) of any Securities that have been previously cancelled, that Securityholders have converted (other than Securities converted after being called for mandatory redemption), that the Company has delivered to the Trustee for cancellation or that the Company has redeemed other than pursuant to this paragraph. The Company may so subtract the same Security only once.

7.   Additional Optional Redemption. In addition to redemptions pursuant to paragraph 6, the Company may redeem not more than $_____ principal amount of the Securities on _____ and on each _____ thereafter through _____ at a redemption price of 100% of principal amount, plus accrued interest to the redemption date.

8.   Notice of Redemption. Notice of redemption will be mailed at least 30 days but not more than 60 days before the redemption date to each holder of Securities to be redeemed at his registered address.

9.   Conversion. A holder of a Security may convert it into Common Stock of the Company at any time before the close of business on _____. If a Security is called for redemption, the holder may convert it at any time before the close of business on the Business Day prior to the redemption date (unless the redemption date is an interest record date in which event it may be converted through the record date). The initial conversion price is $_____ per share, subject to adjustment in certain events. In certain circumstances the right to convert a Security into Common Stock may be

changed into a right to convert it into securities, cash or other assets of the Company or another.

To determine the number of shares issuable upon conversion of a Security, divide the principal amount to be converted by the conversion price in effect on the conversion date. On conversion no payment or adjustment for interest will be made. The Company will deliver a check for cash in lieu of any fractional share.

To convert a Security a Holder must comply with Section 10.02 of the Indenture, which requires the Holder to (1) complete and sign the conversion notice on the back of the Security, (2) surrender the Security to a Conversion Agent, (3) furnish appropriate endorsements and transfer documents if required by the Paying Agent or Conversion Agent, (4) pay any transfer or similar tax if required, and (5) provide funds, if applicable, required pursuant to Section 10.02 of the Indenture. A holder may convert a portion of a Security if the portion is $1000 or a whole multiple of $1000.

10.   Subordination. The Securities are subordinated to Senior Debt as defined in the Indenture. To the extent provided in the Indenture, Senior Debt must be paid before the Securities may be paid. The Company agrees, and each Securityholder by accepting a Security agrees, to the subordination and authorizes the Trustee to give it effect.

11.   Denominations, Transfer, Exchange. The Securities are in registered form without coupons in denominations of $1000 and whole multiples of $1000. The transfer of Securities may be registered and Securities may be exchanged as provided in the Indenture. The Registrar may require a holder, among other things, to furnish appropriate endorsements and transfer documents and to pay any taxes required by law. The Registrar need not exchange or register the transfer of any Security or portion of a Security selected for redemption. Also, it need not exchange or register the transfer of any Securities for a period of 15 days before a selection of Securities to be redeemed.

12.   Persons Deemed Owners. Subject to Section 6.11, the registered holder of a Security may be treated as its owner for all purposes.

13.   Amendments and Waivers. Subject to certain exceptions, the Indenture or the Securities may be amended, and any Default may be waived, with the consent of the holders of a majority in Principal amount of the Securities. Without the consent of any Securityholder, the Indenture or the Securities may be amended to cure any ambiguity, defect or inconsistency, to provide for assumption of Company obligations to Securityholders or to make any change that does not adversely affect the rights of any Securityholder.

14.   Successors. When successors assume all the obligations of the Company under the Securities and the Indenture, the Company will be released from those obligations, except as provided in the Indenture.

15.   Satisfaction and Discharge Prior to Redemption or Maturity. Subject to certain conditions, the Company at any time may terminate some or all of its obligations under the Securities and the Indenture if the Company deposits with the Trustee money or U.S. Government Obligations

for the payment of Principal and interest on the Securities to redemption or maturity.

16.   Defaults and Remedies. Subject to the Indenture, if an Event of Default, as defined in the Indenture, occurs and is continuing, the Trustee or the holders of at least 25% in Principal amount of the Securities may declare all the Securities to be due and payable immediately. Securityholders may not enforce the Indenture or the Securities except as provided in the Indenture. The Trustee may require indemnity satisfactory to it before it enforces the Indenture or the Securities. Subject to certain limitations, holders of a majority in Principal amount of the Securities may direct the Trustee in its exercise of any trust or power. The Trustee may withhold from Securityholders notice of any continuing Default (except a Default in payment of Principal or interest) if it determines that withholding notice is in their interests. The Company must furnish an annual compliance certificate to the Trustee.

17.   Trustee Dealings with Company. Greater Bank and Trust Company, the Trustee under the Indenture, in its individual or any other capacity, may make loans to, accept deposits from, and perform services for the Company or its Affiliates, and may otherwise deal with the Company or its Affiliates, as if it were not Trustee, subject to the Indenture and the Act.

18.   No Recourse Against Others. A director, officer, employee or stockholder, as such, of the Company shall not have any liability for any obligations of the Company under the Securities or the Indenture or for any claim based on, in respect of or by reason of such obligations or their creation. Each Securityholder by accepting a Security waives and releases all such liability. The waiver and release are part of the consideration for the issue of the Securities.

19.   Authentication. This Security shall not be valid until authenticated by a manual signature of the Trustee.

20.   Abbreviations. Customary abbreviations may be used in the name of a Securityholder or an assignee, such as: TEN COM (= tenants in common), TEN ENT (= tenants by the entireties), JT TEN (= joint tenants with right of survivorship and not as tenants in common), CUST (= Custodian), and U/G A (= Uniform Gifts to Minors Act).

The Company will furnish to any Securityholder upon written request and without charge a copy of the Indenture. Requests may be made to: Secretary, Universal Business Corporation, 1 Commerce Plaza, New York, NY 10099.

FORM 2

NOTE PURCHASE AGREEMENT

The Note Purchase Agreement that follows is designed for unsecured long term private placement loans to borrowers of a credit quality of BBB— or better.

Those taking a close look at the negative covenants in § 10 of the Note Purchase Agreement can assume that General Technology, Inc. has the balance sheet as at June 30, 2007, the end of its first fiscal year after the closing of the private placement:

Assets

Cash	$	10,000,000
Accounts receivable		40,000,000
Inventories		50,000,000
P,P & E		120,000,000
Goodwill		30,000,000
Patents		40,000,000
Total	$	290,000,000

Liabilities

Accounts payable	$	50,000,000
Short-term borrowing		30,000,000
Long term debt		80,000,000
Total	$	160,000,000

Shareholders' equity

Common stock	$	130,000,000
Total	$	290,000,000

General Technology, Inc.

$50,000,000

8% Senior Notes due February 1, 2022

———

NOTE PURCHASE AGREEMENT

———

Dated January 27, 2007

Table of Contents

Section

1.   AUTHORIZATION OF NOTES.

2.   SALE AND PURCHASE OF NOTES.

3.   CLOSING.

4.   CONDITIONS TO CLOSING.
  4.1.   Representations and Warranties.
  4.2.   Performance; No Default.
  4.3.   Compliance Certificates.
  4.4.   Opinions of Counsel.
  4.5.   Purchase Permitted By Applicable Law, etc.
  4.6.   Sale of Other Notes.
  4.7.   Payment of Special Counsel Fees.
  4.8.   Private Placement Number.
  4.9.   Changes in Corporate Structure.
  4.10. Proceedings and Documents.

5.   REPRESENTATIONS AND WARRANTIES OF THE COMPANY.
  5.1.   Organization; Power and Authority.
  5.2.   Authorization, etc.
  5.3.   Disclosure.
  5.4.   Organization and Ownership of Shares of Subsidiaries; Affiliates.
  5.5.   Financial Statements.
  5.6   Compliance with Laws, Other Instruments, etc.
  5.7.   Governmental Authorizations, etc.
  5.8.   Litigation; Observance of Agreements, Statutes and Orders.
  5.9.   Taxes.
  5.10. Title to Property; Leases.
  5.11. Licenses, Permits, etc.
  5.12. Compliance with ERISA.
  5.13. Private Offering by the Company.
  5.14. Use of Proceeds; Margin Regulations.
  5.15. Existing Indebtedness; Future Liens.
  5.16. Foreign Assets Control Regulations, etc.
  5.17. Status under Certain Statutes.
  5.18. Environmental Matters.

6.   REPRESENTATIONS OF THE PURCHASER.
  6.1.   Purchase for Investment.
  6.2.   Source of Funds.

7.   INFORMATION AS TO COMPANY.
  7.1.   Financial and Business Information.
  7.2.   Officer's Certificate.
  7.3.   Inspection.

8.   PREPAYMENT OF THE NOTES.
  8.1.   Required Prepayments.
  8.2.   Optional Prepayments with Make–Whole Amount.
  8.3.   Allocation of Partial Prepayments.
  8.4.   Maturity; Surrender, etc.
  8.5.   Purchase of Notes.
  8.6.   Make–Whole Amount.

9.   AFFIRMATIVE COVENANTS.
  9.1.   Compliance with Law.

Section

    9.2.   Insurance.
    9.3.   Maintenance of Properties.
    9.4.   Payment of Taxes and Claims.
    9.5.   Corporate Existence, etc.

10.   NEGATIVE COVENANTS.

11.   EVENTS OF DEFAULT.

12.   REMEDIES ON DEFAULT, ETC.
    12.1.   Acceleration.
    12.2.   Other Remedies.
    12.3.   Rescission.
    12.4.   No Waivers or Election of Remedies, Expenses, etc.

13.   REGISTRATION; EXCHANGE; SUBSTITUTION OF NOTES.
    13.1.   Registration of Notes.
    13.2.   Transfer and Exchange of Notes.
    13.3.   Replacement of Notes.

14.   PAYMENTS ON NOTES.
    14.1.   Place of Payment.
    14.2.   Home Office Payment.

15.   EXPENSES, ETC.
    15.1.   Transaction Expenses.
    15.2.   Survival.

16.   SURVIVAL OF REPRESENTATIONS AND WARRANTIES; ENTIRE AGREEMENT.

17.   AMENDMENT AND WAIVER.
    17.1.   Requirements.
    17.2.   Solicitation of Holders of Notes.
    17.3.   Binding Effect, etc.
    17.4.   Notes held by Company, etc.

18.   NOTICES.

19.   REPRODUCTION OF DOCUMENTS.

20.   CONFIDENTIAL INFORMATION.

21.   SUBSTITUTION OF PURCHASER.

22.   MISCELLANEOUS.
    22.1.   Successors and Assigns.
    22.2.   Payments Due on Non–Business Days.
    22.3.   Severability.
    22.4.   Construction.
    22.5.   Counterparts.
    22.6.   Governing Law.

SCHEDULE A   — INFORMATION RELATING TO PURCHASERS

SCHEDULE B   — DEFINED TERMS

SCHEDULE 4.9   — Changes in Corporate Structure

SCHEDULE 5.3 — Disclosure Materials

SCHEDULE 5.4 — Subsidiaries of the Company and Ownership of Subsidiary Stock

SCHEDULE 5.5 — Financial Statements

SCHEDULE 5.8 — Certain Litigation

SCHEDULE 5.11 — Patents, etc.

SCHEDULE 5.14 — Use of Proceeds

SCHEDULE 5.15 — Existing Indebtedness

SCHEDULE 5.19 — Insurance

EXHIBIT 1 — Form of 8% Senior Note due February 1, 2022

EXHIBIT 4.4(a) — Form of Opinion of Special Counsel for the Company

EXHIBIT 4.4(b) — Form of Opinion of Special Counsel for the Purchasers

1-6, 7.2, 10, 11, 12, A-94

8

NPA

GENERAL TECHNOLOGY, INC.
7777 21st Century Drive
Burns, Stockton 77777

8% Senior Notes due February 1, 2022

January 27, 2007

TO EACH OF THE PURCHASERS LISTED IN THE ATTACHED SCHEDULE A:

Ladies and Gentlemen:

GENERAL TECHNOLOGY, INC., a Delaware corporation (the **"Company"**), agrees with you as follows:

1. AUTHORIZATION OF NOTES.

The Company will authorize the issue and sale of $50,000,000 aggregate principal amount of its 8% Senior Notes due February 1, 2022 (the **"Notes"**, such term to include any such notes issued in substitution therefor pursuant to Section 13 of this Agreement or the Other Agreements (as hereinafter defined)). The Notes shall be substantially in the form set out in Exhibit 1, with such changes therefrom, if any, as may be approved by you and the Company. Certain capitalized terms used in this Agreement are defined in Schedule B; references to a "Schedule" or an "Exhibit" are, unless otherwise specified, to a Schedule or an Exhibit attached to this Agreement.

2. SALE AND PURCHASE OF NOTES.

Subject to the terms and conditions of this Agreement, the Company will issue and sell to you and you will purchase from the Company, at the Closing provided for in Section 3, Notes in the principal amount specified opposite your name in Schedule A at the purchase price of 100% of the principal amount thereof. Contemporaneously with entering into this Agreement, the Company is entering into separate Note Purchase Agreements (the **"Other Agreements"**) identical with this Agreement with each of the other purchasers named in Schedule A (the **"Other Purchasers"**), providing for the sale at such Closing to each of the Other Purchasers of Notes in the principal amount specified opposite its name in Schedule A. Your obligation hereunder and the obligations of the Other Purchasers under the Other Agreements are several and not joint obligations and you shall have no obligation under any Other Agreement and no liability to any Person for the performance or non-performance by any Other Purchaser thereunder.

3. CLOSING.

The sale and purchase of the Notes to be purchased by you and the Other Purchasers shall occur at the offices of Martin & Munson, 77777 Park Avenue, New York, New York, 10077, at 10:00 a.m., Eastern Standard time, at a closing (the **"Closing"**) on February 1, 2007, or on such other Business Day thereafter on or prior to February 10, 2007, as may be agreed upon by the Company and you and the Other Purchasers. At the Closing the Company will deliver to you the Notes to be purchased by you in the form of a single Note (or such greater number of Notes in denominations of at least $100,000 as you may request) dated the date of the Closing and registered in your name (or in the name of your nominee), against delivery by you to the Company or its order of immediately available funds in the amount of the purchase price therefor by wire transfer of immediately available funds for the account of the Company to account number) 7777777777 at Union First Bank, 777 Main Street, Burns, Stockton, ABA number 7777777. If at the Closing the Company shall fail to tender such Notes to you as provided above in this Section 3, or any of the conditions specified in Section 4 shall not have been fulfilled to your satisfaction, you shall, at your election, be relieved of all further obligations under this Agreement, without thereby waiving any rights you may have by reason of such failure or such nonfulfillment.

4. CONDITIONS TO CLOSING.

Your obligation to purchase and pay for the Notes to be sold to you at the Closing is subject to the fulfillment to your satisfaction, prior to or at the Closing, of the following conditions:

4.1. Representations and Warranties. The representations and §5, A-44 warranties of the Company in this Agreement shall be correct when made and at the time of the Closing.

4.2. Performance; No Default. The Company shall have performed and complied with all agreements and conditions contained in this Agreement required to be performed or complied with by it prior to or at the Closing and after giving effect to the issue and sale of the Notes (and the application of the proceeds thereof as contemplated by Schedule 5.14) no Default or Event of Default shall have occurred and be continuing) Neither the Company nor any Subsidiary shall have entered into any transaction since the date of the Memorandum that would have been prohibited by Section 10 hereof had such Section applied since such date.

4.3. Compliance Certificates.

(a) *Officer's Certificate.* The Company shall have delivered to you an — See 7.2, A-54 Officer's Certificate, dated the date of the Closing, certifying that the also certify that conditions specified in Sections 4.1, 4.2 and 4.9 have been fulfilled. certain reps related to

(b) *Secretary's Certificate.* The Company shall have delivered to you a (financials) have been certificate certifying as to the resolutions attached thereto and other met corporate proceedings relating to the authorization, execution and delivery — bylaws, minutes attached of the Notes and the Agreements. are correct

4.4. Opinions of Counsel. You shall have received opinions in form — A-94 and substance satisfactory to you, dated the date of the Closing (a) from — see notes Boggs & Mattingly, counsel for the Company, covering the matters set forth in Exhibit 4.4(a) and covering such other matters incident to the transactions contemplated hereby as you or your counsel may reasonably request (and the Company hereby instructs its counsel to deliver such opinion to you) and (b) from Martin & Munson, your special counsel in connection with such transactions, substantially in the form set forth in

Exhibit 4.4(b) and covering such other matters incident to such transactions as you may reasonably request.

4.5. Purchase Permitted By Applicable Law, etc. On the date of the Closing your purchase of Notes shall (*i*) be permitted by the laws and regulations of each jurisdiction to which you are subject, without recourse to provisions (such as Section 1405(a)(8) of the New York Insurance Law) permitting limited investments by insurance companies without restriction as to the character of the particular investment, (*ii*) not violate any applicable law or regulation (including, without limitation, Regulation G, T or X of the Board of Governors of the Federal Reserve System) and (*iii*) not subject you to any tax, penalty or liability under or pursuant to any applicable law or regulation, which law or regulation was not in effect on the date hereof. If requested by you, you shall have received an Officer's Certificate certifying as to such matters of fact as you may reasonably specify to enable you to determine whether such purchase is so permitted.

4.6. Sale of Other Notes. Contemporaneously with the Closing the Company shall sell to the Other Purchasers and the Other Purchasers shall purchase the Notes to be purchased by them at the Closing as specified in Schedule A.

4.7. Payment of Special Counsel Fees. Without limiting the provisions of Section 15.1, the Company shall have paid on or before the Closing the fees, charges and disbursements of your special counsel referred to in Section 4.4 to the extent reflected in a statement of such counsel rendered to the Company at least one Business Day prior to the Closing.

4.8. Private Placement Number. A Private Placement number issued by Standard & Poor's CUSIP Service Bureau (in cooperation with the Securities Valuation Office of the National Association of Insurance Commissioners) shall have been obtained for the Notes.

4.9. Changes in Corporate Structure. Except as specified in Schedule 4.9, the Company shall not have changed its jurisdiction of incorporation or been a party to any merger or consolidation and shall not have succeeded to all or any substantial part of the liabilities of any other entity, at any time following the date of the most recent financial statements referred to in Schedule 5.5.

4.10. Proceedings and Documents. All corporate and other proceedings in connection with the transactions contemplated by this Agreement and all documents and instruments incident to such transactions shall be satisfactory to you and your special counsel, and you and your special counsel shall have received all such counterpart originals or certified or other copies of such documents as you or they may reasonably request.

5. REPRESENTATIONS AND WARRANTIES OF THE COMPANY.

The Company represents and warrants to you that:

5.1. Organization; Power and Authority. The Company is a corporation duly organized, validly existing and in good standing under the laws of its jurisdiction of incorporation, and is duly qualified as a foreign corporation and is in good standing in each jurisdiction in which such qualification is required by law, other than those jurisdictions as to which the failure to be so qualified or in good standing could not, individually or in the aggregate, reasonably be expected to have a Material Adverse Effect. The Company has the corporate power and authority to own or hold under lease the properties it purports to own or hold under lease, to transact the business it transacts and proposes to transact, to execute and deliver this Agreement and the Other Agreements and the Notes and to perform the provisions hereof and thereof.

5.2. Authorization, etc. This Agreement and the Other Agreements and the Notes have been duly authorized by all necessary corporate action on the part of the Company, and this Agreement constitutes, and upon execution and delivery thereof each Note will constitute, a legal, valid and binding obligation of the Company enforceable against the Company in accordance with its terms, except as such enforceability may be limited by (*i*) applicable bankruptcy, insolvency, reorganization, moratorium or other similar laws affecting the enforcement of creditors' rights generally and (*ii*) general principles of equity (regardless of whether such enforceability is considered in a proceeding in equity or at law).

5.3. Disclosure. The Company, through its agent, W. Street, Brothers, Inc., has delivered to you and each Other Purchaser a copy of a Private Placement Memorandum, dated October 1, 2006 (the **"Memorandum"**), relating to the transactions contemplated hereby. The Memorandum fairly describes, in all material respects, the general nature of the business and principal properties of the Company and its Subsidiaries. Except as disclosed in Schedule 5.3, this Agreement, the Memorandum, the documents, certificates or other writings delivered to you by or on behalf of the Company in connection with the transactions contemplated hereby and the financial statements listed in Schedule 5.5, taken as a whole, do not contain any untrue statement of a material fact or omit to state any material fact necessary to make the statements therein not misleading in light of the circumstances under which they were made. Except as disclosed in the Memorandum or as expressly described in Schedule 5.3, or in one of the documents, certificates or other writings identified therein, or in the financial statements listed in Schedule 5.5, since June 30, 2006, there has been no change in the financial condition, operations, business, properties or prospects of the Company or any Subsidiary except changes that individually or in the aggregate could not reasonably be expected to have a Material Adverse Effect. There is no fact known to the Company that could reasonably be expected to have a Material Adverse Effect that has not been set forth herein or in the Memorandum or in the other documents, certificates and other writings delivered to you by or on behalf of the Company specifically for use in connection with the transactions contemplated hereby.

5.4. Organization and Ownership of Shares of Subsidiaries; Affiliates.

(a) Schedule 5.4 contains (except as noted therein) complete and correct lists (*i*) of the Company's Subsidiaries, showing, as to each Subsidiary, the correct name thereof, the jurisdiction of its organization, and the percentage of shares of each class of its capital stock or similar equity interests outstanding owned by the Company and each other Subsidiary, (ii) of the Company's Affiliates, other than Subsidiaries, and (iii) of the Company's directors and senior officers.

(b) All of the outstanding shares of capital stock or similar equity interests of each Subsidiary shown in Schedule 5.4 as being owned by the Company and its Subsidiaries have been validly issued, are fully paid and nonassessable and are owned by the Company or another Subsidiary free and clear of any Lien (except as otherwise disclosed in Schedule 5.4).

(c) Each Subsidiary identified in Schedule 5.4 is a corporation or other legal entity duly organized, validly existing and in good standing under the laws of its jurisdiction of organization, and is duly qualified as a foreign corporation or other legal entity and is in good standing in each jurisdiction in which such qualification is required by law, other than those jurisdictions as to which the failure to be so qualified or in good standing could not, individually or in the aggregate, reasonably be expected to have a Material Adverse Effect. Each such Subsidiary has the corporate or other power and authority to own or hold under lease the properties it purports to own or hold under lease and to transact the business it transacts and proposes to transact.

(d) No Subsidiary is a party to, or otherwise subject to any legal restriction or any agreement (other than this Agreement, the agreements listed on Schedule 5.4 and customary limitations imposed by corporate law statutes) restricting the ability of such Subsidiary to pay dividends out of profits or make any other similar distributions of profits to the Company or any of its Subsidiaries that owns outstanding shares of capital stock or similar equity interests of such Subsidiary.

5.5. Financial Statements. The Company has delivered to each Purchaser copies of the financial statements of the Company and its Subsidiaries listed on Schedule 5.5. All of said financial statements (including in each case the related schedules and notes) fairly present in all material respects the consolidated financial position of the Company and its Subsidiaries as of the respective dates specified in such Schedule and the consolidated results of their operations and cash flows for the respective periods so specified and have been prepared in accordance with GAAP consistently applied throughout the periods involved except as set forth in the notes thereto (subject, in the case of any interim financial statements, to normal year-end adjustments).

5.6. Compliance with Laws, Other Instruments, etc. The execution, delivery and performance by the Company of this Agreement and the Notes will not (i) contravene, result in any breach of, or constitute a default under, or result in the creation of any Lien in respect of any property of the Company or any Subsidiary under, any indenture, mortgage, deed of trust, loan, purchase or credit agreement, lease, corporate charter or by-laws, or any other agreement or instrument to which the Company or any Subsidiary is bound or by which the Company or any Subsidiary or any of their respective properties may be bound or affected, (ii) conflict with or result in a breach of any of the terms, conditions or provisions of any order, judgment, decree, or ruling of any court, arbitrator or Governmental Authority applicable to the Company or any Subsidiary or (*iii*) violate any provision of any statute or other rule or regulation of any Governmental Authority applicable to the Company or any Subsidiary.

5.7. Governmental Authorizations, etc. No consent, approval or authorization of, or registration, filing or declaration with, any Governmental Authority is required in connection with the execution, delivery or performance by the Company of this Agreement or the Notes.

5.8. Litigation; Observance of Agreements, Statutes and Orders.

(a) Except as disclosed in Schedule 5.8, there are no actions, suits or proceedings pending or, to the knowledge of the Company, threatened against or affecting the Company or any Subsidiary or any property of the Company or any Subsidiary in any court or before any arbitrator of any kind or before or by any Governmental Authority that, individually or in the aggregate, could reasonably be expected to have a Material Adverse Effect.

(b) Neither the Company nor any Subsidiary is in default under any term of any agreement or instrument to which it is a party or by which it is bound, or any order, judgment, decree or ruling of any court, arbitrator or Governmental Authority or is in violation of any applicable law, ordinance, rule or regulation (including without limitation Environmental Laws) of any Governmental Authority, which default or violation, individually or in the aggregate, could reasonably be expected to have a Material Adverse Effect.

5.9. Taxes. The Company and its Subsidiaries have filed all tax returns that are required to have been filed in any jurisdiction, and have paid all taxes shown to be due and payable on such returns and all other taxes and assessments levied upon them or their properties, assets, income or franchises, to the extent such taxes and assessments have become due and payable and before they have become delinquent, except for any taxes and assessments (*i*) the amount of which is not individually or in the aggregate Material or (*ii*) the amount, applicability or validity of which is currently being contested in good faith by appropriate proceedings and with respect to which the Company or a Subsidiary, as the case may be, has established adequate reserves in accordance with GAAP. The Company knows of no basis for any other tax or assessment that could reasonably be expected to have a Material Adverse Effect. The charges, accruals and reserves on the books of the Company and its Subsidiaries in respect of Federal, state or other taxes for all fiscal periods are adequate. The Federal income tax liabilities of the Company and its Subsidiaries have been determined by the Internal Revenue Service and paid for all fiscal years up to and including the fiscal year ended June 30, 2003.

5.10. Title to Property; Leases. The Company and its Subsidiaries have good and sufficient title to their respective properties that individually or in the aggregate are Material, including all such properties reflected in the most recent audited balance sheet referred to in Section 5.5 or purported to have been acquired by the Company or any Subsidiary after said date (except as sold or otherwise disposed of in the ordinary course of business), in each case free and clear of Liens prohibited by this Agreement. All leases that individually or in the aggregate are Material are valid and subsisting and are in full force and effect in all material respects.

Depends on the types of the company

5.11.   Licenses, Permits, etc. Except as disclosed in Schedule 5.11,

(a) the Company and its Subsidiaries own or possess all licenses, permits, franchises, authorizations, patents, copyrights, service marks, trademarks and trade names, or rights thereto, that individually or in the aggregate are Material, without known conflict with the rights of others;

(b) to the best knowledge of the Company, no product of the Company infringes in any material respect any license, permit, franchise, authorization, patent, copyright, service mark, trademark, trade name or other right owned by any other Person; and

(c) to the best knowledge of the Company, there is no Material violation by any Person of any right of the Company or any of its Subsidiaries with respect to any patent, copyright, service mark, trademark, trade name or other right owned or used by the Company or any of its Subsidiaries.

5.12.   Compliance with ERISA.

(a) The Company and each ERISA Affiliate have operated and administered each Plan in compliance with all applicable laws except for such instances of noncompliance as have not resulted in and could not reasonably be expected to result in a Material Adverse Effect. Neither the Company nor any ERISA Affiliate has incurred any liability pursuant to Title I or IV of ERISA or the penalty or excise tax provisions of the Code relating to employee benefit plans (as defined in Section 3 of ERISA), and no event, transaction or condition has occurred or exists that could reasonably be expected to result in the incurrence of any such liability by the Company or any ERISA Affiliate, or in the imposition of any Lien on any of the rights, properties or assets of the Company or any ERISA Affiliate, in either case pursuant to Title I or IV of ERISA or to such penalty or excise tax provisions or to Section 401(a)(29) or 412 of the Code, other than such liabilities or Liens as would not be individually or in the aggregate Material.

(b) The present value of the aggregate benefit liabilities under each of the Plans (other than Multiemployer Plans), determined as of the end of such Plan's most recently ended plan year on the basis of the actuarial assumptions specified for funding purposes in such Plan's most recent actuarial valuation report, did not exceed the aggregate current value of the assets of such Plan allocable to such benefit liabilities by more than $_____ in the case of any single Plan and by more than $_____ in the aggregate for all Plans. The term **"benefit liabilities"** has the meaning specified in section 4001 of ERISA and the terms **"current value"** and **"present value"** have the meaning specified in section 3 of ERISA.

(c) The Company and its ERISA Affiliates have not incurred withdrawal liabilities (and are not subject to contingent withdrawal liabilities) under section 4201 or 4204 of ERISA in respect of Multiemployer Plans that individually or in the aggregate are Material.

(d) The expected postretirement benefit obligation (determined as of the last day of the Company's most recently ended fiscal year in accordance with Financial Accounting Standards Board Statement No. 106, without regard to liabilities attributable to continuation coverage mandated by section 4980B of the Code) of the Company and its Subsidiaries is not Material.

(e) The execution and delivery of this Agreement and the issuance and sale of the Notes hereunder will not involve any transaction that is subject to the prohibitions of section 406 of ERISA or in connection with which a tax could be imposed pursuant to section 4975(c)(1)(A)-(D) of the Code. The representation by the Company in the first sentence of this Section 5.12(e) is made in reliance upon and subject to (i) the accuracy of your representation in Section 6.2 as to the sources of the funds used to pay the purchase price of the Notes to be purchased by you and (ii) the assumption, made solely for the purpose of making such representation, that Department of Labor Interpretive Bulletin 75–2 with respect to prohibited transactions remains valid in the circumstances of the transactions contemplated herein.

5.13. Private Offering by the Company. Neither the Company nor anyone acting on its behalf has offered the Notes or any similar securities for sale to, or solicited any offer to buy any of the same from, or otherwise approached or negotiated in respect thereof with, any person other than you, the Other Purchasers and not more than [__] other Institutional Investors, each of which has been offered the Notes at a private sale for investment. Neither the Company nor anyone acting on its behalf has taken, or will take, any action that would subject the issuance or sale of the Notes to the registration requirements of Section 5 of the Securities Act.

5.14. Use of Proceeds; Margin Regulations. The Company will apply the proceeds of the sale of the Notes as set forth in Schedule 5.14. No part of the proceeds from the sale of the Notes hereunder will be used, directly or indirectly, for the purpose of buying or carrying any margin stock within the meaning of Regulation G of the Board of Governors of the Federal Reserve System (12 CFR 207), or for the purpose of buying or carrying or trading in any securities under such circumstances as to involve the Company in a violation of Regulation X of said Board (12 CFR 224) or to involve any broker or dealer in a violation of Regulation T of said Board (12 CFR 220). Margin stock does not constitute more than 5% of the value of the consolidated assets of the Company and its Subsidiaries and the Company does not have any present intention that margin stock will constitute more than 5% of the value of such assets. As used in this Section, the terms **"margin stock"** and **"purpose of buying or carrying"** shall have the meanings assigned to them in said Regulation G.

5.15. Existing Indebtedness; Future Liens.

(a) Except as described therein, Schedule 5.15 sets forth a complete and correct list of all outstanding Debt of the Company and its Subsidiaries as of December 31, 2006, since which date there has been no Material change in the amounts, interest rates, sinking funds, instalment payments or maturities of the Debt of the Company or its Subsidiaries. Neither the Company nor any Subsidiary is in default and no waiver of default is currently in effect, in the payment of any principal or interest on any Debt of the Company or such Subsidiary and no event or condition exists with respect to any Debt of the Company or any Subsidiary that would permit (or that with notice or the lapse of time, or both, would permit) one or more Persons to cause such Debt to become due and payable before its stated maturity or before its regularly scheduled dates of payment.

(b) Except as disclosed in Schedule 5.15, neither the Company nor any Subsidiary has agreed or consented to cause or permit in the future (upon the happening of a contingency or otherwise) any of its property, whether now owned or hereafter acquired, to be subject to a Lien not permitted by Section 10.3.

5.16. Foreign Assets Control Regulations, etc. Neither the sale of the Notes by the Company hereunder nor its use of the proceeds thereof will violate the Trading with the Enemy Act, as amended, or any of the foreign assets control regulations of the United States Treasury Department (31 CFR, Subtitle B, Chapter V, as amended) or any enabling legislation or executive order relating thereto.

5.17. Status under Certain Statutes. Neither the Company nor any Subsidiary is subject to regulation under the Investment Company Act of 1940, as amended, the Public Utility Holding Company Act of 1935, as amended, the Interstate Commerce Act, as amended, or the Federal Power Act, as amended.

5.18. Environmental Matters. Neither the Company nor any Subsidiary has knowledge of any claim or has received any notice of any claim, and no proceeding has been instituted raising any claim against the Company or any of its Subsidiaries or any of their respective real properties now or formerly owned, leased or operated by any of them or other assets, alleging any damage to the environment or violation of any Environmental Laws, except, in each case, such as could not reasonably be expected to result in a Material Adverse Effect. Except as otherwise disclosed to you in writing,

(a) neither the Company nor any Subsidiary has knowledge of any facts which would give rise to any claim, public or private, of violation of Environmental Laws or damage to the environment emanating from, occurring on or in any way related to real properties now or formerly owned, leased or operated by any of them or to other assets or their use, except, in each case, such as could not reasonably be expected to result in a Material Adverse Effect;

(b) neither the Company nor any of its Subsidiaries has stored any Hazardous Materials on real properties now or formerly owned, leased or operated by any of them and has not disposed of any Hazardous Materials in a manner contrary to any Environmental Laws in each case in any manner that could reasonably be expected to result in a Material Adverse Effect; and

(c) all buildings on all real properties now owned, leased or operated by the Company or any of its Subsidiaries are in compliance with applicable Environmental Laws, except where failure to comply could not reasonably be expected to result in a Material Adverse Effect.

6. REPRESENTATIONS OF THE PURCHASER. *(Representations made by purchaser)*

6.1. Purchase for Investment. You represent that you are purchasing the Notes for your own account or for one or more separate accounts maintained by you or for the account of one or more pension or trust funds and not with a view to the distribution thereof, *provided* that the disposition of your or their property shall at all times be within your or their control. You understand that the Notes have not been registered under the Securities Act and may be resold only if registered pursuant to the provisions of the Securities Act or if an exemption from registration is available, except under circumstances where neither such registration nor such an exemption is required by law, and that the Company is not required to register the Notes.

6.2. Source of Funds. You represent that at least one of the following statements is an accurate representation as to each source of funds (a "Source") to be used by you to pay the purchase price of the Notes to be purchased by you hereunder:

(a) if you are an insurance company, the Source does not include assets allocated to any separate account maintained by you in which any employee benefit plan (or its related trust) has any interest, other than a separate account that is maintained solely in connection with your fixed contractual obligations under which the amounts payable, or credited, to such plan and to any participant or beneficiary of such plan (including any annuitant) are not affected in any manner by the investment performance of the separate account; or

(b) the Source is either (i) an insurance company pooled separate account, within the meaning of Prohibited Transaction Exemption ("PTE") 90–1 (issued January 29, 1990), or (ii) a bank collective investment fund, within the meaning of the PTE 91–38 (issued July 12, 1991) and, except as you have disclosed to the Company in writing pursuant to this paragraph (b), no employee benefit plan or group of plans maintained by the same employer or employee organization beneficially owns more than 10% of all assets allocated to such pooled separate account or collective investment fund; or

(c) the Source constitutes assets of an "investment fund" (within the meaning of Part V of the QPAM Exemption) managed by a "qualified professional asset manager" or "QPAM" (within the meaning of Part V of the QPAM Exemption), no employee benefit plan's assets that are included in such investment fund, when combined with the assets of all other employee benefit plans established or maintained by the same employer or by an affiliate (within the meaning of Section V(c)(1) of the QPAM

Exemption) of such employer or by the same employee organization and managed by such QPAM, exceed 20% of the total client assets managed by such QPAM, the conditions of Part I(c) and (g) of the QPAM Exemption are satisfied, neither the QPAM nor a person controlling or controlled by the QPAM (applying the definition of "control" in Section V(e) of the QPAM Exemption) owns a 5% or more interest in the Company and (*i*) the identity of such QPAM and (*ii*) the names of all employee benefit plans whose assets are included in such investment fund have been disclosed to the Company in writing pursuant to this paragraph (c); or

(d) the Source is a governmental plan; or

(e) the Source is one or more employee benefit plans, or a separate account or trust fund comprised of one or more employee benefit plans, each of which has been identified to the Company in writing pursuant to this paragraph (e); or

(f) the Source does not include assets of any employee benefit plan, other than a plan exempt from the coverage of ERISA.

As used in this Section 6.2, the terms **"employee benefit plan"**, **"governmental plan"**, **"party in interest"** and **"separate account"** shall have the respective meanings assigned to such terms in Section 3 of ERISA.

7.   INFORMATION AS TO COMPANY.

7.1.   Financial and Business Information. The Company shall deliver to each holder of Notes that is an Institutional Investor:

(a) *Quarterly Statements*—within 60 days after the end of each quarterly fiscal period in each fiscal year of the Company (other than the last quarterly fiscal period of each such fiscal year), duplicate copies of,

(i) a consolidated balance sheet of the Company and its Subsidiaries as at the end of such quarter, and

(ii) consolidated statements of income, changes in shareholders' equity and cash flows of the Company and its Subsidiaries, for such quarter and (in the case of the second and third quarters) for the portion of the fiscal year ending with such quarter,

setting forth in each case in comparative form the figures for the corresponding periods in the previous fiscal year, all in reasonable detail, prepared in accordance with GAAP applicable to quarterly financial statements generally, and certified by a Senior Financial Officer as fairly presenting, in all material respects, the financial position of the companies being reported on and their results of operations and cash flows, subject to changes resulting from year-end adjustments, *provided* that delivery within the time period specified above of copies of the Company's Quarterly Report on Form 10–Q prepared in compliance with the requirements therefor and filed with the Securities and Exchange Commission shall be deemed to satisfy the requirements of this Section 7.1(a);

(b) *Annual Statements*—within 105 days after the end of each fiscal year of the Company, duplicate copies of,

(i) a consolidated balance sheet of the Company and its Subsidiaries, as at the end of such year, and

(ii) consolidated statements of income, changes in shareholders' equity and cash flows of the Company and its Subsidiaries, for such year,

setting forth in each case in comparative form the figures for the previous fiscal year, all in reasonable detail, prepared in accordance with GAAP, and accompanied

(A) by an opinion thereon of independent certified public accountants of recognized national standing, which opinion shall state that such financial statements present fairly, in all material respects, the financial position of the companies being reported upon and their results of operations and cash flows and have been prepared in conformity with GAAP, and that the examination of such accountants in connection with such financial statements has been made in accordance with generally accepted auditing standards, and that such audit provides a reasonable basis for such opinion in the circumstances, and

(B) a certificate of such accountants stating that they have reviewed this Agreement and stating further whether, in making their audit, they have become aware of any condition or event that then constitutes a Default or an Event of Default, and, if they are aware that any such condition or event then exists, specifying the nature and period of the existence thereof (it being understood that such accountants shall not be liable, directly or indirectly, for any failure to obtain knowledge of any Default or Event of Default unless such accountants should have obtained knowledge thereof in making an audit in accordance with generally accepted auditing standards or did not make such an audit),

provided that the delivery within the time period specified above of the Company's Annual Report on Form 10–K for such fiscal year (together with the Company's annual report to shareholders, if any, prepared pursuant to Rule 14a–3 under the Exchange Act) prepared in accordance with the requirements therefor and filed with the Securities and Exchange Commission, together with the accountant's certificate described in clause (B) above, shall be deemed to satisfy the requirements of this Section 7.1(b);

(c) *SEC and Other Reports*—promptly upon their becoming available, one copy of (*i*) each financial statement, report, notice or proxy statement sent by the Company or any Subsidiary to public securities holders generally, and (*ii*) each regular or periodic report, each registration statement (without exhibits except as expressly requested by such holder), and each prospectus and all amendments thereto filed by the Company or any Subsidiary with the Securities and Exchange Commission and of all press releases and other statements made available generally by the Company or any Subsidiary to the public concerning developments that are Material;

(d) *Notice of Default or Event of Default*—promptly, and in any event within five days after a Responsible Officer becoming aware of the existence of any Default or Event of Default or that any Person has given any notice or taken any action with respect to a claimed default hereunder or that any Person has given any notice or taken any action with respect to a claimed default of the type referred to in Section 11(f), a written notice specifying the nature and period of existence thereof and what action the Company is taking or proposes to take with respect thereto;

(e) *ERISA Matters*—promptly, and in any event within five days after a Responsible Officer becoming aware of any of the following, a written notice setting forth the nature thereof and the action, if any, that the Company or an ERISA Affiliate proposes to take with respect thereto:

(i) with respect to any Plan, any reportable event, as defined in section 4043(b) of ERISA and the regulations thereunder, for which notice thereof has not been waived pursuant to such regulations as in effect on the date hereof; or

(ii) the taking by the PBGC of steps to institute, or the threatening by the PBGC of the institution of, proceedings under section 4042 of ERISA for the termination of, or the appointment of a trustee to administer, any Plan, or the receipt by the Company or any ERISA Affiliate of a notice from a Multiemployer Plan that such action has been taken by the PBGC with respect to such Multiemployer Plan; or

(iii) any event, transaction or condition that could result in the incurrence of any liability by the Company or any ERISA Affiliate pursuant to Title I or IV of ERISA or the penalty or excise tax provisions of the Code relating to employee benefit plans, or in the imposition of any Lien on any of the rights, properties or assets of the Company or any ERISA Affiliate pursuant to Title I or IV of ERISA or such penalty or excise tax provisions, if such liability or Lien, taken together with any other such liabilities or Liens then existing, could reasonably be expected to have a Material Adverse Effect;

(f) *Notices from Governmental Authority*—promptly, and in any event within 30 days of receipt thereof, copies of any notice to the Company or any Subsidiary from any Federal or state Governmental Authority relating to any order, ruling, statute or other law or regulation that could reasonably be expected to have a Material Adverse Effect; and

(g) *Requested Information*—with reasonable promptness, such other data and information relating to the business, operations, affairs, financial condition, assets or properties of the Company or any of its Subsidiaries or relating to the ability of the Company to perform its obligations hereunder and under the Notes as from time to time may be reasonably requested by any such holder of Notes\

7.2.   Officer's Certificate. Each set of financial statements delivered to a holder of Notes pursuant to Section 7.1(a) or Section 7.1(b) hereof shall be accompanied by a certificate of a Senior Financial Officer setting forth:

(a) *Covenant Compliance*—the information (including detailed calculations) required in order to establish whether the Company was in compliance with the requirements of Section 10.1 through Section 10.10 hereof, inclusive, during the quarterly or annual period covered by the statements then being furnished (including with respect to each such Section, where applicable, the calculations of the maximum or minimum amount, ratio or percentage, as the case may be, permissible under the terms of such Sections, and the calculation of the amount, ratio or percentage then in existence); and

   (b) *Event of Default*—a statement that such officer has reviewed the relevant terms hereof and has made, or caused to be made, under his or her supervision, a review of the transactions and conditions of the Company and its Subsidiaries from the beginning of the quarterly or annual period covered by the statements then being furnished to the date of the certificate and that such review shall not have disclosed the existence during such period of any condition or event that constitutes a Default or an Event of Default or, if any such condition or event existed or exists (including, without limitation, any such event or condition resulting from the failure of the Company or any Subsidiary to comply with any Environmental Law), specifying the nature and period of existence thereof and what action the Company shall have taken or proposes to take with respect thereto.

   7.3.   Inspection. The Company shall permit the representatives of each holder of Notes that is an Institutional Investor:

   (a) *No Default*—if no Default or Event of Default then exists, at the expense of such holder and upon reasonable prior notice to the Company, to visit the principal executive office of the Company, to discuss the affairs, finances and accounts of the Company and its Subsidiaries with the Company's officers, and (with the consent of the Company, which consent will not be unreasonably withheld) its independent public accountants, and (with the consent of the Company, which consent will not be unreasonably withheld) to visit the other offices and properties of the Company and each Subsidiary, all at such reasonable times and as often as may be reasonably requested in writing; and

   (b) *Default*—if a Default or Event of Default then exists, at the expense of the Company to visit and inspect any of the offices or properties of the Company or any Subsidiary, to examine all their respective books of account, records, reports and other papers, to make copies and extracts therefrom, and to discuss their respective affairs, finances and accounts with their respective officers and independent public accountants (and by this provision the Company authorizes said accountants to discuss the affairs, finances and accounts of the Company and its Subsidiaries), all at such times and as often as may be requested.

8.   PREPAYMENT OF THE NOTES.

   8.1.   Required Prepayments. On February 1, 2013 and on each February 1 thereafter to and including February 1, 2022 the Company will prepay $5,000,000 principal amount (or such lesser principal amount as shall then be outstanding) of the Notes at par and without payment of the Make–Whole Amount or any premium, *provided* that upon any partial prepayment of the Notes pursuant to Section 8.2 or purchase of the Notes permitted by Section 8.5 the principal amount of each required prepayment of the Notes becoming due under this Section 8.1 on and after the date of such prepayment or purchase shall be reduced in the same proportion as the aggregate unpaid principal amount of the Notes is reduced as a result of such prepayment or purchase.

8.2. Optional Prepayments with Make–Whole Amount. The Company may, at its option, upon notice as provided below, prepay at any time all, or from time to time any part of, the Notes, in an amount not less than 5% of the aggregate principal amount of the Notes then outstanding in the case of a partial prepayment, at 100% of the principal amount so prepaid, plus the Make–Whole Amount determined for the prepayment date with respect to such principal amount. The Company will give each holder of Notes written notice of each optional prepayment under this Section 8.2 not less than 30 days and not more than 60 days prior to the date fixed for such prepayment. Each such notice shall specify such date, the aggregate principal amount of the Notes to be prepaid on such date, the principal amount of each Note held by such holder to be prepaid (determined in accordance with Section 8.3), and the interest to be paid on the prepayment date with respect to such principal amount being prepaid, and shall be accompanied by a certificate of a Senior Financial Officer as to the estimated Make–Whole Amount due in connection with such prepayment (calculated as if the date of such notice were the date of the prepayment), setting forth the details of such computation. Two Business Days prior to such prepayment, the Company shall deliver to each holder of Notes a certificate of a Senior Financial Officer specifying the calculation of such Make–Whole Amount as of the specified prepayment date.

8.3. Allocation of Partial Prepayments. In the case of each partial prepayment of the Notes, the principal amount of the Notes to be prepaid shall be allocated among all of the Notes at the time outstanding in proportion, as nearly as practicable, to the respective unpaid principal amounts thereof not theretofore called for prepayment.

8.4. Maturity; Surrender, etc. In the case of each prepayment of Notes pursuant to this Section 8, the principal amount of each Note to be prepaid shall mature and become due and payable on the date fixed for such prepayment, together with interest on such principal amount accrued to such date and the applicable Make–Whole Amount, if any. From and after such date, unless the Company shall fail to pay such principal amount when so due and payable, together with the interest and Make–Whole Amount, if any, as aforesaid, interest on such principal amount shall cease to accrue. Any Note paid or prepaid in full shall be surrendered to the Company and cancelled and shall not be reissued, and no Note shall be issued in lieu of any prepaid principal amount of any Note.

8.5. Purchase of Notes. The Company will not and will not permit any Affiliate to purchase, redeem, prepay or otherwise acquire, directly or indirectly, any of the outstanding Notes except upon the payment or prepayment of the Notes in accordance with the terms of this Agreement and the Notes. The Company will promptly cancel all Notes acquired by it or any Affiliate pursuant to any payment, prepayment or purchase of Notes pursuant to any provision of this Agreement and no Notes may be issued in substitution or exchange for any such Notes.

8.6. Make–Whole Amount. The term **"Make–Whole Amount"** means, with respect to any Note, an amount equal to the excess, if any, of the Discounted Value of the Remaining Scheduled Payments with respect to the Called Principal of such Note over the amount of such Called Principal, *provided* that the Make–Whole Amount may in no event be less than zero. For the purposes of determining the Make–Whole Amount, the following terms have the following meanings:

"Called Principal" means, with respect to any Note, the principal of such Note that is to be prepaid pursuant to Section 8.2 or has become or is declared to be immediately due and payable pursuant to Section 12.1, as the context requires.

"Discounted Value" means, with respect to the Called Principal of any Note, the amount obtained by discounting all Remaining Scheduled Payments with respect to such Called Principal from their respective scheduled due dates to the Settlement Date with respect to such Called Principal, in accordance with accepted financial practice and at a discount factor (applied on the same periodic basis as that on which interest on the Notes is payable) equal to the Reinvestment Yield with respect to such Called Principal.

"Reinvestment Yield" means, with respect to the Called Principal of any Note, the yield to maturity implied by (*i*) the yields reported, as of 10:00 A.M. (New York City time) on the second Business Day preceding the Settlement Date with respect to such Called Principal, on the display designated as "Page 678" on the Telerate Access Service (or such other display as may replace Page 678 on Telerate Access Service) for actively traded U.S. Treasury securities having a maturity equal to the Remaining Average Life of such Called Principal as of such Settlement Date, or (*ii*) if such yields are not reported as of such time or the yields reported as of such time are not ascertainable, the Treasury Constant Maturity Series Yields reported, for the latest day for which such yields have been so reported as of the second Business Day preceding the Settlement Date with respect to such Called Principal, in Federal Reserve Statistical Release H.15 (519) (or any comparable successor publication) for actively traded U.S. Treasury securities having a constant maturity equal to the Remaining Average Life of such Called Principal as of such Settlement Date. Such implied yield will be determined, if necessary, by (*a*) converting U.S. Treasury bill quotations to bond-equivalent yields in accordance with accepted financial practice and (*b*) interpolating linearly between (*1*) the actively traded U.S. Treasury security with the duration closest to and greater than the Remaining Average Life and (*2*) the actively traded U.S. Treasury security with the duration closest to and less than the Remaining Average Life.

"Remaining Average Life" means, with respect to any Called Principal, the number of years (calculated to the nearest one-twelfth year) obtained by dividing (*i*) such Called Principal into (*ii*) the sum of the products obtained by multiplying (*a*) the principal component of each Remaining Scheduled Payment with respect to such Called Principal by (*b*) the number of years (calculated to the nearest one-twelfth year) that will elapse between the Settlement Date with respect to such Called Principal and the scheduled due date of such Remaining Scheduled Payment.

"Remaining Scheduled Payments" means, with respect to the Called Principal of any Note, all payments of such Called Principal and interest thereon that would be due after the Settlement Date with respect to such Called Principal if no payment of such Called Principal were made prior to its scheduled due date, *provided* that if such Settlement Date is not a date on which interest payments are due to be made under the terms of the Notes, then the amount of the next succeeding scheduled interest payment will be reduced by the amount of interest accrued to such Settlement Date and required to be paid on such Settlement Date pursuant to Section 8.2 or 12.1.

"Settlement Date" means, with respect to the Called Principal of any Note, the date on which such Called Principal is to be prepaid pursuant to Section 8.2 or has become or is declared to be immediately due and payable pursuant to Section 12.1, as the context requires.

9.   AFFIRMATIVE COVENANTS.

The Company covenants that so long as any of the Notes are outstanding:

9.1.   Compliance With Law. The Company will and will cause each of its Subsidiaries to comply with all laws, ordinances or governmental rules or regulations to which each of them is subject, including, without limitation, Environmental Laws, and will obtain and maintain in effect all licenses, certificates, permits, franchises and other governmental authorizations necessary to the ownership of their respective properties or to the conduct of their respective businesses, in each case to the extent necessary to ensure that non-compliance with such laws, ordinances or governmental rules or regulations or failures to obtain or maintain in effect such licenses, certificates, permits, franchises and other governmental authorizations could not, individually or in the aggregate, reasonably be expected to have a Material Adverse Effect.

9.2.   Insurance. The Company will and will cause each of its Subsidiaries to maintain, with financially sound and reputable insurers, insurance with respect to their respective properties and businesses against such casualties and contingencies, of such types, on such terms and in such amounts (including deductibles, co-insurance and self-insurance, if adequate reserves are maintained with respect thereto) as is customary in the case of entities of established reputations engaged in the same or a similar business and similarly situated.

9.3.   Maintenance of Properties. The Company will and will cause each of its Subsidiaries to maintain and keep, or cause to be maintained and kept, their respective properties in good repair, working order and condition (other than ordinary wear and tear), so that the business carried on in connection therewith may be properly conducted at all times, *provided* that this Section shall not prevent the Company or any Subsidiary from discontinuing the operation and the maintenance of any of its properties if such discontinuance is desirable in the conduct of its business and the Company has concluded that such discontinuance could not, individually or in the aggregate, reasonably be expected to have a Material Adverse Effect.

9.4. Payment of Taxes and Claims. The Company will and will cause each of its Subsidiaries to file all tax returns required to be filed in any jurisdiction and to pay and discharge all taxes shown to be due and payable on such returns and all other taxes, assessments, governmental charges, or levies imposed on them or any of their properties, assets, income or franchises, to the extent such taxes and assessments have become due and payable and before they have become delinquent and all claims for which sums have become due and payable that have or might become a Lien on properties or assets of the Company or any Subsidiary, *provided* that neither the Company nor any Subsidiary need pay any such tax or assessment or claims if (*i*) the amount, applicability or validity thereof is contested by the Company or such Subsidiary on a timely basis in good faith and in appropriate proceedings, and the Company or a Subsidiary has established adequate reserves therefor in accordance with GAAP on the books of the Company or such Subsidiary or (*ii*) the nonpayment of all such taxes and assessments in the aggregate could not reasonably be expected to have a Material Adverse Effect.

9.5. Corporate Existence, etc. The Company will at all times preserve and keep in full force and effect its corporate existence. Subject to Sections 10.10 and 10.11, the Company will at all times preserve and keep in full force and effect the corporate existence of each of its Subsidiaries (unless merged into the Company or a Subsidiary) and all rights and franchises of the Company and its Subsidiaries unless, in the good faith judgment of the Company, the termination of or failure to preserve and keep in full force and effect such corporate existence, right or franchise could not, individually or in the aggregate, have a Material Adverse Effect.

10. NEGATIVE COVENANTS.

The Company covenants that so long as any of the Notes are outstanding:

10.1. Interest Coverage; Current Ratio; Working Capital; Net Worth.

(a) *Interest Charges Coverage Ratio*—The Company will not, at any time, permit the Interest Charges Coverage Ratio to be less than 2 to 1.

(b) *Current Ratio*—The Company will not, at any time, permit the ratio of Consolidated Current Assets to Consolidated Current Liabilities to be less than 1.2 to 1.

(c) *Minimum Working Capital*—Consolidated Current Assets will, at all times, exceed Consolidated Current Liabilities by at least $15,000,000.

(d) *Consolidated Net Worth*—The Company will not, at any time, permit Consolidated Net Worth to be less than $50,000,000.

[handwritten left margin: Consolidated Net worth = shareholder's equity - any intangibles (goodwill, copyright, patent, trademark, etc.)]

10.2. Debt.

(a) *Incurrence of Funded Debt*—The Company will not, and will not permit any Subsidiary to, directly or indirectly, create, incur, assume, guarantee, or otherwise become directly or indirectly liable with respect to, any Funded Debt, *unless* on the date the Company or such Subsidiary becomes liable with respect to any such Debt and immediately after giving effect thereto and the concurrent retirement of any other Debt,

[handwritten left margin: - Funded debt: long-term debt (≥ 1 yr) - Current debt: short-term debt (< 1 yr)]

(1) no Default or Event of Default exists, and

(2) Consolidated Funded Debt does not exceed 90% of Consolidated Net Worth determined as of the then most recently ended fiscal year of the Company. *[handwritten: (If exceeds, must first pay off before add. debt can be incurred)]*

For the purposes of this Section 10.2, any Person becoming a Subsidiary after the date hereof shall be deemed, at the time it becomes a Subsidiary, to have incurred all of its then outstanding Debt, and any Person extending, renewing or refunding any Debt shall be deemed to have incurred such Debt at the time of such extension, renewal or refunding.

[handwritten left margin: Req. for company to pay down current debt once a yr.]

(b) *Clean Down of Current Debt*—The Company will not at any time have any Consolidated Current Debt outstanding *unless* there shall have been during the immediately preceding 12 months a period of at least 60 consecutive days on each of which there shall have been no Consolidated Current Debt outstanding in excess of $10,000,000.

[handwritten left margin: - All borrowing should occur at the parent level; parent borrows & lends to sub - If not, if the sub goes bankrupt, its creditors will get paid first, & then subordinating the creditors of the parent]

(c) *Subsidiary Debt*—The Company will not at any time permit any Subsidiary to, directly or indirectly, create, incur, assume, guarantee, have outstanding, or otherwise become or remain directly or indirectly liable with respect to, any Debt other than:

(i) Debt of a Subsidiary outstanding on the date hereof and disclosed in Schedule 5.15, *provided* that such Debt may not be extended, renewed or refunded except as otherwise permitted by this Agreement;

(ii) Debt of a Subsidiary owed to the Company or a Wholly–Owned Subsidiary; and

(iii) Debt of a Subsidiary outstanding at the time such Subsidiary becomes a Subsidiary, *provided* that (*i*) such Debt shall not have been incurred in contemplation of such Subsidiary becoming a Subsidiary and (*ii*) immediately after such Subsidiary becomes a Subsidiary no Default or Event of Default shall exist, and *provided further* that such Debt may not be extended, renewed or refunded except as otherwise permitted by this Agreement.

[handwritten: See back]

10.3. Liens. The Company will not, and will not permit any of its Subsidiaries to, directly or indirectly create, incur, assume or permit to exist (upon the happening of a contingency or otherwise) any Lien on or with respect to any property or asset (including, without limitation, any document or instrument in respect of goods or accounts receivable) of the Company or any such Subsidiary, whether now owned or held or hereafter acquired, or any income or profits therefrom (whether or not provision is made for the equal and ratable securing of the Notes in accordance with the last paragraph of this Section 10.3), or assign or otherwise convey any right to receive income or profits, except:

(a) Liens for taxes, assessments or other governmental charges which are not yet due and payable or the payment of which is not at the time required by Section 9.4;

(b) statutory Liens of landlords and Liens of carriers, warehousemen, mechanics, materialmen and other similar Liens, in each case, incurred in the ordinary course of business for sums not yet due and payable or the payment of which is not at the time required by Section 9.4;

(c) Liens (other than any Lien imposed by ERISA) incurred or deposits made in the ordinary course of business (*i*) in connection with workers' compensation, unemployment insurance and other types of social security or retirement benefits, or (*ii*) to secure (or to obtain letters of credit that secure) the performance of tenders, statutory obligations, surety bonds, appeal bonds, bids, leases (other than Capital Leases), performance bonds, purchase, construction or sales contracts and other similar obligations, in each case not incurred or made in connection with the borrowing of money, the obtaining of advances or credit or the payment of the deferred purchase price of property;

(d) leases or subleases granted to others, easements, rights-of-way, restrictions and other similar charges or encumbrances, in each case incidental to, and not interfering with, the ordinary conduct of the business of the Company or any of its Subsidiaries, *provided* that such Liens do not, in the aggregate, materially detract from the value of such property;

(e) Liens on property or assets of the Company or any of its Subsidiaries securing Debt owing to the Company or to another Subsidiary;

(f) Liens existing on the date of this Agreement and securing the Debt of the Company and its Subsidiaries referred to in item[s] [___] [and ___] of Schedule 5.15;

(g) any Lien created to secure all or any part of the purchase price, or to secure Debt incurred or assumed to pay all or any part of the purchase price or cost of construction, of tangible property (or any improvement thereon) acquired or constructed by the Company or a Subsidiary after the date of the Closing, *provided* that

(i) any such Lien shall extend solely to the item or items of such property (or improvement thereon) so acquired or constructed and, if required by the terms of the instrument originally creating such Lien, other property (or improvement thereon) which is an improvement to or is acquired for specific use in connection with such acquired or constructed property (or improvement thereon) or which is real property being improved by such acquired or constructed property (or improvement thereon),

(ii) the principal amount of the Debt secured by any such Lien shall at no time exceed an amount equal to 50% (but 100% in the case of property (or improvement thereon) the acquisition of which is financed through a Capital Lease Obligation) of the lesser of (*A*) the cost to the Company or such Subsidiary of the property (or improvement thereon) so acquired or constructed and (B) the Fair Market Value (as determined in good faith by the board of directors of the Company) of such property (or improvement thereon) at the time of such acquisition or construction, and

(iii) any such Lien shall be created contemporaneously with, or within 10 days after, the acquisition or construction of such property; and

(h) any Lien existing on property of a Person immediately prior to its being consolidated with or merged into the Company or a Subsidiary or its becoming a Subsidiary, or any Lien existing on any property acquired by the Company or any Subsidiary at the time such property is so acquired (whether or not the Debt secured thereby shall have been assumed), *provided* that (*i*) no such Lien shall have been created or assumed in contemplation of such consolidation or merger or such Person's becoming a Subsidiary or such acquisition of property, and (*ii*) each such Lien shall extend solely to the item or items of property so acquired and, if required by the terms of the instrument originally creating such Lien, other property which is an improvement to or is acquired for specific use in connection with such acquired property.

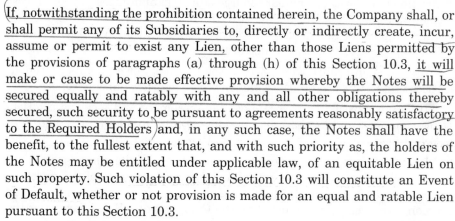

If, notwithstanding the prohibition contained herein, the Company shall, or shall permit any of its Subsidiaries to, directly or indirectly create, incur, assume or permit to exist any Lien, other than those Liens permitted by the provisions of paragraphs (a) through (h) of this Section 10.3, it will make or cause to be made effective provision whereby the Notes will be secured equally and ratably with any and all other obligations thereby secured, such security to be pursuant to agreements reasonably satisfactory to the Required Holders and, in any such case, the Notes shall have the benefit, to the fullest extent that, and with such priority as, the holders of the Notes may be entitled under applicable law, of an equitable Lien on such property. Such violation of this Section 10.3 will constitute an Event of Default, whether or not provision is made for an equal and ratable Lien pursuant to this Section 10.3.

10.4. Leases.

(a) *Long Term Lease Rentals*—The Company will not, at any time, permit Long Term Lease Rentals for any current or future fiscal year of the Company to exceed 33 1/3% of Consolidated Net Worth as of the then most recently ended fiscal year of the Company.

(b) *Sale-and-Leasebacks*—The Company will not, and will not permit any Subsidiary to, enter into any Sale-and-Leaseback Transaction.

10.5. Restricted Investments.

Definition A-88

(a) *Limitation*—The Company will not, and will not permit any of its Subsidiaries to, declare, make or authorize any Restricted Investment *unless* immediately after giving effect to such action:

(i) the aggregate value of all Restricted Investments of the Company and its Subsidiaries (valued immediately after such action) would not exceed the sum of:

(A) $10,000,000, plus

(B) 25% of Consolidated Net Income for the period commencing on July 1, 2006 and ending on the date such Restricted Investment is made (or minus 100% of Consolidated Net Income for such period if Consolidated Net Income for such period is a loss), plus

(C) the aggregate amount of Net Proceeds of Capital Stock for such period;

(ii) no Default or Event of Default would exist; and

(iii) the Company would be permitted by the provisions of Section 10.2 hereof to incur at least $1.00 of additional Funded Debt owing to a Person other than a Subsidiary of the Company.

(b) *Investments of Subsidiaries*—Each Person which becomes a Subsidiary of the Company after the date of the Closing will be deemed to have made, on the date such Person becomes a Subsidiary of the Company, all Restricted Investments of such Person in existence on such date. Investments in any Person that ceases to be a Subsidiary of the Company after the date of the Closing (but in which the Company or another Subsidiary continues to maintain an Investment) will be deemed to have been made on the date on which such Person ceases to be a Subsidiary of the Company.

10.6. Restricted Payments.

[handwritten: Def. A-9]

[handwritten: Related to fraudulent conveyance law; cannot make dividend or gift when it's insolvent or doing so will make it insolvent.]

(a) *Limitation*—The Company will not, and will not permit any of its Subsidiaries to, at any time, declare or make, or incur any liability to declare or make, any Restricted Payment *unless* immediately after giving effect to such action:

(i) the aggregate amount of Restricted Payments of the Company and its Subsidiaries declared or made during the period commencing on July 1, 2006, and ending on the date such Restricted Payment is declared or made, inclusive, would not exceed the sum of

(A) $10,000,000, plus

(B) 50% of Consolidated Net Income for such period (or minus 100% of Consolidated Net Income for such period if Consolidated Net Income for such period is a loss), plus

(C) the aggregate amount of Net Proceeds of Capital Stock for such period;

(ii) no Default or Event of Default would exist; and

(iii) the Company would be permitted by the provisions of Section 10.2 hereof to incur at least $1.00 of additional Funded Debt owing to a Person other than a Subsidiary of the Company.

(b) Time of Payment—The Company will not, nor will it permit any of its Subsidiaries to, authorize a Restricted Payment that is not payable within 60 days of authorization.

10.7.   Transactions with Affiliates. The Company will not and will not permit any Subsidiary to enter into directly or indirectly any transaction or Material group of related transactions (including without limitation the purchase, lease, sale or exchange of properties of any kind or the rendering of any service) with any Affiliate (other than the Company or another Subsidiary), except in the ordinary course and pursuant to the reasonable requirements of the Company's or such Subsidiary's business and upon fair and reasonable terms no less favorable to the Company or such Subsidiary than would be obtainable in a comparable arm's-length transaction with a Person not an Affiliate.

10.8.   Line of Business. The Company will not, and will not permit any of its Subsidiaries to, engage to any substantial extent in any business other than the businesses in which the Company and its Subsidiaries are engaged on the date of this Agreement as described in the Memorandum.

10.9.   Merger, Consolidation, etc. The Company will not consolidate with or merge with any other corporation or convey, transfer or lease substantially all of its assets in a single transaction or series of transactions to any Person unless:

(a) the successor formed by such consolidation or the survivor of such merger or the Person that acquires by conveyance, transfer or lease substantially all of the assets of the Company as an entirety, as the case may be (the "**Successor Corporation**"), shall be a solvent corporation organized and existing under the laws of the United States of America, any State thereof or the District of Columbia;

(b) if the Company is not the Successor Corporation, such corporation shall have executed and delivered to each holder of Notes its assumption of the due and punctual performance and observance of each covenant and condition of this Agreement, the Other Agreements, and the Notes (pursuant to such agreements and instruments as shall be reasonably satisfactory to the Required Holders), and the Company shall have caused to be delivered to each holder of Notes an opinion of nationally recognized independent counsel, or other independent counsel reasonably satisfactory to the Required Holders, to the effect that all agreements or instruments effecting such assumption are enforceable in accordance with their terms and comply with the terms hereof; and

(c) immediately after giving effect to such transaction:

(i) no Default or Event of Default would exist, and

(ii) the Successor Corporation would be permitted by the provisions of Section 10.2 hereof to incur at least $1.00 of additional Funded Debt owing to a Person other than a Subsidiary of the Successor Corporation.

No such conveyance, transfer or lease of substantially all of the assets of the Company shall have the effect of releasing the Company or any Successor Corporation from its liability under this Agreement or the Notes.

successor clause

10.10. Sale of Assets, Etc. Except as permitted under Section 10.9, the Company will not, and will not permit any of its Subsidiaries to, make any Asset Disposition *unless*:

(a) in the good faith opinion of the Company, the Asset Disposition is in exchange for consideration having a Fair Market Value at least equal to that of the property exchanged and is in the best interest of the Company or such Subsidiary;

(b) immediately after giving effect to the Asset Disposition, no Default or Event of Default would exist; and

(c) immediately after giving effect to the Asset Disposition, the Disposition Value of all property that was the subject of any Asset Disposition occurring in the then current fiscal year of the Company would not exceed 10% of Consolidated Assets as of the end of the then most recently ended fiscal year of the Company.

sharon steel clause
- company cannot sell more than 10% of its assets many fiscal

10.11. Disposal of Ownership of a Subsidiary. The Company will not, and will not permit any of its Subsidiaries to, sell or otherwise dispose of any shares of Subsidiary Stock, nor will the Company permit any such Subsidiary to issue, sell or otherwise dispose of any shares of its own Subsidiary Stock, *provided* that the foregoing restrictions do not apply to:

(a) the issue of directors' qualifying shares by any such Subsidiary;

(b) any such Transfer of Subsidiary Stock constituting a Transfer described in clause (a) of the definition of "Asset Disposition"; and

(c) the Transfer of all of the Subsidiary Stock of a Subsidiary of the Company owned by the Company and its other Subsidiaries if:

(i) such Transfer satisfies the requirements of Section 10.10 hereof,

(ii) in connection with such Transfer the entire Investment (whether represented by stock, Debt, claims or otherwise) of the Company and its other Subsidiaries in such Subsidiary is sold, transferred or otherwise disposed of to a Person other than (A) the Company, (B) another Subsidiary not being simultaneously disposed of, or (C) an Affiliate, and

(iii) the Subsidiary being disposed of has no continuing Investment in any other Subsidiary of the Company not being simultaneously disposed of or in the Company.

11. EVENTS OF DEFAULT. *Company usually given time to remedy, except in default in P & I (5 day pmts)*

An **"Event of Default"** shall exist if any of the following conditions or events shall occur and be continuing:

(a) the Company defaults in the payment of any principal or Make-Whole Amount, if any, on any Note when the same becomes due and *no grace period, automatic default* payable, whether at maturity or at a date fixed for prepayment or by declaration or otherwise; or

(b) the Company defaults in the payment of any interest on any Note for more than five Business Days after the same becomes due and payable; or

[handwritten: 5-day grace period for interest → then automatic default]

(c) the Company defaults in the performance of or compliance with any term contained in Sections 7.1(d), 9.5, or 10; or

(d) the Company defaults in the performance of or compliance with any term contained herein (other than those referred to in paragraphs (a), (b) and (c) of this Section 11) and such default is not remedied within 30 days after the earlier of (i) a Responsible Officer obtaining actual knowledge of such default and (ii) the Company receiving written notice of such default from any holder of a Note (any such written notice to be identified as a "notice of default" and to refer specifically to this paragraph (d) of Section 11); or

[handwritten: Defaults besides I & P, if not remedied w/in 30 days]

(e) any representation or warranty made in writing by or on behalf of the Company or by any officer of the Company in this Agreement or in any writing furnished in connection with the transactions contemplated hereby proves to have been false or incorrect in any material respect on the date as of which made; or

[handwritten: Reps & warranties 30 days + other writings]

(f)(i) the Company or any Subsidiary is in default (as principal or as guarantor or other surety) in the payment of any principal of or premium or make-whole amount or interest on any Debt that is outstanding in an aggregate principal amount of at least $1,000,000 beyond any period of grace provided with respect thereto, or (ii) the Company or any Subsidiary is in default in the performance of or compliance with any term of any evidence of any Debt in an aggregate outstanding principal amount of at least $1,000,000 or of any mortgage, indenture or other agreement relating thereto or any other condition exists, and as a consequence of such default or condition such Debt has become, or has been declared (or one or more Persons are entitled to declare such Indebtedness to be), due and payable before its stated maturity or before its regularly scheduled dates of payment, or (iii) as a consequence of the occurrence or continuation of any event or condition (other than the passage of time or the right of the holder of Debt to convert such Debt into equity interests), (x) the Company or any Subsidiary has become obligated to purchase or repay Debt before its regular maturity or before its regularly scheduled dates of payment in an aggregate outstanding principal amount of at least $1,000,000, or (y) one or more Persons have the right to require the Company or any Subsidiary so to purchase or repay such Debt; or

(g) the Company or any Subsidiary (i) is generally not paying, or admits in writing its inability to pay, its debts as they become due, (ii) files, or consents by answer or otherwise to the filing against it of, a petition for relief or reorganization or arrangement or any other petition in bankruptcy, for liquidation or to take advantage of any bankruptcy, insolvency, reorganization, moratorium or other similar law of any jurisdiction, (iii) makes an assignment for the benefit of its creditors, (iv) consents to the

[handwritten: Company not paying, or filing or being filed against in bankruptcy]

appointment of a custodian, receiver, trustee or other officer with similar powers with respect to it or with respect to any substantial part of its property, (*v*) is adjudicated as insolvent or to be liquidated, or (*vi*) takes corporate action for the purpose of any of the foregoing; or)

(h) a court or governmental authority of competent jurisdiction enters an order appointing, without consent by the Company or any of its Subsidiaries, a custodian, receiver, trustee or other officer with similar powers with respect to it or with respect to any substantial part of its property, or constituting an order for relief or approving a petition for relief or reorganization or any other petition in bankruptcy or for liquidation or to take advantage of any bankruptcy or insolvency law of any jurisdiction, or ordering the dissolution, winding-up or liquidation of the Company or any of its Subsidiaries, or any such petition shall be filed against the Company or any of its Subsidiaries and such petition shall not be dismissed within 60 days; or *[handwritten: 60-day grace period to remedy]*

(i) a final judgment or judgments for the payment of money aggregating in excess of $2,500,000 are rendered against one or more of the Company and its Subsidiaries and which judgments are not, within 60 days after entry thereof, bonded, discharged or stayed pending appeal, or are not discharged within 60 days after the expiration of such stay; or

[handwritten margin notes: filing of inv. bankr. against the company.]

[handwritten margin notes: 60 days to appeal; have to have judgment stayed pending appeal; given 60 days to discharge indebtedness or appeal]

(j) if (*i*) any Plan shall fail to satisfy the minimum funding standards of ERISA or the Code for any plan year or part thereof or a waiver of such standards or extension of any amortization period is sought or granted under section 412 of the Code, (*ii*) a notice of intent to terminate any Plan shall have been or is reasonably expected to be filed with the PBGC or the PBGC shall have instituted proceedings under ERISA section 4042 to terminate or appoint a trustee to administer any Plan or the PBGC shall have notified the Company or any ERISA Affiliate that a Plan may become a subject of any such proceedings, (*iii*) the aggregate "amount of unfunded benefit liabilities" (within the meaning of section 4001(a)(18) of ERISA) under all Plans, determined in accordance with Title IV of ERISA, shall exceed $[___], (*iv*) the Company or any ERISA Affiliate shall have incurred or is reasonably expected to incur any liability pursuant to Title I or IV of ERISA or the penalty or excise tax provisions of the Code relating to employee benefit plans, (*v*) the Company or any ERISA Affiliate withdraws from any Multiemployer Plan, or (*vi*) the Company or any Subsidiary establishes or amends any employee welfare benefit plan that provides post-employment welfare benefits in a manner that would increase the liability of the Company or any Subsidiary thereunder; and any such event or events described in clauses (i) through (vi) above, either individually or together with any other such event or events, could reasonably be expected to have a Material Adverse Effect.

As used in Section 11(j), the terms **"employee benefit plan"** and **"employee welfare benefit plan"** shall have the respective meanings assigned to such terms in Section 3 of ERISA.

12. REMEDIES ON DEFAULT, ETC.

12.1. Acceleration.

(a) If an Event of Default with respect to the Company described in paragraph (g) or (h) of Section 11 (other than an Event of Default

[handwritten margin note: filing of vol. or invol. bankruptcy]

described in clause (i) of paragraph (g) or described in clause (vi) of paragraph (g) by virtue of the fact that such clause encompasses clause (i) of paragraph (g)) has occurred, all the Notes then outstanding shall automatically become immediately due and payable.

acceleration by more than 5% holders in principal amt

(b) If any other Event of Default has occurred and is continuing, any holder or holders of more than 5% in principal amount of the Notes at the time outstanding may at any time at its or their option, by notice or notices to the Company, declare all the Notes then outstanding to be immediately due and payable.

(c) If any Event of Default described in paragraph (a) or (b) of Section 11 has occurred and is continuing, any holder or holders of Notes at the time outstanding affected by such Event of Default may at any time, at its or their option, by notice or notices to the Company, declare all the Notes held by it or them to be immediately due and payable.

Upon any Notes becoming due and payable under this Section 12.1, whether automatically or by declaration, such Notes will forthwith mature and the entire unpaid principal amount of such Notes, plus (x) all accrued and unpaid interest thereon and (y) the Make–Whole Amount determined in respect of such principal amount (to the full extent permitted by applicable law), shall all be immediately due and payable, in each and every case without presentment, demand, protest or further notice, all of which are hereby waived. The Company acknowledges, and the parties hereto agree, that each holder of a Note has the right to maintain its investment in the Notes free from repayment by the Company (except as herein specifically provided for) and that the provision for payment of a Make–Whole Amount by the Company in the event that the Notes are prepaid or are accelerated as a result of an Event of Default, is intended to provide compensation for the deprivation of such right under such circumstances.

12.2.   Other Remedies. If any Default or Event of Default has occurred and is continuing, and irrespective of whether any Notes have become or have been declared immediately due and payable under Section 12.1, the holder of any Note at the time outstanding may proceed to protect and enforce the rights of such holder by an action at law, suit in equity or other appropriate proceeding, whether for the specific performance of any agreement contained herein or in any Note, or for an injunction against a violation of any of the terms hereof or thereof, or in aid of the exercise of any power granted hereby or thereby or by law or otherwise.

12.3.   Rescission. At any time after any Notes have been declared due and payable pursuant to clause (b) or (c) of Section 12.1, the holders of not less than 76% in principal amount of the Notes then outstanding, by written notice to the Company, may rescind and annul any such declaration and its consequences if (*a*) the Company has paid all overdue interest on the Notes, all principal of and Make–Whole Amount, if any, on any Notes that are due and payable and are unpaid other than by reason of such declaration, and all interest on such overdue principal and Make–Whole Amount, if any, and (to the extent permitted by applicable law) any overdue interest in respect of the Notes, at the Default Rate, (*b*) all Events of Default and Defaults, other than non-payment of amounts that have become due solely by reason of such declaration, have been cured or have been waived pursuant to Section 17, and (*c*) no judgment or decree has been entered for the payment of any monies due pursuant hereto or to the Notes. No rescission and annulment under this Section 12.3 will extend to or affect any subsequent Event of Default or Default or impair any right consequent thereon.

12.4. No Waivers or Election of Remedies, Expenses, etc. No course of dealing and no delay on the part of any holder of any Note in exercising any right, power or remedy shall operate as a waiver thereof or otherwise prejudice such holder's rights, powers or remedies. No right, power or remedy conferred by this Agreement or by any Note upon any holder thereof shall be exclusive of any other right, power or remedy referred to herein or therein or now or hereafter available at law, in equity, by statute or otherwise. Without limiting the obligations of the Company under Section 15, the Company will pay to the holder of each Note on demand such further amount as shall be sufficient to cover all costs and expenses of such holder incurred in any enforcement or collection under this Section 12, including, without limitation, reasonable attorneys' fees, expenses and disbursements.

13. REGISTRATION; EXCHANGE; SUBSTITUTION OF NOTES.

13.1. Registration of Notes. The Company shall keep at its principal executive office a register for the registration and registration of transfers of Notes. The name and address of each holder of one or more Notes, each transfer thereof and the name and address of each transferee of one or more Notes shall be registered in such register. Prior to due presentment for registration of transfer, the Person in whose name any Note shall be registered shall be deemed and treated as the owner and holder thereof for all purposes hereof, and the Company shall not be affected by any notice or knowledge to the contrary. The Company shall give to any holder of a Note that is an Institutional Investor promptly upon request therefor, a complete and correct copy of the names and addresses of all registered holders of Notes.

13.2. Transfer and Exchange of Notes. Upon surrender of any Note at the principal executive office of the Company for registration of transfer or exchange (and in the case of a surrender for registration of transfer, duly endorsed or accompanied by a written instrument of transfer duly executed by the registered holder of such Note or his attorney duly authorized in writing and accompanied by the address for notices of each transferee of such Note or part thereof), the Company shall execute and deliver, at the Company's expense (except as provided below), one or more new Notes (as requested by the holder thereof) in exchange therefor, in an aggregate principal amount equal to the unpaid principal amount of the surrendered Note. Each such new Note shall be payable to such Person as such holder may request and shall be substantially in the form of Exhibit 1. Each such new Note shall be dated and bear interest from the date to which interest shall have been paid on the surrendered Note or dated the date of the surrendered Note if no interest shall have been paid thereon. The Company may require payment of a sum sufficient to cover any stamp tax or governmental charge imposed in respect of any such transfer of Notes. Notes shall not be transferred in denominations of less than $100,000, *provided* that if necessary to enable the registration of transfer by a holder of its entire holding of Notes, one Note may be in a denomination of less than $100,000. Any transferee, by its acceptance of a Note registered in its name (or the name of its nominee), shall be deemed to have made the representation set forth in Section 6.2.

13.3. Replacement of Notes. Upon receipt by the Company of evidence reasonably satisfactory to it of the ownership of and the loss, theft, destruction or mutilation of any Note (which evidence shall be, in the case of an Institutional Investor, notice from such Institutional Investor of such ownership and such loss, theft, destruction or mutilation), and

(a) in the case of loss, theft or destruction, of indemnity reasonably satisfactory to it (*provided* that if the holder of such Note is, or is a nominee for, an original Purchaser or another holder of a Note with a minimum net worth of at least $[___], such Person's own unsecured agreement of indemnity shall be deemed to be satisfactory), or

(b) in the case of mutilation, upon surrender and cancellation thereof,

the Company at its own expense shall execute and deliver, in lieu thereof, a new Note, dated and bearing interest from the date to which interest shall have been paid on such lost, stolen, destroyed or mutilated Note or dated the date of such lost, stolen, destroyed or mutilated Note if no interest shall have been paid thereon.

14.   PAYMENTS ON NOTES.

14.1. Place of Payment. Subject to Section 14.2, payments of principal, Make–Whole Amount, if any, and interest becoming due and payable on the Notes shall be made in New York, New York at the principal office of Manhattan Chemical Bank, N.A. in such jurisdiction. The Company may at any time, by notice to each holder of a Note, change the place of payment of the Notes so long as such place of payment shall be either the principal office of the Company in such jurisdiction or the principal office of a bank or trust company in such jurisdiction.

14.2. Home Office Payment. So long as you or your nominee shall be the holder of any Note, and notwithstanding anything contained in Section 14.1 or in such Note to the contrary, the Company will pay all sums becoming due on such Note for principal, Make–Whole Amount, if any, and interest by the method and at the address specified for such purpose below your name in Schedule A, or by such other method or at such other address as you shall have from time to time specified to the Company in writing for such purpose, without the presentation or surrender of such Note or the making of any notation thereon, except that upon written request of the Company made concurrently with or reasonably promptly after payment or prepayment in full of any Note, you shall surrender such Note for cancellation, reasonably promptly after any such request, to the Company at its principal executive office or at the place of payment most recently designated by the Company pursuant to Section 14.1. Prior to any sale or other disposition of any Note held by you or your nominee you will, at your election, either endorse thereon the amount of principal paid thereon and the last date to which interest has been paid thereon or surrender such Note to the Company in exchange for a new Note or Notes pursuant to Section 13.2. The Company will afford the benefits of this Section 14.2 to any Institutional Investor that is the direct or indirect transferee of any Note purchased by you under this Agreement and that has made the same agreement relating to such Note as you have made in this Section 14.2.

15. EXPENSES, ETC.

15.1. Transaction Expenses. Whether or not the transactions contemplated hereby are consummated, the Company will pay all costs and expenses (including reasonable attorneys' fees of a special counsel and, if reasonably required, local or other counsel) incurred by you and each Other Purchaser or holder of a Note in connection with such transactions and in connection with any amendments, waivers or consents under or in respect of this Agreement or the Notes (whether or not such amendment, waiver or consent becomes effective), including, without limitation: (*a*) the costs and expenses incurred in enforcing or defending (or determining whether or how to enforce or defend) any rights under this Agreement or the Notes or in responding to any subpoena or other legal process or informal investigative demand issued in connection with this Agreement or the Notes, or by reason of being a holder of any Note, and (*b*) the costs and expenses, including financial advisors' fees, incurred in connection with the insolvency or bankruptcy of the Company or any Subsidiary or in connection with any work-out or restructuring of the transactions contemplated hereby and by the Notes. The Company will pay, and will save you and each other holder of a Note harmless from, all claims in respect of any fees, costs or expenses if any, of brokers and finders (other than those retained by you).

15.2. Survival. The obligations of the Company under this Section 15 will survive the payment or transfer of any Note, the enforcement, amendment or waiver of any provision of this Agreement or the Notes, and the termination of this Agreement.

16. SURVIVAL OF REPRESENTATIONS AND WARRANTIES; ENTIRE AGREEMENT.

All representations and warranties contained herein shall survive the execution and delivery of this Agreement and the Notes, the purchase or transfer by you of any Note or portion thereof or interest therein and the payment of any Note, and may be relied upon by any subsequent holder of a Note, regardless of any investigation made at any time by or on behalf of you or any other holder of a Note. All statements contained in any certificate or other instrument delivered by or on behalf of the Company pursuant to this Agreement shall be deemed representations and warranties of the Company under this Agreement. Subject to the preceding sentence, this Agreement and the Notes embody the entire agreement and understanding between you and the Company and supersede all prior agreements and understandings relating to the subject matter hereof.

17. AMENDMENT AND WAIVER.

[handwritten: 66.66%.]

[handwritten: - Required Holders: def A-88]
[handwritten: - 66.66% in principal amt of the notes at the time outstanding excluding notes owned by company & its affiliates]
[handwritten: - For interest & principal Δ: unanimous.]

17.1.   Requirements. This Agreement and the Notes may be amended, and the observance of any term hereof or of the Notes may be waived (either retroactively or prospectively), with (and only with) the written consent of the Company and the Required Holders, except that (*a*) no amendment or waiver of any of the provisions of Section 1, 2, 3, 4, 5, 6 or 21 hereof, or any defined term (as it is used therein), will be effective as to you unless consented to by you in writing, and (*b*) no such amendment or waiver may, without the written consent of the holder of each Note at the time outstanding affected thereby, (*i*) subject to the provisions of Section 12 relating to acceleration or rescission, change the amount or time of any prepayment or payment of principal of, or reduce the rate or change the time of payment or method of computation of interest or of the Make-Whole Amount on, the Notes, (*ii*) change the percentage of the principal amount of the Notes the holders of which are required to consent to any such amendment or waiver, or (*iii*) amend any of Sections 8, 11(a), 11(b), 12, 17 or 20.

17.2   Solicitation of Holders of Notes.

(a) *Solicitation.* The Company will provide each holder of the Notes (irrespective of the amount of Notes then owned by it) with sufficient information, sufficiently far in advance of the date a decision is required, to enable such holder to make an informed and considered decision with respect to any proposed amendment, waiver or consent in respect of any of the provisions hereof or of the Notes. The Company will deliver executed or true and correct copies of each amendment, waiver or consent effected pursuant to the provisions of this Section 17 to each holder of outstanding Notes promptly following the date on which it is executed and delivered by, or receives the consent or approval of, the requisite holders of Notes.

[handwritten: notRe!]

(b) *Payment.* The Company will not directly or indirectly pay or cause to be paid any remuneration, whether by way of supplemental or additional interest, fee or otherwise, or grant any security, to any holder of Notes as consideration for or as an inducement to the entering into by any holder of Notes or any waiver or amendment of any of the terms and provisions hereof unless such remuneration is concurrently paid, or security is concurrently granted, on the same terms, ratably to each holder of Notes then outstanding even if such holder did not consent to such waiver or amendment.

17.3   Binding Effect, etc. Any amendment or waiver consented to as provided in this Section 17 applies equally to all holders of Notes and is binding upon them and upon each future holder of any Note and upon the Company without regard to whether such Note has been marked to indicate such amendment or waiver. No such amendment or waiver will extend to or affect any obligation, covenant, agreement, Default or Event of Default not expressly amended or waived or impair any right consequent thereon. No course of dealing between the Company and the holder of any

Note nor any delay in exercising any rights hereunder or under any Note shall operate as a waiver of any rights of any holder of such Note. As used herein, the term **"this Agreement"** and references thereto shall mean this Agreement as it may from time to time be amended or supplemented.

17.4. Notes held by Company, etc. Solely for the purpose of determining whether the holders of the requisite percentage of the aggregate principal amount of Notes then outstanding approved or consented to any amendment, waiver or consent to be given under this Agreement or the Notes, or have directed the taking of any action provided herein or in the Notes to be taken upon the direction of the holders of a specified percentage of the aggregate principal amount of Notes then outstanding, <u>Notes directly or indirectly owned by the Company or any of its Affiliates shall be deemed not to be outstanding</u>.

18. NOTICES.

All notices and communications provided for hereunder shall be in writing and sent (*a*) by telecopy if the sender on the same day sends a confirming copy of such notice by a recognized overnight delivery service (charges prepaid), or (*b*) by registered or certified mail with return receipt requested (postage prepaid), or (*c*) by a recognized overnight delivery service (with charges prepaid). Any such notice must be sent:

(i) if to you or your nominee, to you or it at the address specified for such communications in Schedule A, or at such other address as you or it shall have specified to the Company in writing,

(ii) if to any other holder of any Note, to such holder at such address as such other holder shall have specified to the Company in writing, or

(iii) if to the Company, to the Company at its address set forth at the beginning hereof to the attention of [___], or at such other address as the Company shall have specified to the holder of each Note in writing.

Notices under this Section 18 will be deemed given only when actually received.

19. REPRODUCTION OF DOCUMENTS.

This Agreement and all documents relating thereto, including, without limitation, (*a*) consents, waivers and modifications that may hereafter be executed, (*b*) documents received by you at the Closing (except the Notes themselves), and (*c*) financial statements, certificates and other information previously or hereafter furnished to you, may be reproduced by you by any photographic, photostatic, microfilm, microcard, miniature photographic or other similar process and you may destroy any original document so reproduced. The Company agrees and stipulates that, to the extent permitted by applicable law, any such reproduction shall be admissible in evidence as the original itself in any judicial or administrative proceeding (whether or not the original is in existence and whether or not such reproduction was made by you in the regular course of business) and any enlargement, facsimile or further reproduction of such reproduction shall likewise be admissible in evidence. This Section 19 shall not prohibit the Company or any other holder of Notes from contesting any such reproduction to the same extent that it could contest the original, or from introducing evidence to demonstrate the inaccuracy of any such reproduction.

20.   CONFIDENTIAL INFORMATION.

For the purposes of this Section 20, **"Confidential Information"** means information delivered to you by or on behalf of the Company or any Subsidiary in connection with the transactions contemplated by or otherwise pursuant to this Agreement that is proprietary in nature and that was clearly marked or labeled or otherwise adequately identified when received by you as being confidential information of the Company or such Subsidiary, *provided* that such term does not include information that (*a*) was publicly known or otherwise known to you prior to the time of such disclosure, (*b*) subsequently becomes publicly known through no act or omission by you or any person acting on your behalf, (*c*) otherwise becomes known to you other than through disclosure by the Company or any Subsidiary or (*d*) constitutes financial statements delivered to you under Section 7.1 that are otherwise publicly available. You will maintain the confidentiality of such Confidential Information in accordance with procedures adopted by you in good faith to protect confidential information of third parties delivered to you, *provided* that you may deliver or disclose Confidential Information to (*i*) your directors, officers, employees, agents, attorneys and affiliates (to the extent such disclosure reasonably relates to the administration of the investment represented by your Notes), (*ii*) your financial advisors and other professional advisors who agree to hold confidential the Confidential Information substantially in accordance with the terms of this Section 20, (*iii*) any other holder of any Note, (*iv*) any Institutional Investor to which you sell or offer to sell such Note or any part thereof or any participation therein (if such Person has agreed in writing prior to its receipt of such Confidential Information to be bound by the provisions of this Section 20), (*v*) any Person from which you offer to purchase any security of the Company (if such Person has agreed in writing prior to its receipt of such Confidential Information to be bound by the provisions of this Section 20), (*vi*) any federal or state regulatory authority having jurisdiction over you, (*vii*) the National Association of Insurance Commissioners or any similar organization, or any nationally recognized rating agency that requires access to information about your investment portfolio or (*viii*) any other Person to which such delivery or disclosure may be necessary or appropriate (*w*) to effect compliance with any law, rule, regulation or order applicable to you, (*x*) in response to any subpoena or other legal process, (*y*) in connection with any litigation to which you are a party or (*z*) if an Event of Default has occurred and is continuing, to the extent you may reasonably determine such delivery and disclosure to be necessary or appropriate in the enforcement or for the protection of the rights and remedies under your Notes and this Agreement. Each holder of a Note, by its acceptance of a Note, will be deemed to have agreed to be bound by and to be entitled to the benefits of this Section 20 as though it were a party to this Agreement. On reasonable request by the Company in connection with the delivery to any holder of a Note of information required to be delivered to such holder under this Agreement or requested by such holder (other than a holder that is a party to this Agreement or its nominee), such holder will enter into an agreement with the Company embodying the provisions of this Section 20.

21. SUBSTITUTION OF PURCHASER.

You shall have the right to substitute any one of your Affiliates as the purchaser of the Notes that you have agreed to purchase hereunder, by written notice to the Company, which notice shall be signed by both you and such Affiliate, shall contain such Affiliate's agreement to be bound by this Agreement and shall contain a confirmation by such Affiliate of the accuracy with respect to it of the representations set forth in Section 6. Upon receipt of such notice, wherever the word "you" is used in this Agreement (other than in this Section 21), such word shall be deemed to refer to such Affiliate in lieu of you. In the event that such Affiliate is so substituted as a purchaser hereunder and such Affiliate thereafter transfers to you all of the Notes then held by such Affiliate, upon receipt by the Company of notice of such transfer, wherever the word "you" is used in this Agreement (other than in this Section 21), such word shall no longer be deemed to refer to such Affiliate, but shall refer to you, and you shall have all the rights of an original holder of the Notes under this Agreement.

22. MISCELLANEOUS.

22.1. Successors and Assigns. All covenants and other agreements contained in this Agreement by or on behalf of any of the parties hereto bind and inure to the benefit of their respective successors and assigns (including, without limitation, any subsequent holder of a Note) whether so expressed or not.

22.2. Payments Due on Non–Business Days. Anything in this Agreement or the Notes to the contrary notwithstanding, any payment of principal of or Make-whole Amount or interest on any Note that is due on a date other than a Business Day shall be made on the next succeeding Business Day without including the additional days elapsed in the computation of the interest payable on such next succeeding Business Day.

22.3. Severability. Any provision of this Agreement that is prohibited or unenforceable in any jurisdiction shall, as to such jurisdiction, be ineffective to the extent of such prohibition or unenforceability without invalidating the remaining provisions hereof, and any such prohibition or unenforceability in any jurisdiction shall (to the full extent permitted by law) not invalidate or render unenforceable such provision in any other jurisdiction.

22.4. Construction. Each covenant contained herein shall be construed (absent express provision to the contrary) as being independent of each other covenant contained herein, so that compliance with any one covenant shall not (absent such an express contrary provision) be deemed to excuse compliance with any other covenant. Where any provision herein refers to action to be taken by any Person, or which such Person is prohibited from taking, such provision shall be applicable whether such action is taken directly or indirectly by such Person.

22.5. Counterparts. This Agreement may be executed in any number of counterparts, each of which shall be an original but all of which together shall constitute one instrument. Each counterpart may consist of a number of copies hereof, each signed by less than all, but together signed by all, of the parties hereto.

22.6. Governing Law. This Agreement shall be construed and enforced in accordance with, and the rights of the parties shall be governed by, the law of the State of New York excluding choice-of-law principles of the law of such State that would require the application of the laws of a jurisdiction other than such State.

* * *

If you are in agreement with the foregoing, please sign the form of agreement on the accompanying counterpart of this Agreement and return it to the Company, whereupon the foregoing shall become a binding agreement between you and the Company.

Very truly yours,

GENERAL TECHNOLOGY, INC.

By _____

[Title]

The foregoing is hereby agreed to as of the date thereof.

[ADD PURCHASER SIGNATURE BLOCKS]

SCHEDULE A

INFORMATION RELATING TO PURCHASERS

Name and Address of Purchaser	Principal Amount of Notes to be Purchased
[NAME OF PURCHASER]	$

(1)   All payments by wire transfer of immediately available funds to:

     with sufficient information to identify the source and application of such funds.

(2)   All notices of payments and written confirmations of such wire transfers:

(3)   All other communications:

SCHEDULE B

DEFINED TERMS

As used herein, the following terms have the respective meanings set forth below or set forth in the Section hereof following such term:

"Affiliate" means, at any time, and with respect to any Person, (a) any other Person that at such time directly or indirectly through one or more intermediaries Controls, or is Controlled by, or is under common Control with, such first Person, and (b) any Person beneficially owning or holding, directly or indirectly, 10% or more of any class of voting or equity interests of the Company or any Subsidiary or any corporation of which the Company and its Subsidiaries beneficially own or hold, in the aggregate, directly or indirectly, 10% or more of any class of voting or equity interests. As used in this definition, **"Control"** means the possession, directly or indirectly, of the power to direct or cause the direction of the management and policies of a Person, whether through the ownership of voting securities, by contract or otherwise. Unless the context otherwise clearly requires, any reference to an "Affiliate" is a reference to an Affiliate of the Company.

"Asset Disposition" means any Transfer except:

(a) any

(i) Transfer from a Subsidiary to the Company or a Wholly–Owned Subsidiary;

(ii) Transfer from the Company to a Wholly–Owned Subsidiary; and

(iii) Transfer from the Company to a Subsidiary (other than a Wholly–Owned Subsidiary) or from a Subsidiary to another Subsidiary, which in either case is for Fair Market Value,

so long as immediately before and immediately after the consummation of any such Transfer and after giving effect thereto, no Default or Event of Default exists; and

(b) any Transfer made in the ordinary course of business and involving only property that is either (*i*) inventory held for sale or (*ii*) equipment, fixtures, supplies or materials no longer required in the operation of the business of the Company or any of its Subsidiaries or that is obsolete.

"Business Day" means (*a*) for the purposes of Section 8.6 only, any day other than a Saturday, a Sunday or a day on which commercial banks in New York City are required or authorized to be closed, and (*b*) for the purposes of any other provision of this Agreement, any day other than a Saturday, a Sunday or a day on which commercial banks in Burns, Stockton or New York, New York are required or authorized to be closed.

"Capital Lease" means, at any time, a lease with respect to which the lessee is required concurrently to recognize the acquisition of an asset and the incurrence of a liability in accordance with GAAP.

"**Capital Lease Obligation**" means, with respect to any Person and a Capital Lease, the amount of the obligation of such Person as the lessee under such Capital Lease which would, in accordance with GAAP, appear as a liability on a balance sheet of such Person.

"**Closing**" is defined in Section 3.

"**Code**" means the Internal Revenue Code of 1986, as amended from time to time, and the rules and regulations promulgated thereunder from time to time.

"**Company**" means General Technology, Inc., a Delaware corporation.

"**Confidential Information**" is defined in Section 20.

"**Consolidated Assets**" means, at any time, the total assets of the Company and its Subsidiaries which would be shown as assets on a consolidated balance sheet of the Company and its Subsidiaries as of such time prepared in accordance with GAAP, after eliminating all amounts properly attributable to minority interests, if any, in the stock and surplus of Subsidiaries.

"**Consolidated Cash Flow**" means, in respect of any period, the sum of (*a*) Consolidated Net Income for such period and (*b*) the amount of all depreciation and amortization allowances and other non-cash expenses of the Company and its Subsidiaries but only to the extent deducted in the determination of Consolidated Net Income for such period.

"**Consolidated Current Assets**" means, at any time, the total assets of the Company and its Subsidiaries which would be shown as current assets on a balance sheet of the Company and its Subsidiaries prepared in accordance with GAAP at such time, *provided* that in determining such current assets (*a*) notes and accounts receivable shall be included only if good and collectible and payable on demand or within one year from such date (and not by their terms or by the terms of any instrument or agreement relating thereto directly or indirectly renewable or extendible at the option of the obligor beyond such year) and shall be valued at their face value less reserves or accruals for uncollectible accounts determined to be sufficient in accordance with GAAP, (*b*) life insurance policies (other than the cash surrender value of any unencumbered policies that is properly classified as a current asset in accordance with GAAP) shall be excluded, and (*c*) Restricted Investments shall be excluded.

"**Consolidated Current Debt**" means, as of any date of determination, the total of all Current Debt of the Company and its Subsidiaries outstanding on such date, after eliminating all offsetting debits and credits between the Company and its Subsidiaries and all other items required to be eliminated in the course of the preparation of consolidated financial statements of the Company and its Subsidiaries in accordance with GAAP.

"**Consolidated Current Liabilities**" means, at any time, the total liabilities of the Company and its Subsidiaries which would be shown as current liabilities on a balance sheet of the Company and its Subsidiaries prepared in accordance with GAAP at such time, but in any event including as current liabilities, without limitation, Current Maturities of Funded Debt.

"Consolidated Funded Debt" means, as of any date of determination, the total of all Funded Debt of the Company and its Subsidiaries outstanding on such date, after eliminating all offsetting debits and credits between the Company and its Subsidiaries and all other items required to be eliminated in the course of the preparation of consolidated financial statements of the Company and its Subsidiaries in accordance with GAAP.

"Consolidated Income Available for Interest Charges" means, with respect to any period, Consolidated Net Income for such period plus all amounts deducted in the computation thereof on account of (a) Interest Charges and (b) taxes imposed on or measured by income or excess profits.

"Consolidated Net Income" means, with reference to any period, the net income (or loss) of the Company and its Subsidiaries for such period (taken as a cumulative whole), as determined in accordance with GAAP, after eliminating all offsetting debits and credits between the Company and its Subsidiaries and all other items required to be eliminated in the course of the preparation of consolidated financial statements of the Company and its Subsidiaries in accordance with GAAP, *provided* that there shall be excluded:

> (a) the income (or loss) of any Person accrued prior to the date it becomes a Subsidiary or is merged into or consolidated with the Company or a Subsidiary, and the income (or loss) of any Person, substantially all of the assets of which have been acquired in any manner, realized by such other Person prior to the date of acquisition,

> (b) the income (or loss) of any Person (other than a Subsidiary) in which the Company or any Subsidiary has an ownership interest, except to the extent that any such income has been actually received by the Company or such Subsidiary in the form of cash dividends or similar cash distributions,

> (c) the undistributed earnings of any Subsidiary to the extent that the declaration or payment of dividends or similar distributions by such Subsidiary is not at the time permitted by the terms of its charter or any agreement, instrument, judgment, decree, order, statute, rule or governmental regulation applicable to such Subsidiary,

> (d) any restoration to income of any contingency reserve, except to the extent that provision for such reserve was made out of income accrued during such period,

> (e) any aggregate net gain (but not any aggregate net loss) during such period arising from the sale, conversion, exchange or other disposition of capital assets (such term to include, without limitation, (*i*) all non-current assets and, without duplication, (*ii*) the following, whether or not current: all fixed assets, whether tangible or intangible, all inventory sold in conjunction with the disposition of fixed assets, and all Securities),

(f) any gains resulting from any write-up of any assets (but not any loss resulting from any write-down of any assets),

(g) any net gain from the collection of the proceeds of life insurance policies,

(h) any gain arising from the acquisition of any Security, or the extinguishment, under GAAP, of any Debt, of the Company or any Subsidiary,

(i) any net income or gain (but not any net loss) during such period from (*i*) any change in accounting principles in accordance with GAAP, (*ii*) any prior period adjustments resulting from any change in accounting principles in accordance with GAAP, (*iii*) any extraordinary items, or (*iv*) any discontinued operations or the disposition thereof,

(j) any deferred credit representing the excess of equity in any Subsidiary at the date of acquisition over the cost of the investment in such Subsidiary,

(k) in the case of a successor to the Company by consolidation or merger or as a transferee of its assets, any earnings of the successor corporation prior to such consolidation, merger or transfer of assets, and

(*l*) any portion of such net income that cannot be freely converted into United States Dollars.

"**Consolidated Net Worth**" means, at any time,

(a) the total assets of the Company and its Subsidiaries which would be shown as assets on a consolidated balance sheet of the Company and its Subsidiaries as of such time prepared in accordance with GAAP, after eliminating all amounts properly attributable to minority interests, if any, in the stock and surplus of Subsidiaries, *minus*

(b) the total liabilities of the Company and its Subsidiaries which would be shown as liabilities on a consolidated balance sheet of the Company and its Subsidiaries as of such time prepared in accordance with GAAP, *minus*

(c) the net book value of all assets, after deducting any reserves applicable thereto, which would be treated as intangible under GAAP, including, without limitation, good will, trademarks, trade names, service marks, brand names, copyrights, patents and unamortized debt discount and expense, organizational expenses and the excess of the equity in any Subsidiary over the cost of the investment in such Subsidiary, *minus*

(d) any increase in the amount of Consolidated Net Worth attributable to a write-up in the book value of any asset on the books of the Company resulting from a revaluation thereof subsequent to June 30, 2006, *minus*

(e) the amounts, if any, at which any shares of capital stock of the Company or any Subsidiary appear as an asset on the balance sheet from which Consolidated Net Worth is determined for the purposes of this definition, *minus*

> (f) all deferred assets (other than prepaid taxes and other expenses), *minus*

> (g) the book value of all Restricted Investments.

"Current Debt" means, with respect to any Person, all Debt of such Person which by its terms or by the terms of any instrument or agreement relating thereto matures on demand or within one year from the date of the creation thereof and is not directly or indirectly renewable or extendible at the option of the obligor in respect thereof to a date one year or more from such date, *provided* that Debt outstanding under a revolving credit or similar agreement which obligates the lender or lenders to extend credit over a period of one year or more shall constitute Funded Debt and not Current Debt, even though such Debt by its terms matures on demand or within one year from such date.

"Current Maturities of Funded Debt" means, at any time and with respect to any item of Funded Debt, the portion of such Funded Debt outstanding at such time which by the terms of such Funded Debt or the terms of any instrument or agreement relating thereto is due on demand or within one year from such time (whether by sinking fund, other required prepayment or final payment at maturity) and is not directly or indirectly renewable, extendible or refundable at the option of the obligor under an agreement or firm commitment in effect at such time to a date one year or more from such time.

"Debt" means, with respect to any Person, without duplication,

> (a) its liabilities for borrowed money and its redemption obligations in respect of Redeemable Preferred Stock;

trade payable (b) its liabilities for the deferred purchase price of property acquired by such Person (excluding accounts payable arising in the ordinary course of business but including, without limitation, all liabilities created or arising under any conditional sale or other title retention agreement with respect to any such property);

> (c) its Capital Lease Obligations;

> (d) all liabilities for borrowed money secured by any Lien with respect to any property owned by such Person (whether or not it has assumed or otherwise become liable for such liabilities);

> (e) all its liabilities in respect of letters of credit or instruments serving a similar function issued or accepted for its account by banks and other financial institutions (whether or not representing obligations for borrowed money);

> (f) Swaps of such Person; and

> (g) any Guaranty of such Person with respect to liabilities of a type described in any of clauses (a) through (f) hereof.

Debt of any Person shall include all obligations of such Person of the character described in clauses (a) through (g) to the extent such Person remains legally liable in respect thereof notwithstanding that any such obligation is deemed to be extinguished under GAAP.

"Default" means an event or condition the occurrence or existence of which would, with the lapse of time or the giving of notice or both, become an Event of Default.

"Default Rate" means that rate of interest that is the greater of (*i*) 2% per annum above the rate of interest stated in clause (a) of the first paragraph of the Notes or (*ii*) 2% over the rate of interest publicly announced by Chemical Manhattan Bank in New York, New York as its "base" or "prime" rate.

"Disposition Value" means, at any time, with respect to any property

(a) in the case of property that does not constitute Subsidiary Stock, the book value thereof, valued at the time of such disposition in good faith by the Company, and

(b) in the case of property that constitutes Subsidiary Stock, an amount equal to that percentage of book value of the assets of the Subsidiary that issued such stock as is equal to the percentage that the book value of such Subsidiary Stock represents of the book value of all of the outstanding capital stock of such Subsidiary (assuming, in making such calculations, that all Securities convertible into such capital stock are so converted and giving full effect to all transactions that would occur or be required in connection with such conversion) determined at the time of the disposition thereof, in good faith by the Company.

"Distribution" means, in respect of any corporation, association or other business entity:

(a) dividends or other distributions or payments on capital stock or other equity interest of such corporation, association or other business entity (except distributions in such stock or other equity interest); and

(b) the redemption or acquisition of such stock or other equity interests or of warrants, rights or other options to purchase such stock or other equity interests (except when solely in exchange for such stock or other equity interests) unless made, contemporaneously, from the net proceeds of a sale of such stock or other equity interests.

"Environmental Laws" means any and all Federal, state, local, and foreign statutes, laws, regulations, ordinances, rules, judgments, orders, decrees, permits, concessions, grants, franchises, licenses, agreements or governmental restrictions relating to pollution and the protection of the environment or the release of any materials into the environment, including but not limited to those related to hazardous substances or wastes, air emissions and discharges to waste or public systems.

"ERISA" means the Employee Retirement Income Security Act of 1974, as amended from time to time, and the rules and regulations promulgated thereunder from time to time in effect.

"ERISA Affiliate" means any trade or business (whether or not incorporated) that is treated as a single employer together with the Company under section 414 of the Code.

"Event of Default" is defined in Section 11.

"Exchange Act" means the Securities Exchange Act of 1934, as amended.

"Fair Market Value" means, at any time and with respect to any property, the sale value of such property that would be realized in an arm's-length sale at such time between an informed and willing buyer and an informed and willing seller (neither being under a compulsion to buy or sell).

"Funded Debt" means, with respect to any Person, all Debt of such Person which by its terms or by the terms of any instrument or agreement relating thereto matures, or which is otherwise payable or unpaid, one year or more from, or is directly or indirectly renewable or extendible at the option of the obligor in respect thereof to a date one year or more (including, without limitation, an option of such obligor under a revolving credit or similar agreement obligating the lender or lenders to extend credit over a period of one year or more) from, the date of the creation thereof.

"GAAP" means generally accepted accounting principles as in effect from time to time in the United States of America.

"Governmental Authority" means

    (a) the government of

        (i) the United States of America or any State or other political subdivision thereof, or

        (ii) any jurisdiction in which the Company or any Subsidiary conducts all or any part of its business, or which asserts jurisdiction over any properties of the Company or any Subsidiary, or

    (b) any entity exercising executive, legislative, judicial, regulatory or administrative functions of, or pertaining to, any such government.

"Guaranty" means, with respect to any Person, any obligation (except the endorsement in the ordinary course of business of negotiable instruments for deposit or collection) of such Person guaranteeing or in effect guaranteeing any indebtedness, dividend or other obligation of any other Person in any manner, whether directly or indirectly, including (without limitation) obligations incurred through an agreement, contingent or otherwise, by such Person:

    (a) to purchase such indebtedness or obligation or any property constituting security therefor;

    (b) to advance or supply funds (*i*) for the purchase or payment of such indebtedness or obligation, or (*ii*) to maintain any working capital or other balance sheet condition or any income statement condition of any other Person or otherwise to advance or make available funds for the purchase or payment of such indebtedness or obligation;

(c) to lease properties or to purchase properties or services primarily for the purpose of assuring the owner of such indebtedness or obligation of the ability of any other Person to make payment of the indebtedness or obligation; or

(d) otherwise to assure the owner of such indebtedness or obligation against loss in respect thereof.

In any computation of the indebtedness or other liabilities of the obligor under any Guaranty, the indebtedness or other obligations that are the subject of such Guaranty shall be assumed to be direct obligations of such obligor.

"Hazardous Material" means any and all pollutants, toxic or hazardous wastes or any other substances that might pose a hazard to health or safety, the removal of which may be required or the generation, manufacture, refining, production, processing, treatment, storage, handling, transportation, transfer, use, disposal, release, discharge, spillage, seepage, or filtration of which is or shall be restricted, prohibited or penalized by any applicable law (including, without limitation, asbestos, urea formaldehyde foam insulation and polycholorinated biphenyls).

"holder" means, with respect to any Note, the Person in whose name such Note is registered in the register maintained by the Company pursuant to Section 13.1.

"Institutional Investor" means (*a*) any original purchaser of a Note, (*b*) any holder of a Note holding more than 5% of the aggregate principal amount of the Notes then outstanding, and (*c*) any bank, trust company, savings and loan association or other financial institution, any pension plan, any investment company, any insurance company, any broker or dealer, or any other similar financial institution or entity, regardless of legal form.

"Interest Charges" means, with respect to any period, the sum (without duplication) of the following (in each case, eliminating all offsetting debits and credits between the Company and its Subsidiaries and all other items required to be eliminated in the course of the preparation of consolidated financial statements of the Company and its Subsidiaries in accordance with GAAP): (*a*) all interest in respect of Debt of the Company and its Subsidiaries (including imputed interest on Capital Lease Obligations) deducted in determining Consolidated Net Income for such period, and (*b*) all debt discount and expense amortized or required to be amortized in the determination of Consolidated Net Income for such period.

"Interest Charges Coverage Ratio" means, at any time, the ratio of (*a*) Consolidated Income Available for Interest Charges for the fiscal year most recently ended prior to, such time to (*b*) Interest Charges for such year.

"Investment" means any investment, made in cash or by delivery of property, by the Company or any of its Subsidiaries (*i*) in any Person, whether by acquisition of stock, Debt or other obligation or Security, or by loan, Guaranty, advance, capital contribution or otherwise, or (*ii*) in any property.

"Lien" means, with respect to any Person, any mortgage, lien, pledge, charge, security interest or other encumbrance, or any interest or title of any vendor, lessor, lender or other secured party to or of such Person under any conditional sale or other title retention agreement or Capital Lease, upon or with respect to any property or asset of such Person (including in the case of stock, stockholder agreements, voting trust agreements and all similar arrangements).

"Long Term Lease Rentals" means, with respect to any period, the sum of the minimum amount of rental and other obligations required to be paid during such period by the Company or any Subsidiary as lessee under all leases of real or personal property (other than Capital Leases) having a term (including terms of renewal or extension at the option of the lessor or the lessee, whether or not such option has been exercised) expiring more than one year after the commencement of the initial term, *excluding* any amounts required to be paid by the lessee (whether or not therein designated as rental or additional rental) (*a*) which are on account of maintenance and repairs, insurance, taxes, assessments, water rates and similar charges, or (*b*) which are based on profits, revenues or sales realized by the lessee from the leased property or otherwise based on the performance of the lessee.

"Make–Whole Amount" is defined in Section 8.6.

"Material" means material in relation to the business, operations, affairs, financial condition, assets, properties, or prospects of the Company and its Subsidiaries taken as a whole.

"Material Adverse Effect" means a material adverse effect on (*a*) the business, operations, affairs, financial condition, assets or properties of the Company and its Subsidiaries taken as a whole, or (*b*) the ability of the Company to perform its obligations under this Agreement and the Notes, or (*c*) the validity or enforceability of this Agreement or the Notes.

"Memorandum" is defined in Section 5.3.

"Multiemployer Plan" means any Plan that is a "multiemployer plan" (as such term is defined in section 4001(a)(3) of ERISA).

"Net Proceeds Amount" means, with respect to any Transfer of any Property by any Person, an amount equal to the *difference* of

    (a) the aggregate amount of the consideration (valued at the Fair Market Value of such consideration at the time of the consummation of such Transfer) received by such Person in respect of such Transfer, *minus*

    (b) all ordinary and reasonable out-of-pocket costs and expenses actually incurred by such Person in connection with such Transfer.

"Net Proceeds of Capital Stock" means, with respect to any period, cash proceeds (net of all costs and out-of-pocket expenses in connection therewith, including, without limitation, placement, underwriting and brokerage fees and expenses), received by the Company and its Subsidiaries during such period, from the sale of all capital stock (other than Redeemable capital stock) of the Company, including in such net proceeds:

(a) the net amount paid upon issuance and exercise during such period of any right to acquire any capital stock, or paid during such period to convert a convertible debt Security to capital stock (but excluding any amount paid to the Company upon issuance of such convertible debt Security); and

(b) any amount paid to the Company upon issuance of any convertible debt Security issued after June 30, 2006 and thereafter converted to capital stock during such period.

"Notes" is defined in Section 1.

"Officer's Certificate" means a certificate of a Senior Financial Officer or of any other officer of the Company whose responsibilities extend to the subject matter of such certificate.

"Other Agreements" is defined in Section 2.

"Other Purchasers" is defined in Section 2.

"PBGC" means the Pension Benefit Guaranty Corporation referred to and defined in ERISA or any successor thereto.

"Person" means an individual, partnership, corporation, limited liability company, association, trust, unincorporated organization, or a government or agency or political subdivision thereof.

"Plan" means an "employee benefit plan" (as defined in section 3(3) of ERISA) that is or, within the preceding five years, has been established or maintained, or to which contributions are or, within the preceding five years, have been made or required to be made, by the Company or any ERISA Affiliate or with respect to which the Company or any ERISA Affiliate may have any liability.

"Preferred Stock" means any class of capital stock of a corporation that is preferred over any other class of capital stock of such corporation as to the payment of dividends or the payment of any amount upon liquidation or dissolution of such corporation.

"property" or **"properties"** means, unless otherwise specifically limited, real or personal property of any kind, tangible or intangible, choate or inchoate.

"QPAM Exemption" means Prohibited Transaction Class Exemption 84–14 issued by the United States Department of Labor.

"Redeemable" means, with respect to the capital stock of any Person, each share of such Person's capital stock that is:

(a) redeemable, payable or required to be purchased or otherwise retired or extinguished, or convertible into Debt of such Person (i) at a fixed or determinable date, whether by operation of sinking fund or otherwise, (ii) at the option of any Person other than such Person, or (iii) upon the occurrence of a condition not solely within the control of such Person; or

(b) convertible into other Redeemable capital stock.

"Required Holders" means, at any time, the holders of at least 66 2/3% in principal amount of the Notes at the time outstanding (exclusive of Notes then owned by the Company or any of its Affiliates).

"Responsible Officer" means any Senior Financial Officer and any other officer of the Company with responsibility for the administration of the relevant portion of this agreement.

"Restricted Investments" means all Investments except the following:

(a) property to be used in the ordinary course of business of the Company and its Subsidiaries;

(b) current assets arising from the sale of goods and services in the ordinary course of business of the Company and its Subsidiaries;

(c) Investments in one or more Subsidiaries or any Person that concurrently with such Investment becomes a Wholly–Owned Subsidiary;

(d) Investments existing on the date of the Closing and disclosed in Schedule 5.3;

(e) Investments in United States Governmental Securities, *provided* that such obligations mature within 365 days from the date of acquisition thereof;

(f) Investments in certificates of deposit or banker's acceptances issued by an Acceptable Bank, *provided* that such obligations mature within 365 days from the date of acquisition thereof;

(g) Investments in commercial paper given the highest rating by a credit rating agency of recognized national standing and maturing not more than 270 days from the date of creation thereof;

(h) Investments in Repurchase Agreements; and

(i) Investments in tax-exempt obligations of any state of the United States of America, or any municipality of any such state, in each case rated "AA" or better by S & P, "Aa2" or better by Moody's or an equivalent rating by any other credit rating agency of recognized national standing, *provided* that such obligations mature within 365 days from the date of acquisition thereof.

As of any date of determination, each Restricted Investment shall be valued at the greater of:

(x) the amount at which such Restricted Investment is shown on the books of the Company or any of its Subsidiaries (or zero if such Restricted Investment is not shown on any such books); and

(y) either

(i) in the case of any Guaranty of the obligation of any Person, the amount which the Company or any of its Subsidiaries has paid on account of such obligation less any recoupment by the Company or such Subsidiary of any such payments, or

(ii) in the case of any other Restricted Investment, the excess of (x) the greater of (A) the amount originally entered on the books of the Company or any of its Subsidiaries with respect thereto and (B) the cost thereof to the Company or its Subsidiary over (y) any return of capital (after income taxes applicable thereto) upon such Restricted Investment through the sale or other liquidation thereof or part thereof or otherwise.

As used in this definition of "Restricted Investments":

"Acceptable Bank" means any bank or trust company (i) which is organized under the laws of the United States of America or any State thereof, (ii) which has capital, surplus and undivided profits aggregating at least $100,000,000, and (iii) whose long-term unsecured debt obligations (or the long-term unsecured debt obligations of the bank holding company owning all of the capital stock of such bank or trust company) shall have been given a rating of "A" or better by S & P, "A2" or better by Moody's or an equivalent rating by any other credit rating agency of recognized national standing.

"Acceptable Broker–Dealer" means any Person other than a natural person (i) which is registered as a broker or dealer pursuant to the Exchange Act and (ii) whose long-term unsecured debt obligations shall have been given a rating of "A" or better by S & P, "A2" or better by Moody's or an equivalent rating by any other credit rating agency of recognized national standing.

"Moody's" means Moody's Investors Service, Inc.

"Repurchase Agreement" means any written agreement

(a) that provides for (i) the transfer of one or more United States Governmental Securities in an aggregate principal amount at least equal to the amount of the Transfer Price (defined below) to the Company or any of its Subsidiaries from an Acceptable Bank or an Acceptable Broker–Dealer against a transfer of funds (the "Transfer Price") by the Company or such Subsidiary to such Acceptable Bank or Acceptable Broker–Dealer, and (ii) a simultaneous agreement by the Company or such Subsidiary, in connection with such transfer of funds, to transfer to such Acceptable Bank or Acceptable Broker–Dealer the same or substantially similar United States Governmental Securities for a price not less than the Transfer Price plus a reasonable return thereon at a date certain not later than 365 days after such transfer of funds,

(b) in respect of which the Company or such Subsidiary shall have the right, whether by contract or pursuant to applicable law, to liquidate such agreement upon the occurrence of any default thereunder, and

(c) in connection with which the Company or such Subsidiary, or an agent thereof, shall have taken all action required by applicable law or regulations to perfect a Lien in such United States Governmental Securities.

"S & P" means Standard & Poor's Ratings Group, a division of McGraw Hill, Inc.

"United States Governmental Security" means any direct obligation of, or obligation guaranteed by, the United States of America, or any agency controlled or supervised by or acting as an instrumentality of the United States of America pursuant to authority granted by the Congress of the United States of America, so long as such obligation or guarantee shall have the benefit of the full faith and credit of the United States of America which shall have been pledged pursuant to authority granted by the Congress of the United States of America.

"Restricted Payment" means any Distribution in respect of the Company or any Subsidiary of the Company (other than on account of capital stock or other equity interests of a Subsidiary owned legally and beneficially by the Company or another Subsidiary), including, without limitation, any Distribution resulting in the acquisition by the Company of Securities which would constitute treasury stock. For purposes of this Agreement, the amount of any Restricted Payment made in property shall be the greater of (x) the Fair Market Value of such property (as determined in good faith by the board of directors (or equivalent governing body) of the Person making such Restricted Payment) and (y) the net book value thereof on the books of such Person, in each case determined as of the date on which such Restricted Payment is made.

"Sale-and-Leaseback Transaction" means a transaction or series of transactions pursuant to which the Company or any Subsidiary shall sell or transfer to any Person (other than the Company or a Subsidiary) any property, whether now owned or hereafter acquired, and, as part of the same transaction or series of transactions, the Company or any Subsidiary shall rent or lease as lessee (other than pursuant to a Capital Lease), or similarly acquire the right to possession or use of, such property or one or more properties which it intends to use for the same purpose or purposes as such property.

"Securities Act" means the Securities Act of 1933, as amended from time to time.

"Security" has the meaning set forth in section 2(1) of the Securities Act of 1933, as amended.

"Senior Financial Officer" means the chief financial officer, principal accounting officer, treasurer or comptroller of the Company.

"Subsidiary" means, as to any Person, any corporation, association or other business entity in which such Person or one or more of its Subsidiaries or such Person and one or more of its Subsidiaries owns sufficient equity or voting interests to enable it or them (as a group) ordinarily, in the absence of contingencies, to elect a majority of the directors (or Persons performing similar functions) of such entity, and any partnership or joint venture if more than a 50% interest in the profits or capital thereof is owned by such Person or one or more of its Subsidiaries or such Person and one or more of its Subsidiaries (unless such partnership can and does ordinarily take major business actions without the prior approval of such Person or one or more of its Subsidiaries). Unless the context otherwise clearly requires, any reference to a "Subsidiary" is a reference to a Subsidiary of the Company.

"Subsidiary Stock" means, with respect to any Person, the stock (or any options or warrants to purchase stock or other Securities exchangeable for or convertible into stock) of any Subsidiary of such Person.

"Swaps" means, with respect to any Person, payment obligations with respect to interest rate swaps, currency swaps and similar obligations obligating such Person to make payments, whether periodically or upon the happening of a contingency. For the purposes of this Agreement, the amount of the obligation under any Swap shall be the amount determined in respect thereof as of the end of the then most recently ended fiscal quarter of such Person, based on the assumption that such Swap had terminated at the end of such fiscal quarter, and in making such determination, if any agreement relating to such Swap provides for the netting of amounts payable by and to such Person thereunder or if any such agreement provides for the simultaneous payment of amounts by and to such Person, then in each such case, the amount of such obligation shall be the net amount so determined.

"Transfer" means, with respect to any Person, any transaction in which such Person sells, conveys, transfers or leases (as lessor) any of its property, including, without limitation, Subsidiary Stock. For purposes of determining the application of the Net Proceeds Amount in respect of any Transfer, the Company may designate any Transfer as one or more separate Transfers each yielding a separate Net Proceeds Amount.

"Wholly–Owned Subsidiary" means, at any time, any Subsidiary one hundred percent (100%) of all of the equity interests (except directors' qualifying shares) and voting interests of which are owned by any one or more of the Company and the Company's other Wholly–Owned Subsidiaries at such time.

EXHIBIT 1

[FORM OF NOTE]

GENERAL TECHNOLOGY, INC.

8% SENIOR NOTE DUE February 1, 2022

No. [_____]   February 1, 2007
$[_____]   PPN[_____]

FOR VALUE RECEIVED, the undersigned, GENERAL TECHNOLO-GY, INC. (herein called the "Company"), a corporation organized and existing under the laws of the State of Delaware, hereby promises to pay to [_____], or registered assigns, the principal sum of [_____] DOLLARS on February 1, 2022, with interest (computed on the basis of a 360–day year of twelve 30–day months) (*a*) on the unpaid balance thereof at the rate of 8% per annum from the date hereof, payable semiannually, on the 1st day of February and July in each year, commencing with the July 1 next succeeding the date hereof, until the principal hereof shall have become due and payable, and (*b*) to the extent permitted by law on any overdue payment (including any overdue prepayment) of principal, any overdue payment of interest and any overdue payment of any Make–Whole Amount (as defined in the Note Purchase Agreements referred to below), payable [semiannually] as aforesaid (or, at the option of the registered holder hereof, on demand), at a rate per annum from time to time equal to the greater of (*i*) 10% or (*ii*) 2% over the rate of interest publicly announced by Manhattan Chemical Bank from time to time in New York, New York as its "base" or "prime" rate.

Payments of principal of, interest on and any Make–Whole Amount with respect to this Note are to be made in lawful money of the United States of America at New York, New York at the principal office of Manhattan Chemical Bank, N.A. or at such other place as the Company shall have designated by written notice to the holder of this Note as provided in the Note Purchase Agreements referred to below.

This Note is one of a series of Senior Notes (herein called the "Notes") issued pursuant to separate Note Purchase Agreements, dated as of January 27, 2007 (as from time to time amended, the "Note Purchase Agreements"), between the Company and the respective Purchasers named therein and is entitled to the benefits thereof. Each holder of this Note will be deemed, by its acceptance hereof, (*i*) to have agreed to the confidentiality provisions set forth in Section 20 of the Note Purchase Agreements and (*ii*) to have made the representation set forth in Section 6.2 of the Note Purchase Agreements.

This Note is a registered Note and, as provided in the Note Purchase Agreements, upon surrender of this Note for registration of transfer, duly endorsed, or accompanied by a written instrument of transfer duly executed, by the registered holder hereof or such holder's attorney duly authorized in writing, a new Note for a like principal amount will be issued to, and registered in the name of, the transferee. Prior to due presentment for registration of transfer, the Company may treat the person in whose name this Note is registered as the owner hereof for the purpose of receiving payment and for all other purposes, and the Company will not be affected by any notice to the contrary.

The Company will make required prepayments of principal on the dates and in the amounts specified in the Note Purchase Agreements. This Note is also subject to optional prepayment, in whole or from time to time in part, at the times and on the terms specified in the Note Purchase Agreements, but not otherwise.

If an Event of Default, as defined in the Note Purchase Agreements, occurs and is continuing, the principal of this Note may be declared or otherwise become due and payable in the manner, at the price (including any applicable Make–Whole Amount) and with the effect provided in the Note Purchase Agreements.

This Note shall be construed and enforced in accordance with the law of the State of New York excluding choice-of-law principles of the law of such State that would require the application of the laws of a jurisdiction other than such State.

GENERAL TECHNOLOGY, INC.

By _____
[Title]

EXHIBIT 4.4(a)

FORM OF OPINION OF SPECIAL COUNSEL TO THE COMPANY

Matters To Be Covered In *Opinion of Special Counsel to the Company*

1.   Each of the Company and its Subsidiaries being duly incorporated, validly existing and in good standing and having requisite corporate power and authority to issue and sell the Notes and to execute and deliver the documents.

2.   Each of the Company and its Subsidiaries being duly qualified and in good standing as a foreign corporation in appropriate jurisdictions.

3.   Due authorization and execution of the documents and such documents being legal, valid, binding and enforceable.

4.   No conflicts with charter documents, laws or other agreements.

5.   All consents required to issue and sell the Notes and to execute and deliver the documents having been obtained.

6.   No litigation questioning validity of documents.

7.   The Notes not requiring registration under the Securities Act of 1933, as amended; no need to qualify an indenture under the Trust Indenture Act of 1939, as amended.

8.   No violation of Regulations G, T or X of the Federal Reserve Board.

9.   Company not an "investment company", or a company "controlled" by an "investment company", under the Investment Company Act of 1940, as amended.

———

EXHIBIT 4.4(b)

FORM OF OPINION OF SPECIAL COUNSEL TO THE PURCHASERS
[TO BE PROVIDED ON A CASE BY CASE BASIS]

———

FORM 3

PREFERRED STOCK CHARTER PROVISIONS

CERTIFICATE OF INCORPORATION OF
GENERAL TECHNOLOGY, INC.

Pursuant to Section 102 of the General Corporation
Law of the State of Delaware

I, the undersigned, for the purpose of incorporating and organizing a corporation under the General Corporation Law of the State of Delaware, do execute this Certificate of Incorporation and do hereby certify as follows:

FIRST: The name of this corporation is General Technology, Inc.

SECOND: The address of this corporation's current registered office in the State of Delaware is One Rodney Square, 10th Floor, Tenth and King Streets, in the City of Wilmington, County of New Castle, 19801. The name of its registered agent at such address is RL & F Service Corp.

THIRD: The purpose of the corporation is to engage in any lawful act or activity for which corporations may be organized under the General Corporation Law of the State of Delaware.

FOURTH: (a) The aggregate number of shares which this corporation shall have authority to issue is 50,000,000 of which 10,000,000 shares shall be preferred stock without par value, and 40,000,000 shares shall be common stock without par value.

(b) Subject to the provisions of subdivision (c) of this Article 4, the Board of Directors shall have authority at any time or from time to time (i) to divide any or all of the preferred stock into series; (ii) to determine for any such series its designation, number of shares, relative rights, preferences and limitations; (iii) to increase the number of shares of any such series previously determined by it and to decrease such previously determined number of shares to a number not less than that of the shares of such series then outstanding; (iv) to change the designation or number of shares, or the relative rights, preferences and limitations of the shares, of any theretofore established series no shares of which have been issued; and (v) to cause to be executed and filed without further approval of the shareholders such additional provisions of the Certificate of Incorporation as may be required in order to accomplish any of the foregoing. In particular, but without limiting the generality of the foregoing, the Board of Directors shall have authority to determine with respect to any series of preferred stock:

(1) The dividend rate or rates on shares of such series and any restrictions, limitations or conditions upon the payment of such dividends, and whether dividends shall be cumulative and, if so, the date or dates from which dividends shall cumulate, and the dates on which dividends, if declared, shall be payable;

A-95

(2) Whether the shares of such series shall be redeemable and, if so, the time or times and the price or prices at which and the other terms and conditions on which the shares may be redeemed;

(3) The rights of the holders of shares of such series in the event of the liquidation, dissolution or winding upon of the corporation, whether voluntary or involuntary, or any other distribution of its assets;

(4) Whether the shares of such series shall be subject to the operation of a purchase, retirement or sinking fund and, if so, the terms and conditions thereof;

(5) Whether the shares of such series shall be convertible into shares of any other class or classes or of any series of the same or any other class or classes, and if so convertible, the price or prices or the rate or rates of conversion and the method, if any, of adjusting the same, and the other terms and conditions, if any, on which shares shall be so convertible; and

(6) The extent of voting powers, if any, of the shares of such series.

(c) Except as required by law or as determined by the Board of Directors pursuant to subdivision (b) of this Article 4, the exclusive voting power for all purposes shall be vested in the holders of common stock, each share thereof from time to time outstanding having voting power of one vote.

FIFTH: The incorporator of this corporation is _____, whose mailing address is One Rodney Square, P. O. Box 551, Wilmington, Delaware 19899.

SIXTH: The powers of the incorporator are to terminate upon this filing of this certificate of incorporation. The name and mailing address of the persons who are to serve as initial directors of the corporation until the first annual meeting of stockholders of the corporation, or until their successors are elected and qualified are _____.

The undersigned incorporator acknowledges that the foregoing certificate of incorporation is his act and deed on this _____ day of _____ 20__.

_____

Incorporator

RESOLUTION OF BOARD OF DIRECTORS OF GENERAL TECHNOLOGY, INC. PROVIDING FOR THE ISSUE OF SERIES A PREFERRED STOCK

Pursuant to section 151(a) of the General Corporation Law of the State of Delaware, the undersigned hereby certifies:

FIRST: The name of the corporation is General Technology, Inc.

SECOND: On _____, 20XX, the Board of Directors of the corporation duly adopted the following resolution:

"RESOLVED, that, pursuant to the authority granted to the Board of Directors by subdivision (b) of Article 4 of the Certificate of Incorporation of General Technology, Inc., filed _____, 20XX, and by sections 151(a) of the General Corporation Law of the State of Delaware, said Certificate of Incorporation is amended by the insertion of the following new subdivision (d) at the end of said Article 4:

(d) Pursuant to subdivision (b) of this Article 4, there are hereby authorized and established, out of the 10,000,000 shares of preferred stock without par value which the corporation has authority to issue pursuant to subdivision (a) of this Article 4, a series of such preferred stock, designated "Series A Cumulative Preferred Stock" (the "Series A Preferred Stock").

(1) The Series A Preferred Stock shall consist of 1,500,000 shares without par value.

(2) The holders of Series A Preferred Stock shall be entitled to receive, when, as and if declared by the Board of Directors out of funds legally available for the purpose, dividends in cash in the amount of $10 per share per annum, payable quarterly on the first day of each February, May, August and November. Dividends on shares of the Series A Preferred Stock shall begin to accrue and shall be cumulative from the date of their issue. Dividends paid on the shares of Series A Preferred Stock in an amount less than the total amount of dividends at the time accrued and payable on such shares shall be allocated pro rata on a share by share basis among all such shares at the time outstanding. Accrued but unpaid dividends on the Series A Preferred Stock shall not bear interest. The Board of Directors may fix a record date for the determination of holders of Series A Preferred Stock entitled to receive payment of a dividend declared thereon, which record date shall be not more than 60 days prior to the date fixed for the payment thereof.

(3) The holders of Series A Preferred Stock shall be entitled, on all matters submitted for a vote of the holders of common stock, whether pursuant to law or otherwise, to one vote for each share of Series A Preferred Stock held, and on all such matters shall vote together as one class with the holders of common stock and the holders of all other shares of stock entitled to vote with the holders of common stock on such matters. In addition, the holders of Series A Preferred Stock shall have (i) the voting powers provided for by law and (ii) the further voting powers provided for below:

(a) The consent of the holders of a majority of the outstanding shares of Series A Preferred Stock, voting separately as a single class, in person or by proxy, either in writing without a meeting or at a special or annual meeting of shareholders called for the purpose, shall be necessary to (i) authorize any additional class or series of stock ranking, or convertible into shares ranking, prior to or on a parity with (either as to dividends or upon liquidation, dissolution or winding up) the Series A Preferred Stock, or (ii) increase the authorized amount of any class or series of stock so ranking, or convertible into shares so ranking, prior to or on a parity with the Series A Preferred Stock, or (iii) effect a sale of all or substantially all of the assets of the corporation, or (iv) effect any division of the Series A Preferred Stock or any combination thereof with any other class or series of stock, or (v) amend the Certificate of Incorporation to alter materially the relative rights and preferences of the Series A Preferred Stock so as adversely to affect the holders thereof, (vi) effect a consolidation or merger of the corporation with or into any other corporation or other entity or person, or any other corporate reorganization, in which the stockholders of the corporation immediately prior to such consolidation, merger or reorganization, own less than fifty percent (50%) of the corporation's voting power immediately after such consolidation, merger or reorganization, or effect any transaction or series of related transactions to which the corporation is a party in which in excess of fifty percent (50%) of the corporation's voting power is transferred, *provided that* no amendment of the Certificate of Incorporation which reduces any amount payable on the Series A Preferred Stock as dividends, upon redemption or upon liquidation, dissolution or winding up of the corporation, or which postpones the date when any such amount is payable, or which amends this subparagraph (a), shall be effective without the consent of the holders of all the outstanding shares of Series A Preferred Stock.

(b)(i) Whenever quarterly dividends payable on the Series A Preferred Stock as provided in paragraph (2) of this subdivision (d) are in arrears in an aggregate amount at least equal to six full quarterly dividends (which need not be consecutive), the holders of the outstanding Series A Preferred Stock shall have the special right, voting separately as a single class, to elect two directors of the corporation, at the next succeeding annual meeting of shareholders (and at each succeeding annual meeting of shareholders thereafter until such right shall terminate as hereinafter provided).

(ii) At each meeting of shareholders at which the holders of the Series A Preferred Stock shall have the special right, voting separately as a single class, to elect directors as provided in this subparagraph (b), the presence in person or by proxy of the holders of record of one-third of the total number of shares of the Series A Preferred Stock of all series then issued and outstanding shall be necessary and sufficient to constitute a quorum of such class for such election by such shareholders as a class.

(iii) Each director elected by the holders of the Series A Preferred Stock voting separately as a single class as provided in this subparagraph (b) shall hold office until the annual meeting of shareholders next succeeding his election and until his successor, if any, is elected by such holders and qualified.

(iv) In case any vacancy shall occur among the directors elected by the holders of the Series A Preferred Sock voting separately as a single class as provided in this subparagraph (b), such vacancy may be filled for the unexpired portion of the term by vote of the single remaining director theretofore elected by such shareholders, or his successor in office, or by the vote of such shareholders given at a special meeting of such shareholders called for the purpose.

(v) Whenever all dividends accrued and unpaid on the Series A Preferred Stock shall have been paid and dividends thereon for the current quarterly period shall have been paid or declared and provided for, the right of the holders of the Series A Preferred Stock, voting separately as a single class, to elect directors as provided in this subparagraph (b) shall terminate at the next succeeding annual meeting of shareholders, but subject always to the same provisions for the vesting of such special right of the holders of the Series A Preferred Stock, voting separately as a single class, to elect directors in the case of future unpaid dividends as hereinabove set forth.

(c)(i) Whenever any mandatory redemption on the Series A Preferred Stock pursuant to paragraph (7) of this subdivision (d) is in arrears in an aggregate amount at least equal to two full mandatory redemption payments (which need not be consecutive), the holders of the outstanding Series A Preferred Stock shall have the special right, voting separately as a single class, to elect two directors of the corporation, at the next succeeding annual meeting of shareholders (and at each succeeding annual meeting of shareholders thereafter until such right shall terminate as hereinafter provided), *provided that* this subparagraph (c) shall not be given effect at any time when the holders of the outstanding Series A Preferred Stock shall have the right to elect two directors pursuant to subparagraph (b) of this paragraph (3), it being intended that such holders shall not have by reason of this subparagraph (c) the right to elect, voting separately as a single class, more than two directors at any time.

(ii) At each meeting of shareholders at which the holders of the Series A Preferred Stock shall have the special right, voting separately as a single class, to elect directors as provided in this subparagraph (c), the presence in person or by proxy of the holders of record of one-third of the total number of shares of the Series A Preferred Stock then issued and outstanding shall be necessary and sufficient to constitute a quorum of such class for such election by such shareholders as a class.

(iii) Each director elected by the holders of the Series A Preferred Stock voting separately as a single class as provided in this subparagraph (c) shall hold office until the annual meeting of shareholders next succeeding his election and until his successor, if any, is elected by such holders and qualifies.

(iv) In case any vacancy shall occur among the directors elected by the holders of the Series A Preferred Stock voting separately as a single class as provided in this subparagraph (c), such vacancy may be filled for the unexpired portion of the term by vote of the single remaining director theretofore elected by such shareholders, or his successor in office, or by the vote of such shareholders given at a special meeting of such shareholders called for the purpose.

(v) Whenever all mandatory redemption payments which are in arrears shall have been paid, the right of the holders of the Series A Preferred Stock, voting separately as a single class, to elect directors as provided in this subparagraph (c) shall terminate at the next succeeding annual meeting of shareholders, but subject always to the same provisions for the vesting of such special right of the holders of the Series A Preferred Stock, voting separately as a single class, to elect directors in the case of any future mandatory redemption arrears as hereinabove set forth.

(d) In any case in which the holders of the Series A Preferred Stock shall be entitled to vote separately as a single class pursuant to the provisions of this paragraph (3) or pursuant to law, each holder of Series A Preferred Stock of any series shall be entitled to one vote for each such share held.

(4) Whenever quarterly dividends payable on the Series A Preferred Stock as provided in paragraph (2) of this subdivision (d) are in arrears, the corporation shall not (a) pay dividends on, make any other distributions on, or redeem or purchase or otherwise acquire for consideration any stock ranking junior (either as to dividends or upon liquidation, dissolution or winding up) to the Series A Preferred Stock, or (b) pay dividends on or make any other distributions on any stock ranking on a parity (either as to dividends or upon liquidation, dissolution or winding up) with the Series A Preferred Stock, except dividends paid proportionately on the Series A Preferred Stock and all such parity ranking stock on which dividends are payable or in arrears, or (c) redeem or purchase or otherwise acquire for consideration any stock ranking on a parity (either as to dividends or upon liquidation, dissolution or winding up) with the Series A Preferred Stock.

(5) Whenever any mandatory redemption on the Series A Preferred Stock pursuant to paragraph (7) of this subdivision (d) is in arrears, the corporation shall not (a) pay dividends on, make any other distributions on, or redeem or purchase or otherwise acquire for consideration any stock ranking junior (either as to dividends or upon liquidation, dissolution or winding up) to the Series A Preferred Stock, or (b) redeem or purchase or otherwise acquire for consideration any stock ranking on a parity (either as to dividends or upon liquidation, dissolution or winding up) with the Series A Preferred Stock, except mandatory redemptions made proportionately on the Series A Preferred Stock and all other such parity ranking stock on which mandatory redemptions are payable or in arrears.

(6) Upon any liquidation, dissolution or winding up of the corporation, no distribution shall be made (a) to the holders of stock ranking junior (either as to dividends or upon liquidation, dissolution or winding up) to the Series A Preferred Stock unless, prior to the first such distribution, the holders of Series A Preferred Stock shall have received (i) in the event of a voluntary liquidation, dissolution or winding up, an amount per share equal to the amount per share which would be payable upon an optional redemption of the Series A Preferred Stock pursuant to paragraph (8) of this subdivision (e) at the time such amount is paid to the holders of Series A Preferred Stock, or (ii) in the event of an involuntary liquidation, dissolution or winding up, $100 per share, plus, in either such case, dividends accrued and unpaid thereon, whether or not declared, or (b) to the holders of stock ranking on a parity (either as to dividends or upon liquidation, dissolution or winding up) with the Series A Preferred Stock, except distributions made proportionately on the Series A Preferred Stock and all other such parity ranking stock. The merger or consolidation of the corporation or the sale of all or substantially all the assets of the corporation shall not be deemed a liquidation, dissolution or winding up of the corporation for purposes of this paragraph (6).

(7) The corporation shall, on the first day of February in each year beginning with 20XX [sixth anniversary], redeem, out of funds legally available for the purpose, 150,000 shares of the Series A Preferred Stock (or all shares of the Series A Preferred Stock then outstanding if less than 150,000) at the mandatory redemption price of $100 per share plus dividends accrued and unpaid thereon, whether or not declared. The corporation's obligation to make redemptions on any such first day of February as provided in this paragraph (7) shall be cumulative. In addition, the corporation may, at its option, redeem up to an additional 150,000 shares of the Series A Preferred Stock at the mandatory redemption price on the first day of February in any year beginning with 20XX, *provided that* the aggregate number of shares of the Series A Preferred Stock that may be so optionally redeemed shall not exceed 450,000 and the right to effect such optional redemptions shall not be cumulative. No redemption of less than all shares of the Series A Preferred Stock outstanding pursuant to the preceding sentence of this paragraph (7) or pursuant to paragraph (8) or (9) of this subdivision (e) shall relieve the corporation from its obligation to make mandatory redemptions of the Series A Preferred Stock pursuant to the first sentence of this paragraph (7), provided that, in case of the redemption of all shares of the Series A Preferred Stock held by some, but less than all, holders pursuant to paragraph (9) of this subdivision (d), the number of shares of the Series A Preferred Stock subject to mandatory redemption on the first day of each February thereafter shall be reduced in the same proportion as the total number of shares of the Series A Preferred Stock outstanding is reduced by reason of such redemption pursuant to such paragraph (9). The number of shares of the Series A Preferred Stock subject to redemption pursuant to the first and third sentences of this paragraph (7) shall also be adjusted proportionately, as nearly as practicable, to reflect any subdivisions or combinations of the Series A Preferred Stock.

(8) The corporation may redeem the Series A Preferred Stock, at any time in whole or from time to time in part, at the optional redemption price in effect on the date fixed for such redemption, which shall be the then applicable price per share specified below plus dividends accrued and unpaid on the shares to be redeemed, whether or not declared:

During the 12 months ending February 1	Price per share
20XX	$110.00
20XX	109.33
20XX	108.66
20XX	108.00
20XX	107.33
20XX	106.66
20XX	106.00
20XX	105.33
20XX	104.66
20XX	104.00
20XX	103.33
20XX	102.66
20XX	102.00
20XX	101.33
20XX	100.66

Notwithstanding the foregoing, prior to February 1, 20XX, the Series A Preferred Stock shall not be redeemed, in whole or in part, pursuant to this paragraph (8), directly or indirectly, from or in anticipation of all or any part of the proceeds from (a) the incurrence of indebtedness for borrowed money having either an interest rate or an effective interest cost of less than 10% per annum or a weighted average life to maturity which is less than that of the Series A Preferred Stock on the date fixed for such redemption, or (b) the issuance of shares of stock ranking prior (either as to dividends or upon liquidation, dissolution or winding up) to the common stock of the corporation and having either a dividend rate or an effective dividend cost of less than 10% per annum or a weighted average life to maturity which is less than that of the Series A Preferred Stock on the date fixed for such redemption. For purposes of this paragraph (8), the effective interest or dividend cost of any indebtedness or shares of stock shall be determined in accordance with accepted financial practice and the weighted average life to maturity of any indebtedness or shares of stock shall be, in the case of any indebtedness at any date, the number of years obtained by dividing the then outstanding principal amount of such indebtedness into the total of the products obtained by multiplying (i) the amount of each then remaining installment, sinking fund, serial maturity or other required payment, including payment of final maturity, in respect thereof, by (ii) the number of years (calculated to the nearest one-twelfth) which will elapse between such date and the date on which such payment is to be made and, in the case of any stock at any date, the number of years obtained by dividing the then involuntary liquidation value of such stock into the total of the products obtained by multiplying, (x) the amount of each then remaining installment, sinking fund or other required redemption, including redemption at final maturity, in respect thereof, by (y) the number of years (calculated to the nearest one-twelfth) which will elapse between such date and the making of such redemption.

(9) In the event that, pursuant to law or any provision of the Certificate of Incorporation, the consent of the holders of the outstanding shares of Series A Preferred Stock shall be required to authorize an additional class or series of stock ranking on a parity (either as to dividends or upon liquidation, dissolution or winding up) with the Series A Preferred Stock, or to increase the authorized amount of any such class or series of stock, or to effect a merger or consolidation of the corporation or a sale of all or substantially all of its assets. the corporation shall have the right to elect to redeem shares of Series A Preferred Stock to the extent and on the conditions specified below in this paragraph (9). If the corporation shall elect to redeem shares of Series A Preferred Stock pursuant to this paragraph (9), the corporation shall mail to each holder of Series A Preferred Stock, at such holder's address as it appears on the books of the corporation, a written notice (i) specifying a date (the "Determination Date"), which shall be not less than 15 nor more than 60 days after the date on which such notice is mailed, on which a determination will be made as to whether the Series A Preferred Stock is subject to redemption as provided in this paragraph (9), (ii) describing in reasonable detail the corporate action with respect to which the consent of the Series A Preferred Stock is required (and, if applicable, transmitting any proxy statement required to be delivered in connection with such corporate action), (iii) summarizing the voting rights of the holders of the Series A Preferred Stock with respect to such corporate action and (iv) summarizing the respective rights of the corporation and such holder under this paragraph (9). If a vote by the holders of the common stock is to be taken with respect to the corporate action for which the consent of the holders of the Series A Preferred Stock is being sought, the Determination Date shall not be more than three business days prior to the date on which such vote by the holders of common stock is to be taken. If on or before the Determination Date, the corporation shall not have received from the holder of any shares of Series A Preferred Stock a duly authorized and executed instrument which on and after such date will constitute an irrevocable proxy authorizing the corporation (or its nominee) to consent with respect to such shares to the corporate action for which the consent of the holders of the Series A Preferred Stock is being sought, the corporation shall have the right to redeem such shares at the redemption price of $100 per share plus dividends accrued and unpaid thereon, whether or not declared, on the first business day following the Determination Date. A holder of shares of Series A Preferred Stock who wishes to do so may defer the redemption of such shares by delivering to the corporation on or before the Determination Date a duly authorized and executed instrument which on and after such date will constitute an irrevocable proxy authorizing the corporation (or its nominee) to consent with respect to such shares to the corporate action for which the consent of the holders of the Series A Preferred Stock is being

sought and specifying and agreeing that the shares for which such irrevocable proxy is granted shall be redeemed at the redemption price of $100 per share plus dividends accrued and unpaid thereon, whether or not declared, but only (i) upon, and simultaneously with, the consummation of such corporate action on substantially the terms presented to the holders of Series A Preferred Stock for purposes of obtaining their consent thereto and (ii) if the consummation of such corporate action shall take place within 180 days after the Determination Date.

Notwithstanding the foregoing, the corporation shall not have the right to redeem any shares of Series A Preferred Stock pursuant to this paragraph (9) if on the Determination Date the corporation shall have received irrevocable proxies as provided above in this paragraph (9) which are not accompanied by a specification of and agreement to a deferred redemption as provided above in this paragraph (9) and which relate to such number of shares of the Series A Preferred Stock as are sufficient to provide the consent of the holders of the Series A Preferred Stock required for the corporate action for which such consent is being sought.

The corporation shall use its best efforts to mail notice of the date of consummation of the corporate action for which consent is being sought and of the simultaneous redemption of shares of Series A Preferred Stock pursuant to this paragraph (9), at least 5 but not more than 45 days prior to such date, to each bolder of shares of Series A Preferred Stock to be redeemed on such date, at such holder's address as it appears or, the books of the corporation.

Within 20 days after the redemption of any shares of Series A Preferred Stock pursuant to this paragraph (9), the corporation shall mail to each holder of Series A Preferred Stock, at such holder's address as it appears on the books of the corporation, a written notice specifying the number of such shares so redeemed and setting forth the number of shares of Series A Preferred Stock thereafter subject to redemption pursuant to the first and third sentences of paragraph (7) of this clause (A), determined as provided in such paragraph (7).

(10) Notice of any redemption of the Series A Preferred Stock (other than pursuant to paragraph (9) of this subdivision (d)) shall be mailed at least 30, but not more than 60, days prior to the date fixed for such redemption to each holder of Series A Preferred Stock to be redeemed, at such holder's address as it appears on the books of the corporation. In order to facilitate the redemption of the Series A Preferred Stock, the Board of Directors may set a record date for the determination of holders of Series A Preferred Stock to be redeemed, or may cause the transfer books of the corporation to be closed for the transfer of Series A Preferred Stock, not more than 60 days prior to the date fixed for such redemption. If less than all the Series A Preferred Stock outstanding is to be redeemed (other than pursuant to paragraph (9) of this subdivision (d)), the redemption shall be effected, as nearly as practicable, pro rata according to the number of shares held of record, with adjustments to the extent practicable to equalize for prior redemptions, provided that only whole shares of Series A Preferred Stock shall be redeemed.

(11) If on the date fixed for any redemption of the Series A Preferred Stock the full amount of funds necessary to effect the proposed redemption shall have been deposited in a bank or trust company with irrevocable instructions and authority to pay such amount to the holders of shares of Series A Preferred Stock properly called for redemption, then, notwithstanding that the certificates for such shares have not been surrendered for cancellation, from and after such date such shares shall no longer be deemed outstanding, dividends thereon shall cease to accrue and all rights of the holders of such shares shall terminate, except the right to receive the redemption price therefor, without interest.

(12) Notwithstanding any other provision of this subdivision (d), the corporation shall not be required to pay any dividend on, or to pay any amount in respect of any redemption of, the Series A Preferred Stock at a time when, immediately after making such payment the fair market value of the total remaining assets of the corporation would be less than its total liabilities plus the maximum aggregate amount which would be payable on all then outstanding shares of stock ranking (either as to dividends or upon liquidation, dissolution or winding up) prior to or on a parity with the Series A Preferred Stock in the event of a liquidation, dissolution or winding up of the corporation at the date of such payment, *provided that* the obligation of the corporation to make any such payment shall not be extinguished in the event that the foregoing limitation applies.

(13) The corporation shall not, directly or indirectly, redeem or purchase or otherwise acquire any shares of the Series A Preferred Stock except as provided in this subdivision (d) or pursuant to a pro rata offer made in writing, on identical terms, to each holder of Series A Preferred Stock at the time outstanding.

(14) Any shares of the Series A Preferred Stock redeemed or purchased or otherwise acquired by the corporation in any manner whatsoever shall be retired and cancelled promptly after the acquisition thereof; all such shares shall upon their cancellation become authorized but unissued shares of preferred stock, but may not be reissued as shares of Series A Preferred Stock.

(15) Whenever quarterly dividends payable on the Series A Preferred Stock as provided in paragraph (2) of this subdivision (d) are in arrears, and whenever any mandatory redemption on the Series A Preferred Stock pursuant to paragraph (7) of this subdivision (d) is in arrears, the corporation shall not permit any Subsidiary to (a) pay dividends on, make any other distributions on, or redeem or purchase or otherwise acquire for consideration any stock issued by such Subsidiary and held by a Person other than the corporation, (b) pay dividends on, make any other distributions on, or redeem or purchase or otherwise acquire for consideration any stock issued by the corporation and ranking junior (either as to dividends or upon liquidation, dissolution or winding up) to the Series A Preferred Stock, (c) pay dividends on or make any other distributions on any stock issued by the corporation and ranking on a parity (either as to dividends or upon liquidation, dissolution or winding up) with the Series A Preferred Stock, except dividends paid proportionately on the Series A Preferred

Stock and all such parity ranking stock on which dividends are payable or in arrears, or (d) redeem, purchase or otherwise acquire for consideration any stock issued by the corporation and ranking on a parity (either as to dividends or upon liquidation, dissolution or winding up) with the Series A Preferred Stock.

As used in this paragraph (15), Person means an individual, partnership, corporation, limited liability company, association, trust, unincorporated organization, or a government or agency or political subdivision thereof; and Subsidiary means, as to any Person, any corporation, association or other business entity in which such Person or one or more of its Subsidiaries or such Person and one or more of its Subsidiaries owns sufficient equity or voting interests to enable it or them (as a group) ordinarily, in the absence of contingencies, to elect a majority of the directors (or Persons performing similar functions) of such entity, and any partnership or joint venture if more than a 50% interest in the profits or capital thereof is owned by such Person or one or more of its Subsidiaries or such Person and one or more of its Subsidiaries (unless such partnership can and does ordinarily take major business actions without the prior approval of such Person or one or more of its Subsidiaries). Unless the context otherwise clearly requires, any reference to a "Subsidiary" is a reference to a Subsidiary of the Company.

IN WITNESS WHEREOF, General Technology, Inc. has caused this Certificate to be duly executed this __ day of ___, 20XX.

GENERAL TECHNOLOGY, INC.

By _____

Title:

FORM 4

MODEL STOCK PURCHASE AGREEMENT

Prepared by the Committee on Negotiated Acquisitions of the Section of Business Law of the American Bar Association
(1995)

Table of Contents

1.   Definitions
   "ACQUIRED COMPANIES"
   "ADJUSTMENT AMOUNT"
   "APPLICABLE CONTRACT"
   "BALANCE SHEET"
   "BEST EFFORTS"
   "BREACH"
   "BUYER"
   "CLOSING"
   "CLOSING DATE"
   "COMPANY"
   "CONSENT"
   "CONTEMPLATED TRANSACTIONS"
   "CONTRACT"
   "DAMAGES"
   "DISCLOSURE LETTER"
   "EMPLOYMENT AGREEMENTS"
   "ENCUMBRANCE"
   "ENVIRONMENT"
   "ENVIRONMENTAL, HEALTH, AND SAFETY LIABILITIES"
   "ENVIRONMENTAL LAW"
   "ERISA"
   "ESCROW AGREEMENT"
   "FACILITIES"
   "GAAP"
   "GOVERNMENTAL AUTHORIZATION"
   "GOVERNMENTAL BODY"
   "HAZARDOUS ACTIVITY"
   "HAZARDOUS MATERIALS"
   "HSR ACT"
   "INTELLECTUAL PROPERTY ASSETS"
   "INTERIM BALANCE SHEET"
   "IRC"
   "IRS"
   "KNOWLEDGE"
   "LEGAL REQUIREMENT"
   "NONCOMPETITION AGREEMENTS"
   "OCCUPATIONAL SAFETY AND HEALTH LAW"
   "ORDER"
   "ORDINARY COURSE OF BUSINESS"
   "ORGANIZATIONAL DOCUMENTS"
   "PERSON"
   "PLAN"
   "PROCEEDING"
   "PROMISSORY NOTES"
   "RELATED PERSON"
   "RELEASE"
   "REPRESENTATIVE"

"SECURITIES ACT"
"SELLERS"
"SELLERS' RELEASES"
"SHARES"
"SUBSIDIARY"
"TAX"
"TAX RETURN"
"THREAT OF RELEASE"
"THREATENED"

2. Sale and Transfer of Shares; Closing
    2.1   Shares
    2.2   Purchase Price
    2.3   Closing
    2.4   Closing Obligations
    2.5   Adjustment Amount
    2.6   Adjustment Procedure

3. Representations and Warranties of Sellers
    3.1   Organization and Good Standing
    3.2   Authority; No Conflict
    3.3   Capitalization
    3.4   Financial Statements
    3.5   Books and Records
    3.6   Title to Properties; Encumbrances
    3.7   Condition and Sufficiency of Assets
    3.8   Accounts Receivable
    3.9   Inventory
    3.10 No Undisclosed Liabilities
    3.11 Taxes
    3.12 No Material Adverse Change
    3.13 Employee Benefits
    3.14 Compliance With Legal Requirements; Governmental Authorizations
    3.15 Legal Proceedings; Orders
    3.16 Absence of Certain Changes and Events
    3.17 Contracts; No Defaults
    3.18 Insurance
    3.19 Environmental Matters
    3.20 Employees
    3.21 Labor Relations; Compliance
    3.22 Intellectual Property
    3.23 Certain Payments
    3.24 Disclosure
    3.25 Relationships With Related Persons
    3.26 Brokers or Finders

4. Representations and Warranties of Buyer
    4.1   Organization and Good Standing
    4.2   Authority; No Conflict
    4.3   Investment Intent
    4.4   Certain Proceedings
    4.5   Brokers or Finders

5. Covenants of Sellers Prior to Closing Date
    5.1   Access and Investigation
    5.2   Operation of the Businesses of the Acquired Companies
    5.3   Negative Covenant
    5.4   Required Approvals
    5.5   Notification

5.6   Payment of Indebtedness by Related Persons
5.7   No Negotiation
5.8   Best Efforts

6.   Covenants of Buyer Prior to Closing Date
6.1   Approvals of Governmental Bodies
6.2   Best Efforts

7.   Conditions Precedent to Buyer's Obligation to Close
7.1   Accuracy of Representations
7.2   Sellers' Performance
7.3   Consents
7.4   Additional Documents
7.5   No Proceedings
7.6   No Claim Regarding Stock Ownership or Sale Proceeds
7.7   No Prohibition

8.   Conditions Precedent to Sellers' Obligation to Close
8.1   Accuracy of Representations
8.2   Buyer's Performance
8.3   Consents
8.4   Additional Documents
8.5   No Injunction

9.   Termination
9.1   Termination Events
9.2   Effect of Termination

10.   Indemnification; Remedies
10.1   Survival; Right to Indemnification Not Affected By Knowledge
10.2   Indemnification and Payment of Damages by Sellers
10.3   Indemnification and Payment of Damages by Sellers—Environmental
        Matters
10.4   Indemnification and Payment of Damages by Buyer
10.5   Time Limitations
10.6   Limitations on Amount—Sellers
10.7   Limitations on Amount—Buyer
10.8   Escrow; Right of Set–Off
10.9   Procedure for Indemnification—Third Party Claims
10.10   Procedure for Indemnification—Other Claims

11.   General Provisions
11.1   Expenses
11.2   Public Announcements
11.3   Confidentiality
11.4   Notices
11.5   Jurisdiction; Service of Process
11.6   Further Assurances
11.7   Waiver
11.8   Entire Agreement and Modification
11.9   Disclosure Letter
11.10   Assignments, Successors, and no Third–Party Rights
11.11   Severability
11.12   Section Headings, Construction
11.13   Time of Essence
11.14   Governing Law
11.15   Counterparts

Stock Purchase Agreement

This Stock Purchase Agreement ("Agreement") is made as of _____, 199__, by _____, a _____ corporation ("Buyer"), _____, an individual resident in _____ ("A"), and _____, an individual resident in _____ ("B" and, collectively with A, "Sellers").

RECITALS

Sellers desire to sell, and Buyer desires to purchase, all of the issued and outstanding shares (the "Shares") of capital stock of __, a _____ corporation (the "Company"), for the consideration and on the terms set forth in this Agreement.

AGREEMENT

The parties, intending to be legally bound, agree as follows:

1. DEFINITIONS

For purposes of this Agreement, the following terms have the meanings specified or referred to in this Section 1:

"Acquired Companies"—the Company and its Subsidiaries, collectively.

"Adjustment Amount"—as defined in Section 2.5.

"Applicable Contract"—any Contract (a) under which any Acquired Company has or may acquire any rights, (b) under which any Acquired Company has or may become subject to any obligation or liability, or (c) by which any Acquired Company or any of the assets owned or used by it is or may become bound.

"Balance Sheet"—as defined in Section 3.4.

"Best Efforts"—the efforts that a prudent Person desirous of achieving a result would use in similar circumstances to ensure that such result is achieved as expeditiously as possible [; *provided, however,* that an obligation to use Best Efforts under this Agreement does not require the Person subject to that obligation to take actions that would result in a materially adverse change in the benefits to such Person of this Agreement and the Contemplated Transactions].

"Breach"—a "Breach" of a representation, warranty, covenant, obligation, or other provision of this Agreement or any instrument delivered pursuant to this Agreement will be deemed to have occurred if there is or has been (a) any inaccuracy in or breach of, or any failure to perform or comply with, such representation, warranty, covenant, obligation, or other provision, or (b) any claim (by any Person) or other occurrence or circumstance that is or was inconsistent with such representation, warranty, covenant, obligation, or other provision, and the term "Breach" means any such inaccuracy, breach, failure, claim, occurrence, or circumstance.

"Buyer"—as defined in the first paragraph of this Agreement.

"Closing"—as defined in Section 2.3.

"Closing Date"—the date and time as of which the Closing actually takes place.

"Company"—as defined in the Recitals of this Agreement.

"Consent"—any approval, consent, ratification, waiver, or other authorization (including any Governmental Authorization).

"Contemplated Transactions"—all of the transactions contemplated by this Agreement, including:

(a) the sale of the Shares by Sellers to Buyer;

(b) the execution, delivery, and performance of the Promissory Note, the Employment Agreements, the Noncompetition Agreements, the Sellers' Releases, and the Escrow Agreement;

(c) the performance by Buyer and Sellers of their respective covenants and obligations under this Agreement; and

(d) Buyer's acquisition and ownership of the Shares and exercise of control over the Acquired Companies.

"Contract"—any agreement, contract, obligation, promise, or undertaking (whether written or oral and whether express or implied) that is legally binding.

"Damages"—as defined in Section 10.2.

"Disclosure Letter"—the disclosure letter delivered by Sellers to Buyer concurrently with the execution and delivery of this Agreement.

"Employment Agreements"—as defined in Section 2.4(a)(iii).

"Encumbrance"—any charge, claim, community property interest, condition, equitable interest, lien, option, pledge, security interest, right of first refusal, or restriction of any kind, including any restriction on use, voting, transfer, receipt of income, or exercise of any other attribute of ownership.

"Environment"—soil, land surface or subsurface strata, surface waters (including navigable waters, ocean waters, streams, ponds, drainage basins, and wetlands), groundwaters, drinking water supply, stream sediments, ambient air (including indoor air), plant and animal life, and any other environmental medium or natural resource.

"Environmental, Health, and Safety Liabilities"—any cost, damages, expense, liability, obligation, or other responsibility arising from or under Environmental Law or Occupational Safety and Health Law and consisting of or relating to:

(a) any environmental, health, or safety matters or conditions (including on-site or off-site contamination, occupational safety and health, and regulation of chemical substances or products);

(b) fines, penalties, judgments, awards, settlements, legal or administrative proceedings, damages, losses, claims, demands and response, investigative, remedial, or inspection costs and expenses arising under Environmental Law or Occupational Safety and Health Law;

(c) financial responsibility under Environmental Law or Occupational Safety and Health Law for cleanup costs or corrective action, including any investigation, cleanup, removal, containment, or other remediation or response actions ("Cleanup") required by applicable Environmental Law or Occupational Safety and Health Law (whether or not such Cleanup has been required or requested by any Governmental Body or any other Person) and for any natural resource damages; or

(d) any other compliance, corrective, investigative, or remedial measures required under Environmental Law or Occupational Safety and Health Law.

The terms "removal," "remedial," and "response action," include the types of activities covered by the United States Comprehensive Environmental Response, Compensation, and Liability Act, 42 U.S.C. § 9601 et seq., as amended ("CERCLA").

"Environmental Law"—any Legal Requirement that requires or relates to:

(a) advising appropriate authorities, employees, and the public of intended or actual releases of pollutants or hazardous substances or materials, violations of discharge limits, or other prohibitions and of the commencements of activities, such as resource extraction or construction, that could have significant impact on the Environment;

(b) preventing or reducing to acceptable levels the release of pollutants or hazardous substances or materials into the Environment;

(c) reducing the quantities, preventing the release, or minimizing the hazardous characteristics of wastes that are generated;

(d) assuring that products are designed, formulated, packaged, and used so that they do not present unreasonable risks to human health or the Environment when used or disposed of;

(e) protecting resources, species, or ecological amenities;

(f) reducing to acceptable levels the risks inherent in the transportation of hazardous substances, pollutants, oil, or other potentially harmful substances;

(g) cleaning up pollutants that have been released, preventing the threat of release, or paying the costs of such clean up or prevention; or

(h) making responsible parties pay private parties, or groups of them, for damages done to their health or the Environment, or permitting self-appointed representatives of the public interest to recover for injuries done to public assets.

"ERISA"—the Employee Retirement Income Security Act of 1974 or any successor law, and regulations and rules issued pursuant to that Act or any successor law.

"Escrow Agreement"—as defined in Section 2.4.

"Facilities"—any real property, leaseholds, or other interests currently or formerly owned or operated by any Acquired Company and any buildings, plants, structures, or equipment (including motor vehicles, tank cars, and rolling stock) currently or formerly owned or operated by any Acquired Company.

"GAAP"—generally accepted United States accounting principles, applied on a basis consistent with the basis on which the Balance Sheet and the other financial statements referred to in Section 3.4(b) were prepared.

"Governmental Authorization"—any approval, consent, license, permit, waiver, or other authorization issued, granted, given, or otherwise made available by or under the authority of any Governmental Body or pursuant to any Legal Requirement.

"Governmental Body"—any:

(a) nation, state, county, city, town, village, district, or other jurisdiction of any nature;

(b) federal, state, local, municipal, foreign, or other government;

(c) governmental or quasi-governmental authority of any nature (including any governmental agency, branch, department, official, or entity and any court or other tribunal);

(d) multi-national organization or body; or

(e) body exercising, or entitled to exercise, any administrative, executive, judicial, legislative, police, regulatory, or taxing authority or power of any nature.

"Hazardous Activity"—the distribution, generation, handling, importing, management, manufacturing, processing, production, refinement, Release, storage, transfer, transportation, treatment, or use (including any withdrawal or other use of groundwater) of Hazardous Materials in, on, under, about, or from the Facilities or any part thereof into the Environment, and any other act, business, operation, or thing that increases the danger, or risk of danger, or poses an unreasonable risk of harm to persons or property on or off the Facilities, or that may affect the value of the Facilities or the Acquired Companies.

"Hazardous Materials"—any waste or other substance that is listed, defined, designated, or classified as, or otherwise determined to be, hazardous, radioactive, or toxic or a pollutant or a contaminant under or pursuant to any Environmental Law, including any admixture or solution thereof, and specifically including petroleum and all derivatives thereof or synthetic substitutes therefor and asbestos or asbestos-containing materials.

"HSR Act"—the Hart–Scott–Rodino Antitrust Improvements Act of 1976 or any successor law, and regulations and rules issued pursuant to that Act or any successor law.

"Intellectual Property Assets"—as defined in Section 3.22.

"Interim Balance Sheet"—as defined in Section 3.4.

"IRC"—the Internal Revenue Code of 1986 or any successor law, and regulations issued by the IRS pursuant to the Internal Revenue Code or any successor law.

"IRS"—the United States Internal Revenue Service or any successor agency, and, to the extent relevant, the United States Department of the Treasury.

"Knowledge"—an individual will be deemed to have "Knowledge" of a particular fact or other matter if:

(a) such individual is actually aware of such fact or other matter; or

(b) a prudent individual could be expected to discover or otherwise become aware of such fact or other matter in the course of conducting a reasonably comprehensive investigation concerning the existence of such fact or other matter.

A Person (other than an individual) will be deemed to have "Knowledge" of a particular fact or other matter if any individual who is serving, or who has at any time served, as a director, officer, partner, executor, or trustee of such Person (or in any similar capacity) has, or at any time had, Knowledge of such fact or other matter.

"Legal Requirement"—any federal, state, local, municipal, foreign, international, multinational, or other administrative order, constitution, law, ordinance, principle of common law, regulation, statute, or treaty.

"Noncompetition Agreements"—as defined in Section 2.4(a)(iv).

"Occupational Safety and Health Law"—any Legal Requirement designed to provide safe and healthful working conditions and to reduce occupational safety and health hazards, and any program, whether governmental or private (including those promulgated or sponsored by industry associations and insurance companies), designed to provide safe and healthful working conditions.

"Order"—any award, decision, injunction, judgment, order, ruling, subpoena, or verdict entered, issued, made, or rendered by any court, administrative agency, or other Governmental Body or by any arbitrator.

"Ordinary Course of Business"—an action taken by a Person will be deemed to have been taken in the "Ordinary Course of Business" only if:

(a) such action is consistent with the past practices of such Person and is taken in the ordinary course of the normal day-to-day operations of such Person;

(b) such action is not required to be authorized by the board of directors of such Person (or by any Person or group of Persons exercising similar authority) [and is not required to be specifically authorized by the parent company (if any) of such Person]; and

(c) such action is similar in nature and magnitude to actions customarily taken, without any authorization by the board of directors (or by any Person or group of Persons exercising similar authority), in the ordinary course of the normal day-to-day operations of other Persons that are in the same line of business as such Person.

"Organizational Documents"—(a) the articles or certificate of incorporation and the bylaws of a corporation; (b) the partnership agreement and any statement of partnership of a general partnership; (c) the limited partnership agreement and the certificate of limited partnership of a limited partnership; (d) any charter or similar document adopted or filed in connection with the creation, formation, or organization of a Person; and (e) any amendment to any of the foregoing.

"Person"—any individual, corporation (including any non-profit corporation), general or limited partnership, limited liability company, joint venture, estate, trust, association, organization, labor union, or other entity or Governmental Body.

"Plan"—as defined in Section 3.13.

"Proceeding"—any action, arbitration, audit, hearing, investigation, litigation, or suit (whether civil, criminal, administrative, investigative, or informal) commenced, brought, conducted, or heard by or before, or otherwise involving, any Governmental Body or arbitrator.

"Promissory Notes"—as defined in Section 2.4(b)(ii).

"Related Person"—with respect to a particular individual:

(a) each other member of such individual's Family;

(b) any Person that is directly or indirectly controlled by such individual or one or more members of such individual's Family;

(c) any Person in which such individual or members of such individual's Family hold (individually or in the aggregate) a Material Interest; and

(d) any Person with respect to which such individual or one or more members of such individual's Family serves as a director, officer, partner, executor, or trustee (or in a similar capacity).

With respect to a specified Person other than an individual:

(a) any Person that directly or indirectly controls, is directly or indirectly controlled by, or is directly or indirectly under common control with such specified Person;

(b) any Person that holds a Material Interest in such specified Person;

(c) each Person that serves as a director, officer, partner, executor, or trustee of such specified Person (or in a similar capacity);

(d) any Person in which such specified Person holds a Material Interest;

(e) any Person with respect to which such specified Person serves as a general partner or a trustee (or in a similar capacity); and

(f) any Related Person of any individual described in clause (b) or (c).

For purposes of this definition, (a) the "Family" of an individual includes (i) the individual, (ii) the individual's spouse [and former spouses], (iii) any other natural person who is related to the individual or the individual's spouse within the second degree, and (iv) any other natural person who resides with such individual, and (b) "Material Interest" means direct or indirect beneficial ownership (as defined in Rule 13d–3 under the Securities Exchange Act of 1934) of voting securities or other voting interests representing at least __% of the outstanding voting power of a Person or equity securities or other equity interests representing at least __% of the outstanding equity securities or equity interests in a Person.

"Release"—any spilling, leaking, emitting, discharging, depositing, escaping, leaching, dumping, or other releasing into the Environment, whether intentional or unintentional.

"Representative"—with respect to a particular Person, any director, officer, employee, agent, consultant, advisor, or other representative of such Person, including legal counsel, accountants, and financial advisors.

"Securities Act"—the Securities Act of 1933 or any successor law, and regulations and rules issued pursuant to that Act or any successor law.

"Sellers"—as defined in the first paragraph of this Agreement.

"Sellers' Releases"—as defined in Section 2.4.

"Shares"—as defined in the Recitals of this Agreement.

"Subsidiary"—with respect to any Person (the "Owner"), any corporation or other Person of which securities or other interests having the power to elect a majority of that corporation's or other Person's board of directors or similar governing body, or otherwise having the power to direct the business and policies of that corporation or other Person (other than securities or other interests having such power only upon the happening of a contingency that has not occurred) are held by the Owner or one or more of its Subsidiaries; when used without reference to a particular Person, "Subsidiary" means a Subsidiary of the Company.

"Tax Return"—any return (including any information return), report, statement, schedule, notice, form, or other document or information filed with or submitted to, or required to be filed with or submitted to, any Governmental Body in connection with the determination, assessment, collection, or payment of any Tax or in connection with the administration, implementation, or enforcement of or compliance with any Legal Requirement relating to any Tax.

"Threat of Release"—a substantial likelihood of a Release that may require action in order to prevent or mitigate damage to the Environment that may result from such Release.

"Threatened"—a claim, Proceeding, dispute, action, or other matter will be deemed to have been "Threatened" if any demand or statement has been made (orally or in writing) or any notice has been given (orally or in writing), or if any other event has occurred or any other circumstances exist, that would lead a prudent Person to conclude that such a claim, Proceeding, dispute, action, or other matter is likely to be asserted, commenced, taken, or otherwise pursued in the future.

2. SALE AND TRANSFER OF SHARES; CLOSING

2.1 Shares. Subject to the terms and conditions of this Agreement, at the Closing, Sellers will sell and transfer the Shares to Buyer, and Buyer will purchase the Shares from Sellers.

2.2 Purchase Price. The purchase price (the "Purchase Price") for the Shares will be $_____ plus the Adjustment Amount.

2.3 Closing. The purchase and sale (the "Closing") provided for in this Agreement will take place at the offices of Buyer's counsel at _____, at 10:00 a.m. (local time) on the later of (i) _____, 199_ or (ii) the date that is two business days following the termination of the applicable waiting period under the HSR Act, or at such other time and place as the parties may agree. Subject to the provisions of Section 9, failure to consummate the purchase and sale provided for in this Agreement on the date and time and at the place determined pursuant to this Section 2.3 will not result in the termination of this Agreement and will not relieve any party of any obligation under this Agreement.

2.4 Closing Obligations. At the Closing:

(a) Sellers will deliver to Buyer:

(i) certificates representing the Shares, duly endorsed (or accompanied by duly executed stock powers), with signatures guaranteed by a commercial bank or by a member firm of the New York Stock Exchange, for transfer to Buyer;

(ii) releases in the form of Exhibit 2.4(a)(ii) executed by Sellers (collectively, "Sellers' Releases");

(iii) employment agreements in the form of Exhibit 2.4(a)(iii), executed by Sellers (collectively, "Employment Agreements");

(iv) noncompetition agreements in the form of Exhibit 2.4(a)(iv), executed by Sellers (collectively, the "Noncompetition Agreements"); and

(v) a certificate executed by Sellers representing and warranting to Buyer that each of Sellers' representations and warranties in this Agreement was accurate in all respects as of the date of this Agreement and is accurate in all respects as of the Closing Date as if made on the Closing Date (giving full effect to any supplements to the Disclosure Letter that were delivered by Sellers to Buyer prior to the Closing Date in accordance with Section 5.5); and

(b) Buyer will deliver to Sellers:

(i) the following amounts by bank cashier's or certified check payable to the order of [or by wire transfer to accounts specified by] A and B, respectively: $_____ to A and $_____ to B;

(ii) promissory notes payable to A and B in the respective principal amounts of $_____ and $_____ in the form of Exhibit 2.4(b) (the "Promissory Notes");

(iii) the sum of $_____ to the escrow agent referred to in Section 2.4(c) by bank cashier's or certified check;

(iv) a certificate executed by Buyer to the effect that, except as otherwise stated in such certificate, each of Buyer's representations and warranties in this Agreement was accurate in all respects as of the date of this Agreement and is accurate in all respects as of the Closing Date as if made on the Closing Date; and

(v) the Employment Agreements, executed by Buyer.

(c) Buyer and Sellers will enter into an escrow agreement in the form of Exhibit 2.4(c) (the "Escrow Agreement") with _____.

2.5 Adjustment Amount. The Adjustment Amount (which may be a positive or negative number) will be equal to (a) the consolidated stockholders' equity of the Acquired Companies as of the Closing Date determined in accordance with GAAP, minus (b) $_____.

2.6 Adjustment Procedure.

(a) Sellers will prepare and will cause _____, the Company's certified public accountants, to audit consolidated financial statements ("Closing Financial Statements") of the Company as of the Closing Date and for the period from the date of the Balance Sheet through the Closing Date, including a computation of consolidated stockholders' equity as of the Closing Date. Sellers will deliver the Closing Financial Statements to Buyer within sixty days after the Closing Date. If within thirty days following delivery of the Closing Financial Statements, Buyer has not given Sellers notice of its objection to the Closing Financial Statements (such notice must contain a statement of the basis of Buyer's objection), then the consolidated stockholders' equity reflected in the Closing Financial Statements will be used in computing the Adjustment Amount. If Buyer gives such notice of objection, then the issues in dispute will be submitted to _____, certified public accountants (the "Accountants"), for resolution. If issues in dispute are submitted to the Accountants for resolution, (i) each party will furnish to the Accountants such workpapers and other documents and information relating to the disputed issues as the Accountants may request and are available to that party or its Subsidiaries (or its independent public accountants), and will be afforded the opportunity to present to the Accountants any material relating to the determination and to discuss the determination with the Accountants; (ii) the determination by the Accountants, as set forth in a notice delivered to both parties by the Accountants, will be binding and conclusive on the parties; and (iii) Buyer and Sellers will each bear 50% of the fees of the Accountants for such determination.

(b) On the tenth business day following the final determination of the Adjustment Amount, if the Purchase Price is greater than the aggregate of the payments made pursuant to Sections 2.4(b)(i) and 2.4(b)(iii) and the aggregate principal amount of the Promissory Notes, Buyer will pay the difference to Sellers, and if the Purchase Price is less than such aggregate amount, Sellers will pay the difference to Buyer. All payments will be made together with interest at _____% compounded daily beginning on the Closing Date and ending on the date of payment. Payments must be made in immediately available funds. Payments to Sellers must be made in the manner and will be allocated in the proportions set forth in Section 2.4(b)(i). Payments to Buyer must be made by wire transfer to such bank account as Buyer will specify.

3.   REPRESENTATIONS AND WARRANTIES OF SELLERS

Sellers represent and warrant to Buyer as follows:

3.1   Organization and Good Standing.

(a) Part 3.1 of the Disclosure Letter contains a complete and accurate list for each Acquired Company of its name, its jurisdiction of incorporation, other jurisdictions in which it is authorized to do business, and its capitalization (including the identity of each stockholder and the number of shares held by each). Each Acquired Company is a corporation duly organized, validly existing, and in good standing under the laws of its jurisdiction of incorporation, with full corporate power and authority to conduct its business as it is now being conducted, to own or use the properties and assets that it purports to own or use, and to perform all its obligations under Applicable Contracts. Each Acquired Company is duly qualified to do business as a foreign corporation and is in good standing under the laws of each state or other jurisdiction in which either the ownership or use of the properties owned or used by it, or the nature of the activities conducted by it, requires such qualification.

(b) Sellers have delivered to Buyer copies of the Organizational Documents of each Acquired Company, as currently in effect.

3.2   Authority; No Conflict.

(a) This Agreement constitutes the legal, valid, and binding obligation of Sellers, enforceable against Sellers in accordance with its terms. Upon the execution and delivery by Sellers of the Escrow Agreement, the Employment Agreements, the Sellers' Releases, and the Noncompetition Agreements (collectively, the "Sellers' Closing Documents"), the Sellers' Closing Documents will constitute the legal, valid, and binding obligations of Sellers, enforceable against Sellers in accordance with their respective terms. Sellers have the absolute and unrestricted right, power, authority, and capacity to execute and deliver this Agreement and the Sellers' Closing Documents and to perform their obligations under this Agreement and the Sellers' Closing Documents.

(b) Except as set forth in Part 3.2 of the Disclosure Letter, neither the execution and delivery of this Agreement nor the consummation or performance of any of the Contemplated Transactions will, directly or indirectly (with or without notice or lapse of time):

(i) contravene, conflict with, or result in a violation of (A) any provision of the Organizational Documents of the Acquired Companies, or (B) any resolution adopted by the board of directors or the stockholders of any Acquired Company;

(ii) contravene, conflict with, or result in a violation of, or give any Governmental Body or other Person the right to challenge any of the Contemplated Transactions or to exercise any remedy or obtain any relief under, any Legal Requirement or any Order to which any Acquired Company or either Seller, or any of the assets owned or used by any Acquired Company, may be subject;

(iii) contravene, conflict with, or result in a violation of any of the terms or requirements of, or give any Governmental Body the right to revoke, withdraw, suspend, cancel, terminate, or modify, any Governmental Authorization that is held by any Acquired Company or that otherwise relates to the business of, or any of the assets owned or used by, any Acquired Company;

(iv) cause Buyer or any Acquired Company to become subject to, or to become liable for the payment of, any Tax;

(v) cause any of the assets owned by any Acquired Company to be reassessed or revalued by any taxing authority or other Governmental Body;

(vi) contravene, conflict with, or result in a violation or breach of any provision of, or give any Person the right to declare a default or exercise any remedy under, or to accelerate the maturity or performance of, or to cancel, terminate, or modify, any Applicable Contract; or

(vii) result in the imposition or creation of any Encumbrance upon or with respect to any of the assets owned or used by any Acquired Company.

Except as set forth in Part 3.2 of the Disclosure Letter, no Seller or Acquired Company is or will be required to give any notice to or obtain any Consent from any Person in connection with the execution and delivery of this Agreement or the consummation or performance of any of the Contemplated Transactions.

(c) Sellers are acquiring the Promissory Notes for their own account and not with a view to their distribution within the meaning of Section 2(11) of the Securities Act. Each Seller is an "accredited investor" as such term is defined in Rule 501(a) under the Securities Act.

3.3   Capitalization. The authorized equity securities of the Company consist of _____ shares of common stock, par value $_____ per share, of which _____ shares are issued and outstanding and constitute the Shares. Sellers are and will be on the Closing Date the record and beneficial owners and holders of the Shares, free and clear of all Encumbrances. A owns _____ of the Shares and B owns _____ of the Shares. With the exception of the Shares (which are owned by Sellers), all of the outstanding equity securities and other securities of each Acquired Company are owned of record and beneficially by one or more of the Acquired Companies, free and clear of all Encumbrances. No legend or other reference to any purported Encumbrance appears upon any certificate representing equity securities of any Acquired Company. All of the outstanding equity securities of each Acquired Company have been duly authorized and validly issued and are fully paid and nonassessable. There are no Contracts relating to the issuance, sale, or transfer of any equity securities or other securities of any Acquired Company. None of the outstanding equity securities or other securities of any Acquired Company was issued in violation of the Securities Act or any other Legal Requirement. No Acquired Company owns, or has any Contract to acquire, any equity securities or other securities of any Person (other than Acquired Companies) or any direct or indirect equity or ownership interest in any other business.

3.4 Financial Statements. Sellers have delivered to Buyer: (a) [unaudited] consolidated balance sheets of the Acquired Companies as at _____ in each of the years ___ through ___, and the related [unaudited] consolidated statements of income, changes in stockholders' equity, and cash flow for each of the fiscal years then ended, [together with the report thereon of _____, independent certified public accountants,] (b) a consolidated balance sheet of the Acquired Companies as at _____ (including the notes thereto, the "Balance Sheet"), and the related consolidated statements of income, changes in stockholders' equity, and cash flow for the fiscal year then ended, together with the report thereon of _____, independent certified public accountants, and (c) an unaudited consolidated balance sheet of the Acquired Companies as at _____ (the "Interim Balance Sheet") and the related unaudited consolidated statements of income, changes in stockholders' equity, and cash flow for the ___ months then ended, including in each case the notes thereto. Such financial statements and notes fairly present the financial condition and the results of operations, changes in stockholders' equity, and cash flow of the Acquired Companies as at the respective dates of and for the periods referred to in such financial statements, all in accordance with GAAP [, subject, in the case of interim financial statements, to normal recurring year-end adjustments (the effect of which will not, individually or in the aggregate, be materially adverse) and the absence of notes (that, if presented, would not differ materially from those included in the Balance Sheet)]; the financial statements referred to in this Section 3.4 reflect the consistent application of such accounting principles throughout the periods involved [, except as disclosed in the notes to such financial statements]. No financial statements of any Person other than the Acquired Companies are required by GAAP to be included in the consolidated financial statements of the Company.

3.5 Books and Records. The books of account, minute books, stock record books, and other records of the Acquired Companies, all of which have been made available to Buyer, are complete and correct and have been maintained in accordance with sound business practices and the requirements of Section 13(b)(2) of the Securities Exchange Act of 1934, as amended (regardless of whether or not the Acquired Companies are subject to that Section), including the maintenance of an adequate system of internal controls. The minute books of the Acquired Companies contain accurate and complete records of all meetings held of, and corporate action taken by, the stockholders, the Boards of Directors, and committees of the Boards of Directors of the Acquired Companies, and no meeting of any such stockholders, Board of Directors, or committee has been held for which minutes have not been prepared and are not contained in such minute books. At the Closing, all of those books and records will be in the possession of the Acquired Companies.

3.6   Title to Properties; Encumbrances. Part 3.6 of the Disclosure Letter contains a complete and accurate list of all real property, leaseholds, or other interests therein owned by any Acquired Company. [Sellers have delivered or made available to Buyer copies of the deeds and other instruments (as recorded) by which the Acquired Companies acquired such real property and interests, and copies of all title insurance policies, opinions, abstracts, and surveys in the possession of Sellers or the Acquired Companies and relating to such property or interests.] The Acquired Companies own (with good and marketable title in the case of real property, subject only to the matters permitted by the following sentence) all the properties and assets (whether real, personal, or mixed and whether tangible or intangible) that they purport to own [located in the facilities owned or operated by the Acquired Companies or reflected as owned in the books and records of the Acquired Companies], including all of the properties and assets reflected in the Balance Sheet and the Interim Balance Sheet (except for assets held under capitalized leases disclosed or not required to be disclosed in Part 3.6 of the Disclosure Letter and personal property sold since the date of the Balance Sheet and the Interim Balance Sheet, as the case may be, in the Ordinary Course of Business), and all of the properties and assets purchased or otherwise acquired by the Acquired Companies since the date of the Balance Sheet (except for personal property acquired and sold since the date of the Balance Sheet in the Ordinary Course of Business and consistent with past practice) [, which subsequently purchased or acquired properties and assets (other than inventory and short-term investments) are listed in Part 3.6 of the Disclosure Letter]. All material properties and assets reflected in the Balance Sheet and the Interim Balance Sheet are free and clear of all Encumbrances and are not, in the case of real property, subject to any rights of way, building use restrictions, exceptions, variances, reservations, or limitations of any nature except, with respect to all such properties and assets, (a) mortgages or security interests shown on the Balance Sheet or the Interim Balance Sheet as securing specified liabilities or obligations, with respect to which no default (or event that, with notice or lapse of time or both, would constitute a default) exists, (b) mortgages or security interests incurred in connection with the purchase of property or assets after the date of the Interim Balance Sheet (such mortgages and security interests being limited to the property or assets so acquired), with respect to which no default (or event that, with notice or lapse of time or both, would constitute a default) exists, (c) liens for current taxes not yet due, and (d) with respect to real property, (i) minor imperfections of title, if any, none of which is substantial in amount, materially detracts from the value or impairs the use of the property subject thereto, or impairs the operations of any Acquired Company, and (ii) zoning laws and other land use restrictions that do not impair the present or anticipated use of the property subject thereto. All buildings, plants, and structures owned by the Acquired Companies lie wholly within the boundaries of the real property owned by the Acquired Companies and do not encroach upon the property of, or otherwise conflict with the property rights of, any other Person.

3.7   Condition and Sufficiency of Assets. The buildings, plants, structures, and equipment of the Acquired Companies are structurally sound, are in good operating condition and repair, and are adequate for the uses to which they are being put, and none of such buildings, plants, structures, or equipment is in need of maintenance or repairs except for ordinary, routine maintenance and repairs that are not material in nature or cost. The building, plants, structures, and equipment of the Acquired Companies are sufficient for the continued conduct of the Acquired Companies' businesses after the Closing in substantially the same manner as conducted prior to the Closing.

3.8   Accounts Receivable. All accounts receivable of the Acquired Companies that are reflected on the Balance Sheet or the Interim Balance Sheet or on the accounting records of the Acquired Companies as of the Closing Date (collectively, the "Accounts Receivable") represent or will represent valid obligations arising from sales actually made or services actually performed in the Ordinary Course of Business. Unless paid prior to the Closing Date, the Accounts Receivable are or will be as of the Closing Date current and collectible net of the respective reserves shown on the Balance Sheet or the Interim Balance Sheet or on the accounting records of the Acquired Companies as of the Closing Date (which reserves are adequate and calculated consistent with past practice and, in the case of the reserve as of the Closing Date, will not represent a greater percentage of the Accounts Receivable as of the Closing Date than the reserve reflected in the Interim Balance Sheet represented of the Accounts Receivable reflected therein and will not represent a material adverse change in the composition of such Accounts Receivable in terms of aging). Subject to such reserves, each of the Accounts Receivable either has been or will be collected in full, without any set-off, within ninety days after the day on which it first becomes due and payable. There is no contest, claim, or right of set-off, other than returns in the Ordinary Course of Business, under any Contract with any obligor of an Accounts Receivable relating to the amount or validity of such Accounts Receivable. Part 3.8 of the Disclosure Letter contains a complete and accurate list of all Accounts Receivable as of the date of the Interim Balance Sheet, which list sets forth the aging of such Accounts Receivable.

3.9   Inventory. All inventory of the Acquired Companies, whether or not reflected in the Balance Sheet or the Interim Balance Sheet, consists of a quality and quantity usable and salable in the Ordinary Course of Business, except for obsolete items and items of below-standard quality, all of which have been written off or written down to net realizable value in the Balance Sheet or the Interim Balance Sheet or on the accounting records of the Acquired Companies as of the Closing Date, as the case may be. All inventories not written off have been priced at the lower of cost or [market] [net realizable value] on a [last in, first out] [first in, first out] basis. The quantities of each item of inventory (whether raw materials, work-in-process, or finished goods) are not excessive, but are reasonable in the present circumstances of the Acquired Companies.

3.10   No Undisclosed Liabilities. Except as set forth in Part 3.10 of the Disclosure Letter, the Acquired Companies have no liabilities or obligations of any nature (whether known or unknown and whether absolute, accrued, contingent, or otherwise) except for liabilities or obligations reflected or reserved against in the Balance Sheet or the Interim Balance Sheet and current liabilities incurred in the Ordinary Course of Business since the respective dates thereof.

3.11   Taxes.

(a) The Acquired Companies have filed or caused to be filed (on a timely basis since _____) all Tax Returns that are or were required to be filed by or with respect to any of them, either separately or as a member of a group of corporations, pursuant to applicable Legal Requirements. Sellers have delivered [or made available] to Buyer copies of, and Part 3.11 of the Disclosure Letter contains a complete and accurate list of, all such Tax Returns [relating to income or franchise taxes] filed since _____. The Acquired Companies have paid, or made provision for the payment of, all Taxes that have or may have become due pursuant to those Tax Returns or otherwise, or pursuant to any assessment received by Sellers or any Acquired Company, except such Taxes, if any, as are listed in Part 3.11 of the Disclosure Letter and are being contested in good faith and as to which adequate reserves (determined in accordance with GAAP) have been provided in the Balance Sheet and the Interim Balance Sheet.

(b) The United States federal and state income Tax Returns of each Acquired Company subject to such Taxes have been audited by the IRS or relevant state tax authorities or are closed by the applicable statute of limitations for all taxable years through _____. Part 3.11 of the Disclosure Letter contains a complete and accurate list of all audits of all such Tax Returns, including a reasonably detailed description of the nature and outcome of each audit. All deficiencies proposed as a result of such audits have been paid, reserved against, settled, or, as described in Part 3.11 of the Disclosure Letter, are being contested in good faith by appropriate proceedings. Part 3.11 of the Disclosure Letter describes all adjustments to the United States federal income Tax Returns filed by any Acquired Company or any group of corporations including any Acquired Company for all taxable years since _____, and the resulting deficiencies proposed by the IRS. Except as described in Part 3.11 of the Disclosure Letter, no Seller or Acquired Company has given or been requested to give waivers or extensions (or is or would be subject to a waiver or extension given by any other Person) of any statute of limitations relating to the payment of Taxes of any Acquired Company or for which any Acquired Company may be liable.

(c) The charges, accruals, and reserves with respect to Taxes on the respective books of each Acquired Company are adequate (determined in accordance with GAAP) and are at least equal to that Acquired Company's liability for Taxes. There exists no proposed tax assessment against any Acquired Company except as disclosed in the Balance Sheet or in Part 3.11 of the Disclosure Letter. No consent to the application of Section 341(f)(2) of the IRC has been filed with respect to any property or assets held, acquired, or to be acquired by any Acquired Company. All Taxes that any Acquired Company is or was required by Legal Requirements to withhold or collect have been duly withheld or collected and, to the extent required, have been paid to the proper Governmental Body or other Person.

(d) All Tax Returns filed by (or that include on a consolidated basis) any Acquired Company are true, correct, and complete. There is no tax sharing agreement that will require any payment by any Acquired Company after the date of this Agreement. [No Acquired Company is, or within the five-year period preceding the Closing Date has been, an "S" corporation.] [During the consistency period (as defined in Section 338(h)(4) of the IRC with respect to the sale of the Shares to Buyer), no Acquired Company or target affiliate (as defined in Section 338(h)(6) of the IRC with respect to the sale of the Shares to Buyer) has sold or will sell any property or assets to Buyer or to any member of the affiliated group (as defined in Section 338(h)(5) of the IRC) that includes Buyer. Part 3.11 of the Disclosure Letter lists all such target affiliates.]

3.12   No Material Adverse Change. Since the date of the Balance Sheet, there has not been any material adverse change in the business, operations, properties, prospects, assets, or condition of any Acquired Company, and no event has occurred or circumstance exists that may result in such a material adverse change.

3.13   Employee Benefits.

(a) As used in this Section 3.13, the following terms have the meanings set forth below.

"Company Other Benefit Obligation" means an Other Benefit Obligation owed, adopted, or followed by an Acquired Company or an ERISA Affiliate of an Acquired Company.

"Company Plan" means all Plans of which an Acquired Company or an ERISA Affiliate of an Acquired Company is or was a Plan Sponsor, or to which an Acquired Company or an ERISA Affiliate of an Acquired Company otherwise contributes or has contributed, or in which an Acquired Company or an ERISA Affiliate of an Acquired Company otherwise participates or has participated. All references to Plans are to Company Plans unless the context requires otherwise.

"Company VEBA" means a VEBA whose members include employees of any Acquired Company or any ERISA Affiliate of an Acquired Company.

"ERISA Affiliate" means, with respect to an Acquired Company, any other person that, together with the Company, would be treated as a single employer under IRC § 414.

"Multi–Employer Plan" has the meaning given in ERISA § 3(37)(A).

"Other Benefit Obligations" means all obligations, arrangements, or customary practices, whether or not legally enforceable, to provide benefits, other than salary, as compensation for services rendered, to present or former directors, employees, or agents, other than obligations, arrangements, and practices that are Plans. Other Benefit Obligations

include consulting agreements under which the compensation paid does not depend upon the amount of service rendered, sabbatical policies, severance payment policies, and fringe benefits within the meaning of IRC § 132.

"PBGC" means the Pension Benefit Guaranty Corporation, or any successor thereto.

"Pension Plan" has the meaning given in ERISA § 3(2)(A).

"Plan" has the meaning given in ERISA § 3(3).

"Plan Sponsor" has the meaning given in ERISA § 3(16)(B).

"Qualified Plan" means any Plan that meets or purports to meet the requirements of IRC § 401(a).

"Title IV Plans" means all Pension Plans that are subject to Title IV of ERISA, 29 U.S.C. § 1301 et seq., other than Multi–Employer Plans.

"VEBA" means a voluntary employees' beneficiary association under IRC § 501(c)(9).

"Welfare Plan" has the meaning given in ERISA § 3(1).

(b)(i) Part 3.13(i) of the Disclosure Letter contains a complete and accurate list of all Company Plans, Company Other Benefit Obligations, and Company VEBAs, and identifies as such all Company Plans that are (A) defined benefit Pension Plans, (B) Qualified Plans, (C) Title IV Plans, or (D) Multi–Employer Plans.

(ii) Part 3.13(ii) of the Disclosure Letter contains a complete and accurate list of (A) all ERISA Affiliates of each Acquired Company, and (B) all Plans of which any such ERISA Affiliate is or was a Plan Sponsor, in which any such ERISA Affiliate participates or has participated, or to which any such ERISA Affiliate contributes or has contributed.

(iii) Part 3.13(iii) of the Disclosure Letter sets forth, for each Multi–Employer Plan, as of its last valuation date, the amount of potential withdrawal liability of the Acquired Companies and the Acquired Companies' other ERISA Affiliates, calculated according to information made available pursuant to ERISA § 4221(e).

(iv) Part 3.13(iv) of the Disclosure Letter sets forth a calculation of the liability of the Acquired Companies for post-retirement benefits other than pensions, made in accordance with Financial Accounting Statement 106 of the Financial Accounting Standards Board, regardless of whether any Acquired Company is required by this Statement to disclose such information.

(v) Part 3.13(v) of the Disclosure Letter sets forth the financial cost of all obligations owed under any Company Plan or Company Other Benefit Obligation that is not subject to the disclosure and reporting requirements of ERISA.

(c) Sellers have delivered to Buyer, or will deliver to Buyer within ten days of the date of this Agreement:

(i) all documents that set forth the terms of each Company Plan, Company Other Benefit Obligation, or Company VEBA and of any related trust, including (A) all plan descriptions and summary plan descriptions of Company Plans for which Sellers or the Acquired Companies are required to prepare, file, and distribute plan descriptions and summary plan descriptions, and (B) all summaries and descriptions furnished to participants and beneficiaries regarding Company Plans, Company Other Benefit Obligations, and Company VEBAs for which a plan description or summary plan description is not required;

(ii) all personnel, payroll, and employment manuals and policies;

(iii) all collective bargaining agreements pursuant to which contributions have been made or obligations incurred (including both pension and welfare benefits) by the Acquired Companies and the ERISA Affiliates of the Acquired Companies, and all collective bargaining agreements pursuant to which contributions are being made or obligations are owed by such entities;

(iv) a written description of any Company Plan or Company Other Benefit Obligation that is not otherwise in writing;

(v) all registration statements filed with respect to any Company Plan;

(vi) all insurance policies purchased by or to provide benefits under any Company Plan;

(vii) all contracts with third party administrators, actuaries, investment managers, consultants, and other independent contractors that relate to any Company Plan, Company Other Benefit Obligation, or Company VEBA;

(viii) all reports submitted within the four years preceding the date of this Agreement by third party administrators, actuaries, investment managers, consultants, or other independent contractors with respect to any Company Plan, Company Other Benefit Obligation, or Company VEBA;

(ix) all notifications to employees of their rights under ERISA § 601 et seq. and IRC § 4980B;

(x) the Form 5500 filed in each of the most recent three plan years [with respect to each Company Plan], including all schedules thereto and the opinions of independent accountants;

(xi) all notices that were given by any Acquired Company or any ERISA Affiliate of an Acquired Company or any Company Plan to the IRS, the PBGC, or any participant or beneficiary, pursuant to statute, within the four years preceding the date of this Agreement, including notices that are expressly mentioned elsewhere in this Section 3.13;

(xii) all notices that were given by the IRS, the PBGC, or the Department of Labor to any Acquired Company, any ERISA Affiliate of an Acquired Company, or any Company Plan within the four years preceding the date of this Agreement;

(xiii) with respect to Qualified Plans and VEBAs, the most recent determination letter for each Plan of the Acquired Companies that is a Qualified Plan; and

(xiv) with respect to Title IV Plans, the Form PBGC–1 filed for each of the three most recent plan years.

(d) Except as set forth in Part 3.13(vi) of the Disclosure Letter:

(i) The Acquired Companies have performed all of their respective obligations under all Company Plans, Company Other Benefit Obligations, and Company VEBAs. The Acquired Companies have made appropriate entries in their financial records and statements for all obligations and liabilities under such Plans, VEBAs, and Obligations that have accrued but are not due.

(ii) No statement, either written or oral, has been made by any Acquired Company to any Person with regard to any Plan or Other Benefit Obligation that was not in accordance with the Plan or Other Benefit Obligation and that could have an adverse economic consequence to any Acquired Company or to Buyer.

(iii) The Acquired Companies, with respect to all Company Plans, Company Other Benefits Obligations, and Company VEBAs, are, and each Company Plan, Company Other Benefit Obligation, and Company VEBA is, in full compliance with ERISA, the IRC, and other applicable Laws including the provisions of such Laws expressly mentioned in this Section 3.13, and with any applicable collective bargaining agreement.

(A) No transaction prohibited by ERISA § 406 and no "prohibited transaction" under IRC § 4975(c) have occurred with respect to any Company Plan.

(B) No Seller or Acquired Company has any liability to the IRS with respect to any Plan, including any liability imposed by Chapter 43 of the IRC.

(C) No Seller or Acquired Company has any liability to the PBGC with respect to any Plan or has any liability under ERISA § 502 or § 4071.

(D) All filings required by ERISA and the IRC as to each Plan have been timely filed, and all notices and disclosures to participants required by either ERISA or the IRC have been timely provided.

(E) All contributions and payments made or accrued with respect to all Company Plans, Company Other Benefit Obligations, and Company VEBAs are deductible under IRC § 162 or § 404. No amount, or any asset of any Company Plan or Company VEBA, is subject to tax as unrelated business taxable income.

(iv) Each Company Plan can be terminated within thirty days, without payment of any additional contribution or amount and without the vesting or acceleration of any benefits promised by such Plan.

(v) Since _____, 19__, there has been no establishment or amendment of any Company Plan, Company VEBA, or Company Other Benefit Obligation.

(vi) No event has occurred or circumstance exists that could result in a material increase in premium costs of Company Plans and Company Other Benefit Obligations that are insured, or a material increase in benefit costs of such Plans and Obligations that are self-insured.

(vii) Other than claims for benefits submitted by participants or beneficiaries, no claim against, or legal proceeding involving, any Company Plan, Company Other Benefit Obligation, or Company VEBA is pending or, to Sellers' Knowledge, is Threatened.

(viii) No Company Plan is a stock bonus, pension, or profit-sharing plan within the meaning of IRC § 401(a).

(ix) Each Qualified Plan of each Acquired Company is qualified in form and operation under IRC § 401(a); each trust for each such Plan is exempt from federal income tax under IRC § 501(a). Each Company VEBA is exempt from federal income tax. No event has occurred or circumstance exists that will or could give rise to disqualification or loss of tax-exempt status of any such Plan or trust.

(x) Each Acquired Company and each ERISA Affiliate of an Acquired Company has met the minimum funding standard, and has made all contributions required, under ERISA § 302 and IRC § 402.

(xi) No Company Plan is subject to Title IV of ERISA.

(xii) The Acquired Companies have paid all amounts due to the PBGC pursuant to ERISA § 4007.

(xiii) No Acquired Company or any ERISA Affiliate of an Acquired Company has ceased operations at any facility or has withdrawn from any Title IV Plan in a manner that would subject to any entity or Sellers to liability under ERISA § 4062(e), § 4063, or § 4064.

(xiv) No Acquired Company or any ERISA Affiliate of an Acquired Company has filed a notice of intent to terminate any Plan or has adopted any amendment to treat a Plan as terminated. The PBGC has not instituted proceedings to treat any Company Plan as terminated. No event has occurred or circumstance exists that may constitute grounds under ERISA § 4042 for the termination of, or the appointment of a trustee to administer, any Company Plan.

(xv) No amendment has been made, or is reasonably expected to be made, to any Plan that has required or could require the provision of security under ERISA § 307 or IRC § 401(a)(29).

(xvi) No accumulated funding deficiency, whether or not waived, exists with respect to any Company Plan; no event has occurred or circumstance exists that may result in an accumulated funding deficiency as of the last day of the current plan year of any such Plan.

(xvii) The actuarial report for each Pension Plan of each Acquired Company and each ERISA Affiliate of each Acquired Company fairly presents the financial condition and the results of operations of each such Plan in accordance with GAAP.

(xviii) Since the last valuation date for each Pension Plan of each Acquired Company and each ERISA Affiliate of an Acquired Company, no event has occurred or circumstance exists that would increase the amount of benefits under any such Plan or that would cause the excess of Plan assets over benefit liabilities (as defined in ERISA § 4001) to decrease, or the amount by which benefit liabilities exceed assets to increase.

(xiv) No reportable event (as defined in ERISA § 4043 and in regulations issued thereunder) has occurred.

(xx) No Seller or Acquired Company has Knowledge of any facts or circumstances that may give rise to any liability of any Seller, any Acquired Company, or Buyer to the PBGC under Title IV of ERISA.

(xxi) No Acquired Company or any ERISA Affiliate of an Acquired Company has ever established, maintained, or contributed to or otherwise participated in, or had an obligation to maintain, contribute to, or otherwise participate in, any Multi–Employer Plan.

(xxii) No Acquired Company or any ERISA Affiliate of an Acquired Company has withdrawn from any Multi–Employer Plan with respect to which there is any outstanding liability as of the date of this Agreement. No event has occurred or circumstance exists that presents a risk of the occurrence of any withdrawal from, or the participation, termination, reorganization, or insolvency of, any Multi–Employer Plan that could result in any liability of either any Acquired Company or Buyer to a Multi–Employer Plan.

(xxiii) No Acquired Company or any ERISA Affiliate of an Acquired Company has received notice from any Multi–Employer Plan that it is in reorganization or is insolvent, that increased contributions may be required to avoid a reduction in plan benefits or the imposition of any excise tax, or that such Plan intends to terminate or has terminated.

(xxiv) No Multi–Employer Plan to which any Acquired Company or any ERISA Affiliate of an Acquired Company contributes or has contributed is a party to any pending merger or asset or liability transfer or is subject to any proceeding brought by the PBGC.

(xxv) Except to the extent required under ERISA § 601 et seq. and IRC § 4980B, no Acquired Company provides health or welfare benefits for any retired or former employee or is obligated to provide health or welfare benefits to any active employee following such employee's retirement or other termination of service.

(xxvi) Each Acquired Company has the right to modify and terminate benefits to retirees (other than pensions) with respect to both retired and active employees.

(xxii) Sellers and all Acquired Companies have complied with the provisions of ERISA § 601 et seq. and IRC § 4980B.

(xxviii) No payment that is owed or may become due to any director, officer, employee, or agent of any Acquired Company will be non-deductible to the Acquired Companies or subject to tax under IRC § 280G or § 4999; nor will any Acquired Company be required to "gross up" or otherwise compensate any such person because of the imposition of any excise tax on a payment to such person.

(xxiv) The consummation of the Contemplated Transactions will not result in the payment, vesting, or acceleration of any benefit.

3.14 Compliance With Legal Requirements; Governmental Authorizations.

(a) Except as set forth in Part 3.14 of the Disclosure Letter:

(i) each Acquired Company is, and at all times since _____, 19__ has been, in full compliance with each Legal Requirement that is or was applicable to it or to the conduct or operation of its business or the ownership or use of any of its assets;

(ii) no event has occurred or circumstance exists that (with or without notice or lapse of time) (A) may constitute or result in a violation by any Acquired Company of, or a failure on the part of any Acquired Company to comply with, any Legal Requirement, or (B) may give rise to any obligation on the part of any Acquired Company to undertake, or to bear all or any portion of the cost of, any remedial action of any nature; and

(iii) no Acquired Company has received, at any time since _____, 19__, any notice or other communication (whether oral or written) from any Governmental Body or any other Person regarding (A) any actual, alleged, possible, or potential violation of, or failure to comply with, any Legal Requirement, or (B) any actual, alleged, possible, or potential obligation on the part of any Acquired Company to undertake, or to bear all or any portion of the cost of, any remedial action of any nature.

(b) Part 3.14 of the Disclosure Letter contains a complete and accurate list of each Governmental Authorization that is held by any Acquired Company or that otherwise relates to the business of, or to any of the assets owned or used by, any Acquired Company. Each Governmental Authorization listed or required to be listed in Part 3.14 of the Disclosure Letter is valid and in full force and effect. Except as set forth in Part 3.14 of the Disclosure Letter:

(i) each Acquired Company is, and at all times since _____, 19__ has been, in full compliance with all of the terms and requirements of each Governmental Authorization identified or required to be identified in Part 3.14 of the Disclosure Letter;

(ii) no event has occurred or circumstance exists that may (with or without notice or lapse of time) (A) constitute or result directly or indirectly in a violation of or a failure to comply with any term or requirement of any Governmental Authorization listed or required to be listed in Part 3.14 of the Disclosure Letter, or (B) result directly or indirectly in the revocation, withdrawal, suspension, cancellation, or termination of, or any modification to, any Governmental Authorization listed or required to be listed in Part 3.14 of the Disclosure Letter;

(iii) no Acquired Company has received, at any time since _____, 19__, any notice or other communication (whether oral or written) from any Governmental Body or any other Person regarding (A) any actual, alleged, possible, or potential violation of or failure to comply with any term or requirement of any Governmental Authorization, or (B) any actual, proposed, possible, or potential revocation, withdrawal, suspension, cancellation, termination of, or modification to any Governmental Authorization; and

(iv) all applications required to have been filed for the renewal of the Governmental Authorizations listed or required to be listed in Part 3.14 of the Disclosure Letter have been duly filed on a timely basis with the appropriate Governmental Bodies, and all other filings required to have been made with respect to such Governmental Authorizations have been duly made on a timely basis with the appropriate Governmental Bodies.

The Governmental Authorizations listed in Part 3.14 of the Disclosure Letter collectively constitute all of the Governmental Authorizations necessary to permit the Acquired Companies to lawfully conduct and operate their businesses in the manner they currently conduct and operate such businesses and to permit the Acquired Companies to own and use their assets in the manner in which they currently own and use such assets.

3.15 Legal Proceedings; Orders.

(a) Except as set forth in Part 3.15 of the Disclosure Letter, there is no pending Proceeding:

(i) that has been commenced by or against any Acquired Company or that otherwise relates to or may affect the business of, or any of the assets owned or used by, any Acquired Company; or

(ii) that challenges, or that may have the effect of preventing, delaying, making illegal, or otherwise interfering with, any of the Contemplated Transactions.

To the Knowledge of Sellers and the Acquired Companies, (1) no such Proceeding has been Threatened, and (2) no event has occurred or circumstance exists that may give rise to or serve as a basis for the commencement of any such Proceeding. Sellers have delivered to Buyer copies of all pleadings, correspondence, and other documents relating to each Proceeding listed in Part 3.15 of the Disclosure Letter. The Proceedings listed in Part 3.15 of the Disclosure Letter will not have a material adverse effect on the business, operations, assets, condition, or prospects of any Acquired Company.

(b) Except as set forth in Part 3.15 of the Disclosure Letter:

(i) there is no Order to which any of the Acquired Companies, or any of the assets owned or used by any Acquired Company, is subject;

(ii) neither Seller is subject to any Order that relates to the business of, or any of the assets owned or used by, any Acquired Company; and

(iii) [to the Knowledge of Sellers and the Acquired Companies,] no officer, director, agent, or employee of any Acquired Company is subject to any Order that prohibits such officer, director, agent, or employee from engaging in or continuing any conduct, activity, or practice relating to the business of any Acquired Company.

(c) Except as set forth in Part 3.15 of the Disclosure Letter:

(i) each Acquired Company is, and at all times since _____, 19__ has been, in full compliance with all of the terms and requirements of each Order to which it, or any of the assets owned or used by it, is or has been subject;

(ii) no event has occurred or circumstance exists that may constitute or result in (with or without notice or lapse of time) a violation of or failure to comply with any term or requirement of any Order to which any Acquired Company, or any of the assets owned or used by any Acquired Company, is subject; and

(iii) no Acquired Company has received, at any time since _____, 19__, any notice or other communication (whether oral or written) from any Governmental Body or any other Person regarding any actual, alleged, possible, or potential violation of, or failure to comply with, any term or requirement of any Order to which any Acquired Company, or any of the assets owned or used by any Acquired Company, is or has been subject.

3.16 Absence of Certain Changes and Events. Except as set forth in Part 3.16 of the Disclosure Letter, since the date of the Balance Sheet, the Acquired Companies have conducted their businesses only in the Ordinary Course of Business and there has not been any:

(a) change in any Acquired Company's authorized or issued capital stock; grant of any stock option or right to purchase shares of capital stock of any Acquired Company; issuance of any security convertible into such capital stock; grant of any registration rights; purchase, redemption, retirement, or other acquisition by any Acquired Company of any shares of any such capital stock; or declaration or payment of any dividend or other distribution or payment in respect of shares of capital stock;

(b) amendment to the Organizational Documents of any Acquired Company;

(c) payment or increase by any Acquired Company of any bonuses, salaries, or other compensation to any stockholder, director, officer, or (except in the Ordinary Course of Business) employee or entry into any employment, severance, or similar Contract with any director, officer, or employee;

(d) adoption of, or increase in the payments to or benefits under, any profit sharing, bonus, deferred compensation, savings, insurance, pension, retirement, or other employee benefit plan for or with any employees of any Acquired Company;

(e) damage to or destruction or loss of any asset or property of any Acquired Company, whether or not covered by insurance, materially and adversely affecting the properties, assets, business, financial condition, or prospects of the Acquired Companies, taken as a whole;

(f) entry into, termination of, or receipt of notice of termination of (i) any license, distributorship, dealer, sales representative, joint venture, credit, or similar agreement, or (ii) any Contract or transaction involving a total remaining commitment by or to any Acquired Company of at least $_____;

(g) sale (other than sales of inventory in the Ordinary Course of Business), lease, or other disposition of any asset or property of any Acquired Company or mortgage, pledge, or imposition of any lien or other encumbrance on any material asset or property of any Acquired Company, including the sale, lease, or other disposition of any of the Intellectual Property Assets;

(h) cancellation or waiver of any claims or rights with a value to any Acquired Company in excess of $_____;

(i) material change in the accounting methods used by any Acquired Company; or

(j) agreement, whether oral or written, by any Acquired Company to do any of the foregoing.

3.17 Contracts; no Defaults.

(a) Part 3.17(a) of the Disclosure Letter contains a complete and accurate list, and Sellers have delivered to Buyer true and complete copies, of:

(i) each Applicable Contract that involves performance of services or delivery of goods or materials by one or more Acquired Companies of an amount or value in excess of $_____;

(ii) each Applicable Contract that involves performance of services or delivery of goods or materials to one or more Acquired Companies of an amount or value in excess of $_____;

(iii) each Applicable Contract that was not entered into in the Ordinary Course of Business and that involves expenditures or receipts of one or more Acquired Companies in excess of $_____;

(iv) each lease, rental or occupancy agreement, license, installment and conditional sale agreement, and other Applicable Contract affecting the ownership of, leasing of, title to, use of, or any leasehold or other interest in, any real or personal property (except personal property leases and installment and conditional sales agreements having a value per item or aggregate payments of less than $_____ and with terms of less than one year);

(v) each licensing agreement or other Applicable Contract with respect to patents, trademarks, copyrights, or other intellectual property, including agreements with current or former employees, consultants, or contractors regarding the appropriation or the non-disclosure of any of the Intellectual Property Assets;

(vi) each collective bargaining agreement and other Applicable Contract to or with any labor union or other employee representative of a group of employees;

(vii) each joint venture, partnership, and other Applicable Contract (however named) involving a sharing of profits, losses, costs, or liabilities by any Acquired Company with any other Person;

(viii) each Applicable Contract containing covenants that in any way purport to restrict the business activity of any Acquired Company or any Affiliate of an Acquired Company or limit the freedom of any Acquired Company or any Affiliate of an Acquired Company to engage in any line of business or to compete with any Person;

(ix) each Applicable Contract providing for payments to or by any Person based on sales, purchases, or profits, other than direct payments for goods;

(x) each power of attorney that is currently effective and outstanding;

(xi) each Applicable Contract entered into other than in the Ordinary Course of Business that contains or provides for an express undertaking by any Acquired Company to be responsible for consequential damages;

(xii) each Applicable Contract for capital expenditures in excess of $_____;

(xiii) each written warranty, guaranty, and or other similar undertaking with respect to contractual performance extended by any Acquired Company other than in the Ordinary Course of Business; and

(xiv) each amendment, supplement, and modification (whether oral or written) in respect of any of the foregoing.

Part 3.17(a) of the Disclosure Letter sets forth reasonably complete details concerning such Contracts, including the parties to the Contracts, the amount of the remaining commitment of the Acquired Companies under the Contracts, and the Acquired Companies' office where details relating to the Contracts are located.

(b) Except as set forth in Part 3.17(b) of the Disclosure Letter:

(i) neither Seller (and no Related Person of either Seller) has or may acquire any rights under, and neither Seller has or may become subject to any obligation or liability under, any Contract that relates to the business of, or any of the assets owned or used by, any Acquired Company; and

(ii) [to the Knowledge of Sellers and the Acquired Companies,] no officer, director, agent, employee, consultant, or contractor of any Acquired Company is bound by any Contract that purports to limit the ability of such officer, director, agent, employee, consultant, or contractor to (A) engage in or continue any conduct, activity, or practice relating to the business of any Acquired Company, or (B) assign to any Acquired Company or to any other Person any rights to any invention, improvement, or discovery.

(c) Except as set forth in Part 3.17(c) of the Disclosure Letter, each Contract identified or required to be identified in Part 3.17(a) of the Disclosure Letter is in full force and effect and is valid and enforceable in accordance with its terms.

(d) Except as set forth in Part 3.17(d) of the Disclosure Letter:

(i) each Acquired Company is, and at all times since _____, 19__ has been, in full compliance with all applicable terms and requirements of each Contract under which such Acquired Company has or had any obligation or liability or by which such Acquired Company or any of the assets owned or used by such Acquired Company is or was bound;

(ii) each other Person that has or had any obligation or liability under any Contract under which an Acquired Company has or had any rights is, and at all times since _____, 19__ has been, in full compliance with all applicable terms and requirements of such Contract;

(iii) no event has occurred or circumstance exists that (with or without notice or lapse of time) may contravene, conflict with, or result in a violation or breach of, or give any Acquired Company or other Person the right to declare a default or exercise any remedy under, or to accelerate the maturity or performance of, or to cancel, terminate, or modify, any Applicable Contract; and

(iv) no Acquired Company has given to or received from any other Person, at any time since _____, 19__, any notice or other communication (whether oral or written) regarding any actual, alleged, possible, or potential violation or breach of, or default under, any Contract.

(e) There are no renegotiations of, attempts to renegotiate, or outstanding rights to renegotiate any material amounts paid or payable to any Acquired Company under current or completed Contracts with any Person and [, to the Knowledge of Sellers and the Acquired Companies,] no such Person has made written demand for such renegotiation.

(f) The Contracts relating to the sale, design, manufacture, or provision of products or services by the Acquired Companies have been entered into in the Ordinary Course of Business and have been entered into without the commission of any act alone or in concert with any other Person, or any consideration having been paid or promised, that is or would be in violation of any Legal Requirement.

3.18 Insurance.

(a) Sellers have delivered to Buyer:

(i) true and complete copies of all policies of insurance to which any Acquired Company is a party or under which any Acquired Company, or any director of any Acquired Company, is or has been covered at any time within the _____ years preceding the date of this Agreement;

(ii) true and complete copies of all pending applications for policies of insurance; and

(iii) any statement by the auditor of any Acquired Company's financial statements with regard to the adequacy of such entity's coverage or of the reserves for claims.

(b) Part 3.18(b) of the Disclosure Letter describes:

(i) any self-insurance arrangement by or affecting any Acquired Company, including any reserves established thereunder;

(ii) any contract or arrangement, other than a policy of insurance, for the transfer or sharing of any risk by any Acquired Company; and

(iii) all obligations of the Acquired Companies to third parties with respect to insurance (including such obligations under leases and service agreements) and identifies the policy under which such coverage is provided.

(c) Part 3.18(c) of the Disclosure Letter sets forth, by year, for the current policy year and each of the _____ preceding policy years:

(i) a summary of the loss experience under each policy;

(ii) a statement describing each claim under an insurance policy for an amount in excess of $_____, which sets forth:

(A) the name of the claimant;

(B) a description of the policy by insurer, type of insurance, and period of coverage; and

(C) the amount and a brief description of the claim; and

(iii) a statement describing the loss experience for all claims that were self-insured, including the number and aggregate cost of such claims.

(d) Except as set forth on Part 3.18(d) of the Disclosure Letter:

(i) All policies to which any Acquired Company is a party or that provide coverage to either Seller, any Acquired Company, or any director or officer of an Acquired Company:

(A) are valid, outstanding, and enforceable;

(B) are issued by an insurer that is financially sound and reputable;

(C) taken together, provide adequate insurance coverage for the assets and the operations of the Acquired Companies [for all risks normally insured against by a Person carrying on the same business or businesses as the Acquired Companies] [for all risks to which the Acquired Companies are normally exposed];

(D) are sufficient for compliance with all Legal Requirements and Contracts to which any Acquired Company is a party or by which any of them is bound;

(E) will continue in full force and effect following the consummation of the Contemplated Transactions; and

(F) do not provide for any retrospective premium adjustment or other experienced-based liability on the part of any Acquired Company.

(ii) No Seller or Acquired Company has received (A) any refusal of coverage or any notice that a defense will be afforded with reservation of rights, or (B) any notice of cancellation or any other indication that any insurance policy is no longer in full force or effect or will not be renewed or that the issuer of any policy is not willing or able to perform its obligations thereunder.

(iii) The Acquired Companies have paid all premiums due, and have otherwise performed all of their respective obligations, under each policy to which any Acquired Company is a party or that provides coverage to any Acquired Company or director thereof.

(iv) The Acquired Companies have given notice to the insurer of all claims that may be insured thereby.

3.19 Environmental Matters. Except as set forth in part 3.19 of the disclosure letter:

(a) Each Acquired Company is, and at all times has been, in full compliance with, and has not been and is not in violation of or liable under, any Environmental Law. No Seller or Acquired Company has any basis to expect, nor has any of them or any other Person for whose conduct they are or may be held to be responsible received, any actual or Threatened order, notice, or other communication from (i) any Governmental Body or private citizen acting in the public interest, or (ii) the current or prior owner or operator of any Facilities, of any actual or potential violation or failure to comply with any Environmental Law, or of any actual or Threatened obligation to undertake or bear the cost of any Environmental, Health, and Safety Liabilities with respect to any of the Facilities or any other properties or assets (whether real, personal, or mixed) in which Sellers or any Acquired Company has had an interest, or with respect to any property or Facility at or to which Hazardous Materials were generated, manufactured, refined, transferred, imported, used, or processed by Sellers, any Acquired Company, or any other Person for whose conduct they are or may be held responsible, or from which Hazardous Materials have been transported, treated, stored, handled, transferred, disposed, recycled, or received.

(b) There are no pending or, to the Knowledge of Sellers and the Acquired Companies, Threatened claims, Encumbrances, or other restrictions of any nature, resulting from any Environmental, Health, and Safety Liabilities or arising under or pursuant to any Environmental Law, with respect to or affecting any of the Facilities or any other properties and assets (whether real, personal, or mixed) in which Sellers or any Acquired Company has or had an interest.

(c) No Seller or Acquired Company has [Knowledge of] any basis to expect, nor has any of them or any other Person for whose conduct they are or may be held responsible, received, any citation, directive, inquiry, notice,

Order, summons, warning, or other communication that relates to Hazardous Activity, Hazardous Materials, or any alleged, actual, or potential
violation or failure to comply with any Environmental Law, or of any
alleged, actual, or potential obligation to undertake or bear the cost of any
Environmental, Health, and Safety Liabilities with respect to any of the
Facilities or any other properties or assets (whether real, personal, or
mixed) in which Sellers or any Acquired Company had an interest, or with
respect to any property or facility to which Hazardous Materials generated,
manufactured, refined, transferred, imported, used, or processed by Sellers,
any Acquired Company, or any other Person for whose conduct they are or
may be held responsible, have been transported, treated, stored, handled,
transferred, disposed, recycled, or received.

(d) No Seller or Acquired Company, or any other Person for whose
conduct they are or may be held responsible, has any Environmental,
Health, and Safety Liabilities with respect to the Facilities or [, to the
Knowledge of Sellers and the Acquired Companies,] with respect to any
other properties and assets (whether real, personal, or mixed) in which
Sellers or any Acquired Company (or any predecessor), has or had an
interest, or at any property geologically or hydrologically adjoining the
Facilities or any such other property or assets.

(e) There are no Hazardous Materials present on or in the Environment at the Facilities or at any geologically or hydrologically adjoining
property, including any Hazardous Materials contained in barrels, above or
underground storage tanks, landfills, land deposits, dumps, equipment
(whether moveable or fixed) or other containers, either temporary or
permanent, and deposited or located in land, water, sumps, or any other
part of the Facilities or such adjoining property, or incorporated into any
structure therein or thereon. No Seller, Acquired Company, any other
Person for whose conduct they are or may be held responsible, or [to the
Knowledge of Sellers and the Acquired Companies,] any other Person, has
permitted or conducted, or is aware of, any Hazardous Activity conducted
with respect to the Facilities or any other properties or assets (whether
real, personal, or mixed) in which Sellers or any Acquired Company has or
had an interest [except in full compliance with all applicable Environmental Laws].

(f) There has been no Release or, to the Knowledge of Sellers and the
Acquired Companies, Threat of Release, of any Hazardous Materials at or
from the Facilities or at any other locations where any Hazardous Materials were generated, manufactured, refined, transferred, produced, imported, used, or processed from or by the Facilities, or from or by any other
properties and assets (whether real, personal, or mixed) in which Sellers or
any Acquired Company has or had an interest, or [to the Knowledge of
Sellers and the Acquired Companies] any geologically or hydrologically
adjoining property, whether by Sellers, any Acquired Company, or any
other Person.

(g) Sellers have delivered to Buyer true and complete copies and
results of any reports, studies, analyses, tests, or monitoring possessed or
initiated by Sellers or any Acquired Company pertaining to Hazardous

Materials or Hazardous Activities in, on, or under the Facilities, or concerning compliance by Sellers, any Acquired Company, or any other Person for whose conduct they are or may be held responsible, with Environmental Laws.

3.20 Employees.

(a) Part 3.20 of the Disclosure Letter contains a complete and accurate list of the following information for each employee or director of the Acquired Companies, including each employee on leave of absence or layoff status: employer; name; job title; current compensation paid or payable and any change in compensation since _____, 199__; vacation accrued; and service credited for purposes of vesting and eligibility to participate under any Acquired Company's pension, retirement, profit-sharing, thrift-savings, deferred compensation, stock bonus, stock option, cash bonus, employee stock ownership (including investment credit or payroll stock ownership), severance pay, insurance, medical, welfare, or vacation plan, other Employee Pension Benefit Plan or Employee Welfare Benefit Plan, or any other employee benefit plan or any Director Plan.

(b) No employee or director of any Acquired Company is a party to, or is otherwise bound by, any agreement or arrangement, including any confidentiality, noncompetition, or proprietary rights agreement, between such employee or director and any other Person ("Proprietary Rights Agreement") that in any way adversely affects or will affect (i) the performance of his duties as an employee or director of the Acquired Companies, or (ii) the ability of any Acquired Company to conduct its business, including any Proprietary Rights Agreement with Sellers or the Acquired Companies by any such employee or director. To Sellers' Knowledge, no director, officer, or other key employee of any Acquired Company intends to terminate his employment with such Acquired Company.

(c) Part 3.20 of the Disclosure Letter also contains a complete and accurate list of the following information for each retired employee or director of the Acquired Companies, or their dependents, receiving benefits or scheduled to receive benefits in the future: name, pension benefit, pension option election, retiree medical insurance coverage, retiree life insurance coverage, and other benefits.

3.21 Labor Relations; Compliance. Since _____, 19__, no Acquired Company has been or is a party to any collective bargaining or other labor Contract. Since _____, 19__, there has not been, there is not presently pending or existing, and [to Sellers' Knowledge] there is not Threatened, (a) any strike, slowdown, picketing, work stoppage, or employee grievance process, (b) any Proceeding against or affecting any Acquired Company relating to the alleged violation of any Legal Requirement pertaining to labor relations or employment matters, including any charge or complaint filed by an employee or union with the National Labor Relations Board, the Equal Employment Opportunity Commission, or any comparable Governmental Body, organizational activity, or other labor or employment dispute against or affecting any of the Acquired Companies or their premises, or (c) any application for certification of a collective bargaining agent. [To Sellers' Knowledge] No event has occurred or circumstance

exists that could provide the basis for any work stoppage or other labor dispute. There is no lockout of any employees by any Acquired Company, and no such action is contemplated by any Acquired Company. Each Acquired Company has complied in all respects with all Legal Requirements relating to employment, equal employment opportunity, nondiscrimination, immigration, wages, hours, benefits, collective bargaining, the payment of social security and similar taxes, occupational safety and health, and plant closing. No Acquired Company is liable for the payment of any compensation, damages, taxes, fines, penalties, or other amounts, however designated, for failure to comply with any of the foregoing Legal Requirements.

3.22 Intellectual Property.

(a) *Intellectual Property Assets*—The term "Intellectual Property Assets" includes:

(i) the name [the Company's name], all fictional business names, trading names, registered and unregistered trademarks, service marks, and applications (collectively, "Marks");

(ii) all patents, patent applications, and inventions and discoveries that may be patentable (collectively, "Patents");

(iii) all copyrights in both published works and unpublished works (collectively, "Copyrights");

(iv) all rights in mask works (collectively, "Rights in Mask Works"); and

(v) all know-how, trade secrets, confidential information, customer lists, software, technical information, data, process technology, plans, drawings, and blue prints (collectively, "Trade Secrets"); owned, used, or licensed by any Acquired Company as licensee or licensor.

(b) *Agreements*—Part 3.22(b) of the Disclosure Letter contains a complete and accurate list and summary description, including any royalties paid or received by the Acquired Companies, of all Contracts relating to the Intellectual Property Assets to which any Acquired Company is a party or by which any Acquired Company is bound, except for any license implied by the sale of a product and perpetual, paid-up licenses for commonly available software programs with a value of less than $_____ under which an Acquired Company is the licensee. There are no outstanding and, to Sellers' Knowledge, no Threatened disputes or disagreements with respect to any such agreement.

(c) *Know–How Necessary for the Business.*

(i) The Intellectual Property Assets are all those necessary for the operation of the Acquired Companies' businesses as they are currently conducted [or as reflected in the business plan given to Buyer]. One or more of the Acquired Companies is the owner of all right, title, and interest in and to each of the Intellectual Property Assets, free and clear of all liens, security interests, charges, encumbrances, equities, and other adverse claims, and has the right to use without payment to a third party all of the Intellectual Property Assets.

(ii) Except as set forth in Part 3.22(c) of the Disclosure Letter, all former and current employees of each Acquired Company have executed written Contracts with one or more of the Acquired Companies that assign to one or more of the Acquired Companies all rights to any inventions, improvements, discoveries, or information relating to the business of any Acquired Company. No employee of any Acquired Company has entered into any Contract that restricts or limits in any way the scope or type of work in which the employee may be engaged or requires the employee to transfer, assign, or disclose information concerning his work to anyone other than one or more of the Acquired Companies.

(d) *Patents*.

(i) Part 3.22(d) of the Disclosure Letter contains a complete and accurate list and summary description of all Patents. One or more of the Acquired Companies is the owner of all right, title, and interest in and to each of the Patents, free and clear of all liens, security interests, charges, encumbrances, entities, and other adverse claims.

(ii) All of the issued Patents are currently in compliance with formal legal requirements (including payment of filing, examination, and maintenance fees and proofs of working or use), are valid and enforceable, and are not subject to any maintenance fees or taxes or actions falling due within ninety days after the Closing Date.

(iii) No Patent has been or is now involved in any interference, reissue, reexamination, or opposition proceeding. To Sellers' Knowledge, there is no potentially interfering patent or patent application of any third party.

(iv) No Patent is infringed or, to Sellers' Knowledge, has been challenged or threatened in any way. None of the products manufactured and sold, nor any process or know-how used, by any Acquired Company infringes or is alleged to infringe any patent or other proprietary right of any other Person.

(v) All products made, used, or sold under the Patents have been marked with the proper patent notice.

(e) *Trademarks*.

(i) Part 3.22(e) of Disclosure Letter contains a complete and accurate list and summary description of all Marks. One or more of the Acquired Companies is the owner of all right, title, and interest in and to each of the Marks, free and clear of all liens, security interests, charges, encumbrances, equities, and other adverse claims.

(ii) All Marks that have been registered with the United States Patent and Trademark Office are currently in compliance with all formal legal requirements (including the timely post-registration filing of affidavits of use and incontestability and renewal applications), are valid and enforceable, and are not subject to any maintenance fees or taxes or actions falling due within ninety days after the Closing Date.

(iii) No Mark has been or is now involved in any opposition, invalidation, or cancellation and, to Sellers' Knowledge, no such action is Threatened with the respect to any of the Marks.

(iv) To Sellers' Knowledge, there is no potentially interfering trademark or trademark application of any third party.

(v) No Mark is infringed or, to Sellers' Knowledge, has been challenged or threatened in any way. None of the Marks used by any Acquired Company infringes or is alleged to infringe any trade name, trademark, or service mark of any third party.

(vi) All products and materials containing a Mark bear the proper federal registration notice where permitted by law.

(f) *Copyrights*.

(i) Part 3.22(f) of the Disclosure Letter contains a complete and accurate list and summary description of all Copyrights. One or more of the Acquired Companies is the owner of all right, title, and interest in and to each of the Copyrights, free and clear of all liens, security interests, charges, encumbrances, equities, and other adverse claims.

(ii) All the Copyrights have been registered and are currently in compliance with formal legal requirements, are valid and enforceable, and are not subject to any maintenance fees or taxes or actions falling due within ninety days after the date of Closing.

(iii) No Copyright is infringed or, to Sellers' Knowledge, has been challenged or threatened in any way. None of the subject matter of any of the Copyrights infringes or is alleged to infringe any copyright of any third party or is a derivative work based on the work of a third party.

(iv) All works encompassed by the Copyrights have been marked with the proper copyright notice.

(g) *Trade Secrets*.

(i) With respect to each Trade Secret, the documentation relating to such Trade Secret is current, accurate, and sufficient in detail and content to identify and explain it and to allow its full and proper use without reliance on the knowledge or memory of any individual.

(ii) Sellers and the Acquired Companies have taken all reasonable precautions to protect the secrecy, confidentiality, and value of their Trade Secrets.

(iii) One or more of the Acquired Companies has good title and an absolute (but not necessarily exclusive) right to use the Trade Secrets. The Trade Secrets are not part of the public knowledge or literature, and, to Sellers' Knowledge, have not been used, divulged, or appropriated either for the benefit of any Person (other than one or more of the Acquired Companies) or to the detriment of the Acquired Companies. No Trade Secret is subject to any adverse claim or has been challenged or threatened in any way.

3.23   Certain Payments. Since _____, 19_, no Acquired Company or director, officer, agent, or employee of any Acquired Company, or [to Sellers' Knowledge] any other Person associated with or acting for or on behalf of any Acquired Company, has directly or indirectly (a) made any contribution, gift, bribe, rebate, payoff, influence payment, kickback, or other payment to any Person, private or public, regardless of form, whether in money, property, or services (i) to obtain favorable treatment in securing business, (ii) to pay for favorable treatment for business secured, (iii) to obtain special concessions or for special concessions already obtained, for or in respect of any Acquired Company or any Affiliate of an Acquired Company, or (iv) in violation of any Legal Requirement, (b) established or maintained any fund or asset that has not been recorded in the books and records of the Acquired Companies.

3.24   Disclosure.

(a) No representation or warranty of Sellers in this Agreement and no statement in the Disclosure Letter omits to state a material fact necessary to make the statements herein or therein, in light of the circumstances in which they were made, not misleading.

(b) No notice given pursuant to Section 5.5 will contain any untrue statement or omit to state a material fact necessary to make the statements therein or in this Agreement, in light of the circumstances in which they were made, not misleading.

(c) There is no fact known to either Seller that has specific application to either Seller or any Acquired Company (other than general economic or industry conditions) and that materially adversely affects [or, as far as either Seller can reasonably foresee, materially threatens,] the assets, business, prospects, financial condition, or results of operations of the Acquired Companies (on a consolidated basis) that has not been set forth in this Agreement or the Disclosure Letter.

3.25   Relationships With Related Persons. No Seller or any Related Person of Sellers or of any Acquired Company has, or since [the first day of the next to last completed fiscal year of the Acquired Companies] has had, any interest in any property (whether real, personal, or mixed and whether tangible or intangible), used in or pertaining to the Acquired Companies' businesses. No Seller or any Related Person of Sellers or of any Acquired Company is, or since [the first day of the next to last completed fiscal year of the Acquired Companies] has owned (of record or as a beneficial owner) an equity interest or any other financial or profit interest in, a Person that has (i) had business dealings or a material financial interest in any transaction with any Acquired Company [other than business dealings or transactions conducted in the Ordinary Course of Business with the Acquired Companies at substantially prevailing market prices and on substantially prevailing market terms], or (ii) engaged in competition with any Acquired Company with respect to any line of the products or services of such Acquired Company (a "Competing Business") in any market presently served by such Acquired Company [except for less than one percent of the outstanding capital stock of any Competing Business that is publicly traded on any recognized exchange or in the over-the-counter market]. Except as set forth in Part 3.25 of the Disclosure Letter, no Seller or any Related Person of Sellers or of any Acquired Company is a party to any Contract with, or has any claim or right against, any Acquired Company.

3.26 Brokers or Finders. Sellers and their agents have incurred no obligation or liability, contingent or otherwise, for brokerage or finders' fees or agents' commissions or other similar payment in connection with this Agreement.

4. REPRESENTATIONS AND WARRANTIES OF BUYER

Buyer represents and warrants to Sellers as follows:

4.1 Organization and Good Standing. Buyer is a corporation duly organized, validly existing, and in good standing under the laws of the State of _____.

4.2 Authority; No Conflict.

(a) This Agreement constitutes the legal, valid, and binding obligation of Buyer, enforceable against Buyer in accordance with its terms. Upon the execution and delivery by Buyer of the Escrow Agreement, the Employment Agreements, and the Promissory Notes (collectively, the "Buyer's Closing Documents"), the Buyer's Closing Documents will constitute the legal, valid, and binding obligations of Buyer, enforceable against Buyer in accordance with their respective terms. Buyer has the absolute and unrestricted right, power, and authority to execute and deliver this Agreement and the Buyer's Closing Documents and to perform its obligations under this Agreement and the Buyer's Closing Documents.

(b) Except as set forth in Schedule 4.2, neither the execution and delivery of this Agreement [by Buyer] nor the consummation or performance of any of the Contemplated Transactions [by Buyer] will give any Person the right to prevent, delay, or otherwise interfere with any of the Contemplated Transactions pursuant to:

> (i) any provision of Buyer's Organizational Documents;

> (ii) any resolution adopted by the board of directors or the stockholders of Buyer;

> (iii) any Legal Requirement or Order to which Buyer may be subject; or

> (iv) any Contract to which Buyer is a party or by which Buyer may be bound.

Except as set forth in Schedule 4.2, Buyer is not and will not be required to obtain any Consent from any Person in connection with the execution and delivery of this Agreement or the consummation or performance of any of the Contemplated Transactions.

4.3 Investment Intent. Buyer is acquiring the Shares for its own account and not with a view to their distribution within the meaning of Section 2(11) of the Securities Act.

4.4 Certain Proceedings. There is no pending Proceeding that has been commenced against Buyer and that challenges, or may have the effect of preventing, delaying, making illegal, or otherwise interfering with, any of the Contemplated Transactions. To Buyer's Knowledge, no such Proceeding has been Threatened.

4.5 Brokers or Finders. Buyer and its officers and agents have incurred no obligation or liability, contingent or otherwise, for brokerage or finders' fees or agents' commissions or other similar payment in connection with this Agreement and will indemnify and hold Sellers harmless from any such payment alleged to be due by or through Buyer as a result of the action of Buyer or its officers or agents.

5. COVENANTS OF SELLERS PRIOR TO CLOSING DATE

5.1 Access and Investigation. Between the date of this Agreement and the Closing Date, Sellers will, and will cause each Acquired Company and its Representatives to, (a) afford Buyer and its Representatives and prospective lenders and their Representatives (collectively, "Buyer's Advisors") full and free access to each Acquired Company's personnel, properties (including subsurface testing), contracts, books and records, and other documents and data, (b) furnish Buyer and Buyer's Advisors with copies of all such contracts, books and records, and other existing documents and data as Buyer may reasonably request, and (c) furnish Buyer and Buyer's Advisors with such additional financial, operating, and other data and information as Buyer may reasonably request.

5.2 Operation of the Businesses of the Acquired Companies. Between the date of this Agreement and the Closing Date, Sellers will, and will cause each Acquired Company to:

(a) conduct the business of such Acquired Company only in the Ordinary Course of Business;

(b) use their Best Efforts to preserve intact the current business organization of such Acquired Company, keep available the services of the current officers, employees, and agents of such Acquired Company, and maintain the relations and good will with suppliers, customers, landlords, creditors, employees, agents, and others having business relationships with such Acquired Company;

(c) confer with Buyer concerning operational matters of a material nature; and

(d) otherwise report periodically to Buyer concerning the status of the business, operations, and finances of such Acquired Company.

5.3 Negative Covenant. Except as otherwise expressly permitted by this Agreement, between the date of this Agreement and the Closing Date, Sellers will not, and will cause each Acquired Company not to, without the prior consent of Buyer, take any affirmative action, or fail to take any reasonable action within their or its control, as a result of which any of the changes or events listed in Section 3.16 is likely to occur.

5.4   Required Approvals. As promptly as practicable after the date of this Agreement, Sellers will, and will cause each Acquired Company to, make all filings required by Legal Requirements to be made by them in order to consummate the Contemplated Transactions (including all filings under the HSR Act). Between the date of this Agreement and the Closing Date, Sellers will, and will cause each Acquired Company to, (a) cooperate with Buyer with respect to all filings that Buyer elects to make or is required by Legal Requirements to make in connection with the Contemplated Transactions, and (b) cooperate with Buyer in obtaining all consents identified in Schedule 4.2 (including taking all actions requested by Buyer to cause early termination of any applicable waiting period under the HSR Act).

5.5   Notification. Between the date of this Agreement and the Closing Date, each Seller will promptly notify Buyer in writing if such Seller or any Acquired Company becomes aware of any fact or condition that causes or constitutes a Breach of any of Sellers' representations and warranties as of the date of this Agreement, or if such Seller or any Acquired Company becomes aware of the occurrence after the date of this Agreement of any fact or condition that would (except as expressly contemplated by this Agreement) cause or constitute a Breach of any such representation or warranty had such representation or warranty been made as of the time of occurrence or discovery of such fact or condition. Should any such fact or condition require any change in the Disclosure Letter if the Disclosure Letter were dated the date of the occurrence or discovery of any such fact or condition, Sellers will promptly deliver to Buyer a supplement to the Disclosure Letter specifying such change. During the same period, each Seller will promptly notify Buyer of the occurrence of any Breach of any covenant of Sellers in this Section 5 or of the occurrence of any event that may make the satisfaction of the conditions in Section 7 impossible or unlikely.

5.6   Payment of Indebtedness by Related Persons. Except as expressly provided in this Agreement, Sellers will cause all indebtedness owed to an Acquired Company by either Seller or any Related Person of either Seller to be paid in full prior to Closing.

5.7   No Negotiation. Until such time, if any, as this Agreement is terminated pursuant to Section 9, Sellers will not, and will cause each Acquired Company and each of their Representatives not to, directly or indirectly solicit, initiate, or encourage any inquiries or proposals from, discuss or negotiate with, provide any non-public information to, or consider the merits of any unsolicited inquiries or proposals from, any Person (other than Buyer) relating to any transaction involving the sale of the business or assets (other than in the Ordinary Course of Business) of any Acquired Company, or any of the capital stock of any Acquired Company, or any merger, consolidation, business combination, or similar transaction involving any Acquired Company.

5.8   Best Efforts. Between the date of this Agreement and the Closing Date, Sellers will use their Best Efforts to cause the conditions in Sections 7 and 8 to be satisfied.

6.   COVENANTS OF BUYER PRIOR TO CLOSING DATE

6.1   Approvals of Governmental Bodies. As promptly as practicable after the date of this Agreement, Buyer will, and will cause each of its Related Persons to, make all filings required by Legal Requirements to be made by them to consummate the Contemplated Transactions (including all filings under the HSR Act). Between the date of this Agreement and the Closing Date, Buyer will, and will cause each Related Person to, cooperate with Sellers with respect to all filings that Sellers are required by Legal Requirements to make in connection with the Contemplated Transactions, and (ii) cooperate with Sellers in obtaining all consents identified in Part 3.2 of the Disclosure Letter; provided that this Agreement will not require Buyer to dispose of or make any change in any portion of its business or to incur any other burden to obtain a Governmental Authorization.

6.2   Best Efforts. Except as set forth in the proviso to Section 6.1, between the date of this Agreement and the Closing Date, Buyer will use its Best Efforts to cause the conditions in Sections 7 and 8 to be satisfied.

7.   CONDITIONS PRECEDENT TO BUYER'S OBLIGATION TO CLOSE

Buyer's obligation to purchase the Shares and to take the other actions required to be taken by Buyer at the Closing is subject to the satisfaction, at or prior to the Closing, of each of the following conditions (any of which may be waived by Buyer, in whole or in part):

7.1   Accuracy of Representations.

(a) All of Sellers' representations and warranties in this Agreement (considered collectively), and each of these representations and warranties (considered individually), must have been accurate in all material respects as of the date of this Agreement, and must be accurate in all material respects as of the Closing Date as if made on the Closing Date, without giving effect to any supplement to the Disclosure Letter.

(b) Each of Sellers' representations and warranties in Sections [3.3, 3.4, 3.12, and 3.24] must have been accurate in all respects as of the date of this Agreement, and must be accurate in all respects as of the Closing Date as if made on the Closing Date, without giving effect to any supplement to the Disclosure Letter.

7.2   Sellers' Performance.

(a) All of the covenants and obligations that Sellers are required to perform or to comply with pursuant to this Agreement at or prior to the Closing (considered collectively), and each of these covenants and obligations (considered individually), must have been duly performed and complied with in all material respects.

(b) Each document required to be delivered pursuant to Section 2.4 must have been delivered, and each of the other covenants and obligations in Sections [5.4 and 5.8] must have been performed and complied with in all respects.

7.3   Consents. Each of the Consents identified in subparts _____ and _____ of Part 3.2 of the Disclosure Letter, and each Consent identified in Schedule 4.2, must have been obtained and must be in full force and effect.

7.4 Additional Documents. Each of the following documents must have been delivered to Buyer:

(a) an opinion of _____, dated the Closing Date, in the form of Exhibit 7.4(a);

(b) estoppel certificates executed on behalf of _____ and _____, dated as of [a date not more than ___ days prior to] the Closing Date, each in the form of Exhibit 7.4(b); and

(c) such other documents as Buyer may reasonably request for the purpose of (i) enabling its counsel to provide the opinion referred to in Section 8.4(a), (ii) evidencing the accuracy of any of Sellers' representations and warranties, (iii) evidencing the performance by either Seller of, or the compliance by either Seller with, any covenant or obligation required to be performed or complied with by such Seller, (iv) evidencing the satisfaction of any condition referred to in this Section 7, or (v) otherwise facilitating the consummation or performance of any of the Contemplated Transactions.

7.5 No Proceedings. Since the date of this Agreement, there must not have been commenced or Threatened against Buyer, or against any Person affiliated with Buyer, any Proceeding (a) involving any challenge to, or seeking damages or other relief in connection with, any of the Contemplated Transactions, or (b) that may have the effect of preventing, delaying, making illegal, or otherwise interfering with any of the Contemplated Transactions.

7.6 No Claim Regarding Stock Ownership or Sale Proceeds. There must not have been made or Threatened by any Person any claim asserting that such Person (a) is the holder or the beneficial owner of, or has the right to acquire or to obtain beneficial ownership of, any stock of, or any other voting, equity, or ownership interest in, any of the Acquired Companies, or (b) is entitled to all or any portion of the Purchase Price payable for the Shares.

7.7 No Prohibition. Neither the consummation nor the performance of any of the Contemplated Transactions will, directly or indirectly (with or without notice or lapse of time), materially contravene, or conflict with, or result in a material violation of, or cause Buyer or any Person affiliated with Buyer to suffer any material adverse consequence under, (a) any applicable Legal Requirement or Order, or (b) any Legal Requirement or Order that has been published, introduced, or otherwise [formally] proposed by or before any Governmental Body.

8. CONDITIONS PRECEDENT TO SELLERS' OBLIGATION TO CLOSE

Sellers' obligation to sell the Shares and to take the other actions required to be taken by Sellers at the Closing is subject to the satisfaction, at or prior to the Closing, of each of the following conditions (any of which may be waived by Sellers, in whole or in part):

8.1   Accuracy of Representations. All of Buyer's representations and warranties in this Agreement (considered collectively), and each of these representations and warranties (considered individually), must have been accurate in all material respects as of the date of this Agreement and must be accurate in all material respects as of the Closing Date as if made on the Closing Date.

8.2   Buyer's Performance.

(a) All of the covenants and obligations that Buyer is required to perform or to comply with pursuant to this Agreement at or prior to the Closing (considered collectively), and each of these covenants and obligations (considered individually), must have been performed and complied with in all material respects.

(b) Buyer must have delivered each of the documents required to be delivered by Buyer pursuant to Section 2.4 and must have made the cash payments required to be made by Buyer pursuant to Sections 2.4(b)(i) and 2.4(b)(ii).

8.3   Consents. Each of the Consents identified in Subpart _____ of Part 3.2 of the Disclosure Letter must have been obtained and must be in full force and effect.

8.4   Additional Documents. Buyer must have caused the following documents to be delivered to Sellers:

(a) an opinion of _____, dated the Closing Date, in the form of Exhibit 8.4(a); and

(b) such other documents as Sellers may reasonably request for the purpose of (i) enabling their counsel to provide the opinion referred to in Section 7.4(a), (ii) evidencing the accuracy of any representation or warranty of Buyer, (iii) evidencing the performance by Buyer of, or the compliance by Buyer with, any covenant or obligation required to be performed or complied with by Buyer, (ii) evidencing the satisfaction of any condition referred to in this Section 8, or (v) otherwise facilitating the consummation of any of the Contemplated Transactions.

8.5   No Injunction. There must not be in effect any Legal Requirement or any injunction or other Order that (a) prohibits the sale of the Shares by Sellers to Buyer, and (b) has been adopted or issued, or has otherwise become effective, since the date of this Agreement.

9.   TERMINATION

9.1   Termination Events. This Agreement may, by notice given prior to or at the Closing, be terminated:

(a) by either Buyer or Sellers if a material Breach of any provision of this Agreement has been committed by the other party and such Breach has not been waived;

(b)(i) by Buyer if any of the conditions in Section 7 has not been satisfied as of the Closing Date or if satisfaction of such a condition is or becomes impossible (other than through the failure of Buyer to comply with its obligations under this Agreement) and Buyer has not waived such condition on or before the Closing Date; or (ii) by Sellers, if any of the conditions in Section 8 has not been satisfied of the Closing Date or if satisfaction of such a condition is or becomes impossible (other than through the failure of Sellers to comply with their obligations under this Agreement) and Sellers have not waived such condition on or before the Closing Date;

(c) by mutual consent of Buyer and Sellers; or

(d) by either Buyer or Sellers if the Closing has not occurred (other than through the failure of any party seeking to terminate this Agreement to comply fully with its obligations under this Agreement) on or before _____, or such later date as the parties may agree upon.

9.2   Effect of Termination. Each party's right of termination under Section 9.1 is in addition to any other rights it may have under this Agreement or otherwise, and the exercise of a right of termination will not be an election of remedies. If this Agreement is terminated pursuant to Section 9.1, all further obligations of the parties under this Agreement will terminate, except that the obligations in Sections 11.1 and 11.3 will survive; provided, however, that if this Agreement is terminated by a party because of the Breach of the Agreement by the other party or because one or more of the conditions to the terminating party's obligations under this Agreement is not satisfied as a result of the other party's failure to comply with its obligations under this Agreement, the terminating party's right to pursue all legal remedies will survive such termination unimpaired.

10.   INDEMNIFICATION; REMEDIES

10.1   Survival; Right to Indemnification not Affected by Knowledge. All representations, warranties, covenants, and obligations in this Agreement, the Disclosure Letter, the supplements to the Disclosure Letter, the certificate delivered pursuant to Section 2.4(a)(v), and any other certificate or document delivered pursuant to this Agreement will survive the Closing. The right to indemnification, payment of Damages or other remedy based on such representations, warranties, covenants, and obligations will not be affected by any investigation conducted with respect to, or any Knowledge acquired (or capable of being acquired) at any time, whether before or after the execution and delivery of this Agreement or the Closing Date, with respect to the accuracy or inaccuracy of or compliance with, any such representation, warranty, covenant, or obligation. The waiver of any condition based on the accuracy of any representation or warranty, or on the performance of or compliance with any covenant or obligation, will not affect the right to indemnification, payment of Damages, or other remedy based on such representations, warranties, covenants, and obligations.

10.2   Indemnification and Payment of Damages by Sellers. Sellers, jointly and severally, will indemnify and hold harmless Buyer, the Acquired Companies, and their respective Representatives, stockholders, controlling persons, and affiliates (collectively, the "Indemnified Persons") for, and will pay to the Indemnified Persons the amount of, any loss, liability, claim, damage (including incidental and consequential damages), expense (including costs of investigation and defense and reasonable attorneys' fees) or diminution of value, whether or not involving a third-party claim (collectively, "Damages"), arising, directly or indirectly, from or in connection with:

(a) any Breach of any representation or warranty made by Sellers in this Agreement (without giving effect to any supplement to the Disclosure Letter), the Disclosure Letter, the supplements to the Disclosure Letter, or any other certificate or document delivered by Sellers pursuant to this Agreement;

(b) any Breach of any representation or warranty made by Sellers in this Agreement as if such representation or warranty were made on and as of the Closing Date without giving effect to any supplement to the Disclosure Letter, other than any such Breach that is disclosed in a supplement to the Disclosure Letter and is expressly identified in the certificate delivered pursuant to Section 2.4(a)(v) as having caused the condition specified in Section 7.1 not to be satisfied;

(c) any Breach by either Seller of any covenant or obligation of such Seller in this Agreement;

(d) any product shipped or manufactured by, or any services provided by, any Acquired Company prior to the Closing Date;

(e) any matter disclosed in Part _____ of the Disclosure Letter; or

(f) any claim by any Person for brokerage or finder's fees or commissions or similar payments based upon any agreement or understanding alleged to have been made by any such Person with either Seller or any Acquired Company (or any Person acting on their behalf) in connection with any of the Contemplated Transactions.

The remedies provided in this Section 10.2 will not be exclusive of or limit any other remedies that may be available to Buyer or the other Indemnified Persons.

10.3 Indemnification and Payment of Damages by Sellers—Environmental Matters. In addition to the provisions of Section 10.2, Sellers, jointly and severally, will indemnify and hold harmless Buyer, the Acquired Companies, and the other Indemnified Persons for, and will pay to Buyer, the Acquired Companies, and the other Indemnified Persons the amount of, any Damages (including costs of cleanup, containment, or other remediation) arising, directly or indirectly, from or in connection with:

(a) any Environmental, Health, and Safety Liabilities arising out of or relating to: (i) (A) the ownership, operation, or condition at any time on or prior to the Closing Date of the Facilities or any other properties and assets (whether real, personal, or mixed and whether tangible or intangible) in which Sellers or any Acquired Company has or had an interest, or (B) any Hazardous Materials or other contaminants that were present on the Facilities or such other properties and assets at any time on or prior to the Closing Date; or (ii) (A) any Hazardous Materials or other contaminants, wherever located, that were, or were allegedly, generated, transported, stored, treated, Released, or otherwise handled by Sellers or any Acquired

Company or by any other Person for whose conduct they are or may be held responsible at any time on or prior to the Closing Date, or (B) any Hazardous Activities that were, or were allegedly, conducted by Sellers or any Acquired Company or by any other Person for whose conduct they are or may be held responsible; or

(b) any bodily injury (including illness, disability, and death, and regardless of when any such bodily injury occurred, was incurred, or manifested itself), personal injury, property damage (including trespass, nuisance, wrongful eviction, and deprivation of the use of real property), or other damage of or to any Person, including any employee or former employee of Sellers or any Acquired Company or any other Person for whose conduct they are or may be held responsible, in any way arising from or allegedly arising from any Hazardous Activity conducted or allegedly conducted with respect to the Facilities or the operation of the Acquired Companies prior to the Closing Date, or from Hazardous Material that was (i) present or suspected to be present on or before the Closing Date on or at the Facilities (or present or suspected to be present on any other property, if such Hazardous Material emanated or allegedly emanated from any of the Facilities and was present or suspected to be present on any of the Facilities on or prior to the Closing Date) or (ii) Released or allegedly Released by Sellers or any Acquired Company or any other Person for whose conduct they are or may be held responsible, at any time on or prior to the Closing Date.

Buyer will be entitled to control any Cleanup, any related Proceeding, and, except as provided in the following sentence, any other Proceeding with respect to which indemnity may be sought under this Section 10.3. The procedure described in Section 10.9 will apply to any claim solely for monetary damages relating to a matter covered by this Section 10.3.

10.4 Indemnification and Payment of Damages by Buyer. Buyer will indemnify and hold harmless Sellers, and will pay to Sellers the amount of any Damages arising, directly or indirectly, from or in connection with (a) any Breach of any representation or warranty made by Buyer in this Agreement or in any certificate delivered by Buyer pursuant to this Agreement, (b) any Breach by Buyer of any covenant or obligation of Buyer in this Agreement, or (c) any claim by any Person for brokerage or finder's fees or commissions or similar payments based upon any agreement or understanding alleged to have been made by such Person with Buyer (or any Person acting on its behalf) in connection with any of the Contemplated Transactions.

10.5 Time Limitations. If the Closing occurs, Sellers will have no liability (for indemnification or otherwise) with respect to any representation or warranty, or covenant or obligation to be performed and complied with prior to the Closing Date, other than those in Sections 3.3, 3.11, 3.13, and 3.19, unless on or before _____ Buyer notifies Sellers of a claim specifying the factual basis of that claim in reasonable detail to the extent then known by Buyer; a claim with respect to Section 3.3, 3.11, 3.13, or 3.19, or a claim for indemnification or reimbursement not based upon any representation or warranty or any covenant or obligation to be performed and complied with prior to the Closing Date, may be made at any time. If the Closing occurs, Buyer will have no liability (for indemnification or otherwise) with respect to any representation or warranty, or covenant or obligation to be performed and complied with prior to the Closing Date, unless on or before _____ Sellers notify Buyer of a claim specifying the factual basis of that claim in reasonable detail to the extent then known by Sellers.

10.6 Limitations on Amount—Sellers. Sellers will have no liability (for indemnification or otherwise) with respect to the matters described in clause (a), clause (b) or, to the extent relating to any failure to perform or comply prior to the Closing Date, clause (c) of Section 10.2 until the total of all Damages with respect to such matters exceeds $_____, and then only for the amount by which such Damages exceed $_____. Sellers will have no liability (for indemnification or otherwise) with respect to the matters described in clause (d) of Section 10.2 until the total of all Damages with respect to such matters exceeds $_____, and then only for the amount by which such Damages exceed $_____. However, this Section 10.6 will not apply to any Breach of any of Sellers' representations and warranties of which either Seller had Knowledge at any time prior to the date on which such representation and warranty is made or any intentional Breach by either Seller of any covenant or obligation, and Sellers will be jointly and severally liable for all Damages with respect to such Breaches.

10.7 Limitations on Amount—Buyer. Buyer will have no liability (for indemnification or otherwise) with respect to the matters described in clause (a) or (b) of Section 10.4 until the total of all Damages with respect to such matters exceeds $_____, and then only for the amount by which such Damages exceed $_____. However, this Section 10.7 will not apply to any Breach of any of Buyer's representations and warranties of which Buyer had Knowledge at any time prior to the date on which such representation and warranty is made or any intentional Breach by Buyer of any covenant or obligation, and Buyer will be liable for all Damages with respect to such Breaches.

10.8 Escrow; Right of Set–Off. Upon notice to Sellers specifying in reasonable detail the basis for such set-off, Buyer may set off any amount to which it may be entitled under this Section 10 against amounts otherwise payable under the Promissory Notes or may give notice of a Claim in such amount under the Escrow Agreement. The exercise of such right of set-off by Buyer in good faith, whether or not ultimately determined to be justified, will not constitute an event of default under the Promissory Notes or any instrument securing a Promissory Note. Neither the exercise of nor the failure to exercise such right of set-off or to give a notice of a Claim under the Escrow Agreement will constitute an election of remedies or limit Buyer in any manner in the enforcement of any other remedies that may be available to it.

10.9 Procedure for Indemnification—Third Party Claims.

(a) Promptly after receipt by an indemnified party under Section 10.2, 10.4, or (to the extent provided in the last sentence of Section 10.3) Section 10.3 of notice of the commencement of any Proceeding against it, such indemnified party will, if a claim is to be made against an indemnifying party under such Section, give notice to the indemnifying party of the commencement of such claim, but the failure to notify the indemnifying party will not relieve the indemnifying party of any liability that it may have to any indemnified party, except to the extent that the indemnifying party demonstrates that the defense of such action is prejudiced by the indemnifying party's failure to give such notice.

(b) If any Proceeding referred to in Section 10.9(a) is brought against an indemnified party and it gives notice to the indemnifying party of the commencement of such Proceeding, the indemnifying party will, unless the claim involves Taxes, be entitled to participate in such Proceeding and, to the extent that it wishes (unless (i) the indemnifying party is also a party to such Proceeding and the indemnified party determines in good faith that joint representation would be inappropriate, or (ii) the indemnifying party fails to provide reasonable assurance to the indemnified party of its financial capacity to defend such Proceeding and provide indemnification with respect to such Proceeding), to assume the defense of such Proceeding with counsel satisfactory to the indemnified party and, after notice from the indemnifying party to the indemnified party of its election to assume the defense of such Proceeding, the indemnifying party will not, as long as it diligently conducts such defense, be liable to the indemnified party under this Section 10 for any fees of other counsel or any other expenses with respect to the defense of such Proceeding, in each case subsequently incurred by the indemnified party in connection with the defense of such Proceeding, other than reasonable costs of investigation. If the indemnifying party assumes the defense of a Proceeding, (i) it will be conclusively established for purposes of this Agreement that the claims made in that Proceeding are within the scope of and subject to indemnification; (ii) no compromise or settlement of such claims may be effected by the indemnifying party without the indemnified party's consent unless (A) there is no finding or admission of any violation of Legal Requirements or any violation of the rights of any Person and no effect on any other claims that may be made against the indemnified party, and (B) the sole relief provided is monetary damages that are paid in full by the indemnifying party; and (iii) the indemnified party will have no liability with respect to any compromise or settlement of such claims effected without its consent. If notice is given to an indemnifying party of the commencement of any Proceeding and the indemnifying party does not, within ten days after the indemnified party's notice is given, give notice to the indemnified party of its election to assume the defense of such Proceeding, the indemnifying party will be bound by any determination made in such Proceeding or any compromise or settlement effected by the indemnified party.

(c) Notwithstanding the foregoing, if an indemnified party determines in good faith that there is a reasonable probability that a Proceeding may adversely affect it or its affiliates other than as a result of monetary damages for which it would be entitled to indemnification under this Agreement, the indemnified party may, by notice to the indemnifying party, assume the exclusive right to defend, compromise, or settle such Proceeding, but the indemnifying party will not be bound by any determination of a Proceeding so defended or any compromise or settlement effected without its consent (which may not be unreasonably withheld).

(d) Sellers hereby consent to the non-exclusive jurisdiction of any court in which a Proceeding is brought against any Indemnified Person for purposes of any claim that an Indemnified Person may have under this Agreement with respect to such Proceeding or the matters alleged therein, and agree that process may be served on Sellers with respect to such a claim anywhere in the world.

10.10 Procedure for Indemnification—Other Claims. A claim for indemnification for any matter not involving a third-party claim may be asserted by notice to the party from whom indemnification is sought.

11. GENERAL PROVISIONS

11.1 Expenses. Except as otherwise expressly provided in this Agreement, each party to this Agreement will bear its respective expenses incurred in connection with the preparation, execution, and performance of this Agreement and the Contemplated Transactions, including all fees and expenses of agents, representatives, counsel, and accountants. [_____ will pay all amounts payable to [finder or investment banker] in connection with this Agreement and the Contemplated Transactions.] Buyer will pay one-half and Sellers will pay one-half of the HSR Act filing fee. Sellers will cause the Acquired Companies not to incur any out-of-pocket expenses in connection with this Agreement [except for professional fees not in excess of $_____]. In the event of termination of this Agreement, the obligation of each party to pay its own expenses will be subject to any rights of such party arising from a breach of this Agreement by another party.

11.2 Public Announcements. Any public announcement or similar publicity with respect to this Agreement or the Contemplated Transactions will be issued, if at all, at such time and in such manner as Buyer determines. Unless consented to by Buyer in advance or required by Legal Requirements, prior to the Closing Sellers shall, and shall cause the Acquired Companies to, keep this Agreement strictly confidential and may not make any disclosure of this Agreement to any Person. Sellers and Buyer will consult with each other concerning the means by which the Acquired Companies' employees, customers, and suppliers and others having dealings with the Acquired Companies will be informed of the Contemplated Transactions, and Buyer will have the right to be present for any such communication.

11.3 Confidentiality. Between the date of this Agreement and the Closing Date, Buyer and Sellers will maintain in confidence, and will cause the directors, officers, employees, agents, and advisors of Buyer and the Acquired Companies to maintain in confidence, [and not use to the detriment of another party or an Acquired Company] any [written, oral, or other information obtained in confidence from] [written information stamped "confidential" when originally furnished by] another party or an Acquired Company in connection with this Agreement or the Contemplated Transactions, unless (a) such information is already known to such party or to others not bound by a duty of confidentiality or such information becomes publicly available through no fault of such party, (b) the use of such information is necessary or appropriate in making any filing or obtaining any consent or approval required for the consummation of the Contemplated Transactions, or (c) the furnishing or use of such information is required by [or necessary or appropriate in connection with] legal proceedings.

If the Contemplated Transactions are not consummated, each party will return or destroy as much of such written information as the other party may reasonably request. [Whether or not the Closing takes place, Sellers waive, and will upon Buyer's request cause the Acquired Companies to waive, any cause of action, right, or claim arising out of the access of Buyer or its representatives to any trade secrets or other confidential information of the Acquired Companies except for the intentional competitive misuse by Buyer of such trade secrets or confidential information.]

11.4 Notices. All notices, consents, waivers, and other communications under this Agreement must be in writing and will be deemed to have been duly given when (a) delivered by hand (with written confirmation of receipt), (b) sent by telecopier (with written confirmation of receipt), provided that a copy is mailed by registered mail, return receipt requested, or (c) when received by the addressee, if sent by a nationally recognized overnight delivery service (receipt requested), in each case to the appropriate addresses and telecopier numbers set forth below (or to such other addresses and telecopier numbers as a party may designate by notice to the other parties):

Sellers:

Attention: _____

Facsimile No.: _____

with a copy to: _____

Attention: _____

Facsimile No.: _____

Buyer: _____

Attention: _____

Facsimile No.: _____

with a copy to: _____

Attention: _____

Facsimile No.: _____

11.5 Jurisdiction; Service of Process. Any action or proceeding seeking to enforce any provision of, or based on any right arising out of, this Agreement may be brought against any of the parties in the courts of the State of _____, County of _____, or, if it has or can acquire jurisdiction, in the United States District Court for the _____ District of _____, and each of the parties consents to the jurisdiction of such courts (and of the appropriate appellate courts) in any such action or proceeding and waives any objection to venue laid therein. Process in any action or proceeding referred to in the preceding sentence may be served on any party anywhere in the world.

11.6   Further Assurances. The parties agree (a) to furnish upon request to each other such further information, (b) to execute and deliver to each other such other documents, and (c) to do such other acts and things, all as the other party may reasonably request for the purpose of carrying out the intent of this Agreement and the documents referred to in this Agreement.

11.7   Waiver. The rights and remedies of the parties to this Agreement are cumulative and not alternative. Neither the failure nor any delay by any party in exercising any right, power, or privilege under this Agreement or the documents referred to in this Agreement will operate as a waiver of such right, power, or privilege, and no single or partial exercise of any such right, power, or privilege will preclude any other or further exercise of such right, power, or privilege or the exercise of any other right, power, or privilege. To the maximum extent permitted by applicable law, (a) no claim or right arising out of this Agreement or the documents referred to in this Agreement can be discharged by one party, in whole or in part, by a waiver or renunciation of the claim or right unless in writing signed by the other party; (b) no waiver that may be given by a party will be applicable except in the specific instance for which it is given; and (c) no notice to or demand on one party will be deemed to be a waiver of any obligation of such party or of the right of the party giving such notice or demand to take further action without notice or demand as provided in this Agreement or the documents referred to in this Agreement.

11.8   Entire Agreement and Modification. This Agreement supersedes all prior agreements between the parties with respect to its subject matter (including the Letter of Intent between Buyer and Sellers dated _____, 199__) and constitutes (along with the documents referred to in this Agreement) a complete and exclusive statement of the terms of the agreement between the parties with respect to its subject matter. This Agreement may not be amended except by a written agreement executed by the party to be charged with the amendment.

11.9   Disclosure Letter.

(a) The disclosures in the Disclosure Letter, and those in any Supplement thereto, must relate only to the representations and warranties in the Section of the Agreement to which they expressly relate and not to any other representation or warranty in this Agreement.

(b) In the event of any inconsistency between the statements in the body of this Agreement and those in the Disclosure Letter (other than an exception expressly set forth as such in the Disclosure Letter with respect to a specifically identified representation or warranty), the statements in the body of this Agreement will control.

11.10   Assignments, Successors, and no Third–Party Rights. Neither party may assign any of its rights under this Agreement without the prior consent of the other parties[, which will not be unreasonably withheld,] except that Buyer may assign any of its rights under this

Agreement to any Subsidiary of Buyer. Subject to the preceding sentence, this Agreement will apply to, be binding in all respects upon, and inure to the benefit of the successors and permitted assigns of the parties. Nothing expressed or referred to in this Agreement will be construed to give any Person other than the parties to this Agreement any legal or equitable right, remedy, or claim under or with respect to this Agreement or any provision of this Agreement. This Agreement and all of its provisions and conditions are for the sole and exclusive benefit of the parties to this Agreement and their successors and assigns.

11.11   Severability. If any provision of this Agreement is held invalid or unenforceable by any court of competent jurisdiction, the other provisions of this Agreement will remain in full force and effect. Any provision of this Agreement held invalid or unenforceable only in part or degree will remain in full force and effect to the extent not held invalid or unenforceable.

11.12   Section Headings, Construction. The headings of Sections in this Agreement are provided for convenience only and will not affect its construction or interpretation. All references to "Section" or "Sections" refer to the corresponding Section or Sections of this Agreement. All words used in this Agreement will be construed to be of such gender or number as the circumstances require. Unless otherwise expressly provided, the word "including" does not limit the preceding words or terms.

11.13   Time of Essence. With regard to all dates and time periods set forth or referred to in this Agreement, time is of the essence.

11.14   Governing Law. This Agreement will be governed by the laws of the State of _____ without regard to conflicts of laws principles.

ANCILLARY DOCUMENTS

Exhibit 7.4(a)

Opinion of Counsel to Sellers

[DATE]

[Name and Address of Buyer]

Gentlemen:

We have acted as counsel to _____ and _____ (collectively, "Sellers"), _____, a _____ corporation (the "Company") and the Subsidiaries of the Company in connection with the Stock Purchase Agreement dated _____, 199_ (the "Agreement") between the Sellers and _____, a _____ corporation ("Buyer"). This is the opinion contemplated by Section 7.4(a) of the Agreement. All capitalized terms used in this opinion without definition have the respective meanings given to them in the Agreement or the Accord referred to below.

This Opinion Letter is governed by, and shall be interpreted in accordance with, the Legal Opinion Accord (the "Accord") of the ABA Section of Business Law (1991). As a consequence, it is subject to a number of qualifications, exceptions, definitions, limitations on coverage and other limitations, all as more particularly described in the Accord, and this Opinion Letter should be read in conjunction therewith. The law covered by the opinions expressed herein is limited to the Federal Law of the United States and the Law of the State(s) of _____.

Based on the foregoing, our opinion is as follows:

1.   The Agreement, the Escrow Agreement and the Sellers' Releases are enforceable against the Sellers.

2.   The authorized capital stock of the Company consists of ___ shares of common stock, _____ par value, [of which _____ shares] [all of which] are outstanding. Sellers own all of the outstanding Stock of record and beneficially, free and clear of all adverse claims. As a result of the delivery of certificates to Buyer and the payment to Sellers being made at the Closing, Buyer is acquiring ownership of all of the outstanding Stock, free and clear of all adverse claims.

3.   Each Acquired Company is a corporation duly organized, validly existing and in good standing under the laws of its jurisdiction of incorporation as set forth in Part 3.1(a) of the Disclosure Letter, with full corporate power and authority to own its properties and to engage in its business as presently conducted or contemplated, and is duly qualified and in good standing as a foreign corporation under the laws of each other jurisdiction in which it is authorized to do business as set forth in Part 3.1(a) of the Disclosure Letter. All of the outstanding capital stock of each of the Subsidiaries is owned of record [and beneficially] by one or more of the Acquired Companies, free and clear of all adverse claims. All of the outstanding shares of capital stock of each Acquired Company have been duly authorized and validly issued and are fully paid and nonassessable and were not issued in violation of the preemptive rights of any Person.

4. Neither the execution and delivery of the Agreement nor the consummation of any or all of the Contemplated Transactions (a) breaches or constitutes a default (or an event that, with notice or lapse of time or both, would constitute a default) under any agreement or commitment [describe selection criteria] to which either Seller is party or (b) violates any statute, law, regulation or rule, or any judgment, decree or order of any court or other Governmental Body applicable to either Seller.

5. Neither the execution and delivery of the Agreement nor the consummation of any or all of the Contemplated Transactions (a) violates any provision of the certificate of incorporation or bylaws (or other governing instrument) of any Acquired Company, (b) breaches or constitutes a default (or an event that, with notice or lapse of time or both, would constitute a default) under, or results in the termination of, or accelerates the performance required by, or excuses performance by any Person of any of its obligations under, or causes the acceleration of the maturity of any debt or obligation pursuant to, or results in the creation or imposition of any Encumbrance upon any property or assets of any Acquired Company under, any agreement or commitment [describe selection criteria] to which any Acquired Company is a party or by which any of their respective properties or assets are bound, or to which any of the properties or assets of any Acquired Company are subject, or (c) violates any statute, law, regulation, or rule, or any judgment, decree or order of any court or other Governmental Body applicable to any Acquired Company.

6. Except for requirements of the HSR Act, no consent, approval or authorization of, or declaration, filing or registration with, any Governmental Body is required in connection with the execution, delivery and performance of the Agreement or the consummation of the Contemplated Transactions.

We hereby confirm to you that, except as set forth in Part 3.15 of the Disclosure Letter, there is no Proceeding by or before any court or Governmental Body pending or overtly threatened against or involving any Acquired Company or that questions or challenges the validity of the Agreement or any action taken or to be taken by any Acquired Company pursuant to the Agreement or in connection with the Contemplated Transactions, and none of the Acquired Companies is subject to any judgment, order or decree having prospective effect.

The Accord is changed for purposes of this Opinion Letter pursuant to § 21 of the Accord as follows:

(a) The Primary Lawyer Group shall include all lawyers presently at our firm who have given substantive attention to the affairs of any of the Sellers or the Acquired Companies since _____.

(b) Accord § 19(e) and § 19(j) are deleted.

We understand that you are delivering a copy of this opinion to [identify lenders to Buyer] in connection with the financing of the transactions contemplated by the Agreement and agree that [those lenders] may rely on this opinion as if it were addressed to them.

Very truly yours,

_____

Exhibit 8.4

Opinion of Counsel to Buyer

PRELIMINARY NOTE

As is the case with the Buyer's representations in the Model Stock Purchase Agreement, the scope of the opinion required to be delivered to the Sellers by the Buyer's counsel is often limited to matters affecting the validity of the transaction documents. However, where the Buyer is issuing its stock or giving a promissory note for a significant portion of the purchase price, the Sellers may require additional representations from the Buyer and, correspondingly, additional opinions from the Buyer's counsel. See the Commentary to Section 4 of the Model Stock Purchase Agreement.

[DATE]

[Names and Addresses of Sellers]

Gentlemen:

We have acted as counsel to _____, a _____ corporation ("Buyer"), in connection with the Stock Purchase Agreement dated _____, 199_ (the "Agreement") between _____, _____, and Buyer. This is the opinion contemplated by Section 8.4(a) of the Agreement. All capitalized terms used in this opinion without definition have the respective meanings given to them in the Agreement or the Accord referred to below.

This Opinion Letter is governed by, and shall be interpreted in accordance with, the Legal Opinion Accord (the "Accord") of the ABA Section of Business Law (1991). As a consequence, it is subject to a number of qualifications, exceptions, definitions, limitations on coverage and other limitations, all as more particularly described in the Accord, and this Opinion Letter should be read in conjunction therewith. The law covered by the opinions expressed herein is limited to the Federal Law of the United States and the Law of the State(s) of _____.

Based on the foregoing, our opinion is as follows:

1.   The Agreement, the Escrow Agreement and the Promissory Notes are enforceable against Buyer.

2.   Neither the execution and delivery of the Agreement, the Escrow Agreement and the Promissory Notes nor the performance of Buyer's obligations thereunder (a) violates any provision of the certificate of incorporation or bylaws (or other governing instrument) of Buyer, (b) breaches or constitutes a default (or an event that, with notice or lapse of time or both, would constitute a default) under any agreement or commitment [describe selection criteria] to which Buyer is party or (c) violates any statute, law, regulation or rule, or any judgment, decree or order of any court or Governmental Body applicable to Buyer.

Very truly yours,

_____

FORM 5
WACHTELL, LIPTON, ROSEN & KATZ
PREFERRED SHAREHOLDER RIGHTS PLAN
[INTRODUCTION] ...
Terms of Recommended Rights Plan*

Issuance: One right to buy one one-hundredth of a share of a new series of preferred stock as a dividend on each outstanding share of common stock of the company. Until the rights become exercisable, all further issuances of common stock, including common stock issuable upon exercise of outstanding options, would include issuances of rights.

Term: 10 years.

Exercise price: An amount per one one-hundredth of a share of the preferred stock which approximates the board's view of the long-term value of the company's common stock. Factors to be considered in setting the exercise price include the company's business and prospects, its long-term plans and market conditions. The exercise price is subject to certain anti-dilution adjustments. For illustration only, assume an exercise price of $120 per one one-hundredth of a share.

Rights detach and become exercisable: The rights are not exercisable and are not transferable apart from the company's common stock until the tenth day after such time as a person or group acquires beneficial owner-ship of 15% or more of the company's common stock or the tenth business day (or such later time as the board of directors may determine) after a person or group commences a tender or exchange offer the consummation of which would result in beneficial ownership by a person or group of 15% or more of the company's common stock. As soon as practicable after the rights become exercisable, separate right certificates would be issued and the rights would become transferable apart from the company's common stock.

Protection against creeping acquisition/open market purchases: In the event a person or group were to acquire a 15% or greater position in the company, each right then outstanding would "flip in" and become a right to buy that number of shares of common stock of the company which at the time of the 15% acquisition had a market value of two times the exercise price of the rights. The acquiror who triggered the rights would be excluded from the "flip-in" because his rights would have become null and void upon his triggering acquisition. Thus, if the company's common stock at the time of the "flip-in" were trading at $30 per share and the exercise price of the rights at such time were $120, each right would thereafter be exercisable at $120 for eight shares of the company's common stock. The amendment provision of the Rights Agreement provides that the 15% threshold can be

---

* These terms are as they would be set by a company that uses authorized blank check preferred stock, with terms that make 1/100th of a share of the preferred stock the economic equivalent of one share of common stock, as the security for which the rights are exercisable.

lowered to not less than 10%. The board can utilize this provision to provide additional protection against creeping accumulations.

Protection against squeezeout: If, after the rights have been triggered, an acquiring company were to merge or otherwise combine with the company, or the company were to sell 50% or more of its assets or earning power to an acquiring company, each right then outstanding (other than rights held by the acquiring company) would "flip over" and thereby would become a right to buy that number of shares of common stock of the acquiring company-which at the time of such transaction would have a market value of two times the exercise price of the rights. Thus, if the acquiring company's common stock at the time of such transaction were trading at $30 per share and the exercise price of the rights at such time were $120, each right would thereafter be exercisable at $120 for eight shares (i.e., the number of shares that could be purchased for $240, or two times the exercise price of the rights) of the acquiring company's common stock.

Exchange: At any time after the acquisition by a person or group of affiliated or associated persons of beneficial ownership of 15% or more of the outstanding common stock of the company and before the acquisition by a person or group of 50% or more of the outstanding common stock of the company, the board of directors may exchange the rights (other than rights owned by such person or group, which have become void), in whole or in part, at an exchange ratio of one share of the company's common stock (or one one-hundredth of a share of junior participating preferred stock) per right, subject to adjustment.

Redemption: The rights are redeemable by the company's board of directors at a price of $.0l per right at any time prior to the acquisition by a person or group of beneficial ownership of 15% or more of the company's common stock. The redemption of the rights may be made effective at such time, on such basis, and with such conditions as the board of directors in its sole discretion may establish. Thus, the rights would not interfere with a negotiated merger or a white knight transaction, even after a hostile tender offer has been commenced. The rights may prevent a white knight transaction after a 15% acquisition (unless the exchange feature described above is used to eliminate the rights and the white knight's price is adjusted for the issuance of the additional shares).

Voting: The rights would not have any voting rights.

Terms of preferred stock: The preferred stock issuable upon exercise of the rights would be nonredeemable and rank junior to all other series of the company's preferred stock. The dividend, liquidation and voting rights, and non-redemption features of the preferred stock are designed so that the value of the one one-hundredth interest in a share of new preferred stock purchasable with each right will approximate the value of one share of common stock. Each whole share of preferred stock would be entitled to receive a quarterly preferential dividend of $1 per share but would be entitled to receive, in the aggregate, a dividend of 100 times the dividend declared on the common stock. In the event of liquidation, the holders of the new preferred stock would be entitled to receive a preferential liquidation payment of $100 per share but would be entitled to receive, in the aggregate, a liquidation payment equal to 100 times the payment made per share of common stock. Each share of preferred stock would have 100 votes, voting together with the common stock. Finally, in the event of any merger, consolidation or other transaction in which shares of common stock are exchanged for or changed into other stock or securities, cash and/or other property, each share of preferred stock would be entitled to receive 100 times the amount received per share of common stock. The foregoing rights are protected against dilution in the event additional shares of common stock are issued. Since the "out of the money" rights would not be exercisable immediately, registration of the preferred stock issuable upon exercise of the rights with the Securities and Exchange Commission need not be effective until the rights become exercisable and are "in the money" or are so close to being "in the money" so as to make exercise economically possible.

Federal income tax consequences: The Internal Revenue Service has published a revenue ruling holding that the adoption of a rights plan is not a taxable event for the company or its shareholders under the federal income tax laws. The physical distribution of rights certificates upon the rights becoming exercisable should not result in any tax. After such physical distribution, the rights would be treated for tax purposes as capital assets in the hands of most shareholders, the tax basis of each right would be zero in most cases (or, in certain cases, an allocable part of the tax basis of the stock with respect to which the right was issued) and the holding period of each right would include the holding period of the stock with respect to which such right was issued. Upon the rights becoming rights to purchase an acquiror's common stock, holders of rights probably would be taxed even if the rights were not exercised. Upon the rights becoming rights to purchase additional common stock of the company, holders of rights probably would not have a taxable event. The redemption of the rights for cash and, most likely, the acquisition of the rights by the company for its stock would each be taxable events. The use of company stock (with the rights attached) will not interfere with the company's ability to engage in tax-free acquisitions nor will it affect any net operating losses of the company.

Accounting consequences: The initial issuance of the rights has no accounting or financial reporting impact. Since the rights would be "out of the money" when issued, they would not dilute earnings per share. Because the redemption date of the rights is neither fixed nor determinable, the accounting guidelines do not require the redemption amount to be accounted for as a long-term obligation of the company. The rights do not interfere with a company's ability to consummate a pooling transaction so long as the transaction is properly structured.

Miscellaneous: The Rights Agreement provides that the company may not enter into any transaction of the sort which would give rise to the "flip-over" right if, in connection therewith, there are outstanding securities or there are agreements or arrangements intended to counteract the protective provisions of the rights. The Rights Agreement may be amended from time to time in any manner prior to the acquisition of a 15% position (or a 10% position if the board lowers the triggering threshold).

FORM OF PLAN

TABLE OF CONTENTS

Section
1.   Definitions.
2.   Appointment of Rights Agent.
3.   Issue of Right Certificates.
4.   Form of Right Certificates.
5.   Countersignature and Registration.
6.   Transfer, Split Up, Combination and Exchange of Right Certificates; Mutilated, Destroyed, Lost or Stolen Right Certificates.
7.   Exercise of Rights; Purchase Price; Expiration Date of Rights.
8.   Cancellation and Destruction of Right Certificates.
9.   Availability of Preferred Shares.
10. Preferred Shares Record Date.
11. Adjustment of Purchase Price, Number of Shares or Number of Rights.
12. Certificate of Adjusted Purchase Price or Number of Shares.
13. Consolidation, Merger or Sale or Transfer of Assets or Earning Power.
14. Fractional Rights and Fractional Shares.
15. Rights of Action.
16. Agreement of Right Holders.
17. Right Certificate Holder Not Deemed a Stockholder.
18. Concerning the Rights Agent.
19. Merger or Consolidation or Change of Name of Rights Agent.
20. Duties of Rights Agent.
21. Change of Rights Agent.
22. Issuance of New Right Certificates.
23. Redemption.
24. Exchange.
25. Notice of Certain Events.
26. Notices.
27. Supplements and Amendments.
28. Successors.
29. Benefits of this Agreement.
30. Severability.
31. Governing Law.
Signatures.
Exhibit A—Form of Certificate of Designations.
Exhibit B—Form of Right Certificate.
Exhibit C—Summary of Rights to Purchase Preferred Shares.

———

Agreement, dated as of _____, 2000, between _____, Inc., a _____ corporation (the *"Company"*), and _____, as rights agent (the *"Rights Agent"*).

The Board of Directors of the Company has authorized and declared a dividend of one preferred share purchase right (a *"Right"*) for each

Common Share (as hereinafter defined) of the Company outstanding on
___, 2000 (the "Record Date"), each Right representing the right to
purchase one one-hundredth of a Preferred Share (as hereinafter defined),
upon the terms and subject to the conditions herein set forth, and has
further authorized and directed the issuance of one Right with respect to
each Common Share that shall become outstanding between the Record
Date and the earliest of the Distribution Date, the Redemption Date and
the Final Expiration Date (as such terms are hereinafter defined).

Accordingly, in consideration of the premises and the mutual agreements herein set forth, the parties hereby agree as follows:

Section 1. *Definitions.* For purposes of this Agreement, the following
terms have the meanings indicated:

(a) *"Acquiring Person"* shall mean any Person who or which, together
with all Affiliates and Associates of such Person, shall be the Beneficial
Owner of 15% or more of the Common Shares of the Company then
outstanding, but shall not include the Company, any Subsidiary of the
Company, any employee benefit plan of the Company or any Subsidiary of
the Company, or any entity holding Common Shares for or pursuant to the
terms of any such plan. Notwithstanding the foregoing, no Person shall
become an "Acquiring Person" as the result of an acquisition of Common
Shares by the Company which, by reducing the number of Common Shares
of the Company outstanding, increases the proportionate number of Common Shares of the Company beneficially owned by such Person to 15% or
more of the Common Shares of the Company then outstanding; *provided,
however*, that, if a Person shall become the Beneficial Owner of 15% or
more of the Common Shares of the Company then outstanding by reason of
share purchases by the Company and shall, after such share purchases by
the Company, become the Beneficial Owner of any additional Common
Shares of the Company, then such Person shall be deemed to be an
"Acquiring Person." Notwithstanding the foregoing, if the Board of Directors of the Company determines in good faith that a Person who would
otherwise be an "Acquiring Person," as defined pursuant to the foregoing
provisions of this paragraph (a), has become such inadvertently, and such
Person divests as promptly as practicable a sufficient number of Common
Shares so that such Person would no longer be an "Acquiring Person," as
defined pursuant to the foregoing provisions of this paragraph (a), then
such Person shall not be deemed to be an "Acquiring Person" for any
purposes of this Agreement.

(b) *"Affiliate"* shall have the meaning ascribed to such term in Rule
12b–2 of the General Rules and Regulations under the Exchange Act as in
effect on the date of this Agreement.

(c) *"Associate"* shall have the meaning ascribed to such term in Rule
12b–2 of the General Rules and Regulations under the Exchange Act as in
effect on the date of this Agreement.

(d) A Person shall be deemed the "Beneficial Owner" of and shall be
deemed to "beneficially own" any securities:

(i) which such Person or any of such Person's Affiliates or Associates beneficially owns, directly or indirectly;

(ii) which such Person or any of such Person's Affiliates or Associates has (A) the right to acquire (whether such right is exercisable immediately or only after the passage of time) pursuant to any agreement, arrangement or understanding (other than customary agreements with and between underwriters and selling group members with respect to a *bona fide* public offering of securities), or upon the exercise of conversion rights, exchange rights, rights (other than these Rights), warrants or options, or otherwise; *provided, however*, that a Person shall not be deemed the Beneficial Owner of, or to beneficially own, securities tendered pursuant to a tender or exchange offer made by or on behalf of such Person or any of such Person's Affiliates or Associates until such tendered securities are accepted for purchase or exchange; or (B) the right to vote pursuant to any agreement, arrangement or understanding; *provided, however*, that a Person shall not be deemed the Beneficial Owner of, or to beneficially own, any security if the agreement, arrangement or understanding to vote such security (1) arises solely from a revocable proxy or consent given to such Person in response to a public proxy or consent solicitation made pursuant to, and in accordance with, the applicable rules and regulations promulgated under the Exchange Act and (2) is not also then reportable on Schedule 13D under the Exchange Act (or any comparable or successor report); or

(iii) which are beneficially owned, directly or indirectly, by any other Person with which such Person or any of such Person's Affiliates or Associates has any agreement, arrangement or understanding (other than customary agreements with and between underwriters and selling group members with respect to a bona fide public offering of securities) for the purpose of acquiring, holding, voting (except to the extent contemplated by the proviso to Section 1(d)(ii)(B) hereof) or disposing of any securities of the Company.

Notwithstanding anything in this definition of Beneficial Ownership to the contrary, the phrase "then outstanding," when used with reference to a Person's Beneficial Ownership of securities of the Company, shall mean the number of such securities then issued and outstanding together with the number of such securities not then actually issued and outstanding which such Person would be deemed to own beneficially hereunder.

(e) *"Business Day"* shall mean any day other than a Saturday, a Sunday, or a day on which banking institutions in [State of Rights Agent] are authorized or obligated by law or executive order to close.

(f) *"Close of Business"* on any given date shall mean 5:00 P.M., [City of Rights Agent] time, on such date; *provided, however*, that, if such date is not a Business Day, it shall mean 5:00 P.M., [City of Rights Agent] time, on the next succeeding Business Day.

(g) *"Common Shares"* when used with reference to the Company shall mean the shares of common stock, par value $_ per share, of the Company.

"Common Shares" when used with reference to any Person other than the Company shall mean the capital stock (or equity interest) with the greatest voting power of such other Person or, if such other Person is a Subsidiary of another Person, the Person or Persons which ultimately control such first-mentioned Person.

(h) *"Distribution Date"* shall have the meaning set forth in Section 3(a) hereof

(i) *"Exchange Act"* shall mean the Securities Exchange Act of 1934, as amended.

(j) *"Exchange Ratio"* shall have the meaning set forth in Section 24(a) hereof.

(k) *"Final Expiration Date"* shall have the meaning set forth in Section 7(a) hereof.

(*l*) *"NASDAQ"* shall mean the National Association of Securities Dealers, Inc. Automated Quotation System.

(m) *"Person"* shall mean any individual, firm, corporation or other entity, and shall include any successor (by merger or otherwise) of such entity.

(n) *"Preferred Shares"* shall mean shares of Series A Junior Participating Preferred Stock, par value $__ per share, of the Company having the rights and preferences set forth in the Form of Certificate of Designations attached to this Agreement as Exhibit A.

(*o*) *"Purchase Price"* shall have the meaning set forth in Section 4 hereof.

(p) "Record Date" shall have the meaning set forth in the second paragraph hereof.

(q) *"Redemption Date"* shall have the meaning set forth in Section 7(a) hereof.

(r) *"Redemption Price"* shall have the meaning set forth in Section 23(a) hereof.

(s) *"Right"* shall have the meaning set forth in the second paragraph hereof.

(t) *"Right Certificate"* shall have the meaning set forth in Section 3(a) hereof.

(u) *"Shares Acquisition Date"* shall mean the first date of public announcement by the Company or an Acquiring Person that an Acquiring Person has become such.

(v) *"Subsidiary"* of any Person shall mean any corporation or other entity of which a majority of the voting power of the voting equity securities or equity interest is owned, directly or indirectly, by such Person.

(w) *"Summary of Right"* shall have the meaning set forth in Section 3(b) hereof.

(x) *"Trading Day"* shall have the meaning set forth in Section 11 (d) hereof.

Section 2. *Appointment of Rights Agent.* The Company hereby appoints the Rights Agent to act as agent for the Company and the holders of the Rights (who, in accordance with Section 3 hereof, shall, prior to the Distribution Date, also be the holders of the Common Shares of the Company) in accordance with the terms and conditions hereof, and the Rights Agent hereby accepts such appointment. The Company may from time to time appoint such co-Rights Agents as it may deem necessary or desirable.

Section 3. *Issue of Right Certificates.* (a) Until the earlier of (i) the tenth day after the Shares Acquisition Date or (ii) the tenth Business Day (or such later date as may be determined by action of the Board of Directors of the Company prior to such time as any Person becomes an Acquiring Person) after the date of the commencement by any Person (other than the Company, any Subsidiary of the Company, any employee benefit plan of the Company or of any Subsidiary of the Company or any entity holding Common Shares of the Company for or pursuant to the terms of any such plan) of a tender or exchange offer the consummation of which would result in any Person becoming the Beneficial Owner of Common Shares of the Company aggregating 15% or more of the then outstanding Common Shares of the Company (including any such date which is after the date of this Agreement and prior to the issuance of the Rights; the earlier of such dates being herein referred to as the *"Distribution Date"*), (x) the Rights will be evidenced (subject to the provisions of Section 3(b) hereof) by the certificates for Common Shares of the Company registered in the names of the holders thereof (which certificates shall also be deemed to be Right Certificates) and not by separate Right Certificates, and (y) the right to receive Right Certificates will be transferable only in connection with the transfer of Common Shares of the Company. As soon as practicable after the Distribution Date, the Company will prepare and execute, the Rights Agent will countersign, and the Company will send or cause to be sent (and the Rights Agent will, if requested, send) by first-class, insured, postage-prepaid mail, to each record holder of Common Shares of the Company as of the Close of Business on the Distribution Date, at the address of such holder shown on the records of the Company, a Right Certificate, in substantially the form of Exhibit B hereto (a *"Right Certificate"*), evidencing one Right for each Common Share so held. As of the Distribution Date, the Rights will be evidenced solely by such Right Certificates.

(b) On the Record Date, or as soon as practicable thereafter, the Company will send a copy of a Summary of Rights to Purchase Preferred Shares, in substantially the form of Exhibit C hereto (the *"Summary of Rights"*), by first-class, postage-prepaid mail, to each record holder of Common Shares as of the Close of Business on the Record Date, at the address of such holder shown on the records of the Company. With respect to certificates for Common Shares of the Company outstanding as of the Record Date, until the Distribution Date, the Rights will be evidenced by such certificates registered in the names of the holders thereof together with a copy of the Summary of Rights attached thereto. Until the Distribution Date (or the earlier of the Redemption Date or the Final Expiration

Date), the surrender for transfer of any certificate for Common Shares of the Company outstanding on the Record Date, with or without a copy of the Summary of Rights attached thereto, shall also constitute the transfer of the Rights associated with the Common Shares of the Company represented thereby.

(c) Certificates for Common Shares which become outstanding (including, without limitation, reacquired Common Shares referred to in the last sentence of this paragraph (c)) after the Record Date but prior to the earliest of the Distribution Date, the Redemption Date or the Final Expiration Date shall have impressed on, printed on, written on or otherwise affixed to them the following legend:

> This certificate also evidences and entitles the holder hereof to certain rights as set forth in an Agreement between _____, Inc. and _____, dated as of _____, 2000, as it may be amended from time to time (the "Agreement"), the terms of which are hereby incorporated herein by reference and a copy of which is on file at the principal executive offices of _____, Inc. Under certain circumstances, as set forth in the Agreement, such Rights (as defined in the Agreement) will be evidenced by separate certificates and will no longer be evidenced by this certificate _____, Inc. will mail to the holder of this certificate a copy of the Agreement without charge after receipt of a written request therefor. As set forth in the Agreement, Rights beneficially owned by any Person (as defined in the Agreement) who becomes an Acquiring Person (as defined in the Agreement) become null and void.

With respect to such certificates containing the foregoing legend, until the Distribution Date, the Rights associated with the Common Shares of the Company represented by such certificates shall be evidenced by such certificates alone, and the surrender for transfer of any such certificate shall also constitute the transfer of the Rights associated with the Common Shares of the Company represented thereby. In the event that the Company purchases or acquires any Common Shares of the Company after the Record Date but prior to the Distribution Date, any Rights associated with such Common Shares of the Company shall be deemed cancelled and retired so that the Company shall not be entitled to exercise any Rights associated with the Common Shares of the Company which are no longer outstanding.

Section 4. *Form of Right Certificates*. The Right Certificates (and the forms of election to purchase Preferred Shares and of assignment to be printed on the reverse thereof) shall be substantially the same as Exhibit B hereto. . . .

Section 5. *Countersignature and Registration* . . . .

Section 6. *Transfer, Split Up, Combination and Exchange of Right Certificates* . . . . Subject to the provisions of Section 14 hereof, at any time after the Close of Business on the Distribution Date, and at or prior to the Close of Business on the earlier of the Redemption Date or the Final Expiration Date, any Right Certificate or Right Certificates (other than Right Certificates representing Rights that have become void pursuant to

Section 11(a)(ii) hereof or that have been exchanged pursuant to Section 24 hereof) may be transferred, split up, combined or exchanged for another Right Certificate or Right Certificates entitling the registered holder to purchase a like number of one one-hundredths of a Preferred Share as the Right Certificate or Right Certificates surrendered then entitled such holder to purchase. Any registered holder desiring to transfer, split up, combine or exchange any Right Certificate or Right Certificates shall make such request in writing delivered to the Rights Agent, and shall surrender the Right Certificate or Right Certificates to be transferred, split up, combined or exchanged at the principal office of the Rights Agent. Thereupon the Rights Agent shall countersign and deliver to the Person entitled thereto a Right Certificate or Right Certificates, as the case may be, as so requested. The Company may require payment of a sum sufficient to cover any tax or governmental charge that may be imposed in connection with any transfer, split up, combination or exchange of Right Certificates. . . .

Section 7. *Exercise of Rights; Purchase Price; Expiration Date of Rights*. (a) The registered holder of any Right Certificate may exercise the Rights evidenced thereby (except as otherwise provided herein), in whole or in part, at any time after the Distribution Date, upon surrender of the Right Certificate, with the form of election to purchase on the reverse side thereof duly executed, to the Rights Agent at the principal office of the Rights Agent, together with payment of the Purchase Price for each one one-hundredth of a Preferred Share as to which the Rights are exercised, at or prior to the earliest of (i) the Close of Business on _____, 2010 (the "*Final Expiration Date*"), (ii) the time at which the Rights are redeemed as provided in Section 23 hereof (the "*Redemption Date*"), or (iii) the time at which such Rights are exchanged as provided in Section 24 hereof.

(b) The Purchase Price for each one one-hundredth of a Preferred Share purchasable pursuant to the exercise of a Right shall initially be $___, and shall be subject to adjustment from time to time as provided in Section 11 or 13 hereof, and shall be payable in lawful money of the United States of America in accordance with paragraph (c) below. . . .

Section 8. *Cancellation and Destruction of Right Certificates* . . . .

Section 9. *Availability of Preferred Shares*. The Company covenants and agrees that it will cause to be reserved and kept available out of its authorized and unissued Preferred Shares or any Preferred Shares held in its treasury the number of Preferred Shares that will be sufficient to permit the exercise in full of all outstanding Rights in accordance with Section 7 hereof. . . .

Section 10. *Preferred Shares Record Date* . . . .

Section 11. *Adjustment of Purchase Price, Number of Shares or Number of Rights* . . . .

(a)(i) In the event the Company shall at any time after the date of this Agreement (A) declare a dividend on the Preferred Shares payable in Preferred Shares, (B) subdivide the outstanding Preferred Shares, (C) combine the outstanding Preferred Shares into a smaller number of Preferred Shares or (D) issue any shares of its capital stock in a reclassification of the Preferred Shares (including any such reclassification in connection with a consolidation or merger in which the Company is the continuing or surviving corporation), except as otherwise provided in this Section 11(a), the Purchase Price in effect at the time of the record date for such dividend or of the effective date of such subdivision, combination or reclassification, and the number and kind of shares of capital stock issuable on such date, shall be proportionately adjusted so that the holder of any Right exercised after such time shall be entitled to receive the aggregate number and kind of shares of capital stock which, if such Right had been exercised immediately prior to such date and at a time when the Preferred Shares transfer books of the Company were open, such holder would have owned upon such exercise and been entitled to receive by virtue of such dividend, subdivision, combination or reclassification; *provided*, *however*, that in no event shall the consideration to be paid upon the exercise of one Right be less than the aggregate par value of the shares of capital stock of the Company issuable upon exercise of one Right.

(ii) Subject to Section 24 hereof, in the event any Person becomes an Acquiring Person, each holder of a Right shall thereafter have a right to receive, upon exercise thereof at a price equal to the then current Purchase Price multiplied by the number of one one-hundredths of a Preferred Share for which a Right is then exercisable, in accordance with the terms of this Agreement and in lieu of Preferred Shares, such number of Common Shares of the Company as shall equal the result obtained by (A) multiplying the then current Purchase Price by the number of one one-hundredths of a Preferred Share for which a Right is then exercisable and dividing that product by (B) 50% of the then current per share market price of the Common Shares of the Company (determined pursuant to Section 11(d) hereof) on the date of the occurrence of such event. In the event that any Person shall become an Acquiring Person and the Rights shall then be outstanding, the Company shall not take any action which would eliminate or diminish the benefits intended to be afforded by the Rights.

From and after the occurrence of such event, any Rights that are or were acquired or beneficially owned by any Acquiring Person (or any Associate or Affiliate of such Acquiring Person) shall be void, and any holder of such Rights shall thereafter have no right to exercise such Rights under any provision of this Agreement. No Right Certificate shall be issued pursuant to Section 3 hereof that represents Rights beneficially owned by an Acquiring Person whose Rights would be void pursuant to the preceding sentence or any Associate or Affiliate thereof, no Right Certificate shall be issued at any time upon the transfer of any Rights to an Acquiring Person whose Rights would be void pursuant to the preceding sentence or any Associate or Affiliate thereof or to any nominee of such Acquiring Person, Associate or Affiliate; and any Right Certificate delivered to the Rights Agent for transfer to an Acquiring Person whose Rights would be void pursuant to the preceding sentence shall be cancelled. . . .

(d)(i) For the purpose of any computation hereunder, the "current per share market price" of any security (a *"Security"* for the purpose of this Section 11(d)(i)) on any date shall be deemed to be the average of the daily closing prices per share of such Security for the 30 consecutive Trading Days immediately prior to such date. . . .

Section 12. *Certificate of Adjusted Purchase Price or & Number of Shares. . . .*

Section 13. *Consolidation, Merger or Sale or Transfer of Assets or Earning Power.* In the event, directly or indirectly, at any time after a Person has become an Acquiring Person, (a) the Company shall consolidate with, or merge with and into, any other Person, (b) any Person shall consolidate with the Company, or merge with and into the Company and the Company shall be the continuing or surviving corporation of such merger and, in connection with such merger, all or part of the Common Shares shall be changed into or exchanged for stock or other securities of any other Person (or the Company) or cash or any other property, or (c) the Company shall sell or otherwise transfer (or one or more of its Subsidiaries shall sell or otherwise transfer), in one or more transactions, assets or earning power aggregating 50% or more of the assets or earning power of the Company and its Subsidiaries (taken as a whole) to any other Person other than the Company or one or more of its wholly-owned Subsidiaries, then, and in each such case, proper provision shall be made so that (i) each holder of a Right (except as otherwise provided herein) shall thereafter have the right to receive, upon the exercise thereof at a price equal to the then current Purchase Price multiplied by the number of one one-hundredths of a Preferred Share for which a Right is then exercisable, in accordance with the terms of this Agreement and in lieu of Preferred Shares, such number of Common Shares of such other Person (including the Company as successor thereto or as the surviving corporation) as shall equal the result obtained by (A) multiplying the then current Purchase Price by the number of one one-hundredths of a Preferred Share for which a Right is then exercisable and dividing that product by (B) 50% of the then current per share market price of the Common Shares of such other Person (determined pursuant to Section 11(d) hereof) on the date of consummation of such consolidation, merger, sale or transfer; (ii) the issuer of such Common Shares shall thereafter be liable for, and shall assume, by virtue of such consolidation, merger, sale or transfer, all the obligations and duties of the Company pursuant to this Agreement; (iii) the term "Company" shall thereafter be deemed to refer to such issuer; and (iv) such issuer shall take such steps (including, but not limited to, the reservation of a sufficient number of its Common Shares in accordance with Section 9 hereof) in connection with such consummation as may be necessary to assure that the provisions hereof shall thereafter be applicable, as nearly as reasonably may be, in relation to the Common Shares of the Company thereafter deliverable upon the exercise of the Rights. The Company shall not consummate any such consolidation, merger, sale or transfer unless, prior thereto, the Company and such issuer shall have executed and delivered to the Rights Agent a supplemental agreement so providing. The Company shall not enter into any transaction of the kind referred to in this Section 13 if at the time of such transaction there are any rights, warrants, instruments or securities outstanding or any agreements or arrangements which, as a result of the consummation of such transaction, would eliminate or substantially diminish the benefits intended to be afforded by the Rights. The provisions of this Section 13 shall similarly apply to successive mergers or consolidations or sales or other transfers.

Section 14. *Fractional Rights and Fractional Shares.* (a) The Company shall not be required to issue fractions of Rights or to distribute Right Certificates which evidence fractional Rights. In lieu of such fractional Rights, there shall be paid to the registered holders of the Right Certificates with regard to which such fractional Rights would otherwise be issuable, an amount in cash equal to the same fraction of the current market value of a whole Right. For the purposes of this Section 14(a), the current market value of a whole Right shall be the closing price of the Rights for the Trading Day immediately prior to the date on which such fractional Rights would have been otherwise issuable. The closing price for any day shall be the last sale price, regular way, or, in case no such sale takes place on such day, the average of the closing bid and asked prices, regular way, in either case, as reported in the principal consolidated transaction reporting system with respect to securities listed or admitted to trading on the New York Stock Exchange or, if the Rights are not listed or admitted to trading on the New York Stock Exchange, as reported in the principal consolidated transaction reporting system with respect to securities listed on the principal national securities exchange on which the Rights are listed or admitted to trading or, if the Rights are not listed or admitted to trading on any national securities exchange, the last quoted price or, if not so quoted, the average of the high bid and low asked prices in the over-the-counter market, as reported by NASDAQ or such other system then in use or, if on any such date the Rights are not quoted by any such organization, the average of the closing bid and asked prices as furnished by a professional market maker making a market in the Rights selected by the Board of Directors of the Company. If on any such date no such market maker is making a market in the Rights, the fair value of the Rights on such date as determined in good faith by the Board of Directors of the Company shall be used.

(b) The Company shall not be required to issue fractions of Preferred Shares (other than fractions which are integral multiples of one one-hundredth of a Preferred Share) upon exercise of the Rights or to distribute certificates which evidence fractional Preferred Shares (other than fractions which are integral multiples of one one-hundredth of a Preferred Share). Fractions of Preferred Shares in integral multiples of one one-hundredth of a Preferred Share may, at the election of the Company, be evidenced by depositary receipts, pursuant to an appropriate agreement between the Company and a depositary selected by it; *provided* that such agreement shall provide that the holders of such depositary receipts shall have all the rights, privileges and preferences to which they are entitled as beneficial owners of the Preferred Shares represented by such depositary receipts. In lieu of fractional Preferred Shares that are not integral multiples of one one-hundredth of a Preferred Share, the Company shall pay to the registered holders of Right Certificates at the time such Rights are exercised as herein provided an amount in cash equal to the same fraction of the current market value of one Preferred Share. For the purposes of this Section 14(b), the current market value of a Preferred Share shall be the closing price of a Preferred Share (as determined pursuant to the second sentence of Section 11(d)(i) hereof) for the Trading Day immediately prior to the date of such exercise.

(c) The holder of a Right, by the acceptance of the Right, expressly waives such holder's right to receive any fractional Rights or any fractional shares upon exercise of a Right (except as provided above).

Section 15. *Rights of Action.* All rights of action in respect of this Agreement, excepting the rights of action given to the Rights Agent under Section 18 hereof, are vested in the respective registered holders of the Right Certificates (and, prior to the Distribution Date, the registered holders of the Common Shares); and any registered holder of any Right Certificate (or, prior to the Distribution Date, of the Common Shares), without the consent of the Rights Agent or of the holder of any other Right Certificate (or, prior to the Distribution Date, of the Common Shares), may, in such holder's own behalf and for such holder's own benefit, enforce, and may institute and maintain any suit, action or proceeding against the Company to enforce, or otherwise act in respect of, such holder's right to exercise the Rights evidenced by such Right Certificate in the manner provided in such Right Certificate and in this Agreement. Without limiting the foregoing or any remedies available to the holders of Rights, it is specifically acknowledged that the holders of Rights would not have an adequate remedy at law for any breach of this Agreement, and will be entitled to specific performance of the obligations under, and injunctive relief against actual or threatened violations of the obligations of any Person subject to, this Agreement.

Section 16. *Agreement of Right Holders....*

Section 17. *Right Certificate Holder Not Deemed a Stockholder....*

Section 18. *Concerning the Rights Agent....*

Section 19. *Merger or Consolidation or Change of Name of Rights Agent....*

Section 20. *Duties of Rights Agent....*

Section 21. *Change of Rights Agent....*

Section 22. *Issuance of New Right Certificates.* Notwithstanding any of the provisions of this Agreement or of the Rights to the contrary, the Company may, at its option, issue new Right Certificates evidencing Rights in such form as may be approved by the Board of Directors of the Company to reflect any adjustment or change in the Purchase Price and the number or kind or class of shares or other securities or property purchasable under the Right Certificates made in accordance with the provisions of this Agreement.

Section 23. *Redemption.* (a) The Board of Directors of the Company may, at its option, at any time prior to such time as any Person becomes an Acquiring Person, redeem all but not less than all the then outstanding Rights at a redemption price of $.01 per Right, appropriately adjusted to reflect any stock split, stock dividend or similar transaction occurring after the date hereof (such redemption price being hereinafter referred to as the *"Redemption Price"*). The redemption of the Rights by the Board of Directors of the Company may be made effective at such time, on such basis and with such conditions as the Board of Directors of the Company, in its sole discretion, may establish.

(b) Immediately upon the action of the Board of Directors of the Company ordering the redemption of the Rights pursuant to paragraph (a) of this Section 23, and without any further action and without any notice, the right to exercise the Rights will terminate and the only right thereafter of the holders of Rights shall be to receive the Redemption Price.... Neither the Company nor any of its Affiliates or Associates may redeem, acquire or purchase for value any Rights at any time in any manner other than that specifically set forth in this Section 23 or in Section 24 hereof, and other than in connection with the purchase of Common Shares prior to the Distribution Date.

Section 24. *Exchange.* (a) The Board of Directors of the Company may, at its option, at any time after any Person becomes an Acquiring Person, exchange all or part of the then outstanding and exercisable Rights (which shall not include Rights that have become void pursuant to the provisions of Section 11(a)(ii) hereof) for Common Shares at an exchange ratio of one Common Share per Right, appropriately adjusted to reflect any adjustment in the number of Rights pursuant to Section 11(i) (such exchange ratio being hereinafter referred to as the *"Exchange Ratio"*). Notwithstanding the foregoing, the Board of Directors of the Company shall not be empowered to effect such exchange at any time after any Person (other than the Company, any Subsidiary of the Company, any employee benefit plan of the Company or any such Subsidiary, or any entity holding Common Shares for or pursuant to the terms of any such plan), together with all Affiliates and Associates of such Person, becomes the Beneficial Owner of 50% or more of the Common Shares then outstanding.

(b) Immediately upon the action of the Board of Directors of the Company ordering the exchange of any Rights pursuant to paragraph (a) of this Section 24 and without any further action and without any notice, the right to exercise such Rights shall terminate and the only right thereafter of a holder of such Rights shall be to receive that number of Common Shares equal to the number of such Rights held by such holder multiplied by the Exchange Ratio....

Section 25. *Notice of Certain Events....*

Section 26. *Notices....*

Section 27. *Supplements and Amendments.* The Company may from time to time supplement or amend this Agreement without the approval of any holders of Right Certificates in order to cure any ambiguity, to correct or supplement any provision contained herein which may be defective or inconsistent with any other provisions herein, or to make any other provisions with respect to the Rights which the Company may deem necessary or desirable, any such supplement or amendment to be evidenced by a writing signed by the Company and the Rights Agent; *provided, however*, that, from and after such time as any Person becomes an Acquiring Person, this Agreement shall not be amended in any manner which would adversely affect the interests of the holders of Rights. Without limiting the foregoing, the Company may at any time prior to such time as any Person becomes an Acquiring Person amend this Agreement to lower the thresholds set forth in Section 1(a) and 3(a) hereof to not less than 10% (the "Reduced Threshold"); *provided, however*, that no Person who beneficially owns a number of Common Shares equal to or greater than the Reduced Threshold shall become an Acquiring Person unless such Person shall, after the public announcement of the Reduced Threshold, increase its beneficial ownership of the then outstanding Common Shares (other than as a result of an acquisition of Common Shares by the Company) to an amount equal to or greater than the greater of (x) the Reduced Threshold or (y) the sum of (i) the lowest beneficial ownership of such Person as a percentage of the outstanding Common Shares as of any date on or after the date of the public announcement of such Reduced Threshold plus (ii) .0001%.

Section 28. *Successors*. All the covenants and provisions of this Agreement by or for the benefit of the Company or the Rights Agent shall bind and inure to the benefit of their respective successors and assigns hereunder.

Section 29. *Benefits of this Agreement*. Nothing in this Agreement shall be construed to give to any Person other than the Company, the Rights Agent and the registered holders of the Right Certificates (and, prior to the Distribution Date, the Common Shares) any legal or equitable right, remedy or claim under this Agreement; but this Agreement shall be for the sole and exclusive benefit of the Company, the Rights Agent and the registered holders of the Right Certificates (and, prior to the Distribution Date, the Common Shares).

Section 30. *Severability*. If any term, provision, covenant or restriction of this Agreement is held by a court of competent jurisdiction or other authority to be invalid, void or unenforceable, the remainder of the terms, provisions, covenants and restrictions of this Agreement shall remain in full force and effect and shall in no way be affected, impaired or invalidated.

Section 31. *Governing Law*. This Agreement and each Right Certificate issued hereunder shall be deemed to be a contract made under the laws of the State of _____ and for all purposes shall be governed by and construed in accordance with the laws of such state applicable to contracts to be made and performed entirely within such state....

IN WITNESS WHEREOF, the parties hereto have caused this Agreement to be duly executed and attested, all as of the day and year first above written.

Attest: _____, INC.

By: _____   By: _____
    Name: Name:
    Title: Title:

Attest: [Rights Agent]

By: _____   By: _____
    Name: Name:
    Title: Title:

Exhibit A

FORM

of

CERTIFICATE OF DESIGNATIONS

of

SERIES A JUNIOR PARTICIPATING PREFERRED STOCK

of

_____, INC.

(Pursuant to Section 151 of the Delaware General Corporation Law)

_____, Inc., a corporation organized and existing under the General Corporation Law of the State of Delaware (hereinafter called the "Corporation"), hereby certifies that the following resolution was adopted by the Board of Directors of the Corporation as required by Section 151 of the General Corporation Law at a meeting duly called and held on 2000:

RESOLVED, that pursuant to the authority granted to and vested in the Board of Directors of this Corporation (hereinafter called the "Board of Directors" or the "Board") in accordance with the provisions of the Certificate of Incorporation, the Board of Directors hereby creates a series of Preferred Stock, par value $__ per share, of the Corporation (the "Preferred Stock"), and hereby states the designation and number of shares, and fixes the relative rights, preferences, and limitations thereof as follows:

Series A Junior Participating Preferred Stock:

Section 1. *Designation and Amount.* The shares of such series shall be designated as "Series A Junior Participating Preferred Stock" (the "Series A Preferred Stock") and the number of shares constituting the Series A Preferred Stock shall be _____ . . . .

Section 2. *Dividends and Distributions.*

(A) Subject to the rights of the holders of any shares of any series of Preferred Stock (or any similar stock) ranking prior and superior to the

Series. A Preferred Stock with respect to dividends, the holders of shares of Series A Preferred Stock, in preference to the holders of Common Stock, par value $___ per share (the "Common Stock"), of the Corporation, and of any other junior stock, shall be entitled to receive, when, as and if declared by the Board of Directors out of funds legally available for the purpose, quarterly dividends payable in cash on the first day of March, June, September and December in each year (each such date being referred to herein as a "Quarterly Dividend Payment Date"), commencing on the first Quarterly Dividend Payment Date after the first issuance of a share or fraction of a share of Series A Preferred Stock, in an amount per share (rounded to the nearest cent) equal to the greater of (a) $1 or (b) subject to the provision for adjustment hereinafter set forth, 100 times the aggregate per share amount of all cash dividends, and 100 times the aggregate per share amount (payable in kind) of all non-cash dividends or other distributions, other than a dividend payable in shares of Common Stock or a subdivision of the outstanding shares of Common Stock (by reclassification or otherwise), declared on the Common Stock since the immediately preceding Quarterly Dividend Payment Date or, with respect to the first Quarterly Dividend Payment Date, since the first issuance of any share or fraction of a share of Series A Preferred Stock. In the event the Corporation shall at any time declare or pay any dividend on the Common Stock payable in shares of Common Stock, or effect a subdivision or combination or consolidation of the outstanding shares of Common Stock (by reclassification or otherwise than by payment of a dividend in shares of Common Stock) into a greater or lesser number of shares of Common Stock, then in each such case the amount to which holders of shares of Series A Preferred Stock were entitled immediately prior to such event under clause (b) of the preceding sentence shall be adjusted by multiplying such amount by a fraction, the numerator of which is the number of shares of Common Stock outstanding immediately after such event and the denominator of which is the number of shares of Common Stock that were outstanding immediately prior to such event. . . .

Section 3. *Voting Rights.* The holders of shares of Series A Preferred Stock shall have the following voting rights:

(A) Subject to the provision for adjustment hereinafter set forth, each share of Series A Prefer-red Stock shall entitle the holder thereof to 100 votes on all matters submitted to a vote of the stockholders of the Corporation. . . .

Section 4. *Certain Restrictions.*

Section 5. *Reacquired Shares.* . . .

Section 6. *Liquidation, Dissolution or Winding Up.* Upon any liquidation, dissolution or winding up of the Corporation, no distribution shall be made (1) to the holders of shares of stock ranking junior (either as to dividends or upon liquidation, dissolution or winding up) to the Series A Preferred Stock unless, prior thereto, the holders of shares of Series A Preferred Stock shall have received $100 per share, plus an amount equal to accrued and unpaid dividends and distributions thereon, whether or not declared, to the date of such payment, provided that the holders of shares of Series A Preferred Stock shall be entitled to receive an aggregate amount per share, subject to the provision for adjustment hereinafter set forth, equal to 100 times the aggregate amount to be distributed per share to holders of shares of Common Stock, or (2) to the holders of shares of stock ranking on a parity (either as to dividends or upon liquidation, dissolution or winding up) with the Series A Preferred Stock, except distributions made ratably on the Series A Preferred Stock and all such parity stock in proportion to the total amounts to which the holders of all such shares are entitled upon such liquidation, dissolution or winding up. . . .

Section 7. *Consolidation, Merger, etc.* In case the Corporation shall enter into any consolidation, merger, combination or other transaction in which the shares of Common Stock are exchanged for or changed into other stock or securities, cash and/or any other property, then in any such case each share of Series A Preferred Stock shall at the same time be similarly exchanged or changed into an amount per share, subject to the provision for adjustment hereinafter set forth, equal to 100 times the aggregate amount of stock, securities, cash and/or any other property (payable in kind), as the case may be, into which or for which each share of Common Stock is changed or exchanged. . . .

Section 8. *No Redemption.* The shares of Series A Preferred Stock shall not be redeemable.

Section 9. *Rank.* The Series A Preferred Stock shall rank, with respect to the payment of dividends and the distribution of assets, junior to all series of any other class of the Corporation's Preferred Stock.

Section 10. *Amendment.* The Certificate of Incorporation of the Corporation shall not be amended in any manner which would materially alter or change the powers, preferences or special rights of the Series A Preferred Stock so as to affect them adversely without the affirmative vote of the holders of at least two-thirds of the outstanding shares of Series A Preferred Stock, voting together as a single class.

IN WITNESS WHEREOF, this Certificate of Designations is executed on behalf of the Corporation by its Chairman of the Board and attested by its Secretary this ___ day of _____, 2000.

_____
Chairman of the Board

Attest:

_____
Secretary

Exhibit B

Form of Right Certificate

Certificate No. R–   ___ Rights

NOT EXERCISABLE AFTER _____, 2010 OR EARLIER IF REDEMPTION OR EXCHANGE OCCURS. THE RIGHTS ARE SUBJECT TO REDEMPTION AT $.01 PER RIGHT AND TO

EXCHANGE ON THE TERMS SET FORTH IN THE AGREE-
MENT.

Right Certificate

————, INC.

This certifies that ————, or registered assigns, is the registered
owner of the number of Rights set forth above, each of which entitles the
owner thereof, subject to the terms, provisions and conditions of the
Agreement, dated as of ————, 2000 (the "Agreement"), between ————,
Inc., a ———— corporation (the "Company"), and ———— (the "Rights
Agent"), to purchase from the Company at any time after the Distribution
Date (as such term is defined in the Agreement) and prior to 5:00 P.M.,
[City of Rights Agent] time, on ————, 2010 at the principal office of the
Rights Agent, or at the office of its successor as Rights Agent, one one-
hundredth of a fully paid non-assessable share of Series A Junior Participating Preferred Stock, par value $__ per share, of the Company (the
"Preferred Shares"), at a purchase price of $__ per one one-hundredth of
a Preferred Share (the "Purchase Price"), upon presentation and surrender
of this Right Certificate with the Form of Election to Purchase duly
executed. The number of Rights evidenced by this Right Certificate (and
the number of one one-hundredths of a Preferred Share which may be
purchased upon exercise hereof) set forth above, and the Purchase Price set
forth above, are the number and Purchase Price as of ————, 2000, based
on the Preferred Shares as constituted at such date. As provided in the
Agreement, the Purchase Price and the number of one one-hundredths of a
Preferred Share which may be purchased upon the exercise of the Rights
evidenced by this Right Certificate are subject to modification and adjustment upon the happening of certain events.

This Right Certificate is subject to all of the terms, provisions and
conditions of the Agreement, which terms, provisions and conditions are
hereby incorporated herein by reference and made a part hereof and to
which Agreement reference is hereby made for a full description of the
rights, limitations of rights, obligations, duties and immunities hereunder
of the Rights Agent, the Company and the holders of the Right Certificates.
Copies Of the Agreement are on file at the principal executive offices of the
Company and the offices of the Rights Agent. . . .

Subject to the provisions of the Agreement, the Rights evidenced by
this Right Certificate (i) may be redeemed by the Company at a redemption
price of $.01 per Right or (ii) may be exchanged in whole or in part for
Preferred Shares or shares of the Company's Common Stock, par value
$__ per share. . . .

WITNESS the facsimile signature of the proper officers of the Company and its corporate seal. Dated as of ————, ————.

Attest: _____, INC.

_____   By: _____
Name: Name:
Title: Title:
Countersigned:

[Rights Agent]

By: _____
        Name
        Title:

Exhibit C

SUMMARY OF RIGHTS TO PURCHASE PREFERRED SHARES

Introduction

On _____ ___, 2000, the Board of Directors of our Company, _____, Inc., a Delaware corporation, declared a dividend of one preferred share purchase right (a "Right") for each outstanding share of common stock, par value $___ per share. The dividend is payable on _____ ___, 2000 to the stockholders of record on _____ ___, 2000. [These rights will replace rights to purchase common stock that will expire on _____, ___ 2000.]

Our Board has adopted this Rights Agreement to protect stockholders from coercive or otherwise unfair takeover tactics. In general terms, it works by imposing a significant penalty upon any person or group which acquires 15% or more of our outstanding common stock without the approval of our Board. The Rights Agreement should not interfere with any merger or other business combination approved by our Board.

For those interested in the specific terms of the Rights Agreement as made be between our Company and _____, as the Rights Agent, on _____ ___, 2000, we provide the following summary description. Please note, however, that this description is only a summary, and is not complete, and should be read together with the entire Rights Agreement, which has been filed with the Securities and Exchange Commission as an exhibit to a Registration Statement on Form 8–A dated _____ ___, 2000. A copy of the agreement is available free of charge from our Company.

The Rights. Our Board authorized the issuance of a Right with respect to each outstanding share of common stock on _____ ___, 2000. The Rights will initially trade with, and will be inseparable from, the common stock. The Rights are evidenced only by certificates that represent shares of common stock. New Rights will accompany any new shares of common stock we issue after _____ ___, 2000 until the Distribution Date described below.

Exercise Price. Each Right will allow its holder to purchase from our Company one one-hundredth of a share of Series A Junior Participating

Preferred Stock ("Preferred Share") for $___, once the Rights become exercisable. This portion of a Preferred Share will give the stockholder approximately the same dividend, voting, and liquidation rights as would one share of common stock. Prior to exercise, the Right does not give its holder any dividend, voting, or liquidation rights.

Exercisability. The Rights will not be exercisable until

- 10 days after the public announcement that a person or group has become an "Acquiring Person" by obtaining beneficial ownership of 15% or more of our outstanding common stock, or, if earlier,

- 10 business days (or a later date determined by our Board before any person or group becomes an Acquiring Person) after a person or group begins a tender or exchange offer which, if completed, would result in that person or group becoming an Acquiring Person.

We refer to the date when the Rights become exercisable as the "Distribution Date." Until that date, the common stock certificates will also evidence the Rights, and any transfer of shares of common stock will constitute a transfer of Rights. After that date, the Rights will separate from the common stock and be evidenced by book-entry credits or by Rights certificates that we will mail to all eligible holders of common stock. Any Rights held by an Acquiring Person are void and may not be exercised.

Our Board may reduce the threshold at which a person or group becomes an Acquiring Person from 15% to not less than 10% of the outstanding common stock.

Consequences of a Person or Group Becoming an Acquiring Person.

- *Flip In.* If a person or group becomes an Acquiring Person, all holders of Rights except the Acquiring Person may, for $___, purchase shares of our common stock with a market value of $___, based on the market price of the common stock prior to such acquisition.

- *Flip Over.* If our Company is later acquired in a merger or similar transaction after the Rights Distribution Date, all holders of Rights except the Acquiring Person may, for $___, purchase shares of the acquiring corporation with a market value of $___ based on the market price of the acquiring corporation's stock, prior to such merger.

Preferred Share Provisions.

Each one one-hundredth of a Preferred Share, if issued:

- will not be redeemable.

- will entitle holders to quarterly dividend payments of $.01 per share, or an amount equal to the dividend paid on one share of common stock, whichever is greater.

- will entitle holders upon liquidation either to receive $1 per share or an amount equal to the payment made on one share of common stock, whichever is greater.

- will have the same voting power as one share of common stock.

- if shares of our common stock are exchanged via merger, consolidation, or a similar transaction, will entitle holders to a per share payment equal to the Payment made on one share of common stock.

The value of one one-hundredth interest in a Preferred Share should approximate the value of one share of common stock.

Expiration. The Rights will expire on _____ __, 2010.

Redemption. Our Board may redeem the Rights for $.01 per Right at any time before any person or group becomes an Acquiring Person. If our Board redeems any Rights, it must redeem all of the Rights. Once the Rights are redeemed, the only right of the holders of Rights will be to receive the redemption price of $.01 per Right. The redemption price will be adjusted if we have a stock split or stock dividends of our common stock.

Exchange. After a person or group becomes an Acquiring Person, but before an Acquiring Person owns 50% or more of our outstanding common stock, our Board may extinguish the Rights by exchanging one share of common stock or an equivalent security for each Right, other than Rights held by the Acquiring Person.

Anti-Dilution Provisions. Our Board may adjust the purchase price of the Preferred Shares, the number of Preferred Shares issuable and the number of outstanding Rights to prevent dilution that may occur from a stock dividend, a stock split, a reclassification of the Preferred Shares or common stock. No adjustments to the Exercise Price of less than 1% will be made.

Amendments. The terms of the Rights Agreement may be amended by our Board without the consent of the holders of the Rights. However, our Board may not amend the Rights Agreement to lower the threshold at which a person or group becomes an Acquiring Person to below 10% of our outstanding common stock. In addition, the Board may not cause a person or group to become an Acquiring Person by lowering this threshold below the percentage interest that such person or group already owns. After a person or group becomes an Acquiring Person, our Board may not amend the agreement in a way that adversely affects holders of the Rights.

*

STATE CORPORATE CODES

PART 1
PROVISIONS OF THE REVISED MODEL BUSINESS CORPORATION ACT

Contents

CHAPTER 1. GENERAL PROVISIONS

Subchapter A. Short Title and Reservation of Power

Section

* * *

1.02   Reservation of Power to Amend or Repeal

* * *

Subchapter D.   Definitions

1.40   Act Definitions

* * *

1.42   Number of Shareholders

CHAPTER 2.   INCORPORATION

* * *

2.02   Articles of Incorporation

CHAPTER 3.   PURPOSES AND POWERS

* * *

3.02   General Powers

* * *

CHAPTER 6.   SHARES AND DISTRIBUTIONS

Subchapter A.   Shares

6.01   Authorized Shares

6.02   Terms of Class or Series Determined by Board of Directors

6.03   Issued and Outstanding Shares

* * *

Subchapter B.   Issuance of Shares

6.20   Subscription for Shares Before Incorporation

6.21   Issuance of Shares

6.22   Liability of Shareholders

6.23   Share Dividends

6.24   Share Options

Section

6.25 Form and Content of Certificates

6.26 Shares Without Certificates

* * *

6.28 Expense of Issue

Subchapter C. Subsequent Acquisition of Shares
by Shareholders and Corporation

6.30 Shareholders' Preemptive Rights

6.31 Corporation's Acquisition of Its Own Shares

Subchapter D. Distributions

6.40 Distributions to Shareholders

CHAPTER 7. SHAREHOLDERS

* * *

Subchapter B. Voting

* * *

7.21 Voting Entitlement of Shares

* * *

7.25 Quorum and Voting Requirements for Voting Groups

7.26 Action by Single and Multiple Voting Groups

7.27 Greater Quorum or Voting Requirements

7.28 Voting for Directors; Cumulative Voting

* * *

Subchapter C. Voting Trusts and Agreements

7.32 Shareholder Agreements

* * *

CHAPTER 8. DIRECTORS AND OFFICERS

Subchapter A. Board of Directors

8.01 Requirement for and Duties of Board of Directors

* * *

8.04 Election of Directors by Certain Classes of Shareholders

* * *

Subchapter C. Standards of Conduct

8.30 Standards of Conduct for Directors

* * *

8.33 Directors' Liability for Unlawful Distributions

Subchapter D. Officers

8.40 Officers

* * *

Section

8.42   Standards of Conduct for Officers

* * *

CHAPTER 10.   AMENDMENT OF ARTICLES OF INCORPORATION AND BYLAWS

Subchapter A.   Amendment of Articles of Incorporation

10.01   Authority to Amend

10.02   Amendment Before Issuance of Shares

10.03   Amendment by Board of Directors and Shareholders

10.04   Voting on Amendments by Voting Groups

10.05   Amendment by Board of Directors

10.06   Articles of Amendment

10.07   Restated Articles of Incorporation

10.08   Amendment Pursuant to Reorganization

10.09   Effect of Amendment

* * *

Subchapter B.   Amendment of Bylaws

10.20   Amendment by Board of Directors or Shareholders

10.21   Bylaw Increasing Quorum or Voting Requirement for Directors

CHAPTER 11.   MERGER AND SHARE EXCHANGE

11.01   Definitions

11.02   Merger

11.03   Share Exchange

11.04   Action on a Plan of Merger or Share Exchange

11.05   Merger Between Parent and Subsidiary or Between Subsidiaries

11.06   Articles of Merger or Share Exchange

11.07   Effect of Merger or Share Exchange

* * *

CHAPTER 12.   SALE OF ASSETS

12.01   Disposition of Assets Not Requiring Shareholder Approval

12.02   Shareholder Approval of Certain Dispositions

CHAPTER 13.   DISSENTERS' RIGHTS

Subchapter A.

13.01   Definitions

13.02   Right to Appraisal

13.03   Assertion of Rights by Nominees and Beneficial Owners

Subchapter B.   Procedure for Exercise of Dissenters' Rights

13.20   Notice of Appraisal Rights

Section

13.21   Notice of Intent to Demand Payment

13.22   Appraisal Notice and Form

13.23   Perfection of Rights; Right to Withdraw

13.24   Payment

13.25   After–Acquired Shares

13.26   Procedure if Shareholder Dissatisfied With Payment or Offer

Subchapter C.   Judicial Appraisal of Shares

13.30   Court Action

13.31   Court Costs and Counsel Fees

CHAPTER 14.   DISSOLUTION

Subchapter A.   Voluntary Dissolution

* * *

14.02   Dissolution by Board of Directors and Shareholders

14.03   Articles of Dissolution

* * *

14.05   Effect of Dissolution

14.06   Known Claims Against Dissolved Corporation

14.07   Unknown Claims Against Dissolved Corporation

* * *

CHAPTER 16.   RECORDS AND REPORTS

* * *

Subchapter B.   Reports

16.20   Financial Statements for Shareholders

* * *

16.22   Annual Report for Secretary of State

* * *

PART 2.   PROVISIONS OF THE DELAWARE AND NEW YORK STATUTES

Delaware General Corporation Law

Section

151.   Classes and Series of Stock; Rights, etc.

157.   Rights and Options Respecting Stock

203.   Business Combinations With Interested Shareholders

221.   Voting, Inspection and Other Rights of Bondholders and Debenture Holders

242.   Amendment of Certificate of Incorporation After Receipt of Payment for Stock

251.   Merger or Consolidation of Domestic Corporations

253.   Merger of Parent Corporation and Subsidiary or Subsidiaries

Section

262. Appraisal Rights

271. Sale, Lease or Exchange of Assets; Consideration; Procedure

New York Business Corporation Law

Section

501. Authorized Shares

502. Issue of Any Class of Preferred Shares in Series

505. Rights and Options to Purchase Shares; Issue of Rights and Options to Directors, Officers and Employees

518. Corporate Bonds

519. Convertible or Exchangeable Shares and Bonds

623. Procedure to Enforce Shareholder's Right to Receive Payment for Shares

717. Duty of Directors

801. Right to Amend Certificate of Incorporation

803. Authorization of Amendment or Change

804. Class Voting on Amendment

902. Plan of Merger or Consolidation

903. Authorization by Shareholders

909. Sale, Lease, Exchange or Other Disposition of Assets

910. Right of Shareholder to Receive Payment for Shares Upon Merger or Consolidation, or Sale, Lease, Exchange or Other Disposition of Assets, or Share Exchange

912. Requirements Relating to Certain Business Combinations

913. Share Exchanges

* * *

PART I

Provisions of the Revised Model Business Corporation Act
CHAPTER 1. GENERAL PROVISIONS

Subchapter A. Short Title and Reservation of Power

§ 1.02 Reservation of Power to Amend or Repeal

The [name of state legislature] has power to amend or repeal all or part of this Act at any time and all domestic and foreign corporations subject to this Act are governed by the amendment or repeal.

Subchapter D. Definitions

§ 1.40. Act Definitions.

In this Act:

(1) "Articles of incorporation" means the original articles of incorporation, all amendments thereof, and any other documents permitted

or required to be filed by a domestic business corporation with the secretary of state under any provision of this Act except section 16.21. If an amendment of the articles or any other document filed under this Act restates the articles in their entirety, thenceforth the articles shall not include any prior documents.

(2) "Authorized shares" means the shares of all classes a domestic or foreign corporation is authorized to issue.

(3) "Conspicuous" means so written that a reasonable person against whom the writing is to operate should have noticed it. For example, printing in italics or boldface or contrasting color, or typing in capitals or underlined, is conspicuous.

(4) "Corporation," "domestic corporation" or "domestic business corporation" means a corporation for profit, which is not a foreign corporation, incorporated under or subject to the provisions of this Act.

(5) "Deliver" or "delivery" means any method of delivery used in conventional commercial practice, including delivery by hand, mail, commercial delivery, and electronic transmission.

(6) "Distribution" means a direct or indirect transfer of money or other property (except its own shares) or incurrence of indebtedness by a corporation to or for the benefit of its shareholders in respect of any of its shares. A distribution may be in the form of a declaration or payment of a dividend; a purchase, redemption, or other acquisition of shares; a distribution of indebtedness; or otherwise.

(6A) "Domestic unincorporated entity" means an unincorporated entity whose internal affairs are governed by the laws of this state.

(7) "Effective date of notice" is defined in section 1.41.

(7A) "Electronic transmission" or "electronically transmitted" means any process of communication not directly involving the physical transfer of paper that is suitable for the retention, retrieval, and reproduction of information by the recipient.

(7B) "Eligible entity" means a domestic or foreign unincorporated entity or a domestic or foreign nonprofit corporation.

(7C) "Eligible interests" means interests or memberships.

(8) "Employee" includes an officer but not a director. A director may accept duties that make him also an employee.

(9) "Entity" includes domestic and foreign business corporation; domestic and foreign nonprofit corporation; estate; trust; domestic and foreign unincorporated entity; and state, United States, and foreign government.

(9A) The phrase "facts objectively ascertainable outside of a filed document or plan" is defined in section 1.20(k).

(9B) "Filing entity" means an unincorporated entity that is of a type that is created by filing a public organic document.

(10) "Foreign corporation" means a corporation incorporated under a law other than the law of this state; which would be a business corporation if incorporated under the laws of this state.

(10A) "Foreign nonprofit corporation" means a corporation incorporated under a law other than the law of this state, which would be a nonprofit corporation if incorporated under the laws of this state.

(10B) "Foreign unincorporated entity" means an unincorporated entity whose internal affairs are governed by an organic law of a jurisdiction other than this state.

(11) "Governmental subdivision" includes authority, county, district, and municipality.

(12) "Includes" denotes a partial definition.

(13) "Individual" means a natural person.

(13A) "Interest" means either or both of the following rights under the organic law of an unincorporated entity:

(i) the right to receive distributions from the entity either in the ordinary course or upon liquidation; or

(ii) the right to receive notice or vote on issues involving its internal affairs, other than as an agent, assignee, proxy or person responsible for managing its business and affairs.

(13B) "Interest holder" means a person who holds of record an interest.

(14) "Means" denotes an exhaustive definition.

(14A) "Membership" means the rights of a member in a domestic or foreign nonprofit corporation.

(14B) "Nonfiling entity" means an unincorporated entity that is of a type that is not created by filing a public organic document.

(14C) "Nonprofit corporation" or "domestic nonprofit corporation" means a corporation incorporated under the laws of this state and subject to the provisions of the Model Nonprofit Corporation Act.

(15) "Notice" is defined in section 1.41.

(15A) "Organic document" means a public organic document or a private organic document.

(15B) "Organic law" means the statute governing the internal affairs of a domestic or foreign business or nonprofit corporation or unincorporated entity.

(15C) "Owner liability" means personal liability for a debt, obligation or liability of a domestic or foreign business or nonprofit corporation or unincorporated entity that is imposed on a person:

(i) solely by reason of the person's status as a shareholder, member or interest holder; or

(ii) by the articles of incorporation, bylaws or an organic document under a provision of the organic law of an entity authorizing the articles of incorporation, bylaws or an organic document to make one or more specified shareholders, members or interest holders liable in their capacity as shareholders, members or interest holders for all or specified debts, obligations or liabilities of the entity.

(16) "Person" includes an individual and an entity.

(17) "Principal office" means the office (in or out of this state) so designated in the annual report where the principal executive offices of a domestic or foreign corporation are located.

(17A) "Private organic document" means any document (other than the public organic document, if any) that determines the internal governance of an unincorporated entity. Where a private organic document has been amended or restated, the term means the private organic document as last amended or restated.

(17B) "Public organic document" means the document, if any, that is filed of public record to create an unincorporated entity. Where a public organic document has been amended or restated, the term means the public organic document as last amended or restated.

(18) "Proceeding" includes civil suit and criminal, administrative, and investigatory action.

(18A) "Public corporation" means a corporation that has shares listed on a national securities exchange or regularly traded in a market maintained by one or more members of a national or affiliated securities association.

(19) "Record date" means the date established under chapter 6 or 7 on which a corporation determines the identity of its shareholders and their shareholdings for purposes of this Act. The determinations shall be made as of the close of business on the record date unless another time for doing so is specified when the record date is fixed.

(20) "Secretary" means the corporate officer to whom the board of directors has delegated responsibility under section 8.40(c) for custody of the minutes of the meetings of the board of directors and of the shareholders and for authenticating records of the corporation.

(21) "Shareholder" means the person in whose name shares are registered in the records of a corporation or the beneficial owner of shares to the extent of the rights granted by a nominee certificate on file with a corporation.

(22) "Shares" means the units into which the proprietary interests in a corporation are divided.

(22A) "Sign" or "signature" includes any manual, facsimile, conformed or electronic signature.

(23) "State," when referring to a part of the United States, includes a state and commonwealth (and their agencies and governmental subdivisions) and a territory and insular possession (and their agencies and governmental subdivisions) of the United States.

(24) "Subscriber" means a person who subscribes for shares in a corporation, whether before or after incorporation.

(24A) "Unincorporated entity" means an organization or artificial legal person that either has a separate legal existence or has the power to acquire an estate in real property in its own name and that is not any of the following: a domestic or foreign business or nonprofit corporation, an estate, a trust, a state, the United States, or a foreign government. The term includes a general partnership, limited liability company, limited partnership, business trust, joint stock association and unincorporated nonprofit association.

(25) "United States" includes district, authority, bureau, commission, department, and any other agency of the United States.

(26) "Voting group" means all shares of one or more classes or series that under the articles of incorporation or this Act are entitled to vote and be counted together collectively on a matter at a meeting of shareholders. All shares entitled by the articles of incorporation or this Act to vote generally on the matter are for that purpose a single voting group.

(27) "Voting power" means the current power to vote in the election of directors.

§ 1.42 Number of Shareholders

(a) For purposes of this Act, the following identified as a shareholder in a corporation's current record of shareholders constitutes one shareholder:

(1) three or fewer coowners;

(2) a corporation, partnership, trust, estate, or other entity;

(3) the trustees, guardians, custodians, or other fiduciaries of a single trust, estate, or account.

(b) For purposes of this Act, shareholdings registered in substantially similar names constitute one shareholder if it is reasonable to believe that the names represent the same person.

CHAPTER 2.   INCORPORATION

§ 2.02 Articles of Incorporation

(a) The articles of incorporation must set forth:

(1) a corporate name for the corporation that satisfies the requirements of section 4.01;

(2) the number of shares the corporation is authorized to issue;

(3) the street address of the corporation's initial registered office and the name of its initial registered agent at that office; and

(4) the name and address of each incorporator.

(b) The articles of incorporation may set forth:

(1) the names and addresses of the individuals who are to serve as the initial directors;

(2) provisions not inconsistent with law regarding:

(i) the purpose or purposes for which the corporation is organized;

(ii) managing the business and regulating the affairs of the corporation;

(iii) defining, limiting, and regulating the powers of the corporation, its board of directors, and shareholders;

(iv) a par value for authorized shares or classes of shares;

(v) the imposition of personal liability on shareholders for the debts of the corporation to a specified extent and upon specified conditions;

(3) any provision that under this Act is required or permitted to be set forth in the bylaws;

(4) a provision eliminating or limiting the liability of a director to the corporation or its shareholders for money damages for any action taken, or any failure to take any action, as a director, except liability for (A) the amount of a financial benefit received by a director to which he is not entitled; (B) an intentional infliction of harm on the corporation or the shareholders; (C) a violation of section 8.33; or (D) an intentional violation of criminal law; and

(5) a provision permitting or making obligatory indemnification of a director for liability (as defined in section 8.50(5)) to any person for any action taken, or any failure to take any action, as a director, except liability for (A) receipt of a financial benefit to which he is not entitled, (B) an intentional infliction of harm on the corporation or its shareholders, (C) a violation of section 8.33, or (D) an intentional violation of criminal law.

(c) The articles of incorporation need not set forth any of the corporate powers enumerated in this Act.

(d) Provisions of the articles of incorporation may be made dependent upon facts objectively ascertainable outside the articles of incorporation in accordance with section 1.20(k).

CHAPTER 3.   PURPOSES AND POWERS

§ 3.02   General Powers

Unless its articles of incorporation provide otherwise, every corporation has perpetual duration and succession in its corporate name and has the same powers as an individual to do all things necessary or convenient to carry out its business and affairs, including without limitation power:

(1) to sue and be sued, complain and defend in its corporate name;

(2) to have a corporate seal, which may be altered at will, and to use it, or a facsimile of it, by impressing or affixing it or in any other manner reproducing it;

(3) to make and amend bylaws, not inconsistent with its articles of incorporation or with the laws of this state, for managing the business and regulating the affairs of the corporation;

(4) to purchase, receive, lease, or otherwise acquire, and own, hold, improve, use, and otherwise deal with, real or personal property, or any legal or equitable interest in property, wherever located;

(5) to sell, convey, mortgage, pledge, lease, exchange, and otherwise dispose of all or any part of its property;

(6) to purchase, receive, subscribe for, or otherwise acquire; own, hold, vote, use, sell, mortgage, lend, pledge, or otherwise dispose of; and deal in and with shares or other interests in, or obligations of, any other entity;

(7) to make contracts and guarantees, incur liabilities, borrow money, issue its notes, bonds, and other obligations (which may be convertible into or include the option to purchase other securities of the corporation), and secure any of its obligations by mortgage or pledge of any of its property, franchises, or income;

(8) to lend money, invest and reinvest its funds, and receive and hold real and personal property as security for repayment;

(9) to be a promoter, partner, member, associate, or manager of any partnership, joint venture, trust, or other entity;

(10) to conduct its business, locate offices, and exercise the powers granted by this Act within or without this state;

(11) to elect directors and appoint officers, employees, and agents of the corporation, define their duties, fix their compensation, and lend them money and credit;

(12) to pay pensions and establish pension plans, pension trusts, profit sharing plans, share bonus plans, share option plans, and benefit or incentive plans for any or all of its current or former directors, officers, employees, and agents;

(13) to make donations for the public welfare or for charitable, scientific, or educational purposes;

(14) to transact any lawful business that will aid governmental policy;

(15) to make payments or donations, or do any other act, not inconsistent with law, that furthers the business and affairs of the corporation.

CHAPTER 6. SHARES AND DISTRIBUTIONS

Subchapter A. Shares

§ 6.01 Authorized Shares

(a) The articles of incorporation must set forth any classes of shares and series of shares within a class, and the number of shares of each class and series, that the corporation is authorized to issue. If more than one class or series of shares is authorized, the articles of incorporation must prescribe a distinguishing designation for each class or series and must describe, prior to the issuance of shares of a class or series, the terms, including the preferences, rights, and limitations, of that class or series. Except to the extent varied as permitted by this section, all shares of a class or series must have terms, including preferences, rights and limitations, that are identical with those of other shares of the same class or series.

(b) The articles of incorporation must authorize:

(1) one or more classes or series of shares that together have unlimited voting rights, and

(2) one or more classes or series of shares (which may be the same class or classes as those with voting rights) that together are entitled to receive the net assets of the corporation upon dissolution.

(c) The articles of incorporation may authorize one or more classes or series of shares that:

(1) have special, conditional, or limited voting rights, or no right to vote, except to the extent otherwise provided by this Act;

(2) are redeemable or convertible as specified in the articles of incorporation:

(i) at the option of the corporation, the shareholder, or another person or upon the occurrence of a specified event;

(ii) for cash, indebtedness, securities, or other property; and

(iii) at prices and in amounts specified, or determined in accordance with a formula;

(3) entitle the holders to distributions calculated in any manner, including dividends that may be cumulative, noncumulative, or partially cumulative; or

(4) have preference over any other class or series of shares with respect to distributions, including distributions upon the dissolution of the corporation.

(d) Terms of shares may be made dependent upon facts objectively ascertainable outside the articles of incorporation in accordance with section 1.20(k).

(e) Any of the terms of shares may vary among holders of the same class or series so long as such variations are expressly set forth in the articles of incorporation.

(f) The description of the preferences, rights and limitations of classes or series of shares in subsection (c) is not exhaustive.

§ 6.02   Terms of Class or Series Determined by Board of Directors

(a) If the articles of incorporation so provide, the board of directors is authorized, without shareholder approval, to:

(1) classify any unissued shares into one or more classes or into one or more series within a class,

(2) reclassify any unissued shares of any class into one or more classes or into one or more series within one or more classes, or

(3) reclassify any unissued shares of any series of any class into one or more classes or into one or more series within a class.

(b) If the board of directors acts pursuant to subsection (a), it must determine the terms, including the preferences, rights and limitations, to the same extent permitted under section 6.01, of:

(1) any class of shares before the issuance of any shares of that class, or

(2) any series within a class before the issuance of any shares of that series.

(c) Before issuing any shares of a class or series created under this section, the corporation must deliver to the secretary of state for filing articles of amendment setting forth the terms determined under subsection (a).

§ 6.03 Issued and Outstanding Shares

(a) A corporation may issue the number of shares of each class or series authorized by the articles of incorporation. Shares that are issued are outstanding shares until they are reacquired, redeemed, converted, or cancelled.

(b) The reacquisition, redemption, or conversion of outstanding shares is subject to the limitations of subsection (c) of this section and to section 6.40.

(c) At all times that shares of the corporation are outstanding, one or more shares that together have unlimited voting rights and one or more shares that together are entitled to receive the net assets of the corporation upon dissolution must be outstanding.

Subchapter B. Issuance of Shares

§ 6.20 Subscription for Shares Before Incorporation

(a) A subscription for shares entered into before incorporation is irrevocable for six months unless the subscription agreement provides a longer or shorter period or all the subscribers agree to revocation.

(b) The board of directors may determine the payment terms of subscriptions for shares that were entered into before incorporation, unless the subscription agreement specifies them. A call for payment by the board of directors must be uniform so far as practicable as to all shares of the same class or series, unless the subscription agreement specifies otherwise.

(c) Shares issued pursuant to subscriptions entered into before incorporation are fully paid and nonassessable when the corporation receives the consideration specified in the subscription agreement.

(d) If a subscriber defaults in payment of money or property under a subscription agreement entered into before incorporation, the corporation may collect the amount owed as any other debt. Alternatively, unless the subscription agreement provides otherwise, the corporation may rescind the agreement and may sell the shares if the debt remains unpaid more than 20 days after the corporation sends written demand for payment to the subscriber.

(e) A subscription agreement entered into after incorporation is a contract between the subscriber and the corporation subject to section 6.21.

§ 6.21   Issuance of Shares

(a) The powers granted in this section to the board of directors may be reserved to the shareholders by the articles of incorporation.

(b) The board of directors may authorize shares to be issued for consideration consisting of any tangible or intangible property or benefit to the corporation, including cash, promissory notes, services performed, contracts for services to be performed, or other securities of the corporation.

(c) Before the corporation issues shares, the board of directors must determine that the consideration received or to be received for shares to be issued is adequate. That determination by the board of directors is conclusive insofar as the adequacy of consideration for the issuance of shares relates to whether the shares are validly issued, fully paid, and nonassessable.

(d) When the corporation receives the consideration for which the board of directors authorized the issuance of shares, the shares issued therefor are fully paid and nonassessable.

(e) The corporation may place in escrow shares issued for a contract for future services or benefits or a promissory note, or make other arrangements to restrict the transfer of the shares, and may credit distributions in respect of the shares against their purchase price, until the services are performed, the note is paid, or the benefits received. If the services are not performed, the note is not paid, or the benefits are not received, the shares escrowed or restricted and the distributions credited may be cancelled in whole or part.

(f)(1) An issuance of shares or other securities convertible into or rights exercisable for shares, in a transaction or a series of integrated transactions, requires approval of the shareholders, at a meeting at which a quorum exists consisting of at least a majority of the votes entitled to be cast on the matter, if:

(i) the shares, other securities, or rights are issued for consideration other than cash or cash equivalents, and

(ii) the voting power of shares that are issued and issuable as a result of the transaction or series of integrated transactions will comprise more than 20 percent of the voting power of the shares of the corporation that were outstanding immediately before the transaction.

(2) In this subsection:

(i) For purposes of determining the voting power of shares issued and issuable as a result of a transaction or series of integrated transactions, the voting power of shares shall be the greater of (A) the voting power of the shares to be issued, or (B) the voting power of the shares that would be outstanding after giving effect to the conversion of convertible shares and other securities and the exercise of rights to be issued.

(ii) A series of transactions is integrated if consummation of one transaction is made contingent on consummation of one or more of the other transactions.

§ 6.22 Liability of Shareholders

(a) A purchaser from a corporation of its own shares is not liable to the corporation or its creditors with respect to the shares except to pay the consideration for which the shares were authorized to be issued (section 6.21) or specified in the subscription agreement (section 6.20).

(b) Unless otherwise provided in the articles of incorporation, a shareholder of a corporation is not personally liable for the acts or debts of the corporation except that he may become personally liable by reason of his own acts or conduct.

§ 6.23 Share Dividends

(a) Unless the articles of incorporation provide otherwise, shares may be issued pro rata and without consideration to the corporation's shareholders or to the shareholders of one or more classes or series. An issuance of shares under this subsection is a share dividend.

(b) Shares of one class or series may not be issued as a share dividend in respect of shares of another class or series unless (1) the articles of incorporation so authorize, (2) a majority of the votes entitled to be cast by the class or series to be issued approve the issue, or (3) there are no outstanding shares of the class or series to be issued.

(c) If the board of directors does not fix the record date for determining shareholders entitled to a share dividend, it is the date the board of directors authorizes the share dividend.

§ 6.24 Share Options

(a) A corporation may issue rights, options, or warrants for the purchase of shares or other securities of the corporation. The board of directors shall determine (i) the terms upon which the rights, options, or warrants are issued and (ii) the terms, including the consideration for which the shares or other securities are to be issued. The authorization by the board of directors for the corporation to issue such rights, options, or warrants constitutes authorization of the issuance of the shares or other securities for which the rights, options or warrants are exercisable.

(b) The terms and conditions of such rights, options or warrants, including those outstanding on the effective date of this section, may include, without limitation, restrictions or conditions that:

(1) preclude or limit the exercise, transfer or receipt of such rights, options or warrants by any person or persons owning or offering to acquire a specified number or percentage of the outstanding shares

or other securities of the corporation or by any transferee or transferees of any such person or persons, or

(2) invalidate or void such rights, options or warrants held by any
such person or persons or any such transferee or transferees.

§ 6.25 Form and Content of Certificates

(a) Shares may but need not be represented by certificates. Unless this
Act or another statute expressly provides otherwise, the rights and obligations of shareholders are identical whether or not their shares are
represented by certificates.

(b) At a minimum each share certificate must state on its face:

(1) the name of the issuing corporation and that it is organized
under the law of this state;

(2) the name of the person to whom issued; and

(3) the number and class of shares and the designation of the
series, if any, the certificate represents.

(c) If the issuing corporation is authorized to issue different classes of
shares or different series within a class, the designations, relative rights,
preferences, and limitations applicable to each class and the variations in
rights, preferences, and limitations determined for each series (and the
authority of the board of directors to determine variations for future series)
must be summarized on the front or back of each certificate. Alternatively,
each certificate may state conspicuously on its front or back that the
corporation will furnish the shareholder this information on request in
writing and without charge.

(d) Each share certificate (1) must be signed (either manually or in
facsimile) by two officers designated in the bylaws or by the board of
directors and (2) may bear the corporate seal or its facsimile.

(e) If the person who signed (either manually or in facsimile) a share
certificate no longer holds office when the certificate is issued, the certificate is nevertheless valid.

§ 6.26 Shares Without Certificates

(a) Unless the articles of incorporation or bylaws provide otherwise,
the board of directors of a corporation may authorize the issue of some or
all of the shares of any or all of its classes or series without certificates. The
authorization does not affect shares already represented by certificates
until they are surrendered to the corporation.

(b) Within a reasonable time after the issue or transfer of shares
without certificates, the corporation shall send the shareholder a written
statement of the information required on certificates by section 6.25(b) and
(c), and, if applicable, section 6.27.

§ 6.28 Expense of Issue

A corporation may pay the expenses of selling or underwriting its
shares, and of organizing or reorganizing the corporation, from the consideration received for shares.

Subchapter C.   Subsequent Acquisition of Shares
by Shareholders and Corporation

§ 6.30   Shareholders' Preemptive Rights

(a) The shareholders of a corporation do not have a preemptive right to acquire the corporation's unissued shares except to the extent the articles of incorporation so provide.

(b) A statement included in the articles of incorporation that "the corporation elects to have preemptive rights" (or words of similar import) means that the following principles apply except to the extent the articles of incorporation expressly provide otherwise:

(1) The shareholders of the corporation have a preemptive right, granted on uniform terms and conditions prescribed by the board of directors to provide a fair and reasonable opportunity to exercise the right, to acquire proportional amounts of the corporation's unissued shares upon the decision of the board of directors to issue them.

(2) A shareholder may waive his preemptive right. A waiver evidenced by a writing is irrevocable even though it is not supported by consideration.

(3) There is no preemptive right with respect to:

(i) shares issued as compensation to directors, officers, agents, or employees of the corporation, its subsidiaries or affiliates;

(ii) shares issued to satisfy conversion or option rights created to provide compensation to directors, officers, agents, or employees of the corporation, its subsidiaries or affiliates;

(iii) shares authorized in articles of incorporation that are issued within six months from the effective date of incorporation;

(iv) shares sold otherwise than for money.

(4) Holders of shares of any class without general voting rights but with preferential rights to distributions or assets have no preemptive rights with respect to shares of any class.

(5) Holders of shares of any class with general voting rights but without preferential rights to distributions or assets have no preemptive rights with respect to shares of any class with preferential rights to distributions or assets unless the shares with preferential rights are convertible into or carry a right to subscribe for or acquire shares without preferential rights.

(6) Shares subject to preemptive rights that are not acquired by shareholders may be issued to any person for a period of one year after being offered to shareholders at a consideration set by the board of directors that is not lower than the consideration set for the exercise of preemptive rights. An offer at a lower consideration or after the expiration of one year is subject to the shareholders' preemptive rights.

(c) For purposes of this section, "shares" includes a security convertible into or carrying a right to subscribe for or acquire shares.

§ 6.31 Corporation's Acquisition of Its Own Shares

(a) A corporation may acquire its own shares, and shares so acquired constitute authorized but unissued shares.

(b) if the articles of incorporation prohibit the reissue of the acquired shares, the number of authorized shares is reduced by the number of shares acquired.

Subchapter D. Distributions

§ 6.40 Distributions to Shareholders

(a) A board of directors may authorize and the corporation may make distributions to its shareholders subject to restriction by the articles of incorporation and the limitation in subsection (c).

(b) If the board of directors does not fix the record date for determining shareholders entitled to a distribution (other than one involving a purchase, redemption, or other acquisition of the corporation's shares), it is the date the board of directors authorizes the distribution.

(c) No distribution may be made if, after giving it effect:

(1) the corporation would not be able to pay its debts as they become due in the usual course of business; or

(2) the corporation's total assets would be less than the sum of its total liabilities plus (unless the articles of incorporation permit otherwise) the amount that would be needed, if the corporation were to be dissolved at the time of the distribution, to satisfy the preferential rights upon dissolution of shareholders whose preferential rights are superior to those receiving the distribution.

(d) The board of directors may base a determination that a distribution is not prohibited under subsection (c) either on financial statements prepared on the basis of accounting practices and principles that are reasonable in the circumstances or on a fair valuation or other method that is reasonable in the circumstances.

(e) Except as provided in subsection (g), the effect of a distribution under subsection (c) is measured:

(1) in the case of distribution by purchase, redemption, or other acquisition of the corporation's shares, as of the earlier of (i) the date money or other property is transferred or debt incurred by the corporation or (ii) the date the shareholder ceases to be a shareholder with respect to the acquired shares;

(2) in the case of any other distribution of indebtedness, as of the date the indebtedness is distributed; and

(3) in all other cases, as of (i) the date the distribution is authorized if the payment occurs within 120 days after the date of authorization or (ii) the date the payment is made if it occurs more than 120 days after the date of authorization.

(f) A corporation's indebtedness to a shareholder incurred by reason of a distribution made in accordance with this section is at parity with the corporation's indebtedness to its general, unsecured creditors except to the extent subordinated by agreement.

(g) Indebtedness of a corporation, including indebtedness issued as a distribution, is not considered a liability for purposes of determinations under subsection (c) if its terms provide that payment of principal and interest are made only if and to the extent that payment of a distribution to shareholders could then be made under this section. If the indebtedness is issued as a distribution, each payment of principal or interest is treated as a distribution, the effect of which is measured on the date the payment is actually made.

(h) This section shall not apply to distributions in liquidation under chapter 14.

CHAPTER 7. SHAREHOLDERS

Subchapter B. Voting

§ 7.21 Voting Entitlement of Shares

(a) Except as provided in subsections (b) and (c) or unless the articles of incorporation provide otherwise, each outstanding share, regardless of class, is entitled to one vote on each matter voted on at a shareholders' meeting. Only shares are entitled to vote.

(b) Absent special circumstances, the shares of a corporation are not entitled to vote if they are owned, directly or indirectly, by a second corporation, domestic or foreign, and the first corporation owns, directly or indirectly, a majority of the shares entitled to vote for directors of the second corporation.

(c) Subsection (b) does not limit the power of a corporation to vote any shares, including its own shares, held by it in a fiduciary capacity.

(d) Redeemable shares are not entitled to vote after notice of redemption is mailed to the holders and a sum sufficient to redeem the shares has been deposited with a bank, trust company, or other financial institution under an irrevocable obligation to pay the holders the redemption price on surrender of the shares.

§ 7.25 Quorum and Voting Requirements for Voting Groups

(a) Shares entitled to vote as a separate voting group may take action on a matter at a meeting only if a quorum of those shares exists with respect to that matter. Unless the articles of incorporation or this Act provide otherwise, a majority of the votes entitled to be cast on the matter by the voting group constitutes a quorum of that voting group for action on that matter.

(b) Once a share is represented for any purpose at a meeting, it is deemed present for quorum purposes for the remainder of the meeting and for any adjournment of that meeting unless a new record date is or must be set for that adjourned meeting.

(c) If a quorum exists, action on a matter (other than the election of directors) by a voting group is approved if the votes cast within the voting group favoring the action exceed the votes cast opposing the action, unless the articles of incorporation or this Act require a greater number of affirmative votes.

(d) An amendment of articles of incorporation adding, changing, or deleting a quorum or voting requirement for a voting group greater than specified in subsection (a) or (c) is governed by section 7.27.

(e) The election of directors is governed by section 7.28.

§ 7.26   Action by Single and Multiple Voting Groups

(a) If the articles of incorporation or this Act provide for voting by a single voting group on a matter, action on that matter is taken when voted upon by that voting group as provided in section 7.25.

(b) If the articles of incorporation or this Act provide for voting by two or more voting groups on a matter, action on that matter is taken only when voted upon by each of those voting groups counted separately as provided in section 7.25. Action may be taken by one voting group on a matter even though no action is taken by another voting group entitled to vote on the matter.

§ 7.27   Greater Quorum or Voting Requirements

(a) The articles of incorporation may provide for a greater quorum or voting requirement for shareholders (or voting groups of shareholders) than is provided for by this Act.

(b) An amendment to the articles of incorporation that adds, changes, or deletes a greater quorum or voting requirement must meet the same quorum requirement and be adopted by the same vote and voting groups required to take action under the quorum and voting requirements then in effect or proposed to be adopted, whichever is greater.

§ 7.28   Voting for Directors; Cumulative Voting

(a) Unless otherwise provided in the articles of incorporation, directors are elected by a plurality of the votes cast by the shares entitled to vote in the election at a meeting at which a quorum is present.

(b) Shareholders do not have a right to cumulate their votes for directors unless the articles of incorporation so provide.

(c) A statement included in the articles of incorporation that "[all] [a designated voting group of] shareholders are entitled to cumulate their votes for directors" (or words of similar import) means that the shareholders designated are entitled to multiply the number of votes they are entitled to cast by the number of directors for whom they are entitled to vote and cast the product for a single candidate or distribute the product among two or more candidates.

(d) Shares otherwise entitled to vote cumulatively may not be voted cumulatively at a particular meeting unless:

   (1) the meeting notice or proxy statement accompanying the notice states conspicuously that cumulative voting is authorized; or

(2) a shareholder who has the right to cumulate his votes gives notice to the corporation not less than 48 hours before the time set for the meeting of his intent to cumulate his votes during the meeting, and if one shareholder gives this notice all other shareholders in the same voting group participating in the election are entitled to cumulate their votes without giving further notice.

Subchapter C. Voting Trusts and Agreements

§ 7.32 Shareholder Agreements

(a) An agreement among the shareholders of a corporation that complies with this section is effective among the shareholders and the corporation even though it is inconsistent with one or more other provisions of this Act in that it:

(1) eliminates the board of directors or restricts the discretion or powers of the board of directors;

(2) governs the authorization or making of distributions whether or not in proportion to ownership of shares, subject to the limitations in section 6.40;

(3) establishes who shall be directors or officers of the corporation, or their terms of office or manner of selection or removal;

(4) governs, in general or in regard to specific matters, the exercise or division of voting power by or between the shareholders and directors or by or among any of them, including use of weighted voting rights or director proxies;

(5) establishes the terms and conditions of any agreement for the transfer or use of property or the provision of services between the corporation and any shareholder, director, officer or employee of the corporation or among any of them;

(6) transfers to one or more shareholders or other persons all or part of the authority to exercise the corporate powers or to manage the business and affairs of the corporation, including the resolution of any issue about which there exists a deadlock among directors or shareholders;

(7) requires dissolution of the corporation at the request of one or more of the shareholders or upon the occurrence of a specified event or contingency; or

(8) otherwise governs the exercise of the corporate powers or the management of the business and affairs of the corporation or the relationship among the shareholders, the directors and the corporation, or among any of them, and is not contrary to public policy.

(b) An agreement authorized by this section shall be:

(1) set forth (A) in the articles of incorporation or bylaws and approved by all persons who are shareholders at the time of the agreement or (B) in a written agreement that is signed by all persons

who are shareholders at the time of the agreement and is made known to the corporation;

(2) subject to amendment only by all persons who are shareholders at the time of the amendment, unless the agreement provides otherwise; and

(3) valid for 10 years, unless the agreement provides otherwise.

(c) The existence of an agreement authorized by this section shall be noted conspicuously on the front or back of each certificate for outstanding shares or on the information statement required by section 6.26(b). If at the time of the agreement the corporation has shares outstanding represented by certificates, the corporation shall recall the outstanding certificates and issue substitute certificates that comply with this subsection. The failure to note the existence of the agreement on the certificate or information statement shall not affect the validity of the agreement or any action taken pursuant to it. Any purchaser of shares who, at the time of purchase, did not have knowledge of the existence of the agreement shall be entitled to rescission of the purchase. A purchaser shall be deemed to have knowledge of the existence of the agreement if its existence is noted on the certificate or information statement for the shares in compliance with this subsection and, if the shares are not represented by a certificate, the information statement is delivered to the purchaser at or prior to the time of purchase of the shares. An action to enforce the right of rescission authorized by this subsection must be commenced within the earlier of 90 days after discovery of the existence of the agreement or two years after the time of purchase of the shares.

(d) An agreement authorized by this section shall cease to be effective when shares of the corporation are listed on a national securities exchange or regularly traded in a market maintained by one or more members of a national or affiliated securities association. If the agreement ceases to be effective for any reason, the board of directors may, if the agreement is contained or referred to in the corporation's articles of incorporation or bylaws, adopt an amendment to the articles of incorporation or bylaws, without shareholder action, to delete the agreement and any references to it.

(e) An agreement authorized by this section that limits the discretion or powers of the board of directors shall relieve the directors of, and impose upon the person or persons in whom such discretion or powers are vested, liability for acts or omissions imposed by law on directors to the extent that the discretion or powers of the directors are limited by the agreement.

(f) The existence or performance of an agreement authorized by this section shall not be a ground for imposing personal liability on any shareholder for the acts or debts of the corporation even if the agreement or its performance treats the corporation as if it were a partnership or results in failure to observe the corporate formalities otherwise applicable to the matters governed by the agreement.

(g) Incorporators or subscribers for shares may act as shareholders with respect to an agreement authorized by this section if no shares have been issued when the agreement is made.

CHAPTER 8. DIRECTORS AND OFFICERS

Subchapter A. Board of Directors

§ 8.01. Requirement for and Duties of Board of Directors.

(a) Except as provided in section 7.32, each corporation must have a board of directors.

(b) All corporate powers shall be exercised by or under the authority of, and the business and affairs of the corporation managed by or under the direction of, its board of directors, subject to any limitation set forth in the articles of incorporation or in an agreement authorized under section 7.32.

(c) A corporation having 50 or fewer shareholders may dispense with or limit the authority of a board of directors by describing in its articles of incorporation who will perform some or all of the duties of a board of directors.

§ 8.04 Election of Directors by Certain Classes of Shareholders

If the articles of incorporation authorize dividing the shares into classes, the articles may also authorize the election of all or a specified number of directors by the holders of one or more authorized classes of shares. A class (or classes) of shares entitled to elect one or more directors is a separate voting group for purposes of the election of directors.

Subchapter C. Standards of Conduct

§ 8.30. Standards of Conduct for Directors.

(a) Each member of the board of directors, when discharging the duties of a director, shall act: (1) in good faith, and (2) in a manner the director reasonably believes to be in the best interests of the corporation.

(b) The members of the board of directors or a committee of the board, when becoming informed in connection with their decision-making function or devoting attention to their oversight function, shall discharge their duties with the care that a person in a like position would reasonably believe appropriate under similar circumstances.

(c) In discharging board or committee duties a director, who does not have knowledge that makes reliance unwarranted, is entitled to rely on the performance by any of the persons specified in subsection (e)(1) or subsection (e)(3) to whom the board may have delegated, formally or informally by course of conduct, the authority or duty to perform one or more of the board's functions that are delegable under applicable law.

(d) In discharging board or committee duties a director, who does not have knowledge that makes reliance unwarranted, is entitled to rely on information, opinions, reports or statements, including financial statements and other financial data, prepared or presented by any of the persons specified in subsection (e).

(e) A director is entitled to rely, in accordance with subsection (c) or (d), on:

   (1) one or more officers or employees of the corporation whom the director reasonably believes to be reliable and competent in the functions performed or the information, opinions, reports or statements provided;

   (2) legal counsel, public accountants, or other persons retained by the corporation as to matters involving skills or expertise the director reasonably believes are matters (i) within the particular person's professional or expert competence or (ii) as to which the particular person merits confidence; or

   (3) a committee of the board of directors of which the director is not a member if the director reasonably believes the committee merits confidence.

§ 8.33   Directors' Liability for Unlawful Distributions

(a) A director who votes for or assents to a distribution in excess of what may be authorized and made pursuant to section 6.40(a) or 14.09(a) is personally liable to the corporation for the amount of the distribution that exceeds what could have been distributed without violating section 6.40(a) or 14.09(a) if the party asserting liability establishes that when taking the action the director did not comply with section 8.30.

(b) A director held liable under subsection (a) for an unlawful distribution is entitled to:

   (1) contribution from every other director who could be held liable under subsection (a) for the unlawful distribution; and

   (2) recoupment from each shareholder of the pro-rata portion of the amount of the unlawful distribution the shareholder accepted, knowing the distribution was made in violation of section 6.40(a) or 14.09(a).

(c) A proceeding to enforce:

   (1) the liability of a director under subsection (a) is barred unless it is commenced within two years after the date (i) on which the effect of the distribution was measured under section 6.40(e) or (g), (ii) or as of which the violation of section 6.40(a) occurred as the consequence of disregard of a restriction in the articles of incorporation, or (iii) on which the distribution of assets to shareholders under section 14.09 was made; or

   (2) contribution or recoupment under subsection (b) is barred unless it is commenced within one year after the liability of the claimant has been finally adjudicated under subsection (a).

Subchapter D.   Officers

§ 8.40   Officers

(a) A corporation has the offices described in its bylaws or designated by the board of directors in accordance with the bylaws.

(b) The board of directors may elect individuals to fill one or more offices of the corporation. An officer may appoint one or more officers if authorized by the bylaws or the board of directors.

(c) The bylaws or the board of directors shall assign to one of the officers responsibility for preparing minutes of the directors' and shareholders' meetings and for maintaining and authenticating the records of the corporation required to be kept under sections 16.01(a) and 16.01(e).

(d) The same individual may simultaneously hold more than one office in a corporation.

§ 8.42. Standards of Conduct for Officers.

(a) An officer, when performing in such capacity, shall act:

(1) in good faith;

(2) with the care that a person in a like position would reasonably exercise under similar circumstances; and

(3) in a manner the officer reasonably believes to be in the best interests of the corporation.

(b) The duty of an officer includes the obligation:

(1) to inform the superior officer to whom, or the board of directors or the committee thereof to which, the officer reports of information about the affairs of the corporation known to the officer, within the scope of the officer's functions, and known to the officer to be material to such superior officer, board or committee; and

(2) to inform his or her superior officer, or another appropriate person within the corporation, or the board of directors, or a committee thereof, of any actual or probable material violation of law involving the corporation or material breach of duty to the corporation by an officer, employee, or agent of the corporation, that the officer believes has occurred or is about to occur.

(c) In discharging his or her duties, an officer who does not have knowledge that makes reliance unwarranted is entitled to rely on:

(1) the performance of properly delegated responsibilities by one or more employees of the corporation whom the officer reasonably believes to be reliable and competent in performing the responsibilities delegated; or

(2) information, opinions, reports or statements, including financial statements and other financial data, prepared or presented by one or more employees of the corporation whom the officer reasonably believes to be reliable and competent in the matters presented or by legal counsel, public accountants, or other persons retained by the corporation as to matters involving skills or expertise the officer reasonably believes are matters (i) within the particular person's professional or expert competence or (ii) as to which the particular person merits confidence.

(d) An officer shall not be liable to the corporation or its shareholders for any decision to take or not to take action, or any failure to take any action, as an officer, if the duties of the office are performed in compliance with this section. Whether an officer who does not comply with this section shall have liability will depend in such instance on applicable law, including those principles of section 8.31 that have relevance.

CHAPTER 10.   AMENDMENT OF ARTICLES OF INCORPORATION AND BYLAWS

Subchapter A.   Amendment of Articles of Incorporation

§ 10.01   Authority to Amend

(a) A corporation may amend its articles of incorporation at any time to add or change a provision that is required or permitted in the articles of incorporation as of the effective date of the amendment or to delete a provision that is not required to be contained in the articles of incorporation.

(b) A shareholder of the corporation does not have a vested property right resulting from any provision in the articles of incorporation, including provisions relating to management, control, capital structure, dividend entitlement, or purpose or duration of the corporation.

§ 10.02   Amendment Before Issuance of Shares

If a corporation has not yet issued shares, its board of directors, or its incorporators if it has no board of directors, may adopt one or more amendments to the corporation's articles of incorporation.

§ 10.03   Amendment By Board of Directors and Shareholders

If a corporation has issued shares, an amendment to the articles of incorporation shall be adopted in the following manner:

(a) The proposed amendment must be adopted by the board of directors.

(b) Except as provided in sections 10.05, 10.07, and 10.08, after adopting the proposed amendment the board of directors must submit the amendment to the shareholders for their approval. The board of directors must also transmit to the shareholders a recommendation that the shareholders approve the amendment, unless the board of directors makes a determination that because of conflicts of interest or other special circumstances it should not make such a recommendation, in which case the board of directors must transmit to the shareholders the basis for that determination.

(c) The board of directors may condition its submission of the amendment to the shareholders on any basis.

(d) If the amendment is required to be approved by the shareholders, and the approval is to be given at a meeting, the corporation must notify each shareholder, whether or not entitled to vote, of the meeting of shareholders at which the amendment is to be submitted for approval. The notice must state that the purpose, or one of the purposes, of the meeting is to consider the amendment and must contain or be accompanied by a copy of the amendment.

(e) Unless the articles of incorporation, or the board of directors acting pursuant to subsection (c), requires a greater vote or a greater number of shares to be present, approval of the amendment requires the approval of the shareholders at a meeting at which a quorum consisting of at least a majority of the votes entitled to be cast on the amendment exists, and, if any class or series of shares is entitled to vote as a separate group on the amendment, except as provided in section 10.04(c), the approval of each such separate voting group at a meeting at which a quorum of the voting group consisting of at least a majority of the votes entitled to be cast on the amendment by that voting group exists.

§ 10.04 Voting on Amendments By Voting Groups

(a) If a corporation has more than one class of shares outstanding, the holders of the outstanding shares of a class are entitled to vote as a separate voting group (if shareholder voting is otherwise required by this Act) on a proposed amendment to the articles of incorporation if the amendment would:

(1) effect an exchange or reclassification of all or part of the shares of the class into shares of another class;

(2) effect an exchange or reclassification, or create the right of exchange, of all or part of the shares of another class into shares of the class;

(3) change the rights, preferences, or limitations of all or part of the shares of the class;

(4) change the shares of all or part of the class into a different number of shares of the same class;

(5) create a new class of shares having rights or preferences with respect to distributions or to dissolution that are prior or superior to the shares of the class;

(6) increase the rights, preferences, or number of authorized shares of any class that, after giving effect to the amendment, have rights or preferences with respect to distributions or to dissolution that are prior or superior to the shares of the class;

(7) limit or deny an existing preemptive right of all or part of the shares of the class; or

(8) cancel or otherwise affect rights to distributions that have accumulated but not yet been authorized on all or part of the shares of the class.

(b) If a proposed amendment would affect a series of a class of shares in one or more of the ways described in subsection (a), the holders of shares of that series are entitled to vote as a separate voting group on the proposed amendment.

(c) If a proposed amendment that entitles the holders of two or more classes or series of shares to vote as separate voting groups under this section would affect those two or more classes or series in the same or a substantially similar way, the holders of shares of all the classes or series so affected must vote together as a single voting group on the proposed amendment, unless otherwise provided in the articles of incorporation or required by the board of directors.

(d) A class or series of shares is entitled to the voting rights granted by this section although the articles of incorporation provide that the shares are nonvoting shares.

§ 10.05   Amendment By Board of Directors

Unless the articles of incorporation provide otherwise, a corporation's board of directors may adopt amendments to the corporation's articles of incorporation without shareholder approval:

(1) to extend the duration of the corporation if it was incorporated at a time when limited duration was required by law;

(2) to delete the names and addresses of the initial directors;

(3) to delete the name and address of the initial registered agent or registered office, if a statement of change is on file with the secretary of state;

(4) if the corporation has only one class of shares outstanding:

(a) to change each issued and unissued authorized share of the class into a greater number of whole shares of that class; or

(b) to increase the number of authorized shares of the class to the extent necessary to permit the issuance of shares as a share dividend;

(5) to change the corporate name by substituting the word "corporation," "incorporated," "company," "limited," or the abbreviation "corp.," "inc.," "co.," or "ltd.," for a similar word or abbreviation in the name, or by adding, deleting, or changing a geographical attribution for the name;

(6) to reflect a reduction in authorized shares, as a result of the operation of section 6.31(b), when the corporation has acquired its own shares and the articles of incorporation prohibit the reissue of the acquired shares;

(7) to delete a class of shares from the articles of incorporation, as a result of the operation of section 6.31(b), when there are no remaining shares of the class because the corporation has acquired all shares of the class and the articles of incorporation prohibit the reissue of the acquired shares; or

(8) to make any change expressly permitted by section 6.02(a) or (b) to be made without shareholder approval.

§ 10.06   Articles of Amendment

After an amendment to the articles of incorporation has been adopted and approved in the manner required by this Act and by the articles of incorporation, the corporation shall deliver to the secretary of state, for filing, articles of amendment, which shall set forth:

(1) the name of the corporation;

(2) the text of each amendment adopted, or the information required by section 1.20(k)(5);

(3) if an amendment provides for an exchange, reclassification, or cancellation of issued shares, provisions for implementing the amendment (if not contained in the amendment itself), which may be made dependent upon facts objectively ascertainable outside the articles of amendment in accordance with section 1.20(k);

(4) the date of each amendment's adoption; and

(5) if an amendment:

(a) was adopted by the incorporators or board of directors without shareholder approval, a statement that the amendment was duly approved by the incorporators or by the board of directors, as the case may be, and that shareholder approval was not required;

(b) required approval by the shareholders, a statement that the amendment was duly approved by the shareholders in the manner required by this Act and by the articles of incorporation; or

(c) is being filed pursuant to section 1.20(k)(5), a statement to that effect.

§ 10.07   Restated Articles of Incorporation

(a) A corporation's board of directors may restate its articles of incorporation at any time, with or without shareholder approval, to consolidate all amendments into a single document.

(b) If the restated articles include one or more new amendments that require shareholder approval, the amendments must be adopted and approved as provided in section 10.03.

(c) A corporation that restates its articles of incorporation shall deliver to the secretary of state for filing articles of restatement setting forth the name of the corporation and the text of the restated articles of incorporation together with a certificate which states that the restated articles consolidate all amendments into a single document and, if a new amendment is included in the restated articles, which also includes the statements required under section 10.06.

(d) Duly adopted restated articles of incorporation supersede the original articles of incorporation and all amendments thereto.

(e) The secretary of state may certify restated articles of incorporation as the articles of incorporation currently in effect, without including the certificate information required by subsection (c).

§ 10.08   Amendment Pursuant to Reorganization

(a) A corporation's articles of incorporation may be amended without action by the board of directors or shareholders to carry out a plan of reorganization ordered or decreed by a court of competent jurisdiction under the authority of a law of the United States.

(b) The individual or individuals designated by the court shall deliver to the secretary of state for filing articles of amendment setting forth:

(1) the name of the corporation;

(2) the text of each amendment approved by the court;

(3) the date of the court's order or decree approving the articles of amendment;

(4) the title of the reorganization proceeding in which the order or decree was entered; and

(5) a statement that the court had jurisdiction of the proceeding under federal statute.

(c) This section does not apply after entry of a final decree in the reorganization proceeding even though the court retains jurisdiction of the proceeding for limited purposes unrelated to consummation of the reorganization plan.

§ 10.09   Effect of Amendment

An amendment to the articles of incorporation does not affect a cause of action existing against or in favor of the corporation, a proceeding to which the corporation is a party, or the existing rights of persons other than shareholders of the corporation. An amendment changing a corporation's name does not abate a proceeding brought by or against the corporation in its former name.

Subchapter B.   Amendment of Bylaws

§ 10.20   Amendment By Board of Directors or Shareholders

(a) A corporation's shareholders may amend or repeal the corporation's bylaws.

(b) A corporation's board of directors may amend or repeal the corporation's bylaws, unless:

(1) the articles of incorporation or section 10.21 reserve that power exclusively to the shareholders in whole or part; or

(2) the shareholders in amending, repealing, or adopting a bylaw expressly provide that the board of directors may not amend, repeal, or reinstate that bylaw.

§ 10.21   Bylaw Increasing Quorum or Voting Requirement for Directors

(a) A bylaw that increases a quorum or voting requirement for the board of directors may be amended or repealed:

(1) if adopted by the shareholders, only by the shareholders, unless the bylaw otherwise provides;

(2) if adopted by the board of directors, either by the shareholders or by the board of directors.

(b) A bylaw adopted or amended by the shareholders that increases a quorum or voting requirement for the board of directors may provide that it can be amended or repealed only by a specified vote of either the shareholders or the board of directors.

(c) Action by the board of directors under subsection (a) to amend or repeal a bylaw that changes the quorum or voting requirement for the board of directors must meet the same quorum requirement and be adopted by the same vote required to take action under the quorum and voting requirement then in effect or proposed to be adopted, whichever is greater.

CHAPTER 11. MERGERS AND SHARE EXCHANGES

§ 11.01. Definitions.

As used in this chapter:

(a) "Merger" means a business combination pursuant to section 11.02.

(b) "Party to a merger" or "party to a share exchange" means any domestic or foreign corporation or eligible entity that will:

(1) merge under a plan of merger;

(2) acquire shares or eligible interests of another corporation or an eligible entity in a share exchange; or

(3) have all of its shares or eligible interests or all of one or more classes or series of its shares or eligible interests acquired in a share exchange.

(c) "Share exchange" means a business combination pursuant to section 11.03.

(d) "Survivor in a merger" means the corporation or eligible entity into which one or more other corporations or eligible entities are merged. A survivor of a merger may preexist the merger or be created by the merger.

§ 11.02 Merger

(a) One or more domestic business corporations may merge with one or more domestic or foreign business corporations or eligible entities pursuant to a plan of merger, or two or more foreign business corporations or domestic or foreign eligible entities may merge into a new domestic business corporation to be created in the merger in the manner provided in this chapter.

(b) A foreign business corporation, or a foreign eligible entity, may be a party to a merger with a domestic business corporation, or may be created by the terms of the plan of merger, only if the merger is permitted by the foreign business corporation or eligible entity.

(b.1) If the organic law of a domestic eligible entity does not provide procedures for the approval of a merger, a plan of merger may be adopted and approved, the merger effectuated, and appraisal rights exercised in accordance with the procedures in this chapter and chapter 13. For the purposes of applying this chapter and chapter 13:

(1) the eligible entity, its members or interest holders, eligible interests and organic documents taken together shall be deemed to be a domestic business corporation, shareholders, shares and articles of incorporation, respectively and vice versa as the context may require; and

(2) if the business and affairs of the eligible entity are managed by a group of persons that is not identical to the members or interest holders, that group shall be deemed to be the board of directors.

(c) The plan of merger must include:

(1) the name of each domestic or foreign business corporation or eligible entity that will merge and the name of the domestic or foreign business corporation or eligible entity that will be the survivor of the merger;

(2) the terms and conditions of the merger;

(3) the manner and basis of converting the shares of each merging domestic or foreign business corporation and eligible interests of each merging domestic or foreign eligible entity into shares or other securities, eligible interests, obligations, rights to acquire shares, other securities or eligible interests, cash, other property, or any combination of the foregoing;

(4) the articles of incorporation of any domestic or foreign business or nonprofit corporation, or the organic documents of any domestic or foreign unincorporated entity, to be created by the merger, or if a new domestic or foreign business or nonprofit corporation or unincorporated entity is not to be created by the merger, any amendments to the survivor's articles of incorporation or organic documents; and

(5) any other provisions required by the laws under which any party to the merger is organized or by which it is governed, or by the articles of incorporation or organic document of any such party.

(d) Terms of a plan of merger may be made dependent on facts objectively ascertainable outside the plan in accordance with section 1.20(k).

(e) The plan of merger may also include a provision that the plan may be amended prior to filing articles of merger, but if the shareholders of a domestic corporation that is a party to the merger are required or permitted to vote on the plan, the plan must provide that subsequent to approval of the plan by such shareholders the plan may not be amended to change:

(1) the amount or kind of shares or other securities, eligible interests, obligations, rights to acquire shares, other securities or eligible interests, cash, or other property to be received under the plan by the shareholders of or owners of eligible interests in any party to the merger;

(2) the articles of incorporation of any corporation, or the organic documents of any unincorporated entity, that will survive or be created as a result of the merger, except for changes permitted by section 10.05 or by comparable provisions of the organic laws of any such foreign corporation or domestic or foreign unincorporated entity; or

(3) any of the other terms or conditions of the plan if the change would adversely affect such shareholders in any material respect.

(f) Property held in trust or for charitable purposes under the laws of this state by a domestic or foreign eligible entity shall not be diverted by a merger from the objects for which it was donated, granted or devised, unless and until the eligible entity obtains an order of [court] [the attorney general] specifying the disposition of the property to the extent required by and pursuant to [cite state statutory cy pres or other nondiversion statute].

§ 11.03. Share Exchange.

(a) Through a share exchange:

(1) a domestic corporation may acquire all of the shares of one or more classes or series of shares of another domestic or foreign corporation, or all of the interests of one or more classes or series of interests of a domestic or foreign other entity, in exchange for shares or other securities, interests, obligations, rights to acquire shares or other securities, cash, other property, or any combination of the foregoing, pursuant to a plan of share exchange, or

(2) all of the shares of one or more classes or series of shares of a domestic corporation may be acquired by another domestic or foreign corporation or other entity, in exchange for shares or other securities, interests, obligations, rights to acquire shares or other securities, cash, other property, or any combination of the foregoing, pursuant to a plan of share exchange.

(b) A foreign corporation, or eligible entity, may be a party to a share exchange only if the share exchange is permitted by the corporation or other entity is organized or by which it is governed.

(b.1) If the organic law of a domestic other entity does not provide procedures for the approval of a share exchange, a plan of share exchange may be adopted and approved, and the share exchange effectuated, in accordance with the procedures, if any, for a merger. If the organic law of a domestic other entity does not provide procedures for the approval of either a share exchange or a merger, a plan of share exchange may be adopted and approved, the share exchange effectuated, and appraisal rights exercised, in accordance with the procedures in this chapter and chapter 13. For the purposes of applying this chapter and chapter 13:

(1) the other entity, its interest holders, interests and organic documents taken together shall be deemed to be a domestic business corporation, shareholders, shares and articles of incorporation, respectively and vice versa as the context may require; and

(2) if the business and affairs of the other entity are managed by a group of persons that is not identical to the interest holders, that group shall be deemed to be the board of directors.

(c) The plan of share exchange must include:

(1) the name of each corporation or other entity whose shares or interests will be acquired and the name of the corporation or other entity that will acquire those shares or interests;

(2) the terms and conditions of the share exchange;

(3) the manner and basis of exchanging shares of a corporation or interests in an other entity whose shares or interests will be acquired under the share exchange into shares or other securities, interests, obligations, rights to acquire shares, other securities, or interests, cash, other property, or any combination of the foregoing; and

(4) any other provisions required by the laws under which any party to the share exchange is organized or by the articles of incorporation or organic document of any such party.

(d) The terms described in subsections (c)(2) and (c)(3) may be made dependent on facts ascertainable outside the plan of share exchange, provided that those facts are objectively ascertainable. The term facts includes, but is not limited to, the occurrence of any event, including a determination or action by any person or body, including the corporation.

(e) The plan of share exchange may also include a provision that the plan may be amended prior to filing articles of share exchange, but if the shareholders of a domestic corporation that is a party to the share exchange are required or permitted to vote on the plan, the plan must provide that subsequent to approval of the plan by such shareholders the plan may not be amended to change:

(1) the amount or kind of shares or other securities, interests, obligations, rights to acquire shares, other securities or interests, cash, or other property to be issued by the corporation or to be received under the plan by the shareholders of or owners of interests in any party to the share exchange in exchange; or

(2) any of the terms or conditions of the plan if the change would adversely affect such shareholders in any material respect.

(f) Section 11.03 does not limit the power of a domestic corporation to acquire shares of another corporation or interests in another entity in a transaction other than a share exchange.

§ 11.04. Action on a Plan of Merger or Share Exchange.

In the case of a domestic corporation that is a party to a merger or share exchange:

(a) The plan of merger or share exchange must be adopted by the board of directors.

(b) Except as provided in subsection (g) and in section 11.05, after adopting the plan of merger or share exchange the board of directors must submit the plan to the shareholders for their approval. The board of directors must also transmit to the shareholders a recommendation that the shareholders approve the plan, unless the board of directors makes a determination that because of conflicts of interest or other special circumstances it should not make such a recommendation, in which case the board of directors must transmit to the shareholders the basis for that determination.

(c) The board of directors may condition its submission of the plan of merger or share exchange to the shareholders on any basis.

(d) If the plan of merger or share exchange is required to be approved by the shareholders, and if the approval is to be given at a meeting, the corporation must notify each shareholder, whether or not entitled to vote, of the meeting of shareholders at which the plan is to be submitted for approval. The notice must state that the purpose, or one of the purposes, of the meeting is to consider the plan and must contain or be accompanied by a copy or summary of the plan. If the corporation is to be merged into an existing corporation or other entity, the notice shall also include or be accompanied by a copy or summary of the articles of incorporation or organizational documents of that corporation or other entity. If the corporation is to be merged into a corporation or other entity that is to be created pursuant to the merger, the notice shall include or be accompanied by a copy or a summary of the articles of incorporation or organizational documents of the new corporation or other entity.

(e) Unless the articles of incorporation, or the board of directors acting pursuant to subsection (c), requires a greater vote or a greater number of votes to be present, approval of the plan of merger or share exchange requires the approval of the shareholders at a meeting at which a quorum consisting of at least a majority of the votes entitled to be cast on the plan exists, and, if any class or series of shares is entitled to vote as a separate group on the plan of merger or share exchange, the approval of each such separate voting group at a meeting at which a quorum of the voting group consisting of at least a majority of the votes entitled to be cast on the merger or share exchange by that voting group is present.

(f) Separate voting by voting groups is required:

(1) on a plan of merger, by each class or series of shares that: (i) are to be converted under the plan of merger into other securities, interests, obligations, rights to acquire shares, other securities or interests, cash, other property, or any combination of the foregoing; or

(ii) would be entitled to vote as a separate group on a provision in the plan that, if contained in a proposed amendment to articles of incorporation, would require action by separate voting groups under section 10.04;

(2) on a plan of share exchange, by each class or series of shares included in the exchange, with each class or series constituting a separate voting group; and

(3) on a plan of merger or share exchange, if the voting group is entitled under the articles of incorporation to vote as a voting group to approve a plan of merger or share exchange.

(g) Unless the articles of incorporation otherwise provide, approval by the corporation's shareholders of a plan of merger or share exchange is not required if:

(1) the corporation will survive the merger or is the acquiring corporation in a share exchange;

(2) except for amendments permitted by section 10.05, its articles of incorporation will not be changed;

(3) each shareholder of the corporation whose shares were outstanding immediately before the effective date of the merger or share exchange will hold the same number of shares, with identical preferences, limitations, and relative rights, immediately after the effective date of change; and

(4) the issuance in the merger or share exchange of shares or other securities convertible into or rights exercisable for shares does not require a vote under section 6.21(f).

(h) If as a result of a merger or share exchange one or more shareholders of a domestic corporation would become subject to owner liability for the debts, obligations or liabilities of any other person or entity, approval of the plan of merger or share exchange shall require the execution, by each such shareholder, of a separate written consent to become subject to such owner liability.

§ 11.05   Merger Between Parent and Subsidiary or Between Subsidiaries

(a) A domestic parent corporation that owns shares of a domestic or foreign subsidiary corporation that carry at least 90 percent of the voting power of each class and series of the outstanding shares of the subsidiary that have voting power may merge the subsidiary into itself or into another such subsidiary, or merge itself into the subsidiary, without the approval of the board of directors or shareholders of the subsidiary, unless the articles of incorporation of any of the corporations otherwise provide, and unless, in the case of a foreign subsidiary, approval by the subsidiary's board of directors or shareholders is required by the laws under which the subsidiary is organized.

(b) If under subsection (a) approval of a merger by the subsidiary's shareholders is not required, the parent corporation shall, within ten days after the effective date of the merger, notify each of the subsidiary's shareholders that the merger has become effective.

(c) Except as provided in subsections (a) and (b), a merger between a parent and a subsidiary shall be governed by the provisions of chapter 11 applicable to mergers generally.

§ 11.06.   Articles of Merger or Share Exchange.

(a) After a plan of merger or share exchange has been adopted and approved as required by this Act, articles of merger or share exchange shall be executed on behalf of each party to the merger or share exchange by any officer or other duly authorized representative. The articles shall set forth:

(1) the names of the parties to the merger or share exchange and the date on which the merger or share exchange occurred or is to be effective;

(2) if the articles of incorporation of the survivor of a merger are amended, or if a new corporation is created as a result of a merger, the amendments to the survivor's articles of incorporation or the articles of incorporation of the new corporation;

(3) if the plan of merger or share exchange required approval by the shareholders of a domestic corporation that was a party to the merger or share exchange, a statement that the plan was duly approved by the shareholders and, if voting by any separate voting group was required, by each such separate voting group, in the manner required by this Act and the articles of incorporation;

(4) if the plan of merger or share exchange did not require approval by the shareholders of a domestic corporation that was a party to the merger or share exchange, a statement to that effect; and

(5) as to each foreign corporation and each other entity that was a party to the merger or share exchange, a statement that the plan and the performance of its terms were duly authorized by all action required by the laws under which the corporation or other entity is organized, or by which it is governed, and by its articles of incorporation or organizational documents.

(b) Articles of merger or share exchange shall be delivered to the secretary of state for filing by the survivor of the merger or the acquiring corporation in a share exchange and shall take effect on the effective date.

§ 11.07. Effect of Merger or Share Exchange.

(a) When a merger becomes effective:

(1) the corporation or eligible entity that is designated in the plan of merger as the survivor continues or comes into existence, as the case may be;

(2) the separate existence of every corporation or eligible entity that is merged into the survivor ceases;

(3) all property owned by, and every contract right possessed by, each corporation or eligible entity that merges into the survivor is vested in the survivor without reversion or impairment;

(4) all liabilities of each corporation or eligible entity that is merged into the survivor are vested in the survivor;

(5) the name of the survivor may, but need not be, substituted in any pending proceeding for the name of any party to the merger whose separate existence ceased in the merger;

(6) the articles of incorporation or organic documents of the survivor are amended to the extent provided in the plan of merger;

(7) the articles of incorporation or organic documents of a survivor that is created by the merger become effective; and

(8) the shares of each corporation that is a party to the merger, and the interests in an eligible entity that is a party to a merger, that are to be converted under the plan of merger into shares, eligible interests, obligations, rights to acquire securities, other securities, or eligible interests, cash, other property, or any combination of the foregoing, are converted, and the former holders of such shares or eligible interests are entitled only to the rights provided to them in the plan of merger or to any rights they may have under chapter 13 or the organic law of the eligible entity.

(b) When a share exchange becomes effective, the shares of each domestic corporation that are to be exchanged for shares or other securities, interests, obligations, rights to acquire shares or other securities, cash, other property, or any combination of the foregoing, are entitled only to the rights provided to them in the plan of share exchange or to any rights they may have under chapter 13.

(c) A person who becomes subject to owner liability for some or all of the debts, obligations or liabilities of any entity as a result of a merger or share exchange shall have owner liability only to the extent provided in the organic law of the entity and only for those debts, obligations and liabilities that arise after the effective time of the articles of merger or share exchange.

(d) Upon a merger becoming effective, a foreign corporation, or a foreign eligible entity, that is the survivor of the merger is deemed to:

(1) appoint the secretary of state as its agent for service of process in a proceeding to enforce the rights of shareholders of each domestic corporation that is a party to the merger who exercise appraisal rights, and

(2) agree that it will promptly pay the amount, if any, to which such shareholders are entitled under chapter 13.

(e) The effect of a merger or share exchange on the owner liability of a person who had owner liability for some or all of the debts, obligations or liabilities of a party to the merger or share exchange shall be as follows:

(1) The merger or share exchange does not discharge any owner liability under the organic law of the entity in which the person was a shareholder or interest holder to the extent any such owner liability arose before the effective time of the articles of merger or share exchange.

(2) The person shall not have owner liability under the organic law of the entity in which the person was a shareholder or interest holder prior to the merger or share exchange for any debt, obligation or liability that arises after the effective time of the articles of merger or share exchange.

(3) The provisions of the organic law of any entity for which the person had owner liability before the merger or share exchange shall continue to apply to the collection or discharge of any owner liability

preserved by paragraph (1), as if the merger or share exchange had not occurred.

(4) The person shall have whatever rights of contribution from other persons are provided by the organic law of the entity for which the person had owner liability with respect to any owner liability preserved by paragraph (1), as if the merger or share exchange had not occurred.

CHAPTER 12.   DISPOSITION OF ASSETS

§ 12.01   Disposition of Assets Not Requiring Shareholder Approval

No approval of the shareholders of a corporation is required, unless the articles of incorporation otherwise provide:

(1) to sell, lease, exchange, or otherwise dispose of any or all of the corporation's assets in the usual and regular course of business;

(2) to mortgage, pledge, dedicate to the repayment of indebtedness (whether with or without recourse), or otherwise encumber any or all of the corporation's assets, whether or not in the usual and regular course of business;

(3) to transfer any or all of the corporation's assets to one or more corporations or other entities all of the shares or interests of which are owned by the corporation; or

(4) to distribute assets pro rata to the holders of one or more classes or series of the corporation's shares.

§ 12.02   Shareholder Approval of Certain Dispositions

(a) A sale, lease, exchange, or other disposition of assets, other than a disposition described in section 12.01, requires approval of the corporation's shareholders if the disposition would leave the corporation without a significant continuing business activity. If a corporation retains a business activity that represented at least 25 percent of total assets at the end of the most recently completed fiscal year, and 25 percent of either income from continuing operations before taxes or revenues from continuing operations for that fiscal year, in each case of the corporation and its subsidiaries on a consolidated basis, the corporation will conclusively be deemed to have retained a significant continuing business activity.

(b) A disposition that requires approval of the shareholders under subsection (a) shall be initiated by a resolution by the board of directors authorizing the disposition. After adoption of such a resolution, the board of directors shall submit the proposed disposition to the shareholders for their approval. The board of directors shall also transmit to the shareholders a recommendation that the shareholders approve the proposed disposition, unless the board of directors makes a determination that because of conflicts of interest or other special circumstances it should not make such a recommendation, in which case the board of directors shall transmit to the shareholders the basis for that determination.

(c) The board of directors may condition its submission of a disposition to the shareholders under subsection (b) on any basis.

(d) If a disposition is required to be approved by the shareholders under subsection (a), and if the approval is to be given at a meeting, the corporation shall notify each shareholder, whether or not entitled to vote, of the meeting of shareholders at which the disposition is to be submitted for approval. The notice shall state that the purpose, or one of the purposes, of the meeting is to consider the disposition and shall contain a description of the disposition, including the terms and conditions thereof and the consideration to be received by the corporation.

(e) Unless the articles of incorporation or the board of directors acting pursuant to subsection (c) requires a greater vote, or a greater number of votes to be present, the approval of a disposition by the shareholders shall require the approval of the shareholders at a meeting at which a quorum consisting of at least a majority of the votes entitled to be cast on the disposition exists.

(f) After a disposition has been approved by the shareholders under subsection (b), and at any time before the disposition has been consummated, it may be abandoned by the corporation without action by the shareholders, subject to any contractual rights of other parties to the disposition.

(g) A disposition of assets in the course of dissolution under chapter 14 is not governed by this section.

(h) The assets of a direct or indirect consolidated subsidiary shall be deemed the assets of the parent corporation for the purposes of this section.

CHAPTER 13. DISSENTERS' RIGHTS

Subchapter A.

§ 13.01 Definitions

In this chapter:

(1) "Affiliate" means a person that directly or indirectly through one or more intermediaries controls, is controlled by, or is under common control with another person or is a senior executive thereof. For purposes of section 13.02(b)(4), a person is deemed to be an affiliate of its senior executives.

(2) "Beneficial shareholder" means a person who is the beneficial owner of shares held in a voting trust or by a nominee on the beneficial owner's behalf.

(3) "Corporation" means the issuer of the shares held by a shareholder demanding appraisal and, for matters covered in sections 13.22–13.31, includes the surviving entity in a merger.

(4) "Fair value" means the value of the corporation's shares determined:

(i) immediately before the effectuation of the corporate action to which the shareholder objects;

(ii) using customary and current valuation concepts and techniques generally employed for similar businesses in the context of the transaction requiring appraisal; and

(iii) without discounting for lack of marketability or minority status except, if appropriate, for amendments to the articles pursuant to section 13.02(a)(5).

(5) "Interest" means interest from the effective date of the corporate action until the date of payment, at the rate of interest on judgments in this state on the effective date of the corporate action.

(6) "Preferred shares" means a class or series of shares whose holders have preferences over any other class or series with respect to distributions.

(7) "Record shareholder" means the person in whose name shares are registered in the records of the corporation or the beneficial owner of shares to the extent of the rights granted by a nominee certificate on file with the corporation.

(8) "Senior executive" means the chief executive officer, chief operating officer, chief financial officer, and anyone in charge of a principal business unit or function.

(9) "Shareholder" means both a record shareholder and a beneficial shareholder.

§ 13.02.   Right to Appraisal.

(a) A shareholder is entitled to appraisal rights, and to obtain payment of the fair value of that shareholder's shares, in the event of any of the following corporate actions:

(1) consummation of a merger to which the corporation is a party (i) if shareholder approval is required for the merger by section 11.04 and the shareholder is entitled to vote on the merger, except that appraisal rights shall not be available to any shareholder of the corporation with respect to shares of any class or series that remain outstanding after consummation of the merger, or (ii) if the corporation is a subsidiary and the merger is governed by section 11.05;

(2) consummation of a share exchange to which the corporation is a party as the corporation whose shares will be acquired if the shareholder is entitled to vote on the exchange, except that appraisal rights shall not be available to any shareholder of the corporation with respect to any class or series of shares of the corporation that is not exchanged;

(3) consummation of a disposition of assets pursuant to section 12.02 if the shareholder is entitled to vote on the disposition;

(4) an amendment of the articles of incorporation with respect to a class or series of shares that reduces the number of shares of a class or series owned by the shareholder to a fraction of a share if the corporation has the obligation or right to repurchase the fractional share so created;

(5) any other amendment to the articles of incorporation, merger, share exchange or disposition of assets to the extent provided by the articles of incorporation, bylaws or a resolution of the board of directors;

(6) consummation of a domestication if the shareholder does not receive shares in the foreign corporation resulting from the domestication that have terms as favorable to the shareholder in all material respects, and represent at least the same percentage interest of the total voting rights of the outstanding shares of the corporation, as the shares held by the shareholder before the domestication;

(7) consummation of a conversion of the corporation to nonprofit status pursuant to subchapter 9C; or

(8) consummation of a conversion of the corporation to an unincorporated entity pursuant to subchapter 9E.

(b) Notwithstanding subsection (a), the availability of appraisal rights under subsections (a)(1), (2), (3), (4), (6) and (8) shall be limited in accordance with the following provisions:

(1) Appraisal rights shall not be available for the holders of shares of any class or series of shares which is:

(i) listed on the New York Stock Exchange or the American Stock Exchange or designated as a national market system security on an interdealer quotation system by the National Association of Securities Dealers, Inc.; or

(ii) not so listed or designated, but has at least 2,000 shareholders and the outstanding shares of such class or series has a market value of at least $20 million (exclusive of the value of such shares held by its subsidiaries, senior executives, directors and beneficial shareholders owning more than 10 percent of such shares).

(2) The applicability of subsection (b)(1) shall be determined as of:

(i) the record date fixed to determine the shareholders entitled to receive notice of, and to vote at, the meeting of shareholders to act upon the corporate action requiring appraisal rights; or

(ii) the day before the effective date of such corporate action if there is no meeting of shareholders.

(3) Subsection (b)(1) shall not be applicable and appraisal rights shall be available pursuant to subsection (a) for the holders of any class or series of shares who are required by the terms of the corporate action requiring appraisal rights to accept for such shares anything other than cash or shares of any class or any series of shares of any corporation, or any other proprietary interest of any other entity, that satisfies the standards set forth in subsection (b)(1) at the time the corporate action becomes effective.

(4) Subsection (b)(1) shall not be applicable and appraisal rights shall be available pursuant to subsection (a) for the holders of any class or series of shares where:

(i) any of the shares or assets of the corporation are being acquired or converted, whether by merger, share exchange or otherwise, pursuant to the corporate action by a person, or by an affiliate of a person, who:

(A) is, or at any time in the one-year period immediately preceding approval by the board of directors of the corporate action requiring appraisal rights was, the beneficial owner of 20 percent or more of the voting power of the corporation, excluding any shares acquired pursuant to an offer for all shares having voting power if such offer was made within one year prior to the corporate action requiring appraisal rights for consideration of the same kind and of a value equal to or less than that paid in connection with the corporate action; or

(B) directly or indirectly has, or at any time in the one-year period immediately preceding approval by the board of directors of the corporation of the corporate action requiring appraisal rights had, the power, contractually or otherwise, to cause the appointment or election of 25 percent or more of the directors to the board of directors of the corporation; or

(ii) any of the shares or assets of the corporation are being acquired or converted, whether by merger, share exchange or otherwise, pursuant to such corporate action by a person, or by an affiliate of a person, who is, or at any time in the one-year period immediately preceding approval by the board of directors of the corporate action requiring appraisal rights was, a senior executive or director of the corporation or a senior executive of any affiliate thereof, and that senior executive or director will receive, as a result of the corporate action, a financial benefit not generally available to other shareholders as such, other than:

(A) employment, consulting, retirement or similar benefits established separately and not as part of or in contemplation of the corporate action; or

(B) employment, consulting, retirement or similar benefits established in contemplation of, or as part of, the corporate action that are not more favorable than those existing before the corporate action or, if more favorable, that have been approved on behalf of the corporation in the same manner as is provided in section 8.62; or

(C) in the case of a director of the corporation who will, in the corporate action, become a director of the acquiring entity in the corporate action or one of its affiliates, rights and benefits as a director that are provided on the same basis as those afforded by the acquiring entity generally to other directors of such entity or such affiliate.

(5) For the purposes of paragraph (4) only, the term beneficial owner means any person who, directly or indirectly, through any contract, arrangement, or understanding, other than a revocable proxy, has or shares the power to vote, or to direct the voting of, shares, provided that a member of a national securities exchange shall not be deemed to be a beneficial owner of securities held directly or indirectly by it on behalf of another person solely because such member is the record holder of such securities if the member is precluded by the rules of such exchange from voting without instruction on contested matters or matters that may affect substantially the rights or privileges of the holders of the securities to be voted. When two or more persons agree to act together for the purpose of voting their shares of the corporation, each member of the group formed thereby shall be deemed to have acquired beneficial ownership, as of the date of such agreement, of all voting shares of the corporation beneficially owned by any member of the group.

(c) Notwithstanding any other provision of section 13.02, the articles of incorporation as originally filed or any amendment thereto may limit or eliminate appraisal rights for any class or series of preferred shares, but any such limitation or elimination contained in an amendment to the articles of incorporation that limits or eliminates appraisal rights for any of such shares that are outstanding immediately prior to the effective date of such amendment or that the corporation is or may be required to issue or sell thereafter pursuant to any conversion, exchange or other right existing immediately before the effective date of such amendment shall not apply to any corporate action that becomes effective within one year of that date if such action would otherwise afford appraisal rights.

(d) A shareholder entitled to appraisal rights under this chapter may not challenge a completed corporate action for which appraisal rights are available unless such corporate action:

(1) was not effectuated in accordance with the applicable provisions of chapters 10, 11 or 12 or the corporation's articles of incorporation, bylaws or board of directors' resolution authorizing the corporate action; or

(2) was procured as a result of fraud or material misrepresentation.

§ 13.03   Assertion of Rights by Nominees and Beneficial Owners

(a) A record shareholder may assert appraisal rights as to fewer than all the shares registered in the record shareholder's name but owned by a beneficial shareholder only if the record shareholder objects with respect to all shares of the class or series owned by the beneficial shareholder and notifies the corporation in writing of the name and address of each beneficial shareholder on whose behalf appraisal rights are being asserted. The rights of a record shareholder who asserts appraisal rights for only part of the shares held of record in the record shareholder's name under this subsection shall be determined as if the shares as to which the record shareholder objects and the record shareholder's other shares were registered in the names of different record shareholders.

(b) A beneficial shareholder may assert appraisal rights as to shares of any class or series held on behalf of the shareholder only if such shareholder:

(1) submits to the corporation the record shareholder's written consent to the assertion of such rights no later than the date referred to in section 13.22(b)(2)(ii); and

(2) does so with respect to all shares of the class or series that are beneficially owned by the beneficial shareholder.

Subchapter B.   Procedure for Exercise of Appraisal Rights

§ 13.20.   Notice of Appraisal Rights.

(a) If proposed corporate action described in section 13.02(a) is to be submitted to a vote at a shareholders' meeting, the meeting notice must state that the corporation has concluded that shareholders are, are not or may be entitled to assert appraisal rights under this chapter. If the corporation concludes that appraisal rights are or may be available, a copy of this chapter must accompany the meeting notice sent to those record shareholders entitled to exercise appraisal rights.

(b) In a merger pursuant to section 11.05, the parent corporation must notify in writing all record shareholders of the subsidiary who are entitled to assert appraisal rights that the corporate action became effective. Such notice must be sent within ten days after the corporate action became effective and include the materials described in section 13.22.

§ 13.21.   Notice of Intent to Demand Payment.

(a) If proposed corporate action requiring appraisal rights under section 13.02 is submitted to a vote at a shareholders' meeting, a shareholder who wishes to assert appraisal rights with respect to any class or series of shares:

(1) must deliver to the corporation before the vote is taken written notice of the shareholder's intent to demand payment if the proposed action is effectuated; and

(2) must not vote, or cause or permit to be voted, any shares of such class or series in favor of the proposed action.

(b) A shareholder who does not satisfy the requirements of subsection (a) is not entitled to payment under this chapter.

§ 13.22   Appraisal Notice and Form

(a) If proposed corporate action requiring appraisal rights under section 13.02(a) becomes effective, the corporation must deliver a written appraisal notice and form required by subsection (b)(1) to all shareholders who satisfied the requirements of section 13.21. In the case of a merger under section 11.05, the parent must deliver a written appraisal notice and form to all record shareholders who may be entitled to assert appraisal rights.

(b) The appraisal notice must be sent no earlier than the date the corporate action became effective and no later than ten days after such date and must:

(1) supply a form that specifies the date of the first announcement to shareholders of the principal terms of the proposed corporate action and requires the shareholder asserting appraisal rights to certify (i) whether or not beneficial ownership of those shares for which appraisal rights are asserted was acquired before that date and (ii) that the shareholder did not vote for the transaction;

(2) state:

(i) where the form must be sent and where certificates for certificated shares must be deposited and the date by which those certificates must be deposited, which date may not be earlier than the date for receiving the required form under subsection (2)(ii);

(ii) a date by which the corporation must receive the form which date may not be fewer than 40 nor more than 60 days after the date the subsection (a) appraisal notice and form are sent, and state that the shareholder shall have waived the right to demand appraisal with respect to the shares unless the form is received by the corporation by such specified date;

(iii) the corporation's estimate of the fair value of the shares;

(iv) that, if requested in writing, the corporation will provide, to the shareholder so requesting, within ten days after the date specified in subsection (2)(ii) the number of shareholders who return the forms by the specified date and the total number of shares owned by them; and

(v) the date by which the notice to withdraw under section 13.23 must be received, which date must be within 20 days after the date specified in subsection (2)(ii); and

(3) be accompanied by a copy of this chapter.

§ 13.23.   Perfection of Rights; Right to Withdraw.

(a) A shareholder who receives notice pursuant to section 13.22 and who wishes to exercise appraisal rights must certify on the form sent by the corporation whether the beneficial owner of such shares acquired beneficial ownership of the shares before the date required to be set forth in the notice pursuant to section 13.22(b)(1). If a shareholder fails to make this certification, the corporation may elect to treat the shareholder's shares as after-acquired shares under section 13.25. In addition, a shareholder who wishes to exercise appraisal rights must execute and return the form and, in the case of certificated shares, deposits the shareholder's certificates in accordance with the terms of the notice by the date referred to in the notice pursuant to section 13.22(b)(2)(ii). Once a shareholder deposits that shareholder's certificates or, in the case of uncertificated shares, returns the executed forms, that shareholder loses all rights as a shareholder, unless the shareholder withdraws pursuant to subsection (b).

(b) A shareholder who has complied with subsection (a) may nevertheless decline to exercise appraisal rights and withdraw from the appraisal process by so notifying the corporation in writing by the date set forth in the appraisal notice pursuant to section 13.22(b)(2)(v). A shareholder who fails to so withdraw from the appraisal process may not thereafter withdraw without the corporation's written consent.

(c) A shareholder who does not execute and return the form and, in the case of certificated shares, deposit that shareholder's share certificates where required, each by the date set forth in the notice described in section 13.22(b), shall not be entitled to payment under this chapter.

§ 13.24   Payment

(a) Except as provided in section 13.25, within 30 days after the form required by section 13.22(b)(2)(ii) is due, the corporation shall pay in cash to those shareholders who complied with section 13.23(a) the amount the corporation estimates to be the fair value of the shares, plus interest.

(b) The payment to each shareholder pursuant to subsection (a) must be accompanied by:

(1) financial statements of the corporation that issued the shares to be appraised, consisting of a balance sheet as of the end of a fiscal year ending not more than 16 months before the date of payment, an income statement for that year, a statement of changes in shareholders' equity for that year, and the latest available interim financial statements, if any;

(2) a statement of the corporation's estimate of the fair value of the shares, which estimate must equal or exceed the corporation's estimate given pursuant to section 13.22(b)(2)(iii);

(3) a statement that shareholders described in subsection (a) have the right to demand further payment under section 13.26 and that if any such shareholder does not do so within the time period specified therein, such shareholder shall be deemed to have accepted such payment in full satisfaction of the corporation's obligations under this chapter.

§ 13.25   After–Acquired Shares

(a) A corporation may elect to withhold payment required by section 13.24 from any shareholder who did not certify that beneficial ownership of all of the shareholder's shares for which appraisal rights are asserted was acquired before the date set forth in the appraisal notice sent pursuant to section13.22(b)(1).

(b) If the corporation elected to withhold payment under subsection (a), it must, within 30 days after the form required by section 13.22(b)(2)(ii) is due, notify all shareholders who are described in subsection (a):

(1) of the information required by section 13.24(b)(1);

(2) of the corporation's estimate of fair value pursuant to section 13.24(b)(2);

(3) that they may accept the corporation's estimate of fair value, plus interest, in full satisfaction of their demands or demand appraisal under section 13.26;

(4) that those shareholders who wish to accept such offer must so notify the corporation of their acceptance of the corporation's offer within 30 days after receiving the offer; and

(5) that those shareholders who do not satisfy the requirements for demanding appraisal under section 13.26 shall be deemed to have accepted the corporation's offer.

(c) Within ten days after receiving the shareholder's acceptance pursuant to subsection (b), the corporation must pay in cash the amount it offered under subsection (b)(2) to each shareholder who agreed to accept the corporation's offer in full satisfaction of the shareholder's demand.

(d) Within 40 days after sending the notice described in subsection (b), the corporation must pay in cash the amount it offered to pay under subsection (b)(2) to each shareholder described in subsection(b)(5).

§ 13.26   Procedure if Shareholder Dissatisfied With Payment or Offer

(a) A shareholder paid pursuant to section 13.24 who is dissatisfied with the amount of the payment must notify the corporation in writing of that shareholder's estimate of the fair value of the shares and demand payment of that estimate plus interest (less any payment under section 13.24). A shareholder offered payment under section 13.25 who is dissatisfied with that offer must reject the offer and demand payment of the shareholder's stated estimate of the fair value of the shares plus interest.

(b) A shareholder who fails to notify the corporation in writing of that shareholder's demand to be paid the shareholder's stated estimate of the fair value plus interest under subsection (a) within 30 days after receiving the corporation's payment or offer of payment under section 13.24 or section 13.25, respectively, waives the right to demand payment under this section and shall be entitled only to the payment made or offered pursuant to those respective sections.

Subchapter C.   Judicial Appraisal of Shares

§ 13.30   Court Action

(a) If a shareholder makes demand for payment under section 13.26 which remains unsettled, the corporation shall commence a proceeding within 60 days after receiving the payment demand and petition the court to determine the fair value of the shares and accrued interest. If the corporation does not commence the proceeding within the 60–day period, it shall pay in cash to each shareholder the amount the shareholder demanded pursuant to section 13.26 plus interest.

(b) The corporation shall commence the proceeding in the appropriate court of the county where the corporation's principal office (or, if none, its registered office) in this state is located. If the corporation is a foreign corporation without a registered office in this state, it shall commence the proceeding in the county in this state where the principal office or registered office of the domestic corporation merged with the foreign corporation was located at the time of the transaction.

(c) The corporation shall make all shareholders (whether or not residents of this state) whose demands remain unsettled parties to the proceeding as in an action against their shares, and all parties must be served with a copy of the petition. Nonresidents may be served by registered or certified mail or by publication as provided by law.

(d) The jurisdiction of the court in which the proceeding is commenced under subsection (b) is plenary and exclusive. The court may appoint one or more persons as appraisers to receive evidence and recommend a decision on the question of fair value. The appraisers shall have the powers described in the order appointing them, or in any amendment to it. The shareholders demanding appraisal rights are entitled to the same discovery rights as parties in other civil proceedings. There shall be no right to a jury trial.

(e) Each shareholder made a party to the proceeding is entitled to judgment (i) for the amount, if any, by which the court finds the fair value of the shareholder's shares, plus interest, exceeds the amount paid by the corporation to the shareholder for such shares or (ii) for the fair value, plus interest, of the shareholder's shares for which the corporation elected to withhold payment under section 13.25.

§ 13.31 Court Costs and Counsel Fees

(a) The court in an appraisal proceeding commenced under section 13.30 shall determine all costs of the proceeding, including the reasonable compensation and expenses of appraisers appointed by the court. The court shall assess the costs against the corporation, except that the court may assess costs against all or some of the shareholders demanding appraisal, in amounts the court finds equitable, to the extent the court finds such shareholders acted arbitrarily vexatiously, or not in good faith with respect to the rights provided by this chapter.

(b) The court in an appraisal proceeding may also assess the fees and expenses of counsel and experts for the respective parties, in amounts the court finds equitable:

(1) against the corporation and in favor of any or all shareholders demanding appraisal if the court finds the corporation did not substantially comply with the requirements of sections 13.20, 13.22, 13.24 or 13.25; or

(2) against either the corporation or a shareholder demanding appraisal, in favor of any other party, if the court finds that the party against whom the fees and expenses are assessed acted arbitrarily vexatiously, or not in good faith with respect to the rights provided by this chapter.

(c) If the court in an appraisal proceeding finds that the services of counsel for any shareholder were of substantial benefit to other shareholders similarly situated, and that the fees for those services should not be assessed against the corporation, the court may award to such counsel reasonable fees to be paid out of the amounts awarded the shareholders who were benefitted.

(d) To the extent the corporation fails to make a required payment pursuant to sections 13.24, 13.25, or 13.26, the shareholder may sue directly for the amount owed and, to the extent successful, shall be entitled to recover from the corporation all costs and expenses of the suit, including counsel fees.

CHAPTER 14.   DISSOLUTION

Subchapter A.   Voluntary Dissolution

§ 14.02   Dissolution by Board of Directors and Shareholders

(a) A corporation's board of directors may propose dissolution for submission to the shareholders.

(b) For a proposal to dissolve to be adopted:

(1) the board of directors must recommend dissolution to the shareholders unless the board of directors determines that because of conflict of interest or other special circumstances it should make no recommendation and communicates the basis for its determination to the shareholders; and

(2) the shareholders entitled to vote must approve the proposal to dissolve as provided in subsection (e).

(c) The board of directors may condition its submission of the proposal for dissolution on any basis.

(d) The corporation shall notify each shareholder, whether or not entitled to vote, of the proposed shareholders' meeting. The notice must also state that the purpose, or one of the purposes, of the meeting is to consider dissolving the corporation.

(e) Unless the articles of incorporation or the board of directors acting pursuant to subsection (c) require a greater vote, a greater number of shares to be present, or a vote by voting groups, adoption of the proposal to dissolve shall require the approval of the shareholders at a meeting at which a quorum consisting of at least a majority of the votes entitled to be cast exists.

§ 14.03   Articles of Dissolution

(a) At any time after dissolution is authorized, the corporation may dissolve by delivering to the secretary of state for filing articles of dissolution setting forth:

(1) the name of the corporation;

(2) the date dissolution was authorized; and

(3) if dissolution was approved by the shareholders, a statement that the proposal to dissolve was duly approved by the shareholders in the manner required by this Act and by the articles of incorporation.

(b) A corporation is dissolved upon the effective date of its articles of dissolution.

(c) For purposes of this subchapter, "dissolved corporation" means a corporation whose articles of dissolution have become effective and includes a successor entity to which the remaining assets of the corporation are transferred subject to its liabilities for purposes of liquidation.

§ 14.05 Effect of Dissolution

(a) A dissolved corporation continues its corporate existence but may not carry on any business except that appropriate to wind up and liquidate its business and affairs, including:

(1) collecting its assets;

(2) disposing of its properties that will not be distributed in kind to its shareholders;

(3) discharging or making provision for discharging its liabilities;

(4) distributing its remaining property among its shareholders according to their interests; and

(5) doing every other act necessary to wind up and liquidate its business and affairs.

(b) Dissolution of a corporation does not:

(1) transfer title to the corporation's property;

(2) prevent transfer of its shares or securities, although the authorization to dissolve may provide for closing the corporation's share transfer records;

(3) subject its directors or officers to standards of conduct different from those prescribed in chapter 8;

(4) change quorum or voting requirements for its board of directors or shareholders; change provisions for selection, resignation, or removal of its directors or officers or both; or change provisions for amending its bylaws;

(5) prevent commencement of a proceeding by or against the corporation in its corporate name;

(6) abate or suspend a proceeding pending by or against the corporation on the effective date of dissolution; or

(7) terminate the authority of the registered agent of the corporation.

§ 14.06 Known Claims Against Dissolved Corporation

(a) A dissolved corporation may dispose of the known claims against it by notifying its known claimants in writing of the dissolution at any time after its effective date.

(b) The written notice must:

(1) describe information that must be included in a claim;

(2) provide a mailing address where a claim may be sent;

(3) state the deadline, which may not be fewer than 120 days from the effective date of the written notice, by which the dissolved corporation must receive the claim; and

(4) state that the claim will be barred if not received by the deadline.

(c) A claim against the dissolved corporation is barred:

(1) if a claimant who was given written notice under subsection (b) does not deliver the claim to the dissolved corporation by the deadline; or

(2) if a claimant whose claim was rejected by the dissolved corporation does not commence a proceeding to enforce the claim within 90 days from the effective date of the rejection notice.

(d) For purposes of this section, "claim" does not include a contingent liability or a claim based on an event occurring after the effective date of dissolution.

§ 14.07 Other Claims Against Dissolved Corporation

(a) A dissolved corporation may also publish notice of its dissolution and request that persons with claims against the dissolved corporation present them in accordance with the notice.

(b) The notice must:

(1) be published one time in a newspaper of general circulation in the county where the dissolved corporation's principal office (or, if none in this state, its registered office) is or was last located;

(2) describe the information that must be included in a claim and provide a mailing address where the claim may be sent; and

(3) state that a claim against the dissolved corporation will be barred unless a proceeding to enforce the claim is commenced within three years after the publication of the notice.

(c) If the dissolved corporation publishes a newspaper notice in accordance with subsection (b), the claim of each of the following claimants is barred unless the claimant commences a proceeding to enforce the claim against the dissolved corporation within three years after the publication date of the newspaper notice:

(1) a claimant who was not given written notice under section 14.06;

(2) a claimant whose claim was timely sent to the dissolved corporation but not acted on;

(3) a claimant whose claim is contingent or based on an event occurring after the effective date of dissolution.

(d) A claim that is not barred by section 14.06(b) or section 14.07(c) may be enforced:

(1) against the dissolved corporation, to the extent of its undistributed assets; or

(2) except as provided in section 14.08(d), if the assets have been distributed in liquidation, against a shareholder of the dissolved corporation to the extent of the shareholder's pro rata share of the claim or the corporate assets distributed to the shareholder in liquidation, whichever is less, but a shareholder's total liability for all claims under this section may not exceed the total amount of assets distributed to the shareholder.

CHAPTER 16. RECORDS AND REPORTS

Subchapter B. Reports

§ 16.20 Financial Statements for Shareholders

(a) A corporation shall furnish its shareholders annual financial statements, which may be consolidated or combined statements of the corporation and one or more of its subsidiaries, as appropriate, that include a balance sheet as of the end of the fiscal year, an income statement for that year, and a statement of changes in shareholders' equity for the year unless that information appears elsewhere in the financial statements. If financial statements are prepared for the corporation on the basis of generally accepted accounting principles, the annual financial statements must also be prepared on that basis.

(b) If the annual financial statements are reported upon by a public accountant, his report must accompany them. If not, the statements must be accompanied by a statement of the president or the person responsible for the corporation's accounting records:

(1) stating his reasonable belief whether the statements were prepared on the basis of generally accepted accounting principles and, if not, describing the basis of preparation; and

(2) describing any respects in which the statements were not prepared on a basis of accounting consistent with the statements prepared for the preceding year.

(c) A corporation shall mail the annual financial statements to each shareholder within 120 days after the close of each fiscal year. Thereafter, on written request from a shareholder who was not mailed the statements, the corporation shall mail him the latest financial statements.

§ 16.22 Annual Report for Secretary of State

(a) Each domestic corporation, and each foreign corporation authorized to transact business in this state, shall deliver to the secretary of state for filing an annual report that sets forth:

(1) the name of the corporation and the state or country under whose law it is incorporated;

(2) the address of its registered office and the name of its registered agent at that office in this state;

(3) the address of its principal office;

(4) the names and business addresses of its directors and principal officers;

(5) a brief description of the nature of its business;

(6) the total number of authorized shares, itemized by class and series, if any, within each class; and

(7) the total number of issued and outstanding shares, itemized by class and series, if any, within each class.

(b) Information in the annual report must be current as of the date the annual report is executed on behalf of the corporation.

(c) The first annual report must be delivered to the secretary of state between January 1 and April 1 of the year following the calendar year in which a domestic corporation was incorporated or a foreign corporation was authorized to transact business. Subsequent annual reports must be delivered to the secretary of state between January 1 and April 1 of the following calendar years.

(d) If an annual report does not contain the information required by this section, the secretary of state shall promptly notify the reporting domestic or foreign corporation in writing and return the report to it for correction. If the report is corrected to contain the information required by this section and delivered to the secretary of state within 30 days after the effective date of notice, it is deemed to be timely filed.

PART 2
Provisions of the Delaware and New York Statutes
DELAWARE GENERAL CORPORATION LAW
§ 151.   Classes and Series of Stock; Rights, etc.

(a) Every corporation may issue one or more classes of stock or one or pg. 486 more series of stock within any class thereof, any or all of which classes may be of stock with par value or stock without par value and which classes or series may have such voting powers, full or limited, or no voting powers, and such designations, preferences and relative, participating, optional or other special rights, and qualifications, limitations or restrictions thereof, as shall be stated and expressed in the certificate of incorporation or of any amendment thereto, or in the resolution or resolutions providing for the issue of such stock adopted by the board of directors pursuant to authority expressly vested in it by the provisions of its certificate of incorporation. Any of the voting powers, designations, preferences, rights and qualifications, limitations or restrictions of any such class or series of stock may be made dependent upon facts ascertainable outside the certificate of incorporation or of any amendment thereto, or outside the resolution or resolutions providing for the issue of such stock adopted by the board of directors pursuant to authority expressly vested in it by the provisions of its certificate of incorporation, provided that the manner in which such facts shall operate upon the voting powers, designations, preferences, rights and qualifications, limitations or restrictions of such class or series of stock is clearly and expressly set forth in the certificate of incorporation or in the resolution or resolutions providing for the issue of such stock adopted by the board of directors. The term "facts," as used in this subsection, includes, but is not limited to, the occurrence of any event, including a determination or action by any person or body, including the corporation. The power to increase or decrease or otherwise adjust the capital stock as provided in this chapter shall apply to all or any such classes of stock.

(b) Any stock of any class or series may be made subject to redemption by the corporation at its option or at the option of the holders of such stock or upon the happening of a specified event; provided, however, that immediately following any such redemption the corporation shall have outstanding 1 or more shares of 1 or more classes or series of stock, which share, or shares together, shall have full voting powers. Notwithstanding the limitation stated in the foregoing proviso:

(1) Any stock of a regulated investment company registered under the Investment Company Act of 1940, as heretofore or hereafter amended, may be made subject to redemption by the corporation at its option or at the option of the holders of such stock.

(2) Any stock of a corporation which holds (directly or indirectly) a license or franchise from a governmental agency to conduct its business or is a member of a national securities exchange, which license, franchise or membership is conditioned upon some or all of the holders of its stock possessing prescribed qualifications, may be made subject

B-55

to redemption by the corporation to the extent necessary to prevent the loss of such license, franchise or membership or to reinstate it.

Any stock which may be made redeemable under this section may be redeemed for cash, property or rights, including securities of the same or another corporation, at such time or times, price or prices, or rate or rates, and with such adjustments, as shall be stated in the certificate of incorporation or in the resolution or resolutions providing for the issue of such stock adopted by the board of directors pursuant to subsection (a) of this section.

(c) The holders of preferred or special stock of any class or of any series thereof shall be entitled to receive dividends at such rates, on such conditions and at such times as shall be stated in the certificate of incorporation or in the resolution or resolutions providing for the issue of such stock adopted by the board of directors as hereinabove provided, payable in preference to, or in such relation to, the dividends payable on any other class or classes or of any other series of stock, and cumulative or non-cumulative as shall be so stated and expressed. When dividends upon the preferred and special stocks, if any, to the extent of the preference to which such stocks are entitled, shall have been paid or declared and set apart for payment, a dividend on the remaining class or classes or series of stock may then be paid out of the remaining assets of the corporation available for dividends as elsewhere in this chapter provided.

(d) The holders of the preferred or special stock of any class or of any series thereof shall be entitled to such rights upon the dissolution of, or upon any distribution of the assets of, the corporation as shall be stated in the certificate of incorporation or in the resolution or resolutions providing for the issue of such stock adopted by the board of directors as hereinabove provided.

(e) Any stock of any class or of any series thereof may be made convertible into, or exchangeable for, at the option of either the holder or the corporation or upon the happening of a specified event, shares of any other class or classes or any other series of the same or any other class or classes of stock of the corporation, at such price or prices or at such rate or rates of exchange and with such adjustments as shall be stated in the certificate of incorporation or in the resolution or resolutions providing for the issue of such stock adopted by the board of directors as hereinabove provided.

(f) If any corporation shall be authorized to issue more than one class of stock or more than one series of any class, the powers, designations, preferences and relative, participating, optional or other special rights of each class of stock or series thereof and the qualifications, limitations or restrictions of such preferences and/or rights shall be set forth in full or summarized on the face or back of the certificate which the corporation shall issue to represent such class or series of stock, provided that, except as otherwise provided in section 202 of this title, in lieu of the foregoing requirements, there may be set forth on the face or back of the certificate which the corporation shall issue to represent such class or series of stock, a statement that the corporation will furnish without charge to each stockholder who so requests the powers, designations, preferences and relative, participating, optional or other special rights of each class of stock or series thereof and the qualifications, limitations or restrictions of such preferences and/or rights. Within a reasonable time after the issuance or transfer of uncertificated stock, the corporation shall send to the registered owner thereof a written notice containing the information required to be set forth or stated on certificates pursuant to this Section or Sections 156, 202(a) or 218(a) or with respect to this Section a statement that the corporation will furnish without charge to each stockholder who so requests the powers, designations, preferences and relative participating, optional or other special rights of each class of stock or series thereof and the qualifications, limitations or restrictions of such preferences and/or rights. Except as otherwise expressly provided by law, the rights and obligations of the holders of uncertificated stock and the rights and obligations of the holders of certificates representing stock of the same class and series shall be identical.

(g) When any corporation desires to issue any shares of stock of any class or of any series of any class of which the powers, designations, preferences and relative, participating, optional or other rights, if any, or the qualifications, limitations or restrictions thereof, if any, shall not have been set forth in the certificate of incorporation or in any amendment thereto but shall be provided for in a resolution or resolutions adopted by the board of directors pursuant to authority expressly vested in it by the provisions of the certificate of incorporation or any amendment thereto, a certificate of designations setting forth a copy of such resolution or resolutions and the number of shares of stock of such class or series as to which the resolution or resolutions apply shall be executed, acknowledged, filed, and shall become effective, in accordance with § 103 of this Title. Unless otherwise provided in any such resolution or resolutions, the number of shares of stock of any such series to which such resolution or resolutions apply may be increased (but not above the total number of authorized shares of the class) or decreased (but not below the number of shares thereof then outstanding) by a certificate likewise executed, acknowledged and filed setting forth a statement that a specified increase or decrease therein had been authorized and directed by a resolution or resolutions likewise adopted by the board of directors. In case the number of such shares shall be decreased the number of shares so specified in the certificate shall resume the status which they had prior to the adoption of the first resolution or resolutions. When no shares of any such class or series are outstanding, either because none were issued or because no issued shares of any such class or series remain outstanding, a certificate setting forth a resolution or resolutions adopted by the board of directors that none of the authorized shares of such class or series are outstanding, and that none will be issued subject to the certificate of designations previously filed with respect to such class or series, may be executed, acknowledged and filed in accordance with § 103 of this Title and, when such certificate becomes effective, it shall have the effect of eliminating from the certificate of incorporation all matters set forth in the certificate of designations with respect to such class or series of stock. Unless otherwise provided in the certificate of incorporation, if no shares of stock have been issued of a class or series of stock established by a resolution of the board of directors, the voting powers, designations, preferences and relative, participating, optional or other rights, if any, or the qualifications, limitations or restrictions thereof, may be amended by a resolution or resolutions adopted by the board of directors. A certificate which (1) states that no shares of the class or series have been issued, (2) sets forth a copy of the resolution or resolutions and (3) if the designation of the class or series is being changed, indicates the original designation and the new designation, shall be executed, acknowledged and filed, and shall become effective, in accordance with § 103 of this title. When any certificate filed under this subsection becomes effective, it shall have the effect of amending the certificate of incorporation; except that neither the filing of such certificate nor the filing of a restated certificate of incorporation pursuant to § 245 of this title shall prohibit the board of directors from subsequently adopting such resolutions as authorized by this subsection.

§ 157.   Rights and options respecting stock

(a) Subject to any provisions in the certificate of incorporation, every corporation may create and issue, whether or not in connection with the issue and sale of any shares of stock or other securities of the corporation, rights or options entitling the holders thereof to acquire from the corporation any shares of its capital stock of any class or classes, such rights or options to be evidenced by or in such instrument or instruments as shall be approved by the board of directors.

(b) The terms upon which, including the time or times which may be limited or unlimited in duration, at or within which, and the consideration (including a formula by which such consideration may be determined) for which any such shares may be acquired from the corporation upon the exercise of any such right or option, shall be such as shall be stated in the certificate of incorporation, or in a resolution adopted by the board of directors providing for the creation and issue of such rights or options, and, in every case, shall be set forth or incorporated by reference in the instrument or instruments evidencing such rights or options. In the absence of actual fraud in the transaction, the judgment of the directors as to the consideration for the issuance of such rights or options and the sufficiency thereof shall be conclusive.

(c) The board of directors may, by a resolution adopted by the board, authorize 1 or more officers of the corporation to do 1 or both of the following: (i) designate officers and employees of the corporation or of any of its subsidiaries to be recipients of such rights or options created by the corporation, and (ii) determine the number of such rights or options to be received by such officers and employees; provided, however, that the resolution so authorizing such officer or officers shall specify the total number of rights or options such officer or officers may so award. The board of directors may not authorize an officer to designate himself or herself as a recipient of any such rights or options.

(d) In case the shares of stock of the corporation to be issued upon the exercise of such rights or options shall be shares having a par value, the consideration so to be received therefor shall have a value not less than the par value thereof. In case the shares of stock so to be issued shall be shares of stock without par value, the consideration therefor shall be determined in the manner provided in § 153 of this title.

§ 203. Business combinations with interested stockholders

(a) Notwithstanding any other provisions of this chapter, a corporation shall not engage in any business combination with any interested stockholder for a period of 3 years following the time that such stockholder became an interested stockholder, unless:

(1) Prior to such time the board of directors of the corporation approved either the business combination or the transaction which resulted in the stockholder becoming an interested stockholder;

(2) Upon consummation of the transaction which resulted in the stockholder becoming an interested stockholder, the interested stockholder owned at least 85% of the voting stock of the corporation outstanding at the time the transaction commenced, excluding for purposes of determining the voting stock outstanding (but not the outstanding voting stock owned by the interested stockholder) those shares owned (i) by persons who are directors and also officers and (ii) employee stock plans in which employee participants do not have the right to determine confidentially whether shares held subject to the plan will be tendered in a tender or exchange offer; or

(3) At or subsequent to such time the business combination is approved by the board of directors and authorized at an annual or special meeting of stockholders, and not by written consent, by the affirmative vote of at least 66 2/3% of the outstanding voting stock which is not owned by the interested stockholder.

(b) The restrictions contained in this section shall not apply if:

(1) The corporation's original certificate of incorporation contains a provision expressly electing not to be governed by this section;

(2) The corporation, by action of its board of directors, adopts an amendment to its bylaws within 90 days of February 2, 1988, expressly electing not to be governed by this section, which amendment shall not be further amended by the board of directors;

(3) The corporation, by action of its stockholders, adopts an amendment to its certificate of incorporation or bylaws expressly electing not to be governed by this section; provided that, in addition to any other vote required by law, such amendment to the certificate of incorporation or bylaws must be approved by the affirmative vote of a majority of the shares entitled to vote. An amendment adopted pursuant to this paragraph shall be effective immediately in the case of a corporation that both (i) has never had a class of voting stock that falls within any of the 3 categories set out in subsection (b)(4) hereof, and (ii) has not elected by a provision in its original certificate of incorporation or any amendment thereto to be governed by this section. In all other cases, an amendment adopted pursuant to this paragraph shall

not be effective until 12 months after the adoption of such amendment and shall not apply to any business combination between such corporation and any person who became an interested stockholder of such corporation on or prior to such adoption. A bylaw amendment adopted pursuant to this paragraph shall not be further amended by the board of directors;

(4) The corporation does not have a class of voting stock that is: (i) Listed on a national securities exchange; (ii) authorized for quotation on The NASDAQ Stock Market; or (iii) held of record by more than 2,000 stockholders, unless any of the foregoing results from action taken, directly or indirectly, by an interested stockholder or from a transaction in which a person becomes an interested stockholder;

(5) A stockholder becomes an interested stockholder inadvertently and (i) as soon as practicable divests itself of ownership of sufficient shares so that the stockholder ceases to be an interested stockholder; and (ii) would not, at any time within the 3–year period immediately prior to a business combination between the corporation and such stockholder, have been an interested stockholder but for the inadvertent acquisition of ownership;

(6) The business combination is proposed prior to the consummation or abandonment of and subsequent to the earlier of the public announcement or the notice required hereunder of a proposed transaction which (i) constitutes one of the transactions described in the 2nd sentence of this paragraph; (ii) is with or by a person who either was not an interested stockholder during the previous 3 years or who became an interested stockholder with the approval of the corporation's board of directors or during the period described in paragraph (7) of this subsection (b); and (iii) is approved or not opposed by a majority of the members of the board of directors then in office (but not less than 1) who were directors prior to any person becoming an interested stockholder during the previous 3 years or were recommended for election or elected to succeed such directors by a majority of such directors. The proposed transactions referred to in the preceding sentence are limited to (x) a merger or consolidation of the corporation (except for a merger in respect of which, pursuant to § 251(f) of this title, no vote of the stockholders of the corporation is required); (y) a sale, lease, exchange, mortgage, pledge, transfer or other disposition (in 1 transaction or a series of transactions), whether as part of a dissolution or otherwise, of assets of the corporation or of any direct or indirect majority-owned subsidiary of the corporation (other than to any direct or indirect wholly-owned subsidiary or to the corporation) having an aggregate market value equal to 50% or more of either that aggregate market value of all of the assets of the corporation determined on a consolidated basis or the aggregate market value of all the outstanding stock of the corporation; or (z) a proposed tender or exchange offer for 50% or more of the outstanding voting stock of the corporation. The corporation shall give not less than 20 days' notice to all interested stockholders prior to the consummation of any

of the transactions described in clause (x) or (y) of the 2nd sentence of this paragraph; or

(7) The business combination is with an interested stockholder who became an interested stockholder at a time when the restrictions contained in this section did not apply by reason of any of paragraphs (1) through (4) of this subsection (b), provided, however, that this paragraph (7) shall not apply if, at the time such interested stockholder became an interested stockholder, the corporation's certificate of incorporation contained a provision authorized by the last sentence of this subsection (b).

Notwithstanding paragraphs (1), (2), (3) and (4) of this subsection, a corporation may elect by a provision of its original certificate of incorporation or any amendment thereto to be governed by this section; provided that any such amendment to the certificate of incorporation shall not apply to restrict a business combination between the corporation and an interested stockholder of the corporation if the interested stockholder became such prior to the effective date of the amendment.

(c) As used in this section only, the term:

(1) "Affiliate" means a person that directly, or indirectly through 1 or more intermediaries, controls, or is controlled by, or is under common control with, another person.

(2) "Associate," when used to indicate a relationship with any person, means: (i) Any corporation, partnership, unincorporated association or other entity of which such person is a director, officer or partner or is, directly or indirectly, the owner of 20% or more of any class of voting stock; (ii) any trust or other estate in which such person has at least a 20% beneficial interest or as to which such person serves as trustee or in a similar fiduciary capacity; and (iii) any relative or spouse of such person, or any relative of such spouse, who has the same residence as such person.

(3) "Business combination," when used in reference to any corporation and any interested stockholder of such corporation, means:

(i) Any merger or consolidation of the corporation or any direct or indirect majority-owned subsidiary of the corporation with (A) the interested stockholder, or (B) with any other corporation, partnership, unincorporated association or other entity if the merger or consolidation is caused by the interested stockholder and as a result of such merger or consolidation subsection (a) of this section is not applicable to the surviving entity;

(ii) Any sale, lease, exchange, mortgage, pledge, transfer or other disposition (in 1 transaction or a series of transactions), except proportionately as a stockholder of such corporation, to or with the interested stockholder, whether as part of a dissolution or otherwise, of assets of the corporation or of any direct or indirect majority-owned subsidiary of the corporation which assets have an aggregate market value equal to 10% or more of either the aggregate market value of all the assets of the corporation determined on a consolidated basis or the aggregate market value of all the outstanding stock of the corporation;

(iii) Any transaction which results in the issuance or transfer by the corporation or by any direct or indirect majority-owned subsidiary of the corporation of any stock of the corporation or of such subsidiary to the interested stockholder, except: (A) Pursuant to the exercise, exchange or conversion of securities exercisable for, exchangeable for or convertible into stock of such corporation or any such subsidiary which securities were outstanding prior to the time that the interested stockholder became such; (B) pursuant to a merger under § 251(g) of this title; (C) pursuant to a dividend or distribution paid or made, or the exercise, exchange or conversion of securities exercisable for, exchangeable for or convertible into stock of such corporation or any such subsidiary which security is distributed, pro rata to all holders of a class or series of stock of such corporation subsequent to the time the interested stockholder became such; (D) pursuant to an exchange offer by the corporation to purchase stock made on the same terms to all holders of said stock; or (E) any issuance or transfer of stock by the corporation; provided however, that in no case under items (C)-(E) of this subparagraph shall there be an increase in the interested stockholder's proportionate share of the stock of any class or series of the corporation or of the voting stock of the corporation;

(iv) Any transaction involving the corporation or any direct or indirect majority-owned subsidiary of the corporation which has the effect, directly or indirectly, of increasing the proportionate share of the stock of any class or series, or securities convertible into the stock of any class or series, of the corporation or of any such subsidiary which is owned by the interested stockholder, except as a result of immaterial changes due to fractional share adjustments or as a result of any purchase or redemption of any shares of stock not caused, directly or indirectly, by the interested stockholder; or

(v) Any receipt by the interested stockholder of the benefit, directly or indirectly (except proportionately as a stockholder of such corporation), of any loans, advances, guarantees, pledges or other financial benefits (other than those expressly permitted in subparagraphs (i)-(iv) of this paragraph) provided by or through the corporation or any direct or indirect majority-owned subsidiary.

(4) "Control," including the terms "controlling," "controlled by" and "under common control with," means the possession, directly or indirectly, of the power to direct or cause the direction of the management and policies of a person, whether through the ownership of voting stock, by contract or otherwise. A person who is the owner of 20% or more of the outstanding voting stock of any corporation, partnership, unincorporated association or other entity shall be pre-

sumed to have control of such entity, in the absence of proof by a preponderance of the evidence to the contrary; Notwithstanding the foregoing, a presumption of control shall not apply where such person holds voting stock, in good faith and not for the purpose of circumventing this section, as an agent, bank, broker, nominee, custodian or trustee for 1 or more owners who do not individually or as a group have control of such entity.

(5) "Interested stockholder" means any person (other than the corporation and any direct or indirect majority-owned subsidiary of the corporation) that (i) is the owner of 15% or more of the outstanding voting stock of the corporation, or (ii) is an affiliate or associate of the corporation and was the owner of 15% or more of the outstanding voting stock of the corporation at any time within the 3–year period immediately prior to the date on which it is sought to be determined whether such person is an interested stockholder, and the affiliates and associates of such person; provided, however, that the term "interested stockholder" shall not include (x) any person who (A) owned shares in excess of the 15% limitation set forth herein as of, or acquired such shares pursuant to a tender offer commenced prior to, December 23, 1987, or pursuant to an exchange offer announced prior to the aforesaid date and commenced within 90 days thereafter and either (I) continued to own shares in excess of such 15% limitation or would have but for action by the corporation or (II) is an affiliate or associate of the corporation and so continued (or so would have continued but for action by the corporation) to be the owner of 15% or more of the outstanding voting stock of the corporation at any time within the 3–year period immediately prior to the date on which it is sought to be determined whether such a person is an interested stockholder or (B) acquired said shares from a person described in item (A) of this paragraph by gift, inheritance or in a transaction in which no consideration was exchanged; or (y) any person whose ownership of shares in excess of the 15% limitation set forth herein is the result of action taken solely by the corporation; provided that such person shall be an interested stockholder if thereafter such person acquires additional shares of voting stock of the corporation, except as a result of further corporate action not caused, directly or indirectly, by such person. For the purpose of determining whether a person is an interested stockholder, the voting stock of the corporation deemed to be outstanding shall include stock deemed to be owned by the person through application of paragraph (9) of this subsection but shall not include any other unissued stock of such corporation which may be issuable pursuant to any agreement, arrangement or understanding, or upon exercise of conversion rights, warrants or options, or otherwise.

(6) "Person" means any individual, corporation, partnership, unincorporated association or other entity.

(7) "Stock" means, with respect to any corporation, capital stock and, with respect to any other entity, any equity interest.

(8) "Voting stock" means, with respect to any corporation, stock of any class or series entitled to vote generally in the election of directors and, with respect to any entity that is not a corporation, any equity interest entitled to vote generally in the election of the governing body of such entity. Every reference to a percentage of voting stock shall refer to such percentage of the votes of such voting stock.

(9) "Owner," including the terms "own" and "owned," when used with respect to any stock, means a person that individually or with or through any of its affiliates or associates:

(i) Beneficially owns such stock, directly or indirectly; or

(ii) Has (A) the right to acquire such stock (whether such right is exercisable immediately or only after the passage of time) pursuant to any agreement, arrangement or understanding, or upon the exercise of conversion rights, exchange rights, warrants or options, or otherwise; provided, however, that a person shall not be deemed the owner of stock tendered pursuant to a tender or exchange offer made by such person or any of such person's affiliates or associates until such tendered stock is accepted for purchase or exchange; or (B) the right to vote such stock pursuant to any agreement, arrangement or understanding; provided, however, that a person shall not be deemed the owner of any stock because of such person's right to vote such stock if the agreement, arrangement or understanding to vote such stock arises solely from a revocable proxy or consent given in response to a proxy or consent solicitation made to 10 or more persons; or

(iii) Has any agreement, arrangement or understanding for the purpose of acquiring, holding, voting (except voting pursuant to a revocable proxy or consent as described in item (B) of subparagraph (ii) of this paragraph), or disposing of such stock with any other person that beneficially owns, or whose affiliates or associates beneficially own, directly or indirectly, such stock.

(d) No provision of a certificate of incorporation or bylaw shall require, for any vote of stockholders required by this section, a greater vote of stockholders than that specified in this section.

(e) The Court of Chancery is hereby vested with exclusive jurisdiction to hear and determine all matters with respect to this section.

§ 221. Voting, Inspection and Other Rights of Bondholders and Debenture Holders

Every corporation may in its certificate of incorporation confer upon the holders of any bonds, debentures, or other obligations issued or to be issued by the corporation the power to vote in respect to the corporate affairs and management of the corporation to the extent and in the manner provided in the certificate of incorporation, and may confer upon such holders of bonds, debentures or other obligations the same right of inspection of its books, accounts and other records, and also any other rights, which the stockholders of the corporation have or may have by reason of the provisions of this chapter or of its certificate of incorporation. If the certificate of incorporation so provides, such holders of bonds, debentures or other obligations shall be deemed to be stockholders, and their bonds, debentures or other obligations shall be deemed to be shares of stock, for the purpose of any provision of this chapter which requires the vote of stockholders as a prerequisite to any corporate action and the certificate of incorporation may divest the holders of capital stock, in whole or in part, of their right to vote on any corporate matter whatsoever, except as set forth in § 242(b)(2) of this chapter.

§ 242. Amendment of Certificate of Incorporation After Receipt of Payment for Stock ...

(a) After a corporation has received payment for any of its capital stock, it may amend its certificate of incorporation, from time to time, in any and as many respects as may be desired, so long as its certificate of incorporation as amended would contain only such provisions as it would be lawful and proper to insert in an original certificate of incorporation filed at the time of the filing of the amendment; and, if a change in stock or the rights of stockholders, or an exchange, reclassification, subdivision, combination or cancellation of stock or rights of stockholders is to be made, such provisions as may be necessary to effect such change, exchange, reclassification, subdivision, combination or cancellation. In particular, and without limitation upon such general power of amendment, a corporation may amend its certificate of incorporation, from time to time, so as:

(1) To change its corporate name; or

(2) To change, substitute, enlarge or diminish the nature of its business or its corporate powers and purposes; or

(3) To increase or decrease its authorized capital stock or to reclassify the same, by changing the number, par value, designations, preferences, or relative, participating, optional, or other special rights of the shares, or the qualifications, limitations or restrictions of such rights, or by changing shares with par value into shares without par value, or shares without par value into shares with par value either with or without increasing or decreasing the number of shares, or by subdividing or combining the outstanding shares of any class or series of a class of shares into a greater or lesser number of outstanding shares; or

(4) To cancel or otherwise affect the right of the holders of the shares of any class to receive dividends which have accrued but have not been declared; or

(5) To create new classes of stock having rights and preferences either prior and superior or subordinate and inferior to the stock of any class then authorized, whether issued or unissued; or

(6) To change the period of its duration.

Any or all such changes or alterations may be effected by one certificate of amendment.

(b) Every amendment authorized by subsection (a) of this section shall be made and effected in the following manner—

(1) If the corporation has capital stock, its board of directors shall adopt a resolution setting forth the amendment proposed, declaring its advisability, and either calling a special meeting of the stockholders entitled to vote in respect thereof for the consideration of such amendment or directing that the amendment proposed be considered at the next annual meeting of the stockholders. Such special or annual meeting shall be called and held upon notice in accordance with section 222 of this title. The notice shall set forth such amendment in full or a brief summary of the changes to be effected thereby, as the directors shall deem advisable. At the meeting a vote of the stockholders entitled to vote thereon shall be taken for and against the proposed amendment. If a majority of the outstanding stock entitled to vote thereon, and a majority of the outstanding stock of each class entitled to vote thereon as a class has been voted in favor of the amendment, a certificate setting forth the amendment and certifying that such amendment has been duly adopted in accordance with the provisions of this section shall be executed, acknowledged and filed, and shall become effective in accordance with section 103 of this title.

(2) The holders of the outstanding shares of a class shall be entitled to vote as a class upon a proposed amendment, whether or not entitled to vote thereon by the provisions of the certificate of incorporation, if the amendment would increase or decrease the aggregate number of authorized shares of such class, increase or decrease the par value of the shares of such class, or alter or change the powers, preferences or special rights of the shares of such class so as to affect them adversely. If any proposed amendment would alter or change the powers, preferences, or special rights of one or more series of any class so as to affect them adversely, but shall not so affect the entire class, then only the shares of the series so affected by the amendment shall be considered a separate class for the purposes of this paragraph. The number of authorized shares of any such class or classes of stock may be increased or decreased (but not below the number of shares thereof then outstanding) by the affirmative vote of the holders of a majority of the stock of the corporation entitled to vote irrespective of the provisions of this paragraph (b)(2), if so provided in the original certificate of incorporation, in any amendment thereto which created such class or classes of stock or which was adopted prior to the issuance of any shares of such class or classes of stock, or in any amendment thereto which was authorized by a resolution or resolutions adopted by the affirmative vote of the holders of a majority of such class or classes of stock. . . .

(4) Whenever the certificate of incorporation shall require for action by the board of directors, by the holders of any class or series of shares or by the holders of any other securities having voting power the vote of a greater number or proportion than is required by any section of this title, the provision of the certificate of incorporation requiring such greater vote shall not be altered, amended or repealed except by such greater vote.

(c) The resolution authorizing a proposed amendment to the certificate of incorporation may provide that at any time prior to the effectiveness of the filing of the amendment with the Secretary of State, notwithstanding authorization of the proposed amendment by the stockholders of the corporation ... , the board of directors ... may abandon such proposed amendment without further action by the stockholders....

§ 251. Merger or consolidation of domestic corporations and limited liability company

(a) Any 2 or more corporations existing under the laws of this State may merge into a single corporation, which may be any 1 of the constituent corporations or may consolidate into a new corporation formed by the consolidation, pursuant to an agreement of merger or consolidation, as the case may be, complying and approved in accordance with this section.

(b) The board of directors of each corporation which desires to merge or consolidate shall adopt a resolution approving an agreement of merger or consolidation and declaring its advisability. The agreement shall state: (1) The terms and conditions of the merger or consolidation; (2) the mode of carrying the same into effect; (3) in the case of a merger, such amendments or changes in the certificate of incorporation of the surviving corporation as are desired to be effected by the merger, or, if no such amendments or changes are desired, a statement that the certificate of incorporation of the surviving corporation shall be its certificate of incorporation; (4) in the case of a consolidation, that the certificate of incorporation of the resulting corporation shall be as is set forth in an attachment to the agreement; (5) the manner, if any, of converting the shares of each of the constituent corporations into shares or other securities of the corporation surviving or resulting from the merger or consolidation, or of cancelling some or all of such shares, and, if any shares of any of the constituent corporations are not to remain outstanding, to be converted solely into shares or other securities of the surviving or resulting corporation or to be cancelled, the cash, property, rights or securities of any other corporation or entity which the holders of such shares are to receive in exchange for, or upon conversion of such shares and the surrender of any certificates evidencing them, which cash, property, rights or securities of any other corporation or entity may be in addition to or in lieu of shares or other securities of the surviving or resulting corporation; and (6) such other details or provisions as are deemed desirable, including, without limiting the generality of the foregoing, a provision for the payment of cash in lieu of the issuance or recognition of fractional shares, interests or rights, or for any other arrangement with respect thereto, consistent with § 155 of this title. The agreement so adopted shall be executed and acknowledged in accordance with § 103 of this title. Any of the terms of the agreement of merger or consolidation may be made dependent upon facts ascertainable outside of such agreement, provided that the manner in which such facts shall operate upon the terms of the agreement is clearly and expressly set forth in the agreement of merger or consolidation. The term "facts," as used in the preceding sentence, includes, but is not limited to, the occurrence of any event, including a determination or action by any person or body, including the corporation.

(c) The agreement required by subsection (b) of this section shall be submitted to the stockholders of each constituent corporation at an annual or special meeting for the purpose of acting on the agreement. Due notice of the time, place and purpose of the meeting shall be mailed to each holder of stock, whether voting or nonvoting, of the corporation at the stockholder's address as it appears on the records of the corporation, at least 20 days prior to the date of the meeting. The notice shall contain a copy of the agreement or a brief summary thereof, as the directors shall deem advisable. At the meeting, the agreement shall be considered and a vote taken for its adoption or rejection. If a majority of the outstanding stock of the corporation entitled to vote thereon shall be voted for the adoption of the agreement, that fact shall be certified on the agreement by the secretary or assistant secretary of the corporation. If the agreement shall be so adopted and certified by each constituent corporation, it shall then be filed and shall become effective, in accordance with § 103 of this title. In lieu of filing the agreement of merger or consolidation required by this section, the surviving or resulting corporation may file a certificate of merger or consolidation, executed in accordance with § 103 of this title, which states:

(1) The name and state of incorporation of each of the constituent corporations;

(2) That an agreement of merger or consolidation has been approved, adopted, certified, executed and acknowledged by each of the constituent corporations in accordance with this section;

(3) The name of the surviving or resulting corporation;

(4) In the case of a merger, such amendments or changes in the certificate of incorporation of the surviving corporation as are desired to be effected by the merger, or, if no such amendments or changes are desired, a statement that the certificate of incorporation of the surviving corporation shall be its certificate of incorporation;

(5) In the case of a consolidation, that the certificate of incorporation of the resulting corporation shall be as set forth in an attachment to the certificate;

(6) That the executed agreement of consolidation or merger is on file at an office of the surviving corporation, stating the address thereof; and

(7) That a copy of the agreement of consolidation or merger will be furnished by the surviving corporation, on request and without cost, to any stockholder of any constituent corporation.

(d) Any agreement of merger or consolidation may contain a provision that at any time prior to the time that the agreement (or a certificate in lieu thereof) filed with the Secretary of State becomes effective in accordance with § 103 of this title, the agreement may be terminated by the board of directors of any constituent corporation notwithstanding approval of the agreement by the stockholders of all or any of the constituent corporations; in the event the agreement of merger or consolidation is terminated after the filing of the agreement (or a certificate in lieu thereof) with the Secretary of State but before the agreement (or a certificate in lieu thereof) has become effective, a certificate of termination or merger or consolidation shall be filed in accordance with § 103 of this title. Any agreement of merger or consolidation may contain a provision that the boards of directors of the constituent corporations may amend the agreement at any time prior to the time that the agreement (or a certificate in lieu thereof) filed with the Secretary of State becomes effective in accordance with § 103 of this title, provided that an amendment made subsequent to the adoption of the agreement by the stockholders of any constituent corporation shall not (1) alter or change the amount or kind of shares, securities, cash, property and/or rights to be received in exchange for or on conversion of all or any of the shares of any class or series thereof of such constituent corporation, (2) alter or change any term of the certificate of incorporation of the surviving corporation to be effected by the merger or consolidation, or (3) alter or change any of the terms and conditions of the agreement if such alteration or change would adversely affect the holders of any class or series thereof of such constituent corporation; in the event the agreement of merger or consolidation is amended after the filing thereof with the Secretary of State but before the agreement has become effective, a certificate of amendment of merger or consolidation shall be filed in accordance with § 103 of this title.

(e) In the case of a merger, the certificate of incorporation of the surviving corporation shall automatically be amended to the extent, if any, that changes in the certificate of incorporation are set forth in the agreement of merger.

(f) Notwithstanding the requirements of subsection (c) of this section, unless required by its certificate of incorporation, no vote of stockholders of a constituent corporation surviving a merger shall be necessary to authorize a merger if (1) the agreement of merger does not amend in any respect the certificate of incorporation of such constituent corporation, (2) each share of stock of such constituent corporation outstanding immediately prior to the effective date of the merger is to be an identical outstanding or treasury share of the surviving corporation after the effective date of the merger, and (3) either no shares of common stock of the surviving corporation and no shares, securities or obligations convertible into such stock are to be issued or delivered under the plan of merger, or the authorized unissued shares or the treasury shares of common stock of the surviving corporation to be issued or delivered under the plan of merger plus those initially issuable upon conversion of any other shares, securities or obligations to be issued or delivered under such plan do not exceed 20% of the shares of common stock of such constituent corporation outstanding immediately prior to the effective date of the merger. No vote of stockholders of a constituent corporation shall be necessary to authorize a merger or consolidation if no shares of the stock of such corporation shall have been issued prior to the adoption by the board of directors of the resolution approving the agreement of merger or consolidation. If an agreement of merger is adopted by the constituent corporation surviving the merger, by action of its board of directors and without any vote of its stockholders pursuant to this subsection, the secretary or assistant secretary of that corporation shall certify on the agreement that the agreement has been adopted pursuant to this subsection and, (1) if it has been adopted pursuant to the first sentence of this subsection, that the conditions specified in that sentence have been satisfied, or (2) if it has been adopted pursuant to the second sentence of this subsection, that no shares of stock of such corporation were issued prior to the adoption by the board of directors of the resolution approving the agreement of merger or consolidation. The agreement so adopted and certified shall then be filed and shall become effective, in accordance with § 103 of this title. Such filing shall constitute a representation by the person who executes the agreement that the facts stated in the certificate remain true immediately prior to such filing.

(g) Notwithstanding the requirements of subsection (c) of this section, unless expressly required by its certificate of incorporation, no vote of stockholders of a constituent corporation shall be necessary to authorize a merger with or into a single direct or indirect wholly-owned subsidiary of such constituent corporation if: (1) such constituent corporation and the direct or indirect wholly-owned subsidiary of such constituent corporation are the only constituent entities to the merger; (2) each share or fraction of a share of the capital stock of the constituent corporation outstanding immediately prior to the effective time of the merger is converted in the merger into a share or equal fraction of share of capital stock of a holding company having the same designations, rights, powers and preferences, and the qualifications, limitations and restrictions thereof, as the share of stock of the constituent corporation being converted in the merger; (3) the holding company and the constituent corporation are corporations of this State and the direct or indirect wholly-owned subsidiary that is the other constituent entity to the merger is a corporation or limited liability company of this State; (4) the certificate of incorporation and by-laws of the holding company immediately following the effective time of the merger contain provisions identical to the certificate of incorporation and by-laws of the constituent corporation immediately prior to the effective time of the merger (other than provisions, if any, regarding the incorporator or incorporators, the corporate name, the registered office and agent, the initial board of directors and the initial subscribers for shares and such provisions contained in any amendment to the certificate of incorporation as were necessary to effect a change, exchange, reclassification, subdivision, combination or cancellation of stock, if such change, exchange, reclassification, subdivision, combination, or cancellation has become effective); (5) as a result of the merger the constituent corporation or its successor becomes or remains a direct or indirect wholly-owned subsidiary of the holding company; (6) the directors of the constituent corporation become or remain the directors of the holding company upon the effective time of the merger; (7) the organizational documents of the surviving entity immediately following the effective time of the merger contain provisions identical to the certificate of incorporation of the constituent corporation immediately prior to the effective time of the merger (other than provisions, if any, regarding the incorporator or incorporators, the corporate or entity name, the registered office and agent, the initial board of directors and the initial subscribers for shares, references to members rather than stockholders or shareholders, references to interests, units or the like rather than stock or shares, references to managers, managing members or other members of the governing body rather than directors and such provisions contained in any amendment to the certificate of incorporation as were necessary to effect a change, exchange, reclassification, subdivision, combination or cancellation of stock, if such change, exchange, reclassification, subdivision, combination or cancellation has become effective); provided, however, that (i) if the organizational documents of the surviving entity do not contain the following provisions, they shall be amended in the merger to contain provisions requiring that (A) any act or transaction by or involving the surviving entity, other than the election or removal of directors or managers, managing members or other members of the governing body of the surviving entity, that requires for its adoption under this chapter or its organizational documents the approval of the stockholders or members of the surviving entity shall, by specific reference to this subsection, require, in addition, the approval of the stockholders of the holding company (or any successor by merger), by the same vote as is required by this chapter and/or by the organizational documents of the surviving entity; provided, however, that for purposes of this clause (i)(A), any surviving entity that is not a corporation shall include in such amendment a requirement that the approval of the stockholders of the holding company be obtained for any act or transaction by or involving the surviving entity, other than the election or removal of directors or managers, managing members or other members of the governing body of the surviving entity, which would require the approval of the stockholders of the surviving entity if the surviving entity were a corporation subject to this chapter; (B) any amendment of the organizational documents of a surviving entity that is not a corporation, which amendment would, if adopted by a corporation subject to this chapter, be required to be included in the certificate of incorporation of such corporation, shall, by specific reference to this subsection, require, in addition, the approval of the stockholders of the holding company (or any successor by merger), by the same vote as is required by this chapter and/or by the organizational documents of the surviving entity; and (C) the business and affairs of a surviving entity that is not a corporation shall be managed by or under the direction of a board of directors, board of managers or other governing body consisting of individuals who are subject to the same fiduciary duties applicable to, and who are liable for breach of such duties to the same extent as, directors of a corporation subject to this chapter; and (ii) the organizational documents of the surviving entity may be amended in the merger (A) to reduce the number of classes and shares of capital stock or other equity interests or units that the surviving entity is authorized to issue and (B) to eliminate any provision authorized by subsection (d) of § 141 of this title; and (8) the stockholders of the constituent corporation do not recognize gain or loss for United States federal income tax purposes as determined by the board of directors of the constituent corporation. Neither subdivision (g)(7)(i) of this section nor any provision of a surviving entity's organizational documents required by subdivision (g)(7)(i) shall be deemed or construed to require approval of the stockholders of the holding company to elect or remove directors or managers, managing members or other members of the governing body of the surviving entity. The term "organizational documents", as used in subdivision (g)(7) and in the preceding sentence, shall, when used in reference to a corporation, mean the certificate of incorporation of such corporation, and when used in reference to a limited liability company, mean the limited liability company agreement of such limited liability company.

As used in this subsection only, the term "holding company" means a corporation which, from its incorporation until consummation of a merger governed by this subsection, was at all times a direct or indirect wholly-owned subsidiary of the constituent corporation and whose capital stock is issued in such merger. From and after the effective time of a merger adopted by a constituent corporation by action of its board of directors and without any vote of stockholders pursuant to this subsection: (i) to the extent the restrictions of § 203 of this title applied to the constituent corporation and its stockholders at the effective time of the merger, such restrictions shall apply to the holding company and its stockholders immediately after the effective time of the merger as though it were the constituent corporation, and all shares of stock of the holding company acquired in the merger shall for purposes of § 203 of this title be deemed to have been acquired at the time that the shares of stock of the constituent corporation converted in the merger were acquired, and provided further that any stockholder who immediately prior to the effective time of the merger was not an interested stockholder within the meaning of § 203 of this title shall not solely by reason of the merger become an interested stockholder of the holding company, (ii) if the corporate name of the holding company immediately following the effective time of the merger is the same as the corporate name of the constituent corporation immediately prior to the effective time of the merger, the shares of capital stock of the holding company into which the shares of capital stock of the constituent corporation are converted in the merger shall be represented by the stock certificates that previously represented shares of capital stock of the constituent corporation and (iii) to the extent a stockholder of the constituent corporation immediately prior to the merger had standing to institute or maintain derivative litigation on behalf of the constituent corporation, nothing in this section shall be deemed to limit or extinguish such standing. If an agreement of merger is adopted by a constituent corporation by action of its board of directors and without any vote of stockholders pursuant to this subsection, the secretary or assistant secretary of the constituent corporation shall certify on the agreement that the agreement has been adopted pursuant to this subsection and that the conditions specified in the first sentence of this subsection have been satisfied. The agreement so adopted and certified shall then be filed and become effective, in accordance with § 103 of this title. Such filing shall constitute a representation by the person who executes the agreement that the facts stated in the certificate remain true immediately prior to such filing.

§ 253. Merger of parent corporation and subsidiary or subsidiaries

(a) In any case in which at least 90% of the outstanding shares of each class of the stock of a corporation or corporations (other than a corporation which has in its certificate of incorporation the provision required by § 251(g)(7)(i) of this title), of which class there are outstanding shares that, absent this subsection, would be entitled to vote on such merger, is owned by another corporation and 1 of the corporations is a corporation of this State and the other or others are corporations of this State, or any other state or states, or the District of Columbia and the laws of the other state or states, or the District permit a corporation of such jurisdiction to merge with a corporation of another jurisdiction, the corporation having such stock ownership may either merge the other corporation or corporations into itself and assume all of its or their obligations, or merge itself, or itself and 1 or more of such other corporations, into 1 of the other corporations by executing, acknowledging and filing, in accordance with § 103 of this title, a certificate of such ownership and merger setting forth a copy of the resolution of its board of directors to so merge and the date of the adoption; provided, however, that in case the parent corporation shall not own all the outstanding stock of all the subsidiary corporations, parties to a merger as aforesaid, the resolution of the board of directors of the parent corporation shall state the terms and conditions of the merger, including the securities, cash, property, or rights to be issued, paid, delivered or granted by the surviving corporation upon surrender of each share of the subsidiary corporation or corporations not owned by the parent corporation, or the cancellation of some or all of such shares. Any of the terms of the resolution of the board of directors to so merge may be made dependent upon facts ascertainable outside of such resolution, provided that the manner in which such facts shall operate upon the terms of the resolution is clearly and expressly set forth in the resolution. The term "facts," as used in the preceding sentence, includes, but is not limited to, the occurrence of any event, including a determination or action by any person or body, including the corporation. If the parent corporation be not the surviving corporation, the resolution shall include provision for the pro rata issuance of stock of the surviving corporation to the holders of the stock of the parent corporation on surrender of any certificates therefor, and the certificate of ownership and merger shall state that the proposed merger has been approved by a majority of the outstanding stock of the parent corporation entitled to vote thereon at a meeting duly called and held after 20 days' notice of the purpose of the meeting mailed to each such stockholder at the stockholder's address as it appears on the records of the corporation if the parent corporation is a corporation of this State or state that the proposed merger has been adopted, approved, certified, executed and acknowledged by the parent corporation in accordance with the laws under which it is organized if the parent corporation is not a corporation of this State. If the surviving corporation exists under the laws of the District of Columbia or any state or jurisdiction other than this State, subsection (d) of § 252 of this title shall also apply to a merger under this section.

(b) If the surviving corporation is a Delaware corporation, it may change its corporate name by the inclusion of a provision to that effect in the resolution of merger adopted by the directors of the parent corporation and set forth in the certificate of ownership and merger, and upon the effective date of the merger, the name of the corporation shall be so changed.

(c) Subsection (d) of § 251 of this title shall apply to a merger under this section, and subsection (e) of § 251 of this title shall apply to a merger under this section in which the surviving corporation is the subsidiary corporation and is a corporation of this State. References to "agreement of merger" in subsections (d) and (e) of § 251 of this title shall mean for purposes of this subsection the resolution of merger adopted by the board of directors of the parent corporation. Any merger which effects any changes other than those authorized by this section or made applicable by this subsection shall be accomplished under § 251 or § 252 of this title. Section 262 of this title shall not apply to any merger effected under this section, except as provided in subsection (d) of this section.

(d) In the event all of the stock of a subsidiary Delaware corporation party to a merger effected under this section is not owned by the parent corporation immediately prior to the merger, the stockholders of the subsidiary Delaware corporation party to the merger shall have appraisal rights as set forth in § 262 of this title.

(e) A merger may be effected under this section although 1 or more of the corporations parties to the merger is a corporation organized under the laws of a jurisdiction other than 1 of the United States; provided that the laws of such jurisdiction permit a corporation of such jurisdiction to merge with a corporation of another jurisdiction.

§ 262.   Appraisal rights

(a) Any stockholder of a corporation of this State who holds shares of stock on the date of the making of a demand pursuant to subsection (d) of this section with respect to such shares, who continuously holds such shares through the effective date of the merger or consolidation, who has otherwise complied with subsection (d) of this section and who has neither voted in favor of the merger or consolidation nor consented thereto in writing pursuant to § 228 of this title shall be entitled to an appraisal by the Court of Chancery of the fair value of the stockholder's shares of stock under the circumstances described in subsections (b) and (c) of this section. As used in this section, the word "stockholder" means a holder of record of stock in a stock corporation and also a member of record of a nonstock corporation; the words "stock" and "share" mean and include what is ordinarily meant by those words and also membership or membership interest of a member of a nonstock corporation; and the words "depository receipt" mean a receipt or other instrument issued by a depository representing an interest in one or more shares, or fractions thereof, solely of stock of a corporation, which stock is deposited with the depository.

(b) Appraisal rights shall be available for the shares of any class or series of stock of a constituent corporation in a merger or consolidation to be effected pursuant to § 251 (other than a merger effected pursuant to § 251(g) of this title), § 252, § 254, § 257, § 258, § 263 or § 264 of this title:

(1) Provided, however, that no appraisal rights under this section shall be available for the shares of any class or series of stock, which stock, or depository receipts in respect thereof, at the record date fixed to determine the stockholders entitled to receive notice of and to vote at the meeting of stockholders to act upon the agreement of merger or consolidation, were either (i) listed on a national securities exchange or designated as a national market system security on an interdealer quotation system by the National Association of Securities Dealers, Inc. or (ii) held of record by more than 2,000 holders; and further provided that no appraisal rights shall be available for any shares of stock of the constituent corporation surviving a merger if the merger did not require for its approval the vote of the stockholders of the surviving corporation as provided in subsection (f) of § 251 of this title.

(2) Notwithstanding paragraph (1) of this subsection, appraisal rights under this section shall be available for the shares of any class or series of stock of a constituent corporation if the holders thereof are required by the terms of an agreement of merger or consolidation pursuant to §§ 251, 252, 254, 257, 258, 263 and 264 of this title to accept for such stock anything except:

a.　Shares of stock of the corporation surviving or resulting from such merger or consolidation, or depository receipts in respect thereof;

b.　Shares of stock of any other corporation, or depository receipts in respect thereof, which shares of stock (or depository receipts in respect thereof) or depository receipts at the effective date of the merger or consolidation will be either listed on a national securities exchange or designated as a national market system security on an interdealer quotation system by the National Association of Securities Dealers, Inc. or held of record by more than 2,000 holders;

c.　Cash in lieu of fractional shares or fractional depository receipts described in the foregoing subparagraphs a. and b. of this paragraph; or

d.　Any combination of the shares of stock, depository receipts and cash in lieu of fractional shares or fractional depository receipts described in the foregoing subparagraphs a., b. and c. of this paragraph.

(3) In the event all of the stock of a subsidiary Delaware corporation party to a merger effected under § 253 of this title is not owned by the parent corporation immediately prior to the merger, appraisal rights shall be available for the shares of the subsidiary Delaware corporation.

(c) Any corporation may provide in its certificate of incorporation that appraisal rights under this section shall be available for the shares of any class or series of its stock as a result of an amendment to its certificate of incorporation, any merger or consolidation in which the corporation is a constituent corporation or the sale of all or substantially all of the assets of the corporation. If the certificate of incorporation contains such a provision, the procedures of this section, including those set forth in subsections (d) and (e) of this section, shall apply as nearly as is practicable.

(d) Appraisal rights shall be perfected as follows:

(1) If a proposed merger or consolidation for which appraisal rights are provided under this section is to be submitted for approval at a meeting of stockholders, the corporation, not less than 20 days prior to the meeting, shall notify each of its stockholders who was such on the record date for such meeting with respect to shares for which appraisal rights are available pursuant to subsection (b) or (c) hereof that appraisal rights are available for any or all of the shares of the constituent corporations, and shall include in such notice a copy of this section. Each stockholder electing to demand the appraisal of such stockholder's shares shall deliver to the corporation, before the taking of the vote on the merger or consolidation, a written demand for appraisal of such stockholder's shares. Such demand will be sufficient if it reasonably informs the corporation of the identity of the stockholder and that the stockholder intends thereby to demand the appraisal of such stockholder's shares. A proxy or vote against the merger or consolidation shall not constitute such a demand. A stockholder electing to take such action must do so by a separate written demand as herein provided. Within 10 days after the effective date of such merger or consolidation, the surviving or resulting corporation shall notify each stockholder of each constituent corporation who has complied with this subsection and has not voted in favor of or consented to the merger or consolidation of the date that the merger or consolidation has become effective; or

(2) If the merger or consolidation was approved pursuant to § 228 or § 253 of this title, then either a constituent corporation before the effective date of the merger or consolidation or the surviving or resulting corporation within 10 days thereafter shall notify each of the holders of any class or series of stock of such constituent corporation who are entitled to appraisal rights of the approval of the merger or consolidation and that appraisal rights are available for any or all shares of such class or series of stock of such constituent corporation, and shall include in such notice a copy of this section. Such notice may, and, if given on or after the effective date of the merger or consolidation, shall, also notify such stockholders of the effective date of the merger or consolidation. Any stockholder entitled to appraisal rights may, within 20 days after the date of mailing of such notice, demand in writing from the surviving or resulting corporation the appraisal of such holder's shares. Such demand will be sufficient if it reasonably informs the corporation of the identity of the stockholder and that the stockholder intends thereby to demand the appraisal of such holder's shares. If such notice did not notify stockholders of the effective date of

the merger or consolidation, either (i) each such constituent corporation shall send a second notice before the effective date of the merger or consolidation notifying each of the holders of any class or series of stock of such constituent corporation that are entitled to appraisal rights of the effective date of the merger or consolidation or (ii) the surviving or resulting corporation shall send such a second notice to all such holders on or within 10 days after such effective date; provided, however, that if such second notice is sent more than 20 days following the sending of the first notice, such second notice need only be sent to each stockholder who is entitled to appraisal rights and who has demanded appraisal of such holder's shares in accordance with this subsection. An affidavit of the secretary or assistant secretary or of the transfer agent of the corporation that is required to give either notice that such notice has been given shall, in the absence of fraud, be prima facie evidence of the facts stated therein. For purposes of determining the stockholders entitled to receive either notice, each constituent corporation may fix, in advance, a record date that shall be not more than 10 days prior to the date the notice is given, provided, that if the notice is given on or after the effective date of the merger or consolidation, the record date shall be such effective date. If no record date is fixed and the notice is given prior to the effective date, the record date shall be the close of business on the day next preceding the day on which the notice is given.

(e) Within 120 days after the effective date of the merger or consolidation, the surviving or resulting corporation or any stockholder who has complied with subsections (a) and (d) hereof and who is otherwise entitled to appraisal rights, may file a petition in the Court of Chancery demanding a determination of the value of the stock of all such stockholders. Notwithstanding the foregoing, at any time within 60 days after the effective date of the merger or consolidation, any stockholder shall have the right to withdraw such stockholder's demand for appraisal and to accept the terms offered upon the merger or consolidation. Within 120 days after the effective date of the merger or consolidation, any stockholder who has complied with the requirements of subsections (a) and (d) hereof, upon written request, shall be entitled to receive from the corporation surviving the merger or resulting from the consolidation a statement setting forth the aggregate number of shares not voted in favor of the merger or consolidation and with respect to which demands for appraisal have been received and the aggregate number of holders of such shares. Such written statement shall be mailed to the stockholder within 10 days after such stockholder's written request for such a statement is received by the surviving or resulting corporation or within 10 days after expiration of the period for delivery of demands for appraisal under subsection (d) hereof, whichever is later.

(f) Upon the filing of any such petition by a stockholder, service of a copy thereof shall be made upon the surviving or resulting corporation, which shall within 20 days after such service file in the office of the Register in Chancery in which the petition was filed a duly verified list containing the names and addresses of all stockholders who have demanded payment for their shares and with whom agreements as to the value of their shares have not been reached by the surviving or resulting corporation. If the petition shall be filed by the surviving or resulting corporation, the petition shall be accompanied by such a duly verified list. The Register in Chancery, if so ordered by the Court, shall give notice of the time and place fixed for the hearing of such petition by registered or certified mail to the surviving or resulting corporation and to the stockholders shown on the list at the addresses therein stated. Such notice shall also be given by 1 or more publications at least 1 week before the day of the hearing, in a newspaper of general circulation published in the City of Wilmington, Delaware or such publication as the Court deems advisable. The forms of the notices by mail and by publication shall be approved by the Court, and the costs thereof shall be borne by the surviving or resulting corporation.

(g) At the hearing on such petition, the Court shall determine the stockholders who have complied with this section and who have become entitled to appraisal rights. The Court may require the stockholders who have demanded an appraisal for their shares and who hold stock represented by certificates to submit their certificates of stock to the Register in Chancery for notation thereon of the pendency of the appraisal proceedings; and if any stockholder fails to comply with such direction, the Court may dismiss the proceedings as to such stockholder.

(h) After determining the stockholders entitled to an appraisal, the Court shall appraise the shares, determining their fair value exclusive of any element of value arising from the accomplishment or expectation of the merger or consolidation, together with a fair rate of interest, if any, to be paid upon the amount determined to be the fair value. In determining such fair value, the Court shall take into account all relevant factors. In determining the fair rate of interest, the Court may consider all relevant factors, including the rate of interest which the surviving or resulting corporation would have had to pay to borrow money during the pendency of the proceeding. Upon application by the surviving or resulting corporation or by any stockholder entitled to participate in the appraisal proceeding, the Court may, in its discretion, permit discovery or other pretrial proceedings and may proceed to trial upon the appraisal prior to the final determination of the stockholder entitled to an appraisal. Any stockholder whose name appears on the list filed by the surviving or resulting corporation pursuant to subsection (f) of this section and who has submitted such stockholder's certificates of stock to the Register in Chancery, if such is required, may participate fully in all proceedings until it is finally determined that such stockholder is not entitled to appraisal rights under this section.

(i) The Court shall direct the payment of the fair value of the shares, together with interest, if any, by the surviving or resulting corporation to the stockholders entitled thereto. Interest may be simple or compound, as the Court may direct. Payment shall be so made to each such stockholder, in the case of holders of uncertificated stock forthwith, and the case of holders of shares represented by certificates upon the surrender to the corporation of the certificates representing such stock. The Court's decree may be enforced as other decrees in the Court of Chancery may be enforced, whether such surviving or resulting corporation be a corporation of this State or of any state.

(j) The costs of the proceeding may be determined by the Court and taxed upon the parties as the Court deems equitable in the circumstances. Upon application of a stockholder, the Court may order all or a portion of the expenses incurred by any stockholder in connection with the appraisal proceeding, including, without limitation, reasonable attorney's fees and the fees and expenses of experts, to be charged pro rata against the value of all the shares entitled to an appraisal.

(k) From and after the effective date of the merger or consolidation, no stockholder who has demanded appraisal rights as provided in subsection (d) of this section shall be entitled to vote such stock for any purpose or to receive payment of dividends or other distributions on the stock (except dividends or other distributions payable to stockholders of record at a date which is prior to the effective date of the merger or consolidation); provided, however, that if no petition for an appraisal shall be filed within the time provided in subsection (e) of this section, or if such stockholder shall deliver to the surviving or resulting corporation a written withdrawal of such stockholder's demand for an appraisal and an acceptance of the merger or consolidation, either within 60 days after the effective date of the merger or consolidation as provided in subsection (e) of this section or thereafter with the written approval of the corporation, then the right of such stockholder to an appraisal shall cease. Notwithstanding the foregoing, no appraisal proceeding in the Court of Chancery shall be dismissed as to any stockholder without the approval of the Court, and such approval may be conditioned upon such terms as the Court deems just.

(*l*) The shares of the surviving or resulting corporation to which the shares of such objecting stockholders would have been converted had they assented to the merger or consolidation shall have the status of authorized and unissued shares of the surviving or resulting corporation.

§ 271. Sale, lease or exchange of assets; consideration; procedure

(a) Every corporation may at any meeting of its board of directors or governing body sell, lease or exchange all or substantially all of its property and assets, including its goodwill and its corporate franchises, upon such terms and conditions and for such consideration, which may consist in whole or in part of money or other property, including shares of stock in, and/or other securities of, any other corporation or corporations, as its board of directors or governing body deems expedient and for the best interests of the corporation, when and as authorized by a resolution adopted by the holders of a majority of the outstanding stock of the corporation entitled to vote thereon or, if the corporation is a nonstock corporation, by a majority of the members having the right to vote for the election of the members of the governing body, at a meeting duly called upon at least 20 days' notice. The notice of the meeting shall state that such a resolution will be considered.

(b) Notwithstanding authorization or consent to a proposed sale, lease or exchange of a corporation's property and assets by the stockholders or members, the board of directors or governing body may abandon such proposed sale, lease or exchange without further action by the stockholders or members, subject to the rights, if any, of third parties under any contract relating thereto.

(c) For purposes of this section only, the property and assets of the corporation include the property and assets of any subsidiary of the corporation. As used in this subsection, "subsidiary" means any entity wholly-owned and controlled, directly or indirectly, by the corporation and includes, without limitation, corporations, partnerships, limited partnerships, limited liability partnerships, limited liability companies, and/or statutory trusts. Notwithstanding subsection (a) of this section, except to the extent the certificate of incorporation otherwise provides, no resolution by stockholders or members shall be required for a sale, lease or exchange of property and assets of the corporation to a subsidiary.

§ 501. Authorized shares

(a) Every corporation shall have power to create and issue the number of shares stated in its certificate of incorporation. Such shares may be all of one class or may be divided into two or more classes. Each class shall consist of either shares with par value or shares without par value, having such designation and such relative voting, dividend, liquidation and other rights, preferences and limitations, consistent with this chapter, as shall be stated in the certificate of incorporation. The certificate of incorporation may deny, limit or otherwise define the voting rights and may limit or otherwise define the dividend or liquidation rights of shares of any class, but no such denial, limitation or definition of voting rights shall be effective unless at the time one or more classes of outstanding shares or bonds, singly or in the aggregate, are entitled to full voting rights, and no such limitation or definition of dividend or liquidation rights shall be effective unless at the time one or more classes of outstanding shares, singly or in the aggregate, are entitled to unlimited dividend and liquidation rights.

(b) If the shares are divided into two or more classes, the shares of each class shall be designated to distinguish them from the shares of all other classes. Shares which are entitled to preference in the distribution of dividends or assets shall not be designated as common shares. Shares which are not entitled to preference in the distribution of dividends or assets shall be common shares, even if identified by a class or other designation, and shall not be designated as preferred shares.

(c) Subject to the designations, relative rights, preferences and limitations applicable to separate series and except as otherwise permitted by subparagraph two of paragraph (a) of section five hundred five of this article, each share shall be equal to every other share of the same class. With respect to corporations owning or leasing residential premises and operating the same on a cooperative basis, however, provided that (1) liquidation or other distribution rights are substantially equal per share, (2) changes in maintenance charges and general assessments pursuant to a proprietary lease have been and are hereafter fixed and determined on an equal per-share basis or on an equal per-room basis or as an equal percentage of the maintenance charges, and (3) voting rights are substantially equal per share or the certificate of incorporation provides that the shareholders holding the shares allocated to each apartment or dwelling unit owned by the corporation shall be entitled to one vote in the aggregate regardless of the number of shares allocated to the apartment or dwelling unit or the number of shareholders holding such shares, shares of the same class shall not be considered unequal because of variations in fees or charges payable to the corporation upon sale or transfer of shares and appurtenant proprietary leases that are provided for in proprietary leases, occupancy agreements or offering plans or properly approved amendments to the foregoing instruments.

§ 502.   Issue of any class of preferred shares in series

(a) If the certificate of incorporation so provides, a corporation may issue any class of preferred shares in series. Shares of each such series when issued, shall be designated to distinguish them from shares of all other series.

(b) The number of shares included in any or all series of any classes of preferred shares and any or all of the designations, relative rights, preferences and limitations of any or all such series may be fixed in the certificate of incorporation, subject to the limitation that, unless the certificate of incorporation provides otherwise, if the stated dividends and amounts payable on liquidation are not paid in full, the shares of all series of the same class shall share ratably in the payment of dividends including accumulations, if any, in accordance with the sums which would be payable on such shares if all dividends were declared and paid in full, and in any distribution of assets other than by way of dividends in accordance with the sums which would be payable on such distribution if all sums payable were discharged in full.

(c) If any such number of shares or any such designation, relative right, preference or limitation of the shares of any series is not fixed in the certificate of incorporation, it may be fixed by the board, to the extent authorized by the certificate of incorporation. Unless otherwise provided in the certificate of incorporation, the number of preferred shares of any series so fixed by the board may be increased (but not above the total number of authorized shares of the class) or decreased (but not below the number of shares thereof then outstanding) by the board. In case the number of such shares shall be decreased, the number of shares by which the series is decreased shall, unless eliminated pursuant to paragraph (e) of this section, resume the status which they had prior to being designated as part of a series of preferred shares.

(d) Before the issue of any shares of a series established by the board, a certificate of amendment under section 805 (Certificate of amendment; contents) shall be delivered to the department of state. Such certificate shall set forth:

(1) The name of the corporation, and, if it has been changed, the name under which it was formed.

(2) The date the certificate of incorporation was filed by the department of state.

(3) That the certificate of incorporation is thereby amended by the addition of a provision stating the number, designation, relative rights, preferences, and limitations of the shares of the series as fixed by the board, setting forth in full the text of such provision.

(e) Action by the board to increase or decrease the number of preferred shares of any series pursuant to paragraph (c) of this section shall become effective by delivering to the department of state a certificate of amendment under section 805 (Certificate of amendment; contents) which shall set forth:

(1) The name of the corporation, and, if it has been changed, the name under which it was formed.

(2) The date its certificate of incorporation was filed with the department of state.

(3) That the certificate of incorporation is thereby amended to increase or decrease, as the case may be, the number of preferred shares of any series so fixed by the board, setting forth the specific terms of the amendment and the number of shares so authorized following the effectiveness of the amendment.

When no shares of any such series are outstanding, either because none were issued or because no issued shares of any such series remain outstanding, the certificate of amendment under section 805 may also set forth a statement that none of the authorized shares of such series are outstanding and that none will be issued subject to the certificate of incorporation, and, when such certificate becomes accepted for filing, it shall have the effect of eliminating from the certificate of incorporation all matters set forth therein with respect to such series of preferred shares.

§ 505. Rights and options to purchase shares; issue of rights and options to directors, officers and employees

(a)(1) Except as otherwise provided in this section or in the certificate of incorporation, a corporation may create and issue, whether or not in connection with the issue and sale of any of its shares or bonds, rights or options entitling the holders thereof to purchase from the corporation, upon such consideration, terms and conditions as may be fixed by the board, shares of any class or series, whether authorized but unissued shares, treasury shares or shares to be purchased or acquired or assets of the corporation.

(2)(i) In the case of a domestic corporation that has a class of voting stock registered with the Securities and Exchange Commission pursuant to section twelve of the Exchange Act, the terms and conditions of such rights or options may include, without limitation, restrictions or conditions that preclude or limit the exercise, transfer or receipt of such rights or options by an interested shareholder or any transferee of any such interested shareholder or that invalidate or void such rights or options held by any such interested shareholder or any such transferee. For the purpose of this subparagraph, the terms "voting stock", "Exchange Act" and "interested shareholder" shall have the same meanings as set forth in section nine hundred twelve of this chapter;

(ii) Determinations of the board of directors whether to impose, enforce or waive or otherwise render ineffective such limitations or conditions as are permitted by clause (i) of this subparagraph shall be subject to judicial review in an appropriate proceeding in which the courts formulate or apply appropriate standards in order to insure that such limitations or conditions are imposed, enforced or waived in the best long-term interests and short-term interests of the corporation and its shareholders considering, without limitation, the prospects for potential growth, development, productivity and profitability of the corporation.

(b) The consideration for shares to be purchased under any such right or option shall comply with the requirements of section 504 (Consideration and payment for shares).

(c) The terms and conditions of such rights or options, including the time or times at or within which and the price or prices at which they may be exercised and any limitations upon transferability, shall be set forth or incorporated by reference in the instrument or instruments evidencing such rights or options.

(d) The issue of such rights or options to one or more directors, officers or employees of the corporation or a subsidiary or affiliate thereof, as an incentive to service or continued service with the corporation, a subsidiary or affiliate thereof, or to a trustee on behalf of such directors, officers or employees, shall be authorized as required by the policies of all stock exchanges or automated quotation systems on which the corporation's shares are listed or authorized for trading, or if the corporation's shares are not so listed or authorized, by a majority of the votes cast at a meeting of shareholders by the holders of shares entitled to vote thereon, or authorized by and consistent with a plan adopted by such vote of shareholders. If, under the certificate of incorporation, there are preemptive rights to any of the shares to be thus subject to rights or options to purchase, either such issue or such plan, if any shall also be approved by the vote or written consent of the holders of a majority of the shares entitled to exercise preemptive rights with respect to such shares and such vote or written consent shall operate to release the preemptive rights with respect thereto of the holders of all the shares that were entitled to exercise such preemptive rights.

In the absence of preemptive rights, nothing in this paragraph shall require shareholder approval for the issuance of rights or options to purchase shares of the corporation in substitution for, or upon the assumption of, rights or options issued by another corporation, if such substitution or assumption is in connection with such other corporation's merger or consolidation with, or the acquisition of its shares or all or part of its assets by, the corporation or its subsidiary.

(e) A plan adopted by the shareholders for the issue of rights or options to directors, officers or employees shall include the material terms and conditions upon which such rights or options are to be issued, such as, but without limitation thereof, any restrictions on the number of shares that eligible individuals may have the right or option to purchase, the method of administering the plan, the terms and conditions of payment for shares in full or in installments, the issue of certificates for shares to be paid for in installments, any limitations upon the transferability of such shares and the voting and dividend rights to which the holders of such shares may be entitled, though the full amount of the consideration therefor has not been paid; provided that under this section no certificate for shares shall be delivered to a shareholder, prior to full payment therefor, unless the fact that the shares are partly paid is noted conspicuously on the face or back of such certificate.

(f) If there is shareholder approval for the issue of rights or options to individual directors, officers or employees, but not under an approved plan under paragraph (e), the terms and conditions of issue set forth in paragraph (e) shall be permissible except that the grantees of such rights or options shall not be granted voting or dividend rights until the consideration for the shares to which they are entitled under such rights or options has been fully paid.

(g) If there is shareholder approval for the issue of rights and options, such approval may provide that the board is authorized by certificate of amendment under section 805 (Certificate of amendment; contents) to increase the authorized shares of any class or series to such number as will be sufficient, when added to the previously authorized but unissued shares of such class or series, to satisfy any such rights or options entitling the holders thereof to purchase from the corporation authorized but unissued shares of such class or series.

(h) In the absence of fraud in the transaction, the judgment of the board shall be conclusive as to the adequacy of the consideration, tangible or intangible, received or to be received by the corporation for the issue of rights or options for the purchase from the corporation of its shares.

(i) The provisions of this section are inapplicable to the rights of the holders of convertible shares or bonds to acquire shares upon the exercise of conversion privileges under section 519 (Convertible shares and bonds).

§ 518. Corporate bonds

(a) No corporation shall issue bonds except for money or other property, tangible or intangible; labor or services actually received by or performed for the corporation or for its benefit or in its formation or reorganization; a binding obligation to pay the purchase price thereof in cash or other property; a binding obligation to perform services having an agreed value; or a combination thereof. In the absence of fraud in the transaction, the judgment of the board as to the value of the consideration received shall be conclusive.

(b) If a distribution of its own bonds is made by a corporation to holders of any class or series of its outstanding shares, there shall be concurrently transferred to the liabilities of the corporation in respect of such bonds an amount of surplus equal to the principal amount of, and any accrued interest on, such bonds. The amount of the surplus so transferred shall be the consideration for the issue of such bonds.

(c) A corporation may, in its certificate of incorporation, confer upon the holders of any bonds issued or to be issued by the corporation, rights to inspect the corporate books and records and to vote in the election of directors and on any other matters on which shareholders of the corporation may vote.

§ 519. Convertible or exchangeable shares and bonds

(a) Unless otherwise provided in the certificate of incorporation, and subject to the restrictions in section 513 (Purchase, redemption and certain other transactions by a corporation with respect to its own shares) and paragraphs (c) and (d) of this section, a corporation may issue shares or bonds convertible into or exchangeable for, at the option of the holder, the corporation or another person, or upon the happening of a specified event, shares of any class or shares of any series of any class or cash, other property, indebtedness or other securities of the same or another corporation.

(b) If there is shareholder approval for the issue of bonds or shares convertible into, or exchangeable for, shares of the corporation, such approval may provide that the board is authorized by certificate of amendment under section 805 (Certificate of amendment; contents) to increase the authorized shares of any class or series to such number as will be sufficient, when added to the previously authorized but unissued shares of such class or series, to satisfy the conversion or exchange privileges of any such bonds or shares convertible into, or exchangeable for, shares of such class or series.

(c) No issue of bonds or shares convertible into, or exchangeable for, shares of the corporation shall be made unless:

(1) A sufficient number of authorized but unissued shares, or treasury shares, of the appropriate class or series are reserved by the board to be issued only in satisfaction of the conversion or exchange privileges of such convertible or exchangeable bonds or shares when issued;

(2) The aggregate conversion or exchange privileges of such convertible or exchangeable bonds or shares when issued do not exceed the aggregate of any shares reserved under subparagraph (1) and any additional shares which may be authorized by the board under paragraph (b); or

(3) In the case of the conversion or exchange of shares of common stock other than into other shares of common stock, there remains outstanding a class or series of common stock not subject to conversion or exchange other than into other shares of common stock, except in the case of corporations of the type described in the exceptions to the provisions of paragraph (b) of section 512 (Redeemable shares).

(d) No privilege of conversion may be conferred upon, or altered in respect to, any shares or bonds that would result in the receipt by the corporation of less than the minimum consideration required to be received upon the issue of new shares. The consideration for shares issued upon the exercise of a conversion or exchange privilege shall be that provided in paragraph (g) of section 504 (Consideration and payment for shares).

(e) When shares have been converted or exchanged, they shall be cancelled. When bonds have been converted or exchanged, they shall be cancelled and not reissued except upon compliance with the provisions governing the issue of convertible or exchangeable bonds.

§ 623. Procedure to enforce shareholder's right to receive payment for shares

(a) A shareholder intending to enforce his right under a section of this chapter to receive payment for his shares if the proposed corporate action referred to therein is taken shall file with the corporation, before the meeting of shareholders at which the action is submitted to a vote, or at such meeting but before the vote, written objection to the action. The objection shall include a notice of his election to dissent, his name and residence address, the number and classes of shares as to which he dissents and a demand for payment of the fair value of his shares if the action is taken. Such objection is not required from any shareholder to whom the corporation did not give notice of such meeting in accordance with this chapter or where the proposed action is authorized by written consent of shareholders without a meeting.

(b) Within ten days after the shareholders' authorization date, which term as used in this section means the date on which the shareholders' vote authorizing such action was taken, or the date on which such consent without a meeting was obtained from the requisite shareholders, the corporation shall give written notice of such authorization or consent by registered mail to each shareholder who filed written objection or from whom written objection was not required, excepting any shareholder who voted for or consented in writing to the proposed action and who thereby is deemed to have elected not to enforce his right to receive payment for his shares.

(c) Within twenty days after the giving of notice to him, any shareholder from whom written objection was not required and who elects to dissent shall file with the corporation a written notice of such election, stating his name and residence address, the number and classes of shares as to which he dissents and a demand for payment of the fair value of his shares. Any shareholder who elects to dissent from a merger under section 905 (Merger of subsidiary corporation) or paragraph (c) of section 907 (Merger or consolidation of domestic and foreign corporations) or from a share exchange under paragraph (g) of section 913 (Share exchanges) shall file a written notice of such election to dissent within twenty days after the giving to him of a copy of the plan of merger or exchange or an outline of the material features thereof under section 905 or 913.

(d) A shareholder may not dissent as to less than all of the shares, as to which he has a right to dissent, held by him of record, that he owns beneficially. A nominee or fiduciary may not dissent on behalf of any beneficial owner as to less than all of the shares of such owner, as to which such nominee or fiduciary has a right to dissent, held of record by such nominee or fiduciary.

(e) Upon consummation of the corporate action, the shareholder shall cease to have any of the rights of a shareholder except the right to be paid the fair value of his shares and any other rights under this section. A notice of election may be withdrawn by the shareholder at any time prior to his acceptance in writing of an offer made by the corporation, as provided in paragraph (g), but in no case later than sixty days from the date of consummation of the corporate action except that if the corporation fails to make a timely offer, as provided in paragraph (g), the time for withdrawing a notice of election shall be extended until sixty days from the date an offer is made. Upon expiration of such time, withdrawal of a notice of election shall require the written consent of the corporation. In order to be effective, withdrawal of a notice of election must be accompanied by the return to the corporation of any advance payment made to the shareholder as provided in paragraph (g). If a notice of election is withdrawn, or the corporate action is rescinded, or a court shall determine that the shareholder is not entitled to receive payment for his shares, or the shareholder shall otherwise lose his dissenters' rights, he shall not have the right to receive payment for his shares and he shall be reinstated to all his rights as a shareholder as of the consummation of the corporate action, including any intervening preemptive rights and the right to payment of any intervening dividend or other distribution or, if any such rights have expired or any such dividend or distribution other than in cash has been completed, in lieu thereof, at the election of the corporation, the fair value thereof in cash as determined by the board as of the time of such expiration or completion, but without prejudice otherwise to any corporate proceedings that may have been taken in the interim.

(f) At the time of filing the notice of election to dissent or within one month thereafter the shareholder of shares represented by certificates shall submit the certificates representing his shares to the corporation, or to its transfer agent, which shall forthwith note conspicuously thereon that a notice of election has been filed and shall return the certificates to the shareholder or other person who submitted them on his behalf. Any shareholder of shares represented by certificates who fails to submit his certificates for such notation as herein specified shall, at the option of the corporation exercised by written notice to him within forty-five days from the date of filing of such notice of election to dissent, lose his dissenter's rights unless a court, for good cause shown, shall otherwise direct. Upon transfer of a certificate bearing such notation, each new certificate issued therefor shall bear a similar notation together with the name of the original dissenting holder of the shares and a transferee shall acquire no rights in the corporation except those which the original dissenting shareholder had at the time of transfer.

(g) Within fifteen days after the expiration of the period within which shareholders may file their notices of election to dissent, or within fifteen days after the proposed corporate action is consummated, whichever is later (but in no case later than ninety days from the shareholders' authorization date), the corporation or, in the case of a merger or consolidation, the surviving or new corporation, shall make a written offer by registered mail to each shareholder who has filed such notice of election to pay for his shares at a specified price which the corporation considers to be their fair value. Such offer shall be accompanied by a statement setting forth the aggregate number of shares with respect to which notices of election to dissent have been received and the aggregate number of holders of such shares. If the corporate action has been consummated, such offer shall also be accompanied by (1) advance payment to each such shareholder who has submitted the certificates representing his shares to the corporation, as provided in paragraph (f), of an amount equal to eighty percent of the amount of such offer, or (2) as to each shareholder who has not yet submitted his certificates a statement that advance payment to him of an amount equal to eighty percent of the amount of such offer will be made by the corporation promptly upon submission of his certificates. If the corporate action has not been consummated at the time of the making of the offer, such advance payment or statement as to advance payment shall be sent to each shareholder entitled thereto forthwith upon consummation of the corporate action. Every advance payment or statement as to advance payment shall include advice to the shareholder to the effect that acceptance of such payment does not constitute a waiver of any dissenters' rights. If the corporate action has not been consummated upon the expiration of the ninety day period after the shareholders' authorization date, the offer may be conditioned upon the consummation of such action. Such offer shall be made at the same price per share to all dissenting shareholders of the same class, or if divided into series, of the same series and shall be accompanied by a balance sheet of the corporation whose shares the dissenting shareholder holds as of the latest available date, which shall not be earlier than twelve months before the making of such offer, and a profit and loss statement or statements for not less than a twelve month period ended on the date of such balance sheet or, if the corporation was not in existence throughout such twelve month period, for the portion thereof during which it was in existence. Notwithstanding the foregoing, the corporation shall not be required to furnish a balance sheet or profit and loss statement or statements to any shareholder to whom such balance sheet or profit and loss statement or statements were previously furnished, nor if in connection with obtaining the shareholders' authorization for or consent to the proposed corporate action the shareholders were furnished with a proxy or information statement, which included financial statements, pursuant to Regulation 14A or Regulation 14C of the United States Securities and Exchange Commission. If within thirty days after the making of such offer, the corporation making the offer and any shareholder agree upon the price to be paid for his shares, payment therefor shall be made within sixty days after the making of such offer or the consummation of the proposed corporate action, whichever is later, upon the surrender of the certificates for any such shares represented by certificates.

(h) The following procedure shall apply if the corporation fails to make such offer within such period of fifteen days, or if it makes the offer and any dissenting shareholder or shareholders fail to agree with it within the period of thirty days thereafter upon the price to be paid for their shares:

(1) The corporation shall, within twenty days after the expiration of whichever is applicable of the two periods last mentioned, institute a special proceeding in the supreme court in the judicial district in which the office of the corporation is located to determine the rights of dissenting shareholders and to fix the fair value of their shares. If, in the case of merger or consolidation, the surviving or new corporation is a foreign corporation without an office in this state, such proceeding

shall be brought in the county where the office of the domestic corporation, whose shares are to be valued, was located.

(2) If the corporation fails to institute such proceeding within such period of twenty days, any dissenting shareholder may institute such proceeding for the same purpose not later than thirty days after the expiration of such twenty day period. If such proceeding is not instituted within such thirty day period, all dissenter's rights shall be lost unless the supreme court, for good cause shown, shall otherwise direct.

(3) All dissenting shareholders, excepting those who, as provided in paragraph (g), have agreed with the corporation upon the price to be paid for their shares, shall be made parties to such proceeding, which shall have the effect of an action quasi in rem against their shares. The corporation shall serve a copy of the petition in such proceeding upon each dissenting shareholder who is a resident of this state in the manner provided by law for the service of a summons, and upon each nonresident dissenting shareholder either by registered mail and publication, or in such other manner as is permitted by law. The jurisdiction of the court shall be plenary and exclusive.

(4) The court shall determine whether each dissenting shareholder, as to whom the corporation requests the court to make such determination, is entitled to receive payment for his shares. If the corporation does not request any such determination or if the court finds that any dissenting shareholder is so entitled, it shall proceed to fix the value of the shares, which, for the purposes of this section, shall be the fair value as of the close of business on the day prior to the shareholders' authorization date. In fixing the fair value of the shares, the court shall consider the nature of the transaction giving rise to the shareholder's right to receive payment for shares and its effects on the corporation and its shareholders, the concepts and methods then customary in the relevant securities and financial markets for determining fair value of shares of a corporation engaging in a similar transaction under comparable circumstances and all other relevant factors. The court shall determine the fair value of the shares without a jury and without referral to an appraiser or referee. Upon application by the corporation or by any shareholder who is a party to the proceeding, the court may, in its discretion, permit pretrial disclosure, including, but not limited to, disclosure of any expert's reports relating to the fair value of the shares whether or not intended for use at the trial in the proceeding and notwithstanding subdivision (d) of section 3101 of the civil practice law and rules.

(5) The final order in the proceeding shall be entered against the corporation in favor of each dissenting shareholder who is a party to the proceeding and is entitled thereto for the value of his shares so determined.

(6) The final order shall include an allowance for interest at such rate as the court finds to be equitable, from the date the corporate action was consummated to the date of payment. In determining the rate of interest, the court shall consider all relevant factors, including

the rate of interest which the corporation would have had to pay to borrow money during the pendency of the proceeding. If the court finds that the refusal of any shareholder to accept the corporate offer of payment for his shares was arbitrary, vexatious or otherwise not in good faith, no interest shall be allowed to him.

(7) Each party to such proceeding shall bear its own costs and expenses, including the fees and expenses of its counsel and of any experts employed by it. Notwithstanding the foregoing, the court may, in its discretion, apportion and assess all or any part of the costs, expenses and fees incurred by the corporation against any or all of the dissenting shareholders who are parties to the proceeding, including any who have withdrawn their notices of election as provided in paragraph (e), if the court finds that their refusal to accept the corporate offer was arbitrary, vexatious or otherwise not in good faith. The court may, in its discretion, apportion and assess all or any part of the costs, expenses and fees incurred by any or all of the dissenting shareholders who are parties to the proceeding against the corporation if the court finds any of the following: (A) that the fair value of the shares as determined materially exceeds the amount which the corporation offered to pay; (B) that no offer or required advance payment was made by the corporation; (C) that the corporation failed to institute the special proceeding within the period specified therefor; or (D) that the action of the corporation in complying with its obligations as provided in this section was arbitrary, vexatious or otherwise not in good faith. In making any determination as provided in clause (A), the court may consider the dollar amount or the percentage, or both, by which the fair value of the shares as determined exceeds the corporate offer.

(8) Within sixty days after final determination of the proceeding, the corporation shall pay to each dissenting shareholder the amount found to be due him, upon surrender of the certificates for any such shares represented by certificates.

(i) Shares acquired by the corporation upon the payment of the agreed value therefor or of the amount due under the final order, as provided in this section, shall become treasury shares or be cancelled as provided in section 515 (Reacquired shares), except that, in the case of a merger or consolidation, they may be held and disposed of as the plan of merger or consolidation may otherwise provide.

(j) No payment shall be made to a dissenting shareholder under this section at a time when the corporation is insolvent or when such payment would make it insolvent. In such event, the dissenting shareholder shall, at his option:

(1) Withdraw his notice of election, which shall in such event be deemed withdrawn with the written consent of the corporation; or

(2) Retain his status as a claimant against the corporation and, if it is liquidated, be subordinated to the rights of creditors of the corporation, but have rights superior to the non-dissenting sharehold-

ers, and if it is not liquidated, retain his right to be paid for his shares, which right the corporation shall be obliged to satisfy when the restrictions of this paragraph do not apply.

(3) The dissenting shareholder shall exercise such option under subparagraph (1) or (2) by written notice filed with the corporation within thirty days after the corporation has given him written notice that payment for his shares cannot be made because of the restrictions of this paragraph. If the dissenting shareholder fails to exercise such option as provided, the corporation shall exercise the option by written notice given to him within twenty days after the expiration of such period of thirty days.

(k) The enforcement by a shareholder of his right to receive payment for his shares in the manner provided herein shall exclude the enforcement by such shareholder of any other right to which he might otherwise be entitled by virtue of share ownership, except as provided in paragraph (e), and except that this section shall not exclude the right of such shareholder to bring or maintain an appropriate action to obtain relief on the ground that such corporate action will be or is unlawful or fraudulent as to him.

(l) Except as otherwise expressly provided in this section, any notice to be given by a corporation to a shareholder under this section shall be given in the manner provided in section 605 (Notice of meetings of shareholders).

(m) This section shall not apply to foreign corporations except as provided in subparagraph (e)(2) of section 907 (Merger or consolidation of domestic and foreign corporations).

§ 717.   Duty of directors

(a) A director shall perform his duties as a director, including his duties as a member of any committee of the board upon which he may serve, in good faith and with that degree of care which an ordinarily prudent person in a like position would use under similar circumstances. In performing his duties, a director shall be entitled to rely on information, opinions, reports or statements including financial statements and other financial data, in each case prepared or presented by:

(1) one or more officers or employees of the corporation or of any other corporation of which at least fifty percentum of the outstanding shares of stock entitling the holders thereof to vote for the election of directors is owned directly or indirectly by the corporation, whom the director believes to be reliable and competent in the matters presented,

(2) counsel, public accountants or other persons as to matters which the director believes to be within such person's professional or expert competence, or

(3) a committee of the board upon which he does not serve, duly designated in accordance with a provision of the certificate of incorporation or the by-laws, as to matters within its designated authority, which committee the director believes to merit confidence, so long as in so relying he shall be acting in good faith and with such degree of care,

but he shall not be considered to be acting in good faith if he has knowledge concerning the matter in question that would cause such reliance to be unwarranted. A person who so performs his duties shall have no liability by reason of being or having been a director of the corporation.

(b) In taking action, including, without limitation, action which may involve or relate to a change or potential change in the control of the corporation, a director shall be entitled to consider, without limitation, (1) both the long-term and the short-term interests of the corporation and its shareholders and (2) the effects that the corporation's actions may have in the short-term or in the long-term upon any of the following:

(i) the prospects for potential growth, development, productivity and profitability of the corporation;

(ii) the corporation's current employees;

(iii) the corporation's retired employees and other beneficiaries receiving or entitled to receive retirement, welfare or similar benefits from or pursuant to any plan sponsored, or agreement entered into, by the corporation;

(iv) the corporation's customers and creditors; and

(v) the ability of the corporation to provide, as a going concern, goods, services, employment opportunities and employment benefits and otherwise to contribute to the communities in which it does business.

Nothing in this paragraph shall create any duties owed by any director to any person or entity to consider or afford any particular weight to any of the foregoing or abrogate any duty of the directors, either statutory or recognized by common law or court decisions.

For purposes of this paragraph, "control" shall mean the possession, directly or indirectly, of the power to direct or cause the direction of the management and policies of the corporation, whether through the ownership of voting stock, by contract, or otherwise.

§ 801. Right to amend certificate of incorporation

(a) A corporation may amend its certificate of incorporation, from time to time, in any and as many respects as may be desired, if such amendment contains only such provisions as might be lawfully contained in an original certificate of incorporation filed at the time of making such amendment.

(b) In particular, and without limitation upon such general power of amendment, a corporation may amend its certificate of incorporation, from time to time, so as:

(1) To change its corporate name.

(2) To enlarge, limit or otherwise change its corporate purposes.

(3) To specify or change the location of the office of the corporation.

(4) To specify or change the post office address to which the secretary of state shall mail a copy of any process against the corporation served upon him.

(5) To make, revoke or change the designation of a registered agent, or to specify or change the address of its registered agent.

(6) To extend the duration of the corporation or, if the corporation ceased to exist because of the expiration of the duration specified in its certificate of incorporation, to revive its existence.

(7) To increase or decrease the aggregate number of shares, or shares of any class or series, with or without par value, which the corporation shall have authority to issue.

(8) To remove from authorized shares any class of shares, or any shares of any class, whether issued or unissued.

(9) To increase the par value of any authorized shares of any class with par value, whether issued or unissued.

(10) To reduce the par value of any authorized shares of any class with par value, whether issued or unissued.

(11) To change any authorized shares, with or without par value, whether issued or unissued, into a different number of shares of the same class or into the same or a different number of shares of any one or more classes or any series thereof, either with or without par value.

(12) To fix, change or abolish the designation of any authorized class or any series thereof or any of the relative rights, preferences and limitations of any shares of any authorized class or any series thereof, whether issued or unissued, including any provisions in respect of any undeclared dividends, whether or not cumulative or accrued, or the redemption of any shares, or any sinking fund for the redemption or purchase of any shares, or any preemptive right to acquire shares or other securities.

(13) As to the shares of any preferred class, then or theretofore authorized, which may be issued in series, to grant authority to the board or to change or revoke the authority of the board to establish and designate series and to fix the number of shares and the relative rights, preferences and limitation as between series.

(14) To strike out, change or add any provision, not inconsistent with this chapter or any other statute, relating to the business of the corporation, its affairs, its rights or powers, or the rights or powers of its shareholders, directors or officers, including any provision which under this chapter is required or permitted to be set forth in the by-laws, except that a certificate of amendment may not be filed wherein the duration of the corporation shall be reduced.

(c) A corporation created by special act may accomplish any or all amendments permitted in this article, in the manner and subject to the conditions provided in this article.

§ 803. Authorization of amendment or change

(a) Amendment or change of the certificate of incorporation may be authorized by vote of the board, followed by vote of a majority of all outstanding shares entitled to vote thereon at a meeting of shareholders; provided, however, that, whenever the certificate of incorporation requires action by the board of directors, by the holders of any class or series of shares, or by the holders of any other securities having voting power by the vote of a greater number or proportion than is required by any section of this article, the provision of the certificate of incorporation requiring such greater vote shall not be altered, amended, or repealed except by such greater vote; and provided further that an amendment to the certificate of incorporation for the purpose of reducing the requisite vote by the holders of any class or series of shares or by the holders of any other securities having voting power that is otherwise provided for in any section of this chapter that would otherwise require more than a majority of the votes of all outstanding shares entitled to vote thereon shall not be adopted except by the vote of such holders of class or series of shares or by such holders of such other securities having voting power that is at least equal to that which would be required to take the action provided in such other section of this chapter.

(b) Alternatively, any one or more of the following changes may be authorized by or pursuant to authorization of the board:

(1) To specify or change the location of the corporation's office.

(2) To specify or change the post office address to which the secretary of state shall mail a copy of any process against the corporation served upon him.

(3) To make, revoke or change the designation of a registered agent, or to specify or change the address of its registered agent.

(c) This section shall not alter the vote required under any other section for the authorization of an amendment referred to therein, nor alter the authority of the board to authorize amendments under any other section.

(d) Amendment or change of the certificate of incorporation of a corporation which has no shareholders of record, no subscribers for shares whose subscriptions have been accepted and no directors may be authorized by the sole incorporator or a majority of the incorporators.

§ 804. Class voting on amendment

(a) Notwithstanding any provision in the certificate of incorporation, the holders of shares of a class shall be entitled to vote and to vote as a class upon the authorization of an amendment and, in addition to the authorization of the amendment by a majority of the votes of all outstanding shares entitled to vote thereon, the amendment shall be authorized by a majority of the votes of all outstanding shares of the class when a proposed amendment would:

(1) Exclude or limit their right to vote on any matter, except as such right may be limited by voting rights given to new shares then being authorized of any existing or new class or series.

(2) Change their shares under subparagraphs (b) (10), (11) or (12) of section 801 (Right to amend certificate of incorporation) or provide that their shares may be converted into shares of any other class or into shares of any other series of the same class, or alter the terms or conditions upon which their shares are convertible or change the shares issuable upon conversion of their shares, if such action would adversely affect such holders, or

(3) Subordinate their rights, by authorizing shares having preferences which would be in any respect superior to their rights.

(b) If any proposed amendment referred to in paragraph (a) would adversely affect the rights of the holders of shares of only one or more series of any class, but not the entire class, then only the holders of those series whose rights would be affected shall be considered a separate class for the purposes of this section.

§ 902. Plan of merger or consolidation

(a) The board of each corporation proposing to participate in a merger or consolidation under section 901 (Power of merger or consolidation) shall adopt a plan of merger or consolidation, setting forth:

(1) The name of each constituent entity and, if the name of any of them has been changed, the name under which it was formed; and the name of the surviving corporation, or the name, or the method of determining it, of the consolidated corporation.

(2) As to each constituent corporation, the designation and number of outstanding shares of each class and series, specifying the classes and series entitled to vote and further specifying each class and series, if any, entitled to vote as a class; and, if the number of any such shares is subject to change prior to the effective date of the merger or consolidation, the manner in which such change may occur.

(3) The terms and conditions of the proposed merger or consolidation, including the manner and basis of converting the shares of each constituent corporation into shares, bonds or other securities of the surviving or consolidated corporation, or the cash or other consideration to be paid or delivered in exchange for shares of each constituent corporation, or a combination thereof.

(4) In case of merger, a statement of any amendments or changes in the certificate of incorporation of the surviving corporation to be effected by such merger; in case of consolidation, all statements required to be included in a certificate of incorporation for a corporation formed under this chapter, except statements as to facts not available at the time the plan of consolidation is adopted by the board.

(5) Such other provisions with respect to the proposed merger or consolidation as the board considers necessary or desirable.

§ 903. Authorization by shareholders

(a) The board of each constituent corporation, upon adopting such plan of merger or consolidation, shall submit such plan to a vote of shareholders in accordance with the following:

(1) Notice of meeting shall be given to each shareholder of record, as of the record date fixed pursuant to section 604 (Fixing record date), whether or not entitled to vote. A copy of the plan of merger or consolidation or an outline of the material features of the plan shall accompany such notice.

(2) The plan of merger or consolidation shall be adopted at a meeting of shareholders by (i) for corporations in existence on the effective date of this clause the certificate of incorporation of which expressly provides such or corporations incorporated after the effective date of subclause (A) of clause (ii) of this subparagraph, a majority of the votes of the shares entitled to vote thereon or (ii) for other corporations in existence on the effective date of this clause, two-thirds of the votes of all outstanding shares entitled to vote thereon. Notwithstanding any provision in the certificate of incorporation, the holders of shares of a class or series of a class shall be entitled to vote together and to vote as a separate class if both of the following conditions are satisfied:

(A) such shares will remain outstanding after the merger or consolidation or will be converted into the right to receive shares of stock of the surviving or consolidated corporation or another corporation, and

(B) the certificate or articles of incorporation of the surviving or consolidated corporation or of such other corporation immediately after the effectiveness of the merger or consolidation would contain any provision which, is not contained in the certificate of incorporation of the corporation and which, if contained in an amendment to the certificate of incorporation, would entitle the holders of shares of such class or such one or more series to vote and to vote as a separate class thereon pursuant to section 804 (Class voting on amendment).

In such case, in addition to the authorization of the merger or consolidation by the requisite number of votes of all outstanding shares entitled to vote thereon pursuant to the first sentence of this subparagraph (2), the merger or consolidation shall be authorized by a majority of the votes of all outstanding shares of the class entitled to vote as a separate class. If any provision referred to in subclause (B) of clause (ii) of this subparagraph would affect the rights of the holders of shares of only one or more series of any class but not the entire class, then only the holders of those series whose rights would be affected shall together be considered a separate class for purposes of this section.

(b) Notwithstanding shareholder authorization and at any time prior to the filing of the certificate of merger or consolidation, the plan of merger or consolidation may be abandoned pursuant to a provision for such abandonment, if any, contained in the plan of merger or consolidation.

§ 909. Sale, lease, exchange or other disposition of assets

(a) A sale, lease, exchange or other disposition of all or substantially all the assets of a corporation, if not made in the usual or regular course of the business actually conducted by such corporation, shall be authorized only in accordance with the following procedure:

(1) The board shall authorize the proposed sale, lease, exchange or other disposition and direct its submission to a vote of shareholders.

(2) Notice of meeting shall be given to each shareholder of record, whether or not entitled to vote.

(3) The shareholders shall approve such sale, lease, exchange or other disposition and may fix, or may authorize the board to fix, any of the terms and conditions thereof and the consideration to be received by the corporation therefor, which may consist in whole or in part of cash or other property, real or personal, including shares, bonds or other securities of any other domestic or foreign corporation or corporations, by vote at a meeting of shareholders of (A) for corporations in existence on the effective date of this clause the certificate of incorporation of which expressly provides such or corporations incorporated after the effective date of this clause, a majority of the votes of all outstanding shares entitled to vote thereon or (B) for other corporations in existence on the effective date of this clause, two-thirds of the votes of all outstanding shares entitled to vote thereon.

(b) A recital in a deed, lease or other instrument of conveyance executed by a corporation to the effect that the property described therein does not constitute all or substantially all of the assets of the corporation, or that the disposition of the property affected by said instrument was made in the usual or regular course of business of the corporation, or that the shareholders have duly authorized such disposition, shall be presumptive evidence of the fact so recited.

(c) An action to set aside a deed, lease or other instrument of conveyance executed by a corporation affecting real property or real and personal property may not be maintained for failure to comply with the requirements of paragraph (a) unless the action is commenced and a notice of pendency of action is filed within one year after such conveyance, lease or other instrument is recorded or within six months after this subdivision takes effect, whichever date occurs later.

(d) Whenever a transaction of the character described in paragraph (a) involves a sale, lease, exchange or other disposition of all or substantially all the assets of the corporation, including its name, to a new corporation formed under the same name as the existing corporation, upon the expiration of thirty days from the filing of the certificate of incorporation of the new corporation, with the consent of the state tax commission attached, the existing corporation shall be automatically dissolved, unless, before the end of such thirty-day period, such corporation has changed its name. The adjustment and winding up of the affairs of such dissolved corporation shall proceed in accordance with the provisions of article 10 (Non-judicial dissolution).

(e) The certificate of incorporation of a corporation formed under the authority of paragraph (d) shall set forth the name of the existing corporation, the date when its certificate of incorporation was filed by the department of state, and that the shareholders of such corporation have authorized the sale, lease, exchange or other disposition of all or substantially all the assets of such corporation, including its name, to the new corporation to be formed under the same name as the existing corporation.

(f) Notwithstanding shareholder approval, the board may abandon the proposed sale, lease, exchange or other disposition without further action by the shareholders, subject to the rights, if any, of third parties under any contract relating thereto.

§ 910. Right of shareholder to receive payment for shares upon merger or consolidation, or sale, lease, exchange or other disposition of assets, or share exchange

(a) A shareholder of a domestic corporation shall, subject to and by complying with section 623 (Procedure to enforce shareholder's right to receive payment for shares), have the right to receive payment of the fair value of his shares and the other rights and benefits provided by such section, in the following cases:

(1) Any shareholder entitled to vote who does not assent to the taking of an action specified in clauses (A), (B) and (C).

(A) Any plan of merger or consolidation to which the corporation is a party; except that the right to receive payment of the fair value of his shares shall not be available:

(i) To a shareholder of the parent corporation in a merger authorized by section 905 (Merger of parent and subsidiary corporations), or paragraph (c) of section 907 (Merger or consolidation of domestic and foreign corporations); or

(ii) To a shareholder of the surviving corporation in a merger authorized by this article, other than a merger specified in subclause (i), unless such merger effects one or more of the changes specified in subparagraph (b) (6) of section 806 (Provisions as to certain proceedings) in the rights of the shares held by such shareholder; or

(iii) Notwithstanding subclause (ii) of this clause, to a shareholder for the shares of any class or series of stock, which shares or depository receipts in respect thereof, at the record date fixed to determine the shareholders entitled to receive notice of the meeting of shareholders to vote upon the plan of merger or consolidation, were listed on a national securities exchange or designated as a national market system security on an interdealer quotation system by the National Association of Securities Dealers, Inc.

(B) Any sale, lease, exchange or other disposition of all or substantially all of the assets of a corporation which requires shareholder approval under section 909 (Sale, lease, exchange or other disposition of assets) other than a transaction wholly for cash where the shareholders' approval thereof is conditioned upon the dissolution of the corporation and the distribution of substantially all of its net assets to the shareholders in accordance with their respective interests within one year after the date of such transaction.

(C) Any share exchange authorized by section 913 in which the corporation is participating as a subject corporation; except that the right to receive payment of the fair value of his shares shall not be available to a shareholder whose shares have not been acquired in the exchange or to a shareholder for the shares of any class or series of stock, which shares or depository receipt in respect thereof, at the record date fixed to determine the shareholders entitled to receive notice of the meeting of shareholders to vote upon the plan of exchange, were listed on a national securities exchange or designated as a national market system security on an interdealer quotation system by the National Association of Securities Dealers, Inc.

(2) Any shareholder of the subsidiary corporation in a merger authorized by section 905 or paragraph (c) of section 907, or in a share exchange authorized by paragraph (g) of section 913, who files with the corporation a written notice of election to dissent as provided in paragraph (c) of section 623.

(3) Any shareholder, not entitled to vote with respect to a plan of merger or consolidation to which the corporation is a party, whose shares will be cancelled or exchanged in the merger or consolidation for cash or other consideration other than shares of the surviving or consolidated corporation or another corporation.

§ 912. Requirements relating to certain business combinations

(a) For the purposes of this section:

(1) "Affiliate" means a person that directly, or indirectly through one or more intermediaries, controls, or is controlled by, or is under common control with, a specified person.

(2) "Announcement date", when used in reference to any business combination, means the date of the first public announcement of the final, definitive proposal for such business combination.

(3) "Associate", when used to indicate a relationship with any person, means (A) any corporation or organization of which such person is an officer or partner or is, directly or indirectly, the beneficial owner of ten percent or more of any class of voting stock, (B) any trust or other estate in which such person has a substantial beneficial interest or as to which such person serves as trustee or in a similar

fiduciary capacity, and (C) any relative or spouse of such person, or any relative of such spouse, who has the same home as such person.

(4) "Beneficial owner", when used with respect to any stock, means a person:

(A) that, individually or with or through any of its affiliates or associates, beneficially owns such stock, directly or indirectly; or

(B) that, individually or with or through any of its affiliates or associates, has (i) the right to acquire such stock (whether such right is exercisable immediately or only after the passage of time), pursuant to any agreement, arrangement or understanding (whether or not in writing), or upon the exercise of conversion rights, exchange rights, warrants or options, or otherwise; provided, however, that a person shall not be deemed the beneficial owner of stock tendered pursuant to a tender or exchange offer made by such person or any of such person's affiliates or associates until such tendered stock is accepted for purchase or exchange; or (ii) the right to vote such stock pursuant to any agreement, arrangement or understanding (whether or not in writing); provided, however, that a person shall not be deemed the beneficial owner of any stock under this item if the agreement, arrangement or understanding to vote such stock (X) arises solely from a revocable proxy or consent given in response to a proxy or consent solicitation made in accordance with the applicable rules and regulations under the Exchange Act and (Y) is not then reportable on a Schedule 13D under the Exchange Act (or any comparable or successor report); or

(C) that has any agreement, arrangement or understanding (whether or not in writing), for the purpose of acquiring, holding, voting (except voting pursuant to a revocable proxy or consent as described in item (ii) of clause (B) of this subparagraph), or disposing of such stock with any other person that beneficially owns, or whose affiliates or associates beneficially own, directly or indirectly, such stock.

(5) "Business combination", when used in reference to any domestic corporation and any interested shareholder of such corporation, means:

(A) any merger or consolidation of such corporation or any subsidiary of such corporation with (i) such interested shareholder or (ii) any other corporation (whether or not itself an interested shareholder of such corporation) which is, or after such merger or consolidation would be, an affiliate or associate of such interested shareholder;

(B) any sale, lease, exchange, mortgage, pledge, transfer or other disposition (in one transaction or a series of transactions) to or with such interested shareholder or any affiliate or associate of such interested shareholder of assets of such corporation or any subsidiary of such corporation (i) having an aggregate market value equal to ten percent or more of the aggregate market value of all the assets, determined on a consolidated basis, of such corporation, (ii) having an aggregate market value equal to ten percent or more of the aggregate market value of all the outstanding stock of such corporation, or (iii) representing ten percent or more of the earning power or net income determined on a consolidated basis, of such corporation;

(C) the issuance or transfer by such corporation or any subsidiary of such corporation (in one transaction or a series of transactions) of any stock of such corporation or any subsidiary of such corporation which has an aggregate market value equal to five percent or more of the aggregate market value of all the outstanding stock of such corporation to such interested shareholder or any affiliate or associate of such interested shareholder except pursuant to the exercise of warrants or rights to purchase stock offered, or a dividend or distribution paid or made, pro rata to all shareholders of such corporation;

(D) the adoption of any plan or proposal for the liquidation or dissolution of such corporation proposed by, or pursuant to any agreement, arrangement or understanding (whether or not in writing) with, such interested shareholder or any affiliate or associate of such interested shareholder;

(E) any reclassification of securities (including, without limitation, any stock split, stock dividend, or other distribution of stock in respect of stock, or any reverse stock split), or recapitalization of such corporation, or any merger or consolidation of such corporation with any subsidiary of such corporation, or any other transaction (whether or not with or into or otherwise involving such interested shareholder), proposed by, or pursuant to any agreement, arrangement or understanding (whether or not in writing) with, such interested shareholder or any affiliate or associate of such interested shareholder, which has the effect, directly or indirectly, of increasing the proportionate share of the outstanding shares of any class or series of voting stock or securities convertible into voting stock of such corporation or any subsidiary of such corporation which is directly or indirectly owned by such interested shareholder or any affiliate or associate of such interested shareholder, except as a result of immaterial changes due to fractional share adjustments; or

(F) any receipt by such interested shareholder or any affiliate or associate of such interested shareholder of the benefit, directly or indirectly (except proportionately as a shareholder of such corporation) of any loans, advances, guarantees, pledges or other financial assistance or any tax credits or other tax advantages provided by or through such corporation.

(6) "Common stock" means any stock other than preferred stock.

(7) "Consummation date", with respect to any business combination, means the date of consummation of such business combination, or, in the case of a business combination as to which a shareholder vote is taken, the later of the business day prior to the vote or twenty days prior to the date of consummation of such business combination.

(8) "Control", including the terms "controlling", "controlled by" and "under common control with", means the possession, directly or indirectly, of the power to direct or cause the direction of the management and policies of a person, whether through the ownership of voting stock, by contract, or otherwise. A person's beneficial ownership of ten percent or more of a corporation's outstanding voting stock shall create a presumption that such person has control of such corporation. Notwithstanding the foregoing, a person shall not be deemed to have control of a corporation if such person holds voting stock, in good faith and not for the the purpose of circumventing this section, as an agent, bank, broker, nominee, custodian or trustee for one or more beneficial owners who do not individually or as a group have control of such corporation.

(9) "Exchange Act" means the Act of Congress known as the Securities Exchange Act of 1934, as the same has been or hereafter may be amended from time to time.

(10) "Interested shareholder", when used in reference to any domestic corporation, means any person (other than such corporation or any subsidiary of such corporation) that

(A)(i) is the beneficial owner, directly or indirectly, of twenty percent or more of the outstanding voting stock of such corporation; or

(ii) is an affiliate or associate of such corporation and at any time within the five-year period immediately prior to the date in question was the beneficial owner, directly or indirectly, of twenty percent or more of the then outstanding voting stock of such corporation; provided that

(B) for the purpose of determining whether a person is an interested shareholder, the number of shares of voting stock of such corporation deemed to be outstanding shall include shares deemed to be beneficially owned by the person through application of subparagraph four of this paragraph but shall not include any other unissued shares of voting stock of such corporation which may be issuable pursuant to any agreement, arrangement or understanding, or upon exercise of conversion rights, warrants or options, or otherwise.

(11) "Market value", when used in reference to stock or property of any domestic corporation, means:

(A) in the case of stock, the highest closing sale price during the thirty-day period immediately preceding the date in question of a share of such stock on the composite tape for New York stock exchange-listed stocks, or, if such stock is not quoted on such composite tape or if such stock is not listed on such exchange, on the principal United States securities exchange registered under the Exchange Act on which such stock is listed, or, if such stock is not listed on any such exchange, the highest closing bid quotation with respect to a share of such stock during the thirty-day period preceding the date in question on the National Association of Securities Dealers, Inc. Automated Quotations System or any system then in use, or if no such quotations are available, the fair market value on the date in question of a share of such stock as determined by the board of directors of such corporation in good faith; and

(B) in the case of property other than cash or stock, the fair market value of such property on the date in question as determined by the board of directors of such corporation in good faith.

(12) "Preferred stock" means any class or series of stock of a domestic corporation which under the by-laws or certificate of incorporation of such corporation is entitled to receive payment of dividends prior to any payment of dividends on some other class or series of stock, or is entitled in the event of any voluntary liquidation, dissolution or winding up of the corporation to receive payment or distribution of a preferential amount before any payments or distributions are received by some other class or series of stock.

[*(13) Repealed.*]

(14) "Stock" means:

(A) any stock or similar security, any certificate of interest, any participation in any profit sharing agreement, any voting trust certificate, or any certificate of deposit for stock; and

(B) any security convertible, with or without consideration, into stock, or any warrant, call or other option or privilege of buying stock without being bound to do so, or any other security carrying any right to acquire, subscribe to or purchase stock.

(15) "Stock acquisition date", with respect to any person and any domestic corporation, means the date that such person first becomes an interested shareholder of such corporation.

(16) "Subsidiary" of any person means any other corporation of which a majority of the voting stock is owned, directly or indirectly, by such person.

(17) "Voting stock" means shares of capital stock of a corporation entitled to vote generally in the election of directors.

(b) Notwithstanding anything to the contrary contained in this chapter (except the provisions of paragraph (d) of this section), no domestic corporation shall engage in any business combination with any interested shareholder of such corporation for a period of five years following such interested shareholder's stock acquisition date unless such business combination or the purchase of stock made by such interested shareholder on such interested shareholder's stock acquisition date is approved by the board of directors of such corporation prior to such interested shareholder's stock acquisition date. If a good faith proposal is made in writing to the board of directors of such corporation regarding a business combination, the board of directors shall respond, in writing, within thirty days or such shorter period, if any, as may be required by the Exchange Act, setting forth its reasons for its decision regarding such proposal. If a good faith proposal to purchase stock is made in writing to the board of directors of such corporation, the board of directors, unless it responds affirmatively in writing within thirty days or such shorter period, if any, as may be required by the Exchange Act, shall be deemed to have disapproved such stock purchase.

(c) Notwithstanding anything to the contrary contained in this chapter (except the provisions of paragraphs (b) and (d) of this section), no domestic corporation shall engage at any time in any business combination with any interested shareholder of such corporation other than a business combination specified in any one of subparagraph (1), (2) or (3):

(1) A business combination approved by the board of directors of such corporation prior to such interested shareholder's stock acquisition date, or where the purchase of stock made by such interested shareholder on such interested shareholder's stock acquisition date had been approved by the board of directors of such corporation prior to such interested shareholder's stock acquisition date.

(2) A business combination approved by the affirmative vote of the holders of a majority of the outstanding voting stock not beneficially owned by such interested shareholder or any affiliate or associate of such interested shareholder at a meeting called for such purpose no earlier than five years after such interested shareholder's stock acquisition date.

(3) A business combination that meets all of the following conditions:

(A) The aggregate amount of the cash and the market value as of the consummation date of consideration other than cash to be received per share by holders of outstanding shares of common stock of such corporation in such business combination is at least equal to the higher of the following:

(i) the highest per share price paid by such interested shareholder at a time when he was the beneficial owner, directly or indirectly, of five percent or more of the outstanding voting stock of such corporation, for any shares of common stock of the same class or series acquired by it (X) within the five-year period immediately prior to the announcement date with respect to such business combination, or (Y) within the five-year period immediately prior to, or in, the transaction in which such interested shareholder became an interested shareholder, whichever is higher; plus, in either case, interest compounded annually from the earliest date on which such highest per share acquisition price was paid through the consummation date at the rate for one-year United States treasury obligations from time to time in effect; less the aggregate amount of any cash dividends paid, and the market value of any dividends paid other than in cash, per share of common stock since such earliest date, up to the amount of such interest; and

(ii) the market value per share of common stock on the announcement date with respect to such business combination or on such interested shareholder's stock acquisition date, whichever is higher; plus interest compounded annually from such date through the consummation date at the rate for one-year United States treasury obligations from time to time in effect; less the aggregate amount of any cash dividends paid, and the market value of any dividends paid other than in cash, per share of common stock since such date, up to the amount of such interest.

(B) The aggregate amount of the cash and the market value as of the consummation date of consideration other than cash to be received per share by holders of outstanding shares of any class or series of stock, other than common stock, of such corporation is at least equal to the highest of the following (whether or not such interested shareholder has previously acquired any shares of such class or series of stock):

(i) the highest per share price paid by such interested shareholder at a time when he was the beneficial owner, directly or indirectly, of five percent or more of the outstanding voting stock of such corporation, for any shares of such class or series of stock acquired by it (X) within the five-year period immediately prior to the announcement date with respect to such business combination, or (Y) within the five-year period immediately prior to, or in, the transaction in which such interested shareholder became an interested shareholder, whichever is higher; plus, in either case, interest compounded annually from the earliest date on which such highest per share acquisition price was paid through the consummation date at the rate for one-year United States treasury obligations from time to time in effect; less the aggregate amount of any cash dividends paid, and the market value of any dividends paid other than in cash, per share of such class or series of stock since such earliest date, up to the amount of such interest;

(ii) the highest preferential amount per share to which the holders of shares of such class or series of stock are entitled in the event of any voluntary liquidation, dissolution or winding up of such corporation, plus the aggregate amount of any dividends declared or due as to which such holders are entitled prior to payment of dividends on some other class or series of stock (unless the aggregate amount of such dividends is included in such preferential amount); and

(iii) the market value per share of such class or series of stock on the announcement date with respect to such business combination or on such interested shareholder's stock acquisition date, whichever is higher; plus interest compounded annually from such date through the consummation date at the rate for one-year United States treasury obligations from time to time in effect; less the aggregate amount of any cash dividends paid, and the market value of any dividends paid other than in cash, per share of such class or series of stock since such date, up to the amount of such interest.

(C) The consideration to be received by holders of a particular class or series of outstanding stock (including common stock) of such corporation in such business combination is in cash or in the same form as the interested shareholder has used to acquire the largest number of shares of such class or series of stock previously acquired by it, and such consideration shall be distributed promptly.

(D) The holders of all outstanding shares of stock of such corporation not beneficially owned by such interested shareholder immediately prior to the consummation of such business combination are entitled to receive in such business combination cash or other consideration for such shares in compliance with clauses (A), (B) and (C) of this subparagraph.

(E) After such interested shareholder's stock acquisition date and prior to the consummation date with respect to such business combination, such interested shareholder has not become the beneficial owner of any additional shares of voting stock of such corporation except:

(i) as part of the transaction which resulted in such interested shareholder becoming an interested shareholder;

(ii) by virtue of proportionate stock splits, stock dividends or other distributions of stock in respect of stock not constituting a business combination under clause (E) of subparagraph five of paragraph (a) of this section;

(iii) through a business combination meeting all of the conditions of paragraph (b) of this section and this paragraph; or

(iv) through purchase by such interested shareholder at any price which, if such price had been paid in an otherwise permissible business combination the announcement date and consummation date of which were the date of such purchase, would have satisfied the requirements of clauses (A), (B) and (C) of this subparagraph.

(d) The provisions of this section shall not apply:

(1) to any business combination of a domestic corporation that does not have a class of voting stock registered with the Securities and Exchange Commission pursuant to section twelve of the Exchange Act, unless the certificate of incorporation provides otherwise; or

(2) to any business combination of a domestic corporation whose certificate of incorporation has been amended to provide that such corporation shall be subject to the provisions of this section, which did not have a class of voting stock registered with the Securities and Exchange Commission pursuant to section twelve of the Exchange Act on the effective date of such amendment, and which is a business combination with an interested shareholder whose stock acquisition date is prior to the effective date of such amendment; or

(3) to any business combination of a domestic corporation (i) the original certificate of incorporation of which contains a provision expressly electing not to be governed by this section, or (ii) which adopts an amendment to such corporation's by-laws prior to March thirty-first, nineteen hundred eighty-six, expressly electing not to be governed by this section, or (iii) which adopts an amendment to such corporation's by-laws, approved by the affirmative vote of a majority of votes of the outstanding voting stock of such corporation, excluding the voting stock of interested shareholders and their affiliates and associates, expressly electing not to be governed by this section, provided that such amendment to the by-laws shall not be effective until eighteen months after such vote of such corporation's shareholders and shall not apply to any business combination of such corporation with an interested shareholder whose stock acquisition date is on or prior to the effective date of such amendment; or

(4) to any business combination of a domestic corporation with an interested shareholder of such corporation which became an interested shareholder inadvertently, if such interested shareholder (i) as soon as practicable, divests itself of a sufficient amount of the voting stock of such corporation so that it no longer is the beneficial owner, directly or indirectly, of twenty percent or more of the outstanding voting stock of such corporation, and (ii) would not at any time within the five-year period preceding the announcement date with respect to such business combination have been an interested shareholder but for such inadvertent acquisition; or

(5) to any business combination with an interested shareholder who was the beneficial owner, directly or indirectly, of five percent or more of the outstanding voting stock of such corporation on October thirtieth, nineteen hundred eighty-five, and remained so to such interested shareholder's stock acquisition date.

§ 913. Share exchanges

(a)(1) Two domestic corporations may, as provided in this section, participate in the consummation of a plan for binding share exchanges.

(2) Whenever used in this article:

(A) "Acquiring corporation" means a corporation that is participating in a procedure pursuant to which such corporation is acquiring all of the outstanding shares of one or more classes of a subject corporation.

(B) "Subject corporation" means a corporation that is participating in a procedure pursuant to which all of the outstanding shares of one or more classes of such corporation are being acquired by an acquiring corporation.

(b) The board of the acquiring corporation and the board of the subject corporation shall adopt a plan of exchange, setting forth:

(1) The name of the acquiring corporation and the name of the subject corporation, and, if the name of either of them has been changed, the name under which it was formed;

(2) As to the acquiring corporation and the subject corporation, the designation and number of outstanding shares of each class and series, specifying the classes and series entitled to vote and further specifying each class and series, if any, entitled to vote as a class; and, if the number of any such shares is subject to change prior to the effective date of the exchange, the manner in which such change may occur;

(3) The terms and conditions of the proposed exchange, including the manner and basis of exchanging the shares to be acquired for shares, bonds or other securities of the acquiring corporation, or the cash or other consideration to be paid or delivered in exchange for such shares to be acquired, or a combination thereof; and

(4) Such other provisions with respect to the proposed exchange as the board considers necessary or desirable.

(c) The board of the subject corporation, upon adopting the plan of exchange, shall submit such plan, except as provided in paragraph (g) of this section, to a vote of shareholders in accordance with the following:

(1) Notice of meeting shall be given to each shareholder of record, as of the record date fixed pursuant to section 604 (Fixing record date), whether or not entitled to vote. A copy of the plan of exchange or an outline of the material features of the plan shall accompany such notice.

(2)(A) The plan of exchange shall be adopted at a meeting of shareholders by (i) for any corporation in existence on the effective date of subclause (ii) of this clause, two-thirds of the votes of all outstanding shares entitled to vote thereon and (ii) for any corporation in existence on the effective date of this subclause the certificate of incorporation of which expressly provides such and for any corporation incorporated after the effective date of this subclause, a majority of the votes of all outstanding shares entitled to vote thereon. Notwithstanding any provision in the certificate of incorporation, the holders of shares of a class or series of a class shall be entitled to vote together and to vote as a separate class if both of the following conditions are satisfied:

    1.   Such shares will be converted into shares of the acquiring corporation, and

    2.   The certificate or articles of incorporation of the acquiring corporation immediately after the share exchange would contain any provision which is not contained in the certificate of incorporation of the subject corporation and which, if contained in an amendment to the certificate of incorporation of the subject corporation, would entitle the holders of shares of such class or such one or more series to vote and to vote as a separate class thereon pursuant to section 804 (Class voting on amendment).

In such case, in addition to the authorization of the exchange by the proportion of votes indicated above of all outstanding shares entitled to vote thereon, the exchange shall be authorized by a majority of the votes of all outstanding shares of the class entitled to vote as a separate class. If any provision referred to in subclause 2 of this clause (A) would affect the rights of the holders of shares of only one or more series of any class but not the entire class, then only the holders of those series whose rights would be affected shall together be considered a separate class for purposes of this section.

Notwithstanding shareholder authorization and at any time prior to the filing of the certificate of exchange, the plan of exchange may be abandoned pursuant to a provision for such abandonment, if any, contained in the plan of exchange.

    (B) Any corporation may adopt an amendment of the certificate of incorporation which provides that such plan of exchange shall be adopted at a meeting of the shareholders by vote of a specified proportion of the holders of outstanding shares, or class or series of shares, entitled to vote thereon, provided that such proportion may not be less than a majority and subject to the second sentence of clause (A) of this subparagraph (2).

    (d) After adoption of the plan of exchange by the board of the acquiring corporation and the board of the subject corporation and by the shareholders of the subject corporation entitled to vote thereon, unless the exchange is abandoned in accordance with paragraph (c), a certificate of exchange, entitled "Certificate of exchange of shares of . . . . , subject corporation, for shares of . . . . , acquiring corporation, or other consideration, under section 913 of the Business Corporation Law", shall be signed on behalf of each corporation and delivered to the department of state. It shall set forth:

    (1) the statements required by subparagraphs (1) and (2) of paragraph (b) of this section;

    (2) the effective date of the exchange if other than the date of filing of the certificate of exchange by the department of state;

(3) the date when the certificate of incorporation of each corporation was filed by the department of state;

(4) the designation of the shares to be acquired by the acquiring corporation and a statement of the consideration for such shares; and

(5) the manner in which the exchange was authorized with respect to each corporation.

(e) Upon the filing of the certificate of exchange by the department of state or on such date subsequent thereto, not to exceed thirty days, as shall be set forth in such certificate, the exchange shall be effected. When such exchange has been effected, ownership of the shares to be acquired pursuant to the plan of exchange shall vest in the acquiring corporation, whether or not the certificates for such shares have been surrendered for exchange, and the acquiring corporation shall be entitled to have new certificates registered in its name or at its direction. Shareholders whose shares have been so acquired shall become entitled to the shares, bonds or other securities of the acquiring corporation, or the cash or other consideration, required to be paid or delivered in exchange for such shares pursuant to the plan. Subject to any terms of the plan regarding surrender of certificates theretofore evidencing the shares so acquired and regarding whether such certificates shall thereafter evidence securities of the acquiring corporation, such certificates shall thereafter evidence only the right to receive the consideration required to be paid or delivered in exchange for such shares pursuant to the plan or, in the case of dissenting shareholders, their rights under section 910 (Right of shareholder to receive payment for shares upon merger or consolidation, or sale, lease, exchange or other disposition of assets, or share exchange) and section 623 (Procedure to enforce shareholder's right to receive payment for shares).

(f)(1) A foreign corporation and a domestic corporation may participate in a share exchange, but, if the subject corporation is a foreign corporation, only if such exchange is permitted by the laws of the jurisdiction under which such foreign corporation is incorporated. With respect to such exchange, any reference in subparagraph (2) of paragraph (a) of this section to a corporation shall, unless the context otherwise requires, include both domestic and foreign corporations, and the provisions of paragraphs (b), (c), (d) and (e) of this section shall apply, except to the extent otherwise provided in this paragraph.

(2) With respect to procedure, including the requirement of shareholder authorization, a domestic corporation shall comply with the provisions of this chapter relating to share exchanges in which domestic corporations are participating, and a foreign corporation shall comply with the applicable provisions of the law of the jurisdiction under which it is incorporated.

(3) If the subject corporation is a foreign corporation, the certificate of exchange shall set forth, in addition to the matters specified in paragraph (d), the jurisdiction and date of incorporation of such corporation and a statement that the exchange is permitted by the

laws of the jurisdiction of such corporation and is in compliance therewith.

(g)(1) Any corporation owning at least ninety percent of the outstanding common shares, having full voting rights, of another corporation may acquire by exchange the remainder of such outstanding common shares, without the authorization of the shareholders of any such corporation and with the effect provided for in paragraph (e) of this section. The board of the acquiring corporation shall adopt a plan of exchange, setting forth the matters specified in paragraph (b) of this section. A copy of such plan of exchange or an outline of the material features thereof shall be given, personally or by mail, to all holders of shares of the subject corporation that are not owned by the acquiring corporation, unless the giving of such copy or outline has been waived by such holders.

(2) A certificate of exchange, entitled "Certificate of exchange of shares of . . ., subject corporation, for shares of . . ., acquiring corporation, or other consideration, under paragraph (g) of section 913 of the Business Corporation Law" and complying with the provisions of paragraph (d) and, if applicable, subparagraph (3) of paragraph (f) shall be signed, verified and delivered to the department of state by the acquiring corporation, but not less than thirty days after the giving of a copy or outline of the material features of the plan of exchange to shareholders of the subject corporation, or at any time after the waiving thereof by the holders of all the outstanding shares of the subject corporation not owned by the acquiring corporation.

(3) The right of exchange of shares granted by this paragraph to certain corporations shall not preclude the exercise by such corporations of any other right of exchange under this article.

(4) The procedure for the exchange of shares of a subject corporation under this paragraph (g) of this section shall be available where either the subject corporation or the acquiring corporation is a foreign corporation, and, in case the subject corporation is a foreign corporation, where such exchange is permitted by the laws of the jurisdiction under which such foreign corporation is incorporated.

(h) This section does not limit the power of a domestic or foreign corporation to acquire all or part of the shares of one or more classes of another domestic or foreign corporation by means of a voluntary exchange or otherwise.

(i)(1) A binding share exchange pursuant to this section shall constitute a "business combination" pursuant to section nine hundred twelve of this chapter (Requirements relating to certain business combinations) if the subject corporation is a domestic corporation and the acquiring corporation is an "interested shareholder" of the subject corporation, as such term is defined in section nine hundred twelve of this chapter.

(2) With respect to convertible securities and other securities evidencing a right to acquire shares of a subject corporation, a binding share exchange pursuant to this section shall have the same effect on

the rights of the holders of such securities as a merger of the subject corporation.

(3) A binding share exchange pursuant to this section which is effectuated on or after September first, nineteen hundred ninety-one is intended to have the same effect as a "merger" in which the subject corporation is a surviving corporation, within the meaning of any provision of the certificate of incorporation, bylaws or other contract or instrument by which the subject corporation was bound on September first, nineteen hundred eighty-six, unless it is apparent on the face of such instrument that the term "merger" was not intended to include a binding share exchange.

*

THE BANKRUPTCY CODE

THE BANKRUPTCY CODE

SELECTED PROVISIONS

Contents

§ 361. Adequate protection

§ 362. Automatic stay

§ 507. Priorities

§ 1101. Definitions for this chapter

§ 1102. Creditors' and equity security holders' committees

§ 1103. Powers and duties of committees

§ 1104. Appointment of trustee or examiner

§ 1111. Claims and interests

§ 1121. Who may file a plan

§ 1122. Classification of claims or interests

§ 1124. Impairment of claims or interests

§ 1125. Postpetition disclosure and solicitation

§ 1126. Acceptance of plan

§ 1128. Confirmation hearing

§ 1129. Confirmation of plan

§ 361. Adequate protection

When adequate protection is required under section 362, 363, or 364 of this title of an interest of an entity in property, such adequate protection may be provided by—

(1) requiring the trustee to make a cash payment or periodic cash payments to such entity, to the extent that the stay under section 362 of this title, use, sale, or lease under section 363 of this title, or any grant of a lien under section 364 of this title results in a decrease in the value of such entity's interest in such property;

(2) providing to such entity an additional or replacement lien to the extent that such stay, use, sale, lease, or grant results in a decrease in the value of such entity's interest in such property; or

(3) granting such other relief, other than entitling such entity to compensation allowable under section 503(b)(1) of this title as an administrative expense, as will result in the realization by such entity of the indubitable equivalent of such entity's interest in such property.

§ 362. Automatic stay

(a) Except as provided in subsection (b) of this section, a petition filed under section 301, 302, or 303 of this title, or an application filed under section 5(a)(3) of the Securities Investor Protection Act of 1970, operates as a stay, applicable to all entities, of—

(1) the commencement or continuation, including the issuance or employment of process, of a judicial, administrative, or other action or proceeding against the debtor that was or could have been commenced before the commencement of the case under this title, or to recover a claim against the debtor that arose before the commencement of the case under this title;

(2) the enforcement, against the debtor or against property of the estate, of a judgment obtained before the commencement of the case under this title;

(3) any act to obtain possession of property of the estate or of property from the estate or to exercise control over property of the estate;

(4) any act to create, perfect, or enforce any lien against property of the estate;

(5) any act to create, perfect, or enforce against property of the debtor any lien to the extent that such lien secures a claim that arose before the commencement of the case under this title;

(6) any act to collect, assess, or recover a claim against the debtor that arose before the commencement of the case under this title;

(7) the setoff of any debt owing to the debtor that arose before the commencement of the case under this title against any claim against the debtor; and

(8) the commencement or continuation of a proceeding before the United States Tax Court concerning a corporate debtor's tax liability for a taxable period the bankruptcy court may determine or concerning the tax liability of a debtor who is an individual for a taxable period ending before the date of the order for relief under this title.

(b) The filing of a petition under section 301, 302, or 303 of this title, or of an application under section 5(a)(3) of the Securities Investor Protection Act of 1970, does not operate as a stay—

(1) under subsection (a) of this section, of the commencement or continuation of a criminal action or proceeding against the debtor;

(2) under subsection (a)—

(A) of the commencement or continuation of a civil action or proceeding—

(i) for the establishment of paternity;

(ii) for the establishment or modification of an order for domestic support obligations;

(iii) concerning child custody or visitation;

(iv) for the dissolution of a marriage, except to the extent that such proceeding seeks to determine the division of property that is property of the estate; or

(v) regarding domestic violence;

(B) of the collection of a domestic support obligation from property that is not property of the estate;

(C) with respect to the withholding of income that is property of the estate or property of the debtor for payment of a domestic support obligation under a judicial or administrative order or a statute;

(D) of the withholding, suspension, or restriction of a driver's license, a professional or occupational license, or a recreational license, under State law, as specified in section 466(a)(16) of the Social Security Act;

(E) of the reporting of overdue support owed by a parent to any consumer reporting agency as specified in section 466(a)(7) of the Social Security Act;

(F) of the interception of a tax refund, as specified in sections 464 and 466(a)(3) of the Social Security Act or under an analogous State law; or

(G) of the enforcement of a medical obligation, as specified under title IV of the Social Security Act;

(3) under subsection (a) of this section, of any act to perfect, or to maintain or continue the perfection of, an interest in property to the extent that the trustee's rights and powers are subject to such perfection under section 546(b) of this title or to the extent that such act is accomplished within the period provided under section 547(e)(2)(A) of this title;

(4) under paragraph (1), (2), (3), or (6) of subsection (a) of this section, of the commencement or continuation of an action or proceeding by a governmental unit or any organization exercising authority under the Convention on the Prohibition of the Development, Production, Stockpiling and Use of Chemical Weapons and on Their Destruction, opened for signature on January 13, 1993, to enforce such governmental unit's or organization's police and regulatory power, including the enforcement of a judgment other than a money judgment, obtained in an action or proceeding by the governmental unit to enforce such governmental unit's or organization's police or regulatory power;

[(5) Repealed. Pub.L. 105–277, Div. I, Title VI, § 603(1), Oct. 21, 1998, 112 Stat. 2681–886]

(6) under subsection (a) of this section, of the exercise by a commodity broker, forward contract merchant, stockbroker, financial institution, financial participant, or securities clearing agency of any contractual right (as defined in section 555 or 556) under any security agreement or arrangement or other credit enhancement forming a part of or related to any commodity contract, forward contract or securities contract, or of any contractual right (as defined in section 555 or 556) to offset or net out any termination value, payment amount, or other

transfer obligation arising under or in connection with 1 or more such contracts, including any master agreement for such contracts;

(7) under subsection (a) of this section, of the exercise by a repo participant or financial participant of any contractual right (as defined in section 559) under any security agreement or arrangement or other credit enhancement forming a part of or related to any repurchase agreement, or of any contractual right (as defined in section 559) to offset or net out any termination value, payment amount, or other transfer obligation arising under or in connection with 1 or more such agreements, including any master agreement for such agreements;

(8) under subsection (a) of this section, of the commencement of any action by the Secretary of Housing and Urban Development to foreclose a mortgage or deed of trust in any case in which the mortgage or deed of trust held by the Secretary is insured or was formerly insured under the National Housing Act and covers property, or combinations of property, consisting of five or more living units;

(9) under subsection (a), of—

(A) an audit by a governmental unit to determine tax liability;

(B) the issuance to the debtor by a governmental unit of a notice of tax deficiency;

(C) a demand for tax returns; or

(D) the making of an assessment for any tax and issuance of a notice and demand for payment of such an assessment (but any tax lien that would otherwise attach to property of the estate by reason of such an assessment shall not take effect unless such tax is a debt of the debtor that will not be discharged in the case and such property or its proceeds are transferred out of the estate to, or otherwise revested in, the debtor).

(10) under subsection (a) of this section, of any act by a lessor to the debtor under a lease of nonresidential real property that has terminated by the expiration of the stated term of the lease before the commencement of or during a case under this title to obtain possession of such property;

(11) under subsection (a) of this section, of the presentment of a negotiable instrument and the giving of notice of and protesting dishonor of such an instrument;

(12) under subsection (a) of this section, after the date which is 90 days after the filing of such petition, of the commencement or continuation, and conclusion to the entry of final judgment, of an action which involves a debtor subject to reorganization pursuant to chapter 11 of this title and which was brought by the Secretary of Transportation under section 31325 of title 46 (including distribution of any proceeds of sale) to foreclose a preferred ship or fleet mortgage, or a security interest in or relating to a vessel or vessel under construction, held by the Secretary of Transportation under chapter 537 of title 46 or section 109(h) of title 49, or under applicable State law;

(13) under subsection (a) of this section, after the date which is 90 days after the filing of such petition, of the commencement or continuation, and conclusion to the entry of final judgment, of an action which involves a debtor subject to reorganization pursuant to chapter 11 of this title and which was brought by the Secretary of Commerce under section 31325 of title 46 (including distribution of any proceeds of sale) to foreclose a preferred ship or fleet mortgage in a vessel or a mortgage, deed of trust, or other security interest in a fishing facility held by the Secretary of Commerce under chapter 537 of title 46;

(14) under subsection (a) of this section, of any action by an accrediting agency regarding the accreditation status of the debtor as an educational institution;

(15) under subsection (a) of this section, of any action by a State licensing body regarding the licensure of the debtor as an educational institution;

(16) under subsection (a) of this section, of any action by a guaranty agency, as defined in section 435(j) of the Higher Education Act of 1965 or the Secretary of Education regarding the eligibility of the debtor to participate in programs authorized under such Act;

(17) under subsection (a) of this section, of the exercise by a swap participant or financial participant of any contractual right (as defined in section 560) under any security agreement or arrangement or other credit enhancement forming a part of or related to any swap agreement, or of any contractual right (as defined in section 560) to offset or net out any termination value, payment amount, or other transfer obligation arising under or in connection with 1 or more such agreements, including any master agreement for such agreements;

(18) under subsection (a) of the creation or perfection of a statutory lien for an ad valorem property tax, or a special tax or special assessment on real property whether or not ad valorem, imposed by a governmental unit, if such tax or assessment comes due after the date of the filing of the petition;

(19) under subsection (a), of withholding of income from a debtor's wages and collection of amounts withheld, under the debtor's agreement authorizing that withholding and collection for the benefit of a pension, profit-sharing, stock bonus, or other plan established under section 401, 403, 408, 408A, 414, 457, or 501(c) of the Internal Revenue Code of 1986, that is sponsored by the employer of the debtor, or an affiliate, successor, or predecessor of such employer—

(A) to the extent that the amounts withheld and collected are used solely for payments relating to a loan from a plan under section 408(b)(1) of the Employee Retirement Income Security Act of 1974 or is subject to section 72(p) of the Internal Revenue Code of 1986; or

(B) a loan from a thrift savings plan permitted under subchapter III of chapter 84 of title 5, that satisfies the requirements of section 8433(g) of such title;

but nothing in this paragraph may be construed to provide that any loan made under a governmental plan under section 414(d), or a contract or account under section 403(b), of the Internal Revenue Code of 1986 constitutes a claim or a debt under this title;

(20) under subsection (a), of any act to enforce any lien against or security interest in real property following entry of the order under subsection (d)(4) as to such real property in any prior case under this title, for a period of 2 years after the date of the entry of such an order, except that the debtor, in a subsequent case under this title, may move for relief from such order based upon changed circumstances or for other good cause shown, after notice and a hearing;

(21) under subsection (a), of any act to enforce any lien against or security interest in real property—

(A) if the debtor is ineligible under section 109(g) to be a debtor in a case under this title; or

(B) if the case under this title was filed in violation of a bankruptcy court order in a prior case under this title prohibiting the debtor from being a debtor in another case under this title;

(22) subject to subsection (*l*), under subsection (a)(3), of the continuation of any eviction, unlawful detainer action, or similar proceeding by a lessor against a debtor involving residential property in which the debtor resides as a tenant under a lease or rental agreement and with respect to which the lessor has obtained before the date of the filing of the bankruptcy petition, a judgment for possession of such property against the debtor;

(23) subject to subsection (m), under subsection (a)(3), of an eviction action that seeks possession of the residential property in which the debtor resides as a tenant under a lease or rental agreement based on endangerment of such property or the illegal use of controlled substances on such property, but only if the lessor files with the court, and serves upon the debtor, a certification under penalty of perjury that such an eviction action has been filed, or that the debtor, during the 30–day period preceding the date of the filing of the certification, has endangered property or illegally used or allowed to be used a controlled substance on the property;

(24) under subsection (a), of any transfer that is not avoidable under section 544 and that is not avoidable under section 549;

(25) under subsection (a), of—

(A) the commencement or continuation of an investigation or action by a securities self regulatory organization to enforce such organization's regulatory power;

(B) the enforcement of an order or decision, other than for monetary sanctions, obtained in an action by such securities self regulatory organization to enforce such organization's regulatory power; or

(C) any act taken by such securities self regulatory organization to delist, delete, or refuse to permit quotation of any stock that does not meet applicable regulatory requirements;

(26) under subsection (a), of the setoff under applicable nonbankruptcy law of an income tax refund, by a governmental unit, with respect to a taxable period that ended before the date of the order for relief against an income tax liability for a taxable period that also ended before the date of the order for relief, except that in any case in which the setoff of an income tax refund is not permitted under applicable nonbankruptcy law because of a pending action to determine the amount or legality of a tax liability, the governmental unit may hold the refund pending the resolution of the action, unless the court, on the motion of the trustee and after notice and a hearing, grants the taxing authority adequate protection (within the meaning of section 361) for the secured claim of such authority in the setoff under section 506(a);

(27) under subsection (a) of this section, of the exercise by a master netting agreement participant of any contractual right (as defined in section 555, 556, 559, or 560) under any security agreement or arrangement or other credit enhancement forming a part of or related to any master netting agreement, or of any contractual right (as defined in section 555, 556, 559, or 560) to offset or net out any termination value, payment amount, or other transfer obligation arising under or in connection with 1 or more such master netting agreements to the extent that such participant is eligible to exercise such rights under paragraph (6), (7), or (17) for each individual contract covered by the master netting agreement in issue; and

(28) under subsection (a), of the exclusion by the Secretary of Health and Human Services of the debtor from participation in the medicare program or any other Federal health care program (as defined in section 1128B(f) of the Social Security Act pursuant to title XI or XVIII of such Act).

The provisions of paragraphs (12) and (13) of this subsection shall apply with respect to any such petition filed on or before December 31, 1989.

(c) Except as provided in subsections (d), (e), (f), and (h) of this section—

(1) the stay of an act against property of the estate under subsection (a) of this section continues until such property is no longer property of the estate;

(2) the stay of any other act under subsection (a) of this section continues until the earliest of—

(A) the time the case is closed;

(B) the time the case is dismissed; or

(C) if the case is a case under chapter 7 of this title concerning an individual or a case under chapter 9, 11, 12, or 13 of this title, the time a discharge is granted or denied;

(3) if a single or joint case is filed by or against debtor who is an individual in a case under chapter 7, 11, or 13, and if a single or joint case of the debtor was pending within the preceding 1–year period but was dismissed, other than a case refiled under a chapter other than chapter 7 after dismissal under section 707(b)—

(A) the stay under subsection (a) with respect to any action taken with respect to a debt or property securing such debt or with respect to any lease shall terminate with respect to the debtor on the 30th day after the filing of the later case;

(B) on the motion of a party in interest for continuation of the automatic stay and upon notice and a hearing, the court may extend the stay in particular cases as to any or all creditors (subject to such conditions or limitations as the court may then impose) after notice and a hearing completed before the expiration of the 30–day period only if the party in interest demonstrates that the filing of the later case is in good faith as to the creditors to be stayed; and

(C) for purposes of subparagraph (B), a case is presumptively filed not in good faith (but such presumption may be rebutted by clear and convincing evidence to the contrary)—

(i) as to all creditors, if—

(I) more than 1 previous case under any of chapters 7, 11, and 13 in which the individual was a debtor was pending within the preceding 1–year period;

(II) a previous case under any of chapters 7, 11, and 13 in which the individual was a debtor was dismissed within such 1–year period, after the debtor failed to—

(aa) file or amend the petition or other documents as required by this title or the court without substantial excuse (but mere inadvertence or negligence shall not be a substantial excuse unless the dismissal was caused by the negligence of the debtor's attorney);

(bb) provide adequate protection as ordered by the court; or

(cc) perform the terms of a plan confirmed by the court; or

(III) there has not been a substantial change in the financial or personal affairs of the debtor since the dismissal of the next most previous case under chapter 7, 11, or 13 or any other reason to conclude that the later case will be concluded—

(aa) if a case under chapter 7, with a discharge; or

(bb) if a case under chapter 11 or 13, with a confirmed plan that will be fully performed; and

(ii) as to any creditor that commenced an action under subsection (d) in a previous case in which the individual was a debtor if, as of the date of dismissal of such case, that action was still pending or had been resolved by terminating, conditioning, or limiting the stay as to actions of such creditor; and

(4)(A)(i) if a single or joint case is filed by or against a debtor who is an individual under this title, and if 2 or more single or joint cases of the debtor were pending within the previous year but were dismissed, other than a case refiled under section 707(b), the stay under subsection (a) shall not go into effect upon the filing of the later case; and

(ii) on request of a party in interest, the court shall promptly enter an order confirming that no stay is in effect;

(B) if, within 30 days after the filing of the later case, a party in interest requests the court may order the stay to take effect in the case as to any or all creditors (subject to such conditions or limitations as the court may impose), after notice and a hearing, only if the party in interest demonstrates that the filing of the later case is in good faith as to the creditors to be stayed;

(C) a stay imposed under subparagraph (B) shall be effective on the date of the entry of the order allowing the stay to go into effect; and

(D) for purposes of subparagraph (B), a case is presumptively filed not in good faith (but such presumption may be rebutted by clear and convincing evidence to the contrary)—

(i) as to all creditors if—

(I) 2 or more previous cases under this title in which the individual was a debtor were pending within the 1-year period;

(II) a previous case under this title in which the individual was a debtor was dismissed within the time period stated in this paragraph after the debtor failed to file or amend the petition or other documents as required by this title or the court without substantial excuse (but mere inadvertence or negligence shall not be substantial excuse unless the dismissal was caused by the negligence of the debtor's attorney), failed to provide adequate protection as ordered by the court, or failed to perform the terms of a plan confirmed by the court; or

(III) there has not been a substantial change in the financial or personal affairs of the debtor since the dismissal of the next most previous case under this title, or any other reason to conclude that the later case will not be concluded, if a case under chapter 7, with a discharge, and if a case under chapter 11 or 13, with a confirmed plan that will be fully performed; or

(ii) as to any creditor that commenced an action under subsection (d) in a previous case in which the individual was a debtor if, as of the date of dismissal of such case, such action was still pending or had been resolved by terminating, conditioning, or limiting the stay as to such action of such creditor.

(d) On request of a party in interest and after notice and a hearing, the court shall grant relief from the stay provided under subsection (a) of this section, such as by terminating, annulling, modifying, or conditioning such stay—

(1) for cause, including the lack of adequate protection of an interest in property of such party in interest;

(2) with respect to a stay of an act against property under subsection (a) of this section, if—

(A) the debtor does not have an equity in such property; and

(B) such property is not necessary to an effective reorganization;

(3) with respect to a stay of an act against single asset real estate under subsection (a), by a creditor whose claim is secured by an interest in such real estate, unless, not later than the date that is 90 days after the entry of the order for relief (or such later date as the court may determine for cause by order entered within that 90–day period) or 30 days after the court determines that the debtor is subject to this paragraph, whichever is later—

(A) the debtor has filed a plan of reorganization that has a reasonable possibility of being confirmed within a reasonable time; or

(B) the debtor has commenced monthly payments that—

(i) may, in the debtor's sole discretion, notwithstanding section 363(c)(2), be made from rents or other income generated before, on, or after the date of the commencement of the case by or from the property to each creditor whose claim is secured by such real estate (other than a claim secured by a judgment lien or by an unmatured statutory lien); and

(ii) are in an amount equal to interest at the then applicable nondefault contract rate of interest on the value of the creditor's interest in the real estate; or

(4) with respect to a stay of an act against real property under subsection (a), by a creditor whose claim is secured by an interest in such real property, if the court finds that the filing of the petition was part of a scheme to delay, hinder, and defraud creditors that involved either—

(A) transfer of all or part ownership of, or other interest in, such real property without the consent of the secured creditor or court approval; or

(B) multiple bankruptcy filings affecting such real property.

If recorded in compliance with applicable State laws governing notices of interests or liens in real property, an order entered under paragraph (4) shall be binding in any other case under this title purporting to affect such real property filed not later than 2 years after the date of the entry of such order by the court, except that a debtor in a subsequent case under this title may move for relief from such order based upon changed circumstances or for good cause shown, after notice and a hearing. Any Federal, State, or local governmental unit that accepts notices of interests or liens in real property shall accept any certified copy of an order described in this subsection for indexing and recording.

(e)(1) Thirty days after a request under subsection (d) of this section for relief from the stay of any act against property of the estate under subsection (a) of this section, such stay is terminated with respect to the party in interest making such request, unless the court, after notice and a hearing, orders such stay continued in effect pending the conclusion of, or as a result of, a final hearing and determination under subsection (d) of this section. A hearing under this subsection may be a preliminary hearing, or may be consolidated with the final hearing under subsection (d) of this section. The court shall order such stay continued in effect pending the conclusion of the final hearing under subsection (d) of this section if there is a reasonable likelihood that the party opposing relief from such stay will prevail at the conclusion of such final hearing. If the hearing under this subsection is a preliminary hearing, then such final hearing shall be concluded not later than thirty days after the conclusion of such preliminary hearing, unless the 30–day period is extended with the consent of the parties in interest or for a specific time which the court finds is required by compelling circumstances.

(2) Notwithstanding paragraph (1), in a case under chapter 7, 11, or 13 in which the debtor is an individual, the stay under subsection (a) shall terminate on the date that is 60 days after a request is made by a party in interest under subsection (d), unless—

(A) a final decision is rendered by the court during the 60–day period beginning on the date of the request; or

(B) such 60–day period is extended—

(i) by agreement of all parties in interest; or

(ii) by the court for such specific period of time as the court finds is required for good cause, as described in findings made by the court.

(f) Upon request of a party in interest, the court, with or without a hearing, shall grant such relief from the stay provided under subsection (a) of this section as is necessary to prevent irreparable damage to the interest of an entity in property, if such interest will suffer such damage before there is an opportunity for notice and a hearing under subsection (d) or (e) of this section.

(g) In any hearing under subsection (d) or (e) of this section concerning relief from the stay of any act under subsection (a) of this section—

> (1) the party requesting such relief has the burden of proof on the issue of the debtor's equity in property; and

> (2) the party opposing such relief has the burden of proof on all other issues.

(h)(1) In a case in which the debtor is an individual, the stay provided by subsection (a) is terminated with respect to personal property of the estate or of the debtor securing in whole or in part a claim, or subject to an unexpired lease, and such personal property shall no longer be property of the estate if the debtor fails within the applicable time set by section 521(a)(2)—

> (A) to file timely any statement of intention required under section 521(a)(2) with respect to such personal property or to indicate in such statement that the debtor will either surrender such personal property or retain it and, if retaining such personal property, either redeem such personal property pursuant to section 722, enter into an agreement of the kind specified in section 524(c) applicable to the debt secured by such personal property, or assume such unexpired lease pursuant to section 365(p) if the trustee does not do so, as applicable; and

> (B) to take timely the action specified in such statement, as it may be amended before expiration of the period for taking action, unless such statement specifies the debtor's intention to reaffirm such debt on the original contract terms and the creditor refuses to agree to the reaffirmation on such terms.

(2) Paragraph (1) does not apply if the court determines, on the motion of the trustee filed before the expiration of the applicable time set by section 521(a)(2), after notice and a hearing, that such personal property is of consequential value or benefit to the estate, and orders appropriate adequate protection of the creditor's interest, and orders the debtor to deliver any collateral in the debtor's possession to the trustee. If the court does not so determine, the stay provided by subsection (a) shall terminate upon the conclusion of the hearing on the motion.

(i) If a case commenced under chapter 7, 11, or 13 is dismissed due to the creation of a debt repayment plan, for purposes of subsection (c)(3), any subsequent case commenced by the debtor under any such chapter shall not be presumed to be filed not in good faith.

(j) On request of a party in interest, the court shall issue an order under subsection (c) confirming that the automatic stay has been terminated.

(k)(1) Except as provided in paragraph (2), an individual injured by any willful violation of a stay provided by this section shall recover actual damages, including costs and attorneys' fees, and, in appropriate circumstances, may recover punitive damages.

(2) If such violation is based on an action taken by an entity in the good faith belief that subsection (h) applies to the debtor, the recovery under paragraph (1) of this subsection against such entity shall be limited to actual damages.

(*l*)(1) Except as otherwise provided in this subsection, subsection (b) (22) shall apply on the date that is 30 days after the date on which the bankruptcy petition is filed, if the debtor files with the petition and serves upon the lessor a certification under penalty of perjury that—

(A) under nonbankruptcy law applicable in the jurisdiction, there are circumstances under which the debtor would be permitted to cure the entire monetary default that gave rise to the judgment for possession, after that judgment for possession was entered; and

(B) the debtor (or an adult dependent of the debtor) has deposited with the clerk of the court, any rent that would become due during the 30–day period after the filing of the bankruptcy petition.

(2) If, within the 30–day period after the filing of the bankruptcy petition, the debtor (or an adult dependent of the debtor) complies with paragraph (1) and files with the court and serves upon the lessor a further certification under penalty of perjury that the debtor (or an adult dependent of the debtor) has cured, under nonbankruptcy law applicable in the jurisdiction, the entire monetary default that gave rise to the judgment under which possession is sought by the lessor, subsection (b)(22) shall not apply, unless ordered to apply by the court under paragraph (3).

(3)(A) If the lessor files an objection to any certification filed by the debtor under paragraph (1) or (2), and serves such objection upon the debtor, the court shall hold a hearing within 10 days after the filing and service of such objection to determine if the certification filed by the debtor under paragraph (1) or (2) is true.

(B) If the court upholds the objection of the lessor filed under subparagraph (A)—

(i) subsection (b)(22) shall apply immediately and relief from the stay provided under subsection (a)(3) shall not be required to enable the lessor to complete the process to recover full possession of the property; and

(ii) the clerk of the court shall immediately serve upon the lessor and the debtor a certified copy of the court's order upholding the lessor's objection.

(4) If a debtor, in accordance with paragraph (5), indicates on the petition that there was a judgment for possession of the residential

rental property in which the debtor resides and does not file a certification under paragraph (1) or (2)—

    (A) subsection (b)(22) shall apply immediately upon failure to file such certification, and relief from the stay provided under subsection (a)(3) shall not be required to enable the lessor to complete the process to recover full possession of the property; and

    (B) the clerk of the court shall immediately serve upon the lessor and the debtor a certified copy of the docket indicating the absence of a filed certification and the applicability of the exception to the stay under subsection (b)(22).

(5)(A) Where a judgment for possession of residential property in which the debtor resides as a tenant under a lease or rental agreement has been obtained by the lessor, the debtor shall so indicate on the bankruptcy petition and shall provide the name and address of the lessor that obtained that pre-petition judgment on the petition and on any certification filed under this subsection.

    (B) The form of certification filed with the petition, as specified in this subsection, shall provide for the debtor to certify, and the debtor shall certify—

        (i) whether a judgment for possession of residential rental housing in which the debtor resides has been obtained against the debtor before the date of the filing of the petition; and

        (ii) whether the debtor is claiming under paragraph (1) that under nonbankruptcy law applicable in the jurisdiction, there are circumstances under which the debtor would be permitted to cure the entire monetary default that gave rise to the judgment for possession, after that judgment of possession was entered, and has made the appropriate deposit with the court.

    (C) The standard forms (electronic and otherwise) used in a bankruptcy proceeding shall be amended to reflect the requirements of this subsection.

    (D) The clerk of the court shall arrange for the prompt transmittal of the rent deposited in accordance with paragraph (1)(B) to the lessor.

(m)(1) Except as otherwise provided in this subsection, subsection (b)(23) shall apply on the date that is 15 days after the date on which the lessor files and serves a certification described in subsection (b)(23).

    (2)(A) If the debtor files with the court an objection to the truth or legal sufficiency of the certification described in subsection (b)(23) and serves such objection upon the lessor, subsection (b)(23) shall not apply, unless ordered to apply by the court under this subsection.

    (B) If the debtor files and serves the objection under subparagraph (A), the court shall hold a hearing within 10 days after the filing and service of such objection to determine if the situation giving rise to the lessor's certification under paragraph (1) existed or has been remedied.

(C) If the debtor can demonstrate to the satisfaction of the court that the situation giving rise to the lessor's certification under paragraph (1) did not exist or has been remedied, the stay provided under subsection (a)(3) shall remain in effect until the termination of the stay under this section.

(D) If the debtor cannot demonstrate to the satisfaction of the court that the situation giving rise to the lessor's certification under paragraph (1) did not exist or has been remedied—

(i) relief from the stay provided under subsection (a)(3) shall not be required to enable the lessor to proceed with the eviction; and

(ii) the clerk of the court shall immediately serve upon the lessor and the debtor a certified copy of the court's order upholding the lessor's certification.

(3) If the debtor fails to file, within 15 days, an objection under paragraph (2)(A)—

(A) subsection (b)(23) shall apply immediately upon such failure and relief from the stay provided under subsection (a)(3) shall not be required to enable the lessor to complete the process to recover full possession of the property; and

(B) the clerk of the court shall immediately serve upon the lessor and the debtor a certified copy of the docket indicating such failure.

(n)(1) Except as provided in paragraph (2), subsection (a) does not apply in a case in which the debtor—

(A) is a debtor in a small business case pending at the time the petition is filed;

(B) was a debtor in a small business case that was dismissed for any reason by an order that became final in the 2–year period ending on the date of the order for relief entered with respect to the petition;

(C) was a debtor in a small business case in which a plan was confirmed in the 2–year period ending on the date of the order for relief entered with respect to the petition; or

(D) is an entity that has acquired substantially all of the assets or business of a small business debtor described in subparagraph (A), (B), or (C), unless such entity establishes by a preponderance of the evidence that such entity acquired substantially all of the assets or business of such small business debtor in good faith and not for the purpose of evading this paragraph.

(2) Paragraph (1) does not apply—

(A) to an involuntary case involving no collusion by the debtor with creditors; or

(B) to the filing of a petition if—

(i) the debtor proves by a preponderance of the evidence that the filing of the petition resulted from circumstances beyond the control of the debtor not foreseeable at the time the case then pending was filed; and

(ii) it is more likely than not that the court will confirm a feasible plan, but not a liquidating plan, within a reasonable period of time.

(o) The exercise of rights not subject to the stay arising under subsection (a) pursuant to paragraph (6), (7), (17), or (27) of subsection (b) shall not be stayed by any order of a court or administrative agency in any proceeding under this title.

§ 507. Priorities

(a) The following expenses and claims have priority in the following order:

(1) First:

(A) Allowed unsecured claims for domestic support obligations that, as of the date of the filing of the petition in a case under this title, are owed to or recoverable by a spouse, former spouse, or child of the debtor, or such child's parent, legal guardian, or responsible relative, without regard to whether the claim is filed by such person or is filed by a governmental unit on behalf of such person, on the condition that funds received under this paragraph by a governmental unit under this title after the date of the filing of the petition shall be applied and distributed in accordance with applicable nonbankruptcy law.

(B) Subject to claims under subparagraph (A), allowed unsecured claims for domestic support obligations that, as of the date of the filing of the petition, are assigned by a spouse, former spouse, child of the debtor, or such child's parent, legal guardian, or responsible relative to a governmental unit (unless such obligation is assigned voluntarily by the spouse, former spouse, child, parent, legal guardian, or responsible relative of the child for the purpose of collecting the debt) or are owed directly to or recoverable by a governmental unit under applicable nonbankruptcy law, on the condition that funds received under this paragraph by a governmental unit under this title after the date of the filing of the petition be applied and distributed in accordance with applicable nonbankruptcy law.

(C) If a trustee is appointed or elected under section 701, 702, 703, 1104, 1202, or 1302, the administrative expenses of the trustee allowed under paragraphs (1)(A), (2), and (6) of section 503(b) shall be paid before payment of claims under subparagraphs (A) and (B), to the extent that the trustee administers assets that are otherwise available for the payment of such claims.

(2) Second, administrative expenses allowed under section 503(b) of this title, and any fees and charges assessed against the estate under chapter 123 of title 28.

(3) Third, unsecured claims allowed under section 502(f) of this title.

(4) Fourth, allowed unsecured claims, but only to the extent of $10,950 for each individual or corporation, as the case may be, earned within 180 days before the date of the filing of the petition or the date of the cessation of the debtor's business, whichever occurs first, for—

    (A) wages, salaries, or commissions, including vacation, severance, and sick leave pay earned by an individual; or

    (B) sales commissions earned by an individual or by a corporation with only 1 employee, acting as an independent contractor in the sale of goods or services for the debtor in the ordinary course of the debtor's business if, and only if, during the 12 months preceding that date, at least 75 percent of the amount that the individual or corporation earned by acting as an independent contractor in the sale of goods or services was earned from the debtor.

(5) Fifth, allowed unsecured claims for contributions to an employee benefit plan—

    (A) arising from services rendered within 180 days before the date of the filing of the petition or the date of the cessation of the debtor's business, whichever occurs first; but only

    (B) for each such plan, to the extent of—

        (i) the number of employees covered by each such plan multiplied by $10,950; less

        (ii) the aggregate amount paid to such employees under paragraph (4) of this subsection, plus the aggregate amount paid by the estate on behalf of such employees to any other employee benefit plan.

(6) Sixth, allowed unsecured claims of persons—

    (A) engaged in the production or raising of grain, as defined in section 557(b) of this title, against a debtor who owns or operates a grain storage facility, as defined in section 557(b) of this title, for grain or the proceeds of grain, or

    (B) engaged as a United States fisherman against a debtor who has acquired fish or fish produce from a fisherman through a sale or conversion, and who is engaged in operating a fish produce storage or processing facility—

but only to the extent of $5,400 for each such individual.

(7) Seventh, allowed unsecured claims of individuals, to the extent of $2,425 for each such individual, arising from the deposit, before the commencement of the case, of money in connection with the purchase, lease, or rental of property, or the purchase of services, for the

personal, family, or household use of such individuals, that were not delivered or provided.

(8) Eighth, allowed unsecured claims of governmental units, only to the extent that such claims are for—

(A) a tax on or measured by income or gross receipts for a taxable year ending on or before the date of the filing of the petition—

(i) for which a return, if required, is last due, including extensions, after three years before the date of the filing of the petition;

(ii) assessed within 240 days before the date of the filing of the petition, exclusive of—

(I) any time during which an offer in compromise with respect to that tax was pending or in effect during that 240–day period, plus 30 days; and

(II) any time during which a stay of proceedings against collections was in effect in a prior case under this title during that 240–day period, plus 90 days.

(iii) other than a tax of a kind specified in section 523(a)(1)(B) or 523(a)(1)(C) of this title, not assessed before, but assessable, under applicable law or by agreement, after, the commencement of the case;

(B) a property tax incurred before the commencement of the case and last payable without penalty after one year before the date of the filing of the petition;

(C) a tax required to be collected or withheld and for which the debtor is liable in whatever capacity;

(D) an employment tax on a wage, salary, or commission of a kind specified in paragraph (4) of this subsection earned from the debtor before the date of the filing of the petition, whether or not actually paid before such date, for which a return is last due, under applicable law or under any extension, after three years before the date of the filing of the petition;

(E) an excise tax on—

(i) a transaction occurring before the date of the filing of the petition for which a return, if required, is last due, under applicable law or under any extension, after three years before the date of the filing of the petition; or

(ii) if a return is not required, a transaction occurring during the three years immediately preceding the date of the filing of the petition;

(F) a customs duty arising out of the importation of merchandise—

(i) entered for consumption within one year before the date of the filing of the petition;

(ii) covered by an entry liquidated or reliquidated within one year before the date of the filing of the petition; or

(iii) entered for consumption within four years before the date of the filing of the petition but unliquidated on such date, if the Secretary of the Treasury certifies that failure to liquidate such entry was due to an investigation pending on such date into assessment of antidumping or countervailing duties or fraud, or if information needed for the proper appraisement or classification of such merchandise was not available to the appropriate customs officer before such date; or

(G) a penalty related to a claim of a kind specified in this paragraph and in compensation for actual pecuniary loss.

An otherwise applicable time period specified in this paragraph shall be suspended for any period during which a governmental unit is prohibited under applicable nonbankruptcy law from collecting a tax as a result of a request by the debtor for a hearing and an appeal of any collection action taken or proposed against the debtor, plus 90 days; plus any time during which the stay of proceedings was in effect in a prior case under this title or during which collection was precluded by the existence of 1 or more confirmed plans under this title, plus 90 days.

(9) Ninth, allowed unsecured claims based upon any commitment by the debtor to a Federal depository institutions regulatory agency (or predecessor to such agency) to maintain the capital of an insured depository institution.

(10) Tenth, allowed claims for death or personal injury resulting from the operation of a motor vehicle or vessel if such operation was unlawful because the debtor was intoxicated from using alcohol, a drug, or another substance.

(b) If the trustee, under section 362, 363, or 364 of this title, provides adequate protection of the interest of a holder of a claim secured by a lien on property of the debtor and if, notwithstanding such protection, such creditor has a claim allowable under subsection (a)(2) of this section arising from the stay of action against such property under section 362 of this title, from the use, sale, or lease of such property under section 363 of this title, or from the granting of a lien under section 364(d) of this title, then such creditor's claim under such subsection shall have priority over every other claim allowable under such subsection.

(c) For the purpose of subsection (a) of this section, a claim of a governmental unit arising from an erroneous refund or credit of a tax has the same priority as a claim for the tax to which such refund or credit relates.

(d) An entity that is subrogated to the rights of a holder of a claim of a kind specified in subsection (a)(1), (a)(4), (a)(5), (a)(6), (a)(7), (a)(8), or (a)(9) of this section is not subrogated to the right of the holder of such claim to priority under such subsection.

§ 1101.   Definitions for this chapter

In this chapter—

(1) "debtor in possession" means debtor except when a person that has qualified under section 322 of this title is serving as trustee in the case;

(2) "substantial consummation" means—

(A) transfer of all or substantially all of the property proposed by the plan to be transferred;

(B) assumption by the debtor or by the successor to the debtor under the plan of the business or of the management of all or substantially all of the property dealt with by the plan; and

(C) commencement of distribution under the plan.

§ 1102.   Creditors' and equity security holders' committees

(a)(1) Except as provided in paragraph (3), as soon as practicable after the order for relief under chapter 11 of this title, the United States trustee shall appoint a committee of creditors holding unsecured claims and may appoint additional committees of creditors or of equity security holders as the United States trustee deems appropriate.

(2) On request of a party in interest, the court may order the appointment of additional committees of creditors or of equity security holders if necessary to assure adequate representation of creditors or of equity security holders. The United States trustee shall appoint any such committee.

(3) On request of a party in interest in a case in which the debtor is a small business debtor and for cause, the court may order that a committee of creditors not be appointed.

(4) On request of a party in interest and after notice and a hearing, the court may order the United States trustee to change the membership of a committee appointed under this subsection, if the court determines that the change is necessary to ensure adequate representation of creditors or equity security holders. The court may order the United States trustee to increase the number of members of a committee to include a creditor that is a small business concern (as described in section 3(a)(1) of the Small Business Act), if the court determines that the creditor holds claims (of the kind represented by the committee) the aggregate amount of which, in comparison to the annual gross revenue of that creditor, is disproportionately large.

(b)(1) A committee of creditors appointed under subsection (a) of this section shall ordinarily consist of the persons, willing to serve, that hold the seven largest claims against the debtor of the kinds represented on such committee, or of the members of a committee organized by creditors before the commencement of the case under this chapter, if such committee was fairly chosen and is representative of the different kinds of claims to be represented.

(2) A committee of equity security holders appointed under subsection (a)(2) of this section shall ordinarily consist of the persons, willing to serve, that hold the seven largest amounts of equity securities of the debtor of the kinds represented on such committee.

(3) A committee appointed under subsection (a) shall—

(A) provide access to information for creditors who—

(i) hold claims of the kind represented by that committee; and

(ii) are not appointed to the committee;

(B) solicit and receive comments from the creditors described in subparagraph (A); and

(C) be subject to a court order that compels any additional report or disclosure to be made to the creditors described in subparagraph (A).

§ 1103.   Powers and duties of committees

(a) At a scheduled meeting of a committee appointed under section 1102 of this title, at which a majority of the members of such committee are present, and with the court's approval, such committee may select and authorize the employment by such committee of one or more attorneys, accountants, or other agents, to represent or perform services for such committee.

(b) An attorney or accountant employed to represent a committee appointed under section 1102 of this title may not, while employed by such committee, represent any other entity having an adverse interest in connection with the case. Representation of one or more creditors of the same class as represented by the committee shall not per se constitute the representation of an adverse interest.

(c) A committee appointed under section 1102 of this title may—

(1) consult with the trustee or debtor in possession concerning the administration of the case;

(2) investigate the acts, conduct, assets, liabilities, and financial condition of the debtor, the operation of the debtor's business and the desirability of the continuance of such business, and any other matter relevant to the case or to the formulation of a plan;

(3) participate in the formulation of a plan, advise those represented by such committee of such committee's determinations as to any plan formulated, and collect and file with the court acceptances or rejections of a plan;

(4) request the appointment of a trustee or examiner under section 1104 of this title; and

(5) perform such other services as are in the interest of those represented.

(d) As soon as practicable after the appointment of a committee under section 1102 of this title, the trustee shall meet with such committee to transact such business as may be necessary and proper.

§ 1104. Appointment of trustee or examiner

(a) At any time after the commencement of the case but before confirmation of a plan, on request of a party in interest or the United States trustee, and after notice and a hearing, the court shall order the appointment of a trustee—

(1) for cause, including fraud, dishonesty, incompetence, or gross mismanagement of the affairs of the debtor by current management, either before or after the commencement of the case, or similar cause, but not including the number of holders of securities of the debtor or the amount of assets or liabilities of the debtor;

(2) if such appointment is in the interests of creditors, any equity security holders, and other interests of the estate, without regard to the number of holders of securities of the debtor or the amount of assets or liabilities of the debtor; or

(3) if grounds exist to convert or dismiss the case under section 1112, but the court determines that the appointment of a trustee or an examiner is in the best interests of creditors and the estate.

(b)(1) Except as provided in section 1163 of this title, on the request of a party in interest made not later than 30 days after the court orders the appointment of a trustee under subsection (a), the United States trustee shall convene a meeting of creditors for the purpose of electing one disinterested person to serve as trustee in the case. The election of a trustee shall be conducted in the manner provided in subsections (a), (b), and (c) of section 702 of this title.

(2)(A) If an eligible, disinterested trustee is elected at a meeting of creditors under paragraph (1), the United States trustee shall file a report certifying that election.

(B) Upon the filing of a report under subparagraph (A)—

(i) the trustee elected under paragraph (1) shall be considered to have been selected and appointed for purposes of this section; and

(ii) the service of any trustee appointed under subsection (d) shall terminate.

(C) The court shall resolve any dispute arising out of an election described in subparagraph (A).

(c) If the court does not order the appointment of a trustee under this section, then at any time before the confirmation of a plan, on request of a party in interest or the United States trustee, and after notice and a hearing, the court shall order the appointment of an examiner to conduct such an investigation of the debtor as is appropriate, including an investigation of any allegations of fraud, dishonesty, incompetence, misconduct, mismanagement, or irregularity in the management of the affairs of the debtor of or by current or former management of the debtor, if—

(1) such appointment is in the interests of creditors, any equity security holders, and other interests of the estate; or

(2) the debtor's fixed, liquidated, unsecured debts, other than debts for goods, services, or taxes, or owing to an insider, exceed $5,000,000.

(d) If the court orders the appointment of a trustee or an examiner, if a trustee or an examiner dies or resigns during the case or is removed under section 324 of this title, or if a trustee fails to qualify under section 322 of this title, then the United States trustee, after consultation with parties in interest, shall appoint, subject to the court's approval, one disinterested person other than the United States trustee to serve as trustee or examiner, as the case may be, in the case.

(e) The United States trustee shall move for the appointment of a trustee under subsection (a) if there are reasonable grounds to suspect that current members of the governing body of the debtor, the debtor's chief executive or chief financial officer, or members of the governing body who selected the debtor's chief executive or chief financial officer, participated in actual fraud, dishonesty, or criminal conduct in the management of the debtor or the debtor's public financial reporting.

§ 1111. Claims and interests

(a) A proof of claim or interest is deemed filed under section 501 of this title for any claim or interest that appears in the schedules filed under section 521(1) or 1106(a)(2) of this title, except a claim or interest that is scheduled as disputed, contingent, or unliquidated.

(b)(1)(A) A claim secured by a lien on property of the estate shall be allowed or disallowed under section 502 of this title the same as if the holder of such claim had recourse against the debtor on account of such claim, whether or not such holder has such recourse, unless—

(i) the class of which such claim is a part elects, by at least two-thirds in amount and more than half in number of allowed claims of such class, application of paragraph (2) of this subsection; or

(ii) such holder does not have such recourse and such property is sold under section 363 of this title or is to be sold under the plan.

(B) A class of claims may not elect application of paragraph (2) of this subsection if—

(i) the interest on account of such claims of the holders of such claims in such property is of inconsequential value; or

(ii) the holder of a claim of such class has recourse against the debtor on account of such claim and such property is sold under section 363 of this title or is to be sold under the plan.

(2) If such an election is made, then notwithstanding section 506(a) of this title, such claim is a secured claim to the extent that such claim is allowed.

§ 1121.   Who may file a plan

(a) The debtor may file a plan with a petition commencing a voluntary case, or at any time in a voluntary case or an involuntary case.

(b) Except as otherwise provided in this section, only the debtor may file a plan until after 120 days after the date of the order for relief under this chapter.

(c) Any party in interest, including the debtor, the trustee, a creditors' committee, an equity security holders' committee, a creditor, an equity security holder, or any indenture trustee, may file a plan if and only if—

(1) a trustee has been appointed under this chapter;

(2) the debtor has not filed a plan before 120 days after the date of the order for relief under this chapter; or

(3) the debtor has not filed a plan that has been accepted, before 180 days after the date of the order for relief under this chapter, by each class of claims or interests that is impaired under the plan.

(d)(1) Subject to paragraph (2), on request of a party in interest made within the respective periods specified in subsections (b) and (c) of this section and after notice and a hearing, the court may for cause reduce or increase the 120–day period or the 180–day period referred to in this section.

(2)(A) The 120–day period specified in paragraph (1) may not be extended beyond a date that is 18 months after the date of the order for relief under this chapter.

(B) The 180–day period specified in paragraph (1) may not be extended beyond a date that is 20 months after the date of the order for relief under this chapter.

(e) In a small business case—

(1) only the debtor may file a plan until after 180 days after the date of the order for relief, unless that period is—

(A) extended as provided by this subsection, after notice and a hearing; or

(B) the court, for cause, orders otherwise;

(2) the plan and a disclosure statement (if any) shall be filed not later than 300 days after the date of the order for relief; and

(3) the time periods specified in paragraphs (1) and (2), and the time fixed in section 1129(e) within which the plan shall be confirmed, may be extended only if—

(A) the debtor, after providing notice to parties in interest (including the United States trustee), demonstrates by a preponderance of the evidence that it is more likely than not that the court will confirm a plan within a reasonable period of time;

(B) a new deadline is imposed at the time the extension is granted; and

(C) the order extending time is signed before the existing deadline has expired.

§ 1122. Classification of claims or interests

(a) Except as provided in subsection (b) of this section, a plan may place a claim or an interest in a particular class only if such claim or interest is substantially similar to the other claims or interests of such class.

(b) A plan may designate a separate class of claims consisting only of every unsecured claim that is less than or reduced to an amount that the court approves as reasonable and necessary for administrative convenience.

§ 1123. Contents of plan

(a) Notwithstanding any otherwise applicable nonbankruptcy law, a plan shall—

(1) designate, subject to section 1122 of this title, classes of claims, other than claims of a kind specified in section 507(a)(2), 507(a)(3), or 507(a)(8) of this title, and classes of interests;

(2) specify any class of claims or interests that is not impaired under the plan;

(3) specify the treatment of any class of claims or interests that is impaired under the plan;

(4) provide the same treatment for each claim or interest of a particular class, unless the holder of a particular claim or interest agrees to a less favorable treatment of such particular claim or interest;

(5) provide adequate means for the plan's implementation, such as—

(A) retention by the debtor of all or any part of the property of the estate;

(B) transfer of all or any part of the property of the estate to one or more entities, whether organized before or after the confirmation of such plan;

(C) merger or consolidation of the debtor with one or more persons;

(D) sale of all or any part of the property of the estate, either subject to or free of any lien, or the distribution of all or any part of the property of the estate among those having an interest in such property of the estate;

(E) satisfaction or modification of any lien;

(F) cancellation or modification of any indenture or similar instrument;

(G) curing or waiving of any default;

(H) extension of a maturity date or a change in an interest rate or other term of outstanding securities;

(I) amendment of the debtor's charter; or

(J) issuance of securities of the debtor, or of any entity referred to in subparagraph (B) or (C) of this paragraph, for cash, for property, for existing securities, or in exchange for claims or interests, or for any other appropriate purpose;

(6) provide for the inclusion in the charter of the debtor, if the debtor is a corporation, or of any corporation referred to in paragraph (5)(B) or (5)(C) of this subsection, of a provision prohibiting the issuance of nonvoting equity securities, and providing, as to the several classes of securities possessing voting power, an appropriate distribution of such power among such classes, including, in the case of any class of equity securities having a preference over another class of equity securities with respect to dividends, adequate provisions for the election of directors representing such preferred class in the event of default in the payment of such dividends;

(7) contain only provisions that are consistent with the interests of creditors and equity security holders and with public policy with respect to the manner of selection of any officer, director, or trustee under the plan and any successor to such officer, director, or trustee; and

(8) in a case in which the debtor is an individual, provide for the payment to creditors under the plan of all or such portion of earnings from personal services performed by the debtor after the commencement of the case or other future income of the debtor as is necessary for the execution of the plan.

(b) Subject to subsection (a) of this section, a plan may—

(1) impair or leave unimpaired any class of claims, secured or unsecured, or of interests;

(2) subject to section 365 of this title, provide for the assumption, rejection, or assignment of any executory contract or unexpired lease of the debtor not previously rejected under such section;

(3) provide for—

(A) the settlement or adjustment of any claim or interest belonging to the debtor or to the estate; or

(B) the retention and enforcement by the debtor, by the trustee, or by a representative of the estate appointed for such purpose, of any such claim or interest;

(4) provide for the sale of all or substantially all of the property of the estate, and the distribution of the proceeds of such sale among holders of claims or interests;

(5) modify the rights of holders of secured claims, other than a claim secured only by a security interest in real property that is the debtor's principal residence, or of holders of unsecured claims, or leave unaffected the rights of holders of any class of claims; and

(6) include any other appropriate provision not inconsistent with the applicable provisions of this title.

(c) In a case concerning an individual, a plan proposed by an entity other than the debtor may not provide for the use, sale, or lease of property exempted under section 522 of this title, unless the debtor consents to such use, sale, or lease.

(d) Notwithstanding subsection (a) of this section and sections 506(b), 1129(a)(7), and 1129(b) of this title, if it is proposed in a plan to cure a default the amount necessary to cure the default shall be determined in accordance with the underlying agreement and applicable nonbankruptcy law.

§ 1124.   Impairment of claims or interests

Except as provided in section 1123(a)(4) of this title, a class of claims or interests is impaired under a plan unless, with respect to each claim or interest of such class, the plan–

(1) leaves unaltered the legal, equitable, and contractual rights to which such claim or interest entitles the holder of such claim or interest; or

(2) notwithstanding any contractual provision or applicable law that entitles the holder of such claim or interest to demand or receive accelerated payment of such claim or interest after the occurrence of a default—

(A) cures any such default that occurred before or after the commencement of the case under this title, other than a default of a kind specified in section 365(b)(2) of this title or of a kind that section 365(b)(2) expressly does not require to be cured;

(B) reinstates the maturity of such claim or interest as such maturity existed before such default;

(C) compensates the holder of such claim or interest for any damages incurred as a result of any reasonable reliance by such holder on such contractual provision or such applicable law;

(D) if such claim or such interest arises from any failure to perform a nonmonetary obligation, other than a default arising from failure to operate a nonresidential real property lease subject to section 365(b)(1)(A), compensates the holder of such claim or such interest (other than the debtor or an insider) for any actual pecuniary loss incurred by such holder as a result of such failure; and

(E) does not otherwise alter the legal, equitable, or contractual rights to which such claim or interest entitles the holder of such claim or interest.

§ 1125. Postpetition disclosure and solicitation

(a) In this section—

(1) "adequate information" means information of a kind, and in sufficient detail, as far as is reasonably practicable in light of the nature and history of the debtor and the condition of the debtor's books and records, including a discussion of the potential material Federal tax consequences of the plan to the debtor, any successor to the debtor, and a hypothetical investor typical of the holders of claims or interests in the case, that would enable such a hypothetical investor of the relevant class to make an informed judgment about the plan, but adequate information need not include such information about any other possible or proposed plan and in determining whether a disclosure statement provides adequate information, the court shall consider the complexity of the case, the benefit of additional information to creditors and other parties in interest, and the cost of providing additional information; and

(2) "investor typical of holders of claims or interests of the relevant class" means investor having—

(A) a claim or interest of the relevant class;

(B) such a relationship with the debtor as the holders of other claims or interests of such class generally have; and

(C) such ability to obtain such information from sources other than the disclosure required by this section as holders of claims or interests in such class generally have.

(b) An acceptance or rejection of a plan may not be solicited after the commencement of the case under this title from a holder of a claim or interest with respect to such claim or interest, unless, at the time of or before such solicitation, there is transmitted to such holder the plan or a summary of the plan, and a written disclosure statement approved, after notice and a hearing, by the court as containing adequate information. The court may approve a disclosure statement without a valuation of the debtor or an appraisal of the debtor's assets.

(c) The same disclosure statement shall be transmitted to each holder of a claim or interest of a particular class, but there may be transmitted different disclosure statements, differing in amount, detail, or kind of information, as between classes.

(d) Whether a disclosure statement required under subsection (b) of this section contains adequate information is not governed by any otherwise applicable nonbankruptcy law, rule, or regulation, but an agency or official whose duty is to administer or enforce such a law, rule, or regulation may be heard on the issue of whether a disclosure statement contains adequate information. Such an agency or official may not appeal from, or otherwise seek review of, an order approving a disclosure statement.

(e) A person that solicits acceptance or rejection of a plan, in good faith and in compliance with the applicable provisions of this title, or that participates, in good faith and in compliance with the applicable provisions of this title, in the offer, issuance, sale, or purchase of a security, offered or sold under the plan, of the debtor, of an affiliate participating in a joint plan with the debtor, or of a newly organized successor to the debtor under the plan, is not liable, on account of such solicitation or participation, for violation of any applicable law, rule, or regulation governing solicitation of acceptance or rejection of a plan or the offer, issuance, sale, or purchase of securities.

(f) Notwithstanding subsection (b), in a small business case—

(1) the court may determine that the plan itself provides adequate information and that a separate disclosure statement is not necessary;

(2) the court may approve a disclosure statement submitted on standard forms approved by the court or adopted under section 2075 of title 28; and

(3)(A) the court may conditionally approve a disclosure statement subject to final approval after notice and a hearing;

(B) acceptances and rejections of a plan may be solicited based on a conditionally approved disclosure statement if the debtor provides adequate information to each holder of a claim or interest that is solicited, but a conditionally approved disclosure statement shall be mailed not later than 25 days before the date of the hearing on confirmation of the plan; and

(C) the hearing on the disclosure statement may be combined with the hearing on confirmation of a plan.

(g) Notwithstanding subsection (b), an acceptance or rejection of the plan may be solicited from a holder of a claim or interest if such solicitation complies with applicable nonbankruptcy law and if such holder was solicited before the commencement of the case in a manner complying with applicable nonbankruptcy law.

§ 1126. Acceptance of plan

(a) The holder of a claim or interest allowed under section 502 of this title may accept or reject a plan. If the United States is a creditor or equity security holder, the Secretary of the Treasury may accept or reject the plan on behalf of the United States.

(b) For the purposes of subsections (c) and (d) of this section, a holder of a claim or interest that has accepted or rejected the plan before the commencement of the case under this title is deemed to have accepted or rejected such plan, as the case may be, if—

(1) the solicitation of such acceptance or rejection was in compliance with any applicable nonbankruptcy law, rule, or regulation gov-

erning the adequacy of disclosure in connection with such solicitation; or

(2) if there is not any such law, rule, or regulation, such acceptance or rejection was solicited after disclosure to such holder of adequate information, as defined in section 1125(a) of this title.

Creditor

(c) A class of claims has accepted a plan if such plan has been accepted by creditors, other than any entity designated under subsection (e) of this section, that hold at least two-thirds in amount and more than one-half in number of the allowed claims of such class held by creditors, other than any entity designated under subsection (e) of this section, that have accepted or rejected such plan.

equity

(d) A class of interests has accepted a plan if such plan has been accepted by holders of such interests, other than any entity designated under subsection (e) of this section, that hold at least two-thirds in amount of the allowed interests of such class held by holders of such interests, other than any entity designated under subsection (e) of this section, that have accepted or rejected such plan.

(e) On request of a party in interest, and after notice and a hearing, the court may designate any entity whose acceptance or rejection of such plan was not in good faith, or was not solicited or procured in good faith or in accordance with the provisions of this title.

(f) Notwithstanding any other provision of this section, a class that is not impaired under a plan, and each holder of a claim or interest of such class, are conclusively presumed to have accepted the plan, and solicitation of acceptances with respect to such class from the holders of claims or interests of such class is not required.

(g) Notwithstanding any other provision of this section, a class is deemed not to have accepted a plan if such plan provides that the claims or interests of such class do not entitle the holders of such claims or interests to receive or retain any property under the plan on account of such claims or interests.

§ 1128.   Confirmation hearing

(a) After notice, the court shall hold a hearing on confirmation of a plan.

(b) A party in interest may object to confirmation of a plan.

§ 1129.   Confirmation of plan

(a) The court shall confirm a plan only if all of the following requirements are met:

(1) The plan complies with the applicable provisions of this title.

(2) The proponent of the plan complies with the applicable provisions of this title.

(3) The plan has been proposed in good faith and not by any means forbidden by law.

(4) Any payment made or to be made by the proponent, by the debtor, or by a person issuing securities or acquiring property under the plan, for services or for costs and expenses in or in connection with the case, or in connection with the plan and incident to the case, has been approved by, or is subject to the approval of, the court as reasonable.

(5)(A)(i) The proponent of the plan has disclosed the identity and affiliations of any individual proposed to serve, after confirmation of the plan, as a director, officer, or voting trustee of the debtor, an affiliate of the debtor participating in a joint plan with the debtor, or a successor to the debtor under the plan; and

   (ii) the appointment to, or continuance in, such office of such individual, is consistent with the interests of creditors and equity security holders and with public policy; and

(B) the proponent of the plan has disclosed the identity of any insider that will be employed or retained by the reorganized debtor, and the nature of any compensation for such insider.

(6) Any governmental regulatory commission with jurisdiction, after confirmation of the plan, over the rates of the debtor has approved any rate change provided for in the plan, or such rate change is expressly conditioned on such approval.

(7) With respect to each impaired class of claims or interests—

(A) each holder of a claim or interest of such class—

   (i) has accepted the plan; or

   (ii) will receive or retain under the plan on account of such claim or interest property of a value, as of the effective date of the plan, that is not less than the amount that such holder would so receive or retain if the debtor were liquidated under chapter 7 of this title on such date; or

(B) if section 1111(b)(2) of this title applies to the claims of such class, each holder of a claim of such class will receive or retain under the plan on account of such claim property of a value, as of the effective date of the plan, that is not less than the value of such holder's interest in the estate's interest in the property that secures such claims.

(8) With respect to each class of claims or interests—

(A) such class has accepted the plan; or

(B) such class is not impaired under the plan.

(9) Except to the extent that the holder of a particular claim has agreed to a different treatment of such claim, the plan provides that—

(A) with respect to a claim of a kind specified in section 507(a)(2) or 507(a)(3) of this title, on the effective date of the plan, the holder of such claim will receive on account of such claim cash equal to the allowed amount of such claim;

(B) with respect to a class of claims of a kind specified in section 507(a)(1), 507(a)(4), 507(a)(5), 507(a)(6), or 507(a)(7) of this title, each holder of a claim of such class will receive—

(i) if such class has accepted the plan, deferred cash payments of a value, as of the effective date of the plan, equal to the allowed amount of such claim; or

(ii) if such class has not accepted the plan, cash on the effective date of the plan equal to the allowed amount of such claim;

(C) with respect to a claim of a kind specified in section 507(a)(8) of this title, the holder of such claim will receive on account of such claim regular installment payments in cash—

(i) of a total value, as of the effective date of the plan, equal to the allowed amount of such claim;

(ii) over a period ending not later than 5 years after the date of the order for relief under section 301, 302, or 303; and

(iii) in a manner not less favorable than the most favored nonpriority unsecured claim provided for by the plan (other than cash payments made to a class of creditors under section 1122(b)); and

(D) with respect to a secured claim which would otherwise meet the description of an unsecured claim of a governmental unit under section 507(a)(8), but for the secured status of that claim, the holder of that claim will receive on account of that claim, cash payments, in the same manner and over the same period, as prescribed in subparagraph (C).

(10) If a class of claims is impaired under the plan, at least one class of claims that is impaired under the plan has accepted the plan, determined without including any acceptance of the plan by any insider.

(11) Confirmation of the plan is not likely to be followed by the liquidation, or the need for further financial reorganization, of the debtor or any successor to the debtor under the plan, unless such liquidation or reorganization is proposed in the plan.

(12) All fees payable under section 1930 of title 28, as determined by the court at the hearing on confirmation of the plan, have been paid or the plan provides for the payment of all such fees on the effective date of the plan.

(13) The plan provides for the continuation after its effective date of payment of all retiree benefits, as that term is defined in section 1114 of this title, at the level established pursuant to subsection (e)(1)(B) or (g) of section 1114 of this title, at any time prior to confirmation of the plan, for the duration of the period the debtor has obligated itself to provide such benefits.

(14) If the debtor is required by a judicial or administrative order, or by statute, to pay a domestic support obligation, the debtor has paid all amounts payable under such order or such statute for such obligation that first become payable after the date of the filing of the petition.

(15) In a case in which the debtor is an individual and in which the holder of an allowed unsecured claim objects to the confirmation of the plan—

(A) the value, as of the effective date of the plan, of the property to be distributed under the plan on account of such claim is not less than the amount of such claim; or

(B) the value of the property to be distributed under the plan is not less than the projected disposable income of the debtor (as defined in section 1325(b)(2)) to be received during the 5–year period beginning on the date that the first payment is due under the plan, or during the period for which the plan provides payments, whichever is longer.

(16) All transfers of property of the plan shall be made in accordance with any applicable provisions of nonbankruptcy law that govern the transfer of property by a corporation or trust that is not a moneyed, business, or commercial corporation or trust.

(b)(1) Notwithstanding section 510(a) of this title, if all of the applicable requirements of subsection (a) of this section other than paragraph (8) are met with respect to a plan, the court, on request of the proponent of the plan, shall confirm the plan notwithstanding the requirements of such paragraph if the plan does not discriminate unfairly, and is fair and equitable, with respect to each class of claims or interests that is impaired under, and has not accepted, the plan.

(2) For the purpose of this subsection, the condition that a plan be fair and equitable with respect to a class includes the following requirements:

(A) With respect to a class of secured claims, the plan provides—

(i)(I) that the holders of such claims retain the liens securing such claims, whether the property subject to such liens is retained by the debtor or transferred to another entity, to the extent of the allowed amount of such claims; and

(II) that each holder of a claim of such class receive on account of such claim deferred cash payments totaling at least the allowed amount of such claim, of a value, as of the effective date of the plan, of at least the value of such holder's interest in the estate's interest in such property;

(ii) for the sale, subject to section 363(k) of this title, of any property that is subject to the liens securing such claims, free and clear of such liens, with such liens to attach to the proceeds of such sale, and the treatment of such liens on proceeds under clause (i) or (iii) of this subparagraph; or

(iii) for the realization by such holders of the indubitable equivalent of such claims.

(B) With respect to a class of unsecured claims—

(i) the plan provides that each holder of a claim of such class receive or retain on account of such claim property of a value, as of the effective date of the plan, equal to the allowed amount of such claim; or

(ii) the holder of any claim or interest that is junior to the claims of such class will not receive or retain under the plan on account of such junior claim or interest any property, except that in a case in which the debtor is an individual, the debtor may retain property included in the estate under section 1115, subject to the requirements of subsection (a)(14) of this section.

(C) With respect to a class of interests—

(i) the plan provides that each holder of an interest of such class receive or retain on account of such interest property of a value, as of the effective date of the plan, equal to the greatest of the allowed amount of any fixed liquidation preference to which such holder is entitled, any fixed redemption price to which such holder is entitled, or the value of such interest; or

(ii) the holder of any interest that is junior to the interests of such class will not receive or retain under the plan on account of such junior interest any property.

(c) Notwithstanding subsections (a) and (b) of this section and except as provided in section 1127(b) of this title, the court may confirm only one plan, unless the order of confirmation in the case has been revoked under section 1144 of this title. If the requirements of subsections (a) and (b) of this section are met with respect to more than one plan, the court shall consider the preferences of creditors and equity security holders in determining which plan to confirm.

(d) Notwithstanding any other provision of this section, on request of a party in interest that is a governmental unit, the court may not confirm a plan if the principal purpose of the plan is the avoidance of taxes or the avoidance of the application of section 5 of the Securities Act of 1933. In any hearing under this subsection, the governmental unit has the burden of proof on the issue of avoidance.

(e) In a small business case, the court shall confirm a plan that complies with the applicable provisions of this title and that is filed in accordance with section 1121(e) not later than 45 days after the plan is filed unless the time for confirmation is extended in accordance with section 1121(e)(3).

APPENDIX D

PROVISIONS OF THE FEDERAL SECURITIES LAWS AND RULES PROMULGATED THEREUNDER

1. Securities and Exchange Act of 1934 and Rules Promulgated Thereunder

Section 9.

Section 13.

Section 14.

Rule 10b–18. Purchases of certain equity securities by the issuer and others.

Rule 13e–4. Tender Offers by Issuers.

Rule 14d–2. Commencement of a Tender Offer.

Rule 14d–7. Additional Withdrawal Rights.

Rule 14d–8. Exemption From Statutory Pro Rata Requirements.

Rule 14d–10. Equal Treatment of Security Holders.

Rule 14d–11. Subsequent offering period.

Rule 14e–2. Position of Subject Company With Respect to a Tender Offer.

Rule 14e–3. Transactions in Securities on the Basis of Material, Nonpublic Information in the Context of Tender Offers.

2. Trust Indenture Act of 1939

Section 315.

PART 1

SECURITIES AND EXCHANGE ACT OF 1934

Section 9

(a) It shall be unlawful for any person, directly or indirectly, by the use of the mails or any means or instrumentality of interstate commerce, or of any facility of any national securities exchange, or for any member of a national securities exchange—

* * *

(6) To effect either alone or with one or more other persons any series of transactions for the purchase and/or sale of any security registered on a national securities exchange for the purpose of pegging, fixing, or stabilizing the price of such security in contravention of such

rules and regulations as the Commission may prescribe as necessary or appropriate in the public interest or for the protection of investors.
* * *

(e) Any person who willfully participates in any act or transaction in violation of subsections (a), (b), or (c) of this section, shall be liable to any person who shall purchase or sell any security at a price which was affected by such act or transaction, and the person so injured may sue in law or in equity in any court of competent jurisdiction to recover the damages sustained as a result of any such act or transaction. In any such suit the court may, in its discretion, require an undertaking for the payment of the costs of such suit, and assess reasonable costs, including reasonable attorneys' fees, against either party litigant. * * *

Section 13

(d)(1) Any person who, after acquiring directly or indirectly the beneficial ownership of any equity security of a class which is registered pursuant to section 12 of this title, or any equity security of an insurance company which would have been required to be so registered except for the exemption contained in section 12(g)(2)(G) of this title, or any equity security issued by a closed-end investment company registered under the Investment Company Act of 1940 or any equity security issued by a Native Corporation pursuant to Section 37(d)(6) of the Alaska Native Claims Settlement Act, is directly or indirectly the beneficial owner of more than 5 per centum of such class shall, within ten days after such acquisition, send to the issuer of the security at its principal executive office, by registered or certified mail, send to each exchange where the security is traded, and file with the Commission, a statement containing such of the following information, and such additional information, as the Commission may by rules and regulations prescribe as necessary or appropriate in the public interest or for the protection of investors—

> (A) the background, and identity, residence, and citizenship of, and nature of such beneficial ownership by, such person and all other persons by whom or on whose behalf the purchases have been or are to be effected;

> (B) the source and amount of the funds or other consideration used or to be used in making the purchases, and if any part of the purchase price or proposed purchase price is represented or is to be represented by funds or other consideration borrowed or otherwise obtained for the purpose of acquiring, holding, or trading such security, a description of the transaction and the names of the parties thereto, except that where a source of funds is a loan made in the ordinary course of business by a bank, as defined in section 3(a)(6) of this title, if the person filing such statement so requests, the name of the bank shall not be made available to the public;

> (C) if the purpose of the purchases or prospective purchases is to acquire control of the business of the issuer of the securities, any plans or proposals which such persons may have to liquidate such issuer, to

sell its assets to or merge it with any other persons, or to make any other major change in its business or corporate structure;

(D) the number of shares of such security which are beneficially owned, and the number of shares concerning which there is a right to acquire, directly or indirectly, by (i) such person, and (ii) by each associate of such person, giving the background, identity, residence, and citizenship of each such associate; and

(E) information as to any contracts, arrangements, or understandings with any person with respect to any securities of the issuer, including but not limited to transfer of any of the securities, joint ventures, loan or option arrangements, puts or calls, guaranties of loans, guaranties against loss or guaranties of profits, division of losses or profits, or the giving or withholding of proxies, naming the persons with whom such contracts, arrangements, or understandings have been entered into, and giving the details thereof.

* * *

(d)(3) When two or more persons act as a partnership, limited partnership, syndicate, or other group for the purpose of acquiring, holding, or disposing of securities of an issuer, such syndicate or group shall be deemed a "person" for the purposes of this subsection.

* * *

(d)(6) The provisions of this subsection shall not apply to—

(A) any acquisition or offer to acquire securities made or proposed to be made by means of a registration statement under the Securities Act of 1933;

(B) any acquisition of the beneficial ownership of a security which, together with all other acquisitions by the same person of securities of the same class during the preceding twelve months, does not exceed 2 per centum of that class;

(C) any acquisition of an equity security by the issuer of such security;

(D) any acquisition or proposed acquisition of a security which the Commission, by rules or regulations or by order, shall exempt from the provisions of this subsection as not entered into for the purpose of, and not having the effect of, changing or influencing the control of the issuer or otherwise as not comprehended within the purposes of this subsection.

(e)(1) It shall be unlawful for an issuer which has a class of equity securities registered pursuant to section 12 of this title, or which is a closed-end investment company registered under the Investment Company Act of 1940, to purchase any equity security issued by it if such purchase is in contravention of such rules and regulations as the Commission, in the public interest or for the protection of investors, may adopt (A) to define acts and practices which are fraudulent, deceptive, or manipulative, and (B) to prescribe means reasonably designed to prevent such acts and practices. Such rules and regulations may require such issuer to provide holders of equity securities of such class with such information relating to the reasons for such purchase, the source of funds, the number of shares to be purchased, the price to be paid for such securities, the method of purchase, and such additional information, as the Commission deems necessary or appropriate in the public interest or for the protection of investors, or which the Commission deems to be material to a determination whether such security should be sold.

(2) For the purpose of this subsection, a purchase by or for the issuer, or any person controlling, controlled by, or under the common control with the issuer, or a purchase subject to control of the issuer or any such person, shall be deemed to be a purchase by the issuer. * * *

Section 14

(d)(1) It shall be unlawful for any person, directly or indirectly, by use of the mails or by any means or instrumentality of interstate commerce or of any facility of a national securities exchange or otherwise, to make a tender offer for, or a request or invitation for tenders of, any class of any equity security which is registered pursuant to section 12 of this title, or any equity security of an insurance company which would have been required to be so registered except for the exemption contained in section 12(g)(2)(G) of this title, or any equity security issued by a closed-end investment company registered under the Investment Company Act of 1940, if, after consummation thereof, such person would, directly or indirectly, be the beneficial owner of more than 5 per centum of such class, unless at the time copies of the offer or request or invitation are first published or sent or given to security holders such person has filed with the Commission a statement containing such of the information specified in section 13(d) of this title, and such additional information as the Commission may by rules and regulations prescribe as necessary or appropriate in the public interest or for the protection of investors. All requests or invitations for tenders or advertisements making a tender offer or requesting or inviting tenders of such a security shall be filed as a part of such statement and shall contain such of the information contained in such statement as the Commission may by rules and regulations prescribe. Copies of any additional material soliciting or requesting such tender offers subsequent to the initial solicitation or request shall contain such information as the Commission may by rules and regulations prescribe as necessary or appropriate in the public interest or for the protection of investors, and shall be filed with the Commission not later than the time copies of such material are first published or sent or given to security holders. Copies of all statements, in the form in which such material is furnished to security holders and the Commission, shall be sent to the issuer not later than the date such material is first published or sent or given to any security holders.

(d)(2) When two or more persons act as a partnership, limited partnership, syndicate, or other group for the purpose of acquiring, holding, or disposing of securities of an issuer, such syndicate or group shall be deemed a "person" for purposes of this subsection.

* * *

(d)(5) Securities deposited pursuant to a tender offer or request or invitation for tenders may be withdrawn by or on behalf of the depositor at any time until the expiration of seven days after the time definitive copies of the offer or request or invitation are first published or sent or given to security holders, and at any time after sixty days from the date of the original tender offer or request or invitation, except as the Commission may otherwise prescribe by rules, regulations, or order as necessary or appropriate in the public interest or for the protection of investors.

(d)(6) Where any person makes a tender offer, or request or invitation for tenders, for less than all the outstanding equity securities of a class, and where a greater number of securities is deposited pursuant thereto within ten days after copies of the offer or request or invitation are first published or sent or given to security holders than such person is bound or willing to take up and pay for, the securities taken up shall be taken up as nearly as may be pro rata, disregarding fractions, according to the number of securities deposited by each depositor. The provisions of this subsection shall also apply to securities deposited within ten days after notice of an increase in the consideration offered to security holders, as described in paragraph (7), is first published or sent or given to security holders.

(d)(7) Where any person varies the terms of a tender offer or request or invitation for tenders before the expiration thereof by increasing the consideration offered to holders of such securities, such person shall pay the increased consideration to each security holder whose securities are taken up and paid for pursuant to the tender offer or request or invitation for tenders whether or not such securities have been taken up by such person before the variation of the tender offer or request or invitation.

(d)(8) The provisions of this subsection shall not apply to any offer for, or request or invitation for tenders of, any security—

(A) if the acquisition of such security, together with all other acquisitions by the same person of securities of the same class during the preceding twelve months, would not exceed 2 per centum of that class;

(B) by the issuer of such security; or

(C) which the Commission, by rules or regulations or by order, shall exempt from the provisions of this subsection as not entered into for the purpose of, and not having the effect of, changing or influencing the control of the issuer or otherwise as not comprehended within the purposes of this subsection.

(e) It shall be unlawful for any person to make any untrue statement of a material fact or omit to state any material fact necessary in order to make the statements made, in the light of the circumstances under which they are made, not misleading, or to engage in any fraudulent, deceptive, or manipulative acts or practices, in connection with any tender offer or request or invitation for tenders, or any solicitation of security holders in opposition to or in favor of any such offer, request, or invitation. The Commission shall, for the purposes of this subsection, by rules and regulations define, and prescribe means reasonably designed to prevent, such acts and practices as are fraudulent, deceptive, or manipulative.

(f) If, pursuant to any arrangement or understanding with the person or persons acquiring securities in a transaction subject to subsection (d) of this section or subsection (d) of section 13 of this title, any persons are to be elected or designated as directors of the issuer, otherwise than at a meeting of security holders, and the persons so elected or designated will constitute a majority of the directors of the issuer, then, prior to the time any such person takes office as a director, and in accordance with rules and regulations prescribed by the Commission, the issuer shall file with the Commission, and transmit to all holders of record of securities of the issuer who would be entitled to vote at a meeting for election of directors, information substantially equivalent to the information which would be required by subsection (a) or (c) of this section to be transmitted if such person or persons were nominees for election as directors at a meeting of such security holders.

Rule 10b–18. Purchases of certain equity securities by the issuer and others.

Preliminary Notes to Rule 10b–18

1. Section 240.10b–18 provides an issuer (and its affiliated purchasers) with a "safe harbor" from liability for manipulation under sections 9(a)(2) of the Act and § 240.10b–5 under the Act solely by reason of the manner, timing, price, and volume of their repurchases when they repurchase the issuer's common stock in the market in accordance with the section's manner, timing, price, and volume conditions. As a safe harbor, compliance with § 240.10b–18 is voluntary. To come within the safe harbor, however, an issuer's repurchases must satisfy (on a daily basis) each of the section's four conditions. Failure to meet any one of the four conditions will remove all of the issuer's repurchases from the safe harbor for that day. The safe harbor, moreover, is not available for repurchases that, although made in technical compliance with the section, are part of a plan or scheme to evade the federal securities laws.

2. Regardless of whether the repurchases are effected in accordance with § 240.10b–18, reporting issuers must report their repurchasing activity as required by Item 703 of Regulations S–K and S–B and Item 15(e) of Form 20–F (regarding foreign private issuers), and closed-end management investment companies that are registered under the Investment Company Act of 1940 must report their repurchasing activity as required by Item 8 of Form N–CSR.

(a) Definitions. Unless otherwise provided, all terms used in this section shall have the same meaning as in the Act. In addition, the following definitions shall apply:

(1) ADTV means the average daily trading volume reported for the security during the four calendar weeks preceding the week in which the Rule 10b–18 purchase is to be effected.

(2) Affiliate means any person that directly or indirectly controls, is controlled by, or is under common control with, the issuer.

(3) Affiliated purchaser means:

(i) A person acting, directly or indirectly, in concert with the issuer for the purpose of acquiring the issuer's securities; or

(ii) An affiliate who, directly or indirectly, controls the issuer's purchases of such securities, whose purchases are controlled by the issuer, or whose purchases are under common control with those of the issuer; *Provided, however*, that "affiliated purchaser" shall not include a broker, dealer, or other person solely by reason of such broker, dealer, or other person effecting Rule 10b–18 purchases on behalf of the issuer or for its account, and shall not include an officer or director of the issuer solely by reason of that officer or director's participation in the decision to authorize Rule 10b–18 purchases by or on behalf of the issuer.

(4) Agent independent of the issuer has the meaning contained in § 242.100 of this chapter.

(5) Block means a quantity of stock that either:

(i) Has a purchase price of $200,000 or more; or

(ii) Is at least 5,000 shares and has a purchase price of at least $50,000; or

(iii) Is at least 20 round lots of the security and totals 150 percent or more of the trading volume for that security or, in the event that trading volume data are unavailable, is at least 20 round lots of the security and totals at least one-tenth of one percent (.001) of the outstanding shares of the security, exclusive of any shares owned by any affiliate; *Provided, however*, That a block under paragraph (a)(5)(i), (ii), and (iii) shall not include any amount a broker or dealer, acting as principal, has accumulated for the purpose of sale or resale to the issuer or to any affiliated purchaser of the issuer if the issuer or such affiliated purchaser knows or has reason to know that such amount was accumulated for such purpose, nor shall it include any amount that a broker or dealer has sold short to the issuer or to any affiliated purchaser of the issuer if the issuer or such affiliated purchaser knows or has reason to know that the sale was a short sale.

(6) Consolidated system means a consolidated transaction or quotation reporting system that collects and publicly disseminates on a current and continuous basis transaction or quotation information in common equity securities pursuant to an effective transaction reporting plan or an effective national market system plan (as those terms are defined in § 242.600 of this chapter).

(7) Market-wide trading suspension means a market-wide trading halt of 30 minutes or more that is:

(i) Imposed pursuant to the rules of a national securities exchange or a national securities association in response to a market-wide decline during a single trading session; or

(ii) Declared by the Commission pursuant to its authority under section 12(k) of the Act.

(8) Plan has the meaning contained in § 242.100 of this chapter.

(9) Principal market for a security means the single securities market with the largest reported trading volume for the security during the six full calendar months preceding the week in which the Rule 10b–18 purchase is to be effected.

(10) Public float value has the meaning contained in § 242.100 of this chapter.

(11) Purchase price means the price paid per share as reported, exclusive of any commission paid to a broker acting as agent, or commission equivalent, mark-up, or differential paid to a dealer.

(12) Riskless principal transaction means a transaction in which a broker or dealer after having received an order from an issuer to buy its security, buys the security as principal in the market at the same price to satisfy the issuer's buy order. The issuer's buy order must be effected at the same price per-share at which the broker or dealer bought the shares to satisfy the issuer's buy order, exclusive of any explicitly disclosed markup or markdown, commission equivalent, or other fee. In addition, only the first leg of the transaction, when the broker or dealer buys the security in the market as principal, is reported under the rules of a self-regulatory organization or under the Act. For purposes of this section, the broker or dealer must have written policies and procedures in place to assure that, at a minimum, the issuer's buy order was received prior to the offsetting transaction; the offsetting transaction is allocated to a riskless principal account or the issuer's account within 60 seconds of the execution; and the broker or dealer has supervisory systems in place to produce records that enable the broker or dealer to accurately and readily reconstruct, in a time-sequenced manner, all orders effected on a riskless principal basis.

(13) Rule 10b–18 purchase means a purchase (or any bid or limit order that would effect such purchase) of an issuer's common stock (or an equivalent interest, including a unit of beneficial interest in a trust or limited partnership or a depository share) by or for the issuer or any affiliated purchaser (including riskless principal transactions). However, it does not include any purchase of such security:

(i) Effected during the applicable restricted period of a distribution that is subject to § 242.102 of this chapter;

(ii) Effected by or for an issuer plan by an agent independent of the issuer;

(iii) Effected as a fractional share purchase (a fractional interest in a security) evidenced by a script certificate, order form, or similar document;

(iv) Effected during the period from the time of public announcement (as defined in § 230.165(f)) of a merger, acquisition, or similar transaction involving a recapitalization, until the earlier of the completion of such transaction or the completion of the vote by target shareholders. This exclusion does not apply to Rule 10b–18 purchases:

(A) Effected during such transaction in which the consideration is solely cash and there is no valuation period; or

(B) Where:

(1) The total volume of Rule 10b–18 purchases effected on any single day does not exceed the lesser of 25% of the security's four-week ADTV or the issuer's average daily Rule 10b–18 purchases during the three full calendar months preceding the date of the announcement of such transaction;

(2) The issuer's block purchases effected pursuant to paragraph (b)(4) of this section do not exceed the average size and frequency of the issuer's block purchases effected pursuant to paragraph (b)(4) of this section during the three full calendar months preceding the date of the announcement of such transaction; and

(3) Such purchases are not otherwise restricted or prohibited;

(v) Effected pursuant to Rule 13e–1;

(vi) Effected pursuant to a tender offer that is subject to Rule 13e–4 or specifically excepted from Rule 13e–4; or

(vii) Effected pursuant to a tender offer that is subject to section 14(d) of the Act and the rules and regulations thereunder.

(b) Conditions to be met. Rule 10b–18 purchases shall not be deemed to have violated the anti-manipulation provisions of sections 9(a)(2) or 10(b) of the Act, or Rule 10b–5 under the Act, solely by reason of the time, price, or amount of the Rule 10b–18 purchases, or the number of brokers or dealers used in connection with such purchases, if the issuer or affiliated purchaser of the issuer effects the Rule 10b–18 purchases according to each of the following conditions:

(1) One broker or dealer. Rule 10b–18 purchases must be effected from or through only one broker or dealer on any single day; *Provided, however,* that:

(i) The "one broker or dealer" condition shall not apply to Rule 10b–18 purchases that are not solicited by or on behalf of the issuer or its affiliated purchaser(s);

(ii) Where Rule 10b–18 purchases are effected by or on behalf of more than one affiliated purchaser of the issuer (or the issuer and one or more of its affiliated purchasers) on a single day, the issuer and all affiliated purchasers must use the same broker or dealer; and

(iii) Where Rule 10b–18 purchases are effected on behalf of the issuer by a broker-dealer that is not an electronic communication network (ECN) or other alternative trading system (ATS), that broker-dealer can access ECN or other ATS liquidity in order to execute repurchases on behalf of the issuer (or any affiliated purchaser of the issuer) on that day.

(2) Time of purchases. Rule 10b–18 purchases must not be:

(i) The opening (regular way) purchase reported in the consolidated system;

(ii) Effected during the 10 minutes before the scheduled close of the primary trading session in the principal market for the security, and the 10 minutes before the scheduled close of the primary trading session in the market where the purchase is effected, for a security that has an ADTV value of $1 million or more and a public float value of $150 million or more; and

(iii) Effected during the 30 minutes before the scheduled close of the primary trading session in the principal market for the security, and the 30 minutes before the scheduled close of the primary trading session in the market where the purchase is effected, for all other securities;

(iv) However, for purposes of this section, Rule 10b–18 purchases may be effected following the close of the primary trading session until the termination of the period in which last sale prices are reported in the consolidated system so long as such purchases are effected at prices that do not exceed the lower of the closing price of the primary trading session in the principal market for the security and any lower bids or sale prices subsequently reported in the consolidated system, and all of this section's conditions are met. However, for purposes of this section, the issuer may use one broker or dealer to effect Rule 10b–18 purchases during this period that may be different from the broker or dealer that it used during the primary trading session. However, the issuer's Rule 10b–18 purchase may not be the opening transaction of the session following the close of the primary trading session.

(3) Price of purchases. Rule 10b–18 purchases must be effected at a purchase price that:

(i) Does not exceed the highest independent bid or the last independent transaction price, whichever is higher, quoted or reported in the consolidated system at the time the Rule 10b–18 purchase is effected;

(ii) For securities for which bids and transaction prices are not quoted or reported in the consolidated system, Rule 10b–18 purchases must be effected at a purchase price that does not exceed the highest independent bid or the last independent transaction price, whichever is higher, displayed and disseminated on any national securities exchange or on any inter-dealer quotation system (as defined in Rule15c2–11) that displays at least two priced quotations for the security, at the time the Rule 10b–18 purchase is effected; and

(iii) For all other securities, Rule 10b–18 purchases must be effected at a price no higher than the highest independent bid obtained from three independent dealers.

(4) Volume of purchases. The total volume of Rule 10b–18 purchases effected by or for the issuer and any affiliated purchasers effected on any single day must not exceed 25 percent of the ADTV for that security; However, once each week, in lieu of purchasing under the 25 percent of ADTV limit for that day, the issuer or an affiliated purchaser of the issuer may effect one block purchase if:

(i) No other Rule 10b–18 purchases are effected that day, and

(ii) The block purchase is not included when calculating a security's four week ADTV under this section.

(c) Alternative conditions. The conditions of paragraph (b) of this section shall apply in connection with Rule 10b–18 purchases effected during a trading session following the imposition of a market-wide trading suspension, except:

(1) That the time of purchases condition in paragraph (b)(2) of this section shall not apply, either:

(i) From the reopening of trading until the scheduled close of trading on the day that the market-wide trading suspension is imposed; or

(ii) At the opening of trading on the next trading day until the scheduled close of trading that day, if a market-wide trading suspension was in effect at the close of trading on the preceding day; and

(2) The volume of purchases condition in paragraph (b)(4) of this section is modified so that the amount of Rule 10b–18 purchases must not exceed 100 percent of the ADTV for that security.

(d) Other purchases. No presumption shall arise that an issuer or an affiliated purchaser has violated the anti-manipulation provisions of sections 9(a)(2) or 10(b) of the Act, or Rule 10b–5 under the Act, if the Rule 10b–18 purchases of such issuer or affiliated purchaser do not meet the conditions specified in paragraph (b) or (c) of this section.

Rule 13e–4. Tender Offers by Issuers

* * *

(j)(1) It shall be a fraudulent, deceptive or manipulative act or practice, in connection with an issuer tender offer, for an issuer or an affiliate of such issuer, in connection with an issuer tender offer:

(i) to employ any device, scheme or artifice to defraud any person;

(ii) to make any untrue statement of a material fact or to omit to state a material fact necessary in order to make the statements made, in the light of the circumstances under which they were made, not misleading; or

(iii) to engage in any act, practice or course of business which operates or would operate as a fraud or deceit upon any person.

(2) As a means reasonably designed to prevent fraudulent, deceptive or manipulative acts or practices in connection with any issuer tender offer, it shall be unlawful for an issuer or an affiliate of such issuer to make an issuer tender offer unless:

(i) such issuer or affiliate complies with the requirements of paragraphs (c), (d), (e) and (f) of this section, and

(iii) the issuer tender offer is not in violation of paragraph (j)(1) of this section.

Rule 14d–2. Commencement of a Tender Offer.

(a) *Date of commencement*. A bidder will have commenced its tender offer for purposes of section 14(d) of the Act and the rules under that section at 12:01 a.m. on the date when the bidder has first published, sent or given the means to tender to security holders. For purposes of this section, the means to tender includes the transmittal form or a statement regarding how the transmittal form may be obtained.

(b) *Pre–Commencement Communications*. A communication by the bidder will not be deemed to constitute commencement of a tender offer if:

(1) It does not include the means for security holders to tender their shares into the offer; and

(2) All written communications relating to the tender offer, from and including the first public announcement, are filed under cover of Schedule TO with the Commission no later than the date of the communication. The bidder also must deliver to the subject company and any other bidder for the same class of securities the first communication relating to the transaction that is filed, or required to be filed, with the Commission.

(c) *Filing and Other Obligations Triggered by Commencement*. As soon as practicable on the date of commencement, a bidder must comply with the filing requirements of Rule 14d–3(a), the dissemination requirements of Rule 14d–4(a) or (b), and the disclosure requirements of Rule 14d–6(a).

Rule 14d–7. Additional Withdrawal Rights

(a) *Rights*. In addition to the provisions of section 14(d)(5) of the Act, any person who has deposited securities pursuant to a tender offer has the right to withdraw any such securities during the periods such offer request or invitation remains open.

　　　* * *

Rule 14d–8. Exemption From Statutory Pro Rata Requirements

Notwithstanding the pro rata provisions of Section 14(d)(6) of the Act, if any person makes a tender offer or request or invitation for tenders, for less than all of the outstanding equity securities of a class, and if a greater number of securities are deposited pursuant thereto than such person is bound or willing to take up and pay for, the securities taken up and paid for shall be taken up and paid for as nearly as may be pro rata, disregarding fractions, according to the number of securities deposited by each depositor during the period such offer, request or invitation remains open.

Rule 14d–10.   Equal treatment of security holders.

(a) No bidder shall make a tender offer unless:

(1) The tender offer is open to all security holders of the class of securities subject to the tender offer; and

(2) The consideration paid to any security holder for securities tendered in the tender offer is the highest consideration paid to any other security holder for securities tendered in the tender offer.

(b) Paragraph (a)(1) of this section shall not:

(1) Affect dissemination under Rule 14d–4; or

(2) Prohibit a bidder from making a tender offer excluding all security holders in a state where the bidder is prohibited from making the tender offer by administrative or judicial action pursuant to a state statute after a good faith effort by the bidder to comply with such statute.

(c) Paragraph (a)(2) of this section shall not prohibit the offer of more than one type of consideration in a tender offer, *Provided*, That:

(1) Security holders are afforded equal right to elect among each of the types of consideration offered; and

(2) The highest consideration of each type paid to any security holder is paid to any other security holder receiving that type of consideration.

(d)(1) Paragraph (a)(2) of this section shall not prohibit the negotiation, execution or amendment of an employment compensation, severance or other employee benefit arrangement, or payments made or to be made or benefits granted or to be granted according to such an arrangement, with respect to any security holder of the subject company, where the amount payable under the arrangement:

(i) Is being paid or granted as compensation for past services performed, future services to be performed, or future services to be refrained from performing, by the security holder (and matters incidental thereto); and

(ii) Is not calculated based on the number of securities tendered or to be tendered in the tender offer by the security holder.

(2) The provisions of paragraph (d)(1) of this section shall be satisfied and, therefore, pursuant to this non-exclusive safe harbor, the negotiation, execution or amendment of an arrangement and any payments made or to be made or benefits granted or to be granted according to that arrangement shall not be prohibited by paragraph (a)(2) of this section, if the arrangement is approved as an employment compensation, severance or other employee benefit arrangement solely by independent directors as follows:

(i) The compensation committee or a committee of the board of directors that performs functions similar to a compensation committee of the subject company approves the arrangement, regardless of whether the subject company is a party to the arrangement, or, if the bidder is a party to the arrangement, the compensation committee or a committee of the board of directors that performs functions similar to a compensation committee of the bidder approves the arrangement; or

(ii) If the subject company's or bidder's board of directors, as applicable, does not have a compensation committee or a committee of the board of directors that performs functions similar to a compensation committee or if none of the members of the subject company's or bidder's compensation committee or committee that performs functions similar to a compensation committee is independent, a special committee of the board of directors formed to consider and approve the arrangement approves the arrangement; or

(iii) If the subject company or bidder, as applicable, is a foreign private issuer, any or all members of the board of directors or any committee of the board of directors authorized to approve employment compensation, severance or other employee benefit arrangements under the laws or regulations of the home country approves the arrangement.

Instructions to paragraph (d)(2): For purposes of determining whether the members of the committee approving an arrangement in accordance with the provisions of paragraph (d)(2) of this section are independent, the following provisions shall apply:

1. If the bidder or subject company, as applicable, is a listed issuer (as defined in § 240.10A–3 of this chapter) whose securities are listed either on a national securities exchange registered pursuant to section 6(a) of the Exchange Act (15 U.S.C. 78f(a)) or in an inter-dealer quotation system of a national securities association registered pursuant to section 15A(a) of the Exchange Act (15 U.S.C. 78o–3(a)) that has independence requirements for compensation committee members that have been approved by the Commission (as those requirements may be modified or supplemented), apply the bidder's or subject company's definition of independence that it uses for determining that the members of the compensation committee are independent in compliance with the listing standards applicable to compensation committee members of the listed issuer.

2. If the bidder or subject company, as applicable, is not a listed issuer (as defined in § 240.10A–3 of this chapter), apply the independence requirements for compensation committee members of a national securities exchange registered pursuant to section 6(a) of the Exchange Act (15 U.S.C. 78f(a)) or an inter-dealer quotation system of a national securities association registered pursuant to section 15A(a) of the Exchange Act (15 U.S.C. 78o–3(a)) that have been approved by the Commission (as those requirements may be modified or supplemented). Whatever definition the bidder or subject company, as applicable, chooses, it must apply that definition consistently to all members of the committee approving the arrangement.

3. Notwithstanding Instructions 1 and 2 to paragraph (d)(2), if the bidder or subject company, as applicable, is a closed-end investment company registered under the Investment Company Act of 1940, a director is considered to be independent if the director is not, other than in his or her capacity as a member of the board of directors or any board committee, an "interested person" of the investment company, as defined in section 2(a)(19) of the Investment Company Act of 1940 (15 U.S.C. 80a–2(a)(19)).

4. If the bidder or the subject company, as applicable, is a foreign private issuer, apply either the independence standards set forth in Instructions 1 and 2 to paragraph (d)(2) or the independence requirements of the laws, regulations, codes or standards of the home country of the bidder or subject company, as applicable, for members of the board of directors or the committee of the board of directors approving the arrangement.

5. A determination by the bidder's or the subject company's board of directors, as applicable, that the members of the board of directors or the committee of the board of directors, as applicable, approving an arrangement in accordance with the provisions of paragraph (d)(2) are independent in accordance with the provisions of this instruction to paragraph (d)(2) shall satisfy the independence requirements of paragraph (d)(2).

Instruction to paragraph (d): The fact that the provisions of paragraph (d) of this section extend only to employment compensation, severance and other employee benefit arrangements and not to other arrangements, such as commercial arrangements, does not raise any inference that a payment under any such other arrangement constitutes consideration paid for securities in a tender offer.

(e) If the offer and sale of securities constituting consideration offered in a tender offer is prohibited by the appropriate authority of a state after a good faith effort by the bidder to register or qualify the offer and sale of such securities in such state:

(1) The bidder may offer security holders in such state an alternative form of consideration; and

(2) Paragraph (c) of this section shall not operate to require the bidder to offer or pay the alternative form of consideration to security holders in any other state.

(f) This section shall not apply to any tender offer with respect to which the Commission, upon written request or upon its own motion, either unconditionally or on specified terms and conditions, determines that compliance with this section is not necessary or appropriate in the public interest or for the protection of investors.

Rule 14d–11. Subsequent offering period.

A bidder may elect to provide a subsequent offering period of three business days to 20 business days during which tenders will be accepted if:

(a) The initial offering period of at least 20 business days has expired;

(b) The offer is for all outstanding securities of the class that is the subject of the tender offer, and if the bidder is offering security holders a choice of different forms of consideration, there is no ceiling on any form of consideration offered;

(c) The bidder immediately accepts and promptly pays for all securities tendered during the initial offering period;

(d) The bidder announces the results of the tender offer, including the approximate number and percentage of securities deposited to date, no later than 9:00 a.m. Eastern time on the next business day after the expiration date of the initial offering period and immediately begins the subsequent offering period;

(e) The bidder immediately accepts and promptly pays for all securities as they are tendered during the subsequent offering period; and

(f) The bidder offers the same form and amount of consideration to security holders in both the initial and the subsequent offering period.

Note 14d–11: No withdrawal rights apply during the subsequent offering period in accordance with Rule14d–7(a)(2).

Rule 14e–2. Position of Subject Company With Respect to a Tender Offer

(a) *Position of Subject Company.* As a means reasonably designed to prevent fraudulent, deceptive or manipulative acts or practices within the meaning of section 14(e) of the Act, the subject company, no later than 10 business days from the date the tender offer is first published or sent or given, shall publish, send or give to security holders a statement disclosing that the subject company:

(1) Recommends acceptance or rejection of the bidder's tender offer;

(2) Expresses no opinion and is remaining neutral toward the bidder's tender offer; or

(3) Is unable to take a position with respect to the bidder's tender offer.

Such statement shall also include the reason(s) for the position (including the inability to take a position) disclosed therein.

(b) *Material change.* If any material change occurs in the disclosure required by paragraph (a) of this section, the subject company shall promptly publish, send or give a statement disclosing such material change to security holders.

Rule 14e–3. Transactions in Securities on the Basis of Material, Nonpublic Information in the Context of Tender Offers

(a) If any person has taken a substantial step or steps to commence, or has commenced, a tender offer (the "offering person"), it shall constitute a fraudulent, deceptive or manipulative act or practice within the meaning of section 14(e) of the Act for any other person who is in possession of material information relating to such tender offer which information he knows or has reason to know is nonpublic and which he knows or has reason to know has been acquired directly or indirectly from (1) the offering person, (2) the issuer of the securities sought or to be sought by such tender offer, or (3) any officer, director, partner or employee or any other person acting on behalf of the offering person or such issuer, to purchase or sell or cause to be purchased or sold any of such securities or any securities convertible into or exchangeable for any such securities or any option or right to obtain or to dispose of any of the foregoing securities, unless within a reasonable time prior to any purchase or sale such information and its source are publicly disclosed by press release or otherwise.

(b) A person other than a natural person shall not violate paragraph (a) of this section if such person shows that:

(1) The individual(s) making the investment decision on behalf of such person to purchase or sell any security described in paragraph (a) or to cause any such security to be purchased or sold by or on behalf of others did not know the material, nonpublic information; and

(2) Such person had implemented one or a combination of policies and procedures, reasonable under the circumstances, taking into consideration the nature of the person's business, to ensure that individual(s) making investment decision(s) would not violate paragraph (a), which policies and procedures may include, but are not limited to, (i) those which restrict any purchase, sale and causing any purchase and sale of any such security or (ii) those which prevent such individual(s) from knowing such information.

(c) Notwithstanding anything in paragraph (a) to the contrary, the following transactions shall not be violations of paragraph (a) of this section:

(1) Purchase(s) of any security described in paragraph (a) by a broker or by another agent on behalf of an offering person; or

(2) Sale(s) by any person of any security described in paragraph (a) to the offering person.

(d)(1) As a means reasonably designed to prevent fraudulent, deceptive or manipulative acts or practices within the meaning of section 14(e) of the Act, it shall be unlawful for any person described in paragraph (d)(2) of this section to communicate material, nonpublic information relating to a tender offer to any other person under circumstances in which it is reasonably foreseeable that such communication is likely to result in a violation of this section except that this paragraph shall not apply to a communication made in good faith.

(i) To the officers, directors, partners or employees of the offering person, to its advisors or to other persons, involved in the planning, financing, preparation or execution of such tender offer;

(ii) To the issuer whose securities are sought or to be sought by such tender offer, to its officers, directors, partners, employees or advisors or to other persons, involved in the planning, financing, preparation or execution of the activities of the issuer with respect to such tender offer; or

(iii) To any person pursuant to a requirement of any statute or rule or regulation promulgated thereunder.

(d)(2) The persons referred to in paragraph (d)(1) of this section are:

(i) The offering person or its officers, directors, partners, employees or advisors;

(ii) The issuer of the securities sought or to be sought by such tender offer or its officers, directors, partners, employees or advisors;

(iii) Anyone acting on behalf of the persons in paragraph (d)(2)(i) or the issuer or persons in paragraph (d)(2)(ii); and

(iv) Any person in possession of material information relating to a tender offer which information he knows or has reason to know is nonpublic and which he knows or has reason to know has been acquired directly or indirectly from any of the above.

PART 2

TRUST INDENTURE ACT OF 1939 AS AMENDED 1990

Section 315

(a) The indenture to be qualified shall automatically be deemed (unless it is expressly provided therein that any such provision is excluded) to provide that, prior to default (as such term is defined in such indenture)—

(1) the indenture trustee shall not be liable except for the performance of such duties as are specifically set out in such indenture; and

(2) the indenture trustee may conclusively rely, as to the truth of the statements and the correctness of the opinions expressed therein, in the absence of bad faith on the part of such trustee, upon certificates or opinions conforming to the requirements of the indenture;

but the indenture trustee shall examine the evidence furnished to it pursuant to section 314 to determine whether or not such evidence conforms to the requirements of the indenture.

(b) The indenture trustee shall give to the indenture security holders, in the manner and to the extent provided in subsection (c) of section 313, notice of all defaults known to the trustee, within ninety days after the occurrence thereof: Provided, That such indenture shall automatically be deemed (unless it is expressly provided therein that such provision is excluded) to provide that, except in the case of default in the payment of the principal of or interest on any indenture security, or in the payment of any sinking or purchase fund installment, the trustee shall be protected in withholding such notice if and so long as the board of directors, the executive committee, or a trust committee of directors and/or responsible officers, of the trustee in good faith determine that the withholding of such notice is in the interests of the indenture security holders.

(c) The indenture trustee shall exercise in case of default (as such term is defined in such indenture) such of the rights and powers vested in it by such indenture, and to use the same degree of care and skill in their exercise, as a prudent man would exercise or use under the circumstances in the conduct of his own affairs.

(d) The indenture to be qualified shall not contain any provisions relieving the indenture trustee from liability for its own negligent action, its own negligent failure to act, or its own willful misconduct, except that—

(1) such indenture shall automatically be deemed (unless it is expressly provided therein that any such provision is excluded) to contain the provisions authorized by paragraphs (1) and (2) of subsection (a) of this section;

(2) such indenture shall automatically be deemed (unless it is expressly provided therein that any such provision is excluded) to contain provisions protecting the indenture trustee from liability for any error of judgment made in good faith by a responsible officer or officers of such trustee, unless it shall be proved that such trustee was negligent in ascertaining the pertinent facts; and

(3) such indenture shall automatically be deemed (unless it is expressly provided therein that any such provision is excluded) to contain provisions protecting the indenture trustee with respect to any action taken or omitted to be taken by it in good faith in accordance with the direction of the holders of not less than a majority in principal amount of the indenture securities at the time outstanding (determined as provided in subsection (a) of section 316) relating to the time, method, and place of conducting any proceeding for any remedy available to such trustee, or exercising any trust or power conferred upon such trustee, under such indenture.

*

APPENDIX E

THE BINOMIAL AND BLACK-SCHOLES OPTION PRICING MODELS

Alexander, Sharpe, and Bailey, Fundamentals of Investments

3d edition, 2001, pages 618–623, 625–631.

24.5 The Binomial Option Pricing Model

The binomial option pricing model (BOPM) can be used to estimate the fair value of a call or put option. It is best presented using an example in which it is assumed that the options are **European options**, meaning that they can be exercised only on their expiration dates. In addition, it is assumed that the underlying stock does not pay any dividends during the life of the option. The model can be modified to value **American options**, which are options that can be exercised at any time during their life and can also be used to value options on stocks that pay dividends during the life of the option.

24.5.1 CALL OPTIONS

Assume that the price of Widget stock today ($t = 0$) is $100, and that after one year ($t = T$) its stock sells for either $125 or $80, meaning that the stock will either rise by 25% or fall by 20% during the year. In addition, the annual riskfree rate is 8% compounded continuously. Investors can either lend (by purchasing these 8% bonds) or borrow (by short selling the bonds) at this rate.

Now consider a call option on Widget that has an exercise price of $100 and an expiration date of one year from now. On the expiration date the call will have a value of either $25 (if Widget is at $125) or $0 (if Widget is at $80). Panel (a) of Figure 24.5 illustrates the situation using a "price tree," which has two branches that represent prices at the expiration date, thus making the term "binomial" an appropriate title for the model.

E-2

APPENDIX E THE BINOMIAL AND BLACK-SCHOLES OPTION PRICING MODELS

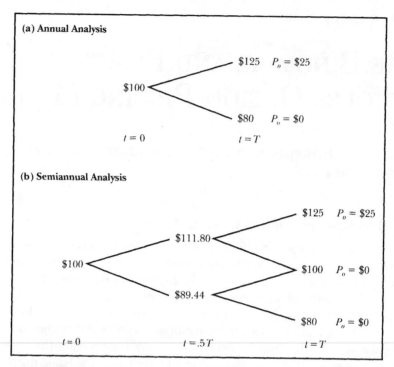

FIGURE 24.5 Binomial Model of Prices for Widget

Valuation

The question that arises is this: What is a fair value for the call at time
0? The binomial option pricing model is designed to answer that question.

Three investments are of interest here: the stock, the option, and a
riskfree bond. The prices and payoffs for the stock and option are known. It
is also known that $100 invested in a riskfree bond will grow to approxi-
mately $108.33 if interest is continuously compounded at an annual rate of
8%. What is to be determined is a fair price that the option should sell for
now.

The key to understanding the situation is the observation that there
are two possible future *states of nature*. The stock's price may go up or
down. For simplicity, these two states are called the "up state" and the
"down state," respectively. This essential information is summarized as
follows:

Security	Payoff in Up State	Payoff in Down State	Current Price
Stock	$125.00	$ 80.00	$100.00
Bond	108.33	108.33	100.00
Call	25.00	0.00	???

Note that at this juncture the current price of the call is unknown.

Replicating Portfolios

Although the Widget call option may seem exotic, its characteristics can in fact be replicated with an appropriate combination of the Widget stock and the riskfree bond. Moreover, the cost of this *replicating portfolio* constitutes the fair value of the option. Why? Because otherwise there would be an *arbitrage opportunity;* an investor could buy the cheaper of the two alternatives and sell the more expensive one, thereby achieving a guaranteed profit. (Just how this transaction is done is revealed shortly.)

The composition of a portfolio that precisely replicates the payoffs of the Widget call option needs to be determined. Consider a portfolio with N_s *shares of Widget stock and* N_b *riskfree bonds. In the* up state such a portfolio has a payoff of $125N_s + $108.33N_b$, whereas in the down state it has a payoff of $80N_s + $108.33N_b$. *Because the call option is worth $25 in the up state,* N_s *and* N_b *need to have values so that*

$$\$125N_s + \$108.33N_b = \$25 \qquad \textbf{(24.3a)}$$

And because the call option is worthless in the down state, N_s *and* N_b need to have values so that

$$\$80N_s + \$108.33N_b = \$0 \qquad \textbf{(24.3b)}$$

These two linear equations, (24.3a) and (24.3b), have two unknowns and can be solved easily. Subtracting the second equation from the first gives

$$(\$125 - \$80)N_s = \$25 \qquad \textbf{(24.3c)}$$

so that N_s *equals .5556. Substituting this value in either Equation (24.3a) or Equation (24.3b) gives the remainder of the solution,* $N_b = -.4103$.

What does this mean in financial terms? It means that an investor can replicate the payoffs from the call by *short selling* $41.03 of the riskfree bonds (note that investing -.4103 in $100 bonds is equivalent to short selling $41.03 of the bonds or borrowing $41.03 at the riskfree rate) and *purchasing* .5556 shares of Widget stock. This is indeed the case, as can be seen here:

Portfolio Component	Payoff in Up State	Payoff in Down State
Stock investment	.5556 × $125 = $69.45	.5556 × $80 = $44.45
Loan repayment	−$41.03 × 1.0833 = −$44.45	−$41.03 × 1.0833 = −$44.45
Net payoff	$25.00	$0.00

Because the replicating portfolio provides the same payoffs as the call, only its cost needs to be calculated to find the fair value of the option. To obtain the portfolio, the investor must spend $55.56 to purchase .5556 shares of Widget stock (at $100 per share). However, $41.03 of this amount is provided by the proceeds from the short sale of the bond, which is equivalent to borrowing $41.03. Thus, only $14.53 ($55.56—$41.03) of the investor's own funds must be spent. Accordingly, this is the fair value of the call option.

More generally, the value of the call option will be

$$V_o = N_s P_s + N_b P_b \qquad (24.4)$$

where V_o represents the value of the option, P_s is the price of the stock, P_b is the price of a riskfree bond, and N_s and N_b are the number of shares and riskfree bonds required to replicate the option's payoffs.

Overpricing

To see that equilibrium will be attained if the call sells for $14.53, consider what a shrewd investor would do if the call were selling for either more or less than this amount. Imagine that the call is selling for $20, so it is overpriced. In this case the investor would consider writing one call, buying .5556 shares, and borrowing $41.03. The net cash flow when this is done (that is, at $t = 0$) would be $5.47 [= $20 − (.5556 × $100) + $41.03], indicating that the investor has a net cash inflow. At the end of the year (that is, at $t = T$) the investor's net cash flow will be as follows:

Portfolio Component	Payoff in Up State	Payoff in Down State
Written call	− $25.00	$0.00
Stock investment	.5556 × $125 = $69.45	.5556 × $80 =$44.45
Loan repayment	− $41.03 × 1.0833 = − $44.45	− $41.03 × 1.0833 = − $44.45
Net payoff	$0.00	$0.00

Because the net aggregate value is zero regardless of the ending stock price, the investor has no risk of loss from this strategy. Thus, the investor currently has a means for generating free cash as long as the call is priced at $20 because the investment strategy does not require any cash from the investor later on. This situation cannot represent equilibrium, because anyone can get free cash by investing similarly.

Underpricing

Next imagine that the call is selling for $10 instead of $20, so it is underpriced. In this case the investor would consider buying one call, short selling .5556 shares, and investing $41.03 at the riskfree rate. The net cash (that is, at $t = 0$) would be $4.53 [=−$10 + (.5556 × $100)−$41.03], indicating that the investor has a net cash inflow. At the end of the year (that is, at $t = T$) the investor's net cash flow will be as follows:

Portfolio Component	Payoff in Up State	Payoff in Down State
Call investment	$25.00	$0.00
Repay shorted stock	−.5556 × $125 = − $69.45	−.5556 × $80 = − $44.45
Riskfree investment	$41.03 × 1.0833 = $44.45	$41.03 × 1.0833 = $44.45
Net payoff	$0.00	$0.00

Once again, the net aggregate value is zero regardless of the ending stock price, indicating that the investor has no risk of loss from this strategy. Hence the investor currently has a means for generating free cash as long as the call is priced at $10. This situation cannot represent equilibrium, however, because anyone can get free cash by investing similarly.

The Hedge Ratio

To replicate the Widget call option, imagine borrowing $41.03 and purchasing .5556 shares of Widget stock. Consider the effect of a change in the price of the stock tomorrow (not a year from now) on the value of the replicating portfolio. Because .5556 shares of stock are included in the portfolio, the value of the portfolio will change by $.5556 for every $1 change in the price of Widget stock. But because the call option and the portfolio should sell for the same price, it follows that the price of the call should also change by $.5556 for every $1 change in the price of the stock. This relationship is defined as the option's **hedge ratio,** denoted h. It equals the value N_s *that was determined in Equation (24.3c).*

In the case of the Widget call option, the hedge ratio was .5556, which equals the value of ($25 − $0)/($125 − $80). Note that the numerator equals the difference between the option's payoffs in the up and down states, and the denominator equals the difference between the stock's payoffs in the two states. More generally, in the binomial model the hedge ratio is

$$h = \frac{P_{ou} - P_{od}}{P_{su} - P_{sd}} \qquad\qquad \textbf{(24.5)}$$

where P represents the end-of-period price and the subscripts indicate the instrument (o for option, s for stock) and the state of nature (u for up, d for down).

To replicate a call option in a binomial world, an investor must purchase h shares of stock and risklessly borrow an amount B by short selling bonds. The amount to be borrowed is

$$B = \text{PV}(hP_{sd} - P_{od}) \qquad\qquad \textbf{(24.6)}$$

where PV refers to the present value of the figure calculated in the following parentheses. (Note that the figure in parentheses is the value of the bond at the end of the period.)

To summarize, the value of a call option is

$$V_o = hP_s - B \qquad\qquad \textbf{(24.7)}$$

where h and B are the hedge ratio and the current value of a short bond position in a portfolio that replicates the payoffs of the call and that are calculated using Equations (24.5) and (24.6).

More Than Two Prices

It is reasonable to wonder about the accuracy of the BOPM if it is based on an assumption that the price of Widget stock can assume only one of two values at the end of a year. Realistically, Widget stock can assume any one of a great number of prices at year-end. This added complexity is not a problem because the model can be extended in a straightforward manner.

In the case of Widget, divide the year into two six-month periods. In the first period, assume that Widget can go up to $111.80 (an 11.80% increase) or down to $89.44 (a 10.56% decrease). For the second six-month period, the price of Widget can again go either up by 11.80% or down by 10.56%. Hence the price of Widget will follow one of the paths of the price tree shown in Figure 24.5(b) during the forthcoming year. Note that Widget can now assume one of three prices at year-end: $125, $100, or $80. The associated value of the call option is also given in the figure for each of these stock prices.

How can the value of the Widget call option at time 0 be calculated from the information given in the figure? The answer is remarkably simple. By breaking the problem into three parts, each is solved in a manner similar to that shown earlier when panel (a) was discussed. The three parts must be approached sequentially by working backward in time.

First, imagine that six months have passed and the price of Widget stock is $111.80. What is the value of the call option at this node in the price tree? The hedge ratio h is calculated to be 1.0 [= ($25 − $0)/ ($125 − $100)], and the amount of the borrowing B is calculated to be $96.08 [= (1 × $100 − $0)/1.0408]. (The 8% riskfree rate compounded continuously corresponds to a discrete discount rate of 4.08% for the six-month period.) Using Equation (24.7), the value of the call is $15.72 (= 1 × $111.80 − $96.08).

Second, again imagine that six months have passed, but the price of Widget is $89.44. Equations (24.5), (24.6), and (24.7) could be used to determine the value of the call at this node in the price tree, but intuition gives the answer in this example more quickly: The call has to be selling for $0. In six months the price of Widget will be either $100 or $80, and regardless of which it is, the call will still be worthless. That is, investors will realize that the call will be worthless at the end of the year if the stock price is at $89.44 after six months, so they will be unwilling to pay anything for the call option.

Third, imagine that no time has elapsed, so that it is time 0. In this case the price tree can be simplified to

Applying Equations (24.5) and (24.6) reveals that the hedge ratio, h, is equal to .7030 [= ($15.72 − $0)/($111.80 − $89.44)], and the amount of borrowing B is equal to $60.41 [= (.7030 × $89.44 − $0)/1.0408]. Applying Equation (24.7) results in a value for the call at $t = 0$ of $9.89 [= (.7030 × $100) − $60.41].

There is no need to stop here. Instead of analyzing 2 six-month periods, 4 quarterly periods can be analyzed, or 12 monthly periods. Note that the number of year-end stock prices for Widget is equal to one more than the number of periods in a year. Hence, when annual periods were used in Figure 24.5(a), there were two year-end prices, and when semiannual prices were used, there were 3 year-end prices. It follows that if quarterly or monthly periods had been used, then there would have been 5 or 13 year-end prices, respectively.

* * *

24.6   The Black–Scholes Model for Call Options

Consider what would happen with the binomial option pricing model if the number of periods before the expiration date were allowed to increase. For example, with Widget's option for which the expiration date was a year in the future, there could be a price tree with periods for each one of the approximately 250 trading days in a year. Hence there would be 251 possible year-end prices for Widget stock. Needless to say, the fair value of any call associated with such a tree would require a computer to perform calculations such as those shown earlier for Widget. If the number of periods were larger, with each one representing a specific hour of each trading day, then there would be about 1,750 ($= 7 \times 250$) hourly periods (and 1,751 possible year-end prices). Note that the number of periods in a year gets larger as the length of each period gets shorter. In the end there will be an infinite number of infinitely small periods (and, consequently, an infinite number of possible year-end prices). In this situation the BOPM given in Equation (24.7) reduces to the Black–Scholes model, so named in honor of its originators.

24.6.1   THE FORMULA

In a world not bothered by taxes and transaction costs, the fair value of a call option can be estimated using the valuation formula developed by Black and Scholes. It has been widely used by those who deal with options to search for situations in which the market price of an option differs substantially from its fair value. A call option found to be selling for substantially less than its Black–Scholes value is a candidate for purchase, whereas one that is found to be selling for substantially more is a candidate for writing. The Black–Scholes formula for estimating the fair value of a call option V_c is

$$V_c = N(d_1)P_s - \frac{E}{e^{RT}} N(d_2) \qquad (24.10)$$

where

$$d_1 = \frac{\ln(P_s/E) + (R + .5\sigma^2)T}{\sigma\sqrt{T}} \qquad (24.11)$$

$$d_2 = \frac{\ln(P_s/E) + (R - .5\sigma^2)T}{\sigma\sqrt{T}} \qquad (24.12a)$$

$$= d_1 - \sigma\sqrt{T} \qquad (24.12b)$$

and where

P_s = current market price of the underlying stock

E = exercise price of the option

R = continuously compounded riskfree rate of return, expressed on an annual basis

T = time remaining before expiration, expressed as a fraction of a year

σ = risk of the underlying common stock, measured by the standard deviation of the continuously compounded annual rate of return on the stock and commonly referred to as **volatility**

Note that E/e^{RT} is the present value of the exercise price where a continuous discount rate is used. The quantity $\ln(P_s/E)$ is the natural logarithm of P_s/E. Finally, $N(d_1)$ and $N(d_2)$ denote the probabilities that outcomes of less than d_1 and d_2, respectively, will occur in a normal distribution that has a mean of 0 and a standard deviation of 1.

Table 24.2 provides values of $N(d_1)$ for various levels of d_1. Only this table and a pocket calculator are needed to use the Black–Scholes formula for valuing a call option. It should be noted that with this formula the interest rate R and the stock volatility & are assumed to be constant over the life of the option. (More recently, formulas have been developed where these assumptions are relaxed.)

For example, consider a call option that expires in three months and has an exercise price of $40 (thus $T = .25$ and $E = \$40$). Furthermore, the current price and the volatility of the underlying common stock are $36 and 50%, respectively, whereas the riskfree rate is 5% (thus $P_s = \$36$, R = .05, and & = .50). Solving Equations (24.11) and (24.12b) provides the following values for d_1 and d_2:

$$d_1 = \frac{\ln(36/40) + [.05 + .5(.50)^2].25}{.50\sqrt{.25}} = -.25$$

$$d_2 = -.25 - .50\sqrt{.25} = -.50$$

Table 24.2 can be used to find the corresponding values of $N(d_1)$ and $N(d_2)$:

$$N(d_1) = N(-.25) = .4013$$

$$N(d_2) = N(-.50) = .3085$$

Finally, Equation (24.10) can be used to estimate the fair value of this call option:

$$V_c = (.4013 \times \$36) - \left(\frac{\$40}{e^{.05 \times .25}} \times .3085 \right)$$

$$= \$14.45 - \$12.19 = \$2.26$$

If this call option is currently selling for $5, the investor should consider writing some of them because they are overpriced according to the Black–Scholes model, suggesting that their price will fall in the near future. Thus, the writer would receive a premium of $5 and would expect to be able to enter a closing buy order later for a lower price, making a profit on the difference. Conversely, if the call option were selling for $1, the investor should consider buying some of them because they are underpriced and can be expected to rise in value in the future.

24.6.2 COMPARISON WITH THE BINOMIAL OPTION PRICING MODEL

At this juncture the BOPM formula [given in Equation (24.7) where V_o is denoted V_o] can be compared with the Black–Scholes option pricing formula [given in Equation (24.10)]:

$$V_c = hP_s - B \qquad\qquad \textbf{(24.7)}$$

$$V_c = N(d_1)P_s - \frac{E}{e^{RT}} N(d_2) \qquad\qquad \textbf{(24.10)}$$

Comparison of the two equations shows the quantity $N(d_1)$ in Equation (24.10) corresponds to h in Equation (24.7). Recall that h is the hedge ratio, so the quantity $N(d_1)$ in the Black–Scholes formula can be interpreted in a similar manner. That is, it corresponds to the number of shares that an investor would need to purchase in executing an investment strategy designed to have the same payoffs as a call option. Similarly, the quantity $EN(d_2)/e^{RT}$ corresponds to B, the amount of money the investor borrows as the other part of the strategy. Consequently, the quantity $EN(d_2)$ corresponds to the face amount of the loan because it is the amount that must be paid back to the lender at time T, the expiration date. Hence e^{RT} is the discount (or present value) factor, indicating that the interest rate on the loan is R per period and that the loan is for T periods. Thus the seemingly complex Black–Scholes formula has an intuitive interpretation. It simply involves calculating the cost of a buy-stock-and-borrow-money investment strategy that has the same payoffs at T as a call option.

TABLE 24.2 Values of $N(d)$ for Selected Values of d

d	$N(d)$	d	$N(d)$	d	$N(d)$
		-1.00	.1587	1.00	.8413
-2.95	.0016	$-.95$	.1711	1.05	.8531
-2.90	.0019	$-.90$	.1841	1.10	.8643
-2.85	.0022	$-.85$	.1977	1.15	.8749
-2.80	.0026	$-.80$	.2119	1.20	.8849
-2.75	.0030	$-.75$	.2266	1.25	.8944
-2.70	.0035	$-.70$	.2420	1.30	.9032
-2.65	.0040	$-.65$	.2578	1.35	.9115
-2.60	.0047	$-.60$	.2743	1.40	.9192
-2.55	.0054	$-.55$	.2912	1.45	.9265
-2.50	.0062	$-.50$	.3085	1.50	.9332
-2.45	.0071	$-.45$	.3264	1.55	.9394
-2.40	.0082	$-.40$	.3446	1.60	.9452
-2.35	.0094	$-.35$	.3632	1.65	.9505
-2.30	.0107	$-.30$	.3821	1.70	.9554
-2.25	.0122	$-.25$	.4013	1.75	.9599
-2.20	.0139	$-.20$	.4207	1.80	.9641
-2.15	.0158	$-.15$	.4404	1.85	.9678
-2.10	.0179	$-.10$	.4602	1.90	.9713
-2.05	.0202	$-.05$	.4801	1.95	.9744
-2.00	.0228	.00	.5000	2.00	.9773
-1.95	.0256	.05	.5199	2.05	.9798
-1.90	.0287	.10	.5398	2.10	.9821
-1.85	.0322	.15	.5596	2.15	.9842
-1.80	.0359	.20	.5793	2.20	.9861
-1.75	.0401	.25	.5987	2.25	.9878
-1.70	.0446	.30	.6179	2.30	.9893
-1.65	.0495	.35	.6368	2.35	.9906
-1.60	.0548	.40	.6554	2.40	.9918
-1.55	.0606	.45	.6736	2.45	.9929
-1.50	.0668	.50	.6915	2.50	.9938
-1.45	.0735	.55	.7088	2.55	.9946
-1.40	.0808	.60	.7257	2.60	.9953
-1.35	.0885	.65	.7422	2.65	.9960
-1.30	.0968	.70	.7580	2.70	.9965
-1.25	.1057	.75	.7734	2.75	.9970
-1.20	.1151	.80	.7881	2.80	.9974
-1.15	.1251	.85	.8023	2.85	.9978
-1.20	.1357	.90	.8159	2.90	.9981
-1.05	.1469	.95	.8289	2.95	.9984

Source: Derived using the NORMSDIST command in Excel.

In the example, $N(d_1)$ was equal to .4013 and $EN(d_2)/e^{RT}$ was equal to $12.19. As a result, an investment strategy that involves buying .4013 shares and borrowing $12.19 at time 0 will have payoffs exactly equal to those associated with buying the call.[14] Because this strategy costs $2.26, it follows that in equilibrium the market price of the call must also be $2.26.

24.6.3 STATIC ANALYSIS

Close scrutiny of the Black–Scholes formula reveals some interesting features of European call option pricing. In particular, the fair value of a call option is dependent on five inputs—the market price of the common stock P_s, *the exercise price of the option* E, *the length of time until the expiration date* T, *the riskfree rate* R, *and the volatility of the common stock* & . *What happens to the fair value of a call option when one of these inputs is changed and the other four remain the same?*

1. The higher the price of the underlying stock P_s, *the higher the value of the call option.*

2. The higher the exercise price E, the lower the value of the call option.

3. The longer the time to the expiration date T, the higher the value of the call option.

4. The higher the riskfree rate R, the higher the value of the call option.

5. The greater the volatility & of the common stock, the higher the value of the call option.

Of these five factors, the first three (P_s, E, and T) are readily determined. The fourth factor, the riskfree rate R, is often estimated by using the yield-to-maturity on a Treasury bill having a maturity date close to the expiration date of the option. The fifth factor, the volatility of the underlying stock & , is not readily observed; consequently various methods for estimating it have been proposed. Two of these methods are presented next.

24.6.4 ESTIMATING A STOCK'S VOLATILITY FROM HISTORICAL PRICES

One method for estimating the volatility of the underlying common stock involves analyzing historical prices of the stock. Initially a set of $n + 1$ market prices on the underlying stock must be obtained from either financial publications or a computer database. These prices are then used to calculate a set of n continuously compounded returns as follows:

$$r_t = \ln \left(\frac{P_{st}}{P_{st-1}} \right) \qquad\qquad (24.13)$$

where P_{st} *and* P_{st-1} denote the market price of the underlying stock at times t and $t-1$, respectively. Here, ln denotes taking the natural logarithm of the quantity P_{st}/P_{st-1}, *which thus results in a continuously compounded return.*

For example, the set of market prices for the stock might consist of the closing price at the end of each of 53 weeks. If the price at the end of one week is $105, and the price at the end of the next week is $107, then the continuously compounded return for the week r_t *equals 1.886% [= ln (107/105)]. Similar calculations will result in a set of 52 weekly returns.*

Once a set of n returns on the stock have been calculated, the next step involves using them to estimate the stock's average return:

$$r_{ave} = \frac{1}{n} \sum_{t=1}^{n} r_t \qquad\qquad (24.14)$$

The average return is used to estimate the per-period variance, which is the square of the per-period standard deviation:

$$s^2 = \frac{1}{n-1} \sum_{t=1}^{n} (r_t - r_{ave})^2 \qquad\qquad (24.15)$$

This value is called the per-period variance because its size depends on the length of time during which each return is measured. In the example, weekly returns were calculated and would lead to the estimation of a weekly variance. Alternatively, daily returns could have been used, leading to a daily variance that would be of smaller magnitude than the weekly variance. However, an annual variance, not a weekly or a daily variance, is needed. This value is obtained by multiplying the per period variance by the number of periods in a year. Thus, an estimated weekly variance is multiplied by 52 to estimate the annual variance $\&^2$ (that is, $\&^2 = 52s^2$).[15]

Alternative methods of estimating a stock's volatility exist. One method involves subjectively estimating possible future stock prices, the corresponding returns, and their probabilities of occurring (see Appendix A to Chapter 7). For any estimate of future uncertainty, historical data are likely to prove more helpful than definitive. And because recent data may prove more helpful than older data, some analysts study daily or weekly price changes for the most recent 6 to 12 months, sometimes giving more weight to more recent data than to earlier ones.

* * *

24.6.6   MORE ON HEDGE RATIOS

The slope of the Black–Scholes curve at any point represents the expected change in the value of the option for each dollar change in the price of the underlying common stock. This amount corresponds to the hedge ratio of the call option and is equal to $N(d_1)$ in Equation (24.10). As Figure 24.6 shows (assuming that the market price of the call is equal to its Black–Scholes value), the slope (that is, the hedge ratio) of the curve is always positive. Note that if the stock has a relatively low market price, the slope will be near zero. For higher stock prices the slope increases, ultimately approaching a value of one for relatively high prices.

Because the hedge ratio is less than 1, a $1 increase in the stock price typically results in an increase in a call option's value of less than $1. However, the percentage change in the value of the call option will generally be greater than the percentage change in the price of the stock. It is this relationship that leads people to say that options offer high leverage.

The reason for referring to the slope of the Black–Scholes curve as the hedge ratio is that a "hedge" portfolio, meaning a nearly riskfree portfolio, can be formed by simultaneously writing one call option and purchasing a number of shares equal to the hedge ratio, $N(d_1)$. For example, assume that the hedge ratio is .5, indicating that the hedge portfolio consists of writing one call and buying .5 shares of stock. If the stock price rises by $1, the value of the call option will rise by approximately $.50. This relationship means that the hedge portfolio will lose approximately $.50 on the written call option but gain $.50 from the rise in the stock's price. Conversely, a $1 decrease in the stock's price results in a $.50 gain on the written call option but a loss of $.50 on the half-share of stock. Overall, the hedge portfolio neither gains nor loses value when the price of the underlying common stock changes by a relatively small amount.

FIGURE 24.6 Option Terminology for Calls

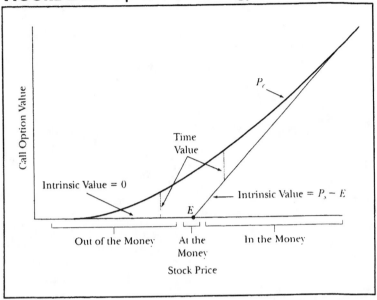

Even if the Black–Scholes model is valid and all the inputs have been correctly specified, risk is not permanently eliminated in the hedge portfolio when the portfolio is first formed (or, for that matter, at any time). There will still be risk because the hedge ratio changes as the stock price changes and as the life of the option decreases with the passage of time. To eliminate risk from the hedge portfolio, the investor has to alter its composition continuously. Altering it less often reduces but does not completely eliminate risk.

*

TABLES

APPENDIX TABLE 1

Discount factors: Present value of $1 to be
received after t years = $1/(1 + r)^t$

Number	Interest rate per year									
of years	1%	2%	3%	4%	5%	6%	7%	8%	9%	10%
1	.990	.980	.971	.962	.952	.943	.935	.926	.917	.909
2	.980	.961	.943	.925	.907	.890	.873	.857	.842	.826
3	.971	.942	.915	.889	.864	.840	.816	.794	.772	.751
4	.961	.924	.888	.855	.823	.792	.763	.735	.708	.683
5	.951	.906	.863	.822	.784	.747	.713	.681	.650	.621
6	.942	.888	.837	.790	.746	.705	.666	.630	.596	.564
7	.933	.871	.813	.760	.711	.665	.623	.583	.547	.513
8	.923	.853	.789	.731	.677	.627	.582	.540	.502	.467
9	.914	.837	.766	.703	.645	.592	.544	.500	.460	.424
10	.905	.820	.744	.676	.614	.558	.508	.463	.422	.386
11	.896	.804	.722	.650	.585	.527	.475	.429	.388	.350
12	.887	.788	.701	.625	.557	.497	.444	.397	.356	.319
13	.879	.773	.681	.601	.530	.469	.415	.368	.326	.290
14	.870	.758	.661	.577	.505	.442	.388	.340	.299	.263
15	.861	.743	.642	.555	.481	.417	.362	.315	.275	.239
16	.853	.728	.623	.534	.458	.394	.339	.292	.252	.218
17	.844	.714	.605	.513	.436	.371	.317	.270	.231	.198
18	.836	.700	.587	.494	.416	.350	.296	.250	.212	.180
19	.828	.686	.570	.475	.396	.331	.277	.232	.194	.164
20	.820	.673	.554	.456	.377	.312	.258	.215	.178	.149
25	.780	.610	.478	.375	.295	.233	.184	.146	.116	.092
30	.742	.552	.412	.308	.231	.174	.131	.099	.075	.057

Number	Interest rate per year									
of years	11%	12%	13%	14%	15%	16%	17%	18%	19%	20%
1	.901	.893	.885	.877	.870	.862	.855	.847	.840	.833
2	.812	.797	.783	.769	.756	.743	.731	.718	.706	.694
3	.731	.712	.693	.675	.658	.641	.624	.609	.593	.579
4	.659	.636	.613	.592	.572	.552	.534	.516	.499	.482
5	.593	.567	.543	.519	.497	.476	.456	.437	.419	.402
6	.535	.507	.480	.456	.432	.410	.390	.370	.352	.335
7	.482	.452	.425	.400	.376	.354	.333	.314	.296	.279
8	.434	.404	.376	.351	.327	.305	.285	.266	.249	.233
9	.391	.361	.333	.308	.284	.263	.243	.225	.209	.194
10	.352	.322	.295	.270	.247	.227	.208	.191	.176	.162
11	.317	.287	.261	.237	.215	.195	.178	.162	.148	.135
12	.286	.257	.231	.208	.187	.168	.152	.137	.124	.112
13	.258	.229	.204	.182	.163	.145	.130	.116	.104	.093
14	.232	.205	.181	.160	.141	.125	.111	.099	.088	.078
15	.209	.183	.160	.140	.123	.108	.095	.084	.074	.065
16	.188	.163	.141	.123	.107	.093	.081	.071	.062	.054
17	.170	.146	.125	.108	.093	.080	.069	.060	.052	.045
18	.153	.130	.111	.095	.081	.069	.059	.051	.044	.038
19	.138	.116	.098	.083	.070	.060	.051	.043	.037	.031
20	.124	.104	.087	.073	.061	.051	.043	.037	.031	.026
25	.074	.059	.047	.038	.030	.024	.020	.016	.013	.010
30	.044	.033	.026	.020	.015	.012	.009	.007	.005	.004

Number	Interest rate per year									
of years	21%	22%	23%	24%	25%	26%	27%	28%	29%	30%
1	.826	.820	.813	.806	.800	.794	.787	.781	.775	.769
2	.683	.672	.661	.650	.640	.630	.620	.610	.601	.592
3	.564	.551	.537	.524	.512	.500	.488	.477	.466	.455
4	.467	.451	.437	.423	.410	.397	.384	.373	.361	.350
5	.386	.370	.355	.341	.328	.315	.303	.291	.280	.269
6	.319	.303	.289	.275	.262	.250	.238	.227	.217	.207
7	.263	.249	.235	.222	.210	.198	.188	.178	.168	.159
8	.218	.204	.191	.179	.168	.157	.148	.139	.130	.123
9	.180	.167	.155	.144	.134	.125	.116	.108	.101	.094
10	.149	.137	.126	.116	.107	.099	.092	.085	.078	.073
11	.123	.112	.103	.094	.086	.079	.072	.066	.061	.056
12	.102	.092	.083	.076	.069	.062	.057	.052	.047	.043
13	.084	.075	.068	.061	.055	.050	.045	.040	.037	.033
14	.069	.062	.055	.049	.044	.039	.035	.032	.028	.025
15	.057	.051	.045	.040	.035	.031	.028	.025	.022	.020
16	.047	.042	.036	.032	.028	.025	.022	.019	.017	.015
17	.039	.034	.030	.026	.023	.020	.017	.015	.013	.012
18	.032	.028	.024	.021	.018	.016	.014	.012	.010	.009
19	.027	.023	.020	.017	.014	.012	.011	.009	.008	.007
20	.022	.019	.016	.014	.012	.010	.008	.007	.006	.005
25	.009	.007	.006	.005	.004	.003	.003	.002	.002	.001
30	.003	.003	.002	.002	.001	.001	.001	.001	.000	.000

E.g.: If the interest rate is 10 percent per year, the present value of $1 received at the end of year 5 is $0.621.

APPENDIX TABLE 2

Future value of $1 by the end of t years $= (1 + r)^{t}$

Number of years	Interest rate per year									
	1%	2%	3%	4%	5%	6%	7%	8%	9%	10%
1	1.010	1.020	1.030	1.040	1.050	1.060	1.070	1.080	1.090	1.100
2	1.020	1.040	1.061	1.082	1.102	1.124	1.145	1.166	1.188	1.210
3	1.030	1.061	1.093	1.125	1.158	1.191	1.225	1.260	1.295	1.331
4	1.041	1.082	1.126	1.170	1.216	1.262	1.311	1.360	1.412	1.464
5	1.051	1.104	1.159	1.217	1.276	1.338	1.403	1.469	1.539	1.611
6	1.062	1.126	1.194	1.265	1.340	1.419	1.501	1.587	1.677	1.772
7	1.072	1.149	1.230	1.316	1.407	1.504	1.606	1.714	1.828	1.949
8	1.083	1.172	1.267	1.369	1.477	1.594	1.718	1.851	1.993	2.144
9	1.094	1.195	1.305	1.423	1.551	1.689	1.838	1.999	2.172	2.358
10	1.105	1.219	1.344	1.480	1.629	1.791	1.967	2.159	2.367	2.594
11	1.116	1.243	1.384	1.539	1.710	1.898	2.105	2.332	2.580	2.853
12	1.127	1.268	1.426	1.601	1.796	2.012	2.252	2.518	2.813	3.138
13	1.138	1.294	1.469	1.665	1.886	2.133	2.410	2.720	3.066	3.452
14	1.149	1.319	1.513	1.732	1.980	2.261	2.579	2.937	3.342	3.797
15	1.161	1.346	1.558	1.801	2.079	2.397	2.759	3.172	3.642	4.177
16	1.173	1.373	1.605	1.873	2.183	2.540	2.952	3.426	3.970	4.595
17	1.184	1.400	1.653	1.948	2.292	2.693	3.159	3.700	4.328	5.054
18	1.196	1.428	1.702	2.026	2.407	2.854	3.380	3.996	4.717	5.560
19	1.208	1.457	1.754	2.107	2.527	3.026	3.617	4.316	5.142	6.116
20	1.220	1.486	1.806	2.191	2.653	3.207	3.870	4.661	5.604	6.727
25	1.282	1.641	2.094	2.666	3.386	4.292	5.427	6.848	8.623	10.83
30	1.348	1.811	2.427	3.243	4.322	5.743	7.612	10.06	13.27	17.45

APPENDIX TABLE 3

Number of years	Interest rate per year									
	11%	**12%**	**13%**	**14%**	**15%**	**16%**	**17%**	**18%**	**19%**	**20%**
1	1.110	1.120	1.130	1.140	1.150	1.160	1.170	1.180	1.190	1.200
2	1.232	1.254	1.277	1.300	1.323	1.346	1.369	1.392	1.416	1.440
3	1.368	1.405	1.443	1.482	1.521	1.561	1.602	1.643	1.685	1.728
4	1.518	1.574	1.630	1.689	1.749	1.811	1.874	1.939	2.005	2.074
5	1.685	1.762	1.842	1.925	2.011	2.100	2.192	2.288	2.386	2.488
6	1.870	1.974	2.082	2.195	2.313	2.436	2.565	2.700	2.840	2.986
7	2.076	2.211	2.353	2.502	2.660	2.826	3.001	3.185	3.379	3.583
8	2.305	2.476	2.658	2.853	3.059	3.278	3.511	3.759	4.021	4.300
9	2.558	2.773	3.004	3.252	3.518	3.803	4.108	4.435	4.785	5.160
10	2.839	3.106	3.395	3.707	4.046	4.411	4.807	5.234	5.695	6.192
11	3.152	3.479	3.836	4.226	4.652	5.117	5.624	6.176	6.777	7.430
12	3.498	3.896	4.335	4.818	5.350	5.936	6.580	7.288	8.064	8.916
13	3.883	4.363	4.898	5.492	6.153	6.886	7.699	8.599	9.596	10.70
14	4.310	4.887	5.535	6.261	7.076	7.988	9.007	10.15	11.42	12.84
15	4.785	5.474	6.254	7.138	8.137	9.266	10.54	11.97	13.59	15.41
16	5.311	6.130	7.067	8.137	9.358	10.75	12.33	14.13	16.17	18.49
17	5.895	6.866	7.986	9.276	10.76	12.47	14.43	16.67	19.24	22.19
18	6.544	7.690	9.024	10.58	12.38	14.46	16.88	19.67	22.90	26.62
19	7.263	8.613	10.20	12.06	14.23	16.78	19.75	23.21	27.25	31.95
20	8.062	9.646	11.52	13.74	16.37	19.46	23.11	27.39	32.43	38.34
25	13.59	17.00	21.23	26.46	32.92	40.87	50.66	62.67	77.39	95.40
30	22.89	29.96	39.12	50.95	66.21	85.85	111.1	143.4	184.7	237.4

Number of years	Interest rate per year									
	21%	**22%**	**23%**	**24%**	**25%**	**26%**	**27%**	**28%**	**29%**	**30%**
1	1.210	1.220	1.230	1.240	1.250	1.260	1.270	1.280	1.290	1.300
2	1.464	1.488	1.513	1.538	1.563	1.588	1.613	1.638	1.664	1.690
3	1.772	1.816	1.861	1.907	1.953	2.000	2.048	2.097	2.147	2.197
4	2.144	2.215	2.289	2.364	2.441	2.520	2.601	2.684	2.769	2.856
5	2.594	2.703	2.815	2.932	3.052	3.176	3.304	3.436	3.572	3.713
6	3.138	3.297	3.463	3.635	3.815	4.002	4.196	4.398	4.608	4.827
7	3.797	4.023	4.259	4.508	4.768	5.042	5.329	5.629	5.945	6.275
8	4.595	4.908	5.239	5.590	5.960	6.353	6.768	7.206	7.669	8.157
9	5.560	5.987	6.444	6.931	7.451	8.005	8.595	9.223	9.893	10.60
10	6.728	7.305	7.926	8.594	9.313	10.09	10.92	11.81	12.76	13.79
11	8.140	8.912	9.749	10.66	11.64	12.71	13.86	15.11	16.46	17.92
12	9.850	10.87	11.99	13.21	14.55	16.01	17.61	19.34	21.24	23.30
13	11.92	13.26	14.75	16.39	18.19	20.18	22.36	24.76	27.39	30.29
14	14.42	16.18	18.14	20.32	22.74	25.42	28.40	31.69	35.34	39.37
15	17.45	19.74	22.31	25.20	28.42	32.03	36.06	40.56	45.59	51.19
16	21.11	24.09	27.45	31.24	35.53	40.36	45.80	51.92	58.81	66.54
17	25.55	29.38	33.76	38.74	44.41	50.85	58.17	66.46	75.86	86.50
18	30.91	35.85	41.52	48.04	55.51	64.07	73.87	85.07	97.86	112.5
19	37.40	43.74	51.07	59.57	69.39	80.73	93.81	108.9	126.2	146.2
20	45.26	53.36	62.82	73.86	86.74	101.7	119.1	139.4	162.9	190.0
25	117.4	144.2	176.9	216.5	264.7	323.0	393.6	478.9	581.8	705.6
30	304.5	389.8	497.9	634.8	807.8	1026	1301	1646	2078	2620

E.g.: If the interest rate is 10 percent per year, the investment of $1 today will be worth $1.611 at the end of year 5.

INDEX

References are to pages

ACCOUNTING
Asset securitization, 292, 294
Mergers, 778
Stock option plans, 710
Valuation, 48

AGENCY COSTS
Asset substitution, 233
Blockholding, 728
Capital structure, 233
Convertible bonds, 554
Dividends, 636, 653
Free cash flow, 304
Mergers, 775
Monitoring, 234
Share repurchases, 671
Underinvestment, 234

ANTITAKEOVER LEGISLATION
Constituency statutes, 1133
Constitutionality, 1125, 1129, 1134
First generation, 1125
Poison pills, 1133
Second generation, 1126, 1129
Third generation, 1132, 1134

APPRAISAL RIGHTS
Asset value, 71
Availability, 14
Capital Asset Pricing Model, 108
Closed-end funds, 6, 13
Comparable companies, 71, 136
Comparative acquisitions, 136
Date, 134
Delaware block, 71, 82
Discounted cash flow, 136
Discounts, 6, 13, 149, 150
Earnings value, 71
Exclusivity, 866, 898
Experts, 82
History, 826
Holding companies, 120
Investment Companies, 6
Judicial role, 111
Preferred stock, 521
Price earnings ratio, 71
Reform, 829
Subsidiaries, 120
Warrants, 595

ASSET SALES
General, 808

ASSET SALES—Cont'd
Covenant, 271
De facto merger, 812, 818
Successor liability, 825

ASSET SECURITIZATION
General, 287, 288
Accounting, 292, 294
Asset risk, 293
Bankruptcy remoteness, 295, 299
Example, 296
Interest rates, 292
Liquidity, 290
Owner trusts, 298
Policy concerns, 304
Risk management, 291

BANKRUPTCY REORGANIZATION
General, 411
Absolute priority, 415, 432, 448
Adequate protection, 444
Best interest of creditors, 430, 447
Claim definition, 428
Classes, 445
Committees, 445
Confirmation, 446
Contracting out, 453, 482
Costs, 231
Creditor control, 468
Debtor in possession, 444
Delaware law, 434
Disclosure, 446
Discrimination, 453
Empirical tests, 454
Executive pay, 476
Feasibility, 447, 453
Forum, 443
Fraudulent conveyances, 393, 394
Full satisfaction, 429
History, 431
Liquidation, 452
New value, 455, 466
Policy, 477
Postpetition interest, 429
Prepackaged, 359
Voting, 448

BEHAVIORAL FINANCE THEORY
Efficient markets, 26
Noise trading, 27
Psychology, 33

BLOCKHOLDING
Comparative corporate governance, 729
Controlling, 741
Control sales, 747
Dual class common, 744
Fiduciary duties, 736, 741, 747
Hedge funds, 733
Monitoring, 728
Noncontrolling, 736
Regulation, 734

BONDS AND BONDHOLDERS
Amendment, 341, 348
Business covenants, 268
Call, 254, 258
Call premium, 255
Corporate trust, 250
Debentures, 240
Default remedies, 267
Discounting, 44
Duration, 243
Event risk, 320, 323, 325
Fiduciary duty, 406
Good faith duties, 323, 335, 343, 348
Hold outs, 356
Indentures, 241, 250
Indenture trustee, 248
Junk bonds, 247
Legal protections, 373
Mortgage bonds, 282
Notes, 240
Priority, 205
Promise to pay, 253
Redemption, 254, 258
Seniority, 212, 286
Subordination, 286
Trust Indenture Act, 248
Workouts, 341, 343, 348

BUSINESS COVENANTS
General, 268
Debt, 270
Dividend, 270, 335
Implied, 323
Interpretation, 274
Investment, 272
Lien, 271
Maintenance, 273
Merger, 271

BUSINESS JUDGMENT
Dividends, 640
Mergers, 919
Tender offer defense, 1037

CAPITAL ASSET PRICING MODEL
Appraisals, 108
Arbitrage, 106, 119
Beta, 100, 104, 106
Derivation, 99
Empirical tests, 105, 116
Equation, 103
Market portfolio, 107
Multiple factor models, 116

CAPITAL BUDGETING
Internal rate of return, 46

CAPITAL BUDGETING—Cont'd
Net present value, 46
Payback, 47

CAPITAL STRUCTURE
Agency costs, 233
Bankruptcy costs, 231
Banks, 380
Blockholding, 728
Cost of capital, 112, 215, 218, 221
Dual class common, 744
Information asymmetries, 235
Institutional constraints, 226
Irrelevance, 214, 221
Legal capital, 383
Leverage, 215, 221
Leveraged restructuring, 304
Margin rules, 378
Pecking order, 236
Regulation, 316, 374
Stock option plans, 705
Taxes, 227, 229

CONTROL SALES
Fiduciary duties, 747
Policy, 837
Venture capital, 596

CONVERTIBLE BONDS
Agency costs, 554
Antidestruction, 559, 584
Antidilution, 559, 561, 563, 577
Call, 551
Common stock dividends, 592
Contracts, 559, 577
Conversion premium, 549
Conversion price, 549
Conversion value, 549
Equity-linked, 555
Features, 548
Floating price, 556
Good faith duties, 579, 584
Hedges, 575
Information asymmetries, 553
Mergers, 584, 594
Original issue discount, 555
Puttable, 555
Redemption, 551
Valuation, 547

CORPORATE REORGANIZATION
See Bankruptcy Reorganization

CORPORATE TRUST
General, 250
Owner trusts, 298

COST OF CAPITAL
See Capital Structure

DEBENTURES
See Bonds and Bondholders

DEBT FINANCING
Agency costs, 233
Bankruptcy reorganization, 411
Concepts, 240
Creditor protection, 373

DEBT FINANCING—Cont'd
Credit ratings, 244
Distress, 341
Fiduciary duty, 406
Lender liability, 329
Leverage, 215
Management discipline, 304
Pecking order, 236
Private placements, 245
Secured, 281
Short term, 247
Taxes, 227
Terms, 240

DERIVATIVES
Counterparties, 174
Credit, 359, 369
Duty of care, 186
Empty voting, 195
Equity swaps, 184
Forward contracts, 156
Futures contracts, 158
Irrelevance hypothesis, 189
Option contracts, 163
Regulation, 173, 202
Swap contracts, 159
Swap dealers, 182
Systemic risk, 196, 199
Transparency, 202

DISCOUNTING
Bond valuation, 44
Capital budgeting, 45
Growth, 146
Terminal value, 146
Time value, 38

DISCOUNTS
Closed-end funds, 6, 23
Marketability, 150
Mergers, 120
Minority, 149

DIVIDENDS
General, 620
Agency costs, 636, 653
Convertible bonds, 592
Corporate opportunity, 644
Disclosure duties, 652, 655
Good faith duty, 645
Information asymmetries, 634
Irrelevance, 632
Pecking order, 634
Policy, 624
Practice, 624, 628
Preferred stock, 495, 502
Puzzle, 629
Share repurchases, 668
Special, 651
Spin offs, 335, 664
Stock dividends, 656
Taxes, 632
Tracking stock, 664
Valuation, 621

DUAL CLASS COMMON CAPITAL STRUCTURE
Recapitalizations, 744
Regulation, 746
Tracking stock, 664

EFFICIENT CAPITAL MARKET HYPOTHESIS
General, 15
Allocative efficiency, 20
Anomalies, 23
Arbitrage, 27, 32
Behavioral finance, 26
Bubbles, 34
Crashes, 34
Empirical testing, 22
Incentive problems, 21
Noise trading, 26
Speculative efficiency, 20

EQUITY FINANCING
Initial public offerings, 239
New issues, 239
Pecking order, 236

EXPECTED RETURNS
Cash flows, 52
Depreciation, 53
Expected value, 69
Growth, 56
Probabilities, 58
Reinvestment, 55
Scrap value, 54

FRAUDULENT CONVEYANCES
General, 392
Constructive fraud, 403
Management buyouts, 394
Remedies, 405
Valuation, 404

FREEZE-OUT MERGERS
General, 832
Appraisal, 866, 898
Business purpose, 843
Coercive, 884
Disclosure, 865
Fairness, 849, 865
Fiduciary Duties, 843, 849, 865, 869, 884
Policy, 833, 892
Short form, 881
Tender offer, 873

FUTURES CONTRACTS
Defined, 158

HEDGE FUNDS
General, 12
Activist, 733
Leverage, 377
Vultures, 358

INVESTMENT COMPANIES
General, 11
Closed–End Funds, 13
Debt ratios, 375
Hedge funds, 12
Investment Company Act of 1940, 11, 375

INVESTMENT COMPANIES—Cont'd
Private equity, 317
Venture capital, 609

LEASING
General, 284

LEGAL CAPITAL RULES
Dividends, 385
Revised approach, 392
Stated capital, 383

LENDER LIABILITY
See Debt Financing

LEVERAGE
See Capital Structure; Debt Financing

LEVERAGED BUYOUTS
See Debt Financing; Fraudulent Convey-
    ances; Management Buyouts; Mergers

MANAGEMENT BUYOUTS
General, 308, 905
Corporate governance, 309
Fairness opinions, 918
Fiduciary duties, 907
Fraudulent conveyances, 394
Legal capital rules, 387
Legal investment laws, 316
Private equity, 317
Taxes, 316

MERGERS
General, 765
Accounting, 778
Appraisal rights, 127, 137, 149, 826
Cash consideration, 807
Classical, 806
Convertible bonds, 584, 594
Covenants, 271
De facto, 812, 818
Disclosure duties, 933, 939, 945
Discounts, 120
Duty of care, 919, 931
Empirical tests, 773
Freeze-out, 832
Gain, 120
History, 767
Management buyouts, 905
Merger Agreement, 791, 793
Motivations, 767, 775
Preferred stock, 521
Premiums, 120, 133
Short form, 807, 881
Small scale, 806
Stock for stock, 806
Taxes, 786
Tender offers, 977, 1016
Triangular, 810, 818
Valuation, 120
Waves, 767, 771

MUTUAL FUNDS
See Investment Companies

NOISE TRADING
Efficient markets, 27

NOTES
See Bonds and Bondholders

OPTIONS
General, 163
Payoffs, 163
Put-call parity, 167
Strategies, 165
Valuation, 171, 173

PORTFOLIO THEORY
General, 84
Analysis, 89
Critical ratio, 94
Diversification, 91
Selection, 89
Separation theorem, 94

PREFERRED STOCK
Amendment, 491, 502
Arrearages, 502
Choice of law, 538
Contract terms, 487
Convertible, 546
Cumulative, 496
Definition, 485
Dividend provisions, 495
Drafting, 533
Exchange offers, 498
Fiduciary duty, 538, 541
Financial analysis, 493
Independent legal significance, 521, 529
Investment value doctrine, 527
Hold ups, 504, 506
Liquidation rights, 502
Mergers, 521
Noncumulative, 497
Principal, 502
Redemption, 510
Venture capital, 596
Voting rights, 489, 501, 536

PRIVATE EQUITY
General, 11
Restructurings, 317

PROBABILITY DISTRIBUTIONS
Capital budgeting, 59
Expected value, 69

RECAPITALIZATION
See Bankruptcy Reorganization; Preferred
    Stock

REDEMPTION
See Bonds and Bondholders; Preferred Stock

RETAINED EARNINGS
Dividend policy, 624
Irrelevance, 630
Retention ratio, 623
Valuation, 54

RISK
Aversion, 115
Derivatives, 196, 199
Dispersion, 64
Diversification, 91

RISK—Cont'd
Duration, 154
Hedging, 153
Neutrality, 115
Premiums, 67
Rates of return, 70
Standard deviation, 70
Systematic, 91
Unsystematic, 91
Variance, 70

SECURITIES MARKETS
Efficiency, 15
Rates of return, 70

SECURITIES REGULATION
Dividend decisions, 652
Margin rules, 378
Materiality, 945, 957
Mergers, 945, 957
Open market repurchases, 689
Repurchase tender offers, 686
Share repurchases, 683
Soft information, 945, 957
Stock dividends, 659
Stock option plans, 711
Tender offers, 998

SECURITIZATION
See Asset Securitization

SHARE EXCHANGES
General, 809

SHARE REPURCHASES
Agency costs, 671, 675
Corporate governance, 694
Fiduciary duties, 677
Greenmail, 684
Information asymmetries, 671
Irrelevance, 669
Manipulation, 690
Motivations, 673
Open market, 668, 689
Regulation, 683
Stock options, 674
Taxes, 671, 686
Tender offer, 668, 686
Volume, 672

SHORT POSITIONS
General, 32
Voting, 190

SPIN OFFS
See Dividends

STOCK DIVIDENDS
General, 656
Disclosure, 659
Fractional shares, 661
Reverse stock splits, 661
Stock splits, 658
Valuation, 656

STOCK OPTION PLANS
Accounting, 710
Backdating, 723

STOCK OPTION PLANS—Cont'd
Drafting, 722
Fiduciary duties, 711, 720
Hedging, 705
Policy, 706
Share repurchases, 674
Spring loading, 726
Stock sales, 705
Taxes, 710
Terms, 699

STOCK SPLITS
See Stock Dividends

SUBORDINATION
See Bonds and Bondholders

SWAPS
See Derivatives

TENDER OFFER DEFENSIVE TACTICS
All cash all shares offers, 1056
Antitakeover legislation, 1124
 Blasius rule, 1052, 1110
Board veto, 988, 1034
Business judgment, 1037
Charter amendments, 1024
Coercion, 1054
Empirical tests, 1034
Fiduciary duty, 1036
Fiduciary out, 1111
Golden parachutes, 1026
Greenmail, 684
Lock ups, 1026, 1111, 1120
Poison pills, 1027, 1030, 1040, 1045, 1051
 Revlon duty, 1058, 1062, 1065, 1066,
  1079, 1096
Shadow pill, 1030
 Unitrin test, 1098, 1105
 Unocal test, 1039, 1040, 1045, 1051,
  1054, 1066, 1110
White knights, 1026

**TENDER OFFER DISCLOSURE REGU-
 LATION**
All holders rule, 1010, 1016
Appraisals, 1006
Bidder disclosure, 999, 1004
Coverage, 1019, 1022
Defensive negotiations, 1006
Equal treatment, 1010
Outside purchases, 1017
Proration, 1008
Target disclosure, 1005
Withdrawal, 1008

TENDER OFFERS
General, 977
Antitakeover legislation, 1124
Bidder incentives, 991
Board veto, 988
Commencement, 1019
Defensive tactics, 1024
Definition, 1019, 1022
Fiduciary duty, 1036
Friendly, 1016
Neutral policy, 989

TENDER OFFERS—Cont'd
Opponent policy, 983
Proponent policy, 979, 982, 993
Repurchase, 668
Securities regulation, 998
Sole owner standard, 996
Street sweeps, 1022

TRACKING STOCK
See Dividends

TRUST INDENTURE ACT
    General, 251
Conflicts of interest, 252

VALUATION
Arbitrage Pricing Model, 119
Bonds, 44
Bubbles, 34
Call options, 171, 173
Capital Asset Pricing Model, 98, 107, 112
Capital budgeting, 45
Capitalization rate, 63, 71, 80
Capital structure, 112
Comparable firms, 71, 112, 136
Comparative acquisition, 136
Convertible bonds, 548
Crashes, 34
Depreciation, 54
Discounted cash flow, 136
Discounting, 38, 146
Discounts, 6, 120, 149
Diversification, 91

VALUATION—Cont'd
Economic value added, 58
Efficient Capital Market Hypothesis, 15
Equity ownership, 697
Expected returns, 47
Firm, 55
Fraudulent conveyances, 404
Gordon Growth Model, 81, 621
Growth, 56, 81, 146
Investment companies, 6
Leverage, 218
Mergers, 120, 773
Multiple factor models, 116
Nonconstant growth, 146
Perpetuities, 43
Portfolio theory, 84
Premiums, 120
Price earnings ratio, 71, 80
Probability distributions, 59
Reinvestment, 54
Risk, 64, 115

VENTURE CAPITAL
Contracts, 610
Control, 612
Investment companies, 609
Preferred stock, 596

WARRANTS
See Convertible Bonds

WORKOUTS
See Bankruptcy Reorganization; Bonds and
    Bondholders

†